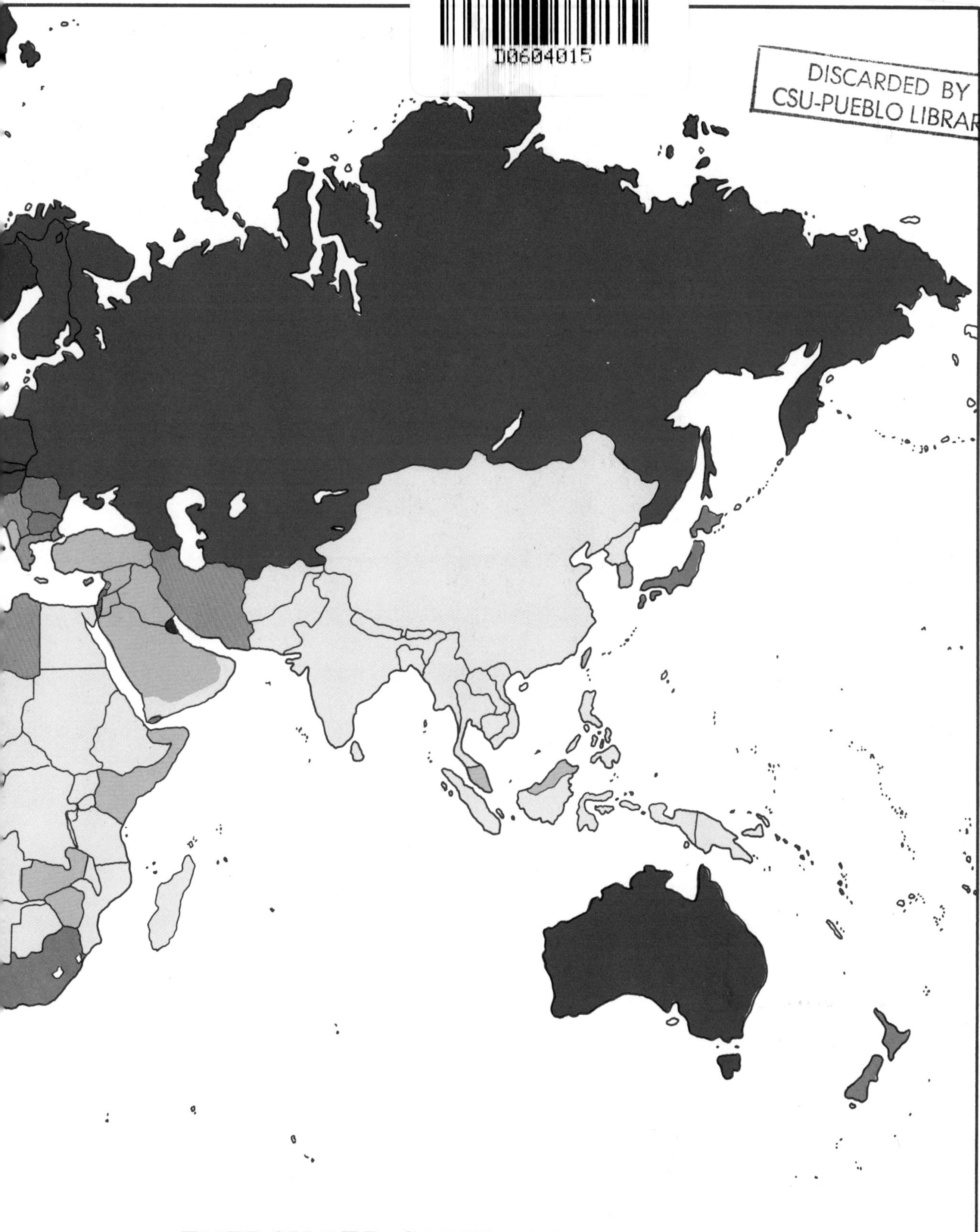

ENERGY PER CAPITA (1967)

(IN KILOGRAMS COAL EQUIVALENT)

ENERGY IN THE WORLD ECONOMY

ENERGY IN THE WORLD ECONOMY

A Statistical Review of Trends in Output, Trade, and Consumption Since 1925

by Joel Darmstadter

with Perry D. Teitelbaum and Jaroslav G. Polach

Published for Resources for the Future, Inc.

by The Johns Hopkins Press
Baltimore and London

RESOURCES FOR THE FUTURE, INC.
1755 Massachusetts Avenue, N.W., Washington, D.C. 20036

Resources for the Future is a nonprofit corporation for research and education in the development, conservation, and use of natural resources and the improvement of the quality of the environment. It was established in 1952 with the cooperation of the Ford Foundation. Part of the work of Resources for the Future is carried out by its resident staff; part is supported by grants to universities and other nonprofit organizations. Unless otherwise stated, interpretations and conclusions in RFF publications are those of the authors; the organization takes responsibility for the selection of significant subjects for study, the competence of the researchers, and their freedom of inquiry.

This book is one of RFF's energy and minerals studies, which are directed by Sam H. Schurr. Joel Darmstadter is a senior research associate with Resources for the Future.

RFF editors: Henry Jarrett, Vera W. Dodds, Nora E. Roots, Tadd Fisher.

Manufactured in the United States of America

The Johns Hopkins Press, Baltimore, Maryland 21218
The Johns Hopkins Press Ltd., London

Library of Congress Catalog Card Number 70-155848

ISBN 0-8018-1282-8

PREFACE AND ACKNOWLEDGMENTS

This book deals with quantitative aspects of long-term trends in energy consumption, production, and foreign trade; and, more particularly, with the transformation, during this century, of the world's fuel base away from coal and toward oil and natural gas. These latter changes, which occurred at different times and rates in the major geographic regions, are particularly important for two reasons: they reflected, as well as facilitated, significant changes which were taking place in the world's industrial life and in economic activity in general; and they gave rise to wholly new patterns of regional economic interdependence. This interdependence is seen most sharply in the strong reliance in petroleum requirements of such industrial countries as Japan and those in Western Europe upon largely underdeveloped regions such as the Middle East and North Africa.

In reviewing these developments, the book sets out to accomplish three main tasks. The first, upon which the others depend, is to assemble statistical series depicting movements in consumption, production, and international trade of energy commodities since 1925 by countries, regions, and the world as a whole. Secondly, these voluminous statistical materials are winnowed in order to bring into sharp focus the main features of those movements. The third task is to relate these main features to other economic variables and, in so doing, to provide an essential springboard for anyone wishing to evaluate prospects for the future.

Part One describes and interprets the significant statistical findings. Part Two presents a series of Statistical Profiles, each dealing with some unique facet of the overall picture. These profiles are derived from the detailed statistics in Part Three. Part Four deals with questions of methodology and definition connected with the detailed statistical series, and also provides country-by-country source notes. Part Five presents selected supplementary materials: on energy and gross national product, matrix tables of international energy flows, and a brief bibliography.

The book represents the product of collaborative effort. Joel Darmstadter, the principal author, is responsible for the final form and content of the study, and is the author of Parts One, Two, and Five. Parts Three and Four involved, in addition, the contributions of Perry D. Teitelbaum (who died in 1966) and Jaroslav G. Polach, both of whom participated at an earlier stage of the project when the initial conception and outline of the quantitative structure of the study were developed. In assembling what were frequently deficient basic data, they grappled with numerous difficult conceptual, methodological, and estimating problems.

Grateful acknowledgment goes to reviewers of the study (or parts thereof) in various of its earlier stages. The following, in particular, are thanked for their time and effort: F. Gerard Adams, University of Pennsylvania; Richard L. Gordon, Pennsylvania State University; Leslie E. Grayson, Harvard University Development Advisory Service; J. A. van den Heuvel, formerly with the Organisation for Economic Cooperation and Development; Vincent E. McKelvey, U.S. Geological Survey; Gerald Manners, University College London, University of London; Warren E. Morrison, U.S. Bureau of Mines; William N. Parker, Yale University; Arthur J. Ramsdell, United Nations Statistical Office; E. F. Schumacher, National Coal Board, London; and Milton F. Searl, U.S. Office of Science and Technology.

Sally Nishiyama's capabilities as a resourceful and persevering research assistant throughout the period of the study contributed greatly to the content, organization, and appearance of the final volume. The research assistance of Elizabeth K. Vogely also proved most valuable. Elizabeth Duenckel did the computer programming and guided along the extensive machine tabulations of Part Three. Helen-Marie Streich provided efficient secretarial help at various stages in the study's progress.

Sam H. Schurr
Director
Energy and Minerals Program
Resources for the Future, Inc.

December 1970

CONTENTS

Introduction

Part One
Major Trends and their Significance– A Summary Discussion

Tables

Part Two
Statistical Profiles: Descriptive Comments, Tables and Charts Based on the Detailed Data

Profile Number

Total Energy Consumption

Energy Consumption, Population, Gross National Product

Consumption of the Different Energy Sources

Production of the Different Energy Sources

Imports and Exports of Energy

Interregional Network of World Energy Trade

Part Three
Detailed Regional and National Energy Statistics

Tables

Part Four
Annotated Guide to the Detailed Energy Statistics of Part Three

I. General Notes

II. Country Notes

Part Five
Supplementary Materials

Tables

ENERGY IN THE WORLD ECONOMY

INTRODUCTION

The objective of this book is to present an essentially quantitative, historical picture of energy in the world economy as reflected in long-term trends in production, foreign trade, and consumption; and in the shifting importance within each of these measures of the different primary energy forms. The heart of the volume presents these indicators in a set of country-by-country statistics as well as regional and worldwide aggregates for the period 1925-65. The surrounding portions of the study provide a descriptive and analytical setting for this material—with selective updating of key data to 1968—as well as the documentation and methodology underlying the statistics.

The study focuses for the most part on primary energy sources (e.g., hard coal or crude oil) rather than energy in its processed or secondary stages (e.g., coke or gasoline). This approach is necessitated by the differing ways in which energy statistics are assembled in the various countries and regions. Because the demand for energy in its end forms and uses is excluded, we shall be little concerned with the processes by which particular primary energy sources are converted into the forms finally consumed. We deal with energy in its aggregate economic setting by looking at measures relating total primary energy demand to overall economic activity, the particular composition of the "energy mix" being less significant in that aggregate context.

The study deals principally with coal, oil, natural gas, and hydroelectricity. Except in passing, it does not cover such energy sources—commonly termed "noncommercial"—as fuelwood, wastes, or the power of draft animals.

It would have been desirable to carry the detailed tabulations beyond 1965. However, the geographic scope of the study as well as publication lags in source materials made this impossible. As noted above, major statistical indicators have been estimated, where possible, for 1968; these are incorporated into a textual review of major findings. The choice of 1925 as the starting year also involved pragmatic considerations: lack of basic data becomes a formidable handicap as one goes back much earlier than this. Also, the further back in time we go, the more widespread becomes the utilization of energy forms, such as fuelwood, not covered here. A longer time span would have made their inclusion imperative; but the estimating problems would have been virtually insurmountable.

Thus, the book is intended to fill a quantitative void in a limited period of twentieth century economic history. That period, however, was one of significant change as regards energy. During these years in many parts of the world there occurred a fundamental shift in primary energy use away from coal toward petroleum. Along with this shift emerged a wholly new degree of reliance on worldwide energy flows as numerous consuming areas (such as Western Europe), which were formerly self-sufficient in energy supplies, began turning to new and distant supply sources (such as the Middle East) to satisfy their fuel requirements. The fact that within a matter of decades the preeminence in world energy output once enjoyed by a country like Great Britain could be matched or exceeded by countries like Venezuela or Kuwait is pointed evidence of this deep-seated transformation. A review of these developments provides the historical backdrop against which contemporary issues of interdependence in world energy supplies can be more readily perceived.

The book should, in addition, assist persons engaged in empirical research having to do with problems of planning and economic development. An intimate connection exists between overall economic growth and primary energy consumption. The quantitative and analytical materials that have been assembled here may help to throw further light on this interrelated process of growth.

Although the preparation of long-term energy projections was not a central purpose of this volume—the subject is treated in a limited fashion—the historical materials presented here should be helpful to those who are engaged in this task. The materials should be useful equally to advanced countries concerned with the adequacy and security of their future fuel supplies, and to less advanced areas in preparing the content and financial requirements of their long-range plans.

Plan of the Book

The volume is divided into the following five parts, of which the extensive tabulations of Part Three constitute the core:

- Part One – Major Trends and Their Significance: A Summary Discussion;
- Part Two – Statistical Profiles: Descriptive Comments, Tables, and Charts Based on the Detailed Data;
- Part Three – Detailed Regional and National Energy Statistics;
- Part Four – Annotated Guide to the Detailed Energy Statistics;
- Part Five – Supplementary Materials (Gross National Product and Energy, Network of World Energy Flows, Bibliographical Suggestions).

As the outline suggests, these five parts become progressively more specialized. Readers who are primarily interested in broad regional trends of world energy consumption, production, and trade, rather than in the underlying statistical detail and its derivation, may wish to concentrate particularly on Parts One and Two. Those who, in addition, are interested in (a) tracing the nature of the basic statistical calculations, (b) adapting the basic data to their own needs, or (c) having on hand a compendium of historical energy statistics for continuing reference, will probably want to examine the content of Parts Three, Four, and Five.

A few remarks will make the distinction among these parts clearer. *Part One* is a summary and interpretive chapter dealing with the major long-term trends in energy consumption, production, and international trade. While heavily dependent on the quantitative materials in ensuing parts of the book, the chapter is essentially a narrative treatment with limited tabular presentations and minimum documentation. While the central statistical portions of the study upon which this chapter draws do not go beyond the year 1965, wherever possible the discussion in Part One considers more recent developments and data, in some cases on the basis of preliminary information.

In *Part Two*, a set of thirty-eight descriptive, tabular, and graphic "profiles" present compressed versions of the much more detailed statistical time series of Part Three. The emphasis in this set of sketches is on broad lines of development and on worldwide and regional aggregates, individual country references being limited in most cases to the principal producing, consuming, and energy-trading countries.

Part Three presents in the form of computer print-out reproductions the detailed statistical series resulting from an elaborate set of machine tabulations. This part of the book is divided into fourteen basic tables, each of which presents national, regional, and worldwide data on some aspect of energy production, trade and bunkering, and consumption during the period 1925-65. Besides aggregates of total energy, separate statistics are given for solid fuels, liquid fuels, natural gas, and hydroelectricity. There are also data on population and on *total* electricity, the only secondary energy form covered in some detail. The statistics are presented in both original physical units (e.g., cubic meters of natural gas) and in a common calorific denominator (metric tons of coal equivalent). Absolute data as well as various derived analytical measures (percentages, ratios, growth rates, per capita figures, etc.) are shown. The regional totals in Part Three are offered in three variants: the first aggregates country data into more or less conventional geographic and/or political groupings and subgroupings, such as total Western Europe, the Common Market, the European Free Trade Association, and "other" Western Europe; at the end of each table, a second regional arrangement presents totals for all non-Communist developed nations, all underdeveloped economies, and the Communist group of nations; following that, a third regional classification scheme divides the world into the Organisation for Economic Cooperation and Development (OECD) grouping, the Communist area, and the rest of the world. These alternative geographic presentations are designed to accommodate a variety of interests and potential uses of the data.

The discussion and notes of *Part Four* serve as a technical back-up to the detailed statistics of Part Three. There are two major sections. The first deals with definitional and conceptual issues, measurement problems and computational procedures, conversion factors, and geographic conventions. The second section comprises a country-by-country listing of sources used in the derivation of the statistics in Part Three.

Part Five of the study presents supplementary statistical materials and analyses not included in the basic tabulations of Part Three. These additional materials, which are drawn on in the discussion of Part One and the profiles of Part Two, include estimates of gross national product and their derivation; a set of energy-GNP regression equations; and matrix tables of world energy flows in physical units and U.S. dollars. In addition, Part Five includes a brief listing of bibliographical suggestions, with special emphasis on recent publications having broad geographic scope and both quantitative and descriptive content.

Some Conceptual, Statistical, and Geographic Ground Rules

In the following paragraphs, we will explain enough of the terminological, geographic, and technical aspects of the assembled energy data to permit the reader to proceed in a reasonably enlightened fashion without the need for frequent forays into the much more detailed explanatory notes of Part Four. These, however, should be consulted by anyone desiring a relatively complete description of the statistical problems involved, and particularly by anyone contemplating extensive adaptation or adoption of the data in Part Three.

Energy Forms Covered

Energy as measured in this study comprises the following primary sources: solid fuels (bituminous coal, anthracite, lignite, and certain minor fuels, including peat); liquid fuels (crude oil and natural gas liquids); natural gas; and hydroelectricity. Nuclear energy—nil or insignificant during the greater part of the period under review—is not considered except in the discussion of future prospects in Part One. Coverage is limited to what are commonly referred to as "commercial" energy sources—so-called because of their dominance in domestic and foreign energy trade and their near-indispensability in modern industrial activity. Such noncommercial energy sources as fuelwood, organic wastes, wind, waterpower (other than for electricity), and the energy of draft animals and human beings are excluded.[1] Some of these noncommercial energy forms remain important in many of the less developed countries, a matter to which we revert from time to time. However, only fragmentary and incomplete data are available concerning these energy sources. The consequence of their omission from the study is to some extent minimized by the very low efficiency with which such fuels are traditionally used.

Measurement of Energy Production, Foreign Trade, and Consumption

For production, only the output of the energy sources at their primary stage is measured. In foreign trade statistics, as well as data on bunkering, primary as well as secondary or processed energy forms (such as coal briquets, diesel fuel, manufactured gas, or thermal electricity) are necessarily included so as to give an accurate measure of total energy consumption.

[1]It has been estimated that in 1956 no more than 1 percent of the world's total (commercial plus noncommercial, animate plus inanimate) energy use represented the physical output of human beings. Organisation for European Economic Cooperation, *Europe's Growing Needs of Energy* (Paris, 1956), p. 13. See *Note* at end of this Introduction.

Accurately defined, energy consumption as used in this study refers to apparent inland consumption of primary energy sources, including, as noted, net imports of secondary as well as primary energy forms. The word "apparent" refers to the fact that inventory accumulation or depletion, which may make an area's actual consumption lower or higher than tabulated, is ignored; and consumption is described as "inland" because fuels absorbed as bunkers for maritime vessels or foreign-bound aircraft are, where possible, excluded from the consumption figures.[2] This procedure seemed to be appropriate for an analysis which relates energy use to an area's gross national product, as in Part One and in Profiles No. 3 and No. 5 of Part Two. Computationally, then,

$$\text{consumption} = \text{production} + \text{imports} - \text{exports} - \text{bunkers}.$$

Conversion of Data into Common Denominator Units of Measurement

The various energy sources are made statistically comparable and additive by converting them to common units based on their respective calorific values. Coal is used as the energy common denominator throughout the study because of widespread international practice rooted in the earlier preeminence of coal, but oil or other energy equivalents could have been used equally well. One metric ton of crude oil contains, on the average, about 1½ times the quantity of British thermal units (Btu's) contained in a metric ton of coal.[3] Therefore, consumption of 1 million tons of oil is expressed as consumption of 1½ million tons coal equivalent.[4]

In the case of the hydroelectric component, we follow the United Nations measurement practice and calculate the coal equivalent of hydroelectricity at the inherent heat value of the electricity generated—i.e., at a

[2]For certain regions (e.g., U.S.S.R.) and years for which bunkers data were not available we were compelled to use a "total consumption" measure. For the world as a whole and for many areas, the addition of bunkers would raise inland consumption by a factor of about 4½ percent in the 1920s and 3 percent in recent years. However, for certain important bunkering areas (e.g., Japan or Egypt while the Suez Canal was in operation), the percentage increase to inland consumption rises considerably.

[3]A Btu is the amount of heat necessary to raise the temperature of one pound of water by 1° Fahrenheit.

[4]Some other equivalents may be noted: at average world specific gravity, 1 metric ton of crude oil = about 7.3 barrels of crude oil; therefore, 1 barrel of crude oil per day = about 50 metric tons of crude oil or 75 metric tons of coal equivalent per year; 1 metric ton of crude oil contains about 41 million Btu's; 1 metric ton of coal contains about 28 million Btu's; 1 cubic meter of natural gas contains about 38,000 Btu's. These are approximate worldwide averages; because of qualitative differences and, in the case of oil, because of variations in specific gravity, these equivalents may vary to some extent from one area to another.

factor of 0.125 metric ton coal equivalent equals 1,000 kwh. This procedure produces some distortion when making energy comparisons between areas having markedly disparate proportions of energy drawn from hydro sources (e.g., Norway vs. the United States). An alternative approach—and one which for certain purposes is preferable—is to convert primary electricity at the prevailing "heat rate" at thermal electric stations (i.e., the amount of boiler fuel needed to generate a given amount of thermal electricity). In 1965 this amounted to approximately 0.40 metric ton of coal per 1,000 kwh (see the discussion under Conversion Factors and Procedures, Part Four). There is no inherently "correct" measurement practice, but for the purposes of our exposition in Part Two (Profiles No. 2 and No. 13) and in Part Three (table XII) we present this alternative formulation. We also refer to it in the discussion of Part One.

While the detailed statistical tables of Part Three present data in original physical units and also in coal equivalents, the summary treatment of these data in Parts One and Two is largely in terms of coal equivalents.

Geographic Classification

On the basis of data collected for as many individual countries or territories as possible, the following regional aggregates were prepared:

- North America
  - Canada
  - United States
- Western Europe
  - European Economic Community
  - European Free Trade Association
  - Western Europe—Other
- Oceania
- U.S.S.R. and Communist Eastern Europe
  - Communist Eastern Europe
  - U.S.S.R.
- Communist Asia
- Latin America
  - Caribbean
    - Caribbean—Oil Producing
    - Caribbean—Other
  - Latin America—Other
- Asia
  - Middle East
    - Middle East—Oil Producing
    - Middle East—Other
  - Far East and Other Asia
- Africa
  - North Africa
  - Tropical Africa
  - South Africa
- World

In the summary discussion and tabulations of Parts One and Two, we do not always show each of these subregions, but only those which underscore the point of the particular presentation. And as explained earlier under the heading "Plan of the Book," in Part Three the foregoing regions are regrouped for analytical purposes into two alternative regional classifications: one distinguishes among developed, underdeveloped, and Communist areas; the other separates the OECD group of countries from the Communist area and the rest of the world.

In order to provide for the continuity and comparability of historical statistical series, pre-World War II data for the present East European Communist countries are aggregated into, and labeled, "Communist Eastern Europe."[5] Similarly, for comparability, numerous nations within Tropical Africa or within Asia have for the most part been grouped throughout the period 1925-65 into regions conforming to their former colonial or other territorial status. This is often the only basis on which their early statistics are published, since in most cases these statistics have not been adjusted to conform to their present national entities. In the case of individual country data available for the entire period, we were generally guided by national frontiers of the year in question, and in a few instances this impairs somewhat the analysis of the time trend for a particular country (though generally not for regions); for example, pre-World War II India includes, while postwar India excludes, data relating to Burma and Pakistan. In each case, the sole basis for the geographic handling of the data was to facilitate description and analysis of long-term trends.

Availability of Unpublished Data by Country and by Years

The tables of Part Three are constructed from data for as many individual countries or territories as could be obtained—about two hundred for recent years. Many of the smaller countries are not represented in the published tables, for the most part because the amounts involved for a given table were nil (or negligible) or the data not available, but also because the available figures were extremely unreliable. Readers interested in obtaining further information about data omissions should write to Resources for the Future.

The tables of Part Three present data only for the following years: 1925, 1929, 1933, 1937, 1938, 1950, 1953, 1955, 1957, and annual figures for 1960-65. However, information on annual data tabulated for the periods 1925-38 and 1949-65 is available from RFF on request.

[5] It was not possible, however, to split off East Germany from the prewar Reich to make this series even more uniform. Nor were we able to construct a completely consistent historical "Communist Asia" series, since separate pre-World War II data were unavailable for North Korea, North Vietnam, and Mongolia.

Terminology

The reader is asked to overlook those numerous occasions when, in order to avoid stylistic monotony, we have been terminologically imprecise. Where we are concerned with broad trends, the term "solid fuels" is used interchangeably with "coal," which is the predominant solid fuel component in most areas. Similarly, "oil" and "liquid fuels" are frequently referred to synonymously, because the latter consists almost wholly of oil and its products except in the few areas where natural gas liquids occur. However, where we wish to single out coal or another solid fuel component from *total* solid fuels, or the crude oil or natural gas liquids portion of *total* liquid fuels, it is so indicated. Energy consumption is referred to interchangeably as energy "use" or "demand." Gross national product (GNP) is referred to as "output" or "national output." Energy "production" and energy "output" are the same. Unless specifically referring to manufactured gas, "gas" is the same as "natural gas." Hydroelectricity receives a variety of labels—"hydro," "waterpower," "hydroelectric power," "hydroelectric energy," or "hydroelectric generation." (Strictly speaking, use of the term "power" should be avoided as it is not the same thing as energy—defined as "the capacity for doing work"—but, rather, the time *rate* at which work is done.)

The reader may find other lapses into murky linguistics but we hope that they and the examples mentioned above will prove to be only a slight nuisance.

NOTE

The dichotomy between commercial and noncommercial energy is admittedly somewhat arbitrary. By solely focusing on commercial energy forms, we may neglect important instances of noncommercial energy consumption in such activities as the use of bagasse in grinding sugar cane, or of locally available firewood in rail and river transportation, and even in electric power generation.

According to rough estimates by the United Nations, as recently as the early 1950s noncommercial energy (in terms of heat content) was more important than the commercial categories in Africa and Asia and nearly as important in South America:

Noncommercial Energy as Percent of Total Energy Consumption

Africa	51%
North America	3
Central America	35
South America	45
Asia	58
Europe	7
Oceania	13
WORLD (non-Communist)	15

Source: United Nations, *Proceedings of the International Conference on the Peaceful Uses of Atomic Energy*, vol. I, *The World's Requirements for Energy* (New York, 1956), pp. 18–20. Communist countries are excluded from the tabulation which comprises fuelwood, vegetal fuels and organic wastes among noncommercial energy; i.e., it excludes wind, water (nonelectric), and animate energy.

In a more recent (though geographically less specific) estimate of the relative importance of the role of noncommercial fuels, the United Nations Economic Commission for Europe finds that, although the noncommercial sources of world energy are slowly declining in importance (representing in 1967 perhaps 4 percent of the worldwide total compared with the 15 percent indicated above for the non-Communist world total in the 1950s), in some countries "as much as 30 or even 50 percent of the total supply of inanimate energy may still be derived from noncommercial fuels." (United Nations, Economic Commission for Europe, *The General Energy Situation in Europe in 1967 and Early 1968 in the Context of Current World Trends*, ST/ECE/Energy/12 [mimeo.], March 3, 1969, p. 5.) A prominent area of noncommercial energy use, for example, is India, where the contribution of cow dung to total energy consumption has variously been estimated as between 32 and 77 percent. (Gunnar Myrdal, *Asian Drama* [Pantheon for Twentieth Century Fund, 1968], vol. I, p. 560.)

One should note that the transformation of subsistence or very low-income economies into progressively more developed and geographically integrated ones typically is accompanied by the replacement of noncommercial by commercial energy. As a result, data on historical changes in energy consumption may present a somewhat misleading picture if the statistical time series only cover (as they do in this volume) commercial energy sources. Specifically, a rapid rate of increase in (measured) commercial energy use may partially reflect a rapid substitution of commercial for (nonmeasured) noncommercial energy. However, the conspicuously low efficiency with which noncommercial fuels are commonly used makes their omission a less serious matter than might be thought.

Part One

MAJOR TRENDS
AND THEIR SIGNIFICANCE:
A SUMMARY DISCUSSION

One

MAJOR TRENDS AND THEIR SIGNIFICANCE: A SUMMARY DISCUSSION

The significance of the contribution to civilization of heat, light, and power—and, hence, of the primary energy resources upon which heat, light, and power are based—is undeniable. Yet, even though primary sources of energy—coal, oil, natural gas, falling water—play an obviously necessary and strategic role in promoting and sustaining economic progress, their inability to achieve that goal without the mobilization of a great many other resources should be equally clear. Availability of cheap and abundant energy within a nation's borders is no more a guarantee of successful development than is its absence a bar to progress. Thus, many countries rich in petroleum resources rank low on the international scale when measured by income; while others—e.g., Denmark, with virtually total dependence on imported fuels—may be among the most prosperous countries in the world. The point need not be labored: for energy-rich countries, the additional provision of other natural resources, of education, technology, and still other endowments constitutes a necessary condition for growth; whereas energy-deficit countries can acquire needed fuel supplies through international trade if their economies possess other resources facilitating development and exports.

However these conditions are met in a particular country, energy consumption and overall economic development go hand in hand. Thus, the major trends in total and per capita energy consumption in different parts of the world since the 1920s reflect, if only approximately, the broader record of economic performance in those geographic regions. We shall now turn to a review of those long-term trends in energy use, deferring to a later section[1] a discussion of their relationship to measures of economic growth in general.

Trends in Total and Per Capita Energy Consumption

The salient features of the statistical story since 1925 are recorded in a set of three summary tabulations (tables 1, 2, and 3) showing, by major world regions, total and per capita energy consumption and percentage growth rates for each of these two indicators. Worldwide energy consumption increased from somewhat under 1½ billion coal equivalent tons in 1925 to nearly 5½ billion tons in 1965, representing a yearly growth rate of around 3⅓ percent. For the post-World War II period (1950-65) growth in total world energy consumption proceeded at the accelerated pace of around 5 percent yearly.

Between 1965 and 1968, when worldwide energy consumption reached an estimated level of 6.3 billion tons, this rapid rate of expansion in world energy use decelerated somewhat, though it was still well in excess of the average growth rate for the four decades as a whole. Moreover, recent slackening in the world energy growth rate was decisively influenced by developments in Mainland China's energy consumption, which has been attributed largely to the internal unrest spurred by the Cultural Revolution. The United Nations Statistical Office figures cited in table 1 apply to Communist Asia as a whole; but Communist China dominates any area-wide statistics. The data show a decline of 70 million tons (or slightly over 20 percent) in the region's energy consumption between 1965 and 1967, with a recovery to the 1965 level barely achieved in 1968. Aside from the effect of the Chinese decline, slower growth in Eastern Europe also contributed to the worldwide deceleration.

With only one exception, all regions shown recorded faster growth in energy consumption during the post-World War II years than for the entire time span. That exception was the Soviet Union, whose post-1950 growth of around 7½ percent per year compares with a 1925-50 rate of 10½ percent and an average of 9 percent for the entire period. Nevertheless, though decelerating in recent years, the Soviet growth rate has persistently exceeded the growth rate for the world as a whole, with the result that the U.S.S.R. share of world-

[1] See pp. 32-40.

Table 1. ENERGY CONSUMPTION, BY MAJOR WORLD REGIONS, SELECTED YEARS, 1925-1968

(All figures based on coal equivalents)

Region	1925	1938	1950	1955	1960	1965	1967	1968
				Million metric tons				
North America	748.9	706.9	1,276.3	1,461.3	1,659.5	2,040.2	2,230	2,359
of which: United States	717.7	669.4	1,201.0	1,370.3	1,550.1	1,881.6	2,055	2,173
Western Europe	517.0	619.2	583.9	748.2	849.5	1,117.2	1,168	1,242
Oceania	15.6	18.1	29.3	37.3	45.8	61.2	67	72
U.S.S.R. & Comm. E. Europe	80.5	244.0	464.1	691.2	934.5	1,255.8	1,376	1,433
U.S.S.R.	25.3	176.3	303.3	461.0	640.6	880.6	989	1,025
Comm. E. Europe[a]	55.1	67.7	160.8	230.2	293.9	375.1	387	408
Communist Asia[a]	23.7	27.3	43.1	98.3	235.3	323.0	255	332
Latin America	24.7	38.7	66.2	105.4	153.5	199.5	224	245
Asia[b]	60.3	112.4	105.8	157.7	247.7	385.1	471	522
Japan	30.5	62.4	45.8	66.5	111.0	188.6	249	280
Other Asia	29.8	50.0	60.0	91.2	136.7	196.5	222	242
Africa	13.9	23.4	42.0	58.8	70.2	92.6	97	102
WORLD	1,484.5	1,790.1	2,610.9	3,358.2	4,196.1	5,474.6	5,888	6,306
				Percentage distribution				
North America	50.4%	39.5%	48.9%	43.5%	39.5%	37.3%	37.9%	37.4%
of which: United States	48.3	37.4	46.0	40.8	36.9	34.4	34.9	34.5
Western Europe	34.8	34.6	22.4	22.3	20.2	20.4	19.8	19.7
Oceania	1.1	1.0	1.1	1.1	1.1	1.1	1.1	1.1
U.S.S.R. & Comm. E. Europe	5.4	13.6	17.8	20.6	22.3	22.9	23.4	22.7
U.S.S.R.	1.7	9.8	11.6	13.7	15.3	16.1	16.8	16.3
Comm. E. Europe[a]	3.7	3.8	6.2	6.9	7.0	6.9	6.6	6.5
Communist Asia[a]	1.6	1.5	1.7	2.9	5.6	5.9	4.3	5.3
Latin America	1.7	2.2	2.5	3.1	3.7	3.6	3.8	3.9
Asia[b]	4.1	6.3	4.1	4.7	5.9	7.0	8.0	8.3
Japan	2.1	3.5	1.8	2.0	2.6	3.4	4.2	4.4
Other Asia	2.0	2.8	2.3	2.7	3.3	3.6	3.8	3.8
Africa	0.9	1.3	1.6	1.8	1.7	1.7	1.6	1.6
WORLD	100.0	100.0	100.0	100.0	100.0	100.0	100.0	100.0

[a]It should be borne in mind that throughout this study pre-World War II data for "Communist Eastern Europe" refer to the present countries of that area with the exception of prewar East Germany which appears (as part of Germany) within Western Europe. Prewar "Communist Asia" refers to Mainland China, while the postwar figures for that region also include North Korea, Mongolia, and (beginning in 1955) North Vietnam.

[b]Throughout this study, unless otherwise specified, "Asia" means non-Communist Asia.

Source: For 1925-65 data, see Part Two, Profile No. 1. Data for 1966-68 are rough estimates derived from United Nations. The latter cites an estimate in *World Energy Supplies*, Series J, nos. 12 and 13 (New York, 1969 and 1970).

Table 2. ENERGY CONSUMPTION PER CAPITA, BY MAJOR WORLD REGIONS, SELECTED YEARS, 1925-1968

(Kilograms coal equivalent)

Region	1925	1938	1950	1955	1960	1965	1967	1968
North America	5,971	4,997	7,686	8,042	8,354	9,524	10,162	10,629
of which: United States	6,196	5,150	7,886	8,258	8,578	9,671	10,333	10,801
Western Europe	1,848	2,035	1,931	2,387	2,602	3,256	3,350	3,543
Oceania	1,721	1,754	2,397	2,703	2,967	3,563	3,727	3,937
U.S.S.R. & Comm. E. Europe	359	899	1,720	2,379	2,987	3,777	4,071	4,191
U.S.S.R.	165	928	1,685	2,350	2,988	3,819	4,197	4,309
Comm. E. Europe	783	832	1,792	2,440	2,985	3,683	3,794	3,920
Communist Asia	54	61	76	158	347	441	338	434
Latin America	252	309	409	569	723	821	872	916
Asia	105	162	131	181	255	354	416	441
Japan	515	885	553	747	1,191	1,926	2,492	2,770
Other Asia	58	80	83	116	156	198	213	224
Africa	100	135	194	241	254	298	299	303
WORLD	785	826	1,042	1,232	1,403	1,668	1,730	1,810

Source: Same as table 1.

Table 3. AVERAGE ANNUAL PERCENTAGE RATES OF CHANGE IN TOTAL AND PER CAPITA ENERGY CONSUMPTION, BY MAJOR WORLD REGIONS, SELECTED PERIODS, 1925-1968

	1925-50	1950-65	1965-68	1925-65	1925-68
			Total energy consumption		
North America	2.2%	3.2%	5.1%	2.5%	2.7%
of which: United States	2.1	3.0	5.0	2.4	2.6
Western Europe	1.0	4.4	3.6	1.9	2.1
Oceania	2.6	5.0	5.6	3.5	3.6
U.S.S.R. & Comm. E. Europe	7.3	6.9	4.5	7.1	6.9
U.S.S.R.	10.4	7.4	5.2	9.3	9.0
Comm. E. Europe	4.4	5.8	2.7	4.9	4.8
Communist Asia	2.4	14.4	0.9	6.7	6.3
Latin America	4.0	7.6	6.9	5.4	5.5
Asia	2.3	9.0	10.5	4.7	5.2
Japan	1.6	9.9	14.1	4.7	5.3
Other Asia	2.8	8.2	6.7	4.8	5.0
Africa	4.5	5.4	3.6	4.8	4.8
WORLD	2.3	5.1	4.8	3.3	3.4
			Per capita energy consumption		
North America	1.0%	1.4%	3.8%	1.2%	1.4%
of which: United States	1.0	1.4	3.8	1.1	1.3
Western Europe	0.2	3.5	2.8	1.4	1.5
Oceania	1.3	2.7	3.4	1.8	1.9
U.S.S.R. & Comm. E. Europe	6.5	5.4	3.5	6.1	5.9
U.S.S.R.	9.7	5.6	4.1	8.2	7.9
Comm. E. Europe	3.4	4.9	1.9	3.9	3.8
Communist Asia	1.4	12.5	-0.5	5.4	5.0
Latin America	2.0	4.8	3.6	3.0	3.0
Asia	0.9	6.8	7.4	3.1	3.4
Japan	0.3	8.7	12.9	3.4	4.0
Other Asia	1.4	6.0	3.7	3.1	3.2
Africa	2.7	2.9	0.9	2.8	2.6
WORLD	1.1	3.2	2.8	1.9	2.0

Source: Same as table 1.

wide energy consumption has risen steadily. This development is one of the striking trends recorded in our statistics. The Soviet Union's share of world energy consumption stood at little over 1½ percent in 1925; just before World War II it was up to 10 percent; and from its early postwar share of 12 percent in 1950, it rose to around 16 percent in 1968. For the Communist group of nations as a whole—Eastern Europe and Communist Asia also raised their world energy share over the long run—the increase was from 7 percent in 1925 to 29 percent in recent years.

Rising shares also occurred elsewhere in the world: Latin America, Africa, and Asia all exhibit long-term increases in their relative world standing. The postwar rise of Asia reflects in part the growing share of the region's developing countries; but to an even greater extent it reflects the phenomenal momentum of energy growth in Japan, whose annual postwar growth rates of 10 to 15 percent have been sustained to the most recent years for which figures are available.

Offsetting these long-term increases in regional shares of worldwide energy consumption has been the declining relative position of North America and Western Europe. In the case of North America, although it retains its leading world share (with the United States occupying the top-ranking country share), that region's proportion of world energy consumption went down from approximately half in 1925 to 37 percent in 1968. Western Europe's decline was from 35 percent in 1925 to 20 percent in 1968.

These distributional shifts in total energy were also accompanied by disparate trends in the growth of per capita energy consumption. Virtually every region of the world has exceeded—in some cases, by a substantial margin—the per capita energy growth of North America and Western Europe, both over the four-decade time span and during the briefer post-World War II period. (North America's accelerated growth rate since 1965 represents a departure from these longer-run trends; but nothing conclusive can be said on the basis of the few additional years.) Nevertheless, while narrowing, regional gaps in per capita energy use remain strikingly wide. In 1968, North America's per capita energy consumption of close to 11,000 kgs coal equivalent was nearly 2½ times larger than that of the Soviet Union (the next ranking area); while the latter, in turn, had a per capita level of energy consumption which was roughly 10 percent above that in Communist Eastern Europe (as well as in Oceania) and

20 percent above that in Western Europe.[2] And the more extreme disparity is reflected in the fact that North American per capita consumption was between forty to fifty times the levels prevailing in Africa and the developing portions of Asia.

If North America's level of per capita energy consumption in 1925 (about 6,000 kgs) had remained unchanged throughout the period, it would still have been some 40 to 50 percent above the next highest region tabulated for the year 1968. A simple computational exercise—one meant to illustrate rather than to forecast—dramatizes these regional trends and disparities. It would take another decade at per capita energy growth of at least 10 percent annually even for a booming Japan to reach North America's *1925* per capita level of consumption. It would take Africa sixty years and an annual per capita growth rate of at least 5 percent—a probably ambitious target—to achieve North America's figure of over four decades ago. Given energy's close—though not fixed and unvarying—relationship to economic development in general (see pp. 32-40), a lag in energy consumption, such as that illustrated for Africa, is yet another sign that substantial improvement in living standards will be difficult.

Interfuel Shifts in Energy Consumption: The Quantitative Picture

Energy consumption cannot be treated in just an aggregative (and in some ways abstract) fashion. Not only does such an aggregation obscure fundamental shifts—of interest in themselves—among the different energy sources, but the size and growth of total energy use is, in fact, affected by the changing role of these different fuels as their individual properties are exploited: for the creation of new products and industries, for the realization of greater efficiency and convenience in use, and, through such changes, for the attainment of higher levels of national well-being. More basic still is the fact that the complexion of different periods of economic history may frequently bear a distinct relationship to the emergence of specific energy sources and forms. The early preeminence of the British iron and steel industry—indeed, the character of the Industrial Revolution as a whole—was closely tied to coal. Early industry in the United States was tied to the location of falling water as a direct source of mechanical energy. Subsequently the development of electricity as a commercial energy form and its distribution to electric motors mounted on industrial machines revolutionized the organization of the factory system. Lighting, first from lamps and then from electricity, was a factor of no small importance in the spread of literacy in the United States and other countries. And who would deny the pervasive influence of the Automotive Age and the fact that its emergence has proceeded hand in hand with the growth of the world petroleum industry?

Looking to the future, atomic fission (and perhaps fusion) may well turn out to be the most profound and enduring scientific development to affect the world of energy during the second half of the twentieth century; and before the year 2000, nuclear energy in a variety of applications (not just as a source of electricity) could take its place as an essential element in new levels and forms of economic activity. Thus far, however, except for radiation and the application of radioisotopes, the civilian use of nuclear energy remains confined to the generation of electricity via thermal processes in large-scale central stations and, even so, is quantitatively slight or nonexistent throughout most of the world.

In terms of commercial energy sources in actual use to date, the major transformation on the twentieth century world energy scene concerns the far-reaching distributional shifts among the different primary energy forms (leaving to one side the emergence of electric energy—a secondary form of the primary sources). Specifically, we refer to the marked long-term decline of solid fuels concurrent with the rising importance of oil and natural gas. Hydroelectricity, though also assuming a greater relative role in energy production over the years, remains nonetheless of minor importance on a worldwide basis.

These historic shifts are shown in table 4. In 1925 coal's 83 percent share of energy consumption had already slipped from the 95 percent level it had reached at the turn of the century, but this share was still preeminent among the four primary commercial energy categories—coal, oil, gas, and hydro—surveyed here.[3] During the ensuing four decades, coal's share dropped steadily until by 1968 it represented only 37 percent of world energy consumption; the greatest slippage took place after World War II. In absolute terms, worldwide solid fuel use *did* increase—by a little over one billion tons between 1925 and 1968; even so, neither for the period as a whole nor for the years since 1950 was this increase markedly higher than worldwide population

[2] Energy consumption comparisons between Communist and non-Communist areas are slightly distorted because the latter exclude energy use for bunkers, while the former (for want of information permitting an "inland" consumption measure) include bunkers. If bunkers figured proportionately to the same degree in Russia as in, say, Western Europe, the Soviet level of total and per capita energy consumption might be overstated by perhaps 5 percent—not sufficient to alter the main thrust of the text observations.

[3] The 1900 estimate comes from P. C. Putnam, *Energy in the Future* (Van Nostrand, 1953), pp. 439-40. It should be noted that in 1900, fuelwood—deducted for purposes of this calculation—is estimated by Putnam to have been far more important than consumption of oil, gas, and hydro taken together.

Table 4. WORLD ENERGY CONSUMPTION, BY SOURCE, SELECTED YEARS, 1925-1968

	1925	1938	1950	1955	1960	1965	1967	1968
	Million metric tons coal equivalent							
Solid fuels	1,230.0	1,291.8	1,593.2	1,816.6	1,998.5	2,290.8	2,209	2,315
Liquid fuels	196.7	375.8	722.2	1,092.7	1,499.0	2,159.1	2,489	2,702
Natural gas	47.9	99.7	252.1	389.6	612.6	912.1	1,064	1,157
Hydroelectricity	9.8	22.8	43.4	59.2	86.0	112.6	126	132
Total	1,484.5	1,790.1	2,610.9	3,358.2	4,196.1	5,474.6	5,888	6,306
	Percentage distribution							
Solid fuels	82.9%	72.2%	61.0%	54.1%	47.6%	41.8%	37.5%	36.7%
Liquid fuels	13.3	21.0	27.7	32.5	35.7	39.4	42.3	42.8
Natural gas	3.2	5.6	9.7	11.6	14.6	16.7	18.1	18.3
Hydroelectricity	0.7	1.3	1.7	1.8	2.0	2.1	2.1	2.1
Total	100.0	100.0	100.0	100.0	100.0	100.0	100.0	100.0

Average annual percentage rates of change

	1925-50	1950-65	1965-68	1925-65	1925-68
Solid fuels	1.0%	2.5%	0.4%	1.3%	1.5%
Liquid fuels	5.3	7.6	7.8	6.2	6.3
Natural gas	6.9	9.0	8.3	7.6	7.7
Hydroelectricity	6.0	6.6	5.4	6.3	6.2
Total	2.3	5.1	4.8	3.3	3.4

Note: As explained in the Introduction (see page 3), the nuclear contribution to total energy is excluded from the statistics except in the case of projections (tables 18-20). The nuclear portion amounted to 6 million coal equivalent tons in 1968, so that its inclusion above would increase world energy consumption to 6,312 million metric tons—that is, by less than 0.1 percent.

Source: For 1925-65 data, see Part Two, Profile No. 2; 1967 and 1968 figures as described in table 1.

Table 5. PER CAPITA ENERGY CONSUMPTION, BY SOURCE AND MAJOR REGION, 1925 AND 1968

(Kilograms coal equivalent)

Region	Solid fuels		Liquid fuels		Natural gas		Hydro-electricity		Total energy	
	1925	1968	1925	1968	1925	1968	1925	1968	1925	1968
North America	4,448	2,329	1,129	4,636	358	3,465	36	198	5,971	10,629
of which: United States	4,597	2,446	1,190	4,648	384	3,564	31	144	6,196	10,801
Western Europe	1,774	1,326	59	1,928	-	165	13	123	1,848	3,543
Oceania	1,594	1,914	119	1,914	-	-	9	109	1,721	3,937
U.S.S.R. & Comm. E. Europe	298	2,226	55	1,170	6	755	-	41	359	4,191
U.S.S.R.	107	1,858	56	1,421	1	975	-	55	165	4,309
Comm. E. Europe	714	3,065	51	596	17	250	1	10	783	3,920
Communist Asia	51	399	3	31	-	-	-	4	54	434
Latin America	95	60	143	647	11	176	4	34	252	916
Asia	87	134	15	274	1	20	2	13	105	441
Japan	476	772	23	1,860	1	40	16	99	515	2,770
Other Asia	43	75	14	126	1	18	-	5	58	224
Africa	92	166	8	125	-	6	-	6	100	303
WORLD	651	664	104	775	25	332	5	38	785	1,810

Source: Data for 1925 derived from Part Three, tables X and XII; data for 1968 same as table 1 above.

growth. As a result, the worldwide per capita level of coal consumption has changed little over the years (see table 5), while for such key energy-consuming areas as North America and Western Europe it has gone down.

Collateral to the declining relative importance of solid fuels, each of the other energy sources—liquid fuels, natural gas, and hydroelectricity—has significantly and progressively raised its share of worldwide energy consumption, as indicated in table 4. Liquid fuels had by 1968 come to occupy the leading place among the energy sources, with a share of 43 percent of world energy consumption, compared with 13 percent in 1925. Incrementally, liquid fuels accounted for over half of the expansion in worldwide energy consumption over this period. Consumption of natural gas went up even more rapidly than that of oil, its long-term annual growth rate of somewhat over 7½ percent per year contrasting with a rate of slightly over 6 percent for liquid fuels. Natural gas accounted for a mere 3 percent of world energy consumption in 1925; by 1950, its share had risen to 10 percent; and by 1968, to 18 percent. Hydro consumption rose as fast as oil over the long run, but its 2 percent share of world energy use in 1968 makes it a minor factor in a global context. Moreover, in recent years the hydro share has shown signs of leveling off as sites available for ready exploitation become fewer; this is especially apparent in parts of the world that have traditionally been in the forefront of waterpower development.

Although the direction of historic shifts in the patterns of fuel consumption in particular regions has paralleled shifts for the world as a whole, the quantitative extent of these regional shifts has varied a good deal. This is clear from table 6, showing for 1925 and 1968 the composition, by energy source, of each principal area's total energy consumption. The lower panel of the table shows, in addition, the geographic distribution of world consumption for each of the four energy categories.

With only one exception, each area shown has reduced the proportion of solids in its energy balance, while increasing the share of liquids, natural gas, and hydropower. The exception relates to the place of oil in Soviet energy consumption, that percentage share having declined very slightly between 1925 and 1968—from 34 to 33 percent. Actually, the role of oil in Soviet energy followed an uneven course (as the more detailed time series of Profile No. 11 in Part Two reveals): the share dropped between the mid-1920s and 1950, reaching 20 percent in that year, after which it rose markedly.[4] Moreover, it should be noted that the role of oil in the Soviet energy balance had already been strikingly high in 1925—the highest recorded, in fact, among all world regions save Latin America.

[4]Part of the explanation is that solid fuels were entering the Soviet commercial energy stream at a rapid pace after 1925, largely in replacement of fuelwood. See U.S. Bureau of the Census, *The Soviet Mineral-Fuel Industries, 1928-1958: A Statistical Survey*, by D. B. Shimkin. International Population Statistics Reports, Series P-90, no. 19 (U.S. Government Printing Office, 1962), pp. 2, 5.

Table 6. WORLD ENERGY CONSUMPTION, BY SOURCE AND MAJOR REGION, 1925 AND 1968

Region	Solid fuels		Liquid fuels		Natural gas		Hydroelectricity	
	1925	1968	1925	1968	1925	1968	1925	1968
	As percent of each area's total energy consumption							
North America	74.5%	21.9%	18.9%	43.6%	6.0%	32.6%	0.6%	1.9%
of which: United States	74.2	22.6	19.2	43.0	6.2	33.0	0.5	1.3
Western Europe	96.0	37.3	3.2	54.3	-	4.7	0.7	3.5
Oceania	92.6	48.6	6.9	48.6	-	-	0.5	2.8
U.S.S.R. & Comm. E. Europe	82.9	53.1	15.2	27.9	1.7	18.0	0.1	1.0
U.S.S.R.	64.9	43.1	34.2	33.0	0.7	22.6	0.1	1.3
Comm. E. Europe	91.2	78.2	6.5	15.2	2.2	6.4	0.1	0.2
Communist Asia	94.0	91.9	6.0	7.2	-	-	-	0.9
Latin America	37.6	6.5	56.6	70.6	4.2	19.2	1.6	3.7
Asia	83.1	30.5	14.4	62.1	0.8	4.6	1.7	2.9
Japan	92.4	27.9	4.4	67.1	0.1	1.4	3.1	3.6
Other Asia	73.7	33.5	24.6	56.2	1.5	8.3	0.2	2.1
Africa	91.6	54.9	8.3	41.2	-	2.0	0.1	2.0
WORLD	82.9	36.7	13.3	42.8	3.2	18.3	0.7	2.1
	As percent of world consumption of each energy source							
North America	45.4%	22.3%	71.9%	38.1%	93.9%	66.5%	45.0%	33.3%
of which: United States	43.3	21.3	69.9	34.6	92.6	62.0	34.0	22.0
Western Europe	40.4	20.1	8.5	25.0	-	5.0	39.2	32.6
Oceania	1.2	1.5	0.5	1.3	-	-	0.8	1.5
U.S.S.R. & Comm. E. Europe	5.4	32.9	6.2	14.8	2.9	22.3	0.8	10.6
U.S.S.R.	1.3	19.1	4.4	12.5	0.4	20.1	0.3	9.8
Comm. E. Europe	4.1	13.8	1.8	2.3	2.5	2.2	0.4	0.8
Communist Asia	1.8	13.2	0.7	0.9	-	-	-	2.3
Latin America	0.8	0.7	7.1	6.4	2.1	4.1	4.0	6.8
Asia	4.1	6.9	4.4	12.0	1.0	2.1	10.1	11.4
Japan	2.3	3.4	0.7	7.0	0.1	0.3	9.7	7.6
Other Asia	1.8	3.5	3.7	5.0	0.9	1.7	0.5	3.8
Africa	1.0	2.4	0.6	1.6	-	0.2	0.1	1.5
WORLD	100.0	100.0	100.0	100.0	100.0	100.0	100.0	100.0
WORLD (mill. tons coal equiv.)	(1,230.0)	(2,315.0)	(196.7)	(2,702.0)	(47.9)	(1,157.0)	(9.8)	(132.0)

Source: For 1925 figures, see Part Two, Profile No. 9. Data for 1968 as in table 1 above.

Table 6 discloses substantial variability in changing regional energy patterns. To point this up, consider the percentage share of coal in the energy consumption of different regions in 1925 in comparison with the percentages prevailing in 1968. In 1925, as noted earlier, coal contributed 83 percent to worldwide energy consumption. The corresponding regional shares of coal in total energy were rather narrowly dispersed around this figure. With the conspicuous exception of Latin America (whose 38 percent coal share reflected the Caribbean area's early prominence in world oil), these regional coal shares ranged from 65 percent in the U.S.S.R. to 96 percent in Western Europe. By 1968, the worldwide average of 37 percent was accompanied by shares ranging from over 90 percent in Communist Asia and of nearly 80 percent in Communist Eastern Europe—where coal displayed remarkable staying power—to as little as 22 percent in North America, not to mention the uncommonly low share of 6½ percent for total Latin America. The point is that in the 1920s choices as to alternative fuel sources were severely circumscribed, coal being the only widely available energy resource and the one, consequently, around which most energy-using activities and industries were organized. All this has obviously changed over the years as discoveries of reserves of other fuels and associated developments in transporting them have widened the choice of fuels available to satisfy the requirements of different areas. Of course, these changes have also resulted from, and been influenced by, the rapid growth of economic activities essentially captive to a given fuel (e.g., automotive transport), and from the substitution of other energy sources for coal in its traditional markets such as railroad transportation and residences. This is especially true in the United States but in recent years has become common in Western Europe and other parts of the world. Even though automotive transport in particular is captive to liquid fuels, there can be little doubt that on an overall basis the circumstances underlying interfuel patterns were much more flexible in the 1960s than they had been in the 1920s.

Just as regional reliance on coal has declined in varying degrees, so has each region's dependence on oil, gas, and hydro risen in different degrees of importance. In oil, drastic long-term changes were recorded by Western Europe (up from 3 percent of total energy consumption in 1925 to 54 percent in 1968) and Japan (up from 4 to 67 percent). By comparison, the rising contribution of liquid fuels to North American energy consumption (up from somewhat under 20 percent in 1925 to a bit short of 45 percent in 1968) was, in relative terms, not quite as dramatic, though very large in an absolute sense. Indeed, the absolute rise in North American liquid fuels consumption between 1925 and 1968 (nearly 900 million tons coal equivalent or roughly 600 million tons of oil) is nearly twice the volume of liquid fuels consumed in Western Europe and Japan combined in recent years.

In natural gas, by 1968 only three areas were drawing on this fuel for significant portions of their total energy requirements: these were North America, where use of gas in total energy went up from 6 percent in 1925 to over 30 percent in 1968; the U.S.S.R., with an increase from under 1 percent to 23 percent (and representing an average annual long-term growth rate of nearly 20 percent—see Part Two, Profile No. 8); and Latin America, from 4 to 20 percent. Together, the United States and the U.S.S.R. have in recent years accounted for over 80 percent of the world's natural gas consumption.

As noted earlier, the hydroelectric portion of energy consumption remains relatively insignificant in most regions even though, in particular countries, the shares prevailing in recent years stayed high. For example, for Norway the 1965 share was 44 percent; for Switzerland, 18 percent; Sweden and New Zealand, 16 percent; and Canada, 9 percent.[5] In recent years, the hydroelectric shares of total energy consumption have tended to rise noticeably in the less developed regions of the world. In the most industrialized areas they have become more or less stable, and in the case of Japan the share has actually declined steadily for over a decade.

Changes in the geographic distribution of worldwide coal, oil, gas, and hydro consumption (shown in the lower panel of table 6) reflect differences in regional growth rates in total energy consumption and the changing shares of the different fuels in that total from one region to another. One notable development revealed by these figures is that what was earlier seen to be the case with energy consumption in the aggregate (see table 1, above) also holds for each of the primary energy forms: that is, the marked reduction in the North American (essentially the United States) proportion of world consumption and the conspicuous increase in the share accounted for by the U.S.S.R. The North American drop was particularly sharp in the case of solid fuels, from 45 percent to 22 percent; and in the case of liquid fuels, down from 72 percent to less than 40 percent. The Soviet surge was most notable in coal and natural gas, each of whose shares started near zero forty years ago and reached 20 percent of the respective world totals by 1968. Note that for liquid fuels, gas, and hydro, North America's falling world share occurred in spite of the increasing relative contribution each of these energy sources was making to North American energy consumption. The reason lies in the fact that North American energy consumption as a whole grew less rapidly than

[5] See Part Two, Profile No. 13. The alternative way of calculating the coal equivalent of hydroelectricity (discussed in the Introduction) would raise these percentages considerably higher.

that for the world—2.7 compared with 3.4 percent annually—and that in the case of oil and gas on a worldwide basis, the relative contribution of each to total energy consumption advanced more sharply than in North America.

Several other long-term trends are observable in the bottom panel of table 6. Western Europe experienced a sizable long-term decline in its share of world coal consumption; along with a more modest reduction of the region's share of world hydroelectric power consumption, this was sufficient to reduce substantially Western Europe's share of world energy consumption in the aggregate (seen in table 1 to have gone from 35 percent in 1925 to 20 percent in 1968), in spite of the fact that the area recorded a striking increase in its share of world petroleum consumption. The Eastern European group of countries and Communist Asia each accounted for markedly higher percentages of world solid fuel consumption. A rising share of world liquid fuels consumption in Asia, particularly Japan, also was a notable development.

Interfuel Shifts in Energy Consumption: Some Underlying Factors

In what has been essentially a factual review, the preceding paragraphs have examined the long-term quantitative shifts in the relative contribution of the different primary fuels to total energy consumption. In spite of the regional exceptions noted, the basic historical story is that of the declining position of coal and the ascendancy of oil and natural gas. If one were to try and account for the many underlying forces that have helped shape or have prominently figured in this long-term transformation, it would entail analysis going well beyond the confines of this summary discussion. In the rundown that follows, therefore, only a few of the more readily apparent causal factors will be touched upon.

As we indicated when summarizing the statistical picture, coal in the mid-1920s was still the principal commercial energy source. In some places in the world and in some uses this supremacy in the world fuel and power base was, it is true, already being noticeably challenged. By and large, however, coal was in most regions the dominant fuel in most sectors of economic life—households, industry, and transport and commerce. Nowhere except in Latin America did it occupy less than a 65 percent share of total energy consumption.[6] Among the circumstances supporting coal's position in the 1920s was the continued use of the steam locomotive; railroad dieselization lay ahead. In waterborne transport, coal-burning steamships were still commonplace, though they were beginning to be displaced by oil-fired vessels. Coal was the preponderant fuel in thermal electricity generation. And among the primary commercial fuels coal had a virtually complete grip on space heating. Automotive transport was growing rapidly in North America, but worldwide its use of motor gasoline made only modest inroads into coal's dominant energy share.

Although the pace and extent of the ensuing changes were to vary from one part of the world to another, all these conditions favorable to coal were to erode substantially in the following four decades. A clear manifestation of these changes was the disproportionately fast growth of economic activities, industries, and technological processes oriented to the use of the emergent energy forms. Automotive transport, railroad dieselization, oil and natural gas heating, petrochemicals, are examples. Fundamental to the shifts in primary energy consumption were the more advantageous physical properties of oil and gas (compared with solid fuels) and the impact on changing relative fuel prices of major discoveries of oil and gas and of the development of the necessary transportation techniques and facilities. We shall note a few of the changing supply-side characteristics of the different fuels, and then speculate about some of the ways in which patterns of interfuel substitution or the growth of different economic activities contributed to the observed shifts.

The convenience of distinguishing between supply effects, on the one hand, and demand effects, on the other, is not meant to underemphasize the role of *interacting* forces at work. The development of motor transport in the twentieth century forms one leading historical example of a new industry responding to but also stimulating the growth of a new energy source.

Growth of Oil and Gas Supplies

World crude oil supplies were being boosted by major new supply sources. (The broader topic of how long-term trends in the location of world energy output contrast with trends in the major location of consumption will be taken up in the next section, beginning on page 20.) It is appropriate to underscore the comparatively recent nature of this development. Six of the world's ten leading oil-producing countries in 1968 had virtually no recorded output in 1925. Many of the bigger Middle Eastern oil discoveries date only from the late 1930s or beyond. Although a handful of countries (principally the United States, Venezuela, and the Soviet Union) were prominent in world oil production in the early years, it was only with the pervasive impact of oil supplies surging from the newer oil fields after World War II that established fuel patterns began their widespread change. With respect to natural gas, enormous expansion of output took place in North America and in Soviet Russia—

[6] Oil from the Caribbean was responsible for coal's 38 percent share of total energy consumed by Latin America as a whole. This share was regionally unequally divided, however, with the Caribbean area's coal-energy share amounting to around one-fifth and the rest of Latin America to over 50 percent.

much of it, especially in the U.S.S.R., occurring after World War II. As to Western Europe's onshore and offshore natural gas production, in the late 1960s this had still to produce a sizable dent in established energy consumption patterns, having got started only during the past decade.

Advantages of Oil and Gas

This growing abundance of oil and natural gas presented energy users with fuels having a number of highly desirable properties. Oil offered outstanding advantages in transportability. Since a ton of oil combined the dual virtue of possessing less volume than a ton of coal while yielding 50 percent more energy, the ton-mile cost of moving energy in the form of oil tended in general to fall substantially below that of coal. (See remarks below on transport.) Due to its form, it could be conveniently handled in loading, unloading, and storage; it was far less subject to damage in transit than coal. It burned more cleanly and in a more controllable fashion than coal; and in numerous applications its thermal efficiency was higher. Many of the desirable features of oil held as well, and sometimes better, for natural gas: especially the factors of cleanliness, ease of use, and–when compared with manufactured gas, which it began to replace–high calorific value relative to volume; a nonpollutant, it promises to offer newly valued advantages.

The alternative energy costs cited relate to volumes and distances for the respective fuels and modes of transport which tend to depict each category in an optimum light. For example, coal by rail and oil by large tanker relate in the table to distances of 1,500 to 2,000 miles, which, especially in the case of oil, reflect a more advantageous scale than very much shorter distances would. The choice of distance as a basis for making standardized comparisons is critical because the point at which economies of scale become operative differs according to the fuel and mode of transport. As an extreme example, truck transport–prohibitively costly over long distances–would be cheaper for short hauls than any mode of transport shown in the table. However, short hauls have little effect on the international aspects of energy transport with which this study mainly deals.

Thus, however approximately, table 7 conveys the changing cost relationships of alternative transport modes at points in time some two decades apart. Note, for example, the sharply improved competitiveness of natural gas pipeline transmission relative to rail shipments of coal. The two means of transport were essentially equal in cost in the latter part of the 1930s; by the mid-1950s, natural gas transport costs had fallen to less than half those of coal. Marked relative improvement had also occurred in charges for oil-pipeline shipments.

The pre- and post-World War II comparison suggests that the disparity between ocean-transport costs for oil,

Table 7. PRE- AND POST-WORLD WAR II ENERGY TRANSPORT-COST COMPARISON

Fuel	Transport means	Prewar (about 1937) Index numbers (coal by rail = 100)	Postwar (about 1955) Index numbers (coal by rail = 100)	Postwar (about 1955) Cost (cents per coal-equiv. met. ton/100 mi.)
Oil	tanker	8	7	5.6¢
Oil	pipeline	23	15	11.2
Coal	collier	28	37	27.5
Coal	rail	100	100	75.0
Natural gas	pipeline	100	46	34.4

Source: Prewar data adapted from U.S. Department of State, *Energy Resources of the World* (U.S. Government Printing Office, 1949), p. 26; postwar data from John Davis, *Canadian Energy Prospects*, Royal Commission on Canada's Economic Prospects (Ottawa: Queen's Printer, 1957), p. 348. The data above are midpoints based on ranges shown in the indicated sources. The prewar data are not identified as to the region to which they apply (although the author's discussion suggests that they relate mostly to U.S. experience). The postwar data refer to actual or hypothetical energy-cost alternatives in Canada; the last column being expressed in Canadian cents per short ton.

Energy Transport Development

The rapid extension of oil and gas pipeline networks with progressively larger diameters and the ever-increasing size of oil tankers, culminating in recent years in the arrival of the super-tanker of several hundred thousand deadweight capacity, are all parts of the energy transport story. Some illustrative cost statistics reflecting a few of these developments, pre- and post-World War II in the United States and Canada, are shown in table 7.

on the one hand, and those for coal, on the other, have remained wide–perhaps even have widened. However, there were sharp annual fluctuations in ocean freight rates in the early and mid-1950s, which were by no means always parallel as between the two fuels,[7] and it is likely that if one could construct a more "representative period average" (an impossibility given the nature of

[7] See the time series on ocean freight rates published periodically in the United Nations' *Statistical Yearbook*.

the data), a narrower gap might be indicated. In any case, based on freight charges on two common sea routes—but different from those in the table—a still more recent transport-cost comparison[8] shows the cost (per unit of energy content per mile) of hauling coal to North Sea ports of Western Europe from the U.S. East Coast to be a bit under twice the cost of shipping oil from Mediterranean ports to the same delivery area.[9] Though still significant, this disparity was considerably narrower than the fivefold gap indicated in the table for earlier in the postwar period.

In this connection, we should recognize that many significant developments have been taking place in the field of energy transport in more recent years. With transport costs a significant proportion of the price of delivered energy, these developments will continue to influence the relative price position of the different energy sources. In coal, for example, witness the development of the "unit train," shuttling exclusively and on a prescribed schedule between a fixed coal mine and fixed terminal point (generally an electric utility). By lowering rolling stock idling time and spreading fixed costs over the maximum number of annual ton-miles, this innovation is serving to improve or restore a degree of competitiveness for coal, especially in thermal electric generation.

Another notable development is the growing size of ocean vessels. In the international coal trade, a continuing trend toward larger-sized, lower unit-cost bulk cargo vessels has lowered the cost of ocean transport during the last decade and contributed to the competitive advantage of U.S. coal in foreign markets.[10] More dramatic still is the emergence in world oil movements of super-tankers whose size ranges upward to 300,000 deadweight tons. Around the mid-1950s the world's tankship fleet averaged about 16,000 dwt per tanker, while vessels then under construction averaged about 29,000 dwt. About a decade later, the average in service had risen to 29,000 dwt; those on order averaged 60,000 dwt and ranged up to well over the 200,000 dwt mark.[11] With scale economies in construction costs, increasing size of ships has meant falling capital costs per unit of oil carried—to the point where overall transport costs on the long Cape of Good Hope route from the Middle East to Western Europe can begin to compete with freight costs formerly incurred on the much shorter Suez Canal route.

Declining Competitiveness of Coal

On balance, as a result of evolving supply conditions at both the extractive and transport stages, an earlier cost advantage of coal relative to oil appears to have receded in many areas. With respect to Western Europe, where coal's preeminence endured well into the post-World War II years, an analysis published in 1966 stated: "The one plain conclusion to be drawn . . . is that at present prices, including taxes, fuel oil is competitive with indigenous or imported coal in the greater part of OECD Europe. This is already clear when comparing prices per unit of heat content; it becomes even more obvious if allowance is made for differences in the efficiency of utilisation. It is probably also the case that natural gas from indigenous sources is highly competitive in most of the region."[12]

In the case of Europe, one factor is especially relevant. The area's coal mining, particularly in comparison with mining in the United States, has increasingly drawn upon high-cost marginal deposits and, in addition, is rather lagging in degree of mechanization. The U.S. experience in coal has been one of rapid productivity improvement, only relatively modest advances in unit labor costs, and retention of competitive standing in export markets[13] and domestic utility use. In Europe, by contrast, strong wage pressures have not been sufficiently offset by productivity advances to maintain coal's competitive attractiveness. In Western Europe, moreover, the competitive weakness of coal has been compounded by the industry's more traditional style of behavior in the marketplace (e.g., poor marketing, inflexible pricing); by its long history of poor labor relations; because of a fragmented production-supply situation (compared with oil, where the producers also market most of their products and own a good deal of the transport facilities in between); and because of the burden of historically negotiated freight rates.

Efforts to mitigate coal's decline—often undertaken under political pressure—have taken the form of fuel

[8] Organisation for Economic Cooperation and Development, *Energy Policy* (Paris, 1966), p. 68.

[9] The cost disparity will vary depending on different assumptions regarding tanker and collier sizes. The comparison in the text assumes a 77,000-deadweight-ton tanker and a 35,000-deadweight-ton collier.

[10] See U.S. Bureau of Mines, *International Coal Trade*, February 1966, pp. 12-13. It is possible that the remaining and substantial disparity between coal and oil transportation costs (see table 7 and the accompanying discussion, above) could shrink further if coal shippers were to adopt the scale and efficiency attained by tankers.

[11] Data from Sun Oil Company, Economics Department, *Analysis of World Tank Ship Fleet, December 31, 1966* (Philadelphia, 1967).

[12] OECD, *Energy Policy*, p. 54.

[13] The competitive advantage of American coal in Western Europe, in the judgment of M. A. Adelman, could be more significant still were railroad freight rates in the United States reduced. The rigidity of these rates is ascribed to monopolistic pricing and the recognition that a substantial part of U.S. coal exports to Europe represents metallurgical coal, which is not easily substitutable. Adelman argues, however, that without some softening of the price a search for alternative technological processes will curb the European market for U.S. coking coal. "American Coal in Western Europe," *Journal of Industrial Economics*, June 1966, pp. 210-11.

import tariffs and other forms of government subsidization. And government-assisted rationalization measures directed at closing the less profitable mines, while to some extent successful at stimulating faster productivity *growth rates* in coal mining (e.g., in West Germany), nonetheless have to cope with productivity *levels* which are conspicuously below those in the United States. The uneconomical status of West European coal is paralleled in Japan. And, despite a still high share of coal in total energy consumption, some East European Communist countries—particularly Hungary and Czechoslovakia—are significantly plagued by unproductive undertakings.

As a result of supply-side factors such as those briefly described, fuel consumption patterns have shifted along lines indicated earlier. Two sorts of situations might loosely be distinguished in characterizing these shifts in the demand for the respective primary energy sources: first, changing primary interfuel patterns arising from *substitution* among different energy sources; and second, the results of *changing industrial structure*. In addition to being interrelated, both situations are associated to some degree with developments in the efficiency with which energy is used.

Substitution

In the case of substitution, even if the composition of national output of goods and services were to remain unchanged, the pattern of fuel use would change in response to factors such as relative price, technological considerations, or such intangibles as convenience. Replacement of coal by oil in railroad locomotives and in ships' boilers, or by oil or gas in residential or industrial heating, are examples. Substitution, it is seen, could bring about changes in primary fuel patterns as a result of a switch from direct use of a primary energy source (e.g., coal) to consumption of a secondary form of energy (e.g., fuel oil).

An outstanding instance of substitution relates to railroad dieselization. In the United States, for example, 99 percent of all railroad engines in service in 1925 were steam locomotives; in 1965, the same proportion (of a smaller total, however) was diesel electric. The turnabout in fuels received by railroads was only slightly less extreme: in coal equivalents, 90 percent represented coal in 1925, while 90 percent represented oil in the early 1960s.[14] An interesting aspect of railroad dieselization is that comparative fuel economy was not the motivating force. Instead, other improvements in operating efficiency made possible by the diesel engine led to its substitution for the steam locomotive, and, with this change, the use of liquid fuels rather than coal as the energy source.

The development of American merchant shipping since the 1920s tells a similar, though less sharply drawn, story of substitution. In 1921, oil-fired vessels for the first time exceeded (in tonnage terms) coal-burning steamships. Nonetheless, in the mid-1920s, over one-third of U.S. registered shipping consisted of coal-burning rather than oil-fired or motorized vessels. In recent years coal-burning ships have dwindled to insignificance; in fact, none is reported to have been built anywhere in the world since the end of World War II.

In manufacturing similar changes have occurred. Though severely limited in time span and country coverage, the figures below do suggest a strong element of interfuel substitution in a wide range of industrial uses, particularly in the more advanced countries.[15]

Oil Products Consumed as Percent of Energy Consumed, Selected Manufacturing Industries and Countries

Country	*Base year*	*Terminal year*	*Industry*	Oil as percent of energy consumed: *Base year*	Oil as percent of energy consumed: *Terminal year*
Austria	1954	1958	Basic metals	4.5%	6.1%
			Metal products	16.7	28.4
			Textiles	22.6	25.5
			Paper	18.1	22.5
Canada	1948	1958	Chemicals	28.4	31.0
			Nonmetallic minerals	17.2	22.1
			Metal mining	15.6	26.1
			Textiles	8.5	35.3
Denmark	1939	1958	Basic metal products	22.6	65.1
			Clothing	6.4	60.0
India	1948	1958	Chemicals	15.0	13.7
			Textiles	11.4	12.0
Sweden	1938	1958	Chemicals	5.5	57.6
			Paper	0.3	56.5
			Wood and wood products	1.8	18.4
			Food, beverages, tobacco	4.9	69.8

[14]The numbers accompanying the illustrations in this and the succeeding three paragraphs are largely based on data in U.S. Bureau of the Census, *Historical Statistics of the United States, Colonial Times to 1957* (U.S. Government Printing Office, 1960) and *Historical Statistics of the United States, Continuation to 1962 and Revisions* (U.S. Government Printing Office, 1965); Sam H. Schurr, Bruce C. Netschert, *et al.*, *Energy in the American Economy, 1850-1975* (Johns Hopkins Press for Resources for the Future, 1960); and Organisation for Economic Cooperation and Development, *Basic Statistics of Energy, 1951-1965* (Paris, 1967).

[15]United Nations, *The Growth of World Industry, 1938-1961*, National Tables (New York, 1963). Oil used to generate purchased electricity is not included. For U.S. manufacturing, where widespread substitution of oil and gas for coal occurred earlier than in most other parts of the world, a precisely comparable tabulation to that shown above cannot be derived.

In the 1920s coal had virtually a complete grip on space heating. Though retaining a fairly important position elsewhere in the world, coal for space heating in the United States has become relatively insignificant.

In the mid-1920s coal was the preponderant fuel used in U.S. thermal electricity generation, accounting for close to 90 percent of all fuels consumed at power stations. In the mid-1960s the share—though still substantial and, as we shall see below, a mainstay of world coal over the years—was down to around two-thirds.

"Industry Mix" Changes

Interfuel shifts also reflect changing industrial structure. That is, the disparate movements of industries or activities requiring different specific fuels will produce compositional changes among primary energy sources; for example, a relatively faster growth of oil-using automotive travel or of petrochemical production than, say, of coal-using steel output would produce such a result. Where some of the newer outlets for oil constituted "captive" markets (road and air transport precluded opportunities for other fuels) this effect would be particularly marked.

In an indirect fashion, table 8 suggests the way in which the shifting demand away from coal was associated with the rise of certain activities linked to the newer fuels. The element of indirectness comes in by the fact that energy-using activities are identified by the nature of the energy commodities (e.g., gasoline, coking coal) rather than by the industrial origin of the demand. The various items shown in the table accounted for 57 percent of primary energy output[16] in 1965; and they accounted for close to 70 percent of the expansion in primary energy output since 1929.[17]

Predictably, motor gasoline has markedly increased its relative claim on total primary energy supplies. So has kerosine, particularly in the period (since 1950) during which jet aircraft came into use; its share of total energy output remains modest, however. Coking coal is of declining relative importance in terms of primary energy output. The fact that enhanced economies in blast-furnace operations contributed to the falling relative role of coking coal serves to remind us that not only industry-mix changes, but to some extent efficiency changes as well, are reflected in the tabulation.

Table 8 shows the rapid growth of electricity[18] since 1929. Coal, as we have seen, is the preeminent fuel in electricity generation—the sole major sector of economic activity that has provided a really significant stimulus to worldwide coal consumption. In 1929 about 7 percent of world energy output represented steam-raising coal used at thermal power stations; in 1965 the figure was 12 percent. A related statistic is the proportion of world coal output going into electricity. In 1929 the figure was about 9 percent, and in 1965 it was about 29 percent. As a percentage of the thirty-six-year *increment* to world coal output, the share works out to around 65 percent. (Its use in electric power generation constituted a particularly important stimulus to coal in the United States.) Yet even in electric power, of all the fossil fuels used at generating plants the relative share of coal has declined in importance, particularly since World War II. The converse of the increased share of world coal output going into electric power is, of course, the declining share serving markets outside electric generation. In these uses even the absolute amounts increased only slightly—from about 1.3 billion tons to 1.6 billion tons during a period of over three and one-half decades.

Trends in Production Compared with Those in Consumption[19]

The declining world role of coal and the growing importance of petroleum has been accompanied by dramatic changes both in the geographic distribution of world energy output and in regional energy supply-demand balances.[20] A summary of these changes appears in table 9. As has been shown to be the case with changes in the geographic distribution of world energy consumption, regional shares of world output have likewise shifted markedly away from the advanced parts of the non-Communist world. An important part of the offset to these regions' declining relative importance as producers has been the emerging prominence of the

[16]Even though this section deals with trends in consumption, output seemed the appropriate measure for table 8 which attempts to exhaust all uses of energy production, including bunkers—the latter being excluded from our measure of (inland) consumption. It should be recalled that in our tabulations, consumption (inland) equals production plus imports minus exports minus bunkers.

[17]However, not all of these reflect just the changing industrial structure phenomenon. As we have seen, the switch from coal to oil bunkers and the growing demand for diesel fuel and other oil products (both showing conspicuously rapid growth in the table) are more aptly considered cases of energy substitution in given economic activities.

[18]As pointed out in fn. [a], table 8, we here refer to primary energy consumed in electric power rather than the considerably faster growth in electric power production. The more detailed figures quoted in this paragraph appear in Part Two, Profile No. 7.

[19]Changing regional trends in consumption relative to production reflect, of course, concomitant trends in foreign trade; developments in foreign trade are taken up explicitly in the next section.

[20]In discussing trends in energy production, this section will be largely concerned with coal and oil. Developments in natural gas and hydroelectricity, the remaining primary energy categories, were covered earlier in the discussion of interfuel shifts in consumption. And since foreign trade in gas and electricity were of negligible importance during the period in question, regional trends in production were virtually identical to those in consumption.

Table 8. DISPOSITION OF WORLDWIDE PRIMARY ENERGY OUTPUT, IN TERMS OF SELECTED ENERGY PRODUCTS, 1929, 1950, 1965

Raw material and product	Million metric tons coal equivalent 1929	1950	1965	Percent of primary energy production 1929	1950	1965	Avg. annual percent. rate of change, 1929–65
Primary energy production							
Solid fuels	1,437.6	1,608.6	2,292.7	77.8%	59.2%	40.5%	1.3%
Liquid fuels	318.7	813.2	2,342.8	17.2	29.9	41.4	5.7
Natural gas	77.0	252.0	912.2	4.2	9.3	16.1	7.1
Hydroelectricity	14.7	43.4	112.6	0.8	1.6	2.0	5.8
Total	1,847.9	2,717.1	5,660.4	100.0	100.0	100.0	3.2
Selected energy products							
Electricity[a]	145.0	367.0	1,037.3	7.8	13.5	18.3	5.6
Fuel and diesel oil for heat and transport (excl. bunkers)	109.6	296.7	972.6	5.9	10.9	17.2	6.3
Gasoline	105.0	255.0	605.0	5.7	9.4	10.7	5.0
Coking coal	132.0	168.0	273.3	7.1	6.2	4.8	2.0
Kerosine	21.0	48.0	178.6	1.1	1.8	3.2	6.1
Bunkers	73.9	85.0	157.5	4.0	3.1	2.8	2.1
Coal	41.0	12.2	1.2	2.2	0.4	-	-9.4
Oil	32.9	72.8	156.3	1.8	2.7	2.8	4.4
Total above	586.5	1,219.7	3,224.3	31.7	44.9	57.0	4.8
All other	1,261.4	1,497.4	2,436.1	68.3	55.1	43.0	1.8

[a]It is important to note that electricity here refers to primary fuel input into electric generation (including the calorific value of hydro) rather than electricity produced. Owing to progressive improvements in the heat rate, electricity generated has increased at the long-term rate of about 7½% annually, compared with the 5.6% in primary fuel input tabulated above.

Source: See Part Two, Profile No. 7.

newer oil-producing regions, particularly the Middle East and, to a lesser extent, Africa. Soviet Russia's share of world energy output also advanced markedly; the Caribbean's percentage rose moderately.

North America, Western Europe, Oceania, and Japan accounted for nearly 90 percent of world energy production in 1925; by 1967 their share had dropped by about one-half to 45 percent. This declining relative position in world energy output, largely associated with the stagnation of coal mining in these regions, was considerably more severe than their falling share of world energy consumption; in the case of Japan the proportion of world consumption actually rose.

Consequently, as is apparent from the comparison of 1925 energy production and consumption, on the one hand, with that in 1967 on the other, the demand-supply position of these areas has changed conspicuously. The least change was experienced by North America where the U.S. switch from net oil exporter to net oil importer was sufficiently modest to make little change in the region's overall degree of energy self-sufficiency.

The counterpart to the declining shares of world energy production of these advanced, non-Communist regions consisted of two major developments: first, the sharp increase of the Communist part of the world, up from 7 percent of world energy production in 1925 to 28 percent in 1967. Spearheaded by the growing energy-producing capability of the Soviet Union, the Communist area's growing world share applies to energy production in the aggregate as well as to each individual primary energy commodity. The second major factor was the vast expansion of output in the oil-rich countries of the Middle East and, to a lesser extent, North Africa. Accounting for one-half of one percent of world energy output in 1925, the percentage for the combined areas had risen to 16 percent by 1967.

As background to these developments, we should recall that energy use in the mid-1920s was still heavily dominated by solid fuels, which accounted for over 80 percent of world energy consumption. (The output from North American and West European coalfields alone contributed nearly 75 percent to world energy consumption from *all* sources, a share down to a bare 15 percent in recent years.) Although proportions lower than this four-fifths share prevailed in the United States and Soviet Russia, the contribution of coal to total energy use was well over 90 percent in such regions as Western Europe, Eastern Europe, and Japan—the first two of these being then prolific coal-producing regions which met not only their own regional energy requirements but served export markets as well. Indeed, it is striking how, in 1925, virtually all the major energy-consuming regions of the world accounted for similar shares of world consumption and world production; or, what is the same thing, how each of these regions met practically the whole of its energy needs from indigenous supplies. North America consumed approximately one-half the

Table 9. ENERGY PRODUCTION AND CONSUMPTION, BY MAJOR REGIONS, 1925 AND 1967

(All data based on coal equivalents)

Region	Production		Consumption		Ratio of production to consumption
	Million met. tons	Percent of world	Million met. tons	Percent of world	
			1925		
North America	779.0	49.7%	748.9	50.4%	1.04
of which: United States	765.0	48.8	717.7	48.3	1.07
Western Europe	532.4	34.0	517.0	34.8	1.03
Oceania	16.0	1.0	15.6	1.1	1.03
U.S.S.R. & Comm. E. Europe	92.1	5.9	80.5	5.4	1.15
U.S.S.R.	27.0	1.7	25.3	1.7	1.07
Comm. E. Europe	65.1	4.2	55.1	3.7	1.18
Communist Asia	22.6	1.4	23.7	1.6	0.95
Latin America	39.9	2.5	24.7	1.7	1.62
Caribbean	33.9	2.2	11.4	0.8	2.98
Other Latin America	6.0	0.4	13.3	0.9	0.45
Asia	71.1	4.5	60.3	4.1	1.18
Middle East	7.7	0.5	2.3	0.2	3.32
Japan	32.9	2.1	30.5	2.1	1.08
Other Asia	30.5	1.9	27.5	1.9	1.11
Africa	13.6	0.9	13.9	0.9	0.98
North Africa	0.3	–	3.0	0.2	0.10
Other Africa	13.3	0.8	10.9	0.7	1.22
WORLD[a]	1,566.6	100.0	1,484.5	100.0	1.06
			1967		
North America	2,114	34.4%	2,230	37.9%	0.95
of which: United States	1,947	31.7	2,055	34.9	0.95
Western Europe	540	8.8	1,168	19.8	0.46
Oceania	46	0.7	67	1.1	0.69
U.S.S.R. & Comm. E. Europe	1,489	24.2	1,376	23.4	1.08
U.S.S.R.	1,124	18.3	989	16.8	1.14
Comm. E. Europe	365	5.9	387	6.6	0.94
Communist Asia	255	4.1	255	4.3	1.00
Latin America	451	7.3	224	3.8	2.01
Caribbean	383	6.2	126	2.1	3.04
Other Latin America	68	1.1	98	1.7	0.69
Asia	966	15.7	471	8.0	2.05
Middle East	764	12.4	68	1.2	11.24
Japan	61	1.0	249	4.2	0.24
Other Asia	141	2.3	154	2.6	0.92
Africa	284	4.6	97	1.6	2.93
North Africa	200	3.3	20	0.3	10.00
Other Africa	84	0.1	77	1.3	1.09
WORLD[a]	6,145	100.0	5,888	100.0	1.04

[a]World production totals differ somewhat from world consumption totals because (1) bunkers are included in production and excluded from consumption (which refers to inland consumption); and (2) because of unexplained statistical discrepancies, as discussed in Part Four of this volume.

Source: Data for 1925 from Part Three, tables X and XIV; data for 1967 are estimates, derived from United Nations, *Statistical Yearbook, 1968* (New York, 1969).

world energy total and produced a like share. For Western Europe, the world share of consumption or production was a bit over one-third; for the combined group of present-day Communist countries, around 7 percent. Except for Latin America and the then insignificant Middle East production—the 1925 share of world output of both regions substantially exceeded their percentage of world consumption—this pattern of roughly similar portions of world energy consumption and production prevailed for the other areas listed in table 9. Of course, this tendency toward equality between *total* fuel output and consumption did not apply to liquid fuels except in the case of the United States (at that time a net oil exporter) and the U.S.S.R. (then, as in recent years, a net oil exporter); but it did apply to coal which exerted a decisive weight on the world energy total and most of the regional energy totals.

Four decades later, regional self-sufficiency persisted only in the Communist group, where it was at least partly a consequence of autarkic policies. Elsewhere, marked regional imbalances had appeared—notably in Western Europe, its roughly one-fifth share of world consumption being over twice its share of world production. As the table shows, the absolute level of total energy output scarcely increased in Western Europe between 1925 and 1967 (although there were, of course, ups and downs during the intervening years); and, due to declining indigenous coal output, West European total energy production has in recent years been falling markedly. The Far East has evolved into another energy-deficit region, the 1967 consumption and production figures being, respectively, 7 and 3 percent. Japan, in particular, reflects a drastic long-term change in its production-consumption position—the sharpest such change shown in the table: the country's ratio of production to consumption was 1.1:1 in 1925; by 1967, it was down to under 0.25. As mentioned above, the North American position in 1967 (34 percent of world energy production, 38 percent of consumption) reflected only a modest deficit status. Other deficit regions were non-Caribbean Latin America and Oceania. The former had been persistently deficient in energy supplies throughout the period under review; and the latter—though still in a deficit position in the late sixties—may in a matter of a few years revert to surplus status or at least a balanced situation, given Australia's rising oil and gas discoveries in recent years as well as an expanding volume of coal exports.

The counterpart development to the emerging deficit areas was, of course, the growth of the oil-producing surplus areas. This part of the story is pictured in table 10, which shows oil output of the principal producing countries since 1925. This was a period during which the regional center of gravity of world oil was gradually shifting eastward from the Western Hemisphere (principally the United States)—primarily to the Middle East, but also to the Soviet Union and, most recently, Africa. In 1925 the two leading producing countries represented over 80 percent of world oil output—the United States with 70 percent and Mexico with 12 percent. Along with Venezuela's 5 percent, the Western Hemisphere contributed 87 percent of the world total, the balance being shared by three countries—Soviet Russia, Indonesia, and Iran.

Table 10. SHARE OF PRINCIPAL PRODUCING COUNTRIES IN WORLD LIQUID FUELS OUTPUT, SELECTED YEARS, 1925-1968

(Percentage distribution)

Country	1925	1938	1950	1955	1960	1965	1968
United States	70.9%	60.8%	52.7%	45.3%	34.9%	27.4%	25.5%
U.S.S.R.	4.7	10.8	7.2	9.1	13.8	15.6	15.6
Venezuela	1.9	9.8	14.5	14.1	13.7	11.7	9.6
Iran	3.1	3.7	6.0	2.0	4.8	6.0	7.2
Saudi Arabia	–	–	4.9	5.9	5.7	6.5	7.1
Libya	–	–	–	–	–	3.8	6.3
Kuwait	–	–	3.2	6.8	7.5	7.0	6.1
Iraq	–	1.6	1.2	4.2	4.3	4.1	3.7
Canada	–	0.3	0.7	2.2	2.4	2.7	3.0
Algeria	–	–	–	–	0.8	1.7	2.2
Indonesia	2.1	2.7	1.2	1.5	1.9	1.5	1.4
Abu Dhabi[a]	–	–	–	–	–	0.9	1.2
Kuwait Neutral Zone	–	–	–	0.2	0.7	1.2	1.1
Mexico	11.6	2.0	1.9	1.6	1.4	1.2	1.1
Above 14 countries	94.3	91.7	93.5	92.9	91.9	91.3	91.1
All other countries	5.7	8.3	6.5	7.1	8.1	8.7	8.9
WORLD	100.0	100.0	100.0	100.0	100.0	100.0	100.0
WORLD (million tons):							
Original units	152.0	280.9	542.1	803.9	1,094.1	1,561.9	1,985
Coal equivalents	228.0	421.3	813.2	1,205.8	1,641.2	2,342.8	2,978
Addendum: oil output of 14 listed countries as percent of world total energy output	13.2%	20.7%	28.0%	32.1%	34.7%	37.8%	41.5%[b]

[a]Carried under "Trucial Oman" in the tables of Part Three.
[b]Partly estimated.

Note: Countries are ranked according to 1968 production and showing countries accounting for at least 1% of the 1968 world total. (Nigeria's output—1.2% of the world total in 1966—declined subsequently due to the civil war; however, following cessation of fighting, production in the first half of 1970 was estimated to be running at a rate of nearly 50 million tons of oil per year, or well in excess of 2% of world output in that year.)

Fuels include crude oil and natural gas liquids—the latter limited largely to the United States and Canada.

Source: Data for 1925-65 from Part Three, tables I and II. Data for 1968 from British Petroleum Co., *Statistical Review of the World Oil Industry, 1968* (London, 1969), adjusted slightly to conform with the 1925-65 series in this volume.

Although U.S. oil production has risen persistently over the years—from 160 million tons in 1925 to over 500 million tons in 1968, or at an average annual rate of growth of 3½ percent yearly[21]—the nation's share of world oil production has declined steadily and sharply, as table 10 shows. From 70 percent in 1925, the U.S. share of the world total was down to 25 percent in 1968. At the same time, the Soviet Union share rose from 5 to 15 percent. The most interesting story, however, concerns the new oil-producing countries, chiefly in the Middle East and Africa. Eight of the fourteen leading world producers in 1968 recorded no output, or virtually none, in 1925; and these eight—Saudi Arabia, Libya, Kuwait, Iraq, Canada, Algeria, Abu Dhabi, and the Kuwait Neutral Zone[22]—accounted for over 30 percent of the world's oil production in 1968.

In the Middle East there had been only two oil discoveries prior to 1925—in Iran in 1908 and in Iraq in 1923; and the latter case did not lead to consequential production for some years. Three Arab states which alone accounted for over 20 percent of worldwide oil output in 1968 began producing their first recorded crude oil in the comparatively recent years of 1936 (Saudi Arabia), 1946 (Kuwait), and 1961 (Libya).[23] With Canada starting to develop her major oil fields only in the late 1940s, and the Soviet Union doubling its already considerable level of output within the five-year period 1955-60, it has really been principally since World War II that the world oil industry has grown to its present enormous size, and that the prewar dominance of the United States in world oil production began to slip to a considerably less lofty position.

The critical role of the fourteen oil-producing countries listed in table 10 is reflected in a statistic added on the bottom line: in 1968 over 40 percent of the world's total energy consumption, irrespective of source, originated in the oil output of these relatively few countries.

One might finally take note of a few other countries which, over the years, have receded in their world oil-output ranking. The most conspicuous is Mexico whose 1925 world share of 12 percent was second only to the United States. Mexico's subsequent long-term decline to scarcely more than 1 percent in 1968 has been roughly compensated by the equal and opposite long-term rise of Venezuela, although—under the impact of Western Europe's historic shift in reliance upon cheaper crude oil from the Middle East and Africa as well as a result of U.S. import quotas dating from the mid-1950s—Venezuela's world share has also been declining in recent years. Indonesia's relatively meager share in 1925 nonetheless put it among the list of the more important oil producers; its share has tended to fall over the years, but there are prospects for relatively substantial growth in output in the years ahead. Romania's share (not shown in table 10) has also fallen over the years—down from 1½ percent in 1925 to under 1 percent in recent years.

The comparative movements of production and consumption just summarized have, of course, been accompanied by vast changes in world energy trade.

The Growth of International Trade

World energy trade has risen rapidly since the 1920s. As shown in table 11, the pace (of close to 5½ percent yearly) has exceeded that in total energy consumption. In 1925 about 14 percent of the primary energy consumed had crossed foreign borders; by 1968 the proportion was up to 33 percent. Because total energy trade in the earlier part of this period was characterized to a substantial extent by *intra*regional trade—particularly exchanges of coal among proximate European countries—the long-term, petroleum-dominated expansion of *inter*regional trade alone was even more rapid. For the interval for which comparable data exist, 1929-65, world energy consumption increased at the average annual rate of 3.2 percent, total world energy trade rose by 4.8 percent a year, while interregional trade among the principal areas of the world went up by over 6 percent yearly. Relatedly, around one-half of total international energy trade in 1929 involved trade within major world regions; only about one-quarter consisted of intraregional trade in 1965.[24]

World energy trade (this time based on value rather than tonnage) has also grown faster than the aggregate dollar value of all world trade. Energy's share in the value of world trade was somewhat over 6 percent in 1929. (It had been under 5 percent prior to the outbreak of World War I.) By 1967 it had risen to approximately 10 percent, being valued at about $21 billion.[25] As in the case of the volumetric data cited above, it seems probable that the percentage share of energy in world trade would show a still more marked increase if the figures could be adjusted to exclude trade *within* major regions.

The dominant force in the expansion of world energy trade has clearly been liquid fuels; comprising under one-

[21]See Part Three, tables II and XIV; and, for 1968, table 10.

[22]Abu Dhabi is one of the so-called Trucial States on the Persian Gulf. Though treated as a separate statistical unit, the Kuwait Neutral Zone, also on the Gulf, has an uncertain political status, its oil output being shared by Saudi Arabia and Kuwait.

[23]By 1969, Libya had moved ahead of Saudi Arabia in the world production standings, thus becoming the leading Arab oil-producing nation, and the fifth highest in the world—behind the United States, U.S.S.R., Venezuela, and Iran. British Petroleum Co., *Statistical Review of the World Oil Industry, 1969* (London, 1970).

[24]See Part Two, Profile No. 35.

[25]Value data from Part Two, Profile No. 23; and United Nations, *Monthly Bulletin of Statistics*, March 1969.

Table 11. WORLD ENERGY EXPORTS BY SOURCE, SELECTED YEARS, 1925-1968

	1925	1938	1950	1955	1960	1965	1967	1968
				Million metric tons coal equivalent				
Solid fuels	145.8	129.7	120.2	157.2	133.0	158.7	159.3	168.5
Liquid fuels	67.9	169.4	375.6	606.9	871.7	1,395.4	1,657.7	1,852.0
Gas	0.005	0.1	1.3	1.3	6.4	18.4	24.3	30.4
Electricity	0.2	0.5	0.5	0.9	1.4	1.7	2.5	2.8
Total energy	214.0	299.6	497.6	766.4	1,012.3	1,574.2	1,843.8	2,053.7
				Percent of world exports				
Solid fuels	68.2%	43.3%	24.2%	20.5%	13.1%	10.1%	8.6%	8.2%
Liquid fuels	31.7	56.5	75.5	79.2	86.1	88.6	89.9	90.2
Gas	–	–	0.2	0.2	0.6	1.2	1.3	1.5
Electricity	0.1	0.2	0.1	0.1	0.1	0.1	0.1	0.1
Total energy	100.0	100.0	100.0	100.0	100.0	100.0	100.0	100.0
				Exports as percent of world consumption of indicated energy source				
Solid fuels	11.9%	10.0%	7.5%	8.7%	6.7%	6.9%	7.2%	7.3%
Liquid fuels	34.5	45.1	52.0	55.5	58.2	64.6	66.6	68.5
Gas	–	–	0.5	0.3	1.0	2.0	2.3	2.6
Electricity	2.0	2.0	1.2	1.5	1.6	1.5	2.0	2.1
Total energy	14.4	16.7	19.1	22.8	24.1	28.8	31.3	32.6

	Average annual percentage rates of change			
	1925-50	1950-60	1960-68	1925-68
Solid fuels	-0.8%	1.0%	3.0%	0.3%
Liquid fuels	7.1	8.8	9.9	8.0
Gas	24.9	17.2	21.5	22.4
Electricity	2.6	11.5	9.1	6.3
Total energy	3.4	7.3	9.2	5.4

Notes and source: Figures include trade in primary as well as secondary energy sources (such as coke, gasoline, manufactured gas, and thermal electricity). For sources to the period 1925-65 and additional notes, see Part Two, Profile No. 23. Data for 1967-68 were estimated on the basis of United Nations, *World Energy Supplies*, Statistical Papers, Series J, Nos. 12 and 13 (New York, 1969 and 1970).

third of world energy exports in 1925, they rose steadily, reaching 90 percent in 1968. *Incrementally*, liquid fuels accounted for virtually the entire increase in energy trade over the four decades.

As to the commodity composition of the trade in liquid fuels, the dominant component in the 1920s comprised refined petroleum products (gasoline, kerosine, fuel oils, and lubricants). These accounted for around 55 percent of the world liquid fuels trade, while crude oil represented 45 percent of the total. Over the years, crude oil moved to the forefront, and in recent years accounted for around three-quarters of the total, refined products slipping to one-fourth.[26] By definition, this historic shift from products to crude oil in the international liquid fuels trade reflected the growth of refining capacity in major consuming areas, such as Western Europe and Japan. For example, the latter two areas possessed 5 percent of the world's crude oil processing capacity in 1937 and 27 percent in 1965. (See Part Two, Profile No. 30.) For a number of economic reasons, no doubt reinforced by considerations of political strategy, refinery location has gradually come to be centered in the major industrial oil-importing areas of the world rather than close to the point of crude oil production, as had once been the case. A principal exception to the historical shift in the international liquid fuels trade from refined to crude petroleum relates to U.S. imports; being an oil producer of its own, the country had early established substantial refining capacity to process the imported crude oil which constituted the predominant part of its liquid fuels imports in the 1920s. In fact, contrary to the long-term trend elsewhere in the world, the proportion of crude oil in U.S. liquid fuels imports has fallen over the years; by 1967 less than one-half the liquid fuels shipped into the country was crude oil, the balance being predominantly made up of residual fuel oil from the Caribbean.[27] Aside from the longer-term forces producing this pattern of U.S. imports, the nature of the more recently evolving mandatory oil import program, dating from 1959, has also

[26]Data on the commodity composition of liquid fuels trade are tabulated in summary form in Part Two, Profile No. 30.

[27]Figures for 1967 appear in United Nations, *World Energy Supplies*, Statistical Papers, Series J, No. 12 (New York, 1969).

been a contributory factor. For, under that program, residual fuel oil is exempt from quotas, being domestically produced in very limited volume.

As liquid fuels rose to dominance in world energy trade, solid fuels, conversely, fell sharply; from two-thirds of the world total in 1925, they declined to 8 percent in 1968. As table 11 shows, coal in absolute terms exhibited little long-term change in tonnage traded.

Gas and electricity, largely limited to natural gas and electricity exchanges between Canada and the United States, and electricity sales within Western Europe, have historically accounted for only trivial shares of international energy trade. Movements of pipeline gas within Europe and slowly rising ocean transport of liquefied natural gas (LNG) may alter that situation in years to come.

The shifting composition of world energy trade from coal to oil has radically transformed the geographic complexion of this trade. In particular, Western Europe and the United States have greatly receded in their share of total world energy exports, while—as in the case of energy production—the oil-rich Middle East has become a major force in energy exports. The West European decline is associated with the area's vanishing role as a coal exporter; while in the case of the United States, even a moderately rapid rise in coal exports (particularly in recent years) was insufficient to overcome the country's declining oil exports and the tremendous expansion of oil shipments from other parts of the world.

Long-term trends in world energy imports are highlighted by the steadily rising position of Western Europe and Japan—both almost entirely deficient in indigenous crude oil. The present-day Communist countries, considered as a group, have over the long run become a declining relative factor in both world energy imports and exports.[28] But the Communist area's relative decline in world imports was sharper than in the case of exports, a trend reflected in the total region's emergence as a substantial net exporter. An estimate of these changes is shown in the following tabulation, in which intraregional trade within the ten areas listed is excluded.[29]

Shares of World Interregional Energy

	Imports		*Exports*	
	1929	*1965*	*1929*	*1965*
Canada	20.2%	4.9%	0.8%	2.2%
United States	17.0	16.5	37.3	5.1
Western Europe	30.9	52.2	12.0	0.6
Oceania	2.5	2.6	–	0.6
Communist Area	5.2	0.2	17.2	8.0
Caribbean	3.2	1.9	23.8	20.7
Other Latin America	8.2	3.2	0.9	–
Middle East	0.5	0.3	3.4	47.4
Far East	6.8	13.8	4.0	1.4
Africa	5.6	4.4	0.8	14.1
WORLD	100.0	100.0	100.0	100.0

The long-run trends suggested by the preceding tabulation are traced more fully, though using a different statistical indicator, in table 12; there net trade balances for major regions are recorded at bench mark intervals for the period 1925-67. The table discloses a number of fundamental changes. The United States shifted from net energy exporter to importer following World War II. The change turned upon oil alone: in coal, the country achieved a continually growing, if modest, export surplus. With the rise of its oil and gas discoveries, Canada's net import balances began falling in the years following World War II. From a zero energy trade balance in 1925, Japan's net imports have skyrocketed over the years, particularly in the last decade or so: its 200 million coal equivalent tons of net imports in 1967 made it the world's leading energy importing nation. Soviet Russia has developed into a significant net exporter, while the East European Communist area's net exports in the 1920s (attributable largely to Polish coal) have been overtaken by imports arising from oil. Finally, table 12 depicts the tremendous expansion in net exports from the Middle East and North Africa—for the combined areas up from practically nothing in 1925 to 850 million coal equivalent tons of net energy exports (virtually all of it petroleum) in 1967. Expansion in net oil exports in each of these two regions has outpaced the rate of growth of shipments from the Caribbean; however, by absolute standards the latter remains of great importance in world oil exports.

A still more meaningful way of portraying the changing net energy trade picture in different parts of the world is presented in table 13. Regional net import balances, shown as a percentage of energy consumption, suggest the overall degree of import dependence, while regional net export balances are shown as a percentage share of production in order to denote export capacity.[30] Increased import dependence was experienced

[28] Not considering exchanges among the Communist countries themselves.

[29] The tabulation, and the discussion relating to it, refers to inter-area trade since that is viewed as providing a clearer picture than one which would, for example, include also the intra-regional shipments of refined oil products (made from imported crude oil) within Western Europe. The result would be a double-counting kind of distortion. However, only 1929 and 1965 figures could be constructed in the above presentation. The data are taken from the first two columns of Profile No. 35 in Part Two. World imports and exports based on inter-area as well as intra-area trade are tabulated in Part Two, Profile No. 26. See also the explanatory note on foreign trade terminology appended to Profile No. 23 in Part Two.

[30] Both measures relate, of course, to statistics which reflect the prevailing economic and policy circumstances for the area and year in question. Policy changes in such matters as import controls, fuel taxes, shut-in productive capacity, or subsidies can bring about a different statistical picture of net foreign "dependence."

Table 12. NET ENERGY IMPORTS OR EXPORTS (-), BY MAJOR REGIONS, SELECTED YEARS, 1925-1967

(Million metric tons coal equivalent)

Region[a]	1925	1938	1950	1955	1960	1965	1967
North America	-4.7	-17.7	66.6	67.7	133.5	171.6	161.0
United States	-23.4	-37.8	19.9	27.9	102.1	152.8	147.4
Canada	18.7	20.0	46.7	39.7	31.3	18.6	13.6
Western Europe	10.1	47.2	93.4	204.4	318.0	591.1	710.5
Oceania	1.2	4.2	8.5	14.6	18.2	23.1	26.7
U.S.S.R. & Comm. E. Europe	-11.5	-17.9	-11.5	-22.3	-59.4	-95.7	-111.8
U.S.S.R.	-1.6	-1.0	11.2	-0.9	-53.1	-112.8	-131.0
Comm. E. Europe	-9.9	-16.9	-22.7	-21.4	-6.3	17.2	19.2
Communist Asia	1.6	-2.0	n.a.	1.0	4.4	-0.1	-0.3
Latin America	-10.9	-31.5	-86.4	-117.1	-162.6	-200.9	-204.5
Caribbean	-18.9	-40.2	-104.9	-147.5	-192.3	-232.1	-235.3
Other Latin America	8.0	8.7	18.5	30.5	29.8	31.2	30.8
Asia	-4.0	-8.8	-105.4	-186.8	-285.6	-399.9	-442.6
Middle East	-5.0	-15.9	-109.6	-212.6	-346.8	-560.5	-670.9
Japan	-	11.8	3.1	18.4	56.2	142.5	200.3
Other Asia	1.0	-4.7	1.1	7.4	5.0	18.1	27.9
Africa	4.0	9.0	12.6	23.6	12.2	-81.5	-174.2
North Africa	3.9	5.8	6.3	9.7	-2.5	-120.7	-176.0
Tropical Africa	1.5	2.5	5.4	9.7	10.2	-4.7	-9.0
South Africa	-1.4	0.7	0.9	4.1	4.5	8.0	11.7

[a]Net imports equal total imports minus total exports for each indicated region or subregion, irrespective of the direction of that trade. Thus, the net exports of, say, the Middle East (a subregion under "Asia") refers to the Middle East's net trade, whether within Asia (say, shipments to Japan) or outside Asia.

Source: Data for 1925-65 from Part Three, table XIV; data for 1967 estimated on the basis of United Nations, *World Energy Supplies*, Statistical Papers, Series J, No. 12 (New York, 1969).

Table 13. NET ENERGY IMPORTS OR EXPORTS IN RELATION TO CONSUMPTION OR PRODUCTION, BY REGION, 1925 AND 1967

Region	1925				1967			
	Net imports or exports (–) of:			Percent of net imports in energy consumption; or net exports (–) in production	Net imports or exports (–) of:			Percent of net imports in energy consumption; or net exports (–) in production
	Solid fuels	Liquid fuels	Total energy[a]		Solid fuels	Liquid fuels	Total energy[a]	
	(million metric tons coal equivalent)				(million metric tons coal equivalent)			
North America	-3.7	-1.0	-4.7	-0.6%	-32.2	198.4	161.0	7.2%
of which: United States	-18.5	-5.1	-23.4	-3.1	-45.8	181.3	147.4	7.2
Western Europe	-8.1	18.2	10.1	2.0	37.6	671.3	710.5	60.8
Oceania	-0.2	1.4	1.2	7.4	-9.2	35.9	26.7	39.9
U.S.S.R. & Comm. E. Europe	-8.4	-3.1	-11.5	-12.5	-25.0	-87.2	-111.8	-7.5
U.S.S.R.	0.3	-2.0	-1.6	-6.1	-17.2	-115.9	-131.0	-11.7
Comm. E. Europe	-8.7	-1.2	-9.9	-15.2	-7.8	28.7	19.2	5.0
Communist Asia	0.2	1.4	1.6	6.8	-2.0	1.7	-0.3	-0.1
Latin America	7.2	-18.1	-10.9	-27.3	3.2	-206.2	-204.5	-45.3
Caribbean	1.4	-20.4	-18.9	-55.9	0.5	-234.3	-235.3	-61.4
Other Latin America	5.8	2.2	8.0	60.3	2.7	28.1	30.8	31.4
Asia	1.0	-5.1	-4.0	-5.7	26.6	-468.9	-442.6	-45.8
Middle East	0.1	-5.1	-5.0	-64.9	-	-670.9	-670.9	-87.8
Japan	-1.0	1.0	-	-	25.6	174.7	200.3	80.4
Other Asia	1.9	-1.0	1.0	3.4	1.0	27.3	27.9	18.1
Africa	2.7	1.3	4.0	28.5	-0.1	-172.5	-174.2	-61.3
North Africa	3.3	0.6	3.9	131.3[b]	0.7	-175.1	-176.0	-88.0
Tropical Africa	1.0	0.5	1.5	80.7	0.5	-10.4	-9.0	-26.5
South Africa	-1.6	0.2	-1.4	-11.4	-1.3	13.0	11.7	20.2

[a]Including gas and electricity, not shown separately.

[b]Net imports exceeded consumption. It should be recalled that consumption refers to "inland" consumption, being measured exclusive of bunkers. Since North African consumption in 1925 was almost wholly dependent on foreign fuels (a moderate part of which went into bunkers after importation), this excess of net imports over consumption becomes arithmetically possible.

Source: For 1925, see Part Two, Profiles No. 33 and No. 34. Data for 1967 were estimated on the basis of United Nations, *World Energy Supplies*, Statistical Papers, Series J, No. 12 (New York, 1969).

by such relatively developed parts of the non-Communist world as North America, Western Europe, Japan, Oceania, and South Africa. The increase in import dependence was fairly modest in the case of North America: in 1925, a very small share of total production—around one-half of 1 percent—was exported; in 1967, a bit over 7 percent of consumption was accounted for by net imports.[31] (The recently prevailing North American share has actually been somewhat higher—in the neighborhood of 8½ percent; the 1967 figure was less, due to reduced net imports associated with the Middle East conflict.) Among the major energy-consuming regions of the world, North America and the Communist area as a whole came closest in recent years to energy self-sufficiency, as represented by these statistical measures.

The increase in the net import/consumption share for Western Europe between 1925 and 1967 was enormously greater than that for North America. The region's net import/consumption share had been only 2 percent back in 1925; by 1967 it had risen to 60 percent. Of the areas shown in table 13, Japan exhibited the most dramatic change of all, a zero trade balance in 1925 giving way four decades later to an import/consumption share of 80 percent. Among the major industrialized countries, only Italy has in recent years been faced with a still higher degree of net import dependence. (See Part Two, Profile No. 34.) Other areas with heightened net import dependence in 1967 as compared with 1925 include Communist Eastern Europe and the less-developed countries of Asia outside the Middle East.

The converse to the foregoing changes has, of course, been the increased export capability of the oil-producing nations of the Middle East, whose net export share of output rose from 65 percent in 1925 to nearly 90 percent of an enormously expanded output in recent years. North Africa and Tropical Africa both made a huge quantum jump from deficit to surplus areas—although the latter's role, involving primarily Nigerian oil, has so far remained relatively small in terms of recent levels of net exports. Soviet Russia's net export/production share of 6 percent in 1925 had doubled by 1967. Non-Caribbean Latin America *decreased* the net import component of its consumption between these years, though, with over a 30 percent net import dependence in 1967, the improvement nevertheless left the area with very substantial deficit status.

The Network of International Energy Flows

The long-term shift from coal to petroleum was seen in the preceding section to have been accompanied by a growing geographical imbalance between the location of energy supply sources, on the one hand, and the central areas of energy demand, on the other. In looking at the directional pattern of world energy flows that has emerged in fulfilling this web of interdependence, it is well to keep in mind the geopolitical issues bearing on this characteristic of the world energy economy. For it has produced for numerous fuel-deficient regions and countries a sense of anxiety about the reliability and adequacy—under various circumstances—of their sources of energy supplies, while for major producing areas, such as the Middle East, North Africa, and the Caribbean, the assurances of stable and growing markets are a critical element in their aspirations for economic development. In view of recurrent political crises in the Middle East as well as an almost chronic uncertainty over contractual relationships between host-country governments and the concessionary international oil companies, such considerations have assumed heightened importance in recent years. The quantitative backdrop to such issues is evident in table 14, which shows, among other things, the extent to which the world's inter-area movements of energy[32] have come to be dominated by Middle Eastern (and additionally, in recent years, African) petroleum.

It has earlier been pointed out that foreign trade played a far smaller role in the world energy economy four decades ago than it has in recent times. Moreover, of the international energy movements that *did* take place in the 1920s, a preponderant share was accounted for by intra- rather than inter-area trade. Thus, over 70 percent of the 1929 energy imports of West European countries originated right *within* Western Europe, compared with about 15 percent in 1965. The turnabout reflects, of course, the wholesale shift to foreign oil from coal indigenous to the region.

The interregional energy movements highlighted in table 14 refer to all flows of coal and of oil amounting to 1 percent or more of worldwide interregional energy trade (both fuels combined), and tabulated in order of importance in each of the two years shown. One quickly notes, first, the concentrated importance within world inter-area energy trade of a handful of particular regional flows (see columns 4 and 5); and, second, the important role of such flows within the energy exports or imports of certain areas (columns 6 and 7). In terms of world energy movements, at the head of the 1929 list were Caribbean oil exports to the United States; these represented 16 percent of world energy flows in that year, two-thirds of the Caribbean area exports, and virtually the whole of U.S. energy imports. U.S. coal shipments to

[31] However, this relatively mild degree of import dependence was supported by U.S. policy, placing severe restrictions on oil imports.

[32] Unless otherwise indicated, the discussion of energy movements in this section refers throughout to solid and liquid fuels. That is, it excludes the negligible inter-area exchanges of gas and electricity.

Table 14. MAJOR INTERREGIONAL EXCHANGES OF SOLID AND LIQUID FUELS, BY ORIGIN AND DESTINATION, 1929 AND 1965

Exports from:	Imports to:	Fuel category	Million met. tons coal equiv.	Percent of: Total world inter-regional exports	Percent of: Exporting region's total energy exports	Percent of: Importing region's total energy imports
(1)	(2)	(3)	(4)	(5)	(6)	(7)
	1929					
Caribbean	United States	liquid	21.7	16.0%	67.2%	94.3%
United States	Canada	solid	17.7	13.1	35.0	64.6
United States	Western Europe	liquid	12.3	9.0	24.4	29.4
U.S.S.R. & Comm. E. Europe	Western Europe	solid	11.5	8.5	57.8	27.4
Caribbean	Western Europe	liquid	6.9	5.1	21.4	16.5
United States	Canada	liquid	6.2	4.6	12.3	22.6
U.S.S.R. & Comm. E. Europe	Western Europe	liquid	6.0	4.4	30.2	14.3
Western Europe	Other Latin America	solid	5.9	4.3	36.4	53.2
Western Europe	Africa	solid	5.4	4.0	33.3	71.1
Middle East	Western Europe	liquid	3.7	2.7	80.4	8.8
Communist Asia	Far East	solid	3.5	2.6	100.0	38.0
United States	Caribbean	liquid	3.0	2.2	5.9	68.2
Western Europe	U.S.S.R. & Comm. E. Europe	solid	3.0	2.2	18.5	96.8
United States	Far East	liquid	2.9	2.1	5.7	31.5
United States	Other Latin America	liquid	2.7	2.0	5.3	24.3
Far East	Communist Asia	solid	2.2	1.6	40.7	53.7
Caribbean	Canada	liquid	1.8	1.3	5.6	6.6
Caribbean	Other Latin America	liquid	1.7	1.3	5.3	15.3
United States	Oceania	liquid	1.4	1.1	2.8	41.2
Sum of above			119.5	88.0	–	–
All other solid fuels			6.4	4.7	–	–
All other liquid fuels			9.8	7.2	–	–
Total world interregional			135.6	100.0	–	–
	1965					
Middle East	Western Europe	liquid	303.2	26.2%	55.3%	50.2%
Africa	Western Europe	liquid	151.6	13.1	92.8	25.1
Middle East	Far East	liquid	132.8	11.5	24.2	83.2
Caribbean	United States	liquid	124.8	10.8	52.3	65.3
Caribbean	Western Europe	liquid	57.1	4.9	23.9	9.5
Total Communist area	Western Europe	liquid	41.3	3.6	44.8	6.8
Middle East	Africa	liquid	36.2	3.1	6.6	71.3
Caribbean	Canada	liquid	30.4	2.6	12.7	53.5
Middle East	United States	liquid	29.6	2.6	5.4	15.5
Canada	United States	liquid	24.4	2.1	95.3	12.8
United States	Western Europe	solid	22.6	2.0	38.4	3.7
Middle East	Oceania	liquid	21.9	1.9	4.0	72.8
Total Communist area	Western Europe	solid	21.8	1.9	23.7	3.6
United States	Canada	solid	15.3	1.3	26.0	26.9
Caribbean	Other Latin America	liquid	15.0	1.3	6.3	41.0
Total Communist area	Caribbean	liquid	13.8	1.2	15.0	62.4
Sum of above			1,041.8	90.1	–	–
All other solid fuels			22.5	1.9	–	–
All other liquid fuels			92.2	8.0	–	–
Total world interregional			1,156.6	100.0	–	–

Note: (a) Ranked according to percentage of world interregional exports, and (b) natural gas and electricity flows excluded; most significant among such flows were Canadian natural gas shipments to the United States, amounting to about 15 million coal equivalent tons (or 35% of Canada's energy exports) in 1965.

Source: Derived from Part Two, Profiles No. 35 and No. 36; and Part Five, tables III-1 and III-2.

Canada ranked next in importance and constituted significant shares of both U.S. energy exports and Canadian imports. The next three most important movements in 1929 were West European imports of U.S. petroleum, of present-day Communist-area coal, and of Caribbean petroleum. Together, these represented about 30 percent of world inter-area energy trade and 70 percent of Western Europe's imports.

However, as noted already, net energy imports from foreign regions did not figure importantly in Western Europe's energy *consumption* in the 1920s. That situation changed decisively during the ensuing four decades; and, in the mid-1960s, Western Europe's imports of Middle Eastern and African oil are seen to have alone contributed 40 percent of world energy flows, three-fourths of Western Europe's energy imports, and dominant shares of the exporting area's oil shipments. Since, in recent years, net imports have risen to paramount importance in relation to West European energy use, oil imports from just these two areas have contributed 40 percent to Western Europe's *total energy consumption from all fuel sources*.[33] While the Middle East has figured significantly in West European energy imports for the greater part of the post-World War II period, the rapidly expanding role of Africa—particularly North Africa, and within North Africa, Libya—dates primarily from the past decade. Libyan petroleum contributed practically nothing to Western Europe's energy imports and consumption in 1961; by 1969, due in part to the continued closure of the Suez Canal, that country alone provided around one-fourth of Western Europe's energy imports, with the African share as a whole up to around 40 percent.[34]

Table 14 reveals the Middle East's emergence as the preeminent energy export area throughout the world: in 1965, the region's liquid fuels exports to five other areas—Western Europe, the Far East, the United States, Oceania, and Africa—accounted for 45 percent of the world's interregional energy trade (i.e., the trade in liquid *and* solid fuels). If African oil exports to Western Europe are added, the figure rises to nearly 60 percent. Note especially the Far East's (chiefly Japan's) paramount reliance on the Middle East relative to total energy imports, with a 1965 figure of well over 80 percent. And Middle Eastern oil accounted for one-half of Western Europe's total energy imports, or, if combined with African oil shipments, for the 75 percent share noted above.

A few other principal changes between 1929 and 1965 in world energy movements might be noted. The relative importance of the present-day Communist area's coal shipments to Western Europe declined sharply—whether measured by proportion of world energy trade, by a share of the Communist area's energy exports, or by a share of Western Europe's energy imports. However, using these same criteria, Communist (essentially Soviet) oil shipments to Western Europe have remained of some considerable significance.[35] (While there is beginning to be some doubt concerning the Soviet Union's capacity to sustain crude oil exports to the West for the long term, emergent signs point to the probability of substantial marketing of Russian natural gas in Western Europe. Agreements to this effect were, for example, reached with Italy and West Germany in 1969.)

U.S. coal exports to Canada ceased to be of much importance in world energy movements. The Caribbean area's oil movements held up better; its exports to the United States represented 16 percent of world energy flows in 1929, and 11 percent in 1965. Moreover, Caribbean oil exports to the United States continued in 1965 to comprise preponderant shares of both Caribbean energy exports and U.S. energy imports.

Among regional energy exchanges that have disappeared as a factor of any importance in the world's interregional energy trade, there are West European coal shipments. For example, that region's coal exports to non-Caribbean Latin America, Africa, and today's Communist Europe (including the U.S.S.R.) represented nearly 15 percent of world energy movements in 1929. Similarly, the United States had been a notable oil exporter in 1929, shipping significant quantities to Canada, Western Europe, and numerous other regions; these U.S. oil exports accounted for over one-fifth of aggregate worldwide energy flows in 1929. By 1965, U.S. oil exports—except for small quantities of specialized products—had essentially disappeared from the world scene.[36] Ample and lower-cost alternatives to U.S. oil were available elsewhere.

* * * * *

A brief word may be added on the *dollar magnitude* of world energy flows corresponding in an approximate

[33]See Part Two, Profile No. 38, which relates a region's energy consumption to its supply dependence upon given parts of the world.

[34]The 1969 figures are estimated from British Petroleum Company, *Statistical Review of the World Oil Industry, 1969*.

[35]Italy has been a leading market for Russian oil: in 1968, one-eighth of Italian crude oil imports came from the U.S.S.R. United Nations, *World Energy Supplies*, Statistical Papers, Series J, No. 13 (New York, 1970).

[36]The role of the United States as a potential exporter of oil in an emergency should, however, be noted. Surplus U.S. productive capacity has in the past facilitated such a role. For example, in 1967 (the year of the Arab-Israeli conflict) the United States cut down on its crude oil imports from 62 to 57 million tons while raising its crude oil exports from virtually zero to over 3½ million tons. United Nations, *World Energy Supplies, 1964-1967*, Statistical Papers, Series J, No. 12 (New York, 1969).

Energy Trade as a Share of the Total Trade of and Between Selected Regions, Selected Years, 1950–1967
(Percents based on value)

	1950	*1955*	*1960*	*1965*	*1967*
Total trade (interregional plus intraregional):					
Total world	9.5%	10.7%	9.8%	9.4%	9.6%
From developed countries	4.4	5.0	3.9	3.2	3.3
To developed countries	8.5	10.4	10.2	10.1	10.2
From underdeveloped countries	19.4	24.2	27.4	30.4	33.0
To underdeveloped countries	12.0	12.2	10.2	8.7	8.6
From Communist countries	n.a.	12.1	10.9	10.6	9.8
To Communist countries	n.a.	8.7	7.1	6.5	6.0
Interregional trade between indicated groups of countries:					
From developed to underdeveloped countries	2.8	3.2	2.6	1.6	1.6
From underdeveloped to developed countries	14.8	20.6	26.1	31.9	34.2
From Communist countries to underdeveloped countries	n.a.	0.8	0.7	0.7	7.5
From underdeveloped countries to Communist countries	n.a.	–	–	–	0.4

way to the volumetric regional movements that have been reviewed above.[37] As mentioned earlier, the overall value of world energy trade in 1967 amounted to about $21 billion, of which–if 1965 relationships prevailed[38]–interregional trade conforming to the tonnage flows discussed above came to perhaps $15 billion. As with the tonnage figures, the most important regional flows involved Middle Eastern exports to Western Europe amounting to approximately $3½ billion and African exports to Western Europe of nearly $2 billion. Other major flows included Middle Eastern exports to Japan of nearly $1½ billion and Latin American exports to the United States of $1 billion. Japan's energy imports from all areas approximated $2 billion, the largest such figure for an individual country anywhere. The $2 billion represented over 20 percent of Japan's total merchandise imports.

A somewhat different perspective on the value of world energy trade appears in the summary tabulation above,[39] which shows world energy flows in relation to the value of world merchandise trade as a whole.

A particularly striking statistic is energy's continuously rising share of the total exports of underdeveloped countries to developed regions of the world. From 15 percent in 1950, this figure has risen steadily, reaching over one-third in 1967. The absolute value of energy flows from underdeveloped to developed areas in 1967–virtually all due to petroleum–is estimated at $10 billion, one-half of it originating in the Middle East. Only a portion of this amount, of course, is retained by the host country in the form of taxes, royalties, and other earnings. The data nonetheless testify to the extent to which oil dominates an important sector of world trade. Particularly, the figures suggest the need for caution in dealing aggregatively with the export potential of the world's underdeveloped countries taken as a group, because so large a portion of that potential reflects only a single commodity originating in only limited parts of the world. Indeed, a recent analysis of trends in world trade finds that

> . . . the developing countries' share in world exports of primary commodities has fallen continuously since 1953. If fuel exports are excluded, this trend is still more striking. World exports of fuels have grown at almost twice the rate of other primary commodities and the developing countries have managed to capture an increasing share of these exports. The developing countries' exports of nonfuel primary commodities have grown less than half as fast as world exports of these commodities. *Therefore, except for the fuel component, the decline in the developing countries' share of world primary exports would have been quite precipitous.*[40]

One final percentage in the tabulation deserves mention. Only a handful of underdeveloped countries are net exporters of energy. Much of the underdeveloped world

[37]Unlike the discussion in the preceding paragraphs of the present section, where tonnage figures on "energy" referred to coal and oil, references to the *value* of energy shipments cover all mineral fuels included in Standard International Trade Classification, No. 3.

[38]The 1965 data appear in Part Two, Profile No. 37. The 1967 data cited above are based on United Nations, *Monthly Bulletin of Statistics*, March 1969.

[39]From United Nations, *Statistical Yearbook*, various issues, and *Monthly Bulletin of Statistics*, March 1969.

[40]"International Trade Policies–The Export Performance of Developing Countries," *Monthly Review*, Federal Reserve Bank of Kansas City, July-August 1969, pp. 11-12. Italics added.

is energy-deficient and the nearly 9 percent or close to \$4 billion of underdeveloped nations' total merchandise imports accounted for by energy imports places a not inconsequential foreign exchange burden on such countries. Subject to the development of refining capacity—which to some extent can be foreign exchange saving—and/or new discoveries in these countries, foreign currency requirements for fuel imports seem destined to grow rapidly in the years ahead and will constitute an important cost factor in programs for economic development.

Energy Consumption and Gross National Product

In turning to an examination of the relationship between comparative levels and trends in energy consumption, on the one hand, with levels and trends in overall economic development, on the other, we enter into a somewhat more conjectural phase of our discussion—and one, moreover, which is somewhat peripheral to the central purpose of this volume. There are statistical difficulties relating to the construction and interpretation of data; and in such a broad-brush review little more than some suggestive points can be advanced.

A prominent characteristic of per capita consumption of commercial energy forms is its systematic and quantitatively close association with indicators of general economic development, measured here by per capita GNP—that is, an area's production of all goods and services per person.[41] This relationship between GNP and energy holds both cross-sectionally and historically: the higher a nation's income or output on the current international scale, the higher, in general, its level of energy consumption; as its GNP rises over time, so does its energy consumption—in close, even if not proportionate, conformity.

Although the connection between energy consumption and GNP may be more or less self-evident, the chain of causation between these two factors is less distinct, for there are clearly two-directional forces at work: some amount of electric generating capacity is obviously required in order to support a modern industrialized economy or one on the move toward it. This "input" of energy may, for example, take the form of an increase in motorized capital equipment, endowing each worker with more horsepower with which to increase his productivity.

Conversely, advancing living standards involve new wants the fulfillment of which is made possible by fuels and power. We have only to note the role of the private passenger car, of comfort heat and air conditioning, of numerous household appliances, of air travel and countless other products and services to appreciate the claims on energy arising from high and growing levels of personal income.

Cross-Sectional Comparison

The data in table 15, showing worldwide distribution of GNP, energy consumption, and population, hold few surprises. North America's 37 percent share of world energy consumption in 1965 was virtually matched by its 33 percent share of world GNP.[42] At the other extreme, Africa's share of both indicators lay between 1½ and 2 percent. Relative to a particular region's percentage share of world population, the table shows sharp disparities in the distribution both of energy use and of GNP: the developed regions (North America, Western Europe, Oceania, Japan, and South Africa),[43] with one-fifth of the world's population, accounted for two-thirds of energy consumption and of total GNP; the (non-Communist) less-developed areas, with around 45 percent of global population, consumed around 8 percent of the world's energy in 1965 and accounted for one-tenth of worldwide GNP. The spread of per capita GNP and energy consumption in the different regions reflects these disparities: per capita GNP ranges from \$3,400 in North America to \$140 in Africa, and per capita energy consumption ranges between 9,500 and 300 kilograms (coal equivalent) in these respective areas.

Broadly speaking, the Communist part of the world also divides sharply into the disparate patterns noted above. Energy consumption and GNP in the Soviet Union and Eastern Europe (treating the two in the aggregate) account for double that area's proportion of world population; while the estimated 1965 figures show Com-

[41]We can synonymously relate per capita energy use to per capita GNP or total energy use to total GNP; and for our purposes, per capita GNP is a serviceable, if somewhat imprecise, proxy for per capita income or per capita living standards.

[42]As discussed in greater detail in Part Five, Section I, there are great conceptual and measurement difficulties in constructing comparative GNP estimates for different parts of the world. (Aware of such difficulties, a few economists propose, in fact, that consideration be given to abandoning international GNP comparisons in favor of international "welfare" indicators based on such measures as energy consumption; see, e.g., W. Beckerman, *International Comparison of Real Income* (Paris: Organisation for Economic Cooperation and Development, 1966). The figures cited in this section are most approximate, and their use should be conditioned by this cautionary note.

[43]The "developed-underdeveloped" split follows essentially that employed in the United Nations publications (e.g., *1968 Statistical Yearbook*). While determined essentially by relative levels of per capita income, the classification is at least partly governed also by statistical convenience. Thus, *all* of Western Europe (a high per capita income area, on the whole) is included in the developed area total, even though certain individual countries (e.g., Portugal) have per capita income levels well below countries belonging to regions defined as underdeveloped because of their low overall per capita incomes. Argentina (in Latin America) and Israel (in the Middle East) are examples.

Table 15. GROSS NATIONAL PRODUCT, ENERGY CONSUMPTION, AND POPULATION, BY MAJOR REGIONS, 1965

Region	GNP ($ billion)	Energy consumption (million metric tons coal equiv.)	Population (million)	Percentage distribution: GNP	Percentage distribution: Energy consumption	Percentage distribution: Population	GNP per capita ($)	Energy consumption (kgs coal equiv.): Per capita	Energy consumption (kgs coal equiv.): Per $1 of GNP
North America	736.2	2,040.2	214.2	33.3%	37.3%	6.5%	3,437	9,524	2.77
Western Europe	578.2	1,117.2	343.1	26.1	20.4	10.5	1,685	3,256	1.93
Oceania	27.7	61.2	17.2	1.3	1.1	0.5	1,613	3,563	2.21
U.S.S.R. & Comm. E. Europe	422.0	1,255.8	334.2	19.1	22.9	10.1	1,269	3,778	2.98
Communist Asia	81.0	323.0	732.2	3.7	5.9	22.3	111	441	3.99
Latin America	95.9	199.5	243.0	4.3	3.6	7.4	395	821	2.08
Asia (other than Communist)	228.5	385.1	1,088.7	10.3	7.0	33.2	210	354	1.69
Africa	43.0	92.6	310.3	1.9	1.7	9.5	139	298	2.15
WORLD	2,212.5	5,474.6	3,281.2	100.0	100.0	100.0	674	1,668	2.47
of which Non-Communist:									
Developed regions	1,472.5	3,462.5	692.5	66.6	63.2	21.1	2,126	5,000	2.35
Underdeveloped regions	237.0	433.3	1,524.1	10.7	7.9	46.4	156	284	1.83

Note: "Developed" regions comprise North America, Western Europe, Oceania, South Africa, and Japan; "underdeveloped" regions comprise all other non-Communist regions of the world. See text fn. 43.

Source: See Part Two, Profile No. 3.

munist Asia (dominated by China) still to be characteristic of the poorest regions of the earth, as judged by its meager level of energy consumption and GNP in comparison to the size of its population.

Looking at the Communist area figures more closely, however, it is worth noting that for both broad regions their levels of energy consumption per capita are relatively high as compared to their levels of per capita GNP.[44] Indeed, the Soviet Union-Eastern Europe figure on per capita energy consumption exceeds that for Western Europe. As a result, both of the Communist regions rank high in terms of another ratio introduced in the table: energy consumption per $1 of GNP. This measure—which can be viewed as reflecting an area's "intensiveness" of energy use—is more suitably discussed in connection with table 16, showing 1965 country rankings in per capita GNP, per capita energy consumption, and energy per $1 of GNP.

Table 16 shows a generally close cross-sectional relationship between per capita GNP and per capita energy consumption. A graphic representation of these data, which accompanies Profile No. 4 in Part Two, shows that when the two indicators are plotted against each other, the resulting scatter of points falls within a fairly narrow band along the left-to-right, upward-sloping regression line. The close association is reflected in a correlation coefficient of 0.87. Of the twenty top-ranking nations in terms of per capita GNP, fifteen are also among the top twenty in terms of energy consumption per capita; of the ten lowest in GNP per capita, eight are among the ten lowest in energy consumption.

There are nonetheless sufficient exceptions (and a few outright anomalies) to warrant a somewhat closer look at the data. A good way of analyzing these less typical cases is by means of the ratios showing energy consumption per unit of gross national product—the measure of energy intensiveness mentioned above. Here, the rankings are noticeably less orderly than in the case of the two per capita indicators, even though a high energy-GNP ratio is more commonly associated with a highly developed and high-income economy than with a poorer country. This was also clear in the preceding regional table where, for developed regions, energy consumption per $1 of GNP was significantly above the ratio for less-developed parts of the world.

One apparent paradox, which finds a number of countries (e.g., Norway, Sweden, Switzerland) noticeably higher in the per-capita-GNP than in the per-capita-energy columns, and conspicuously far down in the energy-GNP ratio, is to a large extent explained by a measurement quirk. As mentioned in the Introduction and for reasons discussed in the technical notes of Part Five, the hydro component of energy consumption is translated into coal equivalents by the calorific value of the generated electricity rather than by the amount of fuel inputs that would, otherwise, have been required at a thermal power station to produce the same amount of

[44] The questionable quality of energy estimates for Mainland China should be kept in mind. According to United Nations, *1968 Statistical Yearbook* (New York, 1969), total Chinese energy consumption dropped by a disastrous 27 percent in 1967 after having risen 9 percent in 1966. (The second year of the "Cultural Revolution," 1967, was reportedly a time of widespread political and economic disruption.) This change would imply over a 20 percent drop between 1965 and 1967 in the level of Mainland China's per capita energy consumption.

Table 16. PER CAPITA GNP, PER CAPITA ENERGY CONSUMPTION, AND ENERGY CONSUMPTION PER DOLLAR OF GNP, SELECTED COUNTRIES, 1965

Country	GNP per capita		Energy consumption: Per capita		Energy consumption: Per dollar of GNP	
	Dollars	Rank	Kgs coal equiv.	Rank	Kgs coal equiv.	Rank
United States	3,515	1	9,671	1	2.75	10
Canada	2,658	2	8,077	2	3.04	7
Sweden	2,495	3	4,604	9	1.85	25
Denmark	2,333	4	4,149	10	1.78	27
Switzerland	2,331	5	2,699	21	1.16	45
West Germany	2,195	6	4,625	8	2.11	20
France	2,104	7	3,309	16	1.57	37
Norway	2,015	8	3,621	13	1.80	26
United Kingdom	1,992	9	5,307	5	2.66	11
Belgium-Luxembourg	1,991	10	5,152	6	2.59	12
New Zealand	1,970	11	2,603	22	1.32	40
Australia	1,910	12	4,697	7	2.46	13
Netherlands	1,839	13	3,749	12	2.04	22
Finland	1,750	14	2,825	19	1.61	33
East Germany	1,562	15	5,534	4	3.54	6
Czechoslovakia	1,561	16	5,870	3	3.76	3
Austria	1,365	17	2,584	23	1.89	24
U.S.S.R.	1,340	18	3,819	11	2.85	9
Israel	1,325	19	2,248	25	1.70	30
Italy	1,254	20	1,940	28	1.55	38
Japan	1,222	21	1,926	29	1.58	34
Hungary	1,094	22	3,188	18	2.91	8
Puerto Rico	1,094	23	2,126	26	1.94	23
Ireland	981	24	2,359	24	2.41	16
Poland	980	25	3,552	14	3.62	5
Venezuela	882	26	3,246	17	3.68	4
Bulgaria	829	27	2,011	27	2.43	15
Romania	778	28	1,916	30	2.46	14
Greece	772	29	904	39	1.17	44
Yugoslavia	743	30	1,217	32	1.65	32
Argentina	718	31	1,471	31	2.05	21
Cyprus	702	32	927	38	1.32	41
Spain	686	33	1,080	36	1.57	35
Trinidad and Tobago	646	34	3,505	15	5.43	1
Uruguay	573	35	958	37	1.67	31
Libya	542	36	613	42	1.13	46
South Africa	535	37	2,761	20	5.16	2
Nicaragua	527	38	247	48	0.70	49
Chile	497	39	1,119	33	2.25	18
Panama	495	40	1,112	34	2.25	19
Jamaica	492	41	873	40	1.77	28
Mexico	475	42	1,104	35	2.33	17
Lebanon	438	43	770	41	1.76	29
Hong Kong	421	44	605	43	1.44	39
Costa Rica	414	45	317	47	0.77	48
Portugal	396	46	520	45	1.31	42
Peru	367	47	577	44	1.57	36
Malaysia and Singapore	332	48	424	46	1.28	43
Guatemala	318	49	188	49	0.59	47

Source: See Part Two, Profile No. 4.

electric output.[45] The resulting measurement of energy consumption in countries where hydro looms large as a component of total energy input tends to be understated in comparison with areas where it is relatively low or negligible.

We have, however, also calculated energy consumption by an alternative formulation, which uses the theoretical boiler fuel input equivalent of the hydroelectricity. The resulting detailed tabulations appear in Part Two, Profiles No. 2 and No. 13, and Part Three, table XII. For the present purpose it is sufficient to note that, using this second procedure, the rankings in energy consumption per capita and, to a greater degree, those in the energy-GNP ratios take on what may be considered as a more reasonable order. For example, Norway's per capita energy consumption in 1965 would move from the 3,621 kgs shown in the table to 6,850 kgs, thus becoming the third highest in the world; and its energy-GNP ratio would become 3.41 kgs–an advance from 26th place in the standings to third place. A similar, though quantitatively less dramatic, reordering would take place for such countries as Sweden, Switzerland, and New Zealand–the latter, for example, moving from 40th place in energy consumption per unit of GNP to around 25th place. This alternative approach to hydro and total energy measurement thus improves the already close fit between energy per capita and GNP per capita, the correlation coefficient rising still higher; and the energy-GNP ratios, measuring energy intensiveness, show fewer erratic deviations.

Other deviations in the figures on energy consumption per unit of GNP are rooted in more substantive factors. A clearcut example–though modest in terms of exerting a decisive weight on country variations in the energy-GNP ratios which show up in the table–is climate; this will obviously produce some differences in fuel consumption, irrespective of income levels.

Then, too, differences in the thermal efficiency with which fuels are converted or used in different sectors of the economy will have some effect on national energy-GNP ratios. For example, in terms of coal-equivalent requirements per kwh of electricity, Czechoslovakia's power plants are only 80 percent as efficient as those of West Germany.[46] And, of course, though a prominent part of the national economy, the electric power sector is not the only one subject to varying thermal efficiencies among countries.

A far more important reason arises from the enormous variability in the energy needs of different industries. While the energy-GNP ratio is likely to be rather low in predominantly agricultural economies, energy per unit of national output tends to be high where a country's industry "mix" is heavily characterized by activities with relatively large energy requirements such as metallurgy or mining (e.g., Canada, Belgium-Luxembourg, Norway, South Africa, United Kingdom), chemicals (East Germany), or petroleum refining (Venezuela, Trinidad, and Tobago). Thus, compared with a country like Denmark, Canada consumes a far greater quantity of energy per capita than could be explained by the relatively slight per capita income differences between the two nations. This is because Canada–partly as a result of low-cost hydroelectric energy–has an energy-intensive industry mix oriented to such activities as metallurgy, electro-process industries, chemicals, pulp and paper, and mining. These industries, consuming energy per $1 of value added ranging from 4 kgs to 6 kgs coal equivalent, represent nearly 30 percent of Canada's value added in manufacturing; the share within Denmark's manufacturing sector (which is fully as important relative to the national economy as is Canada's) is under half of that.[47]

In order to pin down the role of industry mix somewhat more precisely, a statistical test was made to account for variations in the tabulated ratios of energy consumption per $1 of GNP; the results showed a reasonable correlation with the degree to which industrial structure was weighted towards energy-using industries.[48] More often than not, the energy-intensive economies so characterized were also among the higher-income countries of the world. Exceptions include South Africa and Trinidad and Tobago where a metal-mining-based economy and the role of petroleum refining,[49] respectively, yield the highest energy-GNP ratios in the world.[50]

[45]The main reason for having adopted the conversion procedure followed is that the United Nations Statistical Office, an important source of international energy statistics, uses this particular practice. Another reason is that in hydro-based countries electricity will often be used for purposes, such as space heating, which in other countries would entail the thermally more efficient use of fuels burned directly. As a consequence, there being no inherently "correct" hydro conversion technique, we have followed the U.N. procedure in order to avoid problems of lack of comparability with a standard source.

[46]Based on data in United Nations, Economic Commission for Europe, *Annual Bulletin of Electric Energy Statistics for Europe, 1965* (Geneva, 1966).

[47]Data are for 1963; from United Nations, *The Growth of World Industry, 1953-1965* (New York, 1967).

[48]Details on this test appear in Part Five, Section II. The dependent variable was energy consumption per $1 of GNP; the independent variable was value added in four energy-using manufacturing industries (paper, chemicals, petroleum and coal products, and basic metals) as percent of total manufacturing value added. The simple correlation coefficient was 0.59.

[49]This refers to energy consumed in the course of refinery operations, not to the crude oil subject to processing.

[50]Statistical anomalies, particularly in the measurement of

Historical Comparison

The final aspect of the relationship between energy consumption and national output considered here relates to changes over time. In table 17 average annual percentage growth rates in energy consumption and gross national product (based on constant prices) are shown for world regions and selected countries for the period 1950-65. Unavailability of GNP statistics makes it difficult to record trends over a longer historical time span than this, but what pre-1950 data we have been able to gather appear in Part Two, Profile No. 5.

A third column in table 17 introduces another measure—that of the energy-GNP "elasticity coefficient," which simply refers to the ratio of percentage increases in energy consumption to percentage increases in GNP. (An elasticity coefficient of more than 1 means that energy per $1 of GNP—the measure of energy intensiveness presented in table 16—has been rising.) As seen later (pp. 41-42), projected trends in elasticity provide a convenient, if rather crude, way of estimating the volume of future energy consumption associated with expected levels of gross national product.[51]

Looking at broad world areas, the right-hand panel of table 17 discloses average 1950-65 elasticities to be generally related to the stage of regional economic development, at least as measured by per capita output levels. Thus, in the most advanced areas of North America and Western Europe elasticities of under 1.0 signify energy consumption growth rates falling below national output growth rates, while for the low per capita income regions of the world elasticities range upward of 1.2 with the average for the less-developed parts of the world in the aggregate coming to about 1.7.[52] This much having been said as a very broad generalization, one must quickly add some qualifying observations.

Among regional energy-GNP elasticities, one is struck by the roughly similar value of coefficients for such disparate (in terms of per capita living standards) areas as Oceania, Africa, and the combined area of the U.S.S.R. and Communist Eastern Europe. And, looking at individual country data, we find marked variations in elasticities of ratios in the same general per capita output grouping. Note Switzerland's or Sweden's far higher coefficient than that of the United States, in the top income class; or Italy's figure, more than 100 percent higher than Japan's, in the second grouping.

A full explanation of these phenomena would require intensive country-by-country study. It is plain, however, that comparative stages in per capita GNP in many cases do not provide a ready guide to the rate at which a given country's energy demand will grow compared with its GNP growth. Some of the reasons are fairly obvious. By world standards, Italy, for example, is a relatively prosperous country; yet it is far from an industrially "mature" economy, as the sustained postwar movement from agriculture into industry attests. In other words, the scope for industrial growth of a type that implies a large expansion in energy requirements relative to national output growth is a function of a country's stage and pattern of development; per capita income levels serve at best only as proximate indicators.

Among the Communist countries, too, the ratio of energy growth to GNP growth varies for numerous reasons. Some Communist countries, such as China, exhibit the characteristically high elasticities of low-income countries. Others (e.g., Bulgaria) are still industrially developing rather than industrially advanced

GNP for these countries, cannot be ruled out as contributing to these results.

[51]Analysis of energy consumption trends via elasticities needs to be qualified not only because the aggregate nature of this measure is apt to obscure underlying factors (as seen in the ensuing text discussion), but also because in its very construction the elasticity coefficient lacks a certain degree of mathematical rigor. This arises because *annual* elasticities as calculated here and average *period* elasticities frequently calculated by others both differ somewhat from results (using differential calculus) based on *instantaneous* elasticity measurement. These problems are fully discussed by Richard L. Gordon, in "Forecasting and Policymaking—The Case of European Energy," an Italian translation of which appeared in *Economia Internazionale delle Fonti di Energia*, January 1969; it is also dealt with in Gordon's *The Evolution of Energy Policy in Western Europe: The Reluctant Retreat from Coal* (New York: Praeger, 1971).

[52]Although nothing conclusive can be inferred from an additional three-year period, more recent regional trends than those shown in the table seem generally to conform to this pattern. However, Oceania's elasticity since 1965 seems exceptionally high; it may have to do with accelerated growth in Australia's mining sector.

Average annual percentage growth rates, 1965-1968

	Energy consumption	*GNP*	*Elasticity*
North America	5.1%	4.6%	1.11
Western Europe	3.6	3.8	0.95
Oceania	5.6	3.4	1.65
Latin America (1965-67)	6.0	4.5	1.33
Japan	14.1	11.9	1.18

(GNP growth rates based on U.S. Department of State, Agency for International Development, *Gross National Product, Growth Rates and Trend Data by Region and Country*, release dated April 25, 1969; energy growth rates from table 3, herein.)

Table 17. AVERAGE ANNUAL PERCENTAGE GROWTH RATES, ENERGY CONSUMPTION, AND REAL GNP, SELECTED COUNTRIES AND REGIONS, 1950–1965

Per capita GNP range in 1965	Country[a]	Energy consumption	GNP	Energy-GNP elasticity coefficient
Over $1,800	United States	3.0	3.7	0.81
	Canada	5.1	4.5	1.13
	Sweden	6.2	3.9	1.59
	Denmark	5.5	4.0	1.38
	Switzerland	7.7	4.7	1.64
	West Germany	5.2	6.8	0.76
	France	4.7	4.7	1.00
	Norway	5.1	4.1	1.24
	United Kingdom	1.8	2.9	0.62
	Belgium-Luxembourg	3.4	3.6	0.94
	Australia	5.1	4.2	1.21
	Netherlands	5.6	4.8	1.17
$1,000 to $1,800	East Germany	4.4	5.0	0.88
	Czechoslovakia	5.6	3.8	1.47
	Austria	4.5	5.4	0.83
	U.S.S.R.	7.4	5.9	1.25
	Israel	12.1	10.7	1.13
	Italy	11.9	5.5	2.16
	Japan	9.9	9.9	1.00
	Hungary	7.8	4.8	1.62
	Puerto Rico	15.6	8.1	1.93
$700 to $1,000	Venezuela	11.4	7.1	1.61
	Bulgaria	14.1	6.6	2.14
	Romania	9.6	6.0	1.60
	Greece	10.3	7.3	1.41
	Yugoslavia	7.3	6.2	1.18
	Argentina	5.6	3.1	1.81
Under $700	Spain	5.1	6.1	0.84
	South Africa	5.1	4.7	1.09
	Chile	5.8	3.8	1.53
	Mexico	6.9	6.1	1.13
	Costa Rica	7.0	5.6	1.25

Region	Energy consumption	GNP	Energy-GNP elasticity coefficient
North America	3.2	3.8	0.84
Western Europe	4.4	4.8	0.92
Oceania	5.0	4.2	1.19
U.S.S.R. & Comm. E. Europe	6.9	5.6	1.23
Communist Asia	14.4	5.8	2.48
Latin America	7.6	4.9	1.55
Asia	9.0	6.8	1.32
Africa	5.4	4.4	1.23
WORLD	5.1	4.8	1.06
of which Non-Communist:			
Developed regions[b]	3.9	4.6	0.85
Underdev. regions	7.7	4.6	1.67

[a]Countries are listed according to their 1965 per capita GNP ranking.

[b]The indicated results for developed countries in the *aggregate* is heavily influenced by the dominant weight of the United States with its elasticity of 0.8. A regression plotted for fifteen developed countries (in Part Two, Profile No. 5) yields an elasticity of slightly over 1.0.

Note: "Real" GNP is based on constant prices.

Source: See Part Two, Profile No. 5.

economies. But beyond that, a general commitment toward heavy industry and electrification and post-World War II reconstruction—reinforced in some areas by thermally inefficient energy use—also contributes to high but widely varying energy-GNP elasticity coefficients throughout the Communist world.

In other cases a high energy-GNP elasticity among certain high-ranking per capita income countries, for example Sweden and Switzerland, is accounted for by other factors. Both of these countries experienced a post-World War II decline in the substantial share of their total energy consumption accounted for by hydroelectricity. As was pointed out on p. 35, hydroelectricity has been expressed in coal equivalents by its inherent thermal content rather than by the calorific value of the fuels with which it would have had to be replaced in thermal power stations. Consequently, as a falling hydro share in a country's energy consumption is offset by rising shares for other fuels, the nation's *measured* growth rate in energy consumption will be higher than under conditions of an unchanged hydro share. Indeed, Switzerland's 1950-65 yearly energy consumption growth of 7.7 percent and Sweden's 6.2 percent (see table 17) fall to 5.7 and 5.3 percent, respectively, when hydroelectricity is translated into prevailing central station boiler-fuel requirements.[53] The resulting energy-GNP elasticities drop to 1.21 for Switzerland (compared with 1.64 in table 17) and to 1.35 for Sweden (compared with 1.59 in table 17).

Also contributing to the relatively high elasticities recorded by these two countries is a phenomenon more commonly associated with developing countries where per capita income is lower. Where there is significant substitution of (measured) commercial fuels for (nonmeasured) noncommercial fuels, the recorded increases in energy consumption and in energy consumption per unit of national output are accentuated. But substitution is not unknown in advanced countries. For example, fuelwood, which is not classed as a commercial fuel in this study, has been estimated at 12 percent of Switzerland's total (i.e., commercial plus noncommercial) energy consumption in 1950, with a reduction to 3½ percent by 1965. Fuelwood's replacement, largely by liquid fuels, contributed to Switzerland's high energy-GNP elasticity coefficient shown in table 17. Sweden's high energy-GNP elasticity coefficient in part reflects a similar phenomenon.[54]

In view of such formidable qualifications, generalizations which one might be tempted to make about systematic tendencies in energy-GNP elasticity coefficients are easily suspect. It is true that among the thirty-two countries arrayed in order of per capita GNP in the left-hand part of table 17, nine had elasticities of 1.0 or below, and of those, seven were in the top rather than bottom half of the per capita GNP standings, making it possible that high per capita GNP countries might by and large be expected to display lower elasticities than low-income countries—perhaps as a result of factors similar to those cited in the cross-sectional presentation in table 16. One could hypothesize that in advanced industrial economies such as the United States and the United Kingdom, the evolving industry mix characteristics reflect the growth of sectors of relatively low energy demand per unit of output—services, for example. On the other hand, the changing industrial structure in other countries—primarily low-income, developing nations but also those with significant potential for more intensive industrialization, as we have seen—typically involves a shift away from agriculture (with relatively low energy requirements per unit of output) towards nonfarm industrial sectors (demanding relatively large amounts of energy for each dollar of total output).

This latter pattern characterized U.S. development prior to the 1920s; thereafter energy growth began falling persistently below GNP growth. Energy consumption per dollar of U.S. GNP[55] was 3.60 kgs coal equivalent in 1925 and down to 2.75 kgs in 1965. (See Part Two, Profile No. 5.) Conversely, energy use in the United States between 1880 and 1925 grew by about 5.2 percent annually while GNP rose by only 3½ percent; the resultant elasticity coefficient of approximately 1.5 conforms roughly to post-World War II elasticities for Greece, Chile, and Venezuela.[56]

Some advanced countries—in Western Europe, notably Great Britain, Belgium, and West Germany—appear to exhibit long-term declines in energy per unit of output similar to trends in the United States. Others, such as France and perhaps also Japan, may be approaching that point in their development. While these observations regarding long-term trends are not invalidated by developments over just a few years, it may be noted that in the most recent four-year period for which we have data (1965-69) the falling historical trend in the declining U.S. energy-GNP elasticity coefficient was apparently reversed. One reason for the reversal was a

[53] Alternative energy consumption growth rates based on the two conversion procedures appear in Part Three, table XIII, lines 12 and 13.

[54] For data on Switzerland, see United Nations, Economic Commission for Europe, *Factors Affecting the Accuracy of Energy Planning and Forecasting* (Geneva, April 9, 1968, mimeo.), p. 27. For data on Sweden, see "Sweden's Energy Policy," *The OECD Observer* (Paris), June 1969, p. 43.

[55] GNP refers to figures based on 1965 purchasing power.

[56] The 1880-1925 U.S. data (excluding fuelwood in the case of energy) are derived from Schurr, Netschert, *et al.*, *Energy in the American Economy*, pp. 516-17, 524-25.

sharp slowdown to the historic increases in efficiency improvements in thermal electric generation.[57]

Implications for Analysis and Methodology

The somewhat inconclusive note upon which the preceding discussion ends raises the question of whether there is utility (or futility) in analyzing observed changes in an area's energy consumption vis-à-vis changes in its aggregate output of goods and services, particularly if such analysis serves, as is often the case, as the springboard for projections of future energy requirements. (For example, see the following section on projections.)

Other studies, which deal with this question at some length,[58] recognize that such so-called "global" estimates of growth in aggregate energy consumption relative to GNP growth fulfill a legitimate analytical purpose so long as their inherent limitations are recognized, and especially when they are used as a quasi-independent check on energy demand projections arrived at by disaggregated, or "sectoral," methods.[59] The latter case, where forecasts of total energy demand are based on a separate examination of the main categories of consumption (within the perspective of an assumed rate of economic growth), recommends itself most to analysis and projections in individual countries; more may be at stake under such circumstances in terms of the policy use—and hence the required precision—of the numbers.

But even in a broader geographical context, and one where exactitude may be less critical, the sectoral approach is a useful complement to analysis emphasizing changes in energy-GNP elasticity coefficients. The 1966 study of the Organisation for Economic Cooperation and Development,[60] analyzing the energy outlook in North America, the OECD portion of Western Europe, and Japan, illustrates the nature of a limited sectoral approach—limited because the available data permitted consideration of only the following broad economic sectors: the iron and steel industry, other industry, transport, and "domestic and miscellaneous" (i.e., commerce, agriculture, public administration).[61]

Yet even these very broad sectoral groupings pointed up implications for energy demand which, in a more aggregative setting, might have been considered far less explicitly. Some examples follow:

- The OECD analysis underlines the major importance of the iron and steel industry as a consumer of energy. In the Common Market it is estimated that energy demand of the iron and steel industry represents approximately 45 percent of the total for all other manufacturing industries together.
- It is noted that in the industrial sector as a whole, energy demand tends to grow less fast than total output; however, industrial consumption of electricity rises much more rapidly than does industrial output. Because electricity not

[57] Some experts see enduring implications in this short-term reversal. (Both energy consumption and GNP grew at the average annual rate of 4.2 percent between 1965 and 1969 making for an elasticity of 1.0.) In their study, *An Energy Model for the United States* (U.S. Department of the Interior, Bureau of Mines Information Circular 8384 [Government Printing Office, 1968]), Warren E. Morrison and Charles L. Readling attribute the reversal of the historical trend of the energy-GNP elasticity coefficient in the United States to shifts in energy by form within major consuming sectors, and in particular to the displacement of direct fuels by purchased electricity—the latter requiring a higher input of energy resources per unit of secondary (kilowatt-hour) output than fossil fuels used directly. The growth of air conditioning would be one important element in this trend. (See p. 50 of their study.)

It is worth noting that the phenomenon of long-term decline in energy-GNP elasticity coefficients has been interpreted in yet another light. It has been argued that interfuel shifts in energy consumption, such as from coal to petroleum, reflect at the same time shifts from relatively inefficient to efficient uses of energy. "As substitution between fuels proceeds and GNP grows over time, the estimated energy elasticity is downward biased. This appears to be the main reason for the unexpectedly low energy elasticities which have been obtained in past empirical studies." (F. Gerard Adams and Peter Miovic, "On Relative Fuel Efficiency and the Output Elasticity of Energy Consumption in Western Europe," *Journal of Industrial Economics*, November 1968, p. 53.) However, even if the authors' suggested "efficiency-adjusted" measure of energy consumption would reverse the indicated decline in Western European elasticities, there is no particular reason to expect changes in the *relative* position of different countries of the world with respect to their energy-GNP elasticities, since all of them presumably benefit from efficiency-enhancing interfuel shifts. Moreover, the authors' adjustment excludes efficiency improvements associated with a *given* energy source (e.g., in coal burned at electric power plants). By analogy, one could argue that a measured decline in the capital-output ratio which stems from productivity-enhancing shifts—say, from plant to equipment—should be adjusted for efficiency changes, even though, misleadingly, this might leave the capital-output ratio unchanged.

[58] Three studies providing useful insight in this respect are: OECD, *Energy Policy* (1966), particularly pp. 19-42; United Nations, Economic Commission for Europe, *Methods and Principles for Projecting Future Energy Requirements*, ST/ECE/ENERGY/2, mimeo. (New York, 1964); and "The Demand for Energy," *National Institute Economic Review*, May 1967. These three publications deal respectively with comparative analysis of three areas (North America, Western Europe, Japan); of a number of specific Western and Eastern European countries; and of British experience alone.

[59] Of course, the two methods are not wholly independent of each other since assumptions about overall economic growth are common to both. Also, both approaches may be comprehended within a single estimating technique, as, for example, where a multiple regression equation determines energy consumption as a function of GNP, and a host of other variables and parameters representing the sectoral influences.

[60] OECD, *Energy Policy* (1966), pp. 19-21. Ensuing references and quotations are taken from these pages.

[61] For each of the three OECD constituent geographic areas, every sector's past and projected total energy requirement was estimated. In addition, each region's (but not sector's) energy requirement was broken down into the principal primary energy sources and into the demand for these selected secondary energy sources: electricity, coking coal, and refined liquid fuels.

only replaces other fuels but in the form of power replaces labor and increases productivity, the result is increased primary energy consumption at power stations.

- Fuel demand for both commercial and personal transport seems to be closely tied to overall economic growth. In the past, the former has been affected by the replacement of coal by diesel and electric locomotives in the railways; while, in many parts of the OECD area, the latter has been one "of the most dynamic elements of the changing structure of energy demand."

With attention focused on these and other developments (e.g., efficiency improvements and technical innovations) within and among different sectors of economic activity, one is less prepared to offer succinct interpretation of the link between *overall* changes in energy demand and gross national product. Reverting to the observation above about the desirability of independent approaches to estimates of future energy consumption, we might note how, in the OECD analysis, projections covering the period 1964-80 differed, using the global (energy-GNP elasticity) method on the one hand, and the sectoral procedure on the other:[62]

Per Annum Growth Rates in Energy Consumption, 1964-1980

	Japan	*North America*	*OECD Europe*
Sectoral. . .	8.0%	3.7%	4.1%
Global. . . .	7.2	3.9	3.9

Evidently, the two approaches yielded quite close agreement in the case of North America and Europe. Japan, the most dynamic and economically least advanced area in this particular comparison, produced the widest range of estimates.[63]

While, for a number of economically advanced regions, the relationship between growth in energy consumption and national output might thus exhibit behavior that is sufficiently systematic to warrant cautious analytical use, far greater circumspection is required when turning to less-developed areas. There, even though one is tempted to look for historical parallels, it is problematical whether evolving trends in energy and GNP growth in different parts of the world will necessarily follow the historical path of development once taken by the industrialized countries of today. As just one example, let us recall that the United States, during those years in the late nineteenth and early twentieth centuries when its energy per unit of GNP was rising rapidly, was still tied to conditions of energy use that will not be repeated in present-day developing economies. Then, factory mechanical power was based on steam engines rather than electric motors, and the automobile had not yet become a common mode of transport. It is hazardous to place too great a reliance on "stages of growth" in matters relating to energy consumption no less than in general economic development.

Projections of Energy Consumption

It is the primary purpose of this volume to set forth a quantitative record of long-term historical developments in patterns of energy consumption, output, and foreign trade in different parts of the world, with some subsidiary attention to the relationship between energy consumption and overall economic activity. One possible use that readers may make of the materials is to assist with analyses and projections of future energy demands and supplies. We ourselves, however, have stopped short of dealing at length with energy projections. The observations on likely future developments and their implications, offered in this section, are derived to a considerable extent from the author's recent analysis in a Rand-RFF volume dealing with international oil problems.[64]

Since energy resources are depletable, unequally distributed around the world, and an essential ingredient in economic growth, their prospective demand and availability in the years ahead are obviously a matter of considerable concern and significance. In focusing on trends a decade or so ahead, as we do here, the question of whether projected levels of 1980 energy demand worldwide can be met from world energy reserves that will then be at hand is judged to be of no urgency. What is already known today or what can reasonably be inferred about the energy reserve situation makes the issue of worldwide energy scarcity something that is more suitably cast in a much longer time horizon, say the year 2000 or beyond.

Based essentially upon experience since World War II, and especially developments during the past decade or so, the projected growth in world energy demand (the implicit result of separate projections for each of the areas shown in table 18) comes to slightly more than 5 percent per year during the period 1965-80. This rate

[62]OECD, *Energy Policy*, pp. 26-27, 32-33, 38-39.

[63]A retrospective analysis of energy projections for Britain during the period 1959-1965 finds that, as against a realized growth rate of energy consumption of 2.8 percent yearly, the projected rate using sectoral analysis was 2.1 percent, while the energy-GNP coefficient projection yielded the still lower figure of 1.9 percent. Interestingly, even the sectoral approach underestimated the dynamism of expanding energy demand for personal transport and in households. See *National Institute Economic Review*, May 1967, pp. 55-60.

[64]Contained in the Statistical Appendix to Sam H. Schurr, Paul T. Homan, *et al.*, *Middle Eastern Oil and the Western World: Prospects and Problems* (American Elsevier, 1971).

Table 18. PROJECTED GROWTH IN WORLD ENERGY CONSUMPTION, BY MAJOR REGIONS, 1965-1980

Region	Average annual percentage rate of change		Million metric tons coal equiv.		Million metric tons oil equiv.		Percent of world total	
	1950-65	1965-80	1965	1980	1965	1980	1965	1980
United States	3.0%	3.5%	1,790	3,000	1,194	2,000	34.2%	26.8%
Canada	5.1	5.5	150	335	100	223	2.9	3.0
Western Europe	4.4	4.0	1,045	1,882	697	1,255	20.0	16.8
Japan	9.9	7.9	175	547	117	365	3.3	4.9
Middle East	10.2	9.4	45	173	30	115	0.9	1.5
Other Asia	7.6	8.2	148	483	99	322	2.8	4.3
Oceania	5.0	4.8	62	125	41	83	1.2	1.1
Latin America	7.6	7.4	184	538	123	359	3.5	4.8
Caribbean	8.6	8.4	104	349	69	233	2.0	3.1
Other Latin America	6.5	5.9	80	189	53	126	1.5	1.7
Africa	5.4	6.5	88	226	59	151	1.7	2.0
North Africa	4.6	5.6	16	36	11	24	0.3	0.3
Other Africa	5.6	6.7	72	190	48	127	1.4	1.7
U.S.S.R.	7.4	6.5	833	2,142	555	1,428	15.9	19.1
Communist Eastern Europe	5.8	4.6	372	730	248	487	7.1	6.5
Communist Asia	14.4	7.6	338	1,014	225	676	6.5	9.1
WORLD	5.1	5.2	5,231	11,195	3,488	7,464	100.0	100.0
Excluding Communist area	4.2	4.7	3,688	7,309	2,459	4,873	70.5	65.3

Note: 1965 data above differ slightly from 1965 data employed elsewhere in this volume. See text fn. 65.

Source: Sam H. Schurr, Paul T. Homan, *et al.*, *Middle Eastern Oil and the Western World: Prospects and Problems* (American Elsevier, 1971), statistical appendix.

conforms closely to that achieved between 1950 and 1965. In terms of tonnage, world energy consumption in 1980 is projected at more than 11 billion coal equivalent tons (or 7½ billion tons expressed in oil equivalents)—over twice the level recorded in 1965.[65]

As pointed out earlier (pp. 38 ff.), energy demand projections anchored to projected GNP growth via "elasticity coefficients" may rest on a somewhat less than secure analytical base. Nevertheless, because we are largely concerned with broad geographic regions and general orders of magnitude, this approach is not out of place here. These projections of total energy consumption therefore follow essentially from assumptions regarding growth in total regional output of all goods and services (GNP) and prospective trends in elasticities relating the growth of energy use to that in gross national product. A summary tabulation of the relevant historical and projected figures[66] appears on page 42.

For the most part we have allowed for a continuation of the moderately downward historical trends in elasticities, though at a dampened pace, especially where the ratio has already reached a fairly low level as it has in the United States. This assumption signifies growth in total energy consumption at a rate near or below that of GNP growth for most of the highly industrialized countries; while an elasticity still substantially in excess of 1.0 for the less advanced regions reflects, among other things, accelerated mechanization, a disproportionately fast rise of energy-intensive industries such as manufacturing and transport (conversely, a relative decline of agriculture), and patterns of consumption associated with increased uses of electricity. In addition, numerous developing areas are still undergoing a transition from a fairly heavy dependence on so-called noncommercial energy forms (e.g., firewood, vegetable wastes, dung) to predominant reliance upon the commercial energy sources covered in this study. This would result in relatively high (commercial) energy-GNP elasticities for such areas.

[65] The historical and projected data cited here differ somewhat from comparable statistics tabulated or referred to earlier in this discussion. For example, worldwide energy consumption in table 15, above, came to 5,475 million tons in 1965 compared with a total of 5,231 million tons shown in table 18. These discrepancies arise largely from the use of different underlying source materials and, relatedly, somewhat different definitional practices. For example, the Schurr-Homan study upon which the accompanying projection tables are based placed primary reliance on the series appearing in the United Nations, *World Energy Supplies*, Statistical Papers, Series J. In the latter publication, data on crude oil do not enter into the calculation of liquid fuels consumption which, rather, refers to the consumption of refined liquid fuels. As a result, that portion of crude oil production going into petrochemical feedstocks and other nonenergy uses (as well as crude oil subject to refinery losses) is excluded from the United Nations liquid fuels consumption measure, while it is included in the figures cited earlier in our discussion as well as in the data in Parts Two and Three of this volume. There are other sources of difference, but the one just described is major. (See also Comparison of Statistical Aggregates with Other Publications, Part Four.)

[66] Sam H. Schurr, Paul T. Homan, *et al.*, *Middle Eastern Oil and the Western World: Prospects and Problems* (American Elsevier, 1971), taken from the Statistical Appendix prepared by Joel Darmstadter. The reader is referred to the earlier discussion on elasticity (pp. 36-40), above; and to Part Two, Profile No. 5.

	Average annual percentage growth in GNP		*Elasticity: percentage growth in energy consumption divided by percentage growth in GNP*		*Average annual percentage growth in energy consumption*	
	1950–65	*1965–80*	*1950–65*	*1965–80*	*1950–65*	*1965–80*
United States	3.7%	4.4%	0.81%	0.80%	3.0%	3.5%
Canada	4.5	5.0	1.13	1.10	5.1	5.5
Western Europe	4.8	4.5	0.92	0.90	4.4	4.0
Japan	9.9	7.5	1.00	1.05	9.9	7.9
Middle East	5.8	6.3	1.76	1.50	10.2	9.4
Other Asia	4.1	5.1	1.75	1.60	7.6	8.2
Oceania	4.2	4.2	1.19	1.15	5.0	4.8
Latin America	4.9	5.0	1.55	1.48	7.6	7.4
Caribbean	n.a.	5.8	n.a.	1.45	8.6	8.4
Other Latin America	4.3	4.4	1.51	1.35	6.5	5.9
Africa	4.4	5.0	1.23	1.30	5.4	6.5
North Africa	n.a.	n.a.	n.a.	n.a.	4.6	5.6
Other Africa	n.a.	n.a.	n.a.	n.a.	5.6	6.7
U.S.S.R.	5.9	5.4	1.25	1.20	7.4	6.5
Communist Eastern Europe	4.9	4.2	1.18	1.10	5.8	4.6
Communist Asia	5.8	4.6	2.48	1.65	14.4	7.6

The coupling of projected GNP growth rates and projected elasticities yields the regional estimates of future energy demand shown in table 18. The share of world energy consumption accounted for by the advanced, non-Communist part of the world is, in the aggregate, projected as declining (the combined total for North America, Western Europe, and Oceania is projected to go from 58 percent of the world total in 1965 to 48 percent in 1980) though particular areas, notably Japan, may be expected to raise their share of world energy consumption. Taken as a group, the Communist area increases its share (the slight relative decline projected for Eastern Europe being more than offset by relative gains for Soviet Russia and Communist Asia), as do most of the less-developed regions of the world. For the latter group, annual growth of energy consumption works out to a bit more than 7½ percent yearly. This could be a generous assumption, because in many fuel-deficient, less-developed countries, much will depend on their ability to finance energy imports. However, even taking this 7½ percent growth rate,[67] the per capita level of energy use in less-developed areas would still remain very low. Specifically, the implied 1980 level is barely 900 kilograms of coal equivalent—a figure representing less than one-half of what was achieved in Western Europe in the 1920s.

Turning to projected shifts in the shares represented by the different energy sources, as shown in table 19, it is necessary (even more than for the energy totals) to underscore their conjectural nature. A major reason why a projection of individual energy sources presents greater difficulties than one for total energy consumption is that there is much substitutability among the different primary fuels in various uses—especially in the generation of electric power and in the provision of space and process heat. Which primary source will be used will depend upon relative prices as these are affected and modified by new supply sources, governmental policies, and technological advances. All of these factors are of necessity highly speculative. The accompanying figures should therefore be viewed as rough indicators embedded within a very substantial area of uncertainty. Representing judgments about the most reasonable trends that can be extrapolated at the time of writing (mid-1969), the projected shares are only *one* of a number of alternative lines of development, some with perhaps as good a chance of being realized as those which have been postulated. Moreover, crucial underlying elements could be considered only partially or implicitly in the RFF study from which the figures have been taken.

If the facts were available to support such an exercise, it would have been desirable to specify the relevant price, policy, or technological assumptions consistent with the projected demand for particular fuels. In their absence, the projections are essentially trend extrapolations in which such elements are implicit in the historical data employed as background. It is true that in certain ways the projections go beyond a mere mechanical running out into the future of the available statistical time series. That is, they take into consideration actual developments or judgments about probable developments that are as yet barely indicated in any historical data. Announcements of planned nuclear power plant construction, of North Sea gas developments, and Australian petroleum discoveries are examples of such factors that have been taken into account. Nevertheless, the figures cited remain trend extrapolations insofar as they do not allow for certain major economic or technological break-

[67]Composed of a 5 percent annual growth rate in per capita consumption and a 2½ percent rate of population growth.

throughs up to 1980 (e.g., North American Arctic oil production, competitive exploitation of North American oil shale and tar sands, or liquefaction and gasification of coal) which might seriously affect prospective interfuel energy patterns in various parts of the world. Nor do they allow for major changes in governmental policy, such as that restricting oil imports into the United States.

The projected energy shares point to a continued slippage in the share of solid fuels—particularly in the areas where, in the recent past, they have continued to figure prominently—generally offset by rising shares for each of the other energy sources except hydro, whose proportion remains unchanged. In absolute terms, however, all fuel categories gain—including coal which in the latter part of the 1960s has tended to recede in terms of worldwide tonnage consumed. The specifics of these changes obviously vary from region to region. The United States is seen as altering its interfuel pattern least, the American transition to an oil- and gas-oriented economy having occurred many years ago. A modest decline in coal's contribution to U.S. energy demand, chiefly through electric generation, is the result of the sharply rising nuclear proportion—up from zero in 1965 to an estimated 4 percent of total energy consumption in 1980. Western Europe's coal consumption is projected as continuing its past absolute decline. As table 20 shows, it is the only region projected with an actual decrease in physical as well as percentage terms; consumption is assumed to decline from approximately 515 million tons in 1965 to 340 million tons in 1980. Few observers of the Western European coal scene are sanguine about the industry's chances of improving its competitive position vis-à-vis other fuels. A similar outlook applies to Japan where only a slight absolute increase in tons of coal consumed is in sight. Solid fuels shares are likely to fall in the Soviet Union and Communist Eastern Europe; even so, the latter's projected 1980 coal share will still exceed the solid fuels energy share in the United States in the mid-1930s. There is sparse knowledge regarding Mainland China's solid fuels and liquid fuels reserves, making projections of energy shares for Communist Asia a matter of considerable speculation. Coal, however, seems destined to continue as the mainstay of that nation's fuel and power base for some time.

The converse to falling coal shares is primarily rising proportions of liquid fuels in most areas. Although some leveling-off may occur within a decade or so, the worldwide liquid fuels share of total energy consumption is expected to continue rising. The Communist Eastern European countries, Japan, and—to a somewhat lesser extent—Western Europe are all projected as areas with marked increases in the liquid fuels proportion of total energy use.

Natural gas shows a significantly rising share in Western Europe and Oceania, the consequences of Dutch and North Sea gas (plus gas imports) in the first case, and of Australian discoveries in the latter case. Further

Table 19. PROJECTED SHARES OF THE DIFFERENT ENERGY SOURCES IN REGIONAL ENERGY CONSUMPTION, 1965-1980

Region	Solid fuels		Liquid fuels		Natural gas		Hydro-electricity		Nuclear	
	1965	1980	1965	1980	1965	1980	1965	1980	1965	1980
	Percent of each region's total energy consumption									
United States	23.7%	20.9%	40.4%	38.9%	34.5%	34.7%	1.4%	1.4%	–	4.1%
Canada	15.5	10.2	47.5	43.9	27.2	35.7	9.8	8.2	–	2.0
Western Europe	49.3	18.1	44.3	61.2	2.7	13.5	3.5	3.0	0.2%	4.2
Japan	36.9	12.7	56.5	80.5	1.5	2.0	5.1	2.5	–	2.4
Middle East	12.8[a]	8.0[a]	74.8	75.9	11.6	14.4	0.8	1.7	–	–
Other Asia	58.1	55.5	34.8	34.7	4.8	6.3	2.3	3.0	–	0.5
Oceania	55.0	38.0	41.5	44.3	–	13.2	3.5	3.9	–	0.6
Caribbean	4.4	2.8	69.2	65.1	24.5	29.8	1.9	2.3	–	–
Other Latin America	7.5	6.3	74.3	68.2	12.7	17.7	5.5	7.5	–	0.3
North Africa	5.7	2.0	83.2	68.6	8.5	25.0	2.6	4.4	–	–
Other Africa	72.2	58.0	25.9	33.1	0.2	6.0	1.7	2.9	–	–
U.S.S.R.	49.8	33.3	28.7	30.1	20.3	34.6	1.2	1.7	n.a.	0.2
Communist Eastern Europe	82.8	61.9	9.9	25.0	6.9	12.0	0.4	0.4	–	0.7
Communist Asia	94.9	90.5	4.4	9.0	–	–	0.7	0.5	–	0.1
WORLD	43.2	32.3	36.7	41.3	17.8	22.2	2.2	2.1	0.1	2.1
WORLD (million metric tons):										
Coal equivalent	2,261	3,615	1,921	4,622	933	2,485	113	237	3	236
Oil equivalent	1,508	2,410	1,281	3,082	622	1,657	75	158	2	157

[a]The solid fuels entry for the Middle East arises largely from coal output and use in Turkey and Iran.

Note and source: Same as for table 18.

Table 20. PROJECTED LEVELS OF ENERGY CONSUMPTION, BY SOURCE AND MAJOR REGION, 1965 AND 1980

(Million metric tons coal equivalent)

Region	Solid fuels		Liquid fuels		Natural gas		Hydro-electricity		Nuclear	
	1965	1980	1965	1980	1965	1980	1965	1980	1965	1980
United States	425.2	626.0	723.2	1,167.2	616.8	1,041.3	24.6	42.9	0.5	122.6
Canada	23.3	34.2	71.3	147.1	40.8	119.6	14.6	27.5	0.02	6.7
Western Europe	515.4	340.0	462.7	1,151.0	28.0	255.0	36.6	57.0	2.5	79.0
Japan	64.5	69.6	98.8	440.1	2.7	10.7	8.9	13.5	–	13.1
Middle East[a]	5.7	13.8	33.6	131.3	5.2	24.9	0.4	2.9	–	–
Other Asia	85.8	268.1	51.4	167.6	7.1	30.4	3.3	14.5	–	2.0
Oceania	34.3	47.5	25.9	55.4	–	16.5	2.2	4.9	–	0.8
Caribbean	4.6	9.8	72.2	227.2	25.5	104.0	2.0	8.0	–	–
Other Latin America	6.0	11.9	59.6	129.0	10.2	33.4	4.4	14.2	–	0.5
North Africa	0.9	0.7	13.4	24.7	1.4	9.0	0.4	1.6	–	–
Other Africa	52.0	110.2	18.7	62.9	0.1	11.4	1.2	5.5	–	–
U.S.S.R.	414.5	713.9	238.8	645.2	169.5	741.5	10.0	36.4	n.a.	5.0
Communist Eastern Europe	308.6	452.0	37.0	182.5	25.6	87.6	1.4	2.9	–	5.0
Communist Asia	320.4	917.7	14.8	91.3	–	–	2.6	5.1	–	0.9
WORLD (million metric tons):										
Coal equivalent	2,261	3,615	1,921	4,622	933	2,485	113	237	3	236
Oil equivalent	1,508	2,410	1,281	3,082	622	1,657	75	158	2	157

Notes and source: Same as for table 19.

exploitation of Siberian gas fields is likely to push up not only the Soviet Union's own natural gas share but also that of areas supplied with Soviet gas. Principally, this would mean Communist Eastern Europe, although sales of Russian gas in Western Europe are also in prospect. More generally, the rapidly developing international market for natural gas, made possible by improved technology of liquefaction, will broaden use of this primary energy source on a wide geographic front. For example, Japan began importing Alaskan gas in 1969, and in the same year contracted for substantial amounts from Brunei in the years ahead; North African gas is being shipped to Western Europe in rapidly expanding volume.

Nuclear energy—projected as the fastest-growing energy source, starting, as it does, from a negligible current level—is expected to increase markedly for a number of advanced regions. It should be strongly emphasized that the realism of the nuclear power plans of many individual countries is quite hard to assess; our indicated total of *world* nuclear energy consumption, equivalent to roughly 235 million tons of coal in 1980, compares reasonably closely with estimates of the International Atomic Energy Agency, which imply coal equivalents of 263 million tons in 1980.[68] The relative magnitude of our nuclear projections can be appreciated from the fact that 235 million coal-equivalent tons would be about equal in importance to worldwide hydroelectricity at that time, and that it would represent the electrical output which could be furnished by some 360 nuclear power plants of, say, 750 megawatts of capacity each.[69] Nevertheless, as table 19 indicates, this would still amount to little more than 2 percent of world energy consumption in 1980.

The aforementioned shifts in regional patterns of interfuel use also signify changes in the geographic distribution of world consumption of each energy category. In summary form, these are as shown in the tabulation on page 45.

Notable among these projected changes are: the continued diminishing role of Western Europe in world coal consumption, as opposed to a substantially larger share for the Communist area; a falling share of world oil and natural gas consumption in North America (though increases in real terms that will be much larger than for most other regions) as compared to rising or essentially stable proportions of the world totals everywhere else; Western Europe's declining share of world hydroelectric consumption, and the growing proportion accounted for by the Communist countries and the (less developed) rest of the world; and in nuclear power, the relinquishment of Western Europe's hitherto commanding lead to the United States.

[68] International Atomic Energy Agency (Vienna), press release dated December 18, 1968.

[69] Worldwide nuclear generating capacity in 1980 of 270,000 megawatts would be the same as 360 plants of 750 megawatts each. The calculation by which the 270,000-megawatt world total is translated into coal equivalents runs as follows: a plant factor of 80 percent (or 7,000 hours) implies electric generation of 1,890 billion kwh. Applying a conversion factor of 0.125 metric tons of coal per 1,000 kwh (that is, the calorific value of the electricity generated), one obtains a worldwide coal equivalent of 236 million tons.

Percent of World Consumption of Each Energy Source

	Solid fuels		*Liquid fuels*		*Natural gas*		*Hydro*		*Nuclear*	
	1965	*1980*	*1965*	*1980*	*1965*	*1980*	*1965*	*1980*	*1965*	*1980*
United States.	18.8%	17.3%	37.6%	25.3%	66.1%	41.9%	21.9%	18.1%	15.1%	52.0%
Canada	1.0	0.9	3.7	3.2	4.4	4.8	13.0	11.6	0.5	2.8
Western Europe . . .	22.8	9.4	24.1	24.9	3.0	10.3	32.5	24.1	84.4	33.5
Japan	2.9	1.9	5.1	9.5	0.3	0.4	7.9	5.7	–	5.6
Oceania	1.5	1.3	1.3	1.2	–	0.7	2.0	2.1	–	0.3
Total Comm. area . .	46.1	57.6	15.1	19.9	20.9	33.3	12.4	18.7	n.a.	4.6
Rest of world	6.9	11.6	13.1	16.0	5.3	8.6	10.3	19.7	–	1.2
WORLD	100.0	100.0	100.0	100.0	100.0	100.0	100.0	100.0	100.0	100.0

World Energy Reserves

The foregoing projections of energy consumption carry implications regarding the availability and costs of energy supplies. Without examining the complex set of economic, institutional, technological, and geological factors that will affect the pattern of supply—a subject not dealt with explicitly in this study—it may be useful to comment briefly, and very broadly, on one element in this combination of factors—the reserve picture as it looks for the different energy forms, with particular attention to coal and to petroleum.

In going from judgments about projected levels of energy consumption to the question regarding energy reserves or resources, one is not "leaving conjecture behind and entering the realm of hard geological fact."[70]

> . . . Actually there is no true measure of the world's endowment of energy resources, nor, in the nature of things, is there ever likely to be one. Cost alone would prohibit a comprehensive probing of the earth's crust to provide anything approaching a true measure of resources. More to the point, society's interest is confined to resources that are exploitable now or seem likely to be in the future. As time passes the standards of exploitability keep changing, mainly as a result of advances in technology and changes in economic circumstances. Consequently resource-supply estimates are subject to at least as many uncertainties as energy-demand estimates. Although resource estimates embody some actual measurements of the contents of known deposits, they are based chiefly on geological inference.

Nor is there any standard conceptual framework within which this variety of resource estimates can be treated with terminological precision. There are problems of definition when dealing with alternative estimates for a given energy form; and even greater problems when trying to relate resource concepts applicable to, say, coal to some appropriately corresponding concepts for petroleum. Nevertheless, some steps at conceptualization have been taken, as have attempts to provide some practical definitional distinctions among alternative resource measurements.[71] Here we will merely mention a few of these basic distinctions, as a guide to some quantitative estimates to be cited in the discussion of coal and of oil and gas, below.

The most widely employed concept applying to oil, as well as to natural gas, is that of known "proved reserves." Figures on proved oil reserves represent a basic minimum estimate of potential world oil resources. They refer to the amount of oil remaining in the ground which, on the basis of geological and engineering information, can with reasonable certainty be assumed recoverable in the future from known reservoirs and under current *economic and technological circumstances*. For purposes of assessing very long-term adequacy, the measure of proved reserve is regarded as too restrictive a concept and is augmented by estimates of "unproved reserves," which may comprehend knowledge about probable and possible reserves: that is, the amount of petroleum which can reasonably be assumed recoverable under today's economic conditions but which can only be approximated on the basis of incomplete geological, geophysical, and other data. As one progressively relaxes both the economic and technological assumptions (e.g., to include an allowance for higher-cost marginal deposits or to allow for new recovery techniques) as well as assumptions about the degree of certainty (so as to allow for still undiscovered resources) still much higher estimates of total resources or "ultimate probable reserves"[72] can be derived.

[70]Both quoted excerpts are from Sam H. Schurr, "Energy," *Scientific American*, September 1963, p. 114. The ensuing discussion draws to a considerable extent on this article.

[71]A good summary of these issues appears in Schurr, Netschert, *et al.*, *Energy in the American Economy*, pp. 295-301. See also the proposed scheme of resource-estimate classification by Vincent E. McKelvey, "Contradictions in Energy Resource Estimates," in *Energy*, Proceedings of the Seventh Biennial Gas Dynamics Symposium, edited by Lawrence B. Holmes (Northwestern University Press, 1968), pp. 13-25.

[72]Except for proved reserves of oil, which exclude the estimated volume of past production, estimates conforming to the other—much broader—concepts frequently apply to "totals originally in place": that is, they do not net out what has already come out of the ground. Since the latter is, to date, such a small proportion of these larger reserve estimates, the resulting distortion is not serious.

Most coal deposits lie at relatively shallow depth, and they commonly provide surface evidence of their presence. As a result, for coal the problem of estimation generally is not that of "proving out" a reserve. Rather, a commonly accepted concept of potential coal resources defines the deposit in terms of certain physical parameters (e.g., depth, thickness of seam, recoverability), usually as circumscribed by the existing state of mining technology. This enables the estimator to specify the physical factors governing his particular coal-resource estimate. Also, by either greatly relaxing or severely restricting these physical conditions, thereby implicitly introducing higher or lower cost assumptions, it enables him to derive correspondingly higher or lower figures of potential availability. In the discussion below, we shall cite coal resource estimates that illustrate these points.

Coal

In the case of coal,[73] the range of estimated world resources will vary depending on such factors as the minimum thickness of coal included, the size of the overburden, and the degree of inference that an estimator will allow himself on the basis of available geologic and exploratory information. Some of these factors can be illustrated by looking at the estimate of world coal resources tabulated below.[74]

	Coal resources determined by mapping and exploration	*Probable additional resources in unmapped and unexplored areas*	*Estimated total resources*
	(In billion metric tons)		
North America	1,560	2,520	4,080
of which:			
United States	1,420	1,490	2,910
Europe	560	190	750
Oceania	50	70	120
U.S.S.R.	5,900	2,720	8,620
Latin America	20	10	30
Asia	450	910	1,360
Africa	70	150	220
WORLD	8,610	6,570	15,180

The estimated resources included in the tabulation refer to coal seams 12 inches or more thick occurring, for the most part, less than 4,000 feet below the surface. Although over one-half of the staggering world total of 15 trillion tons is credited to coal formations "determined by mapping and exploration," a large portion (45 percent) is assumed to occur in "unmapped and unexplored" areas—generally by extension of information about the mapped and explored category. It is important to note, however, that out of the roughly 8½ trillion tons said to be determined by mapping and exploration, only a relatively small amount (between 5 and 10 percent) consists of "measured" resources, with the preponderant share made up of "indicated" and "inferred" resources. In the United States, for example, some 8 percent of the 1.4 trillion tons represents measured resources, while 27 percent refers to indicated and 65 percent to inferred resources.[75]

An adjustment that should be made in appraising future adequacy of coal resources is to estimate the quantity judged to be recoverable under given technological conditions. Recoverability of 50 percent—a factor generally consistent with current underground mining experience in the United States—is commonly used to pare down estimates of world resources, as shown in the first column of the above tabulation. For the world as a whole, this yields an estimate of the recoverable coal resources determined by mapping and exploration of 4.3 trillion tons, distributed regionally as follows:

	In billion metric tons	*As percent of world*
North America	780	18.1%
of which:		
United States	710	16.5
Europe	280	6.5
Oceania	25	0.6
U.S.S.R.	2,950	68.5
Latin America	10	0.2
Asia	225	5.2
Africa	35	0.8
WORLD	4,305	100.0

[73] In the following discussion bituminous coal and anthracite, as well as brown coal, are all included in cited totals and figured in at hard coal equivalents.

[74] Paul Averitt, *Coal Resources of the United States, January 1, 1967*, Geological Survey Bulletin 1275 (U.S. Government Printing Office, 1969), pp. 12, 82. The figures have been converted from short to metric tons. "Asia" includes the region's Communist countries; "Europe" includes Communist Eastern Europe. For some of the areas outside the United States, the figures refer to "original" resources—that is, resources in the ground before the beginning of mining. Strictly speaking, what we are concerned with here are "resources remaining in the ground." In practice, owing to the minor fraction of the total thus far mined, there is little difference between the two sets of figures.

[75] In World Power Conference, *Survey of Energy Resources, 1968* (London: Central Office of the World Power Conference, 1968), coal resource estimates by country are divided into "measured" resources, on the one hand, and "indicated" and "inferred" resources, on the other. Averitt (*Coal Resources*, p. 25) provides these definitions of the three categories of estimates: "Measured" resources refer to those whose observation and measurement are so closely spaced, and the thickness and extent of the coal so well defined that the computed tonnage is judged to be accurate within 20 percent. "Indicated" resources are estimated partly from specific measurements and partly from projection of visible data for a reasonable distance on the basis of geologic evidence. "Inferred" resources, while still applying to coal occurring within overall

It is possible to introduce restrictive assumptions leading to still more conservative estimates. For example, in more detailed estimates for the United States alone, Averitt[76] considers *economically* recoverable measured or proved resources to be only about 50 billion tons, having reduced the technologically recoverable 710 billion tons shown above to that portion comprising coal beds of 28 or more inches thick and 1,000 feet or less below the surface. A similar adjustment for the world as a whole would yield economical recoverable resources of around 300 billion tons—still representing a century and a half at today's (declining) consumption levels.[77] But, though it includes an indeterminate quantity of submarginal deposits, the higher 4.3 trillion-ton resource figure seems the more appropriate one to use in judging future adequacy.

The above figures indicate that more than two-thirds of the world's potential coal resources are concentrated in the U.S.S.R., with the United States occupying an important, though far lower, second place. Communist China, an important coal producer, accounts for most of the Asian figure of 225 billion tons. The predominant portion of the figure for Europe (which comprises both Western Europe and the Communist countries) refers to Western Europe. Not only does all of Europe comprise a relatively small portion of world coal resources, but reference to the tabulation on page 46 discloses that in comparison with numerous other world regions its potentials have been well established by mapping and exploration and that firmer estimates are not likely to be much larger as a result of future work.

Worldwide potential resources of coal available to help meet future energy consumption are judged to be enormous. If energy consumption from *all* fuels were to grow to the end of the present century at the annual 5 percent rate at which it was projected to 1980 (see page 41), cumulative energy requirements to the end of the century (rising from a recent annual level of 6 billion tons to one of perhaps 26 billion tons in the year 2000) might amount to 400 billion tons of coal equivalent. Not only could the estimated 4.3 trillion tons of estimated recoverable coal resources meet this entire growth of energy demand, but in the year 2000, at then prevailing rates of total energy consumption, enough coal would be left in the ground to meet the entire energy bill for a century and a half beyond.

mapped and explored areas, are those for which "quantitative estimates are based largely on broad knowledge of the geologic character of the bed or region and for which measurements of bed thickness are available." See also *ibid*, p. 35.

[76] *Ibid.*, p. 90.

[77] This might be viewed as a kind of minimum estimate—analogous, in a sense, to the "proved reserve" concept in the case of oil, taken up later.

These hypothetical excursions do not look at the resource pinch that may occur earlier in particular regions. And they ignore the fact that at present trends in patterns of energy consumption, coal accounts for well under a 40 percent share and seems destined to account for progressively lower percentages in the years ahead (see table 4). But as Sam Schurr has expressed it:

> . . . The huge coal reserve is reassuring, nevertheless, because with few exceptions coal, used as such or in the generation of electricity, could be satisfactorily substituted for oil and gas in most applications, although perhaps at some added cost. And if a serious pinch were to develop in oil supplies, coal could be converted, at a price, into liquid motor fuels.[78]

The prospective feasibility of producing pipeline-quality gas from coal underscores still further the significance of the coal resource picture.

Oil and Gas

As noted at the outset of this discussion of reserves, in the assessment of future world supplies of petroleum terminological difficulties are compounded by the fact that concepts of potential resources differ from those used in connection with coal. The most widely cited and basic minimum estimate of potential world oil resources—that of proved reserves—at the end of 1968 added up to approximately 63 billion tons, which translates into nearly 95 billion tons in coal equivalents, or a relatively modest thirty-three-year supply at recent rates of worldwide oil consumption. For natural gas, the corresponding figure is nearly fifty years. Proved world reserves of oil and natural gas are tabulated by region on page 48.[79]

Proved oil reserves are strikingly concentrated in a few major areas, especially the Middle East. In 1968 that region possessed nearly 60 percent of world reserves compared with a 28 percent share of world oil production, resulting in a ratio of proved reserves to current production of over 60 to 1. By contrast the U.S. ratio, tending downward in recent years, is roughly 10 to 1; and the Communist area, another major oil reserve region (primarily the U.S.S.R.), has a ratio of about 25 to 1.

Because natural gas often occurs in association with crude oil, the major regions of world proved oil reserves

[78] Schurr, "Energy," p. 116.

[79] Oil reserves from British Petroleum Co., *Statistical Review of the World Oil Industry, 1968*, p. 5. Natural gas reserves from *Oil and Gas Journal*, December 30, 1968, pp. 102–3. The U.S. and Canadian oil figures include natural gas liquids (totalling for both countries somewhat over 1 billion tons) and are therefore not strictly additive to the natural gas reserve estimates, which refer to the wet production prior to separation of liquids. The worldwide *coal-equivalent* combined total for oil and gas therefore works out to 143.2 billion rather than the apparent total of 144.7 billion tons.

Proved World Oil and Natural Gas Reserves, End of 1968

	Oil		*Natural gas*	
	Billion metric tons	*Percent*	*Trillion* m^3	*Percent*
United States	5.0	8.0%	8.33	22.1%
Canada	1.3	2.1	1.32	3.5
Caribbean	2.6	4.0	1.23	3.3
Other Latin America	1.5	2.4	0.55	1.5
Western Europe	0.4	0.6	4.00	10.6
Africa	5.9	9.4	4.77	12.6
Middle East	36.8	58.5	6.34	16.8
Other non-Communist	1.8	2.9	1.49	3.9
Total Communist area	7.6	12.1	9.71	25.7
WORLD	62.9	100.0	37.74	100.0
WORLD (Bill. met. tons coal equiv.)	94.4	-	50.3	-

are also those prominently endowed with gas—that is, North America, Soviet Russia, Latin America, the Middle East, and Africa. (In recent years natural gas discoveries in Holland, the North Sea, and Australia have broadened the geographic scope of world gas reserves.) However, since the gas resources of such less-developed areas as the Middle East have remained largely untapped—lacking means of transport to consuming regions—regional reserve-to-production ratios in natural gas display far greater variability than in the case of oil. Thus, North America, which produces and consumes around 70 percent of the world's natural gas, has in recent years had proved reserves equal to just twenty years' production; this was one of the lowest such ratios in the world and one, moreover, which has been declining throughout most of the past two decades for a number of reasons which have not yet been clearly sorted out. By contrast, at current rates of output, the Middle East's proved reserves (with over 20 percent of the world total) are estimated at equal to nearly 900 years. Up to now, much natural gas occurring in Middle Eastern and other oil-producing areas has been wasted through venting or flaring, except for those portions used for repressuring purposes and for small amounts used in petroleum company operations. The emergence of new technology leading to the transportation of natural gas in liquid form and its reconstitution to gas in the consuming countries suggests greater possibilities of shipping natural gas to leading world markets from regions hitherto excluded for technical reasons. In addition, the gradual development of the gas-using industry in producing areas—a natural gas-using ammonia fertilizer plant in Kuwait is an example—points to greater possibilities of local natural gas use.

Even in well-defined regions, proved reserve figures do not begin to exhaust petroleum and natural gas resources; and on a world scale reserves have tended to more than keep up with production. In the case of oil this is well illustrated by the accompanying diagram which shows, first of all, how cumulative production of oil since the mid-19th century was, as of 1950, just a bit short of the size of estimated proved reserves in that year. As post-World War II output growth steadily eroded the 1950 reserves, the latter were more than compensated for by the new additions to proved reserves occurring between 1950 and 1968. All told, between 1950 and 1968 proved oil reserves increased by a multiple of 5.2 (i.e., 420 percent), while worldwide oil production went up 3.8 times (i.e., 280 percent). It is true that in the course of the 1960s a reversal occurred: output expansion began to outstrip the growth of worldwide proved oil reserves. But before the end of the sixties Arctic discoveries gave promise of additional reserves.

In any event, a meaningful measure of petroleum and natural gas resources must go beyond the "proved reserve" concept. The reasoning runs as follows:

> . . . reserves cannot be proved without drilling wells, and wells are costly. Reserves are only proved, therefore, in response to explicit commercial needs. In the U.S., for example, proved reserves are essentially a working inventory of natural stocks. Consequently proved reserve figures—which indicate that U.S. reserves will last for perhaps 12 years [now reduced to 10:1]—are virtually useless for an analysis of the long-term adequacy of resources. . . .
>
> For both oil and natural gas, therefore, it is necessary to estimate "unproved" resources to obtain a figure comparable to that presented for world coal resources. [The coal resource figure developed earlier was 4.3 trillion tons.] Estimates of such unproved resources have generally been revised upward over the years, but even today there are wide differences on the subject.[80]

One such estimate of ultimate world petroleum reserves, involving a complex set of geological assumptions and, particularly, statistical calculations, was prepared in

[80]Schurr, "Energy," pp. 116, 118.

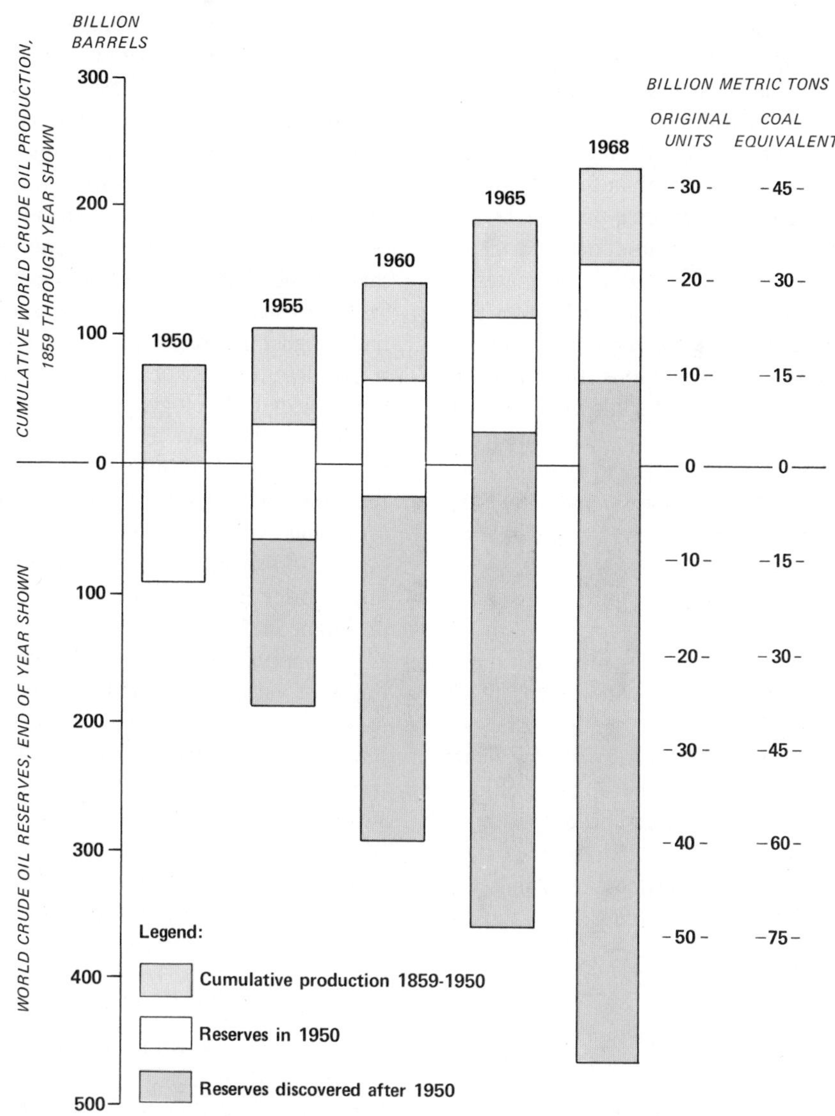

Historical Trends in World Crude Oil Production and Proved Reserves. Adapted from British Petroleum Co., Statistical Review of the World Oil Industry *(London: various editions). Cumulative post-1950 production partly obtained from Part Three, table I.*

the early 1960s by M. King Hubbert.[81] His results show ultimate world reserves of oil amounting to some 170 billion metric tons; of natural gas, 212 trillion cubic meters; and of natural gas liquids, roughly 25 billion metric tons. In terms of coal equivalents, these components add to around 570 billion tons, compared with the approximately 145 billion coal-equivalent tons of proved oil and gas reserves (and the 4.3 trillion tons of coal resources alone) cited earlier. (See pages 46 and 48.)[82]

An interesting aspect of Hubbert's analysis is the geo-

[81]M. King Hubbert, *Energy Resources*, A Report to the Committee on Natural Resources, Publication No. 1000-D, National Academy of Sciences-National Research Council, 1962, pp. 74, 87. Since Hubbert sums the cited estimates for particular energy sources, his natural gas estimate presumably excludes his separately estimated natural gas liquid estimate.

[82]See also Hubbert's later study, "Energy Resources," *Resources and Man*, Committee on Resources and Man, National Academy of Sciences-National Research Council (San Francisco: W. H. Freeman for National Academy of Sciences, 1969), see particularly pp. 194-97. In this more recent analysis, however, Hubbert confines himself to a critical survey of energy resource estimates made in the past few years by others. He

graphic distribution of ultimate world oil resources. Compared with the regional breakdown of proved reserves in which the Middle East looms so prominently (nearly 60 percent of the world total), in Hubbert's estimates that area plus North Africa is credited with no higher a level of *ultimate* oil reserves than the roughly 42 billion tons of *proved* reserves tabulated on page 48; the result is to give the area only around one-quarter of ultimate world oil reserves in Hubbert's estimates—a somewhat puzzling finding. Both the United States and the U.S.S.R. assume somewhat greater relative importance in the ultimate reserve calculations. But the most important element in Hubbert's geographic breakdown is the assignment of a regionally unallocated 30 percent share to the world's offshore areas (other than offshore areas of the United States) which, incidentally, are accounting for a steadily rising portion of worldwide oil and gas output.[83]

Employing less binding economic and technological assumptions, others have developed far higher estimates of ultimate world oil and gas resources. For example, a 1965 U.S. Geological Survey report[84] showed worldwide "possible ultimate discoveries" for crude oil, natural gas, and natural gas liquids, whose total in coal equivalents works out to 2.1 trillion tons,[85] or more than 3½ times Hubbert's 570-billion-ton figure, noted above.[86]

These differing estimates of world resources stem principally from differing assumptions regarding the potential resources of the United States; for it is by extending analysis regarding the United States (about which most is known from a geological point of view) that most estimates for other world areas are drawn up. In Hubbert's comparatively low estimates, assumptions about factors that will determine as yet unproved oil resources are more conservative than in the U.S. Geological Survey estimates.[87] For example, the former's assessment builds in current experience with respect to the share of oil that is recovered (about one-third), whereas improved recovery technology could yield a substantially higher figure. More significant, Hubbert's analysis is based upon statistical curves of discovery experience that reflect technology, policy framework, and price relationships that have existed in the United States, while the U.S. Geological Survey calculations include deposits that are submarginal by today's standards, and whose economic exploitation implies improved exploration and production technology and, quite possibly, accompanying oil price increases in comparison with circumstances prevailing in the past.

No matter whether one focuses on lower or upper limits of estimated *total* fossil fuel resources (coal, oil, gas), the picture that emerges is one of vast quantities implying worldwide abundance of energy sources far into the distant future. Moreover, enormous additional supplies are contained in oil shale and bituminous tar sands, which—future technology and costs permitting—will further strengthen the world's fossil fuel resource base.[88] The outlook is far more restrictive, however, where petroleum and natural gas alone are concerned.

Hydro and Nuclear Fuels

This brief discussion of world energy resources has concentrated on coal, oil, and gas. Hydroelectricity has been neglected due to its relatively small actual and potential significance. The untapped hydro sites in in-

concludes by citing that range of estimates of ultimate world resources which he regards as the most accurate available. Interestingly, even the low end of the range shown in these newer figures exceeds Hubbert's earlier estimates. Specifically, the more recent estimates show ultimate world oil resources of from 180 to 280 billion tons; natural gas, 230–340 billion cubic meters; and natural gas liquids, 30–50 billion tons. In coal equivalents, all these aggregate to a range of 625–945 billion tons. A revision of such magnitude within the span of seven years attests to the dynamic character of resource assessments.

Another recent study, but limited to North America, was prepared in 1969 by the geological consulting firm of DeGolyer and MacNaughton for the Office of Science and Technology in the Executive Office of the President. See *Report on Estimates of Additional Recoverable Reserves of Oil and Gas for the United States and Canada* (Dallas, June 30, 1969). Particular emphasis is given to the new Alaskan (North Slope) discoveries.

[83]In Hubbert's 1969 study (*ibid.*) the offshore component is not calculated separately. But the Middle East and Africa receive considerably more weight than they did in his 1962 study.

[84]T. A. Hendricks, *Resources of Oil, Gas, and Natural Gas Liquids in the United States and the World*, U.S. Geological Survey, Circular 522 (U.S. Government Printing Office, 1965), p. 17.

[85]The underlying figures, in original units (but converted from barrels of oil and natural gas liquids and cubic feet of natural gas) are: oil, 838 billion tons; natural gas, 541 trillion cubic meters; and natural gas liquids, 60 billion tons.

[86]And substantially larger also than the 1969 estimates reported on by Hubbert (see fn. 82).

[87]It is important to note, however, that the USGS does present data from which one could construct a *range* of estimates; this would permit one, in turn, to derive a figure on oil reserves closer to Hubbert's 1962 figure even without satisfactorily reconciling all the differences between the two sets of estimates. For example, if one were to apply the U.S. Geological Survey's percentage of *economically recoverable* oil only (i.e., exclude submarginal oil), the resulting reserve estimate would fall considerably below the USGS figures we have cited. (See Hendricks, *Resources of Oil, Gas, and . . .* , USGS Circular 522, p. 12.)

[88]World resources of shale oil and oil in bituminous rock have been estimated at 190 billion barrels of "known recoverable reserves" (say, 40 billion tons coal equivalent); and at 15 *trillion* barrels of "undiscovered and/or marginal and submarginal resources"—about 3 trillion tons coal equivalent. See V. E. McKelvey and D. C. Duncan, "United States and World Resources of Energy," paper presented at Symposium on Fuel and Energy Economics, American Chemical Society Meeting (Detroit, 1965), p. 7. This paper also provides resource estimates for the traditional energy resources and for nuclear fuels, and comments on the less conventional sources of energy excluded from our discussion.

dustrialized regions are regarded as insufficient to contribute significantly to the future energy requirements of those regions. A somewhat more promising outlook is justified for developing areas, where fairly substantial hydroelectric potential remains to be brought into use. For example, in numerous Asian and Latin American countries, the proportion of theoretical hydropower potential actually used is well under 5 percent—far below comparable percentages in advanced countries. However, such indicators must be used cautiously; to a large extent they reflect waterpower sites situated long distances from electricity-using markets, or characterized by disadvantageous topographical and streamflow characteristics which it might be prohibitively costly to modify. As with the higher range of the fossil-fuel resource estimates discussed earlier, it may be only with changing technological or economic circumstances that these hydro potentials could seriously figure in the world's energy resource picture.

As for the reserves of nuclear fuels, the adequacy of fissionable raw materials is not likely to be a critical factor as one looks several decades or more into the future. Probably more important than the known magnitudes of economically recoverable reserves of uranium or thorium ores will be the development of conversion technology for advanced reactors, including the likely development of breeders. The latter achievement would reduce the problem of nuclear raw materials to insignificance for a long time to come, since it enhances raw material use by a factor of 50 or more compared with nonbreeder systems. If—looking still further ahead—we assume that nuclear fusion can be controlled to produce power economically, the availability of the required resources (deuterium and lithium) appears to be still more staggering.

* * * * *

While the specter of absolute physical exhaustion of world energy resources has ceased to be a matter of chronic anxiety, other issues will continue to command close attention. The technology and the economic cost of exploiting various energy resources and their respective degrees of utilization, and the environmental constraints governing such utilization will pose significant questions. Another matter, not emphasized by the global perspective in which we have framed our discussion, is the uncertain prospect for fuel-deficit regions of the world. Because of spotty geographical occurrence, particularly of liquids, the world totals we have cited cannot be expected to relieve the concern of regions whose satisfaction of fuel and power needs may periodically be jeopardized by supply interruptions such as have occurred in the past, or whose dependence on energy sources from abroad may impose severe foreign exchange burdens. Indeed, these very uncertainties may in themselves prompt energy-deficit areas to engage in the search for fuel deposits which could, in unforeseen ways, alter the world's energy resource picture as it appears today.

Part Two

STATISTICAL PROFILES: Descriptive Comments, Tables, and Charts Based on the Detailed Data

Two
Profile No. 1

TOTAL AND PER CAPITA ENERGY CONSUMPTION, BY MAJOR WORLD REGIONS, SELECTED YEARS, 1925-1965

This profile depicts the long-term growth of total primary energy consumption for major geographical regions of the world.[1] As in all the profiles, the energy forms measured within total consumption comprise solid fuels (bituminous coal and anthracite, lignite, and certain minor fuels including peat); liquid fuels (crude oil and natural gas liquids); natural gas; and hydroelectricity. Nuclear power–nil or insignificant during the greater part of the period under review–is not considered. A more elaborate treatment of definitional and measurement issues appears in Part Four (pp. 818-822).

Two further clarifying points, already mentioned in Part One, are worth repeating here: (1) Energy "consumption" might, for greater precision, be more fully labeled "apparent inland energy consumption"–"apparent" consumption because inventory accumulation or depletion, which may make actual consumption lower or higher than shown, is ignored; and "inland" consumption because fuels absorbed as bunkers for maritime vessels or foreign-bound aircraft are, where possible, excluded from the consumption measure.[2] (2) Coverage is limited to what are commonly referred to as "commercial" energy sources–so called because of their dominance in domestic and foreign energy trade and their near-indispensability in modern industrial activity. For reasons explained in the Introduction (p. 3), such "noncommercial" energy sources as animal waste, firewood, and animate energy or windpower are excluded.

Total world energy consumption increased from 1½ billion coal equivalent tons in 1925 to 5½ billion tons in 1965, or by an average annual growth rate of somewhat over 3 percent. This reflects sluggish growth during depression and war (averaging out to 2.3 percent between 1925 and 1950) followed by marked acceleration (averaging 5 percent yearly since 1950). Among the geographic areas tabulated, only in the Soviet Union, which registered the highest 1925-65 rate, did postwar growth slacken–if "slacken" describes a deceleration from 9½ to 7½ percent yearly.

Energy consumption for each major region shown except North America and Western Europe has exceeded the worldwide growth rate, whether viewed over the long term or only since 1950. The shifting regional distribution of world energy consumption reflects this disparity in growth rates–for example, North America's forty-year decline from one-half to three-eighths of the world total; the Soviet Union's rise from under 2 percent to 16 percent; the more-than-doubling of Latin America's relative standing from roughly 1½ to 3½ percent. Among the factors explaining these shifts, there is the rapid industrial transformation of the Communist countries,[3] which has been accompanied by a pronounced emphasis on electric power and on such basic fuel-using industries as iron and steel. Developmental advance of low-income countries has often progressed from such a meager industrial base that a disproportionately fast rise in the use of modern energy forms (for, say, transportation and electrification) is almost inevitable. Thus, the recorded (as opposed to actual) shift has, no doubt, been partly accentuated by the shift from the use of (nonmeasured) noncommercial energy sources to increased reliance on (measured) commercial

[1] The world regions tabulated throughout these profiles may vary somewhat depending on the particular question highlighted. United States and Soviet figures, prominent in numerous tabulations, will often be shown separately even where a table is primarily designed to compare geographic or other multi-country groupings. Japan is also frequently singled out since its relatively advanced economic status differs so sharply from the Far East region in which it would otherwise be included.

[2] For certain regions (e.g., U.S.S.R.) and years, the fact that bunkers data were not available compelled us to use a "total consumption" measure.

[3] For historical comparability, pre-World War II "Communist" (so labeled for convenience) figures refer to the present (1965) Communist countries, with these exceptions: prewar East Germany is included within total prewar Germany under Western Europe; prewar Communist Asia refers to Mainland China only, while postwar Communist Asia includes also Mongolia, North Korea, and North Vietnam (beginning in 1954). Cuba is always included under Latin America, and Yugoslavia under Western Europe.

energy forms. The relatively modest growth of energy consumption in the most advanced industrial regions of the world may reflect the fact that their period of intensive industrialization has given, or is giving, way to an economic "mix" less demanding of rapid energy growth. This is touched on again in Profiles No. 4 and No. 5.

Looking at historical changes in per capita energy consumption levels, it may be seen that regional differences remain profound even though considerable convergence has occurred. Relative to North America's index of 100 for all years, Communist Europe's per capita consumption level has moved from 6 to 40, Japan's from under 10 to 20, Latin America's from 4 to nearly 9. Yet it is quite remarkable that, by 1965, even the most highly developed areas outside North America only ranged between 35 and 40 percent of North America's per capita energy consumption. Indeed, forty years later North America's 1925 per capita consumption level of 5,970 kilograms (coal equivalent) had been reached nowhere else.

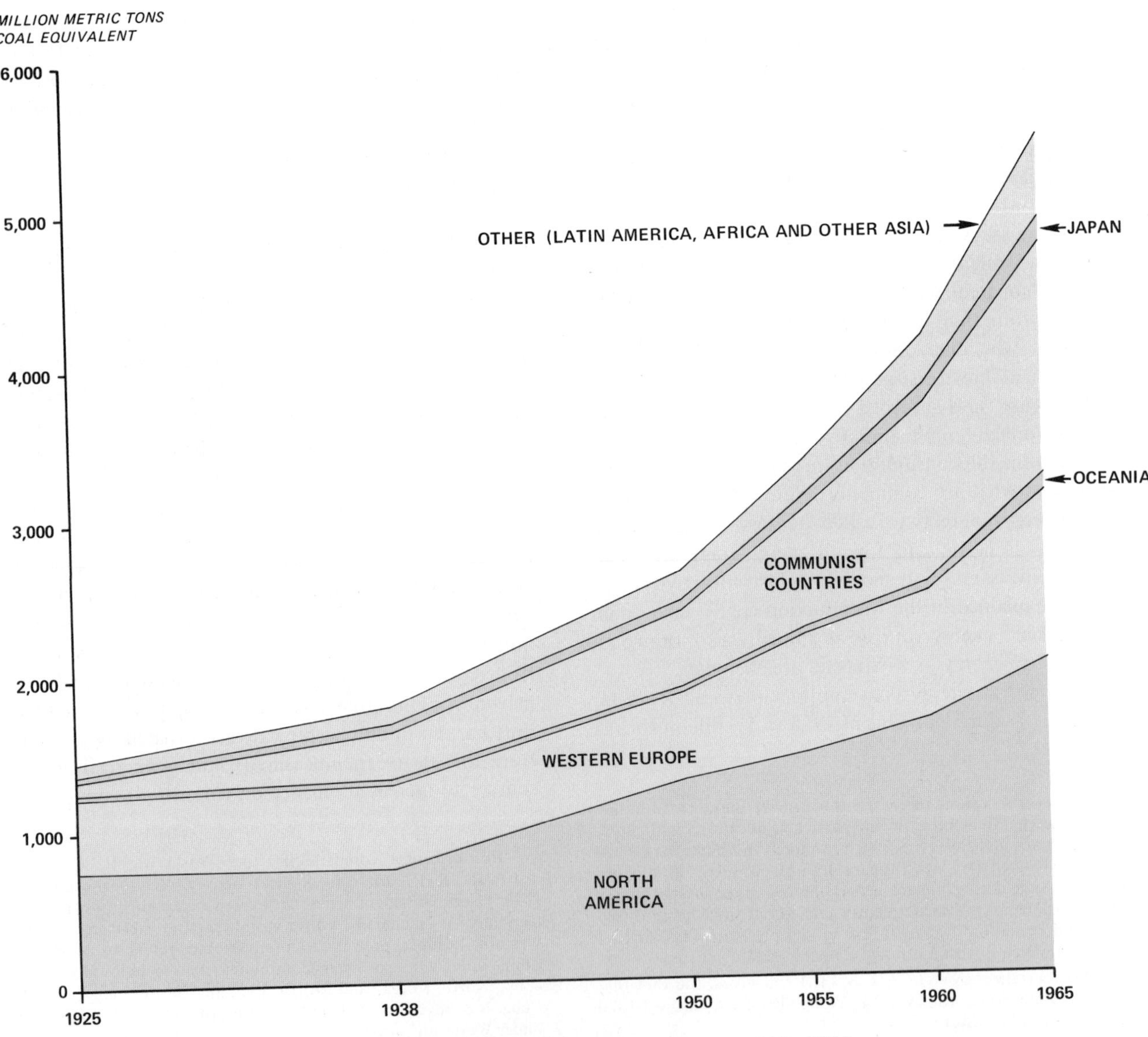

World energy consumption, by major regions, 1925-1965.

TOTAL AND PER CAPITA ENERGY CONSUMPTION, BY MAJOR WORLD REGIONS, SELECTED YEARS, 1925–1965

(All figures based on coal equivalents)

Year	North America		Western Europe	Oceania	U.S.S.R. and Comm. E. Europe			Comm. Asia	Latin America	Asia			Africa	World
	Total	United States			Total	U.S.S.R.	E. Europe			Total	Japan	Other		
					A. Total consumption in million metric tons									
1925	748.9	717.7	517.0	15.6	80.5	25.3	55.1	23.7	24.7	60.3	30.5	29.8	13.9	1,484.5
1938	706.9	669.4	619.2	18.1	244.0	176.3	67.7	27.3	38.7	112.4	62.4	50.0	23.4	1,790.1
1950	1,276.3	1,201.0	583.9	29.3	464.1	303.3	160.8	43.1	66.2	105.8	45.8	60.0	42.0	2,610.9
1955	1,461.3	1,370.3	748.2	37.3	691.2	461.0	230.2	98.3	105.4	157.7	66.5	91.2	58.8	3,358.2
1960	1,659.5	1,550.1	849.5	45.8	934.5	640.6	293.9	235.3	153.5	247.7	111.0	136.7	70.2	4,196.1
1965	2,040.2	1,881.6	1,117.2	61.2	1,255.8	880.6	375.1	323.0	199.5	385.1	188.6	196.5	92.6	5,474.6
					B. Total consumption: percentage distribution									
1925	50.4%	48.3%	34.8%	1.1%	5.4%	1.7%	3.7%	1.6%	1.7%	4.1%	2.1%	2.0%	0.9%	100.0%
1938	39.5	37.4	34.6	1.0	13.6	9.8	3.8	1.5	2.2	6.3	3.5	2.8	1.3	100.0
1950	48.9	46.0	22.4	1.1	17.8	11.6	6.2	1.7	2.5	4.1	1.8	2.3	1.6	100.0
1955	43.5	40.8	22.3	1.1	20.6	13.7	6.9	2.9	3.1	4.7	2.0	2.7	1.8	100.0
1960	39.5	36.9	20.2	1.1	22.3	15.3	7.0	5.6	3.7	5.9	2.6	3.3	1.7	100.0
1965	37.3	34.4	20.4	1.1	22.9	16.1	6.9	5.9	3.6	7.0	3.4	3.6	1.7	100.0
					C. Per capita consumption in kilograms									
1925	5,971	6,196	1,848	1,721	359	165	783	54	252	105	515	58	100	785
1938	4,997	5,150	2,035	1,754	899	928	832	61	309	162	885	80	135	826
1950	7,686	7,886	1,931	2,397	1,720	1,685	1,792	76	409	131	553	83	194	1,042
1955	8,042	8,258	2,387	2,703	2,379	2,350	2,440	158	569	181	747	116	241	1,232
1960	8,354	8,578	2,602	2,967	2,987	2,988	2,985	347	723	255	1,191	156	254	1,403
1965	9,524	9,671	3,256	3,563	3,777	3,819	3,683	441	821	354	1,926	198	298	1,668
					D. Indexes of per capita consumption (North America = 100)									
1925	100.0	103.8	30.9	28.8	6.0	2.8	13.1	0.9	4.2	1.8	8.6	1.0	1.7	13.1
1938	100.0	103.1	40.7	35.1	18.0	18.6	16.6	1.2	6.2	3.2	17.7	1.6	2.7	16.5
1950	100.0	102.6	25.1	31.2	22.4	21.9	23.3	1.0	5.3	1.7	7.2	1.1	2.5	13.6
1955	100.0	102.7	29.7	33.6	29.6	29.2	30.3	2.0	7.1	2.3	9.3	1.4	3.0	15.3
1960	100.0	102.7	31.1	35.5	35.8	35.8	35.7	4.2	8.7	3.1	14.3	1.9	3.0	16.8
1965	100.0	101.5	34.2	37.4	39.7	40.1	38.7	4.6	8.6	3.7	20.2	2.1	3.1	17.5
					E. Average annual percentage growth rate in total consumption									
1925–65	2.5%	2.4%	1.9%	3.5%	7.1%	9.3%	4.9%	6.7%	5.4%	4.7%	4.7%	4.8%	4.8%	3.3%
1950–65	3.2	3.0	4.4	5.0	6.9	7.4	5.8	14.4	7.6	9.0	9.9	8.2	5.4	5.1
					F. Average annual percentage growth rate in per capita consumption									
1925–65	1.2%	1.1%	1.4%	1.8%	6.1%	8.2%	3.9%	5.4%	3.0%	3.1%	3.4%	3.1%	2.8%	1.9%
1950–65	1.4	1.4	3.5	2.7	5.4	5.6	4.9	12.5	4.8	6.8	8.7	6.0	2.9	3.2

Source: Taken or adapted from data in Part Three, tables XI and XIII.

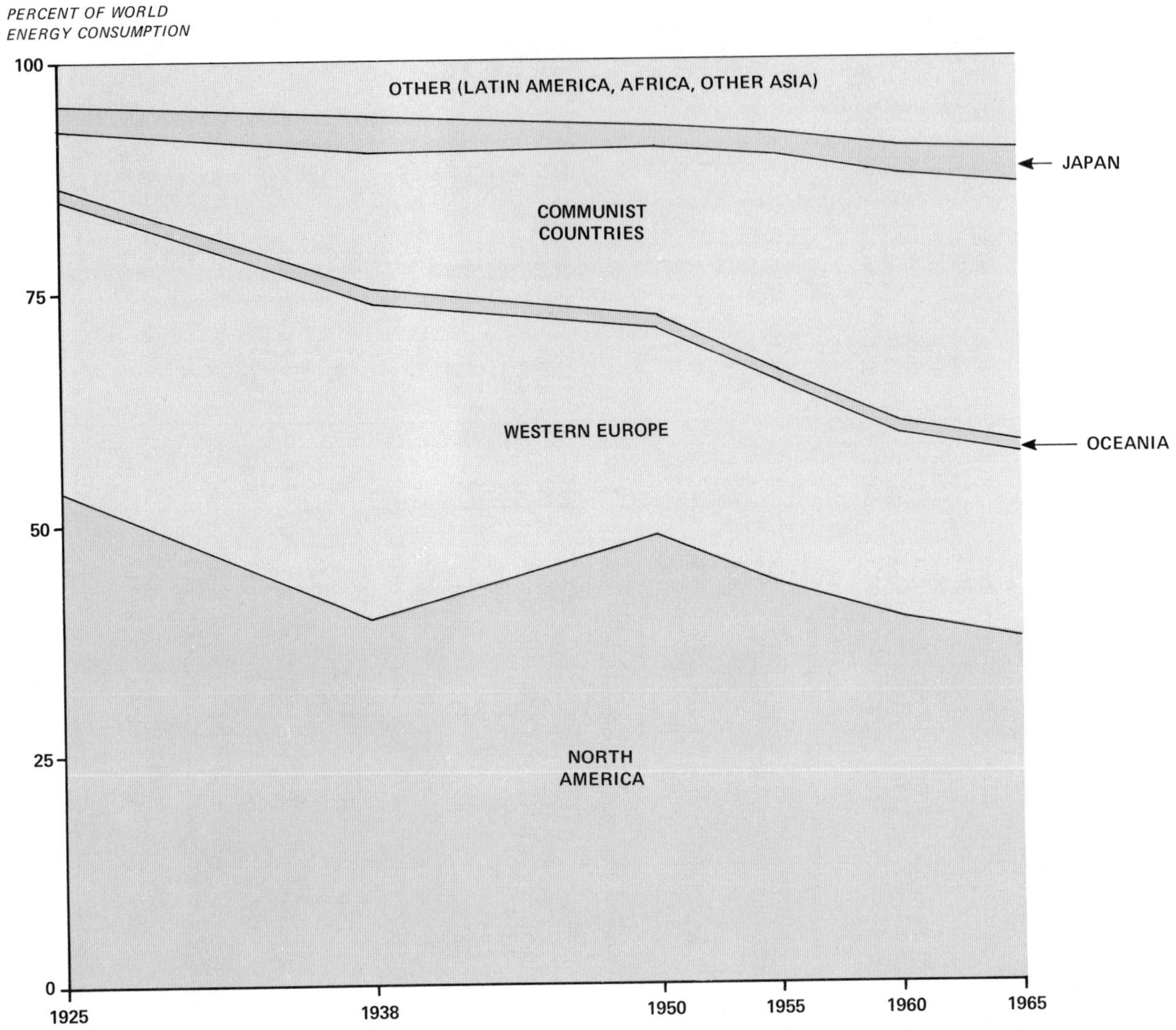

PERCENT OF WORLD
ENERGY CONSUMPTION
100
75
50
25
0
OTHER (LATIN AMERICA, AFRICA, OTHER ASIA)
JAPAN
COMMUNIST
COUNTRIES
WESTERN EUROPE
OCEANIA
NORTH
AMERICA
1925
1938
1950
1955
1960
1965

Total energy consumption, percentage distribution by major world regions, 1925–1965.

40
20
0
1925
1938
1950
1955
1960
1965
WESTERN EUROPE
OCEANIA
U.S.S.R. & COMM.
EASTERN EUROPE
COMMUNIST
ASIA
JAPAN
LATIN AMERICA,
AFRICA, AND
OTHER ASIA
WORLD

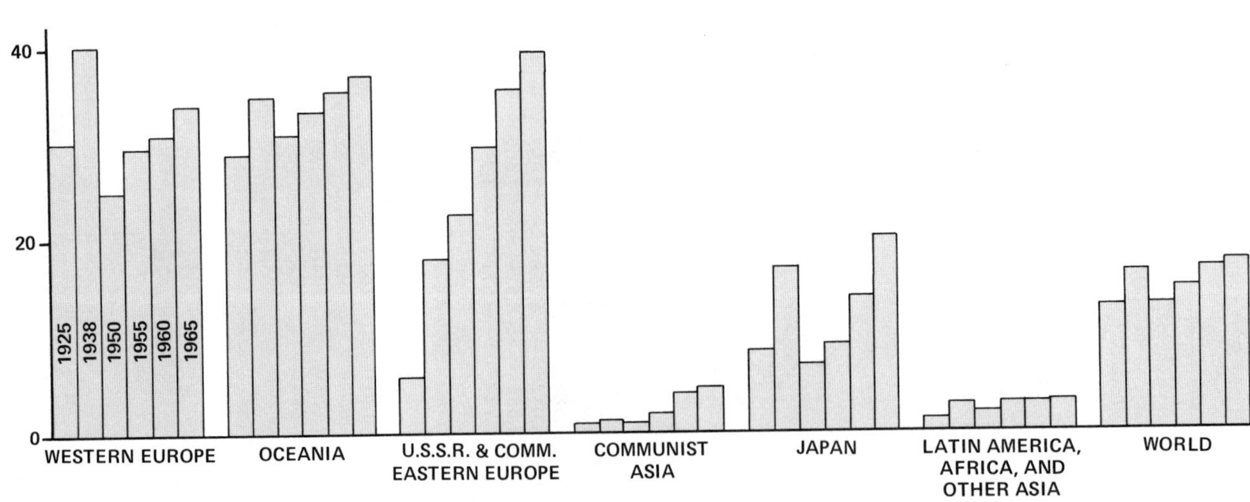

Indexes of per capita energy consumption, selected years (North America = 100).

Profile No. 2

ENERGY CONSUMPTION, BY MAJOR REGIONS AND SELECTED COUNTRIES, USING ALTERNATIVE MEASURES OF HYDROELECTRICITY, 1925, 1950, AND 1965

The conversion of data on primary energy sources from original physical units into a common-denominator unit of measure poses a number of difficulties, one of which is highlighted by this profile. (Problems of conversion and different solutions are discussed in some detail in Part Four, pp. 827-31, especially pp. 829-31.) Dissimilar fuels are made statistically comparable and hence additive by taking account of their relative heat content. For example, one ton of crude oil contains about 1½ times the quantity of British thermal units (Btu) of one ton of coal. Therefore, using coal as the common denominator as is done throughout this study, consumption of 1 million tons of oil is expressed as consumption of 1½ million tons coal equivalent.

The major conversion problem relates to the treatment of hydroelectricity, which is ordinarily converted in one of two ways: (A) Using the actual thermal content of electricity (3,412 Btu per kwh) and of coal (about 27 million Btu per ton), one comes up with a conversion factor of 1,000 kwh of hydroelectricity equal to about 0.125 tons of coal. This relationship serves as the basis for the conversion procedure practiced by the United Nations; except in a few tables it has been applied in this volume. (B) An alternative approach answers the hypothetical question: How much coal, or other boiler fuel expressed in coal equivalents, would have been needed at a steam power plant to produce electricity equal to a given amount of hydro? The answer varies over time and place, but—because of inescapable conversion losses—invariably results in a higher coal equivalent than under the first procedure. (According to estimates in Part Four [p. 830], 1,000 kwh of electricity would have required about 0.40 tons of coal instead of 0.125 tons under average central thermal station efficiencies prevailing in 1965; the 1925 requirement would have been 1.00.)

This profile seeks to illustrate the effects of using one or the other conversion procedure. Clearly, for a region or country lacking significant hydroelectric capacity, the measure of total energy consumption will not vary greatly no matter which practice is followed. Where hydro looms large, however, total energy will be heavily affected by which measurement is used. An outstanding example is Norway, whose 1965 level of total energy use is seen to rise by 90 percent when its large hydroelectric output is measured using the alternative conversion technique. Other important hydro countries are Sweden, Switzerland, and New Zealand, all of whose energy consumption would be measured at a more than 30 percent higher level, if the power station fuel-input equivalent were used rather than the heat-content calculation of hydroelectricity generated. Canada's energy consumption would rise about 20 percent under the alternative procedure; and in the case of Japan, where hydro's role, once important, has recently been diminishing, the figure would rise by roughly 10 percent.

There is no "true" or ideal way to make this particular conversion from hydro to thermal equivalents, but only one which bears on the particular problem being studied. If Norway's total energy consumption is understated using the "A" approach, then the "B" approach may be criticized for its hypothetical character and for possible overstatement, in that electricity is employed in uses in which—were the electricity thermally produced—the direct burning of fuels would be far more economical. In the case of Norway, abundant waterpower and cheap electricity permits electricity's use not only for electro-process industries, such as aluminum, but also for purposes (e.g., residential heating) which would otherwise be met by processes less lavish in their use of fuel. Hence, it is unrealistic to cite the higher energy consumption figure as one which would prevail to the extent shown without the presence of hydro.

For the broad sorts of topics dealt with in these profiles—with particular stress on regional as opposed to national trends—this issue of measuring hydroelectricity need not detain us. In a few special cases (e.g., Profiles No. 4 and No. 13), we shall revert to this aspect of measuring trends in energy consumption. One point may be added, however: the generation of electricity through nuclear energy will pose measurement issues of a somewhat different though similarly "insoluble" character–issues which we have been able to ignore because of nuclear's negligible past contribution to energy consumption. Obviously, an analogous treatment to the calculation of fossil fuel consumption–which would make the measurement at the nuclear raw material stage–makes little sense since the critical phase of nuclear energy production occurs within the reactor and progress in nuclear energy uses is heavily dependent on developments in reactor technology. On the other hand, to measure nuclear-based electricity by the calorific value of the electricity generated (as is done under the "A" procedure for hydro above)[1] would ignore the fact that the nuclear cycle, similar to conventional thermal electricity, is governed by efficiency losses, as the steam heat produced is transferred to a turbine generator; just as primary energy consumption measures the use of coal (or its equivalents), gross of efficiency losses at power stations, so, presumably, would nuclear energy be figured prior to the conversion of heat into electricity. Moreover, in prospective dual-use nuclear power station operations, nuclear energy is a potential source of process steam for desalting processes, for the chemical industry, and for other uses such as photographic film manufacture; in Sweden, a small amount of nuclear-produced steam is used for space heating.

An operationally suitable way of handling the nuclear share of energy consumption might therefore be the calculation of the estimated quantity of fuel required, on the average, to generate the same amount of electricity at thermal-power stations for the year in question (analogous to the "B" approach, described above, for hydro). The OECD conforms closely to this practice by translating nuclear-based electricity into coal equivalents for 1965 by assuming an efficiency of 25 percent from nuclear heat released to kilowatt-hours generated (compared with a roughly 33 percent efficiency factor indicated for 1965 at conventional thermal-power stations); for the years ahead, the OECD assumes that future "efficiency of nuclear plant will probably gradually approach that of conventional equipment."[2]

[1]The United Nations figures nuclear energy output in this way; and in the projections of Part One (pp. 40–45), which are cast within the United Nations statistical framework, the nuclear share of primary energy consumption is therefore also calculated by the thermal content of the electricity generated.

[2]Organisation for Economic Cooperation and Development, *Energy Policy* (Paris, 1966), p. 168.

ENERGY CONSUMPTION, BY MAJOR REGIONS AND SELECTED COUNTRIES, USING ALTERNATIVE MEASURES OF HYDROELECTRICITY, 1925, 1950, 1965

(A = hydro portion of total energy measured by heat content;
B = hydro measured by energy content of fuels consumed at thermal electric stations)

	Total energy consumption in million metric tons coal equivalent						1965		
							Per capita energy consumption in kgs coal equiv.		
	1925		1950		1965				B as percent of A
Region and country	A	B	A	B	A	B	A	B	
World	1,484.5	1,553.5	2,610.9	2,758.5	5,474.6	5,704.3	1,668	1,738	104.2%
North America	748.9	779.9	1,276.3	1,341.4	2,040.2	2,120.1	9,524	9,897	103.9
of which:									
Canada	31.1	38.7	75.3	96.7	158.4	188.1	8,077	9,596	118.8
Western Europe	517.0	544.0	583.9	631.2	1,117.2	1,192.2	3,256	3,474	106.7
of which:									
Austria	7.1	8.2	9.7	11.6	18.7	21.9	2,584	3,013	116.6
Norway	3.6	9.0	6.0	12.8	13.5	25.5	3,621	6,853	189.3
Sweden	5.3	8.3	14.4	21.7	35.6	47.2	4,604	6,109	132.7
Switzerland	3.3	6.0	5.3	9.5	16.1	21.9	2,699	3,666	135.8
Finland	0.8	1.1	3.2	4.8	13.0	15.6	2,825	3,381	119.7
Oceania	15.6	16.1	29.3	31.2	61.2	65.6	3,563	3,820	107.2
of which:									
New Zealand	2.6	2.8	3.8	5.0	6.9	9.1	2,603	3,433	131.9
Communist countries	104.2	104.7	507.2	515.8	1,578.8	1,607.3	1,483	1,510	101.8
Latin America	24.7	27.4	66.2	72.3	199.5	212.6	821	875	106.6
Asia	60.3	67.3	105.8	124.0	385.1	410.5	354	377	106.5
of which:									
Japan	30.1	37.1	45.8	62.1	188.6	206.7	1,926	2,110	109.6
Africa	13.9	14.0	42.0	42.6	92.6	96.0	298	309	103.7
of which:									
Rhodesia	n.a.	n.a.	1.4	1.4	2.9	3.4	670	790	117.9

Source: Part Three, table XII.

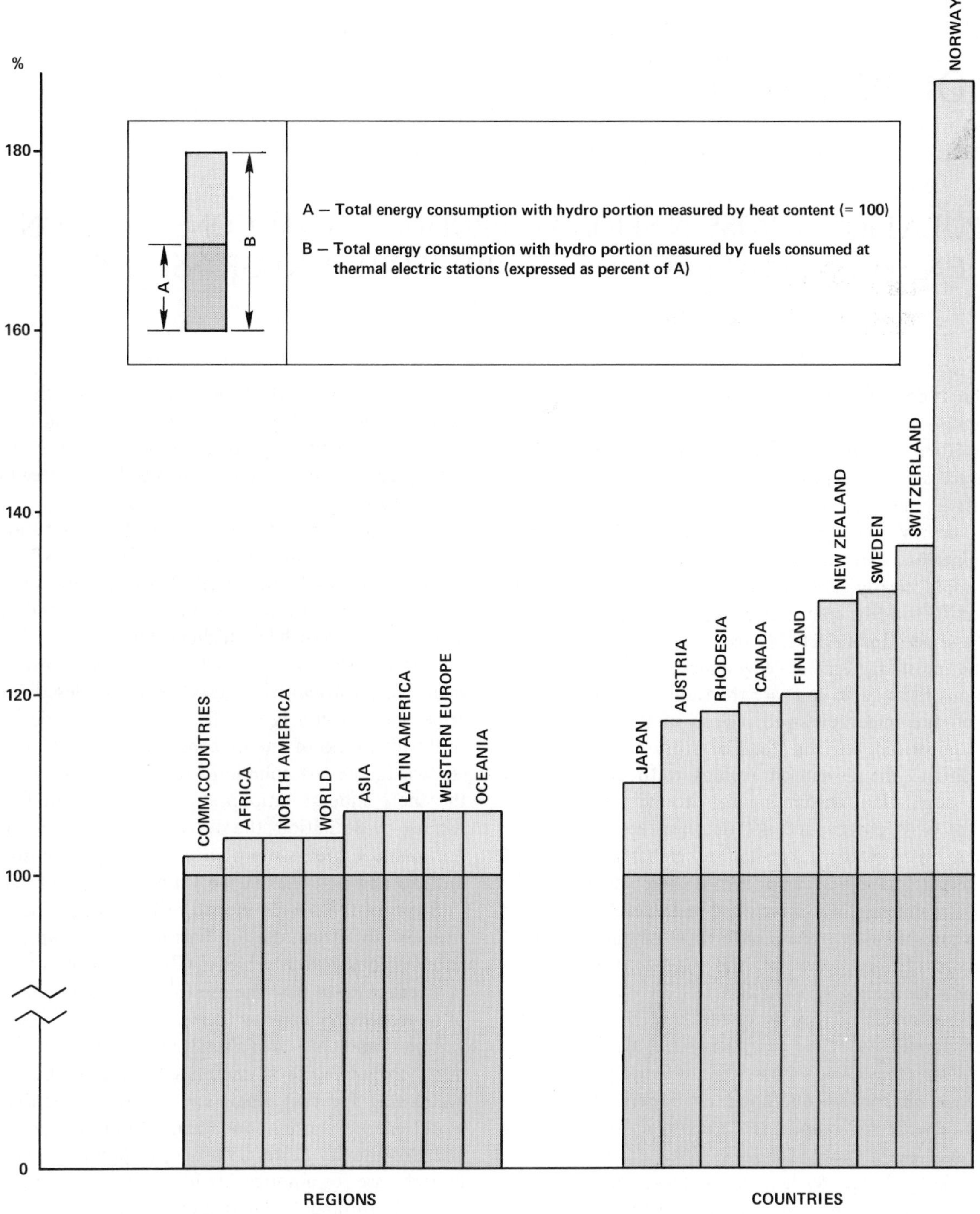

Energy consumption, by major regions and selected countries, using alternative measures of hydroelectricity, 1965.

Profile No. 3

POPULATION, GROSS NATIONAL PRODUCT, AND CONSUMPTION OF ENERGY AND ELECTRICITY, BY WORLD REGIONS, 1965

The 1965 regional distribution of worldwide energy consumption is viewed in this profile in the context of three other categories: regional shares of world population, gross national product, and total electricity consumption—the last representing a major end-use of primary energy. The per capita disparities in energy consumption, remarked upon in Profile No. 1 and here seen more clearly, are found, by and large, to be reflected in roughly comparable disparities in per capita GNP and per capita electricity use.

The most aggregated geographic groupings at the bottom of the table compare the (non-Communist) developed and underdeveloped regions of the world, and this comparison tells the familiar story of worldwide inequalities: the developed regions, with one-fifth of world population, accounting for around a two-thirds share of GNP, energy, and electricity; the less developed regions, with close to one-half of global population, accounting for 10 percent or less of these yardsticks of relative well-being. The developed-underdeveloped contrast shows up also in sharp differences within the Communist-controlled part of the world: Communist Europe's (including the U.S.S.R.) GNP,[1] energy, and electricity shares of roughly one-fifth of the world are about double its 10 percent world population share; while Communist Asia's 22 percent of world population consumes in the neighborhood of 5 percent of the world's energy and output, and a markedly smaller proportion of world electricity.

As far as broad tendencies go, these observations, treating GNP, energy, and electricity in their collective relationship to population, are fair enough. When the figures are looked at more closely, the picture of generally similar regional distributions of GNP, energy use, and electricity must be refined somewhat. For example, each of the (non-Communist) developed areas shown accounts for a greater portion of electricity than of energy use—a fact which may, among other things, be associated with a degree of mechanization and patterns of industrial activity particularly oriented to electricity use. Elsewhere in the world, energy shares exceed electricity shares.

A comparison of the percentage distribution of energy consumption, on the one hand, and GNP, on the other, discloses that the North America shares of world GNP and energy are not too markedly apart (the energy percentage is somewhat higher); by contrast, Western Europe's GNP share exceeds its energy consumption share fairly substantially. Another way of describing the same phenomenon is to refer to North America's relatively high ratio of energy consumption per $1 of GNP (shown in the last column of the table) compared with the more modest ratio prevailing in Western Europe. Almost by definition, the difference reflects the disproportionately great importance of energy-intensive industries and activities in the United States and Canada.

Some of the less developed regions (e.g., Africa aside from South Africa, the Far East aside from Japan) have an even conspicuously higher GNP than energy share, a fact reflecting in part the use (not recorded in our data) of noncommercial energy forms.

The Communist area's traditional emphasis on energy in its economic life is undoubtedly one of the factors accounting for that region's relatively greater share of world energy consumption than GNP. Communist Asia and Communist Eastern Europe, in particular, account in each case for a noticeably higher share of energy than GNP. In turning to interregional variations of the per capita figures, we see that Communist Eastern Europe and Soviet Russia's per capita energy consumption, while only about 40 percent of the level prevailing in North America, surpasses the level of Western Europe.

Profile No. 1 has already touched upon regional differences and historical changes in per capita levels of energy consumption. Greater insight into the relationship between energy use and national output emerges from looking beneath such regional aggregates. Profiles No. 4 and No. 5 examine specific country experience cross-sectionally and historically.

[1] The Communist GNP figures, as well as those for most nonindustrial Western countries, should be regarded as very crude estimates; see the discussion in Part Five, section I.

POPULATION, GROSS NATIONAL PRODUCT, AND CONSUMPTION OF ENERGY AND ELECTRICITY, BY WORLD REGIONS, 1965

Region	Population *(million)*	GNP *($ billion)*	Consumption of: Total energy *(million metric tons coal equiv.)*	Consumption of: Electricity *(billion kwh)*	Percentage distribution: Population	Percentage distribution: GNP	Percentage distribution: Consumption of: Total energy	Percentage distribution: Consumption of: Electricity	Per capita: GNP *($)*	Per capita: Consumption of: Total energy *(kgs coal equiv.)*	Per capita: Consumption of: Electricity *(kwh)*	Energy consumption per $1 of GNP *(kgs coal equiv.)*
North America	214.2	736.2	2,040.2	1,298.0	6.5%	33.3%	37.3%	38.8%	3,437	9,524	6,059	2.77
of which: United States	194.6	683.9	1,881.6	1,157.1	5.9	30.9	34.4	34.6	3,515	9,671	5,947	2.75
Western Europe	343.1	578.2	1,117.2	822.7	10.5	26.1	20.4	24.6	1,685	3,256	2,398	1.93
Oceania	17.2	27.7	61.2	48.5	0.5	1.3	1.1	1.5	1,613	3,563	2,825	2.21
U.S.S.R. & Comm. E. Europe	332.4	422.0	1,255.8	677.1	10.1	19.1	22.9	20.3	1,269	3,778	2,037	2.98
U.S.S.R.	230.6	309.0	880.6	505.2	7.0	14.0	16.1	15.1	1,340	3,819	2,191	2.85
Eastern Europe	101.9	113.0	375.1	171.9	3.1	5.1	6.9	5.1	1,109	3,683	1,687	3.32
Communist Asia	732.2	81.0	323.0	59.2	22.3	3.7	5.9	1.8	111	441	81	3.99
Latin America	243.0	95.9	199.5	105.1	7.4	4.3	3.6	3.1	395	821	433	2.08
Asia	1,088.7	228.5	385.1	273.3	33.2	10.3	7.0	8.2	210	354	251	1.69
Middle East	90.1	24.8	57.1	16.3	2.7	1.1	1.0	0.5	275	634	181	2.30
Israel	3.4	3.4	5.8	4.1	0.1	0.2	0.1	0.1	1,325	2,249	1,617	1.70
Other Middle East	87.5	21.4	51.3	12.2	2.7	1.0	0.9	0.4	245	586	139	2.40
Far East & Other Asia	998.7	203.7	328.0	256.9	30.4	9.2	6.0	7.7	204	328	257	1.61
Japan	98.0	119.7	188.6	188.2	3.0	5.4	3.4	5.6	1,222	1,926	1,921	1.58
Other Far East	900.7	84.0	139.4	68.7	27.4	3.8	2.5	2.1	93	155	76	1.66
Africa	310.3	43.0	92.6	58.4	9.5	1.9	1.7	1.7	139	298	188	2.15
South Africa	20.0	10.7	55.3	35.3	0.6	0.5	1.0	1.1	535	2,761	1,763	5.16
Other Africa	290.3	32.3	37.3	23.1	8.8	1.5	0.7	0.7	111	129	80	1.15
WORLD	3,281.2	2,212.5	5,474.6	3,342.2	100.0	100.0	100.0	100.0	674	1,668	1,019	2.47
Addendum												
Non-Communist regions:												
Developed	692.5	1,472.5	3,462.5	2,392.7	21.1	66.6	63.2	71.6	2,126	5,000	3,455	2.35
Underdeveloped	1,524.1	237.0	433.3	213.3	46.4	10.7	7.9	6.4	156	284	140	1.83
OECD: Europe	341.2	563.2	1,091.8	791.5	10.4	25.5	19.9	23.7	1,651	3,200	2,320	1.94
OECD: Total	653.3	1,418.9	3,230.5	2,277.6	19.9	64.1	60.7	68.1	2,172	5,083	3,486	2.34

Source: Population, energy, and electricity from Part Three, table XI; GNP from Part Five, tables I-1 and I-2.

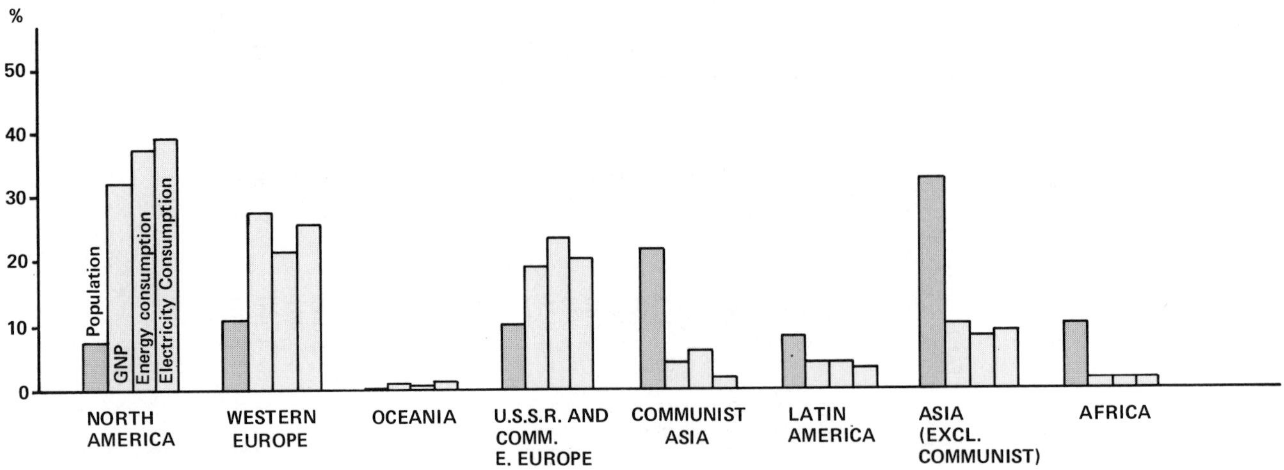

Regional distribution of population, GNP, energy and electricity consumption, 1965 (percent of world totals).

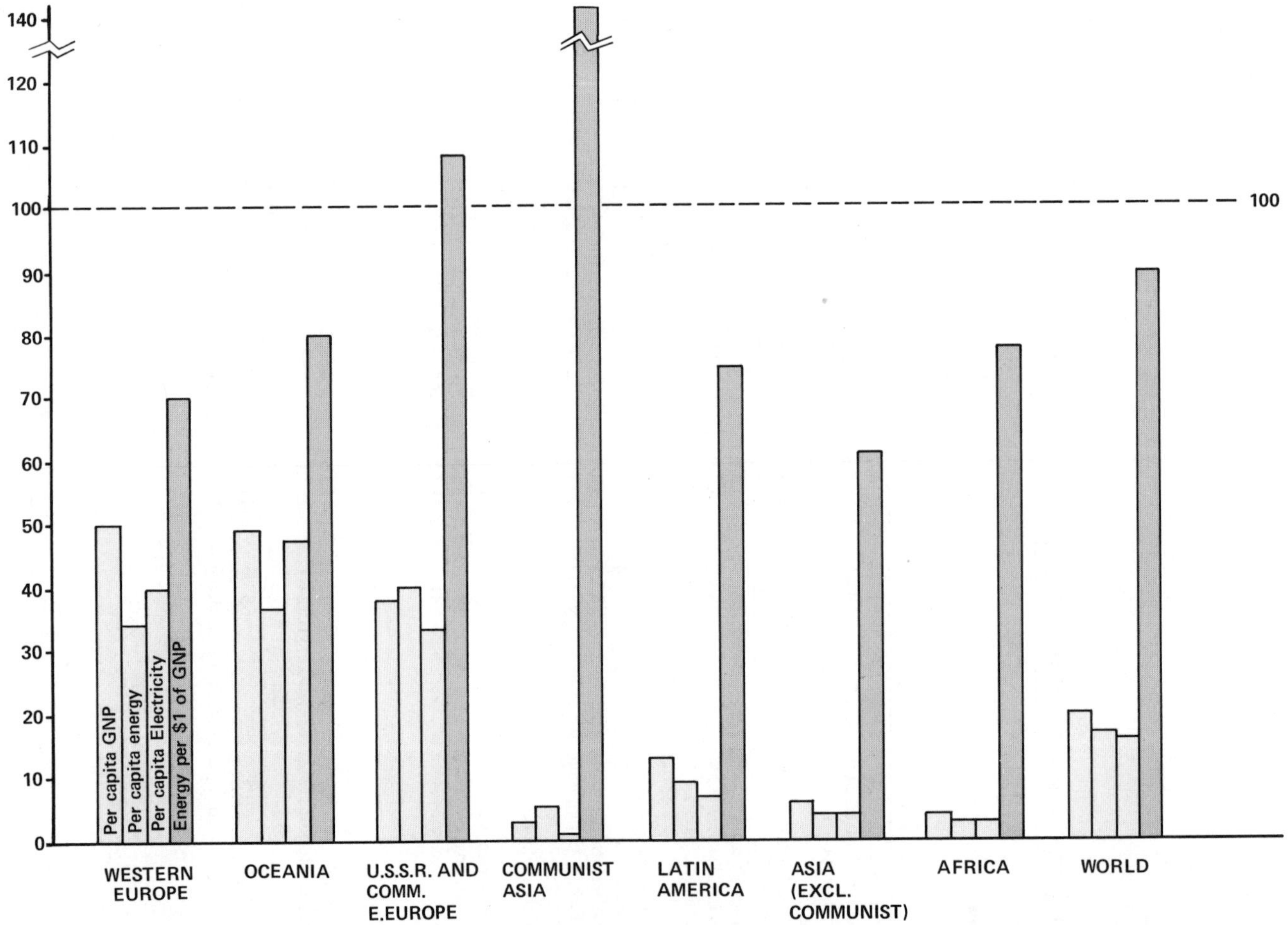

Per capita GNP, energy and electricity consumption, and energy consumption relative to GNP, 1965: index numbers by world regions (North America = 100).

Profile No.4

GNP PER CAPITA, ENERGY CONSUMPTION PER CAPITA AND PER UNIT OF GNP: 49 SELECTED COUNTRIES, 1965

The predictably close connection between levels of general economic activity (measured by gross national product) and energy consumption holds both cross-sectionally and (as we shall see in Profile No. 5) historically: the higher a nation's income or output, the higher its level of energy use; correlation coefficients testing this relationship are invariably and reliably high. And, as a country's GNP rises, so does its energy consumption—in close, if not proportionate, conformity. There is nothing startling about these assertions. Energy's importance—its necessary, if insufficient, role in promoting and sustaining economic growth—is self-evident if viewed merely from the standpoint of such factors as the mechanization of industry and agriculture, or the electric generating capacity and transport facilities needed to support a modern economy. Conversely, advancing living standards are synonymous with wants whose satisfaction requires the use of fuels and power in substantial amounts.

The table and chart in this profile show the relationship of energy consumption per capita to GNP per capita for forty-nine countries in 1965. The table also shows energy consumption per $1 of GNP; and it includes country rankings for each of these three indicators. When per capita energy consumption and per capita GNP are plotted against each other, the resulting points fall within a fairly narrow band along the left-to-right, upward-sloping scattergram. The indicated regression equation yields a correlation coefficient of 0.87, pointing up the close association. (Statistical measures relating energy to GNP are presented in more detail in Part Five, section II.) The correlation is improved somewhat further, rising to 0.89, when hydro is figured at its higher value (see Profile No. 2, alternative "B"). This lifts per capita energy levels of a number of countries which are now rather conspicuously below the regression line—e.g., Switzerland and New Zealand. A few—e.g., Norway—are pushed substantially above the regression line, but on balance the fit is improved.

High-income countries appear to consume more energy for each dollar of GNP than do low-income countries. Graphically, this is reflected in the fact that the regression line is steeper than the 45° line which would indicate no differences among countries in this ratio. However, both the chart and the last column of the table disclose numerous departures from a neat and ordered ranking in the energy-GNP ratios. Consider these apparent incongruities: Trinidad and Tobago, South Africa, and Venezuela (none an especially high-income nation) with the first, second, and fourth world rank, respectively, in energy consumption per $1 of GNP; five Eastern Europe Communist countries among the top ten countries; the United Kingdom surpassing by a wide margin the per capita energy consumption of France, even though both countries have roughly comparable income levels.

Although flaws in the data should not be ruled out as contributing to such seemingly anomalous results, variability in energy-GNP ratios can reasonably be accounted for (even if not easily measured) by a number of factors. A simple example is the effect of climate: at given income levels, a cold country will burn more fuel for residential and other heating (hence consume more primary energy) than one with a more moderate climate. The efficiency with which primary energy forms are used or converted also plays a role. Thus, the very high levels of energy consumption (relative to GNP) in Czechoslovakia and East Germany may in part reflect a pronounced thermal inefficiency in electric generation. This inefficiency appears to stem, in turn, from the fact that utilities in the two countries rely heavily on lignite, a fuel with poor combustion properties. But probably the major explanation for differences in energy-GNP ratios has to do with industrial structure. There is enormous variation in the energy requirements of different industries. Take Canada, for example—a country with a high ratio of energy per $1 of GNP. The nation's

(Text continued on p. 68.)

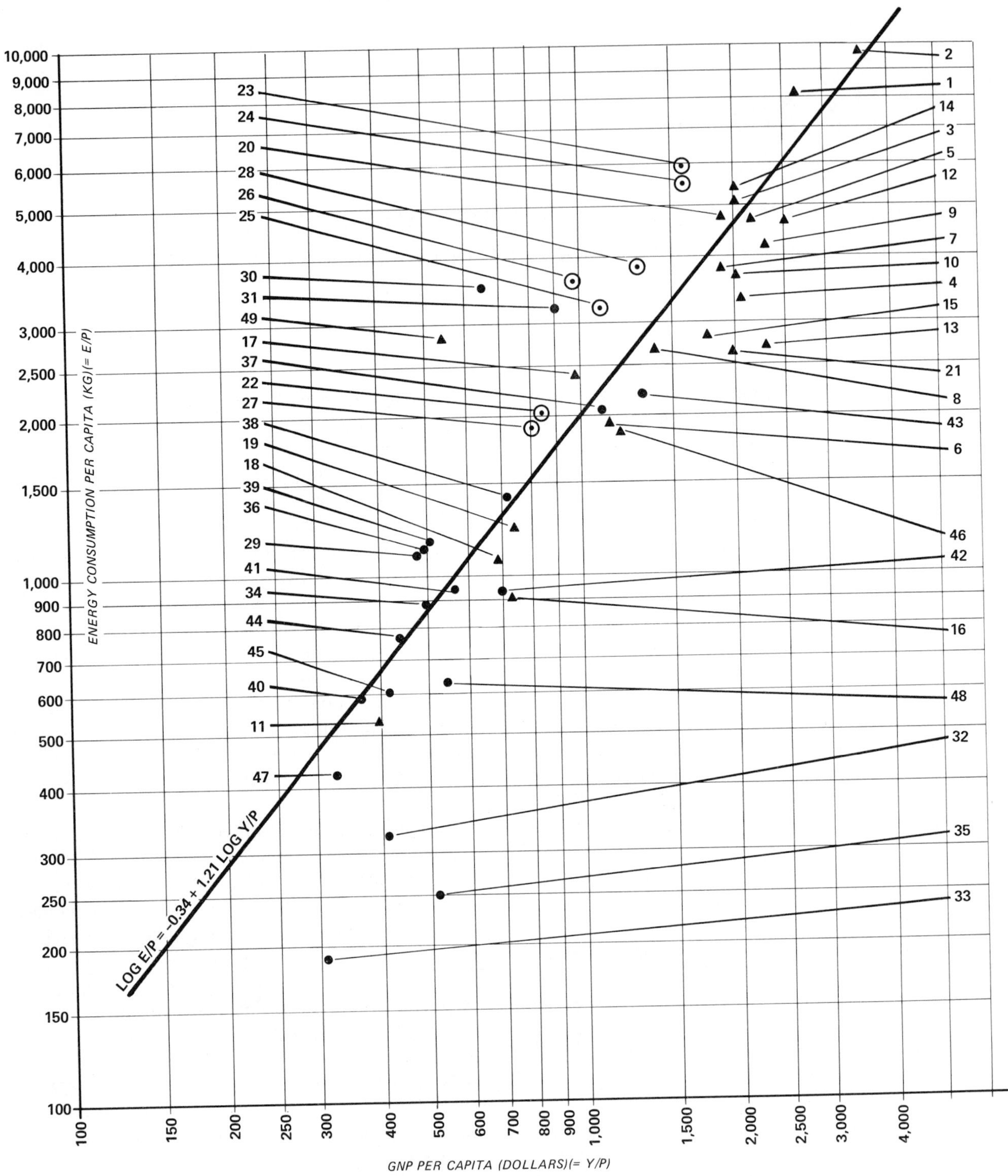

GNP per capita and energy consumption per capita: 49 selected countries, 1965.

GNP PER CAPITA, ENERGY CONSUMPTION PER CAPITA AND PER UNIT OF GNP: FORTY-NINE SELECTED COUNTRIES, 1965

Country	Number on chart	GNP per capita: Dollars	GNP per capita: Rank	Energy consumption, Per capita: Kgs coal equiv.	Energy consumption, Per capita: Rank	Energy consumption, Per $1 of GNP: Kgs coal equiv.	Energy consumption, Per $1 of GNP: Rank
North America							
Canada	1	2,658	2	8,077	2	3.04	7
United States	2	3,515	1	9,671	1	2.75	10
Western Europe							
Belgium-Luxembourg	3	1,991	10	5,152	6	2.59	12
France	4	2,104	7	3,309	16	1.57	37
West Germany	5	2,195	6	4,625	8	2.11	20
Italy	6	1,254	20	1,940	28	1.55	38
Netherlands	7	1,839	13	3,749	12	2.04	22
Austria	8	1,365	17	2,584	23	1.89	24
Denmark	9	2,333	4	4,149	10	1.78	27
Norway	10	2,015	8	3,621	13	1.80	26
Portugal	11	396	46	520	45	1.31	42
Sweden	12	2,495	3	4,604	9	1.85	25
Switzerland	13	2,331	5	2,699	21	1.16	45
United Kingdom	14	1,992	9	5,307	5	2.66	11
Finland	15	1,750	14	2,825	19	1.61	33
Greece	16	772	29	904	39	1.17	44
Ireland	17	981	24	2,359	24	2.41	16
Spain	18	686	33	1,080	36	1.57	35
Yugoslavia	19	743	30	1,217	32	1.65	32
Oceania							
Australia	20	1,910	12	4,697	7	2.46	13
New Zealand	21	1,970	11	2,603	22	1.32	40
U.S.S.R. & Comm. E. Europe							
Bulgaria	22	829	27	2,011	27	2.43	15
Czechoslovakia	23	1,561	16	5,870	3	3.76	3
East Germany	24	1,562	15	5,534	4	3.54	6
Hungary	25	1,094	22	3,188	18	2.91	8
Poland	26	980	25	3,552	14	3.62	5
Romania	27	778	28	1,916	30	2.46	14
U.S.S.R.	28	1,340	18	3,819	11	2.85	9
Latin America							
Mexico	29	475	42	1,104	35	2.33	17
Trinidad & Tobago	30	646	34	3,505	15	5.43	1
Venezuela	31	882	26	3,246	17	3.68	4
Costa Rica	32	414	45	317	47	0.77	48
Guatemala	33	318	49	188	49	0.59	47
Jamaica	34	492	41	873	40	1.77	28
Nicaragua	35	527	38	247	48	0.70	49
Panama	36	495	40	1,112	34	2.25	19
Puerto Rico	37	1,094	23	2,126	26	1.94	23
Argentina	38	718	31	1,471	31	2.05	21
Chile	39	497	39	1,119	33	2.25	18
Peru	40	367	47	577	44	1.57	36
Uruguay	41	573	35	958	37	1.67	31
Asia							
Cyprus	42	702	32	927	38	1.32	41
Israel	43	1,325	19	2,248	25	1.70	30
Lebanon	44	438	43	770	41	1.76	29
Hong Kong	45	421	44	605	43	1.44	39
Japan	46	1,222	21	1,926	29	1.58	34
Malaysia[a] and Singapore	47	332	48	424	46	1.28	43
Africa							
Libya	48	542	36	613	42	1.13	46
South Africa	49	535	37	2,761	20	5.16	2

[a]Including Sabah and Sarawak.

Source: Energy consumption and population from Part Three, table XI (except for several countries included in the totals of table XI, but not shown separately); GNP from Part Five, section I.

textile and food-processing industries require, respectively, about 1.80 and 1.30 kilograms energy (coal equivalent) per $1 of value added, while, by contrast, the respective ratios for chemicals, paper, and basic metals—all industries which are prominent within the nationwide economy—are 3.90, 6.30, and 3.60.[1] Thus, where a country's "industry mix" is dominated by or weighted towards activities with heavy energy content per unit of output, such as mining and metallurgy (e.g., Canada, South Africa, United Kingdom), chemicals (e.g., East Germany), or petroleum refining (e.g., Venezuela, Trinidad and Tobago),[2] energy per unit of national output is apt to be relatively high, while, in a predominantly agricultural economy, it is likely to be rather low. We tested this relationship between energy-GNP ratios and industry mix[3] and found a rather significant (0.59) correlation.

Notwithstanding cases such as Trinidad and Tobago (where petroleum refining dominates a small industrial base), nations with industries oriented towards heavy energy requirements relative to total production tend normally to be relatively high-income countries as well. This fact shows up in a high intercorrelation between per capita income and industry mix. Consequently, if the simple regression relating energy-GNP ratios to industry mix is expanded to a multiple regression taking in *both* industry mix and per capita income levels as independent variables, the correlation coefficient rises only from 0.59 to 0.60.

In summary: a cross-sectional view presents clear-cut evidence that high per capita income countries are high per capita energy users; and much more qualifiedly, and with some notable exceptions, it suggests that high per capita income countries tend, in fact, to be *disproportionately* high per capita energy users.

[1]Data are for 1963; from United Nations, *The Growth of World Industry, 1953-1965* (New York, 1967).

[2]Refers to energy required in the refining operation, not the crude oil subject to processing.

[3]"Industry mix" was measured by the share in total manufacturing value added of the following energy-intensive industrial groups: paper, chemicals, basic metals, and coal and petroleum products. See Part Five, Section II.

Profile No. 5

DATA ON ENERGY-GNP RELATIONSHIP, BY REGIONS AND SELECTED COUNTRIES, SELECTED YEARS, 1925-1965

This profile compares historical trends in energy consumption with trends in gross national product. The indicators shown are: ratios of energy consumption per $1 of GNP—a measure, introduced in Profile No. 4, which reflects the "energy-intensiveness" of an economy; growth rates in energy consumption and in GNP; and the quotient of the last two indicators—commonly termed the "energy-GNP elasticity coefficient"—which shows what percentage growth in energy consumption accompanies each percentage increase in GNP. These indicators are interrelated: an energy growth rate higher than a GNP growth rate implies a rising ratio of energy consumption per $1 of GNP and an elasticity coefficient of greater than 1.0. The energy-GNP ratio has the virtue of describing the absolute level of a country's energy-intensiveness at each point in time, while the elasticity coefficient refers only to changes over time.

Although data gaps for years prior to 1950 make it more difficult to describe the forty-year trends than the briefer post-World War II developments, the principal features of the longer time span can be reasonably well identified. Countries for which we have statistics display a distinct convergence of energy-GNP ratios since 1925. A handful of countries with very high energy-GNP ratios in the pre-Depression period (e.g., United States, United Kingdom, Belgium) experienced subsequent long-term declines; nevertheless, the level of their 1965 ratios remains among the highest in the world. Countries with particularly low ratios of energy consumption relative to output in 1925 (e.g., the Soviet Union, Italy, Sweden) tended to increase theirs over the years that followed—though France is a notable exception, its ratio having drifted slightly downward from a low starting level. The corresponding energy-GNP elasticities reflect these contrasting trends: the United Kingdom and United States with the relatively low elasticities of 0.57 and 0.77, respectively; the U.S.S.R. and Italy with elasticities of around 1.90 each. The United States is one of the few countries whose ratio of energy consumption per $1 of GNP fell for each successive bench-mark year shown in the table.

If the forty-year record suggests that nations undergoing rapid industrialization tend to increase their energy use faster than their total output, the post-World War II data are even more persuasive. In this shorter period, countries with elasticities of over 1.50 (i.e., countries whose energy use rose at least 50 percent faster than GNP) include Puerto Rico, Mexico, Venezuela, Chile, and Italy, along with a number of Eastern Europe and Asiatic Communist countries. The picture is not without apparent anomalies: Sweden's energy-GNP elasticity of 1.6 contrasted with Spain's of 0.8.[1] However, by and large the dominant pattern was one in which rapid industrialization was prominently associated with high energy-GNP elasticity coefficients, while the more modest and diversified growth of the most advanced countries resulted in relatively low elasticities. Thus, five of the seven countries with elasticities of below 1.0 appear among the top fifteen out of forty-nine countries ranked in terms of GNP per capita (see Profile No. 4).

Aggregatively, the 0.85 energy-GNP elasticity of all non-Communist developed countries of the world combined (not just the individually tabulated countries) compares with a figure for all underdeveloped countries of 1.67 for the period 1950-65. The comparison is influenced by the dominant weight of the United States in the "developed" category, but it is striking nonetheless. The accompanying pair of scattergrams, plotting GNP growth rates against energy growth rates for each of a group of developed countries for 1925-65 and 1950-65, helps overcome the distorting influence of aggregation; the charts yield regressions suggesting

(Text continued on p. 73.)

[1] A somewhat narrower though still conspicuous spread would result if Sweden's hydro component (whose relative importance has been falling) were translated into coal equivalents in terms of thermal station fuel requirements rather than in terms of the caloric value of the hydroelectricity generated (see Profile No. 2). In that case, Sweden's energy growth rate would be 5.3 instead of 6.2 percent, and the resulting elasticity 1.35 instead of 1.6.

DATA ON ENERGY-GNP RELATIONSHIP, BY REGIONS AND SELECTED COUNTRIES, SELECTED YEARS, 1925-1965

Region and country	Ratio: energy consumption per $1 of GNP (kilograms coal equivalent)						1925-1965: Average annual percentage rate of growth		1925-1965	1950-1965[a]: Average annual percentage rate of growth		1950-1965[a]
	1925	1938	1950	1955	1960	1965	Energy consumption	GNP	Energy-GNP elasticity coefficient	Energy consumption	GNP	Energy-GNP elasticity coefficient
North America	3.59	3.11	3.03	2.81	2.86	2.77	2.5%	3.2%	0.78	3.2%	3.8%	0.84
Canada	2.91	2.73	2.80	2.70	2.75	3.04	4.1	4.0	1.03	5.1	4.5	1.13
United States	3.62	3.13	3.05	2.82	2.87	2.75	2.4	3.1	0.77	3.0	3.7	0.81
Western Europe	n.a.	n.a.	2.05	2.04	1.87	1.93	1.9	n.a.	n.a.	4.4	4.8	0.92
Belgium-Luxembourg	3.87	3.21	2.67	2.65	2.46	2.59	1.2	2.3	0.52	3.4	3.6	0.94
France	1.73	1.80	1.58	1.55	1.51	1.57	1.9	2.2	0.86	4.7	4.7	1.00
West Germany	n.a.	n.a.	2.67	2.41	2.00	2.11	n.a.	n.a.	n.a.	5.2	6.8	0.76
Italy	0.60	0.70	0.65	0.97	1.15	1.55	5.2	2.8	1.86	11.9	5.5	2.16
Netherlands	1.53	1.76	1.84	1.82	1.79	2.04	3.6	2.8	1.29	5.6	4.8	1.17
Austria	n.a.	n.a.	2.16	2.20	1.94	1.89	2.5	n.a.	n.a.	4.5	5.4	0.83
Denmark	1.38	1.49	1.42	1.77	1.55	1.78	3.7	3.0	1.23	5.5	4.0	1.38
Norway	1.77	1.68	1.55	1.66	1.76	1.80	3.3	3.3	1.00	5.1	4.1	1.24
Sweden	1.07	1.47	1.34	1.60	1.76	1.85	4.9	3.5	1.40	6.2	3.9	1.59
Switzerland	0.76	0.84	0.75	0.81	0.97	1.16	4.0	2.9	1.38	7.7	4.7	1.64
United Kingdom	3.89	3.33	3.17	3.23	2.78	2.66	1.2	2.1	0.57	1.8	2.9	0.62
Greece	n.a.	n.a.	0.77	0.83	1.01	1.17	5.7	n.a.	n.a.	10.3	7.3	1.41
Spain	n.a.	n.a.	1.84	1.55	1.71	1.57	3.5	n.a.	n.a.	5.1	6.1	0.84
Yugoslavia	0.82	0.79	1.40	1.36	1.64	1.64	5.5	3.7	1.49	7.3	6.2	1.18
Oceania	n.a.	n.a.	1.97	2.07	2.09	2.21	3.5	n.a.	n.a.	5.0	4.2	1.19
Australia	n.a.	n.a.	2.16	2.29	2.32	2.46	3.6	n.a.	n.a.	5.1	4.2	1.21
U.S.S.R. & Comm. E. Europe	n.a.	n.a.	2.50	2.74	2.81	2.98	7.1	n.a.	n.a.	6.9	5.6	1.23
Bulgaria	n.a.	n.a.	0.88	1.13	1.43	2.43	9.2	n.a.	n.a.	14.1	6.6	2.14
Czechoslovakia	n.a.	n.a.	2.93	3.27	3.20	3.76	3.3	n.a.	n.a.	5.6	3.8	1.47
East Germany	n.a.	n.a.	3.91	3.90	3.55	3.54	n.a.	n.a.	n.a.	4.4	5.0	0.88
Hungary	n.a.	n.a.	1.91	2.64	2.65	2.91	4.8	n.a.	n.a.	7.8	4.8	1.62
Poland	n.a.	n.a.	3.49	3.77	3.85	3.62	4.1	n.a.	n.a.	5.2	5.0	1.04
Romania	n.a.	n.a.	1.49	1.82	2.09	2.46	5.1	n.a.	n.a.	9.6	6.0	1.60
U.S.S.R.	0.56	1.80	2.32	2.56	2.67	2.85	9.3	4.9	1.90	7.4	5.9	1.25
Communist Asia	n.a.	n.a.	1.23	1.56	2.77	3.99	6.7	n.a.	n.a.	14.4	5.8	2.48

Latin America	n.a.	n.a.	1.41	1.75	2.01	2.08	5.4	n.a.	n.a.	7.6	4.9	1.55
Mexico	n.a.	n.a.	2.06	2.15	2.48	2.33	4.8	n.a.	n.a.	6.9	6.1	1.13
Venezuela	n.a.	n.a.	2.03	2.62	3.59	3.68	11.5	n.a.	n.a.	11.4	7.1	1.61
Costa Rica	n.a.	n.a.	0.62	0.54	0.54	0.77	4.7	n.a.	n.a.	7.0	5.6	1.25
Puerto Rico	n.a.	n.a.	n.a.	1.00	1.78	1.94	n.a.	n.a.	n.a.	15.6	8.1	1.93
Argentina	n.a.	n.a.	1.44	1.66	1.81	2.05	4.6	n.a.	n.a.	5.6	3.1	1.81
Chile	n.a.	n.a.	1.69	1.94	1.91	2.25	3.3	n.a.	n.a.	5.8	3.8	1.53
Asia	n.a.	n.a.	1.24	1.38	1.56	1.69	4.7	n.a.	n.a.	9.0	6.8	1.32
Israel	n.a.	n.a.	1.40	1.67	1.34	1.70	n.a.	n.a.	n.a.	12.1	10.7	1.13
Japan	1.32	1.58	1.57	1.47	1.54	1.58	4.7	4.2	1.12	9.9	9.9	1.00
Other Asia	n.a.	n.a.	1.06	1.30	1.34	1.81	4.8	n.a.	n.a.	8.1	4.4	1.84
Africa	n.a.	n.a.	1.85	2.05	2.02	2.15	4.8	n.a.	n.a.	5.4	4.4	1.23
South Africa	n.a.	n.a.	4.86	5.36	5.22	5.16	4.6	n.a.	n.a.	5.1	4.7	1.09
Other Africa	n.a.	n.a.	0.91	1.05	1.06	1.15	5.3	n.a.	n.a.	5.9	4.2	1.40
WORLD	n.a.	n.a.	2.38	2.36	2.40	2.47	3.3	n.a.	n.a.	5.1	4.8	1.06
Addendum												
Non-Communist regions:												
Developed	n.a.	n.a.	2.60	2.46	2.38	2.35	2.4	n.a.	n.a.	3.9	4.6	0.85
Underdeveloped	n.a.	n.a.	1.18	1.45	1.68	1.83	5.1	n.a.	n.a.	7.7	4.6	1.67
OECD: Europe	n.a.	n.a.	2.07	2.06	1.87	1.94	1.9	n.a.	n.a.	4.4	4.8	0.92
OECD: Total	n.a.	n.a.	2.61	2.46	2.37	2.34	2.4	n.a.	n.a.	3.8	4.5	0.84

[a]Puerto Rico is an exception; its figures apply to 1955–65.

Note: Some regions include country data not shown separately.

Source: Energy consumption based on data in Part Three, tables XI and XIII; GNP based on data in Part Five, section I.

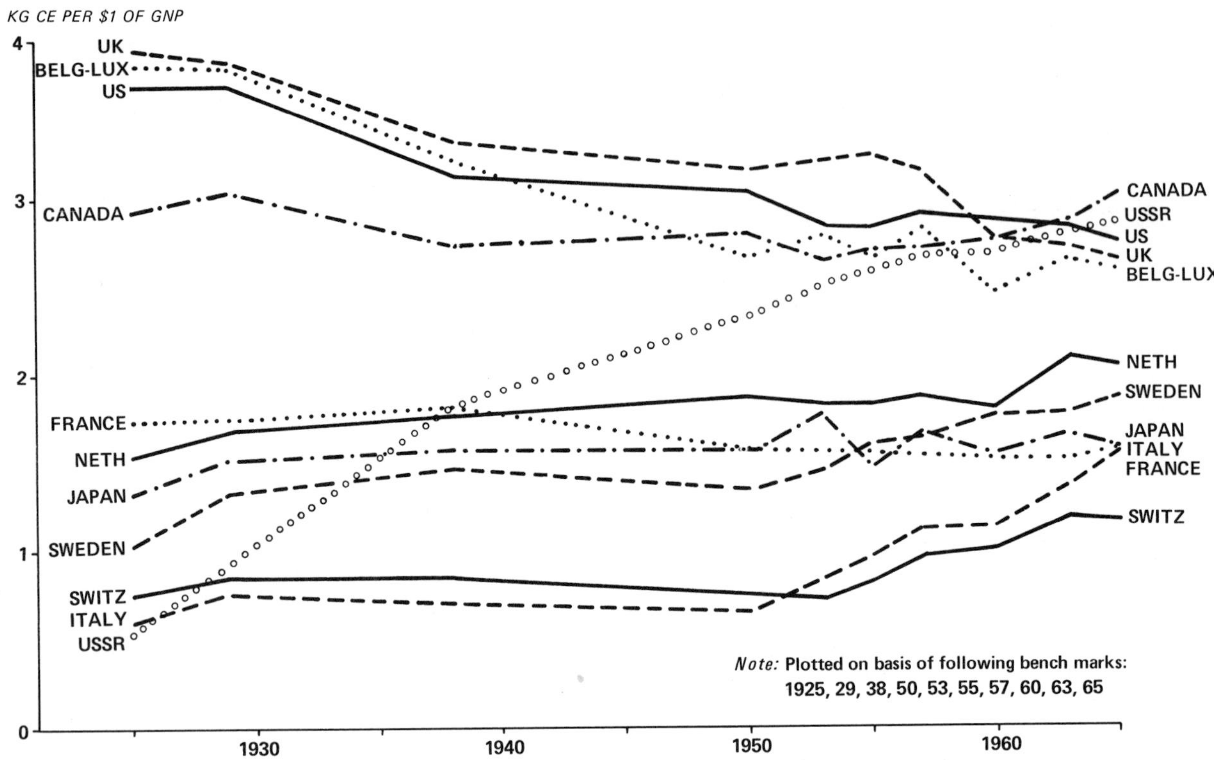

Trends in ratio of energy consumption to GNP, 11 selected countries, 1925–1965 (energy consumption in kg coal equivalent per $1 of GNP in 1965 prices).

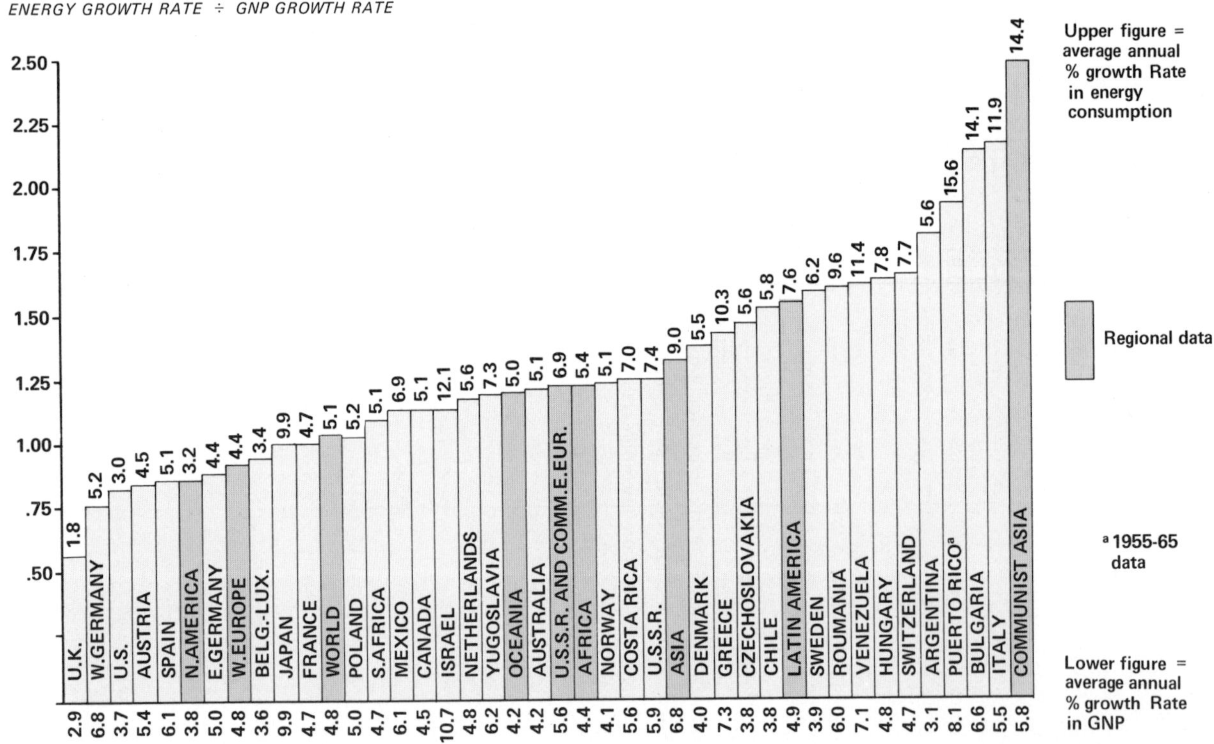

Energy-GNP elasticity coefficients: selected countries and regions, 1950–1965 (average annual percentage rate of growth in energy consumption divided by average annual percentage rate of growth in GNP).

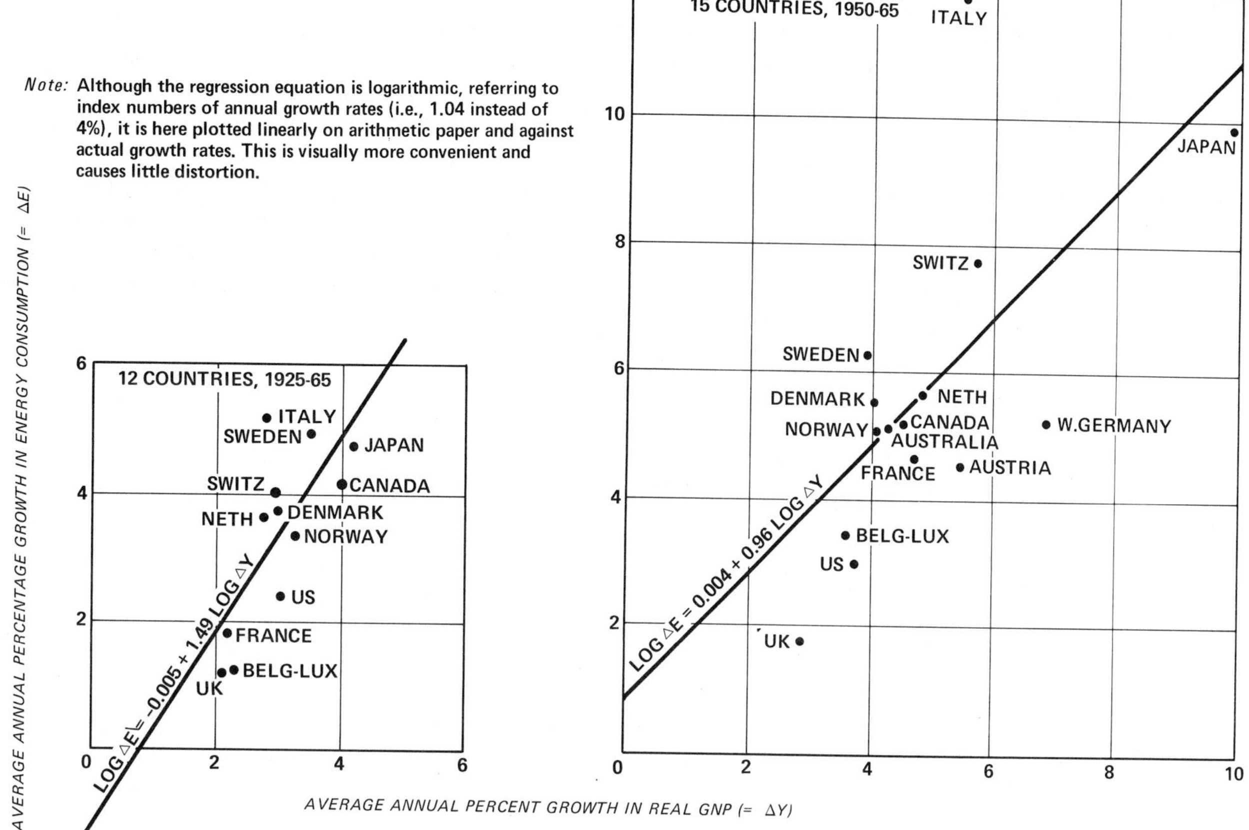

Average annual percentage growth rates in real GNP and energy consumption, selected developed countries, 1925-1965 and 1950-1965.

energy growth rates which tend to diverge little from GNP growth rates—that is, they are characterized by elasticities of close to 1.0.

What can be said about these statistical findings? Factors analogous to those which help explain the significance of the cross-sectional comparisons of Profile No. 4 also shed light on these historical trends. Thus, the changing industrial structure of developing countries involves a shift away from agriculture, with its relatively low energy requirements per unit of output, towards nonfarm industrial sectors, which demand relatively large amounts of energy for each dollar of product. Preceding the declining U.S. energy-GNP ratio shown in our tables, U.S. experience during the forty-year period (1880-1920) of intensive industrialization had been one of a markedly rising ratio. Yearly energy growth was 5.6 percent and GNP growth was 3.4 percent, resulting in an elasticity coefficient of 1.65 and an energy-GNP ratio rising from 1.90 kg per $1 of GNP to 4.30 kg in 1920 prior to declining to 3.60 kg in 1925. Another similarity between earlier U.S. experience and more recent trends in developing countries involves the replacement of the more primitive energy forms. We know that the sharply rising U.S. energy-GNP ratio during 1880-1920 would be somewhat dampened if fuelwood were figured in as a primary energy source. In the same way, post-World War II energy growth among the poorer countries would probably be less if their use of noncommercial fuels (generally declining) were measured in their energy consumption.

Although such a parallel between earlier U.S. experience and that of present-day developing economies is probably not fortuitous, the similarity should not be overdrawn; the United States during the late nineteenth and early twentieth centuries was being transformed under conditions of energy use that today would be considered inefficient and that need not be repeated in developing countries.

A tidy cataloguing of historical trends is also flawed by patterns in the Communist countries. To some extent, they have the characteristics of industrially developing economies, as in the case of Bulgaria. Yet even some of the most developed Communist countries (e.g., Czechoslovakia) display sharp postwar rises in energy-GNP ratios. Perhaps the combination of postwar reconstruction along with a bias in favor of heavy industry and power, reinforced by thermal inefficiency in electric generation, is an important factor here.

One wonders about the emerging and prospective trends of the more mature Western-type economies. With industrialization relatively far advanced and benefitting from steady improvements in thermal efficiency, these countries' records may come increasingly to resemble the decline in energy per unit of output typified by the United States after the first World War. Some countries (e.g., Great Britain, Belgium, West Germany) seem already to have entered this stage, while others (e.g., Japan) may be approaching it. However, there are nations such as Italy which, although relatively prosperous by world standards in terms of per capita income levels, are still undergoing a marked industrial transformation with particularly rapid growth of the manufacturing sector of the economy. Under such circumstances, high rates of growth in energy consumption relative to GNP might be expected to endure for some years.

Profile No.6

WORLD ENERGY CONSUMPTION, BY SOURCE, SELECTED YEARS, 1925-1965

In dealing with primary energy forms in the aggregate rather than with separate fuel categories, the preceding profiles have sought to provide some broad perspective on the comparative position of total energy within the economy of different regions and countries. Plainly, however, energy cannot be viewed simply as an abstract total. Not only does such a total obscure fundamental shifts among the different energy sources, but the size and growth of total energy use itself is affected by the changing role of these different fuels, as their individual properties are exploited for the creation of new products and industries, for the realization of greater efficiency, and for higher levels of national well-being. In other words, the character of different periods of economic history bears a distinct relationship to the emergence of specific energy forms.

Beginning with this profile, and in most of the ensuing ones, we shall compare trends among the individual energy sources. The overview provided by the accompanying table and charts shows the absolute and relative trends in world consumption of solid fuels, liquid fuels, natural gas, and hydroelectricity since 1925.[1] The dominant change during the forty-year period is the relative decline of coal and the ascendancy of each of the other energy forms—especially oil and gas. Although increasing in absolute terms by a billion tons (an increase greater than the absolute rise in either gas or hydro), the solid fuels share of world energy consumption declined by one-half—from somewhat over 80 percent to a bit over 40 percent, or to about the same proportion held by oil in 1965. It also represented only slightly more than one-fourth of the expansion in world energy consumption over the four decades. The shares of the different energy forms in the absolute increase in total energy consumption were:

	1925–1965 change	
	Million metric tons coal equivalent	*Percent of change*
Solid fuels	1,061	27%
Liquid fuels	1,962	49
Natural gas	864	22
Hydroelectricity	103	3
Total	3,990	100%

Liquid fuels, natural gas, and hydro consumption all recorded impressive growth rates during each of the subperiods and the total time span shown in the table. For each energy source as for total energy consumption, postwar rates of change considerably exceeded the long-term rates, but the pace of advance for the various primary fuels ranked in essentially the same relationship to one another as for the entire period. (Hydro is an exception: it grew at roughly the same pace as oil over the long run, and somewhat below oil since 1950.) The 9 percent postwar growth rate in natural gas consumption was especially dramatic; it reflected the fact that utilization of natural gas had to await the availability of economical pipeline transport facilities—in a historical context, a relatively recent development.

[1] For convenience, we shall often refer to solid fuels as simply "coal," and to liquid fuels as "oil" or "petroleum."

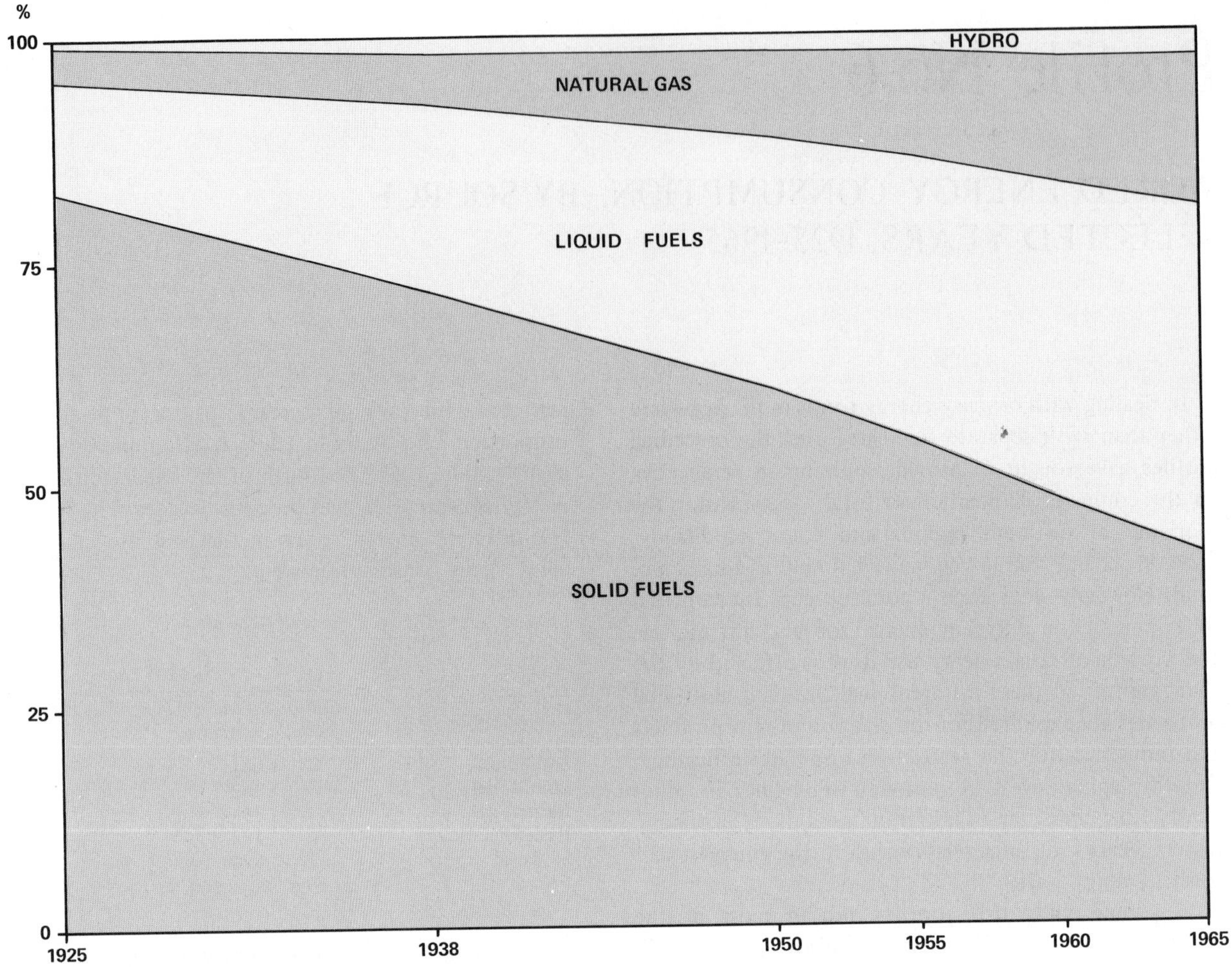

%
100
75
50
25
0
HYDRO
NATURAL GAS
LIQUID FUELS
SOLID FUELS
1925
1938
1950
1955
1960
1965

World energy consumption, percentage distribution by fuel, 1925-1965.

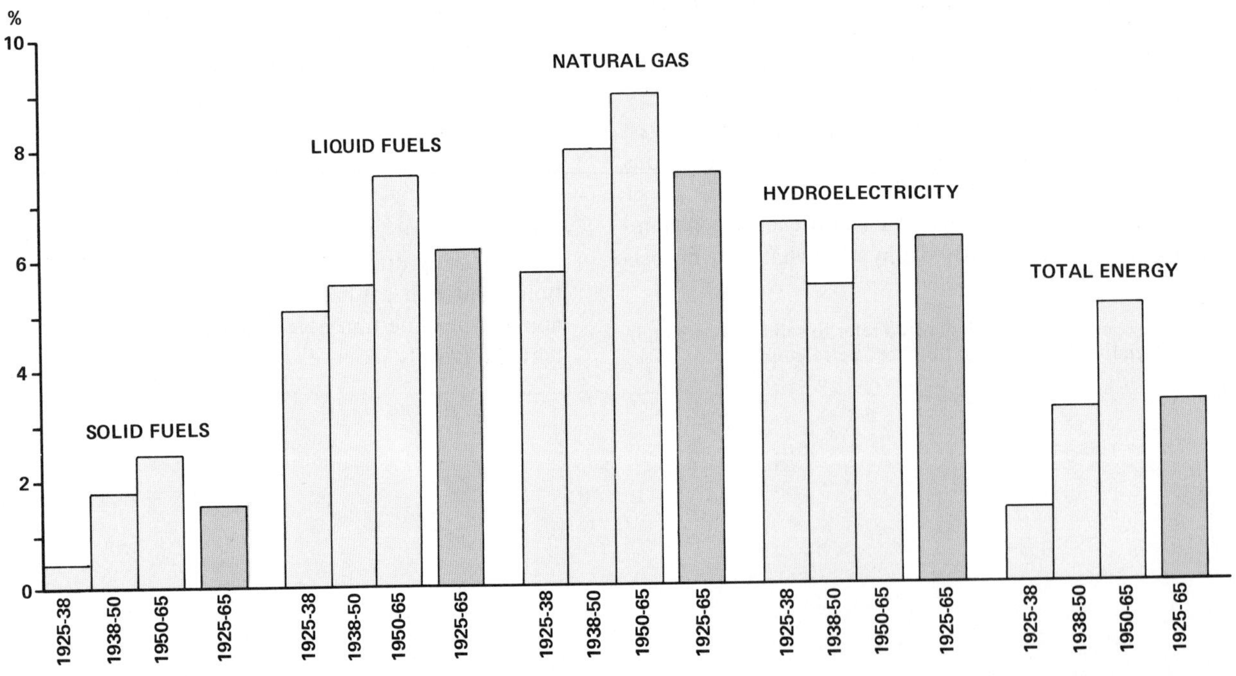

%
10
8
6
4
2
0
SOLID FUELS
LIQUID FUELS
NATURAL GAS
HYDROELECTRICITY
TOTAL ENERGY
1925-38
1938-50
1950-65
1925-65

World energy consumption, average annual percentage rates of change, 1925-38, 1938-50, 1950-65, 1925-65.

WORLD ENERGY CONSUMPTION, BY SOURCE, SELECTED YEARS, 1925-1965

	1925	1938	1950	1955	1960	1965
			A. *Million metric tons coal equivalent*			
Solid fuels	1,230.0	1,291.8	1,593.2	1,816.6	1,998.5	2,290.8
Liquid fuels	196.7	375.8	722.2	1,092.7	1,499.0	2,159.1
Natural gas	47.9	99.7	252.1	389.6	612.6	912.1
Hydroelectricity . . .	9.8	22.8	43.4	59.2	86.0	112.6
Total	1,484.5	1,790.1	2,610.9	3,358.2	4,196.1	5,474.6
			B. *Percentage distribution*			
Solid fuels	82.9%	72.2%	61.0%	54.1%	47.6%	41.8%
Liquid fuels	13.3	21.0	27.7	32.5	35.7	39.4
Natural gas	3.2	5.6	9.7	11.6	14.6	16.7
Hydroelectricity . . .	0.7	1.3	1.7	1.8	2.0	2.1
Total	100.0	100.0	100.0	100.0	100.0	100.0

C. *Average annual percentage rates of change*

	1925-38	1938-50	1950-65	1925-65
Solid fuels	0.4%	1.8%	2.5%	1.6%
Liquid fuels	5.1	5.6	7.6	6.2
Natural gas	5.8	8.0	9.0	7.6
Hydroelectricity . . .	6.7	5.5	6.6	6.3
Total	1.4	3.2	5.1	3.3

Source: Part Three, tables X, XI, and XIII.

Profile No. 7

DISPOSITION OF WORLDWIDE PRIMARY ENERGY OUTPUT, BY SELECTED SECONDARY ENERGY PRODUCTS, 1929, 1950, AND 1965

The dominant concern throughout this study is with data and trends relating to the primary energy forms. Relative shifts occurring among the primary fuel categories would, however, be cast in a more vivid setting were it possible to show how these shifts have interacted with accompanying changes in the different end uses for energy products. How does the diminishing long-term role of coal relate to the decline of the steam locomotive? How does the rise of oil compare with the development of automotive transport? These and other questions could be more meaningfully pursued given information on ultimate energy requirements according to end-use sectors.

This profile is intended as a limited substitute for the worldwide data (largely unavailable) which would be necessary to explore these points. The table and chart call attention to the long-run changes in the disposition of primary energy output among leading processed energy products, such as gasoline; or among primary products identifiable in terms of their particular uses (e.g., coking coal or coal bunkers). In this way, we obtain some indirect clue as to the shifting economic activities towards which primary energy output[1] has been directed since the late 1920s—"indirect" because the industrial origin of the demand for these items can only be inferred. The various items shown in the table accounted for 57 percent of the disposition of primary energy output in 1965; and they accounted for close to 70 percent of the *expansion* in primary energy output since 1929.

Primary energy sources used to generate electricity more than doubled their relative position, rising from 8 to 18 percent; fuel for *thermal* electricity alone (obtained after deducting hydro from the upper panel of the table) rose from 7 to 16 percent. Specific fuels consumed in thermal electric generation (not shown in the tabulation below) can be very roughly estimated by piecing together information from a variety of sources.

	As percent of primary energy output	
	1929	*1965*
Thermal electricity . . .	7.0%	16.3%
Coal	6.7	11.7
Oil	0.2	2.2
Gas	0.1	2.4

The most interesting result of this calculation is that it enables us to estimate the 1929 and 1965 proportions of world coal output which went into electricity. In 1929, the figure was about 9 percent, and in 1965 it was about 29 percent. As a percentage of the thirty-six-year *increment* to world coal output, the share works out to around 65 percent. Clearly, electricity was a mainstay of the world coal industry during this period. Nonetheless, as the above text figures indicate, coal consumed at thermal power stations declined in importance relative to the other fuels used in electric generation.

Coking coal and coal bunkers constitute falling shares, the latter declining to an absolute level close to zero. Enhanced economies in blast-furnace operations have contributed to the decreasing role of coking coal, while the virtual disappearance of coal-burning steamships has led to the nearly total replacement of coal bunkers by oil. Changing patterns of transport to a large extent explain the shifting component shares shown in the table. Automotive transport, jet aircraft, and railroad dieselization account for the predictably rising importance, within aggregate primary energy supplies, of motor gasoline, kerosine, and diesel and fuel oil for transport and heating. However, the "diesel and fuel oil" category, the fastest growing component of those shown, includes, as indicated, liquid space and process

[1]The profile shows a breakdown of total primary energy *output* rather than of total primary energy *consumption*; this is because in the accompanying table on the disposition of primary energy production we wish to account for bunkers, which are excluded from the "inland consumption" definition used in this book.

heating fuels as well, and these too must be credited with having contributed to the rapid growth rate of this necessarily "catchall" category.

Among the secondary products identified in the table, all the items whose relative importance rose between 1929 and 1965 also raised their percentage standing during both of the sub-periods shown, 1929-1950 and 1950-1965; while the two items of declining relative importance (coking coal and bunkering coal) fell in each of the two periods. The indicated trends were therefore of an enduring nature over these years. In the time span covered here, kerosine, having been important in the very early days of the oil industry as an illuminant, recorded quantitatively meaningful growth primarily after 1950 (understandably, because of the advent of jet aircraft).

DISPOSITION OF WORLDWIDE PRIMARY ENERGY OUTPUT, BY SELECTED SECONDARY ENERGY PRODUCTS, 1929, 1950, 1965

	In million metric tons coal equivalent			Percent of primary energy production			Average annual percentage rate of change, 1929-65
	1929	1950	1965	1929	1950	1965	
Primary energy production							
Solid fuels	1,437.6	1,608.6	2,292.7	77.8%	59.2%	40.5%	1.3%
Liquid fuels	318.7	813.2	2,342.8	17.2	29.9	41.4	5.7
Natural gas	77.0	252.0	912.2	4.2	9.3	16.1	7.1
Hydroelectricity	14.7	43.4	112.6	0.8	1.6	2.0	5.8
Total	1,847.9	2,717.1	5,660.4	100.0	100.0	100.0	3.2
Selected secondary energy products[a]							
Electricity[b].	145.0	367.0	1,037.3	7.8	13.5	18.3	5.6
Fuel and diesel oil for heating and transport (excl. bunkers)	109.6	296.7	972.6	5.9	10.9	17.2	6.3
Gasoline	105.0	255.0	605.0	5.7	9.4	10.7	5.0
Coking coal.	132.0	168.0	273.3	7.1	6.2	4.8	2.0
Kerosine	21.0	48.0	178.6	1.1	1.8	3.2	6.1
Bunkers.	73.9	85.0	157.5	4.0	3.1	2.8	2.1
of which: Coal	41.0	12.2	1.2	2.2	0.4	-	-9.4
Oil.	32.9	72.8	156.3	1.8	2.7	2.8	4.4
Total above . . .	586.5	1,219.7	3,224.3	31.7	44.9	57.0	4.8
All others[c]	1,261.4	1,497.4	2,436.1	68.3	55.1	43.0	1.8

[a]Electricity based on energy content of hydro and assumed prevailing "world average" heat rate for thermal electricity, as shown in Part Four, p. 830. For other items, the primary input equivalent could not be similarly calculated, so that refinery losses are included in the "all others" line. However, since transformation losses in the production of secondary energy other than electricity are quite low, this treatment creates negligible distortion. Some of the components are not strictly secondary fuels, but are included because they are direct use items or because of the clue they give as to ultimate industrial uses. Coking coal, coal bunkers, coal and gas as heating or electric station boiler fuels (not shown separately) are cases in point.

[b]It is important to note that electricity here refers to primary fuel input into electric generation (including the calorific value of hydro) rather than electricity produced. Owing to progressive improvements in the heat rate, electricity generated has increased at the long-term rate of about 7½% annually, compared with the 5.6% in primary fuel input tabulated above.

[c]Includes principally: diversion to petrochemical feedstocks, other nonenergy products, coal and natural gas for heating, and refinery losses.

Source: Primary energy data from Part Three, table II. Secondary energy data derived and partially estimated from United Nations, *World Energy Supplies*, Statistical Papers, Series J, various numbers. Fuel oil in thermal electric generation (which had to be estimated in order to show the "fuel and diesel oil" line exclusive of utility fuel) was estimated very roughly from partial geographic coverage in OECD and other publications.

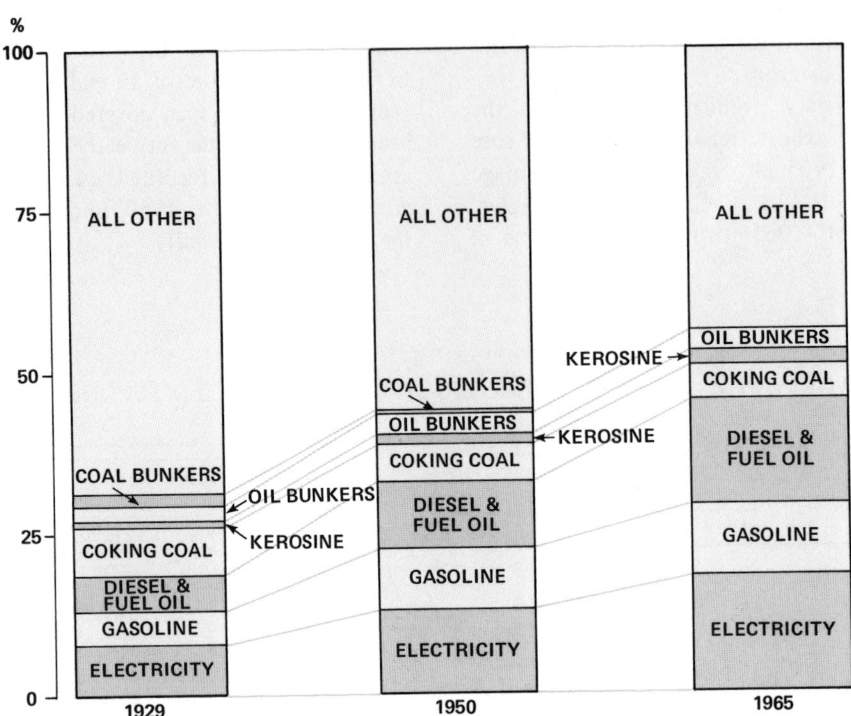

Selected secondary energy products as share of world primary energy output, 1929, 1950, 1965.

Profile No.8

WORLD ENERGY CONSUMPTION, BY SOURCE AND MAJOR REGIONS: AVERAGE ANNUAL PERCENTAGE RATES OF CHANGE, 1925-1965 AND 1950-1965

This tabulation reveals widely divergent growth rates for consumption of the different energy forms in various regions of the world. Because of large differences in the absolute numbers to which these figures refer, the rates of change cannot all be readily compared with one another; and some of the extreme growth rates—e.g., Africa's yearly increase of 45 percent (from a base-year level of practically zero) in postwar natural gas consumption or Japan's yearly increase of 25 percent—are very misleading in comparison with other changes shown. This difficulty is overcome somewhat in the charts, where growth rates are related to the importance of the particular energy form measured. (See also Profile No. 9.)

Conspicuous figures include North American (largely U.S.) coal consumption for which long-term as well as postwar declines constitute the only cases of absolute decrease in the entire table. (In terms of per capita levels of coal consumption, declines also occurred in Western Europe; see Part Three, table XIII.) Among the highest rates of increase in coal consumption for both the 1925-65 and 1950-65 time spans were those recorded by the three Communist areas shown.

The major spotlight, however, falls on oil and natural gas. In Western Europe oil's long-term rate of increase, 9 percent per year, compares with a growth rate in the region's total energy consumption of around 2 percent; for the shorter post-World War II period, the respective rates were 13½ and 4½ percent. In North America and the U.S.S.R. natural gas throughout both periods has constituted the fastest growing fuel in use.

WORLD ENERGY CONSUMPTION, BY SOURCE AND MAJOR REGIONS: AVERAGE ANNUAL PERCENTAGE RATES OF CHANGE, 1925-1965 AND 1950-1965

Region	1925-1965					1950-1965				
	Solid fuels	Liquid fuels	Natural gas	Hydro-elec.	Total energy	Solid fuels	Liquid fuels	Natural gas	Hydro-elec.	Total energy
North America	-0.4%	4.7%	6.8%	5.6%	2.5%	-0.9%	4.2%	7.0%	4.9%	3.2%
of which: United States	-0.4	4.5	6.7	5.1	2.4	-0.7	3.9	6.6	4.4	3.0
Western Europe	0.1	9.0	22.2	5.8	1.9	0.5	13.5	20.0	6.7	4.4
Oceania	2.0	8.4	*	8.6	3.5	2.7	8.9	*	9.5	5.0
U.S.S.R. & Comm. E. Europe	6.2	8.5	13.1	13.4	7.1	4.5	10.7	21.0	12.9	6.9
U.S.S.R.	8.5	9.0	18.6	15.5	9.3	4.2	10.5	23.0	13.1	7.4
Comm. E. Europe	4.6	6.5	7.5	9.1	4.9	4.9	12.5	13.4	11.5	5.8
Communist Asia	6.7	6.4	*	*	6.7	14.0	36.8	*	9.6	14.4
Latin America	0.8	6.0	9.5	7.2	5.4	2.6	7.4	11.8	8.9	7.6
Asia	2.7	8.3	9.6	6.5	4.7	4.7	4.8	16.6	5.8	9.0
Japan	2.2	11.7	11.8	5.7	4.7	3.8	27.7	25.6	4.2	9.9
Other Asia	3.2	6.7	9.4	11.5	4.8	5.6	10.1	15.8	13.2	8.2
Africa	3.6	9.0	*	14.2	4.8	4.2	6.9	45.4	16.3	5.4
WORLD	1.6	6.2	7.6	6.3	3.3	2.5	7.6	9.0	6.6	5.1

*Not computable because of zero in numerator and/or denominator.

Source: Part Three, tables X and XIII.

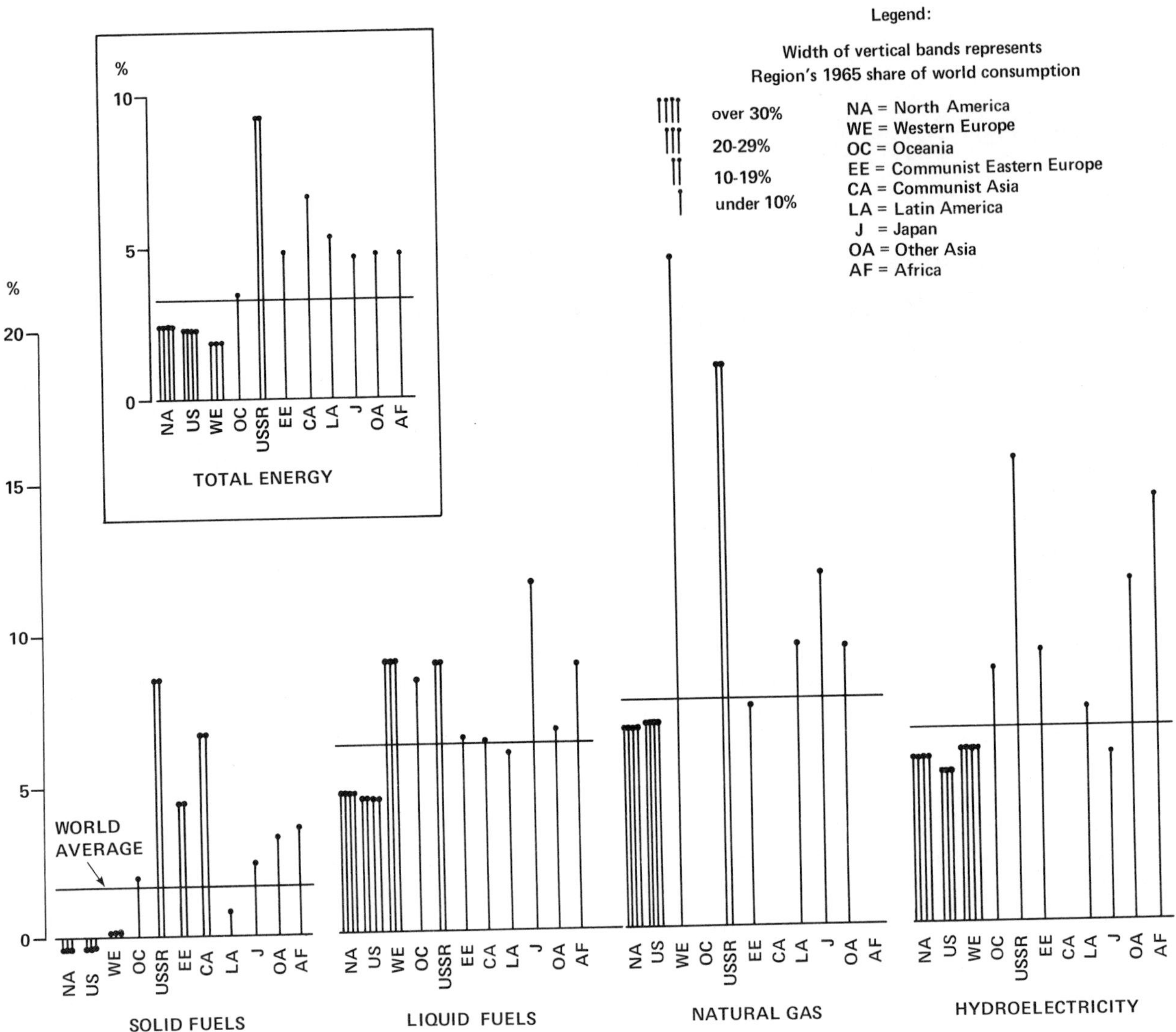

Average annual percentage rates of change in world energy consumption, by source and major region, 1925–1965.

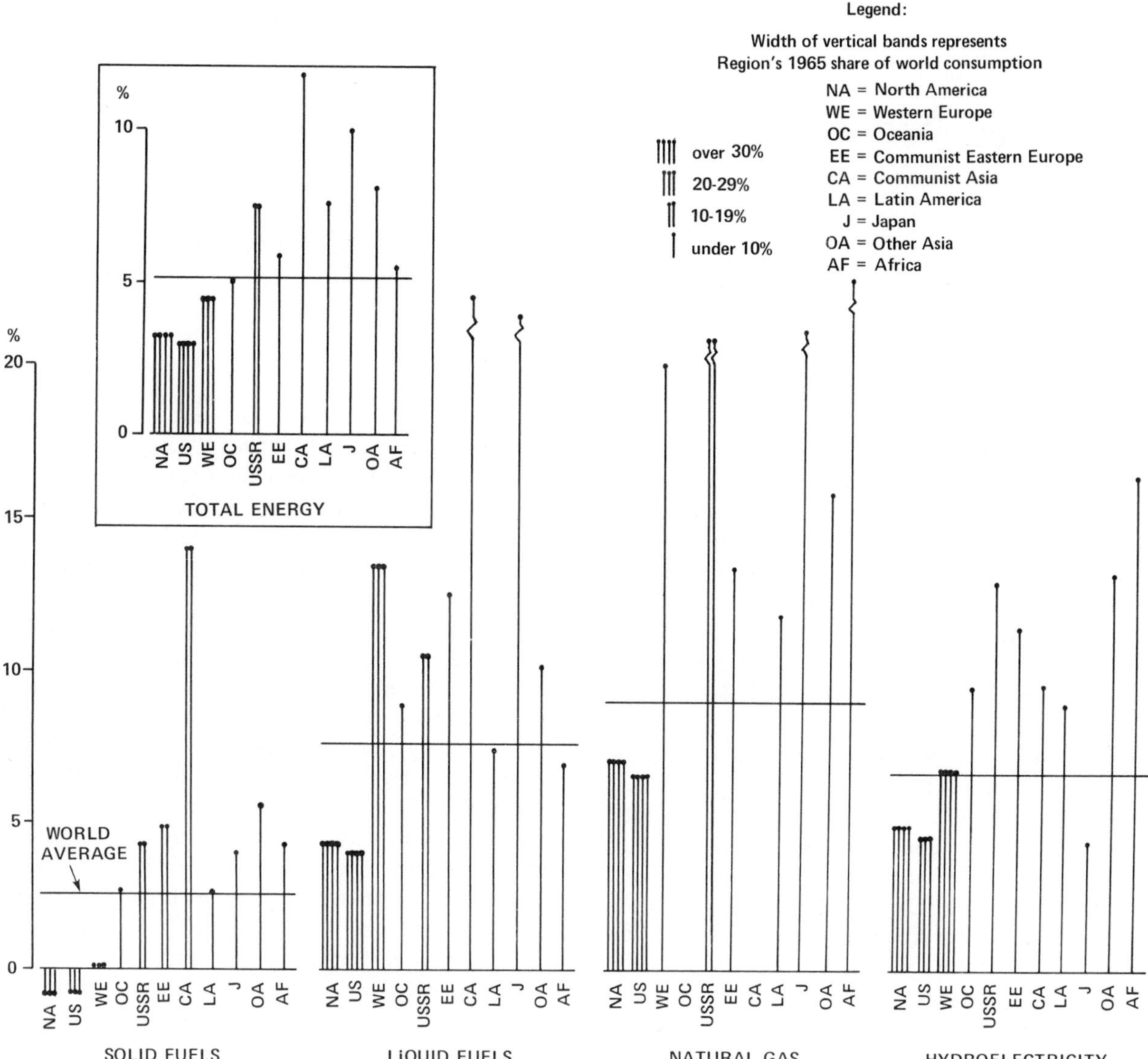

Average annual percentage rates of change in world energy consumption, by source and major region, 1950–1965.

Profile No.9

WORLD ENERGY CONSUMPTION, PERCENTAGE DISTRIBUTION BY SOURCE AND MAJOR REGION, 1925, 1950, AND 1965

We have already sketched (in Profile No. 6) the relative decline of coal and the proportionate rise of each other energy form in overall world energy consumption, and indicated (in Profile No. 1) how the regional concentration of total energy use has changed over the years.

Here, where we look at each region in terms of a specific fuel category, a more varied picture emerges. Clearly, the changing contribution of a particular fuel category to total regional energy use will deviate from that fuel's changing share in total world energy consumption (panel A of the table); similarly, changes in the regional share of world consumption of a particular energy source will differ from that region's share of total world energy consumption (panel B).

As compared with the worldwide average of 83 percent, solid fuels in 1925 contributed about a three-fourths share to North American energy use, while providing over 95 percent for Western Europe. Conversely, oil and natural gas enjoyed a proportionately far more prominent place in the North American energy balance than did these two sources elsewhere.

The regional importance of different fuels within world totals varied accordingly in 1925. North America—with half of world energy consumption—accounted for about 45 percent of world solid fuels consumption, but for over 70 percent of oil and for almost all of global natural gas consumption. At the same time, Western Europe consumed a considerably higher share of worldwide solid fuels than it did of world energy as a whole.

Developments over the ensuing four decades are pictured in greater detail for each fuel category in Profiles Nos. 10 through 13. Several major trends are apparent from the broader historical perspective of the present profile. With respect to the fuel composition of each region's energy consumption (panel A), the significance of coal between 1925 and 1965 declined precipitously in North America and Latin America, modestly in (non-Soviet) Communist Europe, and retained its position in Communist Asia as the almost exclusive energy source. The share of oil in total energy rose in dramatic fashion in Western Europe (from 3 to 47 percent) and in Oceania (from 7 to 45 percent). The natural gas portion of total energy, starting usually from a low share, rose markedly in a number of areas, but most strikingly in the Soviet Union where it climbed from under 1 percent of total energy consumption in 1925 to nearly 20 percent in 1965. Hydro's share of total energy consumption remained fairly modest within the respective regions; for example, North America, where hydro had contributed about 0.5 percent to total energy use in 1925, still received barely 2 percent of its energy from that source in 1965. Nevertheless, this accounted for one-third of the world's hydro consumption in that year.

As to regional shares of world consumption (panel B), the pattern is fairly clear-cut. North America's share declined for each energy source as it did for total energy. Perhaps the most concise way to sum up trends for the other areas shown is to point out that out of a possible thirty-six cases (9 regions X 4 fuel categories) twenty-eight showed a rise in their 1965 world shares of an energy source over their shares in 1925. This reflects the sizable offsetting relative decline in North America's world shares of the different fuels and also the widely diffused and impressive energy growth registered throughout most of the rest of the world. The most significant case of a *declining* world share outside of North America was Western Europe's sharply reduced proportion of world coal use which, along with a modest reduction in its world hydro share, was sufficient to produce a decline in Western Europe's total energy share.

WORLD ENERGY CONSUMPTION, PERCENTAGE DISTRIBUTION BY SOURCE AND MAJOR REGION, 1925, 1950, 1965

Region	Solid fuels			Liquid fuels			Natural gas			Hydroelectricity			Total		
	1925	1950	1965	1925	1950	1965	1925	1950	1965	1925	1950	1965	1925	1950	1965
A. As percent of each region's total energy consumption															
North America	74.5%	43.0%	23.6%	18.9%	37.5%	43.4%	6.0%	18.0%	31.1%	0.6%	1.5%	1.9%	100.0%	100.0%	100.0%
of which:															
United States	74.2	42.3	24.3	19.2	37.7	42.9	6.2	18.9	31.5	0.5	1.1	1.3	100.0	100.0	100.0
Western Europe	96.0	83.8	47.1	3.2	13.5	47.1	-	0.3	2.5	0.7	2.4	3.3	100.0	100.0	100.0
Oceania	92.6	72.0	51.7	6.9	26.1	44.7	-	-	-	0.5	1.9	3.5	100.0	100.0	100.0
U.S.S.R. & Comm. E. Europe	82.9	82.5	58.7	15.2	14.8	25.1	1.7	2.3	15.2	0.1	0.4	0.9	100.0	100.0	100.0
U.S.S.R.	64.9	76.9	48.9	34.2	20.0	30.7	0.7	2.5	19.3	0.1	0.5	1.1	100.0	100.0	100.0
Comm. E. Europe	91.2	93.0	81.9	6.5	4.8	12.0	2.2	2.0	5.7	0.1	0.2	0.4	100.0	100.0	100.0
Communist Asia	94.0	98.1	94.1	6.0	0.3	5.1	-	-	-	-	1.5	0.8	100.0	100.0	100.0
Latin America	37.6	13.0	6.4	56.6	73.2	70.9	4.2	11.0	19.5	1.6	2.7	3.2	100.0	100.0	100.0
Asia	83.1	68.4	37.6	14.4	24.8	54.2	0.8	1.8	5.0	1.7	5.1	3.2	100.0	100.0	100.0
Japan	92.4	83.2	35.5	4.4	6.1	58.4	0.1	0.2	1.4	3.1	10.4	4.7	100.0	100.0	100.0
Other Asia	73.7	57.0	39.6	24.6	39.0	50.2	1.5	3.0	8.4	0.2	0.9	1.8	100.0	100.0	100.0
Africa	91.6	67.7	57.2	8.3	31.9	39.4	-	-	1.6	0.1	0.4	1.8	100.0	100.0	100.0
WORLD	82.9	61.0	41.8	13.3	27.7	39.4	3.2	9.7	16.7	0.7	1.7	2.1	100.0	100.0	100.0
B. As percent of world consumption of each energy source															
North America	45.4%	34.4%	21.0%	71.9%	66.3%	41.0%	93.9%	91.3%	69.5%	45.0%	44.1%	34.8%	50.4%	48.9%	37.3%
of which:															
United States	43.3	31.9	20.0	69.9	62.7	37.3	92.6	90.2	65.0	34.0	29.6	21.9	48.3	46.0	34.4
Western Europe	40.4	30.7	23.0	8.5	10.9	24.4	-	0.7	3.1	39.2	32.0	32.6	34.8	22.4	20.4
Oceania	1.2	1.3	1.4	0.5	1.1	1.3	-	-	-	0.8	1.3	1.9	1.1	1.1	1.1
U.S.S.R. & Comm. E. Europe	5.4	24.0	32.2	6.2	9.5	14.6	2.9	4.3	20.9	0.8	4.3	10.1	5.4	17.8	22.9
U.S.S.R.	1.3	14.6	18.8	4.4	8.4	12.5	0.4	3.0	18.6	0.3	3.7	8.9	1.7	11.6	16.1
Comm. E. Europe	4.1	9.4	13.4	1.8	1.1	2.1	2.5	1.3	2.3	0.4	0.6	1.2	3.7	6.2	6.9
Communist Asia	1.8	2.7	13.3	0.7	-	0.8	-	-	-	-	1.5	2.3	1.6	1.7	5.9
Latin America	0.8	0.5	0.6	7.1	6.7	6.6	2.1	2.9	4.3	4.0	4.1	5.7	1.7	2.5	3.6
Asia	4.1	4.5	6.3	4.4	3.6	9.7	1.0	0.8	2.1	10.1	12.3	11.1	4.1	4.1	7.0
Japan	2.3	2.4	2.9	0.7	0.4	5.1	0.1	-	0.3	9.7	11.0	7.8	2.1	1.8	3.4
Other Asia	1.8	2.1	3.4	3.7	3.2	4.6	0.9	0.7	1.8	0.5	1.3	3.2	2.0	2.3	3.6
Africa	1.0	1.8	2.3	0.6	1.9	1.7	-	-	0.2	0.1	0.4	1.5	0.9	1.6	1.7
WORLD	100.0	100.0	100.0	100.0	100.0	100.0	100.0	100.0	100.0	100.0	100.0	100.0	100.0	100.0	100.0
WORLD (mill. met. tons coal equiv.)	(1,230.0)	(1,593.2)	(2,290.8)	(196.7)	(722.2)	(2,159.1)	(47.9)	(252.1)	(912.1)	(9.8)	(43.4)	(112.6)	(1,484.5)	(2,610.9)	(5,474.6)

Source: Part Three, tables X and XI.

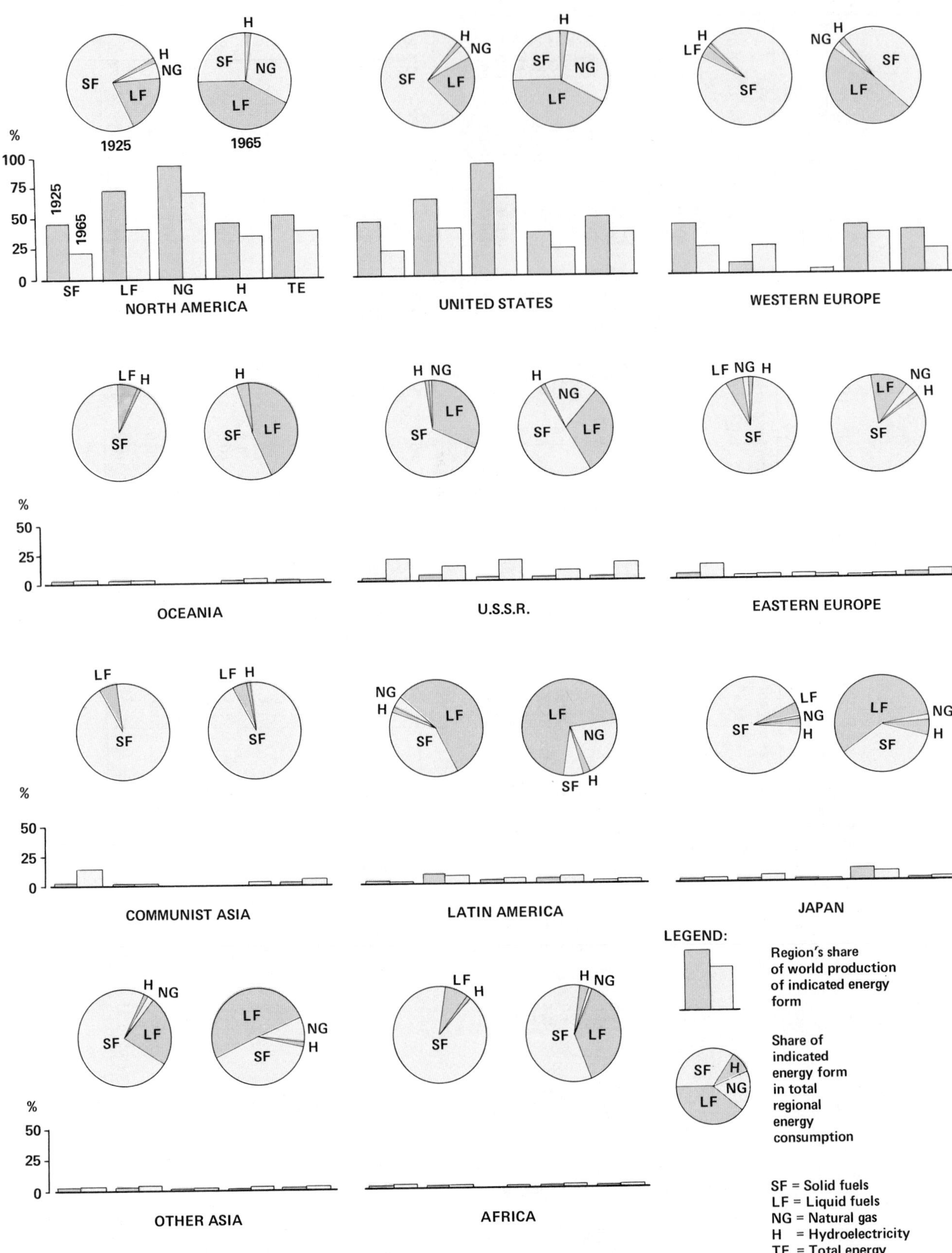

World energy consumption, by source and major region, 1925 and 1965.

Profile No. 10

CONSUMPTION OF SOLID FUELS, BY MAJOR REGIONS, SELECTED YEARS, 1925-1965

The principal long-term regional trends in solid fuels consumption are unmistakable. Except for Communist Asia (essentially Mainland China), coal has dropped relative to each region's total energy consumption. The extent of the relative decline has varied greatly, however: it was particularly sharp for North America, Western Europe, Latin America, and Japan; more moderate for Oceania and the Soviet Union; and least for Communist Eastern Europe. The proportionate role of coal in Communist Asia's energy consumption remained essentially unchanged during the forty years covered here. These disparate changes have left coal with widely differing energy shares in the different regions; in 1965 the shares ranged from a high of 94 percent in Communist Asia to a low of 6 percent in Latin America. Concurrently with these developments, the regional distribution of world coal consumption has shifted drastically away from North America and Western Europe, and towards the rest of the world—where energy consumption as a whole was increasing faster. Thus, the most striking changes recorded in the lower panel of the table show for North America and Western Europe combined a share of world coal consumption falling from around 85 percent in 1925 to 45 percent in 1965, while the Communist group's share was rising from under 10 to over 45 percent during the same period.

For the most part, these changes proceeded fairly steadily throughout the period. The decline of coal within North American energy use displays a reasonably smooth trend for the greater part of the forty-year period; following the mid-1950s, however, a levelling-off has occurred. For the other major regions, coal's declining energy share has been particularly pronounced since 1950. Communist Europe's 1925-50 trend was actually sidewise or upward, partly as a result of the Soviet Union's substitution of solid fuels for firewood during this period.[1] Changing regional shares of world solid fuels consumption, too, have proceeded at a reasonably steady long-term pace. During the past decade or so, the falling North American share appears to have levelled off, as has Communist Europe's rising share.

Factors accounting for coal's declining significance in energy consumption over these forty years are largely those which also explain interfuel shifts towards the other energy forms—particularly oil and gas, with which solid fuels could be replaced over a wide range of uses. We shall check off only a few of these factors. Consider the position of coal in 1925. Although its supremacy in the world fuel and power base was already being challenged, coal in the mid-1920s was still the indisputable leader among commercial energy sources in virtually every sector of economic life—households, industry, transport, and commerce—and in almost every region of the world. (Nowhere except in Latin America did it occupy less than a 65 percent share of energy consumption; Latin America's 38 percent share reflected the dual circumstance that the Caribbean was a prolific oil-producing area, while for the energy-deficient remainder of Latin America the transport cost of imported oil was relatively cheap.) Various circumstances sheltered coal's position. The steam locomotive was still preeminent; in merchant shipping oil-fired vessels had only recently begun to displace coal-burning ships. Coal was the preponderant fuel in thermal electricity generation, and it had virtually a complete grip on space and process heating. Automotive transport was growing rapidly in the 1920s in North America, but worldwide the effect of motor gasoline on coal's dominant energy share was still modest.

Conditions favorable to coal were to erode to a greater or lesser degree among regions in subsequent years. Pipeline gas transport was to become technically feasible during the next several decades. World crude oil supplies were boosted by major Middle East discoveries. In cases of fuel substitutability, oil did not necessarily signal direct and immediate cost advantages over coal; but it did offer numerous attributes of convenience, transportability, and combustibility which frequently

[1] See U.S. Bureau of the Census, *The Soviet Mineral-Fuels Industries, 1928-1958: A Statistical Survey* by D. B. Shimkin, International Population Statistics Reports, Series P-90, No. 19 (U.S. Government Printing Office, 1962), pp. 2-5.

tended to compensate for a higher price. In areas lacking significant indigenous resources of either coal or petroleum the heavy transportation costs of imported coal, relative to energy content, was an added incentive for switching to liquid fuels. And, of course, oil provided a stimulus to industries and to technical developments, such as automobiles and railroad dieselization. Expanding markets for oil, in turn, served to bring about relative price improvements through scale economies which would then enhance the attractiveness of oil still further.

Under the impact of these trends the position of coal was bound to lose supremacy. But coal is hardly extinct, even though part of its survival depends, in different parts of the world, on subsidization. In 1965 it retained over a 40 percent share of worldwide energy consumption and (as shown in Profile No. 7) continued to be the dominant fuel supplier in electric power stations.

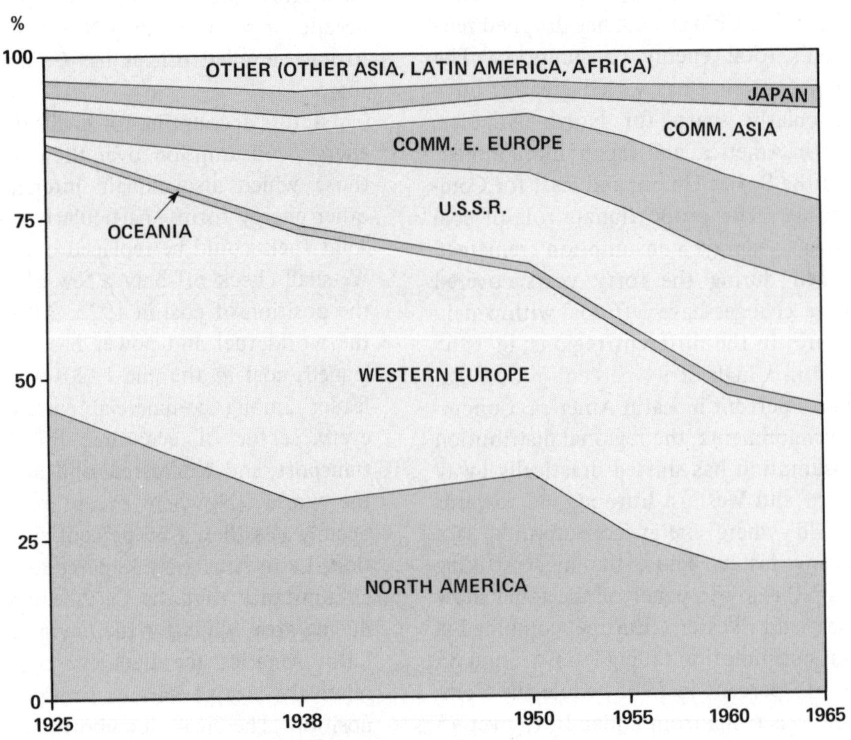

Regional shares of world solid fuels consumption, 1925–1965.

CONSUMPTION OF SOLID FUELS, BY MAJOR REGIONS, SELECTED YEARS, 1925-1965

Region	1925	1938	1950	1955	1960	1965
	A. *As percent of each region's total energy consumption*					
North America	74.5%	54.9%	43.0%	30.7%	24.2%	23.6%
of which: United States	74.2	54.4	42.3	30.6	24.6	24.3
Western Europe	96.0	91.0	83.8	75.6	62.4	47.1
Oceania	92.6	76.9	72.0	64.1	59.7	51.7
U.S.S.R. & Comm. E. Europe	82.9	76.9	82.5	79.4	69.3	58.7
U.S.S.R.	64.9	73.1	76.9	73.9	61.0	48.9
Comm. E. Europe	91.2	86.8	93.0	90.4	87.4	81.9
Communist Asia	94.0	94.5	98.1	95.6	93.2	94.1
Latin America	37.6	24.0	13.0	9.6	7.3	6.4
Asia	83.1	75.5	68.4	55.2	47.8	37.6
Japan	92.4	83.6	83.2	68.4	54.1	35.5
Other Asia	73.7	65.5	57.0	46.0	42.7	39.6
Africa	91.6	81.4	67.7	64.6	61.4	57.2
WORLD	82.9	72.2	61.0	54.1	47.6	41.8
	B. *As percent of world solid fuels consumption*					
North America	45.4%	30.0%	34.4%	24.7%	20.1%	21.0%
of which: United States	43.3	28.2	31.9	23.1	19.1	20.0
Western Europe	40.4	43.6	30.7	31.1	26.5	23.0
Oceania	1.2	1.1	1.3	1.3	1.4	1.4
U.S.S.R. & Comm. E. Europe	5.4	14.5	24.0	30.2	32.4	32.2
U.S.S.R.	1.3	10.0	14.6	18.8	19.6	18.8
Comm. E. Europe	4.1	4.5	9.4	11.5	12.8	13.4
Communist Asia	1.8	2.0	2.7	5.2	11.0	13.3
Latin America	0.8	0.7	0.5	0.6	0.6	0.6
Asia	4.1	6.6	4.5	4.8	5.9	6.3
Japan	2.3	4.0	2.4	2.5	3.0	2.9
Other Asia	1.8	2.5	2.1	2.3	2.9	3.4
Africa	1.0	1.5	1.8	2.1	2.2	2.3
WORLD	100.0	100.0	100.0	100.0	100.0	100.0
WORLD (mill. met. tons coal equiv.)	(1,230.0)	(1,291.8)	(1,593.2)	(1,816.6)	(1,998.5)	(2,290.8)

Source: Part Three, tables X and XI.

Profile No. 11

CONSUMPTION OF LIQUID FUELS, BY MAJOR REGIONS, SELECTED YEARS, 1925-1965

Between 1925 and 1965, the share of liquid fuels in worldwide energy consumption rose from under 15 to around 40 percent; to a greater or lesser extent, almost all regions listed in the top panel of the table increased their proportion of oil in total energy. The exceptions were Communist Asia, where a low liquid fuels energy share of 5-6 percent persisted throughout these years; and the Soviet Union, where roughly 35 percent, one of the highest proportions prevailing anywhere in the world in the 1920s, declined sharply by the outbreak of World War II and subsequently did not quite recover its original share of Soviet energy consumption. A major reason for the relative decline in prewar Soviet Russia was the large-scale replacement of fuelwood (not included in our study) by solid fuels, whose share of commercial energy consumption was rising during the same period (see Profile No. 10); while, after World War II, oil shared the Soviet energy scene with the rapidly rising use of natural gas. (See Profile No. 12.)

Dramatic increases in the liquid fuels share of energy consumption were recorded by Western Europe—up from under 5 percent in 1925 to nearly 50 percent forty years later—and by Japan, where a slightly lower starting share rose to nearly 60 percent in 1965. The greater part of these increases occurred after World War II. In North America, where liquid fuels represented somewhat under 20 percent of energy use in 1925, the rise to nearly 45 percent in 1965 was more modest. For one thing, North America was further ahead than these other areas in the utilization of oil in a wide range of activities, particularly as reflected in the vanguard position of the U.S. automotive market. Then, too, natural gas was claiming a large portion of the increase in energy consumption. Generally speaking, the areas in panel A where liquid fuels shares are shown to be highest in 1925 are those where production was indigenous or where geographically proximate oil supplies could be obtained at lower transport costs than for coal.

The rising contribution of oil to energy consumption during these four decades reflected various factors. On the *demand* side, energy-using activities were developing in which oil commanded "captive" markets; the emergence of road and air transport meant exclusive markets, while—particularly in the period since World War II—oil made significant inroads into such competitive markets as rail transport, now virtually a "captive" market in many countries. In addition, oil became a preferred fuel in home heating and in various industrial uses. On the *supply* side, there was the simple fact of an enormously increased supply stemming from major discoveries in the Middle East, North America, and elsewhere; and this led to the enjoyment of relative price advantages for oil. Besides its physically desirable properties as compared with solid fuels, oil could be shipped more cheaply than coal (per unit of energy content). Improved technology in pipeline construction and tanker size made overland and ocean shipment of petroleum more attractive.

Towards the end of the period covered, the relative role of liquid fuels in the energy economy of most of the areas were tending toward a degree of convergence; for example, North America, Western Europe, and Oceania ranged between 43½ and 47 percent in their 1965 liquid fuel shares.

Changes in the worldwide distribution of liquid fuels consumption, shown in the lower panel of the table, reflect divergent growth rates in total energy consumption and regional variations in the changing shares of liquid fuels in that total, as discussed above. The forty-year picture that emerges here is clear-cut: a marked decline in North America's share of worldwide oil consumption, offset by rising proportions for every other area shown except Latin America. Although this region's total energy growth rate was relatively high (see Profile No. 8), it was not sufficient to reinforce a relatively modest long-term rise in the share of liquid fuels in the region's total energy consumption. But then, Latin America's liquid fuels share of energy had already in 1925 been the highest among regions of the world.

CONSUMPTION OF LIQUID FUELS, BY MAJOR REGIONS, SELECTED YEARS, 1925-1965

Region	1925	1938	1950	1955	1960	1965
	A. *As percent of each region's total energy consumption*					
North America	18.9%	31.5%	37.5%	43.9%	44.5%	43.5%
of which: United States	19.2	31.8	37.7	43.4	43.7	42.9
Western Europe	3.2	7.7	13.5	20.8	32.3	47.1
Oceania	6.9	21.6	26.1	33.7	37.6	44.7
U.S.S.R. & Comm. E. Europe	15.2	20.3	14.8	17.4	22.2	25.1
U.S.S.R.	34.2	24.9	20.0	22.9	28.6	30.7
Comm. E. Europe	6.5	8.2	4.8	6.3	8.3	12.0
Communist Asia	6.0	5.5	0.3	3.6	5.8	5.1
Latin America	56.6	62.1	73.2	76.2	74.2	70.9
Asia	14.4	20.0	24.8	37.3	43.3	54.2
Japan	4.4	11.5	6.1	22.1	38.3	58.4
Other Asia	24.6	30.6	39.0	48.0	47.4	50.2
Africa	8.3	18.4	31.9	34.6	37.3	39.4
WORLD	13.3	21.0	27.7	32.5	35.7	39.4
	B. *As percent of world liquid fuels consumption*					
North America	71.9%	59.2%	66.3%	58.7%	49.3%	41.0%
of which: United States	69.9	56.6	62.7	54.4	45.2	37.3
Western Europe	8.5	12.7	10.9	14.2	18.3	24.4
Oceania	0.5	1.0	1.1	1.1	1.1	1.3
U.S.S.R. & Comm. E. Europe	6.2	13.2	9.5	11.0	13.8	14.6
U.S.S.R.	4.4	11.7	8.4	9.7	12.2	12.5
Comm. E. Europe	1.8	1.5	1.1	1.3	1.6	2.1
Communist Asia	0.7	0.4	–	0.3	0.9	0.8
Latin America	7.1	6.4	6.7	7.4	7.6	6.6
Asia	4.4	6.0	3.6	5.4	7.2	9.7
Japan	0.7	1.9	0.4	1.3	2.8	5.1
Other Asia	3.7	4.1	3.2	4.0	4.3	4.6
Africa	0.6	1.1	1.9	1.9	1.7	1.7
WORLD	100.0	100.0	100.0	100.0	100.0	100.0
WORLD (mill. met. tons coal equiv.)	(196.7)	(375.8)	(722.2)	(1,092.7)	(1,499.0)	(2,159.1)

Source: Part Three, tables X and XI.

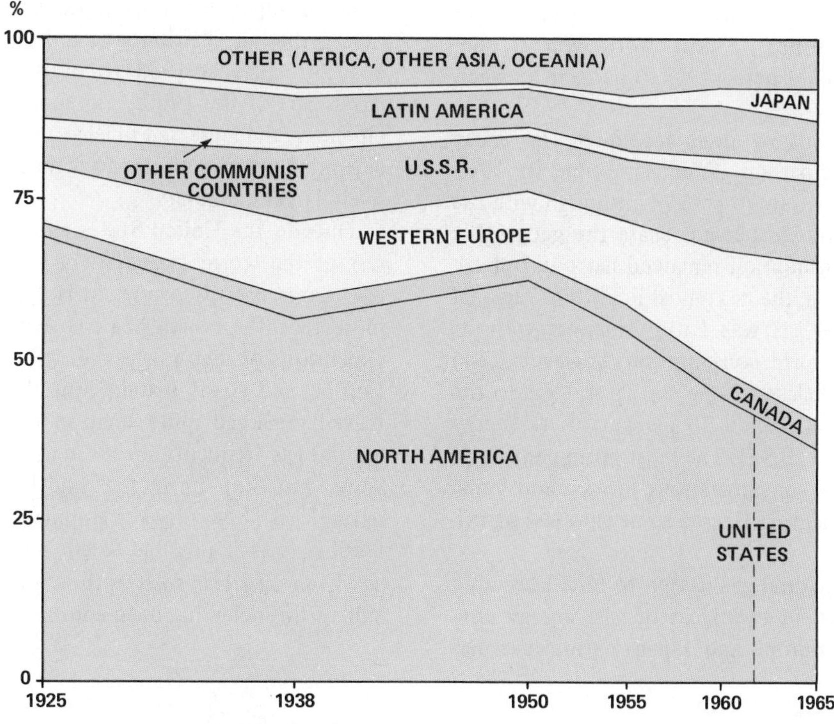

Regional shares of world liquid fuel consumption, 1925-1965.

Profile No. 12

CONSUMPTION OF NATURAL GAS, BY MAJOR REGIONS, SELECTED YEARS, 1925-1965

Of the four primary energy categories covered in this forty-year survey, the fastest rising has been natural gas[1]—a fuel having outstanding qualities of cleanliness, ease of use, and, compared with manufactured gas which it replaces in various regions, high calorific value relative to volume. For the world, its share of total energy consumption increased from 3 percent in 1925 to about 17 percent in 1965. Almost all of the regions listed in the top panel of the table raised the natural gas share of their total energy consumption, but a look at the bottom panel of the table discloses that world consumption remains heavily concentrated in North America.

The increase in North American gas use has risen remarkably. Between 1925 and 1950, it went from 6 percent of energy consumption to 18 percent; and in the postwar period, it continued to increase, reaching 31 percent in 1965. In the Soviet case, the rising natural gas share was almost entirely a post-World War II phenomenon, going from 2 percent to 20 percent between 1950 and 1965.

In 1925 North America alone accounted for nearly 95 percent of world natural gas consumption. By 1965 this figure had dropped to 70 percent, although with the Soviet Union's nearly 20 percent share the geographic spread of world consumption remained narrow. Indeed, after the Soviet Union, the next most important regional consumer of natural gas was Latin America; with its mere 4 percent of world consumption, however, Latin America was nevertheless relying on natural gas to the same relative extent (roughly 20 percent of its energy consumption) as the U.S.S.R. The most prominent Latin American natural gas consumers were Mexico and Venezuela; Chile and Argentina figured somewhat less significantly.

For most areas natural gas is seen to be a latecomer on the energy scene: in two areas of vast energy consumption—Western Europe and Japan—natural gas percentagewise contributed less to total 1965 energy use than it had in the U.S. energy economy of 1925. The early and prolonged world leadership of North America in natural gas use (and this meant largely the United States, until the large Canadian oil and gas discoveries of the late 1940s) is explained by the fact that the oil and gas fields in this region had overland access to major consuming centers and also enjoyed the transport facilities necessary to move the gas to market. Abetted by the development of welded seamless high-pressure pipe and powerful new pipe-laying equipment, U.S. pipeline technology made rapid strides in the 1920s and 1930s. And the acquisition in the 1940s of two major wartime petroleum lines for long-distance gas transmission further strengthened the market potential of southwestern gas in the Northeast region of the United States. Total gas pipeline mileage in the United States, including field gathering, distribution, and transmission, rose from 265,000 miles in 1935 to over 800,000 miles in the latter part of the 1960s; moreover, as in the case of oil pipelines, the increased mileage does not fully reflect the expanded volume of piped gas made possible by progressively larger diameters.[2]

Outside the United States and the Soviet Union, the rest of the world lagged for a long time in natural gas use. Large gas discoveries in Holland a decade ago and, more recently, North Sea gas, have now spurred rapid expansion of natural gas distribution in Continental Europe and Great Britain. But the amounts of gas involved remained quite small in 1965. Large volumes of natural gas frequently occur in association with oil reservoirs, but not until the mid-1960s, when liquefied natural gas (LNG) tanker shipments became technically feasible, was it possible to consider transporting gas by sea from oil fields such as those in North Africa. The result of this delay has been enormous waste of natural gas

[1]Growth rate comparisons appear in Profile No. 8.

[2]OECD, *Pipelines in the United States and Europe* (Paris, 1969), p. 21.

flared or vented in the oil fields, except for those portions used for repressuring purposes and for small amounts used in petroleum company operations. Apparently just entering the competitive threshold, such shipments—principally to Western Europe, but prospectively to Japan from Brunei, Alaska, and elsewhere—are only now beginning to figure in the picture. The fact that formerly wasted natural gas is being used in Kuwait to distill seawater illustrates the changes taking place. And the construction of a natural gas-using ammonia plant in Kuwait and of a projected aluminum smelter in Bahrein powered by natural gas-based electricity also point to greater possibilities of natural gas use in otherwise limited market areas.

CONSUMPTION OF NATURAL GAS, BY MAJOR REGIONS, SELECTED YEARS, 1925-1965

Region	1925	1938	1950	1955	1960	1965
		A. *As percent of each region's total energy consumption*				
North America	6.0%	12.4%	18.0%	23.7%	29.4%	31.1%
of which: United States	6.2	12.9	18.9	24.9	30.4	31.5
Western Europe	–	–	0.3	1.0	1.9	2.5
Oceania	–	–	–	–	–	–
U.S.S.R. & Comm. E. Europe	1.7	2.5	2.3	2.7	7.7	15.2
U.S.S.R.	0.7	1.7	2.5	2.6	9.4	19.3
Comm. E. Europe	2.2	4.8	2.0	3.0	4.1	5.7
Communist Asia	–	–	–	–	–	–
Latin America	4.2	11.9	11.0	11.6	15.7	19.5
Asia	0.8	1.3	1.8	3.0	5.1	5.0
Japan	0.1	0.1	0.2	0.3	1.0	1.4
Other Asia	1.5	2.7	3.0	4.9	8.5	8.4
Africa	–	–	–	–	0.1	1.6
WORLD	3.2	5.6	9.7	11.6	14.6	16.7
		B. *As percent of world natural gas consumption*				
North America	93.9%	87.7%	91.3%	89.0%	79.6%	69.5%
of which: United States	92.6	86.4	90.2	87.5	77.0	65.0
Western Europe	–	–	0.7	1.9	2.6	3.1
Oceania	–	–	–	–	–	–
U.S.S.R. & Comm. E. Europe	2.9	6.2	4.3	4.8	11.7	20.9
U.S.S.R.	0.4	3.0	3.0	3.0	9.8	18.6
Comm. E. Europe	2.5	3.3	1.3	1.8	2.0	2.3
Communist Asia	–	–	–	–	–	–
Latin America	2.1	4.6	2.9	3.1	3.9	4.3
Asia	1.0	1.4	0.8	1.2	2.1	2.1
Japan	0.1	0.1	–	0.1	0.2	0.3
Other Asia	0.9	1.3	0.7	1.2	1.9	1.8
Africa	–	–	–	–	–	0.2
WORLD	100.0	100.0	100.0	100.0	100.0	100.0
WORLD (mill. met. tons coal equiv.)	(47.9)	(99.7)	(252.1)	(389.6)	(612.6)	(912.1)

Source: Part Three, tables X and XI.

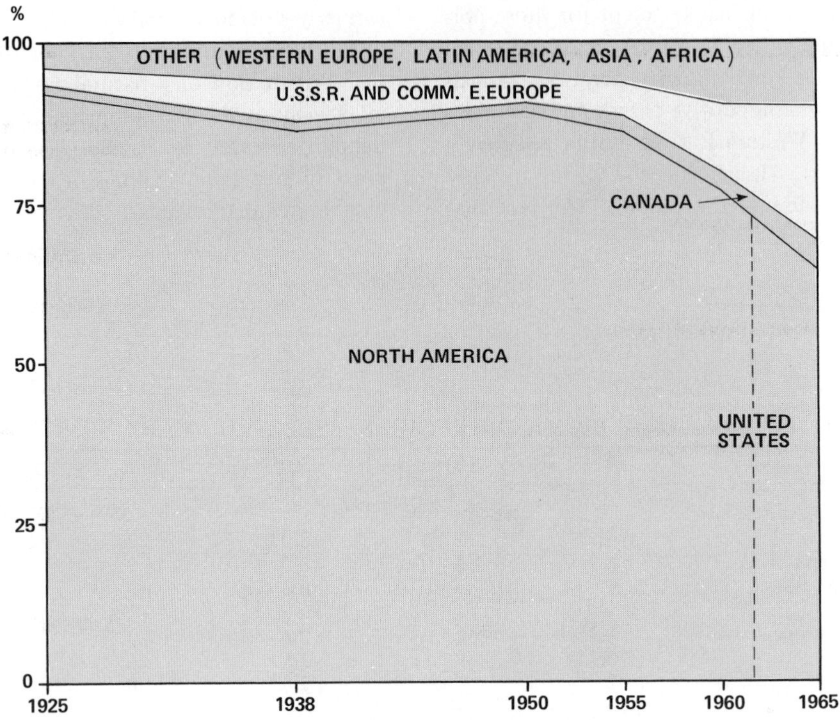

Regional shares of world natural gas consumption, 1925–1965.

Profile No. 13

CONSUMPTION OF HYDROELECTRICITY, BY MAJOR REGIONS, SELECTED YEARS, 1925-1965

As is the case with oil and natural gas, hydropower's share in primary energy consumption has risen over the years throughout most of the world. However, its contribution to total worldwide energy use (a bit over 2 percent in 1965, up from 0.7 percent in 1925) remains negligible. Moreover, the rising hydro share has shown signs of flattening out in recent years. The most conspicuous post-World War II increases in the hydro share of energy have been in Africa and the less developed parts of Asia.

The worldwide total of hydro consumption is concentrated among a limited number of areas in most of which it accounts for only a small portion of energy consumption. In 1965 some 85 percent of world hydro use was confined to Western Europe, Japan, the Soviet Union, and North America (with over one-fifth in the United States alone and 13 percent in Canada); in 1925 these areas, exclusive of Russia, had consumed around 95 percent of the total. Among the places identified in the table, Canada and Japan have relied particularly heavily on hydro in their fuel balance, with 1965 shares of 9 percent and 5 percent respectively. Under an alternative, and in some ways more appropriate, way of converting kilowatts of hydro into coal equivalents, these 1965 Canadian and Japanese figures rise to 24 percent and 13 percent respectively; both of these figures are below their post-World War II peak, especially in the case of Japan, where hydro's relative role has been on the decline. (See Profile No. 2.)

Of course, hydro remains an important factor in the energy economy of numerous smaller countries not individually tabulated here[1]—among them Norway (44 percent of total Norwegian energy consumption in 1965), Switzerland (18 percent), and Sweden and New Zealand (16 percent each).[2] As in the case of Japan, the hydro shares of energy in a number of these countries, such as Switzerland and Sweden, have been tending to decline or, at best, to no more than hold their own. The reason is that the rapid growth of electrification in industrially advanced areas has led to the harnessing of the more accessible and economic portion of hydro resources. In places where exploitation is far advanced, hydro may increasingly come to be utilized for purposes of meeting peak electricity demand in order to complement base-load supplies of conventional or nuclear generating plants; the growth of pumped storage schemes represents one development associated with this trend. (However, there are also other ways of meeting auxiliary power needs and complex cost considerations enter into the picture.)

While hydropower is not considered to contribute significantly to the growth in energy requirements of the present industrialized world, a somewhat more promising outlook is warranted for developing regions, where a fairly substantial hydroelectric potential remains to be tapped. The Volta (Ghana), Mekong (Thailand and Indo-China), Aswan (Egypt), and other water power projects illustrate the significance of prospects for this energy source in particular areas. In the detailed data of table XI in Part Three, the hydro share of total energy in Rhodesia and Zambia (taken together) is seen to have gone from nothing in 1960 to around 13 percent in 1965 following the development of the Kariba Dam, whose output is shared by both countries.

In numerous Asian and Latin American countries (in the latter, notably Brazil, Chile, and Argentina), the proportion of the theoretical hydropower potential which exists in the form of actual capacity is well under 5 percent—far below comparable shares in advanced countries.[3] However, such theoretical indicators of hydro potential give an exaggerated picture since they say nothing about economic feasibility within a prospective

[1] See Part Three, table XI for detailed country data.

[2] The figures refer to the lower of the alternative hydro computations. See preceding paragraph above.

[3] Data of actual and potential hydro capacity appear in World Power Conference, *Survey of Energy Resources, 1968* (London: Central Office of the World Power Conference, 1968).

time horizon. That is, the figures depict physical rather than economic characteristics. For example, quite aside from the large costs associated with the minimum scale at which a project may be feasible, costs may be decisively influenced by the topographical and geological features of the hydro site. There may be a costly investment need to modify stream characteristics so as to maximize the availability of dependable power. And the matter of distances to, and size of, electricity-using markets is critical.

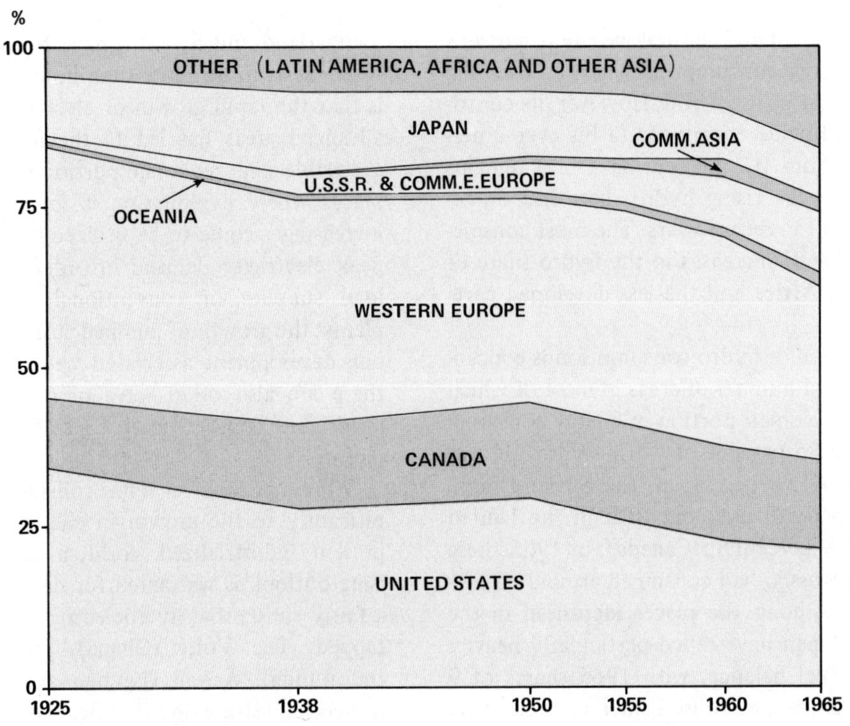

Regional shares of world hydroelectric consumption, 1925–1965.

CONSUMPTION OF HYDROELECTRICITY, BY MAJOR REGIONS, SELECTED YEARS, 1925-1965

Region	1925[a]	1938[a]	1950[a]	1955[a]	1960[a]	1965 a	1965 b
			A. *As percent of each region's total energy consumption*				
North America	0.6%	1.1%	1.5%	1.6%	1.9%	1.9%	5.6%
Canada	3.5	8.0	8.4	9.9	11.5	9.2	23.6
United States	0.5	0.9	1.1	1.1	1.2	1.3	3.9
Western Europe	0.7	1.3	2.4	2.7	3.4	3.3	9.4
Oceania	0.5	1.4	1.9	2.2	3.7	3.5	10.0
U.S.S.R. & Comm. E. Europe	0.1	0.3	0.4	0.5	0.8	0.9	2.7
U.S.S.R.	0.1	0.4	0.5	0.6	1.0	1.1	3.4
Comm. E. Europe	0.1	0.2	0.2	0.2	0.3	0.4	1.1
Communist Asia	-	-	1.5	0.8	1.0	0.8	2.4
Latin America	1.6	2.0	2.7	2.6	2.9	3.2	9.2
Asia	1.7	3.2	5.1	4.5	3.7	3.2	9.2
Japan	3.1	4.8	10.4	9.1	6.6	4.7	13.0
Other Asia	0.2	1.2	0.9	1.1	1.4	1.8	5.4
Africa	0.1	0.3	0.4	0.7	1.2	1.8	5.2
WORLD	0.7	1.3	1.7	1.8	2.0	2.1	6.0
			B. *As percent of world hydroelectric consumption*				
North America	45.0%	40.1%	44.1%	40.6%	37.0%	34.8%	
Canada	11.0	13.1	14.5	15.2	14.6	13.0	
United States	34.0	27.0	29.6	25.4	22.4	21.9	
Western Europe	39.2	36.0	32.0	33.7	33.6	32.6	
Oceania	0.8	1.1	1.3	1.4	1.4	1.9	
U.S.S.R. & Comm. E. Europe	0.8	3.3	4.3	5.8	8.3	10.1	
U.S.S.R.	0.3	2.8	3.7	4.9	7.4	8.9	
Comm. E. Europe	0.4	0.5	0.6	0.9	0.9	1.2	
Communist Asia	-	-	1.5	1.3	2.8	2.3	
Latin America	4.0	3.5	4.1	4.6	5.1	5.7	
Asia	10.1	15.7	12.3	11.9	10.7	11.1	
Japan	9.7	13.0	11.0	10.2	8.5	7.8	
Other Asia	0.5	2.7	1.3	1.6	2.2	3.2	
Africa	0.1	0.3	0.4	0.7	1.0	1.5	
WORLD	100.0	100.0	100.0	100.0	100.0	100.0	
WORLD (mill. metric tons coal equiv.)	(9.9)	(22.9)	(43.4)	(59.2)	(86.0)	(112.6)	(342.4)

[a]Hydro measured by calorific value of the hydroelectricity generated.

[b]Hydro measured by "heat rate" (i.e., energy content of fuels consumed at thermal electric stations). Assuming the same heat rate for all regions (as is done, for convenience, in this calculation), the percentages in the lower panel of the table are the same no matter which of the two methods is used to measure hydro.

Source: Part Three, tables X, XI, and XII.

Profile No. 14

REGIONAL SHARES OF WORLD HYDROELECTRICITY AND TOTAL ELECTRICITY CONSUMPTION, 1925, 1950, AND 1965

The direction of long-term trends in the geographic distribution of worldwide hydroelectricity consumption has paralleled that in *total* electricity use. Comparing 1925 and 1965, all areas shown in the table (except Japan) with falling shares of world electricity consumption likewise accounted for diminishing portions of world hydro consumption. Prominent in this group were North America and Western Europe, whose share of world hydro consumption fell from 84 percent to 67 percent while the percentage of total electricity went from 85 to 63. Most conspicuous among areas with rising proportions of both world hydro and world electricity was the combined group of Communist countries: their roughly 5 percent share of total electricity in 1925 rose to 22 percent in 1965, while their world hydro share went from under 1 to 12 percent. The other areas with rising percentages in both categories were Oceania, Africa, developing Asia, and Latin America. In the case of Japan, that country's percentage of total electricity rose while the share of world waterpower consumption declined.

A few areas accounting for increasing percentages of both categories achieved a relatively greater gain in their portion of world hydro consumption. These areas–most of them containing substantial waterpower potentials–include Oceania, the Soviet Union, Latin America, Africa, developing Asia (i.e., the "Other Asia" region in the table), and Communist Asia. Another way of picturing the same development is to show the changing role of hydroelectricity in total electricity for the world as a whole and for different regions. Such a comparison is tabulated in Profile No. 15.

REGIONAL SHARES OF WORLD HYDROELECTRICITY AND TOTAL ELECTRICITY CONSUMPTION, 1925, 1950, 1965

Region	1925		1950		1965	
	Hydro-electricity	Total electricity	Hydro-electricity	Total electricity	Hydro-electricity	Total electricity
North America	45.0%	47.9%	44.1%	46.9%	34.8%	38.8%
Canada	11.0	4.9	14.5	5.6	13.0	4.2
United States	34.0	42.9	29.6	41.3	21.9	34.6
Western Europe	39.2	37.2	32.0	26.3	32.6	24.6
Oceania	0.8	1.0	1.3	1.3	1.9	1.5
U.S.S.R. & Comm. E. Europe	0.7	3.8	4.3	14.1	10.1	20.3
U.S.S.R.	0.3	1.5	3.7	9.6	8.9	15.1
Comm. E. Europe	0.4	2.3	0.6	4.5	1.2	5.1
Communist Asia	–	1.0	1.5	1.0	2.3	1.8
Latin America	4.0	2.4	4.1	2.7	5.7	3.1
Asia	10.1	5.5	12.3	6.0	11.1	8.2
Japan	9.7	4.3	11.0	4.7	7.8	5.6
Other Asia	0.4	1.2	1.3	1.3	3.3	2.6
Africa	0.1	1.2	0.4	1.6	1.5	1.7
WORLD	100.0	100.0	100.0	100.0	100.0	100.0
WORLD (million kwh)	(78,794)	(188,933)	(347,378)	(945,852)	(901,104)	(3,342,245)

Source: Hydroelectricity based on data in Part Three, table X; total electricity based on data in Part Three, table XI.

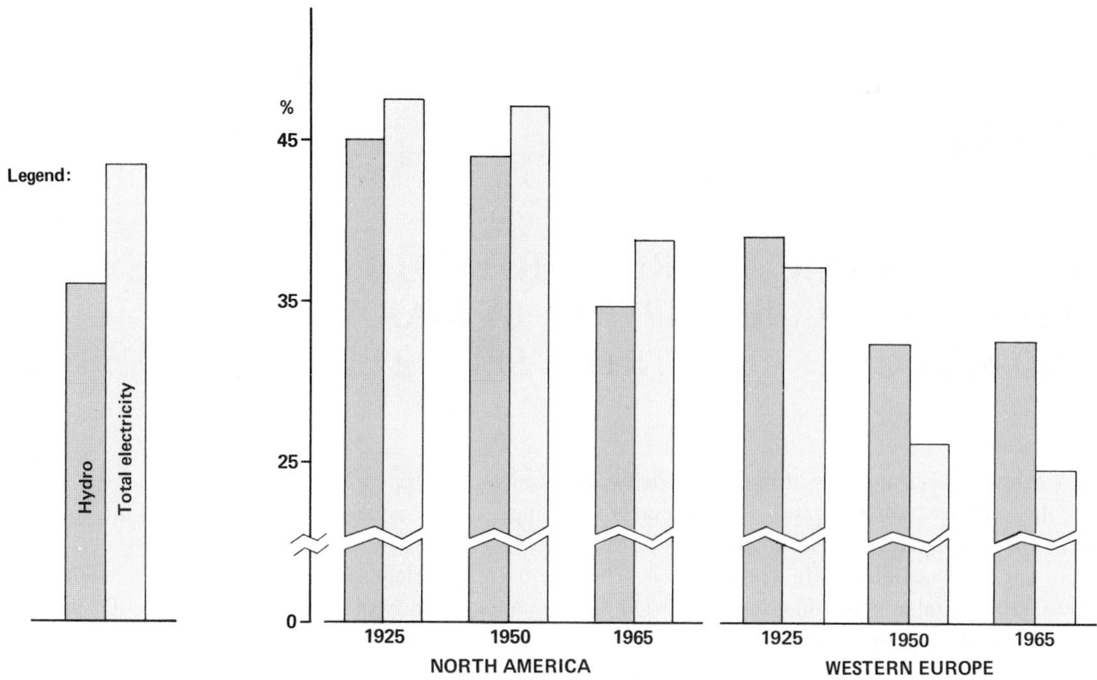

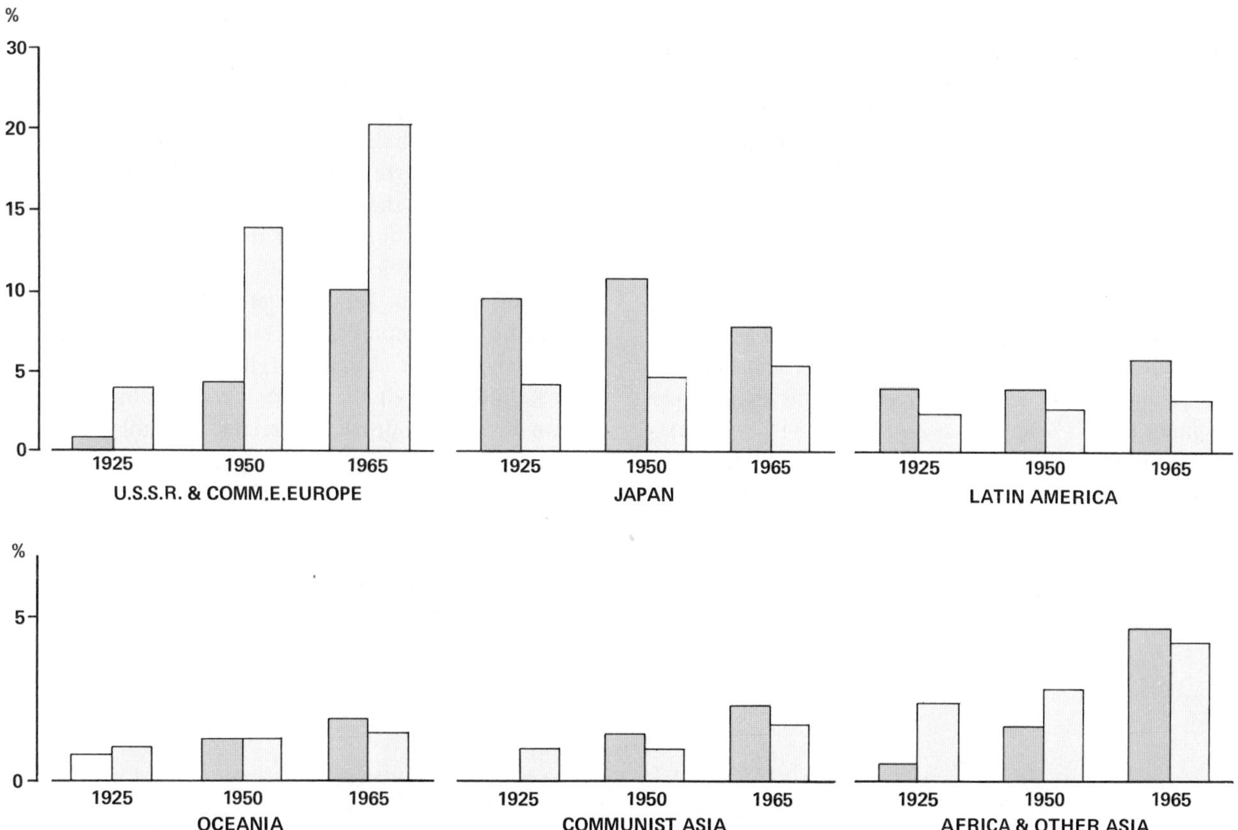

Regional shares of world hydroelectricity and total electricity consumption, 1925, 1950, 1965.

Profile No.15

HYDROELECTRIC SHARE IN TOTAL ELECTRICITY CONSUMPTION, BY MAJOR REGIONS AND SELECTED COUNTRIES, SELECTED YEARS, 1925-1965

Worldwide consumption of hydroelectricity increased at the average annual rate of 6.3 percent during 1925-65—moderately lower than the 7.4 percent rate recorded by *total* electricity consumption. The gap in these growth rates was wider in the period following World War II, when total electricity use grew at over 8½ percent yearly, with no appreciable departure in hydro from the 1925-65 rate. (Growth rates appear in Part Three, table XIII.) These differential growth rates are reflected in the declining worldwide role of hydro in total electricity, shown in this profile. Some 42 percent of world electricity consumption was furnished by waterpower in 1925; this was down to 27 percent in 1965, the largest part of the decline occurring in the years after 1950.

The data for particular regions and countries display a wide range of dispersion around these worldwide proportions of hydro in total electricity—both with respect to changing shares over time and the hydro proportion at a given point in time. Thus, while for the world as a whole the hydroelectric share of total electricity consumption was dropping from 42 to 27 percent, a somewhat steeper decline (33 to 17 percent) occurred in the United States while, in the case of Japan, the fall in the hydro share (from 93 to 38 percent) was even more severe. In Western Europe's electricity consumption, the share of hydro dropped relatively less than it did worldwide. And, as the table shows, a number of individual European countries and also Canada continued during the postwar years to rely on hydro as virtually their exclusive or most important generating source. Of the countries listed, Italy shows the most abrupt historical change. That country, almost solely dependent on hydro in 1925, continued its heavy hydro reliance into the post-World War II period; but by 1965 the proportion of hydro had dropped to 55 percent—the greatest decline occurring only after 1960, when most of a vast expansion of electric generating capacity came from thermal installations.

Areas going against the long-term downward trend for the world as a whole include Africa (up from 3 percent in 1925 to 23 percent in 1965), developing Asia (17 to 38 percent), and the Soviet Union (9 to 16 percent). In the Soviet Union the greatest rise in relative reliance on hydro occurred prior to 1950. After World War II the share of hydro in total Soviet electricity did not rise markedly. This more or less stable trend and the comparatively modest (16 percent) hydro share in 1965 may not be indicative of the future in view of the U.S.S.R.'s prominence in hydroelectric-related technology (e.g., in the size of plant and in long-distance, high-voltage, direct-current transmission) and given the country's vast hydroelectric potentials.

HYDROELECTRIC SHARE IN TOTAL ELECTRICITY CONSUMPTION, BY MAJOR REGIONS AND SELECTED COUNTRIES, SELECTED YEARS, 1925-1965

Region and country	1925	1938	1950	1955	1960	1965
North America	39.2%	43.3%	34.5%	27.0%	26.6%	24.2%
of which:						
Canada	92.9	89.1	94.6	91.6	92.2	82.9
United States	33.0	34.6	26.3	19.0	18.2	17.0
Western Europe	44.0	40.5	44.8	41.0	40.6	35.7
of which:						
France	44.8	52.7	49.5	51.9	56.4	46.1
Italy	95.1	96.7	92.4	85.7	85.7	56.5
Austria	61.6	77.4	75.9	70.6	71.0	63.3
Norway	99.0	98.9	99.7	99.0	99.3	99.5
Sweden	91.5	89.6	95.3	87.6	89.3	93.6
Switzerland	100.0	99.4	98.5	99.7	98.6	96.4
Finland	71.0	79.0	87.4	90.8	63.1	65.5
Oceania	34.6	35.8	35.1	31.2	31.0	35.7
of which:						
New Zealand	90.0	97.9	92.8	92.4	78.7	79.7
U.S.S.R. & Comm. E. Europe	8.1	12.0	11.1	11.3	14.1	13.4
U.S.S.R.	8.6	12.9	14.0	13.6	17.4	15.8
Comm. E. Europe	7.8	8.9	5.0	5.9	5.6	6.4
Communist Asia[a]	-	-	57.4	39.8	28.4	35.5
Latin America	70.0	58.3	55.3	50.3	49.0	48.9
Caribbean	55.7	62.3	45.3	38.8	33.4	34.5
Other Latin America	80.7	56.0	60.3	57.4	58.8	60.5
Asia	76.7	71.1	75.4	63.0	46.2	36.5
Middle East	11.2	5.4	4.5	4.1	11.1	16.7
Far East & Other Asia	77.8	72.2	78.1	66.6	48.7	37.7
Japan	93.1	72.6	85.2	76.4	52.4	37.6
Other	16.9	70.0	45.2	36.5	37.4	38.1
Africa	2.9	6.6	8.8	13.0	16.8	22.6
North Africa	6.2	20.1	22.3	31.6	29.5	39.3
Tropical Africa	35.4	48.9	33.9	41.1	52.4	67.7
South Africa	-	-	-	-	-	-
WORLD	41.7	40.5	36.7	30.8	29.9	26.9

[a]Covering Mainland China (1925-65), Mongolia and North Korea (1950-65), and North Vietnam (1955-65). The addition of North Korean hydroelectricity accounts for a large portion of the 1950 figure.

Notes and sources: With two exceptions, the shares were obtained by taking hydroelectric consumption (Part Three, table X) as a percentage of total electricity (Part Three, table XI). Some inconsistency between numerator and denominator arises where the hydroelectric figure (table X) has been adjusted from a net to gross figure without a similar adjustment having been made for total electricity (table XI). The distorting influence of this inconsistency applies primarily to *levels* of the hydro share, which, in a few cases, may be slightly overstated; the effect on *trends* is minor. In the case of Norway, this yielded a hydroelectric share which, in some years, was slightly over 100 percent. For purposes of the table, this prompted us to make an appropriate upward adjustment in the total Norway electricity figure. A second exception relates to Italy where an unexplained inconsistency between the hydro and total electricity figures for 1925 (apparently stemming from the use of divergent sources) led us to substitute a 1925 share based on data obtained from "Developments in the Use for Fuels for Thermal Power Generation in Italy," paper presented at World Power Conference meeting, Melbourne, 1962.

An additional inconsistency (though slight where it occurs) stems from the fact that net electricity imports are assigned to a country's hydro consumption irrespective of generating mode used.

On these points, see also the remarks in Part Four, pp. 822-23.

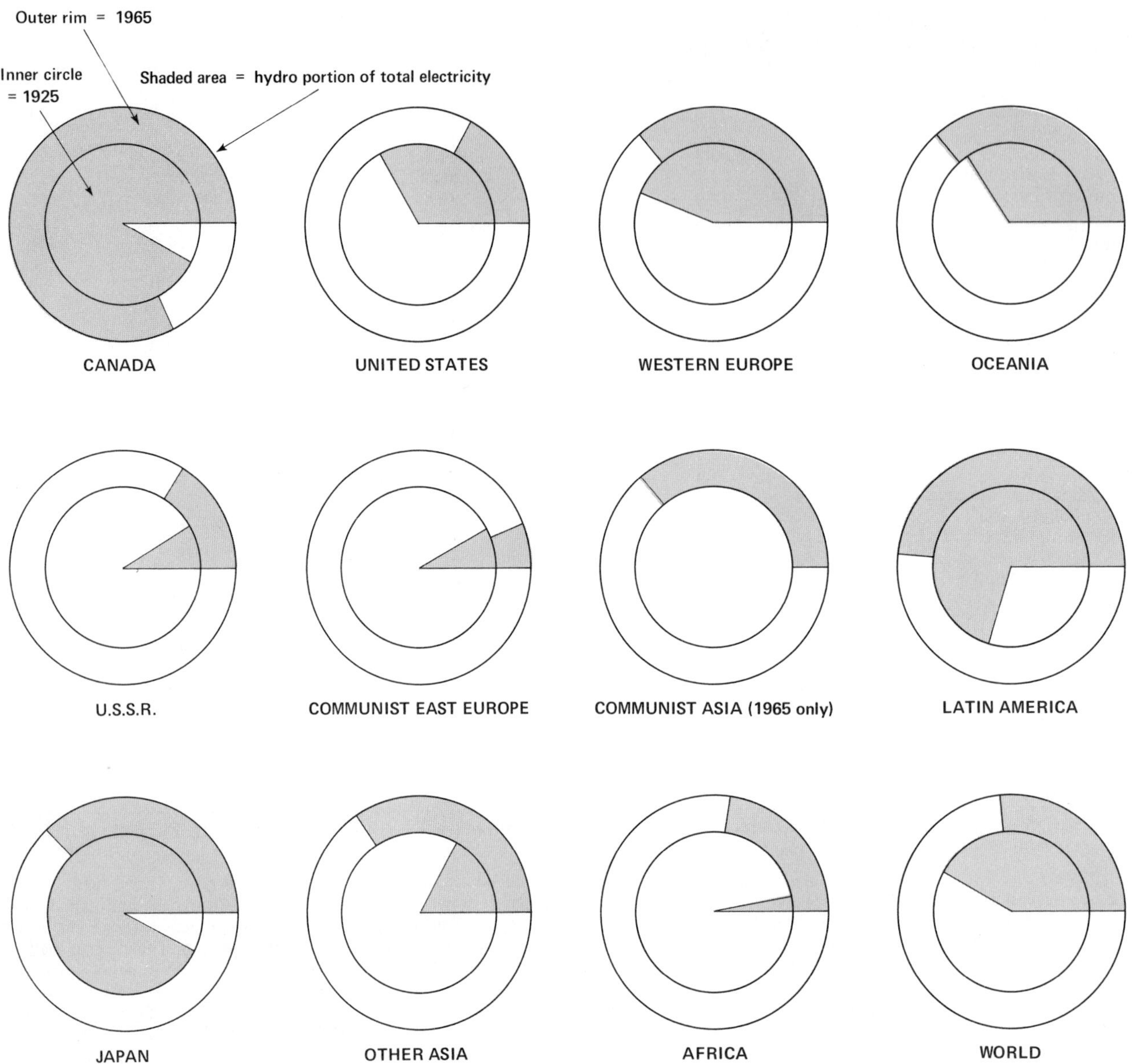

Hydroelectric share of total electricity consumption, by region, 1925 and 1965.

Profile No. 16

WORLD ENERGY CONSUMPTION, LEADING COUNTRIES, 1925, 1950, AND 1965

Previous profiles have sketched energy consumption trends and patterns largely in terms of major world *regions*. This profile and Profile No. 17 present summary data on energy use for leading individual consuming countries.

World energy consumption was highly concentrated among a limited group of countries in the mid-1920s, and it was only slightly less concentrated forty years later. The fourteen nations listed in the table accounted for nearly 85 percent of world energy use in 1965. All but two of the fourteen countries were consumers of energy in far greater proportions than their respective shares of world population. The twelve leading countries consumed over 75 percent of the world's energy with

WORLD ENERGY CONSUMPTION, LEADING COUNTRIES, 1925, 1950, AND 1965

	Percent of world energy consumption			1965			
Country[a]	1925	1950	1965	Percent of world population	Energy consumption *(million metric tons coal equiv.)*	Population *(millions)*	Energy consumption per capita *(kgs coal equiv.)*
United States	48.3%	46.0%	34.4%	5.9%	1,881.6	194.6	9,671
U.S.S.R.	1.7	11.6	16.1	7.0	880.6	230.6	3,819
United Kingdom	12.3	8.5	5.3	1.7	290.3	54.7	5,307
West Germany[b]	10.9	4.9	5.0	1.8	273.1	59.0	4,625
Japan	2.1	1.8	3.4	3.0	188.6	98.0	1,926
France	5.1	3.1	3.0	1.5	161.9	48.9	3,309
Canada	2.1	2.9	2.9	0.6	158.4	19.6	8,077
Poland	1.5	2.0	2.0	1.0	111.6	31.4	3,552
Italy	0.9	0.7	1.8	1.6	100.1	51.6	1,940
East Germany[b]	–	1.9	1.7	0.5	94.2	17.0	5,534
Czechoslovakia	1.5	1.4	1.5	0.4	83.1	14.2	5,870
South Africa	0.6	1.0	1.0	0.6	55.3	20.0	2,761
Total above 12	87.0	85.9	76.5	25.6	4,188.9	839.7	4,989
Communist Asia[c]	1.6	1.7	5.9	22.3	323.0	732.2	441
India	1.3	1.2	1.3	14.8	72.8	487.0	150
Total above 2	2.9	2.8	7.2	37.2	395.8	1,219.1	325
Total above 14	89.9	88.7	83.7	62.7	4,584.8	2,058.8	2,227
All other countries	10.1	11.3	16.3	37.3	889.8	1,222.4	728
WORLD	100.0	100.0	100.0	100.0	5,474.6	3,281.2	1,668

[a]Countries shown comprise all those accounting for 1% or more of world energy consumption in 1965.

[b]West Germany figure for 1925 applies to all of pre-World War II Germany.

[c]Comprises Mainland China (1925, 1950, 1965), Mongolia, and North Korea (1950, 1965), and North Vietnam (1965). Mainland China, for which no separate data are available for 1950 and 1965, dominates the Communist Asia total for those years.

Source: Part Three, table XI.

about one-fourth of the world's population, while the combined percentages for Mainland China[1] and India were: population, 37 percent; energy, 7 percent.

Among the changes that have occurred in the shares of individual countries, the most striking involve the sharply declining relative—though in absolute terms still preeminent—position of the leading Western industrial powers (United States, United Kingdom, France, West Germany[2]) and the ascendant position of the Soviet Union. The latter rose from under 2 percent in world energy consumption in 1925 to 16 percent in 1965. Nevertheless, in terms of its absolute per capita consumption level, the U.S.S.R. in 1965 was not markedly above that for, say, Poland; and it was substantially below per capita consumption in East Germany or Czechoslovakia. (Historical data on Soviet per capita energy consumption appear in Profile No. 1; per capita data for all countries appear in Part Three, table XI.) After 1950 Mainland China also increased its share of world energy consumption, but that country's per capita consumption level in 1965 remained exceedingly low.

Increasing shares of world energy consumption were registered by such important non-Communist countries as Japan, Canada, Italy, and South Africa.

[1]Individual Communist Asia country data are not available; therefore, the comments on Mainland China refer to data that include the other Communist Asian countries. Because of China's immense size relative to North Korea, North Vietnam, and Mongolia, very little distortion results from applying the regional data to a discussion of China alone.

[2]West Germany shows a declining share even allowing for the fact that the 1925 figure refers to *all* of pre-World War II Germany.

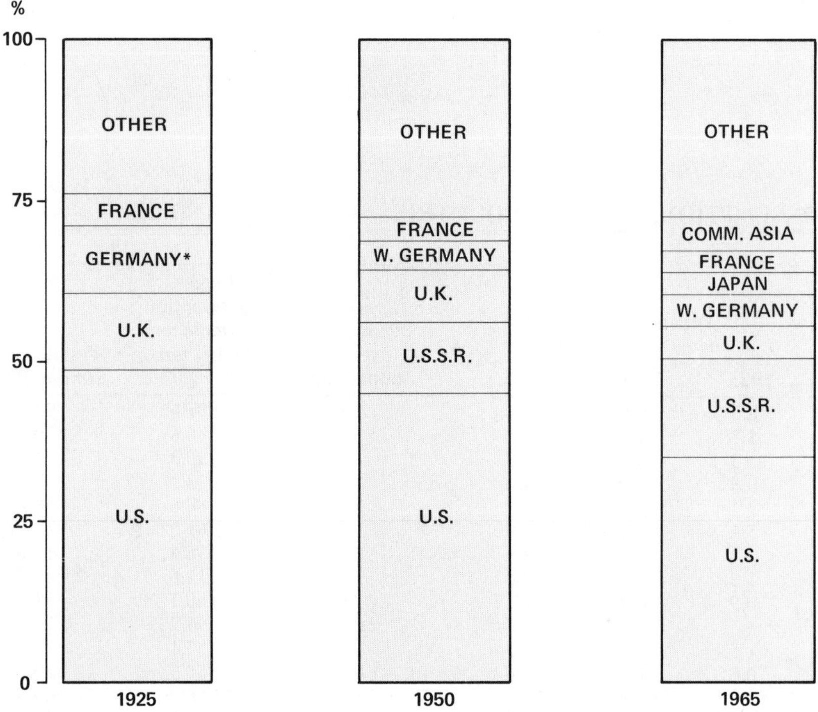

Share of world energy consumption by leading country, 1925, 1950, 1965.

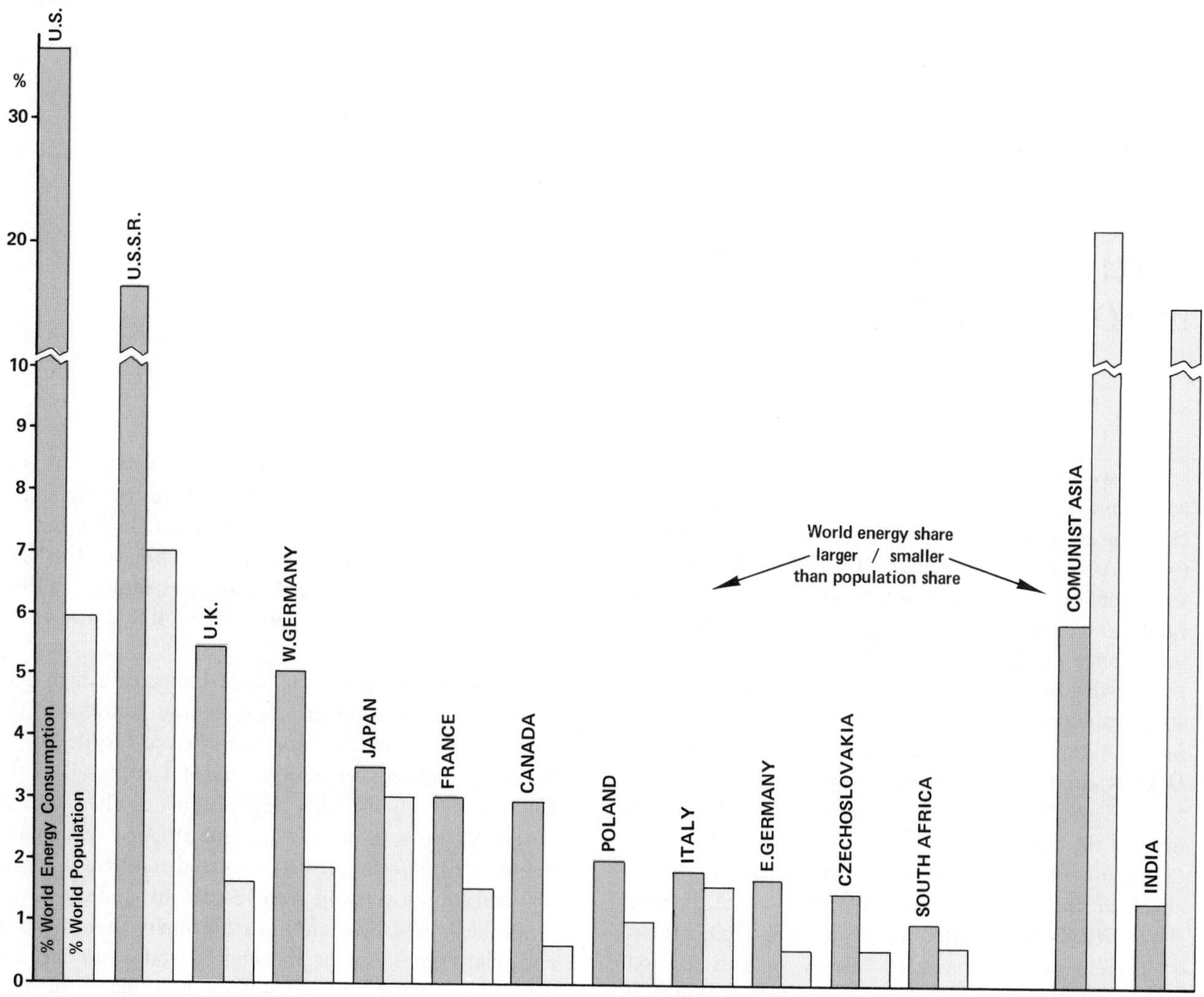

Shares of world energy consumption and world population, 14 leading energy-consuming countries, 1965.

Profile No. 17

WORLD ENERGY CONSUMPTION, BY SOURCE AND COUNTRY, 1925, 1950, AND 1965

The world's leading energy-consuming countries listed in the previous profile are here shown in terms of the changing composition of their total energy consumption (panel A of table), and their shares of worldwide consumption of each energy source (panel B). The overriding trend plainly seen in panel A is the declining importance of solid fuels, compensated particularly by the growing share of oil. Natural gas and hydroelectricity shares did generally increase, but—except for the phenomenal growth of natural gas in the United States, the U.S.S.R., and Canada—these energy categories still contributed relatively small portions to total energy use in most of the countries.

Nonetheless there are some marked national differences in the extent of interfuel shifts. One extreme shows Italy's coal consumption declining from around 85 percent of its total energy use in 1925 to approximately 10 percent in 1965, and its oil share rising from about 10 percent to 75 percent. At the other extreme, there are the Communist countries of Poland, East Germany, and Czechoslovakia, which, up to 1965 at least, had undergone rather little change in the composition of their total energy balance, so that solid fuels retained their preeminent energy share throughout the entire period. Due in part to a pre-World War II replacement of fuelwood by coal, the Soviet Union's solid fuels share increased up to 1950 but declined thereafter in the wake of rapid expansion in both oil and gas output.

Countries faced with the choice of abandoning indigenous coal for imported liquid fuels tended to preserve a significant role for solid fuels. In both West Germany and Great Britain the 1965 solid fuels shares were still well over 50 percent. Countries endowed with indigenous petroleum were not similarly motivated; note the 1965 combined oil and natural gas shares of 75 percent for both the United States and Canada. In the case of countries needing to import large volumes of energy irrespective of form, the end result was similar; in 1965 Japan's oil share was 60 percent and Italy's nearly 75 percent noted above.

The lower panel of the table indicates a high geographic concentration of each energy source for the fourteen countries taken together, just as Profile No. 16 showed a high concentration for total energy. But the distribution among the top countries has altered markedly. For example, Communist Asia (essentially Mainland China) has greatly increased its share of world coal consumption (from 2 to 13 percent) and the Soviet Union has raised its share in each primary fuel category. The relative position of the United States has declined noticeably though still occupying first place for each energy source.

Throughout the forty-year period, natural gas has been the fuel with the most concentrated geographic distribution; in 1965 three countries– the United States (65 percent), the U.S.S.R. (19 percent), and Canada (4½ percent)—accounted for nearly 90 percent of worldwide consumption. (Profile No. 12 notes that this situation is not likely to endure.) Consumption of hydropower is less markedly concentrated in its distribution around the world than the other three primary fuels; in 1965 the roughly 165 countries comprising the "all other" component of the bottom panel of the table accounted for 30 percent of world hydropower consumption compared with 37 percent of world population and a 16 percent share of total world energy use. (See Profile No. 16.)

WORLD ENERGY CONSUMPTION, BY SOURCE AND COUNTRY, 1925, 1950, AND 1965

Country[a]	Solid fuels			Liquid fuels			Natural gas			Hydroelectricity			Total		
	1925	1950	1965	1925	1950	1965	1925	1950	1965	1925	1950	1965	1925	1950	1965
A. As percent of each country's total energy consumption															
United States	74.2%	42.3%	24.3%	19.2%	37.7%	42.8%	6.2%	18.9%	31.5%	0.5%	1.1%	1.3%	100.0%	100.0%	100.0%
U.S.S.R.	64.9	76.9	48.9	34.2	20.0	30.7	0.7	2.5	19.3	0.1	0.5	1.1	100.0	100.0	100.0
United Kingdom	96.2	89.5	64.0	3.8	10.4	35.5	-	-	0.4	0.2	0.1	0.2	100.0	100.0	100.0
West Germany[b]	98.7	94.6	56.9	1.1	4.4	40.7	-	-	1.5	-	1.0	0.9	100.0	100.0	100.0
Japan	92.4	83.2	35.5	4.4	6.1	58.4	0.1	0.2	1.4	3.1	10.4	4.7	100.0	100.0	100.0
France	95.5	77.3	42.5	3.7	19.7	49.4	-	0.4	4.4	0.8	2.5	3.7	100.0	100.0	100.0
Canada	81.9	53.0	14.8	12.5	35.0	50.2	2.1	3.7	25.8	3.5	8.4	9.2	100.0	100.0	100.0
Poland	93.2	97.5	91.6	3.6	1.9	6.3	3.2	0.5	2.1	-	0.1	0.1	100.0	100.0	100.0
Italy	83.9	49.2	11.2	9.2	31.8	72.8	-	3.6	10.4	6.9	15.4	5.7	100.0	100.0	100.0
East Germany[b]	-	99.6	93.2	-	0.3	6.5	-	0.1	0.2	-	-	0.1			
Czechoslovakia	98.5	96.7	87.0	1.4	2.8	10.9	-	0.1	1.4	0.1	0.4	0.8	100.0	100.0	100.0
South Africa	97.9	89.7	85.4	2.1	10.3	14.6	-	-	-	-	-	-	100.0	100.0	100.0
Total above 12	83.0	61.2	39.9	12.8	26.7	38.9	3.6	10.7	19.5	0.6	1.4	1.7	100.0	100.0	100.0
Communist Asia[c]	94.0	98.1	94.1	6.0	0.3	5.1	-	-	-	-	1.5	0.8	100.0	100.0	100.0
India	85.1	83.2	73.4	14.8	15.8	22.9	-	-	0.7	0.1	1.0	3.0	100.0	100.0	100.0
Total above 2	90.1	92.0	90.3	9.9	6.7	8.4	-	-	0.1	0.1	1.3	1.2	100.0	100.0	100.0
Total above 14	83.3	62.2	44.2	12.7	26.1	36.3	3.4	10.3	17.8	0.5	1.4	1.7	100.0	100.0	100.0
All other countries	79.0	51.9	28.0	18.0	40.2	57.8	1.3	4.3	9.9	1.7	3.5	4.3	100.0	100.0	100.0
WORLD	82.9	61.0	41.8	13.3	27.7	39.4	3.2	9.7	16.7	0.7	1.7	2.1	100.0	100.0	100.0
B. As percent of world consumption of each energy source															
United States	43.3	31.9%	20.0%	69.9%	62.7%	37.3%	92.6%	90.2%	65.0%	34.0%	29.6%	21.9%	48.3%	46.0%	34.4%
U.S.S.R.	1.3	14.6	18.8	4.4	8.4	12.5	0.4	3.0	18.6	0.3	3.7	8.9	1.7	11.6	16.1
United Kingdom	14.3	12.5	8.1	3.5	3.2	4.8	-	-	0.1	-	0.4	0.5	12.3	8.5	5.3
West Germany[b]	13.0	7.6	6.8	0.9	0.8	5.1	-	-	0.5	3.9	2.9	2.2	10.9	4.9	5.0
Japan	2.3	2.4	2.9	0.7	0.4	5.1	0.1	-	0.3	9.7	11.0	7.8	2.1	1.8	3.4
France	5.9	3.9	3.0	1.4	2.2	3.7	-	0.1	0.8	5.8	4.7	5.3	5.1	3.1	3.0
Canada	2.1	2.5	1.0	2.0	3.7	3.7	1.3	1.1	4.5	11.0	14.5	13.0	2.1	2.9	2.9
Poland	1.7	3.2	4.5	0.4	0.1	0.3	1.5	0.1	0.3	0.1	0.1	0.1	1.5	2.0	2.0
Italy	0.9	0.6	0.5	0.6	0.8	3.4	-	0.3	1.1	9.0	6.6	5.0	0.9	0.7	1.8
East Germany[b]	-	3.1	3.8	-	-	0.3	-	-	-	-	-	0.1	-	1.9	1.7
Czechoslovakia	1.8	2.2	3.2	0.2	0.1	0.4	-	-	0.1	0.2	0.3	0.6	1.5	1.4	1.5
South Africa	0.7	1.5	2.1	0.1	0.4	0.4	-	-	-	-	-	-	0.6	1.0	1.0
Total above 12	87.2	86.1	74.6	84.1	82.8	77.1	95.9	94.9	91.2	74.1	73.8	65.2	87.0	85.9	76.5
Communist Asia[c]	1.8	2.7	13.3	0.7	-	0.8	-	-	-	-	1.5	2.3	1.6	1.7	5.9
India	1.3	1.6	2.3	1.4	0.7	0.8	-	-	0.1	0.2	0.7	1.9	1.3	1.2	1.3
Total above 2	3.1	4.2	15.6	2.1	0.7	1.5	-	-	0.1	0.2	2.2	4.2	2.9	2.8	7.2
Total above 14	90.3	90.4	90.2	86.2	83.5	78.6	95.9	94.9	91.3	74.3	76.1	69.5	89.9	88.7	83.7
All other countries	9.7	9.6	9.8	13.8	16.5	21.4	4.1	5.1	8.7	25.7	23.9	30.5	10.1	11.3	16.3
WORLD	100.0	100.0	100.0	100.0	100.0	100.0	100.0	100.0	100.0	100.0	100.0	100.0	100.0	100.0	100.0

[a]Countries shown comprise all those accounting for 1% or more of world energy consumption in 1965. The first twelve countries, listed in descending order according to their 1965 percentage share, accounted for a greater share of energy than of population; the energy share of the other two areas (India and Communist Asia) was below their population share.

[b]West Germany figure for 1925 applies to *all* of pre–World War II Germany.

[c]Comprises Mainland China (1925, 1950, 1965), Mongolia and North Korea (1950, 1965), and North Vietnam (1965). Mainland China, for which no separate data are available for 1950 and 1965, dominates the Communist Asia total for those years.

Source: Part Three, tables X and XI.

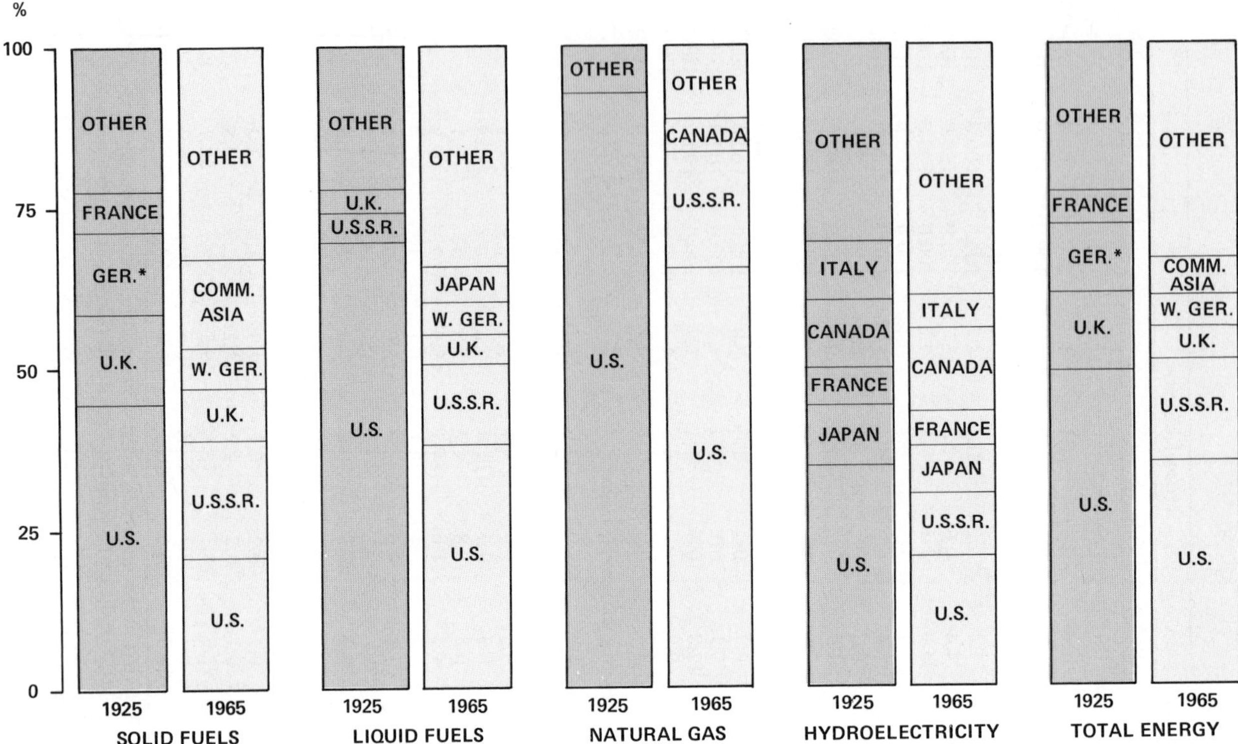

Share of world consumption of each energy source, 1925 and 1965.

Profile No. 18

ENERGY CONSUMPTION AND PRODUCTION, VARIOUS MEASURES, BY MAJOR WORLD REGIONS, 1925, 1950, AND 1965

This comparison of trends in total energy production and consumption around the world bridges the preceding set of profiles on consumption with those that follow dealing with production of the different energy forms. Implied in such a comparison, of course, are the corresponding trends in net imports or exports and in self-sufficiency. Beginning with Profile No. 23, but particularly in Profiles No. 33 and No. 34, the foreign trade aspect is covered as a separate topic.

It is striking how in 1925 virtually all the major energy-consuming regions of the world accounted for similar shares of world consumption and world production, or, what is the same thing, that each of these regions met practically the whole of its energy needs from indigenous supplies. North America consumed approximately one-half the world energy total and produced a like share. For Western Europe, the world share of consumption or production was a bit over one-third; for the combined group of present-day Communist countries, it was around 7 percent. Except for Latin America and the Middle East, where in each case the 1925 share of world output substantially exceeded the share of world consumption, this pattern of roughly similar portions of world energy consumption and production prevailed for the other areas listed in the table. The tendency toward equality between total fuel output and consumption generally did not apply to liquid fuels (except in the case of the United States), but it did apply to coal; and the latter energy form exerted a decisive weight in most regions where total energy production and consumption were roughly in balance.

Four decades later, regional self-sufficiency persisted only in the Communist group, where it was at least partly a consequence of regional autarkic policies. Elsewhere, marked regional imbalances had appeared—notably in Western Europe, its one-fifth share of world consumption being nearly twice its share of world production, and in the Far East (including Japan), where the consumption and production figures were, respectively, 6 percent and 3½ percent. In Western Europe, as panel B of the table shows, total energy output barely increased absolutely between the terminal years of 1925 and 1965 and rose by under 1 percent yearly following 1950. The North American picture in 1965 (37 percent of world consumption and 33 percent of world output) was only mildly one of deficit—a situation supported by the government's oil import policy in the United States. Other deficit regions were non-Caribbean Latin America, which had been persistently deficient in energy supplies throughout the period under review, and Oceania. The latter may in time achieve surplus status, in view of the outlook for Australia based on recent oil discoveries.

The counterpart development to these emerging deficit areas was, of course, the emergence of the oil-producing surplus areas. Their importance is reflected in the long-term average annual growth rates of total energy output—6 percent for the Caribbean and nearly 12 percent for the Middle East—irrespective of whether one looks at the forty-year trend or only the period after 1950. In 1965 consumption and production shares of the world energy total were 2 percent and 6½ percent, respectively, for the Caribbean; and 1 percent and 11 percent for the Middle East. Africa (of growing significance primarily because of Libyan, Nigerian, and Algerian oil output) consumed about 1½ percent of the world's energy and produced nearly 4 percent. Incrementally, the role of these three regions in satisfying the continually expanding energy needs of the world loom even larger: by 1925 and 1965 over one-fourth of the increase in the world's total energy consumption (oil, coal, gas, hydroelectricity) was met by oil supplies from the Middle East, Caribbean, and Africa; and during the post-World War II years alone, the proportion is close to 30 percent.

ENERGY CONSUMPTION AND PRODUCTION, VARIOUS MEASURES, BY MAJOR WORLD REGIONS, 1925, 1950, AND 1965

	North America		Western Europe	Oceania	U.S.S.R. & Comm. E. Europe			Comm. Asia	Latin America			Asia				Africa	WORLD[a]
	Total	U.S.A.			Total	U.S.S.R.	E. Europe		Total	Carib.	Other	Total	Mid. East	Japan	Other		
A. Percent of world consumption and production																	
1925																	
Consumption	50.4%	48.3%	34.8%	1.1%	5.4%	1.7%	3.7%	1.6%	1.7%	0.8%	0.9%	4.1%	0.2%	2.1%	1.9%	0.9%	100.0%
Production	49.7	48.9	34.0	1.0	5.9	1.7	4.2	1.4	2.5	2.2	0.4	4.5	0.5	2.1	1.9	0.9	100.0
1950																	
Consumption	48.9	46.0	22.4	1.1	17.8	11.6	6.2	1.7	2.5	1.3	1.3	4.1	0.5	1.8	1.8	1.6	100.0
Production	45.5	44.4	18.8	0.8	17.5	10.8	6.8	1.6	6.2	5.6	0.6	8.3	4.9	1.6	1.8	1.3	100.0
1965																	
Consumption	37.3	34.4	20.4	1.1	22.9	16.1	6.9	5.9	3.6	2.1	1.6	7.0	1.0	3.4	2.5	1.7	100.0
Production	33.4	30.9	10.2	0.7	23.9	17.6	6.3	5.7	7.5	6.5	1.0	14.7	11.3	1.1	2.3	3.9	100.0
B. Average annual percentage growth rates in production and consumption																	
1925–65																	
Consumption	2.5%	2.4%	1.9%	3.5%	7.1%	9.3%	4.9%	6.7%	5.4%	3.5%	2.5%	4.7%	8.4%	4.7%	4.1%	4.8%	3.3%
Production	2.2	2.1	0.2	2.4	6.9	9.4	4.4	6.9	6.1	6.1	5.8	6.3	11.7	1.6	3.7	7.2	3.3
1950–65																	
Consumption	3.2	3.0	4.4	5.0	6.9	7.4	5.8	14.4	7.6	5.5	3.8	9.0	10.2	9.9	7.5	5.4	5.1
Production	2.9	2.5	0.8	4.5	7.2	8.5	4.5	14.3	6.3	6.0	8.6	9.1	11.0	2.3	6.7	13.2	5.0
C. Ratios of production to consumption																	
1925	1.04	1.07	1.03	1.03	1.15	1.07	1.18	0.95	1.62	2.98	0.45	1.18	3.32	1.08	1.11	0.98	1.06
1950	0.97	1.00	0.87	0.73	1.03	0.96	1.14	1.01	2.54	4.58	0.49	2.14	10.02	0.97	1.05	0.82	1.04
1965	0.93	0.93	0.52	0.68	1.08	1.13	0.96	1.00	2.11	3.20	0.66	2.16	11.22	0.33	0.93	2.36	1.03

[a]Levels and changes in world production totals may differ slightly from world consumption totals (1) because bunker fuels are included in the former and excluded from the latter; and (2) because of discrepancies in world import and export totals. (See notes in Part Four, pp. 820–22.)

Source: Part Three, tables X, XIII, and XIV.

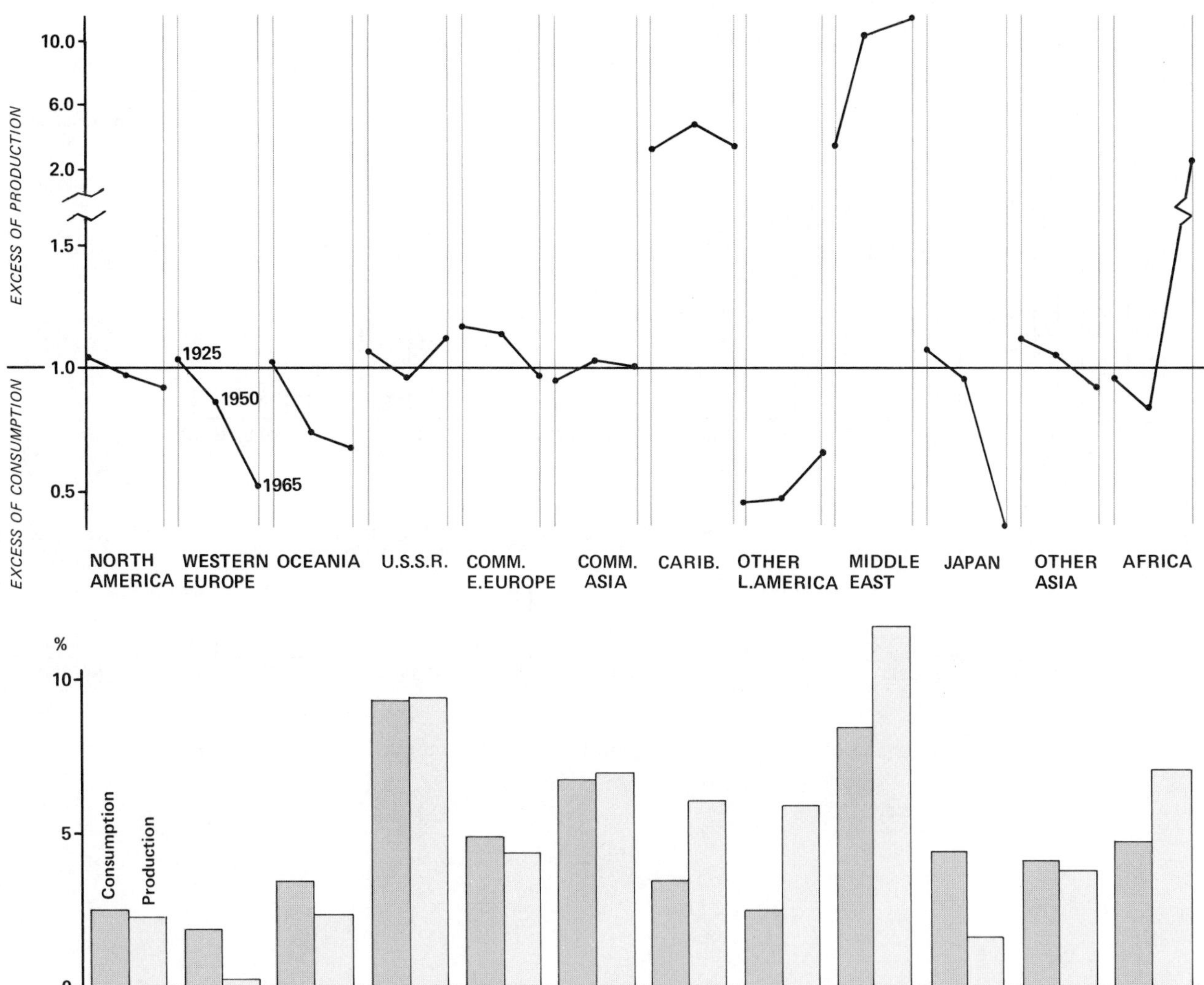

Above: Ratios of energy production to consumption, by region, 1925, 1950, 1965.
Below: Average annual percentage growth rates in energy production and consumption, by region, 1925-1965.

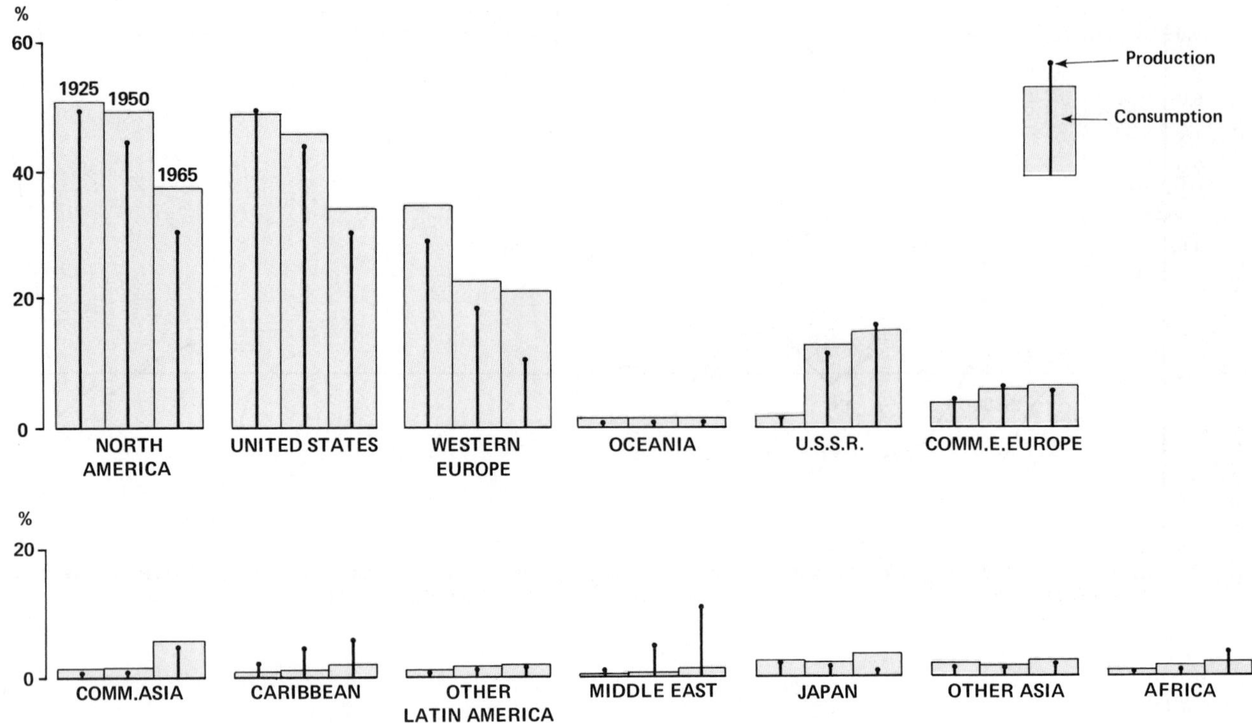

Regional shares of world energy consumption and production, 1925, 1950, 1965.

Profile No. 19

WORLD ENERGY PRODUCTION, BY SOURCE AND MAJOR REGIONS, AVERAGE ANNUAL PERCENTAGE RATES OF CHANGE, 1925-1965 AND 1950-1965

This tabulation of rates of change in production of the different energy sources in regions of the world shows a wide range of diversity. A meaningful appreciation of these differences in growth rates must take into account the size of the absolute figures to which they refer. For example, Western Europe's high growth rate for liquid fuels output still signified only trivial quantities of indigenous oil in 1965. The accompanying chart provides some of this needed perspective, as does also Profile No. 20.

Worldwide,[1] over both the forty-year and the 1950–65 time spans natural gas output grew fastest, with oil and hydro (the latter relatively insignificant as to the absolute quantities involved) trailing closely behind. Coal production rose far less than total energy production in both periods—worldwide as well as for practically every region shown. It did register notable increases in the three Communist areas, in each of which it continued in recent years as a significant energy source. But it also constitutes the only case of declining growth rates in the table—witness the falling levels of coal output in both Western Europe and North America over the forty years as a whole as well as after World War II. This decline in the old coal strongholds of the world compares with annual rates of increase in oil production in the Middle East and Caribbean of around 11 percent and 6 percent, respectively, for both the periods tabulated. These contrasting trends in coal output in the industrial West and oil production in the Middle East and Caribbean Latin America denote one of the fundamental developments in world energy of the last forty years.

Some modest resurgence, it should be added, has occurred in U.S. coal production during the 1960s. Key factors have been expanding sales to electric power stations and a strong export market. But chances for an enduring comeback even for U.S. coal are quite uncertain.

[1] Except for statistical differences arising from minor definitional reasons and from the manner of computation, worldwide production essentially equals worldwide consumption of the different energy forms. Since trends in worldwide consumption have been covered in the preceding set of profiles, little needs therefore to be said about production for the world as a whole. For particular regions, the near-equality of production and consumption also applies to natural gas and hydroelectricity, there being (in the period under review) only modest international exchanges of gas and electricity.

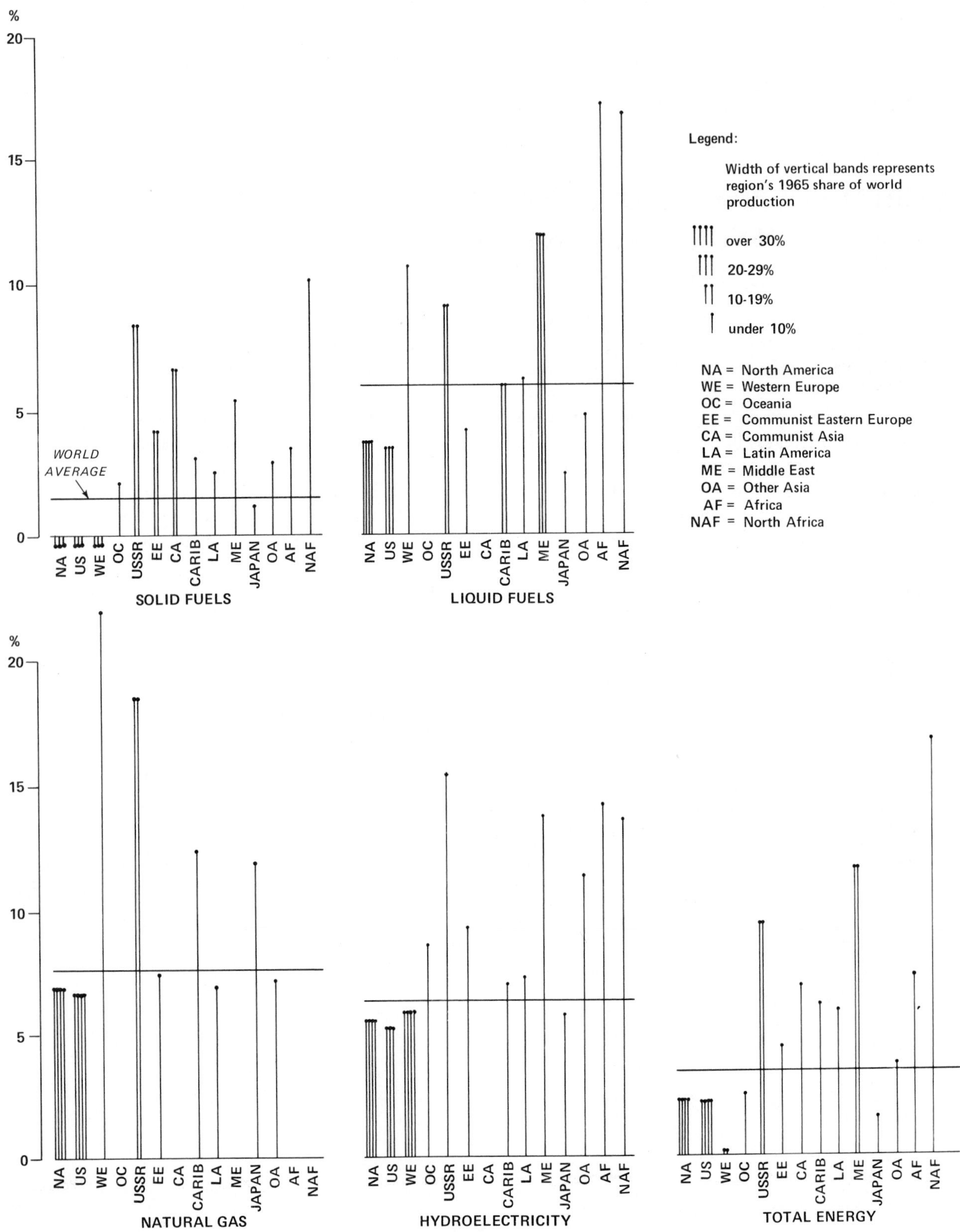

Average annual percentage rates of change in world energy production, by source and major region, 1925–1965.

WORLD ENERGY PRODUCTION, BY SOURCE AND MAJOR REGIONS, AVERAGE ANNUAL PERCENTAGE RATES OF CHANGE, 1925-1965 AND 1950-1965

	1925-1965					1950-1965				
Region	Solid fuels	Liquid fuels	Natural gas	Hydroelec-tricity	Total energy	Solid fuels	Liquid fuels	Natural gas	Hydroelec-tricity	Total energy
North America	-0.2%	3.8%	6.8%	5.6%	2.2%	-0.5%	3.3%	6.9%	4.9%	2.9%
of which: United States	-0.2	3.5	6.6	5.2	2.1	-0.4	2.7	6.4	4.6	2.5
West Europe	-0.2	10.7	22.0	5.8	0.2	-0.1	11.6	20.0	6.7	0.8
Oceania	2.2	*	*	8.6	2.4	4.3	47.4	*	9.5	4.5
U.S.S.R. & Comm. E. Europe	6.0	8.4	13.1	13.8	6.9	4.4	12.4	21.1	12.7	7.2
U.S.S.R.	8.7	9.2	18.6	15.6	9.4	4.7	13.0	22.9	13.2	8.5
Comm. E. Europe	4.2	4.2	7.4	9.3	4.4	4.1	6.8	13.4	9.8	4.5
Communist Asia	6.7	*	*	*	6.9	14.0	29.8	*	9.6	14.3
Latin America	2.8	6.0	9.6	7.2	6.1	3.7	5.9	13.0	8.9	6.3
Caribbean	3.1	6.0	12.3	7.0	6.1	6.8	5.6	13.5	10.1	6.0
Other Latin America	2.6	6.2	6.9	7.3	5.8	1.4	9.8	11.8	8.5	8.6
Asia	2.1	10.0	9.6	6.5	6.3	3.8	10.7	16.6	5.8	9.1
Middle East	5.5	11.9	*	13.7	11.7	3.7	11.1	19.1	25.0	11.1
Japan	1.2	2.4	11.8	5.7	1.6	1.6	5.8	25.6	4.2	2.3
Other Asia	2.9	4.8	7.2	11.4	3.7	5.9	7.1	13.2	12.6	6.7
Africa	3.5	17.3	*	14.2	7.2	3.9	27.9	*	16.3	13.2
North Africa	10.1	16.8	*	13.7	16.8	-2.1	26.7	*	14.9	25.5
Tropical Africa	3.9	*	*	14.4	8.7	3.0	*	*	16.9	16.2
South Africa	3.5	*	*	*	3.5	4.1	*	*	*	4.1
WORLD	1.5	6.0	7.6	6.3	3.3	2.4	7.3	9.0	6.6	5.0

*Not computable because of zero in numerator and/or denominator.

Source: Part Three, tables X and XIII.

Profile No. 20

WORLD ENERGY PRODUCTION, PERCENTAGE DISTRIBUTION BY SOURCE AND MAJOR REGIONS, AND PRODUCTION-CONSUMPTION RATIOS, 1925 AND 1965

For most world areas the mix of regional energy consumption was seen in earlier profiles to have gravitated in pronounced fashion from solid fuels to liquid fuels during the forty years under review. By contrast, changes in the regional composition of energy production (shown in panel A of the table) for the most part have been more modest. Conditioned by the happenstance of geological occurrence, such changes result either from new discoveries or—possibly through advances in technology—from the further exploitation of existing resources. One area where the interfuel pattern of output did change strikingly was North America, where U.S. and Canadian oil and gas discoveries brought about compositional changes in the fuel production mix as marked as those in consumption. The rising share of gas in Soviet energy production and the enormous jump in the oil share of African energy output are other instances of substantial change. Although large-scale Middle Eastern oil discoveries dramatically increased the magnitude of output, that region's energy output pattern was not much altered from that of the 1920s when oil already was preeminent. However, by 1965 the magnitude of Middle Eastern oil had come to exert such a decisive weight on overall Asian energy output—which in 1925 had been dominated by Japanese coal—that for all of Asia, the share of liquids in total energy output had jumped from 20 percent to 80 percent.

Areas in which the proportions of the different energy sources (particularly comparing coal and oil) in total output did not change fundamentally include: Western Europe, Oceania, the Caribbean area, Eastern Europe, Communist Asia, and Japan. In all these regions except the Caribbean, coal dominated production throughout the period, while in the Caribbean (or Latin America as a whole), oil was the prevailing leader in energy output over the years. The fairly significant rise in Latin America's natural gas share should be noted.

Shifts in the importance of different regions in worldwide output of the various energy sources are shown in panel B for 1925 and 1965. In this tabulation, North America's declining shares of world production of each energy source stand in vivid contrast to the steeply rising shares for the Communist group—especially the Soviet Union, whose share of world solid fuels output rose from 1 to 20 percent; oil, from 5 to 15 percent; natural gas, from under 1 to nearly 20 percent; and hydroelectricity, from virtually zero to nearly 10 percent. It is particularly interesting to note that the U.S.S.R.'s rising share of world oil production compares with North America's sharply declining share (from 70 to 30 percent)—and this in spite of the fact that (as shown in panel A) liquids rose as a percentage of North American energy output while declining slightly for the Soviet Union. The explanation lies in the Soviet Union's much more rapid growth in total energy output during 1925-65—about 9½ percent per year on the average compared with a bit over 2 percent for North America. (See Profile No. 19 for growth rates.) Other notable changes recorded in panel B are Western Europe's declining share of world coal output as well as of total energy output (down from 40 to 20 percent, and from about 35 to 10 percent, respectively), and the Middle East's rising share of world oil and of total world energy (up from 3 to over 25 percent, and from ½ to over 10 percent, respectively). Africa's share of world oil production went from practically nothing in 1925 to nearly 7 percent in 1965.

The growth of Middle Eastern and, to a lesser extent, African oil output also produces the more conspicuous changes in production-consumption ratios shown in panel C of the table. Between 1925 and 1965, the oil production-consumption ratio went from 4 to nearly 15 for the Middle East and from 0.2 to nearly 5 for Africa. Total energy production-consumption ratios also showed very large increases for these areas. Note that the sharply declining production-consumption ratios in total energy for Western Europe and Japan were not associated with dramatic ratio change for individual fuel categories; in both years each area was almost totally deficient in oil and rather well supplied with coal. The explanation lies in the big shift to liquids in European and Japanese total energy consumption.

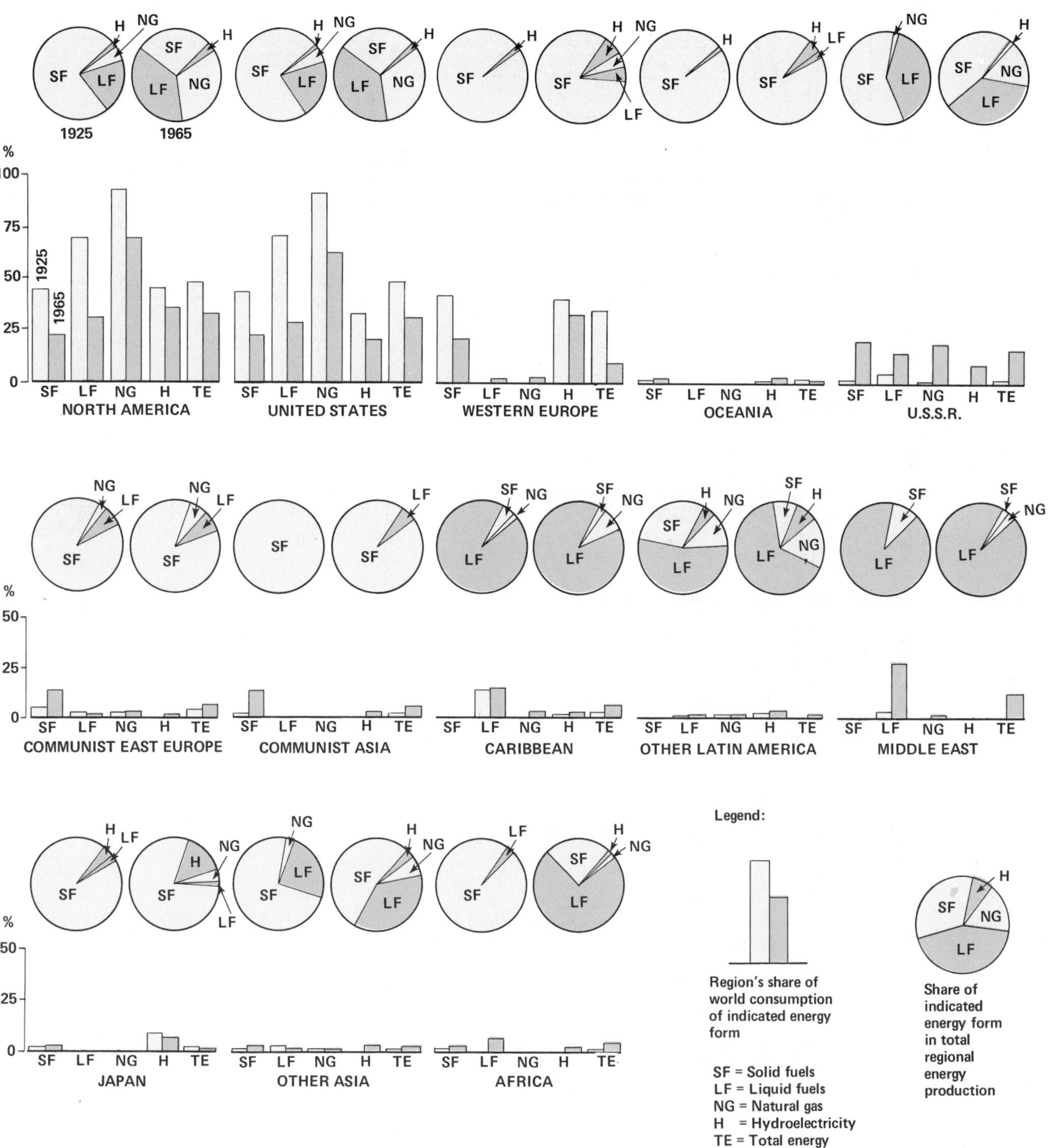

World energy production, by source and major region, 1925 and 1965.

WORLD ENERGY PRODUCTION, PERCENTAGE DISTRIBUTION BY SOURCE AND MAJOR REGIONS, AND PRODUCTION-CONSUMPTION RATIOS, 1925 AND 1965

Region	Solid fuels		Liquid fuels		Natural gas		Hydroelectricity		Total energy	
	1925	1965	1925	1965	1925	1965	1925	1965	1925	1965
A. *As percent of each region's total energy production*										
North America	72.9%	27.2%	20.8%	37.4%	5.8%	33.4%	0.6%	2.1%	100.0%	100.0%
of which: United States	72.7	28.9	21.1	36.7	5.8	33.0	0.4	1.4	100.0	100.0
Western Europe	99.2	83.6	0.1	5.5	-	4.6	0.7	6.3	100.0	100.0
Oceania	99.5	93.5	-	1.2	-	-	0.5	5.2	100.0	100.0
U.S.S.R. & Comm. E. Europe	81.7	56.3	16.7	28.8	1.5	14.1	0.1	0.8	100.0	100.0
U.S.S.R.	59.8	45.2	39.4	36.7	0.7	17.1	0.1	1.0	100.0	100.0
Comm. E. Europe	90.8	87.0	7.3	6.8	1.9	5.8	0.1	0.3	100.0	100.0
Communist Asia	100.0	94.5	-	4.7	-	-	-	0.8	100.0	100.0
Latin America	8.3	2.4	88.2	86.5	2.6	9.6	1.0	1.5	100.0	100.0
Caribbean	4.6	1.4	94.1	89.8	0.9	8.2	0.4	0.5	100.0	100.0
Other Latin America	28.8	8.6	54.5	64.9	12.3	18.7	4.4	7.8	100.0	100.0
Asia	77.0	15.2	20.9	80.9	0.7	2.3	1.4	1.5	100.0	100.0
Middle East	8.8	0.9	91.1	97.6	-	1.4	-	0.1	100.0	100.0
Japan	95.8	79.9	1.2	1.6	0.1	4.3	2.9	14.2	100.0	100.0
Other Asia	73.8	54.8	24.5	36.9	1.5	5.7	0.1	2.5	100.0	100.0
Africa	97.9	24.4	2.0	73.6	-	1.2	0.1	0.8	100.0	100.0
North Africa	3.5	0.3	95.6	97.6	-	1.8	0.9	0.3	100.0	100.0
Tropical Africa	99.4	15.8	-	79.7	-	0.3	0.6	4.2	100.0	100.0
South Africa	100.0	100.0	-	-	-	-	-	-	100.0	100.0
WORLD	81.8	40.5	14.6	41.4	3.1	16.1	0.6	2.0	100.0	100.0
B. *As percent of world production of each energy source*										
North America	44.3%	22.4%	70.9%	30.2%	93.9%	69.3%	45.1%	34.8%	49.7%	33.4%
of which: United States	43.5	22.0	70.9	27.4	92.6	63.2	32.4	21.9	48.9	30.9
Western Europe	41.2	21.1	0.2	1.3	-	2.9	39.2	32.6	34.0	10.2
Oceania	1.2	1.7	-	-	-	-	0.8	1.9	1.0	0.7
U.S.S.R. & Comm. E. Europe	5.9	33.2	6.8	16.6	2.9	20.9	0.7	10.1	5.9	23.9
U.S.S.R.	1.3	19.6	4.7	15.6	0.4	18.6	0.3	9.0	1.7	17.6
Comm. E. Europe	4.6	13.6	2.1	1.0	2.5	2.3	0.3	1.1	4.2	6.3
Communist Asia	1.8	13.3	-	0.6	-	-	-	2.3	1.4	5.7
Latin America	0.3	0.4	15.4	15.6	2.1	4.4	4.0	5.7	2.5	7.5
Caribbean	0.1	0.2	14.0	14.0	0.6	3.3	1.4	1.8	2.2	6.5
Other Latin America	0.1	0.2	1.4	1.6	1.5	1.2	2.7	3.9	0.4	1.0
Asia	4.3	5.5	6.5	28.8	1.0	2.1	10.1	11.1	4.5	14.7
Middle East	0.1	0.2	3.1	26.7	-	1.0	-	0.3	0.5	11.3
Japan	2.5	2.2	0.2	-	0.1	0.3	9.7	7.9	2.1	1.1
Other Asia	1.8	3.1	3.4	2.1	0.9	0.8	0.4	2.9	1.9	2.3
Africa	1.0	2.3	0.1	6.9	-	0.3	0.1	1.5	0.9	3.9
North Africa	-	-	0.1	5.9	-	0.3	-	0.4	-	2.5
Tropical Africa	0.1	0.2	-	1.0	-	-	0.1	1.1	0.1	0.5
South Africa	1.0	2.1	-	-	-	-	-	-	0.8	0.9
WORLD	100.0	100.0	100.0	100.0	100.0	100.0	100.0	100.0	100.0	100.0
WORLD (mill. met. tons										

North America.	1.02	1.07	1.14	0.80	1.00	1.00	1.00	1.00	1.04	0.93
of which: United States.	1.05	1.10	1.18	0.80	1.00	0.97	0.95	1.00	1.07	0.93
Western Europe	1.06	0.92	0.03	0.06	1.00	0.96	1.00	1.00	1.03	0.52
Oceania	1.10	1.22	-	0.02	-	1.00	1.00	1.00	1.03	0.68
U.S.S.R. & Comm. E. Europe . . .	1.13	1.03	1.26	1.23	1.00	1.00	0.88	1.00	1.15	1.08
U.S.S.R.	0.98	1.04	1.23	1.35	1.00	1.00	1.00	1.02	1.07	1.13
Comm E. Europe	1.18	1.01	1.33	0.54	1.00	0.98	0.80	0.87	1.18	0.96
Communist Asia	1.01	1.00	-	0.91	-	-	-	1.00	0.95	1.00
Latin America	0.36	0.80	2.51	2.58	1.00	1.00	1.00	1.00	1.62	2.11
Caribbean	0.66	0.92	3.73	4.20	0.99	1.06	1.00	1.00	2.98	3.20
Other Latin America	0.25	0.70	0.60	0.58	1.00	1.00	1.00	1.00	0.45	0.66
Asia	1.09	0.88	1.71	3.23	1.00	1.00	1.00	1.00	1.18	2.16
Middle East	0.99	1.00	4.29	14.94	-	1.00	1.00	1.00	3.32	11.22
Japan	1.12	0.74	0.29	0.01	1.00	1.00	1.00	1.00	1.08	0.33
Other Asia	1.06	0.99	1.31	0.85	1.00	1.01	1.00	1.00	1.11	0.93
Africa	1.04	1.01	0.24	4.41	-	1.76	1.00	1.00	0.98	2.36
North Africa	-	0.50	0.39	8.81	-	1.81	1.00	1.00	0.10	7.69
Tropical Africa	0.64	0.96	-	1.82	-	1.00	1.00	1.00	0.55	1.54
South Africa	1.38	1.02	-	-	-	-	-	-	1.35	0.88
WORLD[a]	1.04	1.00	1.16	1.08	1.00	1.00	1.00	1.00	1.06	1.03

[a]Reasons for departures in these worldwide ratios from unity (or, what is the same thing, differences between worldwide production and consumption levels) are noted in footnote[a], Profile No. 18.

Source: Part Three, tables III, X, and XIV.

Profile No. 21

COAL, LIGNITE, AND TOTAL SOLID FUELS PRODUCTION: PERCENTAGE DISTRIBUTION BY MAJOR WORLD REGIONS AND BY SELECTED COUNTRIES, 1925, 1950, AND 1965

Between them, the Western industrial powers of North America and Western Europe, on the one hand, and today's Communist regions, on the other, have dominated worldwide solid fuels production, accounting for 90 percent or more of the world total throughout the forty-year period under review. But there has been a drastic redistribution in the share of output contributed by the two groupings: the combined share of North America and Western Europe fell from 85 percent in 1925 to under 45 percent in 1965—the *absolute level* of solid fuels output of the two regions falling by 100 million tons;[1] at the same time, the Communist share climbed from under 8 percent to 46 percent of world production.

Output has been concentrated among a limited group of countries, as panel B of the table indicates. The thirteen nations listed accounted for well over 90 percent of world solid fuels production for each of the three benchmark years shown. As with the regional changes noted above, a significant redistribution has occurred in individual country shares. The combined shares of the United States, Great Britain, and West Germany[2] fell from 78 percent in 1925 to 37 percent in 1965, while the Soviet Union and Mainland China rose from 3 to 32 percent. The rising Chinese share has been mostly a post-World War II phenomenon.

In terms of *absolute levels* of output, the important West European producers (United Kingdom, West Germany, France, Belgium) began experiencing post-World War II declines in production beginning in the 1950s, and these declines have shown no sign of abating. Policy measures in aid of coal mining (such as subsidies and taxes on competing fuels) have averted sharper output cutbacks than have occurred. In the United States, less burdened by uneconomic mining operations, postwar production declines actually gave way to moderate rates of expansion beginning around 1960.

Thus, in the United States, solid fuels production attained a post-World War II peak in 1947 of about 660 million metric tons, following which it declined steadily—reaching little more than 400 million tons in 1961. Production then recovered rather markedly, however, with output by 1965 amounting to somewhat over 500 million tons.[3] By contrast, Great Britain's output fell virtually without interruption after 1952; West Germany's, after 1956; France's, after 1958; and that for Belgium-Luxembourg, after 1955.

The trends commented upon above refer to *total* solid fuels: hard coal, lignite (or brown coal), and some lesser components, such as peat.[4] However, hard coal has always enjoyed a predominant (if slightly falling) weight in total solid fuels (all expressed in calorific terms), so that the trends are largely applicable to hard coal as well. The position of the various solid fuels categories in worldwide solid fuels output have been as follows:

	Percent of world solid fuels production		
	1925	*1950*	*1965*
Hard coal . . .	94.2%	89.6%	86.0%
Lignite	5.2	8.9	12.6
Other	0.6	1.5	1.4
Total . . .	100.0	100.0	100.0

[1] For absolute figures, see Part Three, table II.

[2] The analysis of West German trends is slightly impaired by the prewar inclusion of the eastern part of the country. The latter, though a major world producer of lignite, figures much more modestly in total solid fuels, expressed in coal equivalents.

[3] The 1947 figure for production of anthracite, bituminous coal, and lignite was derived from U.S. Bureau of Mines, *Minerals Yearbook 1965*, vol. II (U.S. Government Printing Office, 1967), and then converted into hard coal equivalents. The 1961 figure appears in Part Three, table II.

[4] A terminological clarification: Following international usage, this study (e.g., Part Three, tables I to III) denotes the combination of anthracite and bituminous coal as "hard coal," whereas in the United States, anthracite is normally labeled "hard coal" and bituminous coal "soft coal." (Anthracite is relatively insignificant outside the United States.) In various publications, lignite is often referred to synonymously as "brown coal," although in some cases, particularly in Europe, a distinction is sometimes made depending on the geological age of the deposit—the older formation being termed "hard lignite" and the more recent formation called just "brown coal."

Lignite warrants a few words—on two grounds. First, its rate of output growth has greatly outdistanced that for coal; between 1925 and 1965 lignite production rose over three times as fast as hard coal (3.8 percent compared with 1.2 percent yearly), and between 1950 and 1965 it rose over twice as fast—4.8 percent compared with 2.1 percent. Second, the worldwide distribution of lignite output differs markedly from that of hard coal (or solid fuels in the aggregate), being even more disproportionately concentrated in the U.S.S.R. and Communist Eastern Europe. The latter two areas accounted for over 75 percent of world lignite output in 1965 and for nearly 90 percent of the expansion in world lignite production since 1950. East Germany and Czechoslovakia produced over 40 percent of the world total in 1965.

Lignite's rapid increase and its importance in parts of the Communist world (in Eastern Europe its output, on a calorific basis, exceeded that of hard coal in 1965) are interrelated. Reconstruction and rapid post-World War II industrial growth required intensive use of available energy resources of which lignite was a leading one. But the growth it has experienced may not signify great future potentialities. It is a fuel with an uneconomic heat content-weight ratio and poor combustion properties; and, though at a pace slower than in the West, Eastern Europe also is tending to become increasingly oriented to petroleum in a diverse range of economic activities.

COAL, LIGNITE, AND TOTAL SOLID FUELS PRODUCTION: PERCENTAGE DISTRIBUTION BY MAJOR WORLD REGIONS AND BY SELECTED COUNTRIES, 1925, 1950, AND 1965

(Data based on coal equivalents)

Region and country	1925			1950			1965		
	Hard coal	Lignite	Total	Hard coal	Lignite	Total	Hard coal	Lignite	Total
	A. *Regions as percent of world production of indicated fuel*								
North America	46.8%	1.4%	44.3%	38.0%	1.6%	34.4%	25.9%	0.7%	22.4%
Western Europe	39.6	72.1	41.2	31.3	23.6	30.3	21.5	19.1	21.1
Oceania	1.2	0.5	1.2	1.2	1.4	1.3	1.5	1.8	1.7
U.S.S.R. & Comm. E. Europe	4.7	25.8	5.9	19.2	72.1	24.6	26.2	76.8	33.2
U.S.S.R.	1.1	1.1	1.3	12.2	23.3	14.0	18.4	22.3	19.6
Comm. E. Europe	3.5	24.8	4.6	7.0	48.8	10.7	7.8	54.5	13.6
Communist Asia	1.9	–	1.8	2.9	0.3	2.6	15.4	0.4	13.3
Latin America	0.3	0.1	0.3	0.4	–	0.4	0.5	–	0.4
Asia	4.5	0.1	4.3	4.9	0.9	4.5	6.3	1.1	5.5
Japan	2.6	0.1	2.5	2.7	0.4	2.4	2.5	0.1	2.2
Other Asia	1.9	–	1.8	2.3	0.4	2.1	3.8	1.0	3.4
Africa	1.1	–	1.0	2.1	–	1.9	2.7	–	2.3
WORLD	100.0	100.0	100.0	100.0	100.0	100.0	100.0	100.0	100.0
WORLD (mill. met. tons coal equiv.)	(1,206.6)	(66.2)	(1,280.9)	(1,441.7)	(143.6)	(1,608.6)	(1,972.1)	(288.6)	(2,292.7)
WORLD (mill. met. tons, original units)	(1,184.2)	(181.9)	–	(1,431.0)	(380.7)	–	(2,038.2)	(748.7)	–
	B. *Selected countries*[a] *as percent of world production of indicated fuel*								
United States	46.1%	1.0%	43.5%	37.1%	0.7%	33.4%	25.6%	0.3%	22.0%
U.S.S.R.	1.1	1.1	1.3	12.2	23.3	14.0	18.4	22.3	19.6
Mainland China	1.9	–	1.8	2.8	–	2.5	14.5	–	12.4
United Kingdom	20.5	–	19.3	15.2	–	13.7	9.7	–	8.3
West Germany[b]	12.1	64.9	14.8	8.8	16.4	9.4	6.9	10.9	7.3
Poland	2.4	–	2.3	5.4	1.0	4.9	6.0	2.4	5.5
East Germany[b]	–	–	–	0.2	28.6	2.7	0.1	26.1	3.4
Czechoslovakia	1.0	16.8	1.9	1.3	11.5	2.2	1.4	15.2	3.1
India	1.4	–	1.3	1.8	–	1.6	2.7	0.2	2.4
France	3.9	0.9	3.7	3.5	0.7	3.2	2.6	0.6	2.3
Japan	2.6	0.1	2.5	2.7	0.4	2.4	2.5	0.1	2.2
South Africa	1.0	–	1.0	1.8	–	1.6	2.5	–	2.1
Australia	1.1	0.3	1.1	1.1	1.3	1.1	1.5	1.8	1.6
Total above 13	95.1	85.2	94.2	94.0	84.0	92.8	94.2	79.9	92.3
All other countries	4.9	14.8	5.8	6.0	16.0	7.2	5.8	20.1	7.7
WORLD	100.0	100.0	100.0	100.0	100.0	100.0	100.0	100.0	100.0

[a]The thirteen countries shown comprise all those accounting for 1% or more of world solid fuels production in 1965; the countries are listed in descending order according to their 1965 percentage shares.

[b]West Germany figures for 1925 apply to all of pre-World War II Germany.

Source: Part Three, table II. (In the case of Mainland China, for which many data are not available, separate figures do not appear in Part Three; see the country source notes of Part Four.)

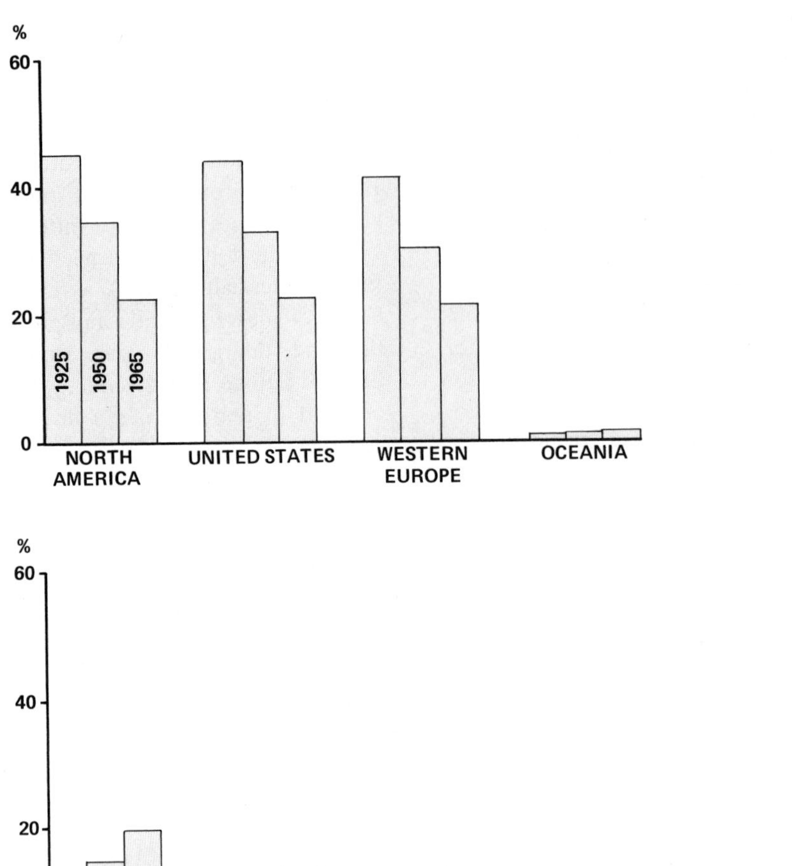

Regional percentage distribution of world solid fuels production, 1925, 1950, 1965.

Profile No.22

LIQUID FUELS PRODUCTION: PERCENTAGE DISTRIBUTION BY MAJOR WORLD REGIONS AND BY SELECTED COUNTRIES, SELECTED YEARS, 1925-1965

This profile depicts the changing regional and national shares of world liquid fuels[1] production from 1925 to 1965. The forty years during which output of liquid fuels expanded four times as rapidly as coal (6 percent yearly on the average, compared with 1½ percent) was a period, also, of marked transformation in the geographic sources of that output, the relative importance of the Eastern Hemisphere (notably the Middle East) gaining at the expense of the Western Hemisphere. In 1925 North America accounted for 70 percent of world oil output, as against a mere 8 percent for the aggregate of the Middle East (3.0 percent), U.S.S.R. (4.7 percent) and Africa (0.1 percent). By 1965 the North American share had fallen to 30 percent, while that of the three Eastern Hemisphere areas had risen to over 50 percent–27 percent for the Middle East, 7 percent for Africa, and 16 percent for the Soviet Union. The Western Hemisphere remains a powerful factor in world oil production; down from an 85 percent world share in 1925 to a 1965 proportion of somewhat over 45 percent, its relative importance would have shrunk more had it not been sustained by reasonably long-term stability in the share of world production contributed by Caribbean Latin America. That region's share of world output was an even 14 percent in both 1925 and 1965. However, this 1965 share reflects a steady drop-off from an earlier post-World War II share of 18 percent–a trend symptomatic, in turn, of (1) the cheaper-cost crude available to Western Europe from other producers; and (2) the imposition of U.S. import quotas dating from the late 1950s.

Significant long-term changes have occurred in country shares of world output. Six of the leading producers in 1965 had virtually no recorded output in 1925. The six in question–Kuwait, Saudi Arabia, Iraq, Libya, Canada, and Algeria–accounted for over one quarter of the world's oil production in 1965.

In the Middle East, only two oil discoveries had been made prior to 1925–in Iran in 1908 and in Iraq in 1923, and the latter case did not lead to consequential production for some years.[2] Three Arab states, which alone accounted for over 17 percent of worldwide output in 1965, began producing their first recorded crude oil in the comparatively recent years of 1936 (Saudi Arabia), 1946 (Kuwait), and 1961 (Libya). With Canada discovering major oil and gas fields only in the late 1940s, and the Soviet Union doubling its already considerable level of output between 1955 and 1960, it has been primarily since World War II that the world oil industry has grown to its present enormous size and that the prewar dominance of the United States in world oil output began to slip to a considerably less lofty position of leadership.

A few other countries over the years have receded in their world oil output ranking. The most conspicuous is Mexico whose 1925 world share of 12 percent was second only to the United States. Mexico's subsequent long-term decline, to scarcely more than 1 percent in 1965, has just about been compensated by the long-term rise of Venezuela, and this, in spite of the decline in recent years already noted, has served to hold up the

[1]"Liquid fuels" refers largely to crude oil, and for convenience, we tend in fact to use the two terms interchangeably. However, it should be noted that the total liquid fuels category comprises, in addition to crude oil, production of natural gas liquids (NGL)–the latter consisting, in turn, principally of natural gasoline and liquefied petroleum gases (LPG). As a proportion of worldwide liquid fuels output, NGL has shown the following trend: 1925, 2.2 percent; 1938, 2.7 percent; 1950, 3.7 percent; 1960, 3.4 percent; and 1965, 3.2 percent. The United States has always been the world's leading NGL producer, accounting for 95 percent of world output in 1925 and 85 percent in 1965. In the latter year, NGL represented 10 percent of U.S. liquid fuels output. Canada was the next ranking NGL producer in 1965 (6 percent of world NGL output, and around 8 percent of Canada's liquid fuels production). These NGL figures can be derived from Part Three, table II.

[2]See S. H. Longrigg, *Oil in the Middle East–Its Discovery and Development* (London: Oxford University Press, 1968), pp. 18, 66.

total Caribbean share over the long run. Indonesia's relatively meager share in 1925 nonetheless put it among the list of the more important oil producers; its share has tended to fall over the years. So has Romania's (not tabulated here)—down from 1½ percent in 1925 to 0.8 percent in 1965.

It will be seen that a substantial part of the historic expansion in world oil output occurred in such geographic areas as North Africa and the Middle East, which themselves consumed only small quantities of this newly discovered resource. Practically all production has been for export. The vast changes in the structure of world energy trade brought about by these circumstances form the subject of subsequent profiles.

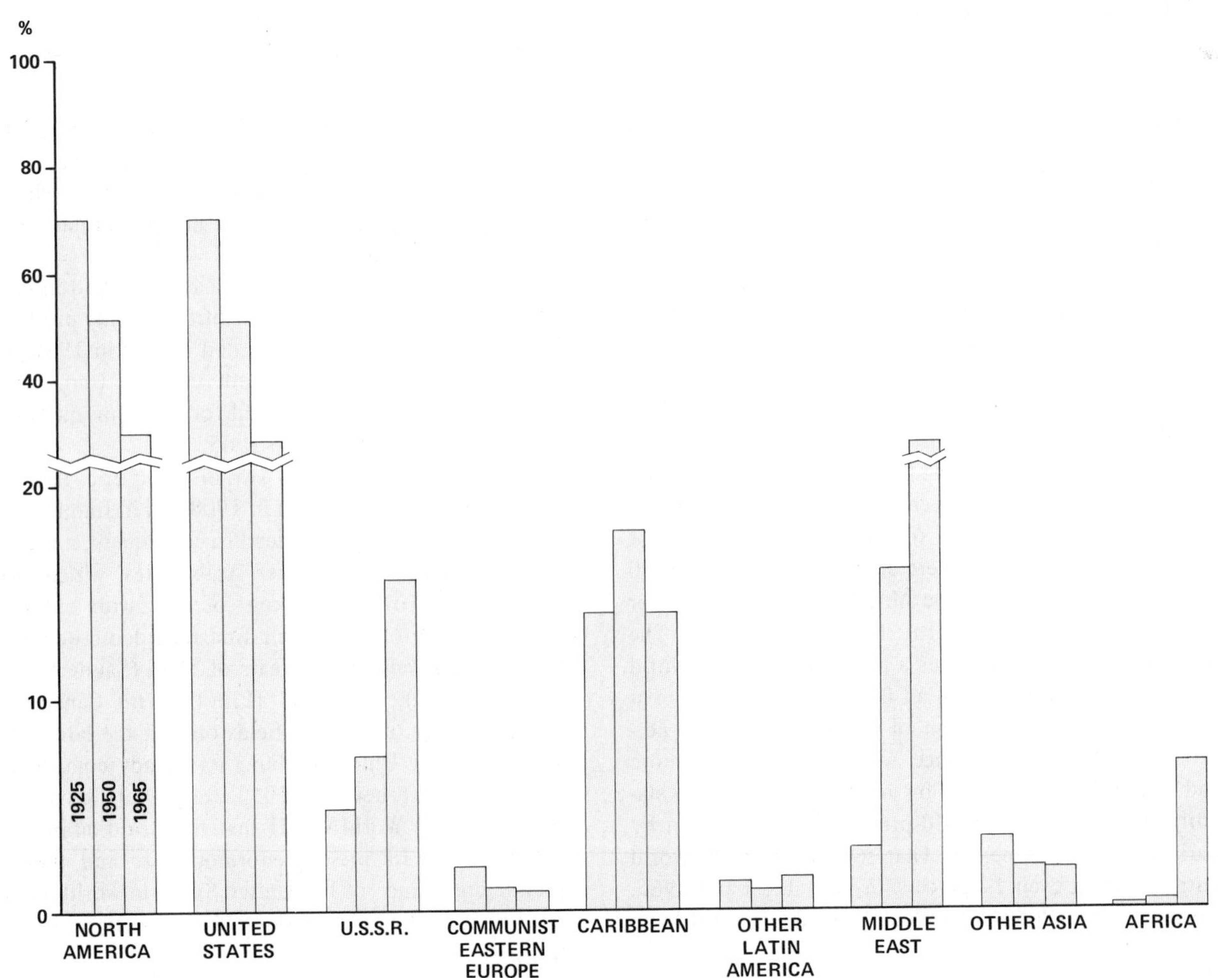

Note: Regions not shown (Oceania, Communist Asia) nil or negligible during 1925-65.

Regional percentage distribution of world liquid fuels production, 1925–1965.

LIQUID FUELS PRODUCTION: PERCENTAGE DISTRIBUTION BY MAJOR WORLD REGIONS AND BY SELECTED COUNTRIES, SELECTED YEARS, 1925-1965

Region and country	1925	1938	1950	1955	1960	1965
			A. Regions as percent of world production			
North America	70.9%	61.1%	53.5%	47.5%	37.3%	30.2%
Western Europe	0.2	0.3	0.7	1.2	1.4	1.3
Oceania	–	–	–	–	–	–
U.S.S.R. & Comm. E. Europe	6.8	13.5	8.3	10.7	15.1	16.6
U.S.S.R.	4.7	10.8	7.2	9.1	13.8	15.6
Comm. E. Europe	2.1	2.7	1.1	1.6	1.3	1.0
Communist Asia	–	0.1	–	0.1	0.5	0.6
Latin America	15.4	15.5	18.9	17.9	18.0	15.6
Caribbean	14.0	13.8	17.8	16.9	16.4	14.0
Other Latin America	1.4	1.8	1.1	1.0	1.6	1.6
Asia	6.5	9.3	18.0	22.3	26.4	28.8
Middle East	3.0	5.7	15.8	20.0	23.9	26.7
Other Asia	3.5	3.6	2.2	2.3	2.5	2.1
Africa	0.1	0.1	0.5	0.3	1.3	6.9
North Africa	0.1	0.1	0.5	0.2	1.1	5.9
Other Africa	–	–	–	–	0.2	1.0
WORLD	100.0	100.0	100.0	100.0	100.0	100.0
WORLD (mill. metric tons coal equiv.)	(228.0)	(421.3)	(813.2)	(1,205.8)	(1,641.2)	(2,342.8)
WORLD (mill. metric tons original units)	(152.0)	(280.9)	(542.1)	(803.9)	(1,094.1)	(1,561.9)
			B. Selected countries[a] as percent of world production			
United States	70.9%	60.8%	52.7%	45.3%	34.9%	27.4%
U.S.S.R.	4.7	10.8	7.2	9.1	13.8	15.6
Venezuela	1.9	9.8	14.5	14.1	13.7	11.7
Kuwait	–	–	3.2	6.8	7.5	7.0
Saudi Arabia	–	–	4.9	5.9	5.7	6.5
Iran	3.1	3.7	6.0	2.0	4.8	6.0
Iraq	–	1.6	1.2	4.2	4.3	4.1
Libya	–	–	–	–	–	3.8
Canada	–	0.3	0.7	2.2	2.4	2.7
Algeria	–	–	–	–	0.8	1.7
Indonesia	2.1	2.7	1.2	1.5	1.9	1.5
Kuwait Neutral Zone	–	–	–	0.2	0.7	1.2
Mexico	11.6	2.0	1.9	1.6	1.4	1.2
Total above 13	94.3	91.7	93.5	92.9	91.9	90.4
All other countries	5.7	8.3	6.5	7.1	8.1	9.6
WORLD	100.0	100.0	100.0	100.0	100.0	100.0

[a]The thirteen countries shown comprise all those accounting for 1% or more of world liquid fuels production in 1965; the countries are listed in descending order according to their 1965 percentage shares.

Source: Part Three, table II.

Profile No. 23

WORLD ENERGY TRADE, BY SOURCE, SELECTED YEARS, 1925-1965

International trade in energy commodities increased rapidly between 1925 and 1965, rising considerably faster throughout the period than did total energy consumption. For the forty years as a whole, world energy trade, as measured by total exports, went up by a little over 5 percent annually, compared with somewhat over 3 percent for energy consumption. (Consumption growth rates appear in Profile No. 1.) In 1925 about 14 percent of total energy consumption crossed international frontiers; by 1965 that proportion had precisely doubled. As for oil alone, foreign shipments represented one-third of worldwide consumption in 1925 and two-thirds by 1965.

Since energy trade in the early years of this period was characterized to a substantial degree by *intra*regional trade–particularly exchanges of coal among proximate European countries–the long-term, petroleum-dominated expansion of *inter*regional trade was even more rapid, increasing by more than 6 percent per annum.[1]

Just as the physical volume of world energy trade has grown faster than the volume of energy consumption, so has world energy trade expressed in value terms tended to grow faster than the aggregate dollar value of world trade in general. The few figures available on this score do not conform to the bench marks in the accompanying tabulation, but the story they tell is worth recording:

Energy Trade as a Share of Total World Trade[2]

Year	Share
1913	4.8%
1929	6.3
1937	7.5
1953	9.0
1965	9.6

As in the tonnage comparison of energy trade and energy consumption, it seems highly probable that percentage shares of the value of energy commodities in world trade would show a still more striking increase if they could be adjusted to exclude trade *within* major regions.

The dominant force in the expansion of world energy trade has clearly been liquid fuels; comprising under one-third of world energy exports in 1925, they rose steadily, reaching nearly 90 percent in 1965. (Incrementally, liquid fuels accounted for 98 percent of increased energy trade over the four decades.) Conversely, coal slipped from two-thirds of the world total in 1925 to around one-tenth in 1965; it exhibited relatively little long-term change in absolute level of shipments. Gas and electricity, largely limited to natural gas and electricity exchanges between Canada and the United States and electricity sales within Western Europe, have historically accounted for only trivial shares of international energy trade. Slowly rising ocean transport of liquefied natural gas (LNG) and pipeline transport within Europe appear likely to alter that situation in the years to come.

A Note on Foreign Trade Terminology

In the following profiles (No. 23 through No. 38) dealing with world energy flows, different foreign trade measures are used, the choice in each case depending on the particular aspect of international energy shipments being reviewed. The following diagram may help to distinguish among these various measures. Picture the world as consisting of four countries and two regions: countries 1 and 2 constitute Region A; countries 3 and 4 constitute Region B. All countries trade with one another–magnitudes and directions being denoted by the arrows on the illustration. Results, using different foreign trade measures such as those cited in this study, appear at the bottom of the diagram.

Total imports or exports of a region refer to the sum of each country's imports or exports, regardless of whether those

[1] A rough estimate; taken from Profile No. 35, and based on the period 1929-65.

[2] Figures for 1913-37 and energy trade in 1953 from P. Lamartine Yates, *Forty Years of Foreign Trade* (Macmillan, 1959), pp. 123, 223; world exports in 1953 from United Nations, *Statistical Yearbook, 1967* (New York, 1968), p. 385; 1965 data from United Nations, *Monthly Bulletin of Statistics*, March 1968, pp. xviii, xxiv.

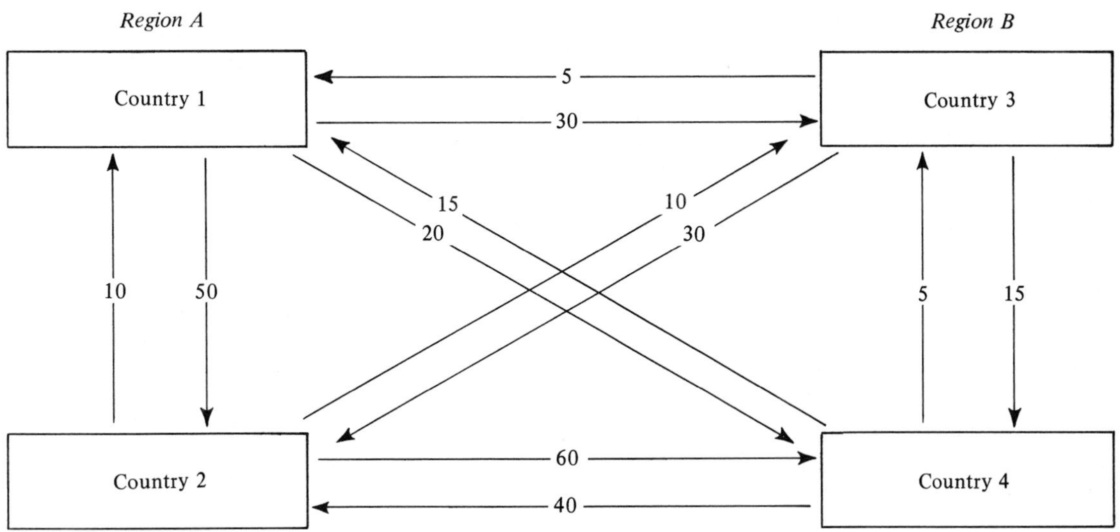

Total Trade

Country 1: total imports = 10 + 15 + 5 = 30
total exports = 50 + 30 + 20 = 100
net imports = –70

Country 2: total imports = 50 + 30 + 40 = 120
total exports = 10 + 60 + 10 = 80
net imports = 40

Region A total imports = 150
Region A total exports = 180
Region A net imports = –30

Country 3: total imports = 30 + 10 + 5 = 45
total exports = 5 + 30 + 15 = 50
net imports = –5

Country 4: total imports = 20 + 60 + 15 = 95
total exports = 15 + 40 + 5 = 60
net imports = 35

Region B total imports = 140
Region B total exports = 110
Region B net imports = 30

World total imports = 150 + 140 = 290
World total exports = 180 + 110 = 290
World net imports = –30 + 30 = 0

Interregional Trade

Region A interregional imports = 90
Region A interregional exports = 120
Region A net imports = –30

Region B interregional imports = 120
Region B interregional exports = 90
Region B net imports = 30

World interregional imports = 90 + 120 = 210
World interregional exports = 120 + 90 = 210
World net imports = –30 + 30 = 0

Intraregional Trade

Region A (imports or exports) = 60

Region B (imports or exports) = 20

Worldwide intraregional trade (imports or exports) = 80

imports or exports are within the region or outside the region. Thus Region A imports equal 150. Of this 150 in total imports, 60 are intraregional flows and 90 are interregional imports. Region A aggregate exports are 180, which after deduction of the same 60 in intraregional shipments yields interregional exports of 120.

Interregional imports or exports are a useful measure when analyzing the direction of energy flows among major parts of the world. For example, if we were to take the Caribbean area total–rather than merely interregional–exports of oil, we would use a figure which aggregates Venezuela's exports of crude oil to the Netherlands Antilles refineries together with the latter's exports (to the United States and elsewhere) of refined fuels made from Venezuelan crude. Where such quasi-doublecounting might distort the analysis, a measure of exports, excluding these intraregional flows, is frequently appropriate. It is obvious that world totals of interregional exports or imports depend on the number of regions used in a tabulation. Where interregional data are used we may, because of statistical necessity or analytical desirability, depart from the regional classification used elsewhere. Wherever this occurs it will be noted.

Net imports equal imports less exports. That is, a net export figure is preceded by a minus (–) sign; and where the phrase "net trade" is used, a figure without a sign refers to net imports, while a negative figure refers to exports. In principle, net imports are the same whether derived by subtracting total exports from total imports or whether obtained by subtracting interregional exports from interregional imports (the same amount having been deducted from total imports or total exports to get interregional imports or interregional exports). In practice, the net trade figures derived from these two bases will frequently vary because of differences in statistical sources.

In principle, also, total world imports should equal total world exports; and worldwide interregional imports should equal interregional exports. Here again discrepancies arise from source differences and because of measurement problems.

WORLD ENERGY TRADE BY SOURCE, SELECTED YEARS, 1925-1965

	1925	1938	1950	1955	1960	1965
A. *Exports[a] in million metric tons coal equivalent*						
Solid fuels	145.8	129.7	120.2	157.2	133.0	158.7
Liquid fuels . . .	67.9	169.4	375.6	606.9	871.7	1,395.4
Gas	-	0.1	1.3	1.3	6.4	18.4
Electricity	0.2	0.5	0.5	0.9	1.4	1.7
Total	214.0	299.6	497.6	766.4	1,012.3	1,574.2
B. *Percentage distribution*						
Solid fuels	68.2%	43.3%	24.2%	20.5%	13.1%	10.1%
Liquid fuels . . .	31.7	56.5	75.5	79.2	86.1	88.6
Gas	-	-	0.2	0.2	0.6	1.2
Electricity	0.1	0.2	0.1	0.1	0.1	0.1
Total	100.0	100.0	100.0	100.0	100.0	100.0
C. *As percent of world consumption*						
Solid fuels	11.9%	10.0%	7.5%	8.7%	6.7%	6.9%
Liquid fuels . . .	34.5	45.1	52.0	55.5	58.2	64.6
Gas	-	-	0.5	0.3	1.0	2.0
Electricity	2.0	2.0	1.2	1.5	1.6	1.5
Total	14.4	16.7	19.1	22.8	24.1	28.8

D. *Average annual percentage rates of change*

	1925-1938	1938-1950	1950-1965	1925-1965
Solid fuels	-0.9%	-0.6%	1.9%	0.2%
Liquid fuels . . .	7.3	6.9	9.1	7.9
Gas	21.7	28.4	19.3	22.7
Electricity	5.1	-	9.1	5.0
Total	2.6	4.3	8.0	5.1

[a]Representing sum of *total* exports of solid and liquid fuels; sum of *net* exports of gas and electricity for which country figures on a gross basis were unavailable.

Note: In this and subsequent profiles dealing with foreign trade, "gas" refers to foreign trade of natural as well as manufactured gas; and "electricity" refers to foreign trade of hydro as well as thermal electricity. However, the denominator of panel C refers to consumption of natural gas and hydroelectricity.

Source: Part Three, tables VI, X, and XIII.

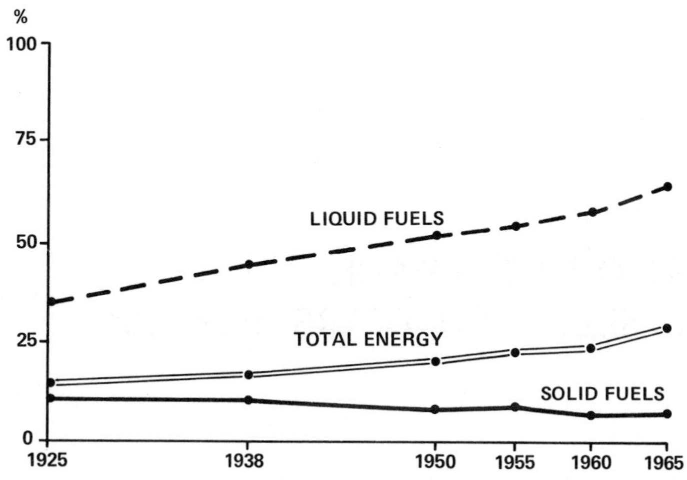

World energy exports as share of world energy consumption, 1925-1965.

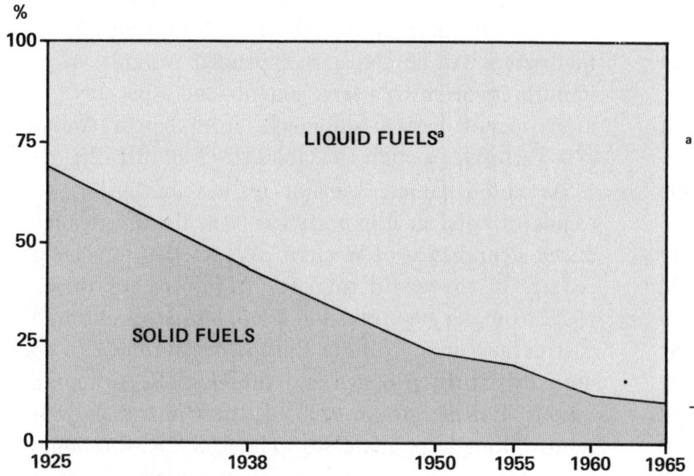

[a] Including gas and electricity exports: 1938, 0.2%; 1950, 0.3%; 1955, 0.3%; 1960, 0.7%; 1965, 1.3%.

Percentage distribution, by source, of world energy exports, 1925-1965.

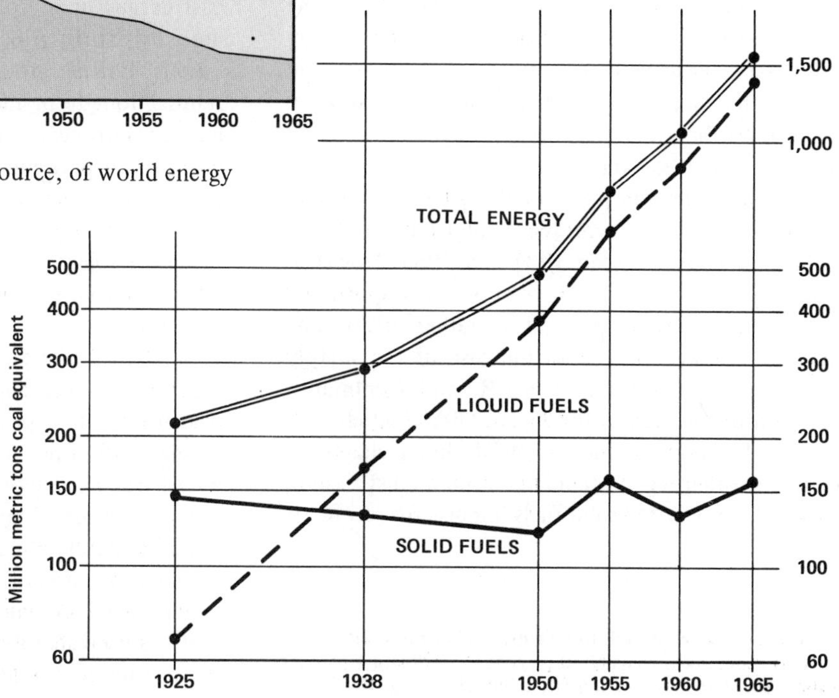

World energy exports, 1925-1965.

Profile No. 24

WORLD IMPORTS, EXPORTS, AND NET TRADE IN SOLID FUELS, BY REGION, SELECTED YEARS, 1925-1965

The regional totals of solid fuels imports and exports (tabulated in panels A and B of the table) comprise the aggregate shipments to and from the areas shown, irrespective of whether this trade was within, or external to, the area. (See the explanatory note on different foreign trade measures included in Profile No. 23.) For example, Western Europe's pronounced decline in its share of world coal exports (from 70 percent in 1925 to 24 percent in 1965) would be even sharper were we to exclude intra-European coal trade and consider merely interregional shipments.[1] However, data that show only interregional flows (as in Profiles No. 35 to No. 38) permit far less extensive time series comparison than those on total trade, as tabulated here. Of course, the net trade figures comprising panel C of the accompanying table necessarily cancel out the imports and exports within the indicated regions, making that series in some ways the more useful one for observing significant trends in an area's trade.

Referring to the top panel of the table, we see that the absolute volume of worldwide solid fuels trade did not change greatly between 1925 and 1965. However, the geographic composition of world coal imports did undergo redistribution—some of it rather erratic and some of it conspicuous, as in the case of the sharply rising shares for both the U.S.S.R. and Communist Eastern Europe as well as for Japan. Offsetting changes were brought about by moderately declining shares for most of the other regions tabulated. Communist Eastern Europe's share of world solid fuels imports rose from 2½ percent in 1925 to close to 20 percent in 1965; Japan's share went up from 1 to 10 percent between these two points. In the former case, most of the increase represented coal trade among the East European countries themselves; while Japan's expanded volume of coal imports involved to a large extent—and especially in the more recent period—shipments from North America. (See Part Five, section III, tables III-1 and III-2.)

As noted earlier, a major feature in the long-term trends of total coal exports has been the drastically reduced significance of Western Europe: that region's percentage of the world total fell from over two-thirds in 1925 to under one-fourth in 1965. Moreover, during the past decade or so Western Europe began to be exceeded both by North America and the U.S.S.R.-Communist Eastern Europe group, each of whose shares show substantial long-term increases. The U.S.S.R.-Communist Eastern Europe share of world solid fuels exports has displayed a particularly strong long-term upward trend, going from 9 percent in 1925 to 37 percent in 1965; after 1950, however, the group's increasing share was sustained solely by the U.S.S.R., the proportion of the East European countries having fallen off between 1950 and 1965.

Western Europe's eclipse as the dominant factor in the international coal export trade also meant the replacement of a positive West European coal export balance with a net import balance in the years following World War II, as shown in the lower panel. Japan's emergence as a net importer of coal is of much longer standing, dating almost from the beginning of the period spanned by our study. But, as in the growth of its energy requirements in general, Japan's net import position in coal has risen sharply in recent years, due in large part to the coking coal requirements needed for its burgeoning steel industry.

[1] To be precise, Western Europe's share of world interregional solid fuels exports was roughly 30 percent in 1929 and 1 percent in 1965. (See Part Five, section III, tables III-1 and III-2; also Profiles No. 35 and No. 36.)

WORLD IMPORTS, EXPORTS, AND NET TRADE IN SOLID FUELS, BY REGION, SELECTED YEARS, 1925-1965

Region	Million metric tons coal equivalent				Percent of world total			
	1925	1950	1955	1965	1925	1950	1955	1965
				A. Total imports				
North America	16.7	25.7	18.8	15.8	12.2%	22.0%	12.1%	10.0%
of which: United States	1.1	0.7	0.4	0.2	0.8	0.6	0.3	0.2
Western Europe	93.9	61.2	98.7	80.6	68.7	52.4	63.6	51.0
Oceania	0.7	0.7	0.3	0.3	0.5	0.6	0.2	0.2
U.S.S.R. & Comm. E. Europe	4.1	20.6	26.0	36.7	3.0	17.6	16.8	23.2
U.S.S.R.	0.7	11.4	9.1	7.4	0.5	9.8	5.8	4.7
Comm. E. Europe	3.4	9.2	17.0	29.3	2.5	7.8	10.9	18.6
Communist Asia	2.8	n.a.	0.1	0.1	2.1	–	0.1	0.1
Latin America	7.2	2.9	2.8	2.6	5.3	2.5	1.8	1.6
Asia	6.5	3.1	5.9	19.0	4.8	2.7	3.8	12.0
Japan	1.8	0.8	2.9	17.1	1.3	0.7	1.8	10.8
Other Asia	4.7	2.3	3.0	1.9	3.5	2.0	2.0	1.2
Africa	4.6	2.8	2.5	2.8	3.4	2.4	1.6	1.8
WORLD[a]	136.6	116.9	155.1	157.9	100.0	100.0	100.0	100.0
				B. Total exports				
North America	20.3	27.8	50.5	48.2	13.9%	23.1%	32.1%	30.4%
of which: United States	19.6	27.2	49.9	47.0	13.4	22.6	31.7	29.6
Western Europe	102.2	53.7	61.8	37.4	69.9	44.7	39.3	23.6
Oceania	1.0	0.1	0.2	7.3	0.7	0.1	0.2	4.6
U.S.S.R. & Comm. E. Europe	12.5	33.1	39.4	59.3	8.6	27.5	25.0	37.4
U.S.S.R.	0.4	2.6	5.8	14.7	0.3	2.2	3.7	16.3
Comm. E. Europe	12.1	30.5	33.6	33.5	8.3	25.4	21.4	21.1
Communist Asia	2.6	n.a.	1.1	1.8	1.8	–	0.7	1.1
Latin America	–	0.1	0.1	–	–	0.1	–	–
Asia	5.5	1.7	2.0	1.3	3.8	1.4	1.3	0.8
Japan	2.7	0.5	0.4	0.1	1.9	0.4	0.3	0.1
Other Asia	2.8	1.2	1.6	1.2	1.9	1.0	1.0	0.7
Africa	1.9	3.7	2.1	3.3	1.3	3.0	1.3	2.1
WORLD[a]	145.8	120.2	157.2	158.7	100.0	100.0	100.0	100.0

C. *Net imports or net exports (-)*
(million metric tons coal equivalent)

Region	1925	1938	1950	1955	1960	1965
North America	-3.7	0.8	-2.2	-31.8	-22.8	-32.4
of which: United States	-18.5	-11.0	-26.4	-49.5	-34.5	-46.8
Western Europe	-8.1	-4.3	7.5	36.9	31.2	43.2
Oceania	-0.2	-0.1	0.6	–	-1.4	-7.0
U.S.S.R. & Comm. E. Europe	-8.4	-10.9	-12.5	-13.3	-18.9	-22.6
U.S.S.R.	0.3	0.7	8.8	3.3	-9.3	-18.4
Comm. E. Europe	-8.7	-11.6	-21.3	-16.6	-9.6	-4.2
Communist Asia	0.2	-3.1	n.a.	-1.0	-0.9	-1.6
Latin America	7.2	5.4	2.8	2.7	3.0	2.6
Asia	1.0	4.8	1.4	3.8	9.1	17.7
Japan	-1.0	5.0	0.3	2.5	8.3	17.0
Other Asia	2.0	-0.2	1.1	0.7	0.8	0.6
Africa	2.7	3.3	-0.9	0.4	-0.1	-0.5
WORLD[a]	-9.2	-4.0	-3.2	-2.2	-0.8	-0.8

[a]Worldwide imports and exports, though equal in principle (and yielding net imports of zero), differ because of various estimating problems, as discussed in the notes of Part Four, p. 821.

Source: Part Three, tables VI and VII.

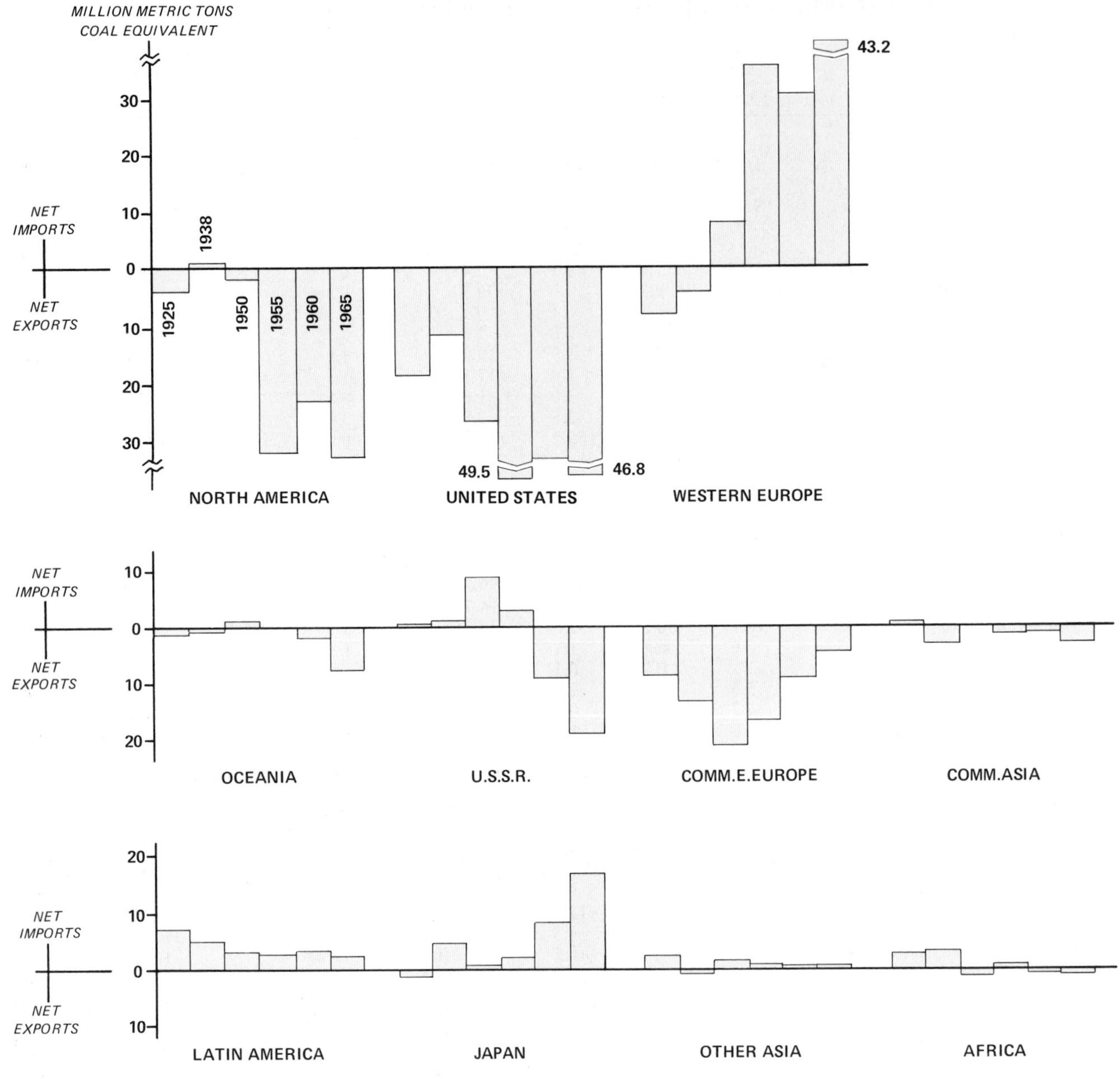

Net imports or exports of solid fuels, 1925-1965.

Profile No.25

WORLD IMPORTS, EXPORTS, AND NET TRADE IN LIQUID FUELS, BY REGION, SELECTED YEARS, 1925-1965

As in Profile No. 24 dealing with solid fuels, the accompanying figures in panels A and B of the table on total imports and exports of liquid fuels comprise the aggregate of each region's and the world's total trade: that is, interregional as well as intraregional movements which, in the case of Caribbean oil imports, for example, includes Venezuelan crude oil shipped to the Dutch West Indies for refining. To the extent that an analysis of trends may be slightly marred on that account, the *net* oil trade figures in panel C provide a picture of regional trade free of exchanges within the region.

In the distribution of world oil imports, Western Europe and Japan have both increased their relative standing substantially. At first glance, the relatively declining North American (essentially U.S.) share in total world imports of liquid fuels seems anomalous, given the area's rising net import dependence (see panel C). The explanation arises from the region's even more precipitous decline in the percentage of world exports (panel B).

In liquid fuels exports (panel B), the most prominent long-term changes concern the positions of the Caribbean, Middle East, and, as noted, North America. North America's share of world oil exports dropped from one-third in 1925 to a mere 2 percent in 1965; and, in the course of this decline, the region moved from a position of net oil exporter to one of net importer. The Caribbean's 1925 share of 42 percent had given it and North America a combined world export proportion of 75 percent; the Caribbean's world share peaked with a nearly 50 percent figure in 1950, following which it declined steadily, reaching 25 percent in 1965. That decline reflected in part the progressively greater importance of the Middle East whose share of world oil exports was under one-tenth in 1925, around one-third in 1950, and well over 40 percent in 1965. Other areas with rising shares of world liquid fuels exports are, first, the Soviet Union (whose renewed growth after the war began with under 1 percent and then reached 7 percent in 1965) and, second, North Africa (whose growth from virtual insignificance to nearly 10 percent of the world total occurred primarily in just the five years 1960-1965).

Long-term trends in net liquid fuels trade (panel C), reflecting the developments noted above, thus disclose some fundamental changes: North America's transition from an essentially balanced picture in 1925 (actually, net exports of one million coal equivalent tons, or roughly 700,000 tons of oil) to one of a substantial net import balance (some 200 million coal equivalent tons, or some 135 million tons of oil) in 1965; Western Europe's rising net oil imports (up by a factor of 30); huge increases in oil imports for Japan; the Middle East's export balance up 100 times; and the Soviet oil export balance up nearly 50 times.

WORLD IMPORTS, EXPORTS, AND NET TRADE IN LIQUID FUELS, BY REGION, SELECTED YEARS, 1925-1965

Region	Million metric tons coal equivalent				Percent of world total			
	1925	1950	1955	1965	1925	1950	1955	1965
				A. *Total imports*				
North America	21.4	89.1	125.8	236.0	34.1%	24.9%	21.2%	17.3%
of which: United States	17.3	66.7	100.0	193.5	27.5	18.7	16.8	14.1
Western Europe	19.4	99.8	210.8	637.7	30.9	27.9	35.5	46.6
Oceania	1.4	8.9	15.0	32.0	2.2	2.5	2.5	2.3
U.S.S.R. & Comm. E. Europe	0.6	6.8	13.6	38.1	0.9	1.9	2.3	2.8
U.S.S.R.	0.1	4.1	7.9	2.7	0.2	1.1	1.3	0.2
Comm. E. Europe	0.5	2.7	5.6	35.4	0.7	0.8	1.0	2.6
Communist Asia	1.4	n.a.	2.1	1.5	2.2	n.a.	0.3	0.1
Latin America	11.8	94.9	118.4	150.6	18.7	26.6	19.9	11.0
Caribbean	8.1	77.5	88.8	119.4	12.9	21.7	14.9	8.7
Other Latin America	3.7	17.5	29.7	31.2	5.8	4.9	5.0	2.3
Asia	5.3	44.4	85.1	231.3	8.5	12.4	14.3	16.9
Middle East	0.6	16.9	28.7	38.9	1.0	4.7	4.9	2.9
Japan	1.0	2.8	16.0	126.8	1.6	0.8	2.7	9.3
Other Asia	3.7	24.8	40.4	65.7	5.9	6.9	6.7	4.7
Africa	1.6	13.4	23.5	40.7	2.5	3.8	4.0	3.0
North Africa	0.9	5.5	9.5	11.4	1.4	1.5	1.6	0.8
Tropical Africa	0.5	4.5	9.2	19.6	0.8	1.3	1.5	1.4
South Africa	0.2	3.4	4.8	9.8	0.3	1.0	0.8	0.7
WORLD[a]	62.8	357.5	594.4	1,368.0	100.0	100.0	100.0	100.0
				B. *Total exports*				
North America	22.4	19.5	25.5	33.6	33.0%	5.2%	4.2%	2.4%
of which: United States	22.4	19.5	22.4	10.2	32.9	5.2	3.7	0.7
Western Europe	1.2	14.1	43.1	91.0	1.7	3.7	7.1	6.5
Oceania	–	–	0.5	1.9	–	–	0.1	0.1
U.S.S.R. & Comm. E. Europe	3.7	5.8	22.6	111.1	5.4	1.5	3.7	8.0
U.S.S.R.	2.1	1.6	11.9	96.4	3.0	0.4	2.0	6.9
Comm. E. Europe	1.6	4.2	10.6	14.7	2.4	1.1	1.8	1.1
Communist Asia	–	n.a.	–	–	–	n.a.	–	–
Latin America	29.9	185.0	239.0	352.3	44.0	49.3	39.4	25.3
Caribbean	28.5	183.4	237.3	350.2	41.9	48.8	39.1	25.1
Other Latin America	1.4	1.6	1.7	2.1	2.1	0.4	0.3	0.2
Asia	10.4	151.2	275.8	648.8	15.3	40.3	45.4	46.5
Middle East	5.7	126.7	241.3	599.4	8.4	33.8	39.7	43.0
Japan	–	–	–	1.3	–	–	–	0.1
Other Asia	4.6	24.6	34.5	48.1	6.9	6.5	5.7	3.4
Africa	0.3	–	0.4	156.5	0.5	–	0.1	11.2
North Africa	0.3	–	0.1	131.4	0.5	–	–	9.4
Tropical Africa	–	–	0.1	24.5	–	–	–	1.8
South Africa	–	–	0.2	0.6	–	–	–	–
WORLD[a]	67.9	375.6	606.9	1,395.4	100.0	100.0	100.0	100.0

WORLD IMPORTS, EXPORTS, AND NET TRADE IN LIQUID FUELS, BY REGION, SELECTED YEARS, 1925-1965 (Continued)

Region	Million metric tons coal equivalent				Percent of world total			
	1925	1950	1955	1965	1925	1950	1955	1965

C. *Net imports or net exports (-)*
(Million metric tons coal equivalent)

Region	1925	1938	1950	1955	1960	1965
North America	1.0	-18.5	69.7	100.3	154.8	202.4
of which: United States	-5.1	-26.9	47.2	77.7	130.6	183.4
Western Europe	18.2	51.6	85.8	167.7	286.8	546.7
Oceania	1.4	4.3	8.9	14.6	19.6	30.1
U.S.S.R. & Comm. E. Europe	-3.1	-7.0	1.0	-9.0	-40.5	-73.0
U.S.S.R.	-2.0	-1.7	2.4	-4.0	-43.4	-93.7
Comm. E. Europe	-1.2	-5.3	-1.4	-5.0	2.9	20.7
Communist Asia	1.4	1.1	n.a.	2.1	5.4	1.5
Latin America	-18.1	-37.0	-90.1	-120.6	-164.1	-201.8
Caribbean	-20.4	-41.0	-105.9	-148.5	-190.0	-230.8
Other Latin America	2.2	3.9	15.8	27.9	26.9	29.1
Asia	-5.1	-13.6	-106.8	-190.6	-294.7	-417.5
Middle East	-5.1	-15.9	-109.8	-212.7	-346.9	-560.5
Japan	1.0	6.8	2.8	16.0	48.0	125.5
Other Asia	-0.9	-4.5	0.2	6.1	4.2	17.6
Africa	1.3	5.7	13.4	23.2	12.4	-115.8
North Africa	0.6	2.5	5.5	9.4	-3.0	-120.1
Tropical Africa	0.5	1.6	4.5	9.0	9.9	-5.0
South Africa	0.2	1.6	3.4	4.7	5.5	9.2
WORLD[a]	-5.1	-13.4	-18.2	-12.5	-20.4	-27.4

[a]Worldwide imports and exports, though equal in principle (and yielding net imports of zero), differ because of various estimating problems, as discussed in the notes of Part Four, p. 821.

Source: Part Three, tables VI and VII.

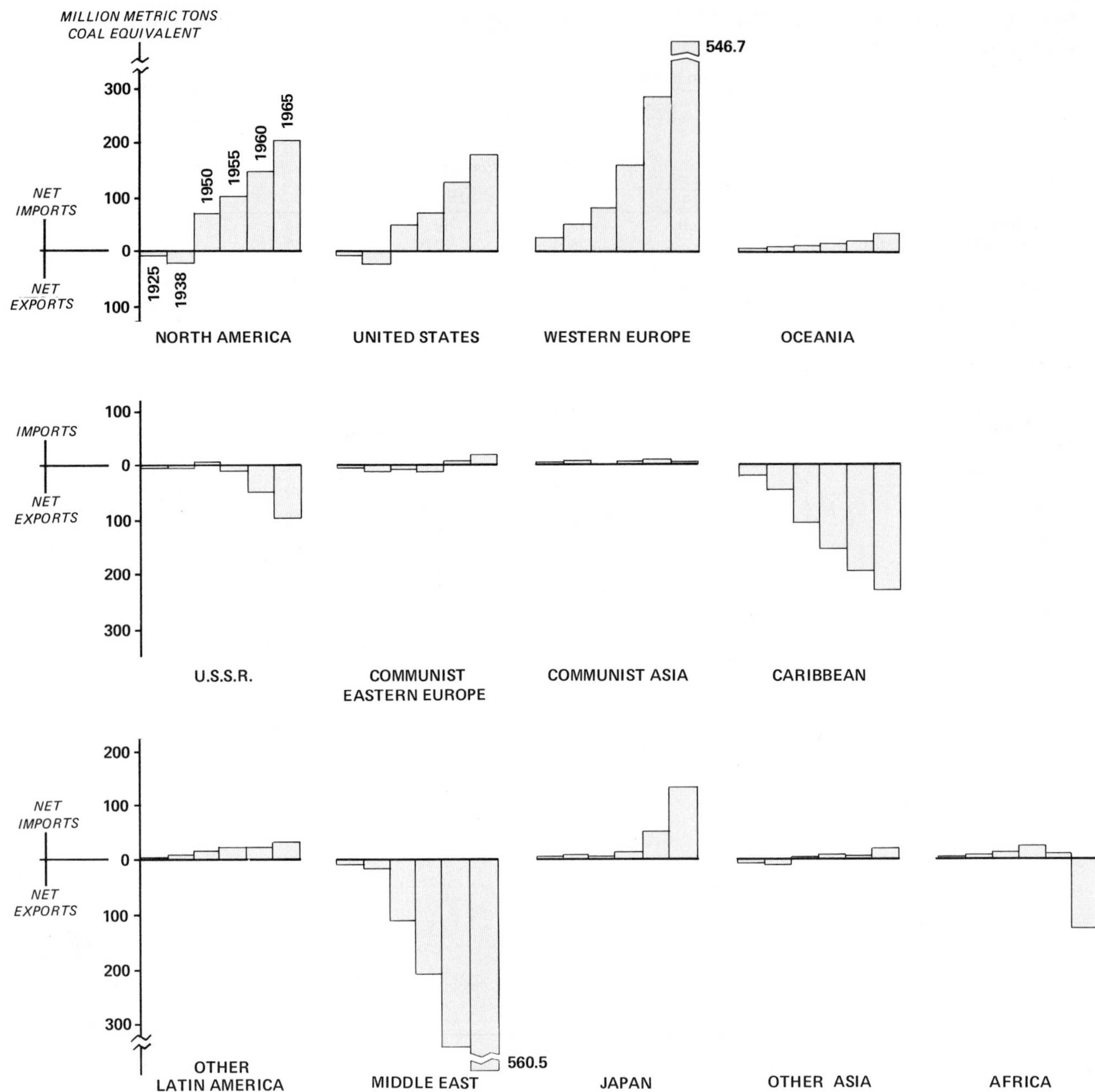

Net imports or exports of liquid fuels, selected years, 1925–1965.

Profile No. 26

WORLD IMPORTS, EXPORTS, AND NET TRADE IN TOTAL ENERGY, BY REGION, SELECTED YEARS, 1925-1965

As in Profiles No. 24 on coal and No. 25 on oil, interpretation of the tabulation dealing with regional trends in total energy trade[1] suffers somewhat from the fact that the total import and total export panels include intraregional as well as interregional trade. (See the explanatory note on foreign trade measures appended to Profile No. 23.) Thus, the reason why Western Europe's share of total world energy imports does not show the expected rise, but is recorded as having fallen (from 57 percent in 1925 to 47 percent in 1965) is because 1925 imports were dominated by coal shipments within Western Europe while 1965 imports largely represented oil from outside the region. (In Profile No. 35 a tabulation restricted to world *interregional* movements of energy produces the predictably marked increase in Western Europe's share of the world total.)

Changing regional shares in total energy exports (panel B of the table) reflect the expanding weight of liquid fuels in world energy trade, so that the long-term gainers have been the Middle East, to a large extent the Caribbean, North Africa, and the U.S.S.R. Almost all other regions have declined to a greater or lesser extent in their shares of world energy exports.

The regional distribution of total world energy exports also reflects an area's interregional plus intra-regional trade, though to a lesser extent than does that of imports. Major focus might therefore be put on the net trade figures of panel C, which have the virtue of cancelling out intraregional energy movements. This part of the tabulation discloses long-term changes largely brought about by the growth of world petroleum. We see, on the net import side, enormous growth in net energy imports for Western Europe and Japan, North America's post-World War II emergence as a net energy importer (resulting from net oil flows into the United States from outside North America), and Eastern Europe's more recent reversal of its net export status; and on the net export side, vast increases from the Middle East and a significant expansion from the Caribbean, substantial growth of net exports from Russia, and, during the past decade, rapidly growing net exports from the oil-producing regions of Africa.

These developments in net energy trade can be put into a different, and perhaps sharper, perspective by looking at the changing trend in the ratio of exports to imports. That ratio is obtained by dividing the tonnage figures in panel B by those in panel A. The results are as follows:

	Ratio of total energy exports to total energy imports		*1965 ratio as percent of 1925 ratio*
	1925	*1965*	*(1925 = 100)*
North America.	1.12	0.36	32%
Western Europe	0.91	0.18	20
Oceania	0.48	0.29	60
U.S.S.R. & Comm. E. Europe.	3.45	2.26	66
U.S.S.R.	3.00	12.18	406
Comm. E. Europe . . .	3.54	0.74	21
Communist Asia	0.62	1.06	171
Latin America	1.57	2.31	147
Caribbean. . . .	3.00	2.94	98
Other Latin America. . .	0.15	0.06	40
Asia	1.34	2.60	194
Middle East. . .	6.56	15.41	235
Japan	1.00	0.01	1
Other Asia . . .	0.89	0.73	82
Africa	0.35	3.67	1,049

When the figures are cast into the above form, Japan is seen to have experienced the greatest deterioration in its energy trade balance, followed by Western Europe, North America, and Eastern Europe.

[1] In addition to solid and liquid fuels, total energy trade includes movements of gas and electricity; in most parts of the world, these have been minor.

WORLD IMPORTS, EXPORTS, AND NET TRADE IN TOTAL ENERGY, BY REGION, SELECTED YEARS, 1925-1965

Region	Million metric tons coal equivalent				Percent of world total			
	1925	1950	1955	1965	1925	1950	1955	1965
				A. *Total imports*				
North America	38.2	115.2	145.1	268.1	19.2%	24.2%	19.3%	17.3%
of which: United States	18.5	67.6	100.9	210.0	9.3	14.2	13.4	13.6
Western Europe	113.4	161.5	309.9	720.8	56.8	33.9	41.2	46.6
Oceania	2.1	9.6	15.3	32.3	1.1	2.0	2.0	2.1
U.S.S.R. & Comm. E. Europe	4.7	27.4	39.8	75.9	2.3	5.8	5.3	4.9
U.S.S.R.	0.8	15.4	17.0	10.1	0.4	3.2	2.3	0.7
Comm. E. Europe	3.9	12.0	22.9	65.7	1.9	2.5	3.0	4.3
Communist Asia	4.2	n.a.	2.1	1.7	2.1	n.a.	0.3	0.1
Latin America	19.0	98.8	122.0	153.2	9.5	20.7	16.2	9.9
Caribbean	9.5	78.5	89.7	119.8	4.8	16.4	11.9	7.7
Other Latin America	9.5	20.3	32.3	33.3	4.7	4.3	4.3	2.2
Asia	11.9	47.6	91.1	250.3	5.9	10.0	12.1	16.2
Middle East	0.9	17.0	28.7	38.9	0.5	3.6	3.8	2.5
Japan	2.8	3.6	18.9	143.9	1.4	0.8	2.5	9.3
Other Asia	8.2	27.0	43.5	67.5	4.0	5.6	5.8	4.4
Africa	6.2	16.2	26.1	43.9	3.1	3.4	3.5	2.8
North Africa	4.2	6.5	10.2	11.9	2.1	1.4	1.4	0.8
Tropical Africa	1.8	6.2	11.0	22.0	0.9	1.3	1.5	1.4
South Africa	0.2	3.5	4.9	10.0	0.1	0.7	0.7	0.6
WORLD[a]	199.7	476.3	751.5	1,546.0	100.0	100.0	100.0	100.0
				B. *Total exports*				
North America	42.9	48.6	77.4	96.5	20.1%	9.8%	10.1%	6.1%
of which: United States	42.0	47.7	73.0	57.2	19.6	9.6	9.5	3.6
Western Europe	103.2	68.1	105.5	129.7	48.2	13.7	13.8	8.2
Oceania	1.0	0.1	0.7	9.3	0.5	–	0.1	0.6
U.S.S.R. & Comm. E. Europe	16.2	39.0	62.1	171.5	7.6	7.8	8.1	10.9
U.S.S.R.	2.4	4.3	17.9	123.0	1.1	0.9	2.3	7.8
Comm. E. Europe	13.8	34.7	44.2	48.6	6.4	7.0	5.8	3.1
Communist Asia	2.6	n.a.	1.1	1.8	1.2	n.a.	0.1	0.1
Latin America	29.9	185.2	239.1	354.0	14.0	37.2	31.2	22.5
Caribbean	28.5	183.4	237.3	351.9	13.3	36.9	31.0	22.4
Other Latin America	1.4	1.8	1.8	2.1	0.7	0.4	0.2	0.1
Asia	15.9	153.0	277.9	650.1	7.4	30.8	36.3	41.3
Middle East	5.9	126.7	241.3	599.4	2.7	25.5	31.5	38.1
Japan	2.8	0.5	0.4	1.4	1.3	0.1	0.1	0.1
Other Asia	7.3	25.8	238.4	49.4	3.4	5.2	4.7	3.1
Africa	2.2	3.7	2.5	161.3	1.0	0.7	0.3	10.2
North Africa	0.3	0.2	0.5	132.7	0.2	–	0.1	8.4
Tropical Africa	0.3	0.9	1.2	26.7	0.1	0.2	0.2	1.7
South Africa	1.6	1.9	0.8	1.9	0.8	0.5	0.1	0.1
WORLD[a]	214.0	497.6	766.4	1,574.2	100.0	100.0	100.0	100.0

WORLD IMPORTS, EXPORTS, AND NET TRADE IN TOTAL ENERGY, BY REGION, SELECTED YEARS, 1925-1965 (Continued)

Region	Million metric tons coal equivalent				Percent of world total			
	1925	1950	1955	1965	1925	1950	1955	1965

C. Net imports or exports (-)
(million metric tons coal equivalent)

Region	1925	1938	1950	1955	1960	1965
North America	-4.7	-17.7	66.6	67.7	133.5	171.6
of which: United States	-23.4	-37.8	19.9	27.9	102.1	152.8
Western Europe	10.1	47.2	93.4	204.4	318.0	591.1
Oceania	1.2	4.2	9.5	14.6	18.2	23.1
U.S.S.R. & Comm. E. Europe	-11.5	-17.9	-11.5	-22.3	-59.4	-95.7
U.S.S.R.	-1.6	-1.0	11.2	-0.9	-53.1	-112.8
Comm. E. Europe	-9.9	-16.9	-22.7	-21.4	-6.3	17.2
Communist Asia	1.6	-2.0	n.a.	1.0	4.4	-0.1
Latin America	-10.9	-31.5	-86.4	-117.1	-162.6	-200.9
Caribbean	-18.9	-40.2	-104.9	-147.5	-192.3	-232.1
Other Latin America	8.0	8.7	18.5	30.5	29.8	31.2
Asia	-4.0	-8.8	-105.4	-186.8	-285.6	-399.9
Middle East	-5.0	-15.9	-109.6	-212.6	-346.8	-560.5
Japan	-	11.8	3.1	18.4	56.2	142.5
Other Asia	0.9	-4.7	1.2	7.4	5.0	18.1
Africa	4.0	9.0	12.6	23.6	12.2	-117.4
North Africa	3.9	5.8	6.3	9.7	-2.5	-120.7
Tropical Africa	1.5	2.5	5.4	9.7	10.2	-4.7
South Africa	-1.4	0.7	0.9	4.1	4.5	8.0
WORLD[a]	-14.3	-17.4	-21.3	-14.9	-21.3	-28.2

[a]Worldwide imports and exports, though equal in principle (and yielding net imports of zero), differ because of various estimating problems, as discussed in the notes of Part Four, p. 821.

Source: Part Three, tables VI and VII.

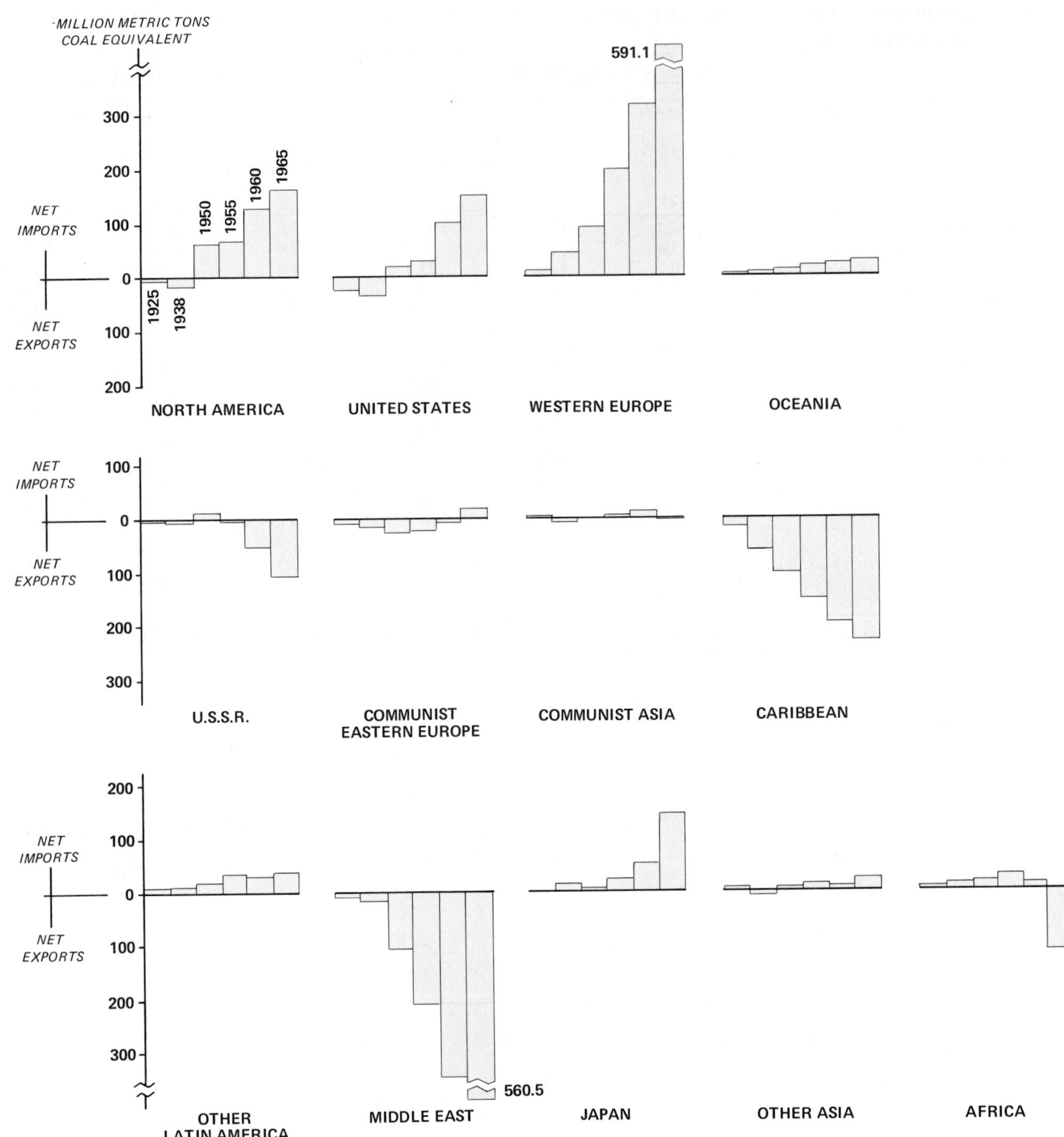

Net imports or exports of total energy, selected years, 1925–1965.

Profile No. 27

DISTRIBUTION OF REGIONAL IMPORTS AND EXPORTS, BY ENERGY SOURCE, 1925, 1950, AND 1965

Almost without exception, each area's foreign energy trade—whether total imports or exports—underwent a similar and basic transformation between 1925 and 1965: liquids replaced solids as the dominant component. All separate areas shown in the tabulation reduced the proportion of solids in their total energy imports—most of them to a substantial extent. The U.S.S.R. is the only case where coal remained the dominant category in energy imports throughout the period; however, given the country's large indigenous energy resources and output, the magnitude of total Soviet imports of energy commodities was always negligible.

On the regional export side a few more exceptions to the coal-oil shift are evident than is the case with imports. For example, coal's share in North American exports increased somewhat, to a point where it comprised exactly half the export total in 1965. Coal also remained the preponderant component of East European exports.

The reader should view these compositional changes in the context of the *absolute* quantities recorded in the right-hand panel of the table. Thus, Western Europe's rising proportion of liquids in total energy exports relates to an export total of relatively modest size and relatively little long-term growth; moreover, the region's liquid exports involve to a large extent the *intra*-West European shipments of refined oil products (e.g., from British or Dutch refineries) made from imported crude.

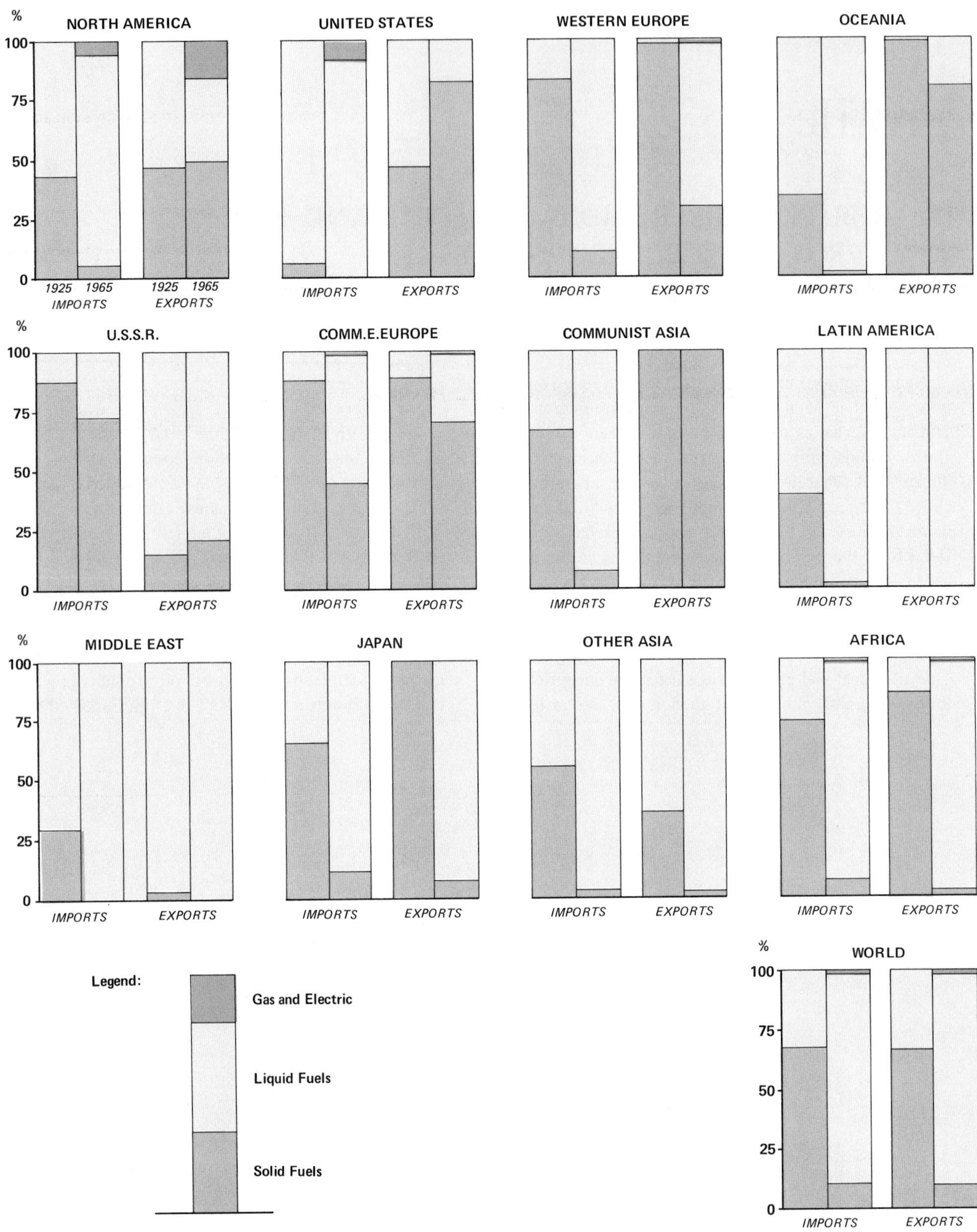

Percentage distribution, by energy source, of regional imports and exports, 1925 and 1965.

DISTRIBUTION OF REGIONAL IMPORTS AND EXPORTS, BY ENERGY SOURCE, 1925, 1950, AND 1965

Region	Percent of region						Million metric tons coal equivalent		
	Solid fuels			Liquid fuels			Total energy		
	1925	1950	1965	1925	1950	1965	1925	1950	1965
				A. *Imports*					
North America	43.6%	22.3%	5.9%	55.9%	77.4%	88.0%	38.2	115.2	268.1
of which: United States	5.8	1.1	0.1	93.3	98.6	92.1	18.5	67.6	210.0
Western Europe	82.8	37.9	11.2	17.1	61.8	88.5	113.4	161.5	720.8
Oceania	35.0	6.9	1.0	65.0	93.1	99.0	2.1	9.6	32.3
U.S.S.R. & Comm. E. Europe	87.8	75.0	48.4	12.0	24.7	50.2	4.7	27.4	75.9
U.S.S.R.	87.7	73.8	73.1	12.3	26.2	26.9	0.8	15.4	10.1
Comm. E. Europe	87.8	76.5	44.6	12.0	22.7	53.8	3.9	12.0	65.7
Communist Asia	66.5	n.a.	8.3	33.5	n.a.	91.7	4.2	n.a.	1.7
Latin America	38.1	3.0	1.7	61.9	96.1	98.3	19.0	98.8	153.2
Asia	55.2	6.5	7.6	44.8	93.3	92.4	11.9	47.6	250.3
Middle East	29.2	0.9	0.1	70.3	99.0	99.9	0.9	17.0	38.9
Japan	64.5	23.2	11.9	35.5	76.8	88.1	2.8	3.6	143.9
Other Asia	54.8	7.8	2.7	45.1	91.9	97.3	8.2	27.0	67.5
Africa	74.4	17.1	6.4	25.6	82.8	92.9	6.2	16.2	43.9
WORLD[a]	68.4	24.5	10.2	31.5	75.1	88.5	199.7	476.3	1,546.0
				B. *Exports*					
North America	47.4%	57.2%	50.0%	52.2%	40.1%	34.9%	42.9	48.6	96.5
of which: United States	46.7	56.9	82.2	53.3	40.8	17.8	42.0	47.7	57.2
Western Europe	98.8	78.9	28.9	1.1	20.7	70.1	103.2	68.1	129.7
Oceania	99.1	82.2	79.1	0.9	17.8	20.9	1.0	0.1	9.3
U.S.S.R. & Comm. E. Europe	77.2	84.9	34.6	22.8	14.9	64.8	16.2	39.0	171.5
U.S.S.R.	15.1	60.7	21.0	84.9	38.5	78.4	2.4	4.3	123.0
Comm. E. Europe	88.1	87.9	69.1	11.9	12.0	30.2	13.8	34.7	48.6
Communist Asia	100.0	n.a.	100.0	–	n.a.	–	2.6	n.a.	1.8
Latin America	0.1	0.1	–	99.9	99.9	99.5	29.9	185.2	354.0
Asia	34.6	1.1	0.2	65.4	98.9	86.4	15.9	153.0	650.1
Middle East	2.6	–	–	97.4	100.0	100.0	5.9	126.7	599.4
Japan	99.2	100.0	6.8	0.8	–	93.2	2.8	0.5	1.4
Other Asia	36.0	4.5	2.3	64.0	95.2	97.5	7.3	25.8	49.4
Africa	85.7	99.9	2.1	14.3	0.1	97.1	2.2	3.7	161.3
WORLD[a]	68.2	24.2	10.1	31.7	75.5	88.6	214.0	497.6	1,574.2

[a]Worldwide imports (both percentages and absolutes), though equal in principle, differ because of various estimating problems, as discussed in the notes of Part Four, p. 821.

[b]The percentages may fall short of 100 because gas and electricity are not shown separately. Where there *is* a gas and/or electricity component, it always refers to *net* imports in panel A and to *net* exports in panel B.

Source: Part Three, tables VI and VIII.

Profile No. 28

WORLD SOLID FUELS TRADE: PERCENTAGE DISTRIBUTION BY LEADING COUNTRIES, SELECTED YEARS, 1925-1965

This profile highlights changes in individual country shares of the world coal trade. Long-term developments on the import side (tabulated in panel A of the table) are less dramatic than those in exports. Among coal importers, Japan in 1965 was the front-ranking nation, with over 10 percent of world imports (representing about 17 million tons) as well as the country with the sharpest rising percentage share; back in 1925, Japan had accounted for around 1 percent of world coal imports—a bit higher than the immediate post-World War II percentage at the start of the country's remarkable period of reconstruction and industrial expansion. Large-scale coke requirements for steel making, coupled with domestic scarcity of high-quality coking coal reserves and the decline of Japan's own (high-cost) coal mines, have helped spur the expanding volume of solid fuels imports.

Most of the West European countries have tended to take diminishing portions of world coal imports, with France's historic decline particularly conspicuous in this regard. The Communist countries have all accounted for rising percentages of world imports.

The export panel exhibits some fairly spectacular cases of long-term change—the foremost being Great Britain's steady decline from 38 percent of world coal exports in 1925 to a mere 3 percent in 1965. In absolute terms, no less than percentagewise, the historic drop was large and persistent, the peak volume having been recorded as long ago as 1929:

British Solid Fuels Exports[1]
(in million metric tons coal equivalent)

Year	
1925	55.0
1929	65.4
1938	38.8
1950	16.1
1955	14.4
1960	6.7
1965	4.8

[1]From Part Three, table VI.

In the post-World War II period, the sharpest break occurred between 1955 and 1960. It was during this period that the West European urge to preserve a strong indigenous output capability tended to recede. In the ensuing years of production cutbacks (not always sufficient to preclude the buildup of excessive inventories) and increasing competition from U.S. coal, Great Britain's falling exports became symptomatic of the general malaise of European coal. The following figures illustrate how U.S. and British coal compared in certain markets between 1955 and 1965:

British and U.S. Coal Exports in Selected European Markets[2]
(in million metric tons coal equivalent)

		1955	*1965*
France	United Kingdom	1.0	0.8
	United States	1.0	1.9
Belgium-Luxembourg	United Kingdom	0.5	0.3
	United States	1.0	2.0
West Germany	United Kingdom	1.2	0.6
	United States	6.1	4.3
Ireland	United Kingdom	1.9	0.4
	United States	-	0.3
Italy	United Kingdom	0.8	-
	United States	6.0	8.1
Netherlands	United Kingdom	0.8	1.0
	United States	4.5	3.1
Sweden	United Kingdom	1.0	0.3
	United States	0.6	0.8

U.S. coal exports have followed a somewhat erratic long-term course. This is evident in the trend of its percentage shares as well as in its volumetric trend. The latter series shows a pre-World War II decline from around 20 million tons in 1925 to 12 million tons in 1938; a rising trend during the first postwar decade, with

[2]From United Nations, *World Energy Supplies*, Series J, various numbers.

a figure going from around 30 million tons to a peak of 74 million tons during the 1957 Suez crisis; a subsequent fall to around 34 million tons in the early 1960s, which was then reversed, and, coinciding with the indicated upsurge in the U.S. percentage share, went up to around 47 million tons in 1965.[3]

[3]The absolute figures cited appear in Part Three, table VI.

Other countries whose positions in worldwide solid fuels exports have shifted markedly over the years include: West Germany—in general, downward; the Soviet Union and Poland—both up over the long run, although Poland's early postwar high had receded by the 1960s; and Australia—expanding exports to Japan were a principal factor in the country's rising share from a bit over 1 percent in 1960 to over 4½ percent in 1965.

WORLD SOLID FUELS TRADE: PERCENTAGE DISTRIBUTION BY LEADING COUNTRIES, SELECTED YEARS, 1925-1965

Country[a]	1925	1938	1950	1955	1960	1965
			A. *Imports*			
Japan	1.3%	5.4%	0.7%	1.8%	6.3%	10.8%
France	21.4	17.5	11.5	10.4	11.6	10.6
Canada	11.4	9.6	21.3	11.8	9.5	9.8
East Germany[b]	–	–	5.5	6.4	9.1	8.9
Belgium-Luxembourg	8.3	5.3	3.0	4.7	6.1	6.9
West Germany[b]	6.0	5.4	1.8	9.8	7.8	6.8
Italy	7.6	9.6	7.1	6.7	7.8	6.8
Netherlands	6.6	6.7	4.2	5.7	5.9	4.7
U.S.S.R.	0.5	0.8	9.8	5.8	4.1	4.7
Czechoslovakia	1.3	0.7	1.5	2.7	2.2	3.2
Austria	3.7	3.0	4.5	3.2	3.8	2.9
Denmark	2.9	4.3	4.9	4.7	4.0	2.7
Hungary	0.8	0.4	0.6	1.2	2.0	2.6
Finland	0.4	1.4	1.6	1.7	2.4	2.1
Sweden	3.1	6.2	5.7	3.6	2.7	1.9
Bulgaria	–	–	n.a.	0.1	0.2	1.8
Yugoslavia	0.4	0.4	0.4	0.7	1.3	1.4
Spain	1.6	0.3	0.9	0.4	0.3	1.1
Poland	0.2	0.1	–	0.1	0.9	1.1
Romania	0.2	0.1	0.2	0.4	0.8	1.0
Total above 20	77.7	77.2	85.2	81.9	88.8	91.8
All other countries	22.3	22.8	14.8	18.1	11.2	8.2
WORLD	100.0	100.0	100.0	100.0	100.0	100.0
WORLD (mill. metric tons coal equivalent)[c]	(136.6)	(125.7)	(116.9)	(155.1)	(132.1)	(157.9)
			B. *Exports*			
United States	13.4%	9.0%	22.6%	31.7%	26.2%	29.6%
U.S.S.R.	0.3	0.3	2.2	3.7	11.1	16.3
Poland	5.6	7.8	23.6	17.4	15.8	15.7
West Germany[b]	25.9	29.7	25.6	18.8	21.9	14.8
Australia	0.7	0.3	0.1	0.2	1.3	4.6
Netherlands	2.2	4.6	0.9	1.8	3.6	3.2
United Kingdom	37.7	29.9	13.4	9.2	5.1	3.0
Czechoslovakia	2.4	2.3	0.8	1.5	3.2	2.8
East Germany[b]	–	–	0.9	2.3	3.2	2.6
Belgium-Luxembourg	2.6	4.8	2.6	5.3	2.3	1.5
Communist Asia[d]	1.8	3.2	n.a.	0.7	0.8	1.1
Rhodesia	0.2	0.4	0.7	0.6	1.0	1.1
Total above 12	92.8	92.3	93.4	93.2	95.5	96.3
All other countries	7.2	7.7	6.6	6.8	4.5	3.7
WORLD	100.0	100.0	100.0	100.0	100.0	100.0
WORLD (mill. metric tons coal equivalent)[c]	(145.8)	(129.7)	(120.2)	(157.2)	(133.0)	(158.7)

[a]The countries shown are those accounting for 1% or more of solid fuels imports or exports in 1965; the countries are listed in descending order according to their 1965 percentage shares.

[b]West Germany figures for 1925 and 1938 apply to *all* of pre-World War II Germany.

[c]Worldwide imports and exports, though equal in principle, differ because of various estimating problems, as discussed in the notes of Part Four, p. 821.

[d]Comprises Mainland China (1925-65), Mongolia and North Korea (1950-65), and North Vietnam (1955-65). Mainland China, for which no separate data are available for 1950-65, undoubtedly dominates the Communist Asia total for that period.

Source: Part Three, table VI.

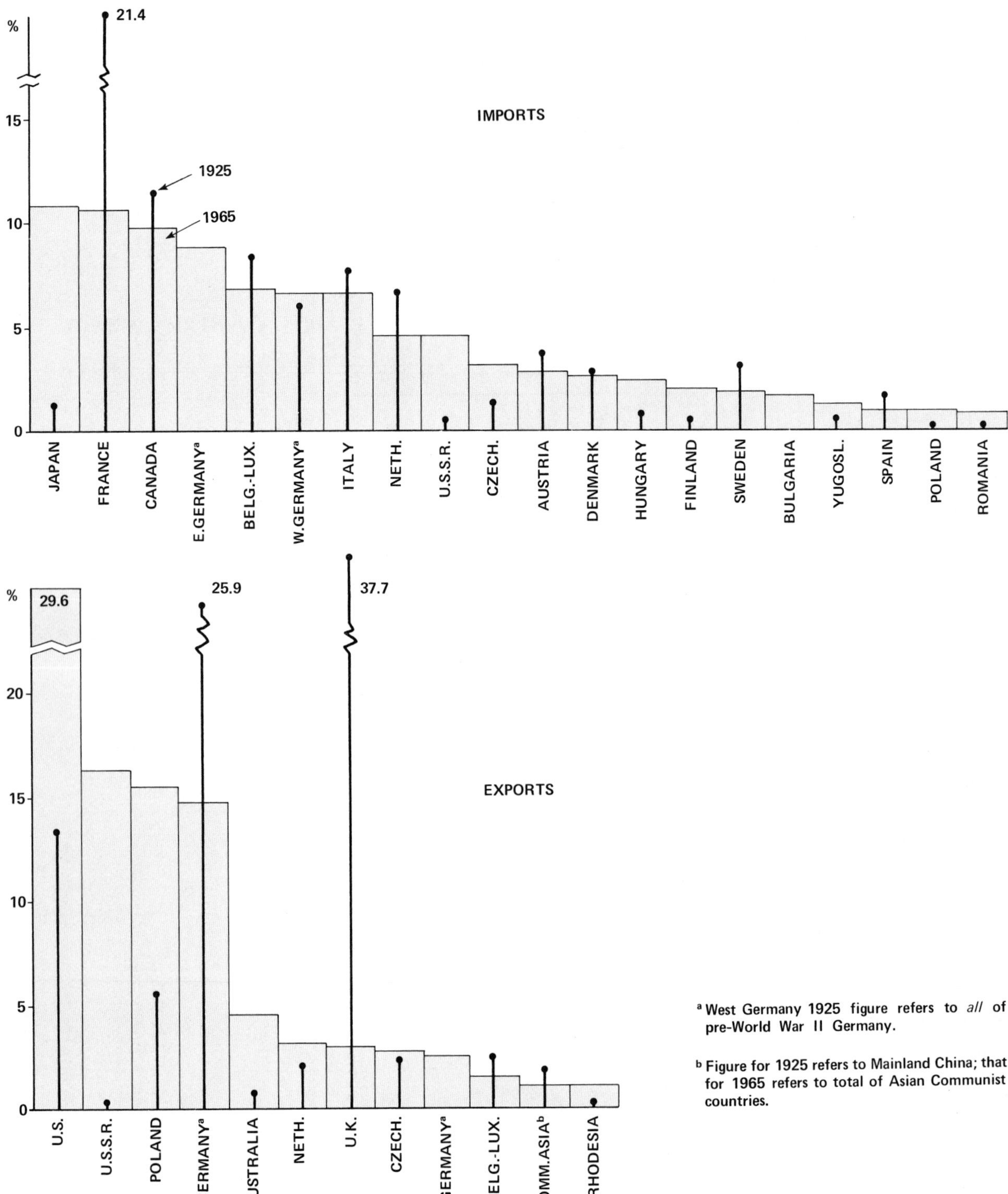

World solid fuels trade, percentage distribution by leading countries, 1925 and 1965.

Profile No.29

WORLD LIQUID FUELS TRADE: PERCENTAGE DISTRIBUTION BY LEADING COUNTRIES, SELECTED YEARS, 1925-1965

While there has been considerable reshuffling in their order of importance, the world's principal oil importers[1] of 1925 by and large maintained their places among the top-ranking group of importing countries over the ensuing four decades. Of the ten leading importers in 1925, nine remained among the top ten of 1965, with the United States and United Kingdom holding the first and second spots in both years. However, Great Britain's 1965 share of 9.3 percent of world imports tied her with Japan which, with a share of under 1 percent in 1950, was the most rapidly advancing oil importer.

Although the United States and Great Britain alone accounted for 42 percent of world liquid fuels imports in 1925, the circumstances of these two countries with respect to oil differed. As shown in Profile No. 17, in the United States oil had already attained a respectable portion (19 percent) of total energy consumption by 1925. Moreover, the United States was then a net *exporter* of oil (see Profile No. 25). The U.S. share of world oil imports subsequently dropped even as the U.S. net export position declined and vanished. In the United Kingdom oil in 1925 accounted for under 4 percent of energy consumption, all of which had to be imported. However, the United Kingdom was by European standards already a relatively motorized country and, in addition, required a fairly large amount of oil–some 20 percent of liquid fuels imports–as bunkers for the maritime trade.[2]

[1]A few countries (e.g., the Netherlands Antilles and Trinidad) owe their places among the leading oil importers as well as exporters not to their roles as producers or consumers, but rather to their positions as refiners and exporters of petroleum products made from imported crude oil. This also explains the appearance of France and Great Britain among leading oil exporters.

While the United Kingdom's share dropped off somewhat, a number of countries raised their shares of world oil imports over the years–among them the leading West European countries. Canada's share dropped, as virtually total reliance on imported liquids in 1925 was partially reduced through availability of indigenous supplies after World War II. The country nonetheless remained a net oil importer for the entire period covered by this study. It is notable that no Communist country appears on the list of leading oil importers; the Soviet Union's absence is explained by the availability of domestic oil, while the absence of the other countries is due to the sustained preeminence of coal in their economies.

Shifts in the export rankings have been far more striking. Note that two nations alone, the United States and Mexico, shared between themselves, in a roughly 50-50 ratio, close to two-thirds of world exports in 1925. By 1965 the two together accounted for just 1 percent of the total. (Following intervening declines, Mexico's oil output in 1965 was no higher than it had been in 1925; and the latter year, in turn, represented a sharp falling off from a peak reached around 1920.) Over one-third of world oil exports in 1965 came from just four countries–Kuwait, Saudi Arabia, Iraq, and Libya–none of which had exported any oil in 1925. Indonesia's share of world oil exports had been nearly as important as Venezuela's back in the mid-1920s, but by 1965 its share had dropped to below 2 percent. Nevertheless, Indonesia's potential oil resources are believed to be large enough to justify expectations for renewed importance in the future.

[2]Data on bunkers appear in Part Three, table IX.

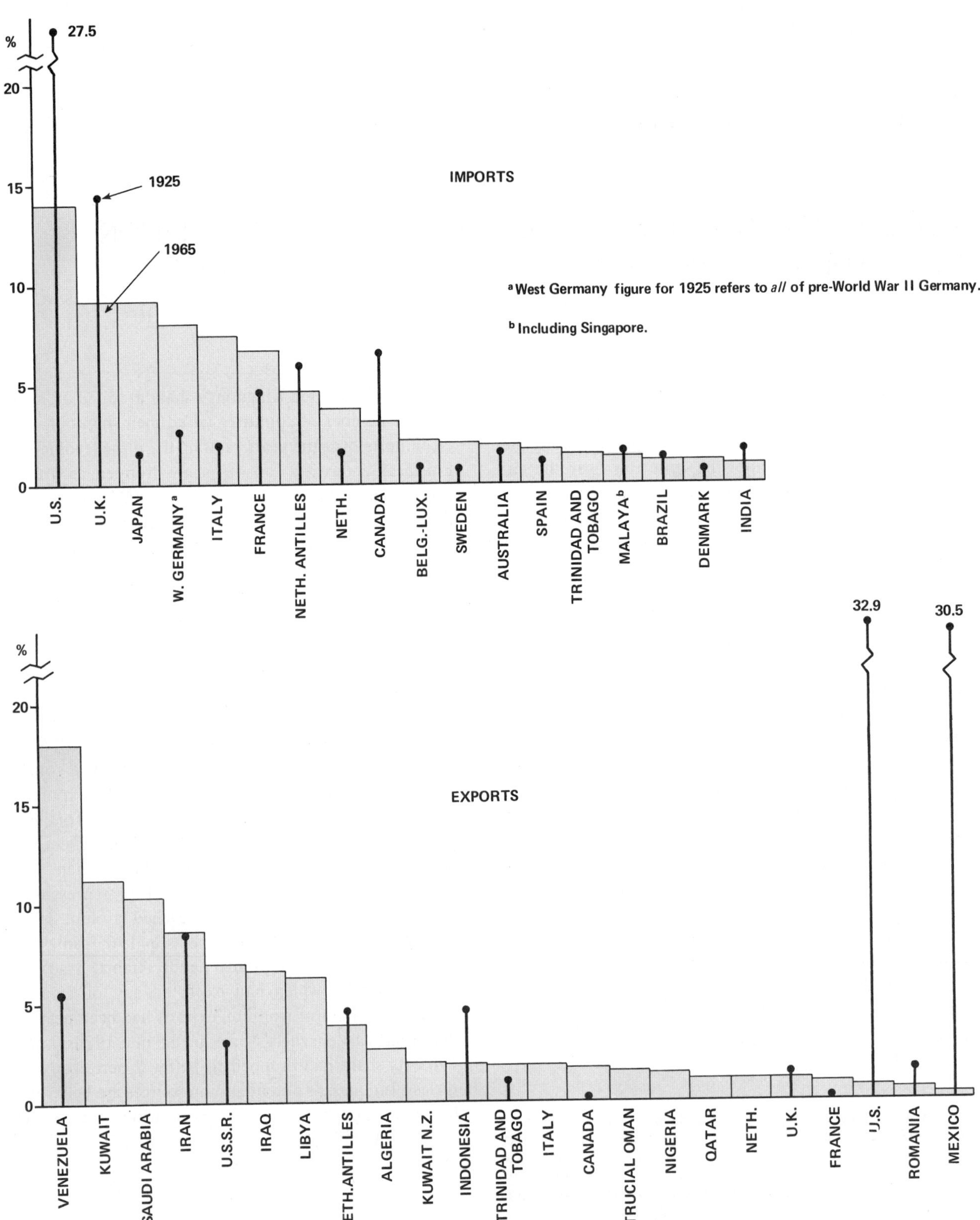

World liquid fuels trade, percentage distribution by leading countries, 1925 and 1965.

WORLD LIQUID FUELS TRADE: PERCENTAGE DISTRIBUTION BY LEADING COUNTRIES, SELECTED YEARS, 1925–1965

Country[a]	1925	1938	1950	1955	1960	1965
			A. *Imports*			
United States	27.5%	7.7%	18.7%	16.8%	16.8%	14.1%
United Kingdom	14.5	11.3	8.1	9.3	10.4	9.3
Japan	1.6	4.5	0.8	2.7	5.7	9.3
West Germany[b]	2.7	4.2	1.2	2.5	5.3	8.2
Italy	1.9	2.5	2.2	4.4	5.4	7.6
France	4.7	7.9	6.1	6.5	5.9	6.8
Netherlands Antilles	5.9	25.7	18.7	11.8	7.2	4.7
Netherlands	1.6	2.0	2.5	3.6	4.0	3.8
Canada	6.5	5.5	6.3	4.3	3.9	3.1
Belgium-Luxembourg	0.8	1.0	1.0	1.8	1.8	2.2
Sweden	0.7	1.3	1.5	2.0	2.3	2.1
Australia	1.6	2.1	2.0	2.1	2.2	2.0
Spain	1.1	1.1	1.6	1.6	1.6	1.7
Trinidad and Tobago	–	0.1	0.7	0.6	1.0	1.4
Malaya (including Singapore)[c]	1.6	1.2	1.5	1.7	1.2	1.3
Brazil	1.3	1.1	1.8	2.2	1.8	1.2
Denmark	0.7	0.8	0.8	0.8	0.9	1.2
India	1.7	1.8	1.2	1.2	1.3	1.0
Total above 18	76.4	81.8	76.7	75.9	78.7	81.0
All other countries	23.6	18.2	23.3	24.1	21.3	19.0
WORLD	100.0	100.0	100.0	100.0	100.0	100.0
WORLD (mill. metric tons coal equivalent)[d]	(62.8)	(156.0)	(357.5)	(594.4)	(851.3)	(1,368.0)
WORLD (mill. metric tons original units)[d]	(41.9)	(104.0)	(238.3)	(396.2)	(567.5)	(912.0)
			B. *Exports*			
Venezuela	5.9%	24.4%	30.1%	26.3%	23.6%	18.0%
Kuwait	–	–	6.5	13.1	13.3	11.2
Saudi Arabia	–	–	9.9	11.1	10.0	10.4
Iran	8.4	6.3	11.6	3.2	7.7	8.7
U.S.S.R.	3.0	1.3	0.4	2.0	5.7	6.9
Iraq	–	3.7	2.5	7.9	7.8	6.6
Libya	–	–	–	–	–	6.3
Netherlands Antilles	4.5	20.1	15.0	9.7	5.7	3.9
Algeria	–	–	–	–	1.4	2.7
Kuwait Neutral Zone	–	–	n.a.	0.3	1.1	2.0
Indonesia	4.6	5.0	2.4	2.2	2.9	1.9
Trinidad and Tobago	1.0	1.5	1.1	1.0	1.6	1.8
Italy	–	0.1	0.3	1.2	1.2	1.8
Canada	0.1	–	–	0.5	1.1	1.7
Trucial Oman	–	–	–	–	–	1.5
Nigeria	–	–	–	–	0.2	1.4
Qatar	–	–	0.6	1.3	1.4	1.2
Netherlands	–	–	1.1	1.8	1.9	1.2
United Kingdom	1.4	0.4	0.5	1.6	1.6	1.2
France	0.1	0.5	1.3	1.3	1.1	1.0
United States	32.9	22.9	5.2	3.7	1.5	0.7
Romania	1.7	3.6	1.0	1.4	1.0	0.6
Mexico	30.5	1.6	0.9	1.0	0.2	0.3
Total above 23	94.1	91.4	90.4	90.6	92.0	93.0
All other countries	5.9	8.6	9.6	9.4	8.0	7.0
WORLD	100.0	100.0	100.0	100.0	100.0	100.0
WORLD (mill. metric tons coal equivalent)[d]	(67.9)	(169.4)	(375.6)	(606.9)	(871.7)	(1,395.4)
WORLD (mill. metric tons original units)[d]	(45.3)	(112.9)	(250.4)	(404.6)	(581.1)	(930.2)

[a]The countries shown are those accounting for 1% or more of liquid fuel imports or exports in 1965. Exceptions are United States, Romania, and Mexico exports–listed because of their past importance. The countries are listed in descending order according to their 1965 percentage shares.

[b]West Germany figures for 1925 and 1938 apply to *all* of pre-World War II Germany.

[c]Excluding Malaysian states of Sabah and Sarawak.

[d]Worldwide imports and exports, though equal in principle, differ because of various estimating problems, as discussed in the notes of Part Four, p. 821.

Note: Several of the importing and exporting countries shown owe their position in the ranking to their role as refiners of crude oil and exporters of the refined fuels. The Netherlands Antilles is the major example.

Source: Part Three, tables IV and VI.

Profile No. 30

LIQUID FUELS TRADE, BY TYPE OF FUEL AND MAJOR REGION, 1925 AND 1965

This profile contrasts the composition of regional and worldwide trade in types of liquid fuels at widely separated points in time. The historic shift with which we are most concerned here, and which is immediately evident, has to do with the rising proportion of crude oil and the declining proportion of refined products within the total international liquid fuels trade. Within refined products, in turn, worldwide trade in fuel oils (including diesel fuel) has risen somewhat relative to trade in the other three product groups shown (gasoline, kerosine, and lubricants). That shift is probably due to the combined effect of railroad dieselization, the growth of fuel oil for bunkers and as a generating-station boiler fuel, and the impact of oil heating.[1]

With the exceptions of North America and Soviet Russia, where already existing refineries processing indigenous crude for the domestic market could also handle imported crude, each region shown in panel A of the table imported the bulk of its 1925 liquids in the form of refined products rather than crude oil. The composition of 1925 exports (shown in panel B) was similar, with the exception of the Caribbean which, as the region largely supplying existing refineries in the North American market, shipped a bit less than two-thirds in the form of crude oil and the balance as refined products.

By 1965, the earlier picture had essentially reversed itself for a number of significant oil-trading areas; and worldwide, nearly three-fourths of total world exports (or imports) consisted of crude oil—double the proportion of 1925. Among the exceptions was the United States (though, because of Canadian crude exports to the United States, not North America as a whole), whose insignificant liquid fuels exports took the form largely of specialized refined products. The crude oil share of Caribbean exports had dropped a bit by 1965; and since these figures measure intraregional as well as interregional exports, if we exclude Venezuelan crude oil shipments to the Netherlands Antilles prior to their being exported as refined products (heavily dominated by residual fuel oil to the North American market), the ratio would tip even further towards refined items from the Caribbean.[2] Similarly, the fact that Western Europe and a few other areas continued to export liquids mostly in the form of products is explained largely by the intraregional exports of refined products made from imported crude.

By definition, the historic shift from crude oil to products in the international liquid fuels trade reflected the growth of refining capacity in major consuming areas such as Western Europe. (See also Profile No. 31.) Among the underlying reasons for this development, improvements in refining technology form the first part of a suggested explanation.[3] With progressively better distillation techniques reducing from 25-50 percent to 5-10 percent the losses associated with the processing of crude oil, there was an advantage (or, at least, less of a disadvantage) in bringing about a gradual shift of refinery location from raw material source to markets. Second, larger markets, permitting the realization of economies of scale at point of delivery or utilization, tended to encourage increased shipment of crude over refined products. Third, both tanker size as well as handling characteristics of the cargo favored crude oil

[1]This study is concerned with energy production and consumption measured, if possible, at the primary stage and thus does not specifically consider output and the consumption of secondary fuels such as refined petroleum products. However, the latter must be taken into account in foreign energy trade in order to obtain a proper measure of both trade, in which they figure prominently, and consumption in those countries in which foreign trade is an important element in supply.

[2]The sum of Caribbean *net* exports of crude oil plus *net* exports of refined products in 1965 broke down with 40 percent for the former and 60 percent for the latter. (See Part Three, table VI.) An explanatory note appended to Profile No. 23 discusses different foreign trade measures used in this study.

[3]The indicated explanations are suggested by Gerald Manners, *The Geography of Energy* (London: Hutchinson University Library, 1964), pp. 183 ff.

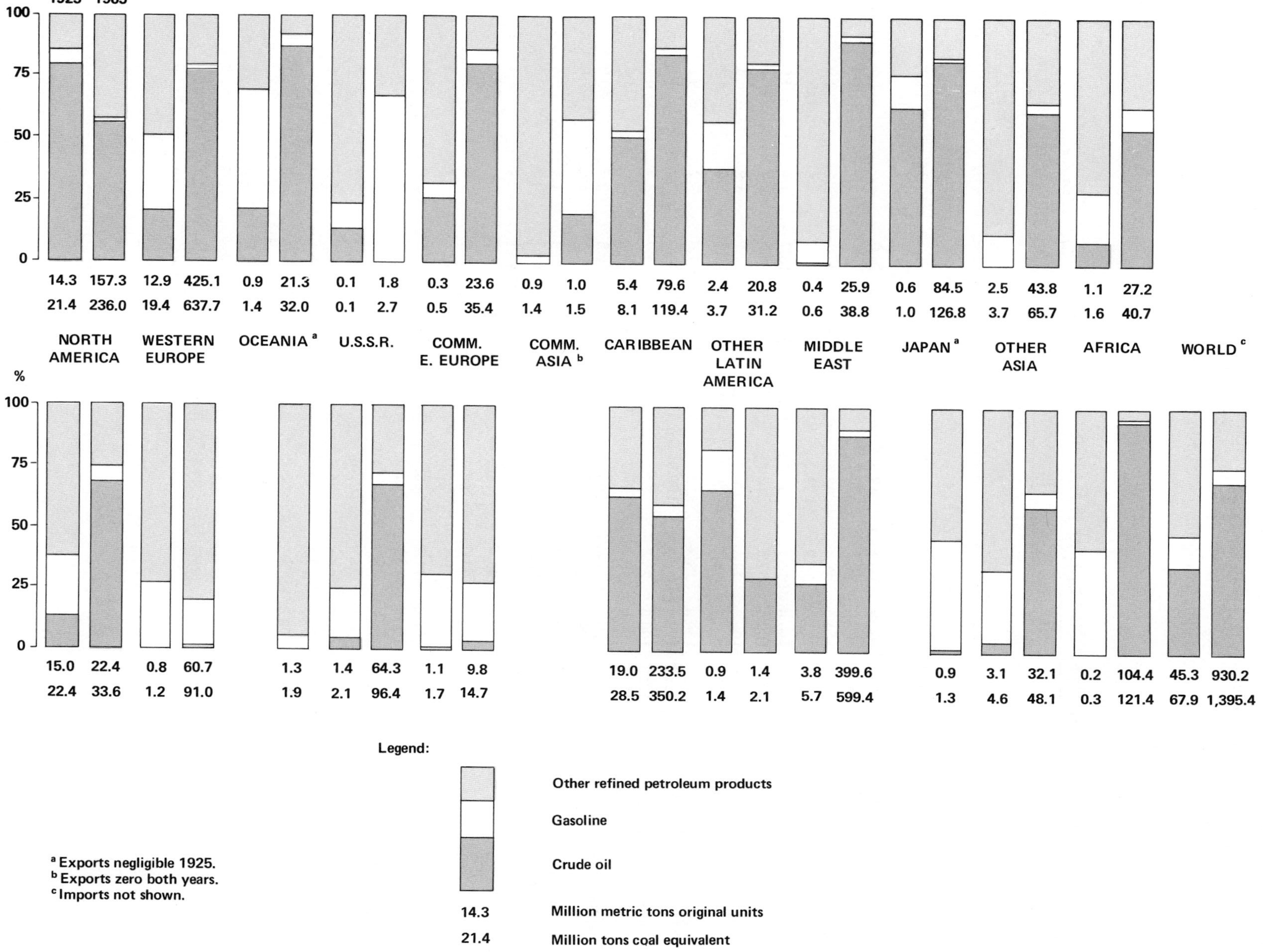

Percentage distribution, by type of fuel, of regional liquid fuel imports and exports, 1925 and 1965.

over refined fuels. Fourth, there was an advantage in permitting refineries the flexibility of switching among different geographical sources of crude as market conditions dictated, and this could be best achieved by locating refineries near the point of consumption rather than near the oil fields. Finally—and particularly with respect to Western European countries—political-strategic factors, as well as the dollar shortage in the earlier post-World War II years, contributed to decisions to build refineries close at hand.

LIQUID FUELS TRADE, BY TYPE OF FUEL AND MAJOR REGION, 1925 AND 1965

Region and year		Percent of liquid fuels								Total liquid fuels *(mill. metric tons)*	
				Refined petroleum products							
		Total liquid fuels	Crude oil	Total[a]	Gasoline	Kerosine	Fuel oils	Lubes & greases		Original units	Coal equiv.
				A. Total imports							
North America	1925	100.0%	80.6%	19.4%	5.1%	0.1%	13.9%	0.3%		14.3	21.4
	1965	100.0	56.9	43.1	1.1	2.7	38.6	0.2		157.3	236.0
of which: United States	1925	100.0	80.1	19.9	3.9	–	16.0	–		11.5	17.3
	1965	100.0	53.8	46.2	1.2	3.1	41.5	–		129.0	193.5
Western Europe	1925	100.0	21.6	78.4	29.3	13.2	25.3	10.6		12.9	19.4
	1965	100.0	76.8	23.2	3.1	1.3	18.2	0.4		425.1	637.7
Oceania	1925	100.0	22.1	77.9	48.5	13.8	10.2	5.4		0.9	1.4
	1965	100.0	87.5	12.5	5.7	2.4	3.5	0.9		21.3	32.0
U.S.S.R. & Comm. E. Europe	1925	100.0	23.5	76.5	7.2	23.5	5.1	4.8		0.4	0.6
	1965	100.0	74.4	25.6	10.4	1.9	12.7	0.6		25.4	38.1
U.S.S.R.	1925	100.0	13.8	86.2	10.8	61.5	4.6	9.2		0.1	0.1
	1965	100.0	–	100.0	67.2	9.3	15.2	8.3		1.8	2.7
Comm. E. Europe	1925	100.0	25.6	74.4	6.5	15.5	5.2	3.9		0.3	0.5
	1965	100.0	80.1	19.9	6.0	1.3	12.5	–		23.6	35.4
Communist Asia	1925	100.0	–	100.0	2.7	84.4	10.3	2.7		0.9	1.4
	1965	100.0	20.4	79.6	38.3	7.8	33.5	n.a.		1.0	1.5
Latin America	1925	100.0	47.3	52.6	7.3	3.5	40.4	1.4		7.8	11.8
	1965	100.0	84.2	15.8	2.4	1.2	10.7	0.5		100.4	150.6
Caribbean	1925	100.0	51.6	48.3	1.9	0.9	45.1	0.4		5.4	8.1
	1965	100.0	85.4	14.6	2.4	1.1	10.2	–		79.6	119.4
Other Latin America	1925	100.0	37.8	62.2	19.5	9.2	30.0	3.6		2.4	3.7
	1965	100.0	79.5	20.5	2.2	2.0	12.8	1.7		20.8	31.2
Asia	1925	100.0	11.9	88.1	11.9	28.0	43.1	5.0		3.5	5.3
	1965	100.0	78.1	21.9	1.8	2.2	16.9	0.6		154.2	231.3
Middle East	1925	100.0	0.3	99.7	8.5	37.0	53.9	0.5		0.4	0.6
	1965	100.0	91.0	9.0	1.6	0.5	6.4	0.4		25.9	38.8
Japan	1925	100.0	64.8	35.3	11.7	15.4	3.9	4.3		0.6	1.0
	1965	100.0	82.5	17.5	0.6	–	16.0	0.3		84.5	126.8
Other Asia	1925	100.0	–	100.0	12.6	29.8	51.6	6.0		2.5	3.7
	1965	100.0	62.1	37.9	4.4	7.3	24.9	1.2		43.8	65.7
Africa	1925	100.0	9.3	90.7	20.0	36.6	25.2	5.8		1.1	1.6
	1965	100.0	55.9	44.1	9.5	5.3	27.5	1.7		27.2	40.7
WORLD[b]	1925	100.0	44.9	55.1	14.9	10.5	24.9	4.4		41.9	62.8
	1965	100.0	73.9	26.1	2.9	1.9	20.5	0.5		912.0	1,368.0

LIQUID FUELS TRADE, BY TYPE OF FUEL AND MAJOR REGION, 1925 AND 1965 (Continued)

Region and year		Percent of liquid fuels								Total liquid fuels (mill. metric tons)	
		Total liquid fuels	Crude oil	Refined petroleum products						Original units	Coal equiv.
				Total[a]	Gasoline	Kerosine	Fuel oils	Lubes & greases			
						B. Total exports					
North America	1925	100.0%	12.9%	87.1%	25.0%	18.3%	34.5%	9.3%		15.0	22.4
	1965	100.0	65.8	34.2	3.5	0.5	13.7	10.6		22.4	33.6
of which: United States	1925	100.0	12.8	87.2	25.0	18.4	34.6	9.3		14.9	22.4
	1965	100.0	2.3	97.7	11.2	1.5	40.2	35.2		6.8	10.2
Western Europe	1925	100.0	-	100.0	25.4	11.0	50.1	13.5		0.8	1.2
	1965	100.0	0.7	99.3	19.8	5.6	69.3	2.8		60.7	91.0
Oceania	1925[c]	100.0	16.7	83.3	33.3	16.7	16.7	16.7		-	-
	1965	100.0	-	100.0	5.2	4.3	86.5	4.1		1.3	1.9
U.S.S.R. & Comm. E. Europe	1925	100.0	2.7	97.3	24.7	34.8	28.6	8.9		2.5	3.7
	1965	100.0	59.1	40.9	6.3	2.0	31.8	0.8		74.1	111.1
U.S.S.R.	1925	100.0	4.6	95.4	20.3	33.1	34.8	7.3		1.4	2.1
	1965	100.0	67.5	32.4	3.7	1.8	26.5	0.4		64.3	96.4
Comm. E. Europe	1925	100.0	0.4	99.7	30.3	37.1	20.8	10.9		1.1	1.7
	1965	100.0	3.9	96.1	23.9	2.9	66.1	3.1		9.8	14.7
Communist Asia	1925	-	-	-	-	-	-	-		-	-
	1965	-	-	-	-	-	-	-		-	-
Latin America	1925	100.0	63.7	36.3	4.4	0.9	30.7	0.4		19.9	29.9
	1965	100.0	55.5	44.5	4.4	3.4	36.0	0.5		234.9	352.3
Caribbean	1925	100.0	63.6	36.4	3.8	0.8	31.5	0.4		19.0	28.5
	1965	100.0	55.7	44.3	4.4	3.4	35.8	0.5		233.5	350.2
Other Latin America	1925	100.0	66.8	33.2	15.6	2.7	14.7	0.1		0.9	1.4
	1965	100.0	29.5	70.5	-	0.1	67.7	0.3		1.4	2.1
Asia	1925	100.0	17.4	82.6	17.2	8.1	56.7	0.6		6.9	10.4
	1965	100.0	86.5	13.5	2.1	1.6	9.5	-		432.5	648.8
Middle East	1925	100.0	27.6	72.4	8.2	3.0	61.2	-		3.8	5.7
	1965	100.0	88.8	11.2	1.7	1.3	7.9	-		399.6	599.4
Japan	1925[c]	100.0	-	100.0	-	52.2	26.1	21.7		-	-
	1965	100.0	0.7	99.3	45.3	20.9	23.0	9.0		0.9	1.3
Other Asia	1925	100.0	5.0	95.0	28.3	14.2	51.2	1.4		3.1	4.6
	1965	100.0	60.6	39.4	6.3	4.6	28.3	0.2		32.1	48.1
Africa	1925	100.0	-	100.0	42.3	49.3	8.0	0.5		0.2	0.3
	1965	100.0	94.9	5.1	1.1	0.2	3.8	-		104.4	121.4
WORLD[b]	1925	100.0	35.1	64.9	14.8	10.0	36.0	4.0		45.3	67.9
	1965	100.0	71.2	28.8	4.1	2.2	21.4	0.7		930.2	1,395.4

[a]Includes liquefied petroleum gases, not shown separately.

[b]Worldwide imports and exports (both in volume and percentage distribution by type of fuel), though equal in principle, may differ because of various estimating problems, as discussed in the notes of Part Four, p. 821.

[c]Exports amounted to less than the minimum 50,000 recorded in the last two columns above.

Source: Part Three, tables IV and VI.

Profile No. 31

CRUDE OIL PROCESSING CAPACITY OF WORLD REFINERIES, BY MAJOR REGIONS, 1937 AND 1965

The long-term rise in the share of crude oil and the diminishing share of refined product shipments in international trade (as shown in Profile No. 30) is seen here to have coincided with a large expansion of crude oil processing facilities in such major liquid fuels consuming and importing areas of the world as Western Europe, Japan, and Oceania. The share of world refining capacity for these three regions went up from around 5½ percent in 1937 to nearly 30 percent in 1965.[1] Expansion of their refining capacity grew faster than their rise in liquid fuels consumption. For example, in 1937 Western Europe already accounted for about 12 percent of the world's oil consumption, while possessing only 5 percent of worldwide refining capacity. In 1965, the area's share was roughly one-fifth in both cases.

In absolute terms, all regions shown expanded their refining capacity substantially. North America raised its capacity from around 175 million tons in 1937 to nearly 600 million tons in 1965—representing an average annual growth rate of 5½ percent. Nonetheless, this increase, being relatively smaller than the worldwide rise in refinery capacity, resulted in a substantial drop of North America's share of the worldwide total. This relative decline is explained by the fact that development of North American refinery capacity, compared, say, with that in Western Europe or Japan, got an early start arising from the presence of large quantities of indigenous crude oil.

The Communist group of countries (essentially the U.S.S.R.) did not significantly change its percentage share of world refining capacity. Historically a negligible importer of crude oil, and hence, as in the case of the United States, an early refiner of its own crude, the Soviet Union's rise in refinery capacity conforms very closely to its changing level of crude oil production for the period.

[1] Unavailability of earlier data made it necessary to make this comparison using the years 1937 and 1965 rather than 1925 and 1965, as was done in the Profile No. 30. However, even though the crude oil share of the worldwide liquid fuels trade had risen to some extent between 1925 and 1937, refined products still constituted well over half the total in the latter year. (See Part Three, table VI.)

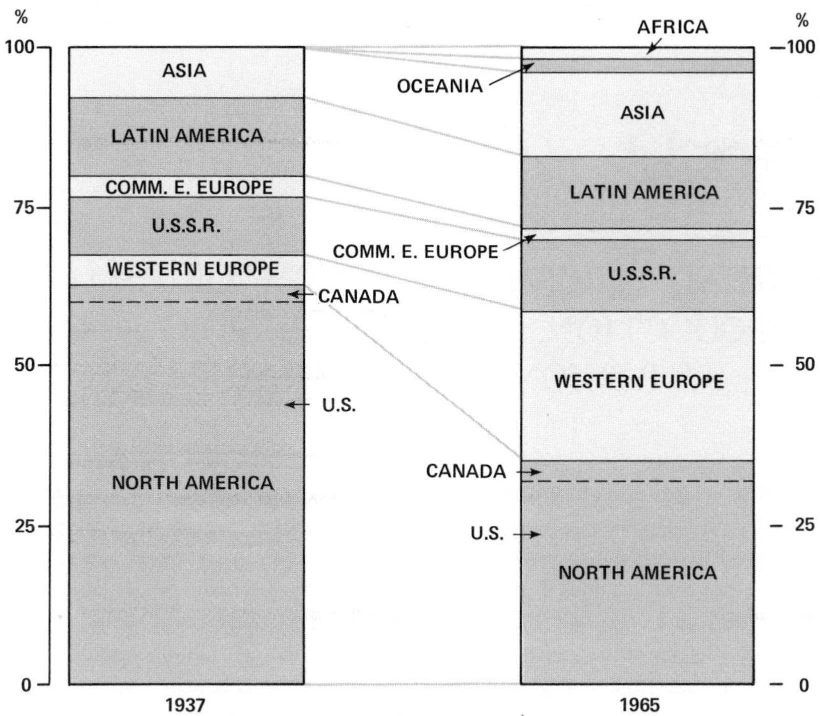

CRUDE OIL PROCESSING CAPACITY OF WORLD REFINERIES, BY MAJOR REGIONS, 1937 AND 1965

Region	1937 Million metric tons	1937 Percent	1965 Million metric tons	1965 Percent
North America	176.2	62.4%	591.3	35.3%
of which: United States	170.2	60.2	536.7	32.0
Western Europe	13.3	4.7	381.5	22.8
Oceania	0.3	0.1	23.5	1.4
U.S.S.R. & Comm. E. Europe	35.6	12.6	232.1	13.9
U.S.S.R.	27.8	9.8	200.0	11.9
Comm. E. Europe	7.8	2.8	32.1	1.9
Communist Asia	0.2	0.1	5.8	0.3
Latin America	35.2	12.5	198.3	11.8
Caribbean	31.3	11.1	151.9	9.1
Other Latin America	3.9	1.4	46.4	2.8
Asia	21.4	7.6	216.7	12.9
Middle East	10.5	3.7	92.4	5.5
Far East and Other Asia	10.9	3.8	124.2	7.4
Japan	1.6	0.6	77.3	4.6
Other Asia	9.3	3.3	46.9	2.8
Africa	0.3	0.1	25.8	1.5
North Africa	0.3	0.1	13.9	0.8
Other Africa	–	–	11.9	0.7
WORLD	282.5	100.0	1,674.9	100.0

Notes and sources: Data for 1937 from U.S. Department of State, *Energy Resources of the World*, Publication 3428 (U.S. Government Printing Office, 1949), p. 65. The figures are shown in the cited document in terms of "oil equivalents," since minor components such as shale oil and natural gasoline had been converted to a crude-oil calorific basis. Also, the 1937 figures refer to actual refinery inputs of oil rather than refinery capacity. The latter would probably be somewhat higher than the indicated figures–particularly with 1937 a year of depressed industrial activity.

Data for 1965 from International Petroleum Institute, *International Petroleum Industry* (New York, 1965 and 1967), vol. I, pp. 22–23, and vol. II, various pages. The figures (published in terms of barrels per day) have here been converted into metric tons per year by multiplying by 50.

Profile No. 32

AVERAGE ANNUAL PERCENTAGE RATES OF CHANGE IN ENERGY PRODUCTION, IMPORTS, EXPORTS, AND CONSUMPTION, BY REGION, 1925 - 1965 AND 1950 - 1965

This summary tabulation of regional growth rates in energy production, imports, exports, and consumption is intended primarily as a convenience for those who wish to be able to view data in other profile tables in terms of the underlying average annual percentage growth rates.

In using these rates of change, the reader should recognize that a rate of increase in consumption exceeding that in production need not mean that a given region has become a net importer, just as a faster growth in production than in consumption does not signify an area having become a net exporter. The rates merely indicate regional *trends in the direction* of rising or falling consumption-production relationships. Whether a region has actually become a net importer or exporter requires knowledge of the situation prevailing in the base year, as presented, for example, in Profile No. 33.

AVERAGE ANNUAL PERCENTAGE RATES OF CHANGE IN ENERGY PRODUCTION, IMPORTS, EXPORTS, AND CONSUMPTION, BY REGION, 1925-1965 AND 1950-1965

Region	1925-1965				1950-1965			
	Production	Imports	Exports	Consumption	Production	Imports	Exports	Consumption
North America	2.2%	5.0%	2.0%	2.5%	2.9%	5.8%	4.7%	3.2%
of which: United States	2.1	6.3	0.8	2.4	2.5	7.8	1.2	3.0
Western Europe	0.2	4.7	0.6	1.9	0.8	10.5	4.4	4.4
Oceania	2.4	7.0	5.8	3.5	4.5	8.4	36.0	5.0
U.S.S.R. & Comm. E. Europe	6.9	7.2	6.1	7.1	7.2	7.0	10.4	6.9
U.S.S.R.	9.4	6.6	10.3	9.3	8.5	-2.8	25.1	7.4
Comm. E. Europe	4.4	7.3	3.2	4.9	4.5	12.0	2.3	5.8
Communist Asia	6.9	-2.3	-1.0	6.7	14.3	n.a.	n.a.	14.4
Latin America	6.1	5.4	6.4	5.4	6.3	3.0	4.4	7.6
Caribbean	6.1	6.5	6.5	5.9	6.0	2.9	4.4	8.6
Other Latin America	5.8	3.2	1.0	4.8	8.6	3.4	1.2	6.5
Asia	6.3	7.9	9.7	4.7	9.1	11.7	10.1	9.0
Middle East	11.7	9.8	12.2	8.4	11.0	5.6	10.9	10.2
Japan	1.6	10.4	-1.7	4.7	2.3	27.9	7.0	9.9
Other Asia	3.7	5.4	4.9	4.1	6.7	6.3	4.4	7.6
Africa	7.2	5.0	11.3	4.8	13.2	6.9	28.7	5.4
North Africa	16.8	2.6	16.1	4.7	25.5	4.1	54.4	4.6
Tropical Africa	8.7	6.5	11.9	6.0	16.2	8.8	25.7	7.5
South Africa	3.5	10.3	0.5	4.6	4.1	7.2	-2.0	5.1
WORLD[a]	3.3	5.3	5.1	3.3	5.0	8.2	8.0	5.1

[a]Worldwide rates of change in imports and exports, though equal in principle, may differ because of various estimating problems, as discussed in the notes of Part Four, p. 821. The same comment applies to production and consumption, although in that case an additional reason for a discrepancy arises when bunkers grow at a different rate from production. (It should be recalled that production plus imports minus exports minus bunkers equals consumption, and that, throughout, consumption refers to "inland" consumption.)

Source: Part Three, table XIII.

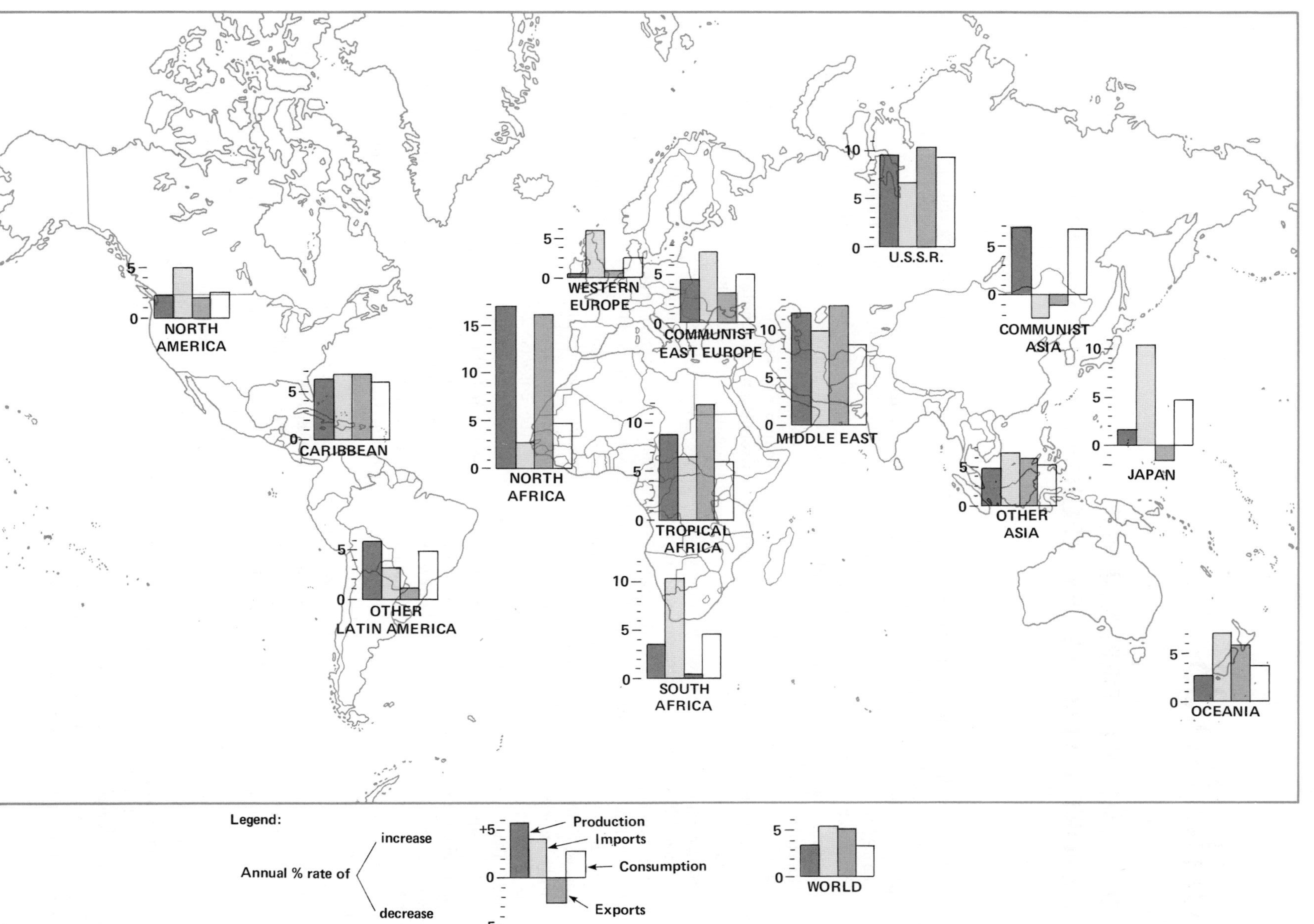

Average annual percentage rates of change in energy production, imports, exports, and consumption, by region, 1925–1965.

Profile No. 33

ENERGY IMPORT DEPENDENCE OR EXPORT CAPACITY, BY REGION, 1925 AND 1965

The major point of this profile is conveyed by the last columns of the 1925 and 1965 panels of the table. The figures appearing there relate regional energy trade balances to a region's total energy consumption or production. Specifically, a regional net import balance is shown as a percentage of consumption in order to denote "import dependence"; and a regional net export balance is shown as a percentage share of production to represent "export capacity." Comparison of the two years indicates the extent to which an area–in the context of its total energy supplies–has become more or less import dependent, has achieved greater or lesser surplus capability for exports, or has reversed the sign of its trade balance altogether. (However, it should be clear that a change in sign–e.g., a movement from net exports to net imports, as in the case of North America–can be quantitatively far less significant than a growing import balance, as in the case of Western Europe.)

The shift from coal to oil, a dominant feature of many of the earlier profiles, was one which did not merely bring about fundamental changes in the fuel base of different regions; it also produced a wholly new order of reliance on foreign trade in the worldwide satisfaction of energy requirements. (Profile No. 23 highlighted this development by indicating the significant long-term increase in the share of world energy trade in world energy consumption.) Increased import dependence (as defined above) was experienced by all parts of the industrial West, along with Japan, and also by Oceania and South Africa. This increase in import dependence was fairly mild in the case of North America: in 1925 a very small portion (around one-half of 1 percent) was available for export; in 1965 approximately 8½ percent of consumption was accounted for by net imports. (However, this relatively mild degree of import dependence was supported by U.S. policy which placed severe restrictions on oil imports.) Among the major energy consuming regions of the world, North America and the Communist group as a whole came closest in 1965 to energy self-sufficiency, as expressed by these statistical measures.[1]

The change for Western Europe was much greater than for North America. Western Europe's import-consumption share had been only 2 percent in 1925; by 1965 it had risen to well over 50 percent. For Japan the change was most dramatic of all: an essentially balanced production-consumption picture in 1925–or, what is essentially the same thing, a net trade balance of zero–gave way forty years later to an import component in total consumption of 75 percent. Other areas with heightened import dependence in 1965 include Communist Eastern Europe (net exports as a share of production, 15 percent in 1925; net imports in consumption, about 5 percent in 1965) and developing Asia outside the Middle East.

The converse to the foregoing changes was the increased petroleum export capability of the Middle East, whose net export proportion of output rose from 65 percent in 1925 to nearly 90 percent of a greatly enlarged total in 1965. Both North Africa and Tropical Africa, chiefly due to Nigerian oil, made huge quantum jumps from deficit to surplus areas–though the latter's role remained relatively small as a world component even in terms of its 1965 volume of exports. The Soviet Union's net export production share of 6 percent in 1925 had doubled by 1965. Non-Caribbean Latin America decreased the import portion of its energy consumption between these years, though with a 36 percent import dependence in 1965 the improvement still left the area in a very substantial deficit status.

[1] A broader concept of "self-sufficiency" would need to consider the question of reserves and of standby productive capacity as well as the consequences of alternative foreign trade policies.

ENERGY IMPORT DEPENDENCE OR EXPORT CAPACITY, BY REGION, 1925 AND 1965

Region	1925						1965					
	Net imports or exports (-) (*mill. met. tons coal equiv.)*			Total energy (*mill. met. tons coal equiv.)*		Percent net imports in energy consumption; or net exports (-) in production	Net imports or exports (-) (*mill. met. tons coal equiv.)*			Total energy (*mill. met. tons coal equiv.)*		Percent net imports in energy consumption; or net exports (-) in production
	Solid fuels	Liquid fuels	Total energy[a]	Consumption	Production		Solid fuels	Liquid fuels	Total energy[a]	Consumption	Production	
North America	-3.7	-1.0	-4.7	748.9	779.0	-0.6%	-32.4	202.4	171.6	2,040.2	1,892.9	8.4%
of which: United States	-18.5	-5.1	-23.4	717.7	765.9	-3.1	-46.8	183.4	152.8	1,881.6	1,749.1	8.1
Western Europe	-8.1	18.2	10.1	517.0	532.4	2.0	43.2	546.7	591.1	1,117.2	577.9	52.9
Oceania	-0.2	1.4	1.2	15.6	16.0	7.4	-7.0	30.1	23.1	61.2	41.4	37.7
U.S.S.R. & Comm. E. Europe	-8.4	-3.1	-11.5	80.5	92.1	-12.5	-22.6	-73.0	-95.7	1,255.8	1,351.7	-7.1
U.S.S.R.	0.3	-2.0	-1.6	25.3	27.0	-6.1	-18.4	-93.7	-112.8	880.6	993.5	-11.4
Comm. E. Europe	-8.7	-1.2	-9.9	55.1	65.1	-15.2	-4.2	20.7	17.2	375.1	358.3	4.8
Communist Asia	0.2	1.4	1.6	23.7	22.6	6.8	-1.6	1.5	-0.1	323.0	323.1	(-)
Latin America	7.2	-18.1	-10.9	24.7	39.9	-27.3	2.6	-201.8	-200.9	199.5	421.8	-47.6
Caribbean	1.4	-20.4	-18.9	11.4	33.9	-55.9	0.4	-230.8	-232.1	114.0	365.3	-63.5
Other Latin America	5.8	2.2	8.0	13.3	6.0	60.3	2.1	29.1	31.2	85.5	56.5	36.5
Asia	1.0	-5.1	-4.0	60.3	71.1	-5.7	17.7	-417.5	-399.9	385.1	832.7	-48.5
Middle East	0.1	-5.1	-5.0	2.3	7.7	-64.9	-	-560.5	-560.5	57.1	640.1	-87.6
Japan	-1.0	1.0	(-)	30.5	32.9	(-)	17.0	125.5	142.5	188.6	62.4	75.5
Other Asia	1.9	-1.0	1.0	27.5	30.5	3.4	0.6	17.5	18.1	139.4	130.2	13.0
Africa	2.7	1.3	4.0	13.9	13.6	28.5	-0.5	-115.8	-117.4	92.6	218.9	-53.6
North Africa	3.3	0.6	3.9[b]	3.0	0.3	131.3[b]	0.5	-120.1	-120.7	18.4	141.2	-85.5
Tropical Africa	1.0	0.5	1.5	1.8	1.0	80.7	0.2	-5.0	-4.7	18.9	29.2	-16.2
South Africa	-1.6	0.2	-1.4	9.1	12.3	-11.4	-1.2	9.2	8.0	55.3	48.4	16.6

[a]Including gas and electricity, not shown separately. Total net energy trade is not precisely equivalent to the difference between production and consumption, since that difference also includes bunkers.

[b]Net imports exceeded consumption (which, throughout these tables, refers to "inland" consumption) because of the insignificance of production coupled with large outflows in the form of bunkers—the latter not being recorded in export statistics.

Source: Taken or calculated from Part Three, table XIV.

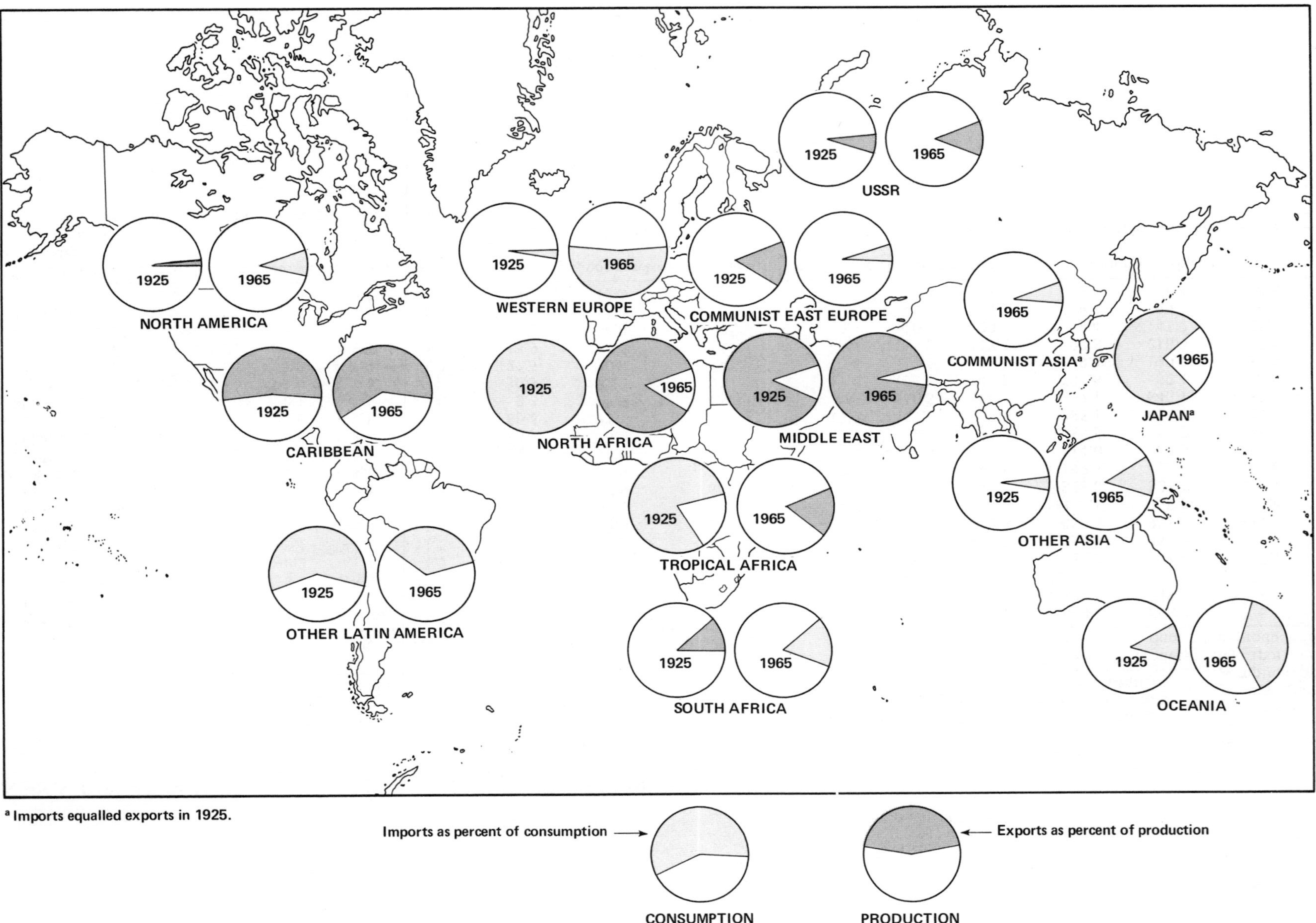

Energy import dependence or export capacity, by region, 1925 and 1965.

Profile No. 34

ENERGY IMPORT DEPENDENCE OR EXPORT CAPACITY, BY SELECTED COUNTRIES, 1925 AND 1965

This profile is analogous to Profile No. 33, but deals with individual country rankings rather than with major world regions. The table lists nations according to their 1965 degree of import dependence (measured by net imports as a percentage of consumption) or by their export capacity (measured by net exports as a percentage of production), proceeding from the country with the largest proportionate energy deficit to that with the largest proportionate surplus. The listing, headed by Italy with a net import-consumption share of over 90 percent, reveals striking trends: out of twelve net importers in 1965, ten had been either net exporters forty years earlier (e.g., United Kingdom, Germany) or had held a much less relative deficit position (e.g., France).

Aside from Venezuela and the Middle Eastern oil-producing countries, only Soviet Russia and Poland recorded net exports in both years; by 1965 the former's relative net export position had doubled, while Poland's relative net export margin had diminished. For the United States, the turnabout from net exporter to net importer was relatively mild compared with the marked increase in import dependence of the other advanced industrial countries; its net exports came to 3 percent of production in 1925; its net import-consumption ratio was 8 percent in 1965. Nonetheless, in absolute terms the U.S. net deficit in 1965 (amounting to over 150 million coal-equivalent tons) was the largest among all countries, exceeding by over 10 million tons the volume of net energy imports into Japan—a country whose net imports made up 75 percent of total energy consumption.

The pattern of world energy flows that has emerged in fulfilling this web of interdependence is described in the next set of profiles.

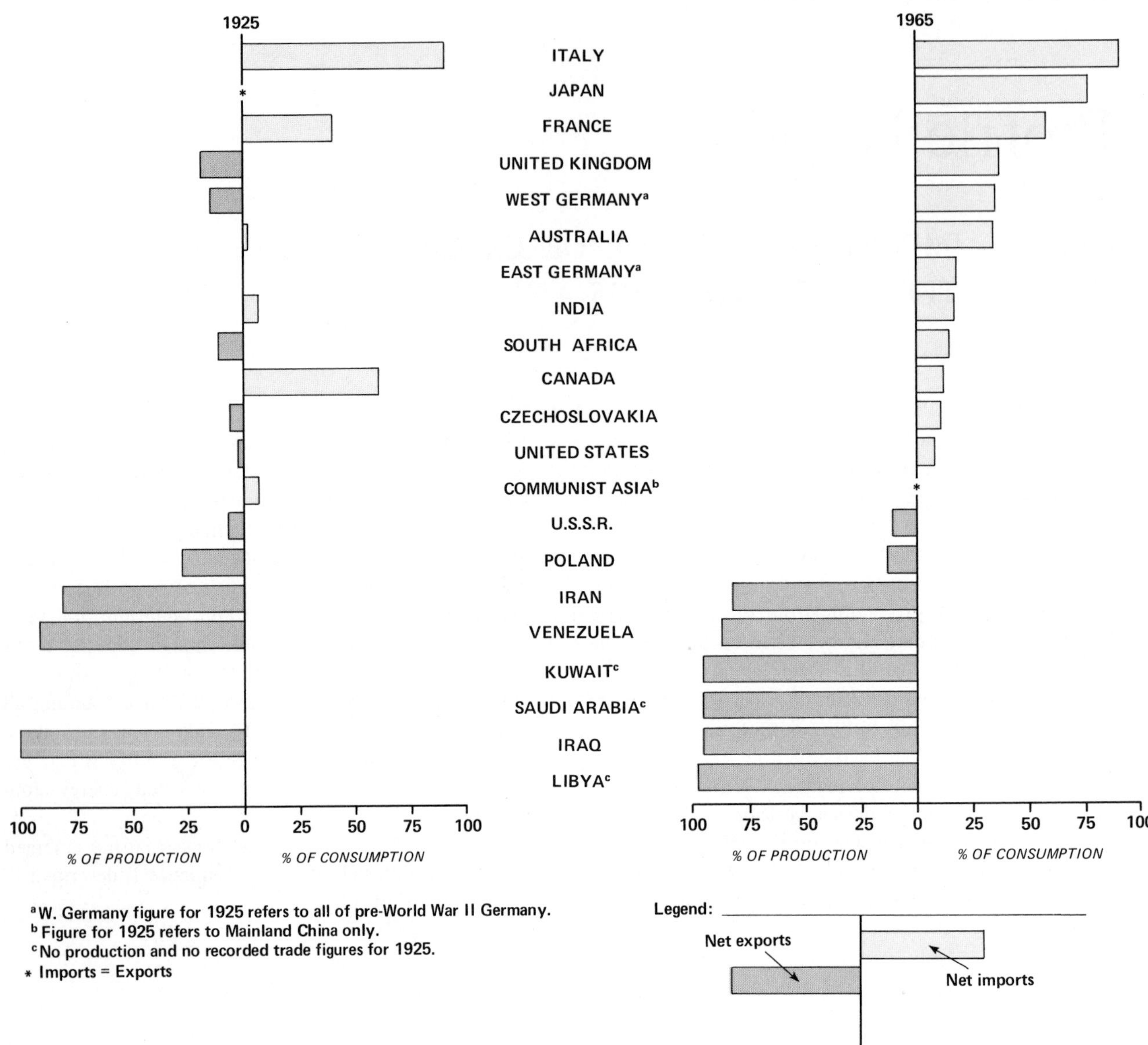

Energy import dependence or export capacity, selected countries, 1925 and 1965.

ENERGY IMPORT DEPENDENCE OR EXPORT CAPACITY, BY SELECTED COUNTRIES, 1925 AND 1965

Country[a]	1925						1965					
	Net imports or exports (-) *(mill. met. tons coal equiv.)*			Total energy *(mill. met. tons coal equiv.)*		Percent net imports in energy consumption; or net exports (-) in production	Net imports or exports (-) *(mill. met. tons coal equiv.)*			Total energy *(mill. met. tons coal equiv.)*		Percent net imports in energy consumption; or net exports (-) in production
	Solid fuels	Liquid fuels	Total energy[d]	Consumption	Production		Solid fuels	Liquid fuels	Total energy[d]	Consumption	Production	
Italy	10.4	1.2	11.6	12.9	1.4	89.5%	10.6	80.0	90.6	100.1	20.0	90.5%
Japan	-1.0	1.0	(-)	30.5	32.9	(-)	17.0	125.5	142.5	188.6	62.4	75.5
France	27.3	2.8	30.1	75.5	48.3	39.9	15.8	78.6	94.9	161.9	70.5	58.6
United Kingdom	-54.9	8.1	-46.8	182.3	247.4	-18.9	-4.8	111.2	107.3	290.3	191.5	36.9
West Germany[b]	-29.6	1.6	-28.0	161.7	189.8	-14.7	-12.7	105.1	92.7	273.1	186.3	34.0
Australia	-0.9	1.0	0.1	12.9	14.1	0.9	-7.3	25.2	17.9	53.4	38.1	33.5
East Germany[b]	-	-	-	-	-	-	9.9	6.1	16.1	94.2	78.1	17.1
India	0.3	1.0	1.3	19.0	18.8	6.8	-0.9	13.0	12.1	72.8	61.6	16.6
South Africa	-1.6	0.2	-1.4	9.1	12.3	-11.4	-1.2	9.2	8.0	55.3	48.4	14.5
Canada	14.8	4.0	18.7	31.1	13.1	60.1	14.4	18.9	18.6	158.4	143.7	11.7
Czechoslovakia	-1.8	0.3	-1.5	22.3	23.8	-6.4	0.6	8.8	9.5	83.1	73.6	11.3
United States	-18.5	-5.1	-23.4	717.7	765.9	-3.1	-46.8	183.4	152.8	1,881.6	1,749.1	8.1
Communist Asia[c]	0.2	1.4	1.6	23.7	22.6	6.8	-1.6	1.5	-0.1	323.0	323.1	(-)
U.S.S.R.	0.3	-2.0	-1.6	25.3	27.0	-6.1	-18.4	-93.7	-112.8	880.6	993.5	-11.4
Poland	-7.9	-0.4	-8.3	22.6	31.1	-26.8	-23.2	6.5	-16.2	111.6	128.1	-12.7
Iran	-	-5.7	-5.7	1.3	7.0	-81.1	-	-120.7	-120.7	19.4	144.9	-83.3
Venezuela	-	-4.0	-4.0	0.4	4.4	-91.6	0.2	-250.6	-250.4	28.3	283.3	-88.4
Kuwait	-	-	-	-	-	-	-	-156.9	-156.9	3.4	166.0	-94.6
Saudi Arabia	-	-	-	-	-	-	-	-144.6	-144.6	3.7	152.8	-94.6
Iraq	-	0.1	0.1	0.1	-	100.0	-	-92.5	-92.5	5.2	97.7	-94.6
Libya	-	-	-	-	-	-	-	-87.0	-87.0	1.0	88.2	-98.7

[a]Countries are listed according to their degree of energy import dependence in 1965—beginning with the country having the highest percentage of imports in energy consumption, and ending with the country having the highest percentage of exports in energy production. All countries accounting for at least 1% of world energy consumption or production in 1965 are listed. In the aggregate, they accounted for 91% of consumption and 93% of production in 1925, and 88% of consumption and 90% of production in 1965.

[b]1925 figures refer to *all* of pre-World War II Germany.

[c]1925 figures refer to Mainland China only; 1965 figures—though dominated by Mainland China—include also Mongolia, North Vietnam, and North Korea. Separate Mainland China figures are not available for 1965.

[d]Including gas and electricity, not shown separately. Total net energy trade is not precisely equivalent to the difference between production and consumption, since that difference also includes bunkers.

Source: Taken or calculated from Part Three, table XIV.

Profile No.35

EXPORTS AND IMPORTS OF SOLID AND LIQUID FUELS: INTERREGIONAL FLOWS BY DESTINATION AND ORIGIN, 1929 AND 1965

The long-term shift from solid fuels to liquid fuels has resulted in a world energy economy characterized by a growing geographical imbalance between the location of energy supplies and the location of energy consumption. Owing to balance-of-payments considerations and, more particularly, to chronic political instability in many of the supplying regions, this situation has raised for numerous regions and countries a legitimate and vital concern about the reliability of their sources of energy supplies or, conversely, about the assurance of their markets. Data on long-term trends in the network of world energy trade, contained in this and the three following profiles, provide at least part of the empirical context in which such evolving issues can be brought into focus. Unfortunately, these limited materials on the *direction* of world energy flows could not be developed within the precise quantitative framework of Part Three, which serves as the basis for most of the other tabulations in our profiles. Therefore some statistical discrepancies will be apparent between the figures in Part Three and those in Profiles No. 35 through No. 38.

In the accompanying table[1] it was feasible to assemble data for only the two years 1929 and 1965. The table thus encompasses a period of somewhat shorter duration than that spanned elsewhere in this study. Having been built up from a variety of source materials of varying and, in some cases, uncertain reliability, these data (especially those for 1929) are somewhat shaky, though not, we believe, enough to obscure or invalidate identification of the major trends in which we are interested. Limitations in the sources also made it necessary to adopt geographical groupings somewhat different from those used elsewhere, though, in the case of North America, our decision to treat Canada and the United States individually was prompted by the special interest that attaches to problems of trade between these two nations. Finally, the table aggregates exchanges of solid and liquid fuels only, since only meager amounts of gas and electricity moved between the regions specified. The primary exception relates to Canadian-United States exchanges of these two energy forms; the quantitative effect that their inclusion would have appears in a footnote to the table and is represented in the chart.

Except for the last line of the top and bottom panels of the table, the data presented here (and in Profiles No. 36, No. 37, and No. 38) cover chiefly *inter*regional exports and imports of energy. By contrast (as explained in greater detail in the note appended to Profile No. 23), our earlier profiles on foreign trade dealt with regions' total exports and total imports—measures which include intraregional as well as interregional movements of energy. Consequently, by aggregating successive stages of processing or re-exporting which frequently occur *within* a region, they overstate to a degree the importance of that region in trade with other parts of the world.[2] As examples, within the Caribbean area Venezuelan crude oil exports get added on to exports of refined products (made from Venezuelan crude) from the Netherlands West Indies; and in Western Europe the shipments of refined oil (or re-exported crude oil) from Dutch and Belgian refineries or entrepôt points somewhat distort the oil export picture for the region.

Further, from the standpoint of interdependence among regions of the world in energy supply and consumption—the main point to be conveyed by the statistics in this profile—trade in fuels among proximate countries within a region can be pretty much ignored not only as a matter of simplification but also because of its secondary policy significance in today's world.

The qualifying phrase "in today's world" deserves brief amplification. For trade among nearby countries, historically and continuing well into the interwar period, had both major quantitative as well as policy signifi-

[1] Derived from the more detailed matrix tables in Part Five, section III, tables III-1 and III-2.

[2] The total export and import data were nevertheless the ones we were obliged to use in those earlier profiles since only they provide the requisite detail in terms of years covered, detailed geographic breakdown, and specific fuel categories.

cance. The numerical facts of the case can be summarized as follows:[3]

- The 1929 share of total worldwide energy trade represented by intraregional movements was around 55 percent; by 1965, the intraregional share of world trade was down to approximately 25 percent.
- Of course, such percentages as these depend on the definition and also the number of regions considered. (The more numerous the regions, the lower the intraregional percentage share in total world trade.) In most of our tabulations on the direction of world energy trade, we deal with ten basic regions, two of which are individual countries: Canada, United States, Western Europe, Oceania, the Communist area, Caribbean, Other Latin America, Middle East, Far East and Other Asia, and Africa. This breakdown, though designed to point up the role of geographic groupings having major economic and/or political importance, also was determined to some extent by data availability.
- The predominant portion of world intraregional trade in 1929—some 75 percent—was accounted for by shipments within Western Europe. By 1965, the intra-West European share of intraregional trade was down to about 30 percent, largely offset by the rising relative importance of exchanges among Communist countries as well as intra-Caribbean movements from oil fields to refineries.
- Another way of looking at the West European picture is to note that over 70 percent of Western Europe's 1929 imports originated right *in* Western Europe, as compared with about 15 percent in 1965. The turnabout reflects, of course, the wholesale shift from coal to oil.
- Compared with oil, world trade in solid fuels has always been dominated to a relatively large degree by intraregional movements. There were, it is true, early examples of long-distance coal haulage (e.g., West European shipments to South America). But around 70 percent of the world coal trade in 1929 was intraregional, as against 30 percent for liquids. In 1965, a bit under one-half of total world coal shipments represented intraregional movements, compared with an intraregional share of under 25 percent for the world oil trade.

As for the political aspects, one need only recall old national rivalries over the control of European coalfields or the fierce trade competition among certain European coal exporters during the Great Depression to appreciate the fact that policy issues arising out of the nearby location of energy supplies, particularly of coal, were at one time of overwhelming international importance.

But the declining relative importance of coal and the movement towards European unity beginning with the European Coal and Steel Community have resulted in a shift in the focus of policy concern to fuel movements between, rather than within, the regions. The table reveals a number of interesting developments, a few of which will be highlighted here, while a more specific look is presented in Profile No. 36. A particularly far-reaching distributional change occurred in the geographic origin of energy movements. (See first two columns, panel B of the table.) Some two-thirds of the worldwide interregional total in 1929 originated in the United States, Western Europe, and today's Communist countries; by 1965, the combined share of these three areas was down to about 14 percent. In 1929, under 25 percent of the world total was accounted for by exports from the Caribbean, with the addition of the Middle East and Africa raising the figure only slightly, to 28 percent. By 1965, well over 80 percent of the world's interregional exports of energy[4] was obtained from these three areas.

These changes in the geographic origin of world energy flows reflect, of course, the almost exclusive takeover by oil—most of it from newly discovered fields—in the interregional trading network. In 1929 around 40 percent of interregional energy flows had consisted of solid fuels and about 60 percent of liquid fuels; by 1965 the solid fuels share was down to 8 percent, while the liquid fuels share was up to 92 percent.[5] The region whose geographic sources of energy imports shifted most fundamentally and concurrently with these developments was Western Europe. The Middle East and Africa, which provided only a bit over 10 percent of West European energy imports in 1929, had risen to a 75 percent share by 1965. The United States was among areas supplying diminishing shares of Western Europe's imports. Some 30 percent of Western Europe's 1929 interregional imports came from the United States; the United States was then still a net oil exporter and these

(Text continued on p. 170.)

[3]These summary data are based on the interregional tabulation in Part Five, section III, tables III-1 and III-2; and on the total (interregional plus intraregional) trade figures in Part Three, table VI.

[4]The addition of gas and electricity scarcely alters this conclusion; see the comment above and the lower panel of the *Note* to the table.

[5]In terms of total (i.e., intraregional plus interregional) trade, the reversal of the solid-liquid proportions was, predictably, more dramatic: in 1929, 60 percent of total world energy trade represented solid fuels and 40 percent liquid fuels; the respective 1965 shares were 10 and 90 percent. (Total trade figures appear in Part Three, table VI and are summarized and discussed in Profile No. 23; detailed interregional flows are tabulated in Part Five, section III, tables III-1 and III-2.)

EXPORTS AND IMPORTS OF SOLID AND LIQUID FUELS: INTERREGIONAL FLOWS BY DESTINATION AND ORIGIN, 1929 AND 1965

(Data based on coal equivalents)

Region	World		Canada		United States		Western Europe		Oceania		Communist Countries	
	1929	1965	1929	1965	1929	1965	1929	1965	1929	1965	1929	1965
					A. Percentage distribution of exports to regions listed at left							
Destination												
Canada	20.2%	4.9%	-	-	47.4%	28.9%	4.9%	4.6%	-	-	-	-
United States	17.0	16.5	93.1%	96.2%	-	-	0.1	3.6	-	-	-	-
Western Europe	30.9	52.2	5.9	-	25.3	44.2	-	-	-	-	75.1%	68.5%
Oceania	2.5	2.6	-	-	2.8	-	3.5	0.3	-	-	-	-
Communist Countries	5.2	0.2	1.0	-	2.0	0.4	19.2	18.2	-	-	-	-
Caribbean	3.2	1.9	-	-	8.5	5.5	0.5	3.1	-	-	-	15.1
Other Latin America	8.2	3.2	-	-	6.5	3.1	36.2	5.7	-	-	0.6	7.2
Middle East	0.5	0.3	-	-	-	-	1.2	9.4	-	-	1.7	0.7
Far East and Other Asia	6.8	13.8	-	3.8	5.7	17.2	1.0	1.4	100.0%	100.0%	18.8	6.0
Africa	5.6	4.4	-	-	1.8	0.6	33.5	53.6	-	-	3.8	2.5
WORLD	100.0	100.0	100.0	100.0	100.0	100.0	100.0	100.0	100.0	100.0	100.0	100.0
WORLD (mill. met. tons)	(135.6)	(1,156.6)	(1.0)	(25.6)	(50.5)	(58.8)	(16.2)	(6.6)	(0.1)	(7.0)	(23.0)	(92.1)
WORLD (mill. met. tons incl. intraregional)[a]	(295.4)	(1,554.1)	(1.0)	(24.7)	(51.2)	(57.3)	(126.2)	(128.4)	(0.4)	(9.3)	(33.6)	(172.2)
					B. Percentage distribution of imports from regions listed at left							
Origin												
Canada	0.8%	2.2%	-	-	4.1%	12.9%	0.1%	-	-	-	0.1%	-
United States	37.3	5.1	87.6%	30.0%	-	-	30.5	4.3%	42.7%	-	14.0	9.1%
Western Europe	12.0	0.6	2.9	0.5	-	0.1	-	-	16.9	0.1%	44.1	51.9
Oceania	-	0.6	-	-	-	-	-	-	-	-	-	-
Communist Countries	17.2	8.0	-	-	-	-	41.7	10.4	-	-	-	-
Caribbean	23.8	20.7	6.7	53.5	94.5	65.3	16.4	9.5	-	-	-	-
Other Latin America	0.9	-	2.9	-	1.3	-	0.3	-	-	-	-	-
Middle East	3.4	47.4	-	15.6	0.1	15.5	8.8	50.2	3.6	72.6	-	-
Far East and Other Asia	4.0	1.4	-	0.4	-	2.6	2.1	0.4	36.8	27.3	41.7	-
Africa	0.8	14.1	-	-	-	3.6	-	25.2	-	-	-	39.0
WORLD	100.0	100.0	100.0	100.0	100.0	100.0	100.0	100.0	100.0	100.0	100.0	100.0
WORLD (mill. met. tons)	(135.6)	(1,156.6)	(27.4)	(56.8)	(23.0)	(191.2)	(41.9)	(603.6)	(3.4)	(30.1)	(7.1)	(2.3)
WORLD (mill. met. tons incl. intraregional)[a]	(277.2)	(1,525.9)	(25.9)	(57.9)	(24.8)	(193.8)	(147.3)	(718.3)	(3.6)	(32.3)	(11.4)	(76.5)

EXPORTS AND IMPORTS OF SOLID AND LIQUID FUELS: INTERREGIONAL FLOWS BY DESTINATION AND ORIGIN, 1929 AND 1965 (Continued)

(Data based on coal equivalents)

Region	Caribbean		Other Latin America		Middle East		Far East & Other Asia		Africa	
	1929	1965	1929	1965	1929	1965	1929	1965	1929	1965
	A. *Percentage distribution of exports to regions listed at left*									
Destination										
Canada	5.7%	12.7%	65.5%	-	-	1.6%	-	1.4%	-	-
United States	67.5	52.3	24.4	-	0.4%	5.4	-	30.4	-	4.3%
Western Europe	21.3	23.9	10.1	-	79.7	55.4	16.3%	12.9	-	93.1
Oceania	-	-	-	-	2.6	4.0	23.0	50.0	-	-
Communist Countries	-	-	-	-	-	-	54.7	-	-	0.6
Caribbean	-	-	-	-	-	0.9	-	-	-	-
Other Latin America	5.4	6.3	-	-	-	1.9	-	-	-	1.4
Middle East	-	0.1	-	-	-	-	0.7	5.5	-	0.5
Far East and Other Asia	-	1.2	-	-	14.7	24.2	-	-	100.0%	0.3
Africa	0.1	3.5	-	-	2.6	6.6	5.2	-	-	-
WORLD	100.0	100.0	100.0	-	100.0	100.0	100.0	100.0	100.0	100.0
WORLD (mill. met. tons)	(32.2)	(238.8)	(1.2)	-	(4.6)	(547.8)	(5.4)	(16.5)	(1.0)	(163.4)
WORLD (mill. met. tons incl. intraregional)[a]	(56.4)	(350.2)	(2.5)	(2.1)	(8.4)	(599.4)	(12.9)	(50.7)	(2.6)	(159.9)
	B. *Percentage distribution of imports from regions listed at left*									
Origin										
Canada	-	-	-	-	-	-	-	0.6%	-	-
United States	98.2%	14.7%	29.9%	5.0%	1.5%	-	31.3%	6.3	11.6%	0.7%
Western Europe	1.8	0.9	53.0	1.0	30.8	19.2	1.7	0.1	71.1	6.9
Oceania	-	-	-	-	-	-	0.7	4.4	-	-
Communist Countries	-	62.7	1.4	18.1	61.5	20.6	47.7	3.4	11.5	4.5
Caribbean	-	-	15.7	41.0	-	9.3	-	1.8	0.5	16.7
Other Latin America	-	-	-	-	-	-	-	-	-	-
Middle East	-	21.7	-	28.7	-	-	7.4	83.1	1.6	71.1
Far East and Other Asia	-	-	-	-	6.2	27.8	-	-	3.7	-
Africa	-	-	-	6.1	-	23.2	11.2	0.3	-	-
WORLD	100.0	100.0	100.0	100.0	100.0	100.0	100.0	100.0	100.0	100.0
WORLD (mill. met. tons)	(4.4)	(22.1)	(11.1)	(36.6)	(0.7)	(3.2)	(9.2)	(159.7)	(7.6)	(50.8)
WORLD (mill. met. tons incl. intraregional)[a]	(25.2)	(119.8)	(12.2)	(33.3)	(1.4)	(38.9)	(16.6)	(211.4)	(9.1)	(43.6)

See *Notes* on following page.

NOTES TO PROFILE NO. 35 TABLE:

[a]Except for 1965 exchanges of gas and electricity in a few areas, the table virtually exhausts *inter*regional flows of *total* energy, using the regional classification system of the table (in which the United States and Canada are treated as separate regions). The only significant 1965 interregional trade in gas and electricity (in thousand metric tons coal equivalent) was as follows:*

Canada gas to United States	15,309
Canada electricity to United States	444
United States gas to Canada	666
United States gas to Mexico	154
United States electricity to Canada	448
United States electricity to Mexico	15
Mexico gas to United States	1,797
Africa gas to Western Europe	1,412
Total	20,245

*Data taken from United Nations, *World Energy Supplies*, Statistical Papers, Series J, No. 11; OECD, *Basic Statistics of Energy, 1951–1965*; and United Nations ECE, *Annual Bulletin of Electric Energy Statistics for Europe, 1965*.

The addition of these 1965 interregional gas and electricity flows to the data in the table produces the following modified percentage distributions for the affected regions:

	Exports of:				
	World	*Canada*	*United States*	*Caribbean*	*Africa*
Destination					
Canada	4.9%	-	30.2%	12.6%	-
United States	17.7	97.6%	-	52.6	4.2%
Western Europe	51.4	-	43.2	23.7	93.1
Oceania	2.6	-	-	-	-
Communist Countries	0.2	-	0.3	-	0.5
Caribbean	1.9	-	5.7	-	-
Other Latin America	3.1	-	3.1	6.2	1.4
Middle East	0.3	-	-	0.1	0.5
Far East	13.6	2.4	16.8	1.2	0.3
Africa	4.3	-	0.6	3.5	-
WORLD	100.0	100.0	100.0	100.0	100.0
WORLD (mill. met. tons)[b]	(1,176.8)	(41.3)	(60.1)	(240.6)	(164.8)

	Imports of:				
	World	*Canada*	*United States*	*West Europe*	*Caribbean*
Origin					
Canada	3.5%	-	19.3%	-	-
United States	5.1	31.3%	-	4.3%	15.3%
Western Europe	0.6	0.5	0.1	-	0.9
Oceania	0.6	-	-	-	-
Communist Countries	7.8	-	-	10.4	62.2
Caribbean	20.4	52.5	60.6	9.4	-
Other Latin America	-	-	-	-	-
Middle East	46.6	15.3	14.2	50.1	21.5
Far East	1.4	0.4	2.4	0.3	-
Africa	14.0	-	3.3	25.4	-
WORLD	100.0	100.0	100.0	100.0	100.0
WORLD (mill. met. tons)[b]	(1,176.8)	(57.9)	(208.8)	(22.3)	(605.0)

[b]The bottom line of figures in parentheses refers to total trade–that is, including intraregional as well as interregional shipments. If the inclusion of intraregional shipments were the only difference from the interregional totals of the preceding line, then the balance of imports minus exports should be identical in the two lines. Also, the two sets of figures should be identical in the case of Canada and the United States where (each country being treated as a separate region) intraregional trade is not involved. Finally, the last line should obviously always be equal to, or greater than, the total of interregional shipments only–a condition which is violated in a few cases, such as in the case of Africa for 1965. Reasons for such discrepancies, arising largely from the use of different source materials, are discussed in the tables of Part Five, section III.

Source: Derived from data in Part Five, section III, tables III-1 and III-2. For 1929, Part Five, table III-1 shows Mainland China separately. In the present table Mainland China has been consolidated into the overall Communist country grouping, with the result that the 1929 trade between Mainland China and the U.S.S.R.-Eastern Europe grouping (as shown in Part Five, table III-1) washes out. The last line of each panel (i.e., data including intraregional) comes from Part Three, table VI.

West European imports represented nearly all liquid fuels. Only 4 percent of Western Europe's 1965 imports came from the United States—this time almost entirely coal. The share of the present-day Communist area also fell sharply as a geographic source of West European energy imports—down from over 40 percent in 1929 to 10 percent in 1965. Imports from the Caribbean declined from 16 to 10 percent.

Some other regions also exhibited major changes. The United States declined markedly as a supplier of Canadian imports (becoming itself a net importer from Canada), largely to be supplanted by the Caribbean area. Non-Caribbean Latin America greatly decreased the proportion of its imports coming from the United States and Western Europe, and increased the percentage contribution of the Caribbean and Middle East. The Middle East share of the Far East imports rose from under 10 to over 80 percent, while conversely the combined U.S. and Communist shares of imports in the Far East dropped by much the same proportion.

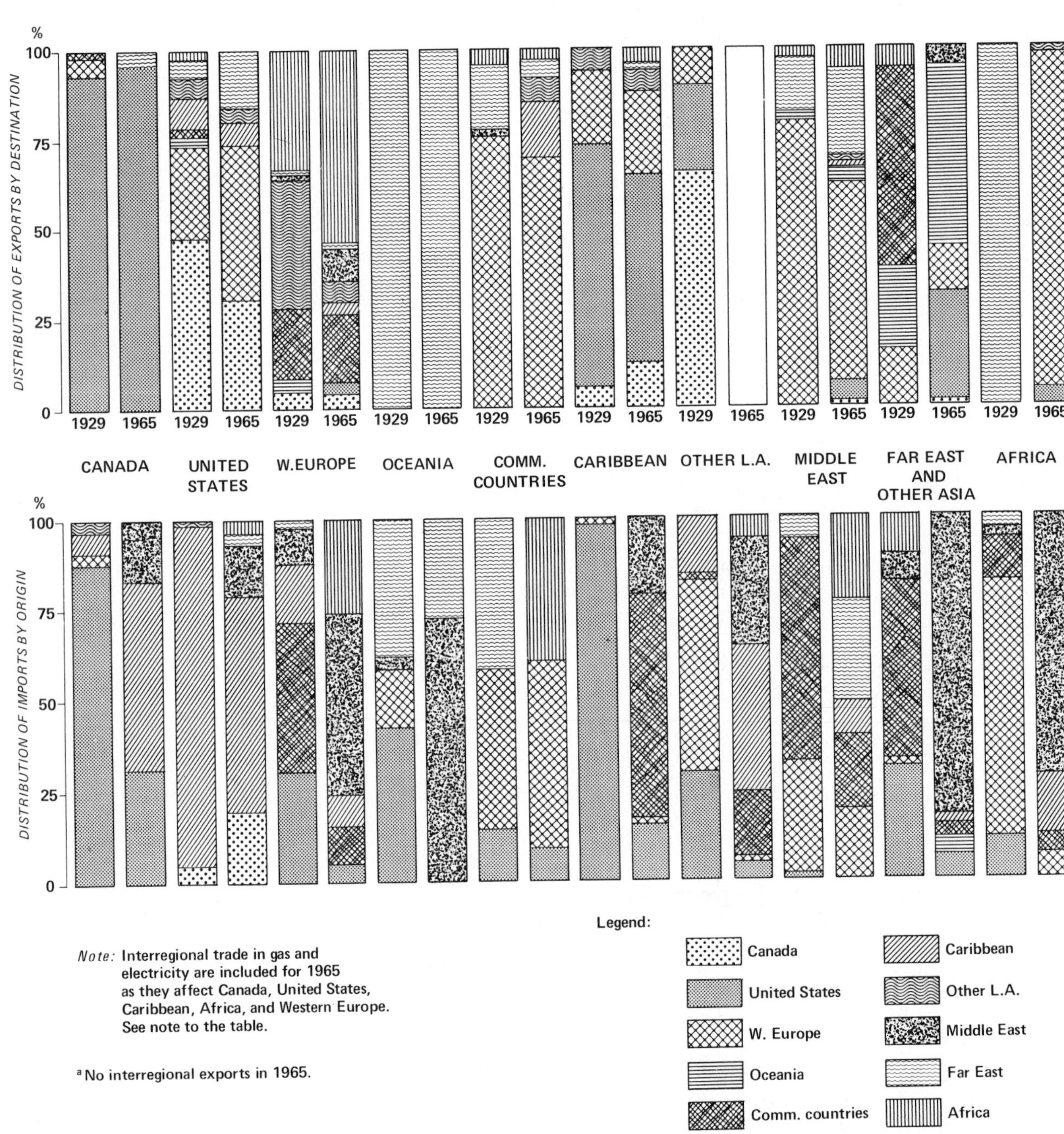

Note: Interregional trade in gas and electricity are included for 1965 as they affect Canada, United States, Caribbean, Africa, and Western Europe. See note to the table.

[a] No interregional exports in 1965.

Direction of interregional trade in solid and liquid fuels, 1929 and 1965.

Profile No. 36

MAJOR INTERREGIONAL MOVEMENTS OF SOLID AND LIQUID FUELS, BY REGIONS OF ORIGIN AND DESTINATION, 1929 AND 1965

In this profile worldwide interregional trade in solid and liquid fuels in 1929 and 1965 is apportioned by the major separate flows between sets of regional trading "partners." Flows amounting to 1 percent or more of total interregional trade in both fuels combined are tabulated in order of importance for each of the two years.

One immediately becomes aware of the concentrated importance within world interregional flows of a handful of regional trading relationships. Out of nineteen different regional pairings listed for 1929, the top five accounted for over one-half of the world's interregional trade in coal and oil. At the head of the list were Caribbean oil exports to the United States (16 percent of the world total) and U.S. coal shipments to Canada (13 percent). The next three most important movements in 1929 comprised Western Europe imports of U.S. liquid fuels, present-day Communist area coal, and Caribbean liquid fuels.

In 1965, sixteen sets of regional flows met the "1 percent and over" criterion laid down above. Of these, just the top three—Middle Eastern and African oil shipments to Western Europe, and Middle Eastern oil shipments to the Far East (including Japan)—exhausted over 50 percent of the worldwide interregional total.

Certain patterns in the direction of trade persisted between 1929 and 1965, although the relative importance of most regional flows shifted markedly. For example, Middle Eastern oil exports to Western Europe "qualified" for the 1929 listing with roughly 3 percent of world trade; in 1965 this particular flow accounted for 26 percent of the total. Indeed, the table reveals the Middle East's emergence as the preeminent energy supplier throughout the world: in 1965 that region's liquid fuels exports to five other areas—Western Europe, the Far East, the United States, Oceania, and Africa—accounted for 45 percent of the world interregional trade in liquid *and* solid fuels. (African oil exports to Western Europe raise the figure to 58 percent.)

Regional exchanges showing a substantial relative decline between 1929 and 1965 include present-day Communist area coal shipments to Western Europe—8½ percent in 1929 down to 2 percent of the world total in 1965; and U.S. coal exports to Canada—13 percent in 1929 down to 1 percent in 1965. The Caribbean area's interregional oil shipments held up better. Its exports to the United States in 1929 represented 16 percent of interregional energy trade, and this declined to 11 percent in 1965. Likewise, Caribbean shipments to Western Europe amounted to 5 percent of interregional trade in both years.

Finally, one must note those interregional exchanges which have completely disappeared as a factor of any importance in the world's interregional energy trade. Western Europe coal shipments to non-Caribbean Latin America, Africa, and the Communist area accounted for over 10 percent of the 1929 total, but failed entirely to make the list in 1965. Similarly, the United States had been a notable oil exporter in 1929, shipping significant quantities to Canada, Western Europe, and numerous other regions; these U.S. exports represented over 20 percent of the 1929 worldwide total. By 1965 U.S. oil exports had essentially disappeared from the scene.

In fact, coal exports to Canada and Western Europe are the only U.S. entries to appear on the 1965 tabulation. These two flows together amounted to 3 percent of the world's interregional energy flows in 1965, a steep drop from the 13 percent share that U.S. coal exports to Canada alone had constituted back in 1929.

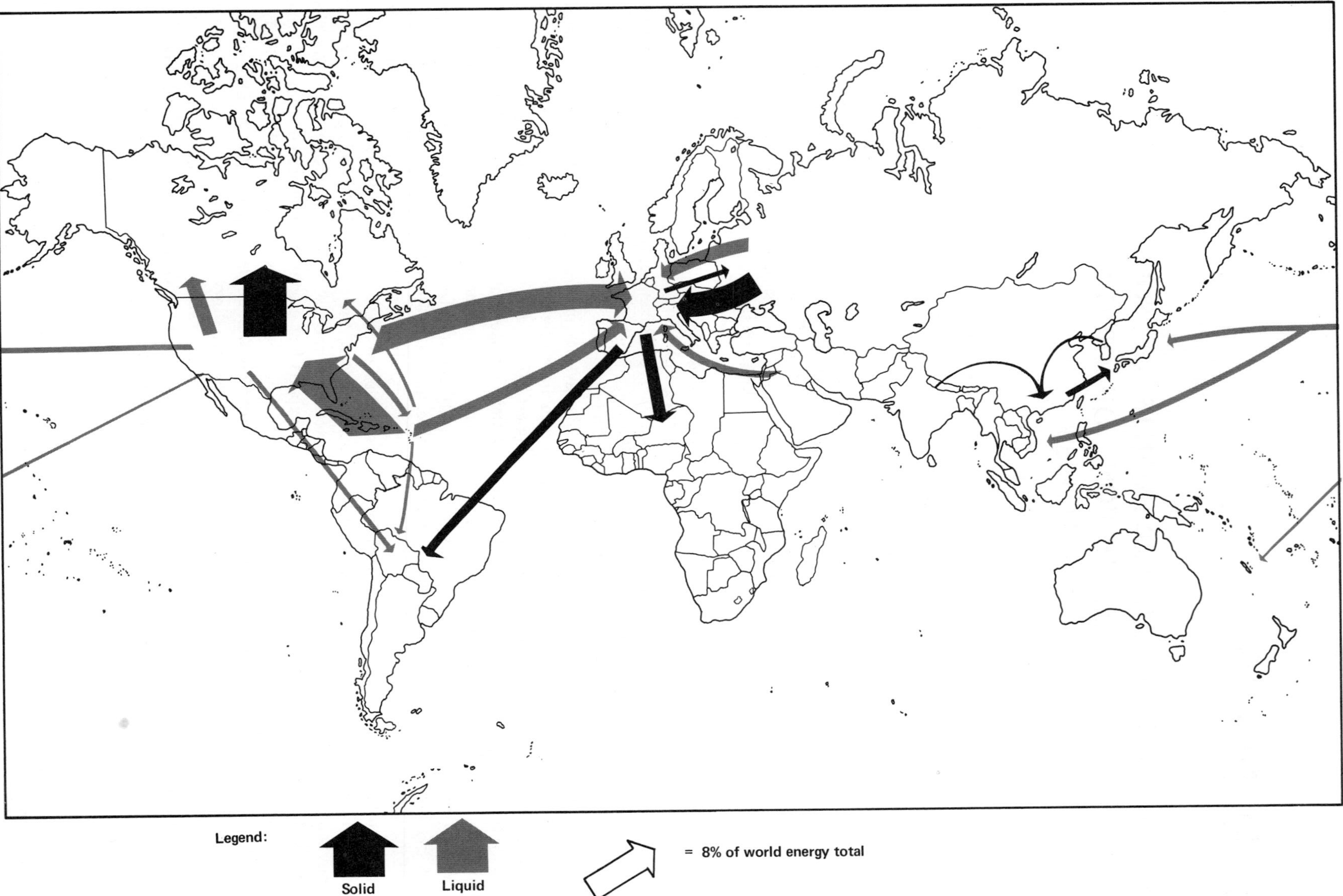

Major interregional exchanges of solid and liquid fuels, 1929.

MAJOR INTERREGIONAL MOVEMENTS OF SOLID AND LIQUID FUELS, BY REGIONS OF ORIGIN AND DESTINATION, 1929 AND 1965

Origin	Destination	Fuel category	Amount shipped[a]: Million metric tons coal equivalent[b]	Amount shipped[a]: Percent of world total
		1929		
Caribbean	United States	Liquid	21.7 (14.5)	16.0%
United States	Canada	Solid	17.7	13.1
United States	Western Europe	Liquid	12.3 (8.2)	9.0
U.S.S.R. & Comm. E. Europe	Western Europe	Solid	11.5	8.5
Caribbean	Western Europe	Liquid	6.9 (4.6)	5.1
United States	Canada	Liquid	6.2 (4.1)	4.6
U.S.S.R. & Comm. E. Europe	Western Europe	Liquid	6.0 (4.0)	4.4
Western Europe	Other Latin America	Solid	5.9	4.3
Western Europe	Africa	Solid	5.4	4.0
Middle East	Western Europe	Liquid	3.7 (2.5)	2.7
Communist Asia[c]	Far East	Solid	3.5	2.6
United States	Caribbean	Liquid	3.0 (2.0)	2.2
Western Europe	U.S.S.R. & Comm. E. Europe	Solid	3.0	2.2
United States	Far East	Liquid	2.9 (1.9)	2.1
United States	Other Latin America	Liquid	2.7 (1.8)	2.0
Far East	Communist Asia	Solid	2.2	1.6
Caribbean	Canada	Liquid	1.8 (1.2)	1.3
Caribbean	Other Latin America	Liquid	1.7 (1.1)	1.3
United States	Oceania	Liquid	1.4 (0.9)	1.1
Total of above			119.5	88.0
All other solid fuels trade			6.4	4.7
All other liquid fuels trade			9.8 (6.5)	7.2
Total world interregional trade			135.6	100.0
		1965		
Middle East	Western Europe	Liquid	303.2 (202.1)	26.2%
Africa	Western Europe	Liquid	151.6 (101.1)	13.1
Middle East	Far East	Liquid	132.8 (88.5)	11.5
Caribbean	United States	Liquid	124.8 (83.2)	10.8
Caribbean	Western Europe	Liquid	57.1 (38.1)	4.9
Communist Countries	Western Europe	Liquid	41.3 (27.5)	3.6
Middle East	Africa	Liquid	36.2 (24.1)	3.1
Caribbean	Canada	Liquid	30.4 (20.3)	2.6
Middle East	United States	Liquid	29.6 (19.7)	2.6
Canada	United States	Liquid	24.4 (16.3)	2.1
United States	Western Europe	Solid	22.6	2.0
Middle East	Oceania	Liquid	21.9 (14.6)	1.9
Communist Countries	Western Europe	Solid	21.8	1.9
United States	Canada	Solid	15.3	1.3
Caribbean	Other Latin America	Liquid	15.0 (10.0)	1.3
Communist Countries	Caribbean	Liquid	13.8 (9.2)	1.2
Total of above			1,041.8	90.1
All other solid fuels trade			22.5	1.9
All other liquid fuels trade			92.2 (61.5)	8.0
Total world interregional trade			1,156.6	100.0

[a]Table lists exchanges accounting for at least 1% of world total.
[b]In the case of liquid fuels, parenthetical figures refer to million tons of original units.
[c]Mainland China only.

Source: Part Five, section III, tables III-1 and III-2. Notes accompanying tables in that section describe derivation and nature of these estimates.

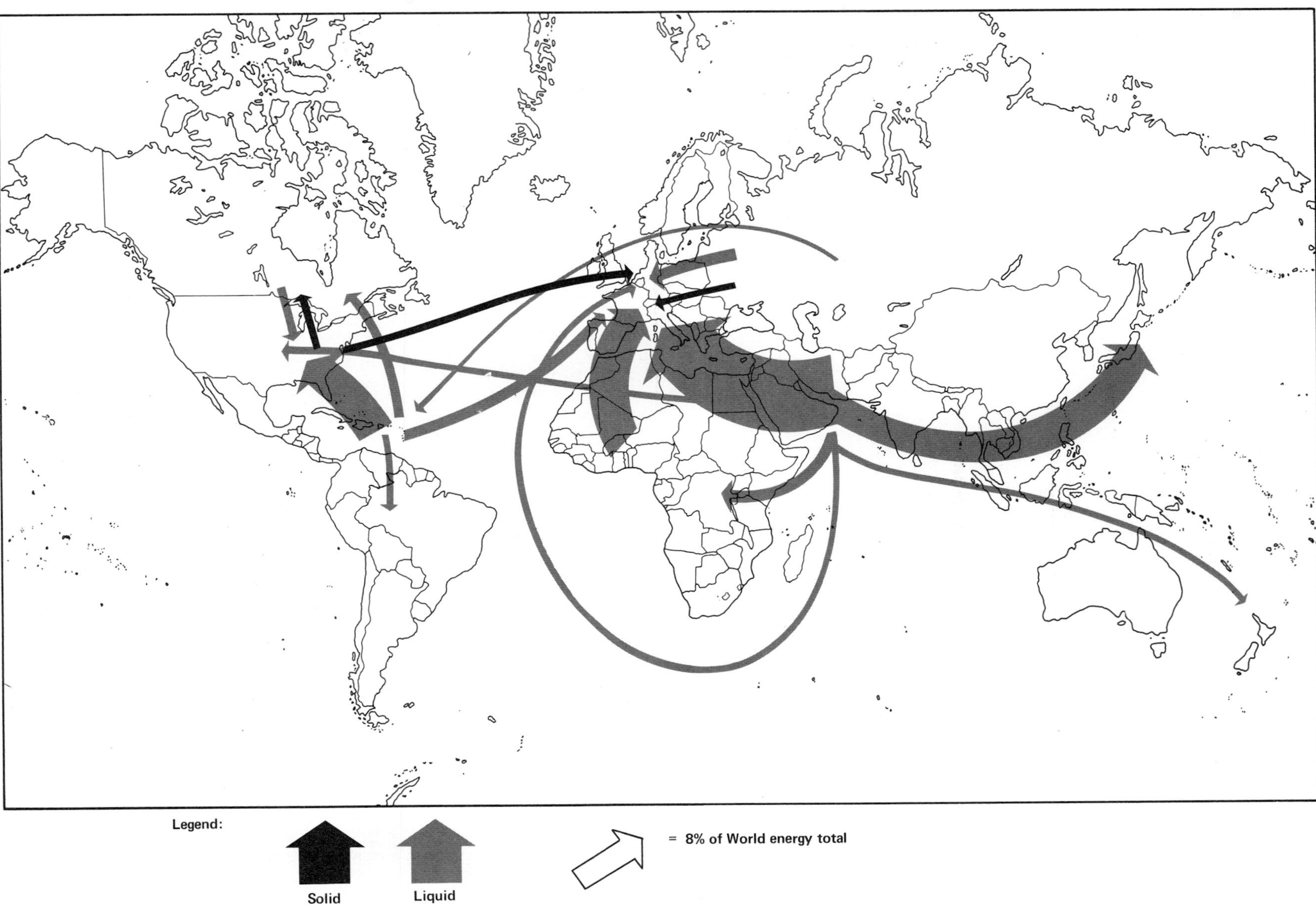

Major interregional exchanges of solid and liquid fuels, 1965.

Profile No. 37

MAJOR INTERREGIONAL EXCHANGES OF ENERGY IN DOLLARS AND IN COAL EQUIVALENTS, BY REGIONS OF ORIGIN AND DESTINATION, 1965

World energy trade in 1965 was valued at approximately $17 billion, of which $11½ billion was accounted for by interregional flows.[1] (As indicated in Profile No. 23, the $17 billion in worldwide energy exports represented about 10 percent of all international trade in 1965.) The ranking of major regional trade flows in terms of value conforms closely to the order of importance based on tonnage in energy units (coal equivalents). Movements of energy from the Middle East to Western Europe head the listing with $2.7 billion or 25 percent of interregional dollar flows, twice as high as the next most important flow—that representing shipments from Africa to Western Europe valued at nearly $1½ billion. The third most important set of regional flows was Middle East shipments to the Far East; these exports were valued at $1.2 billion, of which about $900 million, or three-fourths, comprised Middle East shipments to Japan alone. Representing nearly 20 percent of Japan's imports of all kinds, this gave Japan one of the highest relative fuel-import bills (valued f.o.b.) in the world, the average for all industrial areas in 1965 being about 11 percent.[2]

The total value of interregional energy exports from underdeveloped regions (and this means almost exclusively oil) was estimated at about $9 billion in 1965. These shipments from developing areas represented about 80 percent of total interregional energy trade of $11½ billion. Energy commodities (again essentially oil) also bulk increasingly large as a share of the total exports of all kinds from underdeveloped regions to economically advanced areas. The figure in 1965 was 30 percent, double what it had been in 1950.[3]

A caveat should be added regarding the accompanying table. The side-by-side listing of values and physical units is provided as a matter of general interest. As is pointed out in a cautionary note to the table, the juxtaposition of value and tonnage figures does not mean that these two sets of data can be reliably used to construct faithful estimates of the average f.o.b. unit cost of energy exported from different parts of the world. One difficulty in interpreting the meaning of average unit value is the fact that the recorded value of crude oil shipments in international trade statistics often involves transfer prices within integrated companies based upon "posted" values rather than upon actual market prices as set in arm's-length transactions; the divergence between the two is thought frequently to be substantial. Also, a unit cost calculation would reflect the weighted effect of the underlying product mix; coal, crude oil, refined liquids, and, in United States-Canadian trade, gas and electricity enter into the tonnage figures in varying proportions in different regional exports. This makes it difficult to conclude whether unit cost differentials stem from the kinds of valuation problems noted above or from product-mix differences. The table, for example, implies a unit value of about $10 per coal equivalent ton for the world interregional movement of energy; while the 412 million coal equivalent tons traded *intra*regionally yields a value of $13.50 per coal equivalent ton of energy. A difference of this magnitude, however, very likely reflects more than valuation quirks, and may in large part be due to the relatively important share which the higher-value refined oil products represent in intraregional energy movements, as, for example, within Western Europe.

[1]Except for the consolidation of Caribbean and non-Caribbean Latin America into the single region "Latin America," the regional classification on which the accompanying table is based follows that of the preceding two profiles. The *intra*regional flows of $5½ billion shown in the table were dominated by trade within Western Europe ($2.3 billion), the Communist area ($1.4 billion), and Latin America ($1.0 billion). See Part Five, section III, table III-3.

[2]Some of the figures cited in these two paragraphs are not shown directly in the accompanying table; they are taken from the indicated source to the value figures in the table and from United Nations, *Statistical Yearbook, 1965*.

[3]*Ibid.*

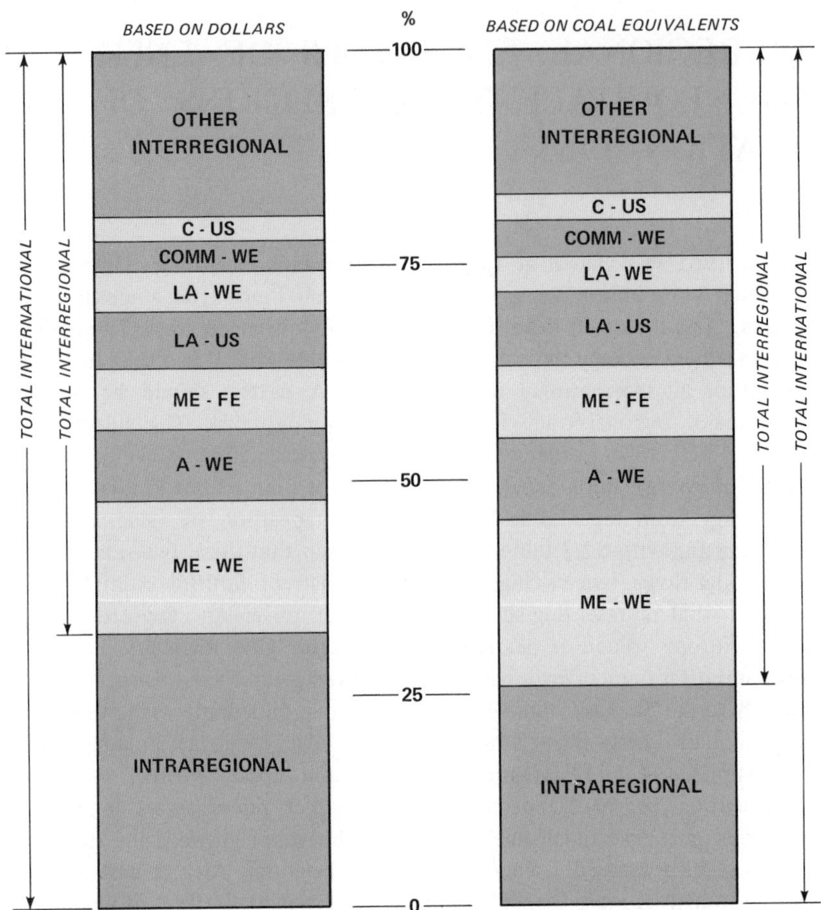

Legend:
ME = Middle East, WE = Western Europe,
A = Africa, FE = Far East and
Other Asia, LA = Latin America,
COMM = Communist countries, C = Canada,
1st Region = Exporter, 2nd Region =
Importer; e.g. LA-US refers to
Latin American shipments to U.S.

Major interregional energy flows, 1965, as percentage of total international energy exports.

MAJOR INTERREGIONAL EXCHANGES OF ENERGY IN DOLLARS AND IN COAL EQUIVALENTS, BY REGIONS OF ORIGIN AND DESTINATION, 1965

Interregional exports		Absolute data[a]		Percent of			
		Million dollars f.o.b.	Million metric tons coal equivalent	Interregional trade		International trade	
From	To			Value	Tonnage	Value	Tonnage
Middle East	Western Europe	2,710	303.2	23.5%	26.1%	15.9%	19.3%
Africa	Western Europe	1,418	153.5	12.3	13.2	8.3	9.8
Middle East	Far East and Other Asia. . .	1,230	132.8	10.7	11.4	7.2	8.4
Latin America	United States.	1,189	126.6	10.3	10.9	7.0	8.1
Latin America	Western Europe	752	57.1	6.5	4.9	4.4	3.6
Communist Countries	Western Europe	625	63.1	5.4	5.4	3.7	4.0
Canada	United States.	400	40.4	3.5	3.5	2.3	2.6
United States	Western Europe	365	26.0	3.2	2.2	2.1	1.7
Latin America	Canada	308	30.4	2.7	2.6	1.8	1.9
Middle East	United States.	290	29.6	2.5	2.5	1.7	1.9
United States	Canada	215	18.1	1.9	1.6	1.3	1.2
United States	Far East and Other Asia. . .	194	10.1	1.7	0.9	1.1	0.6
Middle East	Oceania	166	21.9	1.4	1.9	1.0	1.4
Total above		9,862	1,012.8	85.5	87.3	57.7	64.5
Other interregional		1,681	149.1	14.5	12.7	9.8	9.5
Total interregional		11,543	1,161.8	100.0	100.0	67.5	73.9
Total intraregional		5,547	412.4	–	–	32.5	26.2
Total international energy exports		17,090	1,574.2	–	–	100.0	100.0

[a]The value and coal equivalent tonnage figures (though shown side by side for general interest) are too rough to permit derivation of accurate estimates of the unit price of energy exported from different parts of the world.

Note: The value figures refer to Standard International Trade Classification (SITC), section 3, "mineral fuels, lubricants, and related materials." The interregional tonnage figures cover trade in solid fuels and liquid fuels plus Canadian-United States and Mexican-United States gas and electricity exchanges, and African gas shipments to Western Europe. With these additions, the interregional tonnage figures exhaust virtually *all* energy exchanges between the indicated regions.

Source: Value figures from Part Five, section III, table III-3 and notes thereto.

Interregional coal equivalents from Part Five, section III, table III-2 and from *Note* to the table in Profile No. 35. In the adaptation of figures from Part Five, table III-2, shipments between the Caribbean and Other Latin America have been eliminated so as to conform to the consolidated Latin America classification in the value figures.

The total international (i.e., interregional plus intraregional) coal equivalent figure (including trade in *all* primary energy sources) from Part Three, table VI. The intraregional coal equivalent figure was then derived as a residual between total interregional and total international trade. Because of numerous inconsistencies between the interregional and international estimates (as explained in the notes in Part Five, tables III-1 and III-2, and in the notes accompanying Profile No. 35), this residual must be viewed as a very approximate estimate.

Profile No. 38

DIRECTION OF NET SOLID AND LIQUID FUELS TRADE RELATED TO TOTAL ENERGY CONSUMPTION AND PRODUCTION, BY MAJOR REGIONS, 1929 AND 1965

In this overview we bring together data on energy consumption, production, and trade by geographic direction. The figures on consumption or production, based on Part Three of this volume, have been reviewed in earlier sets of profiles (No. 6 to No. 17 and No. 18 to No. 22), while data on the geographic direction of trade were dealt with in Profiles No. 35 to No. 37. Here for 1929 and 1965 we group world areas into either net energy importing regions or net exporting regions. (Foreign trade terminology is explained in some detail in the note appended to Profile No. 23.) For the net energy importers—i.e., regions whose total imports exceed their exports—we calculate as a percentage of the area's total energy consumption not only the area's total net imports, but also the net imports originating in particular geographic parts of the world. Conversely, for the net energy exporters—i.e., those with an excess of total exports over imports—we calculate total net exports and also net exports by specific regional destinations as a percentage of the area's total energy production. To avoid confusion, it is necessary to remember that although a region may be an overall net importer, it may still be a net exporter to specific other regions—as in the case of U.S. net exports to Western Europe in 1965. Conversely, Africa's overall net energy exports in 1965 are seen to have included net imports from the Middle East.[1]

The purpose of this kind of tabulation is obvious: it permits us to relate a region's total energy consumption to its supply dependence upon given parts of the world, just as it enables us to gauge the stake of a particular regional export market in a supplying region's aggregate output. The table thus gives answers to such questions as: how much of Japan's energy consumption depends on supplies from the Middle East; or, how much of the Communist countries' output is destined for Western Europe?

In bringing together the data on the direction of trade and those on production and consumption certain obstacles relating to statistical consistency and comparability between the two sets of data had to be waived. For example, net trade derived from the basic tabulations of Part Three (table VI) differs to some extent from the net trade estimates obtained from the direction-of-trade computations appearing in Part Five (tables III-1 and III-2). Although both sets of net trade figures are shown in lines (1) and (2) of the accompanying tabulation, it is the direction-of-trade figures in line (2) on which we must rely in this profile. These difficulties do not, however, obscure the more significant points conveyed by the figures.

The principal developments between 1929 and 1965 recorded in the table center on (a) the elimination of U.S. net exports and the consequent virtual disappearance of the United States as a factor of importance in the energy supply of several regions; (b) the Caribbean area's ability to accommodate to the growing U.S. net import requirements and to those of regions formerly served by the United States; (c) the vast increase in Western Europe's net import position; and (d) the capacity of Middle Eastern (and lately, African) suppliers to meet large parts of the growing energy needs in Western Europe and elsewhere.

It may be useful to highlight some of the more pronounced changes revolving around these long-term trends. Among net energy importers in 1929, Canada recorded the highest percentage of energy consumption provided by a given supplying region. Well over one-half of its consumption was in the form of net imports from the United States (primarily coal, but also a substantial amount of oil, as we saw in Profile No. 36). Other regions whose 1929 consumption of energy was heavily dominated by a single supplying region included non-

(Text continued on p. 182.)

[1] In the accompanying table parentheses denote cases where a region that is a net importer overall has net energy exports to a particular area, or, conversely, where a region that is a net exporter in the aggregate receives net imports from a particular part of the world.

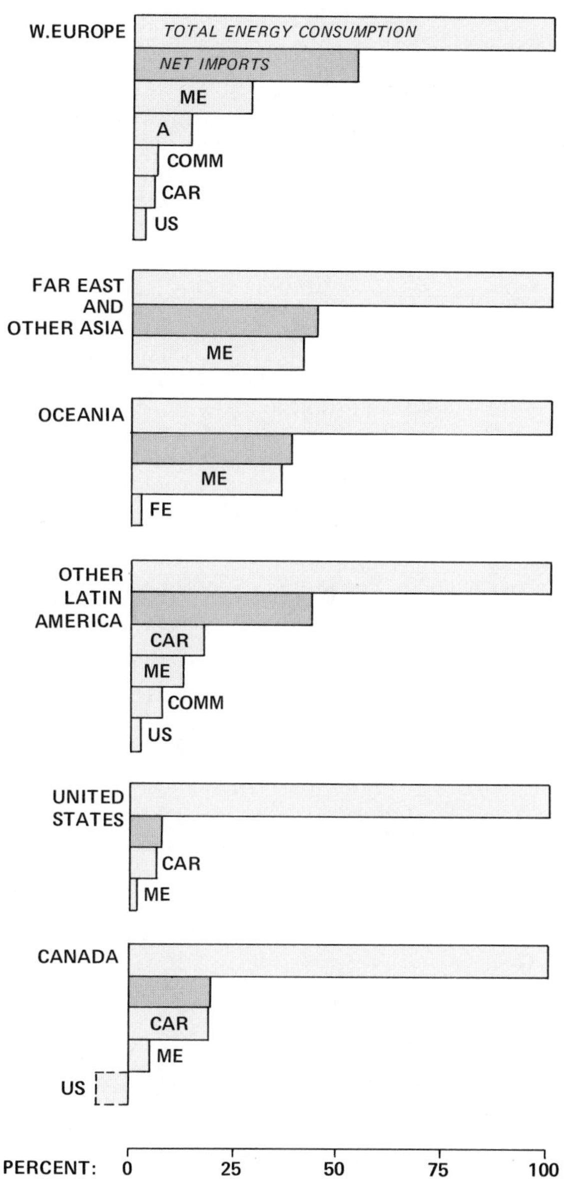

Share of net imports from selected regions in 1965 energy consumption of net importing regions.

Notes: For Western Europe, United States, Canada, Caribbean and Africa, the percentages used are those shown in footnote to table. A broken bar extending to the left signifies net exports of net importing regions or net imports of net exporting regions.
C = Canada; WE = Western Europe; O = Oceania; LA = Other Latin America; FE = Far East and Other Asia; COMM = Communist Countries; CAR = Caribbean; ME = Middle East; A = Africa.

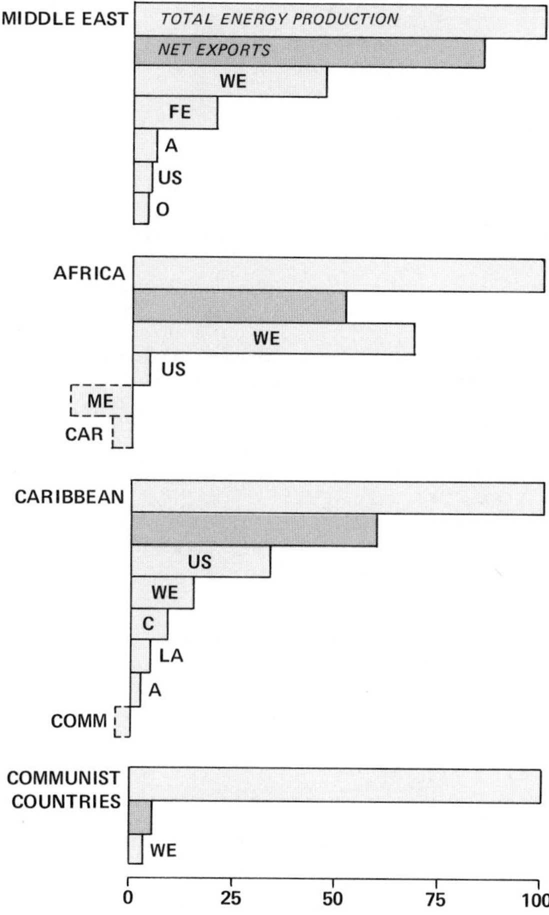

Share of net exports to selected regions in 1965 energy production of net exporting regions.

DIRECTION OF NET SOLID AND LIQUID FUELS TRADE RELATED TO TOTAL ENERGY CONSUMPTION AND PRODUCTION, BY MAJOR REGIONS, 1929 AND 1965

A. 1929

	Net importing regions[a]						
	Canada	Western Europe	Oceania	Communist Asia	Other Latin America	Far East and Other Asia	Africa
Total energy consumption (mill. met. tons coal equiv.)	42.6	603.6	15.3	23.8	17.4	70.8	17.1
Net solid and liquid fuels imports (mill. met. tons coal equiv.)[b]							
(1)	24.9	21.0	3.2	0.4	9.7	3.6	6.5
(2)	26.3	25.7	3.3	0.6	9.9	3.8	6.6
Net imports (as percent of consumption)[b]							
(1)	58.5%	3.5%	20.9%	1.6%	55.6%	5.1%	37.8%
(2)	61.9	4.3	21.6	2.3	56.9	5.4	38.5
By region of origin:							
Canada	–	(0.1)	–	–	(4.5)	–	–
United States	54.1	2.1	9.4	4.1	17.4	4.1	5.2
Western Europe	1.7	–	3.7	0.1	33.1	(1.0)	31.7
Oceania	–	(0.1)	–	–	–	(1.7)	–
U.S.S.R. & Comm. E. Europe	–	2.4	–	0.5	0.9	1.2	5.1
Communist Asia	(–)	(–)	–	–	–	0.8	–
Caribbean	4.3	1.1	–	–	10.0	–	0.2
Other Latin America	1.8	(1.0)	–	–	–	–	–
Middle East	–	0.6	0.8	–	–	0.9	0.7
Far East and Other Asia	–	0.1	7.7	(2.4)	–	–	(4.4)
Africa	–	(0.9)	–	–	–	1.1	–

	Net exporting regions[a]			
	United States	U.S.S.R. & Comm. E. Europe	Caribbean	Middle East
Total energy production (mill. met. tons coal equiv.)	874.6	153.0	49.2	9.5
Net solid and liquid fuels exports (mill. met. tons coal equiv.)[b]				
(1)	26.5	22.6	31.3	7.0
(2)	27.5	16.8	27.9	4.0
Net exports (as percent of production)[b]				
(1)	3.0%	14.8%	63.6%	73.6%
(2)	3.1	11.0	56.7	42.0
By destination:				
Canada	2.6	–	3.7	–
United States	–	(–)	35.5	0.1
Western Europe	1.5	9.4	13.8	36.8
Oceania	0.2	–	–	1.3
U.S.S.R. & Comm. E. Europe	–	–	–	(4.2)
Communist Asia[c]	0.1	0.1	–	–
Caribbean	(2.0)	–	–	–
Other Latin America	0.3	0.1	3.5	–
Middle East	(–)	0.3	–	–
Far East and Other Asia	0.3	0.6	–	6.7
Africa	0.1	0.6	0.1	1.3

[a]The net interregional flows of solid and liquid fuels shown in the table virtually exhaust interregional flows of *total energy*; this is because gas and electricity trade is mostly intraregional. In terms of the regions shown in the table, the only quantitatively significant 1965 net gas and electricity flows (in thousand metric tons coal equivalent) were: Canadian gas to the United States, 14,643; Mexican gas to the United States, 1,643; U.S. electricity to Canada, 4; U.S. electricity to Mexico, 15; Algerian gas to Western Europe, 1,412. Inclusion of these flows in the percentages of panel B of the table (1965) would have the following effect:

	Percent shown in table	*Percent after adding gas and/or electricity*
Canada, net imports	19.7%	10.4%
United States	(4.8)	(14.1)
United States, net imports	7.0	7.9
Canada	0.4	1.2
Caribbean	6.5	6.6
Western Europe, net imports	53.4	53.6
Africa	13.3	13.5
Caribbean, net exports	59.3	59.8
United States	33.3	33.8
Africa, net exports	51.4	52.1
Western Europe	67.9	68.6

DIRECTION OF NET SOLID AND LIQUID FUELS TRADE RELATED TO TOTAL ENERGY CONSUMPTION AND PRODUCTION, BY MAJOR REGIONS, 1929 AND 1965 (CONTINUED)

B. 1965

	Net importing regions[a]					
	Canada	United States	Western Europe	Oceania	Other Latin America	Far East and Other Asia
Total energy consumption (mill. met. tons coal equiv.)	158.4	1,881.6	1,117.2	61.2	85.5	328.0
Net solid and liquid fuels imports (mill. met. tons coal equiv.)[b]						
(1)	33.2	136.6	589.9	23.1	31.2	160.7
(2)	31.2	132.4	597.0	23.1	36.6	143.3
Net imports (as percent of consumption)[b]						
(1)	21.0%	7.3%	52.8%	37.7%	36.5%	49.0%
(2)	19.7	7.0	53.4	37.8	42.8	43.7
By region of origin:						
Canada	-	0.4	(-)	-	-	0.2
United States	(4.8)	-	2.3	-	2.2	1.6
Western Europe	0.2	(1.4)	-	-	0.4	(0.6)
Oceania	-	(-)	(-)	-	-	(0.4)
Communist Countries	-	(-)	5.5	-	7.8	1.7
Caribbean	19.2	6.5	5.1	-	17.5	0.9
Other Latin America	-	(0.1)	(-)	-	-	-
Middle East	5.6	1.6	27.1	35.7	12.3	40.2
Far East and Other Asia	(0.5)	(0.3)	0.2	2.0	-	-
Africa	-	0.4	13.3	-	2.6	0.1

	Net exporting regions[a]			
	Communist Countries	Caribbean	Middle East	Africa
Total energy production (mill. met. tons coal equiv.)	1,674.8	365.3	640.1	218.9
Net solid and liquid fuels exports (mill. met. tons coal equiv.)[b]				
(1)	92.7	230.4	560.5	116.3
(2)	89.8	216.7	544.6	112.6
Net exports (as percent of production)[b]				
(1)	5.5%	63.1%	87.6%	53.1%
(2)	5.4	59.3	85.1	51.4
By destination:				
Canada	-	8.3	1.4	-
United States	(-)	33.3	4.6	3.0
Western Europe	3.7	15.6	47.3	67.9
Oceania	-	-	3.4	-
Communist Countries	-	(3.8)	(0.1)	(0.6)
Caribbean	0.8	-	0.7	(3.9)
Other Latin America	0.4	4.1	1.6	1.0
Middle East	-	(1.2)	-	(16.2)
Far East and Other Asia	0.3	0.8	20.6	0.2
Africa	0.1	2.3	5.5	-

[b]Two figures are given for net trade: line (1) refers to data in Part Three, tables VI or XIV; line (2) refers to estimates constructed in Part Five, tables III-1 and III-2. The percentages for trade by region of origin and destination refer to figure (2). See Part Five, notes to tables III-1 and III-2 concerning differences between the two sets of net trade estimates.

[c]Mainland China only.

Note: Parentheses under "net importing regions" signify net exports; parentheses under "net exporting regions" signify net imports.

Source: Consumption, production, and alternative (1) of net trade from Part Three, table XIV; alternative (2) of net trade and data on origin and destination of trade from Part Five, tables III-1 and III-2.

Caribbean Latin America, one-third of whose energy supplies emanated from Western Europe; and Africa, 30 percent of whose consumption likewise represented net imports from Western Europe.

Western Europe was only a modest net energy importer in 1929. Its most important foreign supplier (today's Communist area) accounted for under 2½ percent of its total consumption. By 1965 Western Europe had become the largest net importing region in the world, and the share of its total energy supplies coming from a single region (27 percent from the Middle East) was topped only by the Far East (40 percent of total consumption composed of net imports from the Middle East), and Oceania (35 percent from the Middle East). More modest 1965 percentages were the nearly 20 percent of Canadian consumption dependent on the Caribbean, and 18 percent of non-Caribbean Latin America originating in the same area. Among U.S. suppliers, the largest share (6½ percent of U.S. energy consumption) was again provided by the Caribbean region.

Turning to net energy exporters, the orientation of total production towards the needs of a single regional market strongly characterizes the Middle East and Caribbean in both years. In 1929 the 36 percent share of Caribbean production destined for the United States was almost precisely the percentage of Middle East output exported to Western Europe. In 1965 these two markets—the United States and Western Europe—remained paramount in Caribbean and Middle East production, the United States taking one-third of the former's output, and Western Europe close to one-half of the latter's. Among producing areas, other 1965 examples of major dependence on specific regional markets are Africa (by now a net exporter), two-thirds of whose output went to Western Europe; and the Middle East's shipments to its second most important market, the Far East, whose imports in 1965 accounted for 20 percent of Middle East production.

Part Three

DETAILED REGIONAL AND NATIONAL ENERGY STATISTICS

A Note on the Computational Steps in the Derivation of Data in Tables I–XIV

For those who wish to be able to trace the derivation of data appearing in the following basic set of fourteen tables, a column-by-column procedural guide precedes each table. Those derivations marked "source" refer to data obtained from sources described under the Country Notes section of Part Four. Computational steps accompanied by an asterisk (*) refer to the application of conversion factors discussed in the paragraphs on Conversion Factors and Procedures under the General Notes section of Part Four.

Three

DERIVATION OF TABLE I

Column	*Derivation*
(1)	Sources
(2)	Sources
(3)	Sources (may contain peat, sub-bituminous coal, pitch or asphaltite)
(4)	Sum of col. (5) and natural gas liquids (from sources) not shown separately
(5)	Sources (may contain shale oil)
(6)	Sources
(7)	Sources

Table I. PRIMARY ENERGY PRODUCTION, SELECTED YEARS, 1925-1965

(Original units)

Region, country, year	Solid fuels (10^3 m.t.)			Liquid fuels (10^3 m.t.)		Natural gas (10^6 c.m.)	Hydro-electric power (10^6 kwh)
	Hard coal	Lignite	Other	Total	Crude oil		
	(1)	(2)	(3)	(4)	(5)	(6)	(7)
WORLD							
1925	1184201	181939	14572	151997	148688	35977	78678
1929	1323596	227481	18107	212445	205823	57823	117239
1933	995961	172861	22930	202107	197385	50637	127090
1937	1298141	249194	34755	287205	280083	77964	177901
1938	1207102	259811	36676	280884	273416	74824	182377
1950	1431011	380741	48814	542117	522082	189179	347178
1953	1489221	464548	51633	685093	659359	256595	414518
1955	1592270	535060	63718	803894	774027	292497	475003
1957	1729440	593076	57893	918856	887431	348242	553986
1960	1779889	640192	66204	1094121	1056867	459924	687912
1961	1805170	663978	63766	1165410	1125436	496679	722752
1962	1849330	686977	47147	1262072	1220818	543251	759456
1963	1919639	721826	70968	1354452	1309395	587704	795952
1964	1987998	752053	73922	1457913	1409628	641925	824742
1965	2038231	748699	73840	1561860	1511108	684864	900763
NORTH AMERICA							
1925	534539	2359	2893	107831	104675	33791	35479
1929	561936	3186	3072	144496	138244	54223	55269
1933	353460	2745	2212	126766	122680	44657	54247

Table I. PRIMARY ENERGY PRODUCTION, SELECTED YEARS, 1925-1965

(Original units)

Region, country, year	Solid fuels (10^3 m.t.)			Liquid fuels (10^3 m.t.)		Natural gas (10^6 c.m.)	Hydro-electric power (10^6 kwh)
	Hard coal	Lignite	Other	Total	Crude oil		
	(1)	(2)	(3)	(4)	(5)	(6)	(7)
NORTH AMERICA (CONTINUED)							
1937	459320	3875	2397	179556	173232	69048	73435
1938	365115	3649	2224	171695	164980	65674	72996
1950	517676	5056	3013	289783	270580	173447	153197
1953	450758	4420	2177	354127	329469	232290	176863
1955	451657	4953	2123	381946	353239	260757	192736
1957	475823	4406	1714	408122	378223	298344	217009
1960	398176	4460	1398	407883	373590	364887	255398
1961	384890	4742	1235	420900	384150	381936	259549
1962	401473	4818	1358	432663	394653	407440	276136
1963	436885	4154	1501	448529	406928	430242	272822
1964	461284	4485	1910	458296	413700	457338	293646
1965	481530	4631	2318	471343	424650	474489	313713
CANADA							
1925	8628	395	2893	53	53	479	9949
1929	12273	528	3072	140	140	804	17695
1933	7742	845	2212	164	144	655	17006
1937	11014	955	2397	438	367	917	27180
1938	9815	929	2224	927	873	947	25691
1950	12351	1999	3013	3924	3871	1921	52175
1953	10414	1834	2177	11004	10933	2860	67069
1955	9231	2081	2123	17595	17493	4269	76200
1957	8211	2041	1714	24779	24575	6230	83373
1960	6622	1969	1398	26241	25614	14809	105883
1961	6194	2004	1235	30878	29845	18569	103919
1962	5925	2047	1358	34234	32993	26808	104050
1963	6394	1700	1501	37112	34925	31642	103832
1964	6550	1809	1910	40066	37091	39845	113344
1965	6323	1871	2318	42917	39704	41628	116712
UNITED STATES							
1925	525909	1964	-	107778	104622	33312	25530
1929	549659	2658	-	144356	138104	53419	37574
1933	345713	1900	-	126602	122536	44002	37241
1937	448300	2920	-	179118	172865	68131	46255
1938	355293	2720	-	170768	164107	64727	47305
1950	505318	3057	-	285859	266709	171526	101022
1953	440337	2586	-	343123	318536	229430	109794
1955	442410	2872	-	364351	335746	256488	116536
1957	467595	2365	-	383343	353648	292114	133636
1960	391526	2491	-	381642	347976	350078	149515
1961	378664	2738	-	390022	354305	363367	155630
1962	395522	2771	-	398429	361660	380632	172086
1963	430451	2454	-	411417	372003	398600	168990
1964	454710	2676	-	418230	376609	417493	180302
1965	475187	2760	-	428426	384946	432861	197001
WESTERN EUROPE							
1925	477494	148559	5421	364	364	7	30833
1929	540251	184614	5730	363	363	9	42689
1933	423382	134353	5559	476	476	15	46861

Table I. PRIMARY ENERGY PRODUCTION, SELECTED YEARS, 1925–1965

(Original units)

Region, country, year	Solid fuels (10^3 m.t.)			Liquid fuels (10^3 m.t.)		Natural gas (10^6 c.m.)	Hydro-electric power (10^6 kwh)
	Hard coal	Lignite	Other	Total	Crude oil		
	(1)	(2)	(3)	(4)	(5)	(6)	(7)
WESTERN EUROPE (CONTINUED)							
1937	522118	193647	6075	710	710	38	64462
1938	515359	204498	5801	837	837	19	65849
1950	451314	96941	6366	4022	4005	1310	110867
1953	480960	106646	6857	7185	7120	3384	138954
1955	487742	117406	6800	9525	9453	5514	160848
1957	493174	130045	7263	12173	12081	7305	175286
1960	448146	133474	6594	15460	15155	12226	230447
1961	440872	137365	5938	16710	16422	14105	239233
1962	443573	143017	6305	17675	17339	15629	243170
1963	438459	151449	5846	18699	18404	16524	264159
1964	440483	157097	6963	20576	20195	18282	260611
1965	424482	149938	5921	21005	20619	20169	293550
EUROPEAN ECONOMIC COMMUNITY (EEC)							
1925	223112	140990	1041	157	157	7	14086
1929	269544	175222	1370	188	188	7	20205
1933	205348	127150	1218	349	349	14	22877
1937	273976	185434	1492	544	544	36	32964
1938	277236	195536	1525	646	646	17	32526
1950	217768	78608	1562	1998	1983	825	47736
1953	238304	87647	1683	3545	3482	2796	60379
1955	247609	93210	1817	5329	5260	4720	70607
1957	249205	100127	1811	8265	8177	6475	71232
1960	234925	99292	1783	11748	11449	10625	102142
1961	230872	101698	1763	12685	12402	12398	96037
1962	227760	105909	1760	13456	13125	13780	90503
1963	224061	110499	1841	14191	13904	14475	105366
1964	228990	114387	1869	15827	15458	16066	89996
1965	218433	105613	1735	15865	15496	17926	108388
BELGIUM-LUXEMBOURG							
1925	23097	-	-	-	-	-	20
1929	26940	-	-	-	-	-	20
1933	25300	-	-	-	-	-	20
1937	29859	-	-	-	-	-	57
1938	29585	-	-	-	-	-	44
1950	27321	-	-	-	-	14	64
1953	30060	-	-	-	-	55	93
1955	29978	-	-	-	-	80	132
1957	29001	-	-	-	-	106	176
1960	22469	-	-	-	-	70	193
1961	21536	-	-	-	-	70	248
1962	21226	-	-	-	-	70	211
1963	21418	-	-	-	-	69	633
1964	21305	-	-	-	-	66	919
1965	19786	-	-	-	-	79	1187
FRANCE							
1925	47097	993	-	70	70	-	4313
1929	53780	1197	-	79	79	-	6600
1933	46887	1094	-	85	85	-	7400
1937	44319	1015	-	79	79	-	10980

Table I. PRIMARY ENERGY PRODUCTION, SELECTED YEARS, 1925-1965

(Original units)

Region, country, year	Solid fuels (10^3 m.t.) Hard coal	Lignite	Other	Liquid fuels (10^3 m.t.) Total	Crude oil	Natural gas (10^6 c.m.)	Hydro-electric power (10^6 kwh)
	(1)	(2)	(3)	(4)	(5)	(6)	(7)
FRANCE (CONTINUED)							
1938	46504	1058	-	81	81	-	10400
1950	50835	1686	-	164	151	230	16233
1953	52596	1948	-	400	388	233	21251
1955	55336	2053	-	897	885	256	25794
1957	56799	2293	-	1432	1410	439	25078
1960	55966	2278	-	2212	1983	2846	40747
1961	52358	2906	-	2377	2164	4072	38596
1962	52370	2882	-	2634	2370	4740	36137
1963	47763	2475	-	2742	2522	4861	43821
1964	53030	2241	-	3142	2846	5090	35062
1965	51348	2689	-	3310	2988	5048	46893
GERMANY							
1925	145612	138684	1041	79	79	-	2852
1929	177020	173086	1370	103	103	-	3564
1933	120253	125576	1218	238	238	-	4090
1937	184513	183217	1492	451	451	21	6904
1938	186179	193434	1525	552	552	NA	7299
GERMANY, FEDERAL REPUBLIC							
1950	126334	75947	1562	1119	1119	63	8658
1953	142220	84689	1683	2189	2189	205	9358
1955	149265	90483	1817	3147	3147	617	12022
1957	151005	97152	1811	3982	3982	789	12318
1960	143255	96216	1783	5561	5550	919	12992
1961	143615	97267	1763	6233	6220	927	12919
1962	141899	101251	1760	6790	6778	1294	12546
1963	142786	106658	1841	7395	7383	1680	12378
1964	142704	110945	1869	7683	7673	2362	12160
1965	135464	101906	1735	7892	7884	3219	15365
ITALY							
1925	189	1105	-	8	8	7	6901
1929	223	782	-	6	6	7	10021
1933	334	383	-	26	26	14	11367
1937	964	1059	-	14	14	15	15023
1938	1480	873	-	13	13	17	14783
1950	1031	781	-	10	8	510	22781
1953	1131	758	-	136	85	2280	29677
1955	1135	419	-	261	204	3627	32659
1957	1024	394	-	1328	1262	4987	33660
1960	737	794	-	2057	1998	6447	48210
1961	742	1525	-	2029	1972	6863	44274
1962	692	1776	-	1875	1820	7150	41609
1963	585	1366	-	1839	1784	7267	48534
1964	471	1201	-	2732	2669	7684	41855
1965	389	1018	-	2268	2229	7800	44943
NETHERLANDS							
1925	7117	208	-	-	-	-	-

Table I. PRIMARY ENERGY PRODUCTION, SELECTED YEARS, 1925-1965

(Original units)

Region, country, year	Solid fuels (10^3 m.t.)			Liquid fuels (10^3 m.t.)		Natural gas (10^6 c.m.)	Hydro-electric power (10^6 kwh)
	Hard coal	Lignite	Other	Total	Crude oil		
	(1)	(2)	(3)	(4)	(5)	(6)	(7)
NETHERLANDS (CONTINUED)							
1929	11581	157	-	-	-	-	-
1933	12574	97	-	-	-	-	-
1937	14321	143	-	-	-	-	-
1938	13488	171	-	-	-	-	-
1950	12247	194	-	705	705	8	-
1953	12297	252	-	820	820	23	-
1955	11895	255	-	1024	1024	140	-
1957	11376	288	-	1523	1523	154	-
1960	12498	4	-	1918	1918	343	-
1961	12621	-	-	2046	2046	466	-
1962	11573	-	-	2157	2157	526	-
1963	11509	-	-	2215	2215	598	-
1964	11480	-	-	2270	2270	864	-
1965	11446	-	-	2395	2395	1780	-
EUROPEAN FREE TRADE ASSOCIATION (EFTA)							
1925	248008	3050	804	201	201	-	14668
1929	263103	3554	716	169	169	-	19392
1933	211549	3026	773	121	121	-	19557
1937	245502	3300	914	159	159	-	26398
1938	231904	3393	858	184	184	-	27827
1950	221102	5172	1490	1911	1911	471	52580
1953	229169	6443	1117	3449	3449	564	63831
1955	226372	7508	1251	3901	3901	760	71242
1957	228570	9621	1304	3436	3436	788	82752
1960	197947	8438	596	2698	2698	1548	99483
1961	194690	8313	510	2614	2614	1638	111642
1962	201722	8421	365	2624	2624	1754	118075
1963	199971	8707	371	2826	2824	1858	119125
1964	197817	8057	394	2875	2873	1942	131667
1965	191499	7668	350	2997	2995	1913	144765
AUSTRIA							
1925	145	3033	-	-	-	-	1330
1929	208	3525	-	-	-	-	1750
1933	239	3014	9	1	1	-	1950
1937	230	3242	50	33	33	-	2392
1938	227	3340	50	57	57	-	2400
1950	183	4308	50	1699	1699	470	4988
1953	162	5574	50	3221	3221	555	6430
1955	171	6619	40	3666	3666	748	7905
1957	152	6877	36	3186	3186	759	9320
1960	132	5973	36	2448	2448	1469	11882
1961	106	5661	5	2356	2356	1556	11664
1962	99	5712	5	2394	2394	1635	12127
1963	104	6053	5	2622	2620	1699	11955
1964	103	5761	5	2665	2663	1764	13179
1965	59	5450	5	2857	2855	1724	16083
DENMARK							
1925	-	-	424	-	-	-	-
1929	-	-	336	-	-	-	-

Table I. PRIMARY ENERGY PRODUCTION, SELECTED YEARS, 1925–1965

(Original units)

Region, country, year	Solid fuels (10^3 m.t.)			Liquid fuels (10^3 m.t.)		Natural gas (10^6 c.m.)	Hydro-electric power (10^6 kwh)
	Hard coal	Lignite	Other	Total	Crude oil		
	(1)	(2)	(3)	(4)	(5)	(6)	(7)
DENMARK (CONTINUED)							
1933	-	-	348	-	-	-	-
1937	-	35	480	-	-	-	-
1938	-	35	432	-	-	-	-
1950	-	770	902	-	-	-	25
1953	-	798	574	-	-	-	30
1955	-	801	712	-	-	-	30
1957	-	2560	734	-	-	-	30
1960	-	2309	170	-	-	-	20
1961	-	2494	113	-	-	-	26
1962	-	2556	61	-	-	-	26
1963	-	2512	50	-	-	-	25
1964	-	2195	36	-	-	-	25
1965	-	2128	20	-	-	-	25
NORWAY							
1925	390	-	350	-	-	-	6187
1929	251	-	350	-	-	-	7516
1933	295	-	350	-	-	-	7322
1937	297	-	350	-	-	-	9257
1938	299	-	350	-	-	-	9918
1950	364	-	361	-	-	-	17882
1953	427	-	253	-	-	-	19640
1955	322	-	239	-	-	-	22680
1957	384	-	249	-	-	-	25820
1960	404	-	180	-	-	-	31223
1961	369	-	163	-	-	-	33720
1962	444	-	146	-	-	-	38000
1963	393	-	104	-	-	-	39656
1964	442	-	104	-	-	-	44216
1965	435	-	105	-	-	-	49347
PORTUGAL							
1925	123	17	-	-	-	-	45
1929	197	29	-	-	-	-	73
1933	228	12	-	-	-	-	98
1937	259	23	-	-	-	-	139
1938	308	18	-	-	-	-	127
1950	419	94	-	-	-	-	437
1953	478	71	-	-	-	-	999
1955	404	88	-	-	-	-	1726
1957	499	184	-	-	-	-	1841
1960	434	156	-	-	-	-	3105
1961	470	158	-	-	-	-	3422
1962	405	153	-	-	-	-	3511
1963	416	142	-	-	-	-	4002
1964	444	101	-	-	-	-	4220
1965	428	90	-	-	-	-	3983
SWEDEN							
1925	264	-	30	-	-	-	3380
1929	395	-	30	-	-	-	4577
1933	349	-	30	-	-	-	4895

Table I. PRIMARY ENERGY PRODUCTION, SELECTED YEARS, 1925-1965

(Original units)

Region, country, year	Solid fuels (10^3 m.t.)			Liquid fuels (10^3 m.t.)		Natural gas (10^6 c.m.)	Hydro-electric power (10^6 kwh)
	Hard coal	Lignite	Other	Total	Crude oil		
	(1)	(2)	(3)	(4)	(5)	(6)	(7)
SWEDEN (CONTINUED)							
1937	460	-	34	-	-	-	6971
1938	431	-	26	-	-	-	7307
1950	309	-	177	53	53	-	17338
1953	285	-	240	66	66	-	21281
1955	282	-	260	83	83	-	21650
1957	304	-	285	95	95	-	27112
1960	251	-	210	102	102	-	31090
1961	200	-	229	107	107	-	36537
1962	148	-	153	101	101	-	39099
1963	99	-	212	79	79	-	37908
1964	84	-	249	81	81	-	43093
1965	59	-	220	56	56	-	46423
SWITZERLAND							
1925	7	-	-	-	-	-	3705
1929	7	-	-	-	-	-	5311
1933	2	-	-	-	-	-	4961
1937	4	-	-	-	-	-	6884
1938	3	-	-	-	-	-	7087
1950	30	-	-	-	-	-	10431
1953	10	-	-	-	-	-	13554
1955	10	-	-	-	-	-	15550
1957	10	-	-	-	-	-	15877
1960	10	-	-	-	-	-	19030
1961	10	-	-	-	-	-	22421
1962	10	-	-	-	-	-	21387
1963	10	-	-	-	-	-	21916
1964	10	-	-	-	-	-	22912
1965	10	-	-	-	-	-	24279
UNITED KINGDOM							
1925	247079	-	-	201	201	-	21
1929	262045	-	-	169	169	-	165
1933	210436	-	-	120	120	-	331
1937	244252	-	-	126	126	-	755
1938	230636	-	-	127	127	-	988
1950	219797	-	-	159	159	1	1479
1953	227807	-	-	162	162	9	1897
1955	225183	-	-	152	152	12	1701
1957	227221	-	-	155	155	29	2752
1960	196716	-	-	148	148	79	3133
1961	193535	-	-	151	151	82	3852
1962	200616	-	-	129	129	119	3925
1963	198949	-	-	125	125	159	3663
1964	196734	-	-	129	129	178	4022
1965	190508	-	-	84	84	189	4625
WESTERN EUROPE - OTHER							
1925	6374	4519	3576	6	6	-	2079
1929	7604	5838	3644	6	6	2	3092
1933	6485	4177	3568	6	6	1	4427
1937	2640	4913	3669	7	7	2	5100

Table I. PRIMARY ENERGY PRODUCTION, SELECTED YEARS, 1925-1965

(Original units)

Region, country, year	Solid fuels (10^3 m.t.)			Liquid fuels (10^3 m.t.)		Natural gas (10^6 c.m.)	Hydro-electric power (10^6 kwh)
	Hard coal	Lignite	Other	Total	Crude oil		
	(1)	(2)	(3)	(4)	(5)	(6)	(7)
WESTERN EUROPE - OTHER (CONTINUED)							
1938	6219	5569	3418	7	7	2	5496
1950	12444	13161	3314	113	111	14	10551
1953	13487	12556	4057	191	189	24	14744
1955	13761	16688	3732	295	292	34	18999
1957	15399	20297	4148	472	468	42	21302
1960	15274	25744	4215	1014	1008	53	28822
1961	15310	27354	3665	1411	1406	69	31554
1962	14091	28687	4180	1595	1590	95	34592
1963	14427	32243	3634	1682	1676	191	39668
1964	13676	34653	4700	1874	1864	274	38948
1965	14550	36657	3836	2143	2128	330	40397
FINLAND							
1925	-	-	20	-	-	-	384
1929	-	-	20	-	-	-	789
1933	-	-	18	-	-	-	1244
1937	-	-	22	-	-	-	2066
1938	-	-	25	-	-	-	2456
1950	-	-	197	-	-	-	3650
1953	-	-	196	-	-	-	4979
1955	-	-	160	-	-	-	6190
1957	-	-	179	-	-	-	6616
1960	-	-	120	-	-	-	5269
1961	-	-	116	-	-	-	8023
1962	-	-	62	-	-	-	9770
1963	-	-	80	-	-	-	8374
1964	-	-	72	-	-	-	8501
1965	-	-	65	-	-	-	9488
GREECE							
1925	-	142	-	-	-	-	8
1929	-	156	-	-	-	-	8
1933	-	99	-	-	-	-	12
1937	-	131	-	-	-	-	12
1938	-	108	-	-	-	-	13
1950	-	180	-	-	-	-	10
1953	-	444	-	-	-	-	31
1955	-	782	-	-	-	-	332
1957	-	998	-	-	-	-	360
1960	-	2551	-	-	-	-	469
1961	-	2504	-	-	-	-	554
1962	-	2694	-	-	-	-	614
1963	-	3516	-	-	-	-	806
1964	-	3802	-	-	-	-	749
1965	-	5009	-	-	-	-	748
ICELAND							
1925	-	-	-	-	-	-	6
1929	-	-	-	-	-	-	6
1933	-	-	-	-	-	-	8
1937	-	-	-	-	-	-	15
1938	-	-	-	-	-	-	23

Table I. PRIMARY ENERGY PRODUCTION, SELECTED YEARS, 1925-1965

(Original units)

Region, country, year	Solid fuels (10^3 m.t.)			Liquid fuels (10^3 m.t.)		Natural gas (10^6 c.m.)	Hydro-electric power (10^6 kwh)
	Hard coal	Lignite	Other	Total	Crude oil		
	(1)	(2)	(3)	(4)	(5)	(6)	(7)
ICELAND (CONTINUED)							
1950	-	-	3	-	-	-	168
1953	-	-	1	-	-	-	198
1955	-	-	-	-	-	-	379
1957	-	-	-	-	-	-	415
1960	-	-	-	-	-	-	523
1961	-	-	-	-	-	-	576
1962	-	-	-	-	-	-	593
1963	-	-	-	-	-	-	629
1964	-	-	-	-	-	-	653
1965	-	-	-	-	-	-	641
IRELAND							
1925	79	-	3556	-	-	-	10
1929	87	-	3624	-	-	-	31
1933	107	-	3550	-	-	-	113
1937	128	-	3647	-	-	-	249
1938	120	-	3393	-	-	-	296
1950	172	-	3114	-	-	-	466
1953	167	-	3860	-	-	-	533
1955	201	-	3572	-	-	-	487
1957	241	-	3969	-	-	-	702
1960	208	-	4095	-	-	-	932
1961	201	-	3549	-	-	-	737
1962	208	-	4118	-	-	-	660
1963	233	-	3554	-	-	-	656
1964	217	-	4628	-	-	-	783
1965	178	-	3771	-	-	-	939
SPAIN							
1925	6117	403	-	6	6	-	1370
1929	7108	439	-	6	6	-	1982
1933	5999	301	-	5	5	-	2646
1937	2084	208	-	6	6	-	2306
1938	5649	166	-	6	6	-	2236
1950	11118	1316	-	1	1	-	5079
1953	12395	1791	-	17	17	-	7500
1955	12426	1836	-	35	35	-	8991
1957	13931	2519	-	72	72	-	9670
1960	13783	1762	-	64	64	-	15624
1961	13796	2089	-	65	65	-	15980
1962	12695	2488	-	65	65	-	16073
1963	12908	2591	-	65	65	-	21139
1964	12196	2604	-	65	65	-	20646
1965	13180	2860	-	65	65	-	19550
YUGOSLAVIA							
1925	178	3974	-	-	-	-	300
1929	409	5243	-	-	-	2	275
1933	379	3777	-	1	1	1	403
1937	428	4574	-	1	1	2	450
1938	450	5287	-	1	1	2	470
1950	1154	11665	-	112	110	14	1175

Table I. PRIMARY ENERGY PRODUCTION, SELECTED YEARS, 1925-1965

(Original units)

Region, country, year	Solid fuels (10^3 m.t.)			Liquid fuels (10^3 m.t.)		Natural gas (10^6 c.m.)	Hydro-electric power (10^6 kwh)
	Hard coal	Lignite	Other	Total	Crude oil		
	(1)	(2)	(3)	(4)	(5)	(6)	(7)
YUGOSLAVIA (CONTINUED)							
1953	925	10321	-	174	172	24	1500
1955	1134	14070	-	260	257	34	2610
1957	1227	16780	-	400	396	42	3522
1960	1283	21431	-	950	944	53	5984
1961	1313	22761	-	1346	1341	69	5658
1962	1188	23505	-	1530	1525	95	6851
1963	1286	26136	-	1617	1611	191	8028
1964	1263	28247	-	1809	1799	274	7575
1965	1192	28788	-	2078	2063	330	8985
OCEANIA							
1925	14921	1052	926	-	-	-	649
1929	11941	1890	1066	-	-	-	1087
1933	10095	2740	874	1	1	-	1388
1937	13254	3571	1205	1	1	-	1956
1938	12862	3868	1130	1	1	-	2065
1950	16776	7730	2467	1	1	-	4439
1953	17903	8594	3158	1	1	-	5700
1955	18772	10461	3224	1	1	-	6603
1957	19439	11095	3273	1	1	-	8571
1960	21835	15370	3993	1	1	-	9960
1961	23173	16699	4032	1	1	-	10627
1962	23141	17563	4161	1	1	-	12175
1963	23359	18916	4519	1	1	3	13933
1964	25603	19499	4962	190	190	3	15019
1965	29390	21204	5059	336	336	4	17336
AUSTRALIA							
1925	13845	891	-	-	-	-	343
1929	10531	1769	-	-	-	-	440
1933	9238	2621	-	-	-	-	533
1937	12268	3448	-	-	-	-	716
1938	11868	3734	-	-	-	-	679
1950	15840	7445	975	-	-	-	1491
1953	17117	8390	1590	-	-	-	1691
1955	17976	10275	1608	-	-	-	1988
1957	18594	10914	1645	-	-	-	3093
1960	21023	15207	1908	-	-	-	4051
1961	22404	16540	1988	-	-	-	4271
1962	22429	17412	2433	-	-	-	4969
1963	22687	18752	2568	-	-	3	6652
1964	24910	19340	2891	189	189	3	6898
1965	28716	21044	3192	335	335	4	8367
NEW ZEALAND							
1925	1061	161	926	-	-	-	306
1929	1389	121	1066	-	-	-	647
1933	857	119	874	1	1	-	855
1937	986	123	1205	1	1	-	1240
1938	994	134	1130	1	1	-	1386
1950	936	285	1492	1	1	-	2864
1953	786	204	1568	1	1	-	3942

Table I. PRIMARY ENERGY PRODUCTION, SELECTED YEARS, 1925–1965

(Original units)

Region, country, year	Solid fuels (10^3 m.t.) Hard coal	Lignite	Other	Liquid fuels (10^3 m.t.) Total	Crude oil	Natural gas (10^6 c.m.)	Hydro-electric power (10^6 kwh)
	(1)	(2)	(3)	(4)	(5)	(6)	(7)
NEW ZEALAND (CONTINUED)							
1955	796	186	1616	1	1	-	4530
1957	845	181	1628	1	1	-	5382
1960	812	163	2085	1	1	-	5512
1961	769	159	2044	1	1	-	5946
1962	712	151	1728	1	1	-	6779
1963	672	164	1951	1	1	-	6852
1964	693	159	2071	1	1	-	7753
1965	674	160	1867	1	1	-	8588
USSR AND COMMUNIST EASTERN EUROPE							
1925	57719	29589	4917	10268	10238	1045	519
1929	100622	37409	7567	19294	19215	1606	927
1933	106431	32679	14063	29716	29505	3075	1633
1937	164109	47674	24440	36805	36460	4722	5070
1938	170201	47314	27035	38007	37690	4663	6029
1950	286264	266595	36499	45013	44845	8143	15037
1953	337049	341157	39086	64859	64641	11404	21860
1955	397593	397540	51277	86118	85894	14064	27348
1957	450808	441229	55391	114267	114025	24818	43860
1960	512045	478672	54125	165369	165035	54007	57182
1961	516541	496795	52482	184253	183912	68499	65393
1962	530117	512848	35245	205336	204982	84591	78883
1963	543713	537019	59013	226087	225705	102626	82235
1964	561920	560024	60011	239582	239200	122591	83683
1965	581999	561228	60465	259237	258822	143364	90915
COMMUNIST EASTERN EUROPE							
1925	42816	27972	-	3182	3152	905	268
1929	64033	33931	-	5605	5526	1276	370
1933	38964	23813	-	8159	7948	1965	470
1937	54231	29584	-	8112	7767	2543	879
1938	55473	28779	-	7592	7275	2453	938
1950	101039	190731	500	6085	5917	2382	2346
1953	112734	245050	500	10582	10364	4536	2659
1955	120978	282896	500	13025	12801	5083	4183
1957	122306	306261	500	13161	12919	6235	4431
1960	137120	340411	500	14310	13976	8704	6269
1961	139522	363279	500	14715	14374	9518	6271
1962	143685	381872	500	15222	14868	11066	6939
1963	148581	400429	500	15688	15306	12794	6376
1964	153050	414897	500	15979	15597	14025	6322
1965	154118	411378	500	16349	15934	15698	9484
ALBANIA							
1925	-	1	-	-	-	-	-
1929	-	4	-	-	-	-	-
1933	-	3	-	2	2	-	-
1937	-	4	-	93	93	-	-
1938	-	4	-	112	112	-	-
1950	-	41	-	132	132	-	-
1953	-	105	-	149	149	-	20
1955	-	195	-	208	208	-	27

Table I. PRIMARY ENERGY PRODUCTION, SELECTED YEARS, 1925-1965

(Original units)

Region, country, year	Solid fuels (10^3 m.t.)			Liquid fuels (10^3 m.t.)		Natural gas (10^6 c.m.)	Hydro-electric power (10^6 kwh)
	Hard coal	Lignite	Other	Total	Crude oil		
	(1)	(2)	(3)	(4)	(5)	(6)	(7)
ALBANIA (CONTINUED)							
1957	-	236	-	490	490	-	60
1960	-	291	-	728	728	-	121
1961	-	289	-	771	771	-	108
1962	-	301	-	785	785	-	118
1963	-	252	-	751	751	-	168
1964	-	292	-	764	764	-	203
1965	-	350	-	800	800	-	250
BULGARIA							
192[illegible]	57	1166	-	-	-	-	17
1929	79	1573	-	-	-	-	49
1933	81	1493	-	-	-	-	77
1937	121	1732	-	-	-	-	134
1938	146	1942	-	-	-	-	141
1950	157	5771	-	-	-	-	306
1953	269	8077	-	-	-	-	453
1955	293	9758	-	150	150	-	648
1957	385	10730	-	285	285	-	850
1960	570	15416	-	200	200	-	1886
1961	591	16966	-	207	207	-	1796
1962	636	19104	-	199	199	-	1695
1963	658	20275	-	173	173	-	2086
1964	609	23751	-	160	160	-	1471
1965	552	24490	-	229	229	-	2000
CZECHOSLOVAKIA							
1925	12559	18605	-	23	23	-	175
1929	16521	22561	-	14	14	2	216
1933	10532	15063	-	18	18	1	235
1937	16672	17895	-	18	18	1	557
1938	15836	16027	-	19	19	1	600
1950	18456	27509	-	64	64	19	1100
1953	18925	34350	-	122	122	168	1014
1955	20643	40751	-	107	107	173	1930
1957	22543	51016	-	108	108	772	2121
1960	26214	58403	-	137	137	1294	2495
1961	26233	65303	-	154	154	1263	2524
1962	27149	69485	-	177	177	1068	3007
1963	28180	73303	-	180	180	998	2289
1964	28202	75605	-	195	195	943	2727
1965	27731	73216	-	192	192	850	4456
GERMANY, EAST							
1950	2805	137050	500	-	-	-	270
1953	2638	172752	500	-	-	-	410
1955	2682	200612	500	-	-	-	500
1957	2754	212595	500	-	-	-	483
1960	2721	225465	500	-	-	-	617
1961	2671	236926	500	-	-	-	676
1962	2575	246992	500	-	-	-	611
1963	2483	254219	500	-	-	101	547
1964	2340	256926	500	-	-	108	536

Table I. PRIMARY ENERGY PRODUCTION, SELECTED YEARS, 1925-1965

(Original units)

Region, country, year	Solid fuels (10^3 m.t.)			Liquid fuels (10^3 m.t.)		Natural gas (10^6 c.m.)	Hydro-electric power (10^6 kwh)
	Hard coal	Lignite	Other	Total	Crude oil		
	(1)	(2)	(3)	(4)	(5)	(6)	(7)
GERMANY, EAST (CONTINUED)							
1965	2212	251301	500	-	-	133	785
HUNGARY							
1925	805	5519	-	-	-	-	5
1929	826	7044	-	-	-	-	9
1933	800	5907	-	-	-	2	12
1937	917	8055	-	2	2	4	15
1938	1042	8318	-	43	43	8	20
1950	1400	11868	-	512	512	381	70
1953	1993	19016	-	846	846	549	44
1955	2692	19623	-	1601	1601	545	46
1957	2277	18926	-	675	675	411	42
1960	2847	23676	-	1244	1217	342	94
1961	3071	25104	-	1470	1457	324	82
1962	3341	25310	-	1654	1641	340	82
1963	3710	26769	-	1770	1757	611	81
1964	4125	27423	-	1811	1801	784	74
1965	4362	27075	-	1812	1802	1107	75
POLAND							
1925	29081	66	-	832	812	535	20
1929	46236	74	-	709	675	467	35
1933	27356	33	-	593	551	462	35
1937	36218	18	-	540	501	531	48
1938	38104	10	-	548	507	584	50
1950	78001	4836	-	177	162	182	400
1953	88719	5633	-	207	189	319	498
1955	94476	6045	-	200	180	393	709
1957	94096	5954	-	200	181	419	575
1960	104438	9327	-	213	194	549	659
1961	106606	10338	-	223	203	734	619
1962	109604	11091	-	223	202	821	774
1963	113150	15344	-	232	212	983	668
1964	117354	20280	-	302	282	1230	726
1965	118831	22626	-	364	340	1378	913
ROMANIA							
1925	314	2615	-	2327	2317	370	51
1929	371	2675	-	4882	4837	807	61
1933	195	1314	-	7546	7377	1500	111
1937	303	1880	-	7459	7153	2007	125
1938	345	2478	-	6870	6594	1860	127
1950	220	3656	-	5200	5047	1800	200
1953	190	5117	-	9258	9058	3500	220
1955	192	5912	-	10759	10555	3972	323
1957	251	6804	-	11403	11180	4633	300
1960	330	7833	-	11788	11500	6519	397
1961	350	8353	-	11890	11582	7197	466
1962	380	9589	-	12184	11864	8837	652
1963	400	10267	-	12582	12233	10101	537
1964	420	10620	-	12747	12395	10960	585
1965	430	12320	-	12952	12571	12230	1005

Table I. PRIMARY ENERGY PRODUCTION, SELECTED YEARS, 1925-1965

(Original units)

Region, country, year	Solid fuels (10^3 m.t.)			Liquid fuels (10^3 m.t.)		Natural gas (10^6 c.m.)	Hydro-electric power (10^6 kwh)
	Hard coal	Lignite	Other	Total	Crude oil		
	(1)	(2)	(3)	(4)	(5)	(6)	(7)
USSR (INCLUDING ESTONIA, LATVIA, LITHUANIA)							
1925	14903	1617	4917	7086	7086	140	251
1929	36589	3478	7567	13689	13689	330	557
1933	67467	8866	14063	21557	21557	1110	1163
1937	109878	18090	24440	28693	28693	2179	4191
1938	114728	18535	27035	30415	30415	2210	5091
1950	185225	75864	35999	38928	38928	5761	12691
1953	224315	96107	38586	54277	54277	6868	19201
1955	276615	114644	50777	73093	73093	8981	23165
1957	328502	134968	54891	101106	101106	18583	39429
1960	374925	138261	53625	151059	151059	45303	50913
1961	377019	133516	51982	169538	169538	58981	59122
1962	386432	130976	34745	190114	190114	73525	71944
1963	395132	136590	58513	210399	210399	89832	75859
1964	408870	145127	59511	223603	223603	108566	77361
1965	427881	149850	59965	242888	242888	127666	81431
COMMUNIST ASIA							
1925	24255	-	-	-	-	-	-
1929	25845	-	-	5	5	-	-
1933	28379	-	-	91	91	-	-
1937	36910	-	-	200	200	-	-
1938	31940	-	-	280	280	-	-
1950	45115	1572	-	200	200	-	5280
1953	70211	402	-	622	622	-	2560
1955	101562	1307	-	966	966	-	6200
1957	135267	1941	-	1481	1481	-	10302
1960	230192	3842	-	5529	5529	-	19304
1961	261078	4290	-	6226	6226	-	16500
1962	263328	4200	-	6823	6823	-	17000
1963	283915	4340	-	7519	7519	-	17500
1964	305310	4300	-	8518	8518	-	19000
1965	319390	4300	-	10016	10016	-	21000
LATIN AMERICA							
1925	3316	200	-	23444	23431	770	3155
1929	3078	200	-	34712	34571	1470	3950
1933	2780	198	-	29723	29519	1986	4589
1937	4331	190	-	44119	43876	3168	5901
1938	4347	190	-	43668	43430	3407	6294
1950	6075	270	47	102714	102165	4840	14222
1953	7087	267	14	118914	118132	7113	18405
1955	7652	229	15	143773	142977	8611	21699
1957	7627	173	22	180965	179853	11311	27309
1960	8476	68	12	196692	194488	19223	34666
1961	8932	91	6	205202	202823	21403	36051
1962	9516	84	5	222870	220605	23463	38992
1963	9738	85	16	227587	225144	25472	41369
1964	10454	79	8	237316	234786	29113	45290
1965	10660	75	9	243130	240462	30424	51370
LATIN AMERICA - CARIBBEAN							
1925	1569	-	-	21266	21264	217	1070

Table I. PRIMARY ENERGY PRODUCTION, SELECTED YEARS, 1925-1965

(Original units)

Region, country, year	Solid fuels (10^3 m.t.)			Liquid fuels (10^3 m.t.)		Natural gas (10^6 c.m.)	Hydro-electric power (10^6 kwh)
	Hard coal	Lignite	Other	Total	Crude oil		
	(1)	(2)	(3)	(4)	(5)	(6)	(7)
LATIN AMERICA - CARIBBEAN (CONTINUED)							
1929	1179	-	-	31276	31230	684	1395
1933	764	-	-	25639	25562	993	1628
1937	1671	-	-	39028	38935	1891	2356
1938	1511	-	-	38676	38574	2201	2470
1950	1947	-	-	96665	96248	3348	3769
1953	2691	-	-	111787	111164	5322	4906
1955	3223	-	-	135527	134892	6642	6287
1957	3456	-	-	170596	169655	8795	7035
1960	4407	-	-	179193	177135	15422	9408
1961	4499	-	-	183837	181618	16279	9364
1962	4920	-	-	199211	197136	17159	10477
1963	5313	-	-	203483	201251	18519	12146
1964	5163	-	-	212709	210435	21764	13850
1965	5237	-	-	218695	216357	22507	16029
CARIBBEAN - OIL PRODUCING							
1925	1569	-	-	21266	21264	217	941
1929	1179	-	-	31276	31230	684	1231
1933	764	-	-	25634	25559	993	1406
1937	1671	-	-	39019	38931	1891	2037
1938	1511	-	-	38659	38564	2201	2129
1950	1947	-	-	96643	96228	3346	2886
1953	2691	-	-	111784	111162	5318	3963
1955	3223	-	-	135477	134843	6638	5177
1957	3456	-	-	170545	169604	8792	5893
1960	4407	-	-	179179	177121	15420	7856
1961	4499	-	-	183827	181608	16276	7773
1962	4920	-	-	199199	197124	17156	8893
1963	5313	-	-	203452	201220	18515	10348
1964	5163	-	-	212672	210398	21761	12019
1965	5237	-	-	218658	216320	22504	13878
COLOMBIA							
1925	100	-	-	144	144	-	92
1929	100	-	-	2911	2911	-	100
1933	112	-	-	1834	1834	-	108
1937	422	-	-	2807	2807	-	181
1938	412	-	-	2984	2984	-	206
1950	1010	-	-	4711	4711	-	725
1953	1230	-	-	5454	5454	-	1008
1955	1850	-	-	5493	5493	-	1480
1957	2000	-	-	6327	6327	-	2013
1960	2600	-	-	7695	7584	404	2587
1961	2650	-	-	7346	7238	417	2513
1962	3000	-	-	7162	7059	592	2762
1963	3200	-	-	8329	8228	702	3218
1964	3000	-	-	8649	8597	834	3721
1965	3200	-	-	10170	10124	917	3900
MEXICO							
1925	1444	-	-	17628	17626	150	828
1929	1054	-	-	6713	6700	220	1106

Table I. PRIMARY ENERGY PRODUCTION, SELECTED YEARS, 1925-1965

(Original units)

Region, country, year	Solid fuels (10^3 m.t.)			Liquid fuels (10^3 m.t.)		Natural gas (10^6 c.m.)	Hydro-electric power (10^6 kwh)
	Hard coal	Lignite	Other	Total	Crude oil		
	(1)	(2)	(3)	(4)	(5)	(6)	(7)
MEXICO (CONTINUED)							
1933	647	-	-	5112	5087	313	1269
1937	1242	-	-	6745	6711	976	1822
1938	1093	-	-	5550	5510	1109	1871
1950	912	-	-	10535	10363	1754	1949
1953	1432	-	-	10558	10362	2645	2622
1955	1342	-	-	13018	12786	3392	3447
1957	1421	-	-	13089	12627	4568	3720
1960	1772	-	-	15315	14171	9665	5174
1961	1818	-	-	16459	15278	10210	5110
1962	1893	-	-	17147	16002	10516	5480
1963	2071	-	-	17723	16433	11371	6024
1964	2127	-	-	18173	16535	13735	7075
1965	2006	-	-	18542	16874	13965	8609
TRINIDAD AND TOBAGO							
1925	-	-	-	610	610	67	-
1929	-	-	-	1217	1217	134	-
1933	-	-	-	1345	1345	148	-
1937	-	-	-	2243	2243	247	-
1938	-	-	-	2566	2566	282	-
1950	-	-	-	2941	2919	475	-
1953	-	-	-	3193	3162	501	-
1955	-	-	-	3555	3523	498	-
1957	-	-	-	4851	4820	600	-
1960	-	-	-	6018	5994	766	-
1961	-	-	-	6499	6476	832	-
1962	-	-	-	6939	6916	850	-
1963	-	-	-	6908	6888	832	-
1964	-	-	-	7060	7036	1089	-
1965	-	-	-	6936	6913	1174	-
VENEZUELA							
1925	25	-	-	2884	2884	-	21
1929	25	-	-	20435	20402	330	25
1933	5	-	-	17343	17293	532	29
1937	7	-	-	27224	27170	668	34
1938	6	-	-	27559	27504	810	52
1950	25	-	-	78456	78235	1117	212
1953	29	-	-	92579	92184	2172	333
1955	31	-	-	113411	113041	2748	250
1957	35	-	-	146278	145830	3624	160
1960	35	-	-	150151	149372	4585	95
1961	31	-	-	153523	152616	4817	150
1962	27	-	-	167951	167147	5198	651
1963	42	-	-	170492	169671	5610	1106
1964	36	-	-	178790	178230	6103	1223
1965	31	-	-	183010	182409	6448	1369
CARIBBEAN - OTHER							
1925	-	-	-	-	-	-	129
1929	-	-	-	-	-	-	164

Table I. PRIMARY ENERGY PRODUCTION, SELECTED YEARS, 1925-1965

(Original units)

Region, country, year	Solid fuels (10^3 m.t.)			Liquid fuels (10^3 m.t.)		Natural gas (10^6 c.m.)	Hydro-electric power (10^6 kwh)
	Hard coal	Lignite	Other	Total	Crude oil		
	(1)	(2)	(3)	(4)	(5)	(6)	(7)
CARIBBEAN - OTHER (CONTINUED)							
1933	-	-	-	5	3	-	222
1937	-	-	-	9	4	-	319
1938	-	-	-	17	10	-	341
1950	-	-	-	22	20	2	883
1953	-	-	-	3	2	4	943
1955	-	-	-	50	49	4	1110
1957	-	-	-	51	51	3	1142
1960	-	-	-	14	14	2	1552
1961	-	-	-	10	10	3	1591
1962	-	-	-	12	12	3	1584
1963	-	-	-	31	31	4	1798
1964	-	-	-	37	37	3	1831
1965	-	-	-	37	37	3	2151
CUBA							
1925	-	-	-	-	-	-	15
1929	-	-	-	-	-	-	15
1933	-	-	-	5	3	-	14
1937	-	-	-	9	4	-	19
1938	-	-	-	17	10	-	19
1950	-	-	-	22	20	-	13
1953	-	-	-	3	2	-	16
1955	-	-	-	50	49	-	20
1957	-	-	-	51	51	-	20
1960	-	-	-	14	14	-	20
1961	-	-	-	10	10	-	22
1962	-	-	-	12	12	-	25
1963	-	-	-	31	31	-	50
1964	-	-	-	37	37	-	100
1965	-	-	-	37	37	-	110
PANAMA CANAL ZONE							
1925	-	-	-	-	-	-	65
1929	-	-	-	-	-	-	62
1933	-	-	-	-	-	-	61
1937	-	-	-	-	-	-	80
1938	-	-	-	-	-	-	83
1950	-	-	-	-	-	-	251
1953	-	-	-	-	-	-	266
1955	-	-	-	-	-	-	252
1957	-	-	-	-	-	-	235
1960	-	-	-	-	-	-	245
1961	-	-	-	-	-	-	256
1962	-	-	-	-	-	-	259
1963	-	-	-	-	-	-	293
1964	-	-	-	-	-	-	263
1965	-	-	-	-	-	-	275
PUERTO RICO							
1925	-	-	-	-	-	-	-
1929	-	-	-	-	-	-	20

Table I. PRIMARY ENERGY PRODUCTION, SELECTED YEARS, 1925-1965

(Original units)

Region, country, year	Solid fuels (10^3 m.t.) Hard coal	Lignite	Other	Liquid fuels (10^3 m.t.) Total	Crude oil	Natural gas (10^6 c.m.)	Hydro-electric power (10^6 kwh)
	(1)	(2)	(3)	(4)	(5)	(6)	(7)
PUERTO RICO (CONTINUED)							
1933	-	-	-	-	-	-	56
1937	-	-	-	-	-	-	93
1938	-	-	-	-	-	-	103
1950	-	-	-	-	-	-	244
1953	-	-	-	-	-	-	180
1955	-	-	-	-	-	-	209
1957	-	-	-	-	-	-	173
1960	-	-	-	-	-	-	243
1961	-	-	-	-	-	-	268
1962	-	-	-	-	-	-	207
1963	-	-	-	-	-	-	277
1964	-	-	-	-	-	-	152
1965	-	-	-	-	-	-	236
LATIN AMERICA - OTHER							
1925	1747	200	-	2178	2167	553	2085
1929	1899	200	-	3436	3341	786	2555
1933	2016	198	-	4084	3957	993	2961
1937	2660	190	-	5091	4941	1277	3545
1938	2836	190	-	4992	4856	1206	3824
1950	4128	270	47	6049	5917	1492	10453
1953	4396	267	14	7127	6968	1791	13499
1955	4429	229	15	8246	8085	1969	15412
1957	4171	173	22	10369	10198	2516	20274
1960	4069	68	12	17499	17353	3801	25258
1961	4433	91	6	21365	21205	5124	26687
1962	4596	84	5	23659	23469	6304	28515
1963	4425	85	16	24104	23893	6953	29223
1964	5291	79	8	24607	24351	7349	31440
1965	5423	75	9	24435	24105	7917	35341
ARGENTINA							
1925	-	-	-	924	924	119	64
1929	-	-	-	1381	1365	212	108
1933	-	-	-	1973	1951	330	86
1937	-	-	-	2363	2340	421	97
1938	-	-	-	2462	2444	407	84
1950	26	-	47	3365	3357	533	190
1953	82	-	14	4088	4078	698	358
1955	136	-	15	4373	4365	719	300
1957	209	-	22	4868	4858	852	580
1960	280	-	12	9145	9138	1383	927
1961	344	-	6	12091	12085	2357	1086
1962	286	-	5	14063	14053	2978	1167
1963	207	-	16	13912	13900	3406	1186
1964	335	-	8	14360	14349	3751	1236
1965	374	-	9	14075	14062	4264	1238
BOLIVIA							
1925	-	-	-	-	-	-	9
1929	-	-	-	3	3	-	20
1933	-	-	-	14	14	-	26

Table I. PRIMARY ENERGY PRODUCTION, SELECTED YEARS, 1925-1965

(Original units)

Region, country, year	Solid fuels (10^3 m.t.)			Liquid fuels (10^3 m.t.)		Natural gas (10^6 c.m.)	Hydro-electric power (10^6 kwh)
	Hard coal	Lignite	Other	Total	Crude oil		
	(1)	(2)	(3)	(4)	(5)	(6)	(7)
BOLIVIA (CONTINUED)							
1937	-	-	-	16	16	-	32
1938	-	-	-	18	18	-	45
1950	-	-	-	80	80	-	190
1953	-	-	-	78	78	-	250
1955	-	-	-	351	351	6	290
1957	-	-	-	466	466	8	350
1960	-	-	-	466	466	6	389
1961	-	-	-	390	390	16	390
1962	-	-	-	364	364	27	377
1963	-	-	-	412	412	54	409
1964	-	-	-	408	408	85	421
1965	-	-	-	433	433	100	430
BRAZIL							
1925	392	-	-	-	-	-	1460
1929	373	-	-	-	-	-	1770
1933	646	-	-	-	-	-	2085
1937	763	-	-	-	-	-	2400
1938	907	-	-	-	-	-	2600
1950	1959	-	-	44	44	5	7198
1953	2025	-	-	120	120	27	9223
1955	2268	-	-	264	264	62	10605
1957	2073	-	-	1321	1321	159	14876
1960	2330	-	-	3870	3870	535	18384
1961	2390	-	-	4549	4549	527	18946
1962	2508	-	-	4366	4366	511	20662
1963	2571	-	-	4667	4667	503	20728
1964	3246	-	-	4353	4353	532	22097
1965	3383	-	-	4488	4488	683	25515
CHILE							
1925	1253	200	-	-	-	-	378
1929	1308	200	-	-	-	-	483
1933	1340	198	-	-	-	-	548
1937	1798	190	-	-	-	-	757
1938	1854	190	-	-	-	-	750
1950	1947	270	-	82	82	100	1651
1953	2079	267	-	171	164	130	2035
1955	1889	229	-	343	336	210	2328
1957	1748	173	-	579	565	350	2505
1960	1297	68	-	959	943	890	2977
1961	1532	91	-	1233	1208	1260	3141
1962	1639	84	-	1576	1524	1760	3312
1963	1516	85	-	1824	1722	1920	3404
1964	1595	79	-	1906	1784	1780	3723
1965	1582	75	-	1851	1656	1770	3954
ECUADOR							
1925	-	-	-	23	23	-	24
1929	-	-	-	196	196	-	24
1933	-	-	-	230	230	9	24
1937	-	-	-	289	285	46	24

Table I. PRIMARY ENERGY PRODUCTION, SELECTED YEARS, 1925-1965

(Original units)

Region, country, year	Solid fuels (10^3 m.t.)			Liquid fuels (10^3 m.t.)		Natural gas (10^6 c.m.)	Hydro-electric power (10^6 kwh)
	Hard coal	Lignite	Other	Total	Crude oil		
	(1)	(2)	(3)	(4)	(5)	(6)	(7)
ECUADOR (CONTINUED)							
1938	-	-	-	301	297	55	25
1950	-	-	-	359	347	132	86
1953	-	-	-	408	391	150	92
1955	-	-	-	486	466	150	120
1957	-	-	-	440	421	150	143
1960	-	-	-	380	364	150	175
1961	-	-	-	402	386	150	200
1962	-	-	-	354	340	150	222
1963	-	-	-	339	325	150	239
1964	-	-	-	384	369	150	248
1965	-	-	-	401	385	150	249
PERU							
1925	102	-	-	1231	1220	434	150
1929	218	-	-	1856	1777	574	150
1933	30	-	-	1867	1762	654	192
1937	99	-	-	2423	2300	810	235
1938	75	-	-	2211	2097	744	320
1950	196	-	-	2119	2007	721	611
1953	210	-	-	2262	2137	786	940
1955	136	-	-	2429	2303	822	1091
1957	141	-	-	2695	2567	997	1270
1960	162	-	-	2679	2572	837	1730
1961	167	-	-	2700	2587	814	1878
1962	163	-	-	2936	2822	878	1946
1963	131	-	-	2950	2867	920	2159
1964	115	-	-	3196	3088	1051	2448
1965	84	-	-	3187	3081	950	2625
URUGUAY							
1925	-	-	-	-	-	-	-
1929	-	-	-	-	-	-	-
1933	-	-	-	-	-	-	-
1937	-	-	-	-	-	-	-
1938	-	-	-	-	-	-	-
1950	-	-	-	-	-	1	527
1953	-	-	-	-	-	-	601
1955	-	-	-	-	-	-	678
1957	-	-	-	-	-	-	550
1960	-	-	-	-	-	-	676
1961	-	-	-	-	-	-	1046
1962	-	-	-	-	-	-	829
1963	-	-	-	-	-	-	1098
1964	-	-	-	-	-	-	1267
1965	-	-	-	-	-	-	1330
ASIA							
1925	58610	180	415	9908	9798	364	7978
1929	65379	182	672	13300	13150	515	13234
1933	59904	146	222	15094	14873	904	18149
1937	81035	237	638	25641	25431	988	26615
1938	89394	292	486	26162	25964	1061	28656

Table I. PRIMARY ENERGY PRODUCTION, SELECTED YEARS, 1925-1965

(Original units)

Region, country, year	Solid fuels (10^3 m.t.)			Liquid fuels (10^3 m.t.)		Natural gas (10^6 c.m.)	Hydro-electric power (10^6 kwh)
	Hard coal	Lignite	Other	Total	Crude oil		
	(1)	(2)	(3)	(4)	(5)	(6)	(7)
ASIA (CONTINUED)							
1950	77754	2536	422	97703	97616	1439	42772
1953	92122	3062	341	136465	136460	2399	48129
1955	89646	3164	279	179542	179480	3539	56315
1957	106390	4187	230	199139	199065	6455	66858
1960	117738	4306	82	289303	289231	9551	73668
1961	125552	3996	73	308278	308207	10483	86073
1962	132641	4447	73	337595	337517	11747	82566
1963	136976	5863	73	368687	368599	12369	92873
1964	133503	6569	68	410775	410682	13702	95370
1965	137269	7323	68	449352	449288	14485	99671
MIDDLE EAST							
1925	671	5	-	4652	4652	-	19
1929	995	12	-	5670	5670	-	19
1933	1311	30	-	7319	7319	-	19
1937	1615	116	-	15655	15655	-	34
1938	1744	146	-	15922	15922	-	35
1950	3032	747	-	85976	85976	506	94
1953	3819	942	-	120095	120095	853	168
1955	3743	1188	-	160746	160746	1330	209
1957	4145	1891	-	176210	176210	3313	498
1960	3883	1911	-	261870	261870	5263	1141
1961	3970	1594	-	280461	280461	5731	1479
1962	4053	1995	-	307890	307890	6240	1417
1963	4346	2570	-	339179	339179	5963	2493
1964	4723	2991	-	380203	380203	6596	2073
1965	4665	3094	-	416593	416593	6896	2720
MIDDLE EAST - OIL PRODUCING							
1925	-	-	-	4652	4652	-	-
1929	-	-	-	5670	5670	-	-
1933	9	-	-	7319	7319	-	-
1937	-	-	-	15655	15655	-	-
1938	-	-	-	15922	15922	-	-
1950	200	-	-	85959	85959	506	-
1953	155	-	-	120069	120069	853	-
1955	245	-	-	160566	160566	1330	-
1957	176	-	-	175858	175858	3313	-
1960	230	-	-	261366	261366	5263	-
1961	198	-	-	279884	279884	5728	-
1962	160	-	-	307160	307160	6229	-
1963	193	-	-	338283	338283	5953	-
1964	274	-	-	379083	379083	6567	-
1965	275	-	-	414858	414858	6824	-
BAHRAIN							
1925	-	-	-	-	-	-	-
1929	-	-	-	-	-	-	-
1933	-	-	-	4	4	-	-
1937	-	-	-	1061	1061	-	-
1938	-	-	-	1133	1133	-	-
1950	-	-	-	1506	1506	-	-

Table I. PRIMARY ENERGY PRODUCTION, SELECTED YEARS, 1925-1965

(Original units)

Region, country, year	Solid fuels (10^3 m.t.)			Liquid fuels (10^3 m.t.)		Natural gas (10^6 c.m.)	Hydro-electric power (10^6 kwh)
	Hard coal	Lignite	Other	Total	Crude oil		
	(1)	(2)	(3)	(4)	(5)	(6)	(7)
BAHRAIN (CONTINUED)							
1953	-	-	-	1501	1501	-	-
1955	-	-	-	1502	1502	-	-
1957	-	-	-	1599	1599	-	-
1960	-	-	-	2256	2256	-	-
1961	-	-	-	2248	2248	-	-
1962	-	-	-	2249	2249	-	-
1963	-	-	-	2256	2256	-	-
1964	-	-	-	2461	2461	-	-
1965	-	-	-	2842	2842	-	-
IRAN							
1925	-	-	-	4652	4652	-	-
1929	-	-	-	5549	5549	-	-
1933	9	-	-	7200	7200	-	-
1937	-	-	-	10331	10331	-	-
1938	-	-	-	10359	10359	-	-
1950	200	-	-	32259	32259	-	-
1953	155	-	-	1489	1489	54	-
1955	245	-	-	16356	16356	592	-
1957	176	-	-	36020	36020	1787	-
1960	230	-	-	52392	52392	2797	-
1961	198	-	-	58982	58982	2792	-
1962	160	-	-	65338	65338	2872	-
1963	193	-	-	73031	73031	2907	-
1964	274	-	-	84006	84006	3280	-
1965	275	-	-	93454	93454	3310	-
IRAQ							
1925	-	-	-	-	-	-	-
1929	-	-	-	121	121	-	-
1933	-	-	-	115	115	-	-
1937	-	-	-	4255	4255	-	-
1938	-	-	-	4363	4363	-	-
1950	-	-	-	6650	6650	-	-
1953	-	-	-	28186	28186	303	-
1955	-	-	-	33681	33681	314	-
1957	-	-	-	21904	21904	255	-
1960	-	-	-	47281	47281	571	-
1961	-	-	-	48826	48826	616	-
1962	-	-	-	48988	48988	637	-
1963	-	-	-	56469	56469	720	-
1964	-	-	-	61626	61626	760	-
1965	-	-	-	64473	64473	770	-
KUWAIT							
1925	-	-	-	-	-	-	-
1929	-	-	-	-	-	-	-
1933	-	-	-	-	-	-	-
1937	-	-	-	-	-	-	-
1938	-	-	-	-	-	-	-
1950	-	-	-	17291	17291	-	-
1953	-	-	-	43287	43287	-	-

Table I. PRIMARY ENERGY PRODUCTION, SELECTED YEARS, 1925-1965

(Original units)

Region, country, year	Solid fuels (10^3 m.t.)			Liquid fuels (10^3 m.t.)		Natural gas (10^6 c.m.)	Hydro-electric power (10^6 kwh)
	Hard coal	Lignite	Other	Total	Crude oil		
	(1)	(2)	(3)	(4)	(5)	(6)	(7)
KUWAIT (CONTINUED)							
1955	-	-	-	54759	54759	-	-
1957	-	-	-	57281	57281	-	-
1960	-	-	-	81867	81867	1160	-
1961	-	-	-	82715	82715	1560	-
1962	-	-	-	92177	92177	1930	-
1963	-	-	-	97202	97202	1516	-
1964	-	-	-	106719	106719	1677	-
1965	-	-	-	109045	109045	1794	-
KUWAIT NEUTRAL ZONE							
1925	-	-	-	-	-	-	-
1929	-	-	-	-	-	-	-
1933	-	-	-	-	-	-	-
1937	-	-	-	-	-	-	-
1938	-	-	-	-	-	-	-
1950	-	-	-	-	-	-	-
1953	-	-	-	-	-	-	-
1955	-	-	-	1294	1294	-	-
1957	-	-	-	3402	3402	-	-
1960	-	-	-	7290	7290	-	-
1961	-	-	-	9499	9499	-	-
1962	-	-	-	13052	13052	NA	-
1963	-	-	-	16752	16752	NA	-
1964	-	-	-	19222	19222	NA	-
1965	-	-	-	19349	19349	NA	-
QATAR							
1925	-	-	-	-	-	-	-
1929	-	-	-	-	-	-	-
1933	-	-	-	-	-	-	-
1937	-	-	-	-	-	-	-
1938	-	-	-	-	-	-	-
1950	-	-	-	1636	1636	-	-
1953	-	-	-	4062	4062	-	-
1955	-	-	-	5438	5438	-	-
1957	-	-	-	6648	6648	-	-
1960	-	-	-	8212	8212	-	-
1961	-	-	-	8382	8382	-	-
1962	-	-	-	8808	8808	-	-
1963	-	-	-	9095	9095	-	-
1964	-	-	-	10136	10136	NA	-
1965	-	-	-	10961	10961	NA	-
SAUDI ARABIA							
1925	-	-	-	-	-	-	-
1929	-	-	-	-	-	-	-
1933	-	-	-	-	-	-	-
1937	-	-	-	8	8	-	-
1938	-	-	-	67	67	-	-
1950	-	-	-	26617	26617	506	-
1953	-	-	-	41544	41544	496	-
1955	-	-	-	47536	47536	424	-

Table I. PRIMARY ENERGY PRODUCTION, SELECTED YEARS, 1925-1965

(Original units)

Region, country, year	Solid fuels (10^3 m.t.) Hard coal	Lignite	Other	Liquid fuels (10^3 m.t.) Total	Crude oil	Natural gas (10^6 c.m.)	Hydro-electric power (10^6 kwh)
	(1)	(2)	(3)	(4)	(5)	(6)	(7)
SAUDI ARABIA (CONTINUED)							
1957	-	-	-	49004	49004	1271	-
1960	-	-	-	62068	62068	735	-
1961	-	-	-	69232	69232	760	-
1962	-	-	-	75751	75751	790	-
1963	-	-	-	81049	81049	810	-
1964	-	-	-	85798	85798	850	-
1965	-	-	-	101033	101033	950	-
TRUCIAL OMAN							
1950	-	-	-	-	-	-	-
1953	-	-	-	-	-	-	-
1955	-	-	-	-	-	-	-
1957	-	-	-	-	-	-	-
1960	-	-	-	-	-	-	-
1961	-	-	-	-	-	-	-
1962	-	-	-	797	797	-	-
1963	-	-	-	2429	2429	-	-
1964	-	-	-	9115	9115	-	-
1965	-	-	-	13701	13701	-	-
MIDDLE EAST - OTHER							
1925	671	5	-	-	-	-	19
1929	995	12	-	-	-	-	19
1933	1302	30	-	-	-	-	19
1937	1615	116	-	-	-	-	34
1938	1744	146	-	-	-	-	35
1950	2832	747	-	17	17	-	94
1953	3664	942	-	26	26	-	168
1955	3498	1188	-	180	180	-	209
1957	3969	1891	-	352	352	-	498
1960	3653	1911	-	504	504	-	1141
1961	3772	1594	-	577	577	3	1479
1962	3893	1995	-	730	730	11	1417
1963	4153	2570	-	896	896	10	2493
1964	4449	2991	-	1120	1120	29	2073
1965	4390	3094	-	1735	1735	72	2720
ISRAEL							
1950	-	-	-	-	-	-	-
1953	-	-	-	-	-	-	-
1955	-	-	-	1	1	-	-
1957	-	-	-	54	54	-	-
1960	-	-	-	129	129	-	-
1961	-	-	-	135	135	3	-
1962	-	-	-	135	135	11	-
1963	-	-	-	151	151	10	-
1964	-	-	-	199	199	29	-
1965	-	-	-	203	203	72	-
LEBANON-SYRIA							
1925	-	-	-	-	-	-	19

Table I. PRIMARY ENERGY PRODUCTION, SELECTED YEARS, 1925-1965

(Original units)

Region, country, year	Solid fuels (10^3 m.t.) Hard coal	Lignite	Other	Liquid fuels (10^3 m.t.) Total	Crude oil	Natural gas (10^6 c.m.)	Hydro-electric power (10^6 kwh)
	(1)	(2)	(3)	(4)	(5)	(6)	(7)
LEBANON - SYRIA (CONTINUED)							
1929	-	-	-	-	-	-	19
1933	-	-	-	-	-	-	19
1937	-	-	-	-	-	-	33
1938	-	-	-	-	-	-	34
LEBANON							
1950	-	-	-	-	-	-	64
1953	-	-	-	-	-	-	101
1955	-	-	-	-	-	-	110
1957	-	-	-	-	-	-	167
1960	-	-	-	-	-	-	109
1961	-	-	-	-	-	-	174
1962	-	-	-	-	-	-	251
1963	-	-	-	-	-	-	350
1964	-	-	-	-	-	-	375
1965	-	-	-	-	-	-	505
SYRIA							
1950	-	-	-	-	-	-	-
1953	-	-	-	-	-	-	-
1955	-	-	-	-	-	-	10
1957	-	-	-	-	-	-	20
1960	-	-	-	-	-	-	30
1961	-	-	-	-	-	-	40
1962	-	-	-	-	-	-	42
1963	-	-	-	-	-	-	44
1964	-	-	-	-	-	-	46
1965	-	-	-	-	-	-	48
TURKEY							
1925	671	5	-	-	-	-	-
1929	995	12	-	-	-	-	-
1933	1302	30	-	-	-	-	-
1937	1615	116	-	-	-	-	1
1938	1744	146	-	-	-	-	1
1950	2832	747	-	17	17	-	30
1953	3664	942	-	26	26	-	67
1955	3498	1188	-	179	179	-	89
1957	3969	1891	-	298	298	-	311
1960	3653	1911	-	375	375	-	1002
1961	3772	1594	-	442	442	-	1265
1962	3893	1995	-	595	595	-	1124
1963	4153	2570	-	745	745	-	2099
1964	4449	2991	-	921	921	-	1652
1965	4390	3094	-	1532	1532	-	2167
FAR EAST AND OTHER ASIA							
1925	57939	175	415	5256	5146	364	7959
1929	64384	170	672	7630	7480	515	13215
1933	58593	116	222	7775	7554	904	18130
1937	79420	121	638	9986	9776	988	26581

Table I. PRIMARY ENERGY PRODUCTION, SELECTED YEARS, 1925-1965

(Original units)

Region, country, year	Solid fuels (10^3 m.t.) Hard coal	Lignite	Other	Liquid fuels (10^3 m.t.) Total	Crude oil	Natural gas (10^6 c.m.)	Hydro-electric power (10^6 kwh)
	(1)	(2)	(3)	(4)	(5)	(6)	(7)
FAR EAST AND OTHER ASIA (CONTINUED)							
1938	87650	146	486	10240	10042	1061	28621
1950	74722	1789	422	11727	11640	933	42678
1953	88303	2120	341	16370	16365	1546	47961
1955	85903	1976	279	18796	18734	2209	56106
1957	102245	2296	230	22929	22855	3142	66360
1960	113855	2395	82	27433	27361	4288	72527
1961	121582	2402	73	27817	27746	4752	84594
1962	128588	2452	73	29705	29627	5507	81149
1963	132630	3293	73	29508	29420	6406	90380
1964	128780	3578	68	30572	30479	7106	93297
1965	132604	4229	68	32759	32695	7589	96951
BORNEO (FORMER BRITISH)							
1925	101	-	-	617	613	-	-
1929	73	-	-	764	760	-	-
1933	-	-	-	615	611	2	-
1937	1	-	-	790	786	21	-
1938	1	-	-	914	910	30	-
1950	-	-	-	4174	4174	52	-
1953	-	-	-	4931	4931	59	-
1955	-	-	-	5377	5320	77	-
1957	-	-	-	5685	5614	192	-
1960	-	-	-	4709	4643	215	-
1961	-	-	-	4248	4184	210	-
1962	-	-	-	3915	3849	209	-
1963	-	-	-	3558	3490	198	-
1964	-	-	-	3659	3593	173	-
1965	-	-	-	4042	3985	211	-
BRUNEI							
1950	-	-	-	4116	4116	NA	-
1953	-	-	-	4881	4881	59	-
1955	-	-	-	5310	5253	77	-
1957	-	-	-	5595	5524	192	-
1960	-	-	-	4649	4583	215	-
1961	-	-	-	4188	4124	210	-
1962	-	-	-	3856	3790	209	-
1963	-	-	-	3506	3438	198	-
1964	-	-	-	3610	3544	173	-
1965	-	-	-	3993	3936	211	-
SARAWAK							
1950	-	-	-	58	58	-	-
1953	-	-	-	50	50	-	-
1955	-	-	-	67	67	-	-
1957	-	-	-	67	67	-	-
1960	-	-	-	60	60	-	-
1961	-	-	-	60	60	-	-
1962	-	-	-	59	59	-	-
1963	-	-	-	52	52	-	-
1964	-	-	-	49	49	-	-
1965	-	-	-	49	49	-	-

Table I. PRIMARY ENERGY PRODUCTION, SELECTED YEARS, 1925–1965

(Original units)

Region, country, year	Solid fuels (10^3 m.t.)			Liquid fuels (10^3 m.t.)		Natural gas (10^6 c.m.)	Hydro-electric power (10^6 kwh)
	Hard coal	Lignite	Other	Total	Crude oil		
	(1)	(2)	(3)	(4)	(5)	(6)	(7)
BURMA							
1950	-	-	-	70	70	-	-
1953	-	-	-	141	141	-	-
1955	7	-	-	211	211	3	-
1957	1	-	-	395	395	6	-
1960	1	-	-	545	545	21	160
1961	2	-	-	564	564	15	187
1962	3	-	-	584	584	18	212
1963	3	-	-	638	638	16	236
1964	10	-	-	558	558	10	280
1965	10	-	-	542	542	10	280
CEYLON							
1925	-	-	-	-	-	-	1
1929	-	-	-	-	-	-	1
1933	-	-	-	-	-	-	1
1937	-	-	-	-	-	-	1
1938	-	-	-	-	-	-	1
1950	-	-	-	-	-	-	9
1953	-	-	-	-	-	-	113
1955	-	-	-	-	-	-	130
1957	-	-	-	-	-	-	153
1960	-	-	-	-	-	-	272
1961	-	-	-	-	-	-	277
1962	-	-	-	-	-	-	320
1963	-	-	-	-	-	-	327
1964	-	-	-	-	-	-	338
1965	-	-	-	-	-	-	332
INDIA							
1925	21239	-	-	1201	1201	-	188
1929	23795	-	-	1201	1201	-	500
1933	20610	-	-	1228	1201	-	812
1937	26074	-	-	1408	1374	-	1125
1938	29518	-	-	1411	1377	-	1200
1950	32825	30	-	256	256	-	2520
1953	36557	40	-	271	271	-	2929
1955	38839	30	-	346	346	-	3753
1957	44204	10	-	429	429	128	5083
1960	52593	47	-	449	449	139	7847
1961	56065	64	-	510	510	107	9824
1962	61370	211	-	1077	1077	214	11515
1963	65956	999	-	1653	1653	268	13665
1964	62440	1569	-	2212	2212	322	15710
1965	67161	2300	-	3022	3022	400	17270
INDO-CHINA							
1925	1363	6	-	-	-	-	-
1929	1941	31	-	-	-	-	-
1933	1568	-	-	-	-	-	-
1937	2308	-	-	-	-	-	-
1938	2331	4	-	-	-	-	-
1950	497	-	-	-	-	-	-

Table I. PRIMARY ENERGY PRODUCTION, SELECTED YEARS, 1925-1965

(Original units)

Region, country, year	Solid fuels (10³ m.t.) Hard coal	Lignite	Other	Liquid fuels (10³ m.t.) Total	Crude oil	Natural gas (10⁶ c.m.)	Hydro-electric power (10⁶ kwh)
	(1)	(2)	(3)	(4)	(5)	(6)	(7)
INDO-CHINA (CONTINUED)							
1953	887	-	-	-	-	-	-
1955	-	-	-	-	-	-	4
1957	12	-	-	-	-	-	3
1960	27	-	-	-	-	-	7
1961	57	-	-	-	-	-	10
1962	71	-	-	-	-	-	10
1963	104	-	-	-	-	-	10
1964	77	-	-	-	-	-	42
1965	75	-	-	-	-	-	58
VIETNAM, SOUTH							
1955	-	-	-	-	-	-	4
1957	12	-	-	-	-	-	3
1960	27	-	-	-	-	-	7
1961	57	-	-	-	-	-	10
1962	71	-	-	-	-	-	10
1963	104	-	-	-	-	-	10
1964	77	-	-	-	-	-	42
1965	75	-	-	-	-	-	58
INDONESIA							
1925	1401	-	-	3172	3066	319	88
1929	1832	-	-	5384	5238	417	100
1933	1035	-	-	5725	5535	788	159
1937	1373	-	-	7434	7262	884	210
1938	1457	-	-	7558	7398	952	235
1950	804	-	-	6757	6673	791	300
1953	897	-	-	10487	10487	1366	454
1955	814	-	-	12264	12264	1908	570
1957	717	-	-	15800	15800	2168	620
1960	658	-	-	20844	20844	2431	810
1961	549	-	-	21451	21451	2561	775
1962	471	-	-	22908	22908	2712	715
1963	591	-	-	22381	22381	2798	715
1964	446	-	-	22951	22951	2930	710
1965	281	-	-	23925	23925	3010	710
JAPAN							
1925	31459	169	-	262	262	23	7610
1929	34258	139	-	270	270	29	12400
1933	32524	116	-	196	196	47	16114
1937	45258	121	-	350	350	53	22278
1938	48684	142	-	353	353	51	23741
1950	38459	1287	-	295	293	66	38258
1953	46531	1486	50	300	296	101	41762
1955	42423	1368	70	318	314	156	48547
1957	51732	1662	75	324	321	329	56687
1960	51067	1409	75	532	526	824	58471
1961	54484	1309	73	663	657	1052	67956
1962	54399	1111	73	771	760	1367	62373
1963	52052	914	73	804	785	1886	69168
1964	50929	691	68	684	657	2073	68957

Table I. PRIMARY ENERGY PRODUCTION, SELECTED YEARS, 1925-1965

(Original units)

Region, country, year	Solid fuels (10^3 m.t.)			Liquid fuels (10^3 m.t.)		Natural gas (10^6 c.m.)	Hydro-electric power (10^6 kwh)
	Hard coal	Lignite	Other	Total	Crude oil		
	(1)	(2)	(3)	(4)	(5)	(6)	(7)
JAPAN (CONTINUED)							
1965	49534	573	68	683	676	2018	70739
KOREA							
1925	622	-	-	-	-	-	-
1929	938	-	-	-	-	-	-
1933	1307	-	-	-	-	-	538
1937	2431	-	-	-	-	-	2087
1938	3419	-	-	-	-	-	2438
KOREA, REPUBLIC OF							
1950	564	28	-	-	-	-	97
1953	867	-	-	-	-	-	395
1955	1308	-	-	-	-	-	478
1957	2441	-	-	-	-	-	419
1960	5350	-	-	-	-	-	580
1961	5884	-	-	-	-	-	652
1962	7444	-	-	-	-	-	702
1963	8858	-	-	-	-	-	727
1964	9622	-	-	-	-	-	750
1965	10248	-	-	-	-	-	710
MALAYA AND SINGAPORE							
1925	-	-	415	-	-	-	21
1929	-	-	672	-	-	-	38
1933	-	-	222	-	-	-	95
1937	-	-	638	-	-	-	235
1938	-	-	486	-	-	-	229
1950	-	-	422	-	-	-	253
1953	-	-	291	-	-	-	255
1955	-	-	209	-	-	-	234
1957	-	-	155	-	-	-	249
1960	-	-	7	-	-	-	195
1961	-	-	-	-	-	-	216
1962	-	-	-	-	-	-	235
1963	-	-	-	-	-	-	317
1964	-	-	-	-	-	-	544
1965	-	-	-	-	-	-	587
PAKISTAN							
1950	-	444	-	171	171	-	65
1953	-	593	-	237	237	-	240
1955	-	537	-	276	276	39	400
1957	-	524	-	294	294	290	520
1960	-	831	-	352	352	633	680
1961	-	921	-	378	378	770	940
1962	-	995	-	447	447	949	1400
1963	-	1243	-	470	470	1189	1570
1964	-	1214	-	499	499	1429	1820
1965	-	1231	-	526	526	1630	1967

Table I. PRIMARY ENERGY PRODUCTION, SELECTED YEARS, 1925-1965

(Original units)

Region, country, year	Solid fuels (10^3 m.t.) Hard coal	Lignite	Other	Liquid fuels (10^3 m.t.) Total	Crude oil	Natural gas (10^6 c.m.)	Hydro-electric power (10^6 kwh)
	(1)	(2)	(3)	(4)	(5)	(6)	(7)
PHILIPPINES							
1925	49	-	-	-	-	-	36
1929	17	-	-	-	-	-	50
1933	16	-	-	-	-	-	63
1937	22	-	-	-	-	-	76
1938	41	-	-	-	-	-	84
1950	159	-	-	-	-	-	191
1953	155	-	-	-	-	-	332
1955	130	-	-	-	-	-	430
1957	191	-	-	-	-	-	640
1960	148	-	-	-	-	-	1320
1961	152	-	-	-	-	-	1290
1962	163	-	-	-	-	-	1350
1963	157	-	-	-	-	-	1540
1964	115	-	-	-	-	-	1600
1965	95	-	-	-	-	-	1509
TAIWAN							
1925	1705	-	-	4	4	22	15
1929	1530	-	-	11	11	69	126
1933	1533	-	-	11	11	67	348
1937	1953	-	-	4	4	30	569
1938	2199	-	-	4	4	28	693
1950	1405	-	-	4	3	24	972
1953	2393	-	-	3	2	20	1466
1955	2359	-	-	4	3	26	1531
1957	2916	-	-	2	2	29	1938
1960	3962	-	-	2	2	25	2065
1961	4322	-	-	3	2	37	2339
1962	4554	-	-	3	2	38	2161
1963	4810	-	-	4	3	51	1931
1964	5028	-	-	9	9	169	2359
1965	5054	-	-	19	19	310	2585
THAILAND							
1925	-	-	-	-	-	-	-
1929	-	-	-	-	-	-	-
1933	-	-	-	-	-	-	-
1937	-	-	-	-	-	-	-
1938	-	-	-	-	-	-	-
1950	-	-	-	-	-	-	-
1953	-	1	-	-	-	-	-
1955	-	41	-	-	-	-	-
1957	-	100	-	-	-	-	-
1960	-	108	-	-	-	-	-
1961	-	108	-	-	-	-	-
1962	-	135	-	-	-	-	-
1963	-	137	-	-	-	-	-
1964	-	104	-	-	-	-	-
1965	-	125	-	-	-	-	-
AFRICA							
1925	13347	-	-	182	182	-	65

Table I. PRIMARY ENERGY PRODUCTION, SELECTED YEARS, 1925-1965

(Original units)

Region, country, year	Solid fuels (10^3 m.t.) Hard coal	Lignite	Other	Liquid fuels (10^3 m.t.) Total	Crude oil	Natural gas (10^6 c.m.)	Hydro-electric power (10^6 kwh)
	(1)	(2)	(3)	(4)	(5)	(6)	(7)
AFRICA (CONTINUED)							
1929	14544	-	-	275	275	-	83
1933	11530	-	-	240	240	-	223
1937	17064	-	-	173	173	-	462
1938	17884	-	-	234	234	-	488
1950	30037	41	-	2681	2670	-	1364
1953	33131	-	-	2920	2914	5	2047
1955	37646	-	-	2023	2017	12	3254
1957	40912	-	-	2708	2702	9	4791
1960	43281	-	-	13884	13838	30	7287
1961	44132	-	-	23840	23695	253	9326
1962	45541	-	-	39109	38898	381	10534
1963	46594	-	-	57343	57095	468	11061
1964	49441	-	-	82660	82357	896	12123
1965	53511	-	-	107441	106915	1929	13208
NORTH AFRICA							
1925	10	-	-	182	182	-	20
1929	16	-	-	275	275	-	38
1933	57	-	-	240	240	-	84
1937	121	-	-	173	173	-	164
1938	136	-	-	229	229	-	164
1950	626	41	-	2645	2634	-	416
1953	860	-	-	2883	2877	5	552
1955	769	-	-	1986	1980	12	1115
1957	757	-	-	2499	2493	9	1218
1960	531	-	-	12089	12043	23	1586
1961	488	-	-	20580	20435	246	2235
1962	423	-	-	34360	34149	370	2469
1963	442	-	-	51772	51524	419	2646
1964	446	-	-	74660	74357	829	3124
1965	464	-	-	91913	91387	1858	3351
ALGERIA							
1925	10	-	-	2	2	-	20
1929	16	-	-	3	3	-	20
1933	30	-	-	1	1	-	25
1937	14	-	-	-	-	-	36
1938	13	-	-	-	-	-	41
1950	258	-	-	3	3	-	131
1953	295	-	-	85	85	-	227
1955	302	-	-	58	58	-	288
1957	236	-	-	21	21	-	327
1960	119	-	-	8668	8632	7	348
1961	78	-	-	15796	15660	231	253
1962	53	-	-	20700	20498	353	258
1963	38	-	-	23882	23641	400	256
1964	46	-	-	26527	26231	809	284
1965	45	-	-	26546	26025	1839	400
EGYPT UAR							
1925	-	-	-	180	180	-	-
1929	-	-	-	272	272	-	-

Table I. PRIMARY ENERGY PRODUCTION, SELECTED YEARS, 1925–1965

(Original units)

Region, country, year	Solid fuels (10^3 m.t.) Hard coal	Lignite	Other	Liquid fuels (10^3 m.t.) Total	Crude oil	Natural gas (10^6 c.m.)	Hydro-electric power (10^6 kwh)
	(1)	(2)	(3)	(4)	(5)	(6)	(7)
EGYPT UAR (CONTINUED)							
1933	-	-	-	238	238	-	-
1937	-	-	-	171	171	-	-
1938	-	-	-	226	226	-	-
1950	-	-	-	2603	2592	-	7
1953	-	-	-	2696	2690	-	7
1955	-	-	-	1825	1819	-	7
1957	-	-	-	2403	2397	-	7
1960	-	-	-	3329	3319	-	260
1961	-	-	-	3828	3819	-	1012
1962	-	-	-	4685	4676	-	1172
1963	-	-	-	5599	5592	-	1280
1964	-	-	-	6361	6354	-	1670
1965	-	-	-	6492	6487	-	1750
LIBYA							
1925	-	-	-	-	-	-	-
1929	-	-	-	-	-	-	-
1933	-	-	-	-	-	-	-
1937	-	-	-	-	-	-	-
1938	-	-	-	-	-	-	-
1950	-	-	-	-	-	-	-
1953	-	-	-	-	-	-	-
1955	-	-	-	-	-	-	-
1957	-	-	-	-	-	-	-
1960	-	-	-	-	-	-	-
1961	-	-	-	876	876	-	-
1962	-	-	-	8848	8848	-	-
1963	-	-	-	22141	22141	-	-
1964	-	-	-	41652	41652	-	-
1965	-	-	-	58772	58772	-	-
MOROCCO							
1925	-	-	-	-	-	-	-
1929	-	-	-	-	-	-	18
1933	27	-	-	1	1	-	59
1937	107	-	-	2	2	-	128
1938	123	-	-	3	3	-	123
1950	368	-	-	39	39	-	278
1953	565	-	-	102	102	5	318
1955	467	-	-	103	103	8	820
1957	521	-	-	75	75	3	858
1960	412	-	-	92	92	9	931
1961	410	-	-	80	80	8	951
1962	370	-	-	127	127	10	1020
1963	404	-	-	150	150	12	1080
1964	400	-	-	120	120	12	1132
1965	419	-	-	103	103	11	1159
TUNISIA							
1925	-	-	-	-	-	-	-
1929	-	-	-	-	-	-	-
1933	-	-	-	-	-	-	-

Table I. PRIMARY ENERGY PRODUCTION, SELECTED YEARS, 1925-1965

(Original units)

Region, country, year	Solid fuels (10³ m.t.)			Liquid fuels (10³ m.t.)		Natural gas	Hydro-electric power
	Hard coal	Lignite	Other	Total	Crude oil	(10^6 c.m.)	(10^6 kwh)
	(1)	(2)	(3)	(4)	(5)	(6)	(7)
TUNISIA (CONTINUED)							
1937	-	-	-	-	-	-	-
1938	-	-	-	-	-	-	-
1950	-	41	-	-	-	-	-
1953	-	-	-	-	-	-	-
1955	-	-	-	-	-	4	-
1957	-	-	-	-	-	6	26
1960	-	-	-	-	-	7	47
1961	-	-	-	-	-	7	19
1962	-	-	-	-	-	7	19
1963	-	-	-	-	-	7	30
1964	-	-	-	-	-	8	38
1965	-	-	-	-	-	8	42
TROPICAL AFRICA							
1925	1015	-	-	-	-	-	45
1929	1510	-	-	-	-	-	45
1933	759	-	-	-	-	-	139
1937	1453	-	-	-	-	-	298
1938	1464	-	-	-	-	-	324
1950	2938	-	-	-	-	-	948
1953	3812	-	-	-	-	-	1495
1955	4730	-	-	-	-	-	2139
1957	5386	-	-	184	184	-	3573
1960	4565	-	-	1770	1770	7	5701
1961	4078	-	-	3254	3254	7	7091
1962	3837	-	-	4749	4749	11	8065
1963	3696	-	-	5571	5571	49	8415
1964	4089	-	-	8000	8000	67	8999
1965	4603	-	-	15528	15528	71	9857
CONGO, DEMOCRATIC REPUBLIC							
1925	65	-	-	-	-	-	30
1929	117	-	-	-	-	-	30
1933	20	-	-	-	-	-	98
1937	36	-	-	-	-	-	220
1938	42	-	-	-	-	-	233
1950	160	-	-	-	-	-	588
1953	315	-	-	-	-	-	992
1955	480	-	-	-	-	-	1330
1957	433	-	-	-	-	-	2375
1960	163	-	-	-	-	-	2310
1961	73	-	-	-	-	-	2380
1962	76	-	-	-	-	-	2520
1963	92	-	-	-	-	-	2235
1964	100	-	-	-	-	-	2255
1965	114	-	-	-	-	-	2470
EAST AFRICA							
1925	-	-	-	-	-	-	10
1929	-	-	-	-	-	-	10
1933	-	-	-	-	-	-	16
1937	-	-	-	-	-	-	24

Table I. PRIMARY ENERGY PRODUCTION, SELECTED YEARS, 1925-1965

(Original units)

Region, country, year	Solid fuels (10^3 m.t.)			Liquid fuels (10^3 m.t.)		Natural gas (10^6 c.m.)	Hydro-electric power (10^6 kwh)
	Hard coal	Lignite	Other	Total	Crude oil		
	(1)	(2)	(3)	(4)	(5)	(6)	(7)
EAST AFRICA (CONTINUED)							
1938	-	-	-	-	-	-	26
1950	-	-	-	-	-	-	72
1953	-	-	-	-	-	-	110
1955	1	-	-	-	-	-	310
1957	1	-	-	-	-	-	414
1960	2	-	-	-	-	-	637
1961	2	-	-	-	-	-	660
1962	3	-	-	-	-	-	713
1963	2	-	-	-	-	-	764
1964	1	-	-	-	-	-	857
1965	2	-	-	-	-	-	948
EQUATORIAL AFRICA							
1925	-	-	-	-	-	-	-
1929	-	-	-	-	-	-	-
1933	-	-	-	-	-	-	-
1937	-	-	-	-	-	-	-
1938	-	-	-	-	-	-	-
1950	-	-	-	-	-	-	-
1953	-	-	-	-	-	-	7
1955	-	-	-	-	-	-	33
1957	-	-	-	173	173	-	30
1960	-	-	-	852	852	7	30
1961	-	-	-	877	877	7	30
1962	-	-	-	950	950	9	30
1963	-	-	-	999	999	9	50
1964	-	-	-	1142	1142	10	50
1965	-	-	-	1335	1335	11	50
GHANA							
1960	-	-	-	-	-	-	-
1961	-	-	-	-	-	-	-
1962	-	-	-	-	-	-	-
1963	-	-	-	-	-	-	-
1964	-	-	-	-	-	-	-
1965	-	-	-	-	-	-	107
LIBERIA							
1950	-	-	-	-	-	-	8
1953	-	-	-	-	-	-	10
1955	-	-	-	-	-	-	11
1957	-	-	-	-	-	-	14
1960	-	-	-	-	-	-	17
1961	-	-	-	-	-	-	17
1962	-	-	-	-	-	-	17
1963	-	-	-	-	-	-	17
1964	-	-	-	-	-	-	17
1965	-	-	-	-	-	-	17

Table I. PRIMARY ENERGY PRODUCTION, SELECTED YEARS, 1925-1965

(Original units)

Region, country, year	Solid fuels (10^3 m.t.)			Liquid fuels (10^3 m.t.)		Natural gas (10^6 c.m.)	Hydro-electric power (10^6 kwh)
	Hard coal	Lignite	Other	Total	Crude oil		
	(1)	(2)	(3)	(4)	(5)	(6)	(7)
NIGERIA							
1925	243	-	-	-	-	-	-
1929	350	-	-	-	-	-	-
1933	239	-	-	-	-	-	-
1937	369	-	-	-	-	-	-
1938	368	-	-	-	-	-	-
1950	592	-	-	-	-	-	52
1953	711	-	-	-	-	-	64
1955	761	-	-	-	-	-	73
1957	828	-	-	1	1	-	88
1960	571	-	-	850	850	-	91
1961	607	-	-	2271	2271	-	101
1962	634	-	-	3328	3328	2	108
1963	577	-	-	3772	3772	40	118
1964	699	-	-	5953	5953	57	126
1965	740	-	-	13538	13538	60	132
RHODESIAN FEDERATION							
1925	689	-	-	-	-	-	-
1929	1037	-	-	-	-	-	-
1933	484	-	-	-	-	-	20
1937	1029	-	-	-	-	-	40
1938	1044	-	-	-	-	-	45
1950	2128	-	-	-	-	-	155
1953	2619	-	-	-	-	-	197
1955	3315	-	-	-	-	-	222
1957	3853	-	-	-	-	-	231
1960	3559	-	-	-	-	-	1310
1961	3073	-	-	-	-	-	2440
1962	2826	-	-	-	-	-	2980
1963	2740	-	-	-	-	-	3460
1964	3044	-	-	-	-	-	3885
1965	3509	-	-	-	-	-	4152
MALAWI							
1950	-	-	-	-	-	-	-
1953	-	-	-	-	-	-	2
1955	-	-	-	-	-	-	1
1957	-	-	-	-	-	-	2
1960	-	-	-	-	-	-	3
1961	-	-	-	-	-	-	2
1962	-	-	-	-	-	-	12
1963	-	-	-	-	-	-	7
1964	-	-	-	-	-	-	9
1965	-	-	-	-	-	-	12
ZAMBIA							
1950	-	-	-	-	-	-	NA
1953	-	-	-	-	-	-	187
1955	-	-	-	-	-	-	217
1957	-	-	-	-	-	-	225
1960	-	-	-	-	-	-	NA
1961	-	-	-	-	-	-	NA

Table I. PRIMARY ENERGY PRODUCTION, SELECTED YEARS, 1925-1965

(Original units)

Region, country, year	Solid fuels (10^3 m.t.)			Liquid fuels (10^3 m.t.)		Natural gas (10^6 c.m.)	Hydro-electric power (10^6 kwh)
	Hard coal	Lignite	Other	Total	Crude oil		
	(1)	(2)	(3)	(4)	(5)	(6)	(7)
ZAMBIA (CONTINUED)							
1962	-	-	-	-	-	-	297
1963	-	-	-	-	-	-	311
1964	-	-	-	-	-	-	305
1965	-	-	-	-	-	-	276
RHODESIA							
1950	2128	-	-	-	-	-	NA
1953	2618	-	-	-	-	-	10
1955	3315	-	-	-	-	-	2
1957	3853	-	-	-	-	-	2
1960	3559	-	-	-	-	-	1046
1961	3073	-	-	-	-	-	2206
1962	2826	-	-	-	-	-	2736
1963	2740	-	-	-	-	-	3142
1964	3044	-	-	-	-	-	3571
1965	3509	-	-	-	-	-	3864
WEST AFRICA							
1950	-	-	-	-	-	-	1
1953	-	-	-	-	-	-	6
1955	-	-	-	-	-	-	9
1957	-	-	-	-	-	-	16
1960	-	-	-	1	1	-	60
1961	-	-	-	2	2	-	80
1962	-	-	-	-	-	-	100
1963	-	-	-	-	-	-	120
1964	-	-	-	-	-	-	103
1965	-	-	-	-	-	-	141
SOUTH AFRICA							
1925	12322	-	-	-	-	-	-
1929	13018	-	-	-	-	-	-
1933	10714	-	-	-	-	-	-
1937	15490	-	-	-	-	-	-
1938	16284	-	-	5	5	-	-
1950	26473	-	-	36	36	-	-
1953	28459	-	-	37	37	-	-
1955	32147	-	-	37	37	-	-
1957	34769	-	-	25	25	-	-
1960	38185	-	-	25	25	-	-
1961	39566	-	-	6	6	-	-
1962	41281	-	-	-	-	-	-
1963	42456	-	-	-	-	-	-
1964	44906	-	-	-	-	-	-
1965	48444	-	-	-	-	-	-
DEVELOPED COUNTRIES							
1925	1070735	152139	9240	108457	105301	33821	74571
1929	1161404	189829	9868	145129	138877	54261	111445
1933	830175	139954	8645	127439	123353	44719	118610
1937	1055440	201214	9677	180617	174293	69139	162131

Table I. PRIMARY ENERGY PRODUCTION, SELECTED YEARS, 1925-1965

(Original units)

Region, country, year	Solid fuels (10^3 m.t.) Hard coal	Lignite	Other	Liquid fuels (10^3 m.t.) Total	Crude oil	Natural gas (10^6 c.m.)	Hydro-electric power (10^6 kwh)
	(1)	(2)	(3)	(4)	(5)	(6)	(7)
DEVELOPED COUNTRIES (CONTINUED)							
1938	958304	212157	9155	172891	166176	65744	164651
1950	1050698	111014	11846	294137	274915	174823	306761
1953	1024611	121146	12242	361650	336923	235775	363279
1955	1032741	134188	12217	391827	363044	266427	408734
1957	1074937	147208	12325	420645	390651	305978	457553
1960	957409	154713	12060	423901	389297	377937	554276
1961	942985	160115	11278	438280	401236	397093	577365
1962	963867	166509	11897	451110	412753	424436	593854
1963	993211	175433	11939	468033	426118	448655	620082
1964	1023205	181772	13903	479746	434742	477696	638233
1965	1033380	176346	13366	493367	446281	496680	695338
UNDERDEVELOPED COUNTRIES							
1925	31492	211	415	33272	33149	1111	3588
1929	35725	243	672	48017	47726	1956	4867
1933	30976	228	222	44861	44436	2843	6847
1937	41682	306	638	69583	69130	4103	10700
1938	46657	340	486	69706	69270	4417	11697
1950	48934	1560	469	202767	202122	6213	20100
1953	57350	1843	305	257962	257173	9416	26819
1955	60374	2025	224	324983	324123	12006	32721
1957	68428	2698	177	382463	381274	17446	42271
1960	80243	2965	19	499322	497006	27980	57150
1961	84566	2778	6	536651	534062	31087	63494
1962	92018	3420	5	598803	596260	34224	69719
1963	98800	5034	16	652813	650053	36423	76135
1964	97563	5957	8	730067	727168	41638	83826
1965	103462	6825	9	799240	795989	44820	93510
COMMUNIST COUNTRIES							
1925	81974	29589	4917	10268	10238	1045	519
1929	126467	37409	7567	19299	19220	1606	927
1933	134810	32679	14063	29807	29596	3075	1633
1937	201019	47674	24440	37005	36660	4722	5070
1938	202141	47314	27035	38287	37970	4663	6029
1950	331379	268167	36499	45213	45045	8143	20317
1953	407260	341559	39086	65481	65263	11404	24420
1955	499155	398847	51277	87084	86860	14064	33548
1957	586075	443170	55391	115748	115506	24818	54162
1960	742237	482514	54125	170898	170564	54007	76486
1961	777619	501085	52482	190479	190138	68499	81893
1962	793445	517048	35245	212159	211805	84591	95883
1963	827628	541359	59013	233606	233224	102626	99735
1964	867230	564324	60011	248100	247718	122591	102683
1965	901389	565528	60465	269253	268838	143364	111915
USSR							
1925	14903	1617	4917	7086	7086	140	251
1929	36589	3478	7567	13689	13689	330	557
1933	67467	8866	14063	21557	21557	1110	1163
1937	109878	18090	24440	28693	28693	2179	4191
1938	114728	18535	27035	30415	30415	2210	5091

Table I. PRIMARY ENERGY PRODUCTION, SELECTED YEARS, 1925-1965

(Original units)

Region, country, year	Solid fuels (10^3 m.t.)			Liquid fuels (10^3 m.t.)		Natural gas (10^6 c.m.)	Hydro-electric power (10^6 kwh)
	Hard coal	Lignite	Other	Total	Crude oil		
	(1)	(2)	(3)	(4)	(5)	(6)	(7)
USSR (CONTINUED)							
1950	185225	75864	35999	38928	38928	5761	12691
1953	224315	96107	38586	54277	54277	6868	19201
1955	276615	114644	50777	73093	73093	8981	23165
1957	328502	134968	54891	101106	101106	18583	39429
1960	374925	138261	53625	151059	151059	45303	50913
1961	377019	133516	51982	169538	169538	58981	59122
1962	386432	130976	34745	190114	190114	73525	71944
1963	395132	136590	58513	210399	210399	89832	75859
1964	408870	145127	59511	223603	223603	108566	77361
1965	427881	149850	59965	242888	242888	127666	81431
COMMUNIST EASTERN EUROPE							
1925	42816	27972	-	3182	3152	905	268
1929	64033	33931	-	5605	5526	1276	370
1933	38964	23813	-	8159	7948	1965	470
1937	54231	29584	-	8112	7767	2543	879
1938	55473	28779	-	7592	7275	2453	938
1950	101039	190731	500	6085	5917	2382	2346
1953	112734	245050	500	10582	10364	4536	2659
1955	120978	282896	500	13025	12801	5083	4183
1957	122306	306261	500	13161	12919	6235	4431
1960	137120	340411	500	14310	13976	8704	6269
1961	139522	363279	500	14715	14374	9518	6271
1962	143685	381872	500	15222	14868	11066	6939
1963	148581	400429	500	15688	15306	12794	6376
1964	153050	414897	500	15979	15597	14025	6322
1965	154118	411378	500	16349	15934	15698	9484
COMMUNIST ASIA							
1925	24255	-	-	-	-	-	-
1929	25845	-	-	5	5	-	-
1933	28379	-	-	91	91	-	-
1937	36910	-	-	200	200	-	-
1938	31940	-	-	280	280	-	-
1950	45115	1572	-	200	200	-	5280
1953	70211	402	-	622	622	-	2560
1955	101562	1307	-	966	966	-	6200
1957	135267	1941	-	1481	1481	-	10302
1960	230192	3842	-	5529	5529	-	19304
1961	261078	4290	-	6226	6226	-	16500
1962	263328	4200	-	6823	6823	-	17000
1963	283915	4340	-	7519	7519	-	17500
1964	305310	4300	-	8518	8518	-	19000
1965	319390	4300	-	10016	10016	-	21000
ORGANISATION FOR ECONOMIC CO-OPERATION AND DEVELOPMENT (OECD)							
1925	1043983	147118	8294	108457	105301	33821	73237
1929	1137027	182708	8782	145129	138877	54259	109293
1933	810284	133467	7753	127437	123351	44718	115574
1937	1027877	193185	8450	180615	174291	69137	157658
1938	930445	203140	8000	172884	166169	65742	159659
1950	1009120	92366	9182	294005	274785	174809	297524

Table I. PRIMARY ENERGY PRODUCTION, SELECTED YEARS, 1925-1965

(Original units)

Region, country, year	Solid fuels (10^3 m.t.)			Liquid fuels (10^3 m.t.)		Natural gas (10^6 c.m.)	Hydro-electric power (10^6 kwh)
	Hard coal	Lignite	Other	Total	Crude oil		
	(1)	(2)	(3)	(4)	(5)	(6)	(7)
ORGANISATION FOR ECONOMIC CO-OPERATION AND DEVELOPMENT (OECD) (CONTINUED)							
1953	980981	103173	8888	361464	336739	235751	351164
1955	984170	110845	8833	391708	362928	266393	393410
1957	1023454	121224	8873	420517	390527	305936	439138
1960	899731	119823	7947	423300	388702	377884	534044
1961	882673	122249	7130	437369	400330	397024	554296
1962	902124	127436	7674	450174	411822	424341	566151
1963	930223	132951	7340	467160	425251	448461	591810
1964	955858	137017	8869	478668	433674	477419	608749
1965	958724	129448	8242	492485	445414	496346	661650
COMMUNIST COUNTRIES							
1925	81974	29589	4917	10268	10238	1045	519
1929	126467	37409	7567	19299	19220	1606	927
1933	134810	32679	14063	29807	29596	3075	1633
1937	201019	47674	24440	37005	36660	4722	5070
1938	202141	47314	27035	38287	37970	4663	6029
1950	331379	268167	36499	45213	45045	8143	20317
1953	407260	341559	39086	65481	65263	11404	24420
1955	499155	398847	51277	87084	86860	14064	33548
1957	586075	443170	55391	115748	115506	24818	54162
1960	742237	482514	54125	170898	170564	54007	76486
1961	777619	501085	52482	190479	190138	68499	81893
1962	793445	517048	35245	212159	211805	84591	95883
1963	827628	541359	59013	233606	233224	102626	99735
1964	867230	564324	60011	248100	247718	122591	102683
1965	901389	565528	60465	269253	268838	143364	111915
WORLD EXCLUDING OECD AND COMMUNIST COUNTRIES							
1925	58244	5232	1361	33272	33149	1111	4922
1929	60102	7364	1758	48017	47726	1958	7019
1933	50867	6715	1114	44863	44438	2844	9883
1937	69245	8335	1865	69585	69132	4105	15173
1938	74516	9357	1641	69713	69277	4419	16689
1950	90512	20208	3133	202899	202252	6227	29337
1953	100980	19816	3659	258148	257357	9440	38934
1955	108945	25368	3608	325102	324239	12040	48045
1957	119911	28682	3629	382591	381398	17488	60686
1960	137921	37855	4132	499923	497601	28033	77382
1961	144878	40644	4154	537562	534968	31156	86563
1962	153761	42493	4228	599739	597191	34319	97422
1963	161788	47516	4615	653686	650920	36617	104407
1964	164910	50712	5042	731145	728236	41915	113310
1965	178118	53723	5133	800122	796856	45154	127198

DERIVATION OF TABLE II

Column	*Derivation*
(1)	Sum of cols. (2), (6), (8), and (9)
(2)	Sum of cols. (3), (4), and (5)
(3) (4) (5)	Cols. (1), (2), and (3) of table I, respectively, converted into coal equivalents using appropriate conversion factors*
(6) (7)	Cols. (4) and (5) of table I, respectively, multiplied by 1.5*
(8)	Col. (6) of table I multiplied by 1.332*
(9)	Col. (7) of table I multiplied by 0.125*

Table II. PRIMARY ENERGY PRODUCTION, SELECTED YEARS, 1925-1965

(Thousand metric tons coal equivalent)

Region, country, year	Total primary energy production	Solid fuels				Liquid fuels		Natural gas	Hydro-electric power
		Total	Hard coal	Lignite	Other	Total	Crude oil		
	(1)	(2)	(3)	(4)	(5)	(6)	(7)	(8)	(9)
WORLD									
1925	1566644	1280893	1206587	66248	8058	227995	223032	47921	9835
1929	1847910	1437567	1345066	82593	9908	318668	308735	77020	14655
1933	1466198	1079703	1005169	63187	11347	303161	296078	67448	15886
1937	1974278	1417385	1310787	89865	16733	430808	420125	103848	22238
1938	1867563	1323774	1213358	93056	17360	421326	410124	99666	22797
1950	2717137	1608578	1441678	143645	23256	813176	783123	251986	43397
1953	3114468	1693229	1492827	176041	24361	1027640	989039	341785	51815
1955	3480857	1826035	1593949	202688	29398	1205841	1161041	389606	59375
1957	3879104	1967713	1710002	226690	31021	1378284	1331147	463858	69248
1960	4341320	2001531	1726938	245745	28848	1641182	1585301	612619	85989
1961	4529153	2029118	1746315	255383	27420	1748115	1688154	661576	90344
1962	4788572	2076922	1791866	263933	21123	1893108	1831227	723610	94932
1963	5081633	2167639	1859843	277497	30299	2031678	1964093	782822	99494
1964	5391092	2246086	1925113	289051	31922	2186870	2114442	855044	103093
1965	5660354	2292730	1972103	288645	31983	2342790	2266662	912239	112595
NORTH AMERICA									
1925	779000	567809	564677	905	2228	161747	157013	45010	4435
1929	893071	597194	593608	1220	2365	216744	207366	72225	6909
1933	632749	376336	373457	1176	1703	190149	184020	59483	6781

Table II. PRIMARY ENERGY PRODUCTION, SELECTED YEARS, 1925-1965

(Thousand metric tons coal equivalent)

Region, country, year	Total primary energy production	Solid fuels				Liquid fuels		Natural gas	Hydro-electric power
		Total	Hard coal	Lignite	Other	Total	Crude oil		
	(1)	(2)	(3)	(4)	(5)	(6)	(7)	(8)	(9)
NORTH AMERICA (CONTINUED)									
1937	859857	489371	485941	1584	1846	269334	259848	91972	9179
1938	743722	389577	386363	1501	1712	257543	247470	87478	9125
1950	1237415	552559	547931	2308	2320	434675	405870	231031	19150
1953	1343711	481002	477281	2045	1676	531191	494204	309410	22108
1955	1426922	482582	478647	2300	1635	572919	529859	347328	24092
1957	1544060	507356	503930	2107	1320	612183	567335	397394	27126
1960	1555109	425330	422152	2102	1076	611825	560385	486029	31925
1961	1583958	411426	408268	2206	951	631350	576225	508739	32444
1962	1655452	429230	425940	2245	1046	648995	591980	542710	34517
1963	1746156	466178	463107	1915	1156	672794	610392	573082	34103
1964	1825960	492636	489106	2059	1471	687444	620550	609174	36706
1965	1892893	514645	510733	2127	1785	707015	636975	632019	39214
CANADA									
1925	13074	11112	8628	257	2228	80	80	638	1244
1929	18474	14982	12273	343	2365	210	210	1071	2212
1933	13239	9994	7742	549	1703	246	216	872	2126
1937	18756	13480	11014	621	1846	657	551	1221	3398
1938	17995	12131	9815	604	1712	1391	1310	1261	3211
1950	30937	15970	12351	1299	2320	5886	5807	2559	6522
1953	41982	13282	10414	1192	1676	16506	16400	3810	8384
1955	53822	12218	9231	1353	1635	26393	26240	5686	9525
1957	66746	10857	8211	1327	1320	37169	36863	8298	10422
1960	81301	8978	6622	1280	1076	39362	38421	19726	13235
1961	92488	8448	6194	1303	951	46317	44768	24734	12990
1962	108367	8301	5925	1331	1046	51351	49490	35708	13006
1963	119449	8655	6394	1105	1156	55668	52388	42147	12979
1964	136537	9197	6550	1176	1471	60099	55637	53074	14168
1965	143737	9324	6323	1216	1785	64376	59556	55448	14589
UNITED STATES									
1925	765925	556695	556047	648	-	161667	156933	44372	3191
1929	874593	582208	581331	877	-	216534	207156	71154	4697
1933	619506	366337	365710	627	-	189903	183804	58611	4655
1937	841094	475885	474921	964	-	268677	259298	90750	5782
1938	725720	377439	376541	898	-	256152	246161	86216	5913
1950	1206471	536582	535573	1009	-	428789	400064	228473	12628
1953	1301723	467713	466860	853	-	514685	477804	305601	13724
1955	1373083	470348	469400	948	-	546527	503619	341642	14567
1957	1477297	496482	495702	780	-	575015	530472	389096	16705
1960	1473780	416324	415502	822	-	572463	521964	466304	18689
1961	1491507	403016	402112	904	-	585033	531458	484005	19454
1962	1547060	420903	419989	914	-	597644	542490	507002	21511
1963	1626667	457483	456673	810	-	617126	558005	530935	21124
1964	1689399	483415	482532	883	-	627345	564914	556101	22538
1965	1749136	505301	504390	911	-	642639	577419	576571	24625
WESTERN EUROPE									
1925	532387	527978	477377	47772	2828	546	546	9	3854
1929	608389	602496	540088	59357	3051	545	545	12	5336
1933	476055	469464	423211	43333	2920	714	714	20	5858
1937	596055	586881	521787	61870	3224	1065	1065	51	8058

Table II. PRIMARY ENERGY PRODUCTION, SELECTED YEARS, 1925-1965

(Thousand metric tons coal equivalent)

Region, country, year	Total primary energy production	Solid fuels: Total	Solid fuels: Hard coal	Solid fuels: Lignite	Solid fuels: Other	Liquid fuels: Total	Liquid fuels: Crude oil	Natural gas	Hydro-electric power
	(1)	(2)	(3)	(4)	(5)	(6)	(7)	(8)	(9)
WESTERN EUROPE (CONTINUED)									
1938	592935	583423	514934	65390	3099	1256	1256	25	8231
1950	509832	488196	451015	33858	3322	6033	6008	1745	13858
1953	554002	521347	480648	37065	3634	10778	10680	4507	17369
1955	574199	532461	487430	41421	3609	14288	14180	7345	20106
1957	592743	542842	492878	46128	3837	18260	18122	9730	21911
1960	567820	499539	447923	48039	3576	23190	22733	16285	28806
1961	567337	493580	440664	49664	3253	25065	24633	18788	29904
1962	576227	498500	443390	51667	3443	26513	26009	20818	30396
1963	579526	496448	438312	54906	3229	28049	27606	22010	33020
1964	588942	501150	440364	56992	3794	30864	30293	24352	32576
1965	577931	482864	424387	55225	3253	31508	30929	26865	36694
EUROPEAN ECONOMIC COMMUNITY (EEC)									
1925	269765	267760	223074	43988	697	236	236	9	1761
1929	327896	325079	26[illegible]499	54661	918	282	282	9	2526
1933	249231	245829	205281	39732	816	524	524	19	2860
1937	337538	332554	273783	57771	1000	815	816	48	4121
1938	343937	338879	276940	60918	1022	969	969	23	4066
1950	253525	243462	217562	24853	1047	2997	2975	1099	5967
1953	283528	266938	238078	27733	1128	5318	5223	3724	7547
1955	301197	278091	247382	29491	1217	7994	7890	6287	8826
1957	311846	281920	249000	31706	1213	12398	12266	8625	8904
1960	311948	267405	234778	31433	1195	17622	17174	14153	12768
1961	311805	264259	230724	32354	1181	19028	18603	16514	12005
1962	312302	262451	227622	33650	1179	20184	19688	18355	11313
1963	313874	260136	223944	34959	1233	21287	20856	19281	13171
1964	322636	266246	228896	36098	1252	23741	23187	21400	11250
1965	314251	253027	218355	33510	1162	23798	23244	23877	13549
BELGIUM-LUXEMBOURG									
1925	23100	23097	23097	-	-	-	-	-	3
1929	26943	26940	26940	-	-	-	-	-	3
1933	25303	25300	25300	-	-	-	-	-	3
1937	29866	29859	29859	-	-	-	-	-	7
1938	29591	29585	29585	-	-	-	-	-	6
1950	27348	27321	27321	-	-	-	-	19	8
1953	30145	30060	30060	-	-	-	-	73	12
1955	30101	29978	29978	-	-	-	-	107	17
1957	29164	29001	29001	-	-	-	-	141	22
1960	22586	22469	22469	-	-	-	-	93	24
1961	21660	21536	21536	-	-	-	-	93	31
1962	21346	21226	21226	-	-	-	-	93	26
1963	21589	21418	21418	-	-	-	-	92	79
1964	21508	21305	21305	-	-	-	-	88	115
1965	20040	19786	19786	-	-	-	-	105	148
FRANCE									
1925	48337	47693	47097	596	-	105	105	-	539
1929	55442	54498	53780	718	-	119	119	-	825
1933	48596	47543	46887	656	-	128	128	-	925
1937	46419	44928	44319	609	-	119	119	-	1373
1938	48560	47139	46504	635	-	122	122	-	1300

Table II. PRIMARY ENERGY PRODUCTION, SELECTED YEARS, 1925-1965

(Thousand metric tons coal equivalent)

Region, country, year	Total primary energy production	Solid fuels				Liquid fuels		Natural gas	Hydro-electric power
		Total	Hard coal	Lignite	Other	Total	Crude oil		
	(1)	(2)	(3)	(4)	(5)	(6)	(7)	(8)	(9)
FRANCE (CONTINUED)									
1950	54428	51847	50835	1012	-	246	227	306	2029
1953	57332	53765	52596	1169	-	600	582	310	2656
1955	61479	56568	55336	1232	-	1346	1328	341	3224
1957	64042	58175	56799	1376	-	2148	2115	585	3135
1960	69535	57333	55966	1367	-	3318	2975	3791	5093
1961	67916	54102	52358	1744	-	3566	3246	5424	4825
1962	68881	54099	52370	1729	-	3951	3555	6314	4517
1963	65313	49248	47763	1485	-	4113	3783	6475	5478
1964	70250	54375	53030	1345	-	4713	4269	6780	4383
1965	70512	52961	51348	1613	-	4965	4482	6724	5862
GERMANY									
1925	189777	189302	145612	42992	697	119	119	-	357
1929	232195	231595	177020	53657	918	155	155	-	446
1933	160866	159998	120253	38929	816	357	357	-	511
1937	243877	242310	184513	56797	1000	677	677	28	863
1938	248906	247165	186179	59965	1022	828	828	NA	912
GERMANY, FEDERAL REPUBLIC									
1950	153769	150924	126334	23544	1047	1679	1679	84	1082
1953	174328	169601	142220	26254	1128	3284	3284	273	1170
1955	185577	178532	149265	28050	1217	4721	4721	822	1503
1957	190899	182335	151005	30117	1213	5973	5973	1051	1540
1960	185466	174277	143255	29827	1195	8342	8325	1224	1624
1961	187148	174949	143615	30153	1181	9350	9330	1235	1615
1962	187943	174466	141899	31388	1179	10185	10167	1724	1568
1963	191961	177083	142786	33064	1233	11093	11075	2238	1547
1964	194540	178349	142704	34393	1252	11525	11510	3146	1520
1965	186264	168217	135464	31591	1162	11838	11826	4288	1921
ITALY									
1925	1367	483	151	332	-	12	12	9	863
1929	1684	413	178	235	-	9	9	9	1253
1933	1861	382	267	115	-	39	39	19	1421
1937	3008	1089	771	318	-	21	21	20	1878
1938	3336	1446	1184	262	-	20	20	23	1848
1950	4601	1059	825	234	-	15	12	679	2848
1953	8083	1132	905	227	-	204	128	3037	3710
1955	10339	1034	908	126	-	392	306	4831	4082
1957	13780	937	819	118	-	1992	1893	6643	4208
1960	18527	828	590	238	-	3086	2997	8587	6026
1961	18770	1051	594	458	-	3044	2958	9142	5534
1962	18624	1086	554	533	-	2813	2730	9524	5201
1963	19383	878	468	410	-	2759	2676	9680	6067
1964	20302	737	377	360	-	4098	4004	10235	5232
1965	20026	617	311	305	-	3402	3344	10390	5618
NETHERLANDS									
1925	7186	7186	7117	69	-	-	-	-	-
1929	11633	11633	11581	52	-	-	-	-	-
1933	12606	12606	12574	32	-	-	-	-	-

Table II. PRIMARY ENERGY PRODUCTION, SELECTED YEARS, 1925-1965

(Thousand metric tons coal equivalent)

Region, country, year	Total primary energy production	Solid fuels				Liquid fuels		Natural gas	Hydro-electric power
		Total	Hard coal	Lignite	Other	Total	Crude oil		
	(1)	(2)	(3)	(4)	(5)	(6)	(7)	(8)	(9)
NETHERLANDS (CONTINUED)									
1937	14368	14368	14321	47	-	-	-	-	-
1938	13544	13544	13488	56	-	-	-	-	-
1950	13379	12311	12247	64	-	1058	1058	11	-
1953	13641	12380	12297	83	-	1230	1230	31	-
1955	13702	11979	11895	84	-	1536	1536	186	-
1957	13961	11471	11376	95	-	2285	2285	205	-
1960	15833	12499	12498	1	-	2877	2877	457	-
1961	16311	12621	12621	-	-	3069	3069	621	-
1962	15509	11573	11573	-	-	3236	3236	701	-
1963	15628	11509	11509	-	-	3323	3323	797	-
1964	16036	11480	11480	-	-	3405	3405	1151	-
1965	17409	11446	11446	-	-	3593	3593	2371	-
EUROPEAN FREE TRADE ASSOCIATION (EFTA)									
1925	251931	249796	247929	1525	343	302	302	-	1834
1929	267750	265072	262985	1777	311	254	254	-	2424
1933	215903	213277	211444	1513	320	182	182	-	2445
1937	250935	247396	245364	1643	390	239	239	-	3300
1938	237587	233832	231775	1689	369	276	276	-	3478
1950	234119	224052	221009	2424	619	2867	2867	627	6573
1953	246519	232616	229084	3054	478	5174	5174	751	7979
1955	246168	230399	226287	3586	526	5852	5852	1012	8905
1957	249849	233301	228479	4273	549	5154	5154	1050	10344
1960	220424	201880	197872	3734	274	4047	4047	2062	12435
1961	218560	198502	194630	3633	239	3921	3921	2182	13955
1962	226557	205525	201678	3674	174	3936	3936	2336	14759
1963	225550	203946	199941	3826	179	4239	4236	2475	14891
1964	224909	201551	197792	3568	192	4313	4310	2587	16458
1965	220180	195041	191481	3387	172	4496	4493	2548	18096
AUSTRIA									
1925	1828	1662	145	1517	-	-	-	-	166
1929	2189	1971	208	1763	-	-	-	-	219
1933	1996	1751	239	1507	5	2	2	-	244
1937	2225	1876	230	1621	25	50	50	-	299
1938	2308	1922	227	1670	25	86	86	-	300
1950	6160	2362	183	2154	25	2549	2549	626	624
1953	9349	2974	162	2787	25	4832	4832	739	804
1955	10984	3501	171	3310	20	5499	5499	996	988
1957	10563	3609	152	3439	18	4779	4779	1011	1165
1960	10250	3137	132	2987	18	3672	3672	1957	1485
1961	10004	2939	106	2831	3	3534	3534	2073	1458
1962	10242	2958	99	2856	3	3591	3591	2178	1516
1963	10823	3133	104	3027	3	3933	3930	2263	1494
1964	10981	2986	103	2881	3	3998	3995	2350	1647
1965	11379	2787	59	2725	3	4286	4283	2296	2010
DENMARK									
1925	153	153	-	-	153	-	-	-	-
1929	121	121	-	-	121	-	-	-	-
1933	125	125	-	-	125	-	-	-	-
1937	183	183	-	10	173	-	-	-	-

Table II. PRIMARY ENERGY PRODUCTION, SELECTED YEARS, 1925-1965

(Thousand metric tons coal equivalent)

Region, country, year	Total primary energy production	Solid fuels				Liquid fuels		Natural gas	Hydro-electric power
		Total	Hard coal	Lignite	Other	Total	Crude oil		
	(1)	(2)	(3)	(4)	(5)	(6)	(7)	(8)	(9)
DENMARK (CONTINUED)									
1938	166	166	-	10	156	-	-	-	-
1950	551	548	-	223	325	-	-	-	3
1953	442	438	-	231	207	-	-	-	4
1955	492	489	-	232	256	-	-	-	4
1957	1010	1007	-	742	264	-	-	-	4
1960	733	731	-	670	61	-	-	-	3
1961	767	764	-	723	41	-	-	-	3
1962	766	763	-	741	22	-	-	-	3
1963	750	746	-	728	18	-	-	-	3
1964	653	650	-	637	13	-	-	-	3
1965	627	624	-	617	7	-	-	-	3
NORWAY									
1925	1338	565	390	-	175	-	-	-	773
1929	1366	426	251	-	175	-	-	-	940
1933	1385	470	295	-	175	-	-	-	915
1937	1629	472	297	-	175	-	-	-	1157
1938	1714	474	299	-	175	-	-	-	1240
1950	2780	545	364	-	181	-	-	-	2235
1953	3009	554	427	-	127	-	-	-	2455
1955	3277	442	322	-	120	-	-	-	2835
1957	3736	509	384	-	125	-	-	-	3228
1960	4397	494	404	-	90	-	-	-	3903
1961	4666	451	369	-	82	-	-	-	4215
1962	5267	517	444	-	73	-	-	-	4750
1963	5402	445	393	-	52	-	-	-	4957
1964	6021	494	442	-	52	-	-	-	5527
1965	6656	488	435	-	53	-	-	-	6168
PORTUGAL									
1925	137	132	123	9	-	-	-	-	6
1929	221	212	197	15	-	-	-	-	9
1933	246	234	228	6	-	-	-	-	12
1937	288	271	259	12	-	-	-	-	17
1938	333	317	308	9	-	-	-	-	16
1950	521	466	419	47	-	-	-	-	55
1953	638	514	478	36	-	-	-	-	125
1955	664	448	404	44	-	-	-	-	216
1957	821	591	499	92	-	-	-	-	230
1960	900	512	434	78	-	-	-	-	388
1961	977	549	470	79	-	-	-	-	428
1962	920	482	405	77	-	-	-	-	439
1963	987	487	416	71	-	-	-	-	500
1964	1022	495	444	51	-	-	-	-	528
1965	971	473	428	45	-	-	-	-	498
SWEDEN									
1925	622	200	185	-	15	-	-	-	423
1929	864	292	277	-	15	-	-	-	572
1933	871	259	244	-	15	-	-	-	612
1937	1210	339	322	-	17	-	-	-	871
1938	1228	315	302	-	13	-	-	-	913

Table II. PRIMARY ENERGY PRODUCTION, SELECTED YEARS, 1925-1965

(Thousand metric tons coal equivalent)

Region, country, year	Total primary energy production	Solid fuels				Liquid fuels		Natural gas	Hydro-electric power
		Total	Hard coal	Lignite	Other	Total	Crude oil		
	(1)	(2)	(3)	(4)	(5)	(6)	(7)	(8)	(9)
SWEDEN (CONTINUED)									
1950	2552	305	216	-	89	80	80	-	2167
1953	3079	320	200	-	120	99	99	-	2660
1955	3158	327	197	-	130	125	125	-	2706
1957	3887	355	213	-	143	143	143	-	3389
1960	4320	281	176	-	105	153	153	-	3886
1961	4982	255	140	-	115	161	161	-	4567
1962	5219	180	104	-	77	152	152	-	4887
1963	5032	175	69	-	106	119	119	-	4739
1964	5691	183	59	-	125	122	122	-	5387
1965	6038	151	41	-	110	84	84	-	5803
SWITZERLAND									
1925	470	7	7	-	-	-	-	-	463
1929	671	7	7	-	-	-	-	-	664
1933	622	2	2	-	-	-	-	-	620
1937	865	4	4	-	-	-	-	-	861
1938	889	3	3	-	-	-	-	-	886
1950	1334	30	30	-	-	-	-	-	1304
1953	1704	10	10	-	-	-	-	-	1694
1955	1954	10	10	-	-	-	-	-	1944
1957	1995	10	10	-	-	-	-	-	1985
1960	2389	10	10	-	-	-	-	-	2379
1961	2813	10	10	-	-	-	-	-	2803
1962	2683	10	10	-	-	-	-	-	2673
1963	2750	10	10	-	-	-	-	-	2740
1964	2874	10	10	-	-	-	-	-	2864
1965	3045	10	10	-	-	-	-	-	3035
UNITED KINGDOM									
1925	247383	247079	247079	-	-	302	302	-	3
1929	262319	262045	262045	-	-	254	254	-	21
1933	210657	210436	210436	-	-	180	180	-	41
1937	244535	244252	244252	-	-	189	189	-	94
1938	230950	230636	230636	-	-	191	191	-	124
1950	220222	219797	219797	-	-	239	239	1	185
1953	228299	227807	227807	-	-	243	243	12	237
1955	225640	225183	225183	-	-	228	228	16	213
1957	227836	227221	227221	-	-	233	233	39	344
1960	197435	196716	196716	-	-	222	222	105	392
1961	194352	193535	193535	-	-	227	227	109	482
1962	201459	200616	200616	-	-	194	194	159	491
1963	199806	198949	198949	-	-	188	188	212	458
1964	197667	196734	196734	-	-	194	194	237	503
1965	191464	190508	190508	-	-	126	126	252	578
WESTERN EUROPE - OTHER									
1925	10690	10422	6374	2260	1788	9	9	-	260
1929	12743	12345	7604	2919	1822	9	9	3	387
1933	10921	10358	6485	2089	1784	9	9	1	553
1937	7582	6931	2640	2457	1835	11	11	3	638
1938	11411	10711	6219	2783	1709	11	11	3	687
1950	22189	20682	12444	6581	1657	170	167	19	1319

Table II. PRIMARY ENERGY PRODUCTION, SELECTED YEARS, 1925-1965

(Thousand metric tons coal equivalent)

Region, country, year	Total primary energy production	Solid fuels				Liquid fuels		Natural gas	Hydro-electric power
		Total	Hard coal	Lignite	Other	Total	Crude oil		
	(1)	(2)	(3)	(4)	(5)	(6)	(7)	(8)	(9)
WESTERN EUROPE - OTHER (CONTINUED)									
1953	23955	21794	13487	6278	2029	287	284	32	1843
1955	26834	23971	13761	8344	1866	443	438	45	2375
1957	31048	27622	15399	10149	2074	708	702	56	2663
1960	35448	30254	15274	12872	2108	1521	1512	71	3603
1961	36972	30820	15310	13677	1833	2117	2109	92	3944
1962	37368	30525	14091	14344	2090	2393	2385	127	4324
1963	40101	32366	14427	16122	1817	2523	2514	254	4959
1964	41397	33353	13676	17327	2350	2811	2796	365	4869
1965	43500	34797	14550	18329	1918	3215	3192	440	5050
FINLAND									
1925	58	10	-	-	10	-	-	-	48
1929	109	10	-	-	10	-	-	-	99
1933	165	9	-	-	9	-	-	-	156
1937	269	11	-	-	11	-	-	-	258
1938	320	13	-	-	13	-	-	-	307
1950	555	99	-	-	99	-	-	-	456
1953	720	98	-	-	98	-	-	-	622
1955	854	80	-	-	80	-	-	-	774
1957	917	90	-	-	90	-	-	-	827
1960	719	60	-	-	60	-	-	-	659
1961	1061	58	-	-	58	-	-	-	1003
1962	1252	31	-	-	31	-	-	-	1221
1963	1087	40	-	-	40	-	-	-	1047
1964	1099	36	-	-	36	-	-	-	1063
1965	1219	33	-	-	33	-	-	-	1186
GREECE									
1925	72	71	-	71	-	-	-	-	1
1929	79	78	-	78	-	-	-	-	1
1933	51	50	-	50	-	-	-	-	2
1937	67	66	-	66	-	-	-	-	2
1938	56	54	-	54	-	-	-	-	2
1950	91	90	-	90	-	-	-	-	1
1953	226	222	-	222	-	-	-	-	4
1955	433	391	-	391	-	-	-	-	42
1957	544	499	-	499	-	-	-	-	45
1960	1334	1276	-	1276	-	-	-	-	59
1961	1321	1252	-	1252	-	-	-	-	69
1962	1424	1347	-	1347	-	-	-	-	77
1963	1859	1758	-	1758	-	-	-	-	101
1964	1995	1901	-	1901	-	-	-	-	94
1965	2598	2505	-	2505	-	-	-	-	94
ICELAND									
1925	1	-	-	-	-	-	-	-	1
1929	1	-	-	-	-	-	-	-	1
1933	1	-	-	-	-	-	-	-	1
1937	2	-	-	-	-	-	-	-	2
1938	3	-	-	-	-	-	-	-	3
1950	23	2	-	-	2	-	-	-	21
1953	25	1	-	-	1	-	-	-	25

Table II. PRIMARY ENERGY PRODUCTION, SELECTED YEARS, 1925-1965

(Thousand metric tons coal equivalent)

Region, country, year	Total primary energy production	Solid fuels				Liquid fuels		Natural gas	Hydro-electric power
		Total	Hard coal	Lignite	Other	Total	Crude oil		
	(1)	(2)	(3)	(4)	(5)	(6)	(7)	(8)	(9)
ICELAND (CONTINUED)									
1955	47	-	-	-	-	-	-	-	47
1957	52	-	-	-	-	-	-	-	52
1960	65	-	-	-	-	-	-	-	65
1961	72	-	-	-	-	-	-	-	72
1962	74	-	-	-	-	-	-	-	74
1963	79	-	-	-	-	-	-	-	79
1964	82	-	-	-	-	-	-	-	82
1965	80	-	-	-	-	-	-	-	80
IRELAND									
1925	1858	1857	79	-	1778	-	-	-	1
1929	1903	1899	87	-	1812	-	-	-	4
1933	1896	1882	107	-	1775	-	-	-	14
1937	1983	1952	128	-	1824	-	-	-	31
1938	1854	1817	120	-	1697	-	-	-	37
1950	1787	1729	172	-	1557	-	-	-	58
1953	2164	2097	167	-	1930	-	-	-	67
1955	2048	1987	201	-	1786	-	-	-	61
1957	2313	2226	241	-	1985	-	-	-	88
1960	2372	2256	208	-	2048	-	-	-	117
1961	2068	1976	201	-	1775	-	-	-	92
1962	2350	2267	208	-	2059	-	-	-	83
1963	2092	2010	233	-	1777	-	-	-	82
1964	2629	2531	217	-	2314	-	-	-	98
1965	2181	2064	178	-	1886	-	-	-	117
SPAIN									
1925	6499	6319	6117	202	-	9	9	-	171
1929	7584	7328	7108	220	-	9	9	-	248
1933	6488	6150	5999	151	-	8	8	-	331
1937	2485	2188	2084	104	-	9	9	-	288
1938	6021	5732	5649	83	-	9	9	-	280
1950	12412	11776	11118	658	-	2	2	-	635
1953	14254	13291	12395	896	-	26	26	-	938
1955	14520	13344	12426	918	-	53	53	-	1124
1957	16507	15191	13931	1260	-	108	108	-	1209
1960	16713	14664	13783	881	-	96	96	-	1953
1961	16936	14841	13796	1045	-	98	98	-	1998
1962	16046	13939	12695	1244	-	98	98	-	2009
1963	16943	14204	12908	1296	-	98	98	-	2642
1964	16176	13498	12196	1302	-	98	98	-	2581
1965	17151	14610	13180	1430	-	98	98	-	2444
YUGOSLAVIA									
1925	2203	2165	178	1987	-	-	-	-	38
1929	3068	3031	409	2622	-	-	-	3	34
1933	2321	2268	379	1889	-	2	2	1	50
1937	2775	2715	428	2287	-	2	2	3	56
1938	3156	3094	450	2644	-	2	2	3	59
1950	7320	6987	1154	5833	-	168	165	19	147
1953	6566	6086	925	5161	-	261	258	32	188
1955	8931	8169	1134	7035	-	390	386	45	326

Table II. PRIMARY ENERGY PRODUCTION, SELECTED YEARS, 1925-1965

(Thousand metric tons coal equivalent)

Region, country, year	Total primary energy production	Solid fuels				Liquid fuels		Natural gas	Hydro-electric power
		Total	Hard coal	Lignite	Other	Total	Crude oil		
	(1)	(2)	(3)	(4)	(5)	(6)	(7)	(8)	(9)
YUGOSLAVIA (CONTINUED)									
1957	10713	9617	1227	8390	-	600	594	56	440
1960	14242	11999	1283	10716	-	1425	1416	71	748
1961	15512	12694	1313	11381	-	2019	2012	92	707
1962	16218	12941	1188	11753	-	2295	2288	127	856
1963	18037	14354	1286	13068	-	2426	2417	254	1004
1964	19412	15387	1263	14124	-	2714	2699	365	947
1965	20266	15586	1192	14394	-	3117	3095	440	1123
OCEANIA									
1925	16000	15919	14921	303	695	-	-	-	81
1929	13379	13243	11941	503	800	-	-	-	136
1933	11640	11465	10095	715	656	2	2	-	174
1937	15327	15081	13254	924	904	2	2	-	245
1938	14970	14710	12862	1001	848	2	2	-	258
1950	21235	20679	16776	2004	1899	2	2	-	555
1953	23265	22551	17903	2200	2448	2	2	-	713
1955	24759	23932	18772	2662	2498	2	2	-	825
1957	25868	24795	19439	2819	2537	2	2	-	1071
1960	30055	28808	21835	3883	3090	2	2	-	1245
1961	31841	30511	23173	4215	3123	2	2	-	1328
1962	32335	30812	23141	4429	3242	2	2	-	1522
1963	33394	31647	23359	4770	3518	2	2	4	1742
1964	36550	34384	25603	4915	3866	285	285	4	1877
1965	41361	38685	29390	5341	3954	504	504	5	2167
AUSTRALIA									
1925	14111	14068	13845	223	-	-	-	-	43
1929	11028	10973	10531	442	-	-	-	-	55
1933	9960	9893	9238	655	-	-	-	-	67
1937	13220	13130	12268	862	-	-	-	-	90
1938	12886	12802	11868	934	-	-	-	-	85
1950	18668	18481	15840	1861	780	-	-	-	186
1953	20698	20487	17117	2098	1272	-	-	-	211
1955	22080	21831	17976	2569	1286	-	-	-	249
1957	23025	22639	18594	2729	1316	-	-	-	387
1960	26858	26351	21023	3802	1526	-	-	-	506
1961	28663	28129	22404	4135	1590	-	-	-	534
1962	29350	28728	22429	4353	1946	-	-	-	621
1963	30265	29429	22687	4688	2054	-	-	4	832
1964	33208	32058	24910	4835	2313	284	284	4	862
1965	38084	36531	28716	5261	2554	503	503	5	1046
NEW ZEALAND									
1925	1874	1836	1061	81	695	-	-	-	38
1929	2330	2249	1389	61	800	-	-	-	81
1933	1680	1572	857	60	656	2	2	-	107
1937	2108	1951	986	62	904	2	2	-	155
1938	2083	1909	994	67	848	2	2	-	173
1950	2557	2198	936	143	1119	2	2	-	358
1953	2558	2064	786	102	1176	2	2	-	493
1955	2669	2101	796	93	1212	2	2	-	566
1957	2831	2157	845	91	1221	2	2	-	673

Table II. PRIMARY ENERGY PRODUCTION, SELECTED YEARS, 1925-1965

(Thousand metric tons coal equivalent)

Region, country, year	Total primary energy production	Solid fuels				Liquid fuels		Natural gas	Hydro-electric power
		Total	Hard coal	Lignite	Other	Total	Crude oil		
	(1)	(2)	(3)	(4)	(5)	(6)	(7)	(8)	(9)
NEW ZEALAND (CONTINUED)									
1960	3148	2457	812	82	1564	2	2	-	689
1961	3126	2382	769	80	1533	2	2	-	743
1962	2932	2084	712	76	1296	2	2	-	847
1963	3075	2217	672	82	1463	2	2	-	857
1964	3296	2326	693	80	1553	2	2	-	969
1965	3229	2154	674	80	1400	2	2	-	1074
USSR AND COMMUNIST EASTERN EUROPE									
1925	92097	75238	56116	17113	2008	15402	15357	1392	65
1929	153002	121806	97233	21364	3208	28941	28823	2139	116
1933	174676	125802	102064	17830	5908	44574	44258	4096	204
1937	256187	194056	158431	25325	10300	55208	54690	6290	634
1938	264280	200305	163973	24981	11350	57011	56535	6211	754
1950	476173	395927	276939	103638	15351	67520	67268	10846	1880
1953	591576	476365	327034	132981	16350	97289	96962	15190	2733
1955	714751	563422	387678	154294	21451	129177	128841	18733	3419
1957	828147	618206	422006	173050	23151	171401	171038	33058	5483
1960	994064	666926	457420	188455	21051	248054	247553	71937	7148
1961	1050636	674841	458822	195969	20050	276380	275868	91241	8174
1962	1119812	689272	473785	202137	13351	308004	307473	112675	9860
1963	1205520	719412	485181	211881	22351	339131	338558	136698	10279
1964	1275847	742723	499050	220922	22751	359373	358800	163291	10460
1965	1351716	760535	516018	221567	22951	388856	388233	190961	11364
COMMUNIST EASTERN EUROPE									
1925	65141	59129	42816	16413	108	4773	4728	1205	34
1929	94150	83997	64033	19864	108	8408	8289	1700	46
1933	67808	52894	38964	13830	108	12239	11922	2617	59
1937	87121	71456	54231	17225	200	12168	11651	3387	110
1938	86927	72154	55473	16681	250	11388	10913	3267	117
1950	184021	171427	101039	70138	251	9128	8876	3173	293
1953	226312	204065	112734	91081	250	15873	15546	6042	332
1955	252853	226022	120978	104794	251	19538	19202	6771	523
1957	266107	237506	122306	114950	251	19742	19379	8305	554
1960	300368	266526	137120	129155	251	21465	20964	11594	784
1961	313976	278441	139522	138669	250	22073	21561	12678	784
1962	328313	289872	143685	145937	251	22833	22302	14740	867
1963	343483	302112	148581	153281	251	23532	22959	17042	797
1964	355363	311923	153050	158622	251	23969	23396	18681	790
1965	358254	311635	154118	157267	251	24524	23901	20910	1186
ALBANIA									
1925	1	1	-	1	-	-	-	-	-
1929	2	2	-	2	-	-	-	-	-
1933	5	2	-	2	-	3	3	-	-
1937	142	2	-	2	-	140	140	-	-
1938	170	2	-	2	-	168	168	-	-
1950	219	21	-	21	-	198	198	-	-
1953	279	53	-	53	-	224	224	-	3
1955	413	98	-	98	-	312	312	-	3
1957	861	118	-	118	-	735	735	-	8
1960	1253	146	-	146	-	1092	1092	-	15

Table II. PRIMARY ENERGY PRODUCTION, SELECTED YEARS, 1925-1965

(Thousand metric tons coal equivalent)

Region, country, year	Total primary energy production	Solid fuels				Liquid fuels		Natural gas	Hydro-electric power
		Total	Hard coal	Lignite	Other	Total	Crude oil		
	(1)	(2)	(3)	(4)	(5)	(6)	(7)	(8)	(9)
ALBANIA (CONTINUED)									
1961	1315	145	-	145	-	1157	1157	-	14
1962	1343	151	-	151	-	1178	1178	-	15
1963	1274	126	-	126	-	1127	1127	-	21
1964	1317	146	-	146	-	1146	1146	-	25
1965	1406	175	-	175	-	1200	1200	-	31
BULGARIA									
1925	409	407	57	350	-	-	-	-	2
1929	557	551	79	472	-	-	-	-	6
1933	539	529	81	448	-	-	-	-	10
1937	657	641	121	520	-	-	-	-	17
1938	746	729	146	583	-	-	-	-	18
1950	1927	1888	157	1731	-	-	-	-	38
1953	2749	2692	269	2423	-	-	-	-	57
1955	3526	3220	293	2927	-	225	225	-	81
1957	4138	3604	385	3219	-	428	428	-	106
1960	5731	5195	570	4625	-	300	300	-	236
1961	6216	5681	591	5090	-	311	311	-	225
1962	6878	6367	636	5731	-	299	299	-	212
1963	7261	6741	658	6083	-	260	260	-	261
1964	8158	7734	609	7125	-	240	240	-	184
1965	8493	7899	552	7347	-	344	344	-	250
CZECHOSLOVAKIA									
1925	23778	23722	12559	11163	-	35	35	-	22
1929	30108	30058	16521	13537	-	21	21	3	27
1933	19628	19570	10532	9038	-	27	27	1	29
1937	27507	27409	16672	10737	-	27	27	1	70
1938	25557	25452	15836	9616	-	29	29	1	75
1950	35220	34961	18456	16505	-	96	96	25	138
1953	40069	39535	18925	20610	-	183	183	224	127
1955	45726	45094	20643	24451	-	161	161	230	241
1957	54608	53153	22543	30610	-	162	162	1028	265
1960	63497	61256	26214	35042	-	206	206	1724	312
1961	67644	65415	26233	39182	-	231	231	1682	316
1962	70904	68840	27149	41691	-	266	266	1423	376
1963	74047	72162	28180	43982	-	270	270	1329	286
1964	75454	73565	28202	45363	-	293	293	1256	341
1965	73638	71661	27731	43930	-	288	288	1132	557
GERMANY, EAST									
1950	44204	44170	2805	41115	250	-	-	-	34
1953	54765	54714	2638	51826	250	-	-	-	51
1955	63178	63116	2682	60184	250	-	-	-	63
1957	66843	66783	2754	63779	250	-	-	-	60
1960	70688	70611	2721	67640	250	-	-	-	77
1961	74083	73999	2671	71078	250	-	-	-	85
1962	76999	76923	2575	74098	250	-	-	-	76
1963	79202	78999	2483	76266	250	-	-	135	68
1964	79879	79668	2340	77078	250	-	-	144	67
1965	78128	77852	2212	75390	250	-	-	177	98

Table II. PRIMARY ENERGY PRODUCTION, SELECTED YEARS, 1925-1965

(Thousand metric tons coal equivalent)

Region, country, year	Total primary energy production	Solid fuels: Total	Solid fuels: Hard coal	Solid fuels: Lignite	Solid fuels: Other	Liquid fuels: Total	Liquid fuels: Crude oil	Natural gas	Hydro-electric power
	(1)	(2)	(3)	(4)	(5)	(6)	(7)	(8)	(9)
HUNGARY									
1925	4117	4116	805	3311	-	-	-	-	1
1929	5054	5052	826	4226	-	-	-	-	1
1933	4348	4344	800	3544	-	-	-	3	2
1937	5760	5750	917	4833	-	3	3	5	2
1938	6110	6033	1042	4991	-	65	65	11	3
1950	9805	8521	1400	7121	-	768	768	507	9
1953	15408	13403	1993	11410	-	1269	1269	731	6
1955	17599	14466	2692	11774	-	2402	2402	726	6
1957	15198	13633	2277	11356	-	1013	1013	547	5
1960	19386	17053	2847	14206	-	1866	1826	456	12
1961	20780	18133	3071	15062	-	2205	2186	432	10
1962	21471	18527	3341	15186	-	2481	2462	453	10
1963	23250	19771	3710	16061	-	2655	2636	814	10
1964	24349	20579	4125	16454	-	2717	2702	1044	9
1965	24809	20607	4362	16245	-	2718	2703	1475	9
POLAND									
1925	31064	29101	29081	20	-	1248	1218	713	3
1929	47948	46258	46236	22	-	1064	1013	622	4
1933	28875	27366	27356	10	-	890	827	615	4
1937	37747	36223	36218	5	-	810	752	707	6
1938	39713	38107	38104	3	-	822	761	778	6
1950	80010	79452	78001	1451	-	266	243	242	50
1953	91207	90409	88719	1690	-	311	284	425	62
1955	97202	96290	94476	1814	-	300	270	523	89
1957	96812	95882	94096	1786	-	300	272	558	72
1960	108369	107236	104438	2798	-	320	291	731	82
1961	111097	109707	106606	3101	-	335	305	978	77
1962	114456	112931	109604	3327	-	335	303	1094	97
1963	119494	117753	113150	4603	-	348	318	1309	84
1964	125620	123438	117354	6084	-	453	423	1638	91
1965	128114	125619	118831	6788	-	546	510	1835	114
ROMANIA									
1925	5873	1883	314	1569	-	3491	3476	493	6
1929	10382	1976	371	1605	-	7323	7256	1075	8
1933	14314	983	195	788	-	11319	11066	1998	14
1937	15308	1431	303	1128	-	11189	10730	2673	16
1938	14630	1832	345	1487	-	10305	9891	2478	16
1950	12636	2414	220	2194	-	7800	7571	2398	25
1953	21837	3260	190	3070	-	13887	13587	4662	28
1955	25209	3739	192	3547	-	16139	15833	5291	40
1957	27647	4333	251	4082	-	17105	16770	6171	38
1960	31445	5030	330	4700	-	17682	17250	8683	50
1961	32841	5362	350	5012	-	17835	17373	9586	58
1962	36262	6133	380	5753	-	18276	17796	11771	82
1963	38955	6560	400	6160	-	18873	18350	13455	67
1964	40584	6792	420	6372	-	19121	18593	14599	73
1965	43666	7822	430	7392	-	19428	18857	16290	126
USSR (INCLUDING ESTONIA, LATVIA, LITHUANIA)									
1925	26955	16109	13300	700	1900	10629	10629	186	31

Table II. PRIMARY ENERGY PRODUCTION, SELECTED YEARS, 1925-1965

(Thousand metric tons coal equivalent)

Region, country, year	Total primary energy production	Solid fuels				Liquid fuels		Natural gas	Hydro-electric power
		Total	Hard coal	Lignite	Other	Total	Crude oil		
	(1)	(2)	(3)	(4)	(5)	(6)	(7)	(8)	(9)
USSR (INCLUDING ESTONIA, LATVIA, LITHUANIA) (CONTINUED)									
1929	58851	37809	33200	1500	3100	20534	20534	440	70
1933	106868	72909	63100	4000	5800	32336	32336	1479	145
1937	169066	122600	104200	8100	10100	43040	43040	2902	524
1938	177353	128151	108500	8300	11100	45623	45623	2944	636
1950	292152	224500	175900	33500	15100	58392	58392	7674	1586
1953	365264	272300	214300	41900	16100	81416	81416	9148	2400
1955	461898	337400	266700	49500	21200	109640	109640	11963	2896
1957	562040	380700	299700	58100	22900	151659	151659	24753	4929
1960	693696	400400	320300	59300	20800	226589	226589	60344	6364
1961	736660	396400	319300	57300	19800	254307	254307	78563	7390
1962	791499	399400	330100	56200	13100	285171	285171	97935	8993
1963	862037	417300	336600	58600	22100	315599	315599	119656	9482
1964	920485	430800	346000	62300	22500	335405	335405	144610	9670
1965	993462	448900	361900	64300	22700	364332	364332	170051	10179
COMMUNIST ASIA									
1925	22557	22557	22557	-	-	-	-	-	-
1929	24043	24036	24036	-	-	8	8	-	-
1933	26529	26392	26392	-	-	137	137	-	-
1937	34626	34326	34326	-	-	300	300	-	-
1938	30124	29704	29704	-	-	420	420	-	-
1950	43480	42520	42049	472	-	300	300	-	660
1953	66651	65398	65277	121	-	933	933	-	320
1955	97247	95023	94631	392	-	1449	1449	-	775
1957	130105	126596	126014	582	-	2222	2222	-	1288
1960	230886	220180	219027	1153	-	8294	8294	-	2413
1961	261079	249678	248391	1287	-	9339	9339	-	2063
1962	264233	251873	250613	1260	-	10235	10235	-	2125
1963	284972	271506	270204	1302	-	11279	11279	-	2188
1964	307075	291923	290633	1290	-	12777	12777	-	2375
1965	323082	305433	304143	1290	-	15024	15024	-	2625
LATIN AMERICA									
1925	39882	3296	3230	66	-	35166	35147	1026	394
1929	57582	3062	2996	66	-	52068	51857	1958	494
1933	50507	2703	2638	65	-	44585	44279	2645	574
1937	75362	4226	4163	63	-	66179	65814	4220	738
1938	75037	4210	4147	63	-	65502	65145	4538	787
1950	168187	5891	5742	89	60	154071	153248	6447	1778
1953	196995	6849	6743	88	18	178371	177198	9475	2301
1955	237203	7361	7266	76	19	215660	214466	11470	2712
1957	297287	7360	7275	57	28	271448	269780	15066	3414
1960	333091	8115	8080	22	13	295038	291732	25605	4333
1961	349381	8562	8526	30	7	307803	304235	28509	4506
1962	379554	9122	9090	28	5	334305	330908	31253	4874
1963	389819	9339	9301	28	10	341381	337716	33929	5171
1964	410348	9935	9902	26	6	355974	352179	38779	5661
1965	421757	10117	10085	25	7	364695	360693	40525	6421
LATIN AMERICA - CARIBBEAN									
1925	33891	1569	1569	-	-	31899	31896	289	134
1929	49178	1179	1179	-	-	46914	46845	911	174

Table II. PRIMARY ENERGY PRODUCTION, SELECTED YEARS, 1925-1965

(Thousand metric tons coal equivalent)

Region, country, year	Total primary energy production	Solid fuels				Liquid fuels		Natural gas	Hydro-electric power
		Total	Hard coal	Lignite	Other	Total	Crude oil		
	(1)	(2)	(3)	(4)	(5)	(6)	(7)	(8)	(9)
LATIN AMERICA - CARIBBEAN (CONTINUED)									
1933	40749	764	764	-	-	38459	38343	1323	204
1937	63026	1671	1671	-	-	58542	58403	2519	295
1938	62765	1511	1511	-	-	58014	57861	2932	309
1950	151875	1947	1947	-	-	144998	144372	4460	471
1953	178074	2691	2691	-	-	167681	166746	7089	613
1955	216147	3223	3223	-	-	203291	202338	8847	786
1957	271944	3456	3456	-	-	255894	254483	11715	879
1960	294915	4407	4407	-	-	268790	265703	20542	1176
1961	303109	4499	4499	-	-	275756	272427	21684	1171
1962	327902	4920	4920	-	-	298817	295704	22856	1310
1963	336723	5313	5313	-	-	305225	301877	24667	1518
1964	354947	5163	5163	-	-	319064	315653	28990	1731
1965	365262	5237	5237	-	-	328043	324536	29979	2004
CARIBBEAN - OIL PRODUCING									
1925	33875	1569	1569	-	-	31899	31896	289	118
1929	49158	1179	1179	-	-	46914	46845	911	154
1933	40713	764	764	-	-	38451	38339	1323	176
1937	62973	1671	1671	-	-	58529	58397	2519	255
1938	62697	1511	1511	-	-	57989	57846	2932	266
1950	151729	1947	1947	-	-	144965	144342	4457	361
1953	177946	2691	2691	-	-	167676	166743	7084	495
1955	215927	3223	3223	-	-	203216	202265	8842	647
1957	271721	3456	3456	-	-	255818	254406	11711	737
1960	294697	4407	4407	-	-	268769	265682	20539	982
1961	302891	4499	4499	-	-	275741	272412	21680	972
1962	327682	4920	4920	-	-	298799	295686	22852	1112
1963	336446	5313	5313	-	-	305178	301830	24662	1294
1964	354659	5163	5163	-	-	319008	315597	28986	1502
1965	364934	5237	5237	-	-	327987	324480	29975	1735
COLOMBIA									
1925	328	100	100	-	-	216	216	-	12
1929	4479	100	100	-	-	4367	4367	-	13
1933	2877	112	112	-	-	2751	2751	-	14
1937	4655	422	422	-	-	4211	4211	-	23
1938	4914	412	412	-	-	4476	4476	-	26
1950	8167	1010	1010	-	-	7067	7067	-	91
1953	9537	1230	1230	-	-	8181	8181	-	126
1955	10275	1850	1850	-	-	8240	8240	-	185
1957	11742	2000	2000	-	-	9491	9491	-	252
1960	15004	2600	2600	-	-	11543	11376	538	323
1961	14539	2650	2650	-	-	11019	10857	555	314
1962	14877	3000	3000	-	-	10743	10589	789	345
1963	17031	3200	3200	-	-	12494	12342	935	402
1964	17550	3000	3000	-	-	12974	12896	1111	465
1965	20164	3200	3200	-	-	15255	15186	1221	488
MEXICO									
1925	28189	1444	1444	-	-	26442	26439	200	104
1929	11555	1054	1054	-	-	10070	10050	293	138
1933	8891	647	647	-	-	7668	7631	417	159

Table II. PRIMARY ENERGY PRODUCTION, SELECTED YEARS, 1925-1965

(Thousand metric tons coal equivalent)

Region, country, year	Total primary energy production	Solid fuels: Total	Solid fuels: Hard coal	Solid fuels: Lignite	Solid fuels: Other	Liquid fuels: Total	Liquid fuels: Crude oil	Natural gas	Hydro-electric power
	(1)	(2)	(3)	(4)	(5)	(6)	(7)	(8)	(9)
MEXICO (CONTINUED)									
1937	12887	1242	1242	-	-	10118	10067	1300	228
1938	11129	1093	1093	-	-	8325	8265	1477	234
1950	19294	912	912	-	-	15803	15545	2336	244
1953	21120	1432	1432	-	-	15837	15543	3523	328
1955	25818	1342	1342	-	-	19527	19179	4518	431
1957	27604	1421	1421	-	-	19634	18941	6085	465
1960	38265	1772	1772	-	-	22973	21257	12874	647
1961	40745	1818	1818	-	-	24689	22917	13600	639
1962	42306	1893	1893	-	-	25721	24003	14007	685
1963	44555	2071	2071	-	-	26585	24650	15146	753
1964	48566	2127	2127	-	-	27260	24803	18295	884
1965	49497	2006	2006	-	-	27813	25311	18601	1076
TRINIDAD AND TOBAGO									
1925	1004	-	-	-	-	915	915	89	-
1929	2004	-	-	-	-	1826	1826	178	-
1933	2215	-	-	-	-	2018	2018	197	-
1937	3694	-	-	-	-	3365	3365	329	-
1938	4225	-	-	-	-	3849	3849	376	-
1950	5044	-	-	-	-	4412	4379	633	-
1953	5457	-	-	-	-	4790	4743	667	-
1955	5996	-	-	-	-	5333	5285	663	-
1957	8076	-	-	-	-	7277	7230	799	-
1960	10047	-	-	-	-	9027	8991	1020	-
1961	10857	-	-	-	-	9749	9714	1108	-
1962	11541	-	-	-	-	10409	10374	1132	-
1963	11470	-	-	-	-	10362	10332	1108	-
1964	12041	-	-	-	-	10590	10554	1451	-
1965	11968	-	-	-	-	10404	10370	1564	-
VENEZUELA									
1925	4354	25	25	-	-	4326	4326	-	3
1929	31120	25	25	-	-	30653	30603	440	3
1933	26732	5	5	-	-	26015	25940	709	4
1937	41737	7	7	-	-	40836	40755	890	4
1938	42430	6	6	-	-	41339	41256	1079	7
1950	119223	25	25	-	-	117684	117353	1488	27
1953	141832	29	29	-	-	138869	138276	2893	42
1955	173839	31	31	-	-	170117	169562	3660	31
1957	224299	35	35	-	-	219417	218745	4827	20
1960	231381	35	35	-	-	225227	224058	6107	12
1961	236750	31	31	-	-	230285	228924	6416	19
1962	258959	27	27	-	-	251927	250721	6924	81
1963	263391	42	42	-	-	255738	254507	7473	138
1964	276503	36	36	-	-	268185	267345	8129	153
1965	283306	31	31	-	-	274515	273614	8589	171
CARIBBEAN - OTHER									
1925	16	-	-	-	-	-	-	-	16
1929	21	-	-	-	-	-	-	-	21
1933	35	-	-	-	-	8	5	-	28
1937	53	-	-	-	-	14	6	-	40

Table II. PRIMARY ENERGY PRODUCTION, SELECTED YEARS, 1925-1965

(Thousand metric tons coal equivalent)

Region, country, year	Total primary energy production	Solid fuels				Liquid fuels		Natural gas	Hydro-electric power
		Total	Hard coal	Lignite	Other	Total	Crude oil		
	(1)	(2)	(3)	(4)	(5)	(6)	(7)	(8)	(9)
CARIBBEAN - OTHER (CONTINUED)									
1938	68	-	-	-	-	26	15	-	43
1950	146	-	-	-	-	33	30	3	110
1953	128	-	-	-	-	5	3	5	118
1955	219	-	-	-	-	75	74	5	139
1957	223	-	-	-	-	77	77	4	143
1960	218	-	-	-	-	21	21	3	194
1961	218	-	-	-	-	15	15	4	199
1962	220	-	-	-	-	18	18	4	198
1963	277	-	-	-	-	47	47	5	225
1964	288	-	-	-	-	56	56	4	229
1965	328	-	-	-	-	56	56	4	269
CUBA									
1925	2	-	-	-	-	-	-	-	2
1929	2	-	-	-	-	-	-	-	2
1933	9	-	-	-	-	8	5	-	2
1937	16	-	-	-	-	14	6	-	2
1938	28	-	-	-	-	26	15	-	2
1950	35	-	-	-	-	33	30	-	2
1953	7	-	-	-	-	5	3	-	2
1955	78	-	-	-	-	75	74	-	3
1957	79	-	-	-	-	77	77	-	3
1960	24	-	-	-	-	21	21	-	3
1961	18	-	-	-	-	15	15	-	3
1962	21	-	-	-	-	18	18	-	3
1963	53	-	-	-	-	47	47	-	6
1964	68	-	-	-	-	56	56	-	13
1965	69	-	-	-	-	56	56	-	14
PANAMA CANAL ZONE									
1925	8	-	-	-	-	-	-	-	8
1929	8	-	-	-	-	-	-	-	8
1933	8	-	-	-	-	-	-	-	8
1937	10	-	-	-	-	-	-	-	10
1938	10	-	-	-	-	-	-	-	10
1950	31	-	-	-	-	-	-	-	31
1953	33	-	-	-	-	-	-	-	33
1955	32	-	-	-	-	-	-	-	32
1957	29	-	-	-	-	-	-	-	29
1960	31	-	-	-	-	-	-	-	31
1961	32	-	-	-	-	-	-	-	32
1962	32	-	-	-	-	-	-	-	32
1963	37	-	-	-	-	-	-	-	37
1964	33	-	-	-	-	-	-	-	33
1965	34	-	-	-	-	-	-	-	34
PUERTO RICO									
1925	-	-	-	-	-	-	-	-	-
1929	3	-	-	-	-	-	-	-	3
1933	7	-	-	-	-	-	-	-	7
1937	12	-	-	-	-	-	-	-	12
1938	13	-	-	-	-	-	-	-	13

Table II. PRIMARY ENERGY PRODUCTION, SELECTED YEARS, 1925-1965

(Thousand metric tons coal equivalent)

Region, country, year	Total primary energy production	Solid fuels: Total	Solid fuels: Hard coal	Solid fuels: Lignite	Solid fuels: Other	Liquid fuels: Total	Liquid fuels: Crude oil	Natural gas	Hydro-electric power
	(1)	(2)	(3)	(4)	(5)	(6)	(7)	(8)	(9)
PUERTO RICO (CONTINUED)									
1950	31	-	-	-	-	-	-	-	31
1953	23	-	-	-	-	-	-	-	23
1955	26	-	-	-	-	-	-	-	26
1957	22	-	-	-	-	-	-	-	22
1960	30	-	-	-	-	-	-	-	30
1961	34	-	-	-	-	-	-	-	34
1962	26	-	-	-	-	-	-	-	26
1963	35	-	-	-	-	-	-	-	35
1964	19	-	-	-	-	-	-	-	19
1965	30	-	-	-	-	-	-	-	30
LATIN AMERICA - OTHER									
1925	5991	1727	1661	66	-	3267	3251	737	261
1929	8403	1883	1817	66	-	5154	5012	1047	319
1933	9758	1939	1874	65	-	6126	5936	1323	370
1937	12335	2555	2492	63	-	7637	7412	1701	443
1938	12272	2699	2636	63	-	7488	7284	1606	478
1950	16312	3944	3795	89	60	9074	8876	1987	1307
1953	18921	4158	4052	88	18	10691	10452	2386	1687
1955	21056	4138	4043	76	19	12369	12128	2623	1927
1957	25343	3904	3819	57	28	15554	15297	3351	2534
1960	38177	3708	3673	22	13	26249	26030	5063	3157
1961	46272	4063	4027	30	7	32048	31808	6825	3336
1962	51652	4202	4170	28	5	35489	35204	8397	3564
1963	53096	4026	3988	28	10	36156	35840	9261	3653
1964	55401	4772	4739	26	6	36911	36527	9789	3930
1965	56495	4880	4848	25	7	36653	36158	10545	4418
ARGENTINA									
1925	1553	-	-	-	-	1386	1386	159	8
1929	2367	-	-	-	-	2072	2048	282	14
1933	3410	-	-	-	-	2960	2927	440	11
1937	4117	-	-	-	-	3545	3510	561	12
1938	4246	-	-	-	-	3693	3666	542	11
1950	5867	86	26	-	60	5048	5036	710	24
1953	7206	100	82	-	18	6132	6117	930	45
1955	7710	155	136	-	19	6560	6548	958	38
1957	8747	237	209	-	28	7302	7287	1135	73
1960	15968	293	280	-	13	13718	13707	1842	116
1961	21763	351	344	-	7	18137	18128	3140	136
1962	25498	291	286	-	5	21095	21080	3967	146
1963	25770	217	207	-	10	20868	20850	4537	148
1964	27032	341	335	-	6	21540	21524	4996	155
1965	27328	381	374	-	7	21113	21093	5680	155
BOLIVIA									
1925	1	-	-	-	-	-	-	-	1
1929	7	-	-	-	-	5	5	-	3
1933	24	-	-	-	-	21	21	-	3
1937	28	-	-	-	-	24	24	-	4
1938	33	-	-	-	-	27	27	-	6
1950	144	-	-	-	-	120	120	-	24

Table II. PRIMARY ENERGY PRODUCTION, SELECTED YEARS, 1925-1965

(Thousand metric tons coal equivalent)

Region, country, year	Total primary energy production	Solid fuels				Liquid fuels		Natural gas	Hydro-electric power
		Total	Hard coal	Lignite	Other	Total	Crude oil		
	(1)	(2)	(3)	(4)	(5)	(6)	(7)	(8)	(9)
BOLIVIA (CONTINUED)									
1953	148	-	-	-	-	117	117	-	31
1955	571	-	-	-	-	527	527	8	36
1957	753	-	-	-	-	699	699	11	44
1960	756	-	-	-	-	699	699	8	49
1961	655	-	-	-	-	585	585	21	49
1962	629	-	-	-	-	546	546	36	47
1963	741	-	-	-	-	618	618	72	51
1964	778	-	-	-	-	612	612	113	53
1965	836	-	-	-	-	650	650	133	54
BRAZIL									
1925	488	306	306	-	-	-	-	-	183
1929	512	291	291	-	-	-	-	-	221
1933	765	504	504	-	-	-	-	-	261
1937	895	595	595	-	-	-	-	-	300
1938	1032	707	707	-	-	-	-	-	325
1950	2598	1626	1626	-	-	66	66	7	900
1953	3050	1681	1681	-	-	180	180	36	1153
1955	3687	1882	1882	-	-	396	396	83	1326
1957	5773	1721	1721	-	-	1982	1982	212	1860
1960	10750	1934	1934	-	-	5805	5805	713	2298
1961	11877	1984	1984	-	-	6824	6824	702	2368
1962	11894	2082	2082	-	-	6549	6549	681	2583
1963	12395	2134	2134	-	-	7001	7001	670	2591
1964	12694	2694	2694	-	-	6530	6530	709	2762
1965	13639	2808	2808	-	-	6732	6732	910	3189
CHILE									
1925	1366	1319	1253	66	-	-	-	-	47
1929	1434	1374	1308	66	-	-	-	-	60
1933	1474	1405	1340	65	-	-	-	-	69
1937	1955	1861	1798	63	-	-	-	-	95
1938	2010	1917	1854	63	-	-	-	-	94
1950	2499	2036	1947	89	-	123	123	133	206
1953	2851	2167	2079	88	-	257	246	173	254
1955	3050	1965	1889	76	-	515	504	280	291
1957	3453	1805	1748	57	-	869	848	466	313
1960	4316	1319	1297	22	-	1439	1415	1185	372
1961	5482	1562	1532	30	-	1850	1812	1678	393
1962	6789	1667	1639	28	-	2364	2286	2344	414
1963	7263	1544	1516	28	-	2736	2583	2557	426
1964	7316	1621	1595	26	-	2859	2676	2371	465
1965	7235	1607	1582	25	-	2777	2484	2358	494
ECUADOR									
1925	38	-	-	-	-	35	35	-	3
1929	297	-	-	-	-	294	294	-	3
1933	360	-	-	-	-	345	345	12	3
1937	498	-	-	-	-	434	428	61	3
1938	528	-	-	-	-	452	446	73	3
1950	725	-	-	-	-	539	521	176	11
1953	823	-	-	-	-	612	587	200	12

Table II. PRIMARY ENERGY PRODUCTION, SELECTED YEARS, 1925-1965

(Thousand metric tons coal equivalent)

Region, country, year	Total primary energy production	Solid fuels				Liquid fuels		Natural gas	Hydro-electric power
		Total	Hard coal	Lignite	Other	Total	Crude oil		
	(1)	(2)	(3)	(4)	(5)	(6)	(7)	(8)	(9)
ECUADOR (CONTINUED)									
1955	944	-	-	-	-	729	699	200	15
1957	878	-	-	-	-	660	632	200	18
1960	792	-	-	-	-	570	546	200	22
1961	828	-	-	-	-	603	579	200	25
1962	759	-	-	-	-	531	510	200	28
1963	738	-	-	-	-	509	488	200	30
1964	807	-	-	-	-	576	554	200	31
1965	832	-	-	-	-	602	578	200	31
PERU									
1925	2545	102	102	-	-	1847	1830	578	19
1929	3785	218	218	-	-	2784	2666	765	19
1933	3726	30	30	-	-	2801	2643	871	24
1937	4842	99	99	-	-	3635	3450	1079	29
1938	4423	75	75	-	-	3317	3146	991	40
1950	4411	196	196	-	-	3179	3011	960	76
1953	4767	210	210	-	-	3393	3206	1047	118
1955	5011	136	136	-	-	3644	3455	1095	136
1957	5670	141	141	-	-	4043	3851	1328	159
1960	5512	162	162	-	-	4019	3858	1115	216
1961	5536	167	167	-	-	4050	3881	1084	235
1962	5980	163	163	-	-	4404	4233	1169	243
1963	6051	131	131	-	-	4425	4301	1225	270
1964	6615	115	115	-	-	4794	4632	1400	306
1965	6458	84	84	-	-	4781	4622	1265	328
URUGUAY									
1925	-	-	-	-	-	-	-	-	-
1929	-	-	-	-	-	-	-	-	-
1933	-	-	-	-	-	-	-	-	-
1937	-	-	-	-	-	-	-	-	-
1938	-	-	-	-	-	-	-	-	-
1950	67	-	-	-	-	-	-	1	66
1953	75	-	-	-	-	-	-	-	75
1955	85	-	-	-	-	-	-	-	85
1957	69	-	-	-	-	-	-	-	69
1960	85	-	-	-	-	-	-	-	85
1961	131	-	-	-	-	-	-	-	131
1962	104	-	-	-	-	-	-	-	104
1963	137	-	-	-	-	-	-	-	137
1964	158	-	-	-	-	-	-	-	158
1965	166	-	-	-	-	-	-	-	166
ASIA									
1925	71093	54749	54362	88	299	14862	14697	485	997
1929	83477	61187	60620	83	484	19950	19725	686	1654
1933	82123	56010	55782	68	160	22641	22310	1204	2269
1937	119483	76378	75820	99	459	38462	38147	1316	3327
1938	128199	83961	83490	120	350	39243	38946	1413	3582
1950	226573	72755	71189	1263	304	146555	146424	1917	5347
1953	300495	86586	84811	1541	235	204698	204690	3195	6016
1955	364673	83607	81878	1543	185	269313	269220	4714	7039

Table II. PRIMARY ENERGY PRODUCTION, SELECTED YEARS, 1925-1965

(Thousand metric tons coal equivalent)

Region, country, year	Total primary energy production	Solid fuels				Liquid fuels		Natural gas	Hydro-electric power
		Total	Hard coal	Lignite	Other	Total	Crude oil		
	(1)	(2)	(3)	(4)	(5)	(6)	(7)	(8)	(9)
ASIA (CONTINUED)									
1957	415309	99646	97549	1947	149	298709	298598	8598	8357
1960	565237	109352	107219	2090	43	433955	433847	12722	9209
1961	603527	116388	114339	2012	37	462417	462311	13963	10759
1962	654931	122571	120367	2168	37	506393	506276	15647	10321
1963	707632	126516	123785	2695	37	553031	552899	16476	11609
1964	770231	123896	121015	2847	34	616163	616023	18251	11921
1965	832722	126941	123837	3070	34	674028	673932	19294	12459
MIDDLE EAST									
1925	7653	673	671	2	-	6978	6978	-	2
1929	9506	999	995	4	-	8505	8505	-	2
1933	12302	1321	1311	10	-	10979	10979	-	2
1937	25140	1653	1615	38	-	23483	23483	-	4
1938	25680	1792	1744	48	-	23883	23883	-	4
1950	132928	3279	3032	247	-	128964	128964	674	12
1953	185430	4130	3819	311	-	180143	180143	1136	21
1955	247052	4135	3743	392	-	241119	241119	1772	26
1957	273559	4769	4145	624	-	264315	264315	4413	62
1960	404472	4514	3883	631	-	392805	392805	7010	143
1961	433006	4496	3970	526	-	420692	420692	7634	185
1962	475035	4711	4053	658	-	461835	461835	8312	177
1963	522217	5194	4346	848	-	508769	508769	7943	312
1964	585060	5710	4723	987	-	570305	570305	8786	259
1965	640101	5686	4665	1021	-	624890	624890	9185	340
MIDDLE EAST - OIL PRODUCING									
1925	6978	-	-	-	-	6978	6978	-	-
1929	8505	-	-	-	-	8505	8505	-	-
1933	10988	9	9	-	-	10979	10979	-	-
1937	23483	-	-	-	-	23483	23483	-	-
1938	23883	-	-	-	-	23883	23883	-	-
1950	129812	200	200	-	-	128939	128939	674	-
1953	181395	155	155	-	-	180104	180104	1136	-
1955	242866	245	245	-	-	240849	240849	1772	-
1957	268376	176	176	-	-	263787	263787	4413	-
1960	399289	230	230	-	-	392049	392049	7010	-
1961	427654	198	198	-	-	419826	419826	7630	-
1962	469197	160	160	-	-	460740	460740	8297	-
1963	515547	193	193	-	-	507425	507425	7929	-
1964	577646	274	274	-	-	568625	568625	8747	-
1965	631652	275	275	-	-	622287	622287	9090	-
BAHRAIN									
1925	-	-	-	-	-	-	-	-	-
1929	-	-	-	-	-	-	-	-	-
1933	6	-	-	-	-	6	6	-	-
1937	1592	-	-	-	-	1592	1592	-	-
1938	1700	-	-	-	-	1700	1700	-	-
1950	2259	-	-	-	-	2259	2259	-	-
1953	2252	-	-	-	-	2252	2252	-	-
1955	2253	-	-	-	-	2253	2253	-	-
1957	2399	-	-	-	-	2399	2399	-	-

Table II. PRIMARY ENERGY PRODUCTION, SELECTED YEARS, 1925-1965

(Thousand metric tons coal equivalent)

Region, country, year	Total primary energy production	Solid fuels: Total	Solid fuels: Hard coal	Solid fuels: Lignite	Solid fuels: Other	Liquid fuels: Total	Liquid fuels: Crude oil	Natural gas	Hydro-electric power
	(1)	(2)	(3)	(4)	(5)	(6)	(7)	(8)	(9)
BAHRAIN (CONTINUED)									
1960	3384	-	-	-	-	3384	3384	-	-
1961	3372	-	-	-	-	3372	3372	-	-
1962	3374	-	-	-	-	3374	3374	-	-
1963	3384	-	-	-	-	3384	3384	-	-
1964	3692	-	-	-	-	3692	3692	-	-
1965	4263	-	-	-	-	4263	4263	-	-
IRAN									
1925	6978	-	-	-	-	6978	6978	-	-
1929	8324	-	-	-	-	8324	8324	-	-
1933	10809	9	9	-	-	10800	10800	-	-
1937	15497	-	-	-	-	15497	15497	-	-
1938	15539	-	-	-	-	15539	15539	-	-
1950	48589	200	200	-	-	48389	48389	-	-
1953	2460	155	155	-	-	2234	2234	72	-
1955	25568	245	245	-	-	24534	24534	789	-
1957	56586	176	176	-	-	54030	54030	2380	-
1960	82544	230	230	-	-	78588	78588	3726	-
1961	92390	198	198	-	-	88473	88473	3719	-
1962	101993	160	160	-	-	98007	98007	3826	-
1963	113612	193	193	-	-	109547	109547	3872	-
1964	130652	274	274	-	-	126009	126009	4369	-
1965	144865	275	275	-	-	140181	140181	4409	-
IRAQ									
1925	-	-	-	-	-	-	-	-	-
1929	182	-	-	-	-	182	182	-	-
1933	173	-	-	-	-	173	173	-	-
1937	6383	-	-	-	-	6383	6383	-	-
1938	6545	-	-	-	-	6545	6545	-	-
1950	9975	-	-	-	-	9975	9975	-	-
1953	42683	-	-	-	-	42279	42279	404	-
1955	50940	-	-	-	-	50522	50522	418	-
1957	33196	-	-	-	-	32856	32856	340	-
1960	71682	-	-	-	-	70922	70922	761	-
1961	74060	-	-	-	-	73239	73239	821	-
1962	74330	-	-	-	-	73482	73482	848	-
1963	85663	-	-	-	-	84704	84704	959	-
1964	93451	-	-	-	-	92439	92439	1012	-
1965	97735	-	-	-	-	96710	96710	1026	-
KUWAIT									
1925	-	-	-	-	-	-	-	-	-
1929	-	-	-	-	-	-	-	-	-
1933	-	-	-	-	-	-	-	-	-
1937	-	-	-	-	-	-	-	-	-
1938	-	-	-	-	-	-	-	-	-
1950	25937	-	-	-	-	25937	25937	-	-
1953	64931	-	-	-	-	64931	64931	-	-
1955	82139	-	-	-	-	82139	82139	-	-
1957	85922	-	-	-	-	85922	85922	-	-
1960	124346	-	-	-	-	122801	122801	1545	-

Table II. PRIMARY ENERGY PRODUCTION, SELECTED YEARS, 1925-1965

(Thousand metric tons coal equivalent)

Region, country, year	Total primary energy production	Solid fuels				Liquid fuels		Natural gas	Hydro-electric power
		Total	Hard coal	Lignite	Other	Total	Crude oil		
	(1)	(2)	(3)	(4)	(5)	(6)	(7)	(8)	(9)
KUWAIT (CONTINUED)									
1961	126150	-	-	-	-	124073	124073	2078	-
1962	140836	-	-	-	-	138266	138266	2571	-
1963	147822	-	-	-	-	145803	145803	2019	-
1964	162312	-	-	-	-	160079	160079	2234	-
1965	165957	-	-	-	-	163568	163568	2390	-
KUWAIT NEUTRAL ZONE									
1925	-	-	-	-	-	-	-	-	-
1929	-	-	-	-	-	-	-	-	-
1933	-	-	-	-	-	-	-	-	-
1937	-	-	-	-	-	-	-	-	-
1938	-	-	-	-	-	-	-	-	-
1950	-	-	-	-	-	-	-	-	-
1953	-	-	-	-	-	-	-	-	-
1955	1941	-	-	-	-	1941	1941	-	-
1957	5103	-	-	-	-	5103	5103	-	-
1960	10935	-	-	-	-	10935	10935	-	-
1961	14249	-	-	-	-	14249	14249	-	-
1962	19578	-	-	-	-	19578	19578	NA	-
1963	25128	-	-	-	-	25128	25128	NA	-
1964	28833	-	-	-	-	28833	28833	NA	-
1965	29023	-	-	-	-	29024	29024	NA	-
QATAR									
1925	-	-	-	-	-	-	-	-	-
1929	-	-	-	-	-	-	-	-	-
1933	-	-	-	-	-	-	-	-	-
1937	-	-	-	-	-	-	-	-	-
1938	-	-	-	-	-	-	-	-	-
1950	2454	-	-	-	-	2454	2454	-	-
1953	6093	-	-	-	-	6093	6093	-	-
1955	8157	-	-	-	-	8157	8157	-	-
1957	9972	-	-	-	-	9972	9972	-	-
1960	12318	-	-	-	-	12318	12318	-	-
1961	12573	-	-	-	-	12573	12573	-	-
1962	13212	-	-	-	-	13212	13212	-	-
1963	13643	-	-	-	-	13643	13643	-	-
1964	15204	-	-	-	-	15204	15204	NA	-
1965	16441	-	-	-	-	16442	16442	NA	-
SAUDI ARABIA									
1925	-	-	-	-	-	-	-	-	-
1929	-	-	-	-	-	-	-	-	-
1933	-	-	-	-	-	-	-	-	-
1937	12	-	-	-	-	12	12	-	-
1938	101	-	-	-	-	101	101	-	-
1950	40599	-	-	-	-	39926	39926	674	-
1953	62977	-	-	-	-	62316	62316	661	-
1955	71869	-	-	-	-	71304	71304	565	-
1957	75199	-	-	-	-	73506	73506	1693	-
1960	94081	-	-	-	-	93102	93102	979	-
1961	104860	-	-	-	-	103848	103848	1012	-

Table II. PRIMARY ENERGY PRODUCTION, SELECTED YEARS, 1925-1965

(Thousand metric tons coal equivalent)

Region, country, year	Total primary energy production	Solid fuels				Liquid fuels		Natural gas	Hydro-electric power
		Total	Hard coal	Lignite	Other	Total	Crude oil		
	(1)	(2)	(3)	(4)	(5)	(6)	(7)	(8)	(9)
SAUDI ARABIA (CONTINUED)									
1962	114679	-	-	-	-	113627	113627	1052	-
1963	122652	-	-	-	-	121574	121574	1079	-
1964	129829	-	-	-	-	128697	128697	1132	-
1965	152815	-	-	-	-	151550	151550	1265	-
TRUCIAL OMAN									
1950	-	-	-	-	-	-	-	-	-
1953	-	-	-	-	-	-	-	-	-
1955	-	-	-	-	-	-	-	-	-
1957	-	-	-	-	-	-	-	-	-
1960	-	-	-	-	-	-	-	-	-
1961	-	-	-	-	-	-	-	-	-
1962	1196	-	-	-	-	1196	1196	-	-
1963	3644	-	-	-	-	3644	3644	-	-
1964	13673	-	-	-	-	13673	13673	-	-
1965	20552	-	-	-	-	20552	20552	-	-
MIDDLE EAST - OTHER									
1925	675	673	671	2	-	-	-	-	2
1929	1001	999	995	4	-	-	-	-	2
1933	1314	1312	1302	10	-	-	-	-	2
1937	1658	1653	1615	38	-	-	-	-	4
1938	1797	1792	1744	48	-	-	-	-	4
1950	3116	3079	2832	247	-	26	26	-	12
1953	4035	3975	3664	311	-	39	39	-	21
1955	4186	3890	3498	392	-	270	270	-	26
1957	5183	4593	3969	624	-	528	528	-	62
1960	5182	4284	3653	631	-	756	756	-	143
1961	5352	4298	3772	526	-	865	866	4	185
1962	5838	4551	3893	658	-	1095	1095	15	177
1963	6670	5001	4153	848	-	1344	1344	13	312
1964	7414	5436	4449	987	-	1680	1680	39	259
1965	8449	5411	4390	1021	-	2603	2603	96	340
ISRAEL									
1950	-	-	-	-	-	-	-	-	-
1953	-	-	-	-	-	-	-	-	-
1955	2	-	-	-	-	2	2	-	-
1957	81	-	-	-	-	81	81	-	-
1960	194	-	-	-	-	194	194	-	-
1961	206	-	-	-	-	203	203	4	-
1962	217	-	-	-	-	203	203	15	-
1963	240	-	-	-	-	227	227	13	-
1964	337	-	-	-	-	299	299	39	-
1965	400	-	-	-	-	305	305	96	-
LEBANON-SYRIA									
1925	2	-	-	-	-	-	-	-	2
1929	2	-	-	-	-	-	-	-	2
1933	2	-	-	-	-	-	-	-	2
1937	4	-	-	-	-	-	-	-	4

Table II. PRIMARY ENERGY PRODUCTION, SELECTED YEARS, 1925-1965

(Thousand metric tons coal equivalent)

Region, country, year	Total primary energy production	Solid fuels				Liquid fuels		Natural gas	Hydro-electric power
		Total	Hard coal	Lignite	Other	Total	Crude oil		
	(1)	(2)	(3)	(4)	(5)	(6)	(7)	(8)	(9)
LEBANON - SYRIA (CONTINUED)									
1938	4	-	-	-	-	-	-	-	4
LEBANON									
1950	8	-	-	-	-	-	-	-	8
1953	13	-	-	-	-	-	-	-	13
1955	14	-	-	-	-	-	-	-	14
1957	21	-	-	-	-	-	-	-	21
1960	14	-	-	-	-	-	-	-	14
1961	22	-	-	-	-	-	-	-	22
1962	31	-	-	-	-	-	-	-	31
1963	44	-	-	-	-	-	-	-	44
1964	47	-	-	-	-	-	-	-	47
1965	63	-	-	-	-	-	-	-	63
SYRIA									
1950	-	-	-	-	-	-	-	-	-
1953	-	-	-	-	-	-	-	-	-
1955	1	-	-	-	-	-	-	-	1
1957	3	-	-	-	-	-	-	-	3
1960	4	-	-	-	-	-	-	-	4
1961	5	-	-	-	-	-	-	-	5
1962	5	-	-	-	-	-	-	-	5
1963	6	-	-	-	-	-	-	-	6
1964	6	-	-	-	-	-	-	-	6
1965	6	-	-	-	-	-	-	-	6
TURKEY									
1925	673	673	671	2	-	-	-	-	-
1929	999	999	995	4	-	-	-	-	-
1933	1312	1312	1302	10	-	-	-	-	-
1937	1653	1653	1615	38	-	-	-	-	-
1938	1792	1792	1744	48	-	-	-	-	-
1950	3108	3079	2832	247	-	26	26	-	4
1953	4022	3975	3664	311	-	39	39	-	8
1955	4170	3890	3498	392	-	269	269	-	11
1957	5079	4593	3969	624	-	447	447	-	39
1960	4971	4284	3653	631	-	563	563	-	125
1961	5119	4298	3772	526	-	663	663	-	158
1962	5584	4551	3893	658	-	893	893	-	141
1963	6381	5001	4153	848	-	1118	1118	-	262
1964	7024	5436	4449	987	-	1382	1382	-	207
1965	7980	5411	4390	1021	-	2298	2298	-	271
FAR EAST AND OTHER ASIA									
1925	63440	54076	53691	86	299	7884	7719	485	995
1929	73970	60188	59625	79	484	11445	11220	686	1652
1933	69822	54689	54471	58	160	11663	11331	1204	2266
1937	94343	74725	74205	61	459	14979	14664	1316	3323
1938	102519	82169	81746	72	350	15360	15063	1413	3578
1950	93645	69477	68157	1016	304	17591	17460	1243	5335

Table II. PRIMARY ENERGY PRODUCTION, SELECTED YEARS, 1925-1965

(Thousand metric tons coal equivalent)

Region, country, year	Total primary energy production	Solid fuels: Total	Solid fuels: Hard coal	Solid fuels: Lignite	Solid fuels: Other	Liquid fuels: Total	Liquid fuels: Crude oil	Natural gas	Hydro-electric power
	(1)	(2)	(3)	(4)	(5)	(6)	(7)	(8)	(9)
FAR EAST AND OTHER ASIA (CONTINUED)									
1953	115066	82456	80992	1230	235	24555	24548	2059	5995
1955	117622	79472	78135	1151	185	28194	28101	2942	7013
1957	141750	94877	93404	1323	149	34394	34283	4185	8295
1960	160765	104838	103336	1459	43	41150	41042	5712	9066
1961	170521	111892	110369	1486	37	41726	41619	6330	10574
1962	179896	117860	116314	1509	37	44558	44441	7335	10144
1963	185415	121322	119439	1847	37	44262	44130	8533	11298
1964	185172	118186	116292	1860	34	45858	45719	9465	11662
1965	192621	121255	119172	2049	34	49139	49043	10109	12119
BORNEO (FORMER BRITISH)									
1925	1027	101	101	-	-	926	920	-	-
1929	1219	73	73	-	-	1146	1140	-	-
1933	925	-	-	-	-	923	917	3	-
1937	1214	1	1	-	-	1185	1179	28	-
1938	1412	1	1	-	-	1371	1365	40	-
1950	6330	-	-	-	-	6261	6261	69	-
1953	7475	-	-	-	-	7397	7397	79	-
1955	8168	-	-	-	-	8066	7980	103	-
1957	8783	-	-	-	-	8528	8421	256	-
1960	7350	-	-	-	-	7064	6965	286	-
1961	6652	-	-	-	-	6372	6276	280	-
1962	6151	-	-	-	-	5873	5774	278	-
1963	5601	-	-	-	-	5337	5235	264	-
1964	5719	-	-	-	-	5489	5390	230	-
1965	6344	-	-	-	-	6063	5978	281	-
BRUNEI									
1950	6174	-	-	-	-	6174	6174	NA	-
1953	7400	-	-	-	-	7322	7322	79	-
1955	8068	-	-	-	-	7965	7880	103	-
1957	8648	-	-	-	-	8393	8286	256	-
1960	7260	-	-	-	-	6974	6875	286	-
1961	6562	-	-	-	-	6282	6186	280	-
1962	6062	-	-	-	-	5784	5685	278	-
1963	5523	-	-	-	-	5259	5157	264	-
1964	5645	-	-	-	-	5415	5316	230	-
1965	6271	-	-	-	-	5990	5904	281	-
SARAWAK									
1950	87	-	-	-	-	87	87	-	-
1953	75	-	-	-	-	75	75	-	-
1955	101	-	-	-	-	101	101	-	-
1957	101	-	-	-	-	101	101	-	-
1960	90	-	-	-	-	90	90	-	-
1961	90	-	-	-	-	90	90	-	-
1962	89	-	-	-	-	89	89	-	-
1963	78	-	-	-	-	78	78	-	-
1964	74	-	-	-	-	74	74	-	-
1965	74	-	-	-	-	74	74	-	-

Table II. PRIMARY ENERGY PRODUCTION, SELECTED YEARS, 1925-1965

(Thousand metric tons coal equivalent)

Region, country, year	Total primary energy production	Solid fuels				Liquid fuels		Natural gas	Hydro-electric power
		Total	Hard coal	Lignite	Other	Total	Crude oil		
	(1)	(2)	(3)	(4)	(5)	(6)	(7)	(8)	(9)
BURMA (1949-1965)									
1950	105	-	-	-	-	105	105	-	-
1953	212	-	-	-	-	212	212	-	-
1955	327	7	7	-	-	317	317	4	-
1957	601	1	1	-	-	593	593	8	-
1960	866	1	1	-	-	818	818	28	20
1961	891	2	2	-	-	846	846	20	23
1962	929	3	3	-	-	876	876	24	27
1963	1011	3	3	-	-	957	957	21	30
1964	895	10	10	-	-	837	837	13	35
1965	871	10	10	-	-	813	813	13	35
CEYLON									
1925	-	-	-	-	-	-	-	-	-
1929	-	-	-	-	-	-	-	-	-
1933	-	-	-	-	-	-	-	-	-
1937	-	-	-	-	-	-	-	-	-
1938	-	-	-	-	-	-	-	-	-
1950	1	-	-	-	-	-	-	-	1
1953	14	-	-	-	-	-	-	-	14
1955	16	-	-	-	-	-	-	-	16
1957	19	-	-	-	-	-	-	-	19
1960	34	-	-	-	-	-	-	-	34
1961	35	-	-	-	-	-	-	-	35
1962	40	-	-	-	-	-	-	-	40
1963	41	-	-	-	-	-	-	-	41
1964	42	-	-	-	-	-	-	-	42
1965	42	-	-	-	-	-	-	-	42
INDIA									
1925	18816	16991	16991	-	-	1802	1802	-	24
1929	20900	19036	19036	-	-	1802	1802	-	63
1933	18432	16488	16488	-	-	1842	1802	-	102
1937	23112	20859	20859	-	-	2112	2061	-	141
1938	25881	23614	23614	-	-	2117	2066	-	150
1950	26968	26269	26260	9	-	384	384	-	315
1953	30030	29258	29246	12	-	407	407	-	366
1955	32068	31080	31071	9	-	519	519	-	469
1957	36816	35366	35363	3	-	644	644	170	635
1960	43928	42089	42074	14	-	674	674	185	981
1961	47007	44871	44852	19	-	765	765	143	1228
1962	52499	49159	49096	63	-	1615	1616	285	1439
1963	57609	53065	52765	300	-	2480	2480	357	1708
1964	56133	50423	49952	471	-	3318	3318	429	1964
1965	61643	54419	53729	690	-	4533	4533	533	2159
INDO-CHINA									
1925	1365	1365	1363	2	-	-	-	-	-
1929	1950	1950	1941	9	-	-	-	-	-
1933	1568	1568	1568	-	-	-	-	-	-
1937	2308	2308	2308	-	-	-	-	-	-
1938	2332	2332	2331	1	-	-	-	-	-
1950	497	497	497	-	-	-	-	-	-

Table II. PRIMARY ENERGY PRODUCTION, SELECTED YEARS, 1925-1965

(Thousand metric tons coal equivalent)

Region, country, year	Total primary energy production	Solid fuels: Total	Solid fuels: Hard coal	Solid fuels: Lignite	Solid fuels: Other	Liquid fuels: Total	Liquid fuels: Crude oil	Natural gas	Hydro-electric power
	(1)	(2)	(3)	(4)	(5)	(6)	(7)	(8)	(9)
INDO-CHINA (CONTINUED)									
1953	887	887	887	-	-	-	-	-	-
1955	1	-	-	-	-	-	-	-	1
1957	12	12	12	-	-	-	-	-	-
1960	28	27	27	-	-	-	-	-	1
1961	58	57	57	-	-	-	-	-	1
1962	72	71	71	-	-	-	-	-	1
1963	105	104	104	-	-	-	-	-	1
1964	82	77	77	-	-	-	-	-	5
1965	82	75	75	-	-	-	-	-	7
VIETNAM, SOUTH									
1955	1	-	-	-	-	-	-	-	1
1957	12	12	12	-	-	-	-	-	-
1960	28	27	27	-	-	-	-	-	1
1961	58	57	57	-	-	-	-	-	1
1962	72	71	71	-	-	-	-	-	1
1963	105	104	104	-	-	-	-	-	1
1964	82	77	77	-	-	-	-	-	5
1965	82	75	75	-	-	-	-	-	7
INDONESIA									
1925	6595	1401	1401	-	-	4758	4599	425	11
1929	10476	1832	1832	-	-	8076	7857	555	13
1933	10692	1035	1035	-	-	8588	8303	1050	20
1937	13728	1373	1373	-	-	11151	10893	1177	26
1938	14091	1457	1457	-	-	11337	11097	1268	29
1950	12031	804	804	-	-	10136	10010	1054	38
1953	18504	897	897	-	-	15731	15731	1820	57
1955	21823	814	814	-	-	18396	18396	2541	71
1957	27382	717	717	-	-	23700	23700	2888	78
1960	35263	658	658	-	-	31266	31266	3238	101
1961	36234	549	549	-	-	32177	32177	3411	97
1962	38535	471	471	-	-	34362	34362	3612	89
1963	37979	591	591	-	-	33572	33572	3727	89
1964	38864	446	446	-	-	34427	34427	3903	89
1965	40267	281	281	-	-	35888	35888	4009	89
JAPAN									
1925	32918	31544	31459	85	-	393	393	31	951
1929	36321	34328	34258	70	-	405	405	39	1550
1933	34953	32582	32524	58	-	294	294	63	2014
1937	48699	45319	45258	61	-	525	525	71	2785
1938	52320	48755	48684	71	-	530	530	68	2968
1950	44415	39103	38459	644	-	443	440	88	4782
1953	53104	47299	46531	743	25	450	444	135	5220
1955	49895	43142	42423	684	35	477	471	208	6068
1957	60611	52601	51732	831	38	486	482	438	7086
1960	61013	51809	51067	705	38	798	789	1098	7309
1961	66065	55175	54484	655	37	995	986	1401	8495
1962	65765	54991	54399	556	37	1157	1140	1821	7797
1963	64910	52546	52052	457	37	1206	1178	2512	8646
1964	63715	51309	50929	346	34	1026	986	2761	8620

Table II. PRIMARY ENERGY PRODUCTION, SELECTED YEARS, 1925-1965

(Thousand metric tons coal equivalent)

Region, country, year	Total primary energy production	Solid fuels				Liquid fuels		Natural gas	Hydro-electric power
		Total	Hard coal	Lignite	Other	Total	Crude oil		
	(1)	(2)	(3)	(4)	(5)	(6)	(7)	(8)	(9)
JAPAN (CONTINUED)									
1965	62409	49855	49534	287	34	1025	1014	2688	8842
KOREA									
1925	622	622	622	-	-	-	-	-	-
1929	938	938	938	-	-	-	-	-	-
1933	1374	1307	1307	-	-	-	-	-	67
1937	2692	2431	2431	-	-	-	-	-	261
1938	3724	3419	3419	-	-	-	-	-	305
KOREA, REPUBLIC OF									
1950	585	572	564	8	-	-	-	-	12
1953	916	867	867	-	-	-	-	-	49
1955	1368	1308	1308	-	-	-	-	-	60
1957	2493	2441	2441	-	-	-	-	-	52
1960	5423	5350	5350	-	-	-	-	-	73
1961	5966	5884	5884	-	-	-	-	-	82
1962	7532	7444	7444	-	-	-	-	-	88
1963	8949	8858	8858	-	-	-	-	-	91
1964	9716	9622	9622	-	-	-	-	-	94
1965	10337	10248	10248	-	-	-	-	-	89
MALAYA AND SINGAPORE									
1925	301	299	-	-	299	-	-	-	3
1929	489	484	-	-	484	-	-	-	5
1933	172	160	-	-	160	-	-	-	12
1937	489	459	-	-	459	-	-	-	29
1938	379	350	-	-	350	-	-	-	29
1950	335	304	-	-	304	-	-	-	32
1953	241	210	-	-	210	-	-	-	32
1955	180	150	-	-	150	-	-	-	29
1957	143	112	-	-	112	-	-	-	31
1960	29	5	-	-	5	-	-	-	24
1961	27	-	-	-	-	-	-	-	27
1962	29	-	-	-	-	-	-	-	29
1963	40	-	-	-	-	-	-	-	40
1964	68	-	-	-	-	-	-	-	68
1965	73	-	-	-	-	-	-	-	73
PAKISTAN									
1950	620	355	-	355	-	257	257	-	8
1953	860	474	-	474	-	356	356	-	30
1955	946	430	-	430	-	414	414	52	50
1957	1311	419	-	419	-	441	441	386	65
1960	2121	665	-	665	-	528	528	843	85
1961	2447	737	-	737	-	567	567	1026	118
1962	2906	796	-	796	-	671	671	1264	175
1963	3479	994	-	994	-	705	705	1584	196
1964	3851	971	-	971	-	749	749	1903	228
1965	4191	985	-	985	-	789	789	2171	246

Table II. PRIMARY ENERGY PRODUCTION, SELECTED YEARS, 1925-1965

(Thousand metric tons coal equivalent)

Region, country, year	Total primary energy production	Solid fuels				Liquid fuels		Natural gas	Hydro-electric power
		Total	Hard coal	Lignite	Other	Total	Crude oil		
	(1)	(2)	(3)	(4)	(5)	(6)	(7)	(8)	(9)
PHILIPPINES									
1925	54	49	49	-	-	-	-	-	5
1929	23	17	17	-	-	-	-	-	6
1933	24	16	16	-	-	-	-	-	8
1937	32	22	22	-	-	-	-	-	10
1938	52	41	41	-	-	-	-	-	11
1950	183	159	159	-	-	-	-	-	24
1953	197	155	155	-	-	-	-	-	42
1955	184	130	130	-	-	-	-	-	54
1957	271	191	191	-	-	-	-	-	80
1960	313	148	148	-	-	-	-	-	165
1961	313	152	152	-	-	-	-	-	161
1962	332	163	163	-	-	-	-	-	169
1963	350	157	157	-	-	-	-	-	193
1964	315	115	115	-	-	-	-	-	200
1965	284	95	95	-	-	-	-	-	189
TAIWAN									
1925	1742	1705	1705	-	-	6	6	29	2
1929	1654	1530	1530	-	-	17	17	92	16
1933	1682	1533	1533	-	-	17	17	89	44
1937	2070	1953	1953	-	-	6	6	40	71
1938	2329	2199	2199	-	-	6	6	37	87
1950	1564	1405	1405	-	-	6	5	32	122
1953	2607	2393	2393	-	-	5	3	27	183
1955	2591	2359	2359	-	-	6	5	35	191
1957	3200	2916	2916	-	-	3	3	39	242
1960	4256	3962	3962	-	-	3	3	33	258
1961	4668	4322	4322	-	-	5	3	49	292
1962	4879	4554	4554	-	-	5	3	51	270
1963	5125	4810	4810	-	-	6	5	68	241
1964	5561	5028	5028	-	-	14	14	225	295
1965	5819	5054	5054	-	-	29	29	413	323
THAILAND									
1925	-	-	-	-	-	-	-	-	-
1929	-	-	-	-	-	-	-	-	-
1933	-	-	-	-	-	-	-	-	-
1937	-	-	-	-	-	-	-	-	-
1938	-	-	-	-	-	-	-	-	-
1950	-	-	-	-	-	-	-	-	-
1953	1	1	-	1	-	-	-	-	-
1955	29	29	-	29	-	-	-	-	-
1957	70	70	-	70	-	-	-	-	-
1960	76	76	-	76	-	-	-	-	-
1961	76	76	-	76	-	-	-	-	-
1962	95	95	-	95	-	-	-	-	-
1963	96	96	-	96	-	-	-	-	-
1964	73	73	-	73	-	-	-	-	-
1965	88	88	-	88	-	-	-	-	-
AFRICA									
1925	13628	13347	13347	-	-	273	273	-	8

Table II. PRIMARY ENERGY PRODUCTION, SELECTED YEARS, 1925-1965

(Thousand metric tons coal equivalent)

Region, country, year	Total primary energy production	Solid fuels				Liquid fuels		Natural gas	Hydro-electric power
		Total	Hard coal	Lignite	Other	Total	Crude oil		
	(1)	(2)	(3)	(4)	(5)	(6)	(7)	(8)	(9)
AFRICA (CONTINUED)									
1929	14967	14544	14544	-	-	413	413	-	10
1933	11918	11530	11530	-	-	360	360	-	28
1937	17381	17064	17064	-	-	260	260	-	58
1938	18296	17884	17884	-	-	351	351	-	61
1950	34243	30051	30037	14	-	4022	4005	-	171
1953	37774	33131	33131	-	-	4380	4371	7	256
1955	41103	37646	37646	-	-	3035	3026	16	407
1957	45585	40912	40912	-	-	4062	4053	12	599
1960	65058	43281	43281	-	-	20825	20757	40	911
1961	81395	44132	44132	-	-	35760	35543	337	1166
1962	106029	45541	45541	-	-	58664	58347	507	1317
1963	134615	46594	46594	-	-	86015	85643	623	1383
1964	176140	49441	49441	-	-	123990	123536	1193	1515
1965	218893	53511	53511	-	-	161162	160373	2569	1651
NORTH AFRICA									
1925	286	10	10	-	-	273	273	-	3
1929	433	16	16	-	-	413	413	-	5
1933	428	57	57	-	-	360	360	-	11
1937	401	121	121	-	-	260	260	-	21
1938	500	136	136	-	-	344	344	-	21
1950	4659	640	626	14	-	3968	3951	-	52
1953	5260	860	860	-	-	4325	4316	7	69
1955	3903	769	769	-	-	2979	2970	16	139
1957	4670	757	757	-	-	3749	3740	12	152
1960	18893	531	531	-	-	18134	18065	31	198
1961	31965	488	488	-	-	30870	30653	328	279
1962	52764	423	423	-	-	51540	51224	493	309
1963	78989	442	442	-	-	77658	77286	558	331
1964	113931	446	446	-	-	111990	111536	1104	391
1965	141227	464	464	-	-	137870	137081	2475	419
ALGERIA									
1925	16	10	10	-	-	3	3	-	3
1929	23	16	16	-	-	5	5	-	3
1933	35	30	30	-	-	2	2	-	3
1937	19	14	14	-	-	-	-	-	5
1938	18	13	13	-	-	-	-	-	5
1950	279	258	258	-	-	5	5	-	16
1953	451	295	295	-	-	128	128	-	28
1955	425	302	302	-	-	87	87	-	36
1957	308	236	236	-	-	32	32	-	41
1960	13174	119	119	-	-	13002	12948	9	44
1961	24111	78	78	-	-	23694	23490	308	32
1962	31605	53	53	-	-	31050	30747	470	32
1963	36426	38	38	-	-	35823	35462	533	32
1964	40950	46	46	-	-	39791	39347	1078	36
1965	42364	45	45	-	-	39819	39038	2450	50
EGYPT UAR									
1925	270	-	-	-	-	270	270	-	-
1929	408	-	-	-	-	408	408	-	-

Table II. PRIMARY ENERGY PRODUCTION, SELECTED YEARS, 1925-1965

(Thousand metric tons coal equivalent)

Region, country, year	Total primary energy production	Solid fuels: Total	Solid fuels: Hard coal	Solid fuels: Lignite	Solid fuels: Other	Liquid fuels: Total	Liquid fuels: Crude oil	Natural gas	Hydro-electric power
	(1)	(2)	(3)	(4)	(5)	(6)	(7)	(8)	(9)
EGYPT UAR (CONTINUED)									
1933	357	-	-	-	-	357	357	-	-
1937	257	-	-	-	-	257	257	-	-
1938	339	-	-	-	-	339	339	-	-
1950	3905	-	-	-	-	3905	3888	-	1
1953	4045	-	-	-	-	4044	4035	-	1
1955	2738	-	-	-	-	2738	2729	-	1
1957	3605	-	-	-	-	3605	3596	-	1
1960	5026	-	-	-	-	4994	4979	-	33
1961	5869	-	-	-	-	5742	5729	-	127
1962	7174	-	-	-	-	7028	7014	-	147
1963	8559	-	-	-	-	8399	8388	-	160
1964	9750	-	-	-	-	9542	9531	-	209
1965	9957	-	-	-	-	9738	9731	-	219
LIBYA									
1925	-	-	-	-	-	-	-	-	-
1929	-	-	-	-	-	-	-	-	-
1933	-	-	-	-	-	-	-	-	-
1937	-	-	-	-	-	-	-	-	-
1938	-	-	-	-	-	-	-	-	-
1950	-	-	-	-	-	-	-	-	-
1953	-	-	-	-	-	-	-	-	-
1955	-	-	-	-	-	-	-	-	-
1957	-	-	-	-	-	-	-	-	-
1960	-	-	-	-	-	-	-	-	-
1961	1314	-	-	-	-	1314	1314	-	-
1962	13272	-	-	-	-	13272	13272	-	-
1963	33212	-	-	-	-	33212	33212	-	-
1964	62478	-	-	-	-	62478	62478	-	-
1965	88158	-	-	-	-	88158	88158	-	-
MOROCCO									
1925	-	-	-	-	-	-	-	-	-
1929	2	-	-	-	-	-	-	-	2
1933	36	27	27	-	-	2	2	-	7
1937	126	107	107	-	-	3	3	-	16
1938	143	123	123	-	-	5	5	-	15
1950	461	368	368	-	-	59	59	-	35
1953	764	565	565	-	-	153	153	7	40
1955	735	467	467	-	-	155	155	11	103
1957	745	521	521	-	-	113	113	4	107
1960	678	412	412	-	-	138	138	12	116
1961	660	410	410	-	-	120	120	11	119
1962	701	370	370	-	-	191	191	13	128
1963	780	404	404	-	-	225	225	16	135
1964	737	400	400	-	-	180	180	16	142
1965	733	419	419	-	-	155	155	15	145
TUNISIA									
1925	-	-	-	-	-	-	-	-	-
1929	-	-	-	-	-	-	-	-	-
1933	-	-	-	-	-	-	-	-	-

Table II. PRIMARY ENERGY PRODUCTION, SELECTED YEARS, 1925-1965

(Thousand metric tons coal equivalent)

Region, country, year	Total primary energy production	Solid fuels				Liquid fuels		Natural gas	Hydro-electric power
		Total	Hard coal	Lignite	Other	Total	Crude oil		
	(1)	(2)	(3)	(4)	(5)	(6)	(7)	(8)	(9)
TUNISIA (CONTINUED)									
1937	-	-	-	-	-	-	-	-	-
1938	-	-	-	-	-	-	-	-	-
1950	14	14	-	14	-	-	-	-	-
1953	-	-	-	-	-	-	-	-	-
1955	5	-	-	-	-	-	-	5	-
1957	11	-	-	-	-	-	-	8	3
1960	15	-	-	-	-	-	-	9	6
1961	12	-	-	-	-	-	-	9	2
1962	12	-	-	-	-	-	-	9	2
1963	13	-	-	-	-	-	-	9	4
1964	15	-	-	-	-	-	-	11	5
1965	16	-	-	-	-	-	-	11	5
TROPICAL AFRICA									
1925	1021	1015	1015	-	-	-	-	-	6
1929	1516	1510	1510	-	-	-	-	-	6
1933	776	759	759	-	-	-	-	-	17
1937	1490	1453	1453	-	-	-	-	-	37
1938	1505	1464	1464	-	-	-	-	-	41
1950	3057	2938	2938	-	-	-	-	-	119
1953	3999	3812	3812	-	-	-	-	-	187
1955	4997	4730	4730	-	-	-	-	-	267
1957	6109	5386	5386	-	-	276	276	-	447
1960	7942	4565	4565	-	-	2655	2655	9	713
1961	9855	4078	4078	-	-	4881	4881	9	886
1962	11983	3837	3837	-	-	7124	7124	15	1008
1963	13170	3696	3696	-	-	8357	8357	65	1052
1964	17303	4089	4089	-	-	12000	12000	89	1125
1965	29222	4603	4603	-	-	23292	23292	95	1232
CONGO, DEMOCRATIC REPUBLIC									
1925	69	65	65	-	-	-	-	-	4
1929	121	117	117	-	-	-	-	-	4
1933	32	20	20	-	-	-	-	-	12
1937	64	36	36	-	-	-	-	-	28
1938	71	42	42	-	-	-	-	-	29
1950	234	160	160	-	-	-	-	-	74
1953	439	315	315	-	-	-	-	-	124
1955	646	480	480	-	-	-	-	-	166
1957	730	433	433	-	-	-	-	-	297
1960	452	163	163	-	-	-	-	-	289
1961	371	73	73	-	-	-	-	-	298
1962	391	76	76	-	-	-	-	-	315
1963	371	92	92	-	-	-	-	-	279
1964	382	100	100	-	-	-	-	-	282
1965	423	114	114	-	-	-	-	-	309
EAST AFRICA									
1925	1	-	-	-	-	-	-	-	1
1929	1	-	-	-	-	-	-	-	1
1933	2	-	-	-	-	-	-	-	2
1937	3	-	-	-	-	-	-	-	3

Table II. PRIMARY ENERGY PRODUCTION, SELECTED YEARS, 1925-1965

(Thousand metric tons coal equivalent)

Region, country, year	Total primary energy production	Solid fuels				Liquid fuels		Natural gas	Hydro-electric power
		Total	Hard coal	Lignite	Other	Total	Crude oil		
	(1)	(2)	(3)	(4)	(5)	(6)	(7)	(8)	(9)
EAST AFRICA (CONTINUED)									
1938	3	-	-	-	-	-	-	-	3
1950	9	-	-	-	-	-	-	-	9
1953	14	-	-	-	-	-	-	-	14
1955	40	1	1	-	-	-	-	-	39
1957	53	1	1	-	-	-	-	-	52
1960	82	2	2	-	-	-	-	-	80
1961	85	2	2	-	-	-	-	-	83
1962	92	3	3	-	-	-	-	-	89
1963	98	2	2	-	-	-	-	-	96
1964	108	1	1	-	-	-	-	-	107
1965	121	2	2	-	-	-	-	-	119
EQUATORIAL AFRICA									
1925	-	-	-	-	-	-	-	-	-
1929	-	-	-	-	-	-	-	-	-
1933	-	-	-	-	-	-	-	-	-
1937	-	-	-	-	-	-	-	-	-
1938	-	-	-	-	-	-	-	-	-
1950	-	-	-	-	-	-	-	-	-
1953	1	-	-	-	-	-	-	-	1
1955	4	-	-	-	-	-	-	-	4
1957	263	-	-	-	-	260	260	-	4
1960	1291	-	-	-	-	1278	1278	9	4
1961	1329	-	-	-	-	1316	1316	9	4
1962	1441	-	-	-	-	1425	1425	12	4
1963	1517	-	-	-	-	1499	1499	12	6
1964	1733	-	-	-	-	1713	1713	13	6
1965	2023	-	-	-	-	2003	2003	15	6
GHANA									
1960	-	-	-	-	-	-	-	-	-
1961	-	-	-	-	-	-	-	-	-
1962	-	-	-	-	-	-	-	-	-
1963	-	-	-	-	-	-	-	-	-
1964	-	-	-	-	-	-	-	-	-
1965	13	-	-	-	-	-	-	-	13
LIBERIA									
1950	1	-	-	-	-	-	-	-	1
1953	1	-	-	-	-	-	-	-	1
1955	1	-	-	-	-	-	-	-	1
1957	2	-	-	-	-	-	-	-	2
1960	2	-	-	-	-	-	-	-	2
1961	2	-	-	-	-	-	-	-	2
1962	2	-	-	-	-	-	-	-	2
1963	2	-	-	-	-	-	-	-	2
1964	2	-	-	-	-	-	-	-	2
1965	2	-	-	-	-	-	-	-	2

Table II. PRIMARY ENERGY PRODUCTION, SELECTED YEARS, 1925-1965

(Thousand metric tons coal equivalent)

Region, country, year	Total primary energy production	Solid fuels				Liquid fuels		Natural gas	Hydro-electric power
		Total	Hard coal	Lignite	Other	Total	Crude oil		
	(1)	(2)	(3)	(4)	(5)	(6)	(7)	(8)	(9)
NIGERIA									
1925	243	243	243	-	-	-	-	-	-
1929	350	350	350	-	-	-	-	-	-
1933	239	239	239	-	-	-	-	-	-
1937	369	369	369	-	-	-	-	-	-
1938	368	368	368	-	-	-	-	-	-
1950	599	592	592	-	-	-	-	-	7
1953	719	711	711	-	-	-	-	-	8
1955	770	761	761	-	-	-	-	-	9
1957	841	828	828	-	-	2	2	-	11
1960	1857	571	571	-	-	1275	1275	-	11
1961	4026	607	607	-	-	3407	3407	-	13
1962	5642	634	634	-	-	4992	4992	3	14
1963	6303	577	577	-	-	5658	5658	53	15
1964	9720	699	699	-	-	8930	8930	76	16
1965	21143	740	740	-	-	20307	20307	80	17
RHODESIAN FEDERATION									
1925	689	689	689	-	-	-	-	-	-
1929	1037	1037	1037	-	-	-	-	-	-
1933	487	484	484	-	-	-	-	-	3
1937	1034	1029	1029	-	-	-	-	-	5
1938	1050	1044	1044	-	-	-	-	-	6
1950	2147	2128	2128	-	-	-	-	-	19
1953	2644	2619	2619	-	-	-	-	-	25
1955	3343	3315	3315	-	-	-	-	-	28
1957	3882	3853	3853	-	-	-	-	-	29
1960	3723	3559	3559	-	-	-	-	-	164
1961	3378	3073	3073	-	-	-	-	-	305
1962	3199	2826	2826	-	-	-	-	-	373
1963	3173	2740	2740	-	-	-	-	-	433
1964	3530	3044	3044	-	-	-	-	-	486
1965	4028	3509	3509	-	-	-	-	-	519
MALAWI									
1950	-	-	-	-	-	-	-	-	-
1953	-	-	-	-	-	-	-	-	-
1955	-	-	-	-	-	-	-	-	-
1957	-	-	-	-	-	-	-	-	-
1960	-	-	-	-	-	-	-	-	-
1961	-	-	-	-	-	-	-	-	-
1962	2	-	-	-	-	-	-	-	2
1963	1	-	-	-	-	-	-	-	1
1964	1	-	-	-	-	-	-	-	1
1965	2	-	-	-	-	-	-	-	2
ZAMBIA									
1950	NA	-	-	-	-	-	-	-	NA
1953	23	-	-	-	-	-	-	-	23
1955	27	-	-	-	-	-	-	-	27
1957	28	-	-	-	-	-	-	-	28
1960	NA	-	-	-	-	-	-	-	NA
1961	NA	-	-	-	-	-	-	-	NA

Table II. PRIMARY ENERGY PRODUCTION, SELECTED YEARS, 1925-1965

(Thousand metric tons coal equivalent)

Region, country, year	Total primary energy production	Solid fuels				Liquid fuels		Natural gas	Hydro-electric power
		Total	Hard coal	Lignite	Other	Total	Crude oil		
	(1)	(2)	(3)	(4)	(5)	(6)	(7)	(8)	(9)
ZAMBIA (CONTINUED)									
1962	37	-	-	-	-	-	-	-	37
1963	39	-	-	-	-	-	-	-	39
1964	38	-	-	-	-	-	-	-	38
1965	35	-	-	-	-	-	-	-	35
RHODESIA									
1950	2128	2128	2128	-	-	-	-	-	NA
1953	2619	2618	2618	-	-	-	-	-	1
1955	3315	3315	3315	-	-	-	-	-	-
1957	3853	3853	3853	-	-	-	-	-	-
1960	3690	3559	3559	-	-	-	-	-	131
1961	3349	3073	3073	-	-	-	-	-	276
1962	3168	2826	2826	-	-	-	-	-	342
1963	3133	2740	2740	-	-	-	-	-	393
1964	3490	3044	3044	-	-	-	-	-	446
1965	3992	3509	3509	-	-	-	-	-	483
WEST AFRICA									
1950	-	-	-	-	-	-	-	-	-
1953	1	-	-	-	-	-	-	-	1
1955	1	-	-	-	-	-	-	-	1
1957	2	-	-	-	-	-	-	-	2
1960	9	-	-	-	-	2	2	-	8
1961	13	-	-	-	-	3	3	-	10
1962	13	-	-	-	-	-	-	-	13
1963	15	-	-	-	-	-	-	-	15
1964	13	-	-	-	-	-	-	-	13
1965	18	-	-	-	-	-	-	-	18
SOUTH AFRICA									
1925	12322	12322	12322	-	-	-	-	-	-
1929	13018	13018	13018	-	-	-	-	-	-
1933	10714	10714	10714	-	-	-	-	-	-
1937	15490	15490	15490	-	-	-	-	-	-
1938	16292	16284	16284	-	-	8	8	-	-
1950	26527	26473	26473	-	-	54	54	-	-
1953	28515	28459	28459	-	-	56	56	-	-
1955	32203	32147	32147	-	-	56	56	-	-
1957	34807	34769	34769	-	-	38	38	-	-
1960	38223	38185	38185	-	-	38	38	-	-
1961	39575	39566	39566	-	-	9	9	-	-
1962	41281	41281	41281	-	-	-	-	-	-
1963	42456	42456	42456	-	-	-	-	-	-
1964	44906	44906	44906	-	-	-	-	-	-
1965	48444	48444	48444	-	-	-	-	-	-
DEVELOPED COUNTRIES									
1925	1372628	1155571	1100756	49065	5750	162686	157952	45050	9321
1929	1564178	1260278	1192913	61150	6216	217694	208316	72276	13931
1933	1166112	900561	850001	45282	5279	191159	185030	59566	14826
1937	1535428	1152143	1081731	64439	5973	270926	261440	92093	20266

Table II. PRIMARY ENERGY PRODUCTION, SELECTED YEARS, 1925-1965

(Thousand metric tons coal equivalent)

Region, country, year	Total primary energy production	Solid fuels				Liquid fuels		Natural gas	Hydro-electric power
		Total	Hard coal	Lignite	Other	Total	Crude oil		
	(1)	(2)	(3)	(4)	(5)	(6)	(7)	(8)	(9)
DEVELOPED COUNTRIES (CONTINUED)									
1938	1420238	1052749	979127	67963	5659	259337	249264	87571	20581
1950	1839424	1127009	1080654	38814	7541	441206	412373	232864	38345
1953	2002595	1100658	1050822	42053	7784	542475	505385	314052	45410
1955	2107977	1114264	1059420	47067	7777	587741	544566	354881	51092
1957	2258087	1162363	1102748	51885	7731	630968	585977	407563	57194
1960	2252220	1043672	981162	54729	7780	635852	583946	503412	69285
1961	2288776	1030258	966155	56739	7364	657420	601854	528928	72171
1962	2371060	1054815	988151	58896	7768	676665	619130	565349	74232
1963	2466442	1089273	1019286	62048	7939	702050	639177	597608	77510
1964	2560072	1124383	1050908	64311	9165	719619	652113	636291	79779
1965	2623038	1134493	1062488	62980	9025	740051	669422	661578	86917
UNDERDEVELOPED COUNTRIES									
1925	79363	27526	27158	69	299	49908	49724	1480	449
1929	106686	31447	30884	79	484	72026	71589	2605	608
1933	98881	26947	26712	75	160	67292	66654	3787	856
1937	148037	36860	36299	101	459	104375	103695	5465	1338
1938	152920	41016	40554	112	350	104559	103905	5883	1462
1950	358060	43122	42036	722	364	304151	303183	8276	2513
1953	453645	50808	49694	886	227	386943	385760	12542	3352
1955	560882	53325	52221	935	170	487475	486185	15992	4090
1957	662764	60548	59235	1173	140	573695	571911	23238	5284
1960	864150	70753	69328	1408	18	748983	745509	37269	7144
1961	928662	74341	72947	1388	7	804977	801093	41408	7937
1962	1033468	80962	79318	1640	5	898205	894390	45586	8715
1963	1124700	87448	85172	2266	10	979220	975080	48515	9517
1964	1248098	87057	84523	2528	6	1095101	1090752	55462	10478
1965	1362519	92270	89455	2808	7	1198860	1193984	59700	11689
COMMUNIST COUNTRIES									
1925	114654	97795	78673	17113	2008	15402	15357	1392	65
1929	177045	145841	121269	21364	3208	28949	28830	2139	116
1933	201205	152195	128456	17830	5908	44711	44394	4096	204
1937	290813	228382	192757	25325	10300	55508	54990	6290	634
1938	294404	230009	193677	24981	11350	57431	56955	6211	754
1950	519653	438447	318988	104109	15351	67820	67568	10846	2540
1953	658227	541763	392311	133102	16350	98222	97895	15190	3053
1955	811998	658445	482309	154686	21451	130626	130290	18733	4194
1957	958252	744802	548020	173632	23151	173622	173259	33058	6770
1960	1224951	887106	676447	189608	21051	256347	255846	71937	9561
1961	1311715	924519	707213	197256	20050	285719	285207	91241	10237
1962	1384044	941145	724398	203397	13351	318239	317708	112675	11985
1963	1490492	990918	755385	213183	22351	350409	349836	136698	12467
1964	1582922	1034645	789683	222212	22751	372150	371577	163291	12835
1965	1674797	1065968	820161	222857	22951	403880	403257	190961	13989
USSR									
1925	26955	16109	13300	700	1900	10629	10629	186	31
1929	58851	37809	33200	1500	3100	20534	20534	440	70
1933	106868	72909	63100	4000	5800	32336	32336	1479	145
1937	169066	122600	104200	8100	10100	43040	43040	2902	524
1938	177353	128151	108500	8300	11100	45623	45623	2944	636

Table II. PRIMARY ENERGY PRODUCTION, SELECTED YEARS, 1925-1965

(Thousand metric tons coal equivalent)

Region, country, year	Total primary energy production	Solid fuels				Liquid fuels		Natural gas	Hydro-electric power
		Total	Hard coal	Lignite	Other	Total	Crude oil		
	(1)	(2)	(3)	(4)	(5)	(6)	(7)	(8)	(9)
USSR (CONTINUED)									
1950	292152	224500	175900	33500	15100	58392	58392	7674	1586
1953	365264	272300	214300	41900	16100	81416	81416	9148	2400
1955	461898	337400	266700	49500	21200	109640	109640	11963	2896
1957	562040	380700	299700	58100	22900	151659	151659	24753	4929
1960	693696	400400	320300	59300	20800	226589	226589	60344	6364
1961	736660	396400	319300	57300	19800	254307	254307	78563	7390
1962	791499	399400	330100	56200	13100	285171	285171	97935	8993
1963	862037	417300	336600	58600	22100	315599	315599	119656	9482
1964	920485	430800	346000	62300	22500	335405	335405	144610	9670
1965	993462	448900	361900	64300	22700	364332	364332	170051	10179
COMMUNIST EASTERN EUROPE									
1925	65141	59129	42816	16413	108	4773	4728	1205	34
1929	94150	83997	64033	19864	108	8408	8289	1700	46
1933	67808	52894	38964	13830	108	12239	11922	2617	59
1937	87121	71456	54231	17225	200	12168	11651	3387	110
1938	86927	72154	55473	16681	250	11388	10913	3267	117
1950	184021	171427	101039	70138	251	9128	8876	3173	293
1953	226312	204065	112734	91081	250	15873	15546	6042	332
1955	252853	226022	120978	104794	251	19538	19202	6771	523
1957	266107	237506	122306	114950	251	19742	19379	8305	554
1960	300368	266526	137120	129155	251	21465	20964	11594	784
1961	313976	278441	139522	138669	250	22073	21561	12678	784
1962	328313	289872	143685	145937	251	22833	22302	14740	867
1963	343483	302112	148581	153281	251	23532	22959	17042	797
1964	355363	311923	153050	158622	251	23969	23396	18681	790
1965	358254	311635	154118	157267	251	24524	23901	20910	1186
COMMUNIST ASIA									
1925	22557	22557	22557	-	-	-	-	-	-
1929	24043	24036	24036	-	-	8	8	-	-
1933	26529	26392	26392	-	-	137	137	-	-
1937	34626	34326	34326	-	-	300	300	-	-
1938	30124	29704	29704	-	-	420	420	-	-
1950	43480	42520	42049	472	-	300	300	-	660
1953	66651	65398	65277	121	-	933	933	-	320
1955	97247	95023	94631	392	-	1449	1449	-	775
1957	130105	126596	126014	582	-	2222	2222	-	1288
1960	230886	220180	219027	1153	-	8294	8294	-	2413
1961	261079	249678	248391	1287	-	9339	9339	-	2063
1962	264233	251873	250613	1260	-	10235	10235	-	2125
1963	284972	271506	270204	1302	-	11279	11279	-	2188
1964	307075	291923	290633	1290	-	12777	12777	-	2375
1965	323082	305433	304143	1290	-	15024	15024	-	2625
ORGANISATION FOR ECONOMIC CO-OPERATION AND DEVELOPMENT (OECD)									
1925	1342716	1125826	1074004	46776	5046	162686	157952	45050	9155
1929	1535600	1231972	1168536	58030	5406	217694	208316	72273	13662
1933	1142579	877413	830110	42689	4614	191155	185027	59564	14447
1937	1503213	1120492	1054167	61266	5059	270923	261437	92090	19707
1938	1387283	1020431	951268	64364	4799	259326	249254	87568	19957
1950	1786887	1075844	1039076	31224	5544	441008	412178	232846	37191

Table II. PRIMARY ENERGY PRODUCTION, SELECTED YEARS, 1925-1965

(Thousand metric tons coal equivalent)

Region, country, year	Total primary energy production	Solid fuels				Liquid fuels		Natural gas	Hydro-electric power
		Total	Hard coal	Lignite	Other	Total	Crude oil		
	(1)	(2)	(3)	(4)	(5)	(6)	(7)	(8)	(9)
ORGANISATION FOR ECONOMIC CO-OPERATION AND DEVELOPMENT (OECD) (CONTINUED)									
1953	1947545	1047434	1007192	35004	5238	542196	505109	314020	43896
1955	2045384	1053810	1010848	37763	5199	587562	544392	354835	49176
1957	2190844	1097669	1051265	41300	5104	630776	585791	407507	54892
1960	2173922	968875	923484	40761	4630	634950	583053	503341	66756
1961	2205941	951765	905913	41670	4182	656054	600495	528836	69287
1962	2285528	974276	926408	43373	4494	675261	617733	565222	70769
1963	2377804	1005738	956298	45058	4381	700740	637877	597350	73976
1964	2465101	1035083	983561	46260	5263	718002	650511	635922	76094
1965	2519703	1037136	987832	44266	5039	738728	668121	661133	82706
COMMUNIST COUNTRIES									
1925	114654	97795	78673	17113	2008	15402	15357	1392	65
1929	177045	145841	121269	21364	3208	28949	28830	2139	116
1933	201205	152195	128456	17830	5908	44711	44394	4096	204
1937	290813	228382	192757	25325	10300	55508	54990	6290	634
1938	294404	230009	193677	24981	11350	57431	56955	6211	754
1950	519653	438447	318988	104109	15351	67820	67568	10846	2540
1953	658227	541763	392311	133102	16350	98222	97895	15190	3053
1955	811998	658445	482309	154686	21451	130626	130290	18733	4194
1957	958252	744802	548020	173632	23151	173622	173259	33058	6770
1960	1224951	887106	676447	189608	21051	256347	255846	71937	9561
1961	1311715	924519	707213	197256	20050	285719	285207	91241	10237
1962	1384044	941145	724398	203397	13351	318239	317708	112675	11985
1963	1490492	990918	755385	213183	22351	350409	349836	136698	12467
1964	1582922	1034645	789683	222212	22751	372150	371577	163291	12835
1965	1674797	1065968	820161	222857	22951	403880	403257	190961	13989
WORLD EXCLUDING OECD AND COMMUNIST COUNTRIES									
1925	109274	57271	53910	2358	1003	49908	49724	1480	615
1929	135265	59754	55261	3200	1293	72026	71589	2608	877
1933	122414	50096	46603	2669	824	67295	66657	3788	1235
1937	180252	68510	63863	3273	1374	104378	103698	5468	1897
1938	185875	73333	68413	3710	1210	104570	103916	5886	2086
1950	410597	94287	83614	8311	2361	304349	303378	8294	3667
1953	508695	104033	93324	7935	2773	387222	386036	12574	4867
1955	623475	113780	100792	10240	2748	487653	486359	16037	6006
1957	730008	125242	110717	11758	2766	573887	572097	23294	7586
1960	942447	145550	127006	15376	3168	749885	746402	37340	9673
1961	1011497	152834	133189	16457	3188	806343	802452	41500	10820
1962	1119000	161501	141060	17163	3278	899609	895787	45713	12178
1963	1213337	170984	148160	19256	3568	980529	976380	48774	13051
1964	1343069	176357	151870	20579	3908	1096718	1092354	55831	14164
1965	1465854	189626	164111	21522	3993	1200183	1195284	60145	15900

DERIVATION OF TABLE III

Column	*Derivation*
(1)	Col. (1) table II as percent of col. (1) table II (= 100)
(2)	Col. (2) table II as percent of col. (1) table II
(3)	Col. (3) table II as percent of col. (1) table II
(4)	Col. (6) table II as percent of col. (1) table II
(5)	Col. (7) table II as percent of col. (1) table II
(6)	Col. (8) table II as percent of col. (1) table II
(7)	Col. (9) table II as percent of col. (1) table II

Table III. PRIMARY ENERGY PRODUCTION PERCENTAGE DISTRIBUTION, SELECTED YEARS, 1925-1965

(Based on coal equivalents)

Region, country, year	Total primary energy production	Solid fuels		Liquid fuels		Natural gas	Hydro-electric power
		Total	Hard coal	Total	Crude oil		
	(1)	(2)	(3)	(4)	(5)	(6)	(7)
WORLD							
1925	100.0	81.8	77.0	14.6	14.2	3.1	0.6
1929	100.0	77.8	72.8	17.2	16.7	4.2	0.8
1933	100.0	73.6	68.5	20.7	20.2	4.6	1.1
1937	100.0	71.8	66.4	21.8	21.3	5.3	1.1
1938	100.0	70.9	65.0	22.6	22.0	5.3	1.2
1950	100.0	59.2	53.1	29.9	28.8	9.3	1.6
1953	100.0	54.4	47.9	33.0	31.8	11.0	1.7
1955	100.0	52.5	45.8	34.6	33.4	11.2	1.7
1957	100.0	50.7	44.1	35.5	34.3	12.0	1.8
1960	100.0	46.1	39.8	37.8	36.5	14.1	2.0
1961	100.0	44.8	38.6	38.6	37.3	14.6	2.0
1962	100.0	43.4	37.4	39.5	38.2	15.1	2.0
1963	100.0	42.7	36.5	40.0	38.7	15.4	2.0
1964	100.0	41.7	35.7	40.6	39.2	15.9	1.9
1965	100.0	40.5	34.8	41.4	40.0	16.1	2.0
NORTH AMERICA							
1925	100.0	72.9	72.5	20.8	20.2	5.8	0.6
1929	100.0	66.9	66.5	24.3	23.2	8.1	0.8
1933	100.0	59.5	59.0	30.1	29.1	9.4	1.1

Table III. PRIMARY ENERGY PRODUCTION PERCENTAGE DISTRIBUTION, SELECTED YEARS, 1925-1965

(Based on coal equivalents)

Region, country, year	Total primary energy production	Solid fuels		Liquid fuels		Natural gas	Hydro-electric power
		Total	Hard coal	Total	Crude oil		
	(1)	(2)	(3)	(4)	(5)	(6)	(7)
NORTH AMERICA (CONTINUED)							
1937	100.0	56.9	56.5	31.3	30.2	10.7	1.1
1938	100.0	52.4	51.9	34.6	33.3	11.8	1.2
1950	100.0	44.7	44.3	35.1	32.8	18.7	1.5
1953	100.0	35.8	35.5	39.5	36.8	23.0	1.6
1955	100.0	33.8	33.5	40.2	37.1	24.3	1.7
1957	100.0	32.9	32.6	39.6	36.7	25.7	1.8
1960	100.0	27.4	27.1	39.3	36.0	31.3	2.1
1961	100.0	26.0	25.8	39.9	36.4	32.1	2.0
1962	100.0	25.9	25.7	39.2	35.8	32.8	2.1
1963	100.0	26.7	26.5	38.5	35.0	32.8	2.0
1964	100.0	27.0	26.8	37.6	34.0	33.4	2.0
1965	100.0	27.2	27.0	37.4	33.7	33.4	2.1
CANADA							
1925	100.0	85.0	66.0	0.6	0.6	4.9	9.5
1929	100.0	81.1	66.4	1.1	1.1	5.8	12.0
1933	100.0	75.5	58.5	1.9	1.6	6.6	16.1
1937	100.0	71.9	58.7	3.5	2.9	6.5	18.1
1938	100.0	67.4	54.5	7.7	7.3	7.0	17.8
1950	100.0	51.6	39.9	19.0	18.8	8.3	21.1
1953	100.0	31.6	24.8	39.3	39.1	9.1	20.0
1955	100.0	22.7	17.2	49.0	48.8	10.6	17.7
1957	100.0	16.3	12.3	55.7	55.2	12.4	15.6
1960	100.0	11.0	8.1	48.4	47.3	24.3	16.3
1961	100.0	9.1	6.7	50.1	48.4	26.7	14.0
1962	100.0	7.7	5.5	47.4	45.7	33.0	12.0
1963	100.0	7.2	5.4	46.6	43.9	35.3	10.9
1964	100.0	6.7	4.8	44.0	40.7	38.9	10.4
1965	100.0	6.5	4.4	44.8	41.4	38.6	10.1
UNITED STATES							
1925	100.0	72.7	72.6	21.1	20.5	5.8	0.4
1929	100.0	66.6	66.5	24.8	23.7	8.1	0.5
1933	100.0	59.1	59.0	30.7	29.7	9.5	0.8
1937	100.0	56.6	56.5	31.9	30.8	10.8	0.7
1938	100.0	52.0	51.9	35.3	33.9	11.9	0.8
1950	100.0	44.5	44.4	35.5	33.2	18.9	1.0
1953	100.0	35.9	35.9	39.5	36.7	23.5	1.1
1955	100.0	34.3	34.2	39.8	36.7	24.9	1.1
1957	100.0	33.6	33.6	38.9	35.9	26.3	1.1
1960	100.0	28.2	28.2	38.8	35.4	31.6	1.3
1961	100.0	27.0	27.0	39.2	35.6	32.5	1.3
1962	100.0	27.2	27.1	38.6	35.1	32.8	1.4
1963	100.0	28.1	28.1	37.9	34.3	32.6	1.3
1964	100.0	28.6	28.6	37.1	33.4	32.9	1.3
1965	100.0	28.9	28.8	36.7	33.0	33.0	1.4
WESTERN EUROPE							
1925	100.0	99.2	89.7	0.1	0.1	-	0.7
1929	100.0	99.0	88.8	0.1	0.1	-	0.9

Table III. PRIMARY ENERGY PRODUCTION PERCENTAGE DISTRIBUTION, SELECTED YEARS, 1925-1965

(Based on coal equivalents)

Region, country, year	Total primary energy production	Solid fuels		Liquid fuels		Natural gas	Hydro-electric power
		Total	Hard coal	Total	Crude oil		
	(1)	(2)	(3)	(4)	(5)	(6)	(7)
WESTERN EUROPE (CONTINUED)							
1933	100.0	98.6	88.9	0.1	0.1	-	1.2
1937	100.0	98.5	87.5	0.2	0.2	-	1.4
1938	100.0	98.4	86.8	0.2	0.2	-	1.4
1950	100.0	95.8	88.5	1.2	1.2	0.3	2.7
1953	100.0	94.1	86.8	1.9	1.9	0.8	3.1
1955	100.0	92.7	84.9	2.5	2.5	1.3	3.5
1957	100.0	91.6	83.2	3.1	3.1	1.6	3.7
1960	100.0	88.0	78.9	4.1	4.0	2.9	5.1
1961	100.0	87.0	77.7	4.4	4.3	3.3	5.3
1962	100.0	86.5	76.9	4.6	4.5	3.6	5.3
1963	100.0	85.7	75.6	4.8	4.8	3.8	5.7
1964	100.0	85.1	74.8	5.2	5.1	4.1	5.5
1965	100.0	83.6	73.4	5.5	5.4	4.6	6.3
EUROPEAN ECONOMIC COMMUNITY (EEC)							
1925	100.0	99.3	82.7	0.1	0.1	-	0.7
1929	100.0	99.1	82.2	0.1	0.1	-	0.8
1933	100.0	98.6	82.4	0.2	0.2	-	1.1
1937	100.0	98.5	81.1	0.2	0.2	-	1.2
1938	100.0	98.5	80.5	0.3	0.3	-	1.2
1950	100.0	96.0	85.8	1.2	1.2	0.4	2.4
1953	100.0	94.1	84.0	1.9	1.8	1.3	2.7
1955	100.0	92.3	82.1	2.7	2.6	2.1	2.9
1957	100.0	90.4	79.8	4.0	3.9	2.8	2.9
1960	100.0	85.7	75.3	5.6	5.5	4.5	4.1
1961	100.0	84.8	74.0	6.1	6.0	5.3	3.9
1962	100.0	84.0	72.9	6.5	6.3	5.9	3.6
1963	100.0	82.9	71.3	6.8	6.6	6.1	4.2
1964	100.0	82.5	70.9	7.4	7.2	6.6	3.5
1965	100.0	80.5	69.5	7.6	7.4	7.6	4.3
BELGIUM-LUXEMBOURG							
1925	100.0	100.0	100.0	-	-	-	-
1929	100.0	100.0	100.0	-	-	-	-
1933	100.0	100.0	100.0	-	-	-	-
1937	100.0	100.0	100.0	-	-	-	-
1938	100.0	100.0	100.0	-	-	-	-
1950	100.0	99.9	99.9	-	-	0.1	-
1953	100.0	99.7	99.7	-	-	0.2	-
1955	100.0	99.6	99.6	-	-	0.4	0.1
1957	100.0	99.4	99.4	-	-	0.5	0.1
1960	100.0	99.5	99.5	-	-	0.4	0.1
1961	100.0	99.4	99.4	-	-	0.4	0.1
1962	100.0	99.4	99.4	-	-	0.4	0.1
1963	100.0	99.2	99.2	-	-	0.4	0.4
1964	100.0	99.1	99.1	-	-	0.4	0.5
1965	100.0	98.7	98.7	-	-	0.5	0.7
FRANCE							
1925	100.0	98.7	97.4	0.2	0.2	-	1.1

Table III. PRIMARY ENERGY PRODUCTION PERCENTAGE DISTRIBUTION, SELECTED YEARS, 1925-1965

(Based on coal equivalents)

Region, country, year	Total primary energy production	Solid fuels		Liquid fuels		Natural gas	Hydro-electric power
		Total	Hard coal	Total	Crude oil		
	(1)	(2)	(3)	(4)	(5)	(6)	(7)
FRANCE (CONTINUED)							
1929	100.0	98.3	97.0	0.2	0.2	-	1.5
1933	100.0	97.8	96.5	0.3	0.3	-	1.9
1937	100.0	96.8	95.5	0.3	0.3	-	3.0
1938	100.0	97.1	95.8	0.3	0.3	-	2.7
1950	100.0	95.3	93.4	0.5	0.4	0.6	3.7
1953	100.0	93.8	91.7	1.0	1.0	0.5	4.6
1955	100.0	92.0	90.0	2.2	2.2	0.6	5.2
1957	100.0	90.8	88.7	3.4	3.3	0.9	4.9
1960	100.0	82.5	80.5	4.8	4.3	5.5	7.3
1961	100.0	79.7	77.1	5.2	4.8	8.0	7.1
1962	100.0	78.5	76.0	5.7	5.2	9.2	6.6
1963	100.0	75.4	73.1	6.3	5.8	9.9	8.4
1964	100.0	77.4	75.5	6.7	6.1	9.7	6.2
1965	100.0	75.1	72.8	7.0	6.4	9.5	8.3
GERMANY							
1925	100.0	99.7	76.7	0.1	0.1	-	0.2
1929	100.0	99.7	76.2	0.1	0.1	-	0.2
1933	100.0	99.5	74.8	0.2	0.2	-	0.3
1937	100.0	99.4	75.7	0.3	0.3	-	0.4
1938	100.0	99.3	74.8	0.3	0.3	NA	0.4
GERMANY, FEDERAL REPUBLIC							
1950	100.0	98.2	82.2	1.1	1.1	0.1	0.7
1953	100.0	97.3	81.6	1.9	1.9	0.2	0.7
1955	100.0	96.2	80.4	2.5	2.5	0.4	0.8
1957	100.0	95.5	79.1	3.1	3.1	0.6	0.8
1960	100.0	94.0	77.2	4.5	4.5	0.7	0.9
1961	100.0	93.5	76.7	5.0	5.0	0.7	0.9
1962	100.0	92.8	75.5	5.4	5.4	0.9	0.8
1963	100.0	92.2	74.4	5.8	5.8	1.2	0.8
1964	100.0	91.7	73.4	5.9	5.9	1.6	0.8
1965	100.0	90.3	72.7	6.4	6.3	2.3	1.0
ITALY							
1925	100.0	35.3	11.1	0.9	0.9	0.7	63.1
1929	100.0	24.5	10.6	0.5	0.5	0.6	74.4
1933	100.0	20.5	14.4	2.1	2.1	1.0	76.4
1937	100.0	36.2	25.6	0.7	0.7	0.7	62.4
1938	100.0	43.3	35.5	0.6	0.6	0.7	55.4
1950	100.0	23.0	17.9	0.3	0.3	14.8	61.9
1953	100.0	14.0	11.2	2.5	1.6	37.6	45.9
1955	100.0	10.0	8.8	3.8	3.0	46.7	39.5
1957	100.0	6.8	5.9	14.5	13.7	48.2	30.5
1960	100.0	4.5	3.2	16.7	16.2	46.4	32.5
1961	100.0	5.6	3.2	16.2	15.8	48.7	29.5
1962	100.0	5.8	3.0	15.1	14.7	51.1	27.9
1963	100.0	4.5	2.4	14.2	13.8	49.9	31.3
1964	100.0	3.6	1.9	20.2	19.7	50.4	25.8
1965	100.0	3.1	1.6	17.0	16.7	51.9	28.1

Table III. PRIMARY ENERGY PRODUCTION PERCENTAGE DISTRIBUTION, SELECTED YEARS, 1925-1965

(Based on coal equivalents)

Region, country, year	Total primary energy production	Solid fuels		Liquid fuels		Natural gas	Hydro-electric power
		Total	Hard coal	Total	Crude oil		
	(1)	(2)	(3)	(4)	(5)	(6)	(7)
NETHERLANDS							
1925	100.0	100.0	99.0	-	-	-	-
1929	100.0	100.0	99.6	-	-	-	-
1933	100.0	100.0	99.7	-	-	-	-
1937	100.0	100.0	99.7	-	-	-	-
1938	100.0	100.0	99.6	-	-	-	-
1950	100.0	92.0	91.5	7.9	7.9	0.1	-
1953	100.0	90.8	90.1	9.0	9.0	0.2	-
1955	100.0	87.4	86.8	11.2	11.2	1.4	-
1957	100.0	82.2	81.5	16.4	16.4	1.5	-
1960	100.0	78.9	78.9	18.2	18.2	2.9	-
1961	100.0	77.4	77.4	18.8	18.8	3.8	-
1962	100.0	74.6	74.6	20.9	20.9	4.5	-
1963	100.0	73.6	73.6	21.3	21.3	5.1	-
1964	100.0	71.6	71.6	21.2	21.2	7.2	-
1965	100.0	65.7	65.7	20.6	20.6	13.6	-
EUROPEAN FREE TRADE ASSOCIATION (EFTA)							
1925	100.0	99.2	98.4	0.1	0.1	-	0.7
1929	100.0	99.0	98.2	0.1	0.1	-	0.9
1933	100.0	98.8	97.9	0.1	0.1	-	1.1
1937	100.0	98.6	97.8	0.1	0.1	-	1.3
1938	100.0	98.4	97.6	0.1	0.1	-	1.5
1950	100.0	95.7	94.4	1.2	1.2	0.3	2.8
1953	100.0	94.4	92.9	2.1	2.1	0.3	3.2
1955	100.0	93.6	91.9	2.4	2.4	0.4	3.6
1957	100.0	93.4	91.4	2.1	2.1	0.4	4.1
1960	100.0	91.6	89.8	1.8	1.8	0.9	5.6
1961	100.0	90.8	89.1	1.8	1.8	1.0	6.4
1962	100.0	90.7	89.0	1.7	1.7	1.0	6.5
1963	100.0	90.4	88.6	1.9	1.9	1.1	6.6
1964	100.0	89.6	87.9	1.9	1.9	1.2	7.3
1965	100.0	88.6	87.0	2.0	2.0	1.2	8.2
AUSTRIA							
1925	100.0	90.9	7.9	-	-	-	9.1
1929	100.0	90.0	9.5	-	-	-	10.0
1933	100.0	87.7	12.0	0.1	0.1	-	12.2
1937	100.0	84.3	10.3	2.2	2.2	-	13.4
1938	100.0	83.3	9.8	3.7	3.7	-	13.0
1950	100.0	38.3	3.0	41.4	41.4	10.2	10.1
1953	100.0	31.8	1.7	51.7	51.7	7.9	8.6
1955	100.0	31.9	1.6	50.1	50.1	9.1	9.0
1957	100.0	34.2	1.4	45.2	45.2	9.6	11.0
1960	100.0	30.6	1.3	35.8	35.8	19.1	14.5
1961	100.0	29.4	1.1	35.3	35.3	20.7	14.6
1962	100.0	28.9	1.0	35.1	35.1	21.3	14.8
1963	100.0	28.9	1.0	36.3	36.3	20.9	13.8
1964	100.0	27.2	0.9	36.4	36.4	21.4	15.0
1965	100.0	24.5	0.5	37.7	37.6	20.2	17.7

Table III. PRIMARY ENERGY PRODUCTION PERCENTAGE DISTRIBUTION, SELECTED YEARS, 1925-1965

(Based on coal equivalents)

Region, country, year	Total primary energy production	Solid fuels		Liquid fuels		Natural gas	Hydro-electric power
		Total	Hard coal	Total	Crude oil		
	(1)	(2)	(3)	(4)	(5)	(6)	(7)
DENMARK							
1925	100.0	100.0	-	-	-	-	-
1929	100.0	100.0	-	-	-	-	-
1933	100.0	100.0	-	-	-	-	-
1937	100.0	100.0	-	-	-	-	-
1938	100.0	100.0	-	-	-	-	-
1950	100.0	99.4	-	-	-	-	0.6
1953	100.0	99.2	-	-	-	-	0.8
1955	100.0	99.2	-	-	-	-	0.8
1957	100.0	99.6	-	-	-	-	0.4
1960	100.0	99.7	-	-	-	-	0.3
1961	100.0	99.6	-	-	-	-	0.4
1962	100.0	99.6	-	-	-	-	0.4
1963	100.0	99.6	-	-	-	-	0.4
1964	100.0	99.5	-	-	-	-	0.5
1965	100.0	99.5	-	-	-	-	0.5
NORWAY							
1925	100.0	42.2	29.1	-	-	-	57.8
1929	100.0	31.2	18.4	-	-	-	68.8
1933	100.0	33.9	21.3	-	-	-	66.1
1937	100.0	29.0	18.2	-	-	-	71.0
1938	100.0	27.7	17.4	-	-	-	72.3
1950	100.0	19.6	13.1	-	-	-	80.4
1953	100.0	18.4	14.2	-	-	-	81.6
1955	100.0	13.5	9.8	-	-	-	86.5
1957	100.0	13.6	10.3	-	-	-	86.4
1960	100.0	11.2	9.2	-	-	-	88.8
1961	100.0	9.7	7.9	-	-	-	90.3
1962	100.0	9.8	8.4	-	-	-	90.2
1963	100.0	8.2	7.3	-	-	-	91.8
1964	100.0	8.2	7.3	-	-	-	91.8
1965	100.0	7.3	6.5	-	-	-	92.7
PORTUGAL							
1925	100.0	95.9	89.7	-	-	-	4.1
1929	100.0	95.9	89.3	-	-	-	4.1
1933	100.0	95.0	92.6	-	-	-	5.0
1937	100.0	94.0	90.0	-	-	-	6.0
1938	100.0	95.2	92.5	-	-	-	4.8
1950	100.0	89.5	80.5	-	-	-	10.5
1953	100.0	80.4	74.9	-	-	-	19.6
1955	100.0	67.5	60.9	-	-	-	32.5
1957	100.0	72.0	60.8	-	-	-	28.0
1960	100.0	56.9	48.2	-	-	-	43.1
1961	100.0	56.2	48.1	-	-	-	43.8
1962	100.0	52.3	44.0	-	-	-	47.7
1963	100.0	49.3	42.1	-	-	-	50.7
1964	100.0	48.4	43.4	-	-	-	51.6
1965	100.0	48.7	44.1	-	-	-	51.3

Table III. PRIMARY ENERGY PRODUCTION PERCENTAGE DISTRIBUTION, SELECTED YEARS, 1925-1965

(Based on coal equivalents)

Region, country, year	Total primary energy production	Solid fuels		Liquid fuels		Natural gas	Hydro-electric power
		Total	Hard coal	Total	Crude oil		
	(1)	(2)	(3)	(4)	(5)	(6)	(7)
SWEDEN							
1925	100.0	32.1	29.7	-	-	-	67.9
1929	100.0	33.8	32.0	-	-	-	66.2
1933	100.0	29.8	28.0	-	-	-	70.2
1937	100.0	28.0	26.6	-	-	-	72.0
1938	100.0	25.6	24.6	-	-	-	74.4
1950	100.0	11.9	8.5	3.1	3.1	-	84.9
1953	100.0	10.4	6.5	3.2	3.2	-	86.4
1955	100.0	10.4	6.3	3.9	3.9	-	85.7
1957	100.0	9.1	5.5	3.7	3.7	-	87.2
1960	100.0	6.5	4.1	3.5	3.5	-	90.0
1961	100.0	5.1	2.8	3.2	3.2	-	91.7
1962	100.0	3.5	2.0	2.9	2.9	-	93.6
1963	100.0	3.5	1.4	2.4	2.4	-	94.2
1964	100.0	3.2	1.0	2.1	2.1	-	94.6
1965	100.0	2.5	0.7	1.4	1.4	-	96.1
SWITZERLAND							
1925	100.0	1.5	1.5	-	-	-	98.5
1929	100.0	1.0	1.0	-	-	-	99.0
1933	100.0	0.3	0.3	-	-	-	99.7
1937	100.0	0.5	0.5	-	-	-	99.5
1938	100.0	0.3	0.3	-	-	-	99.7
1950	100.0	2.2	2.2	-	-	-	97.8
1953	100.0	0.6	0.6	-	-	-	99.4
1955	100.0	0.5	0.5	-	-	-	99.5
1957	100.0	0.5	0.5	-	-	-	99.5
1960	100.0	0.4	0.4	-	-	-	99.6
1961	100.0	0.4	0.4	-	-	-	99.6
1962	100.0	0.4	0.4	-	-	-	99.6
1963	100.0	0.4	0.4	-	-	-	99.6
1964	100.0	0.3	0.3	-	-	-	99.7
1965	100.0	0.3	0.3	-	-	-	99.7
UNITED KINGDOM							
1925	100.0	99.9	99.9	0.1	0.1	-	-
1929	100.0	99.9	99.9	0.1	0.1	-	-
1933	100.0	99.9	99.9	0.1	0.1	-	-
1937	100.0	99.9	99.9	0.1	0.1	-	-
1938	100.0	99.9	99.9	0.1	0.1	-	0.1
1950	100.0	99.8	99.8	0.1	0.1	-	0.1
1953	100.0	99.8	99.8	0.1	0.1	-	0.1
1955	100.0	99.8	99.8	0.1	0.1	-	0.1
1957	100.0	99.7	99.7	0.1	0.1	-	0.2
1960	100.0	99.6	99.6	0.1	0.1	0.1	0.2
1961	100.0	99.6	99.6	0.1	0.1	0.1	0.2
1962	100.0	99.6	99.6	0.1	0.1	0.1	0.2
1963	100.0	99.6	99.6	0.1	0.1	0.1	0.2
1964	100.0	99.5	99.5	0.1	0.1	0.1	0.3
1965	100.0	99.5	99.5	0.1	0.1	0.1	0.3

Table III. PRIMARY ENERGY PRODUCTION PERCENTAGE DISTRIBUTION, SELECTED YEARS, 1925-1965

(Based on coal equivalents)

Region, country, year	Total primary energy production	Solid fuels		Liquid fuels		Natural gas	Hydro-electric power
		Total	Hard coal	Total	Crude oil		
	(1)	(2)	(3)	(4)	(5)	(6)	(7)
WESTERN EUROPE - OTHER							
1925	100.0	97.5	59.6	0.1	0.1	-	2.4
1929	100.0	96.9	59.7	0.1	0.1	-	3.0
1933	100.0	94.8	59.4	0.1	0.1	-	5.1
1937	100.0	91.4	34.8	0.1	0.1	-	8.4
1938	100.0	93.9	54.5	0.1	0.1	-	6.0
1950	100.0	93.2	56.1	0.8	0.8	0.1	5.9
1953	100.0	91.0	56.3	1.2	1.2	0.1	7.7
1955	100.0	89.3	51.3	1.6	1.6	0.2	8.9
1957	100.0	89.0	49.6	2.3	2.3	0.2	8.6
1960	100.0	85.3	43.1	4.3	4.3	0.2	10.2
1961	100.0	83.4	41.4	5.7	5.7	0.2	10.7
1962	100.0	81.7	37.7	6.4	6.4	0.3	11.6
1963	100.0	80.7	36.0	6.3	6.3	0.6	12.4
1964	100.0	80.6	33.0	6.8	6.8	0.9	11.8
1965	100.0	80.0	33.4	7.4	7.3	1.0	11.6
FINLAND							
1925	100.0	17.2	-	-	-	-	82.8
1929	100.0	9.2	-	-	-	-	90.8
1933	100.0	5.5	-	-	-	-	94.5
1937	100.0	4.1	-	-	-	-	95.9
1938	100.0	3.9	-	-	-	-	96.1
1950	100.0	17.8	-	-	-	-	82.2
1953	100.0	13.6	-	-	-	-	86.4
1955	100.0	9.4	-	-	-	-	90.6
1957	100.0	9.8	-	-	-	-	90.2
1960	100.0	8.3	-	-	-	-	91.7
1961	100.0	5.5	-	-	-	-	94.5
1962	100.0	2.5	-	-	-	-	97.5
1963	100.0	3.7	-	-	-	-	96.3
1964	100.0	3.3	-	-	-	-	96.7
1965	100.0	2.7	-	-	-	-	97.3
GREECE							
1925	100.0	98.6	-	-	-	-	1.4
1929	100.0	98.7	-	-	-	-	1.3
1933	100.0	97.1	-	-	-	-	2.9
1937	100.0	97.8	-	-	-	-	2.2
1938	100.0	97.1	-	-	-	-	2.9
1950	100.0	98.6	-	-	-	-	1.4
1953	100.0	98.3	-	-	-	-	1.7
1955	100.0	90.4	-	-	-	-	9.6
1957	100.0	91.7	-	-	-	-	8.3
1960	100.0	95.6	-	-	-	-	4.4
1961	100.0	94.8	-	-	-	-	5.2
1962	100.0	94.6	-	-	-	-	5.4
1963	100.0	94.6	-	-	-	-	5.4
1964	100.0	95.3	-	-	-	-	4.7
1965	100.0	96.4	-	-	-	-	3.6

Table III. PRIMARY ENERGY PRODUCTION PERCENTAGE DISTRIBUTION, SELECTED YEARS, 1925-1965

(Based on coal equivalents)

Region, country, year	Total primary energy production	Solid fuels		Liquid fuels		Natural gas	Hydro-electric power
		Total	Hard coal	Total	Crude oil		
	(1)	(2)	(3)	(4)	(5)	(6)	(7)
ICELAND							
1925	100.0	-	-	-	-	-	100.0
1929	100.0	-	-	-	-	-	100.0
1933	100.0	-	-	-	-	-	100.0
1937	100.0	-	-	-	-	-	100.0
1938	100.0	-	-	-	-	-	100.0
1950	100.0	6.7	-	-	-	-	93.3
1953	100.0	2.0	-	-	-	-	98.0
1955	100.0	-	-	-	-	-	100.0
1957	100.0	-	-	-	-	-	100.0
1960	100.0	-	-	-	-	-	100.0
1961	100.0	-	-	-	-	-	100.0
1962	100.0	-	-	-	-	-	100.0
1963	100.0	-	-	-	-	-	100.0
1964	100.0	-	-	-	-	-	100.0
1965	100.0	-	-	-	-	-	100.0
IRELAND							
1925	100.0	99.9	4.3	-	-	-	0.1
1929	100.0	99.8	4.6	-	-	-	0.2
1933	100.0	99.3	5.6	-	-	-	0.7
1937	100.0	98.4	6.5	-	-	-	1.6
1938	100.0	98.0	6.5	-	-	-	2.0
1950	100.0	96.7	9.6	-	-	-	3.3
1953	100.0	96.9	7.7	-	-	-	3.1
1955	100.0	97.0	9.8	-	-	-	3.0
1957	100.0	96.2	10.4	-	-	-	3.8
1960	100.0	95.1	8.8	-	-	-	4.9
1961	100.0	95.5	9.7	-	-	-	4.5
1962	100.0	96.5	8.9	-	-	-	3.5
1963	100.0	96.1	11.1	-	-	-	3.9
1964	100.0	96.3	8.3	-	-	-	3.7
1965	100.0	94.6	8.2	-	-	-	5.4
SPAIN							
1925	100.0	97.2	94.1	0.1	0.1	-	2.6
1929	100.0	96.6	93.7	0.1	0.1	-	3.3
1933	100.0	94.8	92.5	0.1	0.1	-	5.1
1937	100.0	88.0	83.9	0.4	0.4	-	11.6
1938	100.0	95.2	93.8	0.1	0.1	-	4.6
1950	100.0	94.9	89.6	-	-	-	5.1
1953	100.0	93.2	87.0	0.2	0.2	-	6.6
1955	100.0	91.9	85.6	0.4	0.4	-	7.7
1957	100.0	92.0	84.4	0.7	0.7	-	7.3
1960	100.0	87.7	82.5	0.6	0.6	-	11.7
1961	100.0	87.6	81.5	0.6	0.6	-	11.8
1962	100.0	86.9	79.1	0.6	0.6	-	12.5
1963	100.0	83.8	76.2	0.6	0.6	-	15.6
1964	100.0	83.4	75.4	0.6	0.6	-	16.0
1965	100.0	85.2	76.8	0.6	0.6	-	14.2

Table III. PRIMARY ENERGY PRODUCTION PERCENTAGE DISTRIBUTION, SELECTED YEARS, 1925-1965

(Based on coal equivalents)

Region, country, year	Total primary energy production	Solid fuels		Liquid fuels		Natural gas	Hydro-electric power
		Total	Hard coal	Total	Crude oil		
	(1)	(2)	(3)	(4)	(5)	(6)	(7)
YUGOSLAVIA							
1925	100.0	98.3	8.1	-	-	-	1.7
1929	100.0	98.8	13.3	-	-	0.1	1.1
1933	100.0	97.7	16.3	0.1	0.1	0.1	2.2
1937	100.0	97.8	15.4	0.1	0.1	0.1	2.0
1938	100.0	98.0	14.3	-	-	0.1	1.9
1950	100.0	95.4	15.8	2.3	2.3	0.3	2.0
1953	100.0	92.7	14.1	4.0	3.9	0.5	2.9
1955	100.0	91.5	12.7	4.4	4.3	0.5	3.7
1957	100.0	89.8	11.5	5.6	5.5	0.5	4.1
1960	100.0	84.2	9.0	10.0	9.9	0.5	5.3
1961	100.0	81.8	8.5	13.0	13.0	0.6	4.6
1962	100.0	79.8	7.3	14.2	14.1	0.8	5.3
1963	100.0	79.6	7.1	13.4	13.4	1.4	5.6
1964	100.0	79.3	6.5	14.0	13.9	1.9	4.9
1965	100.0	76.9	5.9	15.4	15.3	2.2	5.5
OCEANIA							
1925	100.0	99.5	93.3	-	-	-	0.5
1929	100.0	99.0	89.3	-	-	-	1.0
1933	100.0	98.5	86.7	-	-	-	1.5
1937	100.0	98.4	86.5	-	-	-	1.6
1938	100.0	98.3	85.9	-	-	-	1.7
1950	100.0	97.4	79.0	-	-	-	2.6
1953	100.0	96.9	77.0	-	-	-	3.1
1955	100.0	96.7	75.8	-	-	-	3.3
1957	100.0	95.9	75.1	-	-	-	4.1
1960	100.0	95.9	72.7	-	-	-	4.1
1961	100.0	95.8	72.8	-	-	-	4.2
1962	100.0	95.3	71.6	-	-	-	4.7
1963	100.0	94.8	70.0	-	-	-	5.2
1964	100.0	94.1	70.0	0.8	0.8	-	5.1
1965	100.0	93.5	71.1	1.2	1.2	-	5.2
AUSTRALIA							
1925	100.0	99.7	98.1	-	-	-	0.3
1929	100.0	99.5	95.5	-	-	-	0.5
1933	100.0	99.3	92.8	-	-	-	0.7
1937	100.0	99.3	92.8	-	-	-	0.7
1938	100.0	99.3	92.1	-	-	-	0.7
1950	100.0	99.0	84.9	-	-	-	1.0
1953	100.0	99.0	82.7	-	-	-	1.0
1955	100.0	98.9	81.4	-	-	-	1.1
1957	100.0	98.3	80.8	-	-	-	1.7
1960	100.0	98.1	78.3	-	-	-	1.9
1961	100.0	98.1	78.2	-	-	-	1.9
1962	100.0	97.9	76.4	-	-	-	2.1
1963	100.0	97.2	75.0	-	-	-	2.7
1964	100.0	96.5	75.0	0.9	0.9	-	2.6
1965	100.0	95.9	75.4	1.3	1.3	-	2.7

Table III. PRIMARY ENERGY PRODUCTION PERCENTAGE DISTRIBUTION, SELECTED YEARS, 1925-1965

(Based on coal equivalents)

Region, country, year	Total primary energy production	Solid fuels		Liquid fuels		Natural gas	Hydro-electric power
		Total	Hard coal	Total	Crude oil		
	(1)	(2)	(3)	(4)	(5)	(6)	(7)
NEW ZEALAND							
1925	100.0	98.0	56.6	-	-	-	2.0
1929	100.0	96.5	59.6	-	-	-	3.5
1933	100.0	93.6	51.0	0.1	0.1	-	6.4
1937	100.0	92.6	46.8	0.1	0.1	-	7.4
1938	100.0	91.6	47.7	0.1	0.1	-	8.3
1950	100.0	85.9	36.6	0.1	0.1	-	14.0
1953	100.0	80.7	30.7	0.1	0.1	-	19.3
1955	100.0	78.7	29.8	0.1	0.1	-	21.2
1957	100.0	76.2	29.9	0.1	0.1	-	23.8
1960	100.0	78.1	25.8	-	-	-	21.9
1961	100.0	76.2	24.6	-	-	-	23.8
1962	100.0	71.1	24.3	0.1	0.1	-	28.9
1963	100.0	72.1	21.9	-	-	-	27.9
1964	100.0	70.6	21.0	-	-	-	29.4
1965	100.0	66.7	20.9	-	-	-	33.2
USSR AND COMMUNIST EASTERN EUROPE							
1925	100.0	81.7	60.9	16.7	16.7	1.5	0.1
1929	100.0	79.6	63.6	18.9	18.8	1.4	0.1
1933	100.0	72.0	58.4	25.5	25.3	2.3	0.1
1937	100.0	75.7	61.8	21.5	21.3	2.5	0.2
1938	100.0	75.8	62.0	21.6	21.4	2.4	0.3
1950	100.0	83.1	58.2	14.2	14.1	2.3	0.4
1953	100.0	80.5	55.3	16.4	16.4	2.6	0.5
1955	100.0	78.8	54.2	18.1	18.0	2.6	0.5
1957	100.0	74.6	51.0	20.7	20.7	4.0	0.7
1960	100.0	67.1	46.0	25.0	24.9	7.2	0.7
1961	100.0	64.2	43.7	26.3	26.3	8.7	0.8
1962	100.0	61.6	42.3	27.5	27.5	10.1	0.9
1963	100.0	59.7	40.2	28.1	28.1	11.3	0.9
1964	100.0	58.2	39.1	28.2	28.1	12.8	0.8
1965	100.0	56.3	38.2	28.8	28.7	14.1	0.8
COMMUNIST EASTERN EUROPE							
1925	100.0	90.8	65.7	7.3	7.3	1.9	0.1
1929	100.0	89.2	68.0	8.9	8.8	1.8	-
1933	100.0	78.0	57.5	18.0	17.6	3.9	0.1
1937	100.0	82.0	62.2	14.0	13.4	3.9	0.1
1938	100.0	83.0	63.8	13.1	12.6	3.8	0.1
1950	100.0	93.2	54.9	5.0	4.8	1.7	0.2
1953	100.0	90.2	49.8	7.0	6.9	2.7	0.1
1955	100.0	89.4	47.8	7.7	7.6	2.7	0.2
1957	100.0	89.3	46.0	7.4	7.3	3.1	0.2
1960	100.0	88.7	45.7	7.1	7.0	3.9	0.3
1961	100.0	88.7	44.4	7.0	6.9	4.0	0.2
1962	100.0	88.3	43.8	7.0	6.8	4.5	0.3
1963	100.0	88.0	43.3	6.9	6.7	5.0	0.2
1964	100.0	87.8	43.1	6.7	6.6	5.3	0.2
1965	100.0	87.0	43.0	6.8	6.7	5.8	0.3

Table III. PRIMARY ENERGY PRODUCTION PERCENTAGE DISTRIBUTION, SELECTED YEARS, 1925-1965

(Based on coal equivalents)

Region, country, year	Total primary energy production	Solid fuels		Liquid fuels		Natural gas	Hydro-electric power
		Total	Hard coal	Total	Crude oil		
	(1)	(2)	(3)	(4)	(5)	(6)	(7)
ALBANIA							
1925	100.0	100.0	-	-	-	-	-
1929	100.0	100.0	-	-	-	-	-
1933	100.0	33.3	-	66.7	66.7	-	-
1937	100.0	1.4	-	98.6	98.6	-	-
1938	100.0	1.2	-	98.8	98.8	-	-
1950	100.0	9.4	-	90.6	90.6	-	-
1953	100.0	18.9	-	80.3	80.3	-	0.9
1955	100.0	23.6	-	75.6	75.6	-	0.8
1957	100.0	13.7	-	85.4	85.4	-	0.9
1960	100.0	11.6	-	87.2	87.2	-	1.2
1961	100.0	11.0	-	88.0	88.0	-	1.0
1962	100.0	11.2	-	87.7	87.7	-	1.1
1963	100.0	9.9	-	88.5	88.5	-	1.6
1964	100.0	11.1	-	87.0	87.0	-	1.9
1965	100.0	12.4	-	85.3	85.3	-	2.2
BULGARIA							
1925	100.0	99.5	13.9	-	-	-	0.5
1929	100.0	98.9	14.2	-	-	-	1.1
1933	100.0	98.2	15.0	-	-	-	1.8
1937	100.0	97.5	18.4	-	-	-	2.5
1938	100.0	97.6	19.6	-	-	-	2.4
1950	100.0	98.0	8.1	-	-	-	2.0
1953	100.0	97.9	9.8	-	-	-	2.1
1955	100.0	91.3	8.3	6.4	6.4	-	2.3
1957	100.0	87.1	9.3	10.3	10.3	-	2.6
1960	100.0	90.7	9.9	5.2	5.2	-	4.1
1961	100.0	91.4	9.5	5.0	5.0	-	3.6
1962	100.0	92.6	9.2	4.3	4.3	-	3.1
1963	100.0	92.8	9.1	3.6	3.6	-	3.6
1964	100.0	94.8	7.5	2.9	2.9	-	2.3
1965	100.0	93.0	6.5	4.0	4.0	-	2.9
CZECHOSLOVAKIA							
1925	100.0	99.8	52.8	0.1	0.1	-	0.1
1929	100.0	99.8	54.9	0.1	0.1	-	0.1
1933	100.0	99.7	53.7	0.1	0.1	-	0.1
1937	100.0	99.6	60.6	0.1	0.1	-	0.3
1938	100.0	99.6	62.0	0.1	0.1	-	0.3
1950	100.0	99.3	52.4	0.3	0.3	0.1	0.4
1953	100.0	98.7	47.2	0.5	0.5	0.6	0.3
1955	100.0	98.6	45.1	0.4	0.4	0.5	0.5
1957	100.0	97.3	41.3	0.3	0.3	1.9	0.5
1960	100.0	96.5	41.3	0.3	0.3	2.7	0.5
1961	100.0	96.7	38.8	0.3	0.3	2.5	0.5
1962	100.0	97.1	38.3	0.4	0.4	2.0	0.5
1963	100.0	97.5	38.1	0.4	0.4	1.8	0.4
1964	100.0	97.5	37.4	0.4	0.4	1.7	0.5
1965	100.0	97.3	37.7	0.4	0.4	1.5	0.8

Table III. PRIMARY ENERGY PRODUCTION PERCENTAGE DISTRIBUTION, SELECTED YEARS, 1925-1965

(Based on coal equivalents)

Region, country, year	Total primary energy production	Solid fuels		Liquid fuels		Natural gas	Hydro-electric power
		Total	Hard coal	Total	Crude oil		
	(1)	(2)	(3)	(4)	(5)	(6)	(7)
GERMANY, EAST							
1950	100.0	99.9	6.3	-	-	-	0.1
1953	100.0	99.9	4.8	-	-	-	0.1
1955	100.0	99.9	4.2	-	-	-	0.1
1957	100.0	99.9	4.1	-	-	-	0.1
1960	100.0	99.9	3.8	-	-	-	0.1
1961	100.0	99.9	3.6	-	-	-	0.1
1962	100.0	99.9	3.3	-	-	-	0.1
1963	100.0	99.7	3.1	-	-	0.2	0.1
1964	100.0	99.7	2.9	-	-	0.2	0.1
1965	100.0	99.6	2.8	-	-	0.2	0.1
HUNGARY							
1925	100.0	100.0	19.6	-	-	-	-
1929	100.0	100.0	16.3	-	-	-	-
1933	100.0	99.9	18.4	-	-	0.1	-
1937	100.0	99.8	15.9	0.1	0.1	0.1	-
1938	100.0	98.7	17.1	1.1	1.1	0.2	-
1950	100.0	86.9	14.3	7.8	7.8	5.2	0.1
1953	100.0	87.0	12.9	8.2	8.2	4.7	-
1955	100.0	82.2	15.3	13.6	13.6	4.1	-
1957	100.0	89.7	15.0	6.7	6.7	3.6	-
1960	100.0	88.0	14.7	9.6	9.4	2.3	0.1
1961	100.0	87.3	14.8	10.6	10.5	2.1	-
1962	100.0	86.3	15.6	11.6	11.5	2.1	-
1963	100.0	85.0	16.0	11.4	11.3	3.5	-
1964	100.0	84.5	16.9	11.2	11.1	4.3	-
1965	100.0	83.1	17.6	11.0	10.9	5.9	-
POLAND							
1925	100.0	93.7	93.6	4.0	3.9	2.3	-
1929	100.0	96.5	96.4	2.2	2.1	1.3	-
1933	100.0	94.8	94.7	3.1	2.9	2.1	-
1937	100.0	96.0	96.0	2.1	2.0	1.9	-
1938	100.0	96.0	95.9	2.1	1.9	2.0	-
1950	100.0	99.3	97.5	0.3	0.3	0.3	0.1
1953	100.0	99.1	97.3	0.3	0.3	0.5	0.1
1955	100.0	99.1	97.2	0.3	0.3	0.5	0.1
1957	100.0	99.0	97.2	0.3	0.3	0.6	0.1
1960	100.0	99.0	96.4	0.3	0.3	0.7	0.1
1961	100.0	98.7	96.0	0.3	0.3	0.9	0.1
1962	100.0	98.7	95.8	0.3	0.3	1.0	0.1
1963	100.0	98.5	94.7	0.3	0.3	1.1	0.1
1964	100.0	98.3	93.4	0.4	0.3	1.3	0.1
1965	100.0	98.1	92.8	0.4	0.4	1.4	0.1
ROMANIA							
1925	100.0	32.1	5.3	59.4	59.2	8.4	0.1
1929	100.0	19.0	3.6	70.5	69.9	10.4	0.1
1933	100.0	6.9	1.4	79.1	77.3	14.0	0.1
1937	100.0	9.3	2.0	73.1	70.1	17.5	0.1
1938	100.0	12.5	2.4	70.4	67.6	16.9	0.1

Table III. PRIMARY ENERGY PRODUCTION PERCENTAGE DISTRIBUTION, SELECTED YEARS, 1925-1965

(Based on coal equivalents)

Region, country, year	Total primary energy production	Solid fuels		Liquid fuels		Natural gas	Hydro-electric power
		Total	Hard coal	Total	Crude oil		
	(1)	(2)	(3)	(4)	(5)	(6)	(7)
ROMANIA (CONTINUED)							
1950	100.0	19.1	1.7	61.7	59.9	19.0	0.2
1953	100.0	14.9	0.9	63.6	62.2	21.3	0.1
1955	100.0	14.8	0.8	64.0	62.8	21.0	0.2
1957	100.0	15.7	0.9	61.9	60.7	22.3	0.1
1960	100.0	16.0	1.0	56.2	54.9	27.6	0.2
1961	100.0	16.3	1.1	54.3	52.9	29.2	0.2
1962	100.0	16.9	1.0	50.4	49.1	32.5	0.2
1963	100.0	16.8	1.0	48.4	47.1	34.5	0.2
1964	100.0	16.7	1.0	47.1	45.8	36.0	0.2
1965	100.0	17.9	1.0	44.5	43.2	37.3	0.3
USSR (INCLUDING ESTONIA, LATVIA, LITHUANIA)							
1925	100.0	59.8	49.3	39.4	39.4	0.7	0.1
1929	100.0	64.2	56.4	34.9	34.9	0.7	0.1
1933	100.0	68.2	59.0	30.3	30.3	1.4	0.1
1937	100.0	72.5	61.6	25.5	25.5	1.7	0.3
1938	100.0	72.3	61.2	25.7	25.7	1.7	0.4
1950	100.0	76.8	60.2	20.0	20.0	2.6	0.5
1953	100.0	74.5	58.7	22.3	22.3	2.5	0.7
1955	100.0	73.0	57.7	23.7	23.7	2.6	0.6
1957	100.0	67.7	53.3	27.0	27.0	4.4	0.9
1960	100.0	57.7	46.2	32.7	32.7	8.7	0.9
1961	100.0	53.8	43.3	34.5	34.5	10.7	1.0
1962	100.0	50.5	41.7	36.0	36.0	12.4	1.1
1963	100.0	48.4	39.0	36.6	36.6	13.9	1.1
1964	100.0	46.8	37.6	36.4	36.4	15.7	1.1
1965	100.0	45.2	36.4	36.7	36.7	17.1	1.0
COMMUNIST ASIA							
1925	100.0	100.0	100.0	-	-	-	-
1929	100.0	100.0	100.0	-	-	-	-
1933	100.0	99.5	99.5	0.5	0.5	-	-
1937	100.0	99.1	99.1	0.9	0.9	-	-
1938	100.0	98.6	98.6	1.4	1.4	-	-
1950	100.0	97.8	96.7	0.7	0.7	-	1.5
1953	100.0	98.1	97.9	1.4	1.4	-	0.5
1955	100.0	97.7	97.3	1.5	1.5	-	0.8
1957	100.0	97.3	96.9	1.7	1.7	-	1.0
1960	100.0	95.4	94.9	3.6	3.6	-	1.0
1961	100.0	95.6	95.1	3.6	3.6	-	0.8
1962	100.0	95.3	94.8	3.9	3.9	-	0.8
1963	100.0	95.3	94.8	4.0	4.0	-	0.8
1964	100.0	95.1	94.6	4.2	4.2	-	0.8
1965	100.0	94.5	94.1	4.7	4.7	-	0.8
LATIN AMERICA							
1925	100.0	8.3	8.1	88.2	88.1	2.6	1.0
1929	100.0	5.3	5.2	90.4	90.1	3.4	0.9
1933	100.0	5.4	5.2	88.3	87.7	5.2	1.1
1937	100.0	5.6	5.5	87.8	87.3	5.6	1.0
1938	100.0	5.6	5.5	87.3	86.8	6.0	1.0
1950	100.0	3.5	3.4	91.6	91.1	3.8	1.1

Table III. PRIMARY ENERGY PRODUCTION PERCENTAGE DISTRIBUTION, SELECTED YEARS, 1925-1965

(Based on coal equivalents)

Region, country, year	Total primary energy production	Solid fuels		Liquid fuels		Natural gas	Hydro-electric power
		Total	Hard coal	Total	Crude oil		
	(1)	(2)	(3)	(4)	(5)	(6)	(7)
LATIN AMERICA (CONTINUED)							
1953	100.0	3.5	3.4	90.5	90.0	4.8	1.2
1955	100.0	3.1	3.1	90.9	90.4	4.8	1.1
1957	100.0	2.5	2.4	91.3	90.7	5.1	1.1
1960	100.0	2.4	2.4	88.6	87.6	7.7	1.3
1961	100.0	2.5	2.4	88.1	87.1	8.2	1.3
1962	100.0	2.4	2.4	88.1	87.2	8.2	1.3
1963	100.0	2.4	2.4	87.6	86.6	8.7	1.3
1964	100.0	2.4	2.4	86.7	85.8	9.5	1.4
1965	100.0	2.4	2.4	86.5	85.5	9.6	1.5
LATIN AMERICA - CARIBBEAN							
1925	100.0	4.6	4.6	94.1	94.1	0.9	0.4
1929	100.0	2.4	2.4	95.4	95.3	1.9	0.4
1933	100.0	1.9	1.9	94.4	94.1	3.2	0.5
1937	100.0	2.7	2.7	92.9	92.7	4.0	0.5
1938	100.0	2.4	2.4	92.4	92.2	4.7	0.5
1950	100.0	1.3	1.3	95.5	95.1	2.9	0.3
1953	100.0	1.5	1.5	94.2	93.6	4.0	0.3
1955	100.0	1.5	1.5	94.1	93.6	4.1	0.4
1957	100.0	1.3	1.3	94.1	93.6	4.3	0.3
1960	100.0	1.5	1.5	91.1	90.1	7.0	0.4
1961	100.0	1.5	1.5	91.0	89.9	7.2	0.4
1962	100.0	1.5	1.5	91.1	90.2	7.0	0.4
1963	100.0	1.6	1.6	90.6	89.7	7.3	0.5
1964	100.0	1.5	1.5	89.9	88.9	8.2	0.5
1965	100.0	1.4	1.4	89.8	88.8	8.2	0.5
CARIBBEAN - OIL PRODUCING							
1925	100.0	4.6	4.6	94.2	94.2	0.9	0.3
1929	100.0	2.4	2.4	95.4	95.3	1.9	0.3
1933	100.0	1.9	1.9	94.4	94.2	3.2	0.4
1937	100.0	2.7	2.7	92.9	92.7	4.0	0.4
1938	100.0	2.4	2.4	92.5	92.3	4.7	0.4
1950	100.0	1.3	1.3	95.5	95.1	2.9	0.2
1953	100.0	1.5	1.5	94.2	93.7	4.0	0.3
1955	100.0	1.5	1.5	94.1	93.7	4.1	0.3
1957	100.0	1.3	1.3	94.1	93.6	4.3	0.3
1960	100.0	1.5	1.5	91.2	90.2	7.0	0.3
1961	100.0	1.5	1.5	91.0	89.9	7.2	0.3
1962	100.0	1.5	1.5	91.2	90.2	7.0	0.3
1963	100.0	1.6	1.6	90.7	89.7	7.3	0.4
1964	100.0	1.5	1.5	89.9	89.0	8.2	0.4
1965	100.0	1.4	1.4	89.9	88.9	8.2	0.5
COLOMBIA							
1925	100.0	30.5	30.5	66.0	66.0	-	3.5
1929	100.0	2.2	2.2	97.5	97.5	-	0.3
1933	100.0	3.9	3.9	95.6	95.6	-	0.5
1937	100.0	9.1	9.1	90.4	90.4	-	0.5
1938	100.0	8.4	8.4	91.1	91.1	-	0.5

Table III. PRIMARY ENERGY PRODUCTION PERCENTAGE DISTRIBUTION, SELECTED YEARS, 1925-1965

(Based on coal equivalents)

Region, country, year	Total primary energy production	Solid fuels: Total	Solid fuels: Hard coal	Liquid fuels: Total	Liquid fuels: Crude oil	Natural gas	Hydro-electric power
	(1)	(2)	(3)	(4)	(5)	(6)	(7)
COLOMBIA (CONTINUED)							
1950	100.0	12.4	12.4	86.5	86.5	-	1.1
1953	100.0	12.9	12.9	85.8	85.8	-	1.3
1955	100.0	18.0	18.0	80.2	80.2	-	1.8
1957	100.0	17.0	17.0	80.8	80.8	-	2.1
1960	100.0	17.3	17.3	76.9	75.8	3.6	2.2
1961	100.0	18.2	18.2	75.8	74.7	3.8	2.2
1962	100.0	20.2	20.2	72.2	71.2	5.3	2.3
1963	100.0	18.8	18.8	73.4	72.5	5.5	2.4
1964	100.0	17.1	17.1	73.9	73.5	6.3	2.7
1965	100.0	15.9	15.9	75.7	75.3	6.1	2.4
MEXICO							
1925	100.0	5.1	5.1	93.8	93.8	0.7	0.4
1929	100.0	9.1	9.1	87.1	87.0	2.5	1.2
1933	100.0	7.3	7.3	86.2	85.8	4.7	1.8
1937	100.0	9.6	9.6	78.5	78.1	10.1	1.8
1938	100.0	9.8	9.8	74.8	74.3	13.3	2.1
1950	100.0	4.7	4.7	81.9	80.6	12.1	1.3
1953	100.0	6.8	6.8	75.0	73.6	16.7	1.6
1955	100.0	5.2	5.2	75.6	74.3	17.5	1.7
1957	100.0	5.1	5.1	71.1	68.6	22.0	1.7
1960	100.0	4.6	4.6	60.0	55.6	33.6	1.7
1961	100.0	4.5	4.5	60.6	56.2	33.4	1.6
1962	100.0	4.5	4.5	60.8	56.7	33.1	1.6
1963	100.0	4.6	4.6	59.7	55.3	34.0	1.7
1964	100.0	4.4	4.4	56.1	51.1	37.7	1.8
1965	100.0	4.1	4.1	56.2	51.1	37.6	2.2
TRINIDAD AND TOBAGO							
1925	100.0	-	-	91.1	91.1	8.9	-
1929	100.0	-	-	91.1	91.1	8.9	-
1933	100.0	-	-	91.1	91.1	8.9	-
1937	100.0	-	-	91.1	91.1	8.9	-
1938	100.0	-	-	91.1	91.1	8.9	-
1950	100.0	-	-	87.5	86.8	12.5	-
1953	100.0	-	-	87.8	86.9	12.2	-
1955	100.0	-	-	88.9	88.1	11.1	-
1957	100.0	-	-	90.1	89.5	9.9	-
1960	100.0	-	-	89.8	89.5	10.2	-
1961	100.0	-	-	89.8	89.5	10.2	-
1962	100.0	-	-	90.2	89.9	9.8	-
1963	100.0	-	-	90.3	90.1	9.7	-
1964	100.0	-	-	88.0	87.7	12.0	-
1965	100.0	-	-	86.9	86.6	13.1	-
VENEZUELA							
1925	100.0	0.6	0.6	99.4	99.4	-	0.1
1929	100.0	0.1	0.1	98.5	98.3	1.4	-
1933	100.0	-	-	97.3	97.0	2.7	-
1937	100.0	-	-	97.8	97.6	2.1	-
1938	100.0	-	-	97.4	97.2	2.5	-

Table III. PRIMARY ENERGY PRODUCTION PERCENTAGE DISTRIBUTION, SELECTED YEARS, 1925-1965

(Based on coal equivalents)

Region, country, year	Total primary energy production	Solid fuels		Liquid fuels		Natural gas	Hydro-electric power
		Total	Hard coal	Total	Crude oil		
	(1)	(2)	(3)	(4)	(5)	(6)	(7)
VENEZUELA (CONTINUED)							
1950	100.0	-	-	98.7	98.4	1.2	-
1953	100.0	-	-	97.9	97.5	2.0	-
1955	100.0	-	-	97.9	97.5	2.1	-
1957	100.0	-	-	97.8	97.5	2.2	-
1960	100.0	-	-	97.3	96.8	2.6	-
1961	100.0	-	-	97.3	96.7	2.7	-
1962	100.0	-	-	97.3	96.8	2.7	-
1963	100.0	-	-	97.1	96.6	2.8	0.1
1964	100.0	-	-	97.0	96.7	2.9	0.1
1965	100.0	-	-	96.9	96.6	3.0	0.1
CARIBBEAN - OTHER							
1925	100.0	-	-	-	-	-	100.0
1929	100.0	-	-	-	-	-	100.0
1933	100.0	-	-	21.3	12.8	-	78.7
1937	100.0	-	-	25.3	11.2	-	74.7
1938	100.0	-	-	37.4	22.0	-	62.6
1950	100.0	-	-	22.6	20.5	1.8	75.6
1953	100.0	-	-	3.5	2.3	4.2	92.3
1955	100.0	-	-	34.2	33.5	2.4	63.3
1957	100.0	-	-	34.3	34.3	1.8	63.9
1960	100.0	-	-	9.6	9.6	1.2	89.1
1961	100.0	-	-	6.9	6.9	1.8	91.3
1962	100.0	-	-	8.2	8.2	1.8	90.0
1963	100.0	-	-	16.8	16.8	1.9	81.3
1964	100.0	-	-	19.2	19.2	1.4	79.4
1965	100.0	-	-	16.9	16.9	1.2	81.9
CUBA							
1925	100.0	-	-	-	-	-	100.0
1929	100.0	-	-	-	-	-	100.0
1933	100.0	-	-	81.1	48.6	-	18.9
1937	100.0	-	-	85.0	37.8	-	15.0
1938	100.0	-	-	91.5	53.8	-	8.5
1950	100.0	-	-	95.3	86.6	-	4.7
1953	100.0	-	-	69.2	46.2	-	30.8
1955	100.0	-	-	96.8	94.8	-	3.2
1957	100.0	-	-	96.8	96.8	-	3.2
1960	100.0	-	-	89.4	89.4	-	10.6
1961	100.0	-	-	84.5	84.5	-	15.5
1962	100.0	-	-	85.2	85.2	-	14.8
1963	100.0	-	-	88.2	88.2	-	11.8
1964	100.0	-	-	81.6	81.6	-	18.4
1965	100.0	-	-	80.1	80.1	-	19.9
PANAMA CANAL ZONE							
1925	100.0	-	-	-	-	-	100.0
1929	100.0	-	-	-	-	-	100.0
1933	100.0	-	-	-	-	-	100.0
1937	100.0	-	-	-	-	-	100.0
1938	100.0	-	-	-	-	-	100.0

Table III. PRIMARY ENERGY PRODUCTION PERCENTAGE DISTRIBUTION, SELECTED YEARS, 1925-1965

(Based on coal equivalents)

Region, country, year	Total primary energy production	Solid fuels		Liquid fuels		Natural gas	Hydro-electric power
		Total	Hard coal	Total	Crude oil		
	(1)	(2)	(3)	(4)	(5)	(6)	(7)
PANAMA CANAL ZONE (CONTINUED)							
1950	100.0	-	-	-	-	-	100.0
1953	100.0	-	-	-	-	-	100.0
1955	100.0	-	-	-	-	-	100.0
1957	100.0	-	-	-	-	-	100.0
1960	100.0	-	-	-	-	-	100.0
1961	100.0	-	-	-	-	-	100.0
1962	100.0	-	-	-	-	-	100.0
1963	100.0	-	-	-	-	-	100.0
1964	100.0	-	-	-	-	-	100.0
1965	100.0	-	-	-	-	-	100.0
PUERTO RICO							
1925	-	-	-	-	-	-	-
1929	100.0	-	-	-	-	-	100.0
1933	100.0	-	-	-	-	-	100.0
1937	100.0	-	-	-	-	-	100.0
1938	100.0	-	-	-	-	-	100.0
1950	100.0	-	-	-	-	-	100.0
1953	100.0	-	-	-	-	-	100.0
1955	100.0	-	-	-	-	-	100.0
1957	100.0	-	-	-	-	-	100.0
1960	100.0	-	-	-	-	-	100.0
1961	100.0	-	-	-	-	-	100.0
1962	100.0	-	-	-	-	-	100.0
1963	100.0	-	-	-	-	-	100.0
1964	100.0	-	-	-	-	-	100.0
1965	100.0	-	-	-	-	-	100.0
LATIN AMERICA - OTHER							
1925	100.0	28.8	27.7	54.5	54.3	12.3	4.4
1929	100.0	22.4	21.6	61.3	59.6	12.5	3.8
1933	100.0	19.9	19.2	62.8	60.8	13.6	3.8
1937	100.0	20.7	20.2	61.9	60.1	13.8	3.6
1938	100.0	22.0	21.5	61.0	59.4	13.1	3.9
1950	100.0	24.2	23.3	55.6	54.4	12.2	8.0
1953	100.0	22.0	21.4	56.5	55.2	12.6	8.9
1955	100.0	19.7	19.2	58.7	57.6	12.5	9.1
1957	100.0	15.4	15.1	61.4	60.4	13.2	10.0
1960	100.0	9.7	9.6	68.8	68.2	13.3	8.3
1961	100.0	8.8	8.7	69.3	68.7	14.8	7.2
1962	100.0	8.1	8.1	68.7	68.2	16.3	6.9
1963	100.0	7.6	7.5	68.1	67.5	17.4	6.9
1964	100.0	8.6	8.6	66.6	65.9	17.7	7.1
1965	100.0	8.6	8.6	64.9	64.0	18.7	7.8
ARGENTINA							
1925	100.0	-	-	89.3	89.3	10.2	0.5
1929	100.0	-	-	87.5	86.5	11.9	0.6
1933	100.0	-	-	86.8	85.8	12.9	0.3
1937	100.0	-	-	86.1	85.2	13.6	0.3
1938	100.0	-	-	87.0	86.3	12.8	0.2

Table III. PRIMARY ENERGY PRODUCTION PERCENTAGE DISTRIBUTION, SELECTED YEARS, 1925-1965

(Based on coal equivalents)

Region, country, year	Total primary energy production	Solid fuels: Total	Solid fuels: Hard coal	Liquid fuels: Total	Liquid fuels: Crude oil	Natural gas	Hydro-electric power
	(1)	(2)	(3)	(4)	(5)	(6)	(7)
ARGENTINA (CONTINUED)							
1950	100.0	1.5	0.4	86.0	85.8	12.1	0.4
1953	100.0	1.4	1.1	85.1	84.9	12.9	0.6
1955	100.0	2.0	1.8	85.1	84.9	12.4	0.5
1957	100.0	2.7	2.4	83.5	83.3	13.0	0.8
1960	100.0	1.8	1.8	85.9	85.8	11.5	0.7
1961	100.0	1.6	1.6	83.3	83.3	14.4	0.6
1962	100.0	1.1	1.1	82.7	82.7	15.6	0.6
1963	100.0	0.8	0.8	81.0	80.9	17.6	0.6
1964	100.0	1.3	1.2	79.7	79.6	18.5	0.6
1965	100.0	1.4	1.4	77.3	77.2	20.8	0.6
BOLIVIA							
1925	100.0	-	-	-	-	-	100.0
1929	100.0	-	-	64.3	64.3	-	35.7
1933	100.0	-	-	86.6	86.6	-	13.4
1937	100.0	-	-	85.7	85.7	-	14.3
1938	100.0	-	-	82.8	82.8	-	17.2
1950	100.0	-	-	83.5	83.5	-	16.5
1953	100.0	-	-	78.9	78.9	-	21.1
1955	100.0	-	-	92.2	92.2	1.4	6.4
1957	100.0	-	-	92.8	92.8	1.4	5.8
1960	100.0	-	-	92.5	92.5	1.1	6.4
1961	100.0	-	-	89.3	89.3	3.3	7.4
1962	100.0	-	-	86.8	86.8	5.7	7.5
1963	100.0	-	-	83.4	83.4	9.7	6.9
1964	100.0	-	-	78.7	78.7	14.6	6.8
1965	100.0	-	-	77.6	77.6	15.9	6.4
BRAZIL							
1925	100.0	62.6	62.6	-	-	-	37.4
1929	100.0	56.8	56.8	-	-	-	43.2
1933	100.0	65.9	65.9	-	-	-	34.1
1937	100.0	66.5	66.5	-	-	-	33.5
1938	100.0	68.5	68.5	-	-	-	31.5
1950	100.0	62.6	62.6	2.5	2.5	0.3	34.6
1953	100.0	55.1	55.1	5.9	5.9	1.2	37.8
1955	100.0	51.1	51.1	10.7	10.7	2.2	36.0
1957	100.0	29.8	29.8	34.3	34.3	3.7	32.2
1960	100.0	18.0	18.0	54.0	54.0	6.6	21.4
1961	100.0	16.7	16.7	57.4	57.4	5.9	19.9
1962	100.0	17.5	17.5	55.1	55.1	5.7	21.7
1963	100.0	17.2	17.2	56.5	56.5	5.4	20.9
1964	100.0	21.2	21.2	51.4	51.4	5.6	21.8
1965	100.0	20.6	20.6	49.4	49.4	6.7	23.4
CHILE							
1925	100.0	96.5	91.7	-	-	-	3.5
1929	100.0	95.8	91.2	-	-	-	4.2
1933	100.0	95.4	90.9	-	-	-	4.6
1937	100.0	95.2	92.0	-	-	-	4.8
1938	100.0	95.3	92.2	-	-	-	4.7

Table III. PRIMARY ENERGY PRODUCTION PERCENTAGE DISTRIBUTION, SELECTED YEARS, 1925-1965

(Based on coal equivalents)

Region, country, year	Total primary energy production	Solid fuels		Liquid fuels		Natural gas	Hydro-electric power
		Total	Hard coal	Total	Crude oil		
	(1)	(2)	(3)	(4)	(5)	(6)	(7)
CHILE (CONTINUED)							
1950	100.0	81.5	77.9	4.9	4.9	5.3	8.3
1953	100.0	76.0	72.9	9.0	8.6	6.1	8.9
1955	100.0	64.4	61.9	16.9	16.5	9.2	9.5
1957	100.0	52.3	50.6	25.2	24.5	13.5	9.1
1960	100.0	30.6	30.1	33.3	32.8	27.5	8.6
1961	100.0	28.5	27.9	33.7	33.1	30.6	7.2
1962	100.0	24.6	24.1	34.8	33.7	34.5	6.1
1963	100.0	21.3	20.9	37.7	35.6	35.2	5.9
1964	100.0	22.2	21.8	39.1	36.6	32.4	6.4
1965	100.0	22.2	21.9	38.4	34.3	32.6	6.8
ECUADOR							
1925	100.0	-	-	92.0	92.0	-	8.0
1929	100.0	-	-	99.0	99.0	-	1.0
1933	100.0	-	-	95.8	95.8	3.3	0.8
1937	100.0	-	-	87.1	85.9	12.3	0.6
1938	100.0	-	-	85.5	84.4	13.9	0.6
1950	100.0	-	-	74.3	71.8	24.2	1.5
1953	100.0	-	-	74.3	71.2	24.3	1.4
1955	100.0	-	-	77.2	74.1	21.2	1.6
1957	100.0	-	-	75.2	72.0	22.8	2.0
1960	100.0	-	-	72.0	69.0	25.2	2.8
1961	100.0	-	-	72.8	69.9	24.1	3.0
1962	100.0	-	-	70.0	67.2	26.3	3.7
1963	100.0	-	-	68.9	66.0	27.1	4.0
1964	100.0	-	-	71.4	68.6	24.8	3.8
1965	100.0	-	-	72.3	69.4	24.0	3.7
PERU							
1925	100.0	4.0	4.0	72.5	71.9	22.7	0.7
1929	100.0	5.8	5.8	73.5	70.4	20.2	0.5
1933	100.0	0.8	0.8	75.2	70.9	23.4	0.6
1937	100.0	2.0	2.0	75.1	71.3	22.3	0.6
1938	100.0	1.7	1.7	75.0	71.1	22.4	0.9
1950	100.0	4.4	4.4	72.1	68.2	21.8	1.7
1953	100.0	4.4	4.4	71.2	67.2	22.0	2.5
1955	100.0	2.7	2.7	72.7	68.9	21.9	2.7
1957	100.0	2.5	2.5	71.3	67.9	23.4	2.8
1960	100.0	2.9	2.9	72.9	70.0	20.2	3.9
1961	100.0	3.0	3.0	73.2	70.1	19.6	4.2
1962	100.0	2.7	2.7	73.6	70.8	19.6	4.1
1963	100.0	2.2	2.2	73.1	71.1	20.3	4.5
1964	100.0	1.7	1.7	72.5	70.0	21.2	4.6
1965	100.0	1.3	1.3	74.0	71.6	19.6	5.1
URUGUAY							
1925	-	-	-	-	-	-	-
1929	-	-	-	-	-	-	-
1933	-	-	-	-	-	-	-
1937	-	-	-	-	-	-	-
1938	-	-	-	-	-	-	-
1950	100.0	-	-	-	-	2.0	98.0

Table III. PRIMARY ENERGY PRODUCTION PERCENTAGE DISTRIBUTION, SELECTED YEARS, 1925-1965

(Based on coal equivalents)

Region, country, year	Total primary energy production	Solid fuels		Liquid fuels		Natural gas	Hydro-electric power
		Total	Hard coal	Total	Crude oil		
	(1)	(2)	(3)	(4)	(5)	(6)	(7)
URUGUAY (CONTINUED)							
1953	100.0	-	-	-	-	-	100.0
1955	100.0	-	-	-	-	-	100.0
1957	100.0	-	-	-	-	-	100.0
1960	100.0	-	-	-	-	-	100.0
1961	100.0	-	-	-	-	-	100.0
1962	100.0	-	-	-	-	-	100.0
1963	100.0	-	-	-	-	-	100.0
1964	100.0	-	-	-	-	-	100.0
1965	100.0	-	-	-	-	-	100.0
ASIA							
1925	100.0	77.0	76.5	20.9	20.7	0.7	1.4
1929	100.0	73.3	72.6	23.9	23.6	0.8	2.0
1933	100.0	68.2	67.9	27.6	27.2	1.5	2.8
1937	100.0	63.9	63.5	32.2	31.9	1.1	2.8
1938	100.0	65.5	65.1	30.6	30.4	1.1	2.8
1950	100.0	32.1	31.4	64.7	64.6	0.8	2.4
1953	100.0	28.8	28.2	68.1	68.1	1.1	2.0
1955	100.0	22.9	22.5	73.9	73.8	1.3	1.9
1957	100.0	24.0	23.5	71.9	71.9	2.1	2.0
1960	100.0	19.3	19.0	76.8	76.8	2.3	1.6
1961	100.0	19.3	18.9	76.6	76.6	2.3	1.8
1962	100.0	18.7	18.4	77.3	77.3	2.4	1.6
1963	100.0	17.9	17.5	78.2	78.1	2.3	1.6
1964	100.0	16.1	15.7	80.0	80.0	2.4	1.5
1965	100.0	15.2	14.9	80.9	80.9	2.3	1.5
MIDDLE EAST							
1925	100.0	8.8	8.8	91.2	91.2	-	-
1929	100.0	10.5	10.5	89.5	89.5	-	-
1933	100.0	10.7	10.7	89.2	89.2	-	-
1937	100.0	6.6	6.4	93.4	93.4	-	-
1938	100.0	7.0	6.8	93.0	93.0	-	-
1950	100.0	2.5	2.3	97.0	97.0	0.5	-
1953	100.0	2.2	2.1	97.1	97.1	0.6	-
1955	100.0	1.7	1.5	97.6	97.6	0.7	-
1957	100.0	1.7	1.5	96.6	96.6	1.6	-
1960	100.0	1.1	1.0	97.1	97.1	1.7	-
1961	100.0	1.0	0.9	97.2	97.2	1.8	-
1962	100.0	1.0	0.9	97.2	97.2	1.7	-
1963	100.0	1.0	0.8	97.4	97.4	1.5	0.1
1964	100.0	1.0	0.8	97.5	97.5	1.5	-
1965	100.0	0.9	0.7	97.6	97.6	1.4	0.1
MIDDLE EAST - OIL PRODUCING							
1925	100.0	-	-	100.0	100.0	-	-
1929	100.0	-	-	100.0	100.0	-	-
1933	100.0	0.1	0.1	99.9	99.9	-	-
1937	100.0	-	-	100.0	100.0	-	-
1938	100.0	-	-	100.0	100.0	-	-

Table III. PRIMARY ENERGY PRODUCTION PERCENTAGE DISTRIBUTION, SELECTED YEARS, 1925-1965

(Based on coal equivalents)

Region, country, year	Total primary energy production	Solid fuels: Total	Solid fuels: Hard coal	Liquid fuels: Total	Liquid fuels: Crude oil	Natural gas	Hydro-electric power
	(1)	(2)	(3)	(4)	(5)	(6)	(7)
MIDDLE EAST - OIL PRODUCING (CONTINUED)							
1950	100.0	0.2	0.2	99.3	99.3	0.5	-
1953	100.0	0.1	0.1	99.3	99.3	0.6	-
1955	100.0	0.1	0.1	99.2	99.2	0.7	-
1957	100.0	0.1	0.1	98.3	98.3	1.6	-
1960	100.0	0.1	0.1	98.2	98.2	1.8	-
1961	100.0	-	-	98.2	98.2	1.8	-
1962	100.0	-	-	98.2	98.2	1.8	-
1963	100.0	-	-	98.4	98.4	1.5	-
1964	100.0	-	-	98.4	98.4	1.5	-
1965	100.0	-	-	98.5	98.5	1.4	-
BAHRAIN							
1925	-	-	-	-	-	-	-
1929	-	-	-	-	-	-	-
1933	100.0	-	-	100.0	100.0	-	-
1937	100.0	-	-	100.0	100.0	-	-
1938	100.0	-	-	100.0	100.0	-	-
1950	100.0	-	-	100.0	100.0	-	-
1953	100.0	-	-	100.0	100.0	-	-
1955	100.0	-	-	100.0	100.0	-	-
1957	100.0	-	-	100.0	100.0	-	-
1960	100.0	-	-	100.0	100.0	-	-
1961	100.0	-	-	100.0	100.0	-	-
1962	100.0	-	-	100.0	100.0	-	-
1963	100.0	-	-	100.0	100.0	-	-
1964	100.0	-	-	100.0	100.0	-	-
1965	100.0	-	-	100.0	100.0	-	-
IRAN							
1925	100.0	-	-	100.0	100.0	-	-
1929	100.0	-	-	100.0	100.0	-	-
1933	100.0	0.1	0.1	99.9	99.9	-	-
1937	100.0	-	-	100.0	100.0	-	-
1938	100.0	-	-	100.0	100.0	-	-
1950	100.0	0.4	0.4	99.6	99.6	-	-
1953	100.0	6.3	6.3	90.8	90.8	2.9	-
1955	100.0	1.0	1.0	96.0	96.0	3.1	-
1957	100.0	0.3	0.3	95.5	95.5	4.2	-
1960	100.0	0.3	0.3	95.2	95.2	4.5	-
1961	100.0	0.2	0.2	95.8	95.8	4.0	-
1962	100.0	0.2	0.2	96.1	96.1	3.8	-
1963	100.0	0.2	0.2	96.4	96.4	3.4	-
1964	100.0	0.2	0.2	96.4	96.4	3.3	-
1965	100.0	0.2	0.2	96.8	96.8	3.0	-
IRAQ							
1925	-	-	-	-	-	-	-
1929	100.0	-	-	100.0	100.0	-	-
1933	100.0	-	-	100.0	100.0	-	-
1937	100.0	-	-	100.0	100.0	-	-
1938	100.0	-	-	100.0	100.0	-	-

Table III. PRIMARY ENERGY PRODUCTION PERCENTAGE DISTRIBUTION, SELECTED YEARS, 1925-1965

(Based on coal equivalents)

Region, country, year	Total primary energy production	Solid fuels		Liquid fuels		Natural gas	Hydro-electric power
		Total	Hard coal	Total	Crude oil		
	(1)	(2)	(3)	(4)	(5)	(6)	(7)
IRAQ (CONTINUED)							
1950	100.0	-	-	100.0	100.0	-	-
1953	100.0	-	-	99.1	99.1	0.9	-
1955	100.0	-	-	99.2	99.2	0.8	-
1957	100.0	-	-	99.0	99.0	1.0	-
1960	100.0	-	-	98.9	98.9	1.1	-
1961	100.0	-	-	98.9	98.9	1.1	-
1962	100.0	-	-	98.9	98.9	1.1	-
1963	100.0	-	-	98.9	98.9	1.1	-
1964	100.0	-	-	98.9	98.9	1.1	-
1965	100.0	-	-	99.0	99.0	1.0	-
KUWAIT							
1925	-	-	-	-	-	-	-
1929	-	-	-	-	-	-	-
1933	-	-	-	-	-	-	-
1937	-	-	-	-	-	-	-
1938	-	-	-	-	-	-	-
1950	100.0	-	-	100.0	100.0	-	-
1953	100.0	-	-	100.0	100.0	-	-
1955	100.0	-	-	100.0	100.0	-	-
1957	100.0	-	-	100.0	100.0	-	-
1960	100.0	-	-	98.8	98.8	1.2	-
1961	100.0	-	-	98.4	98.4	1.6	-
1962	100.0	-	-	98.2	98.2	1.8	-
1963	100.0	-	-	98.6	98.6	1.4	-
1964	100.0	-	-	98.6	98.6	1.4	-
1965	100.0	-	-	98.6	98.6	1.4	-
KUWAIT NEUTRAL ZONE							
1925	-	-	-	-	-	-	-
1929	-	-	-	-	-	-	-
1933	-	-	-	-	-	-	-
1937	-	-	-	-	-	-	-
1938	-	-	-	-	-	-	-
1950	-	-	-	-	-	-	-
1953	-	-	-	-	-	-	-
1955	100.0	-	-	100.0	100.0	-	-
1957	100.0	-	-	100.0	100.0	-	-
1960	100.0	-	-	100.0	100.0	-	-
1961	100.0	-	-	100.0	100.0	-	-
1962	100.0	-	-	100.0	100.0	NA	-
1963	100.0	-	-	100.0	100.0	NA	-
1964	100.0	-	-	100.0	100.0	NA	-
1965	100.0	-	-	100.0	100.0	NA	-
QATAR							
1925	-	-	-	-	-	-	-
1929	-	-	-	-	-	-	-
1933	-	-	-	-	-	-	-
1937	-	-	-	-	-	-	-
1938	-	-	-	-	-	-	-

Table III. PRIMARY ENERGY PRODUCTION PERCENTAGE DISTRIBUTION, SELECTED YEARS, 1925-1965

(Based on coal equivalents)

Region, country, year	Total primary energy production	Solid fuels		Liquid fuels		Natural gas	Hydro-electric power
		Total	Hard coal	Total	Crude oil		
	(1)	(2)	(3)	(4)	(5)	(6)	(7)
QATAR (CONTINUED)							
1950	100.0	-	-	100.0	100.0	-	-
1953	100.0	-	-	100.0	100.0	-	-
1955	100.0	-	-	100.0	100.0	-	-
1957	100.0	-	-	100.0	100.0	-	-
1960	100.0	-	-	100.0	100.0	-	-
1961	100.0	-	-	100.0	100.0	-	-
1962	100.0	-	-	100.0	100.0	-	-
1963	100.0	-	-	100.0	100.0	-	-
1964	100.0	-	-	100.0	100.0	NA	-
1965	100.0	-	-	100.0	100.0	NA	-
SAUDI ARABIA							
1925	-	-	-	-	-	-	-
1929	-	-	-	-	-	-	-
1933	-	-	-	-	-	-	-
1937	100.0	-	-	100.0	100.0	-	-
1938	100.0	-	-	100.0	100.0	-	-
1950	100.0	-	-	98.3	98.3	1.7	-
1953	100.0	-	-	99.0	99.0	1.0	-
1955	100.0	-	-	99.2	99.2	0.8	-
1957	100.0	-	-	97.7	97.7	2.3	-
1960	100.0	-	-	99.0	99.0	1.0	-
1961	100.0	-	-	99.0	99.0	1.0	-
1962	100.0	-	-	99.1	99.1	0.9	-
1963	100.0	-	-	99.1	99.1	0.9	-
1964	100.0	-	-	99.1	99.1	0.9	-
1965	100.0	-	-	99.2	99.2	0.8	-
TRUCIAL OMAN							
1950	-	-	-	-	-	-	-
1953	-	-	-	-	-	-	-
1955	-	-	-	-	-	-	-
1957	-	-	-	-	-	-	-
1960	-	-	-	-	-	-	-
1961	-	-	-	-	-	-	-
1962	100.0	-	-	100.0	100.0	-	-
1963	100.0	-	-	100.0	100.0	-	-
1964	100.0	-	-	100.0	100.0	-	-
1965	100.0	-	-	100.0	100.0	-	-
MIDDLE EAST - OTHER							
1925	100.0	99.6	99.4	-	-	-	0.4
1929	100.0	99.8	99.4	-	-	-	0.2
1933	100.0	99.8	99.1	-	-	-	0.2
1937	100.0	99.7	97.4	-	-	-	0.3
1938	100.0	99.8	97.1	-	-	-	0.2
1950	100.0	98.8	90.9	0.8	0.8	-	0.4
1953	100.0	98.5	90.8	1.0	1.0	-	0.5
1955	100.0	92.9	83.6	6.4	6.4	-	0.6
1957	100.0	88.6	76.6	10.2	10.2	-	1.2
1960	100.0	82.7	70.5	14.6	14.6	-	2.8

Table III. PRIMARY ENERGY PRODUCTION PERCENTAGE DISTRIBUTION, SELECTED YEARS, 1925-1965

(Based on coal equivalents)

Region, country, year	Total primary energy production	Solid fuels		Liquid fuels		Natural gas	Hydro-electric power
		Total	Hard coal	Total	Crude oil		
	(1)	(2)	(3)	(4)	(5)	(6)	(7)
MIDDLE EAST - OTHER (CONTINUED)							
1961	100.0	80.3	70.5	16.2	16.2	0.1	3.5
1962	100.0	78.0	66.7	18.8	18.8	0.3	3.0
1963	100.0	75.0	62.3	20.1	20.1	0.2	4.7
1964	100.0	73.3	60.0	22.7	22.7	0.5	3.5
1965	100.0	64.0	52.0	30.8	30.8	1.1	4.0
ISRAEL							
1950	-	-	-	-	-	-	-
1953	-	-	-	-	-	-	-
1955	100.0	-	-	100.0	100.0	-	-
1957	100.0	-	-	100.0	100.0	-	-
1960	100.0	-	-	100.0	100.0	-	-
1961	100.0	-	-	98.1	98.1	1.9	-
1962	100.0	-	-	93.3	93.3	6.7	-
1963	100.0	-	-	94.4	94.4	5.6	-
1964	100.0	-	-	88.5	88.5	11.5	-
1965	100.0	-	-	76.0	76.0	24.0	-
LEBANON-SYRIA							
1925	100.0	-	-	-	-	-	100.0
1929	100.0	-	-	-	-	-	100.0
1933	100.0	-	-	-	-	-	100.0
1937	100.0	-	-	-	-	-	100.0
1938	100.0	-	-	-	-	-	100.0
LEBANON							
1950	100.0	-	-	-	-	-	100.0
1953	100.0	-	-	-	-	-	100.0
1955	100.0	-	-	-	-	-	100.0
1957	100.0	-	-	-	-	-	100.0
1960	100.0	-	-	-	-	-	100.0
1961	100.0	-	-	-	-	-	100.0
1962	100.0	-	-	-	-	-	100.0
1963	100.0	-	-	-	-	-	100.0
1964	100.0	-	-	-	-	-	100.0
1965	100.0	-	-	-	-	-	100.0
SYRIA							
1950	-	-	-	-	-	-	-
1953	-	-	-	-	-	-	-
1955	100.0	-	-	-	-	-	100.0
1957	100.0	-	-	-	-	-	100.0
1960	100.0	-	-	-	-	-	100.0
1961	100.0	-	-	-	-	-	100.0
1962	100.0	-	-	-	-	-	100.0
1963	100.0	-	-	-	-	-	100.0
1964	100.0	-	-	-	-	-	100.0
1965	100.0	-	-	-	-	-	100.0

Table III. PRIMARY ENERGY PRODUCTION PERCENTAGE DISTRIBUTION, SELECTED YEARS, 1925-1965

(Based on coal equivalents)

Region, country, year	Total primary energy production	Solid fuels		Liquid fuels		Natural gas	Hydro-electric power
		Total	Hard coal	Total	Crude oil		
	(1)	(2)	(3)	(4)	(5)	(6)	(7)
TURKEY							
1925	100.0	100.0	99.8	-	-	-	-
1929	100.0	100.0	99.6	-	-	-	-
1933	100.0	100.0	99.2	-	-	-	-
1937	100.0	100.0	97.7	-	-	-	-
1938	100.0	100.0	97.3	-	-	-	-
1950	100.0	99.1	91.1	0.8	0.8	-	0.1
1953	100.0	98.8	91.1	1.0	1.0	-	0.2
1955	100.0	93.3	83.9	6.4	6.4	-	0.3
1957	100.0	90.4	78.1	8.8	8.8	-	0.8
1960	100.0	86.2	73.5	11.3	11.3	-	2.5
1961	100.0	84.0	73.7	13.0	13.0	-	3.1
1962	100.0	81.5	69.7	16.0	16.0	-	2.5
1963	100.0	78.4	65.1	17.5	17.5	-	4.1
1964	100.0	77.4	63.3	19.7	19.7	-	2.9
1965	100.0	67.8	55.0	28.8	28.8	-	3.4
FAR EAST AND OTHER ASIA							
1925	100.0	85.2	84.6	12.4	12.2	0.8	1.6
1929	100.0	81.4	80.6	15.5	15.2	0.9	2.2
1933	100.0	78.3	78.0	16.7	16.2	1.7	3.2
1937	100.0	79.2	78.7	15.9	15.5	1.4	3.5
1938	100.0	80.1	79.7	15.0	14.7	1.4	3.5
1950	100.0	74.2	72.8	18.8	18.6	1.3	5.7
1953	100.0	71.7	70.4	21.3	21.3	1.8	5.2
1955	100.0	67.6	66.4	24.0	23.9	2.5	6.0
1957	100.0	66.9	65.9	24.3	24.2	3.0	5.9
1960	100.0	65.2	64.3	25.6	25.5	3.6	5.6
1961	100.0	65.6	64.7	24.5	24.4	3.7	6.2
1962	100.0	65.5	64.7	24.8	24.7	4.1	5.6
1963	100.0	65.4	64.4	23.9	23.8	4.6	6.1
1964	100.0	63.8	62.8	24.8	24.7	5.1	6.3
1965	100.0	62.9	61.9	25.5	25.5	5.2	6.3
BORNEO (FORMER BRITISH)							
1925	100.0	9.8	9.8	90.2	89.6	-	-
1929	100.0	6.0	6.0	94.0	93.5	-	-
1933	100.0	-	-	99.7	99.1	0.3	-
1937	100.0	0.1	0.1	97.6	97.1	2.3	-
1938	100.0	0.1	0.1	97.1	96.7	2.8	-
1950	100.0	-	-	98.9	98.9	1.1	-
1953	100.0	-	-	98.9	98.9	1.1	-
1955	100.0	-	-	98.7	97.7	1.3	-
1957	100.0	-	-	97.1	95.9	2.9	-
1960	100.0	-	-	96.1	94.8	3.9	-
1961	100.0	-	-	95.8	94.4	4.2	-
1962	100.0	-	-	95.5	93.9	4.5	-
1963	100.0	-	-	95.3	93.5	4.7	-
1964	100.0	-	-	96.0	94.2	4.0	-
1965	100.0	-	-	95.6	94.2	4.4	-

Table III. PRIMARY ENERGY PRODUCTION PERCENTAGE DISTRIBUTION, SELECTED YEARS, 1925-1965

(Based on coal equivalents)

Region, country, year	Total primary energy production	Solid fuels		Liquid fuels		Natural gas	Hydro-electric power
		Total	Hard coal	Total	Crude oil		
	(1)	(2)	(3)	(4)	(5)	(6)	(7)
BRUNEI							
1950	100.0	-	-	100.0	100.0	NA	-
1953	100.0	-	-	98.9	98.9	1.1	-
1955	100.0	-	-	98.7	97.7	1.3	-
1957	100.0	-	-	97.0	95.8	3.0	-
1960	100.0	-	-	96.1	94.7	3.9	-
1961	100.0	-	-	95.7	94.3	4.3	-
1962	100.0	-	-	95.4	93.8	4.6	-
1963	100.0	-	-	95.2	93.4	4.8	-
1964	100.0	-	-	95.9	94.2	4.1	-
1965	100.0	-	-	95.5	94.2	4.5	-
SARAWAK							
1950	100.0	-	-	100.0	100.0	-	-
1953	100.0	-	-	100.0	100.0	-	-
1955	100.0	-	-	100.0	100.0	-	-
1957	100.0	-	-	100.0	100.0	-	-
1960	100.0	-	-	100.0	100.0	-	-
1961	100.0	-	-	100.0	100.0	-	-
1962	100.0	-	-	100.0	100.0	-	-
1963	100.0	-	-	100.0	100.0	-	-
1964	100.0	-	-	100.0	100.0	-	-
1965	100.0	-	-	100.0	100.0	-	-
BURMA							
1950	100.0	-	-	100.0	100.0	-	-
1953	100.0	-	-	100.0	100.0	-	-
1955	100.0	2.1	2.1	96.6	96.6	1.2	-
1957	100.0	0.2	0.2	98.5	98.5	1.3	-
1960	100.0	0.1	0.1	94.3	94.3	3.2	2.3
1961	100.0	0.2	0.2	94.9	94.9	2.2	2.6
1962	100.0	0.3	0.3	94.2	94.2	2.6	2.9
1963	100.0	0.3	0.3	94.7	94.7	2.1	2.9
1964	100.0	1.1	1.1	93.5	93.5	1.5	3.9
1965	100.0	1.1	1.1	93.3	93.3	1.5	4.0
CEYLON							
1925	-	-	-	-	-	-	-
1929	-	-	-	-	-	-	-
1933	-	-	-	-	-	-	-
1937	-	-	-	-	-	-	-
1938	-	-	-	-	-	-	-
1950	100.0	-	-	-	-	-	100.0
1953	100.0	-	-	-	-	-	100.0
1955	100.0	-	-	-	-	-	100.0
1957	100.0	-	-	-	-	-	100.0
1960	100.0	-	-	-	-	-	100.0
1961	100.0	-	-	-	-	-	100.0
1962	100.0	-	-	-	-	-	100.0
1963	100.0	-	-	-	-	-	100.0
1964	100.0	-	-	-	-	-	100.0
1965	100.0	-	-	-	-	-	100.0

Table III. PRIMARY ENERGY PRODUCTION PERCENTAGE DISTRIBUTION, SELECTED YEARS, 1925-1965

(Based on coal equivalents)

Region, country, year	Total primary energy production	Solid fuels		Liquid fuels		Natural gas	Hydro-electric power
		Total	Hard coal	Total	Crude oil		
	(1)	(2)	(3)	(4)	(5)	(6)	(7)
INDIA							
1925	100.0	90.3	90.3	9.6	9.6	-	0.1
1929	100.0	91.1	91.1	8.6	8.6	-	0.3
1933	100.0	89.5	89.5	10.0	9.8	-	0.6
1937	100.0	90.3	90.3	9.1	8.9	-	0.6
1938	100.0	91.2	91.2	8.2	8.0	-	0.6
1950	100.0	97.4	97.4	1.4	1.4	-	1.2
1953	100.0	97.4	97.4	1.4	1.4	-	1.2
1955	100.0	96.9	96.9	1.6	1.6	-	1.5
1957	100.0	96.1	96.1	1.7	1.7	0.5	1.7
1960	100.0	95.8	95.8	1.5	1.5	0.4	2.2
1961	100.0	95.5	95.4	1.6	1.6	0.3	2.6
1962	100.0	93.6	93.5	3.1	3.1	0.5	2.7
1963	100.0	92.1	91.6	4.3	4.3	0.6	3.0
1964	100.0	89.8	89.0	5.9	5.9	0.8	3.5
1965	100.0	88.3	87.2	7.4	7.4	0.9	3.5
INDO-CHINA							
1925	100.0	100.0	99.9	-	-	-	-
1929	100.0	100.0	99.5	-	-	-	-
1933	100.0	100.0	100.0	-	-	-	-
1937	100.0	100.0	100.0	-	-	-	-
1938	100.0	100.0	99.9	-	-	-	-
1950	100.0	100.0	100.0	-	-	-	-
1953	100.0	100.0	100.0	-	-	-	-
1955	100.0	-	-	-	-	-	100.0
1957	100.0	97.0	97.0	-	-	-	3.0
1960	100.0	96.9	96.9	-	-	-	3.1
1961	100.0	97.9	97.9	-	-	-	2.1
1962	100.0	98.3	98.3	-	-	-	1.7
1963	100.0	98.8	98.8	-	-	-	1.2
1964	100.0	93.6	93.6	-	-	-	6.4
1965	100.0	91.2	91.2	-	-	-	8.8
VIETNAM, SOUTH							
1955	100.0	-	-	-	-	-	100.0
1957	100.0	97.0	97.0	-	-	-	3.0
1960	100.0	96.9	96.9	-	-	-	3.1
1961	100.0	97.9	97.9	-	-	-	2.1
1962	100.0	98.3	98.3	-	-	-	1.7
1963	100.0	98.8	98.8	-	-	-	1.2
1964	100.0	93.6	93.6	-	-	-	6.4
1965	100.0	91.2	91.2	-	-	-	8.8
INDONESIA							
1925	100.0	21.2	21.2	72.1	69.7	6.4	0.2
1929	100.0	17.5	17.5	77.1	75.0	5.3	0.1
1933	100.0	9.7	9.7	80.3	77.7	9.8	0.2
1937	100.0	10.0	10.0	81.2	79.4	8.6	0.2
1938	100.0	10.3	10.3	80.5	78.7	9.0	0.2
1950	100.0	6.7	6.7	84.2	83.2	8.8	0.3

Table III. PRIMARY ENERGY PRODUCTION PERCENTAGE DISTRIBUTION, SELECTED YEARS, 1925-1965

(Based on coal equivalents)

Region, country, year	Total primary energy production	Solid fuels		Liquid fuels		Natural gas	Hydro-electric power
		Total	Hard coal	Total	Crude oil		
	(1)	(2)	(3)	(4)	(5)	(6)	(7)
INDONESIA (CONTINUED)							
1953	100.0	4.8	4.8	85.0	85.0	9.8	0.3
1955	100.0	3.7	3.7	84.3	84.3	11.6	0.3
1957	100.0	2.6	2.6	86.6	86.6	10.5	0.3
1960	100.0	1.9	1.9	88.7	88.7	9.2	0.3
1961	100.0	1.5	1.5	88.8	88.8	9.4	0.3
1962	100.0	1.2	1.2	89.2	89.2	9.4	0.2
1963	100.0	1.6	1.6	88.4	88.4	9.8	0.2
1964	100.0	1.1	1.1	88.6	88.6	10.0	0.2
1965	100.0	0.7	0.7	89.1	89.1	10.0	0.2
JAPAN							
1925	100.0	95.8	95.6	1.2	1.2	0.1	2.9
1929	100.0	94.5	94.3	1.1	1.1	0.1	4.3
1933	100.0	93.2	93.1	0.8	0.8	0.2	5.8
1937	100.0	93.1	92.9	1.1	1.1	0.1	5.7
1938	100.0	93.2	93.1	1.0	1.0	0.1	5.7
1950	100.0	88.0	86.6	1.0	1.0	0.2	10.8
1953	100.0	89.1	87.6	0.8	0.8	0.3	9.8
1955	100.0	86.5	85.0	1.0	0.9	0.4	12.2
1957	100.0	86.8	85.4	0.8	0.8	0.7	11.7
1960	100.0	84.9	83.7	1.3	1 3	1.8	12.0
1961	100.0	83.5	82.5	1.5	1.5	2.1	12.9
1962	100.0	83.6	82.7	1.8	1.7	2.8	11.9
1963	100.0	81.0	80.2	1.9	1.8	3.9	13.3
1964	100.0	80.5	79.9	1.6	1.5	4.3	13.5
1965	100.0	79.9	79.4	1.6	1.6	4.3	14.2
KOREA							
1925	100.0	100.0	100.0	-	-	-	-
1929	100.0	100.0	100.0	-	-	-	-
1933	100.0	95.1	95.1	-	-	-	4.9
1937	100.0	90.3	90.3	-	-	-	9.7
1938	100.0	91.8	91.8	-	-	-	8.2
KOREA, REPUBLIC OF							
1950	100.0	97.9	96.5	-	-	-	2.1
1953	100.0	94.6	94.6	-	-	-	5.4
1955	100.0	95.6	95.6	-	-	-	4.4
1957	100.0	97.9	97.9	-	-	-	2.1
1960	100.0	98.7	98.7	-	-	-	1.3
1961	100.0	98.6	98.6	-	-	-	1.4
1962	100.0	98.8	98.8	-	-	-	1.2
1963	100.0	99.0	99.0	-	-	-	1.0
1964	100.0	99.0	99.0	-	-	-	1.0
1965	100.0	99.1	99.1	-	-	-	0.9
MALAYA AND SINGAPORE							
1925	100.0	99.1	-	-	-	-	0.9
1929	100.0	99.0	-	-	-	-	1.0

Table III. PRIMARY ENERGY PRODUCTION PERCENTAGE DISTRIBUTION, SELECTED YEARS, 1925-1965

(Based on coal equivalents)

Region, country, year	Total primary energy production	Solid fuels		Liquid fuels		Natural gas	Hydro-electric power
		Total	Hard coal	Total	Crude oil		
	(1)	(2)	(3)	(4)	(5)	(6)	(7)
MALAYA AND SINGAPORE (CONTINUED)							
1933	100.0	93.1	-	-	-	-	6.9
1937	100.0	94.0	-	-	-	-	6.0
1938	100.0	92.4	-	-	-	-	7.6
1950	100.0	90.6	-	-	-	-	9.4
1953	100.0	86.8	-	-	-	-	13.2
1955	100.0	83.7	-	-	-	-	16.3
1957	100.0	78.2	-	-	-	-	21.8
1960	100.0	17.1	-	-	-	-	82.9
1961	100.0	-	-	-	-	-	100.0
1962	100.0	-	-	-	-	-	100.0
1963	100.0	-	-	-	-	-	100.0
1964	100.0	-	-	-	-	-	100.0
1965	100.0	-	-	-	-	-	100.0
PAKISTAN							
1950	100.0	57.3	-	41.4	41.4	-	1.3
1953	100.0	55.2	-	41.3	41.3	-	3.5
1955	100.0	45.4	-	43.8	43.8	5.5	5.3
1957	100.0	32.0	-	33.6	33.6	29.5	5.0
1960	100.0	31.3	-	24.9	24.9	39.8	4.0
1961	100.0	30.1	-	23.2	23.2	41.9	4.8
1962	100.0	27.4	-	23.1	23.1	43.5	6.0
1963	100.0	28.6	-	20.3	20.3	45.5	5.6
1964	100.0	25.2	-	19.4	19.4	49.4	5.9
1965	100.0	23.5	-	18.8	18.8	51.8	5.9
PHILIPPINES							
1925	100.0	91.6	91.6	-	-	-	8.4
1929	100.0	73.1	73.1	-	-	-	26.9
1933	100.0	67.0	67.0	-	-	-	33.0
1937	100.0	69.8	69.8	-	-	-	30.2
1938	100.0	79.6	79.6	-	-	-	20.4
1950	100.0	86.9	86.9	-	-	-	13.1
1953	100.0	78.9	78.9	-	-	-	21.1
1955	100.0	70.7	70.7	-	-	-	29.3
1957	100.0	70.5	70.5	-	-	-	29.5
1960	100.0	47.3	47.3	-	-	-	52.7
1961	100.0	48.5	48.5	-	-	-	51.5
1962	100.0	49.1	49.1	-	-	-	50.9
1963	100.0	44.9	44.9	-	-	-	55.1
1964	100.0	36.5	36.5	-	-	-	63.5
1965	100.0	33.5	33.5	-	-	-	66.5
TAIWAN							
1925	100.0	97.9	97.9	0.3	0.3	1.7	0.1
1929	100.0	92.5	92.5	1.0	1.0	5.6	1.0
1933	100.0	91.1	91.1	1.0	1.0	5.3	2.6
1937	100.0	94.3	94.3	0.3	0.3	1.9	3.4
1938	100.0	94.4	94.4	0.3	0.3	1.6	3.7
1950	100.0	89.8	89.8	0.4	0.3	2.0	7.8

Table III. PRIMARY ENERGY PRODUCTION PERCENTAGE DISTRIBUTION, SELECTED YEARS, 1925-1965

(Based on coal equivalents)

Region, country, year	Total primary energy production	Solid fuels		Liquid fuels		Natural gas	Hydro-electric power
		Total	Hard coal	Total	Crude oil		
	(1)	(2)	(3)	(4)	(5)	(6)	(7)
TAIWAN (CONTINUED)							
1953	100.0	91.8	91.8	0.2	0.1	1.0	7.0
1955	100.0	91.0	91.0	0.2	0.2	1.3	7.4
1957	100.0	91.1	91.1	0.1	0.1	1.2	7.6
1960	100.0	93.1	93.1	0.1	0.1	0.8	6.1
1961	100.0	92.6	92.6	0.1	0.1	1.1	6.3
1962	100.0	93.3	93.3	0.1	0.1	1.0	5.5
1963	100.0	93.8	93.8	0.1	0.1	1.3	4.7
1964	100.0	90.4	90.4	0.2	0.2	4.0	5.3
1965	100.0	86.9	86.9	0.5	0.5	7.1	5.6
THAILAND							
1925	-	-	-	-	-	-	-
1929	-	-	-	-	-	-	-
1933	-	-	-	-	-	-	-
1937	-	-	-	-	-	-	-
1938	-	-	-	-	-	-	-
1950	-	-	-	-	-	-	-
1953	100.0	100.0	-	-	-	-	-
1955	100.0	100.0	-	-	-	-	-
1957	100.0	100.0	-	-	-	-	-
1960	100.0	100.0	-	-	-	-	-
1961	100.0	100.0	-	-	-	-	-
1962	100.0	100.0	-	-	-	-	-
1963	100.0	100.0	-	-	-	-	-
1964	100.0	100.0	-	-	-	-	-
1965	100.0	100.0	-	-	-	-	-
AFRICA							
1925	100.0	97.9	97.9	2.0	2.0	-	0.1
1929	100.0	97.2	97.2	2.8	2.8	-	0.1
1933	100.0	96.7	96.7	3.0	3.0	-	0.2
1937	100.0	98.2	98.2	1.5	1.5	-	0.3
1938	100.0	97.7	97.7	1.9	1.9	-	0.3
1950	100.0	87.8	87.7	11.7	11.7	-	0.5
1953	100.0	87.7	87.7	11.6	11.6	-	0.7
1955	100.0	91.6	91.6	7.4	7.4	-	1.0
1957	100.0	89.7	89.7	8.9	8.9	-	1.3
1960	100.0	66.5	66.5	32.0	31.9	0.1	1.4
1961	100.0	54.2	54.2	43.9	43.7	0.4	1.4
1962	100.0	43.0	43.0	55.3	55.0	0.5	1.2
1963	100.0	34.6	34.6	63.9	63.6	0.5	1.0
1964	100.0	28.1	28.1	70.4	70.1	0.7	0.9
1965	100.0	24.4	24.4	73.6	73.3	1.2	0.8
NORTH AFRICA							
1925	100.0	3.5	3.5	95.6	95.6	-	0.9
1929	100.0	3.7	3.7	95.2	95.2	-	1.1
1933	100.0	13.3	13.3	84.2	84.2	-	2.5
1937	100.0	30.2	30.2	64.7	64.7	-	5.1
1938	100.0	27.2	27.2	68.7	68.7	-	4.1
1950	100.0	13.7	13.4	85.2	84.8	-	1.1

Table III. PRIMARY ENERGY PRODUCTION PERCENTAGE DISTRIBUTION, SELECTED YEARS, 1925-1965

(Based on coal equivalents)

Region, country, year	Total primary energy production	Solid fuels		Liquid fuels		Natural gas	Hydro-electric power
		Total	Hard coal	Total	Crude oil		
	(1)	(2)	(3)	(4)	(5)	(6)	(7)
NORTH AFRICA (CONTINUED)							
1953	100.0	16.3	16.3	82.2	82.0	0.1	1.3
1955	100.0	19.7	19.7	76.3	76.1	0.4	3.6
1957	100.0	16.2	16.2	80.3	80.1	0.3	3.3
1960	100.0	2.8	2.8	96.0	95.6	0.2	1.0
1961	100.0	1.5	1.5	96.6	95.9	1.0	0.9
1962	100.0	0.8	0.8	97.7	97.1	0.9	0.6
1963	100.0	0.6	0.6	98.3	97.8	0.7	0.4
1964	100.0	0.4	0.4	98.3	97.9	1.0	0.3
1965	100.0	0.3	0.3	97.6	97.1	1.8	0.3
ALGERIA							
1925	100.0	64.5	64.5	19.4	19.4	-	16.1
1929	100.0	69.6	69.6	19.6	19.6	-	10.9
1933	100.0	86.6	86.6	4.3	4.3	-	9.0
1937	100.0	75.7	75.7	-	-	-	24.3
1938	100.0	71.7	71.7	-	-	-	28.3
1950	100.0	92.5	92.5	1.6	1.6	-	5.9
1953	100.0	65.4	65.4	28.3	28.3	-	6.3
1955	100.0	71.1	71.1	20.5	20.5	-	8.5
1957	100.0	76.5	76.5	10.2	10.2	-	13.3
1960	100.0	0.9	0.9	98.7	98.3	0.1	0.3
1961	100.0	0.3	0.3	98.3	97.4	1.3	0.1
1962	100.0	0.2	0.2	98.2	97.3	1.5	0.1
1963	100.0	0.1	0.1	98.3	97.4	1.5	0.1
1964	100.0	0.1	0.1	97.2	96.1	2.6	0.1
1965	100.0	0.1	0.1	94.0	92.1	5.8	0.1
EGYPT UAR							
1925	100.0	-	-	100.0	100.0	-	-
1929	100.0	-	-	100.0	100.0	-	-
1933	100.0	-	-	100.0	100.0	-	-
1937	100.0	-	-	100.0	100.0	-	-
1938	100.0	-	-	100.0	100.0	-	-
1950	100.0	-	-	100.0	99.6	-	-
1953	100.0	-	-	100.0	99.8	-	-
1955	100.0	-	-	100.0	99.6	-	-
1957	100.0	-	-	100.0	99.7	-	-
1960	100.0	-	-	99.4	99.1	-	0.6
1961	100.0	-	-	97.8	97.6	-	2.2
1962	100.0	-	-	98.0	97.8	-	2.0
1963	100.0	-	-	98.1	98.0	-	1.9
1964	100.0	-	-	97.9	97.8	-	2.1
1965	100.0	-	-	97.8	97.7	-	2.2
LIBYA							
1925	-	-	-	-	-	-	-
1929	-	-	-	-	-	-	-
1933	-	-	-	-	-	-	-
1937	-	-	-	-	-	-	-
1938	-	-	-	-	-	-	-

Table III. PRIMARY ENERGY PRODUCTION PERCENTAGE DISTRIBUTION, SELECTED YEARS, 1925-1965

(Based on coal equivalents)

Region, country, year	Total primary energy production	Solid fuels		Liquid fuels		Natural gas	Hydro-electric power
		Total	Hard coal	Total	Crude oil		
	(1)	(2)	(3)	(4)	(5)	(6)	(7)
LIBYA (CONTINUED)							
1950	-	-	-	-	-	-	-
1953	-	-	-	-	-	-	-
1955	-	-	-	-	-	-	-
1957	-	-	-	-	-	-	-
1960	-	-	-	-	-	-	-
1961	100.0	-	-	100.0	100.0	-	-
1962	100.0	-	-	100.0	100.0	-	-
1963	100.0	-	-	100.0	100.0	-	-
1964	100.0	-	-	100.0	100.0	-	-
1965	100.0	-	-	100.0	100.0	-	-
MOROCCO							
1925	-	-	-	-	-	-	-
1929	100.0	-	-	-	-	-	100.0
1933	100.0	75.3	75.3	4.2	4.2	-	20.6
1937	100.0	84.9	84.9	2.4	2.4	-	12.7
1938	100.0	86.1	86.1	3.1	3.1	-	10.8
1950	100.0	79.8	79.8	12.7	12.7	-	7.5
1953	100.0	73.9	73.9	20.0	20.0	0.9	5.2
1955	100.0	63.6	63.6	21.0	21.0	1.5	14.0
1957	100.0	70.0	70.0	15.1	15.1	0.5	14.4
1960	100.0	60.7	60.7	20.3	20.3	1.8	17.2
1961	100.0	62.2	62.2	18.2	18.2	1.6	18.0
1962	100.0	52.8	52.8	27.2	27.2	1.9	18.2
1963	100.0	51.8	51.8	28.8	28.8	2.0	17.3
1964	100.0	54.2	54.2	24.4	24.4	2.2	19.2
1965	100.0	57.2	57.2	21.1	21.1	2.0	19.8
TUNISIA							
1925	-	-	-	-	-	-	-
1929	-	-	-	-	-	-	-
1933	-	-	-	-	-	-	-
1937	-	-	-	-	-	-	-
1938	-	-	-	-	-	-	-
1950	100.0	100.0	-	-	-	-	-
1953	-	-	-	-	-	-	-
1955	100.0	-	-	-	-	100.0	-
1957	100.0	-	-	-	-	71.1	28.9
1960	100.0	-	-	-	-	61.3	38.7
1961	100.0	-	-	-	-	79.7	20.3
1962	100.0	-	-	-	-	79.7	20.3
1963	100.0	-	-	-	-	71.3	28.7
1964	100.0	-	-	-	-	69.2	30.8
1965	100.0	-	-	-	-	67.0	33.0
TROPICAL AFRICA							
1925	100.0	99.4	99.4	-	-	-	0.6
1929	100.0	99.6	99.6	-	-	-	0.4
1933	100.0	97.8	97.8	-	-	-	2.2
1937	100.0	97.5	97.5	-	-	-	2.5
1938	100.0	97.3	97.3	-	-	-	2.7

Table III. PRIMARY ENERGY PRODUCTION PERCENTAGE DISTRIBUTION, SELECTED YEARS, 1925-1965

(Based on coal equivalents)

Region, country, year	Total primary energy production	Solid fuels		Liquid fuels		Natural gas	Hydro-electric power
		Total	Hard coal	Total	Crude oil		
	(1)	(2)	(3)	(4)	(5)	(6)	(7)
TROPICAL AFRICA (CONTINUED)							
1950	100.0	96.1	96.1	-	-	-	3.9
1953	100.0	95.3	95.3	-	-	-	4.7
1955	100.0	94.6	94.6	-	-	-	5.4
1957	100.0	88.2	88.2	4.5	4.5	-	7.3
1960	100.0	57.5	57.5	33.4	33.4	0.1	9.0
1961	100.0	41.4	41.4	49.5	49.5	0.1	9.0
1962	100.0	32.0	32.0	59.4	59.4	0.1	8.4
1963	100.0	28.1	28.1	63.5	63.5	0.5	8.0
1964	100.0	23.6	23.6	69.4	69.4	0.5	6.5
1965	100.0	15.8	15.8	79.7	79.7	0.3	4.2
CONGO, DEMOCRATIC REPUBLIC							
1925	100.0	94.5	94.5	-	-	-	5.5
1929	100.0	96.9	96.9	-	-	-	3.1
1933	100.0	62.0	62.0	-	-	-	38.0
1937	100.0	56.7	56.7	-	-	-	43.3
1938	100.0	59.1	59.1	-	-	-	40.9
1950	100.0	68.5	68.5	-	-	-	31.5
1953	100.0	71.8	71.8	-	-	-	28.2
1955	100.0	74.3	74.3	-	-	-	25.7
1957	100.0	59.3	59.3	-	-	-	40.7
1960	100.0	36.1	36.1	-	-	-	63.9
1961	100.0	19.7	19.7	-	-	-	80.3
1962	100.0	19.4	19.4	-	-	-	80.6
1963	100.0	24.8	24.8	-	-	-	75.2
1964	100.0	26.2	26.2	-	-	-	73.8
1965	100.0	27.0	27.0	-	-	-	73.0
EAST AFRICA							
1925	100.0	-	-	-	-	-	100.0
1929	100.0	-	-	-	-	-	100.0
1933	100.0	-	-	-	-	-	100.0
1937	100.0	-	-	-	-	-	100.0
1938	100.0	-	-	-	-	-	100.0
1950	100.0	-	-	-	-	-	100.0
1953	100.0	-	-	-	-	-	100.0
1955	100.0	2.5	2.5	-	-	-	97.5
1957	100.0	1.9	1.9	-	-	-	98.1
1960	100.0	2.5	2.5	-	-	-	97.5
1961	100.0	2.4	2.4	-	-	-	97.6
1962	100.0	3.3	3.3	-	-	-	96.7
1963	100.0	2.1	2.1	-	-	-	97.9
1964	100.0	0.9	0.9	-	-	-	99.1
1965	100.0	1.7	1.7	-	-	-	98.3
EQUATORIAL AFRICA							
1925	-	-	-	-	-	-	-
1929	-	-	-	-	-	-	-
1933	-	-	-	-	-	-	-
1937	-	-	-	-	-	-	-
1938	-	-	-	-	-	-	-

Table III. PRIMARY ENERGY PRODUCTION PERCENTAGE DISTRIBUTION, SELECTED YEARS, 1925-1965

(Based on coal equivalents)

Region, country, year	Total primary energy production	Solid fuels		Liquid fuels		Natural gas	Hydro-electric power
		Total	Hard coal	Total	Crude oil		
	(1)	(2)	(3)	(4)	(5)	(6)	(7)
EQUATORIAL AFRICA (CONTINUED)							
1950	-	-	-	-	-	-	-
1953	100.0	-	-	-	-	-	100.0
1955	100.0	-	-	-	-	-	100.0
1957	100.0	-	-	98.6	98.6	-	1.4
1960	100.0	-	-	99.0	99.0	0.7	0.3
1961	100.0	-	-	99.0	99.0	0.7	0.3
1962	100.0	-	-	98.9	98.9	0.8	0.3
1963	100.0	-	-	98.8	98.8	0.8	0.4
1964	100.0	-	-	98.9	98.9	0.8	0.4
1965	100.0	-	-	99.0	99.0	0.7	0.3
GHANA							
1960	-	-	-	-	-	-	-
1961	-	-	-	-	-	-	-
1962	-	-	-	-	-	-	-
1963	-	-	-	-	-	-	-
1964	-	-	-	-	-	-	-
1965	100.0	-	-	-	-	-	100.0
LIBERIA							
1950	100.0	-	-	-	-	-	100.0
1953	100.0	-	-	-	-	-	100.0
1955	100.0	-	-	-	-	-	100.0
1957	100.0	-	-	-	-	-	100.0
1960	100.0	-	-	-	-	-	100.0
1961	100.0	-	-	-	-	-	100.0
1962	100.0	-	-	-	-	-	100.0
1963	100.0	-	-	-	-	-	100.0
1964	100.0	-	-	-	-	-	100.0
1965	100.0	-	-	-	-	-	100.0
NIGERIA							
1925	100.0	100.0	100.0	-	-	-	-
1929	100.0	100.0	100.0	-	-	-	-
1933	100.0	100.0	100.0	-	-	-	-
1937	100.0	100.0	100.0	-	-	-	-
1938	100.0	100.0	100.0	-	-	-	-
1950	100.0	98.9	98.9	-	-	-	1.1
1953	100.0	98.9	98.9	-	-	-	1.1
1955	100.0	98.8	98.8	-	-	-	1.2
1957	100.0	98.5	98.5	0.2	0.2	-	1.3
1960	100.0	30.7	30.7	68.6	68.6	-	0.6
1961	100.0	15.1	15.1	84.6	84.6	-	0.3
1962	100.0	11.2	11.2	88.5	88.5	-	0.2
1963	100.0	9.2	9.2	89.8	89.8	0.8	0.2
1964	100.0	7.2	7.2	91.9	91.9	0.8	0.2
1965	100.0	3.5	3.5	96.0	96.0	0.4	0.1

Table III. PRIMARY ENERGY PRODUCTION PERCENTAGE DISTRIBUTION, SELECTED YEARS, 1925-1965

(Based on coal equivalents)

Region, country, year	Total primary energy production	Solid fuels		Liquid fuels		Natural gas	Hydro-electric power
		Total	Hard coal	Total	Crude oil		
	(1)	(2)	(3)	(4)	(5)	(6)	(7)
RHODESIAN FEDERATION							
1925	100.0	100.0	100.0	-	-	-	-
1929	100.0	100.0	100.0	-	-	-	-
1933	100.0	99.5	99.5	-	-	-	0.5
1937	100.0	99.5	99.5	-	-	-	0.5
1938	100.0	99.5	99.5	-	-	-	0.5
1950	100.0	99.1	99.1	-	-	-	0.9
1953	100.0	99.1	99.1	-	-	-	0.9
1955	100.0	99.2	99.2	-	-	-	0.8
1957	100.0	99.3	99.3	-	-	-	0.7
1960	100.0	95.6	95.6	-	-	-	4.4
1961	100.0	91.0	91.0	-	-	-	9.0
1962	100.0	88.4	88.4	-	-	-	11.6
1963	100.0	86.4	86.4	-	-	-	13.6
1964	100.0	86.2	86.2	-	-	-	13.8
1965	100.0	87.1	87.1	-	-	-	12.9
MALAWI							
1950	-	-	-	-	-	-	-
1953	-	-	-	-	-	-	-
1955	-	-	-	-	-	-	-
1957	-	-	-	-	-	-	-
1960	-	-	-	-	-	-	-
1961	-	-	-	-	-	-	-
1962	100.0	-	-	-	-	-	100.0
1963	100.0	-	-	-	-	-	100.0
1964	100.0	-	-	-	-	-	100.0
1965	100.0	-	-	-	-	-	100.0
ZAMBIA							
1950	NA	NA	NA	NA	NA	NA	NA
1953	100.0	-	-	-	-	-	100.0
1955	100.0	-	-	-	-	-	100.0
1957	100.0	-	-	-	-	-	100.0
1960	NA	NA	NA	NA	NA	NA	NA
1961	NA	NA	NA	NA	NA	NA	NA
1962	100.0	-	-	-	-	-	100.0
1963	100.0	-	-	-	-	-	100.0
1964	100.0	-	-	-	-	-	100.0
1965	100.0	-	-	-	-	-	100.0
RHODESIA							
1950	100.0	100.0	100.0	-	-	-	NA
1953	100.0	100.0	100.0	-	-	-	-
1955	100.0	100.0	100.0	-	-	-	-
1957	100.0	100.0	100.0	-	-	-	-
1960	100.0	96.5	96.5	-	-	-	3.5
1961	100.0	91.8	91.8	-	-	-	8.2
1962	100.0	89.2	89.2	-	-	-	10.8
1963	100.0	87.5	87.5	-	-	-	12.5
1964	100.0	87.2	87.2	-	-	-	12.8
1965	100.0	87.9	87.9	-	-	-	12.1

Table III. PRIMARY ENERGY PRODUCTION PERCENTAGE DISTRIBUTION, SELECTED YEARS, 1925-1965

(Based on coal equivalents)

Region, country, year	Total primary energy production	Solid fuels		Liquid fuels		Natural gas	Hydro-electric power
		Total	Hard coal	Total	Crude oil		
	(1)	(2)	(3)	(4)	(5)	(6)	(7)
WEST AFRICA							
1950	-	-	-	-	-	-	-
1953	100.0	-	-	-	-	-	100.0
1955	100.0	-	-	-	-	-	100.0
1957	100.0	-	-	-	-	-	100.0
1960	100.0	-	-	16.7	16.7	-	83.3
1961	100.0	-	-	23.1	23.1	-	76.9
1962	100.0	-	-	-	-	-	100.0
1963	100.0	-	-	-	-	-	100.0
1964	100.0	-	-	-	-	-	100.0
1965	100.0	-	-	-	-	-	100.0
SOUTH AFRICA							
1925	100.0	100.0	100.0	-	-	-	-
1929	100.0	100.0	100.0	-	-	-	-
1933	100.0	100.0	100.0	-	-	-	-
1937	100.0	100.0	100.0	-	-	-	-
1938	100.0	100.0	100.0	-	-	-	-
1950	100.0	99.8	99.8	0.2	0.2	-	-
1953	100.0	99.8	99.8	0.2	0.2	-	-
1955	100.0	99.8	99.8	0.2	0.2	-	-
1957	100.0	99.9	99.9	0.1	0.1	-	-
1960	100.0	99.9	99.9	0.1	0.1	-	-
1961	100.0	100.0	100.0	-	-	-	-
1962	100.0	100.0	100.0	-	-	-	-
1963	100.0	100.0	100.0	-	-	-	-
1964	100.0	100.0	100.0	-	-	-	-
1965	100.0	100.0	100.0	-	-	-	-
DEVELOPED COUNTRIES							
1925	100.0	84.2	80.2	11.9	11.5	3.3	0.7
1929	100.0	80.6	76.3	13.9	13.3	4.6	0.9
1933	100.0	77.2	72.9	16.4	15.9	5.1	1.3
1937	100.0	75.0	70.5	17.6	17.0	6.0	1.3
1938	100.0	74.1	68.9	18.3	17.6	6.2	1.4
1950	100.0	61.3	58.7	24.0	22.4	12.7	2.1
1953	100.0	55.0	52.5	27.1	25.2	15.7	2.3
1955	100.0	52.9	50.3	27.9	25.8	16.8	2.4
1957	100.0	51.5	48.8	27.9	26.0	18.0	2.5
1960	100.0	46.3	43.6	28.2	25.9	22.4	3.1
1961	100.0	45.0	42.2	28.7	26.3	23.1	3.2
1962	100.0	44.5	41.7	28.5	26.1	23.8	3.1
1963	100.0	44.2	41.3	28.5	25.9	24.2	3.1
1964	100.0	43.9	41.0	28.1	25.5	24.9	3.1
1965	100.0	43.3	40.5	28.2	25.5	25.2	3.3
UNDERDEVELOPED COUNTRIES							
1925	100.0	34.7	34.2	62.9	62.7	1.9	0.6
1929	100.0	29.5	28.9	67.5	67.1	2.4	0.6
1933	100.0	27.3	27.0	68.1	67.4	3.8	0.9
1937	100.0	24.9	24.5	70.5	70.0	3.7	0.9
1938	100.0	26.8	26.5	68.4	67.9	3.8	1.0

Table III. PRIMARY ENERGY PRODUCTION PERCENTAGE DISTRIBUTION, SELECTED YEARS, 1925-1965

(Based on coal equivalents)

Region, country, year	Total primary energy production	Solid fuels		Liquid fuels		Natural gas	Hydro-electric power
		Total	Hard coal	Total	Crude oil		
	(1)	(2)	(3)	(4)	(5)	(6)	(7)
UNDERDEVELOPED COUNTRIES (CONTINUED)							
1950	100.0	12.0	11.7	84.9	84.7	2.3	0.7
1953	100.0	11.2	11.0	85.3	85.0	2.8	0.7
1955	100.0	9.5	9.3	86.9	86.7	2.9	0.7
1957	100.0	9.1	8.9	86.6	86.3	3.5	0.8
1960	100.0	8.2	8.0	86.7	86.3	4.3	0.8
1961	100.0	8.0	7.9	86.7	86.3	4.5	0.9
1962	100.0	7.8	7.7	86.9	86.5	4.4	0.8
1963	100.0	7.8	7.6	87.1	86.7	4.3	0.8
1964	100.0	7.0	6.8	87.7	87.4	4.4	0.8
1965	100.0	6.8	6.6	88.0	87.6	4.4	0.9
COMMUNIST COUNTRIES							
1925	100.0	85.3	68.6	13.4	13.4	1.2	0.1
1929	100.0	82.4	68.5	16.4	16.3	1.2	0.1
1933	100.0	75.6	63.8	22.2	22.1	2.0	0.1
1937	100.0	78.5	66.3	19.1	18.9	2.2	0.2
1938	100.0	78.1	65.8	19.5	19.3	2.1	0.3
1950	100.0	84.4	61.4	13.1	13.0	2.1	0.5
1953	100.0	82.3	59.6	14.9	14.9	2.3	0.5
1955	100.0	81.1	59.4	16.1	16.0	2.3	0.5
1957	100.0	77.7	57.2	18.1	18.1	3.4	0.7
1960	100.0	72.4	55.2	20.9	20.9	5.9	0.8
1961	100.0	70.5	53.9	21.8	21.7	7.0	0.8
1962	100.0	68.0	52.3	23.0	23.0	8.1	0.9
1963	100.0	66.5	50.7	23.5	23.5	9.2	0.8
1964	100.0	65.4	49.9	23.5	23.5	10.3	0.8
1965	100.0	63.6	49.0	24.1	24.1	11.4	0.8
USSR							
1925	100.0	59.8	49.3	39.4	39.4	0.7	0.1
1929	100.0	64.2	56.4	34.9	34.9	0.7	0.1
1933	100.0	68.2	59.0	30.3	30.3	1.4	0.1
1937	100.0	72.5	61.6	25.5	25.5	1.7	0.3
1938	100.0	72.3	61.2	25.7	25.7	1.7	0.4
1950	100.0	76.8	60.2	20.0	20.0	2.6	0.5
1953	100.0	74.5	58.7	22.3	22.3	2.5	0.7
1955	100.0	73.0	57.7	23.7	23.7	2.6	0.6
1957	100.0	67.7	53.3	27.0	27.0	4.4	0.9
1960	100.0	57.7	46.2	32.7	32.7	8.7	0.9
1961	100.0	53.8	43.3	34.5	34.5	10.7	1.0
1962	100.0	50.5	41.7	36.0	36.0	12.4	1.1
1963	100.0	48.4	39.0	36.6	36.6	13.9	1.1
1964	100.0	46.8	37.6	36.4	36.4	15.7	1.1
1965	100.0	45.2	36.4	36.7	36.7	17.1	1.0
COMMUNIST EASTERN EUROPE							
1925	100.0	90.8	65.7	7.3	7.3	1.9	0.1
1929	100.0	89.2	68.0	8.9	8.8	1.8	-
1933	100.0	78.0	57.5	18.0	17.6	3.9	0.1
1937	100.0	82.0	62.2	14.0	13.4	3.9	0.1
1938	100.0	83.0	63.8	13.1	12.6	3.8	0.1

Table III. PRIMARY ENERGY PRODUCTION PERCENTAGE DISTRIBUTION, SELECTED YEARS, 1925-1965

(Based on coal equivalents)

Region, country, year	Total primary energy production	Solid fuels		Liquid fuels		Natural gas	Hydro-electric power
		Total	Hard coal	Total	Crude oil		
	(1)	(2)	(3)	(4)	(5)	(6)	(7)
COMMUNIST EASTERN EUROPE (CONTINUED)							
1950	100.0	93.2	54.9	5.0	4.8	1.7	0.2
1953	100.0	90.2	49.8	7.0	6.9	2.7	0.1
1955	100.0	89.4	47.8	7.7	7.6	2.7	0.2
1957	100.0	89.3	46.0	7.4	7.3	3.1	0.2
1960	100.0	88.7	45.7	7.1	7.0	3.9	0.3
1961	100.0	88.7	44.4	7.0	6.9	4.0	0.2
1962	100.0	88.3	43.8	7.0	6.8	4.5	0.3
1963	100.0	88.0	43.3	6.9	6.7	5.0	0.2
1964	100.0	87.8	43.1	6.7	6.6	5.3	0.2
1965	100.0	87.0	43.0	6.8	6.7	5.8	0.3
COMMUNIST ASIA							
1925	100.0	100.0	100.0	-	-	-	-
1929	100.0	100.0	100.0	-	-	-	-
1933	100.0	99.5	99.5	0.5	0.5	-	-
1937	100.0	99.1	99.1	0.9	0.9	-	-
1938	100.0	98.6	98.6	1.4	1.4	-	-
1950	100.0	97.8	96.7	0.7	0.7	-	1.5
1953	100.0	98.1	97.9	1.4	1.4	-	0.5
1955	100.0	97.7	97.3	1.5	1.5	-	0.8
1957	100.0	97.3	96.9	1.7	1.7	-	1.0
1960	100.0	95.4	94.9	3.6	3.6	-	1.0
1961	100.0	95.6	95.1	3.6	3.6	-	0.8
1962	100.0	95.3	94.8	3.9	3.9	-	0.8
1963	100.0	95.3	94.8	4.0	4.0	-	0.8
1964	100.0	95.1	94.6	4.2	4.2	-	0.8
1965	100.0	94.5	94.1	4.7	4.7	-	0.8
ORGANISATION FOR ECONOMIC CO-OPERATION AND DEVELOPMENT (OECD)							
1925	100.0	83.8	80.0	12.1	11.8	3.4	0.7
1929	100.0	80.2	76.1	14.2	13.6	4.7	0.9
1933	100.0	76.8	72.7	16.7	16.2	5.2	1.3
1937	100.0	74.5	70.1	18.0	17.4	6.1	1.3
1938	100.0	73.6	68.6	18.7	18.0	6.3	1.4
1950	100.0	60.2	58.2	24.7	23.1	13.0	2.1
1953	100.0	53.8	51.7	27.8	25.9	16.1	2.3
1955	100.0	51.5	49.4	28.7	26.6	17.3	2.4
1957	100.0	50.1	48.0	28.8	26.7	18.6	2.5
1960	100.0	44.6	42.5	29.2	26.8	23.2	3.1
1961	100.0	43.1	41.1	29.7	27.2	24.0	3.1
1962	100.0	42.6	40.5	29.5	27.0	24.7	3.1
1963	100.0	42.3	40.2	29.5	26.8	25.1	3.1
1964	100.0	42.0	39.9	29.1	26.4	25.8	3.1
1965	100.0	41.2	39.2	29.3	26.5	26.2	3.3
COMMUNIST COUNTRIES							
1925	100.0	85.3	68.6	13.4	13.4	1.2	0.1
1929	100.0	82.4	68.5	16.4	16.3	1.2	0.1
1933	100.0	75.6	63.8	22.2	22.1	2.0	0.1
1937	100.0	78.5	66.3	19.1	18.9	2.2	0.2
1938	100.0	78.1	65.8	19.5	19.3	2.1	0.3

Table III. PRIMARY ENERGY PRODUCTION PERCENTAGE DISTRIBUTION, SELECTED YEARS, 1925-1965

(Based on coal equivalents)

Region, country, year	Total primary energy production	Solid fuels		Liquid fuels		Natural gas	Hydro-electric power
		Total	Hard coal	Total	Crude oil		
	(1)	(2)	(3)	(4)	(5)	(6)	(7)
COMMUNIST COUNTRIES (CONTINUED)							
1950	100.0	84.4	61.4	13.1	13.0	2.1	0.5
1953	100.0	82.3	59.6	14.9	14.9	2.3	0.5
1955	100.0	81.1	59.4	16.1	16.0	2.3	0.5
1957	100.0	77.7	57.2	18.1	18.1	3.4	0.7
1960	100.0	72.4	55.2	20.9	20.9	5.9	0.8
1961	100.0	70.5	53.9	21.8	21.7	7.0	0.8
1962	100.0	68.0	52.3	23.0	23.0	8.1	0.9
1963	100.0	66.5	50.7	23.5	23.5	9.2	0.8
1964	100.0	65.4	49.9	23.5	23.5	10.3	0.8
1965	100.0	63.6	49.0	24.1	24.1	11.4	0.8
WORLD EXCLUDING OECD AND COMMUNIST COUNTRIES							
1925	100.0	52.4	49.3	45.7	45.5	1.4	0.6
1929	100.0	44.2	40.9	53.2	52.9	1.9	0.6
1933	100.0	40.9	38.1	55.0	54.5	3.1	1.0
1937	100.0	38.0	35.4	57.9	57.5	3.0	1.1
1938	100.0	39.5	36.8	56.3	55.9	3.2	1.1
1950	100.0	23.0	20.4	74.1	73.9	2.0	0.9
1953	100.0	20.5	18.3	76.1	75.9	2.5	1.0
1955	100.0	18.2	16.2	78.2	78.0	2.6	1.0
1957	100.0	17.2	15.2	78.6	78.4	3.2	1.0
1960	100.0	15.4	13.5	79.6	79.2	4.0	1.0
1961	100.0	15.1	13.2	79.7	79.3	4.1	1.1
1962	100.0	14.4	12.6	80.4	80.1	4.1	1.1
1963	100.0	14.1	12.2	80.8	80.5	4.0	1.1
1964	100.0	13.1	11.3	81.7	81.3	4.2	1.1
1965	100.0	12.9	11.2	81.9	81.5	4.1	1.1

DERIVATION OF TABLE IV

Column	*Derivation*
(1)	Sources
(2)	Sum of cols. (3) and (4)
(3)	Sources
(4)	Sum of cols. (5), (6), (7), (8), and liquefied petroleum gases from sources
(5)	Sources
(6)	Sources
(7)	Sources
(8)	Sources
(9), (10)	Sources. For both gas and electricity, represents net imports or net exports

Table IV. ENERGY IMPORTS AND EXPORTS, SELECTED YEARS, 1925-1965

(Original units)

Region, country, year	Solid fuels (10^3 m.t. coal equiv.)	Liquid fuels (10^3 m.t.)							Gas (10^6 c.m.)	Electricity (10^6 kwh)
				Refined petroleum products						
		Total	Crude oil	Total	Gasoline	Kerosine	Fuel oils	Lubes and greases		
	(1)	(2)	(3)	(4)	(5)	(6)	(7)	(8)	(9)	(10)
WORLD								IMPORTS		
1925	136597	41867	18802	23065	6231	4387	10419	1852	4	2085
1929	168343	72664	36024	36640	12574	5610	15765	2479	7	2499
1933	113488	68438	32187	36251	11814	4276	18205	1710	59	2177
1937	142341	99379	50456	48923	14338	4500	26619	2261	136	3474
1938	125691	103967	52988	50980	15989	4576	26761	2104	49	3487
1950	116920	238316	144627	93689	20793	6923	61331	2451	1058	3930
1953	128839	318722	205372	113350	23919	8795	74952	2550	851	4102
1955	155061	396235	257398	138837	27314	11314	96131	3414	979	6130
1957	158291	459214	298579	160635	29938	11123	115247	3539	817	6530
1960	132112	567522	384539	182983	31881	11402	134768	3928	4728	11020
1961	133888	621548	431475	190073	31878	11729	141078	4164	6571	11020
1962	143000	688328	480728	207600	30197	15254	156064	4393	11613	9447
1963	158247	752906	533907	218999	29730	16022	166495	4804	11722	9207
1964	160872	830058	605739	224319	28417	15401	173277	4839	12748	11843
1965	157916	912000	673974	238026	26832	16891	186741	4279	13730	14117
WORLD								EXPORTS		
1925	145845	45260	15902	29359	6686	4529	16307	1830	4	1969
1929	178539	77886	31951	45934	14245	6289	23072	2317	7	2588
1933	120246	75633	31198	44435	13102	4347	25099	1883	59	2300

Table IV. ENERGY IMPORTS AND EXPORTS, SELECTED YEARS, 1925-1965

(Original units)

Region, country, year	Solid fuels (10^3 m.t. coal equiv.)	Liquid fuels (10^3 m.t.) Total	Crude oil	Refined petroleum products Total	Gasoline	Kerosine	Fuel oils	Lubes and greases	Gas (10^6 c.m.)	Electricity (10^6 kwh)
	(1)	(2)	(3)	(4)	(5)	(6)	(7)	(8)	(9)	(10)
WORLD (CONTINUED)							EXPORTS			
1937	150331	110506	47553	62953	15788	5077	39464	2622	136	3746
1938	129685	112904	49656	63248	17611	5024	38303	2308	49	3754
1950	120162	250424	139327	111097	22083	7477	78161	2562	975	3730
1953	128135	334608	200601	134007	27085	9529	90738	3002	878	5087
1955	157228	404594	253896	150698	30255	12323	103533	3921	1006	7230
1957	167356	467918	300649	167269	31830	14159	116673	3825	946	8580
1960	132950	581104	382066	199038	34643	15638	142556	5051	4769	11060
1961	136700	630595	423268	207327	34498	16544	149697	5202	6608	12445
1962	145780	707114	476563	230551	35355	17676	170170	5668	11645	8488
1963	161450	771882	528455	243427	36055	17373	181949	5993	11743	8387
1964	160447	852774	602010	250764	35957	18085	187853	6175	12816	12759
1965	158700	930234	662753	267481	38251	20187	199325	6090	13837	13776
NORTH AMERICA							IMPORTS			
1925	16689	14257	11485	2772	729	21	1979	42	2	1273
1929	18706	21285	16314	4971	1622	44	3222	81	3	1423
1933	11487	11281	8760	2521	191	6	2282	42	-	967
1937	14573	14575	10654	3921	313	9	3532	67	-	1827
1938	12836	13636	9727	3909	435	22	3381	71	-	1808
1950	25666	59419	37436	21983	1105	402	20327	78	149	1670
1953	21890	70853	46219	24634	1031	494	22839	151	-	2115
1955	18760	83868	55053	28815	1277	514	26733	190	-	4070
1957	18720	102672	69515	33157	2187	580	30118	173	266	3810
1960	12940	117839	73743	44096	3169	593	40145	176	4081	4560
1961	11690	122256	76596	45660	3165	414	41910	163	5892	2254
1962	12020	131476	82216	49260	1810	2555	44529	165	10923	722
1963	12740	135826	84127	51699	2195	3433	45673	171	11023	154
1964	14240	144078	87536	56542	2029	3351	50595	203	12000	1094
1965	15797	157336	89586	67750	1805	4259	60784	242	12203	13
NORTH AMERICA							EXPORTS			
1925	20344	14951	1931	13020	3733	2743	5161	1383	4	1273
1929	20828	20922	3871	17051	7317	2588	5595	1551	7	1423
1933	9967	14024	5270	8754	3464	1160	2956	1174	59	988
1937	14515	23229	9604	13625	4519	1149	6384	1573	136	1846
1938	12050	25939	11036	14903	5912	971	6672	1348	49	1826
1950	27822	12983	4975	8008	2448	245	3222	1954	806	1830
1953	33969	16959	3169	13790	3860	915	7000	1760	593	2332
1955	50540	17028	3658	13370	3410	411	7222	1962	577	4270
1957	74480	32581	14709	17872	3914	798	10874	1896	108	4260
1960	35700	14638	6149	8489	1629	89	4192	2202	2923	5130
1961	34510	16350	9274	7076	1033	27	3181	2389	4604	2786
1962	37920	19791	12632	7159	819	40	3320	2474	9766	1293
1963	47100	21274	12525	8749	879	136	4575	2569	9901	745
1964	46630	22298	13879	8419	1069	44	3902	2602	10838	1241
1965	48220	22425	14749	7676	787	104	3074	2388	10990	73
CANADA							IMPORTS			
1925	15601	2733	2257	476	280	19	140	37	2	-
1929	17619	5495	4683	812	583	17	137	75	3	-
1933	10698	4599	4065	534	189	6	297	42	-	-
1937	13690	6179	5649	530	246	9	209	66	-	-

Table IV. ENERGY IMPORTS AND EXPORTS, SELECTED YEARS, 1925-1965

(Original units)

Region, country, year	Solid fuels (10^3 m.t. coal equiv.)	Liquid fuels (10^3 m.t.): Total	Liquid fuels: Crude oil	Refined petroleum products: Total	Refined petroleum products: Gasoline	Refined petroleum products: Kerosine	Refined petroleum products: Fuel oils	Refined petroleum products: Lubes and greases	Gas (10^6 c.m.)	Electricity (10^6 kwh)
	(1)	(2)	(3)	(4)	(5)	(6)	(7)	(8)	(9)	(10)
CANADA (CONTINUED)							IMPORTS			
1938	12126	5677	4971	706	397	22	217	70	-	-
1950	24927	14957	11607	3350	1021	370	1810	78	149	-
1953	21518	16101	11814	4287	963	494	2560	151	-	-
1955	18320	17151	12500	4651	677	513	3170	190	-	-
1957	18270	20301	16087	4214	690	575	2677	173	266	-
1960	12560	22206	17749	4457	310	583	3376	175	-	-
1961	11410	22333	18664	3669	210	356	2932	163	-	-
1962	11650	22706	18850	3856	173	319	3197	160	-	-
1963	12330	24930	20645	4285	290	386	3432	167	-	-
1964	13860	25590	20216	5374	304	348	4517	197	-	-
1965	15530	28223	20192	8031	279	300	7206	237	-	13
CANADA							EXPORTS			
1925	754	43	26	17	5	6	6	-	-	1273
1929	803	122	99	23	16	5	2	-	-	1423
1933	251	115	44	71	14	4	53	-	-	988
1937	353	69	-	69	14	3	47	5	6	1846
1938	346	31	-	31	17	3	8	3	7	1826
1950	667	5	-	5	-	1	4	-	-	1830
1953	357	346	322	24	1	-	23	-	52	2332
1955	630	2126	2005	121	43	-	78	-	5	4270
1957	450	7985	7531	454	142	139	171	2	-	4260
1960	880	6102	5708	394	160	2	112	1	2923	5130
1961	990	9182	8814	368	67	-	160	-	4604	2786
1962	920	12974	12376	598	114	-	307	5	9766	1293
1963	980	12857	12282	575	57	26	289	9	9901	745
1964	1240	14499	13684	815	123	-	347	5	10838	1241
1965	1170	15651	14592	1059	30	-	348	6	10990	-
UNITED STATES							IMPORTS			
1925	1082	11523	9228	2295	449	2	1839	5	-	1273
1929	1081	15788	11631	4157	1039	27	3085	6	-	1423
1933	777	6681	4695	1986	2	-	1984	-	-	967
1937	859	8394	5005	3389	66	-	3322	1	-	1827
1938	684	7958	4756	3202	38	-	3163	1	-	1808
1950	727	44462	25829	18633	84	32	18517	-	-	1670
1953	362	54749	34405	20344	65	-	20279	-	-	2115
1955	410	66672	42553	24119	598	-	23521	-	-	4070
1957	430	82334	53428	28906	1495	4	27407	-	-	3810
1960	350	95587	55994	39593	2856	9	36728	-	4081	4560
1961	260	99844	57932	41912	2952	55	38905	-	5892	2254
1962	350	108704	63366	45338	1633	2234	41273	4	10923	722
1963	380	110822	63482	47340	1901	3044	42175	3	11023	154
1964	360	118392	67320	51072	1721	3000	45990	5	12000	1094
1965	250	129007	69394	59613	1520	3951	53487	4	12203	-
UNITED STATES							EXPORTS			
1925	19590	14908	1905	13003	3728	2737	5155	1383	4	-
1929	20025	20800	3772	17028	7301	2583	5593	1551	7	-
1933	9716	13909	5226	8683	3450	1156	2903	1174	59	-
1937	14162	23160	9604	13556	4505	1146	6337	1568	130	-
1938	11704	25908	11036	14872	5895	968	6664	1345	42	-

Table IV. ENERGY IMPORTS AND EXPORTS, SELECTED YEARS, 1925-1965

(Original units)

Region, country, year	Solid fuels (10^3 m.t. coal equiv.)	Liquid fuels (10^3 m.t.): Total	Liquid fuels: Crude oil	Refined petroleum products: Total	Gasoline	Kerosine	Fuel oils	Lubes and greases	Gas (10^6 c.m.)	Electricity (10^6 kwh)
	(1)	(2)	(3)	(4)	(5)	(6)	(7)	(8)	(9)	(10)
UNITED STATES (CONTINUED)							EXPORTS			
1950	27155	12978	4975	8003	2448	244	3218	1954	806	-
1953	33612	16613	2847	13766	3859	915	6977	1760	541	-
1955	49910	14902	1653	13249	3367	411	7144	1962	572	-
1957	74030	24596	7178	17418	3772	659	10703	1894	108	-
1960	34810	8536	441	8095	1469	87	4080	2201	-	-
1961	33510	7168	460	6708	966	27	3021	2389	-	-
1962	37000	6817	256	6561	705	40	3013	2469	-	-
1963	46120	8417	243	8174	822	110	4286	2560	-	-
1964	45390	7799	195	7604	946	44	3555	2597	-	-
1965	47050	6774	157	6617	757	104	2726	2382	-	73
WESTERN EUROPE							IMPORTS			
1925	93882	12930	2790	10140	3793	1704	3268	1366	-	743
1929	118034	19480	2806	16674	7452	2152	5341	1729	-	1007
1933	80696	24821	5520	19301	8832	1628	7655	1186	-	1172
1937	101034	33681	11136	22545	8852	1787	10409	1497	-	1613
1938	86422	36044	12827	23217	9571	1676	10597	1373	-	1661
1950	61209	66561	39781	26780	7992	2376	15201	1211	141	1950
1953	69274	108774	80547	28227	6145	2710	18245	1122	137	1587
1955	98685	140519	100442	40077	7066	2933	28424	1443	190	1550
1957	103627	162216	109335	52881	8567	2898	39733	1391	267	1740
1960	76883	233150	168187	64963	9442	2458	51095	1548	98	4960
1961	75564	258280	193730	64550	9776	2299	50302	1650	99	5694
1962	81405	295295	215531	79764	11337	3559	62503	1783	104	5398
1963	94350	332490	244573	87917	11380	4431	69654	1798	118	5197
1964	88779	374827	282890	91937	12378	5208	71546	2032	166	6446
1965	80605	425140	326428	98712	12982	5531	77269	1825	946	9514
WESTERN EUROPE							EXPORTS			
1925	101998	775	-	775	197	85	388	105	-	696
1929	125237	659	2	656	158	72	276	150	-	1165
1933	85411	754	37	717	213	67	278	159	-	1308
1937	106940	1659	1	1658	432	187	748	291	-	1900
1938	90757	1637	-	1637	495	169	682	291	-	1928
1950	53676	9380	1079	8301	1649	249	6111	292	90	1500
1953	53457	26888	2100	24788	5925	1154	17160	531	132	2566
1955	61758	28748	1556	27192	7078	1531	17429	932	217	2770
1957	52496	28322	1221	27101	7018	1583	17236	941	419	3040
1960	45720	41951	1678	40273	9172	2554	26785	1242	153	4460
1961	46180	44125	1617	42508	9725	2858	28076	1226	131	7047
1962	45980	48756	2395	46361	10309	3016	30980	1412	136	4881
1963	49730	50605	2667	47938	10100	3348	32297	1418	144	4855
1964	42675	50833	699	50134	10451	3198	33981	1651	122	7262
1965	37433	60655	449	60206	12034	3404	42027	1678	118	9121
EUROPEAN ECONOMIC COMMUNITY (EEC)							IMPORTS			
1925	68197	4882	357	4525	1904	792	972	857	-	723
1929	84335	8358	564	7794	3639	798	2207	1150	-	972
1933	54482	11438	3375	8063	3791	527	3111	634	-	1158
1937	67662	17094	8571	8523	2521	412	4767	823	-	1598
1938	56009	18427	9964	8463	2705	335	4686	737	-	1637
1950	32244	31281	25864	5417	1186	224	3600	407	141	1770

Table IV. ENERGY IMPORTS AND EXPORTS, SELECTED YEARS, 1925-1965

(Original units)

Region, country, year	Solid fuels (10^3 m.t. coal equiv.)	Liquid fuels (10^3 m.t.)		Refined petroleum products					Gas (10^6 c.m.)	Electricity (10^6 kwh)
		Total	Crude oil	Total	Gasoline	Kerosine	Fuel oils	Lubes and greases		
	(1)	(2)	(3)	(4)	(5)	(6)	(7)	(8)	(9)	(10)
EUROPEAN ECONOMIC COMMUNITY (EEC) (CONTINUED)							IMPORTS			
1953	42428	55043	49241	5802	995	211	4248	346	137	1291
1955	57808	74448	65284	9164	1299	244	5887	589	190	1370
1957	73516	86509	71177	15332	1722	271	12579	562	267	1360
1960	51900	126855	106477	20378	2209	467	16847	562	94	4300
1961	51700	146204	124998	21206	2118	435	17664	619	99	4629
1962	56160	168161	139045	29116	2755	488	24743	706	104	4333
1963	68130	194120	162842	31278	2633	674	26778	725	118	4380
1964	62770	224509	192506	32003	2993	686	27002	821	76	4589
1965	56672	260646	226759	33887	3207	683	28852	654	302	6302
EUROPEAN ECONOMIC COMMUNITY (EEC)							EXPORTS			
1925	46793	119	-	119	23	6	20	70	-	-
1929	59550	225	2	223	49	7	49	118	-	-
1933	42476	387	37	350	55	20	149	126	-	20
1937	62715	1047	1	1046	221	99	496	230	-	-
1938	51915	1056	-	1056	302	120	419	215	-	-
1950	37316	7041	9	7032	1512	219	5150	151	90	40
1953	37511	17144	-	17144	4834	1001	10969	322	132	130
1955	46958	20422	37	20385	5569	1267	12792	544	217	150
1957	42346	20017	75	19942	5210	1254	12680	493	419	580
1960	38570	29761	624	29137	6996	1776	19234	648	153	230
1961	38560	32917	553	32364	7751	1900	21506	625	131	282
1962	39060	33078	339	32739	7810	2007	21614	693	136	1137
1963	39230	34806	179	34627	8072	2292	22811	732	144	3
1964	34865	36390	6	36384	8238	2257	24204	883	122	-
1965	32143	44785	32	44753	9501	2391	30894	942	118	-
BELGIUM-LUXEMBOURG							IMPORTS			
1925	11380	343	8	335	156	86	21	72	-	-
1929	15127	429	1	428	193	71	90	74	-	-
1933	7305	447	86	361	231	30	65	35	-	-
1937	9547	1130	281	849	310	9	347	183	-	8
1938	6605	1072	308	764	301	8	298	157	-	5
1950	3485	2437	442	1995	682	33	1135	145	-	60
1953	5317	4903	2933	1970	551	55	1241	123	-	-
1955	7340	7095	4712	2383	354	29	1732	184	-	90
1957	9180	8561	5474	3087	389	29	2381	184	-	-
1960	8100	10051	6861	3190	380	24	2471	158	-	20
1961	8280	11250	7838	3412	369	26	2628	172	-	-
1962	8840	12887	8536	4351	430	41	3423	199	-	-
1963	11500	16339	12152	4187	349	22	3344	209	-	-
1964	11290	18094	13284	4810	273	29	4003	224	-	381
1965	10900	19988	15467	4521	330	17	3716	212	-	723
BELGIUM-LUXEMBOURG							EXPORTS			
1925	3750	13	-	13	1	1	-	11	-	-
1929	4840	4	-	4	-	-	-	4	-	-
1933	4639	40	37	3	-	-	1	2	-	20
1937	6059	292	-	292	13	3	187	89	-	-
1938	6197	244	-	244	9	3	153	79	-	-
1950	3127	148	-	148	32	2	53	61	9	-
1953	5084	1493	-	1493	284	41	1099	51	10	58

Table IV. ENERGY IMPORTS AND EXPORTS, SELECTED YEARS, 1925-1965

(Original units)

Region, country, year	Solid fuels (10^3 m.t. coal equiv.)	Liquid fuels (10^3 m.t.)		Refined petroleum products					Gas (10^6 c.m.)	Electricity (10^6 kwh)
		Total	Crude oil	Total	Gasoline	Kerosine	Fuel oils	Lubes and greases		
	(1)	(2)	(3)	(4)	(5)	(6)	(7)	(8)	(9)	(10)
BELGIUM-LUXEMBOURG (CONTINUED)							EXPORTS			
1955	8270	1845	32	1813	311	106	1295	89	23	-
1957	5310	2120	49	2071	304	123	1543	87	32	140
1960	3080	2519	-	2519	486	217	1701	98	27	-
1961	3490	2141	-	2141	374	157	1483	105	27	282
1962	3430	2163	2	2161	433	175	1416	113	23	364
1963	3090	3463	-	3463	842	201	2246	125	27	3
1964	2940	3253	-	3253	622	384	2067	132	23	-
1965	2440	3328	-	3328	862	412	1847	157	23	-
FRANCE							IMPORTS			
1925	29253	1955	102	1853	1008	249	240	356	-	267
1929	35315	3163	175	2988	1766	221	722	279	-	486
1933	25146	5764	2799	2965	1890	74	808	193	-	510
1937	29713	7720	6140	1580	650	1	827	102	-	571
1938	22030	8246	6968	1278	704	-	482	92	-	570
1950	13500	14639	14133	506	62	-	380	64	9	240
1953	14621	22377	22001	376	138	5	200	33	37	-
1955	16050	25608	24814	794	426	16	315	37	59	-
1957	24340	26520	24084	2436	562	48	1793	33	131	270
1960	15290	33503	31022	2481	824	22	1590	15	90	-
1961	15070	37136	35016	2120	717	14	1351	10	90	94
1962	15310	39808	37160	2648	761	7	1829	19	95	-
1963	22050	47069	43258	3811	700	20	3004	20	104	570
1964	19750	53356	49274	4082	604	20	3365	26	72	2228
1965	16808	61987	58556	3431	502	18	2820	29	302	973
FRANCE							EXPORTS			
1925	1999	55	-	55	18	5	5	27	-	-
1929	3643	88	-	88	39	7	10	32	-	-
1933	1593	217	-	217	45	20	115	37	-	-
1937	967	476	1	475	129	75	243	28	-	-
1938	1149	525	-	525	221	95	176	33	-	-
1950	2200	3214	9	3205	619	89	2473	24	-	-
1953	2521	6595	-	6595	1559	268	4695	73	-	11
1955	6250	5374	-	5374	1270	488	3387	159	-	70
1957	2290	3674	20	3654	983	411	2082	108	-	-
1960	1540	6347	1	6346	1668	638	3715	189	-	100
1961	1440	7228	-	7228	1777	702	4398	182	-	-
1962	1440	7042	-	7042	1434	607	4642	187	-	753
1963	1060	7628	-	7628	1395	860	4932	220	-	-
1964	980	7743	-	7743	1491	684	5024	256	-	-
1965	970	9615	-	9615	1889	490	6609	235	-	-
GERMANY							IMPORTS			
1925	8128	1133	53	1080	437	146	191	306	-	229
1929	8913	2505	90	2415	1066	149	542	658	-	220
1933	4986	2437	281	2156	1005	97	778	276	-	450
1937	6426	3841	732	3109	1058	48	1588	415	-	800
1938	6807	4418	778	3640	1357	22	1873	388	-	800

Table IV. ENERGY IMPORTS AND EXPORTS, SELECTED YEARS, 1925-1965

(Original units)

Region, country, year	Solid fuels (10^3 m.t. coal equiv.)	Liquid fuels (10^3 m.t.)		Refined petroleum products					Gas (10^6 c.m.)	Electricity (10^6 kwh)
		Total	Crude oil	Total	Gasoline	Kerosine	Fuel oils	Lubes and greases		
	(1)	(2)	(3)	(4)	(5)	(6)	(7)	(8)	(9)	(10)
GERMANY (CONTINUED)							EXPORTS			
1925	37767	36	-	36	4	-	1	31	-	-
1929	45347	93	-	93	8	-	9	76	-	-
1933	30664	90	-	90	8	-	5	77	-	-
1937	48830	124	-	124	12	-	6	106	-	-
1938	38536	115	-	115	6	-	13	96	-	-
GERMANY, FEDERAL REPUBLIC							IMPORTS			
1950	2100	2838	1933	905	240	3	650	12	32	1270
1953	7219	5607	4560	1047	120	-	870	57	91	1291
1955	15198	9979	7111	2868	275	35	2435	109	117	1240
1957	18456	14153	8158	5995	556	34	5255	131	122	630
1960	10360	30100	23244	6856	784	238	5671	152	-	4160
1961	10300	36322	29388	6934	801	174	5770	173	-	4324
1962	11370	45796	33201	12595	1329	199	10823	219	-	3064
1963	12100	54087	40077	14010	1339	165	12290	178	-	2465
1964	11225	65325	51276	14049	1673	262	11827	246	-	960
1965	10804	74651	59068	15583	1857	272	13194	193	-	4241
GERMANY, FEDERAL REPUBLIC							EXPORTS			
1950	30785	83	-	83	-	-	79	4	81	-
1953	28312	440	-	440	185	34	100	121	122	-
1955	29518	840	-	840	333	27	369	58	194	80
1957	31466	716	-	716	223	2	326	62	387	360
1960	29070	2527	9	2518	545	22	1698	69	126	-
1961	28390	4495	24	4471	1174	18	2968	81	104	-
1962	29050	3801	-	3801	1206	228	2064	75	113	-
1963	29650	4777	-	4777	1227	169	3070	89	117	-
1964	25790	5428	-	5428	1297	148	3679	99	99	-
1965	23533	4609	21	4588	1131	41	3124	100	95	-
ITALY							IMPORTS			
1925	10434	786	37	749	189	116	363	81	-	227
1929	14540	1283	60	1223	387	162	593	81	-	244
1933	9513	1714	135	1579	291	137	1084	67	-	177
1937	12867	2579	936	1643	261	95	1216	71	-	194
1938	12099	2637	1477	1160	100	52	964	44	-	244
1950	8278	5311	4556	755	22	7	630	96	-	200
1953	9260	13359	12850	509	10	-	450	49	-	-
1955	10400	17496	17006	490	76	-	323	54	-	20
1957	11710	20761	19923	838	27	-	719	47	-	460
1960	10320	30491	28862	1629	90	-	1423	80	-	-
1961	10240	35601	33470	2131	116	1	1864	110	-	168
1962	11020	43111	40220	2891	124	2	2611	122	-	1269
1963	11630	49583	46465	3118	121	126	2695	158	-	1299
1964	10770	57124	55234	1890	159	11	1564	146	-	1002
1965	10700	69620	67289	2331	109	9	2108	95	-	331
ITALY							EXPORTS			
1925	53	1	-	1	-	-	1	-	-	-
1929	35	13	-	13	2	-	6	5	-	-
1933	36	13	-	13	2	-	2	9	-	-

Table IV. ENERGY IMPORTS AND EXPORTS, SELECTED YEARS, 1925-1965

(Original units)

Region, country, year	Solid fuels (10^3 m.t. coal equiv.)	Liquid fuels (10^3 m.t.)		Refined petroleum products					Gas (10^6 c.m.)	Electricity (10^6 kwh)
		Total	Crude oil	Total	Gasoline	Kerosine	Fuel oils	Lubes and greases		
	(1)	(2)	(3)	(4)	(5)	(6)	(7)	(8)	(9)	(10)
ITALY (CONTINUED)								EXPORTS		
1937	16	133	-	133	67	21	40	5	-	-
1938	18	146	-	146	64	21	55	6	-	-
1950	63	770	-	770	246	114	410	-	-	-
1953	88	4308	-	4308	1329	457	2515	7	-	48
1955	70	4976	5	4971	1699	458	2738	74	-	-
1957	100	4983	6	4977	1478	327	3137	27	-	-
1960	110	7103	605	6498	1851	324	4269	41	-	130
1961	90	7830	529	7301	1796	397	5064	30	-	-
1962	160	8564	334	8230	1874	376	5913	50	-	-
1963	160	9335	179	9156	1814	485	6755	55	-	-
1964	95	10156	-	10156	1866	406	7747	81	-	-
1965	110	16315	-	16315	2503	764	12759	144	-	-
NETHERLANDS								IMPORTS		
1925	9002	665	157	508	114	195	157	42	-	-
1929	10440	978	238	740	227	195	260	58	-	22
1933	7532	1076	74	1002	374	189	376	63	-	21
1937	9109	1824	482	1342	242	259	789	52	-	25
1938	8468	2054	433	1621	243	253	1069	56	-	18
1950	4881	6056	4800	1256	180	181	805	90	100	-
1953	6011	8797	6897	1900	176	151	1487	84	9	-
1955	8820	14270	11641	2629	168	164	2082	205	14	20
1957	9830	16514	13538	2976	188	160	2431	167	14	-
1960	7830	22710	16488	6222	131	183	5692	157	4	120
1961	7810	25895	19286	6609	115	220	6051	154	9	43
1962	9620	26559	19928	6631	111	239	6057	147	9	-
1963	10850	27042	20890	6152	124	341	5445	160	14	46
1964	9735	30610	23438	7172	284	364	6243	179	4	18
1965	7460	34400	26379	8021	409	367	7014	125	-	34
NETHERLANDS								EXPORTS		
1925	3224	14	-	14	-	-	13	1	-	-
1929	5685	27	2	25	-	-	24	1	-	-
1933	5544	27	-	27	-	-	26	1	-	-
1937	6843	22	-	22	-	-	20	2	-	-
1938	6015	26	-	26	2	1	22	1	-	-
1950	1141	2826	-	2826	615	14	2135	62	-	40
1953	1506	4308	-	4308	1477	201	2560	70	-	13
1955	2850	7387	-	7387	1956	188	5003	164	-	-
1957	3180	8524	-	8524	2222	391	5592	209	-	80
1960	4770	11265	9	11256	2446	575	7851	251	-	-
1961	5150	11223	-	11223	2630	626	7593	227	-	-
1962	4980	11508	3	11505	2863	621	7579	268	-	20
1963	5270	9603	-	9603	2794	577	5808	243	-	-
1964	5060	9810	6	9804	2962	635	5687	315	-	-
1965	5090	10918	11	10907	3116	684	6555	306	-	-
EUROPEAN FREE TRADE ASSOCIATION (EFTA)								IMPORTS		
1925	19191	7202	2397	4805	1618	763	1987	437	-	20
1929	25594	9741	2098	7643	3297	1184	2665	497	-	35
1933	20685	11484	1871	9613	4441	933	3743	496	-	14
1937	26420	14474	2346	12128	5688	1131	4715	594	-	15

Table IV. ENERGY IMPORTS AND EXPORTS, SELECTED YEARS, 1925-1965

(Original units)

Region, country, year	Solid fuels (10³ m.t. coal equiv.)	Liquid fuels (10³ m.t.) Total	Liquid fuels: Crude oil	Refined petroleum products: Total	Refined: Gasoline	Refined: Kerosine	Refined: Fuel oils	Refined: Lubes and greases	Gas (10⁶ c.m.)	Electricity (10⁶ kwh)
	(1)	(2)	(3)	(4)	(5)	(6)	(7)	(8)	(9)	(10)
EUROPEAN FREE TRADE ASSOCIATION (EFTA) (CONTINUED)							IMPORTS			
1938	24063	15411	2603	12808	6194	1101	4952	561	-	24
1950	22949	28150	10612	17538	5755	1885	9218	680	-	180
1953	20875	44420	27692	16728	4015	2168	9907	635	-	296
1955	34110	54840	31225	23615	4528	2279	16034	710	-	120
1957	23060	60343	31797	28546	5688	2230	19859	689	-	380
1960	17890	88579	49925	38654	6906	1686	29103	849	4	230
1961	16650	93215	56137	37078	7341	1536	27165	895	-	890
1962	17130	104902	61214	43688	8228	2682	31720	911	-	983
1963	18380	114189	64729	49460	8468	3303	36595	934	-	480
1964	17020	123379	70798	52581	9056	3995	38311	995	90	819
1965	14937	134325	78605	55720	9400	4299	40633	1009	644	2226
EUROPEAN FREE TRADE ASSOCIATION (EFTA)							EXPORTS			
1925	55113	655	-	655	173	79	368	35	-	696
1929	65527	431	-	430	107	65	226	32	-	1165
1933	42879	358	-	358	156	46	123	33	-	1288
1937	44178	560	-	560	209	88	202	61	-	1900
1938	38809	529	-	529	191	49	213	76	-	1928
1950	16173	2313	1070	1243	134	30	938	141	-	1460
1953	15775	9697	2100	7597	1089	153	6148	207	-	2401
1955	14630	8172	1519	6653	1436	238	4583	387	-	2570
1957	9910	7907	1145	6762	1630	275	4408	437	-	2280
1960	6970	10794	1054	9740	1911	691	6533	587	-	3990
1961	7370	9814	885	8929	1690	889	5731	591	-	6428
1962	6750	13662	1495	12167	2087	946	8422	694	-	3333
1963	10280	14030	1983	12047	1754	985	8640	639	-	3728
1964	7550	12587	343	12244	1914	816	8759	722	-	5690
1965	5090	13849	272	13577	2168	893	9783	706	-	8487
AUSTRIA							IMPORTS			
1925	5060	123	18	105	47	25	20	13	-	-
1929	6417	229	51	178	104	31	32	11	-	-
1933	3046	313	198	115	50	9	50	6	-	-
1937	3319	321	106	215	81	39	88	7	-	-
1938	3773	329	155	174	72	23	71	8	-	-
1950	5254	63	-	63	49	-	6	8	-	-
1953	4223	11	-	11	1	-	-	10	-	-
1955	4970	326	-	326	97	-	207	22	-	-
1957	5630	375	-	375	148	-	200	26	-	-
1960	4970	1652	535	1117	303	-	771	35	-	-
1961	4540	1855	541	1314	422	-	847	38	-	-
1962	4810	2171	628	1543	528	7	952	39	-	-
1963	5350	2499	825	1674	523	7	1093	44	-	-
1964	5130	2647	788	1859	476	7	1323	49	-	-
1965	4555	2489	661	1828	467	7	1300	50	-	-
AUSTRIA							EXPORTS			
1925	-	-	-	-	-	-	-	-	-	30
1929	-	-	-	-	-	-	-	-	-	120
1933	-	-	-	-	-	-	-	-	-	301
1937	-	-	-	-	-	-	-	-	-	342
1938	-	-	-	-	-	-	-	-	-	367

Table IV. ENERGY IMPORTS AND EXPORTS, SELECTED YEARS, 1925–1965

(Original units)

Region, country, year	Solid fuels (10^3 m.t. coal equiv.)	Liquid fuels (10^3 m.t.)							Gas (10^6 c.m.)	Electricity (10^6 kwh)
				Refined petroleum products						
		Total	Crude oil	Total	Gasoline	Kerosine	Fuel oils	Lubes and greases		
	(1)	(2)	(3)	(4)	(5)	(6)	(7)	(8)	(9)	(10)
AUSTRIA (CONTINUED)							EXPORTS			
1950	11	1118	1070	48	-	-	48	-	-	690
1953	-	2175	2100	75	-	-	75	-	-	1090
1955	20	1603	1450	153	12	15	124	2	-	1080
1957	20	1405	1124	281	-	10	270	1	-	1240
1960	20	1151	1003	148	-	-	140	8	-	1900
1961	20	862	773	89	-	-	84	5	-	1949
1962	20	702	496	206	-	-	195	11	-	2099
1963	10	764	543	221	-	-	206	15	-	1693
1964	10	208	-	208	-	-	131	77	-	2708
1965	10	274	-	274	-	-	200	74	-	3870
DENMARK							IMPORTS			
1925	4022	299	1	298	98	97	80	23	-	20
1929	5500	428	3	425	174	89	140	22	-	35
1933	4902	571	-	571	219	90	236	26	-	14
1937	6024	706	-	706	303	90	288	25	-	15
1938	5396	860	11	849	336	117	369	27	-	24
1950	5731	1804	34	1770	513	69	1149	39	-	180
1953	6059	2115	21	2094	562	95	1401	36	-	296
1955	7360	3236	30	3206	693	133	2268	52	-	-
1957	4430	3918	30	3888	782	132	2848	51	-	380
1960	5290	5189	35	5154	998	271	3734	66	-	100
1961	4980	5861	237	5624	1099	318	4031	72	-	881
1962	5310	7369	1256	6113	1179	324	4435	82	-	895
1963	5380	8314	1990	6324	945	416	4810	69	-	432
1964	4830	9848	3040	6808	1059	392	5188	88	-	819
1965	4235	10938	3676	7262	1130	413	5548	85	-	1736
DENMARK							EXPORTS			
1925	-	1	-	1	-	-	-	1	-	-
1929	-	1	-	-	-	-	-	-	-	-
1933	-	-	-	-	-	-	-	-	-	-
1937	-	-	-	-	-	-	-	-	-	-
1938	-	-	-	-	-	-	-	-	-	-
1950	-	-	-	-	-	-	-	-	-	-
1953	-	-	-	-	-	-	-	-	-	-
1955	20	2	-	2	-	-	-	2	-	110
1957	20	2	-	2	-	-	-	2	-	-
1960	30	13	-	13	1	-	-	6	-	-
1961	50	63	-	63	3	1	40	5	-	-
1962	50	544	-	544	143	8	387	4	-	-
1963	80	375	-	375	87	19	262	6	-	-
1964	70	621	-	621	177	7	425	9	-	-
1965	45	694	-	694	264	5	410	12	-	-
NORWAY							IMPORTS			
1925	2140	194	18	176	36	43	86	11	-	-
1929	2769	277	23	254	77	38	128	11	-	-
1933	2368	445	21	424	98	34	279	13	-	-
1937	3191	552	17	535	166	39	316	14	-	-
1938	2660	592	37	555	176	30	337	12	-	-
1950	1696	1428	16	1412	257	38	1088	29	-	-

Table IV. ENERGY IMPORTS AND EXPORTS, SELECTED YEARS, 1925-1965

(Original units)

Region, country, year	Solid fuels (10^3 m.t. coal equiv.)	Liquid fuels (10^3 m.t.)							Gas (10^6 c.m.)	Electricity (10^6 kwh)
				Refined petroleum products						
		Total	Crude oil	Total	Gasoline	Kerosine	Fuel oils	Lubes and greases		
	(1)	(2)	(3)	(4)	(5)	(6)	(7)	(8)	(9)	(10)
NORWAY (CONTINUED)							IMPORTS			
1953	1384	2187	75	2112	319	78	1687	28	-	-
1955	1260	2851	96	2755	337	111	2275	31	-	-
1957	1050	2983	116	2867	357	160	2312	37	-	-
1960	990	3671	220	3451	458	201	2752	38	-	130
1961	920	4463	1739	2724	336	206	2142	39	-	8
1962	860	5178	2354	2824	465	181	2137	40	-	-
1963	970	5600	2535	3065	446	213	2363	42	-	-
1964	970	6258	2931	3327	441	215	2623	47	-	-
1965	980	5897	2822	3075	498	226	2326	24	-	-
NORWAY							EXPORTS			
1925	152	-	-	-	-	-	-	-	-	-
1929	92	-	-	-	-	-	-	-	-	-
1933	55	3	-	3	-	-	-	3	-	-
1937	15	2	-	2	-	-	-	2	-	-
1938	13	3	-	3	-	-	-	3	-	-
1950	-	-	-	-	-	-	-	-	-	-
1953	-	3	-	3	-	-	-	3	-	-
1955	130	12	-	12	1	-	2	9	-	-
1957	220	11	-	11	1	-	1	9	-	-
1960	170	18	-	18	1	1	-	16	-	-
1961	160	658	-	658	73	5	556	16	-	-
1962	180	1227	-	1227	149	13	1034	18	-	287
1963	170	1239	-	1239	126	8	1077	19	-	945
1964	90	1470	-	1470	231	6	1203	21	-	1391
1965	230	1246	-	1246	106	6	1071	47	-	2162
PORTUGAL							IMPORTS			
1925	998	61	-	61	14	24	20	3	-	-
1929	1147	111	-	111	40	35	36	-	-	-
1933	1109	142	-	142	51	48	43	-	-	-
1937	1360	195	-	195	73	52	58	12	-	-
1938	1152	196	-	196	74	50	61	11	-	-
1950	817	784	265	519	64	53	390	12	-	-
1953	578	1131	132	999	130	121	730	16	-	-
1955	510	1639	910	729	82	56	568	22	-	-
1957	560	1838	1108	730	88	55	561	26	-	-
1960	390	2120	1301	819	78	33	675	31	-	-
1961	550	2188	1306	882	69	25	742	35	-	1
1962	530	2273	1334	939	67	40	780	33	-	1
1963	620	2469	1497	972	60	20	829	35	-	-
1964	630	2634	1519	1115	97	23	896	40	-	-
1965	620	2928	1705	1223	127	23	937	47	-	432
PORTUGAL							EXPORTS			
1925	3	1	-	1	-	-	1	-	-	-
1929	1	-	-	-	-	-	-	-	-	-
1933	-	1	-	1	-	-	1	-	-	-
1937	3	2	-	2	-	-	2	-	-	-
1938	-	1	-	1	-	-	1	-	-	-
1950	-	3	-	3	-	-	3	-	-	-
1953	-	5	-	5	2	-	3	-	-	-

Table IV. ENERGY IMPORTS AND EXPORTS, SELECTED YEARS, 1925-1965

(Original units)

Region, country, year	Solid fuels (10^3 m.t. coal equiv.)	Liquid fuels (10^3 m.t.) Total	Crude oil	Refined petroleum products Total	Gasoline	Kerosine	Fuel oils	Lubes and greases	Gas (10^6 c.m.)	Electricity (10^6 kwh)
	(1)	(2)	(3)	(4)	(5)	(6)	(7)	(8)	(9)	(10)
PORTUGAL (CONTINUED)							EXPORTS			
1955	10	212	-	212	92	15	104	1	-	-
1957	-	187	-	187	70	27	88	2	-	-
1960	-	278	-	278	91	14	171	2	-	-
1961	-	221	-	221	77	42	100	2	-	-
1962	-	151	-	151	47	28	74	2	-	-
1963	-	213	-	213	48	45	118	2	-	55
1964	-	189	-	189	58	17	111	3	-	12
1965	-	176	-	176	44	85	42	4	-	-
SWEDEN							IMPORTS			
1925	4256	301	-	301	139	63	63	36	-	-
1929	6275	481	-	481	250	69	118	44	-	-
1933	6060	773	57	716	329	93	252	42	-	-
1937	8962	1178	80	1098	487	104	450	57	-	-
1938	7733	1326	92	1234	543	112	517	62	-	-
1950	6630	3676	903	2773	520	220	1970	63	-	-
1953	5571	5542	1421	4121	780	370	2913	58	-	-
1955	5560	8079	1889	6190	927	371	4806	86	-	120
1957	4920	9394	1994	7400	1211	304	5787	98	-	-
1960	3580	13212	2646	10566	1529	374	8541	119	-	-
1961	3300	13350	2592	10758	1551	339	8746	117	-	-
1962	3270	14813	2460	12353	1878	376	9959	133	-	-
1963	3240	16136	2748	13388	2013	416	10827	126	-	48
1964	3480	17999	3557	14442	2240	420	11624	154	-	-
1965	2970	19011	3725	15286	2424	413	12288	158	-	-
SWEDEN							EXPORTS			
1925	-	5	-	5	2	2	-	1	-	20
1929	-	5	-	5	-	4	-	1	-	35
1933	-	20	-	20	1	12	6	1	-	14
1937	-	32	-	32	3	2	25	2	-	15
1938	-	32	-	32	1	4	25	2	-	24
1950	27	37	-	37	19	1	17	-	-	180
1953	28	2	-	2	1	-	-	1	-	298
1955	30	11	-	11	-	3	-	1	-	-
1957	10	29	-	29	-	-	10	11	-	390
1960	10	114	-	114	8	17	49	32	-	770
1961	40	98	-	98	3	3	51	37	-	997
1962	30	126	-	126	13	-	70	41	-	797
1963	30	223	-	223	65	8	105	42	-	-
1964	20	321	-	321	130	7	134	48	-	205
1965	10	327	-	327	131	8	140	48	-	805
SWITZERLAND							IMPORTS			
1925	2701	148	-	148	70	25	38	15	-	-
1929	3463	261	-	261	140	27	73	21	-	-
1933	3165	393	-	393	195	24	154	20	-	-
1937	3486	397	-	397	194	20	163	20	-	-
1938	3337	411	-	411	201	20	171	19	-	-
1950	2550	1003	-	1003	302	66	595	40	-	-
1953	2204	1235	-	1235	388	102	716	28	-	-
1955	2640	1927	-	1927	541	41	1299	44	-	-

Table IV. ENERGY IMPORTS AND EXPORTS, SELECTED YEARS, 1925-1965

(Original units)

Region, country, year	Solid fuels (10^3 m.t. coal equiv.)	Liquid fuels (10^3 m.t.) Total	Crude oil	Refined petroleum products Total	Gasoline	Kerosine	Fuel oils	Lubes and greases	Gas (10^6 c.m.)	Electricity (10^6 kwh)
	(1)	(2)	(3)	(4)	(5)	(6)	(7)	(8)	(9)	(10)
SWITZERLAND (CONTINUED)							IMPORTS			
1957	3330	2595	-	2595	656	62	1820	54	-	-
1960	2600	3842	-	3842	990	55	2731	59	-	-
1961	2260	4169	-	4169	1151	58	2890	68	-	-
1962	2330	4827	-	4827	1352	49	3355	70	-	-
1963	2820	6510	359	6151	1273	78	4712	79	-	-
1964	1980	6765	838	5927	1295	87	4459	75	-	-
1965	1572	7940	1209	6731	1335	79	5231	73	-	-
SWITZERLAND							EXPORTS			
1925	-	-	-	-	-	-	-	-	-	646
1929	-	-	-	-	-	-	-	-	-	1010
1933	-	-	-	-	-	-	-	-	-	973
1937	-	-	-	-	-	-	-	-	-	1543
1938	-	2	-	2	-	-	2	-	-	1537
1950	1	3	-	3	3	-	-	-	-	590
1953	-	-	-	-	-	-	-	-	-	1013
1955	30	-	-	-	-	-	-	-	-	1380
1957	10	-	-	-	-	-	-	-	-	650
1960	-	-	-	-	-	-	-	-	-	1320
1961	-	2	-	2	-	1	-	1	-	3478
1962	-	1	-	1	-	-	-	1	-	150
1963	-	2	-	2	1	-	1	-	-	1024
1964	-	79	-	79	12	3	63	1	-	1164
1965	-	133	-	133	22	4	106	1	-	1650
UNITED KINGDOM							IMPORTS			
1925	14	6076	2360	3716	1214	486	1680	336	-	-
1929	23	7954	2021	5933	2512	895	2138	388	-	-
1933	35	8847	1595	7252	3499	635	2729	389	-	-
1937	78	11125	2143	8982	4384	787	3352	459	-	-
1938	12	11697	2308	9389	4792	749	3426	422	-	-
1950	271	19392	9394	9998	4050	1439	4020	489	-	-
1953	856	32199	26043	6156	1835	1402	2460	459	-	-
1955	11810	36782	28300	8482	1851	1567	4611	453	-	-
1957	3140	39240	28549	10691	2446	1517	6331	397	-	-
1960	70	58893	45188	13705	2550	752	9899	501	4	-
1961	100	61329	49722	11607	2713	590	7767	526	-	-
1962	20	68271	53182	15089	2759	1705	10102	514	-	87
1963	-	72661	54775	17886	3208	2153	11961	539	-	-
1964	-	77228	58125	19103	3448	2851	12198	542	90	-
1965	5	85122	64807	20315	3419	3138	13003	572	644	58
UNITED KINGDOM							EXPORTS			
1925	54958	648	-	648	171	77	367	33	-	-
1929	65434	425	-	425	107	61	226	31	-	-
1933	42824	334	-	334	155	34	116	29	-	-
1937	44160	524	-	524	206	86	175	57	-	-
1938	38796	491	-	491	190	45	185	71	-	-
1950	16134	1152	-	1152	112	29	870	141	-	-
1953	15747	7512	-	7512	1086	153	6070	203	-	-
1955	14390	6332	69	6263	1331	205	4353	372	-	-
1957	9630	6273	21	6252	1559	238	4039	412	-	-

Table IV. ENERGY IMPORTS AND EXPORTS, SELECTED YEARS, 1925-1965

(Original units)

Region, country, year	Solid fuels (10^3 m.t. coal equiv.)	Liquid fuels (10^3 m.t.)		Refined petroleum products					Gas (10^6 c.m.)	Electricity (10^6 kwh)
		Total	Crude oil	Total	Gasoline	Kerosine	Fuel oils	Lubes and greases		
	(1)	(2)	(3)	(4)	(5)	(6)	(7)	(8)	(9)	(10)
UNITED KINGDOM (CONTINUED)							EXPORTS			
1960	6740	9220	51	9169	1810	659	6173	523	-	-
1961	7100	7910	112	7798	1534	837	4900	525	-	4
1962	6470	10911	999	9912	1735	897	6662	617	-	-
1963	9990	11214	1440	9774	1427	905	6871	555	-	11
1964	7360	9699	343	9356	1306	776	6692	563	-	210
1965	4795	10999	272	10727	1601	785	7814	520	-	-
WESTERN EUROPE - OTHER							IMPORTS			
1925	6494	846	36	810	271	149	309	72	-	-
1929	8105	1381	144	1237	516	170	469	82	-	-
1933	5529	1899	274	1625	600	168	801	56	-	-
1937	6952	2113	219	1894	643	244	927	80	-	-
1938	6350	2206	260	1946	672	240	959	75	-	-
1950	6016	7130	3305	3825	1051	267	2383	124	-	-
1953	5971	9311	3614	5697	1135	331	4090	141	-	-
1955	6767	11231	3933	7298	1239	410	5503	144	-	60
1957	7051	15364	6361	9003	1157	397	7295	140	-	-
1960	7093	17716	11785	5931	327	305	5145	137	-	430
1961	7214	18861	12595	6266	317	328	5473	136	-	175
1962	8115	22232	15272	6960	354	389	6040	166	-	82
1963	7840	24181	17002	7179	279	454	6281	139	-	337
1964	8989	26939	19586	7353	329	527	6233	216	-	1038
1965	8996	30169	21064	9105	375	549	7784	162	-	986
WESTERN EUROPE - OTHER							EXPORTS			
1925	92	1	-	1	1	-	-	-	-	-
1929	160	3	-	3	2	-	1	-	-	-
1933	56	9	-	9	2	1	6	-	-	-
1937	47	52	-	52	2	-	50	-	-	-
1938	33	52	-	52	2	-	50	-	-	-
1950	187	26	-	26	3	-	23	-	-	-
1953	171	47	-	47	2	-	43	2	-	35
1955	170	154	-	154	73	26	54	1	-	50
1957	240	398	1	397	178	54	148	11	-	180
1960	180	1396	-	1396	265	87	1018	7	-	240
1961	250	1394	179	1215	284	69	839	10	-	337
1962	170	2016	561	1455	412	63	944	25	-	411
1963	220	1769	505	1264	274	71	846	47	-	1124
1964	260	1856	350	1506	299	125	1018	46	-	1572
1965	200	2021	145	1876	365	120	1350	30	-	634
FINLAND							IMPORTS			
1925	612	76	9	67	29	29	-	9	-	-
1929	1170	129	13	116	68	36	-	12	-	-
1933	1138	119	14	105	60	36	-	9	-	-
1937	2235	223	27	196	117	65	-	14	-	-
1938	1784	248	32	216	137	65	-	14	-	-
1950	1929	489	-	489	244	67	158	20	-	-
1953	1980	720	-	720	304	72	332	12	-	-
1955	2630	1110	-	1110	359	75	653	23	-	-
1957	3040	1882	216	1666	349	60	1228	29	-	-
1960	3150	2693	1137	1556	46	32	1441	37	-	420

Table IV. ENERGY IMPORTS AND EXPORTS, SELECTED YEARS, 1925-1965

(Original units)

Region, country, year	Solid fuels (10^3 m.t. coal equiv.)	Liquid fuels (10^3 m.t.) Total	Crude oil	Refined petroleum products Total	Gasoline	Kerosine	Fuel oils	Lubes and greases	Gas (10^6 c.m.)	Electricity (10^6 kwh)
	(1)	(2)	(3)	(4)	(5)	(6)	(7)	(8)	(9)	(10)
FINLAND (CONTINUED)							IMPORTS			
1961	3020	2973	1383	1590	34	27	1483	46	-	175
1962	2950	3498	1512	1986	18	25	1893	50	-	82
1963	2500	4269	2230	2039	20	27	1944	48	-	337
1964	3220	4905	2580	2325	13	23	2228	60	-	696
1965	3265	5696	2700	2996	20	26	2884	65	-	569
FINLAND							EXPORTS			
1925	-	-	-	-	-	-	-	-	-	-
1929	-	-	-	-	-	-	-	-	-	-
1933	-	-	-	-	-	-	-	-	-	-
1937	-	-	-	-	-	-	-	-	-	-
1938	-	-	-	-	-	-	-	-	-	-
1950	-	-	-	-	-	-	-	-	-	-
1953	-	-	-	-	-	-	-	-	-	5
1955	-	-	-	-	-	-	-	-	-	-
1957	-	1	-	1	-	-	-	-	-	-
1960	10	3	-	3	-	-	-	-	-	-
1961	20	2	-	2	-	-	-	-	-	-
1962	10	-	-	-	-	-	-	-	-	-
1963	30	-	-	-	-	-	-	-	-	-
1964	30	-	-	-	-	-	-	-	-	-
1965	30	1	-	1	-	-	-	-	-	-
GREECE							IMPORTS			
1925	663	64	-	64	24	14	21	5	-	-
1929	814	147	-	147	46	29	64	8	-	-
1933	638	183	-	183	46	19	112	6	-	-
1937	969	323	-	323	64	19	227	13	-	-
1938	975	345	-	345	71	21	243	10	-	-
1950	302	1086	-	1086	228	74	768	16	-	-
1953	277	1254	-	1254	249	87	900	18	-	-
1955	320	1511	-	1511	303	95	1094	19	-	-
1957	280	1624	-	1624	238	106	1256	17	-	-
1960	230	2392	1732	660	14	4	614	20	-	10
1961	230	2643	1840	803	14	1	760	22	-	-
1962	210	2993	1820	1173	27	55	1066	24	-	-
1963	270	3422	1843	1579	59	85	1408	27	-	-
1964	290	3349	1882	1467	86	109	1240	32	-	-
1965	410	4123	1830	2293	116	125	2010	38	-	22
GREECE							EXPORTS			
1960	-	-	-	-	-	-	-	-	-	-
1961	-	-	-	-	-	-	-	-	-	14
1962	-	30	-	30	-	-	27	-	-	2
1963	-	26	-	26	-	-	20	-	-	6
1964	-	25	-	25	-	-	21	-	-	15
1965	-	8	-	8	-	-	4	-	-	-
ICELAND							IMPORTS			
1925	-	9	-	9	-	-	-	-	-	-

Table IV. ENERGY IMPORTS AND EXPORTS, SELECTED YEARS, 1925-1965

(Original units)

Region, country, year	Solid fuels (10^3 m.t. coal equiv.)	Liquid fuels (10^3 m.t.)		Refined petroleum products					Gas (10^6 c.m.)	Electricity (10^6 kwh)
		Total	Crude oil	Total	Gasoline	Kerosine	Fuel oils	Lubes and greases		
	(1)	(2)	(3)	(4)	(5)	(6)	(7)	(8)	(9)	(10)
ICELAND (CONTINUED)							IMPORTS			
1929	-	15	-	15	3	5	7	-	-	-
1933	-	14	-	14	10	3	-	1	-	-
1937	-	19	-	19	15	3	-	1	-	-
1938	-	20	-	20	6	2	11	1	-	-
1950	96	248	-	248	42	3	200	3	-	-
1953	49	381	-	381	54	3	320	4	-	-
1955	60	347	-	347	57	2	284	4	-	-
1957	30	400	-	400	63	2	331	4	-	-
1960	20	466	-	466	56	9	397	4	-	-
1961	20	427	-	427	50	8	365	4	-	-
1962	20	453	-	453	57	4	387	5	-	-
1963	10	423	-	423	62	8	349	4	-	-
1964	10	423	-	423	58	9	352	4	-	-
1965	10	468	-	468	64	18	381	5	-	-
IRELAND							IMPORTS			
1925	2286	119	1	118	52	46	11	9	-	-
1929	2518	165	-	165	87	43	25	10	-	-
1933	2320	189	-	189	108	51	21	9	-	-
1937	2623	243	-	243	127	66	39	11	-	-
1938	2541	251	-	251	135	62	43	11	-	-
1950	1994	597	-	597	250	78	255	14	-	-
1953	1770	773	-	773	320	109	328	16	-	-
1955	1940	1120	-	1120	371	125	602	20	-	-
1957	1270	1105	-	1105	352	114	617	15	-	-
1960	1680	1815	1431	384	74	136	148	19	-	-
1961	1810	1900	1455	445	59	184	175	23	-	-
1962	1520	1989	1515	474	51	183	211	23	-	-
1963	1470	2157	1632	525	30	190	274	23	-	-
1964	1320	2347	1745	602	50	216	298	28	-	-
1965	1300	2746	2031	715	32	215	435	24	-	-
IRELAND							EXPORTS			
1925	2	-	-	-	-	-	-	-	-	-
1929	21	-	-	-	-	-	-	-	-	-
1933	22	-	-	-	-	-	-	-	-	-
1937	3	-	-	-	-	-	-	-	-	-
1938	2	-	-	-	-	-	-	-	-	-
1950	-	-	-	-	-	-	-	-	-	-
1953	12	-	-	-	-	-	-	-	-	-
1955	-	-	-	-	-	-	-	-	-	-
1957	20	-	-	-	-	-	-	-	-	-
1960	20	495	-	495	6	-	489	-	-	-
1961	60	397	-	397	4	-	390	-	-	-
1962	40	264	-	264	7	-	254	-	-	-
1963	50	199	-	199	7	-	186	-	-	-
1964	40	172	-	172	7	-	159	-	-	-
1965	50	293	-	293	10	-	281	-	-	-
SPAIN							IMPORTS			
1925	2134	468	15	453	143	21	251	38	-	-
1929	2770	767	28	739	305	21	368	45	-	-

Table IV. ENERGY IMPORTS AND EXPORTS, SELECTED YEARS, 1925-1965

(Original units)

Region, country, year	Solid fuels (10^3 m.t. coal equiv.)	Liquid fuels (10^3 m.t.) Total	Crude oil	Refined petroleum products Total	Gasoline	Kerosine	Fuel oils	Lubes and greases	Gas (10^6 c.m.)	Electricity (10^6 kwh)
	(1)	(2)	(3)	(4)	(5)	(6)	(7)	(8)	(9)	(10)
SPAIN (CONTINUED)							IMPORTS			
1933	1063	1234	163	1071	359	24	660	28	-	-
1937	566	1145	100	1045	308	61	640	36	-	-
1938	428	1142	100	1042	308	61	640	33	-	-
1950	1033	3767	2900	867	200	22	594	51	-	-
1953	1164	5160	3160	2000	100	24	1804	72	-	-
1955	640	6153	3450	2703	65	66	2500	72	-	60
1957	630	8967	5496	3471	77	44	3290	60	-	-
1960	340	9361	7050	2311	68	46	2160	37	-	-
1961	470	10083	7630	2453	96	37	2305	15	-	-
1962	1820	11872	9678	2194	150	54	1948	40	-	-
1963	1910	12506	10519	1987	52	60	1849	11	-	-
1964	1940	14334	12619	1715	58	86	1500	36	-	-
1965	1720	15393	13396	1997	73	93	1600	13	-	-
SPAIN							EXPORTS			
1925	9	1	-	1	1	-	-	-	-	-
1929	70	3	-	3	2	-	1	-	-	-
1933	6	9	-	9	2	1	6	-	-	-
1937	-	52	-	52	2	-	50	-	-	-
1938	-	52	-	52	2	-	50	-	-	-
1950	68	-	-	-	-	-	-	NA	-	-
1953	49	2	-	2	-	-	-	2	-	-
1955	90	111	-	111	71	24	15	1	-	-
1957	140	293	1	292	132	47	102	11	-	30
1960	40	812	-	812	223	87	492	NA	-	150
1961	60	704	-	704	247	69	383	NA	-	245
1962	20	878	-	878	379	63	432	NA	-	253
1963	20	958	50	908	256	69	570	NA	-	823
1964	50	1177	34	1143	250	125	761	NA	-	1557
1965	10	1318	-	1318	297	110	910	-	-	634
YUGOSLAVIA							IMPORTS			
1925	543	85	11	74	13	39	11	11	-	-
1929	651	138	103	35	5	21	2	7	-	-
1933	292	121	97	24	5	14	2	3	-	-
1937	413	113	92	21	1	13	2	5	-	-
1938	495	152	128	24	5	9	4	6	-	-
1950	417	479	405	74	55	-	-	19	-	-
1953	664	527	454	73	55	-	-	18	-	-
1955	1110	523	483	40	35	-	-	5	-	-
1957	1750	681	649	32	18	-	-	14	-	-
1960	1660	612	435	177	24	7	128	18	-	-
1961	1650	457	287	170	11	10	125	24	-	-
1962	1590	1041	747	294	17	5	252	20	-	-
1963	1670	957	778	179	11	5	140	22	-	-
1964	2200	1104	760	344	24	6	263	51	-	342
1965	2285	1289	1107	182	28	3	137	14	-	395
YUGOSLAVIA							EXPORTS			
1925	80	-	-	-	-	-	-	-	-	-
1929	68	-	-	-	-	-	-	-	-	-
1933	27	-	-	-	-	-	-	-	-	-

Table IV. ENERGY IMPORTS AND EXPORTS, SELECTED YEARS, 1925-1965

(Original units)

Region, country, year	Solid fuels (10³ m.t. coal equiv.)	Liquid fuels (10³ m.t.) Total	Crude oil	Refined petroleum products Total	Gasoline	Kerosine	Fuel oils	Lubes and greases	Gas (10⁶ c.m.)	Electricity (10⁶ kwh)
	(1)	(2)	(3)	(4)	(5)	(6)	(7)	(8)	(9)	(10)
YUGOSLAVIA (CONTINUED)							EXPORTS			
1937	44	-	-	-	-	-	-	-	-	-
1938	31	-	-	-	-	-	-	-	-	-
1950	119	26	-	26	3	-	23	-	-	-
1953	110	45	-	45	2	-	43	-	-	30
1955	80	43	-	43	2	2	39	-	-	50
1957	80	100	-	100	42	7	46	-	-	150
1960	110	81	-	81	31	-	37	7	-	90
1961	110	274	179	95	16	-	66	10	-	78
1962	100	844	561	283	26	-	231	25	-	156
1963	120	586	455	131	11	2	70	47	-	295
1964	140	482	316	166	42	-	77	46	-	-
1965	110	400	145	255	57	10	155	30	-	-
OCEANIA							IMPORTS			
1925	744	922	204	718	447	127	94	50	-	-
1929	884	1792	453	1339	955	175	123	86	-	-
1933	217	1663	248	1415	805	140	407	63	-	-
1937	319	2608	284	2324	1327	226	679	92	-	-
1938	366	2835	253	2583	1465	219	818	80	-	-
1950	657	5953	797	5156	2344	474	2173	165	-	-
1953	176	6561	900	5661	2847	494	2222	98	-	-
1955	272	10033	4890	5143	2627	584	1713	219	-	-
1957	380	11839	8650	3189	1511	474	987	217	-	-
1960	272	14746	11265	3481	1779	495	925	281	-	-
1961	273	16003	12405	3598	1694	555	1057	291	-	-
1962	175	16774	12934	3840	1810	530	1241	258	-	-
1963	193	18892	14861	4031	1970	482	1228	350	-	-
1964	304	19940	16159	3781	1887	388	1260	245	-	-
1965	318	21342	18682	2660	1209	506	753	190	-	-
OCEANIA							EXPORTS			
1925	962	6	1	5	2	1	1	1	-	-
1929	354	11	1	10	-	7	1	2	-	-
1933	299	-	-	-	-	-	-	-	-	-
1937	405	2	-	2	-	-	1	1	-	-
1938	460	1	-	1	-	-	1	-	-	-
1950	76	11	-	11	1	5	2	3	-	-
1953	405	8	-	8	2	1	2	3	-	-
1955	240	318	-	318	128	5	184	1	-	-
1957	940	878	-	878	129	12	734	3	-	-
1960	1710	1648	-	1648	135	66	1446	1	-	-
1961	3000	1937	-	1937	217	167	1547	6	-	-
1962	3050	2367	-	2367	114	75	2173	5	-	-
1963	3290	2477	-	2477	184	99	2179	15	-	-
1964	5000	1837	-	1837	178	55	1553	51	-	-
1965	7335	1292	-	1292	67	55	1117	53	-	-
AUSTRALIA							IMPORTS			
1925	55	683	204	479	333	106	-	40	-	-
1929	554	1415	453	962	738	148	4	72	-	-
1933	5	1319	248	1071	613	122	284	52	-	-
1937	28	2077	284	1793	1028	216	476	73	-	-

Table IV. ENERGY IMPORTS AND EXPORTS, SELECTED YEARS, 1925-1965

(Original units)

Region, country, year	Solid fuels (10^3 m.t. coal equiv.)	Liquid fuels (10^3 m.t.)		Refined petroleum products					Gas (10^6 c.m.)	Electricity (10^6 kwh)
		Total	Crude oil	Total	Gasoline	Kerosine	Fuel oils	Lubes and greases		
	(1)	(2)	(3)	(4)	(5)	(6)	(7)	(8)	(9)	(10)
AUSTRALIA (CONTINUED)							IMPORTS			
1938	82	2149	253	1896	1109	208	514	65	-	-
1950	523	4817	797	4020	1839	441	1608	132	-	-
1953	22	5308	900	4408	2131	464	1742	71	-	-
1955	10	8433	4890	3543	1800	541	1026	176	-	-
1957	20	9968	8650	1318	552	416	174	176	-	-
1960	-	12688	11265	1423	740	379	103	201	-	-
1961	10	13766	12405	1361	581	410	159	211	-	-
1962	10	14515	12934	1581	724	386	284	187	-	-
1963	10	16363	14861	1502	784	328	151	239	-	-
1964	10	16786	15114	1672	914	216	355	187	-	-
1965	10	17848	16300	1548	856	286	284	122	-	-
AUSTRALIA							EXPORTS			
1925	952	6	1	5	2	1	1	1	-	-
1929	304	11	1	10	-	7	1	2	-	-
1933	299	-	-	-	-	-	-	-	-	-
1937	405	2	-	2	-	-	1	1	-	-
1938	447	1	-	1	-	-	1	-	-	-
1950	72	11	-	11	1	5	2	3	-	-
1953	405	8	-	8	2	1	2	3	-	-
1955	240	315	-	315	128	4	182	1	-	-
1957	940	870	-	870	124	11	732	3	-	-
1960	1690	1627	-	1627	126	63	1437	1	-	-
1961	2990	1920	-	1920	213	160	1541	6	-	-
1962	3050	2352	-	2352	108	70	2169	5	-	-
1963	3290	2464	-	2464	178	95	2176	15	-	-
1964	5000	1605	-	1605	172	52	1330	51	-	-
1965	7335	1046	-	1046	61	49	883	53	-	-
NEW ZEALAND							IMPORTS			
1925	576	234	-	234	111	19	94	10	-	-
1929	216	366	-	366	208	26	119	13	-	-
1933	102	332	-	332	185	17	120	10	-	-
1937	119	501	-	501	285	6	193	17	-	-
1938	112	652	-	652	341	7	291	13	-	-
1950	49	1079	-	1079	482	29	537	31	-	-
1953	1	1144	-	1144	665	20	440	19	-	-
1955	10	1438	-	1438	765	29	611	33	-	-
1957	10	1663	-	1663	872	40	715	36	-	-
1960	-	1754	-	1754	943	68	696	47	-	-
1961	10	1883	-	1883	1022	83	733	45	-	-
1962	10	1933	-	1933	990	90	804	49	-	-
1963	-	2128	-	2128	1083	96	907	42	-	-
1964	-	2648	1045	1603	853	99	609	42	-	-
1965	-	2967	2382	585	237	128	172	48	-	-
NEW ZEALAND							EXPORTS			
1925	10	-	-	-	-	-	-	-	-	-
1929	50	-	-	-	-	-	-	-	-	-
1933	-	-	-	-	-	-	-	-	-	-
1937	-	-	-	-	-	-	-	-	-	-
1938	13	-	-	-	-	-	-	-	-	-

Table IV. ENERGY IMPORTS AND EXPORTS, SELECTED YEARS, 1925–1965

(Original units)

Region, country, year	Solid fuels (10^3 m.t. coal equiv.)	Liquid fuels (10^3 m.t.)							Gas (10^6 c.m.)	Electricity (10^6 kwh)
				Refined petroleum products						
		Total	Crude oil	Total	Gasoline	Kerosine	Fuel oils	Lubes and greases		
	(1)	(2)	(3)	(4)	(5)	(6)	(7)	(8)	(9)	(10)
NEW ZEALAND (CONTINUED)							EXPORTS			
1950	4	-	-	-	-	-	-	-	-	-
1953	-	-	-	-	-	-	-	-	-	-
1955	-	-	-	-	-	-	-	-	-	-
1957	-	-	-	-	-	-	-	-	-	-
1960	20	9	-	9	3	2	4	-	-	-
1961	10	7	-	7	1	6	-	-	-	-
1962	-	6	-	6	2	4	-	-	-	-
1963	-	5	-	5	2	3	-	-	-	-
1964	-	225	-	225	3	2	220	-	-	-
1965	-	238	-	238	3	5	230	-	-	-
USSR AND COMMUNIST EASTERN EUROPE							IMPORTS			
1925	4090	374	88	286	27	88	19	18	-	69
1929	6283	771	312	459	64	104	52	32	-	69
1933	2722	696	278	418	25	83	48	16	-	17
1937	3291	1128	540	588	191	94	85	26	-	15
1938	2779	970	421	549	183	94	81	27	-	-
1950	20572	4515	1995	2520	300	225	795	-	56	180
1953	24881	7802	3212	4590	360	260	970	-	116	168
1955	26030	9033	3445	5588	2511	811	2157	109	162	320
1957	20230	10157	5212	4945	2887	504	1467	87	216	570
1960	25470	14155	7544	6611	3733	741	1960	177	473	860
1961	27610	15264	8117	7147	3647	668	2618	214	504	811
1962	30440	17049	9419	7630	3497	619	3395	117	514	819
1963	33300	19824	11618	8206	3541	590	3843	230	527	1224
1964	36650	22560	14975	7585	3169	476	3779	155	532	1934
1965	36714	25397	18895	6502	2643	480	3227	150	581	2149
USSR AND COMMUNIST EASTERN EUROPE							EXPORTS			
1925	12503	2462	67	2396	608	858	704	219	-	-
1929	20002	6680	315	6365	1937	1612	2487	319	-	-
1933	13641	10318	769	9549	3104	1562	4536	343	-	4
1937	16057	7269	654	6615	2289	1201	2855	268	-	-
1938	13632	5643	670	4973	1903	1038	1833	197	-	-
1950	33101	3870	410	3460	1265	615	780	-	25	400
1953	34587	10680	2170	8510	2010	1025	1975	-	95	170
1955	39350	15059	3312	11747	4081	1513	5990	152	140	170
1957	33320	20386	6376	14010	4494	1573	7726	214	171	570
1960	44400	41183	18267	22916	5828	1781	14680	608	446	700
1961	47510	49450	23805	25645	6271	1711	16959	685	477	820
1962	52670	54014	26668	27346	5750	1902	19021	658	509	349
1963	55580	60196	30633	29563	5896	1703	21275	680	509	753
1964	59840	65849	37026	28823	5187	1232	21785	612	504	2019
1965	59345	74078	43811	30267	4691	1445	23532	584	594	2191
COMMUNIST EASTERN EUROPE							IMPORTS			
1925	3398	309	79	230	20	48	16	12	-	69
1929	5186	669	295	374	45	55	43	24	-	69
1933	1924	599	275	324	11	25	33	9	-	17
1937	2222	839	527	312	15	30	59	16	-	15
1938	1729	675	406	269	15	21	51	18	-	-
1950	9172	1815	495	1320	300	225	795	-	56	180

Table IV. ENERGY IMPORTS AND EXPORTS, SELECTED YEARS, 1925–1965

(Original units)

Region, country, year	Solid fuels (10^3 m.t. coal equiv.)	Liquid fuels (10^3 m.t.)		Refined petroleum products					Gas (10^6 c.m.)	Electricity (10^6 kwh)
		Total	Crude oil	Total	Gasoline	Kerosine	Fuel oils	Lubes and greases		
	(1)	(2)	(3)	(4)	(5)	(6)	(7)	(8)	(9)	(10)
COMMUNIST EASTERN EUROPE (CONTINUED)							IMPORTS			
1953	14981	3002	1412	1590	360	260	970	-	116	168
1955	16960	3762	1870	1892	523	262	1107	-	162	310
1957	16470	6066	3881	2185	864	210	1111	-	216	570
1960	20100	9996	6378	3618	1559	436	1569	54	473	860
1961	22290	11863	7229	4634	1867	395	2304	68	504	811
1962	24960	14341	8923	5418	1916	375	3125	-	514	819
1963	27610	17103	11075	6028	2006	386	3551	83	527	1224
1964	30950	20585	14975	5610	1783	325	3496	-	532	1934
1965	29319	23580	18895	4685	1422	311	2950	-	581	2149
COMMUNIST EASTERN EUROPE							EXPORTS			
1925	12136	1090	4	1087	330	404	227	119	-	-
1929	18663	2816	3	2813	840	824	1037	102	-	-
1933	11823	5416	237	5179	1806	992	2287	90	-	4
1937	14745	5297	531	4766	1869	957	1890	48	-	-
1938	13306	4196	440	3756	1589	827	1296	42	-	-
1950	30501	2770	110	2660	1265	615	780	-	-	400
1953	30187	5180	170	5010	2010	1025	1975	-	-	170
1955	33580	7097	396	6701	2676	872	3142	-	-	170
1957	22570	6756	453	6303	2789	665	2834	12	-	570
1960	29700	8077	442	7635	3010	688	3690	228	203	670
1961	29680	8420	417	8003	2682	635	4405	262	207	746
1962	30330	8722	389	8333	2595	607	4897	219	207	117
1963	30800	8890	390	8500	2554	434	5210	293	207	6
1964	32610	9318	335	8983	2440	342	5877	317	211	715
1965	33545	9782	379	9403	2338	280	6462	308	202	690
ALBANIA							IMPORTS			
1925	-	5	3	2	1	-	1	-	-	-
1929	-	7	3	4	3	-	1	-	-	-
1933	-	8	2	6	4	-	2	-	-	-
1937	-	8	2	6	3	-	3	-	-	-
1938	4	9	2	7	3	-	4	-	-	-
1950	10	20	-	20	15	-	5	-	-	-
1953	20	20	-	20	15	-	5	-	-	-
1955	-	21	-	21	17	-	4	-	-	-
1957	10	13	-	13	10	2	1	-	-	-
1960	10	10	-	10	5	3	2	-	-	-
1961	10	11	-	11	5	3	3	-	-	-
1962	20	19	-	19	12	4	3	-	-	-
1963	10	14	-	14	10	4	-	-	-	-
1964	10	31	-	31	13	4	14	-	-	-
1965	15	14	-	14	11	3	-	-	-	-
ALBANIA							EXPORTS			
1925	-	-	-	-	-	-	-	-	-	-
1929	-	-	-	-	-	-	-	-	-	-
1933	-	-	-	-	-	-	-	-	-	-
1937	-	59	59	-	-	-	-	-	-	-
1938	-	105	105	-	-	-	-	-	-	-
1950	-	60	60	-	-	-	-	-	-	-
1953	-	70	70	-	-	-	-	-	-	-

Table IV. ENERGY IMPORTS AND EXPORTS, SELECTED YEARS, 1925-1965

(Original units)

Region, country, year	Solid fuels (10³ m.t. coal equiv.)	Liquid fuels (10³ m.t.) Total	Crude oil	Refined petroleum products Total	Gasoline	Kerosine	Fuel oils	Lubes and greases	Gas (10⁶ c.m.)	Electricity (10⁶ kwh)
	(1)	(2)	(3)	(4)	(5)	(6)	(7)	(8)	(9)	(10)
ALBANIA (CONTINUED)							EXPORTS			
1955	20	124	124	-	-	-	-	-	-	-
1957	10	218	218	-	-	-	-	-	-	-
1960	-	329	329	-	-	-	-	-	-	-
1961	-	291	291	-	-	-	-	-	-	-
1962	-	273	273	-	-	-	-	-	-	-
1963	-	320	310	10	-	-	10	-	-	-
1964	-	294	294	-	-	-	-	-	-	-
1965	-	375	375	-	-	-	-	-	-	-
BULGARIA							IMPORTS			
1925	18	43	-	43	4	26	9	4	-	-
1929	9	84	-	84	11	33	32	8	-	-
1933	5	66	-	66	7	25	30	4	-	-
1937	3	88	19	69	10	30	21	8	-	-
1938	4	88	29	59	11	21	19	8	-	-
1950	NA	240	20	220	60	40	120	-	-	-
1953	NA	335	20	315	85	60	170	-	-	-
1955	120	337	-	337	105	47	185	-	-	-
1957	140	513	-	513	196	58	259	-	-	-
1960	320	889	12	877	335	20	522	-	-	-
1961	810	1165	22	1143	392	20	731	-	-	-
1962	1230	1626	15	1611	430	19	1162	-	-	68
1963	1570	2105	451	1654	430	18	1206	-	-	83
1964	2300	3101	1811	1290	224	10	1056	-	-	-
1965	2838	3521	2200	1321	157	11	1153	-	-	-
BULGARIA							EXPORTS			
1925	2	-	-	-	-	-	-	-	-	-
1929	11	-	-	-	-	-	-	-	-	-
1933	1	-	-	-	-	-	-	-	-	-
1937	3	1	-	1	-	-	1	-	-	-
1938	16	-	-	-	-	-	-	-	-	-
1950	NA	-	-	-	-	-	-	-	-	-
1953	NA	-	-	-	-	-	-	-	-	-
1955	20	117	116	1	-	-	1	-	-	-
1957	190	266	202	64	-	-	64	-	-	-
1960	60	100	80	20	-	-	20	-	-	-
1961	60	127	126	1	-	-	1	-	-	-
1962	50	119	116	3	-	-	3	-	-	-
1963	50	80	80	-	-	-	-	-	-	-
1964	-	59	41	18	-	-	18	-	-	24
1965	-	74	4	70	-	-	70	-	-	2
CZECHOSLOVAKIA							IMPORTS			
1925	1751	191	57	134	NA	NA	NA	NA	-	19
1929	2778	363	156	207	NA	NA	NA	NA	-	20
1933	1351	347	101	246	NA	NA	NA	NA	-	17
1937	1381	460	268	192	NA	NA	NA	NA	-	15
1938	928	365	201	164	NA	NA	NA	NA	-	-
1950	1740	630	130	500	35	140	325	-	-	100
1953	3220	885	380	505	35	140	330	-	-	38
1955	4200	1015	445	570	70	150	350	-	-	-

Table IV. ENERGY IMPORTS AND EXPORTS, SELECTED YEARS, 1925-1965

(Original units)

Region, country, year	Solid fuels (10^3 m.t. coal equiv.)	Liquid fuels (10^3 m.t.)							Gas (10^6 c.m.)	Electricity (10^6 kwh)
		Total	Crude oil	Refined petroleum products						
				Total	Gasoline	Kerosine	Fuel oils	Lubes and greases		
	(1)	(2)	(3)	(4)	(5)	(6)	(7)	(8)	(9)	(10)
CZECHOSLOVAKIA (CONTINUED)							IMPORTS			
1957	2290	1551	1221	330	80	100	150	-	-	-
1960	2950	2689	2255	434	127	212	95	-	-	-
1961	3930	3317	2785	532	127	220	185	-	-	-
1962	4600	4233	3675	558	124	244	190	-	-	66
1963	5280	4764	4217	547	116	271	160	-	-	142
1964	5590	5699	5170	529	118	241	170	-	-	702
1965	5111	6591	6096	495	156	243	96	-	-	762
CZECHOSLOVAKIA							EXPORTS			
1925	3540	10	4	7	NA	NA	NA	NA	NA	NA
1929	4683	10	-	10	NA	NA	NA	NA	NA	NA
1933	2669	4	-	4	NA	NA	NA	NA	NA	NA
1937	4345	2	-	2	NA	NA	NA	NA	NA	NA
1938	2960	2	-	2	NA	NA	NA	NA	NA	NA
1950	970	-	-	-	-	-	-	-	-	-
1953	1800	-	-	-	-	-	-	-	-	-
1955	2350	24	-	24	6	1	14	-	-	130
1957	2750	95	-	95	10	-	85	-	-	230
1960	4270	164	-	164	51	-	107	-	-	270
1961	4590	232	-	232	75	-	152	-	4	335
1962	4750	373	-	373	105	-	259	-	4	-
1963	5020	558	-	558	144	-	409	-	4	-
1964	4835	522	-	522	142	-	373	-	4	-
1965	4470	757	-	757	150	-	592	-	4	-
GERMANY, EAST							IMPORTS			
1950	6392	250	50	200	75	-	125	-	36	-
1953	9401	500	400	100	25	-	75	-	36	-
1955	9930	648	648	-	-	-	-	-	36	-
1957	9420	1007	997	10	-	-	10	-	54	-
1960	11960	2415	1941	474	228	148	98	-	54	-
1961	12280	2839	2270	569	240	106	223	-	40	-
1962	13270	3155	2591	564	220	50	294	-	32	-
1963	13490	3846	3163	683	252	40	391	-	23	-
1964	15020	4733	4260	473	187	20	266	-	14	147
1965	14070	5601	5132	469	130	-	339	-	9	92
GERMANY, EAST							EXPORTS			
1950	1051	150	-	150	60	-	90	-	-	400
1953	1991	250	-	250	100	-	150	-	-	170
1955	3540	548	-	548	255	1	288	-	-	10
1957	3280	640	-	640	310	-	330	-	-	330
1960	4320	878	-	878	392	-	475	-	-	370
1961	4240	988	-	988	434	-	543	-	-	372
1962	4500	1007	-	1007	498	-	505	-	-	84
1963	4750	1125	-	1125	532	-	589	-	-	2
1964	4640	1214	-	1214	519	-	695	-	-	-
1965	4080	1539	-	1539	594	-	945	-	-	-

Table IV. ENERGY IMPORTS AND EXPORTS, SELECTED YEARS, 1925–1965

(Original units)

Region, country, year	Solid fuels (10^3 m.t. coal equiv.)	Liquid fuels (10^3 m.t.)							Gas (10^6 c.m.)	Electricity (10^6 kwh)
		Total	Crude oil	Refined petroleum products						
				Total	Gasoline	Kerosine	Fuel oils	Lubes and greases		
	(1)	(2)	(3)	(4)	(5)	(6)	(7)	(8)	(9)	(10)
HUNGARY							IMPORTS			
1925	1153	66	19	47	15	22	5	5	-	-
1929	1845	205	136	69	31	21	9	8	-	-
1933	327	175	172	3	-	-	1	2	-	-
1937	579	280	238	42	2	-	35	5	-	-
1938	523	210	174	36	1	-	28	7	-	-
1950	760	160	100	60	20	5	35	-	-	-
1953	1730	280	200	80	30	10	40	-	-	130
1955	1910	338	232	106	11	15	80	-	-	250
1957	3360	1249	1033	216	28	-	188	-	-	310
1960	2680	1557	1456	101	11	-	90	-	185	540
1961	3020	1643	1412	231	57	-	174	-	203	498
1962	2920	1790	1540	250	63	-	187	-	203	562
1963	3950	2234	1828	406	90	-	316	-	207	930
1964	4730	2579	2026	553	123	-	430	-	225	1081
1965	4070	2621	2251	370	108	-	262	-	198	1295
HUNGARY							EXPORTS			
1925	427	-	-	-	-	-	-	-	-	-
1929	292	-	-	-	-	-	-	-	-	-
1933	164	-	-	-	-	-	-	-	-	-
1937	169	-	-	-	-	-	-	-	-	-
1938	189	-	-	-	-	-	-	-	-	-
1950	150	110	50	60	5	15	40	NA	-	-
1953	340	180	100	80	10	25	45	NA	-	-
1955	260	340	156	184	15	30	139	NA	-	-
1957	20	235	33	202	69	15	106	12	-	-
1960	40	533	33	500	101	-	386	13	-	-
1961	50	509	-	509	96	10	390	13	-	-
1962	100	591	-	591	118	-	459	14	-	-
1963	230	489	-	489	82	-	393	14	-	-
1964	145	568	-	568	124	-	430	14	-	-
1965	140	496	-	496	150	-	332	14	-	-
POLAND							IMPORTS			
1925	242	3	-	3	-	-	1	2	-	50
1929	315	6	-	6	-	1	1	4	-	49
1933	173	1	-	1	-	-	-	1	-	-
1937	182	1	-	1	-	-	-	1	-	-
1938	180	1	-	1	-	-	-	1	-	-
1950	50	515	195	320	95	40	185	-	20	80
1953	80	982	412	570	170	50	350	-	80	-
1955	130	1403	545	858	320	50	488	NA	126	60
1957	480	1733	630	1103	550	50	503	NA	162	260
1960	1170	2436	714	1722	853	53	762	54	234	320
1961	1370	2888	740	2148	1046	46	988	68	261	313
1962	1520	3518	1102	2416	1067	58	1289	NA	279	123
1963	1790	4140	1416	2724	1108	53	1478	83	297	69
1964	1730	4442	1708	2734	1118	50	1560	NA	293	-
1965	1670	5232	3216	2016	860	54	1100	NA	374	-
POLAND							EXPORTS			
1925	8145	298	-	298	65	74	81	78	-	-

Table IV. ENERGY IMPORTS AND EXPORTS, SELECTED YEARS, 1925-1965

(Original units)

Region, country, year	Solid fuels (10^3 m.t. coal equiv.)	Liquid fuels (10^3 m.t.)		Refined petroleum products					Gas (10^6 c.m.)	Electricity (10^6 kwh)
		Total	Crude oil	Total	Gasoline	Kerosine	Fuel oils	Lubes and greases		
	(1)	(2)	(3)	(4)	(5)	(6)	(7)	(8)	(9)	(10)
POLAND (CONTINUED)							EXPORTS			
1929	13643	181	-	181	38	51	52	40	-	-
1933	8982	155	-	155	50	45	28	32	-	4
1937	10228	79	-	79	41	9	15	14	-	-
1938	10141	9	-	9	5	-	2	2	-	-
1950	28330	50	-	50	-	-	50	-	-	-
1953	26056	80	-	80	-	-	80	-	-	-
1955	27390	104	-	104	-	-	100	NA	-	-
1957	16320	52	-	52	-	-	49	NA	-	-
1960	21010	204	-	204	-	12	186	4	-	-
1961	20740	258	-	258	-	8	247	3	-	-
1962	20930	564	-	564	3	5	555	NA	-	-
1963	20730	577	-	577	3	15	555	4	-	-
1964	22910	571	-	571	-	4	567	NA	-	691
1965	24855	905	-	905	-	-	905	NA	-	357
ROMANIA							IMPORTS			
1925	234	1	-	1	-	-	-	1	-	-
1929	239	4	-	4	-	-	-	4	-	-
1933	68	2	-	2	-	-	-	2	-	-
1937	77	2	-	2	-	-	-	2	-	-
1938	90	2	-	2	-	-	-	2	-	-
1950	220	-	-	-	-	-	-	-	-	-
1953	530	-	-	-	-	-	-	-	-	-
1955	670	-	-	-	-	-	-	-	-	-
1957	770	-	-	-	-	-	-	-	-	-
1960	1010	-	-	-	-	-	-	-	-	-
1961	870	-	-	-	-	-	-	-	-	-
1962	1400	-	-	-	-	-	-	-	-	-
1963	1520	-	-	-	-	-	-	-	-	-
1964	1570	-	-	-	-	-	-	-	-	4
1965	1545	-	-	-	-	-	-	-	-	-
ROMANIA							EXPORTS			
1925	22	782	-	782	265	330	146	41	-	-
1929	34	2625	3	2622	802	773	985	62	-	-
1933	7	5257	237	5020	1756	947	2259	58	-	-
1937	-	5156	472	4684	1828	948	1874	34	-	-
1938	-	4080	335	3745	1584	827	1294	40	-	-
1950	-	2400	-	2400	1200	600	600	NA	-	-
1953	-	4600	-	4600	1900	1000	1700	NA	-	-
1955	-	5840	-	5840	2400	840	2600	NA	-	30
1957	-	5250	-	5250	2400	650	2200	NA	-	10
1960	-	5869	-	5869	2466	676	2516	211	203	30
1961	-	6015	-	6015	2077	617	3072	246	203	39
1962	-	5795	-	5795	1871	602	3116	205	203	33
1963	20	5741	-	5741	1793	419	3254	275	203	4
1964	80	6090	-	6090	1655	338	3794	303	207	-
1965	-	5636	-	5636	1444	280	3618	294	198	331
USSR (INCLUDING ESTONIA, LATVIA, LITHUANIA)							IMPORTS			
1925	692	65	9	56	7	40	3	6	-	-
1929	1097	102	17	85	19	49	9	8	-	-

Table IV. ENERGY IMPORTS AND EXPORTS, SELECTED YEARS, 1925-1965

(Original units)

Region, country, year	Solid fuels (10³ m.t. coal equiv.)	Liquid fuels (10³ m.t.) Total	Crude oil	Refined petroleum products Total	Gasoline	Kerosine	Fuel oils	Lubes and greases	Gas (10⁶ c.m.)	Electricity (10⁶ kwh)
	(1)	(2)	(3)	(4)	(5)	(6)	(7)	(8)	(9)	(10)
USSR (INCLUDING ESTONIA, LATVIA, LITHUANIA) (CONTINUED)							IMPORTS			
1933	798	97	3	94	14	58	15	7	-	-
1937	1069	289	13	276	176	64	26	10	-	-
1938	1050	295	15	280	168	73	30	9	-	-
1950	11400	2700	1500	1200	NA	NA	NA	NA	-	-
1953	9900	4800	1800	3000	NA	NA	NA	NA	-	-
1955	9070	5271	1575	3696	1988	549	1050	109	-	10
1957	3760	4091	1331	2760	2023	294	356	87	-	-
1960	5370	4159	1166	2993	2174	305	391	123	-	-
1961	5320	3401	888	2513	1780	273	314	146	-	-
1962	5480	2708	496	2212	1581	244	270	117	-	-
1963	5690	2721	543	2178	1535	204	292	147	-	-
1964	5700	1975	-	1975	1386	151	283	155	-	-
1965	7395	1817	-	1817	1221	169	277	150	-	-
USSR (INCLUDING ESTONIA, LATVIA, LITHUANIA)							EXPORTS			
1925	367	1372	63	1309	278	454	477	100	-	-
1929	1339	3864	312	3552	1097	788	1450	217	-	-
1933	1818	4902	532	4370	1298	570	2249	253	-	-
1937	1312	1972	123	1849	420	244	965	220	-	-
1938	326	1447	230	1217	314	211	537	155	-	-
1950	2600	1100	300	800	NA	NA	NA	NA	25	-
1953	4400	5500	2000	3500	NA	NA	NA	NA	95	-
1955	5770	7962	2916	5046	1405	641	2848	152	140	-
1957	10750	13630	5923	7707	1705	908	4892	202	171	-
1960	14700	33106	17825	15281	2818	1093	10990	380	243	30
1961	17830	41030	23388	17642	3589	1076	12554	423	270	74
1962	22340	45292	26279	19013	3155	1295	14124	439	302	232
1963	24780	51306	30243	21063	3342	1269	16065	387	302	747
1964	27230	56531	36691	19840	2747	890	15908	295	293	1304
1965	25800	64296	43432	20864	2353	1165	17070	276	392	1501
COMMUNIST ASIA							IMPORTS			
1925	2802	941	-	941	25	794	97	25	-	-
1929	2323	1071	-	1071	80	735	207	49	-	-
1933	1527	1154	-	1154	122	610	368	54	-	-
1937	435	1135	158	977	202	433	280	62	-	-
1938	1140	803	160	643	139	275	187	42	-	-
1950	NA	NA	NA	NA	NA	NA	NA	NA	NA	NA
1953	NA	NA	NA	NA	NA	NA	NA	NA	NA	NA
1955	80	1375	400	975	260	320	395	NA	NA	NA
1957	100	2300	425	1875	840	445	590	NA	NA	NA
1960	110	3570	610	2960	1440	500	1020	NA	NA	NA
1961	80	3380	80	3300	1625	560	1115	NA	NA	NA
1962	210	2495	140	2355	1115	525	715	NA	NA	NA
1963	40	2255	150	2105	925	530	650	NA	NA	NA
1964	280	1455	200	1255	645	220	390	NA	NA	NA
1965	140	1030	210	820	395	80	345	NA	NA	NA
COMMUNIST ASIA							EXPORTS			
1925	2601	-	-	-	-	-	-	-	-	-
1929	3544	-	-	-	-	-	-	-	-	-
1933	4165	54	51	3	2	1	-	-	-	-

Table IV. ENERGY IMPORTS AND EXPORTS, SELECTED YEARS, 1925-1965

(Original units)

Region, country, year	Solid fuels (10³ m.t. coal equiv.)	Liquid fuels (10³ m.t.)							Gas (10⁶ c.m.)	Electricity (10⁶ kwh)
				Refined petroleum products						
		Total	Crude oil	Total	Gasoline	Kerosine	Fuel oils	Lubes and greases		
	(1)	(2)	(3)	(4)	(5)	(6)	(7)	(8)	(9)	(10)
COMMUNIST ASIA (CONTINUED)							EXPORTS			
1937	4855	62	62	-	-	-	-	-	-	-
1938	4192	85	85	-	-	-	-	-	-	-
1950	NA	NA	NA	NA	NA	NA	NA	NA	NA	NA
1953	NA	NA	NA	NA	NA	NA	NA	NA	NA	NA
1955	1100	-	-	-	-	-	-	NA	NA	NA
1957	1840	4	-	4	4	-	-	NA	NA	NA
1960	1030	-	-	-	-	-	-	NA	NA	NA
1961	1200	-	-	-	-	-	-	NA	NA	NA
1962	1430	-	-	-	-	-	-	NA	NA	NA
1963	1470	-	-	-	-	-	-	NA	NA	NA
1964	1500	-	-	-	-	-	-	NA	NA	NA
1965	1755	-	-	-	-	-	-	NA	NA	NA
LATIN AMERICA							IMPORTS			
1925	7238	7842	3713	4129	576	273	3169	111	2	-
1929	7556	19868	14268	5600	1124	288	4034	154	4	-
1933	4752	19244	14467	4777	534	171	3991	81	59	21
1937	6145	30480	23567	6913	971	206	5617	119	136	19
1938	5497	33611	25486	8125	1754	435	5820	116	49	18
1950	2932	63287	49427	13860	3613	422	9462	363	654	130
1953	2410	68674	51253	17421	5587	717	10641	476	540	217
1955	2810	78947	57129	21818	5522	1458	13977	537	559	170
1957	2860	82762	60761	22001	5459	1422	14241	532	-	410
1960	3070	80420	62690	17730	3881	1180	11668	527	-	450
1961	2520	85798	67806	17992	4118	1445	11328	520	-	455
1962	1990	90090	72938	17152	3495	1304	11085	566	-	528
1963	2314	91655	74653	17002	3051	1000	11729	461	-	591
1964	2489	98315	80286	18029	2627	1000	13085	487	-	147
1965	2567	100392	84524	15868	2373	1252	10791	455	-	60
LATIN AMERICA							EXPORTS			
1925	15	19928	12698	7230	867	177	6110	76	-	-
1929	25	39297	25901	13396	1930	244	10988	234	-	-
1933	122	37606	22655	14951	3137	403	11244	167	-	-
1937	55	55446	31442	24004	4049	485	19082	388	-	-
1938	58	58302	32595	25707	4407	745	20203	352	-	-
1950	142	123345	74812	48533	7379	2127	38907	245	-	-
1953	37	137860	78832	59028	8109	3451	46972	616	-	-
1955	70	159337	96012	63325	7504	4327	50644	782	-	-
1957	100	184158	117170	66988	7797	5249	53140	738	176	-
1960	50	189805	111832	77973	8457	5321	63023	946	1171	-
1961	-	197713	114814	82899	8867	5990	66906	863	1320	-
1962	10	215130	123445	91685	8917	6387	74918	1074	1158	-
1963	10	221138	124029	97109	9581	5994	80295	876	1126	-
1964	12	231574	130218	101356	9198	7054	83560	1112	1212	-
1965	7	234899	130395	104504	10247	8001	84613	1237	1248	-
LATIN AMERICA - CARIBBEAN							IMPORTS			
1925	1411	5406	2792	2614	102	50	2439	23	2	-
1929	1425	15831	12788	3043	340	53	2622	28	4	-
1933	617	16830	14127	2703	124	38	2519	22	59	21
1937	779	26341	22209	4132	438	49	3599	46	136	19

Table IV. ENERGY IMPORTS AND EXPORTS, SELECTED YEARS, 1925-1965

(Original units)

Region, country, year	Solid fuels (10^3 m.t. coal equiv.)	Liquid fuels (10^3 m.t.)		Refined petroleum products					Gas (10^6 c.m.)	Electricity (10^6 kwh)
		Total	Crude oil	Total	Gasoline	Kerosine	Fuel oils	Lubes and greases		
	(1)	(2)	(3)	(4)	(5)	(6)	(7)	(8)	(9)	(10)
LATIN AMERICA - CARIBBEAN (CONTINUED)							IMPORTS			
1938	661	29080	24035	5045	1257	313	3435	40	49	18
1950	119	51646	46026	5620	1408	128	3925	159	654	130
1953	146	54138	46347	7791	2621	203	4776	191	540	217
1955	200	59180	48327	10853	3831	514	5991	225	559	170
1957	250	60695	48122	12573	4313	746	6971	221	-	410
1960	110	60953	51645	9308	2691	479	5648	176	-	450
1961	120	67527	56413	11114	3004	647	6863	239	-	455
1962	240	71716	59454	12262	2840	637	8237	149	-	528
1963	284	74257	61200	13057	2271	622	9589	111	-	591
1964	359	79197	65579	13618	2102	631	10272	104	-	147
1965	427	79587	67993	11594	1914	837	8129	101	-	60
LATIN AMERICA - CARIBBEAN							EXPORTS			
1925	-	18979	12064	6915	719	151	5970	75	-	-
1929	4	37622	24723	12899	1613	220	10834	232	-	-
1933	-	35915	21510	14405	2782	372	11085	166	-	-
1937	-	53176	29656	23520	3735	393	19005	387	-	-
1938	-	56384	31138	25246	4129	640	20125	352	-	-
1950	2	122246	74243	48003	7085	2086	38713	244	-	-
1953	1	136864	78201	58663	7962	3414	46793	614	-	-
1955	-	158185	95443	62742	7284	4229	50384	779	-	-
1957	10	182637	116389	66248	7611	5116	52721	736	176	-
1960	-	188248	110774	77474	8372	5237	62702	946	1171	-
1961	-	195761	113308	82453	8846	5952	66530	863	1320	-
1962	-	213157	122437	90720	8891	6361	74133	1073	1158	-
1963	-	219291	123081	96210	9533	5986	79517	873	1126	-
1964	2	230342	129736	100606	9177	7054	82895	1111	1212	-
1965	2	233472	129974	103498	10247	8000	83647	1233	1248	-
CARIBBEAN - OIL PRODUCING							IMPORTS			
1925	137	2856	2630	226	34	7	168	17	2	-
1929	178	13162	12518	644	104	11	508	21	4	-
1933	78	15178	14066	1112	16	3	1083	10	59	21
1937	89	24138	22017	2121	241	3	1852	25	136	19
1938	86	27074	23876	3198	1050	266	1857	25	49	18
1950	58	46855	45543	1312	644	47	511	110	653	130
1953	58	48521	45703	2818	1564	85	1036	133	540	217
1955	60	52150	47639	4511	2342	247	1519	135	559	170
1957	70	50213	44085	6128	2819	485	2404	135	-	410
1960	50	47757	44566	3191	1421	50	1323	124	-	450
1961	70	52886	49620	3266	1727	155	884	185	-	455
1962	180	54305	50308	3997	1330	100	2116	96	-	528
1963	190	54759	49959	4800	1125	66	3144	53	-	591
1964	240	57565	52722	4843	1145	121	3073	45	-	147
1965	295	57219	53893	3326	1073	250	1405	37	-	60
CARIBBEAN - OIL PRODUCING							EXPORTS			
1925	-	18979	12064	6915	719	151	5970	75	-	-
1929	4	37622	24723	12899	1613	220	10834	232	-	-
1933	-	35915	21510	14405	2782	372	11085	166	-	-
1937	-	53176	29656	23520	3735	393	19005	387	-	-
1938	-	56384	31138	25246	4129	640	20125	352	-	-

Table IV. ENERGY IMPORTS AND EXPORTS, SELECTED YEARS, 1925-1965

(Original units)

Region, country, year	Solid fuels (10^3 m.t. coal equiv.)	Liquid fuels (10^3 m.t.) Total	Crude oil	Refined petroleum products Total	Gasoline	Kerosine	Fuel oils	Lubes and greases	Gas (10^6 c.m.)	Electricity (10^6 kwh)
	(1)	(2)	(3)	(4)	(5)	(6)	(7)	(8)	(9)	(10)
CARIBBEAN - OIL PRODUCING (CONTINUED)							EXPORTS			
1950	2	122246	74243	48003	7085	2086	38588	244	-	-
1953	1	136864	78201	58663	7962	3414	46673	614	-	-
1955	-	157896	95443	62453	7190	4205	50213	779	-	-
1957	10	181209	116389	64820	7331	5081	51609	736	176	-
1960	-	186026	110774	75252	7520	5196	61374	946	1171	-
1961	-	193366	113308	80058	7729	5887	65318	863	1320	-
1962	-	210137	122437	87700	7641	6233	72493	1073	1158	-
1963	-	215064	123081	91983	8237	5878	76698	873	1126	-
1964	2	226098	129736	96362	7937	6957	79991	1111	1212	-
1965	2	229268	129974	99294	8879	7853	80963	1233	1248	-
ANTILLES, NETHERLANDS							IMPORTS			
1925	-	2478	2454	24	-	-	24	-	-	-
1929	1	12699	12331	368	13	1	354	-	-	-
1933	3	14884	13954	930	-	-	929	1	-	-
1937	3	23778	21941	1837	213	2	1620	2	-	-
1938	3	26764	23789	2975	1032	262	1679	2	-	-
1950	-	44505	43910	595	230	40	320	5	-	-
1953	-	44634	43360	1274	720	20	530	4	-	-
1955	-	46952	45117	1835	1222	5	538	3	-	-
1957	-	44684	41281	3403	1659	128	1535	3	-	-
1960	-	40991	38833	2158	927	29	1118	29	-	-
1961	-	43144	40846	2298	1374	133	653	93	-	-
1962	-	44534	41342	3192	1071	84	1956	17	-	-
1963	-	44299	40210	4089	1042	48	2933	-	-	-
1964	-	44642	40834	3808	993	102	2651	2	-	-
1965	-	43288	40811	2477	1027	234	1130	10	-	-
ANTILLES, NETHERLANDS							EXPORTS			
1925	NA	2038	1129	909	107	5	740	57	-	-
1929	1	11455	516	10939	1222	21	9527	169	-	-
1933	NA	12813	1204	11609	2218	285	8989	117	-	-
1937	-	20156	762	19394	2858	288	15918	330	-	-
1938	NA	22709	1082	21627	3483	608	17197	339	-	-
1950	-	37522	1140	36382	5483	1436	29220	243	-	-
1953	-	39062	720	38342	5407	2241	30180	514	-	-
1955	-	39332	2946	36386	4475	2801	28460	646	-	-
1957	-	36181	926	35255	3933	3139	27571	612	-	-
1960	-	33219	945	32274	4047	3036	24455	735	-	-
1961	-	34469	1436	33033	4042	3267	25058	666	-	-
1962	-	36363	1430	34933	4090	3143	26873	827	-	-
1963	-	36300	940	35360	4136	3291	27324	609	-	-
1964	-	36958	486	36472	4453	3739	27458	822	-	-
1965	-	36076	375	35701	4608	3781	26358	954	-	-
COLOMBIA							IMPORTS			
1925	3	9	-	9	7	-	-	2	-	-
1929	1	52	5	47	28	1	14	4	-	-
1933	2	22	-	22	10	-	10	2	-	-
1937	1	23	-	23	6	-	14	3	-	-
1938	-	23	-	23	7	-	13	3	-	-
1950	-	199	-	199	157	-	41	1	-	-

Table IV. ENERGY IMPORTS AND EXPORTS, SELECTED YEARS, 1925-1965

(Original units)

Region, country, year	Solid fuels (10^3 m.t. coal equiv.)	Liquid fuels (10^3 m.t.): Total	Crude oil	Refined petroleum products: Total	Gasoline	Kerosine	Fuel oils	Lubes and greases	Gas (10^6 c.m.)	Electricity (10^6 kwh)
	(1)	(2)	(3)	(4)	(5)	(6)	(7)	(8)	(9)	(10)
COLOMBIA (CONTINUED)							IMPORTS			
1953	-	506	-	506	358	60	73	15	-	-
1955	-	483	-	483	312	63	79	29	-	-
1957	-	340	-	340	230	39	41	30	-	-
1960	-	104	-	104	61	3	10	30	-	-
1961	-	197	-	197	124	6	32	35	-	-
1962	-	222	-	222	185	-	2	35	-	-
1963	-	65	-	65	36	1	-	28	-	-
1964	-	60	-	60	43	1	-	16	-	-
1965	-	22	-	22	12	-	-	10	-	-
COLOMBIA							EXPORTS			
1925	-	-	-	-	-	-	-	-	-	-
1929	-	2539	2539	-	-	-	-	-	-	-
1933	-	1695	1695	-	-	-	-	-	-	-
1937	-	2546	2546	-	-	-	-	-	-	-
1938	-	2648	2648	-	-	-	-	-	-	-
1950	-	4103	4103	-	-	-	-	-	-	-
1953	-	4607	4607	-	-	-	-	-	-	-
1955	-	3810	3594	216	-	-	216	-	-	-
1957	10	4304	4030	274	-	-	274	-	-	-
1960	-	4940	4353	587	-	-	587	-	-	-
1961	-	4286	3861	425	36	-	389	-	-	-
1962	-	4015	3402	613	-	-	613	-	-	-
1963	-	4736	4364	372	2	3	367	-	-	-
1964	2	4963	4248	715	13	-	702	-	-	-
1965	2	6339	5610	729	16	-	713	-	-	-
MEXICO							IMPORTS			
1925	66	359	176	183	20	5	144	14	2	-
1929	65	400	182	218	60	7	135	16	4	-
1933	12	206	51	155	5	3	141	6	59	21
1937	13	262	13	249	15	1	218	15	136	19
1938	14	192	9	183	9	-	165	9	49	18
1950	31	442	-	442	220	7	150	65	653	130
1953	42	906	-	906	400	5	430	71	540	217
1955	60	2073	-	2073	744	179	902	47	559	170
1957	70	2471	188	2283	909	314	828	25	-	410
1960	50	831	-	831	390	18	188	17	-	450
1961	60	746	25	721	211	16	199	25	-	455
1962	60	519	-	519	57	16	138	17	-	528
1963	60	637	21	616	33	17	211	9	-	591
1964	80	972	83	889	39	18	422	11	-	147
1965	110	817	-	817	30	16	275	11	-	60
MEXICO							EXPORTS			
1925	-	13796	8211	5585	567	136	4864	18	-	-
1929	3	3517	2321	1196	210	192	731	63	-	-
1933	-	3134	1730	1404	268	76	1011	49	-	-
1937	-	3103	1148	1955	517	89	1292	57	-	-
1938	-	1784	705	1079	193	18	855	13	-	-
1950	-	2321	1700	621	52	128	440	1	-	-
1953	-	2362	534	1828	5	3	1820	-	-	-

Table IV. ENERGY IMPORTS AND EXPORTS, SELECTED YEARS, 1925-1965

(Original units)

Region, country, year	Solid fuels (10^3 m.t. coal equiv.)	Liquid fuels (10^3 m.t.)							Gas (10^6 c.m.)	Electricity (10^6 kwh)
				Refined petroleum products						
		Total	Crude oil	Total	Gasoline	Kerosine	Fuel oils	Lubes and greases		
	(1)	(2)	(3)	(4)	(5)	(6)	(7)	(8)	(9)	(10)
MEXICO (CONTINUED)							EXPORTS			
1955	-	4190	797	3393	5	4	3384	-	-	-
1957	-	2326	445	1881	38	2	1841	-	176	-
1960	-	1202	150	1052	5	-	1047	-	1171	-
1961	-	2157	928	1229	42	-	1187	-	1320	-
1962	-	2735	1055	1680	3	-	1677	-	1158	-
1963	-	2706	1005	1701	21	-	1680	-	1126	-
1964	-	2564	1116	1448	6	-	1442	-	1212	-
1965	-	2618	1040	1578	1	-	1577	-	1248	-
TRINIDAD AND TOBAGO							IMPORTS			
1925	44	2	-	2	-	1	-	1	-	-
1929	87	6	-	6	-	1	4	1	-	-
1933	50	64	61	3	-	-	2	1	-	-
1937	62	65	63	2	-	-	-	2	-	-
1938	53	80	78	2	-	-	-	2	-	-
1950	26	1636	1633	3	-	-	-	3	-	-
1953	15	2379	2343	36	30	-	3	3	-	-
1955	-	2526	2522	4	-	-	-	4	-	-
1957	-	2629	2616	13	-	4	-	9	-	-
1960	-	5747	5733	14	-	-	7	7	-	-
1961	-	8756	8749	7	-	-	-	7	-	-
1962	-	8998	8966	32	5	-	20	7	-	-
1963	-	9750	9728	22	14	-	-	8	-	-
1964	-	11867	11805	62	54	-	-	8	-	-
1965	-	13082	13082	NA	-	-	-	NA	-	-
TRINIDAD AND TOBAGO							EXPORTS			
1925	-	463	42	421	45	10	366	-	-	-
1929	-	850	127	723	163	7	553	-	-	-
1933	-	718	163	555	250	11	294	-	-	-
1937	-	1400	87	1313	352	16	945	-	-	-
1938	-	1744	92	1652	453	14	1185	-	-	-
1950	-	2868	340	2528	370	510	1648	-	-	-
1953	1	3603	330	3273	520	900	1853	-	-	-
1955	-	4219	406	3813	560	800	2453	-	-	-
1957	-	5211	488	4723	710	990	3023	-	-	-
1960	-	9323	698	8625	1180	1160	6285	-	-	-
1961	-	12247	803	11444	1500	1460	8484	-	-	-
1962	-	13184	967	12217	1437	1350	9430	-	-	-
1963	-	14569	1052	13517	1581	1134	10802	-	-	-
1964	-	16320	1501	14819	1555	1358	11854	52	-	-
1965	-	17152	1559	15593	1426	1842	12315	NA	-	-
VENEZUELA							IMPORTS			
1925	24	8	-	8	7	1	-	-	-	-
1929	24	5	-	5	3	1	1	-	-	-
1933	11	2	-	2	1	-	1	-	-	-
1937	10	10	-	10	7	-	-	3	-	-
1938	16	15	-	15	2	4	-	9	-	-
1950	1	73	-	73	37	-	-	36	-	-
1953	1	96	-	96	56	-	-	40	-	-
1955	-	116	-	116	64	-	-	52	-	-

Table IV. ENERGY IMPORTS AND EXPORTS, SELECTED YEARS, 1925-1965

(Original units)

Region, country, year	Solid fuels (10^3 m.t. coal equiv.)	Liquid fuels (10^3 m.t.) Total	Crude oil	Refined petroleum products Total	Gasoline	Kerosine	Fuel oils	Lubes and greases	Gas (10^6 c.m.)	Electricity (10^6 kwh)
	(1)	(2)	(3)	(4)	(5)	(6)	(7)	(8)	(9)	(10)
VENEZUELA (CONTINUED)							IMPORTS			
1957	-	89	-	89	21	-	-	68	-	-
1960	-	84	-	84	43	-	-	41	-	-
1961	10	43	-	43	18	-	-	25	-	-
1962	120	32	-	32	12	-	-	20	-	-
1963	130	8	-	8	-	-	-	8	-	-
1964	160	24	-	24	16	-	-	8	-	-
1965	185	10	-	10	4	-	-	6	-	-
VENEZUELA							EXPORTS			
1925	-	2682	2682	-	-	-	-	-	-	-
1929	-	19261	19220	41	18	-	23	-	-	-
1933	-	17555	16718	837	46	-	791	-	-	-
1937	-	25971	25113	858	8	-	850	-	-	-
1938	-	27499	26611	888	-	-	888	-	-	-
1950	2	75432	66960	8472	1180	12	7280	-	-	-
1953	-	87230	72010	15220	2030	270	12820	100	-	-
1955	-	106345	87700	18645	2150	600	15700	133	-	-
1957	-	133187	110500	22687	2650	950	18900	124	-	-
1960	-	137342	104628	32714	2288	1000	29000	211	-	-
1961	-	140207	106280	33927	2109	1160	30200	197	-	-
1962	-	153840	115583	38257	2111	1740	33900	246	-	-
1963	-	156753	115720	41033	2497	1450	36525	264	-	-
1964	-	165293	122385	42908	1910	1860	38535	237	-	-
1965	-	167083	121390	45693	2828	2230	40000	279	-	-
CARIBBEAN - OTHER							IMPORTS			
1925	1274	2550	162	2388	68	43	2271	6	-	-
1929	1247	2669	270	2399	236	42	2114	7	-	-
1933	539	1652	61	1591	108	35	1436	12	-	-
1937	690	2203	192	2011	197	46	1747	21	-	-
1938	575	2006	159	1847	207	47	1578	15	-	-
1950	61	4791	483	4308	764	81	3414	49	1	-
1953	88	5617	644	4973	1057	118	3740	58	-	-
1955	140	7030	688	6342	1489	267	4472	90	-	-
1957	180	10482	4037	6445	1494	261	4567	86	-	-
1960	60	13196	7079	6117	1270	429	4325	52	-	-
1961	50	14641	6793	7848	1277	492	5979	54	-	-
1962	60	17411	9146	8265	1510	537	6121	53	-	-
1963	94	19498	11241	8257	1146	556	6445	58	-	-
1964	119	21632	12857	8775	957	510	7199	59	-	-
1965	132	22368	14100	8268	841	587	6724	64	-	-
CARIBBEAN - OTHER							EXPORTS			
1925	-	-	-	-	-	-	-	-	-	-
1929	-	-	-	-	-	-	-	-	-	-
1933	-	-	-	-	-	-	-	-	-	-
1937	-	-	-	-	-	-	-	-	-	-
1938	-	-	-	-	-	-	-	-	-	-
1950	-	-	-	-	-	-	125	-	-	-
1953	-	-	-	-	-	-	120	-	-	-
1955	-	289	-	289	94	24	171	-	-	-
1957	-	1428	-	1428	280	35	1112	-	-	-

Table IV. ENERGY IMPORTS AND EXPORTS, SELECTED YEARS, 1925-1965

(Original units)

Region, country, year	Solid fuels (10^3 m.t. coal equiv.)	Liquid fuels (10^3 m.t.)							Gas (10^6 c.m.)	Electricity (10^6 kwh)
				Refined petroleum products						
		Total	Crude oil	Total	Gasoline	Kerosine	Fuel oils	Lubes and greases		
	(1)	(2)	(3)	(4)	(5)	(6)	(7)	(8)	(9)	(10)
CARIBBEAN - OTHER (CONTINUED)							EXPORTS			
1960	-	2222	-	2222	852	41	1328	-	-	-
1961	-	2395	-	2395	1117	65	1212	-	-	-
1962	-	3020	-	3020	1250	128	1640	-	-	-
1963	-	4227	-	4227	1296	108	2819	-	-	-
1964	-	4244	-	4244	1240	97	2904	-	-	-
1965	-	4204	-	4204	1368	147	2684	-	-	-
CUBA							IMPORTS			
1925	659	1263	108	1155	22	-	1133	-	-	-
1929	632	1076	203	873	139	-	734	-	-	-
1933	296	308	24	284	32	-	245	7	-	-
1937	381	753	133	620	70	-	542	8	-	-
1938	342	581	88	493	75	-	411	7	-	-
1950	35	2476	280	2196	370	-	1800	26	-	-
1953	58	2690	500	2190	400	-	1760	30	-	-
1955	130	2688	487	2201	460	3	1672	53	-	-
1957	180	4014	2100	1914	380	8	1466	39	-	-
1960	60	4187	3280	907	83	66	754	NA	-	-
1961	50	4340	2980	1360	104	67	1184	NA	-	-
1962	60	4838	3720	1118	228	69	820	NA	-	-
1963	94	4422	3709	713	212	35	466	NA	-	-
1964	119	4771	3469	1302	159	24	1119	NA	-	-
1965	132	4779	3513	1266	147	22	1097	NA	-	-
CUBA							EXPORTS			
1955	-	NA	-	NA	NA	NA	NA	NA	NA	NA
1957	-	603	-	603	3	-	600	-	-	-
1960	-	169	-	169	25	-	144	-	-	-
1961	-	-	-	-	-	-	NA	-	-	-
1962	-	-	-	-	-	-	NA	-	-	-
1963	-	4	-	4	-	-	4	-	-	-
1964	-	22	-	22	-	-	22	-	-	-
1965	-	3	-	3	-	-	3	-	-	-
PANAMA CANAL ZONE							IMPORTS			
1925	331	922	-	922	4	2	916	-	-	-
1929	272	1089	-	1089	8	3	1078	-	-	-
1933	28	865	-	865	8	3	854	-	-	-
1937	113	771	-	771	11	5	755	-	-	-
1938	45	780	-	780	10	4	766	-	-	-
1950	-	865	-	865	40	5	820	-	-	-
1953	-	935	-	935	100	5	830	-	-	-
1955	-	955	-	955	50	25	880	-	-	-
1957	-	1287	-	1287	110	27	1150	-	-	-
1960	-	1137	-	1137	147	48	930	-	-	-
1961	-	1410	-	1410	178	64	1153	-	-	-
1962	-	1674	-	1674	130	69	1459	-	-	-
1963	-	2508	-	2508	113	39	2342	-	-	-
1964	-	2692	-	2692	89	13	2574	-	-	-
1965	-	2919	-	2919	87	34	2780	-	-	-

Table IV. ENERGY IMPORTS AND EXPORTS, SELECTED YEARS, 1925-1965

(Original units)

Region, country, year	Solid fuels (10^3 m.t. coal equiv.)	Liquid fuels (10^3 m.t.)							Gas (10^6 c.m.)	Electricity (10^6 kwh)
				Refined petroleum products						
		Total	Crude oil	Total	Gasoline	Kerosine	Fuel oils	Lubes and greases		
	(1)	(2)	(3)	(4)	(5)	(6)	(7)	(8)	(9)	(10)
PANAMA CANAL ZONE (CONTINUED)							EXPORTS			
1950	-	NA	-	NA	NA	NA	125	-	-	-
1953	-	NA	-	NA	NA	NA	120	-	-	-
1955	-	241	-	241	78	23	140	-	-	-
1957	-	256	-	256	91	25	140	-	-	-
1960	-	254	-	254	114	38	101	-	-	-
1961	-	291	-	291	116	63	111	-	-	-
1962	-	286	-	286	107	67	110	-	-	-
1963	-	213	-	213	76	38	99	-	-	-
1964	-	160	-	160	50	10	100	-	-	-
1965	-	189	-	189	49	30	110	-	-	-
PUERTO RICO							IMPORTS			
1950	NA	NA	NA	NA	NA	NA	NA	NA	NA	NA
1953	6	NA	NA	NA	NA	NA	NA	NA	NA	NA
1955	-	994	-	994	339	94	560	-	-	-
1957	-	2510	1930	580	190	44	345	-	-	-
1960	-	4141	3788	353	130	22	197	-	-	-
1961	-	4076	3789	287	75	7	204	-	-	-
1962	-	4751	4314	437	252	4	181	-	-	-
1963	-	5139	4838	301	-	82	216	-	-	-
1964	-	5688	5393	295	-	157	137	-	-	-
1965	-	6226	5780	446	20	270	155	-	-	-
PUERTO RICO							EXPORTS			
1950	-	NA	NA	NA	NA	NA	NA	NA	NA	NA
1953	-	NA	NA	NA	NA	NA	NA	NA	NA	NA
1955	-	45	-	45	15	-	30	-	-	-
1957	-	565	-	565	185	8	371	-	-	-
1960	-	1794	-	1794	711	1	1082	-	-	-
1961	-	2100	-	2100	1000	1	1099	-	-	-
1962	-	2076	-	2076	1003	13	1060	-	-	-
1963	-	2419	-	2419	1011	4	1404	-	-	-
1964	-	2505	-	2505	998	1	1506	-	-	-
1965	-	2446	-	2446	1031	12	1400	-	-	-
LATIN AMERICA - OTHER							IMPORTS			
1925	5827	2436	921	1515	474	223	730	88	-	-
1929	6131	4037	1480	2557	784	235	1412	126	-	-
1933	4135	2414	340	2074	410	133	1472	59	-	-
1937	5366	4139	1358	2781	533	157	2018	73	-	-
1938	4836	4531	1451	3080	497	122	2385	76	-	-
1950	2813	11641	3401	8240	2205	294	5537	204	-	-
1953	2264	14536	4906	9630	2966	514	5865	285	-	-
1955	2610	19767	8802	10965	1691	944	7986	312	-	-
1957	2610	22067	12639	9428	1146	676	7270	311	-	-
1960	2960	19467	11045	8422	1190	701	6020	351	-	-
1961	2400	18271	11393	6878	1114	798	4465	281	-	-
1962	1750	18374	13484	4890	655	667	2848	417	-	-
1963	2030	17398	13453	3945	780	378	2140	350	-	-
1964	2130	19118	14707	4411	525	369	2813	383	-	-
1965	2140	20805	16531	4274	459	415	2662	354	-	-

Table IV. ENERGY IMPORTS AND EXPORTS, SELECTED YEARS, 1925-1965

(Original units)

Region, country, year	Solid fuels (10^3 m.t. coal equiv.)	Liquid fuels (10^3 m.t.) Total	Crude oil	Refined petroleum products Total	Gasoline	Kerosine	Fuel oils	Lubes and greases	Gas (10^6 c.m.)	Electricity (10^6 kwh)
	(1)	(2)	(3)	(4)	(5)	(6)	(7)	(8)	(9)	(10)
LATIN AMERICA - OTHER (CONTINUED)							EXPORTS			
1925	15	949	634	315	148	26	140	1	-	-
1929	21	1675	1178	497	317	24	154	2	-	-
1933	122	1691	1145	546	355	31	159	1	-	-
1937	55	2270	1786	484	314	92	77	1	-	-
1938	58	1918	1457	461	278	105	78	-	-	-
1950	140	1099	569	530	294	41	194	1	-	-
1953	36	996	631	365	147	37	179	2	-	-
1955	70	1152	569	583	220	98	260	3	-	-
1957	90	1521	781	740	186	133	419	2	-	-
1960	50	1557	1058	499	85	84	321	-	-	-
1961	-	1952	1506	446	21	38	376	-	-	-
1962	10	1973	1008	965	26	26	785	1	-	-
1963	10	1847	948	899	48	8	778	3	-	-
1964	10	1232	482	750	21	-	665	1	-	-
1965	5	1427	421	1006	-	1	966	4	-	-
ARGENTINA							IMPORTS			
1925	3179	715	76	639	255	68	285	31	-	-
1929	3176	1712	488	1224	312	60	799	53	-	-
1933	2458	1010	156	854	43	8	785	18	-	-
1937	3164	1734	569	1165	21	-	1134	10	-	-
1938	2859	2104	663	1441	2	-	1430	9	-	-
1950	1467	5380	2954	2426	250	8	2124	44	-	-
1953	1224	6103	3599	2504	110	9	2320	65	-	-
1955	1260	7144	3714	3430	112	161	3116	39	-	-
1957	1280	9336	6154	3182	126	113	2904	39	-	-
1960	1460	5082	3315	1767	44	485	1141	64	-	-
1961	1260	3394	1800	1594	68	529	878	35	-	-
1962	640	2624	1115	1509	51	333	961	112	-	-
1963	770	1502	869	633	35	31	461	74	-	-
1964	750	2724	1478	1246	28	16	1047	69	-	-
1965	730	4534	3552	982	64	13	586	107	-	-
ARGENTINA							EXPORTS			
1925	-	-	-	-	-	-	-	-	-	-
1929	-	9	-	9	-	-	9	-	-	-
1933	-	-	-	-	-	-	-	-	-	-
1937	-	1	-	1	-	-	1	-	-	-
1938	-	-	-	-	-	-	-	-	-	-
1950	-	-	-	-	-	-	-	-	-	-
1953	-	-	-	-	-	-	-	-	-	-
1955	-	-	-	-	-	-	-	-	-	-
1957	-	1	-	1	1	-	-	-	-	-
1960	-	2	-	2	-	-	2	-	-	-
1961	-	71	32	39	4	2	33	-	-	-
1962	-	895	254	641	20	25	496	-	-	-
1963	-	831	102	729	48	8	654	-	-	-
1964	-	515	16	499	21	-	477	-	-	-
1965	-	894	-	894	-	1	892	-	-	-
BOLIVIA							IMPORTS			
1925	16	22	-	22	2	1	17	2	-	-

Table IV. ENERGY IMPORTS AND EXPORTS, SELECTED YEARS, 1925–1965

(Original units)

Region, country, year	Solid fuels (10^3 m.t. coal equiv.)	Liquid fuels (10^3 m.t.): Total	Crude oil	Refined petroleum products: Total	Gasoline	Kerosine	Fuel oils	Lubes and greases	Gas (10^6 c.m.)	Electricity (10^6 kwh)
	(1)	(2)	(3)	(4)	(5)	(6)	(7)	(8)	(9)	(10)
BOLIVIA (CONTINUED)							IMPORTS			
1929	19	40	-	40	6	2	30	2	-	-
1933	8	20	-	20	4	1	14	1	-	-
1937	31	40	-	40	7	2	28	3	-	-
1938	33	45	-	45	8	2	33	2	-	-
1950	2	71	58	13	10	-	-	3	-	-
1953	5	109	73	36	26	6	-	4	-	-
1955	-	47	8	39	24	3	8	4	-	-
1957	-	24	-	24	6	-	11	7	-	-
1960	-	39	-	39	11	-	25	3	-	-
1961	-	27	-	27	10	-	15	2	-	-
1962	-	63	42	21	11	-	7	3	-	-
1963	-	11	-	11	10	-	-	1	-	-
1964	-	14	-	14	13	-	-	1	-	-
1965	5	17	-	17	15	1	-	1	-	-
BOLIVIA							EXPORTS			
1950	-	3	3	-	-	-	-	-	-	-
1953	-	1	1	-	-	-	-	-	-	-
1955	-	79	62	17	15	1	1	-	-	-
1957	-	159	134	25	23	1	1	-	-	-
1960	-	138	133	5	4	-	1	-	-	-
1961	-	93	85	8	7	-	1	-	-	-
1962	-	66	65	1	1	-	-	-	-	-
1963	-	69	69	-	-	-	-	-	-	-
1964	-	42	36	6	-	-	-	-	-	-
1965	-	39	35	4	-	-	-	-	-	-
BRAZIL							IMPORTS			
1925	1927	542	-	542	143	103	261	35	-	-
1929	2325	793	-	793	294	117	337	45	-	-
1933	1292	787	-	787	236	81	442	28	-	-
1937	1708	1105	38	1067	357	114	557	39	-	-
1938	1576	1178	48	1130	361	99	632	38	-	-
1950	1119	4333	59	4274	1618	236	2304	116	-	-
1953	746	5525	30	5495	2446	408	2478	163	-	-
1955	1120	8715	3513	5202	1170	546	3256	200	-	-
1957	940	8629	4846	3783	703	392	2473	190	-	-
1960	1060	9993	5684	4309	891	98	2981	212	-	-
1961	900	10706	7549	3157	810	138	1889	184	-	-
1962	920	11272	9961	1311	419	239	162	242	-	-
1963	1040	11696	10375	1321	523	254	54	228	-	-
1964	1155	11883	10803	1080	293	249	40	265	-	-
1965	1240	11083	10247	836	163	278	20	210	-	-
BRAZIL							EXPORTS			
1955	-	-	-	-	-	-	-	-	-	-
1957	-	143	-	143	-	-	143	-	-	-
1960	-	647	587	60	-	-	60	-	-	-
1961	-	1127	1052	75	-	-	75	-	-	-
1962	-	375	298	77	-	-	77	-	-	-
1963	-	392	360	32	-	-	32	-	-	-
1964	-	122	-	122	-	-	122	-	-	-

Table IV. ENERGY IMPORTS AND EXPORTS, SELECTED YEARS, 1925-1965

(Original units)

Region, country, year	Solid fuels (10^3 m.t. coal equiv.)	Liquid fuels (10^3 m.t.)		Refined petroleum products					Gas (10^6 c.m.)	Electricity (10^6 kwh)
		Total	Crude oil	Total	Gasoline	Kerosine	Fuel oils	Lubes and greases		
	(1)	(2)	(3)	(4)	(5)	(6)	(7)	(8)	(9)	(10)
BRAZIL (CONTINUED)							EXPORTS			
1965	-	-	-	-	-	-	-	-	-	-
CHILE							IMPORTS			
1925	264	918	845	73	41	21	NA	11	-	-
1929	72	1121	992	129	94	19	NA	16	-	-
1933	3	279	183	96	54	7	30	5	-	-
1937	12	767	634	133	75	9	37	12	-	-
1938	7	724	574	150	90	7	40	13	-	-
1950	84	1154	-	1154	226	39	870	19	-	-
1953	201	1124	-	1124	286	74	740	24	-	-
1955	140	1638	306	1332	190	154	954	34	-	-
1957	290	1560	450	1110	81	143	854	32	-	-
1960	350	1406	513	893	38	77	757	21	-	-
1961	160	1297	491	806	44	83	660	19	-	-
1962	120	1405	607	798	31	35	720	12	-	-
1963	160	1207	419	788	40	38	710	NA	-	-
1964	170	1246	441	805	15	45	745	NA	-	-
1965	115	1544	650	894	31	50	810	NA	-	-
CHILE							EXPORTS			
1925	15	11	11	-	-	-	-	-	-	-
1929	21	1	1	-	-	-	-	-	-	-
1933	122	2	1	1	-	-	1	-	-	-
1937	55	1	1	-	-	-	-	-	-	-
1938	58	-	-	-	-	-	-	-	-	-
1950	82	56	56	-	-	-	-	-	-	-
1953	-	150	150	-	-	-	-	-	-	-
1955	70	2	-	2	-	-	-	-	-	-
1957	60	47	47	-	-	-	-	-	-	-
1960	30	9	-	9	-	-	-	-	-	-
1961	-	11	-	11	-	-	-	-	-	-
1962	-	18	-	18	-	-	-	-	-	-
1963	-	38	-	38	-	-	-	-	-	-
1964	-	50	-	50	-	-	-	-	-	-
1965	-	30	-	30	-	-	-	-	-	-
ECUADOR							IMPORTS			
1925	-	13	-	13	1	1	10	1	-	-
1929	-	22	-	22	2	1	18	1	-	-
1933	-	15	-	15	-	-	14	1	-	-
1937	-	2	-	2	-	-	1	1	-	-
1938	-	37	-	37	-	-	36	1	-	-
1950	-	10	-	10	8	-	-	2	-	-
1953	-	18	-	18	16	-	-	2	-	-
1955	-	93	16	77	56	-	17	4	-	-
1957	-	131	-	131	75	1	51	4	-	-
1960	-	231	214	17	10	1	1	5	-	-
1961	-	208	189	19	11	2	-	6	-	-
1962	-	209	190	19	11	2	1	5	-	-
1963	-	288	250	38	30	-	1	7	-	-
1964	-	404	375	29	10	9	-	10	-	-
1965	-	414	380	34	12	12	-	10	-	-

Table IV. ENERGY IMPORTS AND EXPORTS, SELECTED YEARS, 1925–1965

(Original units)

Region, country, year	Solid fuels (10^3 m.t. coal equiv.)	Liquid fuels (10^3 m.t.)							Gas (10^6 c.m.)	Electricity (10^6 kwh)
				Refined petroleum products						
		Total	Crude oil	Total	Gasoline	Kerosine	Fuel oils	Lubes and greases		
	(1)	(2)	(3)	(4)	(5)	(6)	(7)	(8)	(9)	(10)
ECUADOR (CONTINUED)							EXPORTS			
1925	-	5	5	-	-	-	-	-	-	-
1929	-	157	157	-	-	-	-	-	-	-
1933	-	153	153	-	-	-	-	-	-	-
1937	-	252	252	-	-	-	-	-	-	-
1938	-	246	245	1	1	-	-	-	-	-
1950	-	136	136	-	-	-	-	-	-	-
1953	-	172	172	-	-	-	-	-	-	-
1955	-	194	194	-	-	-	-	-	-	-
1957	-	166	166	-	-	-	-	-	-	-
1960	-	-	-	-	-	-	-	-	-	-
1961	-	-	-	-	-	-	-	-	-	-
1962	-	23	23	-	-	-	-	-	-	-
1963	-	25	25	-	-	-	-	-	-	-
1964	-	70	70	-	-	-	-	-	-	-
1965	-	60	60	-	-	-	-	-	-	-
PARAGUAY							IMPORTS			
1925	NA	NA	-	NA	NA	NA	NA	NA	-	-
1929	NA	NA	-	NA	NA	NA	NA	NA	-	-
1933	3	4	-	4	3	1	-	-	-	-
1937	NA	7	-	7	5	2	-	-	-	-
1938	NA	8	-	8	5	2	1	-	-	-
1950	-	22	-	22	14	4	3	1	-	-
1953	-	47	-	47	22	8	15	2	-	-
1955	-	63	-	63	27	10	24	2	-	-
1957	-	68	-	68	28	10	28	2	-	-
1960	-	103	-	103	36	18	46	3	-	-
1961	-	118	-	118	37	15	64	2	-	-
1962	-	123	-	123	40	18	62	3	-	-
1963	-	134	-	134	41	19	71	3	-	-
1964	-	139	-	139	42	18	77	2	-	-
1965	-	177	-	177	42	24	108	3	-	-
PERU							IMPORTS			
1925	39	4	-	4	1	-	-	3	-	-
1929	41	4	-	4	-	-	-	4	-	-
1933	18	1	-	1	-	-	-	1	-	-
1937	15	32	26	6	3	-	-	3	-	-
1938	13	23	16	7	3	-	-	4	-	-
1950	1	38	-	38	31	-	-	7	-	-
1953	1	42	-	42	30	-	-	12	-	-
1955	-	244	-	244	53	-	177	14	-	-
1957	-	346	-	346	84	-	242	20	-	-
1960	10	574	-	574	108	-	448	18	-	-
1961	20	580	14	566	53	-	497	16	-	-
1962	20	683	99	584	43	-	522	19	-	-
1963	10	657	100	557	53	4	483	17	-	-
1964	5	672	75	597	61	-	520	16	-	-
1965	10	641	112	529	66	1	458	4	-	-
PERU							EXPORTS			
1925	-	933	618	315	148	26	140	1	-	-

Table IV. ENERGY IMPORTS AND EXPORTS, SELECTED YEARS, 1925-1965

(Original units)

Region, country, year	Solid fuels (10³ m.t. coal equiv.)	Liquid fuels (10³ m.t.)		Refined petroleum products					Gas (10⁶ c.m.)	Electricity (10⁶ kwh)
		Total	Crude oil	Total	Gasoline	Kerosine	Fuel oils	Lubes and greases		
	(1)	(2)	(3)	(4)	(5)	(6)	(7)	(8)	(9)	(10)
PERU (CONTINUED)							EXPORTS			
1929	-	1508	1020	488	317	24	145	2	-	-
1933	-	1536	991	545	355	31	158	1	-	-
1937	-	2016	1533	483	314	92	76	1	-	-
1938	-	1672	1212	460	277	105	78	-	-	-
1950	58	904	374	530	294	41	194	1	-	-
1953	36	673	308	365	147	37	179	2	-	-
1955	-	877	313	564	205	97	259	3	-	-
1957	30	1005	434	571	162	132	275	2	-	-
1960	20	761	338	423	81	84	258	-	-	-
1961	-	643	337	306	10	36	260	-	-	-
1962	10	587	368	219	5	1	212	1	-	-
1963	10	487	392	95	-	-	92	3	-	-
1964	10	427	360	67	-	-	66	1	-	-
1965	5	404	326	78	-	-	74	4	-	-
URUGUAY							IMPORTS			
1925	363	215	-	215	29	26	155	5	-	-
1929	474	336	-	336	74	33	224	5	-	-
1933	344	286	-	286	67	32	182	5	-	-
1937	418	404	83	321	61	26	230	4	-	-
1938	334	376	138	238	22	8	200	8	-	-
1950	129	376	330	46	31	-	5	10	-	-
1953	83	1259	1204	55	7	-	37	11	-	-
1955	90	1437	1245	192	30	57	94	11	-	-
1957	100	1562	1189	373	10	-	349	14	-	-
1960	80	1579	1319	260	8	-	233	19	-	-
1961	60	1486	1350	136	32	8	85	11	-	-
1962	50	1565	1470	95	5	14	62	14	-	-
1963	50	1494	1440	54	4	8	28	13	-	-
1964	50	1598	1535	63	17	7	25	14	-	-
1965	40	1756	1590	166	18	6	130	11	-	-
URUGUAY							EXPORTS			
1960	-	-	-	-	-	-	-	-	-	-
1961	-	7	-	7	-	-	7	-	-	-
1962	-	9	-	9	-	-	-	-	-	-
1963	-	5	-	5	-	-	-	-	-	-
1964	-	6	-	6	-	-	-	-	-	-
1965	-	-	-	-	-	-	-	-	-	-
ASIA							IMPORTS			
1925	6539	3541	423	3118	422	992	1526	178	-	-
1929	8394	6423	1749	4674	620	1487	2325	240	-	-
1933	7986	7223	2836	4387	641	1185	2385	176	-	-
1937	11327	11346	4010	7336	1259	1218	3571	275	-	-
1938	11754	12205	4008	8197	1312	1320	3903	277	-	-
1950	3106	29620	15191	14429	2960	1850	8317	382	54	-
1953	7942	44091	23166	20925	4640	2603	13220	462	58	-
1955	5880	56763	34087	22676	4441	2967	14722	544	68	-
1957	9660	69723	42439	27284	4576	3194	18744	763	68	-
1960	10894	84331	56934	27397	4510	3627	18390	859	76	-

Table IV. ENERGY IMPORTS AND EXPORTS, SELECTED YEARS, 1925–1965

(Original units)

Region, country, year	Solid fuels (10^3 m.t. coal equiv.)	Liquid fuels (10^3 m.t.)							Gas (10^6 c.m.)	Electricity (10^6 kwh)
				Refined petroleum products						
		Total	Crude oil	Total	Gasoline	Kerosine	Fuel oils	Lubes and greases		
	(1)	(2)	(3)	(4)	(5)	(6)	(7)	(8)	(9)	(10)
ASIA (CONTINUED)							IMPORTS			
1961	13520	99507	67733	31774	3950	3968	22909	931	76	-
1962	14430	112852	81619	31233	3120	4284	22600	1107	72	-
1963	13140	127966	95746	32220	2999	3768	23831	1399	54	-
1964	15445	141954	109434	32520	2950	3144	24780	1278	50	-
1965	18950	154208	120473	33735	2845	3355	26102	952	-	-
ASIA							EXPORTS			
1925	5505	6925	1205	5720	1189	560	3926	45	-	-
1929	6289	10063	1861	8202	2783	1687	3673	59	-	-
1933	5580	12816	2415	10401	3141	1153	6068	39	-	-
1937	6038	22802	5789	17013	4470	2052	10390	101	-	-
1938	6940	21256	5267	15989	4862	2099	8908	120	-	-
1950	1681	100833	58051	42782	9340	4236	29139	67	54	-
1953	3165	142105	114223	27882	7178	2983	17629	92	58	-
1955	2050	183840	149294	34546	7979	4516	21959	92	72	-
1957	1890	201005	160779	40226	8393	4918	26881	32	72	-
1960	1750	280822	233560	47262	9219	5759	32225	52	76	-
1961	1490	299579	253053	46526	8138	5735	32595	33	76	-
1962	1580	330124	276061	54063	8861	6197	38841	45	76	-
1963	1350	360035	304667	55368	8998	5966	39669	435	63	-
1964	1710	399463	343834	55629	8998	6313	39592	147	50	-
1965	1265	432530	374276	58254	9288	7020	41002	149	54	-
MIDDLE EAST							IMPORTS			
1925	270	425	1	424	36	157	229	2	-	-
1929	344	736	3	733	90	164	469	10	-	-
1933	238	911	11	900	69	105	714	12	-	-
1937	423	1305	17	1288	141	154	971	22	-	-
1938	338	1489	16	1473	152	145	1155	21	-	-
1950	162	11254	6812	4442	533	393	3456	60	-	-
1953	76	14506	9569	4937	619	461	3756	101	-	-
1955	60	19113	14837	4276	672	624	2872	107	-	-
1957	60	19142	13984	5158	697	539	3789	128	-	-
1960	50	19901	15057	4844	674	518	3525	118	-	-
1961	60	21907	17318	4589	636	433	3391	121	-	-
1962	50	25222	22245	2977	288	236	2296	146	-	-
1963	30	26278	23044	3234	316	161	2576	161	-	-
1964	40	26550	23323	3227	349	145	2630	121	-	-
1965	35	25894	23576	2318	414	135	1651	116	-	-
MIDDLE EAST							EXPORTS			
1925	154	3815	1051	2764	314	114	2336	-	-	-
1929	455	5326	1664	3662	1223	920	1519	-	-	-
1933	532	7297	1573	5724	1528	446	3750	-	-	-
1937	293	14428	5117	9311	1929	597	6778	7	-	-
1938	342	12117	4497	7620	2087	587	4935	11	-	-
1950	-	84461	51572	32889	6599	3406	22884	-	-	-
1953	8	120618	104426	16192	3661	1752	10779	-	-	-
1955	-	160883	137636	23247	4828	3403	15016	-	-	-
1957	-	172517	143877	28640	5111	3926	19601	-	-	-
1960	30	251144	215357	35787	5786	4566	25428	-	-	-
1961	-	270211	234586	35625	5119	4537	25944	-	-	-

Table IV. ENERGY IMPORTS AND EXPORTS, SELECTED YEARS, 1925-1965

(Original units)

Region, country, year	Solid fuels (10^3 m.t. coal equiv.)	Liquid fuels (10^3 m.t.)		Refined petroleum products					Gas (10^6 c.m.)	Electricity (10^6 kwh)
		Total	Crude oil	Total	Gasoline	Kerosine	Fuel oils	Lubes and greases		
	(1)	(2)	(3)	(4)	(5)	(6)	(7)	(8)	(9)	(10)
MIDDLE EAST (CONTINUED)							EXPORTS			
1962	-	298021	256571	41450	5952	4893	30487	-	-	-
1963	10	328513	285695	42818	6064	4712	31744	-	-	-
1964	20	367815	324095	43720	6331	5134	31679	-	-	-
1965	10	399576	354825	44751	6866	5370	31729	-	-	-
MIDDLE EAST - OIL PRODUCING							IMPORTS			
1925	5	92	-	92	7	50	34	1	-	-
1929	8	100	-	100	15	40	40	5	-	-
1933	3	93	-	93	8	25	53	7	-	-
1937	4	126	1	125	16	31	65	13	-	-
1938	4	110	-	110	14	14	68	14	-	-
1950	2	6415	6125	290	26	55	196	13	-	-
1953	-	8390	8259	131	1	1	109	20	-	-
1955	-	8939	8558	381	30	15	314	22	-	-
1957	-	9045	7428	1617	61	15	1511	30	-	-
1960	-	8173	8031	142	77	13	24	28	-	-
1961	20	8731	8567	164	84	11	40	29	-	-
1962	-	9853	9728	125	61	12	25	27	-	-
1963	-	9161	8980	181	127	16	29	9	-	-
1964	-	7912	7697	215	160	17	33	5	-	-
1965	-	6972	6740	232	182	13	31	6	-	-
MIDDLE EAST - OIL PRODUCING							EXPORTS			
1925	-	3814	1051	2763	314	113	2336	-	-	-
1929	-	5325	1664	3661	1223	919	1519	-	-	-
1933	-	7297	1573	5724	1528	446	3750	-	-	-
1937	-	14419	5117	9302	1929	597	6769	7	-	-
1938	-	12117	4497	7620	2087	587	4935	11	-	-
1950	-	84461	51572	32889	6599	3406	22884	-	-	-
1953	-	120610	104426	16184	3661	1752	10771	-	-	-
1955	-	158224	137636	20588	4091	2902	13595	-	-	-
1957	-	169712	143877	25835	4403	3560	17871	-	-	-
1960	-	248911	215357	33554	5213	4247	24090	-	-	-
1961	-	266963	234586	32377	4289	4038	24029	-	-	-
1962	-	293886	256571	37315	5029	4328	27845	-	-	-
1963	-	323461	285695	37766	5139	4100	28236	-	-	-
1964	-	362390	324095	38295	5233	4441	28049	-	-	-
1965	-	394243	354825	39418	5626	4738	28270	-	-	-
BAHRAIN							IMPORTS			
1925	-	-	-	-	-	-	-	-	-	-
1929	-	-	-	-	-	-	-	-	-	-
1933	-	-	-	-	-	-	-	-	-	-
1937	-	3	-	3	1	2	-	-	-	-
1938	-	2	-	2	1	1	-	-	-	-
1950	-	6125	6125	-	-	-	-	-	-	-
1953	-	8259	8259	-	-	-	-	-	-	-
1955	-	8558	8558	-	-	-	-	-	-	-
1957	-	7428	7428	-	-	-	-	-	-	-
1960	-	8091	8031	60	57	-	3	-	-	-
1961	-	8656	8567	89	65	1	23	-	-	-
1962	-	9769	9728	41	41	-	-	-	-	-

Table IV. ENERGY IMPORTS AND EXPORTS, SELECTED YEARS, 1925-1965

(Original units)

Region, country, year	Solid fuels (10^3 m.t. coal equiv.)	Liquid fuels (10^3 m.t.)		Refined petroleum products					Gas (10^6 c.m.)	Electricity (10^6 kwh)
		Total	Crude oil	Total	Gasoline	Kerosine	Fuel oils	Lubes and greases		
	(1)	(2)	(3)	(4)	(5)	(6)	(7)	(8)	(9)	(10)
BAHRAIN (CONTINUED)							IMPORTS			
1963	-	9085	8980	105	105	-	-	-	-	-
1964	-	7833	7697	136	136	-	-	-	-	-
1965	-	6879	6740	139	139	-	-	-	-	-
BAHRAIN							EXPORTS			
1925	-	-	-	-	-	-	-	-	-	-
1929	-	-	-	-	-	-	-	-	-	-
1933	-	4	4	-	-	-	-	-	-	-
1937	-	961	627	334	71	35	228	-	-	-
1938	-	778	46	732	266	109	357	-	-	-
1950	-	6496	-	6496	1752	680	4064	-	-	-
1953	-	7876	-	7876	2047	784	5045	-	-	-
1955	-	8400	280	8120	1970	1050	5100	-	-	-
1957	-	7611	15	7596	1261	935	5400	-	-	-
1960	-	8766	-	8766	1694	1182	5890	-	-	-
1961	-	9188	-	9188	1606	1222	6360	-	-	-
1962	-	10253	-	10253	1904	1286	7063	-	-	-
1963	-	9792	-	9792	1930	1132	6730	-	-	-
1964	-	8428	-	8428	1995	1218	5215	-	-	-
1965	-	7950	-	7950	1765	1410	4775	-	-	-
IRAN							IMPORTS			
1925	5	36	-	36	2	30	4	-	-	-
1929	1	51	-	51	14	31	3	3	-	-
1933	1	30	-	30	4	20	3	3	-	-
1937	1	52	1	51	8	20	15	8	-	-
1938	1	26	-	26	6	4	8	8	-	-
1950	-	4	-	4	-	-	-	4	-	-
1953	-	7	-	7	-	-	-	7	-	-
1955	-	5	-	5	-	-	-	5	-	-
1957	-	13	-	13	-	-	-	13	-	-
1960	-	26	-	26	-	-	-	26	-	-
1961	-	26	-	26	-	-	-	26	-	-
1962	-	25	-	25	-	-	-	25	-	-
1963	-	8	-	8	-	-	-	8	-	-
1964	-	4	-	4	-	-	-	4	-	-
1965	-	1	-	1	-	-	-	1	-	-
IRAN							EXPORTS			
1925	-	3814	1051	2763	314	113	2336	-	-	-
1929	-	5325	1664	3661	1223	919	1519	-	-	-
1933	-	7292	1569	5723	1527	446	3750	-	-	-
1937	-	9467	499	8968	1858	562	6541	7	-	-
1938	-	7159	271	6888	1821	478	4578	11	-	-
1950	-	29092	6606	22486	4146	2320	16020	-	-	-
1953	-	239	42	197	147	-	50	-	-	-
1955	-	13110	8330	4780	930	900	2950	-	-	-
1957	-	30420	19200	11220	2250	1770	7200	-	-	-
1960	-	44945	33425	11520	2530	2045	6945	-	-	-
1961	-	50980	41550	9430	1790	1720	5920	-	-	-
1962	-	57475	46025	11450	2205	2090	7155	-	-	-
1963	-	64180	52935	11245	2090	1995	7160	-	-	-

Table IV. ENERGY IMPORTS AND EXPORTS, SELECTED YEARS, 1925–1965

(Original units)

Region, country, year	Solid fuels (10³ m.t. coal equiv.)	Liquid fuels (10³ m.t.)		Refined petroleum products					Gas (10⁶ c.m.)	Electricity (10⁶ kwh)
		Total	Crude oil	Total	Gasoline	Kerosine	Fuel oils	Lubes and greases		
	(1)	(2)	(3)	(4)	(5)	(6)	(7)	(8)	(9)	(10)
IRAN (CONTINUED)							EXPORTS			
1964	-	73650	62585	11065	1940	2185	6940	-	-	-
1965	-	80490	69290	11200	2035	2140	7025	-	-	-
IRAQ							IMPORTS			
1925	-	56	-	56	5	20	30	1	-	-
1929	7	49	-	49	1	9	37	2	-	-
1933	2	63	-	63	4	5	50	4	-	-
1937	3	71	-	71	7	9	50	5	-	-
1938	3	82	-	82	7	9	60	6	-	-
1950	2	286	-	286	26	55	196	9	-	-
1953	NA	15	-	15	1	1	-	13	-	-
1955	-	17	-	17	-	-	-	17	-	-
1957	-	17	-	17	-	-	-	17	NA	NA
1960	-	2	-	2	-	-	-	2	NA	NA
1961	20	3	-	3	-	-	-	3	-	-
1962	-	2	-	2	-	-	-	2	NA	NA
1963	-	1	-	1	-	-	-	1	NA	NA
1964	-	1	-	1	-	-	-	1	NA	NA
1965	-	5	-	5	-	-	-	5	NA	NA
IRAQ							EXPORTS			
1925	-	-	-	-	-	-	-	-	-	-
1929	-	-	-	-	-	-	-	-	-	-
1933	-	1	-	1	1	-	-	-	-	-
1937	-	3991	3991	-	-	-	-	-	-	-
1938	-	4180	4180	-	-	-	-	-	-	-
1950	-	6151	6144	7	1	6	-	-	-	-
1953	-	27421	27419	2	1	1	-	-	-	-
1955	-	32153	32150	3	1	1	1	-	-	-
1957	-	20253	20253	-	-	-	-	-	-	-
1960	-	45205	45204	1	1	-	-	-	-	-
1961	-	46585	46585	-	-	-	-	-	-	-
1962	-	46681	46673	8	-	-	8	-	-	-
1963	-	54119	54110	9	2	-	7	-	-	-
1964	-	59208	59180	28	-	-	28	-	-	-
1965	-	61660	61645	15	-	-	15	-	-	-
KUWAIT							IMPORTS			
1950	-	-	-	-	-	-	-	-	-	-
1953	-	109	-	109	-	-	109	-	-	-
1955	-	274	-	274	-	-	274	-	-	-
1957	-	1500	-	1500	29	-	1471	-	-	-
1960	-	-	-	-	-	-	-	-	-	-
1961	-	-	-	-	-	-	-	-	-	-
1962	-	-	-	-	-	-	-	-	-	-
1963	-	3	-	3	-	3	-	-	-	-
1964	-	4	-	4	-	4	-	-	-	-
1965	-	-	-	-	-	-	-	-	-	-

Table IV. ENERGY IMPORTS AND EXPORTS, SELECTED YEARS, 1925-1965

(Original units)

Region, country, year	Solid fuels (10^3 m.t. coal equiv.)	Liquid fuels (10^3 m.t.) Total	Crude oil	Refined petroleum products Total	Gasoline	Kerosine	Fuel oils	Lubes and greases	Gas (10^6 c.m.)	Electricity (10^6 kwh)
	(1)	(2)	(3)	(4)	(5)	(6)	(7)	(8)	(9)	(10)
KUWAIT (CONTINUED)							EXPORTS			
1950	-	16351	16051	300	-	-	300	-	-	-
1953	-	41929	41693	236	-	-	236	-	-	-
1955	-	53026	52832	194	-	-	194	-	-	-
1957	-	55518	55407	111	-	-	111	-	-	-
1960	-	77015	72100	4915	5	-	4910	-	-	-
1961	-	77875	73600	4275	-	-	4275	-	-	-
1962	-	86759	81990	4769	130	-	4558	-	-	-
1963	-	91166	86025	5141	72	-	4922	-	-	-
1964	-	101366	95235	6131	3	-	5881	-	-	-
1965	-	104611	97800	6811	26	-	6400	-	-	-
KUWAIT NEUTRAL ZONE							IMPORTS			
1955	-	19	-	19	4	5	10	-	-	-
1957	-	19	-	19	4	5	10	-	-	-
1960	-	9	-	9	4	5	-	-	-	-
1961	-	9	-	9	4	5	-	-	-	-
1962	-	9	-	9	4	5	-	-	-	-
1963	-	10	-	10	4	6	-	-	-	-
1964	-	10	-	10	4	6	-	-	-	-
1965	-	10	-	10	4	6	-	-	-	-
KUWAIT NEUTRAL ZONE							EXPORTS			
1955	-	1223	1223	-	-	-	-	-	-	-
1957	-	3320	3320	-	-	-	-	-	-	-
1960	-	6480	5740	740	-	-	740	-	-	-
1961	-	8584	7640	944	-	-	944	-	-	-
1962	-	11788	9222	2566	-	-	2566	-	-	-
1963	-	16037	13590	2447	-	-	2447	-	-	-
1964	-	18725	15900	2825	-	-	2825	-	-	-
1965	-	18470	15900	2570	-	-	2570	-	-	-
QATAR							IMPORTS			
1950	-	-	-	-	-	-	-	-	-	-
1953	-	-	-	-	-	-	-	-	-	-
1955	-	50	-	50	10	10	30	-	-	-
1957	-	50	-	50	10	10	30	-	-	-
1960	-	32	-	32	7	7	18	-	-	-
1961	-	28	-	28	11	4	13	-	-	-
1962	-	36	-	36	11	5	20	-	-	-
1963	-	36	-	36	11	5	20	-	-	-
1964	-	36	-	36	11	5	20	-	-	-
1965	-	33	-	33	11	5	17	-	-	-
QATAR							EXPORTS			
1950	-	1577	1577	-	-	-	-	-	-	-
1953	-	3965	3965	-	-	-	-	-	-	-
1955	-	5347	5347	-	-	-	-	-	-	-
1957	-	6550	6550	-	-	-	-	-	-	-
1960	-	8140	8140	-	-	-	-	-	-	-
1961	-	8360	8360	-	-	-	-	-	-	-

Table IV. ENERGY IMPORTS AND EXPORTS, SELECTED YEARS, 1925-1965

(Original units)

Region, country, year	Solid fuels (10³ m.t. coal equiv.)	Liquid fuels (10³ m.t.)		Refined petroleum products					Gas (10⁶ c.m.)	Electricity (10⁶ kwh)
		Total	Crude oil	Total	Gasoline	Kerosine	Fuel oils	Lubes and greases		
	(1)	(2)	(3)	(4)	(5)	(6)	(7)	(8)	(9)	(10)
QATAR (CONTINUED)							EXPORTS			
1962	-	8780	8780	-	-	-	-	-	-	-
1963	-	9070	9070	-	-	-	-	-	-	-
1964	-	10110	10110	-	-	-	-	-	-	-
1965	-	10930	10930	-	-	-	-	-	-	-
SAUDI ARABIA							IMPORTS			
1950	-	-	-	-	-	-	-	-	-	-
1953	-	-	-	-	-	-	-	-	-	-
1955	-	16	-	16	16	-	-	-	-	-
1957	-	18	-	18	18	-	-	-	-	-
1960	-	7	-	7	7	-	-	-	-	-
1961	-	1	-	1	1	-	-	-	-	-
1962	-	1	-	1	1	-	-	-	-	-
1963	-	-	-	-	-	-	-	-	-	-
1964	-	-	-	-	-	-	-	-	-	-
1965	-	18	-	18	18	-	-	-	-	-
SAUDI ARABIA							EXPORTS			
1950	-	24794	21194	3600	700	400	2500	-	-	-
1953	-	39180	31307	7873	1466	967	5440	-	-	-
1955	-	44965	37474	7491	1190	951	5350	-	-	-
1957	-	46040	39132	6908	892	855	5160	-	-	-
1960	-	58360	50748	7612	983	1020	5605	-	-	-
1961	-	65391	56851	8540	893	1096	6530	-	-	-
1962	-	71352	63083	8269	790	952	6495	-	-	-
1963	-	76667	67535	9132	1045	973	6970	-	-	-
1964	-	81788	71970	9818	1295	1038	7160	-	-	-
1965	-	96432	85560	10872	1800	1188	7485	-	-	-
TRUCIAL OMAN							IMPORTS			
1960	-	6	-	6	2	1	3	-	-	-
1961	-	8	-	8	3	1	4	-	-	-
1962	-	11	-	11	4	2	5	-	-	-
1963	-	18	-	18	7	2	9	-	-	-
1964	-	24	-	24	9	2	13	-	-	-
1965	-	26	-	26	10	2	14	-	-	-
TRUCIAL OMAN							EXPORTS			
1960	-	-	-	-	-	-	-	-	-	-
1961	-	-	-	-	-	-	-	-	-	-
1962	-	798	798	-	-	-	-	-	-	-
1963	-	2430	2430	-	-	-	-	-	-	-
1964	-	9115	9115	-	-	-	-	-	-	-
1965	-	13700	13700	-	-	-	-	-	-	-
MIDDLE EAST - OTHER							IMPORTS			
1925	265	333	1	332	29	107	195	1	-	-
1929	336	636	3	633	75	124	429	5	-	-

Table IV. ENERGY IMPORTS AND EXPORTS, SELECTED YEARS, 1925–1965

(Original units)

Region, country, year	Solid fuels (10^3 m.t. coal equiv.)	Liquid fuels (10^3 m.t.)		Refined petroleum products					Gas (10^6 c.m.)	Electricity (10^6 kwh)
		Total	Crude oil	Total	Gasoline	Kerosine	Fuel oils	Lubes and greases		
	(1)	(2)	(3)	(4)	(5)	(6)	(7)	(8)	(9)	(10)
MIDDLE EAST - OTHER (CONTINUED)							IMPORTS			
1933	235	818	11	807	61	80	661	5	-	-
1937	419	1179	16	1163	125	123	906	9	-	-
1938	334	1379	16	1363	138	131	1087	7	-	-
1950	160	4839	687	4152	507	338	3260	47	-	-
1953	76	6116	1310	4806	618	460	3647	81	-	-
1955	60	10174	6279	3895	642	609	2558	85	-	-
1957	60	10097	6556	3541	636	524	2278	98	-	-
1960	50	11728	7026	4702	597	505	3501	90	-	-
1961	40	13176	8751	4425	552	422	3351	92	-	-
1962	50	15369	12517	2852	227	224	2271	119	-	-
1963	30	17117	14064	3053	189	145	2547	152	-	-
1964	40	18638	15626	3012	189	128	2597	116	-	-
1965	35	18922	16836	2086	232	122	1620	110	-	-
MIDDLE EAST - OTHER							EXPORTS			
1925	154	1	-	1	-	1	-	-	-	-
1929	455	1	-	1	-	1	-	-	-	-
1933	532	-	-	-	-	-	-	-	-	-
1937	293	9	-	9	-	-	9	-	-	-
1938	342	-	-	-	-	-	-	-	-	-
1950	-	-	-	-	-	-	-	-	-	-
1953	8	8	-	8	-	-	8	-	-	-
1955	-	2659	-	2659	737	501	1421	-	-	-
1957	-	2805	-	2805	708	366	1730	-	-	-
1960	30	2233	-	2233	573	319	1338	-	-	-
1961	-	3248	-	3248	830	499	1915	-	-	-
1962	-	4135	-	4135	923	565	2642	-	-	-
1963	10	5052	-	5052	925	612	3508	-	-	-
1964	20	5425	-	5425	1098	693	3630	-	-	-
1965	10	5333	-	5333	1240	632	3459	-	-	-
PALESTINE							IMPORTS			
1925	22	28	-	28	4	19	4	1	-	-
1929	33	50	-	50	10	31	7	2	-	-
1933	58	77	-	77	20	34	21	2	-	-
1937	98	182	-	182	41	49	88	4	-	-
1938	58	156	-	156	39	48	66	3	-	-
ISRAEL							IMPORTS			
1950	34	731	196	535	126	69	331	9	-	-
1953	29	1117	765	352	26	42	277	7	-	-
1955	20	1596	1038	558	15	136	400	7	-	-
1957	40	1505	1015	490	25	23	430	12	-	-
1960	50	1874	1325	549	18	-	520	10	-	-
1961	40	2115	1455	660	25	1	620	14	-	-
1962	40	2474	2055	419	10	2	390	17	-	-
1963	20	2740	2350	390	5	-	367	18	-	-
1964	30	3081	2650	431	10	-	402	19	-	-
1965	15	4207	3890	317	10	-	290	17	-	-

Table IV. ENERGY IMPORTS AND EXPORTS, SELECTED YEARS, 1925–1965

(Original units)

Region, country, year	Solid fuels (10^3 m.t. coal equiv.)	Liquid fuels (10^3 m.t.)		Refined petroleum products					Gas (10^6 c.m.)	Electricity (10^6 kwh)
		Total	Crude oil	Total	Gasoline	Kerosine	Fuel oils	Lubes and greases		
	(1)	(2)	(3)	(4)	(5)	(6)	(7)	(8)	(9)	(10)
ISRAEL (CONTINUED)							EXPORTS			
1960	-	42	-	42	-	-	42	-	-	-
1961	-	97	-	97	7	-	88	-	-	-
1962	-	198	-	198	52	3	143	-	-	-
1963	-	381	-	381	53	3	323	-	-	-
1964	-	492	-	492	78	-	412	-	-	-
1965	-	513	-	513	108	3	401	-	-	-
JORDAN							IMPORTS			
1950	-	57	-	57	22	24	10	1	-	-
1953	-	71	-	71	22	24	23	2	-	-
1955	-	126	13	113	30	32	48	3	-	-
1957	-	146	-	146	37	34	72	3	-	-
1960	-	221	-	221	45	56	115	5	-	-
1961	-	297	207	90	6	20	60	4	-	-
1962	-	329	252	77	2	17	52	6	-	-
1963	-	383	329	54	1	16	32	5	-	-
1964	-	387	359	28	5	11	6	6	-	-
1965	-	449	410	39	10	23	-	6	-	-
LEBANON-SYRIA							IMPORTS			
1925	52	38	-	38	12	24	2	-	-	-
1929	49	68	-	68	28	35	3	2	-	-
1933	67	74	-	74	30	31	10	3	-	-
1937	142	91	-	91	38	29	20	4	-	-
1938	145	94	-	94	42	32	17	3	-	-
LEBANON							IMPORTS			
1950	11	609	491	118	30	26	60	2	-	-
1953	-	710	545	165	50	37	75	3	-	-
1955	10	1068	894	174	36	25	107	5	-	-
1957	10	1254	1053	201	20	26	146	6	-	-
1960	-	927	733	194	55	25	105	7	-	-
1961	-	958	733	225	76	40	100	4	-	-
1962	10	1033	840	193	81	25	80	1	-	-
1963	10	1179	1018	161	65	12	60	9	-	-
1964	10	1306	1306	NA	14	2	NA	9	-	-
1965	10	1482	1482	NA	NA	NA	NA	7	-	-
LEBANON							EXPORTS			
1950	-	-	-	-	-	-	NA	-	-	-
1953	-	-	-	-	-	-	NA	-	-	-
1955	-	395	-	395	65	70	260	-	-	-
1957	-	434	-	434	52	82	300	-	-	-
1960	-	-	-	-	-	-	-	-	-	-
1961	-	-	-	-	-	-	-	-	-	-
1962	-	-	-	-	-	-	-	-	-	-
1963	-	1	-	1	-	-	-	-	-	-
1964	-	-	-	-	-	-	-	-	-	-
1965	-	-	-	-	-	-	-	-	-	-

Table IV. ENERGY IMPORTS AND EXPORTS, SELECTED YEARS, 1925-1965

(Original units)

Region, country, year	Solid fuels (10^3 m.t. coal equiv.)	Liquid fuels (10^3 m.t.)		Refined petroleum products					Gas (10^6 c.m.)	Electricity (10^6 kwh)
		Total	Crude oil	Total	Gasoline	Kerosine	Fuel oils	Lubes and greases		
	(1)	(2)	(3)	(4)	(5)	(6)	(7)	(8)	(9)	(10)
SYRIA							IMPORTS			
1950	2	225	-	225	76	46	96	7	-	-
1953	3	404	-	404	86	51	260	7	-	-
1955	-	510	-	510	83	56	360	11	-	-
1957	-	606	-	606	96	71	427	11	-	-
1960	-	1003	695	308	9	16	270	12	-	-
1961	-	983	768	215	6	6	190	13	-	-
1962	-	1042	786	256	6	6	220	22	-	-
1963	-	1137	881	256	8	7	223	17	-	-
1964	-	1374	1015	359	8	8	332	11	-	-
1965	5	1186	1017	169	10	9	132	18	-	-
SYRIA							EXPORTS			
1950	-	-	-	-	-	-	-	-	-	-
1953	-	8	-	8	-	-	8	-	-	-
1955	-	8	-	8	-	-	8	-	-	-
1957	-	-	-	-	-	-	-	-	-	-
1960	-	-	-	-	-	-	-	-	-	-
1961	-	29	-	29	29	-	-	-	-	-
1962	-	51	-	51	51	-	-	-	-	-
1963	-	26	-	26	26	-	-	-	-	-
1964	-	13	-	13	13	-	-	-	-	-
1965	-	50	-	50	50	-	-	-	-	-
TURKEY							IMPORTS			
1925	75	80	-	80	11	58	11	-	-	-
1929	108	107	-	107	32	53	22	-	-	-
1933	59	88	8	80	7	12	61	-	-	-
1937	40	134	-	134	38	40	56	-	-	-
1938	87	165	-	165	50	47	68	-	-	-
1950	-	605	-	605	230	150	200	25	-	-
1953	-	1158	-	1158	380	280	440	58	-	-
1955	-	1133	-	1133	375	316	390	52	-	-
1957	-	1134	-	1134	310	296	470	58	-	-
1960	-	1248	-	1248	358	303	536	48	-	-
1961	-	1486	219	1267	343	295	579	49	-	-
1962	-	2662	2269	393	23	127	180	63	-	-
1963	-	3216	3080	136	5	39	-	92	-	-
1964	-	3521	3430	91	3	27	-	61	-	-
1965	5	3142	3051	91	5	34	-	52	-	-
TURKEY							EXPORTS			
1925	154	-	-	-	-	-	-	-	-	-
1929	455	-	-	-	-	-	-	-	-	-
1933	532	-	-	-	-	-	-	-	-	-
1937	293	-	-	-	-	-	-	-	-	-
1938	342	-	-	-	-	-	-	-	-	-
1950	-	-	-	-	-	-	-	-	-	-
1953	7	-	-	-	-	-	-	-	-	-
1955	-	-	-	-	-	-	-	-	-	-
1957	-	-	-	-	-	-	-	-	-	-
1960	30	-	-	-	-	-	-	-	-	-
1961	-	24	-	24	-	-	24	-	-	-

Table IV. ENERGY IMPORTS AND EXPORTS, SELECTED YEARS, 1925-1965

(Original units)

Region, country, year	Solid fuels (10^3 m.t. coal equiv.)	Liquid fuels (10^3 m.t.)		Refined petroleum products					Gas (10^6 c.m.)	Electricity (10^6 kwh)
		Total	Crude oil	Total	Gasoline	Kerosine	Fuel oils	Lubes and greases		
	(1)	(2)	(3)	(4)	(5)	(6)	(7)	(8)	(9)	(10)
TURKEY (CONTINUED)							EXPORTS			
1962	-	544	-	544	-	-	540	-	-	-
1963	10	740	-	740	42	-	695	-	-	-
1964	20	754	-	754	47	-	705	-	-	-
1965	10	517	-	517	18	-	498	-	-	-
FAR EAST AND OTHER ASIA							IMPORTS			
1925	6269	3116	422	2694	386	835	1297	176	-	-
1929	8050	5687	1746	3941	530	1323	1856	230	-	-
1933	7748	6312	2825	3487	572	1080	1671	164	-	-
1937	10904	10041	3993	6048	1118	1064	2600	253	-	-
1938	11416	10716	3992	6724	1160	1175	2748	256	-	-
1950	2944	18366	8379	9987	2427	1457	4861	322	54	-
1953	7866	29585	13597	15988	4021	2142	9464	361	58	-
1955	5820	37650	19250	18400	3769	2343	11850	437	68	-
1957	9600	50581	28455	22126	3879	2655	14955	635	68	-
1960	10844	64430	41877	22553	3836	3109	14865	741	76	-
1961	13460	77600	50415	27185	3314	3535	19518	810	76	-
1962	14380	87630	59374	28256	2832	4048	20304	961	72	-
1963	13110	101688	72702	28986	2683	3607	21255	1238	54	-
1964	15405	115404	86111	29293	2601	2999	22150	1157	50	-
1965	18915	128314	96897	31417	2431	3220	24451	836	-	-
FAR EAST AND OTHER ASIA							EXPORTS			
1925	5351	3110	154	2956	875	446	1590	45	-	-
1929	5834	4737	197	4540	1560	767	2154	59	-	-
1933	5048	5519	842	4677	1613	707	2318	39	-	-
1937	5745	8374	672	7702	2541	1455	3612	94	-	-
1938	6598	9139	770	8369	2775	1512	3973	109	-	-
1950	1681	16372	6479	9893	2741	830	6255	67	54	-
1953	3157	21487	9797	11690	3517	1231	6850	92	58	-
1955	2050	22957	11658	11299	3151	1113	6943	92	72	-
1957	1890	28488	16902	11586	3282	992	7280	32	72	-
1960	1720	29678	18203	11475	3433	1193	6797	52	76	-
1961	1490	29368	18467	10901	3019	1198	6651	33	76	-
1962	1580	32103	19490	12613	2909	1304	8354	45	76	-
1963	1340	31522	18972	12550	2934	1254	7925	435	63	-
1964	1690	31648	19739	11909	2667	1179	7913	147	50	-
1965	1255	32954	19451	13503	2422	1650	9273	149	54	-
BORNEO (FORMER BRITISH)							IMPORTS			
1925	1	3	-	3	-	3	-	-	-	-
1929	-	11	-	11	2	6	-	1	-	-
1933	1	284	281	3	-	3	-	-	-	-
1937	-	630	574	56	2	5	48	1	-	-
1938	1	739	703	36	2	5	28	1	-	-
1950	-	4162	4123	39	9	9	17	4	54	-
1953	-	4935	4876	59	19	10	26	4	58	-
1955	-	5318	5258	60	15	12	27	6	68	-
1957	-	5610	5529	81	28	13	34	6	68	-
1960	-	4690	4577	113	28	21	57	7	76	-
1961	-	3889	3768	121	31	19	65	6	76	-
1962	-	4046	3902	144	38	23	74	9	72	-

Table IV. ENERGY IMPORTS AND EXPORTS, SELECTED YEARS, 1925–1965

(Original units)

Region, country, year	Solid fuels (10³ m.t. coal equiv.)	Liquid fuels (10³ m.t.)		Refined petroleum products					Gas (10⁶ c.m.)	Electricity (10⁶ kwh)
		Total	Crude oil	Total	Gasoline	Kerosine	Fuel oils	Lubes and greases		
	(1)	(2)	(3)	(4)	(5)	(6)	(7)	(8)	(9)	(10)
BORNEO (FORMER BRITISH) (CONTINUED)							IMPORTS			
1963	-	3601	3437	164	40	29	88	7	54	-
1964	-	3744	3550	194	47	44	97	6	50	-
1965	-	4128	3888	240	57	59	114	10	-	-
BORNEO (FORMER BRITISH)							EXPORTS			
1925	50	558	154	404	93	104	207	-	-	-
1929	47	746	155	591	234	65	292	-	-	-
1933	5	863	416	447	80	35	332	-	-	-
1937	-	1356	559	797	65	45	687	-	-	-
1938	-	1607	696	911	96	64	751	-	-	-
1950	-	8142	6471	1671	232	-	1439	-	54	-
1953	-	9632	7711	1921	313	-	1608	-	58	-
1955	-	10326	8481	1845	137	-	1708	-	72	-
1957	-	10952	9131	1821	210	-	1611	-	72	-
1960	-	9082	7092	1990	347	4	1639	-	76	-
1961	-	7742	6025	1717	245	2	1470	-	76	-
1962	-	7720	5719	2001	297	2	1702	-	76	-
1963	-	6870	5019	1851	267	16	1568	-	63	-
1964	-	7034	4638	2396	388	155	1853	-	50	-
1965	-	7653	5202	2451	273	163	2015	-	54	-
BRUNEI							IMPORTS			
1925	1	-	-	-	-	-	-	-	-	-
1929	-	-	-	-	-	-	-	-	-	-
1933	-	-	-	-	-	-	-	-	-	-
1937	-	1	-	1	-	1	-	-	-	-
1938	-	1	-	1	-	1	-	-	-	-
1950	-	12	-	12	3	1	6	2	-	-
1953	-	21	-	21	7	1	11	2	-	-
1955	-	9	-	9	2	1	3	3	-	-
1957	-	12	-	12	5	1	3	3	-	-
1960	-	6	-	6	1	2	2	1	-	-
1961	-	5	-	5	1	1	2	1	-	-
1962	-	8	-	8	1	2	3	2	-	-
1963	-	8	-	8	1	2	4	1	-	-
1964	-	5	-	5	1	2	1	1	-	-
1965	-	5	-	5	1	1	2	1	-	-
BRUNEI							EXPORTS			
1925	-	-	-	-	-	-	-	-	-	-
1929	-	-	-	-	-	-	-	-	-	-
1933	-	285	285	-	-	-	-	-	-	-
1937	-	559	559	-	-	-	-	-	-	-
1938	-	696	696	-	-	-	-	-	-	-
1950	-	4076	4076	-	-	-	-	-	54	-
1953	-	4877	4877	-	-	-	-	-	58	-
1955	-	5247	5247	-	-	-	-	-	72	-
1957	-	5528	5528	-	-	-	-	-	72	-
1960	-	4577	4577	-	-	-	-	-	76	-
1961	-	4115	4115	-	-	-	-	-	76	-
1962	-	3817	3817	-	-	-	-	-	76	-
1963	-	3479	3479	-	-	-	-	-	63	-

Table IV. ENERGY IMPORTS AND EXPORTS, SELECTED YEARS, 1925-1965

(Original units)

Region, country, year	Solid fuels (10^3 m.t. coal equiv.)	Liquid fuels (10^3 m.t.) Total	Crude oil	Refined petroleum products Total	Gasoline	Kerosine	Fuel oils	Lubes and greases	Gas (10^6 c.m.)	Electricity (10^6 kwh)
	(1)	(2)	(3)	(4)	(5)	(6)	(7)	(8)	(9)	(10)
BRUNEI (CONTINUED)							EXPORTS			
1964	-	3518	3518	-	-	-	-	-	50	-
1965	-	3931	3931	-	-	-	-	-	54	-
SABAH							IMPORTS			
1925	-	-	-	-	-	-	-	-	-	-
1929	-	2	-	2	1	2	-	-	-	-
1933	1	1	-	1	-	1	-	-	-	-
1937	-	2	-	2	1	1	-	-	-	-
1938	1	2	-	2	1	1	-	-	-	-
1950	-	14	-	14	4	3	6	1	-	-
1953	-	19	-	19	7	3	8	1	-	-
1955	-	24	-	24	6	4	13	1	-	-
1957	-	35	-	35	12	4	18	1	-	-
1960	-	62	-	62	14	9	35	4	-	-
1961	-	64	-	64	17	7	37	3	-	-
1962	-	81	-	81	23	10	44	4	-	-
1963	-	94	-	94	24	13	54	3	-	-
1964	-	113	-	113	28	23	59	3	-	-
1965	-	124	-	124	28	25	66	5	-	-
SABAH							EXPORTS			
1925	50	-	-	-	-	-	-	-	-	-
1929	47	-	-	-	-	-	-	-	-	-
1933	5	-	-	-	-	-	-	-	-	-
1937	-	-	-	-	-	-	-	-	-	-
1938	-	-	-	-	-	-	-	-	-	-
1950	-	-	-	-	-	-	-	-	-	-
1953	-	-	-	-	-	-	-	-	-	-
1955	-	-	-	-	-	-	-	-	-	-
1957	-	3	-	3	2	-	1	-	-	-
1960	-	8	-	8	1	4	3	-	-	-
1961	-	6	-	6	2	2	2	-	-	-
1962	-	6	-	6	2	2	2	-	-	-
1963	-	6	-	6	2	2	2	-	-	-
1964	-	6	-	6	2	3	1	-	-	-
1965	-	4	-	4	1	1	2	-	-	-
SARAWAK							IMPORTS			
1925	-	3	-	3	-	3	-	-	-	-
1929	-	6	-	6	1	4	-	1	-	-
1933	-	283	281	2	-	2	-	-	-	-
1937	-	627	574	53	1	3	48	1	-	-
1938	-	736	703	33	1	3	28	1	-	-
1950	-	4136	4123	13	2	5	5	1	54	-
1953	-	4895	4876	19	5	6	7	1	58	-
1955	-	5285	5258	27	7	7	11	2	68	-
1957	-	5563	5529	34	11	8	13	2	68	-
1960	-	4622	4577	45	13	10	20	2	76	-
1961	-	3820	3768	52	13	11	26	2	76	-
1962	-	3957	3902	55	14	11	27	3	72	-
1963	-	3499	3437	62	15	14	30	3	54	-
1964	-	3626	3550	76	18	19	37	2	50	-

Table IV. ENERGY IMPORTS AND EXPORTS, SELECTED YEARS, 1925-1965

(Original units)

Region, country, year	Solid fuels (10^3 m.t. coal equiv.)	Liquid fuels (10^3 m.t.)		Refined petroleum products					Gas (10^6 c.m.)	Electricity (10^6 kwh)
		Total	Crude oil	Total	Gasoline	Kerosine	Fuel oils	Lubes and greases		
	(1)	(2)	(3)	(4)	(5)	(6)	(7)	(8)	(9)	(10)
SARAWAK (CONTINUED)							IMPORTS			
1965	-	4001	3888	113	29	34	46	4	NA	-
SARAWAK							EXPORTS			
1925	-	558	154	404	93	104	207	-	-	-
1929	-	746	155	591	234	65	292	-	-	-
1933	-	578	131	447	80	35	332	-	-	-
1937	-	797	-	797	65	45	687	-	-	-
1938	-	911	-	911	96	64	751	-	-	-
1950	-	4066	2395	1671	232	-	1439	-	-	-
1953	-	4755	2834	1921	313	-	1608	-	-	-
1955	-	5079	3234	1845	137	-	1708	-	-	-
1957	-	5421	3603	1818	208	-	1610	-	-	-
1960	-	4497	2515	1982	346	-	1636	-	-	-
1961	-	3621	1910	1711	243	-	1468	-	-	-
1962	-	3897	1902	1995	295	-	1700	-	-	-
1963	-	3385	1540	1845	265	14	1566	-	-	-
1964	-	3510	1120	2390	386	152	1852	-	-	-
1965	-	3718	1271	2447	272	162	2013	-	-	-
BURMA							IMPORTS			
1950	NA	110	-	110	60	20	30	NA	-	-
1953	251	110	-	110	64	21	16	9	-	-
1955	200	152	-	152	77	18	47	10	-	-
1957	280	84	-	84	27	3	47	7	-	-
1960	350	67	-	67	14	4	33	16	-	-
1961	260	90	12	78	11	8	38	21	-	-
1962	340	92	-	92	15	16	46	15	-	-
1963	210	52	-	52	10	13	22	7	-	-
1964	215	158	120	38	-	-	22	16	-	-
1965	140	175	160	15	-	-	-	15	-	-
CEYLON							IMPORTS			
1925	827	206	-	206	14	26	164	2	-	-
1929	827	291	-	291	35	31	221	4	-	-
1933	412	342	-	342	25	27	287	3	-	-
1937	582	414	-	414	47	31	332	4	-	-
1938	391	492	-	492	41	30	418	3	-	-
1950	374	780	-	780	91	44	639	6	-	-
1953	390	839	-	839	132	72	630	5	-	-
1955	190	959	-	959	136	94	720	9	-	-
1957	280	1392	-	1392	191	112	1079	10	-	-
1960	260	891	-	891	162	147	573	9	-	-
1961	140	1060	-	1060	172	157	721	10	-	-
1962	140	1037	-	1037	140	179	705	13	-	-
1963	150	909	-	909	142	139	611	17	-	-
1964	180	839	-	839	106	154	569	10	-	-
1965	140	1016	-	1016	176	184	641	15	-	-
CEYLON							EXPORTS			
1953	-	-	-	-	-	-	-	-	-	-

Table IV. ENERGY IMPORTS AND EXPORTS, SELECTED YEARS, 1925-1965

(Original units)

Region, country, year	Solid fuels (10³ m.t. coal equiv.)	Liquid fuels (10³ m.t.)							Gas (10⁶ c.m.)	Electricity (10⁶ kwh)
				Refined petroleum products						
		Total	Crude oil	Total	Gasoline	Kerosine	Fuel oils	Lubes and greases		
	(1)	(2)	(3)	(4)	(5)	(6)	(7)	(8)	(9)	(10)
CEYLON (CONTINUED)							EXPORTS			
1955	-	13	-	13	-	-	13	-	-	-
1957	-	-	-	-	-	-	-	-	-	-
1960	-	-	-	-	-	-	-	-	-	-
1961	-	6	-	6	-	-	6	-	-	-
1962	-	-	-	-	-	-	-	-	-	-
1963	-	-	-	-	-	-	-	-	-	-
1964	-	-	-	-	-	-	-	-	-	-
1965	-	1	-	1	-	1	-	-	-	-
HONG KONG							IMPORTS			
1925	1094	345	-	345	10	131	197	7	-	-
1929	740	289	-	289	20	91	173	5	-	-
1933	916	308	-	308	40	56	204	8	-	-
1937	914	355	-	355	70	83	175	27	-	-
1938	753	368	-	368	48	58	250	12	-	-
1950	325	625	-	625	79	38	503	5	-	-
1953	213	658	-	658	54	43	558	3	-	-
1955	250	835	-	835	60	68	700	7	-	-
1957	260	1081	-	1081	65	86	920	10	-	-
1960	240	1240	-	1240	79	138	1012	11	-	-
1961	250	1365	-	1365	81	166	1107	11	-	-
1962	220	1551	-	1551	66	219	1250	16	-	-
1963	200	1784	-	1784	75	256	1439	14	-	-
1964	180	1867	-	1867	71	236	1539	21	-	-
1965	180	2100	-	2100	76	298	1711	15	-	-
HONG KONG							EXPORTS			
1925	134	88	-	88	3	39	41	5	-	-
1929	98	108	-	108	11	51	39	7	-	-
1933	149	200	-	200	28	55	111	6	-	-
1937	35	213	-	213	44	77	78	14	-	-
1938	57	180	-	180	36	53	77	14	-	-
1950	54	136	-	136	53	27	56	-	-	-
1953	9	9	-	9	2	2	4	1	-	-
1955	-	10	-	10	1	3	6	-	-	-
1957	10	10	-	10	1	2	6	1	-	-
1960	10	13	-	13	1	2	9	1	-	-
1961	10	21	-	21	6	3	11	1	-	-
1962	-	25	-	25	2	4	17	2	-	-
1963	-	30	-	30	2	4	20	4	-	-
1964	-	40	-	40	2	4	25	9	-	-
1965	10	44	-	44	3	5	26	10	-	-
INDIA							IMPORTS			
1925	496	721	-	721	-	261	367	93	-	-
1929	222	994	-	994	1	382	498	113	-	-
1933	69	759	-	759	8	213	455	83	-	-
1937	326	1654	-	1654	292	604	616	142	-	-
1938	506	1823	-	1823	291	698	681	153	-	-
1950	1	2969	1318	1651	653	822	NA	176	-	-
1953	1	3356	1367	1989	872	948	NA	169	-	-
1955	-	4567	2755	1812	376	979	292	165	-	-

Table IV. ENERGY IMPORTS AND EXPORTS, SELECTED YEARS, 1925-1965

(Original units)

Region, country, year	Solid fuels (10^3 m.t. coal equiv.)	Liquid fuels (10^3 m.t.)							Gas (10^6 c.m.)	Electricity (10^6 kwh)
				Refined petroleum products						
		Total	Crude oil	Total	Gasoline	Kerosine	Fuel oils	Lubes and greases		
	(1)	(2)	(3)	(4)	(5)	(6)	(7)	(8)	(9)	(10)
INDIA (CONTINUED)							IMPORTS			
1957	-	6291	4300	1991	178	1199	315	299	-	-
1960	10	7495	5685	1810	111	989	395	315	-	-
1961	10	7857	5910	1947	115	1093	502	237	-	-
1962	10	8444	6021	2423	84	1456	606	277	-	-
1963	-	8828	6314	2514	80	1321	726	387	-	-
1964	-	8789	6500	2289	80	1010	913	286	-	-
1965	-	8962	6800	2162	64	838	960	300	-	-
INDIA							EXPORTS			
1925	220	46	-	46	43	3	-	-	-	-
1929	738	19	16	3	-	3	-	-	-	-
1933	433	17	13	4	2	2	-	-	-	-
1937	887	565	18	547	130	350	46	21	-	-
1938	1365	785	22	763	189	502	49	23	-	-
1950	933	-	-	-	-	-	-	-	-	-
1953	1976	-	-	-	-	-	-	-	-	-
1955	1540	104	-	104	60	-	44	-	-	-
1957	1690	375	-	375	184	-	191	-	-	-
1960	1360	239	-	239	239	-	-	-	-	-
1961	940	165	-	165	165	-	-	-	-	-
1962	1070	64	-	64	64	-	-	-	-	-
1963	870	394	-	394	394	-	-	-	-	-
1964	1250	390	-	390	362	11	17	-	-	-
1965	930	296	-	296	260	12	24	-	-	-
INDO-CHINA							IMPORTS			
1925	37	66	-	66	11	47	-	8	-	-
1929	42	117	-	117	31	62	4	20	-	-
1933	16	87	-	87	29	42	10	6	-	-
1937	14	94	-	94	32	39	18	5	-	-
1938	14	104	-	104	38	37	24	5	-	-
1950	12	126	-	126	70	24	27	5	-	-
1953	6	350	-	350	155	42	143	10	-	-
1955	30	362	-	362	152	51	151	8	-	-
1957	50	490	-	490	208	70	201	11	-	-
1960	10	640	-	640	221	92	310	16	-	-
1961	10	732	-	732	219	87	410	15	-	-
1962	20	736	-	736	221	90	406	18	-	-
1963	10	854	-	854	244	111	475	22	-	-
1964	20	821	-	821	206	110	501	3	-	-
1965	45	973	-	973	231	128	612	-	-	-
INDO-CHINA							EXPORTS			
1925	702	-	-	-	-	-	-	-	-	-
1929	1351	-	-	-	-	-	-	-	-	-
1933	1263	-	-	-	-	-	-	-	-	-
1937	1525	-	-	-	-	-	-	-	-	-
1938	1532	-	-	-	-	-	-	-	-	-
1950	59	-	-	-	-	-	-	-	-	-
1953	306	-	-	-	-	-	-	-	-	-
1955	-	-	-	-	-	-	-	-	-	-
1957	-	-	-	-	-	-	-	-	-	-

Table IV. ENERGY IMPORTS AND EXPORTS, SELECTED YEARS, 1925-1965

(Original units)

Region, country, year	Solid fuels (10^3 m.t. coal equiv.)	Liquid fuels (10^3 m.t.) Total	Crude oil	Refined petroleum products Total	Gasoline	Kerosine	Fuel oils	Lubes and greases	Gas (10^6 c.m.)	Electricity (10^6 kwh)
	(1)	(2)	(3)	(4)	(5)	(6)	(7)	(8)	(9)	(10)
INDO-CHINA (CONTINUED) EXPORTS										
1960	-	-	-	-	-	-	-	-	-	-
1961	-	1	-	1	-	-	1	-	-	-
1962	-	1	-	1	-	-	1	-	-	-
1963	-	2	-	2	-	-	2	-	-	-
1964	-	-	-	-	-	-	-	-	-	-
1965	-	-	-	-	-	-	-	-	-	-
CAMBODIA IMPORTS										
1955	-	56	-	56	26	10	20	-	-	-
1957	-	85	-	85	39	13	33	-	-	-
1960	-	112	-	112	54	15	43	-	-	-
1961	-	144	-	144	60	20	64	-	-	-
1962	-	154	-	154	58	22	74	-	-	-
1963	-	200	-	200	70	26	104	-	-	-
1964	-	175	-	175	43	25	107	-	-	-
1965	30	178	-	178	36	28	114	-	-	-
CAMBODIA EXPORTS										
1955	-	-	-	-	-	-	-	-	-	-
1957	-	-	-	-	-	-	-	-	-	-
1960	-	-	-	-	-	-	-	-	-	-
1961	-	1	-	1	-	-	1	-	-	-
1962	-	1	-	1	-	-	1	-	-	-
1963	-	2	-	2	-	-	2	-	-	-
1964	-	-	-	-	-	-	-	-	-	-
1965	-	-	-	-	-	-	-	-	-	-
LAOS IMPORTS										
1955	-	9	-	9	6	1	1	1	-	-
1957	-	19	-	19	14	2	3	NA	-	-
1960	-	28	-	28	17	2	7	2	-	-
1961	-	38	-	38	24	2	11	1	-	-
1962	-	44	-	44	33	3	7	1	-	-
1963	-	51	-	51	34	5	11	1	-	-
1964	-	60	-	60	38	5	14	3	-	-
1965	-	58	-	58	35	5	18	NA	-	-
VIETNAM, SOUTH IMPORTS										
1955	30	297	-	297	120	40	130	7	-	-
1957	50	386	-	386	155	55	165	11	-	-
1960	10	500	-	500	150	75	260	14	-	-
1961	10	550	-	550	135	65	335	14	-	-
1962	20	538	-	538	130	65	325	17	-	-
1963	10	603	-	603	140	80	360	21	-	-
1964	20	586	-	586	125	80	380	NA	-	-
1965	15	737	-	737	160	95	480	NA	-	-

Table IV. ENERGY IMPORTS AND EXPORTS, SELECTED YEARS, 1925-1965

(Original units)

Region, country, year	Solid fuels (10^3 m.t. coal equiv.)	Liquid fuels (10^3 m.t.): Total	Crude oil	Refined petroleum products: Total	Gasoline	Kerosine	Fuel oils	Lubes and greases	Gas (10^6 c.m.)	Electricity (10^6 kwh)
	(1)	(2)	(3)	(4)	(5)	(6)	(7)	(8)	(9)	(10)
INDONESIA							IMPORTS			
1925	171	44	1	43	1	31	4	7	-	-
1929	168	215	-	215	12	86	100	17	-	-
1933	56	120	-	120	43	15	53	9	-	-
1937	60	143	-	143	48	11	71	13	-	-
1938	84	148	-	148	93	27	16	12	-	-
1950	27	1618	1575	43	3	4	4	32	-	-
1953	56	2349	2279	70	12	8	13	37	-	-
1955	30	2867	2678	189	115	2	22	50	-	-
1957	40	3855	3416	439	360	4	26	49	-	-
1960	30	2391	1800	591	485	33	26	47	-	-
1961	30	2804	2142	662	391	188	17	66	-	-
1962	20	1756	1393	363	228	36	16	83	-	-
1963	10	1555	1247	308	217	4	20	67	-	-
1964	10	236	-	236	145	4	15	72	-	-
1965	5	NA	NA	NA	16	4	15	NA	-	-
INDONESIA							EXPORTS			
1925	373	2098	-	2098	543	228	1302	25	-	-
1929	497	3450	23	3427	1118	537	1733	39	-	-
1933	265	3978	413	3565	1242	531	1771	21	-	-
1937	296	5454	95	5359	1960	848	2527	24	-	-
1938	328	5601	52	5549	2069	712	2751	17	-	-
1950	62	6021	8	6013	1816	573	3561	63	-	-
1953	133	8972	2086	6886	2067	689	4044	86	-	-
1955	50	9034	3176	5858	1731	600	3441	86	-	-
1957	40	13285	6986	6299	1640	515	4120	24	-	-
1960	10	16891	10880	6011	1501	492	3976	42	-	-
1961	-	16673	11660	5013	1168	435	3390	20	-	-
1962	-	18510	12455	6055	1166	492	4370	27	-	-
1963	-	17899	12690	5209	954	394	3861	NA	-	-
1964	-	17965	14845	3120	550	270	2300	NA	-	-
1965	-	17500	14000	3500	400	400	2700	NA	-	-
JAPAN							IMPORTS			
1925	1775	650	421	229	76	100	25	28	-	-
1929	3604	2134	1718	416	33	335	27	21	-	-
1933	4285	3039	2504	535	2	507	17	9	-	-
1937	6197	4400	3387	1013	-	NA	NA	NA	-	-
1938	6850	4642	3257	1385	-	NA	NA	NA	-	-
1950	832	1841	1233	608	31	4	538	35	-	-
1953	4921	8056	5075	2981	275	3	2670	33	-	-
1955	2860	10666	7279	3387	250	32	3076	28	-	-
1957	6500	17882	12742	5140	120	17	4918	85	-	-
1960	8290	32413	27056	5357	112	49	5043	153	-	-
1961	11320	42703	33879	8824	94	84	8413	227	-	-
1962	12040	49758	40084	9674	100	79	9096	290	-	-
1963	11140	62765	51894	10871	85	109	10072	407	-	-
1964	13230	74973	62320	12653	417	28	11382	445	-	-
1965	17125	84522	69691	14831	484	26	13528	290	-	-
JAPAN							EXPORTS			
1925	2738	15	-	15	-	8	4	3	-	-

Table IV. ENERGY IMPORTS AND EXPORTS, SELECTED YEARS, 1925-1965

(Original units)

Region, country, year	Solid fuels (10^3 m.t. coal equiv.)	Liquid fuels (10^3 m.t.)							Gas (10^6 c.m.)	Electricity (10^6 kwh)
				Refined petroleum products						
		Total	Crude oil	Total	Gasoline	Kerosine	Fuel oils	Lubes and greases		
	(1)	(2)	(3)	(4)	(5)	(6)	(7)	(8)	(9)	(10)
JAPAN (CONTINUED)							EXPORTS			
1929	2412	18	-	18	-	7	4	7	-	-
1933	2115	42	-	42	-	15	20	7	-	-
1937	1928	107	-	107	-	40	40	27	-	-
1938	1831	140	-	140	13	45	45	37	-	-
1950	508	-	-	-	-	-	-	-	-	-
1953	486	-	-	-	-	-	-	-	-	-
1955	410	3	1	2	-	-	2	-	-	-
1957	120	12	-	12	12	-	-	-	-	-
1960	30	428	-	428	266	73	84	5	-	-
1961	60	617	-	617	470	41	99	7	-	-
1962	80	533	-	533	365	69	87	11	-	-
1963	110	815	-	815	243	86	76	408	-	-
1964	80	739	2	737	267	178	197	92	-	-
1965	95	866	6	860	392	181	200	78	-	-
KOREA							IMPORTS			
1925	695	52	-	52	5	43	-	4	-	-
1929	922	111	-	111	20	50	31	10	-	-
1933	1099	127	-	127	31	33	49	14	-	-
1937	1705	384	-	384	60	56	250	18	-	-
1938	1969	404	-	404	60	56	270	18	-	-
KOREA							EXPORTS			
1925	216	-	-	-	-	-	-	-	-	-
1929	292	-	-	-	-	-	-	-	-	-
1933	478	-	-	-	-	-	-	-	-	-
1937	661	17	-	17	5	5	3	4	-	-
1938	982	48	-	48	6	15	13	14	-	-
KOREA, REPUBLIC OF							IMPORTS			
1950	219	100	-	100	20	10	70	NA	-	-
1953	679	330	-	330	70	40	220	NA	-	-
1955	1060	364	-	364	90	35	239	NA	-	-
1957	740	474	-	474	145	31	298	NA	-	-
1960	220	695	-	695	144	36	499	16	-	-
1961	290	757	-	757	126	43	579	9	-	-
1962	180	1021	32	989	83	50	842	14	-	-
1963	130	1372	46	1326	75	52	1166	33	-	-
1964	170	1291	803	488	5	10	470	3	-	-
1965	115	1572	1400	172	8	-	160	4	-	-
KOREA, REPUBLIC OF							EXPORTS			
1950	-	-	-	-	-	-	-	-	-	-
1953	36	-	-	-	-	-	-	-	-	-
1955	-	-	-	-	-	-	-	-	-	-
1957	-	-	-	-	-	-	-	-	-	-
1960	120	-	-	-	-	-	-	-	-	-
1961	240	-	-	-	-	-	-	-	-	-
1962	300	-	-	-	-	-	-	-	-	-
1963	260	-	-	-	-	-	-	-	-	-
1964	250	-	-	-	-	-	-	-	-	-

Table IV. ENERGY IMPORTS AND EXPORTS, SELECTED YEARS, 1925-1965

(Original units)

Region, country, year	Solid fuels (10^3 m.t. coal equiv.)	Liquid fuels (10^3 m.t.) Total	Crude oil	Refined petroleum products Total	Gasoline	Kerosine	Fuel oils	Lubes and greases	Gas (10^6 c.m.)	Electricity (10^6 kwh)
	(1)	(2)	(3)	(4)	(5)	(6)	(7)	(8)	(9)	(10)
KOREA, REPUBLIC OF (CONTINUED)							EXPORTS			
1965	205	-	-	-	-	-	-	-	-	-
MALAYA AND SINGAPORE							IMPORTS			
1925	644	663	-	663	230	112	309	12	-	-
1929	852	1013	-	1013	285	156	556	16	-	-
1933	567	734	-	734	310	101	312	11	-	-
1937	749	1294	-	1294	441	127	712	14	-	-
1938	488	1277	-	1277	456	165	642	14	-	-
1950	101	3458	-	3458	850	290	2295	23	-	-
1953	89	5705	-	5705	1550	520	3612	23	-	-
1955	70	6896	-	6896	1705	560	4595	36	-	-
1957	90	7712	857	6855	1557	601	4659	38	-	-
1960	4	6575	284	6291	1298	872	4082	39	-	-
1961	60	8552	1297	7255	1163	981	5068	43	-	-
1962	40	10084	3318	6766	975	1025	4713	53	-	-
1963	40	9606	3000	6606	989	835	4713	69	-	-
1964	40	10848	4526	6322	814	593	4844	71	-	-
1965	25	12104	4914	7190	706	966	5420	98	-	-
MALAYA AND SINGAPORE							EXPORTS			
1925	11	305	-	305	193	64	36	12	-	-
1929	3	391	-	391	197	102	86	6	-	-
1933	4	417	-	417	261	68	84	4	-	-
1937	5	661	-	661	337	90	231	3	-	-
1938	3	777	-	777	366	121	287	3	-	-
1950	-	2073	-	2073	640	230	1199	4	-	-
1953	-	2874	-	2874	1135	540	1194	5	-	-
1955	-	3435	-	3435	1220	510	1699	6	-	-
1957	-	3815	785	3030	1212	471	1340	7	-	-
1960	-	2983	231	2752	1063	618	1067	4	-	-
1961	-	4065	782	3283	940	714	1624	5	-	-
1962	-	5145	1316	3829	979	735	2110	5	-	-
1963	-	5360	1263	4097	1024	754	2296	23	-	-
1964	-	5117	254	4863	1015	560	3242	46	-	-
1965	-	6379	243	6136	1051	884	4141	60	-	-
SINGAPORE							IMPORTS			
1960	-	NA	NA	5159	1084	780	3256	39	-	-
1961	10	NA	NA	5986	938	865	4140	43	-	-
1962	10	NA	NA	5450	756	906	3735	53	-	-
1963	10	NA	NA	5507	828	726	3884	69	-	-
1964	10	NA	NA	5852	736	530	4515	71	-	-
1965	5	NA	NA	6794	700	870	5126	98	-	-
SINGAPORE							EXPORTS			
1960	-	NA	NA	2715	1048	616	1047	4	-	50
1961	-	NA	NA	3240	928	711	1596	5	-	55
1962	-	NA	NA	3778	963	731	2079	5	-	60
1963	-	NA	NA	4001	1001	748	2229	23	-	32

Table IV. ENERGY IMPORTS AND EXPORTS, SELECTED YEARS, 1925-1965

(Original units)

Region, country, year	Solid fuels (10^3 m.t. coal equiv.)	Liquid fuels (10^3 m.t.)		Refined petroleum products					Gas (10^6 c.m.)	Electricity (10^6 kwh)
		Total	Crude oil	Total	Gasoline	Kerosine	Fuel oils	Lubes and greases		
	(1)	(2)	(3)	(4)	(5)	(6)	(7)	(8)	(9)	(10)
SINGAPORE (CONTINUED)							EXPORTS			
1964	-	NA	NA	4357	936	526	2849	46	-	-
1965	-	NA	NA	5567	948	816	3743	60	-	-
PAKISTAN							IMPORTS			
1950	1025	920	-	920	NA	NA	NA	NA	NA	NA
1953	1211	1048	-	1048	110	230	680	28	-	-
1955	1080	1291	-	1291	150	205	900	36	-	-
1957	1330	1517	-	1517	175	210	1100	32	-	-
1960	1410	2093	-	2093	195	343	1555	NA	-	-
1961	1070	2224	-	2224	185	420	1570	49	-	-
1962	1360	2414	330	2084	167	476	1393	48	-	-
1963	1200	2818	1600	1218	67	375	690	86	-	-
1964	1340	3168	2115	1053	82	408	509	54	-	-
1965	1100	3140	2440	700	160	220	320	NA	-	-
PAKISTAN							EXPORTS			
1950	-	-	-	-	-	-	-	-	-	-
1953	-	-	-	-	-	-	-	-	-	-
1955	-	-	-	-	-	-	-	-	-	-
1957	-	8	-	8	5	1	2	-	-	-
1960	-	23	-	23	10	3	10	-	-	-
1961	-	18	-	18	6	2	10	-	-	-
1962	-	17	-	17	5	2	10	-	-	-
1963	-	48	-	48	48	-	-	-	-	-
1964	-	155	-	155	80	-	75	-	-	-
1965	-	-	-	-	-	-	-	-	-	-
PHILIPPINES							IMPORTS			
1925	472	306	-	306	33	49	215	9	-	-
1929	603	358	-	358	71	69	208	10	-	-
1933	273	368	-	368	67	41	251	9	-	-
1937	266	439	-	439	97	57	273	12	-	-
1938	259	467	-	467	100	45	301	21	-	-
1950	7	1264	-	1264	471	152	608	33	-	-
1953	5	1321	-	1321	466	145	676	34	-	-
1955	10	1920	667	1253	376	134	700	43	-	-
1957	10	2215	879	1336	361	135	797	43	-	-
1960	10	2656	1415	1241	440	167	568	66	-	-
1961	10	2765	2285	480	178	41	195	66	-	-
1962	10	3323	3036	287	107	19	114	47	-	-
1963	10	3766	3617	149	38	6	45	60	-	-
1964	10	4355	4216	139	1	38	11	89	-	-
1965	10	4752	4610	142	52	19	71	NA	-	-
PHILIPPINES							EXPORTS			
1960	-	-	-	-	-	-	-	-	-	-
1961	-	-	-	-	-	-	-	-	-	-
1962	-	24	-	24	-	-	24	-	-	-
1963	-	51	-	51	-	-	51	-	-	-
1964	-	74	-	74	1	1	72	-	-	-

Table IV. ENERGY IMPORTS AND EXPORTS, SELECTED YEARS, 1925-1965

(Original units)

Region, country, year	Solid fuels (10^3 m.t. coal equiv.)	Liquid fuels (10^3 m.t.)							Gas (10^6 c.m.)	Electricity (10^6 kwh)
				Refined petroleum products						
		Total	Crude oil	Total	Gasoline	Kerosine	Fuel oils	Lubes and greases		
	(1)	(2)	(3)	(4)	(5)	(6)	(7)	(8)	(9)	(10)
PHILIPPINES (CONTINUED)							EXPORTS			
1965	-	141	-	141	10	1	130	-	-	-
TAIWAN							IMPORTS			
1925	19	18	-	18	-	15	-	3	-	-
1929	18	58	28	30	3	18	1	8	-	-
1933	31	67	40	27	5	14	1	7	-	-
1937	41	122	32	90	10	20	50	10	-	-
1938	45	135	32	103	10	22	60	11	-	-
1950	1	153	130	23	10	-	10	3	-	-
1953	-	68	-	68	62	-	-	6	-	-
1955	-	687	613	74	1	50	10	13	-	-
1957	-	846	732	114	33	56	15	10	-	-
1960	-	1099	1060	39	-	30	-	9	-	-
1961	-	1169	1122	47	-	30	-	17	-	-
1962	-	1321	1258	63	-	37	-	26	-	-
1963	-	1547	1493	54	-	35	-	19	-	-
1964	-	1353	1286	67	-	42	-	25	-	-
1965	20	1832	1785	47	-	-	20	27	-	-
TAIWAN							EXPORTS			
1925	907	-	-	-	-	-	-	-	-	-
1929	396	5	3	2	-	2	-	-	-	-
1933	336	2	-	2	-	1	-	1	-	-
1937	408	1	-	1	-	-	-	1	-	-
1938	500	1	-	1	-	-	-	1	-	-
1950	65	-	-	-	-	-	-	-	-	-
1953	211	-	-	-	-	-	-	-	-	-
1955	50	30	-	30	-	-	30	-	-	-
1957	30	10	-	10	-	-	10	-	-	-
1960	190	13	-	13	1	-	12	-	-	-
1961	240	51	-	51	11	-	40	-	-	-
1962	130	60	-	60	27	-	33	-	-	-
1963	100	51	-	51	-	-	51	-	-	-
1964	110	82	-	82	-	-	82	-	-	-
1965	15	42	-	42	4	-	37	1	-	-
THAILAND							IMPORTS			
1925	38	42	-	42	6	17	16	3	-	-
1929	52	96	-	96	17	37	37	5	-	-
1933	23	77	-	77	12	28	32	5	-	-
1937	50	112	-	112	19	31	55	7	-	-
1938	56	117	-	117	21	32	58	6	-	-
1950	20	240	-	240	80	40	120	NA	-	-
1953	44	460	-	460	180	60	220	NA	-	-
1955	40	718	-	718	250	80	362	26	-	-
1957	20	930	-	930	335	87	473	35	-	-
1960	10	1169	-	1169	411	138	583	37	-	-
1961	-	1287	-	1287	399	162	693	33	-	-
1962	-	1622	-	1622	423	267	880	52	-	-
1963	-	1776	54	1722	424	240	1014	43	-	-
1964	-	2472	675	1797	413	238	1089	56	-	-
1965	-	2491	1209	1282	174	387	659	62	-	-

Table IV. ENERGY IMPORTS AND EXPORTS, SELECTED YEARS, 1925-1965

(Original units)

Region, country, year	Solid fuels (10^3 m.t. coal equiv.)	Liquid fuels (10^3 m.t.): Total	Crude oil	Refined petroleum products: Total	Gasoline	Kerosine	Fuel oils	Lubes and greases	Gas (10^6 c.m.)	Electricity (10^6 kwh)
	(1)	(2)	(3)	(4)	(5)	(6)	(7)	(8)	(9)	(10)
THAILAND (CONTINUED)							EXPORTS			
1953	-	-	-	-	-	-	-	-	-	-
1955	-	2	-	2	2	-	-	-	-	-
1957	-	21	-	21	18	3	-	-	-	-
1960	-	6	-	6	5	1	-	-	-	-
1961	-	9	-	9	8	1	-	-	-	-
1962	-	4	-	4	4	-	-	-	-	-
1963	-	2	-	2	2	-	-	-	-	-
1964	-	52	-	52	2	-	50	-	-	-
1965	-	32	-	32	29	3	-	-	-	-
AFRICA							IMPORTS			
1925	4613	1060	99	961	212	388	267	62	-	-
1929	6163	1974	122	1852	657	625	461	108	-	-
1933	4101	2356	78	2278	664	453	1069	92	-	-
1937	5217	4426	107	4319	1223	527	2446	123	-	-
1938	4897	3863	106	3757	1130	535	1974	118	-	-
1950	2778	8961	-	8961	2479	1174	5056	252	4	-
1953	2266	11967	75	11892	3309	1517	6815	241	-	15
1955	2544	15697	1952	13745	3610	1727	8010	372	-	20
1957	2714	17545	2242	15303	3911	1606	9367	376	-	-
1960	2473	19311	3566	15745	3927	1808	9565	360	-	190
1961	2631	21060	5008	16052	3903	1820	9839	395	-	1806
1962	2330	22297	5931	16366	4013	1878	9996	397	-	1980
1963	2170	23998	8179	15819	3669	1788	9887	395	-	2041
1964	2685	26929	14259	12670	2732	1614	7842	439	-	2222
1965	2825	27155	15176	11979	2580	1428	7470	465	-	2381
AFRICA							EXPORTS			
1925	1917	213	-	213	90	105	17	1	-	-
1929	2260	254	-	254	120	79	52	2	-	-
1933	1061	61	1	60	41	1	17	1	-	-
1937	1466	37	1	36	29	3	4	-	-	-
1938	1596	41	3	38	32	2	4	-	-	-
1950	3664	2	-	2	1	-	-	1	-	-
1953	2515	108	107	1	1	-	-	-	-	19
1955	2120	264	64	200	75	20	105	-	-	20
1957	2290	584	394	190	81	26	82	1	-	710
1960	2590	11057	10580	477	203	68	205	-	-	770
1961	2810	21441	20705	736	247	56	433	-	-	1792
1962	3140	36932	35362	1570	585	59	917	-	-	1965
1963	2920	56157	53934	2223	417	127	1659	-	-	2034
1964	3080	80920	76354	4566	876	189	3480	-	90	2237
1965	3340	104355	99073	5282	1137	158	3960	1	833	2391
NORTH AFRICA							IMPORTS			
1925	3316	602	99	503	97	291	79	36	-	-
1929	4241	1015	122	893	285	461	94	53	-	-
1933	3248	1292	78	1214	295	360	509	50	-	-
1937	3418	1648	107	1541	303	371	820	47	-	-
1938	3333	1727	106	1621	353	393	828	47	-	-
1950	984	3671	-	3671	567	584	2443	77	4	-
1953	552	4391	46	4345	834	714	2716	71	-	-

Table IV. ENERGY IMPORTS AND EXPORTS, SELECTED YEARS, 1925-1965

(Original units)

Region, country, year	Solid fuels (10³ m.t. coal equiv.)	Liquid fuels (10³ m.t.) Total	Crude oil	Refined petroleum products Total	Gasoline	Kerosine	Fuel oils	Lubes and greases	Gas (10⁶ c.m.)	Electricity (10⁶ kwh)
	(1)	(2)	(3)	(4)	(5)	(6)	(7)	(8)	(9)	(10)
NORTH AFRICA (CONTINUED) — IMPORTS										
1955	640	6358	1012	5346	958	783	3487	94	-	-
1957	880	5490	1173	4317	1022	635	2528	95	-	-
1960	670	7113	2167	4946	790	719	3265	105	-	10
1961	690	7582	2914	4668	738	681	3050	121	-	14
1962	500	8376	3915	4461	784	646	2882	88	-	15
1963	470	9243	5119	4124	587	482	2873	124	-	7
1964	730	8725	6174	2551	287	251	1875	117	-	2
1965	575	7575	5572	2003	227	234	1435	93	-	1
NORTH AFRICA — EXPORTS										
1925	20	213	-	213	90	105	17	1	-	-
1929	19	253	-	253	120	79	52	2	-	-
1933	28	61	1	60	41	1	17	1	-	-
1937	97	37	1	36	29	3	4	-	-	-
1938	111	41	3	38	32	2	4	-	-	-
1950	194	2	-	2	1	-	-	1	-	-
1953	268	108	107	1	1	-	-	-	-	4
1955	340	74	64	10	3	1	6	-	-	20
1957	290	258	251	7	2	3	2	-	-	10
1960	190	9087	8911	176	88	15	72	-	-	10
1961	200	17876	17599	277	84	9	184	-	-	-
1962	160	32154	31055	1099	397	7	686	-	-	-
1963	180	50629	49135	1494	228	6	1240	-	-	-
1964	140	71844	69331	2513	635	43	1818	-	90	-
1965	105	87629	84493	3136	754	28	2334	-	833	-
ALGERIA — IMPORTS										
1925	1547	73	-	73	41	18	4	10	-	-
1929	2399	176	-	176	101	44	17	14	-	-
1933	1596	439	-	439	132	49	243	15	-	-
1937	1491	662	-	662	114	39	497	12	-	-
1938	1296	670	-	670	122	38	498	12	-	-
1950	500	1103	-	1103	190	50	840	23	4	-
1953	271	1487	-	1487	270	70	1120	17	-	-
1955	310	1763	-	1763	347	95	1278	28	-	-
1957	500	1953	-	1953	520	95	1280	33	-	-
1960	350	1980	-	1980	361	116	1423	29	-	10
1961	210	1939	-	1939	362	125	1362	29	-	5
1962	100	1839	-	1839	450	118	1202	20	-	7
1963	50	1852	-	1852	324	126	1337	20	-	4
1964	70	791	-	791	83	33	643	20	-	1
1965	20	400	-	400	30	2	351	15	-	-
ALGERIA — EXPORTS										
1925	15	-	-	-	-	-	-	-	-	-
1929	16	4	-	4	3	-	1	-	-	-
1933	11	2	1	1	-	-	1	-	-	-
1937	19	-	-	-	-	-	-	-	-	-
1938	1	1	-	1	1	-	-	-	-	-
1950	45	-	-	-	-	-	-	-	-	-
1953	91	77	77	-	-	-	-	-	-	4
1955	40	64	64	-	-	-	-	-	-	10

Table IV. ENERGY IMPORTS AND EXPORTS, SELECTED YEARS, 1925-1965

(Original units)

Region, country, year	Solid fuels (10^3 m.t. coal equiv.)	Liquid fuels (10^3 m.t.)							Gas (10^6 c.m.)	Electricity (10^6 kwh)
				Refined petroleum products						
		Total	Crude oil	Total	Gasoline	Kerosine	Fuel oils	Lubes and greases		
	(1)	(2)	(3)	(4)	(5)	(6)	(7)	(8)	(9)	(10)
ALGERIA (CONTINUED)							EXPORTS			
1957	20	11	11	-	-	-	-	-	-	10
1960	-	8043	8043	-	-	-	-	-	-	-
1961	-	15283	15097	186	36	1	149	-	-	-
1962	-	20988	20355	633	130	1	493	-	-	-
1963	-	24150	23655	495	80	-	397	-	-	-
1964	-	25677	24825	852	150	15	670	-	90	-
1965	-	25252	24400	852	250	12	570	-	833	-
EGYPT UAR							IMPORTS			
1925	1408	452	99	353	18	251	67	17	-	-
1929	1383	648	122	526	89	364	50	23	-	-
1933	1204	611	78	533	20	269	224	20	-	-
1937	1504	696	107	589	30	291	246	22	-	-
1938	1608	706	106	600	36	311	232	21	-	-
1950	217	1746	-	1746	72	441	1200	33	-	-
1953	78	1551	46	1505	80	495	900	30	-	-
1955	110	3097	1012	2085	96	510	1445	34	-	-
1957	180	2160	1146	1014	66	400	510	38	-	-
1960	160	3502	2077	1425	47	434	903	41	-	-
1961	300	3963	2785	1178	28	386	711	53	-	-
1962	270	5085	3709	1376	21	373	947	35	-	-
1963	270	5509	4323	1186	37	206	876	67	-	-
1964	500	5779	4750	1029	21	92	858	58	-	-
1965	440	4953	3981	972	21	109	800	42	-	-
EGYPT UAR							EXPORTS			
1925	5	213	-	213	90	105	17	1	-	-
1929	3	249	-	249	117	79	51	2	-	-
1933	15	59	-	59	41	1	16	1	-	-
1937	4	36	-	36	29	3	4	-	-	-
1938	7	37	-	37	31	2	4	-	-	-
1950	-	2	-	2	1	-	-	1	-	-
1953	-	1	-	1	1	-	-	-	-	-
1955	-	10	-	10	3	1	6	-	-	-
1957	-	246	240	6	1	3	2	-	-	-
1960	-	1042	868	174	87	14	72	-	-	-
1961	-	1900	1810	90	48	7	35	-	-	-
1962	-	3309	2848	461	267	4	190	-	-	-
1963	-	4438	3441	997	148	4	843	-	-	-
1964	-	4667	3030	1637	478	13	1146	-	-	-
1965	-	3899	1618	2281	504	16	1761	-	-	-
LIBYA							IMPORTS			
1925	17	10	-	10	6	2	1	1	-	-
1929	21	17	-	17	9	3	3	2	-	-
1933	37	33	-	33	15	4	12	2	-	-
1937	44	49	-	49	17	5	25	2	-	-
1938	55	64	-	64	17	7	37	3	-	-
1950	NA	97	-	97	27	40	29	1	-	-
1953	-	134	-	134	45	52	35	2	-	-
1955	70	204	-	204	100	60	40	4	-	-
1957	30	266	-	266	125	65	70	5	-	-

Table IV. ENERGY IMPORTS AND EXPORTS, SELECTED YEARS, 1925-1965

(Original units)

Region, country, year	Solid fuels (10^3 m.t. coal equiv.)	Liquid fuels (10^3 m.t.)		Refined petroleum products					Gas (10^6 c.m.)	Electricity (10^6 kwh)
		Total	Crude oil	Total	Gasoline	Kerosine	Fuel oils	Lubes and greases		
	(1)	(2)	(3)	(4)	(5)	(6)	(7)	(8)	(9)	(10)
LIBYA (CONTINUED)							IMPORTS			
1960	30	344	-	344	120	75	140	7	-	-
1961	40	323	-	323	110	75	130	6	-	-
1962	10	344	-	344	130	75	130	7	-	-
1963	10	379	-	379	140	80	145	8	-	-
1964	-	441	-	441	160	85	180	12	-	-
1965	10	449	-	449	165	90	181	9	-	-
LIBYA							EXPORTS			
1960	-	-	-	-	-	-	-	-	-	-
1961	-	692	692	-	-	-	-	-	-	-
1962	-	7852	7852	-	-	-	-	-	-	-
1963	-	22039	22039	-	-	-	-	-	-	-
1964	-	41476	41476	-	-	-	-	-	-	-
1965	-	58475	58475	-	-	-	-	-	-	-
MOROCCO							IMPORTS			
1925	121	36	-	36	23	7	1	5	-	-
1929	181	94	-	94	57	21	8	8	-	-
1933	196	116	-	116	84	12	12	8	-	-
1937	161	138	-	138	99	12	21	6	-	-
1938	136	181	-	181	132	13	30	6	-	-
1950	94	495	-	495	209	25	249	12	-	-
1953	119	878	-	878	355	62	445	16	-	-
1955	110	852	-	852	329	81	416	20	-	-
1957	80	731	27	704	238	39	408	12	-	-
1960	90	825	90	735	185	49	473	19	-	-
1961	90	872	129	743	168	48	498	19	-	9
1962	80	601	200	401	108	30	242	17	-	8
1963	100	870	710	160	9	19	114	18	-	3
1964	120	950	805	145	5	23	100	14	-	1
1965	55	1074	910	164	9	31	101	16	-	1
MOROCCO							EXPORTS			
1925	-	-	-	-	-	-	-	-	-	-
1929	-	-	-	-	-	-	-	-	-	-
1933	2	-	-	-	-	-	-	-	-	-
1937	74	1	1	-	-	-	-	-	-	-
1938	103	3	3	-	-	-	-	-	-	-
1950	149	-	-	-	-	-	-	-	-	-
1953	177	30	30	-	-	-	-	-	-	-
1955	300	-	-	-	-	-	-	-	-	10
1957	270	1	-	1	1	-	-	-	-	-
1960	190	2	-	2	1	1	-	-	-	10
1961	200	1	-	1	-	1	-	-	-	-
1962	160	5	-	5	-	2	3	-	-	-
1963	180	2	-	2	-	2	-	-	-	-
1964	140	18	-	18	1	15	2	-	-	-
1965	105	3	-	3	-	-	3	-	-	-

Table IV. ENERGY IMPORTS AND EXPORTS, SELECTED YEARS, 1925-1965

(Original units)

Region, country, year	Solid fuels (10^3 m.t. coal equiv.)	Liquid fuels (10^3 m.t.)		Refined petroleum products					Gas (10^6 c.m.)	Electricity (10^6 kwh)
		Total	Crude oil	Total	Gasoline	Kerosine	Fuel oils	Lubes and greases		
	(1)	(2)	(3)	(4)	(5)	(6)	(7)	(8)	(9)	(10)
TUNISIA							IMPORTS			
1925	223	31	-	31	9	13	6	3	-	-
1929	257	80	-	80	29	29	16	6	-	-
1933	215	93	-	93	44	26	18	5	-	-
1937	218	103	-	103	43	24	31	5	-	-
1938	238	106	-	106	46	24	31	5	-	-
1950	173	230	-	230	69	28	125	8	-	-
1953	84	341	-	341	84	35	216	6	-	-
1955	40	442	-	442	86	37	308	8	-	-
1957	90	380	-	380	73	36	260	7	-	-
1960	40	462	-	462	77	45	326	9	-	-
1961	50	485	-	485	70	47	349	14	-	-
1962	40	507	6	501	75	50	361	9	-	-
1963	40	633	86	547	77	51	401	11	-	-
1964	40	764	619	145	18	18	94	13	-	-
1965	50	699	681	18	2	2	2	11	-	-
TROPICAL AFRICA							IMPORTS			
1925	1290	329	-	329	46	56	186	9	-	-
1929	1918	579	-	579	149	91	312	26	-	-
1933	853	657	-	657	125	51	464	17	-	-
1937	1774	1806	-	1806	454	96	1226	30	-	-
1938	1540	1052	-	1052	263	84	673	32	-	-
1950	1730	2993	-	2993	825	238	1828	102	-	-
1953	1686	5063	-	5063	1207	333	3431	92	-	15
1955	1804	6110	-	6110	1572	463	3927	146	-	20
1957	1784	7925	-	7925	1812	503	5457	147	-	-
1960	1803	8449	118	8331	1963	679	5526	145	-	180
1961	1941	9387	612	8775	1941	732	5937	148	-	1792
1962	1770	9597	399	9198	1981	841	6196	159	-	1965
1963	1650	10166	870	9296	1975	900	6237	162	-	2034
1964	1855	11705	3235	8470	1769	907	5602	170	-	2220
1965	2105	13037	4929	8108	1637	804	5461	184	-	2380
TROPICAL AFRICA							EXPORTS			
1925	293	-	-	-	-	-	-	-	-	-
1929	585	1	-	1	-	-	-	-	-	-
1933	251	-	-	-	-	-	-	-	-	-
1937	550	-	-	-	-	-	-	-	-	-
1938	584	-	-	-	-	-	-	-	-	-
1950	860	-	-	-	-	-	-	-	-	-
1953	1035	-	-	-	-	-	-	-	-	15
1955	1120	86	-	86	51	16	19	-	-	-
1957	1400	247	143	104	56	21	26	1	-	700
1960	1440	1870	1669	201	103	38	60	-	-	760
1961	1550	3548	3106	442	160	45	237	-	-	1792
1962	1320	4772	4307	465	184	51	230	-	-	1965
1963	1340	5454	4799	655	188	111	356	-	-	2034
1964	1560	8375	7023	1352	235	127	988	-	-	2237
1965	1890	16341	14580	1761	381	118	1256	1	-	2391
CONGO, DEMOCRATIC REPUBLIC							IMPORTS			
1925	294	14	-	14	4	2	8	-	-	-

Table IV. ENERGY IMPORTS AND EXPORTS, SELECTED YEARS, 1925-1965

(Original units)

Region, country, year	Solid fuels (10^3 m.t. coal equiv.)	Liquid fuels (10^3 m.t.)		Refined petroleum products					Gas (10^6 c.m.)	Electricity (10^6 kwh)
		Total	Crude oil	Total	Gasoline	Kerosine	Fuel oils	Lubes and greases		
	(1)	(2)	(3)	(4)	(5)	(6)	(7)	(8)	(9)	(10)
CONGO, DEMOCRATIC REPUBLIC (CONTINUED)							IMPORTS			
1929	466	43	-	43	18	3	18	4	-	-
1933	45	17	-	17	11	1	3	2	-	-
1937	165	42	-	42	30	2	6	4	-	-
1938	133	31	-	31	20	3	4	4	-	-
1950	208	158	-	158	105	13	32	8	-	-
1953	200	285	-	285	173	23	75	14	-	-
1955	290	408	-	408	212	28	144	22	-	20
1957	240	461	-	461	224	35	178	20	-	-
1960	230	428	-	428	201	44	179	NA	-	-
1961	330	454	-	454	218	47	185	NA	-	-
1962	240	461	-	461	208	57	192	NA	-	-
1963	220	502	-	502	230	74	196	NA	-	-
1964	255	373	-	373	149	56	166	NA	-	-
1965	330	450	-	450	209	63	176	NA	-	-
CONGO, DEMOCRATIC REPUBLIC							EXPORTS			
1925	-	-	-	-	-	-	-	-	-	-
1929	-	1	-	1	-	-	-	-	-	-
1933	-	-	-	-	-	-	-	-	-	-
1937	-	-	-	-	-	-	-	-	-	-
1938	-	-	-	-	-	-	-	-	-	-
1950	-	-	-	-	-	-	-	-	-	-
1953	-	-	-	-	-	-	-	-	-	-
1955	-	-	-	-	-	-	-	-	-	-
1957	-	-	-	-	-	-	-	-	-	690
1960	-	-	-	-	-	-	-	-	-	520
1961	-	-	-	-	-	-	-	-	-	463
1962	-	-	-	-	-	-	-	-	-	470
1963	-	-	-	-	-	-	-	-	-	275
1964	-	-	-	-	-	-	-	-	-	212
1965	-	-	-	-	-	-	-	-	-	275
EAST AFRICA							IMPORTS			
1925	76	47	-	47	7	12	26	2	-	-
1929	111	99	-	99	31	21	42	5	-	-
1933	95	72	-	72	15	10	45	2	-	-
1937	166	135	-	135	36	17	78	4	-	-
1938	152	163	-	163	47	17	94	5	-	-
1950	44	590	-	590	139	39	398	14	-	-
1953	14	839	-	839	189	63	575	12	-	15
1955	26	1043	-	1043	255	77	686	25	-	-
1957	36	1208	-	1208	260	90	840	18	-	-
1960	40	1348	-	1348	311	131	884	21	-	180
1961	40	1292	-	1292	297	145	821	27	-	214
1962	40	1405	-	1405	322	180	873	28	-	210
1963	40	1579	221	1358	298	181	858	19	-	206
1964	30	2187	1500	687	183	133	350	20	-	188
1965	60	2517	1845	672	181	105	358	27	-	190
EAST AFRICA							EXPORTS			
1950	-	-	-	-	-	-	-	-	-	-
1953	-	-	-	-	-	-	-	-	-	15

Table IV. ENERGY IMPORTS AND EXPORTS, SELECTED YEARS, 1925-1965

(Original units)

Region, country, year	Solid fuels (10^3 m.t. coal equiv.)	Liquid fuels (10^3 m.t.)		Refined petroleum products					Gas (10^6 c.m.)	Electricity (10^6 kwh)
		Total	Crude oil	Total	Gasoline	Kerosine	Fuel oils	Lubes and greases		
	(1)	(2)	(3)	(4)	(5)	(6)	(7)	(8)	(9)	(10)
EAST AFRICA (CONTINUED)							EXPORTS			
1955	-	-	-	-	-	-	-	-	-	-
1957	-	-	-	-	-	-	-	-	-	-
1960	-	86	-	86	44	12	30	-	-	180
1961	-	83	-	83	49	12	22	-	-	214
1962	-	96	-	96	56	15	25	-	-	210
1963	-	174	-	174	53	75	46	-	-	206
1964	-	775	-	775	106	103	564	-	-	188
1965	-	983	-	983	195	88	694	1	-	190
EQUATORIAL AFRICA							IMPORTS			
1925	2	2	-	2	2	-	-	-	-	-
1929	1	5	-	5	3	1	1	-	-	-
1933	2	7	-	7	5	1	-	1	-	-
1937	21	12	-	12	6	2	3	1	-	-
1938	11	13	-	13	8	2	2	1	-	-
1950	7	55	-	55	36	4	11	4	-	-
1953	4	84	-	84	44	9	28	3	-	-
1955	-	94	-	94	55	10	23	6	-	-
1957	-	126	-	126	60	10	50	6	-	-
1960	-	185	-	185	81	17	79	7	-	-
1961	-	183	-	183	78	15	81	8	-	-
1962	-	189	-	189	80	16	85	7	-	-
1963	-	192	-	192	74	20	90	7	-	-
1964	-	226	-	226	78	38	102	7	-	-
1965	-	231	-	231	74	36	113	7	-	-
EQUATORIAL AFRICA							EXPORTS			
1955	-	-	-	-	-	-	-	-	-	-
1957	-	143	143	-	-	-	-	-	-	-
1960	-	809	809	-	-	-	-	-	-	-
1961	-	837	831	6	6	-	-	-	-	-
1962	-	954	953	1	1	-	-	-	-	-
1963	-	1045	1045	-	-	-	-	-	-	-
1964	-	1147	1147	-	-	-	-	-	-	-
1965	-	1352	1352	-	-	-	-	-	-	-
GHANA							IMPORTS			
1925	54	19	-	19	9	8	1	1	-	-
1929	73	35	-	35	20	11	2	2	-	-
1933	27	25	-	25	13	6	4	2	-	-
1937	72	80	-	80	25	13	39	3	-	-
1938	77	89	-	89	22	9	56	2	-	-
1950	63	191	-	191	64	21	99	7	-	-
1953	99	233	-	233	87	30	111	5	-	-
1955	120	326	-	326	113	36	165	12	-	-
1957	110	369	-	369	146	41	171	11	-	-
1960	40	451	-	451	141	53	243	14	-	-
1961	50	419	-	419	108	42	256	13	-	-
1962	30	480	-	480	140	62	262	16	-	-
1963	40	584	194	390	100	41	233	16	-	-
1964	40	879	835	44	7	13	8	16	-	-
1965	30	853	800	53	2	18	11	22	-	-

Table IV. ENERGY IMPORTS AND EXPORTS, SELECTED YEARS, 1925-1965

(Original units)

Region, country, year	Solid fuels (10^3 m.t. coal equiv.)	Liquid fuels (10^3 m.t.) Total	Crude oil	Refined petroleum products Total	Gasoline	Kerosine	Fuel oils	Lubes and greases	Gas (10^6 c.m.)	Electricity (10^6 kwh)
	(1)	(2)	(3)	(4)	(5)	(6)	(7)	(8)	(9)	(10)
GHANA (CONTINUED)							EXPORTS			
1953	-	-	-	-	-	-	-	-	-	-
1955	-	-	-	-	-	-	-	-	-	-
1957	-	1	-	1	-	-	-	1	-	-
1960	-	1	-	1	1	-	-	-	-	-
1961	-	-	-	-	-	-	-	-	-	-
1962	-	-	-	-	-	-	-	-	-	-
1963	-	36	-	36	-	-	36	-	-	-
1964	-	232	-	232	14	2	216	-	-	-
1965	-	241	-	241	6	3	232	-	-	-
LIBERIA							IMPORTS			
1925	-	-	-	-	-	-	-	-	-	-
1929	-	-	-	-	-	-	-	-	-	-
1933	-	-	-	-	-	-	-	-	-	-
1937	-	1	-	1	1	-	-	-	-	-
1938	-	2	-	2	1	1	-	-	-	-
1950	-	16	-	16	7	3	6	-	-	-
1953	-	18	-	18	8	3	6	1	-	-
1955	-	61	-	61	11	43	6	1	-	-
1957	-	32	-	32	19	4	7	2	-	-
1960	-	59	-	59	21	7	29	2	-	-
1961	-	60	-	60	26	4	28	2	-	-
1962	-	92	-	92	19	8	61	4	-	-
1963	-	133	-	133	24	15	90	4	-	-
1964	-	193	-	193	28	32	128	5	-	-
1965	-	218	-	218	26	32	155	5	-	-
NIGERIA							IMPORTS			
1925	20	23	-	23	6	15	1	1	-	-
1929	22	35	-	35	13	19	1	2	-	-
1933	28	16	-	16	7	7	1	1	-	-
1937	40	38	-	38	21	11	4	2	-	-
1938	39	40	-	40	23	11	4	2	-	-
1950	63	165	-	165	96	36	28	5	-	-
1953	27	229	-	229	124	45	55	5	-	-
1955	-	399	-	399	206	72	110	11	-	-
1957	-	510	-	510	252	89	156	13	-	-
1960	-	723	-	723	286	128	287	19	-	-
1961	-	915	-	915	297	163	433	19	-	-
1962	-	873	-	873	278	174	396	21	-	-
1963	-	1018	-	1018	308	200	482	23	-	-
1964	-	1138	-	1138	321	244	543	25	-	-
1965	-	1178	-	1178	325	223	600	23	-	-
NIGERIA							EXPORTS			
1925	23	-	-	-	-	-	-	-	-	-
1929	42	-	-	-	-	-	-	-	-	-
1933	24	-	-	-	-	-	-	-	-	-
1937	45	-	-	-	-	-	-	-	-	-
1938	53	-	-	-	-	-	-	-	-	-
1950	2	-	-	-	-	-	-	-	-	-
1953	4	-	-	-	-	-	-	-	-	-

Table IV. ENERGY IMPORTS AND EXPORTS, SELECTED YEARS, 1925-1965

(Original units)

Region, country, year	Solid fuels (10^3 m.t. coal equiv.)	Liquid fuels (10^3 m.t.) Total	Crude oil	Refined petroleum products Total	Gasoline	Kerosine	Fuel oils	Lubes and greases	Gas (10^6 c.m.)	Electricity (10^6 kwh)
	(1)	(2)	(3)	(4)	(5)	(6)	(7)	(8)	(9)	(10)
NIGERIA (CONTINUED) — EXPORTS										
1955	100	86	-	86	51	16	19	-	-	-
1957	100	103	-	103	56	21	26	-	-	-
1960	30	974	860	114	58	26	30	-	-	-
1961	50	2407	2275	132	55	33	44	-	-	-
1962	30	3492	3354	138	45	35	58	-	-	-
1963	40	3894	3754	140	47	35	58	-	-	-
1964	60	5961	5876	85	25	20	40	-	-	-
1965	35	13359	13228	131	40	21	70	-	-	-
RHODESIAN FEDERATION — IMPORTS										
1925	42	6	-	6	4	1	-	1	-	-
1929	145	20	-	20	14	3	-	3	-	-
1933	180	24	-	24	17	1	5	1	-	-
1937	346	52	-	52	30	2	16	4	-	-
1938	409	55	-	55	33	2	16	4	-	-
1950	683	170	-	170	120	28	13	9	-	-
1953	869	267	-	267	163	36	58	10	-	-
1955	931	361	-	361	210	40	90	21	-	-
1957	997	464	-	464	240	40	160	24	-	-
1960	1102	533	-	533	260	60	190	23	-	-
1961	1150	539	-	539	263	70	186	20	-	1578
1962	1060	579	-	579	270	79	205	24	-	1755
1963	1010	577	-	577	253	84	216	22	-	1828
1964	1110	606	-	606	259	88	236	21	-	2032
1965	1305	942	510	432	184	73	147	27	-	2190
RHODESIAN FEDERATION — EXPORTS										
1925	268	-	-	-	-	-	-	-	-	-
1929	541	-	-	-	-	-	-	-	-	-
1933	225	-	-	-	-	-	-	-	-	-
1937	498	-	-	-	-	-	-	-	-	-
1938	524	-	-	-	-	-	-	-	-	-
1950	852	-	-	-	-	-	-	-	-	-
1953	967	-	-	-	-	-	-	-	-	-
1955	1000	-	-	-	-	-	-	-	-	-
1957	1270	-	-	-	-	-	-	-	-	-
1960	1350	-	-	-	-	-	-	-	-	-
1961	1440	5	-	5	2	-	3	-	-	1054
1962	1240	11	-	11	7	1	3	-	-	1216
1963	1240	8	-	8	4	1	3	-	-	1479
1964	1440	13	-	13	6	2	5	-	-	1751
1965	1765	112	-	112	55	6	51	-	-	1851
MALAWI — IMPORTS										
1925	-	1	-	1	1	-	-	-	-	-
1929	3	1	-	1	1	-	-	-	-	-
1933	3	2	-	2	2	-	-	-	-	-
1937	5	2	-	2	2	-	-	-	-	-
1938	4	3	-	3	2	-	1	-	-	-
1950	25	15	-	15	8	2	5	-	-	-
1953	37	18	-	18	10	2	6	-	-	-
1955	42	30	-	30	20	-	10	-	-	-

Table IV. ENERGY IMPORTS AND EXPORTS, SELECTED YEARS, 1925-1965

(Original units)

Region, country, year	Solid fuels (10^3 m.t. coal equiv.)	Liquid fuels (10^3 m.t.)		Refined petroleum products					Gas (10^6 c.m.)	Electricity (10^6 kwh)
		Total	Crude oil	Total	Gasoline	Kerosine	Fuel oils	Lubes and greases		
	(1)	(2)	(3)	(4)	(5)	(6)	(7)	(8)	(9)	(10)
MALAWI (CONTINUED)							IMPORTS			
1957	47	40	-	40	20	-	20	-	-	-
1960	57	50	-	50	20	10	20	-	-	-
1961	60	43	-	43	18	5	20	-	-	-
1962	60	47	-	47	19	6	22	-	-	-
1963	60	51	-	51	20	7	24	-	-	-
1964	60	56	-	56	22	8	26	-	-	-
1965	80	59	-	59	23	9	27	-	-	-
ZAMBIA							IMPORTS			
1925	42	-	-	1	-	-	-	-	-	-
1929	142	4	-	4	3	-	-	1	-	-
1933	177	3	-	3	3	-	-	-	-	-
1937	341	5	-	5	4	-	-	1	-	-
1938	405	6	-	6	5	-	-	1	-	-
1950	654	40	-	40	26	6	6	2	-	-
1953	823	69	-	69	41	7	17	4	-	-
1955	880	90	-	90	50	10	30	NA	-	-
1957	940	110	-	110	60	10	40	NA	-	-
1960	1035	130	-	130	70	10	50	NA	-	-
1961	1080	133	-	133	78	12	43	NA	-	1578
1962	990	138	-	138	78	13	47	NA	-	1755
1963	940	140	-	140	76	13	50	NA	-	1828
1964	1040	153	-	153	77	14	54	7	-	2032
1965	1215	202	-	202	99	19	72	11	-	2190
RHODESIA							IMPORTS			
1925	-	5	-	5	3	1	-	1	-	-
1929	-	15	-	15	10	3	-	2	-	-
1933	-	19	-	19	12	1	5	1	-	-
1937	-	45	-	45	24	2	16	3	-	-
1938	-	46	-	46	26	2	15	3	-	-
1950	4	115	-	115	86	20	2	7	-	-
1953	9	180	-	180	112	27	35	6	-	-
1955	9	241	-	241	140	30	50	21	-	-
1957	10	314	-	314	160	30	100	24	-	-
1960	10	353	-	353	170	40	120	23	-	-
1961	10	363	-	363	167	53	123	20	-	-
1962	10	394	-	394	173	60	136	24	-	-
1963	10	386	-	386	157	64	142	22	-	-
1964	10	397	-	397	160	66	156	14	-	-
1965	10	681	510	171	62	45	48	16	-	-
RHODESIA							EXPORTS			
1925	268	-	-	-	-	-	-	-	-	-
1929	541	-	-	-	-	-	-	-	-	-
1933	225	-	-	-	-	-	-	-	-	-
1937	498	-	-	-	-	-	-	-	-	-
1938	524	-	-	-	-	-	-	-	-	-
1950	852	-	-	-	-	-	-	-	-	-
1953	967	-	-	-	-	-	-	-	-	-
1955	1000	-	-	-	-	-	-	-	-	-
1957	1270	-	-	-	-	-	-	-	-	-

Table IV. ENERGY IMPORTS AND EXPORTS, SELECTED YEARS, 1925–1965

(Original units)

Region, country, year	Solid fuels (10^3 m.t. coal equiv.)	Liquid fuels (10^3 m.t.)							Gas (10^6 c.m.)	Electricity (10^6 kwh)
				Refined petroleum products						
		Total	Crude oil	Total	Gasoline	Kerosine	Fuel oils	Lubes and greases		
	(1)	(2)	(3)	(4)	(5)	(6)	(7)	(8)	(9)	(10)
RHODESIA (CONTINUED)							EXPORTS			
1960	1350	-	-	-	-	-	-	-	-	-
1961	1440	3	-	3	1	-	2	-	-	1054
1962	1240	8	-	8	5	1	2	-	-	1216
1963	1240	4	-	4	2	1	1	-	-	1479
1964	1440	6	-	6	3	1	2	-	-	1751
1965	1765	107	-	107	53	5	49	-	-	1851
WEST AFRICA							IMPORTS			
1925	181	30	-	30	NA	NA	NA	NA	-	-
1929	296	119	-	119	13	7	94	5	-	-
1933	115	270	-	270	15	4	249	2	-	-
1937	399	719	-	719	29	8	678	4	-	-
1938	98	55	-	55	28	8	15	4	-	-
1950	165	818	-	818	80	30	670	38	-	-
1953	56	1408	-	1408	133	38	1225	12	-	-
1955	30	1476	-	1476	160	60	1240	16	-	-
1957	1	2263	-	2263	200	70	1980	13	-	-
1960	1	1752	-	1752	256	79	1398	15	-	-
1961	1	1736	-	1736	259	80	1379	14	-	-
1962	-	1842	-	1842	268	82	1472	16	-	-
1963	-	1876	18	1858	266	94	1477	17	-	-
1964	-	1998	290	1708	268	92	1326	18	-	-
1965	-	2185	654	1531	216	84	1210	19	-	-
SOUTH AFRICA							IMPORTS			
1925	7	129	-	129	69	41	2	17	-	-
1929	4	380	-	380	223	73	55	29	-	-
1933	-	407	-	407	244	42	96	25	-	-
1937	25	972	-	972	466	60	400	46	-	-
1938	24	1084	-	1084	514	58	473	39	-	-
1950	64	2297	-	2297	1087	352	785	73	-	-
1953	28	2513	29	2484	1268	470	668	78	-	-
1955	100	3229	940	2289	1080	481	596	132	-	-
1957	50	4130	1069	3061	1077	468	1382	134	-	-
1960	-	3749	1281	2468	1174	410	774	110	-	-
1961	-	4091	1482	2609	1224	407	852	126	-	-
1962	60	4324	1617	2707	1248	391	918	150	-	-
1963	50	4589	2190	2399	1107	406	777	109	-	-
1964	100	6499	4850	1649	676	456	365	152	-	-
1965	145	6543	4675	1868	716	390	574	188	-	-
SOUTH AFRICA							EXPORTS			
1925	1604	-	-	-	-	-	-	-	-	-
1929	1656	-	-	-	-	-	-	-	-	-
1933	782	-	-	-	-	-	-	-	-	-
1937	819	-	-	-	-	-	-	-	-	-
1938	901	-	-	-	-	-	-	-	-	-
1950	2610	-	-	-	-	-	-	-	-	-
1953	1212	-	-	-	-	-	-	-	-	-
1955	660	104	-	104	21	3	80	-	-	-
1957	600	79	-	79	23	2	54	-	-	-
1960	960	100	-	100	12	15	73	-	-	-

Table IV. ENERGY IMPORTS AND EXPORTS, SELECTED YEARS, 1925-1965

(Original units)

Region, country, year	Solid fuels (10^3 m.t. coal equiv.)	Liquid fuels (10^3 m.t.)		Refined petroleum products					Gas (10^6 c.m.)	Electricity (10^6 kwh)
		Total	Crude oil	Total	Gasoline	Kerosine	Fuel oils	Lubes and greases		
	(1)	(2)	(3)	(4)	(5)	(6)	(7)	(8)	(9)	(10)
SOUTH AFRICA (CONTINUED)							EXPORTS			
1961	1060	17	-	17	3	2	12	-	-	-
1962	1660	6	-	6	4	1	1	-	-	-
1963	1400	74	-	74	1	10	63	-	-	-
1964	1380	701	-	701	6	19	674	-	-	-
1965	1345	385	-	385	2	12	370	-	-	-
DEVELOPED COUNTRIES							IMPORTS			
1925	113097	28888	14900	13988	5114	1993	5368	1503	2	2016
1929	141232	45071	21291	23780	10285	2779	8768	1946	3	2430
1933	96685	41211	17032	24179	10074	2323	10457	1325	-	2139
1937	122148	56236	25461	30775	10958	2082	15020	1702	-	3440
1938	106498	58241	26064	32178	11985	1975	15269	1563	-	3469
1950	88428	136071	79247	56824	12559	3608	39024	1562	290	3620
1953	96289	196757	132770	63987	11566	4171	46644	1482	137	3702
1955	120677	248315	168604	79711	12300	4544	60542	2012	190	5620
1957	129277	298739	201311	97428	13462	4437	77138	2000	533	5550
1960	98385	401897	281532	120365	15676	4005	97982	2268	4179	9520
1961	98847	443333	318092	125241	15953	3759	102534	2457	5991	7948
1962	105700	497627	352382	145245	16305	7114	118287	2646	11027	6120
1963	118473	554562	397645	156917	16737	8861	127404	2835	11141	5351
1964	116653	620317	453755	166562	17387	9431	135148	3077	12166	7540
1965	113990	694883	509062	185821	17196	10712	152908	2735	13149	9527
DEVELOPED COUNTRIES							EXPORTS			
1925	127646	15747	1932	13815	3932	2837	5554	1492	4	1969
1929	150487	21610	3874	17735	7475	2674	5876	1710	7	2588
1933	98574	14820	5307	9513	3677	1242	3254	1340	59	2296
1937	124607	24997	9605	15392	4951	1376	7173	1892	136	3746
1938	105999	27717	11036	16681	6420	1185	7400	1676	49	3754
1950	84692	22374	6054	16320	4098	499	9335	2249	896	3330
1953	89529	43855	5269	38586	9787	2070	24162	2294	725	4898
1955	113608	46201	5215	40986	10637	1950	24917	2895	794	7040
1957	128636	61872	15930	45942	11096	2395	28898	2840	527	7300
1960	84120	58765	7827	50938	11214	2797	32580	3450	3076	9590
1961	84810	63046	10891	52155	11448	3095	32915	3628	4735	9833
1962	88690	71453	15027	56426	11611	3201	36561	3902	9902	6174
1963	101630	75245	15192	60053	11407	3679	39190	4410	10045	5600
1964	95765	76408	14580	61828	11971	3494	40307	4396	10960	8503
1965	94428	85623	15204	70419	13282	3756	46788	4197	11108	9194
UNDERDEVELOPED COUNTRIES							IMPORTS			
1925	16608	11664	3814	7850	1065	1512	4935	306	2	-
1929	18505	25751	14421	11330	2145	1992	6738	452	4	-
1933	12554	25377	14877	10500	1593	1260	7332	315	59	21
1937	16467	40880	24297	16583	2987	1891	11234	471	136	19
1938	15274	43953	26343	17610	3682	2232	11224	472	49	18
1950	7920	97730	63385	34345	7934	3090	21512	889	712	130
1953	7669	114163	69390	44773	11993	4364	27338	1068	598	232
1955	8274	137512	84949	52563	12243	5639	33037	1293	627	190
1957	8684	148018	91631	56387	12749	5737	36052	1452	68	410
1960	8147	147900	94853	53047	11032	6156	33806	1483	76	640
1961	7351	159571	105186	54385	10653	6742	34811	1493	76	2261

Table IV. ENERGY IMPORTS AND EXPORTS, SELECTED YEARS, 1925–1965

(Original units)

Region, country, year	Solid fuels (10^3 m.t. coal equiv.)	Liquid fuels (10^3 m.t.)		Refined petroleum products					Gas (10^6 c.m.)	Electricity (10^6 kwh)
		Total	Crude oil	Total	Gasoline	Kerosine	Fuel oils	Lubes and greases		
	(1)	(2)	(3)	(4)	(5)	(6)	(7)	(8)	(9)	(10)
UNDERDEVELOPED COUNTRIES (CONTINUED)							IMPORTS			
1962	6650	171157	118787	52370	9280	6996	33667	1630	72	2508
1963	6434	176265	124494	51771	8527	6041	34598	1739	54	2632
1964	7289	185726	136809	48917	7216	5274	33960	1607	50	2369
1965	7072	190690	145807	44883	6598	5619	30261	1394	-	2441
UNDERDEVELOPED COUNTRIES							EXPORTS			
1925	3095	27051	13903	13148	2146	834	10049	119	-	-
1929	4506	49596	27762	21834	4833	2003	14709	288	-	-
1933	3866	50441	25071	25370	6319	1542	17309	200	-	-
1937	4812	78178	37232	40946	8548	2500	29436	462	-	-
1938	5862	79459	37865	41594	9288	2801	29070	435	-	-
1950	2369	224180	132863	91317	16720	6363	68046	313	54	-
1953	4019	280073	193162	86911	15288	6434	64601	708	58	19
1955	3170	343334	245369	97965	15537	8860	72626	874	72	20
1957	3560	385656	278343	107313	16236	10191	80049	771	248	710
1960	3400	481156	355972	125184	17601	11060	95296	993	1247	770
1961	3180	518099	388572	129527	16779	11738	99823	889	1396	1792
1962	2990	581647	434868	146779	17994	12573	114588	1108	1234	1965
1963	2770	636441	482630	153811	18752	11991	121484	903	1189	2034
1964	3342	710517	550404	160113	18799	13359	125761	1167	1352	2237
1965	3172	770533	603738	166795	20278	14986	129005	1309	2135	2391
COMMUNIST COUNTRIES							IMPORTS			
1925	6892	1315	88	1227	52	882	116	43	-	69
1929	8606	1842	312	1530	144	839	259	81	-	69
1933	4249	1850	278	1572	147	693	416	70	-	17
1937	3726	2263	698	1565	393	527	365	88	-	15
1938	3919	1773	581	1192	322	369	268	69	-	-
1950	20572	4515	1995	2520	300	225	795	-	56	180
1953	24881	7802	3212	4590	360	260	970	-	116	168
1955	26110	10408	3845	6563	2771	1131	2552	109	162	320
1957	20330	12457	5637	6820	3727	949	2057	87	216	570
1960	25580	17725	8154	9571	5173	1241	2980	177	473	860
1961	27690	18644	8197	10447	5272	1228	3733	214	504	811
1962	30650	19544	9559	9985	4612	1144	4110	117	514	819
1963	33340	22079	11768	10311	4466	1120	4493	230	527	1224
1964	36930	24015	15175	8840	3814	696	4169	155	532	1934
1965	36854	26427	19105	7322	3038	560	3572	150	581	2149
COMMUNIST COUNTRIES							EXPORTS			
1925	15104	2462	67	2396	608	858	704	219	-	-
1929	23546	6680	315	6365	1937	1612	2487	319	-	-
1933	17806	10372	820	9552	3106	1563	4536	343	-	4
1937	20912	7331	716	6615	2289	1201	2855	268	-	-
1938	17824	5728	755	4973	1903	1038	1833	197	-	-
1950	33101	3870	410	3460	1265	615	780	-	25	400
1953	34587	10680	2170	8510	2010	1025	1975	-	95	170
1955	40450	15059	3312	11747	4081	1513	5990	152	140	170
1957	35160	20390	6376	14014	4498	1573	7726	214	171	570
1960	45430	41183	18267	22916	5828	1781	14680	608	446	700
1961	48710	49450	23805	25645	6271	1711	16959	685	477	820
1962	54100	54014	26668	27346	5750	1902	19021	658	509	349

Table IV. ENERGY IMPORTS AND EXPORTS, SELECTED YEARS, 1925–1965

(Original units)

Region, country, year	Solid fuels (10^3 m.t. coal equiv.)	Liquid fuels (10^3 m.t.): Total	Crude oil	Refined petroleum products: Total	Gasoline	Kerosine	Fuel oils	Lubes and greases	Gas (10^6 c.m.)	Electricity (10^6 kwh)
	(1)	(2)	(3)	(4)	(5)	(6)	(7)	(8)	(9)	(10)
COMMUNIST COUNTRIES (CONTINUED)							EXPORTS			
1963	57050	60196	30633	29563	5896	1703	21275	680	509	753
1964	61340	65849	37026	28823	5187	1232	21785	612	504	2019
1965	61100	74078	43811	30267	4691	1445	23532	584	594	2191
USSR							IMPORTS			
1925	692	65	9	56	7	40	3	6	-	-
1929	1097	102	17	85	19	49	9	8	-	-
1933	798	97	3	94	14	58	15	7	-	-
1937	1069	289	13	276	176	64	26	10	-	-
1938	1050	295	15	280	168	73	30	9	-	-
1950	11400	2700	1500	1200	NA	NA	NA	NA	-	-
1953	9900	4800	1800	3000	NA	NA	NA	NA	-	-
1955	9070	5271	1575	3696	1988	549	1050	109	-	10
1957	3760	4091	1331	2760	2023	294	356	87	-	-
1960	5370	4159	1166	2993	2174	305	391	123	-	-
1961	5320	3401	888	2513	1780	273	314	146	-	-
1962	5480	2708	496	2212	1581	244	270	117	-	-
1963	5690	2721	543	2178	1535	204	292	147	-	-
1964	5700	1975	-	1975	1386	151	283	155	-	-
1965	7395	1817	-	1817	1221	169	277	150	-	-
USSR							EXPORTS			
1925	367	1372	63	1309	278	454	477	100	-	-
1929	1339	3864	312	3552	1097	788	1450	217	-	-
1933	1818	4902	532	4370	1298	570	2249	253	-	-
1937	1312	1972	123	1849	420	244	965	220	-	-
1938	326	1447	230	1217	314	211	537	155	-	-
1950	2600	1100	300	800	NA	NA	NA	NA	25	-
1953	4400	5500	2000	3500	NA	NA	NA	NA	95	-
1955	5770	7962	2916	5046	1405	641	2848	152	140	-
1957	10750	13630	5923	7707	1705	908	4892	202	171	-
1960	14700	33106	17825	15281	2818	1093	10990	380	243	30
1961	17830	41030	23388	17642	3589	1076	12554	423	270	74
1962	22340	45292	26279	19013	3155	1295	14124	439	302	232
1963	24780	51306	30243	21063	3342	1269	16065	387	302	747
1964	27230	56531	36691	19840	2747	890	15908	295	293	1304
1965	25800	64296	43432	20864	2353	1165	17070	276	392	1501
COMMUNIST EASTERN EUROPE							IMPORTS			
1925	3398	309	79	230	20	48	16	12	-	69
1929	5186	669	295	374	45	55	43	24	-	69
1933	1924	599	275	324	11	25	33	9	-	17
1937	2222	839	527	312	15	30	59	16	-	15
1938	1729	675	406	269	15	21	51	18	-	-
1950	9172	1815	495	1320	300	225	795	-	56	180
1953	14981	3002	1412	1590	360	260	970	-	116	168
1955	16960	3762	1870	1892	523	262	1107	-	162	310
1957	16470	6066	3881	2185	864	210	1111	-	216	570
1960	20100	9996	6378	3618	1559	436	1569	54	473	860
1961	22290	11863	7229	4634	1867	395	2304	68	504	811
1962	24960	14341	8923	5418	1916	375	3125	-	514	819
1963	27610	17103	11075	6028	2006	386	3551	83	527	1224

Table IV. ENERGY IMPORTS AND EXPORTS, SELECTED YEARS, 1925-1965

(Original units)

Region, country, year	Solid fuels (10^3 m.t. coal equiv.)	Liquid fuels (10^3 m.t.)		Refined petroleum products					Gas (10^6 c.m.)	Electricity (10^6 kwh)
		Total	Crude oil	Total	Gasoline	Kerosine	Fuel oils	Lubes and greases		
	(1)	(2)	(3)	(4)	(5)	(6)	(7)	(8)	(9)	(10)
COMMUNIST EASTERN EUROPE (CONTINUED)							IMPORTS			
1964	30950	20585	14975	5610	1783	325	3496	-	532	1934
1965	29319	23580	18895	4685	1422	311	2950	-	581	2149
COMMUNIST EASTERN EUROPE							EXPORTS			
1925	12136	1090	4	1087	330	404	227	119	-	-
1929	18663	2816	3	2813	840	824	1037	102	-	-
1933	11823	5416	237	5179	1806	992	2287	90	-	4
1937	14745	5297	531	4766	1869	957	1890	48	-	-
1938	13306	4196	440	3756	1589	827	1296	42	-	-
1950	30501	2770	110	2660	1265	615	780	-	-	400
1953	30187	5180	170	5010	2010	1025	1975	-	-	170
1955	33580	7097	396	6701	2676	872	3142	-	-	170
1957	22570	6756	453	6303	2789	665	2834	12	-	570
1960	29700	8077	442	7635	3010	688	3690	228	203	670
1961	29680	8420	417	8003	2682	635	4405	262	207	746
1962	30330	8722	389	8333	2595	607	4897	219	207	117
1963	30800	8890	390	8500	2554	434	5210	293	207	6
1964	32610	9318	335	8983	2440	342	5877	317	211	715
1965	33545	9782	379	9403	2338	280	6462	308	202	690
COMMUNIST ASIA							IMPORTS			
1925	2802	941	-	941	25	794	97	25	-	-
1929	2323	1071	-	1071	80	735	207	49	-	-
1933	1527	1154	-	1154	122	610	368	54	-	-
1937	435	1135	158	977	202	433	280	62	-	-
1938	1140	803	160	643	139	275	187	42	-	-
1950	NA	NA	NA	NA	NA	NA	NA	NA	NA	NA
1953	NA	NA	NA	NA	NA	NA	NA	NA	NA	NA
1955	80	1375	400	975	260	320	395	NA	NA	NA
1957	100	2300	425	1875	840	445	590	NA	NA	NA
1960	110	3570	610	2960	1440	500	1020	NA	NA	NA
1961	80	3380	80	3300	1625	560	1115	NA	NA	NA
1962	210	2495	140	2355	1115	525	715	NA	NA	NA
1963	40	2255	150	2105	925	530	650	NA	NA	NA
1964	280	1455	200	1255	645	220	390	NA	NA	NA
1965	140	1030	210	820	395	80	345	NA	NA	NA
COMMUNIST ASIA							EXPORTS			
1925	2601	-	-	-	-	-	-	-	-	-
1929	3544	-	-	-	-	-	-	-	-	-
1933	4165	54	51	3	2	1	-	-	-	-
1937	4855	62	62	-	-	-	-	-	-	-
1938	4192	85	85	-	-	-	-	-	-	-
1950	NA	NA	NA	NA	NA	NA	NA	NA	NA	NA
1953	NA	NA	NA	NA	NA	NA	NA	NA	NA	NA
1955	1100	-	-	-	-	-	-	NA	NA	NA
1957	1840	4	-	4	4	-	-	NA	NA	NA
1960	1030	-	-	-	-	-	-	NA	NA	NA
1961	1200	-	-	-	-	-	-	NA	NA	NA
1962	1430	-	-	-	-	-	-	NA	NA	NA
1963	1470	-	-	-	-	-	-	NA	NA	NA

Table IV. ENERGY IMPORTS AND EXPORTS, SELECTED YEARS, 1925-1965

(Original units)

Region, country, year	Solid fuels (10^3 m.t. coal equiv.)	Liquid fuels (10^3 m.t.)							Gas (10^6 c.m.)	Electricity (10^6 kwh)
				Refined petroleum products						
		Total	Crude oil	Total	Gasoline	Kerosine	Fuel oils	Lubes and greases		
	(1)	(2)	(3)	(4)	(5)	(6)	(7)	(8)	(9)	(10)
COMMUNIST ASIA (CONTINUED)								EXPORTS		
1964	1500	-	-	-	-	-	-	NA	NA	NA
1965	1755	-	-	-	-	-	-	NA	NA	NA
ORGANISATION FOR ECONOMIC CO-OPERATION AND DEVELOPMENT (OECD)								IMPORTS		
1925	111004	27730	14676	13054	4557	1815	5257	1416	2	2016
1929	138443	42717	20722	21995	9064	2512	8607	1812	3	2430
1933	95007	38949	16681	22268	8955	2082	10006	1225	-	2139
1937	119026	52405	25058	27347	9073	1741	13975	1545	-	3440
1938	103763	54038	25651	28387	9904	1651	14023	1424	-	3469
1950	85104	126994	78045	48949	9027	2842	35700	1309	290	3620
1953	93364	187095	131387	55708	7416	3379	43456	1333	137	3702
1955	116468	234041	162291	71750	8523	3672	57558	1684	190	5620
1957	123986	280599	190727	89872	10755	3659	73404	1663	533	5550
1960	93260	380922	267414	113508	12963	3292	94952	1867	4179	9100
1961	93870	420838	302754	118084	13277	2991	99263	2017	5991	7773
1962	100900	474200	337841	136359	13197	6225	113821	2226	11027	6038
1963	114020	528550	380666	147884	13585	7898	122932	2393	11141	5014
1964	110800	590817	432836	157981	14746	8504	130592	2624	12166	6502
1965	107959	662595	484949	177646	15180	9744	148132	2326	13149	8563
ORGANISATION FOR ECONOMIC CO-OPERATION AND DEVELOPMENT (OECD)								EXPORTS		
1925	125153	15741	1931	13810	3930	2836	5553	1491	4	1969
1929	148863	21599	3873	17725	7475	2667	5875	1708	7	2588
1933	97997	14820	5307	9513	3677	1242	3254	1340	59	2296
1937	123632	24995	9605	15390	4951	1376	7172	1891	136	3746
1938	104949	27716	11036	16680	6420	1185	7399	1676	49	3754
1950	81887	22337	6054	16283	4094	494	9310	2246	896	3330
1953	87809	43802	5269	38533	9783	2069	24117	2291	725	4863
1955	112628	45736	5215	40521	10486	1940	24614	2894	794	6990
1957	127016	60810	15930	44880	10898	2374	28064	2837	527	7150
1960	81350	56928	7827	49101	11031	2716	31024	3442	3076	9500
1961	80610	60823	10712	50111	11195	2926	31314	3612	4735	9755
1962	83870	68780	14466	54314	11467	3125	34696	3872	9902	6018
1963	96800	72848	14737	58111	11253	3568	37573	4348	10045	5305
1964	89235	74142	14264	59878	11792	3420	38708	4299	10960	8503
1965	85618	84061	15059	69002	13173	3679	45644	4114	11108	9194
COMMUNIST COUNTRIES								IMPORTS		
1925	6892	1315	88	1227	52	882	116	43	-	69
1929	8606	1842	312	1530	144	839	259	81	-	69
1933	4249	1850	278	1572	147	693	416	70	-	17
1937	3726	2263	698	1565	393	527	365	88	-	15
1938	3919	1773	581	1192	322	369	268	69	-	-
1950	20572	4515	1995	2520	300	225	795	-	56	180
1953	24881	7802	3212	4590	360	260	970	-	116	168
1955	26110	10408	3845	6563	2771	1131	2552	109	162	320
1957	20330	12457	5637	6820	3727	949	2057	87	216	570
1960	25580	17725	8154	9571	5173	1241	2980	177	473	860
1961	27690	18644	8197	10447	5272	1228	3733	214	504	811
1962	30650	19544	9559	9985	4612	1144	4110	117	514	819
1963	33340	22079	11768	10311	4466	1120	4493	230	527	1224
1964	36930	24015	15175	8840	3814	696	4169	155	532	1934

Table IV. ENERGY IMPORTS AND EXPORTS, SELECTED YEARS, 1925-1965

(Original units)

Region, country, year	Solid fuels (10^3 m.t. coal equiv.)	Liquid fuels (10^3 m.t.)							Gas (10^6 c.m.)	Electricity (10^6 kwh)
				Refined petroleum products						
		Total	Crude oil	Total	Gasoline	Kerosine	Fuel oils	Lubes and greases		
	(1)	(2)	(3)	(4)	(5)	(6)	(7)	(8)	(9)	(10)
COMMUNIST COUNTRIES (CONTINUED)							IMPORTS			
1965	36854	26427	19105	7322	3038	560	3572	150	581	2149
COMMUNIST COUNTRIES							EXPORTS			
1925	15104	2462	67	2396	608	858	704	219	-	-
1929	23546	6680	315	6365	1937	1612	2487	319	-	-
1933	17806	10372	820	9552	3106	1563	4536	343	-	4
1937	20912	7331	716	6615	2289	1201	2855	268	-	-
1938	17824	5728	755	4973	1903	1038	1833	197	-	-
1950	33101	3870	410	3460	1265	615	780	-	25	400
1953	34587	10680	2170	8510	2010	1025	1975	-	95	170
1955	40450	15059	3312	11747	4081	1513	5990	152	140	170
1957	35160	20390	6376	14014	4498	1573	7726	214	171	570
1960	45430	41183	18267	22916	5828	1781	14680	608	446	700
1961	48710	49450	23805	25645	6271	1711	16959	685	477	820
1962	54100	54014	26668	27346	5750	1902	19021	658	509	349
1963	57050	60196	30633	29563	5896	1703	21275	680	509	753
1964	61340	65849	37026	28823	5187	1232	21785	612	504	2019
1965	61100	74078	43811	30267	4691	1445	23532	584	594	2191
WORLD EXCLUDING OECD AND COMMUNIST COUNTRIES							IMPORTS			
1925	18701	12822	4038	8784	1622	1690	5046	393	2	-
1929	21294	28105	14990	13115	3366	2259	6899	586	4	-
1933	14232	27639	15228	12411	2712	1501	7783	415	59	21
1937	19589	44711	24700	20011	4872	2232	12279	628	136	19
1938	18009	48156	26755	21401	5763	2556	12470	611	49	18
1950	11244	106807	64587	42220	11466	3856	24836	1142	712	130
1953	10594	123825	70773	53052	16143	5156	30526	1217	598	232
1955	12483	151786	91262	60524	16020	6511	36021	1621	627	190
1957	13975	166158	102215	63943	15456	6515	39786	1789	68	410
1960	13272	168875	108971	59904	13745	6869	36836	1884	76	1060
1961	12328	182066	120524	61542	13329	7510	38082	1933	76	2436
1962	11450	194584	133328	61256	12388	7885	38133	2050	72	2590
1963	10887	202277	141473	60804	11679	7004	39070	2181	54	2969
1964	13142	215226	157728	57498	9857	6201	38516	2060	50	3407
1965	13103	222978	169920	53058	8614	6587	35037	1803	-	3405
WORLD EXCLUDING OECD AND COMMUNIST COUNTRIES							EXPORTS			
1925	5588	27057	13904	13153	2148	835	10050	120	-	-
1929	6130	49607	27763	21844	4833	2010	14710	290	-	-
1933	4443	50441	25071	25370	6319	1542	17309	200	-	-
1937	5787	78180	37232	40948	8548	2500	29437	463	-	-
1938	6912	79460	37865	41595	9288	2801	29071	435	-	-
1950	5174	224217	132863	91354	16724	6368	68071	316	54	-
1953	5739	280126	193162	86964	15292	6435	64646	711	58	54
1955	4150	343799	245369	98430	15688	8870	72929	875	72	70
1957	5180	386718	278343	108375	16434	10212	80883	774	248	860
1960	6170	482993	355972	127021	17784	11141	96852	1001	1247	860
1961	7380	520322	388751	131571	17032	11907	101424	905	1396	1870
1962	7810	584320	435429	148891	18138	12649	116453	1138	1234	2121
1963	7600	638838	483085	155753	18906	12102	123101	965	1189	2329
1964	9872	712783	550720	162063	18978	13433	127360	1264	1352	2237
1965	11982	772095	603883	168212	20387	15063	130149	1392	2135	2391

DERIVATION OF TABLE V

For each year, imports minus exports from correspondingly numbered columns in table IV.

Table V. NET ENERGY IMPORTS OR EXPORTS, SELECTED YEARS, 1925-1965

(Original units; minus sign [-] = net exports)

Region, country, year	Solid fuels (10^3 m.t. coal equiv.)	Liquid fuels (10^3 m.t.)							Gas (10^6 c.m.)	Electricity (10^6 kwh)
				Refined petroleum products						
		Total	Crude oil	Total	Gasoline	Kerosine	Fuel oils	Lubes and greases		
	(1)	(2)	(3)	(4)	(5)	(6)	(7)	(8)	(9)	(10)
WORLD										
1925	-9248	-3393	2900	-6294	-455	-142	-5888	22	-	116
1929	-10196	-5222	4073	-9294	-1671	-679	-7307	162	-	-89
1933	-6758	-7195	989	-8184	-1288	-71	-6894	-173	-	-123
1937	-7990	-11127	2903	-14030	-1450	-577	-12845	-361	-	-272
1938	-3994	-8937	3332	-12268	-1622	-448	-11542	-204	-	-267
1950	-3242	-12108	5300	-17408	-1290	-554	-16830	-111	83	200
1953	704	-15886	4771	-20657	-3166	-734	-15786	-452	-27	-985
1955	-2167	-8359	3502	-11861	-2941	-1009	-7402	-507	-27	-1100
1957	-9065	-8704	-2070	-6634	-1892	-3036	-1426	-286	-129	-2050
1960	-838	-13582	2473	-16055	-2762	-4236	-7788	-1123	-41	-40
1961	-2812	-9047	8207	-17254	-2620	-4815	-8619	-1038	-37	-1425
1962	-2780	-18786	4165	-22951	-5158	-2422	-14106	-1275	-32	959
1963	-3203	-18976	5452	-24428	-6325	-1351	-15454	-1189	-21	820
1964	425	-22716	3729	-26445	-7540	-2684	-14576	-1336	-68	-916
1965	-784	-18234	11221	-29455	-11419	-3296	-12584	-1811	-107	341
NORTH AMERICA										
1925	-3655	-694	9554	-10248	-3004	-2722	-3182	-1341	-2	-
1929	-2122	363	12443	-12080	-5695	-2544	-2373	-1470	-4	-
1933	1520	-2743	3490	-6233	-3273	-1154	-674	-1132	-59	-21

Table V. NET ENERGY IMPORTS OR EXPORTS, SELECTED YEARS, 1925-1965

(Original units; minus sign [-] = net exports)

Region, country, year	Solid fuels (10^3 m.t. coal equiv.)	Liquid fuels (10^3 m.t.)							Gas (10^6 c.m.)	Electricity (10^6 kwh)
				Refined petroleum products						
		Total	Crude oil	Total	Gasoline	Kerosine	Fuel oils	Lubes and greases		
	(1)	(2)	(3)	(4)	(5)	(6)	(7)	(8)	(9)	(10)
NORTH AMERICA (CONTINUED)										
1937	58	-8654	1050	-9704	-4206	-1140	-2852	-1506	-136	-19
1938	786	-12303	-1309	-10994	-5477	-949	-3291	-1277	-49	-18
1950	-2156	46436	32461	13975	-1343	157	17105	-1876	-657	-160
1953	-12079	53894	43050	10844	-2829	-421	15839	-1609	-593	-217
1955	-31780	66840	51395	15445	-2133	103	19511	-1772	-577	-200
1957	-55760	70091	54806	15285	-1727	-218	19244	-1723	158	-450
1960	-22760	103201	67594	35607	1540	504	35953	-2026	1158	-570
1961	-22820	105906	67322	38584	2132	387	38729	-2226	1288	-532
1962	-25900	111685	69584	42101	991	2515	41209	-2309	1157	-571
1963	-34360	114552	71602	42950	1316	3297	41098	-2398	1122	-591
1964	-32390	121780	73657	48123	960	3307	45693	-2399	1162	-147
1965	-32423	134911	74837	60074	1018	4155	57710	-2146	1213	-60
CANADA										
1925	14847	2690	2231	459	275	13	134	37	2	-1273
1929	16816	5373	4584	789	567	12	135	75	3	-1423
1933	10447	4484	4021	463	175	2	244	42	-	-988
1937	13337	6110	5649	461	232	6	162	61	-6	-1846
1938	11780	5646	4971	675	380	19	209	67	-7	-1826
1950	24260	14952	11607	3345	1021	369	1806	78	149	-1830
1953	21161	15755	11492	4263	962	494	2537	151	-52	-2332
1955	17690	15025	10495	4530	634	513	3092	190	-5	-4270
1957	17820	12316	8556	3760	548	436	2506	171	266	-4260
1960	11680	16104	12041	4063	150	581	3264	174	-2923	-5130
1961	10420	13151	9850	3301	143	356	2772	163	-4604	-2786
1962	10730	9732	6474	3258	59	319	2890	155	-9766	-1293
1963	11350	12073	8363	3710	233	360	3143	158	-9901	-745
1964	12620	11091	6532	4559	181	348	4170	192	-10838	-1241
1965	14360	12572	5600	6972	249	300	6858	231	-10990	13
UNITED STATES										
1925	-18508	-3385	7323	-10708	-3279	-2735	-3316	-1378	-4	1273
1929	-18944	-5012	7859	-12871	-6262	-2556	-2508	-1545	-7	1423
1933	-8939	-7228	-531	-6697	-3448	-1156	-919	-1174	-59	967
1937	-13303	-14766	-4599	-10167	-4439	-1146	-3015	-1567	-130	1827
1938	-11020	-17950	-6280	-11670	-5857	-968	-3501	-1344	-42	1808
1950	-26428	31484	20854	10630	-2364	-212	15299	-1954	-806	1670
1953	-33250	38136	31558	6578	-3794	-915	13302	-1760	-541	2115
1955	-49500	51770	40900	10870	-2769	-411	16377	-1962	-572	4070
1957	-73600	57738	46250	11488	-2277	-655	16704	-1894	-108	3810
1960	-34460	87051	55553	31498	1387	-78	32648	-2201	4081	4560
1961	-33250	92676	57472	35204	1986	28	35884	-2389	5892	2254
1962	-36650	101887	63110	38777	928	2194	38260	-2465	10923	722
1963	-45740	102405	63239	39166	1079	2934	37889	-2557	11023	154
1964	-45030	110593	67125	43468	775	2956	42435	-2592	12000	1094
1965	-46800	122233	69237	52996	763	3847	50761	-2378	12203	-73
WESTERN EUROPE										
1925	-8116	12155	2790	9365	3596	1619	2880	1261	-	47
1929	-7203	18821	2804	16018	7294	2080	5065	1579	-	-158

Table V. NET ENERGY IMPORTS OR EXPORTS, SELECTED YEARS, 1925-1965

(Original units; minus sign [-] = net exports)

Region, country, year	Solid fuels (10^3 m.t. coal equiv.)	Liquid fuels (10^3 m.t.)		Refined petroleum products					Gas (10^6 c.m.)	Electricity (10^6 kwh)
		Total	Crude oil	Total	Gasoline	Kerosine	Fuel oils	Lubes and greases		
	(1)	(2)	(3)	(4)	(5)	(6)	(7)	(8)	(9)	(10)
WESTERN EUROPE (CONTINUED)										
1933	-4715	24067	5483	18584	8619	1561	7377	1027	-	-136
1937	-5906	32022	11135	20887	8420	1600	9661	1206	-	-287
1938	-4335	34407	12827	21580	9076	1507	9915	1082	-	-267
1950	7533	57181	38702	18479	6343	2127	9090	919	51	450
1953	15817	81886	78447	3439	220	1556	1085	591	5	-979
1955	36927	111771	98886	12885	-12	1402	10995	511	-27	-1220
1957	51131	133894	108114	25780	1549	1315	22497	450	-152	-1300
1960	31163	191199	166509	24690	270	-96	24310	306	-55	500
1961	29384	214155	192113	22042	51	-559	22226	424	-32	-1353
1962	35425	246539	213136	33403	1028	543	31523	371	-32	517
1963	44620	281885	241906	39979	1280	1083	37357	380	-26	342
1964	46104	323994	282191	41803	1927	2010	37565	381	44	-816
1965	43172	364485	325979	38506	948	2127	35242	147	828	393
EUROPEAN ECONOMIC COMMUNITY (EEC)										
1925	21404	4763	357	4406	1881	786	952	787	-	723
1929	24785	8133	562	7571	3590	791	2158	1032	-	972
1933	12006	11051	3338	7713	3736	507	2962	508	-	1138
1937	4947	16047	8570	7477	2300	313	4271	593	-	1598
1938	4094	17371	9964	7407	2403	215	4267	522	-	1637
1950	-5072	24240	25855	-1615	-326	5	-1550	256	51	1730
1953	4917	37899	49241	-11342	-3839	-790	-6721	24	5	1161
1955	10850	54026	65247	-11221	-4270	-1023	-5905	45	-27	1220
1957	31170	66492	71102	-4610	-3488	-983	-101	69	-152	780
1960	13330	97094	105853	-8759	-4787	-1309	-2387	-86	-59	4070
1961	13140	113287	124445	-11158	-5633	-1465	-3842	-6	-32	4347
1962	17100	135083	138706	-3623	-5055	-1519	3129	13	-32	3196
1963	28900	159314	162663	-3349	-5439	-1618	3967	-7	-26	4377
1964	27905	188119	192500	-4381	-5245	-1571	2798	-62	-46	4589
1965	24529	215861	226727	-10866	-6294	-1708	-2042	-288	184	6302
BELGIUM-LUXEMBOURG										
1925	7630	330	8	322	155	85	21	61	-	-
1929	10287	425	1	424	193	71	90	70	-	-
1933	2666	407	49	358	231	30	64	33	-	-20
1937	3488	838	281	557	297	6	160	94	-	8
1938	408	828	308	520	292	5	145	78	-	5
1950	358	2289	442	1847	650	31	1082	84	-9	60
1953	233	3410	2933	477	267	14	142	72	-10	-58
1955	-930	5250	4680	570	43	-77	437	95	-23	90
1957	3870	6441	5425	1016	85	-94	838	97	-32	-140
1960	5020	7532	6861	671	-106	-193	770	60	-27	20
1961	4790	9109	7838	1271	-5	-131	1145	67	-27	-282
1962	5410	10724	8534	2190	-3	-134	2007	86	-23	-364
1963	8410	12876	12152	724	-493	-179	1098	84	-27	-3
1964	8350	14841	13284	1557	-349	-355	1936	92	-23	381
1965	8460	16660	15467	1193	-532	-395	1869	55	-23	723
FRANCE										
1925	27254	1900	102	1798	990	244	235	329	-	267

Table V. NET ENERGY IMPORTS OR EXPORTS, SELECTED YEARS, 1925-1965

(Original units; minus sign [-] = net exports)

Region, country, year	Solid fuels (10^3 m.t. coal equiv.)	Liquid fuels (10^3 m.t.)							Gas (10^6 c.m.)	Electricity (10^6 kwh)
				Refined petroleum products						
		Total	Crude oil	Total	Gasoline	Kerosine	Fuel oils	Lubes and greases		
	(1)	(2)	(3)	(4)	(5)	(6)	(7)	(8)	(9)	(10)
FRANCE (CONTINUED)										
1929	31672	3075	175	2900	1727	214	712	247	-	486
1933	23553	5547	2799	2748	1845	54	693	156	-	510
1937	28746	7244	6139	1105	521	-74	584	74	-	571
1938	20881	7721	6968	753	483	-95	306	59	-	570
1950	11300	11425	14124	-2699	-557	-89	-2093	40	9	240
1953	12100	15782	22001	-6219	-1421	-263	-4495	-40	37	-11
1955	9800	20234	24814	-4580	-844	-472	-3072	-122	59	-70
1957	22050	22846	24064	-1218	-421	-363	-289	-75	131	270
1960	13750	27156	31021	-3865	-844	-616	-2125	-174	90	-100
1961	13630	29908	35016	-5108	-1060	-688	-3047	-172	90	94
1962	13870	32766	37160	-4394	-673	-600	-2813	-168	95	-753
1963	20990	39441	43258	-3817	-695	-840	-1928	-200	104	570
1964	18770	45613	49274	-3661	-887	-664	-1659	-230	72	2228
1965	15838	52372	58556	-6184	-1387	-472	-3789	-206	302	973
GERMANY										
1925	-29639	1097	53	1044	433	146	190	275	-	229
1929	-36434	2412	90	2322	1058	149	533	582	-	220
1933	-25678	2347	281	2066	997	97	773	199	-	450
1937	-42404	3717	732	2985	1046	48	1582	309	-	800
1938	-31729	4303	778	3525	1351	22	1860	292	-	800
GERMANY, FEDERAL REPUBLIC										
1950	-28685	2755	1933	822	240	3	571	8	-49	1270
1953	-21093	5167	4560	607	-65	-34	770	-64	-31	1291
1955	-14320	9139	7111	2028	-58	8	2066	51	-77	1160
1957	-13010	13437	8158	5279	333	32	4929	69	-265	270
1960	-18710	27573	23235	4338	239	216	3973	83	-126	4160
1961	-18090	31827	29364	2463	-373	156	2802	92	-104	4324
1962	-17680	41995	33201	8794	123	-29	8759	144	-113	3064
1963	-17550	49310	40077	9233	112	-4	9220	89	-117	2465
1964	-14565	59897	51276	8621	376	114	8148	147	-99	960
1965	-12729	70042	59047	10995	726	231	10070	93	-95	4241
ITALY										
1925	10381	785	37	748	189	116	362	81	-	227
1929	14505	1270	60	1210	385	162	587	76	-	244
1933	9477	1701	135	1566	289	137	1082	58	-	177
1937	12851	2446	936	1510	194	74	1176	66	-	194
1938	12081	2491	1477	1014	36	31	909	38	-	244
1950	8215	4541	4556	-15	-224	-107	220	96	-	200
1953	9172	9051	12850	-3799	-1319	-457	-2065	42	-	-48
1955	10330	12520	17001	-4481	-1623	-458	-2415	-20	-	20
1957	11610	15778	19917	-4139	-1451	-327	-2418	20	-	460
1960	10210	23388	28257	-4869	-1761	-324	-2846	39	-	-130
1961	10150	27771	32941	-5170	-1680	-396	-3200	80	-	168
1962	10860	34547	39886	-5339	-1750	-374	-3302	72	-	1269
1963	11470	40248	46286	-6038	-1693	-359	-4060	103	-	1299
1964	10675	46968	55234	-8266	-1707	-395	-6183	65	-	1002
1965	10590	53305	67289	-13984	-2394	-755	-10651	-49	-	331

Table V. NET ENERGY IMPORTS OR EXPORTS, SELECTED YEARS, 1925-1965

(Original units; minus sign [–] = net exports)

Region, country, year	Solid fuels (10^3 m.t. coal equiv.)	Liquid fuels (10^3 m.t.) Total	Crude oil	Refined petroleum products Total	Gasoline	Kerosine	Fuel oils	Lubes and greases	Gas (10^6 c.m.)	Electricity (10^6 kwh)
	(1)	(2)	(3)	(4)	(5)	(6)	(7)	(8)	(9)	(10)
NETHERLANDS										
1925	5778	651	157	494	114	195	144	41	-	-
1929	4755	951	236	715	227	195	236	57	-	22
1933	1988	1049	74	975	374	189	350	62	-	21
1937	2266	1802	482	1320	242	259	769	50	-	25
1938	2453	2028	433	1595	241	252	1047	55	-	18
1950	3740	3230	4800	-1570	-435	167	-1330	28	100	-40
1953	4505	4489	6897	-2408	-1301	-50	-1073	14	9	-13
1955	5970	6883	11641	-4758	-1788	-24	-2921	41	14	20
1957	6650	7990	13538	-5548	-2034	-231	-3161	-42	14	-80
1960	3060	11445	16479	-5034	-2315	-392	-2159	-94	4	120
1961	2660	14672	19286	-4614	-2515	-406	-1542	-73	9	43
1962	4640	15051	19925	-4874	-2752	-382	-1522	-121	9	-20
1963	5580	17439	20890	-3451	-2670	-236	-363	-83	14	46
1964	4675	20800	23432	-2632	-2678	-271	556	-136	4	18
1965	2370	23482	26368	-2886	-2707	-317	459	-181	-	34
EUROPEAN FREE TRADE ASSOCIATION (EFTA)										
1925	-35922	6547	2397	4150	1445	684	1619	402	-	-676
1929	-39933	9310	2098	7213	3190	1119	2439	465	-	-1130
1933	-22194	11126	1871	9255	4285	887	3620	463	-	-1274
1937	-17758	13914	2346	11568	5479	1043	4513	533	-	-1885
1938	-14746	14882	2603	12279	6003	1052	4739	485	-	-1904
1950	6776	25837	9542	16295	5621	1855	8280	539	-	-1280
1953	5100	34723	25592	9131	2926	2015	3759	428	-	-2105
1955	19480	46668	29706	16962	3092	2041	11451	323	-	-2450
1957	13150	52436	30652	21784	4058	1955	15451	252	-	-1900
1960	10920	77785	48871	28914	4995	995	22570	262	4	-3760
1961	9280	83401	55252	28149	5651	647	21434	304	-	-5538
1962	10380	91240	59719	31521	6141	1736	23298	217	-	-2350
1963	8100	100159	62746	37413	6714	2318	27955	295	-	-3248
1964	9470	110792	70455	40337	7142	3179	29552	273	90	-4871
1965	9847	120476	78333	42143	7232	3406	30850	303	644	-6261
AUSTRIA										
1925	5060	123	18	105	47	25	20	13	-	-30
1929	6417	229	51	178	104	31	32	11	-	-120
1933	3046	313	198	115	50	9	50	6	-	-301
1937	3319	321	106	215	81	39	88	7	-	-342
1938	3773	329	155	174	72	23	71	8	-	-367
1950	5243	-1055	-1070	15	49	-	-42	8	-	-690
1953	4223	-2164	-2100	-64	1	-	-75	10	-	-1090
1955	4950	-1277	-1450	173	85	-15	83	20	-	-1080
1957	5610	-1030	-1124	94	148	-10	-70	25	-	-1240
1960	4950	501	-468	969	303	-	631	27	-	-1900
1961	4520	993	-232	1225	422	-	763	33	-	-1949
1962	4790	1469	132	1337	528	7	757	28	-	-2099
1963	5340	1735	282	1453	523	7	887	29	-	-1693
1964	5120	2439	788	1651	476	7	1192	-28	-	-2708
1965	4545	2215	661	1554	467	7	1100	-24	-	-3870

Table V. NET ENERGY IMPORTS OR EXPORTS, SELECTED YEARS, 1925-1965

(Original units; minus sign [-] = net exports)

Region, country, year	Solid fuels (10^3 m.t. coal equiv.)	Liquid fuels (10^3 m.t.)		Refined petroleum products					Gas (10^6 c.m.)	Electricity (10^6 kwh)
		Total	Crude oil	Total	Gasoline	Kerosine	Fuel oils	Lubes and greases		
	(1)	(2)	(3)	(4)	(5)	(6)	(7)	(8)	(9)	(10)
DENMARK										
1925	4022	298	1	297	98	97	80	22	-	20
1929	5500	427	3	425	174	89	140	22	-	35
1933	4902	571	-	571	219	90	236	26	-	14
1937	6024	706	-	706	303	90	288	25	-	15
1938	5396	860	11	849	336	117	369	27	-	24
1950	5731	1804	34	1770	513	69	1149	39	-	180
1953	6059	2115	21	2094	562	95	1401	36	-	296
1955	7340	3234	30	3204	693	133	2268	50	-	-110
1957	4410	3916	30	3886	782	132	2848	49	-	380
1960	5260	5176	35	5141	997	271	3734	60	-	100
1961	4930	5798	237	5561	1096	317	3991	67	-	881
1962	5260	6825	1256	5569	1036	316	4048	78	-	895
1963	5300	7939	1990	5949	858	397	4548	63	-	432
1964	4760	9227	3040	6187	882	385	4763	79	-	819
1965	4190	10244	3676	6568	866	408	5138	73	-	1736
NORWAY										
1925	1988	194	18	176	36	43	86	11	-	-
1929	2677	277	23	254	77	38	128	11	-	-
1933	2313	442	21	421	98	34	279	10	-	-
1937	3176	550	17	533	166	39	316	12	-	-
1938	2647	589	37	552	176	30	337	9	-	-
1950	1696	1428	16	1412	257	38	1088	29	-	-
1953	1384	2184	75	2109	319	78	1687	25	-	-
1955	1130	2839	96	2743	336	111	2273	22	-	-
1957	830	2972	116	2856	356	160	2311	28	-	-
1960	820	3653	220	3433	457	200	2752	22	-	130
1961	760	3805	1739	2066	263	201	1586	23	-	8
1962	680	3951	2354	1597	316	168	1103	22	-	-287
1963	800	4361	2535	1826	320	205	1286	23	-	-945
1964	880	4788	2931	1857	210	209	1420	26	-	-1391
1965	750	4651	2822	1829	392	220	1255	-23	-	-2162
PORTUGAL										
1925	995	60	-	60	14	24	19	3	-	-
1929	1146	111	-	111	40	35	36	-	-	-
1933	1109	141	-	141	51	48	42	-	-	-
1937	1357	193	-	193	73	52	56	12	-	-
1938	1152	195	-	195	74	50	60	11	-	-
1950	817	781	265	516	64	53	387	12	-	-
1953	578	1126	132	994	128	121	727	16	-	-
1955	500	1427	910	517	-10	41	464	21	-	-
1957	560	1651	1108	543	18	28	473	24	-	-
1960	390	1842	1301	541	-13	19	504	29	-	-
1961	550	1967	1306	661	-8	-17	642	33	-	1
1962	530	2122	1334	788	20	12	706	31	-	1
1963	620	2256	1497	759	12	-25	711	33	-	-55
1964	630	2445	1519	926	39	6	785	37	-	-12
1965	620	2752	1705	1047	83	-62	895	43	-	432

Table V. NET ENERGY IMPORTS OR EXPORTS, SELECTED YEARS, 1925-1965

(Original units; minus sign [–] = net exports)

Region, country, year	Solid fuels (10^3 m.t. coal equiv.)	Liquid fuels (10^3 m.t.)		Refined petroleum products					Gas (10^6 c.m.)	Electricity (10^6 kwh)
		Total	Crude oil	Total	Gasoline	Kerosine	Fuel oils	Lubes and greases		
	(1)	(2)	(3)	(4)	(5)	(6)	(7)	(8)	(9)	(10)
SWEDEN										
1925	4256	296	-	296	137	61	63	35	-	-20
1929	6275	476	-	476	250	65	118	43	-	-35
1933	6060	753	57	696	328	81	246	41	-	-14
1937	8962	1146	80	1066	484	102	425	55	-	-15
1938	7733	1294	92	1202	542	108	492	60	-	-24
1950	6603	3639	903	2736	501	219	1953	63	-	-180
1953	5543	5540	1421	4119	779	370	2913	57	-	-298
1955	5530	8068	1889	6179	927	368	4806	85	-	120
1957	4910	9365	1994	7371	1211	304	5777	87	-	-390
1960	3570	13098	2646	10452	1521	357	8492	87	-	-770
1961	3260	13252	2592	10660	1548	336	8695	80	-	-997
1962	3240	14687	2460	12227	1865	376	9889	92	-	-797
1963	3210	15913	2748	13165	1948	408	10722	84	-	48
1964	3460	17678	3557	14121	2110	413	11490	106	-	-205
1965	2960	18684	3725	14959	2293	405	12148	110	-	-805
SWITZERLAND										
1925	2701	148	-	148	70	25	38	15	-	-646
1929	3463	261	-	261	140	27	73	21	-	-1010
1933	3165	393	-	393	195	24	154	20	-	-973
1937	3486	397	-	397	194	20	163	20	-	-1543
1938	3337	409	-	409	201	20	169	19	-	-1537
1950	2549	1000	-	1000	299	66	595	40	-	-590
1953	2204	1235	-	1235	388	102	716	28	-	-1013
1955	2610	1927	-	1927	541	41	1299	44	-	-1380
1957	3320	2595	-	2595	656	62	1820	54	-	-650
1960	2600	3842	-	3842	990	55	2731	59	-	-1320
1961	2260	4167	-	4167	1151	57	2890	67	-	-3478
1962	2330	4826	-	4826	1352	49	3355	69	-	-150
1963	2820	6508	359	6149	1272	78	4711	79	-	-1024
1964	1980	6686	838	5848	1283	84	4396	74	-	-1164
1965	1572	7807	1209	6598	1313	75	5125	72	-	-1650
UNITED KINGDOM										
1925	-54944	5428	2360	3068	1043	409	1313	303	-	-
1929	-65411	7529	2021	5508	2405	834	1912	357	-	-
1933	-42789	8513	1595	6918	3344	601	2613	360	-	-
1937	-44082	10601	2143	8458	4178	701	3177	402	-	-
1938	-38784	11206	2308	8898	4602	704	3241	351	-	-
1950	-15863	18240	9394	8846	3938	1410	3150	348	-	-
1953	-14891	24687	26043	-1356	749	1249	-3610	256	-	-
1955	-2580	30450	28231	2219	520	1362	258	81	-	-
1957	-6490	32967	28528	4439	887	1279	2292	-15	-	-
1960	-6670	49673	45137	4536	740	93	3726	-22	4	-
1961	-7000	53419	49610	3809	1179	-247	2867	1	-	-4
1962	-6450	57360	52183	5177	1024	808	3440	-103	-	87
1963	-9990	61447	53335	8112	1781	1248	5090	-16	-	-11
1964	-7360	67529	57782	9747	2142	2075	5506	-21	90	-210
1965	-4790	74123	64535	9588	1818	2353	5189	52	644	58

Table V. NET ENERGY IMPORTS OR EXPORTS, SELECTED YEARS, 1925-1965

(Original units; minus sign [-] = net exports)

Region, country, year	Solid fuels (10^3 m.t. coal equiv.)	Liquid fuels (10^3 m.t.) Total	Crude oil	Refined petroleum products Total	Gasoline	Kerosine	Fuel oils	Lubes and greases	Gas (10^6 c.m.)	Electricity (10^6 kwh)
	(1)	(2)	(3)	(4)	(5)	(6)	(7)	(8)	(9)	(10)
WESTERN EUROPE - OTHER										
1925	6402	845	36	809	270	149	309	72	-	-
1929	7945	1378	144	1234	514	170	468	82	-	-
1933	5473	1890	274	1616	598	167	795	56	-	-
1937	6905	2061	219	1842	641	244	877	80	-	-
1938	6317	2154	260	1894	670	240	909	75	-	-
1950	5829	7104	3305	3799	1048	267	2360	124	-	-
1953	5800	9264	3614	5650	1133	331	4047	139	-	-35
1955	6597	11077	3933	7144	1166	384	5449	143	-	10
1957	6811	14966	6360	8606	979	343	7147	129	-	-180
1960	6913	16320	11785	4535	62	218	4127	130	-	190
1961	6964	17467	12416	5051	33	259	4634	126	-	-162
1962	7945	20216	14711	5505	-58	326	5096	141	-	-329
1963	7620	22412	16497	5915	5	383	5435	92	-	-787
1964	8729	25083	19236	5847	30	402	5215	170	-	-534
1965	8796	28148	20919	7229	10	429	6434	132	-	352
FINLAND										
1925	612	76	9	67	29	29	-	9	-	-
1929	1170	129	13	116	68	36	-	12	-	-
1933	1138	119	14	105	60	36	-	9	-	-
1937	2235	223	27	196	117	65	-	14	-	-
1938	1784	248	32	216	137	65	-	14	-	-
1950	1929	489	-	489	244	67	158	20	-	-
1953	1980	720	-	720	304	72	332	12	-	-5
1955	2630	1110	-	1110	359	75	653	23	-	-
1957	3040	1881	216	1665	349	60	1228	29	-	-
1960	3140	2690	1137	1553	46	32	1441	37	-	420
1961	3000	2971	1383	1588	34	27	1483	46	-	175
1962	2940	3498	1512	1986	18	25	1893	50	-	82
1963	2470	4269	2230	2039	20	27	1944	48	-	337
1964	3190	4905	2580	2325	13	23	2228	60	-	696
1965	3235	5695	2700	2995	20	26	2884	65	-	569
GREECE										
1925	663	64	-	64	24	14	21	5	-	-
1929	814	147	-	147	46	29	64	8	-	-
1933	638	183	-	183	46	19	112	6	-	-
1937	969	323	-	323	64	19	227	13	-	-
1938	975	345	-	345	71	21	243	10	-	-
1950	302	1086	-	1086	228	74	768	16	-	-
1953	277	1254	-	1254	249	87	900	18	-	-
1955	320	1511	-	1511	303	95	1094	19	-	-
1957	280	1624	-	1624	238	106	1256	17	-	-
1960	230	2392	1732	660	14	4	614	20	-	10
1961	230	2643	1840	803	14	1	760	22	-	-14
1962	210	2963	1820	1143	27	55	1039	24	-	-2
1963	270	3396	1843	1553	59	85	1388	27	-	-6
1964	290	3324	1882	1442	86	109	1219	32	-	-15
1965	410	4115	1830	2285	116	125	2006	38	-	22

Table V. NET ENERGY IMPORTS OR EXPORTS, SELECTED YEARS, 1925-1965

(Original units; minus sign [–] = net exports)

Region, country, year	Solid fuels (10^3 m.t. coal equiv.)	Liquid fuels (10^3 m.t.)		Refined petroleum products					Gas (10^6 c.m.)	Electricity (10^6 kwh)
		Total	Crude oil	Total	Gasoline	Kerosine	Fuel oils	Lubes and greases		
	(1)	(2)	(3)	(4)	(5)	(6)	(7)	(8)	(9)	(10)
ICELAND										
1925	-	9	-	9	-	-	-	-	-	-
1929	-	15	-	15	3	5	7	-	-	-
1933	-	14	-	14	10	3	-	1	-	-
1937	-	19	-	19	15	3	-	1	-	-
1938	-	20	-	20	6	2	11	1	-	-
1950	96	248	-	248	42	3	200	3	-	-
1953	49	381	-	381	54	3	320	4	-	-
1955	60	347	-	347	57	2	284	4	-	-
1957	30	400	-	400	63	2	331	4	-	-
1960	20	466	-	466	56	9	397	4	-	-
1961	20	427	-	427	50	8	365	4	-	-
1962	20	453	-	453	57	4	387	5	-	-
1963	10	423	-	423	62	8	349	4	-	-
1964	10	423	-	423	58	9	352	4	-	-
1965	10	468	-	468	64	18	381	5	-	-
IRELAND										
1925	2284	119	1	118	52	46	11	9	-	-
1929	2497	165	-	165	87	43	25	10	-	-
1933	2298	189	-	189	108	51	21	9	-	-
1937	2620	243	-	243	127	66	39	11	-	-
1938	2539	251	-	251	135	62	43	11	-	-
1950	1994	597	-	597	250	78	255	14	-	-
1953	1758	773	-	773	320	109	328	16	-	-
1955	1940	1120	-	1120	371	125	602	20	-	-
1957	1250	1105	-	1105	352	114	617	15	-	-
1960	1660	1320	1431	-111	68	136	-341	19	-	-
1961	1750	1503	1455	48	55	184	-215	23	-	-
1962	1480	1725	1515	210	44	183	-43	23	-	-
1963	1420	1958	1632	326	23	190	88	23	-	-
1964	1280	2175	1745	430	43	216	139	28	-	-
1965	1250	2453	2031	422	22	215	154	24	-	-
SPAIN										
1925	2125	467	15	452	142	21	251	38	-	-
1929	2700	764	28	736	303	21	367	45	-	-
1933	1057	1225	163	1062	357	23	654	28	-	-
1937	566	1093	100	993	306	61	590	36	-	-
1938	428	1090	100	990	306	61	590	33	-	-
1950	965	3767	2900	867	200	22	594	NA	-	-
1953	1115	5158	3160	1998	100	24	1804	70	-	-
1955	550	6042	3450	2592	-6	42	2485	71	-	60
1957	490	8674	5495	3179	-55	-3	3188	49	-	-30
1960	300	8549	7050	1499	-155	-41	1668	NA	-	-150
1961	410	9379	7630	1749	-151	-32	1922	NA	-	-245
1962	1800	10994	9678	1316	-229	-9	1516	NA	-	-253
1963	1890	11548	10469	1079	-204	-9	1279	NA	-	-823
1964	1890	13157	12585	572	-192	-39	739	NA	-	-1557
1965	1710	14075	13396	679	-224	-17	690	13	-	-634

Table V. NET ENERGY IMPORTS OR EXPORTS, SELECTED YEARS, 1925-1965

(Original units; minus sign [–] = net exports)

Region, country, year	Solid fuels (10^3 m.t. coal equiv.)	Liquid fuels (10^3 m.t.)								Gas (10^6 c.m.)	Electricity (10^6 kwh)
				Refined petroleum products							
		Total	Crude oil	Total	Gasoline	Kerosine	Fuel oils	Lubes and greases			
	(1)	(2)	(3)	(4)	(5)	(6)	(7)	(8)		(9)	(10)
YUGOSLAVIA											
1925	463	85	11	74	13	39	11	11		-	-
1929	583	138	103	35	5	21	2	7		-	-
1933	265	121	97	24	5	14	2	3		-	-
1937	369	113	92	21	1	13	2	5		-	-
1938	464	152	128	24	5	9	4	6		-	-
1950	298	453	405	48	52	-	-23	19		-	-
1953	554	482	454	28	53	-	-43	18		-	-30
1955	1030	480	483	-3	33	-2	-39	5		-	-50
1957	1670	581	649	-68	-24	-7	-46	14		-	-150
1960	1550	531	435	96	-7	7	91	11		-	-90
1961	1540	183	108	75	-5	10	59	14		-	-78
1962	1490	197	186	11	-9	5	21	-5		-	-156
1963	1550	371	323	48	-	3	70	-25		-	-295
1964	2060	622	444	178	-18	6	186	5		-	342
1965	2175	889	962	-73	-29	-7	-18	-16		-	395
OCEANIA											
1925	-218	916	203	713	445	126	93	49		-	-
1929	530	1781	452	1329	955	168	122	84		-	-
1933	-82	1663	248	1415	805	140	407	63		-	-
1937	-86	2606	284	2322	1327	226	678	91		-	-
1938	-94	2834	253	2582	1465	219	817	80		-	-
1950	581	5942	797	5145	2343	469	2171	162		-	-
1953	-229	6553	900	5653	2845	493	2220	95		-	-
1955	32	9715	4890	4825	2499	579	1529	218		-	-
1957	-560	10961	8650	2311	1382	462	253	214		-	-
1960	-1438	13098	11265	1833	1644	429	-521	280		-	-
1961	-2727	14066	12405	1661	1477	388	-490	285		-	-
1962	-2875	14407	12934	1473	1696	455	-932	253		-	-
1963	-3097	16415	14861	1554	1786	383	-951	335		-	-
1964	-4696	18103	16159	1944	1709	333	-293	194		-	-
1965	-7017	20050	18682	1368	1142	451	-364	137		-	-
AUSTRALIA											
1925	-897	677	203	474	331	105	-1	39		-	-
1929	250	1404	452	952	738	141	3	70		-	-
1933	-294	1319	248	1071	613	122	284	52		-	-
1937	-377	2075	284	1791	1028	216	475	72		-	-
1938	-365	2148	253	1895	1109	208	513	65		-	-
1950	451	4806	797	4009	1838	436	1606	129		-	-
1953	-383	5300	900	4400	2129	463	1740	68		-	-
1955	-230	8118	4890	3228	1672	537	844	175		-	-
1957	-920	9098	8650	448	428	405	-558	173		-	-
1960	-1690	11061	11265	-204	614	316	-1334	200		-	-
1961	-2980	11846	12405	-559	368	250	-1382	205		-	-
1962	-3040	12163	12934	-771	616	316	-1885	182		-	-
1963	-3280	13899	14861	-962	606	233	-2025	224		-	-
1964	-4990	15181	15114	67	742	164	-975	136		-	-
1965	-7325	16802	16300	502	795	237	-599	69		-	-

Table V. NET ENERGY IMPORTS OR EXPORTS, SELECTED YEARS, 1925-1965

(Original units; minus sign [–] = net exports)

Region, country, year	Solid fuels (10^3 m.t. coal equiv.)	Liquid fuels (10^3 m.t.)		Refined petroleum products					Gas (10^6 c.m.)	Electricity (10^6 kwh)
		Total	Crude oil	Total	Gasoline	Kerosine	Fuel oils	Lubes and greases		
	(1)	(2)	(3)	(4)	(5)	(6)	(7)	(8)	(9)	(10)
NEW ZEALAND										
1925	566	234	-	234	111	19	94	10	-	-
1929	166	366	-	366	208	26	119	13	-	-
1933	102	332	-	332	185	17	120	10	-	-
1937	119	501	-	501	285	6	193	17	-	-
1938	99	652	-	652	341	7	291	13	-	-
1950	45	1079	-	1079	482	29	537	31	-	-
1953	1	1144	-	1144	665	20	440	19	-	-
1955	10	1438	-	1438	765	29	611	33	-	-
1957	10	1663	-	1663	872	40	715	36	-	-
1960	-20	1745	-	1745	940	66	692	47	-	-
1961	-	1876	-	1876	1021	77	733	45	-	-
1962	10	1927	-	1927	988	86	804	49	-	-
1963	-	2123	-	2123	1081	93	907	42	-	-
1964	-	2423	1045	1378	850	97	389	42	-	-
1965	-	2729	2382	347	234	123	-58	48	-	-
USSR AND COMMUNIST EASTERN EUROPE										
1925	-8413	-2088	21	-2110	-581	-770	-685	-201	-	69
1929	-13719	-5909	-3	-5906	-1873	-1508	-2435	-287	-	69
1933	-10919	-9622	-491	-9131	-3079	-1479	-4488	-327	-	13
1937	-12766	-6141	-114	-6027	-2098	-1107	-2770	-242	-	15
1938	-10853	-4673	-249	-4424	-1720	-944	-1752	-170	-	-
1950	-12529	645	1585	-940	-965	-390	15	-	31	-220
1953	-9706	-2878	1042	-3920	-1650	-765	-1005	-	21	-2
1955	-13320	-6026	133	-6159	-1570	-702	-3833	-43	22	150
1957	-13090	-10229	-1164	-9065	-1607	-1069	-6259	-127	45	-
1960	-18930	-27028	-10723	-16305	-2095	-1040	-12720	-431	27	160
1961	-19900	-34186	-15688	-18498	-2624	-1043	-14341	-471	27	-9
1962	-22230	-36965	-17249	-19716	-2253	-1283	-15626	-541	5	470
1963	-22280	-40372	-19015	-21357	-2355	-1113	-17432	-450	18	471
1964	-23190	-43289	-22051	-21238	-2018	-756	-18006	-457	28	-85
1965	-22631	-48681	-24916	-23765	-2048	-965	-20305	-434	-13	-42
COMMUNIST EASTERN EUROPE										
1925	-8738	-781	75	-857	-310	-356	-211	-107	-	69
1929	-13477	-2147	292	-2439	-795	-769	-994	-78	-	69
1933	-9899	-4817	38	-4855	-1795	-967	-2254	-81	-	13
1937	-12523	-4458	-4	-4454	-1854	-927	-1831	-32	-	15
1938	-11577	-3521	-34	-3487	-1574	-806	-1245	-24	-	-
1950	-21329	-955	385	-1340	-965	-390	15	-	56	-220
1953	-15206	-2178	1242	-3420	-1650	-765	-1005	-	116	-2
1955	-16620	-3335	1474	-4809	-2153	-610	-2035	-	162	140
1957	-6100	-690	3428	-4118	-1925	-455	-1723	-12	216	-
1960	-9600	1919	5936	-4017	-1451	-252	-2121	-174	270	190
1961	-7390	3443	6812	-3369	-815	-240	-2101	-194	297	65
1962	-5370	5619	8534	-2915	-679	-232	-1772	-219	307	702
1963	-3190	8213	10685	-2472	-548	-48	-1659	-210	320	1218
1964	-1660	11267	14640	-3373	-657	-17	-2381	-317	321	1219
1965	-4226	13798	18516	-4718	-916	31	-3512	-308	379	1459

Table V. NET ENERGY IMPORTS OR EXPORTS, SELECTED YEARS, 1925-1965

(Original units; minus sign [-] = net exports)

Region, country, year	Solid fuels (10^3 m.t. coal equiv.)	Liquid fuels (10^3 m.t.)		Refined petroleum products					Gas (10^6 c.m.)	Electricity (10^6 kwh)
		Total	Crude oil	Total	Gasoline	Kerosine	Fuel oils	Lubes and greases		
	(1)	(2)	(3)	(4)	(5)	(6)	(7)	(8)	(9)	(10)
ALBANIA										
1925	-	5	3	2	1	-	1	-	-	-
1929	-	7	3	4	3	-	1	-	-	-
1933	-	8	2	6	4	-	2	-	-	-
1937	-	-51	-57	6	3	-	3	-	-	-
1938	4	-96	-103	7	3	-	4	-	-	-
1950	10	-40	-60	20	15	-	5	-	-	-
1953	20	-50	-70	20	15	-	5	-	-	-
1955	-20	-103	-124	21	17	-	4	-	-	-
1957	-	-205	-218	13	10	2	1	-	-	-
1960	10	-319	-329	10	5	3	2	-	-	-
1961	10	-280	-291	11	5	3	3	-	-	-
1962	20	-254	-273	19	12	4	3	-	-	-
1963	10	-306	-310	4	10	4	-10	-	-	-
1964	10	-263	-294	31	13	4	14	-	-	-
1965	15	-361	-375	14	11	3	-	-	-	-
BULGARIA										
1925	16	43	-	43	4	26	9	4	-	-
1929	-2	84	-	84	11	33	32	8	-	-
1933	4	66	-	66	7	25	30	4	-	-
1937	-	87	19	68	10	30	20	8	-	-
1938	-12	88	29	59	11	21	19	8	-	-
1950	NA	240	20	220	60	40	120	-	-	-
1953	NA	335	20	315	85	60	170	-	-	-
1955	100	220	-116	336	105	47	184	-	-	-
1957	-50	247	-202	449	196	58	195	-	-	-
1960	260	789	-68	857	335	20	502	-	-	-
1961	750	1038	-104	1142	392	20	730	-	-	-
1962	1180	1507	-101	1608	430	19	1159	-	-	68
1963	1520	2025	371	1654	430	18	1206	-	-	83
1964	2300	3042	1770	1272	224	10	1038	-	-	-24
1965	2838	3447	2196	1251	157	11	1083	-	-	-2
CZECHOSLOVAKIA										
1925	-1789	181	53	127	NA	NA	NA	NA	NA	NA
1929	-1905	353	156	197	NA	NA	NA	NA	NA	NA
1933	-1318	343	101	242	NA	NA	NA	NA	NA	NA
1937	-2964	458	268	190	NA	NA	NA	NA	NA	NA
1938	-2032	363	201	162	NA	NA	NA	NA	NA	NA
1950	770	630	130	500	35	140	325	-	-	100
1953	1420	885	380	505	35	140	330	-	-	38
1955	1850	991	445	546	64	149	336	-	-	-130
1957	-460	1456	1221	235	70	100	65	-	-	-230
1960	-1320	2525	2255	270	76	212	-12	-	-	-270
1961	-660	3085	2785	300	52	220	33	-	-4	-335
1962	-150	3860	3675	185	19	244	-69	-	-4	66
1963	260	4206	4217	-11	-28	271	-249	-	-4	142
1964	755	5177	5170	7	-24	241	-203	-	-4	702
1965	641	5834	6096	-262	6	243	-496	-	-4	762

Table V. NET ENERGY IMPORTS OR EXPORTS, SELECTED YEARS, 1925-1965

(Original units; minus sign [-] = net exports)

Region, country, year	Solid fuels (10^3 m.t. coal equiv.)	Liquid fuels (10^3 m.t.)								Gas (10^6 c.m.)	Electricity (10^6 kwh)
		Total	Crude oil	Refined petroleum products							
				Total	Gasoline	Kerosine	Fuel oils	Lubes and greases			
	(1)	(2)	(3)	(4)	(5)	(6)	(7)	(8)		(9)	(10)
GERMANY, EAST											
1950	5341	100	50	50	15	-	35	-		36	-400
1953	7410	250	400	-150	-75	-	-75	-		36	-170
1955	6390	100	648	-548	-255	-1	-288	-		36	-10
1957	6140	367	997	-630	-310	-	-320	-		54	-330
1960	7640	1537	1941	-404	-164	148	-377	-		54	-370
1961	8040	1851	2270	-419	-194	106	-320	-		40	-372
1962	8770	2148	2591	-443	-278	50	-211	-		32	-84
1963	8740	2721	3163	-442	-280	40	-198	-		23	-2
1964	10380	3519	4260	-741	-332	20	-429	-		14	147
1965	9990	4062	5132	-1070	-464	-	-606	-		9	92
HUNGARY											
1925	726	66	19	47	15	22	5	5		-	-
1929	1553	205	136	69	31	21	9	8		-	-
1933	163	175	172	3	-	-	1	2		-	-
1937	410	280	238	42	2	-	35	5		-	-
1938	334	210	174	36	1	-	28	7		-	-
1950	610	50	50	-	15	-10	-5	NA		-	-
1953	1390	100	100	-	20	-15	-5	NA		-	130
1955	1650	-2	76	-78	-4	-15	-59	NA		-	250
1957	3340	1014	1000	14	-41	-15	82	-12		-	310
1960	2640	1024	1423	-399	-90	-	-296	-13		185	540
1961	2970	1134	1412	-278	-39	-10	-216	-13		203	498
1962	2820	1199	1540	-341	-55	-	-272	-14		203	562
1963	3720	1745	1828	-83	8	-	-77	-14		207	930
1964	4585	2011	2026	-15	-1	-	-	-14		225	1081
1965	3930	2125	2251	-126	-42	-	-70	-14		198	1295
POLAND											
1925	-7903	-295	-	-295	-65	-74	-80	-76		-	50
1929	-13328	-175	-	-175	-38	-50	-51	-36		-	49
1933	-8809	-154	-	-154	-50	-45	-28	-31		-	-4
1937	-10046	-78	-	-78	-41	-9	-15	-13		-	-
1938	-9961	-8	-	-8	-5	-	-2	-1		-	-
1950	-28280	465	195	270	95	40	135	-		20	80
1953	-25976	902	412	490	170	50	270	-		80	-
1955	-27260	1299	545	754	320	50	388	NA		126	60
1957	-15840	1681	630	1051	550	50	454	NA		162	260
1960	-19840	2232	714	1518	853	41	576	50		234	320
1961	-19370	2630	740	1890	1046	38	741	65		261	313
1962	-19410	2954	1102	1852	1064	53	734	NA		279	123
1963	-18940	3563	1416	2147	1105	38	923	79		297	69
1964	-21180	3871	1708	2163	1118	46	993	NA		293	-691
1965	-23185	4327	3216	1111	860	54	195	NA		374	-357
ROMANIA											
1925	212	-781	-	-781	-265	-330	-146	-40		-	-
1929	205	-2621	-3	-2618	-802	-773	-985	-58		-	-
1933	61	-5255	-237	-5018	-1756	-947	-2259	-56		-	-
1937	77	-5154	-472	-4682	-1828	-948	-1874	-32		-	-
1938	90	-4078	-335	-3743	-1584	-827	-1294	-38		-	-

Table V. NET ENERGY IMPORTS OR EXPORTS, SELECTED YEARS, 1925-1965

(Original units; minus sign [-] = net exports)

Region, country, year	Solid fuels (10^3 m.t. coal equiv.)	Liquid fuels (10^3 m.t.)		Refined petroleum products					Gas (10^6 c.m.)	Electricity (10^6 kwh)
		Total	Crude oil	Total	Gasoline	Kerosine	Fuel oils	Lubes and greases		
	(1)	(2)	(3)	(4)	(5)	(6)	(7)	(8)	(9)	(10)
ROMANIA (CONTINUED)										
1950	220	-2400	-	-2400	-1200	-600	-600	NA	-	-
1953	530	-4600	-	-4600	-1900	-1000	-1700	NA	-	-
1955	670	-5840	-	-5840	-2400	-840	-2600	NA	-	-30
1957	770	-5250	-	-5250	-2400	-650	-2200	NA	-	-10
1960	1010	-5869	-	-5869	-2466	-676	-2516	-211	-203	-30
1961	870	-6015	-	-6015	-2077	-617	-3072	-246	-203	-39
1962	1400	-5795	-	-5795	-1871	-602	-3116	-205	-203	-33
1963	1500	-5741	-	-5741	-1793	-419	-3254	-275	-203	-4
1964	1490	-6090	-	-6090	-1655	-338	-3794	-303	-207	4
1965	1545	-5636	-	-5636	-1444	-280	-3618	-294	-198	-331
USSR (INCLUDING ESTONIA, LATVIA, LITHUANIA)										
1925	325	-1307	-54	-1253	-271	-414	-474	-94	-	-
1929	-242	-3762	-295	-3467	-1078	-739	-1441	-209	-	-
1933	-1020	-4805	-529	-4276	-1284	-512	-2234	-246	-	-
1937	-243	-1683	-110	-1573	-244	-180	-939	-210	-	-
1938	724	-1152	-215	-937	-146	-138	-507	-146	-	-
1950	8800	1600	1200	400	NA	NA	NA	NA	-25	-
1953	5500	-700	-200	-500	NA	NA	NA	NA	-95	-
1955	3300	-2691	-1341	-1350	583	-92	-1798	-43	-140	10
1957	-6990	-9539	-4592	-4947	318	-614	-4536	-115	-171	-
1960	-9330	-28947	-16659	-12288	-644	-788	-10599	-257	-243	-30
1961	-12510	-37629	-22500	-15129	-1809	-803	-12240	-277	-270	-74
1962	-16860	-42584	-25783	-16801	-1574	-1051	-13854	-322	-302	-232
1963	-19090	-48585	-29700	-18885	-1807	-1065	-15773	-240	-302	-747
1964	-21530	-54556	-36691	-17865	-1361	-739	-15625	-140	-293	-1304
1965	-18405	-62479	-43432	-19047	-1132	-996	-16793	-126	-392	-1501
COMMUNIST ASIA										
1925	201	941	-	941	25	794	97	25	-	-
1929	-1221	1071	-	1071	80	735	207	49	-	-
1933	-2638	1100	-51	1151	120	609	368	54	-	-
1937	-4420	1073	96	977	202	433	280	62	-	-
1938	-3052	718	75	643	139	275	187	42	-	-
1950	NA	NA	NA	NA	NA	NA	NA	NA	NA	NA
1953	NA	NA	NA	NA	NA	NA	NA	NA	NA	NA
1955	-1020	1375	400	975	260	320	395	NA	NA	NA
1957	-1740	2296	425	1871	836	445	590	NA	NA	NA
1960	-920	3570	610	2960	1440	500	1020	NA	NA	NA
1961	-1120	3380	80	3300	1625	560	1115	NA	NA	NA
1962	-1220	2495	140	2355	1115	525	715	NA	NA	NA
1963	-1430	2255	150	2105	925	530	650	NA	NA	NA
1964	-1220	1455	200	1255	645	220	390	NA	NA	NA
1965	-1615	1030	210	820	395	80	345	NA	NA	NA
LATIN AMERICA										
1925	7223	-12086	-8985	-3101	-291	96	-2941	35	2	-
1929	7531	-19429	-11633	-7796	-806	44	-6954	-80	4	-
1933	4630	-18362	-8188	-10174	-2603	-232	-7253	-86	59	21
1937	6090	-24966	-7875	-17091	-3078	-279	-13465	-269	136	19
1938	5439	-24691	-7109	-17582	-2653	-310	-14383	-236	49	18

Table V. NET ENERGY IMPORTS OR EXPORTS, SELECTED YEARS, 1925-1965

(Original units; minus sign [-] = net exports)

Region, country, year	Solid fuels (10^3 m.t. coal equiv.)	Liquid fuels (10^3 m.t.)		Refined petroleum products					Gas (10^6 c.m.)	Electricity (10^6 kwh)
		Total	Crude oil	Total	Gasoline	Kerosine	Fuel oils	Lubes and greases		
	(1)	(2)	(3)	(4)	(5)	(6)	(7)	(8)	(9)	(10)
LATIN AMERICA (CONTINUED)										
1950	2790	-60058	-25385	-34673	-3766	-1705	-29445	118	654	130
1953	2373	-69186	-27579	-41607	-2522	-2734	-36331	-140	540	217
1955	2740	-80390	-38883	-41507	-1982	-2869	-36667	-245	559	170
1957	2760	-101396	-56409	-44987	-2338	-3827	-38899	-206	-176	410
1960	3020	-109385	-49142	-60243	-4576	-4141	-51355	-419	-1171	450
1961	2520	-111915	-47008	-64907	-4749	-4545	-55578	-343	-1320	455
1962	1980	-125040	-50507	-74533	-5422	-5083	-63833	-508	-1158	528
1963	2304	-129483	-49376	-80107	-6530	-4994	-68566	-415	-1126	591
1964	2477	-133259	-49932	-83327	-6571	-6054	-70475	-625	-1212	147
1965	2560	-134507	-45871	-88636	-7874	-6749	-73822	-782	-1248	60
LATIN AMERICA - CARIBBEAN										
1925	1411	-13573	-9272	-4301	-617	-101	-3531	-52	2	-
1929	1421	-21791	-11935	-9856	-1273	-167	-8212	-204	4	-
1933	617	-19085	-7383	-11702	-2658	-334	-8566	-144	59	21
1937	779	-26835	-7447	-19388	-3297	-344	-15406	-341	136	19
1938	661	-27304	-7103	-20201	-2872	-327	-16690	-312	49	18
1950	117	-70600	-28217	-42383	-5677	-1958	-34788	-85	654	130
1953	145	-82726	-31854	-50872	-5341	-3211	-42017	-423	540	217
1955	200	-99005	-47116	-51889	-3453	-3715	-44393	-554	559	170
1957	240	-121942	-68267	-53675	-3298	-4370	-45750	-515	-176	410
1960	110	-127295	-59129	-68166	-5681	-4758	-57054	-770	-1171	450
1961	120	-128234	-56895	-71339	-5842	-5305	-59667	-624	-1320	455
1962	240	-141441	-62983	-78458	-6051	-5724	-65896	-924	-1158	528
1963	284	-145034	-61881	-83153	-7262	-5364	-69928	-762	-1126	591
1964	357	-151145	-64157	-86988	-7075	-6423	-72623	-1007	-1212	147
1965	425	-153885	-61981	-91904	-8333	-7163	-75518	-1132	-1248	60
CARIBBEAN - OIL PRODUCING										
1925	137	-16123	-9434	-6689	-685	-144	-5802	-58	2	-
1929	174	-24460	-12205	-12255	-1509	-209	-10326	-211	4	-
1933	78	-20737	-7444	-13293	-2766	-369	-10002	-156	59	21
1937	89	-29038	-7639	-21399	-3494	-390	-17153	-362	136	19
1938	86	-29310	-7262	-22048	-3079	-374	-18268	-327	49	18
1950	56	-75391	-28700	-46691	-6441	-2039	-38077	-134	653	130
1953	57	-88343	-32498	-55845	-6398	-3329	-45637	-481	540	217
1955	60	-105746	-47804	-57942	-4848	-3958	-48694	-644	559	170
1957	60	-130996	-72304	-58692	-4512	-4596	-49205	-601	-176	410
1960	50	-138269	-66208	-72061	-6099	-5146	-60051	-822	-1171	450
1961	70	-140480	-63688	-76792	-6002	-5732	-64434	-678	-1320	455
1962	180	-155832	-72129	-83703	-6311	-6133	-70377	-977	-1158	528
1963	190	-160305	-73122	-87183	-7112	-5812	-73554	-820	-1126	591
1964	238	-168533	-77014	-91519	-6792	-6836	-76918	-1066	-1212	147
1965	293	-172049	-76081	-95968	-7806	-7603	-79558	-1196	-1248	60
ANTILLES, NETHERLANDS										
1925	NA	440	1325	-885	-107	-5	-716	-57	-	-
1929	-	1244	11815	-10571	-1209	-20	-9173	-169	-	-
1933	NA	2071	12750	-10679	-2218	-285	-8060	-116	-	-
1937	3	3622	21179	-17557	-2645	-286	-14298	-328	-	-
1938	NA	4055	22707	-18652	-2451	-346	-15518	-337	-	-

Table V. NET ENERGY IMPORTS OR EXPORTS, SELECTED YEARS, 1925-1965

(Original units; minus sign [-] = net exports)

Region, country, year	Solid fuels (10^3 m.t. coal equiv.)	Liquid fuels (10^3 m.t.) Total	Crude oil	Refined petroleum products Total	Gasoline	Kerosine	Fuel oils	Lubes and greases	Gas (10^6 c.m.)	Electricity (10^6 kwh)
	(1)	(2)	(3)	(4)	(5)	(6)	(7)	(8)	(9)	(10)
ANTILLES, NETHERLANDS (CONTINUED)										
1950	-	6983	42770	-35787	-5253	-1396	-28900	-238	-	-
1953	-	5572	42640	-37068	-4687	-2221	-29650	-510	-	-
1955	-	7620	42171	-34551	-3253	-2796	-27922	-643	-	-
1957	-	8503	40355	-31852	-2274	-3011	-26036	-609	-	-
1960	-	7772	37888	-30116	-3120	-3007	-23337	-706	-	-
1961	-	8675	39410	-30735	-2668	-3134	-24405	-573	-	-
1962	-	8171	39912	-31741	-3019	-3059	-24917	-810	-	-
1963	-	7999	39270	-31271	-3094	-3243	-24391	-609	-	-
1964	-	7684	40348	-32664	-3460	-3637	-24807	-820	-	-
1965	-	7212	40436	-33224	-3581	-3547	-25228	-944	-	-
COLOMBIA										
1925	3	9	-	9	7	-	-	2	-	-
1929	1	-2487	-2534	47	28	1	14	4	-	-
1933	2	-1673	-1695	22	10	-	10	2	-	-
1937	1	-2523	-2546	23	6	-	14	3	-	-
1938	-	-2625	-2648	23	7	-	13	3	-	-
1950	-	-3904	-4103	199	157	-	41	1	-	-
1953	-	-4101	-4607	506	358	60	73	15	-	-
1955	-	-3327	-3594	267	312	63	-137	29	-	-
1957	-10	-3964	-4030	66	230	39	-233	30	-	-
1960	-	-4836	-4353	-483	61	3	-577	30	-	-
1961	-	-4089	-3861	-228	88	6	-357	35	-	-
1962	-	-3793	-3402	-391	185	-	-611	35	-	-
1963	-	-4671	-4364	-307	34	-2	-367	28	-	-
1964	-2	-4903	-4248	-655	30	1	-702	16	-	-
1965	-2	-6317	-5610	-707	-4	-	-713	10	-	-
MEXICO										
1925	66	-13437	-8035	-5402	-547	-131	-4720	-4	2	-
1929	62	-3117	-2139	-978	-150	-185	-596	-47	4	-
1933	12	-2928	-1679	-1249	-263	-73	-870	-43	59	21
1937	13	-2841	-1135	-1706	-502	-88	-1074	-42	136	19
1938	14	-1592	-696	-896	-184	-18	-690	-4	49	18
1950	31	-1879	-1700	-179	168	-121	-290	64	653	130
1953	42	-1456	-534	-922	395	2	-1390	71	540	217
1955	60	-2117	-797	-1320	739	175	-2482	47	559	170
1957	70	145	-257	402	871	312	-1013	25	-176	410
1960	50	-371	-150	-221	385	18	-859	17	-1171	450
1961	60	-1411	-903	-508	169	16	-988	25	-1320	455
1962	60	-2216	-1055	-1161	54	16	-1539	17	-1158	528
1963	60	-2069	-984	-1085	12	17	-1469	9	-1126	591
1964	80	-1592	-1033	-559	33	18	-1020	11	-1212	147
1965	110	-1801	-1040	-761	29	16	-1302	11	-1248	60
TRINIDAD AND TOBAGO										
1925	44	-461	-42	-419	-45	-9	-366	1	-	-
1929	87	-844	-127	-717	-163	-6	-549	1	-	-
1933	50	-654	-102	-552	-250	-11	-292	1	-	-
1937	62	-1335	-24	-1311	-352	-16	-945	2	-	-
1938	53	-1664	-14	-1650	-453	-14	-1185	2	-	-

Table V. NET ENERGY IMPORTS OR EXPORTS, SELECTED YEARS, 1925-1965

(Original units; minus sign [-] = net exports)

Region, country, year	Solid fuels (10^3 m.t. coal equiv.)	Liquid fuels (10^3 m.t.) Total	Crude oil	Refined petroleum products Total	Gasoline	Kerosine	Fuel oils	Lubes and greases	Gas (10^6 c.m.)	Electricity (10^6 kwh)
	(1)	(2)	(3)	(4)	(5)	(6)	(7)	(8)	(9)	(10)
TRINIDAD AND TOBAGO (CONTINUED)										
1950	26	-1232	1293	-2525	-370	-510	-1648	3	-	-
1953	14	-1224	2013	-3237	-490	-900	-1850	3	-	-
1955	-	-1693	2116	-3809	-560	-800	-2453	4	-	-
1957	-	-2582	2128	-4710	-710	-986	-3023	9	-	-
1960	-	-3576	5035	-8611	-1180	-1160	-6278	7	-	-
1961	-	-3491	7946	-11437	-1500	-1460	-8484	7	-	-
1962	-	-4186	7999	-12185	-1432	-1350	-9410	7	-	-
1963	-	-4819	8676	-13495	-1567	-1134	-10802	8	-	-
1964	-	-4453	10304	-14757	-1501	-1358	-11854	-44	-	-
1965	-	-4070	11523	NA	-1426	-1842	-12315	NA	-	-
VENEZUELA										
1925	24	-2674	-2682	8	7	1	-	-	-	-
1929	24	-19256	-19220	-36	-15	1	-22	-	-	-
1933	11	-17553	-16718	-835	-45	-	-790	-	-	-
1937	10	-25961	-25113	-848	-1	-	-850	3	-	-
1938	16	-27484	-26611	-873	2	4	-888	9	-	-
1950	-1	-75359	-66960	-8399	-1143	-12	-7280	36	-	-
1953	1	-87134	-72010	-15124	-1974	-270	-12820	-60	-	-
1955	-	-106229	-87700	-18529	-2086	-600	-15700	-81	-	-
1957	-	-133098	-110500	-22598	-2629	-950	-18900	-56	-	-
1960	-	-137258	-104628	-32630	-2245	-1000	-29000	-170	-	-
1961	10	-140164	-106280	-33884	-2091	-1160	-30200	-172	-	-
1962	120	-153808	-115583	-38225	-2099	-1740	-33900	-226	-	-
1963	130	-156745	-115720	-41025	-2497	-1450	-36525	-256	-	-
1964	160	-165269	-122385	-42884	-1894	-1860	-38535	-229	-	-
1965	185	-167073	-121390	-45683	-2824	-2230	-40000	-273	-	-
CARIBBEAN - OTHER										
1925	1274	2550	162	2388	68	43	2271	6	-	-
1929	1247	2669	270	2399	236	42	2114	7	-	-
1933	539	1652	61	1591	108	35	1436	12	-	-
1937	690	2203	192	2011	197	46	1747	21	-	-
1938	575	2006	159	1847	207	47	1578	15	-	-
1950	61	4791	483	4308	764	81	3289	49	1	-
1953	88	5617	644	4973	1057	118	3620	58	-	-
1955	140	6741	688	6053	1395	243	4301	90	-	-
1957	180	9054	4037	5017	1214	226	3455	86	-	-
1960	60	10974	7079	3895	418	388	2997	52	-	-
1961	50	12246	6793	5453	160	427	4767	54	-	-
1962	60	14391	9146	5245	260	409	4481	53	-	-
1963	94	15271	11241	4030	-150	448	3626	58	-	-
1964	119	17388	12857	4531	-283	413	4295	59	-	-
1965	132	18164	14100	4064	-527	440	4040	64	-	-
CUBA										
1925	659	1263	108	1155	22	-	1133	-	-	-
1929	632	1076	203	873	139	-	734	-	-	-
1933	296	308	24	284	32	-	245	7	-	-
1937	381	753	133	620	70	-	542	8	-	-
1938	342	581	88	493	75	-	411	7	-	-

Table V. NET ENERGY IMPORTS OR EXPORTS, SELECTED YEARS, 1925-1965

(Original units; minus sign [-] = net exports)

Region, country, year	Solid fuels (10^3 m.t. coal equiv.)	Liquid fuels (10^3 m.t.) Total	Crude oil	Refined petroleum products Total	Gasoline	Kerosine	Fuel oils	Lubes and greases	Gas (10^6 c.m.)	Electricity (10^6 kwh)
	(1)	(2)	(3)	(4)	(5)	(6)	(7)	(8)	(9)	(10)
CUBA (CONTINUED)										
1950	35	NA	280	NA	NA	NA	NA	NA	NA	NA
1953	58	NA	500	NA	NA	NA	NA	NA	NA	NA
1955	130	NA	487	NA	NA	NA	NA	NA	NA	NA
1957	180	3411	2100	1311	377	8	866	39	-	-
1960	60	4018	3280	738	58	66	610	NA	-	-
1961	50	4340	2980	1360	104	67	NA	NA	-	-
1962	60	4838	3720	1118	228	69	NA	NA	-	-
1963	94	4418	3709	709	212	35	462	NA	-	-
1964	119	4749	3469	1280	159	24	1097	NA	-	-
1965	132	4776	3513	1263	147	22	1094	NA	-	-
PANAMA CANAL ZONE										
1925	331	922	-	922	4	2	916	-	-	-
1929	272	1089	-	1089	8	3	1078	-	-	-
1933	28	865	-	865	8	3	854	-	-	-
1937	113	771	-	771	11	5	755	-	-	-
1938	45	780	-	780	10	4	766	-	-	-
1950	-	NA	-	NA	NA	NA	695	-	-	-
1953	-	NA	-	NA	NA	NA	710	-	-	-
1955	-	714	-	714	-28	2	740	-	-	-
1957	-	1031	-	1031	19	2	1010	-	-	-
1960	-	883	-	883	33	10	829	-	-	-
1961	-	1119	-	1119	62	1	1042	-	-	-
1962	-	1388	-	1388	23	2	1349	-	-	-
1963	-	2295	-	2295	37	1	2243	-	-	-
1964	-	2532	-	2532	39	3	2474	-	-	-
1965	-	2730	-	2730	38	4	2670	-	-	-
PUERTO RICO										
1950	NA	NA	NA	NA	NA	NA	NA	NA	NA	NA
1953	6	NA	NA	NA	NA	NA	NA	NA	NA	NA
1955	-	949	-	949	324	94	530	-	-	-
1957	-	1945	1930	15	5	36	-26	-	-	-
1960	-	2347	3788	-1441	-581	21	-885	-	-	-
1961	-	1976	3789	-1813	-925	6	-895	-	-	-
1962	-	2675	4314	-1639	-751	-9	-879	-	-	-
1963	-	2720	4838	-2118	-1011	78	-1188	-	-	-
1964	-	3183	5393	-2210	-998	156	-1369	-	-	-
1965	-	3780	5780	-2000	-1011	258	-1245	-	-	-
LATIN AMERICA - OTHER										
1925	5812	1487	287	1200	326	197	590	87	-	-
1929	6110	2362	302	2060	467	211	1258	124	-	-
1933	4013	723	-805	1528	55	102	1313	58	-	-
1937	5311	1869	-428	2297	219	65	1941	72	-	-
1938	4778	2613	-6	2619	219	17	2307	76	-	-
1950	2673	10542	2832	7710	1911	253	5343	203	-	-
1953	2228	13540	4275	9265	2819	477	5686	283	-	-
1955	2540	18615	8233	10382	1471	846	7726	309	-	-
1957	2520	20546	11858	8688	960	543	6851	309	-	-
1960	2910	17910	9987	7923	1105	617	5699	351	-	-

Table V. NET ENERGY IMPORTS OR EXPORTS, SELECTED YEARS, 1925-1965

(Original units; minus sign [-] = net exports)

Region, country, year	Solid fuels (10^3 m.t. coal equiv.)	Liquid fuels (10^3 m.t.)							Gas (10^6 c.m.)	Electricity (10^6 kwh)
				Refined petroleum products						
		Total	Crude oil	Total	Gasoline	Kerosine	Fuel oils	Lubes and greases		
	(1)	(2)	(3)	(4)	(5)	(6)	(7)	(8)	(9)	(10)
LATIN AMERICA - OTHER (CONTINUED)										
1961	2400	16319	9887	6432	1093	760	4089	281	-	-
1962	1740	16401	12476	3925	629	641	2063	416	-	-
1963	2020	15551	12505	3046	732	370	1362	347	-	-
1964	2120	17886	14225	3661	504	369	2148	382	-	-
1965	2135	19378	16110	3268	459	414	1696	350	-	-
ARGENTINA										
1925	3179	715	76	639	255	68	285	31	-	-
1929	3176	1703	488	1215	312	60	790	53	-	-
1933	2458	1010	156	854	43	8	785	18	-	-
1937	3164	1733	569	1164	21	-	1133	10	-	-
1938	2859	2104	663	1441	2	-	1430	9	-	-
1950	1467	5380	2954	2426	250	8	2124	44	-	-
1953	1224	6103	3599	2504	110	9	2320	65	-	-
1955	1260	7144	3714	3430	112	161	3116	39	-	-
1957	1280	9335	6154	3181	125	113	2904	39	-	-
1960	1460	5080	3315	1765	44	485	1139	64	-	-
1961	1260	3323	1768	1555	64	527	845	35	-	-
1962	640	1729	861	868	31	308	465	112	-	-
1963	770	671	767	-96	-13	23	-193	74	-	-
1964	750	2209	1462	747	7	16	570	69	-	-
1965	730	3640	3552	88	64	12	-306	107	-	-
BOLIVIA										
1925	16	22	-	22	2	1	17	2	-	-
1929	19	40	-	40	6	2	30	2	-	-
1933	8	20	-	20	4	1	14	1	-	-
1937	31	40	-	40	7	2	28	3	-	-
1938	33	45	-	45	8	2	33	2	-	-
1950	2	68	55	13	10	-	-	3	-	-
1953	5	108	72	36	26	6	-	4	-	-
1955	-	-32	-54	22	9	2	7	4	-	-
1957	-	-135	-134	-1	-17	-1	10	7	-	-
1960	-	-99	-133	34	7	-	24	3	-	-
1961	-	-66	-85	19	3	-	14	2	-	-
1962	-	-3	-23	20	10	-	7	3	-	-
1963	-	-58	-69	11	10	-	-	1	-	-
1964	-	-28	-36	8	13	-	-	1	-	-
1965	5	-22	-35	13	15	1	-	1	-	-
BRAZIL										
1925	1927	542	-	542	143	103	261	35	-	-
1929	2325	793	-	793	294	117	337	45	-	-
1933	1292	787	-	787	236	81	442	28	-	-
1937	1708	1105	38	1067	357	114	557	39	-	-
1938	1576	1178	48	1130	361	99	632	38	-	-
1950	1119	4333	59	4274	1618	236	2304	116	-	-
1953	746	5525	30	5495	2446	408	2478	163	-	-
1955	1120	8715	3513	5202	1170	546	3256	200	-	-
1957	940	8486	4846	3640	703	392	2330	190	-	-
1960	1060	9346	5097	4249	891	98	2921	212	-	-

Table V. NET ENERGY IMPORTS OR EXPORTS, SELECTED YEARS, 1925-1965

(Original units; minus sign [-] = net exports)

Region, country, year	Solid fuels (10^3 m.t. coal equiv.)	Liquid fuels (10^3 m.t.)							Gas (10^6 c.m.)	Electricity (10^6 kwh)
				Refined petroleum products						
		Total	Crude oil	Total	Gasoline	Kerosine	Fuel oils	Lubes and greases		
	(1)	(2)	(3)	(4)	(5)	(6)	(7)	(8)	(9)	(10)
BRAZIL (CONTINUED)										
1961	900	9579	6497	3082	810	138	1814	184	-	-
1962	920	10897	9663	1234	419	239	85	242	-	-
1963	1040	11304	10015	1289	523	254	22	228	-	-
1964	1155	11761	10803	958	293	249	-82	265	-	-
1965	1240	11083	10247	836	163	278	20	210	-	-
CHILE										
1925	249	907	834	73	41	21	NA	11	-	-
1929	51	1120	991	129	94	19	NA	16	-	-
1933	-119	277	182	95	54	7	29	5	-	-
1937	-43	766	633	133	75	9	37	12	-	-
1938	-51	724	574	150	90	7	40	13	-	-
1950	2	1098	-56	1154	226	39	870	19	-	-
1953	201	974	-150	1124	286	74	740	24	-	-
1955	70	1636	306	1330	190	154	954	34	-	-
1957	230	1513	403	1110	81	143	854	32	-	-
1960	320	1397	513	884	38	77	757	21	-	-
1961	160	1286	491	795	44	83	660	19	-	-
1962	120	1387	607	780	31	35	720	12	-	-
1963	160	1169	419	750	40	38	710	NA	-	-
1964	170	1196	441	755	15	45	745	NA	-	-
1965	115	1514	650	864	31	50	810	NA	-	-
ECUADOR										
1925	-	8	-5	13	1	1	10	1	-	-
1929	-	-135	-157	22	2	1	18	1	-	-
1933	-	-138	-153	15	-	-	14	1	-	-
1937	-	-250	-252	2	-	-	1	1	-	-
1938	-	-209	-245	36	-1	-	36	1	-	-
1950	-	-126	-136	10	8	-	-	2	-	-
1953	-	-154	-172	18	16	-	-	2	-	-
1955	-	-101	-178	77	56	-	17	4	-	-
1957	-	-35	-166	131	75	1	51	4	-	-
1960	-	231	214	17	10	1	1	5	-	-
1961	-	208	189	19	11	2	-	6	-	-
1962	-	186	167	19	11	2	1	5	-	-
1963	-	263	225	38	30	-	1	7	-	-
1964	-	334	305	29	10	9	-	10	-	-
1965	-	354	320	34	12	12	-	10	-	-
PARAGUAY										
1925	NA	NA	-	NA	NA	NA	NA	NA	-	-
1929	NA	NA	-	NA	NA	NA	NA	NA	-	-
1933	3	4	-	4	3	1	-	-	-	-
1937	NA	7	-	7	5	2	-	-	-	-
1938	NA	8	-	8	5	2	1	-	-	-
1950	-	22	-	22	14	4	3	1	-	-
1953	-	47	-	47	22	8	15	2	-	-
1955	-	63	-	63	27	10	24	2	-	-
1957	-	68	-	68	28	10	28	2	-	-
1960	-	103	-	103	36	18	46	3	-	-

Table V. NET ENERGY IMPORTS OR EXPORTS, SELECTED YEARS, 1925-1965

(Original units; minus sign [-] = net exports)

Region, country, year	Solid fuels (10^3 m.t. coal equiv.)	Liquid fuels (10^3 m.t.)		Refined petroleum products					Gas (10^6 c.m.)	Electricity (10^6 kwh)
		Total	Crude oil	Total	Gasoline	Kerosine	Fuel oils	Lubes and greases		
	(1)	(2)	(3)	(4)	(5)	(6)	(7)	(8)	(9)	(10)
PARAGUAY (CONTINUED)										
1961	-	118	-	118	37	15	64	2	-	-
1962	-	123	-	123	40	18	62	3	-	-
1963	-	134	-	134	41	19	71	3	-	-
1964	-	139	-	139	42	18	77	2	-	-
1965	-	177	-	177	42	24	108	3	-	-
PERU										
1925	39	-929	-618	-311	-147	-26	-140	2	-	-
1929	41	-1504	-1020	-484	-317	-24	-145	2	-	-
1933	18	-1535	-991	-544	-355	-31	-158	-	-	-
1937	15	-1984	-1507	-477	-311	-92	-76	2	-	-
1938	13	-1649	-1196	-453	-274	-105	-78	4	-	-
1950	-57	-866	-374	-492	-263	-41	-194	6	-	-
1953	-35	-631	-308	-323	-117	-37	-179	10	-	-
1955	-	-633	-313	-320	-152	-97	-82	11	-	-
1957	-30	-659	-434	-225	-78	-132	-33	18	-	-
1960	-10	-187	-338	151	27	-84	190	18	-	-
1961	20	-63	-323	260	43	-36	237	16	-	-
1962	10	96	-269	365	38	-1	310	18	-	-
1963	-	170	-292	462	53	4	391	14	-	-
1964	-5	245	-285	530	61	-	454	15	-	-
1965	5	237	-214	451	66	1	384	-	-	-
URUGUAY										
1925	363	215	-	215	29	26	155	5	-	-
1929	474	336	-	336	74	33	224	5	-	-
1933	344	286	-	286	67	32	182	5	-	-
1937	418	404	83	321	61	26	230	4	-	-
1938	334	376	138	238	22	8	200	8	-	-
1950	129	376	330	46	31	-	5	10	-	-
1953	83	1259	1204	55	7	-	37	11	-	-
1955	90	1437	1245	192	30	57	94	11	-	-
1957	100	1562	1189	373	10	-	349	14	-	-
1960	80	1579	1319	260	8	-	233	19	-	-
1961	60	1479	1350	129	32	8	78	11	-	-
1962	50	1556	1470	86	5	14	62	14	-	-
1963	50	1489	1440	49	4	8	28	13	-	-
1964	50	1592	1535	57	17	7	25	14	-	-
1965	40	1756	1590	166	18	6	130	11	-	-
ASIA										
1925	1034	-3384	-782	-2602	-767	432	-2400	133	-	-
1929	2105	-3640	-112	-3528	-2163	-200	-1348	181	-	-
1933	2406	-5593	421	-6014	-2500	32	-3683	137	-	-
1937	5289	-11456	-1779	-9677	-3211	-834	-6819	174	-	-
1938	4814	-9051	-1259	-7792	-3550	-779	-5005	157	-	-
1950	1425	-71213	-42860	-28353	-6380	-2386	-20822	315	-	-
1953	4777	-98014	-91057	-6957	-2538	-380	-4409	370	-	-
1955	3830	-127077	-115207	-11870	-3538	-1549	-7237	452	-4	-
1957	7770	-131282	-118340	-12942	-3817	-1724	-8137	731	-4	-
1960	9144	-196491	-176626	-19865	-4709	-2132	-13835	807	-	-

Table V. NET ENERGY IMPORTS OR EXPORTS, SELECTED YEARS, 1925-1965

(Original units; minus sign [–] = net exports)

Region, country, year	Solid fuels (10^3 m.t. coal equiv.)	Liquid fuels (10^3 m.t.)		Refined petroleum products					Gas (10^6 c.m.)	Electricity (10^6 kwh)
		Total	Crude oil	Total	Gasoline	Kerosine	Fuel oils	Lubes and greases		
	(1)	(2)	(3)	(4)	(5)	(6)	(7)	(8)	(9)	(10)
ASIA (CONTINUED)										
1961	12030	-200072	-185320	-14752	-4188	-1767	-9686	898	-	-
1962	12850	-217272	-194442	-22830	-5741	-1913	-16241	1062	-4	-
1963	11790	-232069	-208921	-23148	-5999	-2198	-15838	964	-9	-
1964	13735	-257509	-234400	-23109	-6048	-3169	-14812	1131	-	-
1965	17685	-278322	-253803	-24519	-6443	-3665	-14900	803	-54	-
MIDDLE EAST										
1925	116	-3390	-1050	-2340	-278	43	-2107	2	-	-
1929	-111	-4590	-1661	-2929	-1133	-756	-1050	10	-	-
1933	-294	-6386	-1562	-4824	-1459	-341	-3036	12	-	-
1937	130	-13123	-5100	-8023	-1788	-443	-5807	15	-	-
1938	-4	-10628	-4481	-6147	-1935	-442	-3780	10	-	-
1950	162	-73207	-44760	-28447	-6066	-3013	-19428	60	-	-
1953	68	-106112	-94857	-11255	-3042	-1291	-7023	101	-	-
1955	60	-141770	-122799	-18971	-4156	-2779	-12144	107	-	-
1957	60	-153375	-129893	-23482	-4414	-3387	-15812	128	-	-
1960	20	-231243	-200300	-30943	-5112	-4048	-21903	118	-	-
1961	60	-248304	-217268	-31036	-4483	-4104	-22553	121	-	-
1962	50	-272799	-234326	-38473	-5664	-4657	-28191	146	-	-
1963	20	-302235	-262651	-39584	-5748	-4551	-29168	161	-	-
1964	20	-341265	-300772	-40493	-5982	-4989	-29049	121	-	-
1965	25	-373682	-331249	-42433	-6452	-5235	-30078	116	-	-
MIDDLE EAST - OIL PRODUCING										
1925	5	-3722	-1051	-2671	-307	-63	-2302	1	-	-
1929	8	-5225	-1664	-3561	-1208	-879	-1479	5	-	-
1933	3	-7204	-1573	-5631	-1520	-421	-3697	7	-	-
1937	4	-14293	-5116	-9177	-1913	-566	-6704	6	-	-
1938	4	-12007	-4497	-7510	-2073	-573	-4867	3	-	-
1950	2	-78046	-45447	-32599	-6573	-3351	-22688	13	-	-
1953	-	-112220	-96167	-16053	-3660	-1751	-10662	20	-	-
1955	-	-149285	-129078	-20207	-4061	-2887	-13281	22	-	-
1957	-	-160667	-136449	-24218	-4342	-3545	-16360	30	-	-
1960	-	-240738	-207326	-33412	-5136	-4234	-24066	28	-	-
1961	20	-258232	-226019	-32213	-4205	-4027	-23989	29	-	-
1962	-	-284033	-246843	-37190	-4968	-4316	-27820	27	-	-
1963	-	-314300	-276715	-37585	-5012	-4084	-28207	9	-	-
1964	-	-354478	-316398	-38080	-5073	-4424	-28016	5	-	-
1965	-	-387271	-348085	-39186	-5444	-4725	-28239	6	-	-
BAHRAIN										
1925	-	-	-	-	-	-	-	-	-	-
1929	-	-	-	-	-	-	-	-	-	-
1933	-	-4	-4	-	-	-	-	-	-	-
1937	-	-958	-627	-331	-70	-33	-228	-	-	-
1938	-	-776	-46	-730	-265	-108	-357	-	-	-
1950	-	-371	6125	-6496	-1752	-680	-4064	-	-	-
1953	-	383	8259	-7876	-2047	-784	-5045	-	-	-
1955	-	158	8278	-8120	-1970	-1050	-5100	-	-	-
1957	-	-183	7413	-7596	-1261	-935	-5400	-	-	-
1960	-	-675	8031	-8706	-1637	-1182	-5887	-	-	-

Table V. NET ENERGY IMPORTS OR EXPORTS, SELECTED YEARS, 1925-1965

(Original units; minus sign [-] = net exports)

Region, country, year	Solid fuels (10³ m.t. coal equiv.)	Liquid fuels (10³ m.t.)		Refined petroleum products					Gas (10⁶ c.m.)	Electricity (10⁶ kwh)
		Total	Crude oil	Total	Gasoline	Kerosine	Fuel oils	Lubes and greases		
	(1)	(2)	(3)	(4)	(5)	(6)	(7)	(8)	(9)	(10)
BAHRAIN (CONTINUED)										
1961	-	-532	8567	-9099	-1541	-1221	-6337	-	-	-
1962	-	-484	9728	-10212	-1863	-1286	-7063	-	-	-
1963	-	-707	8980	-9687	-1825	-1132	-6730	-	-	-
1964	-	-595	7697	-8292	-1859	-1218	-5215	-	-	-
1965	-	-1071	6740	-7811	-1626	-1410	-4775	-	-	-
IRAN										
1925	5	-3778	-1051	-2727	-312	-83	-2332	-	-	-
1929	1	-5274	-1664	-3610	-1209	-888	-1516	3	-	-
1933	1	-7262	-1569	-5693	-1523	-426	-3747	3	-	-
1937	1	-9415	-498	-8917	-1850	-542	-6526	1	-	-
1938	1	-7133	-271	-6862	-1815	-474	-4570	-3	-	-
1950	-	-29088	-6606	-22482	-4146	-2320	-16020	4	-	-
1953	-	-232	-42	-190	-147	-	-50	7	-	-
1955	-	-13105	-8330	-4775	-930	-900	-2950	5	-	-
1957	-	-30407	-19200	-11207	-2250	-1770	-7200	13	-	-
1960	-	-44919	-33425	-11494	-2530	-2045	-6945	26	-	-
1961	-	-50954	-41550	-9404	-1790	-1720	-5920	26	-	-
1962	-	-57450	-46025	-11425	-2205	-2090	-7155	25	-	-
1963	-	-64172	-52935	-11237	-2090	-1995	-7160	8	-	-
1964	-	-73646	-62585	-11061	-1940	-2185	-6940	4	-	-
1965	-	-80489	-69290	-11199	-2035	-2140	-7025	1	-	-
IRAQ										
1925	-	56	-	56	5	20	30	1	-	-
1929	7	49	-	49	1	9	37	2	-	-
1933	2	62	-	62	3	5	50	4	-	-
1937	3	-3920	-3991	71	7	9	50	5	-	-
1938	3	-4098	-4180	82	7	9	60	6	-	-
1950	2	-5865	-6144	279	25	49	196	9	-	-
1953	NA	-27406	-27419	13	-	-	-	13	-	-
1955	-	-32136	-32150	14	-1	-1	-1	17	-	-
1957	-	-20236	-20253	17	-	-	-	17	NA	NA
1960	-	-45203	-45204	1	-1	-	-	2	NA	NA
1961	20	-46582	-46585	3	-	-	-	3	-	-
1962	-	-46679	-46673	-6	-	-	-8	2	NA	NA
1963	-	-54118	-54110	-8	-2	-	-7	1	NA	NA
1964	-	-59207	-59180	-27	-	-	-28	1	NA	NA
1965	-	-61655	-61645	-10	-	-	-15	5	NA	NA
KUWAIT										
1950	-	-16351	-16051	-300	-	-	-300	-	-	-
1953	-	-41820	-41693	-127	-	-	-127	-	-	-
1955	-	-52752	-52832	80	-	-	80	-	-	-
1957	-	-54018	-55407	1389	29	-	1360	-	-	-
1960	-	-77015	-72100	-4915	-5	-	-4910	-	-	-
1961	-	-77875	-73600	-4275	-	-	-4275	-	-	-
1962	-	-86759	-81990	-4769	-130	-	-4558	-	-	-
1963	-	-91163	-86025	-5138	-72	3	-4922	-	-	-
1964	-	-101362	-95235	-6127	-3	4	-5881	-	-	-
1965	-	-104611	-97800	-6811	-26	-	-6400	-	-	-

Table V. NET ENERGY IMPORTS OR EXPORTS, SELECTED YEARS, 1925-1965

(Original units; minus sign [-] = net exports)

Region, country, year	Solid fuels (10^3 m.t. coal equiv.)	Liquid fuels (10^3 m.t.)							Gas (10^6 c.m.)	Electricity (10^6 kwh)
				Refined petroleum products						
		Total	Crude oil	Total	Gasoline	Kerosine	Fuel oils	Lubes and greases		
	(1)	(2)	(3)	(4)	(5)	(6)	(7)	(8)	(9)	(10)
KUWAIT NEUTRAL ZONE										
1955	-	-1204	-1223	19	4	5	10	-	-	-
1957	-	-3301	-3320	19	4	5	10	-	-	-
1960	-	-6471	-5740	-731	4	5	-740	-	-	-
1961	-	-8575	-7640	-935	4	5	-944	-	-	-
1962	-	-11779	-9222	-2557	4	5	-2566	-	-	-
1963	-	-16027	-13590	-2437	4	6	-2447	-	-	-
1964	-	-18715	-15900	-2815	4	6	-2825	-	-	-
1965	-	-18460	-15900	-2560	4	6	-2570	-	-	-
QATAR										
1950	-	-1577	-1577	-	-	-	-	-	-	-
1953	-	-3965	-3965	-	-	-	-	-	-	-
1955	-	-5297	-5347	50	10	10	30	-	-	-
1957	-	-6500	-6550	50	10	10	30	-	-	-
1960	-	-8108	-8140	32	7	7	18	-	-	-
1961	-	-8332	-8360	28	11	4	13	-	-	-
1962	-	-8744	-8780	36	11	5	20	-	-	-
1963	-	-9034	-9070	36	11	5	20	-	-	-
1964	-	-10074	-10110	36	11	5	20	-	-	-
1965	-	-10897	-10930	33	11	5	17	-	-	-
SAUDI ARABIA										
1950	-	-24794	-21194	-3600	-700	-400	-2500	-	-	-
1953	-	-39180	-31307	-7873	-1466	-967	-5440	-	-	-
1955	-	-44949	-37474	-7475	-1174	-951	-5350	-	-	-
1957	-	-46022	-39132	-6890	-874	-855	-5160	-	-	-
1960	-	-58353	-50748	-7605	-976	-1020	-5605	-	-	-
1961	-	-65390	-56851	-8539	-892	-1096	-6530	-	-	-
1962	-	-71351	-63083	-8268	-789	-952	-6495	-	-	-
1963	-	-76667	-67535	-9132	-1045	-973	-6970	-	-	-
1964	-	-81788	-71970	-9818	-1295	-1038	-7160	-	-	-
1965	-	-96414	-85560	-10854	-1782	-1188	-7485	-	-	-
TRUCIAL OMAN										
1960	-	6	-	6	2	1	3	-	-	-
1961	-	8	-	8	3	1	4	-	-	-
1962	-	-787	-798	11	4	2	5	-	-	-
1963	-	-2412	-2430	18	7	2	9	-	-	-
1964	-	-9091	-9115	24	9	2	13	-	-	-
1965	-	-13674	-13700	26	10	2	14	-	-	-
MIDDLE EAST - OTHER										
1925	111	332	1	331	29	106	195	1	-	-
1929	-119	635	3	632	75	123	429	5	-	-
1933	-297	818	11	807	61	80	661	5	-	-
1937	126	1170	16	1154	125	123	897	9	-	-
1938	-8	1379	16	1363	138	131	1087	7	-	-
1950	160	4839	687	4152	507	338	3260	47	-	-

Table V. NET ENERGY IMPORTS OR EXPORTS, SELECTED YEARS, 1925-1965

(Original units; minus sign [-] = net exports)

Region, country, year	Solid fuels (10^3 m.t. coal equiv.)	Liquid fuels (10^3 m.t.)		Refined petroleum products					Gas (10^6 c.m.)	Electricity (10^6 kwh)
		Total	Crude oil	Total	Gasoline	Kerosine	Fuel oils	Lubes and greases		
	(1)	(2)	(3)	(4)	(5)	(6)	(7)	(8)	(9)	(10)
MIDDLE EAST - OTHER (CONTINUED)										
1953	68	6108	1310	4798	618	460	3639	81	-	-
1955	60	7515	6279	1236	-95	108	1137	85	-	-
1957	60	7292	6556	736	-72	158	548	98	-	-
1960	20	9495	7026	2469	24	186	2163	90	-	-
1961	40	9928	8751	1177	-278	-77	1436	92	-	-
1962	50	11234	12517	-1283	-696	-341	-371	119	-	-
1963	20	12065	14064	-1999	-736	-467	-961	152	-	-
1964	20	13213	15626	-2413	-909	-565	-1033	116	-	-
1965	25	13589	16836	-3247	-1008	-510	-1839	110	-	-
PALESTINE										
1925	22	28	-	28	4	19	4	1	-	-
1929	33	50	-	50	10	31	7	2	-	-
1933	58	77	-	77	20	34	21	2	-	-
1937	98	182	-	182	41	49	88	4	-	-
1938	58	156	-	156	39	48	66	3	-	-
ISRAEL										
1950	34	731	196	535	126	69	331	9	-	-
1953	29	1117	765	352	26	42	277	7	-	-
1955	20	1596	1038	558	15	136	400	7	-	-
1957	40	1505	1015	490	25	23	430	12	-	-
1960	50	1832	1325	507	18	-	478	10	-	-
1961	40	2018	1455	563	18	1	532	14	-	-
1962	40	2276	2055	221	-42	-1	247	17	-	-
1963	20	2359	2350	9	-48	-3	44	18	-	-
1964	30	2589	2650	-61	-68	-	-10	19	-	-
1965	15	3694	3890	-196	-98	-3	-111	17	-	-
JORDAN										
1950	-	57	-	57	22	24	10	1	-	-
1953	-	71	-	71	22	24	23	2	-	-
1955	-	126	13	113	30	32	48	3	-	-
1957	-	146	-	146	37	34	72	3	-	-
1960	-	221	-	221	45	56	115	5	-	-
1961	-	297	207	90	6	20	60	4	-	-
1962	-	329	252	77	2	17	52	6	-	-
1963	-	383	329	54	1	16	32	5	-	-
1964	-	387	359	28	5	11	6	6	-	-
1965	-	449	410	39	10	23	-	6	-	-
LEBANON-SYRIA										
1925	52	38	-	38	12	24	2	-	-	-
1929	49	68	-	68	28	35	3	2	-	-
1933	67	74	-	74	30	31	10	3	-	-
1937	142	91	-	91	38	29	20	4	-	-
1938	145	94	-	94	42	32	17	3	-	-

Table V. NET ENERGY IMPORTS OR EXPORTS, SELECTED YEARS, 1925-1965

(Original units; minus sign [-] = net exports)

Region, country, year	Solid fuels (10^3 m.t. coal equiv.)	Liquid fuels (10^3 m.t.) Total	Crude oil	Refined petroleum products Total	Gasoline	Kerosine	Fuel oils	Lubes and greases	Gas (10^6 c.m.)	Electricity (10^6 kwh)
	(1)	(2)	(3)	(4)	(5)	(6)	(7)	(8)	(9)	(10)
LEBANON										
1950	11	609	491	118	30	26	NA	2	-	-
1953	-	710	545	165	50	37	NA	3	-	-
1955	10	673	894	-221	-29	-45	-153	5	-	-
1957	10	820	1053	-233	-32	-56	-154	6	-	-
1960	-	927	733	194	55	25	105	7	-	-
1961	-	958	733	225	76	40	100	4	-	-
1962	10	1033	840	193	81	25	80	1	-	-
1963	10	1178	1018	160	65	12	60	9	-	-
1964	10	1306	1306	NA	14	2	NA	9	-	-
1965	10	1482	1482	NA	NA	NA	NA	7	-	-
SYRIA										
1950	2	225	-	225	76	46	96	7	-	-
1953	3	396	-	396	86	51	252	7	-	-
1955	-	502	-	502	83	56	352	11	-	-
1957	-	606	-	606	96	71	427	11	-	-
1960	-	1003	695	308	9	16	270	12	-	-
1961	-	954	768	186	-23	6	190	13	-	-
1962	-	991	786	205	-45	6	220	22	-	-
1963	-	1111	881	230	-18	7	223	17	-	-
1964	-	1361	1015	346	-5	8	332	11	-	-
1965	5	1136	1017	119	-40	9	132	18	-	-
TURKEY										
1925	-79	80	-	80	11	58	11	-	-	-
1929	-347	107	-	107	32	53	22	-	-	-
1933	-473	88	8	80	7	12	61	-	-	-
1937	-253	134	-	134	38	40	56	-	-	-
1938	-255	165	-	165	50	47	68	-	-	-
1950	-	605	-	605	230	150	200	25	-	-
1953	-7	1158	-	1158	380	280	440	58	-	-
1955	-	1133	-	1133	375	316	390	52	-	-
1957	-	1134	-	1134	310	296	470	58	-	-
1960	-30	1248	-	1248	358	303	536	48	-	-
1961	-	1462	219	1243	343	295	555	49	-	-
1962	-	2118	2269	-151	23	127	-360	63	-	-
1963	-10	2476	3080	-604	-37	39	-695	92	-	-
1964	-20	2767	3430	-663	-44	27	-705	61	-	-
1965	-5	2625	3051	-426	-13	34	-498	52	-	-
FAR EAST AND OTHER ASIA										
1925	918	6	268	-262	-489	389	-293	131	-	-
1929	2216	950	1549	-599	-1030	556	-298	171	-	-
1933	2700	793	1983	-1190	-1041	373	-647	125	-	-
1937	5159	1667	3321	-1654	-1423	-391	-1012	159	-	-
1938	4818	1577	3222	-1645	-1615	-337	-1225	147	-	-
1950	1263	1994	1900	94	-314	627	-1394	255	-	-
1953	4709	8098	3800	4298	504	911	2614	269	-	-
1955	3770	14693	7592	7101	618	1230	4907	345	-4	-
1957	7710	22093	11553	10540	597	1663	7675	603	-4	-
1960	9124	34752	23674	11078	403	1916	8068	689	-	-

Table V. NET ENERGY IMPORTS OR EXPORTS, SELECTED YEARS, 1925-1965

(Original units; minus sign [-] = net exports)

Region, country, year	Solid fuels (10^3 m.t. coal equiv.)	Liquid fuels (10^3 m.t.)		Refined petroleum products					Gas (10^6 c.m.)	Electricity (10^6 kwh)
		Total	Crude oil	Total	Gasoline	Kerosine	Fuel oils	Lubes and greases		
	(1)	(2)	(3)	(4)	(5)	(6)	(7)	(8)	(9)	(10)
FAR EAST AND OTHER ASIA (CONTINUED)										
1961	11970	48232	31948	16284	295	2337	12867	777	-	-
1962	12800	55527	39884	15643	-77	2744	11950	916	-4	-
1963	11770	70166	53730	16436	-251	2353	13330	803	-9	-
1964	13715	83756	66372	17384	-66	1820	14237	1010	-	-
1965	17660	95360	77446	17914	9	1570	15178	687	-54	-
BORNEO (FORMER BRITISH)										
1925	-49	-555	-154	-401	-93	-101	-207	-	-	-
1929	-47	-735	-155	-580	-232	-59	-292	1	-	-
1933	-4	-579	-135	-444	-80	-32	-332	-	-	-
1937	-	-726	15	-741	-63	-40	-639	1	-	-
1938	1	-868	7	-875	-94	-59	-723	1	-	-
1950	-	-3980	-2348	-1632	-223	9	-1422	4	-	-
1953	-	-4697	-2835	-1862	-294	10	-1582	4	-	-
1955	-	-5008	-3223	-1785	-122	12	-1681	6	-4	-
1957	-	-5342	-3602	-1740	-182	13	-1577	6	-4	-
1960	-	-4392	-2515	-1877	-319	17	-1582	7	-	-
1961	-	-3853	-2257	-1596	-214	17	-1405	6	-	-
1962	-	-3674	-1817	-1857	-259	21	-1628	9	-4	-
1963	-	-3269	-1582	-1687	-227	13	-1480	7	-9	-
1964	-	-3290	-1088	-2202	-341	-111	-1756	6	-	-
1965	-	-3525	-1314	-2211	-216	-104	-1901	10	-54	-
BRUNEI										
1925	1	-	-	-	-	-	-	-	-	-
1929	-	-	-	-	-	-	-	-	-	-
1933	-	-285	-285	-	-	-	-	-	-	-
1937	-	-558	-559	1	-	1	-	-	-	-
1938	-	-695	-696	1	-	1	-	-	-	-
1950	-	-4064	-4076	12	3	1	6	2	-54	-
1953	-	-4856	-4877	21	7	1	11	2	-58	-
1955	-	-5238	-5247	9	2	1	3	3	-72	-
1957	-	-5516	-5528	12	5	1	3	3	-72	-
1960	-	-4571	-4577	6	1	2	2	1	-76	-
1961	-	-4110	-4115	5	1	1	2	1	-76	-
1962	-	-3809	-3817	8	1	2	3	2	-76	-
1963	-	-3471	-3479	8	1	2	4	1	-63	-
1964	-	-3513	-3518	5	1	2	1	1	-50	-
1965	-	-3926	-3931	5	1	1	2	1	-54	-
SABAH										
1925	-50	-	-	-	-	-	-	-	-	-
1929	-47	2	-	2	1	2	-	-	-	-
1933	-4	1	-	1	-	1	-	-	-	-
1937	-	2	-	2	1	1	-	-	-	-
1938	1	2	-	2	1	1	-	-	-	-
1950	-	14	-	14	4	3	6	1	-	-
1953	-	19	-	19	7	3	8	1	-	-
1955	-	24	-	24	6	4	13	1	-	-
1957	-	32	-	32	10	4	17	1	-	-
1960	-	54	-	54	13	5	32	4	-	-

Table V. NET ENERGY IMPORTS OR EXPORTS, SELECTED YEARS, 1925-1965

(Original units; minus sign [-] = net exports)

Region, country, year	Solid fuels (10^3 m.t. coal equiv.)	Liquid fuels (10^3 m.t.)		Refined petroleum products					Gas (10^6 c.m.)	Electricity (10^6 kwh)
		Total	Crude oil	Total	Gasoline	Kerosine	Fuel oils	Lubes and greases		
	(1)	(2)	(3)	(4)	(5)	(6)	(7)	(8)	(9)	(10)
SABAH (CONTINUED)										
1961	-	58	-	58	15	5	35	3	-	-
1962	-	75	-	75	21	8	42	4	-	-
1963	-	88	-	88	22	11	52	3	-	-
1964	-	107	-	107	26	20	58	3	-	-
1965	-	120	-	120	27	24	64	5	-	-
SARAWAK										
1925	-	-555	-154	-401	-93	-101	-207	-	-	-
1929	-	-740	-155	-585	-233	-61	-292	1	-	-
1933	-	-295	150	-445	-80	-33	-332	-	-	-
1937	-	-170	574	-744	-64	-42	-639	1	-	-
1938	-	-175	703	-878	-95	-61	-723	1	-	-
1950	-	70	1728	-1658	-230	5	-1434	1	54	-
1953	-	140	2042	-1902	-308	6	-1601	1	58	-
1955	-	206	2024	-1818	-130	7	-1697	2	68	-
1957	-	142	1926	-1784	-197	8	-1597	2	68	-
1960	-	125	2062	-1937	-333	10	-1616	2	76	-
1961	-	199	1858	-1659	-230	11	-1442	2	76	-
1962	-	60	2000	-1940	-281	11	-1673	3	72	-
1963	-	114	1897	-1783	-250	-	-1536	3	54	-
1964	-	116	2430	-2314	-368	-133	-1815	2	50	-
1965	-	283	2617	-2334	-243	-128	-1967	4	NA	-
BURMA										
1950	NA	110	-	110	60	20	30	NA	-	-
1953	251	110	-	110	64	21	16	9	-	-
1955	200	152	-	152	77	18	47	10	-	-
1957	280	84	-	84	27	3	47	7	-	-
1960	350	67	-	67	14	4	33	16	-	-
1961	260	90	12	78	11	8	38	21	-	-
1962	340	92	-	92	15	16	46	15	-	-
1963	210	52	-	52	10	13	22	7	-	-
1964	215	158	120	38	-	-	22	16	-	-
1965	140	175	160	15	-	-	-	15	-	-
CEYLON										
1925	827	206	-	206	14	26	164	2	-	-
1929	827	291	-	291	35	31	221	4	-	-
1933	412	342	-	342	25	27	287	3	-	-
1937	582	414	-	414	47	31	332	4	-	-
1938	391	492	-	492	41	30	418	3	-	-
1950	374	780	-	780	91	44	639	6	-	-
1953	390	839	-	839	132	72	630	5	-	-
1955	190	946	-	946	136	94	707	9	-	-
1957	280	1392	-	1392	191	112	1079	10	-	-
1960	260	891	-	891	162	147	573	9	-	-
1961	140	1054	-	1054	172	157	715	10	-	-
1962	140	1037	-	1037	140	179	705	13	-	-
1963	150	909	-	909	142	139	611	17	-	-
1964	180	839	-	839	106	154	569	10	-	-
1965	140	1015	-	1015	176	183	641	15	-	-

Table V. NET ENERGY IMPORTS OR EXPORTS, SELECTED YEARS, 1925-1965

(Original units; minus sign [–] = net exports)

Region, country, year	Solid fuels (10^3 m.t. coal equiv.)	Liquid fuels (10^3 m.t.) Total	Crude oil	Refined petroleum products Total	Gasoline	Kerosine	Fuel oils	Lubes and greases	Gas (10^6 c.m.)	Electricity (10^6 kwh)
	(1)	(2)	(3)	(4)	(5)	(6)	(7)	(8)	(9)	(10)
HONG KONG										
1925	960	257	-	257	7	92	156	2	-	-
1929	642	181	-	181	9	40	134	-2	-	-
1933	767	108	-	108	12	1	93	2	-	-
1937	879	142	-	142	26	6	97	13	-	-
1938	696	188	-	188	12	5	173	-2	-	-
1950	271	489	-	489	26	11	447	5	-	-
1953	204	649	-	649	52	41	554	2	-	-
1955	250	825	-	825	59	65	694	7	-	-
1957	250	1071	-	1071	64	84	914	9	-	-
1960	230	1227	-	1227	78	136	1003	10	-	-
1961	240	1344	-	1344	75	163	1096	10	-	-
1962	220	1526	-	1526	64	215	1233	14	-	-
1963	200	1754	-	1754	73	252	1419	10	-	-
1964	180	1827	-	1827	69	232	1514	12	-	-
1965	170	2056	-	2056	73	293	1685	5	-	-
INDIA										
1925	276	675	-	675	-43	258	367	93	-	-
1929	-516	975	-16	991	1	379	498	113	-	-
1933	-364	742	-13	755	6	211	455	83	-	-
1937	-561	1089	-18	1107	162	254	570	121	-	-
1938	-859	1038	-22	1060	102	196	632	130	-	-
1950	-932	2969	1318	1651	653	822	NA	176	-	-
1953	-1975	3356	1367	1989	872	948	NA	169	-	-
1955	-1540	4463	2755	1708	316	979	248	165	-	-
1957	-1690	5916	4300	1616	-6	1199	124	299	-	-
1960	-1350	7256	5685	1571	-128	989	395	315	-	-
1961	-930	7692	5910	1782	-50	1093	502	237	-	-
1962	-1060	8380	6021	2359	20	1456	606	277	-	-
1963	-870	8434	6314	2120	-314	1321	726	387	-	-
1964	-1250	8399	6500	1899	-282	999	896	286	-	-
1965	-930	8666	6800	1866	-196	826	936	300	-	-
INDO-CHINA										
1925	-665	66	-	66	11	47	-	8	-	-
1929	-1309	117	-	117	31	62	4	20	-	-
1933	-1247	87	-	87	29	42	10	6	-	-
1937	-1511	94	-	94	32	39	18	5	-	-
1938	-1518	104	-	104	38	37	24	5	-	-
1950	-47	126	-	126	70	24	27	5	-	-
1953	-300	350	-	350	155	42	143	10	-	-
1955	30	362	-	362	152	51	151	8	-	-
1957	50	490	-	490	208	70	201	11	-	-
1960	10	640	-	640	221	92	310	16	-	-
1961	10	731	-	731	219	87	409	15	-	-
1962	20	735	-	735	221	90	405	18	-	-
1963	10	852	-	852	244	111	473	22	-	-
1964	20	821	-	821	206	110	501	3	-	-
1965	45	973	-	973	231	128	612	-	-	-

Table V. NET ENERGY IMPORTS OR EXPORTS, SELECTED YEARS, 1925-1965

(Original units; minus sign [–] = net exports)

Region, country, year	Solid fuels (10^3 m.t. coal equiv.)	Liquid fuels (10^3 m.t.)		Refined petroleum products					Gas (10^6 c.m.)	Electricity (10^6 kwh)
		Total	Crude oil	Total	Gasoline	Kerosine	Fuel oils	Lubes and greases		
	(1)	(2)	(3)	(4)	(5)	(6)	(7)	(8)	(9)	(10)
CAMBODIA										
1955	-	56	-	56	26	10	20	-	-	-
1957	-	85	-	85	39	13	33	-	-	-
1960	-	112	-	112	54	15	43	-	-	-
1961	-	143	-	143	60	20	63	-	-	-
1962	-	153	-	153	58	22	73	-	-	-
1963	-	198	-	198	70	26	102	-	-	-
1964	-	175	-	175	43	25	107	-	-	-
1965	30	178	-	178	36	28	114	-	-	-
LAOS										
1955	-	9	-	9	6	1	1	1	-	-
1957	-	19	-	19	14	2	3	NA	-	-
1960	-	28	-	28	17	2	7	2	-	-
1961	-	38	-	38	24	2	11	1	-	-
1962	-	44	-	44	33	3	7	1	-	-
1963	-	51	-	51	34	5	11	1	-	-
1964	-	60	-	60	38	5	14	3	-	-
1965	-	58	-	58	35	5	18	NA	-	-
VIETNAM, SOUTH										
1955	30	297	-	297	120	40	130	7	-	-
1957	50	386	-	386	155	55	165	11	-	-
1960	10	500	-	500	150	75	260	14	-	-
1961	10	550	-	550	135	65	335	14	-	-
1962	20	538	-	538	130	65	325	17	-	-
1963	10	603	-	603	140	80	360	21	-	-
1964	20	586	-	586	125	80	380	NA	-	-
1965	15	737	-	737	160	95	480	NA	-	-
INDONESIA										
1925	-202	-2054	1	-2055	-542	-197	-1298	-18	-	-
1929	-329	-3235	-23	-3212	-1106	-451	-1633	-22	-	-
1933	-209	-3858	-413	-3445	-1199	-516	-1718	-12	-	-
1937	-236	-5311	-95	-5216	-1912	-837	-2456	-11	-	-
1938	-244	-5453	-52	-5401	-1976	-685	-2735	-5	-	-
1950	-35	-4403	1567	-5970	-1813	-569	-3557	-31	-	-
1953	-77	-6623	193	-6816	-2055	-681	-4031	-49	-	-
1955	-20	-6167	-498	-5669	-1616	-598	-3419	-36	-	-
1957	-	-9430	-3570	-5860	-1280	-511	-4094	25	-	-
1960	20	-14500	-9080	-5420	-1016	-459	-3950	5	-	-
1961	30	-13869	-9518	-4351	-777	-247	-3373	46	-	-
1962	20	-16754	-11062	-5692	-938	-456	-4354	56	-	-
1963	10	-16344	-11443	-4901	-737	-390	-3841	NA	-	-
1964	10	-17729	-14845	-2884	-405	-266	-2285	NA	-	-
1965	5	NA	NA	NA	-384	-396	-2685	NA	-	-
JAPAN										
1925	-963	635	421	214	76	92	21	25	-	-

Table V. NET ENERGY IMPORTS OR EXPORTS, SELECTED YEARS, 1925-1965

(Original units; minus sign [–] = net exports)

Region, country, year	Solid fuels (10^3 m.t. coal equiv.)	Liquid fuels (10^3 m.t.) Total	Crude oil	Refined petroleum products Total	Gasoline	Kerosine	Fuel oils	Lubes and greases	Gas (10^6 c.m.)	Electricity (10^6 kwh)
	(1)	(2)	(3)	(4)	(5)	(6)	(7)	(8)	(9)	(10)
JAPAN (CONTINUED)										
1929	1192	2116	1718	398	33	328	23	14	-	-
1933	2170	2997	2504	493	2	492	-3	2	-	-
1937	4269	4293	3387	906	-	NA	NA	NA	-	-
1938	5019	4502	3257	1245	-13	NA	NA	NA	-	-
1950	324	1841	1233	608	31	4	538	35	-	-
1953	4435	8056	5075	2981	275	3	2670	33	-	-
1955	2450	10663	7278	3385	250	32	3074	28	-	-
1957	6380	17870	12742	5128	108	17	4918	85	-	-
1960	8260	31985	27056	4929	-154	-24	4959	148	-	-
1961	11260	42086	33879	8207	-376	43	8314	220	-	-
1962	11960	49225	40084	9141	-265	10	9009	279	-	-
1963	11030	61950	51894	10056	-158	23	9996	-1	-	-
1964	13150	74234	62318	11916	150	-150	11185	353	-	-
1965	17030	83656	69685	13971	92	-155	13328	212	-	-
KOREA										
1925	479	52	-	52	5	43	-	4	-	-
1929	630	111	-	111	20	50	31	10	-	-
1933	621	127	-	127	31	33	49	14	-	-
1937	1044	367	-	367	55	51	247	14	-	-
1938	987	356	-	356	54	41	257	4	-	-
KOREA, REPUBLIC OF										
1950	219	100	-	100	20	10	70	NA	-	-
1953	643	330	-	330	70	40	220	NA	-	-
1955	1060	364	-	364	90	35	239	NA	-	-
1957	740	474	-	474	145	31	298	NA	-	-
1960	100	695	-	695	144	36	499	16	-	-
1961	50	757	-	757	126	43	579	9	-	-
1962	-120	1021	32	989	83	50	842	14	-	-
1963	-130	1372	46	1326	75	52	1166	33	-	-
1964	-80	1291	803	488	5	10	470	3	-	-
1965	-90	1572	1400	172	8	-	160	4	-	-
MALAYA AND SINGAPORE										
1925	633	358	-	358	37	48	273	-	-	-
1929	849	622	-	622	88	54	470	10	-	-
1933	563	317	-	317	49	33	228	7	-	-
1937	744	633	-	633	104	37	481	11	-	-
1938	485	500	-	500	90	44	355	11	-	-
1950	101	1385	-	1385	210	60	1096	19	-	-
1953	89	2831	-	2831	415	-20	2418	18	-	-
1955	70	3461	-	3461	485	50	2896	30	-	-
1957	90	3897	72	3825	345	130	3319	31	-	-
1960	4	3592	53	3539	235	254	3015	35	-	-
1961	60	4487	515	3972	223	267	3444	38	-	-
1962	40	4939	2002	2937	-4	290	2603	48	-	-
1963	40	4246	1737	2509	-35	81	2417	46	-	-
1964	40	5731	4272	1459	-201	33	1602	25	-	-
1965	25	5725	4671	1054	-345	82	1279	38	-	-

Table V. NET ENERGY IMPORTS OR EXPORTS, SELECTED YEARS, 1925-1965

(Original units; minus sign [–] = net exports)

Region, country, year	Solid fuels (10^3 m.t. coal equiv.)	Liquid fuels (10^3 m.t.)		Refined petroleum products					Gas (10^6 c.m.)	Electricity (10^6 kwh)
		Total	Crude oil	Total	Gasoline	Kerosine	Fuel oils	Lubes and greases		
	(1)	(2)	(3)	(4)	(5)	(6)	(7)	(8)	(9)	(10)
SINGAPORE										
1960	-	NA	NA	2444	36	164	2209	35	-	-50
1961	10	NA	NA	2746	10	154	2544	38	-	-55
1962	10	NA	NA	1672	-207	175	1656	48	-	-60
1963	10	NA	NA	1506	-173	-22	1655	46	-	-32
1964	10	NA	NA	1495	-200	4	1666	25	-	-
1965	5	NA	NA	1227	-248	54	1383	38	-	-
PAKISTAN										
1950	1025	920	-	920	NA	NA	NA	NA	NA	NA
1953	1211	1048	-	1048	110	230	680	28	-	-
1955	1080	1291	-	1291	150	205	900	36	-	-
1957	1330	1509	-	1509	170	209	1098	32	-	-
1960	1410	2070	-	2070	185	340	1545	NA	-	-
1961	1070	2206	-	2206	179	418	1560	49	-	-
1962	1360	2397	330	2067	162	474	1383	48	-	-
1963	1200	2770	1600	1170	19	375	690	86	-	-
1964	1340	3013	2115	898	2	408	434	54	-	-
1965	1100	3140	2440	700	160	220	320	NA	-	-
PHILIPPINES										
1925	472	306	-	306	33	49	215	9	-	-
1929	603	358	-	358	71	69	208	10	-	-
1933	273	368	-	368	67	41	251	9	-	-
1937	266	439	-	439	97	57	273	12	-	-
1938	259	467	-	467	100	45	301	21	-	-
1950	7	1264	-	1264	471	152	608	33	-	-
1953	5	1321	-	1321	466	145	676	34	-	-
1955	10	1920	667	1253	376	134	700	43	-	-
1957	10	2215	879	1336	361	135	797	43	-	-
1960	10	2656	1415	1241	440	167	568	66	-	-
1961	10	2765	2285	480	178	41	195	66	-	-
1962	10	3299	3036	263	107	19	90	47	-	-
1963	10	3715	3617	98	38	6	-6	60	-	-
1964	10	4281	4216	65	-	37	-61	89	-	-
1965	10	4611	4610	1	42	18	-59	NA	-	-
TAIWAN										
1925	-888	18	-	18	-	15	-	3	-	-
1929	-378	53	25	28	3	16	1	8	-	-
1933	-305	65	40	25	5	13	1	6	-	-
1937	-367	121	32	89	10	20	50	9	-	-
1938	-455	134	32	102	10	22	60	10	-	-
1950	-64	153	130	23	10	-	10	3	-	-
1953	-211	68	-	68	62	-	-	6	-	-
1955	-50	657	613	44	1	50	-20	13	-	-
1957	-30	836	732	104	33	56	5	10	-	-
1960	-190	1086	1060	26	-1	30	-12	9	-	-
1961	-240	1118	1122	-4	-11	30	-40	17	-	-
1962	-130	1261	1258	3	-27	37	-33	26	-	-
1963	-100	1496	1493	3	-	35	-51	19	-	-

Table V. NET ENERGY IMPORTS OR EXPORTS, SELECTED YEARS, 1925-1965

(Original units; minus sign [-] = net exports)

Region, country, year	Solid fuels (10^3 m.t. coal equiv.)	Liquid fuels (10^3 m.t.)		Refined petroleum products					Gas (10^6 c.m.)	Electricity (10^6 kwh)
		Total	Crude oil	Total	Gasoline	Kerosine	Fuel oils	Lubes and greases		
	(1)	(2)	(3)	(4)	(5)	(6)	(7)	(8)	(9)	(10)
TAIWAN (CONTINUED)										
1964	-110	1271	1286	-15	-	42	-82	25	-	-
1965	5	1790	1785	5	-4	-	-17	26	-	-
THAILAND										
1925	38	42	-	42	6	17	16	3	-	-
1929	52	96	-	96	17	37	37	5	-	-
1933	23	77	-	77	12	28	32	5	-	-
1937	50	112	-	112	19	31	55	7	-	-
1938	56	117	-	117	21	32	58	6	-	-
1950	20	240	-	240	80	40	120	NA	-	-
1953	44	460	-	460	180	60	220	NA	-	-
1955	40	716	-	716	248	80	362	26	-	-
1957	20	909	-	909	317	84	473	35	-	-
1960	10	1163	-	1163	406	137	583	37	-	-
1961	-	1278	-	1278	391	161	693	33	-	-
1962	-	1618	-	1618	419	267	880	52	-	-
1963	-	1774	54	1720	422	240	1014	43	-	-
1964	-	2420	675	1745	411	238	1039	56	-	-
1965	-	2459	1209	1250	145	384	659	62	-	-
AFRICA										
1925	2696	847	99	748	122	283	250	61	-	-
1929	3903	1720	122	1598	537	546	409	106	-	-
1933	3040	2295	77	2218	623	452	1052	91	-	-
1937	3751	4389	106	4283	1194	524	2442	123	-	-
1938	3301	3822	103	3719	1098	533	1970	118	-	-
1950	-886	8959	-	8959	2478	1174	5056	251	4	-
1953	-249	11859	-32	11891	3308	1517	6815	241	-	-4
1955	424	15433	1888	13545	3535	1707	7905	372	-	-
1957	424	16961	1848	15113	3830	1580	9285	375	-	-710
1960	-117	8254	-7014	15268	3724	1740	9360	360	-	-580
1961	-179	-381	-15697	15316	3656	1764	9406	395	-	14
1962	-810	-14635	-29431	14796	3428	1819	9079	397	-	15
1963	-750	-32159	-45755	13596	3252	1661	8228	395	-	7
1964	-395	-53991	-62095	8104	1856	1425	4362	439	-90	-15
1965	-515	-77200	-83897	6697	1443	1270	3510	464	-833	-10
NORTH AFRICA										
1925	3296	389	99	290	7	186	62	35	-	-
1929	4222	762	122	640	165	382	42	51	-	-
1933	3220	1231	77	1154	254	359	492	49	-	-
1937	3321	1611	106	1505	274	368	816	47	-	-
1938	3222	1686	103	1583	321	391	824	47	-	-
1950	790	3669	-	3669	566	584	2443	76	4	-
1953	284	4283	-61	4344	833	714	2716	71	-	-4
1955	300	6284	948	5336	955	782	3481	94	-	-20
1957	590	5232	922	4310	1020	632	2526	95	-	-10
1960	480	-1974	-6744	4770	702	704	3193	105	-	-
1961	490	-10294	-14685	4391	654	672	2866	121	-	14
1962	340	-23778	-27140	3362	387	639	2196	88	-	15

Table V. NET ENERGY IMPORTS OR EXPORTS, SELECTED YEARS, 1925-1965

(Original units; minus sign [-] = net exports)

Region, country, year	Solid fuels (10^3 m.t. coal equiv.)	Liquid fuels (10^3 m.t.)		Refined petroleum products					Gas (10^6 c.m.)	Electricity (10^6 kwh)
		Total	Crude oil	Total	Gasoline	Kerosine	Fuel oils	Lubes and greases		
	(1)	(2)	(3)	(4)	(5)	(6)	(7)	(8)	(9)	(10)
NORTH AFRICA (CONTINUED)										
1963	290	-41386	-44016	2630	359	476	1633	124	-	7
1964	590	-63119	-63157	38	-348	208	57	117	-90	2
1965	470	-80054	-78921	-1133	-527	206	-899	93	-833	1
ALGERIA										
1925	1532	73	-	73	41	18	4	10	-	-
1929	2383	172	-	172	98	44	16	14	-	-
1933	1585	437	-1	438	132	49	242	15	-	-
1937	1472	662	-	662	114	39	497	12	-	-
1938	1295	669	-	669	121	38	498	12	-	-
1950	455	1103	-	1103	190	50	840	23	4	-
1953	180	1410	-77	1487	270	70	1120	17	-	-4
1955	270	1699	-64	1763	347	95	1278	28	-	-10
1957	480	1942	-11	1953	520	95	1280	33	-	-10
1960	350	-6063	-8043	1980	361	116	1423	29	-	10
1961	210	-13344	-15097	1753	326	124	1213	29	-	5
1962	100	-19149	-20355	1206	320	117	709	20	-	7
1963	50	-22298	-23655	1357	244	126	940	20	-	4
1964	70	-24886	-24825	-61	-67	18	-27	20	-90	1
1965	20	-24852	-24400	-452	-220	-10	-219	15	-833	-
EGYPT UAR										
1925	1403	239	99	140	-72	146	50	16	-	-
1929	1380	399	122	277	-28	285	-1	21	-	-
1933	1189	552	78	474	-21	268	208	19	-	-
1937	1500	660	107	553	1	288	242	22	-	-
1938	1601	669	106	563	5	309	228	21	-	-
1950	217	1744	-	1744	71	441	1200	32	-	-
1953	78	1550	46	1504	79	495	900	30	-	-
1955	110	3087	1012	2075	93	509	1439	34	-	-
1957	180	1914	906	1008	65	397	508	38	-	-
1960	160	2460	1209	1251	-40	420	831	41	-	-
1961	300	2063	975	1088	-20	379	676	53	-	-
1962	270	1776	861	915	-246	369	757	35	-	-
1963	270	1071	882	189	-111	202	33	67	-	-
1964	500	1112	1720	-608	-457	79	-288	58	-	-
1965	440	1054	2363	-1309	-483	93	-961	42	-	-
LIBYA										
1925	17	10	-	10	6	2	1	1	-	-
1929	21	17	-	17	9	3	3	2	-	-
1933	37	33	-	33	15	4	12	2	-	-
1937	44	49	-	49	17	5	25	2	-	-
1938	55	64	-	64	17	7	37	3	-	-
1950	NA	97	-	97	27	40	29	1	-	-
1953	-	134	-	134	45	52	35	2	-	-
1955	70	204	-	204	100	60	40	4	-	-
1957	30	266	-	266	125	65	70	5	-	-
1960	30	344	-	344	120	75	140	7	-	-
1961	40	-369	-692	323	110	75	130	6	-	-

Table V. NET ENERGY IMPORTS OR EXPORTS, SELECTED YEARS, 1925-1965

(Original units; minus sign [-] = net exports)

Region, country, year	Solid fuels (10³ m.t. coal equiv.)	Liquid fuels (10³ m.t.) Total	Crude oil	Refined petroleum products Total	Gasoline	Kerosine	Fuel oils	Lubes and greases	Gas (10⁶ c.m.)	Electricity (10⁶ kwh)
	(1)	(2)	(3)	(4)	(5)	(6)	(7)	(8)	(9)	(10)
LIBYA (CONTINUED)										
1962	10	-7508	-7852	344	130	75	130	7	-	-
1963	10	-21660	-22039	379	140	80	145	8	-	-
1964	-	-41035	-41476	441	160	85	180	12	-	-
1965	10	-58026	-58475	449	165	90	181	9	-	-
MOROCCO										
1925	121	36	-	36	23	7	1	5	-	-
1929	181	94	-	94	57	21	8	8	-	-
1933	194	116	-	116	84	12	12	8	-	-
1937	87	137	-1	138	99	12	21	6	-	-
1938	33	178	-3	181	132	13	30	6	-	-
1950	-55	495	-	495	209	25	249	12	-	-
1953	-58	848	-30	878	355	62	445	16	-	-
1955	-190	852	-	852	329	81	416	20	-	-10
1957	-190	730	27	703	237	39	408	12	-	-
1960	-100	823	90	733	184	48	473	19	-	-10
1961	-110	871	129	742	168	47	498	19	-	9
1962	-80	596	200	396	108	28	239	17	-	8
1963	-80	868	710	158	9	17	114	18	-	3
1964	-20	932	805	127	4	8	98	14	-	1
1965	-50	1071	910	161	9	31	98	16	-	1
TUNISIA										
1925	223	31	-	31	9	13	6	3	-	-
1929	257	80	-	80	29	29	16	6	-	-
1933	215	93	-	93	44	26	18	5	-	-
1937	218	103	-	103	43	24	31	5	-	-
1938	238	106	-	106	46	24	31	5	-	-
1950	173	230	-	230	69	28	125	8	-	-
1953	84	341	-	341	84	35	216	6	-	-
1955	40	442	-	442	86	37	308	8	-	-
1957	90	380	-	380	73	36	260	7	-	-
1960	40	462	-	462	77	45	326	9	-	-
1961	50	485	-	485	70	47	349	14	-	-
1962	40	507	6	501	75	50	361	9	-	-
1963	40	633	86	547	77	51	401	11	-	-
1964	40	758	619	139	12	18	94	13	-	-
1965	50	699	681	18	2	2	2	11	-	-
TROPICAL AFRICA										
1925	997	329	-	329	46	56	186	9	-	-
1929	1333	578	-	578	149	91	312	26	-	-
1933	602	657	-	657	125	51	464	17	-	-
1937	1224	1806	-	1806	454	96	1226	30	-	-
1938	956	1052	-	1052	263	84	673	32	-	-
1950	870	2993	-	2993	825	238	1828	102	-	-
1953	651	5063	-	5063	1207	333	3431	92	-	-
1955	684	6024	-	6024	1521	447	3908	146	-	20
1957	384	7678	-143	7821	1756	482	5431	146	-	-700
1960	363	6579	-1551	8130	1860	641	5466	145	-	-580
1961	391	5839	-2494	8333	1781	687	5700	148	-	-

Table V. NET ENERGY IMPORTS OR EXPORTS, SELECTED YEARS, 1925-1965

(Original units; minus sign [-] = net exports)

Region, country, year	Solid fuels (10^3 m.t. coal equiv.)	Liquid fuels (10^3 m.t.) Total	Liquid fuels: Crude oil	Refined petroleum products: Total	Refined: Gasoline	Refined: Kerosine	Refined: Fuel oils	Refined: Lubes and greases	Gas (10^6 c.m.)	Electricity (10^6 kwh)
	(1)	(2)	(3)	(4)	(5)	(6)	(7)	(8)	(9)	(10)
TROPICAL AFRICA (CONTINUED)										
1962	450	4825	-3908	8733	1797	790	5966	159	-	-
1963	310	4712	-3929	8641	1787	789	5881	162	-	-
1964	295	3330	-3788	7118	1534	780	4614	170	-	-17
1965	215	-3304	-9651	6347	1256	686	4205	183	-	-11
CONGO, DEMOCRATIC REPUBLIC										
1925	294	14	-	14	4	2	8	-	-	-
1929	466	42	-	42	18	3	18	4	-	-
1933	45	17	-	17	11	1	3	2	-	-
1937	165	42	-	42	30	2	6	4	-	-
1938	133	31	-	31	20	3	4	4	-	-
1950	208	158	-	158	105	13	32	8	-	-
1953	200	285	-	285	173	23	75	14	-	-
1955	290	408	-	408	212	28	144	22	-	20
1957	240	461	-	461	224	35	178	20	-	-690
1960	230	428	-	428	201	44	179	NA	-	-520
1961	330	454	-	454	218	47	185	NA	-	-463
1962	240	461	-	461	208	57	192	NA	-	-470
1963	220	502	-	502	230	74	196	NA	-	-275
1964	255	373	-	373	149	56	166	NA	-	-212
1965	330	450	-	450	209	63	176	NA	-	-275
EAST AFRICA										
1925	76	47	-	47	7	12	26	2	-	-
1929	111	99	-	99	31	21	42	5	-	-
1933	95	72	-	72	15	10	45	2	-	-
1937	166	135	-	135	36	17	78	4	-	-
1938	152	163	-	163	47	17	94	5	-	-
1950	44	590	-	590	139	39	398	14	-	-
1953	14	839	-	839	189	63	575	12	-	-
1955	26	1043	-	1043	255	77	686	25	-	-
1957	36	1208	-	1208	260	90	840	18	-	-
1960	40	1262	-	1262	267	119	854	21	-	-
1961	40	1209	-	1209	248	133	799	27	-	-
1962	40	1309	-	1309	266	165	848	28	-	-
1963	40	1405	221	1184	245	106	812	19	-	-
1964	30	1412	1500	-88	77	30	-214	20	-	-
1965	60	1534	1845	-311	-14	17	-336	26	-	-
EQUATORIAL AFRICA										
1925	2	2	-	2	2	-	-	-	-	-
1929	1	5	-	5	3	1	1	-	-	-
1933	2	7	-	7	5	1	-	1	-	-
1937	21	12	-	12	6	2	3	1	-	-
1938	11	13	-	13	8	2	2	1	-	-
1950	7	55	-	55	36	4	11	4	-	-
1953	4	84	-	84	44	9	28	3	-	-
1955	-	94	-	94	55	10	23	6	-	-
1957	-	-17	-143	126	60	10	50	6	-	-
1960	-	-624	-809	185	81	17	79	7	-	-

Table V. NET ENERGY IMPORTS OR EXPORTS, SELECTED YEARS, 1925-1965

(Original units; minus sign [-] = net exports)

Region, country, year	Solid fuels (10^3 m.t. coal equiv.)	Liquid fuels (10^3 m.t.)							Gas (10^6 c.m.)	Electricity (10^6 kwh)
				Refined petroleum products						
		Total	Crude oil	Total	Gasoline	Kerosine	Fuel oils	Lubes and greases		
	(1)	(2)	(3)	(4)	(5)	(6)	(7)	(8)	(9)	(10)
EQUATORIAL AFRICA (CONTINUED)										
1961	-	-654	-831	177	72	15	81	8	-	-
1962	-	-765	-953	188	79	16	85	7	-	-
1963	-	-853	-1045	192	74	20	90	7	-	-
1964	-	-921	-1147	226	78	38	102	7	-	-
1965	-	-1121	-1352	231	74	36	113	7	-	-
GHANA										
1925	54	19	-	19	9	8	1	1	-	-
1929	73	35	-	35	20	11	2	2	-	-
1933	27	25	-	25	13	6	4	2	-	-
1937	72	80	-	80	25	13	39	3	-	-
1938	77	89	-	89	22	9	56	2	-	-
1950	63	191	-	191	64	21	99	7	-	-
1953	99	233	-	233	87	30	111	5	-	-
1955	120	326	-	326	113	36	165	12	-	-
1957	110	368	-	368	146	41	171	10	-	-
1960	40	450	-	450	140	53	243	14	-	-
1961	50	419	-	419	108	42	256	13	-	-
1962	30	480	-	480	140	62	262	16	-	-
1963	40	548	194	354	100	41	197	16	-	-
1964	40	647	835	-188	-7	11	-208	16	-	-
1965	30	612	800	-188	-4	15	-221	22	-	-
LIBERIA										
1925	-	-	-	-	-	-	-	-	-	-
1929	-	-	-	-	-	-	-	-	-	-
1933	-	-	-	-	-	-	-	-	-	-
1937	-	1	-	1	1	-	-	-	-	-
1938	-	2	-	2	1	1	-	-	-	-
1950	-	16	-	16	7	3	6	-	-	-
1953	-	18	-	18	8	3	6	1	-	-
1955	-	61	-	61	11	43	6	1	-	-
1957	-	32	-	32	19	4	7	2	-	-
1960	-	59	-	59	21	7	29	2	-	-
1961	-	60	-	60	26	4	28	2	-	-
1962	-	92	-	92	19	8	61	4	-	-
1963	-	133	-	133	24	15	90	4	-	-
1964	-	193	-	193	28	32	128	5	-	-
1965	-	218	-	218	26	32	155	5	-	-
NIGERIA										
1925	-3	23	-	23	6	15	1	1	-	-
1929	-20	35	-	35	13	19	1	2	-	-
1933	4	16	-	16	7	7	1	1	-	-
1937	-5	38	-	38	21	11	4	2	-	-
1938	-14	40	-	40	23	11	4	2	-	-
1950	61	165	-	165	96	36	28	5	-	-
1953	23	229	-	229	124	45	55	5	-	-
1955	-100	313	-	313	155	56	91	11	-	-
1957	-100	407	-	407	196	68	130	13	-	-
1960	-30	-251	-860	609	228	102	257	19	-	-

Table V. NET ENERGY IMPORTS OR EXPORTS, SELECTED YEARS, 1925-1965

(Original units; minus sign [–] = net exports)

Region, country, year	Solid fuels (10^3 m.t. coal equiv.)	Liquid fuels (10^3 m.t.)							Gas (10^6 c.m.)	Electricity (10^6 kwh)
				Refined petroleum products						
		Total	Crude oil	Total	Gasoline	Kerosine	Fuel oils	Lubes and greases		
	(1)	(2)	(3)	(4)	(5)	(6)	(7)	(8)	(9)	(10)
NIGERIA (CONTINUED)										
1961	-50	-1492	-2275	783	242	130	389	19	-	-
1962	-30	-2619	-3354	735	233	139	338	21	-	-
1963	-40	-2876	-3754	878	261	165	424	23	-	-
1964	-60	-4823	-5876	1053	296	224	503	25	-	-
1965	-35	-12181	-13228	1047	285	202	530	23	-	-
RHODESIAN FEDERATION										
1925	-226	6	-	6	4	1	-	1	-	-
1929	-396	20	-	20	14	3	-	3	-	-
1933	-45	24	-	24	17	1	5	1	-	-
1937	-152	52	-	52	30	2	16	4	-	-
1938	-115	55	-	55	33	2	16	4	-	-
1950	-169	170	-	170	120	28	13	9	-	-
1953	-98	267	-	267	163	36	58	10	-	-
1955	-69	361	-	361	210	40	90	21	-	-
1957	-273	464	-	464	240	40	160	24	-	-
1960	-248	533	-	533	260	60	190	23	-	-
1961	-290	534	-	534	261	70	183	20	-	524
1962	-180	568	-	568	263	78	202	24	-	539
1963	-230	569	-	569	249	83	213	22	-	349
1964	-330	593	-	593	253	86	231	21	-	281
1965	-460	830	510	320	129	67	96	27	-	339
MALAWI										
1925	-	1	-	1	1	-	-	-	-	-
1929	3	1	-	1	1	-	-	-	-	-
1933	3	2	-	2	2	-	-	-	-	-
1937	5	2	-	2	2	-	-	-	-	-
1938	4	3	-	3	2	-	1	-	-	-
1950	25	15	-	15	8	2	5	-	-	-
1953	37	18	-	18	10	2	6	-	-	-
1955	42	30	-	30	20	-	10	-	-	-
1957	47	40	-	40	20	-	20	-	-	-
1960	57	50	-	50	20	10	20	-	-	-
1961	60	41	-	41	17	5	19	-	-	-
1962	60	44	-	44	17	6	21	-	-	-
1963	60	47	-	47	18	7	22	-	-	-
1964	60	49	-	49	19	7	23	-	-	-
1965	80	54	-	54	21	8	25	-	-	-
ZAMBIA										
1925	42	-	-	1	-	-	-	-	-	-
1929	142	4	-	4	3	-	-	1	-	-
1933	177	3	-	3	3	-	-	-	-	-
1937	341	5	-	5	4	-	-	1	-	-
1938	405	6	-	6	5	-	-	1	-	-
1950	654	40	-	40	26	6	6	2	-	-
1953	823	69	-	69	41	7	17	4	-	-
1955	880	90	-	90	50	10	30	NA	-	-
1957	940	110	-	110	60	10	40	NA	-	-
1960	1035	130	-	130	70	10	50	NA	-	-

Table V. NET ENERGY IMPORTS OR EXPORTS, SELECTED YEARS, 1925-1965

(Original units; minus sign [-] = net exports)

Region, country, year	Solid fuels (10^3 m.t. coal equiv.)	Liquid fuels (10^3 m.t.)								Gas (10^6 c.m.)	Electricity (10^6 kwh)
				Refined petroleum products							
		Total	Crude oil	Total	Gasoline	Kerosine	Fuel oils	Lubes and greases			
	(1)	(2)	(3)	(4)	(5)	(6)	(7)	(8)		(9)	(10)
ZAMBIA (CONTINUED)											
1961	1080	133	-	133	78	12	43	NA		-	1578
1962	990	138	-	138	78	13	47	NA		-	1755
1963	940	140	-	140	76	13	50	NA		-	1828
1964	1040	153	-	153	77	14	54	7		-	2032
1965	1215	202	-	202	99	19	72	11		-	2190
RHODESIA											
1925	-268	5	-	5	3	1	-	1		-	-
1929	-541	15	-	15	10	3	-	2		-	-
1933	-225	19	-	19	12	1	5	1		-	-
1937	-498	45	-	45	24	2	16	3		-	-
1938	-524	46	-	46	26	2	15	3		-	-
1950	-848	115	-	115	86	20	2	7		-	-
1953	-958	180	-	180	112	27	35	6		-	-
1955	-991	241	-	241	140	30	50	21		-	-
1957	-1260	314	-	314	160	30	100	24		-	-
1960	-1340	353	-	353	170	40	120	23		-	-
1961	-1430	360	-	360	166	53	121	20		-	-1054
1962	-1230	386	-	386	168	59	134	24		-	-1216
1963	-1230	382	-	382	155	63	141	22		-	-1479
1964	-1430	391	-	391	157	65	154	14		-	-1751
1965	-1755	574	510	64	9	40	-1	16		-	-1851
WEST AFRICA											
1925	181	30	-	30	NA	NA	NA	NA		-	-
1929	296	119	-	119	13	7	94	5		-	-
1933	115	270	-	270	15	4	249	2		-	-
1937	399	719	-	719	29	8	678	4		-	-
1938	98	55	-	55	28	8	15	4		-	-
1950	165	818	-	818	80	30	670	38		-	-
1953	56	1408	-	1408	133	38	1225	12		-	-
1955	30	1476	-	1476	160	60	1240	16		-	-
1957	1	2263	-	2263	200	70	1980	13		-	-
1960	1	1752	-	1752	256	79	1398	15		-	-
1961	1	1736	-	1736	259	80	1379	14		-	-
1962	-	1842	-	1842	268	82	1472	16		-	-
1963	-	1876	18	1858	266	94	1477	17		-	-
1964	-	1998	290	1708	268	92	1326	18		-	-
1965	-	2185	654	1531	216	84	1210	19		-	-
SOUTH AFRICA											
1925	-1597	129	-	129	69	41	2	17		-	-
1929	-1652	380	-	380	223	73	55	29		-	-
1933	-782	407	-	407	244	42	96	25		-	-
1937	-794	972	-	972	466	60	400	46		-	-
1938	-877	1084	-	1084	514	58	473	39		-	-
1950	-2546	2297	-	2297	1087	352	785	73		-	-
1953	-1184	2513	29	2484	1268	470	668	78		-	-
1955	-560	3125	940	2185	1059	478	516	132		-	-
1957	-550	4051	1069	2982	1054	466	1328	134		-	-
1960	-960	3649	1281	2368	1162	395	701	110		-	-

Table V. NET ENERGY IMPORTS OR EXPORTS, SELECTED YEARS, 1925-1965

(Original units; minus sign [-] = net exports)

Region, country, year	Solid fuels (10^3 m.t. coal equiv.)	Liquid fuels (10^3 m.t.)		Refined petroleum products					Gas (10^6 c.m.)	Electricity (10^6 kwh)
		Total	Crude oil	Total	Gasoline	Kerosine	Fuel oils	Lubes and greases		
	(1)	(2)	(3)	(4)	(5)	(6)	(7)	(8)	(9)	(10)
SOUTH AFRICA (CONTINUED)										
1961	-1060	4074	1482	2592	1221	405	840	126	-	-
1962	-1600	4318	1617	2701	1244	390	917	150	-	-
1963	-1350	4515	2190	2325	1106	396	714	109	-	-
1964	-1280	5798	4850	948	670	437	-309	152	-	-
1965	-1200	6158	4675	1483	714	378	204	188	-	-
DEVELOPED COUNTRIES										
1925	-14549	13141	12968	173	1182	-844	-186	11	-2	47
1929	-9255	23461	17417	6045	2810	105	2892	236	-4	-158
1933	-1889	26391	11725	14666	6397	1081	7203	-15	-59	-157
1937	-2459	31239	15856	15383	6007	706	7847	-190	-136	-306
1938	499	30524	15028	15497	5565	790	7869	-113	-49	-285
1950	3736	113697	73193	40504	8461	3109	29689	-687	-606	290
1953	6760	152902	127501	25401	1779	2101	22482	-812	-588	-1196
1955	7069	202114	163389	38725	1663	2594	35625	-883	-604	-1420
1957	641	236867	185381	51486	2366	2042	48240	-840	6	-1750
1960	14265	343132	273705	69427	4462	1208	65402	-1182	1103	-70
1961	14037	380287	307201	73086	4505	664	69619	-1171	1256	-1885
1962	17010	426174	337355	88819	4694	3913	81726	-1256	1125	-54
1963	16843	479317	382453	96864	5330	5182	88214	-1575	1096	-249
1964	20888	543909	439175	104734	5416	5937	94841	-1319	1206	-963
1965	19562	609260	493858	115402	3914	6956	106120	-1462	2041	333
UNDERDEVELOPED COUNTRIES										
1925	13513	-15387	-10089	-5298	-1081	678	-5114	187	2	-
1929	13999	-23845	-13341	-10504	-2688	-11	-7971	164	4	-
1933	8688	-25064	-10194	-14870	-4726	-282	-9977	115	59	21
1937	11655	-37298	-12935	-24363	-5561	-609	-18202	9	136	19
1938	9412	-35506	-11522	-23984	-5606	-569	-17846	37	49	18
1950	5551	-126450	-69478	-56972	-8786	-3273	-46534	576	658	130
1953	3650	-165910	-123772	-42138	-3295	-2070	-37263	360	540	213
1955	5104	-205822	-160420	-45402	-3294	-3221	-39589	419	555	170
1957	5124	-237638	-186712	-50926	-3487	-4454	-43997	681	-180	-300
1960	4747	-333256	-261119	-72137	-6569	-4904	-61490	490	-1171	-130
1961	4171	-358528	-283386	-75142	-6126	-4996	-65012	604	-1320	469
1962	3660	-410490	-316081	-94409	-8714	-5577	-80921	522	-1162	543
1963	3664	-460176	-358136	-102040	-10225	-5950	-86886	836	-1135	598
1964	3947	-524791	-413595	-111196	-11583	-8085	-91801	440	-1302	132
1965	3900	-579843	-457931	-121912	-13680	-9367	-98744	85	-2135	50
COMMUNIST COUNTRIES										
1925	-8212	-1147	21	-1169	-556	24	-588	-176	-	69
1929	-14940	-4838	-3	-4835	-1793	-773	-2228	-238	-	69
1933	-13557	-8522	-542	-7980	-2959	-870	-4120	-273	-	13
1937	-17186	-5068	-18	-5050	-1896	-674	-2490	-180	-	15
1938	-13905	-3955	-174	-3781	-1581	-669	-1565	-128	-	-
1950	-12529	645	1585	-940	-965	-390	15	-	31	-220
1953	-9706	-2878	1042	-3920	-1650	-765	-1005	-	21	-2
1955	-14340	-4651	533	-5184	-1310	-382	-3438	-43	22	150
1957	-14830	-7933	-739	-7194	-771	-624	-5669	-127	45	-
1960	-19850	-23458	-10113	-13345	-655	-540	-11700	-431	27	160

Table V. NET ENERGY IMPORTS OR EXPORTS, SELECTED YEARS, 1925-1965

(Original units; minus sign [-] = net exports)

Region, country, year	Solid fuels (10^3 m.t. coal equiv.)	Liquid fuels (10^3 m.t.)								Gas (10^6 c.m.)	Electricity (10^6 kwh)
				Refined petroleum products							
		Total	Crude oil	Total	Gasoline	Kerosine	Fuel oils	Lubes and greases			
	(1)	(2)	(3)	(4)	(5)	(6)	(7)	(8)		(9)	(10)
COMMUNIST COUNTRIES (CONTINUED)											
1961	-21020	-30806	-15608	-15198	-999	-483	-13226	-471		27	-9
1962	-23450	-34470	-17109	-17361	-1138	-758	-14911	-541		5	470
1963	-23710	-38117	-18865	-19252	-1430	-583	-16782	-450		18	471
1964	-24410	-41834	-21851	-19983	-1373	-536	-17616	-457		28	-85
1965	-24246	-47651	-24706	-22945	-1653	-885	-19960	-434		-13	-42
USSR											
1925	325	-1307	-54	-1253	-271	-414	-474	-94		-	-
1929	-242	-3762	-295	-3467	-1078	-739	-1441	-209		-	-
1933	-1020	-4805	-529	-4276	-1284	-512	-2234	-246		-	-
1937	-243	-1683	-110	-1573	-244	-180	-939	-210		-	-
1938	724	-1152	-215	-937	-146	-138	-507	-146		-	-
1950	8800	1600	1200	400	NA	NA	NA	NA		-25	-
1953	5500	-700	-200	-500	NA	NA	NA	NA		-95	-
1955	3300	-2691	-1341	-1350	583	-92	-1798	-43		-140	10
1957	-6990	-9539	-4592	-4947	318	-614	-4536	-115		-171	-
1960	-9330	-28947	-16659	-12288	-644	-788	-10599	-257		-243	-30
1961	-12510	-37629	-22500	-15129	-1809	-803	-12240	-277		-270	-74
1962	-16860	-42584	-25783	-16801	-1574	-1051	-13854	-322		-302	-232
1963	-19090	-48585	-29700	-18885	-1807	-1065	-15773	-240		-302	-747
1964	-21530	-54556	-36691	-17865	-1361	-739	-15625	-140		-293	-1304
1965	-18405	-62479	-43432	-19047	-1132	-996	-16793	-126		-392	-1501
COMMUNIST EASTERN EUROPE											
1925	-8738	-781	75	-857	-310	-356	-211	-107		-	69
1929	-13477	-2147	292	-2439	-795	-769	-994	-78		-	69
1933	-9899	-4817	38	-4855	-1795	-967	-2254	-81		-	13
1937	-12523	-4458	-4	-4454	-1854	-927	-1831	-32		-	15
1938	-11577	-3521	-34	-3487	-1574	-806	-1245	-24		-	-
1950	-21329	-955	385	-1340	-965	-390	15	-		56	-220
1953	-15206	-2178	1242	-3420	-1650	-765	-1005	-		116	-2
1955	-16620	-3335	1474	-4809	-2153	-610	-2035	-		162	140
1957	-6100	-690	3428	-4118	-1925	-455	-1723	-12		216	-
1960	-9600	1919	5936	-4017	-1451	-252	-2121	-174		270	190
1961	-7390	3443	6812	-3369	-815	-240	-2101	-194		297	65
1962	-5370	5619	8534	-2915	-679	-232	-1772	-219		307	702
1963	-3190	8213	10685	-2472	-548	-48	-1659	-210		320	1218
1964	-1660	11267	14640	-3373	-657	-17	-2381	-317		321	1219
1965	-4226	13798	18516	-4718	-916	31	-3512	-308		379	1459
COMMUNIST ASIA											
1925	201	941	-	941	25	794	97	25		-	-
1929	-1221	1071	-	1071	80	735	207	49		-	-
1933	-2638	1100	-51	1151	120	609	368	54		-	-
1937	-4420	1073	96	977	202	433	280	62		-	-
1938	-3052	718	75	643	139	275	187	42		-	-
1950	NA	NA	NA	NA	NA	NA	NA	NA		NA	NA
1953	NA	NA	NA	NA	NA	NA	NA	NA		NA	NA
1955	-1020	1375	400	975	260	320	395	NA		NA	NA
1957	-1740	2296	425	1871	836	445	590	NA		NA	NA
1960	-920	3570	610	2960	1440	500	1020	NA		NA	NA

Table V. NET ENERGY IMPORTS OR EXPORTS, SELECTED YEARS, 1925-1965

(Original units; minus sign [–] = net exports)

Region, country, year	Solid fuels (10^3 m.t. coal equiv.)	Liquid fuels (10^3 m.t.) Total	Crude oil	Refined petroleum products Total	Gasoline	Kerosine	Fuel oils	Lubes and greases	Gas (10^6 c.m.)	Electricity (10^6 kwh)
	(1)	(2)	(3)	(4)	(5)	(6)	(7)	(8)	(9)	(10)
COMMUNIST ASIA (CONTINUED)										
1961	-1120	3380	80	3300	1625	560	1115	NA	NA	NA
1962	-1220	2495	140	2355	1115	525	715	NA	NA	NA
1963	-1430	2255	150	2105	925	530	650	NA	NA	NA
1964	-1220	1455	200	1255	645	220	390	NA	NA	NA
1965	-1615	1030	210	820	395	80	345	NA	NA	NA
ORGANISATION FOR ECONOMIC CO-OPERATION AND DEVELOPMENT (OECD)										
1925	-14149	11989	12745	-756	627	-1021	-296	-75	-2	47
1929	-10420	21118	16849	4270	1589	-155	2732	104	-4	-158
1933	-2990	24129	11374	12755	5278	840	6752	-115	-59	-157
1937	-4606	27410	15453	11957	4122	365	6803	-346	-136	-306
1938	-1186	26322	14615	11707	3484	466	6624	-252	-49	-285
1950	3217	104657	71991	32666	4933	2348	26390	-937	-606	290
1953	5555	143293	126118	17175	-2367	1310	19339	-958	-588	-1161
1955	3840	188305	157076	31229	-1963	1732	32944	-1210	-604	-1370
1957	-3030	219789	174797	44992	-143	1285	45340	-1174	6	-1600
1960	11910	323994	259587	64407	1932	576	63928	-1575	1103	-400
1961	13260	360015	292042	67973	2082	65	67949	-1595	1256	-1982
1962	17030	405420	323375	82045	1730	3100	79125	-1646	1125	20
1963	17220	455702	365929	89773	2332	4330	85359	-1955	1096	-291
1964	21565	516675	418572	98103	2954	5084	91884	-1675	1206	-2001
1965	22341	578534	469890	108644	2007	6065	102488	-1788	2041	-631
COMMUNIST COUNTRIES										
1925	-8212	-1147	21	-1169	-556	24	-588	-176	-	69
1929	-14940	-4838	-3	-4835	-1793	-773	-2228	-238	-	69
1933	-13557	-8522	-542	-7980	-2959	-870	-4120	-273	-	13
1937	-17186	-5068	-18	-5050	-1896	-674	-2490	-180	-	15
1938	-13905	-3955	-174	-3781	-1581	-669	-1565	-128	-	-
1950	-12529	645	1585	-940	-965	-390	15	-	31	-220
1953	-9706	-2878	1042	-3920	-1650	-765	-1005	-	21	-2
1955	-14340	-4651	533	-5184	-1310	-382	-3438	-43	22	150
1957	-14830	-7933	-739	-7194	-771	-624	-5669	-127	45	-
1960	-19850	-23458	-10113	-13345	-655	-540	-11700	-431	27	160
1961	-21020	-30806	-15608	-15198	-999	-483	-13226	-471	27	-9
1962	-23450	-34470	-17109	-17361	-1138	-758	-14911	-541	5	470
1963	-23710	-38117	-18865	-19252	-1430	-583	-16782	-450	18	471
1964	-24410	-41834	-21851	-19983	-1373	-536	-17616	-457	28	-85
1965	-24246	-47651	-24706	-22945	-1653	-885	-19960	-434	-13	-42
WORLD EXCLUDING OECD AND COMMUNIST COUNTRIES										
1925	13113	-14235	-9866	-4369	-526	855	-5004	273	2	-
1929	15164	-21502	-12773	-8729	-1467	249	-7811	296	4	-
1933	9789	-22802	-9843	-12959	-3607	-41	-9526	215	59	21
1937	13802	-33469	-12532	-20937	-3676	-268	-17158	165	136	19
1938	11097	-31304	-11109	-20194	-3525	-245	-16601	176	49	18
1950	6070	-117410	-68276	-49134	-5258	-2512	-43235	826	658	130
1953	4855	-156301	-122389	-33912	851	-1279	-34120	506	540	178
1955	8333	-192013	-154107	-37906	332	-2359	-36908	746	555	120
1957	8795	-220560	-176128	-44432	-978	-3697	-41097	1015	-180	-450
1960	7102	-314118	-247001	-67117	-4039	-4272	-60016	883	-1171	200

Table V. NET ENERGY IMPORTS OR EXPORTS, SELECTED YEARS, 1925-1965

(Original units; minus sign [-] = net exports)

Region, country, year	Solid fuels (10^3 m.t. coal equiv.)	Liquid fuels (10^3 m.t.)							Gas (10^6 c.m.)	Electricity (10^6 kwh)
				Refined petroleum products						
		Total	Crude oil	Total	Gasoline	Kerosine	Fuel oils	Lubes and greases		
	(1)	(2)	(3)	(4)	(5)	(6)	(7)	(8)	(9)	(10)
WORLD EXCLUDING OECD AND COMMUNIST COUNTRIES (CONTINUED)										
1961	4948	-338256	-268227	-70029	-3703	-4397	-63342	1028	-1320	566
1962	3640	-389736	-302101	-87635	-5750	-4764	-78320	912	-1162	469
1963	3287	-436561	-341612	-94949	-7227	-5098	-84031	1216	-1135	640
1964	3270	-497557	-392992	-104565	-9121	-7232	-88844	796	-1302	1170
1965	1121	-549117	-433963	-115154	-11773	-8476	-95112	411	-2135	1014

DERIVATION OF TABLE VI

Column	*Derivation*
(1)	Sum of cols. (2), (3), (10), and (11)
(2)	From col. (1) of table IV
(3)	Sum of cols. (4) and (5)
(4)	Col. (3) of table IV multiplied by 1.5*
(5)	Col. (4) of table IV multiplied by 1.5*
(6)	Col. (5) of table IV multiplied by 1.5*
(7)	Col. (6) of table IV multiplied by 1.5*
(8)	Col. (7) of table IV multiplied by 1.5*
(9)	Col. (8) of table IV multiplied by 1.5*
(10)	Col. (9) of table IV multiplied by 1.332*
(11)	Col. (10) of table IV multiplied by 0.125*

Table VI. ENERGY IMPORTS AND EXPORTS, SELECTED YEARS, 1925-1965

(Thousand metric tons coal equivalent)

			Liquid fuels								
					Refined petroleum products						
Region, country, year	Total energy	Solid fuels	Total	Crude oil	Total	Gasoline	Kerosine	Fuel oils	Lubes and greases	Gas	Electricity
	(1)	(2)	(3)	(4)	(5)	(6)	(7)	(8)	(9)	(10)	(11)
WORLD								IMPORTS			
1925	199663	136597	62801	28203	34598	9347	6581	15629	2778	5	261
1929	277661	168343	108996	54036	54960	18861	8415	23648	3719	9	312
1933	216496	113488	102657	48281	54377	17721	6414	27308	2565	79	272
1937	292025	142341	149069	75684	73385	21507	6750	39929	3392	181	434
1938	282144	125691	155952	79482	76470	23984	6864	40142	3156	65	436
1950	476295	116920	357474	216941	140534	31190	10385	91997	3677	1409	491
1953	608562	128839	478083	308058	170025	35879	13193	112428	3825	1134	513
1955	751484	155061	594353	386097	208256	40971	16971	144197	5121	1304	766
1957	849016	158291	688821	447869	240953	44907	16685	172871	5308	1088	816
1960	991070	132112	851283	576809	274475	47822	17103	202152	5892	6298	1377
1961	1076340	133888	932322	647213	285110	47817	17594	211617	6246	8753	1377
1962	1192141	143000	1032492	721092	311400	45296	22881	234096	6589	15469	1181
1963	1304371	158247	1129359	800861	328499	44595	24033	249743	7206	15614	1151
1964	1424420	160872	1245087	908609	336479	42626	23102	259916	7258	16980	1480
1965	1545969	157916	1368000	1010961	357039	40248	25337	280112	6418	18288	1765
WORLD								EXPORTS			
1925	213988	145845	67892	23853	44039	10029	6794	24461	2745	5	246
1929	295699	178539	116828	47927	68901	21368	9434	34608	3476	9	324
1933	234062	120246	113450	46797	66653	19653	6521	37649	2825	79	288

Table VI. ENERGY IMPORTS AND EXPORTS, SELECTED YEARS, 1925-1965

(Thousand metric tons coal equivalent)

			Liquid fuels								
					Refined petroleum products						
Region, country, year	Total energy	Solid fuels	Total	Crude oil	Total	Gasoline	Kerosine	Fuel oils	Lubes and greases	Gas	Electricity
	(1)	(2)	(3)	(4)	(5)	(6)	(7)	(8)	(9)	(10)	(11)
WORLD (CONTINUED)								EXPORTS			
1937	316739	150331	165759	71330	94430	23682	7616	59196	3933	181	468
1938	299576	129685	169356	74484	94872	26417	7536	57455	3462	65	469
1950	497563	120162	375636	208991	166646	33125	11216	117242	3843	1299	466
1953	631852	128135	501912	300902	201011	40628	14294	136107	4503	1169	636
1955	766363	157228	606891	380844	226047	45383	18485	155300	5881	1340	904
1957	871566	167356	701877	450974	250904	47745	21239	175010	5737	1260	1072
1960	1012341	132950	871656	573099	298557	51965	23457	213834	7576	6352	1382
1961	1092950	136700	945893	634902	310991	51747	24816	224546	7803	8802	1556
1962	1223023	145780	1060671	714845	345827	53033	26514	255255	8502	15511	1061
1963	1335963	161450	1157823	792683	365141	54083	26060	272924	8989	15642	1048
1964	1458274	160447	1279161	903015	376146	53936	27128	281780	9262	17071	1595
1965	1574204	158700	1395351	994130	401222	57377	30281	298988	9135	18431	1722
NORTH AMERICA								IMPORTS			
1925	38236	16689	21386	17228	4158	1094	32	2969	63	3	159
1929	50815	18706	31928	24471	7457	2433	66	4833	122	4	178
1933	28529	11487	16922	13140	3782	287	9	3423	63	-	121
1937	36664	14573	21863	15981	5882	470	14	5298	101	-	228
1938	33516	12836	20454	14591	5864	653	33	5072	107	-	226
1950	115202	25666	89129	56154	32975	1658	603	30491	117	198	209
1953	128434	21890	106280	69329	36951	1547	741	34259	227	-	264
1955	145071	18760	125802	82580	43223	1916	771	40100	285	-	509
1957	173559	18720	154008	104273	49736	3281	870	45177	260	354	476
1960	195704	12940	176759	110615	66144	4754	890	60218	264	5436	570
1961	203204	11690	183384	114894	68490	4748	621	62865	245	7848	282
1962	223874	12020	197214	123324	73890	2715	3833	66794	248	14549	90
1963	231181	12740	203739	126191	77549	3293	5150	68510	257	14683	19
1964	246478	14240	216117	131304	84813	3044	5027	75893	305	15984	137
1965	268057	15797	236004	134379	101625	2708	6389	91176	363	16254	2
NORTH AMERICA								EXPORTS			
1925	42935	20344	22427	2897	19530	5600	4115	7742	2075	5	159
1929	52398	20828	31383	5807	25577	10976	3882	8393	2327	9	178
1933	31205	9967	21036	7905	13131	5196	1740	4434	1761	79	124
1937	49770	14515	34844	14406	20438	6779	1724	9576	2360	181	231
1938	51252	12050	38909	16554	22355	8868	1457	10008	2022	65	228
1950	48599	27822	19475	7463	12012	3672	368	4833	2931	1074	229
1953	60489	33969	25439	4754	20685	5790	1373	10500	2640	790	292
1955	77384	50540	25542	5487	20055	5115	617	10833	2943	769	534
1957	124028	74480	48872	22064	26808	5871	1197	16311	2844	144	533
1960	62192	35700	21957	9224	12734	2444	134	6288	3303	3893	641
1961	65516	34510	24525	13911	10614	1550	41	4772	3584	6133	348
1962	80776	37920	29687	18948	10739	1229	60	4980	3711	13008	162
1963	92292	47100	31911	18788	13124	1319	204	6863	3854	13188	93
1964	94668	46630	33447	20819	12629	1604	66	5853	3903	14436	155
1965	96505	48220	33638	22124	11514	1181	156	4611	3582	14639	9
CANADA								IMPORTS			
1925	19703	15601	4100	3386	714	420	29	210	56	3	-
1929	25865	17619	8243	7025	1218	875	26	206	113	4	-
1933	17597	10698	6899	6098	801	284	9	446	63	-	-

Table VI. ENERGY IMPORTS AND EXPORTS, SELECTED YEARS, 1925-1965

(Thousand metric tons coal equivalent)

Region, country, year	Total energy	Solid fuels	Liquid fuels: Total	Liquid fuels: Crude oil	Refined petroleum products: Total	Gasoline	Kerosine	Fuel oils	Lubes and greases	Gas	Electricity
	(1)	(2)	(3)	(4)	(5)	(6)	(7)	(8)	(9)	(10)	(11)
CANADA (CONTINUED)								IMPORTS			
1937	22959	13690	9269	8474	795	369	14	314	99	-	-
1938	20642	12126	8516	7457	1059	596	33	326	105	-	-
1950	47561	24927	22436	17411	5025	1532	555	2715	117	198	-
1953	45670	21518	24152	17721	6431	1445	741	3840	227	-	-
1955	44047	18320	25727	18750	6977	1016	770	4755	285	-	-
1957	49076	18270	30452	24131	6321	1035	863	4016	260	354	-
1960	45869	12560	33309	26624	6686	465	875	5064	263	-	-
1961	44910	11410	33500	27996	5504	315	534	4398	245	-	-
1962	45709	11650	34059	28275	5784	260	479	4796	240	-	-
1963	49725	12330	37395	30968	6428	435	579	5148	251	-	-
1964	52245	13860	38385	30324	8061	456	522	6776	296	-	-
1965	57866	15530	42335	30288	12047	419	450	10809	356	-	2
CANADA								EXPORTS			
1925	978	754	65	39	26	8	9	9	-	-	159
1929	1164	803	183	149	35	24	8	3	-	-	178
1933	547	251	173	66	107	21	6	80	-	-	124
1937	695	353	104	-	104	21	5	71	8	8	231
1938	630	346	47	-	47	26	5	12	5	9	228
1950	903	667	8	-	8	-	2	6	-	-	229
1953	1237	357	519	483	36	2	-	35	-	69	292
1955	4359	630	3189	3008	182	65	-	117	-	7	534
1957	12960	450	11978	11297	681	213	209	257	3	-	533
1960	14568	880	9153	8562	591	240	3	168	2	3893	641
1961	21244	990	13773	13221	552	101	-	240	-	6133	348
1962	33551	920	19461	18564	897	171	-	461	8	13008	162
1963	33547	980	19286	18423	863	86	39	434	14	13188	93
1964	37580	1240	21749	20526	1223	185	-	521	8	14436	155
1965	39285	1170	23477	21888	1589	45	-	522	9	14639	-
UNITED STATES								IMPORTS			
1925	18526	1082	17285	13842	3443	674	3	2759	8	-	159
1929	24941	1081	23682	17447	6236	1559	41	4628	9	-	178
1933	10919	777	10022	7043	2979	3	-	2976	-	-	121
1937	13678	859	12591	7508	5084	99	-	4983	2	-	228
1938	12847	684	11937	7134	4803	57	-	4745	2	-	226
1950	67629	727	66693	38744	27950	126	48	27776	-	-	209
1953	82750	362	82124	51608	30516	98	-	30419	-	-	264
1955	100927	410	100008	63830	36179	897	-	35282	-	-	509
1957	124407	430	123501	80142	43359	2243	6	41111	-	-	476
1960	149736	350	143381	83991	59390	4284	14	55092	-	5436	570
1961	158156	260	149766	86898	62868	4428	83	58358	-	7848	282
1962	178046	350	163056	95049	68007	2450	3351	61910	6	14549	90
1963	181315	380	166233	95223	71010	2852	4566	63263	5	14683	19
1964	194069	360	177588	100980	76608	2582	4500	68985	8	15984	137
1965	210015	250	193511	104091	89420	2280	5927	80231	6	16254	-
UNITED STATES								EXPORTS			
1925	41957	19590	22362	2858	19505	5592	4106	7733	2075	5	-
1929	51234	20025	31200	5658	25542	10952	3875	8390	2327	9	-
1933	30658	9716	20864	7839	13025	5175	1734	4355	1761	79	-

Table VI. ENERGY IMPORTS AND EXPORTS, SELECTED YEARS, 1925-1965

(Thousand metric tons coal equivalent)

Region, country, year	Total energy	Solid fuels	Liquid fuels: Total	Liquid fuels: Crude oil	Refined petroleum products: Total	Refined petroleum products: Gasoline	Refined petroleum products: Kerosine	Refined petroleum products: Fuel oils	Refined petroleum products: Lubes and greases	Gas	Electricity
	(1)	(2)	(3)	(4)	(5)	(6)	(7)	(8)	(9)	(10)	(11)
UNITED STATES (CONTINUED)								EXPORTS			
1937	49075	14162	34740	14406	20334	6758	1719	9506	2352	173	-
1938	50622	11704	38862	16554	22308	8843	1452	9996	2018	56	-
1950	47696	27155	19467	7463	12005	3672	366	4827	2931	1074	-
1953	59252	33612	24920	4271	20649	5789	1373	10466	2640	721	-
1955	73025	49910	22353	2480	19874	5051	617	10716	2943	762	-
1957	111068	74030	36894	10767	26127	5658	989	16055	2841	144	-
1960	47614	34810	12804	662	12143	2204	131	6120	3302	-	-
1961	44262	33510	10752	690	10062	1449	41	4532	3584	-	-
1962	47226	37000	10226	384	9842	1058	60	4520	3704	-	-
1963	58746	46120	12626	365	12261	1233	165	6429	3840	-	-
1964	57089	45390	11699	293	11406	1419	66	5333	3896	-	-
1965	57220	47050	10161	236	9926	1136	156	4089	3573	-	9
WESTERN EUROPE								IMPORTS			
1925	113370	93882	19395	4185	15210	5690	2556	4902	2049	-	93
1929	147380	118034	29220	4209	25011	11178	3228	8012	2594	-	126
1933	118074	80696	37232	8280	28952	13248	2442	11483	1779	-	147
1937	151757	101034	50522	16704	33818	13278	2681	15614	2246	-	202
1938	140696	86422	54066	19241	34826	14357	2514	15896	2060	-	208
1950	161482	61209	99842	59672	40170	11988	3564	22802	1817	188	244
1953	232816	69274	163161	120821	42341	9218	4065	27368	1683	182	198
1955	309910	98685	210779	150663	60116	10599	4400	42636	2165	253	194
1957	347524	103627	243324	164003	79322	12851	4347	59600	2087	356	218
1960	427359	76883	349725	252281	97445	14163	3687	76643	2322	131	620
1961	463828	75564	387420	290595	96825	14664	3449	75453	2475	132	712
1962	525161	81405	442943	323297	119646	17006	5339	93755	2675	139	675
1963	593892	94350	498735	366860	131876	17070	6647	104481	2697	157	650
1964	652046	88779	562241	424335	137906	18567	7812	107319	3048	221	806
1965	720764	80605	637710	489642	148068	19473	8297	115904	2738	1260	1189
WESTERN EUROPE								EXPORTS			
1925	103248	101998	1163	-	1163	296	128	582	158	-	87
1929	126370	125237	987	3	984	237	108	414	225	-	146
1933	86706	85411	1131	56	1076	320	101	417	239	-	164
1937	109666	106940	2489	2	2487	648	281	1122	437	-	238
1938	93454	90757	2456	-	2456	743	254	1023	437	-	241
1950	68053	53676	14070	1619	12452	2474	374	9167	438	120	188
1953	94286	53457	40332	3150	37182	8888	1731	25740	797	176	321
1955	105515	61758	43122	2334	40788	10617	2297	26144	1398	289	346
1957	95917	52496	42483	1832	40652	10527	2375	25854	1412	558	380
1960	109408	45720	62927	2517	60410	13758	3831	40178	1863	204	558
1961	113423	46180	66188	2426	63762	14588	4287	42114	1839	174	881
1962	119905	45980	73134	3593	69542	15464	4524	46470	2118	181	610
1963	126436	49730	75908	4001	71907	15150	5022	48446	2127	192	607
1964	119995	42675	76250	1049	75201	15677	4797	50972	2477	163	908
1965	129713	37433	90983	674	90309	18051	5106	63041	2517	157	1140
EUROPEAN ECONOMIC COMMUNITY (EEC)								IMPORTS			
1925	75610	68197	7323	536	6788	2856	1188	1458	1286	-	90
1929	96994	84335	12537	846	11691	5459	1197	3311	1725	-	122
1933	71784	54482	17157	5063	12095	5687	791	4667	951	-	145

Table VI. ENERGY IMPORTS AND EXPORTS, SELECTED YEARS, 1925-1965

(Thousand metric tons coal equivalent)

Region, country, year	Total energy	Solid fuels	Liquid fuels							Gas	Electricity
					Refined petroleum products						
			Total	Crude oil	Total	Gasoline	Kerosine	Fuel oils	Lubes and greases		
	(1)	(2)	(3)	(4)	(5)	(6)	(7)	(8)	(9)	(10)	(11)
EUROPEAN ECONOMIC COMMUNITY (EEC) (CONTINUED)								IMPORTS			
1937	93503	67662	25641	12857	12785	3782	618	7151	1235	-	200
1938	83854	56009	27641	14946	12695	4058	503	7029	1106	-	205
1950	79575	32244	46922	38796	8126	1779	336	5400	611	188	221
1953	125336	42428	82565	73862	8703	1493	317	6372	519	182	161
1955	169904	57808	111672	97926	13746	1949	366	10331	884	253	171
1957	203805	73516	129764	106766	22998	2583	407	18869	843	356	170
1960	242845	51900	190283	159716	30567	3314	701	25271	843	125	538
1961	271716	51700	219306	187497	31809	3177	653	26496	929	132	579
1962	309082	56160	252242	208568	43674	4133	732	37115	1059	139	542
1963	360015	68130	291180	244263	46917	3950	1011	40167	1088	157	548
1964	400208	62770	336764	288759	48005	4490	1029	40503	1232	101	574
1965	448831	56672	390969	340139	50831	4811	1025	43278	981	402	788
EUROPEAN ECONOMIC COMMUNITY (EEC)								EXPORTS			
1925	46972	46793	179	-	179	35	9	30	105	-	-
1929	59888	59550	338	3	335	74	11	74	177	-	-
1933	43059	42476	581	56	525	83	30	224	189	-	3
1937	64286	62715	1571	2	1569	332	149	744	345	-	-
1938	53499	51915	1584	-	1584	453	180	629	323	-	-
1950	48002	37316	10562	14	10548	2268	329	7725	227	120	5
1953	63419	37511	25716	-	25716	7251	1502	16454	483	176	16
1955	77899	46958	30633	56	30578	8354	1901	19188	816	289	19
1957	73002	42346	30026	113	29913	7815	1881	19020	740	558	73
1960	83444	38570	44642	936	43706	10494	2664	28851	972	204	29
1961	88145	38560	49376	830	48546	11627	2850	32259	938	174	35
1962	89000	39060	49617	509	49109	11715	3011	32421	1040	181	142
1963	91631	39230	52209	269	51941	12108	3438	34217	1098	192	-
1964	89613	34865	54585	9	54576	12357	3386	36306	1325	163	-
1965	99478	32143	67178	48	67130	14252	3587	46341	1413	157	-
BELGIUM-LUXEMBOURG								IMPORTS			
1925	11895	11380	515	12	503	234	129	32	108	-	-
1929	15771	15127	644	2	642	290	107	135	111	-	-
1933	7976	7305	671	129	542	347	45	98	53	-	-
1937	11243	9547	1695	422	1274	465	14	521	275	-	1
1938	8214	6605	1608	462	1146	452	12	447	236	-	1
1950	7148	3485	3656	663	2993	1023	50	1703	218	-	8
1953	12672	5317	7355	4400	2955	827	83	1862	185	-	-
1955	17994	7340	10643	7068	3575	531	44	2598	276	-	11
1957	22022	9180	12842	8211	4631	584	44	3572	276	-	-
1960	23179	8100	15077	10292	4785	570	36	3707	237	-	3
1961	25155	8280	16875	11757	5118	554	39	3942	258	-	-
1962	28171	8840	19331	12804	6527	645	62	5135	299	-	-
1963	36009	11500	24509	18228	6281	524	33	5016	314	-	-
1964	38479	11290	27141	19926	7215	410	44	6005	336	-	48
1965	40972	10900	29982	23201	6782	495	26	5574	318	-	90
BELGIUM-LUXEMBOURG								EXPORTS			
1925	3770	3750	20	-	20	2	2	-	17	-	-
1929	4846	4840	6	-	6	-	-	-	6	-	-
1933	4702	4639	60	56	5	-	-	2	3	-	3

Table VI. ENERGY IMPORTS AND EXPORTS, SELECTED YEARS, 1925-1965

(Thousand metric tons coal equivalent)

Region, country, year	Total energy	Solid fuels	Liquid fuels: Total	Liquid fuels: Crude oil	Refined petroleum products: Total	Gasoline	Kerosine	Fuel oils	Lubes and greases	Gas	Electricity
	(1)	(2)	(3)	(4)	(5)	(6)	(7)	(8)	(9)	(10)	(11)
BELGIUM-LUXEMBOURG (CONTINUED)								EXPORTS			
1937	6497	6059	438	-	438	20	5	281	134	-	-
1938	6563	6197	366	-	366	14	5	230	119	-	-
1950	3361	3127	222	-	222	48	3	80	92	12	-
1953	7344	5084	2240	-	2240	426	62	1649	77	13	7
1955	11068	8270	2768	48	2720	467	159	1943	134	31	-
1957	8550	5310	3180	74	3107	456	185	2315	131	43	18
1960	6894	3080	3779	-	3779	729	326	2552	147	36	-
1961	6773	3490	3212	-	3212	561	236	2225	158	36	35
1962	6751	3430	3245	3	3242	650	263	2124	170	31	46
1963	8321	3090	5195	-	5195	1263	302	3369	188	36	-
1964	7850	2940	4880	-	4880	933	576	3101	198	31	-
1965	7463	2440	4992	-	4992	1293	618	2771	236	31	-
FRANCE								IMPORTS			
1925	32219	29253	2933	153	2780	1512	374	360	534	-	33
1929	40120	35315	4745	263	4482	2649	332	1083	419	-	61
1933	33856	25146	8646	4199	4448	2835	111	1212	290	-	64
1937	41364	29713	11580	9210	2370	975	2	1241	153	-	71
1938	34470	22030	12369	10452	1917	1056	-	723	138	-	71
1950	35500	13500	21959	21200	759	93	-	570	96	12	30
1953	48236	14621	33566	33002	564	207	8	300	50	49	-
1955	54541	16050	38412	37221	1191	639	24	473	56	79	-
1957	64328	24340	39780	36126	3654	843	72	2690	50	174	34
1960	65664	15290	50255	46533	3722	1236	33	2385	23	120	-
1961	70906	15070	55704	52524	3180	1076	21	2027	15	120	12
1962	75149	15310	59712	55740	3972	1142	11	2744	29	127	-
1963	92863	22050	70604	64887	5717	1050	30	4506	30	139	71
1964	100158	19750	80034	73911	6123	906	30	5048	39	96	279
1965	110312	16808	92981	87834	5147	753	27	4230	44	402	122
FRANCE								EXPORTS			
1925	2082	1999	83	-	83	27	8	8	41	-	-
1929	3775	3643	132	-	132	59	11	15	48	-	-
1933	1919	1593	326	-	326	68	30	173	56	-	-
1937	1681	967	714	2	713	194	113	365	42	-	-
1938	1937	1149	788	-	788	332	143	264	50	-	-
1950	7021	2200	4821	14	4808	929	134	3710	36	-	-
1953	12415	2521	9893	-	9893	2339	402	7043	110	-	1
1955	14320	6250	8061	-	8061	1905	732	5081	239	-	9
1957	7801	2290	5511	30	5481	1475	617	3123	162	-	-
1960	11073	1540	9521	2	9519	2502	957	5573	284	-	13
1961	12282	1440	10842	-	10842	2666	1053	6597	273	-	-
1962	12097	1440	10563	-	10563	2151	911	6963	281	-	94
1963	12502	1060	11442	-	11442	2093	1290	7398	330	-	-
1964	12595	980	11615	-	11615	2237	1026	7536	384	-	-
1965	15393	970	14423	-	14423	2834	735	9914	353	-	-
GERMANY								IMPORTS			
1925	9856	8128	1700	80	1620	656	219	287	459	-	29
1929	12698	8913	3758	135	3623	1599	224	813	987	-	28
1933	8698	4986	3656	422	3234	1508	146	1167	414	-	56

Table VI. ENERGY IMPORTS AND EXPORTS, SELECTED YEARS, 1925-1965

(Thousand metric tons coal equivalent)

Region, country, year	Total energy	Solid fuels	Liquid fuels: Total	Liquid fuels: Crude oil	Refined petroleum products: Total	Gasoline	Kerosine	Fuel oils	Lubes and greases	Gas	Electricity
	(1)	(2)	(3)	(4)	(5)	(6)	(7)	(8)	(9)	(10)	(11)
GERMANY (CONTINUED) — IMPORTS											
1937	12288	6426	5762	1098	4664	1587	72	2382	623	-	100
1938	13534	6807	6627	1167	5460	2036	33	2810	582	-	100
GERMANY — EXPORTS											
1925	37821	37767	54	-	54	6	-	2	47	-	-
1929	45487	45347	140	-	140	12	-	14	114	-	-
1933	30799	30664	135	-	135	12	-	8	116	-	-
1937	49016	48830	186	-	186	18	-	9	159	-	-
1938	38709	38536	173	-	173	9	-	20	144	-	-
GERMANY, FEDERAL REPUBLIC — IMPORTS											
1950	6558	2100	4257	2900	1358	360	5	975	18	43	159
1953	15912	7219	8411	6840	1571	180	-	1305	86	121	161
1955	30477	15198	14969	10667	4302	413	53	3653	164	156	155
1957	39927	18456	21230	12237	8993	834	51	7883	197	163	79
1960	56030	10360	45150	34866	10284	1176	357	8507	228	-	520
1961	65324	10300	54483	44082	10401	1202	261	8655	260	-	541
1962	80447	11370	68694	49802	18893	1994	299	16235	329	-	383
1963	93539	12100	81131	60116	21015	2009	248	18435	267	-	308
1964	109333	11225	97988	76914	21074	2510	393	17741	369	-	120
1965	123311	10804	111977	88602	23375	2786	408	19791	290	-	530
GERMANY, FEDERAL REPUBLIC — EXPORTS											
1950	31017	30785	125	-	125	-	-	119	6	108	-
1953	29135	28312	660	-	660	278	51	150	182	163	-
1955	31046	29518	1260	-	1260	500	41	554	87	258	10
1957	33100	31466	1074	-	1074	335	3	489	93	515	45
1960	33028	29070	3791	14	3777	818	33	2547	104	168	-
1961	35271	28390	6743	36	6707	1761	27	4452	122	139	-
1962	34902	29050	5702	-	5702	1809	342	3096	113	151	-
1963	36971	29650	7166	-	7166	1841	254	4605	134	156	-
1964	34064	25790	8142	-	8142	1946	222	5519	149	132	-
1965	30573	23533	6914	32	6882	1697	62	4686	150	127	-
ITALY — IMPORTS											
1925	11641	10434	1179	56	1124	284	174	545	122	-	28
1929	16495	14540	1925	90	1835	581	243	890	122	-	31
1933	12106	9513	2571	203	2369	437	206	1626	101	-	22
1937	16760	12867	3869	1404	2465	392	143	1824	107	-	24
1938	16085	12099	3956	2216	1740	150	78	1446	66	-	31
1950	16270	8278	7967	6834	1133	33	11	945	144	-	25
1953	29299	9260	20039	19275	764	15	-	675	74	-	-
1955	36647	10400	26244	25509	735	114	-	485	81	-	3
1957	42909	11710	31142	29885	1257	41	-	1079	71	-	58
1960	56057	10320	45737	43293	2444	135	-	2135	120	-	-
1961	63663	10240	53402	50205	3197	174	2	2796	165	-	21
1962	75845	11020	64667	60330	4337	186	3	3917	183	-	159
1963	86167	11630	74375	69698	4677	182	189	4043	237	-	162
1964	96581	10770	85686	82851	2835	239	17	2346	219	-	125
1965	115171	10700	104430	100934	3497	164	14	3162	143	-	41

Table VI. ENERGY IMPORTS AND EXPORTS, SELECTED YEARS, 1925-1965

(Thousand metric tons coal equivalent)

Region, country, year	Total energy	Solid fuels	Liquid fuels		Refined petroleum products					Gas	Electricity
			Total	Crude oil	Total	Gasoline	Kerosine	Fuel oils	Lubes and greases		
	(1)	(2)	(3)	(4)	(5)	(6)	(7)	(8)	(9)	(10)	(11)
ITALY (CONTINUED)								EXPORTS			
1925	55	53	2	-	2	-	-	2	-	-	-
1929	55	35	20	-	20	3	-	9	8	-	-
1933	56	36	20	-	20	3	-	3	14	-	-
1937	216	16	200	-	200	101	32	60	8	-	-
1938	237	18	219	-	219	96	32	83	9	-	-
1950	1218	63	1155	-	1155	369	171	615	-	-	-
1953	6556	88	6462	-	6462	1994	686	3773	11	-	6
1955	7534	70	7464	8	7457	2549	687	4107	111	-	-
1957	7575	100	7475	9	7466	2217	491	4706	41	-	-
1960	10781	110	10655	908	9747	2777	486	6404	62	-	16
1961	11835	90	11745	794	10952	2694	596	7596	45	-	-
1962	13006	160	12846	501	12345	2811	564	8870	75	-	-
1963	14163	160	14003	269	13734	2721	728	10133	83	-	-
1964	15329	95	15234	-	15234	2799	609	11621	122	-	-
1965	24583	110	24473	-	24473	3755	1146	19139	216	-	-
NETHERLANDS								IMPORTS			
1925	10000	9002	998	236	762	171	293	236	63	-	-
1929	11910	10440	1467	357	1110	341	293	390	87	-	3
1933	9149	7532	1614	111	1503	561	284	564	95	-	3
1937	11848	9109	2736	723	2013	363	389	1184	78	-	3
1938	11551	8468	3081	650	2432	365	380	1604	84	-	2
1950	14098	4881	9084	7200	1884	270	272	1208	135	133	-
1953	19218	6011	13196	10346	2850	264	227	2231	126	12	-
1955	30246	8820	21405	17462	3944	252	246	3123	308	19	3
1957	34620	9830	24771	20307	4464	282	240	3647	251	19	-
1960	41915	7830	34065	24732	9333	197	275	8538	236	5	15
1961	46670	7810	38843	28929	9914	173	330	9077	231	12	5
1962	49470	9620	39839	29892	9947	167	359	9086	221	12	-
1963	51437	10850	40563	31335	9228	186	512	8168	240	19	6
1964	55658	9735	45915	35157	10758	426	546	9365	269	5	2
1965	59064	7460	51600	39569	12032	614	551	10521	188	-	4
NETHERLANDS								EXPORTS			
1925	3245	3224	21	-	21	-	-	20	2	-	-
1929	5726	5685	41	3	38	-	-	36	2	-	-
1933	5585	5544	41	-	41	-	-	39	2	-	-
1937	6876	6843	33	-	33	-	-	30	3	-	-
1938	6054	6015	39	-	39	3	2	33	2	-	-
1950	5385	1141	4239	-	4239	923	21	3203	93	-	5
1953	7970	1506	6462	-	6462	2216	302	3840	105	-	2
1955	13931	2850	11081	-	11081	2934	282	7505	246	-	-
1957	15976	3180	12786	-	12786	3333	587	8388	314	-	10
1960	21668	4770	16898	14	16884	3669	863	11777	377	-	-
1961	21985	5150	16835	-	16835	3945	939	11390	341	-	-
1962	22245	4980	17262	5	17258	4295	932	11369	402	-	3
1963	19675	5270	14405	-	14405	4191	866	8712	365	-	-
1964	19775	5060	14715	9	14706	4443	953	8531	473	-	-
1965	21467	5090	16377	17	16361	4674	1026	9833	459	-	-

Table VI. ENERGY IMPORTS AND EXPORTS, SELECTED YEARS, 1925-1965

(Thousand metric tons coal equivalent)

Region, country, year	Total energy	Solid fuels	Liquid fuels		Liquid fuels: Refined petroleum products					Gas	Electricity
			Total	Crude oil	Total	Gasoline	Kerosine	Fuel oils	Lubes and greases		
	(1)	(2)	(3)	(4)	(5)	(6)	(7)	(8)	(9)	(10)	(11)
EUROPEAN FREE TRADE ASSOCIATION (EFTA)								IMPORTS			
1925	29997	19191	10803	3596	7208	2427	1145	2981	656	-	3
1929	40210	25594	14612	3147	11465	4946	1776	3998	746	-	4
1933	37913	20685	17226	2807	14420	6662	1400	5615	744	-	2
1937	48133	26420	21711	3519	18192	8532	1697	7073	891	-	2
1938	47183	24063	23117	3905	19212	9291	1652	7428	842	-	3
1950	65197	22949	42225	15918	26307	8633	2828	13827	1020	-	23
1953	87542	20875	66630	41538	25092	6023	3252	14861	953	-	37
1955	116385	34110	82260	46838	35423	6792	3419	24051	1065	-	15
1957	113622	23060	90515	47696	42819	8532	3345	29789	1034	-	48
1960	150793	17890	132869	74888	57981	10359	2529	43655	1274	5	29
1961	156584	16650	139823	84206	55617	11012	2304	40748	1343	-	111
1962	174606	17130	157353	91821	65532	12342	4023	47580	1367	-	123
1963	189724	18380	171284	97094	74190	12702	4955	54893	1401	-	60
1964	202311	17020	185069	106197	78872	13584	5993	57467	1493	120	102
1965	217561	14937	201488	117908	83580	14100	6449	60950	1514	858	278
EUROPEAN FREE TRADE ASSOCIATION (EFTA)								EXPORTS			
1925	56183	55113	983	-	983	260	119	552	53	-	87
1929	66318	65527	645	-	645	161	98	339	48	-	146
1933	43577	42879	537	-	537	234	69	185	50	-	161
1937	45256	44178	840	-	840	314	132	303	92	-	238
1938	39844	38809	794	-	794	287	74	320	114	-	241
1950	19825	16173	3470	1605	1865	201	45	1407	212	-	183
1953	30621	15775	14546	3150	11396	1634	230	9222	311	-	300
1955	27209	14630	12258	2279	9980	2154	357	6875	581	-	321
1957	22056	9910	11861	1718	10143	2445	413	6612	656	-	285
1960	23660	6970	16191	1581	14610	2867	1037	9800	881	-	499
1961	22895	7370	14721	1328	13394	2535	1334	8597	887	-	804
1962	27660	6750	20493	2243	18251	3131	1419	12633	1041	-	417
1963	31791	10280	21045	2975	18071	2631	1478	12960	959	-	466
1964	27142	7550	18881	515	18366	2871	1224	13139	1083	-	711
1965	26924	5090	20774	408	20366	3252	1340	14675	1059	-	1061
AUSTRIA								IMPORTS			
1925	5245	5060	185	27	158	71	38	30	20	-	-
1929	6761	6417	344	77	267	156	47	48	17	-	-
1933	3516	3046	470	297	173	75	14	75	9	-	-
1937	3801	3319	482	159	323	122	59	132	11	-	-
1938	4267	3773	494	233	261	108	35	107	12	-	-
1950	5349	5254	95	-	95	74	-	9	12	-	-
1953	4240	4223	17	-	17	2	-	-	15	-	-
1955	5459	4970	489	-	489	146	-	311	33	-	-
1957	6193	5630	563	-	563	222	-	300	39	-	-
1960	7448	4970	2478	803	1676	455	-	1157	53	-	-
1961	7323	4540	2783	812	1971	633	-	1271	57	-	-
1962	8067	4810	3257	942	2315	792	11	1428	59	-	-
1963	9099	5350	3749	1238	2511	785	11	1640	66	-	-
1964	9101	5130	3971	1182	2789	714	11	1985	74	-	-
1965	8289	4555	3734	992	2742	701	11	1950	75	-	-

Table VI. ENERGY IMPORTS AND EXPORTS, SELECTED YEARS, 1925-1965

(Thousand metric tons coal equivalent)

Region, country, year	Total energy	Solid fuels	Liquid fuels: Total	Crude oil	Refined petroleum products: Total	Gasoline	Kerosine	Fuel oils	Lubes and greases	Gas	Electricity
	(1)	(2)	(3)	(4)	(5)	(6)	(7)	(8)	(9)	(10)	(11)
AUSTRIA (CONTINUED) — EXPORTS											
1925	4	-	-	-	-	-	-	-	-	-	4
1929	15	-	-	-	-	-	-	-	-	-	15
1933	38	-	-	-	-	-	-	-	-	-	38
1937	43	-	-	-	-	-	-	-	-	-	43
1938	46	-	-	-	-	-	-	-	-	-	46
1950	1774	11	1677	1605	72	-	-	72	-	-	86
1953	3399	-	3262	3150	113	-	-	113	-	-	136
1955	2560	20	2405	2175	230	18	23	186	3	-	135
1957	2283	20	2108	1686	422	-	15	405	2	-	155
1960	1984	20	1727	1505	222	-	-	210	12	-	238
1961	1557	20	1293	1160	134	-	-	126	8	-	244
1962	1335	20	1053	744	309	-	-	293	17	-	262
1963	1368	10	1146	815	332	-	-	309	23	-	212
1964	661	10	312	-	312	-	-	197	116	-	339
1965	905	10	411	-	411	-	-	300	111	-	484
DENMARK — IMPORTS											
1925	4473	4022	449	2	447	147	146	120	35	-	3
1929	6146	5500	642	5	638	261	134	210	33	-	4
1933	5760	4902	857	-	857	329	135	354	39	-	2
1937	7085	6024	1059	-	1059	455	135	432	38	-	2
1938	6689	5396	1290	17	1274	504	176	554	41	-	3
1950	8460	5731	2706	51	2655	770	104	1724	59	-	23
1953	9269	6059	3173	32	3141	843	143	2102	54	-	37
1955	12214	7360	4854	45	4809	1040	200	3402	78	-	-
1957	10355	4430	5877	45	5832	1173	198	4272	77	-	48
1960	13086	5290	7784	53	7731	1497	407	5601	99	-	13
1961	13882	4980	8792	356	8436	1649	477	6047	108	-	110
1962	16475	5310	11054	1884	9170	1769	486	6653	123	-	112
1963	17905	5380	12471	2985	9486	1418	624	7215	104	-	54
1964	19704	4830	14772	4560	10212	1589	588	7782	132	-	102
1965	20859	4235	16407	5514	10893	1695	620	8322	128	-	217
DENMARK — EXPORTS											
1925	2	-	2	-	2	-	-	-	2	-	-
1929	-	-	-	-	-	-	-	-	-	-	-
1933	-	-	-	-	-	-	-	-	-	-	-
1937	-	-	-	-	-	-	-	-	-	-	-
1938	-	-	-	-	-	-	-	-	-	-	-
1950	-	-	-	-	-	-	-	-	-	-	-
1953	-	-	-	-	-	-	-	-	-	-	-
1955	37	20	3	-	3	-	-	-	3	-	14
1957	23	20	3	-	3	-	-	-	3	-	-
1960	50	30	20	-	20	2	-	-	9	-	-
1961	145	50	95	-	95	5	2	60	8	-	-
1962	866	50	816	-	816	215	12	581	6	-	-
1963	643	80	563	-	563	131	29	393	9	-	-
1964	1002	70	932	-	932	266	11	638	14	-	-
1965	1086	45	1041	-	1041	396	8	615	18	-	-

Table VI. ENERGY IMPORTS AND EXPORTS, SELECTED YEARS, 1925-1965

(Thousand metric tons coal equivalent)

Region, country, year	Total energy	Solid fuels	Liquid fuels: Total	Liquid fuels: Crude oil	Refined petroleum products: Total	Gasoline	Kerosine	Fuel oils	Lubes and greases	Gas	Electricity
	(1)	(2)	(3)	(4)	(5)	(6)	(7)	(8)	(9)	(10)	(11)
NORWAY								IMPORTS			
1925	2431	2140	291	27	264	54	65	129	17	-	-
1929	3185	2769	416	35	381	116	57	192	17	-	-
1933	3036	2368	668	32	636	147	51	419	20	-	-
1937	4019	3191	828	26	803	249	59	474	21	-	-
1938	3548	2660	888	56	833	264	45	506	18	-	-
1950	3838	1696	2142	24	2118	386	57	1632	44	-	-
1953	4665	1384	3281	113	3168	479	117	2531	42	-	-
1955	5537	1260	4277	144	4133	506	167	3413	47	-	-
1957	5525	1050	4475	174	4301	536	240	3468	56	-	-
1960	6513	990	5507	330	5177	687	302	4128	57	-	16
1961	7616	920	6695	2609	4086	504	309	3213	59	-	1
1962	8627	860	7767	3531	4236	698	272	3206	60	-	-
1963	9370	970	8400	3803	4598	669	320	3545	63	-	-
1964	10357	970	9387	4397	4991	662	323	3935	71	-	-
1965	9826	980	8846	4233	4613	747	339	3489	36	-	-
NORWAY								EXPORTS			
1925	152	152	-	-	-	-	-	-	-	-	-
1929	92	92	-	-	-	-	-	-	-	-	-
1933	60	55	5	-	5	-	-	-	5	-	-
1937	18	15	3	-	3	-	-	-	3	-	-
1938	18	13	5	-	5	-	-	-	5	-	-
1950	-	-	-	-	-	-	-	-	-	-	-
1953	5	-	5	-	5	-	-	-	5	-	-
1955	148	130	18	-	18	2	-	3	14	-	-
1957	237	220	17	-	17	2	-	2	14	-	-
1960	197	170	27	-	27	2	2	-	24	-	-
1961	1147	160	987	-	987	110	8	834	24	-	-
1962	2056	180	1841	-	1841	224	20	1551	27	-	36
1963	2147	170	1859	-	1859	189	12	1616	29	-	118
1964	2469	90	2205	-	2205	347	9	1805	32	-	174
1965	2369	230	1869	-	1869	159	9	1607	71	-	270
PORTUGAL								IMPORTS			
1925	1090	998	92	-	92	21	36	30	5	-	-
1929	1314	1147	167	-	167	60	53	54	-	-	-
1933	1322	1109	213	-	213	77	72	65	-	-	-
1937	1653	1360	293	-	293	110	78	87	18	-	-
1938	1446	1152	294	-	294	111	75	92	17	-	-
1950	1993	817	1176	398	779	96	80	585	18	-	-
1953	2275	578	1697	198	1499	195	182	1095	24	-	-
1955	2969	510	2459	1365	1094	123	84	852	33	-	-
1957	3317	560	2757	1662	1095	132	83	842	39	-	-
1960	3570	390	3180	1952	1229	117	50	1013	47	-	-
1961	3832	550	3282	1959	1323	104	38	1113	53	-	-
1962	3940	530	3410	2001	1409	101	60	1170	50	-	-
1963	4324	620	3704	2246	1458	90	30	1244	53	-	-
1964	4581	630	3951	2279	1673	146	35	1344	60	-	-
1965	5066	620	4392	2558	1835	191	35	1406	71	-	54

Table VI. ENERGY IMPORTS AND EXPORTS, SELECTED YEARS, 1925-1965

(Thousand metric tons coal equivalent)

Region, country, year	Total energy	Solid fuels	Liquid fuels: Total	Liquid fuels: Crude oil	Refined petroleum products: Total	Gasoline	Kerosine	Fuel oils	Lubes and greases	Gas	Electricity
	(1)	(2)	(3)	(4)	(5)	(6)	(7)	(8)	(9)	(10)	(11)
PORTUGAL (CONTINUED)								EXPORTS			
1925	5	3	2	-	2	-	-	2	-	-	-
1929	1	1	-	-	-	-	-	-	-	-	-
1933	2	-	2	-	2	-	-	2	-	-	-
1937	6	3	3	-	3	-	-	3	-	-	-
1938	2	-	2	-	2	-	-	2	-	-	-
1950	5	-	5	-	5	-	-	5	-	-	-
1953	8	-	8	-	8	3	-	5	-	-	-
1955	328	10	318	-	318	138	23	156	2	-	-
1957	281	-	281	-	281	105	41	132	3	-	-
1960	417	-	417	-	417	137	21	257	3	-	-
1961	332	-	332	-	332	116	63	150	3	-	-
1962	227	-	227	-	227	71	42	111	3	-	-
1963	326	-	320	-	320	72	68	177	3	-	7
1964	285	-	284	-	284	87	26	167	5	-	2
1965	264	-	264	-	264	66	128	63	6	-	-
SWEDEN								IMPORTS			
1925	4708	4256	452	-	452	209	95	95	54	-	-
1929	6997	6275	722	-	722	375	104	177	66	-	-
1933	7220	6060	1160	86	1074	494	140	378	63	-	-
1937	10729	8962	1767	120	1647	731	156	675	86	-	-
1938	9722	7733	1989	138	1851	815	168	776	93	-	-
1950	12144	6630	5514	1355	4160	780	330	2955	95	-	-
1953	13884	5571	8313	2132	6182	1170	555	4370	87	-	-
1955	17694	5560	12119	2834	9285	1391	557	7209	129	-	15
1957	19011	4920	14091	2991	11100	1817	456	8681	147	-	-
1960	23398	3580	19818	3969	15849	2294	561	12812	179	-	-
1961	23325	3300	20025	3888	16137	2327	509	13119	176	-	-
1962	25490	3270	22220	3690	18530	2817	564	14939	200	-	-
1963	27450	3240	24204	4122	20082	3020	624	16241	189	-	6
1964	30479	3480	26999	5336	21663	3360	630	17436	231	-	-
1965	31487	2970	28517	5588	22929	3636	620	18432	237	-	-
SWEDEN								EXPORTS			
1925	10	-	8	-	8	3	3	-	2	-	3
1929	12	-	8	-	8	-	6	-	2	-	4
1933	32	-	30	-	30	2	18	9	2	-	2
1937	50	-	48	-	48	5	3	38	3	-	2
1938	51	-	48	-	48	2	6	38	3	-	3
1950	105	27	56	-	56	29	2	26	-	-	23
1953	68	28	3	-	3	2	-	-	2	-	37
1955	47	30	17	-	17	-	5	-	2	-	-
1957	102	10	44	-	44	-	-	15	17	-	49
1960	277	10	171	-	171	12	26	74	48	-	96
1961	312	40	147	-	147	5	5	77	56	-	125
1962	319	30	189	-	189	20	-	105	62	-	100
1963	365	30	335	-	335	98	12	158	63	-	-
1964	527	20	482	-	482	195	11	201	72	-	26
1965	601	10	491	-	491	197	12	210	72	-	101

Table VI. ENERGY IMPORTS AND EXPORTS, SELECTED YEARS, 1925-1965

(Thousand metric tons coal equivalent)

Region, country, year	Total energy	Solid fuels	Liquid fuels: Total	Liquid fuels: Crude oil	Refined petroleum products: Total	Gasoline	Kerosine	Fuel oils	Lubes and greases	Gas	Electricity
	(1)	(2)	(3)	(4)	(5)	(6)	(7)	(8)	(9)	(10)	(11)
SWITZERLAND								IMPORTS			
1925	2923	2701	222	-	222	105	38	57	23	-	-
1929	3855	3463	392	-	392	210	41	110	32	-	-
1933	3755	3165	590	-	590	293	36	231	30	-	-
1937	4082	3486	596	-	596	291	30	245	30	-	-
1938	3954	3337	617	-	617	302	30	257	29	-	-
1950	4055	2550	1505	-	1505	453	99	893	60	-	-
1953	4057	2204	1853	-	1853	582	153	1074	42	-	-
1955	5531	2640	2891	-	2891	812	62	1949	66	-	-
1957	7223	3330	3893	-	3893	984	93	2730	81	-	-
1960	8363	2600	5763	-	5763	1485	83	4097	89	-	-
1961	8514	2260	6254	-	6254	1727	87	4335	102	-	-
1962	9571	2330	7241	-	7241	2028	74	5033	105	-	-
1963	12585	2820	9765	539	9227	1910	117	7068	119	-	-
1964	12128	1980	10148	1257	8891	1943	131	6689	113	-	-
1965	13482	1572	11910	1814	10097	2003	119	7847	110	-	-
SWITZERLAND								EXPORTS			
1925	81	-	-	-	-	-	-	-	-	-	81
1929	126	-	-	-	-	-	-	-	-	-	126
1933	122	-	-	-	-	-	-	-	-	-	122
1937	193	-	-	-	-	-	-	-	-	-	193
1938	195	-	3	-	3	-	-	3	-	-	192
1950	79	1	5	-	5	5	-	-	-	-	74
1953	127	-	-	-	-	-	-	-	-	-	127
1955	203	30	-	-	-	-	-	-	-	-	173
1957	91	10	-	-	-	-	-	-	-	-	81
1960	165	-	-	-	-	-	-	-	-	-	165
1961	438	-	3	-	3	-	2	-	2	-	435
1962	20	-	2	-	2	-	-	-	2	-	19
1963	131	-	3	-	3	2	-	2	-	-	128
1964	264	-	119	-	119	18	5	95	2	-	146
1965	406	-	200	-	200	33	6	159	2	-	206
UNITED KINGDOM								IMPORTS			
1925	9128	14	9114	3540	5574	1821	729	2520	504	-	-
1929	11954	23	11931	3032	8900	3768	1343	3207	582	-	-
1933	13306	35	13271	2393	10878	5249	953	4094	584	-	-
1937	16766	78	16688	3215	13473	6576	1181	5028	689	-	-
1938	17558	12	17546	3462	14084	7188	1124	5139	633	-	-
1950	29359	271	29088	14091	14997	6075	2159	6030	734	-	-
1953	49155	856	48299	39065	9234	2753	2103	3690	689	-	-
1955	66983	11810	55173	42450	12723	2777	2351	6917	680	-	-
1957	62000	3140	58860	42824	16037	3669	2276	9497	596	-	-
1960	88415	70	88340	67782	20558	3825	1128	14849	752	5	-
1961	92094	100	91994	74583	17411	4070	885	11651	789	-	-
1962	102437	20	102407	79773	22634	4139	2558	15153	771	-	11
1963	108992	-	108992	82163	26829	4812	3230	17942	809	-	-
1964	115962	-	115842	87188	28655	5172	4277	18297	813	120	-
1965	128553	5	127683	97211	30473	5129	4707	19505	858	858	7

Table VI. ENERGY IMPORTS AND EXPORTS, SELECTED YEARS, 1925-1965

(Thousand metric tons coal equivalent)

Region, country, year	Total energy	Solid fuels	Liquid fuels: Total	Liquid fuels: Crude oil	Refined petroleum products: Total	Gasoline	Kerosine	Fuel oils	Lubes and greases	Gas	Electricity
	(1)	(2)	(3)	(4)	(5)	(6)	(7)	(8)	(9)	(10)	(11)
UNITED KINGDOM (CONTINUED)								EXPORTS			
1925	55930	54958	972	-	972	257	116	551	50	-	-
1929	66072	65434	638	-	638	161	92	339	47	-	-
1933	43325	42824	501	-	501	233	51	174	44	-	-
1937	44946	44160	786	-	786	309	129	263	86	-	-
1938	39533	38796	737	-	737	285	68	278	107	-	-
1950	17862	16134	1728	-	1728	168	44	1305	212	-	-
1953	27015	15747	11268	-	11268	1629	230	9105	305	-	-
1955	23888	14390	9498	104	9395	1997	308	6530	558	-	-
1957	19040	9630	9410	32	9378	2339	357	6059	618	-	-
1960	20570	6740	13830	77	13754	2715	989	9260	785	-	-
1961	18966	7100	11865	168	11697	2301	1256	7350	788	-	1
1962	22837	6470	16367	1499	14868	2603	1346	9993	926	-	-
1963	26812	9990	16821	2160	14661	2141	1358	10307	833	-	1
1964	21935	7360	14549	515	14034	1959	1164	10038	845	-	26
1965	21294	4795	16499	408	16091	2402	1178	11721	780	-	-
WESTERN EUROPE - OTHER								IMPORTS			
1925	7763	6494	1269	54	1215	407	224	464	108	-	-
1929	10177	8105	2072	216	1856	774	255	704	123	-	-
1933	8378	5529	2849	411	2438	900	252	1202	84	-	-
1937	10122	6952	3170	329	2841	965	366	1391	120	-	-
1938	9659	6350	3309	390	2919	1008	360	1439	113	-	-
1950	16711	6016	10695	4958	5738	1577	401	3575	186	-	-
1953	19938	5971	13967	5421	8546	1703	497	6135	212	-	-
1955	23621	6767	16847	5900	10947	1859	615	8255	216	-	8
1957	30097	7051	23046	9542	13505	1736	596	10943	210	-	-
1960	33721	7093	26574	17678	8897	491	458	7718	206	-	54
1961	35527	7214	28292	18893	9399	476	492	8210	204	-	22
1962	41473	8115	33348	22908	10440	531	584	9060	249	-	10
1963	44154	7840	36272	25503	10769	419	681	9422	209	-	42
1964	49527	8989	40409	29379	11030	494	791	9350	324	-	130
1965	54373	8996	45254	31596	13658	563	824	11676	243	-	123
WESTERN EUROPE - OTHER								EXPORTS			
1925	94	92	2	-	2	2	-	-	-	-	-
1929	165	160	5	-	5	3	-	2	-	-	-
1933	70	56	14	-	14	3	2	9	-	-	-
1937	125	47	78	-	78	3	-	75	-	-	-
1938	111	33	78	-	78	3	-	75	-	-	-
1950	226	187	39	-	39	5	-	35	-	-	-
1953	246	171	71	-	71	3	-	65	3	-	4
1955	407	170	231	-	231	110	39	81	2	-	6
1957	860	240	597	2	596	267	81	222	17	-	23
1960	2304	180	2094	-	2094	398	131	1527	11	-	30
1961	2383	250	2091	269	1823	426	104	1259	15	-	42
1962	3245	170	3024	842	2183	618	95	1416	38	-	51
1963	3014	220	2654	758	1896	411	107	1269	71	-	141
1964	3241	260	2784	525	2259	449	188	1527	69	-	197
1965	3311	200	3032	218	2814	548	180	2025	45	-	79

Table VI. ENERGY IMPORTS AND EXPORTS, SELECTED YEARS, 1925-1965

(Thousand metric tons coal equivalent)

Region, country, year	Total energy	Solid fuels	Liquid fuels: Total	Liquid fuels: Crude oil	Refined petroleum products: Total	Gasoline	Kerosine	Fuel oils	Lubes and greases	Gas	Electricity
	(1)	(2)	(3)	(4)	(5)	(6)	(7)	(8)	(9)	(10)	(11)
FINLAND								IMPORTS			
1925	726	612	114	14	101	44	44	-	14	-	-
1929	1364	1170	194	20	174	102	54	-	18	-	-
1933	1317	1138	179	21	158	90	54	-	14	-	-
1937	2570	2235	335	41	294	176	98	-	21	-	-
1938	2156	1784	372	48	324	206	98	-	21	-	-
1950	2663	1929	734	-	734	366	101	237	30	-	-
1953	3060	1980	1080	-	1080	456	108	498	18	-	-
1955	4295	2630	1665	-	1665	539	113	980	35	-	-
1957	5863	3040	2823	324	2499	524	90	1842	44	-	-
1960	7242	3150	4040	1706	2334	69	48	2162	56	-	53
1961	7501	3020	4460	2075	2385	51	41	2225	69	-	22
1962	8207	2950	5247	2268	2979	27	38	2840	75	-	10
1963	8946	2500	6404	3345	3059	30	41	2916	72	-	42
1964	10665	3220	7358	3870	3488	20	35	3342	90	-	87
1965	11880	3265	8544	4050	4494	30	39	4326	98	-	71
FINLAND								EXPORTS			
1925	-	-	-	-	-	-	-	-	-	-	-
1929	-	-	-	-	-	-	-	-	-	-	-
1933	-	-	-	-	-	-	-	-	-	-	-
1937	-	-	-	-	-	-	-	-	-	-	-
1938	-	-	-	-	-	-	-	-	-	-	-
1950	-	-	-	-	-	-	-	-	-	-	-
1953	1	-	-	-	-	-	-	-	-	-	1
1955	-	-	-	-	-	-	-	-	-	-	-
1957	2	-	2	-	2	-	-	-	-	-	-
1960	15	10	5	-	5	-	-	-	-	-	-
1961	23	20	3	-	3	-	-	-	-	-	-
1962	10	10	-	-	-	-	-	-	-	-	-
1963	30	30	-	-	-	-	-	-	-	-	-
1964	30	30	-	-	-	-	-	-	-	-	-
1965	32	30	2	-	2	-	-	-	-	-	-
GREECE								IMPORTS			
1925	759	663	96	-	96	36	21	32	8	-	-
1929	1035	814	221	-	221	69	44	96	12	-	-
1933	913	638	275	-	275	69	29	168	9	-	-
1937	1454	969	485	-	485	96	29	341	20	-	-
1938	1493	975	518	-	518	107	32	365	15	-	-
1950	1931	302	1629	-	1629	342	111	1152	24	-	-
1953	2158	277	1881	-	1881	374	131	1350	27	-	-
1955	2587	320	2267	-	2267	455	143	1641	29	-	-
1957	2716	280	2436	-	2436	357	159	1884	26	-	-
1960	3819	230	3588	2598	990	21	6	921	30	-	1
1961	4195	230	3965	2760	1205	21	2	1140	33	-	-
1962	4700	210	4490	2730	1760	41	83	1599	36	-	-
1963	5403	270	5133	2765	2369	89	128	2112	41	-	-
1964	5314	290	5024	2823	2201	129	164	1860	48	-	-
1965	6597	410	6185	2745	3440	174	188	3015	57	-	3

Table VI. ENERGY IMPORTS AND EXPORTS, SELECTED YEARS, 1925-1965

(Thousand metric tons coal equivalent)

Region, country, year	Total energy	Solid fuels	Liquid fuels: Total	Crude oil	Refined petroleum products: Total	Gasoline	Kerosine	Fuel oils	Lubes and greases	Gas	Electricity
	(1)	(2)	(3)	(4)	(5)	(6)	(7)	(8)	(9)	(10)	(11)
GREECE (CONTINUED)								EXPORTS			
1960	-	-	-	-	-	-	-	-	-	-	-
1961	2	-	-	-	-	-	-	-	-	-	2
1962	45	-	45	-	45	-	-	41	-	-	-
1963	40	-	39	-	39	-	-	30	-	-	1
1964	39	-	38	-	38	-	-	32	-	-	2
1965	12	-	12	-	12	-	-	6	-	-	-
ICELAND								IMPORTS			
1925	14	-	14	-	14	-	-	-	-	-	-
1929	23	-	23	-	23	5	8	11	-	-	-
1933	21	-	21	-	21	15	5	-	2	-	-
1937	29	-	29	-	29	23	5	-	2	-	-
1938	30	-	30	-	30	9	3	17	2	-	-
1950	468	96	372	-	372	63	5	300	5	-	-
1953	621	49	572	-	572	81	5	480	6	-	-
1955	581	60	521	-	521	86	3	426	6	-	-
1957	630	30	600	-	600	95	3	497	6	-	-
1960	719	20	699	-	699	84	14	596	6	-	-
1961	661	20	641	-	641	75	12	548	6	-	-
1962	700	20	680	-	680	86	6	581	8	-	-
1963	645	10	635	-	635	93	12	524	6	-	-
1964	645	10	635	-	635	87	14	528	6	-	-
1965	712	10	702	-	702	96	27	572	8	-	-
IRELAND								IMPORTS			
1925	2465	2286	179	2	177	78	69	17	14	-	-
1929	2766	2518	248	-	248	131	65	38	15	-	-
1933	2604	2320	284	-	284	162	77	32	14	-	-
1937	2988	2623	365	-	365	191	99	59	17	-	-
1938	2918	2541	377	-	377	203	93	65	17	-	-
1950	2890	1994	896	-	896	375	117	383	21	-	-
1953	2930	1770	1160	-	1160	480	164	492	24	-	-
1955	3620	1940	1680	-	1680	557	188	903	30	-	-
1957	2928	1270	1658	-	1658	528	171	926	23	-	-
1960	4403	1680	2723	2147	576	111	204	222	29	-	-
1961	4660	1810	2850	2183	668	89	276	263	35	-	-
1962	4504	1520	2984	2273	711	77	275	317	35	-	-
1963	4706	1470	3236	2448	788	45	285	411	35	-	-
1964	4841	1320	3521	2618	903	75	324	447	42	-	-
1965	5419	1300	4119	3047	1073	48	323	653	36	-	-
IRELAND								EXPORTS			
1925	2	2	-	-	-	-	-	-	-	-	-
1929	21	21	-	-	-	-	-	-	-	-	-
1933	22	22	-	-	-	-	-	-	-	-	-
1937	3	3	-	-	-	-	-	-	-	-	-
1938	2	2	-	-	-	-	-	-	-	-	-
1950	-	-	-	-	-	-	-	-	-	-	-
1953	12	12	-	-	-	-	-	-	-	-	-
1955	-	-	-	-	-	-	-	-	-	-	-
1957	20	20	-	-	-	-	-	-	-	-	-

Table VI. ENERGY IMPORTS AND EXPORTS, SELECTED YEARS, 1925-1965

(Thousand metric tons coal equivalent)

Region, country, year	Total energy	Solid fuels	Liquid fuels: Total	Liquid fuels: Crude oil	Refined petroleum products: Total	Gasoline	Kerosine	Fuel oils	Lubes and greases	Gas	Electricity
	(1)	(2)	(3)	(4)	(5)	(6)	(7)	(8)	(9)	(10)	(11)
IRELAND (CONTINUED)								EXPORTS			
1960	763	20	743	-	743	9	-	734	-	-	-
1961	656	60	596	-	596	6	-	585	-	-	-
1962	436	40	396	-	396	11	-	381	-	-	-
1963	349	50	299	-	299	11	-	279	-	-	-
1964	298	40	258	-	258	11	-	239	-	-	-
1965	490	50	440	-	440	15	-	422	-	-	-
SPAIN								IMPORTS			
1925	2836	2134	702	23	680	215	32	377	57	-	-
1929	3921	2770	1151	42	1109	458	32	552	68	-	-
1933	2914	1063	1851	245	1607	539	36	990	42	-	-
1937	2284	566	1718	150	1568	462	92	960	54	-	-
1938	2141	428	1713	150	1563	462	92	960	50	-	-
1950	6684	1033	5651	4350	1301	300	33	891	77	-	-
1953	8904	1164	7740	4740	3000	150	36	2706	108	-	-
1955	9877	640	9230	5175	4055	98	99	3750	108	-	8
1957	14081	630	13451	8244	5207	116	66	4935	90	-	-
1960	14382	340	14042	10575	3467	102	69	3240	56	-	-
1961	15595	470	15125	11445	3680	144	56	3458	23	-	-
1962	19628	1820	17808	14517	3291	225	81	2922	60	-	-
1963	20669	1910	18759	15779	2981	78	90	2774	17	-	-
1964	23441	1940	21501	18929	2573	87	129	2250	54	-	-
1965	24810	1720	23090	20094	2996	110	140	2400	20	-	-
SPAIN								EXPORTS			
1925	11	9	2	-	2	2	-	-	-	-	-
1929	75	70	5	-	5	3	-	2	-	-	-
1933	20	6	14	-	14	3	2	9	-	-	-
1937	78	-	78	-	78	3	-	75	-	-	-
1938	78	-	78	-	78	3	-	75	-	-	-
1950	68	68	-	-	-	-	-	-	NA	-	-
1953	52	49	3	-	3	-	-	-	3	-	-
1955	257	90	167	-	167	107	36	23	2	-	-
1957	583	140	440	2	438	198	71	153	17	-	4
1960	1277	40	1218	-	1218	335	131	738	NA	-	19
1961	1147	60	1056	-	1056	371	104	575	NA	-	31
1962	1369	20	1317	-	1317	569	95	648	NA	-	32
1963	1560	20	1437	75	1362	384	104	855	NA	-	103
1964	2010	50	1766	51	1715	375	188	1142	NA	-	195
1965	2066	10	1977	-	1977	446	165	1365	-	-	79
YUGOSLAVIA								IMPORTS			
1925	671	543	128	17	111	20	59	17	17	-	-
1929	858	651	207	155	53	8	32	3	11	-	-
1933	474	292	182	146	36	8	21	3	5	-	-
1937	583	413	170	138	32	2	20	3	8	-	-
1938	723	495	228	192	36	8	14	6	9	-	-
1950	1136	417	719	608	111	83	-	-	29	-	-
1953	1455	664	791	681	110	83	-	-	27	-	-
1955	1895	1110	785	725	60	53	-	-	8	-	-
1957	2772	1750	1022	974	48	27	-	-	21	-	-

Table VI. ENERGY IMPORTS AND EXPORTS, SELECTED YEARS, 1925-1965

(Thousand metric tons coal equivalent)

Region, country, year	Total energy	Solid fuels	Liquid fuels: Total	Liquid fuels: Crude oil	Refined petroleum products: Total	Gasoline	Kerosine	Fuel oils	Lubes and greases	Gas	Electricity
	(1)	(2)	(3)	(4)	(5)	(6)	(7)	(8)	(9)	(10)	(11)
YUGOSLAVIA (CONTINUED) — IMPORTS											
1960	2578	1660	918	653	266	36	11	192	27	-	-
1961	2336	1650	686	431	255	17	15	188	36	-	-
1962	3152	1590	1562	1121	441	26	8	378	30	-	-
1963	3106	1670	1436	1167	269	17	8	210	33	-	-
1964	3899	2200	1656	1140	516	36	9	395	77	-	43
1965	4268	2285	1934	1661	273	42	5	206	21	-	49
YUGOSLAVIA — EXPORTS											
1925	80	80	-	-	-	-	-	-	-	-	-
1929	68	68	-	-	-	-	-	-	-	-	-
1933	27	27	-	-	-	-	-	-	-	-	-
1937	44	44	-	-	-	-	-	-	-	-	-
1938	31	31	-	-	-	-	-	-	-	-	-
1950	158	119	39	-	39	5	-	35	-	-	-
1953	181	110	68	-	68	3	-	65	-	-	4
1955	151	80	65	-	65	3	3	59	-	-	6
1957	249	80	150	-	150	63	11	69	-	-	19
1960	243	110	122	-	122	47	-	56	11	-	11
1961	531	110	411	269	143	24	-	99	15	-	10
1962	1386	100	1266	842	425	39	-	347	38	-	20
1963	1036	120	879	683	197	17	3	105	71	-	37
1964	863	140	723	474	249	63	-	116	69	-	-
1965	710	110	600	218	383	86	15	233	45	-	-
OCEANIA — IMPORTS											
1925	2127	744	1383	306	1077	671	191	141	75	-	-
1929	3572	884	2688	680	2009	1433	263	185	129	-	-
1933	2712	217	2495	372	2123	1208	210	611	95	-	-
1937	4231	319	3912	426	3486	1991	339	1019	138	-	-
1938	4620	366	4254	380	3875	2198	329	1227	120	-	-
1950	9587	657	8930	1196	7734	3516	711	3260	248	-	-
1953	10018	176	9842	1350	8492	4271	741	3333	147	-	-
1955	15322	272	15050	7335	7715	3941	876	2570	329	-	-
1957	18139	380	17759	12975	4784	2267	711	1481	326	-	-
1960	22391	272	22119	16898	5222	2669	743	1388	422	-	-
1961	24278	273	24005	18608	5397	2541	833	1586	437	-	-
1962	25336	175	25161	19401	5760	2715	795	1862	387	-	-
1963	28531	193	28338	22292	6047	2955	723	1842	525	-	-
1964	30214	304	29910	24239	5672	2831	582	1890	368	-	-
1965	32331	318	32013	28023	3990	1814	759	1130	285	-	-
OCEANIA — EXPORTS											
1925	971	962	9	2	8	3	2	2	2	-	-
1929	371	354	17	2	15	-	11	2	3	-	-
1933	299	299	-	-	-	-	-	-	-	-	-
1937	408	405	3	-	3	-	-	2	2	-	-
1938	462	460	2	-	2	-	-	2	-	-	-
1950	93	76	17	-	17	2	8	3	5	-	-
1953	417	405	12	-	12	3	2	3	5	-	-
1955	717	240	477	-	477	192	8	276	2	-	-
1957	2257	940	1317	-	1317	194	18	1101	5	-	-

Table VI. ENERGY IMPORTS AND EXPORTS, SELECTED YEARS, 1925-1965

(Thousand metric tons coal equivalent)

Region, country, year	Total energy	Solid fuels	Liquid fuels: Total	Liquid fuels: Crude oil	Refined petroleum products: Total	Gasoline	Kerosine	Fuel oils	Lubes and greases	Gas	Electricity
	(1)	(2)	(3)	(4)	(5)	(6)	(7)	(8)	(9)	(10)	(11)
OCEANIA (CONTINUED)								EXPORTS			
1960	4182	1710	2472	-	2472	203	99	2169	2	-	-
1961	5906	3000	2906	-	2906	326	251	2321	9	-	-
1962	6601	3050	3551	-	3551	171	113	3260	8	-	-
1963	7006	3290	3716	-	3716	276	149	3269	23	-	-
1964	7756	5000	2756	-	2756	267	83	2330	77	-	-
1965	9273	7335	1938	-	1938	101	83	1676	80	-	-
AUSTRALIA								IMPORTS			
1925	1080	55	1025	306	719	500	159	-	60	-	-
1929	2677	554	2123	680	1443	1107	222	6	108	-	-
1933	1984	5	1979	372	1607	920	183	426	78	-	-
1937	3144	28	3116	426	2690	1542	324	714	110	-	-
1938	3306	82	3224	380	2844	1664	312	771	98	-	-
1950	7749	523	7226	1196	6030	2759	662	2412	198	-	-
1953	7984	22	7962	1350	6612	3197	696	2613	107	-	-
1955	12660	10	12650	7335	5315	2700	812	1539	264	-	-
1957	14972	20	14952	12975	1977	828	624	261	264	-	-
1960	19032	-	19032	16898	2135	1110	569	155	302	-	-
1961	20659	10	20649	18608	2042	872	615	239	317	-	-
1962	21783	10	21773	19401	2372	1086	579	426	281	-	-
1963	24555	10	24545	22292	2253	1176	492	227	359	-	-
1964	25189	10	25179	22671	2508	1371	324	533	281	-	-
1965	26782	10	26772	24450	2322	1284	429	426	183	-	-
AUSTRALIA								EXPORTS			
1925	961	952	9	2	8	3	2	2	2	-	-
1929	321	304	17	2	15	-	11	2	3	-	-
1933	299	299	-	-	-	-	-	-	-	-	-
1937	408	405	3	-	3	-	-	2	2	-	-
1938	449	447	2	-	2	-	-	2	-	-	-
1950	89	72	17	-	17	2	8	3	5	-	-
1953	417	405	12	-	12	3	2	3	5	-	-
1955	713	240	473	-	473	192	6	273	2	-	-
1957	2245	940	1305	-	1305	186	17	1098	5	-	-
1960	4131	1690	2441	-	2441	189	95	2156	2	-	-
1961	5870	2990	2880	-	2880	320	240	2312	9	-	-
1962	6578	3050	3528	-	3528	162	105	3254	8	-	-
1963	6986	3290	3696	-	3696	267	143	3264	23	-	-
1964	7408	5000	2408	-	2408	258	78	1995	77	-	-
1965	8904	7335	1569	-	1569	92	74	1325	80	-	-
NEW ZEALAND								IMPORTS			
1925	927	576	351	-	351	167	29	141	15	-	-
1929	765	216	549	-	549	312	39	179	20	-	-
1933	600	102	498	-	498	278	26	180	15	-	-
1937	871	119	752	-	752	428	9	290	26	-	-
1938	1090	112	978	-	978	512	11	437	20	-	-
1950	1668	49	1619	-	1619	723	44	806	47	-	-
1953	1717	1	1716	-	1716	998	30	660	29	-	-
1955	2167	10	2157	-	2157	1148	44	917	50	-	-
1957	2505	10	2495	-	2495	1308	60	1073	54	-	-

Table VI. ENERGY IMPORTS AND EXPORTS, SELECTED YEARS, 1925–1965

(Thousand metric tons coal equivalent)

Region, country, year	Total energy	Solid fuels	Liquid fuels: Total	Crude oil	Refined petroleum products: Total	Gasoline	Kerosine	Fuel oils	Lubes and greases	Gas	Electricity
	(1)	(2)	(3)	(4)	(5)	(6)	(7)	(8)	(9)	(10)	(11)
NEW ZEALAND (CONTINUED)								IMPORTS			
1960	2631	-	2631	-	2631	1415	102	1044	71	-	-
1961	2835	10	2825	-	2825	1533	125	1100	68	-	-
1962	2910	10	2900	-	2900	1485	135	1206	74	-	-
1963	3192	-	3192	-	3192	1625	144	1361	63	-	-
1964	3972	-	3972	1568	2405	1280	149	914	63	-	-
1965	4451	-	4451	3573	878	356	192	258	72	-	-
NEW ZEALAND								EXPORTS			
1925	10	10	-	-	-	-	-	-	-	-	-
1929	50	50	-	-	-	-	-	-	-	-	-
1933	-	-	-	-	-	-	-	-	-	-	-
1937	-	-	-	-	-	-	-	-	-	-	-
1938	13	13	-	-	-	-	-	-	-	-	-
1950	4	4	-	-	-	-	-	-	-	-	-
1953	-	-	-	-	-	-	-	-	-	-	-
1955	-	-	-	-	-	-	-	-	-	-	-
1957	-	-	-	-	-	-	-	-	-	-	-
1960	34	20	14	-	14	5	3	6	-	-	-
1961	21	10	11	-	11	2	9	-	-	-	-
1962	9	-	9	-	9	3	6	-	-	-	-
1963	8	-	8	-	8	3	5	-	-	-	-
1964	338	-	338	-	338	5	3	330	-	-	-
1965	357	-	357	-	357	5	8	345	-	-	-
USSR AND COMMUNIST EASTERN EUROPE								IMPORTS			
1925	4660	4090	561	132	429	41	132	29	27	-	9
1929	7448	6283	1157	468	689	96	156	78	48	-	9
1933	3768	2722	1044	417	627	38	125	72	24	-	2
1937	4985	3291	1692	810	882	287	141	128	39	-	2
1938	4234	2779	1455	632	824	275	141	122	41	-	-
1950	27442	20572	6773	2993	3780	450	338	1193	-	75	23
1953	36760	24881	11703	4818	6885	540	390	1455	-	155	21
1955	39835	26030	13550	5168	8382	3767	1217	3236	164	216	40
1957	35824	20230	15236	7818	7418	4331	756	2201	131	288	71
1960	47440	25470	21233	11316	9917	5600	1112	2940	266	630	108
1961	51279	27610	22896	12176	10721	5471	1002	3927	321	671	101
1962	56801	30440	25574	14129	11445	5246	929	5093	176	685	102
1963	63891	33300	29736	17427	12309	5312	885	5765	345	702	153
1964	71440	36650	33840	22463	11378	4754	714	5669	233	709	242
1965	75852	36714	38096	28343	9753	3965	720	4841	225	774	269
USSR AND COMMUNIST EASTERN EUROPE								EXPORTS			
1925	16198	12503	3695	101	3594	912	1287	1056	329	-	-
1929	30022	20002	10020	473	9548	2906	2418	3731	479	-	-
1933	29119	13641	15477	1154	14324	4656	2343	6804	515	-	1
1937	26961	16057	10904	981	9923	3434	1802	4283	402	-	-
1938	22097	13632	8465	1005	7460	2855	1557	2750	296	-	-
1950	38989	33101	5805	615	5190	1898	923	1170	-	33	50
1953	50755	34587	16020	3255	12765	3015	1538	2963	-	127	21
1955	62146	39350	22589	4968	17621	6122	2270	8985	228	186	21
1957	64198	33320	30579	9564	21015	6741	2360	11589	321	228	71

Table VI. ENERGY IMPORTS AND EXPORTS, SELECTED YEARS, 1925-1965

(Thousand metric tons coal equivalent)

Region, country, year	Total energy	Solid fuels	Liquid fuels: Total	Liquid fuels: Crude oil	Refined petroleum products: Total	Gasoline	Kerosine	Fuel oils	Lubes and greases	Gas	Electricity
	(1)	(2)	(3)	(4)	(5)	(6)	(7)	(8)	(9)	(10)	(11)
USSR AND COMMUNIST EASTERN EUROPE (CONTINUED)								EXPORTS			
1960	106856	44400	61775	27401	34374	8742	2672	22020	912	594	88
1961	122423	47510	74175	35708	38468	9407	2567	25439	1028	635	103
1962	134413	52670	81021	40002	41019	8625	2853	28532	987	678	44
1963	146646	55580	90294	45950	44345	8844	2555	31913	1020	678	94
1964	159537	59840	98774	55539	43235	7781	1848	32678	918	671	252
1965	171527	59345	111117	65717	45401	7037	2168	35298	876	791	274
COMMUNIST EASTERN EUROPE								IMPORTS			
1925	3870	3398	464	119	345	30	72	24	18	-	9
1929	6198	5186	1004	443	561	68	83	65	36	-	9
1933	2825	1924	899	413	486	17	38	50	14	-	2
1937	3482	2222	1259	791	468	23	45	89	24	-	2
1938	2742	1729	1013	609	404	23	32	77	27	-	-
1950	11992	9172	2723	743	1980	450	338	1193	-	75	23
1953	19660	14981	4503	2118	2385	540	390	1455	-	155	21
1955	22858	16960	5643	2805	2838	785	393	1661	-	216	39
1957	25928	16470	9099	5822	3278	1296	315	1667	-	288	71
1960	35832	20100	14994	9567	5427	2339	654	2354	81	630	108
1961	40857	22290	17795	10844	6951	2801	593	3456	102	671	101
1962	47259	24960	21512	13385	8127	2874	563	4688	-	685	102
1963	54119	27610	25655	16613	9042	3009	579	5327	125	702	153
1964	62778	30950	30878	22463	8415	2675	488	5244	-	709	242
1965	65732	29319	35370	28343	7028	2133	467	4425	-	774	269
COMMUNIST EASTERN EUROPE								EXPORTS			
1925	13773	12136	1637	6	1631	495	606	341	179	-	-
1929	22887	18663	4224	5	4220	1260	1236	1556	153	-	-
1933	19948	11823	8124	356	7769	2709	1488	3431	135	-	1
1937	22691	14745	7946	797	7149	2804	1436	2835	72	-	-
1938	19600	13306	6294	660	5634	2384	1241	1944	63	-	-
1950	34706	30501	4155	165	3990	1898	923	1170	-	-	50
1953	37978	30187	7770	255	7515	3015	1538	2963	-	-	21
1955	44247	33580	10646	594	10052	4014	1308	4713	-	-	21
1957	32775	22570	10134	680	9455	4184	998	4251	18	-	71
1960	42170	29700	12116	663	11453	4515	1032	5535	342	270	84
1961	42679	29680	12630	626	12005	4023	953	6608	393	276	93
1962	43703	30330	13083	584	12500	3893	911	7346	329	276	15
1963	44411	30800	13335	585	12750	3831	651	7815	440	276	1
1964	46957	32610	13977	503	13475	3660	513	8816	476	281	89
1965	48573	33545	14673	569	14105	3507	420	9693	462	269	86
ALBANIA								IMPORTS			
1925	8	-	8	5	3	2	-	2	-	-	-
1929	11	-	11	5	6	5	-	2	-	-	-
1933	12	-	12	3	9	6	-	3	-	-	-
1937	12	-	12	3	9	5	-	5	-	-	-
1938	18	4	14	3	11	5	-	6	-	-	-
1950	40	10	30	-	30	23	-	8	-	-	-
1953	50	20	30	-	30	23	-	8	-	-	-
1955	32	-	32	-	32	26	-	6	-	-	-
1957	30	10	20	-	20	15	3	2	-	-	-

Table VI. ENERGY IMPORTS AND EXPORTS, SELECTED YEARS, 1925-1965

(Thousand metric tons coal equivalent)

Region, country, year	Total energy	Solid fuels	Liquid fuels							Gas	Electricity
					Refined petroleum products						
			Total	Crude oil	Total	Gasoline	Kerosine	Fuel oils	Lubes and greases		
	(1)	(2)	(3)	(4)	(5)	(6)	(7)	(8)	(9)	(10)	(11)
ALBANIA (CONTINUED)								IMPORTS			
1960	25	10	15	-	15	8	5	3	-	-	-
1961	27	10	17	-	17	8	5	5	-	-	-
1962	49	20	29	-	29	18	6	5	-	-	-
1963	31	10	21	-	21	15	6	-	-	-	-
1964	57	10	47	-	47	20	6	21	-	-	-
1965	36	15	21	-	21	17	5	-	-	-	-
ALBANIA								EXPORTS			
1925	-	-	-	-	-	-	-	-	-	-	-
1929	-	-	-	-	-	-	-	-	-	-	-
1933	-	-	-	-	-	-	-	-	-	-	-
1937	89	-	89	89	-	-	-	-	-	-	-
1938	158	-	158	158	-	-	-	-	-	-	-
1950	90	-	90	90	-	-	-	-	-	-	-
1953	105	-	105	105	-	-	-	-	-	-	-
1955	206	20	186	186	-	-	-	-	-	-	-
1957	337	10	327	327	-	-	-	-	-	-	-
1960	494	-	494	494	-	-	-	-	-	-	-
1961	437	-	437	437	-	-	-	-	-	-	-
1962	410	-	410	410	-	-	-	-	-	-	-
1963	480	-	480	465	15	-	-	15	-	-	-
1964	441	-	441	441	-	-	-	-	-	-	-
1965	563	-	563	563	-	-	-	-	-	-	-
BULGARIA								IMPORTS			
1925	83	18	65	-	65	6	39	14	6	-	-
1929	135	9	126	-	126	17	50	48	12	-	-
1933	104	5	99	-	99	11	38	45	6	-	-
1937	135	3	132	29	104	15	45	32	12	-	-
1938	136	4	132	44	89	17	32	29	12	-	-
1950	360	NA	360	30	330	90	60	180	-	-	-
1953	503	NA	503	30	473	128	90	255	-	-	-
1955	626	120	506	-	506	158	71	278	-	-	-
1957	910	140	770	-	770	294	87	389	-	-	-
1960	1654	320	1334	18	1316	503	30	783	-	-	-
1961	2558	810	1748	33	1715	588	30	1097	-	-	-
1962	3678	1230	2439	23	2417	645	29	1743	-	-	9
1963	4738	1570	3158	677	2481	645	27	1809	-	-	10
1964	6952	2300	4652	2717	1935	336	15	1584	-	-	-
1965	8120	2838	5282	3300	1982	236	17	1730	-	-	-
BULGARIA								EXPORTS			
1925	2	2	-	-	-	-	-	-	-	-	-
1929	11	11	-	-	-	-	-	-	-	-	-
1933	1	1	-	-	-	-	-	-	-	-	-
1937	5	3	2	-	2	-	-	2	-	-	-
1938	16	16	-	-	-	-	-	-	-	-	-
1950	-	NA	-	-	-	-	-	-	-	-	-
1953	-	NA	-	-	-	-	-	-	-	-	-
1955	196	20	176	174	2	-	-	2	-	-	-
1957	589	190	399	303	96	-	-	96	-	-	-

Table VI. ENERGY IMPORTS AND EXPORTS, SELECTED YEARS, 1925-1965

(Thousand metric tons coal equivalent)

Region, country, year	Total energy	Solid fuels	Liquid fuels: Total	Liquid fuels: Crude oil	Refined petroleum products: Total	Gasoline	Kerosine	Fuel oils	Lubes and greases	Gas	Electricity
	(1)	(2)	(3)	(4)	(5)	(6)	(7)	(8)	(9)	(10)	(11)
BULGARIA (CONTINUED) — EXPORTS											
1960	210	60	150	120	30	-	-	30	-	-	-
1961	251	60	191	189	2	-	-	2	-	-	-
1962	229	50	179	174	5	-	-	5	-	-	-
1963	170	50	120	120	-	-	-	-	-	-	-
1964	92	-	89	62	27	-	-	27	-	-	3
1965	111	-	111	6	105	-	-	105	-	-	-
CZECHOSLOVAKIA — IMPORTS											
1925	2040	1751	287	86	201	NA	NA	NA	NA	-	2
1929	3325	2778	545	234	311	NA	NA	NA	NA	-	3
1933	1874	1351	521	152	369	NA	NA	NA	NA	-	2
1937	2073	1381	690	402	288	NA	NA	NA	NA	-	2
1938	1476	928	548	302	246	NA	NA	NA	NA	-	-
1950	2698	1740	945	195	750	53	210	488	-	-	13
1953	4552	3220	1328	570	758	53	210	495	-	-	5
1955	5723	4200	1523	668	855	105	225	525	-	-	-
1957	4617	2290	2327	1832	495	120	150	225	-	-	-
1960	6984	2950	4034	3383	651	191	318	143	-	-	-
1961	8906	3930	4976	4178	798	191	330	278	-	-	-
1962	10958	4600	6350	5513	837	186	366	285	-	-	8
1963	12444	5280	7146	6326	821	174	407	240	-	-	18
1964	14226	5590	8549	7755	794	177	362	255	-	-	88
1965	15093	5111	9887	9144	743	234	365	144	-	-	95
CZECHOSLOVAKIA — EXPORTS											
1925	3556	3540	17	6	11	NA	NA	NA	NA	NA	NA
1929	4698	4683	15	-	15	NA	NA	NA	NA	NA	NA
1933	2675	2669	6	-	6	NA	NA	NA	NA	NA	NA
1937	4348	4345	3	-	3	NA	NA	NA	NA	NA	NA
1938	2963	2960	3	-	3	NA	NA	NA	NA	NA	NA
1950	970	970	-	-	-	-	-	-	-	-	-
1953	1800	1800	-	-	-	-	-	-	-	-	-
1955	2402	2350	36	-	36	9	2	21	-	-	16
1957	2921	2750	143	-	143	15	-	128	-	-	29
1960	4550	4270	246	-	246	77	-	161	-	-	34
1961	4985	4590	348	-	348	113	-	228	-	5	42
1962	5315	4750	560	-	560	158	-	389	-	5	-
1963	5862	5020	837	-	837	216	-	614	-	5	-
1964	5623	4835	783	-	783	213	-	560	-	5	-
1965	5611	4470	1136	-	1136	225	-	888	-	5	-
GERMANY, EAST — IMPORTS											
1950	6815	6392	375	75	300	113	-	188	-	48	-
1953	10199	9401	750	600	150	38	-	113	-	48	-
1955	10950	9930	972	972	-	-	-	-	-	48	-
1957	11002	9420	1511	1496	15	-	-	15	-	72	-
1960	15654	11960	3623	2912	711	342	222	147	-	72	-
1961	16592	12280	4259	3405	854	360	159	335	-	53	-
1962	18045	13270	4733	3887	846	330	75	441	-	43	-
1963	19290	13490	5769	4745	1025	378	60	587	-	31	-
1964	22157	15020	7100	6390	710	281	30	399	-	19	18

Table VI. ENERGY IMPORTS AND EXPORTS, SELECTED YEARS, 1925-1965

(Thousand metric tons coal equivalent)

Region, country, year	Total energy	Solid fuels	Liquid fuels: Total	Liquid fuels: Crude oil	Refined petroleum products: Total	Gasoline	Kerosine	Fuel oils	Lubes and greases	Gas	Electricity
	(1)	(2)	(3)	(4)	(5)	(6)	(7)	(8)	(9)	(10)	(11)
GERMANY, EAST (CONTINUED)								IMPORTS			
1965	22495	14070	8402	7698	704	195	-	509	-	12	12
GERMANY, EAST								EXPORTS			
1950	1326	1051	225	-	225	90	-	135	-	-	50
1953	2387	1991	375	-	375	150	-	225	-	-	21
1955	4363	3540	822	-	822	383	2	432	-	-	1
1957	4281	3280	960	-	960	465	-	495	-	-	41
1960	5683	4320	1317	-	1317	588	-	713	-	-	46
1961	5769	4240	1482	-	1482	651	-	815	-	-	47
1962	6021	4500	1511	-	1511	747	-	758	-	-	11
1963	6438	4750	1688	-	1688	798	-	884	-	-	-
1964	6461	4640	1821	-	1821	779	-	1043	-	-	-
1965	6389	4080	2309	-	2309	891	-	1418	-	-	-
HUNGARY								IMPORTS			
1925	1252	1153	99	29	71	23	33	8	8	-	-
1929	2153	1845	308	204	104	47	32	14	12	-	-
1933	590	327	263	258	5	-	-	2	3	-	-
1937	999	579	420	357	63	3	-	53	8	-	-
1938	838	523	315	261	54	2	-	42	11	-	-
1950	1000	760	240	150	90	30	8	53	-	-	-
1953	2166	1730	420	300	120	45	15	60	-	-	16
1955	2448	1910	507	348	159	17	23	120	-	-	31
1957	5272	3360	1874	1550	324	42	-	282	-	-	39
1960	5329	2680	2336	2184	152	17	-	135	-	246	68
1961	5817	3020	2465	2118	347	86	-	261	-	270	62
1962	5946	2920	2685	2310	375	95	-	281	-	270	70
1963	7693	3950	3351	2742	609	135	-	474	-	276	116
1964	9033	4730	3869	3039	830	185	-	645	-	300	135
1965	8427	4070	3932	3377	555	162	-	393	-	264	162
HUNGARY								EXPORTS			
1925	427	427	-	-	-	-	-	-	-	-	-
1929	292	292	-	-	-	-	-	-	-	-	-
1933	164	164	-	-	-	-	-	-	-	-	-
1937	169	169	-	-	-	-	-	-	-	-	-
1938	189	189	-	-	-	-	-	-	-	-	-
1950	315	150	165	75	90	8	23	60	NA	-	-
1953	610	340	270	150	120	15	38	68	NA	-	-
1955	770	260	510	234	276	23	45	209	NA	-	-
1957	373	20	353	50	303	104	23	159	18	-	-
1960	840	40	800	50	750	152	-	579	20	-	-
1961	814	50	764	-	764	144	15	585	20	-	-
1962	987	100	887	-	887	177	-	689	21	-	-
1963	964	230	734	-	734	123	-	590	21	-	-
1964	997	145	852	-	852	186	-	645	21	-	-
1965	884	140	744	-	744	225	-	498	21	-	-

Table VI. ENERGY IMPORTS AND EXPORTS, SELECTED YEARS, 1925-1965

(Thousand metric tons coal equivalent)

Region, country, year	Total energy	Solid fuels	Liquid fuels		Refined petroleum products					Gas	Electricity
			Total	Crude oil	Total	Gasoline	Kerosine	Fuel oils	Lubes and greases		
	(1)	(2)	(3)	(4)	(5)	(6)	(7)	(8)	(9)	(10)	(11)
POLAND								IMPORTS			
1925	253	242	5	–	5	–	–	2	3	–	6
1929	330	315	9	–	9	–	2	2	6	–	6
1933	175	173	2	–	2	–	–	–	2	–	–
1937	184	182	2	–	2	–	–	–	2	–	–
1938	182	180	2	–	2	–	–	–	2	–	–
1950	859	50	773	293	480	143	60	278	–	27	10
1953	1660	80	1473	618	855	255	75	525	–	107	–
1955	2410	130	2105	818	1287	480	75	732	NA	168	8
1957	3328	480	2600	945	1655	825	75	755	NA	216	33
1960	5176	1170	3654	1071	2583	1280	80	1143	81	312	40
1961	6089	1370	4332	1110	3222	1569	69	1482	102	348	39
1962	7184	1520	5277	1653	3624	1601	87	1934	NA	372	15
1963	8404	1790	6210	2124	4086	1662	80	2217	125	396	9
1964	8783	1730	6663	2562	4101	1677	75	2340	NA	390	–
1965	10016	1670	7848	4824	3024	1290	81	1650	NA	498	–
POLAND								EXPORTS			
1925	8592	8145	447	–	447	98	111	122	117	–	–
1929	13915	13643	272	–	272	57	77	78	60	–	–
1933	9215	8982	233	–	233	75	68	42	48	–	1
1937	10347	10228	119	–	119	62	14	23	21	–	–
1938	10155	10141	14	–	14	8	–	3	3	–	–
1950	28405	28330	75	–	75	–	–	75	–	–	–
1953	26176	26056	120	–	120	–	–	120	–	–	–
1955	27546	27390	156	–	156	–	–	150	NA	–	–
1957	16398	16320	78	–	78	–	–	74	NA	–	–
1960	21316	21010	306	–	306	–	18	279	6	–	–
1961	21127	20740	387	–	387	–	12	371	5	–	–
1962	21776	20930	846	–	846	5	8	833	NA	–	–
1963	21596	20730	866	–	866	5	23	833	6	–	–
1964	23853	22910	857	–	857	–	6	851	NA	–	86
1965	26257	24855	1358	–	1358	–	–	1358	NA	–	45
ROMANIA								IMPORTS			
1925	236	234	2	–	2	–	–	–	2	–	–
1929	245	239	6	–	6	–	–	–	6	–	–
1933	71	68	3	–	3	–	–	–	3	–	–
1937	80	77	3	–	3	–	–	–	3	–	–
1938	93	90	3	–	3	–	–	–	3	–	–
1950	220	220	–	–	–	–	–	–	–	–	–
1953	530	530	–	–	–	–	–	–	–	–	–
1955	670	670	–	–	–	–	–	–	–	–	–
1957	770	770	–	–	–	–	–	–	–	–	–
1960	1010	1010	–	–	–	–	–	–	–	–	–
1961	870	870	–	–	–	–	–	–	–	–	–
1962	1400	1400	–	–	–	–	–	–	–	–	–
1963	1520	1520	–	–	–	–	–	–	–	–	–
1964	1571	1570	–	–	–	–	–	–	–	–	1
1965	1545	1545	–	–	–	–	–	–	–	–	–

Table VI. ENERGY IMPORTS AND EXPORTS, SELECTED YEARS, 1925-1965

(Thousand metric tons coal equivalent)

Region, country, year	Total energy	Solid fuels	Liquid fuels							Gas	Electricity
					Refined petroleum products						
			Total	Crude oil	Total	Gasoline	Kerosine	Fuel oils	Lubes and greases		
	(1)	(2)	(3)	(4)	(5)	(6)	(7)	(8)	(9)	(10)	(11)
ROMANIA (CONTINUED)								EXPORTS			
1925	1195	22	1173	-	1173	398	495	219	62	-	-
1929	3972	34	3938	5	3933	1203	1160	1478	93	-	-
1933	7893	7	7886	356	7530	2634	1421	3389	87	-	-
1937	7734	-	7734	708	7026	2742	1422	2811	51	-	-
1938	6120	-	6120	503	5618	2376	1241	1941	60	-	-
1950	3600	-	3600	-	3600	1800	900	900	NA	-	-
1953	6900	-	6900	-	6900	2850	1500	2550	NA	-	-
1955	8764	-	8760	-	8760	3600	1260	3900	NA	-	4
1957	7876	-	7875	-	7875	3600	975	3300	NA	-	1
1960	9078	-	8804	-	8804	3699	1014	3774	317	270	4
1961	9298	-	9023	-	9023	3116	926	4608	369	270	5
1962	8967	-	8693	-	8693	2807	903	4674	308	270	4
1963	8902	20	8612	-	8612	2690	629	4881	413	270	1
1964	9491	80	9135	-	9135	2483	507	5691	455	276	-
1965	8759	-	8454	-	8454	2166	420	5427	441	264	41
USSR (INCLUDING ESTONIA, LATVIA, LITHUANIA)								IMPORTS			
1925	790	692	98	14	84	11	60	5	9	-	-
1929	1250	1097	153	26	128	29	74	14	12	-	-
1933	944	798	146	5	141	21	87	23	11	-	-
1937	1503	1069	434	20	414	264	96	39	15	-	-
1938	1493	1050	443	23	420	252	110	45	14	-	-
1950	15450	11400	4050	2250	1800	NA	NA	NA	NA	-	-
1953	17100	9900	7200	2700	4500	NA	NA	NA	NA	-	-
1955	16978	9070	7907	2363	5544	2982	824	1575	164	-	1
1957	9897	3760	6137	1997	4140	3035	441	534	131	-	-
1960	11609	5370	6239	1749	4490	3261	458	587	185	-	-
1961	10422	5320	5102	1332	3770	2670	410	471	219	-	-
1962	9542	5480	4062	744	3318	2372	366	405	176	-	-
1963	9772	5690	4082	815	3267	2303	306	438	221	-	-
1964	8663	5700	2963	-	2963	2079	227	425	233	-	-
1965	10121	7395	2726	-	2726	1832	254	416	225	-	-
USSR (INCLUDING ESTONIA, LATVIA, LITHUANIA)								EXPORTS			
1925	2425	367	2058	95	1964	417	681	716	150	-	-
1929	7135	1339	5796	468	5328	1646	1182	2175	326	-	-
1933	9171	1818	7353	798	6555	1947	855	3374	380	-	-
1937	4270	1312	2958	185	2774	630	366	1448	330	-	-
1938	2497	326	2171	345	1826	471	317	806	233	-	-
1950	4283	2600	1650	450	1200	NA	NA	NA	NA	33	-
1953	12777	4400	8250	3000	5250	NA	NA	NA	NA	127	-
1955	17899	5770	11943	4374	7569	2108	962	4272	228	186	-
1957	31423	10750	20445	8885	11561	2558	1362	7338	303	228	-
1960	64686	14700	49659	26738	22922	4227	1640	16485	570	324	4
1961	79744	17830	61545	35082	26463	5384	1614	18831	635	360	9
1962	90709	22340	67938	39419	28520	4733	1943	21186	659	402	29
1963	102235	24780	76959	45365	31595	5013	1904	24098	581	402	93
1964	112580	27230	84797	55037	29760	4121	1335	23862	443	390	163
1965	122954	25800	96444	65148	31296	3530	1748	25605	414	522	188

Table VI. ENERGY IMPORTS AND EXPORTS, SELECTED YEARS, 1925-1965

(Thousand metric tons coal equivalent)

Region, country, year	Total energy	Solid fuels	Liquid fuels							Gas	Electricity
					Refined petroleum products						
			Total	Crude oil	Total	Gasoline	Kerosine	Fuel oils	Lubes and greases		
	(1)	(2)	(3)	(4)	(5)	(6)	(7)	(8)	(9)	(10)	(11)
COMMUNIST ASIA								IMPORTS			
1925	4214	2802	1412	-	1412	38	1191	146	38	-	-
1929	3930	2323	1607	-	1607	120	1103	311	74	-	-
1933	3258	1527	1731	-	1731	183	915	552	81	-	-
1937	2138	435	1703	237	1466	303	650	420	93	-	-
1938	2345	1140	1205	240	965	209	413	281	63	-	-
1950	NA	NA	NA	NA	NA	NA	NA	NA	NA	NA	NA
1953	NA	NA	NA	NA	NA	NA	NA	NA	NA	NA	NA
1955	2142	80	2063	600	1463	390	480	593	NA	NA	NA
1957	3550	100	3450	638	2813	1260	668	885	NA	NA	NA
1960	5465	110	5355	915	4440	2160	750	1530	NA	NA	NA
1961	5150	80	5070	120	4950	2438	840	1673	NA	NA	NA
1962	3952	210	3743	210	3533	1673	788	1073	NA	NA	NA
1963	3422	40	3383	225	3158	1388	795	975	NA	NA	NA
1964	2462	280	2183	300	1883	968	330	585	NA	NA	NA
1965	1685	140	1545	315	1230	593	120	518	NA	NA	NA
COMMUNIST ASIA								EXPORTS			
1925	2601	2601	-	-	-	-	-	-	-	-	-
1929	3544	3544	-	-	-	-	-	-	-	-	-
1933	4246	4165	81	77	5	3	2	-	-	-	-
1937	4948	4855	93	93	-	-	-	-	-	-	-
1938	4320	4192	128	128	-	-	-	-	-	-	-
1950	NA	NA	NA	NA	NA	NA	NA	NA	NA	NA	NA
1953	NA	NA	NA	NA	NA	NA	NA	NA	NA	NA	NA
1955	1100	1100	-	-	-	-	-	-	NA	NA	NA
1957	1846	1840	6	-	6	6	-	-	NA	NA	NA
1960	1030	1030	-	-	-	-	-	-	NA	NA	NA
1961	1200	1200	-	-	-	-	-	-	NA	NA	NA
1962	1430	1430	-	-	-	-	-	-	NA	NA	NA
1963	1470	1470	-	-	-	-	-	-	NA	NA	NA
1964	1500	1500	-	-	-	-	-	-	NA	NA	NA
1965	1755	1755	-	-	-	-	-	-	NA	NA	NA
LATIN AMERICA								IMPORTS			
1925	19004	7238	11763	5570	6194	864	410	4754	167	3	-
1929	37363	7556	29802	21402	8400	1686	432	6051	231	5	-
1933	33699	4752	28866	21701	7166	801	257	5987	122	79	3
1937	52049	6145	45720	35351	10370	1457	309	8426	179	181	2
1938	55981	5497	50417	38229	12188	2631	653	8730	174	65	2
1950	98750	2932	94931	74141	20790	5420	633	14193	545	871	16
1953	106161	2410	103011	76880	26132	8381	1076	15962	714	719	27
1955	121996	2810	118421	85694	32727	8283	2187	20966	806	745	21
1957	127054	2860	124143	91142	33002	8189	2133	21362	798	-	51
1960	123756	3070	120630	94035	26595	5822	1770	17502	791	-	56
1961	131274	2520	128697	101709	26988	6177	2168	16992	780	-	57
1962	137191	1990	135135	109407	25728	5243	1956	16628	849	-	66
1963	139870	2314	137483	111980	25503	4577	1500	17594	692	-	74
1964	149980	2489	147473	120429	27044	3941	1500	19628	731	-	18
1965	153162	2567	150588	126786	23802	3560	1878	16187	683	-	8

Table VI. ENERGY IMPORTS AND EXPORTS, SELECTED YEARS, 1925-1965

(Thousand metric tons coal equivalent)

Region, country, year	Total energy	Solid fuels	Liquid fuels		Refined petroleum products					Gas	Electricity
			Total	Crude oil	Total	Gasoline	Kerosine	Fuel oils	Lubes and greases		
	(1)	(2)	(3)	(4)	(5)	(6)	(7)	(8)	(9)	(10)	(11)
LATIN AMERICA (CONTINUED)								EXPORTS			
1925	29907	15	29892	19047	10845	1301	266	9165	114	-	-
1929	58971	25	58946	38852	20094	2895	366	16482	351	-	-
1933	56531	122	56409	33983	22427	4706	605	16866	251	-	-
1937	83224	55	83169	47163	36006	6074	728	28623	582	-	-
1938	87511	58	87453	48893	38561	6611	1118	30305	528	-	-
1950	185160	142	185018	112218	72800	11069	3191	58361	368	-	-
1953	206827	37	206790	118248	88542	12164	5177	70458	924	-	-
1955	239076	70	239006	144018	94988	11256	6491	75966	1173	-	-
1957	276571	100	276237	175755	100482	11696	7874	79710	1107	234	-
1960	286317	50	284708	167748	116960	12686	7982	94535	1419	1560	-
1961	298328	-	296570	172221	124349	13301	8985	100359	1295	1758	-
1962	324247	10	322695	185168	137528	13376	9581	112377	1611	1542	-
1963	333217	10	331707	186044	145664	14372	8991	120443	1314	1500	-
1964	348987	12	347361	195327	152034	13797	10581	125340	1668	1614	-
1965	354018	7	352349	195593	156756	15371	12002	126920	1856	1662	-
LATIN AMERICA - CARIBBEAN								IMPORTS			
1925	9523	1411	8109	4188	3921	153	75	3659	35	3	-
1929	25177	1425	23747	19182	4565	510	80	3933	42	5	-
1933	25943	617	25245	21191	4055	186	57	3779	33	79	3
1937	40474	779	39512	33314	6198	657	74	5399	69	181	2
1938	44349	661	43620	36053	7568	1886	470	5153	60	65	2
1950	78475	119	77469	69039	8430	2112	192	5888	239	871	16
1953	82093	146	81207	69521	11687	3932	305	7164	287	719	27
1955	89736	200	88770	72491	16280	5747	771	8987	338	745	21
1957	91344	250	91043	72183	18860	6470	1119	10457	332	-	51
1960	91596	110	91430	77468	13962	4037	719	8472	264	-	56
1961	101467	120	101291	84620	16671	4506	971	10295	359	-	57
1962	107880	240	107574	89181	18393	4260	956	12356	224	-	66
1963	111743	284	111386	91800	19586	3407	933	14384	167	-	74
1964	119173	359	118796	98369	20427	3153	947	15408	156	-	18
1965	119815	427	119380	101990	17391	2871	1256	12194	152	-	8
LATIN AMERICA - CARIBBEAN								EXPORTS			
1925	28469	-	28469	18096	10373	1079	227	8955	113	-	-
1929	56437	4	56433	37085	19349	2420	330	16251	348	-	-
1933	53873	-	53873	32265	21608	4173	558	16628	249	-	-
1937	79764	-	79764	44484	35280	5603	590	28508	581	-	-
1938	84576	-	84576	46707	37869	6194	960	30188	528	-	-
1950	183371	2	183369	111365	72005	10628	3129	58070	366	-	-
1953	205297	1	205296	117302	87995	11943	5121	70190	921	-	-
1955	237278	-	237278	143165	94113	10926	6344	75576	1169	-	-
1957	274200	10	273956	174584	99372	11417	7674	79082	1104	234	-
1960	283932	-	282372	166161	116211	12558	7856	94053	1419	1560	-
1961	295400	-	293642	169962	123680	13269	8928	99795	1295	1758	-
1962	321278	-	319736	183656	136080	13337	9542	111200	1610	1542	-
1963	330436	-	328937	184622	144315	14300	8979	119276	1310	1500	-
1964	347129	2	345513	194604	150909	13766	10581	124343	1667	1614	-
1965	351872	2	350208	194961	155247	15371	12000	125471	1850	1662	-

Table VI. ENERGY IMPORTS AND EXPORTS, SELECTED YEARS, 1925-1965

(Thousand metric tons coal equivalent)

Region, country, year	Total energy	Solid fuels	Liquid fuels		Refined petroleum products					Gas	Electricity
			Total	Crude oil	Total	Gasoline	Kerosine	Fuel oils	Lubes and greases		
	(1)	(2)	(3)	(4)	(5)	(6)	(7)	(8)	(9)	(10)	(11)
CARIBBEAN - OIL PRODUCING								IMPORTS			
1925	4424	137	4284	3945	339	51	11	252	26	3	-
1929	19926	178	19743	18777	966	156	17	762	32	5	-
1933	22926	78	22767	21099	1668	24	5	1625	15	79	3
1937	36480	89	36207	33026	3182	362	5	2778	38	181	2
1938	40765	86	40611	35814	4797	1575	399	2786	38	65	2
1950	71227	58	70283	68315	1968	966	71	767	165	870	16
1953	73586	58	72782	68555	4227	2346	128	1554	200	719	27
1955	79051	60	78225	71459	6767	3513	371	2279	203	745	21
1957	75441	70	75320	66128	9192	4229	728	3606	203	-	51
1960	71742	50	71636	66849	4787	2132	75	1985	186	-	56
1961	79456	70	79329	74430	4899	2591	233	1326	278	-	57
1962	81704	180	81458	75462	5996	1995	150	3174	144	-	66
1963	82402	190	82139	74939	7200	1688	99	4716	80	-	74
1964	86606	240	86348	79083	7265	1718	182	4610	68	-	18
1965	86131	295	85828	80840	4989	1610	375	2108	56	-	8
CARIBBEAN - OIL PRODUCING								EXPORTS			
1925	28469	-	28469	18096	10373	1079	227	8955	113	-	-
1929	56437	4	56433	37085	19349	2420	330	16251	348	-	-
1933	53873	-	53873	32265	21608	4173	558	16628	249	-	-
1937	79764	-	79764	44484	35280	5603	590	28508	581	-	-
1938	84576	-	84576	46707	37869	6194	960	30188	528	-	-
1950	183371	2	183369	111365	72005	10628	3129	57882	366	-	-
1953	205297	1	205296	117302	87995	11943	5121	70010	921	-	-
1955	236844	-	236844	143165	93680	10785	6308	75320	1169	-	-
1957	272058	10	271814	174584	97230	10997	7622	77414	1104	234	-
1960	280599	-	279039	166161	112878	11280	7794	92061	1419	1560	-
1961	291807	-	290049	169962	120087	11594	8831	97977	1295	1758	-
1962	316748	-	315206	183656	131550	11462	9350	108740	1610	1542	-
1963	324096	-	322596	184622	137975	12356	8817	115047	1310	1500	-
1964	340763	2	339147	194604	144543	11906	10436	119987	1667	1614	-
1965	345566	2	343902	194961	148941	13319	11780	121445	1850	1662	-
ANTILLES, NETHERLANDS								IMPORTS			
1925	3717	-	3717	3681	36	-	-	36	-	-	-
1929	19050	1	19049	18497	552	20	2	531	-	-	-
1933	22329	3	22326	20931	1395	-	-	1394	2	-	-
1937	35670	3	35667	32912	2756	320	3	2430	3	-	-
1938	40149	3	40146	35684	4463	1548	393	2519	3	-	-
1950	66758	-	66758	65865	893	345	60	480	8	-	-
1953	66951	-	66951	65040	1911	1080	30	795	6	-	-
1955	70428	-	70428	67676	2753	1833	8	807	5	-	-
1957	67026	-	67026	61922	5105	2489	192	2303	5	-	-
1960	61487	-	61487	58250	3237	1391	44	1677	44	-	-
1961	64716	-	64716	61269	3447	2061	200	980	140	-	-
1962	66801	-	66801	62013	4788	1607	126	2934	26	-	-
1963	66449	-	66449	60315	6134	1563	72	4400	-	-	-
1964	66963	-	66963	61251	5712	1490	153	3977	3	-	-
1965	64932	-	64932	61217	3716	1541	351	1695	15	-	-

Table VI. ENERGY IMPORTS AND EXPORTS, SELECTED YEARS, 1925-1965

(Thousand metric tons coal equivalent)

Region, country, year	Total energy	Solid fuels	Liquid fuels: Total	Liquid fuels: Crude oil	Refined petroleum products: Total	Gasoline	Kerosine	Fuel oils	Lubes and greases	Gas	Electricity
	(1)	(2)	(3)	(4)	(5)	(6)	(7)	(8)	(9)	(10)	(11)
ANTILLES, NETHERLANDS (CONTINUED)								EXPORTS			
1925	3057	NA	3057	1694	1364	161	8	1110	86	-	-
1929	17184	1	17183	774	16409	1833	32	14291	254	-	-
1933	19219	NA	19220	1806	17414	3327	428	13484	176	-	-
1937	30234	-	30234	1143	29091	4287	432	23877	495	-	-
1938	34063	NA	34064	1623	32441	5225	912	25796	509	-	-
1950	56283	-	56283	1710	54573	8225	2154	43830	365	-	-
1953	58593	-	58593	1080	57513	8111	3362	45270	771	-	-
1955	58998	-	58998	4419	54579	6713	4202	42690	969	-	-
1957	54272	-	54272	1389	52883	5900	4709	41357	918	-	-
1960	49829	-	49829	1418	48411	6071	4554	36683	1103	-	-
1961	51704	-	51704	2154	49550	6063	4901	37587	999	-	-
1962	54545	-	54545	2145	52400	6135	4715	40310	1241	-	-
1963	54450	-	54450	1410	53040	6204	4937	40986	914	-	-
1964	55437	-	55437	729	54708	6680	5609	41187	1233	-	-
1965	54114	-	54114	563	53552	6912	5672	39537	1431	-	-
COLOMBIA								IMPORTS			
1925	17	3	14	-	14	11	-	-	3	-	-
1929	79	1	78	8	71	42	2	21	6	-	-
1933	35	2	33	-	33	15	-	15	3	-	-
1937	36	1	35	-	35	9	-	21	5	-	-
1938	35	-	35	-	35	11	-	20	5	-	-
1950	299	-	299	-	299	236	-	62	2	-	-
1953	759	-	759	-	759	537	90	110	23	-	-
1955	725	-	725	-	725	468	95	119	44	-	-
1957	510	-	510	-	510	345	59	62	45	-	-
1960	156	-	156	-	156	92	5	15	45	-	-
1961	296	-	296	-	296	186	9	48	53	-	-
1962	333	-	333	-	333	278	-	3	53	-	-
1963	98	-	98	-	98	54	2	-	42	-	-
1964	90	-	90	-	90	65	2	-	24	-	-
1965	33	-	33	-	33	18	-	-	15	-	-
COLOMBIA								EXPORTS			
1925	-	-	-	-	-	-	-	-	-	-	-
1929	3809	-	3809	3809	-	-	-	-	-	-	-
1933	2543	-	2543	2543	-	-	-	-	-	-	-
1937	3819	-	3819	3819	-	-	-	-	-	-	-
1938	3972	-	3972	3972	-	-	-	-	-	-	-
1950	6155	-	6155	6155	-	-	-	-	-	-	-
1953	6911	-	6911	6911	-	-	-	-	-	-	-
1955	5715	-	5715	5391	324	-	-	324	-	-	-
1957	6466	10	6456	6045	411	-	-	411	-	-	-
1960	7410	-	7410	6530	881	-	-	881	-	-	-
1961	6429	-	6429	5792	638	54	-	584	-	-	-
1962	6023	-	6023	5103	920	-	-	920	-	-	-
1963	7104	-	7104	6546	558	3	5	551	-	-	-
1964	7447	2	7445	6372	1073	20	-	1053	-	-	-
1965	9511	2	9509	8415	1094	24	-	1070	-	-	-

Table VI. ENERGY IMPORTS AND EXPORTS, SELECTED YEARS, 1925-1965

(Thousand metric tons coal equivalent)

Region, country, year	Total energy	Solid fuels	Liquid fuels: Total	Liquid fuels: Crude oil	Refined petroleum products: Total	Gasoline	Kerosine	Fuel oils	Lubes and greases	Gas	Electricity
	(1)	(2)	(3)	(4)	(5)	(6)	(7)	(8)	(9)	(10)	(11)
MEXICO								IMPORTS			
1925	607	66	539	264	275	30	8	216	21	3	-
1929	670	65	600	273	327	90	11	203	24	5	-
1933	402	12	309	77	233	8	5	212	9	79	3
1937	590	13	393	20	374	23	2	327	23	181	2
1938	370	14	288	14	275	14	-	248	14	65	2
1950	1580	31	663	-	663	330	11	225	98	870	16
1953	2147	42	1359	-	1359	600	8	645	107	719	27
1955	3935	60	3110	-	3110	1116	269	1353	71	745	21
1957	3828	70	3707	282	3425	1364	471	1242	38	-	51
1960	1353	50	1247	-	1247	585	27	282	26	-	56
1961	1236	60	1119	38	1082	317	24	299	38	-	57
1962	905	60	779	-	779	86	24	207	26	-	66
1963	1089	60	956	32	924	50	26	317	14	-	74
1964	1556	80	1458	125	1334	59	27	633	17	-	18
1965	1343	110	1226	-	1226	45	24	413	17	-	8
MEXICO								EXPORTS			
1925	20694	-	20694	12317	8378	851	204	7296	27	-	-
1929	5279	3	5276	3482	1794	315	288	1097	95	-	-
1933	4701	-	4701	2595	2106	402	114	1517	74	-	-
1937	4655	-	4655	1722	2933	776	134	1938	86	-	-
1938	2676	-	2676	1058	1619	290	27	1283	20	-	-
1950	3482	-	3482	2550	932	78	192	660	2	-	-
1953	3543	-	3543	801	2742	8	5	2730	-	-	-
1955	6285	-	6285	1196	5090	8	6	5076	-	-	-
1957	3723	-	3489	668	2822	57	3	2762	-	234	-
1960	3363	-	1803	225	1578	8	-	1571	-	1560	-
1961	4994	-	3236	1392	1844	63	-	1781	-	1758	-
1962	5645	-	4103	1583	2520	5	-	2516	-	1542	-
1963	5559	-	4059	1508	2552	32	-	2520	-	1500	-
1964	5460	-	3846	1674	2172	9	-	2163	-	1614	-
1965	5589	-	3927	1560	2367	2	-	2366	-	1662	-
TRINIDAD AND TOBAGO								IMPORTS			
1925	47	44	3	-	3	-	2	-	2	-	-
1929	96	87	9	-	9	-	2	6	2	-	-
1933	146	50	96	92	5	-	-	3	2	-	-
1937	160	62	98	95	3	-	-	-	3	-	-
1938	173	53	120	117	3	-	-	-	3	-	-
1950	2480	26	2454	2450	5	-	-	-	5	-	-
1953	3584	15	3569	3515	54	45	-	5	5	-	-
1955	3789	-	3789	3783	6	-	-	-	6	-	-
1957	3944	-	3944	3924	20	-	6	-	14	-	-
1960	8621	-	8621	8600	21	-	-	11	11	-	-
1961	13134	-	13134	13124	11	-	-	-	11	-	-
1962	13497	-	13497	13449	48	8	-	30	11	-	-
1963	14625	-	14625	14592	33	21	-	-	12	-	-
1964	17801	-	17801	17708	93	81	-	-	12	-	-
1965	19623	-	19623	19623	NA	-	-	-	NA	-	-

Table VI. ENERGY IMPORTS AND EXPORTS, SELECTED YEARS, 1925-1965

(Thousand metric tons coal equivalent)

Region, country, year	Total energy	Solid fuels	Liquid fuels: Total	Crude oil	Refined petroleum products: Total	Gasoline	Kerosine	Fuel oils	Lubes and greases	Gas	Electricity
	(1)	(2)	(3)	(4)	(5)	(6)	(7)	(8)	(9)	(10)	(11)
TRINIDAD AND TOBAGO (CONTINUED)								EXPORTS			
1925	695	-	695	63	632	68	15	549	-	-	-
1929	1275	-	1275	191	1085	245	11	830	-	-	-
1933	1077	-	1077	245	833	375	17	441	-	-	-
1937	2100	-	2100	131	1970	528	24	1418	-	-	-
1938	2616	-	2616	138	2478	680	21	1778	-	-	-
1950	4302	-	4302	510	3792	555	765	2472	-	-	-
1953	5406	1	5405	495	4910	780	1350	2780	-	-	-
1955	6329	-	6329	609	5720	840	1200	3680	-	-	-
1957	7817	-	7817	732	7085	1065	1485	4535	-	-	-
1960	13985	-	13985	1047	12938	1770	1740	9428	-	-	-
1961	18371	-	18371	1205	17166	2250	2190	12726	-	-	-
1962	19776	-	19776	1451	18326	2156	2025	14145	-	-	-
1963	21854	-	21854	1578	20276	2372	1701	16203	-	-	-
1964	24480	-	24480	2252	22229	2333	2037	17781	78	-	-
1965	25728	-	25728	2339	23390	2139	2763	18473	NA	-	-
VENEZUELA								IMPORTS			
1925	36	24	12	-	12	11	2	-	-	-	-
1929	32	24	8	-	8	5	2	2	-	-	-
1933	14	11	3	-	3	2	-	2	-	-	-
1937	25	10	15	-	15	11	-	-	5	-	-
1938	39	16	23	-	23	3	6	-	14	-	-
1950	111	1	110	-	110	56	-	-	54	-	-
1953	145	1	144	-	144	84	-	-	60	-	-
1955	174	-	174	-	174	96	-	-	78	-	-
1957	134	-	134	-	134	32	-	-	102	-	-
1960	126	-	126	-	126	65	-	-	62	-	-
1961	75	10	65	-	65	27	-	-	38	-	-
1962	168	120	48	-	48	18	-	-	30	-	-
1963	142	130	12	-	12	-	-	-	12	-	-
1964	196	160	36	-	36	24	-	-	12	-	-
1965	200	185	15	-	15	6	-	-	9	-	-
VENEZUELA								EXPORTS			
1925	4023	-	4023	4023	-	-	-	-	-	-	-
1929	28892	-	28892	28830	62	27	-	35	-	-	-
1933	26333	-	26333	25077	1256	69	-	1187	-	-	-
1937	38957	-	38957	37670	1287	12	-	1275	-	-	-
1938	41249	-	41249	39917	1332	-	-	1332	-	-	-
1950	113150	2	113148	100440	12708	1770	18	10920	-	-	-
1953	130845	-	130845	108015	22830	3045	405	19230	150	-	-
1955	159518	-	159518	131550	27968	3225	900	23550	200	-	-
1957	199781	-	199781	165750	34031	3975	1425	28350	186	-	-
1960	206013	-	206013	156942	49071	3432	1500	43500	317	-	-
1961	210311	-	210311	159420	50891	3164	1740	45300	296	-	-
1962	230760	-	230760	173375	57386	3167	2610	50850	369	-	-
1963	235130	-	235130	173580	61550	3746	2175	54788	396	-	-
1964	247940	-	247940	183578	64362	2865	2790	57803	356	-	-
1965	250625	-	250625	182085	68540	4242	3345	60000	419	-	-

Table VI. ENERGY IMPORTS AND EXPORTS, SELECTED YEARS, 1925-1965

(Thousand metric tons coal equivalent)

Region, country, year	Total energy	Solid fuels	Liquid fuels: Total	Liquid fuels: Crude oil	Refined petroleum products: Total	Gasoline	Kerosine	Fuel oils	Lubes and greases	Gas	Electricity
	(1)	(2)	(3)	(4)	(5)	(6)	(7)	(8)	(9)	(10)	(11)
CARIBBEAN - OTHER								IMPORTS			
1925	5099	1274	3825	243	3582	102	65	3407	9	-	-
1929	5251	1247	4004	405	3599	354	63	3171	11	-	-
1933	3017	539	2478	92	2387	162	53	2154	18	-	-
1937	3995	690	3305	288	3017	296	69	2621	32	-	-
1938	3584	575	3009	239	2771	311	71	2367	23	-	-
1950	7249	61	7187	725	6462	1146	122	5121	74	1	-
1953	8508	88	8426	966	7460	1586	177	5610	87	-	-
1955	10685	140	10545	1032	9513	2234	401	6708	135	-	-
1957	15903	180	15723	6056	9668	2241	392	6851	129	-	-
1960	19854	60	19794	10619	9176	1905	644	6488	78	-	-
1961	22012	50	21962	10190	11772	1916	738	8969	81	-	-
1962	26177	60	26117	13719	12398	2265	806	9182	80	-	-
1963	29341	94	29247	16862	12386	1719	834	9668	87	-	-
1964	32567	119	32448	19286	13163	1436	765	10799	89	-	-
1965	33684	132	33552	21150	12402	1262	881	10086	96	-	-
CARIBBEAN - OTHER								EXPORTS			
1925	-	-	-	-	-	-	-	-	-	-	-
1929	-	-	-	-	-	-	-	-	-	-	-
1933	-	-	-	-	-	-	-	-	-	-	-
1937	-	-	-	-	-	-	-	-	-	-	-
1938	-	-	-	-	-	-	-	-	-	-	-
1950	-	-	-	-	-	-	-	188	-	-	-
1953	-	-	-	-	-	-	-	180	-	-	-
1955	434	-	434	-	434	141	36	257	-	-	-
1957	2142	-	2142	-	2142	420	53	1668	-	-	-
1960	3333	-	3333	-	3333	1278	62	1992	-	-	-
1961	3593	-	3593	-	3593	1676	98	1818	-	-	-
1962	4530	-	4530	-	4530	1875	192	2460	-	-	-
1963	6341	-	6341	-	6341	1944	162	4229	-	-	-
1964	6366	-	6366	-	6366	1860	146	4356	-	-	-
1965	6306	-	6306	-	6306	2052	221	4026	-	-	-
CUBA								IMPORTS			
1925	2554	659	1895	162	1733	33	-	1700	-	-	-
1929	2246	632	1614	305	1310	209	-	1101	-	-	-
1933	758	296	462	36	426	48	-	368	11	-	-
1937	1511	381	1130	200	930	105	-	813	12	-	-
1938	1214	342	872	132	740	113	-	617	11	-	-
1950	3749	35	3714	420	3294	555	-	2700	39	-	-
1953	4093	58	4035	750	3285	600	-	2640	45	-	-
1955	4162	130	4032	731	3302	690	5	2508	80	-	-
1957	6201	180	6021	3150	2871	570	12	2199	59	-	-
1960	6341	60	6281	4920	1361	125	99	1131	NA	-	-
1961	6560	50	6510	4470	2040	156	101	1776	NA	-	-
1962	7317	60	7257	5580	1677	342	104	1230	NA	-	-
1963	6727	94	6633	5564	1070	318	53	699	NA	-	-
1964	7276	119	7157	5204	1953	239	36	1679	NA	-	-
1965	7301	132	7169	5270	1899	221	33	1646	NA	-	-

Table VI. ENERGY IMPORTS AND EXPORTS, SELECTED YEARS, 1925-1965

(Thousand metric tons coal equivalent)

Region, country, year	Total energy	Solid fuels	Liquid fuels		Refined petroleum products					Gas	Electricity
			Total	Crude oil	Total	Gasoline	Kerosine	Fuel oils	Lubes and greases		
	(1)	(2)	(3)	(4)	(5)	(6)	(7)	(8)	(9)	(10)	(11)
CUBA (CONTINUED)								EXPORTS			
1955	NA	-	NA	-	NA	NA	NA	NA	NA	NA	NA
1957	905	-	905	-	905	5	-	900	-	-	-
1960	254	-	254	-	254	38	-	216	-	-	-
1961	-	-	-	-	-	-	-	NA	-	-	-
1962	-	-	-	-	-	-	-	NA	-	-	-
1963	6	-	6	-	6	-	-	6	-	-	-
1964	33	-	33	-	33	-	-	33	-	-	-
1965	5	-	5	-	5	-	-	5	-	-	-
PANAMA CANAL ZONE								IMPORTS			
1925	1714	331	1383	-	1383	6	3	1374	-	-	-
1929	1906	272	1634	-	1634	12	5	1617	-	-	-
1933	1326	28	1298	-	1298	12	5	1281	-	-	-
1937	1270	113	1157	-	1157	17	8	1133	-	-	-
1938	1215	45	1170	-	1170	15	6	1149	-	-	-
1950	1298	-	1298	-	1298	60	8	1230	-	-	-
1953	1403	-	1403	-	1403	150	8	1245	-	-	-
1955	1433	-	1433	-	1433	75	38	1320	-	-	-
1957	1931	-	1931	-	1931	165	41	1725	-	-	-
1960	1706	-	1706	-	1706	221	72	1395	-	-	-
1961	2115	-	2115	-	2115	267	96	1730	-	-	-
1962	2511	-	2511	-	2511	195	104	2189	-	-	-
1963	3762	-	3762	-	3762	170	59	3513	-	-	-
1964	4038	-	4038	-	4038	134	20	3861	-	-	-
1965	4379	-	4379	-	4379	131	51	4170	-	-	-
PANAMA CANAL ZONE								EXPORTS			
1950	NA	-	NA	-	NA	NA	NA	188	-	-	-
1953	NA	-	NA	-	NA	NA	NA	180	-	-	-
1955	362	-	362	-	362	117	35	210	-	-	-
1957	384	-	384	-	384	137	38	210	-	-	-
1960	381	-	381	-	381	171	57	152	-	-	-
1961	437	-	437	-	437	174	95	167	-	-	-
1962	429	-	429	-	429	161	101	165	-	-	-
1963	320	-	320	-	320	114	57	149	-	-	-
1964	240	-	240	-	240	75	15	150	-	-	-
1965	284	-	284	-	284	74	45	165	-	-	-
PUERTO RICO								IMPORTS			
1950	NA	NA	NA	NA	NA	NA	NA	NA	NA	NA	NA
1953	NA	6	NA	NA	NA	NA	NA	NA	NA	NA	NA
1955	1491	-	1491	-	1491	509	141	840	-	-	-
1957	3765	-	3765	2895	870	285	66	518	-	-	-
1960	6212	-	6212	5682	530	195	33	296	-	-	-
1961	6114	-	6114	5684	431	113	11	306	-	-	-
1962	7127	-	7127	6471	656	378	6	272	-	-	-
1963	7709	-	7709	7257	452	-	123	324	-	-	-
1964	8532	-	8532	8090	443	-	236	206	-	-	-
1965	9339	-	9339	8670	669	30	405	233	-	-	-

Table VI. ENERGY IMPORTS AND EXPORTS, SELECTED YEARS, 1925-1965

(Thousand metric tons coal equivalent)

Region, country, year	Total energy	Solid fuels	Liquid fuels: Total	Crude oil	Refined petroleum products: Total	Gasoline	Kerosine	Fuel oils	Lubes and greases	Gas	Electricity
	(1)	(2)	(3)	(4)	(5)	(6)	(7)	(8)	(9)	(10)	(11)
PUERTO RICO (CONTINUED)								EXPORTS			
1950	NA	-	NA	NA	NA	NA	NA	NA	NA	NA	NA
1953	NA	-	NA	NA	NA	NA	NA	NA	NA	NA	NA
1955	68	-	68	-	68	23	-	45	-	-	-
1957	848	-	848	-	848	278	12	557	-	-	-
1960	2691	-	2691	-	2691	1067	2	1623	-	-	-
1961	3150	-	3150	-	3150	1500	2	1649	-	-	-
1962	3114	-	3114	-	3114	1505	20	1590	-	-	-
1963	3629	-	3629	-	3629	1517	6	2106	-	-	-
1964	3758	-	3758	-	3758	1497	2	2259	-	-	-
1965	3669	-	3669	-	3669	1547	18	2100	-	-	-
LATIN AMERICA - OTHER								IMPORTS			
1925	9481	5827	3654	1382	2273	711	335	1095	132	-	-
1929	12187	6131	6056	2220	3836	1176	353	2118	189	-	-
1933	7756	4135	3621	510	3111	615	200	2208	89	-	-
1937	11575	5366	6209	2037	4172	800	236	3027	110	-	-
1938	11633	4836	6797	2177	4620	746	183	3578	114	-	-
1950	20275	2813	17462	5102	12360	3308	441	8306	306	-	-
1953	24068	2264	21804	7359	14445	4449	771	8798	428	-	-
1955	32261	2610	29651	13203	16448	2537	1416	11979	468	-	-
1957	35711	2610	33101	18959	14142	1719	1014	10905	467	-	-
1960	32161	2960	29201	16568	12633	1785	1052	9030	527	-	-
1961	29807	2400	27407	17090	10317	1671	1197	6698	422	-	-
1962	29311	1750	27561	20226	7335	983	1001	4272	626	-	-
1963	28127	2030	26097	20180	5918	1170	567	3210	525	-	-
1964	30807	2130	28677	22061	6617	788	554	4220	575	-	-
1965	33348	2140	31208	24797	6411	689	623	3993	531	-	-
LATIN AMERICA - OTHER								EXPORTS			
1925	1439	15	1424	951	473	222	39	210	2	-	-
1929	2534	21	2513	1767	746	476	36	231	3	-	-
1933	2659	122	2537	1718	819	533	47	239	2	-	-
1937	3460	55	3405	2679	726	471	138	116	2	-	-
1938	2935	58	2877	2186	692	417	158	117	-	-	-
1950	1789	140	1649	854	795	441	62	291	2	-	-
1953	1530	36	1494	947	548	221	56	269	3	-	-
1955	1798	70	1728	854	875	330	147	390	5	-	-
1957	2372	90	2282	1172	1110	279	200	629	3	-	-
1960	2386	50	2336	1587	749	128	126	482	-	-	-
1961	2928	-	2928	2259	669	32	57	564	-	-	-
1962	2970	10	2960	1512	1448	39	39	1178	2	-	-
1963	2781	10	2771	1422	1349	72	12	1167	5	-	-
1964	1858	10	1848	723	1125	32	-	998	2	-	-
1965	2146	5	2141	632	1509	-	2	1449	6	-	-
ARGENTINA								IMPORTS			
1925	4252	3179	1073	114	959	383	102	428	47	-	-
1929	5744	3176	2568	732	1836	468	90	1199	80	-	-
1933	3973	2458	1515	234	1281	65	12	1178	27	-	-
1937	5765	3164	2601	854	1748	32	-	1701	15	-	-
1938	6015	2859	3156	995	2162	3	-	2145	14	-	-

Table VI. ENERGY IMPORTS AND EXPORTS, SELECTED YEARS, 1925-1965

(Thousand metric tons coal equivalent)

Region, country, year	Total energy	Solid fuels	Liquid fuels: Total	Crude oil	Refined petroleum products: Total	Gasoline	Kerosine	Fuel oils	Lubes and greases	Gas	Electricity
	(1)	(2)	(3)	(4)	(5)	(6)	(7)	(8)	(9)	(10)	(11)
ARGENTINA (CONTINUED)								IMPORTS			
1950	9537	1467	8070	4431	3639	375	12	3186	66	-	-
1953	10379	1224	9155	5399	3756	165	14	3480	98	-	-
1955	11976	1260	10716	5571	5145	168	242	4674	59	-	-
1957	15284	1280	14004	9231	4773	189	170	4356	59	-	-
1960	9083	1460	7623	4973	2651	66	728	1712	96	-	-
1961	6351	1260	5091	2700	2391	102	794	1317	53	-	-
1962	4576	640	3936	1673	2264	77	500	1442	168	-	-
1963	3023	770	2253	1304	950	53	47	692	111	-	-
1964	4836	750	4086	2217	1869	42	24	1571	104	-	-
1965	7531	730	6801	5328	1473	96	20	879	161	-	-
ARGENTINA								EXPORTS			
1925	-	-	-	-	-	-	-	-	-	-	-
1929	14	-	14	-	14	-	-	14	-	-	-
1933	-	-	-	-	-	-	-	-	-	-	-
1937	2	-	2	-	2	-	-	2	-	-	-
1938	-	-	-	-	-	-	-	-	-	-	-
1950	-	-	-	-	-	-	-	-	-	-	-
1953	-	-	-	-	-	-	-	-	-	-	-
1955	-	-	-	-	-	-	-	-	-	-	-
1957	2	-	2	-	2	2	-	-	-	-	-
1960	3	-	3	-	3	-	-	3	-	-	-
1961	107	-	107	48	59	6	3	50	-	-	-
1962	1343	-	1343	381	962	30	38	744	-	-	-
1963	1247	-	1247	153	1094	72	12	981	-	-	-
1964	773	-	773	24	749	32	-	716	-	-	-
1965	1341	-	1341	-	1341	-	2	1338	-	-	-
BOLIVIA								IMPORTS			
1925	49	16	33	-	33	3	2	26	3	-	-
1929	79	19	60	-	60	9	3	45	3	-	-
1933	38	8	30	-	30	6	2	21	2	-	-
1937	91	31	60	-	60	11	3	42	5	-	-
1938	101	33	68	-	68	12	3	50	3	-	-
1950	109	2	107	87	20	15	-	-	5	-	-
1953	169	5	164	110	54	39	9	-	6	-	-
1955	71	-	71	12	59	36	5	12	6	-	-
1957	36	-	36	-	36	9	-	17	11	-	-
1960	59	-	59	-	59	17	-	38	5	-	-
1961	41	-	41	-	41	15	-	23	3	-	-
1962	95	-	95	63	32	17	-	11	5	-	-
1963	17	-	17	-	17	15	-	-	2	-	-
1964	21	-	21	-	21	20	-	-	2	-	-
1965	31	5	26	-	26	23	2	-	2	-	-
BOLIVIA								EXPORTS			
1950	5	-	5	5	-	-	-	-	-	-	-
1953	2	-	2	2	-	-	-	-	-	-	-
1955	119	-	119	93	26	23	2	2	-	-	-
1957	239	-	239	201	38	35	2	2	-	-	-
1960	207	-	207	200	8	6	-	2	-	-	-

Table VI. ENERGY IMPORTS AND EXPORTS, SELECTED YEARS, 1925-1965

(Thousand metric tons coal equivalent)

Region, country, year	Total energy	Solid fuels	Liquid fuels: Total	Crude oil	Refined petroleum products: Total	Gasoline	Kerosine	Fuel oils	Lubes and greases	Gas	Electricity
	(1)	(2)	(3)	(4)	(5)	(6)	(7)	(8)	(9)	(10)	(11)
BOLIVIA (CONTINUED) — EXPORTS											
1961	140	-	140	128	12	11	-	2	-	-	-
1962	99	-	99	98	2	2	-	-	-	-	-
1963	104	-	104	104	-	-	-	-	-	-	-
1964	63	-	63	54	9	-	-	-	-	-	-
1965	59	-	59	53	6	-	-	-	-	-	-
BRAZIL — IMPORTS											
1925	2740	1927	813	-	813	215	155	392	53	-	-
1929	3515	2325	1190	-	1190	441	176	506	68	-	-
1933	2473	1292	1181	-	1181	354	122	663	42	-	-
1937	3366	1708	1658	57	1601	536	171	836	59	-	-
1938	3343	1576	1767	72	1695	542	149	948	57	-	-
1950	7619	1119	6500	89	6411	2427	354	3456	174	-	-
1953	9034	746	8288	45	8243	3669	612	3717	245	-	-
1955	14193	1120	13073	5270	7803	1755	819	4884	300	-	-
1957	13884	940	12944	7269	5675	1055	588	3710	285	-	-
1960	16050	1060	14990	8526	6464	1337	147	4472	318	-	-
1961	16959	900	16059	11324	4736	1215	207	2834	276	-	-
1962	17828	920	16908	14942	1967	629	359	243	363	-	-
1963	18584	1040	17544	15563	1982	785	381	81	342	-	-
1964	18980	1155	17825	16205	1620	440	374	60	398	-	-
1965	17865	1240	16625	15371	1254	245	417	30	315	-	-
BRAZIL — EXPORTS											
1955	-	-	-	-	-	-	-	-	-	-	-
1957	215	-	215	-	215	-	-	215	-	-	-
1960	971	-	971	881	90	-	-	90	-	-	-
1961	1691	-	1691	1578	113	-	-	113	-	-	-
1962	563	-	563	447	116	-	-	116	-	-	-
1963	588	-	588	540	48	-	-	48	-	-	-
1964	183	-	183	-	183	-	-	183	-	-	-
1965	-	-	-	-	-	-	-	-	-	-	-
CHILE — IMPORTS											
1925	1641	264	1377	1268	110	62	32	NA	17	-	-
1929	1754	72	1682	1488	194	141	29	NA	24	-	-
1933	422	3	419	275	144	81	11	45	8	-	-
1937	1163	12	1151	951	200	113	14	56	18	-	-
1938	1093	7	1086	861	225	135	11	60	20	-	-
1950	1815	84	1731	-	1731	339	59	1305	29	-	-
1953	1887	201	1686	-	1686	429	111	1110	36	-	-
1955	2597	140	2457	459	1998	285	231	1431	51	-	-
1957	2630	290	2340	675	1665	122	215	1281	48	-	-
1960	2459	350	2109	770	1340	57	116	1136	32	-	-
1961	2106	160	1946	737	1209	66	125	990	29	-	-
1962	2228	120	2108	911	1197	47	53	1080	18	-	-
1963	1971	160	1811	629	1182	60	57	1065	NA	-	-
1964	2039	170	1869	662	1208	23	68	1118	NA	-	-
1965	2431	115	2316	975	1341	47	75	1215	NA	-	-

Table VI. ENERGY IMPORTS AND EXPORTS, SELECTED YEARS, 1925-1965

(Thousand metric tons coal equivalent)

Region, country, year	Total energy	Solid fuels	Liquid fuels		Refined petroleum products					Gas	Electricity
			Total	Crude oil	Total	Gasoline	Kerosine	Fuel oils	Lubes and greases		
	(1)	(2)	(3)	(4)	(5)	(6)	(7)	(8)	(9)	(10)	(11)
CHILE (CONTINUED)								EXPORTS			
1925	32	15	17	17	-	-	-	-	-	-	-
1929	23	21	2	2	-	-	-	-	-	-	-
1933	125	122	3	2	2	-	-	2	-	-	-
1937	57	55	2	2	-	-	-	-	-	-	-
1938	58	58	-	-	-	-	-	-	-	-	-
1950	166	82	84	84	-	-	-	-	-	-	-
1953	225	-	225	225	-	-	-	-	-	-	-
1955	73	70	3	-	3	-	-	-	-	-	-
1957	131	60	71	71	-	-	-	-	-	-	-
1960	44	30	14	-	14	-	-	-	-	-	-
1961	17	-	17	-	17	-	-	-	-	-	-
1962	27	-	27	-	27	-	-	-	-	-	-
1963	57	-	57	-	57	-	-	-	-	-	-
1964	75	-	75	-	75	-	-	-	-	-	-
1965	45	-	45	-	45	-	-	-	-	-	-
ECUADOR								IMPORTS			
1925	20	-	20	-	20	2	2	15	2	-	-
1929	33	-	33	-	33	3	2	27	2	-	-
1933	23	-	23	-	23	-	-	21	2	-	-
1937	3	-	3	-	3	-	-	2	2	-	-
1938	56	-	56	-	56	-	-	54	2	-	-
1950	15	-	15	-	15	12	-	-	3	-	-
1953	27	-	27	-	27	24	-	-	3	-	-
1955	140	-	140	24	116	84	-	26	6	-	-
1957	197	-	197	-	197	113	2	77	6	-	-
1960	347	-	347	321	26	15	2	2	8	-	-
1961	312	-	312	284	29	17	3	-	9	-	-
1962	314	-	314	285	29	17	3	2	8	-	-
1963	432	-	432	375	57	45	-	2	11	-	-
1964	606	-	606	563	44	15	14	-	15	-	-
1965	621	-	621	570	51	18	18	-	15	-	-
ECUADOR								EXPORTS			
1925	8	-	8	8	-	-	-	-	-	-	-
1929	236	-	236	236	-	-	-	-	-	-	-
1933	230	-	230	230	-	-	-	-	-	-	-
1937	378	-	378	378	-	-	-	-	-	-	-
1938	369	-	369	368	2	2	-	-	-	-	-
1950	204	-	204	204	-	-	-	-	-	-	-
1953	258	-	258	258	-	-	-	-	-	-	-
1955	291	-	291	291	-	-	-	-	-	-	-
1957	249	-	249	249	-	-	-	-	-	-	-
1960	-	-	-	-	-	-	-	-	-	-	-
1961	-	-	-	-	-	-	-	-	-	-	-
1962	35	-	35	35	-	-	-	-	-	-	-
1963	38	-	38	38	-	-	-	-	-	-	-
1964	105	-	105	105	-	-	-	-	-	-	-
1965	90	-	90	90	-	-	-	-	-	-	-

Table VI. ENERGY IMPORTS AND EXPORTS, SELECTED YEARS, 1925-1965

(Thousand metric tons coal equivalent)

Region, country, year	Total energy	Solid fuels	Liquid fuels: Total	Crude oil	Refined petroleum products: Total	Gasoline	Kerosine	Fuel oils	Lubes and greases	Gas	Electricity
	(1)	(2)	(3)	(4)	(5)	(6)	(7)	(8)	(9)	(10)	(11)
PARAGUAY								IMPORTS			
1925	NA	NA	NA	-	NA	NA	NA	NA	NA	-	-
1929	NA	NA	NA	-	NA	NA	NA	NA	NA	-	-
1933	9	3	6	-	6	5	2	-	-	-	-
1937	10	NA	11	-	11	8	3	-	-	-	-
1938	12	NA	12	-	12	8	3	2	-	-	-
1950	33	-	33	-	33	21	6	5	2	-	-
1953	71	-	71	-	71	33	12	23	3	-	-
1955	95	-	95	-	95	41	15	36	3	-	-
1957	102	-	102	-	102	42	15	42	3	-	-
1960	155	-	155	-	155	54	27	69	5	-	-
1961	177	-	177	-	177	56	23	96	3	-	-
1962	185	-	185	-	185	60	27	93	5	-	-
1963	201	-	201	-	201	62	29	107	5	-	-
1964	209	-	209	-	209	63	27	116	3	-	-
1965	266	-	266	-	266	63	36	162	5	-	-
PERU								IMPORTS			
1925	45	39	6	-	6	2	-	-	5	-	-
1929	47	41	6	-	6	-	-	-	6	-	-
1933	20	18	2	-	2	-	-	-	2	-	-
1937	63	15	48	39	9	5	-	-	5	-	-
1938	48	13	35	24	11	5	-	-	6	-	-
1950	58	1	57	-	57	47	-	-	11	-	-
1953	64	1	63	-	63	45	-	-	18	-	-
1955	366	-	366	-	366	80	-	266	21	-	-
1957	519	-	519	-	519	126	-	363	30	-	-
1960	871	10	861	-	861	162	-	672	27	-	-
1961	890	20	870	21	849	80	-	746	24	-	-
1962	1045	20	1025	149	876	65	-	783	29	-	-
1963	996	10	986	150	836	80	6	725	26	-	-
1964	1013	5	1008	113	896	92	-	780	24	-	-
1965	972	10	962	168	794	99	2	687	6	-	-
PERU								EXPORTS			
1925	1400	-	1400	927	473	222	39	210	2	-	-
1929	2262	-	2262	1530	732	476	36	218	3	-	-
1933	2304	-	2304	1487	818	533	47	237	2	-	-
1937	3024	-	3024	2300	725	471	138	114	2	-	-
1938	2508	-	2508	1818	690	416	158	117	-	-	-
1950	1414	58	1356	561	795	441	62	291	2	-	-
1953	1046	36	1010	462	548	221	56	269	3	-	-
1955	1316	-	1316	470	846	308	146	389	5	-	-
1957	1538	30	1508	651	857	243	198	413	3	-	-
1960	1162	20	1142	507	635	122	126	387	-	-	-
1961	965	-	965	506	459	15	54	390	-	-	-
1962	891	10	881	552	329	8	2	318	2	-	-
1963	741	10	731	588	143	-	-	138	5	-	-
1964	651	10	641	540	101	-	-	99	2	-	-
1965	611	5	606	489	117	-	-	111	6	-	-

Table VI. ENERGY IMPORTS AND EXPORTS, SELECTED YEARS, 1925-1965

(Thousand metric tons coal equivalent)

Region, country, year	Total energy	Solid fuels	Liquid fuels: Total	Crude oil	Refined petroleum products: Total	Gasoline	Kerosine	Fuel oils	Lubes and greases	Gas	Electricity
	(1)	(2)	(3)	(4)	(5)	(6)	(7)	(8)	(9)	(10)	(11)
URUGUAY — IMPORTS											
1925	686	363	323	-	323	44	39	233	8	-	-
1929	978	474	504	-	504	111	50	336	8	-	-
1933	773	344	429	-	429	101	48	273	8	-	-
1937	1024	418	606	125	482	92	39	345	6	-	-
1938	898	334	564	207	357	33	12	300	12	-	-
1950	693	129	564	495	69	47	-	8	15	-	-
1953	1972	83	1889	1806	83	11	-	56	17	-	-
1955	2246	90	2156	1868	288	45	86	141	17	-	-
1957	2443	100	2343	1784	560	15	-	524	21	-	-
1960	2449	80	2369	1979	390	12	-	350	29	-	-
1961	2289	60	2229	2025	204	48	12	128	17	-	-
1962	2398	50	2348	2205	143	8	21	93	21	-	-
1963	2291	50	2241	2160	81	6	12	42	20	-	-
1964	2447	50	2397	2303	95	26	11	38	21	-	-
1965	2674	40	2634	2385	249	27	9	195	17	-	-
URUGUAY — EXPORTS											
1960	-	-	-	-	-	-	-	-	-	-	-
1961	11	-	11	-	11	-	-	11	-	-	-
1962	14	-	14	-	14	-	-	-	-	-	-
1963	8	-	8	-	8	-	-	-	-	-	-
1964	9	-	9	-	9	-	-	-	-	-	-
1965	-	-	-	-	-	-	-	-	-	-	-
ASIA — IMPORTS											
1925	11851	6539	5312	635	4677	633	1488	2289	267	-	-
1929	18029	8394	9635	2624	7011	930	2231	3488	360	-	-
1933	18821	7986	10835	4254	6581	962	1778	3578	264	-	-
1937	28346	11327	17019	6015	11004	1889	1827	5357	413	-	-
1938	30062	11754	18308	6012	12296	1968	1980	5855	416	-	-
1950	47608	3106	44430	22787	21644	4440	2775	12476	573	72	-
1953	74156	7942	66137	34749	31388	6960	3905	19830	693	77	-
1955	91115	5880	85145	51131	34014	6662	4451	22083	816	91	-
1957	114335	9660	104585	63659	40926	6864	4791	28116	1145	91	-
1960	137492	10894	126497	85401	41096	6765	5441	27585	1289	101	-
1961	162882	13520	149261	101600	47661	5925	5952	34364	1397	101	-
1962	183804	14430	169278	122429	46850	4680	6426	33900	1661	96	-
1963	205161	13140	191949	143619	48330	4499	5652	35747	2099	72	-
1964	228443	15445	212931	164151	48780	4425	4716	37170	1917	67	-
1965	250262	18950	231312	180710	50603	4268	5033	39153	1428	-	-
ASIA — EXPORTS											
1925	15893	5505	10388	1808	8580	1784	840	5889	68	-	-
1929	21384	6289	15095	2792	12303	4175	2531	5510	89	-	-
1933	24804	5580	19224	3623	15602	4712	1730	9102	59	-	-
1937	40241	6038	34203	8684	25520	6705	3078	15585	152	-	-
1938	38824	6940	31884	7901	23984	7293	3149	13362	180	-	-
1950	153002	1681	151250	87077	64173	14010	6354	43709	101	72	-
1953	216400	3165	213158	171335	41823	10767	4475	26444	138	77	-
1955	277906	2050	275760	223941	51819	11969	6774	32939	138	96	-
1957	303493	1890	301508	241169	60339	12590	7377	40322	48	96	-

Table VI. ENERGY IMPORTS AND EXPORTS, SELECTED YEARS, 1925-1965

(Thousand metric tons coal equivalent)

Region, country, year	Total energy	Solid fuels	Liquid fuels: Total	Liquid fuels: Crude oil	Refined petroleum products: Total	Gasoline	Kerosine	Fuel oils	Lubes and greases	Gas	Electricity
	(1)	(2)	(3)	(4)	(5)	(6)	(7)	(8)	(9)	(10)	(11)
ASIA (CONTINUED)								EXPORTS			
1960	423084	1750	421233	350340	70893	13829	8639	48338	78	101	-
1961	450960	1490	449369	379580	69789	12207	8603	48893	50	101	-
1962	496867	1580	495186	414092	81095	13292	9296	58262	68	101	-
1963	541486	1350	540053	457001	83052	13497	8949	59504	653	84	-
1964	600971	1710	599195	515751	83444	13497	9470	59388	221	67	-
1965	650132	1265	648795	561414	87381	13932	10530	61503	224	72	-
MIDDLE EAST								IMPORTS			
1925	908	270	638	2	636	54	236	344	3	-	-
1929	1448	344	1104	5	1100	135	246	704	15	-	-
1933	1605	238	1367	17	1350	104	158	1071	18	-	-
1937	2381	423	1958	26	1932	212	231	1457	33	-	-
1938	2572	338	2234	24	2210	228	218	1733	32	-	-
1950	17043	162	16881	10218	6663	800	590	5184	90	-	-
1953	21835	76	21759	14354	7406	929	692	5634	152	-	-
1955	28730	60	28670	22256	6414	1008	936	4308	161	-	-
1957	28773	60	28713	20976	7737	1046	809	5684	192	-	-
1960	29902	50	29852	22586	7266	1011	777	5288	177	-	-
1961	32921	60	32861	25977	6884	954	650	5087	182	-	-
1962	37883	50	37833	33368	4466	432	354	3444	219	-	-
1963	39447	30	39417	34566	4851	474	242	3864	242	-	-
1964	39865	40	39825	34985	4841	524	218	3945	182	-	-
1965	38876	35	38841	35364	3477	621	203	2477	174	-	-
MIDDLE EAST								EXPORTS			
1925	5877	154	5723	1577	4146	471	171	3504	-	-	-
1929	8444	455	7989	2496	5493	1835	1380	2279	-	-	-
1933	11478	532	10946	2360	8586	2292	669	5625	-	-	-
1937	21935	293	21642	7676	13967	2894	896	10167	11	-	-
1938	18518	342	18176	6746	11430	3131	881	7403	17	-	-
1950	126692	-	126692	77358	49334	9899	5109	34326	-	-	-
1953	180935	8	180927	156639	24288	5492	2628	16169	-	-	-
1955	241325	-	241325	206454	34871	7242	5105	22524	-	-	-
1957	258776	-	258776	215816	42960	7667	5889	29402	-	-	-
1960	376746	30	376716	323036	53681	8679	6849	38142	-	-	-
1961	405317	-	405317	351879	53438	7679	6806	38916	-	-	-
1962	447032	-	447032	384857	62175	8928	7340	45731	-	-	-
1963	492780	10	492770	428543	64227	9096	7068	47616	-	-	-
1964	551743	20	551723	486143	65580	9497	7701	47519	-	-	-
1965	599374	10	599364	532238	67127	10299	8055	47594	-	-	-
MIDDLE EAST - OIL PRODUCING								IMPORTS			
1925	143	5	138	-	138	11	75	51	2	-	-
1929	158	8	150	-	150	23	60	60	8	-	-
1933	143	3	140	-	140	12	38	80	11	-	-
1937	193	4	189	2	188	24	47	98	20	-	-
1938	169	4	165	-	165	21	21	102	21	-	-
1950	9625	2	9623	9188	435	39	83	294	20	-	-
1953	12585	-	12585	12389	197	2	2	164	30	-	-
1955	13409	-	13409	12837	572	45	23	471	33	-	-
1957	13568	-	13568	11142	2426	92	23	2267	45	-	-

Table VI. ENERGY IMPORTS AND EXPORTS, SELECTED YEARS, 1925-1965

(Thousand metric tons coal equivalent)

Region, country, year	Total energy	Solid fuels	Liquid fuels: Total	Liquid fuels: Crude oil	Refined petroleum products: Total	Gasoline	Kerosine	Fuel oils	Lubes and greases	Gas	Electricity
	(1)	(2)	(3)	(4)	(5)	(6)	(7)	(8)	(9)	(10)	(11)
MIDDLE EAST - OIL PRODUCING (CONTINUED)								IMPORTS			
1960	12260	-	12260	12047	213	116	20	36	42	-	-
1961	13117	20	13097	12851	246	126	17	60	44	-	-
1962	14780	-	14780	14592	188	92	18	38	41	-	-
1963	13742	-	13742	13470	272	191	24	44	14	-	-
1964	11868	-	11868	11546	323	240	26	50	8	-	-
1965	10458	-	10458	10110	348	273	20	47	9	-	-
MIDDLE EAST - OIL PRODUCING								EXPORTS			
1925	5721	-	5721	1577	4145	471	170	3504	-	-	-
1929	7988	-	7988	2496	5492	1835	1379	2279	-	-	-
1933	10946	-	10946	2360	8586	2292	669	5625	-	-	-
1937	21629	-	21629	7676	13953	2894	896	10154	11	-	-
1938	18176	-	18176	6746	11430	3131	881	7403	17	-	-
1950	126692	-	126692	77358	49334	9899	5109	34326	-	-	-
1953	180915	-	180915	156639	24276	5492	2628	16157	-	-	-
1955	237336	-	237336	206454	30882	6137	4353	20393	-	-	-
1957	254568	-	254568	215816	38753	6605	5340	26807	-	-	-
1960	373367	-	373367	323036	50331	7820	6371	36135	-	-	-
1961	400445	-	400445	351879	48566	6434	6057	36044	-	-	-
1962	440829	-	440829	384857	55973	7544	6492	41768	-	-	-
1963	485192	-	485192	428543	56649	7709	6150	42354	-	-	-
1964	543585	-	543585	486143	57443	7850	6662	42074	-	-	-
1965	591365	-	591365	532238	59127	8439	7107	42405	-	-	-
BAHRAIN								IMPORTS			
1925	-	-	-	-	-	-	-	-	-	-	-
1929	-	-	-	-	-	-	-	-	-	-	-
1933	-	-	-	-	-	-	-	-	-	-	-
1937	5	-	5	-	5	2	3	-	-	-	-
1938	3	-	3	-	3	2	2	-	-	-	-
1950	9188	-	9188	9188	-	-	-	-	-	-	-
1953	12389	-	12389	12389	-	-	-	-	-	-	-
1955	12837	-	12837	12837	-	-	-	-	-	-	-
1957	11142	-	11142	11142	-	-	-	-	-	-	-
1960	12137	-	12137	12047	90	86	-	5	-	-	-
1961	12984	-	12984	12851	134	98	2	35	-	-	-
1962	14654	-	14654	14592	62	62	-	-	-	-	-
1963	13628	-	13628	13470	158	158	-	-	-	-	-
1964	11750	-	11750	11546	204	204	-	-	-	-	-
1965	10319	-	10319	10110	209	209	-	-	-	-	-
BAHRAIN								EXPORTS			
1925	-	-	-	-	-	-	-	-	-	-	-
1929	-	-	-	-	-	-	-	-	-	-	-
1933	6	-	6	6	-	-	-	-	-	-	-
1937	1442	-	1442	941	501	107	53	342	-	-	-
1938	1167	-	1167	69	1098	399	164	536	-	-	-
1950	9744	-	9744	-	9744	2628	1020	6096	-	-	-
1953	11814	-	11814	-	11814	3071	1176	7568	-	-	-
1955	12600	-	12600	420	12180	2955	1575	7650	-	-	-
1957	11417	-	11417	23	11394	1892	1403	8100	-	-	-

Table VI. ENERGY IMPORTS AND EXPORTS, SELECTED YEARS, 1925-1965

(Thousand metric tons coal equivalent)

Region, country, year	Total energy	Solid fuels	Liquid fuels: Total	Crude oil	Refined petroleum products: Total	Gasoline	Kerosine	Fuel oils	Lubes and greases	Gas	Electricity
	(1)	(2)	(3)	(4)	(5)	(6)	(7)	(8)	(9)	(10)	(11)
BAHRAIN (CONTINUED)								EXPORTS			
1960	13149	-	13149	-	13149	2541	1773	8835	-	-	-
1961	13782	-	13782	-	13782	2409	1833	9540	-	-	-
1962	15380	-	15380	-	15380	2856	1929	10595	-	-	-
1963	14688	-	14688	-	14688	2895	1698	10095	-	-	-
1964	12642	-	12642	-	12642	2993	1827	7823	-	-	-
1965	11925	-	11925	-	11925	2648	2115	7163	-	-	-
IRAN								IMPORTS			
1925	59	5	54	-	54	3	45	6	-	-	-
1929	78	1	77	-	77	21	47	5	5	-	-
1933	46	1	45	-	45	6	30	5	5	-	-
1937	79	1	78	2	77	12	30	23	12	-	-
1938	40	1	39	-	39	9	6	12	12	-	-
1950	6	-	6	-	6	-	-	-	6	-	-
1953	11	-	11	-	11	-	-	-	11	-	-
1955	8	-	8	-	8	-	-	-	8	-	-
1957	20	-	20	-	20	-	-	-	20	-	-
1960	39	-	39	-	39	-	-	-	39	-	-
1961	39	-	39	-	39	-	-	-	39	-	-
1962	38	-	38	-	38	-	-	-	38	-	-
1963	12	-	12	-	12	-	-	-	12	-	-
1964	6	-	6	-	6	-	-	-	6	-	-
1965	2	-	2	-	2	-	-	-	2	-	-
IRAN								EXPORTS			
1925	5721	-	5721	1577	4145	471	170	3504	-	-	-
1929	7988	-	7988	2496	5492	1835	1379	2279	-	-	-
1933	10938	-	10938	2354	8585	2291	669	5625	-	-	-
1937	14201	-	14201	749	13452	2787	843	9812	11	-	-
1938	10739	-	10739	407	10332	2732	717	6867	17	-	-
1950	43638	-	43638	9909	33729	6219	3480	24030	-	-	-
1953	359	-	359	63	296	221	-	75	-	-	-
1955	19665	-	19665	12495	7170	1395	1350	4425	-	-	-
1957	45630	-	45630	28800	16830	3375	2655	10800	-	-	-
1960	67418	-	67418	50138	17280	3795	3068	10418	-	-	-
1961	76470	-	76470	62325	14145	2685	2580	8880	-	-	-
1962	86213	-	86213	69038	17175	3308	3135	10733	-	-	-
1963	96270	-	96270	79403	16868	3135	2993	10740	-	-	-
1964	110475	-	110475	93878	16598	2910	3278	10410	-	-	-
1965	120735	-	120735	103935	16800	3053	3210	10538	-	-	-
IRAQ								IMPORTS			
1925	84	-	84	-	84	8	30	45	2	-	-
1929	81	7	74	-	74	2	14	56	3	-	-
1933	97	2	95	-	95	6	8	75	6	-	-
1937	110	3	107	-	107	11	14	75	8	-	-
1938	126	3	123	-	123	11	14	90	9	-	-
1950	431	2	429	-	429	39	83	294	14	-	-
1953	22	NA	23	-	23	2	2	-	20	-	-
1955	26	-	26	-	26	-	-	-	26	-	-
1957	25	-	26	-	26	-	-	-	26	NA	NA

Table VI. ENERGY IMPORTS AND EXPORTS, SELECTED YEARS, 1925-1965

(Thousand metric tons coal equivalent)

Region, country, year	Total energy	Solid fuels	Liquid fuels: Total	Liquid fuels: Crude oil	Refined petroleum products: Total	Gasoline	Kerosine	Fuel oils	Lubes and greases	Gas	Electricity
	(1)	(2)	(3)	(4)	(5)	(6)	(7)	(8)	(9)	(10)	(11)
IRAQ (CONTINUED)								IMPORTS			
1960	3	-	3	-	3	-	-	-	3	NA	NA
1961	25	20	5	-	5	-	-	-	5	-	-
1962	3	-	3	-	3	-	-	-	3	NA	NA
1963	1	-	2	-	2	-	-	-	2	NA	NA
1964	1	-	2	-	2	-	-	-	2	NA	NA
1965	7	-	8	-	8	-	-	-	8	NA	NA
IRAQ								EXPORTS			
1925	-	-	-	-	-	-	-	-	-	-	-
1929	-	-	-	-	-	-	-	-	-	-	-
1933	2	-	2	-	2	2	-	-	-	-	-
1937	5987	-	5987	5987	-	-	-	-	-	-	-
1938	6270	-	6270	6270	-	-	-	-	-	-	-
1950	9227	-	9227	9216	11	2	9	-	-	-	-
1953	41132	-	41132	41129	3	2	2	-	-	-	-
1955	48230	-	48230	48225	5	2	2	2	-	-	-
1957	30380	-	30380	30380	-	-	-	-	-	-	-
1960	67808	-	67808	67806	2	2	-	-	-	-	-
1961	69878	-	69878	69878	-	-	-	-	-	-	-
1962	70022	-	70022	70010	12	-	-	12	-	-	-
1963	81179	-	81179	81165	14	3	-	11	-	-	-
1964	88812	-	88812	88770	42	-	-	42	-	-	-
1965	92490	-	92490	92468	23	-	-	23	-	-	-
KUWAIT								IMPORTS			
1950	-	-	-	-	-	-	-	-	-	-	-
1953	164	-	164	-	164	-	-	164	-	-	-
1955	411	-	411	-	411	-	-	411	-	-	-
1957	2250	-	2250	-	2250	44	-	2207	-	-	-
1960	-	-	-	-	-	-	-	-	-	-	-
1961	-	-	-	-	-	-	-	-	-	-	-
1962	-	-	-	-	-	-	-	-	-	-	-
1963	5	-	5	-	5	-	5	-	-	-	-
1964	6	-	6	-	6	-	6	-	-	-	-
1965	-	-	-	-	-	-	-	-	-	-	-
KUWAIT								EXPORTS			
1950	24527	-	24527	24077	450	-	-	450	-	-	-
1953	62894	-	62894	62540	354	-	-	354	-	-	-
1955	79539	-	79539	79248	291	-	-	291	-	-	-
1957	83277	-	83277	83111	167	-	-	167	-	-	-
1960	115523	-	115523	108150	7373	8	-	7365	-	-	-
1961	116813	-	116813	110400	6413	-	-	6413	-	-	-
1962	130139	-	130139	122985	7154	195	-	6837	-	-	-
1963	136749	-	136749	129038	7712	108	-	7383	-	-	-
1964	152049	-	152049	142853	9197	5	-	8822	-	-	-
1965	156917	-	156917	146700	10217	39	-	9600	-	-	-

Table VI. ENERGY IMPORTS AND EXPORTS, SELECTED YEARS, 1925-1965

(Thousand metric tons coal equivalent)

Region, country, year	Total energy	Solid fuels	Liquid fuels: Total	Liquid fuels: Crude oil	Refined petroleum products: Total	Gasoline	Kerosine	Fuel oils	Lubes and greases	Gas	Electricity
	(1)	(2)	(3)	(4)	(5)	(6)	(7)	(8)	(9)	(10)	(11)
KUWAIT NEUTRAL ZONE — IMPORTS											
1955	29	-	29	-	29	6	8	15	-	-	-
1957	29	-	29	-	29	6	8	15	-	-	-
1960	14	-	14	-	14	6	8	-	-	-	-
1961	14	-	14	-	14	6	8	-	-	-	-
1962	14	-	14	-	14	6	8	-	-	-	-
1963	15	-	15	-	15	6	9	-	-	-	-
1964	15	-	15	-	15	6	9	-	-	-	-
1965	15	-	15	-	15	6	9	-	-	-	-
KUWAIT NEUTRAL ZONE — EXPORTS											
1955	1835	-	1835	1835	-	-	-	-	-	-	-
1957	4980	-	4980	4980	-	-	-	-	-	-	-
1960	9720	-	9720	8610	1110	-	-	1110	-	-	-
1961	12876	-	12876	11460	1416	-	-	1416	-	-	-
1962	17682	-	17682	13833	3849	-	-	3849	-	-	-
1963	24056	-	24056	20385	3671	-	-	3671	-	-	-
1964	28088	-	28088	23850	4238	-	-	4238	-	-	-
1965	27705	-	27705	23850	3855	-	-	3855	-	-	-
QATAR — IMPORTS											
1950	-	-	-	-	-	-	-	-	-	-	-
1953	-	-	-	-	-	-	-	-	-	-	-
1955	75	-	75	-	75	15	15	45	-	-	-
1957	75	-	75	-	75	15	15	45	-	-	-
1960	48	-	48	-	48	11	11	27	-	-	-
1961	42	-	42	-	42	17	6	20	-	-	-
1962	54	-	54	-	54	17	8	30	-	-	-
1963	54	-	54	-	54	17	8	30	-	-	-
1964	54	-	54	-	54	17	8	30	-	-	-
1965	50	-	50	-	50	17	8	26	-	-	-
QATAR — EXPORTS											
1950	2366	-	2366	2366	-	-	-	-	-	-	-
1953	5948	-	5948	5948	-	-	-	-	-	-	-
1955	8021	-	8021	8021	-	-	-	-	-	-	-
1957	9825	-	9825	9825	-	-	-	-	-	-	-
1960	12210	-	12210	12210	-	-	-	-	-	-	-
1961	12540	-	12540	12540	-	-	-	-	-	-	-
1962	13170	-	13170	13170	-	-	-	-	-	-	-
1963	13605	-	13605	13605	-	-	-	-	-	-	-
1964	15165	-	15165	15165	-	-	-	-	-	-	-
1965	16395	-	16395	16395	-	-	-	-	-	-	-
SAUDI ARABIA — IMPORTS											
1950	-	-	-	-	-	-	-	-	-	-	-
1953	-	-	-	-	-	-	-	-	-	-	-
1955	24	-	24	-	24	24	-	-	-	-	-
1957	27	-	27	-	27	27	-	-	-	-	-
1960	11	-	11	-	11	11	-	-	-	-	-

Table VI. ENERGY IMPORTS AND EXPORTS, SELECTED YEARS, 1925-1965

(Thousand metric tons coal equivalent)

Region, country, year	Total energy	Solid fuels	Liquid fuels: Total	Liquid fuels: Crude oil	Refined petroleum products: Total	Gasoline	Kerosine	Fuel oils	Lubes and greases	Gas	Electricity
	(1)	(2)	(3)	(4)	(5)	(6)	(7)	(8)	(9)	(10)	(11)
SAUDI ARABIA (CONTINUED)								IMPORTS			
1961	2	-	2	-	2	2	-	-	-	-	-
1962	2	-	2	-	2	2	-	-	-	-	-
1963	-	-	-	-	-	-	-	-	-	-	-
1964	-	-	-	-	-	-	-	-	-	-	-
1965	27	-	27	-	27	27	-	-	-	-	-
SAUDI ARABIA								EXPORTS			
1950	37191	-	37191	31791	5400	1050	600	3750	-	-	-
1953	58770	-	58770	46961	11810	2199	1451	8160	-	-	-
1955	67448	-	67448	56211	11237	1785	1427	8025	-	-	-
1957	69060	-	69060	58698	10362	1338	1283	7740	-	-	-
1960	87540	-	87540	76122	11418	1475	1530	8408	-	-	-
1961	98087	-	98087	85277	12810	1340	1644	9795	-	-	-
1962	107028	-	107028	94625	12404	1185	1428	9743	-	-	-
1963	115001	-	115001	101303	13698	1568	1460	10455	-	-	-
1964	122682	-	122682	107955	14727	1943	1557	10740	-	-	-
1965	144648	-	144648	128340	16308	2700	1782	11228	-	-	-
TRUCIAL OMAN								IMPORTS			
1960	9	-	9	-	9	3	2	5	-	-	-
1961	12	-	12	-	12	5	2	6	-	-	-
1962	17	-	17	-	17	6	3	8	-	-	-
1963	27	-	27	-	27	11	3	14	-	-	-
1964	36	-	36	-	36	14	3	20	-	-	-
1965	39	-	39	-	39	15	3	21	-	-	-
TRUCIAL OMAN								EXPORTS			
1960	-	-	-	-	-	-	-	-	-	-	-
1961	-	-	-	-	-	-	-	-	-	-	-
1962	1197	-	1197	1197	-	-	-	-	-	-	-
1963	3645	-	3645	3645	-	-	-	-	-	-	-
1964	13673	-	13673	13673	-	-	-	-	-	-	-
1965	20550	-	20550	20550	-	-	-	-	-	-	-
MIDDLE EAST - OTHER								IMPORTS			
1925	765	265	500	2	498	44	161	293	2	-	-
1929	1290	336	954	5	950	113	186	644	8	-	-
1933	1462	235	1227	17	1211	92	120	992	8	-	-
1937	2188	419	1769	24	1745	188	185	1359	14	-	-
1938	2403	334	2069	24	2045	207	197	1631	11	-	-
1950	7419	160	7259	1031	6228	761	507	4890	71	-	-
1953	9250	76	9174	1965	7209	927	690	5471	122	-	-
1955	15321	60	15261	9419	5843	963	914	3837	128	-	-
1957	15206	60	15146	9834	5312	954	786	3417	147	-	-
1960	17642	50	17592	10539	7053	896	758	5252	135	-	-
1961	19804	40	19764	13127	6638	828	633	5027	138	-	-
1962	23104	50	23054	18776	4278	341	336	3407	179	-	-
1963	25706	30	25676	21096	4580	284	218	3821	228	-	-
1964	27997	40	27957	23439	4518	284	192	3896	174	-	-

Table VI. ENERGY IMPORTS AND EXPORTS, SELECTED YEARS, 1925-1965

(Thousand metric tons coal equivalent)

Region, country, year	Total energy	Solid fuels	Liquid fuels		Refined petroleum products					Gas	Electricity
			Total	Crude oil	Total	Gasoline	Kerosine	Fuel oils	Lubes and greases		
	(1)	(2)	(3)	(4)	(5)	(6)	(7)	(8)	(9)	(10)	(11)
MIDDLE EAST - OTHER (CONTINUED)								IMPORTS			
1965	28418	35	28383	25254	3129	348	183	2430	165	-	-
MIDDLE EAST - OTHER								EXPORTS			
1925	156	154	2	-	2	-	2	-	-	-	-
1929	457	455	2	-	2	-	2	-	-	-	-
1933	532	532	-	-	-	-	-	-	-	-	-
1937	307	293	14	-	14	-	-	14	-	-	-
1938	342	342	-	-	-	-	-	-	-	-	-
1950	-	-	-	-	-	-	-	-	-	-	-
1953	20	8	12	-	12	-	-	12	-	-	-
1955	3989	-	3989	-	3989	1106	752	2132	-	-	-
1957	4208	-	4208	-	4208	1062	549	2595	-	-	-
1960	3380	30	3350	-	3350	860	479	2007	-	-	-
1961	4872	-	4872	-	4872	1245	749	2873	-	-	-
1962	6203	-	6203	-	6203	1385	848	3963	-	-	-
1963	7588	10	7578	-	7578	1388	918	5262	-	-	-
1964	8158	20	8138	-	8138	1647	1040	5445	-	-	-
1965	8010	10	8000	-	8000	1860	948	5189	-	-	-
PALESTINE								IMPORTS			
1925	64	22	42	-	42	6	29	6	2	-	-
1929	108	33	75	-	75	15	47	11	3	-	-
1933	174	58	116	-	116	30	51	32	3	-	-
1937	371	98	273	-	273	62	74	132	6	-	-
1938	292	58	234	-	234	59	72	99	5	-	-
ISRAEL								IMPORTS			
1950	1131	34	1097	294	803	189	104	497	14	-	-
1953	1705	29	1676	1148	528	39	63	416	11	-	-
1955	2414	20	2394	1557	837	23	204	600	11	-	-
1957	2298	40	2258	1523	735	38	35	645	18	-	-
1960	2861	50	2811	1988	824	27	-	780	15	-	-
1961	3213	40	3173	2183	990	38	2	930	21	-	-
1962	3751	40	3711	3083	629	15	3	585	26	-	-
1963	4130	20	4110	3525	585	8	-	551	27	-	-
1964	4652	30	4622	3975	647	15	-	603	29	-	-
1965	6326	15	6311	5835	476	15	-	435	26	-	-
ISRAEL								EXPORTS			
1960	63	-	63	-	63	-	-	63	-	-	-
1961	146	-	146	-	146	11	-	132	-	-	-
1962	297	-	297	-	297	78	5	215	-	-	-
1963	572	-	572	-	572	80	5	485	-	-	-
1964	738	-	738	-	738	117	-	618	-	-	-
1965	770	-	770	-	770	162	5	602	-	-	-

Table VI. ENERGY IMPORTS AND EXPORTS, SELECTED YEARS, 1925-1965

(Thousand metric tons coal equivalent)

Region, country, year	Total energy	Solid fuels	Liquid fuels		Refined petroleum products					Gas	Electricity
			Total	Crude oil	Total	Gasoline	Kerosine	Fuel oils	Lubes and greases		
	(1)	(2)	(3)	(4)	(5)	(6)	(7)	(8)	(9)	(10)	(11)
JORDAN								IMPORTS			
1950	86	-	86	-	86	33	36	15	2	-	-
1953	107	-	107	-	107	33	36	35	3	-	-
1955	189	-	189	20	170	45	48	72	5	-	-
1957	219	-	219	-	219	56	51	108	5	-	-
1960	332	-	332	-	332	68	84	173	8	-	-
1961	446	-	446	311	135	9	30	90	6	-	-
1962	494	-	494	378	116	3	26	78	9	-	-
1963	575	-	575	494	81	2	24	48	8	-	-
1964	581	-	581	539	42	8	17	9	9	-	-
1965	674	-	674	615	59	15	35	-	9	-	-
LEBANON-SYRIA								IMPORTS			
1925	109	52	57	-	57	18	36	3	-	-	-
1929	151	49	102	-	102	42	53	5	3	-	-
1933	178	67	111	-	111	45	47	15	5	-	-
1937	279	142	137	-	137	57	44	30	6	-	-
1938	286	145	141	-	141	63	48	26	5	-	-
LEBANON								IMPORTS			
1950	925	11	914	737	177	45	39	90	3	-	-
1953	1065	-	1065	818	248	75	56	113	5	-	-
1955	1612	10	1602	1341	261	54	38	161	8	-	-
1957	1891	10	1881	1580	302	30	39	219	9	-	-
1960	1391	-	1391	1100	291	83	38	158	11	-	-
1961	1437	-	1437	1100	338	114	60	150	6	-	-
1962	1560	10	1550	1260	290	122	38	120	2	-	-
1963	1779	10	1769	1527	242	98	18	90	14	-	-
1964	1969	10	1959	1959	NA	21	3	NA	14	-	-
1965	2233	10	2223	2223	NA	NA	NA	NA	11	-	-
LEBANON								EXPORTS			
1950	NA	-	NA	-	NA	-	-	NA	-	-	-
1953	NA	-	NA	-	NA	-	-	NA	-	-	-
1955	593	-	593	-	593	98	105	390	-	-	-
1957	651	-	651	-	651	78	123	450	-	-	-
1960	-	-	-	-	-	-	-	-	-	-	-
1961	-	-	-	-	-	-	-	-	-	-	-
1962	-	-	-	-	-	-	-	-	-	-	-
1963	2	-	2	-	2	-	-	-	-	-	-
1964	-	-	-	-	-	-	-	-	-	-	-
1965	-	-	-	-	-	-	-	-	-	-	-
SYRIA								IMPORTS			
1950	340	2	338	-	338	114	69	144	11	-	-
1953	609	3	606	-	606	129	77	390	11	-	-
1955	765	-	765	-	765	125	84	540	17	-	-
1957	909	-	909	-	909	144	107	641	17	-	-
1960	1505	-	1505	1043	462	14	24	405	18	-	-
1961	1475	-	1475	1152	323	9	9	285	20	-	-
1962	1563	-	1563	1179	384	9	9	330	33	-	-

Table VI. ENERGY IMPORTS AND EXPORTS, SELECTED YEARS, 1925-1965

(Thousand metric tons coal equivalent)

Region, country, year	Total energy	Solid fuels	Liquid fuels: Total	Liquid fuels: Crude oil	Refined petroleum products: Total	Gasoline	Kerosine	Fuel oils	Lubes and greases	Gas	Electricity
	(1)	(2)	(3)	(4)	(5)	(6)	(7)	(8)	(9)	(10)	(11)
SYRIA (CONTINUED)								IMPORTS			
1963	1706	-	1706	1322	384	12	11	335	26	-	-
1964	2061	-	2061	1523	539	12	12	498	17	-	-
1965	1784	5	1779	1526	254	15	14	198	27	-	-
SYRIA								EXPORTS			
1950	-	-	-	-	-	-	-	-	-	-	-
1953	12	-	12	-	12	-	-	12	-	-	-
1955	12	-	12	-	12	-	-	12	-	-	-
1957	-	-	-	-	-	-	-	-	-	-	-
1960	-	-	-	-	-	-	-	-	-	-	-
1961	44	-	44	-	44	44	-	-	-	-	-
1962	77	-	77	-	77	77	-	-	-	-	-
1963	39	-	39	-	39	39	-	-	-	-	-
1964	20	-	20	-	20	20	-	-	-	-	-
1965	75	-	75	-	75	75	-	-	-	-	-
TURKEY								IMPORTS			
1925	195	75	120	-	120	17	87	17	-	-	-
1929	269	108	161	-	161	48	80	33	-	-	-
1933	191	59	132	12	120	11	18	92	-	-	-
1937	241	40	201	-	201	57	60	84	-	-	-
1938	335	87	248	-	248	75	71	102	-	-	-
1950	908	-	908	-	908	345	225	300	38	-	-
1953	1737	-	1737	-	1737	570	420	660	87	-	-
1955	1700	-	1700	-	1700	563	474	585	78	-	-
1957	1701	-	1701	-	1701	465	444	705	87	-	-
1960	1872	-	1872	-	1872	537	455	804	72	-	-
1961	2229	-	2229	329	1901	515	443	869	74	-	-
1962	3993	-	3993	3404	590	35	191	270	95	-	-
1963	4824	-	4824	4620	204	8	59	-	138	-	-
1964	5282	-	5282	5145	137	5	41	-	92	-	-
1965	4718	5	4713	4577	137	8	51	-	78	-	-
TURKEY								EXPORTS			
1925	154	154	-	-	-	-	-	-	-	-	-
1929	455	455	-	-	-	-	-	-	-	-	-
1933	532	532	-	-	-	-	-	-	-	-	-
1937	293	293	-	-	-	-	-	-	-	-	-
1938	342	342	-	-	-	-	-	-	-	-	-
1950	-	-	-	-	-	-	-	-	-	-	-
1953	7	7	-	-	-	-	-	-	-	-	-
1955	-	-	-	-	-	-	-	-	-	-	-
1957	-	-	-	-	-	-	-	-	-	-	-
1960	30	30	-	-	-	-	-	-	-	-	-
1961	36	-	36	-	36	-	-	36	-	-	-
1962	816	-	816	-	816	-	-	810	-	-	-
1963	1120	10	1110	-	1110	63	-	1043	-	-	-
1964	1151	20	1131	-	1131	71	-	1058	-	-	-
1965	786	10	776	-	776	27	-	747	-	-	-

Table VI. ENERGY IMPORTS AND EXPORTS, SELECTED YEARS, 1925-1965

(Thousand metric tons coal equivalent)

Region, country, year	Total energy	Solid fuels	Liquid fuels: Total	Liquid fuels: Crude oil	Refined petroleum products: Total	Gasoline	Kerosine	Fuel oils	Lubes and greases	Gas	Electricity
	(1)	(2)	(3)	(4)	(5)	(6)	(7)	(8)	(9)	(10)	(11)
FAR EAST AND OTHER ASIA								IMPORTS			
1925	10943	6269	4674	633	4041	579	1253	1946	264	-	-
1929	16581	8050	8531	2619	5912	795	1985	2784	345	-	-
1933	17216	7748	9468	4238	5231	858	1620	2507	246	-	-
1937	25966	10904	15062	5990	9072	1677	1596	3900	380	-	-
1938	27490	11416	16074	5988	10086	1740	1763	4122	384	-	-
1950	30565	2944	27549	12569	14981	3641	2186	7292	483	72	-
1953	52321	7866	44378	20396	23982	6032	3213	14196	542	77	-
1955	62386	5820	56475	28875	27600	5654	3515	17775	656	91	-
1957	85562	9600	75872	42683	33189	5819	3983	22433	953	91	-
1960	107590	10844	96645	62816	33830	5754	4664	22298	1112	101	-
1961	129961	13460	116400	75623	40778	4971	5303	29277	1215	101	-
1962	145921	14380	131445	89061	42384	4248	6072	30456	1442	96	-
1963	165714	13110	152532	109053	43479	4025	5411	31883	1857	72	-
1964	188578	15405	173106	129167	43940	3902	4499	33225	1736	67	-
1965	211386	18915	192471	145346	47126	3647	4830	36677	1254	-	-
FAR EAST AND OTHER ASIA								EXPORTS			
1925	10016	5351	4665	231	4434	1313	669	2385	68	-	-
1929	12940	5834	7106	296	6810	2340	1151	3231	89	-	-
1933	13327	5048	8279	1263	7016	2420	1061	3477	59	-	-
1937	18306	5745	12561	1008	11553	3812	2183	5418	141	-	-
1938	20307	6598	13709	1155	12554	4163	2268	5960	164	-	-
1950	26311	1681	24558	9719	14840	4112	1245	9383	101	72	-
1953	35465	3157	32231	14696	17535	5276	1847	10275	138	77	-
1955	36581	2050	34436	17487	16949	4727	1670	10415	138	96	-
1957	44718	1890	42732	25353	17379	4923	1488	10920	48	96	-
1960	46338	1720	44517	27305	17213	5150	1790	10196	78	101	-
1961	45643	1490	44052	27701	16352	4529	1797	9977	50	101	-
1962	49836	1580	48155	29235	18920	4364	1956	12531	68	101	-
1963	48707	1340	47283	28458	18825	4401	1881	11888	653	84	-
1964	49229	1690	47472	29609	17864	4001	1769	11870	221	67	-
1965	50758	1255	49431	29177	20255	3633	2475	13910	224	72	-
BORNEO (FORMER BRITISH)								IMPORTS			
1925	6	1	5	-	5	-	5	-	-	-	-
1929	17	-	17	-	17	3	9	-	2	-	-
1933	427	1	426	422	5	-	5	-	-	-	-
1937	945	-	945	861	84	3	8	72	2	-	-
1938	1110	1	1109	1055	54	3	8	42	2	-	-
1950	6315	-	6243	6185	59	14	14	26	6	72	-
1953	7480	-	7403	7314	89	29	15	39	6	77	-
1955	8068	-	7977	7887	90	23	18	41	9	91	-
1957	8506	-	8415	8294	122	42	20	51	9	91	-
1960	7136	-	7035	6866	170	42	32	86	11	101	-
1961	5935	-	5834	5652	182	47	29	98	9	101	-
1962	6165	-	6069	5853	216	57	35	111	14	96	-
1963	5473	-	5402	5156	246	60	44	132	11	72	-
1964	5683	-	5616	5325	291	71	66	146	9	67	-
1965	6192	-	6192	5832	360	86	89	171	15	-	-

Table VI. ENERGY IMPORTS AND EXPORTS, SELECTED YEARS, 1925-1965

(Thousand metric tons coal equivalent)

Region, country, year	Total energy	Solid fuels	Liquid fuels: Total	Liquid fuels: Crude oil	Refined petroleum products: Total	Gasoline	Kerosine	Fuel oils	Lubes and greases	Gas	Electricity
	(1)	(2)	(3)	(4)	(5)	(6)	(7)	(8)	(9)	(10)	(11)
BORNEO (FORMER BRITISH) (CONTINUED)								EXPORTS			
1925	887	50	837	231	606	140	156	311	-	-	-
1929	1166	47	1119	233	887	351	98	438	-	-	-
1933	1300	5	1295	624	671	120	53	498	-	-	-
1937	2034	-	2034	839	1196	98	68	1031	-	-	-
1938	2411	-	2411	1044	1367	144	96	1127	-	-	-
1950	12285	-	12213	9707	2507	348	-	2159	-	72	-
1953	14525	-	14448	11567	2882	470	-	2412	-	77	-
1955	15585	-	15489	12722	2768	206	-	2562	-	96	-
1957	16524	-	16428	13697	2732	315	-	2417	-	96	-
1960	13724	-	13623	10638	2985	521	6	2459	-	101	-
1961	11714	-	11613	9038	2576	368	3	2205	-	101	-
1962	11681	-	11580	8579	3002	446	3	2553	-	101	-
1963	10389	-	10305	7529	2777	401	24	2352	-	84	-
1964	10618	-	10551	6957	3594	582	233	2780	-	67	-
1965	11551	-	11480	7803	3677	410	245	3023	-	72	-
BRUNEI								IMPORTS			
1925	1	1	-	-	-	-	-	-	-	-	-
1929	-	-	-	-	-	-	-	-	-	-	-
1933	-	-	-	-	-	-	-	-	-	-	-
1937	2	-	2	-	2	-	2	-	-	-	-
1938	2	-	2	-	2	-	2	-	-	-	-
1950	18	-	18	-	18	5	2	9	3	-	-
1953	32	-	32	-	32	11	2	17	3	-	-
1955	14	-	14	-	14	3	2	5	5	-	-
1957	18	-	18	-	18	8	2	5	5	-	-
1960	9	-	9	-	9	2	3	3	2	-	-
1961	8	-	8	-	8	2	2	3	2	-	-
1962	12	-	12	-	12	2	3	5	3	-	-
1963	12	-	12	-	12	2	3	6	2	-	-
1964	8	-	8	-	8	2	3	2	2	-	-
1965	8	-	8	-	8	2	2	3	2	-	-
BRUNEI								EXPORTS			
1925	-	-	-	-	-	-	-	-	-	-	-
1929	-	-	-	-	-	-	-	-	-	-	-
1933	428	-	428	428	-	-	-	-	-	-	-
1937	839	-	839	839	-	-	-	-	-	-	-
1938	1044	-	1044	1044	-	-	-	-	-	-	-
1950	6186	-	6114	6114	-	-	-	-	-	72	-
1953	7393	-	7316	7316	-	-	-	-	-	77	-
1955	7966	-	7871	7871	-	-	-	-	-	96	-
1957	8388	-	8292	8292	-	-	-	-	-	96	-
1960	6967	-	6866	6866	-	-	-	-	-	101	-
1961	6274	-	6173	6173	-	-	-	-	-	101	-
1962	5827	-	5726	5726	-	-	-	-	-	101	-
1963	5302	-	5219	5219	-	-	-	-	-	84	-
1964	5344	-	5277	5277	-	-	-	-	-	67	-
1965	5968	-	5897	5897	-	-	-	-	-	72	-

Table VI. ENERGY IMPORTS AND EXPORTS, SELECTED YEARS, 1925-1965

(Thousand metric tons coal equivalent)

Region, country, year	Total energy	Solid fuels	Liquid fuels		Refined petroleum products					Gas	Electricity
			Total	Crude oil	Total	Gasoline	Kerosine	Fuel oils	Lubes and greases		
	(1)	(2)	(3)	(4)	(5)	(6)	(7)	(8)	(9)	(10)	(11)
SABAH								IMPORTS			
1925	-	-	-	-	-	-	-	-	-	-	-
1929	3	-	3	-	3	2	3	-	-	-	-
1933	3	1	2	-	2	-	2	-	-	-	-
1937	3	-	3	-	3	2	2	-	-	-	-
1938	4	1	3	-	3	2	2	-	-	-	-
1950	21	-	21	-	21	6	5	9	2	-	-
1953	29	-	29	-	29	11	5	12	2	-	-
1955	36	-	36	-	36	9	6	20	2	-	-
1957	53	-	53	-	53	18	6	27	2	-	-
1960	93	-	93	-	93	21	14	53	6	-	-
1961	96	-	96	-	96	26	11	56	5	-	-
1962	122	-	122	-	122	35	15	66	6	-	-
1963	141	-	141	-	141	36	20	81	5	-	-
1964	170	-	170	-	170	42	35	89	5	-	-
1965	186	-	186	-	186	42	38	99	8	-	-
SABAH								EXPORTS			
1925	50	50	-	-	-	-	-	-	-	-	-
1929	47	47	-	-	-	-	-	-	-	-	-
1933	5	5	-	-	-	-	-	-	-	-	-
1937	-	-	-	-	-	-	-	-	-	-	-
1938	-	-	-	-	-	-	-	-	-	-	-
1950	-	-	-	-	-	-	-	-	-	-	-
1953	-	-	-	-	-	-	-	-	-	-	-
1955	-	-	-	-	-	-	-	-	-	-	-
1957	5	-	5	-	5	3	-	2	-	-	-
1960	12	-	12	-	12	2	6	5	-	-	-
1961	9	-	9	-	9	3	3	3	-	-	-
1962	9	-	9	-	9	3	3	3	-	-	-
1963	9	-	9	-	9	3	3	3	-	-	-
1964	9	-	9	-	9	3	5	2	-	-	-
1965	6	-	6	-	6	2	2	3	-	-	-
SARAWAK								IMPORTS			
1925	5	-	5	-	5	-	5	-	-	-	-
1929	9	-	9	-	9	2	6	-	2	-	-
1933	425	-	425	422	3	-	3	-	-	-	-
1937	941	-	941	861	80	2	5	72	2	-	-
1938	1104	-	1104	1055	50	2	5	42	2	-	-
1950	6276	-	6204	6185	20	3	8	8	2	72	-
1953	7420	-	7343	7314	29	8	9	11	2	77	-
1955	8018	-	7928	7887	41	11	11	17	3	91	-
1957	8435	-	8345	8294	51	17	12	20	3	91	-
1960	7034	-	6933	6866	68	20	15	30	3	101	-
1961	5831	-	5730	5652	78	20	17	39	3	101	-
1962	6031	-	5936	5853	83	21	17	41	5	96	-
1963	5320	-	5249	5156	93	23	21	45	5	72	-
1964	5506	-	5439	5325	114	27	29	56	3	67	-
1965	6001	-	6002	5832	170	44	51	69	6	NA	-

Table VI. ENERGY IMPORTS AND EXPORTS, SELECTED YEARS, 1925-1965

(Thousand metric tons coal equivalent)

Region, country, year	Total energy	Solid fuels	Liquid fuels: Total	Liquid fuels: Crude oil	Refined petroleum products: Total	Gasoline	Kerosine	Fuel oils	Lubes and greases	Gas	Electricity
	(1)	(2)	(3)	(4)	(5)	(6)	(7)	(8)	(9)	(10)	(11)
SARAWAK (CONTINUED)								EXPORTS			
1925	837	-	837	231	606	140	156	311	-	-	-
1929	1119	-	1119	233	887	351	98	438	-	-	-
1933	867	-	867	197	671	120	53	498	-	-	-
1937	1196	-	1196	-	1196	98	68	1031	-	-	-
1938	1367	-	1367	-	1367	144	96	1127	-	-	-
1950	6099	-	6099	3593	2507	348	-	2159	-	-	-
1953	7133	-	7133	4251	2882	470	-	2412	-	-	-
1955	7619	-	7619	4851	2768	206	-	2562	-	-	-
1957	8132	-	8132	5405	2727	312	-	2415	-	-	-
1960	6746	-	6746	3773	2973	519	-	2454	-	-	-
1961	5432	-	5432	2865	2567	365	-	2202	-	-	-
1962	5846	-	5846	2853	2993	443	-	2550	-	-	-
1963	5078	-	5078	2310	2768	398	21	2349	-	-	-
1964	5265	-	5265	1680	3585	579	228	2778	-	-	-
1965	5577	-	5577	1907	3671	408	243	3020	-	-	-
BURMA								IMPORTS			
1950	165	NA	165	-	165	90	30	45	NA	-	-
1953	416	251	165	-	165	96	32	24	14	-	-
1955	428	200	228	-	228	116	27	71	15	-	-
1957	406	280	126	-	126	41	5	71	11	-	-
1960	451	350	101	-	101	21	6	50	24	-	-
1961	395	260	135	18	117	17	12	57	32	-	-
1962	478	340	138	-	138	23	24	69	23	-	-
1963	288	210	78	-	78	15	20	33	11	-	-
1964	452	215	237	180	57	-	-	33	24	-	-
1965	403	140	263	240	23	-	-	-	23	-	-
CEYLON								IMPORTS			
1925	1136	827	309	-	309	21	39	246	3	-	-
1929	1264	827	437	-	437	53	47	332	6	-	-
1933	925	412	513	-	513	38	41	431	5	-	-
1937	1203	582	621	-	621	71	47	498	6	-	-
1938	1129	391	738	-	738	62	45	627	5	-	-
1950	1544	374	1170	-	1170	137	66	959	9	-	-
1953	1649	390	1259	-	1259	198	108	945	8	-	-
1955	1629	190	1439	-	1439	204	141	1080	14	-	-
1957	2368	280	2088	-	2088	287	168	1619	15	-	-
1960	1597	260	1337	-	1337	243	221	860	14	-	-
1961	1730	140	1590	-	1590	258	236	1082	15	-	-
1962	1696	140	1556	-	1556	210	269	1058	20	-	-
1963	1514	150	1364	-	1364	213	209	917	26	-	-
1964	1439	180	1259	-	1259	159	231	854	15	-	-
1965	1664	140	1524	-	1524	264	276	962	23	-	-
CEYLON								EXPORTS			
1953	-	-	-	-	-	-	-	-	-	-	-
1955	20	-	20	-	20	-	-	20	-	-	-
1957	-	-	-	-	-	-	-	-	-	-	-
1960	-	-	-	-	-	-	-	-	-	-	-
1961	9	-	9	-	9	-	-	9	-	-	-

Table VI. ENERGY IMPORTS AND EXPORTS, SELECTED YEARS, 1925-1965

(Thousand metric tons coal equivalent)

Region, country, year	Total energy	Solid fuels	Liquid fuels: Total	Liquid fuels: Crude oil	Refined petroleum products: Total	Gasoline	Kerosine	Fuel oils	Lubes and greases	Gas	Electricity
	(1)	(2)	(3)	(4)	(5)	(6)	(7)	(8)	(9)	(10)	(11)
CEYLON (CONTINUED)								EXPORTS			
1962	-	-	-	-	-	-	-	-	-	-	-
1963	-	-	-	-	-	-	-	-	-	-	-
1964	-	-	-	-	-	-	-	-	-	-	-
1965	2	-	2	-	2	-	2	-	-	-	-
HONG KONG								IMPORTS			
1925	1612	1094	518	-	518	15	197	296	11	-	-
1929	1174	740	434	-	434	30	137	260	8	-	-
1933	1378	916	462	-	462	60	84	306	12	-	-
1937	1447	914	533	-	533	105	125	263	41	-	-
1938	1305	753	552	-	552	72	87	375	18	-	-
1950	1263	325	938	-	938	119	57	755	8	-	-
1953	1200	213	987	-	987	81	65	837	5	-	-
1955	1503	250	1253	-	1253	90	102	1050	11	-	-
1957	1882	260	1622	-	1622	98	129	1380	15	-	-
1960	2100	240	1860	-	1860	119	207	1518	17	-	-
1961	2298	250	2048	-	2048	122	249	1661	17	-	-
1962	2547	220	2327	-	2327	99	329	1875	24	-	-
1963	2876	200	2676	-	2676	113	384	2159	21	-	-
1964	2981	180	2801	-	2801	107	354	2309	32	-	-
1965	3330	180	3150	-	3150	114	447	2567	23	-	-
HONG KONG								EXPORTS			
1925	266	134	132	-	132	5	59	62	8	-	-
1929	260	98	162	-	162	17	77	59	11	-	-
1933	449	149	300	-	300	42	83	167	9	-	-
1937	355	35	320	-	320	66	116	117	21	-	-
1938	327	57	270	-	270	54	80	116	21	-	-
1950	258	54	204	-	204	80	41	84	-	-	-
1953	23	9	14	-	14	3	3	6	2	-	-
1955	15	-	15	-	15	2	5	9	-	-	-
1957	25	10	15	-	15	2	3	9	2	-	-
1960	30	10	20	-	20	2	3	14	2	-	-
1961	42	10	32	-	32	9	5	17	2	-	-
1962	38	-	38	-	38	3	6	26	3	-	-
1963	45	-	45	-	45	3	6	30	6	-	-
1964	60	-	60	-	60	3	6	38	14	-	-
1965	76	10	66	-	66	5	8	39	15	-	-
INDIA								IMPORTS			
1925	1578	496	1082	-	1082	-	392	551	140	-	-
1929	1713	222	1491	-	1491	2	573	747	170	-	-
1933	1208	69	1139	-	1139	12	320	683	125	-	-
1937	2807	326	2481	-	2481	438	906	924	213	-	-
1938	3241	506	2735	-	2735	437	1047	1022	230	-	-
1950	4455	1	4454	1977	2477	980	1233	NA	264	-	-
1953	5035	1	5034	2051	2984	1308	1422	NA	254	-	-
1955	6851	-	6851	4133	2718	564	1469	438	248	-	-
1957	9437	-	9437	6450	2987	267	1799	473	449	-	-
1960	11253	10	11243	8528	2715	167	1484	593	473	-	-
1961	11796	10	11786	8865	2921	173	1640	753	356	-	-

Table VI. ENERGY IMPORTS AND EXPORTS, SELECTED YEARS, 1925-1965

(Thousand metric tons coal equivalent)

Region, country, year	Total energy	Solid fuels	Liquid fuels: Total	Crude oil	Refined petroleum products: Total	Gasoline	Kerosine	Fuel oils	Lubes and greases	Gas	Electricity
	(1)	(2)	(3)	(4)	(5)	(6)	(7)	(8)	(9)	(10)	(11)
INDIA (CONTINUED)								IMPORTS			
1962	12676	10	12666	9032	3635	126	2184	909	416	-	-
1963	13242	-	13242	9471	3771	120	1982	1089	581	-	-
1964	13184	-	13184	9750	3434	120	1515	1370	429	-	-
1965	13443	-	13443	10200	3243	96	1257	1440	450	-	-
INDIA								EXPORTS			
1925	289	220	69	-	69	65	5	-	-	-	-
1929	767	738	29	24	5	-	5	-	-	-	-
1933	459	433	26	20	6	3	3	-	-	-	-
1937	1735	887	848	27	821	195	525	69	32	-	-
1938	2543	1365	1178	33	1145	284	753	74	35	-	-
1950	933	933	-	-	-	-	-	-	-	-	-
1953	1976	1976	-	-	-	-	-	-	-	-	-
1955	1696	1540	156	-	156	90	-	66	-	-	-
1957	2253	1690	563	-	563	276	-	287	-	-	-
1960	1719	1360	359	-	359	359	-	-	-	-	-
1961	1188	940	248	-	248	248	-	-	-	-	-
1962	1166	1070	96	-	96	96	-	-	-	-	-
1963	1461	870	591	-	591	591	-	-	-	-	-
1964	1835	1250	585	-	585	543	17	26	-	-	-
1965	1374	930	444	-	444	390	18	36	-	-	-
INDO-CHINA								IMPORTS			
1925	136	37	99	-	99	17	71	-	12	-	-
1929	218	42	176	-	176	47	93	6	30	-	-
1933	147	16	131	-	131	44	63	15	9	-	-
1937	155	14	141	-	141	48	59	27	8	-	-
1938	170	14	156	-	156	57	56	36	8	-	-
1950	201	12	189	-	189	105	36	41	8	-	-
1953	531	6	525	-	525	233	63	215	15	-	-
1955	573	30	543	-	543	228	77	227	12	-	-
1957	785	50	735	-	735	312	105	302	17	-	-
1960	970	10	960	-	960	332	138	465	24	-	-
1961	1108	10	1098	-	1098	329	131	615	23	-	-
1962	1124	20	1104	-	1104	332	135	609	27	-	-
1963	1291	10	1281	-	1281	366	167	713	33	-	-
1964	1252	20	1232	-	1232	309	165	752	5	-	-
1965	1505	45	1460	-	1460	347	192	918	-	-	-
INDO-CHINA								EXPORTS			
1925	702	702	-	-	-	-	-	-	-	-	-
1929	1351	1351	-	-	-	-	-	-	-	-	-
1933	1263	1263	-	-	-	-	-	-	-	-	-
1937	1525	1525	-	-	-	-	-	-	-	-	-
1938	1532	1532	-	-	-	-	-	-	-	-	-
1950	59	59	-	-	-	-	-	-	-	-	-
1953	306	306	-	-	-	-	-	-	-	-	-
1955	-	-	-	-	-	-	-	-	-	-	-
1957	-	-	-	-	-	-	-	-	-	-	-
1960	-	-	-	-	-	-	-	-	-	-	-
1961	2	-	2	-	2	-	-	2	-	-	-

Table VI. ENERGY IMPORTS AND EXPORTS, SELECTED YEARS, 1925-1965

(Thousand metric tons coal equivalent)

Region, country, year	Total energy	Solid fuels	Liquid fuels: Total	Liquid fuels: Crude oil	Refined petroleum products: Total	Gasoline	Kerosine	Fuel oils	Lubes and greases	Gas	Electricity
	(1)	(2)	(3)	(4)	(5)	(6)	(7)	(8)	(9)	(10)	(11)
INDO-CHINA (CONTINUED)								EXPORTS			
1962	2	-	2	-	2	-	-	2	-	-	-
1963	3	-	3	-	3	-	-	3	-	-	-
1964	-	-	-	-	-	-	-	-	-	-	-
1965	-	-	-	-	-	-	-	-	-	-	-
CAMBODIA								IMPORTS			
1955	84	-	84	-	84	39	15	30	-	-	-
1957	128	-	128	-	128	59	20	50	-	-	-
1960	168	-	168	-	168	81	23	65	-	-	-
1961	216	-	216	-	216	90	30	96	-	-	-
1962	231	-	231	-	231	87	33	111	-	-	-
1963	300	-	300	-	300	105	39	156	-	-	-
1964	263	-	263	-	263	65	38	161	-	-	-
1965	297	30	267	-	267	54	42	171	-	-	-
CAMBODIA								EXPORTS			
1955	-	-	-	-	-	-	-	-	-	-	-
1957	-	-	-	-	-	-	-	-	-	-	-
1960	-	-	-	-	-	-	-	-	-	-	-
1961	2	-	2	-	2	-	-	2	-	-	-
1962	2	-	2	-	2	-	-	2	-	-	-
1963	3	-	3	-	3	-	-	3	-	-	-
1964	-	-	-	-	-	-	-	-	-	-	-
1965	-	-	-	-	-	-	-	-	-	-	-
LAOS								IMPORTS			
1955	14	-	14	-	14	9	2	2	2	-	-
1957	29	-	29	-	29	21	3	5	NA	-	-
1960	42	-	42	-	42	26	3	11	3	-	-
1961	57	-	57	-	57	36	3	17	2	-	-
1962	66	-	66	-	66	50	5	11	2	-	-
1963	77	-	77	-	77	51	8	17	2	-	-
1964	90	-	90	-	90	57	8	21	5	-	-
1965	87	-	87	-	87	53	8	27	NA	-	-
VIETNAM, SOUTH								IMPORTS			
1955	476	30	446	-	446	180	60	195	11	-	-
1957	629	50	579	-	579	233	83	248	17	-	-
1960	760	10	750	-	750	225	113	390	21	-	-
1961	835	10	825	-	825	203	98	503	21	-	-
1962	827	20	807	-	807	195	98	488	26	-	-
1963	915	10	905	-	905	210	120	540	32	-	-
1964	899	20	879	-	879	188	120	570	NA	-	-
1965	1121	15	1106	-	1106	240	143	720	NA	-	-
INDONESIA								IMPORTS			
1925	237	171	66	2	65	2	47	6	11	-	-

Table VI. ENERGY IMPORTS AND EXPORTS, SELECTED YEARS, 1925-1965

(Thousand metric tons coal equivalent)

Region, country, year	Total energy	Solid fuels	Liquid fuels: Total	Liquid fuels: Crude oil	Refined petroleum products: Total	Gasoline	Kerosine	Fuel oils	Lubes and greases	Gas	Electricity
	(1)	(2)	(3)	(4)	(5)	(6)	(7)	(8)	(9)	(10)	(11)
INDONESIA (CONTINUED)								IMPORTS			
1929	491	168	323	-	323	18	129	150	26	-	-
1933	236	56	180	-	180	65	23	80	14	-	-
1937	275	60	215	-	215	72	17	107	20	-	-
1938	306	84	222	-	222	140	41	24	18	-	-
1950	2454	27	2427	2363	65	5	6	6	48	-	-
1953	3580	56	3524	3419	105	18	12	20	56	-	-
1955	4331	30	4301	4017	284	173	3	33	75	-	-
1957	5823	40	5783	5124	659	540	6	39	74	-	-
1960	3617	30	3587	2700	887	728	50	39	71	-	-
1961	4236	30	4206	3213	993	587	282	26	99	-	-
1962	2654	20	2634	2090	545	342	54	24	125	-	-
1963	2343	10	2333	1871	462	326	6	30	101	-	-
1964	364	10	354	-	354	218	6	23	108	-	-
1965	5	5	NA	NA	NA	24	6	23	NA	-	-
INDONESIA								EXPORTS			
1925	3520	373	3147	-	3147	815	342	1953	38	-	-
1929	5672	497	5175	35	5141	1677	806	2600	59	-	-
1933	6232	265	5967	620	5348	1863	797	2657	32	-	-
1937	8477	296	8181	143	8039	2940	1272	3791	36	-	-
1938	8730	328	8402	78	8324	3104	1068	4127	26	-	-
1950	9094	62	9032	12	9020	2724	860	5342	95	-	-
1953	13591	133	13458	3129	10329	3101	1034	6066	129	-	-
1955	13601	50	13551	4764	8787	2597	900	5162	129	-	-
1957	19968	40	19928	10479	9449	2460	773	6180	36	-	-
1960	25347	10	25337	16320	9017	2252	738	5964	63	-	-
1961	25010	-	25010	17490	7520	1752	653	5085	30	-	-
1962	27765	-	27765	18683	9083	1749	738	6555	41	-	-
1963	26849	-	26849	19035	7814	1431	591	5792	NA	-	-
1964	26948	-	26948	22268	4680	825	405	3450	NA	-	-
1965	26250	-	26250	21000	5250	600	600	4050	NA	-	-
JAPAN								IMPORTS			
1925	2750	1775	975	632	344	114	150	38	42	-	-
1929	6805	3604	3201	2577	624	50	503	41	32	-	-
1933	8844	4285	4559	3756	803	3	761	26	14	-	-
1937	12797	6197	6600	5081	1520	-	NA	NA	NA	-	-
1938	13813	6850	6963	4886	2078	-	NA	NA	NA	-	-
1950	3594	832	2762	1850	912	47	6	807	53	-	-
1953	17005	4921	12084	7613	4472	413	5	4005	50	-	-
1955	18859	2860	15999	10919	5081	375	48	4614	42	-	-
1957	33323	6500	26823	19113	7710	180	26	7377	128	-	-
1960	56910	8290	48620	40584	8036	168	74	7565	230	-	-
1961	75375	11320	64055	50819	13236	141	126	12620	341	-	-
1962	86677	12040	74637	60126	14511	150	119	13644	435	-	-
1963	105288	11140	94148	77841	16307	128	164	15108	611	-	-
1964	125690	13230	112460	93480	18980	626	42	17073	668	-	-
1965	143908	17125	126783	104537	22247	726	39	20292	435	-	-
JAPAN								EXPORTS			
1925	2761	2738	23	-	23	-	12	6	5	-	-

Table VI. ENERGY IMPORTS AND EXPORTS, SELECTED YEARS, 1925-1965

(Thousand metric tons coal equivalent)

Region, country, year	Total energy	Solid fuels	Liquid fuels: Total	Liquid fuels: Crude oil	Refined petroleum products: Total	Gasoline	Kerosine	Fuel oils	Lubes and greases	Gas	Electricity
	(1)	(2)	(3)	(4)	(5)	(6)	(7)	(8)	(9)	(10)	(11)
JAPAN (CONTINUED)								EXPORTS			
1929	2439	2412	27	-	27	-	11	6	11	-	-
1933	2178	2115	63	-	63	-	23	30	11	-	-
1937	2089	1928	161	-	161	-	60	60	41	-	-
1938	2041	1831	210	-	210	20	68	68	56	-	-
1950	508	508	-	-	-	-	-	-	-	-	-
1953	486	486	-	-	-	-	-	-	-	-	-
1955	415	410	5	2	3	-	-	3	-	-	-
1957	138	120	18	-	18	18	-	-	-	-	-
1960	672	30	642	-	642	399	110	126	8	-	-
1961	986	60	926	-	926	705	62	149	11	-	-
1962	880	80	800	-	800	548	104	131	17	-	-
1963	1333	110	1223	-	1223	365	129	114	612	-	-
1964	1189	80	1109	3	1106	401	267	296	138	-	-
1965	1394	95	1299	9	1290	588	272	300	117	-	-
KOREA								IMPORTS			
1925	773	695	78	-	78	8	65	-	6	-	-
1929	1089	922	167	-	167	30	75	47	15	-	-
1933	1290	1099	191	-	191	47	50	74	21	-	-
1937	2281	1705	576	-	576	90	84	375	27	-	-
1938	2575	1969	606	-	606	90	84	405	27	-	-
KOREA								EXPORTS			
1925	216	216	-	-	-	-	-	-	-	-	-
1929	292	292	-	-	-	-	-	-	-	-	-
1933	478	478	-	-	-	-	-	-	-	-	-
1937	687	661	26	-	26	8	8	5	6	-	-
1938	1054	982	72	-	72	9	23	20	21	-	-
KOREA, REPUBLIC OF								IMPORTS			
1950	369	219	150	-	150	30	15	105	NA	-	-
1953	1174	679	495	-	495	105	60	330	NA	-	-
1955	1606	1060	546	-	546	135	53	359	NA	-	-
1957	1451	740	711	-	711	218	47	447	NA	-	-
1960	1263	220	1043	-	1043	216	54	749	24	-	-
1961	1426	290	1136	-	1136	189	65	869	14	-	-
1962	1712	180	1532	48	1484	125	75	1263	21	-	-
1963	2188	130	2058	69	1989	113	78	1749	50	-	-
1964	2107	170	1937	1205	732	8	15	705	5	-	-
1965	2473	115	2358	2100	258	12	-	240	6	-	-
KOREA, REPUBLIC OF								EXPORTS			
1950	-	-	-	-	-	-	-	-	-	-	-
1953	36	36	-	-	-	-	-	-	-	-	-
1955	-	-	-	-	-	-	-	-	-	-	-
1957	-	-	-	-	-	-	-	-	-	-	-
1960	120	120	-	-	-	-	-	-	-	-	-
1961	240	240	-	-	-	-	-	-	-	-	-
1962	300	300	-	-	-	-	-	-	-	-	-
1963	260	260	-	-	-	-	-	-	-	-	-

Table VI. ENERGY IMPORTS AND EXPORTS, SELECTED YEARS, 1925-1965

(Thousand metric tons coal equivalent)

Region, country, year	Total energy	Solid fuels	Liquid fuels: Total	Liquid fuels: Crude oil	Refined petroleum products: Total	Gasoline	Kerosine	Fuel oils	Lubes and greases	Gas	Electricity
	(1)	(2)	(3)	(4)	(5)	(6)	(7)	(8)	(9)	(10)	(11)
KOREA, REPUBLIC OF (CONTINUED) — EXPORTS											
1964	250	250	-	-	-	-	-	-	-	-	-
1965	205	205	-	-	-	-	-	-	-	-	-
MALAYA AND SINGAPORE — IMPORTS											
1925	1639	644	995	-	995	345	168	464	18	-	-
1929	2372	852	1520	-	1520	428	234	834	24	-	-
1933	1668	567	1101	-	1101	465	152	468	17	-	-
1937	2690	749	1941	-	1941	662	191	1068	21	-	-
1938	2404	488	1916	-	1916	684	248	963	21	-	-
1950	5288	101	5187	-	5187	1275	435	3443	35	-	-
1953	8647	89	8558	-	8558	2325	780	5418	35	-	-
1955	10414	70	10344	-	10344	2558	840	6893	54	-	-
1957	11658	90	11568	1286	10283	2336	902	6989	57	-	-
1960	9867	4	9863	426	9437	1947	1308	6123	59	-	-
1961	12888	60	12828	1946	10883	1745	1472	7602	65	-	-
1962	15166	40	15126	4977	10149	1463	1538	7070	80	-	-
1963	14449	40	14409	4500	9909	1484	1253	7070	104	-	-
1964	16312	40	16272	6789	9483	1221	890	7266	107	-	-
1965	18181	25	18156	7371	10785	1059	1449	8130	147	-	-
MALAYA AND SINGAPORE — EXPORTS											
1925	469	11	458	-	458	290	96	54	18	-	-
1929	590	3	587	-	587	296	153	129	9	-	-
1933	630	4	626	-	626	392	102	126	6	-	-
1937	997	5	992	-	992	506	135	347	5	-	-
1938	1169	3	1166	-	1166	549	182	431	5	-	-
1950	3110	-	3110	-	3110	960	345	1799	6	-	-
1953	4311	-	4311	-	4311	1703	810	1791	8	-	-
1955	5153	-	5153	-	5153	1830	765	2549	9	-	-
1957	5723	-	5723	1178	4545	1818	707	2010	11	-	-
1960	4475	-	4475	347	4128	1595	927	1601	6	-	-
1961	6098	-	6098	1173	4925	1410	1071	2436	8	-	-
1962	7718	-	7718	1974	5744	1469	1103	3165	8	-	-
1963	8040	-	8040	1895	6146	1536	1131	3444	35	-	-
1964	7676	-	7676	381	7295	1523	840	4863	69	-	-
1965	9569	-	9569	365	9204	1577	1326	6212	90	-	-
SINGAPORE — IMPORTS											
1960	7739	-	NA	NA	7739	1626	1170	4884	59	-	-
1961	8989	10	NA	NA	8979	1407	1298	6210	65	-	-
1962	8185	10	NA	NA	8175	1134	1359	5603	80	-	-
1963	8271	10	NA	NA	8261	1242	1089	5826	104	-	-
1964	8788	10	NA	NA	8778	1104	795	6773	107	-	-
1965	10196	5	NA	NA	10191	1050	1305	7689	147	-	-
SINGAPORE — EXPORTS											
1960	4079	-	NA	NA	4073	1572	924	1571	6	-	6
1961	4867	-	NA	NA	4860	1392	1067	2394	8	-	7

Table VI. ENERGY IMPORTS AND EXPORTS, SELECTED YEARS, 1925-1965

(Thousand metric tons coal equivalent)

Region, country, year	Total energy	Solid fuels	Liquid fuels		Refined petroleum products					Gas	Electricity
			Total	Crude oil	Total	Gasoline	Kerosine	Fuel oils	Lubes and greases		
	(1)	(2)	(3)	(4)	(5)	(6)	(7)	(8)	(9)	(10)	(11)
SINGAPORE (CONTINUED)								EXPORTS			
1962	5675	-	NA	NA	5667	1445	1097	3119	8	-	8
1963	6006	-	NA	NA	6002	1502	1122	3344	35	-	4
1964	6536	-	NA	NA	6536	1404	789	4274	69	-	-
1965	8351	-	NA	NA	8351	1422	1224	5615	90	-	-
PAKISTAN								IMPORTS			
1950	2405	1025	1380	-	1380	NA	NA	NA	NA	NA	NA
1953	2783	1211	1572	-	1572	165	345	1020	42	-	-
1955	3017	1080	1937	-	1937	225	308	1350	54	-	-
1957	3606	1330	2276	-	2276	263	315	1650	48	-	-
1960	4550	1410	3140	-	3140	293	515	2333	NA	-	-
1961	4406	1070	3336	-	3336	278	630	2355	74	-	-
1962	4981	1360	3621	495	3126	251	714	2090	72	-	-
1963	5427	1200	4227	2400	1827	101	563	1035	129	-	-
1964	6092	1340	4752	3173	1580	123	612	764	81	-	-
1965	5810	1100	4710	3660	1050	240	330	480	NA	-	-
PAKISTAN								EXPORTS			
1950	-	-	-	-	-	-	-	-	-	-	-
1953	-	-	-	-	-	-	-	-	-	-	-
1955	-	-	-	-	-	-	-	-	-	-	-
1957	12	-	12	-	12	8	2	3	-	-	-
1960	35	-	35	-	35	15	5	15	-	-	-
1961	27	-	27	-	27	9	3	15	-	-	-
1962	26	-	26	-	26	8	3	15	-	-	-
1963	72	-	72	-	72	72	-	-	-	-	-
1964	233	-	233	-	233	120	-	113	-	-	-
1965	-	-	-	-	-	-	-	-	-	-	-
PHILIPPINES								IMPORTS			
1925	931	472	459	-	459	50	74	323	14	-	-
1929	1140	603	537	-	537	107	104	312	15	-	-
1933	825	273	552	-	552	101	62	377	14	-	-
1937	925	266	659	-	659	146	86	410	18	-	-
1938	960	259	701	-	701	150	68	452	32	-	-
1950	1903	7	1896	-	1896	707	228	912	50	-	-
1953	1987	5	1982	-	1982	699	218	1014	51	-	-
1955	2890	10	2880	1001	1880	564	201	1050	65	-	-
1957	3333	10	3323	1319	2004	542	203	1196	65	-	-
1960	3994	10	3984	2123	1862	660	251	852	99	-	-
1961	4158	10	4148	3428	720	267	62	293	99	-	-
1962	4995	10	4985	4554	431	161	29	171	71	-	-
1963	5659	10	5649	5426	224	57	9	68	90	-	-
1964	6543	10	6533	6324	209	2	57	17	134	-	-
1965	7138	10	7128	6915	213	78	29	107	NA	-	-
PHILIPPINES								EXPORTS			
1960	-	-	-	-	-	-	-	-	-	-	-
1961	-	-	-	-	-	-	-	-	-	-	-

Table VI. ENERGY IMPORTS AND EXPORTS, SELECTED YEARS, 1925-1965

(Thousand metric tons coal equivalent)

Region, country, year	Total energy	Solid fuels	Liquid fuels: Total	Liquid fuels: Crude oil	Refined petroleum products: Total	Gasoline	Kerosine	Fuel oils	Lubes and greases	Gas	Electricity
	(1)	(2)	(3)	(4)	(5)	(6)	(7)	(8)	(9)	(10)	(11)
PHILIPPINES (CONTINUED) — EXPORTS											
1962	36	-	36	-	36	-	-	36	-	-	-
1963	77	-	77	-	77	-	-	77	-	-	-
1964	111	-	111	-	111	2	2	108	-	-	-
1965	212	-	212	-	212	15	2	195	-	-	-
TAIWAN — IMPORTS											
1925	46	19	27	-	27	-	23	-	5	-	-
1929	105	18	87	42	45	5	27	2	12	-	-
1933	132	31	101	60	41	8	21	2	11	-	-
1937	224	41	183	48	135	15	30	75	15	-	-
1938	248	45	203	48	155	15	33	90	17	-	-
1950	231	1	230	195	35	15	-	15	5	-	-
1953	102	-	102	-	102	93	-	-	9	-	-
1955	1031	-	1031	920	111	2	75	15	20	-	-
1957	1269	-	1269	1098	171	50	84	23	15	-	-
1960	1649	-	1649	1590	59	-	45	-	14	-	-
1961	1754	-	1754	1683	71	-	45	-	26	-	-
1962	1982	-	1982	1887	95	-	56	-	39	-	-
1963	2321	-	2321	2240	81	-	53	-	29	-	-
1964	2030	-	2030	1929	101	-	63	-	38	-	-
1965	2768	20	2748	2678	71	-	-	30	41	-	-
TAIWAN — EXPORTS											
1925	907	907	-	-	-	-	-	-	-	-	-
1929	404	396	8	5	3	-	3	-	-	-	-
1933	339	336	3	-	3	-	2	-	2	-	-
1937	410	408	2	-	2	-	-	-	2	-	-
1938	502	500	2	-	2	-	-	-	2	-	-
1950	65	65	-	-	-	-	-	-	-	-	-
1953	211	211	-	-	-	-	-	-	-	-	-
1955	95	50	45	-	45	-	-	45	-	-	-
1957	45	30	15	-	15	-	-	15	-	-	-
1960	210	190	20	-	20	2	-	18	-	-	-
1961	317	240	77	-	77	17	-	60	-	-	-
1962	220	130	90	-	90	41	-	50	-	-	-
1963	177	100	77	-	77	-	-	77	-	-	-
1964	233	110	123	-	123	-	-	123	-	-	-
1965	78	15	63	-	63	6	-	56	2	-	-
THAILAND — IMPORTS											
1925	101	38	63	-	63	9	26	24	5	-	-
1929	196	52	144	-	144	26	56	56	8	-	-
1933	139	23	116	-	116	18	42	48	8	-	-
1937	218	50	168	-	168	29	47	83	11	-	-
1938	232	56	176	-	176	32	48	87	9	-	-
1950	380	20	360	-	360	120	60	180	NA	-	-
1953	734	44	690	-	690	270	90	330	NA	-	-
1955	1117	40	1077	-	1077	375	120	543	39	-	-
1957	1415	20	1395	-	1395	503	131	710	53	-	-
1960	1764	10	1754	-	1754	617	207	875	56	-	-
1961	1931	-	1931	-	1931	599	243	1040	50	-	-

Table VI. ENERGY IMPORTS AND EXPORTS, SELECTED YEARS, 1925-1965

(Thousand metric tons coal equivalent)

Region, country, year	Total energy	Solid fuels	Liquid fuels: Total	Liquid fuels: Crude oil	Refined petroleum products: Total	Gasoline	Kerosine	Fuel oils	Lubes and greases	Gas	Electricity
	(1)	(2)	(3)	(4)	(5)	(6)	(7)	(8)	(9)	(10)	(11)
THAILAND (CONTINUED)								IMPORTS			
1962	2433	-	2433	-	2433	635	401	1320	78	-	-
1963	2664	-	2664	81	2583	636	360	1521	65	-	-
1964	3708	-	3708	1013	2696	620	357	1634	84	-	-
1965	3737	-	3737	1814	1923	261	581	989	93	-	-
THAILAND								EXPORTS			
1953	-	-	-	-	-	-	-	-	-	-	-
1955	3	-	3	-	3	3	-	-	-	-	-
1957	32	-	32	-	32	27	5	-	-	-	-
1960	9	-	9	-	9	8	2	-	-	-	-
1961	14	-	14	-	14	12	2	-	-	-	-
1962	6	-	6	-	6	6	-	-	-	-	-
1963	3	-	3	-	3	3	-	-	-	-	-
1964	78	-	78	-	78	3	-	75	-	-	-
1965	48	-	48	-	48	44	5	-	-	-	-
AFRICA								IMPORTS			
1925	6203	4613	1590	149	1442	318	582	401	93	-	-
1929	9124	6163	2961	183	2778	986	938	692	162	-	-
1933	7635	4101	3534	117	3417	996	680	1604	138	-	-
1937	11856	5217	6639	161	6479	1835	791	3669	185	-	-
1938	10692	4897	5795	159	5636	1695	803	2961	177	-	-
1950	16225	2778	13442	-	13442	3719	1761	7584	378	5	-
1953	20218	2266	17951	113	17838	4964	2276	10223	362	-	2
1955	26092	2544	23546	2928	20618	5415	2591	12015	558	-	3
1957	29032	2714	26318	3363	22955	5867	2409	14051	564	-	-
1960	31463	2473	28967	5349	23618	5891	2712	14348	540	-	24
1961	34447	2631	31590	7512	24078	5855	2730	14759	593	-	226
1962	36023	2330	33446	8897	24549	6020	2817	14994	596	-	248
1963	38422	2170	35997	12269	23729	5504	2682	14831	593	-	255
1964	43356	2685	40394	21389	19005	4098	2421	11763	659	-	278
1965	43855	2825	40733	22764	17969	3870	2142	11205	698	-	298
AFRICA								EXPORTS			
1925	2237	1917	320	-	320	135	158	26	2	-	-
1929	2641	2260	381	-	381	180	119	78	3	-	-
1933	1153	1061	92	2	90	62	2	26	2	-	-
1937	1522	1466	56	2	54	44	5	6	-	-	-
1938	1658	1596	62	5	57	48	3	6	-	-	-
1950	3667	3664	3	-	3	2	-	-	2	-	-
1953	2679	2515	162	161	2	2	-	-	-	-	2
1955	2519	2120	396	96	300	113	30	158	-	-	3
1957	3255	2290	876	591	285	122	39	123	2	-	89
1960	19272	2590	16586	15870	716	305	102	308	-	-	96
1961	35196	2810	32162	31058	1104	371	84	650	-	-	224
1962	58784	3140	55398	53043	2355	878	89	1376	-	-	246
1963	87410	2920	84236	80901	3335	626	191	2489	-	-	254
1964	124860	3080	121380	114531	6849	1314	284	5220	-	120	280
1965	161281	3340	156533	148610	7923	1706	237	5940	2	1110	299

Table VI. ENERGY IMPORTS AND EXPORTS, SELECTED YEARS, 1925-1965

(Thousand metric tons coal equivalent)

Region, country, year	Total energy	Solid fuels	Liquid fuels							Gas	Electricity
			Total	Crude oil	Refined petroleum products						
					Total	Gasoline	Kerosine	Fuel oils	Lubes and greases		
	(1)	(2)	(3)	(4)	(5)	(6)	(7)	(8)	(9)	(10)	(11)
NORTH AFRICA								IMPORTS			
1925	4219	3316	903	149	755	146	437	119	54	-	-
1929	5764	4241	1523	183	1340	428	692	141	80	-	-
1933	5186	3248	1938	117	1821	443	540	764	75	-	-
1937	5890	3418	2472	161	2312	455	557	1230	71	-	-
1938	5924	3333	2591	159	2432	530	590	1242	71	-	-
1950	6496	984	5507	-	5507	851	876	3665	116	5	-
1953	7139	552	6587	69	6518	1251	1071	4074	107	-	-
1955	10177	640	9537	1518	8019	1437	1175	5231	141	-	-
1957	9115	880	8235	1760	6476	1533	953	3792	143	-	-
1960	11341	670	10670	3251	7419	1185	1079	4898	158	-	1
1961	12065	690	11373	4371	7002	1107	1022	4575	182	-	2
1962	13066	500	12564	5873	6692	1176	969	4323	132	-	2
1963	14335	470	13865	7679	6186	881	723	4310	186	-	1
1964	13818	730	13088	9261	3827	431	377	2813	176	-	-
1965	11938	575	11363	8358	3005	341	351	2153	140	-	-
NORTH AFRICA								EXPORTS			
1925	340	20	320	-	320	135	158	26	2	-	-
1929	399	19	380	-	380	180	119	78	3	-	-
1933	120	28	92	2	90	62	2	26	2	-	-
1937	153	97	56	2	54	44	5	6	-	-	-
1938	173	111	62	5	57	48	3	6	-	-	-
1950	197	194	3	-	3	2	-	-	2	-	-
1953	431	268	162	161	2	2	-	-	-	-	1
1955	454	340	111	96	15	5	2	9	-	-	3
1957	678	290	387	377	11	3	5	3	-	-	1
1960	13822	190	13631	13367	264	132	23	108	-	-	1
1961	27014	200	26814	26399	416	126	14	276	-	-	-
1962	48391	160	48231	46583	1649	596	11	1029	-	-	-
1963	76124	180	75944	73703	2241	342	9	1860	-	-	-
1964	108026	140	107766	103997	3770	953	65	2727	-	120	-
1965	132658	105	131444	126740	4704	1131	42	3501	-	1110	-
ALGERIA								IMPORTS			
1925	1657	1547	110	-	110	62	27	6	15	-	-
1929	2663	2399	264	-	264	152	66	26	21	-	-
1933	2255	1596	659	-	659	198	74	365	23	-	-
1937	2484	1491	993	-	993	171	59	746	18	-	-
1938	2301	1296	1005	-	1005	183	57	747	18	-	-
1950	2160	500	1655	-	1655	285	75	1260	35	5	-
1953	2502	271	2231	-	2231	405	105	1680	26	-	-
1955	2955	310	2645	-	2645	521	143	1917	42	-	-
1957	3430	500	2930	-	2930	780	143	1920	50	-	-
1960	3321	350	2970	-	2970	542	174	2135	44	-	1
1961	3119	210	2909	-	2909	543	188	2043	44	-	1
1962	2859	100	2759	-	2759	675	177	1803	30	-	1
1963	2829	50	2778	-	2778	486	189	2006	30	-	1
1964	1257	70	1187	-	1187	125	50	965	30	-	-
1965	620	20	600	-	600	45	3	527	23	-	-

Table VI. ENERGY IMPORTS AND EXPORTS, SELECTED YEARS, 1925-1965

(Thousand metric tons coal equivalent)

Region, country, year	Total energy	Solid fuels	Liquid fuels: Total	Liquid fuels: Crude oil	Refined petroleum products: Total	Gasoline	Kerosine	Fuel oils	Lubes and greases	Gas	Electricity
	(1)	(2)	(3)	(4)	(5)	(6)	(7)	(8)	(9)	(10)	(11)
ALGERIA (CONTINUED)								EXPORTS			
1925	15	15	-	-	-	-	-	-	-	-	-
1929	22	16	6	-	6	5	-	2	-	-	-
1933	14	11	3	2	2	-	-	2	-	-	-
1937	19	19	-	-	-	-	-	-	-	-	-
1938	3	1	2	-	2	2	-	-	-	-	-
1950	45	45	-	-	-	-	-	-	-	-	-
1953	207	91	116	116	-	-	-	-	-	-	1
1955	137	40	96	96	-	-	-	-	-	-	1
1957	38	20	17	17	-	-	-	-	-	-	1
1960	12065	-	12065	12065	-	-	-	-	-	-	-
1961	22925	-	22925	22646	279	54	2	224	-	-	-
1962	31482	-	31482	30533	950	195	2	740	-	-	-
1963	36225	-	36225	35483	743	120	-	596	-	-	-
1964	38635	-	38516	37238	1278	225	23	1005	-	120	-
1965	38988	-	37878	36600	1278	375	18	855	-	1110	-
EGYPT UAR								IMPORTS			
1925	2086	1408	678	149	530	27	377	101	26	-	-
1929	2355	1383	972	183	789	134	546	75	35	-	-
1933	2121	1204	917	117	800	30	404	336	30	-	-
1937	2548	1504	1044	161	884	45	437	369	33	-	-
1938	2667	1608	1059	159	900	54	467	348	32	-	-
1950	2836	217	2619	-	2619	108	662	1800	50	-	-
1953	2405	78	2327	69	2258	120	743	1350	45	-	-
1955	4756	110	4646	1518	3128	144	765	2168	51	-	-
1957	3420	180	3240	1719	1521	99	600	765	57	-	-
1960	5413	160	5253	3116	2138	71	651	1355	62	-	-
1961	6245	300	5945	4178	1767	42	579	1067	80	-	-
1962	7898	270	7628	5564	2064	32	560	1421	53	-	-
1963	8534	270	8264	6485	1779	56	309	1314	101	-	-
1964	9169	500	8669	7125	1544	32	138	1287	87	-	-
1965	7870	440	7430	5972	1458	32	164	1200	63	-	-
EGYPT UAR								EXPORTS			
1925	325	5	320	-	320	135	158	26	2	-	-
1929	377	3	374	-	374	176	119	77	3	-	-
1933	104	15	89	-	89	62	2	24	2	-	-
1937	58	4	54	-	54	44	5	6	-	-	-
1938	63	7	56	-	56	47	3	6	-	-	-
1950	3	-	3	-	3	2	-	-	2	-	-
1953	2	-	2	-	2	2	-	-	-	-	-
1955	15	-	15	-	15	5	2	9	-	-	-
1957	369	-	369	360	9	2	5	3	-	-	-
1960	1563	-	1563	1302	261	131	21	108	-	-	-
1961	2850	-	2850	2715	135	72	11	53	-	-	-
1962	4964	-	4964	4272	692	401	6	285	-	-	-
1963	6657	-	6657	5162	1496	222	6	1265	-	-	-
1964	7001	-	7001	4545	2456	717	20	1719	-	-	-
1965	5849	-	5849	2427	3422	756	24	2642	-	-	-

Table VI. ENERGY IMPORTS AND EXPORTS, SELECTED YEARS, 1925-1965

(Thousand metric tons coal equivalent)

Region, country, year	Total energy	Solid fuels	Liquid fuels: Total	Liquid fuels: Crude oil	Refined petroleum products: Total	Gasoline	Kerosine	Fuel oils	Lubes and greases	Gas	Electricity
	(1)	(2)	(3)	(4)	(5)	(6)	(7)	(8)	(9)	(10)	(11)
LIBYA								IMPORTS			
1925	32	17	15	-	15	9	3	2	2	-	-
1929	47	21	26	-	26	14	5	5	3	-	-
1933	87	37	50	-	50	23	6	18	3	-	-
1937	118	44	74	-	74	26	8	38	3	-	-
1938	151	55	96	-	96	26	11	56	5	-	-
1950	145	NA	146	-	146	41	60	44	2	-	-
1953	201	-	201	-	201	68	78	53	3	-	-
1955	376	70	306	-	306	150	90	60	6	-	-
1957	429	30	399	-	399	188	98	105	8	-	-
1960	546	30	516	-	516	180	113	210	11	-	-
1961	525	40	485	-	485	165	113	195	9	-	-
1962	526	10	516	-	516	195	113	195	11	-	-
1963	579	10	569	-	569	210	120	218	12	-	-
1964	662	-	662	-	662	240	128	270	18	-	-
1965	684	10	674	-	674	248	135	272	14	-	-
LIBYA								EXPORTS			
1960	-	-	-	-	-	-	-	-	-	-	-
1961	1038	-	1038	1038	-	-	-	-	-	-	-
1962	11778	-	11778	11778	-	-	-	-	-	-	-
1963	33059	-	33059	33059	-	-	-	-	-	-	-
1964	62214	-	62214	62214	-	-	-	-	-	-	-
1965	87713	-	87713	87713	-	-	-	-	-	-	-
MOROCCO								IMPORTS			
1925	175	121	54	-	54	35	11	2	8	-	-
1929	322	181	141	-	141	86	32	12	12	-	-
1933	370	196	174	-	174	126	18	18	12	-	-
1937	368	161	207	-	207	149	18	32	9	-	-
1938	408	136	272	-	272	198	20	45	9	-	-
1950	837	94	743	-	743	314	38	374	18	-	-
1953	1436	119	1317	-	1317	533	93	668	24	-	-
1955	1388	110	1278	-	1278	494	122	624	30	-	-
1957	1177	80	1097	41	1056	357	59	612	18	-	-
1960	1328	90	1238	135	1103	278	74	710	29	-	-
1961	1399	90	1308	194	1115	252	72	747	29	-	1
1962	983	80	902	300	602	162	45	363	26	-	1
1963	1405	100	1305	1065	240	14	29	171	27	-	-
1964	1545	120	1425	1208	218	8	35	150	21	-	-
1965	1666	55	1611	1365	246	14	47	152	24	-	-
MOROCCO								EXPORTS			
1925	-	-	-	-	-	-	-	-	-	-	-
1929	-	-	-	-	-	-	-	-	-	-	-
1933	2	2	-	-	-	-	-	-	-	-	-
1937	76	74	2	2	-	-	-	-	-	-	-
1938	108	103	5	5	-	-	-	-	-	-	-
1950	149	149	-	-	-	-	-	-	-	-	-
1953	222	177	45	45	-	-	-	-	-	-	-
1955	301	300	-	-	-	-	-	-	-	-	1
1957	272	270	2	-	2	2	-	-	-	-	-

Table VI. ENERGY IMPORTS AND EXPORTS, SELECTED YEARS, 1925-1965

(Thousand metric tons coal equivalent)

Region, country, year	Total energy	Solid fuels	Liquid fuels: Total	Liquid fuels: Crude oil	Refined petroleum products: Total	Gasoline	Kerosine	Fuel oils	Lubes and greases	Gas	Electricity
	(1)	(2)	(3)	(4)	(5)	(6)	(7)	(8)	(9)	(10)	(11)
MOROCCO (CONTINUED)								EXPORTS			
1960	194	190	3	-	3	2	2	-	-	-	1
1961	202	200	2	-	2	-	2	-	-	-	-
1962	168	160	8	-	8	-	3	5	-	-	-
1963	183	180	3	-	3	-	3	-	-	-	-
1964	167	140	27	-	27	2	23	3	-	-	-
1965	110	105	5	-	5	-	-	5	-	-	-
TUNISIA								IMPORTS			
1925	270	223	47	-	47	14	20	9	5	-	-
1929	377	257	120	-	120	44	44	24	9	-	-
1933	355	215	140	-	140	66	39	27	8	-	-
1937	373	218	155	-	155	65	36	47	8	-	-
1938	397	238	159	-	159	69	36	47	8	-	-
1950	518	173	345	-	345	104	42	188	12	-	-
1953	596	84	512	-	512	126	53	324	9	-	-
1955	703	40	663	-	663	129	56	462	12	-	-
1957	660	90	570	-	570	110	54	390	11	-	-
1960	733	40	693	-	693	116	68	489	14	-	-
1961	778	50	728	-	728	105	71	524	21	-	-
1962	801	40	761	9	752	113	75	542	14	-	-
1963	990	40	950	129	821	116	77	602	17	-	-
1964	1186	40	1146	929	218	27	27	141	20	-	-
1965	1099	50	1049	1022	27	3	3	3	17	-	-
TROPICAL AFRICA								IMPORTS			
1925	1784	1290	494	-	494	69	84	279	14	-	-
1929	2787	1918	869	-	869	224	137	468	39	-	-
1933	1839	853	986	-	986	188	77	696	26	-	-
1937	4483	1774	2709	-	2709	681	144	1839	45	-	-
1938	3118	1540	1578	-	1578	395	126	1010	48	-	-
1950	6220	1730	4490	-	4490	1238	357	2742	153	-	-
1953	9282	1686	7595	-	7595	1811	500	5147	138	-	2
1955	10972	1804	9165	-	9165	2358	695	5891	219	-	3
1957	13672	1784	11888	-	11888	2718	755	8186	221	-	-
1960	14499	1803	12674	177	12497	2945	1019	8289	218	-	23
1961	16246	1941	14081	918	13163	2912	1098	8906	222	-	224
1962	16411	1770	14396	599	13797	2972	1262	9294	239	-	246
1963	17153	1650	15249	1305	13944	2963	1350	9356	243	-	254
1964	19690	1855	17558	4853	12705	2654	1361	8403	255	-	278
1965	21958	2105	19556	7394	12162	2456	1206	8192	276	-	298
TROPICAL AFRICA								EXPORTS			
1925	293	293	-	-	-	-	-	-	-	-	-
1929	587	585	2	-	2	-	-	-	-	-	-
1933	251	251	-	-	-	-	-	-	-	-	-
1937	550	550	-	-	-	-	-	-	-	-	-
1938	584	584	-	-	-	-	-	-	-	-	-
1950	860	860	-	-	-	-	-	-	-	-	-
1953	1037	1035	-	-	-	-	-	-	-	-	2
1955	1249	1120	129	-	129	77	24	29	-	-	-
1957	1858	1400	371	215	156	84	32	39	2	-	88

Table VI. ENERGY IMPORTS AND EXPORTS, SELECTED YEARS, 1925-1965

(Thousand metric tons coal equivalent)

Region, country, year	Total energy	Solid fuels	Liquid fuels: Total	Liquid fuels: Crude oil	Refined petroleum products: Total	Gasoline	Kerosine	Fuel oils	Lubes and greases	Gas	Electricity
	(1)	(2)	(3)	(4)	(5)	(6)	(7)	(8)	(9)	(10)	(11)
TROPICAL AFRICA (CONTINUED)								EXPORTS			
1960	4340	1440	2805	2504	302	155	57	90	-	-	95
1961	7096	1550	5322	4659	663	240	68	356	-	-	224
1962	8724	1320	7158	6461	698	276	77	345	-	-	246
1963	9775	1340	8181	7199	983	282	167	534	-	-	254
1964	14402	1560	12563	10535	2028	353	191	1482	-	-	280
1965	26700	1890	24512	21870	2642	572	177	1884	2	-	299
CONGO, DEMOCRATIC REPUBLIC								IMPORTS			
1925	315	294	21	-	21	6	3	12	-	-	-
1929	531	466	65	-	65	27	5	27	6	-	-
1933	71	45	26	-	26	17	2	5	3	-	-
1937	228	165	63	-	63	45	3	9	6	-	-
1938	180	133	47	-	47	30	5	6	6	-	-
1950	445	208	237	-	237	158	20	48	12	-	-
1953	628	200	428	-	428	260	35	113	21	-	-
1955	905	290	612	-	612	318	42	216	33	-	3
1957	932	240	692	-	692	336	53	267	30	-	-
1960	872	230	642	-	642	302	66	269	NA	-	-
1961	1011	330	681	-	681	327	71	278	NA	-	-
1962	932	240	692	-	692	312	86	288	NA	-	-
1963	973	220	753	-	753	345	111	294	NA	-	-
1964	815	255	560	-	560	224	84	249	NA	-	-
1965	1005	330	675	-	675	314	95	264	NA	-	-
CONGO, DEMOCRATIC REPUBLIC								EXPORTS			
1925	-	-	-	-	-	-	-	-	-	-	-
1929	2	-	2	-	2	-	-	-	-	-	-
1933	-	-	-	-	-	-	-	-	-	-	-
1937	-	-	-	-	-	-	-	-	-	-	-
1938	-	-	-	-	-	-	-	-	-	-	-
1950	-	-	-	-	-	-	-	-	-	-	-
1953	-	-	-	-	-	-	-	-	-	-	-
1955	-	-	-	-	-	-	-	-	-	-	-
1957	86	-	-	-	-	-	-	-	-	-	86
1960	65	-	-	-	-	-	-	-	-	-	65
1961	58	-	-	-	-	-	-	-	-	-	58
1962	59	-	-	-	-	-	-	-	-	-	59
1963	34	-	-	-	-	-	-	-	-	-	34
1964	27	-	-	-	-	-	-	-	-	-	27
1965	34	-	-	-	-	-	-	-	-	-	34
EAST AFRICA								IMPORTS			
1925	147	76	71	-	71	11	18	39	3	-	-
1929	260	111	149	-	149	47	32	63	8	-	-
1933	203	95	108	-	108	23	15	68	3	-	-
1937	369	166	203	-	203	54	26	117	6	-	-
1938	397	152	245	-	245	71	26	141	8	-	-
1950	929	44	885	-	885	209	59	597	21	-	-
1953	1274	14	1259	-	1259	284	95	863	18	-	2
1955	1591	26	1565	-	1565	383	116	1029	38	-	-
1957	1848	36	1812	-	1812	390	135	1260	27	-	-

Table VI. ENERGY IMPORTS AND EXPORTS, SELECTED YEARS, 1925-1965

(Thousand metric tons coal equivalent)

Region, country, year	Total energy	Solid fuels	Liquid fuels: Total	Liquid fuels: Crude oil	Refined petroleum products: Total	Gasoline	Kerosine	Fuel oils	Lubes and greases	Gas	Electricity
	(1)	(2)	(3)	(4)	(5)	(6)	(7)	(8)	(9)	(10)	(11)
EAST AFRICA (CONTINUED)								IMPORTS			
1960	2085	40	2022	-	2022	467	197	1326	32	-	23
1961	2005	40	1938	-	1938	446	218	1232	41	-	27
1962	2174	40	2108	-	2108	483	270	1310	42	-	26
1963	2434	40	2369	332	2037	447	272	1287	29	-	26
1964	3334	30	3281	2250	1031	275	200	525	30	-	24
1965	3859	60	3776	2768	1008	272	158	537	41	-	24
EAST AFRICA								EXPORTS			
1950	-	-	-	-	-	-	-	-	-	-	-
1953	2	-	-	-	-	-	-	-	-	-	2
1955	-	-	-	-	-	-	-	-	-	-	-
1957	-	-	-	-	-	-	-	-	-	-	-
1960	152	-	129	-	129	66	18	45	-	-	23
1961	151	-	125	-	125	74	18	33	-	-	27
1962	170	-	144	-	144	84	23	38	-	-	26
1963	287	-	261	-	261	80	113	69	-	-	26
1964	1186	-	1163	-	1163	159	155	846	-	-	24
1965	1498	-	1475	-	1475	293	132	1041	2	-	24
EQUATORIAL AFRICA								IMPORTS			
1925	5	2	3	-	3	3	-	-	-	-	-
1929	9	1	8	-	8	5	2	2	-	-	-
1933	13	2	11	-	11	8	2	-	2	-	-
1937	39	21	18	-	18	9	3	5	2	-	-
1938	31	11	20	-	20	12	3	3	2	-	-
1950	90	7	83	-	83	54	6	17	6	-	-
1953	130	4	126	-	126	66	14	42	5	-	-
1955	141	-	141	-	141	83	15	35	9	-	-
1957	189	-	189	-	189	90	15	75	9	-	-
1960	278	-	278	-	278	122	26	119	11	-	-
1961	275	-	275	-	275	117	23	122	12	-	-
1962	284	-	284	-	284	120	24	128	11	-	-
1963	288	-	288	-	288	111	30	135	11	-	-
1964	339	-	339	-	339	117	57	153	11	-	-
1965	347	-	347	-	347	111	54	170	11	-	-
EQUATORIAL AFRICA								EXPORTS			
1955	-	-	-	-	-	-	-	-	-	-	-
1957	215	-	215	215	-	-	-	-	-	-	-
1960	1214	-	1214	1214	-	-	-	-	-	-	-
1961	1256	-	1256	1247	9	9	-	-	-	-	-
1962	1431	-	1431	1430	2	2	-	-	-	-	-
1963	1568	-	1568	1568	-	-	-	-	-	-	-
1964	1721	-	1721	1721	-	-	-	-	-	-	-
1965	2028	-	2028	2028	-	-	-	-	-	-	-
GHANA								IMPORTS			
1925	83	54	29	-	29	14	12	2	2	-	-
1929	126	73	53	-	53	30	17	3	3	-	-

Table VI. ENERGY IMPORTS AND EXPORTS, SELECTED YEARS, 1925-1965

(Thousand metric tons coal equivalent)

Region, country, year	Total energy	Solid fuels	Liquid fuels: Total	Crude oil	Refined petroleum products: Total	Gasoline	Kerosine	Fuel oils	Lubes and greases	Gas	Electricity
	(1)	(2)	(3)	(4)	(5)	(6)	(7)	(8)	(9)	(10)	(11)
GHANA (CONTINUED) — IMPORTS											
1933	65	27	38	-	38	20	9	6	3	-	-
1937	192	72	120	-	120	38	20	59	5	-	-
1938	211	77	134	-	134	33	14	84	3	-	-
1950	350	63	287	-	287	96	32	149	11	-	-
1953	449	99	350	-	350	131	45	167	8	-	-
1955	609	120	489	-	489	170	54	248	18	-	-
1957	664	110	554	-	554	219	62	257	17	-	-
1960	717	40	677	-	677	212	80	365	21	-	-
1961	679	50	629	-	629	162	63	384	20	-	-
1962	750	30	720	-	720	210	93	393	24	-	-
1963	916	40	876	291	585	150	62	350	24	-	-
1964	1359	40	1319	1253	66	11	20	12	24	-	-
1965	1310	30	1280	1200	80	3	27	17	33	-	-
GHANA — EXPORTS											
1953	-	-	-	-	-	-	-	-	-	-	-
1955	-	-	-	-	-	-	-	-	-	-	-
1957	2	-	2	-	2	-	-	-	2	-	-
1960	2	-	2	-	2	2	-	-	-	-	-
1961	-	-	-	-	-	-	-	-	-	-	-
1962	-	-	-	-	-	-	-	-	-	-	-
1963	54	-	54	-	54	-	-	54	-	-	-
1964	348	-	348	-	348	21	3	324	-	-	-
1965	362	-	362	-	362	9	5	348	-	-	-
LIBERIA — IMPORTS											
1925	-	-	-	-	-	-	-	-	-	-	-
1929	-	-	-	-	-	-	-	-	-	-	-
1933	-	-	-	-	-	-	-	-	-	-	-
1937	2	-	2	-	2	2	-	-	-	-	-
1938	3	-	3	-	3	2	2	-	-	-	-
1950	24	-	24	-	24	11	5	9	-	-	-
1953	27	-	27	-	27	12	5	9	2	-	-
1955	92	-	92	-	92	17	65	9	2	-	-
1957	48	-	48	-	48	29	6	11	3	-	-
1960	89	-	89	-	89	32	11	44	3	-	-
1961	90	-	90	-	90	39	6	42	3	-	-
1962	138	-	138	-	138	29	12	92	6	-	-
1963	200	-	200	-	200	36	23	135	6	-	-
1964	290	-	290	-	290	42	48	192	8	-	-
1965	327	-	327	-	327	39	48	233	8	-	-
NIGERIA — IMPORTS											
1925	55	20	35	-	35	9	23	2	2	-	-
1929	75	22	53	-	53	20	29	2	3	-	-
1933	52	28	24	-	24	11	11	2	2	-	-
1937	97	40	57	-	57	32	17	6	3	-	-
1938	99	39	60	-	60	35	17	6	3	-	-
1950	311	63	248	-	248	144	54	42	8	-	-
1953	371	27	344	-	344	186	68	83	8	-	-
1955	599	-	599	-	599	309	108	165	17	-	-

Table VI. ENERGY IMPORTS AND EXPORTS, SELECTED YEARS, 1925-1965

(Thousand metric tons coal equivalent)

Region, country, year	Total energy	Solid fuels	Liquid fuels: Total	Crude oil	Refined petroleum products: Total	Gasoline	Kerosine	Fuel oils	Lubes and greases	Gas	Electricity
	(1)	(2)	(3)	(4)	(5)	(6)	(7)	(8)	(9)	(10)	(11)
NIGERIA (CONTINUED)								IMPORTS			
1957	765	-	765	-	765	378	134	234	20	-	-
1960	1085	-	1085	-	1085	429	192	431	29	-	-
1961	1373	-	1373	-	1373	446	245	650	29	-	-
1962	1310	-	1310	-	1310	417	261	594	32	-	-
1963	1527	-	1527	-	1527	462	300	723	35	-	-
1964	1707	-	1707	-	1707	482	366	815	38	-	-
1965	1767	-	1767	-	1767	488	335	900	35	-	-
NIGERIA								EXPORTS			
1925	23	23	-	-	-	-	-	-	-	-	-
1929	42	42	-	-	-	-	-	-	-	-	-
1933	24	24	-	-	-	-	-	-	-	-	-
1937	45	45	-	-	-	-	-	-	-	-	-
1938	53	53	-	-	-	-	-	-	-	-	-
1950	2	2	-	-	-	-	-	-	-	-	-
1953	4	4	-	-	-	-	-	-	-	-	-
1955	229	100	129	-	129	77	24	29	-	-	-
1957	255	100	155	-	155	84	32	39	-	-	-
1960	1491	30	1461	1290	171	87	39	45	-	-	-
1961	3661	50	3611	3413	198	83	50	66	-	-	-
1962	5268	30	5238	5031	207	68	53	87	-	-	-
1963	5881	40	5841	5631	210	71	53	87	-	-	-
1964	9002	60	8942	8814	128	38	30	60	-	-	-
1965	20074	35	20039	19842	197	60	32	105	-	-	-
RHODESIAN FEDERATION								IMPORTS			
1925	51	42	9	-	9	6	2	-	2	-	-
1929	175	145	30	-	30	21	5	-	5	-	-
1933	216	180	36	-	36	26	2	8	2	-	-
1937	424	346	78	-	78	45	3	24	6	-	-
1938	492	409	83	-	83	50	3	24	6	-	-
1950	938	683	255	-	255	180	42	20	14	-	-
1953	1270	869	401	-	401	245	54	87	15	-	-
1955	1473	931	542	-	542	315	60	135	32	-	-
1957	1693	997	696	-	696	360	60	240	36	-	-
1960	1902	1102	800	-	800	390	90	285	35	-	-
1961	2156	1150	809	-	809	395	105	279	30	-	197
1962	2148	1060	869	-	869	405	119	308	36	-	219
1963	2104	1010	866	-	866	380	126	324	33	-	229
1964	2273	1110	909	-	909	389	132	354	32	-	254
1965	2992	1305	1413	765	648	276	110	221	41	-	274
RHODESIAN FEDERATION								EXPORTS			
1925	268	268	-	-	-	-	-	-	-	-	-
1929	541	541	-	-	-	-	-	-	-	-	-
1933	225	225	-	-	-	-	-	-	-	-	-
1937	498	498	-	-	-	-	-	-	-	-	-
1938	524	524	-	-	-	-	-	-	-	-	-
1950	852	852	-	-	-	-	-	-	-	-	-
1953	967	967	-	-	-	-	-	-	-	-	-

Table VI. ENERGY IMPORTS AND EXPORTS, SELECTED YEARS, 1925-1965

(Thousand metric tons coal equivalent)

Region, country, year	Total energy	Solid fuels	Liquid fuels: Total	Liquid fuels: Crude oil	Refined petroleum products: Total	Gasoline	Kerosine	Fuel oils	Lubes and greases	Gas	Electricity
	(1)	(2)	(3)	(4)	(5)	(6)	(7)	(8)	(9)	(10)	(11)
RHODESIAN FEDERATION (CONTINUED) — EXPORTS											
1955	1000	1000	-	-	-	-	-	-	-	-	-
1957	1270	1270	-	-	-	-	-	-	-	-	-
1960	1350	1350	-	-	-	-	-	-	-	-	-
1961	1579	1440	8	-	8	3	-	5	-	-	132
1962	1409	1240	17	-	17	11	2	5	-	-	152
1963	1437	1240	12	-	12	6	2	5	-	-	185
1964	1678	1440	20	-	20	9	3	8	-	-	219
1965	2164	1765	168	-	168	83	9	77	-	-	231
MALAWI — IMPORTS											
1925	2	-	2	-	2	2	-	-	-	-	-
1929	5	3	2	-	2	2	-	-	-	-	-
1933	6	3	3	-	3	3	-	-	-	-	-
1937	8	5	3	-	3	3	-	-	-	-	-
1938	9	4	5	-	5	3	-	2	-	-	-
1950	48	25	23	-	23	12	3	8	-	-	-
1953	64	37	27	-	27	15	3	9	-	-	-
1955	87	42	45	-	45	30	-	15	-	-	-
1957	107	47	60	-	60	30	-	30	-	-	-
1960	132	57	75	-	75	30	15	30	-	-	-
1961	125	60	65	-	65	27	8	30	-	-	-
1962	131	60	71	-	71	29	9	33	-	-	-
1963	137	60	77	-	77	30	11	36	-	-	-
1964	144	60	84	-	84	33	12	39	-	-	-
1965	169	80	89	-	89	35	14	41	-	-	-
ZAMBIA — IMPORTS											
1925	44	42	2	-	2	-	-	-	-	-	-
1929	148	142	6	-	6	5	-	-	2	-	-
1933	182	177	5	-	5	5	-	-	-	-	-
1937	349	341	8	-	8	6	-	-	2	-	-
1938	414	405	9	-	9	8	-	-	2	-	-
1950	714	654	60	-	60	39	9	9	3	-	-
1953	927	823	104	-	104	62	11	26	6	-	-
1955	1015	880	135	-	135	75	15	45	NA	-	-
1957	1105	940	165	-	165	90	15	60	NA	-	-
1960	1230	1035	195	-	195	105	15	75	NA	-	-
1961	1477	1080	200	-	200	117	18	65	NA	-	197
1962	1416	990	207	-	207	117	20	71	NA	-	219
1963	1379	940	210	-	210	114	20	75	NA	-	229
1964	1524	1040	230	-	230	116	21	81	11	-	254
1965	1792	1215	303	-	303	149	29	108	17	-	274
RHODESIA — IMPORTS											
1925	8	-	8	-	8	5	2	-	2	-	-
1929	23	-	23	-	23	15	5	-	3	-	-
1933	29	-	29	-	29	18	2	8	2	-	-
1937	68	-	68	-	68	36	3	24	5	-	-
1938	69	-	69	-	69	39	3	23	5	-	-
1950	177	4	173	-	173	129	30	3	11	-	-
1953	279	9	270	-	270	168	41	53	9	-	-
1955	371	9	362	-	362	210	45	75	32	-	-

Table VI. ENERGY IMPORTS AND EXPORTS, SELECTED YEARS, 1925-1965

(Thousand metric tons coal equivalent)

Region, country, year	Total energy	Solid fuels	Liquid fuels: Total	Crude oil	Refined petroleum products: Total	Gasoline	Kerosine	Fuel oils	Lubes and greases	Gas	Electricity
	(1)	(2)	(3)	(4)	(5)	(6)	(7)	(8)	(9)	(10)	(11)
RHODESIA (CONTINUED)								IMPORTS			
1957	481	10	471	-	471	240	45	150	36	-	-
1960	540	10	530	-	530	255	60	180	35	-	-
1961	555	10	545	-	545	251	80	185	30	-	-
1962	601	10	591	-	591	260	90	204	36	-	-
1963	589	10	579	-	579	236	96	213	33	-	-
1964	606	10	596	-	596	240	99	234	21	-	-
1965	1032	10	1022	765	257	93	68	72	24	-	-
RHODESIA								EXPORTS			
1925	268	268	-	-	-	-	-	-	-	-	-
1929	541	541	-	-	-	-	-	-	-	-	-
1933	225	225	-	-	-	-	-	-	-	-	-
1937	498	498	-	-	-	-	-	-	-	-	-
1938	524	524	-	-	-	-	-	-	-	-	-
1950	852	852	-	-	-	-	-	-	-	-	-
1953	967	967	-	-	-	-	-	-	-	-	-
1955	1000	1000	-	-	-	-	-	-	-	-	-
1957	1270	1270	-	-	-	-	-	-	-	-	-
1960	1350	1350	-	-	-	-	-	-	-	-	-
1961	1576	1440	5	-	5	2	-	3	-	-	132
1962	1404	1240	12	-	12	8	2	3	-	-	152
1963	1431	1240	6	-	6	3	2	2	-	-	185
1964	1668	1440	9	-	9	5	2	3	-	-	219
1965	2157	1765	161	-	161	80	8	74	-	-	231
WEST AFRICA								IMPORTS			
1925	226	181	45	-	45	NA	NA	NA	NA	-	-
1929	475	296	179	-	179	20	11	141	8	-	-
1933	520	115	405	-	405	23	6	374	3	-	-
1937	1478	399	1079	-	1079	44	12	1017	6	-	-
1938	181	98	83	-	83	42	12	23	6	-	-
1950	1392	165	1227	-	1227	120	45	1005	57	-	-
1953	2168	56	2112	-	2112	200	57	1838	18	-	-
1955	2244	30	2214	-	2214	240	90	1860	24	-	-
1957	3396	1	3395	-	3395	300	105	2970	20	-	-
1960	2629	1	2628	-	2628	384	119	2097	23	-	-
1961	2605	1	2604	-	2604	389	120	2069	21	-	-
1962	2763	-	2763	-	2763	402	123	2208	24	-	-
1963	2814	-	2814	27	2787	399	141	2216	26	-	-
1964	2997	-	2997	435	2562	402	138	1989	27	-	-
1965	3278	-	3278	981	2297	324	126	1815	29	-	-
SOUTH AFRICA								IMPORTS			
1925	201	7	194	-	194	104	62	3	26	-	-
1929	574	4	570	-	570	335	110	83	44	-	-
1933	611	-	611	-	611	366	63	144	38	-	-
1937	1483	25	1458	-	1458	699	90	600	69	-	-
1938	1650	24	1626	-	1626	771	87	710	59	-	-
1950	3510	64	3446	-	3446	1631	528	1178	110	-	-
1953	3798	28	3770	44	3726	1902	705	1002	117	-	-
1955	4944	100	4844	1410	3434	1620	722	894	198	-	-

Table VI. ENERGY IMPORTS AND EXPORTS, SELECTED YEARS, 1925-1965

(Thousand metric tons coal equivalent)

Region, country, year	Total energy	Solid fuels	Liquid fuels: Total	Crude oil	Refined petroleum products: Total	Gasoline	Kerosine	Fuel oils	Lubes and greases	Gas	Electricity
	(1)	(2)	(3)	(4)	(5)	(6)	(7)	(8)	(9)	(10)	(11)
SOUTH AFRICA (CONTINUED)								IMPORTS			
1957	6245	50	6195	1604	4592	1616	702	2073	201	-	-
1960	5624	-	5624	1922	3702	1761	615	1161	165	-	-
1961	6137	-	6137	2223	3914	1836	611	1278	189	-	-
1962	6546	60	6486	2426	4061	1872	587	1377	225	-	-
1963	6934	50	6884	3285	3599	1661	609	1166	164	-	-
1964	9849	100	9749	7275	2474	1014	684	548	228	-	-
1965	9960	145	9815	7013	2802	1074	585	861	282	-	-
SOUTH AFRICA								EXPORTS			
1925	1604	1604	-	-	-	-	-	-	-	-	-
1929	1656	1656	-	-	-	-	-	-	-	-	-
1933	782	782	-	-	-	-	-	-	-	-	-
1937	819	819	-	-	-	-	-	-	-	-	-
1938	901	901	-	-	-	-	-	-	-	-	-
1950	2610	2610	-	-	-	-	-	-	-	-	-
1953	1212	1212	-	-	-	-	-	-	-	-	-
1955	816	660	156	-	156	32	5	120	-	-	-
1957	719	600	119	-	119	35	3	81	-	-	-
1960	1110	960	150	-	150	18	23	110	-	-	-
1961	1086	1060	26	-	26	5	3	18	-	-	-
1962	1669	1660	9	-	9	6	2	2	-	-	-
1963	1511	1400	111	-	111	2	15	95	-	-	-
1964	2432	1380	1052	-	1052	9	29	1011	-	-	-
1965	1923	1345	578	-	578	3	18	555	-	-	-
DEVELOPED COUNTRIES								IMPORTS			
1925	156684	113097	43332	22350	20982	7671	2990	8052	2255	3	252
1929	209146	141232	67607	31937	35670	15428	4169	13152	2919	4	304
1933	158769	96685	61817	25548	36269	15111	3485	15686	1988	-	267
1937	206932	122148	84354	38192	46163	16437	3123	22530	2553	-	430
1938	194295	106498	87363	39096	48267	17978	2962	22903	2344	-	434
1950	293373	88428	204107	118871	85236	18839	5412	58536	2343	386	453
1953	392070	96289	295136	199155	95981	17349	6257	69966	2223	182	463
1955	494105	120677	372473	252906	119567	18450	6816	90813	3018	253	703
1957	578789	129277	448109	301967	146142	20193	6656	115707	3000	710	694
1960	707987	98385	602846	422298	180548	23514	6008	146973	3402	5566	1190
1961	772820	98847	665000	477138	187862	23930	5639	153801	3686	7980	994
1962	867593	105700	746441	528573	217868	24458	10671	177431	3969	14688	765
1963	965825	118473	831843	596468	235376	25106	13292	191106	4253	14840	669
1964	1064276	116653	930476	680633	249843	26081	14147	202722	4616	16205	943
1965	1175020	113990	1042325	763593	278732	25794	16068	229362	4103	17514	1191
DEVELOPED COUNTRIES								EXPORTS			
1925	151518	127646	23621	2898	20723	5898	4256	8331	2238	5	246
1929	183233	150487	32414	5811	26603	11213	4011	8814	2565	9	324
1933	121170	98574	22230	7961	14270	5516	1863	4881	2010	79	287
1937	162752	124607	37496	14408	23088	7427	2064	10760	2838	181	468
1938	148109	105999	41576	16554	25022	9630	1778	11100	2514	65	469
1950	119863	84692	33561	9081	24480	6147	749	14003	3374	1193	416
1953	156889	89529	65783	7904	57879	14681	3105	36243	3441	966	612
1955	184847	113608	69302	7823	61479	15956	2925	37376	4343	1058	880

Table VI. ENERGY IMPORTS AND EXPORTS, SELECTED YEARS, 1925-1965

(Thousand metric tons coal equivalent)

Region, country, year	Total energy	Solid fuels	Liquid fuels: Total	Liquid fuels: Crude oil	Refined petroleum products: Total	Gasoline	Kerosine	Fuel oils	Lubes and greases	Gas	Electricity
	(1)	(2)	(3)	(4)	(5)	(6)	(7)	(8)	(9)	(10)	(11)
DEVELOPED COUNTRIES (CONTINUED)								EXPORTS			
1957	223058	128636	92808	23895	68913	16644	3593	43347	4260	702	913
1960	177563	84120	88148	11741	76407	16821	4196	48870	5175	4097	1199
1961	186915	84810	94569	16337	78233	17172	4643	49373	5442	6307	1229
1962	209831	88690	107180	22541	84639	17417	4802	54842	5853	13189	772
1963	228577	101630	112868	22788	90080	17111	5519	58785	6615	13380	700
1964	226039	95765	114612	21870	92742	17957	5241	60461	6594	14599	1063
1965	238808	94428	128435	22806	105629	19923	5634	70182	6296	14796	1149
UNDERDEVELOPED COUNTRIES								IMPORTS			
1925	34107	16608	17496	5721	11775	1598	2268	7403	459	3	-
1929	57137	18505	38627	21632	16995	3218	2988	10107	678	5	-
1933	50701	12554	38066	22316	15750	2390	1890	10998	473	79	3
1937	77971	16467	61320	36446	24875	4481	2837	16851	707	181	2
1938	81271	15274	65930	39515	26415	5523	3348	16836	708	65	2
1950	155480	7920	146595	95077	51518	11901	4635	32268	1333	948	16
1953	179733	7669	171245	104085	67160	17989	6546	41007	1602	797	29
1955	215401	8274	206268	127424	78845	18365	8459	49556	1939	835	24
1957	230853	8684	222027	137447	84581	19124	8606	54078	2178	91	51
1960	230178	8147	221850	142280	79571	16548	9234	50709	2224	101	80
1961	247091	7351	239357	157779	81578	15980	10113	52217	2239	101	283
1962	263795	6650	256736	178181	78555	13920	10494	50501	2445	96	314
1963	271232	6434	264398	186741	77657	12791	9062	51897	2608	72	329
1964	286241	7289	278589	205214	73376	10824	7911	50940	2410	67	296
1965	293412	7072	286035	218711	67324	9897	8429	45392	2091	-	305
UNDERDEVELOPED COUNTRIES								EXPORTS			
1925	43672	3095	40577	20855	19722	3219	1251	15074	179	-	-
1929	78900	4506	74394	41643	32751	7250	3005	22064	432	-	-
1933	79528	3866	75662	37607	38055	9479	2313	25964	300	-	-
1937	122079	4812	117267	55848	61419	12822	3750	44154	693	-	-
1938	125051	5862	119189	56798	62391	13932	4202	43605	653	-	-
1950	338711	2369	336270	199295	136976	25080	9545	102069	469	72	-
1953	424208	4019	420110	289743	130366	22932	9651	96901	1062	77	2
1955	518269	3170	515001	368054	146948	23306	13290	108939	1311	96	3
1957	582463	3560	578484	417515	160970	24354	15287	120074	1156	330	89
1960	726891	3400	721734	533958	187776	26402	16590	142944	1489	1661	96
1961	782412	3180	777149	582858	194291	25169	17607	149735	1334	1859	224
1962	877350	2990	872471	652302	220169	26991	18860	171882	1662	1644	246
1963	959269	2770	954662	723945	230717	28128	17987	182226	1355	1584	254
1964	1071198	3342	1065776	825606	240170	28199	20039	188642	1751	1801	280
1965	1162114	3172	1155800	905607	250193	30417	22479	193508	1964	2844	299
COMMUNIST COUNTRIES								IMPORTS			
1925	8873	6892	1973	132	1841	78	1323	174	65	-	9
1929	11378	8606	2763	468	2295	216	1259	389	122	-	9
1933	7026	4249	2775	417	2358	221	1040	624	105	-	2
1937	7122	3726	3395	1047	2348	590	791	548	132	-	2
1938	6579	3919	2660	872	1788	483	554	402	104	-	-
1950	27442	20572	6773	2993	3780	450	338	1193	-	75	23
1953	36760	24881	11703	4818	6885	540	390	1455	-	155	21
1955	41978	26110	15612	5768	9845	4157	1697	3828	163	216	40

Table VI. ENERGY IMPORTS AND EXPORTS, SELECTED YEARS, 1925-1965

(Thousand metric tons coal equivalent)

Region, country, year	Total energy	Solid fuels	Liquid fuels		Refined petroleum products					Gas	Electricity
			Total	Crude oil	Total	Gasoline	Kerosine	Fuel oils	Lubes and greases		
	(1)	(2)	(3)	(4)	(5)	(6)	(7)	(8)	(9)	(10)	(11)
COMMUNIST COUNTRIES (CONTINUED)								IMPORTS			
1957	39374	20330	18686	8456	10230	5591	1424	3086	130	288	71
1960	52905	25580	26588	12231	14357	7760	1862	4470	265	630	107
1961	56429	27690	27966	12296	15671	7908	1842	5600	321	671	101
1962	60753	30650	29316	14339	14978	6918	1716	6165	175	685	102
1963	67313	33340	33119	17652	15467	6699	1680	6740	345	702	153
1964	73903	36930	36023	22763	13260	5721	1044	6254	232	709	242
1965	77537	36854	39641	28658	10983	4557	840	5358	225	774	269
COMMUNIST COUNTRIES								EXPORTS			
1925	18799	15104	3695	101	3594	912	1287	1056	329	-	-
1929	33566	23546	10020	473	9548	2906	2418	3731	479	-	-
1933	33365	17806	15558	1230	14328	4659	2345	6804	515	-	1
1937	31909	20912	10997	1074	9923	3434	1802	4283	402	-	-
1938	26416	17824	8592	1133	7460	2855	1557	2750	296	-	-
1950	38989	33101	5805	615	5190	1898	923	1170	-	33	50
1953	50755	34587	16020	3255	12765	3015	1538	2963	-	127	21
1955	63246	40450	22589	4968	17621	6122	2270	8985	228	186	21
1957	66044	35160	30585	9564	21021	6747	2360	11589	321	228	71
1960	107886	45430	61775	27401	34374	8742	2672	22020	912	594	87
1961	123623	48710	74175	35708	38468	9407	2567	25439	1027	635	102
1962	135843	54100	81021	40002	41019	8625	2853	28532	987	678	44
1963	148116	57050	90294	45950	44345	8844	2555	31913	1020	678	94
1964	161037	61340	98774	55539	43235	7781	1848	32678	918	671	252
1965	173282	61100	111117	65717	45401	7037	2168	35298	876	791	274
USSR								IMPORTS			
1925	790	692	98	14	84	11	60	5	9	-	-
1929	1250	1097	153	26	128	29	74	14	12	-	-
1933	944	798	146	5	141	21	87	23	11	-	-
1937	1503	1069	434	20	414	264	96	39	15	-	-
1938	1493	1050	443	23	420	252	110	45	14	-	-
1950	15450	11400	4050	2250	1800	NA	NA	NA	NA	-	-
1953	17100	9900	7200	2700	4500	NA	NA	NA	NA	-	-
1955	16978	9070	7907	2363	5544	2982	824	1575	164	-	1
1957	9897	3760	6137	1997	4140	3035	441	534	131	-	-
1960	11609	5370	6239	1749	4490	3261	458	587	185	-	-
1961	10422	5320	5102	1332	3770	2670	410	471	219	-	-
1962	9542	5480	4062	744	3318	2372	366	405	176	-	-
1963	9772	5690	4082	815	3267	2303	306	438	221	-	-
1964	8663	5700	2963	-	2963	2079	227	425	233	-	-
1965	10121	7395	2726	-	2726	1832	254	416	225	-	-
USSR								EXPORTS			
1925	2425	367	2058	95	1964	417	681	716	150	-	-
1929	7135	1339	5796	468	5328	1646	1182	2175	326	-	-
1933	9171	1818	7353	798	6555	1947	855	3374	380	-	-
1937	4270	1312	2958	185	2774	630	366	1448	330	-	-
1938	2497	326	2171	345	1826	471	317	806	233	-	-
1950	4283	2600	1650	450	1200	NA	NA	NA	NA	33	-
1953	12777	4400	8250	3000	5250	NA	NA	NA	NA	127	-
1955	17899	5770	11943	4374	7569	2108	962	4272	228	186	-

Table VI. ENERGY IMPORTS AND EXPORTS, SELECTED YEARS, 1925-1965

(Thousand metric tons coal equivalent)

Region, country, year	Total energy	Solid fuels	Liquid fuels: Total	Liquid fuels: Crude oil	Refined petroleum products: Total	Gasoline	Kerosine	Fuel oils	Lubes and greases	Gas	Electricity
	(1)	(2)	(3)	(4)	(5)	(6)	(7)	(8)	(9)	(10)	(11)
USSR (CONTINUED)								EXPORTS			
1957	31423	10750	20445	8885	11561	2558	1362	7338	303	228	-
1960	64686	14700	49659	26738	22922	4227	1640	16485	570	324	4
1961	79744	17830	61545	35082	26463	5384	1614	18831	635	360	9
1962	90709	22340	67938	39419	28520	4733	1943	21186	659	402	29
1963	102235	24780	76959	45365	31595	5013	1904	24098	581	402	93
1964	112580	27230	84797	55037	29760	4121	1335	23862	443	390	163
1965	122954	25800	96444	65148	31296	3530	1748	25605	414	522	188
COMMUNIST EASTERN EUROPE								IMPORTS			
1925	3870	3398	464	119	345	30	72	24	18	-	9
1929	6198	5186	1004	443	561	68	83	65	36	-	9
1933	2825	1924	899	413	486	17	38	50	14	-	2
1937	3482	2222	1259	791	468	23	45	89	24	-	2
1938	2742	1729	1013	609	404	23	32	77	27	-	-
1950	11992	9172	2723	743	1980	450	338	1193	-	75	23
1953	19660	14981	4503	2118	2385	540	390	1455	-	155	21
1955	22858	16960	5643	2805	2838	785	393	1661	-	216	39
1957	25928	16470	9099	5822	3278	1296	315	1667	-	288	71
1960	35832	20100	14994	9567	5427	2339	654	2354	81	630	108
1961	40857	22290	17795	10844	6951	2801	593	3456	102	671	101
1962	47259	24960	21512	13385	8127	2874	563	4688	-	685	102
1963	54119	27610	25655	16613	9042	3009	579	5327	125	702	153
1964	62778	30950	30878	22463	8415	2675	488	5244	-	709	242
1965	65732	29319	35370	28343	7028	2133	467	4425	-	774	269
COMMUNIST EASTERN EUROPE								EXPORTS			
1925	13773	12136	1637	6	1631	495	606	341	179	-	-
1929	22887	18663	4224	5	4220	1260	1236	1556	153	-	-
1933	19948	11823	8124	356	7769	2709	1488	3431	135	-	1
1937	22691	14745	7946	797	7149	2804	1436	2835	72	-	-
1938	19600	13306	6294	660	5634	2384	1241	1944	63	-	-
1950	34706	30501	4155	165	3990	1898	923	1170	-	-	50
1953	37978	30187	7770	255	7515	3015	1538	2963	-	-	21
1955	44247	33580	10646	594	10052	4014	1308	4713	-	-	21
1957	32775	22570	10134	680	9455	4184	998	4251	18	-	71
1960	42170	29700	12116	663	11453	4515	1032	5535	342	270	84
1961	42679	29680	12630	626	12005	4023	953	6608	393	276	93
1962	43703	30330	13083	584	12500	3893	911	7346	329	276	15
1963	44411	30800	13335	585	12750	3831	651	7815	440	276	1
1964	46957	32610	13977	503	13475	3660	513	8816	476	281	89
1965	48573	33545	14673	569	14105	3507	420	9693	462	269	86
COMMUNIST ASIA								IMPORTS			
1925	4214	2802	1412	-	1412	38	1191	146	38	-	-
1929	3930	2323	1607	-	1607	120	1103	311	74	-	-
1933	3258	1527	1731	-	1731	183	915	552	81	-	-
1937	2138	435	1703	237	1466	303	650	420	93	-	-
1938	2345	1140	1205	240	965	209	413	281	63	-	-
1950	NA	NA	NA	NA	NA	NA	NA	NA	NA	NA	NA
1953	NA	NA	NA	NA	NA	NA	NA	NA	NA	NA	NA
1955	2142	80	2063	600	1463	390	480	593	NA	NA	NA

Table VI. ENERGY IMPORTS AND EXPORTS, SELECTED YEARS, 1925-1965

(Thousand metric tons coal equivalent)

Region, country, year	Total energy	Solid fuels	Liquid fuels: Total	Crude oil	Refined petroleum products: Total	Gasoline	Kerosine	Fuel oils	Lubes and greases	Gas	Electricity
	(1)	(2)	(3)	(4)	(5)	(6)	(7)	(8)	(9)	(10)	(11)
COMMUNIST ASIA (CONTINUED)								IMPORTS			
1957	3550	100	3450	638	2813	1260	668	885	NA	NA	NA
1960	5465	110	5355	915	4440	2160	750	1530	NA	NA	NA
1961	5150	80	5070	120	4950	2438	840	1673	NA	NA	NA
1962	3952	210	3743	210	3533	1673	788	1073	NA	NA	NA
1963	3422	40	3383	225	3158	1388	795	975	NA	NA	NA
1964	2462	280	2183	300	1883	968	330	585	NA	NA	NA
1965	1685	140	1545	315	1230	593	120	518	NA	NA	NA
COMMUNIST ASIA								EXPORTS			
1925	2601	2601	-	-	-	-	-	-	-	-	-
1929	3544	3544	-	-	-	-	-	-	-	-	-
1933	4246	4165	81	77	5	3	2	-	-	-	-
1937	4948	4855	93	93	-	-	-	-	-	-	-
1938	4320	4192	128	128	-	-	-	-	-	-	-
1950	NA	NA	NA	NA	NA	NA	NA	NA	NA	NA	NA
1953	NA	NA	NA	NA	NA	NA	NA	NA	NA	NA	NA
1955	1100	1100	-	-	-	-	-	-	NA	NA	NA
1957	1846	1840	6	-	6	6	-	-	NA	NA	NA
1960	1030	1030	-	-	-	-	-	-	NA	NA	NA
1961	1200	1200	-	-	-	-	-	-	NA	NA	NA
1962	1430	1430	-	-	-	-	-	-	NA	NA	NA
1963	1470	1470	-	-	-	-	-	-	NA	NA	NA
1964	1500	1500	-	-	-	-	-	-	NA	NA	NA
1965	1755	1755	-	-	-	-	-	-	NA	NA	NA
ORGANISATION FOR ECONOMIC CO-OPERATION AND DEVELOPMENT (OECD)								IMPORTS			
1925	152854	111004	41595	22014	19581	6836	2723	7886	2124	3	252
1929	202826	138443	64076	31083	32993	13596	3768	12911	2718	4	304
1933	153698	95007	58424	25022	33402	13433	3123	15009	1838	-	267
1937	198064	119026	78608	37587	41021	13610	2611	20962	2317	-	430
1938	185254	103763	81057	38477	42581	14856	2476	21034	2136	-	434
1950	276434	85104	190491	117068	73424	13541	4263	53550	1964	386	453
1953	374652	93364	280643	197081	83562	11124	5069	65184	2000	182	463
1955	468485	116468	351062	243437	107625	12785	5508	86337	2526	253	703
1957	546288	123986	420899	286091	134808	16133	5489	110106	2495	710	694
1960	671347	93260	571383	401121	170262	19445	4938	142428	2801	5566	1138
1961	734079	93870	631257	454131	177126	19916	4487	148895	3026	7980	972
1962	827643	100900	711300	505762	204539	19796	9338	170732	3339	14688	755
1963	922312	114020	792825	570999	221826	20378	11847	184398	3590	14840	627
1964	1014043	110800	886226	649254	236972	22119	12756	195888	3936	16205	813
1965	1120436	107959	993893	727424	266469	22770	14616	222198	3489	17514	1070
ORGANISATION FOR ECONOMIC CO-OPERATION AND DEVELOPMENT (OECD)								EXPORTS			
1925	149016	125153	23612	2897	20715	5895	4254	8330	2237	5	246
1929	181593	148863	32397	5810	26588	11213	4001	8813	2562	9	324
1933	120593	97997	22230	7961	14270	5516	1863	4881	2010	79	287
1937	161774	123632	37493	14408	23085	7427	2064	10758	2837	181	468
1938	147058	104949	41574	16554	25020	9630	1778	11099	2514	65	469
1950	117002	81887	33506	9081	24425	6141	741	13965	3369	1193	416
1953	155086	87809	65703	7904	57800	14675	3104	36176	3437	966	608
1955	183163	112628	68604	7823	60782	15729	2910	36921	4341	1058	874

Table VI. ENERGY IMPORTS AND EXPORTS, SELECTED YEARS, 1925-1965

(Thousand metric tons coal equivalent)

Region, country, year	Total energy	Solid fuels	Liquid fuels							Gas	Electricity
					Refined petroleum products						
			Total	Crude oil	Total	Gasoline	Kerosine	Fuel oils	Lubes and greases		
	(1)	(2)	(3)	(4)	(5)	(6)	(7)	(8)	(9)	(10)	(11)
(OECD) (CONTINUED)								EXPORTS			
1957	219827	127016	91215	23895	67320	16347	3561	42096	4256	702	894
1960	172027	81350	85392	11741	73652	16547	4074	46536	5163	4097	1188
1961	179371	80610	91235	16068	75167	16793	4389	46971	5418	6307	1219
1962	200982	83870	103170	21699	81471	17201	4688	52044	5808	13189	752
1963	220115	96800	109272	22106	87167	16880	5352	56360	6522	13380	663
1964	216110	89235	111213	21396	89817	17688	5130	58062	6448	14599	1063
1965	227655	85618	126092	22589	103503	19760	5519	68466	6171	14796	1149
COMMUNIST COUNTRIES								IMPORTS			
1925	8873	6892	1973	132	1841	78	1323	174	65	-	9
1929	11378	8606	2763	468	2295	216	1259	389	122	-	9
1933	7026	4249	2775	417	2358	221	1040	624	105	-	2
1937	7122	3726	3395	1047	2348	590	791	548	132	-	2
1938	6579	3919	2660	872	1788	483	554	402	104	-	-
1950	27442	20572	6773	2993	3780	450	338	1193	-	75	23
1953	36760	24881	11703	4818	6885	540	390	1455	-	155	21
1955	41978	26110	15612	5768	9845	4157	1697	3828	163	216	40
1957	39374	20330	18686	8456	10230	5591	1424	3086	130	288	71
1960	52905	25580	26588	12231	14357	7760	1862	4470	265	630	107
1961	56429	27690	27966	12296	15671	7908	1842	5600	321	671	101
1962	60753	30650	29316	14339	14978	6918	1716	6165	175	685	102
1963	67313	33340	33119	17652	15467	6699	1680	6740	345	702	153
1964	73903	36930	36023	22763	13260	5721	1044	6254	232	709	242
1965	77537	36854	39641	28658	10983	4557	840	5358	225	774	269
COMMUNIST COUNTRIES								EXPORTS			
1925	18799	15104	3695	101	3594	912	1287	1056	329	-	-
1929	33566	23546	10020	473	9548	2906	2418	3731	479	-	-
1933	33365	17806	15558	1230	14328	4659	2345	6804	515	-	1
1937	31909	20912	10997	1074	9923	3434	1802	4283	402	-	-
1938	26416	17824	8592	1133	7460	2855	1557	2750	296	-	-
1950	38989	33101	5805	615	5190	1898	923	1170	-	33	50
1953	50755	34587	16020	3255	12765	3015	1538	2963	-	127	21
1955	63246	40450	22589	4968	17621	6122	2270	8985	228	186	21
1957	66044	35160	30585	9564	21021	6747	2360	11589	321	228	71
1960	107886	45430	61775	27401	34374	8742	2672	22020	912	594	87
1961	123623	48710	74175	35708	38468	9407	2567	25439	1027	635	102
1962	135843	54100	81021	40002	41019	8625	2853	28532	987	678	44
1963	148116	57050	90294	45950	44345	8844	2555	31913	1020	678	94
1964	161037	61340	98774	55539	43235	7781	1848	32678	918	671	252
1965	173282	61100	111117	65717	45401	7037	2168	35298	876	791	274
WORLD EXCLUDING OECD AND COMMUNIST COUNTRIES								IMPORTS			
1925	37937	18701	19233	6057	13176	2433	2535	7569	590	3	-
1929	63457	21294	42158	22485	19673	5049	3388	10349	879	5	-
1933	55772	14232	41459	22842	18617	4068	2252	11675	623	79	3
1937	86839	19589	67067	37050	30017	7308	3348	18419	942	181	2
1938	90312	18009	72236	40134	32102	8645	3834	18705	917	65	2
1950	172419	11244	160210	96880	63330	17199	5784	37254	1713	948	16
1953	197151	10594	185738	106159	79578	24214	7734	45789	1825	797	29
1955	241021	12483	227679	136893	90786	24030	9767	54032	2431	835	24

Table VI. ENERGY IMPORTS AND EXPORTS, SELECTED YEARS, 1925-1965

(Thousand metric tons coal equivalent)

Region, country, year	Total energy	Solid fuels	Liquid fuels: Total	Liquid fuels: Crude oil	Refined petroleum products: Total	Gasoline	Kerosine	Fuel oils	Lubes and greases	Gas	Electricity
	(1)	(2)	(3)	(4)	(5)	(6)	(7)	(8)	(9)	(10)	(11)
WORLD EXCLUDING OECD AND COMMUNIST COUNTRIES (CONTINUED)								IMPORTS			
1957	263354	13975	249237	153323	95915	23184	9773	59679	2683	91	51
1960	266818	13272	253313	163457	89856	20618	10304	55254	2826	101	133
1961	285833	12328	273099	180786	92313	19994	11265	57123	2899	101	305
1962	303746	11450	291876	199992	91884	18582	11828	57200	3075	96	324
1963	314746	10887	303416	212210	91206	17519	10506	58605	3271	72	371
1964	336473	13142	322839	236592	86247	14786	9302	57774	3090	67	426
1965	347996	13103	334467	254880	79587	12921	9881	52556	2704	-	426
WORLD EXCLUDING OECD AND COMMUNIST COUNTRIES								EXPORTS			
1925	46174	5588	40586	20856	19730	3222	1253	15075	180	-	-
1929	80541	6130	74411	41645	32766	7250	3015	22065	435	-	-
1933	80105	4443	75662	37607	38055	9479	2313	25964	300	-	-
1937	123057	5787	117270	55848	61422	12822	3750	44156	695	-	-
1938	126102	6912	119190	56798	62393	13932	4202	43607	653	-	-
1950	341571	5174	336326	199295	137031	25086	9552	102106	474	72	-
1953	426012	5739	420189	289743	130446	22938	9653	96969	1066	77	7
1955	519953	4150	515699	368054	147645	23532	13305	109394	1312	96	9
1957	585695	5180	580077	417515	162563	24651	15318	121325	1161	330	108
1960	732428	6170	724490	533958	190532	26676	16712	145278	1502	1661	108
1961	789956	7380	780483	583127	197357	25548	17861	152136	1358	1859	234
1962	886199	7810	876480	653144	223337	27207	18974	174680	1707	1644	265
1963	967732	7600	958257	724628	233630	28359	18153	184652	1448	1584	291
1964	1081127	9872	1069175	826080	243095	28467	20150	191040	1896	1801	280
1965	1173267	11982	1158143	905825	252318	30581	22595	195224	2088	2844	299

DERIVATION OF TABLE VII

For each year, imports minus exports from correspondingly numbered columns in table VI.

Table VII. NET ENERGY IMPORTS OR EXPORTS, SELECTED YEARS, 1925-1965

(Thousand metric tons coal equivalent; minus sign [-] = net exports)

Region, country, year	Total energy	Solid fuels	Liquid fuels		Refined petroleum products					Gas	Electricity
			Total	Crude oil	Total	Gasoline	Kerosine	Fuel oils	Lubes and greases		
	(1)	(2)	(3)	(4)	(5)	(6)	(7)	(8)	(9)	(10)	(11)
WORLD											
1925	-14325	-9248	-5091	4350	-9441	-683	-213	-8832	33	-	15
1929	-18039	-10196	-7832	6110	-13941	-2507	-1019	-10961	243	-	-11
1933	-17566	-6758	-10793	1484	-12276	-1932	-107	-10341	-260	-	-15
1937	-24715	-7990	-16691	4355	-21045	-2175	-866	-19268	-542	-	-34
1938	-17431	-3994	-13404	4998	-18402	-2433	-672	-17313	-306	-	-33
1950	-21268	-3242	-18162	7950	-26112	-1935	-831	-25245	-166	111	25
1953	-23290	704	-23829	7156	-30985	-4749	-1101	-23679	-678	-36	-123
1955	-14879	-2167	-12539	5253	-17792	-4412	-1514	-11103	-761	-36	-138
1957	-22549	-9065	-13056	-3105	-9951	-2838	-4554	-2139	-429	-172	-256
1960	-21271	-838	-20373	3710	-24083	-4143	-6354	-11682	-1684	-55	-5
1961	-16610	-2812	-13571	12311	-25881	-3930	-7223	-12929	-1557	-49	-178
1962	-30882	-2780	-28179	6248	-34427	-7737	-3633	-21159	-1913	-43	120
1963	-31592	-3203	-28464	8178	-36642	-9488	-2027	-23181	-1784	-28	103
1964	-33854	425	-34074	5594	-39668	-11310	-4026	-21864	-2004	-91	-115
1965	-28235	-784	-27351	16832	-44183	-17128	-4944	-18876	-2717	-143	43
NORTH AMERICA											
1925	-4699	-3655	-1041	14331	-15372	-4506	-4083	-4773	-2012	-3	-
1929	-1583	-2122	545	18665	-18120	-8543	-3816	-3560	-2205	-5	-
1933	-2676	1520	-4115	5235	-9350	-4910	-1731	-1011	-1698	-79	-3

Table VII. NET ENERGY IMPORTS OR EXPORTS, SELECTED YEARS, 1925-1965

(Thousand metric tons coal equivalent; minus sign [-] = net exports)

Region, country, year	Total energy	Solid fuels	Liquid fuels							Gas	Electricity
					Refined petroleum products						
			Total	Crude oil	Total	Gasoline	Kerosine	Fuel oils	Lubes and greases		
	(1)	(2)	(3)	(4)	(5)	(6)	(7)	(8)	(9)	(10)	(11)
NORTH AMERICA (CONTINUED)											
1937	-13107	58	-12981	1575	-14556	-6309	-1710	-4278	-2259	-181	-2
1938	-17736	786	-18455	-1964	-16491	-8216	-1424	-4937	-1916	-65	-2
1950	66603	-2156	69654	48692	20963	-2015	236	25658	-2814	-875	-20
1953	67945	-12079	80841	64575	16266	-4244	-632	23759	-2414	-790	-27
1955	67686	-31780	100260	77093	23168	-3200	155	29267	-2658	-769	-25
1957	49531	-55760	105137	82209	22928	-2591	-327	28866	-2585	210	-56
1960	133513	-22760	154802	101391	53411	2310	756	53930	-3039	1542	-71
1961	137688	-22820	158859	100983	57876	3198	581	58094	-3339	1716	-67
1962	143097	-25900	167528	104376	63152	1487	3773	61814	-3464	1541	-71
1963	138889	-34360	171828	107403	64425	1974	4946	61647	-3597	1495	-74
1964	151809	-32390	182670	110486	72185	1440	4961	70040	-3599	1548	-18
1965	171552	-32423	202367	112256	90111	1527	6233	86565	-3219	1616	-8
CANADA											
1925	18726	14847	4035	3347	689	413	20	201	56	3	-159
1929	24702	16816	8060	6876	1184	851	18	203	113	4	-178
1933	17050	10447	6726	6032	695	263	3	366	63	-	-124
1937	22263	13337	9165	8474	692	348	9	243	92	-8	-231
1938	20011	11780	8469	7457	1013	570	29	314	101	-9	-228
1950	46658	24260	22428	17411	5018	1532	554	2709	117	198	-229
1953	44433	21161	23633	17238	6395	1443	741	3806	227	-69	-292
1955	39687	17690	22538	15743	6795	951	770	4638	285	-7	-534
1957	36116	17820	18474	12834	5640	822	654	3759	257	354	-533
1960	31301	11680	24156	18062	6095	225	872	4896	261	-3893	-641
1961	23666	10420	19727	14775	4952	215	534	4158	245	-6133	-348
1962	12158	10730	14598	9711	4887	89	479	4335	233	-13008	-162
1963	16178	11350	18110	12545	5565	350	540	4715	237	-13188	-93
1964	14665	12620	16637	9798	6839	272	522	6255	288	-14436	-155
1965	18581	14360	18858	8400	10458	374	450	10287	347	-14639	2
UNITED STATES											
1925	-23432	-18508	-5078	10985	-16062	-4919	-4103	-4974	-2067	-5	159
1929	-26293	-18944	-7518	11789	-19307	-9393	-3834	-3762	-2318	-9	178
1933	-19739	-8939	-10842	-797	-10046	-5172	-1734	-1379	-1761	-79	121
1937	-35397	-13303	-22149	-6899	-15251	-6659	-1719	-4523	-2351	-173	228
1938	-37775	-11020	-26925	-9420	-17505	-8786	-1452	-5252	-2016	-56	226
1950	19933	-26428	47226	31281	15945	-3546	-318	22949	-2931	-1074	209
1953	23498	-33250	57204	47337	9867	-5691	-1373	19953	-2640	-721	264
1955	27902	-49500	77655	61350	16305	-4154	-617	24566	-2943	-762	509
1957	13339	-73600	86607	69375	17232	-3416	-983	25056	-2841	-144	476
1960	102122	-34460	130577	83330	47247	2081	-117	48972	-3302	5436	570
1961	113894	-33250	139014	86208	52806	2979	42	53826	-3584	7848	282
1962	130820	-36650	152831	94665	58166	1392	3291	57390	-3698	14549	90
1963	122569	-45740	153608	94859	58749	1619	4401	56834	-3836	14683	19
1964	136980	-45030	165890	100688	65202	1163	4434	63653	-3888	15984	137
1965	152795	-46800	183350	103856	79494	1145	5771	76142	-3567	16254	-9
WESTERN EUROPE											
1925	10122	-8116	18233	4185	14048	5394	2429	4320	1892	-	6
1929	21010	-7203	28233	4206	24027	10941	3120	7598	2369	-	-20
1933	31369	-4715	36101	8225	27876	12929	2342	11066	1541	-	-17

Table VII. NET ENERGY IMPORTS OR EXPORTS, SELECTED YEARS, 1925-1965

(Thousand metric tons coal equivalent; minus sign [-] = net exports)

Region, country, year	Total energy	Solid fuels	Liquid fuels		Refined petroleum products					Gas	Electricity
			Total	Crude oil	Total	Gasoline	Kerosine	Fuel oils	Lubes and greases		
	(1)	(2)	(3)	(4)	(5)	(6)	(7)	(8)	(9)	(10)	(11)
WESTERN EUROPE (CONTINUED)											
1937	42091	-5906	48033	16703	31331	12630	2400	14492	1809	-	-36
1938	47242	-4335	51611	19241	32370	13614	2261	14873	1623	-	-33
1950	93429	7533	85772	58053	27719	9515	3191	13635	1379	68	56
1953	138530	15817	122829	117671	5159	330	2334	1628	887	7	-122
1955	204395	36927	167657	148329	19328	-18	2103	16493	767	-36	-153
1957	251607	51131	200841	162171	38670	2324	1973	33746	675	-202	-163
1960	317951	31163	286799	249764	37035	405	-144	36465	459	-73	63
1961	350405	29384	321233	288170	33063	77	-839	33339	636	-43	-169
1962	405256	35425	369809	319704	50105	1542	815	47285	557	-43	65
1963	467456	44620	422828	362859	59969	1920	1625	56036	570	-35	43
1964	532052	46104	485991	423287	62705	2891	3015	56348	572	59	-102
1965	591052	43172	546728	488969	57759	1422	3191	52863	221	1103	49
EUROPEAN ECONOMIC COMMUNITY (EEC)											
1925	28639	21404	7145	536	6609	2822	1179	1428	1181	-	90
1929	37106	24785	12200	843	11357	5385	1187	3237	1548	-	122
1933	28725	12006	16577	5007	11570	5604	761	4443	762	-	142
1937	29217	4947	24071	12855	11216	3450	470	6407	890	-	200
1938	30355	4094	26057	14946	11111	3605	323	6401	783	-	205
1950	31572	-5072	36360	38783	-2423	-489	8	-2325	384	68	216
1953	61917	4917	56849	73862	-17013	-5759	-1185	-10082	36	7	145
1955	92006	10850	81039	97871	-16832	-6405	-1535	-8858	68	-36	153
1957	130803	31170	99738	106653	-6915	-5232	-1475	-152	104	-202	98
1960	159401	13330	145641	158780	-13139	-7181	-1964	-3581	-129	-79	509
1961	183571	13140	169931	186668	-16737	-8450	-2198	-5763	-9	-43	543
1962	220081	17100	202625	208059	-5435	-7583	-2279	4694	20	-43	400
1963	268383	28900	238971	243995	-5024	-8159	-2427	5951	-11	-35	547
1964	310596	27905	282179	288750	-6572	-7868	-2357	4197	-93	-61	574
1965	349353	24529	323792	340091	-16299	-9441	-2562	-3063	-432	245	788
BELGIUM-LUXEMBOURG											
1925	8125	7630	495	12	483	233	128	32	92	-	-
1929	10925	10287	638	2	636	290	107	135	105	-	-
1933	3274	2666	611	74	537	347	45	96	50	-	-3
1937	4746	3488	1257	422	836	446	9	240	141	-	1
1938	1651	408	1242	462	780	438	8	218	117	-	1
1950	3787	358	3434	663	2771	975	47	1623	126	-12	8
1953	5327	233	5115	4400	716	401	21	213	108	-13	-7
1955	6926	-930	7875	7020	855	65	-116	656	143	-31	11
1957	13471	3870	9662	8138	1524	128	-141	1257	146	-43	-18
1960	16285	5020	11298	10292	1007	-159	-290	1155	90	-36	3
1961	18382	4790	13664	11757	1907	-8	-197	1718	101	-36	-35
1962	21420	5410	16086	12801	3285	-5	-201	3011	129	-31	-46
1963	27688	8410	19314	18228	1086	-740	-269	1647	126	-36	-
1964	30628	8350	22262	19926	2336	-524	-533	2904	138	-31	48
1965	33510	8460	24990	23201	1790	-798	-593	2804	83	-31	90
FRANCE											
1925	30137	27254	2850	153	2697	1485	366	353	494	-	33
1929	36345	31672	4613	263	4350	2591	321	1068	371	-	61
1933	31937	23553	8321	4199	4122	2768	81	1040	234	-	64

Table VII. NET ENERGY IMPORTS OR EXPORTS, SELECTED YEARS, 1925-1965

(Thousand metric tons coal equivalent; minus sign [-] = net exports)

Region, country, year	Total energy	Solid fuels	Liquid fuels		Refined petroleum products					Gas	Electricity
			Total	Crude oil	Total	Gasoline	Kerosine	Fuel oils	Lubes and greases		
	(1)	(2)	(3)	(4)	(5)	(6)	(7)	(8)	(9)	(10)	(11)
FRANCE (CONTINUED)											
1937	39683	28746	10866	9209	1658	782	-111	876	111	-	71
1938	32534	20881	11582	10452	1130	725	-143	459	89	-	71
1950	28479	11300	17138	21186	-4049	-836	-134	-3140	60	12	30
1953	35821	12100	23673	33002	-9329	-2132	-395	-6743	-60	49	-1
1955	40221	9800	30351	37221	-6870	-1266	-708	-4608	-183	79	-9
1957	56527	22050	34269	36096	-1827	-632	-545	-434	-113	174	34
1960	54591	13750	40734	46532	-5798	-1266	-924	-3188	-261	120	-13
1961	58624	13630	44862	52524	-7662	-1590	-1032	-4571	-258	120	12
1962	63051	13870	49149	55740	-6591	-1010	-900	-4220	-252	127	-94
1963	80361	20990	59162	64887	-5726	-1043	-1260	-2892	-300	139	71
1964	87564	18770	68420	73911	-5492	-1331	-996	-2489	-345	96	279
1965	94920	15838	78558	87834	-9276	-2081	-708	-5684	-309	402	122
GERMANY											
1925	-27965	-29639	1646	80	1566	650	219	285	413	-	29
1929	-32789	-36434	3618	135	3483	1587	224	800	873	-	28
1933	-22101	-25678	3521	422	3099	1496	146	1160	299	-	56
1937	-36729	-42404	5576	1098	4478	1569	72	2373	464	-	100
1938	-25175	-31729	6455	1167	5288	2027	33	2790	438	-	100
GERMANY, FEDERAL REPUBLIC											
1950	-24459	-28685	4133	2900	1233	360	5	857	12	-65	159
1953	-13222	-21093	7751	6840	911	-98	-51	1155	-96	-41	161
1955	-569	-14320	13709	10667	3042	-87	12	3099	77	-103	145
1957	6826	-13010	20156	12237	7919	500	48	7394	104	-353	34
1960	23002	-18710	41360	34853	6507	359	324	5960	125	-168	520
1961	30052	-18090	47741	44046	3695	-560	234	4203	138	-139	541
1962	45545	-17680	62993	49802	13191	185	-44	13139	216	-151	383
1963	56567	-17550	73965	60116	13850	168	-6	13830	134	-156	308
1964	75269	-14565	89846	76914	12932	564	171	12222	221	-132	120
1965	92738	-12729	105063	88571	16493	1089	347	15105	140	-127	530
ITALY											
1925	11587	10381	1178	56	1122	284	174	543	122	-	28
1929	16441	14505	1905	90	1815	578	243	881	114	-	31
1933	12051	9477	2552	203	2349	434	206	1623	87	-	22
1937	16544	12851	3669	1404	2265	291	111	1764	99	-	24
1938	15848	12081	3737	2216	1521	54	47	1364	57	-	31
1950	15052	8215	6812	6834	-23	-336	-161	330	144	-	25
1953	22743	9172	13577	19275	-5699	-1979	-686	-3098	63	-	-6
1955	29113	10330	18780	25502	-6722	-2435	-687	-3623	-30	-	3
1957	35335	11610	23667	29876	-6209	-2177	-491	-3627	30	-	58
1960	45276	10210	35082	42386	-7304	-2642	-486	-4269	59	-	-16
1961	51828	10150	41657	49412	-7755	-2520	-594	-4800	120	-	21
1962	62839	10860	51821	59829	-8009	-2625	-561	-4953	108	-	159
1963	72004	11470	60372	69429	-9057	-2540	-539	-6090	155	-	162
1964	81252	10675	70452	82851	-12399	-2561	-593	-9275	98	-	125
1965	90589	10590	79958	100934	-20976	-3591	-1133	-15977	-74	-	41

Table VII. NET ENERGY IMPORTS OR EXPORTS, SELECTED YEARS, 1925-1965

(Thousand metric tons coal equivalent; minus sign [-] = net exports)

Region, country, year	Total energy	Solid fuels	Liquid fuels: Total	Liquid fuels: Crude oil	Refined petroleum products: Total	Gasoline	Kerosine	Fuel oils	Lubes and greases	Gas	Electricity
	(1)	(2)	(3)	(4)	(5)	(6)	(7)	(8)	(9)	(10)	(11)
NETHERLANDS											
1925	6755	5778	977	236	741	171	293	216	62	-	-
1929	6184	4755	1427	354	1073	341	293	354	86	-	3
1933	3564	1988	1574	111	1463	561	284	525	93	-	3
1937	4972	2266	2703	723	1980	363	389	1154	75	-	3
1938	5497	2453	3042	650	2393	362	378	1571	83	-	2
1950	8713	3740	4845	7200	-2355	-653	251	-1995	42	133	-5
1953	11249	4505	6734	10346	-3612	-1952	-75	-1610	21	12	-2
1955	16316	5970	10325	17462	-7137	-2682	-36	-4382	62	19	3
1957	18644	6650	11985	20307	-8322	-3051	-347	-4742	-63	19	-10
1960	20248	3060	17168	24719	-7551	-3473	-588	-3239	-141	5	15
1961	24685	2660	22008	28929	-6921	-3773	-609	-2313	-110	12	5
1962	27226	4640	22577	29888	-7311	-4128	-573	-2283	-182	12	-3
1963	31763	5580	26159	31335	-5177	-4005	-354	-545	-125	19	6
1964	35883	4675	31200	35148	-3948	-4017	-407	834	-204	5	2
1965	37597	2370	35223	39552	-4329	-4061	-476	689	-272	-	4
EUROPEAN FREE TRADE ASSOCIATION (EFTA)											
1925	-26186	-35922	9821	3596	6225	2168	1026	2429	603	-	-85
1929	-26108	-39933	13967	3147	10820	4785	1679	3659	698	-	-141
1933	-5664	-22194	16689	2807	13883	6428	1331	5430	695	-	-159
1937	2877	-17758	20871	3519	17352	8219	1565	6770	800	-	-236
1938	7339	-14746	22323	3905	18419	9005	1578	7109	728	-	-238
1950	45372	6776	38756	14313	24443	8432	2783	12420	809	-	-160
1953	56921	5100	52085	38388	13697	4389	3023	5639	642	-	-263
1955	89176	19480	70002	44559	25443	4638	3062	17177	485	-	-306
1957	91567	13150	78654	45978	32676	6087	2933	23177	378	-	-238
1960	127133	10920	116678	73307	43371	7493	1493	33855	393	5	-470
1961	133689	9280	125102	82878	42224	8477	971	32151	456	-	-692
1962	146946	10380	136860	89579	47282	9212	2604	34947	326	-	-294
1963	157933	8100	150239	94119	56120	10071	3477	41933	443	-	-406
1964	175169	9470	166188	105683	60506	10713	4769	44328	410	120	-609
1965	190636	9847	180714	117500	63215	10848	5109	46275	455	858	-783
AUSTRIA											
1925	5241	5060	185	27	158	71	38	30	20	-	-4
1929	6746	6417	344	77	267	156	47	48	17	-	-15
1933	3478	3046	470	297	173	75	14	75	9	-	-38
1937	3758	3319	482	159	323	122	59	132	11	-	-43
1938	4221	3773	494	233	261	108	35	107	12	-	-46
1950	3574	5243	-1582	-1605	23	74	-	-63	12	-	-86
1953	841	4223	-3246	-3150	-96	2	-	-113	15	-	-136
1955	2900	4950	-1916	-2175	260	128	-23	125	30	-	-135
1957	3910	5610	-1545	-1686	141	222	-15	-105	38	-	-155
1960	5464	4950	752	-702	1454	455	-	947	41	-	-238
1961	5766	4520	1490	-348	1838	633	-	1145	50	-	-244
1962	6731	4790	2204	198	2006	792	11	1136	42	-	-262
1963	7731	5340	2603	423	2180	785	11	1331	44	-	-212
1964	8440	5120	3659	1182	2477	714	11	1788	-42	-	-339
1965	7384	4545	3323	992	2331	701	11	1650	-36	-	-484

Table VII. NET ENERGY IMPORTS OR EXPORTS, SELECTED YEARS, 1925-1965

(Thousand metric tons coal equivalent; minus sign [-] = net exports)

Region, country, year	Total energy	Solid fuels	Liquid fuels		Refined petroleum products					Gas	Electricity
			Total	Crude oil	Total	Gasoline	Kerosine	Fuel oils	Lubes and greases		
	(1)	(2)	(3)	(4)	(5)	(6)	(7)	(8)	(9)	(10)	(11)
DENMARK											
1925	4472	4022	447	2	446	147	146	120	33	-	3
1929	6146	5500	642	5	638	261	134	210	33	-	4
1933	5760	4902	857	-	857	329	135	354	39	-	2
1937	7085	6024	1059	-	1059	455	135	432	38	-	2
1938	6689	5396	1290	17	1274	504	176	554	41	-	3
1950	8460	5731	2706	51	2655	770	104	1724	59	-	23
1953	9269	6059	3173	32	3141	843	143	2102	54	-	37
1955	12177	7340	4851	45	4806	1040	200	3402	75	-	-14
1957	10332	4410	5874	45	5829	1173	198	4272	74	-	48
1960	13037	5260	7764	53	7712	1496	407	5601	90	-	13
1961	13737	4930	8697	356	8342	1644	476	5987	101	-	110
1962	15609	5260	10238	1884	8354	1554	474	6072	117	-	112
1963	17263	5300	11909	2985	8924	1287	596	6822	95	-	54
1964	18703	4760	13841	4560	9281	1323	578	7145	119	-	102
1965	19773	4190	15366	5514	9852	1299	612	7707	110	-	217
NORWAY											
1925	2279	1988	291	27	264	54	65	129	17	-	-
1929	3093	2677	416	35	381	116	57	192	17	-	-
1933	2976	2313	663	32	632	147	51	419	15	-	-
1937	4001	3176	825	26	800	249	59	474	18	-	-
1938	3531	2647	884	56	828	264	45	506	14	-	-
1950	3838	1696	2142	24	2118	386	57	1632	44	-	-
1953	4660	1384	3276	113	3164	479	117	2531	38	-	-
1955	5389	1130	4259	144	4115	504	167	3410	33	-	-
1957	5288	830	4458	174	4284	534	240	3467	42	-	-
1960	6316	820	5480	330	5150	686	300	4128	33	-	16
1961	6469	760	5708	2609	3099	395	302	2379	35	-	1
1962	6571	680	5927	3531	2396	474	252	1655	33	-	-36
1963	7223	800	6542	3803	2739	480	308	1929	35	-	-118
1964	7888	880	7182	4397	2786	315	314	2130	39	-	-174
1965	7456	750	6977	4233	2744	588	330	1883	-35	-	-270
PORTUGAL											
1925	1085	995	90	-	90	21	36	29	5	-	-
1929	1313	1146	167	-	167	60	53	54	-	-	-
1933	1321	1109	212	-	212	77	72	63	-	-	-
1937	1647	1357	290	-	290	110	78	84	18	-	-
1938	1445	1152	293	-	293	111	75	90	17	-	-
1950	1989	817	1172	398	774	96	80	581	18	-	-
1953	2267	578	1689	198	1491	192	182	1091	24	-	-
1955	2641	500	2141	1365	776	-15	62	696	32	-	-
1957	3037	560	2477	1662	815	27	42	710	36	-	-
1960	3153	390	2763	1952	812	-20	29	756	44	-	-
1961	3501	550	2951	1959	992	-12	-26	963	50	-	-
1962	3713	530	3183	2001	1182	30	18	1059	47	-	-
1963	3997	620	3384	2246	1139	18	-38	1067	50	-	-7
1964	4296	630	3668	2279	1389	59	9	1178	56	-	-2
1965	4802	620	4128	2558	1571	125	-93	1343	65	-	54

Table VII. NET ENERGY IMPORTS OR EXPORTS, SELECTED YEARS, 1925-1965

(Thousand metric tons coal equivalent; minus sign [-] = net exports)

Region, country, year	Total energy	Solid fuels	Liquid fuels: Total	Liquid fuels: Crude oil	Refined petroleum products: Total	Gasoline	Kerosine	Fuel oils	Lubes and greases	Gas	Electricity
	(1)	(2)	(3)	(4)	(5)	(6)	(7)	(8)	(9)	(10)	(11)
SWEDEN											
1925	4698	4256	444	-	444	206	92	95	53	-	-3
1929	6985	6275	714	-	714	375	98	177	65	-	-4
1933	7188	6060	1130	86	1044	492	122	369	62	-	-2
1937	10679	8962	1719	120	1599	726	153	638	83	-	-2
1938	9671	7733	1941	138	1803	813	162	738	90	-	-3
1950	12039	6603	5459	1355	4104	752	329	2930	95	-	-23
1953	13816	5543	8310	2132	6179	1169	555	4370	86	-	-37
1955	17647	5530	12102	2834	9269	1391	552	7209	128	-	15
1957	18909	4910	14048	2991	11057	1817	456	8666	131	-	-49
1960	23121	3570	19647	3969	15678	2282	536	12738	131	-	-96
1961	23013	3260	19878	3888	15990	2322	504	13043	120	-	-125
1962	25171	3240	22031	3690	18341	2798	564	14834	138	-	-100
1963	27086	3210	23870	4122	19748	2922	612	16083	126	-	6
1964	29951	3460	26517	5336	21182	3165	620	17235	159	-	-26
1965	30885	2960	28026	5588	22439	3440	608	18222	165	-	-101
SWITZERLAND											
1925	2842	2701	222	-	222	105	38	57	23	-	-81
1929	3728	3463	392	-	392	210	41	110	32	-	-126
1933	3633	3165	590	-	590	293	36	231	30	-	-122
1937	3889	3486	596	-	596	291	30	245	30	-	-193
1938	3758	3337	614	-	614	302	30	254	29	-	-192
1950	3975	2549	1500	-	1500	449	99	893	60	-	-74
1953	3930	2204	1853	-	1853	582	153	1074	42	-	-127
1955	5328	2610	2891	-	2891	812	62	1949	66	-	-173
1957	7131	3320	3893	-	3893	984	93	2730	81	-	-81
1960	8198	2600	5763	-	5763	1485	83	4097	89	-	-165
1961	8076	2260	6251	-	6251	1727	86	4335	101	-	-435
1962	9550	2330	7239	-	7239	2028	74	5033	104	-	-19
1963	12454	2820	9762	539	9224	1908	117	7067	119	-	-128
1964	11864	1980	10029	1257	8772	1925	126	6594	111	-	-146
1965	13076	1572	11711	1814	9897	1970	113	7688	108	-	-206
UNITED KINGDOM											
1925	-46802	-54944	8142	3540	4602	1565	614	1970	455	-	-
1929	-54118	-65411	11294	3032	8262	3608	1251	2868	536	-	-
1933	-30020	-42789	12770	2393	10377	5016	902	3920	540	-	-
1937	-28181	-44082	15902	3215	12687	6267	1052	4766	603	-	-
1938	-21975	-38784	16809	3462	13347	6903	1056	4862	527	-	-
1950	11497	-15863	27360	14091	13269	5907	2115	4725	522	-	-
1953	22140	-14891	37031	39065	-2034	1124	1874	-5415	384	-	-
1955	43095	-2580	45675	42347	3329	780	2043	387	122	-	-
1957	42961	-6490	49451	42792	6659	1331	1919	3438	-23	-	-
1960	67845	-6670	74510	67706	6804	1110	140	5589	-33	5	-
1961	73128	-7000	80129	74415	5714	1769	-371	4301	2	-	-1
1962	79601	-6450	86040	78275	7766	1536	1212	5160	-155	-	11
1963	82179	-9990	92171	80003	12168	2672	1872	7635	-24	-	-1
1964	94027	-7360	101294	86673	14621	3213	3113	8259	-32	120	-26
1965	107260	-4790	111185	96803	14382	2727	3530	7784	78	858	7

Table VII. NET ENERGY IMPORTS OR EXPORTS, SELECTED YEARS, 1925-1965

(Thousand metric tons coal equivalent; minus sign [-] = net exports)

Region, country, year	Total energy	Solid fuels	Liquid fuels		Refined petroleum products					Gas	Electricity
			Total	Crude oil	Total	Gasoline	Kerosine	Fuel oils	Lubes and greases		
	(1)	(2)	(3)	(4)	(5)	(6)	(7)	(8)	(9)	(10)	(11)
WESTERN EUROPE - OTHER											
1925	7670	6402	1268	54	1214	405	224	464	108	-	-
1929	10012	7945	2067	216	1851	771	255	702	123	-	-
1933	8308	5473	2835	411	2424	897	251	1193	84	-	-
1937	9997	6905	3092	329	2763	962	366	1316	120	-	-
1938	9548	6317	3231	390	2841	1005	360	1364	113	-	-
1950	16485	5829	10656	4958	5699	1572	401	3540	186	-	-
1953	19692	5800	13896	5421	8475	1700	497	6071	209	-	-4
1955	23214	6597	16616	5900	10716	1749	576	8174	215	-	1
1957	29238	6811	22449	9540	12909	1469	515	10721	194	-	-23
1960	31417	6913	24480	17678	6803	93	327	6191	195	-	24
1961	33144	6964	26201	18624	7577	50	389	6951	189	-	-20
1962	38228	7945	30324	22067	8258	-87	489	7644	212	-	-41
1963	41140	7620	33618	24746	8873	8	575	8153	138	-	-98
1964	46287	8729	37625	28854	8771	45	603	7823	255	-	-67
1965	51062	8796	42222	31379	10844	15	644	9651	198	-	44
FINLAND											
1925	726	612	114	14	101	44	44	-	14	-	-
1929	1364	1170	194	20	174	102	54	-	18	-	-
1933	1317	1138	179	21	158	90	54	-	14	-	-
1937	2570	2235	335	41	294	176	98	-	21	-	-
1938	2156	1784	372	48	324	206	98	-	21	-	-
1950	2663	1929	734	-	734	366	101	237	30	-	-
1953	3059	1980	1080	-	1080	456	108	498	18	-	-1
1955	4295	2630	1665	-	1665	539	113	980	35	-	-
1957	5862	3040	2822	324	2498	524	90	1842	44	-	-
1960	7228	3140	4035	1706	2330	69	48	2162	56	-	53
1961	7478	3000	4457	2075	2382	51	41	2225	69	-	22
1962	8197	2940	5247	2268	2979	27	38	2840	75	-	10
1963	8916	2470	6404	3345	3059	30	41	2916	72	-	42
1964	10635	3190	7358	3870	3488	20	35	3342	90	-	87
1965	11849	3235	8543	4050	4493	30	39	4326	98	-	71
GREECE											
1925	759	663	96	-	96	36	21	32	8	-	-
1929	1035	814	221	-	221	69	44	96	12	-	-
1933	913	638	275	-	275	69	29	168	9	-	-
1937	1454	969	485	-	485	96	29	341	20	-	-
1938	1493	975	518	-	518	107	32	365	15	-	-
1950	1931	302	1629	-	1629	342	111	1152	24	-	-
1953	2158	277	1881	-	1881	374	131	1350	27	-	-
1955	2587	320	2267	-	2267	455	143	1641	29	-	-
1957	2716	280	2436	-	2436	357	159	1884	26	-	-
1960	3819	230	3588	2598	990	21	6	921	30	-	1
1961	4193	230	3965	2760	1205	21	2	1140	33	-	-2
1962	4654	210	4445	2730	1715	41	83	1559	36	-	-
1963	5363	270	5094	2765	2330	89	128	2082	41	-	-1
1964	5274	290	4986	2823	2163	129	164	1829	48	-	-2
1965	6585	410	6173	2745	3428	174	188	3009	57	-	3

Table VII. NET ENERGY IMPORTS OR EXPORTS, SELECTED YEARS, 1925-1965

(Thousand metric tons coal equivalent; minus sign [-] = net exports)

Region, country, year	Total energy	Solid fuels	Liquid fuels: Total	Liquid fuels: Crude oil	Refined petroleum products: Total	Gasoline	Kerosine	Fuel oils	Lubes and greases	Gas	Electricity
	(1)	(2)	(3)	(4)	(5)	(6)	(7)	(8)	(9)	(10)	(11)
ICELAND											
1925	14	-	14	-	14	-	-	-	-	-	-
1929	23	-	23	-	23	5	8	11	-	-	-
1933	21	-	21	-	21	15	5	-	2	-	-
1937	29	-	29	-	29	23	5	-	2	-	-
1938	30	-	30	-	30	9	3	17	2	-	-
1950	468	96	372	-	372	63	5	300	5	-	-
1953	621	49	572	-	572	81	5	480	6	-	-
1955	581	60	521	-	521	86	3	426	6	-	-
1957	630	30	600	-	600	95	3	497	6	-	-
1960	719	20	699	-	699	84	14	596	6	-	-
1961	661	20	641	-	641	75	12	548	6	-	-
1962	700	20	680	-	680	86	6	581	8	-	-
1963	645	10	635	-	635	93	12	524	6	-	-
1964	645	10	635	-	635	87	14	528	6	-	-
1965	712	10	702	-	702	96	27	572	8	-	-
IRELAND											
1925	2463	2284	179	2	177	78	69	17	14	-	-
1929	2745	2497	248	-	248	131	65	38	15	-	-
1933	2582	2298	284	-	284	162	77	32	14	-	-
1937	2985	2620	365	-	365	191	99	59	17	-	-
1938	2916	2539	377	-	377	203	93	65	17	-	-
1950	2890	1994	896	-	896	375	117	383	21	-	-
1953	2918	1758	1160	-	1160	480	164	492	24	-	-
1955	3620	1940	1680	-	1680	557	188	903	30	-	-
1957	2908	1250	1658	-	1658	528	171	926	23	-	-
1960	3640	1660	1980	2147	-167	102	204	-512	29	-	-
1961	4005	1750	2255	2183	72	83	276	-323	35	-	-
1962	4068	1480	2588	2273	315	66	275	-65	35	-	-
1963	4357	1420	2937	2448	489	35	285	132	35	-	-
1964	4543	1280	3263	2618	645	65	324	209	42	-	-
1965	4930	1250	3680	3047	633	33	323	231	36	-	-
SPAIN											
1925	2826	2125	701	23	678	213	32	377	57	-	-
1929	3846	2700	1146	42	1104	455	32	551	68	-	-
1933	2895	1057	1838	245	1593	536	35	981	42	-	-
1937	2206	566	1640	150	1490	459	92	885	54	-	-
1938	2063	428	1635	150	1485	459	92	885	50	-	-
1950	6616	965	5651	4350	1301	300	33	891	NA	-	-
1953	8852	1115	7737	4740	2997	150	36	2706	105	-	-
1955	9621	550	9063	5175	3888	-9	63	3728	107	-	8
1957	13497	490	13011	8243	4769	-83	-5	4782	74	-	-4
1960	13105	300	12824	10575	2249	-233	-62	2502	NA	-	-19
1961	14448	410	14069	11445	2624	-227	-48	2883	NA	-	-31
1962	18259	1800	16491	14517	1974	-344	-14	2274	NA	-	-32
1963	19109	1890	17322	15704	1619	-306	-14	1919	NA	-	-103
1964	21431	1890	19736	18878	858	-288	-59	1109	NA	-	-195
1965	22743	1710	21113	20094	1019	-336	-26	1035	20	-	-79

Table VII. NET ENERGY IMPORTS OR EXPORTS, SELECTED YEARS, 1925-1965

(Thousand metric tons coal equivalent; minus sign [-] = net exports)

Region, country, year	Total energy	Solid fuels	Liquid fuels: Total	Liquid fuels: Crude oil	Refined petroleum products: Total	Gasoline	Kerosine	Fuel oils	Lubes and greases	Gas	Electricity
	(1)	(2)	(3)	(4)	(5)	(6)	(7)	(8)	(9)	(10)	(11)
YUGOSLAVIA											
1925	591	463	128	17	111	20	59	17	17	-	-
1929	790	583	207	155	53	8	32	3	11	-	-
1933	447	265	182	146	36	8	21	3	5	-	-
1937	539	369	170	138	32	2	20	3	8	-	-
1938	692	464	228	192	36	8	14	6	9	-	-
1950	978	298	680	608	72	78	-	-35	29	-	-
1953	1273	554	723	681	42	80	-	-65	27	-	-4
1955	1744	1030	720	725	-5	50	-3	-59	8	-	-6
1957	2523	1670	872	974	-102	-36	-11	-69	21	-	-19
1960	2335	1550	797	653	144	-11	11	137	17	-	-11
1961	1805	1540	275	162	113	-8	15	89	21	-	-10
1962	1766	1490	296	279	17	-14	8	32	-8	-	-20
1963	2070	1550	557	485	72	-	5	105	-38	-	-37
1964	3036	2060	933	666	267	-27	9	279	8	-	43
1965	3558	2175	1334	1443	-110	-44	-11	-27	-24	-	49
OCEANIA											
1925	1156	-218	1374	305	1070	668	189	140	74	-	-
1929	3202	530	2672	678	1994	1433	252	183	126	-	-
1933	2413	-82	2495	372	2123	1208	210	611	95	-	-
1937	3823	-86	3909	426	3483	1991	339	1017	137	-	-
1938	4159	-94	4253	380	3873	2198	329	1226	120	-	-
1950	9494	581	8913	1196	7718	3515	704	3257	243	-	-
1953	9601	-229	9830	1350	8480	4268	740	3330	143	-	-
1955	14605	32	14573	7335	7238	3749	869	2294	327	-	-
1957	15882	-560	16442	12975	3467	2073	693	380	321	-	-
1960	18209	-1438	19647	16898	2750	2466	644	-782	420	-	-
1961	18372	-2727	21099	18608	2492	2216	582	-735	428	-	-
1962	18736	-2875	21611	19401	2210	2544	683	-1398	380	-	-
1963	21526	-3097	24623	22292	2331	2679	575	-1427	503	-	-
1964	22459	-4696	27155	24239	2916	2564	500	-440	291	-	-
1965	23058	-7017	30075	28023	2052	1713	677	-546	206	-	-
AUSTRALIA											
1925	119	-897	1016	305	711	497	158	-2	59	-	-
1929	2356	250	2106	678	1428	1107	212	5	105	-	-
1933	1685	-294	1979	372	1607	920	183	426	78	-	-
1937	2736	-377	3113	426	2687	1542	324	713	108	-	-
1938	2857	-365	3222	380	2843	1664	312	770	98	-	-
1950	7660	451	7209	1196	6014	2757	654	2409	194	-	-
1953	7567	-383	7950	1350	6600	3194	695	2610	102	-	-
1955	11947	-230	12177	7335	4842	2508	806	1266	263	-	-
1957	12727	-920	13647	12975	672	642	608	-837	260	-	-
1960	14902	-1690	16592	16898	-306	921	474	-2001	300	-	-
1961	14789	-2980	17769	18608	-839	552	375	-2073	308	-	-
1962	15205	-3040	18245	19401	-1157	924	474	-2828	273	-	-
1963	17569	-3280	20849	22292	-1443	909	350	-3038	336	-	-
1964	17782	-4990	22772	22671	101	1113	246	-1463	204	-	-
1965	17878	-7325	25203	24450	753	1193	356	-899	104	-	-

Table VII. NET ENERGY IMPORTS OR EXPORTS, SELECTED YEARS, 1925-1965

(Thousand metric tons coal equivalent; minus sign [-] = net exports)

Region, country, year	Total energy	Solid fuels	Liquid fuels							Gas	Electricity
					Refined petroleum products						
			Total	Crude oil	Total	Gasoline	Kerosine	Fuel oils	Lubes and greases		
	(1)	(2)	(3)	(4)	(5)	(6)	(7)	(8)	(9)	(10)	(11)
NEW ZEALAND											
1925	917	566	351	-	351	167	29	141	15	-	-
1929	715	166	549	-	549	312	39	179	20	-	-
1933	600	102	498	-	498	278	26	180	15	-	-
1937	871	119	752	-	752	428	9	290	26	-	-
1938	1077	99	978	-	978	512	11	437	20	-	-
1950	1664	45	1619	-	1619	723	44	806	47	-	-
1953	1717	1	1716	-	1716	998	30	660	29	-	-
1955	2167	10	2157	-	2157	1148	44	917	50	-	-
1957	2505	10	2495	-	2495	1308	60	1073	54	-	-
1960	2598	-20	2618	-	2618	1410	99	1038	71	-	-
1961	2814	-	2814	-	2814	1532	116	1100	68	-	-
1962	2901	10	2891	-	2891	1482	129	1206	74	-	-
1963	3185	-	3185	-	3185	1622	140	1361	63	-	-
1964	3635	-	3635	1568	2067	1275	146	584	63	-	-
1965	4094	-	4094	3573	521	351	185	-87	72	-	-
USSR AND COMMUNIST EASTERN EUROPE											
1925	-11538	-8413	-3134	32	-3165	-872	-1155	-1028	-302	-	9
1929	-22574	-13719	-8864	-5	-8859	-2810	-2262	-3653	-431	-	9
1933	-25350	-10919	-14433	-737	-13697	-4619	-2219	-6732	-491	-	2
1937	-21976	-12766	-9212	-171	-9041	-3147	-1661	-4155	-363	-	2
1938	-17863	-10853	-7010	-374	-6636	-2580	-1416	-2628	-255	-	-
1950	-11548	-12529	968	2378	-1410	-1448	-585	22	-	41	-27
1953	-13995	-9706	-4317	1563	-5880	-2475	-1148	-1508	-	28	-
1955	-22311	-13320	-9039	200	-9239	-2355	-1053	-5750	-65	29	19
1957	-28374	-13090	-15344	-1746	-13598	-2411	-1604	-9389	-191	60	-
1960	-59416	-18930	-40542	-16085	-24458	-3143	-1560	-19080	-647	36	20
1961	-71144	-19900	-51279	-23532	-27747	-3936	-1565	-21512	-707	36	-1
1962	-77612	-22230	-55448	-25874	-29574	-3380	-1925	-23439	-812	7	59
1963	-82755	-22280	-60558	-28523	-32036	-3533	-1670	-26148	-675	24	59
1964	-88097	-23190	-64934	-33077	-31857	-3027	-1134	-27009	-686	37	-11
1965	-95675	-22631	-73022	-37374	-35648	-3072	-1448	-30458	-651	-17	-5
COMMUNIST EASTERN EUROPE											
1925	-9902	-8738	-1173	113	-1286	-465	-534	-317	-161	-	9
1929	-16689	-13477	-3221	438	-3659	-1193	-1154	-1491	-117	-	9
1933	-17123	-9899	-7226	57	-7283	-2693	-1451	-3381	-122	-	2
1937	-19208	-12523	-6687	-6	-6681	-2781	-1391	-2747	-48	-	2
1938	-16859	-11577	-5282	-51	-5231	-2361	-1209	-1868	-36	-	-
1950	-22714	-21329	-1432	578	-2010	-1448	-585	22	-	75	-27
1953	-18319	-15206	-3267	1863	-5130	-2475	-1148	-1508	-	155	-
1955	-21389	-16620	-5003	2211	-7214	-3230	-915	-3053	-	216	18
1957	-6847	-6100	-1035	5142	-6177	-2888	-683	-2585	-18	288	-
1960	-6338	-9600	2879	8904	-6026	-2177	-378	-3182	-261	360	24
1961	-1822	-7390	5165	10218	-5054	-1223	-360	-3152	-291	396	8
1962	3555	-5370	8429	12801	-4373	-1019	-348	-2658	-329	409	88
1963	9708	-3190	12320	16028	-3708	-822	-72	-2489	-315	426	152
1964	15820	-1660	16901	21960	-5060	-986	-26	-3572	-476	428	152
1965	17158	-4226	20697	27774	-7077	-1374	47	-5268	-462	505	182

Table VII. NET ENERGY IMPORTS OR EXPORTS, SELECTED YEARS, 1925-1965

(Thousand metric tons coal equivalent; minus sign [-] = net exports)

Region, country, year	Total energy	Solid fuels	Liquid fuels							Gas	Electricity
					Refined petroleum products						
			Total	Crude oil	Total	Gasoline	Kerosine	Fuel oils	Lubes and greases		
	(1)	(2)	(3)	(4)	(5)	(6)	(7)	(8)	(9)	(10)	(11)
ALBANIA											
1925	8	-	8	5	3	2	-	2	-	-	-
1929	11	-	11	5	6	5	-	2	-	-	-
1933	12	-	12	3	9	6	-	3	-	-	-
1937	-77	-	-77	-86	9	5	-	5	-	-	-
1938	-140	4	-144	-155	11	5	-	6	-	-	-
1950	-50	10	-60	-90	30	23	-	8	-	-	-
1953	-55	20	-75	-105	30	23	-	8	-	-	-
1955	-175	-20	-155	-186	32	26	-	6	-	-	-
1957	-308	-	-308	-327	20	15	3	2	-	-	-
1960	-469	10	-479	-494	15	8	5	3	-	-	-
1961	-410	10	-420	-437	17	8	5	5	-	-	-
1962	-361	20	-381	-410	29	18	6	5	-	-	-
1963	-449	10	-459	-465	6	15	6	-15	-	-	-
1964	-385	10	-395	-441	47	20	6	21	-	-	-
1965	-527	15	-542	-563	21	17	5	-	-	-	-
BULGARIA											
1925	81	16	65	-	65	6	39	14	6	-	-
1929	124	-2	126	-	126	17	50	48	12	-	-
1933	103	4	99	-	99	11	38	45	6	-	-
1937	131	-	131	29	102	15	45	30	12	-	-
1938	120	-12	132	44	89	17	32	29	12	-	-
1950	360	NA	360	30	330	90	60	180	-	-	-
1953	502	NA	502	30	472	128	90	255	-	-	-
1955	430	100	330	-174	504	158	71	276	-	-	-
1957	321	-50	371	-303	674	294	87	293	-	-	-
1960	1444	260	1184	-102	1286	503	30	753	-	-	-
1961	2307	750	1557	-156	1713	588	30	1095	-	-	-
1962	3449	1180	2261	-152	2412	645	29	1739	-	-	9
1963	4568	1520	3038	557	2481	645	27	1809	-	-	10
1964	6860	2300	4563	2655	1908	336	15	1557	-	-	-3
1965	8008	2838	5171	3294	1877	236	17	1625	-	-	-
CZECHOSLOVAKIA											
1925	-1517	-1789	270	80	191	NA	NA	NA	NA	NA	NA
1929	-1373	-1905	530	234	296	NA	NA	NA	NA	NA	NA
1933	-801	-1318	515	152	363	NA	NA	NA	NA	NA	NA
1937	-2275	-2964	687	402	285	NA	NA	NA	NA	NA	NA
1938	-1487	-2032	545	302	243	NA	NA	NA	NA	NA	NA
1950	1727	770	945	195	750	53	210	488	-	-	13
1953	2752	1420	1328	570	757	53	210	495	-	-	5
1955	3320	1850	1487	668	819	96	224	504	-	-	-16
1957	1695	-460	2184	1832	353	105	150	98	-	-	-29
1960	2434	-1320	3788	3383	405	114	318	-18	-	-	-34
1961	3920	-660	4628	4178	450	78	330	50	-	-5	-42
1962	5643	-150	5790	5513	278	29	366	-104	-	-5	8
1963	6581	260	6309	6326	-17	-42	407	-374	-	-5	18
1964	8603	755	7766	7755	11	-36	362	-305	-	-5	88
1965	9482	641	8751	9144	-393	9	365	-744	-	-5	95

Table VII. NET ENERGY IMPORTS OR EXPORTS, SELECTED YEARS, 1925-1965

(Thousand metric tons coal equivalent; minus sign [-] = net exports)

Region, country, year	Total energy	Solid fuels	Liquid fuels		Refined petroleum products					Gas	Electricity
			Total	Crude oil	Total	Gasoline	Kerosine	Fuel oils	Lubes and greases		
	(1)	(2)	(3)	(4)	(5)	(6)	(7)	(8)	(9)	(10)	(11)
GERMANY, EAST											
1950	5489	5341	150	75	75	23	-	53	-	48	-50
1953	7812	7410	375	600	-225	-113	-	-113	-	48	-21
1955	6587	6390	150	972	-822	-383	-2	-432	-	48	-1
1957	6721	6140	551	1496	-945	-465	-	-480	-	72	-41
1960	9971	7640	2306	2912	-606	-246	222	-566	-	72	-46
1961	10823	8040	2777	3405	-629	-291	159	-480	-	53	-47
1962	12024	8770	3222	3887	-665	-417	75	-317	-	43	-11
1963	12852	8740	4082	4745	-663	-420	60	-297	-	31	-
1964	15696	10380	5279	6390	-1112	-498	30	-644	-	19	18
1965	16106	9990	6093	7698	-1605	-696	-	-909	-	12	12
HUNGARY											
1925	825	726	99	29	71	23	33	8	8	-	-
1929	1861	1553	308	204	104	47	32	14	12	-	-
1933	426	163	263	258	5	-	-	2	3	-	-
1937	830	410	420	357	63	3	-	53	8	-	-
1938	649	334	315	261	54	2	-	42	11	-	-
1950	685	610	75	75	-	23	-15	-8	NA	-	-
1953	1556	1390	150	150	-	30	-23	-8	NA	-	16
1955	1678	1650	-3	114	-117	-6	-23	-89	NA	-	31
1957	4900	3340	1521	1500	21	-62	-23	123	-18	-	39
1960	4490	2640	1536	2135	-599	-135	-	-444	-20	246	68
1961	5004	2970	1701	2118	-417	-59	-15	-324	-20	270	62
1962	4959	2820	1799	2310	-512	-83	-	-408	-21	270	70
1963	6729	3720	2618	2742	-125	12	-	-116	-21	276	116
1964	8036	4585	3017	3039	-23	-2	-	-	-21	300	135
1965	7543	3930	3188	3377	-189	-63	-	-105	-21	264	162
POLAND											
1925	-8339	-7903	-443	-	-443	-98	-111	-120	-114	-	6
1929	-13584	-13328	-263	-	-263	-57	-75	-77	-54	-	6
1933	-9041	-8809	-231	-	-231	-75	-68	-42	-47	-	-1
1937	-10163	-10046	-117	-	-117	-62	-14	-23	-20	-	-
1938	-9973	-9961	-12	-	-12	-8	-	-3	-2	-	-
1950	-27546	-28280	697	293	405	143	60	203	-	27	10
1953	-24516	-25976	1353	618	735	255	75	405	-	107	-
1955	-25136	-27260	1949	818	1131	480	75	582	NA	168	8
1957	-13070	-15840	2522	945	1577	825	75	681	NA	216	33
1960	-16140	-19840	3348	1071	2277	1280	62	864	75	312	40
1961	-15038	-19370	3945	1110	2835	1569	57	1112	98	348	39
1962	-14592	-19410	4431	1653	2778	1596	80	1101	NA	372	15
1963	-13191	-18940	5345	2124	3221	1658	57	1385	119	396	9
1964	-15070	-21180	5807	2562	3245	1677	69	1490	NA	390	-86
1965	-16241	-23185	6491	4824	1667	1290	81	293	NA	498	-45
ROMANIA											
1925	-960	212	-1172	-	-1172	-398	-495	-219	-60	-	-
1929	-3727	205	-3932	-5	-3927	-1203	-1160	-1478	-87	-	-
1933	-7822	61	-7883	-356	-7527	-2634	-1421	-3389	-84	-	-
1937	-7654	77	-7731	-708	-7023	-2742	-1422	-2811	-48	-	-
1938	-6027	90	-6117	-503	-5615	-2376	-1241	-1941	-57	-	-
1950	-3380	220	-3600	-	-3600	-1800	-900	-900	NA	-	-

Table VII. NET ENERGY IMPORTS OR EXPORTS, SELECTED YEARS, 1925-1965

(Thousand metric tons coal equivalent; minus sign [-] = net exports)

Region, country, year	Total energy	Solid fuels	Liquid fuels: Total	Crude oil	Refined petroleum products: Total	Gasoline	Kerosine	Fuel oils	Lubes and greases	Gas	Electricity
	(1)	(2)	(3)	(4)	(5)	(6)	(7)	(8)	(9)	(10)	(11)
ROMANIA (CONTINUED)											
1953	-6370	530	-6900	-	-6900	-2850	-1500	-2550	NA	-	-
1955	-8094	670	-8760	-	-8760	-3600	-1260	-3900	NA	-	-4
1957	-7106	770	-7875	-	-7875	-3600	-975	-3300	NA	-	-1
1960	-8068	1010	-8804	-	-8804	-3699	-1014	-3774	-317	-270	-4
1961	-8428	870	-9023	-	-9023	-3116	-926	-4608	-369	-270	-5
1962	-7567	1400	-8693	-	-8693	-2807	-903	-4674	-308	-270	-4
1963	-7382	1500	-8612	-	-8612	-2690	-629	-4881	-413	-270	-1
1964	-7920	1490	-9135	-	-9135	-2483	-507	-5691	-455	-276	1
1965	-7214	1545	-8454	-	-8454	-2166	-420	-5427	-441	-264	-41
USSR (INCLUDING ESTONIA, LATVIA, LITHUANIA)											
1925	-1636	325	-1961	-81	-1880	-407	-621	-711	-141	-	-
1929	-5885	-242	-5643	-443	-5201	-1617	-1109	-2162	-314	-	-
1933	-8228	-1020	-7208	-794	-6414	-1926	-768	-3351	-369	-	-
1937	-2768	-243	-2525	-165	-2360	-366	-270	-1409	-315	-	-
1938	-1004	724	-1728	-323	-1406	-219	-207	-761	-219	-	-
1950	11167	8800	2400	1800	600	NA	NA	NA	NA	-33	-
1953	4323	5500	-1050	-300	-750	NA	NA	NA	NA	-127	-
1955	-922	3300	-4037	-2012	-2025	875	-138	-2697	-65	-186	1
1957	-21526	-6990	-14309	-6888	-7421	477	-921	-6804	-173	-228	-
1960	-53078	-9330	-43421	-24989	-18432	-966	-1182	-15899	-386	-324	-4
1961	-69322	-12510	-56444	-33750	-22694	-2714	-1205	-18360	-416	-360	-9
1962	-81167	-16860	-63876	-38675	-25202	-2361	-1577	-20781	-483	-402	-29
1963	-92463	-19090	-72878	-44550	-28328	-2711	-1598	-23660	-360	-402	-93
1964	-103917	-21530	-81834	-55037	-26798	-2042	-1109	-23438	-210	-390	-163
1965	-112833	-18405	-93719	-65148	-28571	-1698	-1494	-25190	-189	-522	-188
COMMUNIST ASIA											
1925	1613	201	1412	-	1412	38	1191	146	38	-	-
1929	386	-1221	1607	-	1607	120	1103	311	74	-	-
1933	-988	-2638	1650	-77	1727	180	914	552	81	-	-
1937	-2811	-4420	1610	144	1466	303	650	420	93	-	-
1938	-1975	-3052	1077	113	965	209	413	281	63	-	-
1950	NA	NA	NA	NA	NA	NA	NA	NA	NA	NA	NA
1953	NA	NA	NA	NA	NA	NA	NA	NA	NA	NA	NA
1955	1043	-1020	2063	600	1463	390	480	593	NA	NA	NA
1957	1704	-1740	3444	638	2807	1254	668	885	NA	NA	NA
1960	4435	-920	5355	915	4440	2160	750	1530	NA	NA	NA
1961	3950	-1120	5070	120	4950	2438	840	1673	NA	NA	NA
1962	2523	-1220	3743	210	3533	1673	788	1073	NA	NA	NA
1963	1953	-1430	3383	225	3158	1388	795	975	NA	NA	NA
1964	963	-1220	2183	300	1883	968	330	585	NA	NA	NA
1965	-70	-1615	1545	315	1230	593	120	518	NA	NA	NA
LATIN AMERICA											
1925	-10903	7223	-18129	-13478	-4652	-437	144	-4412	53	3	-
1929	-21607	7531	-29144	-17450	-11694	-1209	66	-10431	-120	5	-
1933	-22832	4630	-27543	-12282	-15261	-3905	-348	-10880	-129	79	3
1937	-31175	6090	-37449	-11813	-25637	-4617	-419	-20198	-404	181	2
1938	-31530	5439	-37037	-10664	-26373	-3980	-465	-21575	-354	65	2
1950	-86410	2790	-90087	-38078	-52010	-5649	-2558	-44168	177	871	16
1953	-100666	2373	-103779	-41369	-62411	-3783	-4101	-54497	-210	719	27

Table VII. NET ENERGY IMPORTS OR EXPORTS, SELECTED YEARS, 1925-1965

(Thousand metric tons coal equivalent; minus sign [-] = net exports)

Region, country, year	Total energy	Solid fuels	Liquid fuels: Total	Liquid fuels: Crude oil	Refined petroleum products: Total	Gasoline	Kerosine	Fuel oils	Lubes and greases	Gas	Electricity
	(1)	(2)	(3)	(4)	(5)	(6)	(7)	(8)	(9)	(10)	(11)
LATIN AMERICA (CONTINUED)											
1955	-117079	2740	-120585	-58325	-62261	-2973	-4304	-55001	-368	745	21
1957	-149517	2760	-152094	-84614	-67481	-3507	-5741	-58349	-309	-234	51
1960	-162561	3020	-164078	-73713	-90365	-6864	-6212	-77033	-629	-1560	56
1961	-167054	2520	-167873	-70512	-97361	-7124	-6818	-83367	-515	-1758	57
1962	-187056	1980	-187560	-75761	-111800	-8133	-7625	-95750	-762	-1542	66
1963	-193346	2304	-194225	-74064	-120161	-9795	-7491	-102849	-623	-1500	74
1964	-199008	2477	-199889	-74898	-124991	-9857	-9081	-105713	-938	-1614	18
1965	-200855	2560	-201761	-68807	-132954	-11811	-10123	-110733	-1173	-1662	8
LATIN AMERICA - CARIBBEAN											
1925	-18946	1411	-20360	-13908	-6452	-926	-152	-5297	-78	3	-
1929	-31260	1421	-32687	-17903	-14784	-1910	-251	-12318	-306	5	-
1933	-27929	617	-28628	-11075	-17553	-3987	-501	-12849	-216	79	3
1937	-39290	779	-40253	-11171	-29082	-4946	-516	-23109	-512	181	2
1938	-40227	661	-40956	-10655	-30302	-4308	-491	-25035	-468	65	2
1950	-104896	117	-105900	-42326	-63575	-8516	-2937	-52182	-128	871	16
1953	-123204	145	-124089	-47781	-76308	-8012	-4817	-63026	-635	719	27
1955	-147542	200	-148508	-70674	-77834	-5180	-5573	-66590	-831	745	21
1957	-182856	240	-182913	-102401	-80513	-4947	-6555	-68625	-773	-234	51
1960	-192336	110	-190943	-88694	-102249	-8522	-7137	-85581	-1155	-1560	56
1961	-193932	120	-192351	-85343	-107009	-8763	-7958	-89501	-936	-1758	57
1962	-213398	240	-212162	-94475	-117687	-9077	-8586	-98844	-1386	-1542	66
1963	-218693	284	-217551	-92822	-124730	-10893	-8046	-104892	-1143	-1500	74
1964	-227957	357	-226718	-96236	-130482	-10613	-9635	-108935	-1511	-1614	18
1965	-232057	425	-230828	-92972	-137856	-12499	-10744	-113277	-1698	-1662	8
CARIBBEAN - OIL PRODUCING											
1925	-24045	137	-24185	-14151	-10034	-1028	-216	-8703	-87	3	-
1929	-36511	174	-36690	-18308	-18383	-2264	-314	-15489	-317	5	-
1933	-30946	78	-31106	-11166	-19940	-4149	-554	-15003	-234	79	3
1937	-43284	89	-43557	-11459	-32099	-5241	-585	-25730	-543	181	2
1938	-43811	86	-43965	-10893	-33072	-4619	-561	-27402	-491	65	2
1950	-112144	56	-113087	-43050	-70037	-9662	-3059	-57116	-201	870	16
1953	-131711	57	-132515	-48747	-83768	-9597	-4994	-68456	-722	719	27
1955	-157793	60	-158619	-71706	-86913	-7272	-5937	-73041	-966	745	21
1957	-196617	60	-196494	-108456	-88038	-6768	-6894	-73808	-902	-234	51
1960	-208857	50	-207404	-99312	-108092	-9149	-7719	-90077	-1233	-1560	56
1961	-212351	70	-210720	-95532	-115188	-9003	-8598	-96651	-1017	-1758	57
1962	-235044	180	-233748	-108194	-125555	-9467	-9200	-105566	-1466	-1542	66
1963	-241693	190	-240458	-109683	-130775	-10668	-8718	-110331	-1230	-1500	74
1964	-254158	238	-252800	-115521	-137279	-10188	-10254	-115377	-1599	-1614	18
1965	-259435	293	-258074	-114122	-143952	-11709	-11404	-119337	-1794	-1662	8
ANTILLES, NETHERLANDS											
1925	660	NA	660	1988	-1328	-161	-8	-1074	-86	-	-
1929	1866	-	1866	17723	-15857	-1814	-30	-13760	-254	-	-
1933	3110	NA	3107	19125	-16019	-3327	-428	-12090	-174	-	-
1937	5436	3	5433	31769	-26336	-3968	-429	-21447	-492	-	-
1938	6086	NA	6083	34061	-27978	-3677	-519	-23277	-506	-	-
1950	10475	-	10475	64155	-53681	-7880	-2094	-43350	-357	-	-
1953	8358	-	8358	63960	-55602	-7031	-3332	-44475	-765	-	-

Table VII. NET ENERGY IMPORTS OR EXPORTS, SELECTED YEARS, 1925-1965

(Thousand metric tons coal equivalent; minus sign [-] = net exports)

Region, country, year	Total energy	Solid fuels	Liquid fuels							Gas	Electricity
					Refined petroleum products						
			Total	Crude oil	Total	Gasoline	Kerosine	Fuel oils	Lubes and greases		
	(1)	(2)	(3)	(4)	(5)	(6)	(7)	(8)	(9)	(10)	(11)
ANTILLES, NETHERLANDS (CONTINUED)											
1955	11430	-	11430	63257	-51827	-4880	-4194	-41883	-965	-	-
1957	12755	-	12755	60533	-47778	-3411	-4517	-39054	-914	-	-
1960	11658	-	11658	56832	-45174	-4680	-4511	-35006	-1059	-	-
1961	13013	-	13013	59115	-46103	-4002	-4701	-36608	-860	-	-
1962	12257	-	12257	59868	-47612	-4529	-4589	-37376	-1215	-	-
1963	11999	-	11999	58905	-46907	-4641	-4865	-36587	-914	-	-
1964	11526	-	11526	60522	-48996	-5190	-5456	-37211	-1230	-	-
1965	10818	-	10818	60654	-49836	-5372	-5321	-37842	-1416	-	-
COLOMBIA											
1925	17	3	14	-	14	11	-	-	3	-	-
1929	-3730	1	-3731	-3801	71	42	2	21	6	-	-
1933	-2508	2	-2510	-2543	33	15	-	15	3	-	-
1937	-3784	1	-3785	-3819	35	9	-	21	5	-	-
1938	-3938	-	-3938	-3972	35	11	-	20	5	-	-
1950	-5856	-	-5856	-6155	299	236	-	62	2	-	-
1953	-6152	-	-6152	-6911	759	537	90	110	23	-	-
1955	-4991	-	-4991	-5391	401	468	95	-206	44	-	-
1957	-5956	-10	-5946	-6045	99	345	59	-350	45	-	-
1960	-7254	-	-7254	-6530	-725	92	5	-866	45	-	-
1961	-6134	-	-6134	-5792	-342	132	9	-536	53	-	-
1962	-5690	-	-5690	-5103	-587	278	-	-917	53	-	-
1963	-7007	-	-7007	-6546	-461	51	-3	-551	42	-	-
1964	-7357	-2	-7355	-6372	-983	45	2	-1053	24	-	-
1965	-9478	-2	-9476	-8415	-1061	-6	-	-1070	15	-	-
MEXICO											
1925	-20087	66	-20156	-12053	-8103	-821	-197	-7080	-6	3	-
1929	-4608	62	-4676	-3209	-1467	-225	-278	-894	-71	5	-
1933	-4299	12	-4392	-2519	-1874	-395	-110	-1305	-65	79	3
1937	-4065	13	-4262	-1703	-2559	-753	-132	-1611	-63	181	2
1938	-2306	14	-2388	-1044	-1344	-276	-27	-1035	-6	65	2
1950	-1901	31	-2819	-2550	-269	252	-182	-435	96	870	16
1953	-1396	42	-2184	-801	-1383	593	3	-2085	107	719	27
1955	-2350	60	-3176	-1196	-1980	1109	263	-3723	71	745	21
1957	104	70	218	-386	603	1307	468	-1520	38	-234	51
1960	-2010	50	-557	-225	-332	578	27	-1289	26	-1560	56
1961	-3758	60	-2117	-1355	-762	254	24	-1482	38	-1758	57
1962	-4740	60	-3324	-1583	-1742	81	24	-2309	26	-1542	66
1963	-4469	60	-3104	-1476	-1628	18	26	-2204	14	-1500	74
1964	-3904	80	-2388	-1550	-839	50	27	-1530	17	-1614	18
1965	-4246	110	-2702	-1560	-1142	44	24	-1953	17	-1662	8
TRINIDAD AND TOBAGO											
1925	-648	44	-692	-63	-629	-68	-14	-549	2	-	-
1929	-1179	87	-1266	-191	-1076	-245	-9	-824	2	-	-
1933	-931	50	-981	-153	-828	-375	-17	-438	2	-	-
1937	-1941	62	-2003	-36	-1967	-528	-24	-1418	3	-	-
1938	-2443	53	-2496	-21	-2475	-680	-21	-1778	3	-	-
1950	-1822	26	-1848	1940	-3788	-555	-765	-2472	5	-	-
1953	-1822	14	-1836	3020	-4856	-735	-1350	-2775	5	-	-

Table VII. NET ENERGY IMPORTS OR EXPORTS, SELECTED YEARS, 1925-1965

(Thousand metric tons coal equivalent; minus sign [-] = net exports)

Region, country, year	Total energy	Solid fuels	Liquid fuels: Total	Liquid fuels: Crude oil	Refined petroleum products: Total	Gasoline	Kerosine	Fuel oils	Lubes and greases	Gas	Electricity
	(1)	(2)	(3)	(4)	(5)	(6)	(7)	(8)	(9)	(10)	(11)
TRINIDAD AND TOBAGO (CONTINUED)											
1955	-2540	-	-2540	3174	-5714	-840	-1200	-3680	6	-	-
1957	-3873	-	-3873	3192	-7065	-1065	-1479	-4535	14	-	-
1960	-5364	-	-5364	7553	-12917	-1770	-1740	-9417	11	-	-
1961	-5237	-	-5237	11919	-17156	-2250	-2190	-12726	11	-	-
1962	-6279	-	-6279	11999	-18278	-2148	-2025	-14115	11	-	-
1963	-7229	-	-7229	13014	-20243	-2351	-1701	-16203	12	-	-
1964	-6680	-	-6680	15456	-22136	-2252	-2037	-17781	-66	-	-
1965	-6105	-	-6105	17285	NA	-2139	-2763	-18473	NA	-	-
VENEZUELA											
1925	-3987	24	-4011	-4023	12	11	2	-	-	-	-
1929	-28860	24	-28884	-28830	-54	-23	2	-33	-	-	-
1933	-26319	11	-26330	-25077	-1253	-68	-	-1185	-	-	-
1937	-38932	10	-38942	-37670	-1272	-2	-	-1275	5	-	-
1938	-41210	16	-41226	-39917	-1310	3	6	-1332	14	-	-
1950	-113040	-1	-113039	-100440	-12599	-1715	-18	-10920	54	-	-
1953	-130700	1	-130701	-108015	-22686	-2961	-405	-19230	-90	-	-
1955	-159344	-	-159344	-131550	-27794	-3129	-900	-23550	-122	-	-
1957	-199647	-	-199647	-165750	-33897	-3944	-1425	-28350	-84	-	-
1960	-205887	-	-205887	-156942	-48945	-3368	-1500	-43500	-255	-	-
1961	-210236	10	-210246	-159420	-50826	-3137	-1740	-45300	-258	-	-
1962	-230592	120	-230712	-173375	-57338	-3149	-2610	-50850	-339	-	-
1963	-234988	130	-235118	-173580	-61538	-3746	-2175	-54788	-384	-	-
1964	-247744	160	-247904	-183578	-64326	-2841	-2790	-57803	-344	-	-
1965	-250425	185	-250610	-182085	-68525	-4236	-3345	-60000	-410	-	-
CARIBBEAN - OTHER											
1925	5099	1274	3825	243	3582	102	65	3407	9	-	-
1929	5251	1247	4004	405	3599	354	63	3171	11	-	-
1933	3017	539	2478	92	2387	162	53	2154	18	-	-
1937	3995	690	3305	288	3017	296	69	2621	32	-	-
1938	3584	575	3009	239	2771	311	71	2367	23	-	-
1950	7249	61	7187	725	6462	1146	122	4934	74	1	-
1953	8508	88	8426	966	7460	1586	177	5430	87	-	-
1955	10252	140	10112	1032	9080	2093	365	6452	135	-	-
1957	13761	180	13581	6056	7526	1821	339	5183	129	-	-
1960	16521	60	16461	10619	5843	627	582	4496	78	-	-
1961	18419	50	18369	10190	8180	240	641	7151	81	-	-
1962	21647	60	21587	13719	7868	390	614	6722	80	-	-
1963	23001	94	22907	16862	6045	-225	672	5439	87	-	-
1964	26201	119	26082	19286	6797	-425	620	6443	89	-	-
1965	27378	132	27246	21150	6096	-791	660	6060	96	-	-
CUBA											
1925	2554	659	1895	162	1733	33	-	1700	-	-	-
1929	2246	632	1614	305	1310	209	-	1101	-	-	-
1933	758	296	462	36	426	48	-	368	11	-	-
1937	1511	381	1130	200	930	105	-	813	12	-	-
1938	1214	342	872	132	740	113	-	617	11	-	-
1950	NA	35	NA	420	NA	NA	NA	NA	NA	NA	NA
1953	NA	58	NA	750	NA	NA	NA	NA	NA	NA	NA

Table VII. NET ENERGY IMPORTS OR EXPORTS, SELECTED YEARS, 1925-1965

(Thousand metric tons coal equivalent; minus sign [-] = net exports)

Region, country, year	Total energy	Solid fuels	Liquid fuels: Total	Liquid fuels: Crude oil	Refined petroleum products: Total	Gasoline	Kerosine	Fuel oils	Lubes and greases	Gas	Electricity
	(1)	(2)	(3)	(4)	(5)	(6)	(7)	(8)	(9)	(10)	(11)
CUBA (CONTINUED)											
1955	NA	130	NA	731	NA	NA	NA	NA	NA	NA	NA
1957	5297	180	5117	3150	1967	566	12	1299	59	-	-
1960	6087	60	6027	4920	1107	87	99	915	NA	-	-
1961	6560	50	6510	4470	2040	156	101	NA	NA	-	-
1962	7317	60	7257	5580	1677	342	104	NA	NA	-	-
1963	6721	94	6627	5564	1064	318	53	693	NA	-	-
1964	7243	119	7124	5204	1920	239	36	1646	NA	-	-
1965	7296	132	7164	5270	1895	221	33	1641	NA	-	-
PANAMA CANAL ZONE											
1925	1714	331	1383	-	1383	6	3	1374	-	-	-
1929	1906	272	1634	-	1634	12	5	1617	-	-	-
1933	1326	28	1298	-	1298	12	5	1281	-	-	-
1937	1270	113	1157	-	1157	17	8	1133	-	-	-
1938	1215	45	1170	-	1170	15	6	1149	-	-	-
1950	NA	-	NA	-	NA	NA	NA	1043	-	-	-
1953	NA	-	NA	-	NA	NA	NA	1065	-	-	-
1955	1071	-	1071	-	1071	-42	3	1110	-	-	-
1957	1547	-	1547	-	1547	29	3	1515	-	-	-
1960	1325	-	1325	-	1325	50	15	1244	-	-	-
1961	1679	-	1679	-	1679	93	2	1563	-	-	-
1962	2082	-	2082	-	2082	35	3	2024	-	-	-
1963	3443	-	3443	-	3443	56	2	3365	-	-	-
1964	3798	-	3798	-	3798	59	5	3711	-	-	-
1965	4095	-	4095	-	4095	57	6	4005	-	-	-
PUERTO RICO											
1950	NA	NA	NA	NA	NA	NA	NA	NA	NA	NA	NA
1953	NA	6	NA	NA	NA	NA	NA	NA	NA	NA	NA
1955	1424	-	1424	-	1424	486	141	795	-	-	-
1957	2918	-	2918	2895	23	8	54	-39	-	-	-
1960	3521	-	3521	5682	-2162	-872	32	-1328	-	-	-
1961	2964	-	2964	5684	-2720	-1388	9	-1343	-	-	-
1962	4013	-	4013	6471	-2459	-1127	-14	-1319	-	-	-
1963	4080	-	4080	7257	-3177	-1517	117	-1782	-	-	-
1964	4775	-	4775	8090	-3315	-1497	234	-2054	-	-	-
1965	5670	-	5670	8670	-3000	-1517	387	-1868	-	-	-
LATIN AMERICA - OTHER											
1925	8043	5812	2231	431	1800	489	296	885	131	-	-
1929	9653	6110	3543	453	3090	701	317	1887	186	-	-
1933	5098	4013	1085	-1208	2292	83	153	1970	87	-	-
1937	8115	5311	2804	-642	3446	329	98	2912	108	-	-
1938	8698	4778	3920	-9	3929	329	26	3461	114	-	-
1950	18486	2673	15813	4248	11565	2867	380	8015	305	-	-
1953	22538	2228	20310	6413	13898	4229	716	8529	425	-	-
1955	30463	2540	27923	12350	15573	2207	1269	11589	464	-	-
1957	33339	2520	30819	17787	13032	1440	815	10277	464	-	-
1960	29775	2910	26865	14981	11885	1658	926	8549	527	-	-
1961	26879	2400	24479	14831	9648	1640	1140	6134	422	-	-
1962	26342	1740	24602	18714	5888	944	962	3095	624	-	-

Table VII. NET ENERGY IMPORTS OR EXPORTS, SELECTED YEARS, 1925-1965

(Thousand metric tons coal equivalent; minus sign [-] = net exports)

Region, country, year	Total energy	Solid fuels	Liquid fuels: Total	Liquid fuels: Crude oil	Refined petroleum products: Total	Gasoline	Kerosine	Fuel oils	Lubes and greases	Gas	Electricity
	(1)	(2)	(3)	(4)	(5)	(6)	(7)	(8)	(9)	(10)	(11)
LATIN AMERICA - OTHER (CONTINUED)											
1963	25347	2020	23327	18758	4569	1098	555	2043	521	-	-
1964	28949	2120	26829	21338	5492	756	554	3222	573	-	-
1965	31202	2135	29067	24165	4902	689	621	2544	525	-	-
ARGENTINA											
1925	4252	3179	1073	114	959	383	102	428	47	-	-
1929	5731	3176	2555	732	1823	468	90	1185	80	-	-
1933	3973	2458	1515	234	1281	65	12	1178	27	-	-
1937	5764	3164	2600	854	1746	32	-	1700	15	-	-
1938	6015	2859	3156	995	2162	3	-	2145	14	-	-
1950	9537	1467	8070	4431	3639	375	12	3186	66	-	-
1953	10379	1224	9155	5399	3756	165	14	3480	98	-	-
1955	11976	1260	10716	5571	5145	168	242	4674	59	-	-
1957	15283	1280	14003	9231	4772	188	170	4356	59	-	-
1960	9080	1460	7620	4973	2648	66	728	1709	96	-	-
1961	6245	1260	4985	2652	2333	96	791	1268	53	-	-
1962	3234	640	2594	1292	1302	47	462	698	168	-	-
1963	1777	770	1007	1151	-144	-20	35	-290	111	-	-
1964	4064	750	3314	2193	1121	11	24	855	104	-	-
1965	6190	730	5460	5328	132	96	18	-459	161	-	-
BOLIVIA											
1925	49	16	33	-	33	3	2	26	3	-	-
1929	79	19	60	-	60	9	3	45	3	-	-
1933	38	8	30	-	30	6	2	21	2	-	-
1937	91	31	60	-	60	11	3	42	5	-	-
1938	101	33	68	-	68	12	3	50	3	-	-
1950	104	2	102	83	20	15	-	-	5	-	-
1953	167	5	162	108	54	39	9	-	6	-	-
1955	-48	-	-48	-81	33	14	3	11	6	-	-
1957	-203	-	-203	-201	-2	-26	-2	15	11	-	-
1960	-149	-	-149	-200	51	11	-	36	5	-	-
1961	-99	-	-99	-128	29	5	-	21	3	-	-
1962	-5	-	-5	-35	30	15	-	11	5	-	-
1963	-87	-	-87	-104	17	15	-	-	2	-	-
1964	-42	-	-42	-54	12	20	-	-	2	-	-
1965	-28	5	-33	-53	20	23	2	-	2	-	-
BRAZIL											
1925	2740	1927	813	-	813	215	155	392	53	-	-
1929	3515	2325	1190	-	1190	441	176	506	68	-	-
1933	2473	1292	1181	-	1181	354	122	663	42	-	-
1937	3366	1708	1658	57	1601	536	171	836	59	-	-
1938	3343	1576	1767	72	1695	542	149	948	57	-	-
1950	7619	1119	6500	89	6411	2427	354	3456	174	-	-
1953	9034	746	8288	45	8243	3669	612	3717	245	-	-
1955	14193	1120	13073	5270	7803	1755	819	4884	300	-	-
1957	13669	940	12729	7269	5460	1055	588	3495	285	-	-
1960	15079	1060	14019	7646	6374	1337	147	4382	318	-	-
1961	15269	900	14369	9746	4623	1215	207	2721	276	-	-
1962	17266	920	16346	14495	1851	629	359	128	363	-	-

Table VII. NET ENERGY IMPORTS OR EXPORTS, SELECTED YEARS, 1925-1965

(Thousand metric tons coal equivalent; minus sign [-] = net exports)

Region, country, year	Total energy	Solid fuels	Liquid fuels		Refined petroleum products					Gas	Electricity
			Total	Crude oil	Total	Gasoline	Kerosine	Fuel oils	Lubes and greases		
	(1)	(2)	(3)	(4)	(5)	(6)	(7)	(8)	(9)	(10)	(11)
BRAZIL (CONTINUED)											
1963	17996	1040	16956	15023	1934	785	381	33	342	-	-
1964	18797	1155	17642	16205	1437	440	374	-123	398	-	-
1965	17865	1240	16625	15371	1254	245	417	30	315	-	-
CHILE											
1925	1610	249	1361	1251	110	62	32	NA	17	-	-
1929	1731	51	1680	1487	194	141	29	NA	24	-	-
1933	297	-119	416	273	143	81	11	44	8	-	-
1937	1106	-43	1149	950	200	113	14	56	18	-	-
1938	1035	-51	1086	861	225	135	11	60	20	-	-
1950	1649	2	1647	-84	1731	339	59	1305	29	-	-
1953	1662	201	1461	-225	1686	429	111	1110	36	-	-
1955	2524	70	2454	459	1995	285	231	1431	51	-	-
1957	2500	230	2270	605	1665	122	215	1281	48	-	-
1960	2416	320	2096	770	1326	57	116	1136	32	-	-
1961	2089	160	1929	737	1193	66	125	990	29	-	-
1962	2201	120	2081	911	1170	47	53	1080	18	-	-
1963	1914	160	1754	629	1125	60	57	1065	NA	-	-
1964	1964	170	1794	662	1133	23	68	1118	NA	-	-
1965	2386	115	2271	975	1296	47	75	1215	NA	-	-
ECUADOR											
1925	12	-	12	-8	20	2	2	15	2	-	-
1929	-203	-	-203	-236	33	3	2	27	2	-	-
1933	-207	-	-207	-230	23	-	-	21	2	-	-
1937	-375	-	-375	-378	3	-	-	2	2	-	-
1938	-314	-	-314	-368	54	-2	-	54	2	-	-
1950	-189	-	-189	-204	15	12	-	-	3	-	-
1953	-231	-	-231	-258	27	24	-	-	3	-	-
1955	-152	-	-152	-267	116	84	-	26	6	-	-
1957	-53	-	-53	-249	197	113	2	77	6	-	-
1960	347	-	347	321	26	15	2	2	8	-	-
1961	312	-	312	284	29	17	3	-	9	-	-
1962	279	-	279	251	29	17	3	2	8	-	-
1963	395	-	395	338	57	45	-	2	11	-	-
1964	501	-	501	458	44	15	14	-	15	-	-
1965	531	-	531	480	51	18	18	-	15	-	-
PARAGUAY											
1925	NA	NA	NA	-	NA	NA	NA	NA	NA	-	-
1929	NA	NA	NA	-	NA	NA	NA	NA	NA	-	-
1933	9	3	6	-	6	5	2	-	-	-	-
1937	10	NA	11	-	11	8	3	-	-	-	-
1938	12	NA	12	-	12	8	3	2	-	-	-
1950	33	-	33	-	33	21	6	5	2	-	-
1953	71	-	71	-	71	33	12	23	3	-	-
1955	95	-	95	-	95	41	15	36	3	-	-
1957	102	-	102	-	102	42	15	42	3	-	-
1960	155	-	155	-	155	54	27	69	5	-	-
1961	177	-	177	-	177	56	23	96	3	-	-
1962	185	-	185	-	185	60	27	93	5	-	-

Table VII. NET ENERGY IMPORTS OR EXPORTS, SELECTED YEARS, 1925-1965

(Thousand metric tons coal equivalent; minus sign [-] = net exports)

Region, country, year	Total energy	Solid fuels	Liquid fuels: Total	Liquid fuels: Crude oil	Refined petroleum products: Total	Gasoline	Kerosine	Fuel oils	Lubes and greases	Gas	Electricity
	(1)	(2)	(3)	(4)	(5)	(6)	(7)	(8)	(9)	(10)	(11)
PARAGUAY (CONTINUED)											
1963	201	-	201	-	201	62	29	107	5	-	-
1964	209	-	209	-	209	63	27	116	3	-	-
1965	266	-	266	-	266	63	36	162	5	-	-
PERU											
1925	-1355	39	-1394	-927	-467	-221	-39	-210	3	-	-
1929	-2215	41	-2256	-1530	-726	-476	-36	-218	3	-	-
1933	-2285	18	-2303	-1487	-816	-533	-47	-237	-	-	-
1937	-2961	15	-2976	-2261	-716	-467	-138	-114	3	-	-
1938	-2461	13	-2474	-1794	-680	-411	-158	-117	6	-	-
1950	-1356	-57	-1299	-561	-738	-395	-62	-291	9	-	-
1953	-982	-35	-947	-462	-485	-176	-56	-269	15	-	-
1955	-950	-	-950	-470	-480	-228	-146	-123	17	-	-
1957	-1019	-30	-989	-651	-338	-117	-198	-50	27	-	-
1960	-291	-10	-281	-507	227	41	-126	285	27	-	-
1961	-75	20	-95	-485	390	65	-54	356	24	-	-
1962	154	10	144	-404	548	57	-2	465	27	-	-
1963	255	-	255	-438	693	80	6	587	21	-	-
1964	363	-5	368	-428	795	92	-	681	23	-	-
1965	361	5	356	-321	677	99	2	576	-	-	-
URUGUAY											
1925	686	363	323	-	323	44	39	233	8	-	-
1929	978	474	504	-	504	111	50	336	8	-	-
1933	773	344	429	-	429	101	48	273	8	-	-
1937	1024	418	606	125	482	92	39	345	6	-	-
1938	898	334	564	207	357	33	12	300	12	-	-
1950	693	129	564	495	69	47	-	8	15	-	-
1953	1972	83	1889	1806	83	11	-	56	17	-	-
1955	2246	90	2156	1868	288	45	86	141	17	-	-
1957	2443	100	2343	1784	560	15	-	524	21	-	-
1960	2449	80	2369	1979	390	12	-	350	29	-	-
1961	2279	60	2219	2025	194	48	12	117	17	-	-
1962	2384	50	2334	2205	129	8	21	93	21	-	-
1963	2284	50	2234	2160	74	6	12	42	20	-	-
1964	2438	50	2388	2303	86	26	11	38	21	-	-
1965	2674	40	2634	2385	249	27	9	195	17	-	-
ASIA											
1925	-4042	1034	-5076	-1173	-3903	-1151	648	-3600	200	-	-
1929	-3355	2105	-5460	-168	-5292	-3245	-300	-2022	272	-	-
1933	-5984	2406	-8390	632	-9021	-3750	48	-5525	206	-	-
1937	-11895	5289	-17184	-2669	-14516	-4817	-1251	-10229	261	-	-
1938	-8763	4814	-13577	-1889	-11688	-5325	-1169	-7508	236	-	-
1950	-105394	1425	-106820	-64290	-42530	-9570	-3579	-31233	473	-	-
1953	-142244	4777	-147021	-136586	-10436	-3807	-570	-6614	555	-	-
1955	-186791	3830	-190616	-172811	-17805	-5307	-2324	-10856	678	-5	-
1957	-189158	7770	-196923	-177510	-19413	-5726	-2586	-12206	1097	-5	-
1960	-285593	9144	-294737	-264939	-29798	-7064	-3198	-20753	1211	-	-
1961	-288078	12030	-300108	-277980	-22128	-6282	-2651	-14529	1347	-	-
1962	-313063	12850	-325908	-291663	-34245	-8612	-2870	-24362	1593	-5	-

Table VII. NET ENERGY IMPORTS OR EXPORTS, SELECTED YEARS, 1925-1965

(Thousand metric tons coal equivalent; minus sign [-] = net exports)

Region, country, year	Total energy	Solid fuels	Liquid fuels		Refined petroleum products					Gas	Electricity
			Total	Crude oil	Total	Gasoline	Kerosine	Fuel oils	Lubes and greases		
	(1)	(2)	(3)	(4)	(5)	(6)	(7)	(8)	(9)	(10)	(11)
ASIA (CONTINUED)											
1963	-336325	11790	-348104	-313382	-34722	-8999	-3297	-23757	1446	-12	-
1964	-372529	13735	-386264	-351600	-34664	-9072	-4754	-22218	1697	-	-
1965	-399870	17685	-417483	-380705	-36779	-9665	-5498	-22350	1205	-72	-
MIDDLE EAST											
1925	-4969	116	-5085	-1575	-3510	-417	65	-3161	3	-	-
1929	-6996	-111	-6885	-2492	-4394	-1700	-1134	-1575	15	-	-
1933	-9873	-294	-9579	-2343	-7236	-2189	-512	-4554	18	-	-
1937	-19555	130	-19685	-7650	-12035	-2682	-665	-8711	23	-	-
1938	-15946	-4	-15942	-6722	-9221	-2903	-663	-5670	15	-	-
1950	-109649	162	-109811	-67140	-42671	-9099	-4520	-29142	90	-	-
1953	-159100	68	-159168	-142286	-16883	-4563	-1937	-10535	152	-	-
1955	-212595	60	-212655	-184199	-28457	-6234	-4169	-18216	161	-	-
1957	-230003	60	-230063	-194840	-35223	-6621	-5081	-23718	192	-	-
1960	-346845	20	-346865	-300450	-46415	-7668	-6072	-32855	177	-	-
1961	-372396	60	-372456	-325902	-46554	-6725	-6156	-33830	182	-	-
1962	-409149	50	-409199	-351489	-57710	-8496	-6986	-42287	219	-	-
1963	-453333	20	-453353	-393977	-59376	-8622	-6827	-43752	242	-	-
1964	-511878	20	-511898	-451158	-60740	-8973	-7484	-43574	182	-	-
1965	-560498	25	-560523	-496874	-63650	-9678	-7853	-45117	174	-	-
MIDDLE EAST - OIL PRODUCING											
1925	-5578	5	-5583	-1577	-4007	-461	-95	-3453	2	-	-
1929	-7830	8	-7838	-2496	-5342	-1812	-1319	-2219	8	-	-
1933	-10803	3	-10806	-2360	-8447	-2280	-632	-5546	11	-	-
1937	-21436	4	-21440	-7674	-13766	-2870	-849	-10056	9	-	-
1938	-18007	4	-18011	-6746	-11265	-3110	-860	-7301	5	-	-
1950	-117067	2	-117069	-68171	-48899	-9860	-5027	-34032	20	-	-
1953	-168330	-	-168330	-144251	-24080	-5490	-2627	-15993	30	-	-
1955	-223928	-	-223928	-193617	-30311	-6092	-4331	-19922	33	-	-
1957	-241001	-	-241001	-204674	-36327	-6513	-5318	-24540	45	-	-
1960	-361107	-	-361107	-310989	-50118	-7704	-6351	-36099	42	-	-
1961	-387328	20	-387348	-339029	-48320	-6308	-6041	-35984	44	-	-
1962	-426050	-	-426050	-370265	-55785	-7452	-6474	-41730	41	-	-
1963	-471450	-	-471450	-415073	-56378	-7518	-6126	-42311	14	-	-
1964	-531717	-	-531717	-474597	-57120	-7610	-6636	-42024	8	-	-
1965	-580907	-	-580907	-522128	-58779	-8166	-7088	-42359	9	-	-
BAHRAIN											
1925	-	-	-	-	-	-	-	-	-	-	-
1929	-	-	-	-	-	-	-	-	-	-	-
1933	-6	-	-6	-6	-	-	-	-	-	-	-
1937	-1437	-	-1437	-941	-497	-105	-50	-342	-	-	-
1938	-1164	-	-1164	-69	-1095	-398	-162	-536	-	-	-
1950	-557	-	-557	9188	-9744	-2628	-1020	-6096	-	-	-
1953	575	-	575	12389	-11814	-3071	-1176	-7568	-	-	-
1955	237	-	237	12417	-12180	-2955	-1575	-7650	-	-	-
1957	-275	-	-275	11120	-11394	-1892	-1403	-8100	-	-	-
1960	-1013	-	-1013	12047	-13059	-2456	-1773	-8831	-	-	-
1961	-798	-	-798	12851	-13649	-2312	-1832	-9506	-	-	-
1962	-726	-	-726	14592	-15318	-2795	-1929	-10595	-	-	-

Table VII. NET ENERGY IMPORTS OR EXPORTS, SELECTED YEARS, 1925-1965

(Thousand metric tons coal equivalent; minus sign [-] = net exports)

Region, country, year	Total energy	Solid fuels	Liquid fuels		Refined petroleum products					Gas	Electricity
			Total	Crude oil	Total	Gasoline	Kerosine	Fuel oils	Lubes and greases		
	(1)	(2)	(3)	(4)	(5)	(6)	(7)	(8)	(9)	(10)	(11)
BAHRAIN (CONTINUED)											
1963	-1061	-	-1061	13470	-14531	-2738	-1698	-10095	-	-	-
1964	-893	-	-893	11546	-12438	-2789	-1827	-7823	-	-	-
1965	-1607	-	-1607	10110	-11717	-2439	-2115	-7163	-	-	-
IRAN											
1925	-5662	5	-5667	-1577	-4091	-468	-125	-3498	-	-	-
1929	-7910	1	-7911	-2496	-5415	-1814	-1332	-2274	5	-	-
1933	-10892	1	-10893	-2354	-8540	-2285	-639	-5621	5	-	-
1937	-14122	1	-14123	-747	-13376	-2775	-813	-9789	2	-	-
1938	-10699	1	-10700	-407	-10293	-2723	-711	-6855	-5	-	-
1950	-43632	-	-43632	-9909	-33723	-6219	-3480	-24030	6	-	-
1953	-348	-	-348	-63	-285	-221	-	-75	11	-	-
1955	-19658	-	-19658	-12495	-7163	-1395	-1350	-4425	8	-	-
1957	-45611	-	-45611	-28800	-16811	-3375	-2655	-10800	20	-	-
1960	-67379	-	-67379	-50138	-17241	-3795	-3068	-10418	39	-	-
1961	-76431	-	-76431	-62325	-14106	-2685	-2580	-8880	39	-	-
1962	-86175	-	-86175	-69038	-17138	-3308	-3135	-10733	38	-	-
1963	-96258	-	-96258	-79403	-16856	-3135	-2993	-10740	12	-	-
1964	-110469	-	-110469	-93878	-16592	-2910	-3278	-10410	6	-	-
1965	-120734	-	-120734	-103935	-16799	-3053	-3210	-10538	2	-	-
IRAQ											
1925	84	-	84	-	84	8	30	45	2	-	-
1929	81	7	74	-	74	2	14	56	3	-	-
1933	95	2	93	-	93	5	8	75	6	-	-
1937	-5877	3	-5880	-5987	107	11	14	75	8	-	-
1938	-6144	3	-6147	-6270	123	11	14	90	9	-	-
1950	-8796	2	-8798	-9216	419	38	74	294	14	-	-
1953	-41109	NA	-41109	-41129	20	-	-	-	20	-	-
1955	-48204	-	-48204	-48225	21	-2	-2	-2	26	-	-
1957	-30354	-	-30354	-30380	26	-	-	-	26	NA	NA
1960	-67805	-	-67805	-67806	2	-2	-	-	3	NA	NA
1961	-69853	20	-69873	-69878	5	-	-	-	5	-	-
1962	-70019	-	-70019	-70010	-9	-	-	-12	3	NA	NA
1963	-81177	-	-81177	-81165	-12	-3	-	-11	2	NA	NA
1964	-88811	-	-88811	-88770	-41	-	-	-42	2	NA	NA
1965	-92483	-	-92483	-92468	-15	-	-	-23	8	NA	NA
KUWAIT											
1950	-24527	-	-24527	-24077	-450	-	-	-450	-	-	-
1953	-62730	-	-62730	-62540	-191	-	-	-191	-	-	-
1955	-79128	-	-79128	-79248	120	-	-	120	-	-	-
1957	-81027	-	-81027	-83111	2084	44	-	2040	-	-	-
1960	-115523	-	-115523	-108150	-7373	-8	-	-7365	-	-	-
1961	-116813	-	-116813	-110400	-6413	-	-	-6413	-	-	-
1962	-130139	-	-130139	-122985	-7154	-195	-	-6837	-	-	-
1963	-136745	-	-136745	-129038	-7707	-108	5	-7383	-	-	-
1964	-152043	-	-152043	-142853	-9191	-5	6	-8822	-	-	-
1965	-156917	-	-156917	-146700	-10217	-39	-	-9600	-	-	-

Table VII. NET ENERGY IMPORTS OR EXPORTS, SELECTED YEARS, 1925-1965

(Thousand metric tons coal equivalent; minus sign [-] = net exports)

Region, country, year	Total energy	Solid fuels	Liquid fuels: Total	Liquid fuels: Crude oil	Refined petroleum products: Total	Gasoline	Kerosine	Fuel oils	Lubes and greases	Gas	Electricity
	(1)	(2)	(3)	(4)	(5)	(6)	(7)	(8)	(9)	(10)	(11)
KUWAIT NEUTRAL ZONE											
1955	-1806	-	-1806	-1835	29	6	8	15	-	-	-
1957	-4952	-	-4952	-4980	29	6	8	15	-	-	-
1960	-9707	-	-9707	-8610	-1097	6	8	-1110	-	-	-
1961	-12863	-	-12863	-11460	-1403	6	8	-1416	-	-	-
1962	-17669	-	-17669	-13833	-3836	6	8	-3849	-	-	-
1963	-24041	-	-24041	-20385	-3656	6	9	-3671	-	-	-
1964	-28073	-	-28073	-23850	-4223	6	9	-4238	-	-	-
1965	-27690	-	-27690	-23850	-3840	6	9	-3855	-	-	-
QATAR											
1950	-2366	-	-2366	-2366	-	-	-	-	-	-	-
1953	-5948	-	-5948	-5948	-	-	-	-	-	-	-
1955	-7946	-	-7946	-8021	75	15	15	45	-	-	-
1957	-9750	-	-9750	-9825	75	15	15	45	-	-	-
1960	-12162	-	-12162	-12210	48	11	11	27	-	-	-
1961	-12498	-	-12498	-12540	42	17	6	20	-	-	-
1962	-13116	-	-13116	-13170	54	17	8	30	-	-	-
1963	-13551	-	-13551	-13605	54	17	8	30	-	-	-
1964	-15111	-	-15111	-15165	54	17	8	30	-	-	-
1965	-16346	-	-16346	-16395	50	17	8	26	-	-	-
SAUDI ARABIA											
1950	-37191	-	-37191	-31791	-5400	-1050	-600	-3750	-	-	-
1953	-58770	-	-58770	-46961	-11810	-2199	-1451	-8160	-	-	-
1955	-67424	-	-67424	-56211	-11213	-1761	-1427	-8025	-	-	-
1957	-69033	-	-69033	-58698	-10335	-1311	-1283	-7740	-	-	-
1960	-87530	-	-87530	-76122	-11408	-1464	-1530	-8408	-	-	-
1961	-98085	-	-98085	-85277	-12809	-1338	-1644	-9795	-	-	-
1962	-107027	-	-107027	-94625	-12402	-1184	-1428	-9743	-	-	-
1963	-115001	-	-115001	-101303	-13698	-1568	-1460	-10455	-	-	-
1964	-122682	-	-122682	-107955	-14727	-1943	-1557	-10740	-	-	-
1965	-144621	-	-144621	-128340	-16281	-2673	-1782	-11228	-	-	-
TRUCIAL OMAN											
1960	9	-	9	-	9	3	2	5	-	-	-
1961	12	-	12	-	12	5	2	6	-	-	-
1962	-1181	-	-1181	-1197	17	6	3	8	-	-	-
1963	-3618	-	-3618	-3645	27	11	3	14	-	-	-
1964	-13637	-	-13637	-13673	36	14	3	20	-	-	-
1965	-20511	-	-20511	-20550	39	15	3	21	-	-	-
MIDDLE EAST - OTHER											
1925	609	111	498	2	497	44	159	293	2	-	-
1929	834	-119	953	5	948	113	185	644	8	-	-
1933	930	-297	1227	17	1211	92	120	992	8	-	-
1937	1881	126	1755	24	1731	188	185	1346	14	-	-
1938	2061	-8	2069	24	2045	207	197	1631	11	-	-
1950	7419	160	7259	1031	6228	761	507	4890	71	-	-
1953	9230	68	9162	1965	7197	927	690	5459	122	-	-

Table VII. NET ENERGY IMPORTS OR EXPORTS, SELECTED YEARS, 1925-1965

(Thousand metric tons coal equivalent; minus sign [-] = net exports)

Region, country, year	Total energy	Solid fuels	Liquid fuels							Gas	Electricity
					Refined petroleum products						
			Total	Crude oil	Total	Gasoline	Kerosine	Fuel oils	Lubes and greases		
	(1)	(2)	(3)	(4)	(5)	(6)	(7)	(8)	(9)	(10)	(11)
MIDDLE EAST - OTHER (CONTINUED)											
1955	11333	60	11273	9419	1854	-143	162	1706	128	-	-
1957	10998	60	10938	9834	1104	-108	237	822	147	-	-
1960	14263	20	14243	10539	3704	36	279	3245	135	-	-
1961	14932	40	14892	13127	1766	-417	-116	2154	138	-	-
1962	16901	50	16851	18776	-1925	-1044	-512	-557	179	-	-
1963	18118	20	18098	21096	-2999	-1104	-701	-1442	228	-	-
1964	19840	20	19820	23439	-3620	-1364	-848	-1550	174	-	-
1965	20409	25	20384	25254	-4871	-1512	-765	-2759	165	-	-
PALESTINE											
1925	64	22	42	-	42	6	29	6	2	-	-
1929	108	33	75	-	75	15	47	11	3	-	-
1933	174	58	116	-	116	30	51	32	3	-	-
1937	371	98	273	-	273	62	74	132	6	-	-
1938	292	58	234	-	234	59	72	99	5	-	-
ISRAEL											
1950	1131	34	1097	294	803	189	104	497	14	-	-
1953	1705	29	1676	1148	528	39	63	416	11	-	-
1955	2414	20	2394	1557	837	23	204	600	11	-	-
1957	2298	40	2258	1523	735	38	35	645	18	-	-
1960	2798	50	2748	1988	761	27	-	717	15	-	-
1961	3067	40	3027	2183	845	27	2	798	21	-	-
1962	3454	40	3414	3083	332	-63	-2	371	26	-	-
1963	3559	20	3539	3525	14	-72	-5	66	27	-	-
1964	3914	30	3884	3975	-92	-102	-	-15	29	-	-
1965	5556	15	5541	5835	-294	-147	-5	-167	26	-	-
JORDAN											
1950	86	-	86	-	86	33	36	15	2	-	-
1953	107	-	107	-	107	33	36	35	3	-	-
1955	189	-	189	20	170	45	48	72	5	-	-
1957	219	-	219	-	219	56	51	108	5	-	-
1960	332	-	332	-	332	68	84	173	8	-	-
1961	446	-	446	311	135	9	30	90	6	-	-
1962	494	-	494	378	116	3	26	78	9	-	-
1963	575	-	575	494	81	2	24	48	8	-	-
1964	581	-	581	539	42	8	17	9	9	-	-
1965	674	-	674	615	59	15	35	-	9	-	-
LEBANON-SYRIA											
1925	109	52	57	-	57	18	36	3	-	-	-
1929	151	49	102	-	102	42	53	5	3	-	-
1933	178	67	111	-	111	45	47	15	5	-	-
1937	279	142	137	-	137	57	44	30	6	-	-
1938	286	145	141	-	141	63	48	26	5	-	-

Table VII. NET ENERGY IMPORTS OR EXPORTS, SELECTED YEARS, 1925-1965

(Thousand metric tons coal equivalent; minus sign [-] = net exports)

Region, country, year	Total energy	Solid fuels	Liquid fuels: Total	Liquid fuels: Crude oil	Refined petroleum products: Total	Gasoline	Kerosine	Fuel oils	Lubes and greases	Gas	Electricity
	(1)	(2)	(3)	(4)	(5)	(6)	(7)	(8)	(9)	(10)	(11)
LEBANON											
1950	925	11	914	737	177	45	39	NA	3	-	-
1953	1065	-	1065	818	248	75	56	NA	5	-	-
1955	1020	10	1010	1341	-332	-44	-68	-230	8	-	-
1957	1240	10	1230	1580	-350	-48	-84	-231	9	-	-
1960	1391	-	1391	1100	291	83	38	158	11	-	-
1961	1437	-	1437	1100	338	114	60	150	6	-	-
1962	1560	10	1550	1260	290	122	38	120	2	-	-
1963	1777	10	1767	1527	240	98	18	90	14	-	-
1964	1969	10	1959	1959	NA	21	3	NA	14	-	-
1965	2233	10	2223	2223	NA	NA	NA	NA	11	-	-
SYRIA											
1950	340	2	338	-	338	114	69	144	11	-	-
1953	597	3	594	-	594	129	77	378	11	-	-
1955	753	-	753	-	753	125	84	528	17	-	-
1957	909	-	909	-	909	144	107	641	17	-	-
1960	1505	-	1505	1043	462	14	24	405	18	-	-
1961	1431	-	1431	1152	279	-35	9	285	20	-	-
1962	1487	-	1487	1179	308	-68	9	330	33	-	-
1963	1667	-	1667	1322	345	-27	11	335	26	-	-
1964	2042	-	2042	1523	519	-8	12	498	17	-	-
1965	1709	5	1704	1526	179	-60	14	198	27	-	-
TURKEY											
1925	41	-79	120	-	120	17	87	17	-	-	-
1929	-187	-347	161	-	161	48	80	33	-	-	-
1933	-341	-473	132	12	120	11	18	92	-	-	-
1937	-52	-253	201	-	201	57	60	84	-	-	-
1938	-8	-255	248	-	248	75	71	102	-	-	-
1950	908	-	908	-	908	345	225	300	38	-	-
1953	1730	-7	1737	-	1737	570	420	660	87	-	-
1955	1700	-	1700	-	1700	563	474	585	78	-	-
1957	1701	-	1701	-	1701	465	444	705	87	-	-
1960	1842	-30	1872	-	1872	537	455	804	72	-	-
1961	2193	-	2193	329	1865	515	443	833	74	-	-
1962	3177	-	3177	3404	-227	35	191	-540	95	-	-
1963	3704	-10	3714	4620	-906	-56	59	-1043	138	-	-
1964	4131	-20	4151	5145	-995	-66	41	-1058	92	-	-
1965	3933	-5	3938	4577	-639	-20	51	-747	78	-	-
FAR EAST AND OTHER ASIA											
1925	927	918	9	402	-393	-734	584	-440	197	-	-
1929	3641	2216	1425	2324	-899	-1545	834	-447	257	-	-
1933	3890	2700	1190	2975	-1785	-1562	560	-971	188	-	-
1937	7660	5159	2501	4982	-2481	-2135	-587	-1518	239	-	-
1938	7184	4818	2366	4833	-2468	-2423	-506	-1838	221	-	-
1950	4254	1263	2991	2850	141	-471	941	-2091	383	-	-
1953	16856	4709	12147	5700	6447	756	1367	3921	404	-	-
1955	25804	3770	22040	11388	10652	927	1845	7361	518	-5	-
1957	40844	7710	33140	17330	15810	896	2495	11513	905	-5	-
1960	61252	9124	52128	35511	16617	605	2874	12102	1034	-	-
1961	84318	11970	72348	47922	24426	443	3506	19301	1166	-	-

Table VII. NET ENERGY IMPORTS OR EXPORTS, SELECTED YEARS, 1925-1965

(Thousand metric tons coal equivalent; minus sign [-] = net exports)

Region, country, year	Total energy	Solid fuels	Liquid fuels: Total	Liquid fuels: Crude oil	Refined petroleum products: Total	Gasoline	Kerosine	Fuel oils	Lubes and greases	Gas	Electricity
	(1)	(2)	(3)	(4)	(5)	(6)	(7)	(8)	(9)	(10)	(11)
FAR EAST AND OTHER ASIA (CONTINUED)											
1962	96085	12800	83291	59826	23465	-116	4116	17925	1374	-5	-
1963	117007	11770	105249	80595	24654	-377	3530	19995	1205	-12	-
1964	139349	13715	125634	99558	26076	-99	2730	21356	1515	-	-
1965	160628	17660	143040	116169	26871	14	2355	22767	1031	-72	-
BORNEO (FORMER BRITISH)											
1925	-882	-49	-833	-231	-602	-140	-152	-311	-	-	-
1929	-1150	-47	-1103	-233	-870	-348	-89	-438	2	-	-
1933	-873	-4	-869	-203	-666	-120	-48	-498	-	-	-
1937	-1089	-	-1089	23	-1112	-95	-60	-959	2	-	-
1938	-1301	1	-1302	11	-1313	-141	-89	-1085	2	-	-
1950	-5970	-	-5970	-3522	-2448	-335	14	-2133	6	-	-
1953	-7046	-	-7046	-4253	-2793	-441	15	-2373	6	-	-
1955	-7517	-	-7512	-4835	-2678	-183	18	-2522	9	-5	-
1957	-8018	-	-8013	-5403	-2610	-273	20	-2366	9	-5	-
1960	-6588	-	-6588	-3773	-2816	-479	26	-2373	11	-	-
1961	-5780	-	-5780	-3386	-2394	-321	26	-2108	9	-	-
1962	-5516	-	-5511	-2726	-2786	-389	32	-2442	14	-5	-
1963	-4915	-	-4904	-2373	-2531	-341	20	-2220	11	-12	-
1964	-4935	-	-4935	-1632	-3303	-512	-167	-2634	9	-	-
1965	-5359	-	-5288	-1971	-3317	-324	-156	-2852	15	-72	-
BRUNEI											
1925	1	1	-	-	-	-	-	-	-	-	-
1929	-	-	-	-	-	-	-	-	-	-	-
1933	-428	-	-428	-428	-	-	-	-	-	-	-
1937	-837	-	-837	-839	2	-	2	-	-	-	-
1938	-1043	-	-1043	-1044	2	-	2	-	-	-	-
1950	-6168	-	-6096	-6114	18	5	2	9	3	-72	-
1953	-7361	-	-7284	-7316	32	11	2	17	3	-77	-
1955	-7953	-	-7857	-7871	14	3	2	5	5	-96	-
1957	-8370	-	-8274	-8292	18	8	2	5	5	-96	-
1960	-6958	-	-6857	-6866	9	2	3	3	2	-101	-
1961	-6266	-	-6165	-6173	8	2	2	3	2	-101	-
1962	-5815	-	-5714	-5726	12	2	3	5	3	-101	-
1963	-5290	-	-5207	-5219	12	2	3	6	2	-84	-
1964	-5336	-	-5270	-5277	8	2	3	2	2	-67	-
1965	-5961	-	-5889	-5897	8	2	2	3	2	-72	-
SABAH											
1925	-50	-50	-	-	-	-	-	-	-	-	-
1929	-44	-47	3	-	3	2	3	-	-	-	-
1933	-3	-4	2	-	2	-	2	-	-	-	-
1937	3	-	3	-	3	2	2	-	-	-	-
1938	4	1	3	-	3	2	2	-	-	-	-
1950	21	-	21	-	21	6	5	9	2	-	-
1953	29	-	29	-	29	11	5	12	2	-	-
1955	36	-	36	-	36	9	6	20	2	-	-
1957	48	-	48	-	48	15	6	26	2	-	-
1960	81	-	81	-	81	20	8	48	6	-	-
1961	87	-	87	-	87	23	8	53	5	-	-

Table VII. NET ENERGY IMPORTS OR EXPORTS, SELECTED YEARS, 1925-1965

(Thousand metric tons coal equivalent; minus sign [-] = net exports)

Region, country, year	Total energy	Solid fuels	Liquid fuels: Total	Liquid fuels: Crude oil	Refined petroleum products: Total	Gasoline	Kerosine	Fuel oils	Lubes and greases	Gas	Electricity
	(1)	(2)	(3)	(4)	(5)	(6)	(7)	(8)	(9)	(10)	(11)
SABAH (CONTINUED)											
1962	113	-	113	-	113	32	12	63	6	-	-
1963	132	-	132	-	132	33	17	78	5	-	-
1964	161	-	161	-	161	39	30	87	5	-	-
1965	180	-	180	-	180	41	36	96	8	-	-
SARAWAK											
1925	-833	-	-833	-231	-602	-140	-152	-311	-	-	-
1929	-1110	-	-1110	-233	-878	-350	-92	-438	2	-	-
1933	-443	-	-443	225	-668	-120	-50	-498	-	-	-
1937	-255	-	-255	861	-1116	-96	-63	-959	2	-	-
1938	-263	-	-263	1055	-1317	-143	-92	-1085	2	-	-
1950	177	-	105	2592	-2487	-345	8	-2151	2	72	-
1953	287	-	210	3063	-2853	-462	9	-2402	2	77	-
1955	400	-	309	3036	-2727	-195	11	-2546	3	91	-
1957	304	-	213	2889	-2676	-296	12	-2396	3	91	-
1960	289	-	188	3093	-2906	-500	15	-2424	3	101	-
1961	400	-	299	2787	-2489	-345	17	-2163	3	101	-
1962	186	-	90	3000	-2910	-422	17	-2510	5	96	-
1963	243	-	171	2846	-2675	-375	-	-2304	5	72	-
1964	241	-	174	3645	-3471	-552	-200	-2723	3	67	-
1965	424	-	425	3926	-3501	-365	-192	-2951	6	NA	-
BURMA											
1950	165	NA	165	-	165	90	30	45	NA	-	-
1953	416	251	165	-	165	96	32	24	14	-	-
1955	428	200	228	-	228	116	27	71	15	-	-
1957	406	280	126	-	126	41	5	71	11	-	-
1960	451	350	101	-	101	21	6	50	24	-	-
1961	395	260	135	18	117	17	12	57	32	-	-
1962	478	340	138	-	138	23	24	69	23	-	-
1963	288	210	78	-	78	15	20	33	11	-	-
1964	452	215	237	180	57	-	-	33	24	-	-
1965	403	140	263	240	23	-	-	-	23	-	-
CEYLON											
1925	1136	827	309	-	309	21	39	246	3	-	-
1929	1264	827	437	-	437	53	47	332	6	-	-
1933	925	412	513	-	513	38	41	431	5	-	-
1937	1203	582	621	-	621	71	47	498	6	-	-
1938	1129	391	738	-	738	62	45	627	5	-	-
1950	1544	374	1170	-	1170	137	66	959	9	-	-
1953	1649	390	1259	-	1259	198	108	945	8	-	-
1955	1609	190	1419	-	1419	204	141	1061	14	-	-
1957	2368	280	2088	-	2088	287	168	1619	15	-	-
1960	1597	260	1337	-	1337	243	221	860	14	-	-
1961	1721	140	1581	-	1581	258	236	1073	15	-	-
1962	1696	140	1556	-	1556	210	269	1058	20	-	-
1963	1514	150	1364	-	1364	213	209	917	26	-	-
1964	1439	180	1259	-	1259	159	231	854	15	-	-
1965	1663	140	1523	-	1523	264	275	962	23	-	-

Table VII. NET ENERGY IMPORTS OR EXPORTS, SELECTED YEARS, 1925-1965

(Thousand metric tons coal equivalent; minus sign [-] = net exports)

Region, country, year	Total energy	Solid fuels	Liquid fuels							Gas	Electricity
			Total	Crude oil	Refined petroleum products						
					Total	Gasoline	Kerosine	Fuel oils	Lubes and greases		
	(1)	(2)	(3)	(4)	(5)	(6)	(7)	(8)	(9)	(10)	(11)
HONG KONG											
1925	1346	960	386	-	386	11	138	234	3	-	-
1929	914	642	272	-	272	14	60	201	-3	-	-
1933	929	767	162	-	162	18	2	140	3	-	-
1937	1092	879	213	-	213	39	9	146	20	-	-
1938	978	696	282	-	282	18	8	260	-3	-	-
1950	1005	271	734	-	734	39	17	671	8	-	-
1953	1178	204	974	-	974	78	62	831	3	-	-
1955	1488	250	1238	-	1238	89	98	1041	11	-	-
1957	1857	250	1607	-	1607	96	126	1371	14	-	-
1960	2071	230	1841	-	1841	117	204	1505	15	-	-
1961	2256	240	2016	-	2016	113	245	1644	15	-	-
1962	2509	220	2289	-	2289	96	323	1850	21	-	-
1963	2831	200	2631	-	2631	110	378	2129	15	-	-
1964	2921	180	2741	-	2741	104	348	2271	18	-	-
1965	3254	170	3084	-	3084	110	440	2528	8	-	-
INDIA											
1925	1289	276	1013	-	1013	-65	387	551	140	-	-
1929	947	-516	1463	-24	1487	2	569	747	170	-	-
1933	749	-364	1113	-20	1133	9	317	683	125	-	-
1937	1073	-561	1634	-27	1661	243	381	855	182	-	-
1938	698	-859	1557	-33	1590	153	294	948	195	-	-
1950	3522	-932	4454	1977	2477	980	1233	NA	264	-	-
1953	3059	-1975	5034	2051	2984	1308	1422	NA	254	-	-
1955	5155	-1540	6695	4133	2562	474	1469	372	248	-	-
1957	7184	-1690	8874	6450	2424	-9	1799	186	449	-	-
1960	9534	-1350	10884	8528	2357	-192	1484	593	473	-	-
1961	10608	-930	11538	8865	2673	-75	1640	753	356	-	-
1962	11510	-1060	12570	9032	3539	30	2184	909	416	-	-
1963	11781	-870	12651	9471	3180	-471	1982	1089	581	-	-
1964	11349	-1250	12599	9750	2849	-423	1499	1344	429	-	-
1965	12069	-930	12999	10200	2799	-294	1239	1404	450	-	-
INDO-CHINA											
1925	-566	-665	99	-	99	17	71	-	12	-	-
1929	-1134	-1309	176	-	176	47	93	6	30	-	-
1933	-1117	-1247	131	-	131	44	63	15	9	-	-
1937	-1370	-1511	141	-	141	48	59	27	8	-	-
1938	-1362	-1518	156	-	156	57	56	36	8	-	-
1950	142	-47	189	-	189	105	36	41	8	-	-
1953	225	-300	525	-	525	233	63	215	15	-	-
1955	573	30	543	-	543	228	77	227	12	-	-
1957	785	50	735	-	735	312	105	302	17	-	-
1960	970	10	960	-	960	332	138	465	24	-	-
1961	1107	10	1097	-	1097	329	131	614	23	-	-
1962	1123	20	1103	-	1103	332	135	608	27	-	-
1963	1288	10	1278	-	1278	366	167	710	33	-	-
1964	1252	20	1232	-	1232	309	165	752	5	-	-
1965	1505	45	1460	-	1460	347	192	918	-	-	-

Table VII. NET ENERGY IMPORTS OR EXPORTS, SELECTED YEARS, 1925-1965

(Thousand metric tons coal equivalent; minus sign [-] = net exports)

Region, country, year	Total energy	Solid fuels	Liquid fuels: Total	Liquid fuels: Crude oil	Refined petroleum products: Total	Refined petroleum products: Gasoline	Refined petroleum products: Kerosine	Refined petroleum products: Fuel oils	Refined petroleum products: Lubes and greases	Gas	Electricity
	(1)	(2)	(3)	(4)	(5)	(6)	(7)	(8)	(9)	(10)	(11)
CAMBODIA											
1955	84	-	84	-	84	39	15	30	-	-	-
1957	128	-	128	-	128	59	20	50	-	-	-
1960	168	-	168	-	168	81	23	65	-	-	-
1961	215	-	215	-	215	90	30	95	-	-	-
1962	230	-	230	-	230	87	33	110	-	-	-
1963	297	-	297	-	297	105	39	153	-	-	-
1964	263	-	263	-	263	65	38	161	-	-	-
1965	297	30	267	-	267	54	42	171	-	-	-
LAOS											
1955	14	-	14	-	14	9	2	2	2	-	-
1957	29	-	29	-	29	21	3	5	NA	-	-
1960	42	-	42	-	42	26	3	11	3	-	-
1961	57	-	57	-	57	36	3	17	2	-	-
1962	66	-	66	-	66	50	5	11	2	-	-
1963	77	-	77	-	77	51	8	17	2	-	-
1964	90	-	90	-	90	57	8	21	5	-	-
1965	87	-	87	-	87	53	8	27	NA	-	-
VIETNAM, SOUTH											
1955	476	30	446	-	446	180	60	195	11	-	-
1957	629	50	579	-	579	233	83	248	17	-	-
1960	760	10	750	-	750	225	113	390	21	-	-
1961	835	10	825	-	825	203	98	503	21	-	-
1962	827	20	807	-	807	195	98	488	26	-	-
1963	915	10	905	-	905	210	120	540	32	-	-
1964	899	20	879	-	879	188	120	570	NA	-	-
1965	1121	15	1106	-	1106	240	143	720	NA	-	-
INDONESIA											
1925	-3283	-202	-3081	2	-3083	-813	-296	-1947	-27	-	-
1929	-5182	-329	-4853	-35	-4818	-1659	-677	-2450	-33	-	-
1933	-5996	-209	-5787	-620	-5168	-1799	-774	-2577	-18	-	-
1937	-8203	-236	-7967	-143	-7824	-2868	-1256	-3684	-17	-	-
1938	-8424	-244	-8180	-78	-8102	-2964	-1028	-4103	-8	-	-
1950	-6640	-35	-6605	2351	-8955	-2720	-854	-5336	-47	-	-
1953	-10012	-77	-9935	290	-10224	-3083	-1022	-6047	-74	-	-
1955	-9271	-20	-9251	-747	-8504	-2424	-897	-5129	-54	-	-
1957	-14145	-	-14145	-5355	-8790	-1920	-767	-6141	38	-	-
1960	-21730	20	-21750	-13620	-8130	-1524	-689	-5925	8	-	-
1961	-20774	30	-20804	-14277	-6527	-1166	-371	-5060	69	-	-
1962	-25111	20	-25131	-16593	-8538	-1407	-684	-6531	84	-	-
1963	-24506	10	-24516	-17165	-7352	-1106	-585	-5762	NA	-	-
1964	-26584	10	-26594	-22268	-4326	-608	-399	-3428	NA	-	-
1965	-26245	5	NA	NA	NA	-576	-594	-4028	NA	-	-
JAPAN											
1925	-11	-963	953	632	321	114	138	32	38	-	-
1929	4366	1192	3174	2577	597	50	492	35	21	-	-

Table VII. NET ENERGY IMPORTS OR EXPORTS, SELECTED YEARS, 1925-1965

(Thousand metric tons coal equivalent; minus sign [-] = net exports)

Region, country, year	Total energy	Solid fuels	Liquid fuels		Refined petroleum products					Gas	Electricity
			Total	Crude oil	Total	Gasoline	Kerosine	Fuel oils	Lubes and greases		
	(1)	(2)	(3)	(4)	(5)	(6)	(7)	(8)	(9)	(10)	(11)
JAPAN (CONTINUED)											
1933	6666	2170	4496	3756	740	3	738	-5	3	-	-
1937	10709	4269	6440	5081	1359	-	NA	NA	NA	-	-
1938	11772	5019	6753	4886	1868	-20	NA	NA	NA	-	-
1950	3086	324	2762	1850	912	47	6	807	53	-	-
1953	16519	4435	12084	7613	4472	413	5	4005	50	-	-
1955	18445	2450	15995	10917	5078	375	48	4611	42	-	-
1957	33185	6380	26805	19113	7692	162	26	7377	128	-	-
1960	56238	8260	47978	40584	7394	-231	-36	7439	222	-	-
1961	74389	11260	63129	50819	12311	-564	65	12471	330	-	-
1962	85798	11960	73838	60126	13712	-398	15	13514	419	-	-
1963	103955	11030	92925	77841	15084	-237	35	14994	-2	-	-
1964	124501	13150	111351	93477	17874	225	-225	16778	530	-	-
1965	142514	17030	125484	104528	20957	138	-233	19992	318	-	-
KOREA											
1925	557	479	78	-	78	8	65	-	6	-	-
1929	797	630	167	-	167	30	75	47	15	-	-
1933	812	621	191	-	191	47	50	74	21	-	-
1937	1595	1044	551	-	551	83	77	371	21	-	-
1938	1521	987	534	-	534	81	62	386	6	-	-
KOREA, REPUBLIC OF											
1950	369	219	150	-	150	30	15	105	NA	-	-
1953	1138	643	495	-	495	105	60	330	NA	-	-
1955	1606	1060	546	-	546	135	53	359	NA	-	-
1957	1451	740	711	-	711	218	47	447	NA	-	-
1960	1143	100	1043	-	1043	216	54	749	24	-	-
1961	1186	50	1136	-	1136	189	65	869	14	-	-
1962	1412	-120	1532	48	1484	125	75	1263	21	-	-
1963	1928	-130	2058	69	1989	113	78	1749	50	-	-
1964	1857	-80	1937	1205	732	8	15	705	5	-	-
1965	2268	-90	2358	2100	258	12	-	240	6	-	-
MALAYA AND SINGAPORE											
1925	1170	633	537	-	537	56	72	410	-	-	-
1929	1782	849	933	-	933	132	81	705	15	-	-
1933	1039	563	476	-	476	74	50	342	11	-	-
1937	1694	744	950	-	950	156	56	722	17	-	-
1938	1235	485	750	-	750	135	66	533	17	-	-
1950	2179	101	2078	-	2078	315	90	1644	29	-	-
1953	4336	89	4247	-	4247	623	-30	3627	27	-	-
1955	5262	70	5192	-	5192	728	75	4344	45	-	-
1957	5936	90	5846	108	5738	518	195	4979	47	-	-
1960	5392	4	5388	80	5309	353	381	4523	53	-	-
1961	6791	60	6731	773	5958	335	401	5166	57	-	-
1962	7449	40	7409	3003	4406	-6	435	3905	72	-	-
1963	6409	40	6369	2606	3764	-53	122	3626	69	-	-
1964	8637	40	8597	6408	2189	-302	50	2403	38	-	-
1965	8613	25	8588	7007	1581	-518	123	1919	57	-	-

Table VII. NET ENERGY IMPORTS OR EXPORTS, SELECTED YEARS, 1925-1965

(Thousand metric tons coal equivalent; minus sign [-] = net exports)

Region, country, year	Total energy	Solid fuels	Liquid fuels: Total	Crude oil	Refined petroleum products: Total	Gasoline	Kerosine	Fuel oils	Lubes and greases	Gas	Electricity
	(1)	(2)	(3)	(4)	(5)	(6)	(7)	(8)	(9)	(10)	(11)
SINGAPORE											
1960	3660	-	NA	NA	3666	54	246	3314	53	-	-6
1961	4122	10	NA	NA	4119	15	231	3816	57	-	-7
1962	2511	10	NA	NA	2508	-311	263	2484	72	-	-8
1963	2265	10	NA	NA	2259	-260	-33	2483	69	-	-4
1964	2253	10	NA	NA	2243	-300	6	2499	38	-	-
1965	1846	5	NA	NA	1841	-372	81	2075	57	-	-
PAKISTAN											
1950	2405	1025	1380	-	1380	NA	NA	NA	NA	NA	NA
1953	2783	1211	1572	-	1572	165	345	1020	42	-	-
1955	3017	1080	1937	-	1937	225	308	1350	54	-	-
1957	3594	1330	2264	-	2264	255	314	1647	48	-	-
1960	4515	1410	3105	-	3105	278	510	2318	NA	-	-
1961	4379	1070	3309	-	3309	269	627	2340	74	-	-
1962	4956	1360	3596	495	3101	243	711	2075	72	-	-
1963	5355	1200	4155	2400	1755	29	563	1035	129	-	-
1964	5860	1340	4520	3173	1347	3	612	651	81	-	-
1965	5810	1100	4710	3660	1050	240	330	480	NA	-	-
PHILIPPINES											
1925	931	472	459	-	459	50	74	323	14	-	-
1929	1140	603	537	-	537	107	104	312	15	-	-
1933	825	273	552	-	552	101	62	377	14	-	-
1937	925	266	659	-	659	146	86	410	18	-	-
1938	960	259	701	-	701	150	68	452	32	-	-
1950	1903	7	1896	-	1896	707	228	912	50	-	-
1953	1987	5	1982	-	1982	699	218	1014	51	-	-
1955	2890	10	2880	1001	1880	564	201	1050	65	-	-
1957	3333	10	3323	1319	2004	542	203	1196	65	-	-
1960	3994	10	3984	2123	1862	660	251	852	99	-	-
1961	4158	10	4148	3428	720	267	62	293	99	-	-
1962	4959	10	4949	4554	395	161	29	135	71	-	-
1963	5583	10	5573	5426	147	57	9	-9	90	-	-
1964	6432	10	6422	6324	98	-	56	-92	134	-	-
1965	6927	10	6917	6915	2	63	27	-89	NA	-	-
TAIWAN											
1925	-861	-888	27	-	27	-	23	-	5	-	-
1929	-299	-378	80	38	42	5	24	2	12	-	-
1933	-208	-305	98	60	38	8	20	2	9	-	-
1937	-186	-367	182	48	134	15	30	75	14	-	-
1938	-254	-455	201	48	153	15	33	90	15	-	-
1950	166	-64	230	195	35	15	-	15	5	-	-
1953	-109	-211	102	-	102	93	-	-	9	-	-
1955	936	-50	986	920	66	2	75	-30	20	-	-
1957	1224	-30	1254	1098	156	50	84	8	15	-	-
1960	1439	-190	1629	1590	39	-2	45	-18	14	-	-
1961	1437	-240	1677	1683	-6	-17	45	-60	26	-	-
1962	1762	-130	1892	1887	5	-41	56	-50	39	-	-
1963	2144	-100	2244	2240	5	-	53	-77	29	-	-
1964	1797	-110	1907	1929	-23	-	63	-123	38	-	-

Table VII. NET ENERGY IMPORTS OR EXPORTS, SELECTED YEARS, 1925-1965

(Thousand metric tons coal equivalent; minus sign [-] = net exports)

Region, country, year	Total energy	Solid fuels	Liquid fuels		Refined petroleum products					Gas	Electricity
			Total	Crude oil	Total	Gasoline	Kerosine	Fuel oils	Lubes and greases		
	(1)	(2)	(3)	(4)	(5)	(6)	(7)	(8)	(9)	(10)	(11)
TAIWAN (CONTINUED)											
1965	2690	5	2685	2678	8	-6	-	-26	39	-	-
THAILAND											
1925	101	38	63	-	63	9	26	24	5	-	-
1929	196	52	144	-	144	26	56	56	8	-	-
1933	139	23	116	-	116	18	42	48	8	-	-
1937	218	50	168	-	168	29	47	83	11	-	-
1938	232	56	176	-	176	32	48	87	9	-	-
1950	380	20	360	-	360	120	60	180	NA	-	-
1953	734	44	690	-	690	270	90	330	NA	-	-
1955	1114	40	1074	-	1074	372	120	543	39	-	-
1957	1384	20	1364	-	1364	476	126	710	53	-	-
1960	1755	10	1745	-	1745	609	206	875	56	-	-
1961	1917	-	1917	-	1917	587	242	1040	50	-	-
1962	2427	-	2427	-	2427	629	401	1320	78	-	-
1963	2661	-	2661	81	2580	633	360	1521	65	-	-
1964	3630	-	3630	1013	2618	617	357	1559	84	-	-
1965	3689	-	3689	1814	1875	218	576	989	93	-	-
AFRICA											
1925	3967	2696	1271	149	1122	183	425	375	92	-	-
1929	6483	3903	2580	183	2397	806	819	614	159	-	-
1933	6483	3040	3443	116	3327	935	678	1578	137	-	-
1937	10335	3751	6584	159	6425	1791	786	3663	185	-	-
1938	9034	3301	5733	155	5579	1647	800	2955	177	-	-
1950	12558	-886	13439	-	13439	3717	1761	7584	377	5	-
1953	17539	-249	17789	-48	17837	4962	2276	10223	362	-	-1
1955	23574	424	23150	2832	20318	5303	2561	11858	558	-	-
1957	25777	424	25442	2772	22670	5745	2370	13928	563	-	-89
1960	12192	-117	12381	-10521	22902	5586	2610	14040	540	-	-73
1961	-749	-179	-572	-23546	22974	5484	2646	14109	593	-	2
1962	-22761	-810	-21953	-44147	22194	5142	2729	13619	596	-	2
1963	-48988	-750	-48239	-68633	20394	4878	2492	12342	593	-	1
1964	-81503	-395	-80987	-93143	12156	2784	2138	6543	659	-120	-2
1965	-117426	-515	-115800	-125846	10046	2165	1905	5265	696	-1110	-1
NORTH AFRICA											
1925	3880	3296	584	149	435	11	279	93	53	-	-
1929	5365	4222	1143	183	960	248	573	63	77	-	-
1933	5067	3220	1847	116	1731	381	539	738	74	-	-
1937	5738	3321	2417	159	2258	411	552	1224	71	-	-
1938	5751	3222	2529	155	2375	482	587	1236	71	-	-
1950	6299	790	5504	-	5504	849	876	3665	114	5	-
1953	6708	284	6425	-92	6516	1250	1071	4074	107	-	-1
1955	9724	300	9426	1422	8004	1433	1173	5222	141	-	-3
1957	8437	590	7848	1383	6465	1530	948	3789	143	-	-1
1960	-2481	480	-2961	-10116	7155	1053	1056	4790	158	-	-
1961	-14949	490	-15441	-22028	6587	981	1008	4299	182	-	2
1962	-35325	340	-35667	-40710	5043	581	959	3294	132	-	2
1963	-61788	290	-62079	-66024	3945	539	714	2450	186	-	1
1964	-94208	590	-94679	-94736	57	-522	312	86	176	-120	-

Table VII. NET ENERGY IMPORTS OR EXPORTS, SELECTED YEARS, 1925-1965

(Thousand metric tons coal equivalent; minus sign [-] = net exports)

Region, country, year	Total energy	Solid fuels	Liquid fuels							Gas	Electricity
					Refined petroleum products						
			Total	Crude oil	Total	Gasoline	Kerosine	Fuel oils	Lubes and greases		
	(1)	(2)	(3)	(4)	(5)	(6)	(7)	(8)	(9)	(10)	(11)
NORTH AFRICA (CONTINUED)											
1965	-120720	470	-120081	-118382	-1700	-791	309	-1349	140	-1110	-
ALGERIA											
1925	1642	1532	110	-	110	62	27	6	15	-	-
1929	2641	2383	258	-	258	147	66	24	21	-	-
1933	2241	1585	656	-2	657	198	74	363	23	-	-
1937	2465	1472	993	-	993	171	59	746	18	-	-
1938	2299	1295	1004	-	1004	182	57	747	18	-	-
1950	2115	455	1655	-	1655	285	75	1260	35	5	-
1953	2295	180	2115	-116	2231	405	105	1680	26	-	-1
1955	2817	270	2549	-96	2645	521	143	1917	42	-	-1
1957	3392	480	2913	-17	2930	780	143	1920	50	-	-1
1960	-8743	350	-9095	-12065	2970	542	174	2135	44	-	1
1961	-19805	210	-20016	-22646	2630	489	186	1820	44	-	1
1962	-28623	100	-28724	-30533	1809	480	176	1064	30	-	1
1963	-33397	50	-33447	-35483	2036	366	189	1410	30	-	1
1964	-37379	70	-37329	-37238	-92	-101	27	-41	30	-120	-
1965	-38368	20	-37278	-36600	-678	-330	-15	-329	23	-1110	-
EGYPT UAR											
1925	1762	1403	359	149	210	-108	219	75	24	-	-
1929	1979	1380	599	183	416	-42	428	-2	32	-	-
1933	2017	1189	828	117	711	-32	402	312	29	-	-
1937	2490	1500	990	161	830	2	432	363	33	-	-
1938	2605	1601	1004	159	845	8	464	342	32	-	-
1950	2833	217	2616	-	2616	107	662	1800	48	-	-
1953	2403	78	2325	69	2256	119	743	1350	45	-	-
1955	4741	110	4631	1518	3113	140	764	2159	51	-	-
1957	3051	180	2871	1359	1512	98	596	762	57	-	-
1960	3850	160	3690	1814	1877	-60	630	1247	62	-	-
1961	3395	300	3095	1463	1632	-30	569	1014	80	-	-
1962	2934	270	2664	1292	1373	-369	554	1136	53	-	-
1963	1877	270	1607	1323	284	-167	303	50	101	-	-
1964	2168	500	1668	2580	-912	-686	119	-432	87	-	-
1965	2021	440	1581	3545	-1964	-725	140	-1442	63	-	-
LIBYA											
1925	32	17	15	-	15	9	3	2	2	-	-
1929	47	21	26	-	26	14	5	5	3	-	-
1933	87	37	50	-	50	23	6	18	3	-	-
1937	118	44	74	-	74	26	8	38	3	-	-
1938	151	55	96	-	96	26	11	56	5	-	-
1950	145	NA	146	-	146	41	60	44	2	-	-
1953	201	-	201	-	201	68	78	53	3	-	-
1955	376	70	306	-	306	150	90	60	6	-	-
1957	429	30	399	-	399	188	98	105	8	-	-
1960	546	30	516	-	516	180	113	210	11	-	-
1961	-514	40	-554	-1038	485	165	113	195	9	-	-
1962	-11252	10	-11262	-11778	516	195	113	195	11	-	-
1963	-32480	10	-32490	-33059	569	210	120	218	12	-	-
1964	-61553	-	-61553	-62214	662	240	128	270	18	-	-

Table VII. NET ENERGY IMPORTS OR EXPORTS, SELECTED YEARS, 1925-1965

(Thousand metric tons coal equivalent; minus sign [-] = net exports)

Region, country, year	Total energy	Solid fuels	Liquid fuels							Gas	Electricity
					Refined petroleum products						
			Total	Crude oil	Total	Gasoline	Kerosine	Fuel oils	Lubes and greases		
	(1)	(2)	(3)	(4)	(5)	(6)	(7)	(8)	(9)	(10)	(11)
LIBYA (CONTINUED)											
1965	-87029	10	-87039	-87713	674	248	135	272	14	-	-
MOROCCO											
1925	175	121	54	-	54	35	11	2	8	-	-
1929	322	181	141	-	141	86	32	12	12	-	-
1933	368	194	174	-	174	126	18	18	12	-	-
1937	293	87	206	-2	207	149	18	32	9	-	-
1938	300	33	267	-5	272	198	20	45	9	-	-
1950	688	-55	743	-	743	314	38	374	18	-	-
1953	1214	-58	1272	-45	1317	533	93	668	24	-	-
1955	1087	-190	1278	-	1278	494	122	624	30	-	-1
1957	905	-190	1095	41	1055	356	59	612	18	-	-
1960	1133	-100	1235	135	1100	276	72	710	29	-	-1
1961	1198	-110	1307	194	1113	252	71	747	29	-	1
1962	815	-80	894	300	594	162	42	359	26	-	1
1963	1222	-80	1302	1065	237	14	26	171	27	-	-
1964	1378	-20	1398	1208	191	6	12	147	21	-	-
1965	1557	-50	1607	1365	242	14	47	147	24	-	-
TUNISIA											
1925	270	223	47	-	47	14	20	9	5	-	-
1929	377	257	120	-	120	44	44	24	9	-	-
1933	355	215	140	-	140	66	39	27	8	-	-
1937	373	218	155	-	155	65	36	47	8	-	-
1938	397	238	159	-	159	69	36	47	8	-	-
1950	518	173	345	-	345	104	42	188	12	-	-
1953	596	84	512	-	512	126	53	324	9	-	-
1955	703	40	663	-	663	129	56	462	12	-	-
1957	660	90	570	-	570	110	54	390	11	-	-
1960	733	40	693	-	693	116	68	489	14	-	-
1961	778	50	728	-	728	105	71	524	21	-	-
1962	801	40	761	9	752	113	75	542	14	-	-
1963	990	40	950	129	821	116	77	602	17	-	-
1964	1177	40	1137	929	209	18	27	141	20	-	-
1965	1099	50	1049	1022	27	3	3	3	17	-	-
TROPICAL AFRICA											
1925	1491	997	494	-	494	69	84	279	14	-	-
1929	2200	1333	867	-	867	224	137	468	39	-	-
1933	1588	602	986	-	986	188	77	696	26	-	-
1937	3933	1224	2709	-	2709	681	144	1839	45	-	-
1938	2534	956	1578	-	1578	395	126	1010	48	-	-
1950	5360	870	4490	-	4490	1238	357	2742	153	-	-
1953	8246	651	7595	-	7595	1811	500	5147	138	-	-
1955	9723	684	9036	-	9036	2282	671	5862	219	-	3
1957	11814	384	11517	-215	11732	2634	723	8147	219	-	-88
1960	10159	363	9869	-2327	12195	2790	962	8199	218	-	-73
1961	9150	391	8759	-3741	12500	2672	1031	8550	222	-	-
1962	7688	450	7238	-5862	13100	2696	1185	8949	239	-	-
1963	7378	310	7068	-5894	12962	2681	1184	8822	243	-	-
1964	5288	295	4995	-5682	10677	2301	1170	6921	255	-	-2

Table VII. NET ENERGY IMPORTS OR EXPORTS, SELECTED YEARS, 1925-1965

(Thousand metric tons coal equivalent; minus sign [-] = net exports)

			Liquid fuels								
					Refined petroleum products						
Region, country, year	Total energy	Solid fuels	Total	Crude oil	Total	Gasoline	Kerosine	Fuel oils	Lubes and greases	Gas	Electricity
	(1)	(2)	(3)	(4)	(5)	(6)	(7)	(8)	(9)	(10)	(11)
TROPICAL AFRICA (CONTINUED)											
1965	-4742	215	-4956	-14477	9521	1884	1029	6308	275	-	-1
CONGO, DEMOCRATIC REPUBLIC											
1925	315	294	21	-	21	6	3	12	-	-	-
1929	529	466	63	-	63	27	5	27	6	-	-
1933	71	45	26	-	26	17	2	5	3	-	-
1937	228	165	63	-	63	45	3	9	6	-	-
1938	180	133	47	-	47	30	5	6	6	-	-
1950	445	208	237	-	237	158	20	48	12	-	-
1953	628	200	428	-	428	260	35	113	21	-	-
1955	905	290	612	-	612	318	42	216	33	-	3
1957	845	240	692	-	692	336	53	267	30	-	-86
1960	807	230	642	-	642	302	66	269	NA	-	-65
1961	953	330	681	-	681	327	71	278	NA	-	-58
1962	873	240	692	-	692	312	86	288	NA	-	-59
1963	939	220	753	-	753	345	111	294	NA	-	-34
1964	788	255	560	-	560	224	84	249	NA	-	-27
1965	971	330	675	-	675	314	95	264	NA	-	-34
EAST AFRICA											
1925	147	76	71	-	71	11	18	39	3	-	-
1929	260	111	149	-	149	47	32	63	8	-	-
1933	203	95	108	-	108	23	15	68	3	-	-
1937	369	166	203	-	203	54	26	117	6	-	-
1938	397	152	245	-	245	71	26	141	8	-	-
1950	929	44	885	-	885	209	59	597	21	-	-
1953	1273	14	1259	-	1259	284	95	863	18	-	-
1955	1591	26	1565	-	1565	383	116	1029	38	-	-
1957	1848	36	1812	-	1812	390	135	1260	27	-	-
1960	1933	40	1893	-	1893	401	179	1281	32	-	-
1961	1854	40	1814	-	1814	372	200	1199	41	-	-
1962	2004	40	1964	-	1964	399	248	1272	42	-	-
1963	2148	40	2108	332	1776	368	159	1218	29	-	-
1964	2148	30	2118	2250	-132	116	45	-321	30	-	-
1965	2361	60	2301	2768	-467	-21	26	-504	39	-	-
EQUATORIAL AFRICA											
1925	5	2	3	-	3	3	-	-	-	-	-
1929	9	1	8	-	8	5	2	2	-	-	-
1933	13	2	11	-	11	8	2	-	2	-	-
1937	39	21	18	-	18	9	3	5	2	-	-
1938	31	11	20	-	20	12	3	3	2	-	-
1950	90	7	83	-	83	54	6	17	6	-	-
1953	130	4	126	-	126	66	14	42	5	-	-
1955	141	-	141	-	141	83	15	35	9	-	-
1957	-26	-	-26	-215	189	90	15	75	9	-	-
1960	-936	-	-936	-1214	278	122	26	119	11	-	-
1961	-981	-	-981	-1247	266	108	23	122	12	-	-
1962	-1148	-	-1148	-1430	282	119	24	128	11	-	-
1963	-1280	-	-1280	-1568	288	111	30	135	11	-	-
1964	-1382	-	-1382	-1721	339	117	57	153	11	-	-

Table VII. NET ENERGY IMPORTS OR EXPORTS, SELECTED YEARS, 1925-1965

(Thousand metric tons coal equivalent; minus sign [-] = net exports)

Region, country, year	Total energy	Solid fuels	Liquid fuels		Refined petroleum products					Gas	Electricity
			Total	Crude oil	Total	Gasoline	Kerosine	Fuel oils	Lubes and greases		
	(1)	(2)	(3)	(4)	(5)	(6)	(7)	(8)	(9)	(10)	(11)
EQUATORIAL AFRICA (CONTINUED)											
1965	-1682	-	-1682	-2028	347	111	54	170	11	-	-
GHANA											
1925	83	54	29	-	29	14	12	2	2	-	-
1929	126	73	53	-	53	30	17	3	3	-	-
1933	65	27	38	-	38	20	9	6	3	-	-
1937	192	72	120	-	120	38	20	59	5	-	-
1938	211	77	134	-	134	33	14	84	3	-	-
1950	350	63	287	-	287	96	32	149	11	-	-
1953	449	99	350	-	350	131	45	167	8	-	-
1955	609	120	489	-	489	170	54	248	18	-	-
1957	662	110	552	-	552	219	62	257	15	-	-
1960	715	40	675	-	675	210	80	365	21	-	-
1961	679	50	629	-	629	162	63	384	20	-	-
1962	750	30	720	-	720	210	93	393	24	-	-
1963	862	40	822	291	531	150	62	296	24	-	-
1964	1011	40	971	1253	-282	-11	17	-312	24	-	-
1965	948	30	918	1200	-282	-6	23	-332	33	-	-
LIBERIA											
1925	-	-	-	-	-	-	-	-	-	-	-
1929	-	-	-	-	-	-	-	-	-	-	-
1933	-	-	-	-	-	-	-	-	-	-	-
1937	2	-	2	-	2	2	-	-	-	-	-
1938	3	-	3	-	3	2	2	-	-	-	-
1950	24	-	24	-	24	11	5	9	-	-	-
1953	27	-	27	-	27	12	5	9	2	-	-
1955	92	-	92	-	92	17	65	9	2	-	-
1957	48	-	48	-	48	29	6	11	3	-	-
1960	89	-	89	-	89	32	11	44	3	-	-
1961	90	-	90	-	90	39	6	42	3	-	-
1962	138	-	138	-	138	29	12	92	6	-	-
1963	200	-	200	-	200	36	23	135	6	-	-
1964	290	-	290	-	290	42	48	192	8	-	-
1965	327	-	327	-	327	39	48	233	8	-	-
NIGERIA											
1925	32	-3	35	-	35	9	23	2	2	-	-
1929	33	-20	53	-	53	20	29	2	3	-	-
1933	28	4	24	-	24	11	11	2	2	-	-
1937	52	-5	57	-	57	32	17	6	3	-	-
1938	46	-14	60	-	60	35	17	6	3	-	-
1950	309	61	248	-	248	144	54	42	8	-	-
1953	367	23	344	-	344	186	68	83	8	-	-
1955	370	-100	470	-	470	233	84	137	17	-	-
1957	511	-100	611	-	611	294	102	195	20	-	-
1960	-407	-30	-377	-1290	914	342	153	386	29	-	-
1961	-2288	-50	-2238	-3413	1175	363	195	584	29	-	-
1962	-3959	-30	-3929	-5031	1103	350	209	507	32	-	-
1963	-4354	-40	-4314	-5631	1317	392	248	636	35	-	-
1964	-7295	-60	-7235	-8814	1580	444	336	755	38	-	-

Table VII. NET ENERGY IMPORTS OR EXPORTS, SELECTED YEARS, 1925-1965

(Thousand metric tons coal equivalent; minus sign [-] = net exports)

Region, country, year	Total energy	Solid fuels	Liquid fuels: Total	Liquid fuels: Crude oil	Refined petroleum products: Total	Gasoline	Kerosine	Fuel oils	Lubes and greases	Gas	Electricity
	(1)	(2)	(3)	(4)	(5)	(6)	(7)	(8)	(9)	(10)	(11)
NIGERIA (CONTINUED)											
1965	-18307	-35	-18272	-19842	1571	428	303	795	35	-	-
RHODESIAN FEDERATION											
1925	-217	-226	9	-	9	6	2	-	2	-	-
1929	-366	-396	30	-	30	21	5	-	5	-	-
1933	-9	-45	36	-	36	26	2	8	2	-	-
1937	-74	-152	78	-	78	45	3	24	6	-	-
1938	-33	-115	83	-	83	50	3	24	6	-	-
1950	86	-169	255	-	255	180	42	20	14	-	-
1953	303	-98	401	-	401	245	54	87	15	-	-
1955	473	-69	542	-	542	315	60	135	32	-	-
1957	423	-273	696	-	696	360	60	240	36	-	-
1960	552	-248	800	-	800	390	90	285	35	-	-
1961	577	-290	801	-	801	392	105	275	30	-	66
1962	739	-180	852	-	852	395	117	303	36	-	67
1963	667	-230	854	-	854	374	125	320	33	-	44
1964	595	-330	890	-	890	380	129	347	32	-	35
1965	827	-460	1245	765	480	194	101	144	41	-	42
MALAWI											
1925	2	-	2	-	2	2	-	-	-	-	-
1929	5	3	2	-	2	2	-	-	-	-	-
1933	6	3	3	-	3	3	-	-	-	-	-
1937	8	5	3	-	3	3	-	-	-	-	-
1938	9	4	5	-	5	3	-	2	-	-	-
1950	48	25	23	-	23	12	3	8	-	-	-
1953	64	37	27	-	27	15	3	9	-	-	-
1955	87	42	45	-	45	30	-	15	-	-	-
1957	107	47	60	-	60	30	-	30	-	-	-
1960	132	57	75	-	75	30	15	30	-	-	-
1961	122	60	62	-	62	26	8	29	-	-	-
1962	126	60	66	-	66	26	9	32	-	-	-
1963	131	60	71	-	71	27	11	33	-	-	-
1964	134	60	74	-	74	29	11	35	-	-	-
1965	161	80	81	-	81	32	12	38	-	-	-
ZAMBIA											
1925	44	42	2	-	2	-	-	-	-	-	-
1929	148	142	6	-	6	5	-	-	2	-	-
1933	182	177	5	-	5	5	-	-	-	-	-
1937	349	341	8	-	8	6	-	-	2	-	-
1938	414	405	9	-	9	8	-	-	2	-	-
1950	714	654	60	-	60	39	9	9	3	-	-
1953	927	823	104	-	104	62	11	26	6	-	-
1955	1015	880	135	-	135	75	15	45	NA	-	-
1957	1105	940	165	-	165	90	15	60	NA	-	-
1960	1230	1035	195	-	195	105	15	75	NA	-	-
1961	1477	1080	200	-	200	117	18	65	NA	-	197
1962	1416	990	207	-	207	117	20	71	NA	-	219
1963	1379	940	210	-	210	114	20	75	NA	-	229
1964	1524	1040	230	-	230	116	21	81	11	-	254

Table VII. NET ENERGY IMPORTS OR EXPORTS, SELECTED YEARS, 1925-1965

(Thousand metric tons coal equivalent; minus sign [-] = net exports)

Region, country, year	Total energy	Solid fuels	Liquid fuels: Total	Liquid fuels: Crude oil	Refined petroleum products: Total	Gasoline	Kerosine	Fuel oils	Lubes and greases	Gas	Electricity
	(1)	(2)	(3)	(4)	(5)	(6)	(7)	(8)	(9)	(10)	(11)
ZAMBIA (CONTINUED)											
1965	1792	1215	303	-	303	149	29	108	17	-	274
RHODESIA											
1925	-261	-268	8	-	8	5	2	-	2	-	-
1929	-519	-541	23	-	23	15	5	-	3	-	-
1933	-197	-225	29	-	29	18	2	8	2	-	-
1937	-431	-498	68	-	68	36	3	24	5	-	-
1938	-455	-524	69	-	69	39	3	23	5	-	-
1950	-676	-848	173	-	173	129	30	3	11	-	-
1953	-688	-958	270	-	270	168	41	53	9	-	-
1955	-630	-991	362	-	362	210	45	75	32	-	-
1957	-789	-1260	471	-	471	240	45	150	36	-	-
1960	-811	-1340	530	-	530	255	60	180	35	-	-
1961	-1022	-1430	540	-	540	249	80	182	30	-	-132
1962	-803	-1230	579	-	579	252	89	201	36	-	-152
1963	-842	-1230	573	-	573	233	95	212	33	-	-185
1964	-1062	-1430	587	-	587	236	98	231	21	-	-219
1965	-1125	-1755	861	765	96	14	60	-2	24	-	-231
WEST AFRICA											
1925	226	181	45	-	45	NA	NA	NA	NA	-	-
1929	475	296	179	-	179	20	11	141	8	-	-
1933	520	115	405	-	405	23	6	374	3	-	-
1937	1478	399	1079	-	1079	44	12	1017	6	-	-
1938	181	98	83	-	83	42	12	23	6	-	-
1950	1392	165	1227	-	1227	120	45	1005	57	-	-
1953	2168	56	2112	-	2112	200	57	1838	18	-	-
1955	2244	30	2214	-	2214	240	90	1860	24	-	-
1957	3396	1	3395	-	3395	300	105	2970	20	-	-
1960	2629	1	2628	-	2628	384	119	2097	23	-	-
1961	2605	1	2604	-	2604	389	120	2069	21	-	-
1962	2763	-	2763	-	2763	402	123	2208	24	-	-
1963	2814	-	2814	27	2787	399	141	2216	26	-	-
1964	2997	-	2997	435	2562	402	138	1989	27	-	-
1965	3278	-	3278	981	2297	324	126	1815	29	-	-
SOUTH AFRICA											
1925	-1404	-1597	194	-	194	104	62	3	26	-	-
1929	-1082	-1652	570	-	570	335	110	83	44	-	-
1933	-172	-782	611	-	611	366	63	144	38	-	-
1937	664	-794	1458	-	1458	699	90	600	69	-	-
1938	749	-877	1626	-	1626	771	87	710	59	-	-
1950	900	-2546	3446	-	3446	1631	528	1178	110	-	-
1953	2586	-1184	3770	44	3726	1902	705	1002	117	-	-
1955	4128	-560	4688	1410	3278	1589	717	774	198	-	-
1957	5527	-550	6077	1604	4473	1581	699	1992	201	-	-
1960	4514	-960	5474	1922	3552	1743	593	1052	165	-	-
1961	5051	-1060	6111	2223	3888	1832	608	1260	189	-	-
1962	4877	-1600	6477	2426	4052	1866	585	1376	225	-	-
1963	5423	-1350	6773	3285	3488	1659	594	1071	164	-	-
1964	7417	-1280	8697	7275	1422	1005	656	-464	228	-	-

Table VII. NET ENERGY IMPORTS OR EXPORTS, SELECTED YEARS, 1925-1965

(Thousand metric tons coal equivalent; minus sign [-] = net exports)

Region, country, year	Total energy	Solid fuels	Liquid fuels: Total	Liquid fuels: Crude oil	Refined petroleum products: Total	Refined petroleum products: Gasoline	Refined petroleum products: Kerosine	Refined petroleum products: Fuel oils	Refined petroleum products: Lubes and greases	Gas	Electricity
	(1)	(2)	(3)	(4)	(5)	(6)	(7)	(8)	(9)	(10)	(11)
SOUTH AFRICA (CONTINUED)											
1965	8037	-1200	9237	7013	2225	1071	567	306	282	-	-
DEVELOPED COUNTRIES											
1925	5166	-14549	19712	19452	260	1773	-1266	-279	17	-3	6
1929	25913	-9255	35193	26126	9068	4215	158	4338	354	-5	-20
1933	37599	-1889	39587	17588	21999	9596	1622	10805	-23	-79	-20
1937	44180	-2459	46859	23784	23075	9011	1059	11770	-285	-181	-38
1938	46186	499	45788	22542	23246	8348	1185	11803	-170	-65	-36
1950	173511	3736	170546	109790	60756	12692	4664	44534	-1031	-807	36
1953	235180	6760	229353	191252	38102	2669	3152	33723	-1218	-783	-150
1955	309258	7069	303171	245084	58088	2495	3891	53438	-1325	-805	-178
1957	355731	641	355301	278072	77229	3549	3063	72360	-1260	8	-219
1960	530423	14265	514698	410558	104141	6693	1812	98103	-1773	1469	-9
1961	585905	14037	570431	460802	109629	6758	996	104429	-1757	1673	-236
1962	657763	17010	639261	506033	133229	7041	5870	122589	-1884	1499	-7
1963	737247	16843	718976	573680	145296	7995	7773	132321	-2363	1460	-31
1964	838238	20888	815864	658763	157101	8124	8906	142262	-1979	1606	-120
1965	936212	19562	913890	740787	173103	5871	10434	159180	-2193	2719	42
UNDERDEVELOPED COUNTRIES											
1925	-9565	13513	-23081	-15134	-7947	-1622	1017	-7671	281	3	-
1929	-21763	13999	-35768	-20012	-15756	-4032	-17	-11957	246	5	-
1933	-28827	8688	-37596	-15291	-22305	-7089	-423	-14966	173	79	3
1937	-44108	11655	-55947	-19403	-36545	-8342	-913	-27303	14	181	2
1938	-43779	9412	-53259	-17283	-35976	-8409	-853	-26769	56	65	2
1950	-183231	5551	-189675	-104217	-85458	-13179	-4910	-69801	864	876	16
1953	-244475	3650	-248865	-185658	-63207	-4943	-3105	-55894	540	719	27
1955	-302868	5104	-308733	-240630	-68103	-4941	-4832	-59384	629	739	21
1957	-351610	5124	-356457	-280068	-76389	-5231	-6681	-65996	1022	-240	-37
1960	-496713	4747	-499884	-391679	-108206	-9854	-7356	-92235	735	-1560	-16
1961	-535321	4171	-537792	-425079	-112713	-9189	-7494	-97518	906	-1758	59
1962	-613555	3660	-615735	-474122	-141614	-13071	-8366	-121382	783	-1548	68
1963	-688037	3664	-690264	-537204	-153060	-15338	-8925	-130329	1254	-1512	75
1964	-784957	3947	-787187	-620393	-166794	-17375	-12128	-137702	660	-1734	17
1965	-868702	3900	-869765	-686897	-182868	-20520	-14050	-148116	127	-2844	6
COMMUNIST COUNTRIES											
1925	-9925	-8212	-1722	32	-1754	-834	36	-882	-264	-	9
1929	-22188	-14940	-7257	-5	-7253	-2690	-1160	-3342	-357	-	9
1933	-26338	-13557	-12783	-813	-11970	-4439	-1305	-6180	-410	-	2
1937	-24786	-17186	-7602	-27	-7575	-2844	-1011	-3735	-270	-	2
1938	-19838	-13905	-5933	-261	-5672	-2372	-1004	-2348	-192	-	-
1950	-11548	-12529	968	2378	-1410	-1448	-585	22	-	41	-27
1953	-13995	-9706	-4317	1563	-5880	-2475	-1148	-1508	-	28	-
1955	-21268	-14340	-6977	800	-7776	-1965	-573	-5157	-65	29	19
1957	-26670	-14830	-11900	-1109	-10791	-1157	-936	-8504	-191	60	-
1960	-54981	-19850	-35187	-15170	-20018	-983	-810	-17550	-646	36	20
1961	-67194	-21020	-46209	-23412	-22797	-1499	-725	-19839	-707	36	-1
1962	-75090	-23450	-51705	-25664	-26042	-1707	-1137	-22367	-812	7	59
1963	-80803	-23710	-57176	-28298	-28878	-2145	-875	-25173	-675	24	59

Table VII. NET ENERGY IMPORTS OR EXPORTS, SELECTED YEARS, 1925-1965

(Thousand metric tons coal equivalent; minus sign [-] = net exports)

Region, country, year	Total energy	Solid fuels	Liquid fuels		Refined petroleum products					Gas	Electricity
			Total	Crude oil	Total	Gasoline	Kerosine	Fuel oils	Lubes and greases		
	(1)	(2)	(3)	(4)	(5)	(6)	(7)	(8)	(9)	(10)	(11)
COMMUNIST COUNTRIES (CONTINUED)											
1964	-87134	-24410	-62751	-32777	-29975	-2060	-804	-26424	-686	37	-11
1965	-95745	-24246	-71477	-37059	-34418	-2480	-1328	-29940	-651	-17	-5
USSR											
1925	-1636	325	-1961	-81	-1880	-407	-621	-711	-141	-	-
1929	-5885	-242	-5643	-443	-5201	-1617	-1109	-2162	-314	-	-
1933	-8228	-1020	-7208	-794	-6414	-1926	-768	-3351	-369	-	-
1937	-2768	-243	-2525	-165	-2360	-366	-270	-1409	-315	-	-
1938	-1004	724	-1728	-323	-1406	-219	-207	-761	-219	-	-
1950	11167	8800	2400	1800	600	NA	NA	NA	NA	-33	-
1953	4323	5500	-1050	-300	-750	NA	NA	NA	NA	-127	-
1955	-922	3300	-4037	-2012	-2025	875	-138	-2697	-65	-186	1
1957	-21526	-6990	-14309	-6888	-7421	477	-921	-6804	-173	-228	-
1960	-53078	-9330	-43421	-24989	-18432	-966	-1182	-15899	-386	-324	-4
1961	-69322	-12510	-56444	-33750	-22694	-2714	-1205	-18360	-416	-360	-9
1962	-81167	-16860	-63876	-38675	-25202	-2361	-1577	-20781	-483	-402	-29
1963	-92463	-19090	-72878	-44550	-28328	-2711	-1598	-23660	-360	-402	-93
1964	-103917	-21530	-81834	-55037	-26798	-2042	-1109	-23438	-210	-390	-163
1965	-112833	-18405	-93719	-65148	-28571	-1698	-1494	-25190	-189	-522	-188
COMMUNIST EASTERN EUROPE											
1925	-9902	-8738	-1173	113	-1286	-465	-534	-317	-161	-	9
1929	-16689	-13477	-3221	438	-3659	-1193	-1154	-1491	-117	-	9
1933	-17123	-9899	-7226	57	-7283	-2693	-1451	-3381	-122	-	2
1937	-19208	-12523	-6687	-6	-6681	-2781	-1391	-2747	-48	-	2
1938	-16859	-11577	-5282	-51	-5231	-2361	-1209	-1868	-36	-	-
1950	-22714	-21329	-1432	578	-2010	-1448	-585	22	-	75	-27
1953	-18319	-15206	-3267	1863	-5130	-2475	-1148	-1508	-	155	-
1955	-21389	-16620	-5003	2211	-7214	-3230	-915	-3053	-	216	18
1957	-6847	-6100	-1035	5142	-6177	-2888	-683	-2585	-18	288	-
1960	-6338	-9600	2879	8904	-6026	-2177	-378	-3182	-261	360	24
1961	-1822	-7390	5165	10218	-5054	-1223	-360	-3152	-291	396	8
1962	3555	-5370	8429	12801	-4373	-1019	-348	-2658	-329	409	88
1963	9708	-3190	12320	16028	-3708	-822	-72	-2489	-315	426	152
1964	15820	-1660	16901	21960	-5060	-986	-26	-3572	-476	428	152
1965	17158	-4226	20697	27774	-7077	-1374	47	-5268	-462	505	182
COMMUNIST ASIA											
1925	1613	201	1412	-	1412	38	1191	146	38	-	-
1929	386	-1221	1607	-	1607	120	1103	311	74	-	-
1933	-988	-2638	1650	-77	1727	180	914	552	81	-	-
1937	-2811	-4420	1610	144	1466	303	650	420	93	-	-
1938	-1975	-3052	1077	113	965	209	413	281	63	-	-
1950	NA	NA	NA	NA	NA	NA	NA	NA	NA	NA	NA
1953	NA	NA	NA	NA	NA	NA	NA	NA	NA	NA	NA
1955	1043	-1020	2063	600	1463	390	480	593	NA	NA	NA
1957	1704	-1740	3444	638	2807	1254	668	885	NA	NA	NA
1960	4435	-920	5355	915	4440	2160	750	1530	NA	NA	NA
1961	3950	-1120	5070	120	4950	2438	840	1673	NA	NA	NA
1962	2523	-1220	3743	210	3533	1673	788	1073	NA	NA	NA

Table VII. NET ENERGY IMPORTS OR EXPORTS, SELECTED YEARS, 1925-1965

(Thousand metric tons coal equivalent; minus sign [-] = net exports)

Region, country, year	Total energy	Solid fuels	Liquid fuels: Total	Liquid fuels: Crude oil	Refined petroleum products: Total	Gasoline	Kerosine	Fuel oils	Lubes and greases	Gas	Electricity
	(1)	(2)	(3)	(4)	(5)	(6)	(7)	(8)	(9)	(10)	(11)
COMMUNIST ASIA (CONTINUED)											
1963	1953	-1430	3383	225	3158	1388	795	975	NA	NA	NA
1964	963	-1220	2183	300	1883	968	330	585	NA	NA	NA
1965	-70	-1615	1545	315	1230	593	120	518	NA	NA	NA
ORGANISATION FOR ECONOMIC CO-OPERATION AND DEVELOPMENT (OECD)											
1925	3838	-14149	17984	19118	-1134	941	-1532	-444	-113	-3	6
1929	21233	-10420	31679	25274	6405	2384	-233	4098	156	-5	-20
1933	33105	-2990	36194	17061	19133	7917	1260	10128	-173	-79	-20
1937	36290	-4606	41115	23180	17936	6183	547	10204	-519	-181	-38
1938	38196	-1186	39483	21923	17561	5226	699	9936	-378	-65	-36
1950	159432	3217	156986	107987	48999	7400	3522	39585	-1405	-807	36
1953	219566	5555	214940	189177	25763	-3551	1965	29009	-1437	-783	-145
1955	285322	3840	282458	235614	46844	-2945	2598	49416	-1815	-805	-171
1957	326461	-3030	329684	262196	67488	-215	1928	68010	-1761	8	-200
1960	499320	11910	485991	389381	96611	2898	864	95892	-2362	1469	-50
1961	554708	13260	540023	438063	101960	3123	98	101924	-2392	1673	-248
1962	626661	17030	608130	485063	123068	2595	4650	118688	-2469	1499	3
1963	702196	17220	683553	548894	134660	3498	6495	128039	-2932	1460	-36
1964	797934	21565	775013	627858	147155	4431	7626	137826	-2512	1606	-250
1965	892782	22341	867801	704835	162966	3011	9098	153732	-2682	2719	-79
COMMUNIST COUNTRIES											
1925	-9925	-8212	-1722	32	-1754	-834	36	-882	-264	-	9
1929	-22188	-14940	-7257	-5	-7253	-2690	-1160	-3342	-357	-	9
1933	-26338	-13557	-12783	-813	-11970	-4439	-1305	-6180	-410	-	2
1937	-24786	-17186	-7602	-27	-7575	-2844	-1011	-3735	-270	-	2
1938	-19838	-13905	-5933	-261	-5672	-2372	-1004	-2348	-192	-	-
1950	-11548	-12529	968	2378	-1410	-1448	-585	22	-	41	-27
1953	-13995	-9706	-4317	1563	-5880	-2475	-1148	-1508	-	28	-
1955	-21268	-14340	-6977	800	-7776	-1965	-573	-5157	-65	29	19
1957	-26670	-14830	-11900	-1109	-10791	-1157	-936	-8504	-191	60	-
1960	-54981	-19850	-35187	-15170	-20018	-983	-810	-17550	-646	36	20
1961	-67194	-21020	-46209	-23412	-22797	-1499	-725	-19839	-707	36	-1
1962	-75090	-23450	-51705	-25664	-26042	-1707	-1137	-22367	-812	7	59
1963	-80803	-23710	-57176	-28298	-28878	-2145	-875	-25173	-675	24	59
1964	-87134	-24410	-62751	-32777	-29975	-2060	-804	-26424	-686	37	-11
1965	-95745	-24246	-71477	-37059	-34418	-2480	-1328	-29940	-651	-17	-5
WORLD EXCLUDING OECD AND COMMUNIST COUNTRIES											
1925	-8237	13113	-21353	-14799	-6554	-789	1283	-7506	410	3	-
1929	-17084	15164	-32253	-19160	-13094	-2201	373	-11717	444	5	-
1933	-24333	9789	-34203	-14765	-19439	-5411	-62	-14289	323	79	3
1937	-36218	13802	-50204	-18798	-31406	-5514	-402	-25737	248	181	2
1938	-35790	11097	-46955	-16664	-30291	-5288	-367	-24901	264	65	2
1950	-169152	6070	-176115	-102414	-73701	-7887	-3768	-64852	1239	876	16
1953	-228861	4855	-234452	-183584	-50868	1277	-1918	-51180	759	719	22
1955	-278932	8333	-288020	-231161	-56859	498	-3539	-55362	1119	739	15
1957	-322341	8795	-330840	-264192	-66648	-1467	-5546	-61646	1523	-240	-56
1960	-465610	7102	-471177	-370502	-100676	-6059	-6408	-90024	1324	-1560	25

Table VII. NET ENERGY IMPORTS OR EXPORTS, SELECTED YEARS, 1925-1965

(Thousand metric tons coal equivalent; minus sign [-] = net exports)

Region, country, year	Total energy	Solid fuels	Liquid fuels		Refined petroleum products					Gas	Electricity
			Total	Crude oil	Total	Gasoline	Kerosine	Fuel oils	Lubes and greases		
	(1)	(2)	(3)	(4)	(5)	(6)	(7)	(8)	(9)	(10)	(11)
WORLD EXCLUDING OECD AND COMMUNIST COUNTRIES (CONTINUED)											
1961	-504123	4948	-507384	-402341	-105044	-5555	-6596	-95013	1542	-1758	71
1962	-582453	3640	-584604	-453152	-131453	-8625	-7146	-117480	1368	-1548	59
1963	-652986	3287	-654842	-512418	-142424	-10841	-7647	-126047	1824	-1512	80
1964	-744654	3270	-746336	-589488	-156848	-13682	-10848	-133266	1194	-1734	146
1965	-825272	1121	-823676	-650945	-172731	-17659	-12714	-142668	616	-2844	127

DERIVATION OF TABLE VIII

Column	*Derivation*[a]
(1), (6)	Col. (1) table VI as percent of col. (1) table VI (= 100)
(2), (7)	Col. (2) table VI as percent of col. (1) table VI
(3), (8)	Col. (3) table VI as percent of col. (1) table VI
(4), (9)	Col. (4) table VI as percent of col. (1) table VI
(5), (10)	Cols. (3), (8) minus cols. (4), (9) respectively

[a]Cols. (1) through (5) derived from the import panel of table VI.
Cols. (6) through (10) derived from the export panel of table VI.

Table VIII. ENERGY IMPORTS AND EXPORTS PERCENTAGE DISTRIBUTION, SELECTED YEARS, 1925-1965

(Based on coal equivalents)

Region, country, year	Imports					Exports				
	Total	Solid fuels	Total liquid fuels	Crude oil	Refined petroleum products	Total	Solid fuels	Total liquid fuels	Crude oil	Refined petroleum products
	(1)	(2)	(3)	(4)	(5)	(6)	(7)	(8)	(9)	(10)
WORLD										
1925	100.0	68.4	31.5	14.1	17.3	100.0	68.2	31.7	11.1	20.6
1929	100.0	60.6	39.3	19.5	19.8	100.0	60.4	39.5	16.2	23.3
1933	100.0	52.4	47.4	22.3	25.1	100.0	51.4	48.5	20.0	28.5
1937	100.0	48.7	51.0	25.9	25.1	100.0	47.5	52.3	22.5	29.8
1938	100.0	44.5	55.3	28.2	27.1	100.0	43.3	56.5	24.9	31.7
1950	100.0	24.5	75.1	45.5	29.5	100.0	24.2	75.5	42.0	33.5
1953	100.0	21.2	78.6	50.6	27.9	100.0	20.3	79.4	47.6	31.8
1955	100.0	20.6	79.1	51.4	27.7	100.0	20.5	79.2	49.7	29.5
1957	100.0	18.6	81.1	52.8	28.4	100.0	19.2	80.5	51.7	28.8
1960	100.0	13.3	85.9	58.2	27.7	100.0	13.1	86.1	56.6	29.5
1961	100.0	12.4	86.6	60.1	26.5	100.0	12.5	86.5	58.1	28.5
1962	100.0	12.0	86.6	60.5	26.1	100.0	11.9	86.7	58.4	28.3
1963	100.0	12.1	86.6	61.4	25.2	100.0	12.1	86.7	59.3	27.3
1964	100.0	11.3	87.4	63.8	23.6	100.0	11.0	87.7	61.9	25.8
1965	100.0	10.2	88.5	65.4	23.1	100.0	10.1	88.6	63.2	25.5
NORTH AMERICA										
1925	100.0	43.6	55.9	45.1	10.9	100.0	47.4	52.2	6.7	45.5
1929	100.0	36.8	62.8	48.2	14.7	100.0	39.7	59.9	11.1	48.8
1933	100.0	40.3	59.3	46.1	13.3	100.0	31.9	67.4	25.3	42.1

Table VIII. ENERGY IMPORTS AND EXPORTS PERCENTAGE DISTRIBUTION, SELECTED YEARS, 1925-1965

(Based on coal equivalents)

Region, country, year	Imports: Total	Imports: Solid fuels	Imports: Total liquid fuels	Imports: Crude oil	Imports: Refined petroleum products	Exports: Total	Exports: Solid fuels	Exports: Total liquid fuels	Exports: Crude oil	Exports: Refined petroleum products
	(1)	(2)	(3)	(4)	(5)	(6)	(7)	(8)	(9)	(10)
NORTH AMERICA (CONTINUED)										
1937	100.0	39.7	59.6	43.6	16.0	100.0	29.2	70.0	28.9	41.1
1938	100.0	38.3	61.0	43.5	17.5	100.0	23.5	75.9	32.3	43.6
1950	100.0	22.3	77.4	48.7	28.6	100.0	57.2	40.1	15.4	24.7
1953	100.0	17.0	82.8	54.0	28.8	100.0	56.2	42.1	7.9	34.2
1955	100.0	12.9	86.7	56.9	29.8	100.0	65.3	33.0	7.1	25.9
1957	100.0	10.8	88.7	60.1	28.7	100.0	60.1	39.4	17.8	21.6
1960	100.0	6.6	90.3	56.5	33.8	100.0	57.4	35.3	14.8	20.5
1961	100.0	5.8	90.2	56.5	33.7	100.0	52.7	37.4	21.2	16.2
1962	100.0	5.4	88.1	55.1	33.0	100.0	46.9	36.8	23.5	13.3
1963	100.0	5.5	88.1	54.6	33.5	100.0	51.0	34.6	20.4	14.2
1964	100.0	5.8	87.7	53.3	34.4	100.0	49.3	35.3	22.0	13.3
1965	100.0	5.9	88.0	50.1	37.9	100.0	50.0	34.9	22.9	11.9
CANADA										
1925	100.0	79.2	20.8	17.2	3.6	100.0	77.1	6.6	4.0	2.6
1929	100.0	68.1	31.9	27.2	4.7	100.0	69.0	15.7	12.8	3.0
1933	100.0	60.8	39.2	34.7	4.6	100.0	45.9	31.5	12.1	19.5
1937	100.0	59.6	40.4	36.9	3.5	100.0	50.8	14.9	-	14.9
1938	100.0	58.7	41.3	36.1	5.1	100.0	54.9	7.4	-	7.4
1950	100.0	52.4	47.2	36.6	10.6	100.0	73.8	0.8	-	0.8
1953	100.0	47.1	52.9	38.8	14.1	100.0	28.9	42.0	39.1	2.9
1955	100.0	41.6	58.4	42.6	15.8	100.0	14.5	73.2	69.0	4.2
1957	100.0	37.2	62.0	49.2	12.9	100.0	3.5	92.4	87.2	5.3
1960	100.0	27.4	72.6	58.0	14.6	100.0	6.0	62.8	58.8	4.1
1961	100.0	25.4	74.6	62.3	12.3	100.0	4.7	64.8	62.2	2.6
1962	100.0	25.5	74.5	61.9	12.7	100.0	2.7	58.0	55.3	2.7
1963	100.0	24.8	75.2	62.3	12.9	100.0	2.9	57.5	54.9	2.6
1964	100.0	26.5	73.5	58.0	15.4	100.0	3.3	57.9	54.6	3.3
1965	100.0	26.8	73.2	52.3	20.8	100.0	3.0	59.8	55.7	4.0
UNITED STATES										
1925	100.0	5.8	93.3	74.7	18.6	100.0	46.7	53.3	6.8	46.5
1929	100.0	4.3	95.0	70.0	25.0	100.0	39.1	60.9	11.0	49.9
1933	100.0	7.1	91.8	64.5	27.3	100.0	31.7	68.1	25.6	42.5
1937	100.0	6.3	92.1	54.9	37.2	100.0	28.9	70.8	29.4	41.4
1938	100.0	5.3	92.9	55.5	37.4	100.0	23.1	76.8	32.7	44.1
1950	100.0	1.1	98.6	57.3	41.3	100.0	56.9	40.8	15.6	25.2
1953	100.0	0.4	99.2	62.4	36.9	100.0	56.7	42.1	7.2	34.8
1955	100.0	0.4	99.1	63.2	35.8	100.0	68.3	30.6	3.4	27.2
1957	100.0	0.3	99.3	64.4	34.9	100.0	66.7	33.2	9.7	23.5
1960	100.0	0.2	95.8	56.1	39.7	100.0	73.1	26.9	1.4	25.5
1961	100.0	0.2	94.7	54.9	39.8	100.0	75.7	24.3	1.6	22.7
1962	100.0	0.2	91.6	53.4	38.2	100.0	78.3	21.7	0.8	20.8
1963	100.0	0.2	91.7	52.5	39.2	100.0	78.5	21.5	0.6	20.9
1964	100.0	0.2	91.5	52.0	39.5	100.0	79.5	20.5	0.5	20.0
1965	100.0	0.1	92.1	49.6	42.6	100.0	82.2	17.8	0.4	17.3
WESTERN EUROPE										
1925	100.0	82.8	17.1	3.7	13.4	100.0	98.8	1.1	-	1.1
1929	100.0	80.1	19.8	2.9	17.0	100.0	99.1	0.8	-	0.8

Table VIII. ENERGY IMPORTS AND EXPORTS PERCENTAGE DISTRIBUTION, SELECTED YEARS, 1925-1965

(Based on coal equivalents)

Region, country, year	Imports					Exports				
	Total	Solid fuels	Total liquid fuels	Crude oil	Refined petroleum products	Total	Solid fuels	Total liquid fuels	Crude oil	Refined petroleum products
	(1)	(2)	(3)	(4)	(5)	(6)	(7)	(8)	(9)	(10)
WESTERN EUROPE (CONTINUED)										
1933	100.0	68.3	31.5	7.0	24.5	100.0	98.5	1.3	0.1	1.2
1937	100.0	66.6	33.3	11.0	22.3	100.0	97.5	2.3	-	2.3
1938	100.0	61.4	38.4	13.7	24.8	100.0	97.1	2.6	-	2.6
1950	100.0	37.9	61.8	37.0	24.9	100.0	78.9	20.7	2.4	18.3
1953	100.0	29.8	70.1	51.9	18.2	100.0	56.7	42.8	3.3	39.4
1955	100.0	31.8	68.0	48.6	19.4	100.0	58.5	40.9	2.2	38.7
1957	100.0	29.8	70.0	47.2	22.8	100.0	54.7	44.3	1.9	42.4
1960	100.0	18.0	81.8	59.0	22.8	100.0	41.8	57.5	2.3	55.2
1961	100.0	16.3	83.5	62.7	20.9	100.0	40.7	58.4	2.1	56.2
1962	100.0	15.5	84.3	61.6	22.8	100.0	38.3	61.0	3.0	58.0
1963	100.0	15.9	84.0	61.8	22.2	100.0	39.3	60.0	3.2	56.9
1964	100.0	13.6	86.2	65.1	21.1	100.0	35.6	63.5	0.9	62.7
1965	100.0	11.2	88.5	67.9	20.5	100.0	28.9	70.1	0.5	69.6
EUROPEAN ECONOMIC COMMUNITY (EEC)										
1925	100.0	90.2	9.7	0.7	9.0	100.0	99.6	0.4	-	0.4
1929	100.0	86.9	12.9	0.9	12.1	100.0	99.4	0.6	-	0.6
1933	100.0	75.9	23.9	7.1	16.8	100.0	98.6	1.3	0.1	1.2
1937	100.0	72.4	27.4	13.7	13.7	100.0	97.6	2.4	-	2.4
1938	100.0	66.8	33.0	17.8	15.1	100.0	97.0	3.0	-	3.0
1950	100.0	40.5	59.0	48.8	10.2	100.0	77.7	22.0	-	22.0
1953	100.0	33.9	65.9	58.9	6.9	100.0	59.1	40.5	-	40.5
1955	100.0	34.0	65.7	57.6	8.1	100.0	60.3	39.3	0.1	39.3
1957	100.0	36.1	63.7	52.4	11.3	100.0	58.0	41.1	0.2	41.0
1960	100.0	21.4	78.4	65.8	12.6	100.0	46.2	53.5	1.1	52.4
1961	100.0	19.0	80.7	69.0	11.7	100.0	43.7	56.0	0.9	55.1
1962	100.0	18.2	81.6	67.5	14.1	100.0	43.9	55.7	0.6	55.2
1963	100.0	18.9	80.9	67.8	13.0	100.0	42.8	57.0	0.3	56.7
1964	100.0	15.7	84.1	72.2	12.0	100.0	38.9	60.9	-	60.9
1965	100.0	12.6	87.1	75.8	11.3	100.0	32.3	67.5	-	67.5
BELGIUM-LUXEMBOURG										
1925	100.0	95.7	4.3	0.1	4.2	100.0	99.5	0.5	-	0.5
1929	100.0	95.9	4.1	-	4.1	100.0	99.9	0.1	-	0.1
1933	100.0	91.6	8.4	1.6	6.8	100.0	98.7	1.3	1.2	0.1
1937	100.0	84.9	15.1	3.7	11.3	100.0	93.3	6.7	-	6.7
1938	100.0	80.4	19.6	5.6	14.0	100.0	94.4	5.6	-	5.6
1950	100.0	48.8	51.1	9.3	41.9	100.0	93.0	6.6	-	6.6
1953	100.0	42.0	58.0	34.7	23.3	100.0	69.2	30.5	-	30.5
1955	100.0	40.8	59.1	39.3	19.9	100.0	74.7	25.0	0.4	24.6
1957	100.0	41.7	58.3	37.3	21.0	100.0	62.1	37.2	0.9	36.3
1960	100.0	34.9	65.0	44.4	20.6	100.0	44.7	54.8	-	54.8
1961	100.0	32.9	67.1	46.7	20.3	100.0	51.5	47.4	-	47.4
1962	100.0	31.4	68.6	45.5	23.2	100.0	50.8	48.1	-	48.0
1963	100.0	31.9	68.1	50.6	17.4	100.0	37.1	62.4	-	62.4
1964	100.0	29.3	70.5	51.8	18.8	100.0	37.5	62.2	-	62.2
1965	100.0	26.6	73.2	56.6	16.6	100.0	32.7	66.9	-	66.9

Table VIII. ENERGY IMPORTS AND EXPORTS PERCENTAGE DISTRIBUTION, SELECTED YEARS, 1925-1965

(Based on coal equivalents)

Region, country, year	Imports					Exports				
	Total	Solid fuels	Total liquid fuels	Crude oil	Refined petroleum products	Total	Solid fuels	Total liquid fuels	Crude oil	Refined petroleum products
	(1)	(2)	(3)	(4)	(5)	(6)	(7)	(8)	(9)	(10)
FRANCE										
1925	100.0	90.8	9.1	0.5	8.6	100.0	96.0	4.0	-	4.0
1929	100.0	88.0	11.8	0.7	11.2	100.0	96.5	3.5	-	3.5
1933	100.0	74.3	25.5	12.4	13.1	100.0	83.0	17.0	-	17.0
1937	100.0	71.8	28.0	22.3	5.7	100.0	57.5	42.5	0.1	42.4
1938	100.0	63.9	35.9	30.3	5.6	100.0	59.3	40.7	-	40.7
1950	100.0	38.0	61.9	59.7	2.1	100.0	31.3	68.7	0.2	68.5
1953	100.0	30.3	69.6	68.4	1.2	100.0	20.3	79.7	-	79.7
1955	100.0	29.4	70.4	68.2	2.2	100.0	43.6	56.3	-	56.3
1957	100.0	37.8	61.8	56.2	5.7	100.0	29.4	70.6	0.4	70.3
1960	100.0	23.3	76.5	70.9	5.7	100.0	13.9	86.0	-	86.0
1961	100.0	21.3	78.6	74.1	4.5	100.0	11.7	88.3	-	88.3
1962	100.0	20.4	79.5	74.2	5.3	100.0	11.9	87.3	-	87.3
1963	100.0	23.7	76.0	69.9	6.2	100.0	8.5	91.5	-	91.5
1964	100.0	19.7	79.9	73.8	6.1	100.0	7.8	92.2	-	92.2
1965	100.0	15.2	84.3	79.6	4.7	100.0	6.3	93.7	-	93.7
GERMANY										
1925	100.0	82.5	17.2	0.8	16.4	100.0	99.9	0.1	-	0.1
1929	100.0	70.2	29.6	1.1	28.5	100.0	99.7	0.3	-	0.3
1933	100.0	57.3	42.0	4.8	37.2	100.0	99.6	0.4	-	0.4
1937	100.0	52.3	46.9	8.9	38.0	100.0	99.6	0.4	-	0.4
1938	100.0	50.3	49.0	8.6	40.3	100.0	99.6	0.4	-	0.4
GERMANY, FEDERAL REPUBLIC										
1950	100.0	32.0	64.9	44.2	20.7	100.0	99.3	0.4	-	0.4
1953	100.0	45.4	52.9	43.0	9.9	100.0	97.2	2.3	-	2.3
1955	100.0	49.9	49.1	35.0	14.1	100.0	95.1	4.1	-	4.1
1957	100.0	46.2	53.2	30.6	22.5	100.0	95.1	3.2	-	3.2
1960	100.0	18.5	80.6	62.2	18.4	100.0	88.0	11.5	-	11.4
1961	100.0	15.8	83.4	67.5	15.9	100.0	80.5	19.1	0.1	19.0
1962	100.0	14.1	85.4	61.9	23.5	100.0	83.2	16.3	-	16.3
1963	100.0	12.9	86.7	64.3	22.5	100.0	80.2	19.4	-	19.4
1964	100.0	10.3	89.6	70.3	19.3	100.0	75.7	23.9	-	23.9
1965	100.0	8.8	90.8	71.9	19.0	100.0	77.0	22.6	0.1	22.5
ITALY										
1925	100.0	89.6	10.1	0.5	9.7	100.0	97.2	2.8	-	2.8
1929	100.0	88.1	11.7	0.5	11.1	100.0	64.2	35.8	-	35.8
1933	100.0	78.6	21.2	1.7	19.6	100.0	64.9	35.1	-	35.1
1937	100.0	76.8	23.1	8.4	14.7	100.0	7.4	92.6	-	92.6
1938	100.0	75.2	24.6	13.8	10.8	100.0	7.6	92.4	-	92.4
1950	100.0	50.9	49.0	42.0	7.0	100.0	5.2	94.8	-	94.8
1953	100.0	31.6	68.4	65.8	2.6	100.0	1.3	98.6	-	98.6
1955	100.0	28.4	71.6	69.6	2.0	100.0	0.9	99.1	0.1	99.0
1957	100.0	27.3	72.6	69.6	2.9	100.0	1.3	98.7	0.1	98.6
1960	100.0	18.4	81.6	77.2	4.4	100.0	1.0	98.8	8.4	90.4
1961	100.0	16.1	83.9	78.9	5.0	100.0	0.8	99.2	6.7	92.5
1962	100.0	14.5	85.3	79.5	5.7	100.0	1.2	98.8	3.9	94.9
1963	100.0	13.5	86.3	80.9	5.4	100.0	1.1	98.9	1.9	97.0
1964	100.0	11.2	88.7	85.8	2.9	100.0	0.6	99.4	-	99.4
1965	100.0	9.3	90.7	87.6	3.0	100.0	0.4	99.6	-	99.6

Table VIII. ENERGY IMPORTS AND EXPORTS PERCENTAGE DISTRIBUTION, SELECTED YEARS, 1925-1965

(Based on coal equivalents)

Region, country, year	Imports: Total	Imports: Solid fuels	Imports: Total liquid fuels	Imports: Crude oil	Imports: Refined petroleum products	Exports: Total	Exports: Solid fuels	Exports: Total liquid fuels	Exports: Crude oil	Exports: Refined petroleum products
	(1)	(2)	(3)	(4)	(5)	(6)	(7)	(8)	(9)	(10)
NETHERLANDS										
1925	100.0	90.0	10.0	2.4	7.6	100.0	99.4	0.6	-	0.6
1929	100.0	87.7	12.3	3.0	9.3	100.0	99.3	0.7	0.1	0.7
1933	100.0	82.3	17.6	1.2	16.4	100.0	99.3	0.7	-	0.7
1937	100.0	76.9	23.1	6.1	17.0	100.0	99.5	0.5	-	0.5
1938	100.0	73.3	26.7	5.6	21.0	100.0	99.4	0.6	-	0.6
1950	100.0	34.6	64.4	51.1	13.4	100.0	21.2	78.7	-	78.7
1953	100.0	31.3	68.7	53.8	14.8	100.0	18.9	81.1	-	81.1
1955	100.0	29.2	70.8	57.7	13.0	100.0	20.5	79.5	-	79.5
1957	100.0	28.4	71.6	58.7	12.9	100.0	19.9	80.0	-	80.0
1960	100.0	18.7	81.3	59.0	22.3	100.0	22.0	78.0	0.1	77.9
1961	100.0	16.7	83.2	62.0	21.2	100.0	23.4	76.6	-	76.6
1962	100.0	19.4	80.5	60.4	20.1	100.0	22.4	77.6	-	77.6
1963	100.0	21.1	78.9	60.9	17.9	100.0	26.8	73.2	-	73.2
1964	100.0	17.5	82.5	63.2	19.3	100.0	25.6	74.4	-	74.4
1965	100.0	12.6	87.4	67.0	20.4	100.0	23.7	76.3	0.1	76.2
EUROPEAN FREE TRADE ASSOCIATION (EFTA)										
1925	100.0	64.0	36.0	12.0	24.0	100.0	98.1	1.7	-	1.7
1929	100.0	63.7	36.3	7.8	28.5	100.0	98.8	1.0	-	1.0
1933	100.0	54.6	45.4	7.4	38.0	100.0	98.4	1.2	-	1.2
1937	100.0	54.9	45.1	7.3	37.8	100.0	97.6	1.9	-	1.9
1938	100.0	51.0	49.0	8.3	40.7	100.0	97.4	2.0	-	2.0
1950	100.0	35.2	64.8	24.4	40.4	100.0	81.6	17.5	8.1	9.4
1953	100.0	23.8	76.1	47.4	28.7	100.0	51.5	47.5	10.3	37.2
1955	100.0	29.3	70.7	40.2	30.4	100.0	53.8	45.1	8.4	36.7
1957	100.0	20.3	79.7	42.0	37.7	100.0	44.9	53.8	7.8	46.0
1960	100.0	11.9	88.1	49.7	38.5	100.0	29.5	68.4	6.7	61.8
1961	100.0	10.6	89.3	53.8	35.5	100.0	32.2	64.3	5.8	58.5
1962	100.0	9.8	90.1	52.6	37.5	100.0	24.4	74.1	8.1	66.0
1963	100.0	9.7	90.3	51.2	39.1	100.0	32.3	66.2	9.4	56.8
1964	100.0	8.4	91.5	52.5	39.0	100.0	27.8	69.6	1.9	67.7
1965	100.0	6.9	92.6	54.2	38.4	100.0	18.9	77.2	1.5	75.6
AUSTRIA										
1925	100.0	96.5	3.5	0.5	3.0	100.0	-	-	-	-
1929	100.0	94.9	5.1	1.1	3.9	100.0	-	-	-	-
1933	100.0	86.6	13.4	8.4	4.9	100.0	-	-	-	-
1937	100.0	87.3	12.7	4.2	8.5	100.0	-	-	-	-
1938	100.0	88.4	11.6	5.4	6.1	100.0	-	-	-	-
1950	100.0	98.2	1.8	-	1.8	100.0	0.6	94.5	90.5	4.1
1953	100.0	99.6	0.4	-	0.4	100.0	-	96.0	92.7	3.3
1955	100.0	91.0	9.0	-	9.0	100.0	0.8	93.9	85.0	9.0
1957	100.0	90.9	9.1	-	9.1	100.0	0.9	92.3	73.9	18.5
1960	100.0	66.7	33.3	10.8	22.5	100.0	1.0	87.0	75.8	11.2
1961	100.0	62.0	38.0	11.1	26.9	100.0	1.3	83.1	74.5	8.6
1962	100.0	59.6	40.4	11.7	28.7	100.0	1.5	78.9	55.7	23.1
1963	100.0	58.8	41.2	13.6	27.6	100.0	0.7	83.8	59.6	24.2
1964	100.0	56.4	43.6	13.0	30.6	100.0	1.5	47.2	-	47.2
1965	100.0	55.0	45.0	12.0	33.1	100.0	1.1	45.4	-	45.4

Table VIII. ENERGY IMPORTS AND EXPORTS PERCENTAGE DISTRIBUTION, SELECTED YEARS, 1925-1965

(Based on coal equivalents)

Region, country, year	Imports					Exports				
	Total	Solid fuels	Total liquid fuels	Crude oil	Refined petroleum products	Total	Solid fuels	Total liquid fuels	Crude oil	Refined petroleum products
	(1)	(2)	(3)	(4)	(5)	(6)	(7)	(8)	(9)	(10)
DENMARK										
1925	100.0	89.9	10.0	-	10.0	100.0	-	100.0	-	100.0
1929	100.0	89.5	10.4	0.1	10.4	-	-	-	-	-
1933	100.0	85.1	14.9	-	14.9	-	-	-	-	-
1937	100.0	85.0	14.9	-	14.9	-	-	-	-	-
1938	100.0	80.7	19.3	0.2	19.0	-	-	-	-	-
1950	100.0	67.7	32.0	0.6	31.4	-	-	-	-	-
1953	100.0	65.4	34.2	0.3	33.9	-	-	-	-	-
1955	100.0	60.3	39.7	0.4	39.4	100.0	54.4	8.2	-	8.2
1957	100.0	42.8	56.8	0.4	56.3	100.0	87.0	13.0	-	13.0
1960	100.0	40.4	59.5	0.4	59.1	100.0	60.6	39.4	-	39.4
1961	100.0	35.9	63.3	2.6	60.8	100.0	34.6	65.4	-	65.4
1962	100.0	32.2	67.1	11.4	55.7	100.0	5.8	94.2	-	94.2
1963	100.0	30.0	69.7	16.7	53.0	100.0	12.5	87.5	-	87.5
1964	100.0	24.5	75.0	23.1	51.8	100.0	7.0	93.0	-	93.0
1965	100.0	20.3	78.7	26.4	52.2	100.0	4.1	95.9	-	95.9
NORWAY										
1925	100.0	88.0	12.0	1.1	10.9	100.0	100.0	-	-	-
1929	100.0	87.0	13.0	1.1	12.0	100.0	100.0	-	-	-
1933	100.0	78.0	22.0	1.0	21.0	100.0	92.4	7.6	-	7.6
1937	100.0	79.4	20.6	0.6	20.0	100.0	83.3	16.7	-	16.7
1938	100.0	75.0	25.0	1.6	23.5	100.0	74.3	25.7	-	25.7
1950	100.0	44.2	55.8	0.6	55.2	-	-	-	-	-
1953	100.0	29.7	70.3	2.4	67.9	100.0	-	100.0	-	100.0
1955	100.0	22.8	77.2	2.6	74.6	100.0	87.8	12.2	-	12.2
1957	100.0	19.0	81.0	3.1	77.8	100.0	93.0	7.0	-	7.0
1960	100.0	15.2	84.5	5.1	79.5	100.0	86.3	13.7	-	13.7
1961	100.0	12.1	87.9	34.3	53.7	100.0	13.9	86.1	-	86.1
1962	100.0	10.0	90.0	40.9	49.1	100.0	8.8	89.5	-	89.5
1963	100.0	10.4	89.6	40.6	49.1	100.0	7.9	86.6	-	86.6
1964	100.0	9.4	90.6	42.4	48.2	100.0	3.6	89.3	-	89.3
1965	100.0	10.0	90.0	43.1	46.9	100.0	9.7	78.9	-	78.9
PORTUGAL										
1925	100.0	91.6	8.4	-	8.4	100.0	66.7	33.3	-	33.3
1929	100.0	87.3	12.7	-	12.7	100.0	100.0	-	-	-
1933	100.0	83.9	16.1	-	16.1	100.0	-	100.0	-	100.0
1937	100.0	82.3	17.7	-	17.7	100.0	50.0	50.0	-	50.0
1938	100.0	79.7	20.3	-	20.3	100.0	-	100.0	-	100.0
1950	100.0	41.0	59.0	19.9	39.1	100.0	-	100.0	-	100.0
1953	100.0	25.4	74.6	8.7	65.9	100.0	-	100.0	-	100.0
1955	100.0	17.2	82.8	46.0	36.8	100.0	3.0	97.0	-	97.0
1957	100.0	16.9	83.1	50.1	33.0	100.0	-	100.0	-	100.0
1960	100.0	10.9	89.1	54.7	34.4	100.0	-	100.0	-	100.0
1961	100.0	14.4	85.6	51.1	34.5	100.0	-	100.0	-	100.0
1962	100.0	13.5	86.5	50.8	35.8	100.0	-	100.0	-	100.0
1963	100.0	14.3	85.7	51.9	33.7	100.0	-	97.9	-	97.9
1964	100.0	13.8	86.2	49.7	36.5	100.0	-	99.5	-	99.5
1965	100.0	12.2	86.7	50.5	36.2	100.0	-	100.0	-	100.0

Table VIII. ENERGY IMPORTS AND EXPORTS PERCENTAGE DISTRIBUTION, SELECTED YEARS, 1925-1965

(Based on coal equivalents)

Region, country, year	Imports: Total	Imports: Solid fuels	Imports: Total liquid fuels	Imports: Crude oil	Imports: Refined petroleum products	Exports: Total	Exports: Solid fuels	Exports: Total liquid fuels	Exports: Crude oil	Exports: Refined petroleum products
	(1)	(2)	(3)	(4)	(5)	(6)	(7)	(8)	(9)	(10)
SWEDEN										
1925	100.0	90.4	9.6	-	9.6	100.0	-	75.0	-	75.0
1929	100.0	89.7	10.3	-	10.3	100.0	-	63.2	-	63.2
1933	100.0	83.9	16.1	1.2	14.9	100.0	-	94.5	-	94.5
1937	100.0	83.5	16.5	1.1	15.4	100.0	-	96.2	-	96.2
1938	100.0	79.5	20.5	1.4	19.0	100.0	-	94.1	-	94.1
1950	100.0	54.6	45.4	11.2	34.3	100.0	25.7	52.9	-	52.9
1953	100.0	40.1	59.9	15.4	44.5	100.0	41.0	4.4	-	4.4
1955	100.0	31.4	68.5	16.0	52.5	100.0	64.5	35.5	-	35.5
1957	100.0	25.9	74.1	15.7	58.4	100.0	9.8	42.5	-	42.5
1960	100.0	15.3	84.7	17.0	67.7	100.0	3.6	61.7	-	61.7
1961	100.0	14.1	85.9	16.7	69.2	100.0	12.8	47.2	-	47.2
1962	100.0	12.8	87.2	14.5	72.7	100.0	9.4	59.3	-	59.3
1963	100.0	11.8	88.2	15.0	73.2	100.0	8.2	91.8	-	91.8
1964	100.0	11.4	88.6	17.5	71.1	100.0	3.8	91.3	-	91.3
1965	100.0	9.4	90.6	17.7	72.8	100.0	1.7	81.6	-	81.6
SWITZERLAND										
1925	100.0	92.4	7.6	-	7.6	100.0	-	-	-	-
1929	100.0	89.8	10.2	-	10.2	100.0	-	-	-	-
1933	100.0	84.3	15.7	-	15.7	100.0	-	-	-	-
1937	100.0	85.4	14.6	-	14.6	100.0	-	-	-	-
1938	100.0	84.4	15.6	-	15.6	100.0	-	1.5	-	1.5
1950	100.0	62.9	37.1	-	37.1	100.0	1.3	5.7	-	5.7
1953	100.0	54.3	45.7	-	45.7	100.0	-	-	-	-
1955	100.0	47.7	52.3	-	52.3	100.0	14.8	-	-	-
1957	100.0	46.1	53.9	-	53.9	100.0	11.0	-	-	-
1960	100.0	31.1	68.9	-	68.9	100.0	-	-	-	-
1961	100.0	26.5	73.5	-	73.5	100.0	-	0.7	-	0.7
1962	100.0	24.3	75.7	-	75.7	100.0	-	7.4	-	7.4
1963	100.0	22.4	77.6	4.3	73.3	100.0	-	2.3	-	2.3
1964	100.0	16.3	83.7	10.4	73.3	100.0	-	44.9	-	44.9
1965	100.0	11.7	88.3	13.5	74.9	100.0	-	49.2	-	49.2
UNITED KINGDOM										
1925	100.0	0.2	99.8	38.8	61.1	100.0	98.3	1.7	-	1.7
1929	100.0	0.2	99.8	25.4	74.4	100.0	99.0	1.0	-	1.0
1933	100.0	0.3	99.7	18.0	81.8	100.0	98.8	1.2	-	1.2
1937	100.0	0.5	99.5	19.2	80.4	100.0	98.3	1.7	-	1.7
1938	100.0	0.1	99.9	19.7	80.2	100.0	98.1	1.9	-	1.9
1950	100.0	0.9	99.1	48.0	51.1	100.0	90.3	9.7	-	9.7
1953	100.0	1.7	98.3	79.5	18.8	100.0	58.3	41.7	-	41.7
1955	100.0	17.6	82.4	63.4	19.0	100.0	60.2	39.8	0.4	39.3
1957	100.0	5.1	94.9	69.1	25.9	100.0	50.6	49.4	0.2	49.3
1960	100.0	0.1	99.9	76.7	23.3	100.0	32.8	67.2	0.4	66.9
1961	100.0	0.1	99.9	81.0	18.9	100.0	37.4	62.6	0.9	61.7
1962	100.0	-	100.0	77.9	22.1	100.0	28.3	71.7	6.6	65.1
1963	100.0	-	100.0	75.4	24.6	100.0	37.3	62.7	8.1	54.7
1964	100.0	-	99.9	75.2	24.7	100.0	33.6	66.3	2.3	64.0
1965	100.0	-	99.3	75.6	23.7	100.0	22.5	77.5	1.9	75.6

Table VIII. ENERGY IMPORTS AND EXPORTS PERCENTAGE DISTRIBUTION, SELECTED YEARS, 1925-1965

(Based on coal equivalents)

Region, country, year	Imports					Exports				
	Total	Solid fuels	Total liquid fuels	Crude oil	Refined petroleum products	Total	Solid fuels	Total liquid fuels	Crude oil	Refined petroleum products
	(1)	(2)	(3)	(4)	(5)	(6)	(7)	(8)	(9)	(10)
WESTERN EUROPE - OTHER										
1925	100.0	83.7	16.3	0.7	15.7	100.0	98.4	1.6	-	1.6
1929	100.0	79.6	20.4	2.1	18.2	100.0	97.3	2.7	-	2.7
1933	100.0	66.0	34.0	4.9	29.1	100.0	80.6	19.4	-	19.4
1937	100.0	68.7	31.3	3.2	28.1	100.0	37.6	62.4	-	62.4
1938	100.0	65.7	34.3	4.0	30.2	100.0	29.7	70.3	-	70.3
1950	100.0	36.0	64.0	29.7	34.3	100.0	82.7	17.3	-	17.3
1953	100.0	29.9	70.1	27.2	42.9	100.0	69.5	28.7	-	28.7
1955	100.0	28.6	71.3	25.0	46.3	100.0	41.7	56.7	-	56.7
1957	100.0	23.4	76.6	31.7	44.9	100.0	27.9	69.5	0.2	69.3
1960	100.0	21.0	78.8	52.4	26.4	100.0	7.8	90.9	-	90.9
1961	100.0	20.3	79.6	53.2	26.5	100.0	10.5	87.7	11.3	76.5
1962	100.0	19.6	80.4	55.2	25.2	100.0	5.2	93.2	25.9	67.2
1963	100.0	17.8	82.1	57.8	24.4	100.0	7.3	88.0	25.1	62.9
1964	100.0	18.1	81.6	59.3	22.3	100.0	8.0	85.9	16.2	69.7
1965	100.0	16.5	83.2	58.1	25.1	100.0	6.0	91.6	6.6	85.0
FINLAND										
1925	100.0	84.3	15.7	1.9	13.8	-	-	-	-	-
1929	100.0	85.8	14.2	1.4	12.8	-	-	-	-	-
1933	100.0	86.4	13.6	1.6	12.0	-	-	-	-	-
1937	100.0	87.0	13.0	1.6	11.4	-	-	-	-	-
1938	100.0	82.7	17.3	2.2	15.0	-	-	-	-	-
1950	100.0	72.5	27.5	-	27.5	-	-	-	-	-
1953	100.0	64.7	35.3	-	35.3	100.0	-	-	-	-
1955	100.0	61.2	38.8	-	38.8	-	-	-	-	-
1957	100.0	51.9	48.1	5.5	42.6	100.0	-	100.0	-	100.0
1960	100.0	43.5	55.8	23.6	32.2	100.0	69.0	31.0	-	31.0
1961	100.0	40.3	59.4	27.7	31.8	100.0	87.0	13.0	-	13.0
1962	100.0	35.9	63.9	27.6	36.3	100.0	100.0	-	-	-
1963	100.0	27.9	71.6	37.4	34.2	100.0	100.0	-	-	-
1964	100.0	30.2	69.0	36.3	32.7	100.0	100.0	-	-	-
1965	100.0	27.5	71.9	34.1	37.8	100.0	95.2	4.8	-	4.8
GREECE										
1925	100.0	87.4	12.6	-	12.6	-	-	-	-	-
1929	100.0	78.7	21.3	-	21.3	-	-	-	-	-
1933	100.0	69.9	30.1	-	30.1	-	-	-	-	-
1937	100.0	66.7	33.3	-	33.3	-	-	-	-	-
1938	100.0	65.3	34.7	-	34.7	-	-	-	-	-
1950	100.0	15.6	84.4	-	84.4	-	-	-	-	-
1953	100.0	12.8	87.2	-	87.2	-	-	-	-	-
1955	100.0	12.4	87.6	-	87.6	-	-	-	-	-
1957	100.0	10.3	89.7	-	89.7	-	-	-	-	-
1960	100.0	6.0	93.9	68.0	25.9	-	-	-	-	-
1961	100.0	5.5	94.5	65.8	28.7	100.0	-	-	-	-
1962	100.0	4.5	95.5	58.1	37.4	100.0	-	99.4	-	99.4
1963	100.0	5.0	95.0	51.2	43.8	100.0	-	98.1	-	98.1
1964	100.0	5.5	94.5	53.1	41.4	100.0	-	95.2	-	95.2
1965	100.0	6.2	93.7	41.6	52.1	100.0	-	100.0	-	100.0

Table VIII. ENERGY IMPORTS AND EXPORTS PERCENTAGE DISTRIBUTION, SELECTED YEARS, 1925-1965

(Based on coal equivalents)

Region, country, year	Imports: Total	Imports: Solid fuels	Imports: Total liquid fuels	Imports: Crude oil	Imports: Refined petroleum products	Exports: Total	Exports: Solid fuels	Exports: Total liquid fuels	Exports: Crude oil	Exports: Refined petroleum products
	(1)	(2)	(3)	(4)	(5)	(6)	(7)	(8)	(9)	(10)
ICELAND										
1925	100.0	-	100.0	-	100.0	-	-	-	-	-
1929	100.0	-	100.0	-	100.0	-	-	-	-	-
1933	100.0	-	100.0	-	100.0	-	-	-	-	-
1937	100.0	-	100.0	-	100.0	-	-	-	-	-
1938	100.0	-	100.0	-	100.0	-	-	-	-	-
1950	100.0	20.5	79.5	-	79.5	-	-	-	-	-
1953	100.0	7.9	92.1	-	92.1	-	-	-	-	-
1955	100.0	10.3	89.7	-	89.7	-	-	-	-	-
1957	100.0	4.8	95.2	-	95.2	-	-	-	-	-
1960	100.0	2.8	97.2	-	97.2	-	-	-	-	-
1961	100.0	3.0	97.0	-	97.0	-	-	-	-	-
1962	100.0	2.9	97.1	-	97.1	-	-	-	-	-
1963	100.0	1.6	98.4	-	98.4	-	-	-	-	-
1964	100.0	1.6	98.4	-	98.4	-	-	-	-	-
1965	100.0	1.4	98.6	-	98.6	-	-	-	-	-
IRELAND										
1925	100.0	92.8	7.2	0.1	7.2	100.0	100.0	-	-	-
1929	100.0	91.1	8.9	-	8.9	100.0	100.0	-	-	-
1933	100.0	89.1	10.9	-	10.9	100.0	100.0	-	-	-
1937	100.0	87.8	12.2	-	12.2	100.0	100.0	-	-	-
1938	100.0	87.1	12.9	-	12.9	100.0	100.0	-	-	-
1950	100.0	69.0	31.0	-	31.0	-	-	-	-	-
1953	100.0	60.4	39.6	-	39.6	100.0	100.0	-	-	-
1955	100.0	53.6	46.4	-	46.4	-	-	-	-	-
1957	100.0	43.4	56.6	-	56.6	100.0	100.0	-	-	-
1960	100.0	38.2	61.8	48.8	13.1	100.0	2.6	97.4	-	97.4
1961	100.0	38.8	61.2	46.8	14.3	100.0	9.2	90.8	-	90.8
1962	100.0	33.8	66.2	50.5	15.8	100.0	9.2	90.8	-	90.8
1963	100.0	31.2	68.8	52.0	16.7	100.0	14.3	85.7	-	85.7
1964	100.0	27.3	72.7	54.1	18.7	100.0	13.4	86.6	-	86.6
1965	100.0	24.0	76.0	56.2	19.8	100.0	10.2	89.8	-	89.8
SPAIN										
1925	100.0	75.2	24.8	0.8	24.0	100.0	85.7	14.3	-	14.3
1929	100.0	70.7	29.3	1.1	28.3	100.0	94.0	6.0	-	6.0
1933	100.0	36.5	63.5	8.4	55.1	100.0	30.8	69.2	-	69.2
1937	100.0	24.8	75.2	6.6	68.6	100.0	-	100.0	-	100.0
1938	100.0	20.0	80.0	7.0	73.0	100.0	-	100.0	-	100.0
1950	100.0	15.5	84.5	65.1	19.5	100.0	100.0	-	-	-
1953	100.0	13.1	86.9	53.2	33.7	100.0	94.2	5.8	-	5.8
1955	100.0	6.5	93.4	52.4	41.0	100.0	35.1	64.9	-	64.9
1957	100.0	4.5	95.5	58.5	37.0	100.0	24.0	75.4	0.3	75.1
1960	100.0	2.4	97.6	73.5	24.1	100.0	3.1	95.4	-	95.4
1961	100.0	3.0	97.0	73.4	23.6	100.0	5.2	92.1	-	92.1
1962	100.0	9.3	90.7	74.0	16.8	100.0	1.5	96.2	-	96.2
1963	100.0	9.2	90.8	76.3	14.4	100.0	1.3	92.1	4.8	87.3
1964	100.0	8.3	91.7	80.7	11.0	100.0	2.5	87.8	2.5	85.3
1965	100.0	6.9	93.1	81.0	12.1	100.0	0.5	95.7	-	95.7

Table VIII. ENERGY IMPORTS AND EXPORTS PERCENTAGE DISTRIBUTION, SELECTED YEARS, 1925-1965

(Based on coal equivalents)

Region, country, year	Imports					Exports				
	Total	Solid fuels	Total liquid fuels	Crude oil	Refined petroleum products	Total	Solid fuels	Total liquid fuels	Crude oil	Refined petroleum products
	(1)	(2)	(3)	(4)	(5)	(6)	(7)	(8)	(9)	(10)
YUGOSLAVIA										
1925	100.0	81.0	19.0	2.5	16.6	100.0	100.0	-	-	-
1929	100.0	75.9	24.1	18.0	6.1	100.0	100.0	-	-	-
1933	100.0	61.7	38.3	30.7	7.6	100.0	100.0	-	-	-
1937	100.0	70.9	29.1	23.7	5.4	100.0	100.0	-	-	-
1938	100.0	68.5	31.5	26.6	5.0	100.0	100.0	-	-	-
1950	100.0	36.7	63.3	53.5	9.8	100.0	75.3	24.7	-	24.7
1953	100.0	45.7	54.3	46.8	7.5	100.0	60.7	37.2	-	37.2
1955	100.0	58.6	41.4	38.2	3.2	100.0	53.1	42.8	-	42.8
1957	100.0	63.1	36.9	35.1	1.7	100.0	32.2	60.3	-	60.3
1960	100.0	64.4	35.6	25.3	10.3	100.0	45.3	50.1	-	50.1
1961	100.0	70.6	29.4	18.4	10.9	100.0	20.7	77.4	50.6	26.8
1962	100.0	50.5	49.5	35.6	14.0	100.0	7.2	91.4	60.7	30.6
1963	100.0	53.8	46.2	37.6	8.6	100.0	11.6	84.9	65.9	19.0
1964	100.0	56.4	42.5	29.2	13.2	100.0	16.2	83.8	54.9	28.9
1965	100.0	53.5	45.3	38.9	6.4	100.0	15.5	84.5	30.6	53.9
OCEANIA										
1925	100.0	35.0	65.0	14.4	50.6	100.0	99.1	0.9	0.2	0.8
1929	100.0	24.7	75.3	19.0	56.2	100.0	95.5	4.5	0.4	4.0
1933	100.0	8.0	92.0	13.7	78.3	100.0	100.0	-	-	-
1937	100.0	7.5	92.5	10.1	82.4	100.0	99.3	0.7	-	0.7
1938	100.0	7.9	92.1	8.2	83.9	100.0	99.7	0.3	-	0.3
1950	100.0	6.9	93.1	12.5	80.7	100.0	82.2	17.8	-	17.8
1953	100.0	1.8	98.2	13.5	84.8	100.0	97.1	2.9	-	2.9
1955	100.0	1.8	98.2	47.9	50.4	100.0	33.5	66.5	-	66.5
1957	100.0	2.1	97.9	71.5	26.4	100.0	41.6	58.4	-	58.4
1960	100.0	1.2	98.8	75.5	23.3	100.0	40.9	59.1	-	59.1
1961	100.0	1.1	98.9	76.6	22.2	100.0	50.8	49.2	-	49.2
1962	100.0	0.7	99.3	76.6	22.7	100.0	46.2	53.8	-	53.8
1963	100.0	0.7	99.3	78.1	21.2	100.0	47.0	53.0	-	53.0
1964	100.0	1.0	99.0	80.2	18.8	100.0	64.5	35.5	-	35.5
1965	100.0	1.0	99.0	86.7	12.3	100.0	79.1	20.9	-	20.9
AUSTRALIA										
1925	100.0	5.1	94.9	28.3	66.6	100.0	99.1	0.9	0.2	0.8
1929	100.0	20.7	79.3	25.4	53.9	100.0	94.9	5.1	0.5	4.7
1933	100.0	0.3	99.7	18.8	81.0	100.0	100.0	-	-	-
1937	100.0	0.9	99.1	13.6	85.6	100.0	99.3	0.7	-	0.7
1938	100.0	2.5	97.5	11.5	86.0	100.0	99.7	0.3	-	0.3
1950	100.0	6.7	93.3	15.4	77.8	100.0	81.4	18.6	-	18.6
1953	100.0	0.3	99.7	16.9	82.8	100.0	97.1	2.9	-	2.9
1955	100.0	0.1	99.9	57.9	42.0	100.0	33.7	66.3	-	66.3
1957	100.0	0.1	99.9	86.7	13.2	100.0	41.9	58.1	-	58.1
1960	100.0	-	100.0	88.8	11.2	100.0	40.9	59.1	-	59.1
1961	100.0	-	100.0	90.1	9.9	100.0	50.9	49.1	-	49.1
1962	100.0	-	100.0	89.1	10.9	100.0	46.4	53.6	-	53.6
1963	100.0	-	100.0	90.8	9.2	100.0	47.1	52.9	-	52.9
1964	100.0	-	100.0	90.0	10.0	100.0	67.5	32.5	-	32.5
1965	100.0	-	100.0	91.3	8.7	100.0	82.4	17.6	-	17.6

Table VIII. ENERGY IMPORTS AND EXPORTS PERCENTAGE DISTRIBUTION, SELECTED YEARS, 1925-1965

(Based on coal equivalents)

Region, country, year	Imports					Exports				
	Total	Solid fuels	Total liquid fuels	Crude oil	Refined petroleum products	Total	Solid fuels	Total liquid fuels	Crude oil	Refined petroleum products
	(1)	(2)	(3)	(4)	(5)	(6)	(7)	(8)	(9)	(10)
NEW ZEALAND										
1925	100.0	62.1	37.9	-	37.9	100.0	100.0	-	-	-
1929	100.0	28.2	71.8	-	71.8	100.0	100.0	-	-	-
1933	100.0	17.0	83.0	-	83.0	-	-	-	-	-
1937	100.0	13.7	86.3	-	86.3	-	-	-	-	-
1938	100.0	10.3	89.7	-	89.7	100.0	100.0	-	-	-
1950	100.0	2.9	97.1	-	97.1	100.0	100.0	-	-	-
1953	100.0	0.1	99.9	-	99.9	-	-	-	-	-
1955	100.0	0.5	99.5	-	99.5	-	-	-	-	-
1957	100.0	0.4	99.6	-	99.6	-	-	-	-	-
1960	100.0	-	100.0	-	100.0	100.0	59.7	40.3	-	40.3
1961	100.0	0.4	99.6	-	99.6	100.0	48.8	51.2	-	51.2
1962	100.0	0.3	99.7	-	99.7	100.0	-	100.0	-	100.0
1963	100.0	-	100.0	-	100.0	100.0	-	100.0	-	100.0
1964	100.0	-	100.0	39.5	60.5	100.0	-	100.0	-	100.0
1965	100.0	-	100.0	80.3	19.7	100.0	-	100.0	-	100.0
USSR AND COMMUNIST EASTERN EUROPE										
1925	100.0	87.8	12.0	2.8	9.2	100.0	77.2	22.8	0.6	22.2
1929	100.0	84.4	15.5	6.3	9.2	100.0	66.6	33.4	1.6	31.8
1933	100.0	72.2	27.7	11.1	16.6	100.0	46.8	53.2	4.0	49.2
1937	100.0	66.0	33.9	16.2	17.7	100.0	59.6	40.4	3.6	36.8
1938	100.0	65.6	34.4	14.9	19.4	100.0	61.7	38.3	4.5	33.8
1950	100.0	75.0	24.7	10.9	13.8	100.0	84.9	14.9	1.6	13.3
1953	100.0	67.7	31.8	13.1	18.7	100.0	68.1	31.6	6.4	25.2
1955	100.0	65.3	34.0	13.0	21.0	100.0	63.3	36.3	8.0	28.4
1957	100.0	56.5	42.5	21.8	20.7	100.0	51.9	47.6	14.9	32.7
1960	100.0	53.7	44.8	23.9	20.9	100.0	41.6	57.8	25.6	32.2
1961	100.0	53.8	44.7	23.7	20.9	100.0	38.8	60.6	29.2	31.4
1962	100.0	53.6	45.0	24.9	20.1	100.0	39.2	60.3	29.8	30.5
1963	100.0	52.1	46.5	27.3	19.3	100.0	37.9	61.6	31.3	30.2
1964	100.0	51.3	47.4	31.4	15.9	100.0	37.5	61.9	34.8	27.1
1965	100.0	48.4	50.2	37.4	12.9	100.0	34.6	64.8	38.3	26.5
COMMUNIST EASTERN EUROPE										
1925	100.0	87.8	12.0	3.1	8.9	100.0	88.1	11.9	-	11.8
1929	100.0	83.7	16.2	7.1	9.1	100.0	81.5	18.5	-	18.4
1933	100.0	68.1	31.8	14.6	17.2	100.0	59.3	40.7	1.8	38.9
1937	100.0	63.8	36.1	22.7	13.4	100.0	65.0	35.0	3.5	31.5
1938	100.0	63.1	36.9	22.2	14.7	100.0	67.9	32.1	3.4	28.7
1950	100.0	76.5	22.7	6.2	16.5	100.0	87.9	12.0	0.5	11.5
1953	100.0	76.2	22.9	10.8	12.1	100.0	79.5	20.5	0.7	19.8
1955	100.0	74.2	24.7	12.3	12.4	100.0	75.9	24.1	1.3	22.7
1957	100.0	63.5	35.1	22.5	12.6	100.0	68.9	30.9	2.1	28.8
1960	100.0	56.1	41.8	26.7	15.1	100.0	70.4	28.7	1.6	27.2
1961	100.0	54.6	43.6	26.5	17.0	100.0	69.5	29.6	1.5	28.1
1962	100.0	52.8	45.5	28.3	17.2	100.0	59.4	29.9	1.3	28.6
1963	100.0	51.0	47.4	30.7	16.7	100.0	69.4	30.0	1.3	28.7
1964	100.0	49.3	49.2	35.8	13.4	100.0	69.4	29.8	1.1	28.7
1965	100.0	44.6	53.8	43.1	10.7	100.0	69.1	30.2	1.2	29.0

Table VIII. ENERGY IMPORTS AND EXPORTS PERCENTAGE DISTRIBUTION, SELECTED YEARS, 1925-1965

(Based on coal equivalents)

Region, country, year	Imports					Exports				
	Total	Solid fuels	Total liquid fuels	Crude oil	Refined petroleum products	Total	Solid fuels	Total liquid fuels	Crude oil	Refined petroleum products
	(1)	(2)	(3)	(4)	(5)	(6)	(7)	(8)	(9)	(10)
ALBANIA										
1925	100.0	-	100.0	60.0	40.0	-	-	-	-	-
1929	100.0	-	100.0	42.9	57.1	-	-	-	-	-
1933	100.0	-	100.0	25.0	75.0	-	-	-	-	-
1937	100.0	-	100.0	25.0	75.0	100.0	-	100.0	100.0	-
1938	100.0	22.9	77.1	17.1	60.0	100.0	-	100.0	100.0	-
1950	100.0	25.0	75.0	-	75.0	100.0	-	100.0	100.0	-
1953	100.0	40.0	60.0	-	60.0	100.0	-	100.0	100.0	-
1955	100.0	-	100.0	-	100.0	100.0	9.7	90.3	90.3	-
1957	100.0	33.9	66.1	-	66.1	100.0	3.0	97.0	97.0	-
1960	100.0	40.0	60.0	-	60.0	100.0	-	100.0	100.0	-
1961	100.0	37.7	62.3	-	62.3	100.0	-	100.0	100.0	-
1962	100.0	41.2	58.8	-	58.8	100.0	-	100.0	100.0	-
1963	100.0	32.3	67.7	-	67.7	100.0	-	100.0	96.9	3.1
1964	100.0	17.7	82.3	-	82.3	100.0	-	100.0	100.0	-
1965	100.0	41.7	58.3	-	58.3	100.0	-	100.0	100.0	-
BULGARIA										
1925	100.0	21.8	78.2	-	78.2	100.0	100.0	-	-	-
1929	100.0	6.7	93.3	-	93.3	100.0	100.0	-	-	-
1933	100.0	4.8	95.2	-	95.2	100.0	100.0	-	-	-
1937	100.0	2.2	97.8	21.1	76.7	100.0	66.7	33.3	-	33.3
1938	100.0	2.9	97.1	32.0	65.1	100.0	100.0	-	-	-
1950	100.0	NA	100.0	8.3	91.7	-	-	-	-	-
1953	100.0	NA	100.0	6.0	94.0	-	-	-	-	-
1955	100.0	19.2	80.8	-	80.8	100.0	10.2	89.8	89.0	0.8
1957	100.0	15.4	84.6	-	84.6	100.0	32.3	67.7	51.4	16.3
1960	100.0	19.4	80.6	1.1	79.6	100.0	28.6	71.4	57.1	14.3
1961	100.0	31.7	68.3	1.3	67.0	100.0	24.0	76.0	75.4	0.6
1962	100.0	33.4	66.3	0.6	65.7	100.0	21.9	78.1	76.1	2.0
1963	100.0	33.1	66.6	14.3	52.4	100.0	29.4	70.6	70.6	-
1964	100.0	33.1	66.9	39.1	27.8	100.0	-	96.7	67.2	29.5
1965	100.0	35.0	65.0	40.6	24.4	100.0	-	99.8	5.4	94.4
CZECHOSLOVAKIA										
1925	100.0	85.8	14.0	4.2	9.9	100.0	99.5	0.5	0.2	0.3
1929	100.0	83.5	16.4	7.0	9.3	100.0	99.7	0.3	-	0.3
1933	100.0	72.1	27.8	8.1	19.7	100.0	99.8	0.2	-	0.2
1937	100.0	66.6	33.3	19.4	13.9	100.0	99.9	0.1	-	0.1
1938	100.0	62.9	37.1	20.4	16.7	100.0	99.9	0.1	-	0.1
1950	100.0	64.5	35.0	7.2	27.8	100.0	100.0	-	-	-
1953	100.0	70.7	29.2	12.5	16.6	100.0	100.0	-	-	-
1955	100.0	73.4	26.6	11.7	14.9	100.0	97.8	1.5	-	1.5
1957	100.0	49.6	50.4	39.7	10.7	100.0	94.1	4.9	-	4.9
1960	100.0	42.2	57.8	48.4	9.3	100.0	93.9	5.4	-	5.4
1961	100.0	44.1	55.9	46.9	9.0	100.0	92.1	7.0	-	7.0
1962	100.0	42.0	57.9	50.3	7.6	100.0	89.4	10.5	-	10.5
1963	100.0	42.4	57.4	50.8	6.6	100.0	85.6	14.3	-	14.3
1964	100.0	39.3	60.1	54.5	5.6	100.0	86.0	13.9	-	13.9
1965	100.0	33.9	65.5	60.6	4.9	100.0	79.7	20.2	-	20.2

Table VIII. ENERGY IMPORTS AND EXPORTS PERCENTAGE DISTRIBUTION, SELECTED YEARS, 1925-1965

(Based on coal equivalents)

Region, country, year	Imports					Exports				
	Total	Solid fuels	Total liquid fuels	Crude oil	Refined petroleum products	Total	Solid fuels	Total liquid fuels	Crude oil	Refined petroleum products
	(1)	(2)	(3)	(4)	(5)	(6)	(7)	(8)	(9)	(10)
GERMANY, EAST										
1950	100.0	93.8	5.5	1.1	4.4	100.0	79.3	17.0	-	17.0
1953	100.0	92.2	7.4	5.9	1.5	100.0	83.4	15.7	-	15.7
1955	100.0	90.7	8.9	8.9	-	100.0	81.1	18.8	-	18.8
1957	100.0	85.6	13.7	13.6	0.1	100.0	76.6	22.4	-	22.4
1960	100.0	76.4	23.1	18.6	4.5	100.0	76.0	23.2	-	23.2
1961	100.0	74.0	25.7	20.5	5.1	100.0	73.5	25.7	-	25.7
1962	100.0	73.5	26.2	21.5	4.7	100.0	74.7	25.1	-	25.1
1963	100.0	69.9	29.9	24.6	5.3	100.0	73.8	26.2	-	26.2
1964	100.0	67.8	32.0	28.8	3.2	100.0	71.8	28.2	-	28.2
1965	100.0	62.5	37.3	34.2	3.1	100.0	63.9	36.1	-	36.1
HUNGARY										
1925	100.0	92.1	7.9	2.3	5.6	100.0	100.0	-	-	-
1929	100.0	85.7	14.3	9.5	4.8	100.0	100.0	-	-	-
1933	100.0	55.5	44.5	43.8	0.8	100.0	100.0	-	-	-
1937	100.0	58.0	42.0	35.7	6.3	100.0	100.0	-	-	-
1938	100.0	62.4	37.6	31.1	6.4	100.0	100.0	-	-	-
1950	100.0	76.0	24.0	15.0	9.0	100.0	47.6	52.4	23.8	28.6
1953	100.0	79.9	19.4	13.8	5.5	100.0	55.7	44.3	24.6	19.7
1955	100.0	78.0	20.7	14.2	6.5	100.0	33.8	66.2	30.4	35.8
1957	100.0	63.7	35.5	29.4	6.1	100.0	5.4	94.6	13.3	81.3
1960	100.0	50.3	43.8	41.0	2.8	100.0	4.8	95.2	5.9	89.3
1961	100.0	51.9	42.4	36.4	6.0	100.0	6.1	93.9	-	93.9
1962	100.0	49.1	45.2	38.9	6.3	100.0	10.1	89.9	-	89.9
1963	100.0	51.3	43.6	35.6	7.9	100.0	23.9	76.1	-	76.1
1964	100.0	52.4	42.8	33.6	9.2	100.0	14.5	85.5	-	85.5
1965	100.0	48.3	46.7	40.1	6.6	100.0	15.8	84.2	-	84.2
POLAND										
1925	100.0	95.7	1.8	-	1.8	100.0	94.8	5.2	-	5.2
1929	100.0	95.4	2.7	-	2.7	100.0	98.0	2.0	-	2.0
1933	100.0	99.1	0.9	-	0.9	100.0	97.5	2.5	-	2.5
1937	100.0	99.2	0.8	-	0.8	100.0	98.9	1.1	-	1.1
1938	100.0	99.2	0.8	-	0.8	100.0	99.9	0.1	-	0.1
1950	100.0	5.8	89.9	34.0	55.9	100.0	99.7	0.3	-	0.3
1953	100.0	4.8	88.8	37.2	51.5	100.0	99.5	0.5	-	0.5
1955	100.0	5.4	87.3	33.9	53.4	100.0	99.4	0.6	-	0.6
1957	100.0	14.4	78.1	28.4	49.7	100.0	99.5	0.5	-	0.5
1960	100.0	22.6	70.6	20.7	49.9	100.0	98.6	1.4	-	1.4
1961	100.0	22.5	71.1	18.2	52.9	100.0	98.2	1.8	-	1.8
1962	100.0	21.2	73.5	23.0	50.4	100.0	96.1	3.9	-	3.9
1963	100.0	21.3	73.9	25.3	48.6	100.0	96.0	4.0	-	4.0
1964	100.0	19.7	75.9	29.2	46.7	100.0	96.0	3.6	-	3.6
1965	100.0	16.7	78.4	48.2	30.2	100.0	94.7	5.2	-	5.2
ROMANIA										
1925	100.0	99.4	0.6	-	0.6	100.0	1.8	98.2	-	98.2
1929	100.0	97.6	2.4	-	2.4	100.0	0.9	99.1	0.1	99.0
1933	100.0	95.8	4.2	-	4.2	100.0	0.1	99.9	4.5	95.4
1937	100.0	96.3	3.8	-	3.8	100.0	-	100.0	9.2	90.8

Table VIII. ENERGY IMPORTS AND EXPORTS PERCENTAGE DISTRIBUTION, SELECTED YEARS, 1925-1965

(Based on coal equivalents)

Region, country, year	Imports					Exports				
	Total	Solid fuels	Total liquid fuels	Crude oil	Refined petroleum products	Total	Solid fuels	Total liquid fuels	Crude oil	Refined petroleum products
	(1)	(2)	(3)	(4)	(5)	(6)	(7)	(8)	(9)	(10)
ROMANIA (CONTINUED)										
1938	100.0	96.8	3.2	-	3.2	100.0	-	100.0	8.2	91.8
1950	100.0	100.0	-	-	-	100.0	-	100.0	-	100.0
1953	100.0	100.0	-	-	-	100.0	-	100.0	-	100.0
1955	100.0	100.0	-	-	-	100.0	-	100.0	-	100.0
1957	100.0	100.0	-	-	-	100.0	-	100.0	-	100.0
1960	100.0	100.0	-	-	-	100.0	-	97.0	-	97.0
1961	100.0	100.0	-	-	-	100.0	-	97.0	-	97.0
1962	100.0	100.0	-	-	-	100.0	-	96.9	-	96.9
1963	100.0	100.0	-	-	-	100.0	0.2	96.7	-	96.7
1964	100.0	100.0	-	-	-	100.0	0.8	96.3	-	96.3
1965	100.0	100.0	-	-	-	100.0	-	96.5	-	96.5
USSR (INCLUDING ESTONIA, LATVIA, LITHUANIA)										
1925	100.0	87.7	12.3	1.7	10.6	100.0	15.1	84.9	3.9	81.0
1929	100.0	87.8	12.2	2.0	10.2	100.0	18.8	81.2	6.6	74.7
1933	100.0	84.6	15.4	0.5	14.9	100.0	19.8	80.2	8.7	71.5
1937	100.0	71.1	28.9	1.3	27.6	100.0	30.7	69.3	4.3	65.0
1938	100.0	70.4	29.6	1.5	28.1	100.0	13.1	86.9	13.8	73.1
1950	100.0	73.8	26.2	14.6	11.7	100.0	60.7	38.5	10.5	28.0
1953	100.0	57.9	42.1	15.8	26.3	100.0	34.4	64.6	23.5	41.1
1955	100.0	53.4	46.6	13.9	32.7	100.0	32.2	66.7	24.4	42.3
1957	100.0	38.0	62.0	20.2	41.8	100.0	34.2	65.1	28.3	36.8
1960	100.0	46.3	53.7	15.1	38.7	100.0	22.7	76.8	41.3	35.4
1961	100.0	51.0	49.0	12.8	36.2	100.0	22.4	77.2	44.0	33.2
1962	100.0	57.4	42.6	7.8	34.8	100.0	24.6	74.9	43.5	31.4
1963	100.0	58.2	41.8	8.3	33.4	100.0	24.2	75.3	44.4	30.9
1964	100.0	65.8	34.2	-	34.2	100.0	24.2	75.3	48.9	26.4
1965	100.0	73.1	26.9	-	26.9	100.0	21.0	78.4	53.0	25.5
COMMUNIST ASIA										
1925	100.0	66.5	33.5	-	33.5	100.0	100.0	-	-	-
1929	100.0	59.1	40.9	-	40.9	100.0	100.0	-	-	-
1933	100.0	46.9	53.1	-	53.1	100.0	98.1	1.9	1.8	0.1
1937	100.0	20.4	79.6	11.1	68.6	100.0	98.1	1.9	1.9	-
1938	100.0	48.6	51.4	10.2	41.1	100.0	97.0	3.0	3.0	-
1950	NA	NA	NA	NA	NA	NA	NA	NA	NA	NA
1953	NA	NA	NA	NA	NA	NA	NA	NA	NA	NA
1955	100.0	3.7	96.3	28.0	68.3	100.0	100.0	-	-	-
1957	100.0	2.8	97.2	18.0	79.2	100.0	99.7	0.3	-	0.3
1960	100.0	2.0	98.0	16.7	81.2	100.0	100.0	-	-	-
1961	100.0	1.6	98.4	2.3	96.1	100.0	100.0	-	-	-
1962	100.0	5.3	94.7	5.3	89.4	100.0	100.0	-	-	-
1963	100.0	1.2	98.8	6.6	92.3	100.0	100.0	-	-	-
1964	100.0	11.4	88.6	12.2	76.4	100.0	100.0	-	-	-
1965	100.0	8.3	91.7	18.7	73.0	100.0	100.0	-	-	-
LATIN AMERICA										
1925	100.0	38.1	61.9	29.3	32.6	100.0	0.1	99.9	63.7	36.3
1929	100.0	20.2	79.8	57.3	22.5	100.0	-	100.0	65.9	34.1
1933	100.0	14.1	85.7	64.4	21.3	100.0	0.2	99.8	60.1	39.7

Table VIII. ENERGY IMPORTS AND EXPORTS PERCENTAGE DISTRIBUTION, SELECTED YEARS, 1925-1965

(Based on coal equivalents)

Region, country, year	Imports: Total	Imports: Solid fuels	Imports: Total liquid fuels	Imports: Crude oil	Imports: Refined petroleum products	Exports: Total	Exports: Solid fuels	Exports: Total liquid fuels	Exports: Crude oil	Exports: Refined petroleum products
	(1)	(2)	(3)	(4)	(5)	(6)	(7)	(8)	(9)	(10)
LATIN AMERICA (CONTINUED)										
1937	100.0	11.8	87.8	67.9	19.9	100.0	0.1	99.9	56.7	43.3
1938	100.0	9.8	90.1	68.3	21.8	100.0	0.1	99.9	55.9	44.1
1950	100.0	3.0	96.1	75.1	21.1	100.0	0.1	99.9	60.6	39.3
1953	100.0	2.3	97.0	72.4	24.6	100.0	-	100.0	57.2	42.8
1955	100.0	2.3	97.1	70.2	26.8	100.0	-	100.0	60.2	39.7
1957	100.0	2.3	97.7	71.7	26.0	100.0	-	99.9	63.5	36.3
1960	100.0	2.5	97.5	76.0	21.5	100.0	-	99.4	58.6	40.8
1961	100.0	1.9	98.0	77.5	20.6	100.0	-	99.4	57.7	41.7
1962	100.0	1.5	98.5	79.7	18.8	100.0	-	99.5	57.1	42.4
1963	100.0	1.7	98.3	80.1	18.2	100.0	-	99.5	55.8	43.7
1964	100.0	1.7	98.3	80.3	18.0	100.0	-	99.5	56.0	43.6
1965	100.0	1.7	98.3	82.8	15.5	100.0	-	99.5	55.2	44.3
LATIN AMERICA - CARIBBEAN										
1925	100.0	14.8	85.2	44.0	41.2	100.0	-	100.0	63.6	36.4
1929	100.0	5.7	94.3	76.2	18.1	100.0	-	100.0	65.7	34.3
1933	100.0	2.4	97.3	81.7	15.6	100.0	-	100.0	59.9	40.1
1937	100.0	1.9	97.6	82.3	15.3	100.0	-	100.0	55.8	44.2
1938	100.0	1.5	98.4	81.3	17.1	100.0	-	100.0	55.2	44.8
1950	100.0	0.2	98.7	88.0	10.7	100.0	-	100.0	60.7	39.3
1953	100.0	0.2	98.9	84.7	14.2	100.0	-	100.0	57.1	42.9
1955	100.0	0.2	98.9	80.8	18.1	100.0	-	100.0	60.3	39.7
1957	100.0	0.3	99.7	79.0	20.6	100.0	-	99.9	63.7	36.2
1960	100.0	0.1	99.8	84.6	15.2	100.0	-	99.5	58.5	40.9
1961	100.0	0.1	99.8	83.4	16.4	100.0	-	99.4	57.5	41.9
1962	100.0	0.2	99.7	82.7	17.0	100.0	-	99.5	57.2	42.4
1963	100.0	0.3	99.7	82.2	17.5	100.0	-	99.5	55.9	43.7
1964	100.0	0.3	99.7	82.5	17.1	100.0	-	99.5	56.1	43.5
1965	100.0	0.4	99.6	85.1	14.5	100.0	-	99.5	55.4	44.1
CARIBBEAN - OIL PRODUCING										
1925	100.0	3.1	96.8	89.2	7.7	100.0	-	100.0	63.6	36.4
1929	100.0	0.9	99.1	94.2	4.8	100.0	-	100.0	65.7	34.3
1933	100.0	0.3	99.3	92.0	7.3	100.0	-	100.0	59.9	40.1
1937	100.0	0.2	99.3	90.5	8.7	100.0	-	100.0	55.8	44.2
1938	100.0	0.2	99.6	87.9	11.8	100.0	-	100.0	55.2	44.8
1950	100.0	0.1	98.7	95.9	2.8	100.0	-	100.0	60.7	39.3
1953	100.0	0.1	98.9	93.2	5.7	100.0	-	100.0	57.1	42.9
1955	100.0	0.1	99.0	90.4	8.6	100.0	-	100.0	60.4	39.6
1957	100.0	0.1	99.8	87.7	12.2	100.0	-	99.9	64.2	35.7
1960	100.0	0.1	99.9	93.2	6.7	100.0	-	99.4	59.2	40.2
1961	100.0	0.1	99.8	93.7	6.2	100.0	-	99.4	58.2	41.2
1962	100.0	0.2	99.7	92.4	7.3	100.0	-	99.5	58.0	41.5
1963	100.0	0.2	99.7	90.9	8.7	100.0	-	99.5	57.0	42.6
1964	100.0	0.3	99.7	91.3	8.4	100.0	-	99.5	57.1	42.4
1965	100.0	0.3	99.6	93.9	5.8	100.0	-	99.5	56.4	43.1
ANTILLES, NETHERLANDS										
1925	100.0	-	100.0	99.0	1.0	100.0	NA	100.0	55.4	44.6
1929	100.0	-	100.0	97.1	2.9	100.0	-	100.0	4.5	95.5

Table VIII. ENERGY IMPORTS AND EXPORTS PERCENTAGE DISTRIBUTION, SELECTED YEARS, 1925-1965

(Based on coal equivalents)

Region, country, year	Imports: Total	Imports: Solid fuels	Imports: Total liquid fuels	Imports: Crude oil	Imports: Refined petroleum products	Exports: Total	Exports: Solid fuels	Exports: Total liquid fuels	Exports: Crude oil	Exports: Refined petroleum products
	(1)	(2)	(3)	(4)	(5)	(6)	(7)	(8)	(9)	(10)
ANTILLES, NETHERLANDS (CONTINUED)										
1933	100.0	-	100.0	93.7	6.2	100.0	NA	100.0	9.4	90.6
1937	100.0	-	100.0	92.3	7.7	100.0	-	100.0	3.8	96.2
1938	100.0	-	100.0	88.9	11.1	100.0	NA	100.0	4.8	95.2
1950	100.0	-	100.0	98.7	1.3	100.0	-	100.0	3.0	97.0
1953	100.0	-	100.0	97.1	2.9	100.0	-	100.0	1.8	98.2
1955	100.0	-	100.0	96.1	3.9	100.0	-	100.0	7.5	92.5
1957	100.0	-	100.0	92.4	7.6	100.0	-	100.0	2.6	97.4
1960	100.0	-	100.0	94.7	5.3	100.0	-	100.0	2.8	97.2
1961	100.0	-	100.0	94.7	5.3	100.0	-	100.0	4.2	95.8
1962	100.0	-	100.0	92.8	7.2	100.0	-	100.0	3.9	96.1
1963	100.0	-	100.0	90.8	9.2	100.0	-	100.0	2.6	97.4
1964	100.0	-	100.0	91.5	8.5	100.0	-	100.0	1.3	98.7
1965	100.0	-	100.0	94.3	5.7	100.0	-	100.0	1.0	99.0
COLOMBIA										
1925	100.0	18.2	81.8	-	81.8	-	-	-	-	-
1929	100.0	1.3	98.7	9.5	89.2	100.0	-	100.0	100.0	-
1933	100.0	5.7	94.3	-	94.3	100.0	-	100.0	100.0	-
1937	100.0	2.8	97.2	-	97.2	100.0	-	100.0	100.0	-
1938	100.0	-	100.0	-	100.0	100.0	-	100.0	100.0	-
1950	100.0	-	100.0	-	100.0	100.0	-	100.0	100.0	-
1953	100.0	-	100.0	-	100.0	100.0	-	100.0	100.0	-
1955	100.0	-	100.0	-	100.0	100.0	-	100.0	94.3	5.7
1957	100.0	-	100.0	-	100.0	100.0	0.2	99.8	93.5	6.4
1960	100.0	-	100.0	-	100.0	100.0	-	100.0	88.1	11.9
1961	100.0	-	100.0	-	100.0	100.0	-	100.0	90.1	9.9
1962	100.0	-	100.0	-	100.0	100.0	-	100.0	84.7	15.3
1963	100.0	-	100.0	-	100.0	100.0	-	100.0	92.1	7.9
1964	100.0	-	100.0	-	100.0	100.0	-	100.0	85.6	14.4
1965	100.0	-	100.0	-	100.0	100.0	-	100.0	88.5	11.5
MEXICO										
1925	100.0	10.9	88.7	43.5	45.2	100.0	-	100.0	59.5	40.5
1929	100.0	9.7	89.5	40.7	48.8	100.0	0.1	99.9	66.0	34.0
1933	100.0	3.0	76.8	19.0	57.8	100.0	-	100.0	55.2	44.8
1937	100.0	2.2	66.7	3.3	63.4	100.0	-	100.0	37.0	63.0
1938	100.0	3.8	77.9	3.7	74.3	100.0	-	100.0	39.5	60.5
1950	100.0	2.0	42.0	-	42.0	100.0	-	100.0	73.2	26.8
1953	100.0	2.0	63.3	-	63.3	100.0	-	100.0	22.6	77.4
1955	100.0	1.5	79.0	-	79.0	100.0	-	100.0	19.0	81.0
1957	100.0	1.8	96.8	7.4	89.5	100.0	-	93.7	17.9	75.8
1960	100.0	3.7	92.1	-	92.1	100.0	-	53.6	6.7	46.9
1961	100.0	4.9	90.5	3.0	87.5	100.0	-	64.8	27.9	36.9
1962	100.0	6.6	86.1	-	86.1	100.0	-	72.7	28.0	44.6
1963	100.0	5.5	87.7	2.9	84.8	100.0	-	73.0	27.1	45.9
1964	100.0	5.1	93.7	8.0	85.7	100.0	-	70.4	30.7	39.8
1965	100.0	8.2	91.3	-	91.3	100.0	-	70.3	27.9	42.3
TRINIDAD AND TOBAGO										
1925	100.0	93.6	6.4	-	6.4	100.0	-	100.0	9.1	90.9

Table VIII. ENERGY IMPORTS AND EXPORTS PERCENTAGE DISTRIBUTION, SELECTED YEARS, 1925-1965

(Based on coal equivalents)

Region, country, year	Imports: Total	Imports: Solid fuels	Imports: Total liquid fuels	Imports: Crude oil	Imports: Refined petroleum products	Exports: Total	Exports: Solid fuels	Exports: Total liquid fuels	Exports: Crude oil	Exports: Refined petroleum products
	(1)	(2)	(3)	(4)	(5)	(6)	(7)	(8)	(9)	(10)
TRINIDAD AND TOBAGO (CONTINUED)										
1929	100.0	90.6	9.4	-	9.4	100.0	-	100.0	14.9	85.1
1933	100.0	34.2	65.8	62.7	3.1	100.0	-	100.0	22.7	77.3
1937	100.0	38.9	61.1	59.2	1.9	100.0	-	100.0	6.2	93.8
1938	100.0	30.6	69.4	67.6	1.7	100.0	-	100.0	5.3	94.7
1950	100.0	1.0	99.0	98.8	0.2	100.0	-	100.0	11.9	88.1
1953	100.0	0.4	99.6	98.1	1.5	100.0	-	100.0	9.2	90.8
1955	100.0	-	100.0	99.8	0.2	100.0	-	100.0	9.6	90.4
1957	100.0	-	100.0	99.5	0.5	100.0	-	100.0	9.4	90.6
1960	100.0	-	100.0	99.8	0.2	100.0	-	100.0	7.5	92.5
1961	100.0	-	100.0	99.9	0.1	100.0	-	100.0	6.6	93.4
1962	100.0	-	100.0	99.6	0.4	100.0	-	100.0	7.3	92.7
1963	100.0	-	100.0	99.8	0.2	100.0	-	100.0	7.2	92.8
1964	100.0	-	100.0	99.5	0.5	100.0	-	100.0	9.2	90.8
1965	100.0	-	100.0	100.0	NA	100.0	-	100.0	9.1	90.9
VENEZUELA										
1925	100.0	66.7	33.3	-	33.3	100.0	-	100.0	100.0	-
1929	100.0	76.2	23.8	-	23.8	100.0	-	100.0	99.8	0.2
1933	100.0	78.6	21.4	-	21.4	100.0	-	100.0	95.2	4.8
1937	100.0	40.0	60.0	-	60.0	100.0	-	100.0	96.7	3.3
1938	100.0	41.6	58.4	-	58.4	100.0	-	100.0	96.8	3.2
1950	100.0	0.9	99.1	-	99.1	100.0	-	100.0	88.8	11.2
1953	100.0	0.7	99.3	-	99.3	100.0	-	100.0	82.6	17.4
1955	100.0	-	100.0	-	100.0	100.0	-	100.0	82.5	17.5
1957	100.0	-	100.0	-	100.0	100.0	-	100.0	83.0	17.0
1960	100.0	-	100.0	-	100.0	100.0	-	100.0	76.2	23.8
1961	100.0	13.4	86.6	-	86.6	100.0	-	100.0	75.8	24.2
1962	100.0	71.4	28.6	-	28.6	100.0	-	100.0	75.1	24.9
1963	100.0	91.5	8.5	-	8.5	100.0	-	100.0	73.8	26.2
1964	100.0	81.6	18.4	-	18.4	100.0	-	100.0	74.0	26.0
1965	100.0	92.5	7.5	-	7.5	100.0	-	100.0	72.7	27.3
CARIBBEAN - OTHER										
1925	100.0	25.0	75.0	4.8	70.2	-	-	-	-	-
1929	100.0	23.8	76.2	7.7	68.5	-	-	-	-	-
1933	100.0	17.9	82.1	3.0	79.1	-	-	-	-	-
1937	100.0	17.3	82.7	7.2	75.5	-	-	-	-	-
1938	100.0	16.0	84.0	6.7	77.3	-	-	-	-	-
1950	100.0	0.8	99.1	10.0	89.1	-	-	-	-	-
1953	100.0	1.0	99.0	11.4	87.7	-	-	-	-	-
1955	100.0	1.3	98.7	9.7	89.0	100.0	-	100.0	-	100.0
1957	100.0	1.1	98.9	38.1	60.8	100.0	-	100.0	-	100.0
1960	100.0	0.3	99.7	53.5	46.2	100.0	-	100.0	-	100.0
1961	100.0	0.2	99.8	46.3	53.5	100.0	-	100.0	-	100.0
1962	100.0	0.2	99.8	52.4	47.4	100.0	-	100.0	-	100.0
1963	100.0	0.3	99.7	57.5	42.2	100.0	-	100.0	-	100.0
1964	100.0	0.4	99.6	59.2	40.4	100.0	-	100.0	-	100.0
1965	100.0	0.4	99.6	62.8	36.8	100.0	-	100.0	-	100.0

Table VIII. ENERGY IMPORTS AND EXPORTS PERCENTAGE DISTRIBUTION, SELECTED YEARS, 1925-1965

(Based on coal equivalents)

Region, country, year	Imports					Exports				
	Total	Solid fuels	Total liquid fuels	Crude oil	Refined petroleum products	Total	Solid fuels	Total liquid fuels	Crude oil	Refined petroleum products
	(1)	(2)	(3)	(4)	(5)	(6)	(7)	(8)	(9)	(10)
CUBA										
1925	100.0	25.8	74.2	6.3	67.8	-	-	-	-	-
1929	100.0	28.1	71.9	13.6	58.3	-	-	-	-	-
1933	100.0	39.1	60.9	4.7	56.2	-	-	-	-	-
1937	100.0	25.2	74.8	13.2	61.6	-	-	-	-	-
1938	100.0	28.2	71.8	10.9	60.9	-	-	-	-	-
1950	100.0	0.9	99.1	11.2	87.9	NA	NA	NA	NA	NA
1953	100.0	1.4	98.6	18.3	80.3	NA	NA	NA	NA	NA
1955	100.0	3.1	96.9	17.6	79.3	NA	NA	NA	NA	NA
1957	100.0	2.9	97.1	50.8	46.3	100.0	-	100.0	-	100.0
1960	100.0	0.9	99.1	77.6	21.5	100.0	-	100.0	-	100.0
1961	100.0	0.8	99.2	68.1	31.1	-	-	-	-	-
1962	100.0	0.8	99.2	76.3	22.9	-	-	-	-	-
1963	100.0	1.4	98.6	82.7	15.9	100.0	-	100.0	-	100.0
1964	100.0	1.6	98.4	71.5	26.8	100.0	-	100.0	-	100.0
1965	100.0	1.8	98.2	72.2	26.0	100.0	-	100.0	-	100.0
PANAMA CANAL ZONE										
1925	100.0	19.3	80.7	-	80.7	-	-	-	-	-
1929	100.0	14.3	85.7	-	85.7	-	-	-	-	-
1933	100.0	2.1	97.9	-	97.9	-	-	-	-	-
1937	100.0	8.9	91.1	-	91.1	-	-	-	-	-
1938	100.0	3.7	96.3	-	96.3	-	-	-	-	-
1950	100.0	-	100.0	-	100.0	NA	NA	NA	NA	NA
1953	100.0	-	100.0	-	100.0	NA	NA	NA	NA	NA
1955	100.0	-	100.0	-	100.0	100.0	-	100.0	-	100.0
1957	100.0	-	100.0	-	100.0	100.0	-	100.0	-	100.0
1960	100.0	-	100.0	-	100.0	100.0	-	100.0	-	100.0
1961	100.0	-	100.0	-	100.0	100.0	-	100.0	-	100.0
1962	100.0	-	100.0	-	100.0	100.0	-	100.0	-	100.0
1963	100.0	-	100.0	-	100.0	100.0	-	100.0	-	100.0
1964	100.0	-	100.0	-	100.0	100.0	-	100.0	-	100.0
1965	100.0	-	100.0	-	100.0	100.0	-	100.0	-	100.0
PUERTO RICO										
1950	NA	NA	NA	NA	NA	NA	NA	NA	NA	NA
1953	NA	NA	NA	NA	NA	NA	NA	NA	NA	NA
1955	100.0	-	100.0	-	100.0	100.0	-	100.0	-	100.0
1957	100.0	-	100.0	76.9	23.1	100.0	-	100.0	-	100.0
1960	100.0	-	100.0	91.5	8.5	100.0	-	100.0	-	100.0
1961	100.0	-	100.0	93.0	7.0	100.0	-	100.0	-	100.0
1962	100.0	-	100.0	90.8	9.2	100.0	-	100.0	-	100.0
1963	100.0	-	100.0	94.1	5.9	100.0	-	100.0	-	100.0
1964	100.0	-	100.0	94.8	5.2	100.0	-	100.0	-	100.0
1965	100.0	-	100.0	92.8	7.2	100.0	-	100.0	-	100.0
LATIN AMERICA - OTHER										
1925	100.0	61.5	38.5	14.6	24.0	100.0	1.0	99.0	66.1	32.8
1929	100.0	50.3	49.7	18.2	31.5	100.0	0.8	99.2	69.7	29.4
1933	100.0	53.3	46.7	6.6	40.1	100.0	4.6	95.4	64.6	30.8
1937	100.0	46.4	53.6	17.6	36.0	100.0	1.6	98.4	77.4	21.0
1938	100.0	41.6	58.4	18.7	39.7	100.0	2.0	98.0	74.5	23.6

Table VIII. ENERGY IMPORTS AND EXPORTS PERCENTAGE DISTRIBUTION, SELECTED YEARS, 1925-1965

(Based on coal equivalents)

Region, country, year	Imports: Total	Imports: Solid fuels	Imports: Total liquid fuels	Imports: Crude oil	Imports: Refined petroleum products	Exports: Total	Exports: Solid fuels	Exports: Total liquid fuels	Exports: Crude oil	Exports: Refined petroleum products
	(1)	(2)	(3)	(4)	(5)	(6)	(7)	(8)	(9)	(10)
LATIN AMERICA - OTHER (CONTINUED)										
1950	100.0	13.9	86.1	25.2	61.0	100.0	7.8	92.2	47.7	44.5
1953	100.0	9.4	90.6	30.6	60.0	100.0	2.4	97.6	61.9	35.8
1955	100.0	8.1	91.9	40.9	51.0	100.0	3.9	96.1	47.5	48.6
1957	100.0	7.3	92.7	53.1	39.6	100.0	3.8	96.2	49.4	46.8
1960	100.0	9.2	90.8	51.5	39.3	100.0	2.1	97.9	66.5	31.4
1961	100.0	8.1	91.9	57.3	34.6	100.0	-	100.0	77.2	22.8
1962	100.0	6.0	94.0	69.0	25.0	100.0	0.3	99.7	50.9	48.7
1963	100.0	7.2	92.8	71.7	21.0	100.0	0.4	99.6	51.1	48.5
1964	100.0	6.9	93.1	71.6	21.5	100.0	0.5	99.5	38.9	60.5
1965	100.0	6.4	93.6	74.4	19.2	100.0	0.2	99.8	29.4	70.3
ARGENTINA										
1925	100.0	74.8	25.2	2.7	22.5	-	-	-	-	-
1929	100.0	55.3	44.7	12.7	32.0	100.0	-	100.0	-	100.0
1933	100.0	61.9	38.1	5.9	32.2	-	-	-	-	-
1937	100.0	54.9	45.1	14.8	30.3	100.0	-	100.0	-	100.0
1938	100.0	47.5	52.5	16.5	35.9	-	-	-	-	-
1950	100.0	15.4	84.6	46.5	38.2	-	-	-	-	-
1953	100.0	11.8	88.2	52.0	36.2	-	-	-	-	-
1955	100.0	10.5	89.5	46.5	43.0	-	-	-	-	-
1957	100.0	8.4	91.6	60.4	31.2	100.0	-	100.0	-	100.0
1960	100.0	16.1	83.9	54.7	29.2	100.0	-	100.0	-	100.0
1961	100.0	19.8	80.2	42.5	37.6	100.0	-	100.0	45.1	54.9
1962	100.0	14.0	86.0	36.5	49.5	100.0	-	100.0	28.4	71.6
1963	100.0	25.5	74.5	43.1	31.4	100.0	-	100.0	12.3	87.7
1964	100.0	15.5	84.5	45.8	38.6	100.0	-	100.0	3.1	96.9
1965	100.0	9.7	90.3	70.7	19.6	100.0	-	100.0	-	100.0
BOLIVIA										
1925	100.0	32.7	67.3	-	67.3	-	-	-	-	-
1929	100.0	24.1	75.9	-	75.9	-	-	-	-	-
1933	100.0	21.1	78.9	-	78.9	-	-	-	-	-
1937	100.0	34.1	65.9	-	65.9	-	-	-	-	-
1938	100.0	32.8	67.2	-	67.2	-	-	-	-	-
1950	100.0	1.8	98.2	80.2	18.0	100.0	-	100.0	100.0	-
1953	100.0	3.0	97.0	65.0	32.0	100.0	-	100.0	100.0	-
1955	100.0	-	100.0	17.0	83.0	100.0	-	100.0	78.5	21.5
1957	100.0	-	100.0	-	100.0	100.0	-	100.0	84.3	15.7
1960	100.0	-	100.0	-	100.0	100.0	-	100.0	96.4	3.6
1961	100.0	-	100.0	-	100.0	100.0	-	100.0	91.4	8.6
1962	100.0	-	100.0	66.7	33.3	100.0	-	100.0	98.5	1.5
1963	100.0	-	100.0	-	100.0	100.0	-	100.0	100.0	-
1964	100.0	-	100.0	-	100.0	100.0	-	100.0	85.7	14.3
1965	100.0	16.4	83.6	-	83.6	100.0	-	100.0	89.7	10.3
BRAZIL										
1925	100.0	70.3	29.7	-	29.7	-	-	-	-	-
1929	100.0	66.2	33.8	-	33.8	-	-	-	-	-
1933	100.0	52.3	47.7	-	47.7	-	-	-	-	-
1937	100.0	50.8	49.2	1.7	47.6	-	-	-	-	-
1938	100.0	47.1	52.9	2.2	50.7	-	-	-	-	-

Table VIII. ENERGY IMPORTS AND EXPORTS PERCENTAGE DISTRIBUTION, SELECTED YEARS, 1925-1965

(Based on coal equivalents)

Region, country, year	Imports					Exports				
	Total	Solid fuels	Total liquid fuels	Crude oil	Refined petroleum products	Total	Solid fuels	Total liquid fuels	Crude oil	Refined petroleum products
	(1)	(2)	(3)	(4)	(5)	(6)	(7)	(8)	(9)	(10)
BRAZIL (CONTINUED)										
1950	100.0	14.7	85.3	1.2	84.2	-	-	-	-	-
1953	100.0	8.3	91.7	0.5	91.2	-	-	-	-	-
1955	100.0	7.9	92.1	37.1	55.0	-	-	-	-	-
1957	100.0	6.8	93.2	52.4	40.9	100.0	-	100.0	-	100.0
1960	100.0	6.6	93.4	53.1	40.3	100.0	-	100.0	90.7	9.3
1961	100.0	5.3	94.7	66.8	27.9	100.0	-	100.0	93.3	6.7
1962	100.0	5.2	94.8	83.8	11.0	100.0	-	100.0	79.5	20.5
1963	100.0	5.6	94.4	83.7	10.7	100.0	-	100.0	91.8	8.2
1964	100.0	6.1	93.9	85.4	8.5	100.0	-	100.0	-	100.0
1965	100.0	6.9	93.1	86.0	7.0	-	-	-	-	-
CHILE										
1925	100.0	16.1	83.9	77.2	6.7	100.0	47.6	52.4	52.4	-
1929	100.0	4.1	95.9	84.9	11.0	100.0	93.3	6.7	6.7	-
1933	100.0	0.7	99.3	65.1	34.2	100.0	97.6	2.4	1.2	1.2
1937	100.0	1.0	99.0	81.8	17.2	100.0	97.3	2.7	2.7	-
1938	100.0	0.6	99.4	78.8	20.6	100.0	100.0	-	-	-
1950	100.0	4.6	95.4	-	95.4	100.0	49.4	50.6	50.6	-
1953	100.0	10.7	89.3	-	89.3	100.0	-	100.0	100.0	-
1955	100.0	5.4	94.6	17.7	76.9	100.0	95.9	4.1	-	4.1
1957	100.0	11.0	89.0	25.7	63.3	100.0	46.0	54.0	54.0	-
1960	100.0	14.2	85.8	31.3	54.5	100.0	69.0	31.0	-	31.0
1961	100.0	7.6	92.4	35.0	57.4	100.0	-	100.0	-	100.0
1962	100.0	5.4	94.6	40.9	53.7	100.0	-	100.0	-	100.0
1963	100.0	8.1	91.9	31.9	60.0	100.0	-	100.0	-	100.0
1964	100.0	8.3	91.7	32.4	59.2	100.0	-	100.0	-	100.0
1965	100.0	4.7	95.3	40.1	55.2	100.0	-	100.0	-	100.0
ECUADOR										
1925	100.0	-	100.0	-	100.0	100.0	-	100.0	100.0	-
1929	100.0	-	100.0	-	100.0	100.0	-	100.0	100.0	-
1933	100.0	-	100.0	-	100.0	100.0	-	100.0	100.0	-
1937	100.0	-	100.0	-	100.0	100.0	-	100.0	100.0	-
1938	100.0	-	100.0	-	100.0	100.0	-	100.0	99.6	0.4
1950	100.0	-	100.0	-	100.0	100.0	-	100.0	100.0	-
1953	100.0	-	100.0	-	100.0	100.0	-	100.0	100.0	-
1955	100.0	-	100.0	17.2	82.8	100.0	-	100.0	100.0	-
1957	100.0	-	100.0	-	100.0	100.0	-	100.0	100.0	-
1960	100.0	-	100.0	92.6	7.4	-	-	-	-	-
1961	100.0	-	100.0	90.9	9.1	-	-	-	-	-
1962	100.0	-	100.0	90.9	9.1	100.0	-	100.0	100.0	-
1963	100.0	-	100.0	86.8	13.2	100.0	-	100.0	100.0	-
1964	100.0	-	100.0	92.8	7.2	100.0	-	100.0	100.0	-
1965	100.0	-	100.0	91.8	8.2	100.0	-	100.0	100.0	-
PARAGUAY										
1925	NA	NA	NA	NA	NA	-	-	-	-	-
1929	NA	NA	NA	NA	NA	-	-	-	-	-
1933	100.0	33.3	66.7	-	66.7	-	-	-	-	-
1937	100.0	NA	100.0	-	100.0	-	-	-	-	-
1938	100.0	NA	100.0	-	100.0	-	-	-	-	-

Table VIII. ENERGY IMPORTS AND EXPORTS PERCENTAGE DISTRIBUTION, SELECTED YEARS, 1925-1965

(Based on coal equivalents)

Region, country, year	Imports					Exports				
	Total	Solid fuels	Total liquid fuels	Crude oil	Refined petroleum products	Total	Solid fuels	Total liquid fuels	Crude oil	Refined petroleum products
	(1)	(2)	(3)	(4)	(5)	(6)	(7)	(8)	(9)	(10)
PARAGUAY (CONTINUED)										
1950	100.0	-	100.0	-	100.0	-	-	-	-	-
1953	100.0	-	100.0	-	100.0	-	-	-	-	-
1955	100.0	-	100.0	-	100.0	-	-	-	-	-
1957	100.0	-	100.0	-	100.0	-	-	-	-	-
1960	100.0	-	100.0	-	100.0	-	-	-	-	-
1961	100.0	-	100.0	-	100.0	-	-	-	-	-
1962	100.0	-	100.0	-	100.0	-	-	-	-	-
1963	100.0	-	100.0	-	100.0	-	-	-	-	-
1964	100.0	-	100.0	-	100.0	-	-	-	-	-
1965	100.0	-	100.0	-	100.0	-	-	-	-	-
PERU										
1925	100.0	86.7	13.3	-	13.3	100.0	-	100.0	66.2	33.8
1929	100.0	87.2	12.8	-	12.8	100.0	-	100.0	67.6	32.4
1933	100.0	92.3	7.7	-	7.7	100.0	-	100.0	64.5	35.5
1937	100.0	23.8	76.2	61.9	14.3	100.0	-	100.0	76.0	24.0
1938	100.0	27.4	72.6	50.5	22.1	100.0	-	100.0	72.5	27.5
1950	100.0	1.7	98.3	-	98.3	100.0	4.1	95.9	39.7	56.2
1953	100.0	1.6	98.4	-	98.4	100.0	3.4	96.6	44.2	52.4
1955	100.0	-	100.0	-	100.0	100.0	-	100.0	35.7	64.3
1957	100.0	-	100.0	-	100.0	100.0	2.0	98.0	42.3	55.7
1960	100.0	1.1	98.9	-	98.9	100.0	1.7	98.3	43.7	54.6
1961	100.0	2.2	97.8	2.4	95.4	100.0	-	100.0	52.4	47.6
1962	100.0	1.9	98.1	14.2	83.9	100.0	1.1	98.9	62.0	36.9
1963	100.0	1.0	99.0	15.1	83.9	100.0	1.4	98.6	79.4	19.2
1964	100.0	0.5	99.5	11.1	88.4	100.0	1.5	98.5	83.0	15.4
1965	100.0	1.0	99.0	17.3	81.7	100.0	0.8	99.2	80.0	19.1
URUGUAY										
1925	100.0	53.0	47.0	-	47.0	-	-	-	-	-
1929	100.0	48.5	51.5	-	51.5	-	-	-	-	-
1933	100.0	44.5	55.5	-	55.5	-	-	-	-	-
1937	100.0	40.8	59.2	12.2	47.0	-	-	-	-	-
1938	100.0	37.2	62.8	23.1	39.8	-	-	-	-	-
1950	100.0	18.6	81.4	71.4	10.0	-	-	-	-	-
1953	100.0	4.2	95.8	91.6	4.2	-	-	-	-	-
1955	100.0	4.0	96.0	83.2	12.8	-	-	-	-	-
1957	100.0	4.1	95.9	73.0	22.9	-	-	-	-	-
1960	100.0	3.3	96.7	80.8	15.9	-	-	-	-	-
1961	100.0	2.6	97.4	88.5	8.9	100.0	-	100.0	-	100.0
1962	100.0	2.1	97.9	92.0	5.9	100.0	-	100.0	-	100.0
1963	100.0	2.2	97.8	94.3	3.5	100.0	-	100.0	-	100.0
1964	100.0	2.0	98.0	94.1	3.9	100.0	-	100.0	-	100.0
1965	100.0	1.5	98.5	89.2	9.3	-	-	-	-	-
ASIA										
1925	100.0	55.2	44.8	5.4	39.5	100.0	34.6	65.4	11.4	54.0
1929	100.0	46.6	53.4	14.6	38.9	100.0	29.4	70.6	13.1	57.5
1933	100.0	42.4	57.6	22.6	35.0	100.0	22.5	77.5	14.6	62.9
1937	100.0	40.0	60.0	21.2	38.8	100.0	15.0	85.0	21.6	63.4
1938	100.0	39.1	60.9	20.0	40.9	100.0	17.9	82.1	20.3	61.8

Table VIII. ENERGY IMPORTS AND EXPORTS PERCENTAGE DISTRIBUTION, SELECTED YEARS, 1925-1965

(Based on coal equivalents)

Region, country, year	Imports					Exports				
	Total	Solid fuels	Total liquid fuels	Crude oil	Refined petroleum products	Total	Solid fuels	Total liquid fuels	Crude oil	Refined petroleum products
	(1)	(2)	(3)	(4)	(5)	(6)	(7)	(8)	(9)	(10)
ASIA (CONTINUED)										
1950	100.0	6.5	93.3	47.9	45.5	100.0	1.1	98.9	56.9	41.9
1953	100.0	10.7	89.2	46.9	42.3	100.0	1.5	98.5	79.2	19.3
1955	100.0	6.5	93.4	56.1	37.3	100.0	0.7	99.2	80.6	18.6
1957	100.0	8.4	91.5	55.7	35.8	100.0	0.6	99.3	79.5	19.9
1960	100.0	7.9	92.0	62.1	29.9	100.0	0.4	99.6	82.8	16.8
1961	100.0	8.3	91.6	62.4	29.3	100.0	0.3	99.6	84.2	15.5
1962	100.0	7.9	92.1	66.6	25.5	100.0	0.3	99.7	83.3	16.3
1963	100.0	6.4	93.6	70.0	23.6	100.0	0.2	99.7	84.4	15.3
1964	100.0	6.8	93.2	71.9	21.4	100.0	0.3	99.7	85.8	13.9
1965	100.0	7.6	92.4	72.2	20.2	100.0	0.2	99.8	86.4	13.4
MIDDLE EAST										
1925	100.0	29.8	70.2	0.2	70.1	100.0	2.6	97.4	26.8	70.6
1929	100.0	23.8	76.2	0.3	75.9	100.0	5.4	94.6	29.6	65.1
1933	100.0	14.8	85.2	1.0	84.1	100.0	4.6	95.4	20.6	74.8
1937	100.0	17.8	82.2	1.1	81.2	100.0	1.3	98.7	35.0	63.7
1938	100.0	13.1	86.9	0.9	85.9	100.0	1.8	98.2	36.4	61.7
1950	100.0	1.0	99.0	60.0	39.1	100.0	-	100.0	61.1	38.9
1953	100.0	0.3	99.7	65.7	33.9	100.0	-	100.0	86.6	13.4
1955	100.0	0.2	99.8	77.5	22.3	100.0	-	100.0	85.6	14.4
1957	100.0	0.2	99.8	72.9	26.9	100.0	-	100.0	83.4	16.6
1960	100.0	0.2	99.8	75.5	24.3	100.0	-	100.0	85.7	14.2
1961	100.0	0.2	99.8	78.9	20.9	100.0	-	100.0	86.8	13.2
1962	100.0	0.1	99.9	88.1	11.8	100.0	-	100.0	86.1	13.9
1963	100.0	0.1	99.9	87.6	12.3	100.0	-	100.0	87.0	13.0
1964	100.0	0.1	99.9	87.8	12.1	100.0	-	100.0	88.1	11.9
1965	100.0	0.1	99.9	91.0	8.9	100.0	-	100.0	88.8	11.2
MIDDLE EAST - OIL PRODUCING										
1925	100.0	3.5	96.5	-	96.5	100.0	-	100.0	27.6	72.4
1929	100.0	5.1	94.9	-	94.9	100.0	-	100.0	31.2	68.8
1933	100.0	2.1	97.9	-	97.9	100.0	-	100.0	21.6	78.4
1937	100.0	2.1	97.9	0.8	97.2	100.0	-	100.0	35.5	64.5
1938	100.0	2.4	97.6	-	97.6	100.0	-	100.0	37.1	62.9
1950	100.0	-	100.0	95.5	4.5	100.0	-	100.0	61.1	38.9
1953	100.0	-	100.0	98.4	1.6	100.0	-	100.0	86.6	13.4
1955	100.0	-	100.0	95.7	4.3	100.0	-	100.0	87.0	13.0
1957	100.0	-	100.0	82.1	17.9	100.0	-	100.0	84.8	15.2
1960	100.0	-	100.0	98.3	1.7	100.0	-	100.0	86.5	13.5
1961	100.0	0.2	99.8	98.0	1.9	100.0	-	100.0	87.9	12.1
1962	100.0	-	100.0	98.7	1.3	100.0	-	100.0	87.3	12.7
1963	100.0	-	100.0	98.0	2.0	100.0	-	100.0	88.3	11.7
1964	100.0	-	100.0	97.3	2.7	100.0	-	100.0	89.4	10.6
1965	100.0	-	100.0	96.7	3.3	100.0	-	100.0	90.0	10.0
BAHRAIN										
1925	-	-	-	-	-	-	-	-	-	-
1929	-	-	-	-	-	-	-	-	-	-
1933	-	-	-	-	-	100.0	-	100.0	100.0	-
1937	100.0	-	100.0	-	100.0	100.0	-	100.0	65.2	34.8
1938	100.0	-	100.0	-	100.0	100.0	-	100.0	5.9	94.1

Table VIII. ENERGY IMPORTS AND EXPORTS PERCENTAGE DISTRIBUTION, SELECTED YEARS, 1925-1965

(Based on coal equivalents)

Region, country, year	Imports					Exports				
	Total	Solid fuels	Total liquid fuels	Crude oil	Refined petroleum products	Total	Solid fuels	Total liquid fuels	Crude oil	Refined petroleum products
	(1)	(2)	(3)	(4)	(5)	(6)	(7)	(8)	(9)	(10)
BAHRAIN (CONTINUED)										
1950	100.0	-	100.0	100.0	-	100.0	-	100.0	-	100.0
1953	100.0	-	100.0	100.0	-	100.0	-	100.0	-	100.0
1955	100.0	-	100.0	100.0	-	100.0	-	100.0	3.3	96.7
1957	100.0	-	100.0	100.0	-	100.0	-	100.0	0.2	99.8
1960	100.0	-	100.0	99.3	0.7	100.0	-	100.0	-	100.0
1961	100.0	-	100.0	99.0	1.0	100.0	-	100.0	-	100.0
1962	100.0	-	100.0	99.6	0.4	100.0	-	100.0	-	100.0
1963	100.0	-	100.0	98.8	1.2	100.0	-	100.0	-	100.0
1964	100.0	-	100.0	98.3	1.7	100.0	-	100.0	-	100.0
1965	100.0	-	100.0	98.0	2.0	100.0	-	100.0	-	100.0
IRAN										
1925	100.0	8.5	91.5	-	91.5	100.0	-	100.0	27.6	72.4
1929	100.0	1.3	98.7	-	98.7	100.0	-	100.0	31.2	68.8
1933	100.0	2.2	97.8	-	97.8	100.0	-	100.0	21.5	78.5
1937	100.0	1.3	98.7	1.9	96.8	100.0	-	100.0	5.3	94.7
1938	100.0	2.5	97.5	-	97.5	100.0	-	100.0	3.8	96.2
1950	100.0	-	100.0	-	100.0	100.0	-	100.0	22.7	77.3
1953	100.0	-	100.0	-	100.0	100.0	-	100.0	17.6	82.4
1955	100.0	-	100.0	-	100.0	100.0	-	100.0	63.5	36.5
1957	100.0	-	100.0	-	100.0	100.0	-	100.0	63.1	36.9
1960	100.0	-	100.0	-	100.0	100.0	-	100.0	74.4	25.6
1961	100.0	-	100.0	-	100.0	100.0	-	100.0	81.5	18.5
1962	100.0	-	100.0	-	100.0	100.0	-	100.0	80.1	19.9
1963	100.0	-	100.0	-	100.0	100.0	-	100.0	82.5	17.5
1964	100.0	-	100.0	-	100.0	100.0	-	100.0	85.0	15.0
1965	100.0	-	100.0	-	100.0	100.0	-	100.0	86.1	13.9
IRAQ										
1925	100.0	-	100.0	-	100.0	-	-	-	-	-
1929	100.0	8.7	91.3	-	91.3	-	-	-	-	-
1933	100.0	2.1	97.9	-	97.9	100.0	-	100.0	-	100.0
1937	100.0	2.7	97.3	-	97.3	100.0	-	100.0	100.0	-
1938	100.0	2.4	97.6	-	97.6	100.0	-	100.0	100.0	-
1950	100.0	0.5	99.5	-	99.5	100.0	-	100.0	99.9	0.1
1953	100.0	NA	100.0	-	100.0	100.0	-	100.0	100.0	-
1955	100.0	-	100.0	-	100.0	100.0	-	100.0	100.0	-
1957	100.0	-	100.0	-	100.0	100.0	-	100.0	100.0	-
1960	100.0	-	100.0	-	100.0	100.0	-	100.0	100.0	-
1961	100.0	81.6	18.4	-	18.4	100.0	-	100.0	100.0	-
1962	100.0	-	100.0	-	100.0	100.0	-	100.0	100.0	-
1963	100.0	-	100.0	-	100.0	100.0	-	100.0	100.0	-
1964	100.0	-	100.0	-	100.0	100.0	-	100.0	100.0	-
1965	100.0	-	100.0	-	100.0	100.0	-	100.0	100.0	-
KUWAIT										
1950	-	-	-	-	-	100.0	-	100.0	98.2	1.8
1953	100.0	-	100.0	-	100.0	100.0	-	100.0	99.4	0.6
1955	100.0	-	100.0	-	100.0	100.0	-	100.0	99.6	0.4
1957	100.0	-	100.0	-	100.0	100.0	-	100.0	99.8	0.2
1960	-	-	-	-	-	100.0	-	100.0	93.6	6.4

Table VIII. ENERGY IMPORTS AND EXPORTS PERCENTAGE DISTRIBUTION, SELECTED YEARS, 1925-1965

(Based on coal equivalents)

Region, country, year	Imports: Total	Imports: Solid fuels	Imports: Total liquid fuels	Imports: Crude oil	Imports: Refined petroleum products	Exports: Total	Exports: Solid fuels	Exports: Total liquid fuels	Exports: Crude oil	Exports: Refined petroleum products
	(1)	(2)	(3)	(4)	(5)	(6)	(7)	(8)	(9)	(10)
KUWAIT (CONTINUED)										
1961	-	-	-	-	-	100.0	-	100.0	94.5	5.5
1962	-	-	-	-	-	100.0	-	100.0	94.5	5.5
1963	100.0	-	100.0	-	100.0	100.0	-	100.0	94.4	5.6
1964	100.0	-	100.0	-	100.0	100.0	-	100.0	94.0	6.0
1965	-	-	-	-	-	100.0	-	100.0	93.5	6.5
KUWAIT NEUTRAL ZONE										
1955	100.0	-	100.0	-	100.0	100.0	-	100.0	100.0	-
1957	100.0	-	100.0	-	100.0	100.0	-	100.0	100.0	-
1960	100.0	-	100.0	-	100.0	100.0	-	100.0	88.6	11.4
1961	100.0	-	100.0	-	100.0	100.0	-	100.0	89.0	11.0
1962	100.0	-	100.0	-	100.0	100.0	-	100.0	78.2	21.8
1963	100.0	-	100.0	-	100.0	100.0	-	100.0	84.7	15.3
1964	100.0	-	100.0	-	100.0	100.0	-	100.0	84.9	15.1
1965	100.0	-	100.0	-	100.0	100.0	-	100.0	86.1	13.9
QATAR										
1950	-	-	-	-	-	100.0	-	100.0	100.0	-
1953	-	-	-	-	-	100.0	-	100.0	100.0	-
1955	100.0	-	100.0	-	100.0	100.0	-	100.0	100.0	-
1957	100.0	-	100.0	-	100.0	100.0	-	100.0	100.0	-
1960	100.0	-	100.0	-	100.0	100.0	-	100.0	100.0	-
1961	100.0	-	100.0	-	100.0	100.0	-	100.0	100.0	-
1962	100.0	-	100.0	-	100.0	100.0	-	100.0	100.0	-
1963	100.0	-	100.0	-	100.0	100.0	-	100.0	100.0	-
1964	100.0	-	100.0	-	100.0	100.0	-	100.0	100.0	-
1965	100.0	-	100.0	-	100.0	100.0	-	100.0	100.0	-
SAUDI ARABIA										
1950	-	-	-	-	-	100.0	-	100.0	85.5	14.5
1953	-	-	-	-	-	100.0	-	100.0	79.9	20.1
1955	100.0	-	100.0	-	100.0	100.0	-	100.0	83.3	16.7
1957	100.0	-	100.0	-	100.0	100.0	-	100.0	85.0	15.0
1960	100.0	-	100.0	-	100.0	100.0	-	100.0	87.0	13.0
1961	100.0	-	100.0	-	100.0	100.0	-	100.0	86.9	13.1
1962	100.0	-	100.0	-	100.0	100.0	-	100.0	88.4	11.6
1963	-	-	-	-	-	100.0	-	100.0	88.1	11.9
1964	-	-	-	-	-	100.0	-	100.0	88.0	12.0
1965	100.0	-	100.0	-	100.0	100.0	-	100.0	88.7	11.3
TRUCIAL OMAN										
1960	100.0	-	100.0	-	100.0	-	-	-	-	-
1961	100.0	-	100.0	-	100.0	-	-	-	-	-
1962	100.0	-	100.0	-	100.0	100.0	-	100.0	100.0	-
1963	100.0	-	100.0	-	100.0	100.0	-	100.0	100.0	-
1964	100.0	-	100.0	-	100.0	100.0	-	100.0	100.0	-
1965	100.0	-	100.0	-	100.0	100.0	-	100.0	100.0	-

Table VIII. ENERGY IMPORTS AND EXPORTS PERCENTAGE DISTRIBUTION, SELECTED YEARS, 1925-1965

(Based on coal equivalents)

Region, country, year	Imports					Exports				
	Total	Solid fuels	Total liquid fuels	Crude oil	Refined petroleum products	Total	Solid fuels	Total liquid fuels	Crude oil	Refined petroleum products
	(1)	(2)	(3)	(4)	(5)	(6)	(7)	(8)	(9)	(10)
MIDDLE EAST - OTHER										
1925	100.0	34.7	65.3	0.2	65.1	100.0	99.0	1.0	-	1.0
1929	100.0	26.0	74.0	0.3	73.6	100.0	99.7	0.3	-	0.3
1933	100.0	16.1	83.9	1.1	82.8	100.0	100.0	-	-	-
1937	100.0	19.2	80.8	1.1	79.7	100.0	95.6	4.4	-	4.4
1938	100.0	13.9	86.1	1.0	85.1	100.0	100.0	-	-	-
1950	100.0	2.2	97.8	13.9	84.0	-	-	-	-	-
1953	100.0	0.8	99.2	21.2	77.9	100.0	40.0	60.0	-	60.0
1955	100.0	0.4	99.6	61.5	38.1	100.0	-	100.0	-	100.0
1957	100.0	0.4	99.6	64.7	34.9	100.0	-	100.0	-	100.0
1960	100.0	0.3	99.7	59.7	40.0	100.0	0.9	99.1	-	99.1
1961	100.0	0.2	99.8	66.3	33.5	100.0	-	100.0	-	100.0
1962	100.0	0.2	99.8	81.3	18.5	100.0	-	100.0	-	100.0
1963	100.0	0.1	99.9	82.1	17.8	100.0	0.1	99.9	-	99.9
1964	100.0	0.1	99.9	83.7	16.1	100.0	0.2	99.8	-	99.8
1965	100.0	0.1	99.9	88.9	11.0	100.0	0.1	99.9	-	99.9
PALESTINE										
1925	100.0	34.4	65.6	-	65.6	-	-	-	-	-
1929	100.0	30.6	69.4	-	69.4	-	-	-	-	-
1933	100.0	33.4	66.6	-	66.6	-	-	-	-	-
1937	100.0	26.4	73.6	-	73.6	-	-	-	-	-
1938	100.0	19.9	80.1	-	80.1	-	-	-	-	-
ISRAEL										
1950	100.0	3.0	97.0	26.0	71.0	-	-	-	-	-
1953	100.0	1.7	98.3	67.3	31.0	-	-	-	-	-
1955	100.0	0.8	99.2	64.5	34.7	-	-	-	-	-
1957	100.0	1.7	98.3	66.3	32.0	-	-	-	-	-
1960	100.0	1.7	98.3	69.5	28.8	100.0	-	100.0	-	100.0
1961	100.0	1.2	98.8	67.9	30.8	100.0	-	100.0	-	100.0
1962	100.0	1.1	98.9	82.2	16.8	100.0	-	100.0	-	100.0
1963	100.0	0.5	99.5	85.4	14.2	100.0	-	100.0	-	100.0
1964	100.0	0.6	99.4	85.5	13.9	100.0	-	100.0	-	100.0
1965	100.0	0.2	99.8	92.2	7.5	100.0	-	100.0	-	100.0
JORDAN										
1950	100.0	-	100.0	-	100.0	-	-	-	-	-
1953	100.0	-	100.0	-	100.0	-	-	-	-	-
1955	100.0	-	100.0	10.3	89.7	-	-	-	-	-
1957	100.0	-	100.0	-	100.0	-	-	-	-	-
1960	100.0	-	100.0	-	100.0	-	-	-	-	-
1961	100.0	-	100.0	69.7	30.3	-	-	-	-	-
1962	100.0	-	100.0	76.6	23.4	-	-	-	-	-
1963	100.0	-	100.0	85.9	14.1	-	-	-	-	-
1964	100.0	-	100.0	92.8	7.2	-	-	-	-	-
1965	100.0	-	100.0	91.3	8.7	-	-	-	-	-
LEBANON-SYRIA										
1925	100.0	47.7	52.3	-	52.3	-	-	-	-	-

Table VIII. ENERGY IMPORTS AND EXPORTS PERCENTAGE DISTRIBUTION, SELECTED YEARS, 1925-1965

(Based on coal equivalents)

Region, country, year	Imports					Exports				
	Total	Solid fuels	Total liquid fuels	Crude oil	Refined petroleum products	Total	Solid fuels	Total liquid fuels	Crude oil	Refined petroleum products
	(1)	(2)	(3)	(4)	(5)	(6)	(7)	(8)	(9)	(10)
LEBANON - SYRIA (CONTINUED)										
1929	100.0	32.5	67.5	-	67.5	-	-	-	-	-
1933	100.0	37.6	62.4	-	62.4	-	-	-	-	-
1937	100.0	51.0	49.0	-	49.0	-	-	-	-	-
1938	100.0	50.7	49.3	-	49.3	-	-	-	-	-
LEBANON										
1950	100.0	1.2	98.8	79.7	19.1	NA	NA	NA	NA	NA
1953	100.0	-	100.0	76.8	23.2	NA	NA	NA	NA	NA
1955	100.0	0.6	99.4	83.2	16.2	100.0	-	100.0	-	100.0
1957	100.0	0.5	99.5	83.5	15.9	100.0	-	100.0	-	100.0
1960	100.0	-	100.0	79.1	20.9	-	-	-	-	-
1961	100.0	-	100.0	76.5	23.5	-	-	-	-	-
1962	100.0	0.6	99.4	80.8	18.6	-	-	-	-	-
1963	100.0	0.6	99.4	85.9	13.6	100.0	-	100.0	-	100.0
1964	100.0	0.5	99.5	99.5	NA	-	-	-	-	-
1965	100.0	0.4	99.6	99.6	NA	-	-	-	-	-
SYRIA										
1950	100.0	0.6	99.4	-	99.4	-	-	-	-	-
1953	100.0	0.5	99.5	-	99.5	100.0	-	100.0	-	100.0
1955	100.0	-	100.0	-	100.0	100.0	-	100.0	-	100.0
1957	100.0	-	100.0	-	100.0	-	-	-	-	-
1960	100.0	-	100.0	69.3	30.7	-	-	-	-	-
1961	100.0	-	100.0	78.1	21.9	100.0	-	100.0	-	100.0
1962	100.0	-	100.0	75.4	24.6	100.0	-	100.0	-	100.0
1963	100.0	-	100.0	77.5	22.5	100.0	-	100.0	-	100.0
1964	100.0	-	100.0	73.9	26.1	100.0	-	100.0	-	100.0
1965	100.0	0.3	99.7	85.5	14.2	100.0	-	100.0	-	100.0
TURKEY										
1925	100.0	38.5	61.5	-	61.5	100.0	100.0	-	-	-
1929	100.0	40.2	59.8	-	59.8	100.0	100.0	-	-	-
1933	100.0	30.9	69.1	6.3	62.8	100.0	100.0	-	-	-
1937	100.0	16.6	83.4	-	83.4	100.0	100.0	-	-	-
1938	100.0	26.0	74.0	-	74.0	100.0	100.0	-	-	-
1950	100.0	-	100.0	-	100.0	-	-	-	-	-
1953	100.0	-	100.0	-	100.0	100.0	100.0	-	-	-
1955	100.0	-	100.0	-	100.0	-	-	-	-	-
1957	100.0	-	100.0	-	100.0	-	-	-	-	-
1960	100.0	-	100.0	-	100.0	100.0	100.0	-	-	-
1961	100.0	-	100.0	14.7	85.3	100.0	-	100.0	-	100.0
1962	100.0	-	100.0	85.2	14.8	100.0	-	100.0	-	100.0
1963	100.0	-	100.0	95.8	4.2	100.0	0.9	99.1	-	99.1
1964	100.0	-	100.0	97.4	2.6	100.0	1.7	98.3	-	98.3
1965	100.0	0.1	99.9	97.0	2.9	100.0	1.3	98.7	-	98.7
FAR EAST AND OTHER ASIA										
1925	100.0	57.3	42.7	5.8	36.9	100.0	53.4	46.6	2.3	44.3
1929	100.0	48.6	51.4	15.8	35.7	100.0	45.1	54.9	2.3	52.6

Table VIII. ENERGY IMPORTS AND EXPORTS PERCENTAGE DISTRIBUTION, SELECTED YEARS, 1925-1965

(Based on coal equivalents)

	Imports					Exports				
Region, country, year	Total	Solid fuels	Total liquid fuels	Crude oil	Refined petroleum products	Total	Solid fuels	Total liquid fuels	Crude oil	Refined petroleum products
	(1)	(2)	(3)	(4)	(5)	(6)	(7)	(8)	(9)	(10)
FAR EAST AND OTHER ASIA (CONTINUED)										
1933	100.0	45.0	55.0	24.6	30.4	100.0	37.9	62.1	9.5	52.6
1937	100.0	42.0	58.0	23.1	34.9	100.0	31.4	68.6	5.5	63.1
1938	100.0	41.5	58.5	21.8	36.7	100.0	32.5	67.5	5.7	61.8
1950	100.0	9.6	90.1	41.1	49.0	100.0	6.4	93.3	36.9	56.4
1953	100.0	15.0	84.8	39.0	45.8	100.0	8.9	90.9	41.4	49.4
1955	100.0	9.3	90.5	46.3	44.2	100.0	5.6	94.1	47.8	46.3
1957	100.0	11.2	88.7	49.9	38.8	100.0	4.2	95.6	56.7	38.9
1960	100.0	10.1	89.8	58.4	31.4	100.0	3.7	96.1	58.9	37.1
1961	100.0	10.4	89.6	58.2	31.4	100.0	3.3	96.5	60.7	35.8
1962	100.0	9.9	90.1	61.0	29.0	100.0	3.2	96.6	58.7	38.0
1963	100.0	7.9	92.0	65.8	26.2	100.0	2.8	97.1	58.4	38.6
1964	100.0	8.2	91.8	68.5	23.3	100.0	3.4	96.4	60.1	36.3
1965	100.0	8.9	91.1	68.8	22.3	100.0	2.5	97.4	57.5	39.9
BORNEO (FORMER BRITISH)										
1925	100.0	18.2	81.8	-	81.8	100.0	5.6	94.4	26.0	68.3
1929	100.0	-	100.0	-	100.0	100.0	4.0	96.0	19.9	76.0
1933	100.0	0.2	99.8	98.7	1.1	100.0	0.4	99.6	48.0	51.6
1937	100.0	-	100.0	91.1	8.9	100.0	-	100.0	41.2	58.8
1938	100.0	0.1	99.9	95.0	4.9	100.0	-	100.0	43.3	56.7
1950	100.0	-	98.9	97.9	0.9	100.0	-	99.4	79.0	20.4
1953	100.0	-	99.0	97.8	1.2	100.0	-	99.5	79.6	19.8
1955	100.0	-	98.9	97.8	1.1	100.0	-	99.4	81.6	17.8
1957	100.0	-	98.9	97.5	1.4	100.0	-	99.4	82.9	16.5
1960	100.0	-	98.6	96.2	2.4	100.0	-	99.3	77.5	21.7
1961	100.0	-	98.3	95.2	3.1	100.0	-	99.1	77.1	22.0
1962	100.0	-	98.4	94.9	3.5	100.0	-	99.1	73.4	25.7
1963	100.0	-	98.7	94.2	4.5	100.0	-	99.2	72.5	26.7
1964	100.0	-	98.8	93.7	5.1	100.0	-	99.4	65.5	33.8
1965	100.0	-	100.0	94.2	5.8	100.0	-	99.4	67.6	31.8
BRUNEI										
1925	100.0	100.0	-	-	-	-	-	-	-	-
1929	-	-	-	-	-	-	-	-	-	-
1933	-	-	-	-	-	100.0	-	100.0	100.0	-
1937	100.0	-	100.0	-	100.0	100.0	-	100.0	100.0	-
1938	100.0	-	100.0	-	100.0	100.0	-	100.0	100.0	-
1950	100.0	-	100.0	-	100.0	100.0	-	98.8	98.8	-
1953	100.0	-	100.0	-	100.0	100.0	-	99.0	99.0	-
1955	100.0	-	100.0	-	100.0	100.0	-	98.8	98.8	-
1957	100.0	-	100.0	-	100.0	100.0	-	98.9	98.9	-
1960	100.0	-	100.0	-	100.0	100.0	-	98.5	98.5	-
1961	100.0	-	100.0	-	100.0	100.0	-	98.4	98.4	-
1962	100.0	-	100.0	-	100.0	100.0	-	98.3	98.3	-
1963	100.0	-	100.0	-	100.0	100.0	-	98.4	98.4	-
1964	100.0	-	100.0	-	100.0	100.0	-	98.8	98.8	-
1965	100.0	-	100.0	-	100.0	100.0	-	98.8	98.8	-
SABAH										
1925	-	-	-	-	-	100.0	100.0	-	-	-

Table VIII. ENERGY IMPORTS AND EXPORTS PERCENTAGE DISTRIBUTION, SELECTED YEARS, 1925-1965

(Based on coal equivalents)

Region, country, year	Imports					Exports				
	Total	Solid fuels	Total liquid fuels	Crude oil	Refined petroleum products	Total	Solid fuels	Total liquid fuels	Crude oil	Refined petroleum products
	(1)	(2)	(3)	(4)	(5)	(6)	(7)	(8)	(9)	(10)
SABAH (CONTINUED)										
1929	100.0	-	100.0	-	100.0	100.0	100.0	-	-	-
1933	100.0	40.0	60.0	-	60.0	100.0	100.0	-	-	-
1937	100.0	-	100.0	-	100.0	-	-	-	-	-
1938	100.0	25.0	75.0	-	75.0	-	-	-	-	-
1950	100.0	-	100.0	-	100.0	-	-	-	-	-
1953	100.0	-	100.0	-	100.0	-	-	-	-	-
1955	100.0	-	100.0	-	100.0	-	-	-	-	-
1957	100.0	-	100.0	-	100.0	100.0	-	100.0	-	100.0
1960	100.0	-	100.0	-	100.0	100.0	-	100.0	-	100.0
1961	100.0	-	100.0	-	100.0	100.0	-	100.0	-	100.0
1962	100.0	-	100.0	-	100.0	100.0	-	100.0	-	100.0
1963	100.0	-	100.0	-	100.0	100.0	-	100.0	-	100.0
1964	100.0	-	100.0	-	100.0	100.0	-	100.0	-	100.0
1965	100.0	-	100.0	-	100.0	100.0	-	100.0	-	100.0
SARAWAK										
1925	100.0	-	100.0	-	100.0	100.0	-	100.0	27.6	72.4
1929	100.0	-	100.0	-	100.0	100.0	-	100.0	20.8	79.2
1933	100.0	-	100.0	99.3	0.7	100.0	-	100.0	22.7	77.3
1937	100.0	-	100.0	91.5	8.5	100.0	-	100.0	-	100.0
1938	100.0	-	100.0	95.5	4.5	100.0	-	100.0	-	100.0
1950	100.0	-	98.9	98.5	0.3	100.0	-	100.0	58.9	41.1
1953	100.0	-	99.0	98.6	0.4	100.0	-	100.0	59.6	40.4
1955	100.0	-	98.9	98.4	0.5	100.0	-	100.0	63.7	36.3
1957	100.0	-	98.9	98.3	0.6	100.0	-	100.0	66.5	33.5
1960	100.0	-	98.6	97.6	1.0	100.0	-	100.0	55.9	44.1
1961	100.0	-	98.3	96.9	1.3	100.0	-	100.0	52.7	47.3
1962	100.0	-	98.4	97.0	1.4	100.0	-	100.0	48.8	51.2
1963	100.0	-	98.6	96.9	1.7	100.0	-	100.0	45.5	54.5
1964	100.0	-	98.8	96.7	2.1	100.0	-	100.0	31.9	68.1
1965	100.0	-	100.0	97.2	2.8	100.0	-	100.0	34.2	65.8
BURMA										
1950	100.0	NA	100.0	-	100.0	-	-	-	-	-
1953	100.0	60.3	39.7	-	39.7	-	-	-	-	-
1955	100.0	46.7	53.3	-	53.3	-	-	-	-	-
1957	100.0	69.0	31.0	-	31.0	-	-	-	-	-
1960	100.0	77.7	22.3	-	22.3	-	-	-	-	-
1961	100.0	65.8	34.2	4.6	29.6	-	-	-	-	-
1962	100.0	71.1	28.9	-	28.9	-	-	-	-	-
1963	100.0	72.9	27.1	-	27.1	-	-	-	-	-
1964	100.0	47.6	52.4	39.8	12.6	-	-	-	-	-
1965	100.0	34.8	65.2	59.6	5.6	-	-	-	-	-
CEYLON										
1925	100.0	72.8	27.2	-	27.2	-	-	-	-	-
1929	100.0	65.5	34.5	-	34.5	-	-	-	-	-
1933	100.0	44.5	55.5	-	55.5	-	-	-	-	-
1937	100.0	48.4	51.6	-	51.6	-	-	-	-	-
1938	100.0	34.6	65.4	-	65.4	-	-	-	-	-

Table VIII. ENERGY IMPORTS AND EXPORTS PERCENTAGE DISTRIBUTION, SELECTED YEARS, 1925-1965

(Based on coal equivalents)

Region, country, year	Imports					Exports				
	Total	Solid fuels	Total liquid fuels	Crude oil	Refined petroleum products	Total	Solid fuels	Total liquid fuels	Crude oil	Refined petroleum products
	(1)	(2)	(3)	(4)	(5)	(6)	(7)	(8)	(9)	(10)
CEYLON (CONTINUED)										
1950	100.0	24.2	75.8	-	75.8	-	-	-	-	-
1953	100.0	23.7	76.3	-	76.3	-	-	-	-	-
1955	100.0	11.7	88.3	-	88.3	100.0	-	100.0	-	100.0
1957	100.0	11.8	88.2	-	88.2	-	-	-	-	-
1960	100.0	16.3	83.7	-	83.7	-	-	-	-	-
1961	100.0	8.1	91.9	-	91.9	100.0	-	100.0	-	100.0
1962	100.0	8.3	91.7	-	91.7	-	-	-	-	-
1963	100.0	9.9	90.1	-	90.1	-	-	-	-	-
1964	100.0	12.5	87.5	-	87.5	-	-	-	-	-
1965	100.0	8.4	91.6	-	91.6	100.0	-	100.0	-	100.0
HONG KONG										
1925	100.0	67.9	32.1	-	32.1	100.0	50.4	49.6	-	49.6
1929	100.0	63.1	36.9	-	36.9	100.0	37.7	62.3	-	62.3
1933	100.0	66.5	33.5	-	33.5	100.0	33.2	66.8	-	66.8
1937	100.0	63.2	36.8	-	36.8	100.0	9.9	90.1	-	90.1
1938	100.0	57.7	42.3	-	42.3	100.0	17.4	82.6	-	82.6
1950	100.0	25.7	74.3	-	74.3	100.0	20.9	79.1	-	79.1
1953	100.0	17.8	82.3	-	82.3	100.0	40.0	60.0	-	60.0
1955	100.0	16.6	83.4	-	83.4	100.0	-	100.0	-	100.0
1957	100.0	13.8	86.2	-	86.2	100.0	40.0	60.0	-	60.0
1960	100.0	11.4	88.6	-	88.6	100.0	33.9	66.1	-	66.1
1961	100.0	10.9	89.1	-	89.1	100.0	24.1	75.9	-	75.9
1962	100.0	8.6	91.4	-	91.4	100.0	-	100.0	-	100.0
1963	100.0	7.0	93.0	-	93.0	100.0	-	100.0	-	100.0
1964	100.0	6.0	94.0	-	94.0	100.0	-	100.0	-	100.0
1965	100.0	5.4	94.6	-	94.6	100.0	13.2	86.8	-	86.8
INDIA										
1925	100.0	31.4	68.6	-	68.6	100.0	76.1	23.9	-	23.9
1929	100.0	13.0	87.0	-	87.0	100.0	96.3	3.7	3.1	0.6
1933	100.0	5.7	94.3	-	94.3	100.0	94.4	5.6	4.3	1.3
1937	100.0	11.6	88.4	-	88.4	100.0	51.1	48.9	1.6	47.3
1938	100.0	15.6	84.4	-	84.4	100.0	53.7	46.3	1.3	45.0
1950	100.0	-	100.0	44.4	55.6	100.0	100.0	-	-	-
1953	100.0	-	100.0	40.7	59.3	100.0	100.0	-	-	-
1955	100.0	-	100.0	60.3	39.7	100.0	90.8	9.2	-	9.2
1957	100.0	-	100.0	68.4	31.6	100.0	75.0	25.0	-	25.0
1960	100.0	0.1	99.9	75.8	24.1	100.0	79.1	20.9	-	20.9
1961	100.0	0.1	99.9	75.2	24.8	100.0	79.2	20.8	-	20.8
1962	100.0	0.1	99.9	71.2	28.7	100.0	91.8	8.2	-	8.2
1963	100.0	-	100.0	71.5	28.5	100.0	59.5	40.5	-	40.5
1964	100.0	-	100.0	74.0	26.0	100.0	68.1	31.9	-	31.9
1965	100.0	-	100.0	75.9	24.1	100.0	67.7	32.3	-	32.3
INDO-CHINA										
1925	100.0	27.2	72.8	-	72.8	100.0	100.0	-	-	-
1929	100.0	19.3	80.7	-	80.7	100.0	100.0	-	-	-
1933	100.0	10.9	89.1	-	89.1	100.0	100.0	-	-	-
1937	100.0	9.0	91.0	-	91.0	100.0	100.0	-	-	-
1938	100.0	8.2	91.8	-	91.8	100.0	100.0	-	-	-

Table VIII. ENERGY IMPORTS AND EXPORTS PERCENTAGE DISTRIBUTION, SELECTED YEARS, 1925-1965

(Based on coal equivalents)

Region, country, year	Imports					Exports				
	Total	Solid fuels	Total liquid fuels	Crude oil	Refined petroleum products	Total	Solid fuels	Total liquid fuels	Crude oil	Refined petroleum products
	(1)	(2)	(3)	(4)	(5)	(6)	(7)	(8)	(9)	(10)
INDO-CHINA (CONTINUED)										
1950	100.0	6.0	94.0	-	94.0	100.0	100.0	-	-	-
1953	100.0	1.1	98.9	-	98.9	100.0	100.0	-	-	-
1955	100.0	5.2	94.8	-	94.8	-	-	-	-	-
1957	100.0	6.4	93.6	-	93.6	-	-	-	-	-
1960	100.0	1.0	99.0	-	99.0	-	-	-	-	-
1961	100.0	0.9	99.1	-	99.1	100.0	-	100.0	-	100.0
1962	100.0	1.8	98.2	-	98.2	100.0	-	100.0	-	100.0
1963	100.0	0.8	99.2	-	99.2	100.0	-	100.0	-	100.0
1964	100.0	1.6	98.4	-	98.4	-	-	-	-	-
1965	100.0	3.0	97.0	-	97.0	-	-	-	-	-
CAMBODIA										
1955	100.0	-	100.0	-	100.0	-	-	-	-	-
1957	100.0	-	100.0	-	100.0	-	-	-	-	-
1960	100.0	-	100.0	-	100.0	-	-	-	-	-
1961	100.0	-	100.0	-	100.0	100.0	-	100.0	-	100.0
1962	100.0	-	100.0	-	100.0	100.0	-	100.0	-	100.0
1963	100.0	-	100.0	-	100.0	100.0	-	100.0	-	100.0
1964	100.0	-	100.0	-	100.0	-	-	-	-	-
1965	100.0	10.1	89.9	-	89.9	-	-	-	-	-
LAOS										
1955	100.0	-	100.0	-	100.0	-	-	-	-	-
1957	100.0	-	100.0	-	100.0	-	-	-	-	-
1960	100.0	-	100.0	-	100.0	-	-	-	-	-
1961	100.0	-	100.0	-	100.0	-	-	-	-	-
1962	100.0	-	100.0	-	100.0	-	-	-	-	-
1963	100.0	-	100.0	-	100.0	-	-	-	-	-
1964	100.0	-	100.0	-	100.0	-	-	-	-	-
1965	100.0	-	100.0	-	100.0	-	-	-	-	-
VIETNAM, SOUTH										
1955	100.0	6.3	93.7	-	93.7	-	-	-	-	-
1957	100.0	7.9	92.1	-	92.1	-	-	-	-	-
1960	100.0	1.3	98.7	-	98.7	-	-	-	-	-
1961	100.0	1.2	98.8	-	98.8	-	-	-	-	-
1962	100.0	2.4	97.6	-	97.6	-	-	-	-	-
1963	100.0	1.1	98.9	-	98.9	-	-	-	-	-
1964	100.0	2.2	97.8	-	97.8	-	-	-	-	-
1965	100.0	1.3	98.7	-	98.7	-	-	-	-	-
INDONESIA										
1925	100.0	72.2	27.8	0.6	27.2	100.0	10.6	89.4	-	89.4
1929	100.0	34.3	65.7	-	65.7	100.0	8.8	91.2	0.6	90.6
1933	100.0	23.7	76.3	-	76.3	100.0	4.3	95.7	9.9	85.8
1937	100.0	21.9	78.1	-	78.1	100.0	3.5	96.5	1.7	94.8
1938	100.0	27.5	72.5	-	72.5	100.0	3.8	96.2	0.9	95.3
1950	100.0	1.1	98.9	96.3	2.6	100.0	0.7	99.3	0.1	99.2

Table VIII. ENERGY IMPORTS AND EXPORTS PERCENTAGE DISTRIBUTION, SELECTED YEARS, 1925-1965

(Based on coal equivalents)

Region, country, year	Imports					Exports				
	Total	Solid fuels	Total liquid fuels	Crude oil	Refined petroleum products	Total	Solid fuels	Total liquid fuels	Crude oil	Refined petroleum products
	(1)	(2)	(3)	(4)	(5)	(6)	(7)	(8)	(9)	(10)
INDONESIA (CONTINUED)										
1953	100.0	1.6	98.4	95.5	2.9	100.0	1.0	99.0	23.0	76.0
1955	100.0	0.7	99.3	92.8	6.5	100.0	0.4	99.6	35.0	64.6
1957	100.0	0.7	99.3	88.0	11.3	100.0	0.2	99.8	52.5	47.3
1960	100.0	0.8	99.2	74.7	24.5	100.0	-	100.0	64.4	35.6
1961	100.0	0.7	99.3	75.8	23.4	100.0	-	100.0	69.9	30.1
1962	100.0	0.8	99.2	78.7	20.5	100.0	-	100.0	67.3	32.7
1963	100.0	0.4	99.6	79.9	19.7	100.0	-	100.0	70.9	29.1
1964	100.0	2.7	97.3	-	97.3	100.0	-	100.0	82.6	17.4
1965	100.0	100.0	NA	NA	NA	100.0	-	100.0	80.0	20.0
JAPAN										
1925	100.0	64.5	35.5	23.0	12.5	100.0	99.2	0.8	-	0.8
1929	100.0	53.0	47.0	37.9	9.2	100.0	98.9	1.1	-	1.1
1933	100.0	48.5	51.5	42.5	9.1	100.0	97.1	2.9	-	2.9
1937	100.0	48.4	51.6	39.7	11.9	100.0	92.3	7.7	-	7.7
1938	100.0	49.6	50.4	35.4	15.0	100.0	89.7	10.3	-	10.3
1950	100.0	23.2	76.8	51.5	25.4	100.0	100.0	-	-	-
1953	100.0	28.9	71.1	44.8	26.3	100.0	100.0	-	-	-
1955	100.0	15.2	84.8	57.9	26.9	100.0	98.9	1.1	0.4	0.7
1957	100.0	19.5	80.5	57.4	23.1	100.0	87.0	13.0	-	13.0
1960	100.0	14.6	85.4	71.3	14.1	100.0	4.5	95.5	-	95.5
1961	100.0	15.0	85.0	67.4	17.6	100.0	6.1	93.9	-	93.9
1962	100.0	13.9	86.1	69.4	16.7	100.0	9.1	90.9	-	90.9
1963	100.0	10.6	89.4	73.9	15.5	100.0	8.3	91.7	-	91.7
1964	100.0	10.5	89.5	74.4	15.1	100.0	6.7	93.3	0.3	93.0
1965	100.0	11.9	88.1	72.6	15.5	100.0	6.8	93.2	0.6	92.5
KOREA										
1925	100.0	89.9	10.1	-	10.1	100.0	100.0	-	-	-
1929	100.0	84.7	15.3	-	15.3	100.0	100.0	-	-	-
1933	100.0	85.2	14.8	-	14.8	100.0	100.0	-	-	-
1937	100.0	74.7	25.3	-	25.3	100.0	96.3	3.7	-	3.7
1938	100.0	76.5	23.5	-	23.5	100.0	93.2	6.8	-	6.8
KOREA, REPUBLIC OF										
1950	100.0	59.3	40.7	-	40.7	-	-	-	-	-
1953	100.0	57.8	42.2	-	42.2	100.0	100.0	-	-	-
1955	100.0	66.0	34.0	-	34.0	-	-	-	-	-
1957	100.0	51.0	49.0	-	49.0	-	-	-	-	-
1960	100.0	17.4	82.6	-	82.6	100.0	100.0	-	-	-
1961	100.0	20.3	79.7	-	79.7	100.0	100.0	-	-	-
1962	100.0	10.5	89.5	2.8	86.7	100.0	100.0	-	-	-
1963	100.0	5.9	94.1	3.2	90.9	100.0	100.0	-	-	-
1964	100.0	8.1	91.9	57.2	34.7	100.0	100.0	-	-	-
1965	100.0	4.7	95.3	84.9	10.4	100.0	100.0	-	-	-
MALAYA AND SINGAPORE										
1925	100.0	39.3	60.7	-	60.7	100.0	2.3	97.7	-	97.7
1929	100.0	35.9	64.1	-	64.1	100.0	0.5	99.5	-	99.5

Table VIII. ENERGY IMPORTS AND EXPORTS PERCENTAGE DISTRIBUTION, SELECTED YEARS, 1925-1965

(Based on coal equivalents)

Region, country, year	Imports					Exports				
	Total	Solid fuels	Total liquid fuels	Crude oil	Refined petroleum products	Total	Solid fuels	Total liquid fuels	Crude oil	Refined petroleum products
	(1)	(2)	(3)	(4)	(5)	(6)	(7)	(8)	(9)	(10)
MALAYA AND SINGAPORE (CONTINUED)										
1933	100.0	34.0	66.0	-	66.0	100.0	0.6	99.4	-	99.4
1937	100.0	27.8	72.2	-	72.2	100.0	0.5	99.5	-	99.5
1938	100.0	20.3	79.7	-	79.7	100.0	0.3	99.7	-	99.7
1950	100.0	1.9	98.1	-	98.1	100.0	-	100.0	-	100.0
1953	100.0	1.0	99.0	-	99.0	100.0	-	100.0	-	100.0
1955	100.0	0.7	99.3	-	99.3	100.0	-	100.0	-	100.0
1957	100.0	0.8	99.2	11.0	88.2	100.0	-	100.0	20.6	79.4
1960	100.0	-	100.0	4.3	95.6	100.0	-	100.0	7.7	92.3
1961	100.0	0.5	99.5	15.1	84.4	100.0	-	100.0	19.2	80.8
1962	100.0	0.3	99.7	32.8	66.9	100.0	-	100.0	25.6	74.4
1963	100.0	0.3	99.7	31.1	68.6	100.0	-	100.0	23.6	76.4
1964	100.0	0.2	99.8	41.6	58.1	100.0	-	100.0	5.0	95.0
1965	100.0	0.1	99.9	40.5	59.3	100.0	-	100.0	3.8	96.2
SINGAPORE										
1960	100.0	-	NA	NA	100.0	100.0	-	NA	NA	99.8
1961	100.0	0.1	NA	NA	99.9	100.0	-	NA	NA	99.9
1962	100.0	0.1	NA	NA	99.9	100.0	-	NA	NA	99.9
1963	100.0	0.1	NA	NA	99.9	100.0	-	NA	NA	99.9
1964	100.0	0.1	NA	NA	99.9	100.0	-	NA	NA	100.0
1965	100.0	-	NA	NA	100.0	100.0	-	NA	NA	100.0
PAKISTAN										
1950	100.0	42.6	57.4	-	57.4	-	-	-	-	-
1953	100.0	43.5	56.5	-	56.5	-	-	-	-	-
1955	100.0	35.8	64.2	-	64.2	-	-	-	-	-
1957	100.0	36.9	63.1	-	63.1	100.0	-	100.0	-	100.0
1960	100.0	31.0	69.0	-	69.0	100.0	-	100.0	-	100.0
1961	100.0	24.3	75.7	-	75.7	100.0	-	100.0	-	100.0
1962	100.0	27.3	72.7	9.9	62.8	100.0	-	100.0	-	100.0
1963	100.0	22.1	77.9	44.2	33.7	100.0	-	100.0	-	100.0
1964	100.0	22.0	78.0	52.1	25.9	100.0	-	100.0	-	100.0
1965	100.0	18.9	81.1	63.0	18.1	-	-	-	-	-
PHILIPPINES										
1925	100.0	50.7	49.3	-	49.3	-	-	-	-	-
1929	100.0	52.9	47.1	-	47.1	-	-	-	-	-
1933	100.0	33.1	66.9	-	66.9	-	-	-	-	-
1937	100.0	28.8	71.2	-	71.2	-	-	-	-	-
1938	100.0	27.0	73.0	-	73.0	-	-	-	-	-
1950	100.0	0.4	99.6	-	99.6	-	-	-	-	-
1953	100.0	0.3	99.7	-	99.7	-	-	-	-	-
1955	100.0	0.3	99.7	34.6	65.0	-	-	-	-	-
1957	100.0	0.3	99.7	39.6	60.1	-	-	-	-	-
1960	100.0	0.3	99.7	53.1	46.6	-	-	-	-	-
1961	100.0	0.2	99.8	82.4	17.3	-	-	-	-	-
1962	100.0	0.2	99.8	91.2	8.6	100.0	-	100.0	-	100.0
1963	100.0	0.2	99.8	95.9	3.9	100.0	-	100.0	-	100.0
1964	100.0	0.2	99.8	96.7	3.2	100.0	-	100.0	-	100.0
1965	100.0	0.1	99.9	96.9	3.0	100.0	-	100.0	-	100.0

Table VIII. ENERGY IMPORTS AND EXPORTS PERCENTAGE DISTRIBUTION, SELECTED YEARS, 1925-1965

(Based on coal equivalents)

Region, country, year	Imports					Exports				
	Total	Solid fuels	Total liquid fuels	Crude oil	Refined petroleum products	Total	Solid fuels	Total liquid fuels	Crude oil	Refined petroleum products
	(1)	(2)	(3)	(4)	(5)	(6)	(7)	(8)	(9)	(10)
TAIWAN										
1925	100.0	41.3	58.7	-	58.7	100.0	100.0	-	-	-
1929	100.0	17.1	82.9	40.0	42.9	100.0	98.1	1.9	1.1	0.7
1933	100.0	23.6	76.4	45.6	30.8	100.0	99.1	0.9	-	0.9
1937	100.0	18.3	81.7	21.4	60.3	100.0	99.6	0.4	-	0.4
1938	100.0	18.2	81.8	19.4	62.4	100.0	99.7	0.3	-	0.3
1950	100.0	0.4	99.6	84.6	15.0	100.0	100.0	-	-	-
1953	100.0	-	100.0	-	100.0	100.0	100.0	-	-	-
1955	100.0	-	100.0	89.2	10.8	100.0	52.6	47.4	-	47.4
1957	100.0	-	100.0	86.5	13.5	100.0	66.7	33.3	-	33.3
1960	100.0	-	100.0	96.5	3.5	100.0	90.7	9.3	-	9.3
1961	100.0	-	100.0	96.0	4.0	100.0	75.8	24.2	-	24.2
1962	100.0	-	100.0	95.2	4.8	100.0	59.1	40.9	-	40.9
1963	100.0	-	100.0	96.5	3.5	100.0	56.7	43.3	-	43.3
1964	100.0	-	100.0	95.0	5.0	100.0	47.2	52.8	-	52.8
1965	100.0	0.7	99.3	96.7	2.5	100.0	19.2	80.8	-	80.8
THAILAND										
1925	100.0	37.6	62.4	-	62.4	-	-	-	-	-
1929	100.0	26.5	73.5	-	73.5	-	-	-	-	-
1933	100.0	16.6	83.4	-	83.4	-	-	-	-	-
1937	100.0	22.9	77.1	-	77.1	-	-	-	-	-
1938	100.0	24.2	75.8	-	75.8	-	-	-	-	-
1950	100.0	5.3	94.7	-	94.7	-	-	-	-	-
1953	100.0	6.0	94.0	-	94.0	-	-	-	-	-
1955	100.0	3.6	96.4	-	96.4	100.0	-	100.0	-	100.0
1957	100.0	1.4	98.6	-	98.6	100.0	-	100.0	-	100.0
1960	100.0	0.6	99.4	-	99.4	100.0	-	100.0	-	100.0
1961	100.0	-	100.0	-	100.0	100.0	-	100.0	-	100.0
1962	100.0	-	100.0	-	100.0	100.0	-	100.0	-	100.0
1963	100.0	-	100.0	3.0	97.0	100.0	-	100.0	-	100.0
1964	100.0	-	100.0	27.3	72.7	100.0	-	100.0	-	100.0
1965	100.0	-	100.0	48.5	51.5	100.0	-	100.0	-	100.0
AFRICA										
1925	100.0	74.4	25.6	2.4	23.2	100.0	85.7	14.3	-	14.3
1929	100.0	67.5	32.5	2.0	30.4	100.0	85.6	14.4	-	14.4
1933	100.0	53.7	46.3	1.5	44.8	100.0	92.1	7.9	0.1	7.8
1937	100.0	44.0	56.0	1.4	54.6	100.0	96.4	3.6	0.1	3.5
1938	100.0	45.8	54.2	1.5	52.7	100.0	96.3	3.7	0.3	3.4
1950	100.0	17.1	82.8	-	82.8	100.0	99.9	0.1	-	0.1
1953	100.0	11.2	88.8	0.6	88.2	100.0	93.9	6.0	6.0	0.1
1955	100.0	9.8	90.2	11.2	79.0	100.0	84.2	15.7	3.8	11.9
1957	100.0	9.3	90.7	11.6	79.1	100.0	70.4	26.9	18.2	8.8
1960	100.0	7.9	92.1	17.0	75.1	100.0	13.4	86.1	82.3	3.7
1961	100.0	7.6	91.7	21.8	69.9	100.0	8.0	91.4	88.2	3.1
1962	100.0	6.5	92.8	24.7	68.1	100.0	5.3	94.2	90.2	4.0
1963	100.0	5.6	93.7	31.9	61.8	100.0	3.3	96.4	92.6	3.8
1964	100.0	6.2	93.2	49.3	43.8	100.0	2.5	97.2	91.7	5.5
1965	100.0	6.4	92.9	51.9	41.0	100.0	2.1	97.1	92.1	4.9

Table VIII. ENERGY IMPORTS AND EXPORTS PERCENTAGE DISTRIBUTION, SELECTED YEARS, 1925-1965

(Based on coal equivalents)

Region, country, year	Imports					Exports				
	Total	Solid fuels	Total liquid fuels	Crude oil	Refined petroleum products	Total	Solid fuels	Total liquid fuels	Crude oil	Refined petroleum products
	(1)	(2)	(3)	(4)	(5)	(6)	(7)	(8)	(9)	(10)
NORTH AFRICA										
1925	100.0	78.6	21.4	3.5	17.9	100.0	5.9	94.1	-	94.1
1929	100.0	73.6	26.4	3.2	23.2	100.0	4.8	95.2	-	95.2
1933	100.0	62.6	37.4	2.3	35.1	100.0	23.4	76.6	1.3	75.3
1937	100.0	58.0	42.0	2.7	39.2	100.0	63.6	36.4	1.0	35.4
1938	100.0	56.3	43.7	2.7	41.0	100.0	64.3	35.7	2.6	33.0
1950	100.0	15.1	84.8	-	84.8	100.0	98.5	1.5	-	1.5
1953	100.0	7.7	92.3	1.0	91.3	100.0	62.3	37.6	37.3	0.3
1955	100.0	6.3	93.7	14.9	78.8	100.0	75.0	24.5	21.2	3.3
1957	100.0	9.7	90.3	19.3	71.0	100.0	42.8	57.1	55.5	1.5
1960	100.0	5.9	94.1	28.7	65.4	100.0	1.4	98.6	96.7	1.9
1961	100.0	5.7	94.3	36.2	58.0	100.0	0.7	99.3	97.7	1.5
1962	100.0	3.8	96.2	44.9	51.2	100.0	0.3	99.7	96.3	3.4
1963	100.0	3.3	96.7	53.6	43.2	100.0	0.2	99.8	96.8	2.9
1964	100.0	5.3	94.7	67.0	27.7	100.0	0.1	99.8	96.3	3.5
1965	100.0	4.8	95.2	70.0	25.2	100.0	0.1	99.1	95.5	3.5
ALGERIA										
1925	100.0	93.4	6.6	-	6.6	100.0	100.0	-	-	-
1929	100.0	90.1	9.9	-	9.9	100.0	72.7	27.3	-	27.3
1933	100.0	70.8	29.2	-	29.2	100.0	78.6	21.4	10.7	10.7
1937	100.0	60.0	40.0	-	40.0	100.0	100.0	-	-	-
1938	100.0	56.3	43.7	-	43.7	100.0	40.0	60.0	-	60.0
1950	100.0	23.1	76.6	-	76.6	100.0	100.0	-	-	-
1953	100.0	10.8	89.2	-	89.2	100.0	44.0	55.8	55.8	-
1955	100.0	10.5	89.5	-	89.5	100.0	29.1	69.9	69.9	-
1957	100.0	14.6	85.4	-	85.4	100.0	53.0	43.7	43.7	-
1960	100.0	10.5	89.4	-	89.4	100.0	-	100.0	100.0	-
1961	100.0	6.7	93.2	-	93.2	100.0	-	100.0	98.8	1.2
1962	100.0	3.5	96.5	-	96.5	100.0	-	100.0	97.0	3.0
1963	100.0	1.8	98.2	-	98.2	100.0	-	100.0	98.0	2.0
1964	100.0	5.6	94.4	-	94.4	100.0	-	99.7	96.4	3.3
1965	100.0	3.2	96.8	-	96.8	100.0	-	97.2	93.9	3.3
EGYPT UAR										
1925	100.0	67.5	32.5	7.1	25.4	100.0	1.5	98.5	-	98.5
1929	100.0	58.7	41.3	7.8	33.5	100.0	0.8	99.2	-	99.2
1933	100.0	56.8	43.2	5.5	37.7	100.0	14.5	85.5	-	85.5
1937	100.0	59.0	41.0	6.3	34.7	100.0	6.9	93.1	-	93.1
1938	100.0	60.3	39.7	6.0	33.7	100.0	11.2	88.8	-	88.8
1950	100.0	7.7	92.3	-	92.3	100.0	-	100.0	-	100.0
1953	100.0	3.2	96.8	2.9	93.9	100.0	-	100.0	-	100.0
1955	100.0	2.3	97.7	31.9	65.8	100.0	-	100.0	-	100.0
1957	100.0	5.3	94.7	50.3	44.5	100.0	-	100.0	97.6	2.4
1960	100.0	3.0	97.0	57.6	39.5	100.0	-	100.0	83.3	16.7
1961	100.0	4.8	95.2	66.9	28.3	100.0	-	100.0	95.3	4.7
1962	100.0	3.4	96.6	70.4	26.1	100.0	-	100.0	86.1	13.9
1963	100.0	3.2	96.8	76.0	20.8	100.0	-	100.0	77.5	22.5
1964	100.0	5.5	94.5	77.7	16.8	100.0	-	100.0	64.9	35.1
1965	100.0	5.6	94.4	75.9	18.5	100.0	-	100.0	41.5	58.5

Table VIII. ENERGY IMPORTS AND EXPORTS PERCENTAGE DISTRIBUTION, SELECTED YEARS, 1925-1965

(Based on coal equivalents)

Region, country, year	Imports					Exports				
	Total	Solid fuels	Total liquid fuels	Crude oil	Refined petroleum products	Total	Solid fuels	Total liquid fuels	Crude oil	Refined petroleum products
	(1)	(2)	(3)	(4)	(5)	(6)	(7)	(8)	(9)	(10)
LIBYA										
1925	100.0	53.1	46.9	-	46.9	-	-	-	-	-
1929	100.0	45.2	54.8	-	54.8	-	-	-	-	-
1933	100.0	42.8	57.2	-	57.2	-	-	-	-	-
1937	100.0	37.4	62.6	-	62.6	-	-	-	-	-
1938	100.0	36.4	63.6	-	63.6	-	-	-	-	-
1950	100.0	NA	100.0	-	100.0	-	-	-	-	-
1953	100.0	-	100.0	-	100.0	-	-	-	-	-
1955	100.0	18.6	81.4	-	81.4	-	-	-	-	-
1957	100.0	7.0	93.0	-	93.0	-	-	-	-	-
1960	100.0	5.5	94.5	-	94.5	-	-	-	-	-
1961	100.0	7.6	92.4	-	92.4	100.0	-	100.0	100.0	-
1962	100.0	1.9	98.1	-	98.1	100.0	-	100.0	100.0	-
1963	100.0	1.7	98.3	-	98.3	100.0	-	100.0	100.0	-
1964	100.0	-	100.0	-	100.0	100.0	-	100.0	100.0	-
1965	100.0	1.5	98.5	-	98.5	100.0	-	100.0	100.0	-
MOROCCO										
1925	100.0	69.1	30.9	-	30.9	-	-	-	-	-
1929	100.0	56.2	43.8	-	43.8	-	-	-	-	-
1933	100.0	53.0	47.0	-	47.0	100.0	100.0	-	-	-
1937	100.0	43.8	56.3	-	56.3	100.0	98.0	2.0	2.0	-
1938	100.0	33.4	66.6	-	66.6	100.0	95.8	4.2	4.2	-
1950	100.0	11.2	88.8	-	88.8	100.0	100.0	-	-	-
1953	100.0	8.3	91.7	-	91.7	100.0	79.7	20.3	20.3	-
1955	100.0	7.9	92.1	-	92.1	100.0	99.6	-	-	-
1957	100.0	6.8	93.2	3.4	89.8	100.0	99.4	0.6	-	0.6
1960	100.0	6.8	93.2	10.2	83.1	100.0	97.8	1.5	-	1.5
1961	100.0	6.4	93.5	13.8	79.7	100.0	99.3	0.7	-	0.7
1962	100.0	8.1	91.8	30.5	61.2	100.0	95.5	4.5	-	4.5
1963	100.0	7.1	92.9	75.8	17.1	100.0	98.4	1.6	-	1.6
1964	100.0	7.8	92.2	78.1	14.1	100.0	83.8	16.2	-	16.2
1965	100.0	3.3	96.7	81.9	14.8	100.0	95.9	4.1	-	4.1
TUNISIA										
1925	100.0	82.7	17.3	-	17.3	-	-	-	-	-
1929	100.0	68.2	31.8	-	31.8	-	-	-	-	-
1933	100.0	60.6	39.4	-	39.4	-	-	-	-	-
1937	100.0	58.5	41.5	-	41.5	-	-	-	-	-
1938	100.0	59.9	40.1	-	40.1	-	-	-	-	-
1950	100.0	33.4	66.6	-	66.6	-	-	-	-	-
1953	100.0	14.1	85.9	-	85.9	-	-	-	-	-
1955	100.0	5.7	94.3	-	94.3	-	-	-	-	-
1957	100.0	13.6	86.4	-	86.4	-	-	-	-	-
1960	100.0	5.5	94.5	-	94.5	-	-	-	-	-
1961	100.0	6.4	93.6	-	93.6	-	-	-	-	-
1962	100.0	5.0	95.0	1.1	93.9	-	-	-	-	-
1963	100.0	4.0	96.0	13.0	82.9	-	-	-	-	-
1964	100.0	3.4	96.6	78.3	18.3	100.0	-	100.0	-	100.0
1965	100.0	4.6	95.4	93.0	2.5	-	-	-	-	-

Table VIII. ENERGY IMPORTS AND EXPORTS PERCENTAGE DISTRIBUTION, SELECTED YEARS, 1925-1965

(Based on coal equivalents)

Region, country, year	Imports					Exports				
	Total	Solid fuels	Total liquid fuels	Crude oil	Refined petroleum products	Total	Solid fuels	Total liquid fuels	Crude oil	Refined petroleum products
	(1)	(2)	(3)	(4)	(5)	(6)	(7)	(8)	(9)	(10)
TROPICAL AFRICA										
1925	100.0	72.3	27.7	-	27.7	100.0	100.0	-	-	-
1929	100.0	68.8	31.2	-	31.2	100.0	99.7	0.3	-	0.3
1933	100.0	46.4	53.6	-	53.6	100.0	100.0	-	-	-
1937	100.0	39.6	60.4	-	60.4	100.0	100.0	-	-	-
1938	100.0	49.4	50.6	-	50.6	100.0	100.0	-	-	-
1950	100.0	27.8	72.2	-	72.2	100.0	100.0	-	-	-
1953	100.0	18.2	81.8	-	81.8	100.0	99.8	-	-	-
1955	100.0	16.4	83.5	-	83.5	100.0	89.7	10.3	-	10.3
1957	100.0	13.0	87.0	-	87.0	100.0	75.3	19.9	11.5	8.4
1960	100.0	12.4	87.4	1.2	86.2	100.0	33.2	64.6	57.7	6.9
1961	100.0	11.9	86.7	5.7	81.0	100.0	21.8	75.0	65.7	9.3
1962	100.0	10.8	87.7	3.6	84.1	100.0	15.1	82.1	74.1	8.0
1963	100.0	9.6	88.9	7.6	81.3	100.0	13.7	83.7	73.6	10.1
1964	100.0	9.4	89.2	24.6	64.5	100.0	10.8	87.2	73.1	14.1
1965	100.0	9.6	89.1	33.7	55.4	100.0	7.1	91.8	81.9	9.9
CONGO, DEMOCRATIC REPUBLIC										
1925	100.0	93.3	6.7	-	6.7	-	-	-	-	-
1929	100.0	87.8	12.2	-	12.2	100.0	-	100.0	-	100.0
1933	100.0	63.8	36.2	-	36.2	-	-	-	-	-
1937	100.0	72.4	27.6	-	27.6	-	-	-	-	-
1938	100.0	74.1	25.9	-	25.9	-	-	-	-	-
1950	100.0	46.7	53.3	-	53.3	-	-	-	-	-
1953	100.0	31.9	68.1	-	68.1	-	-	-	-	-
1955	100.0	32.1	67.7	-	67.7	-	-	-	-	-
1957	100.0	25.8	74.2	-	74.2	100.0	-	-	-	-
1960	100.0	26.4	73.6	-	73.6	100.0	-	-	-	-
1961	100.0	32.6	67.4	-	67.4	100.0	-	-	-	-
1962	100.0	25.8	74.2	-	74.2	100.0	-	-	-	-
1963	100.0	22.6	77.4	-	77.4	100.0	-	-	-	-
1964	100.0	31.3	68.7	-	68.7	100.0	-	-	-	-
1965	100.0	32.8	67.2	-	67.2	100.0	-	-	-	-
EAST AFRICA										
1925	100.0	51.9	48.1	-	48.1	-	-	-	-	-
1929	100.0	42.8	57.2	-	57.2	-	-	-	-	-
1933	100.0	46.8	53.2	-	53.2	-	-	-	-	-
1937	100.0	45.0	55.0	-	55.0	-	-	-	-	-
1938	100.0	38.3	61.7	-	61.7	-	-	-	-	-
1950	100.0	4.7	95.3	-	95.3	-	-	-	-	-
1953	100.0	1.1	98.8	-	98.8	100.0	-	-	-	-
1955	100.0	1.6	98.4	-	98.4	-	-	-	-	-
1957	100.0	1.9	98.1	-	98.1	-	-	-	-	-
1960	100.0	1.9	97.0	-	97.0	100.0	-	85.1	-	85.1
1961	100.0	2.0	96.7	-	96.7	100.0	-	82.3	-	82.3
1962	100.0	1.8	97.0	-	97.0	100.0	-	84.6	-	84.6
1963	100.0	1.6	97.3	13.6	83.7	100.0	-	91.0	-	91.0
1964	100.0	0.9	98.4	67.5	30.9	100.0	-	98.0	-	98.0
1965	100.0	1.6	97.8	71.7	26.1	100.0	-	98.4	-	98.4

Table VIII. ENERGY IMPORTS AND EXPORTS PERCENTAGE DISTRIBUTION, SELECTED YEARS, 1925-1965

(Based on coal equivalents)

Region, country, year	Imports					Exports				
	Total	Solid fuels	Total liquid fuels	Crude oil	Refined petroleum products	Total	Solid fuels	Total liquid fuels	Crude oil	Refined petroleum products
	(1)	(2)	(3)	(4)	(5)	(6)	(7)	(8)	(9)	(10)
EQUATORIAL AFRICA										
1925	100.0	40.0	60.0	-	60.0	-	-	-	-	-
1929	100.0	11.8	88.2	-	88.2	-	-	-	-	-
1933	100.0	16.0	84.0	-	84.0	-	-	-	-	-
1937	100.0	53.8	46.2	-	46.2	-	-	-	-	-
1938	100.0	36.1	63.9	-	63.9	-	-	-	-	-
1950	100.0	7.8	92.2	-	92.2	-	-	-	-	-
1953	100.0	3.1	96.9	-	96.9	-	-	-	-	-
1955	100.0	-	100.0	-	100.0	-	-	-	-	-
1957	100.0	-	100.0	-	100.0	100.0	-	100.0	100.0	-
1960	100.0	-	100.0	-	100.0	100.0	-	100.0	100.0	-
1961	100.0	-	100.0	-	100.0	100.0	-	100.0	99.3	0.7
1962	100.0	-	100.0	-	100.0	100.0	-	100.0	99.9	0.1
1963	100.0	-	100.0	-	100.0	100.0	-	100.0	100.0	-
1964	100.0	-	100.0	-	100.0	100.0	-	100.0	100.0	-
1965	100.0	-	100.0	-	100.0	100.0	-	100.0	100.0	-
GHANA										
1925	100.0	65.5	34.5	-	34.5	-	-	-	-	-
1929	100.0	58.2	41.8	-	41.8	-	-	-	-	-
1933	100.0	41.9	58.1	-	58.1	-	-	-	-	-
1937	100.0	37.5	62.5	-	62.5	-	-	-	-	-
1938	100.0	36.6	63.4	-	63.4	-	-	-	-	-
1950	100.0	18.0	82.0	-	82.0	-	-	-	-	-
1953	100.0	22.1	77.9	-	77.9	-	-	-	-	-
1955	100.0	19.7	80.3	-	80.3	-	-	-	-	-
1957	100.0	16.6	83.4	-	83.4	100.0	-	100.0	-	100.0
1960	100.0	5.6	94.4	-	94.4	100.0	-	100.0	-	100.0
1961	100.0	7.4	92.6	-	92.6	-	-	-	-	-
1962	100.0	4.0	96.0	-	96.0	-	-	-	-	-
1963	100.0	4.4	95.6	31.8	63.9	100.0	-	100.0	-	100.0
1964	100.0	2.9	97.1	92.2	4.9	100.0	-	100.0	-	100.0
1965	100.0	2.3	97.7	91.6	6.1	100.0	-	100.0	-	100.0
LIBERIA										
1925	-	-	-	-	-	-	-	-	-	-
1929	-	-	-	-	-	-	-	-	-	-
1933	-	-	-	-	-	-	-	-	-	-
1937	100.0	-	100.0	-	100.0	-	-	-	-	-
1938	100.0	-	100.0	-	100.0	-	-	-	-	-
1950	100.0	-	100.0	-	100.0	-	-	-	-	-
1953	100.0	-	100.0	-	100.0	-	-	-	-	-
1955	100.0	-	100.0	-	100.0	-	-	-	-	-
1957	100.0	-	100.0	-	100.0	-	-	-	-	-
1960	100.0	-	100.0	-	100.0	-	-	-	-	-
1961	100.0	-	100.0	-	100.0	-	-	-	-	-
1962	100.0	-	100.0	-	100.0	-	-	-	-	-
1963	100.0	-	100.0	-	100.0	-	-	-	-	-
1964	100.0	-	100.0	-	100.0	-	-	-	-	-
1965	100.0	-	100.0	-	100.0	-	-	-	-	-

Table VIII. ENERGY IMPORTS AND EXPORTS PERCENTAGE DISTRIBUTION, SELECTED YEARS, 1925–1965

(Based on coal equivalents)

Region, country, year	Imports: Total	Imports: Solid fuels	Imports: Total liquid fuels	Imports: Crude oil	Imports: Refined petroleum products	Exports: Total	Exports: Solid fuels	Exports: Total liquid fuels	Exports: Crude oil	Exports: Refined petroleum products
	(1)	(2)	(3)	(4)	(5)	(6)	(7)	(8)	(9)	(10)
NIGERIA										
1925	100.0	36.7	63.3	-	63.3	100.0	100.0	-	-	-
1929	100.0	29.5	70.5	-	70.5	100.0	100.0	-	-	-
1933	100.0	53.8	46.2	-	46.2	100.0	100.0	-	-	-
1937	100.0	41.2	58.8	-	58.8	100.0	100.0	-	-	-
1938	100.0	39.4	60.6	-	60.6	100.0	100.0	-	-	-
1950	100.0	20.3	79.7	-	79.7	100.0	100.0	-	-	-
1953	100.0	7.3	92.7	-	92.7	100.0	100.0	-	-	-
1955	100.0	-	100.0	-	100.0	100.0	43.7	56.3	-	56.3
1957	100.0	-	100.0	-	100.0	100.0	39.3	60.7	-	60.7
1960	100.0	-	100.0	-	100.0	100.0	2.0	98.0	86.5	11.5
1961	100.0	-	100.0	-	100.0	100.0	1.4	98.6	93.2	5.4
1962	100.0	-	100.0	-	100.0	100.0	0.6	99.4	95.5	3.9
1963	100.0	-	100.0	-	100.0	100.0	0.7	99.3	95.7	3.6
1964	100.0	-	100.0	-	100.0	100.0	0.7	99.3	97.9	1.4
1965	100.0	-	100.0	-	100.0	100.0	0.2	99.8	98.8	1.0
RHODESIAN FEDERATION										
1925	100.0	82.4	17.6	-	17.6	100.0	100.0	-	-	-
1929	100.0	82.9	17.1	-	17.1	100.0	100.0	-	-	-
1933	100.0	83.3	16.7	-	16.7	100.0	100.0	-	-	-
1937	100.0	81.6	18.4	-	18.4	100.0	100.0	-	-	-
1938	100.0	83.2	16.8	-	16.8	100.0	100.0	-	-	-
1950	100.0	72.8	27.2	-	27.2	100.0	100.0	-	-	-
1953	100.0	68.5	31.5	-	31.5	100.0	100.0	-	-	-
1955	100.0	63.2	36.8	-	36.8	100.0	100.0	-	-	-
1957	100.0	58.9	41.1	-	41.1	100.0	100.0	-	-	-
1960	100.0	58.0	42.0	-	42.0	100.0	100.0	-	-	-
1961	100.0	53.3	37.5	-	37.5	100.0	91.2	0.5	-	0.5
1962	100.0	49.4	40.4	-	40.4	100.0	88.0	1.2	-	1.2
1963	100.0	48.0	41.1	-	41.1	100.0	86.3	0.8	-	0.8
1964	100.0	48.8	40.0	-	40.0	100.0	85.8	1.2	-	1.2
1965	100.0	43.6	47.2	25.6	21.7	100.0	81.5	7.8	-	7.8
MALAWI										
1925	100.0	-	100.0	-	100.0	-	-	-	-	-
1929	100.0	66.7	33.3	-	33.3	-	-	-	-	-
1933	100.0	50.0	50.0	-	50.0	-	-	-	-	-
1937	100.0	62.5	37.5	-	37.5	-	-	-	-	-
1938	100.0	47.1	52.9	-	52.9	-	-	-	-	-
1950	100.0	52.6	47.4	-	47.4	-	-	-	-	-
1953	100.0	57.8	42.2	-	42.2	-	-	-	-	-
1955	100.0	48.3	51.7	-	51.7	-	-	-	-	-
1957	100.0	43.9	56.1	-	56.1	-	-	-	-	-
1960	100.0	43.2	56.8	-	56.8	-	-	-	-	-
1961	100.0	48.2	51.8	-	51.8	100.0	-	100.0	-	100.0
1962	100.0	46.0	54.0	-	54.0	100.0	-	100.0	-	100.0
1963	100.0	44.0	56.0	-	56.0	100.0	-	100.0	-	100.0
1964	100.0	41.7	58.3	-	58.3	100.0	-	100.0	-	100.0
1965	100.0	47.5	52.5	-	52.5	100.0	-	100.0	-	100.0

Table VIII. ENERGY IMPORTS AND EXPORTS PERCENTAGE DISTRIBUTION, SELECTED YEARS, 1925-1965

(Based on coal equivalents)

Region, country, year	Imports					Exports				
	Total	Solid fuels	Total liquid fuels	Crude oil	Refined petroleum products	Total	Solid fuels	Total liquid fuels	Crude oil	Refined petroleum products
	(1)	(2)	(3)	(4)	(5)	(6)	(7)	(8)	(9)	(10)
ZAMBIA										
1925	100.0	96.6	3.4	-	3.4	-	-	-	-	-
1929	100.0	95.9	4.1	-	4.1	-	-	-	-	-
1933	100.0	97.5	2.5	-	2.5	-	-	-	-	-
1937	100.0	97.8	2.2	-	2.2	-	-	-	-	-
1938	100.0	97.8	2.2	-	2.2	-	-	-	-	-
1950	100.0	91.6	8.4	-	8.4	-	-	-	-	-
1953	100.0	88.8	11.2	-	11.2	-	-	-	-	-
1955	100.0	86.7	13.3	-	13.3	-	-	-	-	-
1957	100.0	85.1	14.9	-	14.9	-	-	-	-	-
1960	100.0	84.1	15.9	-	15.9	-	-	-	-	-
1961	100.0	73.1	13.5	-	13.5	-	-	-	-	-
1962	100.0	69.9	14.6	-	14.6	-	-	-	-	-
1963	100.0	68.2	15.2	-	15.2	-	-	-	-	-
1964	100.0	68.3	15.1	-	15.1	-	-	-	-	-
1965	100.0	67.8	16.9	-	16.9	-	-	-	-	-
RHODESIA										
1925	100.0	-	100.0	-	100.0	100.0	100.0	-	-	-
1929	100.0	-	100.0	-	100.0	100.0	100.0	-	-	-
1933	100.0	-	100.0	-	100.0	100.0	100.0	-	-	-
1937	100.0	-	100.0	-	100.0	100.0	100.0	-	-	-
1938	100.0	-	100.0	-	100.0	100.0	100.0	-	-	-
1950	100.0	2.3	97.7	-	97.7	100.0	100.0	-	-	-
1953	100.0	3.2	96.8	-	96.8	100.0	100.0	-	-	-
1955	100.0	2.4	97.6	-	97.6	100.0	100.0	-	-	-
1957	100.0	2.1	97.9	-	97.9	100.0	100.0	-	-	-
1960	100.0	1.9	98.1	-	98.1	100.0	100.0	-	-	-
1961	100.0	1.8	98.2	-	98.2	100.0	91.4	0.3	-	0.3
1962	100.0	1.7	98.3	-	98.3	100.0	88.3	0.9	-	0.9
1963	100.0	1.7	98.3	-	98.3	100.0	86.7	0.4	-	0.4
1964	100.0	1.7	98.3	-	98.3	100.0	86.3	0.5	-	0.5
1965	100.0	1.0	99.0	74.2	24.9	100.0	81.8	7.4	-	7.4
WEST AFRICA										
1925	100.0	80.1	19.9	-	19.9	-	-	-	-	-
1929	100.0	62.4	37.6	-	37.6	-	-	-	-	-
1933	100.0	22.1	77.9	-	77.9	-	-	-	-	-
1937	100.0	27.0	73.0	-	73.0	-	-	-	-	-
1938	100.0	54.3	45.7	-	45.7	-	-	-	-	-
1950	100.0	11.9	88.1	-	88.1	-	-	-	-	-
1953	100.0	2.6	97.4	-	97.4	-	-	-	-	-
1955	100.0	1.3	98.7	-	98.7	-	-	-	-	-
1957	100.0	-	100.0	-	100.0	-	-	-	-	-
1960	100.0	-	100.0	-	100.0	-	-	-	-	-
1961	100.0	-	100.0	-	100.0	-	-	-	-	-
1962	100.0	-	100.0	-	100.0	-	-	-	-	-
1963	100.0	-	100.0	1.0	99.0	-	-	-	-	-
1964	100.0	-	100.0	14.5	85.5	-	-	-	-	-
1965	100.0	-	100.0	29.9	70.1	-	-	-	-	-

Table VIII. ENERGY IMPORTS AND EXPORTS PERCENTAGE DISTRIBUTION, SELECTED YEARS, 1925-1965

(Based on coal equivalents)

Region, country, year	Imports					Exports				
	Total	Solid fuels	Total liquid fuels	Crude oil	Refined petroleum products	Total	Solid fuels	Total liquid fuels	Crude oil	Refined petroleum products
	(1)	(2)	(3)	(4)	(5)	(6)	(7)	(8)	(9)	(10)
SOUTH AFRICA										
1925	100.0	3.5	96.5	-	96.5	100.0	100.0	-	-	-
1929	100.0	0.7	99.3	-	99.3	100.0	100.0	-	-	-
1933	100.0	-	100.0	-	100.0	100.0	100.0	-	-	-
1937	100.0	1.7	98.3	-	98.3	100.0	100.0	-	-	-
1938	100.0	1.5	98.5	-	98.5	100.0	100.0	-	-	-
1950	100.0	1.8	98.2	-	98.2	100.0	100.0	-	-	-
1953	100.0	0.7	99.3	1.1	98.1	100.0	100.0	-	-	-
1955	100.0	2.0	98.0	28.5	69.5	100.0	80.9	19.1	-	19.1
1957	100.0	0.8	99.2	25.7	73.5	100.0	83.5	16.5	-	16.5
1960	100.0	-	100.0	34.2	65.8	100.0	86.5	13.5	-	13.5
1961	100.0	-	100.0	36.2	63.8	100.0	97.7	2.3	-	2.3
1962	100.0	0.9	99.1	37.1	62.0	100.0	99.5	0.5	-	0.5
1963	100.0	0.7	99.3	47.4	51.9	100.0	92.7	7.3	-	7.3
1964	100.0	1.0	99.0	73.9	25.1	100.0	56.8	43.2	-	43.2
1965	100.0	1.5	98.5	70.4	28.1	100.0	70.0	30.0	-	30.0
DEVELOPED COUNTRIES										
1925	100.0	72.2	27.7	14.3	13.4	100.0	84.2	15.6	1.9	13.7
1929	100.0	67.5	32.3	15.3	17.1	100.0	82.1	17.7	3.2	14.5
1933	100.0	60.9	38.9	16.1	22.8	100.0	81.4	18.3	6.6	11.8
1937	100.0	59.0	40.8	18.5	22.3	100.0	76.6	23.0	8.9	14.2
1938	100.0	54.8	45.0	20.1	24.8	100.0	71.6	28.1	11.2	16.9
1950	100.0	30.1	69.6	40.5	29.1	100.0	70.7	28.0	7.6	20.4
1953	100.0	24.6	75.3	50.8	24.5	100.0	57.1	41.9	5.0	36.9
1955	100.0	24.4	75.4	51.2	24.2	100.0	61.5	37.5	4.2	33.3
1957	100.0	22.3	77.4	52.2	25.2	100.0	57.7	41.6	10.7	30.9
1960	100.0	13.9	85.1	59.6	25.5	100.0	47.4	49.6	6.6	43.0
1961	100.0	12.8	86.0	61.7	24.3	100.0	45.4	50.6	8.7	41.9
1962	100.0	12.2	86.0	60.9	25.1	100.0	42.3	51.1	10.7	40.3
1963	100.0	12.3	86.1	61.8	24.4	100.0	44.5	49.4	10.0	39.4
1964	100.0	11.0	87.4	64.0	23.5	100.0	42.4	50.7	9.7	41.0
1965	100.0	9.7	88.7	65.0	23.7	100.0	39.5	53.8	9.5	44.2
UNDERDEVELOPED COUNTRIES										
1925	100.0	48.7	51.3	16.8	34.5	100.0	7.1	92.9	47.8	45.2
1929	100.0	32.4	67.6	37.9	29.7	100.0	5.7	94.3	52.8	41.5
1933	100.0	24.8	75.1	44.0	31.1	100.0	4.9	95.1	47.3	47.9
1937	100.0	21.1	78.6	46.7	31.9	100.0	3.9	96.1	45.7	50.3
1938	100.0	18.8	81.1	48.6	32.5	100.0	4.7	95.3	45.4	49.9
1950	100.0	5.1	94.3	61.2	33.1	100.0	0.7	99.3	58.8	40.4
1953	100.0	4.3	95.3	57.9	37.4	100.0	0.9	99.0	68.3	30.7
1955	100.0	3.8	95.8	59.2	36.6	100.0	0.6	99.4	71.0	28.4
1957	100.0	3.8	96.2	59.5	36.6	100.0	0.6	99.3	71.7	27.6
1960	100.0	3.5	96.4	61.8	34.6	100.0	0.5	99.3	73.5	25.8
1961	100.0	3.0	96.9	63.9	33.0	100.0	0.4	99.3	74.5	24.8
1962	100.0	2.5	97.3	67.5	29.8	100.0	0.3	99.4	74.3	25.1
1963	100.0	2.4	97.5	68.8	28.6	100.0	0.3	99.5	75.5	24.1
1964	100.0	2.5	97.3	71.7	25.6	100.0	0.3	99.5	77.1	22.4
1965	100.0	2.4	97.5	74.5	22.9	100.0	0.3	99.5	77.9	21.5

Table VIII. ENERGY IMPORTS AND EXPORTS PERCENTAGE DISTRIBUTION, SELECTED YEARS, 1925-1965

(Based on coal equivalents)

Region, country, year	Imports: Total	Imports: Solid fuels	Imports: Total liquid fuels	Imports: Crude oil	Imports: Refined petroleum products	Exports: Total	Exports: Solid fuels	Exports: Total liquid fuels	Exports: Crude oil	Exports: Refined petroleum products
	(1)	(2)	(3)	(4)	(5)	(6)	(7)	(8)	(9)	(10)
COMMUNIST COUNTRIES										
1925	100.0	77.7	22.2	1.5	20.7	100.0	80.3	19.7	0.5	19.1
1929	100.0	75.6	24.3	4.1	20.2	100.0	70.1	29.9	1.4	28.4
1933	100.0	60.5	39.5	5.9	33.6	100.0	53.4	46.6	3.7	42.9
1937	100.0	52.3	47.7	14.7	33.0	100.0	65.5	34.5	3.4	31.1
1938	100.0	59.6	40.4	13.2	27.2	100.0	67.5	32.5	4.3	28.2
1950	100.0	75.0	24.7	10.9	13.8	100.0	84.9	14.9	1.6	13.3
1953	100.0	67.7	31.8	13.1	18.7	100.0	68.1	31.6	6.4	25.2
1955	100.0	62.2	37.2	13.7	23.5	100.0	64.0	35.7	7.9	27.9
1957	100.0	51.6	47.5	21.5	26.0	100.0	53.2	46.3	14.5	31.8
1960	100.0	48.4	50.3	23.1	27.1	100.0	42.1	57.3	25.4	31.9
1961	100.0	49.1	49.6	21.8	27.8	100.0	39.4	60.0	28.9	31.1
1962	100.0	50.5	48.3	23.6	24.7	100.0	39.8	59.6	29.4	30.2
1963	100.0	49.5	49.2	26.2	23.0	100.0	38.5	61.0	31.0	29.9
1964	100.0	50.0	48.7	30.8	17.9	100.0	38.1	61.3	34.5	26.8
1965	100.0	47.5	51.1	37.0	14.2	100.0	35.3	64.1	37.9	26.2
USSR										
1925	100.0	87.7	12.3	1.7	10.6	100.0	15.1	84.9	3.9	81.0
1929	100.0	87.8	12.2	2.0	10.2	100.0	18.8	81.2	6.6	74.7
1933	100.0	84.6	15.4	0.5	14.9	100.0	19.8	80.2	8.7	71.5
1937	100.0	71.1	28.9	1.3	27.6	100.0	30.7	69.3	4.3	65.0
1938	100.0	70.4	29.6	1.5	28.1	100.0	13.1	86.9	13.8	73.1
1950	100.0	73.8	26.2	14.6	11.7	100.0	60.7	38.5	10.5	28.0
1953	100.0	57.9	42.1	15.8	26.3	100.0	34.4	64.6	23.5	41.1
1955	100.0	53.4	46.6	13.9	32.7	100.0	32.2	66.7	24.4	42.3
1957	100.0	38.0	62.0	20.2	41.8	100.0	34.2	65.1	28.3	36.8
1960	100.0	46.3	53.7	15.1	38.7	100.0	22.7	76.8	41.3	35.4
1961	100.0	51.0	49.0	12.8	36.2	100.0	22.4	77.2	44.0	33.2
1962	100.0	57.4	42.6	7.8	34.8	100.0	24.6	74.9	43.5	31.4
1963	100.0	58.2	41.8	8.3	33.4	100.0	24.2	75.3	44.4	30.9
1964	100.0	65.8	34.2	-	34.2	100.0	24.2	75.3	48.9	26.4
1965	100.0	73.1	26.9	-	26.9	100.0	21.0	78.4	53.0	25.5
COMMUNIST EASTERN EUROPE										
1925	100.0	87.8	12.0	3.1	8.9	100.0	88.1	11.9	-	11.8
1929	100.0	83.7	16.2	7.1	9.1	100.0	81.5	18.5	-	18.4
1933	100.0	68.1	31.8	14.6	17.2	100.0	59.3	40.7	1.8	38.9
1937	100.0	63.8	36.1	22.7	13.4	100.0	65.0	35.0	3.5	31.5
1938	100.0	63.1	36.9	22.2	14.7	100.0	67.9	32.1	3.4	28.7
1950	100.0	76.5	22.7	6.2	16.5	100.0	87.9	12.0	0.5	11.5
1953	100.0	76.2	22.9	10.8	12.1	100.0	79.5	20.5	0.7	19.8
1955	100.0	74.2	24.7	12.3	12.4	100.0	75.9	24.1	1.3	22.7
1957	100.0	63.5	35.1	22.5	12.6	100.0	68.9	30.9	2.1	28.8
1960	100.0	56.1	41.8	26.7	15.1	100.0	70.4	28.7	1.6	27.2
1961	100.0	54.6	43.6	26.5	17.0	100.0	69.5	29.6	1.5	28.1
1962	100.0	52.8	45.5	28.3	17.2	100.0	69.4	29.9	1.3	28.6
1963	100.0	51.0	47.4	30.7	16.7	100.0	69.4	30.0	1.3	28.7
1964	100.0	49.3	49.2	35.8	13.4	100.0	69.4	29.8	1.1	28.7
1965	100.0	44.6	53.8	43.1	10.7	100.0	69.1	30.2	1.2	29.0

Table VIII. ENERGY IMPORTS AND EXPORTS PERCENTAGE DISTRIBUTION, SELECTED YEARS, 1925-1965

(Based on coal equivalents)

Region, country, year	Imports: Total	Imports: Solid fuels	Imports: Total liquid fuels	Imports: Crude oil	Imports: Refined petroleum products	Exports: Total	Exports: Solid fuels	Exports: Total liquid fuels	Exports: Crude oil	Exports: Refined petroleum products
	(1)	(2)	(3)	(4)	(5)	(6)	(7)	(8)	(9)	(10)
COMMUNIST ASIA										
1925	100.0	66.5	33.5	-	33.5	100.0	100.0	-	-	-
1929	100.0	59.1	40.9	-	40.9	100.0	100.0	-	-	-
1933	100.0	46.9	53.1	-	53.1	100.0	98.1	1.9	1.8	0.1
1937	100.0	20.4	79.6	11.1	68.6	100.0	98.1	1.9	1.9	-
1938	100.0	48.6	51.4	10.2	41.1	100.0	97.0	3.0	3.0	-
1950	NA	NA	NA	NA	NA	NA	NA	NA	NA	NA
1953	NA	NA	NA	NA	NA	NA	NA	NA	NA	NA
1955	100.0	3.7	96.3	28.0	68.3	100.0	100.0	-	-	-
1957	100.0	2.8	97.2	18.0	79.2	100.0	99.7	0.3	-	0.3
1960	100.0	2.0	98.0	16.7	81.2	100.0	100.0	-	-	-
1961	100.0	1.6	98.4	2.3	96.1	100.0	100.0	-	-	-
1962	100.0	5.3	94.7	5.3	89.4	100.0	100.0	-	-	-
1963	100.0	1.2	98.8	6.6	92.3	100.0	100.0	-	-	-
1964	100.0	11.4	88.6	12.2	76.4	100.0	100.0	-	-	-
1965	100.0	8.3	91.7	18.7	73.0	100.0	100.0	-	-	-
ORGANISATION FOR ECONOMIC CO-OPERATION AND DEVELOPMENT (OECD)										
1925	100.0	72.6	27.2	14.4	12.8	100.0	84.0	15.8	1.9	13.9
1929	100.0	68.3	31.6	15.3	16.3	100.0	82.0	17.8	3.2	14.6
1933	100.0	61.8	38.0	16.3	21.7	100.0	81.3	18.4	6.6	11.8
1937	100.0	60.1	39.7	19.0	20.7	100.0	76.4	23.2	8.9	14.3
1938	100.0	56.0	43.8	20.8	23.0	100.0	71.4	28.3	11.3	17.0
1950	100.0	30.8	68.9	42.3	26.6	100.0	70.0	28.6	7.8	20.9
1953	100.0	24.9	74.9	52.6	22.3	100.0	56.6	42.4	5.1	37.3
1955	100.0	24.9	74.9	52.0	23.0	100.0	61.5	37.5	4.3	33.2
1957	100.0	22.7	77.0	52.4	24.7	100.0	57.8	41.5	10.9	30.6
1960	100.0	13.9	85.1	59.7	25.4	100.0	47.3	49.6	6.8	42.8
1961	100.0	12.8	86.0	61.9	24.1	100.0	44.9	50.9	9.0	41.9
1962	100.0	12.2	85.9	61.2	24.7	100.0	41.7	51.3	10.8	40.5
1963	100.0	12.4	86.0	61.9	24.1	100.0	44.0	49.6	10.0	39.6
1964	100.0	10.9	87.4	64.0	23.4	100.0	41.3	51.5	9.9	41.6
1965	100.0	9.6	88.7	64.9	23.8	100.0	37.6	55.4	9.9	45.5
COMMUNIST COUNTRIES										
1925	100.0	77.7	22.2	1.5	20.7	100.0	80.3	19.7	0.5	19.1
1929	100.0	75.6	24.3	4.1	20.2	100.0	70.1	29.9	1.4	28.4
1933	100.0	60.5	39.5	5.9	33.6	100.0	53.4	46.6	3.7	42.9
1937	100.0	52.3	47.7	14.7	33.0	100.0	65.5	34.5	3.4	31.1
1938	100.0	59.6	40.4	13.2	27.2	100.0	67.5	32.5	4.3	28.2
1950	100.0	75.0	24.7	10.9	13.8	100.0	84.9	14.9	1.6	13.3
1953	100.0	67.7	31.8	13.1	18.7	100.0	68.1	31.6	6.4	25.2
1955	100.0	62.2	37.2	13.7	23.5	100.0	64.0	35.7	7.9	27.9
1957	100.0	51.6	47.5	21.5	26.0	100.0	53.2	46.3	14.5	31.8
1960	100.0	48.4	50.3	23.1	27.1	100.0	42.1	57.3	25.4	31.9
1961	100.0	49.1	49.6	21.8	27.8	100.0	39.4	60.0	28.9	31.1
1962	100.0	50.5	48.3	23.6	24.7	100.0	39.8	59.6	29.4	30.2
1963	100.0	49.5	49.2	26.2	23.0	100.0	38.5	61.0	31.0	29.9
1964	100.0	50.0	48.7	30.8	17.9	100.0	38.1	61.3	34.5	26.8
1965	100.0	47.5	51.1	37.0	14.2	100.0	35.3	64.1	37.9	26.2

Table VIII. ENERGY IMPORTS AND EXPORTS PERCENTAGE DISTRIBUTION, SELECTED YEARS, 1925-1965

(Based on coal equivalents)

Region, country, year	Imports					Exports				
	Total	Solid fuels	Total liquid fuels	Crude oil	Refined petroleum products	Total	Solid fuels	Total liquid fuels	Crude oil	Refined petroleum products
	(1)	(2)	(3)	(4)	(5)	(6)	(7)	(8)	(9)	(10)
WORLD EXCLUDING OECD AND COMMUNIST COUNTRIES										
1925	100.0	49.3	50.7	16.0	34.7	100.0	12.1	87.9	45.2	42.7
1929	100.0	33.6	66.4	35.4	31.0	100.0	7.6	92.4	51.7	40.7
1933	100.0	25.5	74.3	41.0	33.4	100.0	5.5	94.5	46.9	47.5
1937	100.0	22.6	77.2	42.7	34.6	100.0	4.7	95.3	45.4	49.9
1938	100.0	19.9	80.0	44.4	35.5	100.0	5.5	94.5	45.0	49.5
1950	100.0	6.5	92.9	56.2	36.7	100.0	1.5	98.5	58.3	40.1
1953	100.0	5.4	94.2	53.8	40.4	100.0	1.3	98.6	68.0	30.6
1955	100.0	5.2	94.5	56.8	37.7	100.0	0.8	99.2	70.8	28.4
1957	100.0	5.3	94.6	58.2	36.4	100.0	0.9	99.0	71.3	27.8
1960	100.0	5.0	94.9	61.3	33.7	100.0	0.8	98.9	72.9	26.0
1961	100.0	4.3	95.5	63.2	32.3	100.0	0.9	98.8	73.8	25.0
1962	100.0	3.8	96.1	65.8	30.3	100.0	0.9	98.9	73.7	25.2
1963	100.0	3.5	96.4	67.4	29.0	100.0	0.8	99.0	74.9	24.1
1964	100.0	3.9	95.9	70.3	25.6	100.0	0.9	98.9	76.4	22.5
1965	100.0	3.8	96.1	73.2	22.9	100.0	1.0	98.7	77.2	21.5

DERIVATION OF TABLE IX

Column	*Derivation*
(1)	Sum of cols. (2) and (3)
(2)	Sources
(3)	Col. (4) multiplied by 1.5*
(4)	Sources

Table IX. BUNKERS, SELECTED YEARS, 1925-1965

(Thousand metric tons)

Region, country, year	Coal equivalents			Liquid fuels in original units
	Total bunkers	Solid fuels	Liquid fuels	
	(1)	(2)	(3)	(4)
WORLD				
1925	67790	41622	26168	17444
1929	73892	41023	32869	21910
1933	56397	27756	28641	19092
1937	66135	30729	35406	23601
1938	60077	27965	32112	21406
1950	84970	12158	72812	48541
1953	97937	8020	89917	59945
1955	107790	7233	100557	67038
1957	121236	4461	116775	77850
1960	123955	2194	121761	81174
1961	132596	1501	131095	87397
1962	136681	1219	135462	90308
1963	140323	1124	139199	92799
1964	153500	1154	152346	101564
1965	157543	1195	156348	104232
NORTH AMERICA				
1925	25445	6257	19188	12792
1929	28997	5628	23369	15579
1933	18180	2410	15770	10513

Table IX. BUNKERS, SELECTED YEARS, 1925-1965

(Thousand metric tons)

Region, country, year	Coal equivalents			Liquid fuels in original units
	Total bunkers	Solid fuels	Liquid fuels	
	(1)	(2)	(3)	(4)
NORTH AMERICA (CONTINUED)				
1937	22417	3445	18972	12648
1938	19087	2477	16610	11073
1950	27677	2205	25472	16981
1953	33384	2058	31326	20884
1955	33310	1792	31518	21012
1957	36422	1661	34761	23174
1960	29153	1137	28016	18677
1961	26803	940	25863	17242
1962	26510	863	25647	17098
1963	24573	862	23711	15807
1964	26573	885	25688	17125
1965	24287	869	23418	15612
CANADA				
1925	660	450	210	140
1929	626	420	206	137
1933	489	318	171	114
1937	473	318	155	103
1938	563	365	198	132
1950	2303	353	1950	1300
1953	2570	390	2180	1453
1955	2667	432	2235	1490
1957	3229	424	2805	1870
1960	3325	280	3045	2030
1961	3481	241	3240	2160
1962	3675	240	3435	2290
1963	3674	254	3420	2280
1964	3990	240	3750	2500
1965	3968	275	3693	2462
UNITED STATES				
1925	24779	5804	18975	12650
1929	28365	5205	23160	15440
1933	17682	2085	15597	10398
1937	21930	3114	18816	12544
1938	18506	2096	16410	10940
1950	25374	1852	23522	15681
1953	30815	1668	29147	19431
1955	30643	1360	29283	19522
1957	33193	1237	31956	21304
1960	25813	857	24956	16637
1961	23292	699	22593	15062
1962	22820	623	22197	14798
1963	20884	608	20276	13517
1964	22562	645	21917	14611
1965	20303	594	19709	13139
WESTERN EUROPE				
1925	25492	23368	2124	1416
1929	25765	23011	2754	1836
1933	21128	17593	3535	2356
1937	22523	17167	5356	3570
1938	21028	15813	5215	3476

Table IX. BUNKERS, SELECTED YEARS, 1925-1965

(Thousand metric tons)

Region, country, year	Coal equivalents			Liquid fuels in original units
	Total bunkers	Solid fuels	Liquid fuels	
	(1)	(2)	(3)	(4)
WESTERN EUROPE (CONTINUED)				
1950	19355	6527	12828	8551
1953	24932	4475	20457	13637
1955	30405	3736	26669	17779
1957	31051	2440	28611	19074
1960	36247	904	35343	23562
1961	39748	412	39336	26224
1962	41569	257	41312	27541
1963	43246	184	43062	28707
1964	48079	145	47934	31955
1965	51770	100	51670	34446
EUROPEAN ECONOMIC COMMUNITY (EEC)				
1925	5944	5707	237	158
1929	6226	5398	828	552
1933	4824	3495	1329	886
1937	7466	4745	2721	1814
1938	7481	4736	2745	1830
1950	5810	1803	4007	2671
1953	9993	1378	8615	5743
1955	13483	1288	12195	8130
1957	13352	992	12360	8240
1960	18086	446	17640	11760
1961	21406	256	21150	14100
1962	23288	158	23130	15420
1963	24381	118	24263	16175
1964	29017	98	28919	19279
1965	31959	67	31892	21261
BELGIUM-LUXEMBOURG				
1925	272	270	2	1
1929	431	431	-	-
1933	339	337	2	1
1937	306	214	92	61
1938	392	308	84	56
1950	429	69	360	240
1953	776	66	710	473
1955	976	91	885	590
1957	902	62	840	560
1960	981	36	945	630
1961	1241	26	1215	810
1962	1663	28	1635	1090
1963	2026	16	2010	1340
1964	2744	12	2732	1821
1965	3089	5	3084	2056
FRANCE				
1925	2956	2791	165	110
1929	2253	1596	657	438
1933	2354	1274	1080	720
1937	2981	980	2001	1334
1938	2951	1014	1937	1291
1950	1695	328	1367	911
1953	3112	157	2955	1970

Table IX. BUNKERS, SELECTED YEARS, 1925-1965

(Thousand metric tons)

Region, country, year	Coal equivalents			Liquid fuels in original units
	Total bunkers	Solid fuels	Liquid fuels	
	(1)	(2)	(3)	(4)
FRANCE (CONTINUED)				
1955	3565	70	3495	2330
1957	3472	52	3420	2280
1960	2885	20	2865	1910
1961	3305	20	3285	2190
1962	3580	10	3570	2380
1963	3445	10	3435	2290
1964	3625	10	3615	2410
1965	3491	-	3491	2327
GERMANY				
1925	123	123	-	-
1929	299	299	-	-
1933	179	131	48	32
1937	415	389	26	17
1938	364	344	20	13
GERMANY, FEDERAL REPUBLIC				
1950	1040	909	131	87
1953	2211	894	1317	878
1955	3325	835	2490	1660
1957	3410	680	2730	1820
1960	4090	340	3750	2500
1961	4275	180	4095	2730
1962	4675	100	4575	3050
1963	4555	85	4470	2980
1964	5436	75	5361	3574
1965	5918	57	5861	3907
ITALY				
1925	10	10	-	-
1929	13	7	6	4
1933	21	21	-	-
1937	4	4	-	-
1938	10	7	3	2
1950	1004	104	900	600
1953	1703	63	1640	1093
1955	2060	50	2010	1340
1957	1910	35	1875	1250
1960	5630	20	5610	3740
1961	6445	10	6435	4290
1962	6955	10	6945	4630
1963	7870	2	7868	5245
1964	9565	1	9564	6376
1965	10536	-	10536	7024
NETHERLANDS				
1925	2584	2513	71	47
1929	3230	3065	165	110
1933	1932	1732	200	133
1937	3761	3158	603	402
1938	3765	3063	702	468

Table IX. BUNKERS, SELECTED YEARS, 1925-1965

(Thousand metric tons)

Region, country, year	Coal equivalents: Total bunkers	Coal equivalents: Solid fuels	Coal equivalents: Liquid fuels	Liquid fuels in original units
	(1)	(2)	(3)	(4)
NETHERLANDS (CONTINUED)				
1950	1643	393	1250	833
1953	2192	198	1994	1329
1955	3557	242	3315	2210
1957	3658	163	3495	2330
1960	4500	30	4470	2980
1961	6140	20	6120	4080
1962	6415	10	6405	4270
1963	6485	5	6480	4320
1964	7647	-	7647	5098
1965	8926	5	8921	5947
EUROPEAN FREE TRADE ASSOCIATION (EFTA)				
1925	18607	17005	1602	1068
1929	18451	16897	1554	1036
1933	15362	13836	1526	1017
1937	14221	12092	2129	1419
1938	12724	10775	1949	1299
1950	9681	4301	5380	3586
1953	10602	2987	7615	5076
1955	10962	2232	8730	5820
1957	9176	1256	7920	5280
1960	11536	343	11193	7462
1961	11218	142	11076	7384
1962	10979	87	10892	7261
1963	11077	54	11023	7348
1964	11446	39	11407	7604
1965	11905	29	11876	7917
AUSTRIA				
1950	-	-	-	-
1953	2	-	2	1
1955	15	-	15	10
1957	15	-	15	10
1960	15	-	15	10
1961	15	-	15	10
1962	20	-	20	13
1963	20	-	20	13
1964	17	-	17	11
1965	17	-	17	11
DENMARK				
1950	183	-	183	122
1953	329	-	329	219
1955	450	30	420	280
1957	435	15	420	280
1960	443	23	420	280
1961	407	32	375	250
1962	532	37	495	330
1963	579	24	555	370
1964	627	18	609	406
1965	660	15	645	430

Table IX. BUNKERS, SELECTED YEARS, 1925-1965

(Thousand metric tons)

Region, country, year	Coal equivalents			Liquid fuels in original units
	Total bunkers	Solid fuels	Liquid fuels	
	(1)	(2)	(3)	(4)
NORWAY				
1950	248	-	248	165
1953	335	-	335	223
1955	510	-	510	340
1957	525	-	525	350
1960	510	-	510	340
1961	570	-	570	380
1962	600	-	600	400
1963	645	-	645	430
1964	701	-	701	467
1965	630	-	630	420
PORTUGAL				
1925	305	305	-	-
1929	242	242	-	-
1933	163	161	2	1
1937	201	201	-	-
1938	118	118	-	-
1950	478	104	374	249
1953	516	106	410	273
1955	565	40	525	350
1957	530	20	510	340
1960	675	-	675	450
1961	705	-	705	470
1962	720	-	720	480
1963	710	-	710	473
1964	860	-	860	573
1965	860	-	860	573
SWEDEN				
1950	147	-	147	98
1953	257	-	257	171
1955	330	-	330	220
1957	435	-	435	290
1960	795	-	795	530
1961	885	-	885	590
1962	1080	-	1080	720
1963	1185	-	1185	790
1964	1256	-	1256	837
1965	1313	-	1313	875
SWITZERLAND				
1950	39	-	39	26
1953	39	-	39	26
1955	90	-	90	60
1957	45	-	45	30
1960	75	-	75	50
1961	75	-	75	50
1962	30	-	30	20
1963	30	-	30	20
1964	29	-	29	19
1965	29	-	29	19

Table IX. BUNKERS, SELECTED YEARS, 1925-1965

(Thousand metric tons)

Region, country, year	Coal equivalents: Total bunkers	Coal equivalents: Solid fuels	Coal equivalents: Liquid fuels	Liquid fuels in original units
	(1)	(2)	(3)	(4)
UNITED KINGDOM				
1925	18302	16700	1602	1068
1929	18209	16655	1554	1036
1933	15199	13675	1524	1016
1937	14020	11891	2129	1419
1938	12606	10657	1949	1299
1950	8586	4197	4389	2926
1953	9126	2881	6245	4163
1955	9002	2162	6840	4560
1957	7191	1221	5970	3980
1960	9023	320	8703	5802
1961	8561	110	8451	5634
1962	7997	50	7947	5298
1963	7908	30	7878	5252
1964	7958	21	7937	5291
1965	8398	14	8384	5589
WESTERN EUROPE - OTHER				
1925	NA	NA	NA	NA
1929	NA	NA	NA	NA
1933	NA	NA	NA	NA
1937	NA	NA	NA	NA
1938	NA	NA	NA	NA
1950	3864	423	3441	2294
1953	4337	110	4227	2818
1955	5960	216	5744	3829
1957	8523	192	8331	5554
1960	6625	115	6510	4340
1961	7124	14	7110	4740
1962	7302	12	7290	4860
1963	7788	12	7776	5184
1964	7616	8	7608	5072
1965	7906	4	7902	5268
FINLAND				
1950	8	-	8	5
1953	8	-	8	5
1955	15	-	15	10
1957	15	-	15	10
1960	15	-	15	10
1961	15	-	15	10
1962	15	-	15	10
1963	30	-	30	20
1964	32	-	32	21
1965	39	-	39	26
GREECE				
1950	240	-	240	160
1953	207	-	207	138
1955	270	-	270	180
1957	315	-	315	210
1960	810	-	810	540
1961	1020	-	1020	680
1962	1395	-	1395	930

Table IX. BUNKERS, SELECTED YEARS, 1925-1965

(Thousand metric tons)

Region, country, year	Coal equivalents			Liquid fuels in original units
	Total bunkers	Solid fuels	Liquid fuels	
	(1)	(2)	(3)	(4)
GREECE (CONTINUED)				
1963	1590	-	1590	1060
1964	1326	-	1326	884
1965	1455	-	1455	970
ICELAND				
1950	102	-	102	68
1953	185	-	185	123
1955	150	-	150	100
1957	165	-	165	110
1960	150	-	150	100
1961	135	-	135	90
1962	135	-	135	90
1963	36	-	36	24
1964	23	-	23	15
1965	23	-	23	15
IRELAND				
1950	76	1	75	50
1953	131	-	131	87
1955	201	1	200	133
1957	181	1	180	120
1960	330	-	330	220
1961	360	-	360	240
1962	315	-	315	210
1963	315	-	315	210
1964	353	-	353	235
1965	375	-	375	250
SPAIN				
1925	685	400	285	190
1929	929	557	372	248
1933	879	201	678	452
1937	691	196	495	330
1938	682	187	495	330
1950	2653	217	2436	1624
1953	3160	67	3093	2062
1955	4565	39	4526	3017
1957	6792	15	6777	4518
1960	4820	5	4815	3210
1961	5209	4	5205	3470
1962	5057	2	5055	3370
1963	5372	2	5370	3580
1964	5434	2	5432	3621
1965	5583	-	5583	3722
YUGOSLAVIA				
1950	11	-	11	7
1953	21	-	21	14
1955	215	140	75	50
1957	200	140	60	40
1960	160	100	60	40

Table IX. BUNKERS, SELECTED YEARS, 1925-1965

(Thousand metric tons)

Region, country, year	Coal equivalents			Liquid fuels in original units
	Total bunkers	Solid fuels	Liquid fuels	
	(1)	(2)	(3)	(4)
YUGOSLAVIA (CONTINUED)				
1961	70	10	60	40
1962	70	10	60	40
1963	70	10	60	40
1964	72	6	66	44
1965	79	4	75	50
OCEANIA				
1925	1575	1269	306	204
1929	1238	915	323	215
1933	955	605	350	233
1937	1034	665	369	246
1938	1002	672	330	220
1950	1429	157	1272	848
1953	1520	45	1475	983
1955	2042	27	2015	1343
1957	2438	9	2429	1619
1960	2440	10	2430	1620
1961	2554	10	2544	1696
1962	2367	-	2367	1578
1963	2570	2	2568	1712
1964	2939	-	2939	1959
1965	3215	-	3215	2143
AUSTRALIA				
1925	1339	1138	201	134
1929	970	752	218	145
1933	810	571	239	159
1937	896	615	281	187
1938	859	628	231	154
1950	1010	137	873	582
1953	1162	43	1119	746
1955	1676	26	1650	1100
1957	2079	9	2070	1380
1960	2080	10	2070	1380
1961	2140	10	2130	1420
1962	2010	-	2010	1340
1963	2198	2	2196	1464
1964	2456	-	2456	1637
1965	2604	-	2604	1736
NEW ZEALAND				
1925	236	131	105	70
1929	268	163	105	70
1933	145	34	111	74
1937	131	50	81	54
1938	137	44	93	62
1950	410	20	390	260
1953	347	2	345	230
1955	343	1	342	228
1957	329	-	329	219
1960	285	-	285	190
1961	303	-	303	202
1962	263	-	263	175

Table IX. BUNKERS, SELECTED YEARS, 1925-1965

(Thousand metric tons)

Region, country, year	Coal equivalents			Liquid fuels in original units
	Total bunkers	Solid fuels	Liquid fuels	
	(1)	(2)	(3)	(4)
NEW ZEALAND (CONTINUED)				
1963	276	-	276	184
1964	353	-	353	235
1965	450	-	450	300
USSR AND COMMUNIST EASTERN EUROPE				
1925	NA	NA	NA	NA
1929	NA	NA	NA	NA
1933	NA	NA	NA	NA
1937	NA	NA	NA	NA
1938	NA	NA	NA	NA
1950	NA	NA	NA	NA
1953	NA	NA	NA	NA
1955	NA	NA	NA	NA
1957	NA	NA	NA	NA
1960	NA	NA	NA	NA
1961	NA	NA	NA	NA
1962	NA	NA	NA	NA
1963	NA	NA	NA	NA
1964	NA	NA	NA	NA
1965	NA	NA	NA	NA
COMMUNIST EASTERN EUROPE				
1925	103	100	3	2
1929	718	425	293	195
1933	1151	290	861	574
1937	1874	1146	728	485
1938	2379	1806	573	382
1950	NA	NA	NA	NA
1953	NA	NA	NA	NA
1955	NA	NA	NA	NA
1957	NA	NA	NA	NA
1960	NA	NA	NA	NA
1961	NA	NA	NA	NA
1962	NA	NA	NA	NA
1963	NA	NA	NA	NA
1964	NA	NA	NA	NA
1965	NA	NA	NA	NA
POLAND				
1925	100	100	NA	NA
1929	425	425	NA	NA
1933	290	290	NA	NA
1937	1146	1146	NA	NA
1938	1806	1806	NA	NA
1950	510	510	NA	NA
1953	860	860	NA	NA
1955	1250	1250	NA	NA
1957	194	194	NA	NA
1960	135	120	15	10
1961	161	120	41	27
1962	135	90	45	30
1963	123	70	53	35
1964	175	119	56	37

Table IX. BUNKERS, SELECTED YEARS, 1925-1965

(Thousand metric tons)

Region, country, year	Coal equivalents			Liquid fuels in original units
	Total bunkers	Solid fuels	Liquid fuels	
	(1)	(2)	(3)	(4)
POLAND (CONTINUED)				
1965	281	221	60	40
ROMANIA				
1925	3	-	3	2
1929	293	-	293	195
1933	861	-	861	574
1937	728	-	728	485
1938	573	-	573	382
1950	NA	-	NA	NA
1953	NA	-	NA	NA
1955	NA	-	NA	NA
1957	NA	-	NA	NA
1960	NA	-	NA	NA
1961	NA	-	NA	NA
1962	NA	-	NA	NA
1963	NA	-	NA	NA
1964	NA	-	NA	NA
1965	NA	-	NA	NA
COMMUNIST ASIA				
1925	469	469	NA	NA
1929	659	659	NA	NA
1933	606	606	NA	NA
1937	814	814	NA	NA
1938	819	819	NA	NA
1950	350	200	150	100
1953	NA	NA	NA	NA
1955	NA	NA	NA	NA
1957	NA	NA	NA	NA
1960	NA	NA	NA	NA
1961	NA	NA	NA	NA
1962	NA	NA	NA	NA
1963	NA	NA	NA	NA
1964	NA	NA	NA	NA
1965	NA	NA	NA	NA
LATIN AMERICA				
1925	4292	1239	3053	2034
1929	4635	1262	3373	2248
1933	4853	341	4512	3008
1937	5019	549	4470	2979
1938	4807	380	4427	2951
1950	15547	40	15507	10337
1953	14438	20	14418	9611
1955	14748	13	14735	9823
1957	18394	-	18394	12262
1960	17058	-	17058	11372
1961	19791	-	19791	13194
1962	19380	-	19380	12919
1963	19742	-	19742	13160
1964	21059	-	21059	14039
1965	21389	-	21389	14259

Table IX. BUNKERS, SELECTED YEARS, 1925-1965

(Thousand metric tons)

Region, country, year	Coal equivalents: Total bunkers	Coal equivalents: Solid fuels	Coal equivalents: Liquid fuels	Liquid fuels in original units
	(1)	(2)	(3)	(4)
LATIN AMERICA - CARIBBEAN				
1925	3591	599	2992	1994
1929	3937	644	3293	2195
1933	4494	261	4233	2822
1937	4539	317	4222	2814
1938	4505	251	4254	2836
1950	13820	38	13782	9187
1953	12201	20	12181	8120
1955	12765	13	12752	8501
1957	16421	-	16421	10947
1960	15030	-	15030	10020
1961	17805	-	17805	11870
1962	17320	-	17320	11546
1963	17652	-	17652	11767
1964	18866	-	18866	12577
1965	19191	-	19191	12794
CARIBBEAN - OIL PRODUCING				
1925	1738	50	1688	1125
1929	1842	93	1749	1166
1933	3071	41	3030	2020
1937	3191	63	3128	2085
1938	3188	38	3150	2100
1950	12427	21	12406	8270
1953	10300	11	10289	6859
1955	11070	-	11070	7380
1957	14445	-	14445	9630
1960	12150	-	12150	8100
1961	13500	-	13500	9000
1962	12316	-	12316	8210
1963	11311	-	11311	7540
1964	11897	-	11897	7931
1965	11796	-	11796	7864
ANTILLES, NETHERLANDS				
1925	538	20	518	345
1929	1016	23	993	662
1933	1266	3	1263	842
1937	768	-	768	512
1938	996	-	996	664
1950	9113	-	9113	6075
1953	5511	-	5511	3674
1955	5505	-	5505	3670
1957	6330	-	6330	4220
1960	4920	-	4920	3280
1961	5850	-	5850	3900
1962	4725	-	4725	3150
1963	4410	-	4410	2940
1964	4340	-	4340	2893
1965	4368	-	4368	2912
COLOMBIA				
1950	189	-	189	126
1953	53	-	53	35

Table IX. BUNKERS, SELECTED YEARS, 1925-1965

(Thousand metric tons)

Region, country, year	Coal equivalents			Liquid fuels in original units
	Total bunkers	Solid fuels	Liquid fuels	
	(1)	(2)	(3)	(4)
COLOMBIA (CONTINUED)				
1955	60	-	60	40
1957	210	-	210	140
1960	315	-	315	210
1961	330	-	330	220
1962	420	-	420	280
1963	300	-	300	200
1964	282	-	282	188
1965	321	-	321	214
MEXICO				
1925	1071	-	1071	714
1929	257	-	257	171
1933	NA	-	NA	NA
1937	NA	-	NA	NA
1938	NA	-	NA	NA
1950	902	-	902	601
1953	198	-	198	132
1955	225	-	225	150
1957	285	-	285	190
1960	165	-	165	110
1961	90	-	90	60
1962	120	-	120	80
1963	135	-	135	90
1964	92	-	92	61
1965	89	-	89	59
TRINIDAD AND TOBAGO				
1925	129	30	99	66
1929	570	70	500	333
1933	893	38	855	570
1937	963	63	900	600
1938	896	38	858	572
1950	1637	21	1615	1077
1953	2390	11	2379	1586
1955	1935	-	1935	1290
1957	2580	-	2580	1720
1960	2910	-	2910	1940
1961	3435	-	3435	2290
1962	2911	-	2911	1940
1963	2461	-	2461	1640
1964	2881	-	2881	1920
1965	2445	-	2445	1630
VENEZUELA				
1950	587	-	587	391
1953	2148	-	2148	1432
1955	3345	-	3345	2230
1957	5040	-	5040	3360
1960	3840	-	3840	2560
1961	3795	-	3795	2530
1962	4140	-	4140	2760
1963	4005	-	4005	2670
1964	4304	-	4304	2869

Table IX. BUNKERS, SELECTED YEARS, 1925-1965

(Thousand metric tons)

Region, country, year	Coal equivalents			Liquid fuels in original units
	Total bunkers	Solid fuels	Liquid fuels	
	(1)	(2)	(3)	(4)
VENEZUELA (CONTINUED)				
1965	4574		4574	3049
CARIBBEAN - OTHER				
1925	1853	549	1304	869
1929	2095	551	1544	1029
1933	1423	220	1203	802
1937	1348	254	1094	729
1938	1317	213	1104	736
1950	1393	17	1376	917
1953	1901	9	1892	1261
1955	1695	13	1682	1121
1957	1976	-	1976	1317
1960	2880	-	2880	1920
1961	4305	-	4305	2870
1962	5004	-	5004	3336
1963	6341	-	6341	4227
1964	6969	-	6969	4646
1965	7395	-	7395	4930
CUBA				
1950	59	-	59	39
1953	89	-	89	59
1955	60	-	60	40
1957	90	-	90	60
1960	60	-	60	40
1961	75	-	75	50
1962	45	-	45	30
1963	45	-	45	30
1964	53	-	53	35
1965	53	-	53	35
PANAMA CANAL ZONE				
1925	1619	315	1304	869
1929	1800	256	1544	1029
1933	1245	48	1197	798
1937	1173	94	1079	719
1938	1164	64	1100	733
1950	1019	-	1019	679
1953	1080	-	1080	720
1955	1080	-	1080	720
1957	1245	-	1245	830
1960	1185	-	1185	790
1961	1515	-	1515	1010
1962	1950	-	1950	1300
1963	3165	-	3165	2110
1964	3411	-	3411	2274
1965	3836	-	3836	2557
PUERTO RICO				
1950	75	-	75	50
1953	165	-	165	110

Table IX. BUNKERS, SELECTED YEARS, 1925-1965

(Thousand metric tons)

Region, country, year	Coal equivalents: Total bunkers	Coal equivalents: Solid fuels	Coal equivalents: Liquid fuels	Liquid fuels in original units
	(1)	(2)	(3)	(4)
PUERTO RICO (CONTINUED)				
1955	135	-	135	90
1957	180	-	180	120
1960	135	-	135	90
1961	120	-	120	80
1962	120	-	120	80
1963	120	-	120	80
1964	105	-	105	70
1965	101	-	101	67
LATIN AMERICA - OTHER				
1925	NA	NA	NA	NA
1929	NA	NA	NA	NA
1933	NA	NA	NA	NA
1937	NA	NA	NA	NA
1938	NA	NA	NA	NA
1950	1727	2	1725	1150
1953	2237	-	2237	1491
1955	1983	-	1983	1322
1957	1973	-	1973	1315
1960	2028	-	2028	1352
1961	1986	-	1986	1324
1962	2060	-	2060	1373
1963	2090	-	2090	1393
1964	2193	-	2193	1462
1965	2198	-	2198	1465
ARGENTINA				
1925	345	345	-	-
1929	136	136	-	-
1933	220	19	201	134
1937	258	102	156	104
1938	183	63	120	80
1950	834	-	834	556
1953	297	-	297	198
1955	330	-	330	220
1957	375	-	375	250
1960	375	-	375	250
1961	420	-	420	280
1962	375	-	375	250
1963	555	-	555	370
1964	629	-	629	419
1965	636	-	636	424
BOLIVIA				
1950	5	-	5	3
1953	5	-	5	3
1955	15	-	15	10
1957	15	-	15	10
1960	15	-	15	10
1961	15	-	15	10
1962	15	-	15	10
1963	15	-	15	10
1964	11	-	11	7

Table IX. BUNKERS, SELECTED YEARS, 1925-1965

(Thousand metric tons)

Region, country, year	Coal equivalents			Liquid fuels in original units
	Total bunkers	Solid fuels	Liquid fuels	
	(1)	(2)	(3)	(4)
BOLIVIA (CONTINUED)				
1965	11	-	11	7
BRAZIL				
1950	405	-	405	270
1953	609	-	609	406
1955	255	-	255	170
1957	240	-	240	160
1960	240	-	240	160
1961	300	-	300	200
1962	420	-	420	280
1963	420	-	420	280
1964	431	-	431	287
1965	425	-	425	283
CHILE				
1925	330	295	35	23
1929	379	349	30	20
1933	-	-	-	-
1937	-	-	-	-
1938	-	-	-	-
1950	36	-	36	24
1953	63	-	63	42
1955	105	-	105	70
1957	120	-	120	80
1960	90	-	90	60
1961	30	-	30	20
1962	45	-	45	30
1963	45	-	45	30
1964	30	-	30	20
1965	35	-	35	23
ECUADOR				
1950	14	-	14	9
1953	29	-	29	19
1955	30	-	30	20
1957	30	-	30	20
1960	15	-	15	10
1961	30	-	30	20
1962	15	-	15	10
1963	15	-	15	10
1964	17	-	17	11
1965	17	-	17	11
PERU				
1925	26	-	26	17
1929	50	-	50	33
1933	78	-	78	52
1937	62	-	62	41
1938	53	-	53	35
1950	89	2	87	58
1953	98	-	98	65

Table IX. BUNKERS, SELECTED YEARS, 1925-1965

(Thousand metric tons)

Region, country, year	Coal equivalents: Total bunkers	Coal equivalents: Solid fuels	Coal equivalents: Liquid fuels	Liquid fuels in original units
	(1)	(2)	(3)	(4)
PERU (CONTINUED)				
1955	105	-	105	70
1957	90	-	90	60
1960	60	-	60	40
1961	60	-	60	40
1962	45	-	45	30
1963	45	-	45	30
1964	66	-	66	44
1965	98	-	98	65
URUGUAY				
1925	NA	-	NA	NA
1929	133	133	NA	NA
1933	61	61	NA	NA
1937	123	123	NA	NA
1938	66	66	NA	NA
1950	315	-	315	210
1953	318	-	318	212
1955	375	-	375	250
1957	345	-	345	230
1960	405	-	405	270
1961	345	-	345	230
1962	360	-	360	240
1963	210	-	210	140
1964	225	-	225	150
1965	239	-	239	159
ASIA				
1925	6759	5652	1107	738
1929	7578	5414	2164	1442
1933	6256	3932	2324	1549
1937	7307	4446	2861	1907
1938	7027	3853	3174	2116
1950	15335	1821	13514	9009
1953	16909	432	16477	10984
1955	20155	351	19804	13202
1957	24495	109	24386	16257
1960	31915	20	31895	21263
1961	35763	18	35745	23830
1962	38701	8	38693	25795
1963	41827	6	41821	27880
1964	45923	5	45918	30612
1965	47759	4	47755	31836
MIDDLE EAST				
1925	377	110	267	178
1929	733	137	596	397
1933	896	42	854	569
1937	1250	114	1136	757
1938	1326	57	1269	846
1950	10017	133	9884	6589
1953	9938	36	9902	6601
1955	12143	18	12125	8083
1957	13563	15	13548	9032

Table IX. BUNKERS, SELECTED YEARS, 1925-1965

(Thousand metric tons)

Region, country, year	Coal equivalents			Liquid fuels in original units
	Total bunkers	Solid fuels	Liquid fuels	
	(1)	(2)	(3)	(4)
MIDDLE EAST (CONTINUED)				
1960	18795	-	18795	12530
1961	19215	-	19215	12810
1962	20760	-	20760	13840
1963	21725	-	21725	14483
1964	23238	-	23238	15492
1965	22541	-	22541	15027
MIDDLE EAST - OIL PRODUCING				
1925	NA	NA	NA	NA
1929	NA	NA	NA	NA
1933	NA	NA	NA	NA
1937	NA	NA	NA	NA
1938	NA	NA	NA	NA
1950	5534	-	5534	3689
1953	5172	-	5172	3448
1955	6866	-	6866	4577
1957	9786	-	9786	6524
1960	12885	-	12885	8590
1961	13350	-	13350	8900
1962	15000	-	15000	10000
1963	15222	-	15222	10148
1964	16593	-	16593	11062
1965	16889	-	16889	11259
BAHRAIN				
1950	912	-	912	608
1953	1299	-	1299	866
1955	1247	-	1247	831
1957	1350	-	1350	900
1960	1140	-	1140	760
1961	1245	-	1245	830
1962	1275	-	1275	850
1963	1347	-	1347	898
1964	1467	-	1467	978
1965	1415	-	1415	943
IRAN				
1950	2460	-	2460	1640
1953	-	-	-	-
1955	1215	-	1215	810
1957	2265	-	2265	1510
1960	3180	-	3180	2120
1961	3270	-	3270	2180
1962	3795	-	3795	2530
1963	4140	-	4140	2760
1964	4293	-	4293	2862
1965	4742	-	4742	3161
IRAQ				
1950	8	-	8	5
1953	-	-	-	-

Table IX. BUNKERS, SELECTED YEARS, 1925-1965

(Thousand metric tons)

Region, country, year	Coal equivalents			Liquid fuels in original units
	Total bunkers	Solid fuels	Liquid fuels	
	(1)	(2)	(3)	(4)
IRAQ (CONTINUED)				
1955	15	-	15	10
1957	30	-	30	20
1960	30	-	30	20
1961	30	-	30	20
1962	60	-	60	40
1963	45	-	45	30
1964	45	-	45	30
1965	45	-	45	30
KUWAIT				
1950	908	-	908	605
1953	1815	-	1815	1210
1955	2109	-	2109	1406
1957	3816	-	3816	2544
1960	4725	-	4725	3150
1961	4710	-	4710	3140
1962	5535	-	5535	3690
1963	5880	-	5880	3920
1964	6123	-	6123	4082
1965	5639	-	5639	3759
KUWAIT NEUTRAL ZONE				
1955	-	-	-	-
1957	-	-	-	-
1960	660	-	660	440
1961	885	-	885	590
1962	825	-	825	550
1963	660	-	660	440
1964	765	-	765	510
1965	527	-	527	351
SAUDI ARABIA				
1950	1247	-	1247	831
1953	2058	-	2058	1372
1955	2280	-	2280	1520
1957	2325	-	2325	1550
1960	3150	-	3150	2100
1961	3210	-	3210	2140
1962	3510	-	3510	2340
1963	3150	-	3150	2100
1964	3900	-	3900	2600
1965	4523	-	4523	3015
MIDDLE EAST - OTHER				
1925	377	110	267	178
1929	733	137	596	397
1933	896	42	854	569
1937	1250	114	1136	757
1938	1326	57	1269	846
1950	4483	133	4350	2900
1953	4766	36	4730	3153

Table IX. BUNKERS, SELECTED YEARS, 1925-1965

(Thousand metric tons)

Region, country, year	Coal equivalents: Total bunkers	Coal equivalents: Solid fuels	Coal equivalents: Liquid fuels	Liquid fuels in original units
	(1)	(2)	(3)	(4)
MIDDLE EAST - OTHER (CONTINUED)				
1955	5277	18	5259	3506
1957	3777	15	3762	2508
1960	5910	-	5910	3940
1961	5865	-	5865	3910
1962	5760	-	5760	3840
1963	6503	-	6503	4335
1964	6645	-	6645	4430
1965	5652	-	5652	3768
ISRAEL				
1950	89	-	89	59
1953	156	-	156	104
1955	120	-	120	80
1957	120	-	120	80
1960	165	-	165	110
1961	180	-	180	120
1962	180	-	180	120
1963	180	-	180	120
1964	177	-	177	118
1965	194	-	194	129
LEBANON				
1950	9	-	9	6
1953	354	-	354	236
1955	375	-	375	250
1957	315	-	315	210
1960	240	-	240	160
1961	240	-	240	160
1962	240	-	240	160
1963	345	-	345	230
1964	333	-	333	222
1965	326	-	326	217
SYRIA				
1950	8	-	8	5
1953	8	-	8	5
1955	-	-	-	-
1957	-	-	-	-
1960	15	-	15	10
1961	15	-	15	10
1962	15	-	15	10
1963	8	-	8	5
1964	9	-	9	6
1965	8	-	8	5
TURKEY				
1950	98	-	98	65
1953	24	-	24	16
1955	45	-	45	30
1957	120	-	120	80
1960	60	-	60	40

Table IX. BUNKERS, SELECTED YEARS, 1925-1965

(Thousand metric tons)

Region, country, year	Coal equivalents			Liquid fuels in original units
	Total bunkers	Solid fuels	Liquid fuels	
	(1)	(2)	(3)	(4)
TURKEY (CONTINUED)				
1961	60	-	60	40
1962	90	-	90	60
1963	150	-	150	100
1964	171	-	171	114
1965	180	-	180	120
FAR EAST AND OTHER ASIA				
1925	6382	5542	840	560
1929	6845	5277	1568	1045
1933	5360	3890	1470	980
1937	6057	4332	1725	1150
1938	5701	3796	1905	1270
1950	5318	1688	3630	2420
1953	6971	396	6575	4383
1955	8012	333	7679	5119
1957	10932	94	10838	7225
1960	13120	20	13100	8733
1961	16548	18	16530	11020
1962	17941	8	17933	11955
1963	20102	6	20096	13397
1964	22685	5	22680	15120
1965	25218	4	25214	16809
BORNEO (FORMER BRITISH)				
1950	83	-	83	55
1953	185	-	185	123
1955	210	-	210	140
1957	224	-	224	149
1960	240	-	240	160
1961	180	-	180	120
1962	135	-	135	90
1963	105	-	105	70
1964	87	-	87	58
1965	62	-	62	41
SABAH				
1953	-	-	-	-
1955	15	-	15	10
1957	9	-	9	6
1960	15	-	15	10
1961	15	-	15	10
1962	15	-	15	10
1963	30	-	30	20
1964	29	-	29	19
1965	23	-	23	15
SARAWAK				
1950	83	-	83	55
1953	185	-	185	123
1955	195	-	195	130
1957	215	-	215	143
1960	225	-	225	150

Table IX. BUNKERS, SELECTED YEARS, 1925-1965

(Thousand metric tons)

Region, country, year	Coal equivalents			Liquid fuels in original units
	Total bunkers	Solid fuels	Liquid fuels	
	(1)	(2)	(3)	(4)
SARAWAK (CONTINUED)				
1961	165	-	165	110
1962	120	-	120	80
1963	75	-	75	50
1964	59	-	59	39
1965	39	-	39	26
BURMA				
1950	14	-	14	9
1953	15	-	15	10
1955	15	-	15	10
1957	30	-	30	20
1960	60	-	60	40
1961	45	-	45	30
1962	45	-	45	30
1963	45	-	45	30
1964	45	-	45	30
1965	47	-	47	31
CEYLON				
1925	1020	813	207	138
1929	778	515	263	175
1933	578	221	357	238
1937	734	330	404	269
1938	781	229	552	368
1950	955	82	873	582
1953	781	22	759	506
1955	737	14	723	482
1957	963	9	954	636
1960	720	-	720	480
1961	615	-	615	410
1962	481	1	480	320
1963	300	-	300	200
1964	387	-	387	258
1965	404	-	404	269
HONG KONG				
1925	592	457	135	90
1929	603	448	155	103
1933	608	534	74	49
1937	561	451	110	73
1938	520	412	108	72
1950	338	20	318	212
1953	329	-	329	219
1955	525	-	525	350
1957	660	-	660	440
1960	615	-	615	410
1961	615	-	615	410
1962	720	-	720	480
1963	765	-	765	510
1964	875	-	875	583
1965	954	-	954	636

Table IX. BUNKERS, SELECTED YEARS, 1925-1965

(Thousand metric tons)

Region, country, year	Coal equivalents			Liquid fuels in original units
	Total bunkers	Solid fuels	Liquid fuels	
	(1)	(2)	(3)	(4)
INDIA				
1925	1069	1069	NA	NA
1929	948	948	NA	NA
1933	599	516	83	55
1937	789	684	105	70
1938	883	779	104	69
1950	315	235	80	53
1953	487	167	320	213
1955	615	139	476	317
1957	815	20	795	530
1960	745	10	735	490
1961	713	8	705	470
1962	727	7	720	480
1963	726	6	720	480
1964	701	5	696	464
1965	886	4	882	588
INDO-CHINA				
1925	-	-	-	-
1929	-	-	-	-
1933	-	-	-	-
1937	25	25	-	-
1938	44	44	-	-
1950	9	-	9	6
1953	30	-	30	20
1955	-	-	-	-
1957	-	-	-	-
1960	50	-	50	33
1961	60	-	60	40
1962	38	-	38	25
1963	41	-	41	27
1964	39	-	39	26
1965	44	-	44	29
CAMBODIA				
1955	-	-	-	-
1957	-	-	-	-
1960	5	-	5	3
1961	15	-	15	10
1962	15	-	15	10
1963	15	-	15	10
1964	15	-	15	10
1965	17	-	17	11
VIETNAM, SOUTH				
1955	-	-	-	-
1957	-	-	-	-
1960	45	-	45	30
1961	45	-	45	30
1962	23	-	23	15
1963	26	-	26	17
1964	24	-	24	16
1965	27	-	27	18

Table IX. BUNKERS, SELECTED YEARS, 1925-1965

(Thousand metric tons)

Region, country, year	Coal equivalents			Liquid fuels in original units
	Total bunkers	Solid fuels	Liquid fuels	
	(1)	(2)	(3)	(4)
INDONESIA				
1925	266	135	131	87
1929	529	113	416	277
1933	510	9	501	334
1937	531	22	509	339
1938	492	39	453	302
1950	495	-	495	330
1953	1145	3	1142	761
1955	783	-	783	522
1957	807	-	807	538
1960	720	-	720	480
1961	1020	-	1020	680
1962	675	-	675	450
1963	630	-	630	420
1964	632	-	632	421
1965	671	-	671	447
JAPAN				
1925	2425	2419	6	4
1929	2506	2497	9	6
1933	2030	2019	11	7
1937	2147	2088	59	39
1938	1668	1594	74	49
1950	1685	1296	389	259
1953	1196	164	1032	688
1955	1883	131	1752	1168
1957	3385	37	3348	2232
1960	6250	10	6240	4160
1961	8800	10	8790	5860
1962	10065	-	10065	6710
1963	12315	-	12315	8210
1964	14688	-	14688	9792
1965	16281	-	16281	10854
KOREA, REPUBLIC OF				
1950	29	-	29	19
1953	15	15	-	-
1955	30	30	-	-
1957	10	10	-	-
1960	15	-	15	10
1961	15	-	15	10
1962	15	-	15	10
1963	15	-	15	10
1964	21	-	21	14
1965	27	-	27	18
MALAYA AND SINGAPORE				
1925	662	465	197	131
1929	995	572	423	282
1933	600	358	242	161
1937	705	394	311	207
1938	699	349	350	233
1950	969	45	924	616
1953	2226	15	2211	1474

Table IX. BUNKERS, SELECTED YEARS, 1925-1965

(Thousand metric tons)

Region, country, year	Coal equivalents			Liquid fuels in original units
	Total bunkers	Solid fuels	Liquid fuels	
	(1)	(2)	(3)	(4)
MALAYA AND SINGAPORE (CONTINUED)				
1955	2709	9	2700	1800
1957	3428	8	3420	2280
1960	2970	-	2970	1980
1961	3690	-	3690	2460
1962	4095	-	4095	2730
1963	4110	-	4110	2740
1964	3918	-	3918	2612
1965	4530	-	4530	3020
SINGAPORE				
1960	2955	-	2955	1970
1961	3659	-	3659	2439
1962	4055	-	4055	2703
1963	4047	-	4047	2698
1964	3849	-	3849	2566
1965	4461	-	4461	2974
PAKISTAN				
1950	295	10	285	190
1953	280	10	270	180
1955	265	10	255	170
1957	280	10	270	180
1960	420	-	420	280
1961	450	-	450	300
1962	480	-	480	320
1963	510	-	510	340
1964	566	-	566	377
1965	524	-	524	349
PHILIPPINES				
1950	123	-	123	82
1953	264	-	264	176
1955	135	-	135	90
1957	150	-	150	100
1960	75	-	75	50
1961	90	-	90	60
1962	105	-	105	70
1963	135	-	135	90
1964	284	-	284	189
1965	390	-	390	260
TAIWAN				
1925	184	184	-	-
1929	184	184	-	-
1933	233	233	-	-
1937	338	338	-	-
1938	350	350	-	-
1950	-	-	-	-
1953	-	-	-	-
1955	90	-	90	60
1957	75	-	75	50

Table IX. BUNKERS, SELECTED YEARS, 1925-1965

(Thousand metric tons)

Region, country, year	Coal equivalents			Liquid fuels in original units
	Total bunkers	Solid fuels	Liquid fuels	
	(1)	(2)	(3)	(4)
TAIWAN (CONTINUED)				
1960	105	-	105	70
1961	90	-	90	60
1962	90	-	90	60
1963	135	-	135	90
1964	158	-	158	105
1965	251	-	251	167
THAILAND				
1950	11	-	11	7
1953	20	-	20	13
1955	15	-	15	10
1957	60	-	60	40
1960	90	-	90	60
1961	120	-	120	80
1962	210	-	210	140
1963	195	-	195	130
1964	210	-	210	140
1965	54	-	54	36
AFRICA				
1925	3655	3268	387	258
1929	4302	3709	593	395
1933	3268	1979	1289	859
1937	5147	2497	2650	1766
1938	3928	2145	1783	1188
1950	4771	698	4073	2715
1953	5900	130	5770	3846
1955	5883	64	5819	3879
1957	8244	48	8196	5464
1960	7008	3	7005	4670
1961	7777	1	7776	5184
1962	8022	1	8021	5347
1963	8247	-	8247	5498
1964	8756	-	8756	5837
1965	8846	1	8845	5896
NORTH AFRICA				
1925	NA	1049	NA	NA
1929	NA	1576	NA	NA
1933	NA	1001	NA	NA
1937	NA	880	NA	NA
1938	NA	672	NA	NA
1950	1600	116	1484	989
1953	1604	42	1562	1041
1955	1563	27	1536	1024
1957	1444	13	1431	954
1960	1636	1	1635	1090
1961	2085	-	2085	1390
1962	2055	-	2055	1370
1963	2241	-	2241	1494
1964	2214	-	2214	1476
1965	2144	-	2144	1429

Table IX. BUNKERS, SELECTED YEARS, 1925-1965

(Thousand metric tons)

Region, country, year	Coal equivalents			Liquid fuels in original units
	Total bunkers	Solid fuels	Liquid fuels	
	(1)	(2)	(3)	(4)
ALGERIA				
1925	963	963	NA	NA
1929	1513	1513	NA	NA
1933	1254	942	312	208
1937	1474	814	660	440
1938	1276	617	659	439
1950	882	75	807	538
1953	1127	39	1088	725
1955	1090	26	1064	709
1957	1047	13	1034	689
1960	766	1	765	510
1961	780	-	780	520
1962	465	-	465	310
1963	585	-	585	390
1964	533	-	533	355
1965	473	-	473	315
EGYPT UAR				
1925	248	86	162	108
1929	222	63	159	106
1933	218	59	159	106
1937	152	66	86	57
1938	138	55	83	55
1950	541	38	503	335
1953	197	2	195	130
1955	204	1	203	135
1957	23	-	23	15
1960	555	-	555	370
1961	975	-	975	650
1962	1275	-	1275	850
1963	1320	-	1320	880
1964	1353	-	1353	902
1965	1341	-	1341	894
LIBYA				
1950	62	-	62	41
1953	93	-	93	62
1955	105	-	105	70
1957	135	-	135	90
1960	135	-	135	90
1961	135	-	135	90
1962	135	-	135	90
1963	135	-	135	90
1964	138	-	138	92
1965	138	-	138	92
MOROCCO				
1950	78	-	78	52
1953	156	-	156	104
1955	120	-	120	80
1957	195	-	195	130
1960	150	-	150	100
1961	150	-	150	100
1962	135	-	135	90

Table IX. BUNKERS, SELECTED YEARS, 1925-1965

(Thousand metric tons)

Region, country, year	Coal equivalents: Total bunkers	Coal equivalents: Solid fuels	Coal equivalents: Liquid fuels	Liquid fuels in original units
	(1)	(2)	(3)	(4)
MOROCCO (CONTINUED)				
1963	150	-	150	100
1964	134	-	134	89
1965	141	-	141	94
TUNISIA				
1950	38	3	35	23
1953	31	1	30	20
1955	45	-	45	30
1957	45	-	45	30
1960	30	-	30	20
1961	45	-	45	30
1962	45	-	45	30
1963	51	-	51	34
1964	57	-	57	38
1965	51	-	51	34
TROPICAL AFRICA				
1925	663	438	225	150
1929	936	559	377	251
1933	904	152	752	501
1937	2081	473	1608	1072
1938	986	332	654	436
1950	1983	195	1788	1192
1953	3521	9	3512	2341
1955	3576	3	3573	2382
1957	4870	1	4869	3246
1960	4770	-	4770	3180
1961	4926	-	4926	3284
1962	5216	-	5216	3477
1963	5151	-	5151	3434
1964	5265	-	5265	3510
1965	5538	1	5537	3691
CONGO, DEMOCRATIC REPUBLIC				
1953	-	-	-	-
1955	15	-	15	10
1957	15	-	15	10
1960	15	-	15	10
1961	15	-	15	10
1962	15	-	15	10
1963	15	-	15	10
1964	12	-	12	8
1965	14	-	14	9
EAST AFRICA				
1925	2	2	-	-
1929	36	4	32	21
1933	70	4	66	44
1937	87	1	86	57
1938	76	2	74	49
1950	236	18	218	145

Table IX. BUNKERS, SELECTED YEARS, 1925-1965

(Thousand metric tons)

Region, country, year	Coal equivalents: Total bunkers	Coal equivalents: Solid fuels	Coal equivalents: Liquid fuels	Liquid fuels in original units
	(1)	(2)	(3)	(4)
EAST AFRICA (CONTINUED)				
1953	192	-	192	128
1955	158	-	158	105
1957	309	-	309	206
1960	186	-	186	124
1961	263	-	263	175
1962	251	-	251	167
1963	240	-	240	160
1964	179	-	179	119
1965	260	-	260	173
EQUATORIAL AFRICA				
1950	5	-	5	3
1953	8	-	8	5
1955	15	-	15	10
1957	15	-	15	10
1960	-	-	-	-
1961	3	-	3	2
1962	18	-	18	12
1963	8	-	8	5
1964	26	-	26	17
1965	21	-	21	14
GHANA				
1950	48	-	48	32
1953	36	-	36	24
1955	30	-	30	20
1957	27	-	27	18
1960	30	-	30	20
1961	30	-	30	20
1962	30	-	30	20
1963	30	-	30	20
1964	48	-	48	32
1965	26	-	26	17
LIBERIA				
1950	-	-	-	-
1953	-	-	-	-
1955	-	-	-	-
1957	-	-	-	-
1960	15	-	15	10
1961	15	-	15	10
1962	15	-	15	10
1963	15	-	15	10
1964	44	-	44	29
1965	45	-	45	30
NIGERIA				
1925	10	10	-	-
1929	10	10	-	-
1933	10	10	-	-
1937	15	15	-	-
1938	14	14	-	-

Table IX. BUNKERS, SELECTED YEARS, 1925-1965

(Thousand metric tons)

Region, country, year	Coal equivalents: Total bunkers	Coal equivalents: Solid fuels	Coal equivalents: Liquid fuels	Liquid fuels in original units
	(1)	(2)	(3)	(4)
NIGERIA (CONTINUED)				
1950	17	11	6	4
1953	15	1	14	9
1955	20	-	20	13
1957	12	-	12	8
1960	15	-	15	10
1961	30	-	30	20
1962	45	-	45	30
1963	60	-	60	40
1964	96	-	96	64
1965	84	-	84	56
RHODESIAN FEDERATION				
1950	5	-	5	3
1953	6	-	6	4
1955	15	-	15	10
1957	15	-	15	10
1960	15	-	15	10
1961	15	-	15	10
1962	15	-	15	10
1963	15	-	15	10
1964	12	-	12	8
1965	14	-	14	9
RHODESIA				
1950	5	-	5	3
1953	6	-	6	4
1955	15	-	15	10
1957	15	-	15	10
1960	15	-	15	10
1961	15	-	15	10
1962	15	-	15	10
1963	15	-	15	10
1964	12	-	12	8
1965	14	-	14	9
WEST AFRICA				
1925	148	131	17	11
1929	355	218	137	91
1933	434	57	377	251
1937	1252	245	1007	671
1938	121	98	23	15
1950	1024	97	927	618
1953	1665	-	1665	1110
1955	1680	-	1680	1120
1957	2670	-	2670	1780
1960	1682	-	1682	1121
1961	1473	-	1473	982
1962	1535	-	1535	1023
1963	1506	-	1506	1004
1964	1448	-	1448	965
1965	1464	-	1464	976

Table IX. BUNKERS, SELECTED YEARS, 1925-1965

(Thousand metric tons)

Region, country, year	Coal equivalents: Total bunkers	Coal equivalents: Solid fuels	Coal equivalents: Liquid fuels	Liquid fuels in original units
	(1)	(2)	(3)	(4)
SOUTH AFRICA				
1925	1781	1781	-	-
1929	1631	1574	57	38
1933	892	826	66	44
1937	1440	1144	296	197
1938	1528	1141	387	258
1950	1188	387	801	534
1953	775	79	696	464
1955	744	34	710	473
1957	1930	34	1896	1264
1960	602	2	600	400
1961	766	1	765	510
1962	751	1	750	500
1963	855	-	855	570
1964	1277	-	1277	851
1965	1164	-	1164	776
DEVELOPED COUNTRIES				
1925	56718	35094	21624	14416
1929	60137	33625	26512	17674
1933	43185	23453	19732	13153
1937	49561	24509	25052	16700
1938	44313	21697	22616	15076
1950	51334	10572	40762	27173
1953	61807	6821	54986	36656
1955	68384	5720	62664	41775
1957	75226	4181	71045	47363
1960	74692	2063	72629	48419
1961	78671	1373	77298	51532
1962	81262	1121	80141	53427
1963	83559	1048	82511	55006
1964	93556	1030	92526	61682
1965	96717	969	95748	63831
UNDERDEVELOPED COUNTRIES				
1925	10500	5959	4541	3026
1929	12378	6314	6064	4041
1933	11455	3407	8048	5365
1937	13886	4260	9626	6416
1938	12566	3643	8923	5948
1950	32776	876	31900	21268
1953	35270	339	34931	23289
1955	38156	263	37893	25263
1957	45816	86	45730	30487
1960	49128	11	49117	32745
1961	53764	8	53756	35838
1962	55284	8	55276	36851
1963	56641	6	56635	37758
1964	59769	5	59764	39845
1965	60545	5	60540	40361
COMMUNIST COUNTRIES				
1925	NA	NA	NA	NA
1929	NA	NA	NA	NA

Table IX. BUNKERS, SELECTED YEARS, 1925-1965

(Thousand metric tons)

Region, country, year	Coal equivalents			Liquid fuels in original units
	Total bunkers	Solid fuels	Liquid fuels	
	(1)	(2)	(3)	(4)
COMMUNIST COUNTRIES (CONTINUED)				
1933	NA	NA	NA	NA
1937	NA	NA	NA	NA
1938	NA	NA	NA	NA
1950	NA	NA	NA	NA
1953	NA	NA	NA	NA
1955	NA	NA	NA	NA
1957	NA	NA	NA	NA
1960	NA	NA	NA	NA
1961	NA	NA	NA	NA
1962	NA	NA	NA	NA
1963	NA	NA	NA	NA
1964	NA	NA	NA	NA
1965	NA	NA	NA	NA
USSR				
1925	NA	NA	NA	NA
1929	NA	NA	NA	NA
1933	NA	NA	NA	NA
1937	NA	NA	NA	NA
1938	NA	NA	NA	NA
1950	NA	NA	NA	NA
1953	NA	NA	NA	NA
1955	NA	NA	NA	NA
1957	NA	NA	NA	NA
1960	NA	NA	NA	NA
1961	NA	NA	NA	NA
1962	NA	NA	NA	NA
1963	NA	NA	NA	NA
1964	NA	NA	NA	NA
1965	NA	NA	NA	NA
COMMUNIST EASTERN EUROPE				
1925	103	100	3	2
1929	718	425	293	195
1933	1151	290	861	574
1937	1874	1146	728	485
1938	2379	1806	573	382
1950	NA	NA	NA	NA
1953	NA	NA	NA	NA
1955	NA	NA	NA	NA
1957	NA	NA	NA	NA
1960	NA	NA	NA	NA
1961	NA	NA	NA	NA
1962	NA	NA	NA	NA
1963	NA	NA	NA	NA
1964	NA	NA	NA	NA
1965	NA	NA	NA	NA
COMMUNIST ASIA				
1925	469	469	NA	NA
1929	659	659	NA	NA
1933	606	606	NA	NA

Table IX. BUNKERS, SELECTED YEARS, 1925-1965

(Thousand metric tons)

Region, country, year	Coal equivalents			Liquid fuels in original units
	Total bunkers	Solid fuels	Liquid fuels	
	(1)	(2)	(3)	(4)
COMMUNIST ASIA (CONTINUED)				
1937	814	814	NA	NA
1938	819	819	NA	NA
1950	350	200	150	100
1953	NA	NA	NA	NA
1955	NA	NA	NA	NA
1957	NA	NA	NA	NA
1960	NA	NA	NA	NA
1961	NA	NA	NA	NA
1962	NA	NA	NA	NA
1963	NA	NA	NA	NA
1964	NA	NA	NA	NA
1965	NA	NA	NA	NA
ORGANISATION FOR ECONOMIC CO-OPERATION AND DEVELOPMENT (OECD)				
1925	53100	31785	21315	14210
1929	57103	30974	26129	17419
1933	41266	21954	19312	12874
1937	46928	22553	24375	16249
1938	41624	19753	21871	14580
1950	48022	9823	38199	25464
1953	58883	6654	52229	34817
1955	64869	5483	59386	39590
1957	69908	3962	65946	43964
1960	71180	1941	69239	46159
1961	74981	1352	73629	49086
1962	77819	1110	76709	51139
1963	79794	1036	78758	52504
1964	89010	1024	87986	58655
1965	92032	965	91067	60710
COMMUNIST COUNTRIES				
1925	NA	NA	NA	NA
1929	NA	NA	NA	NA
1933	NA	NA	NA	NA
1937	NA	NA	NA	NA
1938	NA	NA	NA	NA
1950	NA	NA	NA	NA
1953	NA	NA	NA	NA
1955	NA	NA	NA	NA
1957	NA	NA	NA	NA
1960	NA	NA	NA	NA
1961	NA	NA	NA	NA
1962	NA	NA	NA	NA
1963	NA	NA	NA	NA
1964	NA	NA	NA	NA
1965	NA	NA	NA	NA
WORLD EXCLUDING OECD AND COMMUNIST COUNTRIES				
1925	14118	9268	4850	3232
1929	15412	8965	6447	4296
1933	13374	4906	8468	5644
1937	16519	6216	10303	6867
1938	15255	5587	9668	6444

Table IX. BUNKERS, SELECTED YEARS, 1925-1965

(Thousand metric tons)

Region, country, year	Coal equivalents			Liquid fuels in original units
	Total bunkers	Solid fuels	Liquid fuels	
	(1)	(2)	(3)	(4)
WORLD EXCLUDING OECD AND COMMUNIST COUNTRIES (CONTINUED)				
1950	36088	1625	34463	22977
1953	38194	506	37688	25128
1955	41671	500	41171	27448
1957	51134	305	50829	33886
1960	52640	133	52507	35005
1961	57454	29	57425	38284
1962	58727	19	58708	39139
1963	60406	18	60388	40260
1964	64315	11	64304	42872
1965	65230	9	65221	43482

DERIVATION OF TABLE X

Column	*Derivation*
(1)	Col. (2) table II plus col. (1) table IV (imports) minus col. (1) table IV (exports) minus col. (2) table IX
(2)	Col. (4) table I plus col. (2) table IV (imports) minus col. (2) table IV (exports) minus col. (4) table IX
(3)	Col. (6) table I plus col. (9) table V
(4)	Col. (7) table I plus col. (10) table V
(5)	Sum of cols. (6) through (9)
(6)	Col. (1)
(7)	Col. (2) multiplied by 1.5*
(8)	Col. (3) multiplied by 1.332*
(9)	Col. (4) multiplied by 0.125*
(10)	Ratio of col. (1) table II to col. (5)
(11)	Ratio of col. (2) table II to col. (6)
(12)	Ratio of col. (6) table II to col. (7)
(13)	Ratio of col. (8) table II to col. (8)
(14)	Ratio of col. (9) table II to col. (9)

Table X. TOTAL ENERGY CONSUMPTION AND RATIO OF PRODUCTION TO CONSUMPTION, SELECTED YEARS, 1925-1965

	Consumption in original units				Consumption in coal equivalents (10^3 m.t.)					Ratio of production to consumption				
Region, country, year	Solid fuels (10^3 m.t. coal equiv.)	Liquid fuels (10^3 m.t.)	Natural gas (10^6 c.m.)	Hydro-electric power (10^6 kwh)	Total	Solid fuels	Liquid fuels	Natural gas	Hydro-electric power	Total	Solid fuels	Liquid fuels	Natural gas	Hydro-electric power
	(1)	(2)	(3)	(4)	(5)	(6)	(7)	(8)	(9)	(10)	(11)	(12)	(13)	(14)
WORLD														
1925	1230023	131160	35977	78794	1484533	1230023	196740	47921	9849	1.055	1.041	1.159	1.000	0.999
1929	1386348	185313	57823	117150	1755981	1386348	277970	77020	14644	1.052	1.037	1.146	1.000	1.001
1933	1045189	175820	50637	126967	1392238	1045189	263730	67448	15871	1.053	1.033	1.150	1.000	1.001
1937	1378666	252477	77964	177629	1883433	1378666	378716	103848	22204	1.048	1.028	1.138	1.000	1.002
1938	1291815	250541	74824	182110	1790056	1291815	375812	99666	22764	1.043	1.025	1.121	1.000	1.001
1950	1593178	481468	189262	347378	2610900	1593178	722202	252097	43422	1.041	1.010	1.126	1.000	0.999
1953	1685913	609262	256568	413533	2993246	1685913	913893	341749	51692	1.040	1.004	1.124	1.000	1.002
1955	1816635	728497	292470	473903	3358188	1816635	1092746	389570	59238	1.037	1.005	1.103	1.000	1.002
1957	1954187	832302	348113	551936	3735319	1954187	1248453	463687	68992	1.038	1.007	1.104	1.000	1.004
1960	1998499	999365	459883	687872	4196095	1998499	1499048	612564	85984	1.035	1.002	1.095	1.000	1.000
1961	2024805	1068966	496642	721327	4379947	2024805	1603449	661527	90166	1.034	1.002	1.090	1.000	1.002
1962	2072923	1152978	543219	760415	4621009	2072923	1729467	723568	95052	1.036	1.002	1.095	1.000	0.999
1963	2163312	1242677	587683	796772	4909718	2163312	1864016	782794	99597	1.035	1.002	1.090	1.000	0.999
1964	2245357	1333633	641857	823826	5203738	2245357	2000450	854954	102978	1.036	1.000	1.093	1.000	1.001
1965	2290751	1439394	684757	901104	5474576	2290751	2159091	912096	112638	1.034	1.001	1.085	1.000	1.000
NORTH AMERICA														
1925	557897	94345	33789	35479	748857	557897	141518	45007	4435	1.040	1.018	1.143	1.000	1.000
1929	589444	129280	54219	55269	852492	589444	193920	72220	6909	1.035	1.013	1.118	1.000	1.000
1933	375446	113510	44598	54226	611894	375446	170265	59405	6778	1.034	1.002	1.117	1.001	1.000

Table X. TOTAL ENERGY CONSUMPTION AND RATIO OF PRODUCTION TO CONSUMPTION, SELECTED YEARS, 1925-1965

Region, country, year	Consumption in original units: Solid fuels (10^3 m.t. coal equiv.)	Liquid fuels (10^3 m.t.)	Natural gas (10^6 c.m.)	Hydro-electric power (10^6 kwh)	Consumption in coal equivalents (10^3 m.t.): Total	Solid fuels	Liquid fuels	Natural gas	Hydro-electric power	Ratio of production to consumption: Total	Solid fuels	Liquid fuels	Natural gas	Hydro-electric power
	(1)	(2)	(3)	(4)	(5)	(6)	(7)	(8)	(9)	(10)	(11)	(12)	(13)	(14)
NORTH AMERICA (CONTINUED)														
1937	485984	158254	68912	73416	824333	485984	237381	91791	9177	1.043	1.007	1.135	1.002	1.000
1938	387886	148319	65625	72978	706900	387886	222479	87413	9122	1.052	1.004	1.158	1.001	1.000
1950	548198	319238	172790	153037	1276341	548198	478857	230156	19130	0.970	1.008	0.908	1.004	1.001
1953	466865	387137	231697	176645	1378272	466865	580706	308620	22081	0.975	1.030	0.915	1.003	1.001
1955	449010	427774	260180	192536	1461298	449010	641661	345560	24067	0.976	1.075	0.893	1.002	1.001
1957	449935	455039	298502	216559	1557168	449935	682559	397605	27070	0.992	1.128	0.897	0.999	1.002
1960	401433	492407	366045	254828	1659469	401433	738611	487572	31854	0.937	1.060	0.828	0.997	1.002
1961	387666	509564	383224	259017	1694843	387666	764346	510454	32377	0.935	1.061	0.826	0.997	1.002
1962	402467	527250	408597	275565	1772039	402467	790875	544251	34446	0.934	1.066	0.821	0.997	1.002
1963	430956	547274	431364	272231	1860472	430956	820911	574577	34029	0.939	1.082	0.820	0.997	1.002
1964	459361	562951	458500	293499	1951195	459361	844427	610722	36687	0.936	1.072	0.814	0.997	1.001
1965	481353	590642	475702	313653	2040158	481353	885963	633635	39207	0.928	1.069	0.798	0.997	1.000
CANADA														
1925	25509	2603	481	8676	31139	25509	3905	641	1085	0.420	0.436	0.020	0.996	1.147
1929	31378	5376	807	16272	42551	31378	8064	1075	2034	0.434	0.477	0.026	0.996	1.087
1933	20123	4534	655	16018	29799	20123	6801	872	2002	0.444	0.497	0.036	1.000	1.052
1937	26499	6445	911	25334	40547	26499	9668	1213	3167	0.463	0.509	0.068	1.007	1.073
1938	23546	6441	940	23865	37443	23546	9662	1252	2983	0.481	0.515	0.144	1.007	1.077
1950	39877	17576	2070	50345	75292	39877	26364	2757	6293	0.411	0.400	0.223	0.928	1.036
1953	34053	25306	2808	64737	83845	34053	37959	3740	8092	0.501	0.390	0.435	1.019	1.036
1955	29476	31130	4264	71930	90842	29476	46695	5680	8991	0.592	0.415	0.565	1.001	1.059
1957	28253	35225	6496	79113	99633	28253	52838	8653	9889	0.670	0.384	0.703	0.959	1.054
1960	20378	40315	11886	100753	109277	20378	60473	15832	12594	0.744	0.441	0.651	1.246	1.051
1961	18627	41869	13965	101133	112673	18627	62804	18601	12642	0.821	0.454	0.737	1.330	1.028
1962	18791	41676	17042	102757	115850	18791	62514	22700	12845	0.927	0.442	0.821	1.573	1.013
1963	19751	46905	21741	103087	131953	19751	70358	28959	12886	0.905	0.438	0.791	1.455	1.007
1964	21577	48657	29007	112103	147212	21577	72986	38637	14013	0.927	0.426	0.823	1.374	1.011
1965	23409	53027	30638	116725	158350	23409	79541	40810	14591	0.908	0.398	0.809	1.359	1.000
UNITED STATES														
1925	532383	91743	33308	26803	717714	532383	137615	44366	3350	1.067	1.046	1.175	1.000	0.953
1929	558059	123904	53412	38997	819935	558059	185856	71145	4875	1.067	1.043	1.165	1.000	0.964
1933	355313	108976	43943	38208	582085	355313	163464	58532	4776	1.064	1.031	1.162	1.001	0.975
1937	459468	151808	68001	48082	783767	459468	227712	90577	6010	1.073	1.036	1.180	1.002	0.962
1938	364323	141878	64685	49113	669439	364323	212817	86160	6139	1.084	1.036	1.204	1.001	0.963
1950	508302	301662	170720	102692	1201030	508302	452493	227399	12837	1.005	1.056	0.948	1.005	0.984
1953	432795	361828	228889	111909	1294406	432795	542742	304880	13989	1.006	1.081	0.948	1.002	0.981
1955	419488	396599	255916	120606	1370342	419488	594899	340880	15076	1.002	1.121	0.919	1.002	0.966
1957	421645	419777	292006	137446	1457444	421645	629666	388952	17181	1.014	1.177	0.913	1.000	0.972
1960	381007	452056	354159	154075	1550090	381007	678084	471740	19259	0.951	1.093	0.844	0.988	0.970
1961	369067	467636	369259	157884	1582109	369067	701454	491853	19736	0.943	1.092	0.834	0.984	0.986
1962	383630	485518	391555	172808	1655060	383630	728277	521551	21601	0.935	1.097	0.821	0.972	0.995
1963	411135	500305	409623	169144	1728353	411135	750458	545618	21143	0.941	1.113	0.822	0.973	0.999
1964	437740	514212	429493	181396	1803817	437740	771318	572085	22675	0.937	1.104	0.813	0.972	0.994
1965	457907	537520	445064	196928	1881628	457907	806280	592825	24616	0.930	1.104	0.797	0.973	1.000
WESTERN EUROPE														
1925	496494	11103	7	30880	517017	496494	16655	9	3860	1.030	1.063	0.033	1.000	0.998
1929	572282	17348	9	42531	603632	572282	26022	12	5316	1.008	1.053	0.021	1.000	1.004
1933	447156	22187	15	46725	486297	447156	33281	20	5841	0.979	1.050	0.021	1.000	1.003
1937	563808	29162	38	64175	615624	563808	43743	51	8022	0.968	1.041	0.024	1.000	1.004
1938	563275	31768	19	65582	619150	563275	47652	25	8198	0.958	1.036	0.026	1.000	1.004
1950	489202	52652	1361	111317	583907	489202	78978	1813	13915	0.873	0.998	0.076	0.963	0.996
1953	532689	75434	3389	137975	657501	532689	113151	4514	17247	0.830	0.979	0.095	0.999	1.007
1955	565652	103517	5487	159628	748189	565652	155276	7309	19954	0.767	0.941	0.092	1.005	1.008
1957	591533	126993	7153	173986	813299	591533	190490	9528	21748	0.729	0.918	0.096	1.021	1.007
1960	529798	183097	12171	230947	849524	529798	274646	16212	28868	0.668	0.943	0.084	1.005	0.998
1961	522552	204641	14073	237880	877994	522552	306962	18745	29735	0.646	0.945	0.082	1.002	1.006
1962	533668	236673	15597	243687	939914	533668	355010	20775	30461	0.613	0.934	0.075	1.002	0.998
1963	540884	271877	16498	264501	1003737	540884	407816	21975	33063	0.577	0.918	0.069	1.002	0.999
1964	547109	312615	18326	259795	1072916	547109	468923	24410	32474	0.549	0.916	0.066	0.998	1.003
1965	525936	351044	20997	293943	1117213	525936	526566	27968	36743	0.517	0.918	0.060	0.961	0.999

Table X. TOTAL ENERGY CONSUMPTION AND RATIO OF PRODUCTION TO CONSUMPTION, SELECTED YEARS, 1925-1965

Region, country, year	Consumption in original units: Solid fuels (10^3 m.t. coal equiv.)	Liquid fuels (10^3 m.t.)	Natural gas (10^6 c.m.)	Hydro-electric power (10^6 kwh)	Consumption in coal equivalents (10^3 m.t.): Total	Solid fuels	Liquid fuels	Natural gas	Hydro-electric power	Ratio of production to consumption: Total	Solid fuels	Liquid fuels	Natural gas	Hydro-electric power
	(1)	(2)	(3)	(4)	(5)	(6)	(7)	(8)	(9)	(10)	(11)	(12)	(13)	(14)
EUROPEAN ECONOMIC COMMUNITY (EEC)														
1925	283457	4762	7	14809	292460	283457	7143	9	1851	0.922	0.945	0.033	1.000	0.951
1929	344466	7769	7	21177	358775	344466	11654	9	2647	0.914	0.944	0.024	1.000	0.954
1933	254340	10514	14	24015	273132	254340	15771	19	3002	0.912	0.967	0.033	1.000	0.953
1937	332756	14777	36	34562	359290	332756	22166	48	4320	0.939	0.999	0.037	1.000	0.954
1938	338237	16187	17	34163	366811	338237	24281	23	4270	0.938	1.002	0.040	1.000	0.952
1950	236587	23567	876	49466	279287	236587	35351	1167	6183	0.908	1.029	0.085	0.942	0.965
1953	270477	35701	2801	61540	335452	270477	53552	3731	7693	0.845	0.987	0.099	0.998	0.981
1955	287653	51225	4693	71827	379720	287653	76838	6251	8978	0.793	0.967	0.104	1.006	0.983
1957	312098	66517	6323	72012	429297	312098	99776	8422	9002	0.726	0.903	0.124	1.024	0.989
1960	280289	97082	10566	106212	453263	280289	145623	14074	13277	0.688	0.954	0.121	1.006	0.952
1961	277143	111872	12366	100384	473970	277143	167808	16472	12548	0.658	0.954	0.113	1.003	0.957
1962	279393	133119	13748	93699	509096	279393	199679	18312	11712	0.613	0.939	0.101	1.002	0.965
1963	288918	157330	14449	109743	557877	288918	235995	19246	13718	0.563	0.900	0.090	1.002	0.960
1964	294053	184667	16020	94585	604215	294053	277001	21339	11823	0.534	0.905	0.086	1.003	0.951
1965	277489	210465	18110	114690	631646	277489	315698	24123	14336	0.498	0.912	0.075	0.990	0.945
BELGIUM-LUXEMBOURG														
1925	30457	329	-	20	30953	30457	494	-	3	0.746	0.758	-	-	1.000
1929	36796	425	-	20	37436	36796	638	-	3	0.720	0.732	-	-	1.000
1933	27629	406	-	-	28238	27629	609	-	-	0.896	0.916	-	-	-
1937	33133	777	-	65	34307	33133	1166	-	8	0.871	0.901	-	-	0.877
1938	29685	772	-	49	30849	29685	1158	-	6	0.959	0.997	-	-	0.898
1950	27610	2049	5	124	30706	27610	3074	7	16	0.891	0.990	-	2.800	0.516
1953	30227	2937	45	35	34597	30227	4406	60	4	0.869	0.994	-	1.222	2.657
1955	28957	4660	57	222	36051	28957	6990	76	28	0.835	1.035	-	1.404	0.595
1957	32809	5881	74	36	41734	32809	8822	99	5	0.699	0.884	-	1.432	4.889
1960	27453	6902	43	213	37890	27453	10353	57	27	0.596	0.818	-	1.628	0.906
1961	26300	8299	43	-34	38802	26300	12449	57	-4	0.558	0.819	-	1.628	-7.294
1962	26608	9634	47	-153	41102	26608	14451	63	-19	0.519	0.798	-	1.489	-1.379
1963	29812	11536	42	630	47251	29812	17304	56	79	0.457	0.718	-	1.643	1.005
1964	29643	13020	43	1300	49393	29643	19530	57	163	0.435	0.719	-	1.535	0.707
1965	28241	14604	56	1910	50460	28241	21906	75	239	0.397	0.701	-	1.411	0.621
FRANCE														
1925	72156	1860	-	4580	75518	72156	2790	-	573	0.640	0.661	0.038	-	0.942
1929	84574	2716	-	7086	89534	84574	4074	-	886	0.619	0.644	0.029	-	0.931
1933	69822	4912	-	7910	78179	69822	7368	-	989	0.622	0.681	0.017	-	0.936
1937	72694	5989	-	11551	83121	72694	8984	-	1444	0.558	0.618	0.013	-	0.951
1938	67006	6511	-	10970	78144	67006	9767	-	1371	0.621	0.704	0.012	-	0.948
1950	62819	10678	239	16473	81213	62819	16017	318	2059	0.670	0.825	0.015	0.962	0.985
1953	65708	14212	270	21240	90040	65708	21318	360	2655	0.637	0.818	0.028	0.863	1.001
1955	66298	18801	315	25724	98134	66298	28202	420	3216	0.626	0.853	0.048	0.813	1.003
1957	80173	21998	570	25348	117098	80173	32997	759	3169	0.547	0.726	0.065	0.770	0.989
1960	71063	27458	2936	40647	121241	71063	41187	3911	5081	0.574	0.807	0.081	0.969	1.002
1961	67712	30095	4162	38690	123234	67712	45143	5544	4836	0.551	0.799	0.079	0.978	0.998
1962	67959	33020	4835	35384	128352	67959	49530	6440	4423	0.537	0.796	0.080	0.980	1.021
1963	70228	39893	4965	44391	142230	70228	59840	6613	5549	0.459	0.701	0.069	0.979	0.987
1964	73135	46345	5162	37290	154189	73135	69518	6876	4661	0.456	0.743	0.068	0.986	0.940
1965	68799	53355	5350	47866	161941	68799	80033	7126	5983	0.435	0.770	0.062	0.944	0.980
GERMANY														
1925	159540	1176	-	3081	161589	159540	1764	-	385	1.174	1.187	0.067	-	0.926
1929	194862	2515	-	3784	199107	194862	3773	-	473	1.166	1.189	0.041	-	0.942
1933	134189	2553	-	4540	138586	134189	3830	-	568	1.161	1.192	0.093	-	0.901
1937	199517	4151	21	7704	206734	199517	6227	28	963	1.180	1.214	0.109	1.000	0.896
1938	215092	4842	NA	8099	223368	215092	7263	NA	1012	1.114	1.149	0.114	NA	0.901
GERMANY, FEDERAL REPUBLIC														
1950	121330	3787	14	9928	128270	121330	5681	19	1241	1.199	1.244	0.295	4.500	0.872
1953	147614	6478	174	10649	158894	147614	9717	232	1331	1.097	1.149	0.338	1.178	0.879
1955	163377	10626	540	13182	181683	163377	15939	719	1648	1.021	1.093	0.296	1.143	0.912
1957	168645	15599	524	12588	194315	168645	23399	698	1574	0.982	1.081	0.255	1.506	0.979
1960	155227	30634	793	17152	204378	155227	45951	1056	2144	0.907	1.123	0.182	1.159	0.757
1961	156679	35330	823	17243	212926	156679	52995	1096	2155	0.879	1.117	0.176	1.126	0.749
1962	156686	45735	1181	15610	228813	156686	68603	1573	1951	0.821	1.113	0.148	1.096	0.804

Table X. TOTAL ENERGY CONSUMPTION AND RATIO OF PRODUCTION TO CONSUMPTION, SELECTED YEARS, 1925-1965

Region, country, year	Consumption in original units: Solid fuels (10^3 m.t. coal equiv.)	Liquid fuels (10^3 m.t.)	Natural gas (10^6 c.m.)	Hydro-electric power (10^6 kwh)	Consumption in coal equivalents (10^3 m.t.): Total	Solid fuels	Liquid fuels	Natural gas	Hydro-electric power	Ratio of production to consumption: Total	Solid fuels	Liquid fuels	Natural gas	Hydro-electric power
	(1)	(2)	(3)	(4)	(5)	(6)	(7)	(8)	(9)	(10)	(11)	(12)	(13)	(14)
GERMANY FEDERAL REPUBLIC (CONTINUED)														
1963	159448	53725	1563	14843	243973	159448	80588	2082	1855	0.787	1.111	0.138	1.075	0.834
1964	163709	64006	2263	13120	254372	163709	96009	3014	1640	0.736	1.089	0.120	1.044	0.927
1965	155431	74027	3124	19606	273084	155431	111041	4161	2451	0.682	1.082	0.107	1.030	0.784
ITALY														
1925	10854	793	7	7128	12944	10854	1190	9	891	0.106	0.044	0.010	1.000	0.968
1929	14911	1272	7	10265	18111	14911	1908	9	1283	0.093	0.028	0.005	1.000	0.975
1933	9838	1727	14	11544	13890	9838	2591	19	1443	0.134	0.039	0.015	1.000	0.985
1937	13936	2460	15	15217	19548	13936	3690	20	1902	0.154	0.078	0.006	1.000	0.987
1938	13520	2502	17	15027	19174	13520	3753	23	1878	0.174	0.107	0.005	1.000	0.984
1950	9170	3951	510	22981	18649	9170	5927	679	2873	0.247	0.115	0.003	1.000	0.991
1953	10241	8094	2280	29629	29123	10241	12141	3037	3704	0.278	0.111	0.017	1.000	1.002
1955	11314	11441	3627	32679	37391	11314	17162	4831	4085	0.277	0.091	0.023	1.000	0.999
1957	12512	15856	4987	34120	47204	12512	23784	6643	4265	0.292	0.075	0.084	1.000	0.987
1960	11018	21705	6447	48080	58173	11018	32558	8587	6010	0.318	0.075	0.095	1.000	1.003
1961	11191	25510	6863	44442	64153	11191	38265	9142	5555	0.293	0.094	0.080	1.000	0.996
1962	11936	31792	7150	42878	74508	11936	47688	9524	5360	0.250	0.091	0.059	1.000	0.970
1963	12346	36842	7267	49833	83518	12346	55263	9680	6229	0.232	0.071	0.050	1.000	0.974
1964	11411	43324	7684	42857	91989	11411	64986	10235	5357	0.221	0.065	0.063	1.000	0.977
1965	11207	48549	7800	45274	100079	11207	72824	10390	5659	0.200	0.055	0.047	1.000	0.993
NETHERLANDS														
1925	10451	604	-	-	11357	10451	906	-	-	0.633	0.688	-	-	-
1929	13323	841	-	22	14587	13323	1262	-	3	0.797	0.873	-	-	-
1933	12862	916	-	21	14239	12862	1374	-	3	0.885	0.980	-	-	-
1937	13476	1400	-	25	15579	13476	2100	-	3	0.922	1.066	-	-	-
1938	12934	1560	-	18	15277	12934	2340	-	2	0.887	1.047	-	-	-
1950	15658	3102	108	-40	20450	15658	4653	144	-5	0.654	0.786	0.227	0.074	-
1953	16687	3980	32	-13	22698	16687	5970	43	-2	0.601	0.742	0.206	0.719	-
1955	17707	5697	154	20	26460	17707	8546	205	3	0.518	0.677	0.180	0.909	-
1957	17958	7183	168	-80	28946	17958	10775	224	-10	0.482	0.639	0.212	0.917	-
1960	15529	10383	347	120	31581	15529	15575	462	15	0.501	0.805	0.185	0.988	-
1961	15261	12638	475	43	34856	15261	18957	633	5	0.468	0.827	0.162	0.981	-
1962	16203	12938	535	-20	36320	16203	19407	713	-3	0.427	0.714	0.167	0.983	-
1963	17084	15334	612	46	40906	17084	23001	815	6	0.382	0.674	0.144	0.977	-
1964	16155	17972	868	18	44271	16155	26958	1156	2	0.362	0.711	0.126	0.995	-
1965	13811	19930	1780	34	46081	13811	29895	2371	4	0.378	0.829	0.120	1.000	-
EUROPEAN FREE TRADE ASSOCIATION (EFTA)														
1925	196869	5680	-	13992	207138	196869	8520	-	1749	1.216	1.269	0.035	-	1.048
1929	208242	8443	-	18262	223190	208242	12665	-	2283	1.200	1.273	0.020	-	1.062
1933	177247	10230	-	18283	194877	177247	15345	-	2285	1.108	1.203	0.012	-	1.070
1937	217546	12654	-	24513	239592	217546	18981	-	3064	1.047	1.137	0.013	-	1.077
1938	208311	13767	-	25923	232202	208311	20651	-	3240	1.023	1.123	0.013	-	1.073
1950	226527	24162	471	51300	269810	226527	36243	627	6413	0.868	0.989	0.079	1.000	1.025
1953	234729	33096	564	61726	292840	234729	49644	751	7716	0.842	0.991	0.104	1.000	1.034
1955	247647	44749	760	68792	324382	247647	67124	1012	8599	0.759	0.930	0.087	1.000	1.036
1957	245195	50592	788	80852	332239	245195	75888	1050	10107	0.752	0.951	0.068	1.000	1.023
1960	212457	73021	1552	95723	336021	212457	109532	2067	11965	0.656	0.950	0.037	0.997	1.039
1961	207640	78631	1638	106104	341031	207640	117947	2182	13263	0.641	0.956	0.033	1.000	1.052
1962	215818	86603	1754	115725	352525	215818	129905	2336	14466	0.625	0.952	0.030	1.000	1.020
1963	211992	95637	1858	115877	372407	211992	143456	2475	14485	0.606	0.962	0.030	1.000	1.028
1964	210982	106063	2032	126796	388633	210982	159095	2707	15850	0.579	0.955	0.027	0.956	1.038
1965	204859	115556	2557	138504	398912	204859	173334	3406	17313	0.552	0.952	0.026	0.748	1.045
AUSTRIA														
1925	6722	123	-	1300	7069	6722	185	-	163	0.259	0.247	-	-	1.023
1929	8388	229	-	1630	8935	8388	344	-	204	0.245	0.235	-	-	1.074
1933	4797	314	-	1649	5474	4797	471	-	206	0.365	0.365	0.003	-	1.183
1937	5195	354	-	2050	5982	5195	531	-	256	0.372	0.361	0.093	-	1.167
1938	5695	386	-	2033	6528	5695	579	-	254	0.353	0.337	0.148	-	1.181
1950	7605	644	470	4298	9734	7605	966	626	537	0.633	0.311	2.638	1.000	1.161
1953	7197	1056	555	5340	10188	7197	1584	739	668	0.918	0.413	3.050	1.000	1.204
1955	8451	2379	748	6825	13868	8451	3569	996	853	0.792	0.414	1.541	1.000	1.158
1957	9219	2146	759	8080	14458	9219	3219	1011	1010	0.731	0.391	1.485	1.000	1.153

Table X. TOTAL ENERGY CONSUMPTION AND RATIO OF PRODUCTION TO CONSUMPTION, SELECTED YEARS, 1925-1965

Region, country, year	Consumption in original units: Solid fuels (10^3 m.t. coal equiv.)	Liquid fuels (10^3 m.t.)	Natural gas (10^6 c.m.)	Hydro-electric power (10^6 kwh)	Consumption in coal equivalents (10^3 m.t.): Total	Solid fuels	Liquid fuels	Natural gas	Hydro-electric power	Ratio of production to consumption: Total	Solid fuels	Liquid fuels	Natural gas	Hydro-electric power
	(1)	(2)	(3)	(4)	(5)	(6)	(7)	(8)	(9)	(10)	(11)	(12)	(13)	(14)
AUSTRIA (CONTINUED)														
1960	8087	2939	1469	9982	15699	8087	4409	1957	1248	0.653	0.388	0.833	1.000	1.190
1961	7459	3339	1556	9715	15754	7459	5009	2073	1214	0.635	0.394	0.706	1.000	1.201
1962	7748	3850	1635	10028	16954	7748	5775	2178	1254	0.604	0.382	0.622	1.000	1.209
1963	8473	4344	1699	10262	18535	8473	6516	2263	1283	0.584	0.370	0.604	1.000	1.165
1964	8106	5093	1764	10471	19404	8106	7640	2350	1309	0.566	0.368	0.523	1.000	1.259
1965	7332	5061	1724	12213	18746	7332	7592	2296	1527	0.607	0.380	0.565	1.000	1.317
DENMARK														
1925	4175	298	-	20	4624	4175	447	-	3	0.033	0.037	-	-	-
1929	5621	427	-	35	6266	5621	641	-	4	0.019	0.022	-	-	-
1933	5027	571	-	14	5886	5027	857	-	2	0.021	0.025	-	-	-
1937	6207	706	-	15	7268	6207	1059	-	2	0.025	0.029	-	-	-
1938	5562	860	-	24	6855	5562	1290	-	3	0.024	0.030	-	-	-
1950	6279	1682	-	205	8828	6279	2523	-	26	0.062	0.087	-	-	0.122
1953	6497	1896	-	326	9382	6497	2844	-	41	0.047	0.067	-	-	0.092
1955	7799	2954	-	-80	12220	7799	4431	-	-10	0.040	0.063	-	-	-0.375
1957	5402	3636	-	410	10907	5402	5454	-	51	0.093	0.186	-	-	0.073
1960	5968	4896	-	120	13327	5968	7344	-	15	0.055	0.122	-	-	0.167
1961	5662	5548	-	907	14097	5662	8322	-	113	0.054	0.135	-	-	0.029
1962	5986	6495	-	921	15844	5986	9743	-	115	0.048	0.127	-	-	0.028
1963	6022	7569	-	457	17433	6022	11354	-	57	0.043	0.124	-	-	0.055
1964	5392	8821	-	844	18729	5392	13232	-	106	0.035	0.120	-	-	0.030
1965	4799	9814	-	1761	19740	4799	14721	-	220	0.032	0.130	-	-	0.014
NORWAY														
1925	2553	194	-	6187	3617	2553	291	-	773	0.370	0.221	-	-	1.000
1929	3103	277	-	7516	4458	3103	416	-	940	0.306	0.137	-	-	1.000
1933	2783	442	-	7322	4361	2783	663	-	915	0.318	0.169	-	-	1.000
1937	3648	550	-	9257	5630	3648	825	-	1157	0.289	0.129	-	-	1.000
1938	3121	589	-	9918	5244	3121	884	-	1240	0.327	0.152	-	-	1.000
1950	2241	1263	-	17882	6370	2241	1895	-	2235	0.436	0.243	-	-	1.000
1953	1938	1961	-	19640	7334	1938	2942	-	2455	0.410	0.286	-	-	1.000
1955	1572	2499	-	22680	8155	1572	3749	-	2835	0.402	0.281	-	-	1.000
1957	1339	2622	-	25820	8499	1339	3933	-	3228	0.440	0.380	-	-	1.000
1960	1314	3313	-	31353	10203	1314	4970	-	3919	0.431	0.376	-	-	0.996
1961	1211	3425	-	33728	10564	1211	5138	-	4216	0.442	0.372	-	-	1.000
1962	1197	3551	-	37713	11238	1197	5327	-	4714	0.469	0.432	-	-	1.008
1963	1245	3931	-	38711	11980	1245	5897	-	4839	0.451	0.357	-	-	1.024
1964	1374	4321	-	42825	13209	1374	6482	-	5353	0.456	0.360	-	-	1.032
1965	1238	4231	-	47185	13482	1238	6347	-	5898	0.494	0.394	-	-	1.046
PORTUGAL														
1925	822	60	-	45	917	822	90	-	6	0.150	0.160	-	-	1.000
1929	1116	111	-	73	1291	1116	167	-	9	0.171	0.190	-	-	1.000
1933	1182	140	-	98	1404	1182	210	-	12	0.175	0.198	-	-	1.000
1937	1427	193	-	139	1733	1427	290	-	17	0.166	0.190	-	-	1.000
1938	1351	195	-	127	1659	1351	293	-	16	0.201	0.235	-	-	1.000
1950	1179	532	-	437	2032	1179	798	-	55	0.256	0.395	-	-	1.000
1953	986	853	-	999	2390	986	1280	-	125	0.267	0.521	-	-	1.000
1955	908	1077	-	1726	2739	908	1616	-	216	0.242	0.493	-	-	1.000
1957	1131	1311	-	1841	3328	1131	1967	-	230	0.247	0.523	-	-	1.000
1960	902	1392	-	3105	3378	902	2088	-	388	0.266	0.568	-	-	1.000
1961	1099	1497	-	3423	3772	1099	2246	-	428	0.259	0.500	-	-	1.000
1962	1012	1642	-	3512	3914	1012	2463	-	439	0.235	0.476	-	-	1.000
1963	1107	1783	-	3947	4275	1107	2675	-	493	0.231	0.440	-	-	1.014
1964	1125	1872	-	4208	4459	1125	2808	-	526	0.229	0.440	-	-	1.003
1965	1093	2179	-	4415	4913	1093	3269	-	552	0.198	0.433	-	-	0.902
SWEDEN														
1925	4456	296	-	3360	5320	4456	444	-	420	0.117	0.045	-	-	1.006
1929	6567	476	-	4542	7848	6567	714	-	568	0.110	0.044	-	-	1.008
1933	6319	753	-	4881	8059	6319	1130	-	610	0.108	0.041	-	-	1.003
1937	9301	1146	-	6956	11890	9301	1719	-	870	0.102	0.036	-	-	1.002
1938	8048	1294	-	7283	10899	8048	1941	-	910	0.113	0.039	-	-	1.003

Table X. TOTAL ENERGY CONSUMPTION AND RATIO OF PRODUCTION TO CONSUMPTION, SELECTED YEARS, 1925-1965

Region, country, year	Consumption in original units: Solid fuels (10^3 m.t. coal equiv.)	Liquid fuels (10^3 m.t.)	Natural gas (10^6 c.m.)	Hydro-electric power (10^6 kwh)	Consumption in coal equivalents (10^3 m.t.): Total	Solid fuels	Liquid fuels	Natural gas	Hydro-electric power	Ratio of production to consumption: Total	Solid fuels	Liquid fuels	Natural gas	Hydro-electric power
	(1)	(2)	(3)	(4)	(5)	(6)	(7)	(8)	(9)	(10)	(11)	(12)	(13)	(14)
SWEDEN (CONTINUED)														
1950	6908	3594	-	17158	14444	6908	5391	-	2145	0.177	0.044	0.015	-	1.010
1953	5863	5435	-	20983	16638	5863	8153	-	2623	0.185	0.054	0.012	-	1.014
1955	5857	7931	-	21770	20475	5857	11897	-	2721	0.154	0.056	0.010	-	0.994
1957	5265	9170	-	26722	22361	5265	13755	-	3340	0.174	0.067	0.010	-	1.015
1960	3851	12670	-	30320	26646	3851	19005	-	3790	0.162	0.073	0.008	-	1.025
1961	3515	12769	-	35540	27111	3515	19154	-	4443	0.184	0.072	0.008	-	1.028
1962	3420	14068	-	38302	29310	3420	21102	-	4788	0.178	0.053	0.007	-	1.021
1963	3385	15202	-	37956	30933	3385	22803	-	4745	0.163	0.052	0.005	-	0.999
1964	3643	16922	-	42888	34387	3643	25383	-	5361	0.166	0.050	0.005	-	1.005
1965	3111	17865	-	45618	35611	3111	26798	-	5702	0.170	0.049	0.003	-	1.018
SWITZERLAND														
1925	2708	148	-	3059	3312	2708	222	-	382	0.142	0.003	-	-	1.211
1929	3470	261	-	4301	4399	3470	392	-	538	0.153	0.002	-	-	1.235
1933	3167	393	-	3988	4255	3167	590	-	499	0.146	0.001	-	-	1.244
1937	3490	397	-	5341	4753	3490	596	-	668	0.182	0.001	-	-	1.289
1938	3340	409	-	5550	4647	3340	614	-	694	0.191	0.001	-	-	1.277
1950	2579	974	-	9841	5270	2579	1461	-	1230	0.253	0.012	-	-	1.060
1953	2214	1209	-	12541	5595	2214	1814	-	1568	0.305	0.005	-	-	1.081
1955	2620	1867	-	14170	7192	2620	2801	-	1771	0.272	0.004	-	-	1.097
1957	3330	2565	-	15227	9081	3330	3848	-	1903	0.220	0.003	-	-	1.043
1960	2610	3792	-	17710	10512	2610	5688	-	2214	0.227	0.004	-	-	1.075
1961	2270	4117	-	18943	10813	2270	6176	-	2368	0.260	0.004	-	-	1.184
1962	2340	4806	-	21237	12204	2340	7209	-	2655	0.220	0.004	-	-	1.007
1963	2830	6488	-	20892	15174	2830	9732	-	2612	0.181	0.004	-	-	1.049
1964	1990	6667	-	21748	14709	1990	10001	-	2719	0.195	0.005	-	-	1.054
1965	1582	7788	-	22629	16093	1582	11682	-	2829	0.189	0.006	-	-	1.073
UNITED KINGDOM														
1925	175435	4561	-	21	182279	175435	6842	-	3	1.357	1.408	0.044	-	1.000
1929	179979	6662	-	165	189993	179979	9993	-	21	1.381	1.456	0.025	-	1.000
1933	153972	7617	-	331	165439	153972	11426	-	41	1.273	1.367	0.016	-	1.000
1937	188279	9308	-	755	202335	188279	13962	-	94	1.209	1.297	0.014	-	1.000
1938	181195	10034	-	988	196370	181195	15051	-	124	1.176	1.273	0.013	-	1.000
1950	199737	15473	1	1479	223133	199737	23210	1	185	0.987	1.100	0.010	1.000	1.000
1953	210035	20686	9	1897	241313	210035	31029	12	237	0.946	1.085	0.008	1.000	1.000
1955	220441	26042	12	1701	259733	220441	39063	16	213	0.869	1.022	0.006	1.000	1.000
1957	219510	29142	29	2752	263606	219510	43713	39	344	0.864	1.035	0.005	1.000	1.000
1960	189726	44019	83	3133	256257	189726	66029	111	392	0.770	1.037	0.003	0.952	1.000
1961	186425	47936	82	3848	258919	186425	71904	109	481	0.751	1.038	0.003	1.000	1.001
1962	194116	52191	119	4012	273063	194116	78287	159	502	0.738	1.033	0.002	1.000	0.978
1963	188929	56320	159	3652	274077	188929	84480	212	457	0.729	1.053	0.002	1.000	1.003
1964	189353	62367	268	3812	283737	189353	93551	357	477	0.697	1.039	0.002	0.664	1.055
1965	185704	68618	833	4683	290326	185704	102927	1110	585	0.659	1.026	0.001	0.227	0.988
WESTERN EUROPE - OTHER														
1925	16168	661	-	2079	17419	16168	992	-	260	0.614	0.645	0.009	-	1.000
1929	19574	1136	2	3092	21667	19574	1704	3	387	0.588	0.631	0.005	1.000	1.000
1933	15569	1443	1	4427	18288	15569	2165	1	553	0.597	0.665	0.004	1.000	1.000
1937	13506	1731	2	5100	16743	13506	2597	3	638	0.453	0.513	0.004	1.000	1.000
1938	16726	1814	2	5496	20137	16726	2721	3	687	0.567	0.640	0.004	1.000	1.000
1950	26088	4923	14	10551	34810	26088	7385	19	1319	0.637	0.793	0.023	1.000	1.000
1953	27484	6637	24	14709	39310	27484	9956	32	1839	0.609	0.793	0.029	1.000	1.002
1955	30352	7543	34	19009	44088	30352	11315	45	2376	0.609	0.790	0.039	1.000	0.999
1957	34241	9884	42	21122	51763	34241	14826	56	2640	0.600	0.807	0.048	1.000	1.009
1960	37052	12994	53	29012	60240	37052	19491	71	3627	0.588	0.817	0.078	1.000	0.993
1961	37770	14138	69	31392	52992	37770	21207	92	3924	0.587	0.816	0.100	1.000	1.005
1962	38458	16951	95	34263	68293	38458	25427	127	4283	0.547	0.794	0.094	1.000	1.010
1963	39974	18910	191	38881	73453	39974	28365	254	4860	0.546	0.810	0.089	1.000	1.020
1964	42074	21885	274	38414	80068	42074	32828	365	4802	0.517	0.793	0.086	1.000	1.014
1965	43589	25023	330	40749	86656	43589	37535	440	5094	0.502	0.798	0.086	1.000	0.991
FINLAND														
1925	622	76	-	384	784	622	114	-	48	0.074	0.016	-	-	1.000
1929	1180	129	-	789	1472	1180	194	-	99	0.074	0.008	-	-	1.000

Table X. TOTAL ENERGY CONSUMPTION AND RATIO OF PRODUCTION TO CONSUMPTION, SELECTED YEARS, 1925-1965

Region, country, year	Consumption in original units: Solid fuels (10^3 m.t. coal equiv.)	Liquid fuels (10^3 m.t.)	Natural gas (10^6 c.m.)	Hydro-electric power (10^6 kwh)	Consumption in coal equivalents (10^3 m.t.): Total	Solid fuels	Liquid fuels	Natural gas	Hydro-electric power	Ratio of production to consumption: Total	Solid fuels	Liquid fuels	Natural gas	Hydro-electric power
	(1)	(2)	(3)	(4)	(5)	(6)	(7)	(8)	(9)	(10)	(11)	(12)	(13)	(14)
FINLAND (CONTINUED)														
1933	1147	119	-	1244	1481	1147	179	-	156	0.111	0.008	-	-	1.000
1937	2246	223	-	2066	2839	2246	335	-	258	0.095	0.005	-	-	1.000
1938	1797	248	-	2456	2476	1797	372	-	307	0.129	0.007	-	-	1.000
1950	2028	484	-	3650	3210	2028	726	-	456	0.173	0.049	-	-	1.000
1953	2078	715	-	4974	3772	2078	1073	-	622	0.191	0.047	-	-	1.001
1955	2710	1100	-	6190	5134	2710	1650	-	774	0.166	0.030	-	-	1.000
1957	3130	1871	-	6616	6763	3130	2807	-	827	0.136	0.029	-	-	1.000
1960	3200	2680	-	5689	7931	3200	4020	-	711	0.091	0.019	-	-	0.926
1961	3058	2961	-	8198	8524	3058	4442	-	1025	0.124	0.019	-	-	0.979
1962	2971	3488	-	9852	9435	2971	5232	-	1232	0.133	0.010	-	-	0.992
1963	2510	4249	-	8711	9972	2510	6374	-	1089	0.109	0.016	-	-	0.961
1964	3226	4884	-	9197	11702	3226	7326	-	1150	0.094	0.011	-	-	0.924
1965	3268	5669	-	10057	13028	3268	8504	-	1257	0.094	0.010	-	-	0.943
GREECE														
1925	734	64	-	8	831	734	96	-	1	0.087	0.097	-	-	1.000
1929	892	147	-	8	1114	892	221	-	1	0.071	0.087	-	-	1.000
1933	688	183	-	12	964	688	275	-	2	0.053	0.072	-	-	1.000
1937	1035	323	-	12	1521	1035	485	-	2	0.044	0.063	-	-	1.000
1938	1029	345	-	13	1548	1029	518	-	2	0.036	0.052	-	-	1.000
1950	392	926	-	10	1782	392	1389	-	1	0.051	0.230	-	-	1.000
1953	499	1116	-	31	2177	499	1674	-	4	0.104	0.445	-	-	1.000
1955	711	1331	-	332	2749	711	1997	-	42	0.157	0.550	-	-	1.000
1957	779	1414	-	360	2945	779	2121	-	45	0.185	0.641	-	-	1.000
1960	1506	1852	-	479	4343	1506	2778	-	60	0.307	0.847	-	-	0.979
1961	1482	1963	-	540	4494	1482	2945	-	68	0.294	0.845	-	-	1.026
1962	1557	2033	-	612	4683	1557	3050	-	77	0.304	0.865	-	-	1.003
1963	2028	2336	-	800	5632	2028	3504	-	100	0.330	0.867	-	-	1.008
1964	2191	2440	-	734	5943	2191	3660	-	92	0.336	0.868	-	-	1.020
1965	2915	3145	-	770	7728	2915	4718	-	96	0.336	0.859	-	-	0.971
ICELAND														
1950	98	180	-	168	389	98	270	-	21	0.058	0.015	-	-	1.000
1953	50	258	-	198	461	50	387	-	25	0.055	0.010	-	-	1.000
1955	60	247	-	379	478	60	371	-	47	0.099	-	-	-	1.000
1957	30	290	-	415	517	30	435	-	52	0.100	-	-	-	1.000
1960	20	366	-	523	634	20	549	-	65	0.103	-	-	-	1.000
1961	20	337	-	576	598	20	506	-	72	0.121	-	-	-	1.000
1962	20	363	-	593	639	20	545	-	74	0.116	-	-	-	1.000
1963	10	399	-	629	687	10	599	-	79	0.114	-	-	-	1.000
1964	10	408	-	653	704	10	612	-	82	0.116	-	-	-	1.000
1965	10	453	-	641	770	10	680	-	80	0.104	-	-	-	1.000
IRELAND														
1925	4141	119	-	10	4321	4141	179	-	1	0.430	0.448	-	-	1.000
1929	4396	165	-	31	4647	4396	248	-	4	0.409	0.432	-	-	1.000
1933	4180	189	-	113	4478	4180	284	-	14	0.423	0.450	-	-	1.000
1937	4572	243	-	249	4967	4572	365	-	31	0.399	0.427	-	-	1.000
1938	4356	251	-	296	4769	4356	377	-	37	0.389	0.417	-	-	1.000
1950	3722	547	-	466	4601	3722	821	-	58	0.388	0.465	-	-	1.000
1953	3855	686	-	533	4951	3855	1029	-	67	0.437	0.544	-	-	1.000
1955	3926	987	-	487	5467	3926	1481	-	61	0.375	0.506	-	-	1.000
1957	3475	985	-	702	5040	3475	1478	-	88	0.459	0.641	-	-	1.000
1960	3916	1100	-	932	5682	3916	1650	-	117	0.417	0.576	-	-	1.000
1961	3726	1263	-	737	5712	3726	1895	-	92	0.362	0.530	-	-	1.000
1962	3747	1515	-	660	6102	3747	2273	-	83	0.385	0.605	-	-	1.000
1963	3430	1748	-	656	6134	3430	2622	-	82	0.341	0.586	-	-	1.000
1964	3811	1940	-	783	6819	3811	2910	-	98	0.386	0.664	-	-	1.000
1965	3314	2203	-	939	6735	3314	3305	-	117	0.324	0.623	-	-	1.000
SPAIN														
1925	8044	283	-	1370	8639	8044	425	-	171	0.752	0.786	0.021	-	1.000
1929	9471	522	-	1982	10501	9471	783	-	248	0.722	0.774	0.011	-	1.000
1933	7006	778	-	2646	8503	7006	1167	-	331	0.763	0.878	0.006	-	1.000
1937	2558	769	-	2306	4000	2558	1154	-	288	0.621	0.855	0.008	-	1.000

Table X. TOTAL ENERGY CONSUMPTION AND RATIO OF PRODUCTION TO CONSUMPTION, SELECTED YEARS, 1925-1965

Region, country, year	Consumption in original units				Consumption in coal equivalents (10^3 m.t.)					Ratio of production to consumption				
	Solid fuels (10^3 m.t. coal equiv.)	Liquid fuels (10^3 m.t.)	Natural gas (10^6 c.m.)	Hydro-electric power (10^6 kwh)	Total	Solid fuels	Liquid fuels	Natural gas	Hydro-electric power	Total	Solid fuels	Liquid fuels	Natural gas	Hydro-electric power
	(1)	(2)	(3)	(4)	(5)	(6)	(7)	(8)	(9)	(10)	(11)	(12)	(13)	(14)
SPAIN (CONTINUED)														
1938	5973	766	-	2236	7402	5973	1149	-	280	0.813	0.960	0.008	-	1.000
1950	12524	2144	-	5079	16375	12524	3216	-	635	0.758	0.940	-	-	1.000
1953	14339	3113	-	7500	19946	14339	4670	-	938	0.715	0.927	0.005	-	1.000
1955	13855	3060	-	9051	19576	13855	4590	-	1131	0.742	0.963	0.011	-	0.993
1957	15666	4228	-	9640	23213	15666	6342	-	1205	0.711	0.970	0.017	-	1.003
1960	14959	5403	-	15474	24998	14959	8105	-	1934	0.669	0.980	0.012	-	1.010
1961	15247	5974	-	15735	26174	15247	8961	-	1967	0.647	0.973	0.011	-	1.016
1962	15737	7689	-	15820	29248	15737	11534	-	1978	0.549	0.886	0.008	-	1.016
1963	16092	8033	-	20316	30681	16092	12050	-	2540	0.552	0.883	0.008	-	1.041
1964	15386	9601	-	19089	32174	15386	14402	-	2386	0.503	0.877	0.007	-	1.082
1965	16320	10418	-	18916	34312	16320	15627	-	2365	0.500	0.895	0.006	-	1.034
YUGOSLAVIA														
1925	2628	85	-	300	2793	2628	128	-	38	0.789	0.824	-	-	1.000
1929	3614	138	2	275	3858	3614	207	3	34	0.795	0.839	-	1.000	1.000
1933	2533	122	1	403	2767	2533	183	1	50	0.839	0.895	0.008	1.000	1.000
1937	3084	114	2	450	3314	3084	171	3	56	0.838	0.880	0.009	1.000	1.000
1938	3558	153	2	470	3848	3558	230	3	59	0.820	0.870	0.007	1.000	1.000
1950	7285	558	14	1175	8287	7285	837	19	147	0.883	0.959	0.201	1.000	1.000
1953	6640	642	24	1470	7818	6640	963	32	184	0.840	0.917	0.271	1.000	1.020
1955	9059	690	34	2560	10459	9059	1035	45	320	0.854	0.902	0.377	1.000	1.020
1957	11147	941	42	3372	13036	11147	1412	56	422	0.822	0.863	0.425	1.000	1.044
1960	13449	1441	53	5894	16417	13449	2162	71	737	0.868	0.892	0.659	1.000	1.015
1961	14224	1489	69	5580	17246	14224	2234	92	698	0.899	0.892	0.904	1.000	1.014
1962	14421	1687	95	6695	17914	14421	2531	127	837	0.905	0.897	0.907	1.000	1.023
1963	15894	1948	191	7733	20037	15894	2922	254	967	0.900	0.903	0.830	1.000	1.038
1964	17441	2387	274	7917	22376	17441	3581	365	990	0.868	0.882	0.758	1.000	0.957
1965	17757	2917	330	9380	23745	17757	4376	440	1173	0.853	0.878	0.712	1.000	0.958
OCEANIA														
1925	14432	712	-	649	15581	14432	1068	-	81	1.027	1.103	-	-	1.000
1929	12858	1566	-	1087	15343	12858	2349	-	136	0.872	1.030	-	-	1.000
1933	10778	1431	-	1388	13098	10778	2147	-	174	0.889	1.064	0.001	-	1.000
1937	14330	2361	-	1956	18116	14330	3542	-	245	0.846	1.052	-	-	1.000
1938	13944	2615	-	2065	18125	13944	3923	-	258	0.826	1.055	-	-	1.000
1950	21103	5095	-	4439	29300	21103	7643	-	555	0.725	0.980	-	-	1.000
1953	22277	5571	-	5700	31346	22277	8357	-	713	0.742	1.012	-	-	1.000
1955	23937	8373	-	6603	37322	23937	12560	-	825	0.663	1.000	-	-	1.000
1957	24226	9343	-	8571	39312	24226	14015	-	1071	0.658	1.023	-	-	1.000
1960	27360	11479	-	9960	45824	27360	17219	-	1245	0.656	1.053	-	-	1.000
1961	27774	12371	-	10627	47659	27774	18557	-	1328	0.668	1.099	-	-	1.000
1962	27937	12830	-	12175	48704	27937	19245	-	1522	0.664	1.103	-	-	1.000
1963	28548	14704	3	13933	52349	28548	22056	4	1742	0.638	1.109	-	1.000	1.000
1964	29688	16334	3	15019	56070	29688	24501	4	1877	0.652	1.158	0.012	1.000	1.000
1965	31668	18243	4	17336	61205	31668	27365	5	2167	0.676	1.222	0.018	1.000	1.000
AUSTRALIA														
1925	12033	543	-	343	12890	12033	815	-	43	1.095	1.169	-	-	1.000
1929	10471	1259	-	440	12415	10471	1889	-	55	0.888	1.048	-	-	1.000
1933	9028	1160	-	533	10835	9028	1740	-	67	0.919	1.096	-	-	1.000
1937	12138	1888	-	716	15060	12138	2832	-	90	0.878	1.082	-	-	1.000
1938	11809	1994	-	679	14884	11809	2991	-	85	0.866	1.084	-	-	1.000
1950	18795	4224	-	1491	25318	18795	6336	-	186	0.737	0.983	-	-	1.000
1953	20061	4554	-	1691	27103	20061	6831	-	211	0.764	1.021	-	-	1.000
1955	21575	7018	-	1988	32351	21575	10527	-	249	0.683	1.012	-	-	1.000
1957	21710	7718	-	3093	33673	21710	11577	-	387	0.684	1.043	-	-	1.000
1960	24651	9681	-	4051	39679	24651	14522	-	506	0.677	1.069	-	-	1.000
1961	25139	10426	-	4271	41312	25139	15639	-	534	0.694	1.119	-	-	1.000
1962	25688	10823	-	4969	42544	25688	16235	-	621	0.690	1.118	-	-	1.000
1963	26147	12435	3	6652	45635	26147	18653	4	832	0.663	1.126	-	1.000	1.000
1964	27068	13733	3	6898	48534	27068	20600	4	862	0.684	1.184	0.014	1.000	1.000
1965	29206	15401	4	8367	53358	29206	23102	5	1046	0.714	1.251	0.022	1.000	1.000

Table X. TOTAL ENERGY CONSUMPTION AND RATIO OF PRODUCTION TO CONSUMPTION, SELECTED YEARS, 1925-1965

	Consumption in original units				Consumption in coal equivalents (10^3 m.t.)					Ratio of production to consumption				
Region, country, year	Solid fuels (10^3 m.t. coal equiv.)	Liquid fuels (10^3 m.t.)	Natural gas (10^6 c.m.)	Hydro-electric power (10^6 kwh)	Total	Solid fuels	Liquid fuels	Natural gas	Hydro-electric power	Total	Solid fuels	Liquid fuels	Natural gas	Hydro-electric power
	(1)	(2)	(3)	(4)	(5)	(6)	(7)	(8)	(9)	(10)	(11)	(12)	(13)	(14)
NEW ZEALAND														
1925	2271	164	-	306	2555	2271	246	-	38	0.733	0.808	-	-	1.000
1929	2252	296	-	647	2777	2252	444	-	81	0.839	0.999	-	-	1.000
1933	1640	259	-	855	2135	1640	389	-	107	0.787	0.959	0.004	-	1.000
1937	2020	448	-	1240	2847	2020	672	-	155	0.740	0.966	0.002	-	1.000
1938	1964	591	-	1386	3023	1964	887	-	173	0.689	0.972	0.002	-	1.000
1950	2223	820	-	2864	3811	2223	1230	-	358	0.671	0.989	0.001	-	1.000
1953	2063	915	-	3942	3928	2063	1373	-	493	0.651	1.000	0.001	-	1.000
1955	2110	1211	-	4530	4493	2110	1817	-	566	0.594	0.996	0.001	-	1.000
1957	2167	1445	-	5382	5007	2167	2168	-	673	0.565	0.995	0.001	-	1.000
1960	2437	1556	-	5512	5460	2437	2334	-	689	0.576	1.008	0.001	-	1.000
1961	2382	1675	-	5946	5637	2382	2513	-	743	0.555	1.000	0.001	-	1.000
1962	2094	1753	-	6779	5570	2094	2630	-	847	0.526	0.995	0.001	-	1.000
1963	2217	1940	-	6852	5984	2217	2910	-	857	0.514	1.000	0.001	-	1.000
1964	2326	2189	-	7753	6578	2326	3284	-	969	0.501	1.000	-	-	1.000
1965	2154	2430	-	8588	6873	2154	3645	-	1074	0.470	1.000	-	-	1.000
USSR AND COMMUNIST EASTERN EUROPE														
1925	66725	8178	1045	588	80457	66725	12267	1392	74	1.145	1.128	1.256	1.000	0.883
1929	107662	13190	1606	996	129710	107662	19785	2139	125	1.180	1.131	1.463	1.000	0.931
1933	114593	19520	3075	1646	148175	114593	29280	4096	206	1.179	1.098	1.522	1.000	0.992
1937	180144	30179	4722	5085	232338	180144	45269	6290	636	1.103	1.077	1.220	1.000	0.997
1938	187646	32952	4663	6029	244039	187646	49428	6211	754	1.083	1.067	1.153	1.000	1.000
1950	382888	45658	8174	14817	464115	382888	68487	10888	1852	1.026	1.034	0.986	0.996	1.015
1953	465799	61981	11425	21858	576721	465799	92972	15218	2732	1.026	1.023	1.046	0.998	1.000
1955	548852	80092	14086	27498	691190	548852	120138	18763	3437	1.034	1.027	1.075	0.998	0.995
1957	604922	104038	24863	43860	799579	604922	156057	33118	5483	1.036	1.022	1.098	0.998	1.000
1960	647876	138331	54034	57342	934513	647876	207497	71973	7168	1.064	1.029	1.195	1.000	0.997
1961	654821	150040	68526	65384	979331	654821	225060	91277	8173	1.073	1.031	1.228	1.000	1.000
1962	666952	168341	84596	79353	1042065	666952	252512	112682	9919	1.075	1.033	1.220	1.000	0.994
1963	697062	185680	102644	82706	1122642	697062	278520	136722	10338	1.074	1.032	1.218	1.000	0.994
1964	719414	196256	122619	83598	1187576	719414	294384	163329	10450	1.074	1.032	1.221	1.000	1.001
1965	737683	210516	143351	90873	1255760	737683	315774	190944	11359	1.076	1.031	1.231	1.000	1.000
COMMUNIST EASTERN EUROPE														
1925	50291	2399	905	337	55138	50291	3599	1205	42	1.181	1.176	1.326	1.000	0.795
1929	70095	3263	1276	439	76744	70095	4895	1700	55	1.227	1.198	1.718	1.000	0.843
1933	42705	2768	1965	483	49534	42705	4152	2617	60	1.369	1.239	2.948	1.000	0.973
1937	57787	3169	2543	894	66040	57787	4754	3387	112	1.319	1.237	2.560	1.000	0.983
1938	58771	3689	2453	938	67690	58771	5534	3267	117	1.284	1.228	2.058	1.000	1.000
1950	149588	5130	2438	2126	160796	149588	7695	3247	266	1.144	1.146	1.186	0.977	1.103
1953	187999	8404	4652	2657	207134	187999	12606	6196	332	1.093	1.085	1.259	0.975	1.001
1955	208152	9690	5245	4323	230214	208152	14535	6986	540	1.098	1.086	1.344	0.969	0.968
1957	231212	12471	6451	4431	259065	231212	18707	8593	554	1.027	1.027	1.055	0.967	1.000
1960	256806	16219	8974	6459	293895	256806	24329	11953	807	1.022	1.038	0.882	0.970	0.971
1961	270931	18131	9815	6336	311993	270931	27197	13074	792	1.006	1.028	0.812	0.970	0.990
1962	284412	20811	11373	7641	331733	284412	31217	15149	955	0.990	1.019	0.731	0.973	0.908
1963	298852	23866	13114	7594	353068	298852	35799	17468	949	0.973	1.011	0.657	0.976	0.840
1964	310144	27209	14346	7541	371008	310144	40814	19109	943	0.958	1.006	0.587	0.978	0.838
1965	307188	30107	16077	10943	375131	307188	45161	21415	1368	0.955	1.014	0.543	0.976	0.867
ALBANIA														
1950	31	92	-	-	168	31	138	-	-	1.297	0.672	1.435	-	-
1953	73	99	-	20	223	73	148	-	3	1.246	0.724	1.505	-	1.000
1955	78	105	-	27	238	78	158	-	3	1.732	1.258	1.981	-	1.000
1957	118	285	-	60	553	118	428	-	8	1.556	1.000	1.719	-	1.000
1960	156	409	-	121	784	156	614	-	15	1.597	0.936	1.780	-	1.000
1961	155	491	-	108	905	155	737	-	14	1.453	0.935	1.570	-	1.000
1962	171	531	-	118	982	171	797	-	15	1.368	0.883	1.478	-	1.000
1963	136	445	-	168	825	136	668	-	21	1.545	0.926	1.688	-	1.000
1964	156	501	-	203	933	156	752	-	25	1.412	0.936	1.525	-	1.000
1965	190	439	-	250	880	190	659	-	31	1.598	0.921	1.822	-	1.000
BULGARIA														
1925	423	43	-	17	489	423	65	-	2	0.836	0.962	-	-	1.000
1929	549	84	-	49	681	549	126	-	6	0.818	1.004	-	-	1.000

Table X. TOTAL ENERGY CONSUMPTION AND RATIO OF PRODUCTION TO CONSUMPTION, SELECTED YEARS, 1925-1965

	Consumption in original units				Consumption in coal equivalents (10^3 m.t.)					Ratio of production to consumption				
Region, country, year	Solid fuels (10^3 m.t. coal equiv.)	Liquid fuels (10^3 m.t.)	Natural gas (10^6 c.m.)	Hydro-electric power (10^6 kwh)	Total	Solid fuels	Liquid fuels	Natural gas	Hydro-electric power	Total	Solid fuels	Liquid fuels	Natural gas	Hydro-electric power
	(1)	(2)	(3)	(4)	(5)	(6)	(7)	(8)	(9)	(10)	(11)	(12)	(13)	(14)
BULGARIA (CONTINUED)														
1933	533	66	-	77	642	533	99	-	10	0.839	0.992	-	-	1.000
1937	641	87	-	134	788	641	131	-	17	0.834	1.000	-	-	1.000
1938	717	88	-	141	866	717	132	-	18	0.861	1.017	-	-	1.000
1950	1888	240	-	306	2287	1888	360	-	38	0.843	1.000	-	-	1.000
1953	2692	335	-	453	3251	2692	503	-	57	0.845	1.000	-	-	1.000
1955	3320	370	-	648	3956	3320	555	-	81	0.891	0.970	0.405	-	1.000
1957	3554	532	-	850	4458	3554	798	-	106	0.928	1.014	0.536	-	1.000
1960	5455	989	-	1886	7174	5455	1484	-	236	0.799	0.952	0.202	-	1.000
1961	6431	1245	-	1796	8523	6431	1868	-	225	0.729	0.883	0.166	-	1.000
1962	7547	1706	-	1763	10327	7547	2559	-	220	0.666	0.844	0.117	-	0.961
1963	8261	2198	-	2169	11829	8261	3297	-	271	0.614	0.816	0.079	-	0.962
1964	10034	3202	-	1447	15018	10034	4803	-	181	0.543	0.771	0.050	-	1.017
1965	10737	3676	-	1998	16501	10737	5514	-	250	0.515	0.736	0.062	-	1.001
CZECHOSLOVAKIA														
1925	21933	204	-	194	22263	21933	306	-	24	1.068	1.082	0.113	-	0.902
1929	28153	367	2	236	28735	28153	551	3	30	1.048	1.068	0.038	1.000	0.915
1933	18252	361	1	252	18826	18252	542	1	32	1.043	1.072	0.050	1.000	0.933
1937	24445	476	1	572	25232	24445	714	1	72	1.090	1.121	0.038	1.000	0.974
1938	23420	382	1	600	24070	23420	573	1	75	1.062	1.087	0.050	1.000	1.000
1950	35731	694	19	1200	36948	35731	1041	25	150	0.953	0.978	0.092	1.000	0.917
1953	40955	1007	168	1052	42821	40955	1510	224	132	0.936	0.965	0.121	1.000	0.964
1955	46944	1098	173	1800	49046	46944	1647	230	225	0.932	0.961	0.097	1.000	1.072
1957	52693	1564	772	1891	56303	52693	2346	1028	236	0.970	1.009	0.069	1.000	1.122
1960	59936	2662	1294	2225	65931	59936	3993	1724	278	0.963	1.022	0.051	1.000	1.121
1961	64755	3239	1259	2189	71564	64755	4859	1677	274	0.945	1.010	0.048	1.003	1.153
1962	68690	4037	1064	3073	76547	68690	6056	1417	384	0.926	1.002	0.044	1.004	0.979
1963	72422	4386	994	2431	80629	72422	6579	1324	304	0.918	0.996	0.041	1.004	0.942
1964	74320	5372	939	3429	84057	74320	8058	1251	429	0.898	0.990	0.036	1.004	0.795
1965	72302	6026	846	5218	83120	72302	9039	1127	652	0.886	0.991	0.032	1.005	0.854
GERMANY, EAST														
1950	49511	100	36	-130	49693	49511	150	48	-16	0.890	0.892	-	-	-2.077
1953	62124	250	36	240	62577	62124	375	48	30	0.875	0.881	-	-	1.708
1955	69506	100	36	490	69765	69506	150	48	61	0.906	0.908	-	-	1.020
1957	72923	367	54	153	73564	72923	551	72	19	0.909	0.916	-	-	3.157
1960	78251	1537	54	247	80659	78251	2306	72	31	0.876	0.902	-	-	2.498
1961	82039	1851	40	304	84907	82039	2777	53	38	0.873	0.902	-	-	2.224
1962	85693	2148	32	527	89023	85693	3222	43	66	0.865	0.898	-	-	1.159
1963	87739	2721	124	545	92053	87739	4082	165	68	0.860	0.900	-	0.815	1.004
1964	90048	3519	122	683	95574	90048	5279	163	85	0.836	0.885	-	0.885	0.785
1965	87842	4062	142	877	94234	87842	6093	189	110	0.829	0.886	-	0.937	0.895
HUNGARY														
1925	4842	66	-	5	4942	4842	99	-	1	0.833	0.850	-	-	1.000
1929	6605	205	-	9	6914	6605	308	-	1	0.731	0.765	-	-	1.000
1933	4507	175	2	12	4774	4507	263	3	2	0.911	0.964	-	1.000	1.000
1937	6160	282	4	15	6590	6160	423	5	2	0.874	0.933	0.007	1.000	1.000
1938	6367	253	8	20	6759	6367	380	11	3	0.904	0.948	0.170	1.000	1.000
1950	9131	562	381	70	10490	9131	843	507	9	0.935	0.933	0.911	1.000	1.000
1953	14793	946	549	174	16965	14793	1419	731	22	0.908	0.906	0.894	1.000	0.253
1955	16116	1599	545	296	19277	16116	2399	726	37	0.913	0.898	1.001	1.000	0.155
1957	16973	1689	411	352	20098	16973	2534	547	44	0.756	0.803	0.400	1.000	0.119
1960	19693	2268	527	634	23876	19693	3402	702	79	0.812	0.866	0.549	0.649	0.148
1961	21103	2604	527	580	25784	21103	3906	702	73	0.806	0.859	0.565	0.615	0.141
1962	21347	2853	543	644	26430	21347	4280	723	81	0.812	0.868	0.580	0.626	0.127
1963	23491	3515	818	1011	29980	23491	5273	1090	126	0.776	0.842	0.504	0.747	0.080
1964	25164	3822	1009	1155	32385	25164	5733	1344	144	0.752	0.818	0.474	0.777	0.064
1965	24537	3937	1305	1370	32352	24537	5906	1738	171	0.767	0.840	0.460	0.848	0.055
POLAND														
1925	21098	537	535	70	22625	21098	806	713	9	1.373	1.379	1.549	1.000	0.286
1929	32505	534	467	84	33939	32505	801	622	11	1.413	1.423	1.328	1.000	0.417
1933	18267	439	462	31	19545	18267	659	615	4	1.477	1.498	1.351	1.000	1.129
1937	25031	462	531	48	26438	25031	693	707	6	1.428	1.447	1.169	1.000	1.000

Table X. TOTAL ENERGY CONSUMPTION AND RATIO OF PRODUCTION TO CONSUMPTION, SELECTED YEARS, 1925-1965

	Consumption in original units				Consumption in coal equivalents (10^3 m.t.)					Ratio of production to consumption				
Region, country, year	Solid fuels (10^3 m.t. coal equiv.)	Liquid fuels (10^3 m.t.)	Natural gas (10^6 c.m.)	Hydro-electric power (10^6 kwh)	Total	Solid fuels	Liquid fuels	Natural gas	Hydro-electric power	Total	Solid fuels	Liquid fuels	Natural gas	Hydro-electric power
	(1)	(2)	(3)	(4)	(5)	(6)	(7)	(8)	(9)	(10)	(11)	(12)	(13)	(14)
POLAND (CONTINUED)														
1938	26340	540	584	50	27934	26340	810	778	6	1.422	1.447	1.015	1.000	1.000
1950	50662	642	202	480	51954	50662	963	269	60	1.540	1.568	0.276	0.901	0.833
1953	63573	1109	399	498	65830	63573	1664	531	62	1.385	1.422	0.187	0.799	1.000
1955	67780	1499	519	769	70815	67780	2249	691	96	1.373	1.421	0.133	0.757	0.922
1957	79848	1881	581	835	83548	79848	2822	774	104	1.159	1.201	0.106	0.721	0.689
1960	87276	2435	783	979	92094	87276	3653	1043	122	1.177	1.229	0.087	0.701	0.673
1961	90217	2826	995	932	95898	90217	4239	1325	117	1.158	1.216	0.079	0.738	0.664
1962	93431	3147	1100	897	99729	93431	4721	1465	112	1.148	1.209	0.071	0.746	0.863
1963	98743	3760	1280	737	106180	98743	5640	1705	92	1.125	1.193	0.062	0.768	0.906
1964	102139	4136	1523	35	110376	102139	6204	2029	4	1.138	1.209	0.073	0.808	20.743
1965	102213	4651	1752	556	111592	102213	6977	2334	70	1.148	1.229	0.078	0.787	1.642
ROMANIA														
1925	2095	1544	370	51	4910	2095	2316	493	6	1.196	0.899	1.507	1.000	1.000
1929	2181	2066	807	61	6363	2181	3099	1075	8	1.632	0.906	2.363	1.000	1.000
1933	1044	1717	1500	111	5632	1044	2576	1998	14	2.542	0.942	4.395	1.000	1.000
1937	1508	1820	2007	125	6927	1508	2730	2673	16	2.210	0.949	4.098	1.000	1.000
1938	1922	2410	1860	127	8030	1922	3615	2478	16	1.822	0.953	2.851	1.000	1.000
1950	2634	2800	1800	200	9256	2634	4200	2398	25	1.365	0.916	1.857	1.000	1.000
1953	3790	4658	3500	220	15467	3790	6987	4662	28	1.412	0.860	1.988	1.000	1.000
1955	4409	4919	3972	293	17115	4409	7379	5291	37	1.473	0.848	2.187	1.000	1.102
1957	5103	6153	4633	290	20540	5103	9230	6171	36	1.346	0.849	1.853	1.000	1.034
1960	6040	5919	6316	367	23377	6040	8879	8413	46	1.345	0.833	1.992	1.032	1.082
1961	6232	5875	6994	427	24414	6232	8813	9316	53	1.345	0.860	2.024	1.029	1.091
1962	7533	6389	8634	619	28695	7533	9584	11500	77	1.264	0.814	1.907	1.024	1.053
1963	8060	6841	9898	533	31572	8060	10262	13184	67	1.234	0.814	1.839	1.021	1.008
1964	8282	6657	10753	589	32664	8282	9986	14323	74	1.242	0.820	1.915	1.019	0.993
1965	9367	7316	12032	674	36452	9367	10974	16027	84	1.198	0.835	1.770	1.016	1.491
USSR (INCLUDING ESTONIA, LATVIA, LITHUANIA)														
1925	16434	5779	140	251	25320	16434	8669	186	31	1.065	0.980	1.226	1.000	1.000
1929	37567	9927	330	557	52966	37567	14891	440	70	1.111	1.006	1.379	1.000	1.000
1933	71889	16752	1110	1163	98640	71889	25128	1479	145	1.083	1.014	1.287	1.000	1.000
1937	122357	27010	2179	4191	166298	122357	40515	2902	524	1.017	1.002	1.062	1.000	1.000
1938	128875	29263	2210	5091	176349	128875	43895	2944	636	1.006	0.994	1.039	1.000	1.000
1950	233300	40528	5736	12691	303319	233300	60792	7640	1586	0.963	0.962	0.961	1.004	1.000
1953	277800	53577	6773	19201	369587	277800	80366	9022	2400	0.988	0.980	1.013	1.014	1.000
1955	340700	70402	8841	23175	460976	340700	105603	11776	2897	1.002	0.990	1.038	1.016	1.000
1957	373710	91567	18412	39429	540514	373710	137351	24525	4929	1.040	1.019	1.104	1.009	1.000
1960	391070	122112	45060	50883	640618	391070	183168	60020	6360	1.083	1.024	1.237	1.005	1.001
1961	383890	131909	58711	59048	667338	383890	197864	78203	7381	1.104	1.033	1.285	1.005	1.001
1962	382540	147530	73223	71712	710332	382540	221295	97533	8964	1.114	1.044	1.289	1.004	1.003
1963	398210	161814	89530	75112	769574	398210	242721	119254	9389	1.120	1.048	1.300	1.003	1.010
1964	409270	169047	108273	76057	816567	409270	253571	144220	9507	1.127	1.053	1.323	1.003	1.017
1965	430495	180409	127274	79930	880629	430495	270614	169529	9991	1.128	1.043	1.346	1.003	1.019
COMMUNIST ASIA														
1925	22289	941	-	-	23701	22289	1412	-	-	0.952	1.012	-	-	-
1929	22156	1076	-	-	23770	22156	1614	-	-	1.012	1.085	0.005	-	-
1933	23148	1191	-	-	24935	23148	1787	-	-	1.064	1.140	0.076	-	-
1937	29092	1273	-	-	31002	29092	1910	-	-	1.117	1.180	0.157	-	-
1938	25833	998	-	-	27330	25833	1497	-	-	1.102	1.150	0.281	-	-
1950	42320	100	-	5280	43130	42320	150	-	660	1.008	1.005	2.000	-	1.000
1953	65398	622	-	2560	66651	65398	933	-	320	1.000	1.000	1.000	-	1.000
1955	94003	2341	-	6200	98290	94003	3512	-	775	0.989	1.011	0.413	-	1.000
1957	124856	3777	-	10302	131809	124856	5666	-	1288	0.987	1.014	0.392	-	1.000
1960	219260	9099	-	19304	235321	219260	13649	-	2413	0.981	1.004	0.608	-	1.000
1961	248558	9606	-	16500	265029	248558	14409	-	2063	0.985	1.005	0.648	-	1.000
1962	250653	9318	-	17000	266755	250653	13977	-	2125	0.991	1.005	0.732	-	1.000
1963	270076	9774	-	17500	286924	270076	14661	-	2188	0.993	1.005	0.769	-	1.000
1964	290703	9973	-	19000	308037	290703	14960	-	2375	0.997	1.004	0.854	-	1.000
1965	303818	11046	-	21000	323012	303818	16569	-	2625	1.000	1.005	0.907	-	1.000

Table X. TOTAL ENERGY CONSUMPTION AND RATIO OF PRODUCTION TO CONSUMPTION, SELECTED YEARS, 1925-1965

Region, country, year	Consumption in original units: Solid fuels (10^3 m.t. coal equiv.)	Liquid fuels (10^3 m.t.)	Natural gas (10^6 c.m.)	Hydro-electric power (10^6 kwh)	Consumption in coal equivalents (10^3 m.t.): Total	Solid fuels	Liquid fuels	Natural gas	Hydro-electric power	Ratio of production to consumption: Total	Solid fuels	Liquid fuels	Natural gas	Hydro-electric power
	(1)	(2)	(3)	(4)	(5)	(6)	(7)	(8)	(9)	(10)	(11)	(12)	(13)	(14)
LATIN AMERICA														
1925	9280	9324	772	3155	24688	9280	13986	1028	394	1.615	0.355	2.514	0.997	1.000
1929	9331	13035	1474	3950	31341	9331	19553	1963	494	1.837	0.328	2.663	0.997	1.000
1933	6992	8353	2045	4610	22822	6992	12530	2724	576	2.213	0.387	3.558	0.971	0.995
1937	9767	16174	3304	5920	39169	9767	24261	4401	740	1.924	0.433	2.728	0.959	0.997
1938	9269	16026	3456	6312	38701	9269	24039	4603	789	1.939	0.454	2.725	0.986	0.997
1950	8641	32319	5494	14352	66232	8641	48479	7318	1794	2.539	0.682	3.178	0.881	0.991
1953	9202	40117	7653	18622	81899	9202	60176	10194	2328	2.405	0.744	2.964	0.929	0.988
1955	10088	53560	9170	21869	105376	10088	80340	12214	2734	2.251	0.730	2.684	0.939	0.992
1957	10120	67307	11135	27719	129377	10120	100961	14832	3465	2.298	0.727	2.689	1.016	0.985
1960	11135	75935	18052	35116	153472	11135	113903	24045	4390	2.170	0.729	2.590	1.065	0.987
1961	11082	80093	20083	36506	162536	11082	120140	26751	4563	2.150	0.773	2.562	1.066	0.988
1962	11102	84911	22305	39520	173119	11102	127367	29710	4940	2.192	0.822	2.625	1.052	0.987
1963	11643	84944	24346	41960	176733	11643	127416	32429	5245	2.206	0.802	2.679	1.046	0.986
1964	12412	90018	27901	45437	190282	12412	135027	37164	5680	2.157	0.800	2.636	1.043	0.997
1965	12677	94364	29176	51430	199514	12677	141546	38862	6429	2.114	0.798	2.577	1.043	0.999
LATIN AMERICA - CARIBBEAN														
1925	2381	5699	219	1070	11355	2381	8549	292	134	2.985	0.659	3.732	0.991	1.000
1929	1956	7290	688	1395	13982	1956	10935	916	174	3.517	0.603	4.290	0.994	1.000
1933	1120	3732	1052	1649	8325	1120	5598	1401	206	4.895	0.682	6.870	0.944	0.987
1937	2133	9379	2027	2375	19198	2133	14069	2700	297	3.283	0.783	4.161	0.933	0.992
1938	1921	8536	2250	2488	18033	1921	12804	2997	311	3.481	0.787	4.531	0.978	0.993
1950	2026	16878	4002	3899	33161	2026	25317	5331	487	4.580	0.961	5.727	0.837	0.967
1953	2816	20941	5862	5123	42676	2816	31412	7808	640	4.173	0.956	5.338	0.908	0.958
1955	3410	28021	7201	6457	55840	3410	42032	9592	807	3.871	0.945	4.837	0.922	0.974
1957	3696	37707	8619	7445	72668	3696	56561	11481	931	3.742	0.935	4.524	1.020	0.945
1960	4517	41878	14251	9858	87549	4517	62817	18982	1232	3.369	0.976	4.279	1.082	0.954
1961	4619	43733	14959	9819	91371	4619	65600	19925	1227	3.317	0.974	4.204	1.088	0.954
1962	5160	46224	16001	11005	97185	5160	69336	21313	1376	3.374	0.953	4.310	1.072	0.952
1963	5597	46682	17393	12737	100380	5597	70023	23167	1592	3.354	0.949	4.359	1.065	0.954
1964	5520	48987	20552	13997	108125	5520	73481	27375	1750	3.283	0.935	4.342	1.059	0.989
1965	5662	52016	21259	16089	114014	5662	78024	28317	2011	3.204	0.925	4.204	1.059	0.996
CARIBBEAN - OIL PRODUCING														
1925	1656	4018	219	941	8092	1656	6027	292	118	4.186	0.947	5.293	0.991	1.000
1929	1260	5650	688	1231	10805	1260	8475	916	154	4.549	0.936	5.536	0.994	1.000
1933	801	2877	1052	1427	6696	801	4316	1401	178	6.080	0.954	8.910	0.944	0.985
1937	1697	7896	2027	2056	16498	1697	11844	2700	257	3.817	0.985	4.942	0.933	0.991
1938	1559	7249	2250	2147	15698	1559	10874	2997	268	3.994	0.969	5.333	0.978	0.992
1950	1982	12982	3999	3016	27159	1982	19473	5327	377	5.587	0.982	7.444	0.837	0.957
1953	2737	16582	5858	4180	35935	2737	24873	7803	523	4.952	0.983	6.741	0.908	0.948
1955	3283	22351	7197	5347	47064	3283	33527	9586	668	4.588	0.982	6.061	0.922	0.968
1957	3516	29919	8616	6303	60659	3516	44879	11477	788	4.479	0.983	5.700	1.020	0.935
1960	4457	32810	14249	8306	73690	4457	49215	18980	1038	3.999	0.989	5.461	1.082	0.946
1961	4569	34347	14956	8228	77039	4569	51521	19921	1029	3.932	0.985	5.352	1.088	0.945
1962	5100	35157	15998	9421	80322	5100	52736	21309	1178	4.080	0.965	5.666	1.072	0.944
1963	5503	35607	17389	10939	83443	5503	53411	23162	1367	4.032	0.965	5.714	1.065	0.946
1964	5401	36208	20549	12166	88605	5401	54312	27371	1521	4.003	0.956	5.874	1.059	0.988
1965	5530	38745	21256	13938	93703	5530	58117	28313	1742	3.895	0.947	5.644	1.059	0.996
COLOMBIA														
1925	103	153	-	92	344	103	230	-	12	0.952	0.971	0.941	-	1.000
1929	101	424	-	100	750	101	636	-	13	5.976	0.990	6.866	-	1.000
1933	114	161	-	108	369	114	242	-	14	7.795	0.982	11.391	-	1.000
1937	423	284	-	181	872	423	426	-	23	5.341	0.998	9.884	-	1.000
1938	412	359	-	206	976	412	539	-	26	5.033	1.000	8.312	-	1.000
1950	1010	681	-	725	2122	1010	1022	-	91	3.849	1.000	6.918	-	1.000
1953	1230	1318	-	1008	3333	1230	1977	-	126	2.861	1.000	4.138	-	1.000
1955	1850	2126	-	1480	5224	1850	3189	-	185	1.967	1.000	2.584	-	1.000
1957	1990	2223	-	2013	5576	1990	3335	-	252	2.106	1.005	2.846	-	1.000
1960	2600	2649	404	2587	7435	2600	3974	538	323	2.018	1.000	2.905	1.000	1.000
1961	2650	3037	417	2513	8075	2650	4556	555	314	1.800	1.000	2.419	1.000	1.000
1962	3000	3089	592	2762	8767	3000	4634	789	345	1.697	1.000	2.319	1.000	1.000
1963	3200	3458	702	3218	9724	3200	5187	935	402	1.751	1.000	2.409	1.000	1.000
1964	2998	3558	834	3721	9911	2998	5337	1111	465	1.771	1.001	2.431	1.000	1.000
1965	3198	3639	917	3900	10365	3198	5459	1221	488	1.945	1.001	2.795	1.000	1.000

Table X. TOTAL ENERGY CONSUMPTION AND RATIO OF PRODUCTION TO CONSUMPTION, SELECTED YEARS, 1925-1965

Region, country, year	Consumption in original units				Consumption in coal equivalents (10^3 m.t.)					Ratio of production to consumption				
	Solid fuels (10^3 m.t. coal equiv.)	Liquid fuels (10^3 m.t.)	Natural gas (10^6 c.m.)	Hydro-electric power (10^6 kwh)	Total	Solid fuels	Liquid fuels	Natural gas	Hydro-electric power	Total	Solid fuels	Liquid fuels	Natural gas	Hydro-electric power
	(1)	(2)	(3)	(4)	(5)	(6)	(7)	(8)	(9)	(10)	(11)	(12)	(13)	(14)
MEXICO														
1925	1510	3477	152	828	7031	1510	5216	202	104	4.009	0.956	5.070	0.987	1.000
1929	1116	3425	224	1106	6690	1116	5138	298	138	1.727	0.944	1.960	0.982	1.000
1933	659	2184	372	1290	4592	659	3276	496	161	1.936	0.982	2.341	0.841	0.984
1937	1255	3904	1112	1841	8822	1255	5856	1481	230	1.461	0.990	1.728	0.878	0.990
1938	1107	3958	1158	1889	8823	1107	5937	1542	236	1.261	0.987	1.402	0.958	0.990
1950	943	8055	2407	2079	16491	943	12083	3206	260	1.170	0.967	1.308	0.729	0.937
1953	1474	8970	3185	2839	19526	1474	13455	4242	355	1.082	0.972	1.177	0.830	0.924
1955	1402	10751	3951	3617	23243	1402	16127	5263	452	1.111	0.957	1.211	0.859	0.953
1957	1491	13044	4392	4130	27423	1491	19566	5850	516	1.007	0.953	1.003	1.040	0.901
1960	1822	14834	8494	5624	36090	1822	22251	11314	703	1.060	0.973	1.032	1.138	0.920
1961	1878	14988	8890	5565	36897	1878	22482	11841	696	1.104	0.968	1.098	1.148	0.918
1962	1953	14851	9358	6008	37445	1953	22277	12465	751	1.130	0.969	1.155	1.124	0.912
1963	2131	15564	10245	6615	39950	2131	23346	13646	827	1.115	0.972	1.139	1.110	0.911
1964	2207	16520	12523	7222	44570	2207	24780	16681	903	1.090	0.964	1.100	1.097	0.980
1965	2116	16682	12717	8669	45162	2116	25023	16939	1084	1.096	0.948	1.111	1.098	0.993
TRINIDAD AND TOBAGO														
1925	14	83	67	-	228	14	125	89	-	4.410	-	7.349	1.000	-
1929	17	40	134	-	255	17	60	178	-	7.844	-	30.425	1.000	-
1933	12	121	148	-	391	12	182	197	-	5.669	-	11.116	1.000	-
1937	-1	308	247	-	790	-1	462	329	-	4.675	-	7.282	1.000	-
1938	15	330	282	-	886	15	495	376	-	4.770	-	7.776	1.000	-
1950	5	632	475	-	1586	5	948	633	-	3.181	-	4.653	1.000	-
1953	3	383	501	-	1245	3	575	667	-	4.384	-	8.337	1.000	-
1955	-	572	498	-	1521	-	858	663	-	3.941	-	6.215	1.000	-
1957	-	549	600	-	1623	-	824	799	-	4.977	-	8.836	1.000	-
1960	-	502	766	-	1773	-	753	1020	-	5.666	-	11.988	1.000	-
1961	-	718	832	-	2185	-	1077	1108	-	4.968	-	9.052	1.000	-
1962	-	813	850	-	2352	-	1220	1132	-	4.907	-	8.535	1.000	-
1963	-	449	832	-	1782	-	674	1108	-	6.438	-	15.385	1.000	-
1964	-	687	1089	-	2481	-	1031	1451	-	4.853	-	10.277	1.000	-
1965	-	1236	1174	-	3418	-	1854	1564	-	3.502	-	5.612	1.000	-
VENEZUELA														
1950	24	2706	1117	212	5597	24	4059	1488	27	21.300	1.042	28.993	1.000	1.000
1953	30	4013	2172	333	8984	30	6020	2893	42	15.787	0.967	23.070	1.000	1.000
1955	31	4952	2748	250	11151	31	7428	3660	31	15.590	1.000	22.902	1.000	1.000
1957	35	9820	3624	160	19612	35	14730	4827	20	11.437	1.000	14.896	1.000	1.000
1960	35	10333	4585	95	21654	35	15500	6107	12	10.686	1.000	14.531	1.000	1.000
1961	41	10829	4817	150	22719	41	16244	6416	19	10.421	0.756	14.177	1.000	1.000
1962	147	11383	5198	651	24227	147	17075	6924	81	10.689	0.184	14.755	1.000	1.000
1963	172	11077	5610	1106	24398	172	16616	7473	138	10.795	0.244	15.392	1.000	1.000
1964	196	10652	6103	1223	24456	196	15978	8129	153	11.306	0.184	16.785	1.000	1.000
1965	216	12888	6448	1369	28308	216	19332	8589	171	10.008	0.144	14.200	1.000	1.000
CARIBBEAN - OTHER														
1925	725	1681	-	129	3263	725	2522	-	16	0.005	-	-	-	1.000
1929	696	1640	-	164	3177	696	2460	-	21	0.006	-	-	-	1.000
1933	319	855	-	222	1629	319	1283	-	28	0.022	-	0.006	-	1.000
1937	436	1483	-	319	2700	436	2225	-	40	0.020	-	0.006	-	1.000
1938	362	1287	-	341	2335	362	1931	-	43	0.029	-	0.013	-	1.000
1950	44	3896	3	883	6002	44	5844	4	110	0.024	-	0.006	0.667	1.000
1953	79	4359	4	943	6741	79	6539	5	118	0.019	-	0.001	1.000	1.000
1955	127	5670	4	1110	8776	127	8505	5	139	0.025	-	0.009	1.000	1.000
1957	180	7788	3	1142	12009	180	11682	4	143	0.019	-	0.007	1.000	1.000
1960	60	9068	2	1552	13859	60	13602	3	194	0.016	-	0.002	1.000	1.000
1961	50	9386	3	1591	14332	50	14079	4	199	0.015	-	0.001	1.000	1.000
1962	60	11067	3	1584	16862	60	16601	4	198	0.013	-	0.001	1.000	1.000
1963	94	11075	4	1798	16937	94	16613	5	225	0.016	-	0.003	1.000	1.000
1964	119	12779	3	1831	19520	119	19169	4	229	0.015	-	0.003	1.000	1.000
1965	132	13271	3	2151	20311	132	19907	4	269	0.016	-	0.003	1.000	1.000
CUBA														
1925	659	1263	-	15	2555	659	1895	-	2	0.001	-	-	-	1.000
1929	632	1076	-	15	2248	632	1614	-	2	0.001	-	-	-	1.000

Table X. TOTAL ENERGY CONSUMPTION AND RATIO OF PRODUCTION TO CONSUMPTION, SELECTED YEARS, 1925-1965

Region, country, year	Consumption in original units: Solid fuels (10^3 m.t. coal equiv.)	Liquid fuels (10^3 m.t.)	Natural gas (10^6 c.m.)	Hydro-electric power (10^6 kwh)	Consumption in coal equivalents (10^3 m.t.): Total	Solid fuels	Liquid fuels	Natural gas	Hydro-electric power	Ratio of production to consumption: Total	Solid fuels	Liquid fuels	Natural gas	Hydro-electric power
	(1)	(2)	(3)	(4)	(5)	(6)	(7)	(8)	(9)	(10)	(11)	(12)	(13)	(14)
CUBA (CONTINUED)														
1933	296	313	-	14	767	296	470	-	2	0.012	-	0.016	-	1.000
1937	381	762	-	19	1526	381	1143	-	2	0.010	-	0.012	-	1.000
1938	342	598	-	19	1241	342	897	-	2	0.022	-	0.028	-	1.000
1950	35	2459	-	13	3725	35	3689	-	2	0.009	-	0.009	-	1.000
1953	58	2634	-	16	4011	58	3951	-	2	0.002	-	0.001	-	1.000
1955	130	2698	-	20	4180	130	4047	-	3	0.019	-	0.019	-	1.000
1957	180	3402	-	20	5286	180	5103	-	3	0.015	-	0.015	-	1.000
1960	60	3992	-	20	6051	60	5988	-	3	0.004	-	0.004	-	1.000
1961	50	4300	-	22	6503	50	6450	-	3	0.003	-	0.002	-	1.000
1962	60	4820	-	25	7293	60	7230	-	3	0.003	-	0.002	-	1.000
1963	94	4419	-	50	6729	94	6629	-	6	0.008	-	0.007	-	1.000
1964	119	4751	-	100	7258	119	7127	-	13	0.009	-	0.008	-	1.000
1965	132	4778	-	110	7313	132	7167	-	14	0.009	-	0.008	-	1.000
PUERTO RICO														
1957	-	1825	-	173	2759	-	2738	-	22	0.008	-	-	-	1.000
1960	-	2257	-	243	3416	-	3386	-	30	0.009	-	-	-	1.000
1961	-	1896	-	268	2878	-	2844	-	34	0.012	-	-	-	1.000
1962	-	2595	-	207	3918	-	3893	-	26	0.007	-	-	-	1.000
1963	-	2640	-	277	3995	-	3960	-	35	0.009	-	-	-	1.000
1964	-	3113	-	152	4689	-	4670	-	19	0.004	-	-	-	1.000
1965	-	3713	-	236	5599	-	5570	-	30	0.005	-	-	-	1.000
LATIN AMERICA - OTHER														
1925	6899	3625	553	2085	13333	6899	5438	737	261	0.449	0.250	0.601	1.000	1.000
1929	7375	5745	786	2555	17359	7375	8618	1047	319	0.484	0.255	0.598	1.000	1.000
1933	5872	4621	993	2961	14497	5872	6932	1323	370	0.673	0.330	0.884	1.000	1.000
1937	7634	6795	1277	3545	19970	7634	10193	1701	443	0.618	0.335	0.749	1.000	1.000
1938	7348	7490	1206	3824	20668	7348	11235	1606	478	0.594	0.367	0.666	1.000	1.000
1950	6615	15441	1492	10453	33071	6615	23162	1987	1307	0.493	0.596	0.392	1.000	1.000
1953	6386	19176	1791	13499	39223	6386	28764	2386	1687	0.482	0.651	0.372	1.000	1.000
1955	6678	25539	1969	15412	49536	6678	38309	2623	1927	0.425	0.620	0.323	1.000	1.000
1957	6424	29600	2516	20274	56709	6424	44400	3351	2534	0.447	0.608	0.350	1.000	1.000
1960	6618	34057	3801	25258	65924	6618	51086	5063	3157	0.579	0.560	0.514	1.000	1.000
1961	6463	36360	5124	26687	71165	6463	54540	6825	3336	0.650	0.629	0.588	1.000	1.000
1962	5942	38687	6304	28515	75934	5942	58031	8397	3564	0.680	0.707	0.612	1.000	1.000
1963	6046	38262	6953	29223	76353	6046	57393	9261	3653	0.695	0.666	0.630	1.000	1.000
1964	6892	41031	7349	31440	82157	6892	61547	9789	3930	0.674	0.692	0.600	1.000	1.000
1965	7015	42348	7917	35341	85500	7015	63522	10545	4418	0.661	0.696	0.577	1.000	1.000
ARGENTINA														
1925	2834	1639	119	64	5459	2834	2459	159	8	0.284	-	0.564	1.000	1.000
1929	3040	3084	212	108	7962	3040	4626	282	14	0.297	-	0.448	1.000	1.000
1933	2439	2849	330	86	7163	2439	4274	440	11	0.476	-	0.693	1.000	1.000
1937	3062	3992	421	97	9623	3062	5988	561	12	0.428	-	0.592	1.000	1.000
1938	2796	4486	407	84	10078	2796	6729	542	11	0.421	-	0.549	1.000	1.000
1950	1553	8189	533	190	14570	1553	12284	710	24	0.403	0.055	0.411	1.000	1.000
1953	1324	9993	698	358	17288	1324	14990	930	45	0.417	0.075	0.409	1.000	1.000
1955	1415	11297	719	300	19356	1415	16946	958	38	0.398	0.110	0.387	1.000	1.000
1957	1517	13953	852	580	23654	1517	20930	1135	73	0.370	0.156	0.349	1.000	1.000
1960	1753	13975	1383	927	24673	1753	20963	1842	116	0.647	0.167	0.654	1.000	1.000
1961	1611	15134	2357	1086	27587	1611	22701	3140	136	0.789	0.218	0.799	1.000	1.000
1962	931	15542	2978	1167	28356	931	23313	3967	146	0.899	0.312	0.905	1.000	1.000
1963	987	14213	3406	1186	26992	987	21320	4537	148	0.955	0.220	0.979	1.000	1.000
1964	1091	16150	3751	1236	30467	1091	24225	4996	155	0.887	0.313	0.889	1.000	1.000
1965	1111	17291	4264	1238	32882	1111	25937	5680	155	0.831	0.343	0.814	1.000	1.000
BOLIVIA														
1925	16	22	-	9	50	16	33	-	1	0.022	-	-	-	1.000
1929	19	43	-	20	86	19	65	-	3	0.081	-	0.070	-	1.000
1933	8	34	-	26	62	8	51	-	3	0.390	-	0.412	-	1.000
1937	31	56	-	32	119	31	84	-	4	0.235	-	0.286	-	1.000
1938	33	63	-	45	133	33	95	-	6	0.245	-	0.286	-	1.000
1950	2	145	-	190	243	2	218	-	24	0.591	-	0.552	-	1.000

Table X. TOTAL ENERGY CONSUMPTION AND RATIO OF PRODUCTION TO CONSUMPTION, SELECTED YEARS, 1925-1965

Region, country, year	Consumption in original units: Solid fuels (10³ m.t. coal equiv.)	Liquid fuels (10³ m.t.)	Natural gas (10⁶ c.m.)	Hydro-electric power (10⁶ kwh)	Consumption in coal equivalents (10³ m.t.): Total	Solid fuels	Liquid fuels	Natural gas	Hydro-electric power	Ratio of production to consumption: Total	Solid fuels	Liquid fuels	Natural gas	Hydro-electric power
	(1)	(2)	(3)	(4)	(5)	(6)	(7)	(8)	(9)	(10)	(11)	(12)	(13)	(14)
BOLIVIA (CONTINUED)														
1953	5	183	-	250	311	5	275	-	31	0.477	-	0.426	-	1.000
1955	-	309	6	290	508	-	464	8	36	1.124	-	1.136	1.000	1.000
1957	-	321	8	350	536	-	482	11	44	1.406	-	1.452	1.000	1.000
1960	-	357	6	389	592	-	536	8	49	1.276	-	1.305	1.000	1.000
1961	-	314	16	390	541	-	471	21	49	1.211	-	1.242	1.000	1.000
1962	-	351	27	377	610	-	527	36	47	1.032	-	1.037	1.000	1.000
1963	-	344	54	409	639	-	516	72	51	1.160	-	1.198	1.000	1.000
1964	-	373	85	421	725	-	560	113	53	1.072	-	1.094	1.000	1.000
1965	5	404	100	430	798	5	606	133	54	1.048	-	1.072	1.000	1.000
BRAZIL														
1925	2233	542	-	1460	3228	2233	813	-	183	0.151	0.137	-	-	1.000
1929	2616	793	-	1770	4027	2616	1190	-	221	0.127	0.111	-	-	1.000
1933	1796	787	-	2085	3237	1796	1181	-	261	0.236	0.281	-	-	1.000
1937	2303	1105	-	2400	4261	2303	1658	-	300	0.210	0.258	-	-	1.000
1938	2283	1178	-	2600	4375	2283	1767	-	325	0.236	0.310	-	-	1.000
1950	2745	4107	5	7198	9812	2745	6161	7	900	0.265	0.592	0.011	1.000	1.000
1953	2427	5239	27	9223	11474	2427	7859	36	1153	0.266	0.693	0.023	1.000	1.000
1955	3002	8809	62	10605	17624	3002	13214	83	1326	0.209	0.627	0.030	1.000	1.000
1957	2661	9647	159	14876	19202	2661	14471	212	1860	0.301	0.647	0.137	1.000	1.000
1960	2994	13056	535	18384	25589	2994	19584	713	2298	0.420	0.646	0.296	1.000	1.000
1961	2884	13928	527	18946	26846	2884	20892	702	2368	0.442	0.688	0.327	1.000	1.000
1962	3002	14983	511	20662	28740	3002	22475	681	2583	0.414	0.694	0.291	1.000	1.000
1963	3174	15691	503	20728	29971	3174	23537	670	2591	0.414	0.672	0.297	1.000	1.000
1964	3849	15827	532	22097	31060	3849	23741	709	2762	0.409	0.700	0.275	1.000	1.000
1965	4048	15288	683	25515	31079	4048	22932	910	3189	0.439	0.694	0.294	1.000	1.000
CHILE														
1925	1273	884	-	378	2646	1273	1326	-	47	0.516	1.036	-	-	1.000
1929	1076	1100	-	483	2786	1076	1650	-	60	0.515	1.277	-	-	1.000
1933	1286	277	-	548	1770	1286	416	-	69	0.833	1.093	-	-	1.000
1937	1818	766	-	757	3061	1818	1149	-	95	0.639	1.024	-	-	1.000
1938	1866	724	-	750	3045	1866	1086	-	94	0.660	1.027	-	-	1.000
1950	2038	1156	100	1651	4112	2038	1734	133	206	0.608	0.999	0.071	1.000	1.000
1953	2368	1103	130	2035	4450	2368	1655	173	254	0.641	0.915	0.155	1.000	1.000
1955	2035	1909	210	2328	5469	2035	2864	280	291	0.558	0.966	0.180	1.000	1.000
1957	2035	2012	350	2505	5832	2035	3018	466	313	0.592	0.887	0.288	1.000	1.000
1960	1639	2296	890	2977	6641	1639	3444	1185	372	0.650	0.805	0.418	1.000	1.000
1961	1722	2499	1260	3141	7541	1722	3749	1678	393	0.727	0.907	0.493	1.000	1.000
1962	1787	2933	1760	3312	8945	1787	4400	2344	414	0.759	0.933	0.537	1.000	1.000
1963	1704	2963	1920	3404	9131	1704	4445	2557	426	0.795	0.906	0.616	1.000	1.000
1964	1791	3082	1780	3723	9250	1791	4623	2371	465	0.791	0.905	0.618	1.000	1.000
1965	1722	3342	1770	3954	9587	1722	5013	2358	494	0.755	0.933	0.554	1.000	1.000
ECUADOR														
1925	-	31	-	24	50	-	47	-	3	0.758	-	0.742	-	1.000
1929	-	61	-	24	95	-	92	-	3	3.143	-	3.213	-	1.000
1933	-	92	9	24	153	-	138	12	3	2.353	-	2.500	1.000	1.000
1937	-	39	46	24	123	-	59	61	3	4.054	-	7.410	1.000	1.000
1938	-	92	55	25	214	-	138	73	3	2.462	-	3.272	1.000	1.000
1950	-	224	132	86	523	-	336	176	11	1.388	-	1.603	1.000	1.000
1953	-	235	150	92	564	-	353	200	12	1.460	-	1.736	1.000	1.000
1955	-	365	150	120	762	-	548	200	15	1.238	-	1.332	1.000	1.000
1957	-	385	150	143	795	-	578	200	18	1.104	-	1.143	1.000	1.000
1960	-	601	150	175	1123	-	902	200	22	0.705	-	0.632	1.000	1.000
1961	-	590	150	200	1110	-	885	200	25	0.746	-	0.681	1.000	1.000
1962	-	530	150	222	1023	-	795	200	28	0.742	-	0.668	1.000	1.000
1963	-	592	150	239	1118	-	888	200	30	0.660	-	0.573	1.000	1.000
1964	-	707	150	248	1291	-	1061	200	31	0.625	-	0.543	1.000	1.000
1965	-	744	150	249	1347	-	1116	200	31	0.618	-	0.539	1.000	1.000
PARAGUAY														
1950	-	22	-	-	33	-	33	-	-	-	-	-	-	-
1953	-	47	-	-	71	-	71	-	-	-	-	-	-	-
1955	-	63	-	-	95	-	95	-	-	-	-	-	-	-

Table X. TOTAL ENERGY CONSUMPTION AND RATIO OF PRODUCTION TO CONSUMPTION, SELECTED YEARS, 1925-1965

Region, country, year	Consumption in original units				Consumption in coal equivalents (10^3 m.t.)					Ratio of production to consumption				
	Solid fuels (10^3 m.t. coal equiv.)	Liquid fuels (10^3 m.t.)	Natural gas (10^6 c.m.)	Hydro-electric power (10^6 kwh)	Total	Solid fuels	Liquid fuels	Natural gas	Hydro-electric power	Total	Solid fuels	Liquid fuels	Natural gas	Hydro-electric power
	(1)	(2)	(3)	(4)	(5)	(6)	(7)	(8)	(9)	(10)	(11)	(12)	(13)	(14)
PARAGUAY (CONTINUED)														
1957	-	68	-	-	102	-	102	-	-	-	-	-	-	-
1960	-	103	-	-	155	-	155	-	-	-	-	-	-	-
1961	-	118	-	-	177	-	177	-	-	-	-	-	-	-
1962	-	123	-	-	185	-	185	-	-	-	-	-	-	-
1963	-	134	-	-	201	-	201	-	-	-	-	-	-	-
1964	-	139	-	-	209	-	209	-	-	-	-	-	-	-
1965	-	177	-	-	266	-	266	-	-	-	-	-	-	-
PERU														
1925	141	285	434	150	1165	141	428	578	19	2.184	0.723	4.319	1.000	1.000
1929	259	319	574	150	1521	259	479	765	19	2.489	0.842	5.818	1.000	1.000
1933	48	280	654	192	1363	48	420	871	24	2.733	0.625	6.668	1.000	1.000
1937	114	398	810	235	1819	114	597	1079	29	2.661	0.868	6.088	1.000	1.000
1938	88	527	744	320	1910	88	791	991	40	2.316	0.852	4.195	1.000	1.000
1950	137	1195	721	611	2966	137	1793	960	76	1.487	1.431	1.773	1.000	1.000
1953	175	1566	786	940	3688	175	2349	1047	118	1.293	1.200	1.444	1.000	1.000
1955	136	1726	822	1091	3956	136	2589	1095	136	1.267	1.000	1.407	1.000	1.000
1957	111	1976	997	1270	4562	111	2964	1328	159	1.243	1.270	1.364	1.000	1.000
1960	152	2452	837	1730	5161	152	3678	1115	216	1.068	1.066	1.093	1.000	1.000
1961	187	2597	814	1878	5401	187	3896	1084	235	1.025	0.893	1.040	1.000	1.000
1962	173	3002	878	1946	6089	173	4503	1169	243	0.982	0.942	0.978	1.000	1.000
1963	131	3090	920	2159	6261	131	4635	1225	270	0.966	1.000	0.955	1.000	1.000
1964	110	3397	1051	2448	6911	110	5096	1400	306	0.957	1.045	0.941	1.000	1.000
1965	89	3359	950	2625	6721	89	5039	1265	328	0.961	0.944	0.949	1.000	1.000
URUGUAY														
1925	363	215	-	-	686	363	323	-	-	-	-	-	-	-
1929	341	336	-	-	845	341	504	-	-	-	-	-	-	-
1933	283	286	-	-	712	283	429	-	-	-	-	-	-	-
1937	295	404	-	-	901	295	606	-	-	-	-	-	-	-
1938	268	376	-	-	832	268	564	-	-	-	-	-	-	-
1950	129	166	1	527	445	129	249	1	66	0.151	-	-	1.000	1.000
1953	83	1047	-	601	1729	83	1571	-	75	0.043	-	-	-	1.000
1955	90	1187	-	678	1955	90	1781	-	85	0.043	-	-	-	1.000
1957	100	1332	-	550	2167	100	1998	-	69	0.032	-	-	-	1.000
1960	80	1309	-	676	2128	80	1964	-	85	0.040	-	-	-	1.000
1961	60	1249	-	1046	2064	60	1874	-	131	0.063	-	-	-	1.000
1962	50	1316	-	829	2128	50	1974	-	104	0.049	-	-	-	1.000
1963	50	1349	-	1098	2211	50	2024	-	137	0.062	-	-	-	1.000
1964	50	1442	-	1267	2371	50	2163	-	158	0.067	-	-	-	1.000
1965	40	1597	-	1330	2602	40	2396	-	166	0.064	-	-	-	1.000
ASIA														
1925	50131	5786	364	7978	60292	50131	8679	485	997	1.179	1.092	1.712	1.000	1.000
1929	57878	8218	515	13234	72545	57878	12327	686	1654	1.151	1.057	1.618	1.000	1.000
1933	54484	7952	904	18149	69884	54484	11928	1204	2269	1.175	1.028	1.898	1.000	1.000
1937	77221	12278	988	26615	100281	77221	18417	1316	3327	1.191	0.989	2.088	1.000	1.000
1938	84922	14995	1061	28656	112409	84922	22493	1413	3582	1.140	0.989	1.745	1.000	1.000
1950	72359	17481	1439	42772	105844	72359	26222	1917	5347	2.141	1.005	5.589	1.000	1.000
1953	90931	27467	2399	48129	141343	90931	41201	3195	6016	2.126	0.952	4.968	1.000	1.000
1955	87086	39263	3535	56315	157729	87086	58895	4709	7039	2.312	0.960	4.573	1.001	1.000
1957	107307	51600	6451	66858	201657	107307	77400	8593	8357	2.059	0.929	3.859	1.001	1.000
1960	118476	71549	9551	73668	247730	118476	107324	12722	9209	2.282	0.923	4.043	1.000	1.000
1961	128400	84376	10483	86073	279686	128400	126564	13963	10759	2.158	0.906	3.654	1.000	1.000
1962	135413	94528	11743	82566	303168	135413	141792	15642	10321	2.160	0.905	3.571	1.000	1.000
1963	138300	108738	12360	92873	329480	138300	163107	16464	11609	2.148	0.915	3.391	1.001	1.000
1964	137626	122654	13702	95370	351780	137626	183981	18251	11921	2.190	0.900	3.349	1.000	1.000
1965	144622	139194	14431	99671	385094	144622	208791	19222	12459	2.162	0.878	3.228	1.004	1.000
MIDDLE EAST														
1925	679	1084	-	19	2307	679	1626	-	2	3.317	0.991	4.292	-	1.000
1929	751	683	-	19	1778	751	1025	-	2	5.347	1.330	8.302	-	1.000
1933	985	364	-	19	1533	985	546	-	2	8.023	1.341	20.107	-	1.000
1937	1669	1775	-	34	4336	1669	2663	-	4	5.798	0.990	8.820	-	1.000
1938	1731	4448	-	35	8408	1731	6672	-	4	3.054	1.035	3.580	-	1.000

Table X. TOTAL ENERGY CONSUMPTION AND RATIO OF PRODUCTION TO CONSUMPTION, SELECTED YEARS, 1925-1965

Region, country, year	Consumption in original units: Solid fuels (10^3 m.t. coal equiv.)	Liquid fuels (10^3 m.t.)	Natural gas (10^6 c.m.)	Hydro-electric power (10^6 kwh)	Consumption in coal equivalents (10^3 m.t.): Total	Solid fuels	Liquid fuels	Natural gas	Hydro-electric power	Ratio of production to consumption: Total	Solid fuels	Liquid fuels	Natural gas	Hydro-electric power
	(1)	(2)	(3)	(4)	(5)	(6)	(7)	(8)	(9)	(10)	(11)	(12)	(13)	(14)
MIDDLE EAST (CONTINUED)														
1950	3308	6180	506	94	13263	3308	9270	674	12	10.022	0.991	13.912	1.000	1.000
1953	4162	7382	853	168	16392	4162	11073	1136	21	11.312	0.992	16.269	1.000	1.000
1955	4177	10893	1330	209	22314	4177	16340	1772	26	11.071	0.990	14.757	1.000	1.000
1957	4814	13803	3313	498	29994	4814	20705	4413	62	9.121	0.991	12.766	1.000	1.000
1960	4534	18097	5263	1141	38832	4534	27146	7010	143	10.416	0.996	14.470	1.000	1.000
1961	4556	19347	5731	1479	41395	4556	29021	7634	185	10.460	0.987	14.496	1.000	1.000
1962	4761	21251	6240	1417	45127	4761	31877	8312	177	10.527	0.989	14.488	1.000	1.000
1963	5214	22461	5963	2493	47160	5214	33692	7943	312	11.073	0.996	15.101	1.000	1.000
1964	5730	23446	6596	2073	49944	5730	35169	8786	259	11.714	0.997	16.216	1.000	1.000
1965	5711	27884	6896	2720	57062	5711	41826	9185	340	11.218	0.996	14.940	1.000	1.000
MIDDLE EAST - OIL PRODUCING														
1925	5	930	-	-	1400	5	1395	-	-	4.984	-	5.002	-	-
1929	8	445	-	-	676	8	668	-	-	12.591	-	12.742	-	-
1933	12	115	-	-	185	12	173	-	-	59.553	0.750	63.643	-	-
1937	4	1362	-	-	2047	4	2043	-	-	11.472	-	11.494	-	-
1938	4	3915	-	-	5877	4	5873	-	-	4.064	-	4.067	-	-
1950	202	4224	506	-	7212	202	6336	674	-	18.000	0.990	20.350	1.000	-
1953	155	4401	853	-	7893	155	6602	1136	-	22.983	1.000	27.282	1.000	-
1955	245	6704	1330	-	12073	245	10056	1772	-	20.117	1.000	23.951	1.000	-
1957	176	8667	3313	-	17589	176	13001	4413	-	15.258	1.000	20.291	1.000	-
1960	230	12038	5263	-	25297	230	18057	7010	-	15.784	1.000	21.712	1.000	-
1961	218	12752	5728	-	26976	218	19128	7630	-	15.853	0.908	21.948	1.000	-
1962	160	13127	6229	-	28148	160	19691	8297	-	16.669	1.000	23.399	1.000	-
1963	193	13835	5953	-	28875	193	20753	7929	-	17.855	1.000	24.451	1.000	-
1964	274	13543	6567	-	29336	274	20315	8747	-	19.691	1.000	27.991	1.000	-
1965	275	16328	6824	-	33857	275	24492	9090	-	18.657	1.000	25.408	1.000	-
IRAN														
1950	200	1531	-	-	2497	200	2297	-	-	19.463	1.000	21.071	-	-
1953	155	1257	54	-	2112	155	1886	72	-	1.165	1.000	1.185	1.000	-
1955	245	2441	592	-	4695	245	3662	789	-	5.446	1.000	6.701	1.000	-
1957	176	4103	1787	-	8711	176	6155	2380	-	6.496	1.000	8.779	1.000	-
1960	230	5353	2797	-	11985	230	8030	3726	-	6.887	1.000	9.787	1.000	-
1961	198	5848	2792	-	12689	198	8772	3719	-	7.281	1.000	10.086	1.000	-
1962	160	5358	2872	-	12023	160	8037	3826	-	8.483	1.000	12.194	1.000	-
1963	193	6099	2907	-	13214	193	9149	3872	-	8.598	1.000	11.974	1.000	-
1964	274	7498	3280	-	15890	274	11247	4369	-	8.222	1.000	11.204	1.000	-
1965	275	9804	3310	-	19390	275	14706	4409	-	7.471	1.000	9.532	1.000	-
IRAQ														
1950	2	780	-	-	1172	2	1170	-	-	8.511	-	8.526	-	-
1953	NA	780	303	-	1574	NA	1170	404	-	27.124	NA	36.136	1.000	-
1955	-	1535	314	-	2721	-	2303	418	-	18.723	-	21.942	1.000	-
1957	-	1648	255	NA	2812	-	2472	340	NA	11.806	-	13.291	1.000	NA
1960	-	2058	571	NA	3848	-	3087	761	NA	18.630	-	22.974	1.000	NA
1961	20	2224	616	-	4177	20	3336	821	-	17.732	-	21.954	1.000	-
1962	-	2269	637	NA	4252	-	3404	848	NA	17.481	-	21.590	1.000	NA
1963	-	2321	720	NA	4441	-	3482	959	NA	19.291	-	24.330	1.000	NA
1964	-	2389	760	NA	4596	-	3584	1012	NA	20.334	-	25.796	1.000	NA
1965	-	2788	770	NA	5208	-	4182	1026	NA	18.768	-	23.125	1.000	NA
MIDDLE EAST - OTHER														
1925	674	154	-	19	907	674	231	-	2	0.744	0.999	-	-	1.000
1929	743	238	-	19	1102	743	357	-	2	0.908	1.345	-	-	1.000
1933	973	249	-	19	1349	973	374	-	2	0.974	1.348	-	-	1.000
1937	1665	413	-	34	2289	1665	620	-	4	0.724	0.993	-	-	1.000
1938	1727	533	-	35	2531	1727	800	-	4	0.710	1.038	-	-	1.000
1950	3106	1956	-	94	6051	3106	2934	-	12	0.515	0.991	0.009	-	1.000
1953	4007	2981	-	168	8499	4007	4472	-	21	0.475	0.992	0.009	-	1.000
1955	3932	4189	-	209	10242	3932	6284	-	26	0.409	0.989	0.043	-	1.000
1957	4638	5136	-	498	12404	4638	7704	-	62	0.418	0.990	0.069	-	1.000
1960	4304	6059	-	1141	13535	4304	9089	-	143	0.383	0.995	0.083	-	1.000
1961	4338	6595	3	1479	14419	4338	9893	4	185	0.371	0.991	0.087	1.000	1.000
1962	4601	8124	11	1417	16979	4601	12186	15	177	0.344	0.989	0.090	1.000	1.000

Table X. TOTAL ENERGY CONSUMPTION AND RATIO OF PRODUCTION TO CONSUMPTION, SELECTED YEARS, 1925-1965

Region, country, year	Consumption in original units				Consumption in coal equivalents (10^3 m.t.)					Ratio of production to consumption				
	Solid fuels (10^3 m.t. coal equiv.)	Liquid fuels (10^3 m.t.)	Natural gas (10^6 c.m.)	Hydro-electric power (10^6 kwh)	Total	Solid fuels	Liquid fuels	Natural gas	Hydro-electric power	Total	Solid fuels	Liquid fuels	Natural gas	Hydro-electric power
	(1)	(2)	(3)	(4)	(5)	(6)	(7)	(8)	(9)	(10)	(11)	(12)	(13)	(14)
MIDDLE EAST - OTHER (CONTINUED)														
1963	5021	8626	10	2493	18285	5021	12939	13	312	0.365	0.996	0.104	1.000	1.000
1964	5456	9903	29	2073	20608	5456	14855	39	259	0.360	0.996	0.113	1.000	1.000
1965	5436	11556	72	2720	23206	5436	17334	96	340	0.364	0.995	0.150	1.000	1.000
PALESTINE														
1925	22	28	-	-	64	22	42	-	-	-	-	-	-	-
1929	33	50	-	-	108	33	75	-	-	-	-	-	-	-
1933	58	77	-	-	174	58	116	-	-	-	-	-	-	-
1937	98	182	-	-	371	98	273	-	-	-	-	-	-	-
1938	58	156	-	-	292	58	234	-	-	-	-	-	-	-
ISRAEL														
1950	34	672	-	-	1042	34	1008	-	-	-	-	-	-	-
1953	29	1013	-	-	1549	29	1520	-	-	-	-	-	-	-
1955	20	1517	-	-	2296	20	2276	-	-	0.001	-	0.001	-	-
1957	40	1479	-	-	2259	40	2219	-	-	0.036	-	0.037	-	-
1960	50	1851	-	-	2827	50	2777	-	-	0.068	-	0.070	-	-
1961	40	2033	3	-	3093	40	3050	4	-	0.067	-	0.066	1.000	-
1962	40	2291	11	-	3491	40	3437	15	-	0.062	-	0.059	1.000	-
1963	20	2390	10	-	3618	20	3585	13	-	0.066	-	0.063	1.000	-
1964	30	2670	29	-	4074	30	4005	39	-	0.083	-	0.075	1.000	-
1965	15	3768	72	-	5763	15	5652	96	-	0.069	-	0.054	1.000	-
JORDAN														
1950	-	57	-	-	86	-	86	-	-	-	-	-	-	-
1953	-	71	-	-	107	-	107	-	-	-	-	-	-	-
1955	-	126	-	-	189	-	189	-	-	-	-	-	-	-
1957	-	146	-	-	219	-	219	-	-	-	-	-	-	-
1960	-	221	-	-	332	-	332	-	-	-	-	-	-	-
1961	-	297	-	-	446	-	446	-	-	-	-	-	-	-
1962	-	329	-	-	494	-	494	-	-	-	-	-	-	-
1963	-	383	-	-	575	-	575	-	-	-	-	-	-	-
1964	-	387	-	-	581	-	581	-	-	-	-	-	-	-
1965	-	449	-	-	674	-	674	-	-	-	-	-	-	-
LEBANON														
1950	11	603	-	64	924	11	905	-	8	0.009	-	-	-	1.000
1953	-	474	-	101	724	-	711	-	13	0.017	-	-	-	1.000
1955	10	423	-	110	658	10	635	-	14	0.021	-	-	-	1.000
1957	10	610	-	167	946	10	915	-	21	0.022	-	-	-	1.000
1960	-	767	-	109	1164	-	1151	-	14	0.012	-	-	-	1.000
1961	-	798	-	174	1219	-	1197	-	22	0.018	-	-	-	1.000
1962	10	873	-	251	1351	10	1310	-	31	0.023	-	-	-	1.000
1963	10	948	-	350	1476	10	1422	-	44	0.030	-	-	-	1.000
1964	10	1084	-	375	1683	10	1626	-	47	0.028	-	-	-	1.000
1965	10	1265	-	505	1971	10	1897	-	63	0.032	-	-	-	1.000
SYRIA														
1950	2	220	-	-	332	2	330	-	-	-	-	-	-	-
1953	3	391	-	-	590	3	587	-	-	-	-	-	-	-
1955	-	502	-	10	754	-	753	-	1	0.002	-	-	-	1.000
1957	-	606	-	20	912	-	909	-	3	0.003	-	-	-	1.000
1960	-	993	-	30	1493	-	1490	-	4	0.003	-	-	-	1.000
1961	-	944	-	40	1421	-	1416	-	5	0.004	-	-	-	1.000
1962	-	981	-	42	1477	-	1472	-	5	0.004	-	-	-	1.000
1963	-	1106	-	44	1665	-	1659	-	6	0.003	-	-	-	1.000
1964	-	1355	-	46	2038	-	2033	-	6	0.003	-	-	-	1.000
1965	5	1131	-	48	1708	5	1697	-	6	0.004	-	-	-	1.000
TURKEY														
1925	594	80	-	-	714	594	120	-	-	0.943	1.133	-	-	-
1929	652	107	-	-	812	652	161	-	-	1.230	1.532	-	-	-

Table X. TOTAL ENERGY CONSUMPTION AND RATIO OF PRODUCTION TO CONSUMPTION, SELECTED YEARS, 1925-1965

Region, country, year	Consumption in original units				Consumption in coal equivalents (10^3 m.t.)					Ratio of production to consumption				
	Solid fuels (10^3 m.t. coal equiv.)	Liquid fuels (10^3 m.t.)	Natural gas (10^6 c.m.)	Hydro-electric power (10^6 kwh)	Total	Solid fuels	Liquid fuels	Natural gas	Hydro-electric power	Total	Solid fuels	Liquid fuels	Natural gas	Hydro-electric power
	(1)	(2)	(3)	(4)	(5)	(6)	(7)	(8)	(9)	(10)	(11)	(12)	(13)	(14)
TURKEY (CONTINUED)														
1933	839	88	-	-	971	839	132	-	-	1.351	1.564	-	-	-
1937	1400	134	-	1	1601	1400	201	-	-	1.032	1.181	-	-	-
1938	1537	165	-	1	1785	1537	248	-	-	1.004	1.166	-	-	-
1950	3079	557	-	30	3918	3079	836	-	4	0.793	1.000	0.031	-	1.000
1953	3968	1168	-	67	5728	3968	1752	-	8	0.702	1.002	0.022	-	1.000
1955	3890	1282	-	89	5824	3890	1923	-	11	0.716	1.000	0.140	-	1.000
1957	4593	1352	-	311	6660	4593	2028	-	39	0.763	1.000	0.220	-	1.000
1960	4254	1583	-	1002	6753	4254	2375	-	125	0.736	1.007	0.237	-	1.000
1961	4298	1864	-	1265	7252	4298	2796	-	158	0.706	1.000	0.237	-	1.000
1962	4551	2653	-	1124	8671	4551	3980	-	141	0.644	1.000	0.224	-	1.000
1963	4991	3121	-	2099	9935	4991	4682	-	262	0.642	1.002	0.239	-	1.000
1964	5416	3574	-	1652	10984	5416	5361	-	207	0.640	1.004	0.258	-	1.000
1965	5406	4037	-	2167	11732	5406	6056	-	271	0.680	1.001	0.379	-	1.000
FAR EAST AND OTHER ASIA														
1925	49452	4702	364	7959	57985	49452	7053	485	995	1.094	1.094	1.118	1.000	1.000
1929	57127	7535	515	13215	70767	57127	11303	686	1652	1.045	1.054	1.013	1.000	1.000
1933	53499	7588	904	18130	68351	53499	11382	1204	2266	1.022	1.022	1.025	1.000	1.000
1937	75552	10503	988	26581	95945	75552	15755	1316	3323	0.983	0.989	0.951	1.000	1.000
1938	83191	10547	1061	28621	104002	83191	15821	1413	3578	0.986	0.988	0.971	1.000	1.000
1950	69052	11301	933	42678	92581	69052	16952	1243	5335	1.011	1.006	1.038	1.000	1.000
1953	86769	20085	1546	47961	124951	86769	30128	2059	5995	0.921	0.950	0.815	1.000	1.000
1955	82909	28370	2205	56106	135414	82909	42555	2937	7013	0.869	0.959	0.663	1.002	1.000
1957	102493	37797	3138	66360	171663	102493	56696	4180	8295	0.826	0.926	0.607	1.001	1.000
1960	113942	53452	4288	72527	208897	113942	80178	5712	9066	0.770	0.920	0.513	1.000	1.000
1961	123844	65029	4752	84594	238291	123844	97544	6330	10574	0.716	0.903	0.428	1.000	1.000
1962	130652	73277	5503	81149	258041	130652	109916	7330	10144	0.697	0.902	0.405	1.001	1.000
1963	133086	86277	6397	90380	282320	133086	129416	8521	11298	0.657	0.912	0.342	1.001	1.000
1964	131896	99208	7106	93297	301836	131896	148812	9465	11662	0.613	0.896	0.308	1.000	1.000
1965	138911	111310	7535	96951	328031	138911	166965	10037	12119	0.587	0.873	0.294	1.007	1.000
BORNEO (FORMER BRITISH)														
1950	-	139	52	-	278	-	209	69	-	22.790	-	30.029	1.000	-
1953	-	111	59	-	245	-	167	79	-	30.500	-	44.423	1.000	-
1955	-	229	73	-	441	-	344	97	-	18.533	-	23.480	1.055	-
1957	-	194	188	-	541	-	291	250	-	16.223	-	29.304	1.021	-
1960	-	157	215	-	522	-	236	286	-	14.083	-	29.994	1.000	-
1961	-	275	210	-	692	-	413	280	-	9.609	-	15.447	1.000	-
1962	-	151	205	-	500	-	227	273	-	12.313	-	25.927	1.020	-
1963	-	219	189	-	580	-	329	252	-	9.652	-	16.247	1.048	-
1964	-	311	173	-	697	-	467	230	-	8.206	-	11.765	1.000	-
1965	-	476	157	-	923	-	714	209	-	6.872	-	8.492	1.344	-
BURMA														
1950	NA	171	-	-	256	NA	257	-	-	0.409	NA	0.409	-	-
1953	251	241	-	-	613	251	362	-	-	0.345	-	0.585	-	-
1955	207	353	3	-	740	207	530	4	-	0.442	0.034	0.598	1.000	-
1957	281	459	6	-	977	281	689	8	-	0.615	0.004	0.861	1.000	-
1960	351	572	21	160	1257	351	858	28	20	0.689	0.003	0.953	1.000	1.000
1961	262	624	15	187	1241	262	936	20	23	0.718	0.008	0.904	1.000	1.000
1962	343	646	18	212	1362	343	969	24	27	0.682	0.009	0.904	1.000	1.000
1963	213	660	16	236	1254	213	990	21	30	0.806	0.014	0.967	1.000	1.000
1964	225	686	10	280	1302	225	1029	13	35	0.687	0.044	0.813	1.000	1.000
1965	150	686	10	280	1227	150	1029	13	35	0.710	0.067	0.790	1.000	1.000
CEYLON														
1925	14	68	-	1	116	14	102	-	-	0.001	-	-	-	-
1929	312	116	-	1	486	312	174	-	-	-	-	-	-	-
1933	191	104	-	1	347	191	156	-	-	-	-	-	-	-
1937	252	145	-	1	470	252	218	-	-	-	-	-	-	-
1938	162	124	-	1	348	162	186	-	-	-	-	-	-	-
1950	292	198	-	9	590	292	297	-	1	0.002	-	-	-	1.000
1953	368	333	-	113	882	368	500	-	14	0.016	-	-	-	1.000
1955	176	464	-	130	888	176	696	-	16	0.018	-	-	-	1.000
1957	271	756	-	153	1424	271	1134	-	19	0.013	-	-	-	1.000

Table X. TOTAL ENERGY CONSUMPTION AND RATIO OF PRODUCTION TO CONSUMPTION, SELECTED YEARS, 1925-1965

	Consumption in original units				Consumption in coal equivalents (10^3 m.t.)					Ratio of production to consumption				
Region, country, year	Solid fuels (10^3 m.t. coal equiv.)	Liquid fuels (10^3 m.t.)	Natural gas (10^6 c.m.)	Hydro-electric power (10^6 kwh)	Total	Solid fuels	Liquid fuels	Natural gas	Hydro-electric power	Total	Solid fuels	Liquid fuels	Natural gas	Hydro-electric power
	(1)	(2)	(3)	(4)	(5)	(6)	(7)	(8)	(9)	(10)	(11)	(12)	(13)	(14)
CEYLON (CONTINUED)														
1960	260	411	-	272	911	260	617	-	34	0.037	-	-	-	1.000
1961	140	644	-	277	1141	140	966	-	35	0.030	-	-	-	1.000
1962	139	717	-	320	1255	139	1076	-	40	0.032	-	-	-	1.000
1963	150	709	-	327	1254	150	1064	-	41	0.033	-	-	-	1.000
1964	180	581	-	338	1094	180	872	-	42	0.039	-	-	-	1.000
1965	140	746	-	332	1301	140	1119	-	42	0.032	-	-	-	1.000
HONG KONG														
1925	503	167	-	-	754	503	251	-	-	-	-	-	-	-
1929	194	78	-	-	311	194	117	-	-	-	-	-	-	-
1933	233	59	-	-	322	233	89	-	-	-	-	-	-	-
1937	428	69	-	-	532	428	104	-	-	-	-	-	-	-
1938	284	116	-	-	458	284	174	-	-	-	-	-	-	-
1950	251	277	-	-	667	251	416	-	-	-	-	-	-	-
1953	204	430	-	-	849	204	645	-	-	-	-	-	-	-
1955	250	475	-	-	963	250	713	-	-	-	-	-	-	-
1957	250	631	-	-	1197	250	947	-	-	-	-	-	-	-
1960	230	817	-	-	1456	230	1226	-	-	-	-	-	-	-
1961	240	934	-	-	1641	240	1401	-	-	-	-	-	-	-
1962	220	1046	-	-	1789	220	1569	-	-	-	-	-	-	-
1963	200	1244	-	-	2066	200	1866	-	-	-	-	-	-	-
1964	180	1244	-	-	2046	180	1866	-	-	-	-	-	-	-
1965	170	1420	-	-	2300	170	2130	-	-	-	-	-	-	-
INDIA														
1925	16198	1876	-	188	19036	16198	2814	-	24	0.988	1.049	0.640	-	1.000
1929	17572	2176	-	500	20899	17572	3264	-	63	1.000	1.083	0.552	-	1.000
1933	15608	1915	-	812	18582	15608	2873	-	102	0.992	1.056	0.641	-	1.000
1937	19614	2427	-	1125	23395	19614	3641	-	141	0.988	1.063	0.580	-	1.000
1938	21976	2380	-	1200	25696	21976	3570	-	150	1.007	1.075	0.593	-	1.000
1950	25102	3172	-	2520	30175	25102	4758	-	315	0.894	1.046	0.081	-	1.000
1953	27116	3414	-	2929	32603	27116	5121	-	366	0.921	1.079	0.079	-	1.000
1955	29401	4492	-	3753	36608	29401	6738	-	469	0.876	1.057	0.077	-	1.000
1957	33656	5815	128	5083	43185	33656	8723	170	635	0.853	1.051	0.074	1.000	1.000
1960	40729	7215	139	7847	52717	40729	10823	185	981	0.833	1.033	0.062	1.000	1.000
1961	43933	7732	107	9824	56902	43933	11598	143	1228	0.826	1.021	0.066	1.000	1.000
1962	48092	8977	214	11515	63282	48092	13466	285	1439	0.830	1.022	0.120	1.000	1.000
1963	52189	9607	268	13665	68664	52189	14411	357	1708	0.839	1.017	0.172	1.000	1.000
1964	49168	10147	322	15710	66781	49168	15221	429	1964	0.841	1.026	0.218	1.000	1.000
1965	53485	11100	400	17270	72826	53485	16650	533	2159	0.846	1.017	0.272	1.000	1.000
INDO-CHINA														
1925	700	66	-	-	799	700	99	-	-	1.709	1.950	-	-	-
1929	641	117	-	-	817	641	176	-	-	2.388	3.041	-	-	-
1933	321	87	-	-	452	321	131	-	-	3.473	4.885	-	-	-
1937	772	94	-	-	913	772	141	-	-	2.528	2.990	-	-	-
1938	770	104	-	-	926	770	156	-	-	2.518	3.028	-	-	-
1950	450	120	-	-	630	450	180	-	-	0.789	1.104	-	-	-
1953	587	330	-	-	1082	587	495	-	-	0.820	1.511	-	-	-
1955	30	362	-	4	574	30	543	-	1	0.001	-	-	-	1.000
1957	62	490	-	3	797	62	735	-	-	0.016	0.194	-	-	-
1960	37	607	-	7	948	37	911	-	1	0.029	0.730	-	-	1.000
1961	67	691	-	10	1105	67	1037	-	1	0.053	0.851	-	-	1.000
1962	91	710	-	10	1157	91	1065	-	1	0.062	0.780	-	-	1.000
1963	114	825	-	10	1353	114	1238	-	1	0.078	0.912	-	-	1.000
1964	97	795	-	42	1295	97	1193	-	5	0.064	0.794	-	-	1.000
1965	120	944	-	58	1543	120	1416	-	7	0.053	0.625	-	-	1.000
CAMBODIA														
1955	-	56	-	-	84	-	84	-	-	-	-	-	-	-
1957	-	85	-	-	128	-	128	-	-	-	-	-	-	-
1960	-	109	-	-	164	-	164	-	-	-	-	-	-	-
1961	-	133	-	-	200	-	200	-	-	-	-	-	-	-
1962	-	143	-	-	215	-	215	-	-	-	-	-	-	-

Table X. TOTAL ENERGY CONSUMPTION AND RATIO OF PRODUCTION TO CONSUMPTION, SELECTED YEARS, 1925-1965

	Consumption in original units				Consumption in coal equivalents (10^3 m.t.)					Ratio of production to consumption				
Region, country, year	Solid fuels (10^3 m.t. coal equiv.)	Liquid fuels (10^3 m.t.)	Natural gas (10^6 c.m.)	Hydro-electric power (10^6 kwh)	Total	Solid fuels	Liquid fuels	Natural gas	Hydro-electric power	Total	Solid fuels	Liquid fuels	Natural gas	Hydro-electric power
	(1)	(2)	(3)	(4)	(5)	(6)	(7)	(8)	(9)	(10)	(11)	(12)	(13)	(14)
CAMBODIA (CONTINUED)														
1963	-	188	-	-	282	-	282	-	-	-	-	-	-	-
1964	-	165	-	-	248	-	248	-	-	-	-	-	-	-
1965	30	167	-	-	281	30	251	-	-	-	-	-	-	-
LAOS														
1955	-	9	-	-	14	-	14	-	-	-	-	-	-	-
1957	-	19	-	-	29	-	29	-	-	-	-	-	-	-
1960	-	28	-	-	42	-	42	-	-	-	-	-	-	-
1961	-	38	-	-	57	-	57	-	-	-	-	-	-	-
1962	-	44	-	-	66	-	66	-	-	-	-	-	-	-
1963	-	51	-	-	77	-	77	-	-	-	-	-	-	-
1964	-	60	-	-	90	-	90	-	-	-	-	-	-	-
1965	-	58	-	-	87	-	87	-	-	-	-	-	-	-
VIETNAM, SOUTH														
1955	30	297	-	4	476	30	446	-	1	0.001	-	-	-	1.000
1957	62	386	-	3	641	62	579	-	-	0.019	0.194	-	-	-
1960	37	470	-	7	743	37	705	-	1	0.038	0.730	-	-	1.000
1961	67	520	-	10	848	67	780	-	1	0.069	0.851	-	-	1.000
1962	91	523	-	10	877	91	785	-	1	0.082	0.780	-	-	1.000
1963	114	586	-	10	994	114	879	-	1	0.106	0.912	-	-	1.000
1964	97	570	-	42	957	97	855	-	5	0.086	0.794	-	-	1.000
1965	90	719	-	58	1176	90	1079	-	7	0.070	0.833	-	-	1.000
INDONESIA														
1925	1064	1031	319	88	3046	1064	1547	425	11	2.165	1.317	3.077	1.000	1.000
1929	1390	1872	417	100	4766	1390	2808	555	13	2.198	1.318	2.876	1.000	1.000
1933	817	1533	788	159	4186	817	2300	1050	20	2.554	1.267	3.735	1.000	1.000
1937	1115	1784	884	210	4995	1115	2676	1177	26	2.748	1.231	4.167	1.000	1.000
1938	1174	1803	952	235	5176	1174	2705	1268	29	2.722	1.241	4.192	1.000	1.000
1950	769	2024	791	300	4896	769	3036	1054	38	2.457	1.046	3.338	1.000	1.000
1953	817	3103	1366	454	7348	817	4655	1820	57	2.518	1.098	3.380	1.000	1.000
1955	794	5575	1908	570	11769	794	8363	2541	71	1.854	1.025	2.200	1.000	1.000
1957	717	5832	2168	620	12430	717	8748	2888	78	2.203	1.000	2.709	1.000	1.000
1960	678	5864	2431	810	12813	678	8796	3238	101	2.752	0.971	3.555	1.000	1.000
1961	579	6902	2561	775	14440	579	10353	3411	97	2.509	0.948	3.108	1.000	1.000
1962	491	5704	2712	715	12749	491	8556	3612	89	3.023	0.959	4.016	1.000	1.000
1963	601	5617	2798	715	12843	601	8426	3727	89	2.957	0.983	3.985	1.000	1.000
1964	456	4801	2930	710	11649	456	7202	3903	89	3.336	0.978	4.780	1.000	1.000
1965	286	5978	3010	710	13351	286	8967	4009	89	3.016	0.983	4.002	1.000	1.000
JAPAN														
1925	28162	893	23	7610	30483	28162	1340	31	951	1.080	1.120	0.293	1.000	1.000
1929	33023	2380	29	12400	38181	33023	3570	39	1550	0.951	1.040	0.113	1.000	1.000
1933	32733	3186	47	16114	39589	32733	4779	63	2014	0.883	0.995	0.062	1.000	1.000
1937	47500	4604	53	22278	57261	47500	6906	71	2785	0.850	0.954	0.076	1.000	1.000
1938	52180	4806	51	23741	62425	52180	7209	68	2968	0.838	0.934	0.073	1.000	1.000
1950	38131	1877	66	38258	45816	38131	2816	88	4782	0.969	1.025	0.157	1.000	1.000
1953	51570	7668	101	41762	68427	51570	11502	135	5220	0.776	0.917	0.039	1.000	1.000
1955	45461	9813	156	48547	66457	45461	14720	208	6068	0.751	0.949	0.032	1.000	1.000
1957	58944	15962	329	56687	90411	58944	23943	438	7086	0.670	0.892	0.020	1.000	1.000
1960	60059	28357	824	58471	111001	60059	42536	1098	7309	0.550	0.863	0.019	1.000	1.000
1961	66425	36889	1052	67956	131654	66425	55334	1401	8495	0.502	0.831	0.018	1.000	1.000
1962	66951	43286	1367	62373	141497	66951	64929	1821	7797	0.465	0.821	0.018	1.000	1.000
1963	63576	54544	1886	69168	156550	63576	81816	2512	8646	0.415	0.827	0.015	1.000	1.000
1964	64459	65126	2073	68957	173528	64459	97689	2761	8620	0.367	0.796	0.011	1.000	1.000
1965	66885	73485	2018	70739	188642	66885	110228	2688	8842	0.331	0.745	0.009	1.000	1.000
KOREA														
1925	1101	52	-	-	1179	1101	78	-	-	0.528	0.565	-	-	-
1929	1568	111	-	-	1735	1568	167	-	-	0.541	0.598	-	-	-
1933	1928	127	-	538	2186	1928	191	-	67	0.629	0.678	-	-	1.000
1937	3475	367	-	2087	4286	3475	551	-	261	0.628	0.700	-	-	1.000

Table X. TOTAL ENERGY CONSUMPTION AND RATIO OF PRODUCTION TO CONSUMPTION, SELECTED YEARS, 1925-1965

	Consumption in original units				Consumption in coal equivalents (10^3 m.t.)					Ratio of production to consumption				
Region, country, year	Solid fuels (10^3 m.t. coal equiv.)	Liquid fuels (10^3 m.t.)	Natural gas (10^6 c.m.)	Hydro-electric power (10^6 kwh)	Total	Solid fuels	Liquid fuels	Natural gas	Hydro-electric power	Total	Solid fuels	Liquid fuels	Natural gas	Hydro-electric power
	(1)	(2)	(3)	(4)	(5)	(6)	(7)	(8)	(9)	(10)	(11)	(12)	(13)	(14)
KOREA (CONTINUED)														
1938	4406	356	-	2438	5245	4406	534	-	305	0.710	0.776	-	-	1.000
KOREA, REPUBLIC OF														
1950	791	81	-	97	925	791	122	-	12	0.632	0.723	-	-	1.000
1953	1495	330	-	395	2039	1495	495	-	49	0.449	0.580	-	-	1.000
1955	2338	364	-	478	2944	2338	546	-	60	0.465	0.559	-	-	1.000
1957	3171	474	-	419	3934	3171	711	-	52	0.634	0.770	-	-	1.000
1960	5450	685	-	580	6550	5450	1028	-	73	0.828	0.982	-	-	1.000
1961	5934	747	-	652	7136	5934	1121	-	82	0.836	0.992	-	-	1.000
1962	7324	1011	-	702	8928	7324	1517	-	88	0.844	1.016	-	-	1.000
1963	8728	1362	-	727	10862	8728	2043	-	91	0.824	1.015	-	-	1.000
1964	9542	1277	-	750	11551	9542	1916	-	94	0.841	1.008	-	-	1.000
1965	10158	1554	-	710	12578	10158	2331	-	89	0.822	1.009	-	-	1.000
MALAYA AND SINGAPORE														
1925	467	227	-	21	810	467	341	-	3	0.372	0.640	-	-	1.000
1929	761	340	-	38	1276	761	510	-	5	0.383	0.636	-	-	1.000
1933	365	156	-	95	611	365	234	-	12	0.281	0.438	-	-	1.000
1937	809	426	-	235	1478	809	639	-	29	0.331	0.568	-	-	1.000
1938	486	267	-	229	915	486	401	-	29	0.414	0.720	-	-	1.000
1950	360	769	-	253	1545	360	1154	-	32	0.217	0.844	-	-	1.000
1953	284	1357	-	255	2351	284	2036	-	32	0.103	0.739	-	-	1.000
1955	211	1661	-	234	2732	211	2492	-	29	0.066	0.712	-	-	1.000
1957	194	1617	-	249	2650	194	2426	-	31	0.054	0.576	-	-	1.000
1960	9	1612	-	195	2451	9	2418	-	24	0.012	0.558	-	-	1.000
1961	60	2027	-	216	3128	60	3041	-	27	0.009	-	-	-	1.000
1962	40	2209	-	235	3383	40	3314	-	29	0.009	-	-	-	1.000
1963	40	1506	-	317	2339	40	2259	-	40	0.017	-	-	-	1.000
1964	40	3119	-	544	4787	40	4679	-	68	0.014	-	-	-	1.000
1965	25	2705	-	587	4156	25	4058	-	73	0.018	-	-	-	1.000
PAKISTAN														
1950	1370	901	NA	65	2730	1370	1352	NA	8	0.227	0.259	0.190	NA	1.000
1953	1675	1105	-	240	3363	1675	1658	-	30	0.256	0.283	0.214	-	1.000
1955	1500	1397	39	400	3697	1500	2096	52	50	0.256	0.286	0.198	1.000	1.000
1957	1739	1623	290	520	4625	1739	2435	386	65	0.284	0.241	0.181	1.000	1.000
1960	2075	2142	633	680	6216	2075	3213	843	85	0.341	0.320	0.164	1.000	1.000
1961	1807	2284	770	940	6376	1807	3426	1026	118	0.384	0.408	0.165	1.000	1.000
1962	2156	2524	949	1400	7381	2156	3786	1264	175	0.394	0.369	0.177	1.000	1.000
1963	2194	2900	1189	1570	8324	2194	4350	1584	196	0.418	0.453	0.162	1.000	1.000
1964	2311	3135	1429	1820	9145	2311	4703	1903	228	0.421	0.420	0.159	1.000	1.000
1965	2085	3317	1630	1967	9477	2085	4976	2171	246	0.442	0.472	0.159	1.000	1.000
PHILIPPINES														
1925	521	306	-	36	985	521	459	-	5	0.054	0.094	-	-	1.000
1929	620	358	-	50	1163	620	537	-	6	0.020	0.027	-	-	1.000
1933	289	368	-	63	849	289	552	-	8	0.028	0.055	-	-	1.000
1937	288	439	-	76	956	288	659	-	10	0.033	0.076	-	-	1.000
1938	300	467	-	84	1011	300	701	-	11	0.051	0.137	-	-	1.000
1950	166	1182	-	191	1963	166	1773	-	24	0.093	0.958	-	-	1.000
1953	160	1145	-	332	1919	160	1718	-	42	0.102	0.969	-	-	1.000
1955	140	1830	-	430	2939	140	2745	-	54	0.063	0.929	-	-	1.000
1957	201	2115	-	640	3454	201	3173	-	80	0.078	0.950	-	-	1.000
1960	158	2606	-	1320	4232	158	3909	-	165	0.074	0.937	-	-	1.000
1961	162	2705	-	1290	4381	162	4058	-	161	0.072	0.938	-	-	1.000
1962	173	3229	-	1350	5185	173	4844	-	169	0.064	0.942	-	-	1.000
1963	167	3625	-	1540	5797	167	5438	-	193	0.060	0.940	-	-	1.000
1964	125	4092	-	1600	6463	125	6138	-	200	0.049	0.920	-	-	1.000
1965	105	4351	-	1509	6820	105	6527	-	189	0.042	0.905	-	-	1.000
TAIWAN														
1925	633	22	22	15	697	633	33	29	2	2.499	2.694	0.182	1.000	1.000
1929	968	64	69	126	1172	968	96	92	16	1.412	1.581	0.172	1.000	1.000

Table X. TOTAL ENERGY CONSUMPTION AND RATIO OF PRODUCTION TO CONSUMPTION, SELECTED YEARS, 1925-1965

Region, country, year	Consumption in original units				Consumption in coal equivalents (10^3 m.t.)					Ratio of production to consumption				
	Solid fuels (10^3 m.t. coal equiv.)	Liquid fuels (10^3 m.t.)	Natural gas (10^6 c.m.)	Hydro-electric power (10^6 kwh)	Total	Solid fuels	Liquid fuels	Natural gas	Hydro-electric power	Total	Solid fuels	Liquid fuels	Natural gas	Hydro-electric power
	(1)	(2)	(3)	(4)	(5)	(6)	(7)	(8)	(9)	(10)	(11)	(12)	(13)	(14)
TAIWAN (CONTINUED)														
1933	995	76	67	348	1242	995	114	89	44	1.355	1.541	0.145	1.000	1.000
1937	1248	125	30	569	1547	1248	188	40	71	1.338	1.565	0.032	1.000	1.000
1938	1394	138	28	693	1725	1394	207	37	87	1.350	1.577	0.029	1.000	1.000
1950	1341	157	24	972	1730	1341	236	32	122	0.904	1.048	0.025	1.000	1.000
1953	2182	71	20	1466	2498	2182	107	27	183	1.044	1.097	0.042	1.000	1.000
1955	2309	601	26	1531	3437	2309	902	35	191	0.754	1.022	0.007	1.000	1.000
1957	2886	788	29	1938	4349	2886	1182	39	242	0.736	1.010	0.003	1.000	1.000
1960	3772	1018	25	2065	5590	3772	1527	33	258	0.761	1.050	0.002	1.000	1.000
1961	4082	1061	37	2339	6015	4082	1592	49	292	0.776	1.059	0.003	1.000	1.000
1962	4424	1204	38	2161	6551	4424	1806	51	270	0.745	1.029	0.002	1.000	1.000
1963	4710	1410	51	1931	7134	4710	2115	68	241	0.718	1.021	0.003	1.000	1.000
1964	4918	1175	169	2359	7200	4918	1763	225	295	0.772	1.022	0.008	1.000	1.000
1965	5059	1642	310	2585	8258	5059	2463	413	323	0.705	0.999	0.012	1.000	1.000
THAILAND														
1925	38	42	-	-	101	38	63	-	-	-	-	-	-	-
1929	52	96	-	-	196	52	144	-	-	-	-	-	-	-
1933	23	77	-	-	139	23	116	-	-	-	-	-	-	-
1937	50	112	-	-	218	50	168	-	-	-	-	-	-	-
1938	56	117	-	-	232	56	176	-	-	-	-	-	-	-
1950	20	233	-	-	370	20	350	-	-	-	-	-	-	-
1953	45	447	-	-	715	45	671	-	-	0.001	0.016	-	-	-
1955	69	706	-	-	1128	69	1059	-	-	0.025	0.418	-	-	-
1957	90	869	-	-	1394	90	1304	-	-	0.050	0.778	-	-	-
1960	86	1103	-	-	1740	86	1655	-	-	0.043	0.883	-	-	-
1961	76	1198	-	-	1873	76	1797	-	-	0.040	1.000	-	-	-
1962	95	1478	-	-	2312	95	2217	-	-	0.041	1.000	-	-	-
1963	96	1644	-	-	2562	96	2466	-	-	0.037	1.000	-	-	-
1964	73	2280	-	-	3493	73	3420	-	-	0.021	1.000	-	-	-
1965	88	2423	-	-	3722	88	3635	-	-	0.024	1.000	-	-	-
AFRICA														
1925	12775	771	-	65	13940	12775	1157	-	8	0.978	1.045	0.236	-	1.000
1929	14738	1600	-	83	17148	14738	2400	-	10	0.873	0.987	0.172	-	1.000
1933	12591	1676	-	223	15133	12591	2514	-	28	0.788	0.916	0.143	-	1.000
1937	18318	2796	-	462	22570	18318	4194	-	58	0.770	0.932	0.062	-	1.000
1938	19040	2868	-	488	23403	19040	4302	-	61	0.782	0.939	0.082	-	1.000
1950	28467	8925	4	1364	42030	28467	13388	5	171	0.815	1.056	0.300	-	1.000
1953	32752	10933	5	2043	49414	32752	16400	7	255	0.764	1.012	0.267	1.000	1.002
1955	38006	13577	12	3254	58794	38006	20366	16	407	0.699	0.991	0.149	1.000	1.000
1957	41288	14205	9	4081	63118	41288	21308	12	510	0.722	0.991	0.191	1.000	1.174
1960	43161	17468	30	6707	70241	43161	26202	40	838	0.926	1.003	0.795	1.000	1.086
1961	43952	18275	253	9340	72869	43952	27413	337	1168	1.117	1.004	1.305	1.000	0.999
1962	44730	19127	381	10549	75247	44730	28691	507	1319	1.409	1.018	2.045	1.000	0.999
1963	45844	19686	468	11068	77380	45844	29529	623	1384	1.740	1.016	2.913	1.000	0.999
1964	49046	22832	806	12108	85881	49046	34248	1074	1514	2.051	1.008	3.620	1.112	1.001
1965	52995	24345	1096	13198	92622	52995	36518	1460	1650	2.363	1.010	4.413	1.760	1.001
NORTH AFRICA														
1925	2257	463	-	20	2954	2257	695	-	3	0.097	0.004	0.393	-	1.000
1929	2662	931	-	38	4063	2662	1397	-	5	0.107	0.006	0.295	-	1.000
1933	2276	1157	-	84	4022	2276	1736	-	11	0.106	0.025	0.207	-	1.000
1937	2562	1287	-	164	4513	2562	1931	-	21	0.089	0.047	0.134	-	1.000
1938	2686	1421	-	164	4838	2686	2132	-	21	0.103	0.051	0.161	-	1.000
1950	1314	5325	4	416	9358	1314	7988	5	52	0.498	0.487	0.497	-	1.000
1953	1102	6125	5	548	10365	1102	9188	7	69	0.508	0.780	0.471	1.000	1.007
1955	1042	7246	12	1095	12064	1042	10869	16	137	0.324	0.738	0.274	1.000	1.018
1957	1334	6777	9	1208	11662	1334	10166	12	151	0.400	0.567	0.369	1.000	1.008
1960	1010	9025	23	1586	14776	1010	13538	31	198	1.279	0.526	1.340	1.000	1.000
1961	978	8896	246	2249	14931	978	13344	328	281	2.141	0.499	2.313	1.000	0.994
1962	763	9212	370	2484	15384	763	13818	493	311	3.430	0.554	3.730	1.000	0.994
1963	732	8892	419	2653	14960	732	13338	558	332	5.280	0.604	5.822	1.000	0.997
1964	1036	10065	739	3126	17509	1036	15098	984	391	6.507	0.431	7.418	1.122	0.999
1965	934	10430	1025	3352	18363	934	15645	1365	419	7.691	0.497	8.812	1.813	1.000

Table X. TOTAL ENERGY CONSUMPTION AND RATIO OF PRODUCTION TO CONSUMPTION, SELECTED YEARS, 1925-1965

Region, country, year	Consumption in original units: Solid fuels (10^3 m.t. coal equiv.)	Liquid fuels (10^3 m.t.)	Natural gas (10^6 c.m.)	Hydro-electric power (10^6 kwh)	Consumption in coal equivalents (10^3 m.t.): Total	Solid fuels	Liquid fuels	Natural gas	Hydro-electric power	Ratio of production to consumption: Total	Solid fuels	Liquid fuels	Natural gas	Hydro-electric power
	(1)	(2)	(3)	(4)	(5)	(6)	(7)	(8)	(9)	(10)	(11)	(12)	(13)	(14)
ALGERIA														
1925	579	75	-	20	694	579	113	-	3	0.022	0.017	0.027	-	1.000
1929	886	175	-	20	1151	886	263	-	3	0.020	0.018	0.017	-	1.000
1933	673	230	-	25	1021	673	345	-	3	0.034	0.045	0.004	-	1.000
1937	672	222	-	36	1010	672	333	-	5	0.018	0.021	-	-	1.000
1938	691	230	-	41	1041	691	345	-	5	0.017	0.019	-	-	1.000
1950	638	568	4	131	1512	638	852	5	16	0.184	0.404	0.005	-	1.000
1953	436	770	-	223	1619	436	1155	-	28	0.279	0.677	0.110	-	1.018
1955	546	1048	-	278	2153	546	1572	-	35	0.197	0.553	0.055	-	1.036
1957	703	1274	-	317	2654	703	1911	-	40	0.116	0.336	0.016	-	1.032
1960	468	2095	7	358	3665	468	3143	9	45	3.595	0.254	4.137	1.000	0.972
1961	288	1932	231	258	3526	288	2898	308	32	6.838	0.271	8.176	1.000	0.981
1962	153	1241	353	265	2518	153	1862	470	33	12.553	0.346	16.680	1.000	0.974
1963	88	1194	400	260	2444	88	1791	533	33	14.902	0.432	20.002	1.000	0.985
1964	116	1286	719	285	3038	116	1929	958	36	13.478	0.397	20.628	1.125	0.996
1965	65	1379	1006	400	3523	65	2069	1340	50	12.023	0.692	19.250	1.828	1.000
EGYPT UAR														
1925	1317	311	-	-	1784	1317	467	-	-	0.151	-	0.579	-	-
1929	1317	565	-	-	2165	1317	848	-	-	0.188	-	0.481	-	-
1933	1130	684	-	-	2156	1130	1026	-	-	0.166	-	0.348	-	-
1937	1434	774	-	-	2595	1434	1161	-	-	0.099	-	0.221	-	-
1938	1546	840	-	-	2806	1546	1260	-	-	0.121	-	0.269	-	-
1950	179	4012	-	7	6198	179	6018	-	1	0.630	-	0.649	-	1.000
1953	76	4116	-	7	6251	76	6174	-	1	0.647	-	0.655	-	1.000
1955	109	4777	-	7	7275	109	7166	-	1	0.376	-	0.382	-	1.000
1957	180	4302	-	7	6634	180	6453	-	1	0.543	-	0.559	-	1.000
1960	160	5419	-	260	8321	160	8129	-	33	0.604	-	0.614	-	1.000
1961	300	5241	-	1012	8288	300	7862	-	127	0.708	-	0.730	-	1.000
1962	270	5611	-	1172	8833	270	8417	-	147	0.812	-	0.835	-	1.000
1963	270	5790	-	1280	9115	270	8685	-	160	0.939	-	0.967	-	1.000
1964	500	6571	-	1670	10565	500	9857	-	209	0.923	-	0.968	-	1.000
1965	440	6652	-	1750	10637	440	9978	-	219	0.936	-	0.976	-	1.000
MOROCCO														
1925	121	36	-	-	175	121	54	-	-	-	-	-	-	-
1929	181	94	-	18	324	181	141	-	2	0.007	-	-	-	1.000
1933	221	117	-	59	404	221	176	-	7	0.089	0.122	0.009	-	1.000
1937	194	139	-	128	419	194	209	-	16	0.301	0.552	0.014	-	1.000
1938	156	181	-	123	443	156	272	-	15	0.323	0.788	0.017	-	1.000
1950	313	482	-	278	1071	313	723	-	35	0.431	1.176	0.081	-	1.000
1953	507	846	5	318	1822	507	1269	7	40	0.419	1.114	0.121	1.000	1.000
1955	277	875	8	810	1701	277	1313	11	101	0.432	1.686	0.118	1.000	1.012
1957	331	675	3	858	1455	331	1013	4	107	0.512	1.574	0.111	1.000	1.000
1960	312	815	9	921	1662	312	1223	12	115	0.408	1.321	0.113	1.000	1.011
1961	300	851	8	960	1707	300	1277	11	120	0.386	1.367	0.094	1.000	0.991
1962	290	633	10	1028	1381	290	950	13	129	0.508	1.276	0.201	1.000	0.992
1963	324	918	12	1083	1852	324	1377	16	135	0.421	1.247	0.163	1.000	0.997
1964	380	963	12	1133	1982	380	1445	16	142	0.372	1.053	0.125	1.000	0.999
1965	369	1080	11	1160	2149	369	1620	15	145	0.341	1.136	0.095	1.000	0.999
TUNISIA														
1925	223	31	-	-	270	223	47	-	-	-	-	-	-	-
1929	257	80	-	-	377	257	120	-	-	-	-	-	-	-
1933	215	93	-	-	355	215	140	-	-	-	-	-	-	-
1937	218	103	-	-	373	218	155	-	-	-	-	-	-	-
1938	238	106	-	-	397	238	159	-	-	-	-	-	-	-
1950	184	207	-	-	494	184	311	-	-	0.027	0.074	-	-	-
1953	83	321	-	-	565	83	482	-	-	-	-	-	-	-
1955	40	412	4	-	663	40	618	5	-	0.008	-	-	1.000	-
1957	90	350	6	26	626	90	525	8	3	0.018	-	-	1.000	1.000
1960	40	442	7	47	718	40	663	9	6	0.021	-	-	1.000	1.000
1961	50	455	7	19	744	50	683	9	2	0.016	-	-	1.000	1.000
1962	40	477	7	19	767	40	716	9	2	0.015	-	-	1.000	1.000
1963	40	599	7	30	952	40	899	9	4	0.014	-	-	1.000	1.000
1964	40	720	8	38	1135	40	1080	11	5	0.014	-	-	1.000	1.000
1965	50	665	8	42	1063	50	998	11	5	0.015	-	-	1.000	1.000

Table X. TOTAL ENERGY CONSUMPTION AND RATIO OF PRODUCTION TO CONSUMPTION, SELECTED YEARS, 1925-1965

Region, country, year	Consumption in original units: Solid fuels (10^3 m.t. coal equiv.)	Liquid fuels (10^3 m.t.)	Natural gas (10^6 c.m.)	Hydro-electric power (10^6 kwh)	Consumption in coal equivalents (10^3 m.t.): Total	Solid fuels	Liquid fuels	Natural gas	Hydro-electric power	Ratio of production to consumption: Total	Solid fuels	Liquid fuels	Natural gas	Hydro-electric power
	(1)	(2)	(3)	(4)	(5)	(6)	(7)	(8)	(9)	(10)	(11)	(12)	(13)	(14)
TROPICAL AFRICA														
1925	1574	179	-	45	1848	1574	269	-	6	0.552	0.645	-	-	1.000
1929	2284	327	-	45	2780	2284	491	-	6	0.545	0.661	-	-	1.000
1933	1209	156	-	139	1460	1209	234	-	17	0.532	0.628	-	-	1.000
1937	2204	734	-	298	3342	2204	1101	-	37	0.446	0.659	-	-	1.000
1938	2088	616	-	324	3053	2088	924	-	41	0.493	0.701	-	-	1.000
1950	3613	1801	-	948	6433	3613	2702	-	119	0.475	0.813	-	-	1.000
1953	4454	2722	-	1495	8724	4454	4083	-	187	0.458	0.856	-	-	1.000
1955	5411	3642	-	2159	11144	5411	5463	-	270	0.448	0.874	-	-	0.991
1957	5769	4616	-	2873	13052	5769	6924	-	359	0.468	0.934	0.040	-	1.244
1960	4928	5169	7	5121	13331	4928	7754	9	640	0.596	0.926	0.342	1.000	1.113
1961	4469	5809	7	7091	14078	4469	8714	9	886	0.700	0.913	0.560	1.000	1.000
1962	4287	6097	11	8065	14455	4287	9146	15	1008	0.829	0.895	0.779	1.000	1.000
1963	4006	6849	49	8415	15397	4006	10274	65	1052	0.855	0.923	0.813	1.000	1.000
1964	4384	7820	67	8982	17326	4384	11730	89	1123	0.999	0.933	1.023	1.000	1.002
1965	4817	8533	71	9846	18942	4817	12800	95	1231	1.543	0.956	1.820	1.000	1.001
CONGO, DEMOCRATIC REPUBLIC														
1925	359	14	-	30	384	359	21	-	4	0.179	0.181	-	-	1.000
1929	583	42	-	30	650	583	63	-	4	0.186	0.201	-	-	1.000
1933	65	17	-	98	103	65	26	-	12	0.314	0.308	-	-	1.000
1937	201	42	-	220	292	201	63	-	28	0.218	0.179	-	-	1.000
1938	175	31	-	233	251	175	47	-	29	0.284	0.240	-	-	1.000
1950	368	158	-	588	679	368	237	-	74	0.344	0.435	-	-	1.000
1953	515	285	-	992	1067	515	428	-	124	0.412	0.612	-	-	1.000
1955	770	398	-	1350	1536	770	597	-	169	0.421	0.623	-	-	0.985
1957	673	451	-	1685	1560	673	677	-	211	0.468	0.643	-	-	1.409
1960	393	418	-	1790	1244	393	627	-	224	0.363	0.415	-	-	1.291
1961	403	444	-	1917	1309	403	666	-	240	0.283	0.181	-	-	1.242
1962	316	451	-	2050	1249	316	677	-	256	0.313	0.241	-	-	1.229
1963	312	492	-	1960	1295	312	738	-	245	0.287	0.295	-	-	1.140
1964	355	365	-	2043	1158	355	548	-	255	0.330	0.282	-	-	1.104
1965	444	441	-	2195	1380	444	662	-	274	0.306	0.257	-	-	1.125
EAST AFRICA														
1925	74	47	-	10	146	74	71	-	1	0.009	-	-	-	1.000
1929	107	78	-	10	225	107	117	-	1	0.006	-	-	-	1.000
1933	91	28	-	16	135	91	42	-	2	0.015	-	-	-	1.000
1937	165	78	-	24	285	165	117	-	3	0.011	-	-	-	1.000
1938	150	114	-	26	324	150	171	-	3	0.010	-	-	-	1.000
1950	26	445	-	72	703	26	668	-	9	0.013	-	-	-	1.000
1953	14	711	-	110	1094	14	1067	-	14	0.013	-	-	-	1.000
1955	27	938	-	310	1473	27	1407	-	39	0.027	0.037	-	-	1.000
1957	37	1002	-	414	1592	37	1503	-	52	0.033	0.027	-	-	1.000
1960	42	1138	-	637	1829	42	1707	-	80	0.045	0.048	-	-	1.000
1961	42	1034	-	660	1676	42	1551	-	83	0.050	0.048	-	-	1.000
1962	43	1142	-	713	1845	43	1713	-	89	0.050	0.070	-	-	1.000
1963	42	1245	-	764	2005	42	1868	-	96	0.049	0.048	-	-	1.000
1964	31	1293	-	857	2078	31	1940	-	107	0.052	0.032	-	-	1.000
1965	62	1361	-	948	2222	62	2042	-	119	0.054	0.032	-	-	1.000
EQUATORIAL AFRICA														
1925	2	2	-	-	5	2	3	-	-	-	-	-	-	-
1929	1	5	-	-	9	1	8	-	-	-	-	-	-	-
1933	2	7	-	-	13	2	11	-	-	-	-	-	-	-
1937	21	12	-	-	39	21	18	-	-	-	-	-	-	-
1938	11	13	-	-	31	11	20	-	-	-	-	-	-	-
1950	7	52	-	-	85	7	78	-	-	-	-	-	-	-
1953	4	79	-	7	123	4	119	-	1	0.007	-	-	-	1.000
1955	-	84	-	33	130	-	126	-	4	0.032	-	-	-	1.000
1957	-	146	-	30	223	-	219	-	4	1.182	-	1.185	-	1.000
1960	-	228	7	30	355	-	342	9	4	3.636	-	3.737	1.000	1.000
1961	-	221	7	30	345	-	332	9	4	3.856	-	3.968	1.000	1.000
1962	-	173	9	30	275	-	260	12	4	5.235	-	5.491	1.000	1.000
1963	-	141	9	50	230	-	212	12	6	6.602	-	7.085	1.000	1.000
1964	-	204	10	50	326	-	306	13	6	5.322	-	5.598	1.000	1.000
1965	-	200	11	50	321	-	300	15	6	6.305	-	6.675	1.000	1.000

Table X. TOTAL ENERGY CONSUMPTION AND RATIO OF PRODUCTION TO CONSUMPTION, SELECTED YEARS, 1925-1965

Region, country, year	Consumption in original units: Solid fuels (10^3 m.t. coal equiv.)	Liquid fuels (10^3 m.t.)	Natural gas (10^6 c.m.)	Hydro-electric power (10^6 kwh)	Consumption in coal equivalents (10^3 m.t.): Total	Solid fuels	Liquid fuels	Natural gas	Hydro-electric power	Ratio of production to consumption: Total	Solid fuels	Liquid fuels	Natural gas	Hydro-electric power
	(1)	(2)	(3)	(4)	(5)	(6)	(7)	(8)	(9)	(10)	(11)	(12)	(13)	(14)
GHANA														
1925	54	19	-	-	83	54	29	-	-	-	-	-	-	-
1929	73	35	-	-	126	73	53	-	-	-	-	-	-	-
1933	27	25	-	-	65	27	38	-	-	-	-	-	-	-
1937	72	80	-	-	192	72	120	-	-	-	-	-	-	-
1938	77	89	-	-	211	77	134	-	-	-	-	-	-	-
1950	63	159	-	-	302	63	239	-	-	-	-	-	-	-
1953	99	209	-	-	413	99	314	-	-	-	-	-	-	-
1955	120	306	-	-	579	120	459	-	-	-	-	-	-	-
1957	110	350	-	-	635	110	525	-	-	-	-	-	-	-
1960	40	430	-	-	685	40	645	-	-	-	-	-	-	-
1961	50	399	-	-	649	50	599	-	-	-	-	-	-	-
1962	30	460	-	-	720	30	690	-	-	-	-	-	-	-
1963	40	528	-	-	832	40	792	-	-	-	-	-	-	-
1964	40	615	-	-	963	40	923	-	-	-	-	-	-	-
1965	30	595	-	107	936	30	893	-	13	0.014	-	-	-	1.000
LIBERIA														
1925	-	-	-	-	-	-	-	-	-	-	-	-	-	-
1929	-	-	-	-	-	-	-	-	-	-	-	-	-	-
1933	-	-	-	-	-	-	-	-	-	-	-	-	-	-
1937	-	1	-	-	2	-	2	-	-	-	-	-	-	-
1938	-	2	-	-	3	-	3	-	-	-	-	-	-	-
1950	-	16	-	8	25	-	24	-	1	0.040	-	-	-	1.000
1953	-	18	-	10	28	-	27	-	1	0.044	-	-	-	1.000
1955	-	61	-	11	93	-	92	-	1	0.015	-	-	-	1.000
1957	-	32	-	14	50	-	48	-	2	0.035	-	-	-	1.000
1960	-	49	-	17	76	-	74	-	2	0.028	-	-	-	1.000
1961	-	50	-	17	77	-	75	-	2	0.028	-	-	-	1.000
1962	-	82	-	17	125	-	123	-	2	0.017	-	-	-	1.000
1963	-	123	-	17	187	-	185	-	2	0.011	-	-	-	1.000
1964	-	164	-	17	248	-	246	-	2	0.009	-	-	-	1.000
1965	-	188	-	17	284	-	282	-	2	0.007	-	-	-	1.000
NIGERIA														
1925	230	23	-	-	265	230	35	-	-	0.919	1.057	-	-	-
1929	320	35	-	-	373	320	53	-	-	0.940	1.094	-	-	-
1933	233	16	-	-	257	233	24	-	-	0.930	1.026	-	-	-
1937	349	38	-	-	406	349	57	-	-	0.909	1.057	-	-	-
1938	340	40	-	-	400	340	60	-	-	0.920	1.082	-	-	-
1950	642	161	-	52	890	642	242	-	7	0.672	0.922	-	-	1.000
1953	733	220	-	64	1071	733	330	-	8	0.671	0.970	-	-	1.000
1955	661	300	-	73	1120	661	450	-	9	0.688	1.151	-	-	1.000
1957	728	400	-	88	1339	728	600	-	11	0.628	1.137	0.002	-	1.000
1960	541	589	-	91	1436	541	884	-	11	1.294	1.055	1.443	-	1.000
1961	557	759	-	101	1708	557	1139	-	13	2.357	1.090	2.992	-	1.000
1962	604	679	2	108	1639	604	1019	3	14	3.443	1.050	4.901	1.000	1.000
1963	537	856	40	118	1889	537	1284	53	15	3.337	1.074	4.407	1.000	1.000
1964	639	1066	57	126	2330	639	1599	76	16	4.172	1.094	5.584	1.000	1.000
1965	705	1301	60	132	2753	705	1952	80	17	7.680	1.050	10.406	1.000	1.000
RHODESIAN FEDERATION														
1925	463	6	-	-	472	463	9	-	-	1.460	1.488	-	-	-
1929	641	20	-	-	671	641	30	-	-	1.545	1.618	-	-	-
1933	439	24	-	20	478	439	36	-	3	1.019	1.103	-	-	1.000
1937	877	52	-	40	960	877	78	-	5	1.077	1.173	-	-	1.000
1938	929	55	-	45	1017	929	83	-	6	1.032	1.124	-	-	1.000
1950	1959	167	-	155	2229	1959	251	-	19	0.963	1.086	-	-	1.000
1953	2521	263	-	197	2940	2521	395	-	25	0.899	1.039	-	-	1.000
1955	3246	351	-	222	3800	3246	527	-	28	0.880	1.021	-	-	1.000
1957	3580	454	-	231	4290	3580	681	-	29	0.905	1.076	-	-	1.000
1960	3311	523	-	1310	4259	3311	785	-	164	0.874	1.075	-	-	1.000
1961	2783	524	-	2964	3940	2783	786	-	371	0.857	1.104	-	-	0.823
1962	2646	558	-	3519	3923	2646	837	-	440	0.815	1.068	-	-	0.847
1963	2510	559	-	3809	3825	2510	839	-	476	0.829	1.092	-	-	0.908
1964	2714	585	-	4166	4112	2714	878	-	521	0.858	1.122	-	-	0.933
1965	3049	821	-	4491	4842	3049	1232	-	561	0.832	1.151	-	-	0.925

Table X. TOTAL ENERGY CONSUMPTION AND RATIO OF PRODUCTION TO CONSUMPTION, SELECTED YEARS, 1925-1965

Region, country, year	Consumption in original units				Consumption in coal equivalents (10^3 m.t.)					Ratio of production to consumption				
	Solid fuels (10^3 m.t. coal equiv.)	Liquid fuels (10^3 m.t.)	Natural gas (10^6 c.m.)	Hydro-electric power (10^6 kwh)	Total	Solid fuels	Liquid fuels	Natural gas	Hydro-electric power	Total	Solid fuels	Liquid fuels	Natural gas	Hydro-electric power
	(1)	(2)	(3)	(4)	(5)	(6)	(7)	(8)	(9)	(10)	(11)	(12)	(13)	(14)
MALAWI														
1925	-	1	-	-	2	-	2	-	-	-	-	-	-	-
1929	3	1	-	-	5	3	2	-	-	-	-	-	-	-
1933	3	2	-	-	6	3	3	-	-	-	-	-	-	-
1937	5	2	-	-	8	5	3	-	-	-	-	-	-	-
1938	4	3	-	-	9	4	5	-	-	-	-	-	-	-
1950	25	15	-	-	48	25	23	-	-	-	-	-	-	-
1953	37	18	-	2	64	37	27	-	-	0.004	-	-	-	-
1955	42	30	-	1	87	42	45	-	-	0.001	-	-	-	-
1957	47	40	-	2	107	47	60	-	-	0.002	-	-	-	-
1960	57	50	-	3	132	57	75	-	-	0.003	-	-	-	-
1961	60	41	-	2	122	60	62	-	-	0.002	-	-	-	-
1962	60	44	-	12	128	60	66	-	2	0.012	-	-	-	1.000
1963	60	47	-	7	131	60	71	-	1	0.007	-	-	-	1.000
1964	60	49	-	9	135	60	74	-	1	0.008	-	-	-	1.000
1965	80	54	-	12	163	80	81	-	2	0.009	-	-	-	1.000
ZAMBIA														
1925	42	-	-	-	42	42	-	-	-	-	-	-	-	-
1929	142	4	-	-	148	142	6	-	-	-	-	-	-	-
1933	177	3	-	-	182	177	5	-	-	-	-	-	-	-
1937	341	5	-	-	349	341	8	-	-	-	-	-	-	-
1938	405	6	-	-	414	405	9	-	-	-	-	-	-	-
1950	654	40	-	NA	714	654	60	-	NA	NA	-	-	-	NA
1953	823	69	-	187	950	823	104	-	23	0.025	-	-	-	1.000
1955	880	90	-	217	1042	880	135	-	27	0.026	-	-	-	1.000
1957	940	110	-	225	1133	940	165	-	28	0.025	-	-	-	1.000
1960	1035	130	-	NA	1230	1035	195	-	NA	NA	-	-	-	NA
1961	1080	133	-	1578	1477	1080	200	-	197	NA	-	-	-	NA
1962	990	138	-	2052	1454	990	207	-	257	0.026	-	-	-	0.145
1963	940	140	-	2139	1417	940	210	-	267	0.027	-	-	-	0.145
1964	1040	153	-	2337	1562	1040	230	-	292	0.024	-	-	-	0.131
1965	1215	202	-	2466	1826	1215	303	-	308	0.019	-	-	-	0.112
RHODESIA														
1950	1280	112	-	NA	1448	1280	168	-	NA	1.470	1.663	-	-	NA
1953	1660	176	-	10	1925	1660	264	-	1	1.360	1.577	-	-	1.000
1955	2324	231	-	2	2671	2324	347	-	-	1.241	1.426	-	-	-
1957	2593	304	-	2	3049	2593	456	-	-	1.264	1.486	-	-	-
1960	2219	343	-	1046	2864	2219	515	-	131	1.288	1.604	-	-	1.000
1961	1643	350	-	1152	2312	1643	525	-	144	1.448	1.870	-	-	1.915
1962	1596	376	-	1520	2350	1596	564	-	190	1.348	1.771	-	-	1.800
1963	1510	372	-	1663	2276	1510	558	-	208	1.377	1.815	-	-	1.889
1964	1614	383	-	1820	2416	1614	575	-	228	1.445	1.886	-	-	1.962
1965	1754	565	-	2013	2853	1754	848	-	252	1.399	2.001	-	-	1.920
WEST AFRICA														
1925	50	19	-	-	79	50	29	-	-	-	-	-	-	-
1929	78	28	-	-	120	78	42	-	-	-	-	-	-	-
1933	58	19	-	-	87	58	29	-	-	-	-	-	-	-
1937	154	48	-	-	226	154	72	-	-	-	-	-	-	-
1938	-	40	-	-	60	-	60	-	-	-	-	-	-	-
1950	68	200	-	1	368	68	300	-	-	-	-	-	-	-
1953	56	298	-	6	504	56	447	-	1	0.001	-	-	-	1.000
1955	30	356	-	9	565	30	534	-	1	0.002	-	-	-	1.000
1957	1	483	-	16	728	1	725	-	2	0.003	-	-	-	1.000
1960	1	632	-	60	957	1	948	-	8	0.009	-	0.002	-	1.000
1961	1	756	-	80	1145	1	1134	-	10	0.011	-	0.003	-	1.000
1962	-	819	-	100	1241	-	1229	-	13	0.010	-	-	-	1.000
1963	-	872	-	120	1323	-	1308	-	15	0.011	-	-	-	1.000
1964	-	1033	-	103	1562	-	1550	-	13	0.008	-	-	-	1.000
1965	-	1209	-	141	1831	-	1814	-	18	0.010	-	-	-	1.000
SOUTH AFRICA														
1925	8944	129	-	-	9138	8944	194	-	-	1.349	1.378	-	-	-
1929	9792	342	-	-	10305	9792	513	-	-	1.263	1.329	-	-	-

Table X. TOTAL ENERGY CONSUMPTION AND RATIO OF PRODUCTION TO CONSUMPTION, SELECTED YEARS, 1925-1965

	Consumption in original units				Consumption in coal equivalents (10^3 m.t.)					Ratio of production to consumption				
Region, country, year	Solid fuels (10^3 m.t. coal equiv.)	Liquid fuels (10^3 m.t.)	Natural gas (10^6 c.m.)	Hydro-electric power (10^6 kwh)	Total	Solid fuels	Liquid fuels	Natural gas	Hydro-electric power	Total	Solid fuels	Liquid fuels	Natural gas	Hydro-electric power
	(1)	(2)	(3)	(4)	(5)	(6)	(7)	(8)	(9)	(10)	(11)	(12)	(13)	(14)
SOUTH AFRICA (CONTINUED)														
1933	9106	363	-	-	9651	9106	545	-	-	1.110	1.177	-	-	-
1937	13552	775	-	-	14715	13552	1163	-	-	1.053	1.143	-	-	-
1938	14266	831	-	-	15513	14266	1247	-	-	1.050	1.141	0.006	-	-
1950	23540	1799	-	-	26239	23540	2699	-	-	1.011	1.125	0.020	-	-
1953	27196	2086	-	-	30325	27196	3129	-	-	0.940	1.046	0.018	-	-
1955	31553	2689	-	-	35587	31553	4034	-	-	0.905	1.019	0.014	-	-
1957	34185	2812	-	-	38403	34185	4218	-	-	0.906	1.017	0.009	-	-
1960	37223	3274	-	-	42134	37223	4911	-	-	0.907	1.026	0.008	-	-
1961	38505	3570	-	-	43860	38505	5355	-	-	0.902	1.028	0.002	-	-
1962	39680	3818	-	-	45407	39680	5727	-	-	0.909	1.040	-	-	-
1963	41106	3945	-	-	47024	41106	5918	-	-	0.903	1.033	-	-	-
1964	43626	4947	-	-	51047	43626	7421	-	-	0.880	1.029	-	-	-
1965	47244	5382	-	-	55317	47244	8073	-	-	0.876	1.025	-	-	-
DEVELOPED COUNTRIES														
1925	1105928	107182	33819	74618	1321075	1105928	160773	45047	9327	1.039	1.045	1.012	1.000	0.999
1929	1217398	150916	54257	111287	1529954	1217398	226374	72270	13911	1.022	1.035	0.962	1.000	1.001
1933	875219	140677	44660	118453	1160529	875219	211016	59487	14807	1.005	1.029	0.906	1.001	1.001
1937	1125175	195156	69003	161825	1530049	1125175	292734	91912	20228	1.004	1.024	0.926	1.002	1.002
1938	1031551	188339	65695	164366	1422111	1031551	282509	87506	20546	0.999	1.021	0.918	1.001	1.002
1950	1120173	380661	174217	307051	1961603	1120173	570992	232057	38381	0.938	1.006	0.773	1.003	0.999
1953	1100597	477896	235187	362083	2175971	1100597	716844	313269	45260	0.920	1.000	0.757	1.003	1.003
1955	1115613	552166	265823	407314	2348853	1115613	828249	354076	50914	0.897	0.999	0.710	1.002	1.003
1957	1158823	610149	305984	455803	2538593	1158823	915224	407571	56975	0.890	1.003	0.689	1.000	1.004
1960	1055874	718614	379040	554206	2707952	1055874	1077921	504881	69276	0.832	0.988	0.590	0.997	1.000
1961	1042922	767035	398349	575480	2796010	1042922	1150553	530601	71935	0.819	0.988	0.571	0.997	1.003
1962	1070704	823857	425561	593800	2947561	1070704	1235786	566847	74225	0.804	0.985	0.548	0.997	1.000
1963	1105068	892344	449751	619833	3120132	1105068	1338516	599068	77479	0.790	0.986	0.524	0.998	1.000
1964	1144241	961973	478902	637270	3304757	1144241	1442960	637897	79659	0.775	0.983	0.499	0.997	1.002
1965	1153086	1038796	498721	695671	3462535	1153086	1558194	664296	86959	0.758	0.984	0.475	0.996	1.000
UNDERDEVELOPED COUNTRIES														
1925	35080	14859	1113	3588	59300	35080	22289	1483	449	1.338	0.785	2.239	0.998	1.000
1929	39132	20131	1960	4867	72548	39132	30197	2611	608	1.471	0.804	2.385	0.998	1.000
1933	32228	14432	2902	6868	58600	32228	21648	3865	859	1.687	0.836	3.108	0.980	0.997
1937	44255	25869	4239	10719	90044	44255	38804	5646	1340	1.644	0.833	2.690	0.968	0.998
1938	46785	28252	4466	11715	96576	46785	42378	5949	1464	1.583	0.877	2.467	0.989	0.998
1950	47797	55049	6871	20230	142051	47797	82573	9152	2529	2.521	0.902	3.683	0.904	0.994
1953	54119	68763	9956	27032	173904	54119	103145	13261	3379	2.609	0.939	3.751	0.946	0.992
1955	58166	93898	12561	32891	219856	58166	140847	16731	4111	2.551	0.917	3.461	0.956	0.995
1957	65586	114338	17266	41971	265338	65586	171507	22998	5246	2.498	0.923	3.345	1.010	1.007
1960	75489	133321	26809	57020	318308	75489	199982	35710	7128	2.715	0.937	3.745	1.044	1.002
1961	78504	142285	29767	63963	339577	78504	213428	39650	7995	2.735	0.947	3.772	1.044	0.993
1962	84614	151462	33062	70262	364628	84614	227193	44039	8783	2.834	0.957	3.953	1.035	0.992
1963	91106	154879	35288	76733	380020	91106	232319	47004	9592	2.960	0.960	4.215	1.032	0.992
1964	90999	165431	40336	83958	403368	90999	248147	53728	10495	3.094	0.957	4.413	1.032	0.998
1965	96165	179036	42685	93560	433270	96165	268554	56856	11695	3.145	0.959	4.464	1.050	0.999
COMMUNIST COUNTRIES														
1925	89014	9119	1045	588	104158	89014	13679	1392	74	1.101	1.092	1.126	1.000	0.883
1929	129817	14266	1606	996	153480	129817	21399	2139	125	1.154	1.114	1.353	1.000	0.931
1933	137742	20711	3075	1646	173110	137742	31067	4096	206	1.162	1.098	1.439	1.000	0.992
1937	209236	31452	4722	5085	263340	209236	47178	6290	636	1.104	1.081	1.177	1.000	0.997
1938	213479	33950	4663	6029	271369	213479	50925	6211	754	1.085	1.064	1.128	1.000	1.000
1950	425208	45758	8174	20097	507245	425208	68637	10888	2512	1.024	1.031	0.988	0.996	1.011
1953	531197	62603	11425	24418	643372	531197	93905	15218	3052	1.023	1.020	1.046	0.998	1.000
1955	642855	82433	14086	33698	789480	642855	123650	18763	4212	1.029	1.024	1.056	0.998	0.996
1957	729778	107815	24863	54162	931389	729778	161723	33118	6770	1.029	1.021	1.074	0.998	1.000
1960	867136	147430	54034	76646	1169835	867136	221145	71973	9581	1.047	1.023	1.159	1.000	0.998
1961	903379	159646	68526	81884	1244360	903379	239469	91277	10236	1.054	1.023	1.193	1.000	1.000
1962	917605	177659	84596	96353	1308820	917605	266489	112682	12044	1.057	1.026	1.194	1.000	0.995
1963	967138	195454	102644	100206	1409567	967138	293181	136722	12526	1.057	1.025	1.195	1.000	0.995
1964	1010116	206229	122619	102598	1495613	1010116	309344	163329	12825	1.058	1.024	1.203	1.000	1.001
1965	1041501	221562	143351	111873	1578771	1041501	332343	190944	13984	1.061	1.023	1.215	1.000	1.000

Table X. TOTAL ENERGY CONSUMPTION AND RATIO OF PRODUCTION TO CONSUMPTION, SELECTED YEARS, 1925-1965

	Consumption in original units				Consumption in coal equivalents (10^3 m.t.)					Ratio of production to consumption				
Region, country, year	Solid fuels (10^3 m.t. coal equiv.)	Liquid fuels (10^3 m.t.)	Natural gas (10^6 c.m.)	Hydro-electric power (10^6 kwh)	Total	Solid fuels	Liquid fuels	Natural gas	Hydro-electric power	Total	Solid fuels	Liquid fuels	Natural gas	Hydro-electric power
	(1)	(2)	(3)	(4)	(5)	(6)	(7)	(8)	(9)	(10)	(11)	(12)	(13)	(14)
USSR														
1925	16434	5779	140	251	25320	16434	8669	186	31	1.065	0.980	1.226	1.000	1.000
1929	37567	9927	330	557	52966	37567	14891	440	70	1.111	1.006	1.379	1.000	1.000
1933	71889	16752	1110	1163	98640	71889	25128	1479	145	1.083	1.014	1.287	1.000	1.000
1937	122357	27010	2179	4191	166298	122357	40515	2902	524	1.017	1.002	1.062	1.000	1.000
1938	128875	29263	2210	5091	176349	128875	43895	2944	636	1.006	0.994	1.039	1.000	1.000
1950	233300	40528	5736	12691	303319	233300	60792	7640	1586	0.963	0.962	0.961	1.004	1.000
1953	277800	53577	6773	19201	359587	277800	80366	9022	2400	0.988	0.980	1.013	1.014	1.000
1955	340700	70402	8841	23175	460976	340700	105603	11776	2897	1.002	0.990	1.038	1.016	1.000
1957	373710	91567	18412	39429	540514	373710	137351	24525	4929	1.040	1.019	1.104	1.009	1.000
1960	391070	122112	45060	50883	640618	391070	183168	60020	6360	1.083	1.024	1.237	1.005	1.001
1961	383890	131909	58711	59048	667338	383890	197864	78203	7381	1.104	1.033	1.285	1.005	1.001
1962	382540	147530	73223	71712	710332	382540	221295	97533	8964	1.114	1.044	1.289	1.004	1.003
1963	398210	161814	89530	75112	769574	398210	242721	119254	9389	1.120	1.048	1.300	1.003	1.010
1964	409270	169047	108273	76057	816567	409270	253571	144220	9507	1.127	1.053	1.323	1.003	1.017
1965	430495	180409	127274	79930	880629	430495	270614	169529	9991	1.128	1.043	1.346	1.003	1.019
COMMUNIST EASTERN EUROPE														
1925	50291	2399	905	337	55138	50291	3599	1205	42	1.181	1.176	1.326	1.000	0.795
1929	70095	3263	1276	439	76744	70095	4895	1700	55	1.227	1.198	1.718	1.000	0.843
1933	42705	2768	1965	483	49534	42705	4152	2617	60	1.369	1.239	2.948	1.000	0.973
1937	57787	3169	2543	894	66040	57787	4754	3387	112	1.319	1.237	2.560	1.000	0.983
1938	58771	3689	2453	938	67690	58771	5534	3267	117	1.284	1.228	2.058	1.000	1.000
1950	149588	5130	2438	2126	160796	149588	7695	3247	266	1.144	1.146	1.186	0.977	1.103
1953	187999	8404	4652	2657	207134	187999	12606	6196	332	1.093	1.085	1.259	0.975	1.001
1955	208152	9690	5245	4323	230214	208152	14535	6986	540	1.098	1.086	1.344	0.969	0.968
1957	231212	12471	6451	4431	259065	231212	18707	8593	554	1.027	1.027	1.055	0.967	1.000
1960	256806	16219	8974	6459	293895	256806	24329	11953	807	1.022	1.038	0.882	0.970	0.971
1961	270931	18131	9815	6336	311993	270931	27197	13074	792	1.006	1.028	0.812	0.970	0.990
1962	284412	20811	11373	7641	331733	284412	31217	15149	955	0.990	1.019	0.731	0.973	0.908
1963	298852	23866	13114	7594	353068	298852	35799	17468	949	0.973	1.011	0.657	0.976	0.840
1964	310144	27209	14346	7541	371008	310144	40814	19109	943	0.958	1.006	0.587	0.978	0.838
1965	307188	30107	16077	10943	375131	307188	45161	21415	1368	0.955	1.014	0.543	0.976	0.867
COMMUNIST ASIA														
1925	22289	941	-	-	23701	22289	1412	-	-	0.952	1.012	-	-	-
1929	22156	1076	-	-	23770	22156	1614	-	-	1.012	1.085	0.005	-	-
1933	23148	1191	-	-	24935	23148	1787	-	-	1.064	1.140	0.076	-	-
1937	29092	1273	-	-	31002	29092	1910	-	-	1.117	1.180	0.157	-	-
1938	25833	998	-	-	27330	25833	1497	-	-	1.102	1.150	0.281	-	-
1950	42320	100	-	5280	43130	42320	150	-	660	1.008	1.005	2.000	-	1.000
1953	65398	622	-	2560	66651	65398	933	-	320	1.000	1.000	1.000	-	1.000
1955	94003	2341	-	6200	98290	94003	3512	-	775	0.989	1.011	0.413	-	1.000
1957	124856	3777	-	10302	131809	124856	5666	-	1288	0.987	1.014	0.392	-	1.000
1960	219260	9099	-	19304	235321	219260	13649	-	2413	0.981	1.004	0.608	-	1.000
1961	248558	9606	-	16500	265029	248558	14409	-	2063	0.985	1.005	0.648	-	1.000
1962	250653	9318	-	17000	266755	250653	13977	-	2125	0.991	1.005	0.732	-	1.000
1963	270076	9774	-	17500	286924	270076	14661	-	2188	0.993	1.005	0.769	-	1.000
1964	290703	9973	-	19000	308037	290703	14960	-	2375	0.997	1.004	0.854	-	1.000
1965	303818	11046	-	21000	323012	303818	16569	-	2625	1.000	1.005	0.907	-	1.000
ORGANISATION FOR ECONOMIC CO-OPERATION AND DEVELOPMENT (OECD)														
1925	1079892	106236	33819	73284	1293454	1079892	159354	45047	9161	1.038	1.043	1.021	1.000	0.999
1929	1190578	148828	54255	109135	1499729	1190578	223242	72268	13642	1.024	1.035	0.975	1.000	1.001
1933	852469	138692	44659	115417	1134420	852469	208038	59486	14427	1.007	1.029	0.919	1.001	1.001
1937	1093333	191776	69001	157352	1492576	1093333	287664	91909	19669	1.007	1.025	0.942	1.002	1.002
1938	999492	184626	65693	159374	1383856	999492	276939	87503	19922	1.002	1.021	0.936	1.001	1.002
1950	1069238	373198	174203	297814	1898300	1069238	559797	232038	37227	0.941	1.006	0.788	1.003	0.999
1953	1046335	469940	235163	350003	2108232	1046335	704910	313237	43750	0.924	1.001	0.769	1.003	1.003
1955	1052167	540423	265789	392040	2265837	1052167	810635	354031	49005	0.903	1.002	0.725	1.002	1.003
1957	1090677	596342	305942	437538	2447397	1090677	894513	407515	54692	0.895	1.006	0.705	1.000	1.004
1960	978844	701135	378987	533644	2602063	978844	1051703	504811	66706	0.835	0.990	0.604	0.997	1.001
1961	963673	748298	398280	552314	2685668	963673	1122447	530509	69039	0.821	0.988	0.584	0.997	1.004
1962	990196	804455	425466	566171	2834370	990196	1206683	566721	70771	0.806	0.984	0.560	0.997	1.000
1963	1021922	870358	449557	591519	3000209	1021922	1305537	598810	73940	0.793	0.984	0.537	0.998	1.000
1964	1055624	936688	478625	606748	3174028	1055624	1405032	637529	75844	0.777	0.981	0.511	0.997	1.003
1965	1058512	1010309	498387	661019	3320455	1058512	1515464	663851	82627	0.759	0.980	0.487	0.996	1.001

Table X. TOTAL ENERGY CONSUMPTION AND RATIO OF PRODUCTION TO CONSUMPTION, SELECTED YEARS, 1925-1965

	Consumption in original units				Consumption in coal equivalents (10^3 m.t.)					Ratio of production to consumption				
Region, country, year	Solid fuels (10^3 m.t. coal equiv.)	Liquid fuels (10^3 m.t.)	Natural gas (10^6 c.m.)	Hydro-electric power (10^6 kwh)	Total	Solid fuels	Liquid fuels	Natural gas	Hydro-electric power	Total	Solid fuels	Liquid fuels	Natural gas	Hydro-electric power
	(1)	(2)	(3)	(4)	(5)	(6)	(7)	(8)	(9)	(10)	(11)	(12)	(13)	(14)
COMMUNIST COUNTRIES														
1925	89014	9119	1045	588	104158	89014	13679	1392	74	1.101	1.092	1.126	1.000	0.883
1929	129817	14266	1606	996	153480	129817	21399	2139	125	1.154	1.114	1.353	1.000	0.931
1933	137742	20711	3075	1646	173110	137742	31067	4096	206	1.162	1.098	1.439	1.000	0.992
1937	209236	31452	4722	5085	263340	209236	47178	6290	636	1.104	1.081	1.177	1.000	0.997
1938	213479	33950	4663	6029	271369	213479	50925	6211	754	1.085	1.064	1.128	1.000	1.000
1950	425208	45758	8174	20097	507245	425208	68637	10888	2512	1.024	1.031	0.988	0.996	1.011
1953	531197	62603	11425	24418	643372	531197	93905	15218	3052	1.023	1.020	1.046	0.998	1.000
1955	642855	82433	14086	33698	789480	642855	123650	18763	4212	1.029	1.024	1.056	0.998	0.995
1957	729778	107815	24863	54162	931389	729778	161723	33118	6770	1.029	1.021	1.074	0.998	1.000
1960	867136	147430	54034	76646	1169835	867136	221145	71973	9581	1.047	1.023	1.159	1.000	0.998
1961	903379	159646	68526	81884	1244360	903379	239469	91277	10236	1.054	1.023	1.193	1.000	1.000
1962	917605	177659	84596	96353	1308820	917605	266489	112682	12044	1.057	1.026	1.194	1.000	0.995
1963	967138	195454	102644	100206	1409567	967138	293181	136722	12526	1.057	1.025	1.195	1.000	0.995
1964	1010116	206229	122619	102598	1495613	1010116	309344	163329	12825	1.058	1.024	1.203	1.000	1.001
1965	1041501	221562	143351	111873	1578771	1041501	332343	190944	13984	1.061	1.023	1.215	1.000	1.000
WORLD EXCLUDING OECD AND COMMUNIST COUNTRIES														
1925	61116	15805	1113	4922	86921	61116	23708	1483	615	1.257	0.937	2.105	0.998	1.000
1929	65953	22219	1962	7019	102772	65953	33329	2613	877	1.316	0.906	2.161	0.998	1.000
1933	54979	16417	2903	9904	84709	54979	24626	3867	1238	1.445	0.911	2.733	0.980	0.998
1937	76096	29249	4241	15192	127518	76096	43874	5649	1899	1.414	0.900	2.379	0.968	0.999
1938	78843	31965	4468	16707	134831	78843	47948	5951	2088	1.379	0.930	2.181	0.989	0.999
1950	98732	62512	6885	29467	205354	98732	93768	9171	3683	1.999	0.955	3.246	0.904	0.996
1953	108382	76719	9980	39112	241642	108382	115079	13293	4889	2.105	0.960	3.365	0.946	0.995
1955	121613	105641	12595	48165	302871	121613	158462	16777	6021	2.059	0.936	3.077	0.956	0.998
1957	133732	128145	17308	60236	356533	133732	192218	23054	7530	2.048	0.937	2.986	1.010	1.007
1960	152519	150800	26862	77582	424197	152519	226200	35780	9698	2.222	0.954	3.315	1.044	0.997
1961	157753	161022	29836	87129	449919	157753	241533	39742	10891	2.248	0.969	3.338	1.044	0.994
1962	165122	170864	33157	97891	477819	165122	256296	44165	12236	2.342	0.978	3.510	1.035	0.995
1963	174253	176865	35482	105047	499943	174253	265298	47262	13131	2.427	0.981	3.696	1.032	0.994
1964	179616	190716	40613	114480	534097	179616	286074	54097	14310	2.515	0.982	3.834	1.032	0.990
1965	190738	207523	43019	128212	575350	190738	311285	57301	16026	2.548	0.994	3.856	1.050	0.992

DERIVATION OF TABLE XI

Column	*Derivation*
(1)	Col. (6) table X as percent of col. (5) table X
(2)	Col. (7) table X as percent of col. (5) table X
(3)	Col. (8) table X as percent of col. (5) table X
(4)	Col. (9) table X as percent of col. (5) table X
(5)	Col. (5) table X as percent of col. (5) table X
(6)	Col. (5) table X
(7)	Sources
(8)	Col. (6) divided by col. (7) times 1,000
(9)	Sources
(10)	Col. (9) divided by col. (7) times 1,000

Table XI. TOTAL ENERGY CONSUMPTION: PERCENTAGE DISTRIBUTION BY FUEL; RELATED DATA ON POPULATION AND ELECTRICITY CONSUMPTION, SELECTED YEARS, 1925-1965

	Percentage distribution of total consumption (based on coal equivalents)								Addendum: Electricity consumption	
Region, country, year	Solid fuels	Liquid fuels	Natural gas	Hydro-electric power	Total	Total consumption (10^3 m.t. coal equiv.)	Population (10^3)	Consumption per capita (kgs)	Total (10^6 kwh)	Per capita (kwh)
	(1)	(2)	(3)	(4)	(5)	(6)	(7)	(8)	(9)	(10)
WORLD										
1925	82.9	13.3	3.2	0.7	100.0	1484533	1890146	785	188933	100
1929	79.0	15.8	4.4	0.8	100.0	1755981	1980968	886	280267	141
1933	75.1	18.9	4.8	1.1	100.0	1392238	2062628	675	286260	139
1937	73.2	20.1	5.5	1.2	100.0	1883433	2145835	878	436246	203
1938	72.2	21.0	5.6	1.3	100.0	1790056	2168037	826	449537	207
1950	61.0	27.7	9.7	1.7	100.0	2610900	2504539	1042	945852	378
1953	56.3	30.5	11.4	1.7	100.0	2993246	2629477	1138	1246820	474
1955	54.1	32.5	11.6	1.8	100.0	3358188	2725562	1232	1540064	565
1957	52.3	33.4	12.4	1.8	100.0	3735319	2827856	1321	1805733	639
1960	47.6	35.7	14.6	2.0	100.0	4196095	2989858	1403	2304323	771
1961	46.2	36.6	15.1	2.1	100.0	4379947	3050762	1436	2433498	798
1962	44.9	37.4	15.7	2.1	100.0	4621009	3104079	1489	2637540	850
1963	44.1	38.0	15.9	2.0	100.0	4909718	3163394	1552	2847778	900
1964	43.1	38.4	16.4	2.0	100.0	5203738	3222098	1615	3104683	964
1965	41.8	39.4	16.7	2.1	100.0	5474576	3281230	1668	3342245	1019
NORTH AMERICA										
1925	74.5	18.9	6.0	0.6	100.0	748857	125410	5971	90485	722
1929	68.3	22.5	8.4	0.8	100.0	862492	132090	6530	137691	1042
1933	61.4	27.8	9.7	1.1	100.0	611894	136641	4478	120364	881

Table XI. TOTAL ENERGY CONSUMPTION: PERCENTAGE DISTRIBUTION BY FUEL; RELATED DATA ON POPULATION AND ELECTRICITY CONSUMPTION, SELECTED YEARS, 1925-1965

Region, country, year	Percentage distribution of total consumption (based on coal equivalents)					Total consumption (10³ m.t. coal equiv.)	Population (10³)	Consumption per capita (kgs)	Addendum: Electricity consumption	
	Solid fuels	Liquid fuels	Natural gas	Hydro-electric power	Total				Total (10⁶ kwh)	Per capita (kwh)
	(1)	(2)	(3)	(4)	(5)	(6)	(7)	(8)	(9)	(10)
NORTH AMERICA (CONTINUED)										
1937	59.0	28.8	11.1	1.1	100.0	824333	140334	5874	174855	1246
1938	54.9	31.5	12.4	1.3	100.0	706900	141451	4997	168732	1193
1950	43.0	37.5	18.0	1.5	100.0	1276341	166055	7686	443550	2671
1953	33.9	42.1	22.4	1.6	100.0	1378272	175119	7870	583988	3335
1955	30.7	43.9	23.7	1.6	100.0	1461298	181719	8042	711976	3918
1957	28.9	43.8	25.5	1.7	100.0	1557168	188715	8251	809086	4287
1960	24.2	44.5	29.4	1.9	100.0	1659469	198651	8354	958042	4823
1961	22.9	45.1	30.1	1.9	100.0	1694843	202084	8387	994715	4922
1962	22.7	44.6	30.7	1.9	100.0	1772039	205317	8631	1063467	5180
1963	23.2	44.1	30.9	1.8	100.0	1860472	208406	8927	1133201	5437
1964	23.5	43.3	31.3	1.9	100.0	1951196	211456	9227	1216629	5754
1965	23.6	43.4	31.1	1.9	100.0	2040158	214221	9524	1297960	6059
CANADA										
1925	81.9	12.5	2.1	3.5	100.0	31139	9559	3258	9343	977
1929	73.7	19.0	2.5	4.8	100.0	42551	10300	4131	17691	1718
1933	67.5	22.8	2.9	6.7	100.0	29799	10919	2729	17709	1622
1937	65.4	23.8	3.0	7.8	100.0	40547	11339	3576	28379	2503
1938	62.9	25.8	3.3	8.0	100.0	37443	11448	3271	26777	2339
1950	53.0	35.0	3.7	8.4	100.0	75292	13737	5481	53204	3873
1953	40.6	45.3	4.5	9.7	100.0	83845	14886	5632	67696	4548
1955	32.4	51.4	6.3	9.9	100.0	90842	15736	5773	78540	4991
1957	28.4	53.0	8.7	9.9	100.0	99633	16677	5974	86790	5204
1960	18.6	55.3	14.5	11.5	100.0	109277	17909	6102	109250	6100
1961	16.5	55.7	16.5	11.2	100.0	112673	18269	6167	110927	6072
1962	16.1	53.5	19.4	11.0	100.0	116850	18600	6282	116175	6246
1963	15.0	53.3	21.9	9.8	100.0	131953	18925	6972	121580	6424
1964	14.7	49.6	26.2	9.5	100.0	147212	19271	7639	133051	6904
1965	14.8	50.2	25.8	9.2	100.0	158350	19604	8077	140821	7183
UNITED STATES										
1925	74.2	19.2	6.2	0.5	100.0	717714	115832	6196	81142	701
1929	68.1	22.7	8.7	0.6	100.0	819935	121770	6733	120000	985
1933	61.0	28.1	10.1	0.8	100.0	582085	125701	4631	102655	817
1937	58.6	29.1	11.6	0.8	100.0	783767	128973	6077	146476	1136
1938	54.4	31.8	12.9	0.9	100.0	669439	129981	5150	141955	1092
1950	42.3	37.7	18.9	1.1	100.0	1201030	152290	7886	390345	2563
1953	33.4	41.9	23.6	1.1	100.0	1294406	160203	8080	516287	3223
1955	30.6	43.4	24.9	1.1	100.0	1370342	165951	8258	633424	3817
1957	28.9	43.2	26.7	1.2	100.0	1457444	172004	8473	722275	4199
1960	24.6	43.7	30.4	1.2	100.0	1550090	180704	8578	848760	4697
1961	23.3	44.3	31.1	1.2	100.0	1582109	183776	8609	883757	4809
1962	23.2	44.0	31.5	1.3	100.0	1655060	186677	8866	947259	5074
1963	23.8	43.4	31.6	1.2	100.0	1728353	189440	9123	1011584	5340
1964	24.3	42.8	31.7	1.3	100.0	1803817	192143	9388	1083538	5639
1965	24.3	42.9	31.5	1.3	100.0	1881628	194572	9671	1157096	5947

Table XI. TOTAL ENERGY CONSUMPTION: PERCENTAGE DISTRIBUTION BY FUEL; RELATED DATA ON POPULATION AND ELECTRICITY CONSUMPTION, SELECTED YEARS, 1925-1965

Region, country, year	Percentage distribution of total consumption (based on coal equivalents)					Total consumption (10^3 m.t. coal equiv.)	Population (10^3)	Consumption per capita (kgs)	Addendum: Electricity consumption	
	Solid fuels	Liquid fuels	Natural gas	Hydro-electric power	Total				Total (10^6 kwh)	Per capita (kwh)
	(1)	(2)	(3)	(4)	(5)	(6)	(7)	(8)	(9)	(10)
WESTERN EUROPE										
1925	96.0	3.2	-	0.7	100.0	517017	279718	1848	70236	251
1929	94.8	4.3	-	0.9	100.0	603632	287319	2101	97903	341
1933	92.0	6.8	-	1.2	100.0	486297	294997	1648	101263	343
1937	91.6	7.1	-	1.3	100.0	615624	302184	2037	151468	501
1938	91.0	7.7	-	1.3	100.0	619150	304201	2035	161989	533
1950	83.8	13.5	0.3	2.4	100.0	583907	302428	1931	248713	822
1953	79.8	16.9	0.7	2.6	100.0	667601	308861	2161	312684	1012
1955	75.6	20.8	1.0	2.7	100.0	748189	313499	2387	389655	1243
1957	72.7	23.4	1.2	2.7	100.0	813299	318536	2553	451306	1417
1960	62.4	32.3	1.9	3.4	100.0	849524	326485	2602	568773	1742
1961	59.5	35.0	2.1	3.4	100.0	877994	329552	2664	610815	1853
1962	56.8	37.8	2.2	3.2	100.0	939914	333095	2822	665032	1997
1963	53.9	40.6	2.2	3.3	100.0	1003737	336548	2982	714974	2124
1964	51.0	43.7	2.3	3.0	100.0	1072916	339563	3160	771009	2271
1965	47.1	47.1	2.5	3.3	100.0	1117213	343126	3256	822722	2398
EUROPEAN ECONOMIC COMMUNITY (EEC)										
1925	96.9	2.4	-	0.6	100.0	292460	157435	1858	40877	260
1929	96.0	3.2	-	0.7	100.0	358776	161627	2220	61929	383
1933	93.1	5.8	-	1.1	100.0	273132	165484	1651	60975	368
1937	92.6	6.2	-	1.2	100.0	359290	168949	2127	94075	557
1938	92.2	6.6	-	1.2	100.0	366811	170018	2157	101105	595
1950	84.7	12.7	0.4	2.2	100.0	279287	157555	1773	122135	775
1953	80.6	16.0	1.1	2.3	100.0	335452	161256	2080	158408	982
1955	75.8	20.2	1.6	2.4	100.0	379720	163951	2316	192020	1171
1957	72.7	23.2	2.0	2.1	100.0	429297	167057	2570	226028	1353
1960	61.8	32.1	3.1	2.9	100.0	453263	171735	2639	284548	1657
1961	58.5	35.4	3.5	2.6	100.0	473970	173470	2732	303944	1752
1962	54.9	39.2	3.6	2.3	100.0	509096	175515	2901	327845	1868
1963	51.8	42.3	3.4	2.5	100.0	557877	177724	3139	355100	1998
1964	48.7	45.8	3.5	2.0	100.0	604215	179665	3363	383500	2135
1965	43.9	50.0	3.8	2.3	100.0	631646	181666	3477	404513	2227
BELGIUM-LUXEMBOURG										
1925	98.4	1.6	-	-	100.0	30953	8046	3847	2274	283
1929	98.3	1.7	-	-	100.0	37436	8324	4497	4043	486
1933	97.8	2.2	-	-	100.0	28238	8533	3309	4333	508
1937	96.6	3.4	-	-	100.0	34307	8645	3968	6112	707
1938	96.2	3.8	-	-	100.0	30849	8675	3556	5740	662
1950	89.9	10.0	-	0.1	100.0	30706	8936	3436	9241	1034
1953	87.1	12.7	0.2	-	100.0	34697	9082	3820	10628	1170
1955	80.3	19.4	0.2	0.1	100.0	36051	9173	3930	12920	1408
1957	78.6	21.1	0.2	-	100.0	41734	9297	4489	14620	1573
1960	72.5	27.3	0.2	0.1	100.0	37890	9467	4002	16640	1758
1961	67.8	32.1	0.1	-	100.0	38802	9501	4084	17345	1826
1962	64.7	35.2	0.2	-	100.0	41102	9543	4307	18715	1961
1963	63.1	36.6	0.1	0.2	100.0	47251	9614	4915	19760	2055
1964	60.0	39.5	0.1	0.3	100.0	49393	9706	5089	21477	2213
1965	56.0	43.4	0.1	0.5	100.0	50460	9795	5152	22405	2287

Table XI. TOTAL ENERGY CONSUMPTION: PERCENTAGE DISTRIBUTION BY FUEL; RELATED DATA ON POPULATION AND ELECTRICITY CONSUMPTION, SELECTED YEARS, 1925-1965

Region, country, year	Percentage distribution of total consumption (based on coal equivalents)					Total consumption (10^3 m.t. coal equiv.)	Population (10^3)	Consumption per capita (kgs)	Addendum: Electricity consumption	
	Solid fuels	Liquid fuels	Natural gas	Hydro-electric power	Total				Total (10^6 kwh)	Per capita (kwh)
	(1)	(2)	(3)	(4)	(5)	(6)	(7)	(8)	(9)	(10)
FRANCE										
1925	95.5	3.7	-	0.8	100.0	75518	40323	1873	10222	254
1929	94.5	4.6	-	1.0	100.0	89534	40825	2193	14352	352
1933	89.3	9.4	-	1.3	100.0	78179	41363	1890	16400	396
1937	87.5	10.8	-	1.7	100.0	83121	41224	2016	20080	487
1938	85.7	12.5	-	1.8	100.0	78144	41124	1900	20800	506
1950	77.4	19.7	0.4	2.5	100.0	81213	41736	1946	33265	797
1953	73.0	23.7	0.4	2.9	100.0	90040	42674	2110	41451	971
1955	67.6	28.7	0.4	3.3	100.0	98134	43449	2259	49560	1141
1957	68.5	28.2	0.6	2.7	100.0	117098	44332	2641	57700	1302
1960	58.6	34.0	3.2	4.2	100.0	121241	45707	2653	72020	1576
1961	54.9	36.6	4.5	3.9	100.0	123234	46185	2668	76583	1658
1962	52.9	38.6	5.0	3.4	100.0	128352	47020	2730	82340	1751
1963	49.4	42.1	4.6	3.9	100.0	142230	47877	2971	88815	1855
1964	47.4	45.1	4.5	3.0	100.0	154189	48434	3183	96007	1982
1965	42.5	49.4	4.4	3.7	100.0	161941	48945	3309	103926	2123
GERMANY										
1925	98.7	1.1	-	0.2	100.0	161689	63166	2560	20832	330
1929	97.9	1.9	-	0.2	100.0	199107	64739	3076	31550	487
1933	96.8	2.8	-	0.4	100.0	138586	66027	2099	26505	401
1937	96.5	3.0	-	0.5	100.0	206734	67831	3048	48969	722
1938	96.3	3.3	NA	0.5	100.0	223368	68558	3258	55333	807
GERMANY, FEDERAL REPUBLIC										
1950	94.6	4.4	-	1.0	100.0	128270	49986	2566	47376	948
1953	92.9	6.1	0.1	0.8	100.0	158894	51386	3092	64168	1249
1955	89.9	8.8	0.4	0.9	100.0	181683	52363	3470	80020	1528
1957	86.8	12.0	0.4	0.8	100.0	194315	53649	3622	97228	1812
1960	76.0	22.5	0.5	1.0	100.0	204378	55423	3688	123148	2222
1961	73.6	24.9	0.5	1.0	100.0	212926	56227	3787	131616	2341
1962	68.5	30.0	0.7	0.9	100.0	228813	56947	4018	141427	2483
1963	65.4	33.0	0.9	0.8	100.0	243973	57607	4235	152852	2653
1964	61.9	36.3	1.1	0.6	100.0	264372	58290	4535	165359	2837
1965	56.9	40.7	1.5	0.9	100.0	273084	59041	4625	172974	2930
ITALY										
1925	83.9	9.2	0.1	6.9	100.0	12944	38534	336	6545	170
1929	82.3	10.5	0.1	7.1	100.0	18111	39958	453	10380	260
1933	70.8	18.6	0.1	10.4	100.0	13890	41324	336	11650	282
1937	71.3	18.9	0.1	9.7	100.0	19548	42651	458	15430	362
1938	70.5	19.6	0.1	9.8	100.0	19174	42977	446	15544	362
1950	49.2	31.8	3.6	15.4	100.0	18649	46783	399	24876	532
1953	35.2	41.7	10.4	12.7	100.0	29123	47621	612	32571	684
1955	30.3	45.9	12.9	10.9	100.0	37391	48215	776	38140	791
1957	26.5	50.4	14.1	9.0	100.0	47204	48758	968	43190	886
1960	18.9	56.0	14.8	10.3	100.0	58173	49658	1171	56110	1130
1961	17.4	59.6	14.2	8.7	100.0	64153	49920	1285	60733	1217
1962	16.0	64.0	12.8	7.2	100.0	74508	50208	1484	66128	1317

Table XI. TOTAL ENERGY CONSUMPTION: PERCENTAGE DISTRIBUTION BY FUEL; RELATED DATA ON POPULATION AND ELECTRICITY CONSUMPTION, SELECTED YEARS, 1925-1965

Region, country, year	Percentage distribution of total consumption (based on coal equivalents)					Total consumption (10^3 m.t. coal equiv.)	Population (10^3)	Consumption per capita (kgs)	Addendum: Electricity consumption	
	Solid fuels	Liquid fuels	Natural gas	Hydro-electric power	Total				Total (10^6 kwh)	Per capita (kwh)
	(1)	(2)	(3)	(4)	(5)	(6)	(7)	(8)	(9)	(10)
ITALY (CONTINUED)										
1963	14.8	66.2	11.6	7.5	100.0	83518	50659	1649	72643	1434
1964	12.4	70.6	11.1	5.8	100.0	91989	51108	1800	77664	1520
1965	11.2	72.8	10.4	5.7	100.0	100079	51593	1940	80180	1554
NETHERLANDS										
1925	92.0	8.0	-	-	100.0	11357	7366	1542	1004	136
1929	91.3	8.6	-	-	100.0	14587	7781	1875	1604	206
1933	90.3	9.6	-	-	100.0	14239	8237	1729	2087	253
1937	86.5	13.5	-	-	100.0	15579	8598	1812	3484	405
1938	84.7	15.3	-	-	100.0	15277	8684	1759	3688	425
1950	76.6	22.8	0.7	-	100.0	20450	10114	2022	7377	729
1953	73.5	26.3	0.2	-	100.0	22698	10493	2163	9590	914
1955	66.9	32.3	0.8	-	100.0	26460	10751	2461	11380	1059
1957	62.0	37.2	0.8	-	100.0	28946	11021	2626	13290	1206
1960	49.2	49.3	1.5	-	100.0	31581	11480	2751	16630	1449
1961	43.8	54.4	1.8	-	100.0	34856	11637	2995	17667	1518
1962	44.6	53.4	2.0	-	100.0	36320	11797	3079	19235	1630
1963	41.8	56.2	2.0	-	100.0	40906	11967	3418	21030	1757
1964	36.5	60.9	2.6	-	100.0	44271	12127	3651	22993	1896
1965	30.0	64.9	5.1	-	100.0	46081	12292	3749	25028	2036
EUROPEAN FREE TRADE ASSOCIATION (EFTA)										
1925	95.0	4.1	-	0.8	100.0	207138	67937	3049	26687	393
1929	93.3	5.7	-	1.0	100.0	223190	68908	3239	31736	461
1933	91.0	7.9	-	1.2	100.0	194877	70177	2777	34312	489
1937	90.8	7.9	-	1.3	100.0	239592	71282	3361	50246	705
1938	89.7	8.9	-	1.4	100.0	232202	71568	3244	52860	739
1950	84.0	13.4	0.2	2.4	100.0	269810	76913	3508	110345	1435
1953	80.2	17.0	0.3	2.6	100.0	292840	77719	3768	132393	1703
1955	76.3	20.7	0.3	2.7	100.0	324382	78397	4138	169185	2158
1957	73.8	22.8	0.3	3.0	100.0	332239	79216	4194	190718	2408
1960	63.2	32.6	0.6	3.6	100.0	336021	80713	4163	239455	2967
1961	60.9	34.6	0.6	3.9	100.0	341031	81411	4189	256444	3150
1962	59.5	35.8	0.6	4.0	100.0	362525	82243	4408	281584	3424
1963	56.9	38.5	0.7	3.9	100.0	372407	82833	4496	298258	3601
1964	54.3	40.9	0.7	4.1	100.0	388633	83505	4654	317968	3808
1965	51.4	43.5	0.9	4.3	100.0	398912	84142	4741	343453	4082
AUSTRIA										
1925	95.1	2.6	-	2.3	100.0	7069	6582	1074	2110	321
1929	93.9	3.8	-	2.3	100.0	8935	6664	1341	2430	365
1933	87.6	8.6	-	3.8	100.0	5474	6745	812	2089	310
1937	86.8	8.9	-	4.3	100.0	5982	6755	886	2549	377
1938	87.2	8.9	-	3.9	100.0	6528	6753	967	2627	389
1950	78.1	9.9	6.4	5.5	100.0	9734	6935	1404	5659	816
1953	70.6	15.5	7.3	6.6	100.0	10188	6960	1464	7674	1103
1955	60.9	25.7	7.2	6.2	100.0	13868	6974	1989	9670	1387
1957	63.8	22.3	7.0	7.0	100.0	14458	6997	2066	11220	1604

Table XI. TOTAL ENERGY CONSUMPTION: PERCENTAGE DISTRIBUTION BY FUEL; RELATED DATA ON POPULATION AND ELECTRICITY CONSUMPTION, SELECTED YEARS, 1925-1965

Region, country, year	Percentage distribution of total consumption (based on coal equivalents)					Total consumption (10^3 m.t. coal equiv.)	Population (10^3)	Consumption per capita (kgs)	Addendum: Electricity consumption	
	Solid fuels	Liquid fuels	Natural gas	Hydro-electric power	Total				Total (10^6 kwh)	Per capita (kwh)
	(1)	(2)	(3)	(4)	(5)	(6)	(7)	(8)	(9)	(10)
AUSTRIA (CONTINUED)										
1960	51.5	28.1	12.5	7.9	100.0	15699	7081	2217	14060	1986
1961	47.3	31.8	13.2	7.7	100.0	15754	7087	2223	14679	2071
1962	45.7	34.1	12.8	7.4	100.0	16954	7130	2378	15708	2203
1963	45.7	35.2	12.2	6.9	100.0	18535	7172	2584	16747	2335
1964	41.8	39.4	12.1	6.7	100.0	19404	7215	2689	17656	2447
1965	39.1	40.5	12.2	8.1	100.0	18746	7255	2584	19285	2658
DENMARK										
1925	90.3	9.7	-	0.1	100.0	4624	3425	1350	380	111
1929	89.7	10.2	-	0.1	100.0	6266	3518	1781	560	159
1933	85.4	14.6	-	-	100.0	5886	3633	1620	750	206
1937	85.4	14.6	-	-	100.0	7268	3749	1939	1104	294
1938	81.1	18.8	-	-	100.0	6855	3777	1815	1142	302
1950	71.1	28.6	-	0.3	100.0	8828	4271	2067	2395	561
1953	69.3	30.3	-	0.4	100.0	9382	4369	2147	3046	697
1955	63.8	36.3	-	-0.1	100.0	12220	4439	2753	3710	836
1957	49.5	50.0	-	0.5	100.0	10907	4488	2430	4080	909
1960	44.8	55.1	-	0.1	100.0	13327	4581	2909	5280	1153
1961	40.2	59.0	-	0.8	100.0	14097	4610	3058	5851	1269
1962	37.8	61.5	-	0.7	100.0	15844	4647	3409	6670	1435
1963	34.5	65.1	-	0.3	100.0	17433	4684	3722	7420	1584
1964	28.8	70.6	-	0.6	100.0	18729	4720	3968	8140	1725
1965	24.3	74.6	-	1.1	100.0	19740	4758	4149	8711	1831
NORWAY										
1925	70.6	8.0	-	21.4	100.0	3617	2747	1317	6187	2252
1929	69.6	9.3	-	21.1	100.0	4458	2795	1595	7516	2689
1933	63.8	15.2	-	21.0	100.0	4361	2858	1526	7250	2537
1937	64.8	14.7	-	20.6	100.0	5630	2919	1929	9006	3085
1938	59.5	16.8	-	23.6	100.0	5244	2936	1786	9638	3283
1950	35.2	29.7	-	35.1	100.0	6370	3265	1951	17761	5440
1953	26.4	40.1	-	33.5	100.0	7334	3362	2181	19583	5825
1955	19.3	46.0	-	34.8	100.0	8155	3427	2380	22680	6618
1957	15.7	46.3	-	38.0	100.0	8499	3492	2434	25840	7400
1960	12.9	48.7	-	38.4	100.0	10203	3581	2849	31250	8727
1961	11.5	48.6	-	39.9	100.0	10564	3610	2926	33602	9308
1962	10.7	47.4	-	41.9	100.0	11238	3639	3088	37415	10282
1963	10.4	49.2	-	40.4	100.0	11980	3667	3267	38515	10503
1964	10.4	49.1	-	40.5	100.0	13209	3694	3576	42553	11519
1965	9.2	47.1	-	43.7	100.0	13482	3723	3621	47400	12732
PORTUGAL										
1925	89.6	9.8	-	0.6	100.0	917	6549	140	120	18
1929	86.4	12.9	-	0.7	100.0	1291	6861	188	240	35
1933	84.2	15.0	-	0.9	100.0	1404	7210	195	302	42
1937	82.3	16.7	-	1.0	100.0	1733	7581	229	406	54
1938	81.4	17.6	-	1.0	100.0	1659	7675	216	426	56

Table XI. TOTAL ENERGY CONSUMPTION: PERCENTAGE DISTRIBUTION BY FUEL; RELATED DATA ON POPULATION AND ELECTRICITY CONSUMPTION, SELECTED YEARS, 1925-1965

Region, country, year	Percentage distribution of total consumption (based on coal equivalents) Solid fuels	Liquid fuels	Natural gas	Hydro-electric power	Total	Total consumption (10^3 m.t. coal equiv.)	Population (10^3)	Consumption per capita (kgs)	Addendum: Electricity consumption Total (10^6 kwh)	Per capita (kwh)
	(1)	(2)	(3)	(4)	(5)	(6)	(7)	(8)	(9)	(10)
PORTUGAL (CONTINUED)										
1950	58.0	39.3	-	2.7	100.0	2032	8550	238	942	110
1953	41.2	53.5	-	5.2	100.0	2390	8695	275	1380	159
1955	33.1	59.0	-	7.9	100.0	2739	8782	312	1890	215
1957	34.0	59.1	-	6.9	100.0	3328	8865	375	2170	245
1960	26.7	61.8	-	11.5	100.0	3378	9025	374	3260	361
1961	29.1	59.5	-	11.3	100.0	3772	9099	415	3612	397
1962	25.8	62.9	-	11.2	100.0	3914	9182	426	3834	418
1963	25.9	62.6	-	11.5	100.0	4275	9255	462	4247	459
1964	25.2	63.0	-	11.8	100.0	4459	9107	490	4749	521
1965	22.2	66.5	-	11.2	100.0	4913	9456	520	4622	489
SWEDEN										
1925	83.8	8.3	-	7.9	100.0	5320	6045	880	3673	608
1929	83.7	9.1	-	7.2	100.0	7848	6113	1284	4967	813
1933	78.4	14.0	-	7.6	100.0	8059	6201	1300	5344	862
1937	78.2	14.5	-	7.3	100.0	11890	6276	1894	7982	1272
1938	73.8	17.8	-	8.4	100.0	10899	6297	1731	8162	1296
1950	47.8	37.3	-	14.8	100.0	14444	7014	2059	17995	2566
1953	35.2	49.0	-	15.8	100.0	16638	7171	2320	22139	3087
1955	28.6	58.1	-	13.3	100.0	20475	7262	2819	24840	3421
1957	23.5	61.5	-	14.9	100.0	22361	7364	3036	28580	3881
1960	14.5	71.3	-	14.2	100.0	26646	7480	3562	33970	4541
1961	13.0	70.6	-	16.4	100.0	27111	7520	3605	37327	4964
1962	11.7	72.0	-	16.3	100.0	29310	7562	3876	39827	5267
1963	10.9	73.7	-	15.3	100.0	30933	7604	4068	40720	5355
1964	10.6	73.8	-	15.6	100.0	34387	7661	4489	45042	5879
1965	8.7	75.3	-	16.0	100.0	35611	7734	4604	48726	6300
SWITZERLAND										
1925	81.8	6.7	-	11.5	100.0	3312	3988	831	3059	767
1929	78.9	8.9	-	12.2	100.0	4399	4054	1085	4301	1061
1933	74.4	13.9	-	11.7	100.0	4255	4127	1031	3915	949
1937	73.4	12.5	-	14.0	100.0	4753	4200	1132	5374	1280
1938	71.9	13.2	-	14.9	100.0	4647	4216	1102	5583	1324
1950	48.9	27.7	-	23.3	100.0	5270	4708	1119	9995	2123
1953	39.6	32.4	-	28.0	100.0	5595	4892	1144	12589	2573
1955	36.4	38.9	-	24.6	100.0	7192	4995	1440	14215	2846
1957	36.7	42.4	-	21.0	100.0	9081	5141	1766	15408	2997
1960	24.8	54.1	-	21.1	100.0	10512	5378	1955	17955	3339
1961	21.0	57.1	-	21.9	100.0	10813	5513	1961	19031	3452
1962	19.2	59.1	-	21.8	100.0	12204	5677	2150	21425	3774
1963	18.7	64.1	-	17.2	100.0	15174	5780	2625	21220	3671
1964	13.5	68.0	-	18.5	100.0	14709	5892	2496	21939	3724
1965	9.8	72.6	-	17.6	100.0	16093	5963	2699	23470	3936
UNITED KINGDOM										
1925	96.2	3.8	-	-	100.0	182279	45150	4037	11278	250
1929	94.7	5.3	-	-	100.0	189993	45764	4152	11962	261

Table XI. TOTAL ENERGY CONSUMPTION: PERCENTAGE DISTRIBUTION BY FUEL; RELATED DATA ON POPULATION AND ELECTRICITY CONSUMPTION, SELECTED YEARS, 1925-1965

Region, country, year	Percentage distribution of total consumption (based on coal equivalents)					Total consumption (10^3 m.t. coal equiv.)	Population (10^3)	Consumption per capita (kgs)	Addendum: Electricity consumption	
	Solid fuels	Liquid fuels	Natural gas	Hydro-electric power	Total				Total (10^6 kwh)	Per capita (kwh)
	(1)	(2)	(3)	(4)	(5)	(6)	(7)	(8)	(9)	(10)
UNITED KINGDOM (CONTINUED)										
1933	93.1	6.9	-	-	100.0	165439	46613	3549	14964	321
1937	93.1	6.9	-	-	100.0	202335	47383	4270	24231	511
1938	92.3	7.7	-	0.1	100.0	196370	47589	4126	25708	540
1950	89.5	10.4	-	0.1	100.0	223133	50720	4399	56540	1115
1953	87.0	12.9	-	0.1	100.0	241313	50965	4735	67362	1322
1955	84.9	15.0	-	0.1	100.0	259733	51300	5063	94070	1834
1957	83.3	16.6	-	0.1	100.0	263606	51734	5095	105590	2041
1960	74.0	25.8	-	0.2	100.0	256257	52612	4871	136940	2603
1961	72.0	27.8	-	0.2	100.0	258919	53071	4879	145954	2750
1962	71.1	28.7	0.1	0.2	100.0	273063	53588	5096	160539	2996
1963	68.9	30.8	0.1	0.2	100.0	274077	53926	5082	173636	3220
1964	66.7	33.0	0.1	0.2	100.0	283737	54323	5223	182638	3362
1965	64.0	35.5	0.4	0.2	100.0	290326	54709	5307	195861	3580
WESTERN EUROPE - OTHER										
1925	92.8	5.7	-	1.5	100.0	17419	54346	321	2672	49
1929	90.3	7.9	-	1.8	100.0	21667	56784	382	4238	75
1933	85.1	11.8	-	3.0	100.0	18288	59336	308	5976	101
1937	80.7	15.5	-	3.8	100.0	16743	61953	270	7147	115
1938	83.1	13.5	-	3.4	100.0	20137	62615	322	8024	128
1950	74.9	21.2	0.1	3.8	100.0	34810	67960	512	16233	239
1953	69.9	25.3	0.1	4.7	100.0	39310	69886	562	21883	313
1955	68.8	25.7	0.1	5.4	100.0	44088	71151	620	28450	400
1957	66.1	28.6	0.1	5.1	100.0	51763	72263	716	34560	478
1960	61.5	32.4	0.1	6.0	100.0	60240	74037	814	44770	605
1961	60.0	33.7	0.1	6.2	100.0	62992	74671	844	50427	675
1962	56.3	37.2	0.2	6.3	100.0	68293	75337	907	55603	738
1963	54.4	38.6	0.3	6.6	100.0	73453	75991	967	61616	811
1964	52.5	41.0	0.5	6.0	100.0	80068	76393	1048	69541	910
1965	50.3	43.3	0.5	5.9	100.0	86656	77318	1121	74756	967
FINLAND										
1925	79.3	14.5	-	6.1	100.0	784	3304	237	541	164
1929	80.2	13.1	-	6.7	100.0	1472	3424	430	995	291
1933	77.4	12.1	-	10.5	100.0	1481	3526	420	1692	480
1937	79.1	11.8	-	9.1	100.0	2839	3626	783	2786	768
1938	72.6	15.0	-	12.4	100.0	2476	3656	677	3108	850
1950	63.2	22.6	-	14.2	100.0	3210	4009	801	4176	1042
1953	55.1	28.4	-	16.5	100.0	3772	4139	911	5398	1304
1955	52.8	32.1	-	15.1	100.0	5134	4235	1212	6820	1610
1957	46.3	41.5	-	12.2	100.0	6763	4324	1564	7700	1781
1960	40.3	50.7	-	9.0	100.0	7931	4430	1790	9020	2036
1961	35.9	52.1	-	12.0	100.0	8524	4467	1908	10645	2383
1962	31.5	55.5	-	13.1	100.0	9435	4505	2094	11698	2597
1963	25.2	63.9	-	10.9	100.0	9972	4543	2195	12162	2677
1964	27.6	62.6	-	9.8	100.0	11702	4580	2555	14332	3129
1965	25.1	65.3	-	9.6	100.0	13028	4612	2825	15357	3330

Table XI. TOTAL ENERGY CONSUMPTION: PERCENTAGE DISTRIBUTION BY FUEL; RELATED DATA ON POPULATION AND ELECTRICITY CONSUMPTION, SELECTED YEARS, 1925-1965

Region, country, year	Percentage distribution of total consumption (based on coal equivalents)					Total consumption (10^3 m.t. coal equiv.)	Population (10^3)	Consumption per capita (kgs)	Addendum: Electricity consumption	
	Solid fuels	Liquid fuels	Natural gas	Hydro-electric power	Total				Total (10^6 kwh)	Per capita (kwh)
	(1)	(2)	(3)	(4)	(5)	(6)	(7)	(8)	(9)	(10)
GREECE										
1925	88.3	11.6	-	0.1	100.0	831	5958	139	NA	NA
1929	80.1	19.8	-	0.1	100.0	1114	6286	177	102	16
1933	71.4	28.5	-	0.2	100.0	964	6624	145	156	24
1937	68.0	31.9	-	0.1	100.0	1521	7029	216	243	35
1938	66.5	33.4	-	0.1	100.0	1548	7122	217	271	38
1950	22.0	77.9	-	0.1	100.0	1782	7566	236	665	88
1953	22.9	76.9	-	0.2	100.0	2177	7817	278	912	117
1955	25.9	72.6	-	1.5	100.0	2749	7966	345	1390	174
1957	26.5	72.0	-	1.5	100.0	2945	8096	364	1690	209
1960	34.7	64.0	-	1.4	100.0	4343	8327	522	2280	274
1961	33.0	65.5	-	1.5	100.0	4494	8398	535	2507	299
1962	33.2	65.1	-	1.6	100.0	4683	8448	554	2812	333
1963	36.0	62.2	-	1.8	100.0	5632	8480	664	3162	373
1964	36.9	61.6	-	1.5	100.0	5943	8510	698	3765	442
1965	37.7	61.0	-	1.2	100.0	7728	8550	904	4343	508
ICELAND										
1950	25.1	69.5	-	5.4	100.0	389	143	2717	193	1350
1953	10.7	83.9	-	5.4	100.0	461	151	3055	230	1523
1955	12.6	77.5	-	9.9	100.0	478	158	3025	410	2595
1957	5.8	84.2	-	10.0	100.0	517	165	3133	440	2667
1960	3.2	86.5	-	10.3	100.0	634	176	3604	550	3125
1961	3.3	84.6	-	12.1	100.0	598	179	3338	604	3374
1962	3.1	85.3	-	11.6	100.0	639	182	3509	621	3412
1963	1.5	87.1	-	11.4	100.0	687	186	3694	656	3527
1964	1.4	87.0	-	11.6	100.0	704	189	3723	681	3603
1965	1.3	88.3	-	10.4	100.0	770	192	4008	710	3698
IRELAND										
1925	95.8	4.1	-	-	100.0	4321	2985	1447	NA	NA
1929	94.6	5.3	-	0.1	100.0	4647	2937	1582	NA	NA
1933	93.4	6.3	-	0.3	100.0	4478	2962	1512	179	60
1937	92.0	7.3	-	0.6	100.0	4967	2948	1685	309	105
1938	91.3	7.9	-	0.8	100.0	4769	2937	1624	354	121
1950	80.9	17.8	-	1.3	100.0	4601	2969	1550	903	304
1953	77.9	20.8	-	1.3	100.0	4951	2949	1679	1246	423
1955	71.8	27.1	-	1.1	100.0	5467	2921	1872	1600	548
1957	68.9	29.3	-	1.7	100.0	5040	2885	1747	1810	627
1960	68.9	29.0	-	2.1	100.0	5682	2834	2005	2260	797
1961	65.2	33.2	-	1.6	100.0	5712	2818	2027	2453	870
1962	61.4	37.2	-	1.4	100.0	6102	2824	2161	2715	961
1963	55.9	42.7	-	1.3	100.0	6134	2841	2159	2900	1021
1964	55.9	42.7	-	1.4	100.0	6819	2849	2393	3230	1134
1965	49.2	49.1	-	1.7	100.0	6735	2855	2359	3537	1239
SPAIN										
1925	93.1	4.9	-	2.0	100.0	8639	22389	386	1611	72
1929	90.2	7.5	-	2.4	100.0	10501	23319	450	2433	104

Table XI. TOTAL ENERGY CONSUMPTION: PERCENTAGE DISTRIBUTION BY FUEL; RELATED DATA ON POPULATION AND ELECTRICITY CONSUMPTION, SELECTED YEARS, 1925-1965

Region, country, year	Percentage distribution of total consumption (based on coal equivalents): Solid fuels	Liquid fuels	Natural gas	Hydro-electric power	Total	Total consumption (10^3 m.t. coal equiv.)	Population (10^3)	Consumption per capita (kgs)	Addendum: Electricity consumption: Total (10^6 kwh)	Per capita (kwh)
	(1)	(2)	(3)	(4)	(5)	(6)	(7)	(8)	(9)	(10)
SPAIN (CONTINUED)										
1933	82.4	13.7	-	3.9	100.0	8503	24241	351	2897	120
1937	64.0	28.8	-	7.2	100.0	4000	25171	159	2472	98
1938	80.7	15.5	-	3.8	100.0	7402	25409	291	2749	108
1950	76.5	19.6	-	3.9	100.0	16375	28009	585	6916	247
1953	71.9	23.4	-	4.7	100.0	19946	28713	695	9711	338
1955	70.8	23.4	-	5.8	100.0	19576	29199	670	11980	410
1957	67.5	27.3	-	5.2	100.0	23213	29692	782	14560	490
1960	59.8	32.4	-	7.7	100.0	24998	30454	821	18460	606
1961	58.2	34.2	-	7.5	100.0	26174	30712	852	20633	672
1962	53.8	39.4	-	6.8	100.0	29248	30971	944	22652	731
1963	52.4	39.3	-	8.3	100.0	30681	31233	982	25074	803
1964	47.8	44.8	-	7.4	100.0	32174	31495	1022	28043	890
1965	47.6	45.5	-	6.9	100.0	34312	31762	1080	30059	946
YUGOSLAVIA										
1925	94.1	4.6	-	1.3	100.0	2793	12796	218	400	31
1929	93.7	5.4	0.1	0.9	100.0	3858	13577	284	460	34
1933	91.5	6.6	-	1.8	100.0	2767	14369	193	740	51
1937	93.1	5.2	0.1	1.7	100.0	3314	15172	218	913	60
1938	92.4	6.0	0.1	1.5	100.0	3848	15384	250	1090	71
1950	87.9	10.1	0.2	1.8	100.0	8287	16346	507	2408	147
1953	84.9	12.3	0.4	2.4	100.0	7818	17048	459	2952	173
1955	86.6	9.9	0.4	3.1	100.0	10459	17519	597	4290	245
1957	85.5	10.8	0.4	3.2	100.0	13036	17859	730	6110	342
1960	81.9	13.2	0.4	4.5	100.0	16417	18402	892	8830	480
1961	82.5	13.0	0.5	4.0	100.0	17246	18607	927	9846	529
1962	80.5	14.1	0.7	4.7	100.0	17914	18837	951	11119	590
1963	79.3	14.6	1.3	4.8	100.0	20037	19065	1051	13240	694
1964	77.9	16.0	1.6	4.4	100.0	22376	19279	1161	14524	753
1965	74.8	18.4	1.9	4.9	100.0	23745	19511	1217	15889	814
OCEANIA										
1925	92.6	6.9	-	0.5	100.0	15581	9056	1721	1877	207
1929	83.8	15.3	-	0.9	100.0	15343	9637	1592	2996	311
1933	82.3	16.4	-	1.3	100.0	13098	9942	1317	3574	359
1937	79.1	19.5	-	1.3	100.0	18116	10241	1769	5225	510
1938	76.9	21.6	-	1.4	100.0	18125	10334	1754	5769	558
1950	72.0	26.1	-	1.9	100.0	29300	12222	2397	12661	1036
1953	71.1	26.7	-	2.3	100.0	31346	13142	2385	16124	1227
1955	64.1	33.7	-	2.2	100.0	37322	13810	2703	21130	1530
1957	61.6	35.6	-	2.7	100.0	39312	14460	2719	25330	1752
1960	59.7	37.6	-	2.7	100.0	45824	15444	2967	32090	2078
1961	58.3	38.9	-	2.8	100.0	47659	15819	3013	33513	2119
1962	57.4	39.5	-	3.1	100.0	48704	16159	3014	36470	2257
1963	54.5	42.1	-	3.3	100.0	52349	16476	3177	40337	2448
1964	52.9	43.7	-	3.3	100.0	56070	16826	3332	44325	2634
1965	51.7	44.7	-	3.5	100.0	61205	17178	3563	48525	2825

Table XI. TOTAL ENERGY CONSUMPTION: PERCENTAGE DISTRIBUTION BY FUEL; RELATED DATA ON POPULATION AND ELECTRICITY CONSUMPTION, SELECTED YEARS, 1925-1965

Region, country, year	Percentage distribution of total consumption (based on coal equivalents)					Total consumption (10^3 m.t. coal equiv.)	Population (10^3)	Consumption per capita (kgs)	Addendum: Electricity consumption	
	Solid fuels	Liquid fuels	Natural gas	Hydro-electric power	Total				Total (10^6 kwh)	Per capita (kwh)
	(1)	(2)	(3)	(4)	(5)	(6)	(7)	(8)	(9)	(10)
AUSTRALIA										
1925	93.3	6.3	-	0.3	100.0	12890	5939	2170	1537	259
1929	84.3	15.2	-	0.4	100.0	12415	6394	1942	2286	358
1933	83.3	16.1	-	0.6	100.0	10835	6630	1634	2716	410
1937	80.6	18.8	-	0.6	100.0	15060	6836	2203	3972	581
1938	79.3	20.1	-	0.6	100.0	14884	6899	2157	4353	631
1950	74.2	25.0	-	0.7	100.0	25318	8179	3095	9509	1163
1953	74.0	25.2	-	0.8	100.0	27103	8815	3075	12045	1366
1955	66.7	32.5	-	0.8	100.0	32351	9200	3516	16090	1749
1957	64.5	34.4	-	1.1	100.0	33673	9640	3493	19160	1988
1960	62.1	36.6	-	1.3	100.0	39679	10275	3862	24490	2383
1961	60.9	37.9	-	1.3	100.0	41312	10508	3932	25460	2423
1962	60.4	38.2	-	1.5	100.0	42544	10705	3974	27815	2598
1963	57.3	40.9	-	1.8	100.0	45635	10916	4181	30640	2807
1964	55.8	42.4	-	1.8	100.0	48534	11136	4358	33909	3045
1965	54.7	43.3	-	2.0	100.0	53358	11360	4697	37208	3275
NEW ZEALAND										
1925	88.9	9.6	-	1.5	100.0	2555	1382	1849	340	246
1929	81.1	16.0	-	2.9	100.0	2777	1471	1888	710	483
1933	76.8	18.2	-	5.0	100.0	2135	1540	1387	858	557
1937	71.0	23.6	-	5.4	100.0	2847	1587	1794	1253	790
1938	64.9	29.3	-	5.7	100.0	3023	1604	1885	1416	883
1950	58.3	32.3	-	9.4	100.0	3811	1908	1997	3085	1617
1953	52.5	34.9	-	12.5	100.0	3928	2047	1919	4018	1963
1955	47.0	40.4	-	12.6	100.0	4493	2136	2103	4900	2294
1957	43.3	43.3	-	13.4	100.0	5007	2229	2246	6000	2692
1960	44.6	42.7	-	12.6	100.0	5460	2372	2302	7000	2951
1961	42.2	44.6	-	13.2	100.0	5637	2420	2329	7550	3120
1962	37.6	47.2	-	15.2	100.0	5570	2485	2242	8120	3268
1963	37.1	48.6	-	14.3	100.0	5984	2538	2358	9140	3601
1964	35.4	49.9	-	14.7	100.0	6578	2594	2536	9900	3816
1965	31.3	53.0	-	15.6	100.0	6873	2640	2603	10776	4082
USSR AND COMMUNIST EASTERN EUROPE										
1925	82.9	15.2	1.7	0.1	100.0	80457	224359	359	7264	32
1929	83.0	15.3	1.6	0.1	100.0	129710	242663	535	13598	56
1933	77.3	19.8	2.8	0.1	100.0	148175	258215	574	22804	88
1937	77.5	19.5	2.7	0.3	100.0	232338	268566	865	46483	173
1938	76.9	20.3	2.5	0.3	100.0	244039	271346	899	50118	185
1950	82.5	14.8	2.3	0.4	100.0	464115	269766	1720	133518	495
1953	80.8	16.1	2.6	0.5	100.0	576721	281843	2046	194246	689
1955	79.4	17.4	2.7	0.5	100.0	691190	290497	2379	243800	839
1957	75.7	19.5	4.1	0.7	100.0	799579	299118	2673	294970	986
1960	69.3	22.2	7.7	0.8	100.0	934513	312859	2987	406620	1300
1961	66.9	23.0	9.3	0.8	100.0	979331	317068	3089	452048	1426
1962	64.0	24.2	10.8	1.0	100.0	1042065	321217	3244	504420	1570
1963	62.1	24.8	12.2	0.9	100.0	1122642	325303	3451	555934	1709
1964	60.6	24.8	13.8	0.9	100.0	1187576	329007	3610	615858	1872
1965	58.7	25.1	15.2	0.9	100.0	1255760	332439	3777	677083	2037

Table XI. TOTAL ENERGY CONSUMPTION: PERCENTAGE DISTRIBUTION BY FUEL; RELATED DATA ON POPULATION AND ELECTRICITY CONSUMPTION, SELECTED YEARS, 1925-1965

Region, country, year	Percentage distribution of total consumption (based on coal equivalents): Solid fuels	Liquid fuels	Natural gas	Hydro-electric power	Total	Total consumption (10^3 m.t. coal equiv.)	Population (10^3)	Consumption per capita (kgs)	Addendum: Electricity consumption: Total (10^6 kwh)	Per capita (kwh)
	(1)	(2)	(3)	(4)	(5)	(6)	(7)	(8)	(9)	(10)
COMMUNIST EASTERN EUROPE										
1925	91.2	6.5	2.2	0.1	100.0	55138	70459	783	4339	62
1929	91.3	6.4	2.2	0.1	100.0	76744	74163	1035	7374	99
1933	86.2	8.4	5.3	0.1	100.0	49534	77615	638	6447	83
1937	87.5	7.2	5.1	0.2	100.0	66040	80566	820	10083	125
1938	86.8	8.2	4.8	0.2	100.0	67690	81346	832	10518	129
1950	93.0	4.8	2.0	0.2	100.0	160796	89716	1792	42618	475
1953	90.8	6.1	3.0	0.2	100.0	207134	92343	2243	59921	649
1955	90.4	6.3	3.0	0.2	100.0	230214	94347	2440	73560	780
1957	89.2	7.2	3.3	0.2	100.0	259065	95968	2699	85280	889
1960	87.4	8.3	4.1	0.3	100.0	293895	98459	2985	114380	1162
1961	86.8	8.7	4.2	0.3	100.0	311993	99068	3149	124511	1257
1962	85.7	9.4	4.6	0.3	100.0	331733	99752	3326	135377	1357
1963	84.6	10.1	4.9	0.3	100.0	353068	100539	3512	144263	1435
1964	83.6	11.0	5.2	0.3	100.0	371008	101320	3662	158260	1562
1965	81.9	12.0	5.7	0.4	100.0	375131	101854	3683	171849	1687
ALBANIA										
1950	18.1	81.9	-	-	100.0	168	1215	139	NA	NA
1953	32.4	66.4	-	1.1	100.0	223	1302	172	49	38
1955	32.5	66.1	-	1.4	100.0	238	1379	173	80	58
1957	21.3	77.3	-	1.4	100.0	553	1462	378	120	82
1960	19.8	78.2	-	1.9	100.0	784	1607	488	190	118
1961	17.1	81.4	-	1.5	100.0	905	1660	545	227	137
1962	17.4	81.1	-	1.5	100.0	982	1711	574	242	141
1963	16.5	81.0	-	2.5	100.0	825	1762	468	258	146
1964	16.7	80.6	-	2.7	100.0	933	1814	514	288	159
1965	21.6	74.9	-	3.6	100.0	880	1865	472	340	182
BULGARIA										
1925	86.4	13.2	-	0.4	100.0	489	5314	92	32	6
1929	80.6	18.5	-	0.9	100.0	681	5660	120	86	15
1933	83.1	15.4	-	1.5	100.0	642	5961	108	128	21
1937	81.3	16.6	-	2.1	100.0	788	6207	127	202	33
1938	82.7	15.2	-	2.0	100.0	866	6253	139	232	37
1950	82.6	15.7	-	1.7	100.0	2287	7251	315	820	113
1953	82.8	15.5	-	1.7	100.0	3251	7346	443	1557	212
1955	83.9	14.0	-	2.0	100.0	3956	7499	528	2110	281
1957	79.7	17.9	-	2.4	100.0	4458	7651	583	2670	349
1960	76.0	20.7	-	3.3	100.0	7174	7867	912	4680	595
1961	75.5	21.9	-	2.6	100.0	8523	7943	1073	5449	686
1962	73.1	24.8	-	2.1	100.0	10327	8013	1289	6112	763
1963	69.8	27.9	-	2.3	100.0	11829	8078	1464	7267	900
1964	66.8	32.0	-	1.2	100.0	15018	8144	1844	8676	1065
1965	65.1	33.4	-	1.5	100.0	16501	8207	2011	10215	1245
CZECHOSLOVAKIA										
1925	98.5	1.4	-	0.1	100.0	22263	13537	1645	1955	144
1929	98.0	1.9	-	0.1	100.0	28735	13884	2070	2967	214

Table XI. TOTAL ENERGY CONSUMPTION: PERCENTAGE DISTRIBUTION BY FUEL; RELATED DATA ON POPULATION AND ELECTRICITY CONSUMPTION, SELECTED YEARS, 1925-1965

Region, country, year	Percentage distribution of total consumption (based on coal equivalents)					Total consumption (10^3 m.t. coal equiv.)	Population (10^3)	Consumption per capita (kgs)	Addendum: Electricity consumption	
	Solid fuels	Liquid fuels	Natural gas	Hydro-electric power	Total				Total (10^6 kwh)	Per capita (kwh)
	(1)	(2)	(3)	(4)	(5)	(6)	(7)	(8)	(9)	(10)
CZECHOSLOVAKIA (CONTINUED)										
1933	96.9	2.9	-	0.2	100.0	18826	14216	1324	2602	183
1937	96.9	2.8	-	0.3	100.0	25232	14429	1749	4115	285
1938	97.3	2.4	-	0.3	100.0	24070	14603	1648	4052	277
1950	96.7	2.8	0.1	0.4	100.0	36948	12389	2982	9400	759
1953	95.6	3.5	0.5	0.3	100.0	42821	12820	3340	12363	964
1955	95.7	3.4	0.5	0.5	100.0	49046	13093	3746	14880	1136
1957	93.6	4.2	1.8	0.4	100.0	56303	13358	4215	17490	1309
1960	90.9	6.1	2.6	0.4	100.0	65931	13654	4829	24180	1771
1961	90.5	6.8	2.3	0.4	100.0	71564	13780	5193	26627	1932
1962	89.7	7.9	1.9	0.5	100.0	76547	13860	5523	28803	2078
1963	89.8	8.2	1.6	0.4	100.0	80629	13952	5779	29986	2149
1964	88.4	9.6	1.5	0.5	100.0	84057	14058	5979	32685	2325
1965	87.0	10.9	1.4	0.8	100.0	83120	14159	5870	34940	2468
GERMANY, EAST										
1950	99.6	0.3	0.1	-	100.0	49693	18388	2702	17900	973
1953	99.3	0.6	0.1	-	100.0	62577	18178	3442	24247	1334
1955	99.6	0.2	0.1	0.1	100.0	69765	17945	3888	28690	1599
1957	99.1	0.7	0.1	-	100.0	73564	17518	4199	32400	1850
1960	97.0	2.9	0.1	-	100.0	80659	17241	4678	39930	2316
1961	96.6	3.3	0.1	-	100.0	84907	17125	4958	42143	2461
1962	96.3	3.6	-	0.1	100.0	89023	17102	5205	44979	2630
1963	95.3	4.4	0.2	0.1	100.0	92053	17155	5366	47448	2766
1964	94.2	5.5	0.2	0.1	100.0	95574	17096	5590	51179	2994
1965	93.2	6.5	0.2	0.1	100.0	94234	17028	5534	53764	3157
HUNGARY										
1925	98.0	2.0	-	-	100.0	4942	8299	595	441	53
1929	95.5	4.4	-	-	100.0	6914	8583	806	703	82
1933	94.4	5.5	0.1	-	100.0	4774	8848	540	729	82
1937	93.5	6.4	0.1	-	100.0	6590	9107	724	1061	117
1938	94.2	5.6	0.2	-	100.0	6759	9167	737	1109	121
1950	87.0	8.0	4.8	0.1	100.0	10490	9338	1123	3000	321
1953	87.2	8.4	4.3	0.1	100.0	16965	9595	1768	4615	481
1955	83.6	12.4	3.8	0.2	100.0	19277	9825	1962	5680	578
1957	84.5	12.6	2.7	0.2	100.0	20098	9840	2042	5760	585
1960	82.5	14.2	2.9	0.3	100.0	23876	9984	2391	8150	816
1961	81.8	15.1	2.7	0.3	100.0	25784	10028	2571	8880	886
1962	80.8	16.2	2.7	0.3	100.0	26430	10061	2627	9681	962
1963	78.4	17.6	3.6	0.4	100.0	29980	10088	2972	10595	1050
1964	77.7	17.7	4.2	0.4	100.0	32385	10120	3200	11657	1152
1965	75.8	18.3	5.4	0.5	100.0	32352	10148	3188	12313	1213
POLAND										
1925	93.3	3.6	3.1	-	100.0	22625	29275	773	1668	57
1929	95.8	2.4	1.8	-	100.0	33939	31084	1092	3048	98
1933	93.5	3.4	3.1	-	100.0	19545	32810	596	2396	73
1937	94.7	2.6	2.7	-	100.0	26438	34359	769	3628	106

Table XI. TOTAL ENERGY CONSUMPTION: PERCENTAGE DISTRIBUTION BY FUEL; RELATED DATA ON POPULATION AND ELECTRICITY CONSUMPTION, SELECTED YEARS, 1925-1965

	Percentage distribution of total consumption (based on coal equivalents)								Addendum: Electricity consumption	
Region, country, year	Solid fuels	Liquid fuels	Natural gas	Hydro-electric power	Total	Total consumption (10^3 m.t. coal equiv.)	Population (10^3)	Consumption per capita (kgs)	Total (10^6 kwh)	Per capita (kwh)
	(1)	(2)	(3)	(4)	(5)	(6)	(7)	(8)	(9)	(10)
POLAND (CONTINUED)										
1938	94.3	2.9	2.8	-	100.0	27934	34682	805	3977	115
1950	97.5	1.9	0.5	0.1	100.0	51954	24824	2093	9298	375
1953	96.6	2.5	0.8	0.1	100.0	65830	26255	2507	13679	521
1955	95.7	3.2	1.0	0.1	100.0	70815	27281	2596	17810	653
1957	95.6	3.4	0.9	0.1	100.0	83548	28310	2951	21410	756
1960	94.8	4.0	1.1	0.1	100.0	92094	29703	3100	29630	998
1961	94.1	4.4	1.4	0.1	100.0	95898	29965	3200	32567	1087
1962	93.7	4.7	1.5	0.1	100.0	99729	30324	3289	35506	1171
1963	93.0	5.3	1.6	0.1	100.0	106180	30691	3460	37031	1207
1964	92.5	5.6	1.8	-	100.0	110376	31161	3542	39920	1281
1965	91.6	6.3	2.1	0.1	100.0	111592	31420	3552	43058	1370
ROMANIA										
1925	42.7	47.2	10.0	0.1	100.0	4910	13209	372	243	18
1929	34.3	48.7	16.9	0.1	100.0	6363	13952	456	570	41
1933	18.5	45.7	35.5	0.2	100.0	5632	14730	382	592	40
1937	21.8	39.4	38.6	0.2	100.0	6927	15434	449	1077	70
1938	23.9	45.0	30.9	0.2	100.0	8030	15601	515	1148	74
1950	28.5	45.4	25.9	0.3	100.0	9256	16311	567	2200	135
1953	24.5	45.2	30.1	0.2	100.0	15467	16847	918	3411	202
1955	25.8	43.1	30.9	0.2	100.0	17115	17325	988	4310	249
1957	24.8	44.9	30.0	0.2	100.0	20540	17829	1152	5430	305
1960	25.8	38.0	36.0	0.2	100.0	23377	18403	1270	7620	414
1961	25.5	36.1	38.2	0.2	100.0	24414	18567	1315	8618	464
1962	26.3	33.4	40.1	0.3	100.0	28695	18681	1536	10054	538
1963	25.5	32.5	41.8	0.2	100.0	31572	18813	1678	11678	621
1964	25.4	30.6	43.8	0.2	100.0	32664	18927	1726	13855	732
1965	25.7	30.1	44.0	0.2	100.0	36452	19027	1916	17219	905
USSR (INCLUDING ESTONIA, LATVIA, LITHUANIA)										
1925	64.9	34.2	0.7	0.1	100.0	25320	153900	165	2925	19
1929	70.9	28.1	0.8	0.1	100.0	52966	168500	314	6224	37
1933	72.9	25.5	1.5	0.1	100.0	98640	180600	546	16357	91
1937	73.6	24.4	1.7	0.3	100.0	166298	188000	885	36400	194
1938	73.1	24.9	1.7	0.4	100.0	176349	190000	928	39600	208
1950	76.9	20.0	2.5	0.5	100.0	303319	180050	1685	90900	505
1953	75.2	21.7	2.4	0.6	100.0	369587	189500	1950	134325	709
1955	73.9	22.9	2.6	0.6	100.0	460976	196150	2350	170240	868
1957	69.1	25.4	4.5	0.9	100.0	540514	203150	2661	209690	1032
1960	61.0	28.6	9.4	1.0	100.0	640618	214400	2988	292240	1363
1961	57.5	29.6	11.7	1.1	100.0	667338	218000	3061	327537	1502
1962	53.9	31.2	13.7	1.3	100.0	710332	221465	3207	369043	1666
1963	51.7	31.5	15.5	1.2	100.0	769574	224764	3424	411671	1832
1964	50.1	31.1	17.7	1.2	100.0	816567	227687	3586	457598	2010
1965	48.9	30.7	19.3	1.1	100.0	880629	230585	3819	505234	2191

Table XI. TOTAL ENERGY CONSUMPTION: PERCENTAGE DISTRIBUTION BY FUEL; RELATED DATA ON POPULATION AND ELECTRICITY CONSUMPTION, SELECTED YEARS, 1925-1965

Region, country, year	Percentage distribution of total consumption (based on coal equivalents)								Addendum: Electricity consumption	
	Solid fuels	Liquid fuels	Natural gas	Hydro-electric power	Total	Total consumption (10^3 m.t. coal equiv.)	Population (10^3)	Consumption per capita (kgs)	Total (10^6 kwh)	Per capita (kwh)
	(1)	(2)	(3)	(4)	(5)	(6)	(7)	(8)	(9)	(10)
COMMUNIST ASIA										
1925	94.0	6.0	-	-	100.0	23701	440000	54	1950	4
1929	93.2	6.8	-	-	100.0	23770	450000	53	2120	5
1933	92.8	7.2	-	-	100.0	24935	450000	55	3070	7
1937	93.8	6.2	-	-	100.0	31002	450000	69	3930	9
1938	94.5	5.5	-	-	100.0	27330	450000	61	4400	10
1950	98.1	0.3	-	1.5	100.0	43130	569830	76	9200	16
1953	98.1	1.4	-	0.5	100.0	66651	592360	113	10900	18
1955	95.6	3.6	-	0.8	100.0	98290	623505	158	15560	25
1957	94.7	4.3	-	1.0	100.0	131809	644988	204	26460	41
1960	93.2	5.8	-	1.0	100.0	235321	677454	347	68000	100
1961	93.8	5.4	-	0.8	100.0	265029	688468	385	39838	58
1962	94.0	5.2	-	0.8	100.0	266755	699398	381	39967	57
1963	94.1	5.1	-	0.8	100.0	286924	710319	404	42372	60
1964	94.4	4.9	-	0.8	100.0	308037	721250	427	53100	74
1965	94.1	5.1	-	0.8	100.0	323012	732204	441	59170	81
LATIN AMERICA										
1925	37.6	56.6	4.2	1.6	100.0	24688	97824	252	4504	46
1929	29.8	62.4	6.3	1.6	100.0	31341	105742	296	5855	55
1933	30.6	54.9	11.9	2.5	100.0	22822	114234	200	6442	56
1937	24.9	61.9	11.2	1.9	100.0	39169	122804	319	10135	83
1938	24.0	62.1	11.9	2.0	100.0	38701	125080	309	10820	87
1950	13.0	73.2	11.0	2.7	100.0	66232	161865	409	25948	160
1953	11.2	73.5	12.4	2.8	100.0	81899	175415	467	33147	189
1955	9.6	76.2	11.6	2.6	100.0	105376	185131	569	43512	235
1957	7.8	78.0	11.5	2.7	100.0	129377	195583	661	55553	284
1960	7.3	74.2	15.7	2.9	100.0	153472	212371	723	71643	337
1961	6.8	73.9	16.5	2.8	100.0	162536	217461	747	77546	357
1962	6.4	73.6	17.2	2.9	100.0	173119	223602	774	84355	377
1963	6.6	72.1	18.3	3.0	100.0	176733	229725	769	90154	392
1964	6.5	71.0	19.5	3.0	100.0	190282	236395	805	98191	415
1965	6.4	70.9	19.5	3.2	100.0	199514	243021	821	105118	433
LATIN AMERICA - CARIBBEAN										
1925	21.0	75.3	2.6	1.2	100.0	11355	40612	280	1921	47
1929	14.0	78.2	6.6	1.2	100.0	13982	43582	321	2378	55
1933	13.5	67.2	16.8	2.5	100.0	8325	47090	177	2430	52
1937	11.1	73.3	14.1	1.5	100.0	19198	50546	380	3816	75
1938	10.7	71.0	16.6	1.7	100.0	18033	51500	350	3994	78
1950	6.1	76.3	16.1	1.5	100.0	33161	67603	491	8611	127
1953	6.6	73.6	18.3	1.5	100.0	42676	73611	580	12095	164
1955	6.1	75.3	17.2	1.4	100.0	55840	77992	716	16640	213
1957	5.1	77.8	15.8	1.3	100.0	72668	82633	879	21880	265
1960	5.2	71.8	21.7	1.4	100.0	87549	90163	971	28709	318
1961	5.1	71.8	21.8	1.3	100.0	91371	92841	984	31245	337
1962	5.3	71.3	21.9	1.4	100.0	97185	95611	1016	34079	356
1963	5.6	69.8	23.1	1.6	100.0	100380	98594	1018	37793	383
1964	5.1	68.0	25.3	1.6	100.0	108125	101667	1064	42503	418
1965	5.0	68.4	24.8	1.8	100.0	114014	104605	1090	46675	446

Table XI. TOTAL ENERGY CONSUMPTION: PERCENTAGE DISTRIBUTION BY FUEL; RELATED DATA ON POPULATION AND ELECTRICITY CONSUMPTION, SELECTED YEARS, 1925-1965

Region, country, year	Percentage distribution of total consumption (based on coal equivalents)					Total consumption (10^3 m.t. coal equiv.)	Population (10^3)	Consumption per capita (kgs)	Addendum: Electricity consumption	
	Solid fuels	Liquid fuels	Natural gas	Hydro-electric power	Total				Total (10^6 kwh)	Per capita (kwh)
	(1)	(2)	(3)	(4)	(5)	(6)	(7)	(8)	(9)	(10)
CARIBBEAN - OIL PRODUCING										
1925	20.5	74.5	3.6	1.5	100.0	8092	25208	321	1500	60
1929	11.7	78.4	8.5	1.4	100.0	10805	27079	399	1890	70
1933	12.0	64.4	20.9	2.7	100.0	6696	29062	230	1850	64
1937	10.3	71.8	16.4	1.6	100.0	16498	31226	528	2920	94
1938	9.9	69.3	19.1	1.7	100.0	15698	31842	493	3030	95
1950	7.3	71.7	19.6	1.4	100.0	27159	42930	633	6220	145
1953	7.6	69.2	21.7	1.5	100.0	35935	47143	762	8780	186
1955	7.0	71.2	20.4	1.4	100.0	47064	50238	937	11950	238
1957	5.8	74.0	18.9	1.3	100.0	60659	53516	1133	15810	295
1960	6.0	66.8	25.8	1.4	100.0	73690	58799	1253	20870	355
1961	5.9	66.9	25.9	1.3	100.0	77039	60672	1270	22530	371
1962	6.3	65.7	26.5	1.5	100.0	80322	62614	1283	24749	395
1963	6.6	64.0	27.8	1.6	100.0	83443	64625	1291	27684	428
1964	6.1	61.3	30.9	1.7	100.0	88605	66706	1328	31237	468
1965	5.9	62.0	30.2	1.9	100.0	93703	68605	1366	34177	498
COLOMBIA										
1925	29.9	66.7	-	3.3	100.0	344	6724	51	130	19
1929	13.5	84.9	-	1.7	100.0	750	7279	103	150	21
1933	30.9	65.4	-	3.7	100.0	369	7880	47	162	21
1937	48.5	48.9	-	2.6	100.0	872	8531	102	290	34
1938	42.2	55.2	-	2.6	100.0	976	8702	112	325	37
1950	47.6	48.1	-	4.3	100.0	2122	11334	187	705	62
1953	36.9	59.3	-	3.8	100.0	3333	12369	269	1300	105
1955	35.4	61.0	-	3.5	100.0	5224	13172	397	2230	169
1957	35.7	59.8	-	4.5	100.0	5576	14028	397	2790	199
1960	35.0	53.4	7.2	4.3	100.0	7435	15416	482	3750	243
1961	32.8	56.4	6.9	3.9	100.0	8075	15908	508	3776	237
1962	34.2	52.8	9.0	3.9	100.0	8767	16417	534	4280	261
1963	32.9	53.3	9.6	4.1	100.0	9724	16941	574	5268	311
1964	30.2	53.8	11.2	4.7	100.0	9911	17482	567	5916	338
1965	30.9	52.7	11.8	4.7	100.0	10365	17787	583	6544	368
MEXICO										
1925	21.5	74.2	2.9	1.5	100.0	7031	15204	462	1220	80
1929	16.7	76.8	4.5	2.1	100.0	6690	16296	411	1560	96
1933	14.4	71.3	10.8	3.5	100.0	4592	17470	263	1529	88
1937	14.2	66.4	16.8	2.6	100.0	8822	18737	471	2480	132
1938	12.5	67.3	17.5	2.7	100.0	8823	19071	463	2512	132
1950	5.7	73.3	19.4	1.6	100.0	16491	25826	639	4548	176
1953	7.5	68.9	21.7	1.8	100.0	19526	28253	691	5920	210
1955	6.0	69.4	22.6	1.9	100.0	23243	30015	774	7170	239
1957	5.4	71.3	21.3	1.9	100.0	27423	31902	860	8870	278
1960	5.0	61.7	31.3	1.9	100.0	36090	34988	1031	11180	320
1961	5.1	60.9	32.1	1.9	100.0	36897	36091	1022	12209	338
1962	5.2	59.5	33.3	2.0	100.0	37445	37233	1006	13125	353
1963	5.3	58.4	34.2	2.1	100.0	39950	38416	1040	14158	369
1964	5.0	55.6	37.4	2.0	100.0	44570	39643	1124	15884	401
1965	4.7	55.4	37.5	2.4	100.0	45162	40913	1104	17404	425

Table XI. TOTAL ENERGY CONSUMPTION: PERCENTAGE DISTRIBUTION BY FUEL; RELATED DATA ON POPULATION AND ELECTRICITY CONSUMPTION, SELECTED YEARS, 1925-1965

Region, country, year	Percentage distribution of total consumption (based on coal equivalents)					Total consumption (10^3 m.t. coal equiv.)	Population (10^3)	Consumption per capita (kgs)	Addendum: Electricity consumption	
	Solid fuels	Liquid fuels	Natural gas	Hydro-electric power	Total				Total (10^6 kwh)	Per capita (kwh)
	(1)	(2)	(3)	(4)	(5)	(6)	(7)	(8)	(9)	(10)
TRINIDAD AND TOBAGO										
1925	6.1	54.7	39.2	-	100.0	228	382	596	NA	NA
1929	6.7	23.5	69.9	-	100.0	255	398	642	NA	NA
1933	3.1	46.5	50.5	-	100.0	391	422	926	4	9
1937	-0.1	58.5	41.6	-	100.0	790	450	1756	5	11
1938	1.7	55.9	42.4	-	100.0	886	458	1934	5	11
1950	0.3	59.8	39.9	-	100.0	1586	632	2509	54	85
1953	0.2	46.2	53.6	-	100.0	1245	678	1836	86	127
1955	-	56.4	43.6	-	100.0	1521	721	2110	280	388
1957	-	50.7	49.3	-	100.0	1623	765	2121	330	431
1960	-	42.5	57.5	-	100.0	1773	841	2109	470	559
1961	-	49.3	50.7	-	100.0	2185	867	2520	504	581
1962	-	51.9	48.1	-	100.0	2352	894	2631	564	631
1963	-	37.8	62.2	-	100.0	1782	922	1932	621	674
1964	-	41.5	58.5	-	100.0	2481	949	2614	817	861
1965	-	54.2	45.8	-	100.0	3418	975	3505	908	931
VENEZUELA										
1950	0.4	72.5	26.6	0.5	100.0	5597	4976	1125	520	105
1953	0.3	67.0	32.2	0.5	100.0	8984	5665	1586	841	148
1955	0.3	66.6	32.8	0.3	100.0	11151	6150	1813	1600	260
1957	0.2	75.1	24.6	0.1	100.0	19612	6636	2955	3100	467
1960	0.2	71.6	28.2	0.1	100.0	21654	7364	2940	4650	631
1961	0.2	71.5	28.2	0.1	100.0	22719	7612	2985	5217	685
1962	0.6	70.5	28.6	0.3	100.0	24227	7872	3078	5923	752
1963	0.7	68.1	30.6	0.6	100.0	24398	8144	2996	6771	831
1964	0.8	65.3	33.2	0.6	100.0	24456	8427	2902	7598	902
1965	0.8	68.3	30.3	0.6	100.0	28308	8722	3246	8241	945
CARIBBEAN - OTHER										
1925	22.2	77.3	-	0.5	100.0	3263	15404	212	421	27
1929	21.9	77.4	-	0.6	100.0	3177	16503	192	488	30
1933	19.6	78.7	-	1.7	100.0	1629	18028	90	580	32
1937	16.1	82.4	-	1.5	100.0	2700	19320	140	896	46
1938	15.5	82.7	-	1.8	100.0	2335	19658	119	964	49
1950	0.7	97.4	0.1	1.8	100.0	6002	24673	243	2391	97
1953	1.2	97.0	0.1	1.7	100.0	6741	26468	255	3315	125
1955	1.4	96.9	0.1	1.6	100.0	8776	27754	316	4690	169
1957	1.5	97.3	-	1.2	100.0	12009	29117	412	6070	208
1960	0.4	98.1	-	1.4	100.0	13859	31364	442	7839	250
1961	0.3	98.2	-	1.4	100.0	14332	32169	446	8715	271
1962	0.4	98.4	-	1.2	100.0	16862	32997	511	9330	283
1963	0.6	98.1	-	1.3	100.0	16937	33969	499	10109	298
1964	0.6	98.2	-	1.2	100.0	19520	34961	558	11266	322
1965	0.6	98.0	-	1.3	100.0	20311	36000	564	12498	347
CUBA										
1925	25.8	74.1	-	0.1	100.0	2555	NA	NA	NA	NA
1929	28.1	71.8	-	0.1	100.0	2248	3608	623	NA	NA

Table XI. TOTAL ENERGY CONSUMPTION: PERCENTAGE DISTRIBUTION BY FUEL; RELATED DATA ON POPULATION AND ELECTRICITY CONSUMPTION, SELECTED YEARS, 1925-1965

Region, country, year	Percentage distribution of total consumption (based on coal equivalents)								Addendum: Electricity consumption	
	Solid fuels	Liquid fuels	Natural gas	Hydro-electric power	Total	Total con-sumption (10^3 m.t. coal equiv.)	Population (10^3)	Con-sumption per capita (kgs)	Total (10^6 kwh)	Per capita (kwh)
	(1)	(2)	(3)	(4)	(5)	(6)	(7)	(8)	(9)	(10)
CUBA (CONTINUED)										
1933	38.6	61.2	-	0.2	100.0	767	4083	188	173	42
1937	25.0	74.9	-	0.2	100.0	1526	4359	350	257	59
1938	27.6	72.3	-	0.2	100.0	1241	4428	280	275	62
1950	0.9	99.0	-	-	100.0	3725	5516	675	758	137
1953	1.4	98.5	-	-	100.0	4011	5886	681	1007	171
1955	3.1	96.8	-	0.1	100.0	4180	6148	680	1900	309
1957	3.4	96.5	-	-	100.0	5286	6414	824	2360	368
1960	1.0	99.0	-	-	100.0	6051	6826	886	2710	397
1961	0.8	99.2	-	-	100.0	6503	6939	937	3030	437
1962	0.8	99.1	-	-	100.0	7293	7068	1032	2998	424
1963	1.4	98.5	-	0.1	100.0	6729	7236	930	3057	422
1964	1.6	98.2	-	0.2	100.0	7258	7434	976	3250	437
1965	1.8	98.0	-	0.2	100.0	7313	7631	958	3700	485
PUERTO RICO										
1957	-	99.2	-	0.8	100.0	2759	2260	1221	1490	659
1960	-	99.1	-	0.9	100.0	3416	2362	1446	2150	910
1961	-	98.8	-	1.2	100.0	2878	2409	1194	2438	1012
1962	-	99.3	-	0.7	100.0	3918	2460	1593	2742	1115
1963	-	99.1	-	0.9	100.0	3995	2520	1585	3164	1256
1964	-	99.6	-	0.4	100.0	4689	2584	1814	3638	1408
1965	-	99.5	-	0.5	100.0	5599	2633	2126	4100	1557
LATIN AMERICA - OTHER										
1925	51.7	40.8	5.5	2.0	100.0	13333	57212	233	2583	45
1929	42.5	49.6	6.0	1.8	100.0	17359	62160	279	3477	56
1933	40.5	47.8	9.1	2.6	100.0	14497	67144	216	4012	60
1937	38.2	51.0	8.5	2.2	100.0	19970	72258	276	6319	87
1938	35.6	54.4	7.8	2.3	100.0	20668	73580	281	6826	93
1950	20.0	70.0	6.0	4.0	100.0	33071	94262	351	17337	184
1953	16.3	73.3	6.1	4.3	100.0	39223	101804	385	21052	207
1955	13.5	77.3	5.3	3.9	100.0	49536	107139	462	26872	251
1957	11.3	78.3	5.9	4.5	100.0	56709	112950	502	33673	298
1960	10.0	77.5	7.7	4.8	100.0	65924	122208	539	42934	351
1961	9.1	76.6	9.6	4.7	100.0	71165	124620	571	46301	372
1962	7.8	76.4	11.1	4.7	100.0	75934	127991	593	50276	393
1963	7.9	75.2	12.1	4.8	100.0	76353	131131	582	52361	399
1964	8.4	74.9	11.9	4.8	100.0	82157	134728	610	55688	413
1965	8.2	74.3	12.3	5.2	100.0	85500	138416	618	58443	422
ARGENTINA										
1925	51.9	45.0	2.9	0.1	100.0	5459	10358	527	1182	114
1929	38.2	58.1	3.5	0.2	100.0	7962	11592	687	1670	144
1933	34.1	59.7	6.1	0.2	100.0	7163	12623	567	1630	129
1937	31.8	62.2	5.8	0.1	100.0	9623	13490	713	2199	163
1938	27.7	66.8	5.4	0.1	100.0	10078	13725	734	2328	170
1950	10.7	84.3	4.9	0.2	100.0	14570	17070	854	4430	260

Table XI. TOTAL ENERGY CONSUMPTION: PERCENTAGE DISTRIBUTION BY FUEL; RELATED DATA ON POPULATION AND ELECTRICITY CONSUMPTION, SELECTED YEARS, 1925-1965

Region, country, year	Percentage distribution of total consumption (based on coal equivalents)					Total consumption (10^3 m.t. coal equiv.)	Population (10^3)	Consumption per capita (kgs)	Addendum: Electricity consumption	
	Solid fuels	Liquid fuels	Natural gas	Hydro-electric power	Total				Total (10^6 kwh)	Per capita (kwh)
	(1)	(2)	(3)	(4)	(5)	(6)	(7)	(8)	(9)	(10)
ARGENTINA (CONTINUED)										
1953	7.7	86.7	5.4	0.3	100.0	17288	18202	950	4927	271
1955	7.3	87.5	4.9	0.2	100.0	19356	18893	1025	6000	318
1957	6.4	88.5	4.8	0.3	100.0	23654	19615	1206	8800	449
1960	7.1	85.0	7.5	0.5	100.0	24673	20669	1194	10460	506
1961	5.8	82.3	11.4	0.5	100.0	27587	21012	1313	11547	550
1962	3.3	82.2	14.0	0.5	100.0	28356	21351	1328	11887	557
1963	3.7	79.0	16.8	0.5	100.0	26992	21688	1245	12449	574
1964	3.6	79.5	16.4	0.5	100.0	30467	22022	1383	13752	624
1965	3.4	78.9	17.3	0.5	100.0	32882	22352	1471	14979	670
BOLIVIA										
1925	31.9	65.8	-	2.2	100.0	50	2263	22	NA	NA
1929	22.1	75.0	-	2.9	100.0	86	2370	36	NA	NA
1933	12.9	81.9	-	5.2	100.0	62	2482	25	NA	NA
1937	26.1	70.6	-	3.4	100.0	119	2599	46	48	18
1938	24.8	71.0	-	4.2	100.0	133	2629	51	67	25
1950	0.8	89.4	-	9.8	100.0	243	3019	81	174	58
1953	1.6	88.3	-	10.1	100.0	311	3147	99	210	67
1955	-	91.3	1.6	7.1	100.0	508	3225	157	220	68
1957	-	89.8	2.0	8.2	100.0	536	3314	162	400	121
1960	-	90.4	1.3	8.2	100.0	592	3453	171	460	133
1961	-	87.1	3.9	9.0	100.0	541	3500	155	463	132
1962	-	86.4	5.9	7.7	100.0	610	3549	172	496	140
1963	-	80.7	11.3	8.0	100.0	639	3597	178	532	148
1964	-	77.1	15.6	7.3	100.0	725	3647	199	534	146
1965	0.6	75.9	16.7	6.7	100.0	798	3697	216	554	150
BRAZIL										
1925	69.2	25.2	-	5.7	100.0	3228	30332	106	NA	NA
1929	65.0	29.5	-	5.5	100.0	4027	32894	122	740	22
1933	55.5	36.5	-	8.1	100.0	3237	35673	91	1020	29
1937	54.1	38.9	-	7.0	100.0	4261	38687	110	2030	52
1938	52.2	40.4	-	7.4	100.0	4375	39480	111	2240	57
1950	28.0	62.8	0.1	9.2	100.0	9812	51944	189	8208	158
1953	21.1	68.5	0.3	10.0	100.0	11474	56741	202	10341	182
1955	17.0	75.0	0.5	7.5	100.0	17624	60183	293	13650	227
1957	13.9	75.4	1.1	9.7	100.0	19202	63833	301	16960	266
1960	11.7	76.5	2.8	9.0	100.0	25589	69730	367	22860	328
1961	10.7	77.8	2.6	8.8	100.0	26846	71868	374	24405	340
1962	10.4	78.2	2.4	9.0	100.0	28740	74096	388	27158	367
1963	10.6	78.5	2.2	8.6	100.0	29971	76409	392	27869	365
1964	12.4	76.4	2.3	8.9	100.0	31060	78809	394	29094	369
1965	13.0	73.8	2.9	10.3	100.0	31079	81301	382	30128	371
CHILE										
1925	48.1	50.1	-	1.8	100.0	2646	4073	650	480	118
1929	38.6	59.2	-	2.2	100.0	2786	4305	647	675	157
1933	72.7	23.5	-	3.9	100.0	1770	4563	388	860	188

Table XI. TOTAL ENERGY CONSUMPTION: PERCENTAGE DISTRIBUTION BY FUEL; RELATED DATA ON POPULATION AND ELECTRICITY CONSUMPTION, SELECTED YEARS, 1925-1965

Region, country, year	Percentage distribution of total consumption (based on coal equivalents): Solid fuels	Liquid fuels	Natural gas	Hydro-electric power	Total	Total consumption (10^3 m.t. coal equiv.)	Population (10^3)	Consumption per capita (kgs)	Addendum: Electricity consumption: Total (10^6 kwh)	Per capita (kwh)
	(1)	(2)	(3)	(4)	(5)	(6)	(7)	(8)	(9)	(10)
CHILE (CONTINUED)										
1937	59.4	37.5	-	3.1	100.0	3061	4842	632	1446	299
1938	61.3	35.7	-	3.1	100.0	3045	4914	620	1560	317
1950	49.6	42.2	3.2	5.0	100.0	4112	6073	677	2903	478
1953	53.2	37.2	3.9	5.7	100.0	4450	6437	691	3263	507
1955	37.2	52.4	5.1	5.3	100.0	5469	6791	805	4100	604
1957	34.9	51.7	8.0	5.4	100.0	5832	7137	817	4190	587
1960	24.7	51.9	17.9	5.6	100.0	6641	7689	864	4590	597
1961	22.8	49.7	22.3	5.2	100.0	7541	7858	960	4880	621
1962	20.0	49.2	26.2	4.6	100.0	8945	8029	1114	5286	658
1963	18.7	48.7	28.0	4.7	100.0	9131	8217	1111	5623	684
1964	19.4	50.0	25.6	5.0	100.0	9250	8492	1089	5932	699
1965	18.0	52.3	24.6	5.2	100.0	9587	8567	1119	6131	716
ECUADOR										
1925	-	93.9	-	6.1	100.0	50	1724	29	NA	NA
1929	-	96.8	-	3.2	100.0	95	1891	50	35	19
1933	-	90.2	7.8	2.0	100.0	153	2095	73	NA	NA
1937	-	47.6	49.9	2.4	100.0	123	2298	53	52	23
1938	-	64.4	34.2	1.5	100.0	214	2355	91	NA	NA
1950	-	64.3	33.6	2.1	100.0	523	3197	163	118	37
1953	-	62.5	35.4	2.0	100.0	564	3502	161	132	38
1955	-	71.8	26.2	2.0	100.0	762	3710	205	240	65
1957	-	72.6	25.1	2.2	100.0	795	3943	202	290	74
1960	-	80.3	17.8	1.9	100.0	1123	4320	260	390	90
1961	-	79.7	18.0	2.3	100.0	1110	4454	249	411	92
1962	-	77.7	19.5	2.7	100.0	1023	4591	223	451	98
1963	-	79.5	17.9	2.7	100.0	1118	4734	236	495	105
1964	-	82.1	15.5	2.4	100.0	1291	4821	268	551	114
1965	-	82.9	14.8	2.3	100.0	1347	5084	265	572	113
PARAGUAY										
1950	-	100.0	-	-	100.0	33	1397	24	44	31
1953	-	100.0	-	-	100.0	71	1496	47	56	37
1955	-	100.0	-	-	100.0	95	1565	60	70	45
1957	-	100.0	-	-	100.0	102	1648	62	70	42
1960	-	100.0	-	-	100.0	155	1751	88	100	57
1961	-	100.0	-	-	100.0	177	1801	98	107	59
1962	-	100.0	-	-	100.0	185	1854	100	120	65
1963	-	100.0	-	-	100.0	201	1910	105	127	66
1964	-	100.0	-	-	100.0	209	1968	106	130	66
1965	-	100.0	-	-	100.0	266	2030	131	136	67
PERU										
1925	12.1	36.7	49.6	1.6	100.0	1165	5579	209	NA	NA
1929	17.0	31.5	50.3	1.2	100.0	1521	5912	257	200	34
1933	3.5	30.8	63.9	1.8	100.0	1363	6283	217	NA	NA
1937	6.3	32.8	59.3	1.6	100.0	1819	6695	272	315	47
1938	4.6	41.4	51.9	2.1	100.0	1910	6805	281	NA	NA

Table XI. TOTAL ENERGY CONSUMPTION: PERCENTAGE DISTRIBUTION BY FUEL; RELATED DATA ON POPULATION AND ELECTRICITY CONSUMPTION, SELECTED YEARS, 1925-1965

Region, country, year	Percentage distribution of total consumption (based on coal equivalents): Solid fuels	Liquid fuels	Natural gas	Hydro-electric power	Total	Total consumption (10^3 m.t. coal equiv.)	Population (10^3)	Consumption per capita (kgs)	Addendum: Electricity consumption: Total (10^6 kwh)	Per capita (kwh)
	(1)	(2)	(3)	(4)	(5)	(6)	(7)	(8)	(9)	(10)
PERU (CONTINUED)										
1950	4.6	60.4	32.4	2.6	100.0	2966	8521	348	800	94
1953	4.7	63.7	28.4	3.2	100.0	3688	9035	408	1219	135
1955	3.4	65.4	27.7	3.4	100.0	3956	9396	421	1480	158
1957	2.4	65.0	29.1	3.5	100.0	4562	9923	460	1670	168
1960	2.9	71.3	21.6	4.2	100.0	5161	10857	475	2660	245
1961	3.5	72.1	20.1	4.3	100.0	5401	10320	523	2945	285
1962	2.8	74.0	19.2	4.0	100.0	6089	10632	573	3067	288
1963	2.1	74.0	19.6	4.3	100.0	6261	10958	571	3419	312
1964	1.6	73.7	20.3	4.4	100.0	6911	11298	612	3689	327
1965	1.3	75.0	18.8	4.9	100.0	6721	11650	577	3839	330
URUGUAY										
1925	53.0	47.0	-	-	100.0	686	1659	413	84	51
1929	40.4	59.6	-	-	100.0	845	1829	462	125	68
1933	39.7	60.3	-	-	100.0	712	1982	359	160	81
1937	32.7	67.3	-	-	100.0	901	2080	433	203	98
1938	32.2	67.8	-	-	100.0	832	2108	395	229	109
1950	29.0	55.9	0.3	14.8	100.0	445	2407	185	616	256
1953	4.8	90.9	-	4.3	100.0	1729	2528	684	845	334
1955	4.6	91.1	-	4.3	100.0	1955	2617	747	1020	390
1957	4.6	92.2	-	3.2	100.0	2167	2726	795	1150	422
1960	3.8	92.3	-	4.0	100.0	2128	2832	751	1240	438
1961	2.9	90.8	-	6.3	100.0	2064	2873	718	1327	462
1962	2.4	92.8	-	4.9	100.0	2128	2914	730	1559	535
1963	2.3	91.5	-	6.2	100.0	2211	2649	835	1578	596
1964	2.1	91.2	-	6.7	100.0	2371	2682	884	1724	643
1965	1.5	92.1	-	6.4	100.0	2602	2715	958	1850	681
ASIA										
1925	83.1	14.4	0.8	1.7	100.0	60292	574614	105	10404	18
1929	79.8	17.0	0.9	2.3	100.0	72545	604122	120	17107	28
1933	78.0	17.1	1.7	3.2	100.0	69884	640169	109	24802	39
1937	77.0	18.4	1.3	3.3	100.0	100281	682041	147	37423	55
1938	75.5	20.0	1.3	3.2	100.0	112409	692603	162	40299	58
1950	68.4	24.8	1.8	5.1	100.0	105844	805397	131	56740	70
1953	64.3	29.1	2.3	4.3	100.0	141343	850725	166	75696	89
1955	55.2	37.3	3.0	4.5	100.0	157729	873638	181	89359	102
1957	53.2	38.4	4.3	4.1	100.0	201657	909993	222	111774	123
1960	47.8	43.3	5.1	3.7	100.0	247730	970559	255	159350	164
1961	45.9	45.3	5.0	3.8	100.0	279686	992998	282	181764	183
1962	44.7	46.8	5.2	3.4	100.0	303168	1016017	298	197760	195
1963	42.0	49.5	5.0	3.5	100.0	329480	1040017	317	221821	213
1964	39.1	52.3	5.2	3.4	100.0	351780	1064425	330	252073	237
1965	37.6	54.2	5.0	3.2	100.0	385094	1088734	354	273264	251
MIDDLE EAST										
1925	29.4	70.5	-	0.1	100.0	2307	37864	61	169	4
1929	42.2	57.6	-	0.1	100.0	1778	40522	44	205	5

Table XI. TOTAL ENERGY CONSUMPTION: PERCENTAGE DISTRIBUTION BY FUEL; RELATED DATA ON POPULATION AND ELECTRICITY CONSUMPTION, SELECTED YEARS, 1925-1965

Region, country, year	Percentage distribution of total consumption (based on coal equivalents)					Total consumption (10^3 m.t. coal equiv.)	Population (10^3)	Consumption per capita (kgs)	Addendum: Electricity consumption	
	Solid fuels	Liquid fuels	Natural gas	Hydro-electric power	Total				Total (10^6 kwh)	Per capita (kwh)
	(1)	(2)	(3)	(4)	(5)	(6)	(7)	(8)	(9)	(10)
MIDDLE EAST (CONTINUED)										
1933	64.2	35.6	-	0.2	100.0	1533	43399	35	371	9
1937	38.5	61.4	-	0.1	100.0	4336	46841	93	618	13
1938	20.6	79.4	-	0.1	100.0	8408	47693	176	652	14
1950	24.9	69.9	5.1	0.1	100.0	13263	60555	219	2072	34
1953	25.4	67.6	6.9	0.1	100.0	16392	65384	251	3385	52
1955	18.7	73.2	7.9	0.1	100.0	22314	69071	323	5068	73
1957	16.1	69.0	14.7	0.2	100.0	29994	72718	412	6191	85
1960	11.7	69.9	18.1	0.4	100.0	38832	78133	497	10310	132
1961	11.0	70.1	18.4	0.4	100.0	41395	80193	516	11201	140
1962	10.6	70.6	18.4	0.4	100.0	45127	82366	548	12599	153
1963	11.1	71.4	16.8	0.7	100.0	47160	85099	554	13623	160
1964	11.5	70.4	17.6	0.5	100.0	49944	87670	570	14896	170
1965	10.0	73.3	16.1	0.6	100.0	57062	90073	634	16328	181
MIDDLE EAST - OIL PRODUCING										
1925	0.4	99.6	-	-	100.0	1400	18000	78	69	4
1929	1.2	98.8	-	-	100.0	676	19260	35	76	4
1933	6.5	93.5	-	-	100.0	185	20600	9	95	5
1937	0.2	99.8	-	-	100.0	2047	22040	93	172	8
1938	0.1	99.9	-	-	100.0	5877	22410	262	188	8
1950	2.8	87.9	9.3	-	100.0	7212	28016	257	592	21
1953	2.0	83.6	14.4	-	100.0	7893	29826	265	1110	37
1955	2.0	83.3	14.7	-	100.0	12073	31117	388	1550	50
1957	1.0	73.9	25.1	-	100.0	17589	32524	541	1825	56
1960	0.9	71.4	27.7	-	100.0	25297	34451	734	3940	114
1961	0.8	70.9	28.3	-	100.0	26976	35331	764	4222	119
1962	0.6	70.0	29.5	-	100.0	28148	36284	776	4498	124
1963	0.7	71.9	27.5	-	100.0	28875	37646	767	4722	125
1964	0.9	69.2	29.8	-	100.0	29336	38739	757	4908	127
1965	0.8	72.3	26.8	-	100.0	33857	39835	850	5116	128
IRAN										
1950	8.0	92.0	-	-	100.0	2497	16276	153	250	15
1953	7.3	89.3	3.4	-	100.0	2112	17476	121	NA	NA
1955	5.2	78.0	16.8	-	100.0	4695	18325	256	570	31
1957	2.0	70.7	27.3	-	100.0	8711	19216	453	660	34
1960	1.9	67.0	31.1	-	100.0	11985	20182	594	2010	100
1961	1.6	69.1	29.3	-	100.0	12689	20678	614	2090	101
1962	1.3	66.8	31.8	-	100.0	12023	21227	566	2150	101
1963	1.5	69.2	29.3	-	100.0	13214	22182	596	2250	101
1964	1.7	70.8	27.5	-	100.0	15890	22860	695	2300	101
1965	1.4	75.8	22.7	-	100.0	19390	23428	828	2350	100
IRAQ										
1950	0.2	99.8	-	-	100.0	1172	5180	226	117	23
1953	NA	74.4	25.6	-	100.0	1574	5620	280	342	61
1955	-	84.6	15.4	-	100.0	2721	5940	458	490	82
1957	-	87.9	12.1	NA	100.0	2812	6340	443	480	76

Table XI. TOTAL ENERGY CONSUMPTION: PERCENTAGE DISTRIBUTION BY FUEL; RELATED DATA ON POPULATION AND ELECTRICITY CONSUMPTION, SELECTED YEARS, 1925-1965

Region, country, year	Percentage distribution of total consumption (based on coal equivalents)					Total consumption (10^3 m.t. coal equiv.)	Population (10^3)	Consumption per capita (kgs)	Addendum: Electricity consumption	
	Solid fuels	Liquid fuels	Natural gas	Hydro-electric power	Total				Total (10^6 kwh)	Per capita (kwh)
	(1)	(2)	(3)	(4)	(5)	(6)	(7)	(8)	(9)	(10)
IRAQ (CONTINUED)										
1960	-	80.2	19.8	NA	100.0	3848	6945	554	850	122
1961	0.5	79.9	19.6	-	100.0	4177	7175	582	939	131
1962	-	80.0	20.0	NA	100.0	4252	7410	574	995	134
1963	-	78.4	21.6	NA	100.0	4441	7660	580	1063	139
1964	-	78.0	22.0	NA	100.0	4596	7910	581	1166	147
1965	-	80.3	19.7	NA	100.0	5208	8262	630	1260	153
MIDDLE EAST - OTHER										
1925	74.3	25.5	-	0.3	100.0	907	19864	46	100	5
1929	67.4	32.4	-	0.2	100.0	1102	21262	52	129	6
1933	72.1	27.7	-	0.2	100.0	1349	22799	59	276	12
1937	72.8	27.1	-	0.2	100.0	2289	24801	92	446	18
1938	68.2	31.6	-	0.2	100.0	2531	25283	100	464	18
1950	51.3	48.5	-	0.2	100.0	6051	32539	186	1480	45
1953	47.1	52.6	-	0.2	100.0	8499	35558	239	2275	64
1955	38.4	61.4	-	0.3	100.0	10242	37954	270	3518	93
1957	37.4	62.1	-	0.5	100.0	12404	40194	309	4366	109
1960	31.8	67.1	-	1.1	100.0	13535	43682	310	6370	146
1961	30.1	68.6	-	1.3	100.0	14419	44862	321	6979	156
1962	27.1	71.8	0.1	1.0	100.0	16979	46082	368	8101	176
1963	27.5	70.8	0.1	1.7	100.0	18285	47453	385	8901	188
1964	26.5	72.1	0.2	1.3	100.0	20608	48931	421	9988	204
1965	23.4	74.7	0.4	1.5	100.0	23206	50238	462	11212	223
PALESTINE										
1925	34.4	65.6	-	-	100.0	64	847	76	NA	NA
1929	30.6	69.4	-	-	100.0	108	960	113	4	4
1933	33.4	66.6	-	-	100.0	174	1105	157	22	20
1937	26.4	73.6	-	-	100.0	371	1383	268	77	56
1938	19.9	80.1	-	-	100.0	292	1419	206	79	56
ISRAEL										
1950	3.3	96.7	-	-	100.0	1042	1258	828	464	369
1953	1.9	98.1	-	-	100.0	1549	1651	938	759	460
1955	0.9	99.1	-	-	100.0	2296	1748	1313	1260	721
1957	1.8	98.2	-	-	100.0	2259	1937	1166	1420	733
1960	1.8	98.2	-	-	100.0	2827	2114	1337	2310	1093
1961	1.3	98.6	0.1	-	100.0	3093	2185	1416	2546	1165
1962	1.1	98.4	0.4	-	100.0	3491	2292	1523	2936	1281
1963	0.6	99.1	0.4	-	100.0	3618	2376	1523	3160	1330
1964	0.7	98.3	0.9	-	100.0	4074	2476	1645	3625	1464
1965	0.3	98.1	1.7	-	100.0	5763	2563	2248	4145	1617
JORDAN										
1950	-	100.0	-	-	100.0	86	1269	67	NA	NA
1953	-	100.0	-	-	100.0	107	1360	78	NA	NA

Table XI. TOTAL ENERGY CONSUMPTION: PERCENTAGE DISTRIBUTION BY FUEL; RELATED DATA ON POPULATION AND ELECTRICITY CONSUMPTION, SELECTED YEARS, 1925-1965

Region, country, year	Percentage distribution of total consumption (based on coal equivalents): Solid fuels	Liquid fuels	Natural gas	Hydro-electric power	Total	Total consumption (10^3 m.t. coal equiv.)	Population (10^3)	Consumption per capita (kgs)	Addendum: Electricity consumption: Total (10^6 kwh)	Per capita (kwh)
	(1)	(2)	(3)	(4)	(5)	(6)	(7)	(8)	(9)	(10)
JORDAN (CONTINUED)										
1955	-	100.0	-	-	100.0	189	1437	132	10	7
1957	-	100.0	-	-	100.0	219	1527	143	20	13
1960	-	100.0	-	-	100.0	332	1695	196	70	41
1961	-	100.0	-	-	100.0	446	1706	261	87	51
1962	-	100.0	-	-	100.0	494	1727	286	104	60
1963	-	100.0	-	-	100.0	575	1827	314	114	62
1964	-	100.0	-	-	100.0	581	1898	306	136	72
1965	-	100.0	-	-	100.0	674	1976	341	156	79
LEBANON										
1950	1.2	97.9	-	0.9	100.0	924	1385	667	114	82
1953	-	98.3	-	1.7	100.0	724	1455	497	164	113
1955	1.5	96.4	-	2.1	100.0	658	1954	337	220	113
1957	1.1	96.7	-	2.2	100.0	946	2043	463	286	140
1960	-	98.8	-	1.2	100.0	1164	2217	525	420	189
1961	-	98.2	-	1.8	100.0	1219	2292	532	475	207
1962	0.7	96.9	-	2.3	100.0	1351	2325	581	551	237
1963	0.7	96.4	-	3.0	100.0	1476	2380	620	624	262
1964	0.6	96.6	-	2.8	100.0	1683	2521	668	692	274
1965	0.5	96.3	-	3.2	100.0	1971	2560	770	765	299
SYRIA										
1950	0.6	99.4	-	-	100.0	332	3215	103	81	25
1953	0.5	99.5	-	-	100.0	590	3545	166	114	32
1955	-	99.8	-	0.2	100.0	754	3861	195	270	70
1957	-	99.7	-	0.3	100.0	912	4150	220	260	63
1960	-	99.7	-	0.3	100.0	1493	4565	327	370	81
1961	-	99.6	-	0.4	100.0	1421	4650	306	431	93
1962	-	99.6	-	0.4	100.0	1477	4800	308	502	105
1963	-	99.7	-	0.3	100.0	1665	5000	333	525	105
1964	-	99.7	-	0.3	100.0	2038	5200	392	574	110
1965	0.3	99.4	-	0.4	100.0	1708	5300	322	616	116
TURKEY										
1925	83.2	16.8	-	-	100.0	714	13800	52	80	6
1929	80.2	19.8	-	-	100.0	812	14705	55	100	7
1933	86.4	13.6	-	-	100.0	971	15658	62	205	13
1937	87.4	12.6	-	-	100.0	1601	16725	96	300	18
1938	86.1	13.9	-	-	100.0	1785	17016	105	312	18
1950	78.6	21.3	-	0.1	100.0	3918	20947	187	790	38
1953	69.3	30.6	-	0.1	100.0	5728	22818	251	1183	52
1955	66.8	33.0	-	0.2	100.0	5824	24065	242	1580	66
1957	69.0	30.5	-	0.6	100.0	6660	25498	261	2060	81
1960	63.0	35.2	-	1.9	100.0	6753	27755	243	2810	101
1961	59.3	38.6	-	2.2	100.0	7252	28602	254	3011	105
1962	52.5	45.9	-	1.6	100.0	8671	29418	295	3560	121
1963	50.2	47.1	-	2.6	100.0	9935	30256	328	3983	132
1964	49.3	48.8	-	1.9	100.0	10984	31118	353	4435	143

Table XI. TOTAL ENERGY CONSUMPTION: PERCENTAGE DISTRIBUTION BY FUEL; RELATED DATA ON POPULATION AND ELECTRICITY CONSUMPTION, SELECTED YEARS, 1925-1965

Region, country, year	Percentage distribution of total consumption (based on coal equivalents)					Total consumption (10^3 m.t. coal equiv.)	Population (10^3)	Consumption per capita (kgs)	Addendum: Electricity consumption	
	Solid fuels	Liquid fuels	Natural gas	Hydro-electric power	Total				Total (10^6 kwh)	Per capita (kwh)
	(1)	(2)	(3)	(4)	(5)	(6)	(7)	(8)	(9)	(10)
TURKEY (CONTINUED)										
1965	46.1	51.6	-	2.3	100.0	11732	32005	367	4941	154
FAR EAST AND OTHER ASIA										
1925	85.3	12.2	0.8	1.7	100.0	57985	536750	108	10235	19
1929	80.7	16.0	1.0	2.3	100.0	70767	563600	126	16902	30
1933	78.3	16.7	1.8	3.3	100.0	68351	596770	115	24431	41
1937	78.7	16.4	1.4	3.5	100.0	95945	635200	151	36805	58
1938	80.0	15.2	1.4	3.4	100.0	104002	644910	161	39647	61
1950	74.6	18.3	1.3	5.8	100.0	92581	744842	124	54668	73
1953	69.4	24.1	1.6	4.8	100.0	124951	785341	159	72311	92
1955	61.2	31.4	2.2	5.2	100.0	135414	804567	168	84291	105
1957	59.7	33.0	2.4	4.8	100.0	171663	837275	205	105583	126
1960	54.5	38.4	2.7	4.3	100.0	208897	892426	234	149040	167
1961	52.0	40.9	2.7	4.4	100.0	238291	912805	261	170563	187
1962	50.6	42.6	2.8	3.9	100.0	258041	933651	276	185161	198
1963	47.1	45.8	3.0	4.0	100.0	282320	954918	296	208198	218
1964	43.7	49.3	3.1	3.9	100.0	301836	976755	309	237177	243
1965	42.3	50.9	3.1	3.7	100.0	328031	998661	328	256936	257
BORNEO (FORMER BRITISH)										
1950	-	75.1	24.9	-	100.0	278	961	289	NA	NA
1953	-	67.9	32.1	-	100.0	245	1047	234	NA	NA
1955	-	77.9	22.1	-	100.0	441	1105	399	NA	NA
1957	-	53.7	46.3	-	100.0	541	1173	462	80	68
1960	-	45.1	54.9	-	100.0	522	1283	407	110	86
1961	-	59.6	40.4	-	100.0	692	1319	525	117	89
1962	-	45.3	54.7	-	100.0	500	1356	368	125	92
1963	-	56.6	43.4	-	100.0	580	1385	419	137	99
1964	-	66.9	33.1	-	100.0	697	1424	489	159	112
1965	-	77.3	22.7	-	100.0	923	1465	630	200	137
BURMA										
1950	NA	100.0	-	-	100.0	256	18849	14	NA	NA
1953	41.0	59.0	-	-	100.0	613	19640	31	120	6
1955	28.0	71.5	0.5	-	100.0	740	20407	36	180	9
1957	28.7	70.4	0.8	-	100.0	977	21174	46	280	13
1960	27.9	68.3	2.2	1.6	100.0	1257	22325	56	430	19
1961	21.1	75.4	1.6	1.9	100.0	1241	22780	54	472	21
1962	25.2	71.1	1.8	1.9	100.0	1362	23253	59	510	22
1963	17.0	79.0	1.7	2.4	100.0	1254	23735	53	539	23
1964	17.3	79.0	1.0	2.7	100.0	1302	24229	54	569	23
1965	12.2	83.8	1.1	2.9	100.0	1227	24732	50	580	23
CEYLON										
1925	12.1	87.8	-	-	100.0	116	4847	24	NA	NA
1929	64.2	35.8	-	-	100.0	486	5172	94	NA	NA

Table XI. TOTAL ENERGY CONSUMPTION: PERCENTAGE DISTRIBUTION BY FUEL; RELATED DATA ON POPULATION AND ELECTRICITY CONSUMPTION, SELECTED YEARS, 1925-1965

Region, country, year	Percentage distribution of total consumption (based on coal equivalents)					Total consumption (10^3 m.t. coal equiv.)	Population (10^3)	Consumption per capita (kgs)	Addendum: Electricity consumption	
	Solid fuels	Liquid fuels	Natural gas	Hydro-electric power	Total				Total (10^6 kwh)	Per capita (kwh)
	(1)	(2)	(3)	(4)	(5)	(6)	(7)	(8)	(9)	(10)
CEYLON (CONTINUED)										
1933	55.0	44.9	-	-	100.0	347	5419	64	NA	NA
1937	53.7	46.3	-	-	100.0	470	5725	82	28	5
1938	46.5	53.4	-	-	100.0	348	5826	60	31	5
1950	49.5	50.3	-	0.2	100.0	590	7678	77	81	11
1953	41.7	56.7	-	1.6	100.0	882	8290	106	144	17
1955	19.8	78.4	-	1.8	100.0	888	8723	102	180	21
1957	19.0	79.6	-	1.3	100.0	1424	9165	155	220	24
1960	28.6	67.7	-	3.7	100.0	911	9896	92	310	31
1961	12.3	84.7	-	3.0	100.0	1141	10168	112	364	36
1962	11.1	85.7	-	3.2	100.0	1255	10443	120	378	36
1963	12.0	84.8	-	3.3	100.0	1254	10625	118	409	38
1964	16.5	79.7	-	3.9	100.0	1094	10965	100	428	39
1965	10.8	86.0	-	3.2	100.0	1301	11232	116	421	37
HONG KONG										
1925	66.8	33.2	-	-	100.0	754	725	1039	NA	NA
1929	62.4	37.6	-	-	100.0	311	785	396	50	64
1933	72.5	27.5	-	-	100.0	322	923	348	NA	NA
1937	80.5	19.5	-	-	100.0	532	1282	415	80	62
1938	62.0	38.0	-	-	100.0	458	1479	310	NA	NA
1950	37.7	62.3	-	-	100.0	667	2360	282	294	125
1953	24.0	76.0	-	-	100.0	849	2242	379	504	225
1955	26.0	74.0	-	-	100.0	963	2490	387	640	257
1957	20.9	79.1	-	-	100.0	1197	2736	437	830	303
1960	15.8	84.2	-	-	100.0	1456	3075	473	1300	423
1961	14.6	85.4	-	-	100.0	1641	3178	516	1542	485
1962	12.3	87.7	-	-	100.0	1789	3410	525	1787	524
1963	9.7	90.3	-	-	100.0	2066	3592	575	2061	574
1964	8.8	91.2	-	-	100.0	2046	3692	554	2387	647
1965	7.4	92.6	-	-	100.0	2300	3804	605	2732	718
INDIA										
1925	85.1	14.8	-	0.1	100.0	19036	333359	57	470	1
1929	84.1	15.6	-	0.3	100.0	20899	346756	60	1200	3
1933	84.0	15.5	-	0.5	100.0	18582	364792	51	1720	5
1937	83.8	15.6	-	0.6	100.0	23395	387051	60	2100	5
1938	85.5	13.9	-	0.6	100.0	25696	392841	65	2250	6
1950	83.2	15.8	-	1.0	100.0	30175	358293	84	5107	14
1953	83.2	15.7	-	1.1	100.0	32603	376079	87	8749	23
1955	80.3	18.4	-	1.3	100.0	36608	390149	94	10860	28
1957	77.9	20.2	0.4	1.5	100.0	43185	405825	106	13140	32
1960	77.3	20.5	0.4	1.9	100.0	52717	432718	122	19830	46
1961	77.2	20.4	0.3	2.2	100.0	56902	442736	129	22470	51
1962	76.0	21.3	0.5	2.3	100.0	63282	453407	140	24730	55
1963	76.0	21.0	0.5	2.5	100.0	68664	464335	148	28800	62
1964	73.6	22.8	0.6	2.9	100.0	66781	475529	140	32730	69
1965	73.4	22.9	0.7	3.0	100.0	72826	486926	150	35980	74

Table XI. TOTAL ENERGY CONSUMPTION: PERCENTAGE DISTRIBUTION BY FUEL; RELATED DATA ON POPULATION AND ELECTRICITY CONSUMPTION, SELECTED YEARS, 1925-1965

Region, country, year	Percentage distribution of total consumption (based on coal equivalents)					Total consumption (10^3 m.t. coal equiv.)	Population (10^3)	Consumption per capita (kgs)	Addendum: Electricity consumption	
	Solid fuels	Liquid fuels	Natural gas	Hydro-electric power	Total				Total (10^6 kwh)	Per capita (kwh)
	(1)	(2)	(3)	(4)	(5)	(6)	(7)	(8)	(9)	(10)
INDO-CHINA										
1925	87.6	12.4	-	-	100.0	799	20050	40	NA	NA
1929	78.5	21.5	-	-	100.0	817	21060	39	63	3
1933	71.1	28.9	-	-	100.0	452	22060	20	62	3
1937	84.6	15.4	-	-	100.0	913	23270	39	75	3
1938	83.2	16.8	-	-	100.0	926	23560	39	83	4
1950	71.4	28.6	-	-	100.0	630	26920	23	181	7
1953	54.3	45.7	-	-	100.0	1082	28250	38	295	10
1955	5.2	94.7	-	0.1	100.0	574	18260	31	240	13
1957	7.8	92.2	-	-	100.0	797	19245	41	350	18
1960	3.9	96.0	-	0.1	100.0	948	21345	44	500	23
1961	6.1	93.8	-	0.1	100.0	1105	21944	50	559	25
1962	7.9	92.0	-	0.1	100.0	1157	22549	51	626	28
1963	8.4	91.5	-	0.1	100.0	1353	23129	58	688	30
1964	7.5	92.1	-	0.4	100.0	1295	23697	55	720	30
1965	7.8	91.8	-	0.5	100.0	1543	24239	64	791	33
CAMBODIA										
1955	-	100.0	-	-	100.0	84	4710	18	30	6
1957	-	100.0	-	-	100.0	128	4990	26	40	8
1960	-	100.0	-	-	100.0	164	5440	30	60	11
1961	-	100.0	-	-	100.0	200	5600	36	71	13
1962	-	100.0	-	-	100.0	215	5740	37	80	14
1963	-	100.0	-	-	100.0	282	5892	48	87	15
1964	-	100.0	-	-	100.0	248	6022	41	83	14
1965	10.7	89.3	-	-	100.0	281	6115	46	80	13
LAOS										
1955	-	100.0	-	-	100.0	14	1550	9	10	6
1957	-	100.0	-	-	100.0	29	1655	17	10	6
1960	-	100.0	-	-	100.0	42	1805	23	10	6
1961	-	100.0	-	-	100.0	57	1850	31	14	8
1962	-	100.0	-	-	100.0	66	1880	35	15	8
1963	-	100.0	-	-	100.0	77	1920	40	16	8
1964	-	100.0	-	-	100.0	90	1960	46	17	9
1965	-	100.0	-	-	100.0	87	2000	44	22	11
VIETNAM, SOUTH										
1955	6.3	93.6	-	0.1	100.0	476	12000	40	200	17
1957	9.7	90.3	-	-	100.0	641	12600	51	300	24
1960	5.0	94.9	-	0.1	100.0	743	14100	53	430	30
1961	7.9	92.0	-	0.1	100.0	848	14494	59	474	33
1962	10.4	89.5	-	0.1	100.0	877	14929	59	531	36
1963	11.5	88.4	-	0.1	100.0	994	15317	65	585	38
1964	10.1	89.3	-	0.5	100.0	957	15715	61	620	39
1965	7.7	91.7	-	0.6	100.0	1176	16124	73	689	43

Table XI. TOTAL ENERGY CONSUMPTION: PERCENTAGE DISTRIBUTION BY FUEL; RELATED DATA ON POPULATION AND ELECTRICITY CONSUMPTION, SELECTED YEARS, 1925-1965

Region, country, year	Percentage distribution of total consumption (based on coal equivalents)					Total consumption (10^3 m.t. coal equiv.)	Population (10^3)	Consumption per capita (kgs)	Addendum: Electricity consumption	
	Solid fuels	Liquid fuels	Natural gas	Hydro-electric power	Total				Total (10^6 kwh)	Per capita (kwh)
	(1)	(2)	(3)	(4)	(5)	(6)	(7)	(8)	(9)	(10)
INDONESIA										
1925	34.9	50.8	13.9	0.4	100.0	3046	56371	54	NA	NA
1929	29.2	58.9	11.7	0.3	100.0	4766	59830	80	260	4
1933	19.5	54.9	25.1	0.5	100.0	4186	63501	66	320	5
1937	22.3	53.6	23.6	0.5	100.0	4995	67398	74	420	6
1938	22.7	52.3	24.5	0.6	100.0	5176	68409	76	450	7
1950	15.7	62.0	21.5	0.8	100.0	4896	76700	64	670	9
1953	11.1	63.3	24.8	0.8	100.0	7348	81151	91	1230	15
1955	6.7	71.1	21.6	0.6	100.0	11769	84558	139	1510	18
1957	5.8	70.4	23.2	0.6	100.0	12430	88214	141	1590	18
1960	5.3	68.6	25.3	0.8	100.0	12813	94206	136	1820	19
1961	4.0	71.7	23.6	0.7	100.0	14440	96355	150	1902	20
1962	3.9	67.1	28.3	0.7	100.0	12749	98515	129	1970	20
1963	4.7	65.6	29.0	0.7	100.0	12843	100795	127	1970	20
1964	3.9	61.8	33.5	0.8	100.0	11649	103000	113	1950	19
1965	2.1	67.2	30.0	0.7	100.0	13351	105300	127	1960	19
JAPAN										
1925	92.4	4.4	0.1	3.1	100.0	30483	59179	515	8172	138
1929	86.5	9.4	0.1	4.1	100.0	38181	62930	607	13312	212
1933	82.7	12.1	0.2	5.1	100.0	39589	66880	592	19657	294
1937	83.0	12.1	0.1	4.9	100.0	57261	70040	818	30391	434
1938	83.6	11.5	0.1	4.8	100.0	62425	70530	885	32679	463
1950	83.2	6.1	0.2	10.4	100.0	45816	82900	553	44890	541
1953	75.4	16.8	0.2	7.6	100.0	68427	86700	789	55698	642
1955	68.4	22.1	0.3	9.1	100.0	66457	89000	747	63560	714
1957	65.2	26.5	0.5	7.8	100.0	90411	90730	996	79520	876
1960	54.1	38.3	1.0	6.6	100.0	111001	93210	1191	111490	1196
1961	50.5	42.0	1.1	6.5	100.0	131654	94050	1400	128316	1364
1962	47.3	45.9	1.3	5.5	100.0	141497	94930	1491	137759	1451
1963	40.6	52.3	1.6	5.5	100.0	156550	95899	1632	154200	1608
1964	37.1	56.3	1.6	5.0	100.0	173528	96906	1791	175891	1815
1965	35.5	58.4	1.4	4.7	100.0	188642	97960	1926	188161	1921
KOREA										
1925	93.4	6.6	-	-	100.0	1179	18081	65	NA	NA
1929	90.4	9.6	-	-	100.0	1735	18726	93	1500	80
1933	88.2	8.7	-	3.1	100.0	2186	20121	109	NA	NA
1937	81.1	12.8	-	6.1	100.0	4286	21528	199	2336	109
1938	84.0	10.2	-	5.8	100.0	5245	22022	238	2695	122
KOREA, REPUBLIC OF										
1950	85.6	13.1	-	1.3	100.0	925	20513	45	421	21
1953	73.3	24.3	-	2.4	100.0	2039	21440	95	736	34
1955	79.4	18.5	-	2.0	100.0	2944	21526	137	880	41
1957	80.6	18.1	-	1.3	100.0	3934	22677	173	1330	59
1960	83.2	15.7	-	1.1	100.0	6550	24695	265	1760	71
1961	83.2	15.7	-	1.1	100.0	7136	25402	281	1840	72
1962	82.0	17.0	-	1.0	100.0	8928	26125	342	2176	83

Table XI. TOTAL ENERGY CONSUMPTION: PERCENTAGE DISTRIBUTION BY FUEL; RELATED DATA ON POPULATION AND ELECTRICITY CONSUMPTION, SELECTED YEARS, 1925-1965

Region, country, year	Percentage distribution of total consumption (based on coal equivalents)					Total consumption (10^3 m.t. coal equiv.)	Population (10^3)	Consumption per capita (kgs)	Addendum: Electricity consumption	
	Solid fuels	Liquid fuels	Natural gas	Hydro-electric power	Total				Total (10^6 kwh)	Per capita (kwh)
	(1)	(2)	(3)	(4)	(5)	(6)	(7)	(8)	(9)	(10)
KOREA, REPUBLIC OF (CONTINUED)										
1963	80.4	18.8	-	0.8	100.0	10862	26868	404	2514	94
1964	82.6	16.6	-	0.8	100.0	11551	27633	418	2966	107
1965	80.8	18.5	-	0.7	100.0	12578	28353	444	3520	124
MALAYA AND SINGAPORE										
1925	57.6	42.0	-	0.3	100.0	810	NA	NA	57	NA
1929	59.6	40.0	-	0.4	100.0	1276	NA	NA	199	NA
1933	59.7	38.3	-	1.9	100.0	611	NA	NA	119	NA
1937	54.8	43.2	-	2.0	100.0	1478	4734	312	521	110
1938	53.1	43.8	-	3.1	100.0	915	5028	182	375	75
1950	23.3	74.7	-	2.0	100.0	1545	6212	249	787	127
1953	12.1	86.6	-	1.4	100.0	2351	6805	345	1052	155
1955	7.7	91.2	-	1.1	100.0	2732	7229	378	1320	183
1957	7.3	91.5	-	1.2	100.0	2650	7725	343	1570	203
1960	0.4	98.6	-	1.0	100.0	2451	8543	287	1850	217
1961	1.9	97.2	-	0.9	100.0	3128	8824	354	2064	234
1962	1.2	97.9	-	0.9	100.0	3383	9109	371	2250	247
1963	1.7	96.6	-	1.7	100.0	2339	9382	249	2445	261
1964	0.8	97.7	-	1.4	100.0	4787	9630	497	2767	287
1965	0.6	97.6	-	1.8	100.0	4156	9904	420	3175	321
PAKISTAN										
1950	50.2	49.5	NA	0.3	100.0	2730	75040	36	290	4
1953	49.8	49.3	-	0.9	100.0	3363	80083	42	720	9
1955	40.6	56.7	1.4	1.4	100.0	3697	83498	44	1020	12
1957	37.6	52.6	8.4	1.4	100.0	4625	87061	53	1440	17
1960	33.4	51.7	13.6	1.4	100.0	6216	92696	67	1950	21
1961	28.3	53.7	16.1	1.8	100.0	6376	94655	67	2300	24
1962	29.2	51.3	17.1	2.4	100.0	7381	96648	76	2800	29
1963	26.4	52.3	19.0	2.4	100.0	8324	98683	84	3380	34
1964	25.3	51.4	20.8	2.5	100.0	9145	100762	91	4000	40
1965	22.0	52.5	22.9	2.6	100.0	9477	102876	92	4616	45
PHILIPPINES										
1925	52.9	46.6	-	0.5	100.0	985	11600	85	65	6
1929	53.3	46.2	-	0.5	100.0	1163	12792	91	90	7
1933	34.0	65.0	-	0.9	100.0	849	14051	60	114	8
1937	30.1	68.9	-	1.0	100.0	956	15445	62	130	8
1938	29.7	69.3	-	1.0	100.0	1011	15814	64	145	9
1950	8.5	90.3	-	1.2	100.0	1963	20275	97	590	29
1953	8.3	89.5	-	2.2	100.0	1919	22191	86	1111	50
1955	4.8	93.4	-	1.8	100.0	2939	23568	125	1340	57
1957	5.8	91.9	-	2.3	100.0	3454	25030	138	1760	70
1960	3.7	92.4	-	3.9	100.0	4232	27410	154	2760	101
1961	3.7	92.6	-	3.7	100.0	4381	28313	155	3095	109
1962	3.3	93.4	-	3.3	100.0	5185	29257	177	3680	126
1963	2.9	93.8	-	3.3	100.0	5797	30241	192	4217	139
1964	1.9	95.0	-	3.1	100.0	6463	31270	207	4611	147

Table XI. TOTAL ENERGY CONSUMPTION: PERCENTAGE DISTRIBUTION BY FUEL; RELATED DATA ON POPULATION AND ELECTRICITY CONSUMPTION, SELECTED YEARS, 1925-1965

Region, country, year	Percentage distribution of total consumption (based on coal equivalents)					Total consumption (10^3 m.t. coal equiv.)	Population (10^3)	Consumption per capita (kgs)	Addendum: Electricity consumption	
	Solid fuels	Liquid fuels	Natural gas	Hydro-electric power	Total				Total (10^6 kwh)	Per capita (kwh)
	(1)	(2)	(3)	(4)	(5)	(6)	(7)	(8)	(9)	(10)
PHILIPPINES (CONTINUED)										
1965	1.5	95.7	-	2.8	100.0	6820	32345	211	4959	153
TAIWAN										
1925	90.8	4.7	4.2	0.3	100.0	697	4095	170	20	5
1929	82.6	8.2	7.8	1.3	100.0	1172	4493	261	150	33
1933	80.1	9.2	7.2	3.5	100.0	1242	4995	249	395	79
1937	80.7	12.1	2.6	4.6	100.0	1547	5530	280	600	108
1938	80.8	12.0	2.2	5.0	100.0	1725	5678	304	720	127
1950	77.5	13.6	1.8	7.0	100.0	1730	7619	227	1040	137
1953	87.3	4.3	1.1	7.3	100.0	2498	8261	302	1564	189
1955	67.2	26.2	1.0	5.6	100.0	3437	8907	386	1970	221
1957	66.4	27.2	0.9	5.6	100.0	4349	9506	457	2680	282
1960	67.5	27.3	0.6	4.6	100.0	5590	10612	527	3800	358
1961	67.9	26.5	0.8	4.9	100.0	6015	10971	548	4243	387
1962	67.5	27.6	0.8	4.1	100.0	6551	11349	577	4848	427
1963	66.0	29.6	1.0	3.4	100.0	7134	11696	610	5157	441
1964	68.3	24.5	3.1	4.1	100.0	7200	12070	597	6071	503
1965	61.3	29.8	5.0	3.9	100.0	8258	12429	664	6627	533
THAILAND										
1925	37.6	62.4	-	-	100.0	101	10542	10	NA	NA
1929	26.5	73.5	-	-	100.0	196	11496	17	20	2
1933	16.6	83.4	-	-	100.0	139	12919	11	NA	NA
1937	22.9	77.1	-	-	100.0	218	14492	15	30	2
1938	24.2	75.8	-	-	100.0	232	14755	16	34	2
1950	5.4	94.6	-	-	100.0	370	19635	19	69	4
1953	6.3	93.8	-	-	100.0	715	21456	33	158	7
1955	6.1	93.9	-	-	100.0	1128	22762	50	320	14
1957	6.5	93.5	-	-	100.0	1394	24148	58	470	19
1960	4.9	95.1	-	-	100.0	1740	26388	66	590	22
1961	4.0	96.0	-	-	100.0	1873	27180	69	701	26
1962	4.1	95.9	-	-	100.0	2312	27995	83	842	30
1963	3.7	96.3	-	-	100.0	2562	28835	89	906	31
1964	2.1	97.9	-	-	100.0	3493	29700	118	1092	37
1965	2.4	97.6	-	-	100.0	3722	30591	122	1406	46
AFRICA										
1925	91.6	8.3	-	0.1	100.0	13940	139165	100	2213	16
1929	85.9	14.0	-	0.1	100.0	17148	149395	115	2997	20
1933	83.2	16.6	-	0.2	100.0	15133	158430	96	3941	25
1937	81.2	18.6	-	0.3	100.0	22570	169665	133	6727	40
1938	81.4	18.4	-	0.3	100.0	23403	173022	135	7410	43
1950	67.7	31.9	-	0.4	100.0	42030	216976	194	15522	72
1953	66.3	33.2	-	0.5	100.0	49414	232012	213	20035	86
1955	64.6	34.6	-	0.7	100.0	58794	243763	241	25072	103
1957	65.4	33.8	-	0.8	100.0	63118	256463	246	31254	122
1960	61.4	37.3	0.1	1.2	100.0	70241	276035	254	39805	144

Table XI. TOTAL ENERGY CONSUMPTION: PERCENTAGE DISTRIBUTION BY FUEL; RELATED DATA ON POPULATION AND ELECTRICITY CONSUMPTION, SELECTED YEARS, 1925-1965

Region, country, year	Percentage distribution of total consumption (based on coal equivalents)					Total consumption (10^3 m.t. coal equiv.)	Population (10^3)	Consumption per capita (kgs)	Addendum: Electricity consumption	
	Solid fuels	Liquid fuels	Natural gas	Hydro-electric power	Total				Total (10^6 kwh)	Per capita (kwh)
	(1)	(2)	(3)	(4)	(5)	(6)	(7)	(8)	(9)	(10)
AFRICA (CONTINUED)										
1961	60.3	37.6	0.5	1.6	100.0	72869	287312	254	43259	151
1962	59.4	38.1	0.7	1.8	100.0	75247	289274	260	46069	159
1963	59.2	38.2	0.8	1.8	100.0	77380	296600	261	48985	165
1964	57.1	39.9	1.3	1.8	100.0	85881	303176	283	53498	176
1965	57.2	39.4	1.6	1.8	100.0	92622	310307	298	58403	188
NORTH AFRICA										
1925	76.4	23.5	-	0.1	100.0	2954	27825	106	325	12
1929	65.5	34.4	-	0.1	100.0	4063	29732	137	501	17
1933	56.6	43.2	-	0.3	100.0	4022	31595	127	630	20
1937	56.8	42.8	-	0.5	100.0	4513	34038	133	765	22
1938	55.5	44.1	-	0.4	100.0	4838	34712	139	815	23
1950	14.0	85.4	0.1	0.6	100.0	9358	41852	224	1862	44
1953	10.6	88.6	0.1	0.7	100.0	10365	44911	231	2506	56
1955	8.6	90.1	0.1	1.1	100.0	12064	48136	251	3470	72
1957	11.4	87.2	0.1	1.3	100.0	11662	50447	231	4100	81
1960	6.8	91.6	0.2	1.3	100.0	14776	54200	273	5370	99
1961	6.6	89.4	2.2	1.9	100.0	14931	55554	269	6616	119
1962	5.0	89.8	3.2	2.0	100.0	15384	56925	270	6856	120
1963	4.9	89.2	3.7	2.2	100.0	14960	58328	256	7231	124
1964	5.9	86.2	5.6	2.2	100.0	17509	59922	292	8089	135
1965	5.1	85.2	7.4	2.3	100.0	18363	61383	299	8538	139
ALGERIA										
1925	83.4	16.2	-	0.4	100.0	694	NA	NA	105	NA
1929	77.0	22.8	-	0.2	100.0	1151	6500	177	195	30
1933	65.9	33.8	-	0.3	100.0	1021	6850	149	212	31
1937	66.6	33.0	-	0.4	100.0	1010	NA	NA	253	NA
1938	66.4	33.1	-	0.5	100.0	1041	NA	NA	278	NA
1950	42.2	56.4	0.4	1.1	100.0	1512	8753	173	585	67
1953	26.9	71.3	-	1.7	100.0	1619	9370	173	767	82
1955	25.4	73.0	-	1.6	100.0	2153	9715	222	870	90
1957	26.5	72.0	-	1.5	100.0	2654	10143	262	1000	99
1960	12.8	85.8	0.3	1.2	100.0	3665	10784	340	1330	123
1961	8.2	82.2	8.7	0.9	100.0	3526	10993	321	1392	127
1962	6.1	73.9	18.7	1.3	100.0	2518	11206	225	1163	104
1963	3.6	73.3	21.8	1.3	100.0	2444	11423	214	1092	96
1964	3.8	63.5	31.5	1.2	100.0	3038	11645	261	1124	97
1965	1.8	58.7	38.0	1.4	100.0	3523	11871	297	1121	94
EGYPT UAR										
1925	73.8	26.2	-	-	100.0	1784	13965	128	167	12
1929	60.8	39.2	-	-	100.0	2165	14602	148	200	14
1933	52.4	47.6	-	-	100.0	2156	15275	141	238	16
1937	55.3	44.7	-	-	100.0	2595	16008	162	285	18
1938	55.1	44.9	-	-	100.0	2806	16295	172	300	18
1950	2.9	97.1	-	-	100.0	6198	20591	301	586	28
1953	1.2	98.8	-	-	100.0	6251	22212	281	730	33

Table XI. TOTAL ENERGY CONSUMPTION: PERCENTAGE DISTRIBUTION BY FUEL; RELATED DATA ON POPULATION AND ELECTRICITY CONSUMPTION, SELECTED YEARS, 1925-1965

Region, country, year	Percentage distribution of total consumption (based on coal equivalents): Solid fuels	Liquid fuels	Natural gas	Hydro-electric power	Total	Total consumption (10^3 m.t. coal equiv.)	Population (10^3)	Consumption per capita (kgs)	Addendum: Electricity consumption: Total (10^6 kwh)	Per capita (kwh)
	(1)	(2)	(3)	(4)	(5)	(6)	(7)	(8)	(9)	(10)
EGYPT UAR (CONTINUED)										
1955	1.5	98.5	-	-	100.0	7275	23278	313	1410	61
1957	2.7	97.3	-	-	100.0	6634	24400	272	1710	70
1960	1.9	97.7	-	0.4	100.0	8321	26207	318	2640	101
1961	3.6	94.9	-	1.5	100.0	8288	26821	309	3723	139
1962	3.1	95.3	-	1.7	100.0	8833	27512	321	4110	149
1963	3.0	95.3	-	1.8	100.0	9115	28242	323	4460	158
1964	4.7	93.3	-	2.0	100.0	10565	29189	362	5106	175
1965	4.1	93.8	-	2.1	100.0	10637	29897	356	5474	183
MOROCCO										
1925	69.1	30.9	-	-	100.0	175	NA	NA	15	NA
1929	55.8	43.5	-	0.7	100.0	324	5750	56	55	10
1933	54.7	43.5	-	1.8	100.0	404	6250	65	114	18
1937	46.4	49.8	-	3.8	100.0	419	7180	58	143	20
1938	35.2	61.3	-	3.5	100.0	443	7400	60	144	19
1950	29.2	67.5	-	3.2	100.0	1071	8953	120	512	57
1953	27.8	69.6	0.4	2.2	100.0	1822	9571	190	748	78
1955	16.3	77.1	0.6	6.0	100.0	1701	10113	168	870	86
1957	22.8	69.6	0.3	7.4	100.0	1455	10688	136	1050	98
1960	18.8	73.6	0.7	6.9	100.0	1662	11626	143	1000	86
1961	17.6	74.8	0.6	7.0	100.0	1707	12030	142	1062	88
1962	21.0	68.7	1.0	9.3	100.0	1381	12360	112	1105	89
1963	17.5	74.3	0.9	7.3	100.0	1852	12665	146	1163	92
1964	19.2	72.9	0.8	7.1	100.0	1982	12959	153	1256	97
1965	17.2	75.4	0.7	6.7	100.0	2149	13323	161	1282	96
TUNISIA										
1925	82.7	17.3	-	-	100.0	270	NA	NA	23	NA
1929	68.2	31.8	-	-	100.0	377	2200	171	33	15
1933	60.6	39.4	-	-	100.0	355	2500	142	45	18
1937	58.5	41.5	-	-	100.0	373	2670	140	59	22
1938	59.9	40.1	-	-	100.0	397	NA	NA	67	NA
1950	37.1	62.9	-	-	100.0	494	3555	139	141	40
1953	14.7	85.3	-	-	100.0	565	3758	150	211	56
1955	6.0	93.2	0.8	-	100.0	663	3901	170	260	67
1957	14.4	83.8	1.3	0.5	100.0	626	4003	156	270	67
1960	5.6	92.3	1.3	0.8	100.0	718	4232	170	300	71
1961	6.7	91.7	1.3	0.3	100.0	744	4310	173	329	76
1962	5.2	93.3	1.2	0.3	100.0	767	4396	175	345	78
1963	4.2	94.4	1.0	0.4	100.0	952	4494	212	367	82
1964	3.5	95.1	0.9	0.4	100.0	1135	4565	249	446	98
1965	4.7	93.8	1.0	0.5	100.0	1063	4675	227	494	106
TROPICAL AFRICA										
1925	85.2	14.5	-	0.3	100.0	1848	102600	18	127	1
1929	82.2	17.6	-	0.2	100.0	2780	110140	25	196	2
1933	82.8	16.0	-	1.2	100.0	1460	116520	13	364	3
1937	65.9	32.9	-	1.1	100.0	3342	124510	27	626	5

Table XI. TOTAL ENERGY CONSUMPTION: PERCENTAGE DISTRIBUTION BY FUEL; RELATED DATA ON POPULATION AND ELECTRICITY CONSUMPTION, SELECTED YEARS, 1925-1965

Region, country, year	Percentage distribution of total consumption (based on coal equivalents)					Total consumption (10^3 m.t. coal equiv.)	Population (10^3)	Consumption per capita (kgs)	Addendum: Electricity consumption	
	Solid fuels	Liquid fuels	Natural gas	Hydro-electric power	Total				Total (10^6 kwh)	Per capita (kwh)
	(1)	(2)	(3)	(4)	(5)	(6)	(7)	(8)	(9)	(10)
TROPICAL AFRICA (CONTINUED)										
1938	68.4	30.3	-	1.3	100.0	3053	127000	24	662	5
1950	56.2	42.0	-	1.8	100.0	6433	161160	40	2793	17
1953	51.1	46.8	-	2.1	100.0	8724	172160	51	4184	24
1955	48.6	49.0	-	2.4	100.0	11144	179910	62	5252	29
1957	44.2	53.0	-	2.8	100.0	13052	189520	69	7044	37
1960	37.0	58.2	0.1	4.8	100.0	13331	203945	65	9765	48
1961	31.7	61.9	0.1	6.3	100.0	14078	213463	66	10583	50
1962	29.7	63.3	0.1	7.0	100.0	14455	213642	68	11523	54
1963	26.0	66.7	0.4	6.8	100.0	15397	219126	70	12254	56
1964	25.3	67.7	0.5	6.5	100.0	17326	223652	77	13194	59
1965	25.4	67.6	0.5	6.5	100.0	18942	228889	83	14544	64
CONGO, DEMOCRATIC REPUBLIC										
1925	93.6	5.5	-	1.0	100.0	384	NA	NA	NA	NA
1929	89.7	9.7	-	0.6	100.0	650	12056	54	30	2
1933	63.3	24.8	-	11.9	100.0	103	12527	8	98	8
1937	69.0	21.6	-	9.4	100.0	292	13780	21	220	16
1938	69.8	18.6	-	11.6	100.0	251	14037	18	233	17
1950	54.2	34.9	-	10.8	100.0	679	15185	45	617	41
1953	48.3	40.1	-	11.6	100.0	1067	16277	66	1073	66
1955	50.1	38.9	-	11.0	100.0	1536	16851	91	1460	87
1957	43.1	43.4	-	13.5	100.0	1560	17682	88	1800	102
1960	31.6	50.4	-	18.0	100.0	1244	19028	65	1910	100
1961	30.8	50.9	-	18.3	100.0	1309	19484	67	2042	105
1962	25.3	54.2	-	20.5	100.0	1249	19946	63	2246	113
1963	24.1	57.0	-	18.9	100.0	1295	20287	64	2177	107
1964	30.7	47.3	-	22.1	100.0	1158	20918	55	2291	110
1965	32.2	47.9	-	19.9	100.0	1380	21537	64	2500	116
EAST AFRICA										
1925	50.8	48.4	-	0.9	100.0	146	10960	13	NA	NA
1929	47.5	51.9	-	0.6	100.0	225	11460	20	17	1
1933	67.4	31.1	-	1.5	100.0	135	11840	11	NA	NA
1937	57.9	41.1	-	1.1	100.0	285	12295	23	36	3
1938	46.3	52.7	-	1.0	100.0	324	12440	26	NA	NA
1950	3.7	95.0	-	1.3	100.0	703	18950	37	145	8
1953	1.3	97.5	-	1.3	100.0	1094	20346	54	297	15
1955	1.8	95.5	-	2.6	100.0	1473	21343	69	400	19
1957	2.3	94.4	-	3.3	100.0	1592	22419	71	550	25
1960	2.3	93.3	-	4.4	100.0	1829	24029	76	790	33
1961	2.5	92.6	-	4.9	100.0	1676	24618	68	849	34
1962	2.3	92.8	-	4.8	100.0	1845	25218	73	908	36
1963	2.1	93.1	-	4.8	100.0	2005	25835	78	979	38
1964	1.5	93.4	-	5.2	100.0	2078	26461	79	1070	40
1965	2.8	91.9	-	5.3	100.0	2222	27095	82	1551	57

Table XI. TOTAL ENERGY CONSUMPTION: PERCENTAGE DISTRIBUTION BY FUEL; RELATED DATA ON POPULATION AND ELECTRICITY CONSUMPTION, SELECTED YEARS, 1925-1965

Region, country, year	Percentage distribution of total consumption (based on coal equivalents)					Total consumption (10^3 m.t. coal equiv.)	Population (10^3)	Consumption per capita (kgs)	Addendum: Electricity consumption	
	Solid fuels	Liquid fuels	Natural gas	Hydro-electric power	Total				Total (10^6 kwh)	Per capita (kwh)
	(1)	(2)	(3)	(4)	(5)	(6)	(7)	(8)	(9)	(10)
EQUATORIAL AFRICA										
1925	40.0	60.0	-	-	100.0	5	NA	NA	NA	NA
1929	11.8	88.2	-	-	100.0	9	NA	NA	NA	NA
1933	16.0	84.0	-	-	100.0	13	3200	4	NA	NA
1937	53.8	46.2	-	-	100.0	39	3500	11	NA	NA
1938	36.1	63.9	-	-	100.0	31	3575	9	NA	NA
1950	8.2	91.8	-	-	100.0	85	4406	19	12	3
1953	3.2	96.0	-	0.7	100.0	123	4556	27	15	3
1955	-	96.8	-	3.2	100.0	130	4708	28	30	6
1957	-	98.3	-	1.7	100.0	223	4863	46	30	6
1960	-	96.3	2.6	1.1	100.0	355	5533	64	70	13
1961	-	96.2	2.7	1.1	100.0	345	5621	61	72	13
1962	-	94.3	4.4	1.4	100.0	275	5732	48	87	15
1963	-	92.1	5.2	2.7	100.0	230	5818	39	104	18
1964	-	94.0	4.1	1.9	100.0	326	5905	55	115	19
1965	-	93.5	4.6	1.9	100.0	321	5961	54	123	21
GHANA										
1925	65.5	34.5	-	-	100.0	83	3470	24	NA	NA
1929	58.2	41.8	-	-	100.0	126	3930	32	6	2
1933	41.9	58.1	-	-	100.0	65	4290	15	NA	NA
1937	37.5	62.5	-	-	100.0	192	4570	42	10	2
1938	36.6	63.4	-	-	100.0	211	4640	45	NA	NA
1950	20.9	79.1	-	-	100.0	302	5600	54	197	35
1953	24.0	76.0	-	-	100.0	413	5870	70	226	39
1955	20.7	79.3	-	-	100.0	579	6050	96	240	40
1957	17.3	82.7	-	-	100.0	635	6250	102	280	45
1960	5.8	94.2	-	-	100.0	685	6777	101	370	55
1961	7.7	92.3	-	-	100.0	649	6960	93	390	56
1962	4.2	95.8	-	-	100.0	720	7148	101	432	60
1963	4.8	95.2	-	-	100.0	832	7340	113	470	64
1964	4.2	95.8	-	-	100.0	963	7537	128	489	65
1965	3.2	95.4	-	1.4	100.0	936	7740	121	528	68
LIBERIA										
1925	-	-	-	-	-	-	NA	NA	NA	NA
1929	-	-	-	-	-	-	NA	NA	NA	NA
1933	-	-	-	-	-	-	NA	NA	NA	NA
1937	-	100.0	-	-	100.0	2	NA	NA	1	NA
1938	-	100.0	-	-	100.0	3	NA	NA	1	NA
1950	-	96.0	-	4.0	100.0	25	NA	NA	12	NA
1953	-	95.6	-	4.4	100.0	28	NA	NA	29	NA
1955	-	98.5	-	1.5	100.0	93	NA	NA	30	NA
1957	-	96.5	-	3.5	100.0	50	NA	NA	50	NA
1960	-	97.2	-	2.8	100.0	76	988	77	100	101
1961	-	97.2	-	2.8	100.0	77	1002	77	115	115
1962	-	98.3	-	1.7	100.0	125	1016	123	134	132
1963	-	98.9	-	1.1	100.0	187	1030	181	182	177
1964	-	99.1	-	0.9	100.0	248	1041	238	212	204
1965	-	99.3	-	0.7	100.0	284	1066	267	278	261

Table XI. TOTAL ENERGY CONSUMPTION: PERCENTAGE DISTRIBUTION BY FUEL; RELATED DATA ON POPULATION AND ELECTRICITY CONSUMPTION, SELECTED YEARS, 1925-1965

Region, country, year	Percentage distribution of total consumption (based on coal equivalents)					Total consumption (10^3 m.t. coal equiv.)	Population (10^3)	Consumption per capita (kgs)	Addendum: Electricity consumption	
	Solid fuels	Liquid fuels	Natural gas	Hydro-electric power	Total				Total (10^6 kwh)	Per capita (kwh)
	(1)	(2)	(3)	(4)	(5)	(6)	(7)	(8)	(9)	(10)
NIGERIA										
1925	87.0	13.0	-	-	100.0	265	NA	NA	NA	NA
1929	85.9	14.1	-	-	100.0	373	NA	NA	NA	NA
1933	90.7	9.3	-	-	100.0	257	NA	NA	NA	NA
1937	86.0	14.0	-	-	100.0	406	NA	NA	15	NA
1938	85.0	15.0	-	-	100.0	400	NA	NA	15	NA
1950	72.1	27.1	-	0.7	100.0	890	NA	NA	117	NA
1953	68.4	30.8	-	0.7	100.0	1071	NA	NA	179	NA
1955	59.0	40.2	-	0.8	100.0	1120	NA	NA	250	NA
1957	54.4	44.8	-	0.8	100.0	1339	49000	27	330	7
1960	37.7	61.5	-	0.8	100.0	1436	52000	28	560	11
1961	32.6	66.7	-	0.7	100.0	1708	53000	32	642	12
1962	36.9	62.2	0.2	0.8	100.0	1639	54000	30	750	14
1963	28.4	68.0	2.8	0.8	100.0	1889	55670	34	893	16
1964	27.4	68.6	3.3	0.7	100.0	2330	56400	41	1024	18
1965	25.6	70.9	2.9	0.6	100.0	2753	57500	48	1177	20
RHODESIAN FEDERATION										
1925	98.1	1.9	-	-	100.0	472	3306	143	NA	NA
1929	95.5	4.5	-	-	100.0	671	3727	180	NA	NA
1933	91.9	7.5	-	0.5	100.0	478	4190	114	NA	NA
1937	91.4	8.1	-	0.5	100.0	960	4443	216	NA	NA
1938	91.3	8.1	-	0.6	100.0	1017	4540	224	NA	NA
1950	87.9	11.2	-	0.9	100.0	2229	6896	323	1340	194
1953	85.7	13.4	-	0.8	100.0	2940	7604	387	2007	264
1955	85.4	13.9	-	0.7	100.0	3800	8430	451	2290	272
1957	83.5	15.9	-	0.7	100.0	4290	8910	481	3020	339
1960	77.7	18.4	-	3.8	100.0	4259	10310	413	3830	371
1961	70.6	20.0	-	9.4	100.0	3940	10620	371	4010	378
1962	67.5	21.3	-	11.2	100.0	3923	10940	359	4222	386
1963	65.6	21.9	-	12.4	100.0	3825	11259	340	4518	401
1964	66.0	21.3	-	12.7	100.0	4112	11640	353	4852	417
1965	63.0	25.4	-	11.6	100.0	4842	11910	407	5192	436
MALAWI										
1925	-	100.0	-	-	100.0	2	1212	1	NA	NA
1929	66.7	33.3	-	-	100.0	5	1363	3	NA	NA
1933	50.0	50.0	-	-	100.0	6	1613	4	NA	NA
1937	62.5	37.5	-	-	100.0	8	1644	5	NA	NA
1938	47.1	52.9	-	-	100.0	9	1674	5	NA	NA
1950	52.6	47.4	-	-	100.0	48	2290	21	2	1
1953	57.6	42.0	-	-	100.0	64	2430	26	NA	NA
1955	48.2	51.6	-	-	100.0	87	2550	34	NA	NA
1957	43.8	55.9	-	-	100.0	107	2650	40	-	-
1960	43.1	56.7	-	-	100.0	132	3460	38	-	-
1961	49.3	50.5	-	-	100.0	122	3560	34	35	10
1962	47.1	51.8	-	1.2	100.0	128	3660	35	51	14
1963	45.7	53.7	-	0.7	100.0	131	3753	35	52	14
1964	44.6	54.6	-	0.8	100.0	135	3900	35	57	15
1965	49.2	49.8	-	0.9	100.0	163	3940	41	66	17

Table XI. TOTAL ENERGY CONSUMPTION: PERCENTAGE DISTRIBUTION BY FUEL; RELATED DATA ON POPULATION AND ELECTRICITY CONSUMPTION, SELECTED YEARS, 1925-1965

Region, country, year	Percentage distribution of total consumption (based on coal equivalents)					Total consumption (10^3 m.t. coal equiv.)	Population (10^3)	Consumption per capita (kgs)	Addendum: Electricity consumption	
	Solid fuels	Liquid fuels	Natural gas	Hydro-electric power	Total				Total (10^6 kwh)	Per capita (kwh)
	(1)	(2)	(3)	(4)	(5)	(6)	(7)	(8)	(9)	(10)
ZAMBIA										
1925	100.0	-	-	-	100.0	42	1130	37	NA	NA
1929	95.9	4.1	-	-	100.0	148	1290	115	NA	NA
1933	97.5	2.5	-	-	100.0	182	1390	131	NA	NA
1937	97.8	2.2	-	-	100.0	349	1440	242	NA	NA
1938	97.8	2.2	-	-	100.0	414	1460	284	NA	NA
1950	91.6	8.4	-	NA	100.0	714	2436	293	832	342
1953	86.6	10.9	-	2.5	100.0	950	2644	359	NA	NA
1955	84.4	13.0	-	2.6	100.0	1042	2790	374	NA	NA
1957	83.0	14.6	-	2.5	100.0	1133	2960	383	NA	NA
1960	84.1	15.9	-	NA	100.0	1230	3210	383	NA	NA
1961	73.1	13.5	-	13.4	100.0	1477	3300	447	2247	681
1962	68.1	14.2	-	17.6	100.0	1454	3400	428	2397	705
1963	66.3	14.8	-	18.9	100.0	1417	3496	405	2576	737
1964	66.6	14.7	-	18.7	100.0	1562	3600	434	2745	763
1965	66.5	16.6	-	16.9	100.0	1826	3710	492	2856	770
RHODESIA										
1950	88.4	11.6	-	NA	100.0	1448	2170	667	506	233
1953	86.2	13.7	-	0.1	100.0	1925	2530	761	NA	NA
1955	87.0	13.0	-	-	100.0	2671	3090	864	NA	NA
1957	85.0	15.0	-	-	100.0	3049	3300	924	NA	NA
1960	77.5	18.0	-	4.6	100.0	2864	3640	787	NA	NA
1961	71.1	22.7	-	6.2	100.0	2312	3760	615	1728	460
1962	67.9	24.0	-	8.1	100.0	2350	3880	606	1774	457
1963	66.3	24.5	-	9.1	100.0	2276	4010	568	1890	471
1964	66.8	23.8	-	9.4	100.0	2416	4140	584	2050	495
1965	61.5	29.7	-	8.8	100.0	2853	4260	670	2270	533
WEST AFRICA										
1925	63.7	36.3	-	-	100.0	79	NA	NA	NA	NA
1929	65.0	35.0	-	-	100.0	120	14267	8	NA	NA
1933	67.1	32.9	-	-	100.0	87	14400	6	6	-
1937	68.1	31.9	-	-	100.0	226	14750	15	9	1
1938	-	100.0	-	-	100.0	60	14950	4	10	1
1950	18.5	81.5	-	-	100.0	368	17600	21	38	2
1953	11.1	88.7	-	0.1	100.0	504	18425	27	62	3
1955	5.3	94.5	-	0.2	100.0	565	19223	29	120	6
1957	0.1	99.6	-	0.3	100.0	728	21000	35	170	8
1960	0.1	99.1	-	0.8	100.0	957	23654	40	360	15
1961	0.1	99.0	-	0.9	100.0	1145	24318	47	448	18
1962	-	99.0	-	1.0	100.0	1241	24909	50	523	21
1963	-	98.9	-	1.1	100.0	1323	25783	51	584	23
1964	-	99.2	-	0.8	100.0	1562	26375	59	661	25
1965	-	99.0	-	1.0	100.0	1831	27026	68	719	27
SOUTH AFRICA										
1925	97.9	2.1	-	-	100.0	9138	8740	1045	1761	201
1929	95.0	5.0	-	-	100.0	10305	9523	1082	2300	242

Table XI. TOTAL ENERGY CONSUMPTION: PERCENTAGE DISTRIBUTION BY FUEL; RELATED DATA ON POPULATION AND ELECTRICITY CONSUMPTION, SELECTED YEARS, 1925-1965

Region, country, year	Percentage distribution of total consumption (based on coal equivalents)					Total consumption (10^3 m.t. coal equiv.)	Population (10^3)	Consumption per capita (kgs)	Addendum: Electricity consumption	
	Solid fuels	Liquid fuels	Natural gas	Hydro-electric power	Total				Total (10^6 kwh)	Per capita (kwh)
	(1)	(2)	(3)	(4)	(5)	(6)	(7)	(8)	(9)	(10)
SOUTH AFRICA (CONTINUED)										
1933	94.4	5.6	-	-	100.0	9651	10315	936	2947	286
1937	92.1	7.9	-	-	100.0	14715	11117	1324	5336	480
1938	92.0	8.0	-	-	100.0	15513	11310	1372	5933	525
1950	89.7	10.3	-	-	100.0	26239	13964	1879	10867	778
1953	89.7	10.3	-	-	100.0	30325	14941	2030	13345	893
1955	88.7	11.3	-	-	100.0	35587	15717	2264	16350	1040
1957	89.0	11.0	-	-	100.0	38403	16496	2328	20110	1219
1960	88.3	11.7	-	-	100.0	42134	17890	2355	24670	1379
1961	87.8	12.2	-	-	100.0	43860	18295	2397	26060	1424
1962	87.4	12.6	-	-	100.0	45407	18707	2427	27690	1480
1963	87.4	12.6	-	-	100.0	47024	19146	2456	29500	1541
1964	85.5	14.5	-	-	100.0	51047	19602	2604	32215	1643
1965	85.4	14.6	-	-	100.0	55317	20035	2761	35321	1763
DEVELOPED COUNTRIES										
1925	83.7	12.2	3.4	0.7	100.0	1321075	482103	2740	172531	358
1929	79.6	14.8	4.7	0.9	100.0	1529954	501499	3051	254202	507
1933	75.4	18.2	5.1	1.3	100.0	1160529	518775	2237	247805	478
1937	73.5	19.1	6.0	1.3	100.0	1530049	533916	2866	367275	688
1938	72.5	19.9	6.2	1.4	100.0	1422111	537826	2644	375102	697
1950	57.1	29.1	11.8	2.0	100.0	1961603	577569	3396	760681	1317
1953	50.6	32.9	14.4	2.1	100.0	2175971	598763	3634	981839	1640
1955	47.5	35.3	15.1	2.2	100.0	2348853	613745	3827	1202671	1960
1957	45.6	36.1	16.1	2.2	100.0	2538593	628937	4036	1385352	2203
1960	39.0	39.8	18.6	2.6	100.0	2707952	651680	4155	1695065	2601
1961	37.3	41.1	19.0	2.6	100.0	2796010	659800	4238	1793419	2718
1962	36.3	41.9	19.2	2.5	100.0	2947561	668208	4411	1930418	2889
1963	35.4	42.9	19.2	2.5	100.0	3120132	676475	4612	2072212	3063
1964	34.6	43.7	19.3	2.4	100.0	3304757	684353	4829	2240069	3273
1965	33.3	45.0	19.2	2.5	100.0	3462535	692520	5000	2392689	3455
UNDERDEVELOPED COUNTRIES										
1925	59.2	37.6	2.5	0.8	100.0	59300	743684	80	7188	10
1929	53.9	41.6	3.6	0.8	100.0	72548	786806	92	10347	13
1933	55.0	36.9	6.6	1.5	100.0	58600	835638	70	12581	15
1937	49.1	43.1	6.3	1.5	100.0	90044	893353	101	18558	21
1938	48.4	43.9	6.2	1.5	100.0	96576	908865	106	19917	22
1950	33.6	58.1	6.4	1.8	100.0	142051	1087374	131	42453	39
1953	31.1	59.3	7.6	1.9	100.0	173904	1155511	150	59835	52
1955	26.5	64.1	7.6	1.9	100.0	219856	1197815	184	78033	65
1957	24.7	64.6	8.7	2.0	100.0	265338	1254813	211	98951	79
1960	23.7	62.8	11.2	2.2	100.0	318308	1347865	236	134638	100
1961	23.1	62.9	11.7	2.4	100.0	339577	1385426	245	148193	107
1962	23.2	62.3	12.1	2.4	100.0	364628	1415256	258	162735	115
1963	24.0	61.1	12.4	2.5	100.0	380020	1451297	262	177260	122
1964	22.6	61.5	13.3	2.6	100.0	403368	1487488	271	195656	132
1965	22.2	62.0	13.1	2.7	100.0	433270	1524067	284	213303	140

Table XI. TOTAL ENERGY CONSUMPTION: PERCENTAGE DISTRIBUTION BY FUEL; RELATED DATA ON POPULATION AND ELECTRICITY CONSUMPTION, SELECTED YEARS, 1925-1965

Region, country, year	Percentage distribution of total consumption (based on coal equivalents)								Addendum: Electricity consumption	
	Solid fuels	Liquid fuels	Natural gas	Hydro-electric power	Total	Total consumption (10^3 m.t. coal equiv.)	Population (10^3)	Consumption per capita (kgs)	Total (10^6 kwh)	Per capita (kwh)
	(1)	(2)	(3)	(4)	(5)	(6)	(7)	(8)	(9)	(10)
COMMUNIST COUNTRIES										
1925	85.5	13.1	1.3	0.1	100.0	104158	664359	157	9214	14
1929	84.6	13.9	1.4	0.1	100.0	153480	692663	222	15718	23
1933	79.6	17.9	2.4	0.1	100.0	173110	708215	244	25874	37
1937	79.5	17.9	2.4	0.2	100.0	263340	718566	366	50413	70
1938	78.7	18.8	2.3	0.3	100.0	271369	721346	376	54518	76
1950	83.8	13.5	2.1	0.5	100.0	507245	839596	604	142718	170
1953	82.6	14.6	2.4	0.5	100.0	643372	874203	736	205146	235
1955	81.4	15.7	2.4	0.5	100.0	789480	914002	864	259360	284
1957	78.4	17.4	3.6	0.7	100.0	931389	944106	987	321430	340
1960	74.1	18.9	6.2	0.8	100.0	1169835	990313	1181	474620	479
1961	72.6	19.2	7.3	0.8	100.0	1244360	1005536	1238	491886	489
1962	70.1	20.4	8.6	0.9	100.0	1308820	1020615	1282	544387	533
1963	68.6	20.8	9.7	0.9	100.0	1409567	1035622	1361	598306	578
1964	67.5	20.7	10.9	0.9	100.0	1495613	1050257	1424	668958	637
1965	66.0	21.1	12.1	0.9	100.0	1578771	1064643	1483	736253	692
USSR										
1925	64.9	34.2	0.7	0.1	100.0	25320	153900	165	2925	19
1929	70.9	28.1	0.8	0.1	100.0	52966	168500	314	6224	37
1933	72.9	25.5	1.5	0.1	100.0	98640	180600	546	16357	91
1937	73.6	24.4	1.7	0.3	100.0	166298	188000	885	36400	194
1938	73.1	24.9	1.7	0.4	100.0	176349	190000	928	39600	208
1950	76.9	20.0	2.5	0.5	100.0	303319	180050	1685	90900	505
1953	75.2	21.7	2.4	0.6	100.0	369587	189500	1950	134325	709
1955	73.9	22.9	2.6	0.6	100.0	460976	196150	2350	170240	868
1957	69.1	25.4	4.5	0.9	100.0	540514	203150	2661	209690	1032
1960	61.0	28.6	9.4	1.0	100.0	640618	214400	2988	292240	1363
1961	57.5	29.6	11.7	1.1	100.0	667338	218000	3061	327537	1502
1962	53.9	31.2	13.7	1.3	100.0	710332	221465	3207	369043	1666
1963	51.7	31.5	15.5	1.2	100.0	769574	224764	3424	411671	1832
1964	50.1	31.1	17.7	1.2	100.0	816567	227687	3586	457598	2010
1965	48.9	30.7	19.3	1.1	100.0	880629	230585	3819	505234	2191
COMMUNIST EASTERN EUROPE										
1925	91.2	6.5	2.2	0.1	100.0	55138	70459	783	4339	62
1929	91.3	6.4	2.2	0.1	100.0	76744	74163	1035	7374	99
1933	86.2	8.4	5.3	0.1	100.0	49534	77615	638	6447	83
1937	87.5	7.2	5.1	0.2	100.0	66040	80566	820	10083	125
1938	86.8	8.2	4.8	0.2	100.0	67690	81346	832	10518	129
1950	93.0	4.8	2.0	0.2	100.0	160796	89716	1792	42618	475
1953	90.8	6.1	3.0	0.2	100.0	207134	92343	2243	59921	649
1955	90.4	6.3	3.0	0.2	100.0	230214	94347	2440	73560	780
1957	89.2	7.2	3.3	0.2	100.0	259065	95968	2699	85280	889
1960	87.4	8.3	4.1	0.3	100.0	293895	98459	2985	114380	1162
1961	86.8	8.7	4.2	0.3	100.0	311993	99068	3149	124511	1257
1962	85.7	9.4	4.6	0.3	100.0	331733	99752	3326	135377	1357
1963	84.6	10.1	4.9	0.3	100.0	353068	100539	3512	144263	1435
1964	83.6	11.0	5.2	0.3	100.0	371008	101320	3662	158260	1562
1965	81.9	12.0	5.7	0.4	100.0	375131	101854	3683	171849	1687

Table XI. TOTAL ENERGY CONSUMPTION: PERCENTAGE DISTRIBUTION BY FUEL; RELATED DATA ON POPULATION AND ELECTRICITY CONSUMPTION, SELECTED YEARS, 1925-1965

Region, country, year	Percentage distribution of total consumption (based on coal equivalents)								Addendum: Electricity consumption	
	Solid fuels	Liquid fuels	Natural gas	Hydro-electric power	Total	Total consumption (10^3 m.t. coal equiv.)	Population (10^3)	Consumption per capita (kgs)	Total (10^6 kwh)	Per capita (kwh)
	(1)	(2)	(3)	(4)	(5)	(6)	(7)	(8)	(9)	(10)
COMMUNIST ASIA										
1925	94.0	6.0	-	-	100.0	23701	440000	54	1950	4
1929	93.2	6.8	-	-	100.0	23770	450000	53	2120	5
1933	92.8	7.2	-	-	100.0	24935	450000	55	3070	7
1937	93.8	6.2	-	-	100.0	31002	450000	69	3930	9
1938	94.5	5.5	-	-	100.0	27330	450000	61	4400	10
1950	98.1	0.3	-	1.5	100.0	43130	569830	76	9200	16
1953	98.1	1.4	-	0.5	100.0	66651	592360	113	10900	18
1955	95.6	3.6	-	0.8	100.0	98290	623505	158	15560	25
1957	94.7	4.3	-	1.0	100.0	131809	644988	204	26460	41
1960	93.2	5.8	-	1.0	100.0	235321	677454	347	68000	100
1961	93.8	5.4	-	0.8	100.0	265029	688468	385	39838	58
1962	94.0	5.2	-	0.8	100.0	266755	699398	381	39967	57
1963	94.1	5.1	-	0.8	100.0	286924	710319	404	42372	60
1964	94.4	4.9	-	0.8	100.0	308037	721250	427	53100	74
1965	94.1	5.1	-	0.8	100.0	323012	732204	441	59170	81
ORGANISATION FOR ECONOMIC CO-OPERATION AND DEVELOPMENT (OECD)										
1925	83.5	12.3	3.5	0.7	100.0	1293454	455173	2842	167912	369
1929	79.4	14.9	4.8	0.9	100.0	1499729	472888	3171	247310	523
1933	75.1	18.3	5.2	1.3	100.0	1134420	488758	2321	238755	488
1937	73.3	19.3	6.2	1.3	100.0	1492576	502573	2970	352907	702
1938	72.2	20.0	6.3	1.4	100.0	1383856	506147	2734	359086	709
1950	56.3	29.5	12.2	2.0	100.0	1898300	543029	3496	730386	1345
1953	49.6	33.4	14.9	2.1	100.0	2108232	563212	3743	943764	1676
1955	46.4	35.8	15.6	2.2	100.0	2265837	577344	3925	1153689	1998
1957	44.6	36.5	16.7	2.2	100.0	2447397	592020	4134	1325891	2240
1960	37.6	40.4	19.4	2.6	100.0	2602063	613817	4239	1619863	2639
1961	35.9	41.8	19.8	2.6	100.0	2685668	621685	4320	1712596	2755
1962	34.9	42.6	20.0	2.5	100.0	2834370	629808	4500	1842982	2926
1963	34.1	43.5	20.0	2.5	100.0	3000209	637817	4704	1976497	3099
1964	33.3	44.3	20.1	2.4	100.0	3174028	645651	4916	2134102	3305
1965	31.9	45.6	20.0	2.5	100.0	3320455	653308	5083	2277634	3486
COMMUNIST COUNTRIES										
1925	85.5	13.1	1.3	0.1	100.0	104158	664359	157	9214	14
1929	84.6	13.9	1.4	0.1	100.0	153480	692663	222	15718	23
1933	79.6	17.9	2.4	0.1	100.0	173110	708215	244	25874	37
1937	79.5	17.9	2.4	0.2	100.0	263340	718566	366	50413	70
1938	78.7	18.8	2.3	0.3	100.0	271369	721346	376	54518	76
1950	83.8	13.5	2.1	0.5	100.0	507245	839596	604	142718	170
1953	82.6	14.6	2.4	0.5	100.0	643372	874203	736	205146	235
1955	81.4	15.7	2.4	0.5	100.0	789480	914002	864	259360	284
1957	78.4	17.4	3.6	0.7	100.0	931389	944106	987	321430	340
1960	74.1	18.9	6.2	0.8	100.0	1169835	990313	1181	474620	479
1961	72.6	19.2	7.3	0.8	100.0	1244360	1005536	1238	491886	489
1962	70.1	20.4	8.6	0.9	100.0	1308820	1020615	1282	544387	533
1963	68.6	20.8	9.7	0.9	100.0	1409567	1035622	1361	598306	578
1964	67.5	20.7	10.9	0.9	100.0	1495613	1050257	1424	668958	637
1965	66.0	21.1	12.1	0.9	100.0	1578771	1064643	1483	736253	692

Table XI. TOTAL ENERGY CONSUMPTION: PERCENTAGE DISTRIBUTION BY FUEL; RELATED DATA ON POPULATION AND ELECTRICITY CONSUMPTION, SELECTED YEARS, 1925-1965

Region, country, year	Percentage distribution of total consumption (based on coal equivalents): Solid fuels	Liquid fuels	Natural gas	Hydro-electric power	Total	Total consumption (10^3 m.t. coal equiv.)	Population (10^3)	Consumption per capita (kgs)	Addendum: Electricity consumption: Total (10^6 kwh)	Per capita (kwh)
	(1)	(2)	(3)	(4)	(5)	(6)	(7)	(8)	(9)	(10)
WORLD EXCLUDING OECD AND COMMUNIST COUNTRIES										
1925	70.3	27.3	1.7	0.7	100.0	86921	770614	113	11807	15
1929	64.2	32.4	2.5	0.9	100.0	102772	815417	126	17239	21
1933	64.9	29.1	4.6	1.5	100.0	84709	865655	98	21631	25
1937	59.7	34.4	4.4	1.5	100.0	127518	924696	138	32926	36
1938	58.5	35.6	4.4	1.5	100.0	134831	940544	143	35933	38
1950	48.1	45.7	4.5	1.8	100.0	205354	1121914	183	72748	65
1953	44.9	47.6	5.5	2.0	100.0	241642	1192062	203	97910	82
1955	40.2	52.3	5.5	2.0	100.0	302871	1234216	245	127015	103
1957	37.5	53.9	6.5	2.1	100.0	356533	1291730	276	158412	123
1960	36.0	53.3	8.4	2.3	100.0	424197	1385728	306	209840	151
1961	35.1	53.7	8.8	2.4	100.0	449919	1423541	316	229016	161
1962	34.6	53.6	9.2	2.6	100.0	477819	1453656	329	250171	172
1963	34.9	53.1	9.5	2.6	100.0	499943	1489955	336	272975	183
1964	33.6	53.6	10.1	2.7	100.0	534097	1526190	350	301623	198
1965	33.2	54.1	10.0	2.8	100.0	575350	1563279	368	328358	210

DERIVATION OF TABLE XII

Column	*Derivation*
(1)	Col. (9) table X
(2)	Col. (4) table X converted into coal equivalents using appropriate conversion factors*
(3)	Col. (5) table X
(4)	Col. (3) plus col. (2) minus col. (1)
(5)	Col. (8) table XI
(6)	Col. (4) divided by col. (7) table XI times 1,000

Table XII. ALTERNATIVE MEASURES OF HYDROELECTRICITY AND TOTAL ENERGY CONSUMPTION, SELECTED YEARS, 1925-1965

(All figures in coal equivalents; A = hydro measured by heat content, B = hydro measured by hypothetical energy content of fuels consumed at thermal electric stations)

Region, country, year	Hydroelectric power consumption (10^3 m.t.)		Energy consumption: Total (10^3 m.t.)		Energy consumption: Per capita (kgs)	
	A	B	A	B	A	B
	(1)	(2)	(3)	(4)	(5)	(6)
WORLD						
1925	9849	78794	1484533	1553478	785	822
1929	14644	99578	1755981	1840915	886	929
1933	15871	97765	1392238	1474132	675	715
1937	22204	126117	1883433	1987346	878	926
1938	22764	127477	1790056	1894769	826	874
1950	43422	191058	2610900	2758535	1042	1101
1953	51692	202631	2993246	3144186	1138	1196
1955	59238	222734	3358188	3521685	1232	1292
1957	68992	248371	3735319	3914698	1321	1384
1960	85984	288906	4196095	4399017	1403	1471
1961	90166	295744	4379947	4585525	1436	1503
1962	95052	304166	4621009	4830124	1489	1556
1963	99597	310741	4909718	5120863	1552	1619
1964	102978	321292	5203738	5422052	1615	1683
1965	112638	342420	5474576	5704358	1668	1738
NORTH AMERICA						
1925	4435	35479	748857	779901	5971	6219
1929	6909	46979	862492	902562	6530	6833
1933	6778	41754	611894	646870	4478	4734

Table XII. ALTERNATIVE MEASURES OF HYDROELECTRICITY AND TOTAL ENERGY CONSUMPTION, SELECTED YEARS, 1925-1965

(All figures in coal equivalents; A = hydro measured by heat content, B = hydro measured by hypothetical energy content of fuels consumed at thermal electric stations)

Region, country, year	Hydroelectric power consumption (10^3 m.t.)		Energy consumption Total (10^3 m.t.)		Per capita (kgs)	
	A	B	A	B	A	B
	(1)	(2)	(3)	(4)	(5)	(6)
NORTH AMERICA (CONTINUED)						
1937	9177	52125	824333	867282	5874	6180
1938	9122	51085	706900	748862	4997	5294
1950	19130	84170	1276341	1341382	7686	8078
1953	22081	86557	1378272	1442748	7870	8239
1955	24067	90492	1461298	1527723	8042	8407
1957	27070	97452	1557168	1627550	8251	8624
1960	31854	107028	1659469	1734644	8354	8732
1961	32377	106197	1694843	1768663	8387	8752
1962	34446	110226	1772039	1847819	8631	9000
1963	34029	106170	1860472	1932614	8927	9273
1964	36687	114465	1951196	2028974	9227	9595
1965	39207	119188	2040158	2120139	9524	9897
CANADA						
1925	1085	8676	31139	38731	3258	4052
1929	2034	13831	42551	54348	4131	5276
1933	2002	12334	29799	40131	2729	3675
1937	3167	17987	40547	55368	3576	4883
1938	2983	16706	37443	51165	3271	4469
1950	6293	27690	75292	96688	5481	7039
1953	8092	31721	83845	107474	5632	7220
1955	8991	33807	90842	115658	5773	7350
1957	9889	35601	99633	125344	5974	7516
1960	12594	42316	109277	138999	6102	7761
1961	12642	41465	112673	141496	6167	7745
1962	12845	41103	116850	145108	6282	7802
1963	12886	40204	131953	159271	6972	8416
1964	14013	43720	147212	176920	7639	9181
1965	14591	44356	158350	188115	8077	9596
UNITED STATES						
1925	3350	26803	717714	741167	6196	6399
1929	4875	33147	819935	848207	6733	6966
1933	4776	29420	582085	606729	4631	4827
1937	6010	34138	783767	811895	6077	6295
1938	6139	34379	669439	697679	5150	5368
1950	12837	56481	1201030	1244674	7886	8173
1953	13989	54835	1294406	1335253	8080	8335
1955	15076	56685	1370342	1411951	8258	8508
1957	17181	61851	1457444	1502114	8473	8733
1960	19259	64712	1550090	1595542	8578	8830
1961	19736	64732	1582109	1627106	8609	8854
1962	21601	69123	1655060	1702582	8866	9120
1963	21143	65966	1728353	1773176	9123	9360
1964	22675	70744	1803817	1851887	9388	9638
1965	24616	74833	1881628	1931845	9671	9929

Table XII. ALTERNATIVE MEASURES OF HYDROELECTRICITY AND TOTAL ENERGY CONSUMPTION, SELECTED YEARS, 1925-1965

(All figures in coal equivalents; A = hydro measured by heat content, B = hydro measured by hypothetical energy content of fuels consumed at thermal electric stations)

Region, country, year	Hydroelectric power consumption (10^3 m.t.)		Energy consumption: Total (10^3 m.t.)		Energy consumption: Per capita (kgs)	
	A	B	A	B	A	B
	(1)	(2)	(3)	(4)	(5)	(6)
WESTERN EUROPE						
1925	3860	30880	517017	544037	1848	1945
1929	5316	36151	603632	634467	2101	2208
1933	5841	35978	486297	516434	1648	1751
1937	8022	45564	615624	653166	2037	2161
1938	8198	45907	619150	656859	2035	2159
1950	13915	61224	583907	631217	1931	2087
1953	17247	67608	667601	717962	2161	2325
1955	19954	75025	748189	803261	2387	2562
1957	21748	78294	813299	869844	2553	2731
1960	28868	96998	849524	917653	2602	2811
1961	29735	97531	877994	945790	2664	2870
1962	30461	97475	939914	1006928	2822	3023
1963	33063	103155	1003737	1073830	2982	3191
1964	32474	101320	1072916	1141761	3160	3362
1965	36743	111698	1117213	1192169	3256	3474
EUROPEAN ECONOMIC COMMUNITY (EEC)						
1925	1851	14809	292460	305418	1858	1940
1929	2647	18000	358776	374129	2220	2315
1933	3002	18492	273132	288621	1651	1744
1937	4320	24539	359290	379508	2127	2246
1938	4270	23914	366811	386455	2157	2273
1950	6183	27206	279287	300310	1773	1906
1953	7693	30155	335452	357914	2080	2220
1955	8978	33759	379720	404500	2316	2467
1957	9002	32405	429297	452701	2570	2710
1960	13277	44609	453263	484595	2639	2822
1961	12548	41157	473970	502580	2732	2897
1962	11712	37480	509096	534863	2901	3047
1963	13718	42800	557877	586959	3139	3303
1964	11823	36888	604215	629280	3363	3503
1965	14336	43582	631646	660892	3477	3638
BELGIUM-LUXEMBOURG						
1925	3	20	30953	30971	3847	3849
1929	3	17	37436	37451	4497	4499
1933	-	-	28238	28238	3309	3309
1937	8	46	34307	34345	3968	3973
1938	6	34	30849	30877	3556	3559
1950	16	68	30706	30758	3436	3442
1953	4	17	34697	34710	3820	3822
1955	28	104	36051	36127	3930	3938
1957	5	16	41734	41745	4489	4490
1960	27	89	37890	37953	4002	4009
1961	-4	-14	38802	38792	4084	4083
1962	-19	-61	41102	41060	4307	4303
1963	79	246	47251	47418	4915	4932
1964	163	507	49393	49737	5089	5124
1965	239	726	50460	50947	5152	5201

Table XII. ALTERNATIVE MEASURES OF HYDROELECTRICITY AND TOTAL ENERGY CONSUMPTION, SELECTED YEARS, 1925-1965

(All figures in coal equivalents; A = hydro measured by heat content, B = hydro measured by hypothetical energy content of fuels consumed at thermal electric stations)

Region, country, year	Hydroelectric power consumption (10^3 m.t.)		Energy consumption: Total (10^3 m.t.)		Energy consumption: Per capita (kgs)	
	A	B	A	B	A	B
	(1)	(2)	(3)	(4)	(5)	(6)
FRANCE						
1925	573	4580	75518	79526	1873	1972
1929	886	6023	89534	94671	2193	2319
1933	989	6091	78179	83281	1890	2013
1937	1444	8201	83121	89879	2016	2180
1938	1371	7679	78144	84451	1900	2054
1950	2059	9060	81213	88214	1946	2114
1953	2655	10408	90040	97793	2110	2292
1955	3216	12090	98134	107009	2259	2463
1957	3169	11407	117098	125336	2641	2827
1960	5081	17072	121241	133232	2653	2915
1961	4836	15863	123234	134261	2668	2907
1962	4423	14154	128352	138083	2730	2937
1963	5549	17312	142230	153993	2971	3216
1964	4661	14543	154189	164071	3183	3388
1965	5983	18189	161941	174147	3309	3558
GERMANY						
1925	385	3081	161689	164385	2560	2602
1929	473	3216	199107	201850	3076	3118
1933	568	3496	138586	141514	2099	2143
1937	963	5470	206734	211241	3048	3114
1938	1012	5669	223368	228025	3258	3326
GERMANY, FEDERAL REPUBLIC						
1950	1241	5460	128270	132490	2566	2651
1953	1331	5218	158894	162781	3092	3168
1955	1648	6196	181683	186231	3470	3557
1957	1574	5665	194315	198407	3622	3698
1960	2144	7204	204378	209438	3688	3779
1961	2155	7070	212926	217840	3787	3874
1962	1951	6244	228813	233106	4018	4093
1963	1855	5789	243973	247907	4235	4303
1964	1640	5117	264372	267849	4535	4595
1965	2451	7450	273084	278083	4625	4710
ITALY						
1925	891	7128	12944	19181	336	498
1929	1283	8725	18111	25554	453	640
1933	1443	8889	13890	21336	336	516
1937	1902	10804	19548	28450	458	667
1938	1878	10519	19174	27814	446	647
1950	2873	12640	18649	28415	399	607
1953	3704	14518	29123	39937	612	839
1955	4085	15359	37391	48665	776	1009
1957	4265	15354	47204	58293	968	1196
1960	6010	20194	58173	72356	1171	1457
1961	5555	18221	64153	76819	1285	1539
1962	5360	17151	74508	86299	1484	1719
1963	6229	19435	83518	96723	1649	1909

Table XII. ALTERNATIVE MEASURES OF HYDROELECTRICITY AND TOTAL ENERGY CONSUMPTION, SELECTED YEARS, 1925-1965

(All figures in coal equivalents; A = hydro measured by heat content, B = hydro measured by hypothetical energy content of fuels consumed at thermal electric stations)

Region, country, year	Hydroelectric power consumption (10^3 m.t.)		Energy consumption: Total (10^3 m.t.)		Per capita (kgs)	
	A	B	A	B	A	B
	(1)	(2)	(3)	(4)	(5)	(6)
ITALY (CONTINUED)						
1964	5357	16714	91989	103346	1800	2022
1965	5659	17204	100079	111624	1940	2164
NETHERLANDS						
1925	-	-	11357	11357	1542	1542
1929	3	19	14587	14603	1875	1877
1933	3	16	14239	14252	1729	1730
1937	3	18	15579	15594	1812	1814
1938	2	13	15277	15287	1759	1760
1950	-5	-22	20450	20433	2022	2020
1953	-2	-6	22698	22693	2163	2163
1955	3	9	26460	26467	2461	2462
1957	-10	-36	28946	28920	2626	2624
1960	15	50	31581	31616	2751	2754
1961	5	18	34856	34868	2995	2996
1962	-3	-8	36320	36315	3079	3078
1963	6	18	40906	40918	3418	3419
1964	2	7	44271	44276	3651	3651
1965	4	13	46081	46090	3749	3750
EUROPEAN FREE TRADE ASSOCIATION (EFTA)						
1925	1749	13992	207138	219381	3049	3229
1929	2283	15523	223190	236430	3239	3431
1933	2285	14078	194877	206670	2777	2945
1937	3064	17404	239592	253932	3361	3562
1938	3240	18146	232202	247108	3244	3453
1950	6413	28215	269810	291613	3508	3791
1953	7716	30246	292840	315370	3768	4058
1955	8599	32332	324382	348115	4138	4440
1957	10107	36383	332239	358516	4194	4526
1960	11965	40204	336021	364259	4163	4513
1961	13263	43503	341031	371271	4189	4560
1962	14466	46290	362525	394349	4408	4795
1963	14485	45192	372407	403114	4496	4867
1964	15850	49450	388633	422234	4654	5056
1965	17313	52632	398912	434230	4741	5161
AUSTRIA						
1925	163	1300	7069	8206	1074	1247
1929	204	1386	8935	10117	1341	1518
1933	206	1270	5474	6537	812	969
1937	256	1456	5982	7182	886	1063
1938	254	1423	6528	7697	967	1140
1950	537	2364	9734	11561	1404	1667
1953	668	2617	10188	12137	1464	1744
1955	853	3208	13868	16223	1989	2326
1957	1010	3636	14458	17084	2066	2442
1960	1248	4192	15699	18644	2217	2633

Table XII. ALTERNATIVE MEASURES OF HYDROELECTRICITY AND TOTAL ENERGY CONSUMPTION, SELECTED YEARS, 1925-1965

(All figures in coal equivalents; A = hydro measured by heat content, B = hydro measured by hypothetical energy content of fuels consumed at thermal electric stations)

Region, country, year	Hydroelectric power consumption (10^3 m.t.)		Energy consumption: Total (10^3 m.t.)		Energy consumption: Per capita (kgs)	
	A	B	A	B	A	B
	(1)	(2)	(3)	(4)	(5)	(6)
AUSTRIA (CONTINUED)						
1961	1214	3983	15754	18523	2223	2614
1962	1254	4011	16954	19712	2378	2765
1963	1283	4002	18535	21254	2584	2964
1964	1309	4084	19404	22179	2689	3074
1965	1527	4641	18746	21860	2584	3013
DENMARK						
1925	3	20	4624	4642	1350	1355
1929	4	30	6266	6291	1781	1788
1933	2	11	5886	5895	1620	1623
1937	2	11	7268	7277	1939	1941
1938	3	17	6855	6868	1815	1818
1950	26	113	8828	8915	2067	2087
1953	41	160	9382	9501	2147	2175
1955	-10	-38	12220	12192	2753	2747
1957	51	185	10907	11040	2430	2460
1960	15	50	13327	13362	2909	2917
1961	113	372	14097	14356	3058	3114
1962	115	368	15844	16097	3409	3464
1963	57	178	17433	17554	3722	3748
1964	106	329	18729	18952	3968	4015
1965	220	669	19740	20190	4149	4243
NORWAY						
1925	773	6187	3617	9031	1317	3288
1929	940	6389	4458	9907	1595	3545
1933	915	5638	4361	9084	1526	3178
1937	1157	6572	5630	11045	1929	3784
1938	1240	6943	5244	10947	1786	3729
1950	2235	9835	6370	13970	1951	4279
1953	2455	9624	7334	14503	2181	4314
1955	2835	10660	8155	15980	2380	4663
1957	3228	11619	8499	16891	2434	4837
1960	3919	13168	10203	19452	2849	5432
1961	4216	13828	10564	20176	2926	5589
1962	4714	15085	11238	21609	3088	5938
1963	4839	15097	11980	22239	3267	6065
1964	5353	16702	13209	24557	3576	6648
1965	5898	17930	13482	25514	3621	6853
PORTUGAL						
1925	6	45	917	957	140	146
1929	9	62	1291	1344	188	196
1933	12	75	1404	1467	195	204
1937	17	99	1733	1815	229	239
1938	16	89	1659	1732	216	226
1950	55	240	2032	2217	238	259
1953	125	490	2390	2755	275	317
1955	216	811	2739	3335	312	380

Table XII. ALTERNATIVE MEASURES OF HYDROELECTRICITY AND TOTAL ENERGY CONSUMPTION, SELECTED YEARS, 1925-1965

(All figures in coal equivalents; A = hydro measured by heat content, B = hydro measured by hypothetical energy content of fuels consumed at thermal electric stations)

Region, country, year	Hydroelectric power consumption (10^3 m.t.)		Energy consumption			
			Total (10^3 m.t.)		Per capita (kgs)	
	A	B	A	B	A	B
	(1)	(2)	(3)	(4)	(5)	(6)
PORTUGAL (CONTINUED)						
1957	230	828	3328	3926	375	443
1960	388	1304	3378	4294	374	476
1961	428	1403	3772	4748	415	522
1962	439	1405	3914	4879	426	531
1963	493	1539	4275	5321	462	575
1964	526	1641	4459	5574	490	612
1965	552	1678	4913	6039	520	639
SWEDEN						
1925	420	3360	5320	8260	880	1366
1929	568	3861	7848	11141	1284	1823
1933	610	3758	8059	11207	1300	1807
1937	870	4939	11890	15959	1894	2543
1938	910	5098	10899	15087	1731	2396
1950	2145	9437	14444	21736	2059	3099
1953	2623	10282	16638	24297	2320	3388
1955	2721	10232	20475	27986	2819	3854
1957	3340	12025	22361	31045	3036	4216
1960	3790	12734	26646	35590	3562	4758
1961	4443	14571	27111	37239	3605	4952
1962	4788	15321	29310	39843	3876	5269
1963	4745	14803	30933	40991	4068	5391
1964	5361	16726	34387	45753	4489	5972
1965	5702	17335	35611	47244	4604	6109
SWITZERLAND						
1925	382	3059	3312	5989	831	1502
1929	538	3656	4399	7517	1085	1854
1933	499	3071	4255	6827	1031	1654
1937	668	3792	4753	7878	1132	1876
1938	694	3885	4647	7839	1102	1859
1950	1230	5413	5270	9453	1119	2008
1953	1568	6145	5595	10173	1144	2079
1955	1771	6660	7192	12080	1440	2418
1957	1903	6852	9081	14030	1766	2729
1960	2214	7438	10512	15736	1955	2926
1961	2368	7767	10813	16212	1961	2941
1962	2655	8495	12204	18044	2150	3178
1963	2612	8148	15174	20710	2625	3583
1964	2719	8482	14709	20472	2496	3475
1965	2829	8599	16093	21863	2699	3666
UNITED KINGDOM						
1925	3	21	182279	182298	4037	4038
1929	21	140	189993	190112	4152	4154
1933	41	255	165439	165652	3549	3554
1937	94	536	202335	202777	4270	4280
1938	124	692	196370	196938	4126	4138

Table XII. ALTERNATIVE MEASURES OF HYDROELECTRICITY AND TOTAL ENERGY CONSUMPTION, SELECTED YEARS, 1925-1965

(All figures in coal equivalents; A = hydro measured by heat content, B = hydro measured by hypothetical energy content of fuels consumed at thermal electric stations)

Region, country, year	Hydroelectric power consumption (10^3 m.t.)		Energy consumption			
			Total (10^3 m.t.)		Per capita (kgs)	
	A	B	A	B	A	B
	(1)	(2)	(3)	(4)	(5)	(6)
UNITED KINGDOM (CONTINUED)						
1950	185	813	223133	223761	4399	4412
1953	237	930	241313	242006	4735	4748
1955	213	799	259733	260319	5063	5074
1957	344	1238	263606	264500	5095	5113
1960	392	1316	256257	257181	4871	4888
1961	481	1578	258919	260016	4879	4899
1962	502	1605	273063	274166	5096	5116
1963	457	1424	274077	275045	5082	5100
1964	477	1487	283737	284747	5223	5242
1965	585	1780	290326	291520	5307	5329
WESTERN EUROPE - OTHER						
1925	260	2079	17419	19238	321	354
1929	387	2628	21667	23909	382	421
1933	553	3409	18288	21143	308	356
1937	638	3621	16743	19726	270	318
1938	687	3847	20137	23297	322	372
1950	1319	5803	34810	39294	512	578
1953	1839	7207	39310	44678	562	639
1955	2376	8934	44088	50646	620	712
1957	2640	9505	51763	58627	716	811
1960	3627	12185	60240	68798	814	929
1961	3924	12871	62992	71939	844	963
1962	4283	13705	68293	77716	907	1032
1963	4860	15164	73453	83757	967	1102
1964	4802	14981	80068	90247	1048	1181
1965	5094	15485	86656	97047	1121	1255
FINLAND						
1925	48	384	784	1120	237	339
1929	99	671	1472	2044	430	597
1933	156	958	1481	2283	420	648
1937	258	1467	2839	4047	783	1116
1938	307	1719	2476	3888	677	1063
1950	456	2008	3210	4761	801	1188
1953	622	2437	3772	5588	911	1350
1955	774	2909	5134	7269	1212	1716
1957	827	2977	6763	8913	1564	2061
1960	711	2389	7931	9609	1790	2169
1961	1025	3361	8524	10861	1908	2431
1962	1232	3941	9435	12144	2094	2696
1963	1089	3397	9972	12281	2195	2703
1964	1150	3587	11702	14139	2555	3087
1965	1257	3822	13028	15593	2825	3381
GREECE						
1925	1	8	831	838	139	141
1929	1	7	1114	1119	177	178
1933	2	9	964	971	145	147

Table XII. ALTERNATIVE MEASURES OF HYDROELECTRICITY AND TOTAL ENERGY CONSUMPTION, SELECTED YEARS, 1925-1965

(All figures in coal equivalents; A = hydro measured by heat content, B = hydro measured by hypothetical energy content of fuels consumed at thermal electric stations)

Region, country, year	Hydroelectric power consumption (10^3 m.t.)		Energy consumption			
			Total (10^3 m.t.)		Per capita (kgs)	
	A	B	A	B	A	B
	(1)	(2)	(3)	(4)	(5)	(6)
GREECE (CONTINUED)						
1937	2	9	1521	1528	216	217
1938	2	9	1548	1556	217	218
1950	1	6	1782	1787	236	236
1953	4	15	2177	2188	278	280
1955	42	156	2749	2864	345	359
1957	45	162	2945	3062	364	378
1960	60	201	4343	4485	522	539
1961	68	221	4494	4648	535	553
1962	77	245	4683	4851	554	574
1963	100	312	5632	5844	664	689
1964	92	286	5943	6137	698	721
1965	96	293	7728	7925	904	927
ICELAND						
1950	21	92	389	460	2717	3216
1953	25	97	461	534	3055	3533
1955	47	178	478	609	3025	3852
1957	52	187	517	652	3133	3950
1960	65	220	634	789	3604	4481
1961	72	236	598	762	3338	4255
1962	74	237	639	802	3509	4405
1963	79	245	687	854	3694	4590
1964	82	255	704	877	3723	4638
1965	80	244	770	933	4008	4860
IRELAND						
1925	1	10	4321	4330	1447	1450
1929	4	26	4647	4670	1582	1590
1933	14	87	4478	4551	1512	1536
1937	31	177	4967	5113	1685	1734
1938	37	207	4769	4939	1624	1682
1950	58	256	4601	4799	1550	1616
1953	67	261	4951	5145	1679	1745
1955	61	229	5467	5635	1872	1929
1957	88	316	5040	5268	1747	1826
1960	117	391	5682	5957	2005	2102
1961	92	302	5712	5922	2027	2102
1962	83	264	6102	6284	2161	2225
1963	82	256	6134	6308	2159	2220
1964	98	305	6819	7026	2393	2466
1965	117	357	6735	6975	2359	2443
SPAIN						
1925	171	1370	8639	9838	386	439
1929	248	1685	10501	11938	450	512
1933	331	2037	8503	10210	351	421
1937	288	1637	4000	5349	159	212
1938	280	1565	7402	8687	291	342

Table XII. ALTERNATIVE MEASURES OF HYDROELECTRICITY AND TOTAL ENERGY CONSUMPTION, SELECTED YEARS, 1925-1965

(All figures in coal equivalents; A = hydro measured by heat content, B = hydro measured by hypothetical energy content of fuels consumed at thermal electric stations)

Region, country, year	Hydroelectric power consumption (10^3 m.t.)		Energy consumption Total (10^3 m.t.)		Energy consumption Per capita (kgs)	
	A	B	A	B	A	B
	(1)	(2)	(3)	(4)	(5)	(6)
SPAIN (CONTINUED)						
1950	635	2793	16375	18533	585	662
1953	938	3675	19946	22683	695	790
1955	1131	4254	19576	22699	670	777
1957	1205	4338	23213	26346	782	887
1960	1934	6499	24998	29563	821	971
1961	1967	6451	26174	30659	852	998
1962	1978	6328	29248	33599	944	1085
1963	2540	7923	30681	36064	982	1155
1964	2386	7445	32174	37232	1022	1182
1965	2365	7188	34312	39135	1080	1232
YUGOSLAVIA						
1925	38	300	2793	3056	218	239
1929	34	234	3858	4057	284	299
1933	50	310	2767	3027	193	211
1937	56	320	3314	3577	218	236
1938	59	329	3848	4119	250	268
1950	147	646	8287	8786	507	538
1953	184	720	7818	8355	459	490
1955	320	1203	10459	11342	597	647
1957	422	1517	13036	14132	730	791
1960	737	2475	16417	18156	892	987
1961	698	2288	17246	18837	927	1012
1962	837	2678	17914	19756	951	1049
1963	967	3016	20037	22086	1051	1158
1964	990	3088	22376	24474	1161	1269
1965	1173	3564	23745	26136	1217	1340
OCEANIA						
1925	81	649	15581	16149	1721	1783
1929	136	924	15343	16131	1592	1674
1933	174	1069	13098	13994	1317	1408
1937	245	1389	18116	19261	1769	1881
1938	258	1446	18125	19312	1754	1869
1950	555	2441	29300	31187	2397	2552
1953	713	2793	31346	33426	2385	2543
1955	825	3103	37322	39600	2703	2867
1957	1071	3857	39312	42097	2719	2911
1960	1245	4183	45824	48762	2967	3157
1961	1328	4357	47659	50687	3013	3204
1962	1522	4870	48704	52052	3014	3221
1963	1742	5434	52349	56042	3177	3401
1964	1877	5857	56070	60050	3332	3569
1965	2167	6588	61205	65625	3563	3820
AUSTRALIA						
1925	43	343	12890	13190	2170	2221
1929	55	374	12415	12734	1942	1992
1933	67	410	10835	11179	1634	1686

Table XII. ALTERNATIVE MEASURES OF HYDROELECTRICITY AND TOTAL ENERGY CONSUMPTION, SELECTED YEARS, 1925-1965

(All figures in coal equivalents; A = hydro measured by heat content, B = hydro measured by hypothetical energy content of fuels consumed at thermal electric stations)

Region, country, year	Hydroelectric power consumption (10^3 m.t.)		Energy consumption Total (10^3 m.t.)		Energy consumption Per capita (kgs)	
	A	B	A	B	A	B
	(1)	(2)	(3)	(4)	(5)	(6)
AUSTRALIA (CONTINUED)						
1937	90	508	15060	15478	2203	2264
1938	85	475	14884	15275	2157	2214
1950	186	820	25318	25951	3095	3173
1953	211	829	27103	27720	3075	3145
1955	249	934	32351	33037	3516	3591
1957	387	1392	33673	34678	3493	3597
1960	506	1701	39679	40874	3862	3978
1961	534	1751	41312	42530	3932	4047
1962	621	1988	42544	43911	3974	4102
1963	832	2594	45635	47398	4181	4342
1964	862	2690	48534	50362	4358	4522
1965	1046	3179	53358	55492	4697	4885
NEW ZEALAND						
1925	38	306	2555	2823	1849	2043
1929	81	550	2777	3246	1888	2207
1933	107	658	2135	2687	1387	1745
1937	155	880	2847	3573	1794	2251
1938	173	970	3023	3820	1885	2382
1950	358	1575	3811	5028	1997	2635
1953	493	1932	3928	5367	1919	2622
1955	566	2129	4493	6056	2103	2835
1957	673	2422	5007	6756	2246	3031
1960	689	2315	5460	7086	2302	2987
1961	743	2438	5637	7332	2329	3030
1962	847	2712	5570	7435	2242	2992
1963	857	2672	5984	7800	2358	3073
1964	969	3024	6578	8633	2536	3328
1965	1074	3263	6873	9063	2603	3433
USSR AND COMMUNIST EASTERN EUROPE						
1925	74	588	80457	80972	359	361
1929	125	847	129710	130432	535	538
1933	206	1267	148175	149237	574	578
1937	636	3610	232338	235313	865	876
1938	754	4220	244039	247505	899	912
1950	1852	8149	464115	470412	1720	1744
1953	2732	10710	576721	584699	2046	2075
1955	3437	12924	691190	700677	2379	2412
1957	5483	19737	799579	813834	2673	2721
1960	7168	24084	934513	951429	2987	3041
1961	8173	26807	979331	997965	3089	3147
1962	9919	31741	1042065	1063887	3244	3312
1963	10338	32255	1122642	1144559	3451	3518
1964	10450	32603	1187576	1209729	3610	3677
1965	11359	34532	1255760	1278932	3777	3847

Table XII. ALTERNATIVE MEASURES OF HYDROELECTRICITY AND TOTAL ENERGY CONSUMPTION, SELECTED YEARS, 1925-1965

(All figures in coal equivalents; A = hydro measured by heat content, B = hydro measured by hypothetical energy content of fuels consumed at thermal electric stations)

Region, country, year	Hydroelectric power consumption (10^3 m.t.)		Energy consumption: Total (10^3 m.t.)		Energy consumption: Per capita (kgs)	
	A	B	A	B	A	B
	(1)	(2)	(3)	(4)	(5)	(6)
COMMUNIST EASTERN EUROPE						
1925	42	337	55138	55432	783	787
1929	55	373	76744	77062	1035	1039
1933	60	372	49534	49846	638	642
1937	112	635	66040	66563	820	826
1938	117	657	67690	68229	832	839
1950	266	1169	160796	161700	1792	1802
1953	332	1302	207134	208103	2243	2254
1955	540	2032	230214	231705	2440	2456
1957	554	1994	259065	260505	2699	2715
1960	807	2713	293895	295801	2985	3004
1961	792	2598	311993	313799	3149	3168
1962	955	3056	331733	333834	3326	3347
1963	949	2962	353068	355081	3512	3532
1964	943	2941	371008	373007	3662	3681
1965	1368	4158	375131	377922	3683	3710
ALBANIA						
1950	-	-	168	168	139	139
1953	3	10	223	231	172	177
1955	3	13	238	248	173	180
1957	8	27	553	573	378	392
1960	15	51	784	820	488	510
1961	14	44	905	935	545	563
1962	15	47	982	1014	574	593
1963	21	66	825	869	468	493
1964	25	79	933	987	514	544
1965	31	95	880	944	472	506
BULGARIA						
1925	2	17	489	504	92	95
1929	6	42	681	717	120	127
1933	10	59	642	691	108	116
1937	17	95	788	866	127	140
1938	18	99	866	947	139	151
1950	38	168	2287	2417	315	333
1953	57	222	3251	3417	443	465
1955	81	305	3956	4180	528	557
1957	106	383	4458	4735	583	619
1960	236	792	7174	7730	912	983
1961	225	736	8523	9035	1073	1137
1962	220	705	10327	10811	1289	1349
1963	271	846	11829	12403	1464	1535
1964	181	564	15018	15402	1844	1891
1965	250	759	16501	17010	2011	2073
CZECHOSLOVAKIA						
1925	24	194	22263	22433	1645	1657
1929	30	201	28735	28906	2070	2082
1933	32	194	18826	18989	1324	1336

Table XII. ALTERNATIVE MEASURES OF HYDROELECTRICITY AND TOTAL ENERGY CONSUMPTION, SELECTED YEARS, 1925-1965

(All figures in coal equivalents; A = hydro measured by heat content, B = hydro measured by hypothetical energy content of fuels consumed at thermal electric stations)

Region, country, year	Hydroelectric power consumption (10^3 m.t.)		Energy consumption: Total (10^3 m.t.)		Energy consumption: Per capita (kgs)	
	A	B	A	B	A	B
	(1)	(2)	(3)	(4)	(5)	(6)
CZECHOSLOVAKIA (CONTINUED)						
1937	72	406	25232	25566	1749	1772
1938	75	420	24070	24415	1648	1672
1950	150	660	36948	37458	2982	3023
1953	132	515	42821	43205	3340	3370
1955	225	846	49046	49667	3746	3793
1957	236	851	56303	56918	4215	4261
1960	278	935	65931	66587	4829	4877
1961	274	897	71564	72188	5193	5239
1962	384	1229	76547	77392	5523	5584
1963	304	948	80629	81273	5779	5825
1964	429	1337	84057	84966	5979	6044
1965	652	1983	83120	84450	5870	5964
GERMANY, EAST						
1950	-16	-72	49693	49637	2702	2699
1953	30	118	62577	62664	3442	3447
1955	61	230	69765	69934	3888	3897
1957	19	69	73564	73614	4199	4202
1960	31	104	80659	80732	4678	4683
1961	38	125	84907	84993	4958	4963
1962	66	211	89023	89168	5205	5214
1963	68	213	92053	92198	5366	5374
1964	85	266	95574	95755	5590	5601
1965	110	333	94234	94458	5534	5547
HUNGARY						
1925	1	5	4942	4946	595	596
1929	1	8	6914	6921	806	806
1933	2	9	4774	4782	540	540
1937	2	11	6590	6599	724	725
1938	3	14	6759	6771	737	739
1950	9	39	10490	10520	1123	1127
1953	22	85	16965	17028	1768	1775
1955	37	139	19277	19379	1962	1972
1957	44	158	20098	20212	2042	2054
1960	79	266	23876	24063	2391	2410
1961	73	238	25784	25949	2571	2588
1962	81	258	26430	26607	2627	2645
1963	126	394	29980	30248	2972	2998
1964	144	450	32385	32691	3200	3230
1965	171	521	32352	32701	3188	3222
POLAND						
1925	9	70	22625	22686	773	775
1929	11	71	33939	34000	1092	1094
1933	4	24	19545	19565	596	596
1937	6	34	26438	26466	769	770
1938	6	35	27934	27963	805	806

Table XII. ALTERNATIVE MEASURES OF HYDROELECTRICITY AND TOTAL ENERGY CONSUMPTION, SELECTED YEARS, 1925-1965

(All figures in coal equivalents; A = hydro measured by heat content, B = hydro measured by hypothetical energy content of fuels consumed at thermal electric stations)

Region, country, year	Hydroelectric power consumption (10^3 m.t.)		Energy consumption: Total (10^3 m.t.)		Energy consumption: Per capita (kgs)	
	A	B	A	B	A	B
	(1)	(2)	(3)	(4)	(5)	(6)
POLAND (CONTINUED)						
1950	60	264	51954	52158	2093	2101
1953	62	244	65830	66012	2507	2514
1955	96	361	70815	71081	2596	2606
1957	104	376	83548	83819	2951	2961
1960	122	411	92094	92383	3100	3110
1961	117	382	95898	96164	3200	3209
1962	112	359	99729	99976	3289	3297
1963	92	287	106180	106376	3460	3466
1964	4	14	110376	110385	3542	3542
1965	70	211	111592	111734	3552	3556
ROMANIA						
1925	6	51	4910	4955	372	375
1929	8	52	6363	6407	456	459
1933	14	85	5632	5703	382	387
1937	16	89	6927	7000	449	454
1938	16	89	8030	8103	515	519
1950	25	110	9256	9341	567	573
1953	28	108	15467	15547	918	923
1955	37	138	17115	17216	988	994
1957	36	131	20540	20635	1152	1157
1960	46	154	23377	23485	1270	1276
1961	53	175	24414	24535	1315	1321
1962	77	248	28695	28865	1536	1545
1963	67	208	31572	31714	1678	1686
1964	74	230	32664	32820	1726	1734
1965	84	256	36452	36624	1916	1925
USSR (INCLUDING ESTONIA, LATVIA, LITHUANIA)						
1925	31	251	25320	25539	165	166
1929	70	473	52966	53370	314	317
1933	145	896	98640	99391	546	550
1937	524	2976	166298	168750	885	898
1938	636	3564	176349	179276	928	944
1950	1586	6980	303319	308712	1685	1715
1953	2400	9408	369587	376596	1950	1987
1955	2897	10892	460976	468971	2350	2391
1957	4929	17743	540514	553328	2661	2724
1960	6360	21371	640618	655629	2988	3058
1961	7381	24210	667338	684166	3061	3138
1962	8964	28685	710332	730053	3207	3296
1963	9389	29294	769574	789479	3424	3512
1964	9507	29662	816567	836722	3586	3675
1965	9991	30373	880629	901011	3819	3907
COMMUNIST ASIA						
1925	-	-	23701	23701	54	54
1929	-	-	23770	23770	53	53
1933	-	-	24935	24935	55	55

Table XII. ALTERNATIVE MEASURES OF HYDROELECTRICITY AND TOTAL ENERGY CONSUMPTION, SELECTED YEARS, 1925-1965

(All figures in coal equivalents; A = hydro measured by heat content, B = hydro measured by hypothetical energy content of fuels consumed at thermal electric stations)

Region, country, year	Hydroelectric power consumption (10^3 m.t.)		Energy consumption: Total (10^3 m.t.)		Energy consumption: Per capita (kgs)	
	A	B	A	B	A	B
	(1)	(2)	(3)	(4)	(5)	(6)
COMMUNIST ASIA (CONTINUED)						
1937	-	-	31002	31002	69	69
1938	-	-	27330	27330	61	61
1950	660	2904	43130	45374	76	80
1953	320	1254	66651	67585	113	114
1955	775	2914	98290	100429	158	161
1957	1288	4636	131809	135158	204	210
1960	2413	8108	235321	241016	347	356
1961	2063	6765	265029	269732	385	392
1962	2125	6800	266755	271430	381	388
1963	2188	6825	286924	291562	404	410
1964	2375	7410	308037	313072	427	434
1965	2625	7980	323012	328367	441	448
LATIN AMERICA						
1925	394	3155	24688	27449	252	281
1929	494	3358	31341	34204	296	323
1933	576	3550	22822	25795	200	226
1937	740	4203	39169	42632	319	347
1938	789	4418	38701	42330	309	338
1950	1794	7894	66232	72331	409	447
1953	2328	9125	81899	88696	467	506
1955	2734	10278	105376	112921	569	610
1957	3465	12474	129377	138386	661	708
1960	4390	14749	153472	163831	723	771
1961	4563	14967	162536	172940	747	795
1962	4940	15808	173119	183987	774	823
1963	5245	16364	176733	187852	769	818
1964	5680	17720	190282	202323	805	856
1965	6429	19543	199514	212628	821	875
LATIN AMERICA - CARIBBEAN						
1925	134	1070	11355	12291	280	303
1929	174	1186	13982	14993	321	344
1933	206	1270	8325	9389	177	199
1937	297	1686	19198	20588	380	407
1938	311	1742	18033	19464	350	378
1950	487	2144	33161	34818	491	515
1953	640	2510	42676	44546	580	605
1955	807	3035	55840	58068	716	745
1957	931	3350	72668	75087	879	909
1960	1232	4140	87549	90457	971	1003
1961	1227	4026	91371	94170	984	1014
1962	1376	4402	97185	100211	1016	1048
1963	1592	4967	100380	103755	1018	1052
1964	1750	5459	108125	111835	1064	1100
1965	2011	6114	114014	118117	1090	1129

Table XII. ALTERNATIVE MEASURES OF HYDROELECTRICITY AND TOTAL ENERGY CONSUMPTION, SELECTED YEARS, 1925-1965

(All figures in coal equivalents; A = hydro measured by heat content, B = hydro measured by hypothetical energy content of fuels consumed at thermal electric stations)

Region, country, year	Hydroelectric power consumption (10^3 m.t.)		Energy consumption: Total (10^3 m.t.)		Energy consumption: Per capita (kgs)	
	A	B	A	B	A	B
	(1)	(2)	(3)	(4)	(5)	(6)
CARIBBEAN - OIL PRODUCING						
1925	118	941	8092	8916	321	354
1929	154	1046	10805	11698	399	432
1933	178	1099	6696	7617	230	262
1937	257	1460	16498	17701	528	567
1938	268	1503	15698	16932	493	532
1950	377	1659	27159	28440	633	662
1953	523	2048	35935	37461	762	795
1955	668	2513	47064	48909	937	974
1957	788	2836	60659	62707	1133	1172
1960	1038	3489	73690	76140	1253	1295
1961	1029	3373	77039	79384	1270	1308
1962	1178	3768	80322	82913	1283	1324
1963	1367	4266	83443	86342	1291	1336
1964	1521	4745	88605	91829	1328	1377
1965	1742	5296	93703	97257	1366	1418
COLOMBIA						
1925	12	92	344	425	51	63
1929	13	85	750	822	103	113
1933	14	83	369	439	47	56
1937	23	129	872	978	102	115
1938	26	144	976	1095	112	126
1950	91	399	2122	2430	187	214
1953	126	494	3333	3701	269	299
1955	185	696	5224	5735	397	435
1957	252	906	5576	6230	397	444
1960	323	1087	7435	8198	482	532
1961	314	1030	8075	8791	508	553
1962	345	1105	8767	9527	534	580
1963	402	1255	9724	10577	574	624
1964	465	1451	9911	10897	567	623
1965	488	1482	10365	11360	583	639
MEXICO						
1925	104	828	7031	7756	462	510
1929	138	940	6690	7492	411	460
1933	161	993	4592	5424	263	310
1937	230	1307	8822	9899	471	528
1938	236	1322	8823	9909	463	520
1950	260	1143	16491	17375	639	673
1953	355	1391	19526	20563	691	728
1955	452	1700	23243	24491	774	816
1957	516	1859	27423	28766	860	902
1960	703	2362	36090	37749	1031	1079
1961	696	2282	36897	38483	1022	1066
1962	751	2403	37445	39098	1006	1050
1963	827	2580	39950	41703	1040	1086
1964	903	2817	44570	46484	1124	1173
1965	1084	3294	45162	47372	1104	1158

Table XII. ALTERNATIVE MEASURES OF HYDROELECTRICITY AND TOTAL ENERGY CONSUMPTION, SELECTED YEARS, 1925-1965

(All figures in coal equivalents; A = hydro measured by heat content, B = hydro measured by hypothetical energy content of fuels consumed at thermal electric stations)

Region, country, year	Hydroelectric power consumption (10^3 m.t.)		Energy consumption: Total (10^3 m.t.)		Energy consumption: Per capita (kgs)	
	A	B	A	B	A	B
	(1)	(2)	(3)	(4)	(5)	(6)
TRINIDAD AND TOBAGO						
1925	-	-	228	228	596	596
1929	-	-	255	255	642	642
1933	-	-	391	391	926	926
1937	-	-	790	790	1756	1756
1938	-	-	886	886	1934	1934
1950	-	-	1586	1586	2509	2509
1953	-	-	1245	1245	1836	1836
1955	-	-	1521	1521	2110	2110
1957	-	-	1623	1623	2121	2121
1960	-	-	1773	1773	2109	2109
1961	-	-	2185	2185	2520	2520
1962	-	-	2352	2352	2631	2631
1963	-	-	1782	1782	1932	1932
1964	-	-	2481	2481	2614	2614
1965	-	-	3418	3418	3505	3505
VENEZUELA						
1950	27	117	5597	5687	1125	1143
1953	42	163	8984	9106	1586	1607
1955	31	118	11151	11237	1813	1827
1957	20	72	19612	19664	2955	2963
1960	12	40	21654	21682	2940	2944
1961	19	62	22719	22762	2985	2990
1962	81	260	24227	24406	3078	3100
1963	138	431	24398	24691	2996	3032
1964	153	477	24456	24780	2902	2941
1965	171	520	28308	28657	3246	3286
CARIBBEAN - OTHER						
1925	16	129	3263	3376	212	219
1929	21	139	3177	3295	192	200
1933	28	171	1629	1772	90	98
1937	40	226	2700	2887	140	149
1938	43	239	2335	2531	119	129
1950	110	486	6002	6378	243	258
1953	118	462	6741	7085	255	268
1955	139	522	8776	9159	316	330
1957	143	514	12009	12380	412	425
1960	194	652	13859	14317	442	456
1961	199	652	14332	14785	446	460
1962	198	634	16862	17298	511	524
1963	225	701	16937	17413	499	513
1964	229	714	19520	20006	558	572
1965	269	817	20311	20860	564	579
CUBA						
1925	2	15	2555	2569	NA	NA
1929	2	13	2248	2259	623	626
1933	2	11	767	776	188	190

Table XII. ALTERNATIVE MEASURES OF HYDROELECTRICITY AND TOTAL ENERGY CONSUMPTION, SELECTED YEARS, 1925-1965

(All figures in coal equivalents; A = hydro measured by heat content, B = hydro measured by hypothetical energy content of fuels consumed at thermal electric stations)

Region, country, year	Hydroelectric power consumption (10^3 m.t.)		Energy consumption			
			Total (10^3 m.t.)		Per capita (kgs)	
	A	B	A	B	A	B
	(1)	(2)	(3)	(4)	(5)	(6)
CUBA (CONTINUED)						
1937	2	13	1526	1537	350	353
1938	2	13	1241	1252	280	283
1950	2	7	3725	3731	675	676
1953	2	8	4011	4017	681	682
1955	3	9	4180	4186	680	681
1957	3	9	5286	5292	824	825
1960	3	8	6051	6056	886	887
1961	3	9	6503	6509	937	938
1962	3	10	7293	7300	1032	1033
1963	6	20	6729	6742	930	932
1964	13	39	7258	7285	976	980
1965	14	42	7313	7341	958	962
PUERTO RICO						
1957	22	78	2759	2815	1221	1246
1960	30	102	3416	3488	1446	1477
1961	34	110	2878	2954	1194	1226
1962	26	83	3918	3975	1593	1616
1963	35	108	3995	4068	1585	1614
1964	19	59	4689	4729	1814	1830
1965	30	90	5599	5659	2126	2149
LATIN AMERICA - OTHER						
1925	261	2085	13333	15158	233	265
1929	319	2172	17359	19211	279	309
1933	370	2280	14497	16406	216	244
1937	443	2517	19970	22044	276	305
1938	478	2677	20668	22866	281	311
1950	1307	5749	33071	37513	351	398
1953	1687	6615	39223	44150	385	434
1955	1927	7244	49536	54853	462	512
1957	2534	9123	56709	63298	502	560
1960	3157	10608	65924	73375	539	600
1961	3336	10942	71165	78770	571	632
1962	3564	11406	75934	83775	593	655
1963	3653	11397	76353	84097	582	641
1964	3930	12262	82157	90489	610	672
1965	4418	13430	85500	94512	618	683
ARGENTINA						
1925	8	64	5459	5515	527	532
1929	14	92	7962	8040	687	694
1933	11	66	7163	7218	567	572
1937	12	69	9623	9680	713	718
1938	11	59	10078	10126	734	738
1950	24	105	14570	14651	854	858
1953	45	175	17288	17419	950	957
1955	38	141	19356	19459	1025	1030

Table XII. ALTERNATIVE MEASURES OF HYDROELECTRICITY AND TOTAL ENERGY CONSUMPTION, SELECTED YEARS, 1925-1965

(All figures in coal equivalents; A = hydro measured by heat content, B = hydro measured by hypothetical energy content of fuels consumed at thermal electric stations)

Region, country, year	Hydroelectric power consumption (10^3 m.t.)		Energy consumption: Total (10^3 m.t.)		Energy consumption: Per capita (kgs)	
	A	B	A	B	A	B
	(1)	(2)	(3)	(4)	(5)	(6)
ARGENTINA (CONTINUED)						
1957	73	261	23654	23843	1206	1216
1960	116	389	24673	24947	1194	1207
1961	136	445	27587	27897	1313	1328
1962	146	467	28356	28677	1328	1343
1963	148	463	26992	27306	1245	1259
1964	155	482	30467	30795	1383	1398
1965	155	470	32882	33197	1471	1485
BOLIVIA						
1925	1	9	50	58	22	26
1929	3	17	86	101	36	42
1933	3	20	62	79	25	32
1937	4	23	119	138	46	53
1938	6	32	133	159	51	60
1950	24	105	243	324	81	107
1953	31	123	311	402	99	128
1955	36	136	508	608	157	188
1957	44	158	536	650	162	196
1960	49	163	592	707	171	205
1961	49	160	541	652	155	186
1962	47	151	610	713	172	201
1963	51	160	639	747	178	208
1964	53	164	725	837	199	229
1965	54	163	798	908	216	245
BRAZIL						
1925	183	1460	3228	4506	106	149
1929	221	1505	4027	5310	122	161
1933	261	1605	3237	4582	91	128
1937	300	1704	4261	5665	110	146
1938	325	1820	4375	5870	111	149
1950	900	3959	9812	12871	189	248
1953	1153	4519	11474	14840	202	262
1955	1326	4984	17624	21283	293	354
1957	1860	6694	19202	24037	301	377
1960	2298	7721	25589	31012	367	445
1961	2368	7768	26846	32246	374	449
1962	2583	8265	28740	34422	388	465
1963	2591	8084	29971	35464	392	464
1964	2762	8618	31060	36916	394	468
1965	3189	9696	31079	37585	382	462
CHILE						
1925	47	378	2646	2977	650	731
1929	60	411	2786	3137	647	729
1933	69	422	1770	2124	388	465
1937	95	537	3061	3504	632	724
1938	94	525	3045	3477	620	708

Table XII. ALTERNATIVE MEASURES OF HYDROELECTRICITY AND TOTAL ENERGY CONSUMPTION, SELECTED YEARS, 1925-1965

(All figures in coal equivalents; A = hydro measured by heat content, B = hydro measured by hypothetical energy content of fuels consumed at thermal electric stations)

Region, country, year	Hydroelectric power consumption (10^3 m.t.)		Energy consumption: Total (10^3 m.t.)		Energy consumption: Per capita (kgs)	
	A	B	A	B	A	B
	(1)	(2)	(3)	(4)	(5)	(6)
CHILE (CONTINUED)						
1950	206	908	4112	4813	677	793
1953	254	997	4450	5193	691	807
1955	291	1094	5469	6272	805	924
1957	313	1127	5832	6647	817	931
1960	372	1250	6641	7519	864	978
1961	393	1288	7541	8437	960	1074
1962	414	1325	8945	9855	1114	1227
1963	426	1328	9131	10034	1111	1221
1964	465	1452	9250	10237	1089	1205
1965	494	1503	9587	10595	1119	1237
ECUADOR						
1925	3	24	50	71	29	41
1929	3	20	95	112	50	59
1933	3	18	153	168	73	80
1937	3	17	123	137	53	60
1938	3	18	214	229	91	97
1950	11	47	523	559	163	175
1953	12	45	564	597	161	171
1955	15	56	762	804	205	217
1957	18	64	795	842	202	213
1960	22	74	1123	1175	260	272
1961	25	82	1110	1167	249	262
1962	28	89	1023	1084	223	236
1963	30	93	1118	1181	236	249
1964	31	97	1291	1357	268	281
1965	31	95	1347	1410	265	277
PARAGUAY						
1950	-	-	33	33	24	24
1953	-	-	71	71	47	47
1955	-	-	95	95	60	60
1957	-	-	102	102	62	62
1960	-	-	155	155	88	88
1961	-	-	177	177	98	98
1962	-	-	185	185	100	100
1963	-	-	201	201	105	105
1964	-	-	209	209	106	106
1965	-	-	266	266	131	131
PERU						
1925	19	150	1165	1297	209	232
1929	19	128	1521	1630	257	276
1933	24	148	1363	1487	217	237
1937	29	167	1819	1957	272	292
1938	40	224	1910	2094	281	308
1950	76	336	2966	3226	348	379
1953	118	461	3688	4032	408	446
1955	136	513	3956	4333	421	461

Table XII. ALTERNATIVE MEASURES OF HYDROELECTRICITY AND TOTAL ENERGY CONSUMPTION, SELECTED YEARS, 1925-1965

(All figures in coal equivalents; A = hydro measured by heat content, B = hydro measured by hypothetical energy content of fuels consumed at thermal electric stations)

Region, country, year	Hydroelectric power consumption (10^3 m.t.)		Energy consumption			
			Total (10^3 m.t.)		Per capita (kgs)	
	A	B	A	B	A	B
	(1)	(2)	(3)	(4)	(5)	(6)
PERU (CONTINUED)						
1957	159	572	4562	4975	460	501
1960	216	727	5161	5671	475	522
1961	235	770	5401	5937	523	575
1962	243	778	6089	6624	573	623
1963	270	842	6261	6833	571	624
1964	306	955	6911	7560	612	669
1965	328	998	6721	7390	577	634
URUGUAY						
1925	-	-	686	686	413	413
1929	-	-	845	845	462	462
1933	-	-	712	712	359	359
1937	-	-	901	901	433	433
1938	-	-	832	832	395	395
1950	66	290	445	669	185	278
1953	75	294	1729	1948	684	771
1955	85	319	1955	2189	747	837
1957	69	248	2167	2346	795	860
1960	85	284	2128	2327	751	822
1961	131	429	2064	2362	718	822
1962	104	332	2128	2356	730	808
1963	137	428	2211	2502	835	944
1964	158	494	2371	2707	884	1009
1965	166	505	2602	2941	958	1083
ASIA						
1925	997	7978	60292	67273	105	117
1929	1654	11249	72545	82139	120	136
1933	2269	13975	69884	81591	109	127
1937	3327	18897	100281	115851	147	170
1938	3582	20059	112409	128887	162	186
1950	5347	23525	105844	124022	131	154
1953	6016	23583	141343	158910	166	187
1955	7039	26468	157729	177157	181	203
1957	8357	30086	201657	223385	222	245
1960	9209	30941	247730	269462	255	278
1961	10759	35290	279686	304217	282	306
1962	10321	33026	303168	325873	298	321
1963	11609	36220	329480	354091	317	340
1964	11921	37194	351780	377053	330	354
1965	12459	37875	385094	410510	354	377
MIDDLE EAST						
1925	2	19	2307	2324	61	61
1929	2	16	1778	1792	44	44
1933	2	15	1533	1546	35	36
1937	4	24	4336	4356	93	93
1938	4	25	8408	8428	176	177

Table XII. ALTERNATIVE MEASURES OF HYDROELECTRICITY AND TOTAL ENERGY CONSUMPTION, SELECTED YEARS, 1925-1965

(All figures in coal equivalents; A = hydro measured by heat content, B = hydro measured by hypothetical energy content of fuels consumed at thermal electric stations)

Region, country, year	Hydroelectric power consumption (10^3 m.t.)		Energy consumption			
			Total (10^3 m.t.)		Per capita (kgs)	
	A	B	A	B	A	B
	(1)	(2)	(3)	(4)	(5)	(6)
MIDDLE EAST (CONTINUED)						
1950	12	52	13263	13303	219	220
1953	21	82	16392	16453	251	252
1955	26	98	22314	22386	323	324
1957	62	224	29994	30156	412	415
1960	143	479	38832	39169	497	501
1961	185	606	41395	41817	516	521
1962	177	567	45127	45516	548	553
1963	312	972	47160	47821	554	562
1964	259	808	49944	50493	570	576
1965	340	1034	57062	57756	634	641
MIDDLE EAST - OIL PRODUCING						
1925	-	-	1400	1400	78	78
1929	-	-	676	676	35	35
1933	-	-	185	185	9	9
1937	-	-	2047	2047	93	93
1938	-	-	5877	5877	262	262
1950	-	-	7212	7212	257	257
1953	-	-	7893	7893	265	265
1955	-	-	12073	12073	388	388
1957	-	-	17589	17589	541	541
1960	-	-	25297	25297	734	734
1961	-	-	26976	26976	764	764
1962	-	-	28148	28148	776	776
1963	-	-	28875	28875	767	767
1964	-	-	29336	29336	757	757
1965	-	-	33857	33857	850	850
IRAN						
1950	-	-	2497	2497	153	153
1953	-	-	2112	2112	121	121
1955	-	-	4695	4695	256	256
1957	-	-	8711	8711	453	453
1960	-	-	11985	11985	594	594
1961	-	-	12689	12689	614	614
1962	-	-	12023	12023	566	566
1963	-	-	13214	13214	596	596
1964	-	-	15890	15890	695	695
1965	-	-	19390	19390	828	828
IRAQ						
1950	-	-	1172	1172	226	226
1953	-	-	1574	1574	280	280
1955	-	-	2721	2721	458	458
1957	NA	NA	2812	2812	443	443
1960	NA	NA	3848	3848	554	554
1961	-	-	4177	4177	582	582
1962	NA	NA	4252	4252	574	574
1963	NA	NA	4441	4441	580	580

Table XII. ALTERNATIVE MEASURES OF HYDROELECTRICITY AND TOTAL ENERGY CONSUMPTION, SELECTED YEARS, 1925-1965

(All figures in coal equivalents; A = hydro measured by heat content, B = hydro measured by hypothetical energy content of fuels consumed at thermal electric stations)

Region, country, year	Hydroelectric power consumption (10^3 m.t.)		Energy consumption: Total (10^3 m.t.)		Energy consumption: Per capita (kgs)	
	A	B	A	B	A	B
	(1)	(2)	(3)	(4)	(5)	(6)
IRAQ (CONTINUED)						
1964	NA	NA	4596	4596	581	581
1965	NA	NA	5208	5208	630	630
MIDDLE EAST - OTHER						
1925	2	19	907	924	46	46
1929	2	16	1102	1116	52	52
1933	2	15	1349	1361	59	60
1937	4	24	2289	2309	92	93
1938	4	25	2531	2551	100	101
1950	12	52	6051	6091	186	187
1953	21	82	8499	8561	239	241
1955	26	98	10242	10314	270	272
1957	62	224	12404	12566	309	313
1960	143	479	13535	13871	310	318
1961	185	606	14419	14841	321	331
1962	177	567	16979	17369	368	377
1963	312	972	18285	18946	385	399
1964	259	808	20608	21158	421	432
1965	340	1034	23206	23900	462	476
PALESTINE						
1925	-	-	64	64	76	76
1929	-	-	108	108	113	113
1933	-	-	174	174	157	157
1937	-	-	371	371	268	268
1938	-	-	292	292	206	206
ISRAEL						
1950	-	-	1042	1042	828	828
1953	-	-	1549	1549	938	938
1955	-	-	2296	2296	1313	1313
1957	-	-	2259	2259	1166	1166
1960	-	-	2827	2827	1337	1337
1961	-	-	3093	3093	1416	1416
1962	-	-	3491	3491	1523	1523
1963	-	-	3618	3618	1523	1523
1964	-	-	4074	4074	1645	1645
1965	-	-	5763	5763	2248	2248
JORDAN						
1950	-	-	86	86	67	67
1953	-	-	107	107	78	78
1955	-	-	189	189	132	132
1957	-	-	219	219	143	143
1960	-	-	332	332	196	196
1961	-	-	446	446	261	261
1962	-	-	494	494	286	286

Table XII. ALTERNATIVE MEASURES OF HYDROELECTRICITY AND TOTAL ENERGY CONSUMPTION, SELECTED YEARS, 1925-1965

(All figures in coal equivalents; A = hydro measured by heat content, B = hydro measured by hypothetical energy content of fuels consumed at thermal electric stations)

Region, country, year	Hydroelectric power consumption (10^3 m.t.)		Energy consumption			
			Total (10^3 m.t.)		Per capita (kgs)	
	A	B	A	B	A	B
	(1)	(2)	(3)	(4)	(5)	(6)
JORDAN (CONTINUED)						
1963	-	-	575	575	314	314
1964	-	-	581	581	306	306
1965	-	-	674	674	341	341
LEBANON						
1950	8	35	924	951	667	686
1953	13	49	724	760	497	523
1955	14	52	658	696	337	356
1957	21	75	946	1000	463	490
1960	14	46	1164	1196	525	540
1961	22	71	1219	1268	532	553
1962	31	100	1351	1420	581	611
1963	44	137	1476	1569	620	659
1964	47	146	1683	1782	668	707
1965	63	192	1971	2099	770	820
SYRIA						
1950	-	-	332	332	103	103
1953	-	-	590	590	166	166
1955	1	5	754	758	195	196
1957	3	9	912	918	220	221
1960	4	13	1493	1502	327	329
1961	5	16	1421	1432	306	308
1962	5	17	1477	1488	308	310
1963	6	17	1665	1676	333	335
1964	6	18	2038	2050	392	394
1965	6	18	1708	1720	322	324
TURKEY						
1925	-	-	714	714	52	52
1929	-	-	812	812	55	55
1933	-	-	971	971	62	62
1937	-	1	1601	1602	96	96
1938	-	1	1785	1785	105	105
1950	4	17	3918	3931	187	188
1953	8	33	5728	5753	251	252
1955	11	42	5824	5855	242	243
1957	39	140	6660	6761	261	265
1960	125	421	6753	7049	243	254
1961	158	519	7252	7613	254	266
1962	141	450	8671	8980	295	305
1963	262	819	9935	10491	328	347
1964	207	644	10984	11421	353	367
1965	271	823	11732	12285	367	384
FAR EAST AND OTHER ASIA						
1925	995	7959	57985	64949	108	121

Table XII. ALTERNATIVE MEASURES OF HYDROELECTRICITY AND TOTAL ENERGY CONSUMPTION, SELECTED YEARS, 1925-1965

(All figures in coal equivalents; A = hydro measured by heat content, B = hydro measured by hypothetical energy content of fuels consumed at thermal electric stations)

Region, country, year	Hydroelectric power consumption (10^3 m.t.)		Energy consumption: Total (10^3 m.t.)		Energy consumption: Per capita (kgs)	
	A	B	A	B	A	B
	(1)	(2)	(3)	(4)	(5)	(6)
FAR EAST AND OTHER ASIA (CONTINUED)						
1929	1652	11233	70767	80348	126	143
1933	2266	13960	68351	80045	115	134
1937	3323	18873	95945	111495	151	176
1938	3578	20035	104002	120459	161	187
1950	5335	23473	92581	110719	124	149
1953	5995	23501	124951	142457	159	181
1955	7013	26370	135414	154771	168	192
1957	8295	29862	171663	193230	205	231
1960	9066	30461	208897	230293	234	258
1961	10574	34684	238291	262400	261	287
1962	10144	32460	258041	280357	276	300
1963	11298	35248	282320	306271	296	321
1964	11662	36386	301836	326559	309	334
1965	12119	36841	328031	352754	328	353
BORNEO (FORMER BRITISH)						
1950	-	-	278	278	289	289
1953	-	-	245	245	234	234
1955	-	-	441	441	399	399
1957	-	-	541	541	462	462
1960	-	-	522	522	407	407
1961	-	-	692	692	525	525
1962	-	-	500	500	368	368
1963	-	-	580	580	419	419
1964	-	-	697	697	489	489
1965	-	-	923	923	630	630
BURMA						
1950	-	-	256	256	14	14
1953	-	-	613	613	31	31
1955	-	-	740	740	36	36
1957	-	-	977	977	46	46
1960	20	67	1257	1304	56	58
1961	23	77	1241	1295	54	57
1962	27	85	1362	1421	59	61
1963	30	92	1254	1316	53	55
1964	35	109	1302	1377	54	57
1965	35	106	1227	1299	50	53
CEYLON						
1925	-	1	116	117	24	24
1929	-	1	486	487	94	94
1933	-	1	347	348	64	64
1937	-	1	470	470	82	82
1938	-	1	348	349	60	60
1950	1	5	590	594	77	77
1953	14	55	882	923	106	111
1955	16	61	888	933	102	107
1957	19	69	1424	1474	155	161

Table XII. ALTERNATIVE MEASURES OF HYDROELECTRICITY AND TOTAL ENERGY CONSUMPTION, SELECTED YEARS, 1925-1965

(All figures in coal equivalents; A = hydro measured by heat content, B = hydro measured by hypothetical energy content of fuels consumed at thermal electric stations)

Region, country, year	Hydroelectric power consumption (10^3 m.t.)		Energy consumption: Total (10^3 m.t.)		Energy consumption: Per capita (kgs)	
	A	B	A	B	A	B
	(1)	(2)	(3)	(4)	(5)	(6)
CEYLON (CONTINUED)						
1960	34	114	911	991	92	100
1961	35	114	1141	1220	112	120
1962	40	128	1255	1343	120	129
1963	41	128	1254	1341	118	126
1964	42	132	1094	1183	100	108
1965	42	126	1301	1385	116	123
HONG KONG						
1925	-	-	754	754	1039	1039
1929	-	-	311	311	396	396
1933	-	-	322	322	348	348
1937	-	-	532	532	415	415
1938	-	-	458	458	310	310
1950	-	-	667	667	282	282
1953	-	-	849	849	379	379
1955	-	-	963	963	387	387
1957	-	-	1197	1197	437	437
1960	-	-	1456	1456	473	473
1961	-	-	1641	1641	516	516
1962	-	-	1789	1789	525	525
1963	-	-	2066	2066	575	575
1964	-	-	2046	2046	554	554
1965	-	-	2300	2300	605	605
INDIA						
1925	24	188	19036	19200	57	58
1929	63	425	20899	21261	60	61
1933	102	625	18582	19106	51	52
1937	141	799	23395	24053	60	62
1938	150	840	25696	26386	65	67
1950	315	1386	30175	31246	84	87
1953	366	1435	32603	33672	87	90
1955	469	1764	36608	37903	94	97
1957	635	2287	43185	44837	106	110
1960	981	3296	52717	55032	122	127
1961	1228	4028	56902	59702	129	135
1962	1439	4606	63282	66449	140	147
1963	1708	5329	68664	72285	148	156
1964	1964	6127	66781	70944	140	149
1965	2159	6563	72826	77230	150	159
INDO-CHINA						
1925	-	-	799	799	40	40
1929	-	-	817	817	39	39
1933	-	-	452	452	20	20
1937	-	-	913	913	39	39
1938	-	-	926	926	39	39
1950	-	-	630	630	23	23

Table XII. ALTERNATIVE MEASURES OF HYDROELECTRICITY AND TOTAL ENERGY CONSUMPTION, SELECTED YEARS, 1925-1965

(All figures in coal equivalents; A = hydro measured by heat content, B = hydro measured by hypothetical energy content of fuels consumed at thermal electric stations)

Region, country, year	Hydroelectric power consumption (10^3 m.t.)		Energy consumption			
			Total (10^3 m.t.)		Per capita (kgs)	
	A	B	A	B	A	B
	(1)	(2)	(3)	(4)	(5)	(6)
INDO-CHINA (CONTINUED)						
1953	-	-	1082	1082	38	38
1955	1	2	574	575	31	31
1957	-	1	797	798	41	41
1960	1	3	948	950	44	45
1961	1	4	1105	1108	50	50
1962	1	4	1157	1160	51	51
1963	1	4	1353	1355	58	59
1964	5	16	1295	1306	55	55
1965	7	22	1543	1558	64	64
CAMBODIA						
1955	-	-	84	84	18	18
1957	-	-	128	128	26	26
1960	-	-	164	164	30	30
1961	-	-	200	200	36	36
1962	-	-	215	215	37	37
1963	-	-	282	282	48	48
1964	-	-	248	248	41	41
1965	-	-	281	281	46	46
LAOS						
1955	-	-	14	14	9	9
1957	-	-	29	29	17	17
1960	-	-	42	42	23	23
1961	-	-	57	57	31	31
1962	-	-	66	66	35	35
1963	-	-	77	77	40	40
1964	-	-	90	90	46	46
1965	-	-	87	87	44	44
VIETNAM, SOUTH						
1955	1	2	476	477	40	40
1957	-	1	641	642	51	51
1960	1	3	743	745	53	53
1961	1	4	848	851	59	59
1962	1	4	877	880	59	59
1963	1	4	994	997	65	65
1964	5	16	957	968	61	62
1965	7	22	1176	1191	73	74
INDONESIA						
1925	11	88	3046	3123	54	55
1929	13	85	4766	4838	80	81
1933	20	122	4186	4289	66	68
1937	26	149	4995	5118	74	76
1938	29	165	5176	5311	76	78

Table XII. ALTERNATIVE MEASURES OF HYDROELECTRICITY AND TOTAL ENERGY CONSUMPTION, SELECTED YEARS, 1925-1965

(All figures in coal equivalents; A = hydro measured by heat content, B = hydro measured by hypothetical energy content of fuels consumed at thermal electric stations)

Region, country, year	Hydroelectric power consumption (10^3 m.t.)		Energy consumption			
			Total (10^3 m.t.)		Per capita (kgs)	
	A	B	A	B	A	B
	(1)	(2)	(3)	(4)	(5)	(6)
INDONESIA (CONTINUED)						
1950	38	165	4896	5024	64	65
1953	57	222	7348	7513	91	93
1955	71	268	11769	11966	139	142
1957	78	279	12430	12632	141	143
1960	101	340	12813	13052	136	139
1961	97	318	14440	14661	150	152
1962	89	286	12749	12945	129	131
1963	89	279	12843	13032	127	129
1964	89	277	11649	11837	113	115
1965	89	270	13351	13532	127	129
JAPAN						
1925	951	7610	30483	37142	515	628
1929	1550	10540	38181	47171	607	750
1933	2014	12408	39589	49982	592	747
1937	2785	15817	57261	70293	818	1004
1938	2968	16619	62425	76076	885	1079
1950	4782	21042	45816	62076	553	749
1953	5220	20463	68427	83670	789	965
1955	6068	22817	66457	83205	747	935
1957	7086	25509	90411	108834	996	1200
1960	7309	24558	111001	128250	1191	1376
1961	8495	27862	131654	151022	1400	1606
1962	7797	24949	141497	158650	1491	1671
1963	8646	26976	156550	174879	1632	1824
1964	8620	26893	173528	191802	1791	1979
1965	8842	26881	188642	206681	1926	2110
KOREA						
1925	-	-	1179	1179	65	65
1929	-	-	1735	1735	93	93
1933	67	414	2186	2533	109	126
1937	261	1482	4286	5507	199	256
1938	305	1707	5245	6647	238	302
KOREA, REPUBLIC OF						
1950	12	53	925	966	45	47
1953	49	194	2039	2184	95	102
1955	60	225	2944	3109	137	144
1957	52	189	3934	4071	173	180
1960	73	244	6550	6721	265	272
1961	82	267	7136	7322	281	288
1962	88	281	8928	9121	342	349
1963	91	284	10862	11055	404	411
1964	94	293	11551	11750	418	425
1965	89	270	12578	12759	444	450

Table XII. ALTERNATIVE MEASURES OF HYDROELECTRICITY AND TOTAL ENERGY CONSUMPTION, SELECTED YEARS, 1925-1965

(All figures in coal equivalents; A = hydro measured by heat content, B = hydro measured by hypothetical energy content of fuels consumed at thermal electric stations)

Region, country, year	Hydroelectric power consumption (10^3 m.t.)		Energy consumption: Total (10^3 m.t.)		Energy consumption: Per capita (kgs)	
	A	B	A	B	A	B
	(1)	(2)	(3)	(4)	(5)	(6)
MALAYA AND SINGAPORE						
1925	3	21	810	828	NA	NA
1929	5	32	1276	1303	NA	NA
1933	12	73	611	672	NA	NA
1937	29	167	1478	1615	312	341
1938	29	160	915	1047	182	208
1950	32	139	1545	1652	249	266
1953	32	125	2351	2444	345	359
1955	29	110	2732	2813	378	389
1957	31	112	2650	2731	343	354
1960	24	82	2451	2509	287	294
1961	27	89	3128	3189	354	361
1962	29	94	3383	3448	371	378
1963	40	124	2339	2423	249	258
1964	68	212	4787	4931	497	512
1965	73	223	4156	4306	420	435
PAKISTAN						
1950	8	36	2730	2757	36	37
1953	30	118	3363	3451	42	43
1955	50	188	3697	3835	44	46
1957	65	234	4625	4794	53	55
1960	85	286	6216	6417	67	69
1961	118	385	6376	6644	67	70
1962	175	560	7381	7766	76	80
1963	196	612	8324	8740	84	89
1964	228	710	9145	9627	91	96
1965	246	747	9477	9979	92	97
PHILIPPINES						
1925	5	36	985	1016	85	88
1929	6	43	1163	1200	91	94
1933	8	49	849	890	60	63
1937	10	54	956	1000	62	65
1938	11	59	1011	1059	64	67
1950	24	105	1963	2044	97	101
1953	42	163	1919	2040	86	92
1955	54	202	2939	3087	125	131
1957	80	288	3454	3662	138	146
1960	165	554	4232	4621	154	169
1961	161	529	4381	4748	155	168
1962	169	540	5185	5557	177	190
1963	193	601	5797	6205	192	205
1964	200	624	6463	6887	207	220
1965	189	573	6820	7205	211	223
TAIWAN						
1925	2	15	697	710	170	173
1929	16	107	1172	1263	261	281
1933	44	268	1242	1466	249	294

Table XII. ALTERNATIVE MEASURES OF HYDROELECTRICITY AND TOTAL ENERGY CONSUMPTION, SELECTED YEARS, 1925-1965

(All figures in coal equivalents; A = hydro measured by heat content, B = hydro measured by hypothetical energy content of fuels consumed at thermal electric stations)

Region, country, year	Hydroelectric power consumption (10^3 m.t.)		Energy consumption: Total (10^3 m.t.)		Energy consumption: Per capita (kgs)	
	A	B	A	B	A	B
	(1)	(2)	(3)	(4)	(5)	(6)
TAIWAN (CONTINUED)						
1937	71	404	1547	1879	280	340
1938	87	485	1725	2123	304	374
1950	122	535	1730	2143	227	281
1953	183	718	2498	3033	302	367
1955	191	720	3437	3965	386	445
1957	242	872	4349	4979	457	524
1960	258	867	5590	6200	527	584
1961	292	959	6015	6682	548	609
1962	270	864	6551	7145	577	630
1963	241	753	7134	7646	610	654
1964	295	920	7200	7826	597	648
1965	323	982	8258	8917	664	717
THAILAND						
1925	-	-	101	101	10	10
1929	-	-	196	196	17	17
1933	-	-	139	139	11	11
1937	-	-	218	218	15	15
1938	-	-	232	232	16	16
1950	-	-	370	370	19	19
1953	-	-	715	715	33	33
1955	-	-	1128	1128	50	50
1957	-	-	1394	1394	58	58
1960	-	-	1740	1740	66	66
1961	-	-	1873	1873	69	69
1962	-	-	2312	2312	83	83
1963	-	-	2562	2562	89	89
1964	-	-	3493	3493	118	118
1965	-	-	3722	3722	122	122
AFRICA						
1925	8	65	13940	13997	100	101
1929	10	71	17148	17209	115	115
1933	28	172	15133	15277	96	96
1937	58	328	22570	22840	133	135
1938	61	342	23403	23684	135	137
1950	171	750	42030	42610	194	196
1953	255	1001	49414	50159	213	216
1955	407	1529	58794	59917	241	246
1957	510	1836	63118	64444	246	251
1960	838	2817	70241	72220	254	262
1961	1168	3829	72869	75531	254	263
1962	1319	4220	75247	78148	260	270
1963	1384	4317	77380	80313	261	271
1964	1514	4722	85881	89090	283	294
1965	1650	5015	92622	95988	298	309

Table XII. ALTERNATIVE MEASURES OF HYDROELECTRICITY AND TOTAL ENERGY CONSUMPTION, SELECTED YEARS, 1925–1965

(All figures in coal equivalents; A = hydro measured by heat content, B = hydro measured by hypothetical energy content of fuels consumed at thermal electric stations)

Region, country, year	Hydroelectric power consumption (10^3 m.t.)		Energy consumption Total (10^3 m.t.)		Energy consumption Per capita (kgs)	
	A	B	A	B	A	B
	(1)	(2)	(3)	(4)	(5)	(6)
NORTH AFRICA						
1925	3	20	2954	2972	106	107
1929	5	32	4063	4091	137	138
1933	11	65	4022	4076	127	129
1937	21	116	4513	4609	133	135
1938	21	115	4838	4932	139	142
1950	52	229	9358	9535	224	228
1953	69	269	10365	10565	231	235
1955	137	515	12064	12442	251	258
1957	151	544	11662	12055	231	239
1960	198	666	14776	15244	273	281
1961	281	922	14931	15572	269	280
1962	311	994	15384	16067	270	282
1963	332	1035	14960	15663	256	269
1964	391	1219	17509	18337	292	306
1965	419	1274	18363	19218	299	313
ALGERIA						
1925	3	20	694	712	NA	NA
1929	3	17	1151	1166	177	179
1933	3	19	1021	1037	149	151
1937	5	26	1010	1031	NA	NA
1938	5	29	1041	1065	NA	NA
1950	16	72	1512	1567	173	179
1953	28	109	1619	1700	173	181
1955	35	131	2153	2249	222	231
1957	40	143	2654	2757	262	272
1960	45	150	3665	3770	340	350
1961	32	106	3526	3599	321	327
1962	33	106	2518	2591	225	231
1963	33	101	2444	2513	214	220
1964	36	111	3038	3114	261	267
1965	50	152	3523	3625	297	305
EGYPT UAR						
1925	-	-	1784	1784	128	128
1929	-	-	2165	2165	148	148
1933	-	-	2156	2156	141	141
1937	-	-	2595	2595	162	162
1938	-	-	2806	2806	172	172
1950	1	4	6198	6201	301	301
1953	1	3	6251	6253	281	282
1955	1	3	7275	7278	313	313
1957	1	3	6634	6636	272	272
1960	33	109	8321	8398	318	320
1961	127	415	8288	8576	309	320
1962	147	469	8833	9155	321	333
1963	160	499	9115	9454	323	335
1964	209	651	10565	11008	362	377
1965	219	665	10637	11083	356	371

Table XII. ALTERNATIVE MEASURES OF HYDROELECTRICITY AND TOTAL ENERGY CONSUMPTION, SELECTED YEARS, 1925-1965

(All figures in coal equivalents; A = hydro measured by heat content, B = hydro measured by hypothetical energy content of fuels consumed at thermal electric stations)

Region, country, year	Hydroelectric power consumption (10^3 m.t.) A	Hydroelectric power consumption (10^3 m.t.) B	Energy consumption Total (10^3 m.t.) A	Energy consumption Total (10^3 m.t.) B	Energy consumption Per capita (kgs) A	Energy consumption Per capita (kgs) B
	(1)	(2)	(3)	(4)	(5)	(6)
MOROCCO						
1925	-	-	175	175	NA	NA
1929	2	15	324	337	56	59
1933	7	45	404	442	65	71
1937	16	91	419	493	58	69
1938	15	86	443	514	60	69
1950	35	153	1071	1189	120	133
1953	40	156	1822	1938	190	203
1955	101	381	1701	1981	168	196
1957	107	386	1455	1734	136	162
1960	115	387	1662	1933	143	166
1961	120	394	1707	1981	142	165
1962	129	411	1381	1664	112	135
1963	135	422	1852	2139	146	169
1964	142	442	1982	2282	153	176
1965	145	441	2149	2444	161	183
TUNISIA						
1925	-	-	270	270	NA	NA
1929	-	-	377	377	171	171
1933	-	-	355	355	142	142
1937	-	-	373	373	140	140
1938	-	-	397	397	NA	NA
1950	-	-	494	494	139	139
1953	-	-	565	565	150	150
1955	-	-	663	663	170	170
1957	3	12	626	635	156	159
1960	6	20	718	732	170	173
1961	2	8	744	750	173	174
1962	2	8	767	772	175	176
1963	4	12	952	960	212	214
1964	5	15	1135	1145	249	251
1965	5	16	1063	1074	227	230
TROPICAL AFRICA						
1925	6	45	1848	1888	18	18
1929	6	38	2780	2813	25	26
1933	17	107	1460	1550	13	13
1937	37	212	3342	3517	27	28
1938	41	227	3053	3239	24	26
1950	119	521	6433	6836	40	42
1953	187	733	8724	9270	51	54
1955	270	1015	11144	11889	62	66
1957	359	1293	13052	13986	69	74
1960	640	2151	13331	14842	65	73
1961	886	2907	14078	16099	66	75
1962	1008	3226	14455	16673	68	78
1963	1052	3282	15397	17627	70	80
1964	1123	3503	17326	19706	77	88
1965	1231	3741	18942	21453	83	94

Table XII. ALTERNATIVE MEASURES OF HYDROELECTRICITY AND TOTAL ENERGY CONSUMPTION, SELECTED YEARS, 1925-1965

(All figures in coal equivalents; A = hydro measured by heat content, B = hydro measured by hypothetical energy content of fuels consumed at thermal electric stations)

Region, country, year	Hydroelectric power consumption (10^3 m.t.)		Energy consumption: Total (10^3 m.t.)		Energy consumption: Per capita (kgs)	
	A	B	A	B	A	B
	(1)	(2)	(3)	(4)	(5)	(6)
CONGO, DEMOCRATIC REPUBLIC						
1925	4	30	384	410	NA	NA
1929	4	26	650	672	54	56
1933	12	75	103	166	8	13
1937	28	156	292	420	21	30
1938	29	163	251	385	18	27
1950	74	323	679	928	45	61
1953	124	486	1067	1429	66	88
1955	169	635	1536	2002	91	119
1957	211	758	1560	2108	88	119
1960	224	752	1244	1772	65	93
1961	240	786	1309	1855	67	95
1962	256	820	1249	1813	63	91
1963	245	764	1295	1814	64	89
1964	255	797	1158	1699	55	81
1965	274	834	1380	1940	64	90
EAST AFRICA						
1925	1	10	146	155	13	14
1929	1	9	225	233	20	20
1933	2	12	135	145	11	12
1937	3	17	285	299	23	24
1938	3	18	324	339	26	27
1950	9	40	703	733	37	39
1953	14	54	1094	1134	54	56
1955	39	146	1473	1580	69	74
1957	52	186	1592	1726	71	77
1960	80	268	1829	2017	76	84
1961	83	271	1676	1864	68	76
1962	89	285	1845	2041	73	81
1963	96	298	2005	2207	78	85
1964	107	334	2078	2305	79	87
1965	119	360	2222	2464	82	91
EQUATORIAL AFRICA						
1925	-	-	5	5	NA	NA
1929	-	-	9	9	NA	NA
1933	-	-	13	13	4	4
1937	-	-	39	39	11	11
1938	-	-	31	31	9	9
1950	-	-	85	85	19	19
1953	1	3	123	126	27	28
1955	4	16	130	142	28	30
1957	4	14	223	233	46	48
1960	4	13	355	364	64	66
1961	4	12	345	353	61	63
1962	4	12	275	283	48	49
1963	6	20	230	243	39	42
1964	6	20	326	339	55	57
1965	6	19	321	334	54	56

Table XII. ALTERNATIVE MEASURES OF HYDROELECTRICITY AND TOTAL ENERGY CONSUMPTION, SELECTED YEARS, 1925-1965

(All figures in coal equivalents; A = hydro measured by heat content, B = hydro measured by hypothetical energy content of fuels consumed at thermal electric stations)

Region, country, year	Hydroelectric power consumption (10^3 m.t.)		Energy consumption: Total (10^3 m.t.)		Energy consumption: Per capita (kgs)	
	A	B	A	B	A	B
	(1)	(2)	(3)	(4)	(5)	(6)
GHANA						
1925	-	-	83	83	24	24
1929	-	-	126	126	32	32
1933	-	-	65	65	15	15
1937	-	-	192	192	42	42
1938	-	-	211	211	45	45
1950	-	-	302	302	54	54
1953	-	-	413	413	70	70
1955	-	-	579	579	96	96
1957	-	-	635	635	102	102
1960	-	-	685	685	101	101
1961	-	-	649	649	93	93
1962	-	-	720	720	101	101
1963	-	-	832	832	113	113
1964	-	-	963	963	128	128
1965	13	41	936	963	121	124
LIBERIA						
1925	-	-	-	-	NA	NA
1929	-	-	-	-	NA	NA
1933	-	-	-	-	NA	NA
1937	-	-	2	2	NA	NA
1938	-	-	3	3	NA	NA
1950	1	4	25	28	NA	NA
1953	1	5	28	32	NA	NA
1955	1	5	93	97	NA	NA
1957	2	6	50	54	NA	NA
1960	2	7	76	81	77	82
1961	2	7	77	82	77	82
1962	2	7	125	130	123	128
1963	2	7	187	191	181	186
1964	2	7	248	253	238	243
1965	2	6	284	288	267	271
NIGERIA						
1925	-	-	265	265	NA	NA
1929	-	-	373	373	NA	NA
1933	-	-	257	257	NA	NA
1937	-	-	406	406	NA	NA
1938	-	-	400	400	NA	NA
1950	7	29	890	912	NA	NA
1953	8	31	1071	1094	NA	NA
1955	9	34	1120	1145	NA	NA
1957	11	40	1339	1368	27	28
1960	11	38	1436	1463	28	28
1961	13	41	1708	1737	32	33
1962	14	43	1639	1668	30	31
1963	15	46	1889	1920	34	34
1964	16	49	2330	2363	41	42
1965	17	50	2753	2787	48	48

Table XII. ALTERNATIVE MEASURES OF HYDROELECTRICITY AND TOTAL ENERGY CONSUMPTION, SELECTED YEARS, 1925-1965

(All figures in coal equivalents; A = hydro measured by heat content, B = hydro measured by hypothetical energy content of fuels consumed at thermal electric stations)

Region, country, year	Hydroelectric power consumption (10^3 m.t.)		Energy consumption: Total (10^3 m.t.)		Energy consumption: Per capita (kgs)	
	A	B	A	B	A	B
	(1)	(2)	(3)	(4)	(5)	(6)
RHODESIAN FEDERATION						
1925	-	-	472	472	143	143
1929	-	-	671	671	180	180
1933	3	15	478	490	114	117
1937	5	28	960	983	216	221
1938	6	32	1017	1043	224	230
1950	19	85	2229	2295	323	333
1953	25	97	2940	3012	387	396
1955	28	104	3800	3877	451	460
1957	29	104	4290	4365	481	490
1960	164	550	4259	4646	413	451
1961	371	1215	3940	4784	371	450
1962	440	1408	3923	4891	359	447
1963	476	1486	3825	4834	340	429
1964	521	1625	4112	5216	353	448
1965	561	1707	4842	5987	407	503
MALAWI						
1925	-	-	2	2	1	1
1929	-	-	5	5	3	3
1933	-	-	6	6	4	4
1937	-	-	8	8	5	5
1938	-	-	9	9	5	5
1950	-	-	48	48	21	21
1953	-	1	64	65	26	27
1955	-	-	87	87	34	34
1957	-	1	107	108	40	41
1960	-	1	132	133	38	39
1961	-	1	122	122	34	34
1962	2	5	128	131	35	36
1963	1	3	131	133	35	35
1964	1	4	135	137	35	35
1965	2	5	163	166	41	42
ZAMBIA						
1925	-	-	42	42	37	37
1929	-	-	148	148	115	115
1933	-	-	182	182	131	131
1937	-	-	349	349	242	242
1938	-	-	414	414	284	284
1950	NA	NA	714	714	293	293
1953	23	92	950	1018	359	385
1955	27	102	1042	1117	374	400
1957	28	101	1133	1206	383	408
1960	NA	NA	1230	1230	383	383
1961	197	647	1477	1926	447	584
1962	257	821	1454	2018	428	593
1963	267	834	1417	1984	405	568
1964	292	911	1562	2181	434	606
1965	308	937	1826	2455	492	662

Table XII. ALTERNATIVE MEASURES OF HYDROELECTRICITY AND TOTAL ENERGY CONSUMPTION, SELECTED YEARS, 1925-1965

(All figures in coal equivalents; A = hydro measured by heat content, B = hydro measured by hypothetical energy content of fuels consumed at thermal electric stations)

Region, country, year	Hydroelectric power consumption (10^3 m.t.)		Energy consumption: Total (10^3 m.t.)		Energy consumption: Per capita (kgs)	
	A	B	A	B	A	B
	(1)	(2)	(3)	(4)	(5)	(6)
RHODESIA						
1950	NA	NA	1448	1448	667	667
1953	1	5	1925	1929	761	762
1955	-	1	2671	2671	864	865
1957	-	1	3049	3050	924	924
1960	131	439	2864	3173	787	872
1961	144	472	2312	2640	615	702
1962	190	608	2350	2768	606	713
1963	208	649	2276	2717	568	677
1964	228	710	2416	2898	584	700
1965	252	765	2853	3366	670	790
WEST AFRICA						
1925	-	-	79	79	NA	NA
1929	-	-	120	120	8	8
1933	-	-	87	87	6	6
1937	-	-	226	226	15	15
1938	-	-	60	60	4	4
1950	-	1	368	369	21	21
1953	1	3	504	506	27	27
1955	1	4	565	568	29	30
1957	2	7	728	733	35	35
1960	8	25	957	974	40	41
1961	10	33	1145	1168	47	48
1962	13	40	1241	1269	50	51
1963	15	47	1323	1355	51	53
1964	13	40	1562	1590	59	60
1965	18	54	1831	1867	68	69
SOUTH AFRICA						
1925	-	-	9138	9138	1045	1045
1929	-	-	10305	10305	1082	1082
1933	-	-	9651	9651	936	936
1937	-	-	14715	14715	1324	1324
1938	-	-	15513	15513	1372	1372
1950	-	-	26239	26239	1879	1879
1953	-	-	30325	30325	2030	2030
1955	-	-	35587	35587	2264	2264
1957	-	-	38403	38403	2328	2328
1960	-	-	42134	42134	2355	2355
1961	-	-	43860	43860	2397	2397
1962	-	-	45407	45407	2427	2427
1963	-	-	47024	47024	2456	2456
1964	-	-	51047	51047	2604	2604
1965	-	-	55317	55317	2761	2761
DEVELOPED COUNTRIES						
1925	9327	74618	1321075	1386366	2740	2876
1929	13911	94594	1529954	1610637	3051	3212
1933	14807	91209	1160529	1236931	2237	2384

Table XII. ALTERNATIVE MEASURES OF HYDROELECTRICITY AND TOTAL ENERGY CONSUMPTION, SELECTED YEARS, 1925-1965

(All figures in coal equivalents; A = hydro measured by heat content, B = hydro measured by hypothetical energy content of fuels consumed at thermal electric stations)

Region, country, year	Hydroelectric power consumption (10^3 m.t.)		Energy consumption: Total (10^3 m.t.)		Energy consumption: Per capita (kgs)	
	A	B	A	B	A	B
	(1)	(2)	(3)	(4)	(5)	(6)
DEVELOPED COUNTRIES (CONTINUED)						
1937	20228	114896	1530049	1624716	2866	3043
1938	20546	115056	1422111	1516621	2644	2820
1950	38381	168878	1961603	2092100	3396	3622
1953	45260	177421	2175971	2308131	3634	3855
1955	50914	191438	2348853	2489376	3827	4056
1957	56975	205111	2538593	2686729	4036	4272
1960	69276	232767	2707952	2871443	4155	4406
1961	71935	235947	2796010	2960022	4238	4486
1962	74225	237520	2947561	3110856	4411	4656
1963	77479	241735	3120132	3284388	4612	4855
1964	79659	248535	3304757	3473634	4829	5076
1965	86959	264355	3462535	3639931	5000	5256
UNDERDEVELOPED COUNTRIES						
1925	449	3588	59300	62439	80	84
1929	608	4137	72548	76076	92	97
1933	859	5288	58600	63030	70	75
1937	1340	7610	90044	96315	101	108
1938	1464	8201	96576	103312	106	114
1950	2529	11127	142051	150649	131	139
1953	3379	13246	173904	183770	150	159
1955	4111	15459	219856	231203	184	193
1957	5246	18887	265338	278978	211	222
1960	7128	23948	318308	335129	236	249
1961	7995	26225	339577	357806	245	258
1962	8783	28105	364628	383950	258	271
1963	9592	29926	380020	400354	262	276
1964	10495	32744	403368	425617	271	286
1965	11695	35553	433270	457128	284	300
COMMUNIST COUNTRIES						
1925	74	588	104158	104673	157	158
1929	125	847	153480	154202	222	223
1933	206	1267	173110	174171	244	246
1937	636	3610	263340	266314	366	371
1938	754	4220	271369	274836	376	381
1950	2512	11053	507245	515786	604	614
1953	3052	11965	643372	652284	736	746
1955	4212	15838	789480	801106	864	876
1957	6770	24373	931389	948991	987	1005
1960	9581	32191	1169835	1192445	1181	1204
1961	10236	33572	1244360	1267697	1238	1261
1962	12044	38541	1308820	1335317	1282	1308
1963	12526	39080	1409567	1436121	1361	1387
1964	12825	40013	1495613	1522801	1424	1450
1965	13984	42512	1578771	1607299	1483	1510

Table XII. ALTERNATIVE MEASURES OF HYDROELECTRICITY AND TOTAL ENERGY CONSUMPTION, SELECTED YEARS, 1925-1965

(All figures in coal equivalents; A = hydro measured by heat content, B = hydro measured by hypothetical energy content of fuels consumed at thermal electric stations)

Region, country, year	Hydroelectric power consumption (10^3 m.t.)		Energy consumption			
			Total (10^3 m.t.)		Per capita (kgs)	
	A	B	A	B	A	B
	(1)	(2)	(3)	(4)	(5)	(6)
USSR						
1925	31	251	25320	25539	165	166
1929	70	473	52966	53370	314	317
1933	145	896	98640	99391	546	550
1937	524	2976	166298	168750	885	898
1938	636	3564	176349	179276	928	944
1950	1586	6980	303319	308712	1685	1715
1953	2400	9408	369587	376596	1950	1987
1955	2897	10892	460976	468971	2350	2391
1957	4929	17743	540514	553328	2661	2724
1960	6360	21371	640618	655629	2988	3058
1961	7381	24210	667338	684166	3061	3138
1962	8964	28685	710332	730053	3207	3296
1963	9389	29294	769574	789479	3424	3512
1964	9507	29662	816567	836722	3586	3675
1965	9991	30373	880629	901011	3819	3907
COMMUNIST EASTERN EUROPE						
1925	42	337	55138	55432	783	787
1929	55	373	76744	77062	1035	1039
1933	60	372	49534	49846	638	642
1937	112	635	66040	66563	820	826
1938	117	657	67690	68229	832	839
1950	266	1169	160796	161700	1792	1802
1953	332	1302	207134	208103	2243	2254
1955	540	2032	230214	231705	2440	2456
1957	554	1994	259065	260505	2699	2715
1960	807	2713	293895	295801	2985	3004
1961	792	2598	311993	313799	3149	3168
1962	955	3056	331733	333834	3326	3347
1963	949	2962	353068	355081	3512	3532
1964	943	2941	371008	373007	3662	3681
1965	1368	4158	375131	377922	3683	3710
COMMUNIST ASIA						
1925	-	-	23701	23701	54	54
1929	-	-	23770	23770	53	53
1933	-	-	24935	24935	55	55
1937	-	-	31002	31002	69	69
1938	-	-	27330	27330	61	61
1950	660	2904	43130	45374	76	80
1953	320	1254	66651	67585	113	114
1955	775	2914	98290	100429	158	161
1957	1288	4636	131809	135158	204	210
1960	2413	8108	235321	241016	347	356
1961	2063	6765	265029	269732	385	392
1962	2125	6800	266755	271430	381	388
1963	2188	6825	286924	291562	404	410
1964	2375	7410	308037	313072	427	434
1965	2625	7980	323012	328367	441	448

Table XII. ALTERNATIVE MEASURES OF HYDROELECTRICITY AND TOTAL ENERGY CONSUMPTION, SELECTED YEARS, 1925-1965

(All figures in coal equivalents; A = hydro measured by heat content, B = hydro measured by hypothetical energy content of fuels consumed at thermal electric stations)

Region, country, year	Hydroelectric power consumption (10^3 m.t.)		Energy consumption			
			Total (10^3 m.t.)		Per capita (kgs)	
	A	B	A	B	A	B
	(1)	(2)	(3)	(4)	(5)	(6)
ORGANISATION FOR ECONOMIC CO-OPERATION AND DEVELOPMENT (OECD)						
1925	9161	73284	1293454	1357577	2842	2983
1929	13642	92765	1499729	1578852	3171	3339
1933	14427	88871	1134420	1208863	2321	2473
1937	19669	111720	1492576	1584627	2970	3153
1938	19922	111562	1383856	1475496	2734	2915
1950	37227	163798	1898300	2024871	3496	3729
1953	43750	171501	2108232	2235983	3743	3970
1955	49005	184259	2265837	2401091	3925	4159
1957	54692	196892	2447397	2589597	4134	4374
1960	66706	224130	2602063	2759488	4239	4496
1961	69039	226449	2685668	2843077	4320	4573
1962	70771	226468	2834370	2990068	4500	4748
1963	73940	230692	3000209	3156961	4704	4950
1964	75844	236632	3174028	3334817	4916	5165
1965	82627	251187	3320455	3489014	5083	5341
COMMUNIST COUNTRIES						
1925	74	588	104158	104673	157	158
1929	125	847	153480	154202	222	223
1933	206	1267	173110	174171	244	246
1937	636	3610	263340	266314	366	371
1938	754	4220	271369	274836	376	381
1950	2512	11053	507245	515786	604	614
1953	3052	11965	643372	652284	736	746
1955	4212	15838	789480	801106	864	876
1957	6770	24373	931389	948991	987	1005
1960	9581	32191	1169835	1192445	1181	1204
1961	10236	33572	1244360	1267697	1238	1261
1962	12044	38541	1308820	1335317	1282	1308
1963	12526	39080	1409567	1436121	1361	1387
1964	12825	40013	1495613	1522801	1424	1450
1965	13984	42512	1578771	1607299	1483	1510
WORLD EXCLUDING OECD AND COMMUNIST COUNTRIES						
1925	615	4922	86921	91228	113	118
1929	877	5966	102772	107861	126	132
1933	1238	7626	84709	91097	98	105
1937	1899	10786	127518	136405	138	148
1938	2088	11695	134831	144437	143	154
1950	3683	16207	205354	217878	183	194
1953	4889	19165	241642	255918	203	215
1955	6021	22638	302871	319488	245	259
1957	7530	27106	356533	376110	276	291
1960	9698	32584	424197	447083	306	323
1961	10891	35723	449919	474750	316	333
1962	12236	39156	477819	504739	329	347
1963	13131	40968	499943	527780	336	354
1964	14310	44647	534097	564434	350	370
1965	16026	48721	575350	608044	368	389

DERIVATION OF TABLE XIII

Row	*Average annual percentage rates of change (using compound interest formula applied to beginning and terminal years of the relevant period) derived:*	
(1)	Col. (1) table II	
(2)	Col. (2) table II	
(3)	Col. (6) table II	
(4)	Col. (8) table II	
(5)	Col. (9) table II	
(6)	Col. (1) table VI	Import panel
(7)	Col. (2) table VI	Import panel
(8)	Col. (3) table VI	Import panel
(9)	Col. (1) table VI	Export panel
(10)	Col. (2) table VI	Export panel
(11)	Col. (3) Table VI	Export panel
(12)	Col. (5) table X	
(13)	Col. (4) table XII	
(14)	Col. (6) table X	
(15)	Col. (7) table X	
(16)	Col. (8) table X	
(17)	Col. (9) table X	
(18)	Col. (9) table XI	
(19)	Col. (7) table XI	
(20)	Row (1) divided by row (19)‡	
(21)	Col. (8) table XI	
(22)	Col. (6) table XII	
(23)	Row (14) divided by row (19)‡	
(24)	Row (15) divided by row (19)‡	
(25)	Row (16) divided by row (19)‡	
(26)	Row (17) divided by row (19)‡	
(27)	Col. (10) table XI	

‡Preceding these divisions, numerator and denominator are first expressed as index numbers by adding 100; and the resulting quotient is converted to growth rates by multiplying and then subtracting 100. E.g., if for a given period, total production rises 5.5 percent annually, and population 2.0 percent annually, then per capita production rises 3.4 percent annually:

$$\frac{5.5 + 100}{2.0 + 100} \times 100 - 100 = \frac{105.5}{102.0} \times 100 - 100$$
$$= 1.034 \times 100 - 100 = 103.4 - 100 = 3.4.$$

Table XIII. AVERAGE ANNUAL PERCENTAGE RATES OF CHANGE IN TOTAL AND PER CAPITA ENERGY PRODUCTION, TRADE, AND CONSUMPTION, SELECTED PERIODS, 1925-1965

Region, country, indicator	1925-29	1929-38	1938-50	1950-55	1955-60	1960-65	1925-38	1950-65	1925-65
	(1)	(2)	(3)	(4)	(5)	(6)	(7)	(8)	(9)
WORLD									
PRODUCTION									
1 TOTAL	4.2	0.1	3.2	5.1	4.5	5.4	1.4	5.0	3.3
2 SOLID FUELS	2.9	-0.9	1.6	2.6	1.9	2.8	0.3	2.4	1.5
3 LIQUID FUELS	8.7	3.2	5.6	8.2	6.4	7.4	4.8	7.3	6.0
4 NATURAL GAS	12.6	2.9	8.0	9.1	9.5	8.3	5.8	9.0	7.6
5 HYDROELECTRIC POWER	10.5	5.0	5.5	6.5	7.7	5.5	6.7	6.6	6.3
IMPORTS									
6 TOTAL	8.6	0.2	4.5	9.5	5.7	9.3	2.7	8.2	5.3
7 SOLID FUELS	5.4	-3.2	-0.6	5.8	-3.2	3.6	-0.6	2.0	0.4
8 LIQUID FUELS	14.8	4.1	7.2	10.7	7.4	10.0	7.2	9.4	8.0
EXPORTS									
9 TOTAL	8.4	0.1	4.3	9.0	5.7	9.2	2.6	8.0	5.1
10 SOLID FUELS	5.2	-3.5	-0.6	5.5	-3.3	3.6	-0.9	1.9	0.2
11 LIQUID FUELS	14.5	4.2	6.9	10.1	7.5	9.9	7.3	9.1	7.9
CONSUMPTION									
12 TOTAL	4.3	0.2	3.2	5.2	4.6	5.5	1.4	5.1	3.3
13 TOTAL - ALTERNATIVE HYDRO	4.3	0.3	3.2	5.0	4.5	5.3	1.5	5.0	3.3
14 SOLID FUELS	3.0	-0.8	1.8	2.7	1.9	2.8	0.4	2.5	1.6
15 LIQUID FUELS	9.0	3.4	5.6	8.6	6.5	7.6	5.1	7.6	6.2
16 NATURAL GAS	12.6	2.9	8.0	9.1	9.5	8.3	5.8	9.0	7.6
17 HYDROELECTRIC POWER	10.4	5.0	5.5	6.4	7.7	5.5	6.7	6.6	6.3
18 ADDENDUM - TOTAL ELECTRICITY	10.4	5.4	6.4	10.2	8.4	7.7	6.9	8.8	7.4
19 POPULATION	1.2	1.0	1.2	1.7	1.9	1.9	1.1	1.8	1.4
20 TOTAL PER CAPITA PRODUCTION	3.0	-0.9	1.9	3.3	2.6	3.5	0.3	3.1	1.8
PER CAPITA CONSUMPTION									
21 TOTAL	3.1	-0.8	2.0	3.4	2.6	3.5	0.4	3.2	1.9
22 TOTAL - ALTERNATIVE HYDRO	3.1	-0.7	1.9	3.2	2.6	3.4	0.5	3.1	1.9
23 SOLID FUELS	1.8	-1.8	0.5	0.9	0.1	0.9	-0.7	0.6	0.2
24 LIQUID FUELS	7.8	2.4	4.3	6.8	4.6	5.6	4.0	5.7	4.7
25 NATURAL GAS	11.3	1.9	6.7	7.3	7.5	6.3	4.7	7.0	6.2
26 HYDROELECTRIC POWER	9.1	4.0	4.3	4.6	5.8	3.6	5.5	4.7	4.8
27 ADDENDUM - TOTAL ELECTRICITY	9.1	4.3	5.1	8.4	6.4	5.7	5.8	6.8	6.0
NORTH AMERICA									
PRODUCTION									
1 TOTAL	3.5	-2.0	4.3	2.9	1.7	4.0	-0.4	2.9	2.2
2 SOLID FUELS	1.3	-4.6	3.0	-2.7	-2.5	3.9	-2.9	-0.5	-0.2
3 LIQUID FUELS	7.6	1.9	4.5	5.7	1.3	2.9	3.6	3.3	3.8
4 NATURAL GAS	12.6	2.2	8.4	8.5	7.0	5.4	5.2	6.9	6.8
5 HYDROELECTRIC POWER	11.7	3.1	6.4	4.7	5.8	4.2	5.7	4.9	5.6
IMPORTS									
6 TOTAL	7.4	-4.5	10.8	4.7	6.2	6.5	-1.0	5.8	5.0
7 SOLID FUELS	2.9	-4.1	5.9	-6.1	-7.2	4.1	-2.0	-3.2	-0.1
8 LIQUID FUELS	10.5	-4.8	13.0	7.1	7.0	6.0	-0.3	6.7	6.2
EXPORTS									
9 TOTAL	5.1	-0.2	-0.4	9.8	-4.3	9.2	1.4	4.7	2.0
10 SOLID FUELS	0.6	-5.9	7.2	12.7	-6.7	6.2	-3.9	3.7	2.2
11 LIQUID FUELS	8.8	2.4	-5.6	5.6	-3.0	8.9	4.3	3.7	1.0
CONSUMPTION									
12 TOTAL	3.6	-2.2	5.0	2.7	2.6	4.2	-0.4	3.2	2.5
13 TOTAL - ALTERNATIVE HYDRO	3.7	-2.1	5.0	2.6	2.6	4.1	-0.3	3.1	2.5
14 SOLID FUELS	1.4	-4.5	2.9	-3.9	-2.2	3.7	-2.8	-0.9	-0.4
15 LIQUID FUELS	8.2	1.5	6.6	6.0	2.9	3.7	3.5	4.2	4.7
16 NATURAL GAS	12.5	2.1	8.4	8.5	7.1	5.4	5.2	7.0	6.8
17 HYDROELECTRIC POWER	11.7	3.1	6.4	4.7	5.8	4.2	5.7	4.9	5.6
18 ADDENDUM - TOTAL ELECTRICITY	11.1	2.3	8.4	9.9	6.1	6.3	4.9	7.4	6.9
19 POPULATION	1.3	0.8	1.3	1.8	1.8	1.5	0.9	1.7	1.3
20 TOTAL PER CAPITA PRODUCTION	2.1	-2.8	2.9	1.1	-0.1	2.5	-1.3	1.1	0.9
PER CAPITA CONSUMPTION									
21 TOTAL	2.3	-2.9	3.7	0.9	0.8	2.7	-1.4	1.4	1.2
22 TOTAL - ALTERNATIVE HYDRO	2.4	-2.8	3.6	0.8	0.8	2.5	-1.2	1.4	1.2
23 SOLID FUELS	0.1	-5.3	1.6	-5.6	-3.9	2.1	-3.7	-2.5	-1.7
24 LIQUID FUELS	6.8	0.8	5.2	4.1	1.0	2.2	2.6	2.4	3.3
25 NATURAL GAS	11.1	1.4	7.0	6.6	5.2	3.8	4.3	5.2	5.4
26 HYDROELECTRIC POWER	10.3	2.4	5.0	2.8	3.9	2.7	4.7	3.1	4.2
27 ADDENDUM - TOTAL ELECTRICITY	9.6	1.5	6.9	8.0	4.2	4.7	3.9	5.6	5.5
CANADA									
PRODUCTION									
1 TOTAL	9.0	-0.3	4.6	11.7	8.6	12.1	2.5	10.8	6.2

Table XIII. AVERAGE ANNUAL PERCENTAGE RATES OF CHANGE IN TOTAL AND PER CAPITA ENERGY PRODUCTION, TRADE, AND CONSUMPTION, SELECTED PERIODS, 1925-1965

Region, country, indicator	1925-29	1929-38	1938-50	1950-55	1955-60	1960-65	1925-38	1950-65	1925-65
	(1)	(2)	(3)	(4)	(5)	(6)	(7)	(8)	(9)
CANADA (CONTINUED)									
PRODUCTION (CONTINUED)									
2 SOLID FUELS	7.8	-2.3	2.3	-5.2	-6.0	0.8	0.7	-3.5	-0.4
3 LIQUID FUELS	27.5	23.4	12.8	35.0	8.3	10.3	24.6	17.3	18.2
4 NATURAL GAS	13.8	1.8	6.1	17.3	28.2	23.0	5.4	22.8	11.8
5 HYDROELECTRIC POWER	15.5	4.2	6.1	7.9	6.8	2.0	7.6	5.5	6.3
IMPORTS									
6 TOTAL	7.0	-2.5	7.2	-1.5	0.8	4.8	0.4	1.3	2.7
7 SOLID FUELS	3.1	-4.1	6.2	-6.0	-7.3	4.3	-1.9	-3.1	-
8 LIQUID FUELS	19.1	0.4	8.4	2.8	5.3	4.9	5.8	4.3	6.0
EXPORTS									
9 TOTAL	4.5	-6.6	3.0	37.0	27.3	21.9	-3.3	28.6	9.7
10 SOLID FUELS	1.6	-8.9	5.6	-1.1	6.9	5.9	-5.8	3.8	1.1
11 LIQUID FUELS	29.8	-14.1	-14.1	235.5	23.5	20.7	-2.5	71.0	15.9
CONSUMPTION									
12 TOTAL	8.1	-1.4	6.0	3.8	3.8	7.7	1.4	5.1	4.1
13 TOTAL - ALTERNATIVE HYDRO	8.8	-0.7	5.4	3.6	3.7	6.2	2.2	4.5	4.0
14 SOLID FUELS	5.3	-3.1	4.5	-5.9	-7.1	2.8	-0.6	-3.5	-0.2
15 LIQUID FUELS	19.9	2.0	8.7	12.1	5.3	5.6	7.2	7.6	7.8
16 NATURAL GAS	13.8	1.7	6.8	15.5	22.8	20.8	5.3	19.7	10.9
17 HYDROELECTRIC POWER	17.0	4.3	6.4	7.4	7.0	3.0	8.1	5.8	6.7
18 ADDENDUM - TOTAL ELECTRICITY	17.3	4.7	5.9	8.1	6.8	5.2	8.4	6.7	7.0
19 POPULATION	1.9	1.2	1.5	2.8	2.6	1.8	1.4	2.4	1.8
20 TOTAL PER CAPITA PRODUCTION	7.0	-1.5	3.0	8.7	5.8	10.1	1.1	8.2	4.3
PER CAPITA CONSUMPTION									
21 TOTAL	6.1	-2.6	4.4	1.0	1.1	5.8	-	2.6	2.3
22 TOTAL - ALTERNATIVE HYDRO	6.8	-1.8	3.9	0.9	1.1	4.3	0.8	2.1	2.2
23 SOLID FUELS	3.4	-4.3	2.9	-8.4	-9.5	1.0	-2.0	-5.8	-2.0
24 LIQUID FUELS	17.7	0.8	7.1	9.1	2.6	3.7	5.7	5.1	5.9
25 NATURAL GAS	11.7	0.5	5.2	12.5	19.6	18.7	3.8	16.9	9.0
26 HYDROELECTRIC POWER	14.9	3.1	4.8	4.5	4.2	1.1	6.6	3.3	4.8
27 ADDENDUM - TOTAL ELECTRICITY	15.1	3.5	4.3	5.2	4.1	3.3	6.9	4.2	5.1
UNITED STATES									
PRODUCTION									
1 TOTAL	3.4	-2.1	4.3	2.6	1.4	3.5	-0.4	2.5	2.1
2 SOLID FUELS	1.1	-4.7	3.0	-2.6	-2.4	3.9	-2.9	-0.4	-0.2
3 LIQUID FUELS	7.6	1.9	4.4	5.0	0.9	2.3	3.6	2.7	3.5
4 NATURAL GAS	12.5	2.2	8.5	8.4	6.4	4.3	5.2	6.4	6.6
5 HYDROELECTRIC POWER	10.1	2.6	6.5	2.9	5.1	5.7	4.9	4.6	5.2
IMPORTS									
6 TOTAL	7.7	-7.1	14.8	8.3	8.2	7.0	-2.8	7.8	6.3
7 SOLID FUELS	-	-5.0	0.5	-10.8	-3.1	-6.5	-3.5	-6.9	-3.6
8 LIQUID FUELS	8.2	-7.3	15.4	8.4	7.5	6.2	-2.8	7.4	6.2
EXPORTS									
9 TOTAL	5.1	-0.1	-0.5	8.9	-8.2	3.7	1.5	1.2	0.8
10 SOLID FUELS	0.6	-5.8	7.3	12.9	-7.0	6.2	-3.9	3.7	2.2
11 LIQUID FUELS	8.7	2.5	-5.6	2.8	-10.5	-4.5	4.3	-4.2	-2.0
CONSUMPTION									
12 TOTAL	3.4	-2.2	5.0	2.7	2.5	4.0	-0.5	3.0	2.4
13 TOTAL - ALTERNATIVE HYDRO	3.4	-2.1	4.9	2.6	2.5	3.9	-0.5	3.0	2.4
14 SOLID FUELS	1.2	-4.6	2.8	-3.8	-1.9	3.7	-2.9	-0.7	-0.4
15 LIQUID FUELS	7.8	1.5	6.5	5.6	2.7	3.5	3.4	3.9	4.5
16 NATURAL GAS	12.5	2.2	8.4	8.4	6.7	4.7	5.2	6.6	6.7
17 HYDROELECTRIC POWER	9.8	2.6	6.3	3.3	5.0	5.0	4.8	4.4	5.1
18 ADDENDUM - TOTAL ELECTRICITY	10.3	1.9	8.8	10.2	6.0	6.4	4.4	7.5	6.9
19 POPULATION	1.3	0.7	1.3	1.7	1.7	1.5	0.9	1.6	1.3
20 TOTAL PER CAPITA PRODUCTION	2.1	-2.8	3.0	0.9	-0.3	2.0	-1.3	0.8	0.8
PER CAPITA CONSUMPTION									
21 TOTAL	2.1	-2.9	3.6	0.9	0.8	2.4	-1.4	1.4	1.1
22 TOTAL - ALTERNATIVE HYDRO	2.1	-2.9	3.6	0.8	0.7	2.4	-1.3	1.3	1.1
23 SOLID FUELS	-0.1	-5.3	1.5	-5.4	-3.6	2.2	-3.7	-2.3	-1.7
24 LIQUID FUELS	6.5	0.8	5.1	3.8	0.9	2.0	2.5	2.2	3.2
25 NATURAL GAS	11.1	1.4	7.0	6.6	4.9	3.1	4.3	4.9	5.3
26 HYDROELECTRIC POWER	8.5	1.9	4.9	1.5	3.2	3.5	3.8	2.7	3.8
27 ADDENDUM - TOTAL ELECTRICITY	8.9	1.1	7.4	8.3	4.2	4.8	3.5	5.8	5.5
WESTERN EUROPE									
PRODUCTION									
1 TOTAL	3.4	-0.3	-1.3	2.4	-0.2	0.4	0.8	0.8	0.2
2 SOLID FUELS	3.4	-0.4	-1.5	1.8	-1.3	-0.7	0.8	-0.1	-0.2
3 LIQUID FUELS	-0.1	9.7	14.0	18.8	10.2	6.3	6.6	11.6	10.7

Table XIII. AVERAGE ANNUAL PERCENTAGE RATES OF CHANGE IN TOTAL AND PER CAPITA ENERGY PRODUCTION, TRADE, AND CONSUMPTION, SELECTED PERIODS, 1925-1965

Region, country, indicator	1925-29	1929-38	1938-50	1950-55	1955-60	1960-65	1925-38	1950-65	1925-65
	(1)	(2)	(3)	(4)	(5)	(6)	(7)	(8)	(9)
WESTERN EUROPE (CONTINUED)									
PRODUCTION (CONTINUED)									
4 NATURAL GAS	6.5	8.7	42.3	33.3	17.3	10.5	8.0	20.0	22.0
5 HYDROELECTRIC POWER	8.5	4.9	4.4	7.7	7.5	5.0	6.0	6.7	5.8
IMPORTS									
6 TOTAL	6.8	-0.5	1.2	13.9	6.6	11.0	1.7	10.5	4.7
7 SOLID FUELS	5.9	-3.4	-2.8	10.0	-4.9	1.0	-0.6	1.9	-0.4
8 LIQUID FUELS	10.8	7.1	5.2	16.1	10.7	12.8	8.2	13.2	9.1
EXPORTS									
9 TOTAL	5.2	-3.3	-2.6	9.2	0.7	3.5	-0.8	4.4	0.6
10 SOLID FUELS	5.3	-3.5	-4.3	2.8	-5.8	-3.9	-0.9	-2.4	-2.5
11 LIQUID FUELS	-4.0	10.7	15.7	25.1	7.9	7.7	5.9	13.3	11.5
CONSUMPTION									
12 TOTAL	3.9	0.3	-0.5	5.1	2.6	5.6	1.4	4.4	1.9
13 TOTAL - ALTERNATIVE HYDRO	3.9	0.4	-0.3	4.9	2.7	5.4	1.5	4.3	2.0
14 SOLID FUELS	3.6	-0.2	-1.2	2.9	-1.3	-0.1	1.0	0.5	0.1
15 LIQUID FUELS	11.8	7.0	4.3	14.5	12.1	13.9	8.4	13.5	9.0
16 NATURAL GAS	6.5	8.7	42.8	32.2	17.3	11.5	8.0	20.0	22.2
17 HYDROELECTRIC POWER	8.3	4.9	4.5	7.5	7.7	4.9	6.0	6.7	5.8
18 ADDENDUM - TOTAL ELECTRICITY	8.7	5.8	3.6	9.4	7.9	7.7	6.6	8.3	6.3
19 POPULATION	0.7	0.6	-	0.7	0.8	1.0	0.6	0.8	0.5
20 TOTAL PER CAPITA PRODUCTION	2.7	-0.9	-1.3	1.7	-1.0	-0.6	0.2	-	-0.3
PER CAPITA CONSUMPTION									
21 TOTAL	3.3	-0.4	-0.4	4.3	1.7	4.6	0.7	3.5	1.4
22 TOTAL - ALTERNATIVE HYDRO	3.2	-0.2	-0.3	4.2	1.9	4.3	0.8	3.5	1.5
23 SOLID FUELS	2.9	-0.8	-1.2	2.2	-2.1	-1.1	0.3	-0.4	-0.4
24 LIQUID FUELS	11.1	6.3	4.3	13.7	11.2	12.8	7.7	12.5	8.5
25 NATURAL GAS	5.8	8.0	42.8	31.2	16.3	10.4	7.3	19.0	21.5
26 HYDROELECTRIC POWER	7.6	4.3	4.5	6.7	6.8	3.9	5.3	5.8	5.3
27 ADDENDUM - TOTAL ELECTRICITY	7.9	5.1	3.6	8.6	7.0	6.6	6.0	7.4	5.8
EUROPEAN ECONOMIC COMMUNITY (EEC)									
PRODUCTION									
1 TOTAL	5.0	0.5	-2.5	3.5	0.7	0.1	1.9	1.4	0.4
2 SOLID FUELS	5.0	0.5	-2.7	2.7	-0.8	-1.1	1.8	0.3	-0.1
3 LIQUID FUELS	4.6	14.7	9.9	21.7	17.1	6.2	11.5	14.8	12.2
4 NATURAL GAS	-	10.4	38.2	41.7	17.6	11.0	7.1	22.8	21.7
5 HYDROELECTRIC POWER	9.4	5.4	3.2	8.1	7.7	1.2	6.6	5.6	5.2
IMPORTS									
6 TOTAL	6.4	-1.6	-0.4	16.4	7.4	13.1	0.8	12.2	4.6
7 SOLID FUELS	5.5	-4.4	-4.5	12.4	-2.1	1.8	-1.5	3.8	-0.5
8 LIQUID FUELS	14.4	9.2	4.5	18.9	11.2	15.5	10.8	15.2	10.5
EXPORTS									
9 TOTAL	6.3	-1.2	-0.9	10.2	1.4	3.6	1.0	5.0	1.9
10 SOLID FUELS	6.2	-1.5	-2.7	4.7	-3.9	-3.6	0.8	-1.0	-0.9
11 LIQUID FUELS	17.3	18.7	17.1	23.7	7.8	8.5	18.3	13.1	16.0
CONSUMPTION									
12 TOTAL	5.2	0.2	-2.2	6.3	3.6	6.9	1.8	5.6	1.9
13 TOTAL - ALTERNATIVE HYDRO	5.2	0.4	-2.1	6.1	3.7	6.4	1.8	5.4	1.9
14 SOLID FUELS	5.0	-0.2	-2.9	4.0	-0.5	-0.2	1.4	1.1	-0.1
15 LIQUID FUELS	13.0	8.5	3.2	16.8	13.6	16.7	9.9	15.7	9.9
16 NATURAL GAS	-	10.4	38.9	39.9	17.6	11.4	7.1	22.4	21.7
17 HYDROELECTRIC POWER	9.4	5.5	3.1	7.7	8.1	1.5	6.6	5.8	5.3
18 ADDENDUM - TOTAL ELECTRICITY	10.9	5.6	1.6	9.5	8.2	7.3	7.2	8.3	5.9
19 POPULATION	0.7	0.6	-0.6	0.8	0.9	1.1	0.6	1.0	0.4
20 TOTAL PER CAPITA PRODUCTION	4.3	-	-1.9	2.7	-0.2	-1.0	1.3	0.5	-
PER CAPITA CONSUMPTION									
21 TOTAL	4.6	-0.3	-1.6	5.5	2.6	5.7	1.2	4.6	1.6
22 TOTAL - ALTERNATIVE HYDRO	4.5	-0.2	-1.5	5.3	2.7	5.2	1.2	4.4	1.6
23 SOLID FUELS	4.3	-0.8	-2.3	3.2	-1.4	-1.3	0.8	0.1	-0.4
24 LIQUID FUELS	12.3	7.9	3.8	15.9	12.6	15.4	9.2	14.6	9.5
25 NATURAL GAS	-0.7	9.7	39.8	38.8	16.5	10.1	6.4	21.2	21.3
26 HYDROELECTRIC POWER	8.6	4.9	3.8	6.9	7.1	0.4	6.0	4.8	4.9
27 ADDENDUM - TOTAL ELECTRICITY	10.2	5.0	2.2	8.6	7.2	6.1	6.6	7.3	5.5
BELGIUM-LUXEMBOURG									
PRODUCTION									
1 TOTAL	3.9	1.0	-0.7	1.9	-5.6	-2.4	1.9	-2.1	-0.4
2 SOLID FUELS	3.9	1.0	-0.7	1.9	-5.6	-2.5	1.9	-2.1	-0.4
3 LIQUID FUELS	*	*	*	*	*	*	*	*	*
4 NATURAL GAS	*	*	*	41.7	-2.6	2.4	*	12.2	*
5 HYDROELECTRIC POWER	-	9.2	3.2	15.6	7.9	43.8	6.3	21.5	10.7

Table XIII. AVERAGE ANNUAL PERCENTAGE RATES OF CHANGE IN TOTAL AND PER CAPITA ENERGY PRODUCTION, TRADE, AND CONSUMPTION, SELECTED PERIODS, 1925-1965

Region, country, indicator	1925-29	1929-38	1938-50	1950-55	1955-60	1960-65	1925-38	1950-65	1925-65
	(1)	(2)	(3)	(4)	(5)	(6)	(7)	(8)	(9)
BELGIUM-LUXEMBOURG (CONTINUED)									
IMPORTS									
6 TOTAL	7.3	-7.0	-1.2	20.3	5.2	12.1	-2.8	12.3	3.1
7 SOLID FUELS	7.4	-8.8	-5.2	16.1	2.0	6.1	-4.1	7.9	-0.1
8 LIQUID FUELS	5.8	10.7	7.1	23.8	7.2	14.7	9.2	15.1	10.7
EXPORTS									
9 TOTAL	6.5	3.4	-5.4	26.9	-9.0	1.6	4.4	5.5	1.7
10 SOLID FUELS	6.6	2.8	-5.5	21.5	-17.9	-4.6	3.9	-1.6	-1.1
11 LIQUID FUELS	-25.5	57.9	-4.1	65.6	6.4	5.7	25.3	23.1	14.9
CONSUMPTION									
12 TOTAL	4.9	-2.1	-	3.3	1.0	5.9	-	3.4	1.2
13 TOTAL - ALTERNATIVE HYDRO	4.9	-2.1	-	3.3	1.0	6.1	-	3.4	1.3
14 SOLID FUELS	4.8	-2.4	-0.6	1.0	-1.1	0.6	-0.2	0.2	-0.2
15 LIQUID FUELS	6.6	6.9	8.5	17.9	8.2	16.2	6.8	14.0	9.9
16 NATURAL GAS	*	*	*	62.7	-5.5	5.4	*	17.5	*
17 HYDROELECTRIC POWER	-	10.5	8.0	12.4	-0.8	55.1	7.1	20.0	12.1
18 ADDENDUM - TOTAL ELECTRICITY	15.5	4.0	4.0	6.9	5.2	6.1	7.4	6.1	5.9
19 POPULATION	0.9	0.5	0.2	0.5	0.6	0.7	0.6	0.6	0.5
20 TOTAL PER CAPITA PRODUCTION	3.0	0.6	-0.9	1.4	-6.2	-3.0	1.3	-2.6	-0.8
PER CAPITA CONSUMPTION									
21 TOTAL	4.0	-2.6	-0.3	2.7	0.4	5.2	-0.6	2.7	0.7
22 TOTAL - ALTERNATIVE HYDRO	4.0	-2.6	-0.3	2.7	0.4	5.3	-0.6	2.8	0.8
23 SOLID FUELS	4.0	-2.8	-0.8	0.4	-1.7	-0.1	-0.8	-0.5	-0.7
24 LIQUID FUELS	5.7	6.4	8.2	17.2	7.5	15.4	6.2	13.3	9.4
25 NATURAL GAS	*	*	*	61.8	-6.1	4.7	*	16.8	*
26 HYDROELECTRIC POWER	-0.8	10.0	7.8	11.8	-1.4	54.0	6.5	19.3	11.5
27 ADDENDUM - TOTAL ELECTRICITY	14.5	3.5	3.8	6.4	4.5	5.4	6.8	5.4	5.4
FRANCE									
PRODUCTION									
1 TOTAL	3.5	-1.5	1.0	2.5	2.5	0.3	-	1.7	0.9
2 SOLID FUELS	3.4	-1.6	0.8	1.8	0.3	-1.6	-0.1	0.1	0.3
3 LIQUID FUELS	3.1	0.3	6.1	40.5	19.8	8.4	1.1	22.2	10.1
4 NATURAL GAS	*	*	*	2.2	61.9	12.1	*	22.9	*
5 HYDROELECTRIC POWER	11.2	5.2	3.8	9.7	9.6	2.8	7.0	7.3	6.1
IMPORTS									
6 TOTAL	5.6	-1.7	0.2	9.0	3.8	10.9	0.5	7.9	3.1
7 SOLID FUELS	4.8	-5.1	-4.0	3.5	-1.0	1.9	-2.2	1.5	-1.4
8 LIQUID FUELS	12.8	11.2	4.9	11.8	5.5	13.1	11.7	10.1	9.0
EXPORTS									
9 TOTAL	16.0	-7.1	11.3	15.3	-5.0	6.8	-0.6	5.4	5.1
10 SOLID FUELS	16.2	-12.0	5.6	23.2	-24.4	-8.8	-4.2	-5.3	-1.8
11 LIQUID FUELS	12.5	22.0	16.3	10.8	3.4	8.7	19.0	7.6	13.8
CONSUMPTION									
12 TOTAL	4.3	-1.5	0.3	3.9	4.3	6.0	0.3	4.7	1.9
13 TOTAL - ALTERNATIVE HYDRO	4.5	-1.3	0.4	3.9	4.5	5.5	0.5	4.6	2.0
14 SOLID FUELS	4.0	-2.6	-0.5	1.1	1.4	-0.6	-0.6	0.6	-0.1
15 LIQUID FUELS	9.9	10.2	4.2	12.0	7.9	14.2	10.1	11.3	8.8
16 NATURAL GAS	*	*	*	5.7	56.3	12.8	*	23.0	*
17 HYDROELECTRIC POWER	11.5	5.0	3.4	9.3	9.6	3.3	6.9	7.4	6.0
18 ADDENDUM - TOTAL ELECTRICITY	8.9	4.2	4.0	8.3	7.8	7.6	5.6	7.9	6.0
19 POPULATION	0.3	0.1	0.1	0.8	1.0	1.4	0.2	1.1	0.5
20 TOTAL PER CAPITA PRODUCTION	3.2	-1.5	0.8	1.6	1.5	-1.1	-0.2	0.7	0.5
PER CAPITA CONSUMPTION									
21 TOTAL	4.0	-1.6	0.2	3.0	3.3	4.5	0.1	3.6	1.4
22 TOTAL - ALTERNATIVE HYDRO	4.1	-1.3	0.2	3.1	3.4	4.1	0.3	3.5	1.5
23 SOLID FUELS	3.7	-2.6	-0.7	0.3	0.4	-2.0	-0.7	-0.5	-0.6
24 LIQUID FUELS	9.6	10.1	4.1	11.1	6.8	12.7	10.0	10.1	8.2
25 NATURAL GAS	*	*	*	4.8	54.7	11.2	*	21.7	*
26 HYDROELECTRIC POWER	11.2	4.9	3.3	8.4	8.5	1.9	6.8	6.2	5.5
27 ADDENDUM - TOTAL ELECTRICITY	8.5	4.1	3.9	7.4	6.7	6.1	5.5	6.8	5.5
GERMANY									
PRODUCTION									
1 TOTAL	5.2	0.8					2.1		
2 SOLID FUELS	5.2	0.7					2.1		
3 LIQUID FUELS	6.9	20.5					16.1		
4 NATURAL GAS	*	*					*		
5 HYDROELECTRIC POWER	5.7	8.3					7.5		
IMPORTS									
6 TOTAL	6.5	0.7					2.5		

Table XIII. AVERAGE ANNUAL PERCENTAGE RATES OF CHANGE IN TOTAL AND PER CAPITA ENERGY PRODUCTION, TRADE, AND CONSUMPTION, SELECTED PERIODS, 1925-1965

Region, country, indicator	1925-29	1929-38	1938-50	1950-55	1955-60	1960-65	1925-38	1950-65	1925-65
	(1)	(2)	(3)	(4)	(5)	(6)	(7)	(8)	(9)
GERMANY (CONTINUED)									
IMPORTS (CONTINUED)									
7 SOLID FUELS	2.3	-3.0					-1.4		
8 LIQUID FUELS	21.9	6.5					11.0		
EXPORTS									
9 TOTAL	4.7	-1.8					0.2		
10 SOLID FUELS	4.7	-1.8					0.2		
11 LIQUID FUELS	26.8	2.4					9.3		
CONSUMPTION									
12 TOTAL	5.3	1.3					2.5		
13 TOTAL - ALTERNATIVE HYDRO	5.3	1.4					2.5		
14 SOLID FUELS	5.1	1.1					2.3		
15 LIQUID FUELS	20.9	7.5					11.5		
16 NATURAL GAS	*	*					*		
17 HYDROELECTRIC POWER	5.3	8.8					7.7		
18 ADDENDUM - TOTAL ELECTRICITY	10.9	6.4					7.8		
19 POPULATION	0.6	0.6					0.6		
20 TOTAL PER CAPITA PRODUCTION	4.5	0.1					1.5		
PER CAPITA CONSUMPTION									
21 TOTAL	4.7	0.6					1.9		
22 TOTAL - ALTERNATIVE HYDRO	4.6	0.7					1.9		
23 SOLID FUELS	4.5	0.5					1.7		
24 LIQUID FUELS	20.2	6.9					10.8		
25 NATURAL GAS	*	*					*		
26 HYDROELECTRIC POWER	4.6	8.1					7.0		
27 ADDENDUM - TOTAL ELECTRICITY	10.3	5.8					7.1		
GERMANY, FEDERAL REPUBLIC									
PRODUCTION									
1 TOTAL				3.8	-	0.1		1.3	
2 SOLID FUELS				3.4	-0.5	-0.7		0.7	
3 LIQUID FUELS				23.0	12.1	7.3		13.9	
4 NATURAL GAS				57.8	8.3	28.5		30.0	
5 HYDROELECTRIC POWER				6.8	1.6	3.4		3.9	
IMPORTS									
6 TOTAL				36.0	13.0	17.1		21.6	
7 SOLID FUELS				48.6	-7.4	0.8		11.5	
8 LIQUID FUELS				28.6	24.7	19.9		24.4	
EXPORTS									
9 TOTAL				-	1.2	-1.5		-0.1	
10 SOLID FUELS				-0.8	-0.3	-4.1		-1.8	
11 LIQUID FUELS				58.9	24.6	12.8		30.7	
CONSUMPTION									
12 TOTAL				7.2	2.4	6.0		5.2	
13 TOTAL - ALTERNATIVE HYDRO				7.0	2.4	5.8		5.1	
14 SOLID FUELS				6.1	-1.0	-		1.7	
15 LIQUID FUELS				22.9	23.6	19.3		21.9	
16 NATURAL GAS				107.6	8.0	31.5		43.4	
17 HYDROELECTRIC POWER				5.8	5.4	2.7		4.6	
18 ADDENDUM - TOTAL ELECTRICITY				11.1	9.0	7.0		9.0	
19 POPULATION				0.9	1.1	1.3		1.1	
20 TOTAL PER CAPITA PRODUCTION				2.9	-1.1	-1.2		0.2	
PER CAPITA CONSUMPTION									
21 TOTAL				6.2	1.2	4.6		4.0	
22 TOTAL - ALTERNATIVE HYDRO				6.1	1.2	4.5		3.9	
23 SOLID FUELS				5.2	-2.1	-1.3		0.5	
24 LIQUID FUELS				21.8	22.2	17.8		20.6	
25 NATURAL GAS				105.7	6.8	29.9		41.8	
26 HYDROELECTRIC POWER				4.9	4.2	1.4		3.5	
27 ADDENDUM - TOTAL ELECTRICITY				10.0	7.8	5.7		7.8	
ITALY									
PRODUCTION									
1 TOTAL	5.4	7.9	2.7	17.6	12.4	1.6	7.1	10.3	6.9
2 SOLID FUELS	-3.8	14.9	-2.6	-0.5	-4.3	-5.7	8.8	-3.5	0.6
3 LIQUID FUELS	-6.9	9.0	-2.2	92.0	51.1	2.0	3.8	43.6	15.2
4 NATURAL GAS	-	10.4	32.8	48.0	12.2	3.9	7.1	19.9	19.2
5 HYDROELECTRIC POWER	9.8	4.4	3.7	7.5	8.1	-1.4	6.0	4.6	4.8
IMPORTS									
6 TOTAL	9.1	-0.3	0.1	17.6	8.9	15.5	2.5	13.9	5.9
7 SOLID FUELS	8.6	-2.0	-3.1	4.7	-0.2	0.7	1.1	1.7	0.1
8 LIQUID FUELS	13.0	8.3	6.0	26.9	11.7	18.0	9.8	18.7	11.9

Table XIII. AVERAGE ANNUAL PERCENTAGE RATES OF CHANGE IN TOTAL AND PER CAPITA ENERGY PRODUCTION, TRADE, AND CONSUMPTION, SELECTED PERIODS, 1925-1965

Region, country, indicator	1925-29	1929-38	1938-50	1950-55	1955-60	1960-65	1925-38	1950-65	1925-65
	(1)	(2)	(3)	(4)	(5)	(6)	(7)	(8)	(9)
ITALY (CONTINUED)									
EXPORTS									
9 TOTAL	-	17.7	14.6	44.0	7.4	17.9	12.0	22.2	16.5
10 SOLID FUELS	-9.9	-7.1	11.0	2.1	9.5	-	-8.0	3.8	1.8
11 LIQUID FUELS	89.9	30.8	14.9	45.2	7.4	18.1	46.7	22.6	27.4
CONSUMPTION									
12 TOTAL	8.8	0.6	-0.2	14.9	9.2	11.5	3.1	11.9	5.2
13 TOTAL - ALTERNATIVE HYDRO	7.4	0.9	0.2	11.4	8.3	9.1	2.9	9.6	4.5
14 SOLID FUELS	8.3	-1.1	-3.2	4.3	-0.5	0.3	1.7	1.3	0.1
15 LIQUID FUELS	12.5	7.8	3.9	23.7	13.7	17.5	9.2	18.2	10.8
16 NATURAL GAS	-	10.4	32.8	48.0	12.2	3.9	7.1	19.9	19.2
17 HYDROELECTRIC POWER	9.5	4.3	3.6	7.3	8.0	-1.2	5.9	4.6	4.7
18 ADDENDUM - TOTAL ELECTRICITY	12.2	4.6	4.0	8.9	8.0	7.4	6.9	8.1	6.5
19 POPULATION	0.9	0.8	0.7	0.6	0.6	0.8	0.8	0.7	0.7
20 TOTAL PER CAPITA PRODUCTION	4.4	7.0	2.0	16.9	11.7	0.8	6.2	9.6	6.2
PER CAPITA CONSUMPTION									
21 TOTAL	7.8	-0.2	-0.9	14.2	8.6	10.6	2.2	11.1	4.5
22 TOTAL - ALTERNATIVE HYDRO	6.5	0.1	-0.5	10.7	7.6	8.2	2.0	8.8	3.7
23 SOLID FUELS	7.3	-1.9	-3.9	3.7	-1.1	-0.4	0.9	0.7	-0.6
24 LIQUID FUELS	11.5	6.9	3.1	23.0	13.0	16.6	8.3	17.4	10.0
25 NATURAL GAS	-0.9	9.5	31.8	47.2	11.5	3.1	6.2	19.2	18.3
26 HYDROELECTRIC POWER	8.6	3.5	2.9	6.7	7.4	-1.9	5.0	3.9	4.0
27 ADDENDUM - TOTAL ELECTRICITY	11.2	3.7	3.3	8.3	7.4	6.6	6.0	7.4	5.7
NETHERLANDS									
PRODUCTION									
1 TOTAL	12.8	1.7	-0.1	0.5	2.9	1.9	5.0	1.8	2.2
2 SOLID FUELS	12.8	1.7	-0.8	-0.5	0.9	-1.7	5.0	-0.5	1.2
3 LIQUID FUELS	*	*	*	7.8	13.4	4.5	*	8.5	*
4 NATURAL GAS	*	*	*	77.3	19.6	39.0	*	43.4	*
5 HYDROELECTRIC POWER	*	*	*	*	*	*	*	*	*
IMPORTS									
6 TOTAL	4.5	-0.3	1.7	16.5	6.7	7.1	1.1	10.0	4.5
7 SOLID FUELS	3.8	-2.3	-4.5	12.6	-2.4	-1.0	-0.5	2.9	-0.5
8 LIQUID FUELS	10.1	8.6	9.4	18.7	9.7	8.7	9.1	12.3	10.4
EXPORTS									
9 TOTAL	15.3	0.6	-1.0	20.9	9.2	-0.2	4.9	9.7	4.8
10 SOLID FUELS	15.2	0.6	-12.9	20.1	10.8	1.3	4.9	10.5	1.1
11 LIQUID FUELS	17.8	-0.4	47.8	21.2	8.8	-0.6	4.9	9.4	18.1
CONSUMPTION									
12 TOTAL	6.5	0.5	2.5	5.3	3.6	7.8	2.3	5.6	3.6
13 TOTAL - ALTERNATIVE HYDRO	6.5	0.5	2.4	5.3	3.6	7.8	2.3	5.6	3.6
14 SOLID FUELS	6.3	-0.3	1.6	2.5	-2.6	-2.3	1.7	-0.8	0.7
15 LIQUID FUELS	8.6	7.1	5.9	12.9	12.8	13.9	7.6	13.2	9.1
16 NATURAL GAS	*	*	*	7.4	17.6	38.7	*	20.5	*
17 HYDROELECTRIC POWER	*	-2.2	*	*	43.1	-22.3	*	*	*
18 ADDENDUM - TOTAL ELECTRICITY	12.4	9.7	5.9	9.1	7.9	8.5	10.5	8.5	8.4
19 POPULATION	1.4	1.2	1.3	1.2	1.3	1.4	1.3	1.3	1.3
20 TOTAL PER CAPITA PRODUCTION	11.3	0.5	-1.4	-0.7	1.6	0.5	3.7	0.5	0.9
PER CAPITA CONSUMPTION									
21 TOTAL	5.0	-0.7	1.2	4.0	2.3	6.4	1.0	4.2	2.2
22 TOTAL - ALTERNATIVE HYDRO	5.0	-0.7	1.2	4.0	2.3	6.4	1.0	4.2	2.2
23 SOLID FUELS	4.8	-1.5	0.3	1.2	-3.9	-3.6	0.4	-2.1	-0.6
24 LIQUID FUELS	7.1	5.8	4.6	11.6	11.3	12.4	6.2	11.7	7.7
25 NATURAL GAS	*	*	*	6.1	16.1	36.8	*	19.0	*
26 HYDROELECTRIC POWER	*	-3.4	*	*	41.2	-23.3	*	*	*
27 ADDENDUM - TOTAL ELECTRICITY	10.9	8.4	4.6	7.7	6.5	7.0	9.1	7.1	7.0
EUROPEAN FREE TRADE ASSOCIATION (EFTA)									
PRODUCTION									
1 TOTAL	1.5	-1.3	-0.1	1.0	-2.2	-	-0.4	-0.4	-0.3
2 SOLID FUELS	1.5	-1.4	-0.4	0.6	-2.6	-0.7	-0.5	-0.9	-0.6
3 LIQUID FUELS	-4.2	0.9	21.5	15.3	-7.1	2.1	-0.7	3.0	7.0
4 NATURAL GAS	*	*	*	10.0	15.3	4.3	*	9.8	*
5 HYDROELECTRIC POWER	7.2	4.1	5.4	6.3	6.9	7.8	5.0	7.0	5.9
IMPORTS									
6 TOTAL	7.6	1.8	2.7	12.3	5.3	7.6	3.5	8.4	5.1
7 SOLID FUELS	7.5	-0.7	-0.4	8.2	-12.1	-3.5	1.8	-2.8	-0.6
8 LIQUID FUELS	7.8	5.2	5.1	14.3	10.1	8.7	6.0	11.0	7.6
EXPORTS									
9 TOTAL	4.2	-5.5	-5.7	6.5	-2.8	2.6	-2.6	2.1	-1.8

Table XIII. AVERAGE ANNUAL PERCENTAGE RATES OF CHANGE IN TOTAL AND PER CAPITA ENERGY PRODUCTION, TRADE, AND CONSUMPTION, SELECTED PERIODS, 1925-1965

Region, country, indicator	1925-29	1929-38	1938-50	1950-55	1955-60	1960-65	1925-38	1950-65	1925-65
	(1)	(2)	(3)	(4)	(5)	(6)	(7)	(8)	(9)
EUROPEAN FREE TRADE ASSOCIATION (EFTA) (CONTINUED)									
EXPORTS (CONTINUED)									
10 SOLID FUELS	4.4	-5.7	-7.0	-2.0	-13.8	-6.1	-2.7	-7.4	-5.8
11 LIQUID FUELS	-10.0	2.3	13.1	28.7	5.7	5.1	-1.6	12.7	7.9
CONSUMPTION									
12 TOTAL	1.9	0.4	1.3	3.8	0.7	3.5	0.9	2.6	1.7
13 TOTAL - ALTERNATIVE HYDRO	1.9	0.5	1.4	3.6	0.9	3.6	0.9	2.7	1.7
14 SOLID FUELS	1.4	-	0.7	1.8	-3.0	-0.7	0.4	-0.7	0.1
15 LIQUID FUELS	10.4	5.6	4.8	13.1	10.3	9.6	7.0	11.0	7.8
16 NATURAL GAS	*	*	*	10.0	15.3	10.5	*	11.9	*
17 HYDROELECTRIC POWER	6.9	4.0	5.9	6.0	6.8	7.7	4.9	6.8	5.9
18 ADDENDUM - TOTAL ELECTRICITY	4.4	5.8	6.3	8.9	7.2	7.5	5.4	7.9	6.6
19 POPULATION	0.4	0.4	0.6	0.4	0.6	0.8	0.4	0.6	0.5
20 TOTAL PER CAPITA PRODUCTION	1.2	-1.7	-0.7	0.6	-2.8	-0.8	-0.8	-1.0	-0.9
PER CAPITA CONSUMPTION									
21 TOTAL	1.5	-	0.7	3.4	0.1	2.6	0.5	2.0	1.1
22 TOTAL - ALTERNATIVE HYDRO	1.5	0.1	0.8	3.2	0.3	2.7	0.5	2.1	1.2
23 SOLID FUELS	1.1	-0.4	0.1	1.4	-3.6	-1.5	-	-1.3	-0.4
24 LIQUID FUELS	10.0	5.1	4.2	12.7	9.6	8.7	6.6	10.3	7.2
25 NATURAL GAS	*	*	*	9.6	14.7	9.6	*	11.3	*
26 HYDROELECTRIC POWER	6.5	3.5	5.2	5.6	6.2	6.8	4.4	6.2	5.3
27 ADDENDUM - TOTAL ELECTRICITY	4.1	5.4	5.7	8.5	6.6	6.6	5.0	7.2	6.0
AUSTRIA									
PRODUCTION									
1 TOTAL	4.6	0.6	8.5	12.3	-1.4	2.1	1.8	4.2	4.7
2 SOLID FUELS	4.4	-0.3	1.7	8.2	-2.2	-2.3	1.1	1.1	1.3
3 LIQUID FUELS	*	*	32.7	16.6	-7.8	3.1	*	3.5	*
4 NATURAL GAS	*	*	*	9.7	14.5	3.3	*	9.1	*
5 HYDROELECTRIC POWER	7.1	3.6	6.3	9.6	8.5	6.2	4.6	8.1	6.4
IMPORTS									
6 TOTAL	6.6	-5.0	1.9	0.4	6.4	2.2	-1.6	3.0	1.2
7 SOLID FUELS	6.1	-5.7	2.8	-1.1	-	-1.7	-2.2	-0.9	-0.3
8 LIQUID FUELS	16.8	4.1	-12.9	38.9	38.3	8.5	7.9	27.8	7.8
EXPORTS									
9 TOTAL	41.4	13.2	35.6	7.6	-5.0	-14.5	21.2	-4.4	14.7
10 SOLID FUELS	*	*	*	12.7	-	-12.9	*	-0.6	*
11 LIQUID FUELS	*	*	*	7.5	-6.4	-25.0	*	-8.9	*
CONSUMPTION									
12 TOTAL	6.0	-3.4	3.4	7.3	2.5	3.6	-0.6	4.5	2.5
13 TOTAL - ALTERNATIVE HYDRO	5.4	-3.0	3.4	7.0	2.8	3.2	-0.5	4.3	2.5
14 SOLID FUELS	5.7	-4.2	2.4	2.1	-0.9	-1.9	-1.3	-0.2	0.2
15 LIQUID FUELS	16.8	6.0	4.4	29.9	4.3	11.5	9.2	14.7	9.7
16 NATURAL GAS	*	*	*	9.7	14.5	3.3	*	9.1	*
17 HYDROELECTRIC POWER	5.8	2.5	6.4	9.7	7.9	4.1	3.5	7.2	5.8
18 ADDENDUM - TOTAL ELECTRICITY	3.6	0.9	6.6	11.3	7.8	6.5	1.7	8.5	5.7
19 POPULATION	0.3	0.1	0.2	0.1	0.3	0.5	0.2	0.3	0.2
20 TOTAL PER CAPITA PRODUCTION	4.3	0.4	8.3	12.1	-1.7	1.6	1.6	3.9	4.4
PER CAPITA CONSUMPTION									
21 TOTAL	5.7	-3.6	3.2	7.2	2.2	3.1	-0.8	4.2	2.2
22 TOTAL - ALTERNATIVE HYDRO	5.0	-3.1	3.2	6.9	2.5	2.7	-0.7	4.0	2.2
23 SOLID FUELS	5.4	-4.4	2.2	2.0	-1.2	-2.4	-1.5	-0.5	-
24 LIQUID FUELS	16.4	5.8	4.1	29.7	4.0	10.9	9.0	14.4	9.5
25 NATURAL GAS	*	*	*	9.6	14.1	2.8	*	8.7	*
26 HYDROELECTRIC POWER	5.5	2.3	6.2	9.6	7.6	3.6	3.3	6.9	5.5
27 ADDENDUM - TOTAL ELECTRICITY	3.3	0.7	6.4	11.2	7.4	6.0	1.5	8.2	5.4
DENMARK									
PRODUCTION									
1 TOTAL	-5.6	3.6	10.5	-2.2	8.3	-3.1	0.6	0.9	3.6
2 SOLID FUELS	-5.6	3.6	10.5	-2.3	8.4	-3.1	0.6	0.9	3.6
3 LIQUID FUELS	*	*	*	*	*	*	*	*	*
4 NATURAL GAS	*	*	*	*	*	*	*	*	*
5 HYDROELECTRIC POWER	*	*	*	3.7	-7.8	4.6	*	-	*
IMPORTS									
6 TOTAL	8.3	0.9	2.0	7.6	1.4	9.8	3.1	6.2	3.9
7 SOLID FUELS	8.1	-0.2	0.5	5.1	-6.4	-4.4	2.3	-2.0	0.1
8 LIQUID FUELS	9.4	8.1	6.4	12.4	9.9	16.1	8.5	12.8	9.4
EXPORTS									
9 TOTAL	*	*	*	*	6.1	85.5	*	*	17.9
10 SOLID FUELS	*	*	*	*	8.4	8.4	*	*	*
11 LIQUID FUELS	*	*	*	*	45.4	121.6	*	*	17.8

Table XIII. AVERAGE ANNUAL PERCENTAGE RATES OF CHANGE IN TOTAL AND PER CAPITA ENERGY PRODUCTION, TRADE, AND CONSUMPTION, SELECTED PERIODS, 1925-1965

Region, country, indicator	1925-29	1929-38	1938-50	1950-55	1955-60	1960-65	1925-38	1950-65	1925-65
	(1)	(2)	(3)	(4)	(5)	(6)	(7)	(8)	(9)
DENMARK (CONTINUED)									
CONSUMPTION									
12 TOTAL	7.9	1.0	2.1	6.7	1.7	8.2	3.1	5.5	3.7
13 TOTAL - ALTERNATIVE HYDRO	7.9	1.0	2.2	6.5	1.8	8.6	3.1	5.6	3.7
14 SOLID FUELS	7.7	-0.1	1.0	4.4	-5.2	-4.3	2.2	-1.8	0.3
15 LIQUID FUELS	9.4	8.1	5.7	11.9	10.6	14.9	8.5	12.5	9.1
16 NATURAL GAS	*	*	*	*	*	*	*	*	*
17 HYDROELECTRIC POWER	15.0	-4.1	19.6	*	*	71.1	1.4	15.4	11.8
18 ADDENDUM - TOTAL ELECTRICITY	10.2	8.2	6.4	9.1	7.3	10.5	8.8	9.0	8.1
19 POPULATION	0.7	0.8	1.0	0.8	0.6	0.8	0.8	0.7	0.8
20 TOTAL PER CAPITA PRODUCTION	-6.3	2.7	9.4	-3.0	7.6	-3.8	-0.1	0.1	2.7
PER CAPITA CONSUMPTION									
21 TOTAL	7.2	0.2	1.1	5.9	1.1	7.4	2.3	4.8	2.8
22 TOTAL - ALTERNATIVE HYDRO	7.2	0.2	1.2	5.6	1.2	7.8	2.3	4.8	2.9
23 SOLID FUELS	7.0	-0.9	-	3.6	-5.8	-5.0	1.5	-2.5	-0.5
24 LIQUID FUELS	8.7	7.2	4.7	11.1	9.9	14.1	7.7	11.7	8.2
25 NATURAL GAS	*	*	*	*	*	*	*	*	*
26 HYDROELECTRIC POWER	14.2	-4.9	18.4	*	*	69.8	0.7	14.6	10.9
27 ADDENDUM - TOTAL ELECTRICITY	9.4	7.4	5.3	8.3	6.6	9.7	8.0	8.2	7.3
NORWAY									
PRODUCTION									
1 TOTAL	0.5	2.6	4.1	3.3	6.1	8.6	1.9	6.0	4.1
2 SOLID FUELS	-6.8	1.2	1.2	-4.1	2.3	-0.3	-1.3	-0.7	-0.4
3 LIQUID FUELS	*	*	*	*	*	*	*	*	*
4 NATURAL GAS	*	*	*	*	*	*	*	*	*
5 HYDROELECTRIC POWER	5.0	3.1	5.0	4.9	6.6	9.6	3.7	7.0	5.3
IMPORTS									
6 TOTAL	7.0	1.2	0.7	7.6	3.3	8.6	3.0	6.5	3.6
7 SOLID FUELS	6.7	-0.4	-3.7	-5.8	-4.7	-0.2	1.7	-3.6	-1.9
8 LIQUID FUELS	9.3	8.8	7.6	14.8	5.2	9.9	9.0	9.9	8.9
EXPORTS									
9 TOTAL	-11.8	-16.8	*	*	5.9	64.4	-15.3	*	7.1
10 SOLID FUELS	-11.8	-19.5	*	*	5.5	6.2	-17.2	*	1.0
11 LIQUID FUELS	*	*	*	*	8.4	133.4	*	*	*
CONSUMPTION									
12 TOTAL	5.4	1.8	1.6	5.1	4.6	5.7	2.9	5.1	3.3
13 TOTAL - ALTERNATIVE HYDRO	2.3	1.1	2.1	2.7	4.0	5.6	1.5	4.1	2.6
14 SOLID FUELS	5.0	0.1	-2.7	-6.8	-3.5	-1.2	1.6	-3.9	-1.8
15 LIQUID FUELS	9.3	8.7	6.6	14.6	5.8	5.0	8.9	8.4	8.0
16 NATURAL GAS	*	*	*	*	*	*	*	*	*
17 HYDROELECTRIC POWER	5.0	3.1	5.0	4.9	6.7	8.5	3.7	6.7	5.2
18 ADDENDUM - TOTAL ELECTRICITY	5.0	2.8	5.2	5.0	6.6	8.7	3.5	6.8	5.2
19 POPULATION	0.4	0.5	0.9	1.0	0.9	0.8	0.5	0.9	0.8
20 TOTAL PER CAPITA PRODUCTION	0.1	2.0	3.2	2.3	5.1	7.8	1.4	5.1	3.3
PER CAPITA ,CONSUMPTION									
21 TOTAL	4.9	1.3	0.7	4.1	3.7	4.9	2.4	4.2	2.6
22 TOTAL - ALTERNATIVE HYDRO	1.9	0.6	1.2	1.7	3.1	4.8	1.0	3.2	1.9
23 SOLID FUELS	4.5	-0.5	-3.6	-7.7	-4.4	-2.0	1.0	-4.7	-2.5
24 LIQUID FUELS	8.8	8.2	5.6	13.5	4.9	4.2	8.4	7.4	7.2
25 NATURAL GAS	*	*	*	*	*	*	*	*	*
26 HYDROELECTRIC POWER	4.5	2.6	4.1	3.9	5.8	7.7	3.2	5.8	4.4
27 ADDENDUM - TOTAL ELECTRICITY	4.5	2.2	4.3	4.0	5.7	7.8	2.9	5.8	4.4
PORTUGAL									
PRODUCTION									
1 TOTAL	12.6	4.7	3.8	5.0	6.3	1.5	7.1	4.2	5.0
2 SOLID FUELS	12.6	4.6	3.3	-0.8	2.7	-1.6	7.0	0.1	3.3
3 LIQUID FUELS	*	*	*	*	*	*	*	*	*
4 NATURAL GAS	*	*	*	*	*	*	*	*	*
5 HYDROELECTRIC POWER	12.9	6.3	10.8	31.6	12.5	5.1	8.3	15.9	11.9
IMPORTS									
6 TOTAL	4.8	1.1	2.7	8.3	3.8	7.3	2.2	6.4	3.9
7 SOLID FUELS	3.5	-	-2.8	-9.0	-5.2	9.7	1.1	-1.8	-1.2
8 LIQUID FUELS	16.1	6.5	12.2	15.9	5.3	6.7	9.4	9.2	10.2
EXPORTS									
9 TOTAL	-31.3	4.6	9.6	135.8	4.9	-8.7	-8.1	31.2	10.7
10 SOLID FUELS	-24.0	*	*	*	*	*	*	*	*
11 LIQUID FUELS	*	*	9.6	134.3	5.6	-8.7	-	31.2	13.8
CONSUMPTION									
12 TOTAL	8.9	2.8	1.7	6.2	4.3	7.8	4.7	6.1	4.3

Table XIII. AVERAGE ANNUAL PERCENTAGE RATES OF CHANGE IN TOTAL AND PER CAPITA ENERGY PRODUCTION, TRADE, AND CONSUMPTION, SELECTED PERIODS, 1925-1965

Region, country, indicator	1925-29	1929-38	1938-50	1950-55	1955-60	1960-65	1925-38	1950-65	1925-65
	(1)	(2)	(3)	(4)	(5)	(6)	(7)	(8)	(9)
PORTUGAL (CONTINUED)									
CONSUMPTION (CONTINUED)									
13 TOTAL - ALTERNATIVE HYDRO	8.9	2.9	2.1	8.5	5.2	7.1	4.7	6.9	4.7
14 SOLID FUELS	7.9	2.2	-1.1	-5.1	-0.1	3.9	3.9	-0.5	0.7
15 LIQUID FUELS	16.6	6.5	8.7	15.1	5.3	9.4	9.5	9.9	9.4
16 NATURAL GAS	*	*	*	*	*	*	*	*	*
17 HYDROELECTRIC POWER	12.9	6.3	10.8	31.6	12.5	7.3	8.3	16.7	12.1
18 ADDENDUM - TOTAL ELECTRICITY	18.9	6.6	6.8	14.9	11.5	7.2	10.2	11.2	9.6
19 POPULATION	1.2	1.3	0.9	0.5	0.5	0.9	1.2	0.7	0.9
20 TOTAL PER CAPITA PRODUCTION	11.3	3.4	2.9	4.4	5.7	0.6	5.8	3.5	4.1
PER CAPITA /CONSUMPTION									
21 TOTAL	7.7	1.6	0.8	5.6	3.7	6.8	3.4	5.4	3.3
22 TOTAL - ALTERNATIVE HYDRO	7.6	1.6	1.2	7.9	4.6	6.1	3.4	6.2	3.8
23 SOLID FUELS	6.7	0.9	-2.0	-5.6	-0.7	3.0	2.6	-1.2	-0.2
24 LIQUID FUELS	15.3	5.1	7.7	14.5	4.7	8.4	8.2	9.1	8.4
25 NATURAL GAS	*	*	*	*	*	*	*	*	*
26 HYDROELECTRIC POWER	11.6	5.0	9.9	30.9	11.8	6.3	7.0	15.9	11.1
27 ADDENDUM - TOTAL ELECTRICITY	17.5	5.3	5.9	14.3	10.9	6.2	8.9	10.4	8.6
SWEDEN									
PRODUCTION									
1 TOTAL	8.5	4.0	6.3	4.4	6.5	6.9	5.4	5.9	5.8
2 SOLID FUELS	9.9	0.9	-0.3	1.4	-3.0	-11.6	3.6	-4.6	-0.7
3 LIQUID FUELS	*	*	*	9.4	4.2	-11.3	*	0.4	*
4 NATURAL GAS	*	*	*	*	*	*	*	*	*
5 HYDROELECTRIC POWER	7.9	5.3	7.5	4.5	7.5	8.3	6.1	6.8	6.8
IMPORTS									
6 TOTAL	10.4	3.7	1.9	7.8	5.7	6.1	5.7	6.6	4.9
7 SOLID FUELS	10.2	2.3	-1.3	-3.5	-8.4	-3.7	4.7	-5.2	-0.9
8 LIQUID FUELS	12.4	11.9	8.9	17.1	10.3	7.5	12.1	11.6	10.9
EXPORTS									
9 TOTAL	4.4	17.6	6.2	-15.0	42.9	16.7	13.4	12.3	10.8
10 SOLID FUELS	*	*	*	2.1	-19.7	-	*	-6.4	*
11 LIQUID FUELS	-	22.9	1.2	-21.5	59.6	23.5	15.3	15.6	11.0
CONSUMPTION									
12 TOTAL	10.2	3.7	2.4	7.2	5.4	6.0	5.7	6.2	4.9
13 TOTAL - ALTERNATIVE HYDRO	7.8	3.4	3.1	5.2	4.9	5.8	4.7	5.3	4.5
14 SOLID FUELS	10.2	2.3	-1.3	-3.2	-8.0	-4.2	4.7	-5.2	-0.9
15 LIQUID FUELS	12.6	11.8	8.9	17.2	9.8	7.1	12.0	11.3	10.8
16 NATURAL GAS	*	*	*	*	*	*	*	*	*
17 HYDROELECTRIC POWER	7.8	5.4	7.4	4.9	6.8	8.5	6.1	6.7	6.7
18 ADDENDUM - TOTAL ELECTRICITY	7.8	5.7	6.8	6.7	6.5	7.5	6.3	6.9	6.7
19 POPULATION	0.3	0.3	0.9	0.7	0.6	0.7	0.3	0.7	0.6
20 TOTAL PER CAPITA PRODUCTION	8.2	3.6	5.3	3.6	5.8	6.2	5.0	5.2	5.2
PER CAPITA /CONSUMPTION									
21 TOTAL	9.9	3.4	1.5	6.5	4.8	5.3	5.3	5.5	4.2
22 TOTAL - ALTERNATIVE HYDRO	7.5	3.1	2.2	4.5	4.3	5.1	4.4	4.6	3.8
23 SOLID FUELS	9.9	1.9	-2.1	-3.9	-8.6	-4.8	4.3	-5.8	-1.5
24 LIQUID FUELS	12.3	11.4	7.9	16.3	9.2	6.4	11.7	10.6	10.1
25 NATURAL GAS	*	*	*	*	*	*	*	*	*
26 HYDROELECTRIC POWER	7.5	5.0	6.4	4.2	6.2	7.8	5.8	6.0	6.1
27 ADDFNDUM - TOTAL ELECTRICITY	7.5	5.3	5.9	5.9	5.8	6.8	6.0	6.2	6.0
SWITZERLAND									
PRODUCTION									
1 TOTAL	9.3	3.2	3.4	7.9	4.1	5.0	5.0	5.7	4.8
2 SOLID FUELS	-	-9.0	21.2	-19.7	-	-	-6.3	-7.1	0.9
3 LIQUID FUELS	*	*	*	*	*	*	*	*	*
4 NATURAL GAS	*	*	*	*	*	*	*	*	*
5 HYDROELECTRIC POWER	9.4	3.3	3.3	8.3	4.1	5.0	5.1	5.8	4.8
IMPORTS									
6 TOTAL	7.2	0.3	0.2	6.4	8.6	10.0	2.4	8.3	3.9
7 SOLID FUELS	6.4	-0.4	-2.2	0.7	-0.3	-9.6	1.6	-3.2	-1.3
8 LIQUID FUELS	15.2	5.2	7.7	14.0	14.8	15.6	8.2	14.8	10.5
EXPORTS									
9 TOTAL	11.8	5.0	-7.2	20.6	-4.0	19.7	7.0	11.5	4.1
10 SOLID FUELS	*	*	*	97.4	*	*	*	*	*
11 LIQUID FUELS	*	*	3.4	*	*	*	*	28.8	*
CONSUMPTION									
12 TOTAL	7.4	0.6	1.1	6.4	7.9	8.9	2.6	7.7	4.0
13 TOTAL - ALTERNATIVE HYDRO	5.8	0.5	1.6	5.0	5.4	6.8	2.1	5.7	3.3
14 SOLID FUELS	6.4	-0.4	-2.1	0.3	-0.1	-9.5	1.6	-3.2	-1.3

Table XIII. AVERAGE ANNUAL PERCENTAGE RATES OF CHANGE IN TOTAL AND PER CAPITA ENERGY PRODUCTION, TRADE, AND CONSUMPTION, SELECTED PERIODS, 1925-1965

Region, country, indicator	1925-29	1929-38	1938-50	1950-55	1955-60	1960-65	1925-38	1950-65	1925-65
	(1)	(2)	(3)	(4)	(5)	(6)	(7)	(8)	(9)
SWITZERLAND (CONTINUED)									
CONSUMPTION (CONTINUED)									
15 LIQUID FUELS	15.2	5.1	7.5	13.9	15.2	15.5	8.1	14.9	10.4
16 NATURAL GAS	*	*	*	*	*	*	*	*	*
17 HYDROELECTRIC POWER	8.9	2.9	4.9	7.6	4.6	5.0	4.7	5.7	5.1
18 ADDENDUM - TOTAL ELECTRICITY	8.9	2.9	5.0	7.3	4.8	5.5	4.7	5.9	5.2
19 POPULATION	0.4	0.4	0.9	1.2	1.5	2.1	0.4	1.6	1.0
20 TOTAL PER CAPITA PRODUCTION	8.8	2.7	2.5	6.7	2.6	2.8	4.6	4.0	3.7
PER CAPITA CONSUMPTION									
21 TOTAL	6.9	0.2	0.1	5.2	6.3	6.7	2.2	6.0	3.0
22 TOTAL - ALTERNATIVE HYDRO	5.4	-	0.6	3.8	3.9	4.6	1.7	4.1	2.3
23 SOLID FUELS	6.0	-0.9	-3.0	-0.9	-1.5	-11.4	1.2	-4.7	-2.3
24 LIQUID FUELS	14.8	4.7	6.5	12.6	13.5	13.1	7.7	13.1	9.3
25 NATURAL GAS	*	*	*	*	*	*	*	*	*
26 HYDROELECTRIC POWER	8.4	2.4	3.9	6.3	3.0	2.9	4.2	4.1	4.1
27 ADDENDUM - TOTAL ELECTRICITY	8.4	2.5	4.0	6.0	3.2	3.3	4.3	4.2	4.2
UNITED KINGDOM									
PRODUCTION									
1 TOTAL	1.5	-1.4	-0.4	0.5	-2.6	-0.6	-0.5	-0.9	-0.6
2 SOLID FUELS	1.5	-1.4	-0.4	0.5	-2.7	-0.6	-0.5	-0.9	-0.6
3 LIQUID FUELS	-4.2	-3.1	1.9	-0.9	-0.5	-10.7	-3.5	-4.2	-2.2
4 NATURAL GAS	*	*	*	64.4	45.8	19.1	*	41.8	*
5 HYDROELECTRIC POWER	67.4	22.0	3.4	2.8	13.0	8.1	34.5	7.9	14.4
IMPORTS									
6 TOTAL	7.0	4.4	4.4	17.9	5.7	7.8	5.2	10.3	6.8
7 SOLID FUELS	13.2	-7.0	29.7	112.7	-64.1	-41.0	-1.2	-23.4	-2.5
8 LIQUID FUELS	7.0	4.4	4.3	13.7	9.9	7.6	5.2	10.4	6.8
EXPORTS									
9 TOTAL	4.3	-5.5	-6.4	6.0	-2.9	0.7	-2.6	1.2	-2.4
10 SOLID FUELS	4.5	-5.6	-7.1	-2.3	-14.1	-6.6	-2.6	-7.8	-5.9
11 LIQUID FUELS	-10.0	1.6	7.4	40.6	7.8	3.6	-2.1	16.2	7.3
CONSUMPTION									
12 TOTAL	1.0	0.4	1.1	3.1	-0.3	2.5	0.6	1.8	1.2
13 TOTAL - ALTERNATIVE HYDRO	1.1	0.4	1.1	3.1	-0.2	2.5	0.6	1.8	1.2
14 SOLID FUELS	0.6	0.1	0.8	2.0	-3.0	-0.4	0.2	-0.5	0.1
15 LIQUID FUELS	9.9	4.7	3.7	11.0	11.1	9.3	6.3	10.4	7.0
16 NATURAL GAS	*	*	*	64.4	47.2	58.6	*	56.6	*
17 HYDROELECTRIC POWER	67.4	22.0	3.4	2.8	13.0	8.4	34.5	8.0	14.5
18 ADDENDUM - TOTAL ELECTRICITY	1.5	8.9	6.8	10.7	7.8	7.4	6.5	8.6	7.4
19 POPULATION	0.3	0.4	0.5	0.2	0.5	0.8	0.4	0.5	0.5
20 TOTAL PER CAPITA PRODUCTION	1.1	-1.8	-0.9	0.3	-3.1	-1.4	-0.9	-1.4	-1.1
PER CAPITA CONSUMPTION									
21 TOTAL	0.7	-0.1	0.5	2.9	-0.8	1.7	0.2	1.3	0.7
22 TOTAL - ALTERNATIVE HYDRO	0.7	-	0.5	2.8	-0.7	1.7	0.2	1.3	0.7
23 SOLID FUELS	0.3	-0.4	0.3	1.8	-3.4	-1.2	-0.2	-1.0	-0.3
24 LIQUID FUELS	9.6	4.2	3.1	10.7	10.5	8.4	5.8	9.9	6.5
25 NATURAL GAS	*	*	*	64.0	46.5	57.4	*	55.8	*
26 HYDROELECTRIC POWER	66.9	21.5	2.9	2.6	12.4	7.5	33.9	7.4	13.9
27 ADDENDUM - TOTAL ELECTRICITY	1.1	8.4	6.2	10.5	7.3	6.6	6.1	8.1	6.9
WESTERN EUROPE - CTHER									
PRODUCTION									
1 TOTAL	4.5	-1.2	5.7	3.9	5.7	4.2	0.5	4.6	3.6
2 SOLID FUELS	4.3	-1.6	5.6	3.0	4.8	2.8	0.2	3.5	3.1
3 LIQUID FUELS	-	1.7	26.1	21.2	28.0	16.1	1.2	21.7	15.8
4 NATURAL GAS	*	-	17.6	19.4	9.3	44.2	*	23.5	*
5 HYDROELECTRIC POWER	10.4	6.6	5.6	12.5	8.7	7.0	7.8	9.4	7.7
IMPORTS									
6 TOTAL	7.0	-0.6	4.7	7.2	7.4	10.0	1.7	8.2	5.0
7 SOLID FUELS	5.7	-2.7	-0.4	2.4	0.9	4.9	-0.2	2.7	0.8
8 LIQUID FUELS	13.0	5.3	10.3	9.5	9.5	11.2	7.7	10.1	9.3
EXPORTS									
9 TOTAL	15.2	-4.3	6.1	12.5	41.4	7.5	1.3	19.6	9.3
10 SOLID FUELS	14.8	-16.1	15.6	-1.9	1.1	2.1	-7.6	0.4	2.0
11 LIQUID FUELS	31.6	37.3	-5.6	42.7	55.4	7.7	35.5	33.7	21.0
CONSUMPTION									
12 TOTAL	5.6	-0.8	4.7	4.8	6.4	7.5	1.1	6.3	4.1
13 TOTAL - ALTERNATIVE HYDRO	5.6	-0.3	4.5	5.2	6.3	7.1	1.5	6.2	4.1
14 SOLID FUELS	4.9	-1.7	3.8	3.1	4.1	3.3	0.3	3.5	2.5
15 LIQUID FUELS	14.5	5.3	8.7	8.9	11.5	14.0	8.1	11.4	9.5
16 NATURAL GAS	*	-	17.6	19.4	9.3	44.2	*	23.5	*

Table XIII. AVERAGE ANNUAL PERCENTAGE RATES OF CHANGE IN TOTAL AND PER CAPITA ENERGY PRODUCTION, TRADE, AND CONSUMPTION, SELECTED PERIODS, 1925-1965

Region, country, indicator	1925-29	1929-38	1938-50	1950-55	1955-60	1960-65	1925-38	1950-65	1925-65
	(1)	(2)	(3)	(4)	(5)	(6)	(7)	(8)	(9)
WESTERN EUROPE - OTHER (CONTINUED)									
CONSUMPTION (CONTINUED)									
17 HYDROELECTRIC POWER	10.4	6.6	5.6	12.5	8.8	7.0	7.8	9.4	7.7
18 ADDENDUM - TOTAL ELECTRICITY	12.2	7.4	6.0	11.9	9.5	10.8	8.8	10.7	8.7
19 POPULATION	1.1	1.1	0.7	0.9	0.8	0.9	1.1	0.9	0.9
20 TOTAL PER CAPITA PRODUCTION	3.3	-2.3	5.0	2.9	4.9	3.3	-0.6	3.7	2.7
PER CAPITA CONSUMPTION									
21 TOTAL	4.5	-1.9	4.0	3.9	5.6	6.6	-	5.4	3.2
22 TOTAL - ALTERNATIVE HYDRO	4.4	-1.4	3.7	4.2	5.5	6.2	0.4	5.3	3.2
23 SOLID FUELS	3.8	-2.8	3.1	2.1	3.2	2.4	-0.8	2.6	1.6
24 LIQUID FUELS	13.2	4.2	7.9	7.9	10.6	13.0	6.9	10.5	8.5
25 NATURAL GAS	*	-1.1	16.8	18.3	8.4	42.9	*	22.4	*
26 HYDROELECTRIC POWER	9.2	5.4	4.9	11.5	8.0	6.1	6.6	8.5	6.8
27 ADDENDUM - TOTAL ELECTRICITY	11.0	6.2	5.3	10.9	8.6	9.8	7.6	9.8	7.7
FINLAND									
PRODUCTION									
1 TOTAL	17.0	12.7	4.7	9.0	-3.4	11.1	14.0	5.4	7.9
2 SOLID FUELS	-	2.5	18.8	-4.1	-5.6	-11.5	1.7	-7.1	3.0
3 LIQUID FUELS	*	*	*	*	*	*	*	*	*
4 NATURAL GAS	*	*	*	*	*	*	*	*	*
5 HYDROELECTRIC POWER	19.7	13.4	3.4	11.1	-3.2	12.5	15.3	6.6	8.3
IMPORTS									
6 TOTAL	17.1	5.2	1.8	10.0	11.0	10.4	8.7	10.5	7.2
7 SOLID FUELS	17.6	4.8	0.7	6.4	3.7	0.7	8.6	3.6	4.3
8 LIQUID FUELS	14.1	7.5	5.8	17.8	19.4	16.2	9.5	17.8	11.4
EXPORTS									
9 TOTAL	*	*	*	*	*	16.8	*	*	*
10 SOLID FUELS	*	*	*	*	*	24.6	*	*	*
11 LIQUID FUELS	*	*	*	*	*	-19.7	*	*	*
CONSUMPTION									
12 TOTAL	17.1	5.9	2.2	9.8	9.1	10.4	9.2	9.8	7.3
13 TOTAL - ALTERNATIVE HYDRO	16.2	7.4	1.7	8.8	5.7	10.2	10.0	8.2	6.8
14 SOLID FUELS	17.4	4.8	1.0	6.0	3.4	0.4	8.5	3.2	4.2
15 LIQUID FUELS	14.1	7.5	5.7	17.8	19.5	16.2	9.5	17.8	11.4
16 NATURAL GAS	*	*	*	*	*	*	*	*	*
17 HYDROELECTRIC POWER	19.7	13.4	3.4	11.1	-1.7	12.1	15.3	7.0	8.5
18 ADDENDUM - TOTAL ELECTRICITY	16.5	13.5	2.5	10.3	5.8	11.2	14.4	9.1	8.7
19 POPULATION	0.9	0.7	0.8	1.1	0.9	0.8	0.8	0.9	0.8
20 TOTAL PER CAPITA PRODUCTION	15.9	11.9	3.9	7.8	-4.3	10.2	13.1	4.4	7.0
PER CAPITA CONSUMPTION									
21 TOTAL	16.0	5.2	1.4	8.6	8.1	9.5	8.4	8.8	6.4
22 TOTAL - ALTERNATIVE HYDRO	15.2	6.6	0.9	7.6	4.8	9.3	9.2	7.2	5.9
23 SOLID FUELS	16.3	4.0	0.2	4.8	2.5	-0.4	7.7	2.3	3.4
24 LIQUID FUELS	13.1	6.8	4.9	16.6	18.4	15.2	8.7	16.7	10.5
25 NATURAL GAS	*	*	*	*	*	*	*	*	*
26 HYDROELECTRIC POWER	18.7	12.6	2.6	9.9	-2.6	11.2	14.4	6.0	7.6
27 ADDENDUM - TOTAL ELECTRICITY	15.4	12.7	1.7	9.1	4.8	10.3	13.5	8.1	7.8
GREECE									
PRODUCTION									
1 TOTAL	2.3	-3.8	4.2	36.5	25.3	14.3	-2.0	25.0	9.4
2 SOLID FUELS	2.4	-4.0	4.3	34.1	26.7	14.4	-2.1	24.8	9.3
3 LIQUID FUELS	*	*	*	*	*	*	*	*	*
4 NATURAL GAS	*	*	*	*	*	*	*	*	*
5 HYDROELECTRIC POWER	-	5.5	-2.2	101.5	7.2	9.8	3.8	33.3	12.0
IMPORTS									
6 TOTAL	8.0	4.2	2.2	6.0	8.1	11.6	5.3	8.5	5.6
7 SOLID FUELS	5.3	2.0	-9.3	1.2	-6.4	12.3	3.0	2.1	-1.2
8 LIQUID FUELS	23.1	9.9	10.0	6.8	9.6	11.5	13.8	9.3	11.0
EXPORTS									
9 TOTAL	*	*	*	*	*	*	*	*	*
10 SOLID FUELS	*	*	*	*	*	*	*	*	*
11 LIQUID FUELS	*	*	*	*	*	*	*	*	*
CONSUMPTION									
12 TOTAL	7.6	3.7	1.2	9.1	9.6	12.2	4.9	10.3	5.7
13 TOTAL - ALTERNATIVE HYDRO	7.5	3.7	1.2	9.9	9.4	12.1	4.9	10.4	5.8
14 SOLID FUELS	5.0	1.6	-7.7	12.6	16.2	14.1	2.6	14.3	3.5
15 LIQUID FUELS	23.1	9.9	8.6	7.5	6.8	11.2	13.8	8.5	10.2
16 NATURAL GAS	*	*	*	*	*	*	*	*	*
17 HYDROELECTRIC POWER	-	5.5	-2.2	101.5	7.6	10.0	3.8	33.6	12.1
18 ADDENDUM - TOTAL ELECTRICITY	NA	11.5	7.8	15.9	10.4	13.8	NA	13.3	NA

Table XIII. AVERAGE ANNUAL PERCENTAGE RATES OF CHANGE IN TOTAL AND PER CAPITA ENERGY PRODUCTION, TRADE, AND CONSUMPTION, SELECTED PERIODS, 1925-1965

Region, country, indicator	1925-29	1929-38	1938-50	1950-55	1955-60	1960-65	1925-38	1950-65	1925-65
	(1)	(2)	(3)	(4)	(5)	(6)	(7)	(8)	(9)
GREECE (CONTINUED)									
19 POPULATION	1.3	1.4	0.5	1.0	0.9	0.5	1.4	0.8	0.9
20 TOTAL PER CAPITA PRODUCTION	1.0	-5.1	3.7	35.1	24.2	13.7	-3.3	24.0	8.4
PER CAPITA CONSUMPTION									
21 TOTAL	6.2	2.3	0.7	7.9	8.6	11.6	3.5	9.4	4.8
22 TOTAL - ALTERNATIVE HYDRO	6.1	2.3	0.7	8.8	8.4	11.5	3.4	9.5	4.8
23 SOLID FUELS	3.6	0.2	-8.2	11.5	15.2	13.5	1.2	13.4	2.6
24 LIQUID FUELS	21.5	8.4	8.0	6.4	5.9	10.6	12.3	7.6	9.2
25 NATURAL GAS	*	*	*	*	*	*	*	*	*
26 HYDROELECTRIC POWER	-1.3	4.1	-2.7	99.4	6.7	9.4	2.4	32.5	11.1
27 ADDENDUM - TOTAL ELECTRICITY	NA	9.9	7.2	14.7	9.4	13.2	NA	12.4	NA
ICELAND									
PRODUCTION									
1 TOTAL	-	16.1	18.7	16.1	6.7	4.2	10.9	8.8	12.4
2 SOLID FUELS	*	*	*	*	*	*	*	*	*
3 LIQUID FUELS	*	*	*	*	*	*	*	*	*
4 NATURAL GAS	*	*	*	*	*	*	*	*	*
5 HYDROELECTRIC POWER	-	16.1	18.0	17.7	6.7	4.2	10.9	9.3	12.4
IMPORTS									
6 TOTAL	13.6	3.2	25.7	4.4	4.4	-0.2	6.3	2.8	10.4
7 SOLID FUELS	*	*	*	-9.0	-19.7	-12.9	*	-14.0	*
8 LIQUID FUELS	13.6	3.2	23.3	6.9	6.1	0.1	6.3	4.3	10.4
EXPORTS									
9 TOTAL	*	*	*	*	*	*	*	*	*
10 SOLID FUELS	*	*	*	*	*	*	*	*	*
11 LIQUID FUELS	*	*	*	*	*	*	*	*	*
CONSUMPTION									
12 TOTAL	13.0	3.9	22.9	4.2	5.8	3.9	6.6	4.7	10.5
13 TOTAL - ALTERNATIVE HYDRO	9.1	5.9	21.1	5.8	5.3	3.4	6.8	4.8	10.2
14 SOLID FUELS	*	*	*	-9.3	-19.7	-12.9	*	-14.1	*
15 LIQUID FUELS	13.6	3.2	20.1	6.5	8.2	4.4	6.3	6.3	10.3
16 NATURAL GAS	*	*	*	*	*	*	*	*	*
17 HYDROELECTRIC POWER	-	16.1	18.0	17.7	6.7	4.2	10.9	9.3	12.4
18 ADDENDUM - TOTAL ELECTRICITY	NA	14.7	19.0	16.3	6.1	5.2	NA	9.1	NA
19 POPULATION	1.7	1.2	1.6	2.0	2.2	1.8	1.4	2.0	1.7
20 TOTAL PER CAPITA PRODUCTION	-1.7	14.7	16.8	13.8	4.4	2.4	9.4	6.7	10.5
PER CAPITA CONSUMPTION									
21 TOTAL	11.1	2.7	20.9	2.2	3.6	2.1	5.2	2.6	8.7
22 TOTAL - ALTERNATIVE HYDRO	7.2	4.6	19.2	3.7	3.1	1.6	5.4	2.8	8.3
23 SOLID FUELS	*	*	*	-11.0	-21.4	-14.4	*	-15.8	*
24 LIQUID FUELS	11.7	2.0	18.2	4.4	5.9	2.6	4.9	4.3	8.5
25 NATURAL GAS	*	*	*	*	*	*	*	*	*
26 HYDROELECTRIC POWER	-1.7	14.7	16.1	15.3	4.4	2.4	9.4	7.2	10.5
27 ADDENDUM - TOTAL ELECTRICITY	NA	13.3	17.1	14.0	3.8	3.4	NA	7.0	NA
IRELAND									
PRODUCTION									
1 TOTAL	0.6	-0.3	-0.3	2.8	3.0	-1.7	-	1.3	0.4
2 SOLID FUELS	0.6	-0.5	-0.4	2.8	2.6	-1.8	-0.2	1.2	0.3
3 LIQUID FUELS	*	*	*	*	*	*	*	*	*
4 NATURAL GAS	*	*	*	*	*	*	*	*	*
5 HYDROELECTRIC POWER	32.7	28.5	3.9	0.9	13.9	0.1	29.8	4.8	12.0
IMPORTS									
6 TOTAL	2.9	0.6	-0.1	4.6	4.0	4.2	1.3	4.3	2.0
7 SOLID FUELS	2.4	0.1	-2.0	-0.5	-2.8	-5.0	0.8	-2.8	-1.4
8 LIQUID FUELS	8.5	4.8	7.5	13.4	10.1	8.6	5.9	10.7	8.2
EXPORTS									
9 TOTAL	80.0	-23.0	*	*	*	-8.5	-	*	14.7
10 SOLID FUELS	80.0	-23.0	*	*	*	20.1	-	*	8.4
11 LIQUID FUELS	*	*	*	*	*	-10.0	*	*	*
CONSUMPTION									
12 TOTAL	1.8	0.3	-0.3	3.5	0.8	3.5	0.8	2.6	1.1
13 TOTAL - ALTERNATIVE HYDRO	1.9	0.6	-0.2	3.3	1.1	3.2	1.0	2.5	1.2
14 SOLID FUELS	1.5	-0.1	-1.3	1.1	-0.1	-3.3	0.4	-0.8	-0.6
15 LIQUID FUELS	8.5	4.8	6.7	12.5	2.2	14.9	5.9	9.7	7.6
16 NATURAL GAS	*	*	*	*	*	*	*	*	*
17 HYDROELECTRIC POWER	32.7	28.5	3.9	0.9	13.9	0.1	29.8	4.8	12.0
18 ADDENDUM - TOTAL ELECTRICITY	NA	NA	8.1	12.1	7.2	9.4	NA	9.5	NA
19 POPULATION	-0.4	-	0.1	-0.3	-0.6	0.1	-0.1	-0.3	-0.1

Table XIII. AVERAGE ANNUAL PERCENTAGE RATES OF CHANGE IN TOTAL AND PER CAPITA ENERGY PRODUCTION, TRADE, AND CONSUMPTION, SELECTED PERIODS, 1925-1965

Region, country, indicator	1925-29	1929-38	1938-50	1950-55	1955-60	1960-65	1925-38	1950-65	1925-65
	(1)	(2)	(3)	(4)	(5)	(6)	(7)	(8)	(9)
IRELAND (CONTINUED)									
20 TOTAL PER CAPITA PRODUCTION	1.0	-0.3	-0.4	3.1	3.6	-1.8	0.1	1.6	0.5
PER CAPITA CONSUMPTION									
21 TOTAL	2.3	0.3	-0.4	3.8	1.4	3.3	0.9	2.8	1.2
22 TOTAL - ALTERNATIVE HYDRO	2.3	0.6	-0.3	3.6	1.7	3.1	1.1	2.8	1.3
23 SOLID FUELS	1.9	-0.1	-1.4	1.4	0.6	-3.4	0.5	-0.5	-0.4
24 LIQUID FUELS	9.0	4.8	6.6	12.9	2.8	14.7	6.0	10.0	7.7
25 NATURAL GAS	*	*	*	*	*	*	*	*	*
26 HYDROELECTRIC POWER	33.2	28.5	3.8	1.2	14.6	-	29.9	5.1	12.2
27 ADDENDUM - TOTAL ELECTRICITY	NA	NA	8.0	12.5	7.8	9.2	NA	9.8	NA
SPAIN									
PRODUCTION									
1 TOTAL	3.9	-2.5	6.2	3.2	2.9	0.5	-0.6	2.2	2.5
2 SOLID FUELS	3.8	-2.7	6.2	2.5	1.9	-0.1	-0.7	1.4	2.1
3 LIQUID FUELS	-	-	-13.9	103.6	12.8	0.3	-	32.1	6.1
4 NATURAL GAS	*	*	*	*	*	*	*	*	*
5 HYDROELECTRIC POWER	9.7	1.3	7.1	12.1	11.7	4.6	3.8	9.4	6.9
IMPORTS									
6 TOTAL	8.4	-6.5	10.0	8.1	7.8	11.5	-2.1	9.1	5.6
7 SOLID FUELS	6.7	-18.7	7.6	-9.1	-11.9	38.3	-11.6	3.5	-0.5
8 LIQUID FUELS	13.1	4.5	10.5	10.3	8.8	10.5	7.1	9.8	9.1
EXPORTS									
9 TOTAL	63.2	0.5	-1.1	30.4	37.8	10.1	16.7	25.6	14.1
10 SOLID FUELS	67.0	*	*	5.8	-15.0	-24.2	*	-12.0	0.3
11 LIQUID FUELS	31.6	37.3	*	*	48.9	10.2	35.5	*	19.7
CONSUMPTION									
12 TOTAL	5.0	-3.8	6.8	3.6	5.0	6.5	-1.2	5.1	3.5
13 TOTAL - ALTERNATIVE HYDRO	5.0	-3.5	6.5	4.1	5.4	5.8	-1.0	5.1	3.5
14 SOLID FUELS	4.2	-5.0	6.4	2.0	1.5	1.8	-2.3	1.8	1.8
15 LIQUID FUELS	16.5	4.4	9.0	7.4	12.0	14.0	8.0	11.1	9.4
16 NATURAL GAS	*	*	*	*	*	*	*	*	*
17 HYDROELECTRIC POWER	9.7	1.3	7.1	12.2	11.3	4.1	3.8	9.2	6.8
18 ADDENDUM - TOTAL ELECTRICITY	10.9	1.4	8.0	11.6	9.0	10.2	4.2	10.3	7.6
19 POPULATION	1.0	1.0	0.8	0.8	0.8	0.8	1.0	0.8	0.9
20 TOTAL PER CAPITA PRODUCTION	2.9	-3.5	5.4	2.3	2.0	-0.3	-1.5	1.3	1.6
PER CAPITA CONSUMPTION									
21 TOTAL	3.9	-4.7	6.0	2.8	4.1	5.6	-2.1	4.2	2.6
22 TOTAL - ALTERNATIVE HYDRO	3.9	-4.4	5.7	3.3	4.5	4.9	-1.9	4.2	2.6
23 SOLID FUELS	3.1	-5.9	5.5	1.2	0.7	0.9	-3.2	0.9	0.9
24 LIQUID FUELS	15.4	3.4	8.1	6.5	11.1	13.1	6.9	10.2	8.5
25 NATURAL GAS	*	*	*	*	*	*	*	*	*
26 HYDROELECTRIC POWER	8.6	0.4	6.2	11.3	10.4	3.2	2.8	8.3	5.9
27 ADDENDUM - TOTAL ELECTRICITY	9.7	0.4	7.1	10.7	8.1	9.3	3.2	9.4	6.7
YUGOSLAVIA									
PRODUCTION									
1 TOTAL	8.6	0.3	7.3	4.1	9.8	7.3	2.8	7.0	5.7
2 SOLID FUELS	8.8	0.2	7.0	3.2	8.0	5.4	2.8	5.5	5.1
3 LIQUID FUELS	*	*	48.2	18.3	29.6	16.9	*	21.5	*
4 NATURAL GAS	*	-	17.6	19.4	9.3	44.2	*	23.5	*
5 HYDROELECTRIC POWER	-2.2	6.1	7.9	17.3	18.1	8.5	3.5	14.5	8.9
IMPORTS									
6 TOTAL	6.4	-1.9	3.8	10.8	6.4	10.6	0.6	9.2	4.7
7 SOLID FUELS	4.6	-3.0	-1.4	21.6	8.4	6.6	-0.7	12.0	3.7
8 LIQUID FUELS	12.9	1.1	10.0	1.8	3.2	16.1	4.6	6.8	7.0
EXPORTS									
9 TOTAL	-4.0	-8.4	14.5	-0.9	10.0	23.9	-7.0	10.5	5.6
10 SOLID FUELS	-4.0	-8.4	11.9	-7.6	6.6	-	-7.0	-0.5	0.8
11 LIQUID FUELS	*	*	*	10.6	13.5	37.6	*	20.0	*
CONSUMPTION									
12 TOTAL	8.4	-	6.6	4.8	9.4	7.7	2.5	7.3	5.5
13 TOTAL - ALTERNATIVE HYDRO	7.3	0.2	6.5	5.2	9.9	7.6	2.3	7.5	5.5
14 SOLID FUELS	8.3	-0.2	6.2	4.5	8.2	5.7	2.4	6.1	4.9
15 LIQUID FUELS	12.9	1.2	11.4	4.3	15.9	15.1	4.6	11.7	9.2
16 NATURAL GAS	*	-	17.6	19.4	9.3	44.2	*	23.5	*
17 HYDROELECTRIC POWER	-2.2	6.1	7.9	16.9	18.2	9.7	3.5	14.9	9.0
18 ADDENDUM - TOTAL ELECTRICITY	3.6	10.1	6.8	12.2	15.5	12.5	8.0	13.4	9.6
19 POPULATION	1.5	1.4	0.5	1.4	1.0	1.2	1.4	1.2	1.1
20 TOTAL PER CAPITA PRODUCTION	7.0	-1.1	6.7	2.6	8.7	6.1	1.4	5.8	4.6

Table XIII. AVERAGE ANNUAL PERCENTAGE RATES OF CHANGE IN TOTAL AND PER CAPITA ENERGY PRODUCTION, TRADE, AND CONSUMPTION, SELECTED PERIODS, 1925-1965

Region, country, indicator	1925-29	1929-38	1938-50	1950-55	1955-60	1960-65	1925-38	1950-65	1925-65
	(1)	(2)	(3)	(4)	(5)	(6)	(7)	(8)	(9)
YUGOSLAVIA (CONTINUED)									
PER CAPITA CONSUMPTION									
21 TOTAL	6.8	-1.4	6.1	3.3	8.4	6.4	1.1	6.0	4.4
22 TOTAL - ALTERNATIVE HYDRO	5.8	-1.2	6.0	3.8	8.8	6.3	0.9	6.3	4.4
23 SOLID FUELS	6.7	-1.5	5.6	3.0	7.2	4.5	0.9	4.9	3.8
24 LIQUID FUELS	11.2	-0.2	10.8	2.9	14.7	13.8	3.2	10.3	8.1
25 NATURAL GAS	*	-1.4	17.0	17.8	8.2	42.5	*	22.0	*
26 HYDROELECTRIC POWER	-3.6	4.7	7.4	15.2	17.0	8.5	2.1	13.5	7.8
27 ADDENDUM - TOTAL ELECTRICITY	2.0	8.5	6.3	10.7	14.4	11.2	6.5	12.1	8.5
OCEANIA									
PRODUCTION									
1 TOTAL	-4.4	1.3	3.0	3.1	4.0	6.6	-0.5	4.5	2.4
2 SOLID FUELS	-4.5	1.2	2.9	3.0	3.8	6.1	-0.6	4.3	2.2
3 LIQUID FUELS	*	*	-	-	-	220.1	*	47.4	*
4 NATURAL GAS	*	*	*	*	*	*	*	*	*
5 HYDROELECTRIC POWER	13.8	7.4	6.6	8.3	8.6	11.7	9.3	9.5	8.6
IMPORTS									
6 TOTAL	13.8	2.9	6.3	9.8	7.9	7.6	6.1	8.4	7.0
7 SOLID FUELS	4.4	-9.3	5.0	-16.2	-	3.2	-5.3	-4.7	-2.1
8 LIQUID FUELS	18.1	5.2	6.4	11.0	8.0	7.7	9.0	8.9	8.2
EXPORTS									
9 TOTAL	-21.4	2.5	-12.5	50.6	42.3	17.3	-5.6	36.0	5.8
10 SOLID FUELS	-22.1	3.0	-13.9	25.9	48.1	33.8	-5.5	35.6	5.2
11 LIQUID FUELS	16.4	-23.4	22.1	96.0	39.0	-4.8	-12.9	37.4	14.4
CONSUMPTION									
12 TOTAL	-0.4	1.9	4.1	5.0	4.2	6.0	1.2	5.0	3.5
13 TOTAL - ALTERNATIVE HYDRO	-	2.0	4.1	4.9	4.3	6.1	1.4	5.1	3.6
14 SOLID FUELS	-2.8	0.9	3.5	2.6	2.7	3.0	-0.3	2.7	2.0
15 LIQUID FUELS	21.8	5.9	5.7	10.4	6.5	9.7	10.5	8.9	8.4
16 NATURAL GAS	*	*	*	*	*	*	*	*	*
17 HYDROELECTRIC POWER	13.8	7.4	6.6	8.3	8.6	11.7	9.3	9.5	8.6
18 ADDENDUM - TOTAL ELECTRICITY	12.4	7.6	6.8	10.8	8.7	8.6	9.0	9.4	8.5
19 POPULATION	1.6	0.8	1.4	2.5	2.3	2.2	1.0	2.3	1.6
20 TOTAL PER CAPITA PRODUCTION	-5.8	0.5	1.5	0.6	1.7	4.4	-1.5	2.2	0.8
PER CAPITA CONSUMPTION									
21 TOTAL	-1.9	1.1	2.6	2.4	1.9	3.7	0.1	2.7	1.8
22 TOTAL - ALTERNATIVE HYDRO	-1.6	1.2	2.6	2.4	1.9	3.9	0.4	2.7	1.9
23 SOLID FUELS	-4.3	0.1	2.1	0.1	0.4	0.8	-1.3	0.4	0.4
24 LIQUID FUELS	19.9	5.0	4.2	7.8	4.2	7.4	9.4	6.4	6.7
25 NATURAL GAS	*	*	*	*	*	*	*	*	*
26 HYDROELECTRIC POWER	12.0	6.6	5.1	5.7	6.2	9.4	8.2	7.1	6.8
27 ADDENDUM - TOTAL ELECTRICITY	10.7	6.7	5.3	8.1	6.3	6.3	7.9	6.9	6.7
AUSTRALIA									
PRODUCTION									
1 TOTAL	-6.0	1.7	3.1	3.4	4.0	7.2	-0.7	4.9	2.5
2 SOLID FUELS	-6.0	1.7	3.1	3.4	3.8	6.8	-0.7	4.6	2.4
3 LIQUID FUELS	*	*	*	*	*	*	*	*	*
4 NATURAL GAS	*	*	*	*	*	*	*	*	*
5 HYDROELECTRIC POWER	6.4	4.9	6.8	5.9	15.3	15.6	5.4	12.2	8.3
IMPORTS									
6 TOTAL	25.5	2.4	7.4	10.3	8.5	7.1	9.0	8.6	8.4
7 SOLID FUELS	78.2	-19.1	16.7	-54.7	*	*	3.1	-23.2	-4.2
8 LIQUID FUELS	20.0	4.8	7.0	11.9	8.5	7.1	9.2	9.1	8.5
EXPORTS									
9 TOTAL	-24.0	3.8	-12.6	51.8	42.1	16.6	-5.7	36.0	5.7
10 SOLID FUELS	-24.8	4.4	-14.1	27.2	47.8	34.1	-5.6	36.1	5.2
11 LIQUID FUELS	16.4	-23.4	22.1	95.6	38.9	-8.5	-12.9	35.5	13.8
CONSUMPTION									
12 TOTAL	-0.9	2.0	4.5	5.0	4.2	6.1	1.1	5.1	3.6
13 TOTAL - ALTERNATIVE HYDRO	-0.9	2.0	4.5	4.9	4.3	6.3	1.1	5.2	3.7
14 SOLID FUELS	-3.4	1.3	3.9	2.8	2.7	3.4	-0.1	3.0	2.2
15 LIQUID FUELS	23.4	5.2	6.5	10.7	6.6	9.7	10.5	9.0	8.7
16 NATURAL GAS	*	*	*	*	*	*	*	*	*
17 HYDROELECTRIC POWER	6.4	4.9	6.8	5.9	15.3	15.6	5.4	12.2	8.3
18 ADDENDUM - TOTAL ELECTRICITY	10.4	7.4	6.7	11.1	8.8	8.7	8.3	9.5	8.3
19 POPULATION	1.9	0.8	1.4	2.4	2.2	2.0	1.2	2.2	1.6
20 TOTAL PER CAPITA PRODUCTION	-7.7	0.9	1.7	1.0	1.7	5.1	-1.8	2.6	0.9
PER CAPITA CONSUMPTION									
21 TOTAL	-2.7	1.2	3.1	2.6	1.9	4.0	-	2.8	1.9

Table XIII. AVERAGE ANNUAL PERCENTAGE RATES OF CHANGE IN TOTAL AND PER CAPITA ENERGY PRODUCTION, TRADE, AND CONSUMPTION, SELECTED PERIODS, 1925-1965

Region, country, indicator	1925-29	1929-38	1938-50	1950-55	1955-60	1960-65	1925-38	1950-65	1925-65
	(1)	(2)	(3)	(4)	(5)	(6)	(7)	(8)	(9)
AUSTRALIA (CONTINUED)									
PER CAPITA CONSUMPTION (CONTINUED)									
22 TOTAL - ALTERNATIVE HYDRO	-2.7	1.2	3.0	2.5	2.1	4.2	-	2.9	2.0
23 SOLID FUELS	-5.2	0.5	2.5	0.4	0.5	1.4	-1.3	0.8	0.6
24 LIQUID FUELS	21.1	4.4	5.0	8.1	4.3	7.5	9.3	6.6	7.0
25 NATURAL GAS	*	*	*	*	*	*	*	*	*
26 HYDROELECTRIC POWER	4.5	4.1	5.3	3.5	12.8	13.3	4.2	9.8	6.6
27 ADDENDUM - TOTAL ELECTRICITY	8.4	6.5	5.2	8.5	6.4	6.6	7.1	7.1	6.6
NEW ZEALAND									
PRODUCTION									
1 TOTAL	5.6	-1.2	1.7	0.9	3.4	0.5	0.8	1.6	1.4
2 SOLID FUELS	5.2	-1.8	1.2	-0.9	3.2	-2.6	0.3	-0.1	0.4
3 LIQUID FUELS	*	*	-	-	-	-	*	-	*
4 NATURAL GAS	*	*	*	*	*	*	*	*	*
5 HYDROELECTRIC POWER	20.6	8.8	6.2	9.6	4.0	9.3	12.3	7.6	8.7
IMPORTS									
6 TOTAL	-4.7	4.0	3.6	5.4	4.0	11.1	1.3	6.8	4.0
7 SOLID FUELS	-21.7	-7.0	-6.7	-27.2	*	*	-11.8	*	*
8 LIQUID FUELS	11.8	6.6	4.3	5.9	4.1	11.1	8.2	7.0	6.6
EXPORTS									
9 TOTAL	49.5	-13.9	-9.4	*	*	60.5	2.0	34.9	9.3
10 SOLID FUELS	49.5	-13.9	-9.4	*	*	*	2.0	*	*
11 LIQUID FUELS	*	*	*	*	*	92.5	*	*	*
CONSUMPTION									
12 TOTAL	2.1	0.9	1.9	3.3	4.0	4.7	1.3	4.0	2.5
13 TOTAL - ALTERNATIVE HYDRO	3.6	1.8	2.3	3.8	3.2	5.0	2.4	4.0	3.0
14 SOLID FUELS	-0.2	-1.5	1.0	-1.0	2.9	-2.4	-1.1	-0.2	-0.1
15 LIQUID FUELS	15.9	8.0	2.8	8.1	5.1	9.3	10.4	7.5	7.0
16 NATURAL GAS	*	*	*	*	*	*	*	*	*
17 HYDROELECTRIC POWER	20.6	8.8	6.2	9.6	4.0	9.3	12.3	7.6	8.7
18 ADDENDUM - TOTAL ELECTRICITY	20.2	8.0	6.7	9.7	7.4	9.0	11.6	8.7	9.0
19 POPULATION	1.6	1.0	1.5	2.3	2.1	2.2	1.2	2.2	1.6
20 TOTAL PER CAPITA PRODUCTION	4.0	-2.2	0.3	-1.4	1.2	-1.6	-0.3	-0.6	-0.3
PER CAPITA CONSUMPTION									
21 TOTAL	0.5	-	0.5	1.0	1.8	2.5	0.1	1.8	0.9
22 TOTAL - ALTERNATIVE HYDRO	1.9	0.9	0.8	1.5	1.1	2.8	1.2	1.8	1.3
23 SOLID FUELS	-1.8	-2.5	-0.4	-3.2	0.8	-4.5	-2.2	-2.3	-1.7
24 LIQUID FUELS	14.1	7.0	1.3	5.7	3.0	7.0	9.1	5.2	5.3
25 NATURAL GAS	*	*	*	*	*	*	*	*	*
26 HYDROELECTRIC POWER	18.7	7.8	4.7	7.2	1.8	7.0	11.0	5.3	6.9
27 ADDENDUM - TOTAL ELECTRICITY	18.4	6.9	5.2	7.2	5.2	6.7	10.3	6.4	7.3
USSR AND COMMUNIST EASTERN EUROPE									
PRODUCTION									
1 TOTAL	13.5	6.3	5.0	8.5	6.8	6.3	8.4	7.2	6.9
2 SOLID FUELS	12.8	5.7	5.8	7.3	3.4	2.7	7.8	4.4	6.0
3 LIQUID FUELS	17.1	7.8	1.4	13.9	13.9	9.4	10.6	12.4	8.4
4 NATURAL GAS	11.3	12.6	4.8	11.5	30.9	21.6	12.2	21.1	13.1
5 HYDROELECTRIC POWER	15.6	23.1	7.9	12.7	15.9	9.7	20.8	12.7	13.8
IMPORTS									
6 TOTAL	12.4	-6.1	16.9	7.7	3.6	9.8	-0.7	7.0	7.2
7 SOLID FUELS	11.3	-8.7	18.2	4.8	-0.4	7.6	-2.9	3.9	5.6
8 LIQUID FUELS	19.8	2.6	13.7	14.9	9.4	12.4	7.6	12.2	11.1
EXPORTS									
9 TOTAL	16.7	-3.3	4.8	9.8	11.4	9.9	2.4	10.4	6.1
10 SOLID FUELS	12.5	-4.2	7.7	3.5	2.4	6.0	0.7	4.0	4.0
11 LIQUID FUELS	28.3	-1.9	-3.1	31.2	22.3	12.5	6.6	21.7	8.9
CONSUMPTION									
12 TOTAL	12.7	7.3	5.5	8.3	6.2	6.1	8.9	6.9	7.1
13 TOTAL - ALTERNATIVE HYDRO	12.7	7.4	5.5	8.3	6.3	6.1	9.0	6.9	7.1
14 SOLID FUELS	12.7	6.4	6.1	7.5	3.4	2.6	8.3	4.5	6.2
15 LIQUID FUELS	12.7	10.7	2.8	11.9	11.5	8.8	11.3	10.7	8.5
16 NATURAL GAS	11.3	12.6	4.8	11.5	30.9	21.5	12.2	21.0	13.1
17 HYDROELECTRIC POWER	14.1	22.1	7.8	13.2	15.8	9.6	19.6	12.9	13.4
18 ADDENDUM - TOTAL ELECTRICITY	17.0	15.6	8.5	12.8	10.8	10.7	16.0	11.4	12.0
19 POPULATION	2.0	1.2	-	1.5	1.5	1.2	1.5	1.4	1.0
20 TOTAL PER CAPITA PRODUCTION	11.3	5.0	5.0	6.9	5.2	5.1	6.9	5.7	5.9
PER CAPITA CONSUMPTION									
21 TOTAL	10.5	6.0	5.6	6.7	4.7	4.8	7.3	5.4	6.1
22 TOTAL - ALTERNATIVE HYDRO	10.5	6.1	5.5	6.7	4.7	4.8	7.4	5.4	6.1
23 SOLID FUELS	10.5	5.1	6.1	5.9	1.9	1.4	6.7	3.0	5.2

Table XIII. AVERAGE ANNUAL PERCENTAGE RATES OF CHANGE IN TOTAL AND PER CAPITA ENERGY PRODUCTION, TRADE, AND CONSUMPTION, SELECTED PERIODS, 1925-1965

Region, country, indicator	1925-29	1929-38	1938-50	1950-55	1955-60	1960-65	1925-38	1950-65	1925-65
	(1)	(2)	(3)	(4)	(5)	(6)	(7)	(8)	(9)
USSR AND COMMUNIST EASTERN EUROPE (CONTINUED)									
PER CAPITA CONSUMPTION (CONTINUED)									
24 LIQUID FUELS	10.5	9.3	2.8	10.3	9.9	7.4	9.7	9.2	7.4
25 NATURAL GAS	9.2	11.2	4.8	9.9	28.9	20.1	10.6	19.4	12.0
26 HYDROELECTRIC POWER	11.9	20.6	7.8	11.5	14.1	8.3	17.9	11.3	12.3
27 ADDENDUM - TOTAL ELECTRICITY	14.7	14.2	8.5	11.1	9.1	9.4	14.3	9.9	10.9
COMMUNIST EASTERN EUROPE									
PRODUCTION									
1 TOTAL	9.6	-0.9	6.4	6.6	3.5	3.6	2.2	4.5	4.4
2 SOLID FUELS	9.2	-1.7	7.5	5.7	3.4	3.2	1.5	4.1	4.2
3 LIQUID FUELS	15.2	3.4	-1.8	16.4	1.9	2.7	6.9	6.8	4.2
4 NATURAL GAS	9.0	7.5	-0.2	16.4	11.4	12.5	8.0	13.4	7.4
5 HYDROELECTRIC POWER	8.4	10.9	7.9	12.3	8.4	8.6	10.1	9.8	9.3
IMPORTS									
6 TOTAL	12.5	-8.7	13.1	13.8	9.4	12.9	-2.6	12.0	7.3
7 SOLID FUELS	11.1	-11.5	14.9	13.1	3.5	7.8	-5.1	8.1	5.5
8 LIQUID FUELS	21.3	0.1	8.6	15.7	21.6	18.7	6.2	18.6	11.4
EXPORTS									
9 TOTAL	13.5	-1.7	4.9	5.0	-1.0	2.9	2.8	2.3	3.2
10 SOLID FUELS	11.4	-3.7	7.2	1.9	-2.4	2.5	0.7	0.6	2.6
11 LIQUID FUELS	26.8	4.5	-3.4	20.7	2.6	3.9	10.9	8.8	5.6
CONSUMPTION									
12 TOTAL	8.6	-1.4	7.5	7.4	5.0	5.0	1.6	5.8	4.9
13 TOTAL - ALTERNATIVE HYDRO	8.6	-1.3	7.5	7.5	5.0	5.0	1.6	5.8	4.9
14 SOLID FUELS	8.7	-1.9	8.1	6.8	4.3	3.6	1.2	4.9	4.6
15 LIQUID FUELS	8.0	1.4	2.8	13.6	10.9	13.2	3.4	12.5	6.5
16 NATURAL GAS	9.0	7.5	-0.1	16.6	11.3	12.4	8.0	13.4	7.5
17 HYDROELECTRIC POWER	6.8	8.8	7.1	15.3	8.4	11.1	8.2	11.5	9.1
18 ADDENDUM - TOTAL ELECTRICITY	14.2	4.0	12.4	11.5	9.2	8.5	7.0	9.7	9.6
19 POPULATION	1.3	1.0	0.8	1.C	0.9	0.7	1.1	0.8	0.9
20 TOTAL PER CAPITA PRODUCTION	8.3	-1.9	5.6	5.5	2.6	2.9	1.1	3.7	3.4
PER CAPITA CONSUMPTION									
21 TOTAL	7.2	-2.4	6.6	6.4	4.1	4.3	0.5	4.9	3.9
22 TOTAL - ALTERNATIVE HYDRO	7.2	-2.4	6.6	6.4	4.1	4.3	0.5	4.9	4.0
23 SOLID FUELS	7.3	-2.9	7.2	5.8	3.4	2.9	0.1	4.0	3.7
24 LIQUID FUELS	6.6	0.3	2.0	12.4	9.9	12.4	2.2	11.6	5.6
25 NATURAL GAS	7.6	6.4	-0.9	15.4	10.4	11.6	6.8	12.4	6.5
26 HYDROELECTRIC POWER	5.5	7.7	6.2	14.1	7.4	10.4	7.0	10.6	8.1
27 ADDENDUM - TOTAL ELECTRICITY	12.7	3.0	11.5	10.4	8.3	7.7	5.9	8.8	8.6
ALBANIA									
PRODUCTION									
1 TOTAL	41.4	63.8	2.1	13.6	24.9	2.3	56.6	13.2	22.0
2 SOLID FUELS	41.4	-	21.4	36.6	8.3	3.8	11.3	15.4	15.8
3 LIQUID FUELS	*	*	1.4	9.5	28.5	1.9	*	12.8	*
4 NATURAL GAS	*	*	*	*	*	*	*	*	*
5 HYDROELECTRIC POWER	*	*	*	*	35.0	15.6	*	*	*
IMPORTS									
6 TOTAL	8.8	5.8	7.1	-4.7	-4.5	7.6	6.7	-0.7	4.0
7 SOLID FUELS	*	*	7.9	*	*	8.4	*	2.7	*
8 LIQUID FUELS	8.8	2.8	6.9	1.0	-13.8	7.0	4.6	-2.3	2.6
EXPORTS									
9 TOTAL	*	*	-4.6	18.0	19.1	2.7	*	13.0	*
10 SOLID FUELS	*	*	*	*	*	*	*	*	*
11 LIQUID FUELS	*	*	-4.6	15.6	21.5	2.7	*	13.0	*
CONSUMPTION									
12 TOTAL	11.8	10.2	15.5	7.2	26.9	2.3	10.7	11.6	12.5
13 TOTAL - ALTERNATIVE HYDRO	11.8	10.2	15.5	8.0	27.0	2.9	10.7	12.2	12.7
14 SOLID FUELS	41.4	13.0	14.5	20.5	14.9	4.1	21.1	13.0	16.0
15 LIQUID FUELS	8.8	9.6	15.7	2.7	31.3	1.4	9.4	11.0	11.8
16 NATURAL GAS	*	*	*	*	*	*	*	*	*
17 HYDROELECTRIC POWER	*	*	*	*	35.0	15.6	*	*	*
18 ADDENDUM - TOTAL ELECTRICITY	NA	NA	NA	NA	18.9	12.3	NA	NA	NA
19 POPULATION	4.9	0.4	1.3	2.6	3.1	3.0	1.8	2.9	2.1
20 TOTAL PER CAPITA PRODUCTION	34.8	63.1	0.8	10.7	21.1	-0.7	53.8	10.0	19.5
PER CAPITA CONSUMPTION									
21 TOTAL	6.6	9.7	14.0	4.5	23.1	-0.7	8.7	8.5	10.2
22 TOTAL - ALTERNATIVE HYDRO	6.6	9.7	14.0	5.3	23.2	-0.2	8.7	9.0	10.4
23 SOLID FUELS	34.8	12.5	13.0	17.5	11.5	1.0	18.9	9.8	13.7
24 LIQUID FUELS	3.7	9.1	14.2	0.1	27.3	-1.6	7.4	7.9	9.6
25 NATURAL GAS	*	*	*	*	*	*	*	*	*

Table XIII. AVERAGE ANNUAL PERCENTAGE RATES OF CHANGE IN TOTAL AND PER CAPITA ENERGY PRODUCTION, TRADE, AND CONSUMPTION, SELECTED PERIODS, 1925-1965

Region, country, indicator	1925-29	1929-38	1938-50	1950-55	1955-60	1960-65	1925-38	1950-65	1925-65
	(1)	(2)	(3)	(4)	(5)	(6)	(7)	(8)	(9)
ALBANIA (CONTINUED)									
PER CAPITA CONSUMPTION (CONTINUED)									
26 HYDROELECTRIC POWER	*	*	*	*	30.9	12.2	*	*	*
27 ADDENDUM - TOTAL ELECTRICITY	NA	NA	NA	NA	15.3	9.0	NA	NA	NA
BULGARIA									
PRODUCTION									
1 TOTAL	8.0	3.3	8.2	12.9	10.2	8.2	4.7	10.4	7.9
2 SOLID FUELS	7.9	3.2	8.3	11.3	10.0	8.7	4.6	10.0	7.7
3 LIQUID FUELS	*	*	*	*	5.9	2.7	*	*	*
4 NATURAL GAS	*	*	*	*	*	*	*	*	*
5 HYDROELECTRIC POWER	30.3	12.5	6.7	16.2	23.8	1.2	17.7	13.3	12.7
IMPORTS									
6 TOTAL	13.1	0.1	8.5	11.7	21.5	37.5	3.9	23.1	12.2
7 SOLID FUELS	-15.9	-8.6	NA	NA	21.7	54.7	-10.9	NA	13.5
8 LIQUID FUELS	18.2	0.5	8.7	7.0	21.4	31.7	5.7	19.6	11.6
EXPORTS									
9 TOTAL	53.1	4.3	*	*	1.4	-11.9	17.3	*	10.6
10 SOLID FUELS	53.1	4.3	NA	NA	24.6	*	17.3	NA	*
11 LIQUID FUELS	*	*	*	*	-3.1	-5.8	*	*	*
CONSUMPTION									
12 TOTAL	8.6	2.7	8.4	11.6	12.6	18.1	4.5	14.1	9.2
13 TOTAL - ALTERNATIVE HYDRO	9.2	3.2	8.1	11.6	13.1	17.1	5.0	13.9	9.2
14 SOLID FUELS	6.7	3.0	8.4	11.9	10.4	14.5	4.1	12.3	8.4
15 LIQUID FUELS	18.2	0.5	8.7	9.0	21.7	30.0	5.7	20.0	11.8
16 NATURAL GAS	*	*	*	*	*	*	*	*	*
17 HYDROELECTRIC POWER	30.3	12.5	6.7	16.2	23.8	1.2	17.7	13.3	12.7
18 ADDENDUM - TOTAL ELECTRICITY	28.0	11.7	11.1	20.8	17.3	16.9	16.5	18.3	15.5
19 POPULATION	1.6	1.1	1.2	0.7	1.0	0.8	1.3	0.8	1.1
20 TOTAL PER CAPITA PRODUCTION	6.3	2.2	6.9	12.1	9.1	7.3	3.4	9.5	6.7
PER CAPITA CONSUMPTION									
21 TOTAL	6.9	1.6	7.1	10.8	11.6	17.1	3.2	13.1	8.0
22 TOTAL - ALTERNATIVE HYDRO	7.5	2.0	6.8	10.8	12.0	16.1	3.7	13.0	8.0
23 SOLID FUELS	5.1	1.9	7.1	11.2	9.4	13.5	2.8	11.4	7.3
24 LIQUID FUELS	16.4	-0.6	7.4	8.3	20.6	28.9	4.3	19.0	10.6
25 NATURAL GAS	*	*	*	*	*	*	*	*	*
26 HYDROELECTRIC POWER	28.3	11.2	5.4	15.4	22.6	0.3	16.2	12.4	11.4
27 ADDENDUM - TOTAL ELECTRICITY	26.0	10.4	9.7	20.0	16.2	15.9	15.0	17.3	14.3
CZECHOSLOVAKIA									
PRODUCTION									
1 TOTAL	6.1	-1.8	2.7	5.4	6.8	3.0	0.6	5.0	2.9
2 SOLID FUELS	6.1	-1.8	2.7	5.2	6.3	3.2	0.5	4.9	2.8
3 LIQUID FUELS	-11.7	3.5	10.7	10.8	5.1	7.0	-1.5	7.6	5.4
4 NATURAL GAS	*	-7.4	27.8	55.5	49.5	-8.1	*	28.8	*
5 HYDROELECTRIC POWER	5.4	12.0	5.2	11.9	5.3	12.3	9.9	9.8	8.4
IMPORTS									
6 TOTAL	13.0	-8.6	5.2	16.2	4.1	16.7	-2.5	12.2	5.1
7 SOLID FUELS	12.2	-11.5	5.4	19.3	-6.8	11.6	-4.8	7.4	2.7
8 LIQUID FUELS	17.4	0.1	4.7	10.0	21.5	19.6	5.1	16.9	9.3
EXPORTS									
9 TOTAL	7.2	-5.0	-8.9	19.9	13.6	4.3	-1.4	12.4	1.1
10 SOLID FUELS	7.2	-5.0	-8.9	19.4	12.7	0.9	-1.4	10.7	0.6
11 LIQUID FUELS	-2.4	-16.4	*	*	46.9	35.8	-12.3	*	11.2
CONSUMPTION									
12 TOTAL	6.6	-1.9	3.6	5.8	6.1	4.7	0.6	5.6	3.3
13 TOTAL - ALTERNATIVE HYDRO	6.5	-1.9	3.6	5.8	6.0	4.9	0.7	5.6	3.4
14 SOLID FUELS	6.4	-2.0	3.6	5.6	5.0	3.8	0.5	4.8	3.0
15 LIQUID FUELS	15.8	0.4	5.1	9.6	19.4	17.8	4.9	15.5	8.8
16 NATURAL GAS	*	-7.4	27.8	55.5	49.5	-8.1	*	28.8	*
17 HYDROELECTRIC POWER	5.0	10.9	5.9	8.4	4.3	18.6	9.1	10.3	8.6
18 ADDENDUM - TOTAL ELECTRICITY	11.0	3.5	7.3	9.6	10.2	7.6	5.8	9.1	7.5
19 POPULATION	0.6	0.6	-1.4	1.1	0.8	0.7	0.6	0.9	0.1
20 TOTAL PER CAPITA PRODUCTION	5.4	-2.4	4.1	4.2	5.9	2.3	-	4.1	2.8
PER CAPITA CONSUMPTION									
21 TOTAL	5.9	-2.5	5.1	4.7	5.2	4.0	-	4.6	3.2
22 TOTAL - ALTERNATIVE HYDRO	5.9	-2.4	5.1	4.6	5.2	4.1	0.1	4.6	3.3
23 SOLID FUELS	5.8	-2.6	5.0	4.4	4.1	3.1	-0.1	3.9	2.9
24 LIQUID FUELS	15.1	-0.1	6.6	8.4	18.4	16.9	4.3	14.5	8.7
25 NATURAL GAS	*	-7.9	29.6	53.8	48.3	-8.8	*	27.7	*
26 HYDROELECTRIC POWER	4.4	10.3	7.4	7.3	3.5	17.7	8.4	9.3	8.5
27 ADDENDUM - TOTAL ELECTRICITY	10.3	2.9	8.7	8.4	9.3	6.9	5.2	8.2	7.4

Table XIII. AVERAGE ANNUAL PERCENTAGE RATES OF CHANGE IN TOTAL AND PER CAPITA ENERGY PRODUCTION, TRADE, AND CONSUMPTION, SELECTED PERIODS, 1925-1965

Region, country, indicator	1925-29	1929-38	1938-50	1950-55	1955-60	1960-65	1925-38	1950-65	1925-65
	(1)	(2)	(3)	(4)	(5)	(6)	(7)	(8)	(9)
GERMANY, EAST									
PRODUCTION									
1 TOTAL				7.4	2.3	2.0		3.9	
2 SOLID FUELS				7.4	2.3	2.0		3.9	
3 LIQUID FUELS				*	*	*		*	
4 NATURAL GAS				*	*	*		*	
5 HYDROELECTRIC POWER				13.1	4.3	4.9		7.4	
IMPORTS									
6 TOTAL				9.9	7.4	7.5		8.3	
7 SOLID FUELS				9.2	3.8	3.3		5.4	
8 LIQUID FUELS				21.0	30.1	18.3		23.0	
EXPORTS									
9 TOTAL				26.9	5.4	2.4		11.1	
10 SOLID FUELS				27.5	4.1	-1.1		9.5	
11 LIQUID FUELS				29.6	9.9	11.9		16.8	
CONSUMPTION									
12 TOTAL				7.0	2.9	3.2		4.4	
13 TOTAL - ALTERNATIVE HYDRO				7.1	2.9	3.2		4.4	
14 SOLID FUELS				7.0	2.4	2.3		3.9	
15 LIQUID FUELS				-	72.7	21.5		28.0	
16 NATURAL GAS				-	8.4	21.3		9.6	
17 HYDROELECTRIC POWER				*	-12.8	28.8		*	
18 ADDENDUM - TOTAL ELECTRICITY				9.9	6.8	6.1		7.6	
19 POPULATION				-0.5	-0.8	-0.2		-0.5	
20 TOTAL PER CAPITA PRODUCTION				7.9	3.1	2.3		4.4	
PER CAPITA CONSUMPTION									
21 TOTAL				7.5	3.8	3.4		4.9	
22 TOTAL - ALTERNATIVE HYDRO				7.6	3.7	3.4		4.9	
23 SOLID FUELS				7.5	3.2	2.6		4.4	
24 LIQUID FUELS				0.5	74.1	21.8		28.7	
25 NATURAL GAS				0.5	9.3	21.6		10.1	
26 HYDROELECTRIC POWER				*	-12.1	29.2		*	
27 ADDENDUM - TOTAL ELECTRICITY				10.4	7.7	6.4		8.2	
HUNGARY									
PRODUCTION									
1 TOTAL	5.3	2.1	4.0	12.4	2.0	5.1	3.1	6.4	4.6
2 SOLID FUELS	5.3	2.0	2.9	11.2	3.3	3.9	3.0	6.1	4.1
3 LIQUID FUELS	*	*	22.9	25.6	-4.9	7.8	*	8.8	*
4 NATURAL GAS	*	*	38.0	7.4	-8.9	26.5	*	7.4	*
5 HYDROELECTRIC POWER	15.8	9.3	11.0	-8.1	15.4	-4.4	11.3	0.5	7.0
IMPORTS									
6 TOTAL	14.5	-10.0	1.5	19.6	16.8	9.6	-3.0	15.3	4.9
7 SOLID FUELS	12.5	-13.1	3.2	20.2	7.0	8.7	-5.9	11.8	3.2
8 LIQUID FUELS	32.8	0.3	-2.2	16.1	35.7	11.0	9.3	20.5	9.6
EXPORTS									
9 TOTAL	-9.1	-4.7	4.3	19.6	1.7	1.0	-6.1	7.1	1.8
10 SOLID FUELS	-9.1	-4.7	-1.9	11.6	-31.2	28.5	-6.1	-0.5	-2.7
11 LIQUID FUELS	*	*	*	25.3	9.4	-1.4	*	10.6	*
CONSUMPTION									
12 TOTAL	8.8	-0.3	3.7	12.9	4.4	6.3	2.4	7.8	4.8
13 TOTAL - ALTERNATIVE HYDRO	8.8	-0.2	3.7	13.0	4.4	6.3	2.4	7.9	4.8
14 SOLID FUELS	8.1	-0.4	3.1	12.0	4.1	4.5	2.1	6.8	4.1
15 LIQUID FUELS	32.8	2.4	6.9	23.3	7.2	11.7	10.9	13.9	10.8
16 NATURAL GAS	*	*	38.0	7.4	-0.7	19.9	*	8.6	*
17 HYDROELECTRIC POWER	15.8	9.3	11.0	33.4	16.5	16.7	11.3	21.9	15.1
18 ADDENDUM - TOTAL ELECTRICITY	12.4	5.2	8.6	13.6	7.5	8.6	7.4	9.9	8.7
19 POPULATION	0.8	0.7	0.2	1.0	0.3	0.3	0.8	0.6	0.5
20 TOTAL PER CAPITA PRODUCTION	4.4	1.4	3.9	11.3	1.6	4.7	2.3	5.8	4.1
PER CAPITA CONSUMPTION									
21 TOTAL	7.8	-1.0	3.6	11.8	4.0	5.9	1.7	7.2	4.3
22 TOTAL - ALTERNATIVE HYDRO	7.8	-1.0	3.6	11.9	4.1	6.0	1.7	7.3	4.3
23 SOLID FUELS	7.2	-1.1	2.9	10.9	3.8	4.2	1.3	6.2	3.6
24 LIQUID FUELS	31.6	1.6	6.7	22.0	6.9	11.3	10.0	13.2	10.2
25 NATURAL GAS	*	*	37.8	6.3	-1.0	19.5	*	8.0	*
26 HYDROELECTRIC POWER	14.9	8.5	10.8	32.1	16.1	16.3	10.4	21.3	14.5
27 ADDENDUM - TOTAL ELECTRICITY	11.4	4.4	8.5	12.5	7.1	8.2	6.5	9.3	8.1
POLAND									
PRODUCTION									
1 TOTAL	11.5	-2.1	6.0	4.0	2.2	3.4	1.9	3.2	3.6

Table XIII. AVERAGE ANNUAL PERCENTAGE RATES OF CHANGE IN TOTAL AND PER CAPITA ENERGY PRODUCTION, TRADE, AND CONSUMPTION, SELECTED PERIODS, 1925-1965

Region, country, indicator	1925-29	1929-38	1938-50	1950-55	1955-60	1960-65	1925-38	1950-65	1925-65
	(1)	(2)	(3)	(4)	(5)	(6)	(7)	(8)	(9)
POLAND (CONTINUED)									
PRODUCTION (CONTINUED)									
2 SOLID FUELS	12.3	-2.1	6.3	3.9	2.2	3.2	2.1	3.1	3.7
3 LIQUID FUELS	-3.9	-2.8	-9.0	2.5	1.3	11.3	-3.2	4.9	-2.0
4 NATURAL GAS	-3.3	2.5	-9.3	16.6	6.9	20.2	0.7	14.4	2.4
5 HYDROELECTRIC POWER	15.0	4.0	18.9	12.1	-1.5	6.7	7.3	5.7	10.0
IMPORTS									
6 TOTAL	6.9	-6.4	13.8	22.9	16.5	14.1	-2.5	17.8	9.6
7 SOLID FUELS	6.8	-6.0	-10.1	21.1	55.2	7.4	-2.3	26.4	4.9
8 LIQUID FUELS	18.9	-18.1	68.3	22.2	11.7	16.5	-8.1	16.7	20.5
EXPORTS									
9 TOTAL	12.8	-3.4	9.0	-0.6	-5.0	4.3	1.3	-0.5	2.8
10 SOLID FUELS	13.8	-3.2	8.9	-0.7	-5.2	3.4	1.7	-0.9	2.8
11 LIQUID FUELS	-11.7	-28.4	15.4	15.8	14.4	34.7	-23.6	21.3	2.8
CONSUMPTION									
12 TOTAL	10.7	-2.1	5.3	6.4	5.4	3.9	1.6	5.2	4.1
13 TOTAL - ALTERNATIVE HYDRO	10.6	-2.1	5.3	6.4	5.4	3.9	1.6	5.2	4.1
14 SOLID FUELS	11.4	-2.3	5.6	6.0	5.2	3.2	1.7	4.8	4.0
15 LIQUID FUELS	-0.1	0.1	1.5	18.5	10.2	13.8	-	14.1	5.5
16 NATURAL GAS	-3.3	2.5	-8.5	20.8	8.6	17.5	0.7	15.5	3.0
17 HYDROELECTRIC POWER	4.7	-5.6	20.7	9.9	4.9	-10.7	-2.6	1.0	5.3
18 ADDENDUM - TOTAL ELECTRICITY	16.3	3.0	7.3	13.9	10.7	7.8	6.9	10.8	8.5
19 POPULATION	1.5	1.2	-2.7	1.9	1.7	1.1	1.3	1.6	0.2
20 TOTAL PER CAPITA PRODUCTION	9.8	-3.3	9.0	2.0	0.5	2.2	0.6	1.6	3.4
PER CAPITA CONSUMPTION									
21 TOTAL	9.0	-3.3	8.3	4.4	3.6	2.8	0.3	3.6	3.9
22 TOTAL - ALTERNATIVE HYDRO	9.0	-3.3	8.3	4.4	3.6	2.7	0.3	3.6	3.9
23 SOLID FUELS	9.8	-3.5	8.6	4.0	3.4	2.1	0.4	3.2	3.8
24 LIQUID FUELS	-1.6	-1.1	4.3	16.3	8.3	12.5	-1.3	12.3	5.4
25 NATURAL GAS	-4.8	1.3	-5.9	18.5	6.7	16.2	-0.6	13.7	2.8
26 HYDROELECTRIC POWER	3.1	-6.7	24.2	7.8	3.2	-11.7	-3.8	-0.6	5.1
27 ADDENDUM - TOTAL ELECTRICITY	14.5	1.8	10.4	11.8	8.8	6.6	5.5	9.0	8.3
ROMANIA									
PRODUCTION									
1 TOTAL	15.3	3.9	-1.2	14.8	4.5	6.8	7.3	8.6	5.1
2 SOLID FUELS	1.2	-0.8	2.3	9.1	6.1	9.2	-0.2	8.2	3.6
3 LIQUID FUELS	20.4	3.9	-2.3	15.7	1.8	1.9	8.7	6.3	4.4
4 NATURAL GAS	21.5	9.7	-0.3	17.2	10.4	13.4	13.2	13.6	9.1
5 HYDROELECTRIC POWER	4.6	8.5	3.9	10.1	4.2	20.4	7.3	11.4	7.7
IMPORTS									
6 TOTAL	1.0	-10.2	7.4	24.9	8.6	8.9	-6.9	13.9	4.8
7 SOLID FUELS	0.5	-10.3	7.7	24.9	8.6	8.9	-7.1	13.9	4.8
8 LIQUID FUELS	41.4	-7.4	*	*	*	*	5.5	*	*
EXPORTS									
9 TOTAL	35.0	4.9	-4.3	19.5	0.7	-0.7	13.4	6.1	5.1
10 SOLID FUELS	11.5	*	*	*	*	*	*	*	*
11 LIQUID FUELS	35.4	5.0	-4.3	19.5	0.1	-0.8	13.6	5.9	5.1
CONSUMPTION									
12 TOTAL	6.7	2.6	1.2	13.1	6.4	9.3	3.9	9.6	5.1
13 TOTAL - ALTERNATIVE HYDRO	6.6	2.6	1.2	13.0	6.4	9.3	3.9	9.5	5.1
14 SOLID FUELS	1.0	-1.4	2.7	10.9	6.5	9.2	-0.7	8.8	3.8
15 LIQUID FUELS	7.6	1.7	1.3	11.9	3.8	4.3	3.5	6.6	4.0
16 NATURAL GAS	21.5	9.7	-0.3	17.2	9.7	13.8	13.2	13.5	9.1
17 HYDROELECTRIC POWER	4.6	8.5	3.9	7.9	4.6	12.9	7.3	8.4	6.7
18 ADDENDUM - TOTAL ELECTRICITY	23.8	8.1	5.6	14.4	12.1	17.7	12.7	14.7	11.2
19 POPULATION	1.4	1.2	0.4	1.2	1.2	0.7	1.3	1.0	0.9
20 TOTAL PER CAPITA PRODUCTION	13.7	2.6	-1.6	13.4	3.3	6.1	5.9	7.5	4.2
PER CAPITA CONSUMPTION									
21 TOTAL	5.2	1.4	0.8	11.7	5.2	8.6	2.5	8.4	4.2
22 TOTAL - ALTERNATIVE HYDRO	5.2	1.4	0.8	11.7	5.1	8.6	2.5	8.4	4.2
23 SOLID FUELS	-0.4	-2.6	2.3	9.5	5.2	8.4	-1.9	7.7	2.9
24 LIQUID FUELS	6.1	0.5	0.9	10.6	2.5	3.6	2.2	5.5	3.0
25 NATURAL GAS	19.9	8.4	-0.6	15.7	8.4	13.0	11.8	12.3	8.1
26 HYDROELECTRIC POWER	3.2	7.2	3.5	6.6	3.4	12.2	5.9	7.3	5.7
27 ADDENDUM - TOTAL ELECTRICITY	22.1	6.8	5.2	13.0	10.7	16.9	11.3	13.5	10.2
USSR (INCLUDING ESTONIA, LATVIA, LITHUANIA)									
PRODUCTION									
1 TOTAL	21.6	13.0	4.2	9.6	8.5	7.4	15.6	8.5	9.4
2 SOLID FUELS	23.8	14.5	4.8	8.5	3.5	2.3	17.3	4.7	8.7
3 LIQUID FUELS	17.9	9.3	2.1	13.4	15.6	10.0	11.9	13.0	9.2

Table XIII. AVERAGE ANNUAL PERCENTAGE RATES OF CHANGE IN TOTAL AND PER CAPITA ENERGY PRODUCTION, TRADE, AND CONSUMPTION, SELECTED PERIODS, 1925-1965

Region, country, indicator	1925-29	1929-38	1938-50	1950-55	1955-60	1960-65	1925-38	1950-65	1925-65
	(1)	(2)	(3)	(4)	(5)	(6)	(7)	(8)	(9)
USSR (INCLUDING ESTONIA, LATVIA, LITHUANIA) (CONTINUED)									
PRODUCTION (CONTINUED)									
4 NATURAL GAS	23.9	23.5	8.3	9.3	38.2	23.0	23.6	22.9	18.6
5 HYDROELECTRIC POWER	22.1	27.9	7.9	12.8	17.1	9.8	26.1	13.2	15.6
IMPORTS									
6 TOTAL	12.2	2.0	21.5	1.9	-7.3	-2.7	5.0	-2.8	6.6
7 SOLID FUELS	12.2	-0.5	22.0	-4.5	-10.0	6.6	3.3	-2.8	6.1
8 LIQUID FUELS	11.9	12.5	20.3	14.3	-4.6	-15.3	12.3	-2.6	8.7
EXPORTS									
9 TOTAL	31.0	-11.0	4.6	33.1	29.3	13.7	0.2	25.1	10.3
10 SOLID FUELS	38.2	-14.5	18.9	17.3	20.6	11.9	-0.9	16.5	11.2
11 LIQUID FUELS	29.5	-10.3	-2.3	48.6	33.0	14.2	0.4	31.2	10.1
CONSUMPTION									
12 TOTAL	20.3	14.3	4.6	8.7	6.8	6.6	16.1	7.4	9.3
13 TOTAL - ALTERNATIVE HYDRO	20.2	14.4	4.6	8.7	6.9	6.6	16.2	7.4	9.3
14 SOLID FUELS	23.0	14.7	5.1	7.9	2.8	1.9	17.2	4.2	8.5
15 LIQUID FUELS	14.5	12.8	2.8	11.7	11.6	8.1	13.3	10.5	9.0
16 NATURAL GAS	23.9	23.5	8.3	9.0	38.5	23.1	23.6	23.0	18.6
17 HYDROELECTRIC POWER	22.1	27.9	7.9	12.8	17.0	9.5	26.1	13.1	15.5
18 ADDENDUM - TOTAL ELECTRICITY	20.8	22.8	7.2	13.4	11.4	11.6	22.2	12.1	13.7
19 POPULATION	2.3	1.3	-0.4	1.7	1.8	1.5	1.6	1.7	1.0
20 TOTAL PER CAPITA PRODUCTION	18.8	11.5	4.7	7.7	6.6	5.9	13.7	6.7	8.3
PER CAPITA CONSUMPTION									
21 TOTAL	17.6	12.8	5.1	6.9	4.9	5.0	14.2	5.6	8.2
22 TOTAL - ALTERNATIVE HYDRO	17.5	12.9	5.1	6.9	5.0	5.0	14.3	5.6	8.2
23 SOLID FUELS	20.2	13.2	5.5	6.0	1.0	0.5	15.3	2.5	7.4
24 LIQUID FUELS	11.9	11.3	3.2	9.8	9.7	6.6	11.5	8.7	7.9
25 NATURAL GAS	21.1	21.9	8.8	7.2	36.1	21.3	21.7	20.9	17.4
26 HYDROELECTRIC POWER	19.3	26.2	8.4	10.9	15.0	7.9	24.0	11.2	14.3
27 ADDENDUM - TOTAL ELECTRICITY	18.1	21.2	7.7	11.4	9.4	10.0	20.2	10.3	12.6
COMMUNIST ASIA									
PRODUCTION									
1 TOTAL	1.6	2.5	3.1	17.5	18.9	7.0	2.3	14.3	6.9
2 SOLID FUELS	1.6	2.4	3.0	17.4	18.3	6.8	2.1	14.0	6.7
3 LIQUID FUELS	*	56.4	-2.8	37.0	41.8	12.6	*	29.8	*
4 NATURAL GAS	*	*	*	*	*	*	*	*	*
5 HYDROELECTRIC POWER	*	*	*	3.3	25.5	1.7	*	9.6	*
IMPORTS									
6 TOTAL	-1.7	-5.6	NA	NA	20.6	-21.0	-4.4	NA	-2.3
7 SOLID FUELS	-4.6	-7.6	NA	NA	6.6	4.9	-6.7	NA	-7.2
8 LIQUID FUELS	3.3	-3.1	NA	NA	21.0	-22.0	-1.2	NA	0.2
EXPORTS									
9 TOTAL	8.0	2.2	NA	NA	-1.3	11.2	4.0	NA	-1.0
10 SOLID FUELS	8.0	1.9	NA	NA	-1.3	11.2	3.7	NA	-1.0
11 LIQUID FUELS	*	*	NA	NA	*	*	*	NA	*
CONSUMPTION									
12 TOTAL	0.1	1.6	3.9	17.9	19.1	6.5	1.1	14.4	6.7
13 TOTAL - ALTERNATIVE HYDRO	0.1	1.6	4.3	17.2	19.1	6.4	1.1	14.1	6.8
14 SOLID FUELS	-0.1	1.7	4.2	17.3	18.5	6.7	1.1	14.0	6.7
15 LIQUID FUELS	3.4	-0.8	-17.4	87.9	31.2	4.0	0.5	36.8	6.4
16 NATURAL GAS	*	*	*	*	*	*	*	*	*
17 HYDROELECTRIC POWER	*	*	*	3.3	25.5	1.7	*	9.6	*
18 ADDENDUM - TOTAL ELECTRICITY	2.1	8.5	6.3	11.1	34.3	-2.7	6.5	13.2	8.9
19 POPULATION	0.6	-	2.0	1.8	1.7	1.6	0.2	1.7	1.3
20 TOTAL PER CAPITA PRODUCTION	1.0	2.5	1.1	15.4	16.9	5.3	2.1	12.4	5.5
PER CAPITA CONSUMPTION									
21 TOTAL	-0.5	1.6	1.9	15.8	17.1	4.9	0.9	12.5	5.4
22 TOTAL - ALTERNATIVE HYDRO	-0.5	1.6	2.3	15.1	17.2	4.7	0.9	12.2	5.4
23 SOLID FUELS	-0.7	1.7	2.2	15.2	16.5	5.1	1.0	12.2	5.4
24 LIQUID FUELS	2.8	-0.8	-19.1	84.5	29.0	2.4	0.3	34.6	5.0
25 NATURAL GAS	*	*	*	*	*	*	*	*	*
26 HYDROELECTRIC POWER	*	*	*	1.4	23.4	0.1	*	7.8	*
27 ADDENDUM - TOTAL ELECTRICITY	1.5	8.5	4.3	9.1	32.1	-4.2	6.3	11.3	7.5
LATIN AMERICA									
PRODUCTION									
1 TOTAL	9.6	3.0	7.0	7.1	7.0	4.8	5.0	6.3	6.1
2 SOLID FUELS	-1.8	3.6	2.8	4.6	2.0	4.5	1.9	3.7	2.8
3 LIQUID FUELS	10.3	2.6	7.4	7.0	6.5	4.3	4.9	5.9	6.0
4 NATURAL GAS	17.5	9.8	3.0	12.2	17.4	9.6	12.1	13.0	9.6
5 HYDROELECTRIC POWER	5.8	5.3	7.0	8.8	9.8	8.2	5.5	8.9	7.2

Table XIII. AVERAGE ANNUAL PERCENTAGE RATES OF CHANGE IN TOTAL AND PER CAPITA ENERGY PRODUCTION, TRADE, AND CONSUMPTION, SELECTED PERIODS, 1925-1965

Region, country, indicator	1925-29	1929-38	1938-50	1950-55	1955-60	1960-65	1925-38	1950-65	1925-65
	(1)	(2)	(3)	(4)	(5)	(6)	(7)	(8)	(9)
LATIN AMERICA (CONTINUED)									
IMPORTS									
6 TOTAL	18.4	4.6	4.8	4.3	0.3	4.4	8.7	3.0	5.4
7 SOLID FUELS	1.1	-3.5	-5.1	-0.8	1.8	-3.5	-2.1	-0.9	-2.6
8 LIQUID FUELS	26.2	6.0	5.4	4.5	0.4	4.5	11.8	3.1	6.6
EXPORTS									
9 TOTAL	18.5	4.5	6.4	5.2	3.7	4.3	8.6	4.4	6.4
10 SOLID FUELS	13.6	9.8	7.7	-13.2	-6.5	-32.5	11.0	-18.2	-1.9
11 LIQUID FUELS	18.5	4.5	6.4	5.3	3.6	4.4	8.6	4.4	6.4
CONSUMPTION									
12 TOTAL	6.1	2.4	4.6	9.7	7.8	5.4	3.5	7.6	5.4
13 TOTAL - ALTERNATIVE HYDRO	5.7	2.4	4.6	9.3	7.7	5.4	3.4	7.5	5.3
14 SOLID FUELS	0.1	-0.1	-0.6	3.1	2.0	2.6	-	2.6	0.8
15 LIQUID FUELS	8.7	2.3	6.0	10.6	7.2	4.4	4.3	7.4	6.0
16 NATURAL GAS	17.5	9.9	3.9	10.8	14.5	10.1	12.2	11.8	9.5
17 HYDROELECTRIC POWER	5.8	5.3	7.1	8.8	9.9	7.9	5.5	8.9	7.2
18 ADDENDUM - TOTAL ELECTRICITY	6.8	7.1	7.6	10.9	10.5	8.0	7.0	9.8	8.2
19 POPULATION	2.0	1.9	2.2	2.7	2.8	2.7	1.9	2.7	2.3
20 TOTAL PER CAPITA PRODUCTION	7.5	1.1	4.7	4.3	4.1	2.0	3.0	3.5	3.7
PER CAPITA CONSUMPTION									
21 TOTAL	4.1	0.5	2.4	6.8	4.9	2.6	1.6	4.8	3.0
22 TOTAL - ALTERNATIVE HYDRO	3.6	0.5	2.3	6.4	4.8	2.5	1.5	4.6	2.9
23 SOLID FUELS	-1.8	-1.9	-2.7	0.4	-0.8	-0.1	-1.9	-0.2	-1.5
24 LIQUID FUELS	6.6	0.4	3.8	7.7	4.3	1.7	2.3	4.5	3.6
25 NATURAL GAS	15.3	7.9	1.7	7.9	11.4	7.1	10.1	8.8	7.0
26 HYDROELECTRIC POWER	3.7	3.4	4.8	5.9	7.0	5.1	3.5	6.0	4.8
27 ADDENDUM - TOTAL ELECTRICITY	4.7	5.1	5.3	8.0	7.5	5.1	5.0	6.8	5.8
LATIN AMERICA - CARIBBEAN									
PRODUCTION									
1 TOTAL	9.8	2.7	7.6	7.3	6.4	4.4	4.9	6.0	6.1
2 SOLID FUELS	-6.9	2.8	2.1	10.6	6.5	3.5	-0.3	6.8	3.1
3 LIQUID FUELS	10.1	2.4	7.9	7.0	5.7	4.1	4.7	5.6	6.0
4 NATURAL GAS	33.2	13.9	3.6	14.7	18.4	7.9	19.5	13.5	12.3
5 HYDROELECTRIC POWER	6.9	6.6	3.6	10.8	8.4	11.2	6.6	10.1	7.0
IMPORTS									
6 TOTAL	27.5	6.5	4.9	2.7	0.4	5.5	12.6	2.9	6.5
7 SOLID FUELS	0.2	-8.2	-13.3	10.9	-11.3	31.2	-5.7	8.9	-2.9
8 LIQUID FUELS	30.8	7.0	4.9	2.8	0.6	5.5	13.8	2.9	7.0
EXPORTS									
9 TOTAL	18.7	4.6	6.7	5.3	3.7	4.4	8.7	4.4	6.5
10 SOLID FUELS	*	*	*	*	*	*	*	-	*
11 LIQUID FUELS	18.7	4.6	6.7	5.3	3.5	4.4	8.7	4.4	6.5
CONSUMPTION									
12 TOTAL	5.3	2.9	5.2	11.0	9.4	5.4	3.6	8.6	5.9
13 TOTAL - ALTERNATIVE HYDRO	5.1	2.9	5.0	10.8	9.3	5.5	3.6	8.5	5.8
14 SOLID FUELS	-4.8	-0.2	0.4	11.0	5.8	4.6	-1.6	7.1	2.2
15 LIQUID FUELS	6.3	1.8	5.8	10.7	8.4	4.4	3.2	7.8	5.7
16 NATURAL GAS	33.1	14.1	4.9	12.5	14.6	8.3	19.6	11.8	12.1
17 HYDROELECTRIC POWER	6.9	6.6	3.8	10.6	8.8	10.3	6.7	9.9	7.0
18 ADDENDUM - TOTAL ELECTRICITY	5.5	5.9	6.6	14.1	11.5	10.2	5.8	11.9	8.3
19 POPULATION	1.8	1.9	2.3	2.9	2.9	3.0	1.8	3.0	2.4
20 TOTAL PER CAPITA PRODUCTION	7.8	0.9	5.2	4.3	3.4	1.3	3.0	3.0	3.6
PER CAPITA CONSUMPTION									
21 TOTAL	3.5	1.0	2.8	7.9	6.3	2.3	1.7	5.5	3.5
22 TOTAL - ALTERNATIVE HYDRO	3.3	1.1	2.6	7.6	6.1	2.4	1.7	5.4	3.3
23 SOLID FUELS	-6.5	-2.0	-1.8	7.8	2.8	1.6	-3.4	4.0	-0.2
24 LIQUID FUELS	4.5	-0.1	3.5	7.6	5.3	1.4	1.3	4.7	3.2
25 NATURAL GAS	30.8	12.0	2.6	9.3	11.4	5.2	17.5	8.6	9.5
26 HYDROELECTRIC POWER	5.0	4.7	1.5	7.5	5.7	7.1	4.8	6.8	4.5
27 ADDENDUM - TOTAL ELECTRICITY	3.6	4.0	4.2	10.9	8.3	7.0	3.9	8.7	5.8
CARIBBEAN - OIL PRODUCING									
PRODUCTION									
1 TOTAL	9.8	2.7	7.6	7.3	6.4	4.4	4.8	6.0	6.1
2 SOLID FUELS	-6.9	2.8	2.1	10.6	6.5	3.5	-0.3	6.8	3.1
3 LIQUID FUELS	10.1	2.4	7.9	7.0	5.8	4.1	4.7	5.6	6.0
4 NATURAL GAS	33.2	13.9	3.6	14.7	18.4	7.9	19.5	13.5	12.3
5 HYDROELECTRIC POWER	6.9	6.3	2.6	12.4	8.7	12.1	6.5	11.0	7.0
IMPORTS									
6 TOTAL	45.7	8.3	4.8	2.1	-1.9	3.7	18.6	1.3	7.7

Table XIII. AVERAGE ANNUAL PERCENTAGE RATES OF CHANGE IN TOTAL AND PER CAPITA ENERGY PRODUCTION, TRADE, AND CONSUMPTION, SELECTED PERIODS, 1925-1965

Region, country, indicator	1925-29	1929-38	1938-50	1950-55	1955-60	1960-65	1925-38	1950-65	1925-65
	(1)	(2)	(3)	(4)	(5)	(6)	(7)	(8)	(9)
CARIBBEAN - OIL PRODUCING (CONTINUED)									
IMPORTS (CONTINUED)									
7 SOLID FUELS	6.8	-7.8	-3.2	0.7	-3.6	42.6	-3.5	11.5	1.9
8 LIQUID FUELS	46.5	8.3	4.7	2.2	-1.7	3.7	18.9	1.3	7.8
EXPORTS									
9 TOTAL	18.7	4.6	6.7	5.3	3.4	4.3	8.7	4.3	6.4
10 SOLID FUELS	*	*	*	*	*	*	*	-	*
11 LIQUID FUELS	18.7	4.6	6.7	5.3	3.3	4.3	8.7	4.3	6.4
CONSUMPTION									
12 TOTAL	7.5	4.2	4.7	11.6	9.4	4.9	5.2	8.6	6.3
13 TOTAL - ALTERNATIVE HYDRO	7.0	4.2	4.4	11.5	9.3	5.0	5.1	8.5	6.2
14 SOLID FUELS	-6.6	2.4	2.0	10.6	6.3	4.4	-0.5	7.1	3.1
15 LIQUID FUELS	8.9	2.8	5.0	11.5	8.0	3.4	4.6	7.6	5.8
16 NATURAL GAS	33.1	14.1	4.9	12.5	14.6	8.3	19.6	11.8	12.1
17 HYDROELECTRIC POWER	6.9	6.4	2.9	12.1	9.2	10.9	6.6	10.7	7.0
18 ADDENDUM - TOTAL ELECTRICITY	5.9	5.4	6.2	14.0	11.8	10.4	5.6	12.0	8.1
19 POPULATION	1.8	1.8	2.5	3.2	3.2	3.1	1.8	3.2	2.5
20 TOTAL PER CAPITA PRODUCTION	7.8	0.9	5.0	4.C	3.1	1.2	3.0	2.8	3.5
PER CAPITA CONSUMPTION									
21 TOTAL	5.6	2.4	2.1	8.2	6.0	1.7	3.4	5.3	3.7
22 TOTAL - ALTERNATIVE HYDRO	5.1	2.3	1.8	8.0	5.9	1.8	3.2	5.2	3.5
23 SOLID FUELS	-8.3	0.6	-0.5	7.2	3.0	1.2	-2.2	3.8	0.5
24 LIQUID FUELS	7.0	1.0	2.4	8.C	4.6	0.2	2.8	4.3	3.2
25 NATURAL GAS	30.8	12.0	2.3	9.0	11.1	5.0	17.5	8.3	9.3
26 HYDROELECTRIC POWER	5.0	4.5	0.3	8.7	5.8	7.5	4.7	7.3	4.3
27 ADDENDUM - TOTAL ELECTRICITY	4.1	3.5	3.6	10.4	8.3	7.0	3.7	8.6	5.5
COLOMBIA									
PRODUCTION									
1 TOTAL	92.3	1.0	4.3	4.7	7.9	6.1	23.2	6.2	10.8
2 SOLID FUELS	-	17.0	7.8	12.9	7.0	4.2	11.5	8.0	9.1
3 LIQUID FUELS	112.0	0.3	3.9	3.1	7.0	5.7	26.3	5.3	11.2
4 NATURAL GAS	*	*	*	*	*	17.8	*	*	*
5 HYDROELECTRIC POWER	2.1	8.4	11.1	15.3	11.8	8.6	6.4	11.9	9.8
IMPORTS									
6 TOTAL	47.9	-8.8	19.7	19.4	-26.4	-26.7	5.8	-13.7	1.7
7 SOLID FUELS	-24.0	*	*	*	*	*	*	*	*
8 LIQUID FUELS	55.0	-8.7	19.7	19.4	-26.4	-26.7	7.5	-13.7	2.3
EXPORTS									
9 TOTAL	*	0.5	3.7	-1.5	5.3	5.1	*	2.9	*
10 SOLID FUELS	*	*	*	*	*	*	*	*	*
11 LIQUID FUELS	*	0.5	3.7	-1.5	5.3	5.1	*	2.9	*
CONSUMPTION									
12 TOTAL	21.5	3.0	6.7	19.7	7.3	6.9	8.4	11.2	8.9
13 TOTAL - ALTERNATIVE HYDRO	18.0	3.2	6.9	18.7	7.4	6.7	7.6	10.8	8.6
14 SOLID FUELS	-0.5	16.9	7.8	12.9	7.0	4.2	11.3	8.0	9.0
15 LIQUID FUELS	29.0	-1.8	5.5	25.6	4.5	6.6	6.8	11.8	8.2
16 NATURAL GAS	*	*	*	*	*	17.8	*	*	*
17 HYDROELECTRIC POWER	2.1	8.4	11.1	15.3	11.8	8.6	6.4	11.9	9.8
18 ADDENDUM - TOTAL ELECTRICITY	3.6	9.0	6.7	25.9	11.0	11.8	7.3	16.0	10.3
19 POPULATION	2.0	2.0	2.2	3.1	3.2	2.9	2.0	3.0	2.5
20 TOTAL PER CAPITA PRODUCTION	88.5	-1.0	2.1	1.6	4.5	3.1	20.7	3.1	8.2
PER CAPITA CONSUMPTION									
21 TOTAL	19.1	1.0	4.4	16.2	4.0	3.9	6.2	7.9	6.3
22 TOTAL - ALTERNATIVE HYDRO	15.6	1.2	4.5	15.2	4.1	3.7	5.4	7.5	6.0
23 SOLID FUELS	-2.4	14.6	5.4	9.5	3.7	1.3	9.1	4.8	6.4
24 LIQUID FUELS	26.5	-3.8	3.2	21.9	1.3	3.6	4.7	8.5	5.6
25 NATURAL GAS	*	*	*	*	*	14.5	*	*	*
26 HYDROELECTRIC POWER	0.1	6.2	8.6	11.9	8.4	5.5	4.3	8.6	7.2
27 ADDENDUM - TOTAL ELECTRICITY	1.6	6.8	4.3	22.2	7.5	8.6	5.2	12.6	7.6
MEXICO									
PRODUCTION									
1 TOTAL	-20.0	-0.4	4.7	6.0	8.2	5.3	-6.9	6.5	1.4
2 SOLID FUELS	-7.6	0.4	-1.5	8.0	5.7	2.5	-2.1	5.4	0.8
3 LIQUID FUELS	-21.4	-2.1	5.5	4.3	3.3	3.9	-8.5	3.8	0.1
4 NATURAL GAS	10.0	19.7	3.9	14.1	23.3	7.6	16.6	14.8	12.0
5 HYDROELECTRIC POWER	7.5	6.0	0.3	12.1	8.5	10.7	6.5	10.4	6.0
IMPORTS									
6 TOTAL	2.5	-6.4	12.9	20.0	-19.2	-0.1	-3.7	-1.1	2.0
7 SOLID FUELS	-0.4	-15.7	6.8	14.1	-3.6	17.1	-11.2	8.8	1.3
8 LIQUID FUELS	2.7	-7.8	7.2	36.2	-16.7	-0.3	-4.7	4.2	2.1

Table XIII. AVERAGE ANNUAL PERCENTAGE RATES OF CHANGE IN TOTAL AND PER CAPITA ENERGY PRODUCTION, TRADE, AND CONSUMPTION, SELECTED PERIODS, 1925-1965

Region, country, indicator	1925-29	1929-38	1938-50	1950-55	1955-60	1960-65	1925-38	1950-65	1925-65
	(1)	(2)	(3)	(4)	(5)	(6)	(7)	(8)	(9)
MEXICO (CONTINUED)									
EXPORTS									
9 TOTAL	-28.9	-7.3	2.2	12.5	-11.8	10.7	-14.6	3.2	-3.2
10 SOLID FUELS	*	*	*	*	*	*	*	*	*
11 LIQUID FUELS	-28.9	-7.3	2.2	12.5	-22.1	16.8	-14.6	0.8	-4.1
CONSUMPTION									
12 TOTAL	-1.2	3.1	5.4	7.1	9.2	4.6	1.8	6.9	4.8
13 TOTAL - ALTERNATIVE HYDRO	-0.9	3.2	4.8	7.1	9.0	4.6	1.9	6.9	4.6
14 SOLID FUELS	-7.3	-0.1	-1.3	8.3	5.4	3.0	-2.4	5.5	0.8
15 LIQUID FUELS	-0.4	1.6	6.1	5.9	6.7	2.4	1.0	5.0	4.0
16 NATURAL GAS	10.2	20.0	6.3	10.4	16.5	8.4	16.9	11.7	11.7
17 HYDROELECTRIC POWER	7.5	6.1	0.8	11.7	9.2	9.0	6.6	10.0	6.0
18 ADDENDUM - TOTAL ELECTRICITY	6.3	5.4	5.1	9.5	9.3	9.3	5.7	9.4	6.9
19 POPULATION	1.7	1.8	2.6	3.1	3.1	3.2	1.8	3.1	2.5
20 TOTAL PER CAPITA PRODUCTION	-21.4	-2.1	2.1	2.9	4.9	2.0	-8.5	3.3	-1.1
PER CAPITA CONSUMPTION									
21 TOTAL	-2.9	1.3	2.7	3.9	5.9	1.4	-	3.7	2.2
22 TOTAL - ALTERNATIVE HYDRO	-2.6	1.4	2.2	3.9	5.7	1.4	0.1	3.7	2.1
23 SOLID FUELS	-8.9	-1.8	-3.8	5.0	2.2	-0.1	-4.0	2.3	-1.6
24 LIQUID FUELS	-2.1	-0.1	3.5	2.8	3.4	-0.8	-0.7	1.8	1.5
25 NATURAL GAS	8.3	17.9	3.6	7.1	13.0	5.1	14.9	8.4	9.0
26 HYDROELECTRIC POWER	5.7	4.3	-1.7	8.4	5.9	5.7	4.7	6.7	3.5
27 ADDENDUM - TOTAL ELECTRICITY	4.5	3.6	2.4	6.3	6.0	5.9	3.9	6.1	4.3
TRINIDAD AND TOBAGO									
PRODUCTION									
1 TOTAL	18.9	8.6	1.5	3.5	10.9	3.6	11.7	5.9	6.4
2 SOLID FUELS	*	*	*	*	*	*	*	*	*
3 LIQUID FUELS	18.8	8.6	1.1	3.9	11.1	2.9	11.7	5.9	6.3
4 NATURAL GAS	18.9	8.6	4.4	1.0	9.0	8.9	11.7	6.2	7.4
5 HYDROELECTRIC POWER	*	*	*	*	*	*	*	*	*
IMPORTS									
6 TOTAL	19.5	6.8	24.8	8.8	17.9	17.9	10.5	14.8	16.3
7 SOLID FUELS	18.6	-5.4	-5.8	*	*	*	1.4	*	*
8 LIQUID FUELS	31.6	33.4	28.6	9.1	17.9	17.9	32.8	14.9	24.6
EXPORTS									
9 TOTAL	16.4	8.3	4.2	8.0	17.2	13.0	10.7	12.7	9.5
10 SOLID FUELS	*	*	*	*	*	*	*	*	*
11 LIQUID FUELS	16.4	8.3	4.2	8.0	17.2	13.0	10.7	12.7	9.5
CONSUMPTION									
12 TOTAL	2.9	14.8	5.0	-0.8	3.1	14.0	11.0	5.3	7.0
13 TOTAL - ALTERNATIVE HYDRO	2.9	14.8	5.0	-0.8	3.1	14.0	11.0	5.3	7.0
14 SOLID FUELS	5.0	-1.4	-8.7	*	*	*	0.5	*	*
15 LIQUID FUELS	-16.7	26.4	5.6	-2.0	-2.6	19.7	11.2	4.6	7.0
16 NATURAL GAS	18.9	8.6	4.4	1.0	9.0	8.9	11.7	6.2	7.4
17 HYDROELECTRIC POWER	*	*	*	*	*	*	*	*	*
18 ADDENDUM - TOTAL ELECTRICITY	NA	NA	21.9	39.0	10.9	14.1	NA	20.7	NA
19 POPULATION	1.0	1.6	2.7	2.7	3.1	3.0	1.4	2.9	2.4
20 TOTAL PER CAPITA PRODUCTION	17.6	7.0	-1.2	0.8	7.5	0.5	10.1	2.9	3.9
PER CAPITA CONSUMPTION									
21 TOTAL	1.9	13.0	2.2	-3.4	-	10.7	9.5	2.3	4.5
22 TOTAL - ALTERNATIVE HYDRO	1.9	13.0	2.2	-3.4	-	10.7	9.5	2.3	4.5
23 SOLID FUELS	3.9	-2.9	-11.2	*	*	*	-0.9	*	*
24 LIQUID FUELS	-17.5	24.5	2.8	-4.5	-5.5	16.3	9.7	1.6	4.5
25 NATURAL GAS	17.7	6.9	1.7	-1.7	5.7	5.7	10.1	3.2	4.9
26 HYDROELECTRIC POWER	*	*	*	*	*	*	*	*	*
27 ADDENDUM - TOTAL ELECTRICITY	NA	NA	18.7	35.4	7.6	10.8	NA	17.3	NA
VENEZUELA									
PRODUCTION									
1 TOTAL	63.5	3.5	9.0	7.8	5.9	4.1	19.1	5.9	11.0
2 SOLID FUELS	-	-14.7	12.6	4.4	2.5	-2.4	-10.4	1.4	0.5
3 LIQUID FUELS	63.2	3.4	9.1	7.6	5.8	4.0	19.0	5.8	10.9
4 NATURAL GAS	*	10.5	2.7	19.7	10.8	7.1	*	12.4	*
5 HYDROELECTRIC POWER	4.5	8.5	12.4	3.4	-17.6	70.5	7.2	13.2	11.0
IMPORTS									
6 TOTAL	-3.3	2.3	9.2	9.5	-6.3	9.7	0.5	4.0	4.4
7 SOLID FUELS	-	-4.4	-20.6	*	*	*	-3.1	41.6	5.2
8 LIQUID FUELS	-11.1	13.0	14.1	9.7	-6.3	-34.7	5.0	-12.4	0.6
EXPORTS									
9 TOTAL	63.7	4.0	8.8	7.1	5.2	4.0	19.6	5.4	10.9

Table XIII. AVERAGE ANNUAL PERCENTAGE RATES OF CHANGE IN TOTAL AND PER CAPITA ENERGY PRODUCTION, TRADE, AND CONSUMPTION, SELECTED PERIODS, 1925-1965

Region, country, indicator	1925-29	1929-38	1938-50	1950-55	1955-60	1960-65	1925-38	1950-65	1925-65
	(1)	(2)	(3)	(4)	(5)	(6)	(7)	(8)	(9)
VENEZUELA (CONTINUED)									
EXPORTS (CONTINUED)									
10 SOLID FUELS	*	*	*	*	*	*	*	*	*
11 LIQUID FUELS	63.7	4.0	8.8	7.1	5.2	4.0	19.6	5.4	10.9
CONSUMPTION									
12 TOTAL	57.6	-6.6	13.5	14.8	14.2	5.5	9.7	11.4	11.5
13 TOTAL - ALTERNATIVE HYDRO	56.0	-6.5	13.5	14.6	14.0	5.7	9.5	11.4	11.4
14 SOLID FUELS	-	-8.5	0.7	5.3	2.5	43.9	-6.0	15.8	3.8
15 LIQUID FUELS	53.9	-26.4	34.8	12.8	15.8	4.5	-7.6	11.0	10.8
16 NATURAL GAS	*	10.5	2.7	19.7	10.8	7.1	*	12.4	*
17 HYDROELECTRIC POWER	4.5	8.5	12.4	3.4	-17.6	70.5	7.2	13.2	11.0
18 ADDENDUM - TOTAL ELECTRICITY	NA	0.6	14.2	25.2	23.8	12.1	NA	20.2	NA
19 POPULATION	1.7	1.6	2.9	4.3	3.7	3.4	1.6	3.8	2.8
20 TOTAL PER CAPITA PRODUCTION	60.8	1.9	5.9	3.4	2.1	0.7	17.2	2.0	7.9
PER CAPITA CONSUMPTION									
21 TOTAL	54.9	-8.1	10.3	10.0	10.2	2.0	7.9	7.3	8.4
22 TOTAL - ALTERNATIVE HYDRO	53.4	-7.9	10.2	9.8	10.0	2.2	7.7	7.3	8.3
23 SOLID FUELS	-1.7	-10.0	-2.2	0.9	-1.2	39.1	-7.5	11.5	0.9
24 LIQUID FUELS	51.3	-27.5	31.0	8.2	11.7	1.0	-9.1	6.9	7.8
25 NATURAL GAS	*	8.7	-0.2	14.8	6.9	3.5	*	8.3	*
26 HYDROELECTRIC POWER	2.7	6.7	9.2	-0.9	-20.5	64.8	5.5	9.1	7.9
27 ADDENDUM - TOTAL ELECTRICITY	NA	-1.0	10.9	20.0	19.4	8.4	NA	15.8	NA
CARIBBEAN - OTHER									
PRODUCTION									
1 TOTAL	6.2	14.3	6.6	8.4	-0.1	8.6	11.7	5.6	7.8
2 SOLID FUELS	*	*	*	*	*	*	*	*	*
3 LIQUID FUELS	*	*	2.2	17.8	-22.5	21.5	*	3.5	*
4 NATURAL GAS	*	*	*	14.9	-12.9	8.4	*	2.7	*
5 HYDROELECTRIC POWER	6.2	8.5	8.3	4.7	6.9	6.7	7.8	6.1	7.3
IMPORTS									
6 TOTAL	0.7	-4.2	6.0	8.1	13.2	11.2	-2.7	10.8	4.8
7 SOLID FUELS	-0.5	-8.2	-17.1	18.1	-15.6	17.1	-5.9	5.3	-5.5
8 LIQUID FUELS	1.1	-3.1	7.5	8.0	13.4	11.1	-1.8	10.8	5.6
EXPORTS									
9 TOTAL	*	*	*	*	50.4	13.6	*	*	*
10 SOLID FUELS	*	*	*	*	*	*	*	*	*
11 LIQUID FUELS	*	*	*	*	50.4	13.6	*	*	*
CONSUMPTION									
12 TOTAL	-0.7	-3.4	8.2	7.9	9.6	7.9	-2.5	8.5	4.7
13 TOTAL - ALTERNATIVE HYDRO	-0.6	-2.9	8.0	7.5	9.3	7.8	-2.2	8.2	4.7
14 SOLID FUELS	-1.0	-7.0	-16.1	23.6	-13.9	17.1	-5.2	7.6	-4.2
15 LIQUID FUELS	-0.6	-2.7	9.7	7.8	9.8	7.9	-2.0	8.5	5.3
16 NATURAL GAS	*	*	*	5.9	-12.9	8.4	*	-	*
17 HYDROELECTRIC POWER	6.2	8.5	8.3	4.7	6.9	6.7	7.8	6.1	7.3
18 ADDENDUM - TOTAL ELECTRICITY	3.8	7.9	7.9	14.4	10.8	9.8	6.6	11.7	8.8
19 POPULATION	1.7	2.0	1.9	2.4	2.5	2.8	1.9	2.6	2.1
20 TOTAL PER CAPITA PRODUCTION	4.4	12.1	4.6	5.9	-2.5	5.6	9.6	2.9	5.6
PER CAPITA CONSUMPTION									
21 TOTAL	-2.4	-5.2	6.2	5.4	6.9	5.0	-4.4	5.8	2.5
22 TOTAL - ALTERNATIVE HYDRO	-2.3	-4.8	6.0	5.0	6.7	4.9	-4.0	5.5	2.5
23 SOLID FUELS	-2.7	-8.8	-17.7	20.7	-16.0	13.9	-7.0	4.9	-6.2
24 LIQUID FUELS	-2.3	-4.5	7.6	5.3	7.2	5.0	-3.9	5.8	3.1
25 NATURAL GAS	*	*	*	3.5	-15.0	5.5	*	-2.5	*
26 HYDROELECTRIC POWER	4.4	6.4	6.2	2.2	4.4	3.8	5.8	3.5	5.0
27 ADDENDUM - TOTAL ELECTRICITY	2.0	5.8	5.8	11.8	8.1	6.8	4.6	8.9	6.6
CUBA									
PRODUCTION									
1 TOTAL	-	35.0	1.8	17.5	-21.2	24.1	23.1	4.7	9.4
2 SOLID FUELS	*	*	*	*	*	*	*	*	*
3 LIQUID FUELS	*	*	2.2	17.8	-22.5	21.5	*	3.5	*
4 NATURAL GAS	*	*	*	*	*	*	*	*	*
5 HYDROELECTRIC POWER	-	2.7	-3.1	9.0	-	40.6	1.8	15.3	5.1
IMPORTS									
6 TOTAL	-3.2	-6.6	9.9	2.1	8.8	2.9	-5.6	4.5	2.7
7 SOLID FUELS	-1.0	-6.6	-17.3	30.0	-14.3	17.1	-4.9	9.3	-3.9
8 LIQUID FUELS	-3.9	-6.6	12.8	1.7	9.3	2.7	-5.8	4.5	3.4
EXPORTS									
9 TOTAL	*	*	*	NA	NA	-55.3	*	NA	*
10 SOLID FUELS	*	*	*	*	*	*	*	*	*
11 LIQUID FUELS	*	*	*	NA	NA	-55.3	*	NA	*

Table XIII. AVERAGE ANNUAL PERCENTAGE RATES OF CHANGE IN TOTAL AND PER CAPITA ENERGY PRODUCTION, TRADE, AND CONSUMPTION, SELECTED PERIODS, 1925-1965

Region, country, indicator	1925-29	1929-38	1938-50	1950-55	1955-60	1960-65	1925-38	1950-65	1925-65
	(1)	(2)	(3)	(4)	(5)	(6)	(7)	(8)	(9)
CUBA (CONTINUED)									
CONSUMPTION									
12 TOTAL	-3.2	-6.4	9.6	2.3	7.7	3.9	-5.4	4.6	2.7
13 TOTAL - ALTERNATIVE HYDRO	-3.2	-6.3	9.5	2.3	7.7	3.9	-5.4	4.6	2.7
14 SOLID FUELS	-1.0	-6.6	-17.3	30.0	-14.3	17.1	-4.9	9.3	-3.9
15 LIQUID FUELS	-3.9	-6.3	12.5	1.9	8.2	3.7	-5.6	4.5	3.4
16 NATURAL GAS	*	*	*	*	*	*	*	*	*
17 HYDROELECTRIC POWER	-	2.7	-3.1	9.0	-	40.6	1.8	15.3	5.1
18 ADDENDUM - TOTAL ELECTRICITY	NA	NA	8.8	20.2	7.4	6.4	NA	11.1	NA
19 POPULATION	NA	2.3	1.8	2.2	2.1	2.3	NA	2.2	NA
20 TOTAL PER CAPITA PRODUCTION	NA	31.9	-	15.0	-22.9	21.4	NA	2.5	NA
PER CAPITA CONSUMPTION									
21 TOTAL	NA	-8.5	7.6	0.1	5.5	1.6	NA	2.4	NA
22 TOTAL - ALTERNATIVE HYDRO	NA	-8.5	7.5	0.1	5.4	1.6	NA	2.4	NA
23 SOLID FUELS	NA	-8.7	-18.8	27.2	-16.1	14.5	NA	6.9	NA
24 LIQUID FUELS	NA	-8.4	10.5	-0.3	5.9	1.4	NA	2.3	NA
25 NATURAL GAS	NA	*	*	*	*	*	NA	*	NA
26 HYDROELECTRIC POWER	NA	0.4	-4.9	6.7	-2.1	37.5	NA	12.8	NA
27 ADDENDUM - TOTAL ELECTRICITY	NA	NA	6.8	17.6	5.1	4.1	NA	8.8	NA
LATIN AMERICA - OTHER									
PRODUCTION									
1 TOTAL	8.8	4.3	2.4	5.2	12.6	8.2	5.7	8.6	5.8
2 SOLID FUELS	2.2	4.1	3.2	1.0	-2.2	5.6	3.5	1.4	2.6
3 LIQUID FUELS	12.1	4.2	1.6	6.4	16.2	6.9	6.6	9.8	6.2
4 NATURAL GAS	9.2	4.9	1.8	5.7	14.1	15.8	6.2	11.8	6.9
5 HYDROELECTRIC POWER	5.2	4.6	8.7	8.1	10.4	6.9	4.8	8.5	7.3
IMPORTS									
6 TOTAL	6.5	-0.5	4.7	9.7	-0.1	0.7	1.6	3.4	3.2
7 SOLID FUELS	1.3	-2.6	-4.4	-1.5	2.5	-6.3	-1.4	-1.8	-2.5
8 LIQUID FUELS	13.5	1.3	8.2	11.2	-0.3	1.3	4.9	3.9	5.5
EXPORTS									
9 TOTAL	15.2	1.6	-4.0	0.1	5.8	-2.1	5.6	1.2	1.0
10 SOLID FUELS	8.8	11.9	7.6	-12.9	-6.5	-36.9	11.0	-19.9	-2.7
11 LIQUID FUELS	15.3	1.5	-4.5	0.9	6.2	-1.7	5.6	1.8	1.0
CONSUMPTION									
12 TOTAL	6.8	2.0	4.0	8.4	5.9	5.3	3.4	6.5	4.8
13 TOTAL - ALTERNATIVE HYDRO	6.1	2.0	4.2	7.9	6.0	5.2	3.2	6.4	4.7
14 SOLID FUELS	1.7	-	-0.9	0.2	-0.2	1.2	0.5	0.4	-
15 LIQUID FUELS	12.2	3.0	6.2	10.6	5.9	4.5	5.7	7.0	6.3
16 NATURAL GAS	9.2	4.9	1.8	5.7	14.1	15.8	6.2	11.8	6.9
17 HYDROELECTRIC POWER	5.2	4.6	8.7	8.1	10.4	6.9	4.8	8.5	7.3
18 ADDENDUM - TOTAL ELECTRICITY	7.7	7.8	8.1	9.2	9.8	6.4	7.8	8.4	8.1
19 POPULATION	2.1	1.9	2.1	2.6	2.7	2.5	2.0	2.6	2.2
20 TOTAL PER CAPITA PRODUCTION	6.6	2.4	0.3	2.6	9.7	5.5	3.6	5.9	3.5
PER CAPITA CONSUMPTION									
21 TOTAL	4.6	0.1	1.9	5.7	3.1	2.7	1.4	3.8	2.5
22 TOTAL - ALTERNATIVE HYDRO	3.9	0.1	2.1	5.2	3.2	2.6	1.2	3.7	2.4
23 SOLID FUELS	-0.4	-1.9	-2.9	-2.3	-2.8	-1.3	-1.4	-2.1	-2.2
24 LIQUID FUELS	9.9	1.1	4.0	7.8	3.2	1.9	3.7	4.3	4.0
25 NATURAL GAS	6.9	2.9	-0.3	3.0	11.1	13.0	4.1	8.9	4.5
26 HYDROELECTRIC POWER	3.1	2.6	6.5	5.3	7.5	4.3	2.8	5.7	5.0
27 ADDENDUM - TOTAL ELECTRICITY	5.5	5.8	5.9	6.4	7.0	3.7	5.7	5.7	5.7
ARGENTINA									
PRODUCTION									
1 TOTAL	11.1	6.7	2.7	5.6	15.7	11.3	8.0	10.8	7.4
2 SOLID FUELS	*	*	*	12.5	13.5	5.4	*	10.4	*
3 LIQUID FUELS	10.6	6.6	2.6	5.4	15.9	9.0	7.8	10.0	7.0
4 NATURAL GAS	15.5	7.5	2.3	6.2	14.0	25.3	9.9	14.9	9.4
5 HYDROELECTRIC POWER	14.0	-2.8	7.0	9.6	25.3	6.0	2.1	13.3	7.7
IMPORTS									
6 TOTAL	7.8	0.5	3.9	4.7	-5.4	-3.7	2.7	-1.6	1.4
7 SOLID FUELS	-	-1.2	-5.4	-3.0	3.0	-12.9	-0.8	-4.5	-3.6
8 LIQUID FUELS	24.4	2.3	8.1	5.8	-6.6	-2.3	8.7	-1.1	4.7
EXPORTS									
9 TOTAL	*	*	*	*	*	238.9	*	*	*
10 SOLID FUELS	*	*	*	*	*	*	*	*	*
11 LIQUID FUELS	*	*	*	*	*	238.9	*	*	*
CONSUMPTION									
12 TOTAL	9.9	2.7	3.1	5.8	5.0	5.9	4.8	5.6	4.6

Table XIII. AVERAGE ANNUAL PERCENTAGE RATES OF CHANGE IN TOTAL AND PER CAPITA ENERGY PRODUCTION, TRADE, AND CONSUMPTION, SELECTED PERIODS, 1925-1965

Region, country, indicator	1925-29	1929-38	1938-50	1950-55	1955-60	1960-65	1925-38	1950-65	1925-65
	(1)	(2)	(3)	(4)	(5)	(6)	(7)	(8)	(9)
ARGENTINA (CONTINUED)									
CONSUMPTION (CONTINUED)									
13 TOTAL - ALTERNATIVE HYDRO	9.9	2.6	3.1	5.8	5.1	5.9	4.8	5.6	4.6
14 SOLID FUELS	1.8	-0.9	-4.8	-1.8	4.4	-8.7	-0.1	-2.2	-2.3
15 LIQUID FUELS	17.1	4.3	5.1	6.6	4.3	4.4	8.1	5.1	6.1
16 NATURAL GAS	15.5	7.5	2.3	6.2	14.0	25.3	9.9	14.9	9.4
17 HYDROELECTRIC POWER	14.0	-2.8	7.0	9.6	25.3	6.0	2.1	13.3	7.7
18 ADDENDUM - TOTAL ELECTRICITY	9.0	3.8	5.5	6.3	11.8	7.4	5.4	8.5	6.6
19 POPULATION	2.9	1.9	1.8	2.1	1.8	1.6	2.2	1.8	1.9
20 TOTAL PER CAPITA PRODUCTION	8.0	4.7	0.9	3.5	13.6	9.6	5.7	8.8	5.4
PER CAPITA CONSUMPTION									
21 TOTAL	6.8	0.7	1.3	3.7	3.1	4.3	2.6	3.7	2.6
22 TOTAL - ALTERNATIVE HYDRO	6.8	0.7	1.3	3.7	3.2	4.2	2.5	3.7	2.6
23 SOLID FUELS	-1.1	-2.8	-6.5	-3.8	2.5	-10.1	-2.2	-4.0	-4.2
24 LIQUID FUELS	13.9	2.3	3.2	4.5	2.5	2.7	5.7	3.2	4.0
25 NATURAL GAS	12.3	5.5	0.4	4.0	11.9	23.3	7.6	12.8	7.3
26 HYDROELECTRIC POWER	10.8	-4.6	5.1	7.4	23.1	4.3	-0.1	11.3	5.6
27 ADDENDUM - TOTAL ELECTRICITY	6.0	1.8	3.6	4.1	9.8	5.8	3.1	6.5	4.5
BOLIVIA									
PRODUCTION									
1 TOTAL	57.9	18.7	13.2	31.8	5.8	2.1	29.6	12.5	18.0
2 SOLID FUELS	*	*	*	*	*	*	*	*	*
3 LIQUID FUELS	*	22.0	13.2	34.4	5.8	-1.5	*	11.9	*
4 NATURAL GAS	*	*	*	*	-	75.5	*	*	*
5 HYDROELECTRIC POWER	22.1	9.4	12.8	8.8	6.0	2.0	13.2	5.6	10.1
IMPORTS									
6 TOTAL	12.7	2.7	0.6	-8.3	-3.7	-12.2	5.7	-8.1	-1.2
7 SOLID FUELS	4.4	6.3	-20.8	*	*	*	5.7	6.3	-2.9
8 LIQUID FUELS	16.1	1.3	3.9	-7.9	-3.7	-15.3	5.7	-9.1	-0.6
EXPORTS									
9 TOTAL	*	*	*	92.4	11.8	-22.3	*	18.6	*
10 SOLID FUELS	*	*	*	*	*	*	*	*	*
11 LIQUID FUELS	*	*	*	92.4	11.8	-22.3	*	18.6	*
CONSUMPTION									
12 TOTAL	14.4	5.0	5.2	15.9	3.1	6.1	7.8	8.2	7.2
13 TOTAL - ALTERNATIVE HYDRO	14.7	5.2	6.1	13.4	3.1	5.1	8.1	7.1	7.1
14 SOLID FUELS	4.4	6.3	-20.8	*	*	*	5.7	6.3	-2.9
15 LIQUID FUELS	18.2	4.3	7.2	16.3	2.9	2.5	8.4	7.1	7.5
16 NATURAL GAS	*	*	*	*	-	75.5	*	*	*
17 HYDROELECTRIC POWER	22.1	9.4	12.8	8.8	6.0	2.0	13.2	5.6	10.1
18 ADDENDUM - TOTAL ELECTRICITY	NA	NA	8.3	4.8	15.9	3.8	NA	8.0	NA
19 POPULATION	1.2	1.2	1.2	1.3	1.4	1.4	1.2	1.4	1.2
20 TOTAL PER CAPITA PRODUCTION	56.1	17.3	11.9	30.0	4.3	0.7	28.1	10.9	16.5
PER CAPITA CONSUMPTION									
21 TOTAL	13.1	3.8	3.9	14.3	1.7	4.7	6.6	6.8	5.9
22 TOTAL - ALTERNATIVE HYDRO	13.4	4.0	4.9	11.9	1.7	3.7	6.8	5.7	5.8
23 SOLID FUELS	3.2	5.1	-21.7	*	*	*	4.5	4.9	-4.1
24 LIQUID FUELS	16.9	3.1	6.0	14.8	1.5	1.1	7.2	5.6	6.2
25 NATURAL GAS	*	*	*	*	-1.4	73.2	*	*	*
26 HYDROELECTRIC POWER	20.7	8.2	11.5	7.4	4.6	0.6	11.9	4.2	8.8
27 ADDENDUM - TOTAL ELECTRICITY	NA	NA	7.0	3.4	14.3	2.4	NA	6.6	NA
BRAZIL									
PRODUCTION									
1 TOTAL	1.2	8.1	8.0	7.2	23.9	4.9	5.9	11.7	8.7
2 SOLID FUELS	-1.2	10.4	7.2	3.0	0.5	7.7	6.7	3.7	5.7
3 LIQUID FUELS	*	*	*	43.1	71.1	3.0	*	36.1	*
4 NATURAL GAS	*	*	*	65.5	53.9	5.0	*	38.8	*
5 HYDROELECTRIC POWER	4.9	4.4	8.9	8.1	11.6	6.8	4.5	8.8	7.4
IMPORTS									
6 TOTAL	6.4	-0.6	7.1	13.2	2.5	2.2	1.5	5.8	4.8
7 SOLID FUELS	4.8	-4.2	-2.8	-	-1.1	3.2	-1.5	0.7	-1.1
8 LIQUID FUELS	10.0	4.5	11.5	15.0	2.8	2.1	6.2	6.5	7.8
EXPORTS									
9 TOTAL	*	*	*	*	*	*	*	*	*
10 SOLID FUELS	*	*	*	*	*	*	*	*	*
11 LIQUID FUELS	*	*	*	*	*	*	*	*	*
CONSUMPTION									
12 TOTAL	5.7	0.9	7.0	12.4	7.7	4.0	2.4	8.0	5.8
13 TOTAL - ALTERNATIVE HYDRO	4.2	1.1	6.8	10.6	7.8	3.9	2.1	7.4	5.4
14 SOLID FUELS	4.0	-1.5	1.5	1.8	-0.1	6.2	0.2	2.6	1.5

Table XIII. AVERAGE ANNUAL PERCENTAGE RATES OF CHANGE IN TOTAL AND PER CAPITA ENERGY PRODUCTION, TRADE, AND CONSUMPTION, SELECTED PERIODS, 1925-1965

Region, country, indicator	1925-29	1929-38	1938-50	1950-55	1955-60	1960-65	1925-38	1950-65	1925-65
	(1)	(2)	(3)	(4)	(5)	(6)	(7)	(8)	(9)
BRAZIL (CONTINUED)									
CONSUMPTION (CONTINUED)									
15 LIQUID FUELS	10.0	4.5	11.0	16.5	8.2	3.2	6.2	9.2	8.7
16 NATURAL GAS	*	*	*	65.5	53.9	5.0	*	38.8	*
17 HYDROELECTRIC POWER	4.9	4.4	8.9	8.1	11.6	6.8	4.5	8.8	7.4
18 ADDENDUM - TOTAL ELECTRICITY	NA	13.1	11.4	10.7	10.9	5.7	NA	9.1	NA
19 POPULATION	2.0	2.0	2.3	3.0	3.0	3.1	2.0	3.0	2.5
20 TOTAL PER CAPITA PRODUCTION	-0.8	5.9	5.6	4.1	20.3	1.7	3.8	8.4	6.0
PER CAPITA CONSUMPTION									
21 TOTAL	3.6	-1.1	4.5	9.2	4.6	0.8	0.3	4.8	3.2
22 TOTAL - ALTERNATIVE HYDRO	2.1	-0.9	4.3	7.4	4.7	0.8	-	4.2	2.9
23 SOLID FUELS	2.0	-3.5	-0.7	-1.1	-3.0	3.0	-1.8	-0.4	-1.0
24 LIQUID FUELS	7.8	2.4	8.5	13.1	5.0	0.1	4.0	5.9	6.1
25 NATURAL GAS	*	*	*	60.7	49.4	1.8	*	34.7	*
26 HYDROELECTRIC POWER	2.8	2.3	6.4	4.9	8.4	3.5	2.4	5.6	4.8
27 ADDENDUM - TOTAL ELECTRICITY	NA	10.8	8.9	7.5	7.6	2.5	NA	5.8	NA
CHILE									
PRODUCTION									
1 TOTAL	1.2	3.8	1.8	4.1	7.2	10.9	3.0	7.3	4.3
2 SOLID FUELS	1.0	3.8	0.5	-0.7	-7.7	4.0	2.9	-1.6	0.5
3 LIQUID FUELS	*	*	*	33.1	22.8	14.1	*	23.1	*
4 NATURAL GAS	*	*	*	16.0	33.5	14.7	*	21.1	*
5 HYDROELECTRIC POWER	6.3	5.0	6.8	7.1	5.0	5.8	5.4	6.0	6.0
IMPORTS									
6 TOTAL	1.7	-5.1	4.3	7.4	-1.1	-0.2	-3.1	2.0	1.0
7 SOLID FUELS	-27.7	-22.8	23.0	10.8	20.1	-20.0	-24.4	2.1	-2.1
8 LIQUID FUELS	5.1	-4.7	4.0	7.3	-3.0	1.9	-1.8	2.0	1.3
EXPORTS									
9 TOTAL	-8.1	11.1	9.2	-15.2	-9.8	0.7	4.8	-8.3	0.9
10 SOLID FUELS	8.8	11.9	2.9	-3.1	-15.6	*	11.0	*	*
11 LIQUID FUELS	-45.1	*	*	-48.6	35.1	27.2	*	-4.1	2.5
CONSUMPTION									
12 TOTAL	1.3	1.0	2.5	5.9	4.0	7.6	1.1	5.8	3.3
13 TOTAL - ALTERNATIVE HYDRO	1.3	1.2	2.7	5.4	3.7	7.1	1.2	5.4	3.2
14 SOLID FUELS	-4.1	6.3	0.7	-	-4.2	1.0	3.0	-1.1	0.8
15 LIQUID FUELS	5.6	-4.5	4.0	10.6	3.8	7.8	-1.5	7.3	3.4
16 NATURAL GAS	*	*	*	16.0	33.5	14.7	*	21.1	*
17 HYDROELECTRIC POWER	6.3	5.0	6.8	7.1	5.0	5.8	5.4	6.0	6.0
18 ADDENDUM - TOTAL ELECTRICITY	8.9	9.8	5.3	7.1	2.3	6.0	9.5	5.1	6.6
19 POPULATION	1.4	1.5	1.8	2.3	2.5	2.2	1.5	2.3	1.9
20 TOTAL PER CAPITA PRODUCTION	-0.2	2.3	-	1.8	4.6	8.5	1.5	4.9	2.3
PER CAPITA CONSUMPTION									
21 TOTAL	-0.1	-0.5	0.7	3.5	1.4	5.3	-0.4	3.4	1.4
22 TOTAL - ALTERNATIVE HYDRO	-0.1	-0.3	1.0	3.1	1.2	4.8	-0.3	3.0	1.3
23 SOLID FUELS	-5.4	4.8	-1.0	-2.2	-6.6	-1.2	1.5	-3.4	-1.1
24 LIQUID FUELS	4.2	-5.9	2.2	8.1	1.2	5.5	-2.9	4.9	1.5
25 NATURAL GAS	*	*	*	13.4	30.2	12.3	*	18.4	*
26 HYDROELECTRIC POWER	4.9	3.5	4.9	4.7	2.5	3.6	3.9	3.6	4.1
27 ADDENDUM - TOTAL ELECTRICITY	7.4	8.2	3.5	4.8	-0.2	3.7	7.9	2.7	4.6
ECUADOR									
PRODUCTION									
1 TOTAL	67.8	6.6	2.7	5.4	-3.5	1.0	22.6	0.9	8.1
2 SOLID FUELS	*	*	*	*	*	*	*	*	*
3 LIQUID FUELS	70.9	4.9	1.5	6.2	-4.8	1.1	21.9	0.7	7.4
4 NATURAL GAS	*	*	7.6	2.6	-	-	*	0.9	*
5 HYDROELECTRIC POWER	-	0.5	10.8	6.9	7.8	7.3	0.3	7.3	6.0
IMPORTS									
6 TOTAL	14.1	5.9	-10.3	56.2	20.0	12.4	8.4	28.2	9.0
7 SOLID FUELS	*	*	*	*	*	*	*	*	*
8 LIQUID FUELS	14.1	5.9	-10.3	56.2	20.0	12.4	8.4	28.2	9.0
EXPORTS									
9 TOTAL	136.7	5.1	-4.8	7.4	*	*	34.9	-5.3	6.4
10 SOLID FUELS	*	*	*	*	*	*	*	*	*
11 LIQUID FUELS	136.7	5.1	-4.8	7.4	*	*	34.9	-5.3	6.4
CONSUMPTION									
12 TOTAL	17.5	9.5	7.7	7.8	8.1	3.7	11.9	6.5	8.6
13 TOTAL - ALTERNATIVE HYDRO	12.2	8.3	7.7	7.5	7.9	3.7	9.5	6.4	7.8
14 SOLID FUELS	*	*	*	*	*	*	*	*	*
15 LIQUID FUELS	18.4	4.7	7.7	10.3	10.5	4.4	8.7	8.3	8.3
16 NATURAL GAS	*	*	7.6	2.6	-	-	*	0.9	*

Table XIII. AVERAGE ANNUAL PERCENTAGE RATES OF CHANGE IN TOTAL AND PER CAPITA ENERGY PRODUCTION, TRADE, AND CONSUMPTION, SELECTED PERIODS, 1925-1965

Region, country, indicator	1925-29	1929-38	1938-50	1950-55	1955-60	1960-65	1925-38	1950-65	1925-65
	(1)	(2)	(3)	(4)	(5)	(6)	(7)	(8)	(9)
ECUADOR (CONTINUED)									
CONSUMPTION (CONTINUED)									
17 HYDROELECTRIC POWER	-	0.5	10.8	6.9	7.8	7.3	0.3	7.3	6.0
18 ADDENDUM - TOTAL ELECTRICITY	NA	NA	NA	15.3	10.2	8.0	NA	11.1	NA
19 POPULATION	2.3	2.5	2.6	3.0	3.1	3.3	2.4	3.1	2.7
20 TOTAL PER CAPITA PRODUCTION	63.9	4.0	0.1	2.3	-6.3	-2.2	19.7	-2.1	5.2
PER CAPITA CONSUMPTION									
21 TOTAL	14.9	6.9	5.0	4.7	4.8	0.4	9.3	3.3	5.7
22 TOTAL - ALTERNATIVE HYDRO	9.7	5.7	5.0	4.4	4.7	0.4	6.9	3.1	4.9
23 SOLID FUELS	*	*	*	*	*	*	*	*	*
24 LIQUID FUELS	15.7	2.2	5.0	7.0	7.2	1.0	6.2	5.0	5.4
25 NATURAL GAS	*	*	4.9	-0.4	-3.0	-3.2	*	-2.2	*
26 HYDROELECTRIC POWER	-2.3	-2.0	8.1	3.8	4.6	3.9	-2.1	4.1	3.2
27 ADDENDUM - TOTAL ELECTRICITY	NA	NA	NA	11.9	6.9	4.5	NA	7.7	NA
PARAGUAY									
PRODUCTION									
1 TOTAL	*	*	*	*	*	*	*	*	*
2 SOLID FUELS	*	*	*	*	*	*	*	*	*
3 LIQUID FUELS	*	*	*	*	*	*	*	*	*
4 NATURAL GAS	*	*	*	*	*	*	*	*	*
5 HYDROELECTRIC POWER	*	*	*	*	*	*	*	*	*
IMPORTS									
6 TOTAL	NA	NA	8.8	23.4	10.3	11.4	NA	14.9	NA
7 SOLID FUELS	NA	NA	NA	*	*	*	NA	*	NA
8 LIQUID FUELS	NA	NA	8.8	23.4	10.3	11.4	NA	14.9	NA
EXPORTS									
9 TOTAL	*	*	*	*	*	*	*	*	*
10 SOLID FUELS	*	*	*	*	*	*	*	*	*
11 LIQUID FUELS	*	*	*	*	*	*	*	*	*
CONSUMPTION									
12 TOTAL	NA	NA	8.8	23.4	10.3	11.4	NA	14.9	NA
13 TOTAL - ALTERNATIVE HYDRO	NA	NA	8.8	23.4	10.3	11.4	NA	14.9	NA
14 SOLID FUELS	NA	NA	NA	*	*	*	NA	*	NA
15 LIQUID FUELS	NA	NA	8.8	23.4	10.3	11.4	NA	14.9	NA
16 NATURAL GAS	*	*	*	*	*	*	*	*	*
17 HYDROELECTRIC POWER	*	*	*	*	*	*	*	*	*
18 ADDENDUM - TOTAL ELECTRICITY	NA	NA	NA	9.7	7.4	6.3	NA	7.8	NA
19 POPULATION	2.3	2.4	2.3	2.3	2.3	3.0	2.3	2.5	2.4
20 TOTAL PER CAPITA PRODUCTION	*	*	*	*	*	*	*	*	*
PER CAPITA CONSUMPTION									
21 TOTAL	NA	NA	6.3	20.6	7.9	8.2	NA	12.1	NA
22 TOTAL - ALTERNATIVE HYDRO	NA	NA	6.3	20.6	7.9	8.2	NA	12.1	NA
23 SOLID FUELS	NA	NA	NA	*	*	*	NA	*	NA
24 LIQUID FUELS	NA	NA	6.3	20.6	7.9	8.2	NA	12.1	NA
25 NATURAL GAS	*	*	*	*	*	*	*	*	*
26 HYDROELECTRIC POWER	*	*	*	*	*	*	*	*	*
27 ADDENDUM - TOTAL ELECTRICITY	NA	NA	NA	7.3	5.0	3.2	NA	5.2	NA
PERU									
PRODUCTION									
1 TOTAL	10.4	1.7	-	2.6	1.9	3.2	4.3	2.6	2.4
2 SOLID FUELS	20.9	-11.2	8.3	-7.0	3.6	-12.3	-2.3	-5.5	-0.5
3 LIQUID FUELS	10.8	2.0	-0.4	2.8	2.0	3.5	4.6	2.8	2.4
4 NATURAL GAS	7.2	2.9	-0.3	2.7	0.4	2.6	4.2	1.9	2.0
5 HYDROELECTRIC POWER	-	8.8	5.5	12.3	9.7	8.7	6.0	10.2	7.4
IMPORTS									
6 TOTAL	1.1	0.1	1.7	44.5	18.9	2.2	0.4	20.7	8.0
7 SOLID FUELS	1.3	-12.0	-19.2	*	*	-	-8.1	16.6	-3.3
8 LIQUID FUELS	-	21.5	4.3	45.1	18.7	2.2	14.4	20.7	13.5
EXPORTS									
9 TOTAL	12.8	1.2	-4.7	-1.4	-2.5	-12.1	4.6	-5.4	-2.1
10 SOLID FUELS	*	*	*	*	*	-24.2	*	-15.1	*
11 LIQUID FUELS	12.8	1.2	-5.0	-0.6	-2.8	-11.9	4.6	-5.2	-2.1
CONSUMPTION									
12 TOTAL	6.9	2.6	3.7	5.9	5.5	5.4	3.9	5.6	4.5
13 TOTAL - ALTERNATIVE HYDRO	5.9	2.8	3.7	6.1	5.5	5.4	3.8	5.7	4.4
14 SOLID FUELS	16.4	-11.3	3.8	-0.1	2.2	-10.2	-3.6	-2.8	-1.1
15 LIQUID FUELS	2.9	5.7	7.1	7.6	7.3	6.5	4.8	7.1	6.4
16 NATURAL GAS	7.2	2.9	-0.3	2.7	0.4	2.6	4.2	1.9	2.0
17 HYDROELECTRIC POWER	-	8.8	5.5	12.3	9.7	8.7	6.0	10.2	7.4
18 ADDENDUM - TOTAL ELECTRICITY	NA	NA	NA	13.1	12.4	7.6	NA	11.0	NA

Table XIII. AVERAGE ANNUAL PERCENTAGE RATES OF CHANGE IN TOTAL AND PER CAPITA ENERGY PRODUCTION, TRADE, AND CONSUMPTION, SELECTED PERIODS, 1925-1965

Region, country, indicator	1925-29	1929-38	1938-50	1950-55	1955-60	1960-65	1925-38	1950-65	1925-65
	(1)	(2)	(3)	(4)	(5)	(6)	(7)	(8)	(9)
PERU (CONTINUED)									
19 POPULATION	1.5	1.6	1.9	2.0	2.9	1.4	1.5	2.1	1.9
20 TOTAL PER CAPITA PRODUCTION	8.8	0.2	-1.9	0.6	-1.0	1.8	2.8	0.5	0.5
PER CAPITA CONSUMPTION									
21 TOTAL	5.3	1.0	1.8	3.9	2.5	3.9	2.3	3.4	2.6
22 TOTAL - ALTERNATIVE HYDRO	4.4	1.2	1.7	4.0	2.5	4.0	2.2	3.5	2.5
23 SOLID FUELS	14.7	-12.7	1.8	-2.1	-0.7	-11.4	-5.0	-4.8	-2.9
24 LIQUID FUELS	1.4	4.1	5.1	5.5	4.2	5.0	3.3	4.9	4.4
25 NATURAL GAS	5.7	1.3	-2.1	0.7	-2.5	1.1	2.7	-0.2	0.1
26 HYDROELECTRIC POWER	-1.4	7.1	3.6	10.1	6.5	7.2	4.4	7.9	5.5
27 ADDENDUM - TOTAL ELECTRICITY	NA	NA	NA	10.9	9.2	6.1	NA	8.7	NA
URUGUAY									
PRODUCTION									
1 TOTAL	*	*	*	4.7	-0.1	14.5	*	6.2	*
2 SOLID FUELS	*	*	*	*	*	*	*	*	*
3 LIQUID FUELS	*	*	*	*	*	*	*	*	*
4 NATURAL GAS	*	*	*	*	*	*	*	*	*
5 HYDROELECTRIC POWER	*	*	*	5.2	-0.1	14.5	*	6.4	*
IMPORTS									
6 TOTAL	9.3	-0.9	-2.1	26.5	1.7	1.8	2.1	9.4	3.5
7 SOLID FUELS	6.9	-3.8	-7.6	-6.9	-2.3	-12.9	-0.6	-7.5	-5.4
8 LIQUID FUELS	11.8	1.3	-	30.8	1.9	2.1	4.4	10.8	5.4
EXPORTS									
9 TOTAL	*	*	*	*	*	*	*	*	*
10 SOLID FUELS	*	*	*	*	*	*	*	*	*
11 LIQUID FUELS	*	*	*	*	*	*	*	*	*
CONSUMPTION									
12 TOTAL	5.4	-0.2	-5.1	34.4	1.7	4.1	1.5	12.5	3.4
13 TOTAL - ALTERNATIVE HYDRO	5.4	-0.2	-1.8	26.7	1.2	4.8	1.5	10.4	3.7
14 SOLID FUELS	-1.6	-2.6	-5.9	-6.9	-2.3	-12.9	-2.3	-7.5	-5.4
15 LIQUID FUELS	11.8	1.3	-6.6	48.2	2.0	4.1	4.4	16.3	5.1
16 NATURAL GAS	*	*	*	*	*	*	*	*	*
17 HYDROELECTRIC POWER	*	*	*	5.2	-0.1	14.5	*	6.4	*
18 ADDENDUM - TOTAL ELECTRICITY	10.4	7.0	8.6	10.6	4.0	8.3	8.0	7.6	8.0
19 POPULATION	2.5	1.6	1.1	1.7	1.6	-0.8	1.9	0.8	1.2
20 TOTAL PER CAPITA PRODUCTION	*	*	*	3.0	-1.6	15.5	*	5.4	*
PER CAPITA CONSUMPTION									
21 TOTAL	2.8	-1.7	-6.1	32.2	0.1	5.0	-0.4	11.6	2.1
22 TOTAL - ALTERNATIVE HYDRO	2.8	-1.7	-2.9	24.6	-0.4	5.7	-0.4	9.5	2.4
23 SOLID FUELS	-3.9	-4.2	-6.9	-8.5	-3.9	-12.2	-4.1	-8.2	-6.5
24 LIQUID FUELS	9.1	-0.3	-7.6	45.7	0.4	4.9	2.5	15.4	3.9
25 NATURAL GAS	*	*	*	*	*	*	*	*	*
26 HYDROELECTRIC POWER	*	*	*	3.4	-1.6	15.5	*	5.5	*
27 ADDENDUM - TOTAL ELECTRICITY	7.8	5.3	7.4	8.8	2.4	9.2	6.0	6.7	6.7
ASIA									
PRODUCTION									
1 TOTAL	4.1	4.9	4.9	10.0	9.2	8.1	4.6	9.1	6.3
2 SOLID FUELS	2.8	3.6	-1.2	2.8	5.5	3.0	3.3	3.8	2.1
3 LIQUID FUELS	7.6	7.8	11.6	12.9	10.0	9.2	7.8	10.7	10.0
4 NATURAL GAS	9.1	8.4	2.6	19.7	22.0	8.7	8.6	16.6	9.6
5 HYDROELECTRIC POWER	13.5	9.0	3.4	5.7	5.5	6.2	10.3	5.8	6.5
IMPORTS									
6 TOTAL	11.1	5.8	3.9	13.9	8.6	12.7	7.4	11.7	7.9
7 SOLID FUELS	6.4	3.8	-10.5	13.6	13.1	11.7	4.6	12.8	2.7
8 LIQUID FUELS	16.1	7.4	7.7	13.9	8.2	12.8	10.0	11.6	9.9
EXPORTS									
9 TOTAL	7.7	6.9	12.1	12.7	8.8	9.0	7.1	10.1	9.7
10 SOLID FUELS	3.4	1.1	-11.1	4.0	-3.1	-6.3	1.8	-1.9	-3.6
11 LIQUID FUELS	9.8	8.7	13.9	12.8	8.8	9.0	9.0	10.2	10.9
CONSUMPTION									
12 TOTAL	4.7	5.0	-0.5	8.3	9.4	9.2	4.9	9.0	4.7
13 TOTAL - ALTERNATIVE HYDRO	5.1	5.1	-0.3	7.4	8.7	8.8	5.1	8.3	4.6
14 SOLID FUELS	3.7	4.4	-1.3	3.8	6.3	4.1	4.1	4.7	2.7
15 LIQUID FUELS	9.2	6.9	1.3	17.6	12.8	14.2	7.6	14.8	8.3
16 NATURAL GAS	9.1	8.4	2.6	19.7	22.0	8.6	8.6	16.6	9.6
17 HYDROELECTRIC POWER	13.5	9.0	3.4	5.7	5.5	6.2	10.3	5.8	6.5
18 ADDENDUM - TOTAL ELECTRICITY	13.2	10.0	2.9	9.5	12.3	11.4	11.0	11.0	8.5
19 POPULATION	1.3	1.5	1.3	1.6	2.1	2.3	1.4	2.0	1.6

Table XIII. AVERAGE ANNUAL PERCENTAGE RATES OF CHANGE IN TOTAL AND PER CAPITA ENERGY PRODUCTION, TRADE, AND CONSUMPTION, SELECTED PERIODS, 1925-1965

Region, country, indicator	1925-29	1929-38	1938-50	1950-55	1955-60	1960-65	1925-38	1950-65	1925-65
	(1)	(2)	(3)	(4)	(5)	(6)	(7)	(8)	(9)
ASIA (CONTINUED)									
20 TOTAL PER CAPITA PRODUCTION	2.8	3.3	3.5	8.2	6.9	5.6	3.1	6.9	4.7
PER CAPITA CONSUMPTION									
21 TOTAL	3.4	3.4	-1.7	6.6	7.2	6.7	3.4	6.8	3.1
22 TOTAL - ALTERNATIVE HYDRO	3.8	3.5	-1.6	5.7	6.5	6.3	3.6	6.2	3.0
23 SOLID FUELS	2.4	2.8	-2.6	2.1	4.1	1.7	2.7	2.6	1.1
24 LIQUID FUELS	7.8	5.3	-	15.7	10.4	11.6	6.1	12.5	6.6
25 NATURAL GAS	7.7	6.7	1.3	17.8	19.5	6.1	7.0	14.3	7.9
26 HYDROELECTRIC POWER	12.1	7.3	2.1	4.0	3.3	3.8	8.8	3.7	4.8
27 ADDENDUM - TOTAL ELECTRICITY	11.8	8.3	1.6	7.7	9.9	8.9	9.4	8.8	6.8
MIDDLE EAST									
PRODUCTION									
1 TOTAL	5.6	11.7	14.7	13.2	10.4	9.6	9.8	11.0	11.7
2 SOLID FUELS	10.4	6.7	5.2	4.8	1.8	4.7	7.8	3.7	5.5
3 LIQUID FUELS	5.1	12.2	15.1	13.3	10.3	9.7	9.9	11.1	11.9
4 NATURAL GAS	*	*	*	21.3	31.7	5.6	*	19.0	*
5 HYDROELECTRIC POWER	-	7.0	8.6	17.3	40.4	19.0	4.8	25.1	13.2
IMPORTS									
6 TOTAL	12.4	6.6	17.1	11.0	0.8	5.4	8.3	5.7	9.8
7 SOLID FUELS	6.2	-0.2	-5.9	-18.0	-3.6	-6.9	1.7	-9.7	-5.0
8 LIQUID FUELS	14.7	8.1	18.4	11.2	0.8	5.4	10.1	5.7	10.8
EXPORTS									
9 TOTAL	9.5	9.1	17.4	13.8	9.3	9.7	9.2	10.9	12.3
10 SOLID FUELS	31.1	-3.1	*	*	*	-19.7	6.3	*	-6.6
11 LIQUID FUELS	8.7	9.6	17.6	13.8	9.3	9.7	9.3	10.9	12.3
CONSUMPTION									
12 TOTAL	-6.3	18.8	3.9	11.0	11.7	8.0	10.5	10.2	8.4
13 TOTAL - ALTERNATIVE HYDRO	-6.3	18.8	3.9	11.0	11.8	8.1	10.4	10.3	8.4
14 SOLID FUELS	2.6	9.7	5.5	4.8	1.7	4.7	7.5	3.7	5.5
15 LIQUID FUELS	-10.9	23.1	2.8	12.0	10.7	9.0	11.5	10.6	8.5
16 NATURAL GAS	*	*	*	21.3	31.7	5.6	*	19.0	*
17 HYDROELECTRIC POWER	-	7.0	8.6	17.3	40.4	19.0	4.8	25.1	13.2
18 ADDENDUM - TOTAL ELECTRICITY	4.9	13.7	10.1	19.6	15.3	9.6	10.9	14.8	12.1
19 POPULATION	1.7	1.8	2.0	2.7	2.5	2.9	1.8	2.7	2.2
20 TOTAL PER CAPITA PRODUCTION	3.8	9.7	12.4	10.3	7.7	6.5	7.8	8.1	9.3
PER CAPITA CONSUMPTION									
21 TOTAL	-7.9	16.7	1.8	8.1	9.0	5.0	8.5	7.3	6.0
22 TOTAL - ALTERNATIVE HYDRO	-7.9	16.6	1.8	8.1	9.1	5.0	8.5	7.4	6.0
23 SOLID FUELS	0.8	7.8	3.5	2.1	-0.8	1.8	5.6	1.0	3.2
24 LIQUID FUELS	-12.4	20.9	0.8	9.1	8.0	6.0	9.5	7.7	6.1
25 NATURAL GAS	*	*	*	18.2	28.5	2.6	*	15.9	*
26 HYDROELECTRIC POWER	-1.7	5.1	6.4	14.3	37.0	15.6	3.0	21.9	10.8
27 ADDENDUM - TOTAL ELECTRICITY	3.2	11.7	7.9	16.5	12.5	6.6	9.0	11.8	9.7
MIDDLE EAST - OIL PRODUCING									
PRODUCTION									
1 TOTAL	5.1	12.2	15.2	13.3	10.5	9.6	9.9	11.1	11.9
2 SOLID FUELS	*	*	*	4.1	-1.3	3.6	*	2.1	*
3 LIQUID FUELS	5.1	12.2	15.1	13.3	10.2	9.7	9.9	11.1	11.9
4 NATURAL GAS	*	*	*	21.3	31.7	5.3	*	18.9	*
5 HYDROELECTRIC POWER	*	*	*	*	*	*	*	*	*
IMPORTS									
6 TOTAL	2.5	0.8	40.1	6.9	-1.8	-3.1	1.3	0.6	11.3
7 SOLID FUELS	12.5	-7.4	-5.6	*	*	*	-1.7	*	*
8 LIQUID FUELS	2.1	1.1	40.3	6.9	-1.8	-3.1	1.4	0.6	11.4
EXPORTS									
9 TOTAL	8.7	9.6	17.6	13.4	9.5	9.6	9.3	10.8	12.3
10 SOLID FUELS	*	*	*	*	*	*	*	*	*
11 LIQUID FUELS	8.7	9.6	17.6	13.4	9.5	9.6	9.3	10.8	12.3
CONSUMPTION									
12 TOTAL	-16.7	27.2	1.7	10.9	15.9	6.0	11.7	10.9	8.3
13 TOTAL - ALTERNATIVE HYDRO	-16.7	27.2	1.7	10.9	15.9	6.0	11.7	10.9	8.3
14 SOLID FUELS	12.5	-7.4	38.7	3.9	-1.3	3.6	-1.7	2.1	10.5
15 LIQUID FUELS	-16.8	27.3	0.6	9.7	12.4	6.3	11.7	9.4	7.4
16 NATURAL GAS	*	*	*	21.3	31.7	5.3	*	18.9	*
17 HYDROELECTRIC POWER	*	*	*	*	*	*	*	*	*
18 ADDENDUM - TOTAL ELECTRICITY	2.4	10.6	10.0	21.2	20.5	5.4	8.0	15.5	11.4
19 POPULATION	1.7	1.7	1.9	2.1	2.1	2.9	1.7	2.4	2.0
20 TOTAL PER CAPITA PRODUCTION	3.3	10.3	13.0	11.0	8.2	6.5	8.1	8.5	9.7

Table XIII. AVERAGE ANNUAL PERCENTAGE RATES OF CHANGE IN TOTAL AND PER CAPITA ENERGY PRODUCTION, TRADE, AND CONSUMPTION, SELECTED PERIODS, 1925-1965

Region, country, indicator	1925-29	1929-38	1938-50	1950-55	1955-60	1960-65	1925-38	1950-65	1925-65
	(1)	(2)	(3)	(4)	(5)	(6)	(7)	(8)	(9)
MIDDLE EAST - OIL PRODUCING (CONTINUED)									
PER CAPITA CONSUMPTION									
21 TOTAL	-18.1	25.0	-0.2	8.6	13.6	3.0	9.8	8.3	6.2
22 TOTAL - ALTERNATIVE HYDRO	-18.1	25.0	-0.2	8.6	13.6	3.0	9.8	8.3	6.2
23 SOLID FUELS	10.6	-9.0	36.1	1.8	-3.2	0.7	-3.3	-0.3	8.4
24 LIQUID FUELS	-18.2	25.2	-1.2	7.4	10.2	3.2	9.8	6.9	5.3
25 NATURAL GAS	*	*	*	18.8	29.0	2.3	*	16.2	*
26 HYDROELECTRIC POWER	*	*	*	*	*	*	*	*	*
27 ADDENDUM - TOTAL ELECTRICITY	0.7	8.7	8.0	18.7	18.1	2.3	6.2	12.8	9.2
MIDDLE EAST - OTHER									
PRODUCTION									
1 TOTAL	10.4	6.7	4.7	6.1	4.4	10.3	7.8	6.9	6.5
2 SOLID FUELS	10.4	6.7	4.6	4.8	1.9	4.8	7.8	3.8	5.4
3 LIQUID FUELS	*	*	*	60.3	22.9	28.0	*	36.1	*
4 NATURAL GAS	*	*	*	*	*	*	*	*	*
5 HYDROELECTRIC POWER	-	7.0	8.6	17.3	40.4	19.0	4.8	25.1	13.2
IMPORTS									
6 TOTAL	14.0	7.2	9.9	15.6	2.9	10.0	9.2	9.4	9.5
7 SOLID FUELS	6.1	-0.1	-5.9	-17.8	-3.6	-6.9	1.8	-9.6	-4.9
8 LIQUID FUELS	17.6	9.0	11.0	16.0	2.9	10.0	11.6	9.5	10.6
EXPORTS									
9 TOTAL	30.9	-3.2	*	*	-3.3	18.8	6.3	*	10.4
10 SOLID FUELS	31.1	-3.1	*	*	*	-19.7	6.3	*	-6.6
11 LIQUID FUELS	-	*	*	*	-3.4	19.0	*	*	23.9
CONSUMPTION									
12 TOTAL	5.0	9.7	7.5	11.1	5.7	11.4	8.2	9.4	8.4
13 TOTAL - ALTERNATIVE HYDRO	4.8	9.6	7.5	11.1	6.1	11.5	8.1	9.5	8.5
14 SOLID FUELS	2.5	9.8	5.0	4.8	1.8	4.8	7.5	3.8	5.4
15 LIQUID FUELS	11.5	9.4	11.4	16.5	7.7	13.8	10.0	12.6	11.4
16 NATURAL GAS	*	*	*	*	*	*	*	*	*
17 HYDROELECTRIC POWER	-	7.0	8.6	17.3	40.4	19.0	4.8	25.1	13.2
18 ADDENDUM - TOTAL ELECTRICITY	6.6	15.3	10.1	18.9	12.6	12.0	12.5	14.5	12.5
19 POPULATION	1.7	1.9	2.1	3.1	2.9	2.8	1.9	2.9	2.3
20 TOTAL PER CAPITA PRODUCTION	8.5	4.7	2.5	2.9	1.5	7.2	5.8	3.8	4.1
PER CAPITA CONSUMPTION									
21 TOTAL	3.2	7.6	5.3	7.7	2.8	8.3	6.2	6.3	6.0
22 TOTAL - ALTERNATIVE HYDRO	3.1	7.5	5.3	7.7	3.2	8.4	6.1	6.4	6.0
23 SOLID FUELS	0.8	7.7	2.8	1.7	-1.0	1.9	5.5	0.8	2.9
24 LIQUID FUELS	9.6	7.3	9.1	12.9	4.7	10.6	8.0	9.4	8.8
25 NATURAL GAS	*	*	*	*	*	*	*	*	*
26 HYDROELECTRIC POWER	-1.7	5.0	6.3	13.8	36.5	15.7	2.9	21.6	10.6
27 ADDENDUM - TOTAL ELECTRICITY	4.8	13.1	7.9	15.3	9.5	8.9	10.5	11.2	9.9
ISRAEL									
PRODUCTION									
1 TOTAL				*	164.3	15.7		*	
2 SOLID FUELS				*	*	*		*	
3 LIQUID FUELS				*	164.3	9.5		*	
4 NATURAL GAS				*	*	*		*	
5 HYDROELECTRIC POWER				*	*	*		*	
IMPORTS									
6 TOTAL				16.4	3.5	17.2		12.2	
7 SOLID FUELS				-10.1	20.1	-21.4		-5.3	
8 LIQUID FUELS				16.9	3.3	17.6		12.4	
EXPORTS									
9 TOTAL				*	*	65.0		*	
10 SOLID FUELS				*	*	*		*	
11 LIQUID FUELS				*	*	65.0		*	
CONSUMPTION									
12 TOTAL				17.1	4.2	15.3		12.1	
13 TOTAL - ALTERNATIVE HYDRO				17.1	4.2	15.3		12.1	
14 SOLID FUELS				-10.1	20.1	-21.4		-5.3	
15 LIQUID FUELS				17.7	4.1	15.3		12.2	
16 NATURAL GAS				*	*	*		*	
17 HYDROELECTRIC POWER				*	*	*		*	
18 ADDENDUM - TOTAL ELECTRICITY				22.1	12.9	12.4		15.7	
19 POPULATION				6.8	3.9	3.9		4.9	
20 TOTAL PER CAPITA PRODUCTION				*	154.5	11.3		*	
PER CAPITA CONSUMPTION									
21 TOTAL				9.7	0.4	11.0		6.9	

Table XIII. AVERAGE ANNUAL PERCENTAGE RATES OF CHANGE IN TOTAL AND PER CAPITA ENERGY PRODUCTION, TRADE, AND CONSUMPTION, SELECTED PERIODS, 1925-1965

Region, country, indicator	1925-29	1929-38	1938-50	1950-55	1955-60	1960-65	1925-38	1950-65	1925-65
	(1)	(2)	(3)	(4)	(5)	(6)	(7)	(8)	(9)
ISRAEL (CONTINUED)									
PER CAPITA CONSUMPTION (CONTINUED)									
22 TOTAL - ALTERNATIVE HYDRO				9.7	0.4	11.0		6.9	
23 SOLID FUELS				-15.8	15.6	-24.4		-9.7	
24 LIQUID FUELS				10.2	0.2	10.9		7.0	
25 NATURAL GAS				*	*	*		*	
26 HYDROELECTRIC POWER				*	*	*		*	
27 ADDENDUM - TOTAL ELECTRICITY				14.3	8.7	8.2		10.4	
TURKEY									
PRODUCTION									
1 TOTAL	10.4	6.7	4.7	6.1	3.6	9.9	7.8	6.5	6.4
2 SOLID FUELS	10.4	6.7	4.6	4.8	1.9	4.8	7.8	3.8	5.4
3 LIQUID FUELS	*	*	*	60.1	15.9	32.5	*	35.0	*
4 NATURAL GAS	*	*	*	*	*	*	*	*	*
5 HYDROELECTRIC POWER	*	*	*	24.3	62.3	16.7	*	33.0	*
IMPORTS									
6 TOTAL	8.3	2.5	8.7	13.4	2.0	20.3	4.2	11.6	8.3
7 SOLID FUELS	9.5	-2.4	*	*	*	*	1.1	*	-6.5
8 LIQUID FUELS	7.5	4.9	11.4	13.4	2.0	20.3	5.7	11.6	9.6
EXPORTS									
9 TOTAL	31.1	-3.1	*	*	*	92.1	6.3	*	4.2
10 SOLID FUELS	31.1	-3.1	*	*	*	-19.7	6.3	*	-6.6
11 LIQUID FUELS	*	*	*	*	*	*	*	*	*
CONSUMPTION									
12 TOTAL	3.3	9.1	6.8	8.3	3.0	11.7	7.3	7.6	7.3
13 TOTAL - ALTERNATIVE HYDRO	3.3	9.1	6.8	8.3	3.8	11.8	7.3	7.9	7.4
14 SOLID FUELS	2.4	10.0	6.0	4.8	1.8	4.9	7.6	3.8	5.7
15 LIQUID FUELS	7.5	4.9	10.7	18.1	4.3	20.6	5.7	14.1	10.3
16 NATURAL GAS	*	*	*	*	*	*	*	*	*
17 HYDROELECTRIC POWER	*	*	*	24.3	62.3	16.7	*	33.0	*
18 ADDENDUM - TOTAL ELECTRICITY	5.7	13.5	8.0	14.9	12.2	11.9	11.0	13.0	10.9
19 POPULATION	1.6	1.6	1.7	2.8	2.9	2.9	1.6	2.9	2.1
20 TOTAL PER CAPITA PRODUCTION	8.7	5.0	2.9	3.2	0.7	6.8	6.1	3.5	4.2
PER CAPITA CONSUMPTION									
21 TOTAL	1.7	7.4	4.9	5.3	0.1	8.5	5.6	4.6	5.0
22 TOTAL - ALTERNATIVE HYDRO	1.7	7.4	5.0	5.3	0.9	8.6	5.6	4.9	5.1
23 SOLID FUELS	0.8	8.2	4.1	1.9	-1.1	2.0	5.9	0.9	3.5
24 LIQUID FUELS	5.8	3.2	8.8	14.9	1.4	17.2	4.0	10.9	8.0
25 NATURAL GAS	*	*	*	*	*	*	*	*	*
26 HYDROELECTRIC POWER	*	*	*	20.9	57.7	13.4	*	29.3	*
27 ADDENDUM - TOTAL ELECTRICITY	4.1	11.7	6.2	11.7	9.0	8.8	9.3	9.9	8.6
FAR EAST AND OTHER ASIA									
PRODUCTION									
1 TOTAL	3.9	3.7	-0.8	4.7	6.4	3.7	3.8	4.9	2.8
2 SOLID FUELS	2.7	3.5	-1.4	2.7	5.7	3.0	3.3	3.8	2.0
3 LIQUID FUELS	9.8	3.3	1.1	9.9	7.9	3.6	5.3	7.1	4.7
4 NATURAL GAS	9.1	8.4	-1.1	18.8	14.2	12.1	8.6	15.0	7.9
5 HYDROELECTRIC POWER	13.5	9.0	3.4	5.6	5.3	6.0	10.3	5.6	6.4
IMPORTS									
6 TOTAL	10.9	5.8	0.9	15.3	11.5	14.5	7.3	13.8	7.7
7 SOLID FUELS	6.5	4.0	-10.7	14.6	13.3	11.8	4.7	13.2	2.8
8 LIQUID FUELS	16.2	7.3	4.6	15.4	11.3	14.8	10.0	13.8	9.7
EXPORTS									
9 TOTAL	6.6	5.1	2.2	6.8	4.8	1.8	5.6	4.5	4.1
10 SOLID FUELS	2.2	1.4	-10.8	4.0	-3.4	-6.1	1.6	-1.9	-3.6
11 LIQUID FUELS	11.1	7.6	5.0	7.0	5.3	2.1	8.6	4.8	6.1
CONSUMPTION									
12 TOTAL	5.1	4.4	-1.0	7.9	9.1	9.4	4.6	8.8	4.4
13 TOTAL - ALTERNATIVE HYDRO	5.5	4.6	-0.7	6.9	8.3	8.9	4.9	8.0	4.3
14 SOLID FUELS	3.7	4.3	-1.5	3.7	6.6	4.0	4.1	4.8	2.6
15 LIQUID FUELS	12.5	3.8	0.6	20.2	13.5	15.8	6.4	16.5	8.2
16 NATURAL GAS	9.1	8.4	-1.1	18.8	14.2	11.9	8.6	14.9	7.9
17 HYDROELECTRIC POWER	13.5	9.0	3.4	5.6	5.3	6.0	10.3	5.6	6.4
18 ADDENDUM - TOTAL ELECTRICITY	13.4	9.9	2.7	9.0	12.1	11.5	11.0	10.9	8.4
19 POPULATION	1.2	1.5	1.2	1.6	2.1	2.3	1.4	2.0	1.6
20 TOTAL PER CAPITA PRODUCTION	2.7	2.2	-1.9	3.1	4.3	1.4	2.3	2.9	1.2
PER CAPITA CONSUMPTION									
21 TOTAL	3.8	2.8	-2.1	6.3	6.8	7.0	3.1	6.7	2.8
22 TOTAL - ALTERNATIVE HYDRO	4.2	3.0	-1.9	5.3	6.1	6.5	3.4	5.9	2.7
23 SOLID FUELS	2.4	2.7	-2.7	2.1	4.4	1.7	2.6	2.7	1.0

Table XIII. AVERAGE ANNUAL PERCENTAGE RATES OF CHANGE IN TOTAL AND PER CAPITA ENERGY PRODUCTION, TRADE, AND CONSUMPTION, SELECTED PERIODS, 1925-1965

Region, country, indicator	1925-29	1929-38	1938-50	1950-55	1955-60	1960-65	1925-38	1950-65	1925-65
	(1)	(2)	(3)	(4)	(5)	(6)	(7)	(8)	(9)
FAR EAST AND OTHER ASIA (CONTINUED)									
PER CAPITA CONSUMPTION (CONTINUED)									
24 LIQUID FUELS	11.1	2.3	-0.6	18.4	11.2	13.2	4.9	14.2	6.6
25 NATURAL GAS	7.7	6.8	-2.2	17.0	11.9	9.4	7.1	12.7	6.2
26 HYDROELECTRIC POWER	12.1	7.3	2.2	4.0	3.1	3.6	8.8	3.6	4.8
27 ADDENDUM - TOTAL ELECTRICITY	12.0	8.3	1.5	7.4	9.8	9.0	9.4	8.7	6.7
BORNEO (FORMER BRITISH)									
PRODUCTION									
1 TOTAL	4.4	1.6	13.3	5.2	-2.1	-2.9	2.5	-	4.7
2 SOLID FUELS	-7.8	-37.9	*	*	*	*	-29.9	*	*
3 LIQUID FUELS	5.5	2.0	13.5	5.2	-2.6	-3.0	3.1	-0.2	4.8
4 NATURAL GAS	*	*	4.7	8.2	22.8	-0.4	*	9.8	*
5 HYDROELECTRIC POWER	*	*	*	*	*	*	*	*	*
IMPORTS									
6 TOTAL	31.6	59.6	15.6	5.0	-2.4	-2.8	50.4	-0.1	19.2
7 SOLID FUELS	*	*	*	*	*	*	-	*	*
8 LIQUID FUELS	38.4	59.6	15.5	5.0	-2.5	-2.5	52.7	-0.1	19.8
EXPORTS									
9 TOTAL	7.1	8.4	14.5	4.9	-2.5	-3.4	8.0	-0.4	6.6
10 SOLID FUELS	-1.5	*	*	*	*	*	*	*	*
11 LIQUID FUELS	7.5	8.9	14.5	4.9	-2.5	-3.4	8.5	-0.4	6.8
CONSUMPTION									
12 TOTAL	-16.8	5.3	7.9	9.7	3.4	12.1	-2.0	8.3	4.7
13 TOTAL - ALTERNATIVE HYDRO	-16.8	5.3	7.9	9.7	3.4	12.1	-2.0	8.3	4.7
14 SOLID FUELS	-15.9	-24.8	*	*	*	*	-22.2	*	*
15 LIQUID FUELS	-17.3	5.3	9.7	10.5	-7.3	24.8	-2.3	8.6	5.2
16 NATURAL GAS	*	*	4.7	7.0	24.1	-6.1	*	7.6	*
17 HYDROELECTRIC POWER	*	*	*	*	*	*	*	*	*
18 ADDENDUM - TOTAL ELECTRICITY	NA	NA	NA	NA	NA	12.7	NA	NA	NA
19 POPULATION	1.9	0.7	1.6	2.8	3.0	2.7	1.0	2.9	1.9
20 TOTAL PER CAPITA PRODUCTION	2.4	1.0	11.5	2.3	-5.0	-5.4	1.4	-2.8	2.7
PER CAPITA CONSUMPTION									
21 TOTAL	-18.4	4.7	6.2	6.7	0.4	9.1	-3.1	5.3	2.8
22 TOTAL - ALTERNATIVE HYDRO	-18.4	4.7	6.2	6.7	0.4	9.1	-3.1	5.3	2.8
23 SOLID FUELS	-17.5	-25.3	*	*	*	*	-23.0	*	*
24 LIQUID FUELS	-18.9	4.6	7.9	7.5	-10.0	21.6	-3.3	5.5	3.3
25 NATURAL GAS	*	*	3.0	4.1	20.5	-8.6	*	4.7	*
26 HYDROELECTRIC POWER	*	*	*	*	*	*	*	*	*
27 ADDENDUM - TOTAL ELECTRICITY	NA	NA	NA	NA	NA	9.8	NA	NA	NA
BURMA									
PRODUCTION									
1 TOTAL				25.5	21.5	0.1		15.2	
2 SOLID FUELS				*	-32.2	58.5		*	
3 LIQUID FUELS				24.7	20.9	-0.1		14.6	
4 NATURAL GAS				*	47.6	-13.8		*	
5 HYDROELECTRIC POWER				*	*	11.8		*	
IMPORTS									
6 TOTAL				21.0	1.0	-2.2		6.1	
7 SOLID FUELS				NA	11.8	-16.7		NA	
8 LIQUID FUELS				6.7	-15.1	21.2		3.1	
EXPORTS									
9 TOTAL				*	*	*		*	
10 SOLID FUELS				*	*	*		*	
11 LIQUID FUELS				*	*	*		*	
CONSUMPTION									
12 TOTAL				23.6	11.2	-0.5		11.0	
13 TOTAL - ALTERNATIVE HYDRO				23.6	12.0	-0.1		11.4	
14 SOLID FUELS				NA	11.1	-15.6		NA	
15 LIQUID FUELS				15.6	10.1	3.7		9.7	
16 NATURAL GAS				*	47.6	-13.8		*	
17 HYDROELECTRIC POWER				*	*	11.8		*	
18 ADDENDUM - TOTAL ELECTRICITY				NA	19.0	6.2		NA	
19 POPULATION				1.6	1.8	2.1		1.8	
20 TOTAL PER CAPITA PRODUCTION				23.6	19.3	-1.9		13.1	
PER CAPITA CONSUMPTION									
21 TOTAL				21.7	9.2	-2.5		9.0	
22 TOTAL - ALTERNATIVE HYDRO				21.7	10.0	-2.1		9.4	
23 SOLID FUELS				NA	9.2	-17.3		NA	
24 LIQUID FUELS				13.8	8.2	1.6		7.7	
25 NATURAL GAS				*	44.9	-15.5		*	

Table XIII. AVERAGE ANNUAL PERCENTAGE RATES OF CHANGE IN TOTAL AND PER CAPITA ENERGY PRODUCTION, TRADE, AND CONSUMPTION, SELECTED PERIODS, 1925-1965

Region, country, indicator	1925-29	1929-38	1938-50	1950-55	1955-60	1960-65	1925-38	1950-65	1925-65
	(1)	(2)	(3)	(4)	(5)	(6)	(7)	(8)	(9)
BURMA (CONTINUED)									
PER CAPITA CONSUMPTION (CONTINUED)									
26 HYDROELECTRIC POWER				*	*	9.6		*	
27 ADDENDUM - TOTAL ELECTRICITY				NA	16.9	4.0		NA	
CEYLON									
PRODUCTION									
1 TOTAL	*	*	*	70.6	15.9	4.1	*	27.2	*
2 SOLID FUELS	*	*	*	*	*	*	*	*	*
3 LIQUID FUELS	*	*	*	*	*	*	*	*	*
4 NATURAL GAS	*	*	*	*	*	*	*	*	*
5 HYDROELECTRIC POWER	*	*	*	70.6	15.9	4.1	*	27.2	*
IMPORTS									
6 TOTAL	2.7	-1.2	2.6	1.1	-0.4	0.8	-	0.5	1.0
7 SOLID FUELS	-	-8.0	-0.4	-12.7	6.5	-11.6	-5.6	-6.3	-4.3
8 LIQUID FUELS	9.0	6.0	3.9	4.2	-1.5	2.7	6.9	1.8	4.1
EXPORTS									
9 TOTAL	*	*	*	*	*	*	*	*	*
10 SOLID FUELS	*	*	*	*	*	*	*	*	*
11 LIQUID FUELS	*	*	*	*	*	*	*	*	*
CONSUMPTION									
12 TOTAL	43.0	-3.6	4.5	8.5	0.5	7.4	8.8	5.4	6.2
13 TOTAL - ALTERNATIVE HYDRO	42.8	-3.6	4.5	9.5	1.2	6.9	8.8	5.8	6.4
14 SOLID FUELS	117.3	-7.0	5.0	-9.6	8.1	-11.6	20.7	-4.8	5.9
15 LIQUID FUELS	14.3	0.7	4.0	18.6	-2.4	12.7	4.7	9.2	6.2
16 NATURAL GAS	*	*	*	*	*	*	*	*	*
17 HYDROELECTRIC POWER	*	*	*	70.6	15.9	4.1	*	27.2	*
18 ADDENDUM - TOTAL ELECTRICITY	NA	NA	8.3	17.3	11.5	6.3	NA	11.6	NA
19 POPULATION	1.6	1.3	2.3	2.6	2.6	2.6	1.4	2.6	2.1
20 TOTAL PER CAPITA PRODUCTION	*	*	*	66.3	13.0	1.5	*	24.0	*
PER CAPITA CONSUMPTION									
21 TOTAL	40.7	-4.9	2.1	5.8	-2.0	4.7	7.3	2.8	4.0
22 TOTAL - ALTERNATIVE HYDRO	40.5	-4.9	2.2	6.7	-1.3	4.3	7.2	3.2	4.2
23 SOLID FUELS	113.8	-8.2	2.6	-11.9	5.4	-13.9	19.0	-7.2	3.7
24 LIQUID FUELS	12.4	-0.6	1.6	15.6	-4.8	9.8	3.3	6.5	4.0
25 NATURAL GAS	*	*	*	*	*	*	*	*	*
26 HYDROELECTRIC POWER	*	*	*	66.3	13.0	1.5	*	24.0	*
27 ADDENDUM - TOTAL ELECTRICITY	NA	NA	5.9	14.4	8.7	3.7	NA	8.8	NA
INDIA									
PRODUCTION									
1 TOTAL	2.7	2.4	0.3	3.5	6.5	7.0	2.5	5.7	3.0
2 SOLID FUELS	2.9	2.4	0.9	3.4	6.3	5.3	2.6	5.0	3.0
3 LIQUID FUELS	-	1.8	-13.3	6.2	5.3	46.4	1.2	17.9	2.3
4 NATURAL GAS	*	*	*	*	*	23.5	*	*	*
5 HYDROELECTRIC POWER	27.7	10.2	6.4	8.3	15.9	17.1	15.3	13.7	12.0
IMPORTS									
6 TOTAL	2.1	7.3	2.7	9.0	10.4	3.6	5.7	7.6	5.5
7 SOLID FUELS	-18.2	9.6	-40.5	*	*	*	0.2	*	*
8 LIQUID FUELS	8.4	7.0	4.1	9.0	10.4	3.6	7.4	7.6	6.5
EXPORTS									
9 TOTAL	27.6	14.3	-8.0	12.7	0.3	-4.4	18.2	2.6	4.0
10 SOLID FUELS	35.3	7.1	-3.1	10.5	-2.5	-7.3	15.1	-	3.7
11 LIQUID FUELS	-19.8	51.2	*	*	18.1	4.4	24.4	*	4.8
CONSUMPTION									
12 TOTAL	2.4	2.3	1.3	3.9	7.6	6.7	2.3	6.0	3.4
13 TOTAL - ALTERNATIVE HYDRO	2.6	2.4	1.4	3.9	7.7	7.0	2.5	6.2	3.5
14 SOLID FUELS	2.1	2.5	1.1	3.2	6.7	5.6	2.4	5.2	3.0
15 LIQUID FUELS	3.8	1.0	2.4	7.2	9.9	9.0	1.8	8.7	4.5
16 NATURAL GAS	*	*	*	*	*	23.5	*	*	*
17 HYDROELECTRIC POWER	27.7	10.2	6.4	8.3	15.9	17.1	15.3	13.7	12.0
18 ADDENDUM - TOTAL ELECTRICITY	26.4	7.2	7.1	16.3	12.8	12.7	12.8	13.9	11.5
19 POPULATION	1.0	1.4	-0.8	1.7	2.1	2.4	1.3	2.1	1.0
20 TOTAL PER CAPITA PRODUCTION	1.7	1.0	1.1	1.8	4.3	4.5	1.2	3.5	2.0
PER CAPITA CONSUMPTION									
21 TOTAL	1.4	0.9	2.1	2.2	5.4	4.2	1.1	3.9	2.4
22 TOTAL - ALTERNATIVE HYDRO	1.6	1.0	2.2	2.2	5.5	4.5	1.2	4.1	2.6
23 SOLID FUELS	1.1	1.1	1.9	1.5	4.5	3.1	1.1	3.0	2.1
24 LIQUID FUELS	2.8	-0.4	3.2	5.4	7.7	6.5	0.6	6.5	3.6
25 NATURAL GAS	*	*	*	*	*	20.7	*	*	*
26 HYDROELECTRIC POWER	26.5	8.7	7.2	6.5	13.5	14.4	13.9	11.4	10.9
27 ADDENDUM - TOTAL ELECTRICITY	25.2	5.8	7.9	14.3	10.5	10.0	11.4	11.6	10.4

Table XIII. AVERAGE ANNUAL PERCENTAGE RATES OF CHANGE IN TOTAL AND PER CAPITA ENERGY PRODUCTION, TRADE, AND CONSUMPTION, SELECTED PERIODS, 1925-1965

Region, country, indicator	1925-29	1929-38	1938-50	1950-55	1955-60	1960-65	1925-38	1950-65	1925-65
	(1)	(2)	(3)	(4)	(5)	(6)	(7)	(8)	(9)
INDO-CHINA									
PRODUCTION									
1 TOTAL	9.3	2.0	-12.1	-74.9	123.5	24.2	4.2	-11.3	-6.8
2 SOLID FUELS	9.3	2.0	-12.1	*	*	22.7	4.2	-11.8	-7.0
3 LIQUID FUELS	*	*	*	*	*	*	*	*	*
4 NATURAL GAS	*	*	*	*	*	*	*	*	*
5 HYDROELECTRIC POWER	*	*	*	*	11.8	52.6	*	*	*
IMPORTS									
6 TOTAL	12.5	-2.7	1.4	23.3	11.1	9.2	1.7	14.4	6.2
7 SOLID FUELS	3.2	-11.5	-1.3	20.1	-19.7	35.1	-7.2	9.2	0.5
8 LIQUID FUELS	15.4	-1.3	1.6	23.5	12.1	8.7	3.6	14.6	7.0
EXPORTS									
9 TOTAL	17.8	1.4	-23.8	*	*	*	6.2	*	*
10 SOLID FUELS	17.8	1.4	-23.8	*	*	*	6.2	*	*
11 LIQUID FUELS	*	*	*	*	*	*	*	*	*
CONSUMPTION									
12 TOTAL	0.6	1.4	-3.2	-1.9	10.6	10.2	1.1	6.2	1.7
13 TOTAL - ALTERNATIVE HYDRO	0.6	1.4	-3.2	-1.8	10.6	10.4	1.1	6.2	1.7
14 SOLID FUELS	-2.2	2.1	-4.4	-41.8	4.3	26.5	0.7	-8.4	-4.3
15 LIQUID FUELS	15.4	-1.3	1.2	24.7	10.9	9.2	3.6	14.7	6.9
16 NATURAL GAS	*	*	*	*	*	*	*	*	*
17 HYDROELECTRIC POWER	*	*	*	*	11.8	52.6	*	*	*
18 ADDENDUM - TOTAL ELECTRICITY	NA	3.1	6.7	5.8	15.8	9.6	NA	10.3	NA
19 POPULATION	1.2	1.3	1.1	-7.5	3.2	2.6	1.2	-0.7	0.5
20 TOTAL PER CAPITA PRODUCTION	8.0	0.7	-13.1	-72.8	116.6	21.0	2.9	-10.7	-7.2
PER CAPITA CONSUMPTION									
21 TOTAL	-0.7	0.2	-4.2	6.1	7.2	7.5	-0.1	6.9	1.2
22 TOTAL - ALTERNATIVE HYDRO	-0.7	0.2	-4.2	6.1	7.2	7.6	-0.1	7.0	1.2
23 SOLID FUELS	-3.4	0.8	-5.4	-37.1	1.1	23.4	-0.5	-7.8	-4.8
24 LIQUID FUELS	14.0	-2.5	0.1	34.8	7.5	6.5	2.3	15.5	6.4
25 NATURAL GAS	*	*	*	*	*	*	*	*	*
26 HYDROELECTRIC POWER	*	*	*	*	8.4	48.8	*	*	*
27 ADDENDUM - TOTAL ELECTRICITY	NA	1.8	5.5	14.3	12.3	6.9	NA	11.1	NA
CAMBODIA									
PRODUCTION									
1 TOTAL					*	*			
2 SOLID FUELS					*	*			
3 LIQUID FUELS					*	*			
4 NATURAL GAS					*	*			
5 HYDROELECTRIC POWER					*	*			
IMPORTS									
6 TOTAL					14.9	12.1			
7 SOLID FUELS					*	*			
8 LIQUID FUELS					14.9	9.7			
EXPORTS									
9 TOTAL					*	*			
10 SOLID FUELS					*	*			
11 LIQUID FUELS					*	*			
CONSUMPTION									
12 TOTAL					14.2	11.4			
13 TOTAL - ALTERNATIVE HYDRO					14.2	11.4			
14 SOLID FUELS					*	*			
15 LIQUID FUELS					14.2	8.9			
16 NATURAL GAS					*	*			
17 HYDROELECTRIC POWER					*	*			
18 ADDENDUM - TOTAL ELECTRICITY					14.9	5.9			
19 POPULATION					2.9	2.4			
20 TOTAL PER CAPITA PRODUCTION					*	*			
PER CAPITA CONSUMPTION									
21 TOTAL					11.0	8.8			
22 TOTAL - ALTERNATIVE HYDRO					11.0	8.8			
23 SOLID FUELS					*	*			
24 LIQUID FUELS					11.0	6.4			
25 NATURAL GAS					*	*			
26 HYDROELECTRIC POWER					*	*			
27 ADDENDUM - TOTAL ELECTRICITY					11.6	3.5			
LAOS									
PRODUCTION									
1 TOTAL					*	*			

Table XIII. AVERAGE ANNUAL PERCENTAGE RATES OF CHANGE IN TOTAL AND PER CAPITA ENERGY PRODUCTION, TRADE, AND CONSUMPTION, SELECTED PERIODS, 1925-1965

Region, country, indicator	1925-29	1929-38	1938-50	1950-55	1955-60	1960-65	1925-38	1950-65	1925-65
	(1)	(2)	(3)	(4)	(5)	(6)	(7)	(8)	(9)
LAOS (CONTINUED)									
PRODUCTION (CONTINUED)									
2 SOLID FUELS					*	*			
3 LIQUID FUELS					*	*			
4 NATURAL GAS					*	*			
5 HYDROELECTRIC POWER					*	*			
IMPORTS									
6 TOTAL					25.5	15.7			
7 SOLID FUELS					*	*			
8 LIQUID FUELS					25.5	15.7			
EXPORTS									
9 TOTAL					*	*			
10 SOLID FUELS					*	*			
11 LIQUID FUELS					*	*			
CONSUMPTION									
12 TOTAL					25.5	15.7			
13 TOTAL - ALTERNATIVE HYDRO					25.5	15.7			
14 SOLID FUELS					*	*			
15 LIQUID FUELS					25.5	15.7			
16 NATURAL GAS					*	*			
17 HYDROELECTRIC POWER					*	*			
18 ADDENDUM - TOTAL ELECTRICITY					-	17.1			
19 POPULATION					3.1	2.1			
20 TOTAL PER CAPITA PRODUCTION					*	*			
PER CAPITA CONSUMPTION									
21 TOTAL					21.7	13.3			
22 TOTAL - ALTERNATIVE HYDRO					21.7	13.3			
23 SOLID FUELS					*	*			
24 LIQUID FUELS					21.7	13.3			
25 NATURAL GAS					*	*			
26 HYDROELECTRIC POWER					*	*			
27 ADDENDUM - TOTAL ELECTRICITY					-3.0	14.7			
VIETNAM, SOUTH									
PRODUCTION									
1 TOTAL					123.5	24.2			
2 SOLID FUELS					*	22.7			
3 LIQUID FUELS					*	*			
4 NATURAL GAS					*	*			
5 HYDROELECTRIC POWER					11.8	52.6			
IMPORTS									
6 TOTAL					9.8	8.1			
7 SOLID FUELS					-19.7	8.4			
8 LIQUID FUELS					11.0	8.1			
EXPORTS									
9 TOTAL					*	*			
10 SOLID FUELS					*	*			
11 LIQUID FUELS					*	*			
CONSUMPTION									
12 TOTAL					9.3	9.6			
13 TOTAL - ALTERNATIVE HYDRO					9.3	9.8			
14 SOLID FUELS					4.3	19.5			
15 LIQUID FUELS					9.6	8.9			
16 NATURAL GAS					*	*			
17 HYDROELECTRIC POWER					11.8	52.6			
18 ADDENDUM - TOTAL ELECTRICITY					16.5	9.9			
19 POPULATION					3.3	2.7			
20 TOTAL PER CAPITA PRODUCTION					116.4	20.9			
PER CAPITA CONSUMPTION									
21 TOTAL					5.8	6.7			
22 TOTAL - ALTERNATIVE HYDRO					5.8	6.9			
23 SOLID FUELS					1.0	16.3			
24 LIQUID FUELS					6.1	6.0			
25 NATURAL GAS					*	*			
26 HYDROELECTRIC POWER					8.3	48.6			
27 ADDENDUM - TOTAL ELECTRICITY					12.8	7.0			
INDONESIA									
PRODUCTION									
1 TOTAL	12.3	3.3	-1.3	12.6	10.1	2.7	6.0	8.4	4.6
2 SOLID FUELS	6.9	-2.5	-4.8	0.2	-4.2	-15.6	0.3	-6.8	-3.9
3 LIQUID FUELS	14.1	3.8	-0.9	12.7	11.2	2.8	6.9	8.8	5.2

Table XIII. AVERAGE ANNUAL PERCENTAGE RATES OF CHANGE IN TOTAL AND PER CAPITA ENERGY PRODUCTION, TRADE, AND CONSUMPTION, SELECTED PERIODS, 1925-1965

Region, country, indicator	1925-29	1929-38	1938-50	1950-55	1955-60	1960-65	1925-38	1950-65	1925-65
	(1)	(2)	(3)	(4)	(5)	(6)	(7)	(8)	(9)
INDONESIA (CONTINUED)									
PRODUCTION (CONTINUED)									
4 NATURAL GAS	6.9	9.6	-1.5	19.3	5.0	4.4	8.8	9.3	5.8
5 HYDROELECTRIC POWER	3.2	10.0	2.1	13.7	7.3	-2.6	7.8	5.9	5.4
IMPORTS									
6 TOTAL	19.9	-5.1	18.9	12.0	-3.5	-73.2	2.0	-33.8	-9.2
7 SOLID FUELS	-0.4	-7.4	-9.0	2.1	-	-30.1	-5.3	-10.6	-8.5
8 LIQUID FUELS	48.7	-4.1	22.1	12.1	-3.6	NA	9.8	NA	NA
EXPORTS									
9 TOTAL	12.7	4.9	0.3	8.4	13.3	0.7	7.2	7.3	5.2
10 SOLID FUELS	7.4	-4.5	-13.0	-4.2	-27.5	*	-1.0	*	*
11 LIQUID FUELS	13.2	5.5	0.6	8.5	13.3	0.7	7.8	7.4	5.4
CONSUMPTION									
12 TOTAL	11.8	0.9	-0.5	19.2	1.7	0.8	4.2	6.9	3.8
13 TOTAL - ALTERNATIVE HYDRO	11.6	1.0	-0.5	19.0	1.8	0.7	4.2	6.8	3.7
14 SOLID FUELS	6.9	-1.9	-3.5	0.6	-3.1	-15.9	0.8	-6.4	-3.2
15 LIQUID FUELS	16.1	-0.4	1.0	22.5	1.0	0.4	4.4	7.5	4.5
16 NATURAL GAS	6.9	9.6	-1.5	19.3	5.0	4.4	8.8	9.3	5.8
17 HYDROELECTRIC POWER	3.2	10.0	2.1	13.7	7.3	-2.6	7.8	5.9	5.4
18 ADDENDUM - TOTAL ELECTRICITY	NA	6.3	3.4	17.6	3.8	1.5	NA	7.4	NA
19 POPULATION	1.5	1.5	1.0	2.0	2.2	2.3	1.5	2.1	1.6
20 TOTAL PER CAPITA PRODUCTION	10.6	1.8	-2.2	10.5	7.7	0.4	4.4	6.1	3.0
PER CAPITA CONSUMPTION									
21 TOTAL	10.2	-0.6	-1.4	16.9	-0.5	-1.4	2.6	4.7	2.2
22 TOTAL - ALTERNATIVE HYDRO	9.9	-0.5	-1.4	16.7	-0.4	-1.5	2.6	4.6	2.1
23 SOLID FUELS	5.3	-3.3	-4.4	-1.3	-5.2	-17.7	-0.7	-8.3	-4.7
24 LIQUID FUELS	14.4	-1.9	-	20.1	-1.1	-1.8	2.9	5.2	2.9
25 NATURAL GAS	5.3	8.0	-2.5	17.0	2.7	2.1	7.2	7.0	4.1
26 HYDROELECTRIC POWER	1.7	8.3	1.1	11.5	5.0	-4.7	6.3	3.7	3.7
27 ADDENDUM - TOTAL ELECTRICITY	NA	4.7	2.4	15.4	1.6	-0.7	NA	5.2	NA
JAPAN									
PRODUCTION									
1 TOTAL	2.5	4.1	-1.4	2.4	4.1	0.5	3.6	2.3	1.6
2 SOLID FUELS	2.1	4.0	-1.8	2.0	3.7	-0.8	3.4	1.6	1.2
3 LIQUID FUELS	0.8	3.0	-1.5	1.5	10.8	5.1	2.3	5.8	2.4
4 NATURAL GAS	6.0	6.5	2.2	18.8	39.5	19.6	6.3	25.6	11.8
5 HYDROELECTRIC POWER	13.0	7.5	4.1	4.9	3.8	3.9	9.1	4.2	5.7
IMPORTS									
6 TOTAL	25.4	8.2	-10.6	39.3	24.7	20.4	13.2	27.9	10.4
7 SOLID FUELS	19.4	7.4	-16.1	28.0	23.7	15.6	10.9	22.3	5.8
8 LIQUID FUELS	34.6	9.0	-7.4	42.1	24.9	21.1	16.3	29.1	12.9
EXPORTS									
9 TOTAL	-3.0	-2.0	-10.9	-4.0	10.1	15.7	-2.3	7.0	-1.7
10 SOLID FUELS	-3.1	-3.0	-10.1	-4.2	-40.7	25.9	-3.0	-10.6	-8.1
11 LIQUID FUELS	4.7	25.6	*	*	169.7	15.1	18.7	*	10.7
CONSUMPTION									
12 TOTAL	5.8	5.6	-2.5	7.7	10.8	11.2	5.7	9.9	4.7
13 TOTAL - ALTERNATIVE HYDRO	6.2	5.5	-1.7	6.0	9.0	10.0	5.7	8.3	4.4
14 SOLID FUELS	4.1	5.2	-2.6	3.6	5.7	2.2	4.9	3.8	2.2
15 LIQUID FUELS	27.8	8.1	-7.5	39.2	23.6	21.0	13.8	27.7	11.7
16 NATURAL GAS	6.0	6.5	2.2	18.8	39.5	19.6	6.3	25.6	11.8
17 HYDROELECTRIC POWER	13.0	7.5	4.1	4.9	3.8	3.9	9.1	4.2	5.7
18 ADDENDUM - TOTAL ELECTRICITY	13.0	10.5	2.7	7.2	11.9	11.0	11.3	10.0	8.2
19 POPULATION	1.5	1.3	1.4	1.4	0.9	1.0	1.4	1.1	1.3
20 TOTAL PER CAPITA PRODUCTION	0.9	2.8	-2.7	0.9	3.1	-0.5	2.2	1.2	0.3
PER CAPITA CONSUMPTION									
21 TOTAL	4.2	4.3	-3.8	6.2	9.8	10.1	4.3	8.7	3.4
22 TOTAL - ALTERNATIVE HYDRO	4.5	4.1	-3.0	4.5	8.0	8.9	4.3	7.2	3.1
23 SOLID FUELS	2.5	3.9	-3.9	2.1	4.8	1.2	3.5	2.7	0.9
24 LIQUID FUELS	25.8	6.8	-8.8	37.2	22.5	19.8	12.3	26.3	10.3
25 NATURAL GAS	4.4	5.1	0.8	17.1	38.2	18.4	4.9	24.2	10.4
26 HYDROELECTRIC POWER	11.3	6.1	2.7	3.4	2.8	2.9	7.7	3.0	4.4
27 ADDENDUM - TOTAL ELECTRICITY	11.3	9.1	1.3	5.7	10.9	9.9	9.8	8.8	6.8
KOREA									
PRODUCTION									
1 TOTAL	10.8	16.6					14.8		
2 SOLID FUELS	10.8	15.5					14.0		
3 LIQUID FUELS	*	*					*		
4 NATURAL GAS	*	*					*		
5 HYDROELECTRIC POWER	*	*					*		

Table XIII. AVERAGE ANNUAL PERCENTAGE RATES OF CHANGE IN TOTAL AND PER CAPITA ENERGY PRODUCTION, TRADE, AND CONSUMPTION, SELECTED PERIODS, 1925-1965

Region, country, indicator	1925-29	1929-38	1938-50	1950-55	1955-60	1960-65	1925-38	1950-65	1925-65
	(1)	(2)	(3)	(4)	(5)	(6)	(7)	(8)	(9)
KOREA (CONTINUED)									
IMPORTS									
6 TOTAL	8.9	10.0					9.7		
7 SOLID FUELS	7.3	8.8					8.3		
8 LIQUID FUELS	20.9	15.4					17.1		
EXPORTS									
9 TOTAL	7.8	15.3					13.0		
10 SOLID FUELS	7.8	14.4					12.4		
11 LIQUID FUELS	*	*					*		
CONSUMPTION									
12 TOTAL	10.1	13.1					12.2		
13 TOTAL - ALTERNATIVE HYDRO	10.1	16.1					14.2		
14 SOLID FUELS	9.2	12.2					11.3		
15 LIQUID FUELS	20.9	13.8					15.9		
16 NATURAL GAS	*	*					*		
17 HYDROELECTRIC POWER	*	*					*		
18 ADDENDUM - TOTAL ELECTRICITY	NA	6.7					NA		
19 POPULATION	0.9	1.8					1.5		
20 TOTAL PER CAPITA PRODUCTION	9.8	14.5					13.0		
PER CAPITA CONSUMPTION									
21 TOTAL	9.2	11.1					10.5		
22 TOTAL - ALTERNATIVE HYDRO	9.2	14.0					12.5		
23 SOLID FUELS	8.3	10.2					9.6		
24 LIQUID FUELS	19.8	11.8					14.2		
25 NATURAL GAS	*	*					*		
26 HYDROELECTRIC POWER	*	*					*		
27 ADDENDUM - TOTAL ELECTRICITY	NA	4.8					NA		
KOREA, REPUBLIC OF									
PRODUCTION									
1 TOTAL				18.5	31.7	13.8		21.1	
2 SOLID FUELS				18.0	32.5	13.9		21.2	
3 LIQUID FUELS				*	*	*		*	
4 NATURAL GAS				*	*	*		*	
5 HYDROELECTRIC POWER				37.6	3.9	4.1		14.2	
IMPORTS									
6 TOTAL				34.2	-4.7	14.4		13.5	
7 SOLID FUELS				37.1	-27.0	-12.2		-4.2	
8 LIQUID FUELS				29.5	13.8	17.7		20.2	
EXPORTS									
9 TOTAL				*	*	11.3		*	
10 SOLID FUELS				*	*	11.3		*	
11 LIQUID FUELS				*	*	*		*	
CONSUMPTION									
12 TOTAL				26.1	17.3	13.9		19.0	
13 TOTAL - ALTERNATIVE HYDRO				26.3	16.7	13.7		18.8	
14 SOLID FUELS				24.2	18.4	13.3		18.5	
15 LIQUID FUELS				35.1	13.5	17.8		21.8	
16 NATURAL GAS				*	*	*		*	
17 HYDROELECTRIC POWER				37.6	3.9	4.1		14.2	
18 ADDENDUM - TOTAL ELECTRICITY				15.9	14.9	14.9		15.2	
19 POPULATION				1.0	2.8	2.8		2.2	
20 TOTAL PER CAPITA PRODUCTION				17.4	28.1	10.7		18.5	
PER CAPITA CONSUMPTION									
21 TOTAL				24.8	14.2	10.8		16.5	
22 TOTAL - ALTERNATIVE HYDRO				25.1	13.5	10.6		16.2	
23 SOLID FUELS				23.0	15.2	10.2		16.0	
24 LIQUID FUELS				33.8	10.4	14.6		19.2	
25 NATURAL GAS				*	*	*		*	
26 HYDROELECTRIC POWER				36.3	1.1	1.3		11.8	
27 ADDENDUM - TOTAL ELECTRICITY				14.8	11.8	11.7		12.7	
MALAYA AND SINGAPORE									
PRODUCTION									
1 TOTAL	12.8	-2.8	-1.0	-11.7	-30.4	20.1	1.8	-9.6	-3.5
2 SOLID FUELS	12.8	-3.5	-1.2	-13.1	-49.3	*	1.2	*	*
3 LIQUID FUELS	*	*	*	*	*	*	*	*	*
4 NATURAL GAS	*	*	*	*	*	*	*	*	*
5 HYDROELECTRIC POWER	16.0	22.1	0.8	-1.5	-3.6	24.7	20.2	5.8	8.7
IMPORTS									
6 TOTAL	9.7	0.1	6.8	14.5	-1.1	13.0	3.0	8.6	6.2

Table XIII. AVERAGE ANNUAL PERCENTAGE RATES OF CHANGE IN TOTAL AND PER CAPITA ENERGY PRODUCTION, TRADE, AND CONSUMPTION, SELECTED PERIODS, 1925-1965

Region, country, indicator	1925-29	1929-38	1938-50	1950-55	1955-60	1960-65	1925-38	1950-65	1925-65
	(1)	(2)	(3)	(4)	(5)	(6)	(7)	(8)	(9)
MALAYA AND SINGAPORE (CONTINUED)									
IMPORTS (CONTINUED)									
7 SOLID FUELS	7.2	-6.0	-12.3	-7.1	-43.6	44.3	-2.1	-8.9	-7.8
8 LIQUID FUELS	11.2	2.6	8.7	14.8	-0.9	13.0	5.2	8.7	7.5
EXPORTS									
9 TOTAL	5.9	7.9	8.5	10.6	-2.8	16.4	7.3	7.8	7.8
10 SOLID FUELS	-27.7	-	*	*	*	*	-9.5	*	*
11 LIQUID FUELS	6.4	7.9	8.5	10.6	-2.8	16.4	7.5	7.8	7.9
CONSUMPTION									
12 TOTAL	12.0	-3.6	4.5	12.1	-2.1	11.1	0.9	6.8	4.2
13 TOTAL - ALTERNATIVE HYDRO	12.0	-2.4	3.9	11.2	-2.3	11.4	1.8	6.6	4.2
14 SOLID FUELS	13.0	-4.9	-2.5	-10.1	-46.8	22.6	0.3	-16.3	-7.1
15 LIQUID FUELS	10.6	-2.6	9.2	16.7	-0.6	10.9	1.3	8.7	6.4
16 NATURAL GAS	*	*	*	*	*	*	*	*	*
17 HYDROELECTRIC POWER	16.0	22.1	0.8	-1.5	-3.6	24.7	20.2	5.8	8.7
18 ADDENDUM - TOTAL ELECTRICITY	36.7	7.3	6.4	10.9	7.0	11.4	15.6	9.7	10.6
19 POPULATION	NA	NA	1.8	3.1	3.4	3.0	NA	3.2	NA
20 TOTAL PER CAPITA PRODUCTION	NA	NA	-2.7	-14.4	-32.7	16.6	NA	-12.4	NA
PER CAPITA CONSUMPTION									
21 TOTAL	NA	NA	2.6	8.7	-5.4	7.9	NA	3.5	NA
22 TOTAL - ALTERNATIVE HYDRO	NA	NA	2.1	7.9	-5.5	8.2	NA	3.3	NA
23 SOLID FUELS	NA	NA	-4.2	-12.8	-48.5	19.0	NA	-18.9	NA
24 LIQUID FUELS	NA	NA	7.3	13.2	-3.9	7.7	NA	5.4	NA
25 NATURAL GAS	NA	NA	*	*	*	*	NA	*	NA
26 HYDROELECTRIC POWER	NA	NA	-0.9	-4.5	-6.7	21.0	NA	2.5	NA
27 ADDENDUM - TOTAL ELECTRICITY	NA	NA	4.5	7.6	3.5	8.2	NA	6.4	NA
PAKISTAN									
PRODUCTION									
1 TOTAL				8.8	17.5	14.6		13.6	
2 SOLID FUELS				3.9	9.1	8.2		7.0	
3 LIQUID FUELS				10.0	5.0	8.4		7.8	
4 NATURAL GAS				*	74.6	20.8		*	
5 HYDROELECTRIC POWER				43.8	11.2	23.7		25.5	
IMPORTS									
6 TOTAL				4.6	8.6	5.0		6.1	
7 SOLID FUELS				1.1	5.5	-4.8		0.5	
8 LIQUID FUELS				7.0	10.1	8.5		8.5	
EXPORTS									
9 TOTAL				*	*	*		*	
10 SOLID FUELS				*	*	*		*	
11 LIQUID FUELS				*	*	*		*	
CONSUMPTION									
12 TOTAL				6.3	11.0	8.8		8.7	
13 TOTAL - ALTERNATIVE HYDRO				6.8	10.8	9.2		9.0	
14 SOLID FUELS				1.8	6.7	0.1		2.8	
15 LIQUID FUELS				9.2	8.9	9.1		9.1	
16 NATURAL GAS				NA	74.6	20.8		NA	
17 HYDROELECTRIC POWER				43.8	11.2	23.7		25.5	
18 ADDENDUM - TOTAL ELECTRICITY				28.6	13.8	18.8		20.3	
19 POPULATION				2.2	2.1	2.1		2.1	
20 TOTAL PER CAPITA PRODUCTION				6.5	15.1	12.2		11.2	
PER CAPITA CONSUMPTION									
21 TOTAL				4.0	8.7	6.6		6.4	
22 TOTAL - ALTERNATIVE HYDRO				4.6	8.5	7.0		6.7	
23 SOLID FUELS				-0.3	4.5	-2.0		0.7	
24 LIQUID FUELS				6.9	6.7	6.9		6.8	
25 NATURAL GAS				NA	71.0	18.3		NA	
26 HYDROELECTRIC POWER				40.8	8.9	21.1		22.9	
27 ADDENDUM - TOTAL ELECTRICITY				25.9	11.5	16.4		17.8	
PHILIPPINES									
PRODUCTION									
1 TOTAL	-18.8	9.2	11.1	0.1	11.2	-2.0	-0.3	3.0	4.3
2 SOLID FUELS	-23.3	10.3	12.0	-3.9	2.6	-8.5	-1.4	-3.4	1.7
3 LIQUID FUELS	*	*	*	*	*	*	*	*	*
4 NATURAL GAS	*	*	*	*	*	*	*	*	*
5 HYDROELECTRIC POWER	8.6	5.9	7.1	17.6	25.1	2.7	6.7	14.8	9.8
IMPORTS									
6 TOTAL	5.2	-1.9	5.9	8.7	6.7	12.3	0.2	9.2	5.2
7 SOLID FUELS	6.3	-9.0	-26.0	7.4	-	-	-4.5	2.4	-9.2
8 LIQUID FUELS	4.0	3.0	8.7	8.7	6.7	12.3	3.3	9.2	7.1

Table XIII. AVERAGE ANNUAL PERCENTAGE RATES OF CHANGE IN TOTAL AND PER CAPITA ENERGY PRODUCTION, TRADE, AND CONSUMPTION, SELECTED PERIODS, 1925-1965

Region, country, indicator	1925-29	1929-38	1938-50	1950-55	1955-60	1960-65	1925-38	1950-65	1925-65
	(1)	(2)	(3)	(4)	(5)	(6)	(7)	(8)	(9)
PHILIPPINES (CONTINUED)									
EXPORTS									
9 TOTAL	*	*	*	*	*	*	*	*	*
10 SOLID FUELS	*	*	*	*	*	*	*	*	*
11 LIQUID FUELS	*	*	*	*	*	*	*	*	*
CONSUMPTION									
12 TOTAL	4.3	-1.5	5.7	8.4	7.6	10.0	0.2	8.7	5.0
13 TOTAL - ALTERNATIVE HYDRO	4.2	-1.4	5.6	8.6	8.4	9.3	0.3	8.8	5.0
14 SOLID FUELS	4.4	-7.7	-4.8	-3.3	2.4	-7.8	-4.2	-3.0	-3.9
15 LIQUID FUELS	4.0	3.0	8.0	9.1	7.3	10.8	3.3	9.1	6.9
16 NATURAL GAS	*	*	*	*	*	*	*	*	*
17 HYDROELECTRIC POWER	8.6	5.9	7.1	17.6	25.1	2.7	6.7	14.8	9.8
18 ADDENDUM - TOTAL ELECTRICITY	8.5	5.4	12.4	17.8	15.5	12.4	6.4	15.2	11.4
19 POPULATION	2.5	2.4	2.1	3.1	3.1	3.4	2.4	3.2	2.6
20 TOTAL PER CAPITA PRODUCTION	-20.8	6.7	8.9	-2.9	7.9	-5.1	-2.6	-0.2	1.6
PER CAPITA CONSUMPTION									
21 TOTAL	1.7	-3.8	3.5	5.2	4.4	6.4	-2.2	5.3	2.3
22 TOTAL - ALTERNATIVE HYDRO	1.7	-3.7	3.5	5.4	5.2	5.7	-2.0	5.4	2.4
23 SOLID FUELS	1.9	-9.9	-6.8	-6.2	-0.6	-10.8	-6.4	-6.0	-6.4
24 LIQUID FUELS	1.5	0.6	5.8	5.9	4.1	7.2	0.9	5.7	4.2
25 NATURAL GAS	*	*	*	*	*	*	*	*	*
26 HYDROELECTRIC POWER	5.9	3.5	4.9	14.1	21.4	-0.6	4.2	11.3	7.0
27 ADDENDUM - TOTAL ELECTRICITY	5.9	3.0	10.1	14.3	12.1	8.8	3.9	11.7	8.6
TAIWAN									
PRODUCTION									
1 TOTAL	-1.3	3.9	-3.3	10.6	10.4	6.5	2.3	9.2	3.1
2 SOLID FUELS	-2.7	4.1	-3.7	10.9	10.9	5.0	2.0	8.9	2.8
3 LIQUID FUELS	28.8	-10.6	-	-	-12.9	56.9	-	10.9	4.0
4 NATURAL GAS	33.1	-9.5	-1.3	1.6	-0.8	65.5	1.9	18.6	6.8
5 HYDROELECTRIC POWER	70.2	20.9	2.9	9.5	6.2	4.6	34.3	6.7	13.7
IMPORTS									
6 TOTAL	22.9	10.0	-0.6	34.9	9.9	10.9	13.8	18.0	10.8
7 SOLID FUELS	-1.3	10.7	-27.2	*	*	*	6.9	22.1	0.1
8 LIQUID FUELS	34.0	9.8	1.0	35.0	9.9	10.8	16.8	18.0	12.3
EXPORTS									
9 TOTAL	-18.3	2.4	-15.7	7.9	17.1	-17.9	-4.5	1.2	-5.9
10 SOLID FUELS	-18.7	2.6	-15.6	-5.1	30.6	-39.8	-4.5	-9.3	-9.7
11 LIQUID FUELS	*	-16.4	*	*	-15.4	26.4	*	*	*
CONSUMPTION									
12 TOTAL	13.9	4.4	-	14.7	10.2	8.1	7.2	11.0	6.4
13 TOTAL - ALTERNATIVE HYDRO	15.5	5.9	0.1	13.1	9.4	7.5	8.8	10.0	6.5
14 SOLID FUELS	11.2	4.1	-0.3	11.5	10.3	6.0	6.3	9.3	5.3
15 LIQUID FUELS	30.6	8.9	1.1	30.8	11.1	10.0	15.2	16.9	11.4
16 NATURAL GAS	33.1	-9.5	-1.3	1.6	-0.8	65.5	1.9	18.6	6.8
17 HYDROELECTRIC POWER	70.2	20.9	2.9	9.5	6.2	4.6	34.3	6.7	13.7
18 ADDENDUM - TOTAL ELECTRICITY	65.5	19.0	3.1	13.6	14.0	11.8	31.7	13.1	15.6
19 POPULATION	2.3	2.6	2.5	3.2	3.6	3.2	2.5	3.3	2.8
20 TOTAL PER CAPITA PRODUCTION	-3.6	1.2	-5.6	7.2	6.6	3.1	-0.3	5.6	0.2
PER CAPITA CONSUMPTION									
21 TOTAL	11.2	1.7	-2.4	11.2	6.4	4.8	4.6	7.4	3.5
22 TOTAL - ALTERNATIVE HYDRO	12.8	3.2	-2.3	9.6	5.6	4.2	6.1	6.4	3.6
23 SOLID FUELS	8.7	1.5	-2.7	8.1	6.5	2.7	3.6	5.7	2.5
24 LIQUID FUELS	27.6	6.1	-1.4	26.8	7.3	6.6	12.3	13.2	8.3
25 NATURAL GAS	30.0	-11.9	-3.7	-1.5	-4.2	60.3	-0.7	14.8	3.9
26 HYDROELECTRIC POWER	66.3	17.8	0.4	6.1	2.5	1.3	31.0	3.3	10.6
27 ADDENDUM - TOTAL ELECTRICITY	61.7	16.0	0.6	10.1	10.1	8.3	28.5	9.5	12.4
THAILAND									
PRODUCTION									
1 TOTAL	*	*	*	*	21.4	3.0	*	*	*
2 SOLID FUELS	*	*	*	*	21.4	3.0	*	*	*
3 LIQUID FUELS	*	*	*	*	*	*	*	*	*
4 NATURAL GAS	*	*	*	*	*	*	*	*	*
5 HYDROELECTRIC POWER	*	*	*	*	*	*	*	*	*
IMPORTS									
6 TOTAL	18.0	1.9	4.2	24.1	9.6	16.2	6.6	16.5	9.4
7 SOLID FUELS	8.2	0.8	-8.2	14.9	-24.2	*	3.0	*	*
8 LIQUID FUELS	23.0	2.2	6.2	24.5	10.2	16.3	8.2	16.9	10.7
EXPORTS									
9 TOTAL	*	*	*	*	24.6	39.8	*	*	*

Table XIII. AVERAGE ANNUAL PERCENTAGE RATES OF CHANGE IN TOTAL AND PER CAPITA ENERGY PRODUCTION, TRADE, AND CONSUMPTION, SELECTED PERIODS, 1925-1965

Region, country, indicator	1925-29	1929-38	1938-50	1950-55	1955-60	1960-65	1925-38	1950-65	1925-65
	(1)	(2)	(3)	(4)	(5)	(6)	(7)	(8)	(9)
THAILAND (CONTINUED)									
EXPORTS (CONTINUED)									
10 SOLID FUELS	*	*	*	*	*	*	*	*	*
11 LIQUID FUELS	*	*	*	*	24.6	39.8	*	*	*
CONSUMPTION									
12 TOTAL	18.0	1.9	4.0	25.0	9.1	16.4	6.6	16.6	9.4
13 TOTAL - ALTERNATIVE HYDRO	18.0	1.9	4.0	25.0	9.1	16.4	6.6	16.6	9.4
14 SOLID FUELS	8.2	0.8	-8.2	28.0	4.5	0.4	3.0	10.3	2.1
15 LIQUID FUELS	23.0	2.2	5.9	24.8	9.3	17.0	8.2	16.9	10.7
16 NATURAL GAS	*	*	*	*	*	*	*	*	*
17 HYDROELECTRIC POWER	*	*	*	*	*	*	*	*	*
18 ADDENDUM - TOTAL ELECTRICITY	NA	6.1	6.1	35.9	13.0	19.0	NA	22.3	NA
19 POPULATION	2.2	2.8	2.4	3.0	3.0	3.0	2.6	3.0	2.7
20 TOTAL PER CAPITA PRODUCTION	*	*	*	*	17.8	-	*	*	*
PER CAPITA CONSUMPTION									
21 TOTAL	15.5	-0.9	1.5	21.4	5.9	13.0	3.9	13.3	6.6
22 TOTAL - ALTERNATIVE HYDRO	15.5	-0.9	1.5	21.4	5.9	13.0	3.9	13.3	6.6
23 SOLID FUELS	5.8	-1.9	-10.4	24.3	1.5	-2.5	0.4	7.1	-0.6
24 LIQUID FUELS	20.3	-0.6	3.4	21.2	6.1	13.6	5.4	13.5	7.8
25 NATURAL GAS	*	*	*	*	*	*	*	*	*
26 HYDROELECTRIC POWER	*	*	*	*	*	*	*	*	*
27 ADDENDUM - TOTAL ELECTRICITY	NA	3.2	3.6	32.0	9.7	15.5	NA	18.7	NA
AFRICA									
PRODUCTION									
1 TOTAL	2.4	2.3	5.4	3.7	9.6	27.5	2.3	13.2	7.2
2 SOLID FUELS	2.2	2.3	4.4	4.6	2.8	4.3	2.3	3.9	3.5
3 LIQUID FUELS	10.9	-1.8	22.5	-5.5	47.0	50.6	2.0	27.9	17.3
4 NATURAL GAS	*	*	*	*	20.1	130.0	*	*	*
5 HYDROELECTRIC POWER	6.3	21.8	8.9	19.0	17.5	12.6	16.8	16.3	14.2
IMPORTS									
6 TOTAL	10.1	1.8	3.5	10.0	3.8	6.9	4.3	6.9	5.0
7 SOLID FUELS	7.5	-2.5	-4.6	-1.7	-0.6	2.7	0.5	0.1	-1.2
8 LIQUID FUELS	16.8	7.7	7.3	11.9	4.2	7.1	10.5	7.7	8.4
EXPORTS									
9 TOTAL	4.2	-5.0	6.8	-7.2	50.2	52.9	-2.3	28.7	11.3
10 SOLID FUELS	4.2	-3.8	7.2	-10.4	4.1	5.2	-1.4	-0.6	1.4
11 LIQUID FUELS	4.5	-18.3	-22.3	165.5	111.1	56.7	-11.9	106.3	16.7
CONSUMPTION									
12 TOTAL	5.3	3.5	5.0	6.9	3.6	5.7	4.1	5.4	4.8
13 TOTAL - ALTERNATIVE HYDRO	5.3	3.6	5.0	7.1	3.8	5.9	4.1	5.6	4.9
14 SOLID FUELS	3.6	2.9	3.4	6.0	2.6	4.2	3.1	4.2	3.6
15 LIQUID FUELS	20.0	6.7	9.9	8.8	5.2	6.9	10.6	6.9	9.0
16 NATURAL GAS	*	*	*	24.6	20.1	105.4	*	45.4	*
17 HYDROELECTRIC POWER	6.3	21.8	8.9	19.0	15.6	14.5	16.8	16.3	14.2
18 ADDENDUM - TOTAL ELECTRICITY	7.9	10.6	6.4	10.1	9.7	8.0	9.7	9.2	8.5
19 POPULATION	1.8	1.6	1.9	2.4	2.5	2.4	1.7	2.4	2.0
20 TOTAL PER CAPITA PRODUCTION	0.6	0.6	3.4	1.3	6.9	24.5	0.6	10.5	5.1
PER CAPITA CONSUMPTION									
21 TOTAL	3.5	1.8	3.0	4.5	1.1	3.2	2.3	2.9	2.8
22 TOTAL - ALTERNATIVE HYDRO	3.4	1.9	3.1	4.6	1.3	3.4	2.4	3.1	2.8
23 SOLID FUELS	1.8	1.2	1.5	3.5	0.1	1.8	1.4	1.8	1.6
24 LIQUID FUELS	17.9	5.0	7.9	6.2	2.6	4.4	8.8	4.4	6.9
25 NATURAL GAS	*	*	*	21.7	17.2	100.6	*	42.0	*
26 HYDROELECTRIC POWER	4.4	19.8	6.9	16.3	12.7	11.8	14.8	13.6	11.9
27 ADDENDUM - TOTAL ELECTRICITY	6.0	8.8	4.4	7.5	7.0	5.5	7.9	6.7	6.4
NORTH AFRICA									
PRODUCTION									
1 TOTAL	11.0	1.6	20.4	-3.5	37.1	49.5	4.4	25.5	16.8
2 SOLID FUELS	12.5	26.8	13.8	3.8	-7.1	-2.7	22.2	-2.1	10.1
3 LIQUID FUELS	10.9	-2.0	22.6	-5.6	43.5	50.0	1.8	26.7	16.8
4 NATURAL GAS	*	*	*	*	13.9	140.7	*	*	*
5 HYDROELECTRIC POWER	17.4	17.6	8.1	21.8	7.3	16.1	17.6	14.9	13.7
IMPORTS									
6 TOTAL	8.1	0.3	0.8	9.4	2.2	1.0	2.6	4.1	2.6
7 SOLID FUELS	6.3	-2.6	-9.7	-8.2	0.9	-3.0	-	-3.5	-4.3
8 LIQUID FUELS	14.0	6.1	6.5	11.6	2.3	1.3	8.4	4.9	6.5
EXPORTS									
9 TOTAL	4.1	-8.9	1.1	18.1	98.1	57.2	-5.1	54.4	16.1
10 SOLID FUELS	-1.3	21.7	4.8	11.9	-11.0	-11.2	14.1	-4.0	4.2
11 LIQUID FUELS	4.4	-18.3	-22.3	105.9	161.7	57.3	-11.9	103.9	16.2

Table XIII. AVERAGE ANNUAL PERCENTAGE RATES OF CHANGE IN TOTAL AND PER CAPITA ENERGY PRODUCTION, TRADE, AND CONSUMPTION, SELECTED PERIODS, 1925-1965

Region, country, indicator	1925-29	1929-38	1938-50	1950-55	1955-60	1960-65	1925-38	1950-65	1925-65
	(1)	(2)	(3)	(4)	(5)	(6)	(7)	(8)	(9)
NORTH AFRICA (CONTINUED)									
CONSUMPTION									
12 TOTAL	8.3	2.0	5.7	5.2	4.1	4.4	3.9	4.6	4.7
13 TOTAL - ALTERNATIVE HYDRO	8.3	2.1	5.6	5.5	4.1	4.7	4.0	4.8	4.8
14 SOLID FUELS	4.2	0.1	-5.8	-4.5	-0.6	-1.6	1.3	-2.2	-2.2
15 LIQUID FUELS	19.1	4.8	11.6	6.4	4.5	2.9	9.0	4.6	8.1
16 NATURAL GAS	*	*	*	24.6	13.9	113.7	*	44.7	*
17 HYDROELECTRIC POWER	17.4	17.6	8.1	21.4	7.7	16.1	17.6	14.9	13.7
18 ADDENDUM - TOTAL ELECTRICITY	11.4	5.6	7.1	13.3	9.1	9.7	7.3	10.7	8.5
19 POPULATION	1.7	1.7	1.6	2.8	2.4	2.5	1.7	2.6	2.0
20 TOTAL PER CAPITA PRODUCTION	9.2	-0.1	18.6	-6.1	33.9	45.9	2.6	22.4	14.5
PER CAPITA CONSUMPTION									
21 TOTAL	6.5	0.2	4.0	2.3	1.7	1.9	2.1	2.0	2.6
22 TOTAL - ALTERNATIVE HYDRO	6.5	0.4	4.0	2.6	1.7	2.2	2.2	2.1	2.7
23 SOLID FUELS	2.5	-1.6	-7.2	-7.2	-3.0	-4.0	-0.4	-4.7	-4.1
24 LIQUID FUELS	17.1	3.0	9.9	3.4	2.0	0.4	7.2	1.9	6.0
25 NATURAL GAS	*	*	*	21.1	11.2	108.4	*	41.1	*
26 HYDROELECTRIC POWER	15.5	15.6	6.4	18.0	5.2	13.3	15.6	12.0	11.4
27 ADDENDUM - TOTAL ELECTRICITY	9.6	3.8	5.5	10.1	6.6	7.0	5.5	7.9	6.4
ALGERIA									
PRODUCTION									
1 TOTAL	10.4	-2.6	25.6	8.8	98.7	26.3	1.2	39.8	21.9
2 SOLID FUELS	12.5	-2.3	28.3	3.2	-17.0	-17.7	2.0	-11.0	3.8
3 LIQUID FUELS	10.7	*	*	80.8	172.2	25.1	*	83.3	26.8
4 NATURAL GAS	*	*	*	*	*	204.7	*	*	*
5 HYDROELECTRIC POWER	-	8.3	10.2	17.1	3.9	2.8	5.7	7.7	7.8
IMPORTS									
6 TOTAL	12.6	-1.6	-0.5	6.5	2.4	-28.5	2.6	-8.0	-2.4
7 SOLID FUELS	11.6	-6.6	-7.6	-9.1	2.5	-43.6	-1.4	-19.3	-10.3
8 LIQUID FUELS	24.6	16.0	4.2	9.8	2.3	-27.4	18.6	-6.5	4.3
EXPORTS									
9 TOTAL	10.0	-21.5	27.2	25.0	144.8	26.4	-12.9	57.0	21.7
10 SOLID FUELS	1.6	-26.5	37.3	-2.3	*	*	-18.8	*	*
11 LIQUID FUELS	*	-14.3	*	*	162.9	25.7	*	*	*
CONSUMPTION									
12 TOTAL	13.5	-1.1	3.2	7.3	11.2	-0.8	3.2	5.8	4.1
13 TOTAL - ALTERNATIVE HYDRO	13.1	-1.0	3.3	7.5	10.9	-0.8	3.1	5.7	4.2
14 SOLID FUELS	11.2	-2.7	-0.7	-3.1	-3.0	-32.6	1.4	-14.1	-5.3
15 LIQUID FUELS	23.6	3.1	7.8	13.0	14.9	-8.0	9.0	6.1	7.6
16 NATURAL GAS	*	*	*	*	*	170.1	*	44.6	*
17 HYDROELECTRIC POWER	-	8.3	10.2	16.2	5.2	2.2	5.7	7.7	7.8
18 ADDENDUM - TOTAL ELECTRICITY	16.7	4.0	6.4	8.3	8.9	-3.4	7.8	4.4	6.1
19 POPULATION	NA	NA	NA	2.1	2.1	1.9	NA	2.1	NA
20 TOTAL PER CAPITA PRODUCTION	NA	NA	NA	6.5	94.6	23.9	NA	37.0	NA
PER CAPITA CONSUMPTION									
21 TOTAL	NA	NA	NA	5.1	8.9	-2.7	NA	3.7	NA
22 TOTAL - ALTERNATIVE HYDRO	NA	NA	NA	5.3	8.6	-2.7	NA	3.6	NA
23 SOLID FUELS	NA	NA	NA	-5.1	-5.0	-33.9	NA	-15.9	NA
24 LIQUID FUELS	NA	NA	NA	10.7	12.5	-9.8	NA	4.0	NA
25 NATURAL GAS	NA	NA	NA	*	*	164.9	NA	41.6	NA
26 HYDROELECTRIC POWER	NA	NA	NA	13.8	3.0	0.3	NA	5.6	NA
27 ADDENDUM - TOTAL ELECTRICITY	NA	NA	NA	6.0	6.6	-5.2	NA	2.3	NA
EGYPT UAR									
PRODUCTION									
1 TOTAL	10.9	-2.0	22.6	-6.9	12.9	14.7	1.8	6.4	9.4
2 SOLID FUELS	*	*	*	*	*	*	*	*	*
3 LIQUID FUELS	10.9	-2.0	22.6	-6.9	12.8	14.3	1.8	6.3	9.4
4 NATURAL GAS	*	*	*	*	*	*	*	*	*
5 HYDROELECTRIC POWER	*	*	*	-	106.1	46.4	*	44.5	*
IMPORTS									
6 TOTAL	3.1	1.4	0.5	10.9	2.6	7.8	1.9	7.0	3.4
7 SOLID FUELS	-0.4	1.7	-15.4	-12.7	7.8	22.4	1.0	4.8	-2.9
8 LIQUID FUELS	9.4	1.0	7.8	12.1	2.5	7.2	3.5	7.2	6.2
EXPORTS									
9 TOTAL	3.8	-18.1	-22.4	38.0	153.3	30.2	-11.9	65.7	7.5
10 SOLID FUELS	-12.0	9.9	*	*	*	*	2.6	*	*
11 LIQUID FUELS	4.0	-19.1	-21.6	38.0	153.3	30.2	-12.6	65.7	7.5
CONSUMPTION									
12 TOTAL	5.0	2.9	6.8	3.3	2.7	5.0	3.5	3.7	4.6

Table XIII. AVERAGE ANNUAL PERCENTAGE RATES OF CHANGE IN TOTAL AND PER CAPITA ENERGY PRODUCTION, TRADE, AND CONSUMPTION, SELECTED PERIODS, 1925-1965

Region, country, indicator	1925-29	1929-38	1938-50	1950-55	1955-60	1960-65	1925-38	1950-65	1925-65
	(1)	(2)	(3)	(4)	(5)	(6)	(7)	(8)	(9)
EGYPT UAR (CONTINUED)									
CONSUMPTION (CONTINUED)									
13 TOTAL - ALTERNATIVE HYDRO	5.0	2.9	6.8	3.3	2.9	5.7	3.5	3.9	4.7
14 SOLID FUELS	-	1.8	-16.4	-9.4	8.0	22.4	1.2	6.2	-2.7
15 LIQUID FUELS	16.1	4.5	13.9	3.6	2.6	4.2	7.9	3.4	8.0
16 NATURAL GAS	*	*	*	*	*	*	*	*	*
17 HYDROELECTRIC POWER	*	*	*	-	106.1	46.4	*	44.5	*
18 ADDENDUM - TOTAL ELECTRICITY	4.6	4.6	5.7	19.2	13.4	15.7	4.6	16.1	9.1
19 POPULATION	1.1	1.2	2.0	2.5	2.4	2.7	1.2	2.5	1.9
20 TOTAL PER CAPITA PRODUCTION	9.6	-3.2	20.2	-9.1	10.3	11.7	0.6	3.8	7.4
PER CAPITA CONSUMPTION									
21 TOTAL	3.8	1.7	4.8	0.8	0.3	2.3	2.3	1.1	2.6
22 TOTAL - ALTERNATIVE HYDRO	3.8	1.7	4.8	0.8	0.5	3.0	2.3	1.4	2.7
23 SOLID FUELS	-1.1	0.6	-18.1	-11.6	5.4	19.2	-	3.6	-4.5
24 LIQUID FUELS	14.8	3.2	11.7	1.0	0.2	1.5	6.7	0.9	5.9
25 NATURAL GAS	*	*	*	*	*	*	*	*	*
26 HYDROELECTRIC POWER	*	*	*	-2.4	101.2	42.6	*	41.0	*
27 ADDENDUM - TOTAL ELECTRICITY	3.5	3.3	3.7	16.3	10.7	12.7	3.4	13.2	7.1
MOROCCO									
PRODUCTION									
1 TOTAL	*	58.6	10.3	9.8	-1.6	1.6	*	3.1	*
2 SOLID FUELS	*	*	9.6	4.9	-2.5	0.3	*	0.9	*
3 LIQUID FUELS	*	*	23.8	21.4	-2.2	2.3	*	6.7	*
4 NATURAL GAS	*	*	*	*	2.4	4.1	*	*	*
5 HYDROELECTRIC POWER	*	23.8	7.0	24.2	2.6	4.5	*	10.0	*
IMPORTS									
6 TOTAL	16.5	2.7	6.2	10.7	-0.9	4.6	6.7	4.7	5.8
7 SOLID FUELS	10.6	-3.1	-3.0	3.2	-3.9	-9.4	0.9	-3.5	-2.0
8 LIQUID FUELS	27.1	7.6	8.7	11.5	-0.6	5.4	13.2	5.3	8.9
EXPORTS									
9 TOTAL	*	*	2.8	15.1	-8.4	-10.8	*	-2.0	*
10 SOLID FUELS	*	*	3.1	15.0	-8.7	-11.2	*	-2.3	*
11 LIQUID FUELS	*	*	*	*	*	8.4	*	*	*
CONSUMPTION									
12 TOTAL	16.7	3.5	7.6	9.7	-0.5	5.3	7.4	4.8	6.5
13 TOTAL - ALTERNATIVE HYDRO	17.8	4.8	7.2	10.7	-0.5	4.8	8.6	4.9	6.8
14 SOLID FUELS	10.6	-1.6	6.0	-2.4	2.4	3.4	2.0	1.1	2.8
15 LIQUID FUELS	27.1	7.6	8.5	12.7	-1.4	5.8	13.2	5.5	8.9
16 NATURAL GAS	*	*	*	*	2.4	4.1	*	*	*
17 HYDROELECTRIC POWER	*	23.8	7.0	23.8	2.6	4.7	*	10.0	*
18 ADDENDUM - TOTAL ELECTRICITY	38.4	11.3	11.1	11.2	2.8	5.1	19.0	6.3	11.8
19 POPULATION	NA	2.8	1.6	2.5	2.8	2.8	NA	2.7	NA
20 TOTAL PER CAPITA PRODUCTION	NA	54.2	8.5	7.1	-4.3	-1.2	NA	0.4	NA
PER CAPITA CONSUMPTION									
21 TOTAL	NA	0.7	5.9	7.1	-3.2	2.4	NA	2.0	NA
22 TOTAL - ALTERNATIVE HYDRO	NA	1.9	5.6	8.1	-3.2	2.0	NA	2.2	NA
23 SOLID FUELS	NA	-4.4	4.3	-4.8	-0.4	0.6	NA	-1.5	NA
24 LIQUID FUELS	NA	4.6	6.8	10.0	-4.1	2.9	NA	2.8	NA
25 NATURAL GAS	NA	*	*	*	-0.4	1.3	NA	*	NA
26 HYDROELECTRIC POWER	NA	20.4	5.3	20.9	-0.2	1.9	NA	7.1	NA
27 ADDENDUM - TOTAL ELECTRICITY	NA	8.2	9.4	8.5	-	2.3	NA	3.5	NA
TUNISIA									
PRODUCTION									
1 TOTAL	*	*	*	-17.0	23.3	0.9	*	1.1	*
2 SOLID FUELS	*	*	*	*	*	*	*	*	*
3 LIQUID FUELS	*	*	*	*	*	*	*	*	*
4 NATURAL GAS	*	*	*	*	11.8	2.7	*	*	*
5 HYDROELECTRIC POWER	*	*	*	*	*	-2.2	*	*	*
IMPORTS									
6 TOTAL	8.8	0.6	2.2	6.3	0.8	8.4	3.0	5.1	3.6
7 SOLID FUELS	3.6	-0.8	-2.6	-25.4	-	4.6	0.5	-7.9	-3.7
8 LIQUID FUELS	26.7	3.2	6.7	14.0	0.9	8.6	9.9	7.7	8.1
EXPORTS									
9 TOTAL	*	*	*	*	*	*	*	*	*
10 SOLID FUELS	*	*	*	*	*	*	*	*	*
11 LIQUID FUELS	*	*	*	*	*	*	*	*	*
CONSUMPTION									
12 TOTAL	8.8	0.6	1.8	6.1	1.6	8.2	3.0	5.2	3.5
13 TOTAL - ALTERNATIVE HYDRO	8.8	0.6	1.8	6.1	2.0	8.0	3.0	5.3	3.5
14 SOLID FUELS	3.6	-0.8	-2.1	-26.3	-	4.6	0.5	-8.3	-3.7

Table XIII. AVERAGE ANNUAL PERCENTAGE RATES OF CHANGE IN TOTAL AND PER CAPITA ENERGY PRODUCTION, TRADE, AND CONSUMPTION, SELECTED PERIODS, 1925-1965

Region, country, indicator	1925-29	1929-38	1938-50	1950-55	1955-60	1960-65	1925-38	1950-65	1925-65
	(1)	(2)	(3)	(4)	(5)	(6)	(7)	(8)	(9)
TUNISIA (CONTINUED)									
CONSUMPTION (CONTINUED)									
15 LIQUID FUELS	26.7	3.2	5.7	14.8	1.4	8.5	9.9	8.1	8.0
16 NATURAL GAS	*	*	*	*	11.8	2.7	*	*	*
17 HYDROELECTRIC POWER	*	*	*	*	*	-2.2	*	*	*
18 ADDENDUM - TOTAL ELECTRICITY	9.4	8.2	6.4	13.0	2.9	10.5	8.6	8.7	8.0
19 POPULATION	NA	NA	NA	1.9	1.6	2.0	NA	1.8	NA
20 TOTAL PER CAPITA PRODUCTION	NA	NA	NA	-18.5	21.3	-1.1	NA	-0.7	NA
PER CAPITA CONSUMPTION									
21 TOTAL	NA	NA	NA	4.1	-	6.0	NA	3.3	NA
22 TOTAL - ALTERNATIVE HYDRO	NA	NA	NA	4.1	0.3	5.8	NA	3.4	NA
23 SOLID FUELS	NA	NA	NA	-27.6	-1.6	2.5	NA	-10.0	NA
24 LIQUID FUELS	NA	NA	NA	12.6	-0.2	6.4	NA	6.1	NA
25 NATURAL GAS	NA	NA	NA	*	10.0	0.7	NA	*	NA
26 HYDROELECTRIC POWER	NA	NA	NA	*	*	-4.2	NA	*	NA
27 ADDENDUM - TOTAL ELECTRICITY	NA	NA	NA	10.9	1.2	8.3	NA	6.8	NA
TROPICAL AFRICA									
PRODUCTION									
1 TOTAL	10.4	-0.1	6.1	10.3	9.7	29.8	3.0	16.2	8.7
2 SOLID FUELS	10.4	-0.3	6.0	10.0	-0.7	0.2	2.9	3.0	3.9
3 LIQUID FUELS	*	*	*	*	*	54.4	*	*	*
4 NATURAL GAS	*	*	*	*	*	58.9	*	*	*
5 HYDROELECTRIC POWER	-	24.5	9.4	17.7	21.7	11.6	16.4	16.9	14.4
IMPORTS									
6 TOTAL	11.8	1.3	5.9	12.0	5.7	8.7	4.4	8.8	6.5
7 SOLID FUELS	10.4	-2.4	1.0	0.8	-	3.1	1.4	1.3	1.2
8 LIQUID FUELS	15.2	6.9	9.1	15.3	6.7	9.1	9.4	10.3	9.6
EXPORTS									
9 TOTAL	18.9	-	3.3	7.7	28.3	43.8	5.4	25.7	11.9
10 SOLID FUELS	18.9	-	3.3	5.4	5.2	5.6	5.4	5.4	4.8
11 LIQUID FUELS	*	*	*	*	85.1	54.3	*	*	*
CONSUMPTION									
12 TOTAL	10.7	1.0	6.4	11.6	3.6	7.3	3.9	7.5	6.0
13 TOTAL - ALTERNATIVE HYDRO	10.5	1.6	6.4	11.7	4.5	7.6	4.2	7.9	6.3
14 SOLID FUELS	9.8	-1.0	4.7	8.4	-1.9	-0.5	2.2	1.9	2.8
15 LIQUID FUELS	16.3	7.3	9.4	15.1	7.3	10.5	10.0	10.9	10.1
16 NATURAL GAS	*	*	*	*	*	58.9	*	*	*
17 HYDROELECTRIC POWER	-	24.5	9.4	17.9	18.9	14.0	16.4	16.9	14.4
18 ADDENDUM - TOTAL ELECTRICITY	11.5	14.5	12.7	13.5	13.2	8.3	13.5	11.6	12.6
19 POPULATION	1.8	1.6	2.0	2.2	2.5	2.3	1.7	2.4	2.0
20 TOTAL PER CAPITA PRODUCTION	8.5	-1.7	4.0	7.9	7.0	26.8	1.4	13.6	6.6
PER CAPITA CONSUMPTION									
21 TOTAL	8.8	-0.5	4.3	9.2	1.1	4.8	2.2	5.0	3.9
22 TOTAL - ALTERNATIVE HYDRO	8.5	-	4.3	9.3	1.9	5.2	2.5	5.4	4.2
23 SOLID FUELS	7.8	-2.5	2.6	6.1	-4.3	-2.7	0.5	-0.4	0.8
24 LIQUID FUELS	14.2	5.6	7.2	12.6	4.6	8.0	8.2	8.4	8.0
25 NATURAL GAS	*	*	*	*	*	55.3	*	*	*
26 HYDROELECTRIC POWER	-1.8	22.6	7.2	15.3	15.9	11.4	14.5	14.2	12.1
27 ADDENDUM - TOTAL ELECTRICITY	9.5	12.7	10.5	11.0	10.4	5.8	11.7	9.0	10.3
CONGO, DEMOCRATIC REPUBLIC									
PRODUCTION									
1 TOTAL	15.1	-5.7	10.4	22.6	-6.9	-1.3	0.3	4.0	4.6
2 SOLID FUELS	15.8	-10.8	11.8	24.6	-19.4	-6.9	-3.3	-2.2	1.4
3 LIQUID FUELS	*	*	*	*	*	*	*	*	*
4 NATURAL GAS	*	*	*	*	*	*	*	*	*
5 HYDROELECTRIC POWER	-	25.6	8.0	17.7	11.7	1.3	17.1	10.0	11.7
IMPORTS									
6 TOTAL	13.9	-11.3	7.9	15.2	-0.7	2.9	-4.2	5.6	2.9
7 SOLID FUELS	12.2	-13.0	3.8	6.9	-4.5	7.5	-5.9	3.1	0.3
8 LIQUID FUELS	32.4	-3.6	14.5	20.9	1.0	1.0	6.3	7.2	9.1
EXPORTS									
9 TOTAL	*	*	*	*	*	-12.0	*	*	*
10 SOLID FUELS	*	*	*	*	*	*	*	*	*
11 LIQUID FUELS	*	*	*	*	*	*	*	*	*
CONSUMPTION									
12 TOTAL	14.1	-10.0	8.7	17.7	-4.1	2.1	-3.2	4.8	3.3
13 TOTAL - ALTERNATIVE HYDRO	13.1	-6.0	7.6	16.6	-2.4	1.8	-0.5	5.0	4.0
14 SOLID FUELS	12.9	-12.5	6.4	15.9	-12.6	2.5	-5.4	1.3	0.5
15 LIQUID FUELS	31.6	-3.3	14.5	20.3	1.0	1.1	6.3	7.1	9.0
16 NATURAL GAS	*	*	*	*	*	*	*	*	*

Table XIII. AVERAGE ANNUAL PERCENTAGE RATES OF CHANGE IN TOTAL AND PER CAPITA ENERGY PRODUCTION, TRADE, AND CONSUMPTION, SELECTED PERIODS, 1925-1965

Region, country, indicator	1925-29	1929-38	1938-50	1950-55	1955-60	1960-65	1925-38	1950-65	1925-65
	(1)	(2)	(3)	(4)	(5)	(6)	(7)	(8)	(9)
CONGO, DEMOCRATIC REPUBLIC (CONTINUED)									
CONSUMPTION (CONTINUED)									
17 HYDROELECTRIC POWER	-	25.6	8.0	18.1	5.8	4.2	17.1	9.2	11.3
18 ADDENDUM - TOTAL ELECTRICITY	NA	25.6	8.5	18.8	5.5	5.5	NA	9.8	NA
19 POPULATION	NA	1.7	0.7	2.1	2.5	2.5	NA	2.4	NA
20 TOTAL PER CAPITA PRODUCTION	NA	-7.3	9.7	20.1	-9.1	-3.7	NA	1.6	NA
PER CAPITA CONSUMPTION									
21 TOTAL	NA	-11.6	7.9	15.3	-6.4	-0.4	NA	2.4	NA
22 TOTAL - ALTERNATIVE HYDRO	NA	-7.6	6.9	14.2	-4.8	-0.7	NA	2.6	NA
23 SOLID FUELS	NA	-14.0	5.7	13.5	-14.7	-	NA	-1.1	NA
24 LIQUID FUELS	NA	-4.9	13.8	17.8	-1.4	-1.4	NA	4.6	NA
25 NATURAL GAS	NA	*	*	*	*	*	NA	*	NA
26 HYDROELECTRIC POWER	NA	23.5	7.3	15.7	3.3	1.6	NA	6.7	NA
27 ADDENDUM - TOTAL ELECTRICITY	NA	23.5	7.7	16.4	3.0	2.9	NA	7.2	NA
EAST AFRICA									
PRODUCTION									
1 TOTAL	-	11.2	8.9	34.6	15.5	8.1	7.6	18.9	12.1
2 SOLID FUELS	*	*	*	*	14.9	-	*	*	*
3 LIQUID FUELS	*	*	*	*	*	*	*	*	*
4 NATURAL GAS	*	*	*	*	*	*	*	*	*
5 HYDROELECTRIC POWER	-	11.2	8.9	33.9	15.5	8.3	7.6	18.7	12.1
IMPORTS									
6 TOTAL	15.4	4.8	7.4	11.4	5.6	13.1	8.0	10.0	8.5
7 SOLID FUELS	9.9	3.6	-9.8	-10.0	9.0	8.4	5.5	2.1	-0.6
8 LIQUID FUELS	20.5	5.7	11.3	12.1	5.3	13.3	10.0	10.2	10.5
EXPORTS									
9 TOTAL	*	*	*	*	*	58.1	*	*	*
10 SOLID FUELS	*	*	*	*	*	*	*	*	*
11 LIQUID FUELS	*	*	*	*	*	62.8	*	*	*
CONSUMPTION									
12 TOTAL	11.5	4.1	6.7	16.0	4.4	4.0	6.3	8.0	7.0
13 TOTAL - ALTERNATIVE HYDRO	10.8	4.3	6.6	16.6	5.0	4.1	6.2	8.4	7.2
14 SOLID FUELS	9.7	3.8	-13.6	0.8	9.2	8.1	5.6	6.0	-0.4
15 LIQUID FUELS	13.5	4.3	12.0	16.1	3.9	3.6	7.1	7.7	8.8
16 NATURAL GAS	*	*	*	*	*	*	*	*	*
17 HYDROELECTRIC POWER	-	11.2	8.9	33.9	15.5	8.3	7.6	18.7	12.1
18 ADDENDUM - TOTAL ELECTRICITY	NA	NA	NA	22.5	14.6	14.4	NA	17.1	NA
19 POPULATION	1.1	0.9	3.6	2.4	2.4	2.4	1.0	2.4	2.3
20 TOTAL PER CAPITA PRODUCTION	-1.1	10.2	5.1	31.4	12.8	5.5	6.6	16.1	9.6
PER CAPITA CONSUMPTION									
21 TOTAL	10.3	3.2	3.0	13.2	2.0	1.5	5.3	5.4	4.7
22 TOTAL - ALTERNATIVE HYDRO	9.5	3.3	3.0	13.9	2.5	1.6	5.2	5.9	4.8
23 SOLID FUELS	8.4	2.9	-16.6	-1.6	6.7	5.5	4.6	3.5	-2.7
24 LIQUID FUELS	12.2	3.4	8.2	13.4	1.5	1.2	6.0	5.2	6.3
25 NATURAL GAS	*	*	*	*	*	*	*	*	*
26 HYDROELECTRIC POWER	-1.1	10.2	5.1	30.8	12.8	5.7	6.6	16.0	9.5
27 ADDENDUM - TOTAL ELECTRICITY	NA	NA	NA	19.6	11.9	11.7	NA	14.4	NA
EQUATORIAL AFRICA									
PRODUCTION									
1 TOTAL	*	*	*	*	215.6	9.4	*	*	*
2 SOLID FUELS	*	*	*	*	*	*	*	*	*
3 LIQUID FUELS	*	*	*	*	*	9.4	*	*	*
4 NATURAL GAS	*	*	*	*	*	9.5	*	*	*
5 HYDROELECTRIC POWER	*	*	*	*	-1.9	10.8	*	*	*
IMPORTS									
6 TOTAL	14.2	15.3	9.4	9.5	14.5	4.5	14.9	9.4	11.2
7 SOLID FUELS	-15.9	30.5	-3.7	*	*	*	14.0	*	*
8 LIQUID FUELS	25.7	11.2	12.8	11.3	14.5	4.5	15.5	10.0	12.6
EXPORTS									
9 TOTAL	*	*	*	*	*	10.8	*	*	*
10 SOLID FUELS	*	*	*	*	*	*	*	*	*
11 LIQUID FUELS	*	*	*	*	*	10.8	*	*	*
CONSUMPTION									
12 TOTAL	14.2	15.3	8.9	8.9	22.2	-2.0	14.9	9.3	11.0
13 TOTAL - ALTERNATIVE HYDRO	14.2	15.3	8.9	10.7	20.8	-1.7	14.9	9.5	11.1
14 SOLID FUELS	-15.9	30.5	-3.7	*	*	*	14.0	*	*
15 LIQUID FUELS	25.7	11.2	12.2	10.1	22.1	-2.6	15.5	9.4	12.2
16 NATURAL GAS	*	*	*	*	*	9.5	*	*	*
17 HYDROELECTRIC POWER	*	*	*	*	-1.9	10.8	*	*	*
18 ADDENDUM - TOTAL ELECTRICITY	NA	NA	NA	20.1	18.5	11.9	NA	16.8	NA

Table XIII. AVERAGE ANNUAL PERCENTAGE RATES OF CHANGE IN TOTAL AND PER CAPITA ENERGY PRODUCTION, TRADE, AND CONSUMPTION, SELECTED PERIODS, 1925-1965

Region, country, indicator	1925-29	1929-38	1938-50	1950-55	1955-60	1960-65	1925-38	1950-65	1925-65
	(1)	(2)	(3)	(4)	(5)	(6)	(7)	(8)	(9)
EQUATORIAL AFRICA (CONTINUED)									
19 POPULATION	NA	NA	1.8	1.3	3.3	1.5	NA	2.0	NA
20 TOTAL PER CAPITA PRODUCTION	NA	NA	*	*	205.5	7.8	NA	*	NA
PER CAPITA CONSUMPTION									
21 TOTAL	NA	NA	7.0	7.5	18.3	-3.5	NA	7.1	NA
22 TOTAL - ALTERNATIVE HYDRO	NA	NA	7.0	9.3	17.0	-3.2	NA	7.4	NA
23 SOLID FUELS	NA	NA	-5.4	*	*	*	NA	*	NA
24 LIQUID FUELS	NA	NA	10.3	8.6	18.2	-4.0	NA	7.2	NA
25 NATURAL GAS	NA	NA	*	*	*	7.8	NA	*	NA
26 HYDROELECTRIC POWER	NA	NA	*	*	-5.0	9.1	NA	*	NA
27 ADDENDUM - TOTAL ELECTRICITY	NA	NA	NA	18.5	14.7	10.3	NA	14.5	NA
GHANA									
PRODUCTION									
1 TOTAL	*	*	*	*	*	*	*	*	*
2 SOLID FUELS	*	*	*	*	*	*	*	*	*
3 LIQUID FUELS	*	*	*	*	*	*	*	*	*
4 NATURAL GAS	*	*	*	*	*	*	*	*	*
5 HYDROELECTRIC POWER	*	*	*	*	*	*	*	*	*
IMPORTS									
6 TOTAL	11.1	5.9	4.3	11.7	3.3	12.8	7.5	9.2	7.2
7 SOLID FUELS	7.8	0.6	-1.7	13.8	-19.7	-5.6	2.8	-4.8	-1.5
8 LIQUID FUELS	16.5	10.9	6.6	11.3	6.7	13.6	12.6	10.5	10.0
EXPORTS									
9 TOTAL	*	*	*	*	*	199.5	*	*	*
10 SOLID FUELS	*	*	*	*	*	*	*	*	*
11 LIQUID FUELS	*	*	*	*	*	199.5	*	*	*
CONSUMPTION									
12 TOTAL	11.1	5.9	3.0	13.9	3.4	6.4	7.5	7.8	6.3
13 TOTAL - ALTERNATIVE HYDRO	11.1	5.9	3.0	13.9	3.4	7.1	7.5	8.1	6.3
14 SOLID FUELS	7.8	0.6	-1.7	13.8	-19.7	-5.6	2.8	-4.8	-1.5
15 LIQUID FUELS	16.5	10.9	5.0	14.0	7.0	6.7	12.6	9.2	9.0
16 NATURAL GAS	*	*	*	*	*	*	*	*	*
17 HYDROELECTRIC POWER	*	*	*	*	*	*	*	*	*
18 ADDENDUM - TOTAL ELECTRICITY	NA	NA	NA	4.0	9.0	7.4	NA	6.8	NA
19 POPULATION	3.2	1.9	1.6	1.6	2.3	2.7	2.3	2.2	2.0
20 TOTAL PER CAPITA PRODUCTION	*	*	*	*	*	*	*	*	*
PER CAPITA CONSUMPTION									
21 TOTAL	7.7	4.0	1.4	12.2	1.1	3.6	5.1	5.5	4.1
22 TOTAL - ALTERNATIVE HYDRO	7.7	4.0	1.4	12.2	1.1	4.2	5.1	5.7	4.2
23 SOLID FUELS	4.5	-1.2	-3.2	12.0	-21.5	-8.1	0.5	-6.9	-3.4
24 LIQUID FUELS	12.9	8.9	3.3	12.2	4.6	3.9	10.1	6.9	6.8
25 NATURAL GAS	*	*	*	*	*	*	*	*	*
26 HYDROELECTRIC POWER	*	*	*	*	*	*	*	*	*
27 ADDENDUM - TOTAL ELECTRICITY	NA	NA	NA	2.4	6.6	4.6	NA	4.5	NA
NIGERIA									
PRODUCTION									
1 TOTAL	9.6	0.6	4.1	5.2	19.3	62.7	3.2	26.8	11.8
2 SOLID FUELS	9.6	0.6	4.0	5.2	-5.6	5.3	3.2	1.5	2.8
3 LIQUID FUELS	*	*	*	*	*	74.0	*	*	*
4 NATURAL GAS	*	*	*	*	*	*	*	*	*
5 HYDROELECTRIC POWER	*	*	*	7.0	4.5	7.7	*	6.4	*
IMPORTS									
6 TOTAL	8.1	3.2	10.0	14.0	12.6	10.3	4.7	12.3	9.1
7 SOLID FUELS	2.4	6.6	4.1	*	*	*	5.3	*	*
8 LIQUID FUELS	11.1	1.5	12.5	19.3	12.6	10.3	4.3	14.0	10.3
EXPORTS									
9 TOTAL	16.2	2.6	-23.9	158.1	45.5	68.2	6.6	84.8	18.4
10 SOLID FUELS	16.2	2.6	-23.9	118.7	-21.4	3.1	6.6	21.0	1.1
11 LIQUID FUELS	*	*	*	*	62.5	68.8	*	*	*
CONSUMPTION									
12 TOTAL	8.9	0.8	6.9	4.7	5.1	13.9	3.2	7.8	6.0
13 TOTAL - ALTERNATIVE HYDRO	8.9	0.8	7.1	4.7	5.0	13.8	3.2	7.7	6.1
14 SOLID FUELS	8.6	0.7	5.4	0.6	-3.9	5.4	3.1	0.6	2.8
15 LIQUID FUELS	11.1	1.5	12.3	13.3	14.4	17.2	4.3	14.9	10.6
16 NATURAL GAS	*	*	*	*	*	*	*	*	*
17 HYDROELECTRIC POWER	*	*	*	7.0	4.5	7.7	*	6.4	*
18 ADDENDUM - TOTAL ELECTRICITY	NA	NA	18.7	16.4	17.5	16.0	NA	16.6	NA
19 POPULATION	NA	NA	NA	NA	NA	2.0	NA	NA	NA

Table XIII. AVERAGE ANNUAL PERCENTAGE RATES OF CHANGE IN TOTAL AND PER CAPITA ENERGY PRODUCTION, TRADE, AND CONSUMPTION, SELECTED PERIODS, 1925-1965

Region, country, indicator	1925-29	1929-38	1938-50	1950-55	1955-60	1960-65	1925-38	1950-65	1925-65
	(1)	(2)	(3)	(4)	(5)	(6)	(7)	(8)	(9)
NIGERIA (CONTINUED)									
20 TOTAL PER CAPITA PRODUCTION	NA	NA	NA	NA	NA	59.4	NA	NA	NA
PER CAPITA CONSUMPTION									
21 TOTAL	NA	NA	NA	NA	NA	11.6	NA	NA	NA
22 TOTAL - ALTERNATIVE HYDRO	NA	NA	NA	NA	NA	11.5	NA	NA	NA
23 SOLID FUELS	NA	NA	NA	NA	NA	3.3	NA	NA	NA
24 LIQUID FUELS	NA	NA	NA	NA	NA	14.8	NA	NA	NA
25 NATURAL GAS	NA	NA	NA	NA	NA	*	NA	NA	NA
26 HYDROELECTRIC POWER	NA	NA	NA	NA	NA	5.6	NA	NA	NA
27 ADDENDUM - TOTAL ELECTRICITY	NA	NA	NA	NA	NA	13.7	NA	NA	NA
RHODESIAN FEDERATION									
PRODUCTION									
1 TOTAL	10.8	0.1	6.1	9.3	2.2	1.6	3.3	4.3	4.5
2 SOLID FUELS	10.8	0.1	6.1	9.3	1.4	-0.3	3.2	3.4	4.2
3 LIQUID FUELS	*	*	*	*	*	*	*	*	*
4 NATURAL GAS	*	*	*	*	*	*	*	*	*
5 HYDROELECTRIC POWER	*	*	10.9	7.4	42.6	25.9	*	24.5	*
IMPORTS									
6 TOTAL	36.1	12.2	5.5	9.4	5.2	9.5	19.0	8.0	10.7
7 SOLID FUELS	36.3	12.2	4.4	6.4	3.4	3.4	19.1	4.4	9.0
8 LIQUID FUELS	35.1	11.9	9.9	16.3	8.1	12.1	18.6	12.1	13.5
EXPORTS									
9 TOTAL	19.2	-0.4	4.1	3.3	6.2	9.9	5.3	6.4	5.4
10 SOLID FUELS	19.2	-0.4	4.1	3.3	6.2	5.5	5.3	5.0	4.8
11 LIQUID FUELS	*	*	*	*	*	*	*	*	*
CONSUMPTION									
12 TOTAL	9.2	4.7	6.8	11.3	2.3	2.6	6.1	5.3	6.0
13 TOTAL - ALTERNATIVE HYDRO	9.2	5.0	6.8	11.1	3.7	5.2	6.3	6.6	6.6
14 SOLID FUELS	8.5	4.2	6.4	10.6	0.4	-1.6	5.5	3.0	4.8
15 LIQUID FUELS	35.1	11.9	9.7	16.0	8.3	9.4	18.6	11.2	13.1
16 NATURAL GAS	*	*	*	*	*	*	*	*	*
17 HYDROELECTRIC POWER	*	*	10.9	7.4	42.6	27.9	*	25.2	*
18 ADDENDUM - TOTAL ELECTRICITY	NA	NA	NA	11.3	10.8	6.3	NA	9.4	NA
19 POPULATION	3.0	2.2	3.5	4.1	4.1	2.9	2.5	3.7	3.3
20 TOTAL PER CAPITA PRODUCTION	7.5	-2.0	2.5	5.0	-1.9	-1.3	0.8	0.6	1.2
PER CAPITA CONSUMPTION									
21 TOTAL	6.0	2.5	3.1	6.9	-1.7	-0.3	3.5	1.5	2.7
22 TOTAL - ALTERNATIVE HYDRO	6.0	2.7	3.1	6.7	-0.4	2.2	3.7	2.8	3.2
23 SOLID FUELS	5.3	1.9	2.8	6.3	-3.6	-4.4	3.0	-0.7	1.5
24 LIQUID FUELS	31.1	9.5	5.9	11.4	4.0	6.3	15.7	7.2	9.5
25 NATURAL GAS	*	*	*	*	*	*	*	*	*
26 HYDROELECTRIC POWER	*	*	7.1	3.2	37.0	24.3	*	20.7	*
27 ADDENDUM - TOTAL ELECTRICITY	NA	NA	NA	6.9	6.5	3.3	NA	5.5	NA
MALAWI									
PRODUCTION									
1 TOTAL	*	*	*	*	*	*	*	*	*
2 SOLID FUELS	*	*	*	*	*	*	*	*	*
3 LIQUID FUELS	*	*	*	*	*	*	*	*	*
4 NATURAL GAS	*	*	*	*	*	*	*	*	*
5 HYDROELECTRIC POWER	*	*	*	*	*	*	*	*	*
IMPORTS									
6 TOTAL	31.6	7.3	15.4	12.9	8.7	5.0	14.3	8.8	12.5
7 SOLID FUELS	*	3.2	16.5	10.9	6.3	7.0	*	8.1	*
8 LIQUID FUELS	-	13.0	14.4	14.9	10.8	3.4	8.8	9.6	10.7
EXPORTS									
9 TOTAL	*	*	*	*	*	*	*	*	*
10 SOLID FUELS	*	*	*	*	*	*	*	*	*
11 LIQUID FUELS	*	*	*	*	*	*	*	*	*
CONSUMPTION									
12 TOTAL	31.6	7.3	15.4	12.9	8.7	4.2	14.3	8.5	12.4
13 TOTAL - ALTERNATIVE HYDRO	31.6	7.3	15.4	13.0	8.8	4.4	14.3	8.7	12.5
14 SOLID FUELS	*	3.2	16.5	10.9	6.3	7.0	*	8.1	*
15 LIQUID FUELS	-	13.0	14.4	14.9	10.8	1.6	8.8	8.9	10.5
16 NATURAL GAS	*	*	*	*	*	*	*	*	*
17 HYDROELECTRIC POWER	*	*	*	*	*	*	*	*	*
18 ADDENDUM - TOTAL ELECTRICITY	NA	NA	NA	NA	NA	*	NA	26.3	NA
19 POPULATION	3.0	2.3	2.6	2.2	6.3	2.6	2.5	3.7	3.0
20 TOTAL PER CAPITA PRODUCTION	*	*	*	*	*	*	*	*	*

Table XIII. AVERAGE ANNUAL PERCENTAGE RATES OF CHANGE IN TOTAL AND PER CAPITA ENERGY PRODUCTION, TRADE, AND CONSUMPTION, SELECTED PERIODS, 1925-1965

Region, country, indicator	1925-29	1929-38	1938-50	1950-55	1955-60	1960-65	1925-38	1950-65	1925-65
	(1)	(2)	(3)	(4)	(5)	(6)	(7)	(8)	(9)
MALAWI (CONTINUED)									
PER CAPITA CONSUMPTION									
21 TOTAL	27.8	4.9	12.4	10.5	2.3	1.5	11.5	4.7	9.2
22 TOTAL - ALTERNATIVE HYDRO	27.8	4.9	12.4	10.6	2.3	1.8	11.5	4.8	9.2
23 SOLID FUELS	*	0.9	13.5	8.6	-	4.3	*	4.2	*
24 LIQUID FUELS	-2.9	10.4	11.4	12.4	4.2	-1.1	6.1	5.0	7.3
25 NATURAL GAS	*	*	*	*	*	*	*	*	*
26 HYDROELECTRIC POWER	*	*	*	*	*	*	*	*	*
27 ADDENDUM - TOTAL ELECTRICITY	NA	NA	NA	NA	NA	*	NA	21.8	NA
ZAMBIA									
PRODUCTION									
1 TOTAL	*	*	*	NA	NA	NA	*	NA	*
2 SOLID FUELS	*	*	*	*	*	*	*	*	*
3 LIQUID FUELS	*	*	*	*	*	*	*	*	*
4 NATURAL GAS	*	*	*	*	*	*	*	*	*
5 HYDROELECTRIC POWER	*	*	*	NA	NA	NA	*	NA	*
IMPORTS									
6 TOTAL	35.8	12.1	4.6	7.3	3.9	7.8	18.9	6.3	9.7
7 SOLID FUELS	35.6	12.4	4.1	6.1	3.3	3.3	19.0	4.2	8.8
8 LIQUID FUELS	41.4	4.6	17.1	17.6	7.6	9.2	14.8	11.4	14.2
EXPORTS									
9 TOTAL	*	*	*	*	*	*	*	*	*
10 SOLID FUELS	*	*	*	*	*	*	*	*	*
11 LIQUID FUELS	*	*	*	*	*	*	*	*	*
CONSUMPTION									
12 TOTAL	37.0	12.1	4.6	7.9	3.4	8.2	19.2	6.5	9.9
13 TOTAL - ALTERNATIVE HYDRO	37.0	12.1	4.6	9.4	1.9	14.8	19.2	8.6	10.7
14 SOLID FUELS	35.6	12.4	4.1	6.1	3.3	3.3	19.0	4.2	8.8
15 LIQUID FUELS	*	4.6	17.1	17.6	7.6	9.2	*	11.4	*
16 NATURAL GAS	*	*	*	*	*	*	*	*	*
17 HYDROELECTRIC POWER	*	*	*	NA	NA	NA	*	NA	*
18 ADDENDUM - TOTAL ELECTRICITY	NA	NA	NA	NA	NA	NA	NA	8.6	NA
19 POPULATION	3.4	1.4	4.4	2.8	2.8	2.9	2.0	2.8	3.0
20 TOTAL PER CAPITA PRODUCTION	*	*	*	NA	NA	NA	*	NA	*
PER CAPITA/CONSUMPTION									
21 TOTAL	32.5	10.6	0.3	5.0	0.5	5.1	16.9	3.5	6.7
22 TOTAL - ALTERNATIVE HYDRO	32.5	10.6	0.3	6.4	-0.9	11.5	16.9	5.6	7.5
23 SOLID FUELS	31.2	10.8	-0.3	3.3	0.4	0.3	16.7	1.3	5.6
24 LIQUID FUELS	*	3.2	12.2	14.5	4.7	6.1	*	8.3	*
25 NATURAL GAS	*	*	*	*	*	*	*	*	*
26 HYDROELECTRIC POWER	*	*	*	NA	NA	NA	*	NA	*
27 ADDENDUM - TOTAL ELECTRICITY	NA	NA	NA	NA	NA	NA	NA	5.6	NA
RHODESIA									
PRODUCTION									
1 TOTAL	*	*	*	9.3	2.2	1.6	*	4.3	*
2 SOLID FUELS	*	*	*	9.3	1.4	-0.3	*	3.4	*
3 LIQUID FUELS	*	*	*	*	*	*	*	*	*
4 NATURAL GAS	*	*	*	*	*	*	*	*	*
5 HYDROELECTRIC POWER	*	*	*	NA	*	29.9	*	NA	*
IMPORTS									
6 TOTAL	31.6	13.3	8.1	16.0	7.8	13.8	18.6	12.5	13.1
7 SOLID FUELS	*	*	*	17.6	2.1	-	*	6.3	*
8 LIQUID FUELS	31.6	13.3	7.9	15.9	7.9	14.0	18.6	12.6	13.1
EXPORTS									
9 TOTAL	19.2	-0.4	4.1	3.3	6.2	9.8	5.3	6.4	5.4
10 SOLID FUELS	19.2	-0.4	4.1	3.3	6.2	5.5	5.3	5.0	4.8
11 LIQUID FUELS	*	*	*	*	*	*	*	*	*
CONSUMPTION									
12 TOTAL	*	*	*	13.0	1.4	-0.1	*	4.6	*
13 TOTAL - ALTERNATIVE HYDRO	*	*	*	13.0	3.5	1.2	*	5.8	*
14 SOLID FUELS	*	*	*	12.7	-0.9	-4.6	*	2.1	*
15 LIQUID FUELS	31.6	13.3	7.7	15.6	8.2	10.5	18.6	11.4	12.5
16 NATURAL GAS	*	*	*	*	*	*	*	*	*
17 HYDROELECTRIC POWER	*	*	*	NA	*	14.0	*	NA	*
18 ADDENDUM - TOTAL ELECTRICITY	NA	NA	16.6	NA	NA	NA	NA	10.5	NA
19 POPULATION	2.7	3.0	3.7	7.3	3.3	3.2	2.9	4.6	3.8
20 TOTAL PER CAPITA PRODUCTION	*	*	*	1.8	-1.1	-1.6	*	-0.3	*
PER CAPITA \CONSUMPTION									
21 TOTAL	*	*	*	5.3	-1.9	-3.2	*	-	*

Table XIII. AVERAGE ANNUAL PERCENTAGE RATES OF CHANGE IN TOTAL AND PER CAPITA ENERGY PRODUCTION, TRADE, AND CONSUMPTION, SELECTED PERIODS, 1925-1965

Region, country, indicator	1925-29	1929-38	1938-50	1950-55	1955-60	1960-65	1925-38	1950-65	1925-65
	(1)	(2)	(3)	(4)	(5)	(6)	(7)	(8)	(9)
RHODESIA (CONTINUED)									
PER CAPITA CONSUMPTION (CONTINUED)									
22 TOTAL - ALTERNATIVE HYDRO	*	*	*	5.3	0.2	-1.9	*	1.1	*
23 SOLID FUELS	*	*	*	5.0	-4.1	-7.5	*	-2.4	*
24 LIQUID FUELS	28.1	9.9	3.9	7.7	4.7	7.1	15.2	6.5	8.4
25 NATURAL GAS	*	*	*	*	*	*	*	*	*
26 HYDROELECTRIC POWER	*	*	*	NA	*	10.5	*	NA	*
27 ADDENDUM - TOTAL ELECTRICITY	NA	NA	12.5	NA	NA	NA	NA	5.7	NA
WEST AFRICA									
PRODUCTION									
1 TOTAL	*	*	*	*	51.6	14.4	*	*	*
2 SOLID FUELS	*	*	*	*	*	*	*	*	*
3 LIQUID FUELS	*	*	*	*	*	*	*	*	*
4 NATURAL GAS	*	*	*	*	*	*	*	*	*
5 HYDROELECTRIC POWER	*	*	*	*	46.1	18.6	*	*	*
IMPORTS									
6 TOTAL	20.4	-10.2	18.6	10.0	3.2	4.5	-1.7	5.9	6.9
7 SOLID FUELS	13.1	-11.6	4.4	-28.9	-49.4	*	-4.6	*	*
8 LIQUID FUELS	41.1	-8.2	25.2	12.5	3.5	4.5	4.8	6.8	11.3
EXPORTS									
9 TOTAL	*	*	*	*	*	*	*	*	*
10 SOLID FUELS	*	*	*	*	*	*	*	*	*
11 LIQUID FUELS	*	*	*	*	*	*	*	*	*
CONSUMPTION									
12 TOTAL	11.2	-7.4	16.3	9.0	11.1	13.9	-2.0	11.3	8.2
13 TOTAL - ALTERNATIVE HYDRO	11.2	-7.4	16.3	9.0	11.4	13.9	-2.0	11.4	8.2
14 SOLID FUELS	11.8	*	*	-15.1	-49.4	*	*	*	*
15 LIQUID FUELS	10.2	4.0	14.4	12.2	12.2	13.9	5.9	12.7	10.9
16 NATURAL GAS	*	*	*	*	*	*	*	*	*
17 HYDROELECTRIC POWER	*	*	*	*	46.1	18.6	*	*	*
18 ADDENDUM - TOTAL ELECTRICITY	NA	NA	11.8	25.9	24.6	14.8	NA	21.7	NA
19 POPULATION	NA	0.5	1.4	1.8	4.2	2.7	NA	2.9	NA
20 TOTAL PER CAPITA PRODUCTION	NA	*	*	*	45.4	11.4	NA	*	NA
PER CAPITA CONSUMPTION									
21 TOTAL	NA	-7.9	14.7	7.0	6.6	10.9	NA	8.2	NA
22 TOTAL - ALTERNATIVE HYDRO	NA	-7.9	14.8	7.1	6.9	10.9	NA	8.3	NA
23 SOLID FUELS	NA	*	*	-16.6	-51.4	*	NA	*	NA
24 LIQUID FUELS	NA	3.5	12.8	10.3	7.6	10.9	NA	9.6	NA
25 NATURAL GAS	NA	*	*	*	*	*	NA	*	NA
26 HYDROELECTRIC POWER	NA	*	*	*	40.2	15.5	NA	*	NA
27 ADDENDUM - TOTAL ELECTRICITY	NA	NA	10.3	23.7	19.5	11.8	NA	18.2	NA
SOUTH AFRICA									
PRODUCTION									
1 TOTAL	1.4	2.5	4.1	4.0	3.5	4.9	2.2	4.1	3.5
2 SOLID FUELS	1.4	2.5	4.1	4.0	3.5	4.9	2.2	4.1	3.5
3 LIQUID FUELS	*	*	17.9	0.5	-7.5	*	*	*	*
4 NATURAL GAS	*	*	*	*	*	*	*	*	*
5 HYDROELECTRIC POWER	*	*	*	*	*	*	*	*	*
IMPORTS									
6 TOTAL	30.1	12.4	6.5	7.1	2.6	12.1	17.6	7.2	10.3
7 SOLID FUELS	-13.1	22.0	8.5	9.3	*	*	9.9	5.6	7.9
8 LIQUID FUELS	31.0	12.4	6.5	7.0	3.0	11.8	17.8	7.2	10.3
EXPORTS									
9 TOTAL	0.8	-6.5	9.3	-20.7	6.3	11.6	-4.3	-2.0	0.5
10 SOLID FUELS	0.8	-6.5	9.3	-24.0	7.8	7.0	-4.3	-4.3	-0.4
11 LIQUID FUELS	*	*	*	*	-0.8	30.9	*	*	*
CONSUMPTION									
12 TOTAL	3.1	4.6	4.5	6.3	3.4	5.6	4.2	5.1	4.6
13 TOTAL - ALTERNATIVE HYDRO	3.1	4.6	4.5	6.3	3.4	5.6	4.2	5.1	4.6
14 SOLID FUELS	2.3	4.3	4.3	6.0	3.4	4.9	3.7	4.8	4.2
15 LIQUID FUELS	27.6	10.4	6.6	8.4	4.0	10.5	15.4	7.6	9.8
16 NATURAL GAS	*	*	*	*	*	*	*	*	*
17 HYDROELECTRIC POWER	*	*	*	*	*	*	*	*	*
18 ADDENDUM - TOTAL ELECTRICITY	6.9	11.1	5.2	8.5	8.6	7.4	9.8	8.2	7.8
19 POPULATION	2.2	1.9	1.8	2.4	2.6	2.3	2.0	2.4	2.1
20 TOTAL PER CAPITA PRODUCTION	-0.8	0.6	2.3	1.5	0.8	2.5	0.2	1.6	1.4
PER CAPITA CONSUMPTION									
21 TOTAL	0.9	2.7	2.7	3.8	0.8	3.2	2.1	2.6	2.5
22 TOTAL - ALTERNATIVE HYDRO	0.9	2.7	2.7	3.8	0.8	3.2	2.1	2.6	2.5
23 SOLID FUELS	0.1	2.3	2.4	3.6	0.7	2.5	1.6	2.3	2.1

Table XIII. AVERAGE ANNUAL PERCENTAGE RATES OF CHANGE IN TOTAL AND PER CAPITA ENERGY PRODUCTION, TRADE, AND CONSUMPTION, SELECTED PERIODS, 1925-1965

Region, country, indicator	1925-29	1929-38	1938-50	1950-55	1955-60	1960-65	1925-38	1950-65	1925-65
	(1)	(2)	(3)	(4)	(5)	(6)	(7)	(8)	(9)
SOUTH AFRICA (CONTINUED)									
PER CAPITA CONSUMPTION (CONTINUED)									
24 LIQUID FUELS	24.9	8.3	4.8	5.8	1.4	8.0	13.1	5.0	7.5
25 NATURAL GAS	*	*	*	*	*	*	*	*	*
26 HYDROELECTRIC POWER	*	*	*	*	*	*	*	*	*
27 ADDENDUM - TOTAL ELECTRICITY	4.6	9.0	3.3	6.0	5.8	5.0	7.6	5.6	5.6
DEVELOPED COUNTRIES									
PRODUCTION									
1 TOTAL	3.3	-1.1	2.2	2.8	1.3	3.1	0.3	2.4	1.6
2 SOLID FUELS	2.2	-2.0	0.6	-0.2	-1.3	1.7	-0.7	-	-
3 LIQUID FUELS	7.6	2.0	4.5	5.9	1.6	3.1	3.7	3.5	3.9
4 NATURAL GAS	12.5	2.2	8.5	8.8	7.2	5.6	5.2	7.2	6.9
5 HYDROELECTRIC POWER	10.6	4.4	5.3	5.9	6.3	4.6	6.3	5.6	5.7
IMPORTS									
6 TOTAL	7.5	-0.8	3.5	11.0	7.5	10.7	1.7	9.7	5.2
7 SOLID FUELS	5.7	-3.1	-1.5	6.4	-4.0	3.0	-0.5	1.7	-
8 LIQUID FUELS	11.8	2.9	7.3	12.8	10.1	11.6	5.5	11.5	8.3
EXPORTS									
9 TOTAL	4.9	-2.3	-1.7	9.1	-0.8	6.1	-0.2	4.7	1.1
10 SOLID FUELS	4.2	-3.8	-1.9	6.1	-5.8	2.3	-1.4	0.7	-0.8
11 LIQUID FUELS	8.2	2.8	-1.8	15.6	4.9	7.8	4.4	9.4	4.3
CONSUMPTION									
12 TOTAL	3.7	-0.8	2.7	3.7	2.9	5.0	0.6	3.9	2.4
13 TOTAL - ALTERNATIVE HYDRO	3.8	-0.7	2.7	3.5	2.9	4.9	0.7	3.8	2.4
14 SOLID FUELS	2.4	-1.8	0.7	-0.1	-1.1	1.8	-0.5	0.2	0.1
15 LIQUID FUELS	8.9	2.5	6.0	7.7	5.4	7.6	4.4	6.9	5.8
16 NATURAL GAS	12.5	2.1	8.5	8.8	7.4	5.6	5.2	7.3	7.0
17 HYDROELECTRIC POWER	10.5	4.4	5.3	5.8	6.4	4.7	6.3	5.6	5.7
18 ADDENDUM - TOTAL ELECTRICITY	10.2	4.4	6.1	9.6	7.1	7.1	6.2	7.9	6.8
19 POPULATION	1.0	0.8	0.6	1.2	1.2	1.2	0.8	1.2	0.9
20 TOTAL PER CAPITA PRODUCTION	2.3	-1.8	1.6	1.5	0.1	1.8	-0.6	1.2	0.7
PER CAPITA CONSUMPTION									
21 TOTAL	2.7	-1.6	2.1	2.4	1.7	3.8	-0.3	2.6	1.5
22 TOTAL - ALTERNATIVE HYDRO	2.8	-1.4	2.1	2.3	1.7	3.6	-0.2	2.5	1.5
23 SOLID FUELS	1.4	-2.6	0.1	-1.3	-2.3	0.5	-1.4	-1.0	-0.8
24 LIQUID FUELS	7.9	1.7	5.4	6.4	4.2	6.3	3.6	5.6	4.9
25 NATURAL GAS	11.4	1.4	7.8	7.5	6.1	4.4	4.4	6.0	6.0
26 HYDROELECTRIC POWER	9.4	3.6	4.7	4.5	5.1	3.4	5.4	4.3	4.8
27 ADDENDUM - TOTAL ELECTRICITY	9.1	3.6	5.4	8.3	5.8	5.8	5.3	6.6	5.8
UNDERDEVELOPED COUNTRIES									
PRODUCTION									
1 TOTAL	7.7	4.1	7.3	9.4	9.0	9.5	5.2	9.3	7.4
2 SOLID FUELS	3.4	3.0	0.4	4.3	5.8	5.5	3.1	5.2	3.1
3 LIQUID FUELS	9.6	4.2	9.3	9.9	9.0	9.9	5.9	9.6	8.3
4 NATURAL GAS	15.2	9.5	2.9	14.1	18.4	9.9	11.2	14.1	9.7
5 HYDROELECTRIC POWER	7.9	10.2	4.6	10.2	11.8	10.3	9.5	10.8	8.5
IMPORTS									
6 TOTAL	13.8	4.0	5.6	6.7	1.3	5.0	6.9	4.3	5.5
7 SOLID FUELS	2.7	-2.1	-5.3	0.9	-0.3	-2.8	-0.6	-0.8	-2.1
8 LIQUID FUELS	21.9	6.1	6.9	7.1	1.5	5.2	10.7	4.6	7.2
EXPORTS									
9 TOTAL	15.9	5.3	8.7	8.9	7.0	9.8	8.4	8.6	8.5
10 SOLID FUELS	9.8	3.0	-7.3	6.0	1.4	-1.4	5.0	2.0	0.1
11 LIQUID FUELS	16.4	5.4	9.0	8.9	7.0	9.9	8.6	8.6	8.7
CONSUMPTION									
12 TOTAL	5.2	3.2	3.3	9.1	7.7	6.4	3.8	7.7	5.1
13 TOTAL - ALTERNATIVE HYDRO	5.1	3.5	3.2	8.9	7.7	6.4	3.9	7.7	5.1
14 SOLID FUELS	2.8	2.0	0.2	4.0	5.4	5.0	2.2	4.8	2.6
15 LIQUID FUELS	7.9	3.8	5.7	11.3	7.3	6.1	5.1	8.2	6.4
16 NATURAL GAS	15.2	9.6	3.7	12.8	16.4	9.7	11.3	12.9	9.5
17 HYDROELECTRIC POWER	7.9	10.3	4.7	10.2	11.6	10.4	9.5	10.7	8.5
18 ADDENDUM - TOTAL ELECTRICITY	9.5	7.5	6.5	12.9	11.5	9.6	8.2	11.4	8.8
19 POPULATION	1.4	1.6	1.5	2.0	2.4	2.5	1.6	2.3	1.8
20 TOTAL PER CAPITA PRODUCTION	6.2	2.4	5.8	7.3	6.5	6.9	3.6	6.9	5.5
PER CAPITA CONSUMPTION									
21 TOTAL	3.7	1.6	1.7	7.0	5.2	3.8	2.2	5.3	3.2
22 TOTAL - ALTERNATIVE HYDRO	3.6	1.8	1.7	6.9	5.2	3.8	2.4	5.3	3.2
23 SOLID FUELS	1.3	0.4	-1.3	2.0	2.9	2.4	0.7	2.4	0.7
24 LIQUID FUELS	6.4	2.2	4.1	9.1	4.8	3.5	3.5	5.8	4.5
25 NATURAL GAS	13.6	7.8	2.1	10.7	13.7	7.1	9.6	10.4	7.6

Table XIII. AVERAGE ANNUAL PERCENTAGE RATES OF CHANGE IN TOTAL AND PER CAPITA ENERGY PRODUCTION, TRADE, AND CONSUMPTION, SELECTED PERIODS, 1925-1965

Region, country, indicator	1925-29	1929-38	1938-50	1950-55	1955-60	1960-65	1925-38	1950-65	1925-65
	(1)	(2)	(3)	(4)	(5)	(6)	(7)	(8)	(9)
UNDERDEVELOPED COUNTRIES (CONTINUED)									
PER CAPITA CONSUMPTION (CONTINUED)									
26 HYDROELECTRIC POWER	6.4	8.5	3.1	8.1	9.0	7.7	7.9	8.3	6.6
27 ADDENDUM - TOTAL ELECTRICITY	8.0	5.8	4.9	10.8	8.9	7.0	6.5	8.9	6.9
COMMUNIST COUNTRIES									
PRODUCTION									
1 TOTAL	11.5	5.8	4.8	9.3	8.6	6.5	7.5	8.1	6.9
2 SOLID FUELS	10.5	5.2	5.5	8.5	6.1	3.7	6.8	6.1	6.2
3 LIQUID FUELS	17.1	7.9	1.4	14.0	14.4	9.5	10.7	12.6	8.5
4 NATURAL GAS	11.3	12.6	4.8	11.5	30.9	21.6	12.2	21.1	13.1
5 HYDROELECTRIC POWER	15.6	23.1	10.7	10.6	17.9	7.9	20.8	12.0	14.4
IMPORTS									
6 TOTAL	6.4	-5.9	12.6	8.9	4.7	7.9	-2.3	7.2	5.6
7 SOLID FUELS	5.7	-8.4	14.8	4.9	-0.4	7.6	-4.2	4.0	4.3
8 LIQUID FUELS	8.8	-0.4	8.1	18.2	11.2	8.3	2.3	12.5	7.8
EXPORTS									
9 TOTAL	15.6	-2.6	3.3	10.2	11.3	9.9	2.7	10.5	5.7
10 SOLID FUELS	11.7	-3.0	5.3	4.1	2.3	6.1	1.3	4.2	3.6
11 LIQUID FUELS	28.3	-1.7	-3.2	31.2	22.3	12.5	6.7	21.7	8.9
CONSUMPTION									
12 TOTAL	10.2	6.5	5.4	9.3	8.2	6.2	7.6	7.9	7.0
13 TOTAL - ALTERNATIVE HYDRO	10.2	6.6	5.4	9.2	8.3	6.2	7.7	7.9	7.1
14 SOLID FUELS	9.9	5.7	5.9	8.6	6.2	3.7	7.0	6.2	6.3
15 LIQUID FUELS	11.8	10.1	2.5	12.5	12.3	8.5	10.6	11.1	8.3
16 NATURAL GAS	11.3	12.6	4.8	11.5	30.9	21.5	12.2	21.0	13.1
17 HYDROELECTRIC POWER	14.1	22.1	10.6	10.9	17.9	7.9	19.6	12.1	14.0
18 ADDENDUM - TOTAL ELECTRICITY	14.3	14.8	8.3	12.7	12.8	9.2	14.7	11.6	11.6
19 POPULATION	1.0	0.5	1.3	1.7	1.6	1.5	0.6	1.6	1.2
20 TOTAL PER CAPITA PRODUCTION	10.3	5.3	3.5	7.5	6.8	4.9	6.8	6.4	5.7
PER CAPITA CONSUMPTION									
21 TOTAL	9.0	6.1	4.0	7.4	6.5	4.7	7.0	6.2	5.8
22 TOTAL - ALTERNATIVE HYDRO	9.0	6.2	4.1	7.4	6.6	4.6	7.0	6.2	5.8
23 SOLID FUELS	8.8	5.2	4.6	6.8	4.5	2.2	6.3	4.5	5.1
24 LIQUID FUELS	10.7	9.6	1.2	10.6	10.5	6.9	9.9	9.3	7.0
25 NATURAL GAS	10.2	12.1	3.5	9.6	28.8	19.8	11.5	19.1	11.8
26 HYDROELECTRIC POWER	12.9	21.6	9.2	9.0	16.0	6.3	18.9	10.4	12.7
27 ADDENDUM - TOTAL ELECTRICITY	13.1	14.3	7.0	10.8	11.1	7.6	13.9	9.8	10.3
USSR									
PRODUCTION									
1 TOTAL	21.6	13.0	4.2	9.6	8.5	7.4	15.6	8.5	9.4
2 SOLID FUELS	23.8	14.5	4.8	8.5	3.5	2.3	17.3	4.7	8.7
3 LIQUID FUELS	17.9	9.3	2.1	13.4	15.6	10.0	11.9	13.0	9.2
4 NATURAL GAS	23.9	23.5	8.3	9.3	38.2	23.0	23.6	22.9	18.6
5 HYDROELECTRIC POWER	22.1	27.9	7.9	12.8	17.1	9.8	26.1	13.2	15.6
IMPORTS									
6 TOTAL	12.2	2.0	21.5	1.9	-7.3	-2.7	5.0	-2.8	6.6
7 SOLID FUELS	12.2	-0.5	22.0	-4.5	-10.0	6.6	3.3	-2.8	6.1
8 LIQUID FUELS	11.9	12.5	20.3	14.3	-4.6	-15.3	12.3	-2.6	8.7
EXPORTS									
9 TOTAL	31.0	-11.0	4.6	33.1	29.3	13.7	0.2	25.1	10.3
10 SOLID FUELS	38.2	-14.5	18.9	17.3	20.6	11.9	-0.9	16.5	11.2
11 LIQUID FUELS	29.5	-10.3	-2.3	48.6	33.0	14.2	0.4	31.2	10.1
CONSUMPTION									
12 TOTAL	20.3	14.3	4.6	8.7	6.8	6.6	16.1	7.4	9.3
13 TOTAL - ALTERNATIVE HYDRO	20.2	14.4	4.6	8.7	6.9	6.6	16.2	7.4	9.3
14 SOLID FUELS	23.0	14.7	5.1	7.9	2.8	1.9	17.2	4.2	8.5
15 LIQUID FUELS	14.5	12.8	2.8	11.7	11.6	8.1	13.3	10.5	9.0
16 NATURAL GAS	23.9	23.5	8.3	9.0	38.5	23.1	23.6	23.0	18.6
17 HYDROELECTRIC POWER	22.1	27.9	7.9	12.8	17.0	9.5	26.1	13.1	15.5
18 ADDENDUM - TOTAL ELECTRICITY	20.8	22.8	7.2	13.4	11.4	11.6	22.2	12.1	13.7
19 POPULATION	2.3	1.3	-0.4	1.7	1.8	1.5	1.6	1.7	1.0
20 TOTAL PER CAPITA PRODUCTION	18.8	11.5	4.7	7.7	6.6	5.9	13.7	6.7	8.3
PER CAPITA CONSUMPTION									
21 TOTAL	17.6	12.8	5.1	6.9	4.9	5.0	14.2	5.6	8.2
22 TOTAL - ALTERNATIVE HYDRO	17.5	12.9	5.1	6.9	5.0	5.0	14.3	5.6	8.2
23 SOLID FUELS	20.2	13.2	5.5	6.0	1.0	0.5	15.3	2.5	7.4
24 LIQUID FUELS	11.9	11.3	3.2	9.8	9.7	6.6	11.5	8.7	7.9
25 NATURAL GAS	21.1	21.9	8.8	7.2	36.1	21.3	21.7	20.9	17.4
26 HYDROELECTRIC POWER	19.3	26.2	8.4	10.9	15.0	7.9	24.0	11.2	14.3
27 ADDENDUM - TOTAL ELECTRICITY	18.1	21.2	7.7	11.4	9.4	10.0	20.2	10.3	12.6

Table XIII. AVERAGE ANNUAL PERCENTAGE RATES OF CHANGE IN TOTAL AND PER CAPITA ENERGY PRODUCTION, TRADE, AND CONSUMPTION, SELECTED PERIODS, 1925-1965

Region, country, indicator	1925-29	1929-38	1938-50	1950-55	1955-60	1960-65	1925-38	1950-65	1925-65
	(1)	(2)	(3)	(4)	(5)	(6)	(7)	(8)	(9)
COMMUNIST EASTERN EUROPE									
PRODUCTION									
1 TOTAL	9.6	-0.9	6.4	6.6	3.5	3.6	2.2	4.5	4.4
2 SOLID FUELS	9.2	-1.7	7.5	5.7	3.4	3.2	1.5	4.1	4.2
3 LIQUID FUELS	15.2	3.4	-1.8	16.4	1.9	2.7	6.9	6.8	4.2
4 NATURAL GAS	9.0	7.5	-0.2	16.4	11.4	12.5	8.0	13.4	7.4
5 HYDROELECTRIC POWER	8.4	10.9	7.9	12.3	8.4	8.6	10.1	9.8	9.3
IMPORTS									
6 TOTAL	12.5	-8.7	13.1	13.8	9.4	12.9	-2.6	12.0	7.3
7 SOLID FUELS	11.1	-11.5	14.9	13.1	3.5	7.8	-5.1	8.1	5.5
8 LIQUID FUELS	21.3	0.1	8.6	15.7	21.6	18.7	6.2	18.6	11.4
EXPORTS									
9 TOTAL	13.5	-1.7	4.9	5.0	-1.0	2.9	2.8	2.3	3.2
10 SOLID FUELS	11.4	-3.7	7.2	1.9	-2.4	2.5	0.7	0.6	2.6
11 LIQUID FUELS	26.8	4.5	-3.4	20.7	2.6	3.9	10.9	8.8	5.6
CONSUMPTION									
12 TOTAL	8.6	-1.4	7.5	7.4	5.0	5.0	1.6	5.8	4.9
13 TOTAL - ALTERNATIVE HYDRO	8.6	-1.3	7.5	7.5	5.0	5.0	1.6	5.8	4.9
14 SOLID FUELS	8.7	-1.9	8.1	6.8	4.3	3.6	1.2	4.9	4.6
15 LIQUID FUELS	8.0	1.4	2.8	13.6	10.9	13.2	3.4	12.5	6.5
16 NATURAL GAS	9.0	7.5	-0.1	16.6	11.3	12.4	8.0	13.4	7.5
17 HYDROELECTRIC POWER	6.8	8.8	7.1	15.3	8.4	11.1	8.2	11.5	9.1
18 ADDENDUM - TOTAL ELECTRICITY	14.2	4.0	12.4	11.5	9.2	8.5	7.0	9.7	9.6
19 POPULATION	1.3	1.0	0.8	1.0	0.9	0.7	1.1	0.8	0.9
20 TOTAL PER CAPITA PRODUCTION	8.3	-1.9	5.6	5.5	2.6	2.9	1.1	3.7	3.4
PER CAPITA CONSUMPTION									
21 TOTAL	7.2	-2.4	6.6	6.4	4.1	4.3	0.5	4.9	3.9
22 TOTAL - ALTERNATIVE HYDRO	7.2	-2.4	6.6	6.4	4.1	4.3	0.5	4.9	4.0
23 SOLID FUELS	7.3	-2.9	7.2	5.8	3.4	2.9	0.1	4.0	3.7
24 LIQUID FUELS	6.6	0.3	2.0	12.4	9.9	12.4	2.2	11.6	5.6
25 NATURAL GAS	7.6	6.4	-0.9	15.4	10.4	11.6	6.8	12.4	6.5
26 HYDROELECTRIC POWER	5.5	7.7	6.2	14.1	7.4	10.4	7.0	10.6	8.1
27 ADDENDUM - TOTAL ELECTRICITY	12.7	3.0	11.5	10.4	8.3	7.7	5.9	8.8	8.6
COMMUNIST ASIA									
PRODUCTION									
1 TOTAL	1.6	2.5	3.1	17.5	18.9	7.0	2.3	14.3	6.9
2 SOLID FUELS	1.6	2.4	3.0	17.4	18.3	6.8	2.1	14.0	6.7
3 LIQUID FUELS	*	56.4	-2.8	37.0	41.8	12.6	*	29.8	*
4 NATURAL GAS	*	*	*	*	*	*	*	*	*
5 HYDROELECTRIC POWER	*	*	*	3.3	25.5	1.7	*	9.6	*
IMPORTS									
6 TOTAL	-1.7	-5.6	NA	NA	20.6	-21.0	-4.4	NA	-2.3
7 SOLID FUELS	-4.6	-7.6	NA	NA	6.6	4.9	-6.7	NA	-7.2
8 LIQUID FUELS	3.3	-3.1	NA	NA	21.0	-22.0	-1.2	NA	0.2
EXPORTS									
9 TOTAL	8.0	2.2	NA	NA	-1.3	11.2	4.0	NA	-1.0
10 SOLID FUELS	8.0	1.9	NA	NA	-1.3	11.2	3.7	NA	-1.0
11 LIQUID FUELS	*	*	NA	NA	*	*	*	NA	*
CONSUMPTION									
12 TOTAL	0.1	1.6	3.9	17.9	19.1	6.5	1.1	14.4	6.7
13 TOTAL - ALTERNATIVE HYDRO	0.1	1.6	4.3	17.2	19.1	6.4	1.1	14.1	6.8
14 SOLID FUELS	-0.1	1.7	4.2	17.3	18.5	6.7	1.1	14.0	6.7
15 LIQUID FUELS	3.4	-0.8	-17.4	87.9	31.2	4.0	0.5	36.8	6.4
16 NATURAL GAS	*	*	*	*	*	*	*	*	*
17 HYDROELECTRIC POWER	*	*	*	3.3	25.5	1.7	*	9.6	*
18 ADDENDUM - TOTAL ELECTRICITY	2.1	8.5	6.3	11.1	34.3	-2.7	6.5	13.2	8.9
19 POPULATION	0.6	-	2.0	1.8	1.7	1.6	0.2	1.7	1.3
20 TOTAL PER CAPITA PRODUCTION	1.0	2.5	1.1	15.4	16.9	5.3	2.1	12.4	5.5
PER CAPITA CONSUMPTION									
21 TOTAL	-0.5	1.6	1.9	15.8	17.1	4.9	0.9	12.5	5.4
22 TOTAL - ALTERNATIVE HYDRO	-0.5	1.6	2.3	15.1	17.2	4.7	0.9	12.2	5.4
23 SOLID FUELS	-0.7	1.7	2.2	15.2	16.5	5.1	1.0	12.2	5.4
24 LIQUID FUELS	2.8	-0.8	-19.1	84.5	29.0	2.4	0.3	34.6	5.0
25 NATURAL GAS	*	*	*	*	*	*	*	*	*
26 HYDROELECTRIC POWER	*	*	*	1.4	23.4	0.1	*	7.8	*
27 ADDENDUM - TOTAL ELECTRICITY	1.5	8.5	4.3	9.1	32.1	-4.2	6.3	11.3	7.5

Table XIII. AVERAGE ANNUAL PERCENTAGE RATES OF CHANGE IN TOTAL AND PER CAPITA ENERGY PRODUCTION, TRADE, AND CONSUMPTION, SELECTED PERIODS, 1925-1965

Region, country, indicator	1925-29	1929-38	1938-50	1950-55	1955-60	1960-65	1925-38	1950-65	1925-65
	(1)	(2)	(3)	(4)	(5)	(6)	(7)	(8)	(9)
ORGANISATION FOR ECONOMIC CO-OPERATION AND DEVELOPMENT (OECD)									
PRODUCTION									
1 TOTAL	3.4	-1.1	2.1	2.7	1.2	3.0	0.3	2.3	1.6
2 SOLID FUELS	2.3	-2.1	0.4	-0.4	-1.7	1.4	-0.8	-0.2	-0.2
3 LIQUID FUELS	7.6	2.0	4.5	5.9	1.6	3.1	3.7	3.5	3.9
4 NATURAL GAS	12.5	2.2	8.5	8.8	7.2	5.6	5.2	7.2	6.9
5 HYDROELECTRIC POWER	10.5	4.3	5.3	5.7	6.3	4.4	6.2	5.5	5.7
IMPORTS									
6 TOTAL	7.3	-1.0	3.4	11.1	7.5	10.8	1.5	9.8	5.1
7 SOLID FUELS	5.7	-3.2	-1.6	6.5	-4.3	3.0	-0.5	1.6	-0.1
8 LIQUID FUELS	11.4	2.6	7.4	13.0	10.2	11.7	5.3	11.6	8.3
EXPORTS									
9 TOTAL	5.1	-2.3	-1.9	9.4	-1.2	5.8	-0.1	4.5	1.1
10 SOLID FUELS	4.4	-3.8	-2.0	6.6	-6.3	1.0	-1.3	0.3	-0.9
11 LIQUID FUELS	8.2	2.8	-1.8	15.4	4.5	8.1	4.4	9.2	4.3
CONSUMPTION									
12 TOTAL	3.8	-0.9	2.7	3.6	2.8	5.0	0.5	3.8	2.4
13 TOTAL - ALTERNATIVE HYDRO	3.8	-0.7	2.7	3.5	2.8	4.8	0.6	3.7	2.4
14 SOLID FUELS	2.5	-1.9	0.6	-0.3	-1.4	1.6	-0.6	-0.1	-
15 LIQUID FUELS	8.8	2.4	6.0	7.7	5.3	7.6	4.3	6.9	5.8
16 NATURAL GAS	12.5	2.1	8.5	8.8	7.4	5.6	5.2	7.3	7.0
17 HYDROELECTRIC POWER	10.5	4.3	5.3	5.7	6.4	4.4	6.2	5.5	5.7
18 ADDENDUM - TOTAL ELECTRICITY	10.2	4.2	6.1	9.6	7.0	7.1	6.0	7.9	6.7
19 POPULATION	1.0	0.8	0.6	1.2	1.2	1.3	0.8	1.2	0.9
20 TOTAL PER CAPITA PRODUCTION	2.4	-1.9	1.5	1.5	-	1.7	-0.6	1.1	0.7
PER CAPITA CONSUMPTION									
21 TOTAL	2.8	-1.6	2.1	2.3	1.6	3.7	-0.3	2.5	1.5
22 TOTAL - ALTERNATIVE HYDRO	2.9	-1.5	2.1	2.2	1.6	3.5	-0.2	2.4	1.5
23 SOLID FUELS	1.5	-2.7	-	-1.5	-2.6	0.3	-1.4	-1.3	-0.9
24 LIQUID FUELS	7.8	1.7	5.4	6.4	4.1	6.2	3.5	5.6	4.8
25 NATURAL GAS	11.5	1.4	7.8	7.5	6.0	4.3	4.4	5.9	6.0
26 HYDROELECTRIC POWER	9.4	3.5	4.7	4.4	5.1	3.1	5.3	4.2	4.7
27 ADDENDUM - TOTAL ELECTRICITY	9.1	3.4	5.5	8.2	5.7	5.7	5.2	6.6	5.8
COMMUNIST COUNTRIES									
PRODUCTION									
1 TOTAL	11.5	5.8	4.8	9.3	8.6	6.5	7.5	8.1	6.9
2 SOLID FUELS	10.5	5.2	5.5	8.5	6.1	3.7	6.8	6.1	6.2
3 LIQUID FUELS	17.1	7.9	1.4	14.0	14.4	9.5	10.7	12.6	8.5
4 NATURAL GAS	11.3	12.6	4.8	11.5	30.9	21.6	12.2	21.1	13.1
5 HYDROELECTRIC POWER	15.6	23.1	10.7	10.6	17.9	7.9	20.8	12.0	14.4
IMPORTS									
6 TOTAL	6.4	-5.9	12.6	8.9	4.7	7.9	-2.3	7.2	5.6
7 SOLID FUELS	5.7	-8.4	14.8	4.9	-0.4	7.6	-4.2	4.0	4.3
8 LIQUID FUELS	8.8	-0.4	8.1	18.2	11.2	8.3	2.3	12.5	7.8
EXPORTS									
9 TOTAL	15.6	-2.6	3.3	10.2	11.3	9.9	2.7	10.5	5.7
10 SOLID FUELS	11.7	-3.0	5.3	4.1	2.3	6.1	1.3	4.2	3.6
11 LIQUID FUELS	28.3	-1.7	-3.2	31.2	22.3	12.5	6.7	21.7	8.9
CONSUMPTION									
12 TOTAL	10.2	6.5	5.4	9.3	8.2	6.2	7.6	7.9	7.0
13 TOTAL - ALTERNATIVE HYDRO	10.2	6.6	5.4	9.2	8.3	6.2	7.7	7.9	7.1
14 SOLID FUELS	9.9	5.7	5.9	8.6	6.2	3.7	7.0	6.2	6.3
15 LIQUID FUELS	11.8	10.1	2.5	12.5	12.3	8.5	10.6	11.1	8.3
16 NATURAL GAS	11.3	12.6	4.8	11.5	30.9	21.5	12.2	21.0	13.1
17 HYDROELECTRIC POWER	14.1	22.1	10.6	10.9	17.9	7.9	19.6	12.1	14.0
18 ADDENDUM - TOTAL ELECTRICITY	14.3	14.8	8.3	12.7	12.8	9.2	14.7	11.6	11.6
19 POPULATION	1.0	0.5	1.3	1.7	1.6	1.5	0.6	1.6	1.2
20 TOTAL PER CAPITA PRODUCTION	10.3	5.3	3.5	7.5	6.8	4.9	6.8	6.4	5.7
PER CAPITA CONSUMPTION									
21 TOTAL	9.0	6.1	4.0	7.4	6.5	4.7	7.0	6.2	5.8
22 TOTAL - ALTERNATIVE HYDRO	9.0	6.2	4.1	7.4	6.6	4.6	7.0	6.2	5.8
23 SOLID FUELS	8.8	5.2	4.6	6.8	4.5	2.2	6.3	4.5	5.1
24 LIQUID FUELS	10.7	9.6	1.2	10.6	10.5	6.9	9.9	9.3	7.0
25 NATURAL GAS	10.2	12.1	3.5	9.6	28.8	19.8	11.5	19.1	11.8
26 HYDROELECTRIC POWER	12.9	21.6	9.2	9.0	16.0	6.3	18.9	10.4	12.7
27 ADDENDUM - TOTAL ELECTRICITY	13.1	14.3	7.0	10.8	11.1	7.6	13.9	9.8	10.3
WORLD EXCLUDING OECD AND COMMUNIST COUNTRIES									
PRODUCTION									
1 TOTAL	5.5	3.6	6.8	8.7	8.6	9.2	4.2	8.9	6.7

Table XIII. AVERAGE ANNUAL PERCENTAGE RATES OF CHANGE IN TOTAL AND PER CAPITA ENERGY PRODUCTION, TRADE, AND CONSUMPTION, SELECTED PERIODS, 1925-1965

Region, country, indicator	1925-29	1929-38	1938-50	1950-55	1955-60	1960-65	1925-38	1950-65	1925-65
	(1)	(2)	(3)	(4)	(5)	(6)	(7)	(8)	(9)
WORLD EXCLUDING OECD AND COMMUNIST COUNTRIES (CONTINUED)									
PRODUCTION (CONTINUED)									
2 SOLID FUELS	1.1	2.3	2.1	3.8	5.0	5.4	1.9	4.8	3.0
3 LIQUID FUELS	9.6	4.2	9.3	9.9	9.0	9.9	5.9	9.6	8.3
4 NATURAL GAS	15.2	9.5	2.9	14.1	18.4	10.0	11.2	14.1	9.7
5 HYDROELECTRIC POWER	9.3	10.1	4.8	10.4	10.0	10.5	9.8	10.3	8.5
IMPORTS									
6 TOTAL	13.7	4.0	5.5	6.9	2.1	5.5	6.9	4.8	5.7
7 SOLID FUELS	3.3	-1.8	-3.8	2.1	1.2	-0.3	-0.3	1.0	-0.9
8 LIQUID FUELS	21.7	6.2	6.9	7.3	2.2	5.7	10.7	5.0	7.4
EXPORTS									
9 TOTAL	14.9	5.1	8.7	8.8	7.1	9.9	8.0	8.6	8.4
10 SOLID FUELS	2.3	1.3	-2.4	-4.3	8.3	14.2	1.6	5.8	1.9
11 LIQUID FUELS	16.4	5.4	9.0	8.9	7.0	9.8	8.6	8.6	8.7
CONSUMPTION									
12 TOTAL	4.3	3.1	3.6	8.1	7.0	6.3	3.4	7.1	4.8
13 TOTAL - ALTERNATIVE HYDRO	4.3	3.3	3.5	8.0	7.0	6.3	3.6	7.1	4.9
14 SOLID FUELS	1.9	2.0	1.9	4.3	4.6	4.6	2.0	4.5	2.9
15 LIQUID FUELS	8.9	4.1	5.7	11.1	7.4	6.6	5.6	8.3	6.6
16 NATURAL GAS	15.2	9.6	3.7	12.8	16.4	9.9	11.3	13.0	9.6
17 HYDROELECTRIC POWER	9.3	10.1	4.8	10.3	10.0	10.6	9.9	10.3	8.5
18 ADDENDUM - TOTAL ELECTRICITY	9.9	8.5	6.1	11.8	10.6	9.4	8.9	10.6	8.7
19 POPULATION	1.4	1.6	1.5	1.9	2.3	2.4	1.5	2.2	1.8
20 TOTAL PER CAPITA PRODUCTION	4.0	2.0	5.3	6.7	6.1	6.6	2.6	6.5	4.8
PER CAPITA CONSUMPTION									
21 TOTAL	2.8	1.4	2.1	6.0	4.5	3.8	1.9	4.8	3.0
22 TOTAL - ALTERNATIVE HYDRO	2.8	1.7	2.0	5.9	4.5	3.8	2.0	4.7	3.0
23 SOLID FUELS	0.5	0.4	0.4	2.3	2.2	2.1	0.4	2.2	1.1
24 LIQUID FUELS	7.4	2.5	4.2	9.0	4.9	4.1	4.0	6.0	4.8
25 NATURAL GAS	13.6	7.9	2.2	10.7	13.7	7.3	9.6	10.5	7.6
26 HYDROELECTRIC POWER	7.7	8.4	3.3	8.2	7.5	7.9	8.2	7.9	6.6
27 ADDENDUM - TOTAL ELECTRICITY	8.4	6.8	4.5	9.7	8.0	6.8	7.3	8.2	6.8

DERIVATION OF TABLE XIV

Column	*Derivation*
(1)	Col. (2) table II
(2)	Col. (2) table VII
(3)	Col. (2) table IX
(4)	Col. (6) table X
(5)	Col. (6) table II
(6)	Col. (3) table VII
(7)	Col. (3) table IX
(8)	Col. (7) table X
(9)	Col. (8) table II
(10)	Col. (8) table X
(11)	Col. (9) table II
(12)	Col. (9) table X
(13)	Col. (1) table II
(14)	Col. (1) table VII
(15)	Col. (1) table IX
(16)	Col. (5) table X

Table XIV. SUMMARY OF ENERGY PRODUCTION, TRADE, AND CONSUMPTION, BY FUEL, SELECTED YEARS, 1925-1965

(Thousand metric tons coal equivalent)

Region, country, year	Solid fuels				Liquid fuels				Natural gas		Hydroelectric power		Total energy			
	Production	Net imports	Bunkers	Consumption	Production	Net imports	Bunkers	Consumption	Production	Consumption	Production	Consumption	Production	Net imports	Bunkers	Consumption
	(1)	(2)	(3)	(4)	(5)	(6)	(7)	(8)	(9)	(10)	(11)	(12)	(13)	(14)	(15)	(16)
WORLD																
1925	1280893	-9248	41622	1230023	227996	-5091	26168	196740	47921	47921	9835	9849	1566644	-14325	67790	1484533
1929	1437567	-10196	41023	1386348	318668	-7832	32869	277970	77020	77020	14655	14644	1847910	-18039	73892	1755981
1933	1079703	-6758	27756	1045189	303161	-10793	28641	263730	67448	67448	15886	15871	1466198	-17566	56397	1392238
1937	1417385	-7990	30729	1378666	430808	-16691	35406	378716	103848	103848	22238	22204	1974278	-24715	66135	1883433
1938	1323774	-3994	27965	1291815	421326	-13404	32112	375812	99666	99666	22797	22764	1867563	-17431	60077	1790056
1950	1608578	-3242	12158	1593178	813176	-18162	72812	722202	251986	252097	43397	43422	2717137	-21268	84970	2610900
1953	1693229	704	8020	1685913	1027640	-23829	89917	913893	341785	341749	51815	51692	3114468	-23290	97937	2993246
1955	1826035	-2167	7233	1816635	1205841	-12539	100557	1092746	389606	389570	59375	59238	3480857	-14879	107790	3358188
1957	1967713	-9065	4461	1954187	1378284	-13056	116775	1248453	463858	463687	69248	68992	3879104	-22549	121236	3735319
1960	2001531	-838	2194	1998499	1641182	-20373	121761	1499048	612619	612564	85989	85984	4341320	-21271	123955	4196095
1961	2029118	-2812	1501	2024805	1748115	-13571	131095	1603449	661576	661527	90344	90166	4529153	-16610	132596	4379947
1962	2076922	-2780	1219	2072923	1893108	-28179	135462	1729467	723610	723568	94932	95052	4788572	-30882	136681	4621009
1963	2167639	-3203	1124	2163312	2031678	-28464	139199	1864016	782822	782794	99494	99597	5081633	-31592	140323	4909718
1964	2246086	425	1154	2245357	2186870	-34074	152346	2000450	855044	854954	103093	102978	5391092	-33854	153500	5203738
1965	2292730	-784	1195	2290751	2342790	-27351	156348	2159091	912239	912096	112595	112638	5660354	-28235	157543	5474576
NORTH AMERICA																
1925	567809	-3655	6257	557897	161747	-1041	19188	141518	45010	45007	4435	4435	779000	-4699	25445	748857
1929	597194	-2122	5628	589444	216744	545	23369	193920	72225	72220	6909	6909	893071	-1583	28997	862492
1933	376336	1520	2410	375446	190149	-4115	15770	170265	59483	59405	6781	6778	632749	-2676	18180	611894

Table XIV. SUMMARY OF ENERGY PRODUCTION, TRADE, AND CONSUMPTION, BY FUEL, SELECTED YEARS, 1925–1965

(Thousand metric tons coal equivalent)

Region, country, year	Solid fuels: Production	Solid fuels: Net imports	Solid fuels: Bunkers	Solid fuels: Consumption	Liquid fuels: Production	Liquid fuels: Net imports	Liquid fuels: Bunkers	Liquid fuels: Consumption	Natural gas: Production	Natural gas: Consumption	Hydroelectric power: Production	Hydroelectric power: Consumption	Total energy: Production	Total energy: Net imports	Total energy: Bunkers	Total energy: Consumption
	(1)	(2)	(3)	(4)	(5)	(6)	(7)	(8)	(9)	(10)	(11)	(12)	(13)	(14)	(15)	(16)
NORTH AMERICA (CONTINUED)																
1937	489371	58	3445	485984	269334	-12981	18972	237381	91972	91791	9179	9177	859857	-13107	22417	824333
1938	389577	786	2477	387886	257543	-18455	16610	222479	87478	87413	9125	9122	743722	-17736	19087	706900
1950	552559	-2156	2205	548198	434675	69654	25472	478857	231031	230156	19150	19130	1237415	66603	27677	1276341
1953	481002	-12079	2058	466865	531191	80841	31326	580706	309410	308620	22108	22081	1343711	67945	33384	1378272
1955	482582	-31780	1792	449010	572919	100260	31518	641661	347328	346560	24092	24067	1426922	67686	33310	1461298
1957	507356	-55760	1661	449935	612183	105137	34761	682559	397394	397605	27126	27070	1544060	49531	36422	1557168
1960	425330	-22760	1137	401433	611825	154802	28016	738611	486029	487572	31925	31854	1555109	133513	29153	1659469
1961	411426	-22820	940	387666	631350	158859	25863	764346	508739	510454	32444	32377	1583958	137688	26803	1694843
1962	429230	-25900	863	402467	648995	167528	25647	790875	542710	544251	34517	34446	1655452	143097	26510	1772039
1963	466178	-34360	862	430956	672794	171828	23711	820911	573082	574577	34103	34029	1746156	138889	24573	1860472
1964	492636	-32390	885	459361	687444	182670	25688	844427	609174	610722	36706	36687	1825960	151809	26573	1951196
1965	514645	-32423	869	481353	707015	202367	23418	885963	632019	633635	39214	39207	1892893	171552	24287	2040158
CANADA																
1925	11112	14847	450	25509	80	4035	210	3905	638	641	1244	1085	13074	18726	660	31139
1929	14982	16816	420	31378	210	8060	206	8064	1071	1075	2212	2034	18474	24702	626	42551
1933	9994	10447	318	20123	246	6726	171	6801	872	872	2126	2002	13239	17050	489	29799
1937	13480	13337	318	26499	657	9165	155	9668	1221	1213	3398	3167	18756	22263	473	40547
1938	12131	11780	365	23546	1391	8469	198	9662	1261	1252	3211	2983	17995	20011	563	37443
1950	15970	24260	353	39877	5886	22428	1950	26364	2559	2757	6522	6293	30937	46658	2303	75292
1953	13282	21161	390	34053	16506	23633	2180	37959	3810	3740	8384	8092	41982	44433	2570	83845
1955	12218	17690	432	29476	26393	22538	2235	46695	5686	5680	9525	8991	53822	39687	2667	90842
1957	10857	17820	424	28253	37169	18474	2805	52838	8298	8653	10422	9889	66746	36116	3229	99633
1960	8978	11680	280	20378	39362	24156	3045	60473	19726	15832	13235	12594	81301	31301	3325	109277
1961	8448	10420	241	18627	46317	19727	3240	62804	24734	18601	12990	12642	92488	23666	3481	112673
1962	8301	10730	240	18791	51351	14598	3435	62514	35708	22700	13006	12845	108367	12158	3675	116850
1963	8655	11350	254	19751	55668	18110	3420	70358	42147	28959	12979	12886	119449	16178	3674	131953
1964	9197	12620	240	21577	60099	16637	3750	72986	53074	38637	14168	14013	136537	14665	3990	147212
1965	9324	14360	275	23409	64376	18858	3693	79541	55448	40810	14589	14591	143737	18581	3968	158350
UNITED STATES																
1925	556695	-18508	5804	532383	161667	-5078	18975	137615	44372	44366	3191	3350	765925	-23432	24779	717714
1929	582208	-18944	5205	558059	216534	-7518	23160	185856	71154	71145	4697	4875	874593	-26293	28365	819935
1933	366337	-8939	2085	355313	189903	-10842	15597	163464	58611	58532	4655	4776	619506	-19739	17682	582085
1937	475885	-13303	3114	459468	268677	-22149	18816	227712	90750	90577	5782	6010	841094	-35397	21930	783767
1938	377439	-11020	2096	364323	256152	-26925	16410	212817	86216	86160	5913	6139	725720	-37775	18506	669439
1950	536582	-26428	1852	508302	428789	47226	23522	452493	228473	227399	12628	12837	1206471	19933	25374	1201030
1953	467713	-33250	1668	432795	514685	57204	29147	542742	305601	304880	13724	13989	1301723	23498	30815	1294406
1955	470348	-49500	1360	419488	546527	77655	29283	594899	341642	340880	14567	15076	1373083	27902	30643	1370342
1957	496482	-73600	1237	421645	575015	86607	31956	629666	389096	388952	16705	17181	1477297	13339	33193	1457444
1960	416324	-34460	857	381007	572463	130577	24956	678084	466304	471740	18689	19259	1473780	102122	25813	1550090
1961	403016	-33250	699	369067	585033	139014	22593	701454	484005	491853	19454	19736	1491507	113894	23292	1582109
1962	420903	-36650	623	383630	597644	152831	22197	728277	507002	521551	21511	21601	1547060	130820	22820	1655060
1963	457483	-45740	608	411135	617126	153608	20276	750458	530935	545618	21124	21143	1626667	122569	20884	1728353
1964	483415	-45030	645	437740	627345	165890	21917	771318	556101	572085	22538	22675	1689399	136980	22562	1803817
1965	505301	-46800	594	457907	642639	183350	19709	806280	576571	592825	24625	24616	1749136	152795	20303	1881628
WESTERN EUROPE																
1925	527978	-8116	23368	496494	546	18233	2124	16655	9	9	3854	3860	532387	10122	25492	517017
1929	602496	-7203	23011	572282	545	28233	2754	26022	12	12	5336	5316	608389	21010	25765	603632
1933	469464	-4715	17593	447156	714	36101	3535	33281	20	20	5858	5841	476055	31369	21128	486297
1937	586881	-5906	17167	563808	1065	48033	5356	43743	51	51	8058	8022	596055	42091	22523	615624
1938	583423	-4335	15813	563275	1256	51611	5215	47652	25	25	8231	8198	592935	47242	21028	619150
1950	488196	7533	6527	489202	6033	85772	12828	78978	1745	1813	13858	13915	509832	93429	19355	583907
1953	521347	15817	4475	532689	10778	122829	20457	113151	4507	4514	17369	17247	554002	138530	24932	667601
1955	532461	36927	3736	565652	14288	167657	26669	155276	7345	7309	20106	19954	574199	204395	30405	748189
1957	542842	51131	2440	591533	18260	200841	28611	190490	9730	9528	21911	21748	592743	251607	31051	813299
1960	499539	31163	904	529798	23190	286799	35343	274646	16285	16212	28806	28868	567820	317951	36247	849524
1961	493580	29384	412	522552	25065	321233	39336	306962	18788	18745	29904	29735	567337	350405	39748	877994
1962	498500	35425	257	533668	26513	369809	41312	355010	20818	20775	30396	30461	576227	405256	41569	939914
1963	496448	44620	184	540884	28049	422828	43062	407816	22010	21975	33020	33063	579526	467456	43246	1003737
1964	501150	46104	145	547109	30864	485991	47934	468923	24352	24410	32576	32474	588942	532052	48079	1072916
1965	482864	43172	100	525936	31508	546728	51670	526566	26865	27968	36694	36743	577931	591052	51770	1117213
EUROPEAN ECONOMIC COMMUNITY (EEC)																
1925	267760	21404	5707	283457	236	7145	237	7143	9	9	1761	1851	269765	28639	5944	292460
1929	325079	24785	5398	344466	282	12200	828	11654	9	9	2526	2647	327896	37106	6226	358776
1933	245829	12006	3495	254340	524	16577	1329	15771	19	19	2860	3002	249231	28725	4824	273132
1937	332554	4947	4745	332756	816	24071	2721	22166	48	48	4121	4320	337538	29217	7466	359290

Table XIV. SUMMARY OF ENERGY PRODUCTION, TRADE, AND CONSUMPTION, BY FUEL, SELECTED YEARS, 1925-1965

(Thousand metric tons coal equivalent)

Region, country, year	Solid fuels				Liquid fuels				Natural gas		Hydroelectric power		Total energy			
	Production	Net imports	Bunkers	Consumption	Production	Net imports	Bunkers	Consumption	Production	Consumption	Production	Consumption	Production	Net imports	Bunkers	Consumption
	(1)	(2)	(3)	(4)	(5)	(6)	(7)	(8)	(9)	(10)	(11)	(12)	(13)	(14)	(15)	(16)
EUROPEAN ECONOMIC COMMUNITY (EEC) (CONTINUED)																
1938	338879	4094	4736	338237	969	26057	2745	24281	23	23	4066	4270	343937	30355	7481	366811
1950	243462	-5072	1803	236587	2997	36360	4007	35351	1099	1167	5967	6183	253525	31572	5810	279287
1953	266938	4917	1378	270477	5318	56849	8615	53552	3724	3731	7547	7693	283528	61917	9993	335452
1955	278091	10850	1288	287653	7994	81039	12195	76838	6287	6251	8826	8978	301197	92006	13483	379720
1957	281920	31170	992	312098	12398	99738	12360	99776	8625	8422	8904	9002	311846	130803	13352	429297
1960	267405	13330	446	280289	17622	145641	17640	145623	14153	14074	12768	13277	311948	159401	18086	453263
1961	264259	13140	256	277143	19028	169931	21150	167808	16514	16472	12005	12548	311805	183571	21406	473970
1962	262451	17100	158	279393	20184	202625	23130	199679	18355	18312	11313	11712	312302	220081	23288	509096
1963	260136	28900	118	288918	21287	238971	24263	235995	19281	19246	13171	13718	313874	268383	24381	557877
1964	266246	27905	98	294053	23741	282179	28919	277001	21400	21339	11250	11823	322636	310596	29017	604215
1965	253027	24529	67	277489	23798	323792	31892	315698	23877	24123	13549	14336	314251	349353	31959	631646
BELGIUM-LUXEMBOURG																
1925	23097	7630	270	30457	-	495	2	494	-	-	3	3	23100	8125	272	30953
1929	26940	10287	431	36796	-	638	-	638	-	-	3	3	26943	10925	431	37436
1933	25300	2666	337	27629	-	611	2	609	-	-	3	-	25303	3274	339	28238
1937	29859	3488	214	33133	-	1257	92	1166	-	-	7	8	29866	4746	306	34307
1938	29585	408	308	29685	-	1242	84	1158	-	-	6	6	29591	1651	392	30849
1950	27321	358	69	27610	-	3434	360	3074	19	7	8	16	27348	3787	429	30706
1953	30060	233	66	30227	-	5115	710	4406	73	60	12	4	30145	5327	776	34697
1955	29978	-930	91	28957	-	7875	885	6990	107	76	17	28	30101	6926	976	36051
1957	29001	3870	62	32809	-	9662	840	8822	141	99	22	5	29164	13471	902	41734
1960	22469	5020	36	27453	-	11298	945	10353	93	57	24	27	22586	16285	981	37890
1961	21536	4790	26	26300	-	13664	1215	12449	93	57	31	-4	21660	18382	1241	38802
1962	21226	5410	28	26608	-	16086	1635	14451	93	63	26	-19	21346	21420	1663	41102
1963	21418	8410	16	29812	-	19314	2010	17304	92	56	79	79	21589	27688	2026	47251
1964	21305	8350	12	29643	-	22262	2732	19530	88	57	115	163	21508	30628	2744	49393
1965	19786	8460	5	28241	-	24990	3084	21906	105	75	148	239	20040	33510	3089	50460
FRANCE																
1925	47693	27254	2791	72156	105	2850	165	2790	-	-	539	573	48337	30137	2956	75518
1929	54498	31672	1596	84574	119	4613	657	4074	-	-	825	886	55442	36345	2253	89534
1933	47543	23553	1274	69822	128	8321	1080	7368	-	-	925	989	48596	31937	2354	78179
1937	44928	28746	980	72694	119	10866	2001	8984	-	-	1373	1444	46419	39683	2981	83121
1938	47139	20881	1014	67006	122	11582	1937	9767	-	-	1300	1371	48560	32534	2951	78144
1950	51847	11300	328	62819	246	17138	1367	16017	306	318	2029	2059	54428	28479	1695	81213
1953	53765	12100	157	65708	600	23673	2955	21318	310	360	2656	2655	57332	35821	3112	90040
1955	56568	9800	70	66298	1346	30351	3495	28202	341	420	3224	3216	61479	40221	3565	98134
1957	58175	22050	52	80173	2148	34269	3420	32997	585	759	3135	3169	64042	56527	3472	117098
1960	57333	13750	20	71063	3318	40734	2865	41187	3791	3911	5093	5081	69535	54591	2885	121241
1961	54102	13630	20	67712	3566	44862	3285	45143	5424	5544	4825	4836	67916	58624	3305	123234
1962	54099	13870	10	67959	3951	49149	3570	49530	6314	6440	4517	4423	68881	63051	3580	128352
1963	49248	20990	10	70228	4113	59162	3435	59840	6475	6613	5478	5549	65313	80361	3445	142230
1964	54375	18770	10	73135	4713	68420	3615	69518	6780	6876	4383	4661	70250	87564	3625	154189
1965	52961	15838	-	68799	4965	78558	3491	80033	6724	7126	5862	5983	70512	94920	3491	161941
GERMANY																
1925	189302	-29639	123	159540	119	1646	-	1764	-	-	357	385	189777	-27965	123	161689
1929	231595	-36434	299	194862	155	3618	-	3773	-	-	446	473	232195	-32789	299	199107
1933	159998	-25678	131	134189	357	3521	48	3830	-	-	511	568	160866	-22101	179	138586
1937	242310	-42404	389	199517	677	5576	26	6227	28	28	863	963	243877	-36729	415	206734
1938	247165	-31729	344	215092	828	6455	20	7263	NA	NA	912	1012	248906	-25175	364	223368
GERMANY, FEDERAL REPUBLIC																
1950	150924	-28685	909	121330	1679	4133	131	5681	84	19	1082	1241	153769	-24459	1040	128270
1953	169601	-21093	894	147614	3284	7751	1317	9717	273	232	1170	1331	174328	-13222	2211	158894
1955	178532	-14320	835	163377	4721	13709	2490	15939	822	719	1503	1648	185577	-569	3325	181683
1957	182335	-13010	680	168645	5973	20156	2730	23399	1051	698	1540	1574	190899	6826	3410	194315
1960	174277	-18710	340	155227	8342	41360	3750	45951	1224	1056	1624	2144	185466	23002	4090	204378
1961	174949	-18090	180	156679	9350	47741	4095	52995	1235	1096	1615	2155	187148	30052	4275	212926
1962	174466	-17680	100	156686	10185	62993	4575	68603	1724	1573	1568	1951	187943	45545	4675	228813
1963	177083	-17550	85	159448	11093	73965	4470	80588	2238	2082	1547	1855	191961	56567	4555	243973
1964	178349	-14565	75	163709	11525	89846	5361	96009	3146	3014	1520	1640	194540	75269	5436	264372
1965	168217	-12729	57	155431	11838	105063	5861	111041	4288	4161	1921	2451	186264	92738	5918	273084
ITALY																
1925	483	10381	10	10854	12	1178	-	1190	9	9	863	891	1367	11587	10	12944

Table XIV. SUMMARY OF ENERGY PRODUCTION, TRADE, AND CONSUMPTION, BY FUEL, SELECTED YEARS, 1925-1965

(Thousand metric tons coal equivalent)

Region, country, year	Solid fuels				Liquid fuels				Natural gas		Hydroelectric power		Total energy			
	Production	Net imports	Bunkers	Consumption	Production	Net imports	Bunkers	Consumption	Production	Consumption	Production	Consumption	Production	Net imports	Bunkers	Consumption
	(1)	(2)	(3)	(4)	(5)	(6)	(7)	(8)	(9)	(10)	(11)	(12)	(13)	(14)	(15)	(16)
ITALY (CONTINUED)																
1929	413	14505	7	14911	9	1905	6	1908	9	9	1253	1283	1684	16441	13	181[illegible]
1933	382	9477	21	9838	39	2552	-	2591	19	19	1421	1443	1861	12051	21	13890
1937	1089	12851	4	13936	21	3669	-	3690	20	20	1878	1902	3008	16544	4	19548
1938	1446	12081	7	13520	20	3737	3	3753	23	23	1848	1878	3336	15848	10	19174
1950	1059	8215	104	9170	15	6812	900	5927	679	679	2848	2873	4601	15052	1004	18649
1953	1132	9172	63	10241	204	13577	1640	12141	3037	3037	3710	3704	8083	22743	1703	29123
1955	1034	10330	50	11314	392	18780	2010	17162	4831	4831	4082	4085	10339	29113	2060	37391
1957	937	11610	35	12512	1992	23667	1875	23784	6643	6643	4208	4265	13780	35335	1910	47204
1960	828	10210	20	11018	3086	35082	5610	32558	8587	8587	6026	6010	18527	45276	5630	58173
1961	1051	10150	10	11191	3044	41657	6435	38265	9142	9142	5534	5555	18770	51828	6445	64153
1962	1086	10860	10	11936	2813	51821	6945	47688	9524	9524	5201	5360	18624	62839	6955	74508
1963	878	11470	2	12346	2759	60372	7868	55263	9680	9680	6067	6229	19383	72004	7870	83518
1964	737	10675	1	11411	4098	70452	9564	64986	10235	10235	5232	5357	20302	81252	9565	91989
1965	617	10590	-	11207	3402	79958	10536	72824	10390	10390	5618	5659	20026	90589	10536	100079
NETHERLANDS																
1925	7186	5778	2513	10451	-	977	71	906	-	-	-	-	7186	6755	2584	11357
1929	11633	4755	3065	13323	-	1427	165	1262	-	-	-	3	11633	6184	3230	14587
1933	12606	1988	1732	12862	-	1574	200	1374	-	-	-	3	12606	3564	1932	14239
1937	14368	2266	3158	13476	-	2703	603	2100	-	-	-	3	14368	4972	3761	15579
1938	13544	2453	3063	12934	-	3042	702	2340	-	-	-	2	13544	5497	3765	15277
1950	12311	3740	393	15658	1058	4845	1250	4653	11	144	-	-5	13379	8713	1643	20450
1953	12380	4505	198	16687	1230	6734	1994	5970	31	43	-	-2	13641	11249	2192	22698
1955	11979	5970	242	17707	1536	10325	3315	8546	186	205	-	3	13702	16316	3557	26460
1957	11471	6650	163	17958	2285	11985	3495	10775	205	224	-	-10	13961	18644	3658	28946
1960	12499	3060	30	15529	2877	17168	4470	15575	457	462	-	15	15833	20248	4500	31581
1961	12621	2660	20	15261	3069	22008	6120	18957	621	633	-	5	16311	24685	6140	34856
1962	11573	4640	10	16203	3236	22577	6405	19407	701	713	-	-3	15509	27226	6415	36320
1963	11509	5580	5	17084	3323	26159	6480	23001	797	815	-	6	15628	31763	6485	40906
1964	11480	4675	-	16155	3405	31200	7647	26958	1151	1156	-	2	16036	35883	7647	44271
1965	11446	2370	5	13811	3593	35223	8921	29895	2371	2371	-	4	17409	37597	8926	46081
EUROPEAN FREE TRADE ASSOCIATION (EFTA)																
1925	249796	-35922	17005	196869	302	9821	1602	8520	-	-	1834	1749	251931	-26186	18607	207138
1929	265072	-39933	16897	208242	254	13967	1554	12665	-	-	2424	2283	267750	-26108	18451	223190
1933	213277	-22194	13836	177247	182	16689	1526	15345	-	-	2445	2285	215903	-5664	15362	194877
1937	247396	-17758	12092	217546	239	20871	2129	18981	-	-	3300	3064	250935	2877	14221	239592
1938	233832	-14746	10775	208311	276	22323	1949	20651	-	-	3478	3240	237587	7339	12724	232202
1950	224052	6776	4301	226527	2867	38756	5380	36243	627	627	6573	6413	234119	45372	9681	269810
1953	232616	5100	2987	234729	5174	52085	7615	49644	751	751	7979	7716	246519	56921	10602	292840
1955	230399	19480	2232	247647	5852	70002	8730	67124	1012	1012	8905	8599	246168	89176	10962	324382
1957	233301	13150	1256	245195	5154	78654	7920	75388	1050	1050	10344	10107	249849	91567	9176	332239
1960	201880	10920	343	212457	4047	116678	11193	109532	2062	2067	12435	11965	220424	127133	11536	336021
1961	198502	9280	142	207640	3921	125102	11076	117947	2182	2182	13955	13263	218560	133689	11218	341031
1962	205525	10380	87	215818	3936	136860	10892	129905	2336	2336	14759	14466	226557	146946	10979	362525
1963	203946	8100	54	211992	4239	150239	11023	143456	2475	2475	14891	14485	225550	157933	11077	372407
1964	201551	9470	39	210982	4313	166188	11407	159095	2587	2707	16458	15850	224909	175169	11446	388633
1965	195041	9847	29	204859	4496	180714	11876	173334	2548	3406	18096	17313	220180	190636	11905	398912
AUSTRIA																
1925	1662	5060	-	6722	-	185	-	185	-	-	166	163	1828	5241	-	7069
1929	1971	6417	-	8388	-	344	-	344	-	-	219	204	2189	6746	-	8935
1933	1751	3046	-	4797	2	470	-	471	-	-	244	206	1996	3478	-	5474
1937	1876	3319	-	5195	50	482	-	531	-	-	299	256	2225	3758	-	5982
1938	1922	3773	-	5695	86	494	-	579	-	-	300	254	2308	4221	-	6528
1950	2362	5243	-	7605	2549	-1582	-	966	626	626	624	537	6160	3574	-	9734
1953	2974	4223	-	7197	4832	-3246	2	1584	739	739	804	668	9349	841	2	10188
1955	3501	4950	-	8451	5499	-1916	15	3569	996	996	988	853	10984	2900	15	13868
1957	3609	5610	-	9219	4779	-1545	15	3219	1011	1011	1165	1010	10563	3910	15	14458
1960	3137	4950	-	8087	3672	752	15	4409	1957	1957	1485	1248	10250	5464	15	15699
1961	2939	4520	-	7459	3534	1490	15	5009	2073	2073	1458	1214	10004	5766	15	15754
1962	2958	4790	-	7748	3591	2204	20	5775	2178	2178	1516	1254	10242	6731	20	16954
1963	3133	5340	-	8473	3933	2603	20	6516	2263	2263	1494	1283	10823	7731	20	18535
1964	2986	5120	-	8106	3998	3659	17	7640	2350	2350	1647	1309	10981	8440	17	19404
1965	2787	4545	-	7332	4286	3323	17	7592	2296	2296	2010	1527	11379	7384	17	18746
DENMARK																
1925	153	4022	NA	4175	-	447	NA	447	-	-	-	3	153	4472	NA	4624
1929	121	5500	NA	5621	-	642	NA	641	-	-	-	4	121	6146	NA	6266

Table XIV. SUMMARY OF ENERGY PRODUCTION, TRADE, AND CONSUMPTION, BY FUEL, SELECTED YEARS, 1925-1965

(Thousand metric tons coal equivalent)

Region, country, year	Solid fuels				Liquid fuels				Natural gas		Hydroelectric power		Total energy			
	Production	Net imports	Bunkers	Consumption	Production	Net imports	Bunkers	Consumption	Production	Consumption	Production	Consumption	Production	Net imports	Bunkers	Consumption
	(1)	(2)	(3)	(4)	(5)	(6)	(7)	(8)	(9)	(10)	(11)	(12)	(13)	(14)	(15)	(16)
DENMARK (CONTINUED)																
1933	125	4902	NA	5027	-	857	NA	857	-	-	-	2	125	5760	NA	5886
1937	183	6024	NA	6207	-	1059	NA	1059	-	-	-	2	183	7085	NA	7268
1938	166	5396	NA	5562	-	1290	NA	1290	-	-	-	3	166	6689	NA	6855
1950	548	5731	-	6279	-	2706	183	2523	-	-	3	26	551	8460	183	8828
1953	438	6059	-	6497	-	3173	329	2844	-	-	4	41	442	9269	329	9382
1955	489	7340	30	7799	-	4851	420	4431	-	-	4	-10	492	12177	450	12220
1957	1007	4410	15	5402	-	5874	420	5454	-	-	4	51	1010	10332	435	10907
1960	731	5260	23	5968	-	7764	420	7344	-	-	3	15	733	13037	443	13327
1961	764	4930	32	5662	-	8697	375	8322	-	-	3	113	767	13737	407	14097
1962	763	5260	37	5986	-	10238	495	9743	-	-	3	115	766	15609	532	15844
1963	746	5300	24	6022	-	11909	555	11354	-	-	3	57	750	17263	579	17433
1964	650	4760	18	5392	-	13841	609	13232	-	-	3	106	653	18703	627	18729
1965	624	4190	15	4799	-	15366	645	14721	-	-	3	220	627	19773	660	19740
NORWAY																
1925	565	1988	NA	2553	-	291	NA	291	-	-	773	773	1338	2279	NA	3617
1929	426	2677	NA	3103	-	416	NA	416	-	-	940	940	1366	3093	NA	4458
1933	470	2313	NA	2783	-	663	NA	663	-	-	915	915	1385	2976	NA	4361
1937	472	3176	NA	3648	-	825	NA	825	-	-	1157	1157	1629	4001	NA	5630
1938	474	2647	NA	3121	-	884	NA	884	-	-	1240	1240	1714	3531	NA	5244
1950	545	1696	-	2241	-	2142	248	1895	-	-	2235	2235	2780	3838	248	6370
1953	554	1384	-	1938	-	3276	335	2942	-	-	2455	2455	3009	4660	335	7334
1955	442	1130	-	1572	-	4259	510	3749	-	-	2835	2835	3277	5389	510	8155
1957	509	830	-	1339	-	4458	525	3933	-	-	3228	3228	3736	5288	525	8499
1960	494	820	-	1314	-	5480	510	4970	-	-	3903	3919	4397	6316	510	10203
1961	451	760	-	1211	-	5708	570	5138	-	-	4215	4216	4666	6469	570	10564
1962	517	680	-	1197	-	5927	600	5327	-	-	4750	4714	5267	6571	600	11238
1963	445	800	-	1245	-	6542	645	5897	-	-	4957	4839	5402	7223	645	11980
1964	494	880	-	1374	-	7182	701	6482	-	-	5527	5353	6021	7888	701	13209
1965	488	750	-	1238	-	6977	630	6347	-	-	6168	5898	6656	7456	630	13482
PORTUGAL																
1925	132	995	305	822	-	90	-	90	-	-	6	6	137	1085	305	917
1929	212	1146	242	1116	-	167	-	167	-	-	9	9	221	1313	242	1291
1933	234	1109	161	1182	-	212	?	210	-	-	12	12	246	1321	163	1404
1937	271	1357	201	1427	-	290	-	290	-	-	17	17	288	1647	201	1733
1938	317	1152	118	1351	-	293	-	293	-	-	16	16	333	1445	118	1659
1950	466	817	104	1179	-	1172	374	798	-	-	55	55	521	1989	478	2032
1953	514	578	106	986	-	1689	410	1280	-	-	125	125	638	2267	516	2390
1955	448	500	40	908	-	2141	525	1616	-	-	216	216	664	2641	565	2739
1957	591	560	20	1131	-	2477	510	1967	-	-	230	230	821	3037	530	3328
1960	512	390	-	902	-	2763	675	2088	-	-	388	388	900	3153	675	3378
1961	549	550	-	1099	-	2951	705	2246	-	-	428	428	977	3501	705	3772
1962	482	530	-	1012	-	3183	720	2463	-	-	439	439	920	3713	720	3914
1963	487	620	-	1107	-	3384	710	2675	-	-	500	493	987	3997	710	4275
1964	495	630	-	1125	-	3668	860	2808	-	-	528	526	1022	4296	860	4459
1965	473	620	-	1093	-	4128	860	3269	-	-	498	552	971	4802	860	4913
SWEDEN																
1925	200	4256	NA	4456	-	444	NA	444	-	-	423	420	622	4698	NA	5320
1929	292	6275	NA	6567	-	714	NA	714	-	-	572	568	864	6985	NA	7848
1933	259	6060	NA	6319	-	1130	NA	1130	-	-	612	610	871	7188	NA	8059
1937	339	8962	NA	9301	-	1719	NA	1719	-	-	871	870	1210	10679	NA	11890
1938	315	7733	NA	8048	-	1941	NA	1941	-	-	913	910	1228	9671	NA	10899
1950	305	6603	-	6908	80	5459	147	5391	-	-	2167	2145	2552	12039	147	14444
1953	320	5543	-	5863	99	8310	257	8153	-	-	2660	2623	3079	13816	257	16638
1955	327	5530	-	5857	125	12102	330	11897	-	-	2706	2721	3158	17647	330	20475
1957	355	4910	-	5265	143	14048	435	13755	-	-	3389	3340	3887	18909	435	22361
1960	281	3570	-	3851	153	19647	795	19005	-	-	3886	3790	4320	23121	795	26646
1961	255	3260	-	3515	161	19878	885	19154	-	-	4567	4443	4982	23013	885	27111
1962	180	3240	-	3420	152	22031	1080	21102	-	-	4887	4788	5219	25171	1080	29310
1963	175	3210	-	3385	119	23870	1185	22803	-	-	4739	4745	5032	27086	1185	30933
1964	183	3460	-	3643	122	26517	1256	25383	-	-	5387	5361	5691	29951	1256	34387
1965	151	2960	-	3111	84	28026	1313	26798	-	-	5803	5702	6038	30885	1313	35611
SWITZERLAND																
1925	7	2701	-	2708	-	222	-	222	-	-	463	382	470	2842	-	3312
1929	7	3463	-	3470	-	392	-	392	-	-	664	538	671	3728	-	4399
1933	2	3165	-	3167	-	590	-	590	-	-	620	499	622	3633	-	4255

Table XIV. SUMMARY OF ENERGY PRODUCTION, TRADE, AND CONSUMPTION, BY FUEL, SELECTED YEARS, 1925-1965

(Thousand metric tons coal equivalent)

Region, country, year	Solid fuels: Production	Solid fuels: Net imports	Solid fuels: Bunkers	Solid fuels: Consumption	Liquid fuels: Production	Liquid fuels: Net imports	Liquid fuels: Bunkers	Liquid fuels: Consumption	Natural gas: Production	Natural gas: Consumption	Hydroelectric power: Production	Hydroelectric power: Consumption	Total energy: Production	Total energy: Net imports	Total energy: Bunkers	Total energy: Consumption
	(1)	(2)	(3)	(4)	(5)	(6)	(7)	(8)	(9)	(10)	(11)	(12)	(13)	(14)	(15)	(16)
SWITZERLAND (CONTINUED)																
1937	4	3486	-	3490	-	596	-	596	-	-	861	668	865	3889	-	4753
1938	3	3337	-	3340	-	614	-	614	-	-	886	694	889	3758	-	4647
1950	30	2549	-	2579	-	1500	39	1461	-	-	1304	1230	1334	3975	39	5270
1953	10	2204	-	2214	-	1853	39	1814	-	-	1694	1568	1704	3930	39	5595
1955	10	2610	-	2620	-	2891	90	2801	-	-	1944	1771	1954	5328	90	7192
1957	10	3320	-	3330	-	3893	45	3848	-	-	1985	1903	1995	7131	45	9081
1960	10	2600	-	2610	-	5763	75	5688	-	-	2379	2214	2389	8198	75	10512
1961	10	2260	-	2270	-	6251	75	6176	-	-	2803	2368	2813	8076	75	10813
1962	10	2330	-	2340	-	7239	30	7209	-	-	2673	2655	2683	9550	30	12204
1963	10	2820	-	2830	-	9762	30	9732	-	-	2740	2612	2750	12454	30	15174
1964	10	1980	-	1990	-	10029	29	10001	-	-	2864	2719	2874	11864	29	14709
1965	10	1572	-	1582	-	11711	29	11682	-	-	3035	2829	3045	13076	29	16093
UNITED KINGDOM																
1925	247079	-54944	16700	175435	302	8142	1602	6842	-	-	3	3	247383	-46802	18302	182279
1929	262045	-65411	16655	179979	254	11294	1554	9993	-	-	21	21	262319	-54118	18209	189993
1933	210436	-42789	13675	153972	180	12770	1524	11426	-	-	41	41	210657	-30020	15199	165439
1937	244252	-44082	11891	188279	189	15902	2129	13962	-	-	94	94	244535	-28181	14020	202335
1938	230636	-38784	10657	181195	191	16809	1949	15051	-	-	124	124	230950	-21975	12606	196370
1950	219797	-15863	4197	199737	239	27360	4389	23210	1	1	185	185	220222	11497	8586	223133
1953	227807	-14891	2881	210035	243	37031	6245	31029	12	12	237	237	228299	22140	9126	241313
1955	225183	-2580	2162	220441	228	45675	6840	39063	16	16	213	213	225640	43095	9002	259733
1957	227221	-6490	1221	219510	233	49451	5970	43713	39	39	344	344	227836	42961	7191	263606
1960	196716	-6670	320	189726	222	74510	8703	66029	105	111	392	392	197435	67845	9023	256257
1961	193535	-7000	110	186425	227	80129	8451	71904	109	109	482	481	194352	73128	8561	258919
1962	200616	-6450	50	194116	194	86040	7947	78287	159	159	491	502	201459	79601	7997	273063
1963	198949	-9990	30	188929	188	92171	7878	84480	212	212	458	457	199806	82179	7908	274077
1964	196734	-7360	21	189353	194	101294	7937	93551	237	357	503	477	197667	94027	7958	283737
1965	190508	-4790	14	185704	126	111185	8384	102927	252	1110	578	585	191464	107260	8398	290326
WESTERN EUROPE - OTHER																
1925	10422	6402	NA	16168	9	1268	NA	992	-	-	260	260	10690	7670	NA	17419
1929	12345	7945	NA	19574	9	2067	NA	1704	3	3	387	387	12743	10012	NA	21667
1933	10358	5473	NA	15569	9	2835	NA	2165	1	1	553	553	10921	8308	NA	18288
1937	6931	6905	NA	13506	11	3092	NA	2597	3	3	638	638	7582	9997	NA	16743
1938	10711	6317	NA	16726	11	3231	NA	2721	3	3	687	687	11411	9548	NA	20137
1950	20682	5829	423	26088	170	10656	3441	7385	19	19	1319	1319	22189	16485	3864	34810
1953	21794	5800	110	27484	287	13896	4227	9956	32	32	1843	1839	23955	19692	4337	39310
1955	23971	6597	216	30352	443	16616	5744	11315	45	45	2375	2376	26834	23214	5960	44088
1957	27622	6811	192	34241	708	22449	8331	14826	56	56	2663	2640	31048	29238	8523	51763
1960	30254	6913	115	37052	1521	24480	6510	19491	71	71	3603	3627	35448	31417	6625	60240
1961	30820	6964	14	37770	2117	26201	7110	21207	92	92	3944	3924	36972	33144	7124	62992
1962	30525	7945	12	38458	2393	30324	7290	25427	127	127	4324	4283	37368	38228	7302	68293
1963	32366	7620	12	39974	2523	33618	7776	28365	254	254	4959	4860	40101	41140	7788	73453
1964	33353	8729	8	42074	2811	37625	7608	32828	365	365	4869	4802	41397	46287	7616	80068
1965	34797	8796	4	43589	3215	42222	7902	37535	440	440	5050	5094	43500	51062	7906	86656
FINLAND																
1925	10	612	-	622	-	114	-	114	-	-	48	48	58	726	-	784
1929	10	1170	-	1180	-	194	-	194	-	-	99	99	109	1364	-	1472
1933	9	1138	-	1147	-	179	-	179	-	-	156	156	165	1317	-	1481
1937	11	2235	-	2246	-	335	-	335	-	-	258	258	269	2570	-	2839
1938	13	1784	-	1797	-	372	-	372	-	-	307	307	320	2156	-	2476
1950	99	1929	-	2028	-	734	8	726	-	-	456	456	555	2663	8	3210
1953	98	1980	-	2078	-	1080	8	1073	-	-	622	622	720	3059	8	3772
1955	80	2630	-	2710	-	1665	15	1650	-	-	774	774	854	4295	15	5134
1957	90	3040	-	3130	-	2822	15	2807	-	-	827	827	917	5862	15	6763
1960	60	3140	-	3200	-	4035	15	4020	-	-	659	711	719	7228	15	7931
1961	58	3000	-	3058	-	4457	15	4442	-	-	1003	1025	1061	7478	15	8524
1962	31	2940	-	2971	-	5247	15	5232	-	-	1221	1232	1252	8197	15	9435
1963	40	2470	-	2510	-	6404	30	6374	-	-	1047	1089	1087	8916	30	9972
1964	36	3190	-	3226	-	7358	32	7326	-	-	1063	1150	1099	10635	32	11702
1965	33	3235	-	3268	-	8543	39	8504	-	-	1186	1257	1219	11849	39	13028
GREECE																
1925	71	663	NA	734	-	96	NA	96	-	-	1	1	72	759	NA	831
1929	78	814	NA	892	-	221	NA	221	-	-	1	1	79	1035	NA	1114
1933	50	638	NA	688	-	275	NA	275	-	-	2	2	51	913	NA	964
1937	66	969	NA	1035	-	485	NA	485	-	-	2	2	67	1454	NA	1521

Table XIV. SUMMARY OF ENERGY PRODUCTION, TRADE, AND CONSUMPTION, BY FUEL, SELECTED YEARS, 1925-1965

(Thousand metric tons coal equivalent)

Region, country, year	Solid fuels				Liquid fuels				Natural gas		Hydroelectric power		Total energy			
	Production	Net imports	Bunkers	Consumption	Production	Net imports	Bunkers	Consumption	Production	Consumption	Production	Consumption	Production	Net imports	Bunkers	Consumption
	(1)	(2)	(3)	(4)	(5)	(6)	(7)	(8)	(9)	(10)	(11)	(12)	(13)	(14)	(15)	(16)
GREECE (CONTINUED)																
1938	54	975	NA	1029	-	518	NA	518	-	-	2	2	56	1493	NA	1548
1950	90	302	-	392	-	1629	240	1389	-	-	1	1	91	1931	240	1782
1953	222	277	-	499	-	1881	207	1674	-	-	4	4	226	2158	207	2177
1955	391	320	-	711	-	2267	270	1997	-	-	42	42	433	2587	270	2749
1957	499	280	-	779	-	2436	315	2121	-	-	45	45	544	2716	315	2945
1960	1276	230	-	1506	-	3588	810	2778	-	-	59	60	1334	3819	810	4343
1961	1252	230	-	1482	-	3965	1020	2945	-	-	69	68	1321	4193	1020	4494
1962	1347	210	-	1557	-	4445	1395	3050	-	-	77	77	1424	4654	1395	4683
1963	1758	270	-	2028	-	5094	1590	3504	-	-	101	100	1859	5363	1590	5632
1964	1901	290	-	2191	-	4986	1326	3660	-	-	94	92	1995	5274	1326	5943
1965	2505	410	-	2915	-	6173	1455	4718	-	-	94	96	2598	6585	1455	7728
ICELAND																
1950	2	96	-	98	-	372	102	270	-	-	21	21	23	468	102	389
1953	1	49	-	50	-	572	185	387	-	-	25	25	25	621	185	461
1955	-	60	-	60	-	521	150	371	-	-	47	47	47	581	150	478
1957	-	30	-	30	-	600	165	435	-	-	52	52	52	630	165	517
1960	-	20	-	20	-	699	150	549	-	-	65	65	65	719	150	634
1961	-	20	-	20	-	641	135	506	-	-	72	72	72	661	135	598
1962	-	20	-	20	-	680	135	545	-	-	74	74	74	700	135	639
1963	-	10	-	10	-	635	36	599	-	-	79	79	79	645	36	687
1964	-	10	-	10	-	635	23	612	-	-	82	82	82	645	23	704
1965	-	10	-	10	-	702	23	680	-	-	80	80	80	712	23	770
IRELAND																
1925	1857	2284	NA	4141	-	179	NA	179	-	-	1	1	1858	2463	NA	4321
1929	1899	2497	NA	4396	-	248	NA	248	-	-	4	4	1903	2745	NA	4647
1933	1882	2298	NA	4180	-	284	NA	284	-	-	14	14	1896	2582	NA	4478
1937	1952	2620	NA	4572	-	365	NA	365	-	-	31	31	1983	2985	NA	4967
1938	1817	2539	NA	4356	-	377	NA	377	-	-	37	37	1854	2916	NA	4769
1950	1729	1994	1	3722	-	896	75	821	-	-	58	58	1787	2890	76	4601
1953	2097	1758	-	3855	-	1160	131	1029	-	-	67	67	2164	2918	131	4951
1955	1987	1940	1	3926	-	1680	200	1481	-	-	61	61	2048	3620	201	5467
1957	2226	1250	1	3475	-	1658	180	1478	-	-	88	88	2313	2908	181	5040
1960	2256	1660	-	3916	-	1980	330	1650	-	-	117	117	2372	3640	330	5682
1961	1976	1750	-	3726	-	2255	360	1895	-	-	92	92	2068	4005	360	5712
1962	2267	1480	-	3747	-	2588	315	2273	-	-	83	83	2350	4068	315	6102
1963	2010	1420	-	3430	-	2937	315	2622	-	-	82	82	2092	4357	315	6134
1964	2531	1280	-	3811	-	3263	353	2910	-	-	98	98	2629	4543	353	6819
1965	2064	1250	-	3314	-	3680	375	3305	-	-	117	117	2181	4930	375	6735
SPAIN																
1925	6319	2125	400	8044	9	701	285	425	-	-	171	171	6499	2826	685	8639
1929	7328	2700	557	9471	9	1146	372	783	-	-	248	248	7584	3846	929	10501
1933	6150	1057	201	7006	8	1838	678	1167	-	-	331	331	6488	2895	879	8503
1937	2188	566	196	2558	9	1640	495	1154	-	-	288	288	2485	2206	691	4000
1938	5732	428	187	5973	9	1635	495	1149	-	-	280	280	6021	2063	682	7402
1950	11776	965	217	12524	2	5651	2436	3216	-	-	635	635	12412	6616	2653	16375
1953	13291	1115	67	14339	26	7737	3093	4670	-	-	938	938	14254	8852	3160	19946
1955	13344	550	39	13855	53	9063	4526	4590	-	-	1124	1131	14520	9621	4565	19576
1957	15191	490	15	15666	108	13011	6777	6342	-	-	1209	1205	16507	13497	6792	23213
1960	14664	300	5	14959	96	12824	4815	8105	-	-	1953	1934	16713	13105	4820	24998
1961	14841	410	4	15247	98	14069	5205	8961	-	-	1998	1967	16936	14448	5209	26174
1962	13939	1800	2	15737	98	16491	5055	11534	-	-	2009	1978	16046	18259	5057	29248
1963	14204	1890	2	16092	98	17322	5370	12050	-	-	2642	2540	16943	19109	5372	30681
1964	13498	1890	2	15386	98	19736	5432	14402	-	-	2581	2386	16176	21431	5434	32174
1965	14610	1710	-	16320	98	21113	5583	15627	-	-	2444	2365	17151	22743	5583	34312
YUGOSLAVIA																
1925	2165	463	-	2628	-	128	-	128	-	-	38	38	2203	591	-	2793
1929	3031	583	-	3614	-	207	-	207	3	3	34	34	3068	790	-	3858
1933	2268	265	-	2533	2	182	-	183	1	1	50	50	2321	447	-	2767
1937	2715	369	-	3084	2	170	-	171	3	3	56	56	2775	539	-	3314
1938	3094	464	-	3558	2	228	-	230	3	3	59	59	3156	692	-	3848
1950	6987	298	-	7285	168	680	11	837	19	19	147	147	7320	978	11	8287
1953	6086	554	-	6640	261	723	21	963	32	32	188	184	6566	1273	21	7818
1955	8169	1030	140	9059	390	720	75	1035	45	45	326	320	8931	1744	215	10459
1957	9617	1670	140	11147	600	872	60	1412	56	56	440	422	10713	2523	200	13036
1960	11999	1550	100	13449	1425	797	60	2162	71	71	748	737	14242	2335	160	16417

Table XIV. SUMMARY OF ENERGY PRODUCTION, TRADE, AND CONSUMPTION, BY FUEL, SELECTED YEARS, 1925-1965

(Thousand metric tons coal equivalent)

Region, country, year	Solid fuels				Liquid fuels				Natural gas		Hydroelectric power		Total energy			
	Production	Net imports	Bunkers	Consumption	Production	Net imports	Bunkers	Consumption	Production	Consumption	Production	Consumption	Production	Net imports	Bunkers	Consumption
	(1)	(2)	(3)	(4)	(5)	(6)	(7)	(8)	(9)	(10)	(11)	(12)	(13)	(14)	(15)	(16)
YUGOSLAVIA (CONTINUED)																
1961	12694	1540	10	14224	2019	275	60	2234	92	92	707	698	15512	1805	70	17246
1962	12941	1490	10	14421	2295	296	60	2531	127	127	856	837	16218	1766	70	17914
1963	14354	1550	10	15894	2426	557	60	2922	254	254	1004	967	18037	2070	70	20037
1964	15387	2060	6	17441	2714	933	66	3581	365	365	947	990	19412	3036	72	22376
1965	15586	2175	4	17757	3117	1334	75	4376	440	440	1123	1173	20266	3558	79	23745
OCEANIA																
1925	15919	-218	1269	14432	-	1374	306	1068	-	-	81	81	16000	1156	1575	15581
1929	13243	530	915	12858	-	2672	323	2349	-	-	136	136	13379	3202	1238	15343
1933	11465	-82	605	10778	2	2495	350	2147	-	-	174	174	11640	2413	955	13098
1937	15081	-86	665	14330	2	3909	369	3542	-	-	245	245	15327	3823	1034	18116
1938	14710	-94	672	13944	2	4253	330	3923	-	-	258	258	14970	4159	1002	18125
1950	20679	581	157	21103	2	8913	1272	7643	-	-	555	555	21235	9494	1429	29300
1953	22551	-229	45	22277	2	9830	1475	8357	-	-	713	713	23265	9601	1520	31346
1955	23932	32	27	23937	2	14573	2015	12560	-	-	825	825	24759	14605	2042	37322
1957	24795	-560	9	24226	2	16442	2429	14015	-	-	1071	1071	25868	15882	2438	39312
1960	28808	-1438	10	27360	2	19647	2430	17219	-	-	1245	1245	30055	18209	2440	45824
1961	30511	-2727	10	27774	2	21099	2544	18557	-	-	1328	1328	31841	18372	2554	47659
1962	30812	-2875	-	27937	2	21611	2367	19245	-	-	1522	1522	32335	18736	2367	48704
1963	31647	-3097	2	28548	2	24623	2568	22056	4	4	1742	1742	33394	21526	2570	52349
1964	34384	-4696	-	29688	285	27155	2939	24501	4	4	1877	1877	36550	22459	2939	56070
1965	38685	-7017	-	31668	504	30075	3215	27365	5	5	2167	2167	41361	23058	3215	61205
AUSTRALIA																
1925	14068	-897	1138	12033	-	1016	201	815	-	-	43	43	14111	119	1339	12890
1929	10973	250	752	10471	-	2106	218	1889	-	-	55	55	11028	2356	970	12415
1933	9893	-294	571	9028	-	1979	239	1740	-	-	67	67	9960	1685	810	10835
1937	13130	-377	615	12138	-	3113	281	2832	-	-	90	90	13220	2736	896	15060
1938	12802	-365	628	11809	-	3222	231	2991	-	-	85	85	12886	2857	859	14884
1950	18481	451	137	18795	-	7209	873	6336	-	-	186	186	18668	7660	1010	25318
1953	20487	-383	43	20061	-	7950	1119	6831	-	-	211	211	20698	7567	1162	27103
1955	21831	-230	26	21575	-	12177	1650	10527	-	-	249	249	22080	11947	1676	32351
1957	22639	-920	9	21710	-	13647	2070	11577	-	-	387	387	23025	12727	2079	33673
1960	26351	-1690	10	24651	-	16592	2070	14522	-	-	506	506	26858	14902	2080	39679
1961	28129	-2980	10	25139	-	17769	2130	15639	-	-	534	534	28663	14789	2140	41312
1962	28728	-3040	-	25688	-	18245	2010	16235	-	-	621	621	29350	15205	2010	42544
1963	29429	-3280	2	26147	-	20849	2196	18653	4	4	832	832	30265	17569	2198	45635
1964	32058	-4990	-	27068	284	22772	2456	20600	4	4	862	862	33208	17782	2456	48534
1965	36531	-7325	-	29206	503	25203	2604	23102	5	5	1046	1046	38084	17878	2604	53358
NEW ZEALAND																
1925	1836	566	131	2271	-	351	105	246	-	-	38	38	1874	917	236	2555
1929	2249	166	163	2252	-	549	105	444	-	-	81	81	2330	715	268	2777
1933	1572	102	34	1640	2	498	111	389	-	-	107	107	1680	600	145	2135
1937	1951	119	50	2020	2	752	81	672	-	-	155	155	2108	871	131	2847
1938	1909	99	44	1964	2	978	93	887	-	-	173	173	2083	1077	137	3023
1950	2198	45	20	2223	2	1619	390	1230	-	-	358	358	2557	1664	410	3811
1953	2064	1	2	2063	2	1716	345	1373	-	-	493	493	2558	1717	347	3928
1955	2101	10	1	2110	2	2157	342	1817	-	-	566	566	2669	2167	343	4493
1957	2157	10	-	2167	2	2495	329	2168	-	-	673	673	2831	2505	329	5007
1960	2457	-20	-	2437	2	2618	285	2334	-	-	689	689	3148	2598	285	5460
1961	2382	-	-	2382	2	2814	303	2513	-	-	743	743	3126	2814	303	5637
1962	2084	10	-	2094	2	2891	263	2630	-	-	847	847	2932	2901	263	5570
1963	2217	-	-	2217	2	3185	276	2910	-	-	857	857	3075	3185	276	5984
1964	2326	-	-	2326	2	3635	353	3284	-	-	969	969	3296	3635	353	6578
1965	2154	-	-	2154	2	4094	450	3645	-	-	1074	1074	3229	4094	450	6873
USSR AND COMMUNIST EASTERN EUROPE																
1925	75238	-8413	NA	66725	15402	-3134	NA	12267	1392	1392	65	74	92097	-11538	NA	80457
1929	121806	-13719	NA	107662	28941	-8864	NA	19785	2139	2139	116	125	153002	-22574	NA	129710
1933	125802	-10919	NA	114593	44574	-14433	NA	29280	4096	4096	204	206	174676	-25350	NA	148175
1937	194056	-12766	NA	180144	55208	-9212	NA	45269	6290	6290	634	636	256187	-21976	NA	232338
1938	200305	-10853	NA	187646	57011	-7010	NA	49428	6211	6211	754	754	264280	-17863	NA	244039
1950	395927	-12529	NA	382888	67520	968	NA	68487	10846	10888	1880	1852	476173	-11548	NA	464115
1953	476365	-9706	NA	465799	97289	-4317	NA	92972	15190	15218	2733	2732	591576	-13995	NA	576721
1955	563422	-13320	NA	548852	129177	-9039	NA	120138	18733	18763	3419	3437	714751	-22311	NA	691190
1957	618206	-13090	NA	604922	171401	-15344	NA	156057	33058	33118	5483	5483	828147	-28374	NA	799579
1960	666926	-18930	NA	647876	248054	-40542	NA	207497	71937	71973	7148	7168	994064	-59416	NA	934513
1961	674841	-19900	NA	654821	276380	-51279	NA	225060	91241	91277	8174	8173	1050636	-71144	NA	979331

Table XIV. SUMMARY OF ENERGY PRODUCTION, TRADE, AND CONSUMPTION, BY FUEL, SELECTED YEARS, 1925-1965

(Thousand metric tons coal equivalent)

Region, country, year	Solid fuels				Liquid fuels				Natural gas		Hydroelectric power		Total energy			
	Production	Net imports	Bunkers	Consumption	Production	Net imports	Bunkers	Consumption	Production	Consumption	Production	Consumption	Production	Net imports	Bunkers	Consumption
	(1)	(2)	(3)	(4)	(5)	(6)	(7)	(8)	(9)	(10)	(11)	(12)	(13)	(14)	(15)	(16)
USSR AND COMMUNIST EASTERN EUROPE (CONTINUED)																
1962	689272	-22230	NA	666952	308004	-55448	NA	252512	112675	112682	9860	9919	1119812	-77612	NA	1042065
1963	719412	-22280	NA	697062	339131	-60558	NA	278520	136698	136722	10279	10338	1205520	-82755	NA	1122642
1964	742723	-23190	NA	719414	359373	-64934	NA	294384	163291	163329	10460	10450	1275847	-88097	NA	1187576
1965	760535	-22631	NA	737683	388856	-73022	NA	315774	190961	190944	11364	11359	1351716	-95675	NA	1255760
COMMUNIST EASTERN EUROPE																
1925	59129	-8738	100	50291	4773	-1173	3	3599	1205	1205	34	42	65141	-9902	103	55138
1929	83997	-13477	425	70095	8408	-3221	293	4895	1700	1700	46	55	94150	-16689	718	76744
1933	52894	-9899	290	42705	12239	-7226	861	4152	2617	2617	59	60	67808	-17123	1151	49534
1937	71456	-12523	1146	57787	12168	-6687	728	4754	3387	3387	110	112	87121	-19208	1874	66040
1938	72154	-11577	1806	58771	11388	-5282	573	5534	3267	3267	117	117	86927	-16859	2379	67690
1950	171427	-21329	NA	149588	9128	-1432	NA	7695	3173	3247	293	266	184021	-22714	NA	160796
1953	204065	-15206	NA	187999	15873	-3267	NA	12606	6042	6196	332	332	226312	-18319	NA	207134
1955	226022	-16620	NA	208152	19538	-5003	NA	14535	6771	6986	523	540	252853	-21389	NA	230214
1957	237506	-6100	NA	231212	19742	-1035	NA	18707	8305	8593	554	554	266107	-6847	NA	259065
1960	266526	-9600	NA	256806	21465	2879	NA	24329	11594	11953	784	807	300368	-6338	NA	293895
1961	278441	-7390	NA	270931	22073	5165	NA	27197	12678	13074	784	792	313976	-1822	NA	311993
1962	289872	-5370	NA	284412	22833	8429	NA	31217	14740	15149	867	955	328313	3555	NA	331733
1963	302112	-3190	NA	298852	23532	12320	NA	35799	17042	17468	797	949	343483	9708	NA	353068
1964	311923	-1660	NA	310144	23969	16901	NA	40814	18681	19109	790	943	355363	15820	NA	371008
1965	311635	-4226	NA	307188	24524	20697	NA	45161	20910	21415	1186	1368	358254	17158	NA	375131
ALBANIA																
1950	21	10	-	31	198	-60	-	138	-	-	-	-	219	-50	-	168
1953	53	20	-	73	224	-75	-	148	-	-	3	3	279	-55	-	223
1955	98	-20	-	78	312	-155	-	158	-	-	3	3	413	-175	-	238
1957	118	-	-	118	735	-308	-	428	-	-	8	8	861	-308	-	553
1960	146	10	-	156	1092	-479	-	614	-	-	15	15	1253	-469	-	784
1961	145	10	-	155	1157	-420	-	737	-	-	14	14	1315	-410	-	905
1962	151	20	-	171	1178	-381	-	797	-	-	15	15	1343	-361	-	982
1963	126	10	-	136	1127	-459	-	668	-	-	21	21	1274	-449	-	825
1964	146	10	-	156	1146	-395	-	752	-	-	25	25	1317	-385	-	933
1965	175	15	-	190	1200	-542	-	659	-	-	31	31	1406	-527	-	880
BULGARIA																
1925	407	16	-	423	-	65	-	65	-	-	2	2	409	81	-	489
1929	551	-2	-	549	-	126	-	126	-	-	6	6	557	124	-	681
1933	529	4	-	533	-	99	-	99	-	-	10	10	539	103	-	642
1937	641	-	-	641	-	131	-	131	-	-	17	17	657	131	-	788
1938	729	-12	-	717	-	132	-	132	-	-	18	18	746	120	-	866
1950	1888	NA	-	1888	-	360	-	360	-	-	38	38	1927	360	-	2287
1953	2692	NA	-	2692	-	502	-	503	-	-	57	57	2749	502	-	3251
1955	3220	100	-	3320	225	330	-	555	-	-	81	81	3526	430	-	3956
1957	3604	-50	-	3554	428	371	-	798	-	-	106	106	4138	321	-	4458
1960	5195	260	-	5455	300	1184	-	1484	-	-	236	236	5731	1444	-	7174
1961	5681	750	-	6431	311	1557	-	1868	-	-	225	225	6216	2307	-	8523
1962	6367	1180	-	7547	299	2261	-	2559	-	-	212	220	6878	3449	-	10327
1963	6741	1520	-	8261	260	3038	-	3297	-	-	261	271	7261	4568	-	11829
1964	7734	2300	-	10034	240	4563	-	4803	-	-	184	181	8158	6860	-	15018
1965	7899	2838	-	10737	344	5171	-	5514	-	-	250	250	8493	8008	-	16501
CZECHOSLOVAKIA																
1925	23722	-1789	-	21933	35	270	-	306	-	-	22	24	23778	-1517	-	22263
1929	30058	-1905	-	28153	21	530	-	551	3	3	27	30	30108	-1373	-	28735
1933	19570	-1318	-	18252	27	515	-	542	1	1	29	32	19628	-801	-	18826
1937	27409	-2964	-	24445	27	687	-	714	1	1	70	72	27507	-2275	-	25232
1938	25452	-2032	-	23420	29	545	-	573	1	1	75	75	25557	-1487	-	24070
1950	34961	770	-	35731	96	945	-	1041	25	25	138	150	35220	1727	-	36948
1953	39535	1420	-	40955	183	1328	-	1510	224	224	127	132	40069	2752	-	42821
1955	45094	1850	-	46944	161	1487	-	1647	230	230	241	225	45726	3320	-	49046
1957	53153	-460	-	52693	162	2184	-	2346	1028	1028	265	236	54608	1695	-	56303
1960	61256	-1320	-	59936	206	3788	-	3993	1724	1724	312	278	63497	2434	-	65931
1961	65415	-660	-	64755	231	4628	-	4859	1682	1677	316	274	67644	3920	-	71564
1962	68840	-150	-	68690	266	5790	-	6056	1423	1417	376	384	70904	5643	-	76547
1963	72162	260	-	72422	270	6309	-	6579	1329	1324	286	304	74047	6581	-	80629
1964	73565	755	-	74320	293	7766	-	8058	1256	1251	341	429	75454	8603	-	84057
1965	71661	641	-	72302	288	8751	-	9039	1132	1127	557	652	73638	9482	-	83120

Table XIV. SUMMARY OF ENERGY PRODUCTION, TRADE, AND CONSUMPTION, BY FUEL, SELECTED YEARS, 1925–1965

(Thousand metric tons coal equivalent)

Region, country, year	Solid fuels: Production (1)	Solid fuels: Net imports (2)	Solid fuels: Bunkers (3)	Solid fuels: Consumption (4)	Liquid fuels: Production (5)	Liquid fuels: Net imports (6)	Liquid fuels: Bunkers (7)	Liquid fuels: Consumption (8)	Natural gas: Production (9)	Natural gas: Consumption (10)	Hydroelectric power: Production (11)	Hydroelectric power: Consumption (12)	Total energy: Production (13)	Total energy: Net imports (14)	Total energy: Bunkers (15)	Total energy: Consumption (16)
GERMANY, EAST																
1950	44170	5341	NA	49511	-	150	NA	150	-	48	34	-16	44204	5489	NA	49693
1953	54714	7410	NA	62124	-	375	NA	375	-	48	51	30	54765	7812	NA	62577
1955	63116	6390	NA	69506	-	150	NA	150	-	48	63	61	63178	6587	NA	69765
1957	66783	6140	NA	72923	-	551	NA	551	-	72	60	19	66843	6721	NA	73564
1960	70611	7640	NA	78251	-	2306	NA	2306	-	72	77	31	70688	9971	NA	80659
1961	73999	8040	NA	82039	-	2777	NA	2777	-	53	85	38	74083	10823	NA	84907
1962	76923	8770	NA	85693	-	3222	NA	3222	-	43	76	66	76999	12024	NA	89023
1963	78999	8740	NA	87739	-	4082	NA	4082	135	165	68	68	79202	12852	NA	92053
1964	79668	10380	NA	90048	-	5279	NA	5279	144	163	67	85	79879	15696	NA	95574
1965	77852	9990	NA	87842	-	6093	NA	6093	177	189	98	110	78128	16106	NA	94234
HUNGARY																
1925	4116	726	-	4842	-	99	-	99	-	-	1	1	4117	825	-	4942
1929	5052	1553	-	6605	-	308	-	308	-	-	1	1	5054	1861	-	6914
1933	4344	163	-	4507	-	263	-	263	3	3	2	2	4348	426	-	4774
1937	5750	410	-	6160	3	420	-	423	5	5	2	2	5760	830	-	6590
1938	6033	334	-	6367	65	315	-	380	11	11	3	3	6110	649	-	6759
1950	8521	610	-	9131	768	75	-	843	507	507	9	9	9805	685	-	10490
1953	13403	1390	-	14793	1269	150	-	1419	731	731	6	22	15408	1556	-	16965
1955	14466	1650	-	16116	2402	-3	-	2399	726	726	6	37	17599	1678	-	19277
1957	13633	3340	-	16973	1013	1521	-	2534	547	547	5	44	15198	4900	-	20098
1960	17053	2640	-	19693	1866	1536	-	3402	456	702	12	79	19386	4490	-	23876
1961	18133	2970	-	21103	2205	1701	-	3906	432	702	10	73	20780	5004	-	25784
1962	18527	2820	-	21347	2481	1799	-	4280	453	723	10	81	21471	4959	-	26430
1963	19771	3720	-	23491	2655	2618	-	5273	814	1090	10	126	23250	6729	-	29980
1964	20579	4585	-	25164	2717	3017	-	5733	1044	1344	9	144	24349	8036	-	32385
1965	20607	3930	-	24537	2718	3188	-	5906	1475	1738	9	171	24809	7543	-	32352
POLAND																
1925	29101	-7903	100	21098	1248	-443	NA	806	713	713	3	9	31064	-8339	100	22625
1929	46258	-13328	425	32505	1064	-263	NA	801	622	622	4	11	47948	-13584	425	33939
1933	27366	-8809	290	18267	890	-231	NA	659	615	615	4	4	28875	-9041	290	19545
1937	36223	-10046	1146	25031	810	-117	NA	693	707	707	6	6	37747	-10163	1146	26438
1938	38107	-9961	1806	26340	822	-12	NA	810	778	778	6	6	39713	-9973	1806	27934
1950	79452	-28280	510	50662	266	697	NA	963	242	269	50	60	80010	-27546	510	51954
1953	90409	-25976	860	63573	311	1353	NA	1664	425	531	62	62	91207	-24516	860	65830
1955	96290	-27260	1250	67780	300	1949	NA	2249	523	691	89	96	97202	-25136	1250	70815
1957	95882	-15840	194	79848	300	2522	NA	2822	558	774	72	104	96812	-13070	194	83548
1960	107236	-19840	120	87276	320	3348	15	3653	731	1043	82	122	108369	-16140	135	92094
1961	109707	-19370	120	90217	335	3945	41	4239	978	1325	77	117	111097	-15038	161	95898
1962	112931	-19410	90	93431	335	4431	45	4721	1094	1465	97	112	114456	-14592	135	99729
1963	117753	-18940	70	98743	348	5345	53	5640	1309	1705	84	92	119494	-13191	123	106180
1964	123438	-21180	119	102139	453	5807	56	6204	1638	2029	91	4	125620	-15070	175	110376
1965	125619	-23185	221	102213	546	6491	60	6977	1835	2334	114	70	128114	-16241	281	111592
ROMANIA																
1925	1883	212	-	2095	3491	-1172	3	2316	493	493	6	6	5873	-960	3	4910
1929	1976	205	-	2181	7323	-3932	293	3099	1075	1075	8	8	10382	-3727	293	6363
1933	983	61	-	1044	11319	-7883	861	2576	1998	1998	14	14	14314	-7822	861	5632
1937	1431	77	-	1508	11189	-7731	728	2730	2673	2673	16	16	15308	-7654	728	6927
1938	1832	90	-	1922	10305	-6117	573	3615	2478	2478	16	16	14630	-6027	573	8030
1950	2414	220	-	2634	7800	-3600	NA	4200	2398	2398	25	25	12636	-3380	NA	9256
1953	3260	530	-	3790	13887	-6900	NA	6987	4662	4662	28	28	21837	-6370	NA	15467
1955	3739	670	-	4409	16139	-8760	NA	7379	5291	5291	40	37	25209	-8094	NA	17115
1957	4333	770	-	5103	17105	-7875	NA	9230	6171	6171	38	36	27647	-7106	NA	20540
1960	5030	1010	-	6040	17682	-8804	NA	8879	8683	8413	50	46	31445	-8068	NA	23377
1961	5362	870	-	6232	17835	-9023	NA	8813	9586	9316	58	53	32841	-8428	NA	24414
1962	6133	1400	-	7533	18276	-8693	NA	9584	11771	11500	82	77	36262	-7567	NA	28695
1963	6560	1500	-	8060	18873	-8612	NA	10262	13455	13184	67	67	38955	-7382	NA	31572
1964	6792	1490	-	8282	19121	-9135	NA	9986	14599	14323	73	74	40584	-7920	NA	32664
1965	7822	1545	-	9367	19428	-8454	NA	10974	16290	16027	126	84	43666	-7214	NA	36452
USSR (INCLUDING ESTONIA, LATVIA, LITHUANIA)																
1925	16109	325	NA	16434	10629	-1961	NA	8669	186	186	31	31	26955	-1636	NA	25320
1929	37809	-242	NA	37567	20534	-5643	NA	14891	440	440	70	70	58851	-5885	NA	52966
1933	72909	-1020	NA	71889	32336	-7208	NA	25128	1479	1479	145	145	106868	-8228	NA	98640
1937	122600	-243	NA	122357	43040	-2525	NA	40515	2902	2902	524	524	169066	-2768	NA	166298
1938	128151	724	NA	128875	45623	-1728	NA	43895	2944	2944	636	636	177353	-1004	NA	176349
1950	224500	8800	NA	233300	58392	2400	NA	60792	7674	7640	1586	1586	292152	11167	NA	303319

Table XIV. SUMMARY OF ENERGY PRODUCTION, TRADE, AND CONSUMPTION, BY FUEL, SELECTED YEARS, 1925-1965

(Thousand metric tons coal equivalent)

Region, country, year	Solid fuels				Liquid fuels				Natural gas		Hydroelectric power		Total energy			
	Production	Net imports	Bunkers	Consumption	Production	Net imports	Bunkers	Consumption	Production	Consumption	Production	Consumption	Production	Net imports	Bunkers	Consumption
	(1)	(2)	(3)	(4)	(5)	(6)	(7)	(8)	(9)	(10)	(11)	(12)	(13)	(14)	(15)	(16)
USSR (INCLUDING ESTONIA, LATVIA, LITHUANIA) (CONTINUED)																
1953	272300	5500	NA	277800	81416	-1050	NA	80366	9148	9022	2400	2400	365264	4323	NA	369587
1955	337400	3300	NA	340700	109640	-4037	NA	105603	11963	11776	2896	2897	461898	-922	NA	460976
1957	380700	-6990	NA	373710	151659	-14309	NA	137351	24753	24525	4929	4929	562040	-21526	NA	540514
1960	400400	-9330	NA	391070	226589	-43421	NA	183168	60344	60020	6364	6360	693696	-53078	NA	640618
1961	396400	-12510	NA	383890	254307	-56444	NA	197864	78563	78203	7390	7381	736660	-69322	NA	667338
1962	399400	-16860	NA	382540	285171	-63876	NA	221295	97935	97533	8993	8964	791499	-81167	NA	710332
1963	417300	-19090	NA	398210	315599	-72878	NA	242721	119656	119254	9482	9389	862037	-92463	NA	769574
1964	430800	-21530	NA	409270	335405	-81834	NA	253571	144610	144220	9670	9507	920485	-103917	NA	816567
1965	448900	-18405	NA	430495	364332	-93719	NA	270614	170051	169529	10179	9991	993462	-112833	NA	880629
COMMUNIST ASIA																
1925	22557	201	469	22289	-	1412	NA	1412	-	-	-	-	22557	1613	469	23701
1929	24036	-1221	659	22156	8	1607	NA	1614	-	-	-	-	24043	386	659	23770
1933	26392	-2638	606	23148	137	1650	NA	1787	-	-	-	-	26529	-988	606	24935
1937	34326	-4420	814	29092	300	1610	NA	1910	-	-	-	-	34626	-2811	814	31002
1938	29704	-3052	819	25833	420	1077	NA	1497	-	-	-	-	30124	-1975	819	27330
1950	42520	NA	200	42320	300	NA	150	150	-	-	660	660	43480	NA	350	43130
1953	65398	NA	NA	65398	933	NA	NA	933	-	-	320	320	66651	NA	NA	66651
1955	95023	-1020	NA	94003	1449	2063	NA	3512	-	-	775	775	97247	1043	NA	98290
1957	126596	-1740	NA	124856	2222	3444	NA	5666	-	-	1288	1288	130105	1704	NA	131809
1960	220180	-920	NA	219260	8294	5355	NA	13649	-	-	2413	2413	230886	4435	NA	235321
1961	249678	-1120	NA	248558	9339	5070	NA	14409	-	-	2063	2063	261079	3950	NA	265029
1962	251873	-1220	NA	250653	10235	3743	NA	13977	-	-	2125	2125	264233	2523	NA	266755
1963	271506	-1430	NA	270076	11279	3383	NA	14661	-	-	2188	2188	284972	1953	NA	286924
1964	291923	-1220	NA	290703	12777	2183	NA	14960	-	-	2375	2375	307075	963	NA	308037
1965	305433	-1615	NA	303818	15024	1545	NA	16569	-	-	2625	2625	323082	-70	NA	323012
LATIN AMERICA																
1925	3296	7223	1239	9280	35166	-18129	3053	13986	1026	1028	394	394	39882	-10903	4292	24688
1929	3062	7531	1262	9331	52068	-29144	3373	19553	1958	1963	494	494	57582	-21607	4635	31341
1933	2703	4630	341	6992	44585	-27543	4512	12530	2645	2724	574	576	50507	-22832	4853	22822
1937	4226	6090	549	9767	66179	-37449	4470	24261	4220	4401	738	740	75362	-31175	5019	39169
1938	4210	5439	380	9269	65502	-37037	4427	24039	4538	4603	787	789	75037	-31530	4807	38701
1950	5891	2790	40	8641	154071	-90087	15507	48479	6447	7318	1778	1794	168187	-86410	15547	66232
1953	6849	2373	20	9202	178371	-103779	14418	60176	9475	10194	2301	2328	196995	-100666	14438	81899
1955	7361	2740	13	10088	215660	-120585	14735	80340	11470	12214	2712	2734	237203	-117079	14748	105376
1957	7360	2760	-	10120	271448	-152094	18394	100961	15066	14832	3414	3465	297287	-149517	18394	129377
1960	8115	3020	-	11135	295038	-164078	17058	113903	25605	24045	4333	4390	333091	-162561	17058	153472
1961	8562	2520	-	11082	307803	-167873	19791	120140	28509	26751	4506	4563	349381	-167054	19791	162536
1962	9122	1980	-	11102	334305	-187560	19380	127367	31253	29710	4874	4940	379554	-187056	19380	173119
1963	9339	2304	-	11643	341381	-194225	19742	127416	33929	32429	5171	5245	389819	-193346	19742	176733
1964	9935	2477	-	12412	355974	-199889	21059	135027	38779	37164	5661	5680	410348	-199008	21059	190282
1965	10117	2560	-	12677	364695	-201761	21389	141546	40525	38862	6421	6429	421757	-200855	21389	199514
LATIN AMERICA - CARIBBEAN																
1925	1569	1411	599	2381	31899	-20360	2992	8549	289	292	134	134	33891	-18946	3591	11355
1929	1179	1421	644	1956	46914	-32687	3293	10935	911	916	174	174	49178	-31260	3937	13982
1933	764	617	261	1120	38459	-28628	4233	5598	1323	1401	204	206	40749	-27929	4494	8325
1937	1671	779	317	2133	58542	-40253	4222	14069	2519	2700	295	297	63026	-39290	4539	19198
1938	1511	661	251	1921	58014	-40956	4254	12804	2932	2997	309	311	62765	-40227	4505	18033
1950	1947	117	38	2026	144998	-105900	13782	25317	4460	5331	471	487	151875	-104896	13820	33161
1953	2691	145	20	2816	167681	-124089	12181	31412	7089	7808	613	640	178074	-123204	12201	42676
1955	3223	200	13	3410	203291	-148508	12752	42032	8847	9592	786	807	216147	-147542	12765	55840
1957	3456	240	-	3696	255894	-182913	16421	56561	11715	11481	879	931	271944	-182856	16421	72668
1960	4407	110	-	4517	268790	-190943	15030	62817	20542	18982	1176	1232	294915	-192336	15030	87549
1961	4459	120	-	4619	275756	-192351	17805	65600	21684	19925	1171	1227	303109	-193932	17805	91371
1962	4920	240	-	5160	298817	-212162	17320	69336	22856	21313	1310	1376	327902	-213398	17320	97185
1963	5313	284	-	5597	305225	-217551	17652	70023	24667	23167	1518	1592	336723	-218693	17652	100380
1964	5163	357	-	5520	319064	-226718	18866	73481	28990	27375	1731	1750	354947	-227957	18866	108125
1965	5237	425	-	5662	328043	-230828	19191	78024	29979	28317	2004	2011	365262	-232057	19191	114014
CARIBBEAN - OIL PRODUCING																
1925	1569	137	50	1656	31899	-24185	1688	6027	289	292	118	118	33875	-24045	1738	8092
1929	1179	174	93	1260	46914	-36690	1749	8475	911	916	154	154	49158	-36511	1842	10805
1933	764	78	41	801	38451	-31106	3030	4316	1323	1401	176	178	40713	-30946	3071	6696
1937	1671	89	63	1697	58529	-43557	3128	11844	2519	2700	255	257	62973	-43284	3191	16498
1938	1511	86	38	1559	57989	-43965	3150	10874	2932	2997	266	268	62697	-43811	3188	15698
1950	1947	56	21	1982	144965	-113087	12406	19473	4457	5327	361	377	151729	-112144	12427	27159
1953	2691	57	11	2737	167676	-132515	10289	24873	7084	7803	495	523	177946	-131711	10300	35935

Table XIV. SUMMARY OF ENERGY PRODUCTION, TRADE, AND CONSUMPTION, BY FUEL, SELECTED YEARS, 1925-1965

(Thousand metric tons coal equivalent)

Region, country, year	Solid fuels				Liquid fuels				Natural gas		Hydroelectric power		Total energy			
	Production	Net imports	Bunkers	Consumption	Production	Net imports	Bunkers	Consumption	Production	Consumption	Production	Consumption	Production	Net imports	Bunkers	Consumption
	(1)	(2)	(3)	(4)	(5)	(6)	(7)	(8)	(9)	(10)	(11)	(12)	(13)	(14)	(15)	(16)
CARIBBEAN - OIL PRODUCING (CONTINUED)																
1955	3223	60	-	3283	203216	-158619	11070	33527	8842	9586	647	668	215927	-157793	11070	47064
1957	3456	60	-	3516	255818	-196494	14445	44879	11711	11477	737	788	271721	-196617	14445	60659
1960	4407	50	-	4457	268769	-207404	12150	49215	20539	18980	982	1038	294697	-208857	12150	73690
1961	4499	70	-	4569	275741	-210720	13500	51521	21680	19921	972	1029	302891	-212351	13500	77039
1962	4920	180	-	5100	298799	-233748	12316	52736	22852	21309	1112	1178	327682	-235044	12316	80322
1963	5313	190	-	5503	305178	-240458	11311	53411	24662	23162	1294	1367	336446	-241693	11311	83443
1964	5163	238	-	5401	319008	-252800	11897	54312	28986	27371	1502	1521	354659	-254158	11897	88605
1965	5237	293	-	5530	327987	-258074	11796	58117	29975	28313	1735	1742	364934	-259435	11796	93703
COLOMBIA																
1925	100	3	NA	103	216	14	NA	230	-	-	12	12	328	17	NA	344
1929	100	1	NA	101	4367	-3731	NA	636	-	-	13	13	4479	-3730	NA	750
1933	112	2	NA	114	2751	-2510	NA	242	-	-	14	14	2877	-2508	NA	369
1937	422	1	NA	423	4211	-3785	NA	426	-	-	23	23	4655	-3784	NA	872
1938	412	-	NA	412	4476	-3938	NA	539	-	-	26	26	4914	-3938	NA	976
1950	1010	-	-	1010	7067	-5856	189	1022	-	-	91	91	8167	-5856	189	2122
1953	1230	-	-	1230	8181	-6152	53	1977	-	-	126	126	9537	-6152	53	3333
1955	1850	-	-	1850	8240	-4991	60	3189	-	-	185	185	10275	-4991	60	5224
1957	2000	-10	-	1990	9491	-5946	210	3335	-	-	252	252	11742	-5956	210	5576
1960	2600	-	-	2600	11543	-7254	315	3974	538	538	323	323	15004	-7254	315	7435
1961	2650	-	-	2650	11019	-6134	330	4556	555	555	314	314	14539	-6134	330	8075
1962	3000	-	-	3000	10743	-5690	420	4634	789	789	345	345	14877	-5690	420	8767
1963	3200	-	-	3200	12494	-7007	300	5187	935	935	402	402	17031	-7007	300	9724
1964	3000	-2	-	2998	12974	-7355	282	5337	1111	1111	465	465	17550	-7357	282	9911
1965	3200	-2	-	3198	15255	-9476	321	5459	1221	1221	488	488	20164	-9478	321	10365
MEXICO																
1925	1444	66	-	1510	26442	-20156	1071	5216	200	202	104	104	28189	-20087	1071	7031
1929	1054	62	-	1116	10070	-4676	257	5138	293	298	138	138	11555	-4608	257	6690
1933	647	12	-	659	7668	-4392	NA	3276	417	496	159	161	8891	-4299	NA	4592
1937	1242	13	-	1255	10118	-4262	NA	5856	1300	1481	228	230	12887	-4065	NA	8822
1938	1093	14	-	1107	8325	-2388	NA	5937	1477	1542	234	236	11129	-2306	NA	8823
1950	912	31	-	943	15803	-2819	902	12083	2336	3206	244	260	19294	-1901	902	16491
1953	1432	42	-	1474	15837	-2184	198	13455	3523	4242	328	355	21120	-1396	198	19526
1955	1342	60	-	1402	19527	-3176	225	16127	4518	5263	431	452	25818	-2350	225	23243
1957	1421	70	-	1491	19634	218	285	19566	6085	5850	465	516	27604	104	285	27423
1960	1772	50	-	1822	22973	-557	165	22251	12874	11314	647	703	38265	-2010	165	36090
1961	1818	60	-	1878	24689	-2117	90	22482	13600	11841	639	696	40745	-3758	90	36897
1962	1893	60	-	1953	25721	-3324	120	22277	14007	12465	685	751	42306	-4740	120	37445
1963	2071	60	-	2131	26585	-3104	135	23346	15146	13646	753	827	44555	-4469	135	39950
1964	2127	80	-	2207	27260	-2388	92	24780	18295	16681	884	903	48566	-3904	92	44570
1965	2006	110	-	2116	27813	-2702	89	25023	18601	16939	1076	1084	49497	-4246	89	45162
TRINIDAD AND TOBAGO																
1925	-	44	30	14	915	-692	99	125	89	89	-	-	1004	-648	129	228
1929	-	87	70	17	1826	-1266	500	60	178	178	-	-	2004	-1179	570	255
1933	-	50	38	12	2018	-981	855	182	197	197	-	-	2215	-931	893	391
1937	-	62	63	-1	3365	-2003	900	462	329	329	-	-	3694	-1941	963	790
1938	-	53	38	15	3849	-2496	858	495	376	376	-	-	4225	-2443	896	886
1950	-	26	21	5	4412	-1848	1615	948	633	633	-	-	5044	-1822	1637	1586
1953	-	14	11	3	4790	-1836	2379	575	667	667	-	-	5457	-1822	2390	1245
1955	-	-	-	-	5333	-2540	1935	858	663	663	-	-	5996	-2540	1935	1521
1957	-	-	-	-	7277	-3873	2580	824	799	799	-	-	8076	-3873	2580	1623
1960	-	-	-	-	9027	-5364	2910	753	1020	1020	-	-	10047	-5364	2910	1773
1961	-	-	-	-	9749	-5237	3435	1077	1108	1108	-	-	10857	-5237	3435	2185
1962	-	-	-	-	10409	-6279	2911	1220	1132	1132	-	-	11541	-6279	2911	2352
1963	-	-	-	-	10362	-7229	2461	674	1108	1108	-	-	11470	-7229	2461	1782
1964	-	-	-	-	10590	-6680	2881	1031	1451	1451	-	-	12041	-6680	2881	2481
1965	-	-	-	-	10404	-6105	2445	1854	1564	1564	-	-	11968	-6105	2445	3418
VENEZUELA																
1950	25	-1	-	24	117684	-113039	587	4059	1488	1488	27	27	119223	-113040	587	5597
1953	29	1	-	30	138869	-130701	2148	6020	2893	2893	42	42	141832	-130700	2148	8984
1955	31	-	-	31	170117	-159344	3345	7428	3660	3660	31	31	173839	-159344	3345	11151
1957	35	-	-	35	219417	-199647	5040	14730	4827	4827	20	20	224299	-199647	5040	19612
1960	35	-	-	35	225227	-205887	3840	15500	6107	6107	12	12	231381	-205887	3840	21654
1961	31	10	-	41	230285	-210246	3795	16244	6416	6416	19	19	236750	-210236	3795	22719
1962	27	120	-	147	251927	-230712	4140	17075	6924	6924	81	81	258959	-230592	4140	24227
1963	42	130	-	172	255738	-235118	4005	16616	7473	7473	138	138	263391	-234988	4005	24398

Table XIV. SUMMARY OF ENERGY PRODUCTION, TRADE, AND CONSUMPTION, BY FUEL, SELECTED YEARS, 1925–1965

(Thousand metric tons coal equivalent)

Region, country, year	Solid fuels				Liquid fuels				Natural gas		Hydroelectric power		Total energy			
	Production	Net imports	Bunkers	Consumption	Production	Net imports	Bunkers	Consumption	Production	Consumption	Production	Consumption	Production	Net imports	Bunkers	Consumption
	(1)	(2)	(3)	(4)	(5)	(6)	(7)	(8)	(9)	(10)	(11)	(12)	(13)	(14)	(15)	(16)
VENEZUELA (CONTINUED)																
1964	36	160	-	196	268185	-247904	4304	15978	8129	8129	153	153	276503	-247744	4304	24456
1965	31	185	-	216	274515	-250610	4574	19332	8589	8589	171	171	283306	-250425	4574	28308
CARIBBEAN - OTHER																
1925	-	1274	549	725	-	3825	1304	2522	-	-	16	16	16	5099	1853	3263
1929	-	1247	551	696	-	4004	1544	2460	-	-	21	21	21	5251	2095	3177
1933	-	539	220	319	8	2478	1203	1283	-	-	28	28	35	3017	1423	1629
1937	-	690	254	436	14	3305	1094	2225	-	-	40	40	53	3995	1348	2700
1938	-	575	213	362	26	3009	1104	1931	-	-	43	43	68	3584	1317	2335
1950	-	61	17	44	33	7187	1376	5844	3	4	110	110	146	7249	1393	6002
1953	-	88	9	79	5	8426	1892	6539	5	5	118	118	128	8508	1901	6741
1955	-	140	13	127	75	10112	1682	8505	5	5	139	139	219	10252	1695	8776
1957	-	180	-	180	77	13581	1976	11682	4	4	143	143	223	13761	1976	12009
1960	-	60	-	60	21	16461	2880	13602	3	3	194	194	218	16521	2880	13859
1961	-	50	-	50	15	18369	4305	14079	4	4	199	199	218	18419	4305	14332
1962	-	60	-	60	18	21587	5004	16601	4	4	198	198	220	21647	5004	16862
1963	-	94	-	94	47	22907	6341	16613	5	5	225	225	277	23001	6341	16937
1964	-	119	-	119	56	26082	6969	19169	4	4	229	229	288	26201	6969	19520
1965	-	132	-	132	56	27246	7395	19907	4	4	269	269	328	27378	7395	20311
CUBA																
1925	-	659	NA	659	-	1895	NA	1895	-	-	2	2	2	2554	NA	2555
1929	-	632	NA	632	-	1614	NA	1614	-	-	2	2	2	2246	NA	2248
1933	-	296	NA	296	8	462	NA	470	-	-	2	2	9	758	NA	767
1937	-	381	NA	381	14	1130	NA	1143	-	-	2	2	16	1511	NA	1526
1938	-	342	NA	342	26	872	NA	897	-	-	2	2	28	1214	NA	1241
1950	-	35	-	35	33	NA	59	3689	-	-	2	2	35	NA	59	3725
1953	-	58	-	58	5	NA	89	3951	-	-	2	2	7	NA	89	4011
1955	-	130	-	130	75	NA	60	4047	-	-	3	3	78	NA	60	4180
1957	-	180	-	180	77	5117	90	5103	-	-	3	3	79	5297	90	5286
1960	-	60	-	60	21	6027	60	5988	-	-	3	3	24	6087	60	6051
1961	-	50	-	50	15	6510	75	6450	-	-	3	3	18	6560	75	6503
1962	-	60	-	60	18	7257	45	7230	-	-	3	3	21	7317	45	7293
1963	-	94	-	94	47	6627	45	6629	-	-	6	6	53	6721	45	6729
1964	-	119	-	119	56	7124	53	7127	-	-	13	13	68	7243	53	7258
1965	-	132	-	132	56	7164	53	7167	-	-	14	14	69	7296	53	7313
PUERTO RICO																
1957	-	-	-	-	-	2918	180	2738	-	-	22	22	22	2918	180	2759
1960	-	-	-	-	-	3521	135	3386	-	-	30	30	30	3521	135	3416
1961	-	-	-	-	-	2964	120	2844	-	-	34	34	34	2964	120	2878
1962	-	-	-	-	-	4013	120	3893	-	-	26	26	26	4013	120	3918
1963	-	-	-	-	-	4080	120	3960	-	-	35	35	35	4080	120	3995
1964	-	-	-	-	-	4775	105	4670	-	-	19	19	19	4775	105	4689
1965	-	-	-	-	-	5670	101	5570	-	-	30	30	30	5670	101	5599
LATIN AMERICA - OTHER																
1925	1727	5812	NA	6899	3267	2231	NA	5438	737	737	261	261	5991	8043	NA	13333
1929	1883	6110	NA	7375	5154	3543	NA	8618	1047	1047	319	319	8403	9653	NA	17359
1933	1939	4013	NA	5872	6126	1085	NA	6932	1323	1323	370	370	9758	5098	NA	14497
1937	2555	5311	NA	7634	7637	2804	NA	10193	1701	1701	443	443	12335	8115	NA	19970
1938	2699	4778	NA	7348	7488	3920	NA	11235	1606	1606	478	478	12272	8698	NA	20668
1950	3944	2673	2	6615	9074	15813	1725	23162	1987	1987	1307	1307	16312	18486	1727	33071
1953	4158	2228	-	6386	10691	20310	2237	28764	2386	2386	1687	1687	18921	22538	2237	39223
1955	4138	2540	-	6678	12369	27923	1983	38309	2623	2623	1927	1927	21056	30463	1983	49536
1957	3904	2520	-	6424	15554	30819	1973	44400	3351	3351	2534	2534	25343	33339	1973	56709
1960	3708	2910	-	6618	26249	26865	2028	51086	5063	5063	3157	3157	38177	29775	2028	65924
1961	4063	2400	-	6463	32048	24479	1986	54540	6825	6825	3336	3336	46272	26879	1986	71165
1962	4202	1740	-	5942	35489	24602	2060	58031	8397	8397	3564	3564	51652	26342	2060	75934
1963	4026	2020	-	6046	36156	23327	2090	57393	9261	9261	3653	3653	53096	25347	2090	76353
1964	4772	2120	-	6892	36911	26829	2193	61547	9789	9789	3930	3930	55401	28949	2193	82157
1965	4880	2135	-	7015	36653	29067	2198	63522	10545	10545	4418	4418	56495	31202	2198	85500
ARGENTINA																
1925	-	3179	345	2834	1386	1073	-	2459	159	159	8	8	1553	4252	345	5459
1929	-	3176	136	3040	2072	2555	-	4626	282	282	14	14	2367	5731	136	7962
1933	-	2458	19	2439	2960	1515	201	4274	440	440	11	11	3410	3973	220	7163

Table XIV. SUMMARY OF ENERGY PRODUCTION, TRADE, AND CONSUMPTION, BY FUEL, SELECTED YEARS, 1925-1965

(Thousand metric tons coal equivalent)

Region, country, year	Solid fuels				Liquid fuels				Natural gas		Hydroelectric power		Total energy			
	Produc-tion (1)	Net imports (2)	Bunkers (3)	Consump-tion (4)	Produc-tion (5)	Net imports (6)	Bunkers (7)	Consump-tion (8)	Produc-tion (9)	Consump-tion (10)	Produc-tion (11)	Consump-tion (12)	Produc-tion (13)	Net imports (14)	Bunkers (15)	Consump-tion (16)
ARGENTINA (CONTINUED)																
1937	-	3164	102	3062	3545	2600	156	5988	561	561	12	12	4117	5764	258	9623
1938	-	2859	63	2796	3693	3156	120	6729	542	542	11	11	4246	6015	183	10078
1950	86	1467	-	1553	5048	8070	834	12284	710	710	24	24	5867	9537	834	14570
1953	100	1224	-	1324	6132	9155	297	14990	930	930	45	45	7206	10379	297	17288
1955	155	1260	-	1415	6560	10716	330	16946	958	958	38	38	7710	11976	330	19356
1957	237	1280	-	1517	7302	14003	375	20930	1135	1135	73	73	8747	15283	375	23654
1960	293	1460	-	1753	13718	7620	375	20963	1842	1842	116	116	15968	9080	375	24673
1961	351	1260	-	1611	18137	4985	420	22701	3140	3140	136	136	21763	6245	420	27587
1962	291	640	-	931	21095	2594	375	23313	3967	3967	146	146	25498	3234	375	28356
1963	217	770	-	987	20868	1007	555	21320	4537	4537	148	148	25770	1777	555	26992
1964	341	750	-	1091	21540	3314	629	24225	4996	4996	155	155	27032	4064	629	30467
1965	381	730	-	1111	21113	5460	636	25937	5680	5680	155	155	27328	6190	636	32882
BOLIVIA																
1925	-	16	-	16	-	33	-	33	-	-	1	1	1	49	-	50
1929	-	19	-	19	5	60	-	65	-	-	3	3	7	79	-	86
1933	-	8	-	8	21	30	-	51	-	-	3	3	24	38	-	62
1937	-	31	-	31	24	60	-	84	-	-	4	4	28	91	-	119
1938	-	33	-	33	27	68	-	95	-	-	6	6	33	101	-	133
1950	-	2	-	2	120	102	5	218	-	-	24	24	144	104	5	243
1953	-	5	-	5	117	162	5	275	-	-	31	31	148	167	5	311
1955	-	-	-	-	527	-48	15	464	8	8	36	36	571	-48	15	508
1957	-	-	-	-	699	-203	15	482	11	11	44	44	753	-203	15	536
1960	-	-	-	-	699	-149	15	536	8	8	49	49	756	-149	15	592
1961	-	-	-	-	585	-99	15	471	21	21	49	49	655	-99	15	541
1962	-	-	-	-	546	-5	15	527	36	36	47	47	629	-5	15	610
1963	-	-	-	-	618	-87	15	516	72	72	51	51	741	-87	15	639
1964	-	-	-	-	612	-42	11	560	113	113	53	53	778	-42	11	725
1965	-	5	-	5	650	-33	11	606	133	133	54	54	836	-28	11	798
BRAZIL																
1925	306	1927	NA	2233	-	813	NA	813	-	-	183	183	488	2740	NA	3228
1929	291	2325	NA	2616	-	1190	NA	1190	-	-	221	221	512	3515	NA	4027
1933	504	1292	NA	1796	-	1181	NA	1181	-	-	261	261	765	2473	NA	3237
1937	595	1708	NA	2303	-	1658	NA	1658	-	-	300	300	895	3366	NA	4261
1938	707	1576	NA	2283	-	1767	NA	1767	-	-	325	325	1032	3343	NA	4375
1950	1626	1119	-	2745	66	6500	405	6161	7	7	900	900	2598	7619	405	9812
1953	1681	746	-	2427	180	8288	609	7859	36	36	1153	1153	3050	9034	609	11474
1955	1882	1120	-	3002	396	13073	255	13214	83	83	1326	1326	3687	14193	255	17624
1957	1721	940	-	2661	1982	12729	240	14471	212	212	1860	1860	5773	13669	240	19202
1960	1934	1060	-	2994	5805	14019	240	19584	713	713	2298	2298	10750	15079	240	25589
1961	1984	900	-	2884	6824	14369	300	20892	702	702	2368	2368	11877	15269	300	26846
1962	2082	920	-	3002	6549	16346	420	22475	681	681	2583	2583	11894	17266	420	28740
1963	2134	1040	-	3174	7001	16956	420	23537	670	670	2591	2591	12395	17996	420	29971
1964	2694	1155	-	3849	6530	17642	431	23741	709	709	2762	2762	12694	18797	431	31060
1965	2808	1240	-	4048	6732	16625	425	22932	910	910	3189	3189	13639	17865	425	31079
CHILE																
1925	1319	249	295	1273	-	1361	35	1326	-	-	47	47	1366	1610	330	2646
1929	1374	51	349	1076	-	1680	30	1650	-	-	60	60	1434	1731	379	2786
1933	1405	-119	-	1286	-	416	-	416	-	-	69	69	1474	297	-	1770
1937	1861	-43	-	1818	-	1149	-	1149	-	-	95	95	1955	1106	-	3061
1938	1917	-51	-	1866	-	1086	-	1086	-	-	94	94	2010	1035	-	3045
1950	2036	2	-	2038	123	1647	36	1734	133	133	206	206	2499	1649	36	4112
1953	2167	201	-	2368	257	1461	63	1655	173	173	254	254	2851	1662	63	4450
1955	1965	70	-	2035	515	2454	105	2864	280	280	291	291	3050	2524	105	5469
1957	1805	230	-	2035	869	2270	120	3018	466	466	313	313	3453	2500	120	5832
1960	1319	320	-	1639	1439	2096	90	3444	1185	1185	372	372	4316	2416	90	6641
1961	1562	160	-	1722	1850	1929	30	3749	1678	1678	393	393	5482	2089	30	7541
1962	1667	120	-	1787	2364	2081	45	4400	2344	2344	414	414	6789	2201	45	8945
1963	1544	160	-	1704	2736	1754	45	4445	2557	2557	426	426	7263	1914	45	9131
1964	1621	170	-	1791	2859	1794	30	4623	2371	2371	465	465	7316	1964	30	9250
1965	1607	115	-	1722	2777	2271	35	5013	2358	2358	494	494	7235	2386	35	9587
ECUADOR																
1925	-	-	-	-	35	12	-	47	-	-	3	3	38	12	-	50
1929	-	-	-	-	294	-203	-	92	-	-	3	3	297	-203	-	95
1933	-	-	-	-	345	-207	-	138	12	12	3	3	360	-207	-	153
1937	-	-	-	-	434	-375	-	59	61	61	3	3	498	-375	-	123

Table XIV. SUMMARY OF ENERGY PRODUCTION, TRADE, AND CONSUMPTION, BY FUEL, SELECTED YEARS, 1925-1965

(Thousand metric tons coal equivalent)

Region, country, year	Solid fuels				Liquid fuels				Natural gas		Hydroelectric power		Total energy			
	Production	Net imports	Bunkers	Consumption	Production	Net imports	Bunkers	Consumption	Production	Consumption	Production	Consumption	Production	Net imports	Bunkers	Consumption
	(1)	(2)	(3)	(4)	(5)	(6)	(7)	(8)	(9)	(10)	(11)	(12)	(13)	(14)	(15)	(16)
ECUADOR (CONTINUED)																
1938	-	-	-	-	452	-314	-	138	73	73	3	3	528	-314	-	214
1950	-	-	-	-	539	-189	14	336	176	176	11	11	725	-189	14	523
1953	-	-	-	-	612	-231	29	353	200	200	12	12	823	-231	29	564
1955	-	-	-	-	729	-152	30	548	200	200	15	15	944	-152	30	762
1957	-	-	-	-	660	-53	30	578	200	200	18	18	878	-53	30	795
1960	-	-	-	-	570	347	15	902	200	200	22	22	792	347	15	1123
1961	-	-	-	-	603	312	30	885	200	200	25	25	828	312	30	1110
1962	-	-	-	-	531	279	15	795	200	200	28	28	759	279	15	1023
1963	-	-	-	-	509	395	15	888	200	200	30	30	738	395	15	1118
1964	-	-	-	-	576	501	17	1061	200	200	31	31	807	501	17	1291
1965	-	-	-	-	602	531	17	1116	200	200	31	31	832	531	17	1347
PARAGUAY																
1950	-	-	-	-	-	33	-	33	-	-	-	-	-	33	-	33
1953	-	-	-	-	-	71	-	71	-	-	-	-	-	71	-	71
1955	-	-	-	-	-	95	-	95	-	-	-	-	-	95	-	95
1957	-	-	-	-	-	102	-	102	-	-	-	-	-	102	-	102
1960	-	-	-	-	-	155	-	155	-	-	-	-	-	155	-	155
1961	-	-	-	-	-	177	-	177	-	-	-	-	-	177	-	177
1962	-	-	-	-	-	185	-	185	-	-	-	-	-	185	-	185
1963	-	-	-	-	-	201	-	201	-	-	-	-	-	201	-	201
1964	-	-	-	-	-	209	-	209	-	-	-	-	-	209	-	209
1965	-	-	-	-	-	266	-	266	-	-	-	-	-	266	-	266
PERU																
1925	102	39	-	141	1847	-1394	26	428	578	578	19	19	2545	-1355	26	1165
1929	218	41	-	259	2784	-2256	50	479	765	765	19	19	3785	-2215	50	1521
1933	30	18	-	48	2801	-2303	78	420	871	871	24	24	3726	-2285	78	1363
1937	99	15	-	114	3635	-2976	62	597	1079	1079	29	29	4842	-2961	62	1819
1938	75	13	-	88	3317	-2474	53	791	991	991	40	40	4423	-2461	53	1910
1950	196	-57	2	137	3179	-1299	87	1793	960	960	76	76	4411	-1356	89	2966
1953	210	-35	-	175	3393	-947	98	2349	1047	1047	118	118	4767	-982	98	3688
1955	136	-	-	136	3644	-950	105	2589	1095	1095	136	136	5011	-950	105	3956
1957	141	-30	-	111	4043	-989	90	2964	1328	1328	159	159	5670	-1019	90	4562
1960	162	-10	-	152	4019	-281	60	3678	1115	1115	216	216	5512	-291	60	5161
1961	167	20	-	187	4050	-95	60	3896	1084	1084	235	235	5536	-75	60	5401
1962	163	10	-	173	4404	144	45	4503	1169	1169	243	243	5980	154	45	6089
1963	131	-	-	131	4425	255	45	4635	1225	1225	270	270	6051	255	45	6261
1964	115	-5	-	110	4794	368	66	5096	1400	1400	306	306	6615	363	66	6911
1965	84	5	-	89	4781	356	98	5039	1265	1265	328	328	6458	361	98	6721
URUGUAY																
1925	-	363	-	363	-	323	NA	323	-	-	-	-	-	686	NA	686
1929	-	474	133	341	-	504	NA	504	-	-	-	-	-	978	133	845
1933	-	344	61	283	-	429	NA	429	-	-	-	-	-	773	61	712
1937	-	418	123	295	-	606	NA	606	-	-	-	-	-	1024	123	901
1938	-	334	66	268	-	564	NA	564	-	-	-	-	-	898	66	832
1950	-	129	-	129	-	564	315	249	1	1	66	66	67	693	315	445
1953	-	83	-	83	-	1889	318	1571	-	-	75	75	75	1972	318	1729
1955	-	90	-	90	-	2156	375	1781	-	-	85	85	85	2246	375	1955
1957	-	100	-	100	-	2343	345	1998	-	-	69	69	69	2443	345	2167
1960	-	80	-	80	-	2369	405	1964	-	-	85	85	85	2449	405	2128
1961	-	60	-	60	-	2219	345	1874	-	-	131	131	131	2279	345	2064
1962	-	50	-	50	-	2334	360	1974	-	-	104	104	104	2384	360	2128
1963	-	50	-	50	-	2234	210	2024	-	-	137	137	137	2284	210	2211
1964	-	50	-	50	-	2388	225	2163	-	-	158	158	158	2438	225	2371
1965	-	40	-	40	-	2634	239	2396	-	-	166	166	166	2674	239	2602
ASIA																
1925	54749	1034	5652	50131	14862	-5076	1107	8679	485	485	997	997	71093	-4042	6759	60292
1929	61187	2105	5414	57878	19950	-5460	2164	12327	686	686	1654	1654	83477	-3355	7578	72545
1933	56010	2406	3932	54484	22641	-8390	2324	11928	1204	1204	2269	2269	82123	-5984	6256	69884
1937	76378	5289	4446	77221	38462	-17184	2861	18417	1316	1316	3327	3327	119483	-11895	7307	100281
1938	83961	4814	3853	84922	39243	-13577	3174	22493	1413	1413	3582	3582	128199	-8763	7027	112409
1950	72755	1425	1821	72359	146555	-106820	13514	26222	1917	1917	5347	5347	226573	-105394	15335	105844
1953	86586	4777	432	90931	204698	-147021	16477	41201	3195	3195	6016	6016	300495	-142244	16909	141343
1955	83607	3830	351	87086	269313	-190616	19804	58895	4714	4709	7039	7039	364673	-186791	20155	157729
1957	99646	7770	109	107307	298709	-196923	24386	77400	8598	8593	8357	8357	415309	-189158	24495	201657
1960	109352	9144	20	118476	433955	-294737	31895	107324	12722	12722	9209	9209	565237	-285593	31915	247730

Table XIV. SUMMARY OF ENERGY PRODUCTION, TRADE, AND CONSUMPTION, BY FUEL, SELECTED YEARS, 1925-1965

(Thousand metric tons coal equivalent)

Region, country, year	Solid fuels: Production	Solid fuels: Net imports	Solid fuels: Bunkers	Solid fuels: Consumption	Liquid fuels: Production	Liquid fuels: Net imports	Liquid fuels: Bunkers	Liquid fuels: Consumption	Natural gas: Production	Natural gas: Consumption	Hydroelectric power: Production	Hydroelectric power: Consumption	Total energy: Production	Total energy: Net imports	Total energy: Bunkers	Total energy: Consumption
	(1)	(2)	(3)	(4)	(5)	(6)	(7)	(8)	(9)	(10)	(11)	(12)	(13)	(14)	(15)	(16)
ASIA (CONTINUED)																
1961	116388	12030	18	128400	462417	-300108	35745	126564	13963	13963	10759	10759	603527	-288078	35763	279686
1962	122571	12850	8	135413	506393	-325908	38693	141792	15647	15642	10321	10321	654931	-313063	38701	303168
1963	126516	11790	6	138300	553031	-348104	41821	163107	16476	16464	11609	11609	707632	-336325	41827	329480
1964	123896	13735	5	137626	616163	-386264	45918	183981	18251	18251	11921	11921	770231	-372529	45923	351780
1965	126941	17685	4	144622	674028	-417483	47755	208791	19294	19222	12459	12459	832722	-399870	47759	385094
MIDDLE EAST																
1925	673	116	110	679	6978	-5085	267	1626	-	-	2	2	7653	-4969	377	2307
1929	999	-111	137	751	8505	-6885	596	1025	-	-	2	2	9506	-6996	733	1778
1933	1321	-294	42	985	10979	-9579	854	546	-	-	2	2	12302	-9873	896	1533
1937	1653	130	114	1669	23483	-19685	1136	2663	-	-	4	4	25140	-19555	1250	4336
1938	1792	-4	57	1731	23883	-15942	1269	6672	-	-	4	4	25680	-15946	1326	8408
1950	3279	162	133	3308	128964	-109811	9884	9270	674	674	12	12	132928	-109649	10017	13263
1953	4130	68	36	4162	180143	-159168	9902	11073	1136	1136	21	21	185430	-159100	9938	16392
1955	4135	60	18	4177	241119	-212655	12125	16340	1772	1772	26	26	247052	-212595	12143	22314
1957	4769	60	15	4814	264315	-230063	13548	20705	4413	4413	62	62	273559	-230003	13563	29994
1960	4514	20	-	4534	392805	-346865	18795	27146	7010	7010	143	143	404472	-346845	18795	38832
1961	4496	60	-	4556	420692	-372456	19215	29021	7634	7634	185	185	433006	-372396	19215	41395
1962	4711	50	-	4761	461835	-409199	20760	31877	8312	8312	177	177	475035	-409149	20760	45127
1963	5194	20	-	5214	508769	-453353	21725	33692	7943	7943	312	312	522217	-453333	21725	47160
1964	5710	20	-	5730	570305	-511898	23238	35169	8786	8786	259	259	585060	-511878	23238	49944
1965	5686	25	-	5711	624890	-560523	22541	41826	9185	9185	340	340	640101	-560498	22541	57062
MIDDLE EAST - OIL PRODUCING																
1925	-	5	NA	5	6978	-5583	NA	1395	-	-	-	-	6978	-5578	NA	1400
1929	-	8	NA	8	8505	-7838	NA	668	-	-	-	-	8505	-7830	NA	676
1933	9	3	NA	12	10979	-10806	NA	173	-	-	-	-	10988	-10803	NA	185
1937	-	4	NA	4	23483	-21440	NA	2043	-	-	-	-	23483	-21436	NA	2047
1938	-	4	NA	4	23883	-18011	NA	5873	-	-	-	-	23883	-18007	NA	5877
1950	200	2	-	202	128939	-117069	5534	6336	674	674	-	-	129812	-117067	5534	7212
1953	155	-	-	155	180104	-168330	5172	6602	1136	1136	-	-	181395	-168330	5172	7893
1955	245	-	-	245	240849	-223928	6866	10056	1772	1772	-	-	242866	-223928	6866	12073
1957	176	-	-	176	263787	-241001	9786	13001	4413	4413	-	-	268376	-241001	9786	17589
1960	230	-	-	230	392049	-361107	12885	18057	7010	7010	-	-	399289	-361107	12885	25297
1961	198	20	-	218	419826	-387348	13350	19128	7630	7630	-	-	427654	-387328	13350	26976
1962	160	-	-	160	460740	-426050	15000	19691	8297	8297	-	-	469197	-426050	15000	28148
1963	193	-	-	193	507425	-471450	15222	20753	7929	7929	-	-	515547	-471450	15222	28875
1964	274	-	-	274	568625	-531717	16593	20315	8747	8747	-	-	577646	-531717	16593	29336
1965	275	-	-	275	622287	-580907	16889	24492	9090	9090	-	-	631652	-580907	16889	33857
IRAN																
1950	200	-	-	200	48389	-43632	2460	2297	-	-	-	-	48589	-43632	2460	2497
1953	155	-	-	155	2234	-348	-	1886	72	72	-	-	2460	-348	-	2112
1955	245	-	-	245	24534	-19658	1215	3662	789	789	-	-	25568	-19658	1215	4695
1957	176	-	-	176	54030	-45611	2265	6155	2380	2380	-	-	56586	-45611	2265	8711
1960	230	-	-	230	78588	-67379	3180	8030	3726	3726	-	-	82544	-67379	3180	11985
1961	198	-	-	198	88473	-76431	3270	8772	3719	3719	-	-	92390	-76431	3270	12689
1962	160	-	-	160	98007	-86175	3795	8037	3826	3826	-	-	101993	-86175	3795	12023
1963	193	-	-	193	109547	-96258	4140	9149	3872	3872	-	-	113612	-96258	4140	13214
1964	274	-	-	274	126009	-110469	4293	11247	4369	4369	-	-	130652	-110469	4293	15890
1965	275	-	-	275	140181	-120734	4742	14706	4409	4409	-	-	144865	-120734	4742	19390
IRAQ																
1950	-	2	-	2	9975	-8798	8	1170	-	-	-	-	9975	-8796	8	1172
1953	-	NA	-	NA	42279	-41109	-	1170	404	404	-	-	42683	-41109	-	1574
1955	-	-	-	-	50522	-48204	15	2303	418	418	-	-	50940	-48204	15	2721
1957	-	-	-	-	32856	-30354	30	2472	340	340	-	NA	33196	-30354	30	2812
1960	-	-	-	-	70922	-67805	30	3087	761	761	-	NA	71682	-67805	30	3848
1961	-	20	-	20	73239	-69873	30	3336	821	821	-	-	74060	-69853	30	4177
1962	-	-	-	-	73482	-70019	60	3404	848	848	-	NA	74330	-70019	60	4252
1963	-	-	-	-	84704	-81177	45	3482	959	959	-	NA	85663	-81177	45	4441
1964	-	-	-	-	92439	-88811	45	3584	1012	1012	-	NA	93451	-88811	45	4596
1965	-	-	-	-	96710	-92483	45	4182	1026	1026	-	NA	97735	-92483	45	5208
MIDDLE EAST - OTHER																
1925	673	111	110	674	-	498	267	231	-	-	2	2	675	609	377	907
1929	999	-119	137	743	-	953	596	357	-	-	2	2	1001	834	733	1102
1933	1312	-297	42	973	-	1227	854	374	-	-	2	2	1314	930	896	1349

Table XIV. SUMMARY OF ENERGY PRODUCTION, TRADE, AND CONSUMPTION, BY FUEL, SELECTED YEARS, 1925–1965

(Thousand metric tons coal equivalent)

Region, country, year	Solid fuels				Liquid fuels				Natural gas		Hydroelectric power		Total energy			
	Production	Net imports	Bunkers	Consumption	Production	Net imports	Bunkers	Consumption	Production	Consumption	Production	Consumption	Production	Net imports	Bunkers	Consumption
	(1)	(2)	(3)	(4)	(5)	(6)	(7)	(8)	(9)	(10)	(11)	(12)	(13)	(14)	(15)	(16)
MIDDLE EAST - OTHER (CONTINUED)																
1937	1653	126	114	1665	-	1755	1136	620	-	-	4	4	1658	1881	1250	2289
1938	1792	-8	57	1727	-	2069	1269	800	-	-	4	4	1797	2061	1326	2531
1950	3079	160	133	3106	26	7259	4350	2934	-	-	12	12	3116	7419	4483	6051
1953	3975	68	36	4007	39	9162	4730	4472	-	-	21	21	4035	9230	4766	8499
1955	3890	60	18	3932	270	11273	5259	6284	-	-	26	26	4186	11333	5277	10242
1957	4593	60	15	4638	528	10938	3762	7704	-	-	62	62	5183	10998	3777	12404
1960	4284	20	-	4304	756	14243	5910	9089	-	-	143	143	5182	14263	5910	13535
1961	4298	40	-	4338	866	14892	5865	9893	4	4	185	185	5352	14932	5865	14419
1962	4551	50	-	4601	1095	16851	5760	12186	15	15	177	177	5838	16901	5760	16979
1963	5001	20	-	5021	1344	18098	6503	12939	13	13	312	312	6670	18118	6503	18285
1964	5436	20	-	5456	1680	19820	6645	14855	39	39	259	259	7414	19840	6645	20608
1965	5411	25	-	5436	2603	20384	5652	17334	96	96	340	340	8449	20409	5652	23206
PALESTINE																
1925	-	22	-	22	-	42	-	42	-	-	-	-	-	64	-	64
1929	-	33	-	33	-	75	-	75	-	-	-	-	-	108	-	108
1933	-	58	-	58	-	116	-	116	-	-	-	-	-	174	-	174
1937	-	98	-	98	-	273	-	273	-	-	-	-	-	371	-	371
1938	-	58	-	58	-	234	-	234	-	-	-	-	-	292	-	292
ISRAEL																
1950	-	34	-	34	-	1097	89	1008	-	-	-	-	-	1131	89	1042
1953	-	29	-	29	-	1676	156	1520	-	-	-	-	-	1705	156	1549
1955	-	20	-	20	2	2394	120	2276	-	-	-	-	2	2414	120	2296
1957	-	40	-	40	81	2258	120	2219	-	-	-	-	81	2298	120	2259
1960	-	50	-	50	194	2748	165	2777	-	-	-	-	194	2798	165	2827
1961	-	40	-	40	203	3027	180	3050	4	4	-	-	206	3067	180	3093
1962	-	40	-	40	203	3414	180	3437	15	15	-	-	217	3454	180	3491
1963	-	20	-	20	227	3539	180	3585	13	13	-	-	240	3559	180	3618
1964	-	30	-	30	299	3884	177	4005	39	39	-	-	337	3914	177	4074
1965	-	15	-	15	305	5541	194	5652	96	96	-	-	400	5556	194	5763
JORDAN																
1950	-	-	-	-	-	86	-	86	-	-	-	-	-	86	-	86
1953	-	-	-	-	-	107	-	107	-	-	-	-	-	107	-	107
1955	-	-	-	-	-	189	-	189	-	-	-	-	-	189	-	189
1957	-	-	-	-	-	219	-	219	-	-	-	-	-	219	-	219
1960	-	-	-	-	-	332	-	332	-	-	-	-	-	332	-	332
1961	-	-	-	-	-	446	-	446	-	-	-	-	-	446	-	446
1962	-	-	-	-	-	494	-	494	-	-	-	-	-	494	-	494
1963	-	-	-	-	-	575	-	575	-	-	-	-	-	575	-	575
1964	-	-	-	-	-	581	-	581	-	-	-	-	-	581	-	581
1965	-	-	-	-	-	674	-	674	-	-	-	-	-	674	-	674
LEBANON																
1950	-	11	-	11	-	914	9	905	-	-	8	8	8	925	9	924
1953	-	-	-	-	-	1065	354	711	-	-	13	13	13	1065	354	724
1955	-	10	-	10	-	1010	375	635	-	-	14	14	14	1020	375	658
1957	-	10	-	10	-	1230	315	915	-	-	21	21	21	1240	315	946
1960	-	-	-	-	-	1391	240	1151	-	-	14	14	14	1391	240	1164
1961	-	-	-	-	-	1437	240	1197	-	-	22	22	22	1437	240	1219
1962	-	10	-	10	-	1550	240	1310	-	-	31	31	31	1560	240	1351
1963	-	10	-	10	-	1767	345	1422	-	-	44	44	44	1777	345	1476
1964	-	10	-	10	-	1959	333	1626	-	-	47	47	47	1969	333	1683
1965	-	10	-	10	-	2223	326	1897	-	-	63	63	63	2233	326	1971
SYRIA																
1950	-	2	-	2	-	338	8	330	-	-	-	-	-	340	8	332
1953	-	3	-	3	-	594	8	587	-	-	-	-	-	597	8	590
1955	-	-	-	-	-	753	-	753	-	-	1	1	1	753	-	754
1957	-	-	-	-	-	909	-	909	-	-	3	3	3	909	-	912
1960	-	-	-	-	-	1505	15	1490	-	-	4	4	4	1505	15	1493
1961	-	-	-	-	-	1431	15	1416	-	-	5	5	5	1431	15	1421
1962	-	-	-	-	-	1487	15	1472	-	-	5	5	5	1487	15	1477
1963	-	-	-	-	-	1667	8	1659	-	-	6	6	6	1667	8	1665
1964	-	-	-	-	-	2042	9	2033	-	-	6	6	6	2042	9	2038
1965	-	5	-	5	-	1704	8	1697	-	-	6	6	6	1709	8	1708

Table XIV. SUMMARY OF ENERGY PRODUCTION, TRADE, AND CONSUMPTION, BY FUEL, SELECTED YEARS, 1925-1965

(Thousand metric tons coal equivalent)

Region, country, year	Solid fuels				Liquid fuels				Natural gas		Hydroelectric power		Total energy			
	Production	Net imports	Bunkers	Consumption	Production	Net imports	Bunkers	Consumption	Production	Consumption	Production	Consumption	Production	Net imports	Bunkers	Consumption
	(1)	(2)	(3)	(4)	(5)	(6)	(7)	(8)	(9)	(10)	(11)	(12)	(13)	(14)	(15)	(16)
TURKEY																
1925	673	-79	NA	594	-	120	NA	120	-	-	-	-	673	41	NA	714
1929	999	-347	NA	652	-	161	NA	161	-	-	-	-	999	-187	NA	812
1933	1312	-473	NA	839	-	132	NA	132	-	-	-	-	1312	-341	NA	971
1937	1653	-253	NA	1400	-	201	NA	201	-	-	-	-	1653	-52	NA	1601
1938	1792	-255	NA	1537	-	248	NA	248	-	-	-	-	1792	-8	NA	1785
1950	3079	-	-	3079	26	908	98	836	-	-	4	4	3108	908	98	3918
1953	3975	-7	-	3968	39	1737	24	1752	-	-	8	8	4022	1730	24	5728
1955	3890	-	-	3890	269	1700	45	1923	-	-	11	11	4170	1700	45	5824
1957	4593	-	-	4593	447	1701	120	2028	-	-	39	39	5079	1701	120	6660
1960	4284	-30	-	4254	563	1872	60	2375	-	-	125	125	4971	1842	60	6753
1961	4298	-	-	4298	663	2193	60	2796	-	-	158	158	5119	2193	60	7252
1962	4551	-	-	4551	893	3177	90	3980	-	-	141	141	5584	3177	90	8671
1963	5001	-10	-	4991	1118	3714	150	4682	-	-	262	262	6381	3704	150	9935
1964	5436	-20	-	5416	1382	4151	171	5361	-	-	207	207	7024	4131	171	10984
1965	5411	-5	-	5406	2298	3938	180	6056	-	-	271	271	7980	3933	180	11732
FAR EAST AND OTHER ASIA																
1925	54076	918	5542	49452	7884	9	840	7053	485	485	995	995	63440	927	6382	57985
1929	60188	2216	5277	57127	11445	1425	1568	11303	686	686	1652	1652	73970	3641	6845	70767
1933	54689	2700	3890	53499	11663	1190	1470	11382	1204	1204	2266	2266	69822	3890	5360	68351
1937	74725	5159	4332	75552	14979	2501	1725	15755	1316	1316	3323	3323	94343	7660	6057	95945
1938	82169	4818	3796	83191	15360	2366	1905	15821	1413	1413	3578	3578	102519	7184	5701	104002
1950	69477	1263	1688	69052	17591	2991	3630	16952	1243	1243	5335	5335	93645	4254	5318	92581
1953	82456	4709	396	86769	24555	12147	6575	30128	2059	2059	5995	5995	115066	16856	6971	124951
1955	79472	3770	333	82909	28194	22040	7679	42555	2942	2937	7013	7013	117622	25804	8012	135414
1957	94877	7710	94	102493	34394	33140	10838	56696	4185	4180	8295	8295	141750	40844	10932	171663
1960	104838	9124	20	113942	41150	52128	13100	80178	5712	5712	9066	9066	160765	61252	13120	208897
1961	111892	11970	18	123844	41726	72348	16530	97544	6330	6330	10574	10574	170521	84318	16548	238291
1962	117860	12800	8	130652	44558	83291	17933	109916	7335	7330	10144	10144	179896	96085	17941	258041
1963	121322	11770	6	133086	44262	105249	20096	129416	8533	8521	11298	11298	185415	117007	20102	282320
1964	118186	13715	5	131896	45858	125634	22680	148812	9465	9465	11662	11662	185172	139349	22685	301836
1965	121255	17660	4	138911	49139	143040	25214	166965	10109	10037	12119	12119	192621	160628	25218	328031
BORNEO (FORMER BRITISH)																
1950	-	-	-	-	6261	-5970	83	209	69	69	-	-	6330	-5970	83	278
1953	-	-	-	-	7397	-7046	185	167	79	79	-	-	7475	-7046	185	245
1955	-	-	-	-	8066	-7512	210	344	103	97	-	-	8168	-7517	210	441
1957	-	-	-	-	8528	-8013	224	291	256	250	-	-	8783	-8018	224	541
1960	-	-	-	-	7064	-6588	240	236	286	286	-	-	7350	-6588	240	522
1961	-	-	-	-	6372	-5780	180	413	280	280	-	-	6652	-5780	180	692
1962	-	-	-	-	5873	-5511	135	227	278	273	-	-	6151	-5516	135	500
1963	-	-	-	-	5337	-4904	105	329	264	252	-	-	5601	-4915	105	580
1964	-	-	-	-	5489	-4935	87	467	230	230	-	-	5719	-4935	87	697
1965	-	-	-	-	6063	-5288	62	714	281	209	-	-	6344	-5359	62	923
BURMA (1949-1965)																
1950	-	NA	-	NA	105	165	14	257	-	-	-	-	105	165	14	256
1953	-	251	-	251	212	165	15	362	-	-	-	-	212	416	15	613
1955	7	200	-	207	317	228	15	530	4	4	-	-	327	428	15	740
1957	1	280	-	281	593	126	30	689	8	8	-	-	601	406	30	977
1960	1	350	-	351	818	101	60	858	28	28	20	20	866	451	60	1257
1961	2	260	-	262	846	135	45	936	20	20	23	23	891	395	45	1241
1962	3	340	-	343	876	138	45	969	24	24	27	27	929	478	45	1362
1963	3	210	-	213	957	78	45	990	21	21	30	30	1011	288	45	1254
1964	10	215	-	225	837	237	45	1029	13	13	35	35	895	452	45	1302
1965	10	140	-	150	813	263	47	1029	13	13	35	35	871	403	47	1227
CEYLON																
1925	-	827	813	14	-	309	207	102	-	-	-	-	-	1136	1020	116
1929	-	827	515	312	-	437	263	174	-	-	-	-	-	1264	778	486
1933	-	412	221	191	-	513	357	156	-	-	-	-	-	925	578	347
1937	-	582	330	252	-	621	404	218	-	-	-	-	-	1203	734	470
1938	-	391	229	162	-	738	552	186	-	-	-	-	-	1129	781	348
1950	-	374	82	292	-	1170	873	297	-	-	1	1	1	1544	955	590
1953	-	390	22	368	-	1259	759	500	-	-	14	14	14	1649	781	882
1955	-	190	14	176	-	1419	723	696	-	-	16	16	16	1609	737	888
1957	-	280	9	271	-	2088	954	1134	-	-	19	19	19	2368	963	1424
1960	-	260	-	260	-	1337	720	617	-	-	34	34	34	1597	720	911
1961	-	140	-	140	-	1581	615	966	-	-	35	35	35	1721	615	1141

Table XIV. SUMMARY OF ENERGY PRODUCTION, TRADE, AND CONSUMPTION, BY FUEL, SELECTED YEARS, 1925-1965

(Thousand metric tons coal equivalent)

Region, country, year	Solid fuels: Production	Solid fuels: Net imports	Solid fuels: Bunkers	Solid fuels: Consumption	Liquid fuels: Production	Liquid fuels: Net imports	Liquid fuels: Bunkers	Liquid fuels: Consumption	Natural gas: Production	Natural gas: Consumption	Hydroelectric power: Production	Hydroelectric power: Consumption	Total energy: Production	Total energy: Net imports	Total energy: Bunkers	Total energy: Consumption
	(1)	(2)	(3)	(4)	(5)	(6)	(7)	(8)	(9)	(10)	(11)	(12)	(13)	(14)	(15)	(16)
CEYLON (CONTINUED)																
1962	-	140	1	139	-	1556	480	1076	-	-	40	40	40	1696	481	1255
1963	-	150	-	150	-	1364	300	1064	-	-	41	41	41	1514	300	1254
1964	-	180	-	180	-	1259	387	872	-	-	42	42	42	1439	387	1094
1965	-	140	-	140	-	1523	404	1119	-	-	42	42	42	1663	404	1301
HONG KONG																
1925	-	960	457	503	-	386	135	251	-	-	-	-	-	1346	592	754
1929	-	642	448	194	-	272	155	117	-	-	-	-	-	914	603	311
1933	-	767	534	233	-	162	74	89	-	-	-	-	-	929	608	322
1937	-	879	451	428	-	213	110	104	-	-	-	-	-	1092	561	532
1938	-	696	412	284	-	282	108	174	-	-	-	-	-	978	520	458
1950	-	271	20	251	-	734	318	416	-	-	-	-	-	1005	338	667
1953	-	204	-	204	-	974	329	645	-	-	-	-	-	1178	329	849
1955	-	250	-	250	-	1238	525	713	-	-	-	-	-	1488	525	963
1957	-	250	-	250	-	1607	660	947	-	-	-	-	-	1857	660	1197
1960	-	230	-	230	-	1841	615	1226	-	-	-	-	-	2071	615	1456
1961	-	240	-	240	-	2016	615	1401	-	-	-	-	-	2256	615	1641
1962	-	220	-	220	-	2289	720	1569	-	-	-	-	-	2509	720	1789
1963	-	200	-	200	-	2631	765	1866	-	-	-	-	-	2831	765	2066
1964	-	180	-	180	-	2741	875	1866	-	-	-	-	-	2921	875	2046
1965	-	170	-	170	-	3084	954	2130	-	-	-	-	-	3254	954	2300
INDIA																
1925	16991	276	1069	16198	1802	1013	NA	2814	-	-	24	24	18816	1289	1069	19036
1929	19036	-516	948	17572	1802	1463	NA	3264	-	-	63	63	20900	947	948	20899
1933	16488	-364	516	15608	1842	1113	83	2873	-	-	102	102	18432	749	599	18582
1937	20859	-561	684	19614	2112	1634	105	3641	-	-	141	141	23112	1073	789	23395
1938	23614	-859	779	21976	2117	1557	104	3570	-	-	150	150	25881	698	883	25696
1950	26269	-932	235	25102	384	4454	80	4758	-	-	315	315	26968	3522	315	30175
1953	29258	-1975	167	27116	407	5034	320	5121	-	-	366	366	30030	3059	487	32603
1955	31080	-1540	139	29401	519	6695	476	6738	-	-	469	469	32068	5155	615	36608
1957	35366	-1690	20	33656	644	8874	795	8723	170	170	635	635	36816	7184	815	43185
1960	42089	-1350	10	40729	674	10884	735	10823	185	185	981	981	43928	9534	745	52717
1961	44871	-930	8	43933	765	11538	705	11598	143	143	1228	1228	47007	10608	713	56902
1962	49159	-1060	7	48092	1616	12570	720	13466	285	285	1439	1439	52499	11510	727	63282
1963	53065	-870	6	52189	2480	12651	720	14411	357	357	1708	1708	57609	11781	726	68664
1964	50423	-1250	5	49168	3318	12599	696	15221	429	429	1964	1964	56133	11349	701	66781
1965	54419	-930	4	53485	4533	12999	882	16650	533	533	2159	2159	61643	12069	886	72826
INDO-CHINA																
1925	1365	-665	-	700	-	99	-	99	-	-	-	-	1365	-566	-	799
1929	1950	-1309	-	641	-	176	-	176	-	-	-	-	1950	-1134	-	817
1933	1568	-1247	-	321	-	131	-	131	-	-	-	-	1568	-1117	-	452
1937	2308	-1511	25	772	-	141	-	141	-	-	-	-	2308	-1370	25	913
1938	2332	-1518	44	770	-	156	-	156	-	-	-	-	2332	-1362	44	926
1950	497	-47	-	450	-	189	9	180	-	-	-	-	497	142	9	630
1953	887	-300	-	587	-	525	30	495	-	-	-	-	887	225	30	1082
1955	-	30	-	30	-	543	-	543	-	-	1	1	1	573	-	574
1957	12	50	-	62	-	735	-	735	-	-	-	-	12	785	-	797
1960	27	10	-	37	-	960	50	911	-	-	1	1	28	970	50	948
1961	57	10	-	67	-	1097	60	1037	-	-	1	1	58	1107	60	1105
1962	71	20	-	91	-	1103	38	1065	-	-	1	1	72	1123	38	1157
1963	104	10	-	114	-	1278	41	1238	-	-	1	1	105	1288	41	1353
1964	77	20	-	97	-	1232	39	1193	-	-	5	5	82	1252	39	1295
1965	75	45	-	120	-	1460	44	1416	-	-	7	7	82	1505	44	1543
CAMBODIA																
1955	-	-	-	-	-	84	-	84	-	-	-	-	-	84	-	84
1957	-	-	-	-	-	128	-	128	-	-	-	-	-	128	-	128
1960	-	-	-	-	-	168	5	164	-	-	-	-	-	168	5	164
1961	-	-	-	-	-	215	15	200	-	-	-	-	-	215	15	200
1962	-	-	-	-	-	230	15	215	-	-	-	-	-	230	15	215
1963	-	-	-	-	-	297	15	282	-	-	-	-	-	297	15	282
1964	-	-	-	-	-	263	15	248	-	-	-	-	-	263	15	248
1965	-	30	-	30	-	267	17	251	-	-	-	-	-	297	17	281

Table XIV. SUMMARY OF ENERGY PRODUCTION, TRADE, AND CONSUMPTION, BY FUEL, SELECTED YEARS, 1925-1965

(Thousand metric tons coal equivalent)

Region, country, year	Solid fuels				Liquid fuels				Natural gas		Hydroelectric power		Total energy			
	Production	Net imports	Bunkers	Consumption	Production	Net imports	Bunkers	Consumption	Production	Consumption	Production	Consumption	Production	Net imports	Bunkers	Consumption
	(1)	(2)	(3)	(4)	(5)	(6)	(7)	(8)	(9)	(10)	(11)	(12)	(13)	(14)	(15)	(16)
LAOS																
1955	-	-	-	-	-	14	-	14	-	-	-	-	-	14	-	14
1957	-	-	-	-	-	29	-	29	-	-	-	-	-	29	-	29
1960	-	-	-	-	-	42	-	42	-	-	-	-	-	42	-	42
1961	-	-	-	-	-	57	-	57	-	-	-	-	-	57	-	57
1962	-	-	-	-	-	66	-	66	-	-	-	-	-	66	-	66
1963	-	-	-	-	-	77	-	77	-	-	-	-	-	77	-	77
1964	-	-	-	-	-	90	-	90	-	-	-	-	-	90	-	90
1965	-	-	-	-	-	87	-	87	-	-	-	-	-	87	-	87
VIETNAM, SOUTH																
1955	-	30	-	30	-	446	-	446	-	-	1	1	1	476	-	476
1957	12	50	-	62	-	579	-	579	-	-	-	-	12	629	-	641
1960	27	10	-	37	-	750	45	705	-	-	1	1	28	760	45	743
1961	57	10	-	67	-	825	45	780	-	-	1	1	58	835	45	848
1962	71	20	-	91	-	807	23	785	-	-	1	1	72	827	23	877
1963	104	10	-	114	-	905	26	879	-	-	1	1	105	915	26	994
1964	77	20	-	97	-	879	24	855	-	-	5	5	82	899	24	957
1965	75	15	-	90	-	1106	27	1079	-	-	7	7	82	1121	27	1176
INDONESIA																
1925	1401	-202	135	1064	4758	-3081	131	1547	425	425	11	11	6595	-3283	266	3046
1929	1832	-329	113	1390	8076	-4853	416	2808	555	555	13	13	10476	-5182	529	4766
1933	1035	-209	9	817	8588	-5787	501	2300	1050	1050	20	20	10692	-5996	510	4186
1937	1373	-236	22	1115	11151	-7967	509	2676	1177	1177	26	26	13728	-8203	531	4995
1938	1457	-244	39	1174	11337	-8180	453	2705	1268	1268	29	29	14091	-8424	492	5176
1950	804	-35	-	769	10136	-6605	495	3036	1054	1054	38	38	12031	-6640	495	4896
1953	897	-77	3	817	15731	-9935	1142	4655	1820	1820	57	57	18504	-10012	1145	7348
1955	814	-20	-	794	18396	-9251	783	8363	2541	2541	71	71	21823	-9271	783	11769
1957	717	-	-	717	23700	-14145	807	8748	2888	2888	78	78	27382	-14145	807	12430
1960	658	20	-	678	31266	-21750	720	8796	3238	3238	101	101	35263	-21730	720	12813
1961	549	30	-	579	32177	-20804	1020	10353	3411	3411	97	97	36234	-20774	1020	14440
1962	471	20	-	491	34362	-25131	675	8556	3612	3612	89	89	38535	-25111	675	12749
1963	591	10	-	601	33572	-24516	630	8426	3727	3727	89	89	37979	-24506	630	12843
1964	446	10	-	456	34427	-26594	632	7202	3903	3903	89	89	38864	-26584	632	11649
1965	281	5	-	286	35888	NA	671	8967	4009	4009	89	89	40267	-26245	671	13351
JAPAN																
1925	31544	-963	2419	28162	393	953	6	1340	31	31	951	951	32918	-11	2425	30483
1929	34328	1192	2497	33023	405	3174	9	3570	39	39	1550	1550	36321	4366	2506	38181
1933	32582	2170	2019	32733	294	4496	11	4779	63	63	2014	2014	34953	6666	2030	39589
1937	45319	4269	2088	47500	525	6440	59	6906	71	71	2785	2785	48699	10709	2147	57261
1938	48755	5019	1594	52180	530	6753	74	7209	68	68	2968	2968	52320	11772	1668	62425
1950	39103	324	1296	38131	443	2762	389	2816	88	88	4782	4782	44415	3086	1685	45816
1953	47299	4435	164	51570	450	12084	1032	11502	135	135	5220	5220	53104	16519	1196	68427
1955	43142	2450	131	45461	477	15995	1752	14720	208	208	6068	6068	49895	18445	1883	66457
1957	52601	6380	37	58944	486	26805	3348	23943	438	438	7086	7086	60611	33185	3385	90411
1960	51809	8260	10	60059	798	47978	6240	42536	1098	1098	7309	7309	61013	56238	6250	111001
1961	55175	11260	10	66425	995	63129	8790	55334	1401	1401	8495	8495	66065	74389	8800	131654
1962	54991	11960	-	66951	1157	73838	10065	64929	1821	1821	7797	7797	65765	85798	10065	141497
1963	52546	11030	-	63576	1206	92925	12315	81816	2512	2512	8646	8646	64910	103955	12315	156550
1964	51309	13150	-	64459	1026	111351	14688	97689	2761	2761	8620	8620	63715	124501	14688	173528
1965	49855	17030	-	66885	1025	125484	16281	110228	2688	2688	8842	8842	62409	142514	16281	188642
KOREA																
1925	622	479	-	1101	-	78	-	78	-	-	-	-	622	557	-	1179
1929	938	630	-	1568	-	167	-	167	-	-	-	-	938	797	-	1735
1933	1307	621	-	1928	-	191	-	191	-	-	67	67	1374	812	-	2186
1937	2431	1044	-	3475	-	551	-	551	-	-	261	261	2692	1595	-	4286
1938	3419	987	-	4406	-	534	-	534	-	-	305	305	3724	1521	-	5245
KOREA, REPUBLIC OF																
1950	572	219	-	791	-	150	29	122	-	-	12	12	585	369	29	925
1953	867	643	15	1495	-	495	-	495	-	-	49	49	916	1138	15	2039
1955	1308	1060	30	2338	-	546	-	546	-	-	60	60	1368	1606	30	2944
1957	2441	740	10	3171	-	711	-	711	-	-	52	52	2493	1451	10	3934
1960	5350	100	-	5450	-	1043	15	1028	-	-	73	73	5423	1143	15	6550
1961	5884	50	-	5934	-	1136	15	1121	-	-	82	82	5966	1186	15	7136

Table XIV. SUMMARY OF ENERGY PRODUCTION, TRADE, AND CONSUMPTION, BY FUEL, SELECTED YEARS, 1925-1965

(Thousand metric tons coal equivalent)

Region, country, year	Solid fuels				Liquid fuels				Natural gas		Hydroelectric power		Total energy			
	Production	Net imports	Bunkers	Consumption	Production	Net imports	Bunkers	Consumption	Production	Consumption	Production	Consumption	Production	Net imports	Bunkers	Consumption
	(1)	(2)	(3)	(4)	(5)	(6)	(7)	(8)	(9)	(10)	(11)	(12)	(13)	(14)	(15)	(16)
KOREA, REPUBLIC OF (CONTINUED)																
1962	7444	-120	-	7324	-	1532	15	1517	-	-	88	88	7532	1412	15	8928
1963	8858	-130	-	8728	-	2058	15	2043	-	-	91	91	8949	1928	15	10862
1964	9622	-80	-	9542	-	1937	21	1916	-	-	94	94	9716	1857	21	11551
1965	10248	-90	-	10158	-	2358	27	2331	-	-	89	89	10337	2268	27	12578
MALAYA AND SINGAPORE																
1925	299	633	465	467	-	537	197	341	-	-	3	3	301	1170	662	810
1929	484	849	572	761	-	933	423	510	-	-	5	5	489	1782	995	1276
1933	160	563	358	365	-	476	242	234	-	-	12	12	172	1039	600	611
1937	459	744	394	809	-	950	311	639	-	-	29	29	489	1694	705	1478
1938	350	485	349	486	-	750	350	401	-	-	29	29	379	1235	699	915
1950	304	101	45	360	-	2078	924	1154	-	-	32	32	335	2179	969	1545
1953	210	89	15	284	-	4247	2211	2036	-	-	32	32	241	4336	2226	2351
1955	150	70	9	211	-	5192	2700	2492	-	-	29	29	180	5262	2709	2732
1957	112	90	8	194	-	5846	3420	2426	-	-	31	31	143	5936	3428	2650
1960	5	4	-	9	-	5388	2970	2418	-	-	24	24	29	5392	2970	2451
1961	-	60	-	60	-	6731	3690	3041	-	-	27	27	27	6791	3690	3128
1962	-	40	-	40	-	7409	4095	3314	-	-	29	29	29	7449	4095	3383
1963	-	40	-	40	-	6369	4110	2259	-	-	40	40	40	6409	4110	2339
1964	-	40	-	40	-	8597	3918	4679	-	-	68	68	68	8637	3918	4787
1965	-	25	-	25	-	8588	4530	4058	-	-	73	73	73	8613	4530	4156
PAKISTAN																
1950	355	1025	10	1370	257	1380	285	1352	-	NA	8	8	620	2405	295	2730
1953	474	1211	10	1675	356	1572	270	1658	-	-	30	30	860	2783	280	3363
1955	430	1080	10	1500	414	1937	255	2096	52	52	50	50	946	3017	265	3697
1957	419	1330	10	1739	441	2264	270	2435	386	386	65	65	1311	3594	280	4625
1960	665	1410	-	2075	528	3105	420	3213	843	843	85	85	2121	4515	420	6216
1961	737	1070	-	1807	567	3309	450	3426	1026	1026	118	118	2447	4379	450	6376
1962	796	1360	-	2156	671	3596	480	3786	1264	1264	175	175	2906	4956	480	7381
1963	994	1200	-	2194	705	4155	510	4350	1584	1584	196	196	3479	5355	510	8324
1964	971	1340	-	2311	749	4520	566	4703	1903	1903	228	228	3851	5860	566	9145
1965	985	1100	-	2085	789	4710	524	4976	2171	2171	246	246	4191	5810	524	9477
PHILIPPINES																
1925	49	472	NA	521	-	459	NA	459	-	-	5	5	54	931	NA	985
1929	17	603	NA	620	-	537	NA	537	-	-	6	6	23	1140	NA	1163
1933	16	273	NA	289	-	552	NA	552	-	-	8	8	24	825	NA	849
1937	22	266	NA	288	-	659	NA	659	-	-	10	10	32	925	NA	956
1938	41	259	NA	300	-	701	NA	701	-	-	11	11	52	960	NA	1011
1950	159	7	-	166	-	1896	123	1773	-	-	24	24	183	1903	123	1963
1953	155	5	-	160	-	1982	264	1718	-	-	42	42	197	1987	264	1919
1955	130	10	-	140	-	2880	135	2745	-	-	54	54	184	2890	135	2939
1957	191	10	-	201	-	3323	150	3173	-	-	80	80	271	3333	150	3454
1960	148	10	-	158	-	3984	75	3909	-	-	165	165	313	3994	75	4232
1961	152	10	-	162	-	4148	90	4058	-	-	161	161	313	4158	90	4381
1962	163	10	-	173	-	4949	105	4844	-	-	169	169	332	4959	105	5185
1963	157	10	-	167	-	5573	135	5438	-	-	193	193	350	5583	135	5797
1964	115	10	-	125	-	6422	284	6138	-	-	200	200	315	6432	284	6463
1965	95	10	-	105	-	6917	390	6527	-	-	189	189	284	6927	390	6820
TAIWAN																
1925	1705	-888	184	633	6	27	-	33	29	29	2	2	1742	-861	184	697
1929	1530	-378	184	968	17	80	-	96	92	92	16	16	1654	-299	184	1172
1933	1533	-305	233	995	17	98	-	114	89	89	44	44	1682	-208	233	1242
1937	1953	-367	338	1248	6	182	-	188	40	40	71	71	2070	-186	338	1547
1938	2199	-455	350	1394	6	201	-	207	37	37	87	87	2329	-254	350	1725
1950	1405	-64	-	1341	6	230	-	236	32	32	122	122	1564	166	-	1730
1953	2393	-211	-	2182	5	102	-	107	27	27	183	183	2607	-109	-	2498
1955	2359	-50	-	2309	6	986	90	902	35	35	191	191	2591	936	90	3437
1957	2916	-30	-	2886	3	1254	75	1182	39	39	242	242	3200	1224	75	4349
1960	3962	-190	-	3772	3	1629	105	1527	33	33	258	258	4256	1439	105	5590
1961	4322	-240	-	4082	5	1677	90	1592	49	49	292	292	4668	1437	90	6015
1962	4554	-130	-	4424	5	1892	90	1806	51	51	270	270	4879	1762	90	6551
1963	4810	-100	-	4710	6	2244	135	2115	68	68	241	241	5125	2144	135	7134
1964	5028	-110	-	4918	14	1907	158	1763	225	225	295	295	5561	1797	158	7200
1965	5054	5	-	5059	29	2685	251	2463	413	413	323	323	5819	2690	251	8258

Table XIV. SUMMARY OF ENERGY PRODUCTION, TRADE, AND CONSUMPTION, BY FUEL, SELECTED YEARS, 1925-1965

(Thousand metric tons coal equivalent)

Region, country, year	Solid fuels				Liquid fuels				Natural gas		Hydroelectric power		Total energy			
	Production	Net imports	Bunkers	Consumption	Production	Net imports	Bunkers	Consumption	Production	Consumption	Production	Consumption	Production	Net imports	Bunkers	Consumption
	(1)	(2)	(3)	(4)	(5)	(6)	(7)	(8)	(9)	(10)	(11)	(12)	(13)	(14)	(15)	(16)
THAILAND																
1925	-	38	NA	38	-	63	NA	63	-	-	-	-	-	101	NA	101
1929	-	52	NA	52	-	144	NA	144	-	-	-	-	-	196	NA	196
1933	-	23	NA	23	-	116	NA	116	-	-	-	-	-	139	NA	139
1937	-	50	NA	50	-	168	NA	168	-	-	-	-	-	218	NA	218
1938	-	56	NA	56	-	176	NA	176	-	-	-	-	-	232	NA	232
1950	-	20	-	20	-	360	11	350	-	-	-	-	-	380	11	370
1953	1	44	-	45	-	690	20	671	-	-	-	-	1	734	20	715
1955	29	40	-	69	-	1074	15	1059	-	-	-	-	29	1114	15	1128
1957	70	20	-	90	-	1364	60	1304	-	-	-	-	70	1384	60	1394
1960	76	10	-	86	-	1745	90	1655	-	-	-	-	76	1755	90	1740
1961	76	-	-	76	-	1917	120	1797	-	-	-	-	76	1917	120	1873
1962	95	-	-	95	-	2427	210	2217	-	-	-	-	95	2427	210	2312
1963	96	-	-	96	-	2661	195	2466	-	-	-	-	96	2661	195	2562
1964	73	-	-	73	-	3630	210	3420	-	-	-	-	73	3630	210	3493
1965	88	-	-	88	-	3689	54	3635	-	-	-	-	88	3689	54	3722
AFRICA																
1925	13347	2696	3268	12775	273	1271	387	1157	-	-	8	8	13628	3967	3655	13940
1929	14544	3903	3709	14738	413	2580	593	2400	-	-	10	10	14967	6483	4302	17148
1933	11530	3040	1979	12591	360	3443	1289	2514	-	-	28	28	11918	6483	3268	15133
1937	17064	3751	2497	18318	260	6584	2650	4194	-	-	58	58	17381	10335	5147	22570
1938	17884	3301	2145	19040	351	5733	1783	4302	-	-	61	61	18296	9034	3928	23403
1950	30051	-886	698	28467	4022	13439	4073	13388	-	5	171	171	34243	12558	4771	42030
1953	33131	-249	130	32752	4380	17789	5770	16400	7	7	256	255	37774	17539	5900	49414
1955	37646	424	64	38006	3035	23150	5819	20366	16	16	407	407	41103	23574	5883	58794
1957	40912	424	48	41288	4062	25442	8196	21308	12	12	599	510	45585	25777	8244	63118
1960	43281	-117	3	43161	20826	12381	7005	26202	40	40	911	838	65058	12192	7008	70241
1961	44132	-179	1	43952	35760	-572	7776	27413	337	337	1166	1168	81395	-749	7777	72869
1962	45541	-810	1	44730	58664	-21953	8021	28691	507	507	1317	1319	106029	-22761	8022	75247
1963	46594	-750	-	45844	86015	-48239	8247	29529	623	623	1383	1384	134615	-48988	8247	77380
1964	49441	-395	-	49046	123990	-80987	8756	34248	1193	1074	1515	1514	176140	-81503	8756	85881
1965	53511	-515	1	52995	161162	-115800	8845	36518	2569	1460	1651	1650	218893	-117426	8846	92622
NORTH AFRICA																
1925	10	3296	1049	2257	273	584	NA	695	-	-	3	3	286	3880	NA	2954
1929	16	4222	1576	2662	413	1143	NA	1397	-	-	5	5	433	5365	NA	4063
1933	57	3220	1001	2276	360	1847	NA	1736	-	-	11	11	428	5067	NA	4022
1937	121	3321	880	2562	260	2417	NA	1931	-	-	21	21	401	5738	NA	4513
1938	136	3222	672	2686	344	2529	NA	2132	-	-	21	21	500	5751	NA	4838
1950	640	790	116	1314	3968	5504	1484	7988	-	5	52	52	4659	6299	1600	9358
1953	860	284	42	1102	4325	6425	1562	9188	7	7	69	69	5260	6708	1604	10365
1955	769	300	27	1042	2979	9426	1536	10869	16	16	139	137	3903	9724	1563	12064
1957	757	590	13	1334	3749	7848	1431	10166	12	12	152	151	4670	8437	1444	11662
1960	531	480	1	1010	18134	-2961	1635	13538	31	31	198	198	18893	-2481	1636	14776
1961	488	490	-	978	30870	-15441	2085	13344	328	328	279	281	31965	-14949	2085	14931
1962	423	340	-	763	51540	-35667	2055	13818	493	493	309	311	52764	-35325	2055	15384
1963	442	290	-	732	77658	-62079	2241	13338	558	558	331	332	78989	-61788	2241	14960
1964	446	590	-	1036	111990	-94679	2214	15098	1104	984	391	391	113931	-94208	2214	17509
1965	464	470	-	934	137870	-120081	2144	15645	2475	1365	419	419	141227	-120720	2144	18363
ALGERIA																
1925	10	1532	963	579	3	110	NA	113	-	-	3	3	16	1642	963	694
1929	16	2383	1513	886	5	258	NA	263	-	-	3	3	23	2641	1513	1151
1933	30	1585	942	673	2	656	312	345	-	-	3	3	35	2241	1254	1021
1937	14	1472	814	672	-	993	660	333	-	-	5	5	19	2465	1474	1010
1938	13	1295	617	691	-	1004	659	345	-	-	5	5	18	2299	1276	1041
1950	258	455	75	638	5	1655	807	852	-	5	16	16	279	2115	882	1512
1953	295	180	39	436	128	2115	1088	1155	-	-	28	28	451	2295	1127	1619
1955	302	270	26	546	87	2549	1064	1572	-	-	36	35	425	2817	1090	2153
1957	236	480	13	703	32	2913	1034	1911	-	-	41	40	308	3392	1047	2654
1960	119	350	1	468	13002	-9095	765	3143	9	9	44	45	13174	-8743	766	3665
1961	78	210	-	288	23694	-20016	780	2898	308	308	32	32	24111	-19805	780	3526
1962	53	100	-	153	31050	-28724	465	1862	470	470	32	33	31605	-28623	465	2518
1963	38	50	-	88	35823	-33447	585	1791	533	533	32	33	36426	-33397	585	2444
1964	46	70	-	116	39791	-37329	533	1929	1078	958	36	36	40950	-37379	533	3038
1965	45	20	-	65	39819	-37278	473	2069	2450	1340	50	50	42364	-38368	473	3523
EGYPT UAR																
1925	-	1403	86	1317	270	359	162	467	-	-	-	-	270	1762	248	1784

Table XIV. SUMMARY OF ENERGY PRODUCTION, TRADE, AND CONSUMPTION, BY FUEL, SELECTED YEARS, 1925-1965

(Thousand metric tons coal equivalent)

Region, country, year	Solid fuels				Liquid fuels				Natural gas		Hydroelectric power		Total energy			
	Production	Net imports	Bunkers	Consumption	Production	Net imports	Bunkers	Consumption	Production	Consumption	Production	Consumption	Production	Net imports	Bunkers	Consumption
	(1)	(2)	(3)	(4)	(5)	(6)	(7)	(8)	(9)	(10)	(11)	(12)	(13)	(14)	(15)	(16)
EGYPT UAR (CONTINUED)																
1929	-	1380	63	1317	408	599	159	848	-	-	-	-	408	1979	222	2165
1933	-	1189	59	1130	357	828	159	1026	-	-	-	-	357	2017	218	2156
1937	-	1500	66	1434	257	990	86	1161	-	-	-	-	257	2490	152	2595
1938	-	1601	55	1546	339	1004	83	1260	-	-	-	-	339	2605	138	2806
1950	-	217	38	179	3905	2616	503	6018	-	-	1	1	3905	2833	541	6198
1953	-	78	2	76	4044	2325	195	6174	-	-	1	1	4045	2403	197	6251
1955	-	110	1	109	2738	4631	203	7166	-	-	1	1	2738	4741	204	7275
1957	-	180	-	180	3605	2871	23	6453	-	-	1	1	3605	3051	23	6634
1960	-	160	-	160	4994	3690	555	8129	-	-	33	33	5026	3850	555	8321
1961	-	300	-	300	5742	3095	975	7862	-	-	127	127	5869	3395	975	8288
1962	-	270	-	270	7028	2664	1275	8417	-	-	147	147	7174	2934	1275	8833
1963	-	270	-	270	8399	1607	1320	8685	-	-	160	160	8559	1877	1320	9115
1964	-	500	-	500	9542	1668	1353	9857	-	-	209	209	9750	2168	1353	10565
1965	-	440	-	440	9738	1581	1341	9978	-	-	219	219	9957	2021	1341	10637
MOROCCO																
1925	-	121	NA	121	-	54	NA	54	-	-	-	-	-	175	NA	175
1929	-	181	NA	181	-	141	NA	141	-	-	2	2	2	322	NA	324
1933	27	194	NA	221	2	174	NA	176	-	-	7	7	36	368	NA	404
1937	107	87	NA	194	3	206	NA	209	-	-	16	16	126	293	NA	419
1938	123	33	NA	156	5	267	NA	272	-	-	15	15	143	300	NA	443
1950	368	-55	-	313	59	743	78	723	-	-	35	35	461	688	78	1071
1953	565	-58	-	507	153	1272	156	1269	7	7	40	40	764	1214	156	1822
1955	467	-190	-	277	155	1278	120	1313	11	11	103	101	735	1087	120	1701
1957	521	-190	-	331	113	1095	195	1013	4	4	107	107	745	905	195	1455
1960	412	-100	-	312	138	1235	150	1223	12	12	116	115	678	1133	150	1662
1961	410	-110	-	300	120	1307	150	1277	11	11	119	120	660	1198	150	1707
1962	370	-80	-	290	191	894	135	950	13	13	128	129	701	815	135	1381
1963	404	-80	-	324	225	1302	150	1377	16	16	135	135	780	1222	150	1852
1964	400	-20	-	380	180	1398	134	1445	16	16	142	142	737	1378	134	1982
1965	419	-50	-	369	155	1607	141	1620	15	15	145	145	733	1557	141	2149
TUNISIA																
1925	-	223	NA	223	-	47	NA	47	-	-	-	-	-	270	NA	270
1929	-	257	NA	257	-	120	NA	120	-	-	-	-	-	377	NA	377
1933	-	215	NA	215	-	140	NA	140	-	-	-	-	-	355	NA	355
1937	-	218	NA	218	-	155	NA	155	-	-	-	-	-	373	NA	373
1938	-	238	NA	238	-	159	NA	159	-	-	-	-	-	397	NA	397
1950	14	173	3	184	-	345	35	311	-	-	-	-	14	518	38	494
1953	-	84	1	83	-	512	30	482	-	-	-	-	-	596	31	565
1955	-	40	-	40	-	663	45	618	5	5	-	-	5	703	45	663
1957	-	90	-	90	-	570	45	525	8	8	3	3	11	660	45	626
1960	-	40	-	40	-	693	30	663	9	9	6	6	15	733	30	718
1961	-	50	-	50	-	728	45	683	9	9	2	2	12	778	45	744
1962	-	40	-	40	-	761	45	716	9	9	2	2	12	801	45	767
1963	-	40	-	40	-	950	51	899	9	9	4	4	13	990	51	952
1964	-	40	-	40	-	1137	57	1080	11	11	5	5	15	1177	57	1135
1965	-	50	-	50	-	1049	51	998	11	11	5	5	16	1099	51	1063
TROPICAL AFRICA																
1925	1015	997	438	1574	-	494	225	269	-	-	6	6	1021	1491	663	1848
1929	1510	1333	559	2284	-	867	377	491	-	-	6	6	1516	2200	936	2780
1933	759	602	152	1209	-	986	752	234	-	-	17	17	776	1588	904	1460
1937	1453	1224	473	2204	-	2709	1608	1101	-	-	37	37	1490	3933	2081	3342
1938	1464	956	332	2088	-	1578	654	924	-	-	41	41	1505	2534	986	3053
1950	2938	870	195	3613	-	4490	1788	2702	-	-	119	119	3057	5360	1983	6433
1953	3812	651	9	4454	-	7595	3512	4083	-	-	187	187	3999	8246	3521	8724
1955	4730	684	3	5411	-	9036	3573	5463	-	-	267	270	4997	9723	3576	11144
1957	5386	384	1	5769	276	11517	4869	6924	-	-	447	359	6109	11814	4870	13052
1960	4565	363	-	4928	2655	9869	4770	7754	9	9	713	640	7942	10159	4770	13331
1961	4078	391	-	4469	4881	8759	4926	8714	9	9	886	886	9855	9150	4926	14078
1962	3837	450	-	4287	7124	7238	5216	9146	15	15	1008	1008	11983	7688	5216	14455
1963	3696	310	-	4006	8357	7068	5151	10274	65	65	1052	1052	13170	7378	5151	15397
1964	4089	295	-	4384	12000	4995	5265	11730	89	89	1125	1123	17303	5288	5265	17326
1965	4603	215	1	4817	23292	-4956	5537	12800	95	95	1232	1231	29222	-4742	5538	18942
CONGO, DEMOCRATIC REPUBLIC																
1925	65	294	-	359	-	21	-	21	-	-	4	4	69	315	-	384
1929	117	466	-	583	-	63	-	63	-	-	4	4	121	529	-	650

Table XIV. SUMMARY OF ENERGY PRODUCTION, TRADE, AND CONSUMPTION, BY FUEL, SELECTED YEARS, 1925-1965

(Thousand metric tons coal equivalent)

Region, country, year	Solid fuels				Liquid fuels				Natural gas		Hydroelectric power		Total energy			
	Production	Net imports	Bunkers	Consumption	Production	Net imports	Bunkers	Consumption	Production	Consumption	Production	Consumption	Production	Net imports	Bunkers	Consumption
	(1)	(2)	(3)	(4)	(5)	(6)	(7)	(8)	(9)	(10)	(11)	(12)	(13)	(14)	(15)	(16)
CONGO, DEMOCRATIC REPUBLIC (CONTINUED)																
1933	20	45	-	65	-	26	-	26	-	-	12	12	32	71	-	103
1937	36	165	-	201	-	63	-	63	-	-	28	28	64	228	-	292
1938	42	133	-	175	-	47	-	47	-	-	29	29	71	180	-	251
1950	160	208	-	368	-	237	-	237	-	-	74	74	234	445	-	679
1953	315	200	-	515	-	428	-	428	-	-	124	124	439	628	-	1067
1955	480	290	-	770	-	612	15	597	-	-	166	169	646	905	15	1536
1957	433	240	-	673	-	692	15	677	-	-	297	211	730	845	15	1560
1960	163	230	-	393	-	642	15	627	-	-	289	224	452	807	15	1244
1961	73	330	-	403	-	681	15	666	-	-	298	240	371	953	15	1309
1962	76	240	-	316	-	692	15	677	-	-	315	256	391	873	15	1249
1963	92	220	-	312	-	753	15	738	-	-	279	245	371	939	15	1295
1964	100	255	-	355	-	560	12	548	-	-	282	255	392	788	12	1158
1965	114	330	-	444	-	675	14	662	-	-	309	274	423	971	14	1380
EAST AFRICA																
1925	-	76	2	74	-	71	-	71	-	-	1	1	1	147	2	146
1929	-	111	4	107	-	149	32	117	-	-	1	1	1	260	36	225
1933	-	95	4	91	-	108	66	42	-	-	2	2	2	203	70	135
1937	-	166	1	165	-	203	86	117	-	-	3	3	3	369	87	285
1938	-	152	2	150	-	245	74	171	-	-	3	3	3	397	76	324
1950	-	44	18	26	-	885	218	668	-	-	9	9	9	929	236	703
1953	-	14	-	14	-	1259	192	1067	-	-	14	14	14	1273	192	1094
1955	1	26	-	27	-	1565	158	1407	-	-	39	39	40	1591	158	1473
1957	1	36	-	37	-	1812	309	1503	-	-	52	52	53	1848	309	1592
1960	2	40	-	42	-	1893	186	1707	-	-	80	80	82	1933	186	1829
1961	2	40	-	42	-	1814	263	1551	-	-	83	83	85	1854	263	1676
1962	3	40	-	43	-	1964	251	1713	-	-	89	89	92	2004	251	1845
1963	2	40	-	42	-	2108	240	1868	-	-	96	96	98	2148	240	2005
1964	1	30	-	31	-	2118	179	1940	-	-	107	107	108	2148	179	2078
1965	2	60	-	62	-	2301	260	2042	-	-	119	119	121	2361	260	2222
EQUATORIAL AFRICA																
1925	-	2	-	2	-	3	-	3	-	-	-	-	-	5	-	5
1929	-	1	-	1	-	8	-	8	-	-	-	-	-	9	-	9
1933	-	2	-	2	-	11	-	11	-	-	-	-	-	13	-	13
1937	-	21	-	21	-	18	-	18	-	-	-	-	-	39	-	39
1938	-	11	-	11	-	20	-	20	-	-	-	-	-	31	-	31
1950	-	7	-	7	-	83	5	78	-	-	-	-	-	90	5	85
1953	-	4	-	4	-	126	8	119	-	-	1	1	1	130	8	123
1955	-	-	-	-	-	141	15	126	-	-	4	4	4	141	15	130
1957	-	-	-	-	260	-26	15	219	-	-	4	4	263	-26	15	223
1960	-	-	-	-	1278	-936	-	342	9	9	4	4	1291	-936	-	355
1961	-	-	-	-	1316	-981	3	332	9	9	4	4	1329	-981	3	345
1962	-	-	-	-	1425	-1148	18	260	12	12	4	4	1441	-1148	18	275
1963	-	-	-	-	1499	-1280	8	212	12	12	6	6	1517	-1280	8	230
1964	-	-	-	-	1713	-1382	26	306	13	13	6	6	1733	-1382	26	326
1965	-	-	-	-	2003	-1682	21	300	15	15	6	6	2023	-1682	21	321
GHANA																
1925	-	54	-	54	-	29	-	29	-	-	-	-	-	83	-	83
1929	-	73	-	73	-	53	-	53	-	-	-	-	-	126	-	126
1933	-	27	-	27	-	38	-	38	-	-	-	-	-	65	-	65
1937	-	72	-	72	-	120	-	120	-	-	-	-	-	192	-	192
1938	-	77	-	77	-	134	-	134	-	-	-	-	-	211	-	211
1950	-	63	-	63	-	287	48	239	-	-	-	-	-	350	48	302
1953	-	99	-	99	-	350	36	314	-	-	-	-	-	449	36	413
1955	-	120	-	120	-	489	30	459	-	-	-	-	-	609	30	579
1957	-	110	-	110	-	552	27	525	-	-	-	-	-	662	27	635
1960	-	40	-	40	-	675	30	645	-	-	-	-	-	715	30	685
1961	-	50	-	50	-	629	30	599	-	-	-	-	-	679	30	649
1962	-	30	-	30	-	720	30	690	-	-	-	-	-	750	30	720
1963	-	40	-	40	-	822	30	792	-	-	-	-	-	862	30	832
1964	-	40	-	40	-	971	48	923	-	-	-	-	-	1011	48	963
1965	-	30	-	30	-	918	26	893	-	-	13	13	13	948	26	936
LIBERIA																
1925	-	-	-	-	-	-	-	-	-	-	-	-	-	-	-	-
1929	-	-	-	-	-	-	-	-	-	-	-	-	-	-	-	-
1933	-	-	-	-	-	-	-	-	-	-	-	-	-	-	-	-

Table XIV. SUMMARY OF ENERGY PRODUCTION, TRADE, AND CONSUMPTION, BY FUEL, SELECTED YEARS, 1925-1965

(Thousand metric tons coal equivalent)

Region, country, year	Solid fuels				Liquid fuels				Natural gas		Hydroelectric power		Total energy			
	Production	Net imports	Bunkers	Consumption	Production	Net imports	Bunkers	Consumption	Production	Consumption	Production	Consumption	Production	Net imports	Bunkers	Consumption
	(1)	(2)	(3)	(4)	(5)	(6)	(7)	(8)	(9)	(10)	(11)	(12)	(13)	(14)	(15)	(16)
LIBERIA (CONTINUED)																
1937	-	-	-	-	-	2	-	2	-	-	-	-	-	2	-	2
1938	-	-	-	-	-	3	-	3	-	-	-	-	-	3	-	3
1950	-	-	-	-	-	24	-	24	-	-	1	1	1	24	-	25
1953	-	-	-	-	-	27	-	27	-	-	1	1	1	27	-	28
1955	-	-	-	-	-	92	-	92	-	-	1	1	1	92	-	93
1957	-	-	-	-	-	48	-	48	-	-	2	2	2	48	-	50
1960	-	-	-	-	-	89	15	74	-	-	2	2	2	89	15	76
1961	-	-	-	-	-	90	15	75	-	-	2	2	2	90	15	77
1962	-	-	-	-	-	138	15	123	-	-	2	2	2	138	15	125
1963	-	-	-	-	-	200	15	185	-	-	2	2	2	200	15	187
1964	-	-	-	-	-	290	44	246	-	-	2	2	2	290	44	248
1965	-	-	-	-	-	327	45	282	-	-	2	2	2	327	45	284
NIGERIA																
1925	243	-3	10	230	-	35	-	35	-	-	-	-	243	32	10	265
1929	350	-20	10	320	-	53	-	53	-	-	-	-	350	33	10	373
1933	239	4	10	233	-	24	-	24	-	-	-	-	239	28	10	257
1937	369	-5	15	349	-	57	-	57	-	-	-	-	369	52	15	406
1938	368	-14	14	340	-	60	-	60	-	-	-	-	368	46	14	400
1950	592	61	11	642	-	248	6	242	-	-	7	7	599	309	17	890
1953	711	23	1	733	-	344	14	330	-	-	8	8	719	367	15	1071
1955	761	-100	-	661	-	470	20	450	-	-	9	9	770	370	20	1120
1957	828	-100	-	728	2	611	12	600	-	-	11	11	841	511	12	1339
1960	571	-30	-	541	1275	-377	15	384	-	-	11	11	1857	-407	15	1436
1961	607	-50	-	557	3407	-2238	30	1139	-	-	13	13	4026	-2288	30	1708
1962	634	-30	-	604	4992	-3929	45	1019	3	3	14	14	5642	-3959	45	1639
1963	577	-40	-	537	5658	-4314	60	1284	53	53	15	15	6303	-4354	60	1889
1964	699	-60	-	639	8930	-7235	96	1599	76	76	16	16	9720	-7295	96	2330
1965	740	-35	-	705	20307	-18272	84	1952	80	80	17	17	21143	-18307	84	2753
RHODESIAN FEDERATION																
1925	689	-226	-	463	-	9	-	9	-	-	-	-	689	-217	-	472
1929	1037	-396	-	641	-	30	-	30	-	-	-	-	1037	-366	-	671
1933	484	-45	-	439	-	36	-	36	-	-	3	3	487	-9	-	478
1937	1029	-152	-	877	-	78	-	78	-	-	5	5	1034	-74	-	960
1938	1044	-115	-	929	-	83	-	83	-	-	6	6	1050	-33	-	1017
1950	2128	-169	-	1959	-	255	5	251	-	-	19	19	2147	86	5	2229
1953	2619	-98	-	2521	-	401	6	395	-	-	25	25	2644	303	6	2940
1955	3315	-69	-	3246	-	542	15	527	-	-	28	28	3343	473	15	3800
1957	3853	-273	-	3580	-	696	15	681	-	-	29	29	3882	423	15	4290
1960	3559	-248	-	3311	-	800	15	785	-	-	164	164	3723	552	15	4259
1961	3073	-290	-	2783	-	801	15	786	-	-	305	371	3378	577	15	3940
1962	2826	-180	-	2646	-	852	15	837	-	-	373	440	3199	739	15	3923
1963	2740	-230	-	2510	-	854	15	839	-	-	433	476	3173	667	15	3825
1964	3044	-330	-	2714	-	890	12	878	-	-	486	521	3530	595	12	4112
1965	3509	-460	-	3049	-	1245	14	1232	-	-	519	561	4028	827	14	4842
MALAWI																
1925	-	-	-	-	-	2	-	2	-	-	-	-	-	2	-	2
1929	-	3	-	3	-	2	-	2	-	-	-	-	-	5	-	5
1933	-	3	-	3	-	3	-	3	-	-	-	-	-	6	-	6
1937	-	5	-	5	-	3	-	3	-	-	-	-	-	8	-	8
1938	-	4	-	4	-	5	-	5	-	-	-	-	-	9	-	9
1950	-	25	-	25	-	23	-	23	-	-	-	-	-	48	-	48
1953	-	37	-	37	-	27	-	27	-	-	-	-	-	64	-	64
1955	-	42	-	42	-	45	-	45	-	-	-	-	-	87	-	87
1957	-	47	-	47	-	60	-	60	-	-	-	-	-	107	-	107
1960	-	57	-	57	-	75	-	75	-	-	-	-	-	132	-	132
1961	-	60	-	60	-	62	-	62	-	-	-	-	-	122	-	122
1962	-	60	-	60	-	66	-	66	-	-	2	2	2	126	-	128
1963	-	60	-	60	-	71	-	71	-	-	1	1	1	131	-	131
1964	-	60	-	60	-	74	-	74	-	-	1	1	1	134	-	135
1965	-	80	-	80	-	81	-	81	-	-	2	2	2	161	-	163
ZAMBIA																
1925	-	42	-	42	-	2	-	-	-	-	-	-	-	44	-	42
1929	-	142	-	142	-	6	-	6	-	-	-	-	-	148	-	148
1933	-	177	-	177	-	5	-	5	-	-	-	-	-	182	-	182
1937	-	341	-	341	-	8	-	8	-	-	-	-	-	349	-	349

Table XIV. SUMMARY OF ENERGY PRODUCTION, TRADE, AND CONSUMPTION, BY FUEL, SELECTED YEARS, 1925-1965

(Thousand metric tons coal equivalent)

Region, country, year	Solid fuels: Production (1)	Solid fuels: Net imports (2)	Solid fuels: Bunkers (3)	Solid fuels: Consumption (4)	Liquid fuels: Production (5)	Liquid fuels: Net imports (6)	Liquid fuels: Bunkers (7)	Liquid fuels: Consumption (8)	Natural gas: Production (9)	Natural gas: Consumption (10)	Hydroelectric power: Production (11)	Hydroelectric power: Consumption (12)	Total energy: Production (13)	Total energy: Net imports (14)	Total energy: Bunkers (15)	Total energy: Consumption (16)
ZAMBIA (CONTINUED)																
1938	-	405	-	405	-	9	-	9	-	-	-	-	-	414	-	414
1950	-	654	-	654	-	60	-	60	-	-	NA	NA	NA	714	-	714
1953	-	823	-	823	-	104	-	104	-	-	23	23	23	927	-	950
1955	-	880	-	880	-	135	-	135	-	-	27	27	27	1015	-	1042
1957	-	940	-	940	-	165	-	165	-	-	28	28	28	1105	-	1133
1960	-	1035	-	1035	-	195	-	195	-	-	NA	NA	NA	1230	-	1230
1961	-	1080	-	1080	-	200	-	200	-	-	NA	197	NA	1477	-	1477
1962	-	990	-	990	-	207	-	207	-	-	37	257	37	1416	-	1454
1963	-	940	-	940	-	210	-	210	-	-	39	267	39	1379	-	1417
1964	-	1040	-	1040	-	230	-	230	-	-	38	292	38	1524	-	1562
1965	-	1215	-	1215	-	303	-	303	-	-	35	308	35	1792	-	1826
RHODESIA																
1950	2128	-848	-	1280	-	173	5	168	-	-	NA	NA	2128	-676	5	1448
1953	2618	-958	-	1660	-	270	6	264	-	-	1	1	2619	-688	6	1925
1955	3315	-991	-	2324	-	362	15	347	-	-	-	-	3315	-630	15	2671
1957	3853	-1260	-	2593	-	471	15	456	-	-	-	-	3853	-789	15	3049
1960	3559	-1340	-	2219	-	530	15	515	-	-	131	131	3690	-811	15	2864
1961	3073	-1430	-	1643	-	540	15	525	-	-	276	144	3349	-1022	15	2312
1962	2826	-1230	-	1596	-	579	15	564	-	-	342	190	3168	-803	15	2350
1963	2740	-1230	-	1510	-	573	15	558	-	-	393	208	3133	-842	15	2276
1964	3044	-1430	-	1614	-	587	12	575	-	-	446	228	3490	-1062	12	2416
1965	3509	-1755	-	1754	-	861	14	848	-	-	483	252	3992	-1125	14	2853
WEST AFRICA																
1925	-	181	131	50	-	45	17	29	-	-	-	-	-	226	148	79
1929	-	296	218	78	-	179	137	42	-	-	-	-	-	475	355	120
1933	-	115	57	58	-	405	377	29	-	-	-	-	-	520	434	87
1937	-	399	245	154	-	1079	1007	72	-	-	-	-	-	1478	1252	226
1938	-	98	98	-	-	83	23	60	-	-	-	-	-	181	121	60
1950	-	165	97	68	-	1227	927	300	-	-	-	-	-	1392	1024	368
1953	-	56	-	56	-	2112	1665	447	-	-	1	1	1	2168	1665	504
1955	-	30	-	30	-	2214	1680	534	-	-	1	1	1	2244	1680	565
1957	-	1	-	1	-	3395	2670	725	-	-	2	2	2	3396	2670	728
1960	-	1	-	1	2	2628	1682	948	-	-	8	8	9	2629	1682	957
1961	-	1	-	1	3	2604	1473	1134	-	-	10	10	13	2605	1473	1145
1962	-	-	-	-	-	2763	1535	1229	-	-	13	13	13	2763	1535	1241
1963	-	-	-	-	-	2814	1506	1308	-	-	15	15	15	2814	1506	1323
1964	-	-	-	-	-	2997	1448	1550	-	-	13	13	13	2997	1448	1562
1965	-	-	-	-	-	3278	1464	1814	-	-	18	18	18	3278	1464	1831
SOUTH AFRICA																
1925	12322	-1597	1781	8944	-	194	-	194	-	-	-	-	12322	-1404	1781	9138
1929	13018	-1652	1574	9792	-	570	57	513	-	-	-	-	13018	-1082	1631	10305
1933	10714	-782	826	9106	-	611	66	545	-	-	-	-	10714	-172	892	9651
1937	15490	-794	1144	13552	-	1458	296	1163	-	-	-	-	15490	664	1440	14715
1938	16284	-877	1141	14266	8	1626	387	1247	-	-	-	-	16292	749	1528	15513
1950	26473	-2546	387	23540	54	3446	801	2699	-	-	-	-	26527	900	1188	26239
1953	28459	-1184	79	27196	56	3770	696	3129	-	-	-	-	28515	2586	775	30325
1955	32147	-560	34	31553	56	4688	710	4034	-	-	-	-	32203	4128	744	35587
1957	34769	-550	34	34185	38	6077	1896	4218	-	-	-	-	34807	5527	1930	38403
1960	38185	-960	2	37223	38	5474	600	4911	-	-	-	-	38223	4514	602	42134
1961	39566	-1060	1	38505	9	6111	765	5355	-	-	-	-	39575	5051	766	43860
1962	41281	-1600	1	39680	-	6477	750	5727	-	-	-	-	41281	4877	751	45407
1963	42456	-1350	-	41106	-	6773	855	5918	-	-	-	-	42456	5423	855	47024
1964	44906	-1280	-	43626	-	8697	1277	7421	-	-	-	-	44906	7417	1277	51047
1965	48444	-1200	-	47244	-	9237	1164	8073	-	-	-	-	48444	8037	1164	55317
DEVELOPED COUNTRIES																
1925	1155571	-14549	35094	1105928	162686	19712	21624	160773	45050	45047	9321	9327	1372628	5166	56718	1321075
1929	1260278	-9255	33625	1217398	217694	35193	26512	226374	72276	72270	13931	13911	1564178	25913	60137	1529954
1933	900561	-1889	23453	875219	191159	39587	19732	211016	59566	59487	14826	14807	1166112	37599	43185	1160529
1937	1152143	-2459	24509	1125175	270926	46859	25052	292734	92093	91912	20266	20228	1535428	44180	49561	1530049
1938	1052749	499	21697	1031551	259337	45788	22616	282509	87571	87506	20581	20546	1420238	46186	44313	1422111
1950	1127009	3736	10572	1120173	441206	170546	40762	570992	232864	232057	38345	38381	1839424	173511	51334	1961603
1953	1100658	6760	6821	1100597	542475	229353	54986	716844	314052	313269	45410	45260	2002595	235180	61807	2175971
1955	1114264	7069	5720	1115613	587741	303171	62664	828249	354881	354076	51092	50914	2107977	309258	68384	2348853
1957	1162363	641	4181	1158823	630968	355301	71045	915224	407563	407571	57194	56975	2258087	355731	75226	2538593
1960	1043672	14265	2063	1055874	635852	514698	72629	1077921	503412	504881	69285	69276	2252220	530423	74692	2707952

Table XIV. SUMMARY OF ENERGY PRODUCTION, TRADE, AND CONSUMPTION, BY FUEL, SELECTED YEARS, 1925–1965

(Thousand metric tons coal equivalent)

Region, country, year	Solid fuels				Liquid fuels				Natural gas		Hydroelectric power		Total energy			
	Production	Net imports	Bunkers	Consumption	Production	Net imports	Bunkers	Consumption	Production	Consumption	Production	Consumption	Production	Net imports	Bunkers	Consumption
	(1)	(2)	(3)	(4)	(5)	(6)	(7)	(8)	(9)	(10)	(11)	(12)	(13)	(14)	(15)	(16)
DEVELOPED COUNTRIES (CONTINUED)																
1961	1030258	14037	1373	1042922	657420	570431	77298	1150553	528928	530601	72171	71935	2288776	585905	78671	2796010
1962	1054815	17010	1121	1070704	676665	639261	80141	1235786	565349	566847	74232	74225	2371060	657763	81262	2947561
1963	1089273	16843	1048	1105068	702050	718976	82511	1338516	597608	599068	77510	77479	2466442	737247	83559	3120132
1964	1124383	20888	1030	1144241	719619	815864	92526	1442960	636291	637897	79779	79659	2560072	838238	93556	3304757
1965	1134493	19562	969	1153086	740051	913890	95748	1558194	661578	664296	86917	86959	2623038	936212	96717	3462535
UNDERDEVELOPED COUNTRIES																
1925	27526	13513	5959	35080	49908	-23081	4541	22289	1480	1483	449	449	79363	-9565	10500	59300
1929	31447	13999	6314	39132	72026	-35768	6064	30197	2605	2611	608	608	106686	-21763	12378	72548
1933	26947	8688	3407	32228	67292	-37596	8048	21648	3787	3865	856	859	98881	-28827	11455	58600
1937	36860	11655	4260	44255	104375	-55947	9626	38804	5465	5646	1338	1340	148037	-44108	13886	90044
1938	41016	9412	3643	46785	104559	-53259	8923	42378	5883	5949	1462	1464	152920	-43779	12566	96576
1950	43122	5551	876	47797	304151	-189675	31900	82573	8276	9152	2513	2529	358060	-183231	32776	142051
1953	50808	3650	339	54119	386943	-248865	34931	103145	12542	13261	3352	3379	453645	-244475	35270	173904
1955	53325	5104	263	58166	487475	-308733	37893	140847	15992	16731	4090	4111	560882	-302868	38156	219856
1957	60548	5124	86	65586	573695	-356457	45730	171507	23238	22998	5284	5246	662764	-351610	45816	265338
1960	70753	4747	11	75489	748983	-499884	49117	199982	37269	35710	7144	7128	864150	-496713	49128	318308
1961	74341	4171	8	78504	804977	-537792	53756	213428	41408	39650	7937	7995	928662	-535321	53764	339577
1962	80962	3660	8	84614	898205	-615735	55276	227193	45586	44039	8715	8783	1033468	-613555	55284	364628
1963	87448	3664	6	91106	979220	-690264	56635	232319	48515	47004	9517	9592	1124700	-688037	56641	380020
1964	87057	3947	5	90999	1095101	-787187	59764	248147	55462	53728	10478	10495	1248098	-784957	59769	403368
1965	92270	3900	5	96165	1198860	-869765	60540	268554	59700	56856	11689	11695	1362519	-868702	60545	433270
COMMUNIST COUNTRIES																
1925	97795	-8212	NA	89014	15402	-1722	NA	13679	1392	1392	65	74	114654	-9925	NA	104158
1929	145841	-14940	NA	129817	28949	-7257	NA	21399	2139	2139	116	125	177045	-22188	NA	153480
1933	152195	-13557	NA	137742	44711	-12783	NA	31067	4096	4096	204	206	201205	-26338	NA	173110
1937	228382	-17186	NA	209236	55508	-7602	NA	47178	6290	6290	634	636	290813	-24786	NA	263340
1938	230009	-13905	NA	213479	57431	-5933	NA	50925	6211	6211	754	754	294404	-19838	NA	271369
1950	438447	-12529	NA	425208	67820	968	NA	68637	10846	10888	2540	2512	519653	-11548	NA	507245
1953	541763	-9706	NA	531197	98222	-4317	NA	93905	15190	15218	3053	3052	658227	-13995	NA	643372
1955	658445	-14340	NA	642855	130626	-6977	NA	123650	18733	18763	4194	4212	811998	-21268	NA	789480
1957	744802	-14830	NA	729778	173622	-11900	NA	161723	33058	33118	6770	6770	958252	-26670	NA	931389
1960	887106	-19850	NA	867136	256347	-35187	NA	221145	71937	71973	9561	9581	1224951	-54981	NA	1169835
1961	924519	-21020	NA	903379	285719	-46209	NA	239469	91241	91277	10237	10236	1311715	-67194	NA	1244360
1962	941145	-23450	NA	917605	318239	-51705	NA	266489	112675	112682	11985	12044	1384044	-75090	NA	1308820
1963	990918	-23710	NA	967138	350409	-57176	NA	293181	136698	136722	12467	12526	1490492	-80803	NA	1409567
1964	1034645	-24410	NA	1010116	372150	-62751	NA	309344	163291	163329	12835	12825	1582922	-87134	NA	1495613
1965	1065968	-24246	NA	1041501	403880	-71477	NA	332343	190961	190944	13989	13984	1674797	-95745	NA	1578771
USSR																
1925	16109	325	NA	16434	10629	-1961	NA	8669	186	186	31	31	26955	-1636	NA	25320
1929	37809	-242	NA	37567	20534	-5643	NA	14891	440	440	70	70	58851	-5885	NA	52966
1933	72909	-1020	NA	71889	32336	-7208	NA	25128	1479	1479	145	145	106868	-8228	NA	98640
1937	122600	-243	NA	122357	43040	-2525	NA	40515	2902	2902	524	524	169066	-2768	NA	166298
1938	128151	724	NA	128875	45623	-1728	NA	43895	2944	2944	636	636	177353	-1004	NA	176349
1950	224500	8800	NA	233300	58392	2400	NA	60792	7674	7640	1586	1586	292152	11167	NA	303319
1953	272300	5500	NA	277800	81416	-1050	NA	80366	9148	9022	2400	2400	365264	4323	NA	369587
1955	337400	3300	NA	340700	109640	-4037	NA	105603	11963	11776	2896	2897	461898	-922	NA	460976
1957	380700	-6990	NA	373710	151659	-14309	NA	137351	24753	24525	4929	4929	562040	-21526	NA	540514
1960	400400	-9330	NA	391070	226589	-43421	NA	183168	60344	60020	6364	6360	693696	-53078	NA	640618
1961	396400	-12510	NA	383890	254307	-56444	NA	197864	78563	78203	7390	7381	736660	-69322	NA	667338
1962	399400	-16860	NA	382540	285171	-63876	NA	221295	97935	97533	8993	8964	791499	-81167	NA	710332
1963	417300	-19090	NA	398210	315599	-72878	NA	242721	119656	119254	9482	9389	862037	-92463	NA	769574
1964	430800	-21530	NA	409270	335405	-81834	NA	253571	144610	144220	9670	9507	920485	-103917	NA	816567
1965	448900	-18405	NA	430495	364332	-93719	NA	270614	170051	169529	10179	9991	993462	-112833	NA	880629
COMMUNIST EASTERN EUROPE																
1925	59129	-8738	100	50291	4773	-1173	3	3599	1205	1205	34	42	65141	-9902	103	55138
1929	83997	-13477	425	70095	8408	-3221	293	4895	1700	1700	46	55	94150	-16689	718	76744
1933	52894	-9899	290	42705	12239	-7226	861	4152	2617	2617	59	60	67808	-17123	1151	49534
1937	71456	-12523	1146	57787	12168	-6687	728	4754	3387	3387	110	112	87121	-19208	1874	66040
1938	72154	-11577	1806	58771	11388	-5282	573	5534	3267	3267	117	117	86927	-16859	2379	67690
1950	171427	-21329	NA	149588	9128	-1432	NA	7695	3173	3247	293	266	184021	-22714	NA	160796
1953	204065	-15206	NA	187999	15873	-3267	NA	12606	6042	6196	332	332	226312	-18319	NA	207134
1955	226022	-16620	NA	208152	19538	-5003	NA	14535	6771	6986	523	540	252853	-21389	NA	230214
1957	237506	-6100	NA	23121[illegible]	19742	-1035	NA	18707	8305	8593	554	554	266107	-6847	NA	259065
1960	266526	-9600	NA	256806	21465	2879	NA	24329	11594	11953	784	807	300368	-6338	NA	293895
1961	278441	-7390	NA	270931	22073	5165	NA	27197	12678	13074	784	792	313976	-1822	NA	311993

Table XIV. SUMMARY OF ENERGY PRODUCTION, TRADE, AND CONSUMPTION, BY FUEL, SELECTED YEARS, 1925-1965

(Thousand metric tons coal equivalent)

Region, country, year	Solid fuels: Production	Solid fuels: Net imports	Solid fuels: Bunkers	Solid fuels: Consumption	Liquid fuels: Production	Liquid fuels: Net imports	Liquid fuels: Bunkers	Liquid fuels: Consumption	Natural gas: Production	Natural gas: Consumption	Hydroelectric power: Production	Hydroelectric power: Consumption	Total energy: Production	Total energy: Net imports	Total energy: Bunkers	Total energy: Consumption
	(1)	(2)	(3)	(4)	(5)	(6)	(7)	(8)	(9)	(10)	(11)	(12)	(13)	(14)	(15)	(16)
COMMUNIST EASTERN EUROPE (CONTINUED)																
1962	289872	-5370	NA	284412	22833	8429	NA	31217	14740	15149	867	955	328313	3555	NA	331733
1963	302112	-3190	NA	298852	23532	12320	NA	35799	17042	17468	797	949	343483	9708	NA	353068
1964	311923	-1660	NA	310144	23969	16901	NA	40814	18681	19109	790	943	355363	15820	NA	371008
1965	311635	-4226	NA	307188	24524	20697	NA	45161	20910	21415	1186	1368	358254	17158	NA	375131
COMMUNIST ASIA																
1925	22557	201	469	22289	-	1412	NA	1412	-	-	-	-	22557	1613	469	23701
1929	24036	-1221	659	22156	8	1607	NA	1614	-	-	-	-	24043	386	659	23770
1933	26392	-2638	606	23148	137	1650	NA	1787	-	-	-	-	26529	-988	606	24935
1937	34326	-4420	814	29092	300	1610	NA	1910	-	-	-	-	34626	-2811	814	31002
1938	29704	-3052	819	25833	420	1077	NA	1497	-	-	-	-	30124	-1975	819	27330
1950	42520	NA	200	42320	300	NA	150	150	-	-	660	660	43480	NA	350	43130
1953	65398	NA	NA	65398	933	NA	NA	933	-	-	320	320	66651	NA	NA	66651
1955	95023	-1020	NA	94003	1449	2063	NA	3512	-	-	775	775	97247	1043	NA	98290
1957	126596	-1740	NA	124856	2222	3444	NA	5666	-	-	1288	1288	130105	1704	NA	131809
1960	220180	-920	NA	219260	8294	5355	NA	13649	-	-	2413	2413	230886	4435	NA	235321
1961	249678	-1120	NA	248558	9339	5070	NA	14409	-	-	2063	2063	261079	3950	NA	265029
1962	251873	-1220	NA	250653	10235	3743	NA	13977	-	-	2125	2125	264233	2523	NA	266755
1963	271506	-1430	NA	270076	11279	3383	NA	14661	-	-	2188	2188	284972	1953	NA	286924
1964	291923	-1220	NA	290703	12777	2183	NA	14960	-	-	2375	2375	307075	963	NA	308037
1965	305433	-1615	NA	303818	15024	1545	NA	16569	-	-	2625	2625	323082	-70	NA	323012
ORGANISATION FOR ECONOMIC CO-OPERATION AND DEVELOPMENT (OECD)																
1925	1125826	-14149	31785	1079892	162686	17984	21315	159354	45050	45047	9155	9161	1342716	3838	53100	1293454
1929	1231972	-10420	30974	1190578	217694	31679	26129	223242	72273	72268	13662	13642	1535600	21233	57103	1499729
1933	877413	-2990	21954	852469	191156	36194	19312	208038	59564	59486	14447	14427	1142579	33105	41266	1134420
1937	1120492	-4606	22553	1093333	270923	41115	24375	287664	92090	91909	19707	19669	1503213	36290	46928	1492576
1938	1020431	-1186	19753	999492	259326	39483	21871	276939	87568	87503	19957	19922	1387283	38196	41624	1383856
1950	1075844	3217	9823	1069238	441008	156986	38199	559797	232846	232038	37191	37227	1786887	159432	48022	1898300
1953	1047434	5555	6654	1046335	542196	214940	52229	704910	314020	313237	43896	43750	1947545	219566	58883	2108232
1955	1053810	3840	5483	1052167	587562	282458	59386	810635	354835	354031	49176	49005	2045384	285322	64869	2265837
1957	1097669	-3030	3962	1090677	630776	329684	65946	894513	407507	407515	54892	54692	2190844	326461	69908	2447397
1960	968875	11910	1941	978844	634950	485991	69239	1051703	503341	504811	66756	66706	2173922	499320	71180	2602063
1961	951765	13260	1352	963673	656054	540023	73629	1122447	528836	530509	69287	69039	2205941	554708	74981	2685668
1962	974276	17030	1110	990196	675261	608130	76709	1206683	565222	566721	70769	70771	2285528	626661	77819	2834370
1963	1005738	17220	1036	1021922	700740	683553	78758	1305537	597350	598810	73976	73940	2377804	702196	79794	3000209
1964	1035083	21565	1024	1055624	718002	775013	87986	1405032	635922	637529	76094	75844	2465101	797934	89010	3174028
1965	1037136	22341	965	1058512	738728	867801	91067	1515464	661133	663851	82706	82627	2519703	892782	92032	3320455
COMMUNIST COUNTRIES																
1925	97795	-8212	NA	89014	15402	-1722	NA	13679	1392	1392	65	74	114654	-9925	NA	104158
1929	145841	-14940	NA	129817	28949	-7257	NA	21399	2139	2139	116	125	177045	-22188	NA	153480
1933	152195	-13557	NA	137742	44711	-12783	NA	31067	4096	4096	204	206	201205	-26338	NA	173110
1937	228382	-17186	NA	209236	55508	-7602	NA	47178	6290	6290	634	636	290813	-24786	NA	263340
1938	230009	-13905	NA	213479	57431	-5933	NA	50925	6211	6211	754	754	294404	-19838	NA	271369
1950	438447	-12529	NA	425208	67820	968	NA	68637	10846	10888	2540	2512	519653	-11548	NA	507245
1953	541763	-9706	NA	531197	98222	-4317	NA	93905	15190	15218	3053	3052	658227	-13995	NA	643372
1955	658445	-14340	NA	642855	130626	-6977	NA	123650	18733	18763	4194	4212	811998	-21268	NA	789480
1957	744802	-14830	NA	729778	173622	-11900	NA	161723	33058	33118	6770	6770	958252	-26670	NA	931389
1960	887106	-19850	NA	867136	256347	-35187	NA	221145	71937	71973	9561	9581	1224951	-54981	NA	1169835
1961	924519	-21020	NA	903379	285719	-46209	NA	239469	91241	91277	10237	10236	1311715	-67194	NA	1244360
1962	941145	-23450	NA	917605	318239	-51705	NA	266489	112675	112682	11985	12044	1384044	-75090	NA	1308820
1963	990918	-23710	NA	967138	350409	-57176	NA	293181	136698	136722	12467	12526	1490492	-80803	NA	1409567
1964	1034645	-24410	NA	1010116	372150	-62751	NA	309344	163291	163329	12835	12825	1582922	-87134	NA	1495613
1965	1065968	-24246	NA	1041501	403880	-71477	NA	332343	190961	190944	13989	13984	1674797	-95745	NA	1578771
WORLD EXCLUDING OECD AND COMMUNIST COUNTRIES																
1925	57271	13113	9268	61116	49908	-21353	4850	23708	1480	1483	615	615	109274	-8237	14118	86921
1929	59754	15164	8965	65953	72026	-32253	6447	33329	2608	2613	877	877	135265	-17084	15412	102772
1933	50096	9789	4906	54979	67295	-34203	8468	24626	3788	3867	1235	1238	122414	-24333	13374	84709
1937	68510	13802	6216	76096	104378	-50204	10303	43874	5468	5649	1897	1899	180252	-36218	16519	127518
1938	73333	11097	5587	78843	104570	-46955	9668	47948	5886	5951	2086	2088	185875	-35790	15255	134831
1950	94287	6070	1625	98732	304349	-176115	34463	93768	8294	9171	3667	3683	410597	-169152	36088	205354
1953	104033	4855	506	108382	387222	-234452	37688	115079	12574	13293	4867	4889	508695	-228861	38194	241642
1955	113780	8333	500	121613	487653	-288020	41171	158462	16037	16777	6006	6021	623475	-278932	41671	302871
1957	125242	8795	305	133732	573887	-330840	50829	192218	23294	23054	7586	7530	730008	-322341	51134	356533
1960	145550	7102	133	152519	749885	-471177	52507	226200	37340	35780	9673	9698	942447	-465610	52640	424197
1961	152834	4948	29	157753	806343	-507384	57425	241533	41500	39742	10820	10891	1011497	-504123	57454	449919
1962	161501	3640	19	165122	899609	-584604	58708	256296	45713	44165	12178	12236	1119000	-582453	58727	477819

Table XIV. SUMMARY OF ENERGY PRODUCTION, TRADE, AND CONSUMPTION, BY FUEL, SELECTED YEARS, 1925-1965

(Thousand metric tons coal equivalent)

Region, country, year	Solid fuels				Liquid fuels				Natural gas		Hydroelectric power		Total energy			
	Production	Net imports	Bunkers	Consumption	Production	Net imports	Bunkers	Consumption	Production	Consumption	Production	Consumption	Production	Net imports	Bunkers	Consumption
	(1)	(2)	(3)	(4)	(5)	(6)	(7)	(8)	(9)	(10)	(11)	(12)	(13)	(14)	(15)	(16)
WORLD EXCLUDING OECD AND COMMUNIST COUNTRIES (CONTINUED)																
1963	170984	3287	18	174253	980529	-654842	60388	265298	48774	47262	13051	13131	1213337	-652986	60406	499943
1964	176357	3270	11	179616	1096718	-746336	64304	286074	55831	54097	14164	14310	1343069	-744654	64315	534097
1965	189626	1121	9	190738	1200183	-823676	65221	311285	60145	57301	15900	16026	1465854	-825272	65230	575350

Part Four

ANNOTATED GUIDE TO THE DETAILED ENERGY STATISTICS OF PART THREE

Four

ANNOTATED GUIDE TO THE DETAILED ENERGY STATISTICS OF PART THREE

I. General Notes[1]

Scope of the Statistical Tables at a Glance

The tables numbered I through XIV, which comprise the detailed statistics of Part Three, offer basic national and regional data on primary energy production, foreign trade, bunkers, and consumption. Along with this information, the set of fourteen tables includes data on population, total electricity consumption, and—for purposes of analysis—a variety of derived measures (ratios, percentage distributions, per capita indicators, and growth rates). This detailed statistical compendium of Part Three constitutes the principal contribution of this volume.

The regional and world totals shown in each table exhaust, so far as available information permitted, all countries and territories of the world, although data for only about 100 (out of some 200) of the more important areas are actually published in this book. However, country data not shown (although included in regional totals) can be made available by special arrangement. (See pp. 827ff. on "Availability of Unpublished Materials.") The criteria for inclusion of the roughly 100 "important" countries revolved, for the most part, around the significance of the area's total or per capita production or consumption of an energy commodity.[2] However, allowance was also made for a country's political importance as well as for its current or prospective developmental position.

The statistics reproduced in Part Three cover the bench-mark years 1925, 1929, 1933, 1937, 1938, 1950, 1953, 1955, 1957, and the annual years 1960-65, except where their inclusion was precluded by nonavailability or extreme unreliability. Also, where for a particular table a country's data consisted entirely of zeros, those pages (or the relevant block of years) were not reproduced in order to economize on space and permit a more attractive presentation. As with data for omitted countries (see pp. 824-26), annual data for the periods 1925-38 and 1949-65 have been compiled in unpublished form, and inquiries about those are invited. (Data for the period 1939-48 were not compiled.) Given the forty-year (1925-65) scope of the study, these bench-mark years were selected so as to provide a reasonable basis for long-term analysis.

Data are presented for the so-called "commercial," inanimate energy forms; that is, they exclude human effort and that of draft animals as well as the output and consumption of vegetal fuels such as firewood and dung. The *primary energy production* data (tables I-III) cover solid fuels (coal, lignite, and an "other" category comprising a variety of minor fuels), liquid fuels (crude oil and natural gas liquids—the latter not shown separately), natural gas, and hydroelectricity. Energy *imports and exports* (tables IV-VIII) are shown for total solid fuels, liquid fuels (crude oil, gasoline, kerosine, fuel oil, liquefied petroleum gases, and lubricants), gas, and electricity. *Bunkers* (table IX) (fuels furnished foreign-bound ships and aircraft irrespective of flag) comprise total solid fuels and liquid fuels. *Apparent consumption* (tables X and XI) is computed by the formula:

$$\text{consumption} = \text{primary energy production} + \text{imports} - \text{exports} - \text{bunkers}.$$

Since inventory accumulation or run-down is not allowed for, consumption is, more accurately, seen to represent an estimate of "apparent inland disappearance of energy supplies." Except to the extent to which imports (or exports and bunkers) of processed energy forms such as gasoline add to (or subtract from) output of primary energy supplies, these statistical data all

[1] Large-scale reliance upon computer calculations and printouts made it expeditious to exclude written notes from the table pages. The present annotation is intended to fill the gap created by the absence of such notes; readers making or contemplating extensive use of the basic tables are advised to read these remarks.

[2] The number included varies somewhat with the particular table in question; for example, for table XIII—a derived table of average annual percentage growth rates—rather less than the 100 countries are shown owing to substantial data gaps and problems of reliability for some of the smaller of the areas.

apply to primary energy input into the economy (such as crude oil) rather than secondary or processed energy (such as motor gasoline). The only secondary energy form for which data are provided is total electricity consumption. Because electricity data were generally available and because electricity is a significant outlet for primary energy, being widely used as an indicator of relative well-being, it was considered appropriate to supplement the primary energy data with this series.

Data are provided in original physical units (e.g., metric tons of coal and crude oil, cubic meters of natural gas, kilowatt-hours of hydroelectricity) and—to permit aggregation as well as comparison of actual contained energy—in hard-coal equivalent units. Instead of coal equivalents, other units such as oil equivalents, British thermal units, kilocalories, or kilowatt-hours could similarly have been arithmetically derived from the energy content of the various primary products, and would all have been equally suitable.

A difficulty encountered in conversion relates to the appropriate conversion factor for hydroelectricity. One has the choice of computing coal equivalents based on the inherent heat value of the electricity or on the fuel that would have been required to generate a corresponding amount of thermal electricity. The present study, conforming to the practice of the United Nations in its energy statistics, follows the former approach. However, to indicate the effect of the conversion procedure adopted, one series (in table XII) computes hydroelectricity consumption and total energy consumption by means of the second approach.

Subsequent sections will cover these and other questions more fully.

Exclusions from the Basic Data: Animate Energy, Noncommercial Fuels, Nuclear Power

Animate energy (draft animal or human) is excluded from the statistical compilation. Nor has any attempt been made to develop statistics on vegetal fuels, such as cow dung or bagasse, or on fuelwood production and consumption, despite the importance of these energy forms in many of the underdeveloped countries as well as (in the case of wood) certain industrialized countries of Europe. The neglect of these so-called "noncommercial" energy forms—in which category we also place windpower and hydropower, where developed for purposes other than electricity generation—represents a deficiency in these tables. Though based on debatable assumptions and involving exceedingly crude approximations, the figures below show that as recently as the early 1950s noncommercial energy, in terms of energy contained, was estimated to be more important than the commercial forms (coal, oil, natural gas, hydropower) in Africa and Asia and nearly as important in South America.

Percent of Total Energy Consumption[3]

	Commercial	*Non-commercial*	*Total*
Africa	49%	51%	100%
North America	97	3	100
Central America	65	35	100
South America	55	45	100
Asia (incl. Middle East)	42	58	100
Europe	93	7	100
Oceania	87	13	100
World	85	15	100

However, all that is available for noncommercial energy are incomplete data for a handful of countries. For analytical purposes, the effect of this exclusion is mitigated by the fact that in relation to their contained energy such fuels are usually used with markedly poorer efficiency than commercial fuels.

Because the basic statistical tabulation is a historical one, terminating with the year 1965, we have—as a matter of historical insignificance—also refrained from introducing nuclear energy under primary energy production, although it is included in total electricity consumption. The relatively minor contribution of nuclear power in 1965 is seen in the tabulation below, which, apart from unavailable Soviet data, covers all countries recording nuclear electric output in that year.

Production of Electricity, 1965 (million kwh)[4]

	Fossil-fueled	*Hydro*	*Nuclear*	*Total*
Belgium	21,384	272	50	21,706
Canada	27,091	117,063	120	144,274
France	54,116	46,429	897	101,442
West Germany	156,861	15,365	117	172,343
Italy	33,351	42,367	3,510	79,228
Japan	117,184	71,168	25	188,377
United Kingdom	175,566	4,625	15,836	196,027
United States	956,733	197,001	3,657	1,157,391
Sweden	2,661	46,423	18	49,102
Others	881,860	356,747	-	1,238,607
World	2,426,807	897,460	24,230	3,348,497

Character of the Basic Data: Problems of Estimation and Meaning

Here we discuss some of the major measurement, definitional, and conceptual issues associated with the development of the basic statistical series. The discussion begins with some general remarks on estimating procedures and data availability. This is followed by com-

[3] United Nations, *Proceedings of the International Conference on the Peaceful Uses of Atomic Energy*, vol. 1, *The World's Requirements for Energy: The Role of Nuclear Energy* (New York, 1956), pp. 18-20. Communist countries are excluded from the tabulation.

[4] From United Nations, *World Energy Supplies*, Statistical Papers, Series J; *Statistical Yearbook*; and information furnished by United Nations Statistical Office.

ments on the nature of the statistics on energy production, imports and exports, bunkers, and consumption.[5]

The Estimating Approach. The general procedure for development of the production, import and export, and bunkers series (which constituted the components for the subsequent derivation of consumption) was to prepare continuous time series stretching back to 1925 for a particular energy commodity and activity based on evaluation of alternative national and international sources available. On the basis of a systematic comparison of alternative series including descriptive notes in the publications consulted,[6] and noting overlapping values, ratios of change in parallel series, simple interpolations and extrapolations, and numerous other relationships, a single time series was selected or otherwise estimated for inclusion in the basic tables of Part Three as representing the "best estimate" of the desired series conforming to the definitions given below. It goes without saying that a substantial portion of our tabulated data represents estimates which we ourselves constructed; these estimates include the filling in of "nonavailable" cells as well as data adjustments necessary for linking and consistency purposes, as just described. But it should also be noted that the documents consulted themselves often contained estimates, rather than merely information reported to the publication or taken from still other sources. Various publications did not follow uniform practices as regards identification of their own estimates, even in the same series over time. In selecting the "best" estimate of the desired series, relatively less credence was given to data that were indicated as estimates, whether this was shown explicitly or through rounded values.

It is, of course, impossible to describe in anything more than these most general terms the numerous estimation techniques adopted in order to derive continuous and, we hope, consistent time series. Country source notes may provide some general indication of the procedure followed in a specific instance for a particular country, but the vast bulk of such estimations could only be appreciated by direct reference to office files containing worksheets for that energy commodity and that country.

[5]Estimates of population and total electricity consumption are in a sense ancillary to the development of these basic series, and are discussed in a separate subsection.

[6]The difficulty of comparing, and choosing among, different sources was compounded by the frequent inadequacy of explanations and definitions. This was particularly true of international compendia containing data taken, in turn, from national sources or representing data furnished by member or reporting countries; moreover, it is no less true of recent than of early years. Two standard publications (Organisation for Economic Cooperation and Development, *Statistics of Energy*, and United Nations, *World Energy Supplies*) are frequently in conflict with respect to figures applying ostensibly to the same year, country, and measure. However, it was impossible to investigate thoroughly each such discrepancy.

Production. The production series represent the "best" set of estimates of annual gross production of primary energy sources (except in the case of natural gas) for essentially every country of the world during the period 1925-65, based on a systematic review, comparison, and analysis of relevant statistical information in the various sources cited. For natural gas we have depended for the most part upon data on actual utilization rather than gross production, in view of the large volumes of gas that are simply flared for lack of effective demand or are reinjected into the ground for purposes of pressure maintenance or to increase ultimate oil recovery. Except for natural gas liquids (NGL), as explained further below, the term "primary energy sources" refers to the several fuels or energy materials in the initial form that they enter the energy economy, including at most only such minor processing as cleaning of coal or drying of lignite and peat.

The production data consist essentially of all the "commercial" energy sources listed below.

Energy Source	*Remarks*
Solid Fuels	
Hard coal	Comprises bituminous coal and anthracite, not shown separately in the tables. (Occasionally some low-grade coal may be included at hard-coal equivalents.) The term "hard coal" follows accepted international usage. (In American practice, "hard coal" refers to anthracite.) Sub-bituminous coal (see below) might have been included under "hard coal" as well, but it was more convenient to handle it along with the other minor solid fuels.
Lignite	Includes lignite and brown coal.
Peat Sub-bituminous Pitch Asphaltite . .	These statistically lesser fuels are not separately identified in the tables, being shown under "other" solid fuels. They are, however, separately identified in the country notes.
Liquid Fuels	Crude oil plus natural gas liquids (not shown separately in the tables).
Crude oil	Includes, where relevant, shale oil; occasionally, also, the natural gasoline component of natural gas liquids.
Natural gas liquids . .	Included in total liquid fuels but not shown separately; derivable by subtraction. Further remarks appear in text below.
Natural Gas	Includes, where relevant, methane gas from coal mines (at natural gas equivalent). Further remarks appear in text below.
Hydroelectricity	Excludes geothermal and nuclear electric power.[7]

[7]Geothermal electric power was included in the Italian hydro data of Part Three while it was not included (for lack of historical

Gross production is shown for each energy source, with the sole exception of natural gas for which "actual utilization" (if available) was shown. Actual utilization is normally defined to exclude natural gas processed at NGL plants so that both the natural gas consumption and the NGL production may be included under the term "primary energy sources" without duplication. In the United States—by far the world's largest natural gas and NGL producer—the published sources, by contrast, normally exclude NGL in deriving a primary energy total, since the "marketed production" concept used already includes all gas intended to be processed for liquids, and hence automatically includes the energy content of the derived NGL as well as the energy content of the residual natural gas, most of which is then consumed as fuel. We have therefore adjusted the U.S. natural gas statistics to deduct the estimated "offtake" for NGL production. The adjustment is described in the U.S. country note.

Insofar as possible, the following definitions apply to the gross production series (alternative definitions in specific instances are given in the country source notes wherever applicable): With respect to solid fuels, gross production of hard coal is measured at the mine after cleaning; it thus excludes dirt and other waste removed in washeries and cleaning plants, but includes coal consumed at the mine by mine operators and coal delivered free to mine employees. The same definitions apply to lignite and peat, except that measurement is made after drying.

In the case of liquid fuels, gross production of crude oil is measured at the well, while NGL is measured at the natural gasoline plant and other liquids-separation plant. NGL is produced in a relatively small number of countries, and where it is produced it normally consists solely of natural gasoline. In a few countries, among them the United States, NGL also includes varying quantities of liquefied petroleum gases (LPG). LPG is produced from (wet) natural gas at natural gas separation plants as well as from crude oil at refineries; however, our LPG data exclude refinery fuel, which is not properly a component of primary energy production.

A word should be added about units of measurement for crude oil. A large number of countries measure and report oil production in units of volume (such as barrels or barrels per day), while others use metric tons, which is our physical measure. Variations in average specific gravity among countries and, to a lesser extent, over time for given countries can produce some distortion when converting oil from units of volume to units of weight. While we have taken into account country differences in specific gravities,[8] we have—for lack of reliable data—ignored year-to-year variations. Nevertheless, the resulting tonnage figures are judged to provide a satisfactory degree of uniformity and direct comparability among countries.

Gross production of hydroelectric power refers to total generation at all public utility and industrial power stations, including stations' own use and transmission losses. In many countries industrial generation is reported as negligible or nil, in which case the reported series for public (utility) hydro generation was taken as approximating the total. In some cases, electric power data are reported on a net generation basis (i.e., net of station use), or else purchaser sales data are given. Where this occurred, estimates of station consumption (1 to 1½ percent of total generation in the case of hydro) and transmission losses (10 to 15 percent) were added in order to approximate gross generation.[9]

Imports and Exports. The foreign trade statistics, as well as bunkers data discussed later, cover the primary energy forms just considered as well as trade in secondary (i.e., processed) fuels. (That this is necessary for the ultimate calculation of a nation's energy balance or consumption is clear from the following example: while the production of gasoline clearly duplicates what is already included in the nation's crude oil production, the import or export of gasoline adds to or subtracts from the country's primary energy supplies that are available for consumption.)

In addition to the items comprising primary energy production, imports and exports include: under solid fuels, hard coal and lignite made into briquettes and coke; under liquid fuels, refinery products[10] consisting of gasoline, kerosine, fuel oil, liquefied petroleum gases (from gas plants as well as refineries), and lubricants and greases; imports and exports of gas combine natural and manufactured gas (expressed as natural gas equivalents),

---

data) in the hydro statistics for either New Zealand (where it is relatively more important than in the case of Italy), or the United States.

[8] Using, for the most part, national specific gravity data shown in United Nations, *Statistical Yearbook* (annual), e.g., pp. 201-2 of the 1966 edition.

[9] Estimates were based on OECD, *Basic Statistics of Energy* and on the judgment of U.S. Federal Power Commission staff.

[10] In classifying all liquid refined products into five categories, terminological distinctions become somewhat imprecise. (Moreover, the nomenclature governing these energy forms varies a good deal around the world, even when expressed in English.) In our tables, "gasoline" includes motor and aviation gasoline and naphtha; "kerosine" includes aviation jet and turbine fuel along with the traditional versions of this product for illuminating and cooking purposes; "fuel oil" covers the lighter, so-called distillate fuels (such as heating oil and diesel oil) as well as residual fuel oil; "liquefied petroleum gases" refer to propane, butane, or a mixture of both. Note that in European and, frequently, international usage, the term "fuel oil" often refers exclusively to residual fuel oil, while the terms "gas oil (for diesel engines)" and "gas oil (for burning)" refer to the diesel oil and to the heating oil components of our fuel oil category.

while international electricity exchanges cover thermally generated as well as other sources of electricity.

Except for the inclusion of lubricants and greases, the indicated import and export items are conventional components of energy trade statistics.[11]

Several points should be made about the treatment of these series in the basic tables on imports and exports. All the different solid fuels, partly for convenience and partly for their availability only in this aggregated form for numerous countries in post-World War II years, have been combined into a single solid fuels category expressed in coal equivalents. Liquefied petroleum gases are included under "total refined petroleum products" without being shown separately. As opposed to the separate series on imports and exports available for solid and liquid fuels, data on foreign trade in gas and electricity were available only on a "net trade" basis; thus, for a given year a country can have net imports (in the import tabulation of tables IV and VI) or net exports (in the export tabulation of tables IV and VI) but never entries on both.[12] Tables V and VII are on a net trade basis for all commodities, however.

A peculiarity resulting from the inclusion of electricity trade should be pointed out. The electricity component of primary energy production relates only to hydro, while international electricity exchanges cover electricity irrespective of fuel. Since consumption (to be discussed below) is defined and calculated as the production of primary energy forms plus the net imports (and minus bunkers where relevant) of primary and processed items, it is possible for a country to record a negative electricity component in its primary energy consumption. This has occasionally happened in years when a country such as Belgium, a producer of virtually no hydroelectricity, has exported net supplies of electricity.

To the extent possible, the import and export statistics are based on the "general" trade system. Under this system, imports are the combined total of (a) imports for domestic consumption, and (b) imports entering bonded warehouses or free foreign trade zones; exports are the combined total of (a) national exports, and (b) reexports. Reexports, in turn, refer to the outward movement—without transformation—of previously imported goods, including those that are shipped out of the country from bonded warehouses and free zones. Direct transit trade, covering transshipments of goods or the transport of goods merely moving through the country, are excluded from these statistics. Bunkers (to be discussed below) are not knowingly tabulated in exports or reexports, even though fuel imports frequently are shipped out again as bunkers. In the latter case, imports balance bunkers, leaving national energy consumption unaffected.

These are somewhat idealized definitions, however. There is little doubt, for example, that the export statistics obtained from published sources occasionally contain some unspecified quantities of bunkers. This, among other things, could be one of the reasons why worldwide totals of refined fuel exports are generally considerably in excess of world imports; the two should nominally be equal. Another, probably more important, reason for this inequality is believed to stem from "military and naval liftings" reported in export statistics but missing from import statistics. Other sources of error are undoubtedly present which can contribute to such overall discrepancies if erroneous treatment does not apply equally to exporting and importing countries. Thus, in the wide variety of sources used to compile the foreign trade statistics one could not always be certain that the general rather than the special trade system (where imports would cover only those fuels destined for domestic consumption and exports would cover only domestic merchandise) prevailed; or that when the special system did prevail, our adjustments to have it conform to the general system were on the mark.[13] With respect to specific liquid fuel categories, there can be no assurance about classification consistency: a country's kerosine exports may be zero because kerosine may be included in fuel oil. Finally, inconsistency among countries as to reporting period and, not least of all, the likelihood that some country data are underreported subject the foreign trade statistics inescapably to some indeterminate degree of inaccuracy.

[11]The inclusion of lubricants and greases nevertheless leaves the treatment of energy-derived "nonenergy" commodities in foreign trade statistics (e.g., asphalt or waxes) suspended in a somewhat inconsistent state. For example, a country producing ten units of crude oil used exclusively for asphalt production consumes (according to usual statistical practice, and assuming no trade and bunkers) ten units of energy. A country producing nothing, but importing ten units of asphalt, would be said to consume zero energy.

[12]In tables IV and VI, note that the net trade treatment of gas and electricity leads to a peculiarity in regional aggregation. Assume, for the sake of illustration, that all trade occurs as a result of net flows from countries A to B, these two comprising and exhausting a region:

	Net imports	*Net exports*
Country A	0	100
Country B	100	0
Regional total	100	100

In other words, the regional aggregate indicated in the tables has still to be netted (i.e., 100 − 100 = 0) as it is in tables V and VII, to be on a basis consistent with the country treatment.

[13]For example, one of the standard sources used and so adjusted is the United Kingdom's annual *Statistical Summary of the Mineral Industry* which for the most part reports fuel trade data on the basis of the special trade system.

Bunkers. These refer to "fuel supplied to foreign-bound ships and aircraft, irrespective of the flag of the vessel or plane."[14] (In principle, this definition may be construed as including coastal and lake navigation in international waters; in practice there appears to be little uniformity in adherence to this component of bunkering.) Bunkers comprise solid fuels (chiefly hard coal and important principally in the earlier years covered by this study) and liquid fuels (chiefly fuel oil, including diesel oil, for steam and motor ships, and aviation gasoline and jet fuel).

For various reasons, information on bunkers was found to be in a highly unsatisfactory state. (a) For numerous years and countries, no published data were available, and estimates had to be constructed. Where the omitted amounts could be presumed to be particularly large, the development of estimated figures was not attempted; the Soviet Union is a case in point. As a result, and in such a case, our estimate of energy consumption refers to "total" rather than "inland" consumption. (b) For a given year, country, and—as far as could be ascertained—identical bunkering concept, it was not unusual to find substantial differences in the bunkers figure reported in two different sources. (c) As mentioned in the foreign trade discussion, bunkers are likely, on occasion, to be erroneously reported as part of exports. (d) There was often no basis for judging whether a reported bunkers figure included or excluded coastal shipping. (e) Published data on the aviation fuel (gasoline or jet fuel) component of liquid fuel bunkers appear often to be incomplete.

For these reasons, the bunkers series which we have constructed, and which is shown in table IX of Part Three, must be viewed as a highly approximate product.

Consumption. Energy consumption is derived from the simple arithmetic formula:

$$\text{consumption} = \text{primary production} + \text{imports} - \text{exports} - \text{bunkers}.$$

In other publications, the fuller term "inland consumption" is sometimes used to indicate that the figure is net of bunkers. While there are undoubtedly advantages in using a total consumption definition (i.e., one gross of bunkers) in connection with an area's overall energy requirements, the inland measure used here is perhaps the one more suitably related to a given area's gross national product, as is done elsewhere in this study.

Because the above formula does not contain the estimate of inventory change necessary to measure actual disappearance, it should be clear that, as figured, our measure of consumption might be more accurately described as a calculated estimate of *apparent* change in domestic energy supply. Without a measure of inventory change, the consumption series is somewhat limited for certain analytical purposes. For example, one's interest in the relationship between energy consumption and gross national product is presumably better served by a measure of energy consumption that includes the net change in stocks. European countries plagued in recent years by unsold accumulations of pithead stocks of coal illustrate this problem. For example, 1964 and 1965 West German solid fuel consumption (expressed in million tons coal equivalent) shows the following alternative measurement:

	1964	*1965*
Consumption as measured in this study	164	155
Inventory change (addition).	4	8
Consumption measured by actual "disappearance" . . .	160	147

It is evident that by our indicator consumption between the two years declined by 9 million tons, whereas—considering that an additional 4 million tons went into inventory accumulation—the decline was 13 million tons or nearly 50 percent greater.

Unfortunately, knowledge about inventory change exists only for solid fuels, and then only for a limited number of countries and years (recent data for large Western European countries being the prime example). Under the circumstances, it was deemed best to stick with a consistent, if somewhat deficient, concept of consumption for all energy forms rather than with the more appropriate one that could have been developed only on a fragmentary basis.

In addition to the matter of stock changes, the reliability of the consumption series is affected by the various uncertainties in the series of which it is composed. Our consumption figures are particularly sensitive to errors in estimating foreign trade or bunkering totals, especially when those totals are large relative to production. The fact that estimates of production, foreign trade, and bunkers were frequently obtained from different sources, whose consistency with one another could not always be checked out, is a reason for occasional erratic movements—usually of a short-term nature—in the calculated consumption series. Such unexplained swings sometimes stand out even more clearly in the consumption-per-capita series. For years where, because of inherent statistical difficulties, no meaningful consumption or consumption-per-capita figure (or growth rates based thereon) could be calculated, they have been omitted (from tables X through XIV).

Approximations in Statistics of Population and Total Electricity Consumption

In the task of assembling data for a study of this scale, it was necessary to operate with some sense of

[14] United Nations, *World Energy Supplies, 1962-1965*, Statistical Papers, Series J, No. 10 (New York, 1967), p. 6. Our historical compilation has been designed to conform to this (latest) concept of bunkers.

priority in the allocation of effort and resources. Major emphasis and care went into the compilation of as accurate and exhaustive a geographic and historical series of primary production, import and export, and bunkers data as could be gathered for the different energy forms. The search for data on population and total electricity consumption as analytical adjuncts to these basic series was given a lesser order of importance.

Population. Data obtained from the major sources (primarily the United Nations *Demographic Yearbooks* and the *Statistical Yearbooks* of the League of Nations and the United Nations) were generally accepted without being subjected to the same degree of critical scrutiny as the energy figures. Thus, there are apparent breaks in the continuity of some of the population series which we made no effort to overcome by smoothing adjustments; such adjustments would have required substantially increased research effort. Also, numerous population figures were unavailable—especially for African and Asian areas in the pre-World War II years of the study; these gaps were generally allowed to remain in the data. However, in order to have a reasonably comprehensive series of area-wide and world population totals, we did—in the absence of the necessary country figures—construct regional population estimates, using as a basis either (a) estimates for closely corresponding regions available for intermittent years from the above-mentioned sources; or (b) crude estimates for the constituent countries of the region (derived usually by interpolation or extrapolation from a limited number of published bench-mark years) which we have nowhere shown separately.

Total Electricity Consumption (gross electricity output plus net imports). This represents the only extensive nonprimary energy flows tabulated in the study. Development of this series frequently required similarly rough-and-ready approaches as those used in getting population estimates, and again primarily for pre-World War II years. During that period a number of regional totals were constructed in the same way as is described for the population data. Also, for the 1925-38 data, the electricity figures usually refer to output rather than to consumption. However, since these two measures are markedly dissimilar only when there is foreign electricity trade, we adjusted the output figures of important electricity-trading countries (such as Austria and Switzerland) for net trade so as to obtain more appropriate estimates of consumption. The electricity data refer generally to gross flows (that is, include generating-center use and transmission losses) and cover electricity originating in both enterprises generating primarily for public use and in industrial establishments. However, there is by no means uniformity of treatment in the published sources in these two respects either as among countries or for a given country over time.

In the country source descriptions it was not feasible to provide for each country detailed documentation of the problems discussed in this general note.

Geographic Treatment

In most cases the basic country statistics refer to national frontiers of the year in question; e.g., Burma and Pakistan are included in India for pre-World War II years. To some extent, therefore, historical comparability of national data is impaired. Where feasible, some territorial adjustments—based on the most recent status of a particular area—were introduced to overcome this problem. Thus, the Saar, which alternated between French and German jurisdiction during the period of the study (even while frequently treated as an autonomous statistical unit), has to the extent possible been included with Germany (1925-38) and West Germany (1949-65);[15] and the three Baltic states (Estonia, Latvia, Lithuania) have been combined with the Soviet Union.

Comparability of time series is, of course, further improved at the level of regional or subregional aggregation. In some cases, however, this necessitated some classification practices which should be noted. For example, pre-World War II data for Albania, Bulgaria, Czechoslovakia, Hungary, Poland, and Romania are all carried under the region "U.S.S.R. and Communist Eastern Europe." (It was not possible to split East Germany off from the prewar Reich so as to make this series even more uniform.) With the purpose of historical continuity similarly in mind, numerous nations within Tropical Africa or within Asia and the Far East, in addition to being tabulated individually for a more limited recent period, have been grouped throughout the period into subregions which conform to their former colonial or other territorial status.[16] Thus, British Borneo (comprising Brunei and the present Malaysian states of Sabah and Sarawak), though no longer a colonial entity, is

[15]As part of this consolidation, the Saar's trade with Germany (or West Germany) was treated as internal and therefore deducted from the total of German and Saar trade. In the case of less significant regional groupings, this internal trade adjustment could not be made. For example, to make the pre-1954 Indo-China foreign trade total completely comparable with the *summed* post-1954 foreign trade total of South Vietnam, Laos, and Cambodia combined, one would have to eliminate post-1954 trade among these countries (or, alternatively, estimate pre-1954 intra-Indo-China trade). This was not attempted. Fuel trade among small, less developed nations can be viewed as having been insignificant throughout the period of the study; and, in any case, *net trade* data presumably wash out these intraregional imports and exports and are therefore historically consistent.

[16]In a few cases certain small African countries, which acquired sovereignty in the last few years covered by the study, are treated as part of the country of which they were formerly a part. For example, Burundi and Rwanda (which prior to 1963 constituted the single nation Ruanda-Urundi, and prior to 1961 were part of the then Belgian Congo) are included in the Congo Democratic Republic. As another example, Tanganyika and Zanzibar, which united in 1964 to form Tanzania, are still treated separately in the study.

carried as a statistical unit for all years.[17] Conversely, the European Economic Community (EEC or Common Market) and the European Free Trade Association (EFTA) groupings have been carried back to years antedating their establishment. Needless to say, the geographic handling of the data was intended solely to facilitate analysis of long-term trends.

The country and regional arrangements of the statistics in Part Three (shown in the list below) deserve brief comment. The so-called "Basic Grouping" comprises continents and a substantial number of lesser regions and subregions; the arrangement is fairly conventional except insofar as it highlights the two prominent oil-producing regions in the Caribbean and in the Middle East. At the end of the Basic Grouping, in each of the fourteen tables of Part Three two additional and somewhat more compact alternative regional arrangements (each of which is exhaustive in terms of world totals) are provided to expand the opportunities for analysis. The first of these—bowing to the reality of the terms in which many worldwide problems are approached—divides the world into Developed, Underdeveloped, and Communist regions. The second classification—acknowledging the prominence in the world economy of the OECD group of nations as well as the functional role of OECD in energy questions and general economic policy—shows totals for OECD, Communist, and all other countries, and should facilitate a statistical bridging between the present volume and OECD statistics.

Inevitably, the effort to satisfy political along with economic criteria (not to mention those of habit, convenience, and common usage) produces a geographic classification that is neither wholly consistent and logical nor universally acceptable. This is true in the basic as well as the two alternative formulations. A few examples make this clear. The exclusion of Yugoslavia from the Communist grouping conforms to widespread statistical practice but is obviously somewhat arbitrary (as is the stretching of Western Europe eastward to make room for that Balkan nation as well as for Greece). Convenience is served by a similarly common but arbitrary procedure which puts Cuba into Latin America rather than the Communist group. And the "developed"-"underdeveloped" dichotomy is no doubt debatable. On strict GNP-per-capita criteria, Israel, for example, would more appropriately belong in the developed category than, say, Greece, while Malta—grouped with the developed nations simply for the convenience of treating the entire Western European region as developed without further computational adjustment—obviously would be more accurately treated in the underdeveloped category.

[17] A number of these subregions, being statistically insignificant, are omitted from the published series, but the relevant data are included as part of the unpublished materials (see p. 827).

Listing of Countries and Regions

A. Basic Grouping

North America
- Canada
- Greenland[a]
- St. Pierre-Miquelon[a]
- United States

Western Europe
- European Economic Community (EEC)
  - Belgium-Luxembourg
  - France
  - Germany (1925–38)
  - Germany, Federal Republic (1949–65)
  - Italy
  - Netherlands
- European Free Trade Association (EFTA)[b]
  - Austria
  - Denmark
  - Norway
  - Portugal
  - Sweden
  - Switzerland
  - United Kingdom
- Western Europe: Other
  - Faeroe Islands[a]
  - Finland[b]
  - Gibraltar[a]
  - Greece
  - Iceland[b]
  - Ireland
  - Malta[a]
  - Spain
  - Yugoslavia

Oceania
- Australia
- Fiji Islands[a]
- Gilbert-Ellice Islands[a]
- Nauru[a]
- New Caledonia[a]
- New Guinea (Australian)[a]
- New Hebrides[a]
- New Zealand
- Oceania (French)[a]
- Papua[a]
- Samoa, Western[a]
- Solomon Islands (British)[a]

U.S.S.R. and Communist Eastern Europe
- Communist Eastern Europe
  - Albania
  - Bulgaria
  - Czechoslovakia
  - Germany, East (1949–65)
  - Hungary
  - Poland
  - Romania
- U.S.S.R. (including Estonia, Latvia, Lithuania) (1925–65)
  - U.S.S.R. (excluding Estonia, Latvia, Lithuania) (1925–38)[a]
  - Estonia[a]
  - Latvia[a]
  - Lithuania[a]

Communist Asia
- China, Mainland[a]
- Korea, North (1949–65)[a]
- Mongolia (1949–65)[a]
- Vietnam, North (1954–65)[a]

Note: See footnotes at end of listing.

- Latin America
  - Caribbean
    - Caribbean: Oil Producing
      - Antilles, Netherlands
      - Colombia
      - Mexico
      - Trinidad and Tobago
      - Venezuela
    - Caribbean: Other
      - Bahamas[a]
      - Barbados[a]
      - Bermuda[a]
      - Costa Rica[a]
      - Cuba
      - Dominican Republic[a]
      - El Salvador[a]
      - Guadeloupe[a]
      - Guatemala[a]
      - Haiti[a]
      - Honduras[a]
      - Honduras, British[a]
      - Jamaica[a]
      - Leeward Islands[a]
      - Martinique[a]
      - Nicaragua[a]
      - Panama[a]
      - Panama Canal Zone
      - Puerto Rico
      - Windward Islands[a]
    - Latin America: Other
      - Antarctic Fisheries[a]
      - Argentina
      - Bolivia
      - Brazil
      - Chile
      - Ecuador
      - Falkland Islands[a]
      - French Guiana[a]
      - Guyana[a]
      - Paraguay
      - Peru
      - Surinam[a]
      - Uruguay
- Asia
  - Middle East
    - Middle East: Oil Producing
      - Bahrain
      - Iran
      - Iraq
      - Kuwait
      - Kuwait Neutral Zone
      - Qatar
      - Saudi Arabia
      - Trucial Oman
    - Middle East: Other
      - Aden[a]
      - Cyprus
      - Palestine (1925-38)
      - Israel (1949-65)
      - Jordan (1949-65)
      - Lebanon-Syria (1925-49)
      - Lebanon (1950-65)
      - Syria (1950-65)
      - Turkey
      - Yemen[a]
  - Far East and Other Asia
    - Afghanistan[a]
    - Borneo (former British)
      - Brunei
      - Sabah
      - Sarawak
    - Burma (1949-65)
    - Ceylon
    - Hong Kong
    - India
    - Indo-China (1925-65)
      - Cambodia (1954-65)
      - Laos (1954-65)
      - Vietnam, South (1954-65)
    - Indonesia
    - Japan
    - Korea (1925-38)
    - Korea, Republic of (1949-65)
    - Macao[a]
    - Malaya and Singapore
      - Singapore (1960-65)
    - Philippines
    - Ryukyu Islands[a]
    - Taiwan
    - Thailand
- Africa
  - North Africa
    - Algeria
    - Egypt (U.A.R.)
    - Libya
    - Morocco
    - Tunisia
  - Tropical Africa
    - Angola[a]
    - Cameroon[a]
    - Cape Verde Island[a]
    - Congo, Democratic Republic
    - East Africa
      - Kenya[a]
      - Uganda[a]
      - Tanganyika[a]
    - Equatorial Africa
      - Central African Republic[a]
      - Chad[a]
      - Congo (Brazzaville)[a]
      - Gabon[a]
    - Ethiopia[a]
    - Gambia[a]
    - Liberia
    - Madagascar[a]
    - Mauritius[a]
    - Mozambique[a]
    - Nigeria
    - Portuguese Guinea[a]
    - Reunion[a]
    - Rhodesian Federation
      - Malawi
      - Zambia
      - Rhodesia
    - Seychelles[a]
    - Sierra Leone[a]
    - Somalia[a]
    - Somaliland, French[a]
    - St. Thomas and Principe[a]
    - Sudan[a]
    - Togo[a]
    - West Africa
      - Dahomey[a]
      - Guinea[a]
      - Ivory Coast[a]
      - Mali[a]
      - Mauritania[a]
      - Niger[a]
      - Senegal[a]
      - Upper Volta[a]
    - Zanzibar[a]
  - South Africa

B. Two Alternate Groupings[c]

Region	*Derivation from basic grouping above*
(1) Developed countries	North America + Western Europe + Oceania + South Africa + Japan.
Underdeveloped countries	World–(Developed countries + Communist countries)
Communist countries. . . .	Sum of the following:
U.S.S.R.	from basic grouping
Comm. E. Europe	(U.S.S.R. and Communist Eastern Europe)–U.S.S.R.
Communist Asia	from basic grouping
(2) Organisation for Economic Cooperation and Development (OECD)[d]	Canada + United States + Western Europe (EEC) + Western Europe (EFTA) + Greece + Iceland + Ireland + Spain + Turkey + Japan
Communist countries. . . .	Same as under (1) above
World excluding OECD and Communist countries	World–(OECD + Communist countries)

[a]Refers to countries or areas for which data, though included in their applicable regional aggregate, are not shown in this volume. (See section below on "Availability of Unpublished Materials," p. 827.) Data for countries not marked with footnote [a] appear in the volume except for those tables (or portions thereof) that are almost entirely zero, unavailable, or very unreliable.

[b]Iceland, which joined EFTA on 1 March 1970, is excluded from the present EFTA classification. Finland is an associate member of EFTA.

[c]The rationale for these groupings is discussed in the accompanying text.

[d]Finland, which joined OECD on 28 January 1969, is excluded from the present OECD classification.

Note: Years shown in parentheses–e.g., "Korea, Republic of (1949-65)"–refer to the period for which basic data for the indicated area were collected. The years do not necessarily coincide with the period of the country's sovereign status (the Republic of Korea dates from 1948); nor do the years refer in all cases to data actually appearing in this volume (in our benchmark tabulations 1949 is omitted).

Comparison of Statistical Aggregates with other Publications

While there are numerous *ad hoc* and continuing publications (those issued by national and international bodies as well as private ones) containing statistics on energy for regions and separate countries, only a few do so on a worldwide basis. The United Nations *World Energy Supplies*, which has been issued annually beginning in 1952, is the most regular and comprehensive of these publications. By using successive editions of *World Energy Supplies*, it is possible to contruct a limited set of statistical series for the years 1929, 1937, and annually from 1949 to date. In doing so, one must allow for some fairly significant breaks in historical continuity of the data, for changes in geographic classification, and for limitations in the scope of particular energy series. Once published, the UN data have only infrequently been revised or adjusted to accord with ensuing releases.

To the extent of its reliance upon and adaptation of UN statistics, the present study tried to overcome some of the deficiencies in the UN historical series–e.g., by linking adjustments and other devices, as noted earlier on pp. 818-19. The UN statistics for the period since the late 1950s are less subject to the problem mentioned; changes in the scope of the various UN series became relatively minor over these years, and the need for successive revisions in a given year's data (so as to insure comparability with subsequent years) was not severe. Consequently, levels and changes in aggregates in our study conform reasonably well to those in recent UN documents. Without entering into comparisons of specific fuels and regions, we show below worldwide energy consumption (in million tons of coal equivalent) from the respective calculations.[18]

	This study	*UN World Energy Supplies*
1957 . . .	3,735	3,532
1960 . . .	4,196	4,230
1962 . . .	4,621	4,417
1963 . . .	4,910	4,716
1964 . . .	5,202	4,990
1965 . . .	5,472	5,231

Reasons for differences between the two series emerge from the discussion of detailed points raised elsewhere under separate subheads. For example, in the conversion to coal equivalents, crude oil gets a somewhat higher calorific value in the present study. Somewhat more detailed conversion factors are used in the present study for solid fuels. Lubricants and greases are included here and are excluded by the United Nations. Unlike our calculation, crude petroleum, as such, is not included in the UN figures on liquid fuels consumption; rather, the United Nations–departing from its procedure for measuring the consumption of other fuels–begins its liquid fuel consumption calculation with figures on production of refined petroleum products. As a result, that portion of crude oil consumption diverted to non-energy uses such as petrochemical feedstocks is excluded from UN data. This appears to be the major explanation for the UN world energy consumption totals falling consistently below ours, as shown above. In addition to these factors, there is the overriding fact that the variety of national and other sources consulted, along with our own estimates in the case of certain unavailable data, is

[18]This study's figures from table X; United Nations data from *World Energy Supplies*, Statistical Papers, Series J, No. 10, 1967.

likely to have yielded somewhat different figures from those published by the United Nations. On balance, however, these differences are of a sort that those using the UN system should find it both analytically useful and manageable to work our figures into a common quantitative frame of reference.

Selected world energy totals have been prepared for two additional studies: (1) United Kingdom Commonwealth Economic Committee, *Sources of Energy* (London: Her Majesty's Stationery Office, 1966); and (2) OECD, *Energy Policy* (Paris, 1966). World energy consumption totals published in the United Kingdom study are entirely consistent with those of the United Nations series (from which they were taken), with the exception that hydroelectricity has been converted at the (higher) central station fuel-input equivalent. (See subsequent discussion under "Conversion Factors and Procedures.") The United Kingdom study therefore shows consistently higher (by about 8 percent) world energy consumption levels than the United Nations document.[19]

The OECD publication also shows higher energy consumption totals than the United Nations. For 1962, the last year for which a comparison is possible, the OECD figure is about 10 percent higher. (The figure in the present study of 4,621 million coal-equivalent tons is about 5 percent higher.) One reason—accounting for perhaps half the difference—arises from the fact that the OECD, like the present study, measures liquid fuel consumption inclusive of crude oil diverted to feedstocks. Another reason—explaining 3 percent of the 10 percent difference—follows from the OECD's inclusion of bunkers in total consumption. A minor reason—1 percent out of the 10 percent—is a higher OECD thermal value for hydro, which, however, results from the addition of efficiency losses associated with the falling water. (See footnote 24, p. 830). There may also be differences stemming from source materials; the OECD study relied on the OECD's own statistics as well as on materials including, but going beyond, the UN data.

Availability of Unpublished Materials

Data have been compiled for countries and territories and for years other than those shown in the present volume. Statistics including about 100 additional countries and territories (allowed for in regional aggregates but not published) and for *each* year (as opposed to the published bench-mark years) in the periods 1925-38 and 1949-65 have been assembled and are retrievable from computer storage. In addition to these materials, notes have been prepared describing the sources of data for countries and years not published.

Were it not for considerations of space, we would have included in this volume all data that were assembled. However, it should be emphasized that the omission of country data from publication is to a large extent explained by their insignificance or by the absence in the basic sources consulted of numerous statistical series covered in the tables of Part Three. For example, very few tropical African countries recorded any fuel production or exports in the pre-World War II years. And there were no population estimates for numerous such areas. In these cases, of course, beyond what already appears in this volume, very little more than zeros or "nonavailable" symbols can be provided. Requests for information about the availability of unpublished materials should be sent to Resources for the Future, Inc.

Conversion Factors and Procedures

In the tables of Part Three, data are expressed both in an initially prepared set of metric system estimates (metric tons of coal and other solid and liquid fuels, cubic meters of natural gas, and kilowatt-hours of hydroelectricity) and in hard-coal equivalents ("coal equivalents," for short). (Metric system data had, at an earlier stage, been converted in many cases from prior worksheet tabulations expressed in U.S. or British measures such as short or long tons; or—in the case of liquids—from units of capacity, such as barrels or gallons, into units of weight.)

The purpose of conversion into coal equivalents is to permit aggregation of, and comparison among, the different energy forms. A common-denominator measure is as indispensable to energy analysis as dollar aggregates of dissimilar components of GNP are to the study of economic growth. Analysis of national energy requirements or of interfuel patterns of competition and use is normally conducted in terms of such a common unit of measure. The usual basis for measurement is in terms of the inherent heat content of the different raw energy forms; and the most common unit for measuring heat is the British thermal unit (Btu), defined as "the heat needed to raise one pound of water by one degree Fahrenheit, at or near the temperature of maximum density." (Two frequently used alternative measures of heat content are the kilocalorie, equal to 4 Btu, and the therm, equal to 100,000 Btu.) Given the Btu content of the various energy forms, the translation of different units of measure into a common unit follows routinely. (A metric ton of hard coal contains approximately 28 million Btu; a metric ton of crude oil contains approximately 41 million Btu; therefore a metric ton of crude oil equals about 1½ metric tons of coal, expressed in terms of coal equivalents.) The decision to use coal

[19]The U.K. conversion factor of 0.6 tons coal = 1,000 kwh hydro appears to us as somewhat too high as a worldwide average for the mid-1960s.

equivalents as the unit of energy measurement conforms to widespread usage. It is, however, an arbitrary practice, and one likely to wane as the future relative position of coal recedes; oil equivalents or kilowatt-hours, though less common, would also have been appropriate, as would such "neutral" heat units as Btu's or kilocalories.[20] Listed below is a summary of the conversion factors generally used in this study. Exceptions and more specific additional information appear in the accompanying tabulations.

Summary of Conversion Factors

Energy commodity	*Original unit of measurement*	*Conversion factor (metric ton of hard coal equivalent per indicated original unit of measurement)*
Hard coal (bituminous coal and anthracite)	metric ton	1.0 (see table for exceptions)
Hard coal briquettes	metric ton	1.0
Lignite and brown coal	metric ton	0.33 (see table for exceptions)
Lignite briquettes	metric ton	0.67
Coke	metric ton	0.9
Crude petroleum	metric ton	1.5
All other liquid fuels	metric ton	1.5
Natural gas[21]	1,000 cubic meters	1.332
Hydroelectricity	1,000 kilowatt-hours	0.125 (measured by heat content of the hydroelectricity; for alternative measure, based on prevailing coal-equivalent fuel requirements at thermal generating plants, see table, p. 830)

[20] It is also possible, of course, to combine different energy forms into an aggregate measure by using constant price weights. The superiority of such a measure has been argued by Ralph Turvey and A. R. Nobay in "On Measuring Energy Consumption," *Economic Journal*, December 1965, pp. 787-93. The choice in such matters is dictated by the use to which the statistics are to be put, and for our purposes a measure which relates energy content, as such, to other economic variables is more appropriate. Moreover, the energy aggregation approach yields results which can readily be fitted in with the body of work that others have done in the field of international energy statistics. It is conceded, however, that these alternative approaches *can* produce considerably different figures. For example, total energy output in the United States during 1899-1939 grew by 3 percent annually when measured in terms of energy content, and by 3.7 percent in terms of price-weighted indexes of physical production. H. Barger and S. H. Schurr, *The Mining Industries, 1899-1939* (National Bureau of Economic Research, 1944), pp. 14, 41.

[21] In the case of foreign trade in natural gas, data were generally obtained from published sources in "manufactured gas equivalent," which we then converted into "natural gas equivalents," at the rate of 1 cubic meter of natural gas = 2.22 cubic meters of manufactured gas. Also, methane from coal mines, where included, was converted into natural gas equivalents.

These conversion factors conform in most respects to those adopted in other publications on energy statistics; they follow closely the conversion factors currently used by the United Nations in what is the most standard and complete available statistical source—its *World Energy Supplies*.[22] The extent to which the present study introduces exceptions to and elaborates in somewhat more detailed fashion upon the UN conversions will be briefly noted.

Solid Fuel Coal Equivalent Conversion Factors
(Metric ton of coal equivalent per metric ton of item shown)

Country	*Coal*	*Sub-bituminous coal*	*Lignite and brown coal*	*Peat*
Albania	n.p.	[a]	0.5	n.p.
Argentina	1.0	1.28[b]	n.p.	0.33
Australia	1.0	0.8	0.25	n.p.
Austria	1.0	[a]	0.5	0.5
Brazil	(0.78–0.83)[c]	[a]	n.p.	n.p.
Bulgaria	1.0	[a]	0.3	n.p.
Canada	1.0	0.77	0.65	n.c.
Chile	1.0	[a]	0.33	n.p.
China, Mainland	(0.93–0.95)[d]	[a]	n.p.	n.p.
Czechoslovakia	1.0	[a]	0.6	n.p.
Denmark	n.p.	n.p.	0.29	0.36
Estonia	n.p.	n.p.	n.p.	0.5
Faeroe Islands	n.p.	n.p.	0.3	n.p.
Finland	n.p.	n.p.	n.p.	0.5
France	1.0	[a]	0.6	n.c.
Germany, East	1.0	[a]	0.3	0.5
Germany, West	1.0	0.67[e]	0.31	n.c.
Greece	n.p.	n.p.	0.5	n.p.
Hungary	1.0	[a]	0.6	n.p.
India	0.8	[a]	0.3	n.p.
Indo-China	1.0	[a]	0.3	n.p.
Ireland	1.0	[a]	n.p.	0.5
Italy	0.8	[a]	0.3	n.c.
Japan	1.0	[a]	0.5	0.5
Korea, North	1.0	[a]	0.3	n.p.
Korea, South	1.0	[a]	0.3	n.p.
Latvia	n.p.	n.p.	n.p.	0.5
Lithuania	n.p.	n.p.	n.p.	0.5
Malaya Federation	n.p.	0.72	n.p.	n.p.
Mongolia	0.75	[a]	n.p.	n.p.
Netherlands	1.0	[a]	0.33	n.c.
New Zealand	1.0	0.75	0.5	n.p.
Norway	1.0	n.p.	n.p.	0.5
Pakistan	0.8	[a]	[f]	n.p.
Poland	1.0	[a]	0.3	n.c.
Portugal	1.0	[a]	0.5	n.p.
Romania	1.0	[a]	0.6	n.p.
Spain	1.0	[a]	0.5	n.c.
Sweden	0.7	[a]	n.p.	0.5
Thailand	n.p.	n.p.	0.7	n.p.
Tunisia	n.p.	n.p.	0.33	n.p.
Turkey	1.0	[a]	0.33	n.p.
United States	[g]	[a]	[g]	n.p.
U.S.S.R.	[h]	[a]	[h]	[h]
Yugoslavia	1.0	[a]	0.5	n.p.

n.p.: No production, or else information regarding production, if any, unavailable. *(Notes continued on p. 829.)*

[22] See, for example, *World Energy Supplies, 1962-1965*, Statistical Papers, Series J, No. 10, 1967, pp. 6-8.

n.c.: Not considered.

[a]Production, if any, assumed to be included under "coal."

[b]Represents asphaltite produced and used as solid fuel.

[c]0.78 for 1925–38, and 0.83 for 1949–65.

[d]0.93 for 1925–57, and 0.95 for 1958–65.

[e]Pitch coal.

[f]Included under "coal."

[g]The average heat value of anthracite in the United States is estimated by the U.S. Bureau of Mines as 12,700 Btu/lb, or approximately 7,060 kcal/kg. The average figure for bituminous coal *and* lignite combined is 13,100 Btu/lb or 7,280 kcal/kg. The coal equivalent totals shown for the United States in table II of Part Three are derived using these average heat values applied respectively to the gross production figures of anthracite, and of bituminous coal and lignite combined. More specifically, to take account of the differences between these heat values (7,060 kcal/kg for anthracite and 7,280 kcal/kg for bituminous coal and lignite) and the 6,880 kcal/kg figure for hard coal (which defines our standard coal-equivalent measure), the conversion factor for anthracite was taken as 1.026 (= 7,060/6,880) and for bituminous coal and lignite as 1.058 (= 7,280/6,880). In order to derive bituminous coal plus anthracite and lignite separately, lignite *alone* is then converted at the rate of 0.33 metric tons of hard coal equivalent per metric ton of lignite (using UN data), while the so-called "hard coal" column of table II (i.e., bituminous coal plus anthracite) is then derived as a residual.

[h]Conversion factors applicable to Soviet coal, lignite, and peat vary over time; for a substantial part of the period covered implicit conversion factors, derived for a limited number of bench-mark years from data already reported in both raw and coal-equivalent terms (in Soviet statistics so-called "standard fuel" units of 7,000 kcal/kg), were used to develop the needed series. Throughout the period as a whole, a ton of peat corresponded to about 0.4 tons of coal equivalent; a ton of lignite, to 0.40–0.45 tons of coal equivalent; and a ton of hard coal, to about 0.9 tons of coal equivalent. The latter figure shows some decline in recent years.

Crude oil in metric tons = 1.5 metric tons coal equivalent. This figure compares with the UN figure of 1.3, and is intended to allow for the full calorific value of crude oil, rather than merely the calorific value of the net refinery output of the major liquid fuels—gasoline, kerosine, and fuel oils. The UN factor includes only about seven-eighths of the calorific content of crude oil, excluding both the energy conversion losses involved in refining crude oil—about 10 percent or more—and the energy content of such refined oil products as liquefied refinery gases, lubricating oils and greases, asphalt, and wax. We have therefore applied to crude oil the same conversion factor of 1.5 applicable to the other liquid fuels—including refined products as well as natural gas liquids.[23]

In the case of solid fuels, we felt it desirable to consider and use somewhat more detailed conversion factors than are used by the United Nations. These factors, shown in the accompanying tabulation, were compiled from a wide number of international and national sources—including, for example, various national papers for the several World Power Conferences, energy studies of the United Nations regional commissions, as well as national publications offering specific information about individual countries. It is believed that the resulting factors are somewhat more reliable than the more general UN factors, although it is readily admitted that major uncertainties regarding factors for specific countries and the stability of such factors over time still exist.

It may also be noted that the United Nations converts all energy commodities to hard-coal equivalent, without explicitly defining the energy content of "hard coal." However, the UN conversion of hydroelectricity to hard-coal equivalent provides a link which permits such definition: the UN conversion factor of 1 kwh = 0.125 kg coal equivalent necessarily implies a value of 27,295,000 Btu per metric ton coal equivalent, because 1 kwh = 3,412 Btu. At 4 Btu = 1 kcal, the foregoing yields a value of 6,880 kcal/kg, slightly less than the rather widely used standard (and rounded) value of 7,000 kcal/kg. However, no effort was, or could be, made to insure that all our coal equivalents represented a uniformly constant heat content. Given the widely differing heat values of "hard coal" in the various countries, as well as within any one of them, and the inadequacy of available information on average heat values, it would indeed have been presumptuous, if not quixotic, to attempt extensive refinements based on this small difference.

One of the more troublesome problems associated with the measurement of energy in a common-denominator unit has to do with the treatment of hydroelectricity. One has the choice of translating hydro in terms of its inherent heat value—i.e., at the rate of 0.125 kg hard coal equals 1,000 kwh of electricity; or, alternatively, hydro can be expressed using the coal-equivalent quantity of fuel required, under prevailing conditions, at thermal generating stations. A roughly calculated worldwide estimate of this hypothetical equivalence is (for recent years) that somewhat under 0.40 kg hard coal equals 1,000 kwh of electricity. (The figure of 0.40, commonly also expressed in Btu, is termed the "heat rate"; the ratio of 0.125 to 0.40—i.e., of output to input—represents the "efficiency" of fuel use in electrical generation, in percentage terms, equalling about 30 percent; while the difference between 0.40 and 0.125 largely represents energy loss arising from the conversion of heat energy into the mechanical energy needed to turn the dynamos.)

In all the coal-equivalent tables of Part Three (except for parts of tables XII and XIII), and following UN practice, we adopted the first of these two conversion procedures—that of translating hydro at the rate of 0.125 kg of coal equals 1,000 kwh (alternative "A"). In tables XII and XIII we include, in addition, estimates of hydroelec-

[23]The natural gasoline component of natural gas liquids (NGL) is appropriately converted at 1.5 while the liquefied petroleum gas component is more correctly converted at a slightly higher rate. For convenience, however, we have applied 1.5 to the entire NGL category.

tricity and total energy consumption using the fuel input-requirement basis of conversion (alternative "B"). The conversion factors used (they obviously change over time as efficiency changes) for this alternative calculation appear in the accompanying tabulation. These are exceedingly rough, and assailable, rates of conversion. (The difficulty of assembling meaningful conversion factors in a worldwide statistical study is one reason for rejecting this conversion procedure; other pros and cons are discussed below.) With the limited objective in mind of illustrating the effect upon total energy consumption of using the "B" approach, we relied upon a single historical series of conversion factors and applied these across the board to all countries and regions covered in the study. Even if these figures were truly a worldwide average—which, in the light of their derivation cannot be claimed—there is no ground for converting, at given years, each country's hydro at the same rate; generating technology and efficiency does vary considerably among countries. Nevertheless, in the light of the fact that the "A" and "B" approaches both have some virtues and some shortcomings, it seemed useful to include figures based on both procedures.

Alternative Conversion Factors for Hydroelectricity[a]

Year	Coal equivalent (metric ton) per 1,000 kwh
1925 . . .	1.00
1926 . . .	0.96
1927 . . .	0.92
1928 . . .	0.88
1929 . . .	0.85
1930 . . .	0.83
1931 . . .	0.81
1932 . . .	0.79
1933 . . .	0.77
1934 . . .	0.75
1935 . . .	0.73
1936 . . .	0.72
1937 . . .	0.71
1938 . . .	0.70
1949 . . .	0.56
1950 . . .	0.55
1951 . . .	0.53
1952 . . .	0.51
1953 . . .	0.49
1954 . . .	0.48
1955 . . .	0.47
1956 . . .	0.46
1957 . . .	0.45
1958 . . .	0.44
1959 . . .	0.43
1960 . . .	0.42
1961 . . .	0.41
1962 . . .	0.40
1963 . . .	0.39
1964 . . .	0.39
1965 . . .	0.38

[a]Applicable to calculation "B" in table XII and to lines 13 and 22 of table XIII. Estimates are based on prevailing coal-equivalent fuel requirements at thermal generating plants. In constructing these estimates, post-World War II rates of change and levels (the latter controlling for the entire period) in the heat rate were derived and aggregated for about twenty-five East and West European countries plus the United States and Canada on the basis of data in European Communities (EEC), *Energy Statistics, 1950-1965*, and various editions of UN-ECE, *Bulletin of Electric Energy Statistics.* Prewar rates are based on changes in the U.S. heat rate (Sam H. Schurr, Bruce C. Netschert, and others, *Energy in the American Economy, 1850-1975* [Johns Hopkins Press, 1960], p. 728). The results accord closely with the UN "world average" shown in the first issue of its *World Energy Supplies*, Statistical Papers, Series J, No. 1, 1952. There the United Nations cites figures of 0.9 kg of coal per 1,000 kwh for 1929, 0.7 for 1937, and 0.6 for 1950.

In an analytical context, the principal objection to the "A" procedure is its distorting effect: it seriously understates the energy production and consumption of countries with substantial proportions of hydroelectric energy. For example, with Norway's hydro measured (as in this study and by the United Nations) at its inherent heat value, the country's 1965 total energy consumption comes to about 13½ million tons coal equivalent; with the hydro component measured at a hypothetical fuel input of 0.38 kg of coal per 1,000 kwh (see tabulation), Norway's aggregate comes to 25½ million coal-equivalent tons, a nearly 90 percent jump.[24]

Another kind of distortion—though infrequent and likely to arise only in the case of very small areas—may result when a large portion of a country's generating capacity suddenly changes from thermal to hydro (or vice versa). The 1960 start-up of the Kariba Hydroelectric station in Rhodesia illustrates the point. "Measured" energy consumption for Rhodesia fell by 21 percent between 1959 and 1961—principally because of a substantial falling-off in coal requirements for an expanding volume of electric generation. Calculated on the fuel-input basis, the country's overall energy consumption still declined, but only by approximately 12 percent over the two-year period.[25]

However, this example by no means establishes an unanswerable case for procedure "B," which makes the

[24]The OECD adopts a method of converting hydroelectric data resulting in coal equivalents (or, in the OECD case, oil equivalents) somewhat higher than if the hydro were converted at calorific value, but considerably below what it would be if measured at central station fuel input. The OECD method introduces an allowance for conversion losses from the falling water to generating station terminals. Since the efficiency assumed (74 percent), however, is much higher than the efficiency of thermal production, the coal equivalent value of hydro still understates hydro's contribution to primary energy. See OECD, *Energy Policy* (Paris, 1966), p. 168.

[25]The decline, even in the second case, may mean that the hypothetical worldwide average heat rate which we are applying to Rhodesian thermal electricity generation is too low.

conversion based on a country's average thermal efficiency to produce electric energy, even though primary energy goes into uses other than electric or mechanical energy—e.g., heat. Norway, endowed with abundant and cheap hydro, uses considerably more of this waterpower for nonelectric purposes, such as space heating, than it would were it forced to rely on thermal generation. In other words, in the absence of its hydro resources, the country would not really require the fuels implied in the 25½ million ton figure just cited. Moreover, quite apart from the problem of measuring hydroelectricity, distortions in energy comparisons arise from the fact that equal quantities of heat content between two countries may, depending on the efficiency and allocation of uses, be put to highly unequal amounts of productively used energy in practice. Logically, this would call for conversion adjustments (i.e., "coefficients of substitution") similar to the hypothetical fuel-input procedure in the case of a hydro country. Nothing of the sort is statistically or conceptually feasible, although adherents of the "B" approach could—with some legitimacy—still point to the hydro measurement problem as being by far the most serious one.

On balance, a strong reason for choosing the "A" conversion is that it is the procedure used in the UN *World Energy Supplies*.[26] It appeared to us appropriate not to depart in such a fundamental way from a standard and widely used source, keeping in mind particularly the likelihood that readers might wish to use the historical material in this study as background in connection with their use of continuing UN releases.

The Handling of Nonavailable Data in Constructing Aggregates

As pointed out in the earlier remarks on "Character of the Basic Data," and as is more specifically indicated in various country source notes below, numerous gaps in published data have been filled by our own estimates, using for this purpose a variety of devices, not excluding that of the educated guess. Nonetheless, considerable unfilled "nonavailable" cells remain in the tables of Part Three; among the more conspicuous omissions, for example, is information regarding bunkers for the European Communist area.

Nonavailability of figures raised the problem of whether, for purposes of aggregation, the omissions were, on the one hand, important enough to bar the summation of series to which the missing figures belong or, on the other hand, could be viewed as relatively insignificant components of such sums, and therefore treated as zero. The problem exists both for country totals and regional totals. Our approach was to meet the issue not by an ironclad rule but judgmentally[27] as the two hypothetical cases below illustrate.

1st Example: Calculation of Consumption

	Production	(+) *Imports*	(-) *Exports*	(-) *Bunkers*	(=) *Consumption*
World	375	100	100	70	305
Region A	175	90	20	n.a.	215
Country 1	150	80	5	30	195
Country 2	15	5	5	n.a.	15
Country 3	10	5	10	n.a.	5
Region B	200	10	80	40	90
Country 4	160	5	60	10	95
Country 5	10	5	0	n.a.	15
Country 6	30	n.a.	20	n.a.	n.a.

2nd Example: Exports of Liquid Refined Products, by Type

	Total Exports	*Gasoline*	*Kerosine*	*Other*[28]
World	1,020	390	420	10
Region X	260	n.a.	n.a.	n.a.
Country (i)	200	n.a.	n.a.	n.a.
Country (ii)	60	40	20	0
Region Y	760	350	400	10
Country (iii)	510	250	250	10
Country (iv)	250	100	150	n.a.

[26] It should be noted that in data prior to 1955 the United Nations had itself used the "B" conversion procedure; as in our case, it did not allow for differences in conversion factors among individual countries.

[27] The way the problem was handled for population and total electricity consumption is discussed on pp. 822–23.

[28] Assumed, for purposes of this illustration, to comprise items shown separately in the tables.

Each example covers situations encountered in the development of the tabulations. In the first example, selected entries for bunkers (Countries 2, 3, 5, and 6) and one entry for imports (Country 6) are used to represent nonavailability. (Production was hardly ever allowed to stand as unavailable.) Four things should be noted: (a) The missing bunkers figure was not deemed significant enough to preclude the calculation of consumption—bunkers being regarded, for this purpose as zero, and consumption being therefore to a degree overstated. (b) The missing import figure for Country 6, on the other hand, *was* judged too important an omission to permit calculation of the country's consumption. Note that for purposes of regional aggregation, however, the missing import figure was treated as zero. Also, when an actual time series suggested (say, from the insignificance of a preceding or following year's *available* data) that the n.a. could be regarded as zero, the country's consumption *was* calculated. (c) The nonavailability of a significant number of individual country bunkers estimates did advise against calculating a regional bunkers total, as in the case of Region A, where two out of three countries are not available. However, these missing figures did not prevent calculation of the best possible larger regional total (in this case, the world)—arrived at by summing the total for Region B and whatever country figure was available for Region A. Nor did the missing figures bar the best estimate that could be made of the calculation of consumption for Region A, in the sense that understatement is minimized by at least considering Country 1's bunkers of 30. (d) Occasionally, a series was available (or could be derived) only for a regional total, rather than for each constituent country, as is the case of the bunkers total for Region B. Region B consumption is therefore "correct" while that for Countries 5 and 6 is overstated (bunkers being treated as zero). As a result, Region B total consumption falls short of the added consumption of Countries 4, 5, and 6.

In the second example, two sorts of nonavailable cells appear. For Country (iv) "Other" exports are not available, but for calculation of Country (iv) total exports and Region Y total "Other" exports, the omission is treated as zero. The more serious gap arises from the fact that the exports of Country (i) (and, therefore, of Region X of which it forms a major part) are available (or could be estimated) only in the aggregate. This poses the problem of whether a larger regional aggregate (in this case, the World) should—as would be most accurate—have the three items appear as not available, or whether figures based on what is available should be provided. In the present example, the maximum available world totals of gasoline, kerosine, and "other" were entered, leaving the horizontal World addition short by the 200 of the missing data for Country (i). In this example, as in the essentially *ad hoc* decisions entering into the tabulations of Part Three, the course followed was to generate aggregates for countries and regions as often as possible—that is, whenever this could be done without producing major distortion in the resulting totals. In other words, we were willing to err on the side of somewhat deficient totals rather than no totals. The subjective and question-begging element in this statement is readily conceded; and interpretive use of the data should be governed by these caveats.

Rounding

It was not deemed feasible to attempt a wholly internally consistent treatment with respect to rounding of data. This derives primarily from variability in "roundedness" in sources from which data were derived, and applies to the handling of different statistical series for a given country as well as to the handling of the same or different series for different countries.

Original data in the tables of Part Three were recorded in—and to the nearest of—the units shown below:

Solid and liquid fuels	thousand metric tons,
Natural gas	million cubic meters,
Hydro and total electricity	million kilowatt-hours,
Population	thousands.

Coal-equivalent units were recorded in—and to the nearest—thousand metric tons.

However, published sources occasionally did not permit us to follow this practice. For example, while hydroelectric production data were generally available in million kwh, the figures for quite a few countries could be obtained only in 10 million kwh (producing the zeros at the end of numerous hydro entries in table I). As a result, year-to-year (absolute or percent) comparisons between countries in these two groups may be somewhat distorted. (A country recording 10 units in two years may be equivalent to another country more precisely recorded as 6 and 14 in two years.) Also, while the principles of "significant figures" would dictate that aggregation of the two kinds of figures must bear the same degree of rounding (that is, the more precise figure rounded in the same way as the more rounded one), our failure to follow this rule might at times yield aggregates (say, regional totals) not wholly faithful to the nature of the sums from which they were constructed.

Occasionally, sources would provide a time series which would suddenly and obviously become less rounded—for example: 10, 10, 10, 20, 20, 27, 29. Changes in such series should be cautiously interpreted.

Conversions from original to coal-equivalent units frequently produce data which likewise depart from strict principles of rounding. Take, as an example, the conversion of lignite. A ton of lignite is commonly converted at a rate of 1 ton lignite = 0.33 tons hard coal. If the original lignite figure appeared as a rounded 100,000 tons (i.e., rounded to the nearest hundred thousand, and representing a possible range of 51,000 to 149,000 tons), the converted figure of 33,000 tons actually reflects a possible range of 17,000 to 49,000; on the other hand, an original figure of, say, 123,000 (i.e., rounded only to the nearest thousand) will yield a coal equivalent of 41,000 tons. In other words, both converted data appear to be correct to the nearest thousand, while in actuality this is only true of the second case. Because all conversions were performed by the computer, it was enormously more convenient to avoid having to program differential rounding procedures. The resulting distortion is minor for purposes of analyzing broad aggregates and long-term movements; it should, however, be borne in mind in cases where the data are used in very specific ways.

Finally, even when data are available in the desired unit, it should be noted that we applied our rounding standards uniformly to large and small countries (i.e., to countries having significant and negligible quantities of a particular item). This obviously requires a country producing, say, 1,000 tons of crude oil to raise its output by 50 percent before a new figure will be entered for that country, the new figure thereupon reflecting a 100 percent increase in output.

Anyone planning extensive use of the data (including, particularly, further manipulations) should bear these points in mind.

Abbreviations and Symbols Used[29]

m.t. . . . . . . metric tons

kgs . . . . kilograms

kwh . . . . . . kilowatt-hours

c.m. . . . . . . cubic meters

CE . . . . hard coal equivalent

- . . . . zero, less than half of unit shown, or not applicable; in the case of table X (columns 10 to 14, dealing with ratios of production to consumption) a dash may signify that numerator alone, or numerator and denominator both, are zero.

NA . . . . data not available or too unreliable to be used

10^3 . . . . . . thousand

10^6 . . . . . . million

* . . . . applies to table XIII, where a zero or negative number in the base or terminal year makes growth-rate calculation impossible

[29]These refer to abbreviations and symbols appearing in the tables of Part Three. Abbreviated references in the country notes to commonly cited sources appear under "Country Notes" (section II, below).

II. Country Notes[30]

Introductory Comment

This portion of Part Four lists, in compressed and abbreviated form, the derivation of the country data which form the ultimate basis for all the statistical tabulations of Part Three. These country notes apply exclusively to the source of data on primary fuel production (table I in Part Three), imports and exports (table IV), bunkers (table IX), and population and total electricity consumption (table XI). The remaining tables in Part Three–coal equivalents, energy consumption, percentages, growth rates, and per capita data–are described under General Notes; their arithmetic derivation is explained prior to each of the fourteen tables in Part Three.

Only the sources for those selected countries shown in Part Three are identified. The derivation of estimates and countries not specifically shown (even though these estimates are included in regional totals) is not included. As explained under "General Notes," inquiries about the availability of data as well as notes on derivation may be directed to Resources for the Future, Inc.

Certain other points about the derivation of country data should be noted:

a) For some periods and for certain groups of ex-colonial countries (e.g., those comprising the former Federation of Rhodesia and Nyasaland) notes will normally appear in the form of a combined entry rather than separate country citations. This treatment often applies to countries which, for part of the period spanned by the study, formed a single statistical or political unit.

b) Estimates (by the RFF staff) are a common citation. A fuller treatment of estimates appears under the subhead "Character of the Basic Data" in the General Notes section of this Part.

c) For countries whose data are reproduced in Part Three, documentation is provided for all years covered by the study–not merely the published bench-mark years. When no years are shown for a particular energy form, the indicated source applies to all years for which there are data in Part Three. Thus, under production for Albania, the entry "Hydro: UNSY" means that the United Nations *Statistical Yearbook* was the source for all years for which hydro production for Albania is estimated in table I. When only part of the historical period covered by the study (1925-38, 1949-65) is documented as to source (as, for example, when crude oil production for Albania is given beginning with the year 1933), the remaining years (in this case 1925-32) are understood to be either zero or not available (NA). The reader can easily determine which of the two it is by referring to the particular table in which the item appears. Only in cases where, for that country, the table (or portions thereof) has been deleted from the published data of Part Three will such a determination be difficult. However, except for bunkers where data were not available for a number of countries (especially Communist countries), deletion was prompted mostly by zero entries.

d) Zero values are generally not identified as to source; i.e., they may either have been so designated in a specific published source or, lacking evidence of mere "nonavailability," we may have presumed to count them at zero.

e) Routine adaptation of data in a published source from one unit of measure to another is not described. This includes, e.g., conversion of coal from long tons into metric tons, or of oil from a volumetric to a weight basis via assumed specific gravities.

f) Following the detail shown in the tables, notes to the solid fuel production statistics often distinguish between hard coal, lignite, and certain other solid fuels. Under imports and exports–where only solid fuels in coal equivalents appear in the tables (having been built up from separate underlying components)– the source notes are correspondingly general.

g) Data generally refer to calendar years. Numerous exceptions prevail, however, and these are *not* noted in the country source notes.

h) Only a general citation to, rather than reference to the specific editions of, a serial publication (e.g., the United Nations *Statistical Yearbook*) is given.

i) In cases where a particular historical series was constructed using a wide variety of sources, a general statement to that effect is made, without attributing specific figures to specific publications.

j) Data obtained from an unpublished source (e.g., the United Nations Statistical Office) are so identified. However, in cases where figures were obtained shortly before their appearance in published form, the published source nonetheless is cited. Sometimes data thus obtained were available in a less rounded form than in the cited document. (Examples: UN data on bunkers and foreign trade for 1961-65.)

k) Data, particularly for the later years, may be preliminary and subject to revision.

l) Because of the standardized and repetitious treatment, as well as because of the expectation that the sources will be consulted primarily for occasional reference, the wording is frequently fragmentary; abbreviations for the most cited publications follow.

[30] See fn. 1 of Part Four, p. 817.

Listing and Abbreviations of Commonly Cited Sources and Organizations[31]

ECAFE Proceedings . . . United Nations, Economic Commission for Asia and the Far East. *Proceedings* of the Second Symposium on the Development of Petroleum Resources of Asia and the Far East. Mineral Resources Development Series no. 18, vol. II. 1963.

ECE . . . . United Nations, Economic Commission for Europe.

ECE-QCS . . . . . United Nations, Economic Commission for Europe. *Quarterly Bulletin of Coal Statistics for Europe.* Geneva, 1952-present.

ECLA . . . . United Nations, Economic Commission for Latin America.

ECLA ELA . . . . United Nations, Economic Commission for Latin America. *Energy in Latin America.* Geneva, 1957.

EEC-EnStat . . . . European Communities (EEC). *Energy Statistics.* Brussels, periodic, 1962-present.

FPC . . . . United States, Federal Power Commission.

Guyol . . . . United States, Department of State. *Energy Resources of the World.* Publication 3428. Washington: Government Printing Office, 1949. Study prepared under the direction of Nathaniel B. Guyol.

ITPP . . . . United States, Department of Commerce. *International Trade in Petroleum and its Products.* Trade Promotion Series. Washington: Government Printing Office, periodic.

Kohlen . . . . Unternehmensverband Ruhrbergbau. *Die Kohlenwirtschaft der Welt in Zahlen.* Essen: Verlag Glückauf GMBH, periodic, 1925-61.

LNITS . . . . League of Nations. *International Trade Statistics.* Annual, 1926-38.

LNSY . . . . League of Nations. *Statistical Year-Book.* Annual, 1926-38.

MY . . . . United States, Department of the Interior, Bureau of Mines. *Minerals Yearbook.* Washington: Government Printing Office, annual, 1925-present.

OECD Stat.En . . Organisation for Economic Cooperation and Development. *Basic Statistics of Energy.* Paris, OECD, annual, 1958-present.

Regul . . . . Rudolf Regul. *Energiequellen der Welt.* Hamburg: Hanseatische Verlagsanstalt, published for the Institut für Konjunkturforschung, 1937.

UKSS . . . . Institute of Geological Sciences, Overseas Division, Mineral Resources Section. *Statistical Summary of the Mineral Industry.* London: Her Majesty's Stationery Office, annual, 1925-present.

UNDY . . . . United Nations. *Demographic Yearbook.* Annual, 1948-present.

UNIPEDE . . . . . Union Internationale des Producteurs et Distributeurs d'Énergie Électrique.

UNITS . . . . United Nations, Department of Economic and Social Affairs, Statistical Office of the United Nations. *Yearbook of International Trade Statistics.* New York: United Nations, annual, 1950-present

UNSY . . . . United Nations. *Statistical Yearbook.* New York: United Nations, annual, 1948-present.

UNWES . . . . . . United Nations. *World Energy Supplies.* Statistical Papers, Series J. New York: United Nations, annual, 1952-present.

USBM . . . . United States, Department of the Interior, Bureau of Mines.

USDC . . . . United States, Department of Commerce.

WPC . . . . Central Office of the World Power Conference. *Statistical Year-Book of the World Power Conference.* London, periodic, 1936-60.

[31]In this listing only the latest or (in the case of discontinued publications) final title and detail of publication is provided; during its history a publication may have undergone changes in both. The description indicates whether a document represents an annual or periodic edition along with which period of our 1925-65 time span it has been published.

est . . . . Signifies estimate or estimates by RFF staff.

LPG . . . . Liquefied petroleum gas.

lubes . . . . Refers to lubricants and greases.

NGL . . . . Natural gas liquids.

Country Notes

Albania

Production
Lignite: 25-38 MY; 49-65 UNSY.
Crude oil: 33-38 MY; 49-65 UNSY.
Hydro: UNSY.
Imports and Exports (For derivation of certain 49-54 estimates see U.S.S.R. source notes.)
Solid fuels: 35-38 UKSS; 49-54 est.; 57-65 UNWES.
Liquid fuels: 25-36 LNITS; 37-38 UKSS; 49-53 est.; 54-60 data furnished by UN Stat. Office; 61-65 UNWES.
Population
25-28, 31-32, 34 based on LNSY (some adjustment in the LNSY figures was necessary to produce approximate consistency with other years); 29, 33 LNSY; 30, 35-38, 49-65 UNDY.
Electricity Consumption
53-54 UNSY; 55-65 UNWES.

Algeria

Production
Hard coal: LNSY and UNSY.
Crude oil: 25-33 LNSY; 49-65 UNSY.
NGL: UNSY.
Natural gas: UNSY.
Hydro: 25-28, 30-32 est.; 29, 33-38, 49-65 UNSY.
Imports and Exports
Solid fuels: 25-30 imports and 25-28 exports estimated as sum of retained imports and bunkers given in Regul; 31-38 imports and 29-38 exports UKSS; 49-50 est. based on UKSS and linked to 51-65 UNWES.
Liquid fuels: lubes all years UKSS; all other liquid fuels 25-28 ITPP, 29-38 UKSS, 49-53 data in UKSS adjusted by linking to 54 UN figure, 54-60 data from UN Stat. Office, 61-65 UNWES.
Gas: UNWES.
Electricity: UNWES.
Bunkers
Solid fuels: 25-36 Regul; 37-38, 55-60 UKSS; 49-54 UNWES.
Liquid fuels: 32-38, 55-59 UKSS; 49-54, 60-65 UNWES.
Population
UNDY.
Electricity Consumption
25-28, 30-32 est. based on LNSY data apparently covering Algiers only; 33-38 UNSY; 29, 49-65 UNWES.

Antilles, Netherlands

Imports and Exports
Solid fuels: UKSS.
Liquid fuels: 25 est.; 26-38 and lubes all years UKSS; other liquid fuels 49-53 UKSS adjusted by linking to 54 UN figure; 54-60 data furnished by UN Stat. Office; 61-65 UNWES.
Bunkers
Solid fuels: 25-28 est.; 29-33 UKSS.
Liquid fuels: 25-28 ITPP; 29-33, 38 est.; 34-37 UKSS; 49-65 UNWES.
Population
UNDY.
Electricity Consumption
UNWES.

Argentina

Production
Hard coal: 49-65 UNSY.
Other (asphaltite and peat): asphaltite est. 50-59; peat est. 60; all other years MY.
Crude oil: 25-33 LNSY; 34-38, 49-65 UNSY.
NGL: 27-38, 49-65 UNSY.
Natural gas: 25-38, 49-50 ECLA *Report of the Latin American Power Seminar*, Mexico City, 1961 (Santiago: 1962) adjusted by linking to 51 UN figure; 51-65 UNSY.
Hydro: 25-28, 30-31 est.; 29 UNWES; 32-38 derived from ECLA ELA; 49-50 est. based on UNWES; 51-54 est. based on UNSY for public hydro data; 55-65 UNWES.
Imports and Exports
Solid fuels: 25-35 Regul; 36-38, 49-50 UKSS; 51-65 UNWES.
Liquid fuels: 25-38 and lubes all years UKSS; 49-53 UKSS adjusted by linking to 54 UN figure; 54-60 data furnished by UN Stat. Office; 61-65 UNWES.
Bunkers
Solid fuels: 25-36 Regul; 37-38 UKSS.
Liquid fuels: 32-36, 38 assumed equal to reported exports (from UKSS); 37 Guyol; 49-65 UNWES.
Population
UNDY.
Electricity Consumption
25-28 est. based on movement of electricity production in Buenos Aires (from LNSY) and adjusted by linking to 29 UNWES; 30-34 LNSY; 35-38 UNSY; 49-65 UNWES.

Australia

Production

Hard coal: UKSS.

Lignite: UNSY.

Other (sub-bituminous): UKSS.

Crude oil: UNSY.

Natural gas: UNSY.

Hydro: 25-38, 49-63 data furnished by Australian Department of National Development; 64-65 UNSY.

Imports and Exports

Solid fuels: 25-38, 49-50 UKSS; 51-65 UNWES.

Liquid fuels: 25-38 and lubes and greases 49-65 UKSS; crude oil 49-53 UNWES (using net import figure–exports known to be zero); other refined petroleum products 49-53 UKSS; all data, except lubes and greases, for 54-60 furnished by UN Stat. Office, 61-65 UNWES.

Bunkers

Solid fuels: 25-26, 30-38, 49-65 UKSS; 27-29 LNITS.

Liquid fuels: 25-38 Australian national trade statistics; 49-65 UNWES.

Population

UNDY (excludes aborigines: 46,638 in 1947; 39,319 in 1954; 40,081 in 1961).

Electricity Consumption

25-38 UNSY; 49-65 UNWES.

Austria

Production

Hard coal: LNSY and UNSY.

Lignite: LNSY and UNSY.

Other (peat): 33-36 WPC; 37-38, 49 est.; 50-65 MY.

Crude oil: UNSY.

NGL: UNSY.

Natural gas: 34 Kohlen; 49 est.; 50-65 UNSY.

Hydro: UNSY.

Imports and Exports

Solid fuels: 25-38 Regul and Kohlen (38 figure adjusted to conform to 1937 boundaries); 49-50 UKSS; 51-65 UNWES.

Liquid fuels: 25-38 UKSS; 49 crude oil exports est. basis of net exports in UNWES (imports known to be negligible); 50-53 crude oil OECD Stat. En.; 54-60 crude oil data furnished by UN Stat. Office; 61-65 crude oil UNWES; 49-65 lubes UKSS; other refined petroleum prods. 49-53 UKSS, 54-65 same source as crude oil.

Electricity: 25-38 constructed from variety of published sources–principally WPC, but including partial estimates and unpublished data furnished by ECE; 49-65 UNWES.

Bunkers

UNWES.

Population

UNDY.

Electricity Consumption

25-38 production figures from UNSY minus net exports from indicated source; 49-65 UNWES.

Bahrain

Production

Crude oil: UNSY.

Imports and Exports

36-38, 49-53 UKSS; 54-60 data furnished by UN Stat. Office; 61-65 UNWES.

Bunkers

49 est.; 50-51, 55-62 UKSS; 52-54, 63-65 UNWES.

Population

UNDY.

Electricity Consumption

UNWES. (Published data for 51-59 excluding industrial generation have been adjusted upward by linking to 60 figure comprising total generation.)

Belgium-Luxembourg

Production

Hard coal: LNSY.

Natural gas: UNSY.

Hydro: 25-32 est.; 33-36 WPC; 37-38, 49-65 UNSY.

Imports and Exports

Solid fuels: 25-38, 49-50 UKSS; 51-65 UNWES.

Liquid fuels: 25-38 and lubes all years UKSS; all other liquid fuels 49-53 UKSS, 54-60 data furnished by UN Stat. Office, 61-65 UNWES.

Gas: UNWES.

Electricity: 31-38 WPC and Guyol; 49-65 UNWES.

Bunkers

Solid fuels: 25-38 UKSS; 49-54 UNWES; 55-59 ECE-QCS; 60-65 UNWES.

Liquid fuels: 25-38 UKSS; 49-65 UNWES.

Population

UNDY.

Electricity Consumption

25-38 LNSY and UNSY (data for 25-32 are for Belgium only); 49-65 UNWES. (Subsequent to completion of final machine tabulations, data for 63-65 have been revised considerably upward–the 65 figure by about 10 percent.)

Bolivia

Production

Crude oil: 28-29 UNSY; 30-33 LNSY; 34-38, 49-65 UNSY.

Natural gas: 55-65 UNSY.

Bolivia (Cont'd.)

Hydro: 29, 37 UNWES; 25-28, 30-36 est.; 38, 49-50, 57-65 UNSY; 51 est.; 52, 54 derived from data in ECLA ELA.

Imports and Exports

Solid fuels: 25-33 LNITS; 34-38, 49-50 UKSS; 51-65 UNWES.

Liquid fuels: 25-38 UKSS (except 25-27 lubes LNSY); lubes 49-65 UKSS; all other liquid fuels 49-54 UKSS, 55-60 data furnished by UN Stat. Office, 61-65 UNWES.

Bunkers

UNWES.

Population

UNDY.

Electricity Consumption

37-38, 49-54 UNSY; 55-65 UNWES.

Borneo, British

(comprising Brunei, Sabah, and Sarawak)

Production

Solid fuels: 25-38 MY (Sabah only).

Crude oil: LNSY and UNSY. (Until early 1930's, represents primarily Sarawak production; thereafter, primarily Brunei.)

NGL: 25-38 derived and partially est. from WPC; 55-65 UNSY. (25-38 refers to Sarawak NGL production; 55-65 to Brunei.)

Natural gas: 33-38 derived from data in WPC; 49 derived from data in UKSS; 50-65 UNSY. (Data refer to sales rather than gross production and apply exclusively to Brunei; apparent break in series after 1956 impairs historical comparison.)

Imports and Exports

Solid fuels: UKSS and partly estimated.

Liquid fuels: 25-38, 49-53 and lubes all years UKSS; 54-60 data furnished by UN Stat. Office; 61-65 UNWES.

Gas: UNWES. (Brunei net exports, Sarawak net imports; there are slight unexplained differences in the respectively reported data.)

Bunkers

UNWES and UKSS.

Population

UNDY.

Electricity Consumption

UNWES.

Brazil

Production

Hard coal: 25-27 LNSY; 28-38 and 49-65 MY. (A reviewer suggests that the MY data may overstate Brazil's hard coal output because of the inclusion of excessive waste content. However, it was not feasible to adjust for this possibility.)

Crude oil: UNSY.

Natural gas: 49-65 UNSY (gross production, including repressuring and waste).

Hydro: 25-38 est. largely on basis of Rio and São Paulo *total* public production; 49-65 UNSY.

Imports and Exports

Solid fuels: 25-38 LNITS; 49-50 UKSS; 51-65 UNWES.

Liquid fuels: 25-38, 49-55 and lubes all years UKSS; all other liquid fuels 56-60 data furnished by UN Stat. Office, 61-65 UNWES.

Bunkers

49-65 UNWES.

Population

UNDY. (Excludes Indians living in jungle reportedly 45,000 in 1950, 150,000 in 1956.)

Electricity Consumption

28, 30-36, 38 est. using series cited under *Production*; 29, 37, 49-65 UNWES.

Brunei

(see Borneo, British)

Bulgaria

Production

Hard coal: LNSY and UNSY.

Lignite: LNSY and UNSY.

Crude oil: UNSY.

Hydro: 25-27 est.; 28-38, 50-65 UNSY; 49 est. on basis of trends in total public generation.

Imports and Exports (For derivation of certain 49-53 estimates see U.S.S.R. source notes.)

Solid fuels: 25-37 Kohlen; 38 UKSS; 55-65 UNWES.

Liquid fuels: 25-38 UKSS; 49-53 est.; 54-60 data furnished by UN Stat. Office; 61-65 UNWES.

Electricity: UNWES.

Population

UNDY.

Electricity Consumption

25-30 LNSY; 31-38 UNSY; 49-54 UNSY; 55-65 UNWES.

Burma

(1949-65; for period 1925-38 included with India.)

Production

Solid fuels: UNSY.

Crude oil: UNSY.

Natural gas: UNSY.

Hydro: UNSY.

Imports and Exports

Solid fuels: UNWES.

Liquid fuels: lubes and greases 53-65 UKSS; all other liquid fuels 49-52 est., 53 UKSS adjusted by linking to 54 UN data, 55-60 data furnished by UN Stat. Office, 61-65 UNWES.

Bunkers

UNWES.

Population

UNDY.

Electricity Consumption

UNWES. (51-54 data on public generation only adjusted upward to include estimate of industrial.)

Cambodia

(see Indo-China)

Canada

Production

Hard coal: 25-37, 49-58 Kohlen; 38 MY; 59-65 UKSS.

Lignite and other (sub-bituminous): 25-38, 49-58 MY and Kohlen; 59-65 UKSS.

Crude oil: 25, 49-50 UKSS; 26-37 LNSY; 38 UNSY; 51-65 MY.

NGL: UNSY.

Natural gas: 25-38 LNSY and UNSY; 49-65 UNSY.

Hydro: 25-33 LNSY; 34-36 Davis, *Canadian Energy Prospects* (Ottawa: Royal Commission on Canada's Economic Prospects, 1957); 37-38, 56-65 UNSY; 49-55 est. based on "Public" hydro series from UNSY.

Imports and Exports

Solid fuels: UKSS.

Liquid fuels: 25-38 and lubes for all years where shown primarily UKSS but partially estimated (lube exports included under fuel oil 25-34); crude oil and gasoline 49-53 UKSS, 54-60 data furnished by UN Stat. Office; 61-65 UNWES; kerosine and fuel oil 49 est., 50-53 OECD Stat. En. adjusted by linking to 54 UN figure, 55-65 as with crude oil and gasoline.

Gas: 25-38 MY; 49-65 UNWES.

Electricity: 25-38 derived (jointly with the preparation of United States and Mexico trade estimates) from U.S. Census, *Historical Stat. of the U.S.* (1960), WPC, and other sources; 49-65 UNWES.

Bunkers

UKSS and UNWES.

Population

UNDY.

Electricity Consumption

25-28, 30-31 production figures derived from LNSY less net exports from indicated source; 29, 32-38 production from UNSY less net exports; 49-65 UNWES.

Central African Republic

(see Equatorial Africa)

Ceylon

Production

Hydro: UNSY.

Imports and Exports

Solid fuels: 25-38, 49-50 UKSS; 51-65 UNWES.

Liquid fuels: 25-38, 49-53 and lubes all years UKSS; 54-60 data furnished by UN Stat. Office; 61-65 UNWES.

Bunkers

Solid fuels: 25-38, 55-62 UKSS; 49-54, 63-65 UNWES.

Liquid fuels: 25-27 est.; 28-38, 55-62 UKSS; 49-54, 63-65 UNWES.

Population

UNDY.

Electricity Consumption

35-38 UNSY; 49-65 UNWES.

Chad

(see Equatorial Africa)

Chile

Production

Hard coal and lignite: 25-32, 37-38 est. breakdown between coal and lignite on basis of total solid fuel data UKSS, UNSY, LNSY; 33-36 UKSS; 49-50 est.; 51-65 UNSY.

Crude oil: UNSY.

NGL: 49-59 natural gasoline only from UNSY; 60-65 total NGL from MY.

Natural gas: 49-59 *gross production* figures (derived from UNSY, MY and other sources) adjusted substantially downward by linking to UN figure (*utilization*) for 60; 60-65 UNWES.

Hydro: 25-29, 31-38, 49 estimated on basis of ELA; 30, 50-51 US Commerce Dept. *Investment in Chile* (1958); 52-65 UNSY.

Imports and Exports

Solid fuels: 25-36 Regul; 37-38, 49-50 UKSS; 51-65 UNWES.

Liquid fuels: 25-38 and lubes all years UKSS; 49-53 UKSS (fuel oil adjusted by linking to 54 UN figure); 54-60 data supplied by UN Stat. Office; 61-65 UNWES.

Bunkers

25-32 UKSS; 33-38 included with export data; 49-65 UNWES.

Population

UNDY.

Electricity Consumption

Chile (Cont'd.)

29, 37 UNWES; 25-28, 30-36, 38 based on 29 and 37 total/hydro ratios and moved according to hydro series from *Production* table; 49-65 UNWES.

China, Mainland

(see Communist Asia)

Communist Asia

[Comprising Mainland China all years (Manchuria and Kwantung data added where appropriate and possible); North Korea and Mongolia (1949-65), and North Vietnam (1954-65)]

Production

China, Mainland:

Hard coal: 25-34, 61-65 MY; 35-38, 49-57 Yuan-li Wu, *Economic Development and the Use of Energy Resources in Communist China* (New York: Praeger for the Hoover Institution, 1963); 58-60 est.

Crude oil: 29-30 est. based on UKSS; 31-38, 49-59 Wu; 60-65 MY.

Natural gas: Little known about natural gas supplies in Mainland China, and we have arbitrarily marked the series zero rather than not available; fragmentary information, cited in Wu, suggests a possible natural gas output of 600-700 million cubic meters in the early 1960's.

Hydro: 49-51 est. on basis of data given in Wu; 52-60 Wu; 61-65 est. based on series shown in UNWES for total Communist Asia. (Note: Among other things, the sharp break between 60 and 61 makes this series one of very doubtful reliability.)

North Korea:

Hard coal: UNSY.

Lignite: UNSY.

Hydro: 49-54 UNSY; 55-60 derived from Wu and UNWES; 61-65 est. based on series shown in UNWES for total Communist Asia.

Mongolia:

Hard coal: 49-51, 53-54 est.; 52 UNSY; 55-65 MY.

Crude oil: UNSY.

North Vietnam:

Hard coal: UNSY.

Imports and Exports

Solid fuels: 25-38 figures derived from UKSS, Kohlen, and official Chinese foreign trade returns; 55-65 UNWES.

Liquid fuels: 25-37 figures derived from UKSS, Regul, and official Chinese foreign trade returns; 38 est.; 55-60 data furnished by UN Stat. Office; 61-65 UNWES.

Bunkers

Solid fuels: 25-38 UKSS except 34 from official Chinese foreign trade returns. (Note: 33-38 are exclusively Manchuria; 32 the sum of China and Manchuria; 49-50 UNWES refers to bunkers of China Mainland and North Korea.)

Liquid fuels: 49-50 UNWES.

Population

China, Mainland: 25-38 very rough estimates using fragmentary information in LNSY; 49-65 UNDY.

Mongolia, North Korea, North Vietnam: UNDY.

Electricity Consumption (Note: No data available for North Korea 50-52, 54, North Vietnam 54 and Mongolia 49, 51. For these years a rough electricity figure for total Communist Asia includes implicit estimates for these countries.)

China, Mainland: 29, 37 UNWES; other years during 25-38 roughly estimated on basis of UNSY data; 52-60 UNSY. (Note: The geographical scope of the series is quite uncertain.)

Mongolia, North Korea, North Vietnam: UNSY.

Communist Asia TOTAL: 25-38 as under China, Mainland; 49-50, 55-59, 61-65 UNWES; 51-54 est.; 60 UNSY.

Colombia

Production

Solid fuels: 25 est.; 26-32 LNSY; 33 est.; 34-38, 49 ECLA ELA; 50-65 UNSY.

Crude oil: 25-27 LNSY; 28-38, 49-57 UNSY; 58-65 MY. Note: 25-38, 49-57 includes NGL (natural gasoline).

NGL: UNSY.

Natural gas: UNSY.

Hydro: 25-28 est.; 29 UNWES; 30-33 est.; 34-36, 49-50 derived from ECLA ELA; 37-38, 51-65 UNSY.

Imports and Exports

Solid fuels: 25-38 UNSY; 54, 57, 64-65 UNWES.

Liquid fuels: 25-38, 49-54 and lubes all years UKSS; other liquid fuels 55-60 data furnished by UN Stat. Office, 61-65 UNSY.

Bunkers

UNWES.

Population

UNDY.

Electricity Consumption

25-38 est. using 29 and 37 ratios of hydro to total (from UNWES) and movements in hydro from *Production* table; 49-64 UNSY; 65 UNWES.

Congo (Brazzaville)

(see Equatorial Africa)

Congo, Democratic Republic (Kinshasa)

(includes Burundi and Rwanda)

Production

Hard coal: 25-38, 49-65 MY.

Hydro: 29, 37, 49, 59-65 UNWES; 25-28 est.; 30-36, 38, 50-58 UNSY.

Imports and Exports

Solid fuels: 25-38, 49-50 UKSS; 51-65 UNWES.

Liquid fuels: 25-38, 49-53 and lubes all years where shown UKSS; 54-60 data furnished by UN Stat. Office; 61-65 UNWES. (Lube imports 25-26 included under fuel oils.)

Electricity: UNWES.

Bunkers

UNWES.

Population

UNDY.

Electricity Consumption

29, 49-65 UNWES; 30-38 UNSY.

Cuba

Production

Crude oil: 33-38, 49-65 MY.

Hydro: 25-29, 31, 35-36, 38, 51, 53 est.; 30, 32-34 U.S. Commerce Dept., *World Power Manual*; 37, 55-65 UNWES; 49-50, 54 derived from data in ECLA ELA.

Imports and Exports

Solid fuels: 25-38 UKSS; 49-50 UKSS adjusted by linking to 51 UN figure; 51-65 UNWES.

Liquid fuels: Crude oil 25-29 and 31-37 LNITS; 30 est.; 38 UKSS; refined products 25-38 and lubes 49-59 UKSS; all other liquid fuels 49-53 UKSS adjusted by linking to 54 UN figure, 54-60 data furnished by UN Stat. Office, 61-65 UNWES.

Bunkers

UNWES.

Population

UNDY.

Electricity Consumption

31-38 UNSY; 49-65 UNWES.

Czechoslovakia

Production

Hard coal: LNSY and UNSY.

Lignite: 25-36, 38 LNSY and UNSY; 37, 49 MY; 50-65 UNSY.

Crude oil: LNSY and UNSY.

Natural gas: UNSY.

Hydro: 25-27 est. on basis of trends in total generation from LNSY; 28-38, 49-65 UNSY.

Imports and Exports (For derivation of certain 49-54 estimates see U.S.S.R. source notes.)

Solid fuels: 25-38 LNITS, Regul, ECE-QCS, and Kohlen (38 adjusted to 37 territorial coverage); 49-54 imports and 49-53 exports est.; 54 exports UKSS; 55-65 UNWES.

Liquid fuels: Crude oil 25-29 ITPP; 30-38 UKSS; total refined products (breakdown not available) 25, 30-38 UKSS; 26-29 ITPP; all liquid fuels 49-53 est.; 54-60 data furnished by UN Stat. Office; 61-65 UNWES.

Electricity: 25-35 Guyol; 36-38 WPC; 49-50, 55-65 UNWES; 51-53 est.

Gas: UNWES.

Population

UNDY (Note: territorial changes, for which figures are not adjusted, impair to some extent the historical comparability of the series.)

Electricity Consumption

25-38, 51-54 UNSY; 49-50, 55-65 UNWES.

Dahomey

(see West Africa)

Denmark

Production

Lignite: 25-38, 49-55: *Danmarks Energiforsyning, 1900-1958*; 56-65 MY.

Other (peat): 25-38, 49-58 *Danmarks Energiforsyning*; 59-65 MY.

Hydro: UNWES.

Imports and Exports

Solid fuels: 25-38, LNSY and Regul; 49-50 UKSS; 51-65 UNSY.

Liquid fuels: 25-38, 49-53 UKSS; 54-60 data furnished by UN Stat. Office; 61-65 UNWES.

Electricity: 25-38 Guyol; 49-65 UNWES.

Bunkers

Solid fuels: 55-58 *Danmarks Energiforsyning*; 59 est.; 60-65 UNWES.

Liquid fuels: UNWES.

Population

UNDY.

Electricity Consumption

25-38 UNSY and LNSY; 49-65 UNWES.

East Africa

(Comprises Kenya, Uganda, Tanganyika)

Production

Hard coal: MY (Tanganyika).

Hydro: 25-28, 30-36, 38 est.; 29, 37 UNWES; 49-65 UNSY.

Imports and Exports

Solid fuels: 25-38, 49-58 UKSS; 56-58 based on net import data from UNWES (three-country breakdown was estimated); 59-65 UNWES. (All 49-65 trade accounted for by Kenya.)

Liquid fuels: 25-38, 49-55 and lubes all years UKSS; 59-60 data furnished by UN Stat. Office (for all three areas); 61-65 UNWES (for all three areas).

East Africa (Cont'd.)

(Liquid fuels trade largely accounted for by Kenya.)
Electricity: UNWES. (Represents largely Kenya net imports from Uganda.)

Bunkers
Solid fuels: 25-38 UKSS; 49-52 UNWES. (All Kenya.)
Liquid fuels: 29-38, 55-62 UKSS; 49-54, 63-65 UNWES. (Primarily Kenya.)

Population
UNDY.

Electricity Consumption
UNWES.

East Germany (1949-1965)

Production
Hard coal: 49 MY; 50-65 UNSY.
Lignite: 49-50, 52-65 UNSY; 51 UKSS.
Peat: MY.
Natural gas: UNSY.
Hydro: 49-50, 53-54 est. on basis of trend in total generation; 51-52 UNWES; 55-65 UNSY.

Imports and Exports (For derivation of certain 49-54 estimates see U.S.S.R. source notes.)
Solid fuels: 49-53 Kohlen; 54-55 UKSS; 56-65 UNWES.
Liquid fuels: Crude oil 49-53 est., 54-55 UKSS, 56-60 data furnished by UN Stat. Office, 61-65 UNWES; other liquid fuels 49-54 est. (except 54 partially from UKSS), 55-60 data furnished by UN Stat. Office, 61-65 UNWES.
Gas: 49-54 est.; 55-65 UNWES.
Electricity: 49-50, 55-65 UNWES; 51-54 est.

Population
UNDY.

Electricity Consumption
UNWES.

Ecuador

Production
Crude oil: 25-28 LNSY; 29-38, 49-65 UNSY.
NGL: UNSY.
Natural gas: 32-38, 49-51 UNSY; 31 est.; 52-65 est. on basis of relative constancy of both NGL and crude oil production over this period.
Hydro: 25-36, 38 est. on basis of installed capacity data in U.S. Commerce Dept. *World Electrical Markets*; 49-53 est. on basis of FPC-furnished, and other data; 55-65 UNSY.

Imports and Exports
Solid fuels: 28, 30-31 UKSS.
Liquid fuels: 25-27 est.; 28-38, 49-53, and lubes all years UKSS; other liquid fuels 54-60 data furnished by UN Stat. Office, 61-65 UNWES.

Bunkers
UNWES.

Population
UNDY.

Electricity Consumption
UNWES.

Egypt (U.A.R.)

Production
Crude oil: 25-38 UKSS; 49-65 UNSY.
NGL: UNSY.
Hydro: 49-56 est.; 57-64 UNSY; 65 UNWES.

Imports and Exports
Solid fuels: 25-38 Egypt, Ministry of Finance, *Statement of Foreign Trade*; 49-50 UKSS; 51-65 UNWES.
Liquid fuels: 25-38 *Statement of Foreign Trade*; lubes 49-65 UKSS; other fuels 49-53 UKSS (fuel oils 49-53 adjusted by linking to 54 UN figures), 54-60 data from UN Stat. Office, 61-65 UNWES.

Bunkers
Solid fuels: 25-29, 31-38 *Statement of Foreign Trade*; 30 est.; 49-55 UKSS.
Liquid fuels: 25-26, 31-38 *Statement of Foreign Trade*; 27-30 est.; 49-57 Egypt, *Foreign Trade*; 58-59 UKSS; 60-65 UNWES. (Note: Liquid fuels data 60-65 are not comparable with previous years' figures probably because bunkers from transshipments of foreign commodities were (correctly) excluded in the earlier period, and very likely included during 60-65. Completion of the machine tabulations precluded a smoothing of the statistical series.)

Population
UNDY. (Includes "Registered Palestinian Refugees" in Gaza Strip, numbering about 300,000 in 1965.)

Electricity Consumption
25-28, 30-36, 38 est.; 29, 37, 49-65 UNWES.

Equatorial Africa

(Comprising Central African Republic, Chad, Congo [Brazzaville], Gabon)

Production
Crude oil: UNSY and MY.
Natural gas: UNSY.
Hydro: Regional total from UNWES; country data from UNSY.

Imports and Exports
Solid fuels: 25-38, 49-50 UKSS and est.; 51-53 UNWES.
Liquid fuels: 25-38 UKSS and est.; except for lubes and greases (from UKSS 49-65) all liquid fuels for 49-53 UKSS adjusted by linking to 54 UN figure; 54-60 data furnished by UN Stat. Office; 61-65 UNWES.

Bunkers
UNWES and est.
Population
26-38 regional totals est. from fragmentary data in LNSY; 49-65 available country data from UNDY and UN *Monthly Bull. Stat.*; sharp break in Chad series for 1958 precludes comparison with earlier years. Where 49-65 country data were missing, regional total was roughly estimated.
Electricity Consumption
UNWES.

Estonia

(see U.S.S.R.)

Finland

Production
Solid fuels (peat): 25-32, 34-36 est.; 28, 38 from Bror Nordqvist, "Production and Use of Energy in Finland: Development Since 1950 and Prospects of the Future," Paper 51 A/11, Fifth World Power Conference, Vienna, 1956; 33 WPC; 37, 49-65 MY.
Hydro: 25-28 est. on basis of total electric in UNSY; 29-38, 49-65 UNSY.
Imports and Exports
Solid fuels: 25-36 Regul; 37-38 ECE-QCS; 49-50 UKSS; 51-65 UNWES.
Liquid fuels: 25-38, 49-53 and lubes and greases all years UKSS; 54-60 data furnished by UN Stat. Office; 61-65 UNWES.
Electricity: UNWES.
Bunkers
Liquid fuels: UNWES.
Population
UNDY.
Electricity Consumption
25-38 UNSY; 49-65 UNWES.

Formosa

(see Taiwan)

France

(Excluding Saar except for Saar imports and exports in items other than solid fuels prior to 1935 and during 49-59.)

Production
Hard coal: MY.
Lignite: MY.
Crude oil (including shale): UNSY.
NGL: UNSY.
Natural gas: 49-51 UKSS adjusted by linking to 52 UN figure; 52-65 UNSY.
Hydro: 25-28 LNSY adjusted by linking to 29; 29-38, 49-65 UNSY. Published (net production) data adjusted upward to approximate gross production.
Imports and Exports
Solid fuels: 25-38 Kohlen and Regul; 49-50 est. on the basis of movement in UKSS; 51-65 UNWES.
Liquid fuels: 25-38 Direction Général des Douanes, *Tableau Général du Commerce Extérieur*; except for lubes and greases (from UKSS for 49-65) all liquid fuels for 49-53 est. on basis of movements in UKSS; 54-60 data furnished by UN Stat. Office; 61-65 UNWES.
Gas: UNWES.
Electricity: 25-26 est.; 27-38 data furnished by Union Internationale des Producteurs et Distributeurs d'Énergie Électrique (UNIPEDE), (Paris); 49-65 UNWES.
Bunkers
25-38 *Commerce Extérieur*; solid fuels 49-54, 65-66 and liquid fuels 49-65 UNWES; solid fuels 55-59 UKSS.
Population
UNDY.
Electricity Consumption
25-38 UNSY and LNSY; 49-65 UNWES.

Gabon

(see Equatorial Africa)

Germany (1925-38)

(Includes Saar; see note under France.)

Production
Hard coal: UNSY.
Lignite and other (pitch): Kohlen.
Crude oil: LNSY and UNSY.
Natural Gas: UNSY.
Hydro: LNSY and UNSY.
Imports and Exports
Solid fuels: Kohlen and Regul; data adjusted between 25-35 to include Saar trade except for shipments between Saar and Germany.
Liquid fuels: UKSS and Kohlen.
Electricity: 25-37 Guyol and data furnished by UNIPEDE; 38 import figure estimated on basis of net exports from Austria and Switzerland.
Bunkers
25-27 from various national statistics; 28-38 UKSS.
Population
UNDY.
Electricity Consumption
UNSY and LNSY.

Germany, Federal Republic (1949-65)

(Includes West Berlin and Saar; see note under France.)

Germany, Federal Republic of (Cont'd.)

Production
Hard coal: UNSY, MY, and Kohlen.
Lignite: UNSY.
Other (pitch): 49 Kohlen adjusted by linking to 50 UN figure; 50-65 UNSY.
Crude: UNSY (includes shale oil 56-62 from UKSS).
Natural Gas: UNSY and OECD *Gas in Europe* (1958).
NGL: UNSY.
Hydro: UNSY.

Imports and Exports
Solid fuels: Kohlen and UKSS; data adjusted between 49-59 to include Saar trade except for shipments between Saar and Fed. Republic.
Liquid fuels: Lubes UKSS; other liquid fuels 49-53 UKSS adjusted by linking to 54 UN figures, 54-60 data furnished by UN Stat. Office, 61-65 UNWES (exports 51-52 include some bunker fuels).
Gas: UNWES.
Electricity: UNWES.

Bunkers
Solid fuels: 49, 61-62 UNWES; 50-60 Kohlen.
Liquid fuels: UNWES.

Population
UNDY.

Electricity Consumption
UNWES. Excludes West Berlin 49-56; 57-65 West Berlin electricity production added—from UNSY.

Ghana

Production
Hydro: UNWES.

Imports and Exports
Solid fuels: 25-38, 49-50 UKSS; 51-65 UNWES.
Liquid fuels: 25-38, 49-53 and lubes all years UKSS; 54-60 data furnished by UN Stat. Office; 61-65 UNWES.

Bunkers
49, 51, 54, 63-65 UNWES; 50, 53, 55-62 UKSS.

Population
25-30 very rough estimates; 31-38, 49-56 based on UNDY but adjusted upward to link with revised 57-65 data from UNDY.

Electricity Consumption
UNWES.

Greece

Production
Lignite: LNSY and UNSY.
Hydro: 25-28 est.; 29-30 LNSY; 31-38, 49-65 UNSY. Series shown represents public hydro only through 52, and total public and industrial hydro since 53; public hydro in 53 was 21 million kwh.

Imports and Exports
Solid fuels: 25-38, 49-50 UKSS; 51-65 UNWES.
Liquid fuels: 25-38, 49-55 and lubes and greases all years UKSS; other 56-60 data furnished by UN Stat. Office, 61-65 UNWES.
Electricity: UNWES.

Bunkers
Liquid fuels: UNWES.

Population
UNDY. Beginning 49 includes Dodecanese ceded by Italy to Greece in 47 (pop. 115,343 in 47).

Electricity Consumption
29-38 UNSY; 49-65 UNWES.

Guinea

(see West Africa)

Hong Kong

Imports and Exports
Solid fuels: 25, 30 and exports 26-29 Government of Hong Kong *Administrative Reports*; imports 26-29 est.; 31-38, 49-50 UKSS; 51-65 UNWES.
Liquid fuels: 25, 30 and kerosine exports 26-29 *Administrative Reports*; other liquid fuels 26-29 est.; 31-38, 49-53 UKSS, 54-60 data furnished by UN Stat. Office, 61-65 UNWES. Lubes 49-51 est., 52-65 UKSS.

Bunkers
Solid fuels: 25-38 *Administrative Reports*; 49-50 UNWES.
Liquid fuels: 25-38 *Administrative Reports*; 49-65 UNWES.

Population
UNDY.

Electricity Consumption
UNWES.

Hungary

Production
Hard coal and lignite: LNSY and UNSY.
Crude oil: UNSY.
NGL: 58-62 Karl I. Turyn, "Hungary Seeks Oil Sufficiency," *Petroleum Management*, March 1964; 63-65 UNSY.
Natural gas: UNSY (Repressured gas included 49 and after.)
Hydro: 30, 36-38, 49-65 UNSY; 25-29, 31-36 est.

Imports and Exports (For derivation of certain 49-54 estimates see U.S.S.R. source notes.)
Solid fuels: 25-38 LNITS, Regul, and Kohlen; 49-53 est.; 54 UKSS; 55-65 UNWES.
Liquid fuels: 25-38, 54-55 and lubes 57-65 UKSS; 49-53 est.; 56-60 data furnished by UN Stat. Office; 61-65 UNWES.

Gas: UNWES.
Electricity: 49-54 est.; 55-65 UNWES.

Population
UNDY.

Electricity Consumption
25-38, 51-54 UNSY; 49-50, 55-65 UNWES.

Iceland

Production
Solid fuels (peat): MY.
Hydro: 25-27 est.; 28-38, 49-65 UNSY.

Imports and Exports
Solid fuels: 49-50 UKSS; 51-65 UNWES.
Liquid fuels: 25-28 UKSS (specific refined petroleum products not separately available); 29 est.; 30-38 UKSS (fuel oil presumed to be included in gasoline 33-37); lubes and greases 49-65 UKSS; fuel oil 49-53 UKSS adjusted by linking to 54 UN figure; other refined products 49-55 UKSS; fuel oil 54-60 and other (non-lubes) products 56-60 data furnished by UN Stat. Office, 61-65 UNWES.

Bunkers
Liquid fuels: 49-65 UNWES.

Population
UNDY.

Electricity Consumption
28-38 UNSY; 49-65 UNWES.

India

(Includes Goa throughout; Burma and Pakistan for period 1925-38.)

Production
Hard coal: 25-38, 49-50 MY; 51-65 UNSY. (Includes sub-bituminous coal and negligible quantities of lignite in 53-56; data for 31-38 include coal consumed by miners, amounting to 500,000 tons or more annually.)
Lignite: 49-50, 53 est.; 51-52, 54-56 WPC; 57-65 UNSY.
Crude oil: 25-27 derived from data in UKSS; 28-38, 49-65 UNSY. (May include small quantities of NGL; 25-38 data represent largely crude oil production of Burma.)
NGL: UNSY. (Almost all natural gasoline from Burma.)
Natural gas: MY.
Hydro: 25-28, 30-36, 38 est.; 29, 51-52 UNWES; 37 Guyol; 49-50, 53-65 UNSY.

Imports and Exports
Solid fuels: 25-38, 49-50 UKSS; 51-65 UNWES.
Liquid fuels: 25-38, 49-53 and lubes all years UKSS; 54-60 data furnished by UN Stat. Office; 61-65 UNWES. (Fuel oils figures 49-54 include crude oil.)

Bunkers
25-38, 49-56 UKSS; 57-65 UNWES. (25-26 excludes bunkers from Karachi.)

Population
UNDY. (25-38 figures represent sum of separate data for India, Burma, and Pakistan; Pakistan population for 25-30, 32-38 represents estimated interpolations on the basis of 21, 31, and 49 bench marks shown in UNDY.)

Electricity Consumption
25-28, 30-36, 38 est.; 29, 37, 49-65 UNWES.

Indo-China

(Comprising Cambodia, Laos, and South Vietnam; note that Indo-China totals include the area of North Vietnam through 1953. Beginning with 1954 the Indo-China totals are therefore not comparable with those for preceding years.)

Production
Hard coal: UNSY.
Lignite: 25-32, 38 MY.
Hydro: UNSY.

Imports and Exports
Solid fuels: 25-38 Kohlen and UKSS; 49-50 UKSS; 51-65 UNWES.
Liquid fuels: 25-38, 49-54 and lubes all years where shown UKSS; 55-60 data furnished by UN Stat. Office; 61-65 UNWES.

Bunkers
Solid fuels: UKSS.
Liquid fuels: UNWES.

Population
25-38 estimates based on bench marks (from UNDY) for separate member areas of Cambodia, Laos, and Vietnam (North and South); total for 49-52 est.; 53 UNDY figure excluding North Vietnam raised to allow for North Vietnam whose energy data are included in Indo-China in 1953; 54-65 UNDY.

Electricity Consumption
29-38 UNSY; 49-65 UNWES.

Indonesia

(Including West Irian)

Production
Hard coal: LNSY and UNSY.
Crude oil: 25-27 LNSY; 28-38 UNSY; 49-65 UNSY and MY. (53-65 may include NGL.)
NGL: 25-26 est.; 27-30 derived from data in MY; 31-38, 49-52 UNSY.
Natural gas: LNSY and UNSY. (Gross production including gas repressured and wasted.)
Hydro: 25-27, 30-32 est.; 29, 37, 49-65 UNWES.

Indonesia (Cont'd.)

Imports and Exports
Solid fuels: 25-38 Kohlen; 49 est.; 50 UKSS; 51-65 UNWES.
Liquid fuels: 25-38, 49-53 and lubes all years UKSS; 54-60 data furnished by UN Stat. Office; 61-65 UNWES.
Bunkers
Solid fuels: 25 est.; 26-27, 29-38 LNITS; 28 UKSS; 49-54 UNWES.
Liquid fuels: 25 est.; 26-29, 31-38 LNITS; 30, 52-59 UKSS; 49-51, 60-65 UNWES.
Population
UNDY.
Electricity Consumption
28-38, 49-54 data from LNSY, UNSY, and UNWES adjusted upward to include estimate of industrial generation; 55-65 UNWES.

Iraq

Production
Crude oil: UKSS.
Natural gas: ECAFE Proceedings; 62-65 UNWES.
Imports and Exports
Solid fuels: 25-38, 49-50 UKSS; 51-52 UNWES.
Liquid fuels: 25, 28 est.; 26-27 ITPP; 29-38, 49-53 and lubes all years UKSS; all other liquid fuels 54-60 based on data furnished by UN Stat. Office, 61-65 UNWES.
Bunkers
49-65 UNWES.
Population
UNDY.
Electricity Consumption
35-38 UNSY; 49-65 UNWES.

Iran

Production
Hard coal: 33-35 MY; 49-65 UNSY.
Crude oil: 25-31 LNSY; 32-38, 49-65 UNSY.
Natural gas: 53-55 est.; 56-63 derived from USBM Information Circular 8203, *The Petroleum Industry of Iran* (1963); 64-65 MY.
Imports and Exports
Solid fuels: UKSS.
Liquid fuels: 25-38, 49-53 and lubes all years UKSS; other liquid fuels 54-60 data furnished by UN Stat. Office, 61-65 UNWES.
Bunkers
UNWES.
Population
UNDY.
Electricity Consumption
UNWES.

Ireland

Production
Hard coal: 25-38 Irish National Committee, World Power Conference, "The Energy Resources of the Republic of Ireland and Power Developments up to 1955," Fifth World Power Conference, Vienna, 1956, Paper #17 A/2; 49-65 UNSY.
Other (peat): 25-38 WPC Paper #17 A/2; 49-65 MY.
Hydro: 25-38, 49-54 WPC Paper #17 A/2; 55-65 UNSY.
Imports and Exports
Solid fuels: 25-36 LNITS and Regul; 37-38 ECE-QCS; 49-50 UKSS; 51-65 UNWES.
Liquid fuels: 25-38 and lubes and greases 49-65 UKSS; other liquid fuels 49-53 UKSS adjusted by linking to 54 UN figure, 54-60 data furnished by UN Stat. Office, 61-65 UNWES.
Bunkers
Solid fuels: 49-50, 55-58 UKSS.
Liquid fuels: UKSS.
Population
UNDY.
Electricity Consumption
30-38 UNSY; 49-65 UNWES.

Israel (1949-65)

Production
Crude oil: UNSY.
Natural gas: UNSY.
Imports and Exports
Solid fuels: 49-50 UKSS; 51-65 UNWES.
Liquid fuels: 49-53 and lubes 49-65 UKSS; all other liquid fuels 54-60 data furnished by UN Stat. Office, 61-65 UNWES.
Bunkers
UNWES.
Population
UNDY.
Electricity Consumption
UNWES.

Italy

Production
Hard coal: 25-38, 49-63 MY; 64-65 UNSY.
Lignite: 25-38, 53-63 MY; 49-52, 64-65 UNSY.
Crude oil: LNYS and UNSY.
NGL: UNSY.
Natural gas: UKSS.
Hydro (including geothermal): 25-38 (derived partly by estimation in the case of geothermal) from numerous published sources–principally UNSY, UNWES, and EEC-En. Stat.; 49-65 UNSY and UNWES.

Imports and Exports

Solid fuels: 25-38 various sources—principally Regul and UKSS; 49-50 UKSS; 51-65 UNWES.

Liquid fuels: 25-38 various sources—principally UKSS and Italian Government, *Movimento Commerciale*; except for lubes and greases (49-65 from UKSS), all other liquid fuels 49-53 UKSS adjusted by linking to 54 UN figure, 54-60 from UN Stat. Office, 61-65 UNWES.

Electricity: 25-38 Guyol; 49-65 UNWES.

Bunkers

Solid fuels: 25-33, 37-38 from *Movimento Commerciale*; 34-36 UKSS; 49-54, 63-65 UNWES; 55-62 ECE-QCS. (Note: 25-38 data refer to foreign bunkers only.)

Liquid fuels: 25-38 *Movimento Commerciale* (foreign bunkers only); 49-65 UNWES.

Population

UNDY.

Electricity Consumption

25-38 UNSY and LNSY; 49-65 UNWES.

Ivory Coast

(see West Africa)

Japan

(Excluding Korea and Taiwan during period of Imperial rule, and Manchuria and Kwantung Province during period of occupation by Japan.)

Production

Hard coal: LNSY and UNSY.

Lignite: LNSY and UNSY.

Other (peat): 52, 61-65 MY; 53-60 Kohlen.

Crude oil: 25-38 MY and UNSY; 49-65 UNSY.

NGL: 49-65 UNSY. (During 25-38 NGL, if any, probably included with crude oil.)

Natural gas: 25-27 LNSY; 28-38 UNSY; 49-54 WPC; 55-65 UNSY.

Hydro: 25-29 est. on basis of trend in total generation; 30-38, 49-65 UNSY.

Imports and Exports (Note: where necessary data adjusted to treat trade within Japanese Empire similarly to that with rest of world.)

Solid fuels: 25-30, 32, 35-37 Kohlen; 31, 33-34 estimated on basis of data from Japan, Dept. of Finance, *Annual Return of Foreign Trade* and Kohlen; 38, 49-50 UKSS; 51-65 UNWES.

Liquid fuels: lubes all years where shown from UKSS, except small amount of Japan-Taiwan lubes trade (25-38) based on Taiwan official statistics; other liquid fuels 25-36 *Annual Return of Foreign Trade*, 37 est., 38 figure largely derived from MY and UKSS (38 import figure involved estimating the breakdown between crude and refined products and adding an allowance for shipments from Sakhalin), 49 est., 50-53 UKSS, 54-60 data furnished by UN Stat. Office, 61-65 UNWES. (Note: some lube exports 25-34 included under fuel oil; and heavy fuel oil imports 25-38 included with crude oil.)

Bunkers

Solid fuels: 25-34 Regul; 35-38 *Annual Return of Foreign Trade*; 49-52 UNWES; 53-61 UKSS.

Liquid fuels: 25-36 *Annual Return of Foreign Trade*; 37-38 est.; 49-51, 58-65 UNWES; 52-57 UKSS.

Population

UNDY.

Electricity Consumption

25-38 UNSY; 49-65 UNWES.

Jordan (1949-65)

Imports and Exports

Liquid fuels: 49-53 and lubes all years UKSS; all other liquid fuels 54-60 data furnished by UN Stat. Office, 61-65 UNWES. (Following are estimates: gasoline in 51 and 52, fuel oil in 49, lubes in 49 and 51-52.)

Bunkers

UNWES.

Population

UNSY.

Electricity Consumption

UNWES.

Kenya

(see East Africa)

Korea (1925-38)

Production

Hard coal: LNSY and UNSY.

Hydro: 25-36 est.; 37-38 UNSY.

Imports and Exports

Solid fuels: 25-38 Chosen, *Tables of Trade and Shipping*; 29-38 UKSS.

Liquid fuels: 25-28 ITPP; 29-38 UKSS.

Bunkers

none.

Population

UNDY.

Electricity Consumption

29 UNWES; 37-38 UNSY.

Korea, North

(see Communist Asia)

Korea, Republic of (1949-65)

Production

Hard coal: 49, 52-65 UNSY; 50-51 UN Proceedings of the International Conference, *Peaceful Uses of*

Korea, Republic of (Cont'd.)

Atomic Energy, vol. I (Geneva: August 1955), p. 212.
Lignite: UNSY.
Hydro: UNSY.
Imports and Exports
Solid fuels: 49-50 UKSS; 51-65 UNWES.
Liquid fuels: lubes all years UKSS; all other liquid fuels 49-53 est. and linked to 54-60 data furnished by UN Stat. Office, 61-65 UNWES.
Bunkers
Solid fuels: UNWES.
Liquid fuels: UNWES.
Population
UNDY.
Electricity Consumption
UNWES.

Kuwait

Production
Crude oil: UNSY.
NGL: UNSY.
Natural gas: 60-61 ECAFE Proceedings; 62 MY; 63-65 UNSY.
Imports and Exports
49-53 UKSS; 54-60 data furnished by UN Stat. Office; 61-65 UNWES.
Bunkers
UNWES.
Population
UNDY.
Electricity Consumption (includes Kuwait Neutral Zone 60-65)
UNWES. (Data on public generation only adjusted upward to include estimate of industrial.)

Kuwait Neutral Zone

Production
Crude oil: 54-65 UNSY.
Imports and Exports
54-60 data furnished by UN Stat. Office; 61-65 UNWES.
Bunkers
58-65 UNWES.
Electricity Consumption
(Included in Kuwait–52 million kwh in 1965.)

Laos

(see Indo-China)

Latvia

(see U.S.S.R.)

Lebanon (1950-65)

Production
Hydro: 50 UNWES; 51-65 UNSY.
Imports and Exports
Solid fuels: 50-51 UKSS; 52-65 UNWES.
Liquid fuels: 50-53 and lubes all years UKSS; all other liquid fuels 54-60 data furnished by UN Stat. Office, 61-65 UNWES. (50-53 data for gasoline and fuel oil from UKSS adjusted by linking to 54 UN figure.)
Bunkers
Liquid fuels: UNWES.
Population
UNDY. (Includes Palestinian refugees–137,000 in 1960; 1955 change in series impairs comparability with earlier years.)
Electricity Consumption
50-56, 60-65 UNWES; 57-59 UNSY.

Lebanon and Syria (1925-38, 1949)

Production
Hydro: 25-38 derived from data in WPC; 49 UNWES.
Imports and Exports
Solid fuels: 25-27 (Syria only), 29-38 UKSS; 28 est.
Liquid fuels: 25-26 est.; 27-38, 49 UKSS.
Bunkers
UNWES.
Population
UNDY (except Lebanon portion 37-38 est.).
Electricity Consumption
UNWES.

Liberia

Production
Hydro: UNSY.
Imports and Exports
Liquid fuels: 34-38, 49-53 and lubes all years UKSS; 54-60 data furnished by UN Stat. Office; 61-65 UNWES.
Bunkers
Liquid fuels: UNWES.
Population
UNDY.
Electricity Consumption
UNWES.

Libya

Production
Crude oil: MY.
Imports and Exports
Solid fuels: 25-30 Italy, Ministero delle Colonie, *Statistica de Movimento Commerciale Marittimo*; 31-35 est.; 36-38 UKSS; 54-65 UNWES.

Liquid fuels: 25-30 *Statistica de Movimento Commerciale Marittimo*; 31-35 est.; 36-38 UKSS; lubes 49-57 est., 58-65 UKSS; other liquid fuels 49-54 est. based on partial UN net import data (exports assumed zero), 55-60 data furnished by UN Stat. Office, 61-65 UNWES.

Bunkers

Liquid fuels: 49-53 est. in relation to trend in total imports; 54-65 UNWES.

Population

UNDY.

Electricity Consumption

25-38 and 49 very rough estimates assuming relatively little per capita improvement during these years; 50-65 UNWES.

Lithuania

(see U.S.S.R.)

Malawi

(see Rhodesian Federation)

Malaya and Singapore

(Excluding Sabah and Sarawak, included under British Borneo.)

Production

Solid fuels (sub-bituminous coal): LNSY and UNSY.

Hydro: 25-32, 34-38 LNSY and UNSY; 33 U.S. Commerce Dept. *World Power Manual*; 49-65 UNSY.

Imports and Exports

Solid fuels: 25-38 LNSY and UKSS; 49-50 UKSS; 51-65 UNWES.

Liquid fuels: lubes all years UKSS; other liquid fuels 25-38 LNITS; crude oil 49-62 UKSS, 63 est., 64-65 UNWES; gasoline and kerosine 49-55 UKSS data adjusted by linking to 56 UN figure, 56-60 UN Stat. Office, 61-65 UNWES; fuel oil 49-55 UKSS, 56-60 UN Stat. Office, 61-65 UNWES (49-55 fuel oil may include some crude).

Bunkers

Solid fuels: UKSS.

Liquid fuels: 25-38, 49-59 UKSS; 60-65 UNWES.

Population

UNDY.

Electricity Consumption

25-38 UNSY; 49-65 UNWES.

Mali

(see West Africa)

Mauritania

(see West Africa)

Mexico

Production

Hard coal: 25-27 LNSY; 28-38, 49-60 UNSY; 61-65 MY.

Crude oil: 25-33 LNSY; 34 MY; 35-38, 49-65 UNSY.

NGL: 25-26 est.; 27 MY; 28-38, 49-65 UNSY.

Natural Gas: 25-29 est.; 30-38, 49-65 UNSY. (Gross production including gas repressured and wasted.)

Hydro: 25-32 derived from data in ECLA ELA; 33-38, 49-65 UNSY.

Imports and Exports

Solid fuels: 25-38, 49-50 UKSS; 51-65 UNWES.

Liquid fuels: 25-38 UKSS, and Mexico, *Anuario Estadístico de Comercio Exterior*; lubes 49-65 UKSS; other liquid fuels 49-53 UKSS adjusted by linking to 54 UN figure, 54-60 data furnished by UN Stat. Office, 61-65 UNWES.

Gas: 25-38 MY; 49-65 UNWES.

Electricity: 25-30 est.; 31-38 derived (jointly with the preparation of United States and Canada electricity trade estimates) from U.S. Census Bureau, *Historical Statistics of the U.S.* (1960), WPC, and other sources; 49-65 UNWES.

Bunkers

Liquid fuels: 25-31 *Anuario Estadístico de Comercio Exterior*; 32-38 bunkers data not separately available, included in fuel oil exports; 49-65 UNWES.

Population

UNDY.

Electricity Consumption

25, 28-29 based on hydro data from *Production* series; 26-27, 30-33 LNSY; 34-38 UNSY; 49-65 UNWES.

Mongolia

(see Communist Asia)

Morocco

Production

Hard coal: 30-38 MY; 49-65 UNSY.

Crude oil: UNSY.

Natural gas: UNSY.

Hydro: UNSY.

Imports and Exports

Solid fuels: 25-38, 49-50 UKSS; 51-65 UNWES.

Liquid fuels: 25-38 and lubes all years UKSS; 49-53 UKSS (fuel oil 49-53 adjusted by linking to 54 UN figure); 54-60 data furnished by UN Stat. Office; 61-65 UNWES.

Electricity: UNSY.

Bunkers

UNWES.

Morocco (Cont'd.)

Population
UNDY.
Electricity Consumption
25 est.; 26-38 UNSY; 49-65 UNWES.

Netherlands

Production
Hard coal: UNSY.
Lignite: UNSY.
Crude oil: UNSY.
Natural gas: UNSY.
Imports and Exports
Solid fuels: 25-38, 49-50 UKSS; 51-65 UNWES.
Liquid fuels: 25-38 UKSS; except for lubes and greases (49-65 from UKSS), all other liquid fuels 49-53 UKSS, 54-60 data furnished by UN Stat. Office, 61-65 UNWES.
Gas: 49-65 UNWES.
Electricity: 25-38 Guyol; 49-65 UNWES.
Bunkers
Solid fuels: 25-37 LNITS, 38, 55-57 UKSS; 49-54, 58-65 UNWES.
Liquid fuels: 25-38 LNITS; 49, 50, 56 UKSS; 51-55, 57-65 UNWES.
Population
UNDY.
Electricity Consumption
25-38 UNSY and LNSY; 49-65 UNWES.

New Zealand

Production
Hard coal: UNSY.
Lignite: UKSS.
Other (sub-bituminous coal): UKSS.
Crude oil: UNSY.
Hydro: 25-34 LNSY; 35-38, 49-65 UNSY. (Geothermal electric power, amounting to 1,255 million kwh in 1965, is excluded.)
Imports and Exports
Solid fuels: 25-38, 49-50 UKSS; 50-65 UNWES.
Liquid fuels: 25-38, 49-53 and lubes all years UKSS; all other liquid fuels 54-60 data furnished by UN Stat. Office, 61-65 UNWES.
Bunkers
Solid fuels: 25-38, 55-65 UKSS; 49-54 UNWES.
Liquid fuels: 25-26 est.; 27-38 UKSS; 49-65 UNWES.
Population
UNDY.
Electricity Consumption
25-38 UNSY; 49-65 UNWES.

Niger

(see West Africa)

Nigeria

Production
Hard coal: 25-38 MY; 49-65 UNSY.
Crude oil: UNSY.
Natural gas: UNSY.
Hydro: UNSY.
Imports and Exports
Solid fuels: 25-38, 49-50 UKSS; 51-54 UNWES.
Liquid fuels: 25-38, 49-53 and lubes all years UKSS; 54-60 data furnished by UN Stat. Office; 61-65 UNWES.
Bunkers
Solid fuels: 25-33 est.; 34-38 UKSS; 49-53 UNWES.
Liquid fuels: 49-59 UKSS; 60-65 UNWES.
Population
57 UN *Monthly Bulletin of Statistics* (Feb. 1967); 58-65 UNDY.
Electricity Consumption
36-38 UNSY; 49-65 UNWES.

Norway

(Including Spitzbergen)

Production
Hard coal: 25-38 Kohlen; 49-65 MY.
Other (peat): 25-38 est. on basis of figures for peat plus wood in J. Bjerke, "Energy Consumption and Economic Growth in Norway from 1900 to 1939." XIth Sectional Meeting, World Power Conference, Belgrade, 1957, Section A, Paper 22.
Hydro: 25-29 consumption figures given in World Power Conf. paper (above); 30-38, 49-65 UNSY. Figures for 30-36 include small amounts of thermal electricity; for all years, figures adjusted upward to approximate gross generation.
Imports and Exports
Solid fuels: 25-38 LNSY, Kohlen, and ECE-QCS; 49-50 UKSS; 51-65 UNWES.
Liquid fuels: 25-38 UKSS; except for lubes and greases (49-65 from UKSS) all other liquid fuels for 49-53 UKSS, 54-60 data furnished by UN Stat. Office, 61-65 UNWES.
Electricity: UNWES.
Bunkers
UNWES except 50 est.
Population
UNDY.
Electricity Consumption
25-29, 31 from Table I (see note under *Production* above); 30, 32-38 UNSY and LNSY; 49-65 UNWES.

Pakistan

(1949-65; period 1925-38 included with India.)

Production

Lignite: UNSY. (Series comprises both coal and lignite–not separately available.)

Crude oil: UNSY (includes NGL).

Natural gas: UNSY.

Hydro: 49-54 UNSY *public* hydro series adjusted by linking to 55 *total* hydro figure; 55-65 UNWES.

Imports and Exports

Solid fuels: 49-50 UKSS; 51-65 UNWES.

Liquid fuels: Lubes and greases UKSS; all other liquid fuels 49-50 est., 51-53 UKSS adjusted by linking to 54 UN figure, 54-60 data furnished by UN Stat. Office, 61-65 UNWES.

Bunkers

Solid fuels: 49, 51-53, 55-65 UNWES; 50, 54 est.

Liquid fuels: 49-50, 55-65 UNWES; 51-54 est.

Population

UNDY.

Electricity Consumption

UNWES. (49-54 data on public generation only adjusted upward to include estimate of industrial.)

Palestine (1925-38)

Imports and Exports

Solid fuels: UKSS.

Liquid fuels: UKSS.

Population

UNDY.

Electricity Consumption

UNSY.

Panama Canal Zone

Production

Hydro: 29, 32, 37-38, 49-65 UNSY; all other years estimated.

Imports and Exports

Solid fuels: 25-38, Annual Report of the Governor (estimated on the basis of coal purchases).

Liquid fuels: 25-38, Annual Report of the Governor; gasoline imports 49-56 and kerosine imports 49-53 from UNWES assuming net and gross imports equal; 49-53 fuel oil imports and exports estimated on the basis of net trade figures in UNWES; all other years through 1960 from data furnished by UN Stat. Office; 61-65 UNWES.

Bunkers

Solid fuels: 25-38, Annual Report of the Governor.

Liquid fuels: 25-38, Annual Report of the Governor; 49-65 UNWES.

Population

UNDY.

Electricity Consumption

UNWES.

Paraguay

Imports and Exports

Solid fuels: 33 UKSS.

Liquid fuels: 33-35, 37-38, 49-52 and lubes all years UKSS; 36, 53 est.; 54-60 data furnished by UN Stat. Office; 61-65 UNWES.

Population

UNDY.

Electricity Consumption

25-38 UNSY; 49-65 UNWES.

Peru

Production

Hard coal: 25-30 LNSY; 31-38, 49-65 MY.

Crude oil: UNSY.

NGL: 25-27 ITPP; 28-38, 49-65 UNSY.

Natural gas: 25-38, 49-54 est. on basis of movement in crude oil and NGL series; 55-65 UNSY.

Hydro: 25-28, 30-36, 38 est. on basis of data on public hydro only (UNSY); 29, 37 UNWES; 49-51 ECLA ELA; 52 UN, *Estudios Sobre Electricidad en America Latina* (1962); 53 est.; 54-65 UNSY.

Imports and Exports

Solid fuels: 25-27 LNITS; 28-38 LNITS and UKSS; 49-50 UKSS; 51-65 UNWES.

Liquid fuels: 25-38, 49-53 and lubes all years UKSS (for 25-27 naphtha from ITPP added to gasoline); all other liquid fuels 54-60 data furnished by UN Stat. Office, 61-65 UNWES.

Bunkers

Liquid fuels: 25-38 UKSS; 49-65 UNWES. (Data not entirely complete; some bunkers included in exports.)

Solid fuels: 49-50 UNWES.

Population

UNDY.

Electricity Consumption

29, 37, 49-50, 52-65 UNWES; 51 est.

Philippines

Production

Hard coal: 25-28 LNSY; 29-36, 38, 49-65 UNSY; 37 MY.

Hydro: 25-28, 30-36, 38 est. on basis of LNSY and UNSY data for Manila; 29, 37, 49-65 UNWES (65 public only).

Imports and Exports

Solid fuels: 25-38, 49-50 UKSS; 51-65 UNWES.

Liquid fuels: 25-27 ITPP; 28-38, 49-53 and lubes 28-38, 49-65 UKSS; all other fuels 54-60 data furnished by UN Stat. Office, 61-65 UNWES.

Bunkers

UNWES.

Philippines (Cont'd.)

Population
25 est.; 26-38, 49-65 UNDY.
Electricity Consumption
25-38 UNSY; 49-65 UNWES.

Poland

(Largely unadjusted for territorial changes)

Production
Hard coal and lignite: LNSY and UNSY.
Crude oil: LNSY and UNSY.
NGL: 25-26, 49 est.; 27 derived from MY; 28-38, 50-65 UNSY.
Natural gas: LNSY and UNSY (represents gross production).
Hydro: 25-32, 38, 49-50 est. on basis of trends in total production from LNSY and UNSY; 33-36 WPC; 37 Guyol; 51-65 UNSY.
Imports and Exports (For derivation of certain 49-54 estimates see U.S.S.R. source notes.)
Solid fuels: 25-36 Regul; 37-38 Kohlen; exports 49-52, imports 49-54 est.; exports 53-54 UKSS; imports and exports 55-65 UNWES.
Liquid fuels: *Imports* all liquid fuels 25-38, crude petroleum 53, and lubes where shown during 58-65 UKSS; crude 49-52 and other liquid fuels 49-53 est.; all liquid fuels 54-60 data furnished by UN Stat. Office; 61-65 UNWES.
Exports 25-29 ITPP; 30-38 (and lubes where shown during 58-65) UKSS; 49-53 est.; 54-65 as under imports.
Gas: UNWES.
Electricity: 25-28, 30, 32, 49-54 est.; 29, 31, 33-36 U.S. Dept. Commerce, *World Power Manual* and Edison Electric Institute (New York), *Handbook*; 55-65 UNWES.
Bunkers
Solid fuels: 25-27 est. based on Kohlen; 28-36 Regul; 37-38, 53-56 Kohlen; 49-50, 57-65 UNWES; 51-52 est.
Liquid fuels: 59-65 data furnished by UN Stat. Office.
Population
UNDY. (Note: pre- and post-World War II data not readily comparable.)
Electricity Consumption
25-28, 30 LNSY; 29, 31-38, 51-54 UNSY; 49-50, 55-65 UNWES. (Note: Aside from changes in series resulting from territorial changes, these figures may be of questionable accuracy because of variations in the scope of the series, resulting from lack of uniformity regarding inclusion of small-sized plants.)

Portugal

Production
Hard coal: 25-32 MY; 33 UKSS; 34-38, 49-65 UNSY.
Lignite: UNSY.
Hydro: 25-26 est.; 27 LNSY; 28-38, 49-65 UNSY.
Imports and Exports
Solid fuels: 25-38 Regul, LNSY and UKSS; 49-50 UKSS; 51-65 UNWES.
Liquid fuels: 25-38 UKSS, Regul and LNSY; except for lubes and greases (from UKSS for 49-65), all liquid fuels for 49-53 est. basis of movements in UKSS, 54-60 data furnished by UN Stat. Office, 61-65 UNWES.
Electricity: UNWES.
Bunkers
Solid fuels: 25-36 Regul; 37-38 ECE-QCS; 49-59 UNWES.
Liquid fuels: 33-36 UKSS; 49-50 est.; 51-65 UNWES.
Population
UNDY.
Electricity Consumption
25-26 est.; 27-38 UNSY and LNSY; 49-65 UNWES.

Puerto Rico

Production
Hydro: 37-38, 49-65 UNSY. All other years estimated on the basis of 29 total electricity figure and thermal/hydro proportion shown in UNWES.
Imports and Exports
Solid fuels: Included with U.S. 25-38; 49-65 UNWES.
Liquid fuels: 54-60 data furnished by UN Stat. Office; 61-65 UNWES.
Bunkers
Liquid fuels: UNWES.
Population
UNDY.
Electricity Consumption
37-38 UNSY; 49-65 UNWES.

Qatar

Production
Crude oil: UNSY.
Imports and Exports
49-55 UKSS; 56-60 data furnished by UN Stat. Office; 61-65 UNWES.
Population
UNDY.
Electricity Consumption
UNWES.

Rhodesia

(see Rhodesian Federation)

Rhodesian Federation

(Comprises Malawi, Rhodesia, Zambia)

Production
Hard coal: UNSY.
Hydro: 30-36, 38 est.; 37, 49-65 UNSY.
Imports and Exports
(Note: For 54-60, the breakdown of coal and liquid fuel trade by each of the tree parts of the Federation represents an estimate. This estimate includes an allowance for coal shipments from Rhodesia to Zambia. Lube imports were all assigned to Rhodesia.)
Solid fuels: 25-38, 49-60 UKSS; 61-65 UNWES.
Liquid fuels: 25-38, 49-60 and lubes all years where shown UKSS; 61-65 UNWES.
Electricity: UNWES.
Bunkers
UNWES.
Population
UNDY.
Electricity Consumption
25-38 UNSY; 49-65 UNWES.

Romania

Production
Hard coal and lignite: LNSY and UNSY, except 63-65 estimated from trend in related (but different) series in UNWES.
Crude oil: LNSY and UNSY.
NGL: 25-27 est.; 28-38 and 49-65 UNSY.
Natural gas: 25-38, 49-51, 53-57 UKSS; 58-62 MY; 63-65 est.
Hydro: 25-34 LNSY; 35-38 est.; 49-65 UNSY.
Imports and Exports (For derivation of certain 49-54 estimates see U.S.S.R. source notes.)
Solid fuels: 25-36 Regul and Kohlen; 37-38 UKSS; 49-54 est.; 55-65 UNWES.
Liquid fuels: 25-38 various sources—principally official Romania trade returns; 49-53 est.; 54-60 data furnished by UN Stat. Office; 61-65 UNWES, except lubes 58-65 UKSS.
Gas: UNWES.
Electricity: UNWES.
Bunkers
Liquid fuels: Various sources—principally official Romanian trade returns.
Population
UNDY.
Electricity Consumption
25-38, 51-54 UNSY; 49-50, 55-65 UNWES.

Rwanda

(see Congo, Democratic Republic)

Sabah

(see Borneo, British)

Sarawak

(see Borneo, British)

Saudi Arabia

Production
Crude oil: 36-38 UNSY; 49-61 Arabian American Oil Co., *Aramco Handbook* (1960) and *Annual Reports*; 62-65 MY.
Natural gas: 49-53 UKSS adjusted by linking to 54 ECAFE figure; 54-60 ECAFE Proceedings; 61-65 est. on basis of ratio of natural gas to crude oil in previous years.
Imports and Exports
Crude oil: 49-53 UKSS; other liquid fuels 49-53 est., 54-60 (except gasoline 54-65) data furnished by UN Stat. Office, 61-65 UNWES.
Bunkers
49-65 UNWES.
Population
UNSY.
Electricity Consumption
UNWES. (55-58 data on public generation only adjusted upward to include estimate of industrial.)

Senegal

(see West Africa)

Singapore

(Partial data for 1956-65; see combined Malaya and Singapore data.)

Imports and Exports
Solid fuels: 56-60 data furnished by UN Stat. Office; 61-65 UNWES.
Liquid fuels: Lubes UKSS (Malaya-Singapore, total all attributed to Singapore); crude oil not separately available for Singapore, shown only for Malaya-Singapore combined; other liquid fuels 56-60 data furnished by UN Stat. Office, 61-65 UNWES.
Bunkers
UNWES.
Population
UNDY.
Electricity Consumption
UNSY.

South Africa

(Comprises South Africa, South-West Africa, Basutoland [now Lesotho], Bechuanaland [now Botswana], and Swaziland; except for population and slight amounts of coal production [Swaziland] and electricity consumption, data refer almost exclusively to South Africa itself.)

Production
Hard coal: LNSY and UNSY.
Crude oil: UNSY (shale oil).
Imports and Exports
Solid fuels: 25-38, 49-50 UKSS; 51-65 UNWES.
Liquid fuels: 25-38, 49-53 and lubes all years UKSS; other liquid fuels 54-60 data furnished by UN Stat. Office, 61-65 UNWES.
Bunkers
Solid fuels: 25-38 Kohlen; 49-54 UNWES; 55-62 UKSS.
Liquid fuels: 25-27 est.; 28-38, 54-59 UKSS; 49-53, 60-65 UNWES.
Population
UNDY.
Electricity Consumption
25-38 UNSY; 49-65 UNWES.

Spain

(Including Canary Islands, Ceuta, Melilla; no data available for Sp. Morocco—disregarded as insignificant.)

Production
Hard coal: 25-34, 55-65 UNSY; 35-38, 49-54 MY.
Lignite: 25-35, 37-38, 49-63 MY; 36, 64-65 UNSY.
Crude oil (shale): 25-28, 35-36, 53-54 est.; 29-34 UKSS; 37-38, 49-63 UNSY; 64-65 est. on basis of movement of series shown in UNWES.
Hydro: 25-28 est. at 85% of *total* electricity generation (relationship prevailing in subsequent years) from LNSY; 29-38, 49-65 UNSY.
Imports and Exports
Solid fuels: 25-38 largely est. on basis of partial information in *Estadística del Comercio Exterior de España*; 49-53 UKSS; 54-65 UNWES (except exports for 54 est.).
Liquid fuels: 25-38 largely est. on basis of partial information in UKSS; except for lubes and greases (from UKSS for 49-65), all liquid fuels for 49-53 UKSS, adjusted by linking to 54 UN figure, 54-60 data furnished by UN Stat. Office, 61-65 UNWES.
Electricity: 49-65 UNWES.
Bunkers
Solid and liquid fuels 25-38 and 49-59 rough estimates based on numerous national and international sources; solid fuels 60-65 from data furnished by UN Stat. Office; liquid fuels 60-65 UNWES.
Population
UNDY.
Electricity Consumption
25-38 LNSY and UNSY; 49-50 UNSY; 51-65 UNWES.

Sweden

Production
Hard coal: MY.
Other (peat): 25-32 est.; 33-35 WPC; 36-38, 49-65 MY.
Crude oil (shale): 49 est.; 50-51 WPC; 52-65 UNSY.
Hydro: UNSY except 25-28 and 30-35 est. basis of movement in total electric generation.
Imports and Exports
Solid fuels: 25-38 Regul and Kohlen; 49-50 UKSS adjusted by linking to 51 UN figure; 51-65 UNWES.
Liquid fuels: 25-38 UKSS; except for lubes and greases (from UKSS for 49-65) all liquid fuels 49-53 UKSS adjusted by linking to 54 UN figure, 54-60 data furnished by UN Stat. Office, 61-65 UNWES.
Electricity: 25-38 Guyol; 49-65 UNWES.
Bunkers
UNWES.
Population
UNDY.
Electricity Consumption
25-38 UNSY and LNSY; 49-65 UNWES.

Switzerland

(Including Liechtenstein)

Production
Hard coal (incl. lignite for some years): 25-26 est.; 27-38, 49-63 MY; 64-65 est.
Hydro: 25-28 LNSY; 29 UNWES; 30 est.; 31-38, 49-65 UNSY. Published (net production) data adjusted upward to approximate gross production.
Imports and Exports
Solid fuels: 25-38 Regul and Kohlen; 49-50 UKSS adjusted by linking to 51 UN figure; 51-65 UNWES.
Liquid fuels: 25-38 UKSS; except for lubes and greases from UKSS for 49-65, all liquid fuels for 49-53 UKSS adjusted by linking to 54 UN figure, 54-60 data furnished by UN Stat. Office, 61-65 UNWES.
Electricity: 25-38 Union Internationale des Producteurs et Distributeurs d'Énergie Électrique (UNIPEDE, Paris), *Circulaire Périodique*; 49-65 UNWES.
Bunkers
25-38 assumed zero; 49-65 UNWES.
Population
UNDY.

Electricity Consumption

25-38 LNSY and UNSY production data (hydro only for 25-30—thermal known to be negligible and assumed to be zero) less net exports from indicated source; 49-65 UNWES. In all cases, data adjusted to represent gross data (as explained under *Production* above).

Syria (1950-65)

Production

Hydro: UNWES.

Imports and Exports

Solid fuels: 50 UKSS; 51-65 UNWES.

Liquid fuels: 50-53 and lubes all years UKSS; all other liquid fuels 54-60 data furnished by UN Stat. Office, 61-65 UNWES.

Bunkers

UNWES.

Population

UNDY. (Includes Palestinian refugees—127,000 in 1960.)

Electricity Consumption

UNWES.

Taiwan

Production

Hard coal: LNSY and UNSY.

Crude oil: 25-27 MY; 26-38, 49-65 UNSY.

NGL: 49-55 UNSY; 56-61 UKSS; 62-63 est. on basis of trends in natural gas production.

Natural gas: 25-32 est. on basis of trends in crude oil production; 33 WPC; 34-38 LNSY and UNSY; 49-65 UNSY.

Hydro: 25-28, 30-36 est.; 29, 37-38, 49-65 UNSY.

Imports and Exports

(For period of Japanese rule, data adjusted to include shipments to and from Japan and other parts of the Japanese Empire as part of Taiwan imports and exports.)

Solid fuels: 25-37 Taiwan, *Annual Return of the Trade of Taiwan*; 38 est.; 50 UKSS; 51-65 UNWES.

Liquid fuels: 25-36 *Annual Return of Trade of Taiwan*; 37-38 est.; lubes 49-65 UKSS; other fuels 49-53 data from UKSS adjusted by linking to 54-60 data furnished by UN Stat. Office, 61-65 UNWES. (Note: Heavy fuel oil imports 25-38 included under crude oil imports.)

Bunkers

Solid fuels: 25 est.; 26-38 UKSS. (For 49-65, solid fuel bunkers, if any, included with exports.)

Liquid fuels: UNWES.

Population

UNDY.

Electricity Consumption

25-28, 30-36, 38 est.; 29, 37, 49, 50-65 UNWES.

Tanganyika

(see East Africa)

Thailand

Production

Lignite: UNSY.

Hydro: Data inadvertently omitted in study. Recently issued data indicate hydro output commencing in 1964 with 288 million kwh in that year and 841 million kwh in 1965.

Imports and Exports

Solid fuels: 25-37 Kohlen; 38 UKSS; 49-50 est.; 53-65 UNWES.

Liquid fuels: 25-38 and lubes all years UKSS; all other fuels 49-53 data in UKSS adjusted by linking to 54 UN figure, 54-60 data furnished by UN Stat. Office, 61-65 UNWES.

Bunkers

UNWES.

Population

UNDY.

Electricity Consumption

UNWES.

Trinidad-Tobago

Production

Crude oil: 25-27 LNSY; 28-38, 49-65 UNSY.

NGL: 49-65 UNSY.

Natural gas: 25-38 est. based on post-38 ratio of natural gas to crude oil data from UKSS and UNSY; 49-65 UNSY.

Imports and Exports

Solid fuels: 25-38 Trinidad and Tobago, *Trade Statistics*; 49-50 UKSS; 51-65 UNWES.

Liquid fuels: 25-38 *Trade Statistics*; 49-65 lubes and 49-53 crude oil UKSS; 54-60 crude oil data furnished by UN Stat. Office; 49-60 other refined products UKSS adjusted by linking to 61 figure; 61-65 crude oil and other refined products UNWES.

Bunkers

Solid fuels: 25-38 *Trade Statistics*; 49-54 UNWES; 58 UKSS.

Liquid fuels: 25-38 *Trade Statistics*; 49-65 UNWES.

Population

UNDY.

Electricity Consumption

33-38 UNSY; 49-65 UNWES.

Trucial Oman

(Comprising seven Trucial Sheikdoms plus the Sultinate of Muscat and Oman.)

Production

Crude oil: UNSY. (Sheikdom of Abu Dhabi only.)

Imports and Exports

Trucial Oman (Cont'd.)

Liquid fuels: UNWES.

Population

UNDY.

Tunisia

Production

Lignite: UNSY.

Natural gas: UNSY.

Hydro: UNSY.

Imports and Exports

Solid fuels: 25 UKSS; 26-38 Kohlen; 49-50 UKSS; 51-65 UNWES.

Liquid fuels: 25-38, 49-53 and lubes all years UKSS; 54-60 data furnished by UN Stat. Office; 61-65 UNWES.

Bunkers

Solid fuels: UNWES.

Liquid fuels: UNWES.

Population

UNDY.

Electricity Consumption

25-28 est.; 29-38 UNSY; 49-65 UNWES.

Turkey

Production

Hard coal: LNSY and UNSY. (Refers to "marketed" production.)

Lignite: 25 Kohlen; 26-38, 49-65 LNSY and UNSY. (25-38 data labeled "shipments" rather than "production"; also prior to 57, state-owned mines only; in 58 these represented about 70 percent of total production.)

Crude oil: UNSY.

Hydro: 37 UNWES; 38 est.; 49-65 UNSY.

Imports and Exports

Solid fuels: 25-29, 33-38 Turkish statistics; 30-32 UKSS; 65 UNWES.

Liquid fuels: 25 Turkish statistics; 26-38 UKSS; 49-53 UKSS adjusted by linking to 54 UN figure; 54-60 data furnished by UN Stat. Office; 61-65 UNWES. (Lubes included with fuel oil 25-29, 33-38; where shown separately, lubes from UKSS.)

Bunkers

Liquid fuels: 49-56, 61, 63-65 UNWES; 57-60, 62 OECD Stat. En.

Population

UNDY.

Energy Consumption

25-28, 30-36, 38 est. on basis of Istanbul data from LNSY; 29, 49-65 UNWES.

Uganda

(see East Africa)

U.S.S.R.

(Including, to the extent possible, 1925-38 estimates for Estonia, Latvia, and Lithuania.) Unless otherwise indicated, these source notes refer solely to the derivation of data for the U.S.S.R., exclusive of Estonia, Latvia, and Lithuania during 1925-38. (Data for these now-annexed Baltic States are, of course, presumed to be included as part of Soviet statistics since 1949.) Such 1925-38 Baltic States data as could be estimated or were available (being added on to Soviet statistics as described below) were limited to production (almost entirely peat) and imports of solid and liquid fuels. (No attempt was made to cancel out 1925-38 imports which may have originated in the U.S.S.R.) Sources on Baltic States production data were principally MY, WPC, and UKSS; sources on imports were Kohlen, ITPP, and UKSS. Baltic States energy exports were either nil or negligible; while data on bunkers, population, and electricity consumption were not available. In the case of population, an upward adjustment was made in the Soviet series (described above) as an allowance for the inclusion of the three Baltic States.

Production

Hard coal and lignite: 25-38, 49-58 Kohlen; 59-63 UNSY; 64-65 MY.

Other (peat): 25-27 est.; 28-38, 49-58 U.S. Bureau of the Census, *The Soviet Mineral-Fuels Industries, 1925-1958* by D. B. Shimkin (Washington: Govt. Printing Office, 1962); 59-65 MY.

(For note on Soviet solid fuels conversion from original units into coal-equivalent units, see table footnote[h], p. 829, of the General Notes.)

Crude oil: 25-27 UKSS; 28-38, 49-58 Shimkin; 59-65 UNSY. (Includes shale oil which, for 59-63, derived from U.S.S.R., *Soviet Statistical Handbook* and MY, unavailable for 64-65 at time of completion of machine tabulations; shale oil amounted to about 4.5 million tons in 1963. The crude oil series is also assumed to include natural gas liquids.)

Natural gas: 25-27 data in LNSY adjusted by linking to Shimkin 28 figure; 28, 32, 37, 55, 57 Shimkin; 29-31, 33-36, 38 est.; 49 R. W. Campbell, *The Economics of Soviet Oil and Gas* (Baltimore: Johns Hopkins Press for RFF, 1968); 50-54, 58-65 UNSY.

Hydro: 25-27, 30-31, 33-36, 49 est.; 28, 32 *Soviet Statistical Handbook*; 29, 37-38, 50-65 UNSY.

Imports and Exports (Note: The import and export figures described for the period from 1949 to 1953 or 1954 as "estimates" require special mention since they represent substantially more guesswork—and are therefore apt to be far less reliable—than numerous other estimated figures in this study. Data on foreign trade in fuels were almost entirely unavailable for the European Communist countries during these years. Partly to avoid having this vast a gap in our time series and partly to overcome what would otherwise be inconsistencies in regional and world trade aggregates (East European exports to Western Europe during this period would, e.g., be reflected in West European import statistics without appearing in Eastern European export data), we found it desirable to construct the most reasonable set of estimates that, under the circumstances, was possible. Imports and exports for Albania, Bulgaria, Czechoslovakia, East Germany, Hungary, Poland, Romania, and the U.S.S.R. were prepared jointly and within a common procedural context. This approach seemed desirable, since the presumably substantial volume of trade *within* this region could be more easily allocated looking at imports and exports of the various countries concurrently; and since some published foreign trade for this group of countries as a whole provided a constraint on the totals of our estimates.

Although judgment was the principal basis for the development of these figures, fragmentary published materials in UNWES were of some use in the process of linking our 1949-53 or 1949-54 estimates to published data for subsequent years. For example, East German and Polish solid fuel trade data were available; net trade figures for selected countries were available for 1949 and 1950; and net trade data of the Eastern European countries as a whole (that is, net imports or net exports, and therefore relating only to trade with other regions) were available for 1951-54. Also, a very rough check was provided by the degree of balance in world exports and imports before and after the incorporation of these estimates.

Solid fuels: 25-38 UKSS; 49-54 est.; 55-65 UNWES.
Liquid fuels: 25-38 from *Vneshnya ya torgovlya SSSR* ("Foreign Trade of the USSR"), with some reclassification of the refined products on the basis of UKSS; 49-53 est.; 54 crude oil and refined products total UKSS, refined products breakdown est.; 55 (and 55-65 in the case of lubes) UKSS; 56-60 data furnished by UN Stat. Office; 61-65 UNWES.
Gas: 49-54 est.; 55-65 UNWES.
Electricity: UNWES.

Population

25-38 estimates based principally on data in LNSY and UNSY–adjusted roughly [on the basis of data in Joint Economic Committee, U.S. Congress, *Dimensions of Soviet Power* (Washington: Government Printing Office, 1962)] to conform to post-World War II territory (i.e., for acquisition of Baltic States, Poland, and other areas); 49 est.; 50-65 UNDY.

Electricity Consumption

25-38, 49-54 UNSY; 55-65 UNWES.

United Kingdom

(Includes Channel Islands; and Northern Ireland from 1951.)

Production

Hard coal: UNSY; data for No. Ireland from UKSS and MY.
Crude oil (incl. shale oil): UKSS.
Natural gas: 50-55 est. on basis of data in OECD Stat. En.: 56-65 UNSY.
Hydro: 25-27 est. on basis of LNSY data; 28-38, 49-65 UNSY. (The addition of No. Ireland contributed 151 million kwh in 1951.)

Imports and Exports

Solid fuels: UKSS.
Liquid fuels: 25-38, 49-53 and lubes all years UKSS (gasoline and fuel oil 49-53 adjusted by linking to 54 UN figure); 54-60 data furnished by UN Stat. Office; 61-65 UNWES.
Gas: UNWES.
Electricity: UNWES.

Bunkers

Solid fuels: 25-38, 51-62 UKSS; 49-50, 63-65 UNWES.
Liquid fuels: 25-27 LNITS; 28-38 UKSS; 49-65 UNWES.

Population

UNDY.

Electricity Consumption

25-38 UNSY and LNSY; 49-65 UNWES.

United States

(Including, as far as available information permitted, Alaska and Hawaii, Virgin Islands, Guam, Wake Island, and American Samoa; excluding Puerto Rico and Panama Canal Zone, listed separately.)

Production

Hard coal: Bituminous coal 25-35 from Kohlen; bituminous coal all other years and anthracite all years from MY.
Lignite: 25-35 Kohlen; 36-38, 49-65 MY.
(For note on U.S. solid fuels conversion from original units into coal-equivalent units, see table footnote[g], on p. 829 of the General Notes.)
Crude oil: MY.
NGL: MY. (LPG portion up to 38 read off from MY chart and approximate.)
Natural gas: Published data elsewhere refer to marketed production of "wet" natural gas; to avoid doublecounting with NGL, it was necessary to derive an estimated "dry" natural gas series by deducting the approximate offtake for NGL. "Wet" natural gas for 25-30 from Schurr and Netschert, *Energy in the American Economy* (Baltimore: Johns Hopkins Press for RFF, 1960); 31-38, 49-65 UNSY. Deduction

United States (Cont'd.)

for NGL offtake was made at the rate of 34 cubic feet natural gas per gallon of NGL during 25-59 and rising thereafter to 40.6 cubic feet in 1965. These ratios were taken (or derived) from Schurr-Netschert, from U.S. Bureau of Mines Information Circular 8242, *Summary Energy Balances*, by W. E. Morrison (1964), and from MY.

Hydro: 25-38, 49-53 for continental U.S. from Schurr-Netschert (Alaska and Hawaii partially estimated) and UNWES, Guyol, and UNSY; 54-65 all data from UNSY. (Note: Data refer to net generation; geothermal electric power is excluded.)

Imports and Exports

(Note: Solid and liquid fuels import and export data have been adjusted to the maximum extent possible, to conform to the territorial definition shown above, by including trade of continental U.S. and possessions with third countries, and excluding trade between U.S. and possessions.)

Solid fuels: 25-38 MY; 49-50 UKSS; 51-65 UNWES.

Liquid fuels: 25-38 *exports* from *Historical Statistics of the U.S.*, *imports* from MY; 49-65 MY. (Crude oil series includes also unfinished and topped oils.)

Gas: 25-38 MY; 49-65 UNWES.

Electricity: 25-38 derived (jointly with the preparation of Canada and Mexico trade estimates) from *Historical Statistics of the U.S.*, WPC, and other sources; 49-65 UNWES.

Bunkers

Solid fuels: 25-38 UKSS (except Great Lakes bunkers 25-32 from information furnished by Ore and Coal Exchange, Cleveland, Ohio, and 33-38 derived from data in UKSS and MY); 49-65 MY.

Liquid fuels: MY. (The coastal and Great Lakes portion of bunkers for 25-29 were partly estimated.)

Population

UNDY. (Alaska and Hawaii excluded 25-38.)

Electricity Consumption

25 figure in *Historical Statistics of the U.S.* adjusted by linking to 26 LNSY figure; 26-30 LNSY; 31-38 UNSY; 49-65 UNWES. (Alaska and Hawaii excluded prior to 59.)

Upper Volta

(see West Africa)

Uruguay

Production

Natural gas: 49-51 UKSS.

Hydro: 49-62 UNSY; 63-65 UNWES.

Imports and Exports

Solid fuels: 25-38 LNITS; 49-50 UKSS; 51-65 UNWES.

Liquid fuels: 25-38, 49-53 and lubes all years UKSS; all other liquid fuels 54-60 data furnished by UN Stat. Office, 61-65 UNWES.

Bunkers

Solid fuels: 27-38 LNITS and UKSS. (Series identified as "reexports"; assumed to be mainly bunkers.)

Liquid fuels: 49, 51, 56-60 UKSS; 50, 52-55, 61-65 UNWES.

Population

UNDY. Population figures preceding 1963 appear to be overestimated as judged from later census findings. Subsequently revised historical data—available too late to be introduced into the machine tabulations—result in a lowering of the 1962 population by about 300,000 and of the 1950 population by about 200,000. The correspondingly revised annual population growth rate (table XIII) would show 1.4% instead of a decline of 0.8% for 1960-1965; and an increase of 1.7% instead of an increase of 0.8% for 1950-1965.

Electricity Consumption

25-32 LNSY; 33 est.; 34-38 UNSY; 49-65 UNWES; 65 est.

Venezuela

Production

Solid fuels: 25-30, 32-38 MY; 31 LNSY; 49-65 UNSY.

Crude oil: 25-33 MY; 34-38, 49-65 UNSY.

NGL: 25-26 est.; 27-30 derived from MY; 37-38, 49-58 UNSY; 59-65 LPG from MY added to natural gasoline from UNSY.

Natural gas: 27-30 est.; 31 derived from UKSS; 32-38 LNSY; 49-65 UNSY.

Hydro: 25-28, 31-36 est.; 29, 37 UNSY; 38, 49-52, 54 derived from data in ECLA ELA; 53 est. on basis of hydro/thermal capacity split; 55-65 UNSY.

Imports and Exports

Solid fuels: 25-38, 49-50 UKSS; 51-65 UNWES.

Liquid fuels: 25-38 and lubes all years UKSS; 49-53 UKSS adjusted by linking to 54 UN figure; 54-60 data furnished by UN Stat. Office; 61-65 UNWES.

Bunkers

UNWES.

Population

UNDY.

Electricity Consumption

29, 37, 49-65 UNWES; 38 UNSY.

Vietnam, North

(see Communist Asia)

Vietnam, South

(see Indo-China)

West Africa

(Comprises Dahomey, Guinea, Ivory Coast, Mali, Mauritania, Niger, Senegal, Upper Volta)

Production
Crude oil: MY. (Senegal.)
Hydro: 49-57 UNSY; 58-65 UNWES.

Imports and Exports
Solid fuels: 25-38, 49-50, 55-61 UKSS; 51-54 UNWES.
Liquid fuels: 25-38 and lubes all years UKSS; other liquid fuels 48-58 net import data from UNWES (exports assumed zero and component fuels partly estimated), 59-65 summed totals of separate country data from UN Stat. Office and UNWES. (Major portion of liquid fuel imports accounted for by Senegal.)

Bunkers
Solid fuels: 25-26 est. on basis of imports; 27-38 UKSS; 49-54 UNWES.
Liquid fuels: 25-26 est. on basis of imports; 27-38 UKSS; 49-65 UNWES.

Population
UNDY.

Electricity Consumption
31-38 UNSY; 49-65 UNWES.

Yugoslavia

Production
Hard coal and lignite: 25-38 MY; 49-65 UNSY.
Crude oil: UNSY.
NGL: UNSY.
Natural gas: UNSY.
Hydro: 25, 30, 35 C. Milićević, "Bisherige Entwicklung und weitere Möglichkeiten der Energiewirtschaft in Jugoslawien," Fifth World Power Conference, Vienna, 1956, Paper #183 A/32; 26-28, 33, 36 est.; 34 LNSY; 29, 31-32, 37-38, 49-65 UNSY.

Imports and Exports
Solid fuels: 25-38 UKSS and Kohlen; 49 est.; 50 UKSS; 51-65 UNWES.
Liquid fuels: 25-26 ITPP; 27-38 and lubes and greases 49-65 UKSS; 49 crude oil est.; all liquid fuels, except lubes and greases, 50-55 UKSS, 56-60 data furnished by UN Stat. Office, 61-65 UNWES.
Electricity: UNWES.

Bunkers
UNWES.

Population
UNDY.

Electricity Consumption
29, 31, 34-38 UNSY; 25-28, 30, 32-33 est. on basis of data in source to hydro production; 49-65 UNWES.

Zambia

(see Rhodesian Federation)

Five

SUPPLEMENTARY MATERIALS

I. Gross National Product Statistics and Notes on Their Derivation

A cross-sectional and historical look at the significance of total energy consumption in the overall economy of selected nations and regions appears in the Statistical Profiles of Part Two (Nos. 3 through 5). The topic is also touched on in the discussion of Part One. It was necessary, for this purpose, to pull together and adapt estimates of gross national product for a widely differing group of countries.

Worldwide GNP comparisons are beset with immense and well-known difficulties. From a conceptual standpoint, GNP comparisons among different countries can never be wholly satisfactory. The greater the difference in economic systems or organization, the more hazardous the task of constructing comparative GNP statistics and interpreting the results for particular purposes—e.g., measurement of relative living standards. Identical levels of per capita GNP for three countries may reflect, in one case, a centrally planned economy biased toward heavy industrial output and capital formation; in the second case, a feudal economy characterized by a highly unequal distribution of income; or, in the third case, a consumer-oriented market economy. No statistical device can overcome uncomparable situations. For many (though not all) purposes, it is similarly difficult to view as valid comparisons among countries in extremely disparate stages of development. (For this reason, we exclude from the country comparisons those nations having a 1965 per capita GNP of below $300.)

Apart from conceptual problems, there are innumerable statistical problems leading to comparison difficulties. National practices vary in what is included in national output. Though the Western estimates of Communist nations' output adapted here are adjusted to conform to Western concepts, socialist countries exclude (for ideological reasons) certain service sectors. Because of measurement difficulties, developing countries often fail to impute nonmarket activities in their economy; no quantitative indicator exists as to the significance of this exclusion. The price weights used to construct constant price series (in national currencies) may refer to different and outdated weighting periods.

To be meaningful, GNP data obviously have to be reduced to a common currency unit (in our case, U.S. dollars approximating 1965 purchasing power); yet the official exchange rate data available to make this translation from foreign currencies into dollars are often arbitrary or unrealistic, while the construction of purchasing power equivalent rates constitutes an elaborate undertaking which has been attempted by experts only selectively and intermittently.

These and other formidable problems raise real questions about the extent to which worldwide GNP comparisons serve legitimate analytical purposes. In the case of the present study, we feel that—in spite of their sometimes questionable quality—the use of such data helps provide useful insight into understanding historical trends and cross-sectional patterns of energy consumption relative to overall economic activity around the world. However, from what has been said, it should be clear that findings emerging from such statistical approximations are suggestive rather than precise.

Listed below are the principal sources used to construct the GNP series:

1. Stanley H. Cohn. "Soviet Economic Development Over Its First Half Century: Growth, Efficiency, and Structure." Paper presented at a conference sponsored by the Institute for the Study of the U.S.S.R., Munich, Germany, October 1966 (unpublished).
2. Maurice Ernst. "Postwar Economic Growth in Eastern Europe," in *New Directions in the Soviet Economy*. U.S. Congress, Joint Economic Committee, 89th Cong., 2nd sess., 1966.

3. Angus Maddison. *Economic Growth in the West.* New York: Twentieth Century Fund, 1963.

4. United Nations, Economic Commission for Europe. *Some Factors in Economic Growth in Europe During the 1950's.* Geneva, 1964.

5. United Nations, Department of Economic and Social Affairs. Statistical Office, *Statistical Yearbook.* New York, annual, various issues.

6. United States, Agency for International Development. *Gross National Product Growth Rates and Trend Data by Region and Country.* Office of Program Coordination Report No. RC-W-138. Washington, D.C., 31 March 1967.

7. United States, Arms Control and Disarmament Agency. *World-Wide Military Expenditures and Related Data, Calendar Year 1965.* Economics Bureau Research Report 67-6. Washington, D.C., 1967.

8. United States, Department of Commerce, Bureau of the Census. *Long-Term Economic Growth.* Washington, D.C.: Government Printing Office, 1966.

9. United States. *Economic Report of the President.* Washington, D.C.: Government Printing Office, February 1968.

10. United States Congress, Joint Economic Committee. *An Economic Profile of Mainland China.* Studies Prepared for the Committee, 90th Cong., 1st sess. Washington, D.C.: Government Printing Office, 1967.

11. ———. *Soviet Economic Performance: 1966-1967.* Materials Prepared for the Subcommittee on Foreign Economic Policy, 90th Cong., 2nd sess. Washington, D.C.: Government Printing Office, 1968.

In addition to the use of these source materials, advice from Herbert Block—an analyst steeped in the problems of international GNP comparisons—helped greatly in the process of adapting and selecting the most appropriate figures and avoiding some of the pitfalls. (The choice of the final series, however, was made by the author, who is solely responsible for any statistical abuses and faulty judgment.)

Only some brief overall comments on derivation will be given here. The procedure, generally speaking, was to start by obtaining dollar estimates of GNP for 1965 (or a proximate year)—based, where possible, on purchasing power equivalent, rather than official, rates of exchange; express these in U.S. dollars of 1965 purchasing power; and extrapolate these backward (or forward) using index numbers of real GNP for countries or regions. In the relatively few cases where recent-year dollar estimates in the published sources were expressed in other than 1965 prices, the U.S. GNP deflator was used to convert those to the 1965 price level. (Since the most important estimates here presented attempt to approximate comparisons based on purchasing power equivalents, rather than official exchange rates, this procedure implicitly assumes that differences in relative price movements between the United States and elsewhere would be appropriately reflected in offsetting changes in purchasing power equivalent exchange rates.)

For the most part, derivation of the estimates can be conveniently summarized under four geographical headings: (a) the United States; (b) the European and Asiatic Communist countries; (c) Western Europe, Canada, and Japan; and (d) all other countries.

(a) United States GNP was obtained from sources (8) and (9) listed above.

(b) Soviet GNP was based principally on data in source (1) and in chapter I of source (11). The Soviet estimates tend to reflect late-year rather than early-year price weights and are intended to represent purchasing power parities based on geometric means of U.S. and Soviet prices. GNPs of other European Communist countries are based on source (2) and chapter XIII of source (11), likewise reflecting estimated purchasing power equivalent exchange rates. Asiatic Communist GNP, based largely on source (10), is a crude and unreliable series which should be looked upon as provided in order to round out world totals.

(c) Western European, Japanese, and Canadian GNP levels for 1965 (again, based on estimated purchasing power equivalents except for Sweden, Switzerland, and a few smaller countries, which are based on official exchange rates) were obtained principally from sources (1), (2), and (11) since these authors developed their Communist estimates largely in the context of West European and U.S. purchasing power. With some exceptions, their estimates of recent West European GNP levels generally start with OECD estimates of GNP in national currencies; 1965 (or other recent-year) purchasing power equivalent exchange rates are initially based on 1955 ratios[1] moved forward to recent years by indexes of European and U.S. prices. Data for extrapolating the resulting dollar estimates backward to 1950 were taken largely from source (6). Pre-1965 Yugoslavia data are based on data in source (4) and reflect movements in the socialist concept of national product. The Finland figure for 1965 comes from source (7). Pre-World War II figures are based primarily on data in source (3) and, secondarily, in source (8) which contains selected international comparisons. In numerous cases, the pre-World War II data on West European GNP are based on movements in gross *domestic* rather than gross *national* product; this would have some distorting influence on prewar data for countries with disproportionate changes in net income from overseas investments.

[1]From Milton Gilbert and Associates, *Comparative National Products and Price Levels* (Paris: Organisation for Economic Cooperation and Development, 1958).

(d) Data for all other countries came almost exclusively from source (6) and reflect throughout the official exchange rate basis of conversion into U.S. dollars. A few 1965 figures were taken from source (7) (which in turn are described as having been obtained from U.S. Agency for International Development sources), while the Puerto Rico time series was constructed on the basis of figures shown in source (5). The South African figure for 1953 is likewise based on data in source (5); that for 1950 is roughly estimated.

The resulting GNP series appears in the appended set of three tables. Two additional remarks should be made. The regional aggregations in table I-1 are based, to the extent possible, on available individual country data whose derivation has been summarized above. However, the nonavailability of data for a number of countries—particularly for the years prior to 1965—required that regional aggregates be constructed on the basis of incomplete country statistics and on some partial regional output trends tabulated in source (5). The resulting estimates (especially for Africa other than South Africa, and Asia other than Israel and Japan) are crude and should be very cautiously used.

Finally, the juxtaposition of estimates based on both purchasing power equivalent rates of exchange and official exchange rates poses problems of comparability which must be kept in mind in interpretations of the data.

Table I-1. GROSS NATIONAL PRODUCT BY REGIONS, SELECTED YEARS, 1950-1965

(Millions of 1965 dollars)

Region	1950	1955	1960	1965
North America	421,000	519,400	580,900	736,200
Western Europe	285,000	366,000	455,300	578,200
Oceania	14,900	18,000	21,900	27,700
U.S.S.R. & Comm. E. Europe	186,000	252,000	333,000	422,000
U.S.S.R.	131,000	180,000	240,000	309,000
Eastern Europe	54,900	72,400	93,100	113,000
Communist Asia	35,000	63,000	85,000	81,000
Latin America	47,000	60,200	76,400	95,900
Asia	85,500	114,700	158,700	228,500
Middle East	10,600	14,400	18,100	24,800
Israel	743	1,374	2,116	3,397
Other Middle East	9,900	13,000	16,000	21,400
Far East and Other Asia	74,900	100,300	140,600	203,700
Japan	29,100	45,100	71,900	119,700
Other Far East	45,800	55,200	68,700	84,000
Africa	22,700	28,700	34,700	43,000
South Africa	5,400	6,640	8,075	10,720
Other Africa	17,300	22,100	26,600	32,300
WORLD	1,097,130	1,422,000	1,745,900	2,212,500
Addendum:				
A. Non-Communist countries:				
Developed	755,430	955,100	1,138,100	1,472,500
Underdeveloped	120,700	151,900	189,800	237,000
B. OECD:				
European OECD (including Turkey)	278,700	358,000	445,200	563,200
Total OECD	728,700	922,400	1,097,800	1,418,900

Note:

(1) Regional totals may be more rounded than component countries and areas; parts may therefore not add exactly to totals shown.

(2) North America, Western Europe, Communist areas, and Japan reflect 1965 levels largely based on estimated purchasing power equivalent exchange rates, other areas on official rates. See accompanying notes on derivation of historical data.

Table I-2. GROSS NATIONAL PRODUCT, SELECTED COUNTRIES, 1965

(Millions of 1965 dollars)

North America	
Canada	52,100
United States	683,900
Western Europe	
Belgium-Luxembourg	19,500
France	103,000
West Germany	129,600
Italy	64,700
Netherlands	22,600
Austria	9,900
Denmark	11,100
Norway	7,500
Portugal*	3,740
Sweden*	19,300
Switzerland*	13,900
United Kingdom	109,000
Finland*	8,070
Greece	6,600
Ireland*	2,800
Spain*	21,800
Yugoslavia	14,500
Oceania	
Australia*	21,700
New Zealand*	5,200
U.S.S.R. & Comm. E. Europe	
Bulgaria	6,800
Czechoslovakia	22,100
East Germany	26,600
Hungary	11,100
Poland	30,800
Romania	14,800
U.S.S.R.	309,000
Latin America	
Mexico*	19,415
Trinidad and Tobago*	630
Venezuela*	7,691
Costa Rica*	593
Guatemala*	1,410
Jamaica*	873
Nicaragua*	588
Panama*	617
Puerto Rico	2,880
Argentina*	16,050
Chile*	4,257
Peru*	4,281
Uruguay*	1,555
Asia	
Kuwait*	1,518
Cyprus*	417
Israel*	3,397
Lebanon*	1,120
Hong Kong*	1,600
Japan	119,700
Malaysia and Singapore*	3,740
Africa	
Libya*	876
South Africa*	10,720

*GNP converted at official exchange rates; other countries converted at purchasing power equivalent rates. See accompanying notes.

Note: Countries with per capita GNP of below $300 excluded from this listing.

Table I-3. GROSS NATIONAL PRODUCT, SELECTED COUNTRIES AND YEARS, 1925-1965

(Millions of 1965 dollars)

Country	1925	1929	1938	1950	1953	1955	1957	1960	1963	1965
North America										
Canada	10,700	14,000	13,700	26,900	31,900	33,600	36,700	39,800	45,900	52,100
United States	198,000	225,800	213,900	394,000	457,800	485,700	501,800	540,900	611,100	683,900
West Europe										
Belgium-Luxembourg	8,000	10,100	9,600	11,500	12,500	13,600	14,400	15,400	17,800	19,500
France	43,700	51,600	43,300	51,500	57,800	63,500	70,600	80,200	93,900	103,000
West Germany	n.a.	n.a.	n.a.	48,000	62,600	75,400	85,200	102,300	116,100	129,600
Italy	21,600	23,500	27,200	28,900	34,900	38,600	42,500	50,500	61,000	64,700
Netherlands	7,400	8,700	8,700	11,100	12,600	14,500	15,500	17,600	19,600	22,600
Austria	n.a.	n.a.	n.a.	4,500	5,200	6,300	7,000	8,100	9,100	9,900
Denmark	3,360	3,850	4,600	6,200	6,600	6,900	7,400	8,600	9,800	11,100
Norway	2,040	2,410	3,120	4,100	4,600	4,900	5,400	5,800	6,700	7,500
Sweden*	4,970	5,900	7,420	10,800	11,600	12,800	13,700	15,100	17,400	19,300
Switzerland*	4,360	5,270	5,560	7,000	7,900	8,900	9,700	10,800	12,700	13,900
United Kingdom	46,900	50,200	59,000	70,500	74,800	80,400	83,800	92,300	100,800	109,000
Greece	n.a.	n.a.	n.a.	2,300	2,900	3,300	3,900	4,300	5,500	6,600
Spain*	n.a.	n.a.	n.a.	8,900	11,100	12,600	13,800	14,600	18,900	21,800
Yugoslavia	3,400	4,200	4,900	5,900	n.a.	7,700	n.a.	10,000	n.a.	14,500
Oceania										
Australia*	n.a.	n.a.	n.a.	11,700	12,600	14,100	15,100	17,100	19,200	21,700
U.S.S.R. & Comm. E. Europe										
Bulgaria	n.a.	n.a.	n.a.	2,600	n.a.	3,500	n.a.	5,000	6,000	6,800
Czechoslovakia	n.a.	n.a.	n.a.	12,600	n.a.	15,000	n.a.	20,600	21,500	22,100
East Germany	n.a.	n.a.	n.a.	12,700	n.a.	17,900	n.a.	22,700	24,600	26,600
Hungary	n.a.	n.a.	n.a.	5,500	n.a.	7,300	n.a.	9,000	10,400	11,100
Poland	n.a.	n.a.	n.a.	14,900	n.a.	18,800	n.a.	23,900	27,300	30,800
Romania	n.a.	n.a.	n.a.	6,200	n.a.	9,400	n.a.	11,200	12,600	14,800
U.S.S.R.	45,000	58,000	98,000	131,000	148,000	180,000	203,000	240,000	274,000	309,000
Latin America										
Mexico*	n.a.	n.a.	n.a.	8,020	9,020	10,830	12,400	14,530	16,750	19,415
Venezuela*	n.a.	n.a.	n.a.	2,760	3,590	4,256	5,038	6,033	6,751	7,691
Costa Rica*	n.a.	n.a.	n.a.	262	340	378	415	475	536	593
Puerto Rico	n.a.	n.a.	n.a.	n.a.	n.a.	1,320	1,460	1,924	2,452	2,880
Argentina*	n.a.	n.a.	n.a.	10,090	10,530	11,670	12,510	13,600	13,770	16,050
Chile*	n.a.	n.a.	n.a.	2,436	2,844	2,824	3,163	3,469	3,869	4,257
Asia										
Israel*	n.a.	n.a.	n.a.	743	1,007	1,374	1,630	2,116	2,887	3,397
Japan	23,100	25,100	39,600	29,100	38,500	45,100	54,500	71,900	94,900	119,700
Africa										
South Africa*	n.a.	n.a.	n.a.	5,400	6,094	6,640	7,439	8,075	9,653	10,720

*Reflecting 1965 levels converted at official exchange rates; other countries based on purchasing power equivalent rates. See accompanying notes on derivation of historical data.

II. Some Simple Energy-GNP Regression Relationships

Regression number	Dependent variable	Independent variable	Equation	Standard error of: Estimate	Standard error of: Regression coefficient	Correlation coefficient	F Ratio	Significance level
1.	1965 per capita energy consumption	1965 per capita GNP	Log $E/P = -0.34 + 1.21$ Log Y/P *Description*: Cross-sectional regression for 49 countries having per capita GNP of $\geqslant$ \$300; resulting regression line is plotted on scattergram of Profile No. 4, Part Two.	0.20	0.10	0.87	141.1	0.1%
1(a).	1965 per capita energy consumption	1965 per capita GNP	Log $E/P = 0.81 + 0.85$ Log Y/P *Description*: Cross-sectional regression for top 25 countries having per capita GNP of $\geqslant$ \$900.	0.14	0.20	0.67	18.6	0.1%
1(b).	1965 per capita energy consumption	1965 per capita GNP	Log $E/P = -1.93 + 1.79$ Log Y/P *Description*: Cross-sectional regression for next 24 countries having per capita GNP of \$300–\$899.	0.24	0.39	0.70	21.4	0.1%
2.	1965 per capita energy (E_1) consumption	1965 per capita GNP	Log $E_1/P = -0.45 + 1.26$ Log Y/P *Description*: Cross-sectional regression for 49 countries, using energy measure whose hydro component represents alternative "B" in Part Three, table XII.	0.19	0.09	0.89	187.7	0.1%
3.	Average annual percentage growth rate in energy consumption 1925–1965	Average annual percentage growth rate in real GNP 1925–1965	Log $\Delta E_{(25-65)} = -0.004 + 1.4898$ Log $\Delta Y_{(25-65)}$ *Description*: Historical regression for 12 advanced countries; resulting regression line is plotted on scattergram in Profile No. 5, Part Two. As with the preceding regression the equation can be alternatively stated: $\Delta E_{(25-65)} = \Delta Y_{(25-65)}^{1.4898} (1.012)^{-1}$ (where 1.012 is the antilog of 0.0049). This alternative formulation brings into clearer relief a suggestive implication of the regression: namely, that for every 1% increase in real GNP, there tended to be a 1½% rise in energy consumption, offset by a tendency for energy consumption to fall by a bit over 1% yearly.	0.0049	0.46	0.71	10.3	1.0%
4.	Average annual percentage growth rate in energy consumption 1950–1965	Average annual percentage growth rate in real GNP 1950–1965	Log $\Delta E_{(50-65)} = 0.0041 + 0.96$ Log $\Delta Y_{(50-65)}$ *Description*: Historical regression for 15 advanced countries; resulting regression line is plotted on scattergram in Profile No. 5, Part Two. As with the preceding regression the equation can be alternatively stated: $\Delta E_{(50-65)} = \Delta Y_{(50-65)}^{0.96} (1.0095)$ (where 1.0095 is the antilog of 0.0041), suggesting that for every 1% increase in GNP, there was a tendency for energy consumption to go up by 0.96%, reinforced by the further tendency for energy consumption to rise by 0.95% per year.	0.008	0.33	0.63	8.6	5.0%
5.	Energy consumption (E_1) per dollar of GNP in 1965	Value added in energy-using industries as percent of total value added, 1965	$E_1/Y = 1.19 + 0.54X$ *Description*: Cross-sectional (linear) regression for 1965 in which the variation in energy consumption per unit of output of 32 countries is related to the relative importance of major energy-using industries in their manufacturing sector. (Energy measure is that using alternative "B" variant of hydro, as in Regression No. 2, above.)	0.65	0.013	0.59	16.2	0.1%

Part Five

SUPPLEMENTARY MATERIALS

I. Gross National Product Statistics and Notes on Their Derivation

II. Some Simple Energy-GNP Regression Relationships

III. Network of World Energy Flows

IV. Bibliographical Suggestions

Symbols used:

E	Energy consumption in terms of coal equivalents; hydro component of energy measured by heat content.
E_1	Energy consumption in terms of coal equivalents; hydro component of energy measured by central station fuel input requirements (alternative "B" in Part Three, table XII).
P	Population.
Y	GNP in 1965 dollars.
$\Delta E_{(25-65)}$	Index number of average annual percentage growth rate in energy consumption during 1925–65. In this, as well as in the following three growth-rate variables, note that the growth rates (in the form in which they are entered into the equations) are actually expressed as index numbers; thus, a 4% average annual growth rate is signified by 1.04. However, in Profile No. 5 the regression line and points are plotted against actual growth rates rather than their index numbers; also, the chart, while properly logarithmic, is arithmetic for greater visual convenience. Considering the relatively low numbers involved, virtually no distortion is thereby introduced.
$\Delta E_{(50-65)}$	Same as preceding for period 1950–65.
$\Delta Y_{(25-65)}$	Index number of average annual percentage growth rate in constant-dollar GNP during 1925–65.
$\Delta Y_{(50-65)}$	Same as preceding for 1950–65.
X	Value added in heavy energy-using industries (paper, chemicals, petroleum and coal products, and basic metals) as percent of total value added in manufacturing. (Most data refer to 1965 or to nearest preceding year when 1965 figure was not available.)

Sources:

$E, P, E/P$	Part Three, table XI.
$E_1, E_1/P$	Part Three, table XII.
Y	Part Two, Profile No. 4 and table I–2, above.
ΔE and ΔY	Part Two, Profile No. 5.
X	(Not shown elsewhere in the study.) Derived from data in United Nations, Department of Economic and Social Affairs, *The Growth of World Industry, 1953–1965* (New York, 1967).

List of Countries (and regression in which included)

Country	. . . . Regression Number						
	1	*1(a)*	*1(b)*	*2*	*3*	*4*	*5*
Canada	x	x		x	x	x	x
United States	x	x		x	x	x	x
Belgium-Luxembourg	x	x		x	x	x	x
France	x	x		x	x	x	x
West Germany	x	x		x		x	x
Italy	x	x		x	x	x	x
Netherlands	x	x		x	x	x	x
Austria	x	x		x		x	x
Denmark	x	x		x	x	x	x
Norway	x	x		x	x	x	x
Portugal	x		x	x			x
Sweden	x	x		x	x	x	x
Switzerland	x	x		x	x	x	
United Kingdom	x	x		x	x	x	x
Finland	x	x		x			x
Greece	x		x	x			
Ireland	x	x		x			x
Spain	x		x	x			x
Yugoslavia	x		x	x			
Australia	x	x		x		x	x
New Zealand	x	x		x			x
Bulgaria	x		x	x			
Czechoslovakia	x	x		x			
East Germany	x	x		x			
Hungary	x	x		x			
Poland	x	x		x			
Romania	x		x	x			
U.S.S.R.	x	x		x			
Mexico	x		x	x			x
Trinidad & Tobago	x		x	x			
Venezuela	x		x	x			x
Costa Rica	x		x	x			
Guatemala	x		x	x			
Jamaica	x		x	x			x
Nicaragua	x		x	x			
Panama	x		x	x			x
Puerto Rico	x	x		x			x
Argentina	x		x	x			x
Chile	x		x	x			x
Peru	x		x	x			x
Uruguay	x		x	x			x
Cyprus	x		x	x			x
Israel	x	x		x			x
Lebanon	x		x	x			
Hong Kong	x		x	x			
Japan	x	x		x	x	x	x
Malaysia-Singapore	x		x	x			
Libya	x		x	x			x
South Africa	x		x	x			x

III. Network of World Energy Flows

Table III-1. ESTIMATED MAJOR INTERREGIONAL FLOWS OF SOLID AND LIQUID FUELS, BY REGION OF ORIGIN AND DESTINATION, 1929
(Thousand metric tons coal equivalent)

Importing region and fuel category	Exporting region: World	Canada	United States	Western Europe	Oceania	U.S.S.R. & Communist E. Europe	Communist Asia	Caribbean	Other Latin America	Middle East	Far East and Other Asia	Africa
World												
Solid fuels	55,640	840	20,170	16,080	60	11,730	3,530	–	–	–	2,200	1,030
Liquid fuels	80,100	180	30,370	150	–	8,150	–	32,230	1,190	4,640	3,190	–
Total	135,740	1,020	50,540	16,230	60	19,880	3,530	32,230	1,190	4,640	5,390	1,030
Canada												
Solid fuels	18,510	–	17,720	790	–	–	–	–	–	–	–	–
Liquid fuels	8,840	–	6,230	–	–	–	–	1,830	780	–	–	–
Total	27,350	–	23,950	790	–	–	–	1,830	780	–	–	–
United States												
Solid fuels	840	840	–	–	–	–	–	–	–	–	–	–
Liquid fuels	22,170	110	–	10	–	–	–	21,740	290	20	–	–
Total	23,010	950	–	10	–	–	–	21,740	290	20	–	–
Western Europe												
Solid fuels	12,000	–	520	–	–	11,480	–	–	–	–	–	–
Liquid fuels	29,910	60	12,270	–	–	6,000	–	6,880	120	3,700	880	–
Total	41,910	60	12,790	–	–	17,480	–	6,880	120	3,700	880	–
Oceania												
Solid fuels	570	–	–	570	–	–	–	–	–	–	–	–
Liquid fuels	2,800	–	1,440	–	–	–	–	–	–	120	1,240	–
Total	3,370	–	1,440	570	–	–	–	–	–	120	1,240	–
U.S.S.R. & Comm. E. Europe												
Solid fuels	3,000	–	–	3,000	–	–	–	–	–	–	–	–
Liquid fuels	110	–	10	100	–	–	–	–	–	–	–	–
Total	3,110	–	10	3,100	–	–	–	–	–	–	–	–
Communist Asia[a]												
Solid fuels	2,300	–	–	–	–	100	–	–	–	–	2,200	–
Liquid fuels	1,780	10	980	20	–	20	–	–	–	–	750	–
Total	4,080	10	980	20	–	120	–	–	–	–	2,950	–
Caribbean												
Solid fuels	1,340	–	1,260	80	–	–	–	–	–	–	–	–
Liquid fuels	3,020	–	3,020	–	–	–	–	–	–	–	–	–
Total	4,360	–	4,280	80	–	–	–	–	–	–	–	–

Other Latin America												
Solid fuels	6,500	–	630	5,870	–	–	–	–	–	–	–	–
Liquid fuels	4,570	–	2,680	–	–	150	–	1,740	–	–	–	–
Total	11,070	–	3,310	5,870	–	150	–	1,740	–	–	–	–
Middle East												
Solid fuels	200	–	–	200	–	–	–	–	–	–	–	–
Liquid fuels	450	–	10	–	–	400	–	–	–	–	40	–
Total	650	–	10	200	–	400	–	–	–	–	40	–
Far East and Other Asia												
Solid fuels	4,880	–	–	140	60	120	3,530	–	–	–	–	1,030
Liquid fuels	4,310	–	2,880	20	–	730	–	–	–	680	–	–
Total	9,190	–	2,880	160	60	850	3,530	–	–	680	–	1,030
Africa												
Solid fuels	5,500	–	40	5,430	–	30	–	–	–	–	–	–
Liquid fuels	2,140	–	850	–	–	850	–	40	–	120	280	–
Total	7,640	–	890	5,430	–	880	–	40	–	120	280	–

[a]Mainland China only.

Notes and Sources follow table III–2.

Table III-2. ESTIMATED MAJOR INTERREGIONAL[a] FLOWS OF SOLID AND LIQUID FUELS, BY REGION OF ORIGIN AND DESTINATION, 1965

(Thousand metric tons coal equivalent)

Importing region and fuel category	Exporting region[b] World	Canada	United States	Western Europe	Oceania	Communist Countries	Caribbean	Middle East	Far East and Other Asia	Africa
World										
Solid fuels	82,225	1,160	47,040	920	6,990	25,220	–	–	–	895
Liquid fuels	1,074,345	24,435	11,755	5,660	–	66,855	238,835	547,810	16,455	162,540
Total	1,156,570	25,595	58,795	6,580	6,990	92,075	238,835	547,810	16,455	163,435
Canada										
Solid fuels	15,295	–	15,290	5	–	–	–	–	–	–
Liquid fuels	41,475	–	1,725	300	–	–	30,375	8,850	225	–
Total	56,770	–	17,015	305	–	–	30,375	8,850	225	–
United States										
Solid fuels	250	240	–	10	–	–	–	–	–	–
Liquid fuels	190,995	24,375	–	225	–	–	124,800	29,625	4,995	6,975
Total	191,245	24,615	–	235	–	–	124,800	29,625	4,995	6,975
Western Europe										
Solid fuels	44,940	–	22,600	–	–	21,800	–	–	–	540
Liquid fuels	558,640	–	3,375	–	–	41,275	57,075	303,225	2,115	151,575
Total	603,580	–	25,975	–	–	63,075	57,075	303,225	2,115	152,115
Oceania										
Solid fuels	40	–	5	20	–	–	–	–	–	15
Liquid fuels	30,075	–	–	–	–	–	–	21,855	8,220	–
Total	30,115	–	5	20	–	–	–	21,855	8,220	15
Communist Countries										
Solid fuels	660	–	210	450	–	–	–	–	–	–
Liquid fuels	1,650	–	–	750	–	–	–	–	–	900
Total	2,310	–	210	1,200	–	–	–	–	–	900
Caribbean										
Solid fuels	510	–	250	130	–	130	–	–	–	–
Liquid fuels	21,625	–	3,000	75	–	13,750	–	4,800	–	–
Total	22,135	–	3,250	205	–	13,880	–	4,800	–	–
Other Latin America										
Solid fuels	2,130	–	1,840	150	–	140	–	–	–	–
Liquid fuels	34,475	–	–	225	–	6,500	15,000	10,500	–	2,250
Total	36,605	–	1,840	375	–	6,640	15,000	10,500	–	2,250
Middle East										
Solid fuels	460	–	–	20	–	440	–	–	–	–
Liquid fuels	2,775	–	–	600	–	225	300	–	900	750
Total	3,235	–	–	620	–	665	300	–	900	750
Far East and Other Asia										
Solid fuels	17,795	920	6,840	55	6,990	2,650	–	–	–	340
Liquid fuels	141,935	60	3,280	35	–	2,855	2,810	132,805	–	90
Total	159,730	980	10,120	90	6,990	5,505	2,810	132,805	–	430
Africa										
Solid fuels	145	–	5	80	–	60	–	–	–	–
Liquid fuels	50,700	–	375	3,450	–	2,250	8,475	36,150	–	–
Total	50,845	–	380	3,530	–	2,310	8,475	36,150	–	–

[a]Some major *intra*regional flows in 1965 were:

Exports from	*Exports to*	*Fuel category*	*Amount in 1,000 met. tons coal equivalent*
Western Europe	Western Europe	solid fuels	36,380
of which:			
West Germany	Western Europe	solid fuels	22,780
	of which:		
	France	solid fuels	8,700
Communist Countries	Communist Countries	solid fuels	36,030
of which:	of which:		
U.S.S.R.	Eastern Europe	solid fuels	16,480
Poland	U.S.S.R.	solid fuels	7,110
Poland	Eastern Europe	solid fuels	7,595
Indonesia	Japan	liquid fuels (mostly crude)	9,000
Brunei	Far East & Other Asia	liquid fuels (mostly crude)	4,875

Caribbean	Caribbean	liquid fuels (mostly crude)	70,500
Middle East	Middle East	liquid fuels (mostly crude)	22,875
Western Europe of which:	Western Europe	liquid fuels (mostly products)	87,825
West Germany	Western Europe	liquid fuels (mostly products)	16,660
United Kingdom	Western Europe	liquid fuels (mostly products)	16,475

[b]Other Latin America not shown since there were no interregional exports from that area.

For notes and sources to both table III-1 and table III-2, see next page.

Notes and Sources to Tables III-1 and III-2

The totals appearing across the top and in the first column at the left fall below the corresponding regional exports and imports in Part Three, table VI. This is principally due to the fact that the present tables exclude intraregional fuel shipments. However, if the exclusion of intraregional trade were the only difference between the two tables, the net trade (import less export) figures of the present tables should equal the net trade figures of Part Three, table VII. In fact, a comparison indicates that there are numerous and sometimes considerable discrepancies (particularly for 1929) between the net solid and liquid fuels trade balances as shown in the two calculations. For example, table III-1 shows United States 1929 net liquid fuels exports of 8,200 thousand tons (= 30,370 minus 22,170), while table VII shows net exports of 7,518 thousand tons; or, table III-1 estimates 1929 West Europe net solid fuels exports of 4,080 thousand tons (= 16,080 minus 12,000), while table VII shows a figure of 7,203 thousand tons. (The West Europe discrepancy is the most serious one in the comparison; it should, however, be viewed in the context of West Europe *gross* solid fuels exports to 1929 of about 125,000 thousand tons and imports of 118,000 thousand tons.) A comparison of the 1965 net trade balances of table III-2 and table VII discloses far more reasonable differences—probably due to the partial use of common source materials.

Several important reasons suggest themselves as major reasons for differences between the net trade figures of the two tables: (1) Differences in sources; the multi-country publications consulted for the present tables (see citations below) represent much more limited source materials than the extensive international and national data sources used to compile the data in Part Three. (2) A related point is that the matrix arrangement of the present tables necessarily produces regional import (or export) figures as a result of data used for the particular region's trading partner. (It makes no sense to use one figure for A's exports to B and another for B's imports from A.) In Part Three, by contrast, independent sources (that is, the ultimate sources of information—not necessarily independent secondary source documents) are frequently the rule. This, in turn, produces internal inconsistencies *within Part Three*, as discussed in the notes of Part Four, pp. 820-22. (3) Sources for the present tables frequently included geographically unallocable imports or exports; these were not used in construction of our tables, but their exclusion obviously results in a less than complete picture of world flows by region of origin and destination. (4) There was no way to insure that the two tables reflect precise uniformity of treatment with respect (a) to the scope of the particular solid and liquid fuels included; (b) to conversion factors used to translate figures from a volumetric to weight basis and, further, to express the data in coal equivalents; or (c) to the regional classification scheme. (5) With respect to 1929, some of the data in table III-1 were estimated by interpolation or extrapolation in cases where 1929 figures were not shown in the indicated sources.

The three sources used in deriving the 1929 figures in table III-1 were:

Rudolf Regul. *Energiequellen der Welt*. Hamburg: Hanseatische Verlagsanstalt, published for the Instituts für Konjunkturforschung, 1937.

U.S. Department of Commerce. *International Trade in Petroleum and Its Products, 1929*, Trade Promotion Series No. 99. Washington: Government Printing Office, 1930.

Germany. *Statistische Übersicht über die Kohlenwirtschaft im Jahre 1931*. Berlin: Reichskohlenrat, 1932.

Regul and *Kohlenwirtschaft* were both used to estimate solid fuels flows. Regul was also used to estimate liquid fuels trade other than for the United States, while the U.S. Department of Commerce document was used to estimate the regional distribution of U.S. liquid fuels exports and imports as well as to fill in gaps in liquid fuels data not shown by Regul.

For the 1965 estimates of table III-2, solid fuels figures were obtained from United Nations, Department of Economic and Social Affairs, *World Energy Supplies*, Statistical Papers Series J, No. 10 and No. 11 (New York, 1967 and 1968). The liquid fuels data were adapted from a release dated May 1966, U.S. Department of the Interior, Office of Oil and Gas, covering crude oil and refined petroleum products combined. This source expressed data in barrels per day; these were converted into metric tons per year by multiplying by 50. Data on exports by destination and imports by origin for Japan, Other Asia, and Oceania were not separately shown in the cited source and had to be constructed from three additional sources: (1) Crude oil flows for all three areas from United Nations, *World Energy Supplies*; (2) Japanese refined product flows from OECD, *Oil Statistics, 1965* (Paris, 1966); and (3) refined product flow of Other Asia area from U.S. Department of the Interior, Office of Oil and Gas, *1965 Petroleum Supply and Demand in the Free World* (Washington, June 1967). Oceania's insignificant refined product flows were roughly estimated. Some geographic reclassification (done by rough estimation) was necessary to make the May 1966 Office of Oil and Gas release consistent with the scheme used in our other table. Principally, this involved moving Puerto Rico and Jamaica from "Other Latin America" into the "Caribbean" area. Also, Cuba was placed in the Caribbean region and estimated roughly on the basis of figures in UN, *World Energy Supplies*.

Table III-3. ESTIMATED DOLLAR VALUE OF MAJOR INTERREGIONAL[a] ENERGY FLOWS, BY REGION OF ORIGIN AND DESTINATION, 1965

(Million U.S. dollars, f.o.b.)

	Exporting region									
Importing region	World	Canada	United States	Western Europe	Oceania	Communist Countries	Latin America	Middle East	Far East and Other Asia	Africa
World	11,543	411	943	206	79	902	2,384	4,957	172	1,489
Canada	609	–	215	8	–	–	308	76	–	2
United States.	1,985	400	–	12	–	1	1,189	290	49	44
Western Europe[b]. . .	5,904	1	365	–	1	625	752	2,710	32	1,418
Oceania[b]	298	–	13	6	–	–	4	190	84	1
Communist Countries	18	–	3	12	–	–	–	–	–	3
Latin America	429	–	123	17	–	106	–	166	2	15
Middle East	36	–	7	21	–	6	–	–	2	–
Far East and Other Asia	1,743	10	194	37	74	127	65	1,230	–	6
Africa	521	–	23	93	4	37	66	295	3	–

[a]*Intra*regional flows in 1965 were:

	Million $
Western Europe	2,340
Communist Countries. . .	1,358
Latin America	1,004
Far East.	402
Middle East.	335
Africa	100
Oceania	8
Total	5,547

The sum ($17.1 billion) of $5.5 billion in intraregional flows and $11.5 billion (given in the table above) in interregional flows falls about $0.8 billion short of the United Nations' estimate of overall energy flows of $17.9 billion. This is primarily due to the inclusion in the UN figure of bunkers (and some minor items, such as special category exports and ships' stores) which are not geographically allocable.

[b]Western Europe excludes the imports and exports of a few minor countries and possessions—e.g., Malta and Gibraltar; similarly, Oceania (which, in the table, covers only Australia and New Zealand) excludes numerous territories, such as New Guinea, New Caledonia, and the Solomon Islands. Data for the missing areas, which are also omitted from the interregional world total of $11.5 billion (while being included in the grand total of $17.9 billion indicated in the note above), are negligible.

Notes and Sources to Table III-3

Data refer to Standard Industrial Trade Classification (SITC), Section 3: "mineral fuels, lubricants, and related materials." This includes coal, coke, briquettes, and other coal products; crude petroleum; petroleum products; natural and manufactured gas; and electricity. The "petroleum products" category includes mineral jelly, waxes, and a number of other nonenergy items which, generally speaking, are excluded from statistical coverage throughout this study.

Data are described by the United Nations as being based primarily on exporting country statistics and as having been adjusted to approximate the "special" trade system.

The data were obtained primarily from United Nations, *Monthly Bulletin of Statistics*, March 1968, pp. xxiv-xxv. Since the United Nations includes the Netherlands Antilles, Jamaica, and Trinidad and Tobago within a "rest of world" grouping, data for these three countries were obtained separately, taken out of the "rest of world" grouping, and consolidated with Latin America. The sources used were:

Netherlands Antilles: United Nations. *Commodity Trade Statistics, 1965*, Statistical Papers, Series D, vol. XV, no. 1-24.

Jamaica: Jamaica, Department of Statistics. *External Trade of Jamaica, 1965.*

Trinidad and Tobago: Trinidad and Tobago, Central Statistical Office. *Overseas Trade, 1965.*

Imports into these three countries by region of origin relate to c.i.f. rather than f.o.b. values.

IV. Bibliographical Suggestions

This listing of references dealing with quantitative aspects of world energy is highly selective. The emphasis is on breadth of treatment: each work cited relates to all energy forms dealt with comparatively, and embraces worldwide coverage or coverage of major regions. The first group of works cited has interpretive as well as statistical content, while the second group contains strictly serial tabular materials.

A. *Selected Ad Hoc Studies with Both Statistical and Textual-Analytical Content:*

Commission of the European Communities (Common Market). *Tendenzen der Weltenergiewirtschaft.* Serie Energie, No. 1. Brussels: 1968. English translation: *Trends in the World Energy Economy.*

European Coal and Steel Community (ECSC). *Review of the Long-Term Energy Outlook for the European Community.* Bulletin No. 61. Luxembourg: 1966.

_____. *Study on the Long-Term Energy Outlook for the European Community.* Luxembourg, 1964.

Fisher, Joseph L. and Neal Potter. *World Prospects for Natural Resources: Some Projections of Demand and Indicators of Supply to the Year 2000.* Washington: Resources for the Future, 1964.

Gordon, Richard L. *The Evolution of Energy Policy in Western Europe: The Reluctant Retreat from Coal.* New York: Praeger, 1971.

Great Britain, Commonwealth Economic Committee. *Sources of Energy.* London: Her Majesty's Stationery Office, 1966.

Hubbert, M. King. *Energy Resources.* A Report to the Committee on Natural Resources of the National Academy of Sciences–National Research Council, Publication 1000–D. Washington, 1962.

_____. "Energy Resources," in *Resources and Man.* Committee on Resources and Man of the National Academy of Sciences–National Research Council. San Francisco: W. H. Freeman for the National Academy of Sciences, 1969.

Ismail, Salem K. *The Correlation Between Energy Consumption and Gross National Product: A Statistical Analysis.* Vienna: Organization of the Petroleum Exporting Countries (OPEC), 1968.

Jensen, W. G. *Energy in Europe, 1945–1980.* London: G. T. Foulis, 1967.

Lehbert, Ben. *Entwicklungstendenzen in der Westeuropäischen Energiewirtschaft.* Kieler Studien No. 35. Kiel: 1955. English translation: *Trends in the Development of the West European Energy Economy.*

Organisation for Economic Cooperation and Development (OECD)–successor in 1961 to Organisation for European Economic Cooperation (OEEC). *Energy Policy.* Paris, 1966.

Organisation for European Economic Cooperation (OEEC). *Some Aspects of the European Energy Problem.* Paris, June 1955.

_____. *Europe's Growing Needs of Energy–How Can They Be Met?* Paris, May 1956.

_____. *Towards a New Energy Pattern in Europe.* Paris: January 1960.

Schurr, Sam H. "Energy," *Scientific American.* September 1963.

Schurr, Sam H., Bruce C. Netschert and others. *Energy in the American Economy, 1850–1975.* Baltimore: Johns Hopkins Press for Resources for the Future, 1960.

Schurr, Sam H., Paul T. Homan and others. *Middle Eastern Oil and the Western World: A Review of Prospects and Problems.* New York: American Elsevier, 1971. Considerable attention is given to comparative trends among all energy forms.

United Nations, Department of Economic Affairs. *World Energy Supplies in Selected Years, 1929–1950.* Statistical Papers, Series J, No. 1. New York: September 1952. Subsequent editions of this series, included in listing B, below, were entirely devoted to statistical compilations.

_____, Department of Economic and Social Affairs. *Energy in Latin America.* Study prepared by the Secretariat of the Economic Commission for Latin America. Geneva, 1957.

_____, Economic Commission for Asia and the Far East. "Planning for Energy Development," *Economic Bulletin for Asia and the Far East.* Bangkok, December 1965.

_____, Economic Commission for Europe. *Methods and Principles for Projecting Future Energy Requirements.* ST/ECE/ENERGY/2, mimeo. New York, 1964.

_____. *The General Energy Situation in Europe in 1967 and Early 1968 in the Context of Current World Trends.* ST/ECE/ENERGY/12, mimeo. New York: 3 March 1969.

_____. "World Energy Requirements in 1975 and 2000," in *Proceedings of the International Conference on the Peaceful Uses of Atomic Energy,* Vol. 1. Held in Geneva, August 1955. New York, 1956, pp. 3–33.

U.S. Department of State. *Energy Resources of the World.* Prepared by Nathaniel B. Guyol. Publication 3428. Washington, June 1949.

B. *Major Periodical Statistical Publications* (see individual country source listings in Part Four for more extensive references):

Common Market. *Energy Statistics.* Brussels, annual.

Great Britain, Institute of Geological Sciences, Mineral Resources Division. *Statistical Summary of the Mineral Industry*. London, annual.

Organisation for Economic Cooperation and Development (OECD). *Statistics of Energy*. Paris, annual.

United Nations, Department of Economic and Social Affairs, Statistical Office. *World Energy Supplies*. Statistical Papers, Series J. New York, annual.

U.S. Department of the Interior, Bureau of Mines. *Minerals Yearbook, Area Reports: International*. Washington, D.C.: Government Printing Office, annual.

World Power Conference. *Survey of Energy Resources*. London: Central Office of the World Power Conference, periodic; most recent edition dated 1968.

THE JOHNS HOPKINS PRESS

Composed in Press Roman text and display
by Jones Composition Company, Inc.

Printed on 50-lb. Sebago MF Medium
by Universal Lithographers, Inc.

Bound in Holliston Roxite Vellum
by L. H. Jenkins, Inc.

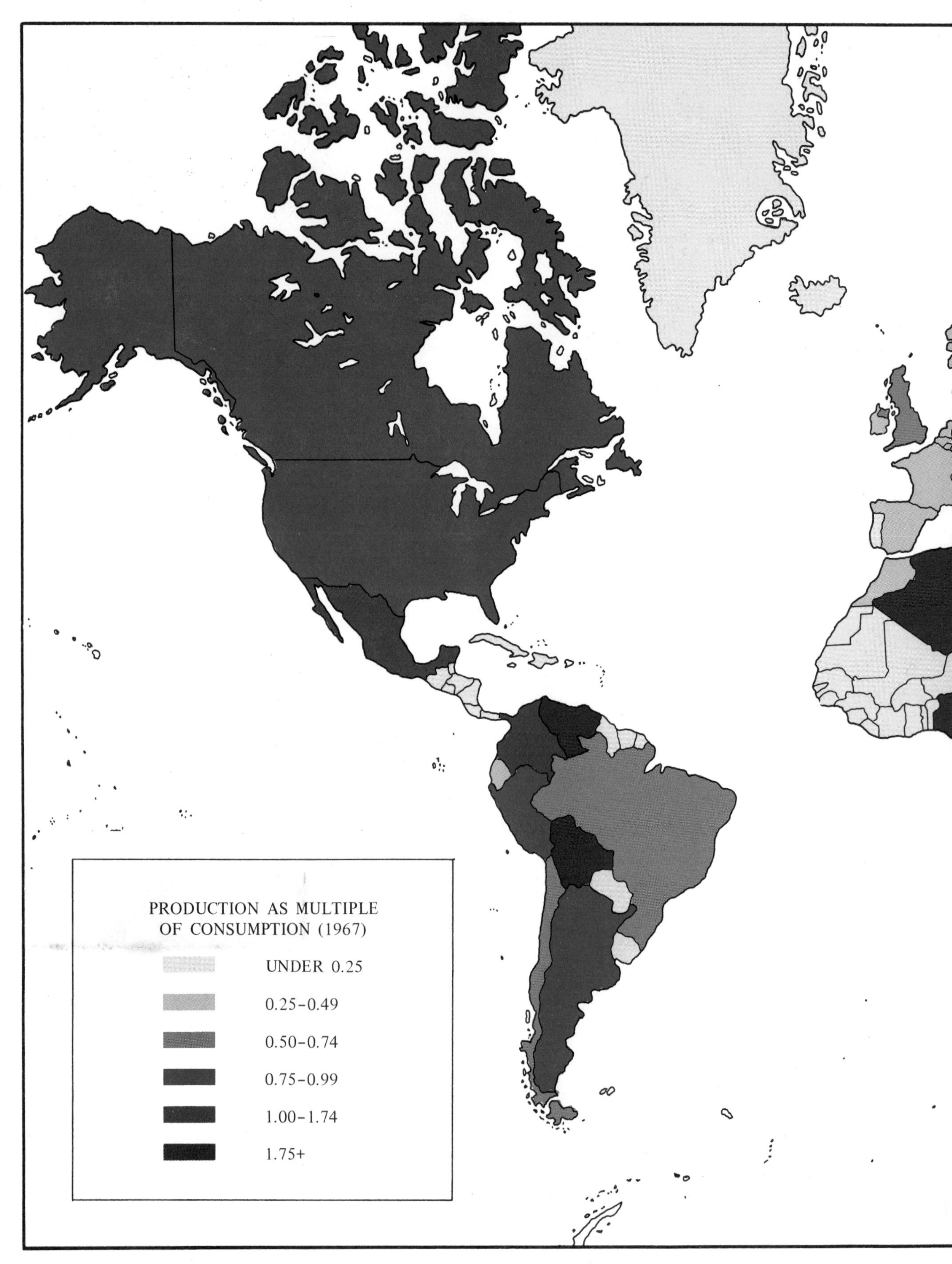
PRODUCTION AS MULTIPLE
OF CONSUMPTION (1967)
UNDER 0.25
0.25–0.49
0.50–0.74
0.75–0.99
1.00–1.74
1.75+